GUIDE TO
REFERENCE BOOKS
Covering Materials from 1985-1990

Contributors

Janet Ayers, *Mudd Library, Northwestern University* : EJ, Engineering

Barbara L. Bell, *Andrews Library, The College of Wooster* : AA, Bibliography

Beki Biefeld, *Syracuse University Library* : CD, Psychology and Psychiatry

John A. Bollier, *Yale Divinity Library* : BB, Religion

Wendy Bousfield, *Syracuse University Library* : C, Social and Behavioral Sciences (various)

Carl Braun, *Syracuse University Library* : CG, Statistics and Demography

Loretta Caren, *Syracuse University Library* : CA, Social and Behavioral Sciences—General Works; Coordinator, Section C

Mary Cargill, *Columbia University Library* : AA, Bibliography; AC, Encyclopedias; AD, Language Dictionaries; AE, Periodicals; AF, Newspapers; AG, Government Publications; AH, Dissertations; AJ, Biography; Coordinator, Section A

Kathe Chipman, *Avery Architectural and Fine Arts Library, Columbia University* : BE, Fine Arts; BF, Applied Arts

Elaine Coppola, *Syracuse University Library* : CJ, Political Science

Lloyd A. Davidson, *Mudd Library, Northwestern University* : EC, Biological Sciences; EH , Agricultural Sciences

Elizabeth A. Davis, *Music Library, Columbia University* : BH, Music

Olha della Cava, *Columbia University Library* : AB, Librarianship and Library Resources

Margaret Durkin, *Yale Law Library* : CK, Law

Cathryn Easterbrook, *John Crerar Library, University of Chicago* : EK, Medical and Health Sciences

Edith Fried, *Syracuse University Library* : CG, Statistics and Demography

Ed Goodman, *Syracuse University Library* : CB, Education; CC, Sociology; CJ, Political Science

Karen Ingeman, *Syracuse University Library* : CB, Education

Patricia McCandless, *The Ohio State University Libraries* : BJ, Sports, Recreation, and Travel

Eileen McIlvaine, *Columbia University Library* : DA-DH, History and Area Studies; Coordinator, Section D

Pamela McLaughlin, *Syracuse University Library* : C, Social and Behavioral Sciences (various)

Robert C. Michaelson, *Mudd Library, Northwestern University* : ED, Chemistry; EG, Physics; EJ, Engineering; Coordinator, Section E

Christa Modschiedler, *John Crerar Library, University of Chicago* : EH, Agricultural Sciences; EK, Medical and Health Sciences

Lee Murray, *Carnegie Library, Syracuse University* : CD, Psychology and Psychiatry

Lesley Pease, *Syracuse University Library* : CC, Sociology

Brenda S. Rice, *John Crerar Library, University of Chicago* : EF, Mathematics; EJ, Engineering

Urmila Sharma, *Syracuse University Library* : CD, Psychology and Psychiatry

Kip Sperry, *Brighham Young University* : AK, Genealogy

Sarah Spurgin, *Columbia University Library* : BD, Literature

Marcella Stark, *Syracuse University Library* : CC, Sociology

Diane Strauss, *University of North Carolina at Chapel Hill Library* : CH, Economics

Mary Anne Waltz, *Syracuse University Library* : BJ, Sports, Recreation, and Travel; CE, Anthropology and Ethnology; CL, Geography

Raymond S. Wright III, *Brigham Young University* : AK, Genealogy

Kathleen A. Zar, *John Crerar Library, University of Chicago* : EA, Science, Technology, and Medicine—General Works; EB, Astronomy; EE, Earth Sciences

Meseratch Zecharias, *Syracuse University Library* : CC, Sociology

Advisors

Terry Plum, *University of Connecticut Library* : Advisor for Databases

Paul Stuehrenberg, *Yale Divinity Library* : Advisor for Cataloging

Project Director

Patricia Sabosik, *Choice Magazine*

GUIDE TO REFERENCE BOOKS

Covering Materials from 1985-1990

SUPPLEMENT TO THE TENTH EDITION

Edited by

Robert Balay

Special Editorial Advisor

Eugene P. Sheehy

AMERICAN LIBRARY ASSOCIATION

Chicago and London 1992

Cover by gordonStromberg design.
Composed by INFORONICS, Inc. in
   Times Roman and Friz Quadrata.
Printed on 50-pound Precision White,
   a pH-neutral stock, and
   bound in KIVAR 9 Cambric cloth
   by Braun-Brumfield, Inc.

Library of Congress Cataloging-in-Publication Data

Guide to reference books, tenth edition. Supplement / edited by
   Robert Balay : special editorial advisor, Eugene P. Sheehy.
        p.   cm.
     Includes index.
     ISBN 0-8389-0588-9
     1. Reference books—Bibliography.   I. Balay, Robert.   II. Sheehy,
Eugene P. (Eugene Paul), 1922-
Z1035.1.S43 1986 Suppl.   92-6463
011′.02—dc20   CIP

Contents

Abbreviations   vi
Preface   vii

A

General Reference Works

AA	Bibliography	1
AB	Librarianship and Library Resources	25
AC	Encyclopedias	36
AD	Language Dictionaries	39
AE	Periodicals	54
AF	Newspapers	63
AG	Government Publications	65
AH	Dissertations	70
AJ	Biography	72
AK	Genealogy	81

B

Humanities

BA	Philosophy	87
BB	Religion	90
BC	Linguistics and Philology	104
BD	Literature	110
BE	Fine Arts	148
BF	Applied Arts	167
BG	Theater and Performing Arts	175
BH	Music	186
BJ	Sports, Recreation, and Travel	201

C

Social and Behavioral Sciences

CA	General Works	207
CB	Education	213
CC	Sociology	228
CD	Psychology and Psychiatry	259
CE	Anthropology and Ethnology	264
CF	Mythology, Folklore, and Popular Culture	267
CG	Statistics and Demography	271
CH	Economics	278
CJ	Political Science	316
CK	Law	349
CL	Geography	360

D

History and Area Studies

DA	General History	368
DB	The Americas	377
DC	Europe	394
DD	Africa	417
DE	Asia	423
DF	Australia and New Zealand	435
DG	Oceania	436
DH	Arctic and Antarctic	438

E

Science, Technology, and Medicine

EA	General Works	440
EB	Astronomy	450
EC	Biological Sciences	452
ED	Chemistry	459
EE	Earth Sciences	463
EF	Mathematics	468
EG	Physics	471
EH	Agricultural Sciences	472
EJ	Engineering	476
EK	Medical and Health Sciences	486

Index   499

Abbreviations

Abbreviations used in the citations and annotations of this
Supplement *conform to those established for the tenth*
edition of the Guide to Reference Books, *pages xiii-xiv.*
Abbreviations listed here are those which have been added for this Supplement.

AMS : *American Mathematical Society*
BCE : *Before Common Era* (preferred to B.C.)
CAS : *Chemical Abstracts Service*
CD-ROM : *Compact disc—read-only memory*
CE : *Common Era* (preferred to A.D.)
CRC : *Chemical Rubber Company*
DNA : *Deoxyribonucleic acid*
enl. : *enlarged*
F (France) : *franc*
H.M.S.O. : *Her Majesty's Stationery Office*
IUPAC : *International Union of Pure and Applied Chemistry*
JANAF : *Joint Army-Navy-Air Force*
JPRS : *Joint Publications Research Service*
Kčs (Czech.) : *koruna*
L (Italy) : *lira*
NATO : *North Atlantic Treaty Organization*
NMR : *Nuclear magnetic resonance*

£ (Eng.) : *pound*
pbk. : *paperback*
R (India) : *rupee*
RISM : *Répertoire internationale des sources musicales*
rub (U.S.S.R.) : *ruble*
SI : *Système internationale des unités*
SIC : *Standard Industrial Classification*
t.p. : *title page*
U.K. : *United Kingdom*
U.N. : *United Nations*
U.S. : *United States*
U.S. Govt. Print. Off. : *United States Government Printing Office*
USP : *United States Pharmacopoeia*
WHO : *World Health Organization*
¥ (Japan) : *yen*
zł. (Poland) : *złoty*

Preface

This version of the *Guide to Reference Books*, like the supplements to earlier editions, bridges the period between the most recent full edition (the 10th, 1986) and the forthcoming edition (the 11th), in anticipation of which this *Supplement* has been prepared. Without attempting to account for titles that are cited in either the contents notes or the annotations for individual entries, this *Supplement* lists 4,668 titles. The period of publishing we have attempted to cover comprehensively begins with the cutoff date for the 10th edition, the end of December 1984, and ends with the final day of December 1990. Some works of merit omitted from the 10th edition but predating its cutoff date are included, as are some bearing a 1991 imprint date that have come to the attention of contributors; the *Guide* is an ongoing publication, and the dates of inclusion will of necessity be somewhat fuzzy at either end.

Although selective, this *Supplement*, like supplements to earlier editions, is more nearly a record of reference publishing over the stated period than is any full edition of the *Guide*. Many titles are so new there has been little opportunity to develop experience in their use, hence the *Guide*'s primary criterion of usefulness does not apply uniformly; contributors have instead been asked to apply their best professional judgment in assessing whether such sources are likely to be of continuing usefulness. As with previous supplements, a good

share of the titles here will be dropped from the next full edition.

Selection

In selecting titles for inclusion in the *Supplement*, contributors were asked to survey the record of publishing for the period that was to be covered, choosing reference sources that had been found, or were likely to prove, useful in reference work. Contributors were to think of themselves as working at the general reference desk of the central library of an academic research institution, a library that covers all academic disciplines and supports an undergraduate curriculum, graduate study, faculty research, and inquiry by educated adults from the general populace. The emphasis therefore continues to lie on reference works for scholarly research, but representative works intended for general readers are included as well. Works primarily or exclusively of interest for the training of candidates for professional work (in law, medicine, the clergy, etc.) are excluded, as are works aimed at the specialized clientele of such institutions as pharmaceutical houses, investment banking firms, hospitals, architectural offices, or aircraft manufacturing plants. No restrictions as to languages have been observed, but for a work intended for use in North America, it is to be expected that English-language sources will predominate. Contributors have also kept in mind the various purposes the *Guide* has traditionally attempted to serve: to assist in developing reference collections, to refresh the memories of working reference librarians, to describe a working reference collection for research purposes, to assist smaller collections in identifying potential sources for verification and interlibrary loan, and to provide a bibliography of reference sources for users who are not librarians. In all this, contributors have been guided by earlier editions of the *Guide*, whose examples set standards for selection, judgment, accuracy, thoroughness, and concision we have tried to follow.

Production

This *Supplement* differs from previous versions in several respects. To begin with, it has been prepared from a database that maintains records in machine-readable form. The 10th edition, published in 1986, was typeset by computer, but the tape used to drive the photocomposition device was created from paper copy, so that the entire text had to be keyboarded. The work of compilation took place entirely outside the computer environment.

With this *Supplement*, further steps have been taken to computerize production. An interactive database of *Guide* records is being maintained by a service bureau, Inforonics, Inc., of Littleton, Massachusetts, where a full database of MARC records is kept and new and revised records loaded weekly from MARC tapes. Records for the *Supplement* have been matched against this MARC file and copied to a separate *Supplement* database. The records are then edited to provide records from which the printed version can be derived. If no match is found, Inforonics staff search other databases to locate records, or records can be keyboarded directly to MARC workforms by *Guide* staff. To print pages, Inforonics uses a software application called INFOCAT that manages the file of records, extracts files in *Guide* order and format, and prints pages.

The decision to compile the *Supplement* from machine-readable records was made in response to urgent requests from the compilers of the 10th edition, who hoped that enlisting the aid of computers would lessen the pain of compilation. To what extent that benefit has been realized is not clear at this writing, but the production of this book from a computer-controlled database provides an object lesson in both the power and the limitations of computers. Records can be copied readily to the *Guide* files, saving many keystrokes; but numerous changes and additions need to be made in every record in order to have bibliographic descriptions that were designed for online or card catalog lookup serve as the basis for a printed bibliography. The index can be compiled readily from MARC-formatted records, avoiding the grim task of creating the index after the file has been closed; but the fields to be indexed must be selected with exquisite care, and supplementary fields must be added to almost every record. The headings that print above sections and subsections can be changed readily, enabling records to be sent to other locations and the text of the headings themselves altered with ease; but all headings must first be loaded into a computer file together with instructions for sorting them into the order prescribed for the *Guide*. Perhaps most significant, computerization may make production of printed pages simpler; but the intellectual work of compilation has still had to be carried out on paper. The contributors had hoped that with the existence of machine-readable records they would have access to the files and could add annotations or make corrections online. At the present stage of development, with the computing and communication resources available, this has simply not as yet been possible.

Entries

One result of this method of production has been that most records for the *Supplement* adhere closely to the MARC format, and since they are derived from Library of Congress records, follow the AACR2 cataloging code as interpreted by LC. This has dictated some changes from previous *Guide* practice. Titles are used more frequently as main entries, for example, and corporate entries are entered under name rather than place (e.g., "University of Chicago. Oriental Institute" replaces the earlier entry "Chicago. University. Oriental Institute"). In the case of works with multiple authors, only the first is shown as main entry, the others appearing in the responsibility statement. As a glance at the following pages will show, some conventions of the International Standard Bibliographic Description have been adopted (e.g., a colon following place of publication, a virgule separating title and responsibility statement).

Some records, however, depart from LC practice, and some have been created strictly for the *Supplement* and have no counterpart in cataloging found elsewhere. In some cases, titles that are cataloged by LC as serials are here treated as monographs, and vice versa. The definition of serial is still open to interpretation by individual catalogers; some titles seem to have been cataloged as serials principally to avoid having to deal with them again. The needs of a printed bibliography and the nature of the contributor's annotation have determined changes in LC practice with regard to serials vs. monographs. Other entries have been created for convenience, usually in those cases when a publisher issues a number of titles in a series, but LC has chosen to catalog each as a discrete title. The *Dictionary of American literary biography* is a case in point; this series now occupies more than 100 volumes, each cataloged separately by LC. For the *Supplement*, an entry is given for the series and individual volumes are shown in a contents note. Although this manufactures a record for which no basis can be found in AACR2 or MARC, since it rests on a series name assigned by the publisher, the record makes better sense in a printed bibliography than would the inclusion of several dozen discrete entries. Another departure from MARC practice is the entry format for databases, about which there is more below.

Databases

Reference works in electronic form (online and CD-ROM databases) occupy a more prominent place here than in prior versions of the *Guide*. The first *Supplement* to the 9th edition listed databases in a separate section, the second *Supplement* listed only database directories, and the 10th edition used a bullet (•) at the end of an entry to indicate the existence of an electronic version of the cited title. In the few years since publication of the 10th edition (1986), reference sources in electronic form have assumed a far more prominent place than they held before. In particular, the advent of CD-ROM has made machine-assisted searching both more accessible and more attractive. The reference department that lacks at least one or two searching stations is now rare, and readers have come virtually overnight to expect that searching electronic sources will be a service their library routinely provides. Reference work without daily access to computer-based sources has become difficult to imagine. Many libraries have converted card catalogs to some version of an online public access catalog, querying bibliographic utilities (OCLC, RLIN, WLN) is routine in day-to-day reference work, and many reference departments search online databases frequently (some have staff members for whom database searching is a primary assignment).

It therefore made sense to the contributors to this *Supplement* to include electronic sources (applying the same criteria that are used in choosing printed sources), to class them by subject with printed materials, and to give each one a full entry of its own. The device of the bullet has been continued, but it precedes the entry rather than following it. Contributors have made an effort to include databases if the 10th edition listed their printed counterparts, and have selected those databases that are important for reference work in research libraries.

Entries for databases depart from MARC practice. Some of the fields present in the MARC database format are of little use for *Guide* purposes (system requirements, for example, which are subject to change) and are treated in considerable detail in the various directories of databases (listed here in section AB). The directories themselves, which have the virtue of being compiled by specialists in the medium, tend toward uniformity in the kinds of information they provide, but their formats vary widely. The information provided by database producers concerning their products has no uniformity, and a single source may provide conflicting information: it is not unusual to encounter CD-ROM databases that show one title on the entry screen, another on the face of the disc itself, a third on the accompanying software, a fourth on the printed user's manual, etc. Confronted by this state of confusion, it seemed best to make database entries as simple as possible. Accordingly, we show here the title of the resource, the standard phrase "[computer file]," the place of production, the name of the producer (not the vendor), and the dates of coverage of the file (if that information can be determined). The notes and annotation treat such matters as file size, updating schedule, format, and vendors. Other information can best be obtained from the database directories.

Index

The index continues to list authors, titles, and subjects in a single alphabet. To distinguish types of entries, however, entries for authors are printed in roman type, titles in italic, and subjects in boldface. The index also has entries for authors and titles that are mentioned in the notes or annotations associated with full entries.

Contributors

This *Supplement* has been compiled by a new group of contributors, only two of whom—Eileen McIlvaine of Columbia and Robert Michaelson of Northwestern—were among the contributors for previous versions of the *Guide*; all the other contributors, including the General Editor, are new with this issue. In addition, the general editorship has passed from the Columbia University Library to the publisher of the *Guide*, the American Library Association.

The specter of computerized processing bears some of the responsibility for these changes. Despite the desire by both the prospective contributors to the forthcoming edition and the publisher to establish a machine-readable file, the prospect of learning and maintaining a computer-based database caused hesitation. At that time, *Choice* magazine (also published by the American Library Association) which had been working with the system that would be used to maintain the *Guide* database and produce its printed pages, and had already acquired the necessary equipment, suggested that *Choice* produce the next version and establish the machine-readable database. This suggestion was embraced by both Columbia and ALA. Before work could begin, however, ALA determined that in the interest of continuity, general editorship of the *Guide* should rest with staff at ALA itself. Since *Choice* already had experience in publishing and had acquired expertise in managing its own machine-readable database, and since I had edited the Reference column for two years and had long experience as a reference librarian, I was chosen General Editor.

This broke two longstanding *Guide* traditions. First, since the second edition of the *Guide*, its General Editor has been the Head of Reference at the Columbia University Library, a distinguished line that includes Isadore Gilbert Mudge, Constance Winchell, and Eugene Sheehy. Second, the *Guide* grew out of the collective experience of the staff of that reference department, both the collections with which they worked and were instrumental in building, and their exposure to queries from the wide range of readers that use a large academic library in one of the nation's most intellectually active cities. In great part, the high reputation the *Guide* has enjoyed rests on its having been compiled by working reference librarians who plied their craft in a large and distinguished collection. The *Guide* represented the considered judgment of working professionals concerning the corpus of reference works available at the time.

In a sense, the present version continues the latter tradition, since all its sections have been compiled by working reference librarians, but the strong Columbia flavor of past editions has faded somewhat. To be sure, a large part of this *Supplement* has been compiled at Columbia, but some forty-five contributors from seven institutions have labored to bring it forth. It may be pointed out that this continues a trend that began with the first *Supplement* to the 9th edition and continued through the 10th edition, in which the Science and Technology sections were prepared by staff of the Kline Science Library at Yale. It seems fair to observe that, in light of the volume of reference publishing and the increasing pressure of reference work, it may be permanently beyond the capabilities of any single reference department to assume full responsibility for compilation of the *Guide*.

So far as the general editorship is concerned, my own role differs from that of my predecessors. I do not conduct business in a research library, but in the office of a publishing firm. As those familiar with editorial offices might expect, my work has been carried out without daily access to a reference collection. Although 17 years as Head of Reference at the Yale University Library acquainted me thoroughly with reference work, I have not had opportunity to work directly under the supervision of a previous editor of the *Guide*—I had no period of apprenticeship. By force of circumstance, therefore, my role has had to be different from that of at least the most recent editor. I have not personally compiled any section of this *Supplement*, but have relied on the judgment of the contributors, and on their access to collections in their own and neighboring libraries. Many of the titles listed here are works that I have not seen; but as in the past, all have been examined by the contributors to the various sections. My role has been that of editor and coordinator rather than contributor, and my energies have been directed toward production of the printed book.

I cannot leave discussion of this point without expressing my profound gratitude to the previous General Editor, Eugene Sheehy. Although he imagined that the torch had been passed, Mr. Sheehy willingly offered advice on many points respecting the compilation and editorship of the *Guide*, attended several editorial meetings (where his comments drew the breathless attention that reveals deep respect), read and commented on a large share of the entries submitted by contributors and on sets of printed pages, and was available on many occasions to answer specific questions concerning practices he had employed in previous versions. His advice and written comments in great measure compensated for my own inexperience and provided a measure of the apprenticeship I had missed.

Acknowledgments

Little remains except to acknowledge my sincere gratitude and appreciation to the contributors of the various sections of this *Supplement,* who are named on the page facing the title page. When we began, few of them imagined the amount of work that would be required to compile even a single section: keeping current with reference publications acquired by their own libraries; visiting other libraries to examine sources not held locally; writing annotations whose aim was to present the intention, arrangement, special features, and usefulness of each work in as few words as possible; making the sheer physical effort to locate and examine a large number of titles; and deciding, often with great difficulty, which titles to include—all balanced against the demands of their regular work. Each of them has managed this impossible task with skill and aplomb.

I extend a special word of appreciation to the Project Director, Patricia Sabosik, who was a ready source of advice and who removed from me the necessity to worry about budgetary matters; to Paul Stuehrenberg of the Yale Divinity Library, who advised concerning cataloging, especially early in the project when mere reference librarians were struggling to penetrate the mysteries of AACR2 and MARC; and to Terry Plum of the University of Connecticut, who advised as to databases, both titles to include and key pieces of information to be included in bibliographic records. Personnel at Publishing Services of ALA have been most helpful, especially Edgar S. McLarin, ALA's Publishing Director, and David Epstein.

Several members of the staff of Inforonics, Inc., to whom this project was unplowed ground, have been from the beginning both of great assistance and a source of fruitful suggestions; I mention especially John Finni, Jonathan Bourne, Candy Verhulst, Merle Downing, Steve Prowten, and Cora Arsenault, and the firm's president, Lawrence Buckland. Without dedicated work by all of them, this *Supplement* would not have seen the light of day.

I would be remiss if I did not also extend my own sincere gratitude and that of the contributors to the administrations of the various libraries with which the contributors are associated. Without the firm and continuing support of their libraries, the contributors could not have completed their work on a project that constantly threatened to invade or overwhelm the normal work of the library. The libraries with which contributors and advisors were associated are:

Brigham Young University : *Lee Library*
The College of Wooster : *Andrews Library*
Columbia University : *Avery Architectural and Fine Arts Library; Butler library; Music Library; School of Library Service Library*
Family History Library of the Church of Jesus Christ of Latter-Day Saints
Northwestern University : *Mudd Library*
The Ohio State University : *University Library*
Syracuse University : *Bird Library; Carnegie Library*
University of Chicago : *Crerar Library*
University of Connecticut : *Babbidge Library*
University of Illinois at Champaign-Urbana : *Applied Life Studies Library*
University of North Carolina at Chapel Hill : *Davis Library*
Yale University : *Law Library; Divinity Library*

We also offer a special note of thanks to the interlibrary loan departments of libraries who have been extraordinarily generous in sending works not locally available so they might be examined in preparing entries for the *Supplement*.

Throughout the project, *Choice* magazine has provided a home for the *Supplement*, making its facilities, equipment, and staff available for our many unanticipated requirements. Especially helpful have been *Choice* editors Virginia Clark, Judith Douville, Claire Dudley, and Helen MacLam, who at the last minute suggested additional entries for three sections of the *Supplement* and stood ready to write annotations had the need arisen.

Finally, my own profound gratitude and affection go out to the selfless and dedicated staff of the *Guide* at the *Choice* office. Without Vee Carrington, who had the cataloging experience I lacked and was a constant source of knowledge, counsel, and gentle correction, and Lana Latrell, who carries the craft of data entry to new heights, this *Supplement* could not only have not been completed, it could not have been begun. I speak for all the contributors in extending Vee and Lana the most heartfelt admiration and appreciation.

ROBERT BALAY

Middletown, Conn.
October 1991

A

General Reference Works

AA

Bibliography

GENERAL WORKS

Guides and manuals

Malclès, Louise-Noëlle. Manuel de bibliographie. 4e éd. rev. et augm. / par Andrée Lhéritier. Paris : Presses universitaires de France, 1985. 448 p.   **AA1**

    3rd ed., 1976 (*Guide* AA7).

    Adheres to the format of the earlier edition, with the addition of information on the new information technologies.

               Z1002.M28

Totok, Wilhelm. Handbuch der bibliographischen Nachschlagewerke / [Wilhelm] Totok, [Rolf] Weitzel ; hrsg. von Hans-Jürgen und Dagmar Kernchen. 6., erw., völlig neu bearb. Aufl. Frankfurt am Main : V. Klostermann, 1985. v. 2. ISBN 3-465-01594-0 (Bd. 2 : Deut. Bibl.).

                            AA2

    For v. 1 and annotation, see *Guide* AA14.

    Contents: v. 2, Fachbibliographien und fachbezogene Nachschlagewerke. Completes the set.

    Vol. 2 has its own author, title, and subject index.

               Z1002.T68

Bibliography of bibliography

Bibliographische Berichte. Jahrg. 1, Heft 1 (1959)–Bd. 30 (1988). Frankfurt am Main : Klostermann, 1959–1988. Annual. ISSN 0006-1506.   **AA3**

    For earlier vols. and annotation, see *Guide* AA19.

    Vol. 30 (1988) is a cumulative subject index to v. 11–29 (1969–87).

Internationale Personalbibliographie, 1944–1975 / begr. von Max Arnim ; fortgef. von Franz Hodes. 2., überarb. u. bis zum Berichtsjahr 1975 fortgef. Aufl. von Bd. 3 (1944–1959) mit Nachtr. zur 2. Aufl. von Bd. 1/2 (1800–1943). Stuttgart : Hiersemann, 1987. Lfg. 19–24. ISBN 3-7772-8138-7 (Lfg 9). (In progress).   **AA4**

    For earlier vols. and annotation, see *Guide* AA27.

    Contents: Lfg. 19–24, S–Z (completes v. 5).

    The index mentioned in *Guide* AA27 has yet to appear.

               Z8001.A1I57

India

Kochukoshy, K. K. A bibliography of Indian bibliographies, 1961–1980. [Calcutta], India : Central Reference Library, Govt. of India, Dept. of Culture, 1985. 146 p. **AA5**

A listing by broad Dewey Decimal classes of some 655 English-language bibliographies, with author/title and subject indexes. Based mainly on entries in the *Indian national bibliography* (*Guide* AA884), 1961–80.   Z3201.A1K63

Iran

Tasbī.hī, Gulām 'Husayn. Nigārishī jāmī bar jahān-i kitābshināsī-yi Īrān. Chāp-i 1. Tabrīz : Nīmā, 1986. 306 p.   **AA6**

Title on added title page: *A comprehensive survey of Persian bibliographies in the world.*

A listing of bibliographies on all subjects published in Persian or about Iran appearing as books or journal articles. Arranged by subject; lacks an index.

Italy

Bosco, Giovanna. Bibliografia di bibliografie, edizioni italiane del XVI secolo / a dura di Giovanna Bosco e Alessandra Pesante. Pisa : Scuola Normale Superiore, 1988. 105 p. : ill. (Mnemosyne: Ricerche sull'arte della memoria, 1.).   **AA7**

A annotated listing by broad subject of 177 bibliographies of early Italian books. Author index.   Z155.3.B5

Latin America

A bibliography of Latin American bibliographies, 1980–1984 : social sciences and humanities / Lionel V. Loroña, ed. Metuchen, N.J. : Scarecrow, 1987. 223 p. ISBN 0-8108-1941-4. $25.00.   **AA8**

"Supplement No. 4 to Arthur E. Gropp's *A bibliography of Latin American bibliographies (Guide* AA77)."—*t.p.*

Consolidates the entries in *Annual report on bibliographic activities* of the Seminar on the Acquisition of Latin American Library Materials for 1980–82, and its successor which appears in the *SALALM bibliography and reference series* for 1983–85. Adheres to the format of the earlier volumes.   Z1601.A2G76

UNIVERSAL

Bibliography

Checklist of bibliographies appearing in the *Bulletin of bibliography* 1897–1987 / ed. by Naomi Caldwell-Wood and Patrick W. Wood. Westport, Conn. : Meckler, c1989. 144 p. ISBN 0-88736-237-0. $75.00.   **AA9**

" . . . covers articles, bibliographies, and selected book reviews as well as editorials of historical or continuing interest."—*Pref.* Supersedes the earlier index (*Guide* AA112 note).   Z1007.B94C45

Library catalogs

National libraries

Biblioteca Nacional (Spain). Catálogo general de libros impresos, hasta 1981 [microform]. [Paris ; Alexandria, Va.] : Chadwyck-Healey, c1989. 4,408 microfiches. ISBN 2-86976-022-1.   **AA10**
Z945.B53

——— Catálogo general de libros impresos, 1982–1987 [microform]. [Paris ; Alexandria, Va.] : Chadwyck-Healey, c1989. [579] microfiches. ISBN 2-86976-023-X.   **AA11**

These two sets list the nearly 2 million printed books in the Biblioteca Nacional. Arranged alphabetically by author, corporate author (since 1964 with place name first), or title, if anonymous. A 56-page *Catalogo de autores y orbra anonimas de la Biblioteca Nacional de Madrid: gúia de consulta* was published in 1990 by Chadwyck-Healey.   Z945.B53

Bibliothèque Nationale (France). Catalogue général des livres imprimés, 1897–1959 : supplément sur fiches [microform]. Paris : Chadwyck-Healey France, 1986. 2890 microfiches.   **AA12**

Supplements the Bibliothèque Nationale's *Catalogue général des livres imprimés : Auteurs (Guide* AA140).

Lists works added to the Bibliothèque Nationale through 1959; as in the printed catalog, only works under names of personal authors are included. Thus the catalog (which, before v. 189, listed works acquired at the time the individual volumes were published) now has uniform coverage.   Z927.P2

——— Catalogue général des livres imprimés. Auteurs, collectivités-auteurs, anonymes, 1970–1979. Série en caractères non latins / Bibliothèque nationale. Paris : La Bibliothèque, 1983–1985. v. 1, pts. 1–3; v. 2–4; v. 5, pts. 1–2; v. 6–8; v. 9, pts. 1–3; v. 10. ISBN 2-7177-1670-X (set). (In progress).   **AA13**

Continues *Catalogue général des livres imprimés : auteurs—collectivités-auteurs, anonymes, 1960–1969 (Guide* AA141).

Contents: t. 1, Caractères cyrilliques: russe (3 v.); t. 2. Caractères cyrilliques: biélorusse, moldave, ukrainien, macédonien; t. 3, Caractères cyrilliques: bulgare; t. 4, Caractères grecs; t. 5, Caractères hébraïques (2 v.); t. 6, Thaï; t. 7, Coréen; t. 8, Japonais; t. 9. Arabe (3 v.); t. 10, Persan.

Z798.P22F7

——— Anonymes 1501–1800 : état au 31 décembre 1986 [microform]. Paris : BN, Livres imprimés, 1986. 9 microfiches : negative.   **AA14**

Supplements the Bibliothèque Nationale's *Catalogue général des livres imprimés: Auteurs (Guide* AA140).

User's guide has title: *Catalogue général des livres imprimés de la Bibliothèque nationale. Anonymes XVIe–XVIIIe siécles.* "Errata de l'index des auteurs": p. [10]–[12] of user's guide.

"Erratum de l'index des lieux d'édition et de la liste des imprimeurs": p. [12] of user's guide.

A listing, arranged alphabetically by title, of some 175,000 anonymous printed books issued from 1501 to 1800 held by the Bibliothèque Nationale as of December 1986. It includes works published without a name on the title page; works issued under a pseudonym which is not a personal name, or under initials, or an occupation; and works by more than five authors. Excludes corporate publications, and anonymous works (e.g., legal documents, liturgical books) listed in special catalogs of the Bibliothèque Nationale.

Bernard, Annick. Guide de l'utilisateur des catalogues des livres imprimés de la Bibliothèque Nationale. Paris : Chadwyck-Healey France ; Alexandria, Va. : Distr. by Chadwyck-Healey, 1986. 60 p. ISBN 2-86976-004-3.
AA15

Offers a useful description of the history and arrangement of the printed and microfiche catalogs of the Bibliothèque Nationale (*Guide* AA140). Z927.P3

British Library. The British Library general catalogue of printed books to 1975. London : C. Bingley ; London ; N.Y. : K.G. Saur, 1985–1987. v. 293–360. ISBN 0-85157-520-X (set). £11,800.00. **AA16**

For earlier vols. and annotation, see *Guide* AA134.

Contents: v. 293–360, Schle–Z. Completes the set.

Two unnumbered indexes to the entries under England (v. 95–100) were published in 1982: an index to the subheadings used, and a title index. This edition is also available in CD-ROM.

Supplemented by: Z921.L553B74

——————— The British Library general catalogue of printed books to 1975 : Supplement. London ; N.Y. : K.G. Saur, 1987–1988. 6 v. ISBN 0-8629-1275-X (set).
AA17

Lists some 85,000 entries "for books published before 1971 which were cataloged by the British Library too late for inclusion in the BLC, or are reprints of entries considerably revised from the form in which they appear there."—*Introd.* "Some *see* references which appear in the Supplement refer to authors and titles in the General Catalog."—*Note to users.* Items in the supplement are not included in the CD-ROM version of the catalog.

Continued by: Z921.L553B74

——————— The British Library general catalogue of printed books, 1976 to 1982. London ; N.Y. : K.G. Saur, 1983. 50 v. ISBN 0-86291-485-X (set). **AA18**
Z921.L553B74

——————— The British Library general catalogue of printed books, 1982 to 1985. London ; N.Y. : Saur, 1986. 26 v. ISBN 0-86291-540-6 (set). **AA19**
Z921.L553B74

——————— The British Library general catalogue of printed books, 1986 to 1987. London ; N.Y. : K.G. Saur, 1988. 22 v. ISBN 0-86291-730-1 (set). **AA20**
Z921.L553B74

——————— The British Library general catalogue of printed books 1988 to 1989. London : Saur, 1990. 28 v. ISBN 3-598-33050-2. £2,800. **AA21**

Although not stated, numerals and diacritics (including some obvious mistakes) are filed before the letter A in the supplements issued for 1976 on. The individual supplements and a 1976–85 cumulation are also available in microfiche. Z921.B

——————— Subject index of modern books acquired, 1971–1975. London : The Library, 1986. 14 v. (8366 p.). ISBN 0-7123-0090-2 (set). **AA22**
Z921.L553B74

——————— The British Library general subject catalogue, 1975 to 1985. London ; N.Y. : K.G. Saur, 1986. 75 v. ISBN 0-86291-650-X. **AA23**

These volumes continue the *Subject index of modern books ...* (*Guide* AA135 and AA136). The 1975–85 cumulation is also available on microfiche. Z921.L553B74

National union catalog. Books [microform]. Jan. 1983– . Wash. : Library of Congress, 1983– . Monthly. ISSN 0734-7650. **AA24**

For complete annotation, see *Guide* AA127.

Superintendent of Documents classification: LC 30.26.

According to the *Library of Congress information bulletin* (18 June 1990, 227), as of 1990, *NUC* will no longer list books from OCLC, the Research Libraries Information Network (RLIN), or the Western Library Network (WLN). The article states that *NUC* "will continue to include Library of Congress cataloging, reports from U.S. libraries that create records on local systems, reports from Canadian libraries, reports of microform masters and reports from other libraries that do not add their cataloging to the three bibliographic utilities."

The Near East national union list / comp. by Dorothy Stehle under the direction of George N. Atiyeh. Wash. : Library of Congress, 1988. v. 1. ISBN 0-8444-0583-3 (v.1). $47.00. (In progress). **AA25**

Contents: v. 1, A.

Superintendent of Documents classification: LC 1.2:N27.

" ... a guide to [pre-1979] publications in Near Eastern languages that have been reported to the National Union Catalog by some 240 libraries in the United States and Canada."— *Pref.* (Beginning with 1979 these titles are listed in the *National union catalog.*) Arranged alphabetically by author or title, if anonymous. All forms of the authors' names are listed at the end of v.1, with cross-references to the main alphabetical section. Title index. Z3015.N4

Nonnational libraries

Bayerische Staatsbibliothek. Alphabetischer Katalog 1501–1840 : BSB-AK 1501–1840. Voraus-Ausg. München ; N.Y. : K.G. Saur, 1987–1990. v. 1–60. ISBN 3-598-30800-0. (In progress). **AA26**

Title on added t.p.: Alphabetical catalogue 1501–1840.

Cover title: BSB-AK 1501–1840.

"Preliminary edition."—English *t.p.*

Contents: v. 1–60, A–Z (completes the preliminary ed.).

Introductory material in English and German.

An author and title listing of some 662,000 items held by the Bavarian State Library, excluding incunabula and journals. "The preliminary edition will contain about 80 percent of all titles edited and recorded during the first work phase. The bulk of the dissertations ... will only be included in the final edition."—*p.v.* Z929.M98B38

United States

New York Public Library. Research Libraries. Dictionary catalog of the Research Libraries : a cumulative list of authors, titles, and subjects representing books and book-like materials added to the collections since January 1, 1971. [N.Y.] : New York Public Library, [1972]. 741 p. **AA27**

For annotation, see *Guide* AA147.

A cumulation for 1972–80 was published in 1980 in 64 v. and a second cumulation covering 1981–88 in 1988 in 73 v. Z881.N59

Festschriften

Leistner, Otto. Internationale Bibliographie der Festschriften von den Anfängen bis 1979 : mit Sachregister = International bibliography of Festschriften from the beginnings until 1979 : with subject-index. 2. erw. Aufl. Osnabrück : Biblio Verlag, 1986. v. 2. ISBN 3-7648-1275-3 (set). **AA28**

> For v. 1 and annotation, see *Guide* AA153.
> Contents: v. 2, L–Z. Completes the set. Z1033.F4L43

Microforms and reproductions

Bibliographic guide to microform publications. 1986– . Boston : G.K. Hall, c1987– . Annual. ISSN 0891-3749. $215.00. **AA29**

> Brings together catalog records for microform publications in the New York Public Library and the Library of Congress, including books, government publications, and pamphlets. Lists microforms made in-house as well as commercial publications. Dictionary arrangement of author, title, and subject entries. Z1033.M5B525

Translations

Canadian translations = Traductions canadiennes. Ottawa : National Library of Canada = Bibliothèque nationale du Canada, 1987– . Annual. ISSN 0835-2291. **AA30**

> Introductory and explanatory matter in English and French.
>
> A record of translations published in Canada and cataloged by the National Library of Canada during the year of coverage. Arranged by broad Universal Decimal Classification, with author/title index incorporating cross-references and added entries. Includes translations in any language, although the great bulk of entries is in French or English. Z1369.C28

Anonyms and pseudonyms

International

Marshall, Alice Kahler. Pen names of women writers : from 1600 to the present. Camp Hill, Penn. : Copies from Alice Marshall Collection, 1985. 181 p. : ill. **AA31**

> Subtitle: A compendium of the literary identities of 2,650 women novelists, playwrights, poets, diarists, journalists and miscellaneous writers, fully cross-referenced.
>
> Includes a bibliography of sources. Z1041.M34

Pseudonyms and nicknames dictionary / Jennifer Mossman, ed. 3rd ed. Detroit : Gale, c1987. 2 v. (2207 p.). ISBN 0-8103-0541-0 (set). $225.00. **AA32**

> 2nd ed., 1982 (*Guide* AA172).
> Subtitle: A guide to aliases, appellations, assumed names, code names, cognomens, cover names, epithets, initialisms, nicknames, noms de guerre, noms de plume, pen names, pseudonyms, sobriquets, and stage names of contemporary and historical persons, including the subjects' real names, basic biographical information, and citations for the sources from which the entries were compiled. Covers actors, aristocrats, artists, athletes, authors, clergymen, criminals, entertainers, film stars, journalists, military leaders, monarchs, musicians, playwrights, poets, politicans, popes, rogues, saints, theatrical figures, and

other prominent personalities of all nations throughout the ages.

> Adheres to the format of the previous edition; includes some 135,000 entries. Supplemented by *New pseudonyms and nicknames* (*Guide* AA173). CT120.P8

United States and Great Britain

Atkinson, Frank. Dictionary of literary pseudonyms : a selection of popular modern writers in English. 4th enl. ed. London : Lib. Assoc. Pub. ; Chicago : Amer. Lib. Assoc., 1987. 299 p. ISBN 0-85157-401-7. **AA33**

> 3rd ed., 1982 (*Guide* AA174).
> Retains the format of the earlier edition but adds more than 2,000 names. Z1065.A83

Bulgaria

Bogdanov, Ivan. Rechnik na bŭlgarskite psevdonimi : pisateli, nauchni rabotnitsi, prevodachi, karikaturisti, publitsisti, zhurnalisti—. 3., osnovno prer. i dop. izd. Sofiĭa : "D-r Petŭr Beron", 1989. 528 p. **AA34**

> 1st ed., 1961; 2nd ed., 1978.
> In three sections: (1) a listing of pseudonyms, (2) a listing of initials and abbreviations, and (3) a listing of nonalphabetical symbols used to sign works. Each entry provides the real name, when and where the pseudonym was used, and the source of the information; sections are divided into Cyrillic and Roman alphabets. Indexed by real name. Z1080.B8B6

Mexico

Ruiz Castañeda, María del Carmen. Catálogo de seudónimos, anagramas, iniciales y otros alias usados por escritores mexicanos y extranjeros que han publicado en México / María del Carmen Ruiz Castañeda ; Sergio Márquez Acevedo, coautor. México, D.F. : Universidad Nacional Autónoma de México, Instituto de Investigaciones Bibliográficas, 1985. lxxi, 290 p. (Instrumenta bibliographica, 6). ISBN 968-837-507-1. **AA35**

> A single alphabetical list of authors (with dates and pseudonyms) and cross-references from pseudonyms to real names. Addenda and bibliography of works consulted. Z1049.M6R84

ANCIENT, MEDIEVAL AND RENAISSANCE MANUSCRIPTS

Catalogs

Bibliography

British Library. Dept. of Manuscripts. Index of manuscripts in the British Library. Cambridge, England ; Teaneck, N.J. : Chadwyck-Healey, 1985–1986. v. 5–10. ISBN 0-85964-140-6. **AA36**

> For v. 1–4 and annotation, see *Guide* AA239.
> Contents: v. 5–10, Grenville–Z. Completes the set. Z921.L553B74x

Kristeller, Paul Oskar. Iter Italicum : a finding list of uncatalogued or incompletely catalogued humanistic manuscripts of the Renaissance in Italian and other libraries.

London : Warburg Institute, 1989–90. v. 4–5. ISBN 90-04-06925-9 (Netherlands : Brill ; v. 3). (In progress). **AA37**

For v. 1–3 and annotation, see *Guide* AA240.

Vol. 4– published: London : Warburg Institute ; Leiden : E.J. Brill.

Contents: v. 4, Great Britain to Spain; v. 5, Sweden to Yugoslavia, Utopia, Supplement to Italy (A–F).

The section entitled "Utopia" "lists pertinent manuscripts owned by private collectors or antiquarian book dealers . . . [who] did not authorize me to disclose their name or address."—*Pref.* Z6611.H8K7

Union lists

Jeudy, Colette. Les manuscrits classiques latins des bibliothèques publiques de France / catalogue établi par Colette Jeudy et Yves-François Riou. Paris : Editions du Centre national de la recherche scientifique, 1989. v. 1 : ill. ISBN 2-222-04089-2 (v. 1). 990F. (In progress). **AA38**

Contents: v. 1, Agen–Évreux.

Offers detailed physical descriptions and provenance of manuscripts of classical texts from the 8th to the 15th century. Arranged by city; excludes collections in private and academic libraries. Each entry has a bibliography of secondary literature. Many indexes, including authors and texts, scribes and illuminators, incipits, etc. Z6605.L3J48

Diplomatics, handwriting, and scripts

Brown, Michelle P. A guide to western historical scripts from antiquity to 1600. London : British Library, 1990. [144] p. : ill. ISBN 0-7123-0177-1. £17.95. **AA39**

Aims "to provide an aid for a wide variety of readers who wish to trace the evolution of scripts in the West from the world of Antiquity to the early modern period."—*Introd.* Indexed.

EARLY AND RARE BOOKS

Incunabula and early printed books

Union lists

Biblioteca Nacional (Spain). Catalogo general de Incunables en bibliotecas españolas / Biblioteca Nacional ; coordinado y dirigido por Francisco García Craviotto. Madrid : Ministerio de Cultura, Dirección General del Libro y Bibliotecas, 1989. v. 1. ISBN 84-7483-461-9 (set). (In progress). **AA40**

Contents: v. 1, A–M.

A listing, arranged alphabetically by author, of incunabula published throughout Europe held in Spanish libraries. Locates copies and provides citations to the standard bibliographies of incunabula. Z240.B6154

Gesamtkatalog der Wiegendrucke / Hrsg. von der Kommission für den Gesamtkatalog der Wiegendrucke. 2. Aufl. Stuttgart : A. Hiersemann ; N.Y. : H.P. Kraus, 1985–91. Bd. 9²⁻⁵. (In progress). **AA41**

For earlier vols. and annotation, see *Guide* AA280.

Contents: Bd. 9²⁻⁵, Friedrich–Grassus. Completes the vol. Z240.A1G47

Indice generale degli incunaboli delle biblioteche d'Italia / a cura del Centro nazionale d'informazioni bibliografiche. Roma : Istituto poligrafico dello Stato, 1981. v. 6 : facsims. (Indici e cataloghi. Nuova serie, 1, etc.). **AA42**

For v. 1–5 and annotation, see *Guide* AA282.

Contents: v. 6, Aggiunte, correzioni, indici. Completes the set.

Includes a list of Hebraic incunabula, p.285–298, and a concordance to entries in Ludwig Hain's *Repertorium bibliographicum* (*Guide* AA269) and *Gesamtkatalog der Wiegendrucke* (above). Z240.I5

Offenberg, A. K. Hebrew incunabula in public collections : a first international census / comp. by A.K. Offenberg, in collaboration with C. Moed-Van Walraven. Nieuwkoop : De Graaf Publishers, 1990. lxxiv, 214 p. (Bibliotheca humanistica & reformatorica, v. 47). ISBN 90-6004-404-5. fl95.40. **AA43**

A descriptive bibliography arranged alphabetically by author, with locations and citations to other catalogs. Includes indexes of places and printers, of Hebrew titles, and of names. Z240.O35

Auction records

Blogie, Jeanne. Répertoire des catalogues de ventes de livres imprimés. Bruxelles : Fl. Tulkens, 1985–88. v. 2–3. (Collection du Centre national de l'archéologie et de l'histoire du livre, 4). (In progress). **AA44**

For v.1 and annotation, see *Guide* AA327.

Contents: v. 2, Catalogues français appartenant à la Bibliothèque Royale Albert Iᵉʳ; v. 3, Catalogues britanniques appartenant à la Bibliothèque Royale Albert Iᵉʳ. Z999.5.B55

PRINTING AND PUBLISHING

General works

Bibliography

Corsten, Severin. Der Buchdruck im 15. Jahrhundert : eine bibliographie / hrsg. von Severin Corsten und Reimar Walter Fuchs ; unter Mitarbeit von Kurt Hans Staub. Stuttgart : A. Hiersemann, 1988. v. 1. (Hiersemanns bibliographische Handbücher, Bd. 7). ISBN 3-7772-8813-6. (In progress). **AA45**

Contents: Teil 1, Bibliographie.

A useful classified bibliography covering such areas as the technical aspects of printing, works on individual authors, and publishing in different countries and cities. Includes books and articles written in the major European languages published from the 18th century to about 1982, the majority of citations being to 20th- century publications. Z127C826b

Encyclopedias

Lexikon des gesamten Buchwesens : LGB² / hrsg. von Severin Corsten, Günther Pflug und Friedrich Adolf Schmidt-Künsemüller, unter Mitwirkung von Bernhard Bischoff... [et al.]. Zweite, völlig neubearbeitete Auflage. Stuttgart : A. Hiersemann, 1985–1991. v. 1–3⁵ : ill. ISBN 3-7772-8527-7 (set). (In progress).   **AA46**
    1st ed., 1935–37 (*Guide* AA361).
    Contents: Bd. 1–2, A–Foster; Bd. 3¹⁻⁵, Foto–Hawaii.
    Greatly revised and expanded, although some entries have been dropped; many articles have illustrations.   Z1006.L464

Dictionaries

Feather, John. A dictionary of book history. N.Y. : Oxford Univ. Pr., 1986. 278 p. ISBN 0-19-520520-0. $39.95.   **AA47**
    Offers short articles, many with brief bibliographies, which explain the "technical language of bibliography... derived largely from that of the book trade, and especially of printing."—*Introd.*   Z1006.F38

Directories

Bibliography

Alternative publications : a guide to directories, indexes, bibliographies, and other sources / ed. by Cathy Seitz Whitaker. Jefferson, N.C. : McFarland, c1990. 90 p. ISBN 0-89950-484-1.   **AA48**
    Prepared by the American Library Association's Social Responsibilities Round Table Task Force on Alternatives in Print.
    Aims "to facilitate identifying and locating small press material."—*Introd.* Differs from the Task Force's earlier publication, *Alternatives in print* (1st–6th eds., 1971–80) "in that it does not list individual titles, but rather cites sources, many ongoing, which in turn list individual titles." A selective bibliography is followed by annotated lists of indexes and abstracts, review sources, subject and trade bibliographies, and alternative mail order outlets. Combined index of authors, titles, publishers, subjects, etc.   Z1033.L73A45

Handbooks

Bell, Herbert W. How to get your book published. Cincinnati, Ohio : Writer's Digest Books, c1985. 250 p. : forms. ISBN 0-89879-193-6. $15.95.   **AA49**
    Intended "to help authors through the complexities of book publishing: preparing acceptable projects, selecting the best publisher, negotiating favorable terms, and ensuring that their manuscripts are published in a satisfactory way."—*Pref.* Offers practical advice in brief chapters dealing with all stages of the work. Brief bibliography; appendix of sample publishing contracts; general index.   PN155.B45

History

American literary publishing houses, 1900–1980. Trade and paperback / ed. by Peter Dzwonkoski. Detroit : Gale, c1986. 465 p. : ill. (Dictionary of literary biography, v. 46). ISBN 0-8103-1724-9.   **AA50**
    Offers signed articles on the history and character of American publishers of literary works in book format. Most articles include references to sources of further information. Two further volumes are planned, one to cover 20th-century small and university publishers of literary works and literary reference works, the other to deal with publishing houses founded before 1900. For other volumes in the series, see *Guide* BD416 and *Supplement* BD52.   Z479.A45

Biography

Munter, Robert. A dictionary of the print trade in Ireland, 1550–1775. N.Y. : Fordham Univ. Pr., 1988. 340 p. ISBN 0-8232-1200-9.   **AA51**
    Intended to supplement existing biographical dictionaries by adding, correcting, and augmenting earlier entries (most of the new information coming from the Stationers' Guild in Dublin), and broadening the scope to include the print trade as well as the book trade. Bibliography, p.315–40.   Z152.6.M86

Renouard, Philippe. Imprimeurs & libraires parisiens du XVIe siècle / ouvrage publié d'après les manuscrits de Philippe Renouard. Paris : Service des travaux historiques de la ville de Paris, 1986. v. 4. : facsims. ISBN 2-85349-004-1 (set). (In progress).   **AA52**
    For earlier vols. and annotation, see *Guide* AA404.
    Contents: v. 4, Binet–Blumenstock.
    Two more unnumbered vols. have been published; "Fasc. Brumen" (1984) and "Fasc. Cavellat/Marnot & Cavellat" (1986).   Z305.R4

Copy preparation

Achtert, Walter S. The MLA style manual / by Walter S. Achtert and Joseph Gibaldi. N.Y. : Modern Language Association of America, 1985. 271 p. ISBN 0-87352-136-6. $17.50 (est.).   **AA53**
    A companion to the *MLA handbook* (*Supplement* AH1), which is intended for students, this guide "attempts to meet the scholar's need for comprehensive guide to publishing in the humanities."—*Pref.*   PN147.A28

Kline, Mary-Jo. A guide to documentary editing. Baltimore : Johns Hopkins Univ. Pr., c1987. 228 p. ISBN 0-8018-3341-8. $29.50.   **AA54**
    At head of title: Prepared for the Association for Documentary Editing.
    A unique and very useful work which provides chapters on the history, techniques, conventions, and applications of textual editing. Of interest to historians and others in nonliterary fields. Includes detailed instructions for preparing editions for printers and publishers, as well as sample form letters to libraries, collectors, and auction houses. General index.   Z113.3.K55

Lindsell, Sheryl L. Proofreading and editing for word processors. N.Y. : Arco, c1985. 120 p. : ill. ISBN 0-668-06088-3. $12.95. ISBN 0-668-06092-1 (pbk.). $6.95.   **AA55**
    Basically a textbook with rules and exercises developed for use in working with word processing software. In three sections: Techniques of proofreading; Mechanics of English;

Proofreading and editing drills and exercises. Not indexed.
Z52.4.L56

Luey, Beth. Handbook for academic authors. Rev. ed. Cambridge ; N.Y. : Cambridge Univ. Pr., 1990. 273 p. : ill. ISBN 0-521-39494-5. ISBN 0-521-39646-8 (pbk.).
AA56

Covers a wide range of publishing practices, with chapters devoted to journal articles, revising a dissertation for publication, finding a publisher for scholarly books and college textbooks, as well as the mechanics of authorship and special problems relating to multiauthor books and anthologies. Classified bibliography p.205–21; general index.   PN146.L84

Miller, Casey. The handbook of nonsexist writing / Casey Miller and Kate Swift. 2nd ed. N.Y. : Harper & Row, c1988. 180 p. ISBN 0-06-181602-7. $15.95. ISBN 0-06-096238-0 (pbk.). $6.95.   **AA57**

1st ed., 1980 (*Guide* AA418).

Follows the format of the 1st ed., and includes "A brief thesaurus" of "words to avoid."   PN218.M5

University of Chicago. Press. Chicago guide to preparing electronic manuscripts : for authors and publishers. Chicago : Univ. of Chicago Pr., 1987. 143 p. : ill. ISBN 0-226-10392-7. ISBN 0-226-10393-5 (pbk.).   **AA58**

"This guide is addressed to authors and publishers who wish to use electronic manuscripts for typesetting.... [The] focus is on manuscript preparation ... and on the procedures that should be followed by author and publisher so that the author's electronic medium can be used for typesetting."—*Pref.* Indexed.   Z286.E43U54

Bibliography

Luey, Beth. Editing documents and texts : an annotated bibliography / comp. for the Association for Documentary Editing by Beth Luey with the assistance of Kathleen Gorman. Madison, Wisc. : Madison House, 1990. 289 p. ISBN 0-945612-13-3. $29.95.   **AA59**

"The rationale for compiling a bibliography on editing historical documents, literary texts, and materials in other fields is based on the belief that editors in all subject areas share certain concerns, commitments, goals, and techniques."—*Introd.* A section of "Suggestions for teaching" precedes the bibliography of books, articles, and parts of books. About 800 items are listed by author or anonymous title; annotations are descriptive rather than evaluative. Subject index.   Z5165.L83

SELECTION OF BOOKS

Guides

The reader's adviser : a layman's guide to literature. 13th ed. N.Y. : Bowker, 1986–1988. ISBN 0-8352-2428-7. $399.95.   **AA60**

12th ed., 1974–1977 (*Guide* AA443).

1st–8th eds. had title *Bookman's manual;* 9th ed., *Reader's adviser and bookman's manual.*

Contents: v. 1, Best in American and British fiction, poetry, essays, literary biography, bibliography, and reference; v. 2, Best in American and British drama and world literature in English translation; v. 3, Best in general reference literature, the social sciences, history, and the arts; v. 4, Best in the literature of philosophy and world religions; v. 5, Best in the literature of science, technology, and medicine; v. 6, Indexes.

Designed for nonspecialists, it "provides annotated bibliographies arranged by subject, with brief biographies of authors, creative artists, and scientists worthy of special mention; in addition it informs the reader of a book's availability, price, and purchasing source."—*Pref.* Each volume has its own name, title, and subject indexes. Vol. 6 has a directory of publishers and cumulated name, title, and subject indexes.   Z1035.B7

The reader's catalog : an annotated selection of more than 40,000 of the best books in print in 208 categories / ed. by Geoffrey O'Brien, with Stephen Wasserstein and Helen Morris. N.Y. : Reader's Catalog, c1989. 1382 p. : ill. ISBN 0-924322-00-4. $24.95.   **AA61**

"... aims to provide access for book buyers to a wide range of titles, many of them hard to find."—*Using the Reader's catalog.* Indexed by author and subject.   Z1035.R26

Books for college students

Books for college libraries : a core collection of 50,000 titles. 3rd ed. Chicago : Amer. Lib. Assoc., 1988. 6 v. ISBN 0-8389-3357-2 (v. 1).   **AA62**

2nd ed., 1975 (*Guide* AA452).

Contents: v. 1, Humanities; v. 2, Language and literature; v. 3, History; v. 4, Social sciences; v. 5, Psychology, science, technology, bibliography; v. 6, Index.

"A project of the Association of College and Research Libraries"—*t.p.*

Offers a "core collection for undergraduate libraries."—*Introd.* Entries contain cataloging and classification information; titles are arranged by Library of Congress call number within each volume. Author, title, and subject indexes.
Z1039.C65B67

Reference books

Barteczko, Ewa. Polskie wydawnictwa informacyjne 1945–1981 / Ewa Barteczko, Joanna Jarzyńska. Warszawa : Biblioteka Narodowa, 1985. 328 p. ISBN 83-7009-007-9. zł120.00.   **AA63**

At head of title: Biblioteka Narodowa. Dział Informacji i Udostępniania Zbiorów.

Attempts to list all major reference works published in Poland, 1945–81. Arranged by Universal Decimal Classification with an author/title index and an alphabetical list of subject headings.   Z1035.6.B37 1985

Guide to New Zealand information sources. [Palmerston North] : Massey Univ., 1982. v. 7. (Massey University library series, no. 17.). (In progress).   **AA64**

For earlier vols. and annotation, see *Guide* AA483.

Contents: v. 7, Geography, comp. by B.A. Allan.
Z4101.B37

Sharma, H. D. Indian reference sources : an annotated guide to Indian reference material / H.D. Sharma ; assisted by L.M.P. Singh, Ramji Singh, and G.C. Kendadamath. 2nd ed. Varanasi : Indian Bibliographic Centre, 1988–1989. 2 v. ISBN 81-85131-02-3 (v. 1). Rs260.00 ($35.00 U.S.). ISBN 81-85131-03-1 (v. 2). Rs280.00 ($40.00 U.S).   **AA65**

1st ed., 1972.

Contents: v.1, Generalia and humanities; v.2, Social sciences, pure sciences & applied sciences.

An annotated listing by broad subject of some 5,500 sources in print or readily available in 1985. Each volume has an author and title index.   Z3206.S483

Spanish-language reference books : an annotated bibliography / comp. by Bibliotecas para la Gente, Reference Committee. Berkeley, Calif. : Chicano Studies Library Publications Unit, Univ. of California at Berkeley, 1989. 45 leaves. ISBN 0-918520-15-0. $10.00.   **AA66**

    A classified list evaluating a core collection of Spanish-language reference books. Author and title index.

                          Z1035.1.S586

Walford, Albert John. Walford's guide to reference material / ed. by A. J. Walford ; with the collaboration of Marilyn Mulley and Priscilla Schlicke, and with the assistance of Charles A. Crossley. 5th ed. Metuchen, N. J. ; N. Y. : K. G. Saur, 1989–90. v. 1–2. ISBN 3-598-10905-9 (v.1). ISBN 0-85365-539-1 (v.2). (In progress).   **AA67**

    4th ed., 1980–87 (*Guide* AA507). Vol. 3, Generalia, language and literature, the arts was publ. 1987 and completes the set.

    Contents: v. 1, Science and technology; v. 2, Social and historical sciences, philosophy and religion, ed. by Alan Day and Joan M. Harvey and publ. by Library Association, London.

    To be published in 3 v. over a three-year period. As in previous editions, the aim "is to provide a signpost to reference books and bibliographies published in recent years. Although international in scope the material is principally in English."—*Introd.* Selection criteria for reference works are generally broader than those of the present *Guide.* Each volume has author/title and subject indexes. The volumes have been completely revised, with some entries dropped; v. 1 now includes some 6,000 entries, v. 2 more than 7,000. Topics new to this edition of v. 1 include biotechnology, artificial intelligence, robots, word processing, pollution control, and biomass energy. Business and management sections have been transferred to v. 2.

SELECTION OF PERIODICALS

Ganly, John. Serials for libraries : an annotated guide to continuations, annuals, yearbooks, almanacs, transactions, proceedings, directories, services / ed. by John V. Ganly and Diane M. Sciattara. 2nd ed. N.Y. : Neal-Schuman Publishers, c1985. 441 p. ISBN 0-918212-85-5. $75.00.   **AA68**

    1st ed., 1979, ed. by Joan K. Marshall (*Guide* AA524).

    " . . . designed as a reference tool for the selection, acquisition, and control of serials. It provides current information on the contents, frequency, and price of serials of interest to school, junior and senior college, and public libraries."—*Introd.* The main section is a classified, annotated list of about 2,000 serials; it is followed by a guide to about 125 serials available online, a "when to buy what" purchasing guide, and title and subject indexes.   Z1035.1.G34

Katz, William A. Magazines for libraries : for the general reader and school, junior college, college, university, and public libraries / Bill Katz and Linda Sternberg Katz. 5th ed. N.Y. : Bowker, 1986. 1057 p. ISBN 0-8352-2217-9.   **AA69**

    4th ed., 1982 (*Guide* AA523).

    Adheres to the format and arrangement of the earlier editions, with the addition of a detailed subject index. Approximately 30% of the titles are new listings. A 6th ed. was published in 1989.

NATIONAL AND TRADE

Bibliography

Bell, Barbara L. An annotated guide to current national bibliographies. Alexandria, Va. : Chadwyck-Healey, 1986. 407 p. ISBN 0-85964-123-6.   **AA70**

    A comprehensive worldwide guide to current national bibliographies, suitable substitutes, or alternative information when no current national bibliography exists. Information from 160 countries is arranged alphabetically by country; annotations provide complete information in a standardized format. "Selective bibliography on current national bibliographies" (p.358–401) includes books, pamphlets, and periodical articles, and is divided into general guides and source materials, and by geographic areas. Analytical table of contents.   Z1002.B4714

Boy, Joachim. Nationalbibliographien Schwarzafrikas : Entwicklungen und heutiger Stand. Köln : Greven, c1981. 156 p. : ill., maps. (Arbeiten aus dem Bibliothekar-Lehrinstitut des Landes Nordrhein-Westfalen, Heft 53). ISBN 3-7743-0553-6.   **AA71**

    Now somewhat out of date, but a good source for information about national bibliographies in the countries of sub-Saharan Africa. Chapter five describes 20 black African national bibliographies in detail. Bibliography; subject, title, and name indexes.   Z3501.B69

Commonwealth national bibliographies : an annotated directory / comp. by the IFLA International Office for UBC. 2nd ed. rev. London : Commonwealth Secretariat, 1982. 69 p. ISBN 0-85092-224-0. (pbk.).   **AA72**

    1st ed., 1977 (*Guide* AA544).

    Follows the plan and practice of the earlier edition, recording "both the appearance of a number of new national bibliographies and many changes that have taken place in existing ones."—*Pref.* Some nonserial bibliographies that appeared in the 1st ed. have been transferred to the companion *Commonwealth retrospective national bibliographies* (below). If no national bibliography exists within a country, state, or dependency, a substitute title may be given.   Z2000.9.C653

Commonwealth retrospective national bibliographies : an annotated directory / comp. by the IFLA International Office for UBC. London : Commonwealth Secretariat, 1981. 128 p. ISBN 0-85092-205-4.   **AA73**

    Companion volume to *Commonwealth national bibliographies: an annotated directory* (above). For Commonwealth current member states, special members, and dependencies of nations (but not former territories), lists publications that provide national bibliographic coverage antedating the member's current national bibliography. "The term 'national' bibliographies . . . should be understood as meaning bibliographies of national scope rather than the 'authoritative and comprehensive records of the national imprint of the country . . . made by a responsible organization.' "—*Introd.* Alphabetically arranged by the English name, entries include a brief historical note, followed by complete descriptive information in a standardized format. An index of variant and former names of Commonwealth members is included at the front.   Z2000.9.C58

Domay, Friedrich. Bibliographie der nationalen Bibliographien = Bibliographie mondiale des bibliographies nationales = A world bibliography of national bibliographies. Stuttgart : A. Hiersemann, 1987. 557 p. (Hiersemanns Bibliographische Handbücher, Bd. 6). ISBN 3-7772-8709-1.   **AA74**

    A useful listing of nearly 3,000 retrospective and current national bibliographies and related works for more than 100 regions or countries. Entries are annotated and arranged alphabetically under continent, region, and country; countries are subdivided by such headings as: bibliography of bibliographies, current national bibliography, maps, periodicals, regional bibliographies. Citations are in the language of publication; most annotations are in German. Name and title index.

§ More thorough than *Inventaire général des bibliographies national rétrospectives* (below), which, for example, lists six titles for entire U.K., while Domay cites more than 40 retrospective guides for England alone. Z1002.D65

Gorman, G. E. Guide to current national bibliographies in the Third World / G.E. Gorman and J.J. Mills. 2nd rev. ed. London; N.Y.: Zell, 1987. 372 p. ISBN 0-905450-34-5. **AA75**

1st ed., 1983 (*Guide* AA545).

A complete revision, but similar in organization to the 1st ed. Lists regional bibliographies, current national bibliographies, and suitable substitute compilations for Third World countries, mid-1970s to 1987. Z1002.G67

Inventaire général des bibliographies nationales rétrospectives = Retrospective national bibliographies : an international directory / ed. by Marcelle Beaudiquez. München; N.Y.: K.G. Saur, 1986. 189 p. (IFLA publications, 35). ISBN 3-598-20399-3. **AA76**

A bibliography of sources that trace the record of publishing in countries of the world, beginning for each country with its first printed book and continuing to the onset of its current national bibliography. Excludes most East European countries. Arranged alphabetically by country, in most cases using the English form of name (e.g., Spain), but for French-speaking countries the French form (e.g., Maroc). Prefatory material, in both French and English, gives a brief summary of each country's publishing history and of attempts at bibliographic control, and a list of sources by dates of coverage. Entries are annotated (in English or French, or for "German-speaking countries," in German). A code with each entry indicates the type of bibliography. Types of bibliographies included are: (1) retrospective bibliographies that list monographs and/or periodicals as well as official publications; (2) those that list documents about a country; (3) special bibliographies about a country that include material published there; and (4) catalogs of certain special libraries and printed catalogs of large national libraries. Z1002.I58

Kuznetsova, T. R. Gosudarstvennye (natsional'nye) bibliograficheskie ukazateli sotsialisticheskikh stran : annotirovannyĭ bibliograficheskiĭ ukazatel' / [sostavitel' T.R. Kuznetsova ; redaktor N.V. Gavrilenko]. Moskva : Gos. biblioteka SSSR im. V.I. Lenina, 1984–1985. v. 1–2. (In progress). **AA77**

Title on added t.p.: National bibliographical indexes of the Socialist countries.

Contents: v. 1–2, Annotated bibliographical index.

Prefatory matter in Russian and English.

Vol. 1 deals with Bulgaria, Hungary, the German Democratic Republic, Cuba, Poland, the U.S.S.R., and Czechoslovakia; v. 2 with Yugoslavia and its constituent republics. Lists and annotates national bibliographies (current and retrospective) by country, then by type of publication (books, periodicals, periodical indexes, dissertations, cartographic publications, printed music, imitative arts, sound recordings, exteriorica, bibliographic aids). Emphasizes bibliographies that record publishing of the period 1945–82, although the output of earlier periods is dealt with. Indexes of names, titles, and corporate authors; abbreviations list; table of types of national bibliographic indexes. Z1975.K89

United States

Early

European Americana : a chronological guide to works printed in Europe relating to the Americas, 1493–1776 / ed. by John Alden with the assistance of Dennis C. Landis. New Canaan, Conn.: Readex Books, 1987–1988. v. 5–6. ISBN 0-918414-00-8. (In progress). **AA78**

For v. 1–2 and annotation, see *Guide* AA556.

At head of title: The John Carter Brown Library.

Contents: v. 5, 1701–1725; v. 6, 1726–1750 (both ed. by Dennis Channing Landis).

Published out of sequence (v.3–4 have yet to appear). " . . . prepared in accordance with the bibliographic and editorial principles developed by John Alden" (*Pref.*) for the earlier volumes. Z1203.E87

Walsh, Jim. Maps contained in the publications of the American bibliography, 1639–1819 : an index and checklist. Metuchen, N.J.: Scarecrow, 1988. 367 p. ISBN 0-8108-2193-1. $37.50. **AA79**

For annotation, see *Supplement* CL43. Z6027.U5W35

19th century

A checklist of American imprints. Metuchen, N.J.: Scarecrow, 1985–1990. v. [6–13], 1835–41. (In progress). **AA80**

For volumes covering 1830–34 and annotation, see *Guide* AA569.

Compiler varies: vols. for 1835–39 comp. by Carol Rinderknecht; vols. for 1840– comp. by Carol Rinderknecht and Scott Bruntjen.

Cumulative indexes published separately: 1820–29, Author index; corrections & sources (1973); 1830–39, Title index (1989. 2 v.); 1830–39, Author index (1989).

When complete, will cover 1820–75. Z1215.C44

Newton, Frances P. American bibliography, a preliminary checklist, 1801 to 1819 : Ralph R. Shaw and Richard H. Shoemaker : printers, publishers, and booksellers index, geographical index, omissions / comp. by Frances P. Newton. Metuchen, N.J.: Scarecrow, 1983. 443 p. **AA81**

For earlier vols. and annotation, see *Guide* AA567.

Completes the set. Z1215.N58

Current

●**Books in print plus** [computer file]. N.Y.: Bowker, 1979– . **AA82**

File size: 1 million records. Updated bimonthly.

Machine-readable version in CD-ROM, updated bimonthly, of the current data in several Bowker publications: *Books in print* title and author sections (*Guide* AA590), *Subject guide to books in print* (*Guide* AA591), *Forthcoming books* (*Guide* AA592), *Children's books in print* (*Guide* AA582). Among the searchable fields are author, title, publisher, subject, ISBN, keyword.

Forthcoming books. v. 1 (Jan. 1966)– . [N. Y.: Bowker], [1966]– . Bimonthly. ISSN 0015-8119. $27.50. **AA83**

For annotation, see *Guide* AA592.

Beginning in 1987, absorbed *Subject guide to forthcoming books* (*Guide* AA592), which ceased Nov. 1986.   Z1219

Words on tape. 1984/1985– . Westport, Conn. : Meckler Pub., c1984– . Biennial. ISSN 8755-3759. $29.95. **AA84**
Subtitle (1990): A guide to the audio cassette market.
The 1990 edition lists more than 20,000 audiocassettes published in the U.S. and Canada. Arranged by title, with author and subject indexes.   Z5347.W67

Albania

Bibliografia kombëtare e librit që botohet në RPS të Shqipërisë / Biblioteka Kombëtare, Sektori i Bibliografisë. Viti 27, 1 (Jan.–Mar. 1986)– . Tiranë : Biblioteka, 1986– . Quarterly. ISSN 0250-5053.   **AA85**
Supersedes *Bibliografia kombëtare e Republikës Popullore Socialiste të Shqipërisë: libri shqip* (*Guide* AA606), which ceased in 1985, and continues its volume numbering and organization. Periodical and newspaper articles are included in *Bibliografia kombëtare e Republikës Popullore Socialiste të Shqipërisë: artikujt e periodikut shqiptar*, 1977– (Tirana : Biblioteka kombëtare, 1977– . Monthly).   Z2854.A5B53

Argentina

Libros argentinos. ISBN. Buenos Aires : Cámara Argentina del Libro, c1984– . Annual.   **AA86**
On t.p. of the 1984 vol.: La pressente edición continene la producción registrada hasta 1984. On t.p. of the 1987 vol.: producción editorial registrada entre 1982 y 1986.
A classified listing (arranged by title within subject classes), with author and title indexes. Includes an alphabetical list of publishers with addresses and ISBN prefix, and another list by ISBN number.   Z1615.L73

Australia

Australian national bibliography, 1901–1950. Canberra : National Library of Australia, 1988. 4 v. ISBN 0-642-10445-X.   **AA87**
A retrospective bibliography that includes about 49,500 entries for books and pamphlets published in Australia, titles by Australian authors published elsewhere, or works with significant content on Australia. Bridges the period between John Ferguson's *Bibliography of Australia 1784–1900* (*Guide* DF6) and *Annual catalogue of Australian publications* (*Guide* AA615), the latter incomplete between 1936 and 1951. Serials and nonprint titles excluded. Arranged by main entry. Vol. 3 is an author/title/series index, v.4 a subject index.   Z4011.A94

Ferguson, John Alexander. Bibliography of Australia : addenda, 1784–1850. Canberra : National Library of Australia, 1986. 706 p. ISBN 0-642-99307-6.   **AA88**
For annotation, see *Supplement* DF5.   Z4011.F47

Brazil

Bibliografia brasileira / Biblioteca Nacional. v. 1, no. 1/2 (1o. e 2o. trim. 1983)– . Rio de Janeiro : A Biblioteca, 1984– . Quarterly (irregular). ISSN 0102-3144.   **AA89**
Supersedes *Boletim bibliográfico da Biblioteca Nacional* (*Guide* AA643), which ceased with n.s., v.27 (covering 1982).

Includes materials received on legal deposit. Classified arrangement using the Dewey Decimal Classification; author, title, and subject indexes in each issue (with no cumulation). The fourth issue of each year includes a list of periodicals (with addresses). For a 1989 thesis suppl., see *Supplement* AH6.   Z1671.B52

Library of Congress. Library of Congress Office, Rio de Janeiro. Accessions list, Brazil and Uruguay. v. 15, no. 1 (Jan./Feb. 1989)– . Rio de Janeiro : Library of Congress Office, [1989]– . Bimonthly. ISSN 1041-1763.   **AA90**
Supersedes *Accessions list, Brazil* (*Guide* AA644) and continues its numbering.
Superintendent of Documents classification: LC 1.30/11:
"... encompasses current Brazilian and Uruguayan materials that are within the scope of the Library's acquisitions policies and hence is not intended to take the place of current national bibliographies."—*Introd.* Divided by country, then by monographs and serials; arranged alphabetically by main entry with preliminary cataloging supplied by the Library's field office. Entries for serials cumulate annually in a supplement.   Z1671.U53a

Bulgaria

Paprikoff, George I. Works of Bulgarian emigrants : an annotated bibliography : books, booklets, dissertations. Chicago : S.K. Paprikoff, 1985. 693 p., [1] leaf of plates : port.   **AA91**
A chronological listing of 1,579 monographs, dissertations, and conference proceedings published in any language and in any country from 1944 through 1983. For each, gives author, title in original and English language, bibliographic details, and often the table of contents. Indexed by author, genre (biographies, calenders, dissertations) or broad topic, language, and country.   Z2891.P36

Burma

Shaw, Graham. The South Asia and Burma retrospective bibliography (SABREB). London : British Library, 1987. v. 1 (554 p.). ISBN 0-7123-0119-4. (In progress).   **AA92**
Contents: Stage 1: 1556–1800.
The "aid is ultimately to provide for the first time a comprehensive standard record of publishing in the subcontinent from the introduction of printing technology in the middle of the sixteenth century up to the close of the nineteenth."—*Pref.* Stage 1 is based primarily on the collection of the British Library and includes almost all forms of printed material (excluding maps and prints) in any language. Arrangement is by date and place of publication, with indexes of names, titles, and subjects. For extant copies, location symbols are given. Stage 2 is to cover 1802–67; Stage 3, 1868–1900.   Z3185.S54

Canada

Canadiana 1867–1900, monographs : Canada's national bibliography = Canadiana 1867–1900, monographies : la bibliographie nationale du Canada [microform]. Microfiche ed. [Ottawa] : National Library of Canada = Bibliothèque nationale du Canada, 1980– . microfiches. ISBN 0-660-50465-0.   **AA93**
Includes more than 48,000 entries for books, pamphlets, leaflets, broadsides, offprints, municipal and county publications, atlases, printed music, reports of annual meetings, and non-Canadian government titles published in French and English in Canada 1867–1900. Also includes works published out-

side Canada written by Canadians, or about Canada or Canadians. Excludes serials, Canadian federal, provincial and territorial government publications (with some exceptions), newspapers, all manuscript material including unpublished theses, maps, audiovisual material, patents. Consists of a register and five indexes: author/title, chronological (by year of publication), publisher/printer, place of publication/printing, subject. Locates copies in Canadian libraries. "Each new issue is a complete re-cumulation of the bibliography with the inclusion of new entries and changes to previous listings."—*Canadiana* [printed guide] *p.12*. Z1365

Chile

Libros chilenos ISBN. 1989– . Santiago, Chile : Cámara Chilena del Libro, 1989– . **AA94**
 A listing of currently available titles with separate sections arranged by Universal Decimal Classification, by author, and by title. Includes a list of publishers arranged by ISBN.
 Z1701.L52

China

Zhongguo guojia shumu. v. 1 (1985)– . Beijing : Shumu Wenxian Chubanshe [Bibliographical and Documentation Publishing House], 1987– . Annual. 50 yuan. **AA95**
 Contents: v. 1, Bibliography; v. 2, Indexes.
 Lists books and serials received by the National Central Library under depository law. Entries are arranged by the Chinese Library Classification system; title and author indexes are alphabetic according to Pinyin transliteration. Will attempt to include in future issues titles published cooperatively between China and other countries, publications in China regardless of language, and publications by Chinese citizens wherever published.

Cyprus

Kypriakē vivliographia. 1983/84– . Leukōsia : Vivliographikē Hetaireia Kyprou, [1985]– . Annual. **AA96**
 Compiler: Nikos Panagiotou.
 Gives full bibliographic information for books, pamphlets, serials (newspapers, periodicals, school publications), government publications, some mimeographed material, offprints, and reprints published in Cyprus during the year of coverage. Lists titles by Cypriots published outside Cyprus, but excludes Turkish Cypriot publications. Entries in Greek are arranged alphabetically within some 50 subject groups; entries in other languages (chiefly English, French, and German) are listed after the Greek entries. Author index. Z3496.K95

Czechoslovakia

Fedor, Michal. Bibliografia slovenských kníh, 1901–1918. Martin : Matica slovenská, 1964. 727 p. (Slovenská národná bibliografia. Séria A: Knihy, 1–3.).
 AA97
 Part of a retrospective effort to cover all of Slovak publishing in books and other formats. Includes a review of Slovakian publishing history and imprints during this time period. Entries in Pt. I listed alphabetically; in Pt. II in classified arrangement. Indexes include names, publishers and printers, reviews listed by periodical title, and tabular presentation of articles in

various subjects. Summaries in Russian, Hungarian, and German.

Voit, Petr. Příspěvky ke knihopisu. Praha : Státní knihovna ČSR, 1985–1988. 10 v. **AA98**
 At head of title: Státní knihovna ČSR-Nositelka rádu republiky.
 Contents: v. 1, Rejstřík autorů, překladatelů a editorů; v. 2, Rejstřík anonymních záhlaví; v. 3, Rejstřík názvový; v. 4, Význam Bartoloměje Netolického pro český knihtisk 16. století / Petr Mašek; v. 5, Moravské prameny z let 1567–1568 k dějinám bibliografie, cenzury, knihtisku a literární historie; v. 6–10, Konkordance koniášových klíčů, indexu, Jungmanna a knihopisu / Bedřiška Wižďálková.
 An index to *Knihopis českých a slovenských tisku od doby nejstarsí až do konce XVIII stoltí (Guide AA709)*. Indexes for v. 1 (incunabula, A) and v. 2, pt. 1 (B–C) were included with the original set; remainder had not been indexed. Z2131.V65

Current

Bibliografický katalog ČSSR. České knihy, 1960, seš. 29 (23.8.1960)– . Praha : Státní knihovna ČSR, Národní knihovna v Praze, 1960– . **AA99**
 For early volumes and annotation, see *Guide* AA716.
 Frequency varies: 1960–1975, weekly; 1976– , monthly (irregular).
 Lists in classified arrangement publications of Bohemia, Moravia, and part of Silesia that are deposited at the Státní Knihovna. Monthly author, illustrator, translator, translated title, title, and subject indexes, cumulating annually. Some issues include *Dodatky* [addenda] and occasional supplements. Other subseries: *České hudebniny a gramofonové desky* [Czech music and gramophone records] and *Soupis Českých bibliografií* [bibliography of Czech bibliography]. For Slovak publications, see:

Slovenská národná bibliografia. Seria A: Knihy. roč.21 (1970)– . Martin : Matica slovenská, 1970– . Monthly (irregular). **AA100**
 Formerly *Bibliograficky katalog ČSSR. Slovenské knihy* (see *Guide* AA716); continues the volume numbering of that set. A classified list of books and pamphlets deposited at the Matica Slovenská. Indexes of names, subjects, and titles, cumulated annually. Includes statistics of the Slovak book trade. Other series of the *Bibliograficky katalog ČSSR* were reorganized in 1980 as follows: Seria B, Periodiká [periodicals]; C, Mapy [maps]; D, Dizertačné práce [theses and dissertations]; E, Špeciálne tlače [special publications]; F, Firemná literatúra [trade catalogs and technical newsletters]; G, Grafika [graphic and fine arts]; H, Hudebniny [sheet music, books on music]; I, Oficiálne dokumenty [official documents]; J, Audiovizuálne dokumenty [audio-visual materials]. Z2124.S56S53

Denmark

19th and 20th centuries

Dansk Bogfortegnelse [for aarene]. Ballerup [etc.] : Bibliotekscentralens Forlag [etc.], 1981–87. 7 v. (In progress). **AA101**
 For earlier cumulations, see *Guide* AA720.
 Contents: 1976–80 (1981. 3 v.); 1981–85 (1987. 4 v.).
 Continues quinquennial cumulation of the author-title and classified lists from the annual volumes, as well as the other lists noted in the annotation for *Guide* AA725.

Also available in microfiche with coverage beginning in 1976. Z2561.D19

Current

Dansk bogfortegnelse : Åarskatalog. 1976– . [Ballerup] : Bibliotekscentralens Forlag [etc.], 1977– . Annual. ISSN 0106-2743. **AA102**
For earlier issues and annotation, see *Guide* AA725.

Annual issues will continue to be cumulated quinquennially in *Dansk Bogfortegnelse* (see above and *Guide* AA720). Other titles that collectively make up the *Danish national bibliography* are: *Dansk anmeldelsesindeks* [reviews], 1979– ; *Dansk artikelindeks. Aviser og tidsskrifter* [articles, newspapers, and periodicals], 1981– ; *Dansk billedfortegnelse* [visual recordings], 1984– ; *Danske grammofonplader og kassetteband* [gramophone records and tapes], 1985– ; *Dansk lydfortegnelse* [sound recordings], 1982– ; *Dansk musikfortegnelse* [music], 1972/73– ; *Bibliografi over Danmarks offentlige publikationer* [government publications], 1948– ; *Dania polyglotta* [foreign publications about Denmark; see *Guide* AA723–724]; *Dansk periodicafortegnelse* [serials], 1977– ; *Artikler i bøger* [articles in books]; *Grønlandsk avis- og tidsskrift-index* [Greenlandic newspapers and periodicals index], 1976– . Z2561.D22

Dominican Republic

Anuario bibliográfico dominicano. 1978– . Santo Domingo : Biblioteca Nacional, 1978– . Irregular. **AA103**
For 1946–47 issues, see *Guide* AA726.

On verso of half-title, 1984: Anuario bibliográfico dominicano 1980–82; de contenido retrospectivo al año 1979 y anteriores.

Assumes the title of the earlier compilation (*Guide* AA726); issues for 1978 called "primero número." The 1984 issue emphasizes publications of the 1980–82 period, but includes many of much earlier date. Lists books, pamphlets, official and government publications, theses and dissertations, and university publications published in the country or about it if published abroad that have been received by the Biblioteca Nacional under depository law; also lists acquisitions by the library. Volumes for 1978 and 1979 arranged by classification; from 1980/82, arranged alphabetically by subject, with author and subject indexes. Projected annual volumes covering 1983 and after have yet to appear. Z1533.A58

Ecuador

Anuario bibliográfico ecuatoriano. 1982– . Cuenca : Banco Central del Ecuador, Centro de Investigación y Cultura, c1984– . Annual. **AA104**
For unannotated entry, see *Guide* AA731.

A listing of books, pamphlets, and periodical articles arranged by broad subject, then alphabetically. Author and corporate author index; subject index. Volume for 1985 has "Indice alfabetico de revistas . . . " and a name and corporate author index. Z1761.E37

Egypt

Nuṣayr, ʿĀydah Ibrāhīm. al-Kutub al-ʿArabīyah allatī nushirat fī Miṣr fī al-qarn al-tāsiʿ ʿashar / iʿdād ʿĀydah Ibrāhīm Nuṣayr. Ṭabʿah 1. al-Qāhirah : Qism al-Nashr bi-al-Jāmiʿah al-Amrīkīyah bi-al-Qāhirah, 1990. 14, 403 p. **AA105**
Introductory material in Arabic and English. Title on added t.p.: *Arabic books published in Egypt in the nineteenth century.*

" . . . covers the period from the first Egyptian printed book published in 1822 up until the end of 1900."—*Introd.* Arranged by Dewey Decimal classification, with author, title, and subject indexes.

Chronological coverage continued by the author's *al-Kutub al-ʿArabīyah allatīnushirat fī miṣrbayna 1900–1925* (1983); his *al-Kutub al-ʿArabīyah allatī nushirat fī miṣrbayna amay 1926–1940* (1980); and by *Dalil al-matbuat al-miṣriyah, 1940–1956* (1975), all published al-Qāhirah : Qism al-Nashr bi-al Jāmiah al-Amrīkīyah bi-al-Qāhirah (American University in Cairo Pr.). Z3658.A4N87

Ethiopia

Ethiopian publications. Addis Ababa : Provisional Military Government of Socialist Ethiopia, Ministry of Culture and Sports, [1980]–[1990?]. (In progress). **AA106**
Includes titles published in Ethiopia which are deposited at the national library, titles published elsewhere about Ethiopia, and selected documents published in or about neighboring countries. Alphabetical arrangement; title index. Prefatory matter in Amharic, English, and French, with bibliographic entries in English. Several volumes have specific themes and appear to be monographs in series. Z3521.E83

Fiji Islands

Fiji national bibliography. Dec. 1970/1978– . Lautoka, Fiji : Library Service of Fiji, Ministry of Social Welfare, 1979– . Annual. **AA107**
Place of publication and publisher vary.

Includes monographs, first issues of serials, theses, official and government publications, maps, films, and microforms published in Fiji; titles published outside Fiji are included if a substantial portion of the work is about Fiji or written by Fiji citizens. The first volume covers 1970–78; most entries in successive annual issues are from the year of coverage, but publications from 1970 (or from 1950 beginning with the 1984 issue) to date are included if not previously listed. Classified arrangement for monographs; periodicals and maps are alphabetically arranged; and legal notices and statutes are listed numerically. Author, title, and series index; subject index. Z4651.F54

Finland

Lisäyksiä Fredrik Wilhelm Pippingin bibliografiaan Luettelo suomeksi präntätyistä kirjoista = Tillägg till Förteckning öfver i tryck utgifna skrifter på finska av Fredrik Wilhelm Pippin / redigerad av Irja Rämä. Helsinki : Helsingin Yliopiston Kirjasto, 1984. 84 p. ISBN 951-45-3287-2. **AA108**
Supplement to F. W. Pippin's *Luettelo suomeksi präntätyistä kirjoista . . .* (*Guide* AA738).

Lists more than 400 titles published 1543–1809. Includes both new entries, chronologically arranged in the Pippin numerical sequence, and additional bibliographic information for titles in the original Pippin list. Indexes of authors, titles of anonymous works, and persons; list of library locations.

Current

●**Fennica** : Suomen kansallisbibliografia = Finlands nationalbibliografi = The Finnish national bibliography [computer file]. Helsinki : Helsingin yliopiston kirjasto ; Kirjastopalvelu Oy, 1977–1989.　　　　**AA109**
Machine-readable version of *Suomen kirjallisuus* (*Guide* AA740).
File size: 141,000 records (monographs). Updated semiannually. Available in CD-ROM (Kirjastopalvelu Oy).
Boolean operators, search keys, and scrolling enable refined searches in most MARC fields. Search languages: Finnish. Swedish, English; instruction manual in Finnish and Swedish. The producers plan to include monographic titles for 1967–71 and 1972–76, which will add 63,000 records.

Suomen kirjallisuus = Finlands litteratur = The Finnish national bibliography. 1544/1877– . Helsinki : Helsingin Yliopiston Kirjasto, [1878]– . Frequency varies. ISSN 0355-001X. ISSN 0355-0001 (annual).　　**AA110**
For earlier issues and annotation, see *Guide* AA740.
No cumulation published for 1969–71.
Since 1978, available on magnetic tape and microfiche. Now also available online as *KOTI* through KDOK/Minttu information retrieval system.　　　　Z2520.S95

France

Early

Moreau, Brigitte. Inventaire chronologique des éditions parisiennes du XVIe siècle / par Brigitte Moreau, d'après les manuscrits de Philippe Renouard. Abbeville : Impr. F. Paillart, 1985. v. 3. (In progress).　**AA111**
For earlier vols. and annotation, see *Guide* AA748.
Contents: v. 3, 1521–30.
Each volume has its own index.　　　Z145.P3M67

Répertoire bibliographique des livres imprimés en France au XVIIe siècle. Baden-Baden : V. Koerner, 1978–1989. 16 v. (Bibliotheca bibliographica Aureliana, 75, 81, 84, 86, 89, 91, 92, 94, 97, 98, 101–103, 110–111, 117). (In progress).　　　　　　　　　　　　**AA112**
Continues the 16th-century coverage provided by *Répertoire bibliographique des livres imprimés en France au seizième siècle . . .* (*Guide* AA749); continued for the 18th century by *Répertoire bibliographique des livres imprimés en France au XVIIIe siècle* (*Supplement* AA114). Arranged by region, then chronologically. Each region begins with a Table des imprimeurs et libraires; each volume has author and title indexes and an abbreviations list. A cooperative effort by various scholars; many volumes are by Louis Desgraves.　Z2162.D47

18th century

Conlon, Pierre M. Le siècle des lumières : bibliographie chronologique. Genève : Droz, 1986–1990. v. 4–7. (Histoire des idées et critique littéraire, vol. 239, 250, 266, 282.). (In progress).　　　　　　　　**AA113**

For v.1–3 and annotation, see *Guide* AA751.
Contents: v. 4, 1737–42; v.5, 1743–47; v.6, 1748–52; v. 7, 1753–56.
Each volume has an introduction and lists of sources and libraries cited. Latin place-name equivalents given. Arranged chronologically, then alphabetically.　　Z7128.E55C66

Desgraves, Louis. Répertoire bibliographique des livres imprimés en France au XVIIIe siècle. Baden-Baden ; Bouxwiller : V. Koerner, 1988–1989. v. 1–3. (Bibliotheca bibliographica Aureliana, 112, 115, 119.). (In progress).　　　　　　　　　　　　**AA114**
Contents: v.1–3, Agen–La Rochelle.
Continues the coverage of *Répertoire bibliographique des livres imprimés en France au seizième siècle . . .* (*Guide* AA749) and *Répertoire bibliographique des livres imprimés en France au XVIIe siècle* (*Supplement* AA112) into the 18th century. Arranged alphabetically by place, then chronologically. Table of places at the beginning of volume and "Table des imprimeurs et libraries" under each place name. A general index and list of abbreviations conclude each volume.　　Z1016.D47

19th and 20th centuries

Catalogue général des ouvrages en langue française, 1926–1929 / publié sous la direction de Bernard Dermineur. München ; N.Y. : K.G. Saur, 1987–89. 9 v. ISBN 3-598-30990-2 (set).　　　　　　　　　**AA115**
Contents: [I] Auteurs (3 v.); [II] Titres (2 v.); [III] Matières (4 v.).
The first state of an effort to close the gap in coverage between Otto H. Lorenz's *Catalogue générale de la librarie française, 1840–1925* (*Guide* AA755) and *Biblio* (*Guide* AA753). Full bibliographical descriptions are given in the author volumes; only title, place, and date of publication (along with the author's name in boldface) are given in the other sections. Another segment covering 1930–33 is promised.
Z2161.C357

Current

●**Bibliographie nationale française depuis 1975 sur CD-ROM** [computer file]. Paris : Bibliothèque Nationale, 1975– .　　　　　　　　　　　　**AA116**
Machine-readable version of *Bibliographie de la France* (*Guide* AA759; since 1990 entitled *Bibliographie nationale française* [below]).
File size: 390,000 records. Each disc cumulates from 1976. Available in CD-ROM (Chadwyck-Healey, Faxon).
Contains all French MARC records for (1) works deposited at the Bibliothèque Nationale since 1975 (for offical publications, since 1987) and listed in *Bibliographie de la France. Livres* and its successor, and since 1987 its *Suppl. II. Publications officielles*; (2) titles issued by international government organizations and published in France; (3) new titles not yet listed in *Bibliographie nationale française*. Boolean operators enable refined searches from some 20 index options. Menus and help screens available in French or English; German and Italian are planned.

Bibliographie nationale française. Livres : notices établies par la Bibliothèque Nationale. 1990, no. 1 (3 janv. 1990)– . Paris : Bibliothèque Nationale, Office général du livre, 1990– . Biweekly. ISSN 1142-3250.
AA117
Also called 179. année– .
Represents a title change for the *Bibliographie de la France* (*Guide* AA759); assumes its numbering. The indexes now cumulate three times a year on microfiche, with an annual printed cumulation. The four supplements still appear: I, Publications

en série (monthly with an annual index); II, Publications officielles (bimonthly with an annual index); III, Musique (three times a year); and IV, Atlas, cartes, et plans (annually).

Z2165.B5725

Germany

Early

British Library. Short-title catalogue of books printed in the German-speaking countries and of German books printed in other countries from 1455 to 1600 now in the British Library. Supplement. London : British Library, 1990. 141 p. ISBN 0-7123-0207-7. £50.00.   **AA118**

For main volume (published 1962), see *Guide* AA768.

Lists more than 1,300 books which were added to the Library after 1962. Includes a list of amendments to the earlier catalogue, and a list of books destroyed during World War II which have been replaced. Printers and publishers index.

Z1014.B67

Verzeichnis der im deutschen Sprachbereich erschienenen Drucke des XVI. Jahrhunderts : VD 16 / herausgegeben von der Bayerischen Staatsbibliothek in München in Verbindung mit der Herzog August Bibliothek in Wolfenbüttel ; [Redaktion, Irmgard Bezzel]. Stuttgart : Hiersemann, 1985–90. v. 4–16. ISBN 3-7772-8319-3 (1. Abt., Bd. 1). (In progress).   **AA119**

For earlier vols. and annotation, see *Guide* AA770.

Contents: v.4–16, Carm–Reh.   Z1014.V47

18th and 19th centuries

Gesamtverzeichnis des deutschsprachigen Schrifttums (GV), 1700–1910 / bearb. unter d. Leitung von Hilmar Schmuck u. Willi Gorzny ; bibliograph. u. red. Beratung, Hans Popst u. Rainer Schöller. München ; N.Y. : K.G. Saur, 1979–1987. v. 131–160. ISBN 3-598-30000-X.   **AA120**

For earlier volumes, see *Guide* AA771. Also available in microfiche.

Contents: v. 131–160, Sch–Zz. A separately published *Nachträge* (München ; N.Y. : K.G. Saur, 1987. 294 p.) completes the set.   Z2221.G469

20th century

Gesamtverzeichnis des deutschsprachigen Schrifttums ausserhalb des Buchhandels (GVB), 1966–1980 / bearb. unter der Leitung von Willemina van der Meer und Hilmar Schmuck. München ; N.Y. : K.G. Saur, 1988–1990. 28 v. ISBN 3-598-31630-5 (Gesamtwerk).   **AA121**

For related series covering publications of earlier periods, see *Guide* AA771, AA777, and *Supplement* AA120.

Contents: v. 1–28, A–Z; Nachträge.

Lists approximately 450,000 titles alphabetically by title, with appropriate subarrangements. Includes "all available German-language titles published outside the booktrade, i.e., all relevant publications—irrespective of place of publication—published in East or West Germany, Austria or German-speaking Switzerland, irrespective of the language in which they are written"—*Introd.* Non-trade publications of societies, associations, communities, clubs, firms, research centers, and authorities are compiled from *Deutsche Bibliographie. Reihe B, Erscheinungen ausserhalb des Verlagsbuchhandels* (*Guide* AA783) 1966–1986; *Deutsche Nationalbibliographie. Reihe B. Neuerscheinungen ausserhalb des Buchhandels* (*Guide* AA778)

1966–1985; *Österreichische Bibliographie* (*Guide* AA621) 1966–1985; *Das Schweizer Buch. Serie B. Veröffentlichungen ausserhalb des Buchhandels* (*Guide* AA1129) 1966–1975; *Deutsche Forschungsberichte/ Forschungsberichte aus Technik und Naturwissenschaften*, 1971–1981; and the database of the Deutsche Bibliothek. Indexed.

Current

Deutsche Nationalbibliographie und Bibliographie der im Ausland erschienenen deutschsprachigen Veröffentlichungen. Amstblatt. [. . .] Verzeichnis / Bearb. und hrsg., Die Deutsche Bibliothek. Frankfurt am Main : Buchhändler-Vereinigung, 1991– .   **AA122**

Formed by the merger of the East and West Germany bibliographies: *Deutsche Nationalbibliographie*, Reihe A–C (*Guide* AA778) which ceased in 1990; and *Deutsche Bibliographie. Wöchentliches Verzeichnis*, Reihe A–C (*Guide* AA783), H (*Guide* AH55), N (*Guide* AA784), M, and T, which ceased 1990.

Titles of sections incorporate frequency, e.g., Wöchentliches Verzeichnis, Vierteljährliches Verzeichnis.

Being published in the following sections: Reihe A, *Monographien und Periodika des Verlagsbuchhandels*, A01– (3 Jan. 1991– . Weekly); Reihe B, *Monographien und Periodika ausserhalb des Verlagsbuchhandels*, B01– (3 Jan. 1991– . Weekly); Reihe C, *Karten*, C01– (28 March 1991– . Quarterly); Reihe H, *Hochschulschriften*, H01– (Jan. 1991– . Monthly), which replaces *Deutsche Bibliographie. Hochschulschriften-Verzeichnis* (*Guide* AH55; ceased 1990); Reihe M, *Musikalien und Musikschriften*, M01– (Jan. 1991– . Monthly); Reihe N, *Vorankündigungen Monographien und Periodika (CIP)*, N01– (3 Jan. 1991– . Weekly), which replaces *Deutsche Bibliographie. Wöchentliches Verzeichnis. Neuerscheinungen Sofortdienst (CIP)* (*Guide* AA784; ceased 1990); and Reihe T, *Musiktonträger*, T01– (Jan. 1991– . Monthly).

Yet to appear are: Reihe D, *Monographien und Periodika. Halbjahresverzeichnis*; Reihe E, *Monographien und Periodika. Fünfjahresverzeichnis (Deutsches Bucherverzeichnis)*; Reihe F, *Periodika. Fünfjahresverzeichnis*; and Reihe G, *Fremdsprachiger Germanica und Übersetzungen Deutschsprachiger Werke. Vierteljährliches Verzeichnis*.

Also being published is *Wöchenregister zu Reihe A und Reihe B*, A01/B01– (3 Jan. 1991– . Weekly; cumulated monthly as *Monatsregister*).

●**Deutsche Bibliographie-aktuell-CD-ROM** [computer file]. Frankfurt am Main : Buchhändler-Vereinigung, 1986– .   **AA123**

Machine-readable version of *Deutsche Bibliographie* (*Guide* AA783) and *Neuerscheinunge Sofortdienst (CIP)* (*Guide* AA784).

File size: more than 500,000 records. Updated three times per year; cumulates from Jan. 1986. Available in CD-ROM (Chadwyck-Healey).

Boolean operators permit refined searches from 19 indexes. Menus and help messages in German, English, or French. Taken from *Deutsche Bibliographie*, Reihe A–C, H, and N; excludes printed music and sound recordings.

Ghana

Ghana national bibliography bi monthly. v. 20, no. 1 (Jan./Feb. 1987)– . [Accra, Ghana] : Research Library on African Affairs, 1987– . Bimonthly.   **AA124**

Supersedes *Ghana : a current bibliography*, v. 1–19 (Sept./ Oct. 1967–Nov./Dec. 1986), and assumes its numbering.

A listing by Dewey Decimal Classification of materials received on legal deposit, new acquisitions of the Research Library on African Affairs originating in Ghana, works by Ghanians or about Ghana published abroad, new serial titles, and selected articles about Ghana appearing in books, pamphlets, periodicals, and newspapers. Author/title/series and subject indexes. The promised annual cumulations have not been forthcoming. Serves in lieu of the *Ghana national bibliography* (*Guide* AA790), which because of financial difficulties was suspended with the volume covering 1974 (publ. 1977).

Z3785.G445

Great Britain

Current

British words on tape. Westport, Conn. : Meckler. Annual. ISSN 1052-3375. $35.00 (institutions). **AA125**
Subtitle: A directory of spoken word cassettes available in the UK.
The 1991 edition lists some 6,700 items arranged by title, with author and subject indexes.

Whitaker's books in print. 1988– . London : J. Whitaker & Sons, c1988– . Annual. ISSN 0953-0398. **AA126**
Represents a change in title for *British books in print* (1874–1987; *Guide* AA832); continues its format. Z2001.R33

Before 1640

Pollard, Alfred W. A short-title catalogue of books printed in England, Scotland, & Ireland and of English books printed abroad, 1475–1640 / first compiled by A. W. Pollard & G. R. Redgrave. 2nd ed. rev. & enl., / begun by W. A. Jackson & F. S. Ferguson, completed by Katharine F. Pantzer. London : Bibliographical Society, 1986–91. v. 1, 3. ISBN 0-19-721789-3 (v. 1). $195.00. ISBN 0-19-721791-5 (v. 3). **AA127**
For v. 2 and annotation, see *Guide* AA802.
Contents: v. 1, A–H; v. 3, A printers' & publishers' index, other indexes & appendices, cumulative addenda & corrigenda. Completes the set. Z2002.P77

17th and 18th centuries

The eighteenth century short title catalogue 1990 [microform]. Microfiche edition. [London] : The British Library, [1990]. 220 microfiches. **AA128**
Supersedes the 1983 microfiche ed.
The *ESTC*, an ambitious project begun at the British Library, and now involving libraries in the U.S. and Germany, is an online union list of the holdings of more than 1,000 libraries throughout the world of material published in Great Britain and its dependencies (including the U.S.) and material in English wherever published from 1701 through 1800. "Publication" is broadly defined; the *ESTC* includes advertisements, shipping lists, society membership lists, transport timetables, the sessional papers of the House of Commons, etc. Periodicals published more than once a year, engraved music, separately published maps, and playbills are excluded. Although called a short-title catalog, it offers detailed bibliographic descriptions; all known locations are listed.
The new microfiche edition is a "snapshot" of the online file as of 1990, and includes nearly 300,000 records. It is arranged by author, or title if anonymous, with date and place of publication indexes, and five genre indexes listing advertisements, almanacs, directories, prospectuses, and single-sheet verse.

The *ESTC* is maintained as part of the RLIN database. The March 1987 issue of *Factotum* (the newsletter issued by the ESTC project), called "Occasional paper 5," is entitled "Searching the *ESTC* on RLIN," and provides a detailed description of the search capabilities and protocols. A rather discursive set of articles discussing various aspects of the *ESTC* appears in *Papers of the Bibliographical Society of America* (Oct./Dec. 1981): 371–400.

Jefcoate, Graham. A catalogue of English books printed before 1801 held by the University Library at Göttingen / comp. by Graham Jefcoate and Karen Kloth ; ed. for the Library by Bernhard Fabian. Hildesheim ; N.Y. : Olms : Weidmann, 1987–1988. 3 v. in 7. ISBN 3-487-07887-2 (v. 1). **AA129**
Contents: Pt. 2, v. 1–2, 1470–1700; Pt. 2, v. 1–4, 1701–1800; Pt. 3, Indices.
At head of title: Niedersächsische Staats- und Universitätsbibliothek Göttingen.
Prepared in cooperation with *Eighteenth century short-title catalogue* (above), Göttingen's 18th-century titles are included in *ESTC*), this publication provides detailed bibliographic descriptions for nearly 20,000 titles in "one of the largest repositories of early English books outside the English-speaking world."—*Pref.* Pt. 1 contains "(1) Books, pamphlets, single sheets and periodical publications printed in any language in the British Isles or English colonies; (2) Books printed in English anywhere . . . ; (3) Books by English-speaking authors or subjects of English-speaking states regardless of language or place of publication . . . ; (4) Translations of works by English-speaking authors . . . ; (5) Works with false imprints purporting to have been printed in an English-speaking country."—*Introd. to Pt. 1.* Arranged alphabetically by author or anonymous title; Pt. 1 includes indexes by Goff, *STC*, and Wing numbers. Pt. 2 adheres to the same criteria. It includes items published in the U.S. and India; advertisements and perspectuses are also listed. Pt. 3 has indexes to prospectuses, to advertisements, to dates of publication, and to places of publication. Z2002.J44

Smith, Hilda L. Women and the literature of the seventeenth century : an annotated bibliography based on Wing's *Short-title catalogue* / comp. by Hilda L. Smith and Susan Cardinale. N.Y. : Greenwood, 1990. 332 p. (Bibliographies and indexes in women's studies, no. 10). ISBN 0-313-22059-X. **AA130**
This excellent bibliography expands the entries in Wing's *Short-title catalogue* (*Guide* AA818–AA819) and the catalog of the Thomason tracts in the British Library (*Guide* AA811) to compensate for the abbreviated form and lack of subject indexing in those works. In two sections: (1) 637 works by women; (2) 973 works for and about women. Entries give reel positions for the *Thomason tracts* and *Early English books* microfilm sets, and annotations provide very useful background information and summaries. The addendum lists 183 works which were not read. A special section lists female booksellers, publishers, and printers (based on Morrison's *Index* to Wing; (*Guide* AA822). Indexed by author, topic, and genre, with a separate chronological index listing works by year of publication. Z2013.5.W6S6

Wing, Donald Goddard. Short-title catalogue of books printed in England, Scotland, Ireland, Wales, and British America, and of English books printed in other countries, 1641–1700. 2nd ed., rev. and enl. N.Y. : Index Committee of the Modern Language Association of America, 1988. v. 3. ISBN 0-87352-046-7 (v. 3). **AA131**
For v. 1–2 and annotation, see *Guide* AA819.
Vol. 3 rev. and ed. by John J. Morrison and Carolyn W. Nelson.
Contents: v. 3, P1–Z28. Completes the set.
For serials published during this period, see *British newspapers and periodicals, 1641–1700* (*Supplement* AE41).
Z2002.W52

19th and 20th centuries

●**BNB on CD-ROM** [computer file]. London : British Library, National Bibliographic Service.   **AA132**
  Machine-readable version of *British national bibliography* (*Guide* AA827).
  Contains all records in the BNBMARC database, 1950–85 (two discs) and 1986– (one disc). Updated quarterly. Available from Chadwyck-Healey.
  Discs cumulate from 1986. Boolean and range operators enable refined searches from 26 index options. Onscsreen instructions and help in English, French, German or Italian.

Nineteenth century short title catalogue. Newcastle-upon-Tyne, England : Avero ; Teaneck, N.J. : Chadwyck-Healey, c1985–91. Ser. 1, v. 3–6; ser. 2, v. 1–22. ISBN 0-907977-10-3 (Series 1; set). ISBN 0-907977-52-9 (Series 2; set). (In progress).   **AA133**
  For earlier vols. and annotation, see *Guide* AA826.
  Contents: Ser. 1, phase 1, v. 3–4, I–Z; v. 5, England, Ireland, Scotland, London, directories, ephemerides & periodical publications; Title index [to v. 5], 1st supplement [and] cumulative imprint and subject indexes to v. 1–4; v. 6, Title index [to v. 1–4 and 1st suppl.]: Ser. 2, phase 1, (1816–70), v. 1–22, A–Kief. Ser. 2 has subject and imprint indexes in every fifth vol.
  With regard to these titles and to volumes already published (see *Guide* AA826), a publisher's brochure notes that "each of the three series of NSTC will be divided into three *phases*: (1) the recordings of the holdings of a number of major libraries; (2) supplementation of this data base from specialist libraries and special collections in other libraries; (3) the eventual accretion of other libraries' holdings as these become available in machine-readable form."
  With the publication of v. 3–4, the author and anonymous title entries for series 1, phase 1 are complete. The categories of publications in v. 5 were "created by the compilers of the British Museum General Catalogue of Printed Books (GK3). Under these categories miscellaneous independent institutions and appendix sections containing relevant anonymous works were gathered together ."—*Introd.* British Library holdings in v. 5 were excluded from v. 1–4, but relevant entries held by other libraries are repeated from those volumes. Each category (e.g., Directories, Ephemerides) is followed by imprint and subject indexes. Also in v. 5 are cumulative imprint and subject indexes to v. 1–5 and a supplement that lists accessions at the British Library through 1975 of imprints dated 1801–1815 (more than 50,000 items). The title index (v. 6) indexes titles in v. 1–4 and in the v. 5 supplement.
  The general plan for series 1 continues in series 2. Entries are prepared from the catalogs, published or on-site, of participating libraries rather than from examination of the books; holdings symbols are shown for participating libraries. "British books . . . include all books published in Britain, its colonies and the United States of America; all books in English wherever published; and all translations from English . . . . [T]he ever increasing proportion of books in English published in the United States of America during this period is reflected in this second series by the inclusion of the relevant holdings of the Library of Congress and Harvard University. This series will consist of fifty volumes"—*Introd.* Some volumes contain special features—e.g., "Index of the book trade," in v. 4 lists references to the book trade in participating libraries' catalogs.   Z2001

Greece

Papadopoulos, Thōmas I. Hellēnikē vivliographia : 1466 ci.-1800. Athēnai : Grapheion Dēmosieumatōn tēs Akadēmias Athēnōn, 1984–86. 2 v. (Pragmateiai tēs Akadēmias Athēnōn, t. 48).   **AA134**
  Contents: v.1, Alphavétikè ai chronologiké anakatataxis; v.2, Prosthetaisympleroseis-diorthoseis.
  Introductory summary in English.
  Includes and supplements items from Emile Legrand's *Bibliographie hellénique* (*Guide* AA842) but does not supersede his descriptions. Vol.1 is an alphabetical listing of titles published in Greece or in Greek throuihout the world, followed by a chronological listing of short titles. Entries in the alphabetical section include brief bibliographic descriptions, reference to other bibliographies, and locations in selected libraries. Printer, place of publication, and country of issue indexes.
  Vol.2 contains detailed bibliographic descriptions with citations to catalogs and selected locations of newly identified titles. (These titles are also included in v. 1.) It is arranged chronologically, with additions and corrections beginning on p.351. Separate indexes for author, or title if anonymous; date; and name, including editors and printers.   Z2282.P36

Current

Hellēnikē vivliographia. 1972– . Athēnai : Vivliographikē Hetaireia tēs Hellados, 1975– . Annual.   **AA135**
  Added t.p.: Greek national bibliography.
  Issues for 1976– published in 2 v.
  Includes books, pamphlets, periodicals, official and government publications, reprints, foreign language publications, and translations into Greek that are published in Greece, most of which are housed at the national library. Alphabetically arranged by subject. Indexes of persons, biographies, corporate bodies, publishers, printers and printing houses. An alphabetical table of contents by subject is given in both Greek and English. The annual volumes are late in appearing, and include addenda to earlier volumes.   Z2281.H44

Guatemala

Figueroa Marroquín, Horacio. Apéndice a la Bibliografía guatemalteca. Guatemala : Tip. Nacional, 1988. 204 p. : ill. (Colección Guatemala, v. 47 ; Serie José Joaquín Pardo, 6).   **AA136**
  A listing of items not included in the *Bibliografía guatemalteca* (*Guide* AA851), which covers the years 1600–1960. Offers detailed annotated descriptions in separate sections for: (1) books and pamphlets; (2) dissertations, mainly in the fields of medicine and pharmacology; and (3) journals published in Guatemala through 1960. Each section is arranged chronologically. Pt. 2 is a listing of undated works arranged by approximate publication date. Lacks an index.   Z1461.F54

Honduras

Anuario bibliográfico hondureño / preparado por Miguel Angel García. 1962–1963– . Tegucigalpa, D.C., Honduras, C.A. : Biblioteca Nacional de Honduras, 1963– . Annual. ISSN 0570-3948.   **AA137**
  Shares title with an annual publication that began 1980 (*Guide* AA862).
  Publisher varies. Suspended 1972–79.

Continues *Bibliográfia hondureña (Guide* AA860) and *Anuario bibliográfico hondureño, 1961–1971 (Guide* AA861). Lists books, pamphlets, official and government publication, and dissertations deposited at the Biblioteca Nacional. Arranged alphabetically by author; issues covering a range of years (e.g., 1981–83) are arranged year by year, then alphabetically. No index. Z1471.H6

Hong Kong

A catalogue of books printed in Hong Kong, [year] : in *Hong Kong government gazette. Special supplement number 4.* Oct./Dec. 1964– . Hong Kong : H. Myers, Government Printer, 1965– . Quarterly. **AA138**
Compiled by New Territories Public Libraries, Cultural Services Department.
Includes titles issued by Hong Kong publishers and received under depository law, and titles printed in Hong Kong for foreign publishers. English and Chinese sections, the English arranged alphabetically, the Chinese by stroke sequence. The fourth-quarter list includes annual English and Chinese author indexes, printers' and publishers' addresses, and English and Chinese periodical supplements which include titles received during the current year.

Hungary

Magyar könyvészet, 1921–1944 : a Magyarországon nyomtatott könyvek szakosított jegyzéke / közreadja az Országos Széchényi Könyvtár ; [szerkesztette Komjáthy Miklósné]. Budapest : [Országos Széchényi Könyvtár], 1984–89. v. 2–3,5. ISBN 963-200-200-8. (In progress). **AA139**
For v.1, 6–7 and annotation, see *Guide* AA867.
Added t.p.: *Bibliographica Hungarica, 1921–1944*.
Contents: v. 2, Társadalomtudományok. 1. Társadalom-politika-közgazdaságtan (1984); v. 3, Társadalomtudományok. 2. Jog-Közigazgatás-népjólét-pedagógia-néprajz (1985); v. 5, Müvészet-sport-földrajz-électrajz-történelem (1989).
Includes books, annuals, school textbooks, official publications, and a selection of characteristic leaflets and offprints. Still to come are v. 4, Natural and applied sciences, and v. 8, Alphabetical index. Z2141.M256

Indonesia

Perpustakaan Nasional (Indonesia). Katalog majalah terbitan Indonesia : kumulasi 1779–1980 (A–Z) = Catalogue of Indonesian serials. [Jakarta] : Perpustakaan Nasional, Departemen Pendidikan dan Kebudayaan, [1985]. 412 p. **AA140**
In Dutch, English, and Indonesian. Introductory material in English and Indonesian.
An alphabetical listing of journals published in Indonesia 1779–1980. Cumulates *Katalog majalah terbitan Indonesia . . .* published in 3 v., 1981–83. Z6958.I45I53

———— Katalog terbitan Indonesia selama pendudukan Jepang, 1942–1945 = Catalogue of Indonesian publications during Japanese occupation, 1942–1945. [Jakarta] : Perpustakaan Nasional, Departemen Pendidikan dan Kebudayaan, [1983]. 101 p. **AA141**
Contains entries in Dutch, English, Japanese, Javanese, and Sundanese.
" . . . a bibliography of Indonesian publications, [including newspapers and journals] during Japanese occupation."—

Introd. Classified arrangement with author and title indexes. Z3271.I47

Iran

Mudabbirī, Maḥmūd. Farhang-i kitābhā-yi Fārsī : az qarn-i chahārum tā 1300. Chāp-i 1. Tihrān : Nashr-i Vīs, 1364 [1985]. v. 1–2. (In progress). **AA142**
Added title page for v. 2: Bibliography of Persian books from 921 to 1921.
Aims to list most of the books published in Persia from 921 to 1921. Does not include collected editions of an individual writer, pamphlets, or translations of European writers; the compilers hope to list the latter in a forthcoming volume. Arranged alphabetically by title, with an author index. A subject listing is planned. Z3366.M73

Iraq

al-Bibliyūghrāfīyah al-waṭanīyah al-'Irāqīyah / Wizārat al-Thaqāfah wa-al-I'lām, Da'irat al-Maktabah al-waṭanīyah. [Baghdād] : al-Qism, 1971– . ISSN 0250-5290. **AA143**
Alternate title: al-Fihris al-waṭanī lil-maṭbū'āt al-'Irāqīyah.
Title and frequency vary.
Title on added title page: Iraqi national bibliography.
Includes titles published in Iraq, those about Iraq, and those written by Iraqi authors but published elsewhere, deposited at the National Library. Separate sections for European languages and for Arabic, with each section divided into several parts, most of them in classified arrangement. Author and title indexes for both sections. Z3036.B5

Ireland

Irish books in print & Leabhair Gaeilge i gCló. 1984– . Wicklow [Wicklow] : S & J Cleary, c1984– . **AA144**
Offers a listing of "current literature from and about Ireland, North and South."—*Introd.* Includes English and Irish titles, excluding textbooks, published in Ireland, and books about Ireland available in the U.S. and Great Britain. English and Irish titles are listed separately; English titles are arranged by author, by title, and by broad subject, Irish titles by author and by title. Includes a list of Irish publishers. Z2031.I75

Israel

Israeli books in print. Tel Aviv : Israel Book and Printing Center, Israel Export Institute ; Jerusalem : Halberstadt Communication, c1986– . **AA145**
Intends to provide "a fair and representative picture of the range of subject matter and variety of languages" to be found in non-Hebrew books published in Israel 1970–86. Lists 1,260 books in classed arrangement with author/editor index. Directory of Israeli publishers. Z3476.I86

Italy

British Library. Catalogue of seventeenth century Italian books in the British Library. London ; Wolfeboro, N.H. : The Library, c1986. 3 v. ISBN 0-7123-0065-1.   **AA146**

Contents: v. 1–2, A–Z; v. 3, Indexes.

Continues and follows the pattern of the *Short-title catalogue of books printed in Italy . . . from 1465 to 1600 . . .* (*Guide* AA900). Aims to include "all those books now in the British Library which were either printed in Italy between 1601 and 1700, or printed outside Italy in the Italian language."—*Pref.* Includes "entries for books of printed and engraved music; for books which may be classified as atlases or roadbooks, though not for sheet maps; and for books of prints or engravings, with or without text."—*Introd.*

Vol. 2 includes an appendix, Books destroyed by enemy action, 1939–1945. There are indexes of publishers and printers; of places of publication; of places shown in imprint without printer or publisher (together with false and fictitious imprints); and of books with no place, printer, or publisher.   Z1015.B75

———— Short-title catalogue of books printed in Italy and of Italian books printed in other countries from 1465 to 1600 now in the British Library. Supplement. London ; Wolfeboro, N.H. : The Library, c1986 (1988 printing). 152 p. ISBN 0-7123-0094-5.   **AA147**

For the main volume and annotation, see *Guide* AA900.

Spine title: *Catalogue of Italian books, 1465–1600.*

Lists more than "1,200 books which have either been added to the Library since 1958, or been found to have been omitted by oversight from the previous work."—*Pref.* A section of corrigenda to the 1958 catalog precedes the new listings. An index of printers and publishers is followed by three indexes which also apply to the main volume: (1) Towns in Italy (with publishers); (2) Non-Italian towns; and (3) False and fictitious imprints. There is also a brief list of books destroyed during World War II which have been replaced since 1958.

Z1014.B67

Le edizioni italiane del XVI secolo : censimento nazionale. Roma : Istituto centrale per il catalogo unico delle biblioteche italiane e per le informazioni bibliografiche, 1985– . v. 1. ISBN 88-7107-010-0 (v. 1). (In progress).   **AA148**

The *Primo catalogo collettivo delle biblioteche italiana* (*Guide* AA143) having ceased publication with v.9, this represents a new effort toward a national union catalog of Italian publications of the 16th century. The first volume lists 3,539 editions held in some 550 Italian libraries. Arranged by author or anonymous title; v.1 has indexes of coauthors, translators and commentators, and of printers/publishers.   Z1014.E35

Michel, Suzanne P. Répertoire des ouvrages imprimés en langue italienne au XVIIe siècle conservés dans les bibliothèques de France. Paris : Éditions du Centre national de la recherche scientifique, 1984. v. 8. ISBN 2-222-03304-7 (v. 8).   **AA149**

For v. 1–7 and annotation, see *Guide* AA904.

Contents: v. 8, T–Z and suppl. Completes the set.

The supplement (p. 157–243) lists additions and corrections for v. 1–7.   Z2342.M5

Jamaica

Jamaican national bibliography. v.1 (Jan./Mar. 1975)– . Kingston, Jamaica : Institute of Jamaica, West India Reference Library, 1975– . Quarterly, with annual cumulations. ISSN 0075-2991. $20.00.   **AA150**

Continues a publication by the same title which ceased with the issue covering 1970; see *Guide* AA914. Bibliographic coverage provided through 1974 by a separately published volume; see *Guide* AA913.

Vols. for 1978– issued by the National Library of Jamaica.

Lists books, pamphlets, first issues or changes of serials, annual reports, government publications, maps and atlases, and audiovisual materials published in Jamaica, as well as works about Jamaica or by Jamaicans published outside the country and received at the National Library of Jamaica. Not based on depository law. Indexed.   Z1541.J27

Japan

●**J-BISC** [computer file]. Tokyo : National Diet Library in cooperation with the Japan Library Association, 1969– .   **AA151**

Available in CD-ROM, one retrospective disc of more than 512,000 records processed Jan. 1969–Dec. 1983 and one current disc of more than 420,000 records processed Jan. 1984– ; current disc updated quarterly.

A commercial version of JAPAN-MARC, containing records of monographs cataloged at the National Diet Library; serials are omitted. Records are displayed in Chinese characters (kanji), and instructions are in Japanese. Bibliographic information follows international standards. Boolean operators permit refined search using 12 indexes: titles, authors, subject headings, classification, publisher, ISBN, etc.

Jordan

al-Bibliyūghrāfiyā al-waṭanīyah al-Urdunnīyah. 1980. ['Ammān] : Mudīrīyat al-Maktabāt wa-al-Wathā'iq al-Waṭanīyah, 1981.   **AA152**

An attempt to produce an official national bibliography. Based on materials deposited at the Mudīrīyat al-Maktabāt wa-al-Wathā'iq al-Waṭanīyah [Department of Libraries, Documentation and National Archives]. Includes titles published in Jordan and selected titles published elsewhere. Separate Western language and Arabic sections, arranged by type of publication, then by subject. Author, title, and subject indexes for both Western and Arabic sections.   Z3471.B524

Korea

Taehan Min'guk ch'ulp'anmul ch'ongmongnok. 1963/1964– . Seoul : Kungnip chungang Tosŏgwan, 1965– . Annual. ISSN 0496-6945.   **AA153**

Added title page: Korean national bibliography.

Continues *Han'guk sŏmok*, 1945/62 (Seoul : Kungnip Chungang Tosŏgwan, 1964).

Includes titles published in the Republic of Korea deposited at the national library. Separate sections for: official publications, general publications, theses and scholarly works, books for children, special publications, and serial publications. Sections for official publications, books for children and special publications are arranged by author or issuing agency; the others are alphabetically arranged under subject headings of the Korean Decimal Classification system. Western-language titles are listed at the end of each section. Title index.   Z3316.T3

Latin America

Current

Libros en venta en Hispanoamérica y España. 5. ed. San Juan, P.R., Melcher Ediciones, 1990. 3 v. **AA154**
2nd ed., 1974 (*Guide* AA935); [4th ed.], 1988.
Contents: v. 1, Autores con guía de editores; v. 2, Títulos; v. 3, Materias.
Lists more than 150,000 titles currently available from some 6,000 publishers in 36 Spanish-speaking countries. A directory of publishers appears at the end of v.1. Vol.3 is a subject index arranged according the the Dewey Decimal Classification system. Kept up to date by supplements. Also available in microfiche. Z1601.L5

Libya

al-Bibliyūghrāfiyah al-'Arabīyah al-Lībīyah. 1972– . Ṭarābulus : Wizārat al-I'lām wa-al-Thaqāfah, al-Idārah al-'Āmmah lil-Thaqāfah, Qism al-Thaqāfah al-Jamāhīrīyah, 1973– . Annual. **AA155**
Added title page: *The Arab bibliography of Libya* ....
Title, place of publication, and publisher vary.
Lists titles published in Libya which come to the attention of the staff of the National Library; depository law is not effective. Arabic and English sections, each divided into classified subsections for trade, official publications, children's books and manuals, periodicals, and foreign publications. Author, title, subject indexes for monographs, and title and subject indexes for serials, although type of index varies from year to year.
Continues *al-Bibliyūghrāfiyah al-Waṭanīyah al-Lībīyah*, covering 1866/71–1971 (1972). Z3971.B53

Madagascar

Bibliographie Nationale de Madagascar. 1983– . Antananarivo : Bibliothèque Nationale, [1984]– . **AA156**
For earlier numbers and annotation, see *Guide* AA943.
Alternate title: Rakitahirinkevi-Pirenen'i Madigasikara.
Frequency varies.
Being compiled in separate sections by the Bibliothèque Nationale, which is responsible for monographs ("ouvrages") and the Université d'Antananarivo, for periodical articles. No volumes have appeared so far from the Université. The Bibliothèque Nationale has issued mimeographed lists irregularly since 1983 that include monographs published in Madagascar as well as selected foreign titles. Classified order with author, series, and subject indexes. There is a lag between publication of the bibliography and the time period covered.
Z3701.B5

Malta

Bibljografija nazzjonali ta' Malta = Malta national bibliography. 1983– . Valletta : National Library of Malta, 1984– . Annual. **AA157**
A classified list, arranged according to the Dewey Decimal Classification, of monographs, pamphlets, first issues and title changes of periodicals, and official and government publications published in Malta during the current year. Also includes works about the Maltese Islands and works by Maltese nationals published abroad. A "Select list of periodical articles" includes items from local sources as well as articles about Malta

or those written by Maltese in foreign periodicals. Index of authors, titles, and series.

Mauritius

"Bibliography of Mauritius ... " : in Mauritius. Archives Department. *Annual report of the Archives Department.* 1950– . Port Louis, Mauritius : Govt Printer, 1950– . Annual. ISSN 0076-5481. **AA158**
Since 1955, a supplement printed with the *Annual report* that lists titles published in Mauritius and selected titles of interest to Mauritius published elsewhere deposited at the Archives Department of Mauritius. Sections: private publications (alphabetical by author); periodicals, newspapers, and other serials (alphabetical by title); government and semi-official publications (by issuing agency); publications issued abroad (by author). No index. CD2355.M3A33

Mexico

Bibliografía mexicana / Biblioteca Nacional e Instituto Bibliografico Mexicano. enero-feb. (1967)– . México, [D.F.] : UNAM, Biblioteca Nacional e Instituto Bibliografico Mexicano. Annual. ISSN 0006-1069. **AA159**
For earlier numbers, see *Guide* AA962.
Frequency varies: Jan./Feb. 1967–Nov./Dec. 1980, bimonthly; Jan.1981–May 1985, monthly; a seven-month number, June/Dec. 1985; 1986– , annual.
Publisher varies.
Appears late, but since 1967 has provided continuous coverage. Includes titles published in Mexico and received through legal deposit at the national library. Some years include supplements. Absorbed *Anuario bibliográfico, 1958–69* (*Guide* AA964). Z1411.B53

Monaco

Lavagna, Paul. Bibliographie nationale de la principauté de Monaco, 1761–1986. Monaco : Impr. Testa, 1988 [i.e. 1989]. 345 p. : ill. **AA160**
Arranged alphabetically by author. Includes a history of publishing and printing in Monaco (p. i–xxii) and lists of printers, publishers, and serial publications. Lacks an index. A supplement and updates are planned. Z2191.L38

Morocco

Bibliographie nationale. 1961– . Rabat : Bibliothèque générale et archives du Maroc, 1962– . ISSN 0483-7991. **AA161**
Title, frequency, and scope vary; before 1984, had title *Bibliographie nationale marocaine*.
Currently includes titles published in or about Morocco and deposited at the national library. Separate French and Arabic sections; classified arrangement. Author, corporate author, title, and subject indexes. With 1985, periodical titles listed separately in *Guide des revues et des journaux marocains courants* (Rabat: Bibliothèque générale et archives, 1985–).
Z3636.B53

Nepal

Nepalese national bibliography for [year] / [comp. by Tribhuvan University Central Library and Nepal Research Centre]. 1981– . Kathmandu : The Library and The Centre, 1983– . Annual.   **AA162**

A listing of Nepalese publications including monographs, official and government publications, and other publications in book form, but excluding periodicals, newspapers, maps, musical scores, textbooks, school books, and ephemeral material such as trade catalogs. Not based on depository law. Arranged by Dewey Decimal Classification, with author, title, and subject indexes. A serial supplement is planned. Also appears in *Journal of the Nepal Research Centre : JNRC*: v.5–6 (1981/82) includes the 1981 bibliography; v.7 (1985) the 1982 bibliography; v.8 (1988) the 1983 bibliography.   Z3210.N44

Netherlands

British Library. Catalogue of books from the Low Countries 1601–1621 in the British Library / compiled by Anna Simoni. London : British Library, 1989. [400] p. : ill. ISBN 0-7123-0066X. £60.00.   **AA163**

Continues *Short-title catalogue of books printed in the Netherlands . . . (Guide AA966)*.

A listing of "books now in the British Library whose text is either wholly or to a large extent in Dutch or which, though in other languages, were printed or published in the Low Countries."—*Introd.* Arranged by author, with an index of printers and publishers and a general index of secondary authors, editors, artists, and translators.

Includes an appendix, Chronological list of news reports, which lists "publications which form part or are assumed to form part of regularly published reports, regardless of variable titles."—*p.721.* Appendix arranged alphabetically by city, then chronologically. printers and publishers

New Zealand

Bagnall, Austin Graham. New Zealand national bibliography to the year 1960. Wellington : Govt. Printer, 1985. v. 5.   **AA164**

For v. 1–4 and annotation, see *Guide* AA979.

Contents: v. 5, Supplement and index. Completes the set.

Vol. 5 is in three sections: (1) Addenda and corrigenda to v. 2–4; (2) Index to v. 2–4, and (3) Addenda and corrigenda to v. 1. Some 2,500 new titles have been addded and are assigned numbers "in closest alphabetical sequence to their hypothetical position in volumes I–IV with the prefix 'S'."—*Note.*   Z4101.B28

Nicaragua

Nicaraguan national bibliography, 1800–1978 = Bibliografía nacional nicaragüense, 1800–1978 / Latin American Bibliographic Foundation [and] Ministerio de Cultura de Nicaragua. Redlands, Calif. : Latin American Bibliographic Foundation ; Managua, D.N., Nicaragua : Biblioteca Nacional Rubén Darío, 1986–87. 3 v. ISBN 0-914369-01-6. $450.00.   **AA165**

General ed., G. F. Elmendorf.

Contents: v. 1–2, A–Z; v. 3, Serials and indexes.

Prefatory matter in English and Spanish.

An ambitious compilation designed to compensate in part for the lack of an official ongoing national bibliography. "These volumes sum up the entire Nicaraguan bibliography, everything that has been published by Nicaraguans or about Nicaragua, whether inside the country or abroad, whether printed or mimeographed and whether a book or a flier, from the time the printing press was introduced into the country in 1829 until 1978."—*Prologue.* Monographs and serials are listed by main entry in separate sections. Only annuals and irregular serials are included, but a "serial history and holding records section" is issue-specific and locates copies in selected U.S. and Nicaraguan libraries. There are separate author, title, and subject indexes in English for both the monographs and the serials, plus an "encabezamientos de materia, monografias y publicaciones en serie" which gives cross-references to the English indexes.   Z1481.N53

Norway

19th and 20th centuries

Norsk bokfortegnelse, 1971–75. Oslo : Universitetsbiblioteket i Oslo, 1984–85. 3 v. ISSN 0029-1870.   **AA166**

For earlier cumulations, see *Guide* AA992.

Current periodicals, printed music, and yearbooks are omitted from these quinquennial volumes; printed music, 1981– , can be found in *Norsk bokfortegnelse. Musikktrykk.* Alphabetic arrangement; classified index. A microfiche edition is available under the title *Norske trykk*; online searches of *Norsk bokfortegnelse* are available through the University Library, Oslo.   Z2591.N865

Current

●**Nasjonalbibliografiske data 1962–1990** [computer file]. Oslo : Universitetsbiblioteket i Oslo, 1962– .   **AA167**

Coverage: books, 1962–90; periodical articles, 1980–90. File size: more than 140,000 records (books); 95,000 records (articles). Updated annually. Available in CD-ROM (producer).

Articles are drawn from 33 Norwegian-language periodicals. Two search formats, for librarians and for general readers. Virtually every MARC tag is searchable.

Oceania

South Pacific bibliography. 1981– . Suva : Univ. of the South Pacific Library, Pacific Information Centre, 1982– . Annual.   **AA168**

Supersedes *Pacific Collection accession list* (v. 1–8; 1975–82), which in turn superseded *Pacific Collection legal deposit accessions* (1972–74).

A cooperative regional bibliography which includes books, pamphlets, government publications, first issues of serials, maps, local language publications, and material related to social and cultural affairs published in the region or related thereto. Also includes titles on the Pacific and indigenous peoples in Australia, Hawaii, and New Zealand. Lists titles received at the Library regardless of date and place of publication, as well as titles published after 1975 not previously included. Monographs are arranged by Dewey Decimal Classification, with author/ title and subject indexes. Separate list of periodicals and legal notices; directory of printers and publishers.   Z4001.S65

Papua New Guinea

Butler, Alan. A New Guinea bibliography. Waigani : Univ. of Papua New Guinea Pr., 1984–1987. v. 1–4. (In progress). **AA169**

For annotation, see *Supplement* DG11. Z4811.B88

Paraguay

Fernández-Caballero, Carlos F. S. The Paraguayan bibliography : a retrospective and enumerative bibliography of printed works of Paraguayan authors. Asunción ; Wash. : Paraguay Arandu Books, 1983. v. 3. (In progress). **AA170**

For v. 1–2, see *Guide* AA1004.

At head of title: Paraguái rembiapolúe ha paraguái rehegúa tembiapo añembokuatiavaekúe.

Prepared also by Marianne Fernández Caballero.

Vol. 3 has title: La bibliografía paraguaya.

An author listing of 3,550 unannotated entries that supplements v. 1–2. Includes additional works by Paraguayans and foreign works on Paraguay published 1975–1982. Some earlier imprints not previously listed are also included. Subject index. Z1821.F45

Paraguay ... años de bibliografía. Asunción, Paraguay : Cromos, 198?– . ISSN 0257-7070. Irregular. **AA171**

Compiler: Margarita Kallsen.

Published at intervals: ... *cinco años de bibliografía, 1980–1984* (publ. 1986); ... *dos años de bibliografía, 1985–1986* (publ. 1987); ... *un año de bibliografía, 1987* (publ. 1988); ... *dos años de bibliografía, 1988–1989* (publ. 1990).

Serie Bibliografía paraguaya, 4–5, 7–8.

Publisher varies.

An annotated bibliography of books, journals, and official publications published in Paraguay or about Paraguay published abroad. The five-year list includes more than 1,400 titles, the first two-year list 450, the one-year list 289. Appendixes list publications omitted from prior lists. Z1821.P37

Peru

Bibliografía nacional. Enero/marzo 1978–nov./dic. 1982. Lima : Biblioteca Nacional, Instituto Nacional de Cultura. **AA172**

For earlier volumes and annotation, see *Guide* AA1008.

Ceased publication.

An attempt to fill the bibliographic gap for the years not yet covered by *Anuario bibliográfico peruano* (*Guide* AA1010). Each issue has author and subject indexes and each volume a cumulated annual index. Z1851.P47a

Poland

Bibliografia polska 1901–1939 = Polish bibliography 1901–1939 / pod redakcją Janiny Wilgat. Wrocław : Zakład Narodowy im. Ossolińskich, 1986–1991. v. 1–2. ISBN 83-04-01899-3 (set). zł1'500.00. (In progress). **AA173**

At head of title : Biblioteka Narodowa. Instytut Bibliograficzny.

Contents: v. 1–2, A–Bok.

Designed to fill the gap between Karol Estreicher's *Bibliografia polska* (below) and the *Przewodnik bibljograficzny* (*Guide* AA1029).

Lists works published in Poland regardless of language, and works by Polish writers and works about Poland published throughout the world, 1901–August 1939. Arranged by author or title (if anonymous); provides brief bibliographic descriptions. If possible, copies are located in major Polish libraries. Each volume has a separately published index of names (excluding names used as main entries) and titles. Z2521.B568

Estreicher, Karol Józef Teofil. Bibliografia polska XIX stulecia. Wyd. 2. Kraków : Państwowe Wydawn. Naukowe, Oddzial w Krakowie, 1987. v. 13–14. (In progress). **AA174**

For v.1–12, see *Guide* AA1025.

Contents: v.13–14, K–Katakumby. Z2521.E85

Portugal

Livros disponíveis. 1987– . Lisboa : Associacão Portuguesa de Editores e Livreiros, 1987– . Annual. ISSN 0870-6093. **AA175**

Issue for 1985–86 entitled *Catalogo dos livros disponíveis*.

Prepared by the Bibliographical Documentation Centre of the Portuguese Publishers' and Booksellers' Association.

Kept up to date with alternate year supplement: *Livros disponíveis, actualizacão e adenda*.

Introductory matter in Portuguese and English.

A listing of currently available books by title, author, and subject. Includes a list of publishers, distributors, and booksellers. Z2715.C38

Qatar

Qā'imat al-intāj al-fikrī al-Qaṭarī li-'ām / Dawlat Qaṭar, Wizārat al-Tarbiyah wa-al-Ta'līm, Dār al-Kutub al-Qaṭarīyah. 1970– . al-Dawḥah [Qatar] : al-Dār, 1971– . Annual. **AA176**

Lists books, pamphlets, dissertations, serials, maps, music, official and government publications, and audiovisual materials written by Qataris and deposited in the National Library. Beginning in 1982, has sections for general publications, government publications, school publications, and children's books in non-Arabic languages. The general and school sections are arranged in classified sequence; the government publications by issuing agency. Author, title, subject, and publisher indexes. Z3038.Q2Q24

Romania

Bibliografia românească modernă, 1831–1918 / prefață de Gabriel Ștrempel ; [coordonare generală, Gabriel Ștrempel ; autori Neonila Onofrei, et al.]. [Bucharest] : Editura Științifică și Enciclopedică : Societatea de Stiințe Filologice din R.S. România, 1984–1989. v. 1–3. (In progress). **AA177**

At head of title: Biblioteca Academiei Republicii Socialiste România.

Contents: [Partea I] v. 1–3, A–Q.

Designed as a continuation of *Bibliografia româneasca veche 1508–1830* (*Guide* AA1044). Pt.I is primarily an author listing with some form headings for anonymous works (e.g., catalogs, catechisms) and cross-references. It includes works by Romanians published outside Romania. Z2921.B59 1984

Current

Bibliografia României: Cărți, albume, hărți. v. 39 (1990)– . [București] : Biblioteca Națională a României, 1990– . Semimonthly.   **AA178**

Represents a change in title and assumes the numbering of part of *Bibliografia Republicii Socialiste România* (*Guide* AA1048), which ceased with v. 39 (1989). Other subseries are *Note muzicale, discrui* (1968–) and *Articole din publicatii periodice si seriale* (1953–).

Arranged by Universal Decimal Classification. A name index is followed by a table of contents, which gives the order of classification.

Russia and the U.S.S.R.

General

Semenovker, B. A. Retrospektivnaĭa gosudarstvennaĭa bibliografiĭa SSSR : spravochnik. Moskva : Izd-vo "Knizhnaĭa palata", 1990. 303 p.   **AA179**

Offers detailed descriptions of retrospective bibliographies produced by the Soviet Union and its union and autonomous republics, covering publications from the 16th century to the present. Indexes by author, title, institution, language, place of publication, and genre.   Z2491.S45

18th century

Svodnyĭ katalog knig na inostrannykh ĭazykakh, izdannykh v Rossii v XVIII veke, 1701–1800 / [redaktsionnaĭa kollegiĭa, V.A. Filov . . . A.I. Kopanev (otv. red.) . . . [et al.] ; otvetstvennye sostaviteli, E.A. Savel'eva, T.P. Shcherbakova]. Leningrad : "Nauka," Leningradskoe otd-nie, 1984–1986. v. 2–3.   **AA180**

For v. 1 and annotation, see *Guide* AA1057.

At head of title: Akademiĭa Nauk SSSR. Ordena Trudovogo Krasnogo Znameni Biblioteka.

Contents: v. 2, H–R; v. 3, S–Z, Prilozheniĭa [Supplements]. Completes the set.

Supplements in v. 3 include: bookseller and library catalogs, St. Petersburg and Moscow; advertisements from St. Petersburg Academy of Sciences and Moscow University; material earlier thought to be published in Russia, including chronological index of materials; and publications with falsified publishing data. Bibliography; list of abbreviations.   Z2491.S9

Scandinavia

Guide to Nordic bibliography / general ed., Erland Munch-Petersen. [Copenhagen] : Nord, c1984. 235 p. : ill. ISBN 87-7303-080-5. Kr.195.00.   **AA181**

For annotation of basic volume and 1988 suppl., see *Supplement* DC181.   Z2551.G84

Senegal

Bibliographie du Sénégal. no. 40 (1972)– . [Dakar : Archives du Sénégal], 1972–. ISSN 0378-9942.   **AA182**

Early volumes issued over agency's former name, Archives du Sénégal. Continues *Bulletin bibliographique des Archives du Sénégal* (Oct. 1964–1971).

Includes publications received by legal deposit, Senegalese works acquired by the Archives, works about Senegal, and those by Senegalese published elsewhere. Beginning with no. 52, employs a classified subject arrangement. Some issues include supplements (e.g.: no. 48, Liste des périodiques Sénégalese reçus aux Archives; no. 52, Thèses et mémoires reçus aux Archives en 1980). Author and title indexes.   Z3711.A73a

Sierra Leone

Sierra Leone. Library Board. Sierra Leone publications. 1962/63– . Freetown : Sierra Leone Library Board, 1964– . Annual. ISSN 0583-2276. $6.00.   **AA183**

A classified subject listing of books, pamphlets, first issues of periodicals, government publications, publications of international government organizations, maps and atlases, reports, and internal documents published in Sierra Leone during the year of coverage and received by the Library Board under depository law. Also includes works by Sierra Leoneans or about Sierra Leone published elsewhere. Earlier issues are printed, later ones mimeographed. Author/title index.   Z3553.S5S5

South Africa

RSANB, 1926–1958 : retrospective South African national bibliography for the period, 1926–1958 = Retrospektiewe Suid-Afrikaanse nasionale bibliografie vir die tydperk, 1926–1958. Pretoria : State Library, 1985. 2 v. : ill. (Bibliographies / the State Library = Bibliografieë / die Staatsbiblioteek, no. 33). ISBN 0-7989-1208-1.   **AA184**

Contents: v. 1, A–Z; v. 2, Index.

Prefatory matter in English and Afrikaans.

Intended to fill the gap between *South African bibliography to the year 1925* (*Guide* DD176) and *SANB: South African national bibliography* (*Guide* AA1075).

Includes material published in South Africa and South West Africa (excluding the High Commission Territories); excludes material in Bantu languages, periodicals and government publications, technical reports, and highly ephemeral material. Arranged alphabetically by main entry. The index includes titles, series, personal and corporate names in a single alphabet.   Z3601.R77

Spain

General

See also Latin America (above).

Palau Claveras, Agustín. Addenda y corrigenda o volumen complementario del tomo primero del Manual del librero hispanoamericano de Antonio Palau y Dulcet. Barcelona : Editorial Palau y Dulcet, 1990. v. 1. ISBN 84-4047595-0. (In progress).   **AA185**

Contents: v. 1, A–Azzavac.

A meticulous elaboration of information appearing in the 2nd ed. of Palau (*Guide* AA1083), supplying omitted material, corrections, and additional entries; it incorporates material from the appendix published with v.7 of the *Indice* (below).

——————— Indice alfabético de títulos-materias, correcciones, conexiones y adiciones del Manual del librero hispanoamericano de Antonio Palau y Dulcet. Gerona : Palacete Palau Dulcet ; Oxford : Dolphin Book, 1985–1987. v. 5–7. ISBN 84-300-4752-2.   **AA186**

For v.1–4 and annotation, see *Guide* AA1084.

Contents: v.5–7, Mil–Z and "Apendice, A–Z". Completes the set.

The appendix includes in a single alphabet corrections, additional information, and some titles from the main body of the index under a second subject heading.   Z2681.P16P34

Early

British Library. Catalogue of books printed in Spain and of Spanish books printed elsewhere in Europe before 1601 now in the British Library. 2nd ed. London : British Library, 1989. 294 p. ISBN 0-7123-0150-X. £50.00.   **AA187**

1st ed., 1921, had title: *Short-title catalogue of books prionted in Spain . . .* (*Guide* AA1091).

" . . . very considerably revised and expanded, and for the first time includes comprehensive indexes of printers, booksellers and towns both within and outside Spain in which books in Spanish were printed."—*Pref.* Entries conform to new cataloging rules of the British Library so that some items appear under headings differing from those of the 1921 ed.   Z2682.B75 1989

Catálogo colectivo del patrimonio bibliográfico español : siglo XVII / Dirección General del Libro y Bibliotecas, Biblioteca Nacional. Madrid : Arco Libros, 1988–98. v. 1–2. ISBN 84-7635-043-0. (In progress).   **AA188**

Contents: v. 1–2, A–Cañ.

A listing by author, or title if anonymous, of books published in Spain or in Spanish during the 17th century held by major libraries in Madrid. Includes detailed bibliographic descriptions and Madrid locations.   Z1015.C37

Laurenti, Joseph L. Hispanic rare books of the Golden Age (1470–1699) in the Newberry Library of Chicago and in selected North American libraries. N.Y. : P. Lang, c1989. 229 p. (American university studies. Series II, Romance languages and literature, vol. 111). ISBN 0-8204-1066-7. $45.00.   **AA189**

A listing of the more than 1,000 Hispanic books published during the Golden Age held by the Newberry Library. Arranged alphabetically by author, with citations to references in other catalogs and locations in major American libraries. Indexed by place name (with publication dates) and by printer, publisher, and bookseller.   Z1029.L37

Sweden

Early

Swedish imprints 1731–1833 : a retrospective national bibliography / prepared at the Center for Bibliographical Studies, Uppsala ; general ed., Rolf E. Du Rietz. Uppsala : Dahlia Books, 1984–90. v. 20–31. (In progress).   **AA190**

For v. 1–19 and annotation, see *Guide* AA1113.

Co-editor, v. 16– : Gun-Britt Du Rietz.

Prefatory material in English and Swedish.

Accompanied by a manual, "Basic information for users of Swedish imprints, 1831–1833." A "second cumulative index" cumulates indexing for v. 1–20, replacing the earlier cumulation covering v. 1–15 and individual indexes in v. 16–20. Indexes: personal names; printing, publishing, and bookselling

firms; entry headings; and supplementary entries which supersede all earlier lists of addenda and corrigenda.   Z2621.S975

Current

Svensk bok-katalog [för aren]. 1971/75. Stockholm : Liberförlag, 1985–86. 3v. (In progress).   **AA191**

For earlier volumes, see *Guide* AA1115.

Contents: v. 1–2, A–Ö; v. 3, Systematisk avdelning.

Scope of the cumulations varies slightly (e.g., treatment of sheet music, maps); cumulations list additional titles excluded from annual volumes (e..g., certain legal deposit material, state and local official publications, society and firm publications).   Z2621.S95

Syria

al-Bibliyūghrāfiyā al-Waṭanīyah al-Sūrīyah. 1984– . Dimashq : al-Maktabat al-Asad, 1985– . Annual.   **AA192**

Continues *al-Nashrah al-Maktabīyah bi-al-Kutub al-Ṣādirah fī al-Jumhūrīyah al-'Arabīyah al-Sūrīyah* covering 1970–1973 (Ministry of National Culture and Guidance, 1971–1974).

At head of title: Jumhuriyah al-'Arabiyah al-Suriyah. Title on added t.p.: The Syrian national bibliography.

A classified arrangement of Arabic language books, pamphlets, serials, government publications, and theses published in Syria and deposited at the Assad Library. Includes some titles published since *al-Nashrah . . .* ceased. Recent volumes include a section for periodicals, newspapers, and irregular serials (alphabetically arranged), and a section for Western language books (in classified arrangement). An additional retrospective volume covering items published 1980–84 was issued in 1984. Author, title, subject, and publisher indexes.   Z3028

al-Bibliyūghrāfiyā al-waṭanīyah al-Sūrīyah al-rāji'ah. Dimashq : Manshūrat Maktabat al-Asad, 1987– . v. 1– .   **AA193**

A retrospective bibliography of titles published in Syria prior to the current national bibliography; also includes titles by Syrians published abroad and titles from other languages translated into Syrian. Classified arrangement; author, title, subject, publisher indexes.   Z3481.M33

Taiwan

Chung-hua min kuo ch'u pan t'u shu mu lu. v.1 (June 1970)– . [T'ai-pei] : Kuo li chung yang t'u shu kuan. Monthly. ISSN 0301-5165.   **AA194**

Cover title: Chinese national bibliography.

Supersedes *Hsin shu chien pao = The monthly list of Chinese books*, v. 1–9, 1960–69. Title varies.

Published monthly, with irregular annual and five-year cumulations.

Lists books and first issues of periodicals published in Taiwan and deposited at the National Central Library. Also includes books acquired by gift or purchase and earlier titles of research value not previously listed. Arrangement varies; recent issues arranged by broad subject. Title and author indexes.   Z3111.C59

Thailand

Bannánukrom hǎěng chát = Thai national bibliography. 1975– . [Krungthêp, i.e. Bangkok, Thailand] : Hosamut hǎěng Chat, Krom Sinlapakon, [1978]– . ISSN 0125-1899.   **AA195**

Introduction and table of contents in Thai and English.

Lists publications received by the National Library of Thailand under depository law and works of national interest published elsewhere. Since 1985, in two sections: books, arranged by Dewey Decimal Classification, with author, title, and cremation books indexes; and serials, arranged alphabetically by title.

Uganda

Uganda national bibliography. v. 1, no. 1 (Mar. 1987)– . [Kampala, Uganda] : Makerere Univ. Library Services, 1987– . Quarterly.   **AA196**

Lists books and first issues of serials published in Uganda, and books about Uganda or by Ugandan authors published in other countries. Arranged by Dewey Decimal Classification, with an author and title index. Does not cumulate.

Z3586.U37

Uruguay

Library of Congress. Library of Congress Office, Rio de Janeiro. Accessions list, Brazil and Uruguay. v. 15, no. 1 (Jan./Feb. 1989)– . Rio de Janeiro : Library of Congress Office, [1989]– . Bimonthly. ISSN 1041-1763.   **AA197**

For annotation, see *Supplement* AA90.   Z1671.U53a

Venezuela

Boletín ISBN, Venezuela. No. 1 (1987)– . Caracas : Instituto Autónomo Biblioteca Nacional y de Servicios de Bibliotecas, Dirección de Formación de Colecciones, Agencia Nacional del ISBN, 1987– . Annual.   **AA198**

A register of Venezuelan publications assigned International Standard Book numbers, the 1987 issue covering 1985–86. Arranged by Dewey Decimal Classification, with indexes by ISBN, authors, and titles. Useful list of publishers with addresses.   Z1911.B64

Drenikoff, Iván. Impresos venezolanos del siglo XIX. Caracas : Instituto Autónomo Biblioteca Nacional y de Servicios de Bibliotecas, 1984. 238 p.   **AA199**

Offers an alphabetical listing of publications, excluding periodicals, but including broadsheets, leaflets, and books, produced in Venezuela, 1808–30. Gives locations in South American and major North American and European libraries. Chronological index and an index of printers arranged by city.

Z213.V45D64

Villasana, Angel Raúl. Nuevo repertorio bibliográfico venezolano : años 1951–1975. Caracas : Instituto Autónomo Biblioteca Nacional y de Servicios de Bibliotecas : Fundación para el Rescate del Acervo Documental Venezolano, 1989– . v. 1. ISBN 980-6016-69-6 (set). (In progress).   **AA200**

Contents: v. 1, A–Ch.

Continues the coverage of the compiler's *Ensayo de un repertorio bibliográfico venezolano* (*Guide* AA1143), which lists works of Venezuelan authors 1808–1950. Like its predecessor,

excludes scientific works. Offers extremely detailed contents and explanatory notes. Indicates the location of the copy described. A list of the major bibliographies consulted appears on p. 563–573.   Z1911.V54

Vietnam

Thư mục quốc gia / Cộng hòa xã hội chủ nghĩa Việt Nam, Thư viện quốc gia. 1954. Hà-nội : Cộng Hòa Xã Hội Chủ Nghĩa Việt Nam, Thư viện quốc gia, 1954– . Monthly (issues often combined), with annual index cumulation.   **AA201**

Although coverage has varied, presently includes books, first issues of periodicals, official and government publications, annual reports, microforms, newspapers, photographs, and drawings deposited in the National Library. Arranged alphabetically within general subject categories. Author and title indexes.   Z3226.T48

Wales

Rees, Eiluned. Libri Walliae : a catalogue of Welsh books and books printed in Wales, 1546–1820 = catalog o lyfrau cymraeg a llyfrau a argraffwyd yng nghymru, 1546–1820. Aberystwyth : National Library of Wales, 1987. 2 v. (923, lxxxx) : ill. ISBN 0-907158-19-6 (set).   **AA202**

Added title page in Welsh. Introductory matter in English and Welsh.

While admitting imperfections, the compiler offers this as "the most comprehensive catalogue to date of Welsh books and books printed in Wales before 1820. Periodicals, newspapers, ephemera and ballads are not included. Ballads are defined . . . as poems for which tunes are provided, although exceptions are made for elegies."—*Guide for the reader.* Arranged by author, issuing body, or key word in title, with five indexes: titles, names, chronological; the book-trade (Wales); the book-trade (outside Wales). Vol. 2 includes an essay on "The Welsh book-trade before 1820" and a section of reproductions of "Some ornaments used by printers of Welsh books." Does not locate copies.   Z2071.L5

Yugoslavia

Bibliografija Jugoslavije. Zbirke i monografske serije / Jugoslovenski bibliografski institut. 1984/1985– . Beograd : Institut, 1986– . Irregular. ISSN 0352-8847.   **AA203**

A companion to *Bibliografija Jugoslavije; knjige, brošure i muzikalije* (*Guide* AA1152).

An alphabetical title listing of some 2,000 collections and monographic series published during the year. Gives place and publisher, but no indication of volume number or beginning date.   Z2951.B38

Srpska bibliografija : knjige, 1868–1944 / urěivački odbor : predsednik Radovan Samardžić . . . et al. ; glavni i odgovorni urednik Milomir Petrović. Beograd : Narodna biblioteka Srbije, 1989. v. 1–2. ISBN 86-7035-024-6 (v. 1). (In progress).   **AA204**

T.p. and introductory material in English and Serbian. Title on added t.p.: *The Serbian bibliography : books, 1868–1944.*

"Edited by the National Library of Serbia."—*t.p.*

Contents: v. 1–2, A–Děs. To be complete in 20 v.

Constitutes Pt. IV of the "Serbian retrospective bibliography," to be published under the auspices of the Council for Science and Culture of Serbia. Also planned are Pt. I, 1494–1700; Pt. II, 1701–1800; Pt. III, 1801–67.

Attempts to list Serbian books published in Serbia, books published by writers of Serbian origin throughout the world in any language, and "books published in Serbo-Croatian in other republics or outside Yugoslavia if they are intended for Serbs."—*p.xxiv*. Arranged alphabetically by author with detailed bibliographic descriptions. Provides locations in Yugoslavian and some European libraries. Each volume has indexes of names (including authors, coauthors, translators, editors, etc.) and subjects; indexes will be cumulated when Pt. IV is complete.   Z2951.S65

Current

Slovenska bibliografija. Knjige. 1985, 1/3– . Ljubljana: Narodna in univerzitetna knjižnica, 1985– .   **AA205**

Continues in part *Slovenska bibliografija* (*Guide* AA1153) which ceased with v. 31, 1977, publ. 1985.

Frequency varies: monthly, 1985; quarterly, 1986– .

A bibliography of Slovenian books arranged by Universal Decimal Classification. Each issue has an author index; an annual author index is issued separately.

For 1978–84, will appear in 4 parts, continuing the numbering of the earlier edition: A, Serijski publikacije; B, Knjige; C, Članki in leposlovni prispevki v serijskih publikacijah in zbornikih; and D, Ostalo in neknjižno gradivo (not yet published). It is not clear whether sections A, C, or D will continue beyond 1985.

Zaire

Bibliographie du Zaire. 1987/88– . [Kinshasa/Gombé: Bibliothèque Nationale du Zaire, 1990–]. Annual.   **AA206**

A new attempt to record titles published in Zaire or elsewhere about Zaire. The initial volume lists internal publications only, and is arranged by Dewey Decimal Classification, with lists of publishers and journals and an author index. Beginning with the volume covering 1989, to be in three annual volumes: Imprimés; Les mémoires et thèses de doctorat; Les documents audio-visuels.

AB

Librarianship and Library Resources

GENERAL WORKS

Bibliography

ARBA guide to library science literature, 1970–1983 / ed. by Donald G. Davis, Jr. and Charles D. Patterson. Littleton, Colo.: Libraries Unlimited, 1987. 682 p. ISBN 0-87287-585-7. $65.00.   **AB1**

A comprehensive, evaluative listing of some 1,700 works in library science, both reference and non-reference, arranged under four broad categories: general works, reference works, works dealing with types of libraries, and works dealing with library services and special topics. Comprises reviews published in *American reference books annual* (*Guide* AA476) and summary reviews prepared specifically for this work; most are signed. Author/title and limited subject indexes.   Z666.A73

Davis, Donald G. American library history: a comprehensive guide to the literature / Donald G. Davis, Jr., John Mark Tucker. Santa Barbara, Calif.: ABC-Clio, c1989. 471 p. ISBN 0-87436-142-7.   **AB2**

A revised and expanded version of Michael H. Harris's *American library history: a bibliography* (Austin: Univ. of Texas Pr., 1978). Includes 7,150 entries, published through 1986, consciously written as history, about libraries and closely related subjects in the U.S. In 15 sections: (1) Historiography and sources, (2) General studies, (3) Private libraries and reading tastes, (4) Predecessors of the public library, (5) Public libraries, (6) Academic libraries, (7) School libraries, (8) State libraries, (9) Special libraries, (10) Archival enterprise, (11) Education for librarianship, (12) Library associations, (13) Special aspects of librarianship, (14) Women in librarianship, (15) Biographies of individual librarians and library benefactors. Indexes of authors, institutions, and essays.   Z731.D38

Herring, Mark Youngblood. Controversial issues in librarianship: an annotated bibliography, 1960–1984. N.Y.: Garland, 1987. 698 p. ISBN 0-8240-8578-7. **AB3**

Coverage extends to controversies regarding collections, library facilities, human factors in libraries, technology, cooperation and networking, library education, reference services, library mangement, librarians and society, and the profession. Non-English material is excluded. Annotations describe the controversy in question and whenever possible, trace it to a conclusion. Entries are arranged alphabetically by subject. Author/name and title indexes.   Z666.H44

Prytherch, Raymond John. Sources of information in librarianship and information science. 2nd ed. Aldershot, England; Brookfield, Vt.: Gower, c1987. 153 p. ISBN 0-566-05509-0. $37.00 (est.).   **AB4**

1st ed., 1983.

A narrative description, illustrated with sample entries, of the principal sources and services (Encyclopedic tools; Theses, dissertations, and reports; Current awareness; and Abstracting and indexing services) that provide access to the literature and to professional knowledge of the field. Emphasis is on English-language materials. Indexed.   Z666.P935

Purcell, Gary R. Reference sources in library and information services : a guide to the literature / Gary R. Purcell with Gail Ann Schlachter. Santa Barbara, Calif. : ABC-Clio, c1984. 359 p. ISBN 0-87436-355-1. $45.00.   **AB5**

An annotated bibliography of separately published, commercially available library-related reference sources. Emphasizes titles issued from the early 1900s through the first half of 1983 in the U.S., Canada, the U.K., Australia, and New Zealand. Some foreign-language titles are also included. In two parts: Pt. 1, General, is divided by type of publication (e.g., bibliographies; biographical and membership directories; sources of library statistics), with subdivisions for format, language, and geographic region, as applicable. Pt. 2 lists, under 103 alphabetically arranged subject sections, 500 reference works that concentrate on one or more library issues, processes, institutions, or techniques. Numerous cross-references; separate author, title, and geographic indexes.   Z666.P96

Current

●**Library literature** [computer file]. Bronx, N.Y. : H.W. Wilson, 1984– .   **AB6**

Machine-readable version of *Library literature* (*Guide* AB14).

File size: 41,000 records. Available online (WILSON-LINE; updated twice weekly) and in CD-ROM (Wilson, Faxon; updated quarterly).

Dissertations

Library and information science : a catalog of selected doctoral dissertation research. Ann Arbor, Mich. : Univ. Microfilms International, [1986]. 83 p.   **AB7**

Editors: Charles H. Davis, Debora Shaw.

A classified list of 1,848 dissertations and master's theses, 1970–1985, available for purchase through University Microfilms International. There are no indexes, but an alphabetical list of subjects with page references serves as a table of contents. Includes ordering information.   Z666.U54

Periodicals

Bowman, Mary Ann. Library and information science journals and serials : an analytical guide. Westport, Conn. : Greenwood, c1985. 140 p. ISBN 0-313-23807-3.   **AB8**

An alphabetically arranged, annotated list of 311 periodicals (including annuals), international in scope, but limited to materials in English. Information was drawn mainly from responses to questionnaires. An appendix lists 56 additional titles for which full information was not available. Geographical, classified title, and publisher indexes.   Z666.B64

Handbooks of Usage

Gates, Jean Key. Guide to the use of libraries and information sources. 6th ed. N.Y. : McGraw-Hill, c1989. 348 p. ISBN 0-07-022999-6. $17.95.   **AB9**

5th ed., 1983 (*Guide* AB29).

Follows the plan of the previous edition.   Z710.G27

Grimsted, Patricia Kennedy. A handbook for archival research in the USSR. [N.Y.?] : International Research and Exchanges Board ; [Wash.] : Kennan Institute for Advanced Russian Studies, c1989. 430 p.   **AB10**

For annotation, see *Supplement* DC201.   CD1711.G68

Encyclopedias

ALA world encyclopedia of library and information services / [Robert Wedgeworth, ed.]. 2nd ed. Chicago : Amer. Lib. Assoc., 1986. 895 p. : ill. ISBN 0-8389-0427-0.   **AB11**

1st ed., 1980 (*Guide* AB32).

Greatly expanded, revised, and updated. The "parallel index" in the margins of the text pages of the first edition has been replaced by an expanded conventional index that ties the *Encyclopedia* to the *ALA yearbook of library and information services* (*Guide* AB110). A review in *Library quarterly* 58 (Apr. 1988) :2 finds that "its size and format uniquely promote comparative study and a coherent understanding of the field, and its kinship to the *ALA yearbook* renders both publications more useful than either would be alone."   Z1006.A18

Encyclopedia of library and information science / Editors: Allen Kent and Harold Lancour. Assistant ed.: William Z. Nasri. N.Y. : M. Dekker, 1985–1990. v. 38–45. ISBN 0-8247-2004-0 (v. 4). (In progress).   **AB12**

For v.1–37 and annotation, see *Guide* AB33.

Contents: v.38–45, supplements 3–10.   Z1006.E57

Wertsman, Vladimir. The librarian's companion : a handbook of thousands of facts and figures on libraries/librarians, books/newspapers, publishers/booksellers. N.Y. : Greenwood, 1987. 166 p. ISBN 0-313-25500-8.   **AB13**

Presents 644 entries referring to some 200 countries, 300 book and periodical titles, and 338 noted people, arranged in two parts. Pt. 1, arranged by country, gives minimal library and publishing facts. Pt. 2 consists of annotated lists: (1) Noted librarians; (2) Who said what on books, libraries, and librarians; (3) Librarians in belle lettres; (4) Books, newspapers and libraries on stamps. Index.   Z670.W39

Dictionaries

Bürger, Erich. Dictionary of information science. Amsterdam ; N.Y. : Elsevier, 1989. 2 v. (903 p.). ISBN 0-444-98904-8 (set). $250.00 (est.).   **AB14**

A listing of information science terms without definitions, arranged on an English base with equivalent terms in German, French, and Russian. Covers computer architecture, hardware and software components, systems engineering, interactive and batch processing, programming, data mangement, artificial intelligence, expert systems, databases, etc. Vol. 2 consists of German, French, and Russian indexes.   Z1006.B94

Harrod, Leonard Montague. Harrod's librarians' glossary of terms used in librarianship, documentation and the book crafts, and reference book. 6th ed, comp. by Ray

Prytherch. Aldershot, England ; Brookfield, Vt. : Gower, c1987. 855 p. ISBN 0-566-03538-3. **AB15**

5th ed., 1984 (*Guide* AB39).

"A terminological reference source for . . . librarianship, information science, archive work, authorship, publishing, the printing industry, the book trade, binding and conservation."—*Pref.* For this edition, listings were revised and expanded to include terms from peripheral, nontraditional fields that now form part of the central ground of these professions and trades. Remains primarily British in scope. Z1006.H32

Rosenberg, Kenyon C. Dictionary of library and educational technology / Kenyon C. Rosenberg and John J. Elsbree. 3rd and enl. ed. Englewood, Colo. : Libraries Unlimited, 1989. 196 p. ISBN 0-87287-623-3. $28.50. **AB16**

2nd ed., 1983 (*Guide* AB41).

Completely revised, updated, and expanded, now including about 1,000 terms. Follows the plan of the previous editions. TS2301.A7R66

Sawoniak, Henryk. New international dictionary of acronyms in library and information science and related fields / Henryk Sawoniak, Maria Witt. München ; N.Y. : K.G. Saur, 1988. 449 p. ISBN 3-598-10697-1. **AB17**

About 17,000 acronyms (including variant and equivalent forms) in library and information science, publishing, printing, archival management, journalism, and reprography. Global coverage. Acronyms are expanded in the language of the official name, when known, otherwise an English form is given and in the case of lesser-known languages, an English translation; Cyrillic alphabet entries are transliterated. For organizations, there are notes concerning country, dates, and, in some instances, focus. Tables of country and language codes precede the principal list. Z1006.S344

Directories

International

Block, David. A directory of vendors of Latin American library materials / David Block and Howard L. Karno. 3rd ed., rev. and enl. Madison, Wis. : Secretariat, Seminar on the Acquisition of Latin American Library Materials, Memorial Library, Univ. of Wisconsin-Madison, c1988. 48 p. ISBN 0-917617-19-3 (pbk.). **AB18**

1st ed., 1983; 2nd ed., 1986.

An alphabetical list of 149 suppliers, giving address, hours, type of materials handled, geographic and subject coverage, catalogues issued, and services provided. Geographic index and list of vendors by country. Z1601.S38 no. 22

International guide to library and information science education : a reference source for educational programs in the information fields world-wide / ed. by Josephine Riss Fang and Paul Nauta with the assistance of Anna J. Fang. München ; N.Y. : K.G. Saur, 1985. 537 p. (IFLA publications, 32). ISBN 0-86291-298-9. **AB19**

Arranged alphabetically by country. For each country, gives a brief introductory sketch of the general educational system, followed by individual library and information science educational institutions alphabetically arranged by place. The profile for each institution includes: name, address, head, year founded, administrative structure, sources of finance, program, teaching staff, physical resources, continuing education, and accreditation information. Index of place names. Z668.I574

Internationales Bibliotheks-Handbuch = World guide to libraries / ed. dir.: Helga Lengenfelder ; editors: Bettina

Bartz, Ruth Lochar, Helmut Opitz. 9th ed. München : K. G. Saur, c1989. 1001 p. ISBN 3-598-20539-2. **AB20**

6th ed., 1983 (*Guide* AB46).

Provides name of institution, address, year founded, name of director, important holdings, and size of collection for 39,887 libraries in 177 countries, including special libraries with more than 5,000 volumes, or national, academic, research, government, school, ecclesiastical, and public libraries with more than 30,000 volumes. Arranged alphabetically by country, then by type of library. Index of libraries. Z721.W7

United States

●**American library directory** : (ALD) [computer file]. N.Y. : Bowker. **AB21**

Machine-readable version of *American library directory* (*Guide* AB52).

Coverage: current. File size: 38,000 records. Updated annually. Available online (NewsNet), and in CD-ROM as part of *Library reference plus* (Bowker).

●**Library reference plus** [computer file]. N.Y. : Bowker. **AB22**

Coverage: current. File size: 130,000 records. Updated annually. Available in CD-ROM (producer).

A machine-readable file covering librarians, libraries, book publishers and distributors, and related organizations as included in publications from Bowker: *The Bowker annual library and book trade almanac* (34th ed., 1989/90– ; *Supplement* AB43); *American book trade directory* (*Guide* AA344); *American library directory* (*Guide* AB52); *Literary market place* (*Guide* AA353); and *Publishers, distributors, and wholesalers of the United States* (3rd ed., 1981–).

Africa

Dube, S. R. Directory of libraries in Zimbabwe / comp. by S.R. Dube and R.G.S. Douglas. 4th ed. Harare : National Archives of Zimbabwe, 1987. 28 p. ISBN 0-908302-04-5. **AB23**

3rd ed., 1981.

This edition lists 243 libraries in four groups: public/subscription libraries, University of Zimbabwe and its branch libraries, government-sponsored special libraries, and other special libraries. School libraries are excluded. Arrangement within each group is alphabetical by place name. Entries include: name, address, founding date, staff, budget, hours, subject fields, size of collection, users, etc. Z857.Z55D83

Australia

Cree, Jan. Directory of special libraries in Australia. 7th ed. Ultimo, N.S.W. : Library Association of Australia Special Libraries Section, 1988. 552 p. ISBN 0-86804-059-2. **AB24**

1st ed., 1954; 6th ed., 1984.

More than 12,000 entries, arranged by state, then alphabetically by name of parent body. A brief list of last-minute name changes, closings, and mergers precedes each state listing. Entries include: name, address, founding date, number of staff, classification used, hours, size of collection, subjects, name of librarian. Indexes: library names (with alternate forms) and subjects derived from terms designated by respondents.

Z870.A1C74

Directory of Australian academic libraries / ed., Alan L. Bundy. 3rd ed. Adelaide: AUSLIB Pr., 1985. 271 p. ISBN 0-9589895-1-6.   **AB25**

1st ed., 1978; 2nd ed., 1981.

Includes libraries of universities, colleges of advanced education, and colleges of technical and continuing education, as well as state libraries. Entries are arranged alphabetically by name of institution (with cross-references when necessary) and include: name, address, size of student body, hours, collection size and budget, collection strengths, publications, staff size, and names of senior staff. A "Guide to collections" lists the libraries under general subject headings.   Z675.U5D5

Great Britain

Aslib directory of information sources in the United Kingdom / ed. by Ellen M. Codlin. 5th ed. London: Aslib, 1982–1984. 2 v. ISBN 0-85142-166-0 (v. 1). ISBN 0-85142-184-9 (v. 2).   **AB26**

4th ed., 1977–80 (*Guide* AB77)

A one-volume version has been published as: *The shorter Aslib directory of information sources in the United Kingdom*, ed. by Ellen M. Codlin (London: Aslib, 1986).

Contents: v. 1, Science, technology, and commerce; v. 2, Social sciences, medicine, and the humanities.

Follows the plan of the previous edition, but includes for the first time an index of abbreviations and acronyms at the end of v. 1. Lists only "the central government and local authority libraries and information offices, the libraries of universities and polytechnics, learned, professional and research institutions, commercial and industrial sources, UK offices of overseas countries and some frequently needed specialized bodies."—*Introd.* Abbreviations and subject index.
    Z791.A1A82

The British library directory. Chicago; London: St. James Pr., c1989. 1 v. (unpaged). ISBN 1-55862-043-5.
    AB27

Lists public and special libraries in the U.K. and Ireland alphabetically—public libraries under the name of the local governing authority, special libraries by city—giving the following information: name of local authority; address; population served; name of committee responsible for libraries; chief librarian; branch libraries, including mobile, picture and video libraries; loan period; collection size; significant special collections; library programs; size of staff; budget. Entries for special libraries also include conditions of use for nonmembers, main subject covered, classification method used, cooperative programs engaged in, and publications issued. A list of abbreviations and a special entry for the British Library precedes the body of the text. Combined subject and name index.
    Z791.A1B77

Directory of American studies librarians in the UK / SCONUL Advisory Committee on American Studies. Wetherby: British Library Lending Division, 1984. 95 p. ISBN 0-7123-2023-7 (pbk).   **AB28**

Intended to supplement Peter Snow's *The United States: a guide to library holdings in the UK* (*Guide* DB41) and Catherine M. Deering's *Union list of American studies periodicals in UK libraries* (Boston Spa, Wetherby, West Yorkshire: British Library Lending Division, 1983), this volume identifies persons responsible for the collections. Arranged alphabetically by city, institution, and personal name. American studies responsibilities and personal interests in American studies are indicated for each person. Name (libraries and persons) and subject index.
    Z675.U5D57

A directory of rare book and special collections in the United Kingdom and the Republic of Ireland / ed. by Moelwyn I. Williams for the Rare Books Group of the Library Association. London: The Association, 1985. 664 p. ISBN 0-85365-646-0. £65.00.   **AB29**

Describes rare book collections, complementary manuscript collections, and special collections housed in public, academic, ecclesiastical, society, and some private libraries. Arrangement is by region, then alphabetically by name of library. Entries include address, hours, admission policy, research facilities, and history of the institution, followed by a description of each collection giving provenance, size, subjects covered, a brief summary of the contents, and references to catalogues and published sources. Lists of abbreviations and acronyms. Name and topical index.   Z791.A1D58

India

Directory of Indian public libraries: a selected list of libraries assisted by the Foundation / ed., B.P. Barua. Calcutta: Naya Prokash, 1986. 520 p. ISBN 81-85109-43-5. Rs160.00.   **AB30**

Lists the names and addresses of some 6,000 libraries that were assisted, between 1972 and 1985, by the Raja Rammohun Roy Library Foundation, which promotes public library services in India. Arranged by state with libraries grouped into three categories: state central libraries, district libraries, and other. Includes general library statistics for each state, a list of abbreviations, and a name index.   Z845.I4D55

Directory of library and information science schools in India / comp. by H.R. Chopra, assisted by P.S.G. Kumar, A. Tejomurty. Chandigarh, India: Arun Pub. House, 1988. 144 p. ISBN 81-85212-00-7. Rs195.00.
    AB31

Lists, in alphabetical order, 93 schools and other institutions offering training in library and information science at various levels. Entries include name of the school, address, year established, head of the program, names and ranks of faculty members, a description of the physical accommodations, admissions procedures, courses offered, tuition fees, and publications issued. Appendixes: list of schools contacted that did not reply, a list of schools by city, and a list of schools by state.
    Z669.5.I5D57

Directory of special and research libraries in India / comp. by IASLIC. 2nd ed. Calcutta: Indian Association of Special Libraries & Information Centres, 1985. 90 p.
    AB32

1st ed., 1962 (*Guide* AB86).

Follows the plan of the previous edition, increasing the number of entries to about 250.   Z845.I4D57

Indian library directory / comp. and ed. by Joginder Singh and A.R. Sethi. 4th ed. Delhi: Indian Library Association, 1985. 251 p. $30.00.   **AB33**

1st ed., 1938; 3rd ed., 1951.

Lists 1,610 university, college, special, government, and public libraries. Arrangement is alphabetical within each category, except for public libraries which are first grouped by state. Entries include name of library, address, founding date, head librarian, size of staff, size of budget, size of collection, special collections, access policy, services, and library hours. Institution, librarian, and state indexes.   Z845.I4I42

Kalia, D. R. Directory of scientific and technical libraries in India / comp. & ed. by D.R. Kalia & Surender Kumar. New Delhi: Reliance Pub. House, 1988. 454 p. ISBN 81-85047-26-X. Rs300.00.   **AB34**

For 465 libraries, gives name, address, year founded, name of librarian in charge, size of budget and of holdings, and system of classification used, plus name and address only for an additional 689 libraries. Arrangement is alphabetical by state and union territory. Institutional, subject, and city indexes.

Z845.I4K25

Indonesia

Directory of special libraries and information sources in Indonesia 1985 = Direktori perpustakaan khusus dan sumber informasi di Indonesia 1985 / comp. and ed. by Sudarisman Dwinarto and Setya Iswanti. 7th ed. Jakarta, Indonesia : Indonesian National Scientific Documentation Center, Indonesian Institute of Sciences, 1987. 1 v. **AB35**

1st ed., 1966; 6th ed., 1983.
English and Indonesian.

An alphabetical listing by city of 581 libraries and information centers covering science and technology, social science, humanities, and life sciences. Includes governmental and business libraries; special subject collections; documentation, data processing and statistical centers. Entries indicate name and address of the institution, person in charge, size of staff, hours, access policy, subjects collected, language of collection, classification used, services offered, budget, and publications. Index of institutions and subjects. Z845.I6D57

Union of Soviet Socialist Republics

Gosudarstvennye arkhivy SSSR : spravochnik / V.N. Avtokratov, F.M. Vaganov (predsedatel redkollegii) ... et al. ; sostaviteli N.M. Andreeva ... I.V. Volkova (otvetstvennyĭ sostavitel) ... [et al.]. Moskva : "Mysl", 1989. 2 v. **AB36**

For annotation, see *Supplement* DC199.   CD1711.G66

Biography

Dale, Doris Cruger. A directory of oral history tapes of librarians in the United States and Canada. Chicago : Amer. Lib. Assoc., 1986. 103 p. ISBN 0-8389-0443-2 (pbk.). $15.00 (est.). **AB37**

A list of 205 recorded interviews held by 40 institutions, arranged alphabetically by institution, then by name of librarian. Entries include a brief biographical sketch of the interviewee, name of interviewer, date and length of interview, subjects covered and names of other librarians mentioned, as well as information regarding copyright, availability of transcript, and permission to cite. Personal name and subject indexes.

Z720.A4D34

Directory of librarians in international development / Elaine Brekke, ed. 2nd ed. Pullman, Wash. : Washington State Univ. Libraries, c1988. 170 leaves. **AB38**

1st ed., 1977.

An alphabetical listing of librarians and information specialists who have served overseas as library consultants to development projects or to a developing country. Entries give individual's title, complete address, education, area of specialization, language proficiency, and project experience as well as the name of the project, host country, and sponsoring agency. Country, language proficiency, and area of specialization indexes. Z720.A4D55

Directory of library & information professionals. Woodbridge, Conn. : Research Publications, c1988. 2 v. ISBN 0-89235-125-X. $345.00. **AB39**

Vol. 1 presents biographical data on nearly 43,000 individuals who are employed in the information field at a professional level or in education or training, or are members of library and information professional associations. Entries appear in alphabetical order and include some or all of the following information: biographee's name, current position, previous positions, education, publications, achievements, honors, memberships, language proficiency, professional expertise or subject specialty, and consulting availability. Vol. 2 contains specialty, employer, consulting/freelance, and geographical indexes.

Z720.A4D57

●**Directory of library & information professionals** : (DLIP) [computer file]. Chicago : Amer. Lib. Assoc., 1988. **AB40**

Machine-readable version of above.
File size: 43,000 records. Available in CD-ROM (producer).

Originally compiled jointly by ALA and Research Publ. (Woodbridge, Conn.). Entries date to 1986–87; there are no plans to update either the printed or machine-readable versions.

Munford, William Arthur. Who was who in British librarianship, 1800–1985 : a dictionary of dates with notes. London : Lib. Assoc., 1987. 91 p. ISBN 0-85365-976-1. £19.50. **AB41**

Includes only chief or deputy librarians. Entries (arranged alphabetically) give, where available, birth and death dates, dates and places of positions held, and other significant achievements. Abbreviations table. Appendix of persons with information limited to place and date of office held.

Z720.A46G7

Sabzwari, Ghaniul Akram. Who's who in library and information science in Pakistan. 2nd ed. Karachi, Pakistan : Library Promotion Bureau, Pakistan and Society for the Promotion and Improvement of Libraries, 1987. 368 p. : ill. ISBN 969-412-069-1. $10.00. **AB42**

1st ed., 1969 (*Guide* AB107), had title *Who's who in librarianship in Pakistan.*

Follows the plan of the previous edition but includes a "Who was who" section. Z720.A46P363

Yearbooks

The Bowker annual library and book trade almanac. 34th ed. (1989/1990)– . N.Y. : Bowker, 1989– . Annual. ISSN 0068-0540. **AB43**

Represents a change of title for *The Bowker annual of library and book trade information* (*Guide* AB111) and assumes its edition numbering. Scope remains the same. Z731.A47

Library and information science annual. v. 3 (1987)–. Littleton, Colo. : Libraries Unlimited, 1987– . Annual. ISSN 8755-2108. **AB44**

Vols. 1–2 (1985–86) had title *Library science annual.*

Intended as a companion to *American reference books annual* (*Guide* AA476). Reviews the previous year's English-language monographs, reference books, and periodicals; provides abstracts of the year's most significant doctoral dissertations; and presents essays on current trends and issues in library and information science. Author/title and subject indexes.

Z666.L45

LIBRARY RESOURCES

International

Guide to the archives of international organizations. Paris : UNESCO, 1984–[1986?]. v. 1–3. (v. 1: Documentation, libraries, and archives. Bibliographies and reference works, 8). ISBN 92-3-102090-0 (pbk. : v. 1). **AB45**
  Compilers vary.
  Contents: v. 1, The United Nations system; v. 2, Archives of international organizations and their former officials in the custody of national and other archival and manuscript repositories; v. 3, Archives of other international inter-governmental organizations and non-governmental organizations.
  Vol. 1 contains chapters describing the administrative histories and archives of the different offices of the U.N. Vol. 2 includes responses to a questionnaire about the holdings of archives relating to the U.N. held by individuals and organizations. The amount of detail varies greatly. Vol. 3 has brief descriptions of the archives of 64 current international organizations who responded to a questionnaire about their holdings.
  JX1995.G85

International directory of archives = Annuaire international des archives. München ; N.Y. : K.G. Saur, 1988. 351 p. (Archivum, v.33). ISBN 3-598-21233-X. $45.00. **AB46**
  1975 ed. (*Guide* AB112).
  Sponsored by the International Council on Archives.
  Entries, compiled from responses to a questionnaire, cover some 151 countries, including, for some, information about federal, state, and a few local (city) archives; for others, adds religious, university, or cultural organizations. Dropped from this edition is the index for types of archives. CD941.I61

United States

Burton, Dennis A. A guide to manuscripts in the Presidential Libraries / comp. and ed. by Dennis A. Burton, James B. Rhoads, Raymond W. Smock. College Park, Md. : Research Materials Corp., c1985. 451 p. : ill. ISBN 0-934-63100-X. $90.00. **AB47**
  Describes the holdings of seven presidential libraries (Hoover, Roosevelt, Truman, Eisenhower, Kennedy, Johnson, Ford). Brief data on the institutions themselves (e.g., address, telephone, hours) are followed by entries for manuscript collections, microfilm, and oral histories, arranged alphabetically by the names of individuals, government agencies and offices, countries, and specific subjects. The entries themselves provide a collection reference number, the name and size of the collection, the holding library, a description of the collection, and the *National union catalog of manuscript collections* number. General index cites collection reference numbers. CD3029.82.B87

Special collections in college and university libraries / comp. by Modoc Press, Inc. N.Y. : Macmillan ; London : Collier Macmillan, c1989. 639 p. ISBN 0-02-921651-6. **AB48**
  "A compilation of detailed, descriptive information concerning special collections, rare books, and manuscripts to be found in the libraries of colleges and universities throughout the United States."—*Pref.* Describes collections at 1,805 four- and two-year institutions. Alphabetically arranged by state, then by institution. General index (personal names, subjects, geographic place names, and titles of books and magazines) and institutional index. Z731.S73

Szucs, Loretto Dennis. The archives : a guide to the National Archives field branches / by Loretto Dennis Szucs & Sandra Hargreaves Luebking. Salt Lake City, Utah : Ancestry Pub., 1988. 340 p. : ill. ISBN 0-916489-23-X. $35.95. **AB49**
  For annotation, see *Supplement* DB22. CD3026

Great Britain

Foster, Janet. British archives : a guide to archive resources in the United Kingdom / Janet Foster & Julia Sheppard. 2nd ed. N.Y. : Stockton Pr., 1989. lviii, 834 p. ISBN 0-93585-974-8. $100.00. **AB50**
  1st ed., 1982 (*Guide* AB141).
  Publ. in U.K. : London : Macmillan.
  This edition has "a substantial number of new entries with additional information, more thorough indexing, expanded sections on publications and useful addresses . . . Entries which appeared in the first edition have, in many cases, been provided with more detailed or accurate descriptions of their holdings."—*Pref.* Contains 1,048 entries. Three appendixes: Institutions which have placed their archives elsewhere; Institutions which reported having no archives; Institutions which did not respond to questionnaire. CD1040.F67

Mexico

Guía de archivos y bibliotecas. [1a coedición]. [Mexico, D.F.] : Universidad Iberoamericana, Departamento de Historia : Ediciones El Caballito, [1984, i.e. 1985]. 167 p. : maps. ISBN 968-60-1158-7. **AB51**
  Lists 24 institutions housing major historical collections. Each entry gives the name of the institution, address, hours, access policy, historical sketch and mission statement, description of holdings, services provided, organizational structure, and situates the institution on a local map. CD3677.M4G85

Union of Soviet Socialist Republics

Grimsted, Patricia Kennedy. Archives and manuscript repositories in the USSR. Ukraine and Moldavia. Princeton, N.J. : Princeton Univ. Pr., c1988. v. 1 : map. ISBN 0-691-05391-X (v.1). $125.00. (In progress). **AB52**
  For annotation, see *Supplement* DC200. CD1735.U4G75

LIBRARY AND INFORMATION SCIENCE

Bibliography

Wei, Karen T. Library and information science in China : an annotated bibliography. N.Y. : Greenwood, 1988. 273 p. (Bibliographies and indexes in library and information science, no. 3). ISBN 0-313-25548-2. **AB53**
  "Designed to meet the needs of scholars, researchers, librarians, and library school students in their search for sources in the field."—*Pref.* About 1,000 entries, with emphasis on English-language materials and titles of great importance in Chinese, French, German, and Japanese published during the past 100 years. 11 topical sections: (1) Bibliography and reference, (2) Books and printing, (3) History, (4) Types of libraries, (5) Technical services activities, (6) Automation and informa-

tion services, (7) Education for librarianship, (8) Publishing and trade, (9) General works, (10) International exchange and activities, and (11) Librarians. Author and subject indexes.

Z845.C5W45

Handbooks

Bryant, E. T. Music librarianship : a practical guide / by E.T. Bryant with the assistance of Guy A. Marco. 2nd ed. Metuchen, N.J. : Scarecrow, 1985. 449 p. ISBN 0-8108-1785-3. **AB54**

1st ed., 1959.

A comprehensive manual of practice in five main sections: (1) Music library administration, (2) Reference books and periodicals, (3) Cataloguing, (4) Classification, and (5) Sound recordings. This edition has been completely rewritten and considerably internationalized. General index and bibliography.

ML111.B83

Gervasi, Anne. Handbook for small, rural, and emerging public libraries / by Anne Gervasi and Betty Kay Seibt. Phoenix : Oryx, 1988. 196 p. ISBN 0-89774-303-2 (pbk.). **AB55**

Aims "to show the breadth and scope of library work and what a library can provide for the community of which it is a part."—*Pref.* Three main sections are directed respectively to builders and planners, the library board, and the library's director and staff. A sample community survey, miscellaneous library forms, and a list of state libraries and the services they offer are included in appendixes. Index. Z679.5.G47

Handbook of medical library practice / Louise Darling, ed., David Bishop, Lois Ann Colaianni, associate editors. 4th ed. Chicago : Medical Library Association, 1988. v. 3 : ill. ISBN 0-912176-21-0. **AB56**

For annotation, see *Supplement* EK1. Z675.M4H33

Larsgaard, Mary Lynette. Map librarianship : an introduction. 2nd ed. Littleton, Colo. : Libraries Unlimited, 1987. 382 p. : ill. ISBN 0-87287-537-7. $43.50. **AB57**

1st ed., 1978 (*Guide* AB174).

This edition treats all forms of cartographic materials (maps, atlases, diagrams, globes, models, profiles, sections, views, and remote sensing imagery), for a much changed and enlarged work. Z692.M3L37

Manual of law librarianship : the use and organization of legal literature / ed. by Elizabeth M. Moys. 2nd ed. Boston : G.K. Hall, 1986. [915] p. ISBN 0-8161-1854-X. $65.00. **AB58**

1st ed., 1976 (*Guide* AB178).

Coverage has been extended beyond the British Isles to other parts of the world. Includes a glossary, index of works cited, and subject index. Z675.L2M27

McMichael, Betty. The church librarian's handbook : a complete guide for the library and resource center in Christian education. Grand Rapids, Mich. : Baker Book House, 1984. 277 p. : ill. ISBN 0-8010-6166-0 (pbk.). $9.95. **AB59**

An expansion and updating of the author's *The library and resource center in Christian education* (Chicago : Moody Pr., 1977). A comprehensive manual of library practice including information on staffing, material selection and processing, library policies, and finances. Directory of suppliers, classification system, and subject headings for church libraries are listed in appendixes. Bibliography and index. Z675.C5M3

Mount, Ellis. University science and engineering libraries. 2nd ed. Westport, Conn. : Greenwood, 1985. 303 p. : ill. (Contributions in librarianship and information science, no. 49). ISBN 0-313-23949-5. **AB60**

1st ed., 1978 (*Guide* AB180).

This edition treats college science and technology libraries more extensively and puts greater emphasis on computer applications and networks. In six main sections: (1) Overview, (2) Management of libraries, (3) Technical services, (4) User services, (5) Collections, and (6) Facilities and equipment. Completed survey forms from selected academic sci-tech libraries appear in Appendix 1. Z675.U5M68

Pruett, Nancy Jones. Scientific and technical libraries / Nancy Jones Pruett ; with contributions by Stephen J. Rollins ... [et al.]. Orlando, Fla. : Academic Pr., 1986. 2 v. : ill. ISBN 0-12-566041-3 (v. 1). ISBN 0-12-566042-1 (v. 2). **AB61**

" ... a guide to the functions and management of scientific and technical ... research libraries, primarily in the United States."—*Pref.* Excludes medical libraries. Vol. 1 covers library functions (information retrieval, current awareness, collection development and control, and document delivery) and addresses major management issues, including space planning, library automation, and equipment. Vol. 2 treats such special formats as conference literature, dissertations, in-house and proprietary information, microforms, numeric data, patents, standards and specifications, and translations. It also discusses libraries for biology, chemistry, engineering, geoscience, mathematics, pharmaceutics, and physics. Bibliography and index.

Z675.T3P69

The smaller academic library : a management handbook / ed. by Gerard B. McCabe. N.Y. : Greenwood, 1988. 380 p. ISBN 0-313-25027-8. **AB62**

A collection of essays by different authors arranged under the following main headings: (1) General administration, (2) Personnel, (3) Budget and finance, (4) The collection, (5) User programs and services, (6) Technical services, and (7) Physical plant. Most essays are accompanied by references. Index.

Z675.U5S57

Acquisitions, collection development, & maintenance

American Library Association. Subcommittee on Guidelines for Collection Development. Guide for written collection policy statements / Subcommittee on Guidelines for Collection Development, Collection Management and Development Committee, Resources Section, Resources and Technical Services Division, American Library Association ; Bonita Bryant, ed. 2nd ed. Chicago : The Association, 1989. 29 p. : ill. (Collection management and development guides, no. 3). ISBN 0-8389-3371-8. $4.25. **AB63**

A revision of the chapter "Guidelines for the formulation of collection development policies" by Sheila Dowd, Thomas Shaughnessy, and Hans Weber, originally published in the Collection Development Committee's *Guidelines for collection development* (*Guide* AB187).

Focus is on the policy statement. Additional sections on the conspectus apparatus, collection levels, language codes and definitions, narrative statements and analysis of special collections. Glossary. Z687.A518

Curley, Arthur. Building library collections / by Arthur Curley and Dorothy Broderick. 6th ed. Metuchen, N.J. : Scarecrow, 1985. 339 p. ISBN 0-8108-1776-4. **AB64**

5th ed., 1979, by Wallace John Bonk and Rose Mary Magrill (*Guide* AB188).

Aimed at practitioners as well as library school students. Text has been "restructured and revised to reflect the major changes in collection development theory and practice ...."—

Introd. Chapters stress community needs, the growth of cooperative collection development in resource-sharing networks, nonbook formats, censorship challenges, and the library's informational role in a new information society.   Z687.C87

Evans, G. Edward. Developing library and information center collections. 2nd ed. Littleton, Colo. : Libraries Unlimited, 1987. 443 p. : ill. ISBN 0-8728-7463-X. $29.50. ISBN 0-8728-7546-6 (pbk.). $22.50.   **AB65**
1st ed., 1979.

A textbook for library school students. Provides "practical information on materials producers and distributors, community survey techniques, [collection development] policies, materials selection, acquisition, weeding and evaluation . . . [and] delves into library cooperation, copyright . . . and censorship as they affect the process in its entirety."—*Pref. 1st ed.* Also includes chapters on serials, government documents, audiovisual materials, fiscal management, automation and preservation. Suggestions for further reading conclude each chapter. Author, title and subject indexes.   Z687.E92

Kim, David U. Policies of publishers : a handbook for order librarians / by David U. Kim and Craig A. Wilson. 4th ed. Metuchen, N.J. : Scarecrow, 1989. 279 p. ISBN 0-8108-2233-4.   **AB66**
3rd ed., 1982 (*Guide* AB192).

Increases the number of publishers' policies to approximately 600 and includes extensive cross-references. Otherwise follows the plan of the previous edition.   Z689.K55

Magrill, Rose Mary. Acquisitions management and collection development in libraries / Rose Mary Magrill and John Corbin. 2nd ed. Chicago : Amer. Lib. Assoc., 1989. 285 p. ISBN 0-8389-0513-7.   **AB67**
1st ed., 1984 (*Guide* AB194).

Follows plan of the previous edition.   Z689.M19

Perryman, Wayne R. International subscription agents : an annotated directory / comp. by Wayne R. Perryman and Lenore Wilkas. 5th ed. Chicago : Amer. Lib. Assoc., 1986. 133 p. ISBN 0-8389-3326-2 (pbk.). $9.00 (est.).   **AB68**
4th ed., 1978 (*Guide* AB189). Compiler varies.

Increases the number of agents to 319. The questionnaire used was expanded to include subscription services starting date, the level of computerization at the operation, and dealings in serial backfiles if any.   Z286.P4P47

Spiller, David. Book selection : an introduction to principles and practice. 4th ed. London : Bingley, 1986. 235 p. ISBN 0-8515-7404-1. £14.75.   **AB69**
1st ed., 1971; 3rd ed., 1980.

A manual for the practicing librarian. Goes beyond being an introductory text to include material on the use of automation, databases, computer software and bibliometrics in the selection process. Bibliographies in each chapter; index.
Z689.S65

Administration

The how-to-do-it manual for small libraries / ed. by Bill Katz. N.Y. : Neal-Schuman, c1988. 387 p. : ill. ISBN 1-55570-016-0.   **AB70**

"Written by and for people working in small rural or urban libraries who must deal with everything from limited staffs and budgets to automation and demand for bestsellers."—*Pref.* Also useful for administrators of small special, school, or academic libraries. Five sections: Managing the small library; Administration; Collection development and technical services; Public services; Computers to lasers. Each chapter represents a

specific author's report on small library issues and experiences. Bibliography for each section.   Z678.H73

The library trustee : a practical guidebook / [ed.] by Virginia G. Young. 4th ed. Chicago : Amer. Lib. Assoc., 1988. 230 p. ISBN 0-8389-0495-5.   **AB71**
1st ed., 1964; 3rd ed., 1978.

A collection of essays on topics of interest to both recent and experienced trustees of small as well as large library systems (e.g., standards, public relations, facilities planning, cooperation with library staff, governmental and legal issues, financial management). Suggestions for further reading conclude each essay. Index.   Z681.5.L5

Stephenson, Mary Sue. Planning library facilities : a selected, annotated bibliography. Metuchen, N.J. : Scarecrow, 1990. 249 p. ISBN 0-8108-2285-7.   **AB72**

Lists 800 references to documents published primarily in the U.S. and Canada, 1970–mid-1988. Three major sections: (1) Facility planning, design, evaluation and renovation; (2) Housing and serving the user; (3) Environmental, mechanical, electrical and security systems. Entries are arranged alphabetically by title within sections. Subject and author indexes.
Z679.5.S73

Archives

Dictionary of archival terminology = Dictionnaire de terminologie archivistique : English and French, with equivalents in Dutch, German, Italian, Russian and Spanish / ed. by Peter Walne. 2nd rev. ed. München ; N.Y. : K.G. Saur, 1988. 212 p. (ICA handbooks series, v. 7.). ISBN 3-598-20279-2.   **AB73**
1st ed., 1984 (*Guide* AB202).

Follows the plan of the previous edition. Where necessary, definitions have been refined and rewritten, some terms deleted, and new ones added. Specifically Austrian terms appear alongside the German equivalents and are identified as such.
CD945.D53

Modern archives administration and records management : a RAMP reader / comp. by Peter Walne with the assistance of a working group of the International Council on Archives ; General Information Programme and UNISIST. Paris : UNESCO, 1985. 587 p. : ill.   **AB74**

A compilation of reading on basic archival and records management topics reprinted from the major journals in the field. International in scope; intended to supplement existing textbooks and manuals, with special applicability to training programs in the developing countries. No index.   CD950.M62

Cataloging

Manuals

Taylor, Arlene G. Cataloging with copy : a decision-maker's handbook / Arlene G. Taylor, with the assistance of Rosanna M. O'Neil. 2nd ed. Englewood, Colo. : Libraries Unlimited, 1988. 355 p. ISBN 0-87287-575-X. $35.00.   **AB75**
1st ed., 1976.

"Attempts to provide a framework to aid individual libraries in coming to grips with the implications of opposing viewpoints" (*Introd.*) as to whether catalogs should be responsive to the needs of local users, or cataloging data from the Library of Congress or elsewhere should be used without change. In nine chapters: (1) Catalogs, procedures and personnel; (2) Description (i.e. descriptive cataloging); (3) Choice of name and title access points; (4) Form of name and title access points; (5) Subject headings; (6) Classification and call numbers; (7) Near and co-op copy; (8) Computer-based copy cataloging; (9) Merits and problems of copy cataloging. Many illustrative examples. Select bibliography and index. Z693.3.C67T38

Wynar, Bohdan S. Introduction to cataloging and classification. 7th ed. / by Arlene G. Taylor. Littleton, Colo. : Libraries Unlimited, 1985. 641 p. ISBN 0-87287-512-1. $35.00. ISBN 0-87287-485-0 (pbk.). $21.50. **AB76**
6th ed., 1980 (*Guide* AB210).

Follows the plan of the previous edition. Takes into consideration such innovations in bibliographic control as online catalogs, AACR2, and cataloging via computer using the MARC format. Chapters have been updated and somewhat rearranged and examples expanded. Suggestions for further reading end each chapter. Includes a listing of cataloging and classification aids, bibliography, glossary, and index. Z693.W94

MARC formats

USMARC format for bibliographic data : including guidelines for content designation / prepared by Network Development and MARC Standards Office. Wash. : Cataloging Distribution Service, Library of Congress, 1988– . 2 v. (looseleaf). ISBN 0-8444-0595-7. **AB77**

Earlier ed. published under title *MARC formats for bibliographic data.*

Incorporates all changes published as updates 1–15 to the 1980 edition (*Guide* AB211). Intended for "personnel involved in the creation and maintenance of bibliographic records, as well as those involved in the design and maintenance of systems for communication and processing of bibliographic records."—*Introd.* Defines the tags, indicators, subfield codes, and coded values that identify the data elements in USMARC bibliographic records. Each field is separately paged to facilitate updating.

§ The 2nd ed. of Walt Crawford's *MARC for library use: understanding the integrated USMARC* (Boston: G.K. Hall, 1989. 359 p.) aims to show "what MARC (specifically USMARC) is, how it works, and how it is changing."—*Introd.* OCLC's *Bibliographic input standards* (4th ed.; Dublin, Ohio : OCLC, c1990. Looseleaf) "provides standards for input of machine-readable cataloging records into the OCLC Online Union Catalog."—*Introd.* The formats of the records are derived from the Library of Congress MARC formats for communication of bibliographic information in machine-readable form. Z699.4.M2U48

Special subjects

Weihs, Jean. Nonbook materials : the organization of integrated collections / Jean Weihs with assistance from Shirley Lewis and in consultation with the CLA/ALA/AECT Advisory Committee on the Cataloguing of Nonbook Materials. 3rd ed. Ottawa : Canadian Lib. Assoc., 1989. 151 p. ISBN 0-88802-240-9. $40.00. **AB78**
2nd ed., 1979 (*Guide* AB218).

" . . . continues to be a manual of practice, but as an interpretation and explication of principles and rules set out in *AACR2, 1988 Revision* [below]. In this respect it is intended to serve as a companion volume to that edition of the Code."—*Foreword.* This edition includes cataloging rules for two additional types of materials (art reproductions and toys), and for component parts of an item. Four appendixes, bibliography, and index. Z695.66W44

Codes

United States

Anglo-American cataloguing rules / prepared under the direction of the Joint Steering Committee for Revision of AACR, a committee of the American Library Association, the Australian Committee on Cataloguing, the British Library, the Canadian Committee on Cataloguing, the Library Association, the Library of Congress ; ed. by Michael Gorman and Paul W. Winkler. 2nd ed., 1988 revision. Ottawa : Canadian Lib. Assoc. ; Chicago : Amer. Lib. Assoc., 1988. 677 p. ISBN 0-8389-3346-7 (ALA). ISBN 0-8389-3360-2 (ALA : pbk.). **AB79**
2nd ed., 1978 (*Guide* AB219).

This revision corrects errors, modifies wording, changes inadequate rules, and adds rules and examples. "It is not a new edition; it has not changed basic concepts."—*Pref.* Includes sets of already published rule revisions from 1982, 1983 and 1985, as well as authorized unpublished revisions since 1985. Appendixes cover capitalization, abbreviations, numerals, and glossary. Index.

§ Guidelines for applying the rules contained in this revision can be found in Margaret Maxwell's *Handbook for AACR2 1988 revision: Explaining and illustrating the Anglo-American cataloguing rules* (Chicago: Amer. Lib. Assoc., 1989. 436 p.). Z694.15.A56A53

Gorman, Michael. The concise AACR2, 1988 revision. Chicago : Amer. Lib. Assoc., 1989. 161 p. ISBN 0-8389-3362-9. **AB80**
2nd ed., 1981 (*Guide* AB221).

An abridgement "intended to convey the essence and basic principles of *AACR2 1988 Revision* [above] without many of that comprehensive work's rules for out-of-the-way and complex materials."—*General introd.* Z694.15.A56G67

Classification

Schedules

Chan, Lois Mai. Immroth's guide to the Library of Congress classification. 4th ed. Englewood, Colo. : Libraries Unlimited, 1990. 436 p. ISBN 0-87287-604-7. $38.50. ISBN 0-87287-763-9 (pbk.). $28.50. **AB81**
3rd ed., 1989 (*Guide* AB233).

Reflects changes in general policies as well as changes and revisions in classification schedules. Follows the plan of the previous edition with the exception of Chapter 4, on tables, which has been reorganized. Examples in the book employ call numbers from LC MARC records. One consolidated bibliography. Z696.U4C47

Dewey, Melvil. Dewey decimal classification and relative index / devised by Melvil Dewey. Ed. 20 / ed. by John P. Comaromi . . . [et al.]. Albany, N.Y. : Forest Pr., a division of OCLC Online Computer Library Center, 1989. 4 v. ISBN 0-910608-37-7 (set). **AB82**
19th ed., 1979 (*Guide* AB234).

"The aim of Edition 20 is user convenience: clearer instructions, more explanations, greater accessibility through expanded summaries, elimination of duplicate provisions for classing single subjects, and the inclusion of a Manual to guide the classifier . . . . The Manual describes policies and practices of the Decimal Classification Division of the L of C, offers advice on classing in difficult areas, and explains how to choose between related numbers."—*New features.* The number of summaries and notes have been increased. Reflects international assistance in the development of the DDC. Both tables and schedules have been revised. This edition's "Relative index" is smaller than the previous edition's as a result of the elimination of unlikely entries and the removal of *see* references.

Z696.D519

Universal decimal classification = Classification décimale universelle = Dezimalklassifikation. International medium ed. English text. London : British Standards Institution, 1985–1988. 2 v. ISBN 0-580-14568-9 (v. 1).   **AB83**

2nd English full ed., 1977 (*Guide* AB238).

Contents: pt. 1, Systematic tables; pt. 2, Alphabetical subject index.

English text published by arrangement with the International Federation of Documentation (FID) as part of the International Medium Edition of the UDC.

Represents a selective edition of UDC that includes modifications authorized in "Extensions and corrections to the UDC" through series 9, no.3 (June 1977).   Z696.U862

Subject headings

Schedules

Sears, Minnie Earl. Sears list of subject headings. 13th ed. / ed. by Carmen Rovira and Caroline Reyes. N.Y. : Wilson, 1986. 681 p. ISBN 0-8242-0730-0.   **AB84**

12th ed., 1982 (*Guide* AB252).

Continues the updating and revision of existing headings, with particular attention to headings in health and environment, computer services, space technology, changing family relationships, minorities and consumerism. Uses new expanded Dewey Decimal Classification schedules as found in the 12th abridged edition of the DDC for data processing and computer science, and computer engineering. Revised and expanded "List of subdivisions."   Z695.S43

Filing and indexing

Cleveland, Donald B. Introduction to indexing and abstracting / Donald B. Cleveland, Ana D. Cleveland. 2nd ed. Englewood, Colo. : Libraries Unlimited, 1990. 329 p. : ill. ISBN 0-87287-677-2. $32.50.   **AB85**

1st ed., 1983.

A comprehensive guide for students and practitioners to the fundamentals of indexing and abstracting. There are chapters on the nature of information, the nature and types of indexes, vocabulary control, indexing methods and procedures, book indexes, index evaluation, nature and types of abstracts, abstracting methods and procedures, automatic methods, indexing and abstracting services, as well as examples of how to index and abstract a document. Includes a glossary, bibliography, and an index.   Z695.9.C592

Rowley, Jennifer E. Abstracting and indexing. 2nd ed. London : Bingley, 1988. 181 p. : ill. ISBN 0-85157-411-4.   **AB86**

1st ed., 1982.

"This book attempts to lay the groundwork for abstracting and indexing practice."—*Pref.* Emphasizes technique rather than theory. Covers the role of computers in abstracting and indexing. Includes an appendix on editing and proofreading an abstracting or indexing publication, a section on further readings and an index.   Z695.9.R68

Information storage and retrieval

Automated library systems

Boss, Richard W. The library manager's guide to automation. 3rd ed. Boston : G.K. Hall, 1990. 202 p. ISBN 0-8161-1942-2. ISBN 0-8161-1943-0 (pbk.).   **AB87**

2nd ed., 1984 (*Guide* AB263).

Follows the plan of the previous edition. Emphasizes multiuser rather than PC-based systems and adds a new chapter on costs of automation. Includes a list of vendors of library automation products, a glossary, a bibliography, and an index.

Z678.9.B66

Saffady, William. Introduction to automation for librarians. 2nd ed. Chicago : Amer. Lib. Assoc., 1989. 363 p. : ill. ISBN 0-8389-0503-X.   **AB88**

1st ed., 1983 (*Guide* AB268).

Format and topics follow the plan of the previous edition, but most chapters have been updated and include treatment of such areas as optical storage technology, pre-written software packages, video-based information systems, optical filing systems, and CD-ROM applications. Index.   Z678.9.S25

Database directories

●**CD-ROM databases** [computer file]. Boston : Worldwide Videotex, 1987– .   **AB89**

Updated monthly. Available online (NewsNet, DIALOG as part of *PTS newsletter database*).

Provides descriptive information concerning CD-ROM databases in all subject areas.

CD-ROMs in print. 1987– . Westport, Conn. : Meckler, c1987– . Annual. ISSN 0891-8198. $30.00.   **AB90**

Includes almost 1,400 titles of commercially available CD-ROMs. An "Optical product directory" lists titles in alphabetical order, giving title, providers, drives, hardware/software, subscription, and description. Indexes of data providers, publishers, U.S. distributors, non-U.S. distributors, software providers, and subjects.   TK7882.C56C34

Computer-readable data bases / comp. and ed. by Martha E. Williams . . . [et al.]. Oct. 1979– . Wash. : American Society for Information Science ; White Plains, N.Y. : Knowledge Industry Publications [distributor], c1979– . Annual, [1991]– .   **AB91**

4th ed., 1985 (*Guide* AB269); 7th ed., 1991.

Available online (DIALOG) and on magnetic tape and diskette (producer). Updated semiannually.

Now a single-volume annual, with coverage expanded to more than 6,000 publicly available databases and subfiles worldwide. The text is in three sections (Database profiles, Database producers, Database vendors), and has three indexes: CD-ROM products, Subjects, and Master index.   Z699.22.W54

●**Cuadra directory of databases** [computer file]. Los Angeles : Cuadra Associates, Inc.   **AB92**

Machine-readable version of *Directory of online databases* (*Guide* AB272).

File size: 5,500 records. Updated quarterly. Available online (Data-Star, ORBIT) and on magnetic tape (producer).

●**Database directory** [computer file]. White Plains, N.Y. : Knowledge Industry Publications, Inc.   **AB93**

Coverage: current. File size: 2,600 records. Updated monthly. Available online (BRS).

Provides descriptions of more than 2,600 databases publicly available in North America. Includes *Data base directory* (*Guide* AB270), its annual supplement, and the most recent 12 issues of *Data base alert* (v. 1, 1983–), a current contents service from the same publisher.

Directory of portable databases. v. 1, no. 1 (Jan. 1990)– . N.Y.: Cuadra/Elsevier, c1990– . Two no. a year. $85.00. **AB94**

Lists 583 portable information sources worldwide in three sections: CD-ROM (409 titles), Diskette (66 titles), and Magnetic tape (108 titles). Entries are arranged alphabetically in each section; an entry represents one or more databases available as a single product on a single medium. Appendixes include listings of: Information providers, Vendors/distributors, Corresponding online databases, and Corresponding information sources. Subject and master indexes. QA76.9.D32D575

Online bibliographic databases : a directory and source-book / by James L. Hall. 4th ed. London : Aslib ; Detroit : Gale, c1986. 509 p. **AB95**

1st ed., 1979; 3rd ed., 1983.

Aimed primarily at librarians, information seekers, and library science students. Provides "a quick-reference inventory of 250 principal English-language online bibliographic databases."—*Pref.* Entries, in alphabetical order by acronym or full name, list the database producer, subject, printed version, online sample record, access charges, and references. Includes an extensive bibliography and three appendixes: Database producers, Online service suppliers, and Subject guide. General index. Z699.22.O58

Scanlan, Jean M. Business online : the professional's guide to electronic information sources / Jean M. Scanlan, Ulla de Stricker, Anne Conway Fernald. N. Y. : Wiley, c1989. 368 p. : ill. ISBN 0-471-60838-6. **AB96**

For annotation, see *Supplement* CH82. HF5548.2.S2635

Interlibrary loan

Allen, G. G. Guide to the availability of theses II : Non-university institutions / [comp. by] G.G. Allen and K. Deubert. München ; N.Y. : K.G. Saur, 1984. 124 p. (IFLA publications, 29). ISBN 3-598-20394-2. **AB97**

Compiled for the International Federation of Library Associations and Institutions Section of University Libraries and other General Research Libraries.

Supplements *Guide to the availability of theses* (*Guide* AB273), listing thesis-producing non-university institutions worldwide. Entries are arranged alphabetically by country, then alphabetically by the official name of the institution. Each entry is in six sections: (1) Degrees awarded, (2) Publishing information; (3) Library access; (4) Copying, purchase, and exchange provisions; (5) Bibliographic control; (6) Other information. "The compilers envisage that a future edition will combine entries for all types of institutions of higher education in the one work."—*Preface.* Subject, geographic, and institution indexes. Z5053.A2A55

A brief guide to centres of international lending and photocopying / comp. and ed. by Richard J. Bennett. 3rd ed. Boston Spa, England : IFLA Office for International Lending : British Library Lending Division, 1984. 153 p. ISBN 0-7123-2020-2. **AB98**

2nd ed., 1979 (*Guide* AB276).

Follows the plan of the previous edition. Based on information obtained from 90 countries. Now includes information on reprographic services. Z672.B67

Interlibrary loan directory / comp. by National Library of Canada. 5th ed. Ottawa : Canadian Lib. Assoc.,

c1989– . 1 v. (looseleaf). ISBN 0-88802-249-2. $120.00. **AB99**

Title on binder: *Interlibrary loan services : an information manual.*

1st ed., 1973; 4th ed., 1986, had title: *Directory of interlibrary loan policies and duplication services in Canadian libraries.*

"Includes most libraries currently listed in National Library's publication, *Symbols of Canadian Libraries* and in the PEB/ILL, the National Library's automated interlibrary loan system."—*Introd.* Combines the entries for these libraries with the policy and service information appearing in the 4th ed. The main record for each library includes name and address, messaging and delivery services, and interlibrary loan policy information. Updated semiannually. Indexes of library names and UTLAS library identifiers (called WHO codes).

Z713.5 C3D57

Morris, Leslie R. Interlibrary loan policies directory / by Leslie R. Morris and Patsy Brautigam. 3rd ed. N.Y. : Neal-Schuman, c1988. 781 p. ISBN 1-55570-024-1 (pbk.). $87.50. **AB100**

2nd ed., 1984 (*Guide* AB278).

Follows the plan of the previous edition. Number of policy entries now more than 1,500, including the U.S., Canada, and Puerto Rico. Survey questionnaire's new categories include: Acceptable methods of transmission; Average turnaround time; Newspapers; Technical reports; Billing procedures; Mailing requirements; Will you lend to foreign libraries? Two new indexes: Libraries with facsimile transmission and receiving capabilities and Libraries charging for book loans. Z713.5.U6M67

Library instruction

The LIRT library instruction handbook / ed. by May Brottman and Mary Loe. Englewood, Colo. : Libraries Unlimited, 1990. 125 p. : ill. ISBN 0-87287-664-0. $26.50. **AB101**

Intends "to provide practical, step-by-step advice to enable institutions to develop programs based on sound theory and to enable practicing instruction librarians to evaluate and improve their own programs."—*Pref.* In six parts: (1) Planning and managing library instruction; (2) Academic libraries; (3) Public libraries; (4) School libraries; (5) Special libraries; (6) Bibliography. Index. Z711.2.L77

Roberts, Anne F. Library instruction for librarians / Anne F. Roberts and Susan G. Blandy. 2nd rev. ed. Englewood, Colo. : Libraries Unlimited, 1989. 257 p. : ill. ISBN 0-87287-628-4. $26.50. **AB102**

1st ed., 1982.

"This textbook provides librarians and students [of library science] with a theoretical, practical, and historical framework for library instruction."—*Pref.* Seven chapters: (1) Introducing the concept; (2) Educating for library instruction; (3) Deciding on a program; (4) Choosing formats; (5) Teaching and library instruction; (6) Keeping instruction going; (7) Shaping instruction for special needs. Suggestions for further reading throughout each chapter. Four appendixes: (1) Policies and guidelines; (2) Checklists for library instruction program; (3) Proficiencies and competencies needed; (4) Recommendations for bibliographic instruction. Annotated bibliography; index.

Z711.2.R6

Wheeler, Helen Rippier. The bibliographic instruction-course handbook : a skills and concepts approach to the undergraduate, research methodology, credit course : for college and university personnel. Metuchen, N.J. : Scarecrow, 1988. 626 p. ISBN 0-8108-2131-1. **AB103**

Intended for librarians and library educators, this is primarily a detailed outline (including model assignments, handouts, instructor's text, and other supporting course materials) for a college-level bibliographic instruction course. Also includes a bibliographic instruction course case study, an extensive bibliography, and lists of pertinent clearinghouses and audiovisuals. Index.   Z711.2.W48

Preservation work

Darling, Pamela W. Preservation planning program : an assisted self-study manual for libraries / prepared by Pamela W. Darling with Duane E. Webster. Expanded 1987 ed. Wash. : Association of Research Libraries, Office of Management Studies, c1987. 117, [41] p. : ill.
AB104

1st ed., 1982 (*Guide* AB287).

Expanded to include new chapters on Staff and user education and Interinstitutional cooperation. Otherwise, follows the plan of the previous edition.   Z701.3.R48D37

Preservation guidelines in ARL libraries. Wash. : Systems and Procedures Exchange Center, Association of Research Libraries, Office of Management Studies, c1987. 110 p. (Spec kit, 137).   **AB105**

Includes unedited ARL library documents (policy statements, manuals, charts, memos, checklists, guidelines, forms, outlines of procedures, etc.), selected for their value to administrators, that illustrate a wide range of alternative approaches to three broad areas of preservation activity in research libraries: establishing policies and priorities; making practical preservation decisions; and dealing with the brittle books problem.
Z701.P725

Preservation organization and staffing / Systems and Procedures Exchange Center. Wash. : Association of Research Libraries, Office of Management Studies, 1990. 135 p. : ill. (SPEC kit, no. 160. ; SPEC flyer, no. 160.).
AB106

A section of ARL preservation statistics is followed by the body of the work—unedited, selected ARL library organization charts, job descriptions, and planning documents (task force and study reports, priority statements, long-range planning documents, and program recommendations).   Z670.A85

Reference work

Katz, William A. Introduction to reference work. 5th ed. N.Y. : McGraw-Hill, c1987. 2 v. ISBN 0-07-033537-0 (v. 1). $28.95. ISBN 0-07-033538-9 (v. 2). $27.95.
AB107

4th ed., 1982 (*Guide* AB298).

Vol. 1, Basic information sources, adds a chapter describing computer-assisted reference services from a nontechnical perspective. In v. 2, Reference services and reference processes, chapters on Reference service and the community, The manual search, The online search, Databases, Bibliographic networks, and Evaluation of reference service have been rewritten, and new chapters added on microcomputers and bibliographic and end user searching instruction. A list of suggested readings ends each chapter; each volume has its own index.

§ A useful companion is *Reference and information services : a reader for today*, comp. by Katz (Metuchen, N.J. : Scarecrow, 1986), a collection of articles published since 1982.
Z711.K32

Puccio, Joseph A. Serials reference work. Englewood, Colo. : Libraries Unlimited, 1989. 228 p. ISBN 0-87287-757-4. $34.50.   **AB108**

" . . . a practical guide to the tools and techniques of serials reference work . . . intended for librarians, library support staff, and library school students."—*Introd.* Basic reference sources

for serials are described, including directories, union lists, and indexes and abstracts. All types of serials are treated, including annuals, irregular serials, conference publications, U.S. government serials, and those of international governmental organizations. Newspapers and reference sources relating to them are given extensive coverage, as is the effect of serials processing and cataloging on serials reference work. Author/title and subject indexes.   Z711.P85

Reprography

Keene, James A. Planning, equipping, and staffing a document reprographic service : a RAMP study with guidelines / prepared by James A. Keene and Michael Roper [for the] General Information Programme and UNISIST. Paris : UNESCO, 1984. 84 p. : ill.   **AB109**

Intends "to provide archivists . . . with a survey of current relevant reprographic technology and with guidelines and standards which they can apply in selecting and introducing the technology [most appropriate to their own specific situations]."—*Introd.* Written with the problems of developing countries (especially those in tropical areas) firmly in mind; in four parts, treating Basic technology; Issues in planning, equipping, and staffing; A three-stage program for establishing an archival reprographic service; and Guidelines. Eight appendixes include job descriptions, facility plans, list of manufacturers and suppliers, glossary, and bibliography.   Z48.K43

Saffady, William. Micrographics. 2nd ed. Littleton, Colo. : Libraries Unlimited, 1985. 254 p. : ill. ISBN 0-87287-453-2. $28.00.   **AB110**

1st ed., 1978.

" . . . a text designed for practicing librarians and library school students who want a systematic presentation of the basic facets of micrographics as applied to library work."—*Pref.* Describes the basic types of microforms and discusses production of microform from source documents as well as from machine-readable data (COM—Computer Output Microfilm). Also treats micropublishing, microform display and printing equipment, bibliographic control of microforms, and microform storage and retrieval. Illustrations; index.   Z692.M5S24

AC

Encyclopedias

AMERICAN AND ENGLISH

The Cambridge encyclopedia. Cambridge ; N.Y. : Cambridge Univ. Pr., 1990. 1334, 128 p., xvi p. of plates :ill. (some col.), maps (some col.). ISBN 0-521-39528-3. **AC1**

Aims to "provide a succinct, systematic, and readable guide to the facts, events, issues, beliefs, and achievements which make up the sum of human knowledge."—*Pref.* The compilers have made an effort to cover recent events, both political and scientific. The brief entries are arranged alphabetically; there are a few illustrations, primarily maps. A ready reference section has a number of useful tables, including a list, arranged alphabetically by country, of political leaders 1900–90.

AG5.C26

The concise Columbia encyclopedia. 2nd ed. N.Y. : Columbia Univ. Pr., c1989. 920 p. ISBN 0-231-06938-3.

AC2

1st ed., 1983 (*Guide* AC9 *note*).

More than a third of the entries have been revised and some 500 new entries have been added.   AG5.C737

●**Electronic encyclopedia** [computer file]. 1990 ed. Danbury, Conn. : Grolier Electronic Publishing, Inc., c1990.

AC3

File size: 33,000 articles. Update frequency: quarterly; 10–20% of encyclopedia articles revised per year. Available on-line as *Academic American encyclopedia* (BRS, CompuServe, Dow Jones News/Retrieval, GEnie, PRODIGY, Q-Link, StarText, U.S. Videotel, VU/TEXT) and in CD-ROM as *Electronic encyclopedia* (Abt Books, Bureau of Electronic Publishing, EBSCO, Faxon, producer).

Contains the text, minus the illustrations, of *Academic American encyclopedia* (*Guide* AC1).

The Harper dictionary of modern thought. New and rev. ed. / ed. by Alan Bullock and Stephen Trombley, assisted by Bruce Eadie. N.Y. : Harper & Row, c1988. 917 p. ISBN 0-06-015869-7. $29.95.   **AC4**

Rev. ed. of *The Harper dictionary of modern thought*, ed. by Alan Bullock and Oliver Stallybrass (N.Y. : Harper & Row, 1977). British ed. has title: *The Fontana dictionary of modern thought* (London : Fontana, 1988).

Aims to steer "a middle course between an ordinary dictionary and an encyclopedia. It takes some 4,000 terms from across the whole range of modern thought, sets them within their context, and offers short explanatory accounts (anything from ten to a thousand words) written by experts, but in language as simple as can be used without *over*-simplification or distortion."—*Pref.* Articles are signed with initials and often include select bibliographies. Some British orientation. A related work is *The Fontana biographical companion to modern thought* (London : Collins, 1983).   AG5.H19

The Longman encyclopedia / ed. in chief, Asa Briggs. Burnt Mill, Harlow, Essex, England : Longman, 1989. 1178 p. ISBN 0-582-91620-8 :c$21.99.   **AC5**

Based on the 1st ed. of *The concise Columbia encyclopedia* (*Guide* AC9 *note*). The editors "went on to review and update each existing article, to add thousands of new ones, and to delete some others."—*Foreword.* Contains alphabetically arranged entries varying in length from a paragraph to a column, many with illustrations. British emphasis.   AE5.L66

The Random House encyclopedia / James Mitchell, ed. in chief ; Jess Stein, ed. dir. New rev. 3rd ed. N.Y. : Random House, c1990. 2781, 130 p. : ill. (some col.), col. maps. ISBN 0-394-58450-3. $129.95.   **AC6**

2nd ed., 1983 (*Guide* AC10).

Follows the arrangement of the 2nd ed. A review in *Choice* 28 (March 1991) : 1091, says it will be "frustrating and infrequently used in academic libraries."   AG5.R25

Guides

Kister, Kenneth F. Kister's concise guide to best encyclopedias. Phoenix : Oryx, 1988. 108 p. ISBN 0-89774-484-5 (pbk.).   **AC7**

Concise in format rather than content; supersedes Kister's *Best encyclopedias: a guide to general and special encyclopedias* (Phoenix : Oryx, 1986). More up-to-date than the same compiler's *Encyclopedia buying guide* (*Guide* AC11), including a number of general encyclopedias not treated in the earlier

work and providing annotated lists of specialized and foreign-language encyclopedias, but offering less detailed treatment of individual encyclopedias than the buying guide. Title index.

AE1.K57

Indexes

Ryan, Joe. First stop : the master index to subject encyclopedias. Phoenix : Oryx, 1989. 1582 p. ISBN 0-89774-397-0.   **AC8**

" . . . a keyword and broad subject index to nearly 40,000 topics contained in 430 of the best sources of background information and topic overviews . . . . Sources include English-language subject encyclopedias, dictionaries, handbooks, comprehensive textbooks, and other standard sources" (*Prefatory note*) in all subject areas.   Z5848.R93

FOREIGN LANGUAGE

Czech

Malá československá encyklopedie / [hlavní redakce československé encyklopedie Bohumil Kvasil et al.]. Vyd. 1. Praha : Academia, 1984–1987. 6 v. : ill.   **AC9**

Editors vary.

A general encyclopedia with well-illustrated, brief, unsigned articles arranged alphabetically. Contains many biographies of Czech nationals.   AE51.M25

French

Encyclopaedia universalis. [3rd ed.]. Paris : Encyclopaedia Universalis France, c1990. 30 v. : ill. ISBN 2-85229-287-4.   **AC10**

1st ed., 1968–74 (*Guide* AC33); [2nd ed.], 1985–88.

Contents: v. 1–23, A–Z; v. 24–26, Symposium; v. 27–30, Thesaurus-index.

Vols. 1–23 contains some 5,000 extended articles on all topics, more than 1,000 of which are new to this edition. The "Thesaurus-index" consists of shorter articles, providing brief factual information. The "Symposium" has nearly 200 essays on recent world developments, and current social, economic, and demographic statistics for all nations.

A 2 v. supplement to the 1st ed. was published in 1980, and a 2nd suppl., also 2 v. (called v. 21–22 of the 1st ed.), was published 1984–85. Another 2 v. suppl. was published in 1990, incorporating new information from the 3rd ed. of the encyclopedia. This can serve as either the 3rd suppl. to the 1968–74 ed., or as the 1st suppl. to the 1985–88 ed. (The purpose is to allow libraries to have current information without having to buy a new edition every few years.) The yearbook *Universalia* (*Guide* AC34) is still being published.   AE25.E3

La grande encyclopédie : [2e supplément]. Paris : Larousse, c1985. 584 p. : ill. (some col.). ISBN 2-03-152300-7 (set). ISBN 2-03-152326-0 (v. 2).   **AC11**

For main set and 1st suppl., see *Guide* AC38.

Covers events of 1977–82, with cross-references to the basic volumes and 1st suppl. Additional supplements are planned at 5-year intervals.   AE25.G69

German

Brockhaus Enzyklopädie : in vierundzwanzig Bänden. 19. völlig neu bearbeitete Aufl. Mannheim : F.A. Brockhaus, 1986–91. v. 1–15. : ill. (some col.). ISBN 3-7653-1100-6. (In progress). **AC12**

Rev. ed. of *Brockhaus Enzyklopädie in zwanzig Bänden*, 17th ed., 1966–81 (*Guide* AC43). The 18th ed., entitled *Der grosse Brockhaus* (12 v., 1977–81), is a rev. ed. of the 16th ed., 1952–63 (*Guide* AC42).

Contents: v. 1–15, A–Nor; Weltatlas.

Follows the format of the 17th ed., with predominantly brief, well-illustrated entries. The longer entries (those on individual countries, for example, run 10–20 pages) include brief, current bibliographies. The 7th ed. of *Der neue Brockhaus* (*Guide* AC42 *note*) was published in 6 v., 1984–85.

AG27.B861

Greek

Ekpaideutikē Hellēnikē Enkyklopaideia. Athens : Ekdotikē Athēnōn, c1983–1990. v. 1–9, pt. 1, v. 10–12, v. 20. (In progress). **AC13**

Contents: v. 1–8, Pankosmio viographiko lexico; v. 9–18, Thetikes epistemes; v. 19–24, Theoretikes epistemes; v. 25–29, Historia; v. 30–34, Grammata kai technes; v. 35, Geniko eyrethrio.

A well-illustrated, thematically arranged general encyclopedia. Some articles have brief bibliographies. To be complete in 35 vols., the last of which will be a general index. AE29.E55

Hebrew

ha-Entsiḳlopedyah ha-Yiśre'elit ha-kelalit : ḥadashah, maḳifah / [rikuz medaʻ va-ʻarikhah, Pozner u-vanav (yoʻatsim) be-ʻe. m.]. Yerushalayim : Keter, c1987–1988. v. 1–3 : ill. (some col.). ISBN 965-07-0010-2. (In progress). **AC14**

Title on added t.p.: *The Israeli general encyclopedia.*

Contents: v. 1, A'eginah–hatashah; v. 2, Ṿagner–Natran; v. 3, Saba–Tat-Pituaḥ.

A general, well-illustrated encyclopedia, with brief, unsigned entries. To be complete in 4 v.; v. 4 will update the first three volumes. AE30.E515

Hungarian

Akadémiai kislexikon / [a szerkesztőség vezetője, Szelle Béla ; főszerkesztők, Beck Mihály, Peschka Vilmos ; szerkesztő, Élesztős László]. Budapest : Akadémiai Kiadó, 1989. v. 1 : ill. (some col.). ISBN 963-05-5279-5 (set). (In progress). **AC15**

Contents: v. 1, A–K.

A well-illustrated general encyclopedia, with very brief entries. Particularly useful for biographical information.

AE31.A38

Italian

Enciclopedia del Novecento. Roma : Istituto della enciclopedia italiana, c1989. v. 8. **AC16**

For v. 1–7 and annotation, see *Guide* AC57.
Contents: v. 8, Supplemento. Completes the set.

AE35.E47

Spanish

Enciclopedia hispanica. Barcelona : Encyclopaedia Britannica Publishers, c1990–1991. 18 v. : ill., maps. ISBN 0-85229-532-4 (set). **AC17**

Contents: v. 1–14, Macropedia; v. I–II [i.e., v. 15–16], Micropedia e índice; [v. 17], Temapedia; [v. 18], Datapedia y atlas.

Divided into the "Micropedia," a 2 v. ready reference tool; the "Macropedia," with in-depth articles; the "Temapedia," with essays on selected topics; and the "Datapedia," with an atlas and current statistical information for all nations.

AE61.E52

Gran enciclopedia Rialp : GER. 5. ed. (revisada). Madrid : Ediciones Rialp, 1989. 25 v. : ill. (some col.). **AC18**

1st ed., 1971–76 (*Guide* AC80).

Contents: v. 1–23, A–Z; v. 24, Cartografia, Indices; v. 25, Supplemento, A–Z, 4th ed.

The 1st (1979), 2nd (1981), and 3rd (1984) reprintings were called the 2nd, 3rd, and 4th editions respectively.

Follows the format of the 1st ed. and in many cases reprints articles and bibliographies without revision. Vol. 25, called a supplement to the 4th ed., contains substantial articles, with brief bibliographies, emphasizing current geographical, political, and biographical information. The supplement has its own detailed subject index, and contains information not found in the main volumes.

Turkish

Yeni Türk ansiklopedisi / Birinci Cilt. [İstanbul] : Ötüken, [1985]. 12 v. : ill. (some col.). **AC19**

A general encyclopedia, some of whose articles are quite long. No bibliography. AE75.Y46

FACT BOOKS AND COMPENDIUMS

The New York Public Library desk reference. N.Y. : Webster's New World : Distr. by Prentice Hall Trade Sales, c1989. 836 p., [16] p. of plates : ill. ISBN 0-13-620444-9. $29.95. **AC20**

With a more tenuous relationship to the New York Public Library than the title might suggest, this volume aims to offer "the kind of basic information on popular subjects that will help . . . find quick, efficient answers to most commonly asked questions."—*Pref.* Sources are not cited; subject index. For a discussion of some of its shortcomings, see *Choice* 27 (Jan. 1990): 774. AG6.N49

AD

Language Dictionaries

ENGLISH LANGUAGE

Bibliography

O'Neill, Robert Keating. English-language dictionaries, 1604–1900: the catalog of the Warren N. and Suzanne B. Cordell collection. N.Y.: Greenwood, 1988. 480 p. (Bibliographies and indexes in library and information science, no. 1). ISBN 0-313-25522-9. **AD1**

A descriptive bibliography of more than 2,000 titles in the collection at Indiana State University (which includes subject as well as language dictionaries), representing "all but a few of the English language dictionary titles known to have been published prior to 1900."—*Pref.* Arranged by author, with a subject index. Z2015.D6O53

Schäfer, Jürgen. Early modern English lexicography. Oxford: Clarendon Pr.; N.Y.: Oxford Univ. Pr., 1989. 2 v. ISBN 0-19-812847-9 (set). $67.50. ISBN 0-19-812849-5 (set: pbk.). $37.50. **AD2**

Contents: v. 1, A survey of monolingual printed glossaries and dictionaries, 1475–1640; v. 2, Additions and corrections to the OED.

"... presents for the first time a census of printed monolingual glossaries and dictionaries .... A second volume compiles additions and corrections to the OED documentation never before published."—*p. preceding t.p.* PE891.S34

American

The Random House dictionary of the English language / Stuart Berg Flexner, ed. in chief. 2nd ed., unabridged. N.Y.: Random House, c1987. 2478, 32 p.: ill. (some col.). ISBN 0-394-50050-4. $79.95. **AD3**

1st ed., 1966 (*Guide* AD9).

"... expanded by some 50,000 new entries and 75,000 new definitions. Sample sentences, Usage notes, Synonym Studies, Synonym and Antonym Lists, illustrations and locator maps have also been increased in number."—*Pref. to the 2nd ed.* This edition also indicates the dates words entered the vocabulary, identifies American words, and provides specific regional labeling for American dialects. Geographic and the somewhat eclectic biographical entries are interfiled with other terms. A supplement includes concise French, Spanish, Italian, and German dictionaries; a style manual; lists of words commonly confused and misspelled; and a world atlas.

The illustrative sentences are not actual quotations but were written by the staff. The example from the publicity brochure illustrating "broadcast" as an adverb ("The vital news was sent broadcast to inform the entire nation") might make some users regret this policy.

Unlike the 1st ed., this edition is completely descriptive, attempting to reflect the language as the editors believe it is actually used—an approach that has not found universal favor. The reviewer in the *New York times book review*, January 3, 1988, 8–9 concludes that "This dictionary is depressingly, even resolutely, antiliterary. If users want to use English with grace, power and precision ... this work is not for them."

PE1625.R3

Desk dictionaries

The American heritage illustrated encyclopedic dictionary. Boston: Houghton Mifflin, c1987. 1920 p.: ill. (some col.). ISBN 0-395-44295-8. **AD4**

Offers definitions, etymologies, usage notes, illustrative quotations, and synonyms for some 200,000 words "with special emphasis on North America."—*Pref.* Includes geographical and biographical entries. Also published in 2 v. as *Reader's Digest illustrated encyclopedic dictionary* (Pleasantville, N.Y.: Readers Digest Association, 1987). PE1628.A624

Webster's New World dictionary of American English / Victoria Neufeldt, ed. in chief; David B. Guralnik, ed. in chief emeritus. 3rd college ed. N.Y.: Webster's New World: Distr. by Prentice Hall Trade, c1988. 1574 p.: ill. ISBN 0-13-947169-3. $16.95. **AD5**

"... a major revision of *Webster's New World dictionary*, 2nd college ed. [*Guide* AD17]."—*verso of t.p.*

Format and arrangement of the prior edition have been retained, but the appendixes now consist of a family tree of Indo-European languages; a guide to Editorial style; and a list of Special signs and symbols. Some 5,000 words, mainly from the business and scientific fields, have been added.

PE1628.W5633

English

The Oxford English dictionary. 2nd ed. / prepared by J.A. Simpson and E.S.C. Weiner. Oxford: Clarendon Pr.; Oxford: N. Y.; Oxford Univ. Pr., 1989. 20 v. ISBN 0-19-861186-2. $2,500.00. **AD6**

1st ed., 1888–1933 (*Guide* AD27); *Supplement*, v. 1–4, 1972–86 (*Guide* AD28).

Combines and partially revises Sir James Murray's *New English dictionary* (frequently called the *NED* or the *OED*; *Guide* AD27) and its *Supplement*, adding some 5,000 words, mainly in the scientific and technical fields. Although the 2nd ed. omits the words "on historical principles" from the title, the purpose (thoroughly described in the 10th ed. of the *Guide to reference books*) remains the same as that of the 1st ed. Briefly, both editions provide the history and development of English words through the last 800 years, excluding only those words which were obsolete by 1150, illustrating them with numerous quotations from the works of some 5,000 authors. A 143-page bibliography of the most frequently quoted works may be found at the end of v. 20.

The 2nd ed. reprints, with minor changes, the "Historical introduction" from the 1933 ed., but does not reprint Sir James Murray's preface nor the prefaces to the *Supplements*. The 2nd ed. has also eliminated Murray's unique pronunciation alphabet in favor of the International Phonetical Alphabet; in many cases pronunciations have been updated. An extensive and generally favorable review in *The review of English studies* n.s. 41 (Feb. 1990): 76–88 notes that changes and additions to entries are not indicated, and that "the etymological sections leave much to be desired. We are never sure what belongs to the dictionary of 1882–1932, and what to the edition of 1989." After noting that some of the quotations have been dropped (and many added), the reviewer states that "a learned library must not sell its *OED* [1st ed.] and *Supplements*."

§ The 1st ed. was published in CD-ROM in 1987 (Tri Star); the University of Waterloo is planning to publish the 2nd ed. on CD-ROM. PE1625.O87

Desk dictionaries

Chambers English dictionary / editors, Catherine Schwarz... [et al.]; assistant editors, Pandora Kerr Frost... [et al.]. Edinburgh: Chambers; Cambridge; N.Y.: Cambridge, c1988. 1792 p. ISBN 1-85296-000-0.
AD7

1st ed., 1901, had title *Chambers's twentieth century dictionary of the English language*; previous ed., 1983, entitled *Chambers 20th century dictionary*.

The reference dictionary for the National Scrabble Championships. This edition has added many new scientific and technical terms. Particularly useful for archaic words. Includes etymologies; British emphasis. PE1628.C43

Collins CoBUILD English language dictionary / [ed. in chief, John Sinclair]. London: Collins, 1987. 1703 p. ISBN 0-00-375021-3. £12.95. **AD8**

Defines some 34,000 of the most frequently used words, based on a computerized examination of material issued in the last 10 years, including books, newspapers, magazines, radio broadcasts, etc. Designed primarily for non-native speakers, it defines words in complete sentences, rather than by synonyms. Provides guidance on usage. British emphasis. PE1628

Abbreviations

Wall, C. Edward. Abbreviations: the comprehensive dictionary of abbreviations and letter symbols for the computer era. Ann Arbor, Mich.: Pierian Pr., 1984. 2 v. ISBN 0-87650-179-X (v. 1). ISBN 0-87650-183-8 (v. 2).
AD9

Contents: v. 1, Abbreviation to word; v. 2, Word to abbreviation.

"The main source... has been primary documents designed for data processing purposes.... This is the first major, comprehensive dictionary of abbreviated words for application in the computer era."—*Introd.* PE1693.W35

Etymology

The American heritage dictionary of Indo-European roots / rev. and ed. by Calvert Watkins. Boston: Houghton Mifflin Co., c1985. 113 p. ISBN 0-395-37888-5. $10.95. ISBN 0-395-36070-6 (pbk.). $5.95. **AD10**

A revised and expanded ed. of the "Appendix of Indo-European roots" from the *American heritage dictionary of the English language* (Boston: Houghton Mifflin, 1969); published as a companion to *American heritage dictionary*, 2nd College ed. (*Guide* AD13).

"... designed and written for the general English-speaking public."—*Pref.* Arranged alphabetically by Indo-European root, with examples of English words derived from that root. Index of English words. P615.A43

The Barnhart dictionary of etymology / Robert K. Barnhart, ed.; Sol Steinmetz, managing ed. [Bronx, N.Y.]: H.W. Wilson Co., 1988. 1284 p. ISBN 0-8242-0745-9. $59.00. **AD11**

"... traces the origins of the basic vocabulary of modern English. It contains over 30,000 entries... [and] examines not only the antecedents of modern English, but emphasizes its development, especially from the point of view of American English."—*Explanatory note.* Includes two brief articles (Short history of the English language, and General statement of proto-Germanic forms and Indo-European roots) and glossaries of language names and linguistic terms and of literary works listed in etymologies. The review in *Language* 65 (Dec. 1989): 848–52 stresses both its scholarship and its accessibility and concludes that it "appears to be the best etymological work now available." PE1580.B35

Beeching, Cyril Leslie. A dictionary of eponyms. 3rd ed. Oxford; N.Y.: Oxford Univ. Pr., 1990. 218 p. ISBN 0-19-282777-4. **AD12**

1st ed., 1979; 2nd ed., 1983.

Offers some 700 descriptions of "'true' eponymic words which have become part of the language... and are taken from the names of people who actually exist."—*Introd.* The areas of engineering, horticulture, and botany "have been generally avoided." Subject index. PE1596.B43

Byrne, Mary. Eureka!: a dictionary of Latin and Greek elements in English words. Newton Abbot: David & Charles, c1987. 224 p. ISBN 0-7153-8831-2. £7.95.
AD13

"Each entry consists of a number of examples derived from a particular Latin or Greek word.... [Entries] are intended to show the route (sometimes obvious, sometimes tortuous) by which the modern meaning of an English word can be traced back to the basic meaning of its Latin or Greek ancestors."—*Introd.* Arranged by Greek and Latin roots. PE1582.L3B97

Claiborne, Robert. The roots of English: a reader's handbook of word origins. N.Y.: Times Books, c1989. 335 p. ISBN 0-8129-1716-2. $18.95. **AD14**

An alphabetical listing of Indo-European sources of English words, with illustrative examples, excluding "roots whose only English descendants are scholarly, rare, or archaic."—*Introd.* The compiler used the *American heritage dictionary of Indo-European roots* (above) but has emphasized "how the roots evolved into English words." Includes an index to English words. PE1580.C56

The concise Oxford dictionary of English etymology / ed. by T.F. Hoad. Oxford; N.Y.: Oxford Univ. Pr., 1986. 552 p. ISBN 0-19-861182-X. $18.20. **AD15**

This abridged version of *Oxford dictionary of etymology*, ed. by C.T. Onions (*Guide* AD44), has some 17,000 headwords as opposed to 24,000. Personal and mythological names, and medical and technical terms have been dropped. "The intention is that each entry should give a concise statement of the route by which its headword entered the English language, together with, where appropriate, a brief account of its development in English."—*Introd.* PE1580.C66

Hendrickson, Robert. The Facts on File encyclopedia of word and phrase origins. N.Y.: Facts on File, c1987. 581 p. ISBN 0-8160-1012-9. **AD16**

Repr. as: *Henry Holt encyclopedia of word and phrase origins* (N.Y.: Holt, 1990).

Offers an alphabetical listing of some 7,500 words and phrases with definitions and origins. Intended for general readers rather than scholars. PE1689.H47

Morris, William. Morris dictionary of word and phrase origins / William and Mary Morris; foreword by Isaac Asimov. 2nd ed. N.Y.: Harper & Row, c1988. 669 p. ISBN 0-06-015862-X. $25.00. **AD17**

1st ed., 1977 (*Guide* AD43).

Words and phrases from the first edition have been repeated, with many new entries. PE1580.M6

Rees, Nigel. Why do we say— ? : words and sayings and where they come from. Poole ; N.Y. : Blandford Pr. ; N.Y. : Distr. by Sterling Pub., 1987. (1988 printing). 224 p. ISBN 0-7137-1944-3. **AD18**

Aims to "sift through the lore and disentangle the misconceptions" (*Pref.*) of many common folk etymologies. British emphasis. PE1574.R44

Room, Adrian. Dictionary of changes in meaning. London ; N.Y. : Routledge & Kegan Paul, 1986. 292 p. ISBN 0-7102-0341-1. £14.95. **AD19**

Offers histories of more than 1,300 words from the first use to the present, illustrated with quotations. No formal etymologies. British emphasis. PE1580.R59

——————— A dictionary of true etymologies. London ; Boston : Routledge & Kegan Paul, 1986. 193 p. ISBN 0-7102-0340-3. $13.00. **AD20**

Repr. as *NTC's dictionary of word origins* (Lincolnwood, Ill. : National Textbook Co., 1991).

Aims to correct popular misconceptions of the origins of some 1,200 words. Includes both popular (i.e., false) and scholarly etymologies. PE1580.R6

Webster's word histories. Springfield, Mass. : Merriam-Webster, c1989. 526 p. ISBN 0-87779-048-5. $14.95. **AD21**

Offers one- to two-page articles on the origins and meanings of some 600 words. PE1580.W35

Idioms and usage

Allusions—cultural, literary, biblical, and historical : a thematic dictionary / Laurence Urdang and Frederick G. Ruffner, Jr., editors, David M. Glixon, assoc. ed. 2nd ed. Detroit : Gale, c1986. 634 p. ISBN 0-8103-1828-8. $68.00. **AD22**

For annotation, see *Supplement* BD32. PN43.A4

Bloomsbury good word guide / ed., Martin H. Manser. 2nd ed. London : Bloomsbury, 1990. 316 p. ISBN 0-7475-0575-6. **AD23**

1st ed., 1988; repr. as *The World Almanac guide to good word usage* (N.Y. : World Almanac, 1989.)

Offers an alphabetical listing of problem words and phrases, providing suggestions on spelling, pronunciation, grammar, and/or usage. British emphasis, although American spelling, pronunciation, and usage are noted. PE1625.B56

Clark, John Owen Edward. Word perfect : a dictionary of current English usage. N.Y. : H. Holt, 1990. 1 v. ISBN 0-8050-1457-8. **AD24**

"Originally published in Great Britain in 1987 by Harrap Ltd."—*verso of t.p.*

" . . . a guide to current English usage, arranged alphabetically . . . . It is intended to be of help to learners of English, to writers and to editors."—*Pref.* PE1460.C485

Freeman, Morton S. A handbook of problem words & phrases. Philadelphia : ISI Pr., c1987. 299 p. ISBN 0-89495-074-6. $19.95. ISBN 0-89495-080-0 (pbk.). $14.95. **AD25**

Reprinted in 1990 by Writer's Digest Press under the title *The wordwatcher's guide to good writing & grammar.*

" . . . designed to present in concise and readable form a clear exposition of problems involving word usage, spelling and pronunciation—and their suggested answers."—*Pref.* PE1460.F654

Schur, Norman W. British English, A to Zed. N.Y. : Facts on File, c1987. 477 p. ISBN 0-8160-1635-6. $35.00. **AD26**

1st ed., 1980, had title *English English* (*Guide* AD64).

Aims to be "a comprehensive glossary of Briticisms for Americans, rather than a dictionary of British English in general."—*Introd.* Appendix 1: General differences between British and American English; Appendix 2: Glossaries and tables. Indexed. PE1704.S38

Shaw, Harry. Dictionary of problem words and expressions. Rev. ed. N.Y. : McGraw-Hill, c1987. 368 p. ISBN 0-07-056517-1. **AD27**

1st ed., 1975.

" . . . selects, defines, explains, and illustrates more than 1500 of the most common mistakes made by speakers and writers of our language."—*To the reader.* PE1460.S5158 1987

Sparkes, Ivan George. Dictionary of collective nouns and group terms. 2nd ed. Detroit : Gale, c1985. 283 p. ISBN 0-8103-2188-2. **AD28**

Subtitle: Being a compendium of more than 1800 collective nouns, group terms, and phrases, that from medieval to modern times have described companies of persons, birds, insects, animals, professions, and objects.

1st ed., 1975.

Index of "things collected." PE1689.S69

Todd, Loreto. International English usage / Loreto Todd & Ian Hancock. N.Y. : New York Univ. Pr., c1987. 520 p. ISBN 0-8147-8176-4. $40.00. **AD29**

Originally publ. London : Croom Helm, 1986; repr.: London : Routledge, 1990.

Aims "to deal objectively with English as a world-wide language with many local varieties, and to distinguish legitimate regional practices from actual errors" (*Introd.*), striking "a balance between *description* and *prescription.*" Dictionary arrangement of grammatical terms, figures and parts of speech, specific words and phrases. Indexed. PE1460.T64

Webster's dictionary of English usage. Springfield, Mass. : Merriam-Webster, c1989. [989 p.]. ISBN 0-87779-032-9. $18.95. **AD30**

" . . . examines and evaluates common problems of confused or disputed English usage from two perspectives: that of historical background . . . and that of present-day usage."—*Pref.* Some 500 words are discussed, illustrated with quotations. PE1460.W425

Williams, Stephen N. The dictionary of British and American homophones. London : Brookside Pr., c1987. 503 p. ISBN 0-85173-011-6. **AD31**

Claims to be "the first and only comprehensive dictionary of British and American homophones."—*Introd.* More than 12,000 are listed, with brief definitions. PE1595.W54

New words

12,000 words : a supplement to *Webster's third new international dictionary.* Springfield, Mass. : Merriam-Webster, c1986. [236] p. ISBN 0-87779-207-0. **AD32**

The most recent "Addenda" section of *Webster's third new international dictionary* (*Guide* AD11). Includes new words and "older words that for various reasons had been passed over in the earlier editing."—*p. 21a.* This appears as the "Addenda" in editions of *Webster's third* printed after 1985. Supersedes *6,000 words,* (1976), and *9,000 words,* (1983; *Guide* AD72). PE1630.A17

Ayto, John. The Longman register of new words. 1989 ed. Burnt Mill, Harlow, Essex, England : Longman, c1989. v. 1. ISBN 0-582-03772-7 (v. 1). £10.95. ISBN 0-582-03771-9 (pbk). $12.95. (In progress).   **AD33**

Vol. 1 defines some 1,200 words that appeared between 1986 and 1988, based primarily on usage in British newspapers and magazines. It "does not set out to be a record of every last coinage . . . but is a representative sample."—*Introd.*

PE1630.A97

Barnhart, David K. The Barnhart dictionary companion—index, 1982–1985. Cold Spring, N.Y.: Lexik House Publishers, c1987. 102 p. ISBN 0-936368-05-5. $36.00.   **AD34**

Cumulates the indexes to *The Barnhart dictionary companion* (*Guide* AD69). Arranged alphabetically with a broad subject index, various "Etymological lists," and a list of "Formative elements of words and phrases."   PE1460.A2B37

-ologies & -isms / Laurence Urdang, ed. in chief; Anne Ryle and Tanya H. Lee, editors. 3rd ed. Detroit: Gale, c1986. 795 p. ISBN 0-8103-1196-8. $90.00.   **AD35**

2nd ed., 1981 (*Guide* AD31).

Subtitle: A unique lexicon of more than 15,000 English words used of and about theories, concepts, doctrines, systems, attitudes, practices, states of mind, and branches of science, focusing especially on words containing the suffixes *-ology, -ism, -ics, -graphy, -metry, -archy, -cide, -philia, -phobia, -mancy, -latry,* et al., including derivative forms of these words, the entries conveniently arranged by thematic categories, and the whole supplemented by an alphabetical index.

Repr. as: *Dictionary of uncommon words: over 17,000 entries often omitted from standard dictionaries* (N.Y.: Wynwood Pr., 1991).

This edition adds about 1,000 new words.   PE1680.O4

The third Barnhart dictionary of new English / [ed. by] Robert K. Barnhart, Sol Steinmetz with Clarence L. Barnhart. Bronx, N.Y.: H.W. Wilson, 1990. 565 p. ISBN 0-8242-0796-3.   **AD36**

Continues *The Barnhart dictionary of new English since 1963* (*Guide* AD70) and *The second Barnhart dictionary of new English* (*Guide* AD71).

Offers "a lexical index of new words of the past decade" (*Pref.*) and new uses of older words, illustrated by quotations. Many of the entries in the first two volumes have been revised, but the earlier vols. have not been completely superseded.

PE1630.B3

Pronunciation

Jones, Daniel. Everyman's English pronouncing dictionary: containing over 59,000 words in international phonetic transcription. 14th ed. London: Dent, c1988. 576 p. ISBN 0-460-03036-1. $18.95.   **AD37**

12th ed., 1963 (*Guide* AD80); 14th ed., 1977.

"Extensively revised and edited by A.C. Gimson . . . with revisions and Supplement by Susan Ramsaran."—*t.p.* This new printing of the 14th ed. adds "a supplement of about a thousand 'new' words . . . [and] several thousand alterations to pronunciation."—*Pref. to the rev. ed.*   PE1137.J55

Rhymes

Wood, Clement. The complete rhyming dictionary and poet's craft book / ed. by Clement Wood; rev. by Ronald J. Bogus. N.Y.: Doubleday, c1990. 627 p. ISBN 0-385-41350-5.   **AD38**

Rev. ed. of *Wood's unabridged rhyming dictionary*, 1943 (*Guide* AD91).

Offers separate chapters for single, double, and triple rhymes; within each chapter words are arranged by vowel sounds, then alphabetically. "The poet's craft book" serves as an introduction to the technical aspects of writing poetry, but the introduction to the earlier edition is still useful for its examples and concise definitions of the different poetic genres.

PE1519.W6

Young, Sue. The new comprehensive American rhyming dictionary. N.Y.: W. Morrow, c1991. 622 p. ISBN 0-688-10360-X. $24.95.   **AD39**

Arranged by vowel sound. Includes phrases.   PE1519.Y68

Slang

Chapman, Robert L. New dictionary of American slang. N.Y.: Harper & Row, c1986. 485 p. ISBN 0-06-181157-2. $21.95.   **AD40**

Based on Harold Wentworth and Stuart Berg Flexner's *Dictionary of American slang*, 2nd supplemented ed., 1975 (*Guide* AD101), the content of that work having been " 'recycled' and its wealth of material retained, altered, or discarded according to the new policies" (*Pref.*) established for the present work, which is intended as "a dictionary of current general American slang." In addition to definitions and indication of parts of speech, entries sometimes include "impact symbols" (indicating social or emotional impact), pronunciation (for unusual pronunciations only), variant forms, dating labels, provenience labels, slang synonyms, examples (but omitting specific sources and dates), and derivation. Although a considerable number of "non-current" terms have been retained, the Wentworth and Flexner volume will continue to be useful for many older terms.

PE2846.C46

Clark, Gregory R. Words of the Vietnam War. Jefferson, N.C.: McFarland, c1990. 604 p. ISBN 0-89950-465-5.   **AD41**

Subtitle: the slang, jargon, abbreviations, acronyms, nomenclature, nicknames, pseudonyms, slogans, specs, euphemisms, double-talk, chants, and names and places of the era of United States involvement in Vietnam.

"The primary focus of this dictionary is the period of direct American involvement in Southeast Asia, from 1961 . . . to the fall of Saigon in 1975."—*Introd.* Some 4,000 entries (plus about 6,000 references) compiled from printed material, interviews with veterans and antiwar antivists, and personal experience. Numerals are filed at the end of the alphabet. No index; liberal use of cross-references.   PE3727.S7C57

Green, Jonathon. Dictionary of jargon. London; N.Y.: Routledge & Kegan Paul, in association with Methuen, 1987. 616 p. ISBN 0-7100-9919-3. £25.00.   **AD42**

A greatly expanded edition of the author's *Newspeak*, 1984. Offers "a collection of some 21,000 words and phrases, acronyms and abbreviations that have been collected from the jargons, or professional slangs and verbal shorthands, of a wide variety of occupations."—*Introd.*   PE1689.G73

Henke, James T. Gutter life and language in the early "street" literature of England. West Cornwall, Conn.: Locust Hill Pr., 1988. 339 p. ISBN 0-933951-17-5. $30.00.   **AD43**

Subtitle: a glossary of terms and topics, chiefly of the sixteenth and seventeenth centuries.

" . . . contains the gleanings from thousands of items of ephemeral British literature published chiefly in London and chiefly during the 16th and 17th centuries."—*Pref.* Dictionary arrangement with broad subject index.   PE3724.O3H44

Holder, R. W. The Faber dictionary of euphemisms. Rev. ed. London; Boston: Faber and Faber, 1989.

408 p. ISBN 0-571-14253-2. $18.95. ISBN 0-571-15125-6 (pbk.). **AD44**

[1st ed.] (Bath : Bath Univ. Pr., 1987) had title: *A dictionary of American and British euphemisms: the language of evasion, hypocrisy, prudery and deceit.*

Arranged alphabetically, with illustrative quotations. Broad subject index. PE1449.H548

Lewin, Esther. The thesaurus of slang / Esther Lewin and Albert E. Lewin. N.Y. : Facts on File, c1988. 435 p. ISBN 0-8160-1742-5. **AD45**

Subtitle: 150,000 uncensored contemporary slang terms, common idioms, and colloquialisms arranged for quick and easy reference.

Repr. as *The Random House thesaurus of slang* (N.Y. : Random House, 1988).

Some 12,000 standard words are listed alphabetically, followed by their slang equivalents. PE3721.L45

McDonald, James,. A dictionary of obscenity, taboo & euphemism. London ; N.Y. : Sphere, 1988. 167 p. ISBN 0-7474-0166-7 (pbk.). £3.99. **AD46**

An "eclectic rather than comprehensive" (*p. xiii*) listing, providing brief histories and, in some cases, quotations from literary sources. PE1691

Neaman, Judith S. Kind words : a thesaurus of euphemisms / Judith S. Neaman and Carole G. Silver. Expanded & rev. ed. N.Y. : Facts on File, c1990. 373 p. ISBN 0-8160-1896-0. $22.95. **AD47**

1st ed., 1983.

Arranged by broad subject headings. Indexed. PE1449.N34

Rawson, Hugh. Wicked words : a treasury of curses, insults, put-downs, and other formerly unprintable terms from Anglo-Saxon times to the present. N.Y. : Crown, c1989. 435 p. ISBN 0-517-57334-2. $24.95. **AD48**

Offers detailed definitions and usage histories of some 1,600 words. PE3721.R38

Synonyms and antonyms

Longman synonym dictionary. Burnt Mill, Harlow, Essex, England : Longman, 1986. 1355 p. ISBN 0-582-89322-4 (pbk.). £14.95. **AD49**

Although it is not specifically stated, this is a slightly expanded edition of Jerome I. Rodale's *The synonym finder*, 1978 (*Guide* AD107). More than one million words are listed. PE1591.L66

The Random House thesaurus / ed. by Jess Stein and Stuart Berg Flexner. College ed. N.Y. : Random House, c1984. 812 p. ISBN 0-394-52949-9. $14.95. **AD50**

"Based upon the Reader's Digest family word finder, c1975."—*verso of t.p.*

Some 11,000 words are arranged alphabetically, with illustrative sentences and lists of synonyms and antonyms. PE1591.R28

Roget's II : the new thesaurus / by the editors of American heritage dictionary. Expanded ed. Boston : Houghton Mifflin, c1988. 1135 p. ISBN 0-395-48317-4. $12.95. **AD51**

1st ed., 1980 (*Guide* AD109)

This edition includes near-synonyms, near-antonyms and antonyms for some words. PE1591.R715

Regional and dialect

American

Dictionary of American regional English / Frederic G. Cassidy, chief ed. Cambridge, Mass. : Belknap Pr. of Harvard Univ. Pr., 1985. v. 1 : ill. ISBN 0-674-20511-1 (v. 1). $65.00. (In progress). **AD52**

Contents: v. 1, Introduction; A–C.

Sponsored by the American Dialect Society. Compiled mainly from responses to a lengthy questionnaire (reprinted in the introduction) administered in 1,002 communities in the U.S. Concentrating on colloquialisms, regional usages, dialect and ethnic terms, and out-of-the-way meanings, "DARE does not treat technical, scientific, or other learned words or phrases—or anything else that could be considered standard."—*Introd.* Entries (mainly single words but including some phrases) indicate parts of speech, variant spellings, etc., and are illustrated with quotations. Many entries have maps indicating geographical distribution of usages. Five volumes are planned; v. 5 is to be a detailed bibliography of quoted sources. PE2843.D52

British

Commonwealth

The Australian concise Oxford dictionary of current English / ed. by George W. Turner. 1st Australian ed. Melbourne ; N.Y. : Oxford Univ. Pr., 1987. 1340 p. ISBN 0-19-554619-9. **AD53**

" . . . a line-by-line revision, from an Australian point of view, of the seventh edition of the *Concise Oxford dictionary* [*of current English*] edited by J.B. Sykes [1982]."—*Pref.* PE3601.Z5A863

The Australian national dictionary : a dictionary of Australianisms on historical principles / ed. by W.S. Ramson. Melbourne ; N.Y. : Oxford Univ. Pr., 1988. 814 p. ISBN 0-19-554736-5. **AD54**

" . . . an Australianism is one of those words and meanings of words which have originated in Australia, which have a greater currency here than elsewhere, or which have a special significance in Australia . . . . The aim of the dictionary is to provide as full an historical record of these as possible."—*Introd.* Includes pronunciations, etymologies, definitions, and illustrative quotations arranged chronologically. Select bibliography of works frequently quoted, p.767–814.

An abridged version, with the entire word list minus some of the illustrative material, was published as *Australian words and their origins* (Melbourne : Oxford Univ. Pr., 1989). PE3601.Z5A865

The Australian pocket Oxford dictionary / ed. by George W. Turner. 2nd ed. Melbourne : Oxford Univ. Pr., 1984. 824 p. ISBN 0-19-554560-5. **AD55**

1st ed., 1976 (*Guide* AD125), ed. by Grahame Johnston.

"In this second edition the standpoint is even more decidedly Australian than in the first."—*Pref. to 2nd ed.* PE3601.Z5A87

Branford, Jean. A dictionary of South African English. 3rd ed., rev. and enl. Cape Town : Oxford Univ. Pr., 1987. 444 p. ISBN 0-19-570427-4. **AD56**

1980 ed. (*Guide* AD121).

"In this second edition the standpoint is even more decidedly Australian than in the first."—*Pref. to 2nd ed.*

PE3601.Z5A87

Branford, Jean. A dictionary of South African English. 3rd ed., rev. and enl. Cape Town : Oxford Univ. Pr., 1987. 444 p. ISBN 0-19-570427-4.   **AD56**

1980 ed. (*Guide* AD121).

Includes new words and definitions, many relating to recent events in South Africa.   PE3451.B7

The South African pocket Oxford dictionary / ed. by William Branford. Cape Town ; Oxford : Oxford Univ. Pr., 1987. 903 p. ISBN 0-19-570503-3.   **AD57**

"Based on *The pocket Oxford dictionary of current English*, 7th ed., [1984]."—*t.p.*

"Some 2,500 South African English entries [have been added] with a corresponding deletion of items judged not to be relevant in South Africa."—*Pref.*   PE3452.S6

Wilkes, G. A. A dictionary of Australian colloquialisms. 2nd ed., rev. and reset. [Sydney] : Sydney Univ. Pr. ; Portland, Or. : Exclusive distributor, ISBS, 1985. 470 p. ISBN 0-424-00113-6. $33.05.   **AD58**

1st ed., 1978 (*Guide* AD127).

" . . . considerably revised and enlarged."—*Pref. to 2nd ed.*

PE3601.Z5W5

Scottish

The concise Scots dictionary / ed. in chief, Mairi Robinson. Aberdeen : Aberdeen Univ. Pr., 1985. 819 p. : ill. ISBN 0-08-028491-4.   **AD59**

Based mainly on the *Scottish national dictionary* (*Guide* AD133) and the *Dictionary of the older Scottish tongue* (*Guide* AD129), it "aims to include what is (or was) wholly or mainly Scots . . . [and] words and usages which . . . were used at least 100 years earlier or later in Scots than in the English of England."—*Introd.* Provides pronunciations, parts of speech, definitions, dates of usage, and geographical distribution.

PE2106.C66

Craigie, William A. *Sir.* A dictionary of the older Scottish tongue : from the twelfth century to the end of the seventeenth. Chicago : The Univ. of Chicago Pr. ; London : H. Milford, Oxford Univ. Pr., 1985-1990. pts. 32-41. (In progress).   **AD60**

For pts. 1-31 and annotation, see *Guide* AD129.

Contents: pts. 32-41, Po-Ro.   PE2116.C7

Stevenson, James A. C. Scoor-oot : a dictionary of Scots words and phrases in current use / James A.C. Stevenson with Iseabail Macleod. London ; Atlantic Highlands, N.J. : Athlone Pr., 1989. 256 p., [10] p. of plates : ill. ISBN 0-485-11373-2. ISBN 0-485-12068-2 (pbk.).   **AD61**

A dictionary, arranged under 15 broad subject headings, of "the most widely-used words and expressions."—*Foreword.* Alphabetical index.   PE2106.S74

Anglo-Norman

Anglo-Norman dictionary. London : Modern Humanities Research Association, 1985-1990. fasc. 4-6. (Publications of the Modern Humanities Research Association, v. 8). ISBN 0-900547-47-2 (fasc. 1). £15.00. (In progress).   **AD62**

For fasc. 1-3 and annotation, see *Guide* AD134.

Contents: fasc. 4-6, M-S.   PC2946.M6

Anglo-Saxon

Dictionary of Old English [microform]. [Toronto] : Published for the Dictionary of Old English Project, Centre for Medieval Studies, Univ. of Toronto by the Pontifical Institute of Mediaeval Studies, [1986-1988]. Fasc. C-D; 10 microfiches. ISBN 0-88844-926-7. (In progress).   **AD63**

When completed this will include all words from *A microfiche concordance to Old English* (Newark : Univ. of Delaware, 1980), excepting Latin words in a Latin context, partial and damaged spellings, and personal and place names. Thus, it complements the *Oxford English dictionary* (*Supplement* AD6), which excludes words not used after 1150. Arranged by late West Saxon spelling (with many cross-references), entries include: grammatical labels; brief definitions; number of occurrences in, and up to 12 citations to, the *Microfiche concordance*; and when appropriate, Latin equivalents and references to the *Oxford English dictionary, Middle English dictionary* (below), etc. Etymologies are not provided. Note that line references in the citations to the *Microfiche concordance* are to the beginning of the sentence in which the word occurs rather than the line in which the word itself appears. A printed preface is available; there are no plans to publish the dictionary in printed form.

PE279D53

Middle English

Middle English dictionary / Hans Kurath, ed. ; Sherman M. Kuhn, associate ed. Ann Arbor, Mich. : Univ. of Michigan Pr. ; London : G. Cumberledge, Oxford Univ. Pr., c1985-1990. v. R$^{4-5}$-S$^{1-14}$. (In progress).   **AD64**

For earlier parts and annotation, see *Guide* AD140.

Suppl. I to the *Plan and bibliography* was published in 1984.   PE679.M54

Foreign words and phrases

Loanwords dictionary / Laurence Urdang, editorial dir. ; Frank R. Abate, ed. Detroit : Gale, c1988. 324 p. ISBN 0-8103-1543-2. $80.00.   **AD65**

Subtitle: a lexicon of more than 6,500 words and phrases encountered in English contexts that are not fully assimilated into English and retain a measure of their foreign orthography, pronunciation, or flavor.

Repr. as: *Dictionary of borrowed words: over 6,500 foreign words and phrases used in English contexts* (N.Y. : Wynwood Pr., 1991).

Aims to "focus on those terms that are likely to be encountered . . . by a person who is attuned to literature, culture, and society."—*Pref.* Does not include botanical or zoological names, quotations, mottoes, or proverbs.   PE1670.L58

Mawson, C. O. Sylvester. The Harper dictionary of foreign terms : based on the original edition by C.O. Sylvester Mawson. 3rd ed. / rev. and ed. by Eugene Ehrlich. N.Y. : Harper & Row, c1987. 423 p. ISBN 0-06-181576-4. $20.00.   **AD66**

1st ed., 1934, and 2nd ed., 1975, had title: *Dictionary of foreign terms.*

Repr. as *Le mot juste: the Penguin dictionary of foreign terms and phrases* (Harmondsworth : Penguin, 1990).

Aims "to create a single-volume source that explains foreign phrases and words likely to be encountered in American and English literature."—*Pref.* Some 7,500 foreign words and phrases are listed alphabetically, with brief explanations of English usage; indexed by English term.   PE1670.M3

FOREIGN LANGUAGES

Bibliography

Dictionaries, encyclopedias, and other word-related books / Annie M. Brewer. 4th ed. Detroit : Gale, c1988. 2 v. (1333 p.). ISBN 0-8103-0440-6. $495.00.   **AD67**
  3rd ed., 1982 (*Guide* AD146).

  Subtitle: A classed guide to dictionaries, encyclopedias, and similar works, based on Library of Congress MARC records, and arranged according to the Library of Congress classification system. Including compilations of acronyms, Americanisms, colloquialisms, etymologies, glossaries, idioms and expressions, orthography, provincialisms, slang, terms and phrases, and vocabularies in English and all other languages.

  English and foreign language titles are interfiled. The characterization of the 2nd ed. from *Booklist* 76:1079 cited in the *Guide* as "expensive and difficult to use" is still applicable.
                         Z5848.D52

Afrikaans

Kritzinger, Matthys Stefanus Benjamin. Groot woordeboek : Afrikaans-Engels, [English-Afrikaans] / vroeëre samestellers, M.S.B. Kritzinger, P.C. Schoonees, U.J. Cronjé. 13e uitg. / versorg deur L.C. Eksteen. Pretoria : J.L. van Schaik, 1986. 1410 p. ISBN 0-627-01491-7.   **AD68**
  12th ed., 1981 (*Guide* AD158).
  "Revised by L.C. Eksteen."—*English t.p.*
  Includes more idiomatic expressions than the previous edition.   PF862.K7

Arabic

Hinds, Martin. A dictionary of Egyptian Arabic : Arabic-English / Martin Hinds, el-Said Badawi. Beirut : Librairie du Liban, 1986. 981 p. : ill.   **AD69**
  Title on added t.p.: *Mu'jam al-lughah al-'Arabīyah al-Miṣrīyah.*
  Concentrates on the spoken language, rather than the more formal written Arabic.   PJ6795.H54

Karmī, Ḥasan Sa'īd. al-Mughni al-akbar : a dictionary of classical and contemporary English : English-Arabic, with illustrations and coloured plates. Beirut : Librairie du Liban, c1987. 1710 p. : ill. (some col.).   **AD70**
  Added t.p. in Arabic.
  English words, phrases, and idioms are defined by "the correct equivalent from classical Arabic," followed "by either modern Arabic equivalents or by explanations in simple language."—*Pref.*   PJ6640.K35

Wörterbuch der klassischen arabischen Sprache / auf Grund der Sammlungen von August Fischer, Theodor N[e]öldeke, Hermann Reckendorf und anderer Quellen hrsg. durch die Deutsche Morgenländische Gesellschaft. Wiesbaden : O. Harrassowitz, 1985–90. Bd. 2¹³⁻¹⁹. (In progress).   **AD71**
  For earlier volumes and annotation, see *Guide* AD171.
  Manfred Ullman became editor with Lfg. 3.
  Contents: Bd. 2, Lfg. 13–19, Lātifun–Laqiya. (Bd. 2, Teil 1 is complete in 11 Lfg., La–Laḍama.)

A 2nd rev. ed. of the *Vorläufiges Literatur-und Abkürzungsverzeichnis zum zweiten Band (Lām)* was issued in 1989 (62 p.).   PJ6635.W63

Aryan

Mann, Stuart E. An Indo-European comparative dictionary. Hamburg : H. Buske, c1984–87. 1682 p. ISBN 3-87118-550-7 (pbk.).   **AD72**
  "The object of the present work is to indicate what words in the living or the dead languages of the Indo-European family appear to have a common origin, and to give them an acceptable prototype form . . . . [T]he author has tried to avoid the German fault of overloading etymologies with irrelevancies, the French fault of trimming the evidence to achieve a neat pattern, and the Anglo-Saxon fault of being content with approximations."—*Introd.*   P725.M36

Assyro-Babylonian

Soden, Wolfram von. Akkadisches Handwörterbuch : unter Benutzung des lexikalischen Nachlasses von Bruno Meissner (1868–1947). 2., um Hinweise auf die Nachträge verm. Aufl. Wiesbaden : Harrassowitz, 1985. v. 1. ISBN 3-447-02613-8 (v. 1). (In progress).   **AD73**
  1st ed., 1959–81 (*Guide* AD193).
  Contents: v. 1, A–L.
  A reprinting of the 1st ed. with the addition of markers in the text referring the reader to the supplement at the end of v. 3.   PJ3540.S63

The Sumerian dictionary of the University Museum of the University of Pennsylvania / ed. by Åke W. Sjöberg with the collaboration of Hermann Behrens . . . [et al.]. Philadelphia, Pa. : Babylonian Section of the Univ. Museum, 1984. v. 2. ISBN 0-934718-63-6 (set). (In progress).   **AD74**
  Contents: v. 2, B.
  The first volume of a Sumerian-English dictionary modelled on the Univ. of Chicago Oriental Institute's *Assyrian dictionary* (*Guide* AD190). "Entries are arranged according to the presumed Sumarian word units."—*Foreword, v.2.* PJ4037.S86

University of Chicago. Oriental Institute. Assyrian dictionary / Editorial board: Ignace J. Gelb [and others]. Chicago : [The Institute], 1982–1989. v. 13, 15, 17, pt. 1. ISBN 0-918986-05-2 (set). (In progress).   **AD75**
  For earlier volumes and annotation, see *Guide* AD190.
  Contents: v. 13, Q; v. 15, S; v. 17, pt. 1, Ša–Šap and "Provisional list of bibliographical abbreviations."   PJ3525.C5

Basque

Aulestia, Gorka. Basque-English dictionary. Reno : Univ. of Nevada Pr., c1989. 108, 558 p. : ill. ISBN 0-87417-126-1. $45.00.   **AD76**
  Compiled at the Basque Studies Program of the Univ. of Nevada, this is the first Basque-English dictionary, listing some 50,000 words from Unified Basque and the five major Basque dialects. Includes a detailed discussion of Basque grammar.   PH5177.E5A95

——————— English-Basque dictionary / Gorka Aulestia and Linda White. Reno : Univ. of Nevada Pr., c1990. 397 p. : map. ISBN 0-87417-156-3. $40.00 (est.).   **AD77**

A companion to the title described above. Provides Unified Basque equivalents for some 25,000 English words.
PH5177.E5A96

Bulgarian

Bŭlgarski etimologichen rechnik / sŭstavili V. I. Georgiev . . . [et al. ; red. Vladimir I. Georgiev]. Sofiiă : BAN, 1985–86. v. 3⁴⁻⁵. (In progress).   **AD78**
For earlier vols. and annotation, see *Guide* AD203.
Contents: v. 3⁴⁻⁵, Lochka–Mingo.   PG963.B8

Rankova, Mariiă. Angliĭsko-bŭlgarski rechnik / Mariiă Rankova, Teodora Atanasova, Ivanka Kharlakova. 1. izd. Sofiiă : Izd-vo Nauka i izkustvo, 1987–1988. 2 v.   **AD79**
Title on added t.p.: *English-Bulgarian dictionary.*
Concentrates on literary and colloquial English, with only a few scientific and technical terms.   PG979.R36

Rechnik na bŭlgarskiiă ezik / [glav. redaktor Kristalina Cholakova ; sŭstaviteli Simeon Boĭădzhiev . . . et al.]. Sofiiă : Izd-vo na Bŭlgarskata akademiiă na naukite, 1984–89. v. 4–5. (In progress).   **AD80**
For earlier vols. and annotation, see *Guide* AD206.
Contents: v. 4–5, Deiatelen–Ziapnuvane.   PG975.R39

Catalan

Corominas, Joan. Diccionari etimològic i complementari de la llengua catalana / per Joan Coromines, amb la col·laboració de Joseph Gulsoy i Max Cahner. Barcelona : Curial Edicions Catalanes : Caixa de Pensions La Caixa, 1986–1988. v. 4–8. ISBN 84-7256-173-9 (set). (In progress).   **AD81**
For v.1–3 and annotation, see *Guide* AD213.
Contents: v.4–8, Fl–Ux. Vol. 9, to be published in 1991, will complete the set.   PC3883.5.C6

Chinese

Han yü ta tz'u tien / chu pien Lo Chu-feng ; Han yü ta tz'u tien pien chi wei yüan hui, Han yü ta tz'u tien pien tsuan ch'u pien tsuan. Ti 1 pan. [Shanghai] : Shang-hai tz'u shu ch'u pan she : Fa hsing Shang-hai tz'u shu ch'u pan she fa hsing so, 1986–90. v. 1–5. (In progress).   **AD82**
Aims to be a comprehensive dictionary of classical and modern Chinese. Lists major people and places; includes etymologies.   PL1420.H349

Czech

Hais, Karel. Velký anglicko-český slovník / Karel Hais, Břetislav Hodek. Vyd. 1. Praha : Academia, 1984–1985. 3 v.   **AD83**
Title on added t.p.: English-Czech dictionary.
On page preceding t.p.: Československá akademia věd.
Replaces Václav Jung's *Slovník anglicko-česky* (1st ed., 1911), previously the most comprehensive English-Czech dictionary available. Lists some 100,000 words, including slang and technical terms.   PG4640.H343

Danish

The standard Danish-English, English-Danish dictionary = Dansk-engelsk, engelsk-dansk ordbok / ed. by Jens Axelsen. Eastbourne, East Sussex : Holt, Rinehart & Winston ; Copenhagen : Gyldendal, 1986. 581 p. ISBN 0-03-910703-5.   **AD84**
1st Gyldendal ed., 1984.
About 65,000 entries in each section, aiming "to cover the general contemporary vocabulary of the two languages" (*Pref.*) including idioms and phrases, slang words, and some terms from business, technology, etc.   PD3640.S74

Dutch

Woordenboek der nederlandsche taal. 's-Gravenhage [etc.] : M. Nijhoff [etc.], 1986–1990. v. 20, pt. 2; v. 22, pt. 2–v. 25¹⁻⁷. (In progress).   **AD85**
For earlier volumes and annotation, see *Guide* AD260.
Contents: v. 20, pt. 2¹⁻²¹, Verscheiden–Verzworen; v. 22, pt. 2¹⁻¹², Voonhouden–Voyant; v. 23⁸⁻¹², Vrijkomen–Vuuster; v. 24, W–Wee (all four volumes complete); v. 25¹⁻⁷, Weelde–Wekker.   PF625.Wö

Ethiopian

Leslau, Wolf. Comparative dictionary of Ge'ez (Classical Ethiopic) : Ge'ez-English, English-Ge'ez, with an index of the Semitic roots. Wiesbaden : Harrassowitz, 1987. 813 p. ISBN 3-447-02592-1. DM248.00.   **AD86**
". . . a comprehensive dictionary of Geez."—*Introd.* Includes etymologies and comparisons with other Semitic languages.   PJ9087.L37

Finnish

Häkkinen, Kaisa. Nykysuomen sanakirja : etymologinen sanakirja. Porvoo : Söderström, c1987. v. 6 : ill. ISBN 951-0-14050-3 (v. 6). (In progress).   **AD87**
An excellent scholarly etymological dictionary of 1,000 of the most frequently used Finnish words. Appears to have been published as v.6 of the 1982–87 reprint of Suomalaisen Kirjallisuuden Seura, *Nykysuomen sanakirja* (*Guide* AD282).
PH263.H35

Wuolle, Aino. The standard Finnish-English English-Finnish dictionary. Eastbourne [East Sussex] : Holt, Rinehart and Winston, 1986. 492, 512 p. ISBN 0-03-910704-3.   **AD88**
Combines Wuolle's *Suomalais-englantilainen sanakirja*, 1978 printing (*Guide* AD287) and *Englantilais-suomalainen koulusanakirja*, 1981 printing (*Guide* AD288) in a single volume.

French

Camion, Jean. Dictionnaire des homonymes de la langue française. Soisy-sous-Montmorency [France] : Gachot, [c1986]. 683 p. ISBN 2-906444-00-6.   **AD89**
Arranged alphabetically, with phrases illustrating the different possible meanings and their parts of speech. Includes a

pronunciation guide and a guide to variant spellings.

PC2595.C26

Dictionnaire de l'Académie française. 9e éd. Paris : Impr. nationale, 1986–1990. Fasc. 1–5. ISBN 2-11-080892-6 (fasc. 1). 50.00F. ISBN 2-11-080920-5 (fasc. 2.). 50.00F. (In progress).   **AD90**

8th éd., 1931–35 (*Guide* AD290).

Contents: Fasc.1–5, A–Encyclique.

Adheres to the form and purpose of the earlier editions; that is, to establish proper French usage. Some 10,000 words not listed in the earlier edition will be included, indicated by asterisks.   PC2625.D455

Imps, Paul. Trésor de la langue française : dictionnaire de la langue du XIXe et du XXe siècle (1789–1960). Paris : Editions du Centre national de la recherche scientifique, 1985–90. v. 11–14. ISBN 2-07-077013-3 (v. 13). (In progress).   **AD91**

For v. 1–10 and annotation, see *Guide* AD295.

Contents: v. 11–14, Lot–Salaud.   PC2625.I4

Petit Larousse illustré, 1990. Paris : Larousse, c1989. 1680 p., [50] p. of plates : ill. (some col.), maps.   **AD92**

Rev. ed. of *Nouveau petit Larousse* (*Guide* AD297).

"83,500 articles, 3,600 illustrations, 269 cartes, et un atlas à la fin de l'ouvrage."—*t.p.*

Adheres to the form and content of the previous edition, with more emphasis on computer science, biology, and medicine.   AG25.P43

Robert, Paul. Dictionnaire alphabétique et analogique de la langue française. 2e éd. entièrement rev. et enrichie / par Alain Rey. Paris : Le Robert, c1985. 9 v. : ill. ISBN 2-85036-099-6 (set).   **AD93**

Previous ed., 1970 (*Guide* AD301).

Revised and enlarged.   PC2625.R552

Bilingual

Harrap's concise French-English dictionary = dictionnaire anglais-français / ed. by Patricia Forbes and Muriel Holland Smith. Rev. / by Helen Knox and Richard Northcott. London : Harrap, 1989. 415, 535 p. ISBN 0-13-383035-7. $16.95. ISBN 0-13-383043-8 (pbk.). $7.95.   **AD94**

1st ed., 1984, had title: *Harrap's concise French and English dictionary.*

Introductory material in French and English.

Aims to provide "an up-to-date practical work . . . giving translations of modern English and French vocabulary."—*Pref.* Includes scientific and technical terms.   PC2640.H27

Robert-Collins dictionnaire français-anglais, anglais-français / par Beryl T. Atkins . . . [et al.]. Nouv. éd. Paris : Le Robert ; London : Collins, 1987. 768, 929 p. ISBN 2-85036-088-0.   **AD95**

1st ed., 1978 (*Guide* AD303)

Added t.p. in English: *Collins-Robert French-English, English-French dictionary*, 2nd ed.

Revised and enlarged by some 20,000 words. Includes a new section of standard phrases and expressions.   PC2640.R63

Etymology

Wartburg, Walther von. Französisches etymologisches Wörterbuch : eine Darstellung des galloromanischen Sprachschatzes / von Walther v. Wartburg. Bonn, etc. : F. Klopp, etc., 1983–1990. (In progress).   **AD96**

For previously published volumes and annotation, see *Guide* AD317.

Publication has proceeded through fasc. (formerly Lfg.) 151 in 1990. Vol. 24 is now complete in 7 fasc. Partially completed volumes are: v. 22, pt. 1^{1-3}; v. 22, pt. 2^1, Materialen unbekannten unsicheren Ursprungs; and v. 25^{2-6}, Architectus–Assulare.   PC2580.W3

Slang

Bernet, Charles. Dictionnaire du français parlé : le monde des expressions familières / Charles Bernet, Pierre Rézeau. Paris : Seuil, c1989. 465 p. ISBN 2-02-010927-1.   **AD97**

Offers definitions, with examples of usage, of more than 700 colloquial terms not found in other French dictionaries.

PC2689.B47

Colin, Jean-Paul. Dictionnaire de l'argot / Jean-Paul Colin, Jean-Pierre Mével, avec la collaboration de Christian Leclère. Paris : Larousse, c1990. 763 p. ISBN 2-03-340323-8.   **AD98**

A scholarly dictionary partially based on Gaston Esnault's *Dictionnaire historique des argots française* (*Guide* AD318). Offers etymologies and historical developments, with examples and sources, of some 6,500 words from the end of the 13th century to the present. "Glossaire français–argot," p. 677–726.

PC3741.C66

Synonyms

Macé, Pierre-Antoine. Le grand dictionnaire des synonymes / Pierre-Antoine Macé et Madeleine Guinard. [Paris] : F. Nathan, c1984. 444 p. : ill. ISBN 2-09-191558-0. 79.00F.   **AD99**

A useful dictionary with sample sentences. Indexed by the synonyms provided for the entry words.   PC2591.M27

New words

Les mots nouveaux apparus depuis 1985 / Gabriel Merle . . . [et al.]. Paris : P. Belfond, c1989. 231 p. ISBN 2-7144-2369-8. 89.00F.   **AD100**

Provides examples of usage through quotations from newspapers and magazines.   PC2680.M68

Old–17th century

Duchesne, Alain. L'obsolète : dictionnaire des mots perdus / Alain Duchesne, Thierry Leguay. Paris : Larousse, c1989. 267 p. : ill. ISBN 2-03-330005-6.   **AD101**

An illustrated dictionary arranged by broad subject. Includes illustrative sentences, mainly from 17th and 18th century authors. Lacks an index.   PC2667.D83

Tobler, Adolf. Altfranzösisches Wörterbuch : Adolf Toblers nachgelassene Materilien / bearb. und hrsg. von Erhard Lommatzsch, weitergeführt von Hans Helmut

Christmann. Stuttgart : F. Steiner Verlag Wiesbaden, 1989. Lfg. 88. ISBN 3-515-05403-0 (v. 11). (In progress).
AD102

For v.1–10 and annotation, see *Guide* AD345.
Contents: v.11¹ (Lfg.88), U–Venteler. Vol.11 ed. by Hans Helmut Christmann.   PC2893.T6

German

Althochdeutsches Wörterbuch / auf Grund d. von Elias von Steinmeyer hinterlassenen Sammlungen im Auftr. d. Sächs. Akad. d. Wiss. zu Leipzig bearb. u. hrsg. von Elisabeth Karg-Gasterstädt u. Theodor Frings. Berlin : Akademie-Verl., 1985–1990. Bd. 3¹⁶/¹⁸–4¹⁻⁸. (In progress).   **AD103**
For earlier vols. and annotation, see *Guide* AD363.
Contents: Bd. 3¹⁶/¹⁸, Forni–Fwra (completes the volume); Bd. 4¹⁻⁸, G–Hage.
Bd. 4, Lfg. 1/2 includes supplementary lists of texts and sources of quotations.   PF3975.A48

Frühneuhochdeutsches Wörterbuch / hrsg. von Robert R. Anderson, Ulrich Goebel, Oskar Reichmann. Berlin ; N.Y. : W. de Gruyter, 1986–1989. v. 1 : ill. ISBN 3-11-010887-9. (In progress).   **AD104**
Contents: v. 1, A–Äpfelkern (issued in 4 Lfg.)
A scholarly German-German dictionary covering the period 1350–1600; includes etymologies, illustrative quotations, and references to secondary sources. Lfg.1 includes a "Verzeichnes der Quellen," p. 165–224, and a "Verzeichnis der Sekundärliteratur," p. 225–285. To be in 10 v.; v. 10 will be an index.   PF4591.F78

Grimm, Jacob. Deutsches Wörterbuch / von Jacob Grimm und Wilhelm Grimm. Hrsg. von der Deutschen Akademie der Wissenschaften zu Berlin in Zusammenarbeit mit der Akademie der Wissenschaften zu Göttingen. Neubearbeitungen. Leipzig : Hirzel, 1983–1990. Bd. 2¹⁻³, 6¹², 7¹⁻⁶. (In progress).   **AD105**
For earlier volumes and annotation, see *Guide* AD362.
Contents: Bd. 2, Lfg. 1–3, Affront–Allmenda; Bd. 6, Lfg. 12, Durchstreiten–D-zug (completes the volume); Bd. 7, Lfg. 1–6, E–Einschlagen.   PF3625.G72

Das Grosse Wörterbuch der deutschen Sprache in 6 Bänden / hrsg. u. bearb. vom Wiss. Rat u. d. Mitarb. d. Dudenred. unter Leitung von Günther Drosdowski ; [Bearb., Rudolf Köster . . . et al.]. Mannheim ; Wien ; Zürich : Bibliographisches Institut, 1976–1981. 6 v. ISBN 3-411-01354-0. DM48.00 (v. 1).   **AD106**
At head of title: Duden.
The first 20th-century unabridged dictionary of the German language published in West Germany. Contains etymologies, grammatical information, usage labels, and illustrative quotations. An earlier unabridged dictionary, *Wörterbuch der deutschen Gegenwartssprache* (1961–76; *Guide* AD371), was published in East Germany; according to an extensive review comparing the two dictionaries in *Modern language review* 80 (April 1985) : 372–86, it has marked ideological bias. The review also discusses a number of serious errors in *Das grosse Wörterbuch* and concludes the two works are "monumental but flawed . . . . [T]here is still no comprehensive dictionary of German to which a user can turn for a reliable, objective account of the German lexis."
§ A one-volume abridgment, without quotations, of *Das grosse Wörterbuch* was published as *Duden, deutsches Universal-Wörterbuch* (1st ed., 1983; 2nd rev. ed., 1989). Many of the errors in the parent work have been corrected in the 2nd ed.   PF3625.G75

Wahrig, Gerhard. Deutsches Wörterbuch : mit einem "Lexikon der Deutschen Sprachlehre" / Gerhard Wahrig; hrsg. in Zusammenarbeit mit zahlreichen Wissenschaftlern und anderen Fachleuten. Völlig überarbeitete Neuausg. München : Mosaik, 1987. 1493 p. ISBN 3-570-03648-0.   **AD107**
Previous ed., 1980 (*Guide* AD369).
Includes some 5,000 new words and meanings, mainly in the sciences.   PF3625.W2

Wörterbuch der mittelhochdeutschen Urkundensprache : auf der Grundlage des Corpus der altdeutschen Originalurkunden bis zum Jahr 1300 / unter Leitung von Bettina Kirschstein und Ursula Schulze. Berlin : E. Schmidt, c1986–1989. v. 1, pt. 1–4. ISBN 3-503-02247-3. (In progress).   **AD108**
At head of title: Veröffentlichungen der Kommission für Deutscheliteratur des Mittelalters der Bayerischen Akademie der Wissenschaften.
Contents: v. 1¹⁻⁴, Ab–Dingen.
Limited to the approximately 10,000 words of the *Corpus der altdeutschen Originalurkunden bus zum Jahr 1300* (Lahr [Baden] : M. Schauenburg, 1929–), this scholarly German-German dictionary is based on legal and business rather than literary sources.   PF4327.W67

Bilingual

The Oxford-Duden German dictionary : English-German/German-English / ed. by the Dudenredaktion and the German Section of the Oxford University Press Dictionary Department ; chief editors, W. Scholze-Stubenrecht, J.B. Sykes. Oxford : Clarendon Pr., 1990. 1696 p. : ill. ISBN 0-19-864141-9. £14.95.   **AD109**
Based on the databases maintained by the Oxford Univ. Pr. and by the Dudenredaktion of the Bibliographisches Institut, Mannheim, "this is the first bilingual dictionary ever to be produced by a team based in both language areas."—*Foreword*. Includes many examples illustrating usage and a number of appendixes discussing grammar, punctuation, etc.   PF3640.O94

Spalding, Keith. An historical dictionary of German figurative usage. Oxford : Blackwell, 1984–89. fasc. 40–48. (In progress).   **AD110**
For fasc. 1–39 and annotation, see *Guide* AD380.
Contents: fasc. 40–48, Pflug–Spiel.   PF3440.S7

Etymology

Etymologisches Wörterbuch des Deutschen / erarbeitet von einem Autorenkollektiv des Zentralinstituts für Sprachwissenschaft unter der Leitung von Wolfgang Pfeifer ; Autoren, Wilhelm Braun . . . [et al.]. Berlin : Akademie-Verlag, 1989. 3 v. ISBN 3-05-000626-9 (set). 98.00M.   **AD111**
On added t.p.: Akademie der Wissenschaften der DDR. Zentralinstitut für Sprachwissenschaft.
Offers detailed etymologies of some 8,000 words.
PF3580.E88

Kluge, Friedrich. Etymologisches Wörterbuch der deutschen Sprache. 22. Aufl. / unter Mithilfe von Max Bürgisser und Bernd Gregor völlig neu bearb. von Elmar Seebold. Berlin ; N.Y. : de Gruyter, 1989. lxv, 822 p. ISBN 3-11-006800-1.   **AD112**
21. Aufl., 1975 (*Guide* AD385).
Completely revised and updated. The *Sachverzeichnis* of the 21. Aufl. has been dropped but will be included in Elmar Seebold's forthcoming *Register und Auswertung zur 22. Auflage*

des etymologischen Wörterbuch von Friedrich Kluge.
PF3580.K5

Slang

Küpper, Heinz. Pons Wörterbuch der deutschen Umgangssprache. Stuttgart : Klett, c1987. 959 p. ISBN 3-12-570600-9. **AD113**
Includes dates of usage. PF5991.K85

Usage

Mackensen, Lutz. Deutsches Wörterbuch : Rechtschreibung, Grammatik, Stil, Worterklärungen, Abkürzungen, Aussprache, Fremdwörterlexikon, Geschichte des deutschen Wortschatzes. 12., völlig neu bearbeitete und stark erw. Aufl. / unter Mitarbeit von Gesine Schwarz-Mackensen. München : Südwest, 1986. 1219 p. ISBN 3-517-00909-1. **AD114**
1st ed., (1952) had title: *Neues deutsches Wörterbuch* (*Guide* AD396).
Revised and expanded. Offers definitions, pronunciations, and usage. PF3625.M25

Greek

Snell, Bruno. Lexikon des frühgriechischen Epos / vorbereitet und hrsg. von Bruno Snell ; verantwortlicher Redaktor, Hans Joachim Mette. Göttingen : Vandenhoeck & Ruprecht, 1987–89. v. 2³⁻⁴. (In progress). **AD115**
For earlier volumes and annotation, see *Guide* AD399.
Contents: v. 2³⁻⁴ (Lfg. 12–13), ξπαμύντωρ–χαπνος. PA445.G4S6

Hausa

Newman, Roxana Ma. An English-Hausa dictionary. New Haven, Conn. : Yale Univ. Pr., c1990. 327 p. ISBN 0-300-04702-9. **AD116**
" . . . a practical dictionary designed for the English-speaking user who wishes to acquire an active control of the modern vocabulary and structure of the Hausa language."—*User's guide.* PL8233.N49

Hebrew

Gesenius, Wilhelm. Hebräisches und aramäisches Handwörterbuch über das Alte Testament / Wilhelm Gesenius ; unter verantwortlicher Mitarbeit von Udo Rüterswörden ; bearb. und hrsg. von Rudolf Meyer und Herbert Donner. 18. Aufl. Berlin ; N.Y. : Springer-Verlag, c1987. Lfg. 1. ISBN 0-387-18206-3 (1. Lfg.). (In progress). **AD117**
17th ed., 1921 (*Guide* AD435).
Contents: Lfg. 1, Alef–Gimel.
A scholarly Hebrew-German dictionary, listing all words, including proper names, found in the Hebrew Bible. Provides etymologies. PJ4835.G5G47

Klein, Ernest David. A comprehensive etymological dictionary of the Hebrew language for readers of English / Ernest David Klein ; [ed., Baruch Sarel]. N.Y. : Macmillan, c1987. 721 p. ISBN 0-02-917431-7. **AD118**
" . . . the first etymological dictionary in the proper sense of Hebrew as a totality, comprising both the vocabulary current in present-day Hebrew . . . as well as medieval words."—*Introd.* PJ4833.K54

Sokoloff, Michael. A dictionary of Jewish Palestinian Aramaic of the Byzantine period. Ramat Gan : Bar Ilan Univ. Pr., 1990. 823 p. (Dictionaries of Talmud, Midrash and Targum, 2). ISBN 965-226-101-7. **AD119**
Aims "to provide students and scholars with a tool for an accurate understanding of the Aramaic dialect of the Jewish Palestinian literature of the Byzantine period [and] to provide a tool for the Aramaist and Semitic linguist by which to see the relationship of this Aramaic dialect to the other ones."—*Pref.*
Includes etymologies. PJ5205.S6

Bilingual

Zilkha, Avraham. Modern Hebrew-English dictionary. New Haven, Conn. : Yale Univ. Pr., c1989. 305 p. ISBN 0-300-04647-2. ISBN 0-300-04648-0 (pbk.). **AD120**
Aims to provide "an up-to-date, easy to use . . . tool . . . [Reflects] the contemporary language of Israel."—*Pref.* PJ4833.Z57

Hittite

Puhvel, Jaan. Hittite etymological dictionary. Berlin ; N.Y. : Mouton, 1991. v. 3. (Trends in linguistics. Documentation, 5). ISBN 3-11-011547-6 (v. 3). ISBN 0-89925-431-4 (v. 3). (In progress). **AD121**
For earlier vols. and annotation, see *Guide* AD457.
Contents: v.3, Words beginning with H. P945.Z8

University of Chicago. Oriental Institute. The Hittite dictionary of the Oriental Institute of the University of Chicago / ed. by Hans G. Güterbock and Harry A. Hoffner. [Chicago] : The Institute, 1983–1989. v. 3, fasc. 1–4. ISBN 0-918986-26-5 (set). (In progress). **AD122**
For earlier vols. and annotation, see *Guide* AD456.
On spine: Chicago Hittite dictionary.
Contents: v. 3 ²⁻⁴, ma f–nutarnu. P945.Z8

Hungarian

Bilingual

Magay, Tamás. A concise Hungarian-English dictionary / by T. Magay, L. Országh ; contributing ed., P.A. Sherwood. Oxford ; N.Y. : Oxford Univ. Pr. by permission of the Akadémiai Kiadó, 1990. 1152 p. ISBN 0-19-864169-9. **AD123**
A previous ed., 1973, ed. by László Országh, had title, *Magyar-angol kéziszótár* (*Guide* AD464).
Introductory material in English and Hungarian.
Revised and expanded. PH2640.M3

Országh, László. A concise English-Hungarian dictionary / ed. in chief, L. Országh ; editor, T. Magay. 14th ed., new impression of the 10th, completely revised ed. Oxford ; N.Y. : Oxford Univ. Pr. ; Budapest : Akadémiai Kiadó, 1990. 1052, [1] p. ISBN 0-19-864170-2. **AD124**

8th ed., 1975 (*Guide* AD463); 10th completely rev. ed., 1981.

This edition, a new impression of the 10th ed., lists some 37,000 words.   PH2640.O6513

Icelandic

Ensk-íslensk orabók : mẽ alfr ẽilegu ívafi / Sören Sörenson [œýddi] ; Jóhann S. Hannesson bjó til prentunar ásamt fleirum. [Reykjavík] : Örn og Örlygur, 1984. 1241 p. : ill.   **AD125**
On t.p.: "Bygg á Scott, Foresman advanced dictionary sem er endurskoú útgáfa af the Thorndike-Barnhart high school dictionary eftir E.L. Thorndike og Clarence L. Barnhart."

English vocabulary is derived from the Thorndike-Barnhart and Scott, Foresman dictionaries mentioned on the title page. Definitions in Icelandic, with some examples of English usage.   PD2437.S6

Indonesian

Echols, John M. An Indonesian-English dictionary / by John M. Echols and Hassan Shadily. 3rd ed. / rev. and ed. by John U. Wolff and James T. Collins in cooperation with Hassan Shadily. Ithaca, N.Y. : Cornell Univ. Pr., 1989. 618 p. ISBN 0-8014-2127-6.   **AD126**
2nd ed., 1963 (*Guide* AD479).

" . . . much-revised and much-expanded."—*Editor's pref. to the 3rd ed.*   PL5076.E35

Irish

Etymology

Vendryes, Joseph. Lexique étymologique de l'irlandais ancien. Dublin : Dublin Institue for Advanced Studies, 1981–1987. fasc. B–C. (In progress).   **AD127**
For earlier parts and annotation, see *Guide* AD489.
                                       PB1288.V4

Italian

Battaglia, Salvatore. Grande dizionario della lingua italiana / [Redazione, direttore: Giorgio Bárberi Squarotti]. [Torino] : Unione tipografico-editrice torinese, 1984–1990. v. 12–15. (In progress).   **AD128**
For v. 1–11 and annotation, see *Guide* AD492.
Contents: v. 12–15, Orad–Ria.

Bilingual

Hofmann Cortesi, Livio. I segreti dell'inglese : bidizionario di falsi sinonimi e vere equivalenze tra italiano e inglese / Livio Hofmann Cortesi, Bona Schmid. Firenze : Sansoni, 1988. 264 p. ISBN 88-383-0831-4. **AD129**
Arranged by English word accompanied by the similar Italian word (which may or may not have the same meaning); definitions in Italian for both are provided.   PC1640.H64

Il Nuovo dizionario Hazon Garzanti : inglese-italiano, italiano-inglese. [Milano] : Garzanti, 1990. 2429 p.
                                       AD130
Rev. ed. of the author's *Garzanti comprehensive Italian-English, English-Italian dictionary*, 1963 (*Guide* AD499).

According to the review in the *Times literary supplement*, 19 April 1991, 11, this complete revision puts this dictionary "once more at the forefront" of modern bilingual dictionaries.
                                       PC1640.N85

Etymology

Cortelazzo, Manlio. Dizionario etimologico della lingua italiana / [di] Manlio Cortelazzo, Paolo Zolli. Bologna : Zanichelli, 1985–1988. v. 4–5.   **AD131**
For v. 1–3 and annotation, see *Guide* AD506.
Contents: v. 4–5, O–Z. Completes the set.   PC1580.C67

Pfister, Max. Lessico etimologico italiano : LEI. Wiesbaden : Reichert, 1987–90. fasc. 9–31. ISBN 3-88226-074-2 (v. 1, fasc. 1). (In progress).   **AD132**
For v. 1 and annotation, see *Guide* AD507.
Contents: v. 2, fasc. 9–17, Albus–Apertura (completes v. 2); v. 3, fasc. 18–31, Apertus–Axiculus.   PC1580.P38

Synonyms

Pittàno, Giuseppe. Sinonimi e contrari : dizionario fraseologico delle parole equivalenti, analoghe e contrarie. Bologna : Zanichelli, c1987. 863 p. ISBN 88-08-03070-9. L42000.   **AD133**
A useful guide.   PC1591.P58

Latin

Thesaurus linguae latinae. Lipsiae : B.G. Teubneri, 1984–88. v. 10, T. 1^{2-4}–T. 2^{4-5}. (In progress).   **AD134**
For earlier vols. and annotation, see *Guide* AD540.
Contents: v. 10, T. 1^{2-4}, Palpebra–Pastor; v. 10, T. 2^{4-5}, Praecipuus–Praepotens.
Additions and corrections in: PA2361.T4

Ferrua, Antonio. Note al Thesaurus linguae latinae : addenda et corrigenda. Bari : Edipuglia, [1986]. v. 1. (In progress).   **AD135**
Contents: v. 1, A–D.   PA2361.T4F4

Thesaurus linguae latinae : Index librorum sciptorum inscriptionum ex quibus exempla afferuntur / editus iussu et auctoritate consilii ab academiis societatibusque diversarum nationum electi. Editio altera. Lipsiae : B.G. Teubneri, 1990. 228 p. ISBN 3-322-00748-0.   **AD136**
Cumulates the 1904 index and its 1958 supplement.
                                       PA2361.T4

Thesaurus linguae latinae : Praemonenda de rationibus et usu operis / editus iussu et auctoritate consilii ab academiis societatibusque diversarum nationum electi. 1. Aufl. Lipsiae : B.G. Teubneri, 1990. 72 p. ISBN 3-322-00000-1.   **AD137**
An introduction to and explanation of the dictionary in Latin, German, English, French, Italian, Spanish, and Russian.
                                       PA2361.T47

Medieval

Arnaldi, Francesco. Latinitatis Italicae Medii Aevi inde ab a. CDLXXVI usque ad a. MXXII Lexicon imperfectum cura et studio . . . Addenda, fasc. 6 (In *Bulletin Du Cange*, v. 44/45; 1985). (In progress). **AD138**
For earlier fasc., see *Guide* AD554.
Contents: Addenda, fasc. 6, Ha–In. PA2889.A7

Latham, R. E. Dictionary of medieval Latin from British sources / prepared by R. E. Latham under the direction of a committee appointed by the British Academy. London : Publ. for the British Academy by Oxford Univ. Pr., 1986–1989. fasc. 3–4. ISBN 0-19-725948-0. (In progress). **AD139**
For earlier parts and annotation, see *Guide* AD556.
Contents: Fasc. 3–4, D–H. PA2891.L28

Mittellateinisches Wörterbuch bis zum ausgehenden 13. [i.e. dreizehnten] Jahrhundert / in Gemeinschaft mit den Akademien der Wissenschaften zu Göttingen, Heidelberg, Leipzig, Mainz, Wien und der Schweizerischen Geisteswissenschaftlichen Gesellschaft hrsg. von der Bayerischen Akademie der Wissenschaften und der Deutschen Akademie der Wissenschaften zu Berlin. München : Beck, 1967; 1985–1991. Bd. 2^{8-9}. (In progress). **AD140**
For earlier vols. and annotation, see *Guide* AD559.
Contents: Bd.2^{8-9} (Lfg. 18–19), Comprovincialis–Conigium. PA2893.G3M48

Novum glossarium mediae latinitatis : ab anno DCCC usque ad annum MCC / Ed. curavit Consilium Academiarum Consociatarum. Hafniae : Munksgaard, 1985–87. 2 v. (In progress). **AD141**
For earlier vols. and annotation, see *Guide* AD561.
Contents: P–Panis, ed. by Yves Lefèvre; Paniscardus–Parrula, ed. by Jacque Monfrin. PA2893.F7N65

Index scriptorum novus mediae latinitatis : ab anno DCCC usque ad annum MCC : Supplementum / qui afferuntur in Novo glossario ab Academiis Consociatis iuris publici facto. Hatniae : E. Munskgaard, 1989. 62 p. **AD142**
Supplements the 1973 basic list (*Guide* AD561). PA2893.F7N65

Norwegian

Kirkeby, Willy. English-Norwegian dictionary = Engelsk-norsk ordbok. [Oslo, Norway] : Norwegian Univ. Pr. ; Oxford : Distr. world-wide excluding Scandinavia by Oxford Univ. Pr., c1989. 809 p. ISBN 82-00-18293-2. **AD143**
Prefatory material in English and Norwegian. Confined to standard Norwegian. Includes guidance in current usage. PD2691.K49

Persian

Āryānpūr Kāshānī, 'Abbās. Farhang-i nuvīn-i payvastah-i Fārsī–Ingilīsī va Ingilīsī–Fārsī / 'Abbās Aryan'pur Kāshānī, Manūchihr Āryān'pūr Kāshānī. Lexington, Ky : Mazdâ Publishers, 1986. 45, 307, 273 p. : ill. ISBN 0-939214-29-6. **AD144**
Title on added t.p.: *The combined new Persian-English and English-Persian dictionary.*

"A combination and rearrangement of our pocket English-Persian and Persian-English dictionaries plus an all-new Etymological Study and the pioneering Guide to Punctuation in Persian."—*Pref. to the first American ed.* PK6379.A694

Polish

Polska Akademia Nauk. Słownik staropolski / [Komitet redakcyjny: Kazimierz Nitsch et al.]. Warszawa : [Polska Akademia Nauk], 1984–1990. v. 9^{3-6}, v. 10 $^{1-3}$. (In progress). **AD145**
For earlier vols. and annotation, see *Guide* AD603.
Contents: v. 9 $^{3-6}$, Tłoka–Używowanie (completes the vol.); v. 10^{1-3}, W–Wjechać. PG6729.P6

Portuguese

Michaelis dicionário prático : inglês–português, português-inglês. São Paulo : Melhoramentos, c1987. 856 p. **AD146**
Includes lists of irregular verbs and standard abbreviations. PC5333.M55

Romanian

Costinescu, Mariana. Dicționarul limbii române literare vechi, 1640–1780 : termèni regionali / Mariana Costinescu, Magdalena Georgescu, Florentina Zgraon. București : Editura Științifică și Enciclopedică, 1987. 330 p. **AD147**
Includes brief etymologies. PC782.C67

Dicționarul limbii române : (DLR) Serie nouă / [Redactori responsabili: Iorgu Iordan și Ion Coteanu]. București : Editura Academiei Republicii Populare Românè, 1982–1987. v. 8, pt. 5; v. 10, pts. 1–2; v. 11, pts. 2–3. (In progress). **AD148**
For earlier vols. and annotation, see *Guide* AD644.
Contents: t. VIII^5, Presin–Puzzolană; t. X$^{1-2}$, S–Semîntărie; t. XI$^{2-3}$, T–Twist. PC775.D48

Romansh

Società Retorumantscha. Disciunari rumantsch grischen / publichà da la Società retorumantscha cul agüd da la Confederaziun, dal chantun Grischen e da la Lia rumantscha. Fundà da Robert de Planta e Florian Melcher; redacziun: Chasper Pult [et al.]. Cuoira : Bischofberger, 1985–1990. v. 7^{18}–v. 8^{1-10} (i.e., fasc. 103–114) : ill. (In progress). **AD149**
For earlier volumes and annotation, see *Guide* AD652.
Contents: v. 7^{18}, Güstamaint–Gyra (completes v. 7); v. 8^{1-10}, H–Indrizzar. PC937.G5S6

Russian

Institut russkogo îazyka (Akademiîa nauk SSSR). Slovarnyĭ sektor. Slovar' russkikh narodnykh govorov / Sostavil F.P. Filin. Leningrad : Nauka [Leningradskoe otdnie], 1985–1990. v. 20–25. (In progress). **AD150**

For earlier volumes and annotation, see *Guide* AD656.
Contents: v. 20–25, Nakuchkat'–Pervachok.   PG2735.A48

Slovar' russkogo iāzyka XI-XVII vv / [glav. redaktor S.G. Barkhudarov]. Moskva : Nauka, 1975–1989. v. 1–15. (In progress).   **AD151**
At head of title : Akademiiā nauk SSSR. Institut russkogo iāzyka.
Vols. 9–10 ed. by F.P. Filin; v. 11–14 by D.N. Shmelev ; v. 15 by G.P. Smolitskaiā.
Contents: v. 1–15, A–Podmyshka.
When complete, this dictionary of obsolete Russian words will contain about 60,000 terms, listing their first appearance and subsequent development. An extensive review in *Language* 52 (Sept. 1976) : 708–17 praises the "rich documentation for the 15th–17th centuries," but calls the scholarship on the whole "disappointing."   PG2742.S5

Bilingual

Bol'shoĭ anglo-russkiĭ slovar' / pod obshchim rukovodst-vom I.R. Gal'perina i É.M. Mednikovoĭ. Izd. 4–e, ispr., s dopolneniem. Moskva : "Russkiĭ iāzyk", 1987–1988. 2 v.   **AD152**
1st ed., 1972 (*Guide* AD662); 3rd ed., 1979.
Title on added t.p.: *New English-Russian dictionary.*
"Fourth improved edition with a supplement."—*added t.p.*
The supplement, separately published in 1980, has been reprinted on p. 929–1072.   PG2640.G3

Macura, Paul. Elsevier's Russian-English dictionary. Amsterdam ; N.Y. : Elsevier ; N.Y. : Distr. [by] Elsevier Science Pub. Co., 1990. 4 v. (3208 p.). ISBN 0-444-88467-X (set).   **AD153**
" ... contains approximately 240,000 key entries, constituting the most extensive listing of vocabulary to date in the areas of humanities, social sciences, and fine arts. It also contains scientific terminology."—*Pref.* Appears to rely heavily on the *Oxford Russian-English dictionary* (*Guide* AD669), although that work is not cited as a source.   Q123.M182

Abbreviations

Scheitz, Edgar. Dictionary of Russian abbreviations : containing about 40,000 abbreviations. Amsterdam ; N.Y. : Elsevier, 1986. 695 p. ISBN 0-444-99554-4. $90.00 (est.).   **AD154**
Originally published in Russian as *Russische Abkürzungen* (Berlin : Verlag Technik, 1985).
Text in Russian.
Includes abbreviations for state authorities, institutions of the Academy of Science, serials, measurements, etc.
PG2693.S28

Bibliography

Aissing, Alena. Russian dictionaries : selected bibliography, 1960–1990. Monroe, N.Y. : Library Research Associates, 1991. 61 p. ISBN 0-912526-52-1. $12.95. **AD155**
A listing of some 300 Russian monolingual, bilingual, and multilingual dictionaries in all subjects. No annotations or evaluations; subject index.   Z2505.D6A38

Sanskrit

An encyclopaedic dictionary of Sanskrit on historical principles / gen. ed., A. M. Ghatage. Poona : Deccan College Post Graduate and Research Institute, 1988. v. 3². (In progress).   **AD156**
For earlier vols. and annotation, see *Guide* AD692.
Contents: v.3², Adhimās-ika–adhyāpana-siddhi.
PK933.E5

Mayrhofer, Manfred. Etymologisches Wörterbuch des Altindoarischen. Heidelberg : C. Winter, 1986–1990. Bd. 1¹⁻⁸. ISBN 3-533-03826-2 (pbk.). (In progress).
AD157
Contents: Bd. 1¹⁻⁸, A–Tārhi.
A scholarly German-Sanskrit dictionary which updates but does not supersede the author's *Kurzgefasstes etymologisches Wörterbuch des Altindischen* (1953–80, *Guide* AD693). The newer work concentrates on word origins, not historical development, and does not include English glosses. A list of works cited in the text appears on p. 7–31 of Lfg. 1, with additions on the back cover of subsequent Lfg.
To be in 3 v. Each volume will be in two sections, the first covering the original Vedic Sanskrit vocabulary and the second, post-Vedic vocabulary.   PK905.M28

Serbo-Croatian

Benson, Morton. An English-SerboCroatian dictionary. 3rd ed. Cambridge ; N.Y. : Cambridge Univ. Pr., 1990. xlix, 722 p. ISBN 0-521-38496-6.   **AD158**
1st ed., 1979 (*Guide* AD697); 2nd ed., 1986.
Title on added t.p.: *Englesko-srpskohrvatski rečnik.*
Introductory material in English and Serbo-Croatian.
Many new technical terms have been added.   PG1376.B38

———————— SerboCroatian-English dictionary / Morton Benson ; with the collaboration of Biljana Šljivić–Šimšić. 3rd ed. Cambridge ; N.Y. : Cambridge Univ. Pr., 1990. lxv, 769 p. ISBN 0-521-38495-8.
AD159
1st ed., 1971 (*Guide* AD698); 2nd ed., 1981.
Title on added t.p.: *Srpskohrvatsko-engleski rečnik.*
Introductory material in English and Serbo-Croatian.
Technical, mainly computer terms have been added.
PG1376.B4

Bujas, Željko. Hrvatsko ili srpsko-engleski enciklo-pedijski rječnik. Zagreb : Grafički zavod Hrvatske, 1983–1989. v. 1–2. (In progress).   **AD160**
Title on added t.p. : *Croatoserbian-English encylopedic dictionary.*
Contents: v.1, A–LJ; v.2, M–O.
Defines some 150,000 words in the Croatian variant of Serbo-Croatian. Includes colloquial and slang terms and selected scientific and technical terms.   PG1377.B82

Shona

Hannan, M. Standard Shona dictionary / comp. for the Literature Bureau by M. Hannan. Rev. ed. with addendum. [Harare : College Pr. in conjunction with the Literature Bureau, 1984]. 1014 p. ISBN 0-86925-549-5 (pbk.).   **AD161**
2nd ed., 1974 (*Guide* AD706).

Includes minor revisions to the 2nd ed. and a brief addendum. Retains the English-Shona index. Reprinted in 1987.

PL8681.4.H3

Slovenian

Inštitut za slovenski jezik (Slovenska akademija znanosti in umetnosti). Slovar slovenskega knjižnega jezika : [Glavni uredniški odbor / Anton Bajec in dr.]. Ljubljana : Slovenska akademija znanosti in umetnosti, Inštitut za slovenski jezik; Državna založba Slovenije, 1985. v. 4. (In progress). **AD162**

For earlier volumes and annotation, see *Guide* AD713.

Contents: v. 4, Preo–Š. PG1888.S5

Somali

Schels, Christa. Vocabulary, English-Somali, Somali-English. Muqdishu : Office of FAO Representative, Food and Agricultural Organization of the United Nations, 1989. 131 p. **AD163**

" . . . compiled to help foreigners who are interested in acquiring some knowledge of the language . . . . It [provides] a basic vocabulary for day-to-day use, but is not meant to be a comprehensive dictionary."—*Pref.* PJ2533.S34

Spanish

Bilingual

The American Heritage Larousse Spanish dictionary : Spanish/English, English/Spanish. Boston : Houghton Mifflin, c1986. 532, 572 p. ISBN 0-395-32429-7. $19.95. **AD164**

Based on the *American Heritage dictionary* (*Guide* AD13) and the *Pequeño Larousse.*

Introductory material in English and Spanish.

Emphasizes "U.S. and Latin American usage."—*Pref.* PC4640.A54

The University of Chicago Spanish dictionary : / comp. by Carlos Castillo & Otto F. Bond, with the assistance of Barbara M. García. 4th ed, rev. and enl. by D. Lincoln Canfield. Chicago : Univ. of Chicago Pr., 1987. 475 p. : maps. ISBN 0-226-10400-1. $19.95. **AD165**

3rd ed., 1977 (*Guide* AD731).

Subtitle: A new concise Spanish-English and English-Spanish dictionary of words and phrases basic to the written and spoken languages of today, plus a list of 500 Spanish idioms and sayings, with variants and English equivalents.

PC4640.U5

Etymology

García de Diego, Vicente. Diccionario etimológico español e hispánico. 2a ed. Madrid : Espasa-Calpe, 1985. 1091 p. ISBN 84-239-6928-2. **AD166**

1st ed., 1954 (*Guide* AD735).

"Considerablemente aumentada con materiales inéditos del autor a cargo de Carmen García de Diego."—*t.p.*

Reprinted without change as the 3rd ed. in 1989.

PC4580.G33

Gómez de Silva, Guido. Elsevier's concise Spanish etymological dictionary : containing 10,000 entries, 1,300 word families. Amsterdam ; N.Y. : Elsevier, 1985. 559 p. : ill. ISBN 0-444-42440-7. Dfl 350.00. **AD167**

Aims "to trace each Spanish word as far back as possible in order to acquaint the reader with the story of the evolution of the Spanish language."—*Introd.* Includes prefixes, suffixes, inflectional endings, and proper names. Definitions and explanations are in English. PC4580.G65

Medieval–18th century

Müller, Bodo. Diccionario del español medieval. Heidelberg : C. Winter, 1987–1990. fasc. 1–5. ISBN 3-533-03879-3 (set). (In progress). **AD168**

Contents: fasc. 1–5, A–Acebuche.

"Bibliografía provisional," fasc. 1, p. viii–xxxii.

A scholarly etymological and historical dictionary, based on some 500 literary and nonliterary texts. Sponsored by the Heidelberger Akademie der Wissenschaften. PC4715.Z5M8

Regional and dialect

Galván, Roberto A. El diccionario del español chicano = The dictionary of Chicano Spanish / comp. by Roberto A. Galván, Richard V. Teschner. Lincolnwood, Ill. : Voluntad Publishers, c1985. 145 p. ISBN 0-8325-9634-5 (pbk.). $7.95. **AD169**

Reprint of the 1977 ed. (Silver Spring, Md. : Institute of Modern Languages), which was a revised and expanded edition of the author's *El diccionario del español de Tejas,* published by the Institute in 1975.

Offers some 8,000 Chicano words and phrases, including slang, to supplement standard Spanish dictionaries. Reprinted without change (Lincolnwood, Ill. : National Textbook Co., 1989). PC4827.G35

Swedish

Svenska akademien. Ordbok öfver svenska språket. Lund : C.W.K. Gleerup, 1985–89. v. 29^2–30. (In progress). **AD170**

For earlier vols. and annotation, see *Guide* AD752.

Contents: v. 29^2 (häfte 309–313), Spelman–Spånta; v. 30 (häfte 314–323), Spar–Stockna. PD5625.S8

Turkish

Eren, Hasan. Türkçe sözlük / [hazırlayanlar, başkan, Hasan Eren ; Nevzat Gözaydın . . . et al.]. Yeni baskı. Ankara : Atatürk Kültür, Dil, ve Tarih Yüksek Kurumu, Türk Dil Kurumu, 1988. 2 v. (1679 p.) : ill. ISBN 975-16-0070-7. 20,000TL. **AD171**

An excellent dictionary of modern Turkish. PL189.E68

Uralic

Rédei, Károly. Uralisches etymologisches Wörterbuch / Károly Rédei, unter Mitarbeit von Marianne Bakró–Nagy . . . [et al.]; [aus dem Ungarischen übersetzt von Mária Káldor]. Wiesbaden : Harrassowitz, 1986–88. v. 1–2. ISBN 3-447-02735-5 (v. 1). ISBN 3-447-02820-3 (v. 2). (In progress). **AD172**

Issued in parts. T.p. of Bd. 1 dated 1988.

Contents: Bd. 1 (Lfg. 1–5), Uralische und finnisch-ugrische Schicht; Bd. 2 (Lfg. 6–7), Finnisch-permische und finnisch-wolgaische Schicht. Urgische Schicht.

A scholarly dictionary prepared at the Akademiai Kiado in Budapest. To be in 3 v.; v. 3 will be a combined alphabetical index.   PH65.R43

Welsh

Geiriadur Prifysgol Cymru : a dictionary of the Welsh language / Golygydd: R.J. Thomas. Cyhoeddwyd ar ran Bwrdd Gwybodau Celtaidd, Prifysgol Cymru. Caerdydd : Gwasg Prifysgol Cymru, 1985–1990. pts. 34–41. (In progress).   **AD173**

For earlier volumes and annotation, see *Guide* AD805.

Contents: pts. 34–41, Lledneisiaf–Obo. Pts. 22–36 make up v. 2.   PB2191.G45

Yiddish

Groyser verterbukh fun der Yidisher shprakh = Great dictionary of the Yiddish language / editors in chief, Judah A. Joffe, Yudel Mark . . . [et al.]. N.Y. : Yiddish Dictionary Committee, 1980. v. 4 : ill. (In progress).   **AD174**

For earlier volumes and annotation, see *Guide* AD807.

Contents: v. 4, opboy–eṡrog.   PJ5117.G7

Bilingual

Harduf, David Mendel. Transliterated English-Yiddish dictionary = Ṭransliṭerirṭer English-Yidisher verṭerbukh. Willowdale, Ont., Canada : Harduf Hebrew Books, c1989–1990. 2 v. ISBN 0-920243-18-5.   **AD175**

Arranged by English word with brief definitions in both transliterated Yiddish and Hebrew characters.   PJ5117.H25

——————— Transliterated Yiddish-English dictionary = Ṭransliṭerirṭer Yidish-Englisher verṭerbukh. Willowdale, Ont., Canada : Harduf Hebrew Books, c1987. 185 p. ISBN 0-920243-17-7.   **AD176**

Arranged alphabetically by Hebrew character; with English and transliterated Yiddish definitions.   PJ5117.H28

Zulu

Doke, Clement Martyn. English-Zulu Zulu-English dictionary. 1st combined ed. Johannesburg : Witwatersrand Univ. Pr., 1990. 1 v.   **AD177**

Combines the author's *Zulu-English dictionary* (1953; *Guide* AD815) and his *English-Zulu dictionary* (1958; *Guide* AD814).

"While recognizing the need to revise and update both volumes, a task that will be the work of several years, the publishers are convinced that these invaluable works must be kept in print."—*Pref. note.*

AE

Periodicals

BIBLIOGRAPHY

Benn's media directory. International. 134th ed. (1986)– . Tonbridge, Kent : Benn Business Information Services, c1985– . Annual.   **AE1**

The change in title reflects expanded coverage of the broadcast media.   P88.8.B46

Directory of periodicals online. 1st ed.– . [Wash.] : Federal Document Retrieval, [c1985–]. Annual. ISSN 0884-0911.   **AE2**

Contents: v. 1, News, law & business; v. 2, Medicine & social science; v.3, Science & technology.

An alphabetical listing of journals available online through "databases available to the general public (not private or restricted databases) or subscribers, accessible through a communications network, and in English. Foreign language periodicals are included when they are part of English-language databases."—*Introd.* Very few of the titles listed are available in full text. Subject index.   Q1.A1D57

Directory of world Jewish press and publications. Mar. 1984– . Jerusalem : The Directory, 1984– . $21.00.   **AE3**

Aims to provide a "current, reliable and comprehensive worldwide listing" (*Introd.*) of some 900 bulletins, newsletters, newspapers, and journals. Based on responses to a questionnaire, the directory provides for each title the mailing address, editor, date founded, publisher, language, frequency, and circulation. Arranged by continent, then country, then alphabetically by title. U.S. publications are subdivided by state. Title index. Effectively supersedes Fraenkel's *The Jewish press of the world* (*Guide* AF7).

Gale international directory of publications. 1st ed. (1989–90)– . Detroit : Gale Research, c1989– . Annual. ISSN 1040-9351. $95.00.   **AE4**

Subtitle: An international guide to more than 4,800 newspapers, magazines, and other periodicals circulating primarily outside the United States and Canada.

Arranged alphabetically by country, then city, then title. Includes publisher's address and phone number, date established, frequency, editorial and advertising contacts, subscription rates, advertising rates, and circulation. Name and keyword index.   Z6941.G27

Hebrew Union College-Jewish Institute of Religion. American Jewish Periodical Center. Jewish newspapers and periodicals on microfilm : available at the American Jewish Periodical Center / ed. by Herbert C. Zafren.

Augm. ed. Cincinnati : The Center, 1984. 158 p. ISBN 0-87820-350-8 (pbk.). **AE5**

1st ed., 1957 (*Guide* AF22).

Follows the arrangement of the 1st edition, but contains more entries, including some South American and Canadian titles, with "somewhat less detail than the earlier catalog."—*p.5*. This edition does not include editors' names or characterization of editorial policy. Z6367.H48

The serials directory : an international reference book. 1986– . Birmingham, Ala. : EBSCO, c1986– . Annual. ISSN 0886-4179. $289.00. **AE6**

Updated quarterly by *Serials directory update*.

Compiled primarily from the CONSER database, with additions from EBSCO's internal subscription database and answers to questionnaires sent to publishers. The 4th ed. lists more than 123,000 titles (including irregular serials and annuals, and some newspapers) under broad subject headings. The information listed, when available, includes variant titles; dates of publication; ISSN; language; frequency; price; publisher and address; telephone; editor; indexing or abstracting services covering the title; Library of Congress, Dewey, and Universal Decimal Classification numbers; and circulation figures. Also indicates which titles are peer-reviewed. Title and ISSN indexes. Includes a list of ceased titles.

An extensive review comparing the 1st ed. of *The serials directory* with *Ulrich's international periodical directory* (*Guide* AE10) appears in *Serials review* 13 (Summer 1987): 5–13. A review of the 2nd ed. concludes that while it "is not a replacement for other standard bibliographic tools, it does have something of value to offer."—*Serials review* 14 no.3 (1988): 71–73. Z6941.S464

Singerman, Robert. Jewish serials of the world : a research bibliography of secondary sources. N.Y. : Greenwood, 1986. 377 p. ISBN 0-313-24493-6. **AE7**

Aims to identify "pertinent source materials for writing a world history of the Jewish press."—*Introd.* General and multinational sections are followed by geographical sections listing studies of the Jewish press on a country-by-country basis. Author and subject indexes. Z6366.S526

Ulrich's international periodicals directory. [1st] ed. (1932)– . N.Y. : Bowker. $280.00. **AE8**

For annotation, see *Guide* AE10.

Beginning with the 27th ed. (1988), absorbed *Irregular serials and annuals* (*Guide* AE7), which ceased with the 13th ed. (1987/88). With the 28th ed. (1989/90), refereed titles are indicated by an italicized note at the end of the entry; the 29th ed. (1990/91) adds an index of refereed serials, and an index of publications available in CD-ROM. Kept up to date by *Ulrich's update* (below). Z6941.U5

●**Ulrich's plus** [computer file]. N.Y. : Bowker. **AE9**

Machine-readable version of *Ulrich's international periodicals directory* (above), *Irregular serials and annuals* (*Guide* AE7), *Sources of serials* (*Guide* AE9), and *Ulrich's quarterly* (*Guide* AE11).

File size: about 160,000 records. Available in CD-ROM (Bowker), updated quarterly. A version, called *Ulrich's international periodicals directory*, is available online (DIALOG, BRS), updated monthly.

Kept up to date by an online file maintained by Bowker, on which other versions are based. Searchable fields include title, publisher, subject, abstracting/indexing services, etc.

Ulrich's update. v. 1, no. 1 (Sept. 1988)– . N.Y. : Bowker, [c1988]– . Quarterly. ISSN 0000-1074. $100.00. **AE10**

Earlier versions called *Ulrich's quarterly* (Spring 1977–Sept. 1985; see *Guide* AE11) and *The Bowker international serials database update* (Dec. 1985–1987).

Subtitle: A quarterly supplement to *Ulrich's international periodicals directory*.

" . . . contains entries for periodicals and other serials newly added to the Bowker International Serials Database. It also contains entries for serials which have changed title since the publication of the base volumes of *Ulrich's international periodicals directory*."—*User's guide*.

UMI article clearinghouse. Ann Arbor, Mich. : Univ. Microfilms International, [1984]– . ISSN 1046-8536. **AE11**

Lists "current details on ordering, pricings and availability" (*Pref.*) of journals whose articles are available from the Clearinghouse. The 1987 edition is an alphabetical list of more than 10,000 journals "for which the Clearinghouse has copy permission from the publisher. Titles with photocopy restrictions are clearly marked."—*p. 7*. Broad subject index and a list of titles covered by major indexes and databases.

Abbreviations

Periodical title abbreviations. [5th ed.]– . Detroit : Gale, 1987– . Irregular. ISSN 0737-7843. **AE12**

4th ed., 1983 (*Guide* AE13).

Kept up to date by an annual supplement: *New periodical title abbreviations*.

Retains the arrangement of the prior edition, but has a 50% increase in coverage, now listing Australian journals and many more scientific and technical titles. Z6945.A2P47

Translations

Journals in translation. 4th ed. Boston Spa, Wetherby, West Yorkshire, U.K. : British Library Document Supply Centre ; Delft, The Netherlands : International Translations Centre, c1988. 218 p. ISBN 0-7123-2038-5. **AE13**

3rd ed., 1982 (*Guide* AE17).

Adheres to the plan and scope of the previous edition. Z6944.T7J68

United States

Bibliography and history

American humor magazines and comic periodicals / ed. by David E.E. Sloane. N.Y. : Greenwood, 1987. 648 p. ISBN 0-313-23956-8. **AE14**

" . . . seeks to provide a comprehensive survey of its field, assessing over two hundred years of publication in this genre through examination of the individual magazines."—*Pref.* Pt. 1 describes more than 100 titles, listed alphabetically. Brief bibliographies, detailed publication histories, and selected locations follow each article. Pt. 2 has 400 briefer entries, again arranged alphabetically by title. Pt. 3 contains two lists: unexamined titles compiled from the *Catalog of copyright entries: serials and periodicals* and a list of other unexamined titles. Pt. 4 contains essays on college humor magazines, scholarly humor magazines, and humor in American almanacs. Name and title index. PN4880.A46

American mass-market magazines / ed. by Alan Nourie and Barbara Nourie. N.Y. : Greenwood, 1990. 611 p. ISBN 0-313-25254-8.   **AE15**

Offers profiles, arranged alphabetically by title, of 106 "of the most significant mass-market or general U.S. periodicals . . . for the most part originating in the late nineteenth and twentieth centuries."—*Introd.* A bibliography, indexes, selected locations, and publication history follow each entry. Also includes a selected bibliography of books and articles discussing American magazines in general. Name and title index.   PN4877.A48

The ethnic press in the United States : a historical analysis and handbook / ed. by Sally M. Miller. N.Y. : Greenwood, 1987. 437 p. ISBN 0-313-23879-0.   **AE16**

Offers ten- to fifteen-page signed articles, each with a brief bibliography, on the press of 28 ethnic groups. Name and title index.   PN4882.E84

Guide to special issues and indexes of periodicals / Miriam Uhlan, ed. 3rd ed. N.Y. : Special Libraries Association, c1985. 160 p. ISBN 0-87111-263-9 (pbk.). $35.00.   **AE17**

2nd ed., 1976 (*Guide* AE21).

Covers 1,362 U.S. and Canadian periodicals. Retains the alphabetical arrangement of earlier editions, adding the name of the publisher and ordering information. Subject index.   Z7164.C81G85

Paine, Fred K. Magazines : a bibliography for their analysis with annotations and study guide / by Fred K. Paine and Nancy E. Paine. Metuchen, N.J. : Scarecrow, 1987. 690 p. ISBN 0-8108-1975-9.   **AE18**

Intended as a supplement to J.H. Schacht's *Bibliography for the study of magazines* (Urbana : College of Communications, Univ. of Illinois, 1979), "this bibliography lists more than 2,200 magazine, newspaper and journal articles, books, and dissertations written about [American] magazines" (*Pref.*), 1979–86. Arranged by broad topic, then alphabetically by author. Subject and magazine title index. Lacks an author index.   Z6940.P24

Periodical directories and bibliographies / Gary C. Tarbert, ed. Detroit : Gale, c1987. 195 p. ISBN 0-8103-1474-6. $75.00.   **AE19**

Subtitle: An annotated guide to approximately 350 directories, bibliographies, and other sources of information about English-language periodicals, from 1850 to the present, including newspapers, journals, magazines, newsletters, yearbooks, and other serial publications.

" . . . identifies approximately 350 directories, bibliographies, and other publications that furnish facts about English-language periodicals, from 1850 to the present . . . . Emphasis is on U.S. and Canadian sources with some representation of foreign materials."—*Introd.* Arranged alphabetically by title; subject index.   Z6941.P47

Riley, Sam G. Magazines of the American South. N.Y. : Greenwood, 1986. 346 p. ISBN 0-313-24337-9.   **AE20**

Offers profiles, arranged alphabetically by title, of some 85 general interest magazines published in the South between 1764 and 1982. Each article discusses the history and contents of the journal, and includes a bibliography of secondary sources and a detailed publishing history. Name and title index.   PN4893.R54

Directories

Directory of literary magazines / prepared by The Coordinating Council of Literary Magazines. 1984– . N.Y. : The Council, c1984– . Annual. ISSN 0884-6006. $5.95.   **AE21**

Formerly *CCLM literary magazine directory* (1983).

Includes little magazines. The 1989/90 edition lists more than 400 magazines alphabetically by title. Information provided includes editor, address, description, beginning publication date, price, and advertising rates.   Z6513.C37

Encyclopedia of associations : association periodicals. 1st ed.– . Detroit : Gale, c1987– . Annual. ISSN 0894-3869.   **AE22**

Contents: v. 1, Business, finance, industry, and trade; v. 2, Science, medicine, and technology; v.3, Social sciences, education, and humanities.

A listing of more than "12,000 periodical publications of national nonprofit membership organizations in the United States . . . arranged alphabetically by assigned primary subject keywords."—*Introd.* Each volume has its own association index and title and keyword index.   Z5055.U4E53

Gale directory of publications and broadcast media. 122nd ed. (1990)– . Detroit : Gale, c1990– . Annual. ISSN 1048-7972.   **AE23**

Subtitle: An annual guide to publications and broadcasting stations including newspapers, magazines, journals, radio stations, television stations, and cable systems.

Earlier titles: 1983–85, *The IMS . . . Ayer directory of publications* (*Guide* AE32); 1986, *The IMS . . . directory of publications*; 1987–89, *Gale directory of publications.*

Covers U.S. and Canada. Arranged alphabetically by state (for Canada, by province), then by city. For print media, information includes publisher, address and telephone, beginning date, description, advertising rates, circulation, etc.; for broadcast media, call letters and frequency, address, format, advertising rates, etc. Special features include: detailed subject index to print media, including type of publication (college, black, women, trade, etc.); subject index to radio station format; list of feature editors of daily newspapers with at least 50,000 circulation, arranged alphabetically by state, then by city. Name and keyword index. "A single-volume directory of new or changed media will be sent to subscribers midway between editions."—*Introd.*   Z6951.A97

Ireland, Sandra L. Jones. Ethnic periodicals in contemporary America : an annotated guide. N.Y. : Greenwood, 1990. 222 p. (Bibliographies and indexes in ethnic studies, no. 3). ISBN 0-313-26817-7.   **AE24**

A list, alphabetical by ethnic group, of 234 current magazines, newspapers, and newsletters "published for and about an audience identified as interested in the social, cultural, religious, economic, education, geographic and political information associated with people who align themselves with a specific ethnic group."—*p. xvii.* Includes detailed information on publication requirements. Title, subject, and editor index.

Z6953.5.A1I74

The national directory of magazines. 1988– . N.Y. : Oxbridge Communications, c1988– . Annual.   **AE25**

Claims to be the "largest single source of information available on the U.S. & Canadian magazine industry."—*Pref.* Includes addresses, circulation figures, and advertising rates. Arranged by subject with a title index.   Z6941.N28

Skidmore, Gail. From radical left to extreme right : a bibliography of current periodicals of protest, controversy, advocacy, or dissent, with dispassionate content-summaries to guide librarians and other educators. 3rd ed., completely rev. / by Gail Skidmore and Theodore Jurgen Spahn. Metuchen, N.J. : Scarecrow, 1987. 491 p. ISBN 0-8108-1967-8.   **AE26**

2nd ed., 1970 (*Guide* AE35).

Does not fully supersede the 2nd ed., which contains many titles not included here. Arranged by broad subject with a geographical index; an index of titles, editors, and publishers; and a subject index.   Z7165.U5S473

Wynar, Lubomyr Roman. Guide to the American ethnic press : Slavic and East European newspapers and periodicals. Kent, Ohio : Center for the Study of Ethnic Publications, School of Library Science, Kent State Univ., 1986. 280 p. **AE27**

An "annotated encyclopedic directory to current Slavic and East European newspapers and periodicals published in the United States."—*Pref.* Based on answers to a questionnaire; lists some 580 titles alphabetically by ethnic group. Includes address, frequency, circulation, and price. Geographic and title indexes. Z6953.5.S62W96

Brazil

Guia de publicações seriadas brasileiras / MCT-Ministério da Ciência e Tecnologia, CNPq-Conselho Nacional de Desenvolvimento Científico e Tecnológico, IBICT-Instituto Brasileiro de Informação em Ciência e Tecnologia. Brasília : IBICT, 1987. 671 p. ISBN 85-7013-010-4. **AE28**

Formerly (1968) *Periódicos brasileiros de cultura,* (*Guide* AE49); supersedes *Periódicos brasileiros de ciência e tecnologia,* 1977; rev. ed. of *ISSN, publicações periódicas brasileiras,* (1983).

Lists more than 1,500 currently published titles by broad subject category. Subject, title, and ISSN indexes. Includes an alphabetical list of publishers and their addresses.

Z6954.B8G84

Canada

Canadian serials directory = Répertoire des publications sériées canadiennes / ed. by Gordon Ripley. 3rd ed. Toronto : Reference Pr., 1987. 396 p. ISBN 0-919981-10-0. $36.00. **AE29**

2nd ed, 1976 (*Guide* AE54).

Continues the scope and arrangement of the previous edition. Z6954.C2C258

China

Chung-kuo pao k'an ta ch'üan / "Chung-kuo pao k'an pao" pien chi pu, Yu tien pu pao k'an fa hsing chü shen chiao. Pei-ching : Jen min yu tien ch'u pan she, [1986?]– . Annual. **AE30**

Offers separate listings of newspapers and magazines currently published in China; both sections are arranged by subject. Each entry provides frequency, beginning date, any title changes, issuing body, distribution, and a brief description of the contents. Province and title indexes. Z6958.C5C5834

Finland

Kurikka, Jussi. Suomen aikakauslehdistön bibliografia 1782–1955 = Bibliografi över Finlands tidskriftslitteratur 1782–1955 = Bibliography of Finnish periodicals, 1782–1955 / Jussi Kurikka, Marketta Takkala. Helsinki : [Helsingin yliopiston kirjasto], 1983. 463 p. (Helsingin yliopiston kirjaston julkaisuja, 47.). ISBN 951-45-3158-2. **AE31**
Z6956.F5K87

Takkala, Marketta. Suomen aikakauslehdistön bibliografia 1956–1977 = Bibliografi över Finlands tidskriftslitteratur 1956–1977 = Bibliography of Finnish periodicals, 1956–1977 / Marketta Takkala, Anna-Maija Ortamo, Päivi Tommila. Helsinki : [Helsingin yliopiston kirjasto], 1986. 632 p. (Helsingin yliopiston kirjaston julkaisuja, 48.). ISBN 951-45-3924-9. **AE32**

Introductory matter in Finnish, Swedish, and English.

Together, these constitute a listing of all periodicals issued at least twice a year published in Finland through 1977. Arranged by title; indexes of editors and publishers.
Z6956.F5T34

France

Bibliothèque Nationale (France). Catalogue général des périodiques du début du XVIIᵉ siècle à 1959. Fichier alphabetique des titres / edité par Chadwyck-Healey France [microform]. [Paris] : Chadwyck-Healey France S.A.R.L., 1988. 1419 microfiches. **AE33**

An alphabetical listing of French and foreign periodicals received by the Bibliothèque Nationale to 1959. Revises much of the information in the *Catalogue collectif des périodiques du début du XVIIᵉ siècle à 1939* (*Guide* AE192) but is not a union list, hence does not supersede that work. Z6945.F72

Sgard, Jean. Bibliographie de la presse classique, 1600–1789. Genève : Slatkine, 1984. 226 p. : ill. ISBN 2-05-100616-4. **AE34**

An alphabetic listing of 1,138 French-language general interest titles published throughout Europe. Information provided includes titles, with variants and subtitles, publication dates, frequency, and editors and founders. Locations and call numbers in major French libraries are also given. Chronological and name indexes. Z6956.F8S48

Germany

Dietzel, Thomas. Deutsche literarische Zeitschriften, 1880–1945 : ein Repertorium / Thomas Dietzel, Hans-Otto Hügel ; hrsg. vom Deutschen Literaturarchiv, Marbach am Neckar. München ; N.Y. : K. G. Saur, 1988. 5 v. ISBN 3-598-10645-9. $470.00. **AE35**

Continues Alfred Estermann's *Die deutschen Literatur-Zeitschriften, 1850–1880* (below); does not list titles covered in that set.

The 3,341 titles, listed alphabetically, include literary, cultural, and general interest journals published in German throughout Europe. Information for each title includes dates, editors, publication history, detailed collation, selected locations, and in many cases, names of the major contributors. Selected bibliographies of secondary sources are provided for many titles. Indexed by editor, by contributor, by publisher, by place of publication, and by type of publication (literary, political, women, film, etc.) Z2233.D37

Estermann, Alfred Adolph. Die deutschen Literatur-Zeitschriften, 1850–1880 : Bibliographien, Programme. München : Saur, c1988–1989. 5 v. ISBN 3-598-10709-9. $750.00. **AE36**

Continues the author's *Die deutschen Literatur-Zeitschriften, 1815–1850* (Nendeln : KTO Press, 1977–1981, 10 v.), and is continued by Thomas Dietzel's *Deutsche literarische Zeitschriften, 1880–1945* (above).

An alphabetical listing of nearly 3,000 literary, cultural, and general interest journals published in German throughout Europe. Each entry includes the title, any variant titles, dates and places of publication, selected locations and call numbers in German and other European libraries, and a detailed collation. In many cases introductions or prospectuses are reprinted. Separate indexes for editors, places of publication, and publishers. Z2225.E87

Hagelweide, Gert. Literatur zur deutschsprachigen Presse : eine Bibliographie. München ; N.Y. : K.G. Saur, 1985–1989. v. 1–3. ISBN 3-598-21284-4 (set). (In progress). **AE37**
Contents: Bd. 1: Handbücher, Lexika, Bibliographien, Pressesammlung und -dokumentation, Organisation der Presse (Verbände), Zeitungs– Publizistik– und Kommunikationswissenschaft, Presse im Wechselspiel der Medien und der Öffentlichkeit; Bd. 2: Presseverlag, Träger der Aussage, Presseinhalt, Formgebung und Gestaltung, Inhaltsbeschaffung und -vermittlung, Nachrichtenwesen; Bd. 3: Technische Herstellung und Vertrieb der Rezipient.
Lists selected books, articles, and dissertations on all aspects of the press throughout the world written primarily in German during the 19th and 20th centuries. Classed arrangement, with a detailed table of contents. To be in 9 v., the last of which will be an index. PN4703.D6

Kirchner, Joachim. Bibliographie der Zeitschriften des deutschen Sprachgebietes bis 1900. Stuttgart : Hiersemann, 1989. v.4. ISBN 3-7772-6617-5. DM30. (In progress). **AE38**
For v.1–3 and annotation, see *Guide* AE77.
Contents: v. 4, pt. 1, Alphabetisches Titelregister.
Includes subtitles, variant titles, etc. Vol. 4, pt.2 will be an index by publisher, place of publication, and editor. Z6956.G3K53

Rösch-Sondermann, Hermann. Bibliographie der lokalen Alternativpresse : vom Volksblatt zum Stadtmagazin. München ; N.Y. : K.G. Saur, 1988. 156 p. ISBN 3-598-10816-8. **AE39**
An alphabetical listing of 930 titles published in West Germany in the 1970s and 1980s. Lists place of publication, beginning and cessation dates as applicable, frequency, and periodical type. Indexed by place of publication. PN5214.U53R6

Current

Deutsche Bibliographie. Zeitschriften-Verzeichnis / bearbeitet von der Deutschen Bibliothek, Frankfurt a. M. 1981–85– . Frankfurt am Main : Buchhändler-Vereinigung, 1989. Irregular. ISSN 0170-1002. **AE40**
For annotation, see *Guide* AE75.
The 1981–85 v. was published in 1989. Z6956.G3F67

Great Britain

Before 1800

Nelson, Carolyn. British newspapers and periodicals, 1641–1700 : a short-title catalogue of serials printed in England, Scotland, Ireland, and British America / comp. by Carolyn Nelson and Matthew Seccombe. N.Y. : Modern Language Association of America, 1987. 724 p. ISBN 0-87352-174-9. $250.00. **AE41**
Subtitle: With a checklist of serials printed 1701–March 1702 and chronological, geographical, foreign language, subject, publishers, and editor indexes, 1641–1702.
The 700 titles are listed alphabetically with detailed bibliographic information for each issue. Includes issue-specific locations in a number of British and American Libraries. "Designed . . . to be compatible with Pollard and Redgrave's *STC*, which includes serials published before 1641, and with Wing's *Catalogue*, which includes annuals but excludes serials pub-

lished at shorter intervals . . . . [The authors] have excluded annuals."—*Pref.* Z6956.G6N44

19th century and after

Doughan, David. Feminist periodicals, 1855–1984 : an annotated critical bibliography of British, Irish, Commonwealth, and international titles / David Doughan, Denise Sanchez. N.Y. : New York Univ. Pr., 1987. 316 p. ISBN 0-8147-1798-5. $95.00. **AE42**
For annotation, see *Supplement* CC271. Z7963.F44D68

Victorian periodicals : a guide to research / Scott Bennett . . . [et al.] ; ed. by J. Don Vann and Rosemary T. VanArsdel. N.Y. : Modern Language Association of America, 1989. v. 2. ISBN 0-87352-264-8 (v. 2). $32.00. ISBN 0-87352-265-6 (pbk.). **AE43**
For v. 1 and annotation, see *Guide* AE88.
"The object of volume 2 is to complement, to build on, and augment the material offered in volume 1."—*Pref.* PN5124.P4V5

Current

Benn's media directory. United Kingdom. 134th ed. (1986)– . Tonbridge, Kent : Benn Business Information Services, c1986– . Annual. **AE44**
Formerly (1978–85) Pt. 1 of *Benn's press directory* (*Guide* AE90).
The change in title reflects expanded coverage of the broadcast media. P88.8.B47

Current British journals: a bibliographic guide. Boston Spa [Yorkshire] : published by the British Library Lending Division in association with the UK Serials Group, 1986. 583 p. **AE45**
3rd ed., 1982 (*Guide* AE91).
Continues the arrangement of the previous edition, but includes 50% more titles and has reintroduced pricing information. Z6956.G6G84

Serials in the British Library. No. 1 (June 1981)– . London : British Library, Bibliographic Services Division, c1981– . Quarterly. ISSN 0260-0005. **AE46**
For earlier information, see *Guide* AE198.
Beginning 1987, published in three quarterly issues and annual printed cumulation.
After 1986, lists alphabetically "titles (including new British serials received through legal deposit) that have been newly acquired for the London-based reference collections of the British Library."—*Pref.* Most titles are new, but retrospective acquisitions are also included. Information provided includes title, dates, publisher, frequency, ISSN, and price. No longer lists additional locations. Keyword-in-title index. Also available in microfiche. Z6945.B874

Walford's guide to current British periodicals in the humanities and social sciences / ed. by A.J. Walford with the assistance of Joan M. Harvey. London : Library Association, 1985. 473 p. ISBN 0-85-365676-2. $50.00. **AE47**
A classified listing of current British periodicals in the broad range of humanities and social sciences. In addition to publication information, there is a brief listing of representative articles and notes on sponsorship, coverage, etc. Subject sections begin with a short survey of the range of publications included, plus listings of abstracting, indexing, and online services in the field. Indexed. Z7165.W36

Hungary

Magyar nemzeti bibliográfia. 1981– . Budapest : Országos Széchényi Könyvtár, 1983– . Annual. ISSN 0231-4592. **AE48**

For annotation, see *Guide* AE97.

A cumulated index for 1981–85 was published in 1988 in 2v.: v.1, Címmutató; v.2, Testületi mutató. The first is a cumulative title index, including title changes and variant titles; the second a cumulative index to the corporate bodies issuing periodicals during the period. Both refer to the appropriate annual volumes. Z6956.H8K87

India

Nagar, Murari Lal. TULIP : the universal list of Indian periodicals / offered by Murari Lal Nagar and Sarla Devi Nagar. Columbia, Mo. : International Library Center, 1986–89. 8 v. ISBN 0-943913-03-9 (v. 3). $45.00. **AE49**

An alphabetical listing of Indian periodicals, including those from Pakistan and Bangladesh, issued in English, Hindi, or Sanskrit before 1980. "It does not locate a title in a specific library, but in some major union catalogs which report the title."—*Introd.* Z6958.I4N33

Susheel Kaur. Directory of periodicals published in India, 1986–87 : a classified guide / comp., Susheel Kaur, assisted by Dinesh Chand, Prem Singh Rawat ; ed. by R.P. Sood. [New Delhi] : Sapra and Sapra, c1988. 353 p. **AE50**

Attempts to update and expand N.N. Gidwani and K. Navalani's *Current Indian periodicals in English (Guide* AE99). Lists by broad subject 5,300 periodicals currently published in India in any language, excluding newspapers and irregular serial titles. Information provided, when available, includes beginning date, frequency, price, address, and circulation. Title index.

Indonesia

Perpustakaan Nasional (Indonesia). Katalog majalah terbitan Indonesia : kumulasi 1779–1980 = Catalogue of Indonesian serials. [Jakarta] : Perpustakaan Nasional, Departemen Pendidikan dan Kebudayaan, [1984]. 476 p. **AE51**

In Dutch, English, and Indonesian.

A classified list, cumulating the 1981–83 volumes. Z6958.I45I53

Zulkarjono, Maesarah. Daftar majalah Indonesia yang telah mempunyai ISSN. Jakarta : Pusat Dokumentasi Ilmiah Nasional, Lembaga Ilmu Pengetahuan Indonesia, 1984. 87 p. **AE52**

A list of currently published Indonesian periodicals arranged alphabetically by publisher. Title index. Z460.4.Z84

Iran

Union catalogue of Persian serials & newspapers in British libraries / Middle East Libraries Committee ; ed. by Ursula Sims-Williams. London : Ithaca Pr., 1985. 149 p. ISBN 0-86372-039-0. **AE53**

" . . . attempts to record all Persian language serials in national, university and government libraries in Great Britain. It includes details of periodicals and newspapers, whether wholly or partially in Persian, Dari, or Tajik, published throughout the world."—*p.xii.* Arranged alphabetically by title. Holdings are issue-specific. Z6958.I65U54

Ireland

North, John S. The Waterloo directory of Irish newspapers and periodicals, 1800–1900. Waterloo, Ont. : North Waterloo Academic Pr., 1986. 838 p. (Waterloo directory series of newspapers and periodicals, England, Ireland, Scotland and Wales, 1800–1900, Phase 2, v. 1). ISBN 0-921-07500-6. **AE54**

Phase II of the Waterloo directory series. For description of Phase I, *Waterloo directory of Victorian periodicals, 1824–1900,* see *Guide* AE89.

"An alphabetical listing and description of publications in Ireland in all fields . . . . The editor has sought to list every newspaper and periodical published in the century."—*Pref.* The 3,932 titles, most examined by the compilers, include the 1,100 Irish titles listed in Phase I. The listings include, when available, title, subtitle, publisher, printer, dates and volume numbers, price, circulation, indexes, description of the contents, and a bibliography of secondary sources. At least one British or Irish location is given for most titles. Includes subject, personal name, and place of publication indexes.

PN5144.W2

Italy

Maini, Roberti. Catalogo dei periodici italiani. [Third ed.]. Milano : Bibliografica ; Ann Arbor, Mich. : Distr. by Bowker, c1988. 732 p. **AE55**

2nd ed., 1983 (*Guide* AE109).

The new edition lists more than 10,000 currently published periodicals. Z6956.I8C18

Kenya

Kenyan periodicals directory. 1984–85– . Nairobi : Kenya National Library Service, National Reference & Bibliographic Dept., c1984– . Biennial. $9.50. **AE56**

Attempts "to list all serial titles published in Kenya. Foreign serials of interest to Kenya, by subject or otherwise, and periodicals produced locally by international and regional intergovernmental and private organizations based in Kenya are also listed."—*Pref.* Classified arrangement with title/agency index. Separate classified list of cessations; directory of publishers. Z6960.K4K43

Latvia

Latviešu periodika : bibliogrāfisks rādītājs / K. Egle . . . [et al.] ; redakcijas koleģija E. Arājs . . . [et al.]. 2., papildināts izdevums. Rīga : Zinātne, 1988–1989. v. 3¹⁻². **AE57**

For v. 1–2, 1768–1940, see *Guide* AE121.

Contents: v. 3, pt. 1, 1920–40; v. 3, pt. 2, 1920–40, Palīgrādītāji. Completes the set.

Prefatory matter in Latvian and Russian.

Vol. 2 lists revolutionary and Soviet titles published 1920–40; v. 3, pt. 1 is an alphabetical listing of all other periodicals published in Latvia during that period. Entries give publication dates, place, publisher, editors, detailed collation, and holdings in the two major Latvian libraries. Vol. 3, pt. 2 includes numerous tables and indexes to v. 3, pt. 1.

Z6956.L36L35

Mexico

Orozco Tenorio, José. Las publicaciones periódicas mexicanas. México : Instituto Tecnológico Autónomo de México, 1986. 190 p.   **AE58**

An alphabetical listing of 546 currently published Mexican journals. Includes address, price, frequency, and circulation. Subject and variant title indexes.   PN4968.O769

Nigeria

Ogbondah, Chris W. The press in Nigeria : an annotated bibliography. N.Y. : Greenwood, 1990. 127 p. (African special bibliographic series, no. 12). ISBN 0-313-26521-6.   **AE59**

Includes "scholarly journal articles, books, conference papers and reports on Nigerian mass communication" (*Introd.*) published from the 1950s to about 1985. Arranged alphabetically by author. Subject index.   Z6940.O34

Poland

Bibliografia wydawnictw ciągłych = Bibliography of Polish serials / Biblioteka Narodowa, Instytut Bibliograficzny. 1981– . Warszawa : Biblioteka, 1984– . Annual. ISSN 0239-4421.   **AE60**

Continues *Bibliografia czasopism i wydawnictw zbiorowych* (*Guide* AE135), which last appeared in 1978, covering 1972/74.

Lists, alphabetically by title, all Polish serials, including newspapers, annuals, and irregular issues, legally deposited at the Biblioteka Narodowa during the year. Classified, organization, and editor indexes.   Z6956.P7B5

Biblioteka Jagiellońska. Katalog czasopism polskich Biblioteki Jagiellońskiej / [pod red. Stanisława Grzeszczuka]. Wyd. 2. Kraków : Nakładem Uniwersytetu Jagiellońskiego, 1986. v. 9. ISBN 83-233-0088-7 (v. 9).   **AE61**

For earlier volumes and annotation, see *Guide* AE137.

Contents: v. 9, Wiadukt–Żywienie. Completes the set.

Includes corrections to v. 1–8.   Z6956.P7K72

Kowalik, Jan. Bibliografia czasopism polskich wydanych poza granicami Kraju od września 1939 roku = World index of Polish periodicals published outside of Poland since September 1939. Wyd. 1. Lublin : Katolicki Uniwersytet Lubelski, 1988. v.5. zł600.00.   **AE62**

For v. 1–4 and annotation, see *Guide* AE136.

Vol. 5 lists 361 titles published 1973–84, and 354 titles supplementing v. 1–4.   Z6956.P7K59

Romania

Publicaţiunile periodice româneşti (ziare, gazete, reviste) : cu o introducere de Ioan Bianu. Bucureşti : Socec, 1987. v. 3. (In progress).   **AE63**

For v. 1–2 and annotation, see *Guide* AE142.

Contents: v. 3, Catalog alfabetic, 1919–1924, descriere bibliografică de Ileana Stancu Desa, Dulcia Morărescu, Ioana Patriche, Adriana Paliade şi Iliana Sulică.

At head of title: Biblioteca Academiei Republicii Socialiste România.   Z2923.P9

Russia and the U.S.S.R.

L'emigration russe : revues et recueils, 1920–1980 : index général des articles / [ouvrage édité sous la direction de Tatiana Gladkova, Tatiana Ossorguine]. Paris : Institut d'études slaves, 1988. 661 p. (Bibliothèque russe de l'Institut d'études slaves , t. 81). ISBN 2-7204-0236-2.

    AE64

Title on added t.p.: Russkaiā émigratsiiā : zhurnaly i sborniki na russkom iāzyke, 1920–1980 : svodnyĭ ukazatel' stateĭ = The Russian emigration : journals and miscellanea, 1920–1980 : general index of articles.

" ... publié par la Bibliothèque russe Tourguenev et la Bibliothèque de documentation internationale contemporaine."—*t.p.*   Text in Russian; introductory material in French, English, and Russian.

An author index to the "contents of 45 Russian language periodicals and 16 collections of general historical and cultural interest" (*Pref.*) published 1920–80, mainly in Paris. Gives the title of the article, the source, and the year and volume number. Index of names mentioned in the articles.   Z6955.E56

Library of Congress. Russian imperial government serials on microfilm in the Library of Congress : a guide to the uncatalogued collection / comp. by Harold M. Leich with the assistance of staff members of the Library of Congress European Division and Preservation Microfilming Office. Wash. : The Library, 1985. 135 p. ISBN 0-8444-0493-4.   **AE65**

Superintendent of Documents classification: LC 43.8:R92.

The 967 titles include "publications of pre-revolutionary Russian governmental bodies and units at various levels ... publications of a large number of general and specialized societies, associations, and institutions ... [and] a group of miscellaneous serials" (*Introd.*) arranged alphabetically by romanized title. It does not include titles which the Library of Congress has cataloged. Information provided includes statement of responsibility, place of publication, related titles, and dates which the Library of Congress has filmed; does not give beginning and ending dates. Indexed by issuing body and by place of publication. (There is a broad subject arrangement under cities with more than 12 titles). Also includes a Summary guide to reels.

Z6956.S65L52

Current

Center for Research Libraries (U.S.). Soviet serials currently received at the Center for Research Libraries. 4th ed. Chicago : The Center, 1990.   **AE66**

1st ed., 1981; 3rd ed., 1988.

Offers an alphabetical listing of "1287 titles of Soviet periodicals, irregular serials, annuals, and numbered monographic series received at CRL as of June 1, 1990."—*Introd.* Monographic series, non-academic serials, and broad subject indexes.

Scotland

North, John S. The Waterloo directory of Scottish newspapers and periodicals, 1800–1900 / John S. North. Waterloo, Ont. : North Waterloo Academic Pr., 1989. 2 v. (2199 p.) : ill. (Waterloo directory series of newspapers and periodicals, England, Ireland, Scotland and Wales, 1800–1900, v. 1–2). ISBN 0-921075-02-2 (v. 1).   **AE67**

Forms part of Phase II of "Waterloo directory series of newspapers and periodicals, England, Ireland, Scotland and Wales, 1600–1900"; for description of Phase I, *Waterloo directory of Victorian periodicals, 1824–1900*, see *Guide* AE89.

Offers "an alphabetical listing, description, and finding list of publications issued in Scotland in all fields."—*Pref.* Lists more than 7,000 titles, including daily and annual publications. The extremely detailed annotations include collation statements, printers, descriptions of content, locations in Great Britain, etc. More than 2,000 title pages are reproduced. Subject, name, and place of publication indexes.   Z6956.S36N67

Senegal

Bibliothèque Nationale (France). Les publications en série éditées au Sénégal, 1856–1982 : liste provisoire / par Marie-Elisabeth Bouscarle. Paris : Bibliothèque Nationale, 1987. 107 p. ISBN 2-7177-1758-7. 100F.   **AE68**

At head of title: Bibliothèque Nationale. Département des livres imprimés. Département des entrées étrangères.

An alphabetical listing of 692 journals held in the Bibliothèque Nationale and in the libraries of Versailles and the Société de Géographie. Detailed holdings and call numbers are given, but publication dates are not included. Subject, editor, and sponsoring body index.   Z3715.B54

Spain

Periódicos y revistas españolas e hispanoamericanas. Barcelona : C.I.L.E.H., 1989. 2 v. (lviii, 1153 p.). ISBN 84-8741-101-0 (set).   **AE69**

Prefatory matter in English, French, German, and Italian.

Aims to list all currently published Spanish-language periodicals, including newspapers and irregular serial titles. Titles in Catalan, Basque, and Galician are listed separately. Information provided includes frequency, beginning date, price, editor, address, and subject. Includes brief biographical entries for editors where possible. Subject index. New editions are promised at two-year intervals.   Z6956.S7P47

Tunisia

Bibliyūghrāfiyā al-qawmīyah al-Tūnisīyah. Dawrīyāt al-ʿArabīyah. al-Bibliyūghrāfiyā al-qawmīyah al-Tūnisīyah / Wizārat al-Shuʾūn al-Thaqāfīyah, Dār al-Kutub al-Waṭanīyah, Maṣlaḥat al-Dawrīyāt. v. 1 (1860–1975)– . Tūnis : al-Maṣlaḥah, 1975– . Decennial.   **AE70**

Contents: v.1, 1860–1975; v.2, 1975–1985 (publ. 1987).

An alphabetical listing of Arabic periodicals published in Tunisia. Information provided includes title, place of publication, publisher and printer, dates, and frequency. Separate indexes for subject, sponsor and/or publisher, date of first publication, printer, and place of publication (excluding Tunis). Vol. 2 lacks place and printer indexes.

UNION LISTS

International

Volkoff, Anne Marie. L'émigration russe en Europe : catalogue collectif des périodiques en langue russe, 1940–1979. 2e éd. ref. Paris : Institut d'études slaves, 1981. 147 p. (Bibliothèque russe de l'Institut d'études slaves , t. 40/2). ISBN 2-7204-0166-8. 69.00F.   **AE71**

2e éd. of v. 2 of *L'émigration russe en Europe, 1940–1970* (*Guide* AE178).

An alphabetical listing of some 500 Russian émigré periodicals indicates holdings in selected French and European libraries.   Z6955.V64

United States

New serial titles / prepared under the sponsorship of the Joint Committee on the Union List of Serials. Began with Jan. 1953– . Wash. : Library of Congress. Eight monthly issues, four quarterly issues and annual cumulations which are self-cumulative through periods of five or ten years. ISSN 0028-6680.   **AE72**

For annotation, see *Guide* AE183.

Superintendent of Documents classification: LC 1.23/4: .

Cumulations for 1981–85 (6v.) and 1986–88 (6v.) were published in 1986 and 1989 respectively.   Z6945.U5S42

Great Britain

Fulton, Richard D. Union list of Victorian serials : a union list of selected nineteenth-century British serials available in United States and Canadian libraries / Richard D. Fulton and C.M. Colee, general editors ; editorial board, Christopher C. Dahl . . . [et al.]. N.Y. : Garland Pub., 1985. 732 p. (Garland reference library of the humanities, vol. 530). ISBN 0-8240-8846-8. $103.00.   **AE73**

Aims to provide a finding list for selected Victorian periodicals in nearly 500 North American libraries. Selection was "based on the list of periodicals included in Volume III of the *New Cambridge bibliography of English literature*, with about 100 titles added in science and technology."—*Introd.* More than 300 librarians and scholars assisted in compiling detailed holdings information and doing actual shelf checks; where only published lists or regional guides had to be relied on, the library name is marked with an asterisk. In addition to libraries with major Victorian collections, local and regional libraries were selected to give broad geographical representation.

Z6956.G6F85

INDEXES

Bibliography

The index and abstract directory : an international guide to services and serial coverage. Premier ed.– . Birmingham, Ala. : Ebsco Pub., c1989– . Irregular. ISSN 1041-1321.   **AE74**

Seeks to provide "one source in which to look for: (1) all serials . . . covered by one or more index/abstract services, and (2) all international index/abstract services, with each service accompanied by a complete list of serials covered by that particular service."—*Pref.* This ambitious goal has not been met; for instance, the directory lists only eight of the hundreds of journals indexed by *Internationale Bibliographie der Zeitschriftenliteratur . . . (Guide* AE222).

Section 1 lists more than 30,000 titles, arranged by subject, then alphabetically by title. Section 2 is an alphabetical list of indexing and abstracting services, with an alphabetical list of serials covered. There is an alphabetical title index to both sections; a subject index to the services; and a combined ISSN index.   Z695.93.I52

United States and Great Britain

The cover story index, 1960–1989 / Robert Skapura, ed. Fort Atkinson, Wis. : Highsmith Pr., 1990. 381 p. ISBN 0-917846-02-8.   **AE75**

A subject index, based on Sears subject headings, of cover stories in *Newsweek, Time,* and *U.S. news & world report.* Includes a chronology of the cover stories and a list of subject headings used.   AP2.C68

Fulltext sources online / BiblioData. Winter 1989– . Needham, Mass. : BiblioData, 1989– . Semiannual. ISSN 1040-8258. $80.00.   **AE76**

Subtitle: For periodicals, newspapers, newsletters & newswires. Covers titles in science, technology, medicine, law, finance, business, industry, the popular press, etc.

Ed. by Ruth M. Orenstein.

"Each edition is complete in itself and replaces all previous editions. Complete new editions are published twice yearly in January and July."—*p.i.* Titles are listed alphabetically, each entry listing the databases in which that title appears. Subject index.

Index to American periodicals of the 1700's : keyed to University Microfilms APS I. [Indianapolis : Computer Indexed Systems, 1986?]. 2 v. $1190.00.   **AE77**

Contents: v. 1, Reels 1–16; v. 2, Reels 17–33.   Z6951.I533

Index to American periodicals of the 1800's : keyed to University Microfilms APS II. Indianapolis : Computer Indexed Systems, 1989–1990. v. 1–11. (In progress).   **AE78**

Contents: v. 1–3, 1800–09; v. 4–11, 1810–25.

A detailed subject index to articles in the magazines included in the microfilm sets *American periodicals: series I, 1741–1800* and *American periodicals: series II, 1800–1850* (both Ann Arbor, Mich.: Univ. Microfilms International). The index points to the reel number of the microfilm set, the title and volume of the journal, and the page number of the article. Hoornstra and Heath's *American periodicals 1741–1900: an index to the microfilm collection (Guide* AE26) is basically an index to the periodical titles in the microfilm series, rather than to their contents.   Z6951.I533

Readers' guide abstracts. Print ed. Aug. 1988–Jan. 1989– . N.Y.: H.W. Wilson, 1989– . Semiannual. ISSN 0899-1553. $229.00.   **AE79**

10 issues a year, cumulated semiannually.

Offers abstracts of some 40% of the articles indexed by the *Readers' guide to periodical literature (Guide* AE231), based on the "substantive nature of the article, its currency and topicality, its reference value, and its relevancy to school and college curricula."—*Pref. note.* Arranged alphabetically by subject.

Also available in microfiche from Sept. 1984; issued 8 times a year. The fiche set cumulates until two years are covered, then the earlier year is dropped. The microfiche abstracts every article indexed by *Readers' guide* except book reviews. Author and subject entries.   Z6941.R38

The Wellesley index to Victorian periodicals, 1824–1900 / Walter E. Houghton, ed. [Toronto] : Univ. of Toronto Pr. ; [London] : Routledge & K. Paul, [c1988–c1989]. v. 4–5. ISBN 0-8020-2688-5 (v.5).   **AE80**

For v. 1–3 and annotation, see *Guide* AE260.

Subtitle for v. 5: Dated bibliographies of all identified authors and their contributions to major quarterlies and monthlies of the period with a separate bibliography of identified pseudonyms and initials.

Vol. 5 ed. by Jean Harris Slingerland.

Vol. 5, Epitome and Index. Completes the set.

Vol. 4 (826 p.) covers an additional eight periodicals and includes an appendix of additions and corrections to the previous three volumes. Vol. 5 (923 p.) serves as an author index to the 43 titles covered in v. 1–4. Under each author, articles are listed chronologically, with the abbreviated title of the journal (if more than one article is from the same journal, the abbreviation appears after the first article); the item number; and the date. Full journal titles with the volume number of the *Wellesley index* in which it appears are listed at the bottom of each page.

The subject and book review indexes mentioned in the introduction to v. 1 appear not to be forthcoming.   AI3.W45

Canada

Canadian periodical index, 1920–1937 : an author and subject index / Grace Heggie . . . [et al.]. Ottawa : Canadian Library Association, 1988. 567 p. ISBN 0-88802-187-9. $200.00.   **AE81**

" . . . a retrospective index to twenty Canadian periodicals covering the years 1920 to 1937" *(Pref.),* the period preceding the annual cumulative volumes of *Canadian periodical index (Guide* AE269). Follows the format of that index.   AI3.C24

Yugoslavia

Jugoslavenski leksikografski zavod. Bibliografija rasprava, članaka i književnih radova. Zagreb : Jugoslavenski leksikografski zavod, 1984–86. v. 6 (in 2 pts.). (In progress.).   **AE82**

For v.1–5 and annotation, see *Guide* AE316.

Vol. 6 (publ. 1984–1986 in 2 pts.) covers music.

       Z2951.Z3

AF

Newspapers

BIBLIOGRAPHIES AND UNION LISTS

United States

United States Newspaper Program national union list [microform]. 3rd ed. Dublin, Ohio : OCLC, 1989. 55 microfiches + 1 booklet (unpaged) in binder. ISBN 1-55653-074-9 (microfiche). **AF1**

1st ed., 1985; 2nd ed., 1987.

This edition is a title listing with volume-specific holdings for more than 77,000 U.S. newspapers held by American libraries participating in the United States Newspaper Program. The information is maintained as part of the OCLC database. Indexed by place of publication, beginning date, and language. A useful description of this important project appears in *Guide to sources in American journalism history* (*Supplement* AF19). Z6945.U6115

Newsletters

Newsletters in print. 4th ed. (1988–89)– . Detroit : Gale, c1988– . Annual. ISSN 0899-0425. $160.00. **AF2**

Represents a 4th edition of *National directory of newsletters and reporting services* (*Guide* AF30); 3rd ed. (1987) had title *Newsletters directory*.

Subtitle: A descriptive guide to more than 10,000 subscription, membership, and free newsletters, bulletins, digests, updates, and similar serial publications issued in the United States and Canada, and available in print or online.

Arranged by broad subjects. For each title, includes address, frequency, circulation, price, and description. Title, publisher, and subject indexes. Z6941.N3

Oxbridge directory of newsletters. 1979– . N.Y. : Oxbridge Communications. Annual. ISSN 0163-7010. **AF3**

Continues *Standard directory of newsletters* (1971).

The 1989 edition lists 17,500 newsletters in 167 subject categories, providing for each: address, frequency, circulation, distribution, and primary readership. Title index. Z6944.N44S82

Canada

Sotiron, Minko. An annotated bibliography of works on daily newspapers in Canada, 1914–1983 = Une bibliographie annotée des ouvrages portant sur les quotidiens canadiens, 1914–1983; Gordon Rabchuk, indexation. Montréal : M. Sotiron, 1987. 288 p. ISBN 0-9693102-0-X. **AF4**

Books and articles are arranged by province, then alphabetically by author. Emphasis is on 20th century newspapers. Author and subject indexes. PN904.S68

Caribbean

Pactor, Howard S. Colonial British Caribbean newspapers : a bibliography and directory. N.Y. : Greenwood, c1990. 144 p. (Bibliographies and indexes in world history, no. 19). ISBN 0-313-27232-8. $45.00. **AF5**

Lists 677 newspapers, published from the 18th century through the gaining of independence, alphabetically by colony, then chronologically. Includes publication dates; editors, publishers and proprietors when they can be determined; and issue-specific locations when available. Notes the existence of microfilmed copies. Title and name indexes. Z6941.P26

China Coast

Library of Congress. Chinese newspapers in the Library of Congress : a bibliography = [Kuo hui t'u shu kuan ts'ang Chung wen pao k'an mu lu] / comp. by Han-chu Huang and Hseo-chin Jen. Wash. : Library of Congress : For sale by the Supt. of Docs., U.S. Govt. Print. Off., 1985. 206 p. ISBN 0-8444-0481-0. $13.00. **AF6**

Superintendent of Documents classification: LC 17.9:C44.

Lists newspapers from the 1870s to the present, both original and microform files. About 1,200 titles; holdings are issue-specific. Title listing with index by place of publication. Z6958.C5L52

Great Britain

Bibliography of British newspapers / [gen. ed., Charles A. Toase]. London : Lib. Assoc., Reference, Special and Information Section, 1975–1991. v. [1–6] : maps. ISBN 0-85365-038-1 (v. [1]). $41.20. (In progress). **AF7**

County editors vary.

Contents: [v. 1], Wiltshire; [v. 2], Nottinghamshire; [v. 3], Kent; [v. 4], Durham and Northumberland; [v. 5], Derbyshire; [v. 6], Cornwall and Devon.

Aims to provide a complete list of all British newspapers with brief notes on dates of publication, title changes, etc., and issue-specific holdings of British (and a few American) libraries. Z6956.G6B5

Ferguson, Joan P. S. Directory of Scottish newspapers. [2nd ed.]. Edinburgh : National Library of Scotland, 1984. 155 p. : ill. ISBN 0-902220-40-3 (pbk.). £10.00. **AF8**

Lists "Scottish newspaper holdings of 57 Scottish libraries and of many Scottish newspaper publishers, as well as approximately 80% of the Scottish newspaper holdings of the British Library Newspaper Library."—*Introd.* 1,178 newspapers published from the 1700s through 1979 are arranged alphabetically by title. Includes detailed holdings and existence of microfilm editions. Indexed by place of publication. Z6956.G6F47

Linton, David. The newspaper press in Britain : an annotated bibliography / ed. by David Linton and Ray Boston. London ; N.Y. : Mansell, 1987. 361 p. ISBN 0-7201-1792-5. $70.00 (est.). **AF9**

Lists (alphabetically by author) books, dissertations, and articles discussing the history of British newspapers from the 17th century through the mid-1980s. Two appendixes: (1) Chronology of British newspaper history, 1476–1986; (2) Loca-

tions of papers and other archives. Subject index.
Z6956.G6L56

Northern Ireland newspapers, 1737–1987 : a checklist with locations. 2nd rev. ed. Belfast : Lib. Assoc. (Northern Ireland Branch) : Public Record Office of Northern Ireland Working Party on Resources for Local Studies, 1987. 63 p. ISBN 0-906066-03-4. **AF10**
1st ed., 1979.
Arranged alphabetically by title. Lists holdings, including microfilmed copies, of more than 250 titles in Irish libraries and the British Library. Z6956.G6N67

Indonesia

Perpustakaan Nasional (Indonesia). Katalog surat kabar : koleksi Perpustakaan Nasional, 1810–1984 = Catalogue of newspapers / disusun oleh Wartini Santoso. Ed. rev. [Jakarta] : Perpustakaan Nasional, Departemen Pendidikan dan Kebudayaan, [1984]. 246 p. **AF11**
Rev. ed. of *Katalogus surat-karab, koleksi Perpustakaan Museum Pusat 1810–1973* [1973].
An alphabetical listing of approximately 1,600 newspapers published 1810–1984 held by the National Library of Indonesia; the majority are Indonesian titles. Indexed by place of publication. Z6958.I45I53

INDEXES

United States

Falk, Byron A. Personal name index to "The New York times index," 1975–1989 supplement / Bryon A. Falk, Jr., Valerie R. Falk. Verdi, Nev. : Roxbury Data Interface, c1990–1991. 5 v. ISBN 0-89902-089-5. (In progress). **AF12**
For main series, see *Guide* AF79.
Supersedes and extends the coverage of the 1975–1979 Suppl. (*Guide* AF79) which appeared as v. 23–25 of the set, and the 1975–84 Suppl., which appeared in 4 v. (1986–88) not numbered consecutively with the parent work. CT104.A1F3

●**Newspaper abstracts ondisc** [computer file]. Louisville, Ky. : UMI/Data courier, 1985– . **AF13**
Two archival discs cover 1985–88. A third disc (1989–90) is updated monthly.
File size: 2.5 million records. Updated monthly. Available in CD-ROM (Univ. Microfilms International). A version is also available online as *Newspaper abstracts* (DIALOG).
Indexes *Atlanta constitution, Boston globe, Chicago tribune, Christian Science monitor, Los Angeles times,* and *Wall Street journal* from 1985; *New York times* from 1987; and *Washington post* from 1989. Searchable fields include newspaper titles, headlines, abstracts, bylines, and subject headings (which use a controlled vocabulary). User's guide and thesaurus are provided with the subscription.

Canada

Burrows, Sandra. Checklist of indexes to Canadian newspapers = Liste de contrôle des index de journaux canadiens / by Sandra Burrows and Franceen Gaudet. Ottawa : National Library of Canada, 1987. 148, 154 p. : ill. ISBN 0-660-53735-4 (pbk.). $20.35. **AF14**
In English and French.
Based on responses to a survey sent to Canadian libraries, archives, newspaper offices, and genealogical and historical societies. Lists in-house indexes, including clipping files, of 19th- and 20th-century newspapers. Arranged by province, then by city. Title and geographical indexes. Z69.54.C2B87

France

Le Monde [Index]. Janv. 1988– . Reading, Eng. : Research Publications Ltd., c1988– . Monthly, with annual cumulations. ISSN 0953-7171. **AF15**
A detailed subject index with brief annotations, providing date, page, and column references. Lists reviews under type (*livre, film,* etc.) Not related to *Index analytique* (*Guide* AF88) which appears to have ceased in 1968.

Great Britain

The Guardian index. v. 1 (Jan. 1986)– . Ann Arbor, Mich. : Univ. Microfilms International, c1986– . 8 monthly and 4 quarterly issues, with annual cumulations. ISSN 0886-4667. $350.00. **AF16**
A detailed alphabetical index referring to date, page, and column, with illustration and article length indicators. Provides brief "abstracts and comprehensive indexing of all significant articles" (*Users' guide*), including editorials and editorial cartoons. Entries are arranged chronologically under each subject heading. Reviews are indexed under form (books, moving pictures, etc.) subdivided by author and by title. Also indexes the *Guardian weekly.* AI21.G8G82

JOURNALISM

Bibliography

Cates, Jo A. Journalism : a guide to the reference literature. Englewood, Colo. : Libraries Unlimited, 1990. 214 p. ISBN 0-87287-716-7. $38.00. **AF17**
"A selected, annotated bibliography and reference guide to the English-language reference literature of print and broadcast journalism" (*Introd.*), listing sources published from the late 1960s through 1988. Some earlier standard works are included. Arranged by broad topic. Author, title, and subject indexes. Z6940.C38

Wolseley, Roland Edgar. The journalist's bookshelf : an annotated and selected bibliography of United States print journalism / Roland E. Wolseley and Isabel Wolseley. 8th ed. Indianapolis : R.J. Berg, 1986. 400 p. ISBN 0-89730-139-0. **AF18**
7th ed., 1961 (*Guide* AF106)
A revised and greatly expanded edition, updated to about 1984. Z6940.W64

History

Guide to sources in American journalism history / ed. and comp. by Lucy Shelton Caswell. N.Y. : Greenwood, 1989. 319 p. (Bibliographies and indexes in mass media and communications, no. 2). ISBN 0-313-26178-4. **AF19**

"Prepared under the auspices of the American Journalism Historians Association"—*t.p.*

In two parts, the first a collection of essays, most with bibliographies, discussing various aspects of research in the history of American journalism. The second part is a guide, arranged by state, to archival and manuscript sources, including many collections of personal papers. The archival guide has a subject index. Z6951.G83

Sloan, W. David. American journalism history : an annotated bibliography. N.Y. : Greenwood, 1989. 344 p. (Bibliographies and indexes in mass media and communications, no. 1). ISBN 0-313-26350-7. **AF20**

Books, articles, and dissertations written primarily in the 20th century and covering all aspects of American journalism history are arranged by broad topic, and within each topic, alphabetically by author. Author and subject index. Z6951.S54

Biography

American magazine journalists, 1741–1850 / ed. by Sam G. Riley. Detroit : Gale, 1988. 430 p. : ill. (Dictionary of literary biography, v. 73). ISBN 0-8103-4551-X. **AF21**
PN4871.A47

American magazine journalists, 1850–1900 / ed. by Sam G. Riley. Detroit : Gale, 1989. 387 p. : ill. (Dictionary of literary biography, v. 79). ISBN 0-8103-4557-9. **AF22**
PN4871.A474

American magazine journalists, 1900–1960 / ed. by Sam G. Riley. Detroit : Gale, 1990. 401 p. : ill. (Dictionary of literary biography, v. 91). ISBN 0-8103-4571-4. **AF23**

These titles in the "Dictionary of literary biography" series provide biographical material about journalists.
PN4871.A475

Biographical dictionary of American journalism / ed. by Joseph P. McKerns. N.Y. : Greenwood, 1989. 820 p. ISBN 0-313-23818-9. **AF24**

Alphabetically arranged entries of one to two pages cover "nearly 500 persons who contributed to the development of American journalism" (*Introd.*) in the fields of newspapers, magazines, radio, and television from 1690 to the present. Each entry includes a brief bibliography. Appendixes include lists of women in journalism, minority and ethnic journalists, and winners of major awards. Subject index. PN4871.B56

Taft, William H. Encyclopedia of twentieth-century journalists. N.Y. : Garland, 1986. 408 p. (Garland reference library of the humanities, vol. 493). ISBN 0-8240-8961-8. $39.95. **AF25**

Contains biographical information on some 600 post-World War II newspaper, magazine, and television journalists. "The majority of persons here are alive" (*Introd.*) and the emphasis is on Americans. Subject index. PN4871.T34

Who's who in the press. 1st ed. (1985)– . Ayr [England] : Carrick, 1984– . Annual. ISSN 0268-165X. **AF26**

Subtitle: A biographical guide to British journalism.

The 2nd ed. (1986/87) offers brief entries for nearly 1,000 print journalists and aims to provide "a comprehensive guide to British journalism."—*Foreword.* PN5122.W43

AG

Government Publications

INTERNATIONAL

Bibliography

Guide to official publications of foreign countries / American Library Association, Government Documents Round Table. [Bethesda, Md.] : Congressional Information Service, c1990. 359 p. **AG1**

Gloria Westfall, ed. in chief.

A very useful selective, annotated bibliography of official publications issued by 157 countries that includes guides to official publications, directories, statistical sources, legislative proceedings, development plans, court reports, etc. Includes acquisition information. Arranged alphabetically by country, then by subject. Z7164.G7G83

Library resources

Directory of government document collections & librarians / Government Documents Round Table, American Library Association. Wash. : Congressional Information Service, 1987. 5th ed. ISSN 0276-959X. $32.50. **AG2**

4th ed., 1984 (*Guide* AG14).

Continues the scope and arrangement of the 4th ed.
Z1223.Z7D57

UNITED STATES

Guides

D'Aleo, Richard J. FEDfind : your key to finding federal government information : a directory of information sources, products, and services. 2nd ed. Springfield, Va. : ICUC Pr., 1986. 480 p. : ill. ISBN 0-910205-03-5. $17.95. ISBN 0-910205-02-7 (pbk.). $9.95. **AG3**

Designed to help individuals locate both products and services, and information from the federal government. Arranged by department with brief descriptions of the different branches and their services and publications. Subject and organization index. Z1223.Z7D3

Robinson, Judith Schiek. Subject guide to U.S. government reference sources. Littleton, Colo. : Libraries Unlimited, 1985. 333 p. ISBN 0-87287-496-6. $40.00. **AG4**

Rev. ed. of Sally Wynkoop's *Subject guide to government reference books*, 1972 (*Guide* AG25).

Adheres to the scope and arrangement of the previous edition. Over half the entries are new. Z1223.Z7R63

Sears, Jean L. Using government publications / by Jean L. Sears, Marilyn Moody. Phoenix : Oryx, 1985–1986. 2 v. ISBN 0-89774-094-7 (v.1). $74.00. **AG5**

Contents: v. 1, Searching by subject and agencies; v. 2, Finding statistics and using special techniques.

Aims to provide "a basic reference to the use of United States government documents."—*Introd.* Vol. 1 is divided into topical chapters (Occupations, Travel information, Genealogy, Climate, etc.), each of which includes "a suggested search strategy, a checklist of sources, and a narrative description of covered sources." Vol. 2 has chapters that describe (1) ways to find statistics related to a specific subject (population, business, crime, etc.) or (2) special techniques related to finding specific types of government publications (treaties, technical reports, etc.). Each volume has its own title and subject index. Z1223OC7S4

Zwirn, Jerrold. Congressional publications and proceedings : research on legislation, budgets, and treaties. 2nd ed. Englewood, Colo. : Libraries Unlimited, 1988. 299 p. ISBN 0-87287-642-X. $27.50. **AG6**

Rev. ed. of *Congressional publications: a research guide to legislation, budgets, and treaties* (1982).

More than a guide to congressional publications, this work attempts to "explore the relationship between the information environment and the legislative process."—*Pref.* 11 topical chapters (e.g., Legislative history, Committee reports, Federal budget) describe, in essay form, publications rising from the various avenues Congress follows in conducting its business. Appendixes include standing committee jurisdiction charts and a topical annotated list of legislative information sources. Document and subject indexes. See also Joe Morehead's *Introduction to United States public documents* (*Guide* AG21). JK1067.Z85

Bibliography

Bailey, William G. Guide to popular U.S. government publications. 2nd ed. Englewood, Colo. : Libraries Unlimited, 1990. 313 p. ISBN 0-87287-796-5. $35.00. **AG7**

Rev. ed. of LeRoy Schwarzkopf's *Guide to popular U.S. government publications* (Littleton, Colo. : Libraries Unlimited, 1986), which in turn revised Walter L. Newsome's *New guide to government publications* (*Guide* AG23).

Includes selected titles issued from June 1985 (Schwarzkopf's cutoff date) through June 1989. Adheres to the scope and arrangement of the earlier editions. Z1223.Z7B35

Government reference books. 1st ed. (1968/69)– . [Littleton, Colo.] : Libraries Unlimited, 1970– . Biennial. ISSN 0072-5188. **AG8**

For earlier editions and annotation, see *Guide* AG28.

Beginning with the 1984/85 ed., most serial titles were withdrawn and listed in LeRoy C. Schwarzkopf's *Government reference serials* (below). Z1223.Z7G68

Major studies & issue briefs of the Congressional Research Service : Cumulative index. 1916–1989. Frederick, Md. : Univ. Publication of Americas, c1989. 2 v. **AG9**

Contents: [v.1] Bibliography & supplementary indexes; [v.2] Index by subjects & names.

"The Congressional Research Service (CRS) is the department . . . [in] the Library of Congress that . . . works exclusively as a reference and research arm for members, committees, and staff of the United States Congress . . . . The index covers over 5,000 documents (most from 1975 to 1989) that are reproduced in the companion UPA microfilm collection."—*Introd.* Vol. 1 includes an annotated list of the documents (arranged in the order in which they appear on the reels) and indexes by title and report numbers. Vol. 2 is an index of names and subjects. Z733.U63C653

Schwarzkopf, LeRoy C. Government reference serials. Englewood, Colo. : Libraries Unlimited, 1988. 344 p. ISBN 0-87287-451-6. $45.00. **AG10**

" . . . a companion and supplementary guide to *Government reference books* [above]."—*Introd.* Serial titles previously listed in earlier editions (see *Guide* AG28) are now listed here. Titles published less frequently than biennially are excluded; only titles distributed to depository libraries are described. Classified arrangement under four main categories: General library reference, Social sciences, Science and technology, and Humanities. Entries, based on the latest issue of the serial available, provide complete bibliographic information and include Superintendent of Documents and *Monthly catalog* numbers, complete publishing history, and detailed annotation. Title, SuDoc class number, author, and subject indexes. Z1223.Z7S338

Catalogs and indexes

The Serial Set

United States congressional serial set catalog. 98th Congress (1983–1984)– . Wash. : Classification and Cataloging Branch, Library Division, Library Programs Service, Supt. of Docs. : For sale by U.S. Govt. Print. Off., 1988– . Biennial. ISSN 0898-1639. **AG11**

Superintendent of Documents classification: GP 3.34.

"Through the 96th Congress, this index had been issued as the *Numerical lists and schedule of volumes* [*Guide* AG55]. In 1985, the title for the records of the 97th Congress was changed to *Monthly catalog—U.S. congressional serial set supplement* [*Guide* AG53] and made part of the *Monthly catalog*. That publication was reviewed and evaluated by the Congressional Serial Set Committee, which issued its report and recommendations to the Public Printer in 1987 . . . . This catalog was prepared using bibliographic records which originally appeared in various issues of the *Monthly catalog of United States government publications*."—*Pref.* Follows the format of the traditional numerical lists, but includes detailed author, title, subject, series, and bill number indexes. Z1223.A18

Legislative branch

CIS index to U.S. Senate executive document & reports : covering documents and reports not printed in the U.S. serial set, 1817–1969. Wash. : Congressional Information Service, c1987. 2 v. ISBN 0-88692-130-9. $695.00. **AG12**

Contents: [v. 1] Reference bibliography; [v. 2] Indexes.

" . . . assembles, describes, and indexes comprehensively all [Senate executive] documents and reports from the earliest items through 1969 . . . . The majority of materials in this collection concern Senate consideration of treaties with foreign governments [including Indian tribes]."—*Introd.* The documents are listed by accession number and have brief annotations. Subject, personal name, and document and report number indexes. A companion microfiche collection, *Senate execu-*

tive documents and reports, is available; most of these items have not been previously available.   KF40.C57

●**Congressional masterfile 1** : 1789–1969 [computer file]. Bethesda, Md. : Congressional Information Service, c1988.   **AG13**

Machine-readable version of the following CIS indexes: *CIS U.S. serial set index, 1789–1969* (*Guide* AG39); *CIS U.S. congressional committee hearings index, 1833–1969* (*Guide* AG66); *CIS index to unpublished U.S. Senate committee hearings, 1823–1968* (*Supplement* AG17); *CIS index to unpublished U.S. House of Representatives committee hearings, 1833–1946* (*Supplement* AG16); *CIS index to U.S. Senate executive documents and reports, 1817–1969* (above); and *CIS U.S. congressional committee prints index, 1830–1969* (*Guide* AG67).

Available in CD-ROM, and online as *CIS* (DIALOG).

●**Congressional masterfile 2** [computer file]. Bethesda, Md. : Congressional Information Service, 1989– . **AG14**

Machine-readable version of *Index to publications of the United States Congress* (*Guide* AG64).

Coverage: 1970– . Updated quarterly. Available on CD-ROM, and online as *CIS* (DIALOG).

Consists of a retrospective disc, 1970–1988, and a current disc, 1989– .

Stubbs, Walter. Congressional committees, 1789–1982 : a checklist. Westport, Conn. : Greenwood, 1985. 210 p. (Bibliographies and indexes in law and political science, no. 6). ISBN 0-313-24539-8.   **AG15**

A listing of more than 1,500 committees, including "standing committees, select and special committees, select and special joint committees, and statutory joint committees. Exceptions to this group are honorary, ceremonial, and housekeeping committees.... Also excluded are political committees, committees of the whole, and conference committees."—*Introd.* Arranged alphabetically by keyword in the title of the committee. The entry for each committee includes beginning and ending dates; citations to the resolution or public law creating and terminating it; later names, if any; and the Superintendent of Documents number, if assigned. Contains a chronological list of committees. Subject index.   JK1029.S78

Congressional committee prints and hearings

CIS index to unpublished U.S. House of Representatives committee hearings, 1833–1936. Bethesda, Md : Congressional Information Service, c1988. 2 v. ISBN 0-88692-152-X (set).   **AG16**

Contents: v. 1, Reference bibliography; v. 2, Index.

"... provides access to some 1,400 House Committee hearings transcripts dated 1833 through 1936 ... that ... were never printed and published .... [T]ranscripts for the last fifty years are currently not available under rules of the House."—*User guide.* Vol. 1 lists the hearings in the order in which they appear in the companion set *CIS unpublished U.S. House of Representatives committee hearings on microfiche.* Vol. 2 includes subject, name (including witnesses), title, and bill number indexes.   KF40.C54

CIS index to unpublished U.S. Senate committee hearings : 18th Congress–88th Congress, 1823–1964. Bethesda, Md. : Congressional Information Service, c1986. 5 v. ISBN 0-88692-089-2 (set). $2,300.00.   **AG17**

Contents: [v. 1–2], Index by subjects and organizations; [v. 3], Index by personal names; [v. 4–5], Reference bibliography.

Lists some 7,300 unpublished hearings found in the National Archives and in the papers of former senators; texts of the hearings are available in the companion set, *CIS unpublished U.S. Senate committee hearings on microfiche.* Arranged by microfiche accession number. Information provided for

each hearing includes title, date, collation, related bill numbers, issuing committee and subcommittee, and witnesses. Separate subject, name (mainly witnesses), title, and bill number indexes.

Supplemented by: KF40.C55

CIS index to unpublished U.S. Senate committee hearings : 89th Congress–90th Congress, 1965–1968. Bethesda, Md. : Congressional Information Service, c1989. 255 p. ISBN 0-88692-174-0. $395.00.   **AG18**

Lists approximately 690 hearings.   KF40.C55

CIS U.S. congressional committee hearings index. Wash. : Congressional Information Service, 1985. 5 v. ISBN 0-88692-004-3 (set).   **AG19**

For pt. II–VIII and annotation, see *Guide* AG66.

Contents: pt. I, 23rd Congress–64th Congress (1985. 5 v.). Completes the set.   KF40.C56

Executive branch

CIS index to presidential executive orders & proclamations. Wash. : Congressional Information Service, c1987. 2 v. in 20. ISBN 0-88692-106-6 (set). $3,500.00 (per pt.).   **AG20**

Contents: Pt. 1, George Washington to Woodrow Wilson (v. 1–10); Pt. 2, Warren Harding to Ronald Reagan (v. 11–20).

KF70.A55

CIS index to presidential executive orders & proclamations : Supplement : Mar. 4, 1921 to Dec. 31, 1983, Warren Harding to Ronald Reagan. Bethesda, Md. : Congressional Information Service, 1987. 2 v.   **AG21**

Lists more than "7,400 orders and proclamations ... together with 3,500 related descriptive attachments and oversized maps acquired and filmed separately. The collection is as comprehensive and complete as it has been possible to make it based upon thorough review and screening of all key source groups of records in major federal archives and public government documents collections."—*User guide.* Each part consists of a reference bibliography, arranged in accession order (roughly chronological), giving the title, date, and other related information; and an index by subject and organizations, a chronological list of orders, an index of personal names, an index of interrelated executive orders and proclamations, and an index of site and document numbers. The "User guide" describes the various printed sources of the available texts; the texts are also available in the companion microfiche collection. The *Supplement* covers "two large series of 1921–1983 presidential pardons and miltary orders that were discovered by CIS editors subsequent to the original publication of Part II."—*User guide.*

KF70.A55

CIS index to U.S. executive branch documents, 1789–1909 : a guide to documents listed in *Checklist of U.S. public documents, 1789–1909*, not printed in the U.S. serial set. Bethesda, Md. : Congressional Information Service, c1990. v. 1. ISBN 0-88692-202-X. (In progress).   **AG22**

Contents: Pt. 1, Treasury Dept., Commerce and Labor Dept.

Indexes the *Checklist of United States public documents, 1789–1909* (*Guide* AG48) by subject, author, title, and agency. To be in 6 v. A companion microfiche set of the documents is available.   CD3030.C57

GAO masterfile, 1976–1989. Alexandria, Va. : Chadwyck-Healey, [1989?]. 15 v.   **AG23**

Kept up to date by annual supplements.

Abstracts of publications issued by the General Accounting Office, most of which are not listed in the *Monthly catalog.* Separate indexes for subject, keyword, author, title, etc. Keyed to the microfiche set of the documents available from the publisher.

§ Also available in CD-ROM format, with annual cumulations.

United States. President. Public papers of the presidents of the United States. Wash. : Office of the Federal Register, National Archives and Records Service, 1986–90. ISSN 0079-7626.   **AG24**

For full citation and annotation, see *Guide* AG74.

Contents: Ronald Reagan, 1984–July 1988. 9 v. (publ. 1986–90; in progress); George Bush, 1989. 1 v. (publ. 1990; in progress).

Superintendent of Documents classification: GS 4.113.
J80.A283

State publications

Bibliography

Dow, Susan L. State document checklists : a historical bibliography. Buffalo, N.Y. : W.S. Hein, 1990. 224 p. ISBN 0-89941-739-6.   **AG25**

" . . . serves as a reference tool for librarians who acquire materials and librarians that provide reference services."—*p. 48.* Arranged alphabetically by state, then chronologically by date covered; title index. "Sources consulted," p. [201]–210.
Z1223.5.A1D68

Guide to the publications of interstate agencies and authorities / comp. by Jack Sulzer and Roberta Palen. Chicago : Amer. Lib. Assoc., 1986. 48 p. ISBN 0-8389-0444-0. $6.00 (est.).   **AG26**

A list of the types and availability of publications issued by interstate agencies, based on the agencies included in the Council of State Goverments' *Interstate compacts and agencies* (Lexington, Ky., 1983). Arranged by broad topic with an index of agencies by states, and an index of agency names.
JK2445.I57G85

Parish, David W. A bibliography of state bibliographies, 1970–1982. Littleton, Colo. : Libraries Unlimited, c1985. 267 p. ISBN 0-87287-466-4. $37.50.   **AG27**

A bibliography of bibliographies that were issued as state documents; a high percentage of entries relate to the state in which the bibliography was published, but many items have no geographical focus or limitation. Arranged by state, then by subject categories; title and subject indexes. Includes some important pre-1970 imprints.   Z1223.5.A1P36

State blue books, legislative manuals, and reference publications : a selective bibliography / Lynn Hellebust, ed. Topeka, Kan. : Government Research Service, c1990. 142 p. ISBN 0-9615227-7-1.   **AG28**

Offers annotated citations to " . . . currently available general reference publications for each of the fifty states, as well as the District of Columbia and Puerto Rico."—*Pref.* Arranged alphabetically by state, each in four sections: Blue books and general reference publications; Legislative handbooks, manuals and directories; State government and politics texts; and Other sources (e.g., registers, telephone directories). Each citation includes a description of the item, price, publisher, address, and telephone as of summer, 1990. A bibliographic appendix provides entries for general state government reference books, directories, and periodicals. No index.

AUSTRALIA

Australian government publications [microform]. Sept. 1988– . Canberra : National Library of Australia, 1988– . ISSN 0067-1878.   **AG29**

Continues publication of the same title, 1961–87, issued on paper; (*Guide* AG94); now available only on microfiche.

Quarterly with annual cumulations.

Fiche sets arranged in 2 sequences: author/title, and subject.

Cook, John. A guide to commonwealth government information sources / John Cook, Nancy Lane, Michael Piggott. Sydney [Australia] : Pergamon Pr., 1988. 89 p. ISBN 0-08-034421-6.   **AG30**

" . . . serves as a guide to the unpublished information . . . available through Commonwealth [i.e. Australian] departments, statutory authorities and agencies. Excluded, however, is the unpublished information extracted and provided by the Parliament, the Courts, Royal Commissions and other enquiries."—*Introd.* Indexed.   Z674.5.A8C66

CANADA

Bibliography

Maillet, Lise. Provincial royal commissions and commissions of inquiry, 1867–1982 : a selective bibliography = Commissions royales provinciales et commissions d'enquête, 1867–1982 : bibliographie sélective / comp. by Lise Maillet. Ottawa : National Library of Canada, 1986. 254 p. ISBN 0-660-53123-2 (pbk.). $15.00 ($18.00 other countries).   **AG31**

For annotation, see *Supplement* CJ158.   Z1373.3.M34

CHILE

Publicaciones oficiales de Chile, 1973–1983 / dirigida por María Teresa Sanz con la colaboración de Manuel Cornejo A., Héctor Gómez F. ; compilada por Manuel Cornejo A. . . . [et al.]. Santiago, Chile : Instituto Profesional de Santiago, Escuela de Bibliotecología y Documentación, 1985. 196 p.   **AG32**

Lists over 4,000 government publications by agency. Author and agency indexes, but no detailed subject approach.
Z1709.P83

EUROPE, WESTERN

Official publications of Western Europe / ed. by Eve Johansson. London : Mansell ; Bronx, N.Y. : H.W. Wilson, 1984–1988. 2 v. : ill. ISBN 0-7201-1623-6 (v.1). $48.00. ISBN 0-7201-1662-7 (v.2).   **AG33**

Contents: v.1, Denmark, Finland, France, Ireland, Italy, Luxembourg, Netherlands, Spain, and Turkey; v.2, Austria, Belgium, Federal Republic of Germany, Greece, Norway, Portugal, Sweden, Switzerland, and United Kingdom.

Designed to give "an overview of the main publications, their indexing and bibliographic control, the languages in which they appear, and their availability."—*Pref.* Arranged by country; indexes of organizations and titles, and of subjects.

Z291.O38

FRANCE

La documentation administrative / sous la direction de Pierre Pelou ; Ministère de l'éducation nationale, de la jeunesse et des sports, Direction générale des enseignements supérieurs et de la recherche, DBMIST. Paris : La Documentation française, 1988. 268 p. ISBN 2-11-002056-3. **AG34**

Offers a survey of French government documents, discussing their organization and availability, with a chapter on the implications of the new technologies. Lacks an index.

JF1352.D625

Répertoire des publications officielles (séries et périodiques) : Administrations centrales françaises, établissements public. 1985. [Paris] : Documentation Française, 1985. 1 v. **AG35**

Supersedes *Répertoire des publications officielles : séries et périodiques* (Paris : Documentation Française, 1979–80. 3 v.); and *Répertoire des publications périodiques et de serie de l'administration française* (Paris : Documentation Française, 1973; *Guide* AG106).

Issued by the Commission de Coordination de la Documentation Administrative as a separate issue of *Bulletin signalétique d'information administrative* for April 1985.

Lists 893 periodicals issued by government ministries and other public institutions, including scientific and cultural organizations. Provides title, address of issuing agency, frequency, summary of the contents, etc. Arranged by ministry, with subject, abbreviation, agency, and title indexes.

GREAT BRITAIN

Guides

Jones, David Lewis. Debates and proceedings of the British parliaments : a guide to printed sources. London : H.M.S.O., 1986. 152 p. (House of Commons Library document, no. 16). ISBN 0-10-850615-0 (pbk). £9.10. **AG36**

Based on holdings of the House of Commons and House of Lords Libraries. Intends "to provide as complete a record as possible of the printed sources" (*Introd.*) for the debates and proceedings from 1278 to the 1980s for the British Parliament; from the 13th century to 1800 for the Parliament of Ireland; and from the 12th century to 1704 for the Parliament of Scotland. Citations to *STC*, Wing, *Eighteenth century short title catalogue*, etc., are noted. Author and title index. Z2009.J65

Bibliography

•**Catalogue of the United Kingdom official publications (UKOP)** [computer file]. Cambridge, England : Chadwyck-Healey, 1980– . **AG37**

Cumulated quarterly. Available in CD-ROM (Chadwyck-Healey).

Includes H.M.S.O. publications, non-H.M.S.O. publications of official organizations, and publications of international organizations available through H.M.S.O.

Printing for Parliament, 1641–1700 / ed. by Sheila Lambert. London : Swift Printers (Sales), 1984. 323 p. (Special series [List & Index Society], v. 20). **AG38**

A chronological list of items ordered to be printed by Parliament. "The loss of titles for the period 1641–48 is of the order of 25%. To minimise this distortion ... this list makes reference to all papers known to have been printed for parliament, whether or not copies have been found."—*p.i.* Detailed bibliographic information, including reference to available copies, is provided. Includes a checklist of titles arranged by Wing number. Z2018.P75

Catalogs and indexes

Great Britain. Her Majesty's Stationery Office. HMSO agency catalogue. 1986–87– . London : H.M.S.O., c1988– . Annual. **AG39**

Previously, 1955–64, *International organisations publications*, a supplement to the Stationery Office's *Government publications* (*Guide* AG133); 1965–1975, entitled *International organisations and overseas agencies publications*; 1976–1984, entitled *International organisations publications*; 1985, entitled *International organisations catalogue*.

" ... lists items placed on sale by HMSO ... for the British, European and international organizations for which HMSO is the United Kingdom agent."—*Introd.* Arranged alphabetically by issuing agency; author and keyword index. Z6464.I6I62

19th and 20th centuries

HMSO monthly catalogue. Feb. 1986– . London : H.M.S.O., c1986– . Monthly. ISSN 0263-7197. **AG40**

Continues: Gt. Brit. Stationery Office. *Government publications monthly list*, also entitled *Government publications of ...* (monthly, 1939–Jan. 1986; *Guide* AG135).

Cumulated by:

HMSO annual catalogue. [London] : H.M.S.O., 1986– . **AG41**

Continues: Great Britain. Stationery Office. *Government publications*, 1922–84 (*Guide* AG133).

Also available in microfiche. Z2009.G822

Cockton, Peter. Subject catalogue of the House of Commons Parliamentary papers, 1801–1900. Cambridge, England ; Alexandria, Va. : Chadwyck-Healey, 1988. 5 v. ISBN 0-85964-133-3 (set). $1,200.00. **AG42**

Contents: v. 1, Central government and administration; national finance and financial institutions; population and demography; statistics, agriculture and rural society; v. 2, Industry and industrial society; trade and commerce; transport and communication; v. 3, Law and order; local government and local finance; poverty and social administration; education; information and recreation; v. 4, Health and housing; Ireland; the churches and religious affairs; India, Ceylon, Burma and Afghanistan; v. 5, The dominions and colonies; slavery and the slave trade; defence and the armed services; foreign affairs and diplomacy.

Aims "to provide a comprehensive listing of the entire output of nineteenth century Parliamentary Papers in the form of a thematic subject catalog."—*Introd.* Earlier indexes generally exclude some areas. Offers a detailed, although somewhat confusing, classified arrangement. Titles "have been slightly shortened in some cases .... Others have been expanded by the insertion of added words, within brackets." Provides citations to both the bound set and the publisher's microfiche set. Includes an index, with cross-references, to the headings used in the classified section.

A review in the *Government publications review* 16 (Sept./Oct, 1989) : 516 concludes that "The *Subject catalogue* complements but does not replace the existing indexes to the nineteenth-century Sessional Papers .... Libraries whose research is done in this area will consider this a basic purchase."

Z2019.C63

Select lists

Ford list of British parliamentary papers, 1974–1983, together with specialist commentaries / ed. by Diana Marshallsay and Peter G. Richards ; with the assistance of Debbie A. Copping. Cambridge, U.K. : Chadwyck-Healey, c1989. 694 p.   **AG43**

Chronological successor to *Ford list of British parliamentary papers 1965–1974* (*Guide* AG144). Follows the scope and arrangement of the earlier volume.   Z2009.F66

KENYA

Kenya National Archives. A guide to government monographs, reports, and research works / Republic of Kenya, Office of the Vice-President and Ministry of Home Affairs, Department of Kenya National Archives. [Nairobi] : The Archives, 1984. 157 p.   **AG44**

In four chapters: (1) Government monographs, arranged alphabetically by title; (2) Reports and other documents from government ministries, departments, and other institutions; (3) Provincial and district annual and quarterly reports, both arranged alphabetically by department; (4) Theses, dissertations and other research reports (including works about Kenya prepared anywhere in the world), arranged alphabetically by author. Lacks an index.   Z3587.K467

MALAYSIA

Arkib Negara Malaysia. Panduan rekod-rekod kerajaan persekutuan di Arkib Negara Malaysia. [Petaling Jaya] : Arkib Negara Malaysia, 1986. 94 p.   **AG45**

Offers a survey of government documents stored at the National Archives of Malaysia issued since independence through 1982. This is a description of record groups, rather than a listing of individual titles. Arranged alphabetically by agency; indexed by keyword in agency title.   CD2291.M34A74

SAUDI ARABIA

Maʻhad al-Idārah al-ʻĀmmah (Riyadh, Saudi Arabia). Markaz al-Wathāʼiq. Qism al-Maṭbūʻāt al-Rasmīyah. al-Maṭbūʻāt al-rasmīyah fī al-Mamlakah al-ʻArabīyah al-al-Saʻūdīyah : bibliyūjrāfīyah mukhtārah min majmūʻāt Qism al-Maṭbūʻāt al-Rasmīyah fī Markaz al-Wathāʼiq. al-Riyāḍ : al-Mamlakah al-ʻArabīyah al-Saʻūdīyah, Maʻhad al-Idārah al-ʻĀmmah, al-Idārah al-ʻĀmmah lil-Maktabāt, Markaz al-Wathāʼiq, 1984. 552 p. : ill.   **AG46**

A retrospective, selective bibliography of government publications, including those issued by public companies, held by the Dept. of Official Publications of the Documentation Center, Riyadh. Arranged by agency with subject and title indexes.   Z3027.M34

SWEDEN

Statliga publikationer, årsbibliografi. 1985– . Stockholm : Riksdagsbiblioteket, 1987– . Annual. ISSN 0283-8826.   **AG47**

Added title: Swedish government publications, annual bibliography.

Continues *Årsbibliografi över Sveriges offentliga publikationer*, 1931/33–1975, (publ. 1934–79; *Guide* AG184) entitled *Sveriges statliga publikationer, bibliografi.*

Arranged by agency, then alphabetically by title. Subject and personal name indexes.   Z2629.S94

AH

Dissertations

GUIDES AND MANUALS

Gibaldi, Joseph. MLA handbook for writers of research papers / Joseph Gibaldi, Walter S. Achtert. 3rd ed. N.Y. : Modern Language Association of America, 1988. 248 p. : ill. ISBN 0-87352-379-2 (pbk.).   **AH1**

2nd ed., 1984 (*Guide* AH7).

Designed "as a supplementary text in writing courses or as a reference book for students."—*Pref.* The major change in this edition is that is includes details "on the ways that computer technology can assist students in preparing research papers" and covers "the problem of documenting nonprint sources."

§ A brief summary of this handbook, not officially endorsed by the MLA, was published by Joseph Trimmer as *A guide to MLA documentation* (Boston : Houghton Mifflin, 1989).   LB2369.G53

Stock, Molly. A practical guide to graduate research. N.Y. : McGraw-Hill, c1985. 168 p. : ill. ISBN 0-07-061583-7 (pbk.). $10.75 (est.).   **AH2**

Intended "to be used independently by graduate students and their faculty advisors (especially those in the natural or physical sciences) and as a text for graduate-level research methods courses."—*Pref.* Thesis-oriented, but includes chapters on preparing grant proposals and giving talks about research. Brief bibliography; index.   Q180.55.M4S86

Turabian, Kate L. A manual for writers of term papers, theses, and dissertations. 5th ed. rev. and exp. by Bonnie Birtwistle Honigsblum. Chicago : Univ. of Chicago Pr., 1987. 300 p. ISBN 0-226-81624-9. ISBN 0-226-81625-7 (pbk.).   **AH3**

4th ed., 1973 (*Guide* AH8).

Includes a new chapter on preparing manuscripts by computer.   LB2369.T8

BIBLIOGRAPHY

Bibliography of Bibliography

Reynolds, Michael M. Guide to theses and dissertations : an international bibliography of bibliographies. Rev. and enl. ed. Phoenix : Oryx, 1985. 263 p. ISBN 0-89774-149-8. $125.00. **AH4**

lst ed., 1975 (*Guide* AH11).

Updates the first edition through 1983 and most of 1984, and follows the plan of the previous ediiton. Z5053.A1R49

Austria

Gesamtverzeichnis österreichischer Dissertationen. [v.]1 (1966)–[v.]19 (1984). Wien : Verlag Notring der Wissenschaftliche Verbände Österreichs, 1967–1989. Annual. ISSN 0072-4165. **AH5**

A classified index to Austrian dissertations, citing entries in the annual bibliography (see *Guide* AH28). Includes subject indexes for names and places. Authors and complete titles are not given. Z 5055.A9 G389

Brazil

Bibliografia brasileira : catalogo de teses : Suplemento ao vol. 6 / Biblioteca Nacional. Rio de Janeiro : A Biblioteca, 1989. 1 v. **AH6**

A list, arranged alphabetically by broad subject, then by author, of social science and history dissertations written at Brazilian institutions from the early 1970s through the mid-1980s. Author/institution, title, and subject indexes. Z1671.B52

Canada

Robitaille, Denis. Theses in Canada : a bibliographic guide = Thèses au Canada : guide bibliographique / Denis Robitaille and Joan Waiser. Ottawa : National Library of Canada, 1986. 72 p. ISBN 0-660-53228-X (pbk.). **AH7**

A list of sources to help identify Canadian theses. Includes general bibliographies, guides published by individual universities, and subject bibliographies, including periodical articles. Author and detailed subject indexes. Z5055.C2R63

Germany

Gesamtverzeichnis deutschsprachiger Hochschulschriften (GVH), 1966–1980 / hrsg. von Willi Gorzny. München ; N.Y. : K.G. Saur, 1984–87. v. 1–24. ISBN 3-598-30600-8 (set). (In progress). **AH8**

Contents: v. 1–24, A–Z, author listing.

A list of dissertations and theses written in German compiled from dissertation lists from Germany, other countries in Western and Eastern Europe, Great Britain, the U.S., and Canada. Vols. 26–40, indexes, not yet published. Z5055.G4G47

Kössler, Franz. Verzeichnis von Programm-Abhandlungen deutscher, österreichischer und schweizerischer Schulen der Jahre 1825–1918 : alphabetisch geordnet nach Verfassern. München ; N.Y. : K.G. Saur, 1987. 4 v. ISBN 3-598-10665-3. **AH9**

A list, arranged alphabetically by author, of more than 55,000 scholarly pamphlets written in German, Austrian, and Swiss schools. No subject access. Z2221.K67x

Great Britain

The BRITS index : an index to the British theses collections, 1971–1987 held at the British Document Supply Centre and London University. Godstone, Surrey : British Theses Service, c1989. 3 v. ISBN 0-576-40018-1 (set). **AH10**

Contents: v. 1, Author index; v. 2, Subject index; v. 3, Title index.

Lists doctoral dissertations available from the British Library Document Supply Centre. Z5055.G69B74

Index to theses with abstracts accepted for higher degrees by the universities of Great Britain and Ireland and the Council for National Academic Awards. v. 35, pt. 1 ([Nov. 1986])– . London : Aslib, c1986– . Quarterly. ISSN 0073-6066. **AH11**

Continues Aslib's *Index to theses accepted for higher degrees ...* (see *Guide* AH61), assumes its numbering, and follows its arrangement and coverage. Now appears quarterly and includes abstracts. The quarterly author and subject indexes do not cumulate. Z5055.G69A84

Hungary

Kállay, István. Kandidátusi és doktori disszertációk. Budapest : Magyar Tudományos Akadémia Könyvtára, 1981–88. nos. 12,19. **AH12**

For earlier numbers and annotation, see *Guide* AH68–69.

Contents: no. 12 (Feb. 1, 1975–Dec. 31, 1979); no. 19 (Jan. 1, 1980–Dec. 31, 1984).

Volumes in this series are numbered issues of *Magyar Tudományos Akadémia Könyvtára Kézirattárának Katalógusai*. Z6621.M25125

India

Bibliography of doctoral dissertations. 1975/76– . New Delhi : Association of Indian Universities. **AH13**

An annual list of doctoral dissertations accepted by Indian universities, issued in separate volumes for Natural & applied sciences and Social sciences & humanities. Classed arrangement with subject and author indexes. Z5055.I57B5

Morocco

Répertoire des thèses et mémoires, 1953–1984. Rabat : Association des auteurs marocains pour la publication, 1987. 374 p. **AH14**

Lists dissertations and theses from Moroccan institutions. Arranged by institution, then by faculty. Separate author indexes for theses written in Arabic and those in European languages. No detailed subject approach. Z5055.M73R46

Nigeria

Nigerian universities dissertation abstracts (NUDA) : a comprehensive listing of dissertations and theses undertaken in the Universities of Nigeria / [ed., Stephen A. Osiobe.]. Port Harcourt : Univ. of Port Harcourt Pr., c1989. 1 v. (In progress).   **AH15**
  Contents: v. 1, 1960–1975.
  A classified listing with author and subject indexes.

  Z5055.N83N5

Ofori, Patrick E. Retrospective index to Nigerian doctoral dissertations and masters theses, 1895–1980 / Patrick E. Ofori, Stephen A. Amune. Zaria : Gaskiya Corp., 1984. v. 1. ISBN 978-194-000-4 (v. 1). (In progress).   **AH16**
  Contents: v.1, Science and technology.
  Attempts to list by broad subject categories all dissertations and theses accepted by Nigerian universities and those by Nigerians in American and British universities. Covers all Nigerian universities through 1977, and foreign and selected Nigerian universities through 1980. Author and detailed subject indexes. Vol.2, Humanities and social sciences, not yet published.

  Z5053.O37

Philippines

Philippines. National Science Development Board. Compilation of graduate theses prepared in the Philippines. Manila : National Science Development Board, 1980. v. 3. (In progress).   **AH17**
  Contents: v. 3, 1966–69.
  Recent Library of Congress cataloging now designates the 1913–60 and 1961–65 compilations (*Guide* AH81) as v. [1–2]. Vol. 3 follows the subject arrangement of the earlier volumes and includes an author index.
  § The 1988 *Philippine national bibliography* (*Guide* AA1022) lists an *Annotated bibliography of theses and dissertations written during the ten year period May 1973 to April 1983* (Manila? : Philippine Association for Graduate Education). That publication was not available for examination. Maria Nena R. Mata and Clarita S. Barbosa edited a *Compilation of graduate theses, 1983–1984* for the Philippine Association of Academic and Research Libraries, Readers' Services Group (Manila : The Libraries[?], 1986. 131 p.).
  Beginning in 1985, the *Philippine national bibliography* is published in two parts; Pt. 2, Theses and dissertations, follows a classed arrangement with author/title and subject indexes. (Pt. 2 for 1985 was published 1989.)   Z5055.P47P47

Romania

Teze de doctorat : lucrări susţinute in ţară de autori romani şi străini şi lucrări susţinute in străinătate de autori romani / [lucrare elaborată in cadrul Serviciului de Informare şi Documentare condus de Ileana Băncilă ; redactor responsabil, Silvia Maruţă]. Bucureşti : Biblioteca Centrală Universitară Bucureşti, 1973–1982. v. 2–3.   **AH18**
  For compilation covering 1948–70, see *Guide* AH83.
  Compiltions have been published covering 1974–76 and 1977–79.   Z5055.R64B878

Rwanda

Université nationale du Rwanda. Centre de bibliographie rwandaise. Bibliographie signalétique des écrits académiques disponibles au Centre de bibliographie rwandaise : thèses, mémoires et essais de 2è cycle. [Butare] : Université national du Rwanda, Bibliothèque centrale, [1985]. 108 leaves.   **AH19**
  Supersedes the 1982 publication with the same title.
  Lists dissertations and other academic theses accepted by Rwandan institutions, about Rwanda and its neighbors, or written by Rwandans in foreign universities from 1976 through 1984. Pt. 1 is a listing by subject; pt. 2 a chronological listing. Includes an author index.   Z3721.U54

AJ

Biography

GENERAL WORKS

Cambridge biographical dictionary / gen. ed., Magnus Magnusson, assistant ed., Rosemary Goring. Cambridge ; N.Y. : Cambridge Univ. Pr., c1990. 1 v. ISBN 0-521-39518-6.   **AJ1**
  Rev. ed. of *Chambers's biographical dictionary*, 1969 (*Guide* AJ31).
  "Published in the U.K. under the title *Chambers's biographical dictionary*"—verso t.p.
  "One of our priorities for this edition was to broaden the work's international coverage. We have also focused far more attention on women, at the same time giving greater prominence to 20th century figures and to personalities from more popular spheres such as sports, media, and jazz."—*Pref.* Some names have been dropped from the earlier edition, but this volume "contains a third more entries than previously."

  CT103.C4

Bibliography

Graves, Diane J. Biographical sources : a guide to dictionaries and reference works / by Diane J. Cimbala, Jennifer Cargill, and Brian Alley. Phoenix : Oryx, 1986. 146 p. ISBN 0-89774-136-6.   **AJ2**
  A classified, annotated listing of English-language biographical sources. Author/title/subject index.   Z5301.G72

Jarboe, Betty. Obituaries : a guide to sources. 2nd ed. Boston : G.K. Hall, 1989. 362 p. ISBN 0-8161-0483-2.   **AJ3**
  1st ed., 1982 (*Guide* AJ4).
  Adheres to the arrangement of the 1st ed., more than doubling the number of sources listed.   Z5305.U5J37

Indexes

Internationaler Nekrolog. 1 (1982)– . Pullach : W. Gorzny, 1984– . Annual. **AJ4**

"Mit einem ausführlichen Pressespiegel vom Nachrufen aus deutschsprachigen Zeitungen und Zeitschriften."—*t.p.*

Persons who died during the year of coverage are listed alphabetically in the "Totenliste," with a biographical note, birth and death dates, and references to obituaries appearing in German newspapers, magazines, and some scholarly journals. Selected obituaries are reproduced in the second part of the volume. Geographical and occupational indexes. CT159.I57

Ireland, Norma Olin. Index to women of the world from ancient to modern times : a supplement. Metuchen, N.J. : Scarecrow, 1988. 774 p. ISBN 0-8108-2092-7. **AJ5**

For basic volume and annotation, see *Guide* AJ16.

Analyzes some 380 collective biographies published from 1971 to about 1985. Z7963.B6I73

Lobies, Jean-Pierre. IBN : Index bio-bibliographicus notorum hominum / edidit Jean-Pierre Lobies, François-Pierre Lobies adiuvante. Osnabrück : Biblio Verlag, 1984–91. v. C, I, 29–30; III, 3–4. (In progress). **AJ6**

For earlier vols. and complete annotation, see *Guide* AJ18.

Edited 1990– by Otto and Wolfram Zeller.

Contents: Pars C, *Corpus alphabeticum* I, Sectio generalis, v. 32–50, Carafa, G.G.–DeConinckx, S. Vols. 29–30 are designated "Supplementum II," Bang–Canelli; "Supplementum III" appears in v. 44–47 and provides additional listings for A Beckett through Czoerning von Czernhausen. Vols. 3–4 (E–Z and Suppl.) of Subsection 3, Sectio armeniaca were publ. 1983–87.

Additional lists of sources (supplements to Pars B) appear in v. 23–25, and v. 40 of Pars C. Z5301.L7

Obituary index. 1988– . Westport, Conn. : Meckler, 1989– . Annual. ISSN 1044-8659. $85.00. **AJ7**

Has companion publication: *New York times obituary index.*

"This volume indexes all obituaries (exclusive of 'death notices') in . . . the *Atlanta constitution, Boston globe, Chicago tribune, Los Angeles times*, the *New York times*, the *Times* (London), and the *Washington post*."—*Introd.*, 1988. CT120.O18

INTERNATIONAL

Biographical dictionary of modern European radicals and socialists / ed. by David Nicholls and Peter Marsh. Sussex : Harvester Pr. ; N.Y. : St. Martin's, 1988. v. 1. ISBN 0-312-01968-8. $30.00 (v. 1). (In progress). **AJ8**

Contents: v. 1, 1780–1815.

A companion to Joseph O. Baylen and Norbert J. Gossman's *Biographical dictionary of modern British radicals* (*Guide* AJ221). Offers two- to three-page signed articles with brief bibliographies on 187 individuals, the majority from France, "who wished to change existing economic, social and political structures by political action and/or theoretical criticism."—*Introd.* HN380.Z9R32

The Continuum dictionary of women's biography / comp. and ed., Jennifer S. Uglow ; assistant ed. on first edition (for science, mathematics, and medicine), Frances Hinton. New expanded ed. N.Y. : Continuum, 1989. 621 p. : ill. ISBN 0-8264-0417-0. **AJ9**

1st ed., 1962 (*Guide* AJ34) had title: *The international dictionary of women's biography.*

Adds some 250 entries, updates entries on contemporary women, and deletes "only a handful."—*Note on 2nd ed.* Published in England by Macmillan as *The Macmillan dictionary of women's biography.* CT3202.C66

Great lives from history. Twentieth century series / ed. by Frank N. Magill. Pasadena, Calif. : Salem Pr., c1990. 5 v. (2527 p.). ISBN 0-89356-565-2 (set). $325.00. **AJ10**

Offers 469 signed articles on 475 significant historical figures as diverse as Adenauer, Akhmatova, Arafat, and Atatürk. For each, a brief note giving dates and facts about career is followed by an essay of about one to three pages on early life and "life's work." Each essay ends with an annotated listing of five or six books. Indexes : names covered (with cross-references), fields or professions, geographical areas. CT120.G69

Nobel prize winners : an H.W. Wilson biographical dictionary / ed., Tyler Wasson ; consultants, Gert H. Brieger . . . [et al.]. N.Y. : H.W. Wilson, 1987. 1165 p. : ports. ISBN 0-8242-0756-4. **AJ11**

Contains "profiles of all 566 men, women, and institutions that have received the Nobel Prize between 1901 and 1986."—*Pref.* The two- to three-page essays, which have a photograph of the recipient, include a list of selected writings and a brief bibliography of secondary sources. "Nobel Prize winners by prize category and year," p. xii–xix. AS911.N9N59

Webster's new biographical dictionary. Springfield, Mass. : Merriam-Webster, c1988. 1130 p. ISBN 0-87779-543-6. **AJ12**

Eds. before 1983 entitled *Webster's biographical dictionary* (*Guide* AJ46).

A pronouncing dictionary with brief factual entries; editions published from 1983 do not include living persons. The 1988 edition lists some 30,000 names, and has greatly expanded the coverage of Africans and Asians. CT103.W4

Windrow, Martin. A concise dictionary of military biography : the careers and campaigns of 200 of the most important military leaders / by Martin Windrow & Francis K. Mason. London : Windrow & Greene, 1990. 1 v. ISBN 0-471-53441-2. **AJ13**

1st ed., 1975.

Publ. in U.S. : N.Y. : Wiley, c1991.

Offers one- to four-page biographies. No sources cited. U51.W53

Contemporary

Contemporary authors autobiography series. v. 1– . Detroit : Gale, c1984– . Irregular. ISSN 0748-0636. **AJ14**

PN453.C63

Contemporary authors bibliographical series. v. 1–. Detroit : Gale, c1986–1989. Irregular. ISSN 0887-3070. **AJ15**

Two spin-offs of the "Contemporary authors" series (*Guide* AJ48–51). Z6519.C64

Current biography. Cumulated index, 1940–1985 / ed. by Mary E. Kiffer. N.Y. : H.W. Wilson, c1986. 125 p. **AJ16**

For series and annotation, see *Guide* AJ52.

Supersedes the 1940–70 cumulated index.

Newsmakers. 1988, issue 2– . Detroit : Gale, c1988– . Three issues yearly, with an annual cumulation. ISSN 0899-0417. $70.00. **AJ17**

Subtitle: The people behind today's headlines.

Previously entitled *Contemporary newsmakers*, 1985–88, issue 1.

Each quarterly issue offers some 50 two- to three-page biographies, with brief bibliographies; each annual volume includes about 200 biographies. The nationality, occupation, subject, and names indexes in the annual volumes cumulate all previous years. A review in *ARBA* 18 (1987): 14 notes the similarities between this publication and *Current biography* (*Guide* AJ52) and concludes that "Librarians who already subscribe to *CB* will need to weigh very carefully the advantages of securing coverage for some additional personalities."   CT120.C663

Répertoire international des médiévistes = International directory of medievalists. 6th ed. Paris; N.Y.: Saur, 1987. 2 v. (1259 p.). ISBN 3-598-10683-1.   **AJ18**
For annotation, see *Supplement* DA52.   D112.R512

Bibliography

Zubatsky, David S. Jewish autobiographies and biographies: an international bibliography of books and dissertations in English. N.Y.: Garland, 1989. 370 p. (Garland reference library of the humanities, vol. 722). ISBN 0-8240-5643-4.   **AJ19**
A listing of autobiographies and biographies of Jews, including converts to Judaism, living from the 1st century CE to the present. Arranged alphabetically by biographee. Topical index.   Z6374.B5Z78

UNITED STATES

American biographical archive: a one-alphabet cumulation of almost 400 of the most important English-language biographical reference works on the United States and Canada originally published between the 18th and the early 20th centuries / managing ed., Laureen Baillie; ed., Gerry Easter. Worters [microform]. London: Bowker-Saur Ltd.; N.Y.: K.G. Saur, [1986?-1990]. 1842 microfiches: negative, ill. ISBN 0-86291-381-0 (set).   **AJ20**
Reproduces in one alphabetical sequence entries from 367 biographical works published from the earliest period to the early 20th century; does not include the *Dictionary of American biography*. A printed index is in preparation.

American reformers / ed., Alden Whitman. N.Y.: H.W. Wilson, 1985. 930 p.: ports. ISBN 0-8242-0705-X. $65.00.   **AJ21**
For annotation, see *Supplement* CC24.   CT215.A67

Black biographical dictionaries, 1790–1950 [microform]. Alexandria, Va.: Chadwyck-Healey Inc., 1987. 1068 microfiches: ill.   **AJ22**
Sponsored by the W.E.B. DuBois Institute for Afro-American Research at Harvard University, the microfiches reproduce some 300 American collective biographies published before 1951. "We have also included all separately published books or pamphlets, whether histories, handbooks, yearbooks, or other works . . . that have an identifiable chapter, section, or appendix devoted to collective biographies . . . . We have also sought to include all variant editions of each title where different biographical sketches are included or new information is given."—*Introd. to the Index.*
Indexed by:

Black biography, 1790–1950: a cumulative index / editors, Randall K. Burkett, Nancy Hall Burkett, Henry Louis Gates, Jr. Alexandria, Va.: Chadwyck-Healey, 1991. 3 v. ISBN 0-89887-085-2.   **AJ23**
Contents: v. 1–2, A–Z; v. 3, Indexes.
An alphabetical listing of all African Americans included in the collective biographies reproduced in the above collection. (The editors included the names of individuals when it could not be determined that they were African Americans.) Provides dates, when available, other brief biographical facts, and cita-

tions to the microfiche collection. A list of sources may be found at the beginning of v. 3. Includes indexes by place of birth, by occupation, and by religion, and an index of women.   Z1361.N39B52

Concise dictionary of American biography. 4th ed. complete to 1970. N.Y.: Scribner's, c1990. 1536 p. ISBN 0-684-19188-1. $125.00.   **AJ24**
3rd ed., 1980 (*Guide* AJ64).
Extends the coverage of the 3rd ed. through the 8th suppl. of the *DAB*. Adheres to the form of the previous edition, but adds an occupational index.   E176.D564

Dictionary of American biography. Supplement eight: with an index guide to the supplements / John A. Garraty, ed. N.Y.: Scribner, 1988. v. 8. ISBN 0-684-15054-9 (Suppl. 3). $45.00.   **AJ25**
For earlier volumes and annotation, see *Guide* AJ63.
Contents: v. 8, 1966–70.   E176.D563

Dictionary of American biography. Comprehensive index: complete through supplement eight. N.Y.: Scribner, c1990. 1001 p. ISBN 0-684-19114-8. $80.00.   **AJ26**
Supersedes the 1937 index (*Guide* AJ63).
Contains 6 separate indexes: (1) Names of subjects of biographies, with authors; (2) Contributors, with subjects of their articles; (3) Birthplaces, arranged alphabetically by (a) states, and (b) foreign countries; (4) Schools and colleges attended by persons included in the dictionary; (5) Occupations; (6) Topics.   E176.D563

Mullaney, Marie Marmo. Biographical directory of the governors of the United States, 1983–1988. Westport, Conn.: Meckler, c1989. 398 p.: ill. ISBN 0-88736-177-3. $55.00.   **AJ27**
Continues *Biographical directory of the governors of the United States, 1789–1978* and its suppl. covering the years 1978–83 (*Guide* AJ62). Offers two- to four-page biographies with brief bibliographies and a photograph. Arranged by state with an index of names.   JK2447.M86

Contemporary

Who's who among Hispanic Americans. 1st ed. (1991–92)– . Detroit: Gale, 1991– . Biennial. ISSN 1052-7354. $89.95.   **AJ28**
The 1st ed. provides information "on more than 5,000 of today's prominent Hispanic leaders."—*Pref.* Indexes by occupation and ethnic/culture heritage.

AFRICA

Lipschutz, Mark R. Dictionary of African historical biography / Mark R. Lipschutz & R. Kent Rasmussen. 2nd ed., expanded and updated. Berkeley: Univ. of California Pr., c1986. 328 p. ISBN 0-520-05179-3. $42.00. ISBN 0-520-06611-1 (pbk.). $12.95.   **AJ29**
1st ed., 1978 (*Guide* AJ104).
Provides biographical information and brief bibliographies for major figures, primarily political, from Africa south of the Sahara, including South Africa, from the earliest period. Besides updating and revising many of the entries in the 1st ed., the authors have included African leaders, 1960–80, in a supplement, p. 258–290. Includes a bibliography of secondary sources, a subject index, and a name index.   DT352.6.L56

ALGERIA

Stora, Benjamin. Dictionnaire biographique de militants nationalistes algériens : E.N.A, P.P.A., M.T.L.D., 1926–1954. Paris : Harmattan, c1985. 404 p., [8] p. of plates : ill. **AJ30**

Offers biographical information ranging from one paragraph to several pages for Algerian nationalists active 1926–54 who held offices in the E.N.A., the P.P.A., or the M.T.L.D., the major political organizations of the Algerian independence movement. Divided into three parts: (1) those active in France; (2) those active in Algeria; and (3) officers of the P.P.A.-M.T.L.D.; then subdivided into other parts. Within each subdivision, entries are arranged alphabetically under the most commonly used name or pseudonym. Sources of information are provided for each entry. Includes a bibliography of archival and secondary sources, p. 365–382. Indexes by biographee and by other names mentioned in the entries. DT294.7.A1S76

ARAB NATIONS

Auchterlonie, Paul. Arabic biographical dictionaries : a summary guide and bibliography. Durham : Middle East Libraries Committee, 1987. 60 p. (Middle East Libraries Committee research guides, 2.). **AJ31**

Offers a classified listing of "the best-known, fullest and most useful biographical dictionaries" (*p. 1*) for the classical and modern periods. Author, editor, translator, and title index. DS39.2.A2A93

ARGENTINA

Nuevo diccionario biografico argentino : (1750–1930) / Vicente Osvaldo Cutolo. Buenos Aires : Editorial Elche, 1985. v. 7. **AJ32**

For earlier vols. and annotation, see *Guide* AJ107.

Contents: v.7, Sc–Z. Completes the set. Note that v. 6 rather than v. 5 covered through Sa. CT653.C87

AUSTRALIA

Australian dictionary of biography. [Melbourne] : Melbourne Univ. Pr. ; London ; N.Y. : Cambridge Univ. Pr., [1986]–1990. v. 10–12. (In progress). **AJ33**

For v. 1–9 and annotation, see *Guide* AJ115.

Gen. ed., v. 1–6. Douglas Pike; v. 7–10, Bede Nairn, Geoffrey Serle; v. 12, John Ritchie.

Contents: v. 10–12, 1891–1939, Lat–Z.

A cumulative list of corrigenda for v.1–6 was issued with v.7; additional lists were issued with each successive volume. An index is promised in 1991 and four volumes "covering those whose *floruit* was after 1939 and who died before 1981 will be published subsequently."—*Pref., v.12.* CT2802.A95

Gibbney, H. J. A biographical register, 1788–1939 : notes from the name index of the *Australian dictionary of biography* / comp. and ed. by H.J. Gibbney and Ann G. Smith. Canberra : Australian Dictionary of Biography, Australian National Univ., 1987. 2 v. ISBN 0-7315-0104-7 (set). **AJ34**

Contains brief biographical information and citations to further sources for individuals about whom the staff of the *Australian dictionary of biography* (above) and found material, but who were not included in that work. "Readers must be cautioned against taking the *Biographical register* entries as fully researched statements . . . rather they should be used as the basis for individual research."—*Introd.* Includes an occupational index. CT2802.G53

AUSTRIA

Kleindel, Walter. Das grosse Buch der Österreicher : 4500 Personendarstellungen in Wort und Bild : Namen, Daten, Fakten / zusammengestellt von Walter Kleindel unter Mitarbeit von Hans Veigl. Wien : Kremayr & Scheriau, c1987. 615 p. : ill. (some col.). ISBN 3-218-00455-1. **AJ35**

A lavishly illustrated dictionary of Austrians, as well as other nationals who lived and worked in Austria, in all fields, from the earliest period to the present day. Many of the entries are quite brief, but some run to several columns. Many cite additional sources. CT905.K57

Neue österreichische Biographie ab 1815. Wien : Amalthea-Verlag, 1987. Bd. 22 : ports. ISBN 3-85002-075-4. **AJ36**

For earlier vols. and annotation, see *Guide* AJ119.

Contents: Bd. 22. CT912.N4

Österreichisches biographisches Lexikon 1815–1950 / Hrsg. von der Österreichischen Akademie der Wissenschaften unter der Leitung von Leo Santifaller, bearb. von Eva Obermeyer-Marnach. Graz : H. Böhlaus Nachf., 1984–90. Lfg. 41–46 : 24 cm. (In progress). **AJ37**

For earlier vols. and annotation, see *Guide* AJ120.

Contents: Bd.9–10¹ (Lfg. 41–46), Rázus–Scheu. CT903.O4

BELGIUM

Académie royale des sciences, des lettres et des beaux-arts de Belgique. Biographie nationale. Bruxelles : H. Thiry-van Buggenhoudt, 1984–86. v. 43²–44. (In progress). **AJ38**

For earlier vols. and annotations, see *Guide* AJ124.

Contents: v. 43²–44 (Suppl. 15²–16).

Each supplementary vol. is an A–Z arrangement. CT1163.A2

CANADA

McMann, Evelyn de R. *Canadian who's who* index, 1898–1984 : incorporating *Canadian men and women of the time.* Toronto ; Buffalo : Univ. of Toronto, c1986. 528 p. ISBN 0-8020-4633-9. $125.00. **AJ39**

Provides a cumulated index to biographical sketches found in *Canadian who's who (Guide* AJ149), 1910–84, together with those appearing in the 1898 and 1912 editions of H. J. Morgan's *Canadian men and women of the time.* F1033.C23

CARIBBEAN

The directory of Caribbean personalities in Britain and North America / ed., Roy Dickson. Kingston, Jamaica : Gleaner Co., 1985. 333 p., [1] leaf of plates : map, ports. ISBN 976-612-000-5.   **AJ40**
Based entirely on information provided by the biographees, the sketches include brief biographical information and a current address. Limited to individuals from the English-speaking islands. Divided into sections for those living in Britain, in Canada, and in the U.S. Lacks an index.   CT366.D57

CHINA

Contemporary

Bartke, Wolfgang. Who's who in the People's Republic of China. 3rd ed. München ; N.Y. : K.G. Saur, 1991. 2 v. : ports. ISBN 3-598-10771-4.   **AJ41**
1st ed., 1981 (*Guide* AJ162); 2nd ed., 1987.
" . . . with more than 2,400 portraits."—*t.p.*
"A publication of the Institute of Asian Affairs, Hamburg."—*verso t.p.*
" . . . contains 4,120 biographies and includes only 40% of the contents of the 2nd ed." (*Pref.*)   DS779.28.B37

Who's who in China. Current leaders / comp. by the Editorial Board of *Who's who in China* = [Chung-kuo jen ming ta tz'u tien. Hsien jen tang cheng chün ling tao jen wu chüan / "Chung-kuo jen ming ta tz'u tien" pien chi pu pien]. Beijing : Foreign Languages Pr. : China International Book Trading Corp. [distributor], c1989. 1126 p. : ill. ISBN 0-8351-2352-9. ISBN 7-119-01093-X.   **AJ42**
In English and Chinese.
Offers biographies and photographs of more than 2,100 "current senior officials at the central level and in the provinces, municipalities and autonomous regions."—*Publishers' note.* Each entry provides birth date, present position, and career summary; current addresses are not listed. Includes an appendix of major organizations and their leading officials, p. 1037–1078.   DS779.28.W46

CZECHOSLOVAKIA

Biographisches Lexikon zur Geschichte der böhmischen Länder / hrsg. im Auftrag des Collegium Carolinum von Heribert Sturm. München : R. Oldenbourg, 1984–89. Bd. 2⁹–3⁵. ISBN 3-486-44051-9. (In progress).   **AJ43**
For earlier vols. and annotation, see *Guide* AJ177.
Contents: Bd.2, Lfg.9 (completes the vol.)–Bd.3, Lfg.5, Me–Re.   CT933.B56

Slovenský biografický slovník : od roku 833 do roku 1990 / [hlavná redakcia Vladimír Mináč, hlavný redaktor . . . et al.]. Martin : Matica slovenská, 1986–1990. v. 1–4. (In progress).   **AJ44**
Contents: v. 1–4, A–Q.
Introductory material in Slovak, Russian, English, and German.
Based on the archives of the Biographical Institute of the Matica Slovenská, this work offers articles, varying in length from one paragraph to several columns, on "the life and work of the personalities of national importance, closely concerning

Slovakia from the period of the Great Moravian Empire till the present from all branches of material and spiritual culture, political, social and economic life . . . . [I]t includes Slovak personalities who were active in Slovakia or abroad, as well as representatives of other nations who lived in Slovakia and played an important role."—*Introd.* Includes citations to secondary and archival sources.   CT'945.S56S55

DENMARK

Dansk biografisk leksikon. 3. Udg. bredaktør Sv. Cedergreen Bech. København : Gyldendal, 1984. v. 15–16. ISBN 87-00-05551-4. ISBN 87-00-05552-2 (pbk.).   **AJ45**
For earlier vols. and annotation, see *Guide* AJ181a.
Contents: v. 15–16, Treschow–Aastrup, Suppl., Register. Completes the set.
In addition to a supplement (p. 249–352), v. 16 includes a list of additions and corrections, indexes of contributors and names (including references to other principal Danish biographical dictionaries), and a chronological index.
                                                     CT1263.D33

DOMINICAN REPUBLIC

Clase, Pablo. 50 biografías de figuras dominicanas. Santo Domingo, R.D. : Libreros Dominicanos Unidos, 1990. 241 p. : ill. (Colección Dominicanos célebres, t. 3).
                                                     AJ46
Offers two- to three-page biographies of living persons. Many of the biographies were originally published in the magazine *Hoy* and the newspaper *Listin diario.*   CT542.C57

Personalidades dominicanas. 1988–89– . Santo Domingo, República Dominicana : Molina Morillo & Asociados, [1989?]– .   **AJ47**
Provides brief biographies, but no current addresses, for individuals in all fields living at the time of compilation.
                                                     CT542.P47

ECUADOR

Pérez Pimentel, Rodolfo. Diccionario biográfico del Ecuador. [Guayaquil, Ecuador] : Litografía e Imp. de la Universidad de Guayaquil, 1987–[1988]. v. 1–5. (In progress).   **AJ48**
Contains two- to three-page essays, most of which previously appeared in Ecuadorian newspapers, of individuals from all areas and periods of Ecuadorian life; no living people are included. Each volume is arranged alphabetically; v. 5 includes a cumulative index, p. ii–xii.   CT712.D53

EUROPE, EASTERN

Who's who in the socialist countries of Europe / ed. by Juliusz Stroynowski. München ; N.Y. : K.G. Saur, 1989. 3 v. (lx, 1367 p.). ISBN 3-598-10636-X (set).   **AJ49**
Subtitle: A biographical encyclopedia of more than 12,600 leading personalities in Albania, Bulgaria, Czechoslovakia, German Democratic Republic, Hungary, Poland, Romania, Yugoslavia.

A companion to Jeanne Vronskaya's *A biographical dictionary of the Soviet Union, 1917–1988* (*Supplement* AJ99).

Offers brief entries for "individuals from the spheres of party, government, military, diplomacy, economics, sciences, literature, religion, art and press."—*Pref.* "Name index arranged by country," *p. xv–lx.* CT1195.W46

FRANCE

Archives biographiques françaises / [ed. by Susan Bradley] [microform]. London : Bowker-Saur Ltd., c1988–1990. 1200 microfiches : negative, ill. ISBN 0-86291-453-1 (silver : set). **AJ50**
Reproduces in a single alphabet entries from nearly 200 biographical sources published from the earliest time to 1914.

Dictionnaire de biographie française / sous la direction de J. Balteau . . . M. Barroux . . . M. Prévost . . . avec le concours de nombreux collaborateurs. Paris : Letouzey et Ané, 1984–90. v. 16^3–18^2. (In progress). **AJ51**
For earlier vols. and annotation, see *Guide* AJ194.
Contents: v.16^3–18^2, Goislard de Monsabert–Jauberthou.
CT143.D5

Dictionnaire des maréchaux de France : du Moyen Age à nos jours / coordination de Geneviéve Maze-Sencier ; avec la collaboration de Christophe Brun . . . [et al.] ; introduction de Joseph Valynseele. [Paris] : Perrin, c1988. 452 p., [32] p. of plates : ports. (some col.). ISBN 2-262-00546-X. 290F. **AJ52**
Offers sketches of some 350 military figures; includes brief bibliographies. DC44.5.D53

Fierro, Alfred. Bibliographie analytique des biographies collectives imprimées de la France contemporaine : 1789–1985. Paris : Libr. H. Champion, 1986. 376 p. (Bibliothèque de l'Ecole des hautes études, IVe section, Sciences historiques et philologiques, fasc. 330.). ISBN 2-85203-021-7. 380F. **AJ53**
A bibliography of collective biographies of French figures of the 1789–1985 period. Works of broader chronological scope are included if they extend to "contemporary" figures; those of international coverage are excluded if less than 25 % of the entries are for French persons; and each work must include three or more biographies. More than 2,500 citations, many with brief descriptive notes, are arranged in three main sections: (1) general works of collective biography subdivided by period; (2) biographical works grouped by profession (with chronological and other subdivisions as appropriate); and (3) works of local and regional coverage. Index of authors and titles. AS162.B6

Hommes et destins : dictionnaire biographique d'outre-mer. Paris : Académie des sciences d'outre-mer, 1984–89. v. 5–9. ISBN 2-900098-03-3 (v. 4). **AJ54**
For v. 1–4 and annotation, see *Guide* AJ196.
Contents: v. 5–9. Completes the set.
Vol. 5 covers Africa and the French West Indies; v. 6, Asia; v. 7, Northern Africa; v. 8, Colonial governors, administrators, and magistrates; and v. 9, Africa south of the Sahara. Each volume has a cumulative index. CT1014.H65

GERMANY

Deutsches biographisches Archiv : eine Kumulation aus 254 der wichtigsten biographischen Nachschlagewerke für den deutschen Bereich bis zum Ausgang des neunzehnten Jahrhunderts / Hrsg. von Bernhard Fabian, bearb. unter der Leitung von Willi Gorzny [microform]. München ; N.Y. : K.G. Saur, c1982. 1437 microfiches. ISBN 3-598-30421-8 (microfiche). ISBN 3-598-30410-2 (microfiche : diazo). **AJ55**
Reproduces in a single alphabetical order 267 German biographical works published between 1700 and 1910. "Quellenverzeichnisse," fiche I–XVI.
Indexed by:

Koch, Hans-Albrecht. Deutscher biographischer Index / hrsg. von Willi Gorzny ; bearb. von Hans-Albrecht Koch, Uta Koch und Angelika Koller. München ; N.Y. : K.G. Saur, 1986. 4 v. ISBN 3-598-30432-3. **AJ56**
Introductory material in English and German.
An alphabetical listing of names, providing dates, vocations, and citations to both the microfiche and printed sources.
Z5305.G3K63

Hänsel, Markus. Die anonym erschienenen autobiographischen Schriften des neunzehnten Jahrhunderts : Bibliographie : mit einem Nachweis für die Bibliotheken Deutschlands. München ; N.Y. : Saur, 1986. 292 p. ISBN 3-598-10643-2. **AJ57**
A listing of 2,358 anonymously published 19th-century German autobiographies. Titles, broad subjects, and authors (if determined) are arranged in a single alphabet, with brief bibliographical information. Copies are located in major German libraries when possible. Z5301.H36

Ihme, Heinrich. Deutsches biographisches Jahrbuch : Reg. zu Bd. 1–5, 10 u. 11. München ; N.Y. ; London ; Oxford ; Paris : Saur, 1986. 99 p. ISBN 3-598-10656-4. **AJ58**
A cumulated index to v. 1–5, 10–11 (the only vols. published) of the *Deutsches biographisches Jahrbuch* (*Guide* AJ204).

Neue deutsche Biographie / hrsg. von der Historischen Kommission bei der Bayerischen Akademie der Wissenschaften. Berlin : Duncker & Humblot, 1985–1990. v. 14–16. (In progress). **AJ59**
For earlier vols. and annotation, see *Guide* AJ207.
Contents: v. 14–16, Laverrenz–Melanchthon.
CT1053.N4

Bibliography

Jessen, Jens Christian. Bibliographie der Autobiographien. München ; N.Y. : K.G. Saur, 1987–1989. v. 1–3. ISBN 3-598-10673-4 (Bd. 1). (In progress). **AJ60**
Contents: v. 1, Selbstzeugnisse, Erinnerungen, Tagebücher und Briefe deutscher Schriftsteller und Künstler; v. 2, Selbstzeugnisse, Erinnerungen, Tagebücher und Briefe deutscher Geisteswissenschaftler; v. 3, Selbstzeugnisse, Erinnerungen, Tagebücher und Briefe deutscher Mathematiker, Naturwissenschaftler und Techniker.
A listing, arranged alphabetically by author, of published autobiographies, diaries, and letters. Most entries have abbreviated citations to standard biographical sources, the keys to which appear at the end of each volume. Z5961.G4J47

GREAT BRITAIN

Banks, Olive. The biographical dictionary of British feminists. N.Y. : New York Univ. Pr., 1985–1990. v.1–2. ISBN 0-8147-1078-6 (v.1). $50.00. (In progress). **AJ61**

Contents: v.1, 1800–1930; v. 2, Supplement, 1900–45.

Aims "to provide biographical sketches of those women and, occasionally, men, who contributed their time, effort and money, and sometimes their health and happiness to forwarding the progress of the women's movement."—*Introd. to v. 1.* Women whose feminist careers began after 1930 or whose main work belongs to the later generation of feminists are not included in v. 1. Vol. 2 focuses on "the years between 1920 and 1945 . . . . [W]omen whose feminist activity did not appear to begin until after 1945 have been excluded."—*Introd. to v. 2.* Principal sources of information are indicated at the end of each article. Alphabetical arrangement; each volume has an index of names (with cross-references) and a topical index.

HQ1123.B36

Barrows, Floyd D. A dictionary of obituaries of modern British radicals / Floyd D. Barrows, David B. Mock. N.Y. : Harvester Wheatsheaf, 1989. 490 p. **AJ62**

Reprints contemporary obituaries "of individuals who have sought to introduce far-reaching change to the political, social, economic, or religious institutions of Great Britain" (*Introd.*) since the 1780s. The radicals chosen are those included in *Biographical dictionary of modern British radicals* (*Guide* AJ221) for whom obituaries were available. Sources of obituaries include *Gentleman's magazine*, *Western mail*, the *Times*, the *New York times*, and *Spectator*. Each entry concludes with a few bibliographical citations. Not indexed.

Bellamy, Joyce M. Dictionary of labour biography / [ed. by] Joyce M. Bellamy and John Saville. London : Macmillan, 1987. v. 8. ISBN 0-333-13180-0. £10.00 (v. 1). (In progress). **AJ63**

For v. 1–7 and annotation, see *Guide* AJ220.

Contents: v. 8. HD8393.A1B43

British biographical archive : a one-alphabet cumulation of 324 of the most important English-language biographical reference works originally published between 1601 and 1929 / managing ed., Laureen Baillie ; ed., Paul Sieveking [microform]. London ; N.Y. : K.G. Saur, c1984. 1236, 16 microfiches : negative. ISBN 0-86291-366-7 (microfiche : silver). ISBN 0-86291-365-9 (microfiche : diazo). **AJ64**

Reproduces in one alphabetical sequence entries from some 320 biographical sources published between 1601 and 1926. Entries from the *Dictionary of national biography* (*Guide* AJ217) are cited but not reproduced.

Indexed by:

British biographical index / ed. by David Bank & Anthony Esposito. London ; N.Y. : Saur, 1990. 4 v. ISBN 0-86291-390-X (set). £498.00. **AJ65**

Useful both as an index to the microfiche set and as an independent resource. The entries provide dates, occupations, and citations to the printed sources as well as to the microfiche.

CT773.B75

The dictionary of national biography, 1981–1985 : with an index covering the years 1901–1985 in one alphabetical series / ed. by Lord Blake and C.S. Nicholls. [Oxford] ; N.Y. : Oxford Univ. Pr., 1990. 518 p. ISBN 0-19-865210-0. $60.00. **AJ66**

For earlier volumes and annotation, see *Guide* AJ217.

Supplements are now to appear every five years.

DA28.D59

Fenwick, Gillian. The contributors' index to the *Dictionary of national biography*, 1885–1901. Winchester : St. Paul's Bibliographies ; Detroit : Omnigraphics, 1989. 413 p. ISBN 1-55888-815-2. **AJ67**

An alphabetical list of contributors to the *Dictionary of national biography* (*Guide* AJ217), excluding the supplements, with an indication of their subjects. DA28.D53F4

Oxbury, Harold. Great Britons : twentieth-century lives. Oxford ; N.Y. : Oxford Univ. Pr., 1985. 370 p. : ill. ISBN 0-19-211599-5. $25.95. **AJ68**

Aims " to portray the history and character of modern Britain through the lives of those men and women who have left the greatest mark on their time . . . . Only British subjects who died between 1915 and 1980 are included."—*Pref.* Does not list additional sources. Occupational index. CT783.O93

HUNGARY

Fekete, Márton. Prominent Hungarians : home and abroad. 4th ed. London : Szepsi Csombor Literary Circle, 1985. 658 p. (Publications of Szepsi Csombor Literary Society : English series, 3). **AJ69**

3rd ed., 1979 (*Guide* AJ251).

"Five thousand, four hundred and sixty seven short biographies."—*t.p.*

Includes a list of deaths since the 3rd ed.

Magyar ki kicsoda 1990 : több mint 6000 élő magyar személy életrajza / Biográf Szerkesztőség. [Budapest] : TEXOFT : Láng, [1990?]. 667 p. ISBN 963-7840-28-1. 579.00Ft. **AJ70**

Provides brief biographical information on more than 6,000 living individuals. CT963.M34

INDIA

Dictionary of national biography. Supplement / ed. by N.R. Ray. Calcutta : Institute of Historical Studies, 1986. v. 1. (In progress). **AJ71**

For main series, see *Guide* AJ256.

Contents: v. 1, A–D.

Aims to present "authentic and well-documented biosketches of prominent personalities [who made] tangible contributions to the making of India during the quarter century since Independence."—*Pref.* Includes individuals still living. When complete (4 v. are planned), will include some 1,400 entries.

CT1502.S46

Who's who, Indian personages / [comp. and ed. by P. Chavda and H.L. Sagar]. New Delhi : Crystal Ship Pub., 1986. v. 1 : ports. (In progress). **AJ72**

Attempts to include people from all fields. "The individuals listed in this volume have furnished their own data and their profiles have been prepared entirely from the information sent by them."—*Verso of t.p.* CT1502.W48

IRELAND

Boylan, Henry. A dictionary of Irish biography. 2nd ed. N.Y. : St. Martin's, 1988. 420 p. ISBN 0-312-02497-5. $35.00 (est.). **AJ73**

1st ed., 1978 (*Guide* AJ261).

This revised and expanded edition adheres to the plan of the 1st ed.; i.e., it aims to provide the important facts for individuals born in Ireland or those born abroad who "had an Irish parent, or were of Irish descent, lived or worked in Ireland or made a considerable contribution to Irish affairs" (*Pref.*); excludes living people. Select bibliography, p. 413–420.

CT862.B69

ITALY

Archivio biografico italiano / a cura di Tommaso Nappo; curatore consigliere Silvio Furlani [microform]. [München ; New York] : Saur, c1987–[1990]. 1024 microfiches : ill., negative. ISBN 3-598-31520-1 (microfiche : silver). ISBN 3-598-31535-X (guide). **AJ74**

Accompanied by printed guide with introd. in Italian, English, and German.

Parallel titles on guide: Italienisches biographisches Archiv = Italian biographical archive.

Reproduces in one alphabetical sequence entries from 321 biographical sources published between 1646 and 1931.

Dizionario biografico degli Italiani : [direttore, Alberto M. Ghisalberti]. Roma : Istituto della Enciclopedia Italiana, 1984–89. v. 30–37. (In progress). **AJ75**

For earlier vols. and annotation, see *Guide* AJ267.

Contents: v. 30–37, Cosattini–Della Volpaia.

CT1123.D5

JAPAN

Who's who in Japan. Hong Kong : International Culture Institute, c1984– . Biennial. **AJ76**

Includes figures "from the fields of government, commerce and industry, medicine, journalism, visual and performing arts and cultural areas such as literature and education."—*Introd.* Information is very brief, often no more than birthdate, education, current position, and address. CT1836.W47

LATIN AMERICA

Biographical dictionary of Latin American and Caribbean political leaders / ed. by Robert J. Alexander. N.Y. : Greenwood, 1988. 509 p. ISBN 0-313-24353-0. $75.00. **AJ77**

For annotation, see *Supplement* CJ193. F1414.2.B48

Mundo Lo, Sara de. Index to Spanish American collective biography. Boston : G.K. Hall, 1982–1985. v. 2–4. ISBN 0-8161-8181-0 (v. 1). (In progress). **AJ78**

For v. 1 and annotation, see *Guide* AJ291.

Contents: v. 2, Mexico; v. 3, The Central American and Caribbean countries; v. 4, The River Plate countries.

Z1609.B6M86

MALAYSIA

New Malaysian who's who. Kuala Lumpur : Kasuya Pub., 1989/1990 [i.e. 1989?]–1990. 2 v. in 3 : ill., map, ports. ISBN 983-9624-00-8 (pt.1). ISBN 983-9624-01-6 (pt. 2, v. 1). **AJ79**

Contents: Pt. 1, Sabah & Sarawak; pt. 2. West Malaysia (2 v.).

Includes a separate listing of Malaysian government officials. CT1566.N48

MEXICO

Camp, Roderic Ai. Who's who in Mexico today. Boulder, Colo. : Westview, 1988. 183 p. ISBN 0-8133-7397-2. $45.00. **AJ80**

Provides "brief, accurate biographical portraits of living Mexican leaders from all sectors of society—military, entrepreneurial, political, social, cultural, and religious."—*Pref.* Dictionary arrangement. CT552.C36

Woods, Richard Donovon. Mexican autobiography : an annotated bibliography = La autobiografía mexicana : una bibliografía razonada / comp. by Richard Donovon Woods ; translated by Josefina Cruz-Meléndez. N.Y. : Greenwood, 1988. 228 p. (Bibliographies and indexes in world history, no. 13). ISBN 0-313-25945-3. **AJ81**

Annotations in Spanish and English.

A listing, arranged alphabetically by author, of 332 autobiographies, "memoirs, collections of letters, diaries, oral autobiographies, interviews, the autobiographical novel, as well as the autobiographical essay."—*Introd.* Title, subject, profession, genre, and chronological indexes. Z5305.M6W6618

NETHERLANDS

Biografisch woordenboek van Nederland / onder eindredactie van J. Charité ; redactiecommissie I. Schöffer . . . [et al.]. 's-Gravenhage : Nijhoff, 1984–89. v. 2–3. ISBN 90-247-2278-0 (v. 1). (In progress). **AJ82**

For v. 1 and annotation, see *Guide* AJ313.

Each volume is arranged alphabetically with a cumulative index to all preceeding volumes. Additional volumes are planned every four years. CT1143.B56

NORWAY

Norsk biografisk leksikon. Kristiania : H. Aschehoug, 1983. v. 19⁴⁻⁵. **AJ83**

For previously published parts and annotation, see *Guide* AJ320.

Contents: v. 19$^{4-5}$ (hft. 94/95), Wolle'–Ø. Completes the set. CT1293.N6

PHILIPPINES

Manuel, E. Arsenio. Dictionary of Philippine biography. Quezon City : Filipiniana Publications, 1970–86. v. 2–3. : ill., ports., facsims. (In progress). **AJ84**
For v.1 and annotation, see *Guide* AJ333.
Vols.2–3 are each A–Z listings similar to the initial work.
DS653.7.M3

POLAND

Biogramy uczonych polskich : materiały o życiu i działalności członków AU w Krakowie, TNW, PAU, PAN / opracowali Andrzej Śródka, Paweł Szczawiński. Wrocław : Zakład Narodowy im. Ossolińskich, 1983–1990. v. 1–6, pt. 1 : ill. ISBN 83-04-01682-6 (set). (In progress). **AJ85**
At head of title: Polska Akademia Nauk. Ośrodek Informacji Naukowej.
Contents: cz. 1, Nauki społeczne; cz. 2, Nauki biologiczne; cz. 3, Nauki ścisłe; cz. 4, Nauki techniczne; cz. 5, Nauki rolnicze i leśne; cz. 6, v. 1, Nauki medyczne, A–L.
Offers biographical information for members of four 19th- and 20th-century scholarly societies (the Polska Akademia Umiejetnosci w Krakowie, the Towarzystwo Naukowe Warszawskie, the Polska Akademia Umiejętnosci, and the Polska Akademia Nauk); no living members are included. Information provided includes mentors, most important publications, and important students, as well as standard biographical information. Each part is arranged alphabetically; each volume (including those with partial alphabetical sequences) has its own name and discipline index. To be complete in 7 volumes.
CT1230.B56

Krzyzanowska, Jadwiga. Członkowie Polskiej Akademii Nauk : informator. Wyd. 5, uaktualnione. Wrocław : Zakład Narodowy im. Ossolińskich, 1990. 194 p. : ports. ISBN 83-04-03678-9. **AJ86**
1st ed., 1979.
A directory of current Polish members of the Polish Academy of Sciences, arranged by division (social sciences, biological sciences, etc.). Entries include a photograph, birth date, position, degrees, awards, and current addresses. Foreign and deceased members are listed separately with brief entries. Name index.
AS248.W37K79

Kto jest kim w Polsce : informator biografiszny / [redaguje zespół Lidia Becela . . . et al.]. Edycja 2. Warszawa : Wydawn. Interpress, 1989. 1584 p. **AJ87**
1st ed., 1984.
Provides brief biographical information and current addresses for some 4,500 contemporary individuals in the fields of government, science, and the arts.

Polska Akademia Umiejętności, Krakow. Polski słownik biograficzny / [Komitet redakcyjny: Władysław Konopczyński, et al.]. Kraków : Skład główny w księg, Gebethnera i Wolffa, 1984–90. v. 28–33². (In progress). **AJ88**
For earlier vols. and annotation, see *Guide* AJ334.
Contents: v.28–33², Potocki, Ignacy–Rozdeiczer-Kryszkowski, T.
CT1230.P65

PUERTO RICO

Fowlie-Flores, Fay. Index to Puerto Rican collective biography. N.Y. : Greenwood, 1987. 214, [1] p. (Bibliographies and indexes in American history, no. 5). ISBN 0-313-25193-2. **AJ89**
Indexes some 140 collective biographies—"reference works, collections of essays, histories, and some anthologies, all published before or during 1985 . . . [of] Puerto Ricans living on the island or on the mainland . . . as well as Americans and other nationals who have lived on the island."—*Pref.* Excludes journal articles. Z5305.P9F68

Reynal, Vicente. Diccionario de hombres y mujeres ilustres de Puerto Rico y de hechos históricos. Rio Piedras : Editorial Edil, 1988. 256, [3] p. : ill. (some col.). ISBN 84-599-9232-2. **AJ90**
Offers brief biographies of people in all fields from the earliest period to the present day. Dictionary arrangement.
CT522.R49

SCANDINAVIA

Scandinavian biographical archive [microform]. London ; N.Y. : K. G. Saur, 1990– . microfiches : negative, ill. **AJ91**
Ed. by David Metherell and Paul Guthrie.
Reproduces entries from more than 350 biographical sources for Denmark, Finland, Iceland, Norway, and Sweden published from the earliest period through the early 20th century. Divided into two alphabetical sections, the first covering Denmark, Norway, and Iceland, and the second Sweden and Finland. Includes a printed list of sources.

SOUTH AFRICA

Dictionary of South African biography / ed. in chief W.J. de Kock. [Pretoria] : Nasional Boekhandel Bpk. for National Council for Social Research, Dept. of Higher Education, 1987. v. 5. (In progress). **AJ92**
For v. 1–4 and annotation, see *Guide* AJ346.
Vol.5 includes some 1,100 biographies, the majority of which treat 20th-century individuals who died before 1983. Includes a cumulative name index to v.1–5. CT1924.D53

SPAIN

Archivo biográfico de España, Portugal e Iberoamérica / direccíon y redaccíon: Victor Herrero Mediavilla, L. Rosa Aguayo Nayle [microform] = Arquivo biográfico de Espanha, Portugal e Ibero-América]. München ; N.Y. : K. G. Saur, c1986. 1105 microfiches : negative + manual (64 p.). **AJ93**
Text of microfiche in Spanish or Portuguese; text of manual in Spanish, Portuguese, English, and German.
Reproduces in one alphabetical sequence entries from 306 biographical sources published from the 17th to the 20th centuries; more than half the entries are from Spain.
Indexed by:

Indice biográfico de España, Portugal e Iberoamérica = Indice biográfico de Espanha, Portugal e Ibero-América = Spanish, Portuguese and Latin American biographical

index / editado e dirigido por Victor Herrero Mediavilla, Lolita Rosa Aguayo Nayle. München ; N.Y. : K.G. Saur, 1990. 4 v. (1429 p.). ISBN 3-598-32061-2 (v. 1).
    AJ94

Introductory material in Spanish, Portuguese, English, and German.

" . . . an alphabetically arranged list of the ca.200,000 biographical entries contained in the microfiche . . . . In addition to the names themselves, IBEPI provides dates of birth and death, profession and geographical sphere of activity, as well as the location in ABEPI and the bibliographical references."—*Note on use.* "List of the evaluated biographies," p. xxxi–xxxvii.   CT1345.I53

Who's who in Spain. 1987– . Milano : Who's Who in Italy S.r.l., c1987– . Biennial.   **AJ95**

The 1990 ed., "provides information on some 7,000 personalities, both Spanish nationals and foreign residents, who are actively engaged in all spheres of Spanish life."—*Pref.* Entries are in English.

SWEDEN

Svenskt biografiskt lexikon. Stockholm : A. Bonnier, 1985–90. v. 25–27² : illus. (ports.). (In progress).   **AJ96**

For earlier vols. and annotation, see *Guide* AJ362.

Contents: v. 25–27² (whole nos. 121–132), Mlmros–Nordenström.   CT1313.S8

TURKEY

Günümüz Türkiyesinde kim kimdir = Who's who in Turkey. 1985–1986– . İstanbul : Profesyonel, c1986– .
    AJ97

Includes Turks living in the U.S. and Cyprus.

     CT1906.G86

UNION OF SOVIET SOCIALIST REPUBLICS

The Soviet Union : a biographical dictionary / ed. by Archie Brown. London : Weidenfeld and Nicolson, c1990. [600] p. ISBN 0-297-82010-9. £40.00.   **AJ98**

Offers brief signed biographies, written by specialists, of "some of the most prominent figures in Soviet public life from 1917 to the present day."—*Introd.* Emphasizes political figures, but individual from all areas have been included.   CT1203

Vronskaya, Jeanne. A biographical dictionary of the Soviet Union, 1917–1988 / by Jeanne Vronskaya with Vladimir Chuguev. London ; N.Y. : K.G. Saur, 1988. 525 p. ISBN 0-86291-470-1. £128.00.   **AJ99**

Offers brief biographies of some 5,000 individuals "covering all fields over the whole Soviet period."—*Pref.* Includes émigrés. Occupational index.   CT1213.V76

Contemporary

The Tauris Soviet directory : the elite of the USSR today / comp. by Romolo Cichero. London : I.B. Tauris, c1989. 713 p. ISBN 1-85043-090-X.   **AJ100**

In two parts: (1) a listing of major officials by government agency; (2) brief biographical information concerning some 2,000 individuals. Includes individuals prominent in a wide range of fields, including arts, sciences, religion, etc., but "the focus is on senior office holders in the major economic, administrative and political hierarchies."—*Pref.* Lacks an index.

     DK37.4.T38

VENEZUELA

Quién es quién en Venezuela. 1988– . Caracas : Editorial Quiénes Somos en Venezuela, 1988– .   **AJ101**

No more published?

Includes a separate listing of government officials and a section illustrating and describing official medals.

YUGOSLAVIA

Hrvatski biografski leksikon / [glavni urednik Nikica Kolumbić]. Zagreb : Jugoslavenski leksikografski zavod, 1983–1989. v. 1–2 : ill. (some col.). (In progress). **AJ102**

Ivo Cecić, direktor, v. 1; Vladimir Pezo, direktor, v. 2.

Contents: v. 1–2, A–C.

Covers figures from all periods, including persons living at time of compilation. Extensive bibliographies.

     CT1457.C76H78

Slovenski biografski leksikon / uredila Izidor Cankar in Franc Ksaver Lukman s sodelovanjem uredniškega odbora. Ljubljana : Založila Zadružna gospodarska banka, 1986. v. 4³. (In progress).   **AJ103**

For earlier volumes and annotation, see *Guide* AJ399.

Contents: v. 4³ (zv. 14), Vode–Zdešar.   DR381.S66S58

AK

Genealogy

INTERNATIONAL

Kemp, Thomas Jay. International vital records handbook. Baltimore : Genealogical Pub. Co., c1990. 355 p. ISBN 0-8063-1264-5.   **AK1**

Provides guidance in requesting birth, marriage, and death certificates. Gives for each state or country cost, addresses of vital records offices, and application forms. Emphasizes the

U.S., but scope is international; describes procedures for obtaining vital records from many foreign countries.   CS24.K44

Morby, John E. Dynasties of the world : a chronological and genealogical handbook. Oxford ; N.Y. : Oxford Univ. Pr., 1989. 254 p. ISBN 0-19-215872-4. $45.00.
                                           AK2
For annotation, see *Supplement* CJ146.   CS27.M67

UNITED STATES

Thorndale, William. Map guide to the U.S. federal censuses, 1790–1920 / William Thorndale and William Dollarhide. Baltimore : Genealogical Pub. Co., 1987. 420 p. : maps ; 23 x 30 cm. ISBN 0-8063-1188-6. $49.95.
                                           AK3
For annotation, see *Supplement* CL60.   G1201.F7T5

Guides

Ancestry's red book : American state, county, and town sources / ed. by Alice Eichholz. Salt Lake City, Utah : Ancestry Pub., 1989. 758 p. ISBN 0-916489-47-7. $39.95 (est.).   **AK4**
    A guide to state and local records of genealogical interest, arranged alphabetically by state with brief descriptions of records. Counties (or, for the New England states, towns) listed alphabetically under state, giving for each: address of the courthouse, year of county formation, parent county, beginning dates for genealogical records (births, marriages, deaths), and land, probate, and court records. County outline maps are provided for each state. Expands and updates much of the information in George B. Everton's *Handy book for genealogists*, 7th ed. (Logan, Utah : Everton Publ., 1981).   CS49.A55

Horowitz, Lois. A bibliography of military name lists from pre-1675 to 1900 : a guide to genealogical sources. Metuchen, N.J. : Scarecrow, 1990. 1080 p. ISBN 0-8108-2166-4.   **AK5**
    A monumental annotated bibliography designed to help genealogists identify individuals through their military service in America through 1900. Includes war records, rolls of soldiers, reports, journals, histories, lists of veterans and pensioners. Arranged by time period and locality. Not comprehensive, but valuable for locating published or typescript U.S. military records. No index.   Z5313.U5H67

Neagles, James C. Confederate research sources : a guide to archive collections. Salt Lake City, Utah : Ancestry Pub., c1986. 286 p. : ill. ISBN 0-916489-11-6. ISBN 0-916489-16-7 (pbk.).   **AK6**
For annotation, see *Supplement* DB32.   Z1242.N3

———— The Library of Congress : a guide to genealogical and historical research / by James C. Neagles ; assisted by Mark C. Neagles. Salt Lake City, Utah : Ancestry Pub., c1990. 381 p. : ill. ISBN 0-916489-48-5.
                                           AK7
For annotation, see *Supplement* DB42.   Z1250.N4

Bibliography

Filby, P. William. Passenger and immigration lists bibliography, 1538–1900 : being a guide to published lists of arrivals in the United States and Canada, by P. William Filby & Dorothy M. Lower. 2nd ed. Detroit : Gale, c1988. 324 p. ISBN 0-8103-2740-6.   **AK8**
    Includes entries from 1st ed. and its supplement (*Guide* AK25) plus more than 750 new lists. Indexed.   Z5313.U5F54

Passenger and immigration lists index. Supplement. Detroit : Gale, c1985– . ISSN 0736-8267.   **AK9**
    For basic set and earlier supplements, see *Guide* AK35.
    Each of these volumes cumulates into a single alphabetical sequence the entries from the supplements issued annually for 1982–85 and 1986–90 respectively.
    With publication of the 1986–90 cumulated *Supplements*, the *Index* with its supplements provides access to data describing more than 1,775,000 immigrants to the U.S.   CS68.P363

Periodical source index / prepared by the staff of the Allen County Public Library, Genealogy Department, Fort Wayne, Indiana. Fort Wayne, Ind. : Allen County Public Library Foundation, c1988– . Annual.   **AK10**
    Also known as *PERSI*.
    A valuable surname, subject, and locality index to more than 2,000 genealogical and local history periodicals. Essential for genealogical research.   CS1.P47

Indexes

The famine immigrants : lists of Irish immigrants arriving at the port of New York, 1846–1851 / Ira A. Glazier, ed. ; Michael Tepper, associate ed. Baltimore : Genealogical Pub. Co., 1985–1986. v. 6–7. ISBN 0-8063-1024-3 (v. 1).   **AK11**
    For v.1–5 and annotation, see *Guide* AK46.
    Contents: v.6–7, June 1850–Dec. 1851. Completes the set.
                                          E184.I6F25

Germans to America : lists of passengers arriving at U.S. ports, 1850 / ed. by Ira A. Glazier and P. William Filby. Wilmington, Del. : Scholarly Resources, c1988–c1991. v. 1–20 : ill. ISBN 0-8420-2279-1 (set). $75.00 (per vol.). (In progress).   **AK12**
    Contents: v.1–20 : Jan. 1850–May 1968.
    Transcriptions of passenger lists for ships arriving at major Atlantic coast ports as well as New Orleans, Galveston, and San Francisco. For 1850–55 includes only lists that contained 80% German passengers; thereafter, covers all ships with German passengers. Age, sex, occupation, place of origin, and destination are provided for each passenger; for some the home town is given, for others only the province of origin. Indexed by surname.
    Supplemented by Zimmerman's *German immigrants* (below).   E184.G3G38

Schenk, Trudy. The Wuerttemberg emigration index / by Trudy Schenk, Ruth Froelke, and Inge Bork. Salt Lake City, Utah : Ancestry Inc., 1986–1988. 4 v. ISBN 0-916489-08-6 (v. 1). $15.95. (In progress).   **AK13**
    Contains names of emigrants from Wuerttemberg to other countries in Europe and elsewhere, ca. 1790–1900; many listed the U.S. as their destination. Provides names, birthdates, birthplaces, emigration dates, destinations, and the call numbers of microfilms from the Family History Library (Salt Lake City, Utah) used in the project.   CS627.W86S34

Zimmerman, Gary J. German immigrants : lists of passengers bound from Bremen to New York [1847–1867], with places of origin / comp. by Gary J. Zimmerman & Marion Wolfert. Baltimore : Genealogical Pub. Co., 1985–1988. 3 v. ISBN 0-8063-1128-2 (v. 1).   **AK14**
Contents: v. 1–3, 1847–1867.
Contains approximately 100,000 names (about 21% of the total) of passengers outbound from Bremen to New York during this period. Provides name, age, residence, year of emigration, and ship name. Lists only passengers who gave a town or district of origin. Valuable because the Bremen passenger lists were destroyed. Supplements *Germans to America* (above) which does not cover the period 1847–49 and is incomplete for 1850–55.   E184.G3Z56

Directories

Bentley, Elizabeth Petty. County courthouse book. Baltimore : Genealogical Pub. Co., c1990. 386 p. ISBN 0-8063-1284-X. $29.95.   **AK15**
A genealogical guide to U.S. courthouses. Gives background on the court system for each state, name of courthouse, address, brief summary of holdings, etc.   KF8700.A19B46

———— The genealogist's address book. Baltimore : Genealogical Pub. Co., c1991. 391 p. ISBN 0-8063-1292-0. $29.95.   **AK16**
A useful directory, giving names and addresses of genealogical and historical societies, state libraries and archives, public libraries, ethnic organizations, and many other institutions.   CS44.B46

Filby, P. William. Directory of American libraries with genealogy or local history collections. Wilmington, Del. : Scholarly Resources Inc., 1988. 319 p. ISBN 0-8420-2286-4. $75.00.   **AK17**
Identifies most libraries with genealogical collections in the U.S. and Canada. Arranged alphabetically by state or province; entries show address, telephone number, and a brief description of collections and services available. Omitted are genealogical and family history collections housed at major academic libraries, such as Harvard and Yale. A helpful feature is the index of libraries with significant out-of-state collections.   Z675.G44F56

Meyer, Mary Keysor. Meyer's directory of genealogical societies in the U.S.A. and Canada. Pasadena, Md. : M. K. Meyer, c1990. 8th ed. ISSN 0732-3395. $15.00.   **AK18**
1st ed., 1976; 7th ed., 1988.
Arranged alphabetically by state, or for Canada, by province. Compiled partially from responses to a questionnaire; gives fuller information about publications, areas of interest, etc., for organizations that responded. Includes a list of specialized, surname, and independent genealogical periodicals that gives address and scope.   CS44.M44

Compendiums

Coldham, Peter Wilson. The complete book of emigrants. Baltimore : Genealogical Pub. Co., 1987–c1990. 2 v. : ill. ISBN 0-8063-1192-4 (v. 1). $29.95. ISBN 0-8063-1282-3 (v. 2).   **AK19**
Contents: v.1, 1607–1660; v.2, 1661–1699.
Contains the names of approximately 50,000 emigrants to America taken from published and manuscript sources available in England. Entries are arranged chronologically and there

is an index of persons and ships at the end of each volume. Bibliography of sources.   E184.B7C59

CANADA

National Archives of Canada. Manuscript Division. Checklist of parish registers, 1986 = Répertoire de registres paroissiaux, 1986. 4th ed. rev. by Patricia Birkett. Ottawa : Manuscript Division, National Archives of Canada, 1987. 205 p. ISBN 0-660-53863-6.   **AK20**
1st ed., 1969, comp. Marielle Campeau; 3rd ed., 1981, rev. Patricia Birkett.
English and French.
A listing of "all registers on microfilm or microfiche at the Public Archives of Canada that may be borrowed through the interlibrary loan service."—*Introd.* Alphabetically arranged by place name within each province or region. Includes a few foreign works. Geographical index.   CD3648.A1N38

FRANCE

Aublet, Robert. Nouveau guide de généalogie. Rennes : Ouest-France, c1986. 189 p. : ill., map. ISBN 2-85882-796-5. 70.00F.   **AK21**
A basic guide to the methods and resources for genealogical research in France. Covers the roles of archives, libraries, and government offices in the research process. Brief appendixes describe paleography, heraldry, computer genealogy, calendars, emigrant genealogy, and vital records. Bibliography; index.   CS10.A93

Bernard, Gildas. Les familles protestantes en France : XVIe siècle–1792 : guide des recherches biographiques et généalogiques. Paris : Archives nationales : Diffusé par La Documentation française, 1987. 699 p. : maps. ISBN 2-86000-130-1. 230F.   **AK22**
Describes records in France that name Protestants. A personal and place name index simplifies searches for specific families and localities. Chapters on colonial records will help those tracing Protestant emigrants; bibliographies provide an introduction to the subject of Protestant family history in France.   Z5313.F8B46

———— Guide des recherches sur l'histoire des familles. Paris : Archives nationales : diffusé par La Documentation française, 1981. 335 p. ISBN 2-86000-059-3.   **AK23**
Describes genealogical sources in France and indicates where these materials are found. The bibliographies list book titles about archives and records seldom cited elsewhere. No index.   Z5313.F8B47

GERMANY

Baxter, Angus. In search of your German roots : a complete guide to tracing your ancestors in the Germanic areas of Europe. 2nd ed. Baltimore : Genealogical Pub. Co., 1991. 116 p. ISBN 0-8063-1311-0 (pbk.). $10.95.   **AK24**
Describes German records commonly used by genealogists and indicates where to find them. Best used in conjunction with Larry O. Jensen's *A genealogical handbook of German research* (below) and Clifford Neal Smith and Anna Pszczan-Czaja Smith's *Encyclopedia of German-American genealogical research* (*Guide* AK54), both of which treat research methods,

historical background, and information sources not included here. This edition reflects changes brought by German unification. Indexed.   CS614.B39

Jensen, Larry O. A genealogical handbook of German research. Rev. ed. Pleasant Grove, Utah : Jensen Publ., c1978, 1983. 2 v. (205 p.) : ill.   **AK25**

Explains the use of German sources to reconstruct families from the 17th century to the present. Emphasizes genealogical research methods and solving specific research problems. Bibliography; index.   CS614.J46

Kludas, Arnold. Die Geschichte der deutschen Passagierschiffahrt. Hamburg : E. Kabel, c1986–1989. v. 1–4 : ill. (some col.). ISBN 3-8225-0037-2 (Bd. 1).   **AK26**

For annotation, see *Supplement* CH191.   HE601.G3K58

Taschenbuch für Familiengeschichtsforschung / [Hrsg.], Wolfgang Ribbe, Eckart Henning; begründet von Friedrich Wecken. 10., erw. und verb. Aufl. Neustadt an der Aisch : Degener, 1990. 479 p. : ill. ISBN 3-7686-1037-3.   **AK27**

A comprehensive handbook, essential for genealogical research in Germany. Manuscript and published sources are discussed as are the uses of genealogy in other disciplines. There are extensive bibliographies on the subject for Europe, North and South America. Other chapters cover terminology, chronology, paleography, genealogical symbols, heraldry, and onomastics. Addresses of archives, libraries, genealogical, and historical societies add to the work's usefulness.   CS18.T36

GREAT BRITAIN

Foster, Janet. British archives : a guide to archive resources in the United Kingdom / Janet Foster & Julia Sheppard. 2nd ed. N.Y. : Stockton Pr., 1989. lviii, 834 p. ISBN 0-93585-974-8. $100.00.   **AK28**

For annotation, see *Supplement* AB50.   CD1040.F67

The Phillimore atlas and index of parish registers / ed. by Cecil R. Humphrey-Smith. Baltimore : Genealogical Pub. Co., 1984. 282 p. : some maps in color; 29 cm. ISBN 0-85033-398-9. $50.00.   **AK29**

Simultaneously published: Chichester, Sussex : Phillimore & Co., 1984.

Includes reproductions of topographical maps from James Bell's *A new and comprehensive gazetteer of England and Wales* (1834).

Contains detailed maps of English parishes and dioceses, indexed for easy use. Bibliography. Essential for locating English parishes.   G1816.E42P5

Guides

Baxter, Angus. In search of your British & Irish roots : a complete guide to tracing your English, Welsh, Scottish, and Irish ancestors. Rev. and updated. Baltimore : Genealogical Pub. Co., 1989. 310 p. : ill. ISBN 0-8063-1127-4. $12.95.   **AK30**

Explains how to find British, Scottish, Irish, and Welsh records containing information about families and individuals. Bibliography; index.   CS414.B38

Harvey, Richard. Genealogy for librarians. London : Bingley, 1983. 166 p. ISBN 0-85157-335-5. £11.50.
                                                      AK31

A guide to books and original records, intended for librarians providing reference service to genealogical patrons of English ancestry. Indexed.   CS9.H35

Hey, David. Family history and local history in England. London ; N.Y. : Longman, 1987. 276 p. : ill. ISBN 0-582-00522-1. ISBN 0-582-49458-3 (pbk.).   **AK32**

Presents a newly popular approach to genealogy that incorporates methods and sources used by local and social historians. The chapter on the Middle Ages covers ground ignored in most recent handbooks. Bibliography; index.   CS414.H49

Markwell, F. C. The A–Z guide to tracing ancestors in Britain / F.C. Markwell & Pauline Saul. Baltimore : Genealogical Pub. Co., 1989. 224 p. : ill. ISBN 0-8063-1252-1.   **AK33**

Rev. ed. of F.C. Markwell's *The family historian's enquire within* (2nd ed., 1986).

A pocket encyclopedia of terms, sources, offices, names, books, and addresses essential to genealogists in search of ancestors from the British Isles. Indexed.   CS414.M37

Moulton, Joy Wade. Genealogical resources in English repositories. Columbus, Ohio : Hampton House, 1988. 614 p. : ill., maps. ISBN 0-944485-00-6.   **AK34**

A guide to repositories (records offices, libraries, and family history societies) and their records of genealogical value. Arranged by county. Indexed.   Z5313.G69M94

Rogers, Colin Darlington. Tracing your English ancestors : a manual for analysing and solving genealogical problems in England and Wales, 1538 to the present day. Manchester ; N.Y. : Manchester Univ. Pr. : Distr. by St. Martin's Pr., 1989. 1 v. ISBN 0-7190-3172-9. $19.95.   **AK35**

Explains which records and methods solve specific research problems encountered in identifying English ancestors. Bibliography; index.   CS414.R64

Bibliography

Weaver, Jack W. Immigrants from Great Britain and Ireland : a guide to archival and manuscript sources in North America / comp. by Jack W. Weaver and DeeGee Lester. Westport, Conn. : Greenwood, 1986. 129 p. (Reference guides to archives and manuscript collections on immigrant culture, no. 1). ISBN 0-313-24342-5.   **AK36**

For annotation, see *Supplement* CC178.   Z1361.B74W43

Dictionaries

Richardson, John. The local historian's encyclopedia. New Barnet : Historical Publications Ltd., 1974. [312] p. : ill. ISBN 0-9503656-0-2. £1.50.   **AK37**

A guide to terms, institutions, and records. Useful in genealogical work. Bibliographies; index.   DA34.R53

IRELAND

Mitchell, Brian. A guide to Irish parish registers. Baltimore : Genealogical Pub. Co., 1988. 134 p. ISBN 0-8063-1215-7.   **AK38**

Contains charts that facilitate identification of taxing districts and parishes in Ireland. Charts, arranged by country, are keyed to: (1) maps in Mitchell's *A new genealogical atlas of Ireland* (below), and (2) maps prepared by the National Library of

Ireland for use with the principal collection of Irish land tax records, called "Griffith's" or "Primary valuation of Ireland." The tax records themselves, some parish records, and the National Library maps are available in microfilm copy at several libraries in the U.S. and Britain. CD1118.5.A1M58

———————— A new genealogical atlas of Ireland. Baltimore : Genealogical Pub. Co., 1986. 123 p. ; 26 cm. ISBN 0-8063-1152-5 (pbk.). $18.95. **AK39**

An atlas of church and civil jurisdictions in Ireland and Northern Ireland. Includes brief descriptions of sources created by church and state that are essential to the study of genealogy in Ireland. No index; meant to be used "in conjunction with . . . *General alphabetical index to the town lands and towns, parishes, and baronies of Ireland* [Dublin : Tham, 1861; repr. Baltimore : Genealogical Pub. Co., 1984]."—*Introd.*

G1831.F7M5

Ryan, James G. Irish records : sources for family & local history. Salt Lake City, Utah : Ancestry Pub., c1988. li, 562 p. : ill., maps. ISBN 0-916489-22-1. $34.95. **AK40**

Indicates content and whereabouts of family history/ genealogical sources in the Republic of Ireland and Northern Ireland. Bibliographies and index. Z5313.I7R83

Yurdan, Marilyn. Irish family history. Baltimore : Genealogical Pub. Co., 1990. 194 p. : ill. ISBN 0-8063-1274-2. **AK41**

Summarizes Irish emigration history and describes the content and use of records in Ireland and other countries needed for Irish genealogical research. Bibliography and index.

CS498.Y87

JEWISH

Sack, Sallyann Amdur. A guide to Jewish genealogical research in Israel. Baltimore : Genealogical Pub. Co., 1987. 110 p. : ill., maps. ISBN 0-8063-1186-X. **AK42**

Spine title: *Genealogical research in Israel.*

Designed for those of Ashkenazi descent visiting Israel to do genealogical research. Provides detailed instruction on how to find and use genealogical sources in Israel. No bibliography or index. Z6374.B5S23

NETHERLANDS

Swierenga, Robert P. Dutch households in U.S. population censuses, 1850, 1860, 1870 : an alphabetical listing by family heads. Wilmington, Del. : Scholarly Resources, 1987. 3 v. (lxiv, 1389 p.). ISBN 0-8420-2237-6. $165.00. **AK43**

An alphabetical list of single persons and household heads of Dutch parentage. Census data is summarized for each entry. Useful for determining a person's place of residence in the U.S. and his or her date of emigration. E184.D9S948

SCOTLAND

Moody, David. Scottish family history. Baltimore : Genealogical Pub. Co., 1990. 219 p. ISBN 0-8063-1268-8.

AK44

Identifies sources that describe individuals, their families, and communities, and demonstrates how these sources can be interpreted to place ancestors in the context of their world.

Shows how to use this information to write accurate, interesting family histories. Bibliography; index. CS463.M66

SWITZERLAND

Familiennamenbuch der Schweiz = Répertoire des noms de famille suisses = Register of Swiss surnames / bearbeitet im Auftrag der Schweizerischen Gesellschaft für Familienforschung von der Arbeitsgemeinschaft Schweizer Familiennamen, Emil und Clothilde Meier . . . [et. al.]. 3., verb. und korrigierte Aufl. Zürich : Schulthess, c1989. 3 v. (2082 p.). ISBN 3-7255-2692-3. 450.00F. **AK45**

A register of Swiss surnames from a 1962 survey. Identifies communities where each surname was found and other towns where the name existed in the past. No bibliography or index. CS2625.F34

WALES

Hamilton-Edwards, Gerald Kenneth Savery. In search of Welsh ancestry. Baltimore : Genealogical Pub. Co., 1986. 95 p. : ill. ISBN 0-85033-563-9. $25.00. **AK46**

Identifies the records needed to trace Welsh ancestors. Includes a bibliography, index, and appendixes with addresses of record offices and family history societies. CS452.H35

Rawlins, Bert J. The parish churches and nonconformist chapels of Wales : their records and where to find them. Salt Lake City, Utah : Celtic Heritage Research, c1987. v. 1 : ill., maps. (In progress). **AK47**

Contents: v. 1, Carmarthenshire, Cardiganshire, and Pembrokeshire.

Lists Church of England parishes and nonconformist chapels. Provides brief notes about the history and records of each parish or chapel, and includes numerous photographs. Bibliography; denominational index; general index. More comprehensive than C.J. Williams's *Parish registers of Wales* (below).

CD1068.A2R39

Williams, C. J. Cofrestri plwyf Cymru = Parish registers of Wales / comp. by C.J. Williams & J. Watts-Williams. [Aberystwyth, Dyfed] : National Library of Wales & Welsh County Archivists' Group in association with the Society of Genealogists, 1986. 217 p., [12] p. of plates : ill. ISBN 0-907158-14-5. £6.95. **AK48**

Identifies Church of England parishes in Wales, the time periods covered by their records, and where records are kept. County maps show parishes but not their boundaries. Index.

CD1068.A2W55

NAMES

Surnames

German

Jones, George Fenwick. German-American names. Baltimore : Genealogical Pub. Co., c1990. 268 p. : ill. ISBN 0-8063-1271-8. $25.00. **AK49**

A dictionary of German given and surnames, including spelling variations found in North America. A 60-page introduction discusses the origins of German names and how they were changed when their bearers emigrated to the U.S.

CS2487.J66

Greek

A lexicon of Greek personal names / ed. by P.M. Fraser and E. Matthews. Oxford : Clarendon Pr. ; N.Y. : Oxford Univ. Pr., 1987. v. 1. ISBN 0-19-864222-9 (v. 1). $90.00. (In progress).   **AK50**
    Contents: v.1, The Aegean Islands, Cyprus, Cyrenaica. (498 p.)   CS2349.L48

B

Humanities

BA

Philosophy

GUIDES

Bynagle, Hans E. Philosophy : a guide to the reference literature. Littleton, Colo. : Libraries Unlimited, 1986. 170 p. ISBN 0-87287-464-8. $35.00.   **BA1**

A bibliography and handbook, "compiled and written with a diversity of users in mind."—*Pref.* Less exhaustive than R.T. De George's *Philosopher's guide* (*Guide* BA2), but covers much the same ground, containing lengthy annotations and citations to more recent works. Organized by resource type, (e.g., general and specialized dictionaries, indexes, abstracting and reviewing journals and serial bibliographies, concordances), with entries arranged alphabetically within each chapter. Core journals and professional societies are also listed.   Reference sources are cited for specific philosophical schools, countries, periods, and individuals, but citations to standard editions of philosophical

works are not included. Emphasis is on English-language materials. Author/title and subject indexes.   Z7125.B97

BIBLIOGRAPHY

Inada, Kenneth K. Guide to Buddhist philosophy. Boston : G.K. Hall, c1985. 226 p. ISBN 0-8161-7899-2. $45.00.   **BA2**

A companion to Frank E. Reynolds's *Guide to Buddhist religion* (*Guide* BB494) and other volumes in the series, this annotated bibliography is intended for undergraduates and their instructors. Lists primarily English-language books, articles, and dissertations on Buddhist philosophy, as well as English translations of Buddhist texts. Arranged in 16 chapters that treat such topics as logic, ethics, history, and comparative philosophy. Author/title and subject indexes.   Z7128.B93I53

Totok, Wilhelm. Bibliographischer Wegweiser der philosophischen Literatur. 2. Aufl. / bearb. von Horst-Dieter Finke. Frankfurt am Main : Klostermann, 1985. 53 p. ISBN 3-465-01677-7.   **BA3**

1st ed., 1959.

Lists 200 citations to reference works, annuals, and periodicals by subject or publication type. Author/editor and title indexes.   Z7125.A1T67

International

Bibliographien zur Philosophie. Köln : Edition Gemini, 1979– . Irregular. ISSN 0173-1831.   **BA4**

Contents: v. 2, Hegel : e. Bibliographie d. Dissertationen aus sieben westeuropäischen Ländern 1885–1975 (c1980. 50 p.); v. 3, Immanuel Kant : ein Verzeichnis der Dissertationen aus den deutschsprachigen Ländern 1900–1980, 2nd enl. ed.

(c1980. 70 p.); v. 4, Die deutsche Philosophie im Spiegel französischer Hochschulschriften, 1885–1975 (c1981. 38 p.); v. 5, Bibliographie österreichischer und schweizerischer Dissertationen zur deutschen Philosophie, 1885–1975 (c1982. 89 p.); v. 6, Canadian theses on German philosophy, 1925–1975 : a bibliography (c1982. 47 p.); v. 7, Leibniz : eine Bibliographie europäischer und nordamerikanischer Hochschulschriften, 1875–1980, 2nd enl. ed. (c1986. 49 p.); v. 8, Index to theses on German philosophy accepted by the universities of Great Britain and Ireland, 1900–1980 (c1984. 50 p.); v. 9, Fichte : ein Verzeichnis westeuropäischer und nordamerikanischer Hochschulschriften 1885–1980 (c1985. 44 p.); v. 11, Schelling, ein Verzeichnis westeuropäischer und nordamerikanischer Hochschulschriften, 1885–1980 (1986. 34 p.); v. 12, Ludwig Wittgenstein : a comprehensive bibliography of international theses and dissertations, 1933–1985 (1988. 60 p.). All vols. comp. by Gernot U. Gabel.

Periodicals

Ruben, Douglas H. Philosophy journals and serials : an analytical guide. Westport, Conn. : Greenwood, 1985. 147 p. ISBN 0-313-23958-4. $36.95.   **BA5**

An annotated list of 335 journals, yearbooks, newsletters, and bulletins, compiled from responses to a survey mailed to the editors of philosophy serials listed in *Ulrich's.* Arranged alphabetically with geographic and subject indexes.   Z7127.R83

Greece

Paquet, Léonce. Les présocratiques : bibliographie analytique, 1879–1980 / par L. Paquet, M. Roussel, Y. Lafrance. Montréal : Éditions Bellarmin, 1988–1989. 2 v.   **BA6**

Contents: v. 1, Des Milésiens à Héraclite; v. 2, D'Alcméon aux auteurs de la Collection hippocratique.

This comprehensive work lists alphabetically by author and annotates books, dissertations, journal articles, and conference proceedings in all languages within a classified arrangement with sections devoted to general studies, specific themes, and individual schools or philosophers. Index of modern authors.   Z7129 G7P36

India

Potter, Karl H. Guide to Indian philosophy / Karl H. Potter with Austin B. Creel and Edwin Gerow. Boston : G.K. Hall, c1988. 159 p. ISBN 0-8161-7904-2.   **BA7**

An annotated bibliography of 884 citations to English-language books and articles from the 20th century. Entries are arranged alphabetically by author and include primary texts translated into English, as well as secondary literature from all areas of philosophy, including "epistemology, logic, metaphysics and ethics, works on aesthetics, philosophy of religion, and social, legal, and political philosophy, and philosophy of education."—*Pref.* Name and subject indexes.   Z7129.I5P68

Latin America

Anuario bibliográfico de historia del pensamiento ibero e iberoamericano. Athens, Ga. : Univ. of Georgia, 1989– . Annual. $50.00.   **BA8**

Lists books and articles on all aspects of Hispanic philosophy, arranged in chapters by country of publication, with name index.   Z7129.S8A58

Netherlands

Bibliographie de l'humanisme des anciens Pays-Bas, avec un répertoire bibliographique des humanistes et poètes néo-latins : supplément 1970–1985, avec compléments à l'édition de A. Gerlo et H.D.L. Vervliet (Bruxelles 1972) / sous la rédaction de Marcus de Schepper ; avec la collaboration de Chris L. Heesakkers. Bruxelles : Koninklijke Academie voor Wetenschappen, Letteren en Schone Kunsten van België, 1988. 439 p. ISBN 90-6569-397-7.   **BA9**

Supplements and greatly expands the coverage of the original volume by Gerlo and Vervliet (*Guide* BA43). Continues the original arrangement and numbering, adding over 5,000 items, including many pre-1970 imprints which were missed in the earlier work. Author index.   Z7029.N4B53

Poortman, J. J. Repertorium der Nederlandse wijsbegeerte. Amsterdam : Wereldbibliotheek, 1983. v.4. ISBN 90-6064-463-8 (v.4). (In progress).   **BA10**

For v. 1–3 and annotation, see *Guide* BA58.

The original arrangement has been abandoned in favor of a classed system of periods and topics. Entries on individual philosophers follow each topical section. Personal name and subject indexes, title index for anonymous publications, and a biographic register of cited authors conclude this volume.   Z7129.D8P6

ENCYCLOPEDIAS

The concise encyclopedia of western philosophy and philosophers / ed. by J.O. Urmson and Jonathan Rée. New ed., completely rev. London ; Boston : Unwin Hyman, 1989. 331 p. ISBN 0-04-445379-5. $16.95 (pbk.).   **BA11**

2nd ed., 1975 (*Guide* BA87).

Includes new articles that treat recent developments or aspects of the field not documented in the earlier editions, together with older articles that are for the most part reproduced here with some corrections and additions. About a tenth of the older material has been deleted.   B41.C66

The encyclopedia of Eastern philosophy and religion : Buddhism, Hinduism, Taoism, Zen / Ingrid Fischer-Schreiber [et al.] ; editors, Stephan Schuhmacher, Gert Woerner. Boston : Shambhala, 1989. 468 p. : ill. ISBN 0-87773-433-X. $39.95.   **BA12**

For annotation, see *Supplement* BB23.   BL1005.L4813

Encyclopedia of Indian philosophies / Ram Shankar Bhattacharya ... [et al.]. Princeton, N.J. : Princeton Univ. Pr., c1987–1990. v. 4–5. (In progress).   **BA13**

For earlier volumes and annotation, see *Guide* BA74.

Contents: v. 4, Sāṃkhya : a dualist tradition in Indian philosophy, ed. Gerald James Larson and Ram Shankar Bhattacharya; v. 5, The philosophy of the Grammarians, ed. Harold G. Coward and K. Kunjunni Raja.   B131.E5

Encyclopédie philosophique universelle / publié sous la direction d'André Jacob. Paris : Presses universitaires de France, 1989–1990. v. 1–2 : ill. ISBN 2-13-041440-0 (set). (In progress).   **BA14**

Contents: v. 1, 1989, L'universe philosophique (ed. André Jacob); v. 2, t. 1–2, 1990, Les notions philosophiques: Dictionnaire; Philosophie occidentale A–Z; Pensées asiatiques; Conceptualisation des sociétés traditionelles; Tables analytiques (ed. Sylvain Auroux).

A comprehensive work with emphasis on current scholarship. In v. 1, chapters by leading scholars, such as Paul Ricoeur and Jacques Ellul, discuss the major themes and problems of philosophical thought, with numerous illustrations, charts, bibliographic references, and concept/theme and personal name indexes. Vol. 2 contains signed essays on concepts and terms; "Pensées asiatiques" are listed alphabetically by transliterated term with some Chinese and other vernacular characters and the French translation. "Conceptualizations" includes topics from African, South American, and other cultures. The tables list terms from all traditions under broad subjects, such as moral or political philosophy. Vol. 3 and 4 are planned to include articles on philosophical works and texts. B51.E52

Filosofskiĭ ėntsiklopedicheskiĭ slovar' / red. kollegiia, S. S. Averintsev... [et al.]. 2. izd. Moskva : "Sovetskaia ėntsiklopediia,", 1989. 814 p. **BA15**

1st ed., 1983.

Biographical and topical articles, some signed, on all aspects of philosophy. Translations of primary sources into Russian and secondary studies are listed at the end of each entry. A table of standard philosophical terms provides Russian translations from Latin and other languages. Arranged alphabetically with a subject/name index. B48.R9F55

Lacey, A. R. A dictionary of philosophy. 2nd ed. London : Routledge & Kegan Paul, 1986. 266 p. ISBN 0-7102-0991-6. £6.95. **BA16**

1st ed., 1976 (*Guide* BA80).

Adds 25 new entries, as well as various cross-references, corrections, and bibliographical citations. Most of the original articles have not been rewritten. B41.L32

DICTIONARIES

Grimes, John A. A concise dictionary of Indian philosophy : Sanskrit terms defined in English. Albany, N.Y. : State Univ. of New York Pr., c1989. 440 p. ISBN 0-7914-0100-6. $39.50. ISBN 0-7914-0101-4 (pbk.). $12.95. **BA17**

An "introduction to the basic terms found in the major schools of Indian philosophy."—*Pref.* Headwords, printed in Sanskrit and in transliteration, are listed in alphabetical order with literal translations and, when necessary, further explanations of usage in various philosophical systems or schools. Includes transliteration and pronunciation guides, an index of major terms, and a useful series of charts depicting the relationships of works, concepts, and categories of individual schools. A similar title, B.N. Singh's *Dictionary of Indian philosophical concepts*, (Varanasi: Asha Prakashan, 1988. 340p.), includes bibliographic citations to source texts along with the definitions. B131.G67

Historisches Wörterbuch der Philosophie / unter Mitwirkung von mehr als 700 Fachgelehrten in Verbindung mit Günther Bien... [et al.]; hrsg. von Joachim Ritter. Völlig neubearbeitete Ausg. des Wörterbuchs der philosophischen Begriffe von Rudolf Eisler. Basel : Schwabe, 1984–1989. v. 6–7. ISBN 3-7965-0115-X (set). 84.00F (v. 1). (In progress). **BA18**

For v. 1–5 and annotation, see *Guide* BA85.

Contents: v. 6, M–O; v. 7, P–Q. Vol. 7 contains errata for v. 1–6. B43.R59

HISTORY

The Cambridge history of Renaissance philosophy / gen. ed., Charles B. Schmitt ; editors, Quentin Skinner, Eckhard Kessler. Cambridge ; N.Y. : Cambridge Univ. Pr., 1988. 968 p. ISBN 0-521-25104-4. **BA19**

Discusses the background and advancement of Renaissance philosophy, metaphysics, psychology, and related fields. Chapters by contributing scholars are organized in three parts: Pt. 1, The intellectual context, which includes sections on humanism, manuscripts, and printing; Pt. 2, Philosophy and its parts, the main body of text; and Pt. 3, which contains appendixes on ancient texts and a history of textbooks, biobibliographies of Renaissance philosophers, and lengthy bibliographies of primary and secondary literature. Name and subject indexes. B775.C25

Grundriss der Geschichte der Philosophie / Friedrich Ueberweg. Völlig neubearbeitete Ausg. Basel : Schwabe, 1988. 2 v. in 3. ISBN 3-7965-0872-3. (In progress). **BA20**

For earlier volumes, see *Guide* BA94.

Contents: Die Philosophie des 17. Jahrhunderts, hrsg. von Jean-Pierre Schobinger. Bd. 3, England (2v.)

Includes seventeenth-century American philosophy. B801.P44

Totok, Wilhelm. Handbuch der Geschichte der Philosophie : unter Mitarbeit von Helmut Schröer. Frankfurt am Main : V. Klostermann, [1986]. v. 5. (In progress). **BA21**

For v. 1–4 and annotation, see *Guide* BA28.

Contents: v. 5, Bibliographie 18. und 19. Jahrhundert, unter Mitarbeit von Horst-Dieter Finke [et al.]. B82.T6

BIOGRAPHY

Dictionnaire des philosophes antiques / publié sous la direction de Richard Goulet. Paris : Éditions du Centre national de la recherche scientifique, 1989. v. 1 : ill. (some col.). ISBN 2-222-04042-6. (In progress). **BA22**

Contents: v. 1, Abam(m)on–Axiothéa.

A comprehensive biographical encyclopedia of philosophers from the beginnings until about the 6th century CE. Signed articles range in length from a paragraph to over 100 pages (e.g., Aristotle). Most include dates, citations to articles in Pauly-Wissowa (*Guide* DA126), a biographical sketch with numerous citations to both ancient and modern sources, a list of works with standard editions and translations and textual histories, and a discussion of the subject's philosophy and influence. An appendix to v. 1, "Académie topographie et archéologie," p. 692–787, provides an overview of the situation, history, religious significance, and importance of the Academy, with several maps and charts. Name, Greek word, and subject indexes in each volume. B112.D53

Dizionario dei filosofi del Novecento. [Firenze] : L.S. Olschki, [1985]. 825 p. ISBN 88-222-3319-0. li.154. **BA23**

At head of title: Centro di studi filosofici de Gallarate.

Some 1,500 unsigned biographical sketches of philosophers and scholars and authors in other fields (mathematics, religion, literature, political science, history, and linguistics) who have drawn on or influenced 20th-century philosophy. Emphasizes Europe and America; a portion of the entries are taken from *Enciclopedia filosofia* (*Guide* BA73). Some bibliographical references. B804.D59

Kersey, Ethel M. Women philosophers : a bio-critical source book / Ethel M. Kersey ; Calvin O. Schrag, consulting ed. N.Y. : Greenwood, 1989. 230 p. ISBN 0-313-25720-5. $49.95.   **BA24**

Approximately 150 biographical sketches and articles on women who have "seriously thought or written in the traditional fields of philosophy, including metaphysics, ethics, aesthetics, and logic."—*Pref.* Entries contain primary and secondary bibliographies, and the lengthy introductory essay provides an overview of women in the history of philosophy and a general bibliography. The appendix consists of an alphabetical table of women, indicating their countries, dates, and disciplines. Personal name index.   B105.W6K47

Metzler Philosophen Lexikon : dreihundert biographisch-werkgeschichtliche Porträts von den Vorsokratikern bis zu den Neuen Philosophen / unter redaktioneller Mitarbeit von Christel Dehlinger . . . [et al.] ; herausgegeben von Bernd Lutz. Stuttgart : J.B. Metzlersche Verlagsbuchhandlung, c1989. 851 p. ISBN 3-476-00639-5.   **BA25**

Consists of 268 signed biographical essays, each of which includes a portrait or photograph and short bibliography. Arranged alphabetically, with name index.   B104.M48

INDIVIDUAL PHILOSOPHERS

Erasmus

Contemporaries of Erasmus : a biographical register of the Renaissance and Reformation / Peter G. Bietenholz, ed. ; Thomas B. Deutscher, assoc. ed. Toronto ; Buffalo : Univ. of Toronto Pr., c1985–c1987. 3 v. : ill. ISBN 0-8020-2507-2 (v.1). $240.00.   **BA26**

Intended to accompany *Collected works of Erasmus* (Toronto : Univ. of Toronto Pr., 1974).   PA8500

Gemeentebibliotheek Rotterdam. Catalogue of the Erasmus collection in the City Library of Rotterdam. N.Y. : Greenwood, c1990. 678 p. (Bibliographies and indexes in philosophy, no. 2). ISBN 0-313-27698-6.   **BA27**

"The Rotterdam City Library holds the world's largest collection of works by and about Desiderius Erasmus (1469–1536), perhaps the city's most famous son."—*Introd.* This volume reproduces the catalog cards for the Erasmus Collection of about 5,000 volumes. The entries, which are fairly easy to read, are arranged in sections of works by, edited by, and about Erasmus, published from the 16th century until 1989. Includes some journal articles and essays. No index.   Z8268.G46

Pythagoros

Navia, Luis E. Pythagoras : an annotated bibliography. N.Y. : Garland, 1990. 381 p. : ill. (Garland reference library of the humanities, vol. 1128). ISBN 0-8240-4380-4. $50.00.   **BA28**

Lists 1,197 books, articles, and dissertations in chapters devoted to topics such as philosophical studies, mathematics, music, and literature. Author and name indexes.   Z8722.3.N38

Socrates

Navia, Luis E. Socrates : an annotated bibliography / Luis E. Navia, Ellen L. Katz. N.Y. : Garland, 1988. 536 p. : ill. (Garland reference library of the humanities, vol. 844). ISBN 0-8240-5740-6. $65.00.   **BA29**

Although by no means as comprehensive as R.D. McKirahan's *Plato and Socrates* (*Guide* BA124), this volume contains almost 2,000 annotated citations to primary and secondary books, articles, and dissertations on the life, philosophy, and influence of Socrates. Arranged alphabetically within broad subject divisions, including a section on the portrayal of Socrates in fiction, poetry, and drama. Author index.   Z8824.34.N38

BB

Religion

GENERAL WORKS

Guides

Kennedy, James R. Library research guide to religion and theology : illustrated search strategy and sources. 2nd ed., rev. Ann Arbor, Mich. : Pierian Pr., 1984. 60 p. : ill. (Library research guides series, no. 1). ISBN 0-87650-185-4. ISBN 0-87650-184-6 (pbk.).   **BB1**

1st ed., 1974 (*Guide* BB2).

Includes new and revised works that have appeared since the 1974 edition and provides information on computerized searching.   BL41.K45

Bibliography

Choquette, Diane. New religious movements in the United States and Canada : a critical assessment and annotated bibliography. Westport, Conn. : Greenwood, 1985. 235 p. (Bibliographies and indexes in religious studies, no. 5). ISBN 0-313-23772-7.   **BB2**

An annotated, classified bibliography of monographic and serial literature, dissertations, and unpublished papers documenting the new religious and human potential movements in North America from the 1960s through 1983. Approximately 90% of the 738 items listed are in the New Religious Movements Research Collection at the Graduate Theological Union Library, Berkeley, and 10% in the libraries of the University of California at Berkeley. Selected list of new religious movement publishers; author/title and subject indexes.   Z7834.U6C46

Cornish, Graham P. Religious periodicals directory. Santa Barbara, Calif. : ABC-Clio, c1986. 330 p. ISBN 0-87436-365-9. $89.00. **BB3**

Provides bibliographic information and contents notes for 1,763 journals in religion/theology and many related fields. Arranged by six geographic regions, by country of publication within each region, and alphabetically by title within each country. Title and subject/geographic indexes. Z7753.C75

Lippy, Charles H. Bibliography of religion in the South. Macon, Ga. : Mercer Univ. Pr., c1985. 498 p. ISBN 0-86554-161-2. $49.95. **BB4**

A comprehensive work, identifying and critically appraising scholarly secondary literature published mainly since 1960. Includes articles, monographs, dissertations, theses. Arranged in chapters dealing with denominational groups and other topics, each chapter opening with a commentary on the literature, followed by a classified bibliography. Detailed table of contents, but no index. Z7778.S59L56

——————— Religious periodicals of the United States : academic and scholarly journals. Westport, Conn. : Greenwood, 1986. 607 p. ISBN 0-313-23420-5. $65.00. **BB5**

Essays by 50 specialists profile more than 100 academic and scholarly journals representative of various religious perspectives and ecclesiastical bodies. Essays, arranged alphabetically by journal title, are followed by endnotes, information sources, and publication history for the journal. Appendixes list journals chronologically by date of first publication and by sponsoring organization or religious orientation. Index of names, titles, and subjects. Serves as a survey of religious publishing in the U.S. PN4888.R4L5

McIver, Tom. Anti-evolution : an annotated bibliography. Jefferson, N.C. : McFarland, c1988. 385 p. ISBN 0-89950-313-5. $39.95. **BB6**

Consists of 1,852 entries, mostly annotated, arranged alphabetically by author. "This bibliography is intended as a guide for the understanding and evaluation of the plethora of anti-evolution books, pamphlets and other literature in circulation today."—*Pref.* "The approach . . . is descriptive rather than polemical."—*Introd.* An invaluable tool for scholars studying this topic. Separate title, author, and subject indexes. Z5322.E9M38

Oster, Richard. A bibliography of ancient Ephesus. [Philadelphia] : American Theological Library Association ; Metuchen, N.J. : Scarecrow, 1987. 155 p. (ATLA bibliography series, no. 19). ISBN 0-8108-1996-1. **BB7**

"The scope of this bibliography is the ancient history, culture and archaeological evidence of Ephesus."—*Introd.* An alphabetically arranged author listing of books, essays, pamphlets, articles, and dissertations, mostly in English, French, and German. The indexing by broad subject headings means that headings such as "Architecture" or "Numismatics" carry as much as half a page of item numbers. Z2304.E58O87

Purvis, James D. Jerusalem, the Holy City : a bibliography. [St. Meinrad, Ind.] : American Theological Library Association ; Metuchen, N.J. : Scarecrow, 1988. 499 p. (ATLA bibliography series, no. 20). ISBN 0-8108-1999-6. **BB8**

A comprehensive list of scholarly books and articles, most in English, 19th century to the present, on the history, archaeology, and geography of Jerusalem. Covers from the biblical period to the present. Classified arrangement. Indexes of authors and subjects. Z3478.J4P87

Religion and American life : resources / ed. by Anne T. Fraker. Urbana : Univ. of Illinois Pr., c1989. 236 p. ISBN 0-252-01588-6. **BB9**

Contains fairly long critical annotations of 116 books and 121 articles selected by 40 contributors who participated in a two-year project at Indiana University-Purdue University at Indianapolis. Books and articles are listed in separate sections, each arranged alphabetically by author. Author and title indexes. Z7757.U5R45

Religious & inspirational books & serials in print. 1985– . N.Y. : Bowker, c1985– . ISSN 0000-0868. $79.95. **BB10**

Continues *Religious books and serials in print*, 1978–1982/83 (*Guide* BB29).

Covers all areas of religion, including devotional and self-help literature. Z7751.R387

Shermis, Michael. Jewish-Christian relations : an annotated bibliography and resource guide. Bloomington : Indiana Univ. Pr., c1988. 291 p. ISBN 0-253-33153-6. **BB11**

A comprehensive listing of books, pamphlets, important articles, journals, congresses, media, syllabi, organizations, and speakers. Covers Jewish-Christian relations from antiquity through the present. Classified arrangement, with critical annotations. Indexes of subjects, names and organizations, titles, and media. Z6370.S53

Thompson, Laurence G. Chinese religion in Western languages : a comprehensive and classified bibliography of publications in English, French, and German through 1980. Tucson, Ariz. : Published for the Association for Asian Studies by the Univ. of Arizona Pr., c1985. 302 p. ISBN 0-8165-0926-3. **BB12**

Updated ed. of Thompson's *Studies of Chinese religion* (Encino, Calif. : Dickenson, 1976).

An extensive unannotated list of monographs and serials with an index of authors, editors, compilers, translators, photographers, and illustrators. Covers Chinese Buddhism as well as Chinese religion exclusive of Buddhism. Intended for specialists. Z7757.C6T55

Yu, David C. Guide to Chinese religion / David C. Yu with contributions by Laurence G. Thompson. Boston : G.K. Hall, c1985. 200 p. ISBN 0-8161-7902-6. **BB13**

A critically annotated, selected bibliography of books, journal articles, and essays through 1977, primarily in English. Deals with religions indigenous to China: Taoism, Confucianism, Lao Tzu, Maoism, archaic religions and folk beliefs; excludes Chinese Buddhism. Detailed classified arrangement, with author/title and subject indexes. Intended for undergraduate and beginning graduate students. Z7757.C6Y8

Periodicals

Fieg, Eugene C. Religion journals and serials : an analytical guide. N.Y. : Greenwood, 1988. 218 p. ISBN 0-313-24513-4. **BB14**

Lists 328 English-language journals representative of Christianity and many other religions. Entries contain bibliographic information and brief descriptive notes. Classified arrangement. Indexes by geography, title, publisher, subject, audience. Z7753.F53

Indexes and abstract journals

Politics and religion : a bibliography selected from the ATLA religion database / ed. by Paul D. Petersen ; Ruth F. Frazer, gen. ed. 2nd rev. ed. Chicago : American Theological Library Association, 1984. 774 p. **BB15**

For annotation, see *Supplement* CJ13.   Z7776.72.P6

●**Religion indexes** [computer file]. Evanston, Ill. : American Theological Library Association, 1975– .   **BB16**
    File size: 358,000 records. Available online as *Religion index* (BRS, DIALOG, WILSONLINE; updated monthly) and in CD-ROM (Wilson; updated annually).
    Machine-readable version of: *Religion index one : periodicals* (*Guide* BB41); *Religion index two : multi-author works* (*Guide* BB42); *Research in ministry* (Chicago : ATLA, 1982–); and *Index to book reviews in religion* (*Supplement* BB21).

●**Religious and theological abstracts** [computer file]. Myerstown, Pa. : Religious and Theological Abstracts, 1958– .   **BB17**
    Machine-readable version of *Religious and theological abstracts* (*Guide* BB43).
    Updated annually. Available in CD-ROM (producer).

South African theological bibliography = Suid-Afrikaanse teologiese bibliografie / editors, C.F.A. Borchardt & W.S. Vorster. Pretoria : Univ. of South Africa, 1989. v. 4. ISBN 0-86981-185-1 (pbk.). (In progress).   **BB18**
    Vol. 4 ed. by C.F.A. Borchardt, J. Kilian, W.S. Vorster.
    An index, with some abstracts, of theological journal and multiauthor works published 1976–88 in South Africa. Includes dissertations and theses submitted to South African institutions. Coverage has been expanded with each volume; volumes now appear annually. Beginning with v. 4, access has been improved by a change from classified to dictionary arrangement.   Z7757.S6S68

Reviews

Critical review of books in religion. 1988– . Atlanta : Journal of the American Academy of Religion and the Journal of Biblical Literature, 1988– . Annual. ISSN 0894-8860. $20.00.   **BB19**
    Several long, critical reviews of a single work or type of work (e.g., *Encyclopedia of religion* in 1989, religious studies textbooks in 1988) fill the first 100 pages (in a total of 500) of each annual volume. The balance contains shorter book reviews by specialists of works selected from the spectrum of religious studies literature. A bibliography of translations and new editions is appended. Indexes of authors and reviewers.   BL1.C75

Index to book reviews in religion : cumulated and revised edition of the book reviews from *Index to religious periodical literature* / ed. by Douglas W. Geyer. Evanston, Ill. : American Theological Library Association, c1990. v. 1. (In progress).   **BB20**
    Subtitle: IBRR : an author, title, and classified index to reviews of books published in and of interest to the field of religion.
    A cumulated and revised reprinting of the book review index sections of *Index to religious periodical literature*, v. 1–4, 1949–59 (*Guide* BB41 note). Two additional volumes, cumulating and revising the book review sections from v. 5–11, 1960–74, are in progress. As these cumulated volumes reach completion, the data in them will be available online and in CD-ROM.   Z7753.I5

Index to book reviews in religion. [Feb. 1986]– . Chicago : American Theological Library Association, c1986– . Bimonthly, with Dec. constituting the annual cumulation. ISSN 0887-1574. $148.00.   **BB21**
    Supersedes the book review index section of *Religion index one* (*Guide* BB41), which last appeared in v.17 (1985). Contains author/editor, title, reviewer, and series indexes to book reviews, review essays, and review articles published in more

than 400 periodicals in the field of religion or of interest to it. The annual index, besides cumulating quarterly indexes, adds a classified index.
    § Indexes to book reviews are included as part of the database *Religion indexes*, available online (BRS, DIALOG, WILSONLINE) and in CD-ROM (Wilson; *Supplement BB16*). Coverage in both formats begins with 1975; the online files are updated monthly, the CD-ROM annually.   Z7753.I5

Dictionaries; Encyclopedias

The dictionary of Bible and religion / William H. Gentz, ed. Nashville : Abingdon, c1986. 1147 p. : ill. ISBN 0-687-10757-1.   **BB22**
    Brief articles, initialed by 28 contributors, with cross-references, treat principally the Bible, but also the history of Christianity, Christian doctrine, world religions, and contemporary religions. Ecumenically Christian in origin; intended for the lay reader. Contains photographs, illustrations, charts, maps in color, and a brief bibliography.   BR95.D46

The encyclopedia of Eastern philosophy and religion : Buddhism, Hinduism, Taoism, Zen / Ingrid Fischer-Schreiber [et al.] ; editors, Stephan Schuhmacher, Gert Woerner. Boston : Shambhala, 1989. 468 p. : ill. ISBN 0-87773-433-X. $39.95.   **BB23**
    Also published as: *The Rider encyclopedia of Eastern philosophy and religion* (London : Rider, [1989]).
    Translation of: *Lexikon der östlichen Weisheitslehren* (Bern : O.W. Barth, [1986]).
    Written by specialists but intended for general readers; attempts to present "the basic terminology and doctrinal systems of the four great wisdom teachings of the East . . . ."—*Introd.* Contains approximately 4,000 unsigned definitions and biographical sketches, arranged alphabetically. Longer entries often include discussions of historical and cultural significance, explanatory parables or *koans*, or references to important translations or studies. A "Ch'an/Zen lineage chart" following the text shows the transmission of the Buddhist tradition through various masters, texts, sects, and philosophies. Concludes with a lengthy classified bibliography that lists primary and secondary sources. No index, but entries contain numerous cross-references and illustrations.   BL1005.L4813

Encyclopedia of religion in the South / ed. by Samuel S. Hill. [Macon, Ga.] : Mercer Univ. Pr., c1984. 878 p. ISBN 0-86554-117-5. $60.00.   **BB24**
    Signed articles with bibliographies that treat a broad range of topics in the religious life and thought of a region consisting of the 13 states of the Confederacy and certain adjoining areas. Detailed subject index; appendix of articles on the colonial period (1607–1798) and the recent period (1940 to the present).   BR535.E52

The encyclopedia of religion / [ed. in chief, Mircea Eliade ; editors, Charles J. Adams . . . et al.]. N.Y. : Macmillan, c1987. 16 v : ill. ISBN 0-02-909480-1. $1,100.00.   **BB25**
    Intended to "introduce educated, non-specialist readers to important ideas, practices and persons in the religious experience of humankind from the Paleolithic past to our day."—*Foreword*. Treats theoretical (e.g., doctrines, myths, theologies, ethics), practical (e.g., cults, sacraments, meditations), and sociological (e.g., religious groups, ecclesiastical forms) aspects of religion; includes extensive coverage of non-Western religions. Signed articles by some 1,400 contributors worldwide end with bibliographies and are arranged in alphabetic order. Many composite entries treat two or more related topics. Vol. 16 provides an alphabetic list of entries, a synoptic outline of contents, and an extensive general index. Has quickly become the

standard work, updating *Encyclopedia of religion and ethics* (ed. by James Hastings, *Guide* BB51). BL31.E46

Encyclopedia of the American religious experience : studies of traditions and movements / Charles H. Lippy and Peter W. Williams, editors. N.Y. : Scribner, c1988. 3 v. (1872 p.). ISBN 0-684-18062-6. $225.00. **BB26**

Consists of 105 long, interpretative essays by leading scholars in the fields of history, religion, theology, American studies, sociology, and philosophy. Arranged logically and topically under nine broad subjects: Approaches to religion in America; North America: contexts and backgrounds; Jewish and Christian traditions; Religions outside the Jewish and Christian traditions; Movements in American religion; American religious thought and literature; Liturgy, worship and the arts; Religion and the political and social orders; The dissemination of American religion. A selected bibliography and cross-references follow each essay. An extensive index provides quick access to topics discussed in one or many articles; there is also an alphabetical list of articles and a list of contributors with institutional affiliations. A comprehensive, authoritative work.

BL20.C5.E53

The encyclopedia of unbelief / Gordon Stein, ed. Buffalo, N.Y. : Prometheus Books, 1985. 2 v. (819 p.). ISBN 0-87975-307-2 (set). **BB27**

Contains 203 signed articles, some of considerable length, with bibliographies, written by 101 scholars worldwide. Scope extends from ancient times to the present and to all areas of the world. Among the articles are biographies of unbelievers, histories of unbelief in various countries or time periods, and surveys of unbelief within the literatures of many countries. Subject index and five appendixes: Bibliography of unbelief; Meetings of unbelievers; Organizations of unbelief; Publishers of unbelief; Periodicals of unbelief. BL2705.E53

MacGregor, Geddes. Dictionary of religion and philosophy. N.Y. : Paragon House, 1989. 696 p. ISBN 1-55778-019-6. $35.00. **BB28**

Intended for students. Emphasizes the Judeo-Christian tradition and philosophical topics related to it, but also includes information on Eastern religions. Brief articles in alphabetical order, without bibliographies or cross-references. Selected classified bibliography at the end of the work.

BL31.M23

Man, myth & magic : the illustrated encyclopedia of mythology, religion, and the unknown / ed. in chief, Richard Cavendish ; editorial board, C.A. Burland . . . [et al.]. New ed., ed. and comp. by Yvonne Deutch. N.Y. : Marshall Cavendish, 1983. 12 v. (3201 p.) : ill. (some col.). ISBN 0-86307-041-8 (set). $349.50. **BB29**

For annotation, see *Supplement* CF4. BF1411.M25

Melton, J. Gordon. The encyclopedia of American religions. 3rd ed. Detroit : Gale, c1989. 1102 p. : ill. ISBN 0-8103-2841-0. $165.00. **BB30**

1st ed., 1978 (*Guide* BB57).

Contains 250 new entries and revisions of most entries from earlier editions. Coverage now extends to Canadian as well as U.S. religious groups. Includes two extensive introductory essays on the history of religion in the U.S. and Canada; 22 essays on all religious families (e.g., Catholic, Protestant, Jewish, Spiritualist, Middle Eastern), and a directory providing historical and current information on individual religious bodies arranged by families. Essays and directory entries have extensive bibliographies. Six indexes: educational institutions; periodicals; geographic; personal name; subject; and religious organizations and institutions. An authoritative source for information on prominent and obscure North American religious groups. BL2525.M449

Directories

Butler, Francis J. Foundation guide for religious grant seekers / Francis J. Butler & Catherine E. Farrell, co-editors. [3rd ed.]. Atlanta : Scholars Pr., [c1987]. 172 p. ISBN 1-55540-121-X (pbk.). **BB31**

3rd ed., 1987 (*Guide* BB67).

A revised and enlarged edition providing information on 407 Protestant, Catholic, Jewish, and interfaith foundations with a history of religious grant making. Appendixes list locations of Foundation Center libraries and area foundation directories. BV774.5.B87

Directory of departments and programs of religious studies in North America / Watson E. Mills, ed. 1987 ed. Macon, Ga. : [Mercer Univ. Pr.], 1987. 410 p. ISBN 0-86554-282-1 (pbk.). $15.95. ISBN 0-86554-283-X. $19.95. **BB32**

At head of title: Council of Societies for the Study of Religion.

Issued annually beginning in 1987.

Provides detailed information on undergraduate and graduate programs in religious studies at four-year colleges, universities, and theological schools. Lists faculty members with their graduate degrees and fields of specialization. BL41.D57

Guide to schools and departments of religion and seminaries in the United States and Canada : degree programs in religious studies / comp. by Modoc Press, Inc. N.Y. : Macmillan, c1987. 609 p. ISBN 0-02-921650-8. $90.00. **BB33**

Gives detailed information on 703 regionally or nationally accredited four-year and graduate institutions. Separate sections for U.S. and Canada. Arranged alphabetically by state or province, then by name of institution. Denomination and institution indexes. BV4030.G85

Biography

Melton, J. Gordon. Biographical dictionary of American cult and sect leaders. N.Y. : Garland, 1986. 354 p. ISBN 0-8240-9037-3. **BB34**

Contains sketches of 300 to 500 words on 213 persons who played leading roles in founding or developing dissident minority religious groups in the U.S. Only persons who died before 1983 are included. A bibliography of works by and about the biographee follows each sketch. Appendix lists biographees by religious tradition they adopted, by birthplace, and by religious backgrounds from which they came. Subject index.

BL2525.M448

Who's who in religion. 3rd ed. Chicago : Marquis Who's Who, 1985. ISSN 0160-3728. **BB35**

For earlier eds. and annotation, see *Guide* BB264.

Contains "biographical information on more than 7,000 religious leaders and religion professionals in North America . . . 4,000 of whom are new to this edition."—*Pref.*

BL2530.U6W48

Sacred books

The Bible

Versions

Bible. O.T. *1985. English.* Tanakh : a new translation of the Holy Scriptures according to the traditional Hebrew text. Philadelphia : Jewish Publication Society, 1985. 1624 p. ISBN 0-8276-0252-9.   **BB36**

The three sections of the English translation of the Hebrew Bible noted in the *Guide*, p. 348, reissued in a single volume. The title derives from the three component sections, the *Torah*, *Nevi'im* (the Prophets), and *Kethuvim* (the Writings).

BS895.J4

Bible. *1988. English. New American.* The New American Bible. Revised New Testament / authorized by the Board of Trustees of the Confraternity of Christian Doctrine and approved by the Administrative Committee/ Board of the National Conference of Catholic Bishops and the United States Catholic Conference. [Rev. ed.]. Northport, N.Y. : Costello Pub. Co. ; Grand Rapids, Mich. : Eerdmans, 1988. 774 p. ISBN 0-918344-27-1. ISBN 0-8028-0417-9 (Eerdmans).   **BB37**

A literal translation conforming to contemporary American English usage, intended for Roman Catholic liturgical proclamation and for private reading and study. Introduces some inclusive language. The introductions and notes have been rewritten and expanded, and the cross-references revised.

BS2092.3.A1G73

Bible. *1989. English. Revised English.* The revised English Bible with the Apocrypha. New Rochelle, N.Y. : Oxford Univ. Pr. : Cambridge Univ. Pr., 1989. [828, 205, 236 p.]. ISBN 0-521-15137-6.   **BB38**

A substantial revision of the *New English Bible* (1970; see *Guide* p. 347–348, no. 4), based on scholarship of the 1980s. Attempts to use idiomatic English while maintaining a fluent style with appropriate dignity for liturgical use. "The revisers have preferred more inclusive gender reference where that has been possible without compromising scholarly integrity or English style."—*Pref.*

BS195.R4

Bible. *1990. English. New Revised Standard.* The Holy Bible : containing the Old and New Testaments with the Apocryphal/Deuterocanonical books. New Revised Standard Version. Nashville : T. Nelson, c1990. 26, 890, 264, 261, 32 p. : ill., map.   **BB39**

The *NRSV* stands in the tradition of the King James (Authorized) Version, 1611; the Revised Version, 1881–85; the American Standard Version, 1901; and the Revised Standard Version, 1952 (*Guide*, p. 347). Intended for public reading, congregational worship, private study, instruction, and meditation, it attempts to be as literal as possible while following standard American English usage, avoids colloquialism, and prefers simple, direct terms and phrases. Uses inclusive language "as far as this can be done without altering passages that reflect the historical situation of ancient patriarchal culture."—*To the Reader.*

BS195.N39

The Old Testament pseudepigrapha / ed. by James H. Charlesworth. Garden City, N.Y. : Doubleday, 1985. v. 2. ISBN 0-385-18813-7 (v. 2).   **BB40**

For v. 1, see *Guide*, p.348.

Contents: v. 2, Expansions of the "Old Testament" and legends, wisdom and philosophical literature, prayers, psalms, and odes, fragments of lost Judeo-Hellenistic works. Completes the set.

This work supersedes *Apocrypha and pseudepigrapha of the Old Testament in English*, ed. by R.H. Charles, (1913, 2 v.; Repr. 1963).   BS1830.A3

Bibliography

Belle, Gilbert van. Johannine bibliography 1966–1985 : a cumulative bibliography on the Fourth Gospel. Louvain : Leuven Univ. Pr. : Uitgeverij Peters, 1988. 563 p. (Bibliotheca Ephemeridum theologicarum Lovaniensium, 82). ISBN 90-6186-285-X.   **BB41**

Contains 6,300 citations, with cross-references, to monographs, multiauthor works, articles, dissertations, and book reviews in detailed classified arrangement. Indexes of miscellanea, festschriften and collected essays; periodicals; biblical references; subjects; and names. Continues coverage provided by Edward Malatesta's *St. John's Gospel, 1920–1965* (Rome: Pontifical Biblical Institute, 1967).   Z7772.M1

Charlesworth, James H. The New Testament apocrypha and pseudepigrapha : a guide to publications, with excursuses on Apocalypses / by James H. Charlesworth, with James R. Mueller. [Chicago] : American Theological Library Association ; Metuchen, N.J. : Scarecrow, 1987. 450 p. (ATLA bibliography series, no. 17). ISBN 0-8108-1845-0. $42.50.   **BB42**

The first comprehensive bibliography of monographic and serial publications on the 99 major works forming the complex New Testament Apocrypha and Pseudepigrapha. Includes three introductory essays: (1) Defining the New Testament Apocrypha and Pseudepigrapha and the history of its study; (2) The theology and impact of the Apocalypse of John; (3) Subsequent apocalypses in the Jewish and Christian traditions. Author index. An invaluable tool for general readers and specialists alike.   Z7772.Z5C45

Mills, Watson E. A bibliography of the periodical literature on the Acts of the Apostles, 1962–1984. Leiden : E.J. Brill, 1986. 115 p. (Supplements to Novum Testamentum, v. 58). ISBN 90-04-08130-5.   **BB43**

Lists relevant articles from approximately 600 scholarly journals. Entries are arranged alphabetically by author. Scripture and subject indexes.   Z7772.N1M55

Wagner, Günter. An exegetical bibliography of the New Testament. Macon, Ga. : Mercer Univ. Pr., c1985–1987. v. 2–3. ISBN 0-86554-013-6 (v. 1). $35.00. (In progress).   **BB44**

For initial volume, see *Guide* BB114.

Contents: v.2, Luke and Acts; v.3, John and 1,2,3 John.

Entries are arranged in the order of chapters and verses of the biblical text, then chronologically. References cite many discussions hidden within more comprehensive works. Most citations refer to publications in English or German, 1950s to time of publication. No indexes. An outstanding contribution to biblical scholarship, but should be used with other standard bibliographies (e.g., *New testament abstracts*, *Guide* BB117). A fourth volume, on the major Pauline epistles, is in preparation.

Z7772.M1W33

Indexes and abstract journals

Elenchus of Biblica. 1985– . Roma : Pontificio Istituto biblico, 1988– . Annual.   **BB45**

Continues *Elenchus bibiographicus biblicus* (*Guide* BB115), which ceased with v. 65, covering publications through 1984. The new series, *Elenchus of biblical bibliography*, which uses the title *Elenchus of Biblica* for each annual volume, still provides the most comprehensive, although not most timely, indexing of journal and monographic literature for biblical studies.

Z7770.E63

Dictionaries; Handbooks

Bijbelse encyclopedie. *English.* The Eerdmans Bible dictionary / revision ed., Allen C. Myers. Grand Rapids, Mich.: Eerdmans, 1987. 1094 p., [12] p. of plates: ill. (some col.). ISBN 0-8028-2402-1. **BB46**

1st ed., (Kampen: Kok, c1950); 2nd ed., c1976.

A revised, augmented translation, by North American scholars, that is evangelical Protestant in orientation, but treats other viewpoints fairly. Bibliographical references for selected articles. Limited number of black-and-white photographs, line drawings, and maps in color. BS440.G7613

Blair, Edward Payson. The illustrated Bible handbook. Nashville: Abingdon Pr., c1987. 538 p.: col. ill. ISBN 0-687-18680-3. **BB47**

A new edition of Blair's *Abingdon Bible handbook*, (*Guide* BB151). Several chapters have been revised as a result of recent scholarship, and greater attention is given to views of conservative as well as liberal scholars. Updated bibliographies and improved graphics. BS475.2.B5

Botterweck, G. Johannes. Theological dictionary of the Old Testament / ed. by G. Johannes Botterweck and Helmer Ringgren. Grand Rapids: Eerdmans, 1986. v. 5. ISBN 0-8028-2338-6 (set). (In progress). **BB48**

For v. 1–4 and annotation, see *Guide* BB153.
Contents: v. 5, hmr–YHWH. BS440.B5713

——————— Theologisches Wörterbuch zum Alten Testament / hrsg. von G. Johannes Botterweck und Helmer Ringgren. Stuttgart: W. Kohlhammer, [1986–1989]. v. 5–6. ISBN 3-17-001209-6 (v. 1). (In progress). **BB49**

For v.1–5$^{1/2}$ and annotation, see *Guide* BB152.
Contents: v. 5, Mrd–'zv; v. 6, 'zz–qwm. BS440.B57

A dictionary of Biblical interpretation / ed. by R.J. Coggins and J.L. Houlden. London: SCM Pr.; Philadelphia: Trinity Pr. International, 1990. 751 p. ISBN 0-334-00294-X. **BB50**

Signed articles by British scholars, with bibliographies, on a wide range of topics dealing with the history of biblical interpretation and current issues in biblical scholarship. Includes a select index of subjects and an index of biblical references. Provides access to many subjects not treated in most Bible dictionaries. BS500.D5

Harper's Bible dictionary / gen. ed., Paul J. Achtemeier. San Francisco: Harper & Row, c1985. 1178 p. ISBN 0-06-069862-4. $29.95. **BB51**

8th ed., 1973 (*Guide* BB173).
Sponsored by Society of Biblical Literature.

A thoroughly revised edition that presents in a form accessible to general readers the consensus of biblical scholarship from a nonsectarian perspective. Signed articles with cross-references by 179 leading scholars treat all the important personal and place names in the Bible, every book of the Bible including the Apocrypha, all major archaeological sites, and all important theological terms. There are also major articles with bibliography on such topics as: Jerusalem; Sociology of the Old and New Testaments; Moses; and Bible texts, versions, manuscripts, and editions. Well illustrated with numerous black-and-white photographs, some color photographs, and line drawings. Maps in color and an index appear at the end of the volume. An excellent one-volume source. BS440.H237

Harper's Bible pronunciation guide / gen. ed., William O. Walker, Jr.; associate editors, Toni Craven, J. Andrew Dearman, with the Society of Biblical Literature. San Francisco: Harper & Row, c1989. 170 p. ISBN 0-06-068951-X. $15.95. **BB52**

Gives the pronunciation of every proper name in the English Bible (including the Apocrypha), many proper names from the ancient world, and technical terms important for biblical study. Words appear in alphabetical order in two sections: "Biblical terms" and "Nonbiblical terms." The pronunciation key is printed at the bottom of each page. BS435.H35

Hughes, John J. Bits, bytes & biblical studies: a resource guide for the use of computers in biblical and classical studies. Grand Rapids, Mich.: Academie Books, c1987. 643 p.: ill. ISBN 0-310-28581-X (pbk.). $29.95. **BB53**

Contains critical reviews of a wide variety of computer programs, arranged in chapters on word processing, Bible concordances, language learning, communications/online services, study of archaeology, and ancient texts, with a bibliography appended to each chapter. Also has an introductory chapter on computers, a list of computer abbreviations and acronyms, a list of trademarks, a glossary, and indexes of proper names and topics. A unique and highly useful encyclopedic work for beginners and specialists. Updated by the newsletter, *Bits & bytes review*, 1986– . BS600.2.H83

Illustrated dictionary & concordance of the Bible / [general ed., Geoffrey Wigoder; editors, Shalom M. Paul, Old Testament, Benedict T. Viviano, New Testament, Ephraim Stern, biblical archeology]. N.Y.: Macmillan, c1986. 1070 p.: ill. (some col.). ISBN 0-02-916380-3. $100.00. **BB54**

A Bible dictionary with entries for every place and person mentioned in the Old and New Testaments and for major religious concepts and general topics. Brief articles by specialists reflecting current scholarship are free of technical jargon. Numerous illustrations in color, but few cross-references and no bibliography. Bible references related to each subject are listed in the margin next the the entry, hence the word "concordance" in the title. BS440.I36

The international standard Bible encyclopedia / gen. ed., Geoffrey W. Bromiley ... [et al.]. Fully rev. Grand Rapids, Mich.: Eerdmans, 1986–c1988. v. 3–4. ISBN 0-8028-8160-2 (set). $29.95 (v. 1). **BB55**

For v. 1–2 and annotation, see *Guide* BB166.
Contents: v. 3–4, K–Z. Completes the set.
No indexes. BS440.I6

The literary guide to the Bible / ed. by Robert Alter and Frank Kermode. Cambridge, Mass.: Belknap Pr. of Harvard Univ. Pr., 1987. 678 p. ISBN 0-674-87530-3. **BB56**

The only commentary now available on the entire Bible that uses the methods of literary rather than historical criticism, emphasizing such matters as allusion, imagery, narrative structure, symbolism, and poetic form. Contributors are Christian, Jewish, and secular scholars affiliated with major universities in the U.S., Great Britain, and Israel. Has sections on individual books and on groups of related books (e.g., The Pauline epistles), followed by seven general essays (e.g., The characteristics of ancient Hebrew poetry), a glossary of biblical and literary terms, and a subject index. Intended for general readers.

BS535.L54

Mercer dictionary of the Bible / gen. ed., Watson E. Mills; associate ed., Roger Bullard ... [et al.]. Macon, Ga.: Mercer Univ. Pr., c1990. 987 p., 62 p. of plates: ill. (some col.). ISBN 0-86554-299-6. ISBN 0-86554-373-9 (pbk.). **BB57**

Signed articles by 225 members of the National Association of Baptist Professors of Religion, intended for college, university, and seminary students. Reflects a broad range of viewpoints. Most articles have bibliographies. Well-illustrated throughout; 62 center plates have maps and photographs in color. BS440.M429

Theologisches Wörterbuch zum Neuen Testament. *English.* Theological dictionary of the New Testament / ed. by Gerhard Kittel and Gerhard Friedrich ; translated by Geoffrey W. Bromiley ; abridged in one volume by Geoffrey W. Bromiley. Grand Rapids, Mich. : Eerdmans, c1985. 1356 p. ISBN 0-8028-2404-8. $44.95.
BB58

Reduced to one-sixth the size of the original (*Guide* BB169). Theological material has been retained as much as possible; philological, archaeological, and other supporting materials have been drastically reduced; footnotes and bibliographies are excluded. Volume and page references at the end of each article direct the reader to the original article in the parent set. Access is facilitated by transliteration of all Greek words, bracketed English translations in the page headings, and alphabetical tables of English keywords and Greek keywords.
PA881.T4713

Concordances

Goodrick, Edward W. The NIV exhaustive concordance / Edward W. Goodrick, John R. Kohlenberger III. Grand Rapids, Mich. : Zondervan Pub. House, c1990. 1853 p. ISBN 0-310-43690-7.
BB59

A 1981 compilation by the same editors had title: *The NIV complete concordance* (*Guide* BB126).

Expands the 1981 edition by identifying the original Hebrew, Aramaic, and Greek words for which the English object words are translations, and by listing in a separate sequence, with biblical citations, the articles, conjunctions, particles, prepositions, and pronouns. Gives frequency count for each word and contexts for each keyword. Contains Hebrew, Aramaic, and Greek concordances and indexes correlating this work to James Strong's *Exhaustive concordance of the Bible* (*Guide* BB134). BS425.G62

Konkordanz zum Novum Testamentum Graece von Nestle-Aland / hrsg. vom Institut für Neutestamentliche Textforschung und vom Rechenzentrum der Universität Münster ; unter besonderer mitwirkung von H. Bachmann und W. A. Slaby. 3. Aufl. Berlin : W. de Gruyter, 1987. 1963 [p.], 63 p. ISBN 3-11-011570-0.
BB60

1st ed., 1980 (*Guide* BB138) and 2nd ed., 1985, had title: *Computer-Kondoranz zum Novum Testamentum Graece.*

Despite the change in title, the three editions vary only slightly. BS2302.K65

Whitaker, Richard E. The Eerdmans analytical concordance to the Revised Standard Version of the Bible. Grand Rapids, Mich. : Eerdmans, c1988. 1548 p. ISBN 0-8028-2403-X. $49.95.
BB61
" . . . with James E. Goehring and research personnel of the Institute for Antiquity and Christianity"—*t.p.*

The only analytical concordance of the whole Revised Standard Version, in that it indicates what word in an original language is being translated in each context. Omits many frequently used prepositions and conjunctions and all personal pronouns. Has Main concordance, Concordance of proper names, and Concordance of numbers. Hebrew, Aramaic, Greek, and Latin indexes at the end of the volume include all words in those languages that are cited in the Main concordance and in the Concordance of proper names. BS425.W48

Quotations

Ehrlich, Eugene. Mene, Mene, Tekel / Eugene Ehrlich, David H. Scott. N.Y. : Harper & Row, 1990. p. ISBN 0-06-016456-5. $18.00.
BB62

Lists in alphabetical order significant words and phrases from the Authorized (King James) Version of the Bible (1611), that have gained wide currency in English. Identifies the source and explains the context and meaning of each entry. Index to scriptural passages. PE1689.E36

Commentaries

The books of the Bible / Bernhard W. Anderson, ed. N.Y. : Scribner's, c1989. 2 v. ISBN 0-684-18487-7 (set). $175.00.
BB63

Contents: v. 1, Old Testament, subject index; v. 2, New Testament, apocryphal writings, comprehensive subject index.

A series of interpretative essays, each followed by a select bibliography, on books of the Bible arranged according to the order of the biblical canon. Focuses on the text as it now stands rather than its historical development. Written from an ecumenical perspective mainly by American and British scholars. Intended for general readers. BS540.B62

Harper's Bible commentary / gen. ed., James L. Mays, with the Society of Biblical Literature. San Francisco : Harper & Row, c1988. 1326 p. ISBN 0-06-065541-0.
BB64

Prior ed., 1962, ed. by William Neil (*Guide* BB202).

The work of 82 contributors and six editors, representing Jewish and Christian scholarship. Designed "to make the best current scholarship available to general audiences for reading and studying the books of the Bible."—*Pref.* Contains numerous introductory essays on the whole Bible and on the seven parts into which the *Commentary* divides it, and provides an introductory essay, concise commentary, and current bibliography for each book, including the Apocrypha. Cross-references to *Harper's Bible dictionary* (*Supplement* BB51). Black-and-white illustrations; plates and maps in color. Index.
BS491.2.H37

Hermeneia : a critical and historical commentary on the Bible. Minneapolis : Fortress, 1971–1991. v. 1–37. (In progress.).
BB65

Most volumes are translations of German works by renowned Protestant scholars, with revisions and updated bibliography. Others were written by American scholars specifically for this series. Offers a high level of technical scholarship, but accessible to general readers. Quotations in ancient languages are translated into English.

The international critical commentary on the Holy Scriptures of the Old and New Testaments. Edinburgh : T. & T. Clark, 1975–88. v. 1–5. (In progress).
BB66

Contents: Romans 1–8 (Romans, v. 1), 1975; Romans 9–16 (Romans, v. 2), 1979, both by C.E.B. Cranfield; Jeremiah 1–25 (Jeremiah, v. 1), 1986, by William McKane; Matthew 1–7 (Matthew, v. 1), 1988, by W.D. Davis and Dale C. Allison.

The previous edition of this important work (*Guide* BB197) was never completed; various volumes have been reprinted, and as recently as 1951 a completely new volume was published (*Kings I and II*, by J.A. Montgomery and H.S. German). This new edition constitutes an extension and revision of the earlier set. Under the new editors, "commentaries on books of the Bible which have not appeared in the ICC before are now in preparation and new editions of many existing volumes are in preparation."—*Publisher's catalog.* The newer works continue the critical and philological emphasis of the earlier titles. BS491.I6

The new Jerome biblical commentary / ed. by Raymond E. Brown, Joseph A. Fitzmyer, Roland E. Murphy. Englewood Cliffs, N.J. : Prentice-Hall, 1990. 1484 p. ISBN 0-13-614934-0. **BB67**
1968 ed. had title *The Jerome biblical commentary* (*Guide* BB194).
Two-thirds new material, contributed by some 70 Catholic scholars, laymen and women as well as clergy, primarily North Americans, who exemplify the sophistication of biblical scholarship and range of exegetical variation in the Catholic Church today. Intended for educated readers, seminarians and clergy. Contains commentary on all the books of the Bible, numerous cross-references to the 20 topical and introductory articles, scholarly bibliographies, a suggested basic bibliography, and an extensive index of subjects and persons. BS491.2.N485

Atlases

The Harper atlas of the Bible / ed. by James B. Pritchard. N.Y. : Harper & Row, c1987. 254 p.; 37 cm. ISBN 0-06-181883-6. $44.95. **BB68**
Some 50 scholars worldwide present the results of recent scholarship in an accessible and highly attractive form. Maps, illustrations, charts, and graphs, all in color, accompanied by concise commentary and notes, chronicle war and conquest, and everyday life and custom. A color-coded chronological chart extending from prehistoric times to 150 CE provides the context for the maps which follow. An index of people who play an important role in the Bible lists biblical citations for each. An index of place names identifies each by area/country, variant name, Arabic name, modern Hebrew name, and map location. G2230.H47

Rasmussen, Carl. Zondervan NIV atlas of the Bible. Grand Rapids, Mich. : Regency Reference Library, c1989. 256 p. : col. ill. ISBN 0-310-25160-5. $39.95. **BB69**
Offers clear, concise, attractive maps, charts, diagrams, and pictures (most in color), accompanied by text. Bible quotations are drawn from the *New International Version* (NIV) (Grand Rapids, Mich.: Zondervan, 1973–78). Geographical section concentrates on areas within Israel and Jordan, but also covers the entire Middle East; historical section covers from the prepatriarchal period to the fall of Jerusalem. Appendixes include endnotes, bibliography, timeline of biblical history, glossary, index of scripture references, index of persons, and gazetteer with index. Intended for the general reader. BS630.R37

Koran

Koran. *English & Arabic.* al-Qur'ān : a contemporary translation / by Ahmed Ali. 2nd rev. ed., Corr. ed. Princeton, N.J. : Princeton Univ. Pr., 1988. [572 p.]. ISBN 0-691-07329-5. $50.00. ISBN 0-691-02046-9 (pbk.). $9.95. **BB70**
1st ed., Karachi : Akrasu, 1984.
An elegant contemporary English translation of the Koran, with English and Arabic in parallel columns. Occasional explanatory footnotes. Subject index and index of the prophets giving English and Qur'anic forms of their names. BP109.1988

Mir, Mustansir. Dictionary of Qur'ānic terms and concepts. N.Y. : Garland, 1987. 244 p. (Garland reference library of the humanities, vol. 693). ISBN 0-8240-8546-9. $40.00. **BB71**

Brief articles are arranged alphabetically by English translation or transliteration of Arabic words or phrases. Most entries contain cross-references. No bibliography. BP133.M57

Prayers

The Oxford book of prayer / gen. ed., George Appleton. Oxford ; N.Y. : Oxford Univ. Pr., 1985. 397 p. ISBN 0-19-213222-9. **BB72**
An anthology of prayers, selected mainly from the Bible and individuals and church liturgies representing the various branches of the Christian tradition, but including a long chapter with prayers from ten other traditions of belief (e.g., Jewish, Indian, Buddhist). An appendix contains "Notes on the development of eucharistic prayers," and the acknowledgements list all the sources from which selections were made. Indexes of authors and sources, and of subjects. BV245.O94

CHRISTIANITY

General Works

West, Edward N. Outward signs : the language of Christian symbolism. N.Y. : Walker, 1989. 237 p. : ill. ISBN 0-8027-1073-5. $30.00. **BB73**
Discusses the origin and meaning of Christian symbols used in liturgy, vestments, and architecture. Classified arrangement. Contains 455 line drawings, glossary, bibliography, and subject index. Intended for general readers. BV150.W418

Bibliography

Birney, Alice L. The literary lives of Jesus : an international bibliography of poetry, drama, fiction, and criticism. N.Y. : Garland, 1989. 187 p. : ill. (Garland reference library of the humanities, vol. 735). ISBN 0-8240-8475-6. **BB74**
For annotation, see *Supplement* BD1. Z6514.C5J473

Blumhofer, Edith Waldvogel. Twentieth-century evangelicalism : a guide to the sources / Edith L. Blumhofer, Joel A. Carpenter. N.Y. : Garland, 1990. 384 p. ISBN 0-8240-3040-0. **BB75**
Contains 1,572 citations, critically annotated by nine specialists, to the literature and the repositories essential for the study of all aspects of American Evangelicalism. Employs a classified arrangement with indexes of authors, institutions and organizations, and subjects. BR1644.U6B48

Church and state in postwar eastern Europe : a bibliographical survey / comp. by Paul Mojzes. N.Y. : Greenwood, [1987]. 109 p. (Bibliographies and indexes in religious studies, no. 11). ISBN 0-313-24002-7. **BB76**
For annotation, see *Supplement* DC12. Z7776.72.C5

Crumb, Lawrence N. The Oxford Movement and its leaders : a bibliography of secondary and lesser primary sources. Metuchen, N.J. : American Theological Library Association : Scarecrow, 1988. 706 p. (ATLA bibliography series, no. 24). ISBN 0-8108-2141-9. $62.50. **BB77**
Contains 5,432 entries on the "Tractarian" generation (1833–50) of the Oxford Movement. Includes books, pamphlets, theses, parts of books, periodical articles, manuscripts, microforms, and tape recordings. Arranged by year, by the form of literature within each year, and alphabetically within

each form. Author, periodical, and subject indexes.

Z7845.O83C78

Evans, James H. Black theology : a critical assessment and annotated bibliography / comp. by James H. Evans, Jr., G.E. Gorman, advisory ed. N.Y. : Greenwood, 1987. 205 p. (Bibliographies and indexes in religious studies, no. 10). ISBN 0-313-24822-2.　　　　**BB78**

An introductory essay is followed by an annotated bibliography of 461 entries listing both monographs and periodical articles. Materials are arranged alphabetically by author in one of three sections: Origins and development of black theology; Liberation, feminism and Marxism; Cultural and global discourse. Indexes of names, titles and subjects.　　　Z7774.E9

Gorman, G. E. Theological and religious reference materials / G.E. Gorman and Lyn Gorman. Westport, Conn. : Greenwood, 1985–1986. v. 2–3. (Bibliographies and indexes in religious studies, no. 2, 7). ISBN 0-313-20924-3 (v. 1). (In progress).　　**BB79**

For v. 1, see *Guide* BB12.

Contents: v. 2, Systematic theology and church history; v. 3, Practical theology.

Although they describe a large quantity of theological materials spanning many periods, fields and languages, these volumes, like v. 1, have classifications too broad for effective browsing or study (440 works are listed under Systematic/doctrinal theology and ethics: handbooks). Other than the preface and introduction in v. 1, there are no interpretive or summarizing essays.　　　　　　　　　　　Z7770.G66

Jones, Charles Edwin. Black holiness : a guide to the study of black participation in Wesleyan perfectionist and glossolalic Pentecostal movements. [Chicago] : American Theological Library Association ; Metuchen, N.J. : Scarecrow, 1987. 388 p. (ATLA bibliography series, no. 18). ISBN 0-8108-1948-1.　　　　**BB80**

Lists in classified order almost 2,400 books and journal articles on the many African-American church bodies and individuals identified with the Holiness Movement. Library locations often given. Historical and biographical notes introduce sections and subsections. Index of subjects and authors.

Z1361.N39J66

Kaske, Robert Earl. Medieval Christian literary imagery : a guide to interpretation / R.E. Kaske, in collaboration with Arthur Groos and Michael W. Twomey. Toronto ; Buffalo : Univ. of Toronto Pr., c1988. 247 p. (Toronto medieval bibliographies, 11). ISBN 0-8020-2636-2. ISBN 0-8020-6663-1 (pbk.).　　　　　**BB81**

For annotation, see *Supplement* BD3.　　PN671.Z99K37

Soukup, Paul A. Christian communication : a bibliographical survey. N.Y. : Greenwood, 1989. 400 p. (Bibliographies and indexes in religious studies, no. 14). ISBN 0-313-25673-X.　　　　　　　　**BB82**

Annotates 1,311 books, journal articles, reports, and dissertations on communication history, theory, and current practice in Christian churches. Treats such topics as rhetoric, interpersonal communication, and mass communication, but excludes homiletics because of its coverage elsewhere. Classified arrangement; name, title, and subject indexes. Z5633.R45S66

Speaking in tongues : a guide to research on glossolalia / ed. by Watson E. Mills. Grand Rapids, Mich. : Eerdmans, c1986. 537 p. ISBN 0-8028-0183-8 (pbk.). **BB83**

A historical introduction by the editor, and a survey of the literature and a bibliography, are followed by 25 reprinted essays, written 1954–80 by theologians, biblical scholars, historians, and psychologists. Indexes of names and of Bible references. Does not "advocate a personal or theological position,"

(*Pref.*) but rather explores "the available methods for evaluating" this phenomenon.　　　　　　　　　BL54.S64

Dictionaries; Encyclopedias

Dictionary of Christianity in America / coordinating ed., Daniel G. Reid ; consulting editors, Robert D. Linder, Bruce L. Shelley, Harry S. Stout. Downers Grove, Ill. : InterVarsity Pr., c1990. 1305 p. ISBN 0-8308-1776-X.

BB84

Authoritative articles, in alphabetical order, by some 500 scholars, cover religious bodies, movements, and individuals and institutions in North America (especially the U.S.). Emphasis is historical rather than contemporary. "Does not attempt to arbitrate in matters of religious convictions, but to report fairly, accurately and objectively the beliefs and practices of the respective groups."—*Pref.* The only work of its kind to date.　　　　　　　　　　　　　　BR515.D53

Dictionnaire de spiritualité : ascétique et mystique, doctrine et histoire / publié sous la direction de Marcel Viller, S.J., assisté de F. Cavallera, et J. de Guibert, S.J., avec le concours d'un grand nombre de collaborateurs. Paris : G. Beauchesne et ses fils, 1986–1990. v. 12²–15. (In progress).　　　　　　　　　　　　　　**BB85**

For earlier parts and annotation, see *Guide* BB239.

Editors vary; principal ed.: v. 3, Charles Baumgartner; v. 4–6, André Rayez.

Contents: v. 12² (fasc. 80–85, 1986)–v. 15 (fasc. 96–98, 1990), Piaristes–Thiers.　　　　　　　　BX841.D67

Encyclopedia of early Christianity / Everett Ferguson, ed. . . . [et al.]. N.Y. : Garland, 1990. 983 p. : ill. (Garland reference library of the humanities, vol. 846). ISBN 0-8240-5745-7.　　　　　　　　　　　　　　**BB86**

Covers persons, places, doctrines, practices, art, liturgy, heresies, and schisms from the time of Jesus to approximately 600 CE. Articles by 135 specialists include bibliographies and cross-references. Extensive subject index. Intended for general readers, students, and professionals in fields outside religion who want information concerning early Christianity.

BR162.2.E53

Evangelisches Kirchenlexikon : EKL : internationale theologische Enzyklopädie / [hrsg. von Erwin Fahlbusch . . . et al.]. Neufassung. Göttingen : Vandenhoeck & Ruprecht, c1986 [i.e. c1985]–1989. v. 1–2. ISBN 3-525-50128-5 (1. Lfg.). (In progress).　　　**BB87**

2nd ed., 1961–62 (*Guide* BB242).

Vol. 1–2, A–K.

An entirely new edition, to be complete in four volumes. A German Protestant work on the life and teachings of the Christian churches, but ecumenical and international in outlook and with strong emphasis on contemporary issues, Third World churches, Roman Catholicism, and Eastern Orthodoxy. Long signed articles, in alphabetical order, contain cross-references and updated bibliographies arranged in chronological order. All articles on individuals and some historical surveys have been omitted.　　　　　　　　　　　　　　BR95.E89

New dictionary of theology / editors, Sinclair B. Ferguson, David F. Wright ; consulting ed., J.I. Packer. Downers Grove, Ill. : InterVarsity Pr., c1988. 738 p. ISBN 0-8308-1400-0.　　　　　　　　　　　　**BB88**

Offers concise, signed articles in alphabetical order, each with numerous cross-references and a select bibliography. The more than 200 British and North American contributors represent the Protestant evangelical viewpoint.　　BR95.N39

The new Westminster dictionary of liturgy and worship / ed. by J.G. Davies. Philadelphia : Westminster Pr., c1986. 544 p. : ill. ISBN 0-664-21270-0. **BB89**

Rev. ed. of Davies's *The Westminster dictionary of worship*, 1972 (*Guide* BB237); publ. in U.K. as *A new dictionary of liturgy and worship*.

About half the articles have been updated from the earlier edition, 70 new articles added, and 50% more space made available; bibliographies have been updated. Numerous cross-references; 90 black-and-white illustrations. Most contributors are British. Not definitive for specialists in liturgical studies, but provides introduction and clarification for general readers.
BV173.N49

Praktisches Lexikon der Spiritualität / hrsg. von Christian Schütz. Freiburg : Herder, c1988. 1503 p. ISBN 3-451-21063-0. **BB90**

Presents more than 500 articles of moderate length written by 210 Catholic and Lutheran specialists on persons, biblical themes, experiences, disciplines, and symbols important for the study and practice of spirituality. Each article has numerous cross-references and a select bibliography of mostly German works. Subject/person index. BV4488.P7

Theologische Realenzyklopädie / in Gemeinschaft mit Horst Robert Balz . . . [et al.] ; hrsg. von Gerhard Krause u. Gerhard Müller. Berlin ; N.Y. : de Gruyter, 1985–1988. Bd. 14–18. ISBN 3-11-006944-X (v. 1). DM220.00 (v. 1). (In progress). **BB91**

Contents: Bd. 14–18, Gottesdienst–Kirchenrecht.

For v. 1–13 and annotation, see *Guide* BB66. BR95.T47

The Westminster dictionary of Christian ethics / ed. by James F. Childress and John Macquarrie. Philadelphia : Westminster Pr., c1986. 678 p. ISBN 0-664-20940-8. $34.95. **BB92**

Rev. ed. of *A dictionary of Christian ethics*, ed. by John Macquarrie, 1967 (*Guide* BB243).

Contains signed articles, with numerous cross-references and brief bibliographies, by approximately 350 scholars from a wide range of traditions, including Protestant, Anglican, Roman Catholic, Orthodox, and Jewish. Articles provide factual information and indicate major options in Christian ethical debate. 60% of the articles are new; the remainder were retained, with revision, from the previous edition. Subject areas include: basic ethical concepts; biblical ethics; theological ethics; philosophical traditions in ethics; major non-Christian religious traditions in ethics; psychological, sociological and political concepts important for Christian ethics; and substantial ethical problems (e.g., abortion, war, unemployment). Individual thinkers are discussed in the context of articles on major traditions, movements, or themes, such as "Aristotelian ethics" or "Augustinian ethics." Index of names. A highly useful tool for general readers and specialists alike. BJ1199.W47

The Westminster dictionary of Christian spirituality / ed. by Gordon S. Wakefield. Philadelphia : Westminster Pr., c1983. 400 p. ISBN 0-664-21396-0. $20.95. **BB93**

Attempts "to give direct access to the whole development and present state of the subject."—*Pref.* Contains concise articles in alphabetical order, with cross-references and bibliography, by more than 150 contributors. Ecumenical in perspective, international in scope; useful for students and scholars.
BV4488.W47

Christian antiquities

Reallexikon für Antike und Christentum : Sachwörterbuch zur Auseinandersetzung des Christentums mit der antiken Welt / In Verbindung mit Franz Joseph Dölger und Hans Lietzmann und unter besonderer Mitwirkung von Jan Hendrik Wasznik und Leopold Wenger hrsg. von Theodor Klauser. Stuttgart : Hiersemann, 1988–1989. v. 13–15 (Lfg. 113–116). (In progress). **BB94**

For earlier volumes and annotation, see *Guide* BB252.

Contents: Bd. 13–14, Gütergemeinschaft–Hexe; Bd.15, (Lfg. 113–116) Hibernia–Hispania. BR131.R4

Reallexikon für Antike und Christentum : Sachwörterbuch zur Auseinandersetzung des Christentums mit der antiken Welt : Supplement / herausgegeben von Theodor Klauser . . . [et al.]. Stuttgart : A. Hiersemann, 1985–1986. 3 Lfg. ISBN 3-7772-8504-8 (v. 1/2). (In progress). **BB95**

Contents: Lfg. 1/2,3,4, Aaron–Athens I.

Contains selected articles reprinted from *Jahrbuch für Antike und Christentum* (1959–), new articles on topics not in the main work, and bibliographic essays updating articles in the main work. BR131.R4

Biography

Saints

The book of saints : a dictionary of servants of God / comp. by the Benedictine monks of St. Augustine's Abbey, Ramsgate. 6th ed., entirely rev. and re-set ; 1st American ed. Wilton, Conn. : Morehouse Pub., 1989. 605 p. : ill. ISBN 0-8192-1501-5. **BB96**

5th ed., 1966 (*Guide* BB269).

An entirely new edition, reflecting changes in the General Calendar of the Roman Catholic Church promulgated in 1969. Notes the removal from the canon of certain saints now considered nonhistorical, and the addition of others, including those recently canonized. Brief biographical entries are arranged alphabetically. Includes photographs; short bibliography; index of emblems; list of patron saints of various professions, trades, arts, states of life; and list of the twelve Sibyls (prophetesses) of the ancient world. BX4655.2.B66

Farmer, David Hugh. The Oxford dictionary of saints. 2nd ed. Oxford ; N.Y. : Oxford Univ. Pr., 1987. 478 p. ISBN 0-19-869149-1. $22.50. **BB97**

1st ed., 1978 (*Guide* BB274).

Approximately 80 articles have been rewritten or substantially revised, and there are new entries both for saints from the British Isles and those of interest to the English-speaking world outside the British Isles. New appendixes list some unsuccessful English candidates for canonization, principal patronages, and principal iconographical emblems. BR1710.F34

Church history and expansion

History

Decrees of the ecumenical councils / ed. by Norman P. Tanner. London : Sheed & Ward ; Wash. : Georgetown Univ. Pr., 1990. 2 v. ISBN 0-87840-490-2 (set). **BB98**

Contents: v. 1, Nicaea I to Lateran V; v. 2, Trent to Vatican II.

An English translation, by 29 British Jesuits, of the decrees of all the Ecumenical Councils of the Catholic Church as they appear in the critical edition, *Conciliorum oecumenicorum decreta* (1972). The original text in Latin or Greek and the English translation appear on facing pages. Ten separate indexes in v. 2: chronological, Bible, councils, Roman Magisterium, Fathers and early church, liturgical books, canon law, proper names, authors, subjects. BX825.A1990

Dotzauer, Winfried. Das Zeitalter der Glaubensspaltung (1500–1618). Darmstadt : Wissenschaftliche Buchgesellschaft, 1987. 182 p. (Quellenkunde zur deutschen Geschichte der Neuzeit von 1500 bis zur Gegenwart, Bd. 1). **BB99**
For annotation, see *Supplement* DC82. Z2237.5.D66x

The Oxford illustrated history of Christianity / ed. by John McManners. Oxford ; N.Y. : Oxford Univ. Pr., 1990. 724 p. ISBN 0-19-8229283. £19.50 (est.). **BB100**
A popular history written by 18 scholars, mostly British. Essays in the first section are arranged chronologically from the earliest Christian communities to 1800. The second section, 1800 to the present, is arranged geographically by continent. A third section treats current issues and future prospects. Includes illustrations, color plates, maps, a chronology, an annotated bibliography for further reading, and a comprehensive subject index. BR145.2.O86

Patrology

Biblia patristica : index des citations et allusions bibliques dans la littérature patristique / Centre d'analyse et de documentation patristiques, équipe de recherche associée au Centre national de la recherche scientifique, J. Allenbach . . . [et al.]. Paris : Editions du Centre national de la recherche scientifique, 1987. v. 4. ISBN 2-222-01802-1 (v. 1). (In progress). **BB101**
For v. 1–3 and annotation, see *Guide* BB305.
Contents: v. 4, Eusèbe de Césarée, Cyrille de Jérusalem, Epiphane de Salamine (1987). BR66.5.U53

Dizionario patristico e di antichità cristiane / diretto da Angelo Di Berardino. 1a ed. Casale Monferrato : Marietti, [1987?]–1988. v. 2–3. ISBN 88-211-6706-2. **BB102**
Now complete; for v. 1, see *Guide* BB310. BR66.5.D58

Quasten, Johannes. Patrology. Westminster, Md. : Newman Pr., 1986. v. 4. **BB103**
Contents: v. 4, The golden age of Latin patristic literature from the Council of Nicea to the Council of Chalcedon / ed. by Angelo di Bernardino.
English translation of the 1978 Italian edition (*Guide* BB312).
Vol. 4 contains a brief introduction by the ailing Quasten and is designated as the final volume of his monumental work (for v. 1–3, see *Guide* BB312). "While following in its general outlines the methodological criteria of Quasten, the work attempts to see the Fathers in their political and social context and to give more space to the problematics of contemporary patristic research."—*Pref.* Contains biographies, summaries of writings, and extensive bibliographies of Church Fathers. Indexes: scripture, ancient writers, authors, subjects. Inferior copy editing does not diminish the volume's scholarly value. BR67.Q3

Missions

Christianity in China : a scholars' guide to resources in the libraries and archives of the United States / Archie R. Crouch . . . [et al.]. Armonk, N.Y. : M.E. Sharpe, c1989. lvi, 709 p. ISBN 0-87332-419-6. $95.00. **BB104**
Lists and describes primary and secondary resources located in 554 repositories. Entries are arranged alphabetically by state, then by city. Also includes: union lists of more than 700 serial titles; 650 oral history interviews; 500 dissertations/theses; bibliography of archival guides and directories; and indexes by subject, personal name, and repository. Z7757.C6C46

Lexikon missionstheologischer Grundbegriffe / hrsg. von Karl Müller und Theo Sundermeier. Berlin : D. Reimer, c1987. 546. ISBN 3-496-00911-X. **BB105**
Contains 110 articles by 91 Protestant, Catholic, and Orthodox theologians, mostly German, supplemented by contributions from a few African, Asian, and Latin American scholars. Contemporary rather than historical emphasis. Articles, arranged in alphabetical order, have cross-references in the text and bibliographies appended. No index. BV2040.L48

Mission handbook : North American Protestant ministries overseas / Samuel Wilson, John Siewart, eds. 13th ed. [Monrovia, Calif.] : Missions Advanced Research and Communication Center, 1986. 626 p. **BB106**
12th ed., 1980 (*Guide* BB320).
Provides data on 764 Protestant mission agencies which support 67,200 overseas representatives. BV2050.D55

Atlases

Atlas zur Kirchengeschichte : die christlichen Kirchen in Geschichte und Gegenwart ; Kommentare Ausführliches Register / hrsg. von Hubert Jedin, Kenneth Scott Latourette, Jochen Martin. Aktualisierte Neuausg. / [bearb. und hrsg. von Jochen Martin]. Freiburg : Herder, c1987. 83, 152 p. ; 35 cm. ISBN 3-451-20869-5. **BB107**
1st ed., 1970 (*Guide* BB329)
Sections dealing with modern and contemporary periods have been extensively revised and enlarged and bibliographies updated. An outstanding church history atlas. G1046.E4A8

Protestant denominations

Lutherans

Biographical directory of clergy : Evangelical Lutheran Church in America. Minneapolis : Augsburg Pub. House/Fortress, 1988. 1498 p. : ill. ISBN 0-8066-2405-1 (pbk.). **BB108**
Rev. ed. of *A biographical directory of clergymen of the American Lutheran Church*, 1972.
Provides brief biographical entries in alphabetical order, many with photographs, for the approximately 17,000 clergy who, as of August 31, 1987, were on the clergy rosters of the three uniting American Lutheran church bodies (the American Lutheran Church, Association of Evangelical Lutheran Churches, and Lutheran Church in America), which in 1987 merged to form the Evangelical Lutheran Church in America. BX8048.3.B56

Evangelical Lutheran Church in America. Yearbook. 1988– . Minneapolis : Publishing House of the Evangel-

ical Lutheran Church in America, 1988– . Annual.
BB109

The official statistical and directorial publication of the ELCA, the church created in 1987 by merger of the American Lutheran Church, the Lutheran Church in America, and the Association of Evangelical Lutheran Churches. The *Yearbook* supersedes those of the first two bodies. The American Lutheran Church *Yearbook* (*Guide* BB77) ceased with the 1987 volume and the Lutheran Church in America *Yearbook* (*Guide* BB378) with the 1986 volume.

Methodists

Rowe, Kenneth E. Methodist union catalog, pre-1976 imprints. Metuchen, N.J. : Scarecrow, 1985. v. 6. ISBN 0-8108-0880-3 (v. 1). (In progress). **BB110**
For v.1–5 and annotation, see *Guide* BB388.
Contents: v. 6, He–I. Z7845.M5R69

Presbyterians

Parker, Harold M. Bibliography of published articles on American Presbyterianism, 1901–1980. Westport, Conn. : Greenwood, 1985. 261 p. (Bibliographies and indexes in religious studies, no. 4). ISBN 0-313-24544-4.
BB111

Lists almost 3,000 articles from the U.S. periodicals, both religious and secular, excluding denominational journals, house organs, or serials published monthly or weekly. Entries are arranged alphabetically by author. Detailed topical index.
Z7845.P9P37

Presbyterian Church (U.S.A.). General Assembly. Minutes. 195th (1983)– . [N.Y. ; Atlanta] : Office of the General Assembly, c1983– . Annual. **BB112**
Contents: pt. 1, Journal; pt. 2, Statistics.

Supersedes annuals published by two denominations which merged in 1983: *Minutes of the General Assembly* of the United Presbyterian Church in the U.S.A. (ceased with volume for 1982, but its numbering is continued by the new series; see *Guide* BB399) and *Minutes* of the Presbyterian Church in the U.S. (ceased with the volume that covered its 125th General Assembly).

Shakers

Henry Francis du Pont Winterthur Museum. The Edward Deming Andrews Memorial Shaker Collection / comp. by E. Richard McKinstry. N.Y. : Garland, 1987. 357 p., [22] p. of plates : ill., ports. ISBN 0-8240-9430-1. $67.00. **BB113**

A detailed guide to an extensive Shaker collection. Printed materials by and about the Shakers are arranged alphabetically by author; manuscripts, written mostly by Shakers, are arranged under 16 subject headings. Includes brief descriptive essays on the collection's photographic materials and artifacts and on the archives of Edward Deming Andrews and Faith Andrews, who assembled this collection. Extensive title, name, and subject index. Z7845.S5H46

Congregationalists—United Church of Christ

Youngs, J. William T. The Congregationalists. N.Y. : Greenwood, c1990. 1 v. (Denominations in America, no. 4). ISBN 0-313-22159-6. **BB114**

Consists of a history of Congregationalism from 16th-century England to 20th-century America and a biographical dictionary of approximately 85 Congregational leaders. Bibliography appended to each biographical entry. Includes a chronology, an extensive bibliographical essay, and a subject index. Useful for both general readers and specialists. BX7135.Y68

Roman Catholic church

Bibliography

Allison, Antony Francis. The contemporary printed literature of the English Counter-Reformation between 1558 and 1640 : an annotated catalogue / by A.F. Allison and D.M. Rogers. Aldershot, England : Scolar Pr. ; Brookfield, Vt. : Gower Pub. Co., 1989. v. 1. ISBN 0-85967-640-4. (In progress). **BB115**
Contents: v. 1, Works in languages other than English, with the collaboration of W. Lottes.

Contains 1,619 bibliographic entries with library location symbols and frequent descriptive notes. Vol. 1 lists "religious literature in Latin and other foreign languages [including translations from English] published abroad by the English Catholics."—*Foreword.* Pt. I (entries 1–1428) is arranged alphabetically by personal name, Pt. II (entries 1429–1619) by 19 subjects, with entries in chronological order, then alphabetically by name under each subject. Separate indexes for titles, publishers and printers, dates of publication, proper names. To be followed by v. 2, which will be a revision of the same editors' *A catalogue of Catholic books in English printed abroad or secretly in England, 1558–1640* (Bognor Regis [England] : Arandel Pr., 1956). Z7830.A46

McCabe, James Patrick. Critical guide to Catholic reference books. 3rd ed. Englewood, Colo. : Libraries Unlimited, Inc., 1989. 323 p. (Research studies in library science, no. 20). ISBN 0-87287-621-7. $45.00. **BB116**
2nd ed., 1980 (*Guide* BB418).

Revises the previous edition, enlarging it by more than 20%. Provides "a critical introduction to over fifteen hundred of the most important reference works in English and foreign languages whose contents or point of view relate in some way to Catholicism."—*Introd.* Areas covered are: general works, theology, the humanities, social sciences, and history. Annotations frequently cite critical reviews. All titles are currently available in the U.S. Appendixes list typical diocesan reference publications and bibliographies consulted. Author, title and subject index. Z7837

Musto, Ronald G. The peace tradition in the Catholic Church : an annotated bibliography. N.Y. : Garland, 1987. 590 p. (Garland reference library of social science, v. 339). ISBN 0-8240-8584-1. $67.00. **BB117**
For annotation, see *Supplement* CJ298. Z7838.P54M87

Dictionaries

The new dictionary of theology / editors, Joseph A. Komonchak, Mary Collins, Dermot A. Lane. Wilmington, Del.: Michael Glazier, 1987. 1112 p. ISBN 0-89453-609-5.　　　　　　　　　　　　　　　　**BB118**

Marking the 25th anniversary of the opening of the Second Vatican Council, this work "represents the first collaborative attempt in English to take stock of the remarkable developments in the church and in theology since the Council."—*Pref.* Summarizes the present state of Catholic theology while demonstrating ecumenical sensitivity. Includes many articles of 10–15 pages on the 24 topics the editors believe constitute "principal themes of the Christian vision of faith," together with numerous articles on liturgy, the Bible, and theology. Articles are signed (most of the 165 contributors are from North America) and most include cross-references and bibliography. Intended for those engaged in secondary and college-level teaching and in preaching.　　　　　　　　　　BR95.N38

History

Catholicism in early modern history : a guide to research / John W. O'Malley, ed. St. Louis : Center for Reformation Research, c1988. 342 p. (Reformation guides to research, 2). ISBN 0-910345-02-3.　　**BB119**

Contains 16 essays by specialists, five on geographical areas in Europe (e.g., Germany, France, Spain) and the rest on various topics (e.g., popular piety, spirituality, preaching). Each essay reviews current scholarship and includes an extensive bibliography.　　　　　　　　　　　BX946.C37

Liturgy and ritual

Lang, Jovian. Dictionary of the liturgy. N.Y. : Catholic Book Pub. Co., c1989. 687 p. ISBN 0-89942-273-X. $10.95.　　　　　　　　　　　　　　　　**BB120**

Treats Catholic liturgy exclusively and its historical development and changes since Vatican II. Select bibliography appended. A popular work intended for general and nonspecialist readers.　　　　　　　　　　　　　　BV173.L26

Popes, cardinals, bishops

Kelly, J. N. D. The Oxford dictionary of Popes. Oxford ; N.Y. : Oxford Univ. Pr., 1986. 347 p. ISBN 0-19-213964-9. $24.95. ISBN 0-19-282085-0 (pbk.). $7.50.　　　　　　　　　　　　　　　　**BB121**

Offers biographical sketches, arranged chronologically, of all 268 popes and 39 antipopes, from St. Peter to John Paul II. Bibliography of primary and secondary sources follows each entry. An alphabetical list of popes and antipopes precedes the text. Subject index.　　　　　　　　BX955.2.K45

BUDDHISM

550 books on Buddhism : translations, studies, and general readings / [ed. by Elizabeth Cook and Ruth Fellhauer]. Berkeley, Calif. : Nyingma Institute : Dharma Pub., c1985. 95 p. : ill. ISBN 0-913546-97-6 (pbk.).　　　　　　　　　　　　　　　　**BB122**

Lists in classified order and often briefly annotates primary and secondary sources in English. Indicates availability and provides ordering information. Intended for beginners.　　　　　　　　　　　　　　　　Z7860.A12

Inada, Kenneth K. Guide to Buddhist philosophy. Boston : G.K. Hall, c1985. 226 p. ISBN 0-8161-7899-2. $45.00.　　　　　　　　　　　　　　　　**BB123**

For annotation, see *Supplement* BA2.　　Z7128.B93I53

HINDUISM

Feuerstein, Georg. Encyclopedic dictionary of yoga. N.Y. : Paragon House, 1990. 430 p. : ill. (The Paragon living traditions series, v. 1). ISBN 1-55778-244-X. $24.95.　　　　　　　　　　　　　　　　**BB124**

Defines and discusses yogic terms, concepts, sages, history, and literature. Arranged alphabetically by English words or by words transliterated from non-Roman alphabets. Numerous cross-references and illustrations; select annotated bibliography. Intended for general readers.　　　B132.Y6F46

ISLAM

The encyclopaedia of Islam. New ed. / prepared by a number of leading orientalists. Ed. by an editorial committee consisting of H.A.R. Gibb [and others]. Leiden : Brill, 1986–1989. v. 5–6 : illus., plates, fold. maps (part col.) diagrs., plans. (In progress).　　　　**BB125**

For previously published parts and annotation, see *Guide* BB524.

Contents: v. 5, Khe–Mahi (1986); v. 6: fasc. 1–6, Maihkama–Mawlid, (1986–89).　　　　DS37.E523

Geddes, C. L. Guide to reference books for Islamic studies. Denver, Colo. : American Institute of Islamic Studies, c1985. 429 p. ISBN 0-933017-00-6. $42.00 (est.).　　　　　　　　　　　　　　　　**BB126**

An annotated, classified bibliography of some 1,200 books and articles on Muslim history, culture, society, and faith from the time of Muhammad to the abolition of the caliphate in 1924. Covers geographical expanse from Spain to China. Titles in non-Western languages appear in their original script with transliterations and English translations. Author/title/subject index.　　　　　　　　　　　Z7835.M6A54

Glasse, Cyril. The concise encyclopedia of Islam. San Francisco : Harper & Row, 1989. 472 p. : col. ill. ISBN 0-06-063123-6. $59.95.　　　　　　　　**BB127**

Offers articles of moderate length with cross-references, arranged alphabetically by English words or transliterations of Arabic words. From a Sunni perspective, focuses on outward religious forms (e.g., commandments, observances, and texts), and on inner religious and metaphysical truths. Contains three sections of photographic color plates and four appendixes: maps illustrating Islamic history; Mecca and the Hajj; branches of Islam; genealogical tables. Chronology and bibliography of primary and secondary sources.　　　　　BP40.G42

JUDAISM

Bibliography

Antisemitism : an annotated bibliography / the Vidal Sassoon International Center for the Study of Antisemitism, the Hebrew University of Jerusalem ; ed. by Susan Sarah Cohen. N.Y. : Garland, 1987. v. 1. ISBN 0-8240-8532-9. (In progress).   **BB128**
    Contents: v. 1, 1984–1985 (392 p. $47.00).
    A comprehensive, classified bibliography of books, dissertations, masters' theses, articles from periodicals, and collections about anti-Semitism from the ancient period to the present. Materials included were published 1984–85 in English, other European languages, Hebrew, and Yiddish. Appendixes list anti-Semitic periodicals and bibliographies on anti-Semitism published before 1984. Author index and detailed subject index.   Z6374.A56A57

The book of Jewish books : a reader's guide to Judaism / ed. by Ruth S. Frank & William Wollheim. San Francisco : Harper & Row, c1986. 320 p. ISBN 0-06-063008-6. ISBN 0-06-063009-4 (pbk.).   **BB129**
    Lists books and periodicals covering all aspects of Jewish history, life, and thought. Includes chapters on topics such as children's books, prayer books, and women. Critically annotated and arranged in classified order; each chapter introduced by a specialist. Intended for general readers, Jewish and non-Jewish. Glossary of Jewish words and index of names and titles.   Z6366.B66

Edelheit, Abraham J. The Jewish world in modern times : a selected, annotated bibliography / Abraham J. Edelheit and Hershel Edelheit. Boulder, Colo. : Westview ; London, England : Mansell, 1988. 569 p. ISBN 0-8133-0572-1. $65.00.   **BB130**
    For annotation, see *Supplement* DA56.   Z6372.E25

Elkin, Judith Laikin. Latin American Jewish studies : an annotated guide to the literature / comp. by Judith Laikin Elkin and Ana Lya Sater. N. Y. : Greenwood , 1990. 238 p. (Bibliographies and indexes in ethnic studies, no. 4). ISBN 0-313-25936-4.   **BB131**
    An introduction to research on the Jewish experience in Latin America. Arranged in four sections: (1) introduction; (2) literature survey, covering bibliography and reference, demography, agriculture, biography, anti-Semitism, identity, and country studies; (3) suggestions for additional research; (4) a directory of scholars, listing names, addresses, institutional affiliation, and research interests. No index.   Z6373.L3E44

Griffiths, David B. A critical bibliography of writings on Judaism. Lewiston, N.Y. : E. Mellen Pr., 1988. 2 v. (804 p.). ISBN 0-88946-257-7 (pt. 2).   **BB132**
    Contents: Pt. 1, Resource apparatus; Judaism in antiquity; Medieval to early modern times; Thought and culture. Pt. 2, Modern Jewish history: The Holocaust; Studies of Zionist thought and history; Modernity and modern thought.
    A comprehensive annotated bibliography of mainly English-language monographic and journal literature, most published since World War II. Arranged in classified order; absence of an index severely impedes access.   Z6370.G75

Karkhanis, Sharad. Jewish heritage in America : an annotated bibliography. N.Y. : Garland, 1988. 434 p. ISBN 0-8240-7538-2.   **BB133**
    A critically annotated, classified bibliography of 1,100 books and articles published in English 1925–87 on all aspects of Jewish life in America. A list of periodical sources and separate indexes by author, title, and subject are appended. The compiler, a Hindu, intends the work "for the use of students,

scholars and general readers—both Jewish and non-Jewish."— *Introd.*   Z6373.U5K37

Korsch, Boris. Soviet publications on Judaism, Zionism, and the State of Israel, 1984–1988 : an annotated bibliography. N.Y. : Garland, 1990. 126 p. (Garland reference library of social science, vol. 482). ISBN 0-8240-4108-9.   **BB134**
    For annotation, see *Supplement* DE72.   Z6366.K67

Singerman, Robert. Judaica Americana : a bibliography of publications to 1900. N.Y. : Greenwood, c1990. 2 v. (1335 p.). (Bibliographies and indexes in American history, no. 14). ISBN 0-313-25023-5 (set).   **BB135**
    Contents: v. 1, Chronological file 1676–1889; v. 2, Chronological file 1890–1900; Union list of nineteenth-century Jewish serials published in the United States; English, French, German, Hebrew, Yiddish serials; Index [of subjects].
    "Sponsored by the Center for the Study of the American Jewish Experience, Hebrew Union College-Jewish Institute of Religion"—*t.p.*
    A comprehensive work listing 6,512 books, pamphlets, and serials with NUC location symbols and some annotations. Gazetteer of Jewish publishers and printers included in the index.   Z6373.U5S58

Dictionaries

A dictionary of the Jewish-Christian dialogue / ed. by Leon Klenicki and Geoffrey Wigoder. N.Y. : Paulist Pr., c1984. 213 p. ISBN 0-8091-2590-0 (pbk.). $7.95.   **BB136**
    Brief essays, presented in pairs, by Jewish and Christian specialists, on 34 English words, such as "covenant," "law," and "messiah," which are used in both religious traditions, but understood differently. The headwords, with their interpretative essays, are arranged in alphabetical order. Index of Hebrew terms and subject index.   BM50.D53

History

The Cambridge history of Judaism / ed. by W.D. Davies, Louis Finkelstein. Cambridge ; N.Y. : Cambridge Univ. Pr., 1989. v. 2. ISBN 0-521-21880-2 (v. 1). (In progress).   **BB137**
    For v. 1 and annotation, see *Guide* BB597.
    Contents: v. 2, The hellenistic age.   BM155.2.C35

Encyclopedia of Jewish history : events and eras of the Jewish people / [ed. of the English edition, Joseph Alpher]. N.Y. : Facts on File, c1986. 287 p. : ill. (some col.). ISBN 0-8160-1220-2. $35.00.   **BB138**
    A popular work by Israeli scholars, writers and educators. Provides concise information about Jewish history and key figures from the earliest times to the present. Contains 100 chronologically arranged entries of about 800 words each. Numerous colored illustrations, photographs, maps, and diagrams. Includes index to text and illustrations and a dozen appendixes on culture and ethnography.   DS118.E465

SHINTOISM

Schwade, Arcadio. Shintō-bibliography in western languages : bibliography on Shintō and religious sects, intellectual schools and movements influenced by Shintōism. Leiden : E.J. Brill, 1986. 124 p. ISBN 90-04-08173-9 (pbk.). **BB139**
　　Lists in alphabetical order 2,006 monographs and articles, most published in English, French, or German in the 20th century. Topical index. Z7835.S5S38

SIKHISM

Rai, Priya Muhar. Sikhism and the Sikhs : an annotated bibliography. N.Y. : Greenwood, 1989. 257 p. (Bibliographies and indexes in religious studies, no. 13). ISBN 0-313-26130-X. **BB140**
　　A classified, annotated bibliography of 1,150 scholarly books and articles written in English since 1965. Author, title, and subject indexes. Z7835.S64R34

BC

Linguistics and Philology

INTERNATIONAL

Bibliography

Beard, Robert. Bibliography of morphology, 1960–1985 / comp. by Robert Beard and Bogdan Szymanek. Amsterdam ; Philadelphia : J. Benjamins, 1988. 193 p. ISBN 90-272-3742-5. $26.00. **BC1**
　　"Rather than an attempt at an exhaustive bibliography of morphology, this is a collection of major and selected minor works of theoretical interest in the broadest sense."—*Introd.* Emphasizes English-language works. Articles and books are listed alphabetically by author, with subject and language indexes. Z7004.M67B43

Eschbach, Achim. Bibliography of semiotics, 1975–1985 / comp. by Achim Eschbach & Viktoria Eschbach-Szabó with the collaboration of Gabi Willenberg. Amsterdam ; Philadelphia : J. Benjamins Pub. Co., 1986. 2 v. (948 p.). (Amsterdam studies in the theory and history of linguistic science. Series V, Library and information sources in linguistics, v. 16). ISBN 90-272-3739-5 (set). $140.00. **BC2**
　　Intended to continue and supplement two of Eschbach's earlier works, *Semiotik-Bibliographie I* (Frankfurt am Main : Antoren- and Verlagsgesellschaft Syndikat, 1976) and *Zeichen, Text, Bedeutung* (München : Fink, 1974). Lists 10,839 monographs, articles, reviews, dissertations, conference proceedings,

and translations in alphabetical order by main entry with subject/name and journal indexes. Z7004.S43E76

Gordon, W. Terrence. Semantics : a bibliography, 1979–1985. Metuchen, N.J. : Scarecrow, 1987. 292 p. ISBN 0-8108-2055-2. $27.50. **BC3**
　　Supplements and continues the numbering of the author's *Semantics* (*Guide* BC13), adding over 2,600 items. "Lexical" and author indexes. Z7004.S4G68

Noppen, J. P. van. Metaphor : a bibliography of post-1970 publications. Amsterdam ; Philadelphia : J. Benjamins Pub. Co., 1985. 497 p. ISBN 90-272-3737-9. $54.00. **BC4**
　　Intended to supplement Warren Shible's *Metaphor: an annotated bibliography and history* (Whitewater, Wis. : Language Pr., 1971). An alphabetical list of more than 2,300 citations, some with annotations. Indexed by name and subject, by theories and uses of metaphor, and by metaphor types. A supplementary index lists recommended texts on various topics for the beginning student. Z7004.M4N66

Renaissance linguistics archive, 1350–1700 : a print-out from the secondary-sources data-base / ed. by Mirko Tavoni. Ferrara : Istituto di studi rinascimentali, 1987–1988. v. 1–2. (In progress). **BC5**
　　At head of title: Istituto di studi rinascimentali.
　　"A bibliographical project in collaboration with the Henry Sweet Society for the History of Linguistic Ideas (Oxford) and the Société d' histoire et d'épistémologie des sciences du langage (Paris)."
　　The result of a cooperative bibliographic project to facilitate "an international and interdisciplinary exchange of bibliographical information among scholars in this large and complex field of research."—*Foreword.* Each of these first two printouts from the RLA database lists approximately 1,000 books, articles, conference proceedings, and book collections published in the 19th and 20th centuries that address the development and study of European languages during the early modern period. Entries are arranged alphabetically, with subject/names, keyword, geographic, and language indexes. Each volume also contains a list of periodicals and collective works that are indexed in the main bibliography. Further volumes are expected as the database grows. Z7001.R46

Troike, Rudolph C. Bibliography of bibliographies of the languages of the world. Amsterdam ; Philadelphia : J. Benjamins Pub. Co., 1990. v. 1. (Amsterdam studies in the theory and history of linguistic science. Series V, Library and information sources in linguistics, v. 19). ISBN 90-272-3743-3 (v. 1). $105.00. (In progress). **BC6**
　　Contents: v. 1, General and Indo-European languages of Europe.
　　Lists 2,480 bibliographies published through 1985, as books, journal articles, and dissertations, in a classed arrangement. Name and subject indexes. Z7001.T78

Encyclopedias

Crystal, David. The Cambridge encyclopedia of language. Cambridge, Eng. ; N.Y. : Cambridge Univ. Pr., 1987. 472 p. : ill. (some col.). ISBN 0-521-26438-3. $39.50. **BC7**
　　" . . . in 11 Parts, comprizing 65 thematic sections. Each section is a self-contained presentation of a major theme in language study, with cross-references included to related section and topics."—*Contents.* Thematic sections cover subjects such as sounds, speech development, and language families, and include numerous illustrations, graphs, charts, and abbreviations,

a table of world languages, and bibliographies of suggested readings. Language, author/name, and subject indexes. P29.C64

An encyclopaedia of language / ed. by N.E. Collinge. London ; N.Y. : Routledge, 1990. 1011 p. : ill. ISBN 0-415-02064-6. **BC8**

Presents 26 signed chapters that discuss current scholarship and provide bibliographies on the nature and social, scientific, logical, and geographical aspects of language. Topics/terms and personal name indexes. P106.A46

Encyclopedic dictionary of semiotics / gen. ed., Thomas A. Sebeok. Berlin ; N.Y. : Mouton de Gruyter, c1986. 3 v. (Approaches to semiotics, 73). ISBN 0-89925-137-4. $238.95. **BC9**

Vols. 1–2 contain signed essays with bibliographic references on terms, themes, persons, and schools of thought. Vol. 3 is a bibliographic companion to the work, arranged alphabetically by author. P99.E65

The world's major languages / ed. by Bernard Comrie. N.Y. : Oxford Univ. Pr., 1987. 1025 p. : ill., maps. ISBN 0-19-520-521-9. $79.00. **BC10**

"Major languages are here defined by criteria such as the number of speakers of individual languages, whether they are official languages of independent states, whether they are widely used in more than one country, whether they are the bearers of long-standing literary traditions."—*Pref.* Signed chapters, which vary in arrangement and emphasis, discuss the history, social context, writing systems, morphology, and phonology of language families and specific languages. Bibliographies are included with each chapter; language index. P371.W6

Dictionaries

Abad Nebot, Francisco. Diccionario de lingüística de la escuela española. Madrid : Gredos, c1986. 281 p. : ill. (Biblioteca románica hispánica. Diccionarios, 12). ISBN 84-249-1043-5. ISBN 84-249-1042-7 (pbk.). **BC11**

Definitions and discussions of terms, themes, and topics from Spanish linguistics, with brief bibliographies at the end of each entry. An "epilogo" describes 20th-century developments and controversies. Short index of additional concepts and terms used within entries. P29.A23

Crystal, David. A dictionary of linguistics and phonetics. 3rd ed. Oxford [England] ; Cambridge, Mass. : B. Blackwell, c1991. 389 p. : ill. ISBN 0-631-17869-4. $45.00. ISBN 0-631-17871-6 (pbk.). $19.95. **BC12**

2nd ed., 1985.

Now twice revised and expanded since its publication as *A first dictionary of linguistics and phonetics* (*Guide* BC62), this volume is now intended both for laymen or undergraduates and for advanced scholars from other related disciplines. Definitions include bibliographic citations for further information. P29.C65

Richards, Jack C. Longman dictionary of applied linguistics / Jack Richards, John Platt, Heidi Weber. Burnt Mill, Harlow, Essex, England : Longman, 1985. 323 p. : ill. ISBN 0-582-55708-9. £6.25. **BC13**

Written "for those with little or no background in linguistics...."—*Introd.* Entries provide pronunciations, definitions, and citations to further reading for some 1,500 terms. P129.R5

Handbooks

Nöth, Winfried. Handbook of semiotics. Bloomington : Indiana Univ. Pr., c1990. 576 p. : ill. ISBN 0-253-34120-5. $57.50. **BC14**

Translation of *Handbuch der Semiotik* (Stuttgart : Matzler, 1985) with substantial revision and expansion.

"... aims at the adventurous goal of a topographical survey of the main areas of theoretical and applied semiotics... [and] intends to be systematic, comprehensive, and up to date."—*Pref.* In eight chapters: (1) History and classics of modern semiotics; (2) Sign and meaning; (3) Semiosis, code, and the semiotic field; (4) Language and language-based codes; (5) From Structuralism to texts, semiotics: schools and major figures; (6) Text semiotics: the field; (7) Nonverbal communication; (8) Aesthetics and visual communication. Each chapter is further subdivided into essays on particular problems, individuals, theories, or concepts. Within the text are numerous cross-references to the extensive bibliography at the end of the volume. Subject/term and name indexes. P99.N6513

Ruhlen, Merritt. A guide to the world's languages. Stanford, Calif. : Stanford Univ. Pr., 1987. v. 1. ISBN 0-8047-1250-6 (v. 1). $42.50. (In progress). **BC15**

Revised and expanded version of the author's *Guide to the languages of the world* (Stanford : Stanford Univ. Pr., 1976). Further volumes are to cover Language data (v. 2) and Language universals (v. 3).

Vol. 1 "discusses the history and present state of the genetic classification of the world's languages and offers a complete classification."—*Pref.* Based in part on Charles and Florence Voegelin's *Classification and index of the world's languages* (*Guide* BC55). In eight main parts: a general section on the principles and methods of language classification; sections on the language families of Europe, Africa, Asia, Oceania, and North and South America; a discussion of areas for future research; classification charts. Bibliographies follow each section; personal name, language group, and language indexes. P203.R8

Translation

Briamonte, Nino. Saggio di bibliografia sui problemi storici, teorici e pratici della traduzione. [Italy?] : Libreria sapere, [1984]. 253 p. **BC16**

Lists books, articles, conference proceedings, and special journal articles published for the most part 1960–80. Arranged in a classified scheme, with a name index. Z7004.T72B74

ENGLISH

Bibliography and history

Alston, R. C. A bibliography of the English language from the invention of printing to the year 1800 : a systematic record of writings on English, and on other languages in English, based on the collections of the principal libraries of the world. Leeds [Eng.] : Printed for the author by E.J. Arnold, 1977–87. v. 11–12. (In progress). **BC17**

For earlier volumes and annotation, see *Guide* BC76.

Contents: v. 11, Place names and personal names (1977); v. 12, pt. 1, The French language: grammar, miscellaneous treatises, dictionaries (1985); v. 12, pt. 2, The Italian, Spanish, Portuguese, and Romansh languages: grammars, dictionaries, miscellaneous treatises (1987).   Z2015.A1A4

Cameron, Angus. Old English word studies : a preliminary author and word index / Angus Cameron, Allison Kingsmill, Ashley Crandell Amos. Toronto ; Buffalo : Published in association with the Centre for Medieval Studies, Univ. of Toronto by Univ. of Toronto Pr., c1983. 192 p. (Toronto Old English series, 8). ISBN 0-8020-5526-5.   **BC18**

Word index: 5 microfiches in pocket.

A useful by-product of the *Dictionary of Old English* (*Supplement* AD63), this bibliography lists "etymological, phonological, morphological, or syntactic studies of Old English vocabulary."—*Introd.* Entries are arranged alphabetically by author, with an index by word on microfiche. The editors plan to publish a revised set of the microfiche index, with cross-references to dictionary entries, after the *Dictionary of Old English* has been completed.   Z2015.S4C35

Fisiak, Jacek. A bibliography of writings for the history of the English language. 2nd ed. Berlin ; N.Y. : Mouton de Gruyter, 1987. 216 p. ISBN 0-89925-057-2. $66.00.   **BC19**

1st ed., 1983.

Lists 3,641 citations to books, articles, and dissertations in a classed arrangement. Author/editor index.   Z2015.A1F57

Höhlein, Helga. Auswahlbibliographie zum Studium der anglistischen Sprachwissenschaft : mit Kommentaren / Helga Höhlein, Peter H. Marsden, Clausdirk Pollner. Tübingen : M. Niemeyer, 1987. 155 p. (Forschung & Studium Anglistik, 2). ISBN 3-484-41002-7.   **BC20**

Lists books and articles in a classed arrangement; most sections include a few titles (one to ten) with lengthy annotations and a longer, supplementary list without annotations. Author/title index.   Z5818.E5H64

Lougheed, W. C. Writings on Canadian English, 1976–1987 : a selective, annotated bibliography. Kingston, Ont. : Strathy Language Unit, Queen's Univ., [1988]. 66 p. ISBN 0-88911-510-9. $5.00.   **BC21**

Updates Walter Avis' *Writings on Canadian English, 1792–1975* (Toronto : Fitzhenry & Whiteside, c1978). Lists alphabetically by main entry approximately 300 items with cursory annotations. Subject index.   Z1379.L68

Markus, Manfred. English-German contrastive linguistics : a bibliography / Manfred Markus, Josef Wallmannsberger. Frankfurt am Main : Peter Lang, 1987. 108 p. ISBN 3-8204-0146-6.   **BC22**

Intended to enable "foreign students/teachers of English and German respectively to bridge the gap between theoretical and applied CL [contrastive linguistics]."—*Introd.* Lists books, articles, and dissertations from the last 30 years. Arranged alphabetically in chapters devoted to particular formats (Bibliographies) or topics (Semantics) with author index.   PE1099.M37

McMillan, James B. Annotated bibliography of Southern American English / James B. McMillan and Michael B. Montgomery. Tuscaloosa : Univ. of Alabama Pr., c1989. 444 p. ISBN 0-8173-0448-7. $32.95.   **BC23**

1st ed., 1971 (*Guide* BC80).

Updates the original volume for items published 1969 through the mid-1980s, and expands coverage to include "peripherally southern areas—Central and West Texas, Oklahoma, the Missouri Ozarks, and Delaware."—*Pref.* Books, theses, and articles are listed in a classed arrangement, with author index.   Z1251.S7M37

Pulsiano, Phillip. An annotated bibliography of North American doctoral dissertations on Old English language and literature. East Lansing, Mich. : Colleagues

Pr., 1988. 317 p. (Medieval texts and studies, no. 3). ISBN 0-937191-06-X.   **BC24**

For annotation, see *Supplement* BD207.   Z2012.P85

Tajima, Matsuji. Old and Middle English language studies : a classified bibliography, 1923–1985. Amsterdam ; Philadelphia : J. Benjamins Pub. Co., 1988. 391 p. (Amsterdam studies in the theory and history of linguistic science. Series V, Library and information sources in linguistics, v. 13). ISBN 90-272-3732-8. $60.00.   **BC25**

Intended to supplement in part A.G. Kennedy's *Bibliography of writings on the English language* (*Guide* BC78). Lists 3,913 books, monographs, dissertations, and articles in a classed arrangement. Most book entries include citations to reviews. Name index.   Z2015.A1T3

Handbooks

Hairston, Maxine. The Scott, Foresman handbook for writers / Maxine Hairston, John J. Ruszkiewicz. Glenview, Ill. : Scott, Foresman, c1988. 848 p. ISBN 0-673-18542-7.   **BC26**

Similar in scope and purpose to the *Harbrace college handbook* (*Supplement* BC29). Intended as both a reference guide and textbook with writing exercises. Endpapers list common editing marks and abbreviations. Subject index.

PE1408.H2968

———————— ———————— Glenview, Ill. : Scott, Foresman, c1988. 848 p. ISBN 0-673-18542-7.   **BC27**

For annotation, see *Supplement* BC26.   PE1408.H2968

Handbook of English and Celtic studies in the United Kingdom and Republic of Ireland / ed. by N.H. Keeble. [london] : Stirling Univ. Pr., 1988. 379 p.   **BC28**

A faculty directory listing departments of English and Celtic language, literature, and linguistics by institution. Compiled by survey; many entries include an individual's birthdate, academic degrees, title of thesis, current position, areas of academic interest and publications, but some list only names of faculty members and their appointments. Name and topic indexes.

PE68.G5H27

Harbrace college handbook / John C. Hodges . . . [et al.]. 11th ed. San Diego, Calif. : Harcourt Brace Jovanovich, c1990. 576, 24 p. ISBN 0-15-531862-4. $14.00.   **BC29**

9th ed., 1984 (*Guide* BC87); 10th ed., 1986.

A "complete revision of the Tenth Edition" (*Pref.*) that offers significant additions to the sections concerning resumes, style sheets, and reasoning.

§ Another recent guide to English style and usage is *Oxford English: a guide to the language* (Oxford; New York : Oxford Univ. Pr., 1986), which contains essays on usage, vocabulary, grammar, slang, authors, and dialects, as well as specialized vocabulary lists.   PE1112.H6

Atlases

Anderson, Peter M. A structural atlas of the English dialects. London ; N.Y. : Croom Helm, c1987. 153 p. ISBN 0-7099-5116-7. £35.00 (est.).   **BC30**

Grew from "a need for information about the structural realities underlying the dialect material presented in the *Survey of English dialects* [Leeds : E.J. Arnold, 1962–]."—*Introd.* 114 maps display the distribution of particular vowels, consonants, or diphthongs over England. Short bibliography; word indexes. Clive Upton's *Word maps* (London; N. Y. : Croom Helm, c1987) also draws on the *Survey*, and contains 200 small black-

and-white maps that show distribution of forms and variants with vocabulary and pronunciation indexes. PE1705.A53

McIntosh, Angus. A linguistic atlas of late mediaeval English / Angus McIntosh, M.L. Samuels, Michael Benskin. [Aberdeen] ; N.Y. : Aberdeen Univ. Pr., 1986. 4 v. : maps ; 35 cm. ISBN 0-08-032437-1. £335.00. **BC31**

Contents: v. 1, General introduction, index of sources, dot maps; v. 2, Item maps; v. 3, Linguistic profiles; v. 4, County dictionary.

Covers England and portions of Wales, roughly 1350–1450, by analyzing local manuscript sources. The "dot maps" of v. 1 show particular linguistic and dialectical variants; the "item maps" of v. 2 discuss the geographical distribution of words or forms used in the survey. Vol. 3 includes the completed survey questionnaires which inventory the linguistic features of each source text; the "county dictionary" of v. 4 indexes the word forms in the linguistic profiles of v. 3 and so provides a printed list of their geographic distribution. Appendixes include a list of southern forms, a key to linguistic profile numbers by county area on maps, a key to geographical abbreviations and the linguistic profiles which are drawn from that area, and maps which plot the exact geographical location of the manuscript sources and their repositories. A *Guide* (Aberdeen : Aberdeen Univ. Pr., 1987) reprints sections from the general introduction and sample maps. PE1705.M35

OTHER GERMANIC LANGUAGES

General works

Braunmüller, Kurt. Deutsch-Skandinavisch im Vergleich : eine Bibliographie zur Linguistik und Lexikologie (1945–1985) / von Kurt Braunmüller ; (unter Mitarbeit von Sabine Stropnicky). Neumünster : K. Wachholtz, 1987. 160 p. (Kieler Beiträge zur deutschen Sprachgeschichte, Bd. 9). ISBN 3-529-04359-4. **BC32**

Lists 478 books, articles, congress proceedings, and dissertations on comparative Scandinavian-German linguistics. Arranged alphabetically within four main sections: bibliographies in comparative linguistics, studies of comparative linguistics, bibliographies of dictionaries, and German/Scandinavian dictionaries (including many polyglot and technical subject dictionaries). Language and subject indexes. Z2235.G7B7

Pasierbsky, Fritz. Deutsche Sprache im Reformationszeitalter : eine geistes– und sozialgeschichtlich orientierte Bibliographie / Fritz Pasierbsky ; bearb. und hrsg. von Edeltrud Büchler und Edmund Dirkschnieder. Tübingen : Niemeyer, 1988. 2 v. (1088 p.). ISBN 3-484-10606-9. **BC33**

Lists books, dissertations, and articles on German philology and the German language in the medieval and early modern periods. Arranged alphabetically by author, with a section that analyzes collective works. Subject index. Z2235.A2P37x

Yiddish

Bratkowsky, Joan Gloria. Yiddish linguistics : a multilingual bibliography. N.Y. : Garland, 1988. 407 p. (Garland reference library of the humanities, vol. 140). ISBN 0-8240-9804-8. **BC34**

Intended to supplement Uriel and Beatrice Weinreich's *Yiddish language and folklore* (*Guide* BC111). Lists almost 2,200 items in a classed arrangement of 12 main chapters: general works, structure of Yiddish, history of Yiddish, dialectology, interaction with other languages, onomastics, stylistics, se-

miotics, history and biography of linguistics and linguists, sociolinguistics, psycholinguistics, and applied linguistics. Name index. Z7038.Y53B7

ROMANCE LANGUAGES

General works

Klingebiel, Kathryn. Bibliographie linguistique de l'ancien occitan (1960–1982). Hamburg : H. Buske, c1986. 185 p. ISBN 3-87118-767-4. **BC35**

Lists alphabetically 802 dictionaries and linguistic and stylistic studies of Provençal language and literature. A "Supplément lexicographique" lists older dictionaries that have been reissued or revised between 1960 and 1982, as well as some reviews of those works. Subject index. Z7033.P8K57

Lexikon der Romanistischen Linguistik : LRL / hrsg. von Günter Holtus, Michael Metzeltin, Christian Schmitt. Tübingen : M. Niemeyer, c1988–89. v. 3–4 : ill., maps. ISBN 3-484-50250-9. (In progress). **BC36**

Contents: v. 3 (1989), pt. VI. Die einzelnen romanischen Sprachen und Sprachgebiete von der Renaissance bis zur Gegenwart. Rumänisch, Dalmatisch/Istroromanisch, Friaulisch, Ladinisch, Bündnerromanisch; v. 4 (1988), Italienisch, Korsisch, Sardisch.

Table of contents in French and German; text in French, German, and Italian.

The first of a projected eight-volume comprehensive history and linguistic analysis of the Romance languages, which is, in effect, a revision of Gustav Gröber's *Grundriss der romanischen Philologie* (*Guide* BC114–115). Arranged in signed chapters with detailed bibliographies, illustrations, charts, and both color and black-and-white maps. PC43.L49

Wexler, Paul. Judeo-Romance linguistics : a bibliography (Latin, Italo-, Gallo, Ibero-, and Rhaeto-Romance except Castilian). N.Y. : Garland, 1989. 174 p. (Garland reference library of the humanities, vol. 890). ISBN 0-8240-4531-9. $25.00. **BC37**

Lists 1,638 works on "all the Judeo-Romance languages attested before the expulsions of the Jews from the Kingdom of France and the Iberian Peninsula (1394 and 1492–8 respectively)—with the exception of Judezmo and Sephardic Ladino."—*Introd.* Arranged in a classified scheme of chapters on Latin, Italian, Gallic, Iberian forms, and comparative studies. Author index. Z7033.J48W49

French

Bassan, Fernande. French language and literature : an annotated bibliography / Fernande Bassan, Donald C. Spinelli, Howard A. Sullivan. N.Y. : Garland, 1989. 365 p. (Garland reference library of the humanities, vol. 954). ISBN 0-8240-4798-2. **BC38**

1st ed., 1976 (*Guide* BC121).

The editors have "made a complete revision and updating of all entries, added a sizeable body of new material, . . . written new annotations for those retained from the earlier work . . . [and] annotated Parts II and III . . . ."—*Pref.* Coverage has been expanded through the first half of 1988. Author/title index. Z2175.A2B39

Dees, Anthonij. Atlas des formes linguistiques des textes littéraires de l'ancien français. Tübingen : M. Niemeyer, 1987. 684 p. : ill., chiefly maps ; 24 cm. (Beihefte zur

Zeitschrift für romanische Philologie, Bd. 212). ISBN 3-484-52212-7.   **BC39**

Contains 517 black-and-white maps that show word forms, vocabulary, and usage variations in over 200 regional French texts from the medieval period. Appendixes list texts by region, words used for each map, and an index of forms and word-types treated in the maps.   PC2833.D43

Sabourin, Conrad. La francité canadienne / Conrad F. Sabourin, Rolande M. Lamarche. Montréal : Université de Montréal, Faculté des sciences de l'éducation, 1985–1987. v. 1–2. (In progress).   **BC40**

Vol. 2 by Conrad F. Sabourin, Rolande M. Lamarche, and Elca Tarrab.

Contents: v. 1, Aspects linguistiques : bibliographie; v. 2, Sociologie et politicologie de la langue.

Lists books, essays, journal articles, theses, dissertations, and government reports in alphabetical order by main entry. Subject index.   Z1380.S22

Italian

Hall, Robert Anderson,. Bibliografia della linguistica italiana : Terzo supplemento decennale, 1976–1986. Firenze : Sansoni, 1988. 620 p. (Orientamenti linguistici, 23).   **BC41**

For 2nd ed., 1958, and supplement 1–2, see *Guide* BC131.

Contains more than 6,000 entries, numbered consecutively with the preceding supplement, plus new editions, republications, and supplements or corrections to previous entries in the entire set.   Z2355.A2H315

Latin

Bibliographie zur lateinischen Wortforschung / hrsg. von Otto Hiltbrunner. Bern : Francke, c1981–1988. v. 1–3. ISBN 3-7720-1543-3 (Bd. 1). 42.00F. (In progress).   **BC42**

Contents: v.1–3, A–Causa.

Lists studies on etymology, word forms, and usage alphabetically by Latin word. Lengthier entries conclude with a brief discussion of the works cited and the history of scholarship on that particular word.   Z7028.E88B52

Sanders, Gabriel. Bibliographie signalétique du latin des chrétiens / par Gabriel Sanders et Marc Van Uytfanghe. Turnholti : Typographi Brepols editores pontificii, 1989. 188 p. (Corpus Christianorum. Lingua patrum, 1). **BC43**

For basic set, see *Guide* BB302.

A list of books and articles on texts, vocabularies, and language use of early Christian authors. Index of Latin words.   BR67.L55 v.1

Steitz, Lothar. Bibliographie zur Aussprache des Latein. Saarbrücken : [Institut für Phonetik, Universität des Saarlandes], 1987. 148 p. (Phonetica Saraviensia, Nr. 9).   **BC44**

In German, Czech, English, French, Hungarian, Italian, Polish, Russian, Spanish, and Ukrainian.

Over 1,400 citations to books, articles, and dissertations on the pronunciation of Latin are arranged alphabetically by author within chapters on particular topics. Author index.   Z7028.P75S73

Tremblay, Florent A. Bibliotheca lexicologiae Medii Aevi. Lewiston, N.Y. : Edwin Mellen Pr., c1988–[1989?]. 10 v. ISBN 0-88946-208-9.   **BC45**

Contents: v. 1, Classics in the Middle Ages, Education in the Middle Ages; v. 2, Lexicons (A–F) in the Middle Ages; v. 3, Lexicons (G–Z) in the Middle Ages; v. 4, Grammars in the Middle Ages; v. 5, Rise of vernacular languages; v. 6, Influence of vulgar Latin; v. 7, Lexicographical manuscripts (A–L); v. 8, Lexicographical manuscripts (M–Z), Journals and periodicals; v. 9, Author index, Title index; v. 10, Geographical index, Abbreviation index, Chronological index, Index on [sic] incipits.

Intended as a companion to Rodrigue LaRue's *Clavis scriptorum Graecorum et Latinorum* (4 v.; Trois-Rivières : Université du Québec à Trois-Rivières, Service de la Bibliothèque, c1985), this computer-generated bibliography lists publications and manuscripts from all time periods that relate to the use and study of Latin in the Middle Ages. The citations, which are arranged alphabetically by author or main entry in the topical volumes (v. 1–8), include references to reviews for modern works, bibliographic descriptions and some holdings information for early printed works, and references to censuses or textual analyses for manuscripts. Although volumes 9 and 10 contain numerous indexes, the lack of a comprehensive subject index, combined with the awkward use of abbreviations instead of volume numbers, makes this comprehensive tool suitable only for advanced scholars and researchers.   Z7028.L47T74

Portuguese

Bibliografia de linguística portuguesa / Núcleo de Estudos da Lingística Contrastiva da Faculdade de Ciências Sociais e Humanas da Universidade Nova de Lisboa. Lisboa : Litoral Edições : Distribuição, Sodilivros, [1987?]. 147 p.   **BC46**

Cites books, articles, conference proceedings, and dissertations in all languages in a classed arrangement.

§A similar work by José de Azevedo Ferreira, *Bibliografia selectiva de la lingua portuguese* (Lisbon : Instituto de Cultura e Lingua Portuguesa, 1989), includes a name and subject index, although a greater quantity of the works it cites are in Portuguese.   Z7001.B53

Chamberlain, Bobby J. Portuguese language and Luso-Brazilian literature : an annotated guide to selected reference works. N.Y. : Modern Language Association of America, 1989. 95 p. (Selected bibliographies in language and literature, 6). ISBN 0-87352-956-1. $22.00. ISBN 0-87352-957-X (pbk.). $14.50 (est.).   **BC47**

A classified list of 538 books with brief annotations. Includes a chapter on Lusophone Africa. Index of authors and editors.   Z2725.A2C45

Spanish

Bibliografía sobre el español del Caribe hispánico / Rafael Angel Rivas D[ugarte]. Caracas : Instituto Universitario Pedagógico de Caracas, Departamento de Castellano, Literatura y Latín : Centro de Investigaciones Lingüísticas y Literarias "Andrés Bello", 1985. 294 p.   **BC48**

Lists some 2,400 books, articles, and dissertations alphabetically by author in sections devoted to the entire region and to individual countries including Colombia, Costa Rica, Cuba, Guatemala, Honduras, Nicaragua, Panama, Puerto Rico, the Dominican Republic, and Venezuela. Some citations are incomplete. Subject index.   Z1609.L3B53

Billick, David J. Lexical studies of medieval Spanish texts : a bibliography of concordances, glossaries, vocabularies and selected word studies / by David J. Billick and Steven N. Dworkin. Madison [Wis.] : Hispanic Seminary of Medieval Studies, 1987. 116 p. ISBN 0-942260-87-2. $12.50 (pbk.). **BC49**

Originally published in the journal *La Corónica* 13/14 (1984/85–85/86), this work indexes "the numerous glossaries, vocabularies, concordances, and word indices appended to or based on scholarly editions of medieval texts."—*Pref.* Intended to point to works that can partially fulfill the need for a comprehensive medieval Spanish lexicon, "the majority of the compilations included in this volume are alphabetically arranged glossaries restricted to words no longer used or which display a meaning unknown in the modern language." Citations to these glossaries, published as journal articles, books, appendixes, and theses, are arranged chronologically by century covered, with separate sections for Judeo-Spanish and Aljamiado texts. Name and title indexes. PC4715.Z5B54

Faitelson-Weiser, Silvia. Diasle : dictionnaire inverse et analyse statistique de la langue espagnole = diccionario inverso y análisis estadístico de la lengua española = reverse dictionary and statistical analysis of the Spanish language. Québec : Presses de l'Université Laval, 1987. 261 p. + 6 microfiches. ISBN 2-7637-7137-8. $55.00. **BC50**

Table of contents and explanatory material in French, Spanish, and English.

A complicated tool for advanced researchers, *Diasle* is an "index of the words contained in 16 lexicographical works of the Spanish language."—*Introd.* Words or word units are listed alphabetically on microfiches in a standard phonological system with codes for parts of speech and bibliographic sources. The printed companion volume contains analytical tables, cross-references to alternative word entries, and lists of words which have been phonetically or grammatically modified, word endings, grammatical categories, and foreign words. PC4691.F34

Heydenreich, Titus. Bibliographie der Hispanistik in der Bundesrepublik Deutschland, Österreich und der deutschsprachigen Schweiz. Frankfurt am Main : Vervuert, 1988–1990. v. 1–2. (Editionen der Iberoamericana. Reihe II, Bibliographische Reihe, 4, etc.). ISBN 3-89354-704-5 (v. 1). (In progress). **BC51**

Contents: v. 1, 1978–81; v. 2, 1982–86.

Lists publications on Spanish, Portuguese, Catalan, Basque, and Galician linguistics, philology, and literature in a classed arrangement. Name index. Z2695.A2H49

Nuessel, Frank H. Theoretical studies in Hispanic linguistics (1960–) : a selected, annotated research bibliography. Bloomington : Indiana Univ. Linguistics Club, c1988. 355 p. **BC52**

"The primary purpose of this reference guide is to provide the scholar in Hispanic linguistics with a basic research tool that will be a starting point for the examination of some of the fundamental issues in the field."—*Pref.* The lengthy introduction and list of "related bibliographies" furnishes an overview of the past 30 years of Spanish linguistic research. Organized alphabetically by author with subject and name indexes. Z2695.A2N84

Viudas Camarasa, Antonio. Dialectología hispánica y geografía lingüística en los estudios locales (1920–1984) : bibliografía crítica y comentada. Cáceres : Institución cultural "El Brocense", 1986. 347 p. (Colección Plenos de la Confederación Espanola de Centros de Estudios Locales, 4). **BC53**

Arranged in sections by dialect, this bibliography lists primarily Spanish-language books, articles, dissertations, and conference proceedings in a classified scheme. Each section contains citations with sometimes quite lengthy annotations and a

more inclusive "Bibliografía complementaria." Subject, geographical, and author indexes. PC4700.Z9V854

CELTIC

Baumgarten, Rolf. Bibliography of Irish linguistics and literature, 1942–71. Dublin : Dublin Institute for Advanced Studies, 1986. 776 p. ISBN 0-901282-81-2. **BC54**

In effect, supplements and continues Richard I. Best's *Bibliography of Irish philology and manuscript literature* (*Guide* BC150). Contains citations to over 9,000 books, articles, theses, and conference proceedings in a classed arrangement. Irish word/name, first line, source and author indexes. A volume covering 1972–86 was in preparation in 1986. Z7012.I73B38

GREEK

Baumbach, Lydia. Studies in Mycenaean inscriptions and dialect, 1965–1978. Roma : Edizioni dell'Ateneo, 1986. 516 p. **BC55**

" . . . a complete bibliography and index incorporating the contents of volumes XI–XXIII [of the journal *Studies in Mycenaean inscriptions and dialect*] published between 1965 and 1978 by the Institute of Classical Studies of the University of London and the British Association of Mycenaean Studies compiled by Lydia Baumbach, from the volumes prepared by L.J.D. Richardson . . . [et al.]."—*t.p.* An earlier volume (1968) cumulated the bibliographies from v. I–X (1953–64). Citations are listed alphabetically by author, with a somewhat confusing classified subject index, and word and tablet indexes. Z7023.I5B38

INDIC

Geetha, K. R. Classified state bibliography of linguistic research on Indian languages. Mysore : Central Institute of Indian Languages, 1983. v. 1. (CIIL occasional monographs series, 28). (In progress). **BC56**

Contents: v. 1, Hindi speaking states (Bihar, Haryana, Himachal Pradesh, Madhya Pradesh, Rajasthan, Uttar Pradesh, Delhi).

Planned to be in 5 v., this work lists citations to linguistic studies by geographic area and language. Vol. 1 contains over 4,250 citations in a classed arrangement with author and journal indexes. Appendixes include tables of languages spoken and sources consulted. Z7049.I3G44

AFRICAN LANGUAGES

African language materials in the Boston University Libraries / comp. by Gretchen Walsh and Jenny Hochstadt. [Updated ed.]. Boston : Boston Univ., African Studies Center, [1988]. [99 p.]. **BC57**

1st ed., 1979 (*Guide* BC181).

Includes a cross-reference table for various dialects and language families. Z7106

Mann, Michael. A thesaurus of African languages : a classified and annotated inventory of the spoken languages of Africa : with an appendix on their written representation / by Michael Mann and David Dalby. London ; N.Y. : Zell, 1987. 325 p. ISBN 0-905450-24-8. $76.00.   **BC58**

Conceived in part as a companion to David Dalby's *Language map of Africa and the adjacent islands* (*Guide* BC183) and follows that work's classification scheme. In four main sections: (1) an inventory listing languages, names, synonyms, and dialects and giving bibliographic references to grammars and studies; (2) a second inventory arranged geographically; (3) a discussion of the universal African alphabet; (4) a complete bibliography of cited sources. Language index.   PL8005.M36

SOUTHEAST ASIAN

Huffman, Franklin E. Bibliography and index of mainland Southeast Asian languages and linguistics. New Haven, Conn. : Yale Univ. Pr., c1986. 640 p. ISBN 0-300-03679-5.   **BC59**

Lists some 10,000 publications, 1960–85, on the Austroasiatic, Tibeto-Burman, Tai-Kadai, Miao-Yao, and mainland Austronesian language families. Arranged alphabetically by author and chronologically within each author listing. Subject index.   Z3221.H82

South-East Asia : languages and literatures : a select guide / ed. by Patricia Herbert & Anthony Milner. Honolulu : Univ. of Hawaii Pr., c1989. 182 p. : ill. ISBN 0-8248-1267-0. $32.00.   **BC60**

For annotation, see *Supplement* BD382.   PL3501.S66

OCEANIC

Cook, Marjorie. Bibliography of the Summer Institute of Linguistics, Philippines, 1953–1984 / comp. by Marjorie Cook, Heather Kilgour, Jeanne Miller. Manila, Philippines : The Institute, [1986?]. 212 p. ISBN 971-1800-17-9 (pbk.).   **BC61**

Lists books, articles, government reports, and dissertations on some 78 languages of the Philippines in a classed arrangement. An appendix lists language name changes; author index.   Z7049.P45C66

BD

Literature

GENERAL WORKS

Bibliography

Birney, Alice L. The literary lives of Jesus : an international bibliography of poetry, drama, fiction, and criticism. N.Y. : Garland, 1989. 187 p. : ill. (Garland reference library of the humanities, vol. 735). ISBN 0-8240-8475-6.   **BD1**

Lists "separately published poetry, drama, and fiction about the life of Jesus Christ and literary criticism on those poems, plays, and stories."—*Pref.* The 1,424 items, written from late antiquity to 1984, are arranged in chapters by genre and time period, with some annotations. Author/editor index.

§ Warren S. Kissinger's *Lives of Jesus* (N.Y. : Garland, 1985) is a discursive bibliography that focuses specifically on biographical, rather than literary, works.   Z6514.C5J473

Hebel, Udo J. Intertextuality, allusion, and quotation : an international bibliography of critical studies. N.Y. : Greenwood, 1989. 175 p. (Bibliographies and indexes in world literature, no. 18). ISBN 0-313-26517-8. $39.95.   **BD2**

Lists 2,033 articles, books, chapters, and dissertations alphabetically by author with indexes to writers and anonymous texts and to subjects.   Z6514.C97H4

Kaske, Robert Earl. Medieval Christian literary imagery : a guide to interpretation / R.E. Kaske, in collaboration with Arthur Groos and Michael W. Twomey. Toronto ; Buffalo : Univ. of Toronto Pr., c1988. 247 p. (Toronto medieval bibliographies, 11). ISBN 0-8020-2636-2. ISBN 0-8020-6663-1 (pbk.).   **BD3**

Designed for "the graduate student or young scholar who is interested in . . . interpreting medieval literature but has little or no guidance in it."—*Introd.* Chapters provide bibliographical essays and suggest research methods on topics such as biblical exegesis, hymns, mythography, and major authors. Subject/medieval author, modern author/editor/translator, manuscript, and translation indexes.   PN671.Z99K37

Kiell, Norman. Psychoanalysis, psychology, and literature, a bibliography : Supplement to the second edition. Metuchen, N.J. : Scarecrow, 1990. 587 p. ISBN 0-8108-2178-8.   **BD4**

For earlier volumes and annotation, see *Guide* BD11.

Continues the arrangement of the original volumes, adding 7,754 new citations to works published for the most part 1980–87.   Z6514.P78K53

Kohl, Benjamin G. Renaissance humanism, 1300–1550 : a bibliography of materials in English. N.Y. : Garland, 1985. 354 p. (Garland reference library of the humanities, vol. 570). ISBN 0-8240-8773-9.   **BD5**

Prepared "with the needs of the undergraduate student in mind ."—*Introd.* Arranged in 18 chapters, which fall into two fairly distinct halves. Chapters 1–8 list reference works, journals, bibliographies, guides, and seminal studies on the various disciplines of Renaissance humanism. Chapters 9–18 cover specific humanists (e.g., Boccaccio) or geographic locations (e.g., Great Britain) in an approximate chronological order. Each chapter is further subdivided for particular topics or types of publication. Works by humanists and other source materials translated into English are listed, as are secondary texts. Review articles, book reviews, and doctoral dissertations are, for the most part, omitted. Author/editor/translator and subject indexes. Z7128.H9K64

Meurs, Jos van. Jungian literary criticism, 1920–1980: an annotated, critical bibliography of works in English (with a selection of titles after 1980) / by Jos van Meurs with John Kidd. Metuchen, N.J.: Scarecrow, 1988. 353 p. ISBN 0-8108-2160-5. **BD6**

Aims to offer "a complete bibliography of all secondary works (books and articles, critical and scholarly), written in English, that apply the psychology of C.G. Jung to the interpretation of literary texts written in English."—*Introd.* Comprehensive 1920–80, with some citations to works published in the early 1980s. In two main sections: (1) a survey of the history and development of Jungian criticism in narrative form; (2) the bibliography of 902 items arranged alphabetically by critic, with author and subject indexes. Z6514.P78M48

Pfeiffer, Joachim. Literaturpsychologie, 1945–1987: eine systematische und annotierte Bibliographie / Joachim Pfeiffer; hrsg. in Verbindung mit Wolfram Mauser und Bernd Urban und mit Unterstützung der Breuninger-Stiftung. Würzburg: Königshausen & Neumann, c1989. 516 p. ISBN 3-88479-394-2. **BD7**

Lists 2,411 books, articles, dissertations, and conference proceedings in a classified arrangement. Some overlap with Kiell (above) but contains many more citations to German-language publications; includes many items which do not strictly pertain to literature. Includes a long section on individual authors. Author and subject indexes. Z6514.P78P47

Current

Cohen, Ralph. New literary history international bibliography of literary theory and criticism / Ralph Cohen, ed.; Jeffrey M. Peck, bibliographical ed.; Christopher Camuto, technical ed.; Charlotte Bowen, supervisory ed. Baltimore: Johns Hopkins Univ. Pr., c1988. 188 p. ISBN 0-8018-3687-5. $30.00. **BD8**

Intended as an "annual compilation in one volume of the massive amount of material considered to be theoretical from all the so-called major and minor literary traditions."—*Introd.* Chapters compiled by contributing scholars list books, articles, and conference proceedings pertaining to specific world literatures and languages, from Arabic to Spanish and Portuguese. Chapters are subdivided into classified arrangements by literary topics or periods. Many citations are annotated. Name index. Z6514.C97C65

●**MLA international bibliography** [computer file]. [N.Y.]: Modern Language Association of America, 1981– . **BD9**

Machine-readable version of *Guide* BD22.

Coverage: 1981– . File size: 950,000 records. Available online (DIALOG, WILSONLINE; updated monthly) and in CD-ROM (Wilson, Faxon; updated quarterly).

Indexes

Harris, Laurie Lanzen. Characters in 20th-century literature. Detroit: Gale, c1990. 480 p. ISBN 0-8103-1847-4. $49.95. **BD10**

Presents "essays that elucidate the function and significance of the most important literary characters from more than 600 works of twentieth-century literature."—*Pref.* Profiles more than 2,000 characters from 250 authors of fiction. Entries are arranged alphabetically by author and include short bibliographies. Character and title indexes.

§ Another recent publication, *Imaginary people* by David Pringle (N.Y.: World Almanac; London: Grafton, c1987), lists characters from film, cartoons, radio and television, as well as from literature. PN56.4.H37

Hazen, Edith P. The Columbia Granger's index to poetry. 9th ed., completely rev., indexing anthologies published through June 30, 1989 / ed. by Edith P. Hazen, Deborah J. Fryer. N.Y.: Columbia Univ. Pr., c1990. 2082 p. ISBN 0-231-07104-3. **BD11**

1st ed., 1904; 8th ed., 1986 (*Guide* BD302).

As with earlier editions, some anthologies have been dropped and more than 150 new anthologies have been added, including over 50 collections translated from other languages.

§ A companion volume to the 9th ed., *Columbia Granger's guide to poetry anthologies* (N.Y.: Columbia Univ. Pr., c1991) lists and annotates collections in chapters devoted to particular topics or regions. Appendixes list recommended titles; general index. PN1022.H39

Research methods

Feldman, Paula R. The wordworthy computer: classroom and research applications in language and literature / Paula R. Feldman and Buford Norman. N.Y.: Random House, c1987. 228 p.: ill. ISBN 0-3943-5623-3. $13.00. **BD12**

As with many reference works on new technology, this volume is sadly out of date only a few years after publication. However, it still offers an idea of the broad range of applications which computers may have in both research and teaching, including bibliographic databases, concordances, stylistic analysis, or scholarly publishing. Selected bibliography; glossary of terms. PN73.F44

Kline, Mary-Jo. A guide to documentary editing. Baltimore: Johns Hopkins Univ. Pr., c1987. 228 p. ISBN 0-8018-3341-8. $29.50. **BD13**

For annotation, see *Supplement* AA54. Z113.3.K55

Miller, R. H. Handbook of literary research. Metuchen, N.J.: Scarecrow, 1987. 110 p. ISBN 0-8108-1959-7. **BD14**

"The purpose of this book is to help you use research time to your best advantage."—*Introd.* Intended for undergraduates, it presents chapters on basic reference sources and selected topics in literature and criticism, in a suggested order of consultation. Author/title index. PR56.M54

Research guide to biography and criticism: [literature] / [ed. by] Walton Beacham. Wash.: Research Pub., c1985. 2 v. (1362 p.). ISBN 0-933833-00-8. $129.00. **BD15**

" . . . designed to assist students in narrowing and researching topics for term papers and essay exams, and to provide librarians with a tool which will help them lead students to valuable, accessible resources."—*Pref.* Deals with "those authors most often studied," giving for each a chronology or biographical sketch, select bibliography, overview and evaluation of biographical sources, autobiographical sources, and an overview and evaluation of critical works.   Z2011.R47

Rudall, B. H. Computers and literature : a practical guide / B.H. Rudall and T.N. Corns. Cambridge, Mass. : Tunbridge Wells, Kent : Abacus Pr., 1987. 129 p. : ill. ISBN 0-85626-340-0.   **BD16**

Though much of the information is now outdated, this volume provides a guide for those doing literary research who wish to adapt "the power and convenience of data management and word-processing procedures" (*Pref.*) to their work. Chapters cover using the computer, programming and the choice of language, managing a bibliographic database, concordances, etc. Glossary of terms. An index is listed in the table of contents, but none is included.   PN73.R83

General collections

Criticism

Classical and medieval literature criticism. v. 1– . Detroit : Gale, 1988– . Annual. ISSN 0896-0011. $80.00.   **BD17**

Subtitle: Excerpts from criticism of the works of world authors from classical antiquity through the fourteenth century, from first appraisals to current evaluations.

Presents "significant passages from the most important criticism published in English to aid students in the location and selection of commentaries on the authors of this period . . . . Each entry in CMLC provides an overview of major criticism on an author or literary work . . . four to six authors in each 500 page volume."—*Pref.* Each entry includes a historical and critical introduction, a list of principal translations, criticism, and additional bibliography. Author, title, and critic indexes.   PN681.5.C57

Critical survey of literary theory / ed. by Frank N. Magill. Pasadena, Calif. : Salem Pr., c1987. 4 v. (1833, 47 p.). ISBN 0-89356-390-0 (set). $300.00.   **BD18**

For each of 247 Western and non-Western theorists, lists principal critical works, indicates the subject's influence as a theorist, provides biographical information and explication of theories and criticism, and cites several secondary critical works. Vol. 4 includes a glossary, 12 essays surveying historical and national trends in literary theory, and an index. Especially useful for undergraduates.   PN45.C74

Gale Research Company. Twentieth-century literary criticism. 1978– . Detroit : Gale, 1978– .   **BD19**

For annotation, see *Guide* BD47.

Annual, 1978–80. Irregular, 1981– .

Vols. 34 and 38 are called Topics volumes, covering topics rather than individual authors.   PN771.G27

Humm, Maggie. An annotated critical bibliography of feminist criticism. Boston : G.K. Hall, 1987. 240 p. ISBN 0-8161-8937-4.   **BD20**

Treats "contemporary feminist criticism: its theories, techniques, debates, and development in America and England."—*Introd.* Covers not only literary criticism, but also psychology, sociology, anthropology, and allied fields. Citations to books are arranged alphabetically by author in chapters on broad subject areas, with subject and author indexes.

§ See also Wendy Frost, *Feminist literary criticism : a bibliography of journal articles, 1975–1981* (N.Y. : Garland, 1988).   Z7963.F44H85

Orr, Leonard. Research in critical theory since 1965 : a classified bibliography. N.Y. : Greenwood, 1989. 465 p.

(Bibliographies and indexes in world literature, no. 21). ISBN 0-313-26388-4.   **BD21**

About 5,500 books, articles, and dissertations in English, French, and German are arranged by school of criticism (e.g., structuralist, reception aesthetics). Index by author and by type of criticism, but not by a specific literary work on which the article may be based.   Z6514.C97O77

Selden, Raman. A reader's guide to contemporary literary theory. 2nd ed. Lexington : Univ. Pr. of Kentucky, c1989. 159 p. ISBN 0-8131-0194-8. $9.00.   **BD22**

1st ed., 1985.

Lucid chapters explain the antecedents, development, and recent trends of critical theory. In six main sections: (1) Russian formalism; (2) Marxist theories; (3) Structuralist theories; (4) Post-structuralist theories; (5) Reader-oriented theories; (6) Feminist criticism. Each section concludes with bibliographies of selected introductory works and further reading. Name index.   PN94.S45

Stevens, Bonnie Klomp. A guide to literary criticism and research / Bonnie Klomp Stevens, Larry L. Stewart. N.Y. : Holt, Rinehart, and Winston, c1987. 176 p. ISBN 0-03-071964-X (pbk.).   **BD23**

Attempts to offer "upper-level students a concise but adequate guide to the range of modern literary criticism and to basic methods of research."—*Pref.* Presents chapters on particular kinds of criticism, (e.g., Formalist studies, Structuralist studies), the influence of other fields upon criticism (e.g., Feminist studies, Psychological studies), elements of critical essays, and methods of literary research. Each chapter includes bibliographies of cited or recommended works. Appendixes provide an annotated bibliography of basic research sources and guidelines and advice on documentation. General index.   PN81.S73

Encyclopedias

Benét's reader's encyclopedia. 3rd ed. N.Y. : Harper & Row, c1987. 1091 p. ISBN 0-06-181088-6. $35.00.   **BD24**

2nd ed., 1965 (*Guide* BD50).

Many of the older entries have been revised or dropped, and a substantial number of new entries added "with an eye to expanding the book's international scope."—*Introd.* Compiled by many hands, the 3rd ed. emphasizes 20th-century and non-Western literatures, with the result that some of the more obscure classical and European authors, characters, works, and motifs have been excluded.   PN41.B4

Dictionnaire historique, thématique et technique des littératures : littératures française et étrangères, anciennes et modernes / sous la direction de Jacques Demougin. Paris : Larousse, c1985–c1986. 2 v. : ill. (some col.). ISBN 2-03-508301-X (v. 1). ISBN 2-03-508302-8 (v. 2).   **BD25**

A work of wide coverage, with entries for authors, titles, and terms from all literatures and periods. Vol. 2 concludes with bibliographies for selected entries.   PN41.D487

Encyclopedia of world literature in the 20th century : index / comp. by Paula Rumaugh Sonntag ; Leonard S. Klein, gen. ed. Rev. ed. N.Y. : Ungar, c1984. 132 p. ISBN 0-8044-3131-0. $40.00.   **BD26**

For basic set and annotation, see *Guide* BD60.

Provides a complete index of personal names and some subject access.   PN771.E5

Frenzel, Elisabeth. Motive der Weltliteratur : ein Lexikon dichtungsgeschichtlicher Längsschnitte. 3.,

überarbeitete und erw. Aufl. Stuttgart : A. Kröner, c1988. 907 p. ISBN 3-520-30103-2. **BD27**
2nd ed., [1980] (*Guide* BD61).
Updates some articles and expands the index. PN43.F7

Le grand atlas des littératures / [réalisé par Encyclopædie Universalis]. [Paris] : Encyclopædia Universalis, c1990. 435 p. : ill. (some col.). ISBN 2-85229-930-5. 630F. **BD28**
Presents signed articles on the history, genres, political and social contexts and influences of world literature. Useful for its extensive color illustrations. PN41.G7

Kindlers neues Literatur Lexikon / herausgegeben von Walter Jens. München : Kindler, c1988–1990. v. 1–11. ISBN 3-463-43001-0 (Bd. 1). (In progress). **BD29**
Contents: v. 1–11, Aa–Mo (1988–90).
A reworking of *Kindlers Literatur Lexikon* (*Guide* BD63), arranged in alphabetical order by author, rather than title of work. While some articles are reprinted verbatim from the earlier set, a great many 20th-century authors have been added. Entries include birth and death dates and places, bibliographical information, and signed articles on each author's major works, with collective entries for shorter genres, such as lyric poetry, short stories, or essays. Literature is here interpreted in the broadest sense and includes history, journalism, and folklore. Planned for 20v., each with an author/title index; v.20 will contain complete indexes. PN44.K54

Wilpert, Gero von. Lexikon der Weltliteratur. 3., neubearbeitete Aufl. Stuttgart : A. Körner, c1988. v. 1. ISBN 3-520-80703-3 (v. 1). (In progress). **BD30**
1st ed., c1963–68; 2nd ed., c1975–80 (2 v.).
Contents: Bd. 1, Biographisch-bibliographisches Handwörterbuch nach Autoren und anonymen Werken. (1677 p.).
Comprehensive coverage of all time periods and literatures; brief entries include primary and secondary bibliographies. PN41.W48

Dictionaries

Abrams, M. H. A glossary of literary terms. 5th ed. N.Y. : Holt, Rinehart, and Winston, c1988. 260 p. ISBN 0-03-011953-7 (pbk.). $12.95. **BD31**
1st ed., 1941; 4th ed., 1981.
Defines "terms, concepts, and points of view that are commonly and profitably used in the history, analysis, interpretation, and criticism of works of literature."—*Pref.* All the articles have been rewritten and many new terms have been added to this 5th ed. In two sections: literary terms and modern theories of literature and criticism. The alphabetically-arranged entries range in length from a paragraph to several hundred words; most have several bibliographic references for further information. General index.
§ Another recent glossary, *The concise Oxford dictionary of literary terms*, (N.Y. : Oxford Univ. Pr., 1990), provides short definitions and illustrative examples. Less comprehensive is the revised and enlarged *A dictionary of modern critical terms*, ed. by Roger Fowler (below). PN41.A184

Allusions—cultural, literary, biblical, and historical : a thematic dictionary / Laurence Urdang and Frederick G. Ruffner, Jr., editors, David M. Glixon, assoc. ed. 2nd ed. Detroit : Gale, c1986. 634 p. ISBN 0-8103-1828-8. $68.00. **BD32**
1st ed., 1982.
Lists and explains 8,700 allusions under 712 themes (e.g., Virility, Joviality). Themes are arranged alphabetically, with a general index. Bibliography of works cited.

§ A more recent work, Elizabeth Webber's *Grand allusions* (Wash. : Farragut Publ. Co., 1990) offers "an eclectic collection of those allusions, figures of speech, terms of art, terms of the trade, foreign language phrases and jargon that appear in our daily reading" and "add color and vigor to language."—*Pref.* Intended for a popular audience. Provides pronunciations for foreign words and examples of usage for most allusions. No index. PN43.A4

Armentier, Louis. Dictionnaire de la théorie et de l'histoire littéraires du XIXe siècle à nos jours. Paris : Retz, c1986. 334, [2] p. : ill. ISBN 2-7256-1153-9. 190F. **BD33**
"Publié avec le concours de la Fonction Publique du Canada (Formation Linguistique)."*t.p.*
In addition to defining terms in literature, poetics, and rhetoric, emphasizes semiotics and the relationship of various literary terms to those used in linguistics, anthropology, psychology, and other fields. PN41.A7

Beckson, Karl E. Literary terms : a dictionary / Karl Beckson and Arthur Ganz. 3rd ed., rev. and enl. N.Y. : Noonday Pr., 1989. 308 p. ISBN 0-374-52177-8. $8.95. **BD34**
2nd ed., 1975 (*Guide* BD49).
Adds new critical terms, updates older entries, and revises bibliographic citations. An appendix lists entries by broad subject areas. PN44.5.B334

Cole, Sylvia. The Facts on File dictionary of twentieth-century allusions : from atom bomb to Ziegfeld girls / Sylvia Cole, Abraham H. Lass. N.Y. : Facts on File, 1990. 287 p. ISBN 0-8160-1915-0. **BD35**
Attempts to provide a handy reference for more than 900 contemporary persons, events, literary figures, facts, phenomena, or events such as "Chappaquiddick" or "Chernobyl." Furnishes some bibliographic references; general index.
§ The same authors have compiled *The Facts on File dictionary of classical, biblical, and literary allusions* (N.Y. : Facts on File, c1987). AG5.C7234

A dictionary of modern critical terms / ed. by Roger Fowler. Rev. and enl. ed. London ; N.Y. : Routledge & K. Paul, 1987. 262 p. ISBN 0-7102-1022-1. $29.95. **BD36**
"The present work is not designed to replace terminological handbooks but to add to and qualify such aids . . . [and] to stimulate curiosity about how literary terms work actively for us."—*Pref.* For some 150 terms covering such topics as farce, feeling, feminist criticism, fiction, figure, foregrounding, there are signed essays by scholars, many with references.
PN41.D4794

Escarpit, Robert. Dictionnaire international des termes littéraires. The Hague : Mouton, 1973–1989. v. 1–6. (In progress). **BD37**
Contents: fasc. 1–6, Académie–Emblème.
A comprehensive work, providing etymologies, semantic analyses, equivalent terms in foreign languages, historical overviews, and bibliographies for each word. A fascicle containing introductory matter was publ. 1973. PN44.5.E8

Grote, David. Common knowledge : a reader's guide to literary allusions. N.Y. : Greenwood, 1987. 437 p. ISBN 0-313-25757-4. **BD38**
Attempts "to present in one place the fundamental names in mythology, theater, literature, religion, history, and popular culture that reasonably educated persons might be expected to know in order to understand most general literature."—*Introd.* Alphabetically arranged. PN43.G68

Holman, C. Hugh. A handbook to literature / C. Hugh Holman and William Harmon. 5th ed. N.Y. : Macmil-

lan ; London : Collier Macmillan, c1986. 647 p. ISBN
0-02-356410-5. $25.00.   **BD39**
    4th ed., 1980 (*Guide* BD62).
    "Based on the original edition by William Flint Thrall and
Addison Hibbard."
    With the editorship passing to William Harmon, this 5th
ed. incorporates much revision of text with some additional entries. Many articles now have at least one bibliographical reference. The appendixes still include an outline of English and
American literature and lists of Nobel prizes for literature and
Pulitzer prizes for fiction, poetry, and drama through 1985.
Index of proper names.   PN41.H6

Prince, Gerald. A dictionary of narratology. Lincoln :
Univ. of Nebraska Pr., c1987. 118 p. : ill. ISBN 0-8032-
3678-6. $17.95.   **BD40**
    Defines and explains terms which are peculiar to or which
have specific meanings in the study of narrative discourse. Definitions tend to be rather technical and contain many cross-
references to other entries; most entries include bibliographic
references for further information.   P302.7.P75

Similes dictionary / Elyse Sommer, ed. dir. ; Mike Sommer, ed. Detroit : Gale, c1988. 950 p. ISBN 0-8103-
4361-4.   **BD41**
    Subtitle: A collection of more than 16,000 comparison
phrases from ancient times to the present, compiled from
books, folklore, magazines, newspapers, plays, politics, stage,
screen, and television and arranged under more than 500 thematic categories.
    A dictionary of phrases as indicated in the subtitle.
    PN6084.S5S55

Directories

**Directory of master's programs in foreign languages, for-
eign literatures, and linguistics.** N.Y. : Modern Language
Association of America, c1987. 173 p. ISBN
0-87352-169-2 (pbk.).   **BD42**
    For annotation, see *Supplement* CB96.   PB38.U6D57

The guide to writers conferences. 1st ed. (1988)– . Coral
Gables, Fla. : Shaw Associates, c1988– . Annual. ISSN
0897-4195. $14.95.   **BD43**
    Describes and lists alphabetically conferences, retreats, res-
idency programs, and organizations. Appendixes include a conference calendar; geographical, specialty, and organization indexes; lists of events for special interest groups, such as women
or students; and a list of those organizations that sponsor prizes
or scholarships.

The writer's advisor / comp. by Leland G. Alkire, Jr. ;
Cheryl I. Westerman, associate editor. Detroit : Gale,
c1985. 452 p. ISBN 0-8103-2093-2.   **BD44**
    Subtitle: A guide to books and articles about writing nov-
els, short stories, poetry, dramatic scripts, screenplays, magazine articles, biographies, technical articles and books, as well
as a guide to information about literary agents, marketing, and
a wide range of legal and business materials of interest to full-
and part-time writers.
    About 4,250 entries are grouped mainly according to the
categories mentioned in the subtitle. Some annotations. Author, title, and subject indexes.   Z5165.W74

Literary awards

Strachan, Anne. Prizewinning literature : UK literary
award winners. London : Library Association, 1989.
267 p. ISBN 0-85365-558-8.   **BD45**
    Provides author/title and publication information for win-
ners of 58 different literary prizes through June 1989. Excludes
juvenile or specialized literary awards.   Z2013.3.S77

Handbooks

Brewer, Ebenezer Cobham. Brewer's dictionary of phrase
and fable. 14th ed. / by Ivor H. Evans. N.Y. : Harper &
Row, c1989. 1220 p. : ill. ISBN 0-06-016200-7. $35.00.
    BD46
    "Centenary ed." [1981] (*Guide* BD89).
    Approximately 300 entries have been added to this indis-
pensable volume and "many existing entries have been updated, expanded and . . . improved."—*Pref.* Some quotations have
been included to illustrate definitions and usage. A selective
index of headwords and cross-references has also been added.
The clear and easy-to-read typography is another improvement
over the previous edition.   PN43.B65

Daemmrich, Horst S. Themes & motifs in western literature : a handbook / Horst S. and Ingrid Daemmrich.
Tübingen : Francke, c1987. 255 p. ISBN 3-7720-1776-2.
ISBN 3-7720-1790-8 (pbk.).   **BD47**
    A "theoretical, historical, and bibliographical guide to liter-
ary motifs and themes."—*Pref.* Alphabetically arranged entries
discuss and provide bibliographies to approximately 150 topics
such as "sea," "twilight," or "heart." No index.   PN43.D34

Dictionary of literary themes and motifs / Jean-Charles
Seigneuret, ed. .. [et al.]. N.Y. : Greenwood, 1988. 2 v.
(1507 p.). ISBN 0-313-22943-0 ($195.00).   **BD48**
    Over 600 scholars examined more than 5,000 works of lit-
erature to determine the 143 themes discussed in these volumes. The themes, which range from "utopia" to "grotesque"
to "marriage," are explored in alphabetically-arranged, signed
essays, which include brief bibliographies. Cross-index of related themes and general index of authors, works, and topics.
    PN43.D48

Park, Karin R. Publication grants for writers & publishers : how to find them, win them, and manage them / by
Karin R. Park & Beth Luey. Phoenix : Oryx, 1991.
105 p. : ill. ISBN 0-89774-557-4. $29.95.   **BD49**
    Written "to help authors and publishers find outside fund-
ing for their publications."—*Introd.* Organized in chapters that
describe publication costs, governmental and nongovernmental
sources, institutional sources, and grant writing techniques.
Brief bibliography; general index.   Z283.P37

Room, Adrian. Dictionary of translated names and titles.
London ; Boston : Routledge & Kegan Paul, 1986. 460 p.
ISBN 0-7100-9953-3. $40.00.   **BD50**
    Lists primary literary names, titles, terms, and places in
French, German, Italian, Spanish, and Russian. Titles here include novels, musical works, films, plays, fairy tales, and books
of the Bible, with a few short stories or poems. Arranged alphabetically in English, with separate language indexes.
    NX80.R66

Thomas, Edmund J. Writers and philosophers : a sourcebook of philosophical influences on literature / Edmund
J. Thomas and Eugene G. Miller. N.Y. : Greenwood,
1990. 269 p. ISBN 0-313-25684-5.   **BD51**

Intended for the beginning researcher; describes the philosophical influences on 123 Western European and American authors. Entries are arranged alphabetically and contain basic biographical and critical information, with brief bibliographies. A second section profiles 77 philosophers whose work is discussed in the author entries. Appendixes include a glossary of philosophical terms and a selected bibliography; general index.

PN49.T447

Biographies of authors

Dictionary of literary biography. Detroit : Gale, 1985–1991. v. 34–112. (In progress). **BD52**

For earlier vols., see *Guide* BD416.

Contents: v. 34, British novelists, 1890–1929 : traditionalists, ed. by Thomas F. Staley; v. 35, Victorian poets after 1850, ed. by William E. Fredeman and Ira B. Nadel; v. 36, British novelists, 1890–1929 : modernists, ed. by Thomas F. Staley; v. 37, American writers of the early republic, ed. by Emory Elliott; v. 38, Afro-American writers after 1955, ed. by Thadious M. Davis and Trudier Harris; v. 39, British novelists, 1660–1800, ed. by Martin C. Battestin (2 v.).

Vol. 40, Poets of Great Britain and Ireland since 1960, ed. by Vincent B. Sherry, Jr. (2 v.); v. 41, Afro-American poets since 1955, ed. by Trudier Harris and Thadious M. Davis; v. 42, American writers for children before 1900, ed. by Glenn E. Estes; v. 43, American newspaper journalists, 1690–1872, ed. by Perry J. Ashley; v. 44, American screenwriters, second series, ed. by Randall Clark; v. 45, American poets, 1880–1945, first series, ed. by Peter Quartermain; v. 46, American literary publishing houses, 1900–1980, trade and paperback, ed. by Peter Dzwonkoski; v. 47, American historians, 1886–1912, ed. by Clyde N. Wilson; v. 48, American poets, 1880–1945, second series, ed. by Peter Quartermain; v. 49, American literary publishing houses, 1638–1899, ed. by Peter Dzwonkoski (2 v.).

Vol. 50, Afro-American writers before the Harlem Renaissance, ed. by Trudier Harris; v. 51, Afro-American writers from the Harlem Renaissance to 1940, ed. by Trudier Harris; v. 52, American writers for children since 1960, fiction, ed. by Glenn E. Estes; v. 53, Canadian writers since 1960, first series, ed. by W.H. New; v. 54, American poets, 1880–1945, third series, ed. by Peter Quartermain (2 v.); v. 55, Victorian prose writers before 1867, ed. by William B. Thesing; v. 56, German fiction writers, 1914–1945, ed. by James Hardin; v. 57, Victorian prose writers after 1867, ed. by William B. Thesing; v. 58, Jacobean and Caroline dramatists, ed. by Fredson Bowers; v. 59, American literary critics and scholars, 1800–1850, ed. by John W. Rathbun and Monica M. Grecu.

Vol. 60, Canadian writers since 1960, second series, ed. by W.H. New; v. 61, American writers for children since 1960, poets, illustrators, and nonfiction authors, ed. by Glenn E. Estes; v. 62, Elizabethan dramatists, ed. by Fredson Bowers; v. 63, Modern American critics, 1920–1955, ed. by Gregory S. Jay; v. 64, American literary critics and scholars, 1850–1880, ed. by John W. Rathbun and Monica M. Grecu; v. 65, French novelists, 1900–1930, ed. by Catharine Savage Brosman; v. 66, German fiction writers, 1885–1913, ed. by James Hardin (2 v.); v. 67, Modern American critics since 1955, ed. by Gregory S. Jay; v. 68, Canadian writers, 1920–1959, ed. by W.H. New; v. 69, Contemporary German fiction writers, ed. by Wolfgang D. Elfe and James Hardin.

Vol. 70, British mystery writers, 1860–1919, ed. by Bernard Benstock and Thomas F. Staley; v. 71, American literary critics and scholars, 1880–1900, ed. by John W. Rathbun and Monica M. Grecu; v. 72, French novelists 1930–1960, ed. by Catharine Savage Brosman; v. 73, American magazine journalists, 1741–1850, ed. by Sam G. Riley; v. 74, American short-story writers before 1880, ed. by Bobby Ellen Kimbel, with the assistance of William E. Grant; v. 75, Contemporary German fiction writers, second series; v. 76, Afro-American writers, 1940–1955, ed. by Trudier Harris; v. 77, British mystery writers, 1920–1939, ed. by Bernard Benstock and Thomas F. Sta-

ley; v. 78, American short-story writers, 1880–1910, ed. by Bobby Ellen Kimbel, with the assistance of William E. Grant; v. 79, American magazine journalists, 1850–1900, ed. by Sam G. Riley.

Vol. 80, Restoration and eighteenth-century dramatists, first series, ed. by Paula R. Backscheider, v. 81, Austrian fiction writers, 1875–1913, ed. by James Hardin and Donald G. Daviau; v. 82, Chicano writers, first series, ed. by Francisco A. Lomerí and Carl R. Shirley; v. 83, French novelists since 1960, ed. by Catharine Savage Brosman; v. 84, Restoration and eighteenth-century dramatists, second series, ed. by Paula R. Backscheider; v. 85, Austrian fiction writers after 1914, ed. by James Hardin and Donald G. Daviau; v. 86, American short-story writers, 1910–1945, first series, ed. by Bobby Ellen Kimbel; v. 87, British mystery and thriller writers since 1940, first series, ed. by Bernard Benstock and Thomas F. Staley; v. 88, Canadian writers, 1920–1959, second series, ed. by W.H. New; v. 89, Restoration and eighteenth-century dramatists, third series, ed. by Paula R. Backscheider.

Vol. 90, German writers in the age of Goethe, first series, 1789–1832, ed. by James Hardin and Christoph Schweitzer; v. 91, American magazine journalists, 1900–1960, first series, ed. by Sam G. Riley; v. 92, Canadian writers, 1890–1920, ed. by W.H. New; v. 93, British romantic poets, 1789–1832, first series, ed. by John R. Greenfield; v. 94, German writers in the age of Goethe : Sturm und Drang to classicism, ed. by James Hardin and Christoph E. Schweitzer; v. 95, Eighteenth-century British poets, first series, ed. by John Sitter; v. 96, British romantic poets, 1789–1832, second series, ed. by John R. Greenfield; v. 97, German writers from the Enlightment to Sturm und Drang, 1720–1764, ed. by James Hardin and Cristoph E. Schweitzer; v. 98, American short-story writers, 1910–1945, second series, ed. by Bobby Ellen Kimbel; v. 99, Canadian writers before 1890, ed. by W.H. New.

Vol. 100, Modern British essayists, second series, ed. by Robert Beum; v. 101, British prose writers, 1660–1800, first series, ed. by Donald T. Siebert; v. 102, American short-story writers, 1910–1945, second series, ed. by Bobby Ellen Kimbel; v. 103, American literary biographers, first series, ed. by Steven Serafin; v. 104, British prose writers, 1660–1800, second series, ed. by Donald T. Siebert; v. 105, American poets since World War II, second series, ed. by R.S. Gwynn; v. 106, British literary publishing houses, 1820–1880, ed. by Patricia J. Anderson and Jonathan Rose; v. 107, British romantic prose writers, 1789–1832, first series, ed. by John R. Greenfield; v. 108, Twentieth-century Spanish poets, ed. by Michael L. Perna; v. 109, Eighteenth-century British poets, second series, ed. by John Sitter.

Vol. 110, British romantic prose writers, 1789–1832, second series, ed. by John R. Greenfield; v. 111, American literary biographers, second series, ed. by Steven Serafin; v. 112, British literary publishing houses, 1881–1965, ed. by Patricia J. Anderson and Jonathan Rose.

Dizionario Bompiani degli autori di tutti i tempi e di tutte le letterature. Milano : Bompiani, 1987. 4 v. (2550 p.). **BD53**

1st ed., 1956–57 (*Guide* BD100) had title: *Dizionario letterario Bompiani degli autori . . . .*

Adds articles on some 3,000 authors to bring the total to almost 9,000. The illustrations have been dropped for this edition.

PN466.D54

European writers / William T.H. Jackson, ed., George Stade, ed. in chief. N.Y. : Scribner, 1985–1990. v. 5–14. ISBN 0-684-17915-6 (v.5–7). $195.00. (In progress). **BD54**

For earlier volumes and annotation, see *Guide* BD102.

Vols. 5–13, Jacques Barzun, ed., George Stade, ed. in chief.

Contents: v. 5–7, The Romantic century; v. 8–13, The twentieth century; v. 14, Index.

PN501.E9

Index to the Wilson authors series. Rev. 1986 ed. N.Y. : H.W. Wilson Co., c1986. 104 p. ISBN 0-8242-0731-9.
    BD55

1st ed., 1976.

Indexes articles on more than 8,600 authors from *American authors 1600–1900* (*Guide* BD417), *British authors before 1800* (*Guide* BD576), *British authors of the 19th century* (*Guide* BD577), *European authors 1000–1900* (*Guide* BD106), *Greek and Latin authors 800 B.C.–A.D. 1000* (*Guide* BD1400), *Twentieth century authors* (*Guide* BD107) and its *First supplement* (*Guide* BD108), *World authors 1950–1970* and *1970–1975* (*Guide* BD113), and *World authors 1975–1980* (*Supplement* CH2574). A new edition is expected in 1991.   PN451.I5

Nobel laureates in literature : a biographical dictionary / ed. by Rado Pribic. N.Y. : Garland, 1990. 473 p. (Garland reference library of the humanities, vol. 849). ISBN 0-8240-5741-4.   **BD56**

Presents signed essays and selected bibliographies on laureates from 1901 through 1988. Arranged alphabetically by laureate, with a chronological list of prizewinners and a general index.   PN452.N6

Quotations

General collections

Andrews, Robert. The concise Columbia dictionary of quotations. N.Y. : Columbia Univ. Pr., c1989. 343 p. ISBN 0-231-06990-1.   **BD57**

Also published as *The Routledge dictionary of quotations* (London: Routledge, c1987).

Witty or provocative quotations, many of recent vintage, arranged by topic from "Absence" or "Absurdity" to "Writing" or "Youth." Gives author of each quote and his or her dates, but not the title of the specific work. Index of subjects.
  PN6081.A653

Bloomsbury dictionary of quotations. London : Bloomsbury, 1987. [448] p. ISBN 0-7475-0043-6. £14.95. **BD58**

Attempts to include "both familiar quotations and perceptive or witty sayings that are less well known . . . especially . . . quotations that reflect contemporary issues as well as those from literature and the Bible."—*Introd.* Arranged alphabetically by author, with brief notes on the author's works or importance. Does not provide exact references, in most instances furnishing only the title of the quoted work. Keyword index. A 2nd ed. is expected in 1991.   PN6081

Boller, Paul F. They never said it : a book of fake quotes, misquotes, and misleading attributions / Paul F. Boller, Jr., John George. N.Y. : Oxford Univ. Pr., 1989. 159 p. ISBN 0-19-505541-1. $15.95.   **BD59**

Two historians discuss and clarify misquotes credited to historical personages, literary authors, and the Bible. Arranged alphabetically by attributed source. Footnotes and author/title index.   PN6081.B635

Douglas, Auriel. Webster's New World best book of aphorisms / Auriel Douglas, Michael Strumpf. N.Y. : Webster's NewWorld : Distr. by Prentice Hall, c1989. 409 p. ISBN 0-13-947128-6. $7.95.   **BD60**

Pithy sayings and apothegms arranged alphabetically by topic/keyword. Author index.   PN6271.D68

The Macmillan dictionary of quotations. N.Y. : Macmillan, c1989. 790 p. ISBN 0-02-511931-1.   **BD61**

More than 20,000 quotations—biographical, thematic, biblical, proverbial, and from nursery rhymes. Source is given,

when known, to author, title, and chapter. Keyword index.
  PN6081.M27

Mottoes : a compilation of more than 9,000 mottoes from around the world and throughout history / Laurence Urdang, ed. dir. ; Ceila Dame Robbins, ed. ; Frank R. Abate, assoc. ed. Detroit : Gale, c1986. 1162 p. ISBN 0-8103-2076-2. $130.00.   **BD62**

Subtitle: A compilation of more than 9,000 mottoes from around the world and throughout history, with foreign examples identified and translated into English, the entries arranged in the text under thematic categories, supplemented by alphabetic indexes of all mottoes and of the families, institutions, individuals, etc., to which they are attributed.

Identifies mottoes appearing on coats of arms, emblems, and seals.   PN6309.M68

O'Clery, Conor. The dictionary of political quotations on Ireland, 1886–1987 : phrases make history here. Boston : G.K. Hall, [1987]. 232 p. ISBN 0-8161-8939-0.   **BD63**

For annotation, see *Supplement* DC151.   DA959.O25

Powell, David. The wisdom of the novel : a dictionary of quotations. N.Y. : Garland, 1985. 729 p. (Garland reference library of the humanities, vol. 459). ISBN 0-8240-9017-9.   **BD64**

Hoping to rectify the scant attention paid to novelists in most quotations collections, this work draws maxims and sayings from "all of the major British and American novels, and hundreds of the lesser ones, from 1470 through 1900."—*Pref.* Arranged in an alphabetical list of subject headings with author/novel and keyword indexes.   PN6083.P58

Respectfully quoted : a dictionary of quotations requested from the Congressional Research Service / ed. by Suzy Platt. Wash. : Library of Congress : For sale by the Supt. of Docs., U.S. Govt. Print. Off., 1989. 520 p. ISBN 0-8444-0538-8.   **BD65**

Superintendent of Documents classification no.: LC 14.2:D56.

Scrupulously researched and satisfyingly thorough, this volume presents 2,100 quotations from the Congressional Reading Room Quotations File developed as result of trying to identify or verify quotations for more than 50 years. Topical arrangement, with author and subject indexes. Sources are given in most instances, with untraceable quotations so marked.   PN6081.R435

Simpson, James Beasley. Simpson's contemporary quotations. Boston : Houghton Mifflin, 1988. 495 p. ISBN 0-395-43085-2. $19.95.   **BD66**

An earlier version was published as *Contemporary quotations* (New York : Crowell, c1964).

"Contemporary" is here defined as the latter half of the 20th century. Arranged in three main categories, The world, Humankind, and Communications and the arts, with subcategories such as sports, travel, or medicine. Exact source citations, in many cases including page numbers, are given for each quote. Source and subject/keyword indexes.   PN6083.S53

Stephens, Meic. A dictionary of literary quotations. London ; N.Y. : Routledge, 1990. 193 p. ISBN 0-415-04129-5. £14.95.   **BD67**

Collects some 3,250 quotations which refer to "literature, writers, writing, books and reading, defined in a fairly broad way and taking in a number of contiguous areas such as journalism and the book trade."—*Pref.* Does not include quotes about specific authors. Arranged in 180 topical areas, such as Bestseller, Editor. Citations are to author and title of work; author and subject indexes.   PN6081.S728

Webster's New World dictionary of quotable definitions / ed. by Eugene E. Brussell. 2nd ed. Englewood Cliffs, N.J. : Prentice Hall, c1988. 674 p. ISBN 0-13-949272-0. $29.95. ISBN 0-13-948159-1 (pbk.). $14.95.　　**BD68**

1st ed., 1970, had title: *Dictionary of quotable definitions.*

Adds some 5,000 new entries and some new subject areas. Arranged alphabetically by subject, with an author index. No sources provided.　　PN6081.B77

Foreign and classical

German

Zitatenlexikon / [hrsg. von] Ursula Eichelberger. [Leipzig] : Bibliographisches Institut Leipzig, 1981. 920 p.　　**BD69**

A topical arrangement of some 12,500 German-language citations, giving for each quotation the author, title, chapter, and page. List of authors with full bibliographic citation to text used. International in coverage, though text is in German.　　PN6092.Z55

Proverbs

Mieder, Wolfgang. International proverb scholarship : an annotated bibliography. Supplement I (1800–1981). N.Y. : Garland, 1990. 436 p. (Garland reference library of the humanities, vol. 1230). ISBN 0-8240-4037-6.　　**BD70**

Updates and expands the coverage of the original volume (*Guide* BD175), and continues its numbering, adding 1,881 new entries.　　Z7191.M543

———————— The Prentice-Hall encyclopedia of world proverbs : a treasury of wit and wisdom through the ages. Englewood Cliffs, N.J. : Prentice-Hall, c1986. 582 p. ISBN 0-13-695586-X.　　**BD71**

A collection assembled by a folklorist that presents proverbs from peoples and languages throughout the world. Arranged by keyword; all proverbs are given in English, with language of origin indicated. About 18,500 entries. Select bibliography.　　PN6405.M54

Whiting, Bartlett Jere. Modern proverbs and proverbial sayings. Cambridge, Mass. : Harvard Univ. Pr., 1989. 709 p. ISBN 0-674-58053-2. $39.95.　　**BD72**

Over 5,500 proverbs collected from writings published primarily from 1930 to early 1980s are listed by keyword, with source citations providing page numbers and dates of publication, as well as references to earlier compilations. Not indexed.　　PN6403.W48

Children's literature

Dunhouse, Mary Beth. International directory of children's literature. N.Y. : Facts on File : c1986. 128 p. ISBN 0-8160-1411-6. $29.95.　　**BD73**

Gives addresses and other information for publishers, magazines, organizations, fairs and conferences, prizes, libraries and special collections, with statistics for 1979–81.　　PN1008.4.D86

Helbig, Alethea. Dictionary of American children's fiction, 1859–1959 : books of recognized merit / Alethea K. Helbig and Agnes Regan Perkins. Westport, Conn. :

Greenwood, 1985. 666 p. ISBN 0-313-22590-7.　　**BD74**
PS374.C454H45

———————— Dictionary of American children's fiction, 1960–1984 : recent books of recognized merit / Alethea K. Helbig and Agnes Regan Perkins. N.Y. : Greenwood, 1986. 914 p. ISBN 0-313-25233-5.　　**BD75**

Taken together, these two volumes provide almost 9,000 sketches on characters, authors, and individual works, with detailed general indexes which include subject entries for topics such as Old persons, Nieces, Fires, or Eighteenth century.　　PS374.C454H45

———————— Dictionary of British children's fiction : books of recognized merit / Alethea K. Helbig and Agnes Regan Perkins. N.Y. : Greenwood, 1989. 2 v. (1632 p.). ISBN 0-313-22591-5 (set).　　**BD76**

Contains "1,626 entries on such elements as titles, authors, characters, and settings based on 387 books published from 1678 to 1985."—*Pref.* General index.　　PR830.C513H4

Lynn, Ruth Nadelman. Fantasy literature for children and young adults : an annotated bibliography. 3rd ed. N.Y. : Bowker Co., c1989. 771 p. ISBN 0-8352-2347-7.　　**BD77**

1st ed., 1979, and 2nd ed., 1983, had title: *Fantasy for children.*

Provides extremely brief annotations to "over 3,300 fantasy novels and story collections for children and young adults in grades 3 through 12, as well as a research guide on the authors who write fantasy for children and young adults."—*Pref.* In two main parts: (1) Annotated bibliography, which presents material in a classified arrangement under topics or themes such as Talking animal fantasy or Travel to other worlds; (2) Research guide, which lists materials on history and criticism, teaching aids and bibliographies. Author/illustrator, title, and subject indexes.　　Z1037.L97

Nakamura, Joyce. Children's authors and illustrators : an index to biographical dictionaries. 4th ed. Detroit : Gale, c1987. lxvi, 799 p. (Gale biographical index series, no. 2). ISBN 0-8103-2525-X. $140.00.　　**BD78**

1st ed., 1976 (*Guide* BD197); 3rd ed., 1981.

Retains "all material included in the previous editions" (*Introd.*), indexing more than 400 reference books.

§ Another volume in the same series is the author's *Writers for young adults : biographies master index* (3rd ed., Detroit : Gale, 1989).　　Z1037.A1N18

Olderr's young adult fiction index. 1987– . Chicago : St. James Pr.,1988–. Annual. ISSN 1052-3472.　　**BD79**

Indexes works of fiction by subject and character, with citations to reviews from library journals. Appendixes: list of "Best books" for the year; directory of publishers and distributors.

Sixth book of junior authors & illustrators / ed. by Sally Holmes Holtze. N.Y. : H.W. Wilson, 1989. 345 p. : ill. ISBN 0-8242-0777-7.　　**BD80**

For earlier editions, see *Guide* BD194–196.

Includes a cumulative index for all volumes.　　PN1009.A1S3936

Trefny, Beverly Robin. Index to children's plays in collections, 1975–1984 / by Beverly Robin Trefny and Eileen C. Palmer. Metuchen, N.J. : Scarecrow, 1986. 108 p. ISBN 0-8108-1893-0.　　**BD81**

2nd ed., 1977 (*Guide* BD213).

Indexes 540 plays from 48 collections, published 1975–84.　　PN1627.T73

Twentieth-century children's writers / ed., Tracy Chevalier ; consulting ed., D.L. Kirkpatrick. 3rd ed. Chicago : St. James Pr., 1989. 1288 p. ISBN 0-912289-95-3. **BD82**
2nd ed., 1983 (*Guide* BD199).

Approximately 100 entries have been added and most of the biographical sketches and bibliographies have been updated. PN1009.A1T9

Writers for children / Jane M. Bingham, ed. N.Y. : Scribner's, 1987. 661 p. ISBN 0-684-18165-7. $75.00. **BD83**

Signed essays, each with a selected bibliography, profile 84 authors who have either written specifically for children or whose works have a largely juvenile audience. All are deceased and continue "to hold either popular or scholarly status."— *Introd.* General index. PN1009.A1W73

Drama

Bibliography

Drury, Francis K. W. Drury's guide to best plays / James M. Salem. 4th ed. Metuchen, N.J. : Scarecrow, 1987. 480 p. ISBN 0-8108-1980-5. **BD84**
3rd ed., 1978 (*Guide* BD201).

Follows the plan of the previous edition providing "information on approximately 1,500 selected, non-musical, full-length plays in English, covering all dramatic periods . . . from 400 B.C. to 1985."—*Foreword.* Z5781.D8

Indexes

Keller, Dean H. Index to plays in periodicals, 1977–1987. Metuchen, N.J. : Scarecrow, 1990. 391 p. ISBN 0-8108-2288-1. **BD85**

Forms a supplement to the compiler's 1979 volume (*Guide* BD212). Indexes 4,605 plays published in 104 periodicals (i.e., those journals from the earlier list which continued to publish plays and which are still in existence, plus several new titles). Z5781.K43

Ottemiller, John H. Ottemiller's index to plays in collections : an author and title index to plays appearing in collections published between 1900 and 1985. 7th ed. / rev. and enl. by Billie M. Connor and Helene G. Mochedlover. Metuchen, N.J. : Scarecrow, 1988. 564 p. ISBN 0-8108-2081-1. $42.50. **BD86**
6th ed., 1976 (*Guide* BD215).

This edition indexes some 6,548 plays by 2,555 different authors in 1,350 collections "published in the English-speaking world from 1900 through 1985."—*Pref.* Follows the plan of the previous edition. Z5781.O8

Criticism

Carpenter, Charles A. Modern drama scholarship and criticism, 1966–1980 : an international bibliography. Toronto ; Buffalo : Univ. of Toronto Pr., c1986. 587 p. ISBN 0-8020-2549-8. $75.00. **BD87**

" . . . a classified, selective list of publications on world drama since Ibsen."—*Introd.* International in scope, but limited to publications in Roman-alphabet languages. About 27,300 items in classed arrangement. Index of playwrights at front; index of names (i.e., authors of critical writings, etc.) at back.

Table of contents, but no subject approach other than through playwrights' names. Z5781.C37

Contemporary dramatists / ed., D.L. Kirkpatrick ; consulting ed., James Vinson. 4th ed. Chicago : St. James Pr., c1988. 785 p. ISBN 0-912289-62-7. **BD88**
3rd ed., 1982 (*Guide* BD222).

An updating, following the plan of the previous edition. Includes an appendix "for some seven writers who have died since the 1950s but whose reputations are essentially contemporary."—*Editor's note.* PR737.C57

Encyclopedias

A companion to the medieval theatre / ed. by Ronald W. Vince. N.Y. : Greenwood, 1989. 420 p. ISBN 0-313-24647-5. **BD89**

A dictionary arrangement of authors, anonymous works, literary styles and forms, regions, and symbols, covering roughly 900–1550. Brief bibliographies at the end of most entries; chronology, name, title, and subject indexes. PN2152.C66

Fiction

Bibliography

Hartman, Donald K. Themes and settings in fiction : a bibliography of bibliographies / comp. by Donald K. Hartman and Jerome Drost. N.Y. : Greenwood, 1988. 223 p. (Bibliographies and indexes in world literature, no. 14). ISBN 0-313-25866-X. **BD90**

Lists bibliographies, bibliographic essays, review articles, and literary surveys of novels and short stories. Covers publications of 1900–85 in English. One-sentence annotations; joint author and subject indexes. Z5916.H28

Husband, Janet. Sequels : an annotated guide to novels in series / Janet Husband and Jonathan F. Husband. 2nd ed. Chicago : Amer. Lib. Assoc., 1990. 576 p. ISBN 0-8389-0533-1. $24.95. **BD91**
1st ed., 1982 (*Guide* BD236).

Adds titles published 1982–89 and the genre of detective fiction. Z5917.S44H87

Menendez, Albert J. The Catholic novel : an annotated bibliography. N.Y. : Garland, 1988. 323 p. (Garland reference library of the humanities, vol. 690). ISBN 0-8240-8534-5. **BD92**

A list of 490 critical works on religious fiction, Catholic novels, and individual authors, followed by an author list of 1,703 representative Catholic novels. Covers English-language works almost exclusively. Title index. Z5917.C47M46

Biobibliography

Contemporary novelists / ed., D.L. Kirkpatrick ; consulting ed., James Vinson. 4th ed. N.Y. : St. Martin's Pr., 1986. 1003 p. ISBN 0-312-16731-8. $70.00. **BD93**
3rd ed., 1982 (*Guide* BD248).

An updating following the plan of the previous edition. The appendix provides entries "for some 11 writers who have died since 1960 but whose reputations are essentially contemporary."—*Editor's note.* PR883.C64

Postmodern fiction : a bio-bibliographical guide / ed. by Larry McCaffery. N.Y. : Greenwood, 1986. 604 p. (Movements in the arts, no. 2). ISBN 0-313-24170-8. $75.00. **BD94**

Provides "biographical and bibliographical information, as well as critical assessments, about many of the important figures in the field of post-modern literature."—*Introd.* In two main sections: (1) Overview articles, which contains 15 chapters by contributing scholars on topics such as realism, journalism, feminist fiction, or Latin American literature; and (2) Authors and critics, signed biographical and critical sketches of more than 100 individual writers. Both sections include bibliographies at the end of each chapter or sketch; citations are for the most part to English-language works. General index.

PN3503.P594

Indexes

Amos, William. The originals : an a–z of fiction's real-life characters. Boston : Little, Brown; London : J. Cape, c1985. 614 p., [24] p. of plates : ill. ISBN 0-316-03741-9. $19.95. **BD95**

Includes characters from essays and poems as well as novels and plays. Entries are for the most part arranged by characters' surnames and aim "to indicate the strength of the identification and extent to which the character is based on the model."—*Foreword.* Emphasizes English and American literature, but includes some French, German, Italian, Russian, etc. Index of persons, with reference to the entries under which they are found. PN56.4.A4

Bold, Alan Norman. Who was really who in fiction / Alan Bold and Robert Giddings. Burnt Mill, Harlow, Essex, England : Longman, 1987. 383 p. ISBN 0-582-89251-1. £9.95. **BD96**

Arranged by character, this work gives much fuller descriptions of character, plot, and prototype than *The originals* (above), as well as providing one or two references in each entry to biographical and critical works. General index. PN41.B57

Cyclopedia of literary characters II / ed. by Frank N. Magill. Pasadena, Calif. : Salem Pr., c1990. 4 v. (1775, lxxxi p.). ISBN 0-89356-517-2 (set). $300.00. **BD97**

Draws on the *Masterplots II* series, and supplements, rather than replaces, the original volume (*Guide* BD92). Signed entries for 1,437 works are arranged alphabetically by title and include descriptions of genre and setting as well as character analyses. Indexes of titles, authors, and characters (there are about 12,000). PN44.M3

Ireland, Norma Olin. Index to fairy tales, 1978–1986, including folklore, legends, and myths in collections : fifth supplement / comp. by Norma Olin Ireland and Joseph W. Sprug. Metuchen, N.J. : Scarecrow, 1989. 575 p. ISBN 0-8108-2194-X. **BD98**

For basic volume and previous suppls., see *Guide* BD244, BD246–247.

Indexes 261 collections "selected on the basis of availability and favorable reviews in professional journals."—*Introd.*

Z5983.F17I732

Criticism

Short story criticism. SSC 1– . Detroit : Gale, 1988– . Annual. ISSN 0895-9439. $70.00. **BD99**

Quotes "significant passages from criticism of the greatest short story writers of all time and provides supplementary materials—biographical and bibliographical—to guide the interested student to a greater understanding of the authors of short fiction."—*Pref.* 15 to 20 authors are included in each volume, with excerpts ranging from four to ten paragraphs drawn from critical works—books, articles, reviews. Criticism is presented in chronological order. Cumulative author and title indexes in successive volumes. PN3373.S386

Walker, Warren S. Twentieth-century short story explication : supplement to third edition : with check lists of books and journals used. Hamden, Conn. : Shoe String Pr., 1984–1989. v. 2–4. ISBN 0-208-02005-5. $39.00. (In progress). **BD100**

For earlier volumes and annotation, see *Guide* BD254.

Contents: Suppl. 2 (1984), 1979–81; Suppl. 3 (1987), 1981–84; Suppl. 4 (1989), 1984–86.

A fifth supplemental volume and cumulative index to the entire set is expected in 1992. Z5917.S5W33

Detective and mystery stories

Barzun, Jacques. A catalogue of crime : being a reader's guide to the literature of mystery, detection, and related genres / Jacques Barzun & Wendell Hertig Taylor. Rev. and enl. ed. N.Y. : Harper & Row, c1989. 952 p. ISBN 0-06-010263-2. $50.00. **BD101**

1st ed., c1971 (*Guide* BD258).

"A comparison between the present catalogue and its first edition would show that a good many authors of the first rank are now represented by all, or nearly all, their works; that the subgenres . . . receive treatment on a par with the older forms; that the search for notable authors . . . has been diligently pursued and has turned up single works of the greatest merit; that continental and Japanese writers have been sampled . . . finally, that certain omissions have been made."—*Pref.* The most notable changes are the removal of ghost stories and supernatural fiction, and the omission of biographical data, both due to recent publications which contain fuller information. Lists and briefly describes 5,044 works, with an author/title index.

§ A similar work, Susan Oleksiw's *A reader's guide to the classic British mystery* (Boston : G.K. Hall, c1988; rpt. N.Y. : Mysterious Pr., 1989), provides synopses for novels and novellas by 121 British authors published 1900–85. Z5917.D5B37

Conquest, John. Trouble is their business : private eyes in fiction, film, and television, 1927–1988. N.Y. : Garland, 1990. liii, 497 p. (Garland reference library of the humanities, vol. 1151). ISBN 0-8240-5947-6. **BD102**

Lists alphabetically and describes authors and characters in private eye fiction, with separate chapters on film, television, and radio, as well as a "yellow pages" section which lists fictional private eyes by geographical location. Somewhat confusing typography and organization. Title index. P96.D4C66

Contento, William. Index to crime and mystery anthologies / William G. Contento with Martin H. Greenberg. Boston : G.K. Hall, 1990. 736 p. ISBN 0-8161-8629-4. **BD103**

" . . . over 1,000 anthologies are indexed by editor and title, their contents are listed, and indexed by author and title."—*Introd.* Covers titles published 1875–1990 in five main parts: (1) Author list: books; (2) Title list: books; (3) Author list: stories; (4) Title list: stories; (5) Book contents, which lists anthologies by editor, rather than title. Entries include publication information, ISBN, and price (for books) and story length and original publication information (for stories). Z2014.F4C58

Cook, Michael L. Mystery, detective, and espionage fiction : a checklist of fiction in U.S. pulp magazines, 1915–1974 / Michael L. Cook and Stephen T. Miller. N.Y. : Garland, 1988. 2 v. (Fiction in the pulp magazines, vol. 1 ; Garland reference library of the humanities, vol. 838). ISBN 0-8240-7539-0 (v. 1). **BD104**

Compiled from a survey of collectors. Vol. 1 lists approximately 200 magazines alphabetically by title, with chronological list of contents and summary publication information; v. 2 lists stories alphabetically by author.   Z1231.D47C66

Hubin, Allen J. 1981–1985 supplement to *Crime fiction, 1749–1980*. N.Y. : Garland, 1988. 260 p. (Garland reference library of the humanities, vol. 766). ISBN 0-8240-7596-X. $32.00.   **BD105**
For earlier volume and annotation, see *Guide* BD261.

Extends coverage through 1985 and adds film adaptations from all periods, with title, settings, series, movie, screenwriter, and director indexes.   Z2014.F4H82

McCormick, Donald. Spy fiction : a connoisseur's guide / Donald McCormick & Katy Fletcher. N.Y. : Facts on File, c1990. 346 p. ISBN 0-8160-2098-1. $23.95. **BD106**
1st ed. had title: *Who's who in spy fiction* (London, Elm Tree Books, 1977).

Approximately 200 American and British authors are profiled here in articles that include pseudonyms, names of major characters, brief biographical sketches, critical analyses, bibliographies, and filmographies. In two sections: alphabetically-arranged entries and eight essays on the history and critical reception of espionage literature. A glossary, general bibliography, and index conclude the volume.   PN3448.S66M3

Menendez, Albert J. The subject is murder : a selective subject guide to mystery fiction. N.Y. : Garland Pub., 1986–90. 2 v. (Garland reference library of the humanities, vol. 627, 1060). ISBN 0-8240-8655-4 (v. 1). ISBN 0-8240-2580-6 (v. 2).   **BD107**
A bibliography of mystery novels published, for the most part, 1950– . Arranged by subjects (e.g., Gardening, Academia, Theater, Amnesia). Vol.2 lists works published since 1985 and adds sections on several new subjects. An appendix to v.1 lists specialty bookshops. Author index; v.2 also has a title index.   Z1231.D47M46

Twentieth-century crime and mystery writers / ed. John M. Reilly. 2nd ed. N.Y. : St. Martin's Pr., c1985. 1094 p. ISBN 0-312-82418-1.   **BD108**
1st ed., 1980 (*Guide* BD263).

Like other volumes in the publisher's "Twentieth-century writers series," offers brief biographical information, lists of writings, and signed critical assessments; often includes comments by the author. Updates biographies and bibliographies through the early 1980s. Title index.   PR888.D4T8

Science fiction, fantasy, and the Gothic

Bibliography

Anatomy of wonder : a critical guide to science fiction / ed. by Neil Barron. 3rd ed. N.Y. : Bowker, 1987. 874 p. ISBN 0-8352-2312-4.   **BD109**
2nd ed., 1981 (*Guide* BD264).   Z5917.S36A52

Fantasy literature : a reader's guide / ed. by Neil Barron. N.Y. : Garland, 1990. 586 p. (Garland reference library of the humanities, v.874). ISBN 0-8240-3148-2. **BD110**
Z5917.F3F36

Horror literature : a reader's guide / ed. by Neil Barron. N.Y. : Garland, 1990. 596 p. (Garland reference library of the humanities, v.1220). ISBN 0-8240-4347-2. **BD111**
Three works that are similar in format and are intended as companions. Signed chapters cover historical periods, research sources, and special topics such as film and television, art, and magazines. Most chapters include annotated bibliographies

and references to other biographical dictionaries and encyclopedias. Each volume concludes with a section listing a recommended core collection, award-winning works, organizations, and works published in series. Author, title, and theme indexes.   Z5917.H65H67

Cottrill, Tim. Science fiction and fantasy series and sequels : a bibliography / Tim Cottrill, Martin H. Greenberg, Charles G. Waugh. N.Y. : Garland, 1986. v. 1. ISBN 0-8240-8671-6 (v. 1). $28.00.   **BD112**
Contents: v. 1, Books.
A "comprehensive checklist of publications comprising extended series, two-volume sequences, sequels to an author's original work by other authors, and other multi-volume book formats ... published between 1700 and 1985."—*Foreword*. Arranged alphabetically by author, with a separate section for anthologies. Series title index.   Z5917.S36C67

Fisher, Benjamin Franklin. The Gothic's Gothic : study aids to the tradition of the tale of terror. N.Y. : Garland, 1988. 485 p. (Garland reference library of the humanities, vol. 567). ISBN 0-8240-8784-4.   **BD113**
Provides 2,614 citations, some with brief annotations, to biographical and critical books and articles published from the late 18th century until the early 1980s. Includes some material on art. In two sections: (1) Authors, which covers more than 100 British, American, and Canadian authors in alphabetical order; (2) Subjects, which lists citations to topics such as "orientalism" or "vampires." Author/artist/subject, title, and critic indexes.   Z5917.G66F57

Frank, Frederick S. The first Gothics : a critical guide to the English Gothic novel. N.Y. : Garland, 1987. 496 p., 14 leaves of plates : ill. (Garland reference library of the humanities, vol. 710). ISBN 0-8240-8501-9.   **BD114**
Synopses of some 500 British Gothic titles. Appendix of terms; bibliography; chronology; indexes of authors, titles, critics.   Z2014.H67F7

——————— Gothic fiction : a master list of twentieth century criticism and research. Westport, Conn. : Meckler, c1988. 193 p. (Meckler's bibliographies on science fiction, fantasy, and horror, 3). ISBN 0-88736-218-4. $39.95.   **BD115**
Z5917.G66F69

——————— Guide to the Gothic : an annotated bibliography of criticism. Metuchen, N.J. : Scarecrow, 1984. 421 p. ISBN 0-8108-1669-5.   **BD116**
Two bibliographies which list an almost identical set of approximately 2,500 citations in topical arrangements with critic and author indexes.   Z5917.G66F7

——————— Through the pale door : a guide to and through the American Gothic. N.Y. : Greenwood, 1990. 338 p. (Bibliographies and indexes in American literature, no. 11). ISBN 0-313-25900-3. $45.00.   **BD117**
A "selected bibliographical census of American Gothic Literature from its origins in the dark visions of Charles Brockden Brown at the end of the Eighteenth Century to its proliferation in the masters of modern American horror."—*Introd.* 509 short stories and novels are listed by author, each with one or more "research sources," a bibliography of secondary literature, and a critical synopsis of the work. Appendixes contain a chronology of Gothic publications and a bibliography of critical sources. Author/critic, title, and subject indexes.
Z1231.G66F7

Justice, Keith L. Science fiction, fantasy, and horror reference : an annotated bibliography of works about literature and film. Jefferson, N.C. : McFarland, c1989. 226 p. ISBN 0-89950-406-X.   **BD118**

Compiled "to help librarians, collectors, researchers, and others with an interest in SF/fantasy/horror reference materials determine what books might be of use or interest to them or their library's patrons."—*Introd.* Provides bibliographic, critical, and evaluative information on 304 titles, which are arranged alphabetically by author in chapters devoted to topics such as Author studies and bibliographies, Encyclopedias, Comics, or Television, film, and radio. Appendixes cover publications in series and provide a list of suggested core materials. Title and author/editor indexes. Z5917.S36J86

Reader's guide to twentieth-century science fiction / comp. and ed. by Marilyn P. Fletcher ; James L. Thorson, consulting ed. Chicago : Amer. Lib. Assoc., 1989. 673 p. ISBN 0-8389-0504-8. **BD119**

A "work was needed which would, first of all, give information on an author's life and works; themes and styles; and plot summaries of award-winning and major works."—*Introd.* Alphabetically-arranged entries provide this as well as bibliographic citations to further resources, for over 125 authors. Appendixes list journals and Nebula and Hugo award winners; title index. PN3433.8.R44

Science fiction, fantasy & horror. 1986– . Oakland, Calif. : Locus Pr. ; Westport, Conn. : Meckler Corp., c1986– . Annual. ISSN 0898-4077. $50.00. **BD120**

Editors: Charles N. Brown and William G. Contento.

Vol. for 1984 published 1990; vol. for 1985 had title *Science fiction in print: 1985* by Charles N. Brown (Oakland, Calif.: Locus Pr., 1986).

Intended to supplement Contento's *Index to science fiction anthologies and collections* (*Guide* BD285–286). Based on a monthly column in *Locus* magazine, this index lists American and British books and short stories in seven sections: books arranged by author and title; new publications in all formats, by author; subjects/formats, by author; short stories, by author and title; and contents lists for anthologies and individual magazine issues. Appendixes include statistical summaries of science fiction publishing, recommended reading, awards, necrology, and a directory of publishers. Z131.F4 C65

Twentieth-century romance and historical writers. 2nd ed. ed., Lesley Henderson ; consulting ed., D.L. Kirkpatrick. Chicago : St. James Pr., 1990. 856 p. ISBN 0-912289-97-X. **BD121**

1st ed., 1982, had title, *Twentieth-century romance and Gothic writers.*

A bio-bibliography of more than 400 authors, from popular romance novelists (e.g., Barbara Cartland and Victoria Holt) to Pulitzer Prize winners (Robert Penn Warren) and Poets Laureate (John Masefield) who have employed historical settings in their work. The signed entries are arranged alphabetically and include exhaustive bibliographies. Title index. PR888.L69T87

Tymn, Marshall B. Science fiction, fantasy, and weird fiction magazines / ed. by Marshall B. Tymn and Mike Ashley. Westport, Conn. : Greenwood, 1985. 970 p. ISBN 0-313-21221-X. **BD122**

The main section, English-language magazines, offers signed profiles of the magazines with publication history and references to additional sources of information (including index sources, reprints, and library locations). Additional sections for: Associational English-language anthologies, Academic periodicals and major fanzines, and Non-English language magazines, by country. Chronology; bibliography; index.

§ An earlier title, Halbert W. Hall's *Science fiction magazines* (San Bernardino, Calif. : Borgo Pr., 1984) based on the collection at Texas A&M, provides publication, volumes and numbering, and indexing information for English and Amrican magazines, with an editor index and an appendix of non-English language titles. PN3433.T9

Indexes

Bleiler, Everett Franklin. Science-fiction, the early years / by Everett F. Bleiler with the assistance of Richard J. Bleiler. Kent, Ohio : Kent State Univ. Pr., c1990. 998 p. ISBN 0-87338-416-4. **BD123**

Subtitle: a full description of more than 3,000 science-fiction stories from earliest times to the appearance of the genre magazines in 1930 : with author, title, and motif indexes.

Includes "novels, novellas, short stories, and occasional plays."—*Pref.* Arranged alphabetically by author, with some biographical information. Z5917.S36B62

Science fiction and fantasy reference index, 1878–1985 : an international author and subject index to history and criticism / ed. by H.W. Hall. Detroit : Gale, c1987. 2 v. (1460 p.). ISBN 0-8103-2129-7. $175.00. **BD124**

Contents: v. 1, Author entries; v. 2, Subject entries.

Draws together and adds to material from previous bibliographies by the same editor, including *Science fiction and fantasy book review index* (below) and *Science fiction and fantasy research index/SFFRI*, (Bryan, Tex.: SFBRI, 1980–84). Some 19,000 books, articles, news reports, and audiovisual items indexed by author and subject. To be supplemented by annual volumes. Z5917.S36S297

Book reviews and criticism

Hall, Halbert W. Science fiction and fantasy book review index, 1980–1984. Detroit : Gale, c1985. 761 p. ISBN 0-8103-1646-3. **BD125**

Earlier edition (*Guide* BD279–280) had title: *Science fiction book review index.*

Associate editor, Science fiction and fantasy research index, Geraldine L. Hutchins.

Lists over 13,800 reviews from more than 70 journals and periodicals. Z5917.S36H36

Science fiction & fantasy book review annual. 1988– . Westport, Conn. : Meckler, c1988– . Annual. ISSN 1040-192X. $65.00. **BD126**

Designed "to provide critics, teachers, researchers, librarians, students, and fans with a comprehensive critical overview of the genres of science fiction, fantasy, and horror ... geared toward the interests of literary historians rather than book collectors."—*Introd.* Approximately 600 short signed reviews of books published in the previous year are arranged alphabetically by author in three sections: Fiction, Young adult fiction, and Non-fiction. Lengthy profiles of specific authors, surveys of publishing trends, and lists of award winners precede the main review sections. Title index; volume for 1989 also has a contributor index. PN3433.8.S35

Biography

Supernatural fiction writers : fantasy and horror / E.F. Bleiler, ed. N.Y. : Scribner, c1985. 2 v. (1169 p.). ISBN 0-684-17808-7. $130.00. **BD127**

Similar in scope and authoritativeness to the same publisher's *Science fiction writers* (*Guide* BD281), these volumes present signed chapters on almost 50 British, American, French, and German authors from Apuleius to Roger Zelazny. Includes authors not primarily known for this genre (e.g., James Thurber, Edith Wharton). Chapters include biographical and critical information, as well as selected primary and secondary bibliographies. General index. PN3435.S96

Weinberg, Robert E. A biographical dictionary of science fiction and fantasy artists. N.Y. : Greenwood, 1988. 346 p. ISBN 0-313-24349-2.   **BD128**
For annotation, see *Supplement* BE89.   NC961.6.W45

Poetry

Bibliography

Brogan, T. V. F. Verseform : a comparative bibliography. Baltimore : Johns Hopkins Univ. Pr., 1989. 122 p. ISBN 0-8018-3362-0.   **BD129**
Updates the author's *English versification* (*Guide* BD635), by expanding coverage to include all the major languages of the world. In two parts: (1) Structures, devices, and forms (e.g., sound patterning, stanza forms, rhythm and visual prosody; (2) Verse systems (e.g., Greek and Latin, English, French, African, etc.). Author index.   Z7156.V6B76

McCullough, Kathleen. Concrete poetry : an annotated international bibliography, with an index of poets and poems. Troy, N.Y. : Whitston Pub. Co., 1989. 1010 p. ISBN 0-87875-332-X.   **BD130**
"Concrete poetry is international in its roots in early Greek and Latin shaped poetry and continuing through the more recent poets Apollinaire, Cummings, Majakovski, Marinetti, and Pound, as examples."—*Introd.* Lists "books of and about concrete poetry, principally in Indo-European languages." Coverage is comprehensive for the 20th century; the introductory essay defines several categories of concrete poetry, suggests a few basic works on the topic, and provides directory information for special collections and archives. Arranged alphabetically by poet, with indexes by title/permuted title/subject, language, and publication date.   Z7156.C64M33

Biobibliography

Contemporary poets / ed., Tracy Chevalier. 5th ed. Chicago : St. James Pr., c1991. 1179 p. ISBN 1-55862-035-4.   **BD131**
3rd ed., c1980 (*Guide* BD639); 4th ed., 1985.
Provides biobibliographical information on more than 1,000 poets currently writing in the English language, chosen by their peers and editors. The signed entries, which are arranged alphabetically, include biographical sketches, addresses, bibliographies of first editions, sound recordings, other publications (e.g., novels or essays), and lists of critical studies. Some entries give locations of manuscript collections. Title index.
PR603.C6

Indexes

Guy, Patricia A. Women's poetry index. Phoenix : Oryx, 1985. 174 p. ISBN 0-89774-173-0.   **BD132**
Compiled because standard indexes such as *Granger's index to poetry* (*Guide* BD302) offer limited access to poems by women. Indexes poems written in English or translated into English in 51 anthologies which are either in print or available in many libraries. In three main parts (1) Author index; (2) Title index, (3) First line index.   PN1024.G89

Hoffman, Herbert H. Hoffman's index to poetry : European and Latin American poetry in anthologies. Metuchen, N.J. : Scarecrow, 1985. 672 p. ISBN 0-8108-1831-0.   **BD133**

Intended to serve as a non-English language supplement to *Granger's index to poetry* (*Guide* BD302). Indexes 110 anthologies by author, title, and first line (the latter subdivided by language: French, German, Italian, Polish, Portuguese, Russian, and Spanish). Reference to the anthology appears in the author section.   PN1022.H627

Dictionaries

Myers, Jack Elliott. Longman dictionary and handbook of poetry / Jack Myers, Michael Simms. N.Y. : Longman, c1985. 366 p. ISBN 0-582-28343-4.   **BD134**
". . . attempts to define a critical vocabulary for the poet and the student of poetry," and claims to be "the most comprehensive list of poetic terms that has yet been compiled."—*Pref.* Includes a number of essays of substantial length. Excerpts from poems illustrate many of the terms defined. The appendixes group the terms topically or according to type of rhetorical or poetical device.   PN1021.M94

Packard, William. The poet's dictionary : a handbook of prosody and poetic devices. N.Y. : Harper & Row, c1989. 221 p. ISBN 0-06-016130-2. $19.95.   **BD135**
Intended for the practicing writer, this handbook describes and gives examples of various meters, techniques, and forms. An appendix lists guidelines for submitting manuscript copy for publication; selected bibliography.   PN44.5.P3

Peters, Robert. Hunting the snark : a compendium of new poetic terminology. N.Y. : Paragon House, 1989. 396 p. ISBN 1-55778-052-8. $39.95.   **BD136**
An individual and at times eccentric dictionary of contemporary poetry. Presents 133 categories or types (e.g., Semantic hang-up poems, Vietnam poems) alphabetically, with definitions, quotations from examples, and citations to collections and journals. General index.   PS323.5.P49

The Princeton handbook of poetic terms / Alex Preminger, ed. ; Frank J. Warnke and O.B. Hardison, Jr., assoc. eds. Princeton, N.J. : Princeton Univ. Pr., c1986. 309 p. ISBN 0-691-06659-0. $32.50.   **BD137**
Articles have been selected from the *Princeton encyclopedia of poetry and poetics* (*Guide* BD314) to form a handbook emphasizing poetic genres, modes and forms. In some cases little change was needed, in others extensive revisions or rewritings occurred. There are also new entries, e.g., Cycle, Psalms, Equivalence. Short bibliographies, often updated, follow each article. Appendixes list recommended readings.   PN1042.P75

Romances, epics, etc.

The Arthurian encyclopedia / Norris J. Lacy, ed. ; with associate editors Geoffrey Ashe . . . [et al.]. N.Y. : Garland, 1986. 649 p., [20] p. of plates : ill. (Garland reference library of the humanities, vol. 585). ISBN 0-8240-8745-3. $39.95.   **BD138**
Offers, "in encyclopedia form, a comprehensive and critical treatment of Arthurian subjects, artists, and works."—*Pref.* Signed articles in dictionary arrangement with cross-references; selected bibliographic references. Includes brief entries devoted to particular subjects, and extended essays on major authors, texts, and topics. Numerous intentional omissions are noted in the preface.
§ A revised and enlarged edition, *The new Arthurian encyclopedia* (N.Y. : Garland, 1991. 577 p.) retains the original format, while adding some 500 entries.   DA152.5.A7A78

Lacy, Norris J. The Arthurian handbook / Norris J. Lacy, Geoffrey Ashe. N.Y. : Garland, 1988. 455 p. : ill.

(Garland reference library of the humanities, vol. 765). ISBN 0-8240-7941-8.   **BD139**

A survey of the Arthurian legend, treating "all periods, from the fifth and sixth centuries through the Middle Ages, and to the present, examining Arthurian origins, the development of the legend in chronicles and other sources, the interpretation of Arthurian themes in literature, and their treatment in the other arts."—*Pref.* In chapters by period, with a glossary, chronology, and bibliography. Lacks an index.   PN685.L3

Stylistics

Bennett, James R. A bibliography of stylistics and related criticism, 1967–83. N.Y. : Modern Language Association of America, 1986. 405 p. ISBN 0-87352-142-0. $30.00. ISBN 0-87352-143-9 (pbk.). $15.00.   **BD140**

"The present bibliography carries forward the work of Hatzfeld [*Guide* BD931–933], Milic [BD330], and Bailey and Burton [BD329] through 1983."—*Description.*   Z6514.S8B46

Wales, Katie. A dictionary of stylistics. London ; N.Y. : Longman, 1989. 504 p. ISBN 0-582-29142-9. $79.95.   **BD141**

Designed for undergraduate or beginning graduate students "both as a dictionary and as a guide-book: not only to explain the meanings of terms, but also overall to give a general picture of the nature and aims of stylistics, its approaches, methodologies and insights, its historical origins and potential developments."—*Introd.*   P301.W35

Speech and rhetoric

Bibliography

CCCC bibliography of composition and rhetoric. 1987– . Carbondale, Ill. : Southern Illinois Univ. Pr., c1990– . Annual. ISSN 1046-0675.   **BD142**

Sponsored by the Conference on College Composition and Communication.

Continues *Longman bibliography of composition and rhetoric* (below), and retains its arrangement. Vol. for 1988 contains 1,798 citations.   PE1404.L66

Houlette, Forrest. Nineteenth-century rhetoric : an enumerative bibliography. N.Y. : Garland, 1989. 308 p. (Garland reference library of the humanities, vol. 787). ISBN 0-8240-6645-6. $42.00.   **BD143**

Lists 3,932 primary and secondary works "published in rhetoric, composition, grammar, and the teaching of English between 1800 and 1920."—*Pref.* Arranged alphabetically by author, with a subject index.   Z2015.R5H68

Longman bibliography of composition and rhetoric / Erika Lindemann. 1984–1985– . N.Y. : Longman, c1987– . Annual. ISSN 0897-3385. $35.95.   **BD144**

The volume for 1984/85 lists and briefly annotates 3,853 citations to books, articles, and dissertations drawn from sources such as *Dissertation abstracts international* (*Guide* AH19), *Resources in education* (*Guide* CB133), and *Current index to journals in education* (*Guide* CB130). Arranged in classified chapters devoted to topics such as writing theory, teacher education, curricula, and testing. The chapter on textbooks and other instructional materials lists video and sound recordings and computer programs, as well as traditional sources. Author index.   Z5818.E5L66

Murphy, James Jerome. Medieval rhetoric : a select bibliography. 2nd ed. Toronto ; Buffalo : Univ. of Toronto Pr., c1989. 198 p. (Toronto medieval bibliographies, 3). ISBN 0-8020-5750-0.   **BD145**

1st ed., 1971.

Designed to "facilitate the study of the perceptive arts of discourse in Europe from the time of Saint Augustine . . . to the rediscovery of complete major classical rhetorical texts in the early fifteenth century."—*Pref.* Lists editions and translations of primary sources and key secondary works in chapters devoted to particular time periods or topics, with some annotations. Name index.   Z7004.R5M87

Noppen, J. P. van. Metaphor : a bibliography of post-1970 publications. Amsterdam ; Philadelphia : J. Benjamins Pub. Co., 1985. 497 p. ISBN 90-272-3737-9. $54.00.   **BD146**

For annotation, see *Supplement* BC4.   Z7004.M4N66

Research in composition and rhetoric : a bibliographic sourcebook / ed. by Michael G. Moran and Ronald F. Lunsford. Westport, Conn. : Greenwood, 1984. 506 p. ISBN 0-313-23308-X. $69.95.   **BD147**

Contains 17 bibliographical essays on research in aspects of college-level composition instruction, including psychology, philosophy, sociology, and literary theory, as well as more practical skill-specific topics such as orthography, punctuation, and usage. Appendixes include chapters on evaluating textbooks and usage handbooks. Author and subject indexes.

Z5818.E5R47

Biography

American orators before 1900 : critical studies and sources / ed. by Bernard K. Duffy and Halford R. Ryan. N.Y. : Greenwood, 1987. 481 p. ISBN 0-313-25129-0.   **BD148**

Each volume presents more than 50 signed essays on individual speakers, providing for each a biographical sketch, a discussion of speaking style with illustrative quotations from the speeches, an evaluation of the person's contribution, a bibliography of information sources, and a chronology of major speeches. Both volumes contain bibliographies of basic research sources, glossaries of rhetorical terms, and general indexes.

PN4055.U5A4

ENGLISH LANGUAGE

American

Guides

Harner, James L. Literary research guide : a guide to reference sources for the study of literatures in English and related topics. N.Y. : Modern Language Association of America, 1989. 737 p. ISBN 0-87352-182-X. $35.00. ISBN 0-87352-183-8 (pbk.). $16.50.   **BD149**

Intended to replace Margaret Patterson's *Literary research guide* (2nd ed., 1984; *Guide* BD360), concentrating more specifically on British and American literature at a level slightly above that necessary for basic undergraduate research. Lists and extensively annotates reference sources, core journals, suggested items for background reading, library collections and catalogs, and computer programs or databases in a classified arrangement. In addition to English literature, includes brief chapters on foreign-language literature, comparative literature, and translation. Name, title, and subject indexes.

§ Another recent publication, Dorothy Kahler's *Problems in literary research* (3rd ed., Metuchen, N.J. : Scarecrow, 1987) provides methodological guidance and bibliographies for the beginning student, along with practice problems and questions.
Z2011.H34

Bibliography

Biographical dictionary of contemporary Catholic American writing / ed. by Daniel J. Tynan. N.Y. : Greenwood, 1989. 341 p. ISBN 0-313-24585-1.   **BD150**
Presents "135 biographical-critical essays on a representative group of contemporary Catholic American poets, dramatists and fiction writers."—*Pref.* Signed articles of evaluation for each author are followed by a bibliography. Indexed.
PS153.C3B5

Blanck, Jacob. Bibliography of American literature / comp. by Jacob Blanck for the Bibliographical Society of America. New Haven : Yale Univ. Pr., 1990. v. 8. (In progress).   **BD151**
For earlier volumes and annotation, see *Guide* BD364.
Contents: v. 8, Charles Warren Stoddard to Susan Bogert Warner, ed. and completed by Michael Winship.   Z1225.B55

Boos, Florence Saunders. Bibliography of women & literature / ed. by Florence Boos with Lynn Miller. N.Y. : Holmes & Meier, c1989. 2 v. ISBN 0-8419-0693-9 (set). $22.00 (est.).   **BD152**
Contents: v. 1, Articles and books (1974–1978) by and about women from 600 to 1975; v. 2, Supplement, articles and books (1979–1981).
Drawn from and supplementing annual bibliographies published in the journal *Women and literature*, these two volumes list, in a classed arrangement, books, articles, and dissertations, concentrating for the most part on literature in English. Author indexes.   Z2014.W65B66

Encyclopedia of American humorists / ed. by Steven H. Gale. N.Y. : Garland, 1988. v. 1. (Garland reference library of the humanities, vol. 633, etc.). ISBN 0-8240-8644-9 (v. 1). (In progress).   **BD153**
Treats American and Canadian humorists of all periods, giving for each an essay by a specialist that includes biographical and literary analysis and a bibliography of primary and secondary material. Vol.1 covers some 135 writers known primarily as humorists; v.2 will treat "serious" literary artists who use humor effectively. Indexed.   PS430.E53

Fifty southern writers before 1900 : a bio-bibliographical sourcebook / ed. by Robert Bain and Joseph M. Flora. N.Y. : Greenwood, c1987. 601 p. ISBN 0-313-24518-5. $32.00.   **BD154**
PS261.F543

Fifty southern writers after 1900 : a bio-bibliographical sourcebook / ed. by Joseph M. Flora and Robert Bain. N.Y. : Greenwood, 1987. 628 p. ISBN 0-313-24519-3. $75.00.   **BD155**
These two substantial volumes provide signed essays which present an overview of the writers' life and works; a biographical sketch, discussion of the author's major themes, assessment of scholarship, chronological list of the author's works, and bibliography of criticism. Arranged alphabetically within each volume, with general indexes. Most of the compilers are southern or teach at universities in the South. A few nonliterary authors, such as Thomas Jefferson, are included.   PS261.F54

First printings of American authors : contributions toward descriptive checklists / Matthew J. Bruccoli, series ed. .. [et al.]. Detroit : Gale, 1987. v. 5 : ill. ISBN 0-8103-0933-5 (v. 1). (In progress).   **BD156**
For v. 1–4 and annotation, see *Guide* BD366.
Vol. 5 ed. by Philip B. Eppard.
Covers 53 additional authors, with a cumulative author index to v. 1–5.   Z1231.F5F57

Hickey, Morgen. The bohemian register : an annotated bibliography of the beat literary movement. Metuchen, N.J. : Scarecrow, 1990. 252 p. : ill. ISBN 0-8108-2397-7.   **BD157**
In three sections: (1) General works and critical studies; (2) Collections and anthologies; (3) The Beats, which lists and annotates magazine and journal articles, books, interviews, letters, and essays by, and biographical and critical writings on, major authors. Covers material published from the late 1940s through 1989; most annotations cite book reviews. Chronology and list of little magazines; general index, which unfortunately does not include critics' names.   Z1231.B4H53

Newman, John. Vietnam War literature : an annotated bibliography of imaginative works about Americans fighting in Vietnam / by John Newman, with Ann Hilfinger. 2nd ed. Metuchen, N.J. : Scarecrow, 1988. 285 p. ISBN 0-8108-2155-9.   **BD158**
1st ed., 1982.
Lists and annotates 752 novels, short stories, poetry, drama, and other works published 1964–88. Based on the Vietnam War Literature Collection at Colorado State University.
§ Another recent publication, Sandra M. Wittman's *Writing about Vietnam* (*Supplement* DE102) also lists creative writings together with autobiographical, biographical, and critical works.   Z1227.N49

Periodicals

American literary magazines : the eighteenth and nineteenth centuries / ed. by Edward E. Chielens. N.Y. : Greenwood, 1986. 503 p. ISBN 0-313-23985-1.   **BD159**
Signed essays profile and provide short bibliographies of 92 magazines. Each essay discusses publishing history, editorial personnel and policies, and influence. Appendixes list and briefly describe minor literary magazine or nonliterary magazines which publish fiction or belle-lettres, and a chronology of publishing and social or literary events. General index.
Z1231.P45A43

Directory of literary magazines / prepared by The Coordinating Council of Literary Magazines. 1984– . N.Y. : The Council, c1984– . Annual. ISSN 0884-6006. $5.95.   **BD160**
For annotation, see *Supplement* AE21.   Z6513.C37

Criticism

Sixteen modern American authors : volume 2, a survey of research and criticism since 1972 / ed. by Jackson R. Bryer. Durham [N.C.] : Duke Univ. Pr., 1990. 810 p. ISBN 0-8223-0976-9.   **BD161**
For basic volume, see *Guide* BD403.
Because of the sheer volume of material published since the original volume in 1973, "it seemed best simply to ask each contributor to prepare a new essay, updating the version in the 1973 edition and incorporating material inadvertently omitted earlier."—*Pref.* As a result, the present volume supplements, rather than replaces, the original work, for the most part includ-

ing material published 1972–85, with some supplements through mid-1988. General index. PS221.S625

Handbooks

The Cambridge handbook of American literature / ed. by Jack Salzman, with Cameron Bardrick . . . [et al.]. Cambridge ; N.Y. : Cambridge Univ. Pr., 1986. 286 p. ISBN 0-521-30703-1. **BD162**

Designed to be compact and succinct, this volume was compiled by members of the Columbia University Center for American Culture Studies. Approximately 750 sketches discuss authors, works, and themes. A useful appendix presents chronologies of American literature and history side by side. Select bibliography; no index. PS21.C36

Handbook of American popular literature / ed. by M. Thomas Inge. N.Y. : Greenwood, 1988. 408 p. ISBN 0-313-25405-2. $55.00. **BD163**

In essence, a supplement and companion to *Handbook of popular culture* (*Supplement* CF34). 15 signed chapters present critical essays and bibliographies on specific genres or topics (e.g., Verse and popular poetry, Historical fiction). Each chapter includes sections on research collections and reference tools, as well as historical outlines, summaries of critical reception, and lengthy bibliographies. General index. Z1231.P74H36

Watson, Edward A. A study of selected English critical terms from 1650–1800 : a constellation. N.Y. : P. Lang, c1987. 677 p. ISBN 0-8204-0518-3. $90.00. **BD164**

"This book is a study of twenty-two words . . . " (*Pref.*) and how they were used in English literary criticism during the 17th and 18th centuries. Terms, such as "nature," "sentiment," and "the sublime," are defined in an outline arrangement, with quotations supporting each definition in chronological order. Most terms have between 10 and 20 definitions. Despite its complicated arrangement, this is a useful work which complements standard dictionaries such as the *Oxford English dictionary* (*Supplement* AD6) and less specialized handbooks of critical terminology. PR73.W38

Outlines

Ludwig, Richard M. Annals of American literature, 1602–1983 / ed. by Richard M. Ludwig and Clifford A. Nault, Jr. N.Y. : Oxford Univ. Pr., 1986. 342 p. ISBN 0-19-503970-X. $29.95. **BD165**

Patterned after *Annals of English literature* (*Guide* BD561). Provides a chronological listing of significant American books, with a side column mentioning new journals, important events of social and political history, and outstanding foreign literary publications. Detailed index. PS94.L83

Rogal, Samuel J. A chronological outline of American literature. N.Y. : Greenwood, 1987. 446 p. (Bibliographies and indexes in American literature, no. 8). ISBN 0-313-25471-0. **BD166**

Covers from the 16th century through 1986. For each year gives names of literary authors and editors who were born or died in that year, two or three political and literary events, and a list of literary works published. Emphasis is on "variety and representation, as well as literary diversity."—*Introd.* Index of authors and events. PS92.R67

History

Columbia literary history of the United States / Emory Elliott, gen. ed. N.Y. : Columbia Univ. Pr., 1988. 1263 p. ISBN 0-231-05812-8. $59.95. **BD167**

A somewhat abbreviated descendant of Spiller's *Literary history of the United States* (*Guide* BD411). This volume presents an editorial outlook which is "mostly post-modern; it acknowledges diversity, complexity, and contradiction."—*Pref.* Divided into five broad time periods, each with a different general editor; signed chapters present essays on literary figures, movements, and criticism, ranging from The native voice to The avante-garde and experimental writing. No bibliography or footnotes; general index. PS92.C64

Biographies of authors

A dictionary of British and American women writers, 1660–1800 / ed. by Janet Todd. Totowa, N.J. : Rowman & Allanheld, 1985. 344 p. ISBN 0-8476-7125-9. $35.00. **BD168**

This biographical dictionary of some 450 writers aims "to stimulate research into female literary history and to indicate the wealth and abundance of female writing."—*Pref.* The introductory essay addresses women's writing, discussing class, education, politics, marriage, motives, genres, and themes. Signed, well-written essays range in length from one column (Ann Chandler) to six (Maria Edgeworth) and nearly all the writers profiled receive more extensive treatment here than in other biographical dictionaries. There are no bibliographies of primary or secondary works, although major works are discussed within each essay. Writers are listed alphabetically by their most commonly known name, with cross-references only in the table of contents. Brief subject index. PR113.D5

Reference guide to American literature / ed., D.L. Kirkpatrick. 2nd ed. Chicago : St. James Pr., 1987. 816 p. ISBN 0-912289-61-9. **BD169**

A combined and updated edition of *American writers to 1900, American writers since 1900* (*Guide* BD415), both ed. by James Vinson, and the chronology portion of *History of American literature* by Walker Marshall (all three publ. Chicago : St. James Pr., 1983).

In three main parts: Writers, Works, and Chronology. Entries for writers provide a biographical sketch, a complete short-title bibliography of the writer's books, a selected bibliography of critical studies, and a signed critical essay. Entries for works consist of short signed essays on particular novels, short stories, poems, or plays. Introductions by Louis Leary (to 1900) and Warren French (since 1900) summarize American literary history. Title index. PS129.R44

Ward, Robert Elmer. A bio-bibliography of German-American writers, 1670–1970. White Plains, N.Y. : Kraus Internat., c1985. 377 p. ISBN 0-527-94444-0. $72.00. **BD170**

Based on the author's *Dictionary of German-American creative writers* (Cleveland : German-American Publ. Co., 1978). Z1229.G3W35

Who's who in writers, editors & poets, United States & Canada. 3rd ed. (1989/1990)– . Highland Park, Ill. : December Pr., c1989– . Biennial. ISSN 1049-8621. $76.80. **BD171**

1st ed., 1986–87, publ. 1987.

The 3rd ed. "contains the biographies of just under 9,500 poets, novelists, short story writers, editors of journals, periodicals and books, journalists, nonfiction writers, translators, critics, playwrights, scriptwriters, and biographers from the United States and Canada."—*Pref.* Biographical data and lists of publications tend to be very full; current addresses are given. Geographical index by state then by city for the U.S.; by city for Canada and other non-U.S. locations.   PS129.W47

Drama

American playwrights since 1945 : a guide to scholarship, criticism, and performance / ed. by Philip C. Kolin. N.Y. : Greenwood, c1989. 595 p. ISBN 0-313-25543-1.   **BD172**

Some 40 playwrights are treated in essays, each discussing achievements and reputation, published work, production history, secondary works, and future research opportunity. Author and title indexes.   Z1231.D7A53

Fiction

Bibliography

Dickinson, A. T. Dickinson's American historical fiction. 5th ed. / Virginia Brokaw Gerhardstein. Metuchen, N.J. : Scarecrow, 1986. 352 p. ISBN 0-8108-1867-1.   **BD173**

4th ed., 1981 (*Guide* BD438).

"A total of 3,048 novels casting light on some aspect of American history are classified into natural chronological periods from Colonial days to the 1970's."—*Pref.* Annotations; author/title and subject indexes. Mainly publications of 1917–84, with some earlier standard works.   Z1231.F4D47

Dictionary of American literary characters / ed. by Benjamin Franklin V ; associate editors, Gary Geer and Judith Haig. N.Y. : Facts on File, 1990. 542 p. ISBN 0-8160-1917-7.   **BD174**

"This book describes the major characters in significant American novels—in addition to those in some uncelebrated novels and in a sampling of bestsellers—from ... [1789] through 1979."—*Pref.* Both purely fictional and historical characters are listed in alphabetical order with one-sentence descriptions. Author index. A *Dictionary of British literary characters* was forthcoming from the same publisher in 1991.   PS374.C43D5

Hanna, Archibald. A mirror for the nation : an annotated bibliography of American social fiction, 1901–1950. N.Y. : Garland, 1985. 472 p. (Garland reference library of the humanities, vol. 595). ISBN 0-8240-8727-5.   **BD175**

Aims "to provide an annotated guide to the large body of fiction published between 1901 and 1950, which is useful as source material for the economic, political and social history of the United States during that period."—*Introd.* Author listing with subject, title, and illustrator indexes. 3,943 items.   Z1231.F4H32

McPheron, William. The bibliography of contemporary American fiction, 1945–1988 : an annotated checklist / William McPheron and Jocelyn Sheppard. Westport, Conn. : Meckler, c1989. 190 p. ISBN 0-88736-167-6. $39.50.   **BD176**

"This checklist records and describes bibliographical accounts of contemporary American fiction writers."—*Pref.* Emphasizes single-author studies and "reference tools that provide substantial coverage of individual novelists and short story writers." Arranged by literary author, with subject and author indexes.   Z1231.F4M36

White, Ray Lewis. Index to *Best American short stories* and O. Henry prize stories. Boston : G.K. Hall, c1988. 183 p. ISBN 0-8161-8955-2.   **BD177**

Provides author and title indexes for *Best American short stories* (1915–86) and *Prize stories: the O. Henry awards* (1919–87), as well as descriptive essays on the history of those two publications. Also lists O. Henry prizewinners by year.   Z1231.F4W52

Poetry

Bibliography

Jason, Philip K. Nineteenth century American poetry : an annotated bibliography. Pasadena, Calif. : Salem Pr., c1989. 257 p. ISBN 0-89356-651-9. $40.00.   **BD178**

Treats 16 poets in chronological order, citing both general studies and books or articles devoted to specific poems. Author index.   Z1231.P7J37

Reardon, Joan. Poetry by American women, 1975–1989 : a bibliography. Metuchen, N.J. : Scarecrow, 1990. 232 p. ISBN 0-8108-2366-7.   **BD179**

Supplements the author's *Poetry by American women, 1900–1975* (Metuchen, N.J. : Scarecrow, 1979) and retains its arrangement. Both volumes list "separately published volumes of poetry by women who are citizens of the United States."—*Introd.* The volume for 1975–89 contains 2,880 titles by 1,565 authors. Title index.   Z1229.W8R42

Indexes

Caskey, Jefferson D. Index to poetry in popular periodicals, 1960–1964. N.Y. : Greenwood, 1988. 232 p. ISBN 0-313-24810-9. $49.95.   **BD180**

A companion to the compiler's *Index to poetry in popular periodicals, 1955–1959* (1984. 269p.). Indexes periodicals included in the *Readers' guide to periodical literature*, since for this period poetry was not indexed therein. Title, first line, author, and subject indexes.   Z1231.P7C372

Chapman, Dorothy Hilton. Index to poetry by black American women. N.Y. : Greenwood, 1986. 424 p. (Bibliographies and indexes in Afro-American and African studies, no. 15). ISBN 0-313-25152-5.   **BD181**

Indexes more than 200 book collections, by title and first line, author, and subject.   Z1229.N39C45

Criticism

Guide to American poetry explication. Boston : G.K. Hall, c1989. 2 v. ISBN 0-8161-8919-6 (v. 1). ISBN 0-8161-8918-8 (v. 2).   **BD182**

Contents: v. 1, Colonial and nineteenth century, ed. by James Ruppert; v. 2, Modern and contemporary, ed. by John R. Leo.

Partially supersedes Joseph M. Kunitz and Nancy C. Martinez's *Poetry explication* (*Guide* BD653), extending coverage through December 1987, and maintaining that volume's arrangement.   Z1231.P7G85

Diaries; Letters

Arksey, Laura. American diaries : an annotated bibliography of published American diaries and journals / Laura Arksey, Nancy Pries, and Marcia Reed. Detroit : Gale, c1987. v. 2. ISBN 0-8103-1801-6 (v.2). $98.00. **BD183**

For v. 1 and annotation, see *Guide* BD473.
Contents: v. 2, Diaries written from 1845 to 1980 (501 p.). Completes the set. Z5305.U5A74

Goodfriend, Joyce D. The published diaries and letters of American women : an annotated bibliography. Boston : G.K. Hall, c1987. 230 p. ISBN 0-8161-8778-9. $30.00. **BD184**

Published collections of letters and diaries by American women written in the U.S., arranged by year of first entry. Most of the diaries are listed in *American diaries* (v.2, above) but the inclusion of letters and identification of materials by women make this bibliography worthwhile. Annotations; author and subject indexes. Z5305.U5G66

African-American literature

Bibliography

Glikin, Ronda. Black American women in literature : a bibliography, 1976 through 1987. Jefferson, N.C. : McFarland, c1989. 251 p. ISBN 0-89950-372-1. **BD185**

Lists "the poetry, short fiction, novels, essays, and plays by, and criticism on, approximately 300 women whose work has been published in periodicals and anthologies between 1976 and 87."—*Introd.* Also cites full-length studies or published books. Arranged by literary author, with appendixes listing general works of criticism and authors by genre. Author/title index. Z1229.N39G57

Page, James A. Selected black American, African, and Caribbean authors : a bio-bibliography / comp. by James A. Page and Jae Min Roh. Littleton, Colo. : Libraries Unlimited, 1985. 388 p. ISBN 0-87287-430-3. $55.00. **BD186**

Represents a revised and enlarged edition of Page's *Selected black American authors* (Boston: G.K. Hall, 1977). Provides biobibliographical information on 632 authors, both literary and nonliterary. Emphasizes African American literature of the U.S.; non-U.S. writers included are those who "have either lived, studied, or been published in the United States."—*Pref.* Bibliography of sources. Nationality, occupational, and title indexes. Z1229.N39P34

Biography

Foster, Mamie Marie Booth. Southern Black creative writers, 1829–1953 : biobibliographies. N.Y. : Greenwood, 1988. 113 p. (Bibliographies and indexes in Afro-American and African studies, no. 22). ISBN 0-313-26207-1. **BD187**

Offers brief biographical notes for some 200 African-American writers who were born or spent time in the South. Each entry includes a list of published writings. Selected bibliography of Southern black writers, p.84–102; appendixes provide author listings by state and by period. Z1229.N39F67

Newby, James Edward. Black authors : a selected annotated bibliography. N.Y. : Garland, 1991. 720 p. (Garland reference library of the humanities, vol. 1260). ISBN 0-8240-3329-9. **BD188**

Attempts "to provide a selected bibliography of works written, coauthored, or edited by black Americans."—*Pref.* Includes some African, Caribbean, and non-black authors. Lists over 3,200 books published for the most part 1973–90 in ten subject sections, which roughly correspond to LC subject classifications. Author/title, but no subject, index. Z1215.N57

Roses, Lorraine Elena. The Harlem Renaissance and beyond : 100 black women writers, 1900–1950 / Lorraine Elena Roses, Ruth Elizabeth Randolph. Boston : G.K. Hall, 1989. 413 p. ISBN 0-8161-8926-9. **BD189**

"It is the purpose of this book to focus attention on black women writers whose work belongs primarily to the early half of the twentieth century and whose achievements or very existence has been little recognized, even within specialized circles."—*Pref.* Profiles of poets, journalists, novelists, essayists, playwrights, scholars, critics, and biographers are arranged alphabetically and include primary and secondary bibliographies. Appendixes list writers by genre, geographical locations, and date; a title index and a general bibliography conclude the volume. PS153.N5R65

Fiction

Werner, Craig Hansen. Black American women novelists : an annotated bibliography. Pasadena, Calif. : Salem Pr., c1989. 286 p. ISBN 0-89356-655-1. $40.00. **BD190**

Lists books and articles on 32 authors, with a general section on basic works that treat African-American culture and history. For most authors covered, citations are given to biographical and critical sources, as well as selected references on specific novels. Author index. Z1229.N39W47

Yancy, Preston M. The Afro-American short story : a comprehensive, annotated index with selected commentaries. Westport, Conn. : Greenwood, 1986. 171 p. (Bibliographies and indexes in Afro-American and African studies, no. 10). ISBN 0-313-24355-7. **BD191**

Indexes more than 850 stories by more than 300 authors published in anthologies, 1950–82. In three main parts: (1) a chronology; (2) an alphabetical list of collections and their contents; (3) commentaries on particular stories. Author and title indexes. Z1229.N39Y36

Ethnic literature

Cheung, King-Kok. Asian American literature : an annotated bibliography / King-Kok Cheung, Stan Yogi. N.Y. : Modern Language Association of America, 1988. 276 p. ISBN 0-87352-960-X. ISBN 0-87352-961-8 (pbk.). **BD192**

A "reference guide to literature written by Asian American writers in the United States and Canada."—*Pref.* Includes "works by writers of Asian descent who have made the United States or Canada their home, regardless of where they were born, when they settled in North America, and how they interpret their experience . . . writers of mixed descent who have one Asian parent . . . as well as authors who may not be permanent North American residents but who have written specifically on the experiences of Asians in the United States or Canada." Includes primary and secondary sources, selected background studies, fiction and poetry collections. Arranged by ethnic group (e.g., Chinese Americans), then by format. Brief annotations; index of names. Z1229.A75C47

Chicano literature : a reference guide / ed. by Julio A. Martínez and Francisco A. Lomelí. Westport, Conn. : Greenwood, 1985. 492 p. ISBN 0-313-23691-7.   **BD193**

Signed articles cover individual authors as well as topics (e.g., Chicano theater, Contemporary Chicano novel), providing literary and historical significance, critical evaluations, and bibliographies of primary and secondary works. Appendixes include information on nonliterary Chicanos, (e.g., Anthony Quinn), a chronology, a glossary, and a general bibliography. General index.   PS153.M4C46

Handbook of American-Jewish literature : an analytical guide to topics, themes, and sources / Lewis Fried, ed. in chief ; Gene Brown, Jules Chametzky, and Louis Harap, advisory editors. N.Y. : Greenwood, 1988. 539 p. ISBN 0-313-24593-2.   **BD194**

In 18 chapters, specialists discuss English-language, German-language, and Yiddish fiction, poetry, drama, and criticism, as well as nonliterary forms such as theology, autobiography, history, and philosophy. Includes chapters on Zionist ideology, the fiction of the Holocaust, and the portrayal of Eastern Europe. Selected bibliographies follow each chapter; chapter 18 comprises a bibliography of European writings on American-Jewish literature. General index.   PS153.J4H365

Kanellos, Nicolás. Biographical dictionary of Hispanic literature in the United States : the literature of Puerto Ricans, Cuban Americans, and other Hispanic writers. N.Y. : Greenwood, 1989. 357 p. ISBN 0-313-24465-0.   **BD195**

For each of the 50 authors covered, a signed essay points up literary significance, then gives a biographical statement, a survey of criticism, and a bibliography of works by and about the biographee. General bibliography and index.

PQ7420.2.K3

Littlefield, Daniel F. A biobibliography of native American writers, 1772–1924 / by Daniel F. Littlefield, Jr. and James W. Parins. Metuchen, N.J. : Scarecrow, 1981. 343 p. (Native American bibliography series, no. 2). ISBN 0-8108-1463-3.   **BD196**

Z1209.2.U5L57

———————— A biobibliography of native American writers, 1772–1924 : a supplement / by Daniel F. Littlefield, Jr. and James W. Parins. Metuchen, N.J. : Scarecrow, 1985. 339 p. (Native American bibliography series, no. 5). ISBN 0-8108-1802-7.   **BD197**

The first volume lists 4,321 works by Native Americans writing in English, with short biographical sketches of identifiable authors. "Not strictly literary in scope, this book lists works of some very different sorts: political essays and addresses, satirical pieces written in various dialects, myths and legends, original poetry and fiction, published letters, historical works, personal reminiscences, and other genres."—*Pref.* The supplement adds 942 new writers and new works by 250 of the authors included in v. 1. Both volumes are indexed by tribal affiliation and subject.   Z1209.2.U5L57

Women authors

Butler, Deborah A. American women writers on Vietnam : unheard voices : a selected annotated bibliography. N.Y. : Garland, 1990. 312 p. (Garland reference library of the humanities, vol. 1278). ISBN 0-8240-3528-3.   **BD198**

For annotation, see *Supplement* DE103.   Z1227.B88

Schwartz, Narda Lacey. Articles on women writers : a bibliography. Santa Barbara, Calif. : ABC-Clio,

c1977–1986. v. 1–2. ISBN 0-87436-252-0 (v. 1). $24.95. (In progress).   **BD199**

Contents: v. 1 (1977), 1960–75; v. 2, (1986), 1976–84.

Covers some 1,000 authors, for the most part American and British, with name indexes.   Z2013.5.W6S37

English

Guides

Bracken, James K. Reference works in British and American literature. Englewood, Colo. : Libraries Unlimited, 1990. v. 1. ISBN 0-87287-699-3. $35.00. (In progress).   **BD200**

Contents: v. 1, English and American literature.

Aims to "respond to the basic needs of literary researchers of all degrees of sophistication."—*Introd.* Describes scope, unique characteristics, and use of 512 reference works, core journals, and principal research centers or associations, in a classified arrangement. Annotations are quite lengthy and often point out the strengths or weaknesses of one tool as measured against another. Author/title and subject indexes. Vol. 2 is planned to cover individual authors.   Z2011.B74

Marcuse, Michael J. A reference guide for English studies. Berkeley : Univ. of California Pr., c1990. lxxii, 790 p. ISBN 0-520-05161-0.   **BD201**

This comprehensive and impressive guide to English and American literature includes considerable information not usually found in guides to English literature: descriptions of important library collections (e.g., The Newberry Library, the Berg Collection); lists of national bibliographies and library catalogs; sections addressing classical and modern literatures; and a chapter devoted to history and ancillae which describes 123 reference works in British and American history, geographies, chronologies, and numerous secondary works. Resembles *Guide to reference books* with longer annotations and smaller type. 24 chapters address topics ranging from literature by country, period and genre, to professional topics, bibliography, biography, serials, and archives and manuscripts. Within each chapter, reference works are grouped by topic, and are followed by lists of periodicals and "frequently recommended works." The descriptive annotations are well written, and nearly all cite additional works. Coverage is through 1985, with some additional titles from 1986 and 1987; the sections of recommended works, although valuable, suffer from being five years out of date. Indexed by author, title, and subject.   PR56.M37

Bibliography

Howard-Hill, T. H. Bibliography of British literary bibliographies. 2nd ed., rev. and enl. Oxford : Clarendon Pr. ; N.Y. : Oxford Univ. Pr., 1986. 886 p. (Index to British literary bibliography, 1). ISBN 0-19-818184-1. $79.00.   **BD202**

For the previous edition, other volumes of the *Index to British literary bibliography*, and annotation, see *Guide* BD494.

"Revision of the *Bibliography of British literary bibliographies* and its resetting by computer has afforded an opportunity to bring its conventions into line with those adopted in later volumes of the *Index*."—*Pref.* Some 1,860 new entries have been added, although coverage has not been expanded beyond the 1890–1969 scope of the 1st ed. Entries are indexed by author, title, and subject in this volume, and in the comprehensive index in v.6.   Z2011.A1H68

Periodicals

British literary magazines / ed. by Alvin Sullivan. Westport, Conn. : Greenwood, 1985–1986. v. 3–4. ISBN 0-313-22871-X (v.1). **BD203**

For previously published volumes and annotation, see *Guide* BD508.

Contents: v. 3, The Victorian and Edwardian age, 1837–1913 (1985); v. 4, The modern age, 1914–1984 (1986).

PN51240C6B74

Old and Middle English

Jost, Jean E. Ten Middle English Arthurian romances : a reference guide. Boston : G.K. Hall, c1986. 162 p. ISBN 0-8161-8611-1. **BD204**

Aims to provide "a comprehensive guide to scholarship and criticism from ca.1800 to 1980 for ten major English Arthurian romances .... Editions and scholarly redactions that contribute significant critical opinion are included."—*Pref.* Descriptive annotations; indexed by author, title, and subject.

Z2014.R6J68

Lewis, Robert E. Index of printed Middle English prose / R.E. Lewis, N.F. Blake, A.S.G. Edwards. N.Y. : Garland, 1985. 362 p. (Garland reference library of the humanities, vol. 537). ISBN 0-8240-8839-5. **BD205**

Serves as a companion to Carleton Brown and Russell H. Robbins's *Index of Middle English verse* (*Guide* BD637), taking "within its orbit everything which is not included in the index of verse, including a few pieces which modern editors now print as prose." Aims "to provide a bibliographic overview of editorial work completed on Middle English prose texts" and "to provide a bibliographic tool of assistance to scholars and students working with Middle English prose materials, particularly with such materials in manuscript form."—*Introd.* Arranged by first lines (usually 20 to 30 words of the text). General index and manuscript index.

Z2014.P795L49

A manual of the writings in Middle English, 1050–1500 / by members of the Middle English Group of the Modern Language Association of America. New Haven : Connecticut Academy of Arts and Sciences, 1986–1989. v. 7–8. ISBN 0-208-02107-8 (v.7). $32.50. (In progress). **BD206**

For earlier volumes and annotation, see *Guide* BD517.

Contents: v. 7, John Gower, *Piers plowman*, Travel and geographical writings, Works of religious and philosophical instruction; v. 8, Chronicles and other historical writing, by Edward Donald Kennedy.

PR255.M3

Pulsiano, Phillip. An annotated bibliography of North American doctoral dissertations on Old English language and literature. East Lansing, Mich. : Colleagues Pr., 1988. 317 p. (Medieval texts and studies, no. 3). ISBN 0-937191-06-X. **BD207**

Includes dissertations completed through 1986 in Canada and the U.S. In two parts: general works, including themes, studies of language and style, and historical and cultural subjects; and poetry, including dissertations on specific Old English poems. Appendix 2 lists homilies that have been edited or translated in dissertations. Author and subject indexes.

Z2012.P85

Rice, Joanne A. Middle English romance : an annotated bibliography, 1955–1985. N.Y. : Garland, 1987. 626 p. (Garland reference library of the humanities, vol. 545). ISBN 0-8240-8830-1. **BD208**

In two sections, verse and prose, each listing criticism within broad categories and under individual romances by title. "Each romance section has two parts: editions and criticism.

The editions, which are not restricted to 1955–1985, as is criticism, are intended to be comprehensive."—*Pref.* Indexed by author and editor. Updates the bibliographies in v. 1 of *A manual of the writings in Middle English, 1050–1500* (*Guide* BD517). Z2014.R6R5

Saito, Toshio. A concordance to Middle English metrical romances / ed. by Toshio Saito and Mitsunori Imai ; computer programmed by Kunihiro Miki. Frankfurt am Main ; N.Y. : Verlag Peter Lang, c1988. 2 v. ISBN 3-8204-1196-8. 298.00F (Switzerland). **BD209**

Contents: v. 1, The matter of England; v. 2, The Breton lays.

In each volume, a complete concordance in keyword in context format is followed by a word index, word list, reverse work list, and frequency list. Compiled by computer.

PR321.S25

18th century

Forster, Antonia. Index to book reviews in England, 1749–1774. Carbondale, Ill. : Southern Illinois Univ. Pr., c1990. 307 p. ISBN 0-8093-1406-1. **BD210**

Lists reviews of 3,023 published works of poetry, fiction, or drama which appeared in 16 English periodicals. Entries are cited alphabetically by author or anonymous title of the work being reviewed and include information concerning format, price, and bookseller's name. A library location, generally the British Library, is given for nearly every title. Z1035.A1F67

Spector, Robert Donald. Backgrounds to restoration and eighteenth-century English literature : an annotated bibliographical guide to modern scholarship. N.Y. : Greenwood, 1989. 553 p. (Bibliographies and indexes in world literature, no. 17). ISBN 0-313-24098-1. $59.95. **BD211**

Offers "a broad and detailed view of the period: ranging from the daily lives of its people, through the institutions that governed their existence, to the cultural, social, scientific, and philosophical foundations of their society."—*Pref.* Annotated citations to books and articles are arranged by topic (e.g., Crime and the law, Women, Philosophy) and indexed by author.

Z2012.S65

19th century

A comprehensive bibliography of Victorian studies : 1970–1984 / comp. & ed. by Brahma Chaudhuri. Edmonton, Alta. : LITIR Database, 1984–85. 3 v. ISBN 0-919237-11-8 (v.1). $140.00/vol. **BD212**

Although not so stated in the preface, these volumes are presumably meant to supersede *Cumulative bibliography of Victorian studies, 1976–1980* (*Guide* BD532), cumulate the book and periodical citations (but not the references to book reviews) from *Annual bibliography of Victorian studies* (*Guide* BD531), and extend coverage back to 1970. Each volume follows the arrangement of the annuals, and each has its own subject, author, and title indexes. Vols. 2–3 include some items missed in the previous volumes. Z2019.A48

20th century

Richardson, Elizabeth P. A Bloomsbury iconography. Winchester, Hampshire : St. Paul's Bibliographies, 1989. 372, 16 p. of plates : ill., ports., facsims. ISBN 0-906795-63-X. £50.00. **BD213**

This guide lists "reproductions of pictures in books, periodicals, and exhibition catalogues ... by alphabetical entry (usually the name of a person) with numbered subentries consisting of pictures in chronological order, generally grouped into separate categories. Subentries conclude with one or more sources of reproductions. There are seven appendixes (one bibliographical) and four ancillary indexes."—*Introd.* Categories include pictures (photographs, paintings, and caricatures of the subject); posthumous pictures; works of artists; autographs; books (dust jackets, facsimile pages, and illustrations); decorations; miscellaneous (solid objects—e.g., eggcups, book plates, negative boxes); and places which do not have their own entries.

Manuscript sources

Early English manuscripts in facsimile. Copenhagen : Rosenkilde and Bagger ; Baltimore : Johns Hopkins Pr., 1988–1991. v. 22–23.   **BD214**
For previously published volumes and annotation, see *Guide* BD545.
Contents: v. 22, The Épinal, Erfurt, Werden, and Corpus glossaries (Épinal Bibliothèque municipale 72 [2]; Erfurt Wissenschaftliche Bibliothek Amplonianus 2⁰ 42; Staatsbibliothek Cgm. 187 III [e.4]; Cambridge Corpus Christi College 144), ed. by Bernhard Bischoff et al., 1988; v. 23, Old English verse texts from many sources : a comprehensive collection, ed. by Fred C. Robinson and E.G. Stanley, 1991.   Z115.E5E2

Index of English literary manuscripts / editorial board, P.J. Croft, Theodore Hofmann, and John Horden ; editorial advisors, Rodney G. Dennis and Stephen Parks. London : Mansell ; N.Y. : Bowker, 1986–[1987?]. v. 2, pt. 1; v. 3, pts. 1–2; v. 4, pt. 2 : ill. ISBN 0-8352-1216-5 (Bowker : set). (In progress).   **BD215**
For previously published parts and annotation, see *Guide* BD546.
Vol. 2, pt. 1 has imprint: London ; New York : Mansell; v. 3, pt. 1; v. 4, pt. 1 have imprint: London ; New York : Mansell ; Bronx, N.Y. : Distr. by Wilson.
Contents: v. 2, 1625–1700, pt. 1, Behn–King, comp. by Peter Beal; v. 3, 1700–1800, pts. 1–2, Addison–Philips, comp. by Margaret M. Smith; v. 4, 1800–1900, pt. 2, Hardy–Lamb, comp. by Barbara Rosenbaum.
In the interest of clarity, some "innovations in printing style and layout have been introduced" (*Pref.*, v.2, pt.1) in recent volumes, and a first-line index to pts. 1–2 of v.3 appears at the end of v.3, pt.2 (in advance of the promised comprehensive indexes of v.5). As previously noted, there have been many departures from the original goal of including all authors listed in the *Concise Cambridge bibliography of English literature*; in the case of v.4, pt.2, A.E. Housman, Leigh Hunt, and Charles Kingsley "were dropped following the theft of the working drafts for much of Part 2 in 1986."—*Pref.*   Z6611.L7I5

Location register of twentieth-century English literary manuscripts and letters : a union list of papers of modern English, Irish, Scottish, and Welsh authors in the British Isles. Boston : G.K. Hall, 1988. 2 v. (1054 p.). ISBN 0-8161-8981-1. $175.00.   **BD216**
" 'British' includes not only English, Irish, Scottish, and Welsh writers who used the English language, but also immigrants, refugees and others who spent a considerable part of their life in the British Isles . . . . 'Literary' includes poets, novelists, dramatists and men and women of letters of all styles and qualities . . . . [and] 'Twentieth-century' has . . . been interpreted to include anyone who lived beyond the year 1899."—*Introd.* Not limited to literary manuscripts and letters, the *Register* also refers to "photographs, tape recordings and floppy diskettes, as well as to proofs of published works. Entries have been made for photostat, xerographic, and microfilm copies of literary papers, whether or not the originals remain in the British Isles. Microfilm copies which are published commercially have also been noted." Within the alphabetical arrangement of authors' names, manuscripts are listed alphabetically, followed by a miscellaneous list of letters in chronological sequence. "For many authors . . . the first entry is a note which may ex-

plain omissions from the entries which follow. The note may outline holdings of papers by repositories overseas [sometimes including *NUCMC* references] . . . but may also describe authors' policies for retention or destruction of their papers and even mishaps and disasters which have befallen them." Appendix giving full addresses of institutions at the end of v.2.
Z6611.L7L63

Criticism

The new Moulton's library of literary criticism / gen. ed., Harold Bloom. N.Y. : Chelsea House Publishers, 1985–1990. 11 v. : 29 cm. ISBN 0-87754-779-3 (v. 1).   **BD217**
Contents: v. 1, Medieval–Early Renaissance; v. 2, William Shakespeare; v. 3, Elizabethan–Caroline; v. 4, Restoration–Early Georgian; v. 5, Georgian; v. 6, Late Georgian–Romantic; v. 7, Early Victorian; v. 8, Mid-Victorian; v. 9, Late Victorian; v. 10, Late Victorian–Edwardian; v. 11, Bibliographical supplement and index.
Designed "to present a concise portrait of the critical heritage of every crucial British and American author."—*Pref.* Both abridges and updates earlier Moulton's collections (*Guide* BD551-552) providing excerpts from criticism written before the 20th century concerning 532 authors and anonymous works written from the 8th century up to 1904. Entries, which include biographies as well as critical information, are arranged chronologically by death date within each volume. Figures covered include nonliterary authors, such as Thomas Jefferson and Charles Darwin. Vol.11 contains bibliographical references and author and critic indexes for the entire set.   PR85.N39

Encyclopedias

The Cambridge guide to literature in English / ed. by Ian Ousby. Cambridge ; N.Y. : Cambridge Univ. Pr. ; London : Hamlyn Pub. Group, 1988. 1109 p. : ill. ISBN 0-521-26751-X. $39.50.   **BD218**
Virtually replaces the *Cambridge guide to English literature* (*Guide* BD554), although this volume makes no mention of that work. Many entries from the earlier work, especially those on fictional characters, have been dropped or shortened; new entries focus on non-British, contemporary, and less well-known figures and works. For a review and history of both volumes, see Claude Rawson, "Coverage and slippage," *Times literary supplement*, no. 4,490 (April 21–27, 1989): 429–430.
PR85.C29

Handbooks

Drabble, Margaret. The Oxford companion to English literature. 5th ed. Oxford ; N.Y. : Oxford Univ. Pr., 1985. 1155 p. ISBN 0-19-866130-4. $29.95.   **BD219**
4th ed., ed. by Paul Harvey, 1967 (*Guide* BD556).
A thorough revision, retaining many of the principal characteristics of the original work. Includes authors born through 1939.   PR19.D73

Prentice Hall guide to English literature : the new authority on English literature / ed. by Marion Wynne-Davies. N.Y. : Prentice Hall, c1990. 1066 p. ISBN 0-13-083619-2. $35.00.   **BD220**
Published in U.K. as *Bloomsbury guide to English literature* (London : Bloomsbury, 1989).
Represents a reworking of Christopher Gillie's *Longman companion to English literature* (1977). In three parts: an essay section (12 chapters on political, social, and historical topics); an alphabetical dictionary of authors, works, themes, historical

and literary figures, places, and events; and a chronology.

PR19.B5

Outlines

Gray, Martin. A chronology of English literature. Burnt Mill, Harlow, Essex, England : Longman, 1989. [288] p. ISBN 0-582-05141-X. £12.95. **BD221**

In three parts: Old English literature; Middle English literature; and Literature 1500–1980. The first two parts are in tabular format, with historical events in one column, and literature in another. From 1500 onwards, annual entries begin with a paragraph describing important political activity and major scientific and artistic achievements in Britain and elsewhere, followed by a very selective list of poetry, prose, and drama published or performed during the year. Indexed by author and title. Appendixes list the 100 books with the highest British public library circulation 1987–88; the winners of the Booker and Whitbread literary prizes; dates and versions of the Bible and Prayer Book; and the Poets Laureate. **PR87**

History

The Oxford history of English literature / ed., Frank Percy Wilson and Bonamy Dobrée. Oxford : Clarendon Pr., 1986–1990. v. 1, pt. 2; v. 11, pt. 1; v. 13. (In progress). **BD222**

For earlier volumes and annotation, see *Guide* BD566.

Contents: v. 1, pt. 2, Middle English literature, by J.A.W. Bennett and Douglas Gray (1986); v. 11, pt. 1, English literature, 1832–1890, excluding the novel, by Paul Turner (1989); v. 13, The Victorian novel, by Alan Horsman (1990).

With the publication of v.13, the volumes in this standard reference history have been renumbered, and many are being reissued with new titles.

Biographies of authors

A biographical dictionary of English women writers, 1580–1720 / [ed. by] Maureen Bell, George Parfitt, Simon Shepherd. Boston : G.K. Hall, c1990. 298 p. ISBN 0-8161-1806-X. $32.50. **BD223**

Aims to include every woman writing in English in the British Isles whose work was published betweed 1580 and 1700, whether during her lifetime or posthumously; and a selection of 17th-century women whose writing is unpublished or was published after 1700. Writers are listed alphabetically; each entry includes brief biographical facts (patronym, places of birth and residence, social status or occupation, religion, husband's name, and husband's social status or occupation) and a paragraph concerning the subject's writings. Entries do not cite secondary sources, but a selection is included in a general bibliography at the beginning of the volume. Appendixes list anonymous and pseudonymous texts and false ascriptions. The volume ends with an essay discussing women's writing before and after 1640, Quaker writers, writers of petitions and letters, and the role of women in the book trade. **PR113.B46**

British women writers : a critical reference guide / ed. by Janet Todd. N.Y. : Continuum, 1989. 762 p. ISBN 0-8044-3334-8. $59.50. **BD224**

PR111.B75

An encyclopedia of British women writers / ed. by Paul Schlueter and June Schlueter. N.Y. : Garland, 1988.

516p. (Garland reference library of the humanities, vol. 818). ISBN 0-8240-8449-7. $75.00. **BD225**

These two biobibliographies are remarkably similar in scope and format. Signed essays arranged alphabetically by writer provide biographical information, critical assessment, and bibliographies of primary and secondary works. Todd includes more writers (440 compared to 370), but the Schlueters provide more complete bibliographies of primary works, often including unpublished manuscripts. There is considerable overlap in coverage, although Todd includes more writers from the early 20th century, and the Schlueters more from the 18th and 19th centuries. Both are indexed by writer and topic (e.g., Sentimental fiction, Regional writing, Working class). Todd includes cross-references only in the table of contents and index, not in the body of the guide. **PR111.E54**

British writers. Supplement / ed. under the auspices of the British Council, Ian Scott-Kilvert, gen. ed. N.Y. : Scribner, 1987. v. 1. ISBN 0-684-18612-8. $75.00. (In progress). **BD226**

For basic set, see *Guide* BD573.

Contents: v. 1, Graham Greene to Tom Stoppard.

PR85.B688

Twentieth-century British literature / gen. ed., Harold Bloom. N.Y. : Chelsea House Publishers, 1985–1987. 6 v. : ports. ISBN 0-87754-809-9. **BD227**

Covers modern authors from the U.K. and its former colonies. Authors are listed alphabetically and for each a brief biographical sketch is followed by excerpts from criticism and evaluations by various writers which appeared in journal articles, memoirs, reviews of individual works, and book-length studies. Some of the longer, essay-like pieces include footnote references. Lists of additional readings appear at the end of v.1–5. Vol.6 includes full lists (with publication dates) of all titles of each author treated; a "Series contents" section that lists the authors and sources of extracts concerning each writer; and an alphabetical index to critics represented in the full set.

PR473.T84

Women authors

Blain, Virginia. The feminist companion to literature in English : women writers from the Middle Ages to the present / Virginia Blain, Patricia Clements, Isobel Grundy. New Haven, Conn. : Yale Univ. Pr., 1990. 1231 p. ISBN 0-300-04854-8. **BD228**

This excellent and comprehensive work includes women writing in English in all national traditions, among them African, American, Asian, Australian, British, Canadian, Caribbean, New Zealand, South Pacific. Primarily a dictionary of authors, although 63 topics, ranging from Abolition to "Women question," are also included. **PR111.B57**

Drama

Bibliography

Berger, Sidney E. Medieval English drama : an annotated bibliography of recent criticism. N.Y. : Garland, 1990. 500 p. (Garland Medieval bibliographies, vol. 2 ; Garland reference library of the humanities, vol. 956). ISBN 0-8240-5790-2. **BD229**

"... focuses only on work which is not already cited in Carl J. Stratman's *Bibliography of medieval drama* [*Guide* BD205]."—*Pref.* In two sections: Editions, listing 87 works alphabetically by editor; and Criticism, listing 1,750 items alphabetically by author. The index cites plays, playwrights, characters, places, and themes or topics. Three appendixes list the

"Cycle plays;" plays by author or anonymous title; and the projected volumes of the "Records of early English drama."

Z2014.D7B43

Critical survey of drama : English language series / ed. by Frank N. Magill. Englewood Cliffs, N.J. : Salem Pr., c1985. 6 v. (2575 p.).   **BD230**

Contents: v. 1–5, Authors; v. 6, Essays; Index.

Similar to the publisher's other series for short fiction, poetry, etc., offering signed commentary, select bibliography, and the like on dramatists of all periods writing in English. The essays in v. 6 range from dramatic genres to drama of specific periods.   PR623.C75

Ellis, James. English drama of the nineteenth century : an index and finding guide / comp. and ed. by James Ellis, assisted by Joseph Donohue, with Louise Allen Zak, editorial associate. New Canaan, Conn. : Readex Books, 1985. 345 p.   **BD231**

Intended primarily "as an index and finding guide to the English plays issued through 1981 in the Readex Microprint Collection *English and American Drama of the Nineteenth Century*" (*Pref.*), but also useful as a bibliography of about 9,000 English plays (including children's plays, opera libretti, translations of continental dramas, etc.). Various useful appendixes. The American portion of the microform collection is indexed by Donald L. Hixon and Don A. Hennessee's *Nineteenth-century American drama* (*Guide* BD425).   Z2014.D7E42

Harbage, Alfred. Annals of English drama, 975–1700 : an analytical record of all plays, extant or lost, chronologically arranged and indexed by authors, titles, dramatic companies & c. / by Alfred Harbage ; rev. by S. Schoenbaum. 3rd ed. / rev. by Sylvia Stoler Wagonheim. London : Rutledge, 1989. 375 p. ISBN 0-415-01099-3. $79.95.   **BD232**

2nd ed., 1964 (*Guide* BD589).

Incorporates "more than 1,000 new entries, clarifications, corrections, and deletions."—*Pref.* The separate lists of editions and dissertations have been eliminated, with that information now listed in the indexes of English playwrights and plays. The chronological tables have also been changed: the column listing last editions now gives abbreviations for the type of editions (e.g., collected edition, individual edition, facsimile reprint) without listing dates. Abbreviations, p. xviii–xix. These alterations are somewhat confusing, and the 2nd ed., though dated, is still useful.

Lidman, Mark J. Studies in Jacobean drama, 1973–1984 : an annotated bibliography. N.Y. : Garland, 1986. 278 p. (Garland reference library of the humanities, vol. 597). ISBN 0-8240-8725-9.   **BD233**

Intended to update Logan and Smith's four-volume series on Renaissance English drama (*Guide* BD594–597). A general section is followed by sections for individual playwrights (Chapman, Dekker, Heywood, Tourneur, Marston, Middleton, Webster, Massinger, Ford, Brome, and Shirley) each listing editions, followed by critical studies listed alphabetically by author. Indexed by author only.

§ A more useful bibliography for comedy is *An annotated critical bibliography of Jacobean and Caroline comedy (excluding Shakespeare)* by Peter Corbin and Douglas Sedge (N.Y.; London : Harvester, 1988. 235p.) Playwrights are treated individually in chapters citing editions, general criticism, and criticism of individual plays. Author index.   Z2014.D7L5

White, D. Jerry. Early English drama, Everyman to 1580 : a reference guide. Boston : G.K. Hall, 1986. 289 p. ISBN 0-8161-8338-4. $50.00.   **BD234**

An annotated bibliography of resources for the study of British drama and dramatists of the period 1495–1580. Sections for bibliographies, collections, and general studies are followed by sections for individual playwrights and plays. Within an author's section entries are subdivided for bibliographies,

studies and editions, and specific plays. Covers studies published 1691–1982, together with many unpublished dissertations. Descriptive annotations for most items. Index for specific authors, titles, and subjects.   Z2014.D7W48

Handbooks

The Cambridge companion to English Renaissance drama / ed. by A.R. Braunmuller and Michael Hattaway. Cambridge [England] ; N.Y. : Cambridge Univ. Pr., 1990. 456 p. : ill., map. ISBN 0-521-34657-6. ISBN 0-521-38662-4 (pbk.).   **BD235**

"The predominant organizing principle of this Companion is generic . . . the essays seek not the be definitive but perhaps to be paradigmatic: to offer the reader examples of recent ways of experiencing texts and performances, to provoke further reading, and above all, to add to the enjoyment of Renaissance dramatic texts in the study and the playhouse."—*Pref.* Ten essays discuss: Playhouses and players; The arts of the dramatist; Drama and society; Private and occasional drama; Political drama; Romance and the heroic play; Pastiche, burlesque, tragicomedy; Comedy; Tragedy; and Caroline drama; with brief bibliographies at the end of each essay. A separate bibliography (p. 381–418) lists reference works, critical studies, biographical sources, and biographies and bibliographies of individual authors. The chronological table lists many (but not all) the plays of the period 1497–1642. Indexed by dramatist, title, and topic (e.g., city comedy); but the bibliographies are not indexed.

PR651.C36

Fiction

Bibliography

Harner, James L. English Renaissance prose fiction, 1500–1660 : an annotated bibliography of criticism, 1976–1983. Boston : G.K. Hall, c1985. 228 p. ISBN 0-8161-8709-6. $50.00.   **BD236**

Constitutes a supplement to Harner's 1978 bibliography (*Guide* BD518a). Emphasis is on scholarship published 1976–83, with some corrections and additions to the earlier volume.   Z2014.F4H372

Paris, Michael. The novels of World War Two : an annotated bibliography of World War Two fiction. London : Library Association, 1990. 184 p. ISBN 0-85365-918-4.   **BD237**

Lists more than 2,000 English-language novels published from September 1939 through 1988 that take World War II, 1939–45, as their central theme. Includes "not only those fictions dealing directly with the experience of men and women on the various battlefields and on the home fronts, but also those novels which explore personal relationships affected by the war or which take place in Wartime."—*Pref.* Novels are listed alphabetically by year of publication with author, title, and subject indexes.

Raven, James. British fiction, 1750–1770 : a chronological check-list of prose fiction printed in Britain and Ireland. Newark : Univ. of Delaware Pr. ; London : Associated Univ. Pr., c1987. 349 p. : ill. ISBN 0-87413-324-6. $39.50.   **BD238**

Continues William Harlin McBurney's *Check list of English prose fiction, 1700–1739* (*Guide* BD618) and Jerry C. Beasley's *Check list of prose fiction published in England, 1740–1749* (*Guide* BD619).

Attempts to identify all works of fiction published in the 1750s and 1760s, whether extant or perished, including translations and reprints of early novels. Provides, where possible, number of copies printed, price, printer, bookseller, references to reviews, secondary references, and notes on authorship, translators, and other editions. Entries are arranged chronologically by year and then alphabetically in three sections: anonymous titles, authors, and miscellanies. Indexed by author, translator, and title. Z2014.F4R34

Sargent, Lyman Tower. British and American utopian literature, 1516–1985 : an annotated, chronological bibliography. N.Y. : Garland, c1988. 559 p. (Garland reference library of the humanities, vol. 831). ISBN 0-8240-0694-1. $75.00. **BD239**

1st ed., 1979 (*Guide* BD62).

Expands and extends through 1985 the chronological list of utopian works, but excludes the section of secondary literature which appeared in the earlier edition. Z2014.U84S28

Vann, J. Don. Victorian novels in serial. N.Y. : Modern Language Association of America, 1985. 181 p. ISBN 0-87352-135-8. $50.00 (est.). **BD240**

Lists the serialized novels of 16 Victorian authors and indicates which part of each novel appeared in a given serial installment. Selected bibliography. Z2014.F4V36

Criticism

English novel explication. Supplement. Hamden, Conn. : Shoe String Pr., 1981–1990. Suppl. II–IV. ISBN 0-208-01464-0 (v. 1). **BD241**

For the original bibliography by Helen H. Palmer and Anne Jane Dyson and Suppl. I of this series, see *Guide* BD630.

Suppl. II (1981. 326 p.), comp. by Christian J.W. Kloesel and Jeffrey R. Smitten, emphasizes material published 1975–79; Suppl. III, (1986. 532 p.), comp. by Christian J.W. Kloesel and Lynn F. Kloesel, concentrates on publications of 1980–85. Suppl. IV, (1990. 351 p.), comp. by Christian J.W. Kloesel, extends coverage from 1986 through the first half of 1989. Z2014.F5P26

Handbooks

Sutherland, John. The Stanford companion to Victorian fiction. Stanford, Calif. : Stanford Univ. Pr., 1989. 696 p. ISBN 0-8047-1528-9. **BD242**

"First published as *The Longman companion to Victorian fiction* by Longman Group UK Ltd"—*t.p. verso.*

Intended as "a source of ready factual information about Victorian fiction and its immediate context."—*Pref.* Some 1,606 entries in alphabetical arrangement deal with novelists, periodicals, synopses of novels (with indication of serialization), publishers, forms of novels, and major illustrators. Abbreviations at the end of author entries signal lists of works in standard bibliographies (e.g., *NCBEL*, British Museum *Catalogue*, *Wellesley index*), and biographical entries (*DNB* and *Who's Who*). Indexes of proper names and pseudonyms, and of maiden and married names. PR871.S87

Poetry

Bibliography

Jackson, J. R. de J. Annals of English verse, 1770–1835 : a preliminary survey of the volumes published. N.Y. : Garland, 1985. 709 p. (Garland reference library of the humanities, vol. 535). ISBN 0-8240-8841-7. $76.00. **BD243**

" . . . based on reports of books rather than on firsthand examination of copies."—*Introd.* Compiled from reviews in periodicals, from the *Cambridge bibliography of English literature*

(*Guide* BD496), and from the British Museum *Catalogue* (*Guide* AA132). Publications are listed by year, then alphabetically by short title. Hymnals, books of songs, publications of less than eight pages, and titles published outside the U.K. are excluded. Author and anonymous title indexes. Z2039.P6J32

Kallich, Martin. British poetry and the American Revolution : a bibliographical survey of books and pamphlets, journals and magazines, newspapers, and prints, 1755–1800. Troy, N.Y. : Whitston Pub. Co., 1988. 2 v. (1731 p.). ISBN 0-87875-318-4 (set). $150.00. **BD244**

Intends "to make readily accessible . . . a substantial part of the poetry published in Great Britain between 1763–1783 about its domestic colonies . . . including selections from 1755 to 1762 and 1784 and 1800."—*Introd.* About 5,600 poems are listed by year, then format (book or pamphlet, serial, broadside, print), then by author or title. Entries include the poem's first line, reviews, and pithy annotations. Verse has been broadly defined to include songs and ballads, satires, even sermons and advertisements. Locations are given for many items. Indexed by author, subject, and verse form. Z2014.P7K34

Reilly, Catherine W. English poetry of the Second World War : a biobibliography. London ; N.Y. : Mansell, 1985. 1 v. ISBN 0-7201-1793-3. $50.00 (est.). **BD245**

Lists "3,072 separate publications, including eighty-seven anthologies, issued during the years 1939–1980. It identifies 2,679 poets . . . 831 of whom are known to have served in the armed forces or other uniformed organizations."—*Introd.* Limited to books of poetry, broadsides, and other published works on the theme of the 1939–45 war written by English, Irish, Scots, and Welsh poets. In two parts: anthologies and individual poets. Includes a title index and a list of war poets of other English-speaking countries. Z2014.P7R45

Ringler, William A. Bibliography and index of English verse printed 1476–1558. London ; N.Y. : Mansell, 1988. 440 p. ISBN 0-7201-1892-1. $153.00. **BD246**

Intended to supplement and carry forward to 1558 Carleton Brown and Russell H. Robbins's *Index of Middle English verse* (*Guide* BD637). In two sections: verse printed 1476–1500, and verse printed 1501–58. Each section has two parts: a bibliography listing indexed books by *STC* number, and a first line index. Entries in the first line index are arranged alphabetically and include author, title, date of composition, number of lines, verse form, and *STC* number of the work containing the verse. Separate indexes for each time period provide access by author, title, subject, and verse form indexes. Z2014.P7R56

Criticism

The English romantic poets : a review of research and criticism / John Clubbe . . . [et al.] ; ed. by Frank Jordan. 4th ed. N.Y. : Modern Language Association of America, 1985. 765 p. ISBN 0-87352-262-1. $30.00 (est.). ISBN 0-87352-263-X (pbk.). $15.00 (est.). **BD247**

3rd rev. ed., 1972 (*Guide* BD650).

Entirely rewritten and presented as a new work. Chapters on the Romantic Movement in England, Blake, Wordsworth, Coleridge, Byron, Shelley, and Keats cover historical and recent scholarship through 1982. Indexed by author and subject. PR590.E5

Ballads

Richmond, W. Edson. Ballad scholarship : an annotated bibliography. N.Y. : Garland, 1989. 356 p. (Garland reference library of the humanities, vol. 499 ; Garland folklore bibliographies, v. 4). ISBN 0-8240-8932-4. **BD248**

Confined largely to studies of ballads (rather than collections) published between 1898 and 1986. Lists and annotates books and articles in 13 chapters devoted to areas of scholarship such as Ballads and history, or Ballad prosody and metrics. Items cited are in all languages although they tend to focus on English and American ballads, and to a lesser extent on Anglo-Saxon, Germanic, and Scandinavian ballads. Author and subject indexes. Z7156.P7R5

Diaries

Cline, Cheryl. Women's diaries, journals, and letters : an annotated bibliography. N.Y. : Garland, 1989. 716 p. (Garland reference library of the humanities, vol. 780). ISBN 0-8240-6637-5. **BD249**

Lists 2,990 "published private writings of appreciable length, including those published as articles or extracts in larger works."—*Pref.* Works are drawn from all periods and are primarily in English or English translation. Arranged alphabetically by author, with profession, subject, geographical, and title indexes. Z7963.B6C55

Havlice, Patricia Pate. And so to bed : a bibliography of diaries published in English. Metuchen, N.J. : Scarecrow, 1987. 698 p. ISBN 0-8108-1923-6. $59.50. **BD250**

Lists, with brief descriptions, 2,509 diaries and journals from 1838 to 1983 "written or translated into English and published as books, chapters in books, or journal articles."—*Pref.* Includes an index by diarist; a merged index to Matthews' bibliographies of American, British, and Canadian diaries; and a general index listing subjects, authors, editors, and titles. Although no selection criteria are given, this is a highly selective listing.

§ Arksey's *American diaries* (*Supplement* BD183) lists 6,046 published diaries and journals through 1980 and is most useful for locating English copies of diaries published in other languages. Z5301.H38

Huff, Cynthia Anne. British women's diaries : a descriptive bibliography of selected nineteenth-century women's manuscript diaries. N.Y. : AMS Pr., c1985. 139 p. (AMS studies in social history, no. 4). **BD251**

Long annotations describe 59 diaries in five categories (Aristocracy, Gentry, Professional-commercial, Intelligentsia, and Religious) with author and subject indexes. Z7964.G7H84

Individual authors

Chaucer

Allen, Mark. The essential Chaucer : an annotated bibliography of major modern studies / Mark Allen and John H. Fisher. Boston : G.K. Hall, c1987. 243 p. ISBN 0-8161-8739-8. **BD252**

An annotated listing of 925 studies written between 1900 and 1984, based on the bibliography in John Fisher's edition of *The complete poetry and prose of Geoffrey Chaucer* (N.Y. : Holt Rinehart & Winston, 1977). Topical arrangement; general subjects (including Biography, Language, Literary relations, Imagery) precede studies of individual works. The section on the *Canterbury tales* has subsections for thematic studies (e.g., Pilgrimage, Order, The marriage question) followed by studies of

the individual tales. Author index with subject entries for topics which do not appear in the table of contents. Z8164.A43

Baird-Lange, Lorrayne Y. A bibliography of Chaucer, 1974–1985 / Lorrayne Y. Baird-Lange and Hildegard Schnuttgen. Hamden, Conn. : Archon Books, 1988. lxxv, 344 p. ISBN 0-208-02134-5. **BD253**

Continues Baird's *Bibliography of Chaucer, 1964–1973* (*Guide* BD679), adding sections on facsimiles, medieval women's studies, and pedagogy. Z8164.B275

Besserman, Lawrence L. Chaucer and the Bible : a critical review of research, indexes, and bibliography. N.Y. : Garland, 1988. 432 p. (Garland reference library of the humanities, vol. 839). ISBN 0-8240-6340-6. **BD254**

In two parts: a list of Chaucer's biblical allusions, arranged by line number; and an index from biblical line to Chaucer. Entries include the line(s) being glossed; a reference to the Douay-Rheims Bible (with references to the King James version in parentheses); intermediate or noncanonical sources; and citations to secondary literature. The index of scriptural references provides a reverse index from biblical line to Chaucer. A review essay on Chaucer and the Bible, and a bibliography of primary and secondary sources complete the volume. PR1933.R4B47

The Chaucer bibliographies. Toronto ; Buffalo : Publ. in association with the Univ. of Rochester by the Univ. of Toronto Pr., 1983–1990. v. 1–3. ISBN 0-8020-2481-5 (v. 1). ISBN 0-8020-2493-9 (v. 2). ISBN 0-8020-2592-7 (v. 3). (In progress). **BD255**

Contents: v. 1, Chaucer's lyrics and Anelida and Arcite: an annotated bibliography 1900 to 1980, by R. A. Peck; v. 2, Chaucer's Romaunt of the rose and Boece, Treatise on the astrolabe, Equatorie of the planetis, lost works, and Chaucerian apocrypha: an annotated bibliography 1900–1985, by R. A. Peck; v. 3, Chaucer's General prologue to the Canterbury tales: an annotated bibliography, 1900–1984, by C. D. Eckhardt.

Aims to "encompass, in a series of sixteen volumes, a complete listing and assessment of scholarship and criticism on the writings of Geoffrey Chaucer, and on his life, times, and historical context."—*Pref.* In each volume, annotated entries are arranged by topic, with many cross-references. Author and subject index.

De Weever, Jacqueline. A Chaucer name dictionary : a guide to astrological, biblical, historical, literary, and mythological names in the works of Geoffrey Chaucer. N.Y. : Garland, 1987. 402 p. : ill. (Garland reference library of the humanities, vol. 709). ISBN 0-8240-8306-7. $40.00. **BD256**

Brings together "information on personal names in Chaucer's works and on the names of gods and goddesses in their mythological and planetary aspects."—*Pref.* Each entry has four paragraphs: the first provides biographical, historical, or mythological information; the second discusses Chaucer's use of the name; the third considers the etymology of the name; and the fourth is a bibliography listing sources consulted for the entry and articles on the person or tale. Entries are listed in alphabetical order, using Chaucer's spelling, with cross-references. Includes a bibliography of primary and secondary sources, a glossary listing astronomical and astrological terms, and six astrological diagrams. PR1903.D4

Leyerle, John. Chaucer, a bibliographical introduction / John Leyerle and Anne Quick. Toronto ; Buffalo : Univ. of Toronto Pr., c1986. 321 p. (Toronto medieval bibliographies, 10). ISBN 0-8020-2375-4. ISBN 0-8020-6408-6 (pbk.). **BD257**

Intended for "readers relatively unfamiliar with the works of Chaucer and their context."—*Pref.* In three main sections: (1) Materials for the study of Chaucer's works (bibliographies, texts and canon, language and versification, sources and influences); (2) Chaucer's works (listing editions, sources, and critical studies for each); and (3) Backgrounds (including fine arts, music, politics, education, philosophy, literature, and science). Lists works published through 1979, with a few from the early 1980s. Topical arrangement with brief annotations and an author index. Z8164.L49

Milton

Klemp, P. J. The essential Milton : an annotated bibliography of major modern studies. Boston : G.K. Hall, c1989. 474 p. ISBN 0-8161-8730-4. **BD258**

Offers long, descriptive annotations of 1,021 studies published 1900–87. Omits highly specialized or narrowly focused studies, theses, dissertations, and works in foreign languages. Indexed by author and subject. Z8578.K57

Patrides, C. A. An annotated critical bibliography of John Milton. N.Y. : St. Martin's, 1987. 200 p. ISBN 0-312-00480-X. $35.00. **BD259**

Highly selective, with brief, evaluative annotations of 1,145 scholarly and critical studies of Milton published through 1984. Topical arrangement with subject and author indexes. Z8578.P37

Shakespeare

Bibliography

Champion, Larry S. The essential Shakespeare : an annotated bibliography of major modern studies. Boston : G.K. Hall, c1986. 463 p. ISBN 0-8161-8731-2. $55.00. **BD260**

About 1,500 entries that attempt "to address the needs and interests both of the casual reader and the student with a specific need and limited agenda. The entries as a body represent what is generally accepted as essential Shakesperean scholarship."—*Pref.* A section for general works is followed by sections for the poems and sonnets, the English history plays, the comedies, the tragedies, the romances (all subdivided for specific plays). Concentrates on 20th-century scholarship. Indexed by author and subject. Z8811.C53

The Garland Shakespeare bibliographies / William Godshalk, gen. ed. N.Y. : Garland, 1980–1991. v. 1–17, 20. (In progress). **BD261**

Contents: v. 1, King Lear, comp. by Larry S. Champion (1980); v. 2, Four plays ascribed to Shakespeare : Edward III, Sir Thomas More, Cardenio, The two noble kinsmen, comp. by G. Harold Metz (1982); v. 3, Cymbeline, comp. by Henry E. Jacobs (1982); v. 4, Henry V, comp. by Joseph Candido and Charles R. Forker (1983); v. 5, King Henry VI, parts 1, 2, and 3, comp. by Judith Hinchcliffe (1984); v. 6, Love's labor's lost, comp. by Nancy Lenz Harvey and Anna Kirwan Carey (1984); v. 7, Hamlet in the 1950s, comp. by Randal F. Robinson (1984); v. 8, As you like it, comp. by Jay L. Halio and Barbara C. Millard (1985); v. 9, Merchant of Venice, comp. by Thomas Wheeler (1985); v. 10, Timon of Athens, comp. by John J. Ruszkiewicz (1986); v. 11, Richard III, comp. by James A. Moore (1986); v. 12, A midsummer night's dream, comp. by D. Allen Carroll and Gary Jay Williams (1986); v. 13, Pericles, comp. by Nancy C. Michael (1987); v. 14, Richard II, comp. by Josephine A. Roberts (1988); v. 15, Henry VIII, comp. by Linda McJ. Micheli (1988); v. 16, Two gentlemen of Verona, comp. by D'Orsay W. Pearson (1988); v. 17, Coriolanus, comp. by Alexander Leggatt and Lois Moren (1989); v. 20, Othello, comp. by Margaret Lael Mikesell and Virginia Mason Vaughn (1990).

Planned as "a series of annotated bibliographies surveying Shakespeare scholarship published from 1940 until the present. Major contributions published before that period would also be included . . . each bibliography would be as comprehensive as possible, fully annotated, cross-referenced, and thoroughly indexed. Each would be divided into major sections that indicate the dominant critical and scholarly concerns of the play being discussed."—*Pref.* A useful and comprehensive series. Arrangement and quality of indexing varies from volume to volume.

McRoberts, J. Paul. Shakespeare and the medieval tradition : an annotated bibliography. N.Y. : Garland, 1985. 256 p. (Garland reference library of the humanities, vol. 603). ISBN 0-8240-8716-X. **BD262**

"Lists books, articles, notes, chapters, letters to editors and (in some cases) introductions to individual plays which concern the criticism of Medieval elements in Shakespearean drama."—*Pref.* Some 900 entries cite general works; criticism of the comedies, histories, romances, or tragedies; and criticism of individual plays. Author, Shakespearean play, medieval, and subject indexes. The subject index lists genres and topics (e.g., allegory, courtly love, women); the medieval index is primarily a list of names and titles (e.g., Bartholomaeus, Chaucer, Everyman); certain terms (fool, devil, Celtic mythology) are listed in both, citing different entries. Z8813.M34

Shakespeare : a bibliographical guide / ed. by Stanley Wells. New ed. Oxford : Clarendon Pr. ; N.Y. : Oxford Univ. Pr., 1990. 431 p. ISBN 0-19-871036-4. $46.50. ISBN 0-19-811213-0 (pbk.). $15.00. **BD263**

A revision and updating of the same editor's 1973 volume (*Guide* BD710). It has been modified to permit the inclusion of two chapters (instead of one) on the English history plays, and one on New approaches to Shakespeare. "Nine of the chapters are entirely new; others have been rewritten by their original authors."—*Introd.* Z8811.S5

Filmography

Rothwell, Kenneth S. Shakespeare on screen : an international filmography and videography / Kenneth S. Rothwell and Annabelle Henkin Melzer. N.Y. : Neal-Schuman, c1990. 404 p. : ill. ISBN 1-55570-049-7. $59.95. **BD264**

Lists and describes more than 750 films and videotapes—including major adaptations, spinoffs, musical and dance versions, abridgments, travesties, and excepts; documentaries; and television performances in the U.S., Great Britain, Europe, and South America—which were produced or released between 1899 and 1989. Entries, listed alphabetically by the title of the play, and chronologically by date, provide basic factual information (dates, location of first showing, medium, authorship, distribution and availability), and several paragraphs of description and evaluation, with quotations from critics. Documentaries on general topics are listed together at the end of the volumes. Separate indexes list plays; series and genres; dates; actors and speakers; members of the production team; and authors, critics, and editors. PR3093.R68

Dictionaries

Onions, C. T. A Shakespeare glossary / C.T. Onions ; enlarged and revised throughout by Robert D. Eagleson. Oxford : Clarendon Pr., 1986. 326 p. ISBN 0-19-811199-1. $34.95. ISBN 0-19-812521-6 (pbk.). $8.95. **BD265**

2nd ed. rev., 1919 (*Guide* BD724).

An expansion of the earlier editions, with some completely new entries, and some additions to existing entries. Every definition is now accompanied with at least one quotation from the text of a play or poem; and foreign words and phrases are included alphabetically in the body of the glossary, not in a separate section at the end. PR2892.O6

Quotations

DeLoach, Charles. The quotable Shakespeare : a topical dictionary. Jefferson, N.C. : McFarland, c1988. 544 p. ISBN 0-89950-303-9. **BD266**

Some 6,500 quotations are given under about 1,000 topical headings in alphabetical sequence. Reference is given to the exact line of the source in *The Riverside Shakespeare*. Title, character, and topical indexes. PR2892.D37

Handbooks

Boyce, Charles. Shakespeare A to Z : the essential reference to his plays, his poems, his life and times, and more / Charles Boyce ; David White, editorial consultant. N.Y. : Facts on File, c1990. 742 p. : ill. ISBN 0-8160-1805-7. $45.00. **BD267**

"This book is not meant as scholarship; my intention has been to assemble conveniently a body of lore for the information and entertainment of the student and general reader."— *Pref.* Entries include synopses of the plays, names of characters, actors, scholars, Shakespeare's contemporaries, place-names, etc. There is a list of suggested readings, but sources of information for the individual articles are not supplied. Cross-references are signalled by use of small capitals in the text of articles. The appendix provides alphabetical lists of names of actors, characters, contemporaries, etc. PR2892.B69

Hotaling, Edward R. Shakespeare and the musical stage : a guide to sources, studies, and first performances. Boston : G.K. Hall, 1990. 517 p. ISBN 0-8161-9070-4. **BD268**

An alphabetical listing by composer giving, when available, the author of the text; type of composition (e.g., opera, Broadway show, etc.); number of acts; language; place and date of premiere; source of information about the premiere; publisher of earliest published vocal score; sources maintaining that the work was based on a Shakespeare play; comments; and cast. At the end of the volume, the information is sorted into lists by title, city, date of premiere, text, and play. There are also lists, with call numbers, of items held by the Library of Congress and the British Library. ML128.O4H68

William Shakespeare : his world, his work, his influence / John F. Andrews, ed. N.Y. : Scribner, c1985. 3 v. : ill. (some col.). ISBN 0-684-17851-6 (set). $180.00. **BD269**

" . . . designed to provide a multifaceted twentieth-century view of Shakespeare for the same kind of audience the compilers of the First Folio addressed in 1623 as 'the great variety of readers.' "—*Introd.* Each volume constitutes a series of signed essays (with selective bibliographies) which together explore "virtually every aspect of the phenomenon we refer to as Shakespeare." The first ten essays in v. 1 deal with major institutions and professions (government, religion, law, education, etc.) while the second ten treat subjects such as travel, dress, fine arts, and sports. In v. 2, the first ten essays are meant to provide a broad background (Shakespeare's life, professional career, language, dramatic method, etc.) for the following ten which deal with the works generically and topically, while v. 3 "offers a variety of perspectives on Shakespeare's reception and influence." Contributors (American and British, with two exceptions) are mainly academics but include names from the theater such as John Gielgud, Jonathan Miller and John Simon. Illustrations are fully described in v. 3, which includes a general index to the set. PR2976.W5354

Irish

Anglo-Irish literature : a bibliography of dissertations, 1873–1989 / comp. by William T. O'Malley. N.Y. : Greenwood, 1990. 299 p. (Bibliographies and indexes in world literature, no. 26). ISBN 0-313-27303-0. **BD270**

Identifies 4,359 dissertations from the U.S., Great Britain, Europe, Commonwealth nations, U.S.S.R., Egypt, Japan, and the Philippines. In two main sections: (1) Author studies, which lists works on 193 Anglo-Irish authors; (2) General and topical studies. Author and subject indexes. Z2037.A54

A biographical dictionary of Irish writers / [ed. by] Anne M. Brady and Brian Cleeve. N.Y. : St. Martin's, 1985. 387 p. ISBN 0-312-07871-4. $35.00. **BD271**

A revised and expanded version of Brian T. Cleeve's *Dictionary of Irish writers* (Cork : Mercier Pr., 1967–1971. 3 v.).

Aims "to offer as much biographical and critical material as possible in the given space, about as many Irish writers as possible, from the time of St. Patrick to the present day."— *Pref.* Separate sections for writers in English and writers in Irish and Latin. Includes nonfiction and academic writers, with particular attention given to contemporary figures. PR8727.B5

Scottish

Bold, Alan Norman. Scotland : a literary guide. London : Routledge, 1989. 327 p. ISBN 0-415-00731-3. **BD272**

Arranged alphabetically by place, with entries for towns, castles, abbeys, lakes, bridges, etc. Includes information on the history and geography of the place, followed by chronological entries for individual authors with quotations from literary works. Author index. PR8531.B65

Welsh

The Oxford companion to the literature of Wales / comp. and ed. by Meic Stephens. Oxford ; N.Y. : Oxford Univ. Pr., 1986. 682 p. ISBN 0-19-211586-3. $16.50. **BD273**

"This book was commissioned by Yr Academi Gymreig (The Welsh Academy)"—*t.p. verso.*

A new addition to the "Oxford companion" series, covering the literature of Wales from the 6th century to the present. "Some 2,825 entries have been included, of which nearly twelve hundred, the core of the work, deal with authors. Most of the authors listed are writing in the Welsh language, but also included is a selection of those Welsh men and women who have written in English, Latin and, in at least two instances, dialects of Norman French."—*Pref.* Cross-references; some brief bibliographies. "Chronology of the history of Wales," p.675–82. PB2202.O94

Commonwealth

Australian

The Oxford literary guide to Australia / gen. ed., Peter Pierce ; assistant ed., Rosemary Hunter ; associate ed., Barry Andrews . . . [et al.]. Melbourne ; N.Y. : Oxford Univ. Pr., 1987. 344 p. : ill., col. maps. ISBN 0-19-554592-3. **BD274**

Entries are grouped geographically (e.g., Australian territories, New South Wales, Queensland, South Australia, Tasmania, Victoria, and Western Australia), then alphabetically by place. Cities are further subdivided by suburbs, institutions, geographical formations, etc. A history of each place is given, followed by its literary associations. Color and black-and-white illustrations. Entries are keyed to maps in the back of the volume. The author index gives brief biographical facts and lists works mentioned in the text. Unfortunately, there is no geographical index. PR9607.O94

Ross, Robert L. Australian literary criticism, 1945–1988 : an annotated bibliography. N.Y. : Garland, 1989. 375 p. (Garland reference library of the humanities, vol. 1075). ISBN 0-8240-1510-X. **BD275**

Lists and annotates 1,397 citations to books, articles, and dissertations in a classified arrangement. Includes sections on special topics (e.g., Aborigines, Fiction about the convict period) as well as film, language, multiculturalism, women's studies, fiction, poetry, drama, and 42 individual authors. Index to critics and authors/subjects. Z4024.C8R67

Wilde, W. H. The Oxford companion to Australian literature / William H. Wilde, Joy Hooton, Barry Andrews. Melbourne ; N.Y. : Oxford Univ. Pr., 1985. 760 p. ISBN 0-19-554233-9. $45.00. **BD276**

Typical of the "Oxford companion" series, with entries for authors, literary works, journals, movements, and a few literary characters. Bibliographical information is limited mainly to lists of author's works (with publication dates), and occasional references to biographies of the writers. PR9600.2.W55

Canadian

The annotated bibliography of Canada's major authors / ed. by Robert Lecker and Jack David. Downsview, Canada : ECW Pr. ; Boston : Distr. by G.K. Hall, 1985–1987. v. 6–7. ISBN 0-920802-08-7 (set). (In progress). **BD277**

For earlier volumes and annotation, see *Guide* BD758.

Contents: v. 6 (1985), Margeret Avison–Phyllis Webb; v. 7 (1987), Marian Engel–Thomas Raddall. Z1375.A56

Literary manuscripts at the National Library of Canada = Les manuscrits littéraires à la Bibliothèque nationale du Canada / by Linda Hoad. 2nd ed. rev. and enl. Ottawa : The Library, 1990. 61 p. ISBN 0-662-57263-7. **BD278**

1st ed., 1984.

Intended "to serve as an introduction to the library's unpublished resources in the field of Canadian literature."—*Introd.* Lists and describes approximately 100 collections, with an index of personal names and a chronological table of collections.

Miska, John P. Ethnic and native Canadian literature : a bibliography. Toronto : Univ. of Toronto Pr., 1990. 445 p. ISBN 0-8020-5852-3. $135.00. **BD279**

Lists 5,497 publications by ethnic immigrants to Canada and by Native Americans in Canada, or about ethnic and native literature in Canada. In three main sections: (1) Reference works; (2) Nationality/language groups, which makes up the main part of the volume; (3) Minorities in Canadian literature, which lists works on the portrayal of immigrants and Native Americans. Name index. Derived in part from the author's *Ethnic and native Canadian literature, 1850–1979* (Lethbridge, Alta. : Microform Biblios, c1980). Z1373.E87M57

Moritz, A. F. The Oxford illustrated literary guide to Canada / Albert & Theresa Moritz. Toronto ; N.Y. : Ox-

ford Univ. Pr., 1987. 246 p. : ill. ISBN 0-19-540596-X. **BD280**

"More than 500 entries detail the literary associations of cities, towns, villages, hamlets, and even rivers and islands . . . [or] describe and provide anecdotes about the careers and residences, and moves from place to place" (*Pref.*) of Canadian writers. Geographical arrangement; personal name index. Portraits outnumber literary sites among the illustrations. PR9187.M67

Weiss, Allan Barry. A comprehensive bibliography of English-Canadian short stories, 1950–1983. Toronto : ECW Pr., c1988. 973 p. ISBN 0-920763-67-7. **BD281**

Records "the appearance of 14,314 short stories in 1,308 different periodicals, anthologies, and radio productions, as well as 391 author collections published in monograph form."—*Introd.* Lists the stories of 4,966 authors alphabetically with a title index. Z1375.W46

Caribbean

Berrian, Brenda F. Bibliography of women writers from the Caribbean. Wash. : Three Continents Pr., c1988. 320 p. ISBN 0-89410-600-7. $25.00. ISBN 0-89410-601-5 (pbk.). $15.00. **BD282**

Lists "creative works—novels, short stories, poetry, folklore, autobiographies, biographies, and children's literature—by women writers of [the] Caribbean . . . and the Guyanes in English, French, Dutch, Spanish, Creole, Sranen Tongo, and Papiamento."—*Introd.* Also includes criticism, cookbooks, and book reviews. In four main sections: (1) English Caribbean and Guyana; (2) French Caribbean and Guyana; (3) Netherlands Caribbean and Suriname; (4) Spanish Caribbean. Within each section items are arranged by genre. Each section has a separate name index. Z1595.B46

Fifty Caribbean writers : a bio-bibliographical critical sourcebook / ed. by Daryl Cumber Dance. N.Y. : Greenwood, 1986. 530 p. ISBN 0-313-23939-8. **BD283**

Essays by contributing scholars treat individual authors according to a uniform pattern: biography, major works and themes, critical reception, honors and awards, and bibliography of editions and studies. Indexed. PR9205.A52F54

Hughes, Roger. Caribbean writing : a checklist. London : Commonwealth Institute Library Services, 1986. 49 p. (Checklists on Commonwealth literature, no. 4). **BD284**

Lists works by and about Caribbean authors, including anthologies, collections, and special issues of journals devoted entirely to Caribbean literature. Excludes articles, referring readers to Jeanette B. Allis's *West Indian literature* (*Guide* BD782). An appendix lists authors by country of origin. Z1501

Wharton-Lake, Beverly D. Creative literature of Trinidad and Tobago : a bibliography. Wash. : Columbus Memorial Library, Organization of American States, 1988. 102 p. (Hipólito Uranue bibliographic series, 4). ISBN 0-8270-2709-5 (pbk.). **BD285**

Lists 842 works, mostly books, by author, with a title index. Does not include criticism. PR9272.Z99W53x

South African

Companion to South African English literature / comp. by David Adey . . . [et al.]. Craighall [South Africa] : Ad. Donker, 1986. 220 p. : ports. ISBN 0-86852-039-X. **BD286**

A dictionary arrangement of mostly biographical entries that also provide general articles for History, African-language literature, Exploration, etc. Treats South Africans by birth or residence, as well as travellers who wrote significantly on South Africa. Short entries, no secondary bibliography. Addendum for writers about whom few details are known.   PR9350.2.C66

GERMANIC LANGUAGES

German

Bibliography

Krewson, Margrit B. Contemporary authors of the German-speaking countries of Europe : a selective bibliography. Wash. : Library of Congress : For sale by the Supt. of Docs., U.S. Govt. Print. Off., 1988. 306 p. ISBN 0-8444-0613-9.   **BD287**
Superintendent of Documents classification: LC 1.12/2:G31/4.
Covers writers from the postwar period up to recent years from Austria, the two Germanies, and Switzerland. Under each country is a section for general reference works, then editions, translations, and criticism on individual authors. Only monographic works cited; no indexes.   Z2233.K79

Dictionaries of authors and literature

Brinker-Gabler, Gisela. Lexikon deutschsprachiger Schriftstellerinnen, 1800–1945 / Gisela Brinker-Gabler, Karola Ludwig, Angela Wöffen. Originalausg. München : Deutscher Taschenbuch Verlag, 1986. 363 p. : ill., ports. ISBN 3-423-03282-0. DM16.80.   **BD288**
Treats 200 women authors from the period, providing biographical and critical sketches, brief bibliographies, and photographs or portraits for most subjects.   PT167.B75

Die deutsche Literatur des Mittelalters : Verfasserlexikon / begr. von Wolfgang Stammler ; fortgeführt von Karl Langosch ; unter Mitarb. zahlr. Fachgelehrter hrsg. von Kurt Ruh zs. mit Gundolf Keil . . . [et al.]. 2., völlig neubearb. Aufl. Berlin ; N.Y. : de Gruyter, 1978⁵–1990. v. 5, Lfg. 3/4–Bd. 8, Lfg. 1. ISBN 3-11-006927-X (v. 1, pt. 1). DM68.00 (v. 1). (In progress).   **BD289**
For earlier volumes and annotation, see *Guide* BD865.
Contents: Bd. 5³/⁴–Bd. 8¹, 1985–90, Lecküchner, Hans–Rudolf von Biberach.   Z2230.S78

Garland, Henry B. The Oxford companion to German literature / by Henry Garland and Mary Garland. 2nd ed. Oxford ; N.Y. : Oxford Univ. Pr., 1986. 1020 p. ISBN 0-19-8661398. $29.25.   **BD290**
1st ed., 1976 (*Guide* BD846).
Preserves the structure and scope of the 1st ed., updating many original entries and adding new author entries. PT41.G3

Kosch, Wilhelm. Deutsches Literatur-Lexikon : Biograph.-bibliograph. Handbuch / Begr. von Wilhelm Kosch. Hrsg. von Bruno Berger u. Heinz Rupp. Ältere Abt.: Bearb. von Heinz Zimmermann. Neuere Abt.: Bearb. von Bruno Berger unter Mitw. von . . . Red.: Siegmar Hohl. 3., völl. neubearb. Aufl. Bern ; München : Francke, 1986–1991. v. 10–13. ISBN 3-7720-0952-2 (4. Bd.). DM88.00 (v. 2). (In progress).   **BD291**

For earlier volumes and annotation, see *Guide* BD848.
Bd. 10–13 (1986–91), Lucius–Salzmann.   Z2231.K663

Reallexikon der deutschen Literaturgeschichte / Begr. von Paul Merker und Wolfgang Stammler. 2 Aufl. Neu bearb. und unter redaktioneller Mitarbeit von Klaus Kanzog, sowie Mitwirkung zahlreicher Fachgelehrter. Hrsg. von Werner Kohlschmidt und Wolfgang Mohr. Berlin : De Gruyter, 1988. v. 5.   **BD292**
For earlier volumes and annotation, see *Guide* BD859.
Contents: Bd. 5 (1988), Sachregister. Completes the set.   PT41.R

Biography

Lexikon deutschsprachiger Schriftsteller : von den Anfängen bis zur Gegenwart / von Günter Albrecht . . . [et al.] ; Leitung und Gesamtredaktion Kurt Böttcher. Leipzig : VEB Bibliographisches Institut, 1987. v. 1. ISBN 3-323-00103-6. (In progress).   **BD293**
Contents: v. 1 (1987), Von den Anfängen bis zum Ausgang des 19. Jahrhunderts.
Contains 640 articles on authors and anonymous works.   PT41.L38

Women writers of Germany, Austria, and Switzerland : an annotated bio-bibliographical guide / ed. by Elke Frederiksen. N.Y. : Greenwood, 1989. 323 p. (Bibliographies and indexes in women's studies, no. 8). ISBN 0-313-24989-X.   **BD294**
Covers women writers, 10th–20th centuries, providing for each a short signed biographical sketch and a bibliography of writings. Title index; list of translated titles.   Z2233.5.W6W66

Drama

Meyer, Reinhart. Bibliographia dramatica et dramaticorum : kommentierte Bibliographie der im ehemaligen deutschen Reichsgebiet gedruckten und gespielten Dramen des 18. Jahrhunderts nebst deren Bearbeitungen und Übersetzungen und ihrer Rezeption bis in die Gegenwart. Tübingen : M. Niemeyer, c1986. 3 v. ISBN 3-484-10481-3 (set).   **BD295**
Primarily a descriptive bibliography of published plays listed by author, with library locations in Europe, The British Museum, and 6 libraries in the U.S.   Z5785.M37

Richel, Veronica C. The German stage, 1767–1890 : a directory of playwrights and plays. N.Y. : Greenwood, 1988. 230 p. (Bibliographies and indexes in the performing arts, no. 7). ISBN 0-313-24990-3. $49.95.   **BD296**
" . . . to facilitate investigation of the working repertory of German theatres between 1767 and 1890 by recording the production of more than four thousand plays."—*Introd.* Some 35 printed sources were consulted to compile the alphabetical list of plays with another 10 biographical reference sources consulted. For each playwright then is given name most frequently used, dates and places of birth and death, references to additional sources of biographical information, title of play, date of publication, city of performance with year of performance. Title index.   PT641.R5

Fiction

O'Pecko, Michael T. The twentieth-century German novel : a bibliography of English language criticism, 1945–1986 / by Michael T. O'Pecko and Eleanore O. Hofstetter. Metuchen, N.J. : Scarecrow, 1989. 810 p. ISBN 0-8108-2262-8. **BD297**

Lists 6,417 translations, books, articles, dissertations, and book reviews alphabetically under author and novel or novella studied, with a short section on the German novel in general. No index. Z2234.F4O63

Individual authors

Goethe

Goethe-Wörterbuch / Hrsg. von der Deutschen Akademie der Wissenschaften zu Berlin, der Akademie der Wissenschaften zu Göttingen und der Heidelberger Akademie der Wissenschaften. Stuttgart : Kohlhammer, 1984–1989. v. 2⁷⁻¹². (In progress). **BD298**

For earlier volumes and annotation, see *Guide* BD886. Contents: v. 2⁷⁻¹², Bleiche–Einweisen. Completes v. 2. PT2239.G6

Inventare des Goethe- und Schiller-Archivs / Redaktor Gerhard Schmid. Weimar : Böhlau, 1989. v. 1. ISBN 3-7400-0046-5. (In progress). **BD299**

Contents: v. 1, Schillersband.

Lists and describes the Archive's holdings of published and unpublished materials by Schiller and his circle in a classified arrangement under personal names. Names index.

Scandinavian

Icelandic

Ober, Kenneth H. Bibliography of modern Icelandic literature in translation. Supplement, 1971–1980. Ithaca : Cornell Univ. Pr., 1990. 332 p. (Islandica, 47). ISBN 0-8014-2475-5. $37.50. **BD300**

Supplements Philip M. Mitchell and Ober's basic bibliography, 1975 (*Guide* BD912), and continues its arrangement. Index of translators, editors, and composers. Z2551.O28

SWISS LITERATURE

Schriftstellerinnen und Schriftsteller der Gegenwart : Schweiz = Ecrivaines et écrivains d'aujourd'hui : Suisse / [Redaktion, Grégoire Boulanger . . . et al. ; Koordination und Schlussredaktion, Otto Böni, Lou Pflüger]. Aarau : Sauerländer, c1988. 286 p. ISBN 3-7941-2933-4. **BD301**

Gives biographical and directory information for 20th-century authors writing in German, French, and Italian. PN849.S9S28

ROMANCE LANGUAGES

African writers (French)

Waters, Harold A. Théâtre noir : encyclopédie des pièces écrites en français par des auteurs noirs. Wash. : Three Continents Pr., c1988. 214 p. ISBN 0-89410-627-9. $30.00. ISBN 0-89410-628-7 (pbk.). $16.00. **BD302**

Covers "the black francophone playwrights of especially Africa, the Indian Ocean, the Caribbean, and French Guiana."—*Introd. (version anglaise)*. Also includes the Louisianian Sejour, Dumas *père* and *fils*, and some African and Haitian expatriates. In three main parts: (1) Encyclopédie, which is organized by geographical area and lists and briefly describes each author's published plays; (2) Documentation, classements, thématique, etc., which lists critical works, reference sources, periodicals, anthologies, library collections, and English translations, and provides a selective thematic index to plays; (3) Indexes of names, geographical areas, titles, and playwrights. Z3508.D7W38

Belgian writers

Frickx, Robert. Lettres françaises de Belgique : dictionnaire des œuvres / Robert Frickx et Raymond Trousson. Paris : Duculot, c1988–c1989. 3 v. ISBN 2-8011-0782-4 (set). **BD303**

Contents: v. 1, Le roman; v. 2, La poésie; v. 3, Le théâtre.

Covers works published 1830–1980, presenting in each section signed essays on the work, arranged alphabetically by title, with author indexes. The poetry and essay sections tend to discuss entire volumes, rather than individual works. PQ3811.Z5

Canadian writers (French)

Hamel, Réginald. Dictionnaire des auteurs de langue française en Amérique du Nord / Réginald Hamel, John Hare, Paul Wyczynski. [Montréal] : Fidès, c1989. 1364 p. : ports. ISBN 2762114756. **BD304**

Provides biographical sketches, bibliographies, and some photographs for more than 1,600 authors, from the late 17th century to the early 1980s. Includes some authors from the U.S. PQ3900.2.H36

Kandiuk, Mary. French-Canadian authors : a bibliography of their works and of English-language criticism. Metuchen, N.J. : Scarecrow, 1990. 222 p. ISBN 0-8108-2362-4. **BD305**

Intends "to include only the major French Canadian authors for whom there existed a substantial body of criticism in English."—*Introd.* Lists works by and about 36 authors, including selected book reviews. Index to critics; an appendix provides addresses for Canadian publishers. Z1377.F8K35

Mezei, Kathy. Bibliography of criticism on English and French literary translations in Canada : 1950–1986, annotated = Bibliographie de la critique des traductions littéraires anglaises et françises au Canada : de 1950 á 1986 avec commentaires / Kathy Mezei ; with the assistance of Patricia Matson and Maureen Hole. [Ottawa] : Univ. of Ottawa Pr., 1988. 177 p. (Cahiers de traductologie, t. 7). ISBN 0-7766-0198-9. $19.95. **BD306**

Lists and annotates 581 books, articles, bibliographies, interviews, book reviews, dissertations, and translators' notes on the art, craft, and theory of translation, as well as on particular translations, in a series of chapters devoted to specific publishing formats. Indexes of authors, translators, titles, and subjects. Annotations are in either French or English, depending on the language of the original.   Z1377.T7M49

French

Guides

Brix, Michel. Guide bibliographique des études d'histoire de la littérature française. 2e éd. rev. et augm. Namur : Bibliothèque universitaire Moretus Plantin : Distribué par Presses universitaires de Namur, 1987. 134 p. ISBN 2-87235-011-X.   **BD307**
1st ed., 1985.
Lists and describes 306 sources in a classified arrangement, with an author/title index. Most items cited are in French; almost a third of the volume is devoted to medieval literature.   Z2171.A1B75

Bibliography

Bassan, Fernande. French language and literature : an annotated bibliography / Fernande Bassan, Donald C. Spinelli, Howard A. Sullivan. N.Y. : Garland, 1989. 365 p. (Garland reference library of the humanities, vol. 954). ISBN 0-8240-4798-2.   **BD308**
For annotation, see *Supplement* BC38.   Z2175.A2B39

Klingebiel, Kathryn. Bibliographie linguistique de l'ancien occitan (1960–1982). Hamburg : H. Buske, c1986. 185 p. ISBN 3-87118-767-4.   **BD309**
For annotation, see *Supplement* BC35.   Z7033.P8K57

Vielliard, Françoise. Manuel bibliographique de la littérature française du Moyen Age de Robert Bossuat. Troisième supplément, 1960–1980 / Françoise Vielliard, Jacques Monfrin. Paris : Editions du Centre national de la recherche scientifique : Diffusion, Presses du CNRS, 1986–1991. 2 v. ISBN 2-222-04324-7 (v. 2). 450F.   **BD310**
For basic volume and Suppl. 1–2, see *Guide* BD970.
Contents: v. 1, Les origines; Les légendes épiques; Le roman courtois; v. 2, L'ancien français (chapitres IV à IX), Le moyen français.   Z2172.B7

Criticism

Gelfand, Elissa D. French feminist criticism : women, language, and literature : an annotated bibliography / Elissa D. Gelfand, Virginia Thorndike Hules. N.Y. : Garland, 1985. lii, 318 p. (Garland reference library of the humanities, vol. 351 ; Garland bibliographies of modern critics and critical schools, v. 9). ISBN 0-8240-9252-X.   **BD311**
Presents 555 items in two main sections: (1) General problematics of feminist criticism, which includes comparative studies and works on feminist criticism in general; (2) French and Francophone voices, which lists works by and about individual critics. An appendix gives contents of special issues of journals; title and subject indexes.   HQ1386.G44

Dictionaries of authors and literature

Beaumarchais, Jean-Pierre de. Dictionnaire des littératures de langue française / J.-P. de Beaumarchais, Daniel Couty, Alain Rey. Paris : Bordas, c1987. 4 v. : ill. (some col.). ISBN 2-04-016351-4. $295.00.   **BD312**
1st ed., 1984–85 (*Guide* BD997).
Adds many new articles, and updates original articles and bibliographies through the 1980s. A comprehensive work, covering: French literature from medieval to contemporary times, with signed entries on authors, terms and themes, titles for anonymous works and literary reviews; other national literatures; and French literatures outside France. Entries for major authors are very full, providing discussion of a writer's life and works, chronological tables, synopses and critiques of important works, and bibliographies of primary and secondary works. Numerous illustrations; v. 4 contains an Index des oeuvres, a chronological table of literary terms, and lists of literary prizes and winners.   PQ41.B4

Dolbow, Sandra W. Dictionary of modern French literature : from the age of reason through realism. N.Y. : Greenwood, 1986. 365 p. ISBN 0-313-23784-0. $45.95.   **BD313**
Aims to provide an " . . . introduction to the major writers, works, and literary movements that flourished during the 180 years from the dawn of eighteenth-century French literature through the age of realism, as well as a starting point for further research."—*Pref.* 1880 is the cutoff date. 300 entries, some quite extensive; short bibliographies conclude each entry, with quite current books and articles cited; cross-references. Appendixes give a chronological list in parallel columns of history and literature, and a list of entries by subject matter or chronological period. General index.   PQ41.D65

History

A new history of French literature / ed. by Denis Hollier with R. Howard Bloch . . . [et al.]. Cambridge, Mass. : Harvard Univ. Pr., 1989. 1150 p. : ill. ISBN 0-674-61565-4. $49.95.   **BD314**
Presents essays by individual scholars built around a particular date and theme, beginning with Roland's death in 778 and ending Sept. 27, 1985, the 500th broadcast of "Apostrophes" on Antenne 2. Covers French literature outside France (e.g., the Négritude movement in Martinique) and political or social events that influenced literature (e.g., the Dreyfus affair). Each essay includes a short bibliography; a chronology, map, and general index conclude the volume.   PQ119.N48

Italian

Buja, Maureen E. Italian Renaissance poetry : a first-line index to Petrarch, Ariosto, Tasso, and others. N.Y. : Garland, 1987. 204 p. (Garland reference library of the humanities, vol. 712). ISBN 0-8240-8581-7. $33.00.   **BD315**
The seven Italian renaissance poets Petrarch, Ariosto, Tasso, Bembo, Strozzi, Cassola, and della Casa, were selected because of the frequency with which they were set to music. Each author is indexed separately with the first line, the poem or canto number, and the stanza number, based on the standard editions.   PQ4210.B8

De Vendittis, Luigi. La letteratura italiana : otto secoli di storia : gli autori, le opere, i movimenti, la critica. Bologna : Zanichelli, 1988. 1113 p. : ill.   **BD316**

A history from the middle ages to the early 1970s. Chronologically arranged chapters treat authors, movements, and time periods, with copious illustrations and some bibliographical references. Appendixes list recommended books "alla formazione di una biblioteca privata di letteratura italiana"; films with literary subjects; and literature on television. Name and title indexes.   PQ4037.D418

Portuguese

Guides

Chamberlain, Bobby J. Portuguese language and Luso-Brazilian literature : an annotated guide to selected reference works. N.Y. : Modern Language Association of America, 1989. 95 p. (Selected bibliographies in language and literature, 6). ISBN 0-87352-956-1. $22.00. ISBN 0-87352-957-X (pbk.). $14.50 (est.).   **BD317**

For annotation, see *Supplement* BC47.   Z2725.A2C45

Brazilian

Dictionary of Brazilian literature / Irwin Stern, ed. in chief. N.Y. : Greenwood, 1988. 402 p. ISBN 0-313-24932-6. $65.00.   **BD318**

Contains "approximately 300 entries in English covering the most significant writers, literary schools, and selected cultural movements in Brazilian literary history with an emphasis on twentieth-century and very contemporary figures."—*Pref.* The volume is "oriented toward the English-reading public"; essays and bibliographies take particular care to identify English-language translations and criticism. In addition to the alphabetically arranged entries, a map, chronology, glossary, and lengthy introductory essay on Brazilian literature in cultural perspective are included. General index.   PQ9506.D53

Foster, David William. Brazilian literature : a research bibliography / David William Foster, Walter Rela. N.Y. : Garland, 1990. 426 p. (Garland reference library of the humanities, vol. 1162). ISBN 0-8240-3442-2.   **BD319**

Lists books and articles in both a general section, which encompasses anthologies, periods of literary history, and particular literary forms, and an authors section, which includes criticisms on 150 Brazilian authors. Names index.   Z1681.F73

Igreja, Francisco. Dicionário de poetas contemporâneos. Rio de Janiero : Oficina Letras & Artes, 1988. 148 p.   **BD320**

A dictionary of living poets, with bibliographies of books, anthology contributions, and some secondary literature. Appendixes include lists of periodicals and literary academies with addresses.   PQ9527.I37

Spanish

Guides

Woodbridge, Hensley Charles. Guide to reference works for the study of the Spanish language and literature and Spanish American literature. N.Y. : Modern Language Association of America, 1987. 183 p. (Selected bibliographies in language and literature, 5). ISBN 0-87352-958-8. $14.50 (est.). ISBN 0-87352-959-6 (pbk.). $7.50 (est.).   **BD321**

A greatly expanded version of the author's *Spanish and Spanish-American literature : an annotated guide to selected bibliographies* (1983). Includes reference books and bibliographies on literature and philology published from 1950 to early 1986. Almost 1,000 citations are listed in a classed arrangement and usually include brief annotations. Indexes to authors/editors/compilers and to individual author bibliographies, glossaries, and concordances.   Z2695.A2W66

Bibliography

Aguilar Piñal, Francisco. Bibliografía de autores españoles del siglo XVIII. Madrid : Consejo Superior de Investigaciones Científicas, Instituto "Miguel de Cervantes", 1981–1991. v. 1–6. ISBN 84-00-05317-6 (set). (In progress).   **BD322**

Contents: v. 1–6, A–Q. To be complete in 10 volumes.
Publisher varies.

Covers authors, 1700–1808, writing in Spanish and published in Spain or the Canary or Balearic Islands. For each author, gives biographical sketch, works listed under the categories of letters, manuscripts, printed works, translations, studies. At least one location in a Spanish library is provided. Anonymous works are to be cataloged in v.9; v.10 is to provide general studies. Cross-references from variant forms, pseudonyms, or anagrams. Each volume is indexed by name, subject, geographical location, play title, and printer. List of libraries consulted.   Z2682.A64

Bibliography of Old Spanish texts / comp. by Charles B. Faulhaber . . . [et al.] (with the assistance of Jean Lentz). 3rd ed. Madison, [Wisc.] : Hispanic Seminary of Medieval Studies, 1984. 341 p. (Hispanic Seminary of Medieval Studies. Bibliographic series, 4.). ISBN 0-942260-43-0.   **BD323**

1st ed., 1975; 2nd ed., 1977 (*Guide* BD1132).

Aims to create "an exhaustive descriptive inventory of the relevant pre-1501 Old Spanish texts" (*Introd.*) from which a selection can be made of the most lexically promising material to use in compiling an Old Spanish dictionary, an ongoing project at the University of Wisconsin—Madison. This edition provides full citations (with indication of present location) for 3,378 items. Indexes of library locations, production dates, authors, titles, production locations, printers or scribes, languages, and bibliographical citations.   Z2682.B52

Moseley, William W. Spanish literature, 1500–1700 : a bibliography of Golden Age studies in Spanish and English, 1925–1980 / comp. by William W. Moseley, Glenroy Emmons, and Marilyn C. Emmons. Westport, Conn. : Greenwood, 1984. lxiii, 765 p. (Bibliographies and indexes in world literature, no. 3). ISBN 0-313-21491-3.   **BD324**

Intended as "a ready-reference source of books and articles for the generalist and the advanced student rather than the specialist."—*Introd.* Nearly 11,200 entries arranged by literary genre, plus sections for general works, general bibliography, and individual authors. Author and subject indexes.   Z2692.M67

Simón Díaz, José. Bibliografía de la literatura hispánica / José Simón Díaz ; prólogo de Joaquín de Entrambasaguas. 3a ed. corr. y actualizada. Madrid : Consejo Superior de Investigaciones Científicas, Instituto "Miguel de Cervantes" de Filología Hispánica, 1987. v. 2. ISBN 84-0005202-1. (In progress).   **BD325**

For v. 1, see *Guide* BD1139 *note*; for earlier editions, see *Guide* BD1138–1139.

Contents: v. 2, Literatura castellana edad media.

Z2691.S5

Women writers of Spain: an annotated bio-bibliographical guide / ed. by Carolyn L. Galerstein ; non-Castilian materials ed. by Kathleen McNerney. N.Y. : Greenwood, 1986. 389 p. (Bibliographies and indexes in women's studies, no. 2). ISBN 0-313-24965-2. $45.00.   **BD326**

Aims "to familiarize readers ... with the content and meaning of selected works by 300 women writers of Spain."—*Pref*. Writers are listed alphabetically; a biographical note for each is followed by annotated lists of writings. Title index.

Z2693.5.W6W65

History

Modern Spanish and Portuguese literatures / comp. and ed. by Marshall J. Schneider, Irwin Stern. N.Y. : Continuum, 1988. 615 p. ISBN 0-8044-3280-5. $75.00.   **BD327**

Like other volumes in the "Library of literary criticism" series (e.g., *Guide* BD1203), this work presents selected critical commentary about some "eighty twentieth-century authors of the Iberian Peninsula, writing in Spanish, Catalan, Galician, and Portuguese."—*Pref*. Selections drawn from books and periodicals, are presented in two main sections, Spain and Portugal; many selections have been translated into English by the editors. Index to critics.   PQ6072.M57

Poetry

Rokiski Lázaro, Gloria. Bibliografía de la poesía española del siglo XIX (1801–1850). Madrid : Consejo Superior de Investigaciones Científicas, 1988. v. 1. ISBN 84-00-06914-5 (set). (In progress).   **BD328**

Contents: v. 1, Obras generales; autores y obras anónimas (A–Ch).

Primarily an author listing of Spanish poetry published in books or journals in Spain, although some Latin American imprints do appear. At least one library location in Spain is given for each item cited; contents are given for collections of poems. Author, subject, and first line index.   Z2694.P7R64

Spanish American

Guides

Handbook of Latin American literature / comp. by David William Foster. N.Y. : Garland, 1987. 608 p. (Garland reference library of the humanities, vol. 669). ISBN 0-8240-8559-0. $50.00.   **BD329**

Aims to provide a "source of information for general readers and non-Hispanists who may require concise information concerning a particular author or work or literary tradition of Latin America ... [and is also] intended to meet the needs of students and researchers ... seeking reliable and comprehen-sive information concerning the various national literatures of Latin America and the features that set one national literature off from another."—*Pref*. Signed essays on various national literatures are followed by brief bibliographies of monographic sources, with a name index.   PQ7081.A1H36

Rela, Walter. A bibliographical guide to Spanish American literature : twentieth-century sources. N.Y. : Greenwood, 1988. 381 p. (Bibliographies and indexes in world literature, no. 13). ISBN 0-313-25861-9. $49.95.   **BD330**

Does not replace or supersede the author's earlier *Guia bibliográfica de la literatura hispano-americana desde siglo XIX hasta 1970* (*Guide* BD1185) or its supplement (*Guide* BD1186). Instead, the present volume aims to provide "a single, rigorously selective inventory of sources that must necessarily serve as an initial point of departure for serious scholarship on Latin American literature."—*Foreword*. Lists and annotates 1,884 items in sections devoted to bibliographies, dictionaries, history and criticism, and anthologies. Each section is subdivided by countries and genres. Author index.   Z1609.L7R438

Bibliography

Cypess, Sandra Messinger. Women authors of modern Hispanic South America : a bibliography of literary criticism and interpretation / Sandra Messinger Cypess, David R. Kohut, Rachelle Moore. Metuchen, N.J. : Scarecrow, 1989. 156 p. ISBN 0-8108-2263-6.   **BD331**

Covers Spanish-speaking portions of South and Central America, the Caribbean, and the U.S., presenting "references to critical and interpretive studies of the literary output of 169 modern women authors."—*Pref*. A brief general section is followed by author studies arranged by country of origin.

Z1609.L7C94

Forster, Merlin H. Vanguardism in Latin American literature : an annotated bibliographical guide / comp. by Merlin H. Forster and K. David Jackson, with the collaboration of Margo Milleret and John F. Day. N.Y. : Greenwood, 1990. 214 p. (Bibliographies and indexes in world literature, no. 27). ISBN 0-313-24861-3.   **BD332**

Aims to provide "an annotated guide to research materials rather then an exhaustive listing of everything ever written by or about Latin American vanguardists."—*Introd*. Covers primary materials published 1920–35 and critical works since 1935 in classed arrangement within both an overview section and sections devoted to particular countries. General index.

Z1609.L7F67

Zubatsky, David S. Latin American literary authors : an annotated guide to bibliographies. Metuchen, N.J. : Scarecrow, 1986. 332 p. ISBN 0-8108-1900-7.   **BD333**

Contains "personal bibliographies of Brazilian and Spanish American writers of novels, drama, poetry, and short stories, as well as essayists, journalists, linguists, and literary critics" (*Pref.*) which have been published in books, journals, dissertations and festschriften. Arranged by author with cross-references from pseudonyms or alternate form of name. A supplement lists bibliographies which treat countries or regions rather than individual authors. No index.   Z1609.L7Z82

Dictionaries of authors

Latin American writers / Carlos A. Solé, ed. in chief, Maria Isabel Abreu, associate ed. N.Y. : Scribner, c1989. 3 v. ISBN 0-684-18463-X. $250.00.   **BD334**

A "comprehensive effort to acquaint the English-speaking world, and other countries where Spanish and Portuguese are not the mother tongue, with the rich and varied literature of Spanish America and Brazil."—*Pref*. 176 writers, 15th–20th centuries, are profiled in signed essays varying in length from 2,500 to 10,000 words. Each essay includes a biographical sketch, a critical appraisal, and a bibliography of primary and secondary works. Arranged chronologically, with a name/subject index and a geographical list of authors. A lengthy introductory essay on the history of Latin American literature and a chronological table of political and cultural events precede the main text. PQ7081.A1L37

Spanish American women writers : a bio-bibliographical source book / ed. by Diane E. Marting. N.Y. : Greenwood, 1990. 645 p. ISBN 0-313-25194-0. **BD335**
Z1609.L7S6

Women writers of Spanish America : an annotated bio-bibliographical guide / ed. by Diane E. Marting. N.Y. : Greenwood, 1987. 448 p. (Bibliographies and indexes in women's studies, no. 5). ISBN 0-313-24969-5. **BD336**

These two volumes from the same editor contain much overlapping information, although they differ significantly in scope and completeness. The earlier work lists more than 1,000 individual writers, giving country of origin and dates, and listing titles of works without any other bibliographical information. Approximately a tenth of the entries include some biographical information and bibliographical annotations. Indexes list authors born before 1900 and authors by country.

In contrast, *Spanish American women writers* concentrates on "fifty of the most important women writers of Latin America from the seventeenth century to the present, representing most Spanish-speaking American nations and a variety of literary genres."—*Pref.* Signed entries provide biographical and critical information, discuss major themes and importance, and conclude with bibliographies of primary and secondary works. Two separate chapters discuss Latin American Indian women writers and Latina writers in the U.S. Lists of authors covered by birth date, country, and genre; title and suibject indexes.
Z1609.L7W63

Drama

Allen, Richard F. Teatro hispanoaméricano : una bibliografía anotada = Spanish American theatre : an annotated bibliography. Boston : G.K. Hall, c1987. 633 p. ISBN 0-8161-8395-3. $39.95. **BD337**

Intended to "aid the serious researcher, professor, critic, student, librarian, or play producer in locating and evaluating sufficient primary sources of the Spanish-American Theatre."—*Introd.* Plays published in books or journals, are arranged alphabetically by author within chapters devoted to specific countries; 13 general anthologies are listed as well. Each entry gives at least one and up to five library locations in North America, with one-act plays designated by an asterisk. Annotations are in Spanish or Portuguese. Author and title indexes.
Z1609.D7A44

Reichenberger, Kurt. Das spanische Drama im Goldenen Zeitalter : ein bibliographisches Handbuch = El teatro Español en los siglos de Oro : inventario de bibliografías / Kurt & Roswitha Reichenberger. Kassel : Edition Reichenberger, 1989. 319 p. (Teatro del Siglo de Oro. Bibliografías y catálogos, 2). **BD338**

Topical arrangement of books, essays, articles, with special collections in libraries and archives listed by country. Personal subject, subject, modern author, and library location indexes.
PQ6105.A1R45

Fiction

Brower, Keith H. Contemporary Latin American fiction : an annotated bibliography. Pasadena, Calif. : Salem Pr., c1989. 218 p. ISBN 0-89356-660-8. $40.00. **BD339**

Lists and annotates more than 600 biographical and critical books, chapters, and journal articles on 23 authors active from 1940 on. Intended for the undergraduate student; aims to "present most of the readily available and accessible English-language criticism."—*Introd.* Arranged alphabetically by author, with general biographical and critical sources followed by items on individual novels or stories. General index.
Z1609.F4B76

Individual countries

Cuban

Dictionary of twentieth-century Cuban literature / ed. by Julio A. Martínez. N.Y. : Greenwood, 1990. 537 p. ISBN 0-313-25185-1. **BD340**

"Designed to serve as a useful, one volume companion to contemporary Cuban literature, this dictionary produces, in a single alphabetical sequence, ready reference information on contemporary Cuban creative writers on the island or in exile as well as essays on literary genes and movements."—*Pref.* Signed articles covering the period 1900 to the mid-1980s include some cited bibliographies of works and secondary sources. An appendix describes nine literary journals. Author/title index.
PQ7378.D53

Maratos, Daniel C. Escritores de la diáspora cubana : manual biobibliográfica = Cuban exile writers : a biobibliographic handbook / by Daniel C. Maratos and Marnesba D. Hill. Metuchen, N.J. : Scarecrow, 1986. 391 p. ISBN 0-8108-1878-7. **BD341**

In Spanish and English.

Treats Cuban literary exiles from 1959 to the present. Offers biobibliographies of about 420 writers. Arranged by author; title index.
Z1520.M37

Honduran

Argueta, Mario. Diccionario de escritores hondureños. [Tegucigalpa] : [Centro Técnico Tipolitográfico Nacional?], 1986. 110 p. **BD342**

Brief biographical notices concerning authors who either were born in or wrote in Honduras.
PQ7500.A64

Mexican

Diccionario de escritores mexicanos, siglo XX : desde las generaciones del Ateneo y novelistas de la Revolución hasta nuestros días / [dirección y asesoría, Aurora M. Ocampo]. México : Universidad Nacional Autónoma de México, Instituto de Investigaciones Filológicas, Centro de Estudios Literarios, 1988. v. 1. (In progress). **BD343**

Contents: v. 1, A–Ch.

Includes both native-born writers and those born elsewhere who wrote in Mexico. For each author gives a biographical sketch, a critical evaluation, and a very full bibliography of works both by and about. Lengthy list of periodicals indexed; general bibliography.

§ Another recent volume, *Diccionario biobibliográfico de escritores contemporaneos de México* (Mexico : Instituto Nacional de Bellas Artes, 1988), gives short biographical and bibliographical information on writers born for the most part 1930–60.   PQ7106.D53

Glazer, Mark. A dictionary of Mexican American proverbs. N.Y. : Greenwood, 1987. 347 p. ISBN 0-313-25385-4.   **BD344**

Lists 986 Chicano proverbs in Spanish (with English translations) alphabetically by Spanish keyword, and provides contexts, sources, and variants for each. Spanish and English keyword indexes. Developed from a folklore study undertaken at the Pan-American University in Edinburg, Tex.

PN6426.3.T4G5

Mendoza-López, Margarita. Teatro mexicano del siglo XX, 1900–1986 : catálogo de obras teatrales / Margarita Mendoza López, Daniel Salazar, Tomás Espinosa. México, D.F. : Instituto Mexicano del Seguro Social, c1987–c1989. 4 v. : ill., ports. ISBN 968-824-418-X (set).   **BD345**

For annotation, see *Supplement* BG22.   PQ7189.M4

Woods, Richard Donovon. Mexican autobiography : an annotated bibliography = La autobiografía mexicana : una bibliografía razonada / comp. by Richard Donovon Woods ; translated by Josefina Cruz-Meléndez. N.Y. : Greenwood, 1988. 228 p. (Bibliographies and indexes in world history, no. 13). ISBN 0-313-25945-3.   **BD346**

For annotation, see *Supplement* AJ81.   Z5305.M6W6618

Uruguayan

Diccionario de literatura uruguaya / [direccíon, Alfredo F. Oreggioni ; coordinacíon, Wilfredo Penco]. Montevideo, Uruguay : Arca : Credisol, [1987]–. 2 v. : ill., facsims., ports. ISBN 84-89267-03-0 (set).   **BD347**

Signed articles provide biographical and critical information, and primary and secondary bibliographies.

PQ8511.D53x

Rela, Walter. Diccionario de escritores uruguayos. Montevideo : Ediciones de la Plaza, [1986]. 397 p.   **BD348**

Brief biographical and critical articles with short bibliographies of author's works appended.   PQ8511.R45

——————— Literatura uruguaya : bilbiografía selectiva. Tempe : Center for Latin American Studies, Arizona State Univ., 1986. 86 p. ISBN 0-87918-060-9 (pbk.). $12.95.   **BD349**

Lists works by and selected works about Uruguayan authors, arranged alphabetically by Uruguayan author's name with author index.

§ Another recent title by Rela, *Literatura uruguaya : tablas cronologicas, 1835–1985* (Montevideo : Univ. Católica del Uruguay, [1986]), presents chronological tables for essays and critical works, drama, poetry, and narratives published 1835–1985 and a list of periodicals published 1838–1986, with a name index.   Z1891.R43

Welch, Thomas L. Bibliografía de la literatura uruguaya. Wash. : Biblioteca Colón, Organización de los Estados Americanos, 1985. 502 p. ISBN 0-8270-2243-3 (pbk.).   **BD350**

Identifies 9,329 volumes of fiction, poetry, plays, criticism, and essays published primarily in the 20th century. Items are arranged alphabetically by author, with name (including editors and personal subjects) and title indexes.   Z1891.W45

SLAVIC AND EAST EUROPEAN LANGUAGES

Albanian

Elsie, Robert. Dictionary of Albanian literature. Westport, Conn. : Greenwood, 1986. 170 p. ISBN 0-313-25186-X.   **BD351**

Aims "to provide the Western reader with basic information on Albanian literature from its origins to the present day. It contains entries on over five hundred Albanian writers and literature-related topics, including in most cases fundamental biographical and bibliographical data."—*Pref.* Indexed.

PG9602.E47

Czech

Čeští spisovatelé 20. století : slovníková příručka / napsal autorský kolektiv za redakce Milana Blahynky. Vyd. 1. Praha : Československý spisovatel, 1985. 830 p.   **BD352**

Forms a supplement to *Čeští spisovatelé 19. a počátku 20. století* (*Guide* BD1272), offering biographical sketches of later 20th-century authors, with an index of names and titles.

PG5004.C47

Kovtun, George J. Czech and Slovak literature in English : a bibliography. 2nd ed. Wash. : European Division, Library of Congress; For sale by the U.S. Govt. Print. Off., 1988. 152 p. ISBN 0-8444-0578-7.   **BD353**

1st ed., 1984.

Superintendent of Documents classification: LC1.12/2:C99.

"Bibliography of translations published in monographical form that includes belles-lettres and folklore. Several items dealing with journalism are also listed because of the close relationship between journalism and literary work ... Children's literature is excluded except for works of special importance or works by poets or prose writers known for significant contributions to adult literature."—*Pref.* The 2nd ed. updates to 1986.

Z2138.L5K68

Russian

Bibliography

Proffer, Carl R. Nineteenth-century Russian literature in English : a bibliography of criticism and translations / comp. by Carl R. Proffer and Ronald Meyer. Ann Arbor, [Mich.] : Ardis, c1990. 188 p. ISBN 0-88233-943-5.

BD354

Covers books, articles, and dissertations published from the 1890s through 1986 on general topics and on 69 individual writers. Arranged alphabetically by writer studied, with a section on general topics. No index.   Z2503.P76

Russkie sovetskie pisateli—poėty : biobibliograficheskiĭ ukazatel' / [sost. I.V. Aleksakhina, kand. filol. nauk. D.A. Berman, F.M. Bykova ... et al.] ; Gos. publ. b-ka im. M.E. Saltykova-Shchedrina. Moskva : Kniga, 1985–1990. v. 8–13 : ports. (In progress).   **BD355**

For v. 1–7 and annotation, see *Guide* BD1343.

Contents: v. 8–13, 1985–90, Esenin–Matueeva.

Z2505.P7R87

Encyclopedias

Kasack, Wolfgang. Dictionary of Russian literature since 1917. N.Y.: Columbia Univ. Pr., 1988. 502 p. ISBN 0-231-052421. $40.00. **BD356**

A translation of Kasack's *Lexikon der russischen Literatur ab 1917* (Stuttgart : Kröner, 1976) and its *Ergänzungsband*, by Maria Carolson and Jane T. Hedges.

"For this translation, all entries were updated and 153 entries were added."—*Pref.* Contains 629 author and 87 subject entries, including coverage of important literary journals, themes, movements, and prizes. Each article includes a selected primary and secondary bibliography; most citations are to German- or Russian-language works. Name and subject indexes. Z2500.K3513

History

The Cambridge history of Russian literature / ed. by Charles A. Moser. Cambridge [England] ; N.Y.: Cambridge Univ. Pr., 1989. 685 p. ISBN 0-521-30994-8. **BD357**

Aims to present "in narrative form a survey of Russian literature from the beginnings to this decade, in sufficient but not overwhelming detail."—*Pref.* Ten chapters by specialists elucidate this history from 988 to approximately 1980, with a lengthy bibliography at the end of the volume. General index. PG2951.C36

Biography

Ionov, E. P. Pisateli Moskvy : biobibliograficheskiĭ spravochnik / sostaviteli E.P. Ionov, S.P. Kolov. Moskva : Moskovskiĭ rabochiĭ, 1987. 541 p. **BD358**

This directory of members of the Moscow writer's organization gives very brief biographical information on authors, critics, translators, and scholars with some selected bibliographies. Arranged alphabetically without index. PG3505.M6I56

Ukranian

Piaseckyj, Oksana. Bibliography of Ukrainian literature in English and French : translations and critical works (1950–1986). Ottawa : Univ. of Ottawa Pr., c1989. 386 p. (University of Ottawa Ukrainian studies, no. 10). ISBN 0-7766-0264-0. **BD359**

Translations and criticism are arranged alphabetically under author or work covered within four major chronological periods. Includes Ukrainian émigré literature. Author index. Z2514.U5P52

Yugoslav

Adresar pisaca Jugoslavije / [priredili Gordana Granić . . . et al.]. Novi Sad : Savez književnika Jugoslavije : Književna zajednica Novog Sada, 1986. 852 p. **BD360**

For contemporary Yugoslav literary authors gives name, date of birth, profession, list of publications, and address. Includes authors of translations and scenarios as well as poets, novelists, etc. PG564.A37

Mihailovich, Vasa D. A comprehensive bibliography of Yugoslav literature in English, 1593–1980 / Vasa D. Mihailovich, Mateja Matejic. Columbus, Ohio : Slavica Publishers, c1984. 586 p. ISBN 0-89357-136-9. **BD361**

Constitutes a 2nd, enl. ed. of the same compilers' *Yugoslav literature in English* (*Guide* BD1370) and, like that volume, includes both translations of the literature and critical works. Coverage is extended through 1980, bringing the number of entries to 5,255. Z2958.L5M53

———— First supplement to *A comprehensive bibliography of Yugoslav literature in English*, 1981–1985. Columbus, Ohio : Slavica Publishers, c1988. 338 p. ISBN 0-89357-188-1 (pbk.). **BD362**

Continues the listings as in the basic volume (above) through 1985 and includes some items previously omitted, for an additional 3,127 entries. Again there are indexes of English and Yugoslav titles, of periodicals and newspapers, and of subjects and names. Z2958.L5M54

Srpska književna periodika 1768–1941 : popis i drugi prilozi / Dragiša Vitošević . . . [et al.]. Beograd : Institut za književnost i umetnost, 1984. 177 p. **BD363**

The offshoot of a history of literary periodicals, this bibliography lists 1,336 literary periodicals by date of first publication, with a separate listing of 35 almanacs. Title and geographical indexes. PN5355.S4S67

CLASSICAL LANGUAGES

General works

Dizionario degli scrittori greci e latini / diretto da Francesco Della Corte. [Milano] : Marzorati Editore, 1988. 3 v. (2433 p.). **BD364**
Contents: v. 1–3, A–V.

Lengthy articles by contributing scholars discuss authors and some literary movements or schools (e.g., Epigrammatici, Peripatetici), with recommended texts and translations, and secondary bibliographies. A name index concludes v. 3, hence the set may be complete. DE5.D5956

Halton, Thomas P. Classical scholarship : an annotated bibliography / Thomas P. Halton and Stella O'Leary. White Plains, N.Y. : Kraus Internat., c1986. 396 p. ISBN 0-527-37436-9. $110.00. **BD365**

Updates and reorders Martin McGuire's *Introduction to classical scholarship, a syllabus and bibliographic guide* (Wash. : Catholic Univ. of America Pr., 1961). An annotated bibliography of books, a few essays, serials, and articles divided into 15 subject areas subdivided into smaller topics. Intended for both beginning and advanced researchers. Author and subject indexes. Z6207.C65H34

Howatson, M. C. The Oxford companion to classical literature. 2nd ed. Oxford ; N.Y. : Oxford Univ. Pr., 1989. 615 p., [10] p. of plates : ill. ISBN 0-19-866121-5. $30.00. **BD366**
1st ed., 1937, ed. by Sir Paul Harvey (*Guide* BD1394).

This revision aims to broaden the volume's scope in order to "pay more attention to the philosophy and political institutions" (*Pref.*) of the ancient world—e.g., Women, position of. Covers literature from the beginnings up to 529 CE (the closing of the philosophy academies in Athens). Cross-references; some pronunciation information; maps. PA31.H69

Greek

Bibliography

Berkowitz, Luci. Thesaurus Linguae Graecae canon of Greek authors and works / Luci Berkowitz, Karl A. Squitier with technical assistance from William A. Johnson. 3rd ed. N.Y.: Oxford Univ. Pr., 1990. lx, 471 p. ISBN 0-19-506037-7.   **BD367**

A printed register of the authors, texts, and editions which comprise the *Thesaurus Linguae Graecae* database (below). Each of almost 3,200 authors is listed alphabetically, followed by an author epithet (e.g., Rhetorician, Historian), date, geographical epithet, and works of that author which have been entered into the *TLG* database, including complete bibliographical information. Indexes by *TLG* author number and work type. Since the *Canon* is included online with the *TLG* itself and can be searched using various software packages, one can identify authors or texts from various geographical areas or time periods in using it.   Z7021.B47

Philippides, Dia Mary L. Census of modern Greek literature: check-list of English-language sources useful in the study of modern Greek literature (1824–1987). New Haven, Conn.: Modern Greek Studies Association, 1990. 248 p. ISBN 0-912105-01-1 (pbk.). $15.00.   **BD368**

"The check-list began... with the idea of providing a means by which speakers of English could approach Modern Greek literature through translations and works of criticism."—*Introd.* Arranged in seven parts: Bibliographical sources; Journals; Special issues of journals; Anthologies; Collected essays; Literary history; Authors. These parts are further divided into sections on particular regions, periods, or genres; the anthologies, collected essays, and author chapters have detailed contents notes. Name/title index.   Z2294.C8P46

●**Thesaurus Linguae Graecae** [computer file]. [Irvine, Calif.]: Univ. of California, Irvine, 1987.   **BD369**

Coverage: 8th century BCE–600 CE. File size: 63 million words. Available in CD-ROM (producer).

A full-text database of Greek literature (in Greek), from Homer through the 10th century CE. The CD-ROM, which can be accessed using several different software packages, can be searched for word or letter strings, phrases, or combinations thereof, making it a vital tool for classical philologists, lexicographers, literary scholars, and historians. Berkowitz's *TLG* canon (above) lists the 9,400 texts and editions that have been loaded into the database. For a history of *TLG*, see Theodore F. Brunner, "Databases for the humanities: learning from the *Thesaurus Linguae Graecae*," *Scholarly communication*, no.7 (Winter 1987): 1, 6–9.

History

Greek literature / ed. by P.E. Easterling and B.M.W. Knox. Cambridge [England]; N.Y.: Cambridge Univ. Pr., 1985. 936 p., [8] p. of plates: ill. (The Cambridge history of classical literature, 1). ISBN 0-521-21042-9. $55.00 (est.).   **BD370**

For v. 2 and annotation, see *Guide* BD1398.

Chapters by specialists discuss authors, genres, and topics with extensive bibliographical references reflecting much recent scholarship in the field. "Appendix of authors and works" includes primary works, critical editions, manuscript traditions, translations, and critical studies; a "Metrical appendix" provides help with basic terms and forms. General index.   PA3052.G73

Latin

Munk Olsen, B. L'étude des auteurs classiques latins aux XIe et XIIe siècles. Paris: Editions du Centre national de la recherche scientifique, 1985–1989. v. 2–3 in 3 v. ISBN 2-222-02803-5 (v. 1). 580F.   **BD371**

For v. 1 and annotation, see *Guide* BD1428.

Contents: v. 2, Catalogue des manuscrits classiques latins copiés du IXe au XIIe siècle, Livius–Vitruvius; Florilèges; Essais de plume; v. 3, 1re pte., Les classiques dans le bibliothèques médiévales; v. 3, 2e pte, Addenda et corrigenda; Tables.

Vol. 3, pt. 2, which completes the set, includes indexes by title, geographical and medieval names, classical and medieval authors, editors, and commentators.   PA2045.M86

AFRICAN LITERATURE

Bibliography

Berrian, Brenda F. Bibliography of African women writers and journalists: ancient Egypt–1984. Wash.: Three Continents Pr., c1985. 279 p. ISBN 0-89410-226-5. ISBN 0-89410-227-3 (pbk.).   **BD372**

Authors and their works are listed in chapters devoted to autobiography, biography, fiction, poetry, drama, miscellaneous prose, journalism, and broadcast literature, with separate chapters for interviews, bibliography, and criticism. Lists of authors by country and genre.   Z3508.L5B47

Lindfors, Bernth. Black African literature in English. 1977–1981 supplement. N.Y.: Africana Pub. Co., 1986. 382 p. ISBN 0-8419-0962-8. $24.50.   **BD373**
    Z3508.L5L56

———— Black African literature in English, 1982–1986. London; N.Y.: Zell, 1989. 444 p. ISBN 0-905450-75-2. £48.00.   **BD374**

For basic volume and annotation, see *Guide* BD746.
    Z3508.L5L562

Strange Library of Africana. Southern African material in anthologies of English literature in the Strange Library of Africana: an index / comp. by Carol Leigh. Johannesburg: City of Johannesburg Public Library, 1988. 330 p.   **BD375**

Provides indexes by author, title, and subject to stories, poems, and essays from approximately 300 anthologies, most of which were published in South Africa.   Z965.S77J64

Encyclopedias

African literatures in the 20th century: a guide. N.Y.: Ungar, c1986. 245 p. ISBN 0-8044-6362-X. $12.95.   **BD376**

Reprints articles from *Encyclopedia of world literature in the 20th century*, rev. ed., 1981–84 (*Guide* BD60), with a "few minor revisions and corrections."—*Pref.* Includes the African continent, Malagasy Republic, Mauritius, and Reunion.   PL8010.A43

ORIENTAL LANGUAGES

Indic

Encyclopaedia of Indian literature / chief ed., Amaresh Datta. New Delhi : Sahitya Akademi, c1987–1991. v. 1–4. (In progress). **BD377**

Contents: v. 1–4, A–Sarvasena.

Designed "to give a fairly clear and comprehensive idea about the growth and development of Indian literature in 22 languages."—*Editorial*. Signed articles discuss authors, epic works, styles, influences, and terms, with bibliographic references. PK2902.E53

Garg, Gaṅgā Rām. International encyclopaedia of Indian literature. Rev. and enl. ed. Delhi, India : Mittal Publications, 1987–[1990?]. v. 1–6. (In progress). **BD378**

Contents: v. 1, pt. 1–2, Sanskrit, Pali, Prakit and Apahramsa; v. 2, Tamil; v. 3, Assamese; v. 4, Kannada; v. 5, Telugu; v. 6, Malayalam.

A revised and expanded version of the author's *Encyclopedia of Indian literature* (Delhi : Mittal, 1982) and *Encyclopedia of world Hindi literature* (New Delhi : Concept, 1986). Short, for the most part biographical, articles on authors of vernacular literature and on Indologists. PK2902.G37

Iranian

Storey, C. A. Persian literature : a bio-bibliographical survey. London : Royal Asiatic Society of Great Britain and Ireland, 1977–1990. v. 2, pt. 3; v. 3, pt. 1–2. (In progress). **BD379**

For v. 1–2, pts. 1–2, and annotation, see *Guide* BD1497.

Contents: v. 2, pt. 3 (1977), Encyclopedias and miscellanies, arts and crafts, science, occult arts; v. 3, pt. 1 (1984), Lexicography, grammmar, prosody and poetics; v. 3, pt. 2 (1990), Rhetoric, riddles and chronograms, ornate prose. Z7085.S88

Japanese

Rimer, J. Thomas. A reader's guide to Japanese literature. Tokyo ; N.Y. : Kodansha International ; N.Y. : Distr. through Harper and Row, 1988. 208 p. ISBN 0-87011-896-X (pbk.). $14.95. **BD380**

Descriptions, plot summaries, critical evaluations, and recommended English translations of 20 classics, written from the 10th to 20th centuries. Brief bibliography; general index. PL717.R551

Bibliography

The Yanagita Kunio guide to the Japanese folk tale / trans. and ed. by Fanny Hagin Mayer. Bloomington : Indiana Univ. Pr., [1986?]. 363 p. : maps, port. ISBN 0-253-36812-X. $27.50. **BD381**

For annotation, see *Supplement* CF36. GR340.N52213

Southeast Asian

South-East Asia : languages and literatures : a select guide / ed. by Patricia Herbert & Anthony Milner. Honolulu : Univ. of Hawaii Pr., c1989. 182 p. : ill. ISBN 0-8248-1267-0. $32.00. **BD382**

"This Guide was conceived by members of the South-East Asia Library Group . . . who felt there was a need for a concise introduction to the history, major languages, scripts, dating systems, manuscripts, printing and publishing histories, and literary genres of South-East Asia."—*Pref*. Chapters, which cover Burma, Thailand, Cambodia, Laos, Vietnam, Malaysia, Indonesia, Philippines, and overseas Chinese, include a historical overview, short essays on the matters mentioned above, and a basic bibliography. PL3501.S66

Turkish

Mitler, Louis. Contemporary Turkish writers : a critical bio-bibliography of leading writers in the Turkish Republican Period up to 1980. Bloomington, Ind. : Indiana Univ., Research Institute for Inner Asian Studies, 1988. 325 p. : ill., ports. (Uralic and Altaic series, v. 146). ISBN 0-933070-14-4. **BD383**

Lists alphabetically writers, 1923–80, providing biographical information, a brief sample of the writer's work in translation, primary and secondary bibliographies, and some photographs. Appendixes give information on the transliteration of the Turkish alphabet, a glossary of Turkish literary terms, lists of major Turkish literary awards, and a general bibliography of works in Western languages. Endpapers have a map of Turkey and locations mentioned in the biographies. No index. PL213.M46

————— Ottoman Turkish writers : a bibliographical dictionary of significant figures in pre-Republican Turkish literature. N.Y. : P. Lang, c1988. 203 p. : 1 map. (American university studies. Series XIX, General literature, vol. 15). ISBN 0-8204-0633-3. $37.00. **BD384**

A work "humbly offered to the rather large body of intellectually curious, literate, non-specialist(s) and [which] does not presume to be yet another learned treatise for the hermetic body of scholars in the field."—*Pref*. Provides biographical sketches, primary and some secondary bibliographies for about 100 poets, novelists, playwrights, essayists, folklorists, and scholars, who wrote from c.1000 CE to the end of World War I. Many of the sketches, which are arranged alphabetically, include samples of an author's work in English translation. The introduction provides an overview of the history of Turkish literature and the volume concludes with a literary glossary, a note on pronunciation and transcription of Turkish, and a selected bibliography of works of criticism by Western authors. PL213.M48

BE

Fine Arts

GENERAL WORKS

Guides

Ehresmann, Donald L. Fine arts : a bibliographic guide to basic reference works, histories, and handbooks / Donald L. Ehresmann. 3rd ed. Littleton, Colo. : Libraries Unlimited, 1990. 1 v. ISBN 0-87287-640-3. $45.00.
BE1

2nd ed., 1979 (*Guide* BE2).

Adds 258 titles published in the past decade and incorporates 72 additional titles published prior to the cutoff date for this edition, for a total of 2,051. Includes a new chapter (Historiography of art history), notes new editions or reprints and volumes in series, and has reorganized the somewhat complex listing of topographical handbooks. Two indexes, author/title and subject. The author plans two additional bibliographies on sculpture and on painting and graphic arts.   Z5931.E47

Jones, Lois Swan. Art information : research methods and resources. 3rd ed. Dubuque, Iowa : Kendall/Hunt Pub. Co., c1990. 373 p. ISBN 0-8403-5713-3.   **BE2**

2nd ed., 1984 (*Guide* BE3) had title: *Art research methods and resources.*

The 19,000 bibliographic citations reflect an increase of roughly 25% over the previous edition. New features: more citations for "early published works ... and numerous foreign-language items" (*Foreword*), a section on "Using this book," an outline of the five major indexes available online, a listing of 275 serials in various subject areas, and expanded regional sections. The four parts have been reorganized into six, the additional two being Specialized resources for various media and disciplines and Iconographical resources. The expanded appendixes include "Databases: their primary subjects and vendors."   N85.J64

Woodhead, Peter. Keyguide to information sources in museum studies / Peter Woodhead and Geoffrey Stansfield. London ; N.Y. : Mansell, 1989. 194 p. ISBN 0-7201-2025-X. $55.00.   **BE3**

"A first source of information about museums" (*Introd.*) in three parts: Overview of museum studies and its literature; Bibliographical listing of sources of information; List of selected organizations (international; arranged by country). Index: authors, titles, subjects, organizations.   AM7.W66

Bibliography

See also BE91, BE95.

Burt, Eugene C. Erotic art : an annotated bibliography with essays. Boston : G.K. Hall, c1989. 396 p. ISBN 0-8161-8957-9.   **BE4**

Erotic art is defined as "art that primarily addresses some aspect(s) of the human sexual experience."—*Introd.* Compiled "over fifteen years by scouring a wide range of information sources including published bibliographies ... periodical indexes ... antiquarian book dealer sales catalogs ... and library card catalogs." The 30 chapters are grouped in seven sections, each beginning with an introductory essay: General background; General surveys; Ancient world; Asia; Ethnoart-Africa, Oceania and the Native Americas; Western world; Modern world [20th century]. The latter two sections cite a total of 318 artists, about a third of whom are photographers. Includes entries not only for scholarly titles but for articles from *Penthouse* or *Playgirl*. Most entries have brief annotations or evaluative comments. Author index.   Z5956.E7B87

Goldman, Shifra M. Arte Chicano : a comprehensive annotated bibliography of Chicano art, 1965–1981 / comp. by Shifra M. Goldman and Tomás Ybarra-Frausto. Berkeley : Chicano Studies Library Publications Unit, Univ. of California, 1985. 778 p. ISBN 0-918520-09-6 (pbk.). $25.50 (est.).   **BE5**

Seven years in compilation, this bibliography integrates material from alternative and little-known publications and from local and regional newspapers with citations to popular and widely-held publications. The 55-page introduction, with sections on Revealing the image and Outline of a theoretical model for the study of Chicano art (theories, definitions, chronology), has its own index. The body of the bibliography consists of 2,500 annotated citations, each listed under subject headings (four per citation) taken from *Chicano thesaurus*, 3rd ed. The citation format matches that used in *Chicano periodical index* (*Guide* CC490–491). Indexes by author/artist and title. Appendixes: Alphabetical list of Chicano artists (about 2,200 names); Periodical titles cited in bibliography (about 300).   Z5961.U5G64

Handbook of Latin American art = Manual de arte latinoamericano : a bibliographic compilation / gen. ed., Joyce Waddell Bailey. Santa Barbara, Calif. : ABC-Clio Information Services, c1986. v. 2 in 2 parts. ISBN 0-87436-386-1 (set). (In progress).   **BE6**

For v. 1 and annotation, see *Guide* BE30.

Regional editors, v. 2: Aracy Abreu Amaral (Brazil), Ramón Gutiérrez and Alberto S.J. de Paula (Southern cone).

Contents: v. 2, Art of the colonial period.

Also known as *HLAA*.

Vol. 2 cites 5,200 titles, has indexes similar to those in v. 1, and also covers architecture.   Z5961.L3H36

Heppner, Irene. Bibliography on portraiture : selected writings on portraiture as an art form and as documentation. Boston : G.K. Hall, c1990. 2 v. : ill. ISBN 0-8161-0481-6. $225.00.   **BE7**

"Covers the portraiture of Western cultures of all times" (*Introd.*), emphasizing American examples, British influences on American trends, and English-language publications. Cites monographs, sections of monographs, periodical articles, museum publications, and theses. The project was undertaken in the library of the National Portrait Gallery in Washington, D.C. The classified arrangement includes such topics as special pose or length, intellectual concepts, and media, and is followed by an index to those topics. The 1,600 pages of the bibliography, which consist of photoreproductions of catalog cards, ten per page, are difficult to read.   Z5939.H465

Kaufmann, Thomas DaCosta. Art and architecture in Central Europe, 1550–1620 : an annotated bibliography. Boston : G.K. Hall, c1988. 316 p. ISBN 0-8161-8594-8.   **BE8**

Covers the area comprising the contemporary states of Germany, Austria, Switzerland, Czechoslovakia, Slovenia, and portions of Poland, corresponding to the area of the Holy Roman Empire. Excludes Hungary, and has little coverage of decorative arts. Arrangement is by general studies, studies of collecting and patronage, and medium, subdivided chronologically. Entries provide annotations and translations of titles for less common languages. An 18-page introduction is followed by information on sources. Author index. Z5936.M34K38

Lincoln, Betty Woelk. Festschriften in art history, 1960–1975 : bibliography and index. N.Y. : Garland, 1988. 220 p. (Garland reference library of the humanities, vol. 745). ISBN 0-8240-8497-7. $40.00. **BE9**

"Fills the lacuna between [Paul Rave's *Kunstgeschichte in Festschriften, Guide* BE45] and *RILA* [*Guide* BE60] with a bibliography and analytical index of Festscriften in art history and related fields from the beginning of the Christian era to the present."—*Introd.* Cites 344 festschriften, 1960–75, and lists their 4,676 essays, followed by indexes of subjects, authors, and dedicatees. Z5931.L52

The museum : a reference guide / ed. by Michael Steven Shapiro, with the assistance of Louis Ward Kemp. N.Y. : Greenwood, c1990. 385 p. ISBN 0-313-23686-0. **BE10**

A critical bibliography for museum studies. The main section, consisting of 11 essays on methodology and museum history by various contributors, is followed by three appendixes: Museum directories; Museum archives and special collections; Museum-related periodicals. Index for significant names, institutions, and events in museum history. Z5052.M93

Pearson, J. D. A bibliography of the architecture, arts, and crafts of Islam by Sir K.A.C. Creswell, C.B.E. Second supplement, Jan. 1972 to Dec. 1980 (with omissions from previous years) / by J.D. Pearson ; assisted by Michael Meinecke, George T. Scanlon. [Cairo] : American Univ. in Cairo Pr., 1984. 578 columns. ISBN 977-424-052-9. **BE11**

For basic volume and 1st supplement, see *Guide* BE21.

Lists 11,000 entries for a nine-year period; *Suppl. 1* had 4,000 entries for a 12-year period. ". . . includes important *lacunae* from the first two volumes" (*Pref.*), a large number of national, regional, and international exhibitions of Islamic art, and additional dissertations, and incorporates citations for Arabic, Persian, and Turkish publications. Excludes explanatory comments. Z5956.I8C74

Repertorium doctoraalscripties 1981–1985 : neerlandistiek en kunstgeschiedenis / Werkgroep Repertorium Doctoraalscripties ; [Bea Pinj-Blom . . . et al.]. 's-Gravenhage : Stichting Bibliographia Neerlandica, 1988. 132 p. ISBN 90-71313-11-5. **BE12**

A bibliography of some 1,555 dissertations completed 1981–85 at 11 Dutch universities, including some 500 art history theses. Arrangement is classified by code for 15 media, period (i.e., century), country of subject. Two indexes: author, subject (places, topics, groups). N6941

Schimmelman, Janice Gayle. American imprints on art through 1865 : books and pamphlets on drawing, painting, sculpture, aesthetics, art criticism, and instruction : an annotated bibliography. Boston : G.K. Hall, 1990. 419 p. ISBN 0-8161-7261-7. **BE13**

". . . identifies 637 titles and covers a broad range of art literature: addresses and essays, biographies of artists, histories of art, descriptions of paintings and sculpture, art journals, trade catalogs of artists' materials, practical handbooks . . . and instructional books . . . with the exception of exhibition catalogs."—*Pref.* No judgment was made as to quality or content. Arrangement of the main section is alphabetical, first by author, then by artist. In addition to standard bibliographical information, variant titles, and description of contents, gives li-

brary locations as identified by the *National union catalog: pre-1956 imprints, Checklist of American imprints for 1830– ,* OCLC, and by six additional sources (but lacks a key to holdings abbreviations). There is a 38-page chronological listing of titles cited, and an index of names and titles. Z5961.U5S34

Schlosser, Julius, *Ritter von.* Die Kunstliteratur : ein Handbuch zur Quellenkunde der neueren Kunstgeschichte. Wien : A. Schroll & Co., 1985. 640 p. ISBN 3-7031-0604-2. **BE14**

Repr. of the 1924 ed. (*Guide* BE48 *note*). The 3rd Italian ed., 1964 (*Guide* BE48) has also been reprinted (Firenze : La nuova Italia, 1977 and 1979), and a French translation incorporates corrections and updates from the 3rd Italian ed. (Paris : Flammarion, 1984; "Idées et recherches" series). N5300.S32

Weisberg, Gabriel P. Japonisme : an annotated bibliography / Gabriel P. Weisberg, Yvonne M.L. Weisberg. New Brunswick, N.J. : Jane Voorhees Zimmerli Art Museum, Rutgers-The State Univ. of New Jersey ; N.Y. : Garland, 1990. 445 p. : ill. (Garland reference library of the humanities, vol. 695). ISBN 0-8240-8545-0. **BE15**

The core of the work consists of 729 citations through 1988 which are accompanied by substantial evaluative annotations and arranged by publication type (books, catalogs, articles, dissertations, reviews, and notes), subdivided by date. Begins with a 20-page essay on "The nature of Japonisme" and concludes with author and subject indexes, the latter also listing journal titles from citations. Z5956.J35W44

Current

Art and archaeology technical abstracts. v. 6– . N.Y. [etc.] : Institute of Fine Arts, New York Univ. [etc.], 1966– . Semiannual (irregular). ISSN 0004-2994. $20.00. **BE16**

For earlier volumes, see *Guide* BE53.

Subtitle: Formerly *IIC abstracts.* Published by the Getty Conservation Institute in association with the International Institute of Conservation of Historic and Artistic Works, London.

Beginning with v. 23 (1986), "compiled and produced through the bibliographic component of the Conservation Information Network, a joint project of the Getty Conservation Institute and the Department of Communications, Canada."—*Acknowledgements, v. 26 no. 1.* Content and arrangement remain the same.

§ Also available online through the Conservation Information Network. Indexes periodical, monographic, and technical report literature pertaining to the technical aspects of conservation and restoration. Component files include: Bibliographic database (BCIN), Materials database (MCIN), Suppliers database (ACIN). AM1.A7

●**Art index** [computer file]. Bronx, N.Y. : H.W. Wilson Co., 1984– . **BE17**

Machine-readable version of *Art index* (*Guide* BE68).

File size: 212,000 records. Available online (WILSONLINE, updated twice weekly) and in CD-ROM (Wilson, updated quarterly).

●**Artbibliographies modern** [computer file]. Santa Barbara, Calif. : ABC-Clio, 1974– . **BE18**

Machine-readable version of *Artbibliographies modern* (*Guide* BE55).

File size: about 110,000 records. Updated semiannually. Available online (DIALOG).

Bibliography of the history of art : BHA = Bibliographie d'histoire de l'art. v. 1/1– . Vandoeuvre-les-Nancy, France : Centre national de la recherche scientifique, Institut de l'information scientifique et technique ; Santa Monica, Calif. : J. Paul Getty Trust, Getty Art History

Information Program, 1991– . Quarterly, with annual cumulative index. ISSN 1150-1588. **BE19**

Combines the services of *RILA* (*Répertoire international de la littérature de l'art*) (below) and *RAA* (*Répertoire d'art et d'archéologie*) (below) in a quarterly publication with bilingual subject indexes and a yearly cumulative index. Coverage will include 4,000 periodical titles and a slightly increased number of citations (some 24,000). It begins with a 1990 volume, covering 1989 imprints and some earlier ones in order to maintain continuous coverage with *RILA* and *RAA*. *BHA* will be available online in the future through DIALOG and FRANCIS.

N1.A1B52

Black arts annual. 1987/88– . N.Y.: Garland, 1989– . Annual. ISSN 1042-7104. **BE20**

Sections treat art, photography, literature, popular music, jazz and classical music, dance, theater, movies, and television. Each section begins with an overview of the season in general, followed by annotated lists "spotlighting individual pieces of work."—*Introd.* The purpose is "to examine and explore, probe and scrutinize, dissect and analyze ... and report on the year's important events in the arts in the African-American community." Vol. 2 (1990) covers Sept. 1, 1988 to Aug. 31, 1989 and in the Art section cites 19 traveling exhibitions and 58 nontraveling exhibitions and gives six biographical profiles. Includes a name index but lacks an index for titles of works, periodicals, institutions, or places. Contributors are Donald Boyle, Tonya Bolden, Herb Boyd, William Moore, Don Palmer, Beth Turner, Deborah Willis, and Judith Wilson.

NX512.3.A35B58

Répertoire d'art et d'archéologie : RAA. t. 1 (1910)–t. 67 (1963); Nouv. sér., t. 1 (1965)–t. 25 no. 4 (1989). Paris : Bibliothèque d'art et d'archéologie, 1910–1989. ISSN 0080-0953. **BE21**

For earlier volumes and annotation, see *Guide* BE59.

Ceased with v. 25 no. 4 (1989). Merged with *Répertoire international de la littérature de l'art (RILA)* (below) to form *Bibliography of the history of art* (above).

§ Also available as: *Répertoire d'art et d'archéologie* [computer file] (Vandoeuvre-les-Nancy Cedex : Centre National de la Recherche Scientifique [CNRS]). Coverage 1973–89. File size: about 200,000 records. Available online (FRANCIS).

Z5937.R4

Répertoire international de la littérature de l'art : RILA = International repertory of the literature of art. v. 1 (1975)–v. 15 no. 2 (1989). N.Y.: College Art Association of America. ISSN 0145-5982. $60.00. **BE22**

For earlier volumes and annotation, see *Guide* BE60.

Ceased with v. 15 no. 2 (1989). Merged with *Répertoire d'art et d'archéologie* (above) form *Bibliography of the history of art (BHA)* (above). A five-year cumulative index for v. 11–15 is forthcoming.

Also available in machine-readable form: Z5937.R16

•**Art literature international** [computer file]. Williamstown, Mass. : J. Paul Getty Trust, Getty Art History Information Program, 1973–1989. **BE23**

File size: 133,000 records. Updated semiannually. Available online (DIALOG).

Library catalogs

Bibliotheca Hertziana, Max-Planck-Institut. Kataloge der Bibliotheca Hertziana in Rom (Max-Planck-Institut). Wiesbaden : L. Reichert, 1985–1990. v. 1–16, 1–15. ISBN 3-88226-300-8 (I, Bd. 1). (In progress). **BE24**

Catalog of a unique library of Italian art, housed in the Palazzo Zuccari at Rome, that emphasizes Rome, the Renaissance, architecture, and guidebooks. To be complete in 55 v.

The first 16 v. constitute the systematic shelflist, of which v. 13–15 list catalogs of libraries and museums, arranged alphabetically by city, then chronologically, and v. 16 lists 1,500 periodicals. These are being followed by 32 v. of the alphabetical catalog (in progress, published through v. 15, 1990, reproducing only eight cards per page), and will conclude with 7 v. of the analytical catalog (an author list of periodical articles). Current through the end of 1984, at which time the library held 147,285 volumes. Introductory material, in German, Italian, and English, covers the history of the library. Includes a four-page bibliography on the library and an outline of the classification scheme.

Z933.R66

Harvard University. Fine Arts Library. Catalog of the Rübel Asiatic Research Collection, Harvard University Fine Arts Library. London : Saur, 1989. 7 v. ISBN 0-86291-862-6. $950.00. **BE25**

Arranged in three main sections: Dictionary catalog; Catalog of reproductions of Chinese and Japanese art; The Mei shu Ts'ung shu and I-shu ts'ung Pien. Covers 12,000 volumes of monographs and periodicals added through Dec. 31, 1985. "Author and title entries for materials in East Asian languages are romanized, but the cards also contain the original characters and an English translation of the title."—*Pref.* Covers the art of "East Asia, Central Asia, Southeast Asia and India. Particularly strong are the holdings on Chinese ritual bronzes, Buddhist arts, Chinese and Japanese painting, Japanese woodblock prints, and East Asian ceramics." The library collection, begun in 1927, has been since July 1978 part of Harvard's Fine Arts Library.

N7260.H37

Metropolitan Museum of Art (New York, N.Y.). Library. Library catalog of the Metropolitan Museum of Art, New York. 2nd ed., rev. and enl. Second supplement. Boston : G.K. Hall, 1985. 4 v. **BE26**

Z881.N6624

———— ———— 2nd ed., rev. and enl. Third supplement, 1983–1986. Boston : G.K. Hall, 1987. 3 v. **BE27**

Z881.N6624

———— ———— 2nd ed., rev. and enl. Fourth supplement, 1987–1989. Boston : G.K. Hall, 1990. 3 v. **BE28**

For 2nd ed., 1st suppl., and annotation, see *Guide* BE62.

The 4th suppl. covers materials cataloged Jan. 1987 through Dec. 1989 (1700 p.) and serves as the 12th supplement to the first edition. Most volumes of the 2nd ed. are also available on microfilm.

Z881.N6624

Robert Gore Rifkind Center for German Expressionist Studies. Bibliography of German Expressionism : catalog of the Library of the Robert Gore Rifkind Center for German Expressionist Studies at the Los Angeles County Museum of Art. Boston : G.K. Hall, c1990. 272 p. : ill. ISBN 0-8161-0494-8. **BE29**

An introduction by Susan C. Trauger covers: history of the Center; the classification scheme and its development; the Library's holdings (more than 4,000 volumes by or about 278 artists, a third of which are early or rare books). Includes all works acquired through 1988; produced from OCLC machine-readable tapes, creating one alphabet of author, title, and subject entries.

Z5961.G4R63

Museum publications

See also BE10 and BE76.

Klos, Sheila M. Historical bibliography of art museum serials from the United States and Canada / ed. by Sheila M. Klos and Christine M. Smith ; editorial committee, Alexandra A. de Luise ... [et al.]. Tucson, Ariz. : Art

Libraries Society of North America, 1987. 58 p. ISBN 0-942740-04-1 (pbk.). **BE30**

Intends "to provide a reference source for the bibliographic verification of art museum serial titles, including their exact publishing history.... [Cites] frequency changes, suspensions and cessations, irregularities in numbering, merges, and continuations, and [gives] a brief description of the content of the serial."—*Introd.* Covers primarily serials from art museums, noncommercial galleries, college and university art museums and galleries, and art associations with permanent collections. Covers art schools, athenaeums, general museums, and state museums selectively. Excludes monographic series. Arrangement is alphabetical by present name of the institution. Entries were compiled from questionnaires, RLIN and OCLC records, and several printed sources. An appendix lists "Institutions which have never published any serials within the scope of this bibliography." Title index. Z5937.K57

Indexes

See also BE86.

Appel, Marsha C. Illustration index VI, 1982–1986. Metuchen, N.J.: Scarecrow, 1988. 531 p. ISBN 0-8108-2146-X. **BE31**

For earlier volumes, see *Guide* BE81–82.

"Follows the patterns of scope, style, and arrangement set in the fourth and fifth volumes."—*Pref.* Contains 35,000 entries, from the same list of periodicals covered in the previous volume; the only material methodically excluded is advertisements. Uses the subject heading and cross-reference format of the *World book encyclopedia* (*Guide* AC22). N7525.A66

Archives

See also BE51.

Archives of American Art. The card catalog of the manuscript collections of the Archives of American Art. Supplement 1981–1984. Wilmington, Del.: Scholarly Resources, 1985. 542 p. ISBN 0-8420-2235-X. **BE32**

For basic set, see *Guide* BE89.

"... contains descriptions of over one thousand new collections and collection additions acquired since October 1980."—*Introd.* Also incorporates revisions for collections "more thoroughly processed or microfilmed since the previous publication." Z6611.A7A72

Encyclopedias

Denvir, Bernard. The Thames and Hudson encyclopaedia of Impressionism. N.Y.: Thames and Hudson, 1990. 240 p.: ill. (some col.). ISBN 0-500-20239-7 (pbk.). $11.95. **BE33**

Aims "to present a concise compendium of information, based for the most part on recently published work, relating to Impressionism, its practitioners, ancillary figures... models, dealers and critics, as well as to relevant general themes."— *Introd.* Entries are illustrated and contain short bibliographies. A so-called subject index precedes the entries and arranges them into groups. Includes a bibliography, chronology (1855–90), and list of primary collections of Impressionist works. N6465.I4D4

Enciclopedia dell'arte antica, classica e orientale. Roma: Istituto della Enciclopedia italiana, 1981–85. v.

[10–11]: illus., col. plates, maps, facsims., plans. (In progress). **BE34**

For v. 1–8 and annotation, see *Guide* BE95; for v. [9] (1970 suppl.), see *Guide* BE95 *note.*

Volumes for 1981 and 1985 serve as v. 10–11 and are edited by Giovanni Pugliese Carratelli. An index volume, covering v. 1–7 and the supplement, was publ. in 1984 (629 p.). N31.E48

Encyclopedia of world art. N.Y.: McGraw-Hill, [1987]. v. 17: illus., maps, plans., plates (part col.). **BE35**

For v. 1–16 and annotation, see *Guide* BE96.

Ed. by Giulio Carlo Argan.

Contents: v. 17, Supplement II, New discoveries and perspectives in the world of art.

Under the auspices of the Fondazione Giorgio Cini in cooperation with Jack Heraty & Associates, Inc., Palatine, Ill.

This supplement in four parts: (1) The origins of art and the ancient world; (2) The Orient and other non-European civilizations; (3) The Middle Ages and the modern era; (4) The twentieth century and problems of contemporary criticism.

Although the two supplements are similar in format and design, their respective coverage is somewhat unclear. Contributors to Suppl. I were Americans; to Suppl. II, Italians. Suppl. II suffers from out-of-date bibliographies (current only to 1977) and a minimal index that includes broad thematic headings and authors, but excludes artists, sites, and titles of works of art. Many of the 176 plates are in color. N31.E4833

Lexikon der Kunst : Architektur, bildende Kunst, angewandte Kunst, Industrieformgestaltung, Kunsttheorie / [begründet von Gerhard Strauss ; hrsg. von Harald Olbrich... et al.]. 1. Aufl., Neubearbeitung. Leipzig : E.A. Seemann, 1987–1991. v. 1–3 : ill. (some col.). ISBN 3-363-00286-6 (set). (In progress). **BE36**

Revision of the 1st ed., 1968–78, 5 v. (*Guide* BE99).

The lengthy entries cover places, movements, media, and broad topics such as "Aesthetics," and are particularly strong on Central and Eastern European art and architecture. Bibliographical references have been updated through the mid-1980s. N33.L47

Lexikon der Kunst : Malerei, Architektur, Bildhauerkunst / [Gesamtleitung, Wolf Stadler ; Redaktion, Eckhart Bergmann... et al.]. Freiburg : Herder, c1987–c1990. 12 v.: ill. (chiefly col.). ISBN 3-451-20662-5 (1. Bd.). **BE37**

Similar in format to the somewhat smaller *McGraw-Hill dictionary of art* (*Guide* BE101). Entries cover artists, concepts, materials, building parts, and are distinguished by color illustrations of reliable quality, particularly in the later volumes. Entries conclude with brief bibliographies, chiefly in German, many current through 1980 or 1985. Some of the illustrations (such as building sections and axonometric views of famous monuments) are useful for instructional purposes. N33.L48

The Oxford dictionary of art / ed. by Ian Chilvers and Harold Osborne ; consultant ed., Dennis Farr. Oxford ; N.Y. : Oxford Univ. Pr., 1988. 548 p. ISBN 0-19-866133-9. $39.95. **BE38**

A descendant of *The Oxford companion to art*, 1970 (*Guide* BE102), *The Oxford companion to twentieth-century art*, 1981 (*Guide* BE103), and *The Oxford companion to the decorative arts*, 1975 (*Guide* BF6). Much of the text has been rewritten and incorporates more than 300 new entries, while excluding the long entries on individual countries and those on architecture and Oriental art. N33.O93

Reallexikon zur deutschen Kunstgeschichte. Stuttgart : J.B. Metzler, 1985–90. Bd. 8⁹⁻¹²–9¹⁻³ (Lfg. 93–99) : illus., ports., diagrs., facsims., plans. (In progress). **BE39**

For earlier volumes and annotation, see *Guide* BE107.

Contents: Bd. 8⁹⁻¹², Figurine–Firnis (completes the vol.

and includes a supplement to "Festaufzug"); Bd. 9¹⁻³, Firstbekrönung–Fischzug. N6861.R4

Wessel, Klaus. Reallexikon zur byzantinischen Kunst / Unter Mitwirkung von Marcell Restle, hrsg. von Klaus Wessel. Stuttgart : A. Hiersemann, 1989–1991. v. 4–5 : illus., maps, plans. (In progress). **BE40**
For earlier parts and annotation, see *Guide* BE106.
Contents: Bd. 4, Lfg. 27–32, Kommagene/Kilikien/Isaurien, Schluss–Kreta, Schluss (1989–90); Bd. 5, Lfg. 33–34, Kreuz I–Kreuzigung Christi (Anfang) (1991). N6250.W45

Dictionaries

Earls, Irene. Renaissance art : a topical dictionary. N.Y. : Greenwood, 1987. 345 p. ISBN 0-313-24658-0. **BE41**
" ... intended to serve as a quick reference source for identifying and understanding Renaissance art of Italy and northern Europe. It contains basic information about topics that were common subjects ... entries on characteristic schools, techniques, media, and other terminology have been included as background information."—*Pref.* The 800 entries are alphabetically arranged and include cross-references; those for iconographical topics cite one work depicting the subject. Concludes with a bibliography of about 110 English-language sources and a name and subject index. N6370.E27

Wa-Ei taishō Nihon bijutsu yōgo jiten = A dictionary of Japanese art terms, bilingual "Japanese & English" / [henshū Wa-Ei Taishō Nihon Bijutsu Yōgo Jiten Henshū Iinkai]. Shohan. Tōkyō : Tōkyō Bijutsu, 1990. 793 p. : ill. ISBN 4-8087-0549-4. Y1800. **BE42**
"Contains about 4,300 terms considered to be necessary in understanding Japanese art" (*Remarks*) including architecture and gardens. Definitions are bilingual, have marks to identify which of ten fields use the term, and cite locations of built works and collections by name of prefecture, giving "old names for provinces" where appropriate. Cross-references and three indexes: Japanese vocabulary by number of strokes; Romanized Japanese vocabulary entries in alphabetical order; English vocabulary entries in alphabetical order. Useful in conjunction with Ki-chien Wang's *Seals of Chinese painters and collectors of the Ming and Ching periods*, rev. ed. with suppl. ([Hong Kong] : Hong Kong Univ. Pr., 1966). N7350.W23

Terms

See also BE130, BE158.

Atkins, Robert. Artspeak : a guide to contemporary ideas, movements, and buzzwords. N.Y. : Abbeville Pr., c1990. 176 p. : ill. (some col.). ISBN 1-55859-127-3. $24.95. ISBN 1-55859-010-2 (pbk.). **BE43**
Follows a modified dictionary format. Despite its subtitle, includes Dada, Expressionism, and Surrealism as well as terms for the period since 1945 that range in currency to Neo-Geo. The main section of 100 entries is preceded by a timeline section ("Artchart" and 23 pages of chronology and illustrations in color) and followed by an index of personal and corporate names, works of art, and concepts, supported by numerous cross-references. Helpful because of its currency and provision of artists' names (the entry for performance art lists 40, of various nationalities). Should be used in conjunction with John A. Walker's *Glossary of art, architecture and design since 1945* (*Guide* BE119). N6490.A87

Thesauruses

Art & architecture thesaurus / Toni Petersen, director. N.Y. : Oxford Univ. Pr. : Published on behalf of the J. Paul Getty Trust, c1990. v. 1–3. ISBN 0-19-506403-8 (set). $250.00. (In progress). **BE44**
A structured set of some 47,000 terms, arranged in three categories: The built environment; Furnishings and equipment; Visual and verbal communication. This edition includes 23 of a projected 40 hierarchies that display terms within context, and the alphabetical list of terms, with synonyms, variants, and some scope notes. Additional sections are expected in 1993. In v.1, prefatory matter provides a history of the *AAT*, guide to use, list of projected hierarchies, application protocol and indexer's guide, field guide to coding for use with USMARC, and a 75-page bibliography.
Also available in machine-readable form: Z695.1.A7A76

●**Art and architecture thesaurus** [computer file]. N.Y. : Oxford Univ. Pr. : Published on behalf of the Getty Art History Information Program, 1990. **BE45**
Coverage: 1983– (online). Available online (RLIN; updated quarterly) and on computer diskettes (publisher).

Quotations

See also BE86.

La Cour, Donna Ward. Artists in quotation : a dictionary of the creative thoughts of painters, sculptors, designers, writers, educators, and others. Jefferson, N.C. : McFarland, c1989. 196 p. ISBN 0-89950-379-9. $29.95. **BE46**
For about 75 artistic and philosophical topics and subtopics, provides up to a dozen quotes, in chronological order. Intends to show that patterns of thinking are "representative of the variety of human activity" (*Pref.*), although with only 1,971 quotes, this is done on an extremely modest scale. Author index gives nationality and dates for some 350 names; subject index provides access to more specific topics. PN6084.A8L3

Directories

International

Art museums of the world / Virginia Jackson, ed. in chief. Westport, Conn. : Greenwood, 1987. 2 v. (1681 p.). ISBN 0-313-21322-4 (set). **BE47**
Consists of a few hundred signed "scholarly articles on the history and collections of the world's major museums."—*Pref.* Arrangement is by country, then by city. Separate bibliographies are included with each museum entry and there is a 25-page topical bibliography in v. 2, along with a brief glossary and name and subject indexes. N410.A78

Directory of museums in Africa = Répertoire des musées en Afrique / Unesco-ICOM Documentation Centre ; ed. by Susanne Peters ... [et al.]. London ; N.Y. : Kegan Paul International, 1990. 1 v. ISBN 0-7103-0378-5. **BE48**
The 503 entries are arranged by country, place, and museum name, and include some illustrations. Indexes: museum name, place, subject (archaeology, contemporary art, ethnography, folk art, geology, history, military history, oceanography, prehistory, transportation, zoology). All entries were checked,

updated, and supplemented with results from a questionnaire. Entries not validated are indicated by an asterisk.   AM80.D57

Hudson, Kenneth. The Cambridge guide to the museums of Britain and Ireland / Kenneth Hudson and Ann Nicholls. Rev. pbk. ed. Cambridge [England] ; N.Y. : Cambridge Univ. Pr., 1989. 452 p., [16] p. of plates : ill., maps (some col.). ISBN 0-521-37892-3.   **BE49**

First published in 1987. Describes nearly 2,000 museums and historic house museums, in a geographical arrangement, giving information on hours, admission fees, handicapped access, tours, public transportation, and refreshments. Unfortunately, "Museums new to this edition" is a separate section rather than being integrated into the main listing. Several regional outline maps show locations of museums. Includes indexes by museum names, subjects, and museums associated with individuals. Broader in scope than Joan Abse's *The art galleries of Britain and Ireland* (*Guide* BE120), which should be consulted for descriptions of major works held by any art museum.   AM41.H79

———————— The directory of museums & living displays / Kenneth Hudson and Ann Nicholls. 3rd ed. N.Y. : Stockton Pr., 1985. 1047 p. ISBN 0-943818-17-6. $150.00.   **BE50**

Rev. ed. of *The directory of world museums*, 1st ed., 1975 (N.Y. : Columbia Univ. Pr.); 2nd ed., 1981 (N.Y. : Facts on File).

The 3rd ed. is justified by the statement that "The number of museums across the world increases by approximately ten per cent every five years . . . ."—*p.[viii]*. Includes nearly 35,000 entries, incorporating zoos, aquaria, botanical gardens, and living history farms, because they are accepted as members of the International Council of Museums. Arrangement is alphabetical within country and the vernacular form of each museum name is supplied after the name in English. Introductory information covers scope and plan of the work, a note on languages and addresses, museums in the context of population and national income, glossary of terms used. Lacks an index.

AM1.H78 1985

Répertoire des dossiers documentaires traitant de l'art et de l'architecture dans les régions représentées á la section ARLIS M/O/Q = Directory of vertical file collections on art and architecture represented by ARLIS M/O/Q. Montreal : ARLIS, 1989. 77 p. ISBN 2-969351-50-X.   **BE51**

A small directory, compiled from responses to a questionnaire (138 of 310 were returned, of which 77 were used) that lists: art galleries; museum, academic, government, corporate, and public libraries; societies; and historic sites. Entries include address, hours, name of contact person, services offered, document types collected, and subject headings used in the vertical file collection. Partially bilingual: the preface, introduction, and subject index are in French and English, while the name index and main list (which has sections for Montreal, Ottawa, and Quebec) " . . . follow the language of response used by the institution."—*Introd.*   Z5961.C35R463

United States

ARTnews international directory of corporate art collections. Largo, Fla. : Publ. by ARTnews & International Art Alliance, c1988– .   **BE52**

The 1990–91 edition (518 p.) lists 833 American and 337 Canadian and overseas corporate collections, in alphabetical order by company name. Entries were compiled from information received from the companies, and have informative explanatory notes covering 17 categories (such as loan policy and governing authority), and including bibliographic references when available. The collections hold paintings, works on paper, prints, photographs, and sculpture. Includes basic information

on the Association of Corporate Art Curators (ACAC) and the National Association for Corporate Art Management (NACAM). Appendixes: Group exhibitions of corporate art collections; Collections which have been transferred or dispersed; Other corporate supported art programs. Indexes: state and country; corporate business; status; media and type of collection; personnel.

Funding for museums, archives, and special collections / ed. by Denise Wallen and Karen Cantrell. Phoenix : Oryx, 1988. 355 p. ISBN 0-89774-347-4.   **BE53**

" . . . designed to facilitate the search for financial support for museums and museum activities and programs" (*Introd.*), museums being defined as nonprofit institutions whose purpose is educational or aesthetic. Lists more than 500 "sources of support, arranged alphabetically by sponsor, including foundations, corporations, government agencies, associations and organizations, and professional societies." For each program gives location, program description, eligibility or limitations, fiscal information, application information, deadlines. Indexes of subject, geographic restrictions, and sponsor type; list of sponsoring organizations; bibliography (current through 1987–88) that includes a two-page section, "Grant funding: online databases."   AM122.F86

Green, Laura R. Money for artists : a guide to grants and awards for individual artists. N.Y. : ACA Books, c1987. 241 p. ISBN 0-915400-58-8. $16.95. ISBN 0-915400-59-6 (pbk.). $9.95.   **BE54**

A joint project of the American Council for the Arts and the Center for Arts Information.

"Profiles organizations, government agencies and foundations which provide financial support" (*How to use this guide*) only to artists. Includes sections for: Literary arts; Media arts; Multidisciplinary arts; Performing arts; Visual arts. Many of the entries are for arts councils. Concludes with information on the Center for Arts Information, a "clearinghouse and research library founded in 1976." Indexes: Awards; Organizations; Organizations by state; Organizations by discipline.   NX398.G75

Katlan, Alexander W. American artists' materials suppliers directory : nineteenth century : New York 1810–1899, Boston 1823–1887. Park Ridge, N.J. : Noyes Pr., c1987. 460 p. : ill., facsims. ISBN 0-8155-5064-2. $64.00.   **BE55**

Intended for use as a first step in the authentication process. In seven parts: (1) Historical background; (2) Artist colormen and supply firms (3,700 in New York, compiled from city directories); (3) Museum reference list; (4) Reference list by artist (615 paintings by 300 artists, citing information observed on those works); (5) Bibliography (seven pages); (6) Illustrations (photographs of stencil-marks and labels on canvases and frames); (7) Checklist of Boston retailers in artist's materials (by Norman E. Muller; first published in 1977 in a journal). Pt. 2, the main section, is an alphabetical listing by firm name, giving location and years of operation.   HD9791.U52K37

Money to work : grants for visual artists. Wash. : Art Resources International, 1988. 107 p. ISBN 0-929665-00-7. $8.00.   **BE56**

The "culmination of an extensive research project conducted by the Center for Arts Information (CAI)" (*About the book*) to analyze data from a regional perspective. Identifies 340 organizations as potential sources, based on questionnaires and telephone interviews. Contents: Introduction ("An assessment of visual artists' fellowships"); Profiles of organizations (national, regional, state, and local); Bibliography and resource organizations. Indexes: Geographical eligibility; Media; National grants; Grants available by nomination; Financial need; Emergency grants index; Acronyms of organizations; Common names of awards.   N347.M6

Shipley, Lloyd W. Information resources in the arts : a directory / comp. by Lloyd W. Shipley (National Referral Center). Wash. : Library of Congress : For sale by the

Supt. of Docs., U.S. Govt. Print. Off. 1986. 161 p. ISBN 0-84440-512-4.   **BE57**

Superintendent of Documents classification: LC 1.2:In3.

Intended to "enable its user to identify easily . . . organizations by most common areas of interest and to compare and contrast groups . . . "—*Introd.* Lists federal, state, and local government agencies; national and regional arts service organizations; arts education programs; dance organizations; theater organizations; music organizations; film organizations; television, video, radio, broadcasting, and cable organizations; international arts organizations; and others. Entries include address and phone number, areas of interest, statement about holdings, information on publications and information services, and contact name. Three indexes: geographic, organizations, subjects. Produced by the National Referral Center of the Library of Congress. The printed version is a "preliminary and experimental edition" (*Pref.*), with a new edition intended.

NX110.S48

Sales

Annuaire des cotes international = International art price annual. 1988– . Paris : ADEC-Production, 1987– . Annual. $160.00.   **BE58**

Assembles an impressive volume of sales information (approximately 116,200 works in the third volume—*ADEC 90*, 1989) for paintings, prints, sculpture, and photographs sold in galleries throughout Europe and some in America. The main section is a 2,112-page alphabetical listing by artists, compiled from information provided by the auction houses. Includes for each work the title (in the artist's language), medium, sale price (in francs, pounds, and dollars), dimensions, date of sale, gallery and lot number. Lacks prefatory material; concludes with "Index of artists mentioned recently in catalogues of public sales and exhibitions and professional catalogues."

Edwards, Gary. International guide to nineteenth-century photographers and their works : based on catalogues of auction houses and dealers. Boston : G.K. Hall, c1988. 591 p. ISBN 0-8161-8938-2.   **BE59**

For annotation, see *Supplement* BF63.   TR15.E48

Index of art sales catalogs, 1981–1985 : a union list from the SCIPIO database. Boston : G.K. Hall, c1987. 2 v. (1253 p.). ISBN 0-8161-0463-8.   **BE60**

Contents: v. 1, Main index (5 Jan. 1981–6 Oct. 1984); v. 2, Main index (7 Oct. 1984–23 Dec. 1985), Subject index.

Derived from the *SCIPIO* database (below), this publication intends to be "the first published union list of art auction catalogs since Harold Lancour's work of 1944 [*American art auction catalogs, 1785–1942*; *Guide* BE143]."—*Pref.* Records for each sale provide: date, city, auction house; type of material; indication of illustrations in catalog; annotation, such as subtitle; sellers' names; library locations. The subject index employs 40 broad terms subdivided by chronology, but lacks access by collectors' names.   Z5956.A66I54

The index of paintings sold in the British Isles during the nineteenth century / ed. by Burton B. Fredericksen ; assisted by Julia I. Armstrong and Doris A. Mendenhall. Santa Barbara, Calif. : ABC-Clio, c1988–1990. v. 1–2. ISBN 0-87436-5244 (v.1). $90.00. (In progress).   **BE61**

Contents: v. 1, 1801–1805; v. 2, pt. 1, 1806–1810, A–N; v. 2, pt. 2, 1806–1810, O–Z and Anonymous.

A monumental index to catalogs of sales of paintings, produced by the Provenance Index of the Getty Art History Information Program, based on its growing computerized database. Each volume covers a five-year period and is in three sections: a chronological index of sales, an alphabetic index of paintings (under the name of the painter, subdivided by sale date and giving specifics of each painting), and an alphabetic index of owners. Catalog citations note known sellers' and buyers' names

and prices, and offer comments on the sale and on annotated copies of the catalog. Incorporates nearly 30% more catalogs than Frits Lugt's *Répertoire des catalogues des ventes publiques* (*Guide* BE144) and goes beyond Algernon Graves's *Art sales from early in the eighteenth century to early in the twentieth century* (3 v., 1918–21; repr. 1970). 20 volumes are projected.

ND47.I5

Leonard's annual price index of art auctions / Auction Index, Inc. West Newton, Mass. : Auction Index, c1982– . ISSN 0747-6566. $195.00.   **BE62**

The 1991 volume covers the 1989–90 auction season and has an introduction summarizing market activity during that year as well as a three-page bibliography. Aims to be "a complete listing of original works of art sold at the major auction houses in the United States."—*Explanatory notes.* Lists roughly 36,000 artworks in the main section under artist's name, giving nationality and dates, title of work, price, indication of signature, medium, dimensions, date and place of sale. Covers painting, sculpture, drawing, and mixed media (but excludes photography and graphic arts) from sales at 36 auction houses, named in a list that cites the date and title of each sale. Recommended over the smaller *Jacobsen's . . . painting and bronze price guide* (Staten Island, N.Y. : A. Jacobsen, 1975–), which covers catalogs from 24 auction galleries in the eastern U.S.

N8602.L46

●**SCIPIO** : Sales Catalog Index Project Input On-line [computer file]. Mountain View, Calif. : Research Libraries Group, Art and Architecture Program, 1980– .   **BE63**

File size: more than 100,000 records, updated several times weekly. Available online (RLIN).

A union list of sales catalogs, 1599 to the present, from nearly 3,000 auction houses. Founded by the Art Institute of Chicago, the Cleveland Museum of Art, and the Metropolitan Museum of Art (N.Y.), later joined by the Getty Center for the History of Art and the Humanities (Santa Monica, Calif.) and the National Gallery of Art (Wash.). Access points include name of auction house, place of sale, date of sale, a coded name or number for the sale, catalog title, collector's name. The years 1981–85 are also available in book form (*Supplement* BE60).

Le semestriel des arts. 1989– . Paris : Van Wilder, [1989]– . Semiannual.   **BE64**

Compiled by C. Ritzenthaler and F. Van Wilder.

Bilingual prefatory matter includes a list of sales by date, list of price commissioners in Paris and regions of France, tables for dimension measurements, a one-page glossary of 15 terms in five languages, tables for exchange rates, a list of professional experts' names, and tax information by country. Artist entries give name and dates, title of each work in the vernacular, whether signed, medium (including photography), dimensions, sale date, place and firm, and price in dollars and francs. Auction houses represented are in Europe and New York (one in Montreal), but France is most heavily represented. In the first four volumes, dates on the spine do not correspond exactly to months included. Similar to *Annuaire des cotes international* (above).

World collectors annuary. v. 1 (1946/49)– . Delft : Brouwer [etc.]. ISSN 0084-1498.   **BE65**

For earlier volumes and annotation, see *Guide* BE146.

Vol. 39 (1988–89), ed. by Hadewych E. van der Lande, lists 37 auction houses and, according to the introduction, is a "selection," a point worth noting in comparison with two new titles—*Annuaire des cotes international* and *Le semestriel des arts* (both above). Includes a provenance index.   ND47.W6

Exhibitions

The annual exhibition record of the Pennsylvania Academy of the Fine Arts / ed. by Peter Hastings Falk. Madison, Conn. : Sound View Pr., 1988–1989. 3 v. : ill. ISBN 0-932087-03-5 (v. 1). $89.00. **BE66**

Contents: v. 1, 1807–1870 (24,000 entries); v. 2, 1876–1913 (21,700 entries); v. 3, 1914–1968 (21,860 entries).

Vol. 1: Reprint with revisions of the 1955 edition of Anna Wells Rutledge's *Cummulative* [sic] *record of exhibition catalogues.*

Based on a computerized database. Vol. 2–3 contain: Analytic chart of the annual exhibitions; Medals and prizes awarded; and indexes of: juries by year, jurors, artists (giving birth and death dates, address for each year, titles of works, and prices when known), and places and last names. There are no subject indexes. A review in *Art documentation* (Spring 1990): 36–37, outlines the shortcomings of this work. N6505.A64

Yarnall, James L. The National Museum of American Art's index to American art exhibition catalogues : from the beginning through the 1876 centennial year / comp. by James L. Yarnall and William H. Gerdts. Boston : G.K. Hall, 1986. 6 v. (4944 p.). ISBN 0-8161-0440-9 (set). **BE67**

Took its impetus from a Bicentennial project, the Inventory of American Paintings Executed Before 1914. Intends "not merely to index the publications of specific institutions, but also to provide insight into what artworks Americans in all parts of the country exhibited and viewed ... includes the exhibition name, location, and date; the names of the artists exhibited, with their addresses if known; the titles of the works; the owners of the works, with addresses; narrative excerpts of catalogue commentary ... and subjects of the works."—*Foreword.* Includes works by artists of all nationalities and schools listed in 952 catalogs. Of 118,012 works listed, 843 are American and 16 Canadian. Excludes auction sales catalogs, but photocopies of these are available at NMAA, "including a large number that do not appear in the standard bibliography of auctions [Harold Lancour's *American art auctions, 1785–1942*; *Guide* BE143]."—*User's guide.* The subject index in v. 6 includes names of individuals, places, and iconographic objects.

§ See also Raymond L. Wilson's *Index of American print exhibitions, 1882–1940* (Supplement BE156) and indexes specific to the Pennsylvania Academy of the Fine Arts (above).
N6507.Y363

Handbooks

Evans, Hilary. Picture researcher's handbook : an international guide to picture sources—and how to use them. 4th ed. / comp.by Hilary and Mary Evans. London : Van Nostrand Reinhold (International), 1989. [480] p. : ill. ISBN 0-7476-0038-4. £24.95. **BE68**

2nd ed., 1979 (*Guide* BE149a); 3rd ed., 1986 (401 p.).

Similar in format to the 1979 ed., but coverage is expanded to 1,066 sources. In four divisions: General; Regional; National; Specialist (including topics such as art, entertainment, natural history, religion, and an interesting "Various"). Endpapers provide handy French, German, Italian, and Spanish translations of "How to use this book." For a directory of picture sources in Britain, see *Picture sources UK* (below). N4000

Mayer, Ralph. The artist's handbook of materials and techniques. 5th ed., rev. and updated / by Steven Sheehan. N.Y. : Viking, 1991. 761 p. : ill. ISBN 0-670-83701-6. $30.00. **BE69**

1982 ed. (*Guide* BE324); 4th ed., 1985.

This edition includes new information, such as changes concerning pigments, and excludes that which is no longer relevant. The preface notes the rapid rate of change in artists' materials in recent years. ND1500.M3

Picture sources UK / ed., Rosemary Eakins ; assoc. ed., Elizabeth Loving. London : Macdonald, 1985. 474 p. ISBN 0-356-10078-2. £45.00. **BE70**

The main section of this directory is a listing of 1,141 collections grouped by general subject and location, then by some 20 subject categories. Indicates size and scope of each collection, the range of dates of photographs, subject matter, access, and conditions information. Includes two essays with a practical purpose: Pictures and the law, about copyright, and An introduction to picture research. Indexes: collections and subcollections, by name; subjects. TR12.P54

History

Gardner, Helen. Gardner's art through the ages / [ed. by] Horst de la Croix, Richard G. Tansey, Diane Kirkpatrick. 9th ed. San Diego, Calif. : Harcourt Brace Jovanovich, c1991. 1135 p. : ill. (some col.). ISBN 0-15-503769-2. **BE71**

7th ed., 1980 (*Guide* BE151); 8th ed., 1986.

This edition has expanded text and images, where warranted by subject matter. Various teaching aids are available in conjunction with this edition. N5300.G25

Janson, H. W. History of art / rev. and expanded by Anthony F. Janson. 4th ed. Englewood Cliffs, N.J. : Prentice Hall ; N.Y. : H.N. Abrams, 1991. 856 p. : ill. (some col.), maps. ISBN 0-13-388463-5 (Prentice-Hall). **BE72**

2nd ed., 1977 (*Guide* BE154); 3rd ed., 1986.

Changes in the 3rd ed. included the addition of two sections and one entire chapter on the history of photography. The 4th ed. "preserves most of the text of the previous one" (*Pref.*), has three times as many color illustrations, plus new diagrams and architectural drawings. Pt. 4 (The modern world) has been reorganized, with a separate chapter on sculpture since 1900.

§ A similar survey also has appeared in a new edition, Frederick Hartt's *Art : a history of painting, sculpture, architecture* (3rd ed. N.Y. : Prentice Hall & Abrams, 1989). N5300.J3

Pelican history of art / ed. by Nikolaus Pevsner. [N.Y.] : Penguin, 1986–87. 2 v. : ill. (In progress). **BE73**

For v. 1–44 and annotation, see *Guide* BE156.

Two titles, both unnumbered, have been added to this series: *The art and architecture of the Indian subcontinent,* by J.C. Harle (1986), and *The art and architecture of Islam : 650–1250,* by Richard Ettinghausen and Oleg Grabar (1987). Several earlier titles have been revised; more titles are planned.

Biography

Allgemeines Künstlerlexikon : die bildenden Künstler aller Zeiten und Völker / erarbeitet, redigiert und hrsg. von Günter Meissner und einem Redaktionskollektiv unter internationaler Mitwirkung. Leipzig : E.A. Seemann, 1983–1986. v. 1–3. ISBN 3-363-00113-4 (set). (In progress). **BE74**

Contents: v. 1–3, Aa–Ardon.

Known as *AKL* and likely to equal Thieme-Becker and Vollmer (*Guide* BE177–178) in thoroughness and quality and to be more than triple their size. Includes painters, graphic artists, sculptors, architects, and decorative artists of all nationalities; excludes photographers. The editorial board for the initial volumes comprises 15 German scholars, and entries are written by a large international group of scholars listed in the front of each volume. Entries provide biographical data and "creative characteristics" (for persons born up to ca.1940); locations of the artist's works; references to writings by the artist; a listing of exhibitions (solo and group); and a bibliography (in v. 3, current through the late 1980s). Each volume averages 950–1,000 pages and provides a list of abbreviations and bibliography. The "How to use this book" information in v. 1 is given in six languages. For a review, see *Art libraries journal* (Spring 1985): 52–54.   N40.A63

Artist biographies master index / Barbara McNeil, ed. Detroit : Gale, c1986. 700 p. (Gale biographical index series, no. 9). ISBN 0-8103-2107-6. $85.00.   **BE75**

A listing of sources for more than 275,000 biographical sketches from about 70 English-language reference books. Covers all nationalities and periods. Lists any name or date exactly as found in the source, with no attempt to reconcile variants. "This index is derived from material that has appeared or will appear in the more comprehensive *Biography and genealogy master index*" (*Introd.*); see *Guide* AJ8. Useful as a starting point or to clarify distinctions between artists' names.

N40.A78

Besemer, Susan P. From museums, galleries, and studios : a guide to artists on film and tape / comp. by Susan P. Besemer and Christopher Crosman. Westport, Conn. : Greenwood, c1984. 199 p. (Art reference collection, no. 6). ISBN 0-313-23881-2.   **BE76**

A listing of over "600 films, videocassettes, and audiocassettes, which document the work of contemporary artists... [limited] to productions in which artists are heard or seen with their work."—*Pref.* In four sections: Individual artists; Multiple artists; Directory of sources for renting or buying [distributors]; Index to persons, museums, galleries, works of art, media, and professions. Entries are based on replies from producers and distributors; and annotations reflect these responses, with some elaborated upon or edited. They contain a "mediagraphic citation followed by a narrative annotation." Excludes listings from the Archives of American Art Oral History Program (*Guide* BE90); may be useful in conjunction with Jack Robertson's *Twentieth-century artists on art* (below).

N368.B47

Biographies of Inuit artists. 3rd ed. [Mississauga, Ont.] : Published by Tuttavik for Arctic Cooperatives, Fédération des coopératives du Nouveau-Québec, Indian and Northern Affairs Canada, 1988. 4 v. ISBN 0-920234-83-6. $100.00.   **BE77**

"... an ongoing project, which since it was first published in 1981, has been revised twice with supplements, in 1982 and 1984. Over 300 biographies have been added since the 1984 edition, bringing the total number... to approximately 1,100."—*Introd.* Biographies are prepared in part in response to suggestions to, or requests for information from, the compilers. Each artist's entry is on a separate looseleaf page and gives birth date, sex, residence, media, and, when applicable, a list of exhibitions, honors, collections, and selected references, as well as the signature. The 3rd ed. includes a new index, sorted by alternate name (married name for female Inuits).   N6548.B58

Contemporary artists / ed., Colin Naylor. 3rd ed. Chicago : St. James Pr., c1989. 1059 p. : ill. ISBN 0-912289-96-1.   **BE78**

2nd ed., 1983 (*Guide* BE164).

This edition treats about 1,000 artists living or deceased after 1960.   N6490.C6567

Dunford, Penny. Biographical dictionary of women artists in Europe and America since 1850. Philadelphia : Univ. of Pennsylvania Pr., c1990. 1 v. ISBN 0-8122-8230-2.   **BE79**

For each of approximately 1,700 artists, provides a paragraph summarizing accomplishments, followed by a short list of collections holding the artist's work and brief citations to mon-

ographs. Includes some illustrations and a six-page bibliography (current through 1989), citing monographs, exhibition catalogs, and journal titles. This well-designed volume is best used in conjunction with other works, such as Chris Petteys's *Dictionary of women artists* (*Guide* BE175), Paula L. Chiarmonte's *Women artists in the United States* (*Supplement* BE91), and Virginia Watson-Jones's *Contemporary American women sculptors* (*Supplement* BE167).   N6757.D86

Hesse, Gritta. Künstler der jungen Generation : Literaturverzeichnis zur Gegenwartskunst in der Amerika-Gedenkbibliothek, Berliner Zentralbibliothek = Artists of the "young generation" : literature on contemporary art in the American Memorial Library, Berlin Central Library / [compilers, Gritta Hesse and Marie Agnes Bingel]. München ; N.Y. : Saur, 1987. 353 p. ISBN 3-598-10693-9.   **BE80**

Emphasizes European artists, largely because the publications held by the library are primarily from German-speaking countries. For most artists, birth date and city of residence are provided; most were born in the 1930s and 1940s. Contains 17,000 entries on some 6,500 artists, including illustrators and photographers; entries give bibliographic data but no annotations. For a comparison of Hesse's work with *Artist biographies master index* (above) and other reference works, see *Art documentation* (Fall 1989): 150–151.   Z5935.5.H47

International dictionary of art and artists / ed.: James Vinson. Chicago : St. James Pr., 1990. 2 v. : ill., ports. ISBN 1-55862-001-X (v.1). £75.00. ISBN 1-55862-000-1 (v.2). £75.00.   **BE81**

The title of this work overstates its scope; it covers only European and American art from the 13th through 20th centuries. Furthermore, some artists are represented in both volumes. The Artists volume is alphabetical and presents information in four parts: "essential facts in the artist's career"; the "most important public and private collections of his work"; a bibliography; and a critical essay of "up to 2000 words which discusses historical and critical aspects of his art."—*Foreword.* The Art volume is chronological, presents 500 individual works of art (with black-and-white illustrations), and "functions as an extended catalogue of the ideal art gallery."   N31.I58

McDonald, Jan. Australian artists' index : a biographical index of Australian artists, craft workers, photographers, and architects. Sydney : Arts Libraries Society / Australia and New Zealand, 1986. 432 p. (ARLIS/ANZ publication, no. 1). ISBN 0-947101-00-4 (pbk.).   **BE82**

For more than 10,000 names, cites references from 416 standard sources for Australian art, including exhibition catalogs and the two most essential reference works, Alan McCulloch's *Encyclopedia of Australian art* (*Guide* BE100) and Max Germaine's *Artists and galleries of Australia* (*Guide* BE124). Supplements are expected at three-year intervals.

N7404.M33

McLeish, Kenneth. The Penguin companion to the arts in the twentieth century. Middlesex, England ; N.Y. : Viking, 1985. 604 p. ISBN 0-670-80127-5. $25.00.   **BE83**

Covers architecture, fiction and poetry, film, music, painting and sculpture, and theater. The introductions to these sections highlight key dates and events; in architecture, for example, function and form, the Chicago Plan, the International Style, and individualism. The author "tried, throughout, to write from the point of view of someone experiencing the [art]... for the first time.... In the end this is a personal book reflecting personal delight."—*Pref.* Entries, arranged alphabetically by artist's name within sections, emphasize creative accomplishments and conclude with a bibliography incorporating brief critical comments. The 16-page "glossary" covers a modest 30 movements in the arts, while the index is quite useful since it includes not only artists and concepts but also individual works by title.   NX456.M4

New York Public Library. The artists file [microform]. Alexandria, Va. : Chadwyck-Healey Inc., [1989]. 11,381 microfiches : ill. $20,000.00. **BE84**

On header: New York Public Library. Artists file.

Original file compiled by and located in the New York Public Library. Largely a clipping file of 1.5 million items on some 76,000 painters, sculptors and architects taken from 19th- and 20th-century material.

An expensive resource that was thoroughly assessed by reviewers in *Art documentation* (Fall 1989): 149–150. The file was begun in 1911. The fiche set includes a printed guide with an index of artists cited. Includes jewellers, furniture and interior designers, handicraft and commercial artists; excludes printmakers, photographers, medalists, and city planners. Material for architect Frank Lloyd Wright ranges from a 1959 article from the *New York times* to a brochure from a Milwaukee church by Wright.

§ A second recent microfiche resource is *The Museum of Modern Art artists scrapbooks microform* (Alexandria, Va. : Chadwyck-Healey, 1986), consisting of 642 fiches in four loose-leaf volumes, limited to 44 artists.

Ogilvie, Grania. The dictionary of South African painters and sculptors, including Namibia / Grania Ogilvie, assisted by Carol Graff. Rosebank, Johannesburg, South Africa : Everard Read, 1988. 799 p., [84] p. of plates : ill. (some col.). ISBN 0-620-12663-9. **BE85**

Lists 1,800 artists from South Africa and Namibia who met these criteria: held a solo exhibition; participated in a major group exhibition; are represented in a public collection or public display; won awards or prizes; or "are an integral part of the South African or Namibian artistic heritage."—*Pref.* For each, gives vital dates, media, education, profile of achievements, exhibitions, awards and honors, publications (books), and bibliographic references. Includes a representative selection of quality color reproductions and a substantial bibliography. The 10-page "Useful addresses" section lists galleries, museums, libraries, associations, art schools, and art centers. Comparable to Esmé Berman's *Art & artists of South Africa* (*Guide* BE161). N7395.6.O35

Robertson, Jack. Twentieth-century artists on art : an index to artists' writings, statements, and interviews. Boston : G.K. Hall, c1985. 488 p. ISBN 0-8161-8714-2. **BE86**

According to the compiler, two distinct types of primary documents are used in art historical research—works of art and the artists' own words; hence, this index covers "495 published sources . . . not otherwise analyzed by individual artist's name."—*Pref.* Entries for some 5,000 artists give dates, nationality, and medium; some figures more prominent in the 19th century are listed to permit inclusion of statements they made in the 20th. 75% of the 14,000 bibliographic citations are in English, the remainder in five Western European languages. They are drawn from anthologies, monographs, group exhibition catalogs, and periodicals, and cite not only statements and interviews but also poems, stories, and group discussions. A bibliography preceding the index gives full descriptions, including OCLC and LC control numbers, for the sources from which the index citations are taken. NX456.R59

Seymour, Nancy N. An index-dictionary of Chinese artists, collectors, and connoisseurs with character identification by modified stroke count. Metuchen, N.J. : Scarecrow, 1988. 987 p. ISBN 0-8108-2091-9. **BE87**

Pt. 1, the Master dictionary, "is intended to be a sourcebook for the researcher to use initially for artist information and identification."—*Introd.* The 5,000 name entries provide both Wade-Giles and Pinyin romanization, dynasty or period, alternate names or signatures, places and dates for biography, a note of characteristic work and subject matter, strokes in surname, bibliographic sources, and full Chinese characters for the name. Pt. 2 "presents a simple methodology for Western scholars to learn to read Chinese characters in order to identify

names." Its sections include: Index of modified stroke count; Index of alternate names; Chronology of Chinese dynasties; Pinyin and Wade-Giles romanizations; Selected bibliography; Character index of Chinese names. N7348.S48

Verzeichnis der bildenden Künstler von 1880 bis heute : ein biographisch-bibliographisches Nachschlagewerk zur Kunst der Gegenwart / [hrsg. und bearb. von] Roger M. Gorenflo. Darmstadt : Brün, 1988. 3 v. (989 p.). ISBN 3-926759-00-3 (set). DM146.00. **BE88**

Similar to *Artist biographies master index* (above), but cites a broader range of sources. Gives date, nationality, medium, and references for nearly 35,000 artists working in the past 100 years. The 600 sources (many of them dating from the mid-1980s) include monographs, biographical dictionaries, who's whos, exhibition catalogs, and a few journals, in all Western languages. N6447.V43

Weinberg, Robert E. A biographical dictionary of science fiction and fantasy artists. N.Y. : Greenwood, 1988. 346 p. ISBN 0-313-24349-2. **BE89**

More than 250 biographies of artists (chiefly American) constitute the main section of this dictionary. Entries include a list of publications in which the artist's work has appeared, citing magazines through the early 1980s, and differentiating between hardcover and softcover publications. The more than 100 magazines cited are all English-language publications. Begins with a historical overview of science fiction illustration and ends with a list of fantasy illustration award winners, a bibliography, and an index of personal names, magazine titles and films, publishers, and related topics. NC961.6.W45

World artists 1980–1990 : a volume in the Wilson biographical series / ed., Claude Marks. N.Y. : H.W. Wilson, 1991. 1 v. ISBN 0-8242-0827-7. **BE90**

A successor to the editor's *World artists, 1950–1980* (*Guide* BE172). Includes 120 new artists. N6489.W67

United States

Chiarmonte, Paula L. Women artists in the United States : a selective bibliography and resource guide on the fine and decorative arts, 1750–1986. Boston : G.K. Hall, 1990. 997 p. ISBN 0-8161-8917-X. **BE91**

More substantial than most recent publications on women artists, this work aims "to foster a more critical analysis of the position of women artists in cultural history by examining the modes of production in which they have excelled."—*Pref.* The 16 contributors were chosen "on the basis of their professional expertise and access to special collections representing their media." In two parts: (1) Critics; Organizations; Manuscript repositories and special collections; (2) [Literature]: Biographical reference tools; Documents on women's art (by type or medium) and on women artists. The documents section consists of about 3,900 annotated bibliographic and archival references, constituting two-thirds of the publication. Sections include introductory essays by the contributors. Indexes are by author/title and artist; both are further subdivided by folk art and minority art (African American, Latina, Native American, and Asian American categories). The only geographical access in Pt. 1 is by state. Z7963.A75W65

Cummings, Paul. Dictionary of contemporary American artists. 5th ed. N.Y. : St. Martin's, c1988. 738 p. : ill. ISBN 0-312-00232-7 (pbk.). **BE92**

4th ed., 1982 (*Guide* BE181).

This edition, current through May 1987 (June 1987 for obituaries), contains extensive revisions: 127 artists have been deleted and 87 added, and most entries updated. Recommended strongly over *Encyclopedia of living artists in America . . .* (2nd ed., Renaissance, Calif. : Directors Guild, 1977), a com-

mercial listing of some 330 artists who recommended themselves for inclusion.   N6512.C854

Falk, Peter H. Who was who in American art. Madison,
Conn. : Sound View Pr., 1985. 707 p. : ill. ISBN 0-
932087-00-0. $115.00.   **BE93**
   Compiled by checking more than 120,000 entries in the
American art annual (*Guide* BE134) and adding "many facts
and dates ... to make this book more useful."—
Acknowledgements. The resulting 25,000 entries present con-
cise information about education, exhibitions, associations, etc.
Well-designed and readable.   N6512.F26

Fielding, Mantle. Mantle Fielding's dictionary of American painters, sculptors & engravers / ed. by Glenn B.
Opitz. 2nd newly-rev., enl., and updated ed. Poughkeep-
sie, N.Y. : Apollo, c1986. 1081 p. ISBN 0-938290-04-5.
$85.00.   **BE94**
   1st ed., 1983 (*Guide* BE183).
   This edition adds almost 2,500 artists' names, for a total of
more than 12,000, updates about 60% of the existing entries,
and makes corrections as necessary. An eight-page bibliography emphasizes mid-19th through early 20th-century publications.   N6536.F5

Tufts, Eleanor. American women artists, past and
present : a selected bibliographic guide. N.Y. : Garland,
1984–89. 2 v. : ill. (Garland reference library of the humanities, vol. 504, 1123). ISBN 0-8240-9070-5 (v. 1).
                                                         BE95
   Vol. 1 treats 500 artists from the early 1700s to contemporary figures born before 1950, of whom half were alive in 1983.
Includes painters, sculptors, graphic artists, photographers, and
conceptual artists, but excludes craftswomen. Arranged alphabetically by artist's name, but lacks an author index. Entries
cite monographs and journal articles, and the introduction includes a bibliography. Vol. 2 states as its purpose " ... to add
more artists ... as well as to supplement (not replace) the first
volume by augmenting the entries of the women previously listed.... The basis for inclusion remains ... continuity and
visibility."—*Introd.* Limited to artists born before 1960. Includes more photographers and ceramic sculptors, for a total of
about 1,000 names.   Z7963.A75T84

Artists' signatures

Castagno, John. American artists : signatures and monograms, 1800–1989. Metuchen, N.J. : Scarecrow, 1990.
826 p. : ill. ISBN 0-8108-2249-0.   **BE96**
   Besides signature facsimiles for 5,100 artists, gives dates,
nationality (Canadians and Latin Americans are included), and
abbreviations for 70 sources used in compilation (e.g., standard
reference works, monographs, journals, collectors, galleries).
                                                         N45.C37

———————— Artists as illustrators : an international
directory with signatures and monograms, 1800–the
present. Metuchen, N.J. : Scarecrow, 1989. 625 p. ISBN
0-8108-2168-0.   **BE97**
   Although the author claims this "is the first definitive book
encompassing the international world of illustration of the last
two centuries" (*Foreword*), it is somewhat overshadowed by
Peter H. Falk's *Dictionary of signatures & monograms of American artists* (below) and earlier works, and overlaps substantially
Castagno's own *American artists : signatures & monograms,
1800–1989* (above). Includes 14,000 names derived from some
95 sources. Two additional volumes are promised over the next
eight years.
   § Related titles include Walter Reed and Roger Reed, *The
illustrator in America* (N.Y. : Madison Square Pr., [1984]) and
Simon Houfe, *The dictionary of British book illustrators and
caricaturists, 1800–1914* (Woodbridge, Eng. : Baron Publ.,

[1978]). Both provide illustrations as well as brief discussions of
artists' work.   NC961.63.C37

———————— European artists : signatures and monograms, 1800–1990, including selected artists from other
parts of the world. Metuchen, N.J. : Scarecrow, c1990.
895 p : ill. ISBN 0-8108-2313-6.   **BE98**
   Includes some "4800 European artists and a selection of artists from other parts of the world, such as Australia, South Africa, and Japan, who have worked from 1800 to the
present."—*Introd.* The main listing provides nationality and
birth and death dates, and cites sources from a list of about 70
reference books, galleries (chiefly Christie's and Sotheby's), and
magazines, and includes some signature facsimiles. Includes
brief sections of name cross-references, monograms by initials,
illegible signatures and symbols, Cyrillic and Greek signatures,
and Chinese and Japanese signatures.   N45.C38

Falk, Peter H. Dictionary of signatures & monograms of
American artists : from the colonial period to the mid
20th century. Madison, Conn. : Sound View Pr. ; Land
O'Lakes, Fla. : Distr. by Dealer's Choice Books, 1988.
556 p., [1] leaf of plates : ill. ISBN 0-932087-04-3.
$115.00.   **BE99**
   A "companion volume to *Who was who in American art*
[*Supplement* BE93]" (*Introd.*), providing media, dates, cross-
references, and multiple examples of signatures where pertinent. Approximately 10,000 signatures (based on photocopies
taken in galleries by the author) are arranged in three main sections: signatures and monograms, initials and monograms, and
shapes and symbols. A lengthy introduction discusses forged
signatures and the detection of forgeries. Most of the artists
were active ca.1860s–1940s.   N45.F35

Self, James. Japanese art signatures : a handbook and
practical guide / James Self and Nobuko Hirose. Rut-
land, Vt. : C.E. Tuttle Co., c1987. 399 p. : ill. ISBN 0-
8048-7021-7. $29.95.   **BE100**
   In eight parts: Introduction on the reading of signatures;
Dictionary of *kaisho* characters; Explanation and tables of key
characters; Explanation of geographical and place names, and
dates; Variant characters, facsimiles, and seals; Catalogue of
names (swordsmiths, metal workers, lacquer artists, netsuke
carvers); Bibliography; Stroke-count index of *kaisho* characters.
                                                         N7358.S45

Symbolism in art

General

Roberts, Helene E. Iconographic index to Old Testament subjects represented in photographs and slides of
paintings in the visual collections, Fine Arts Library,
Harvard University. N.Y. : Garland, 1987. 197 p., [6] p.
of plates : ill. (Garland reference library of the humanities, vol. 729). ISBN 0-8240-8345-8.   **BE101**
   In two parts: (1) Index of concepts, terms, and proper
names; (2) Iconclass classification of Old Testament themes
(based on H. van de Waal's *Iconclass : an iconographic classification system* [Amsterdam : North-Holland, 1973–]), and listing of themes and paintings representing them.
   Came into being in response to questions by users of the
Fine Arts Library slide and photograph collections, which was
organized by medium and culture (i.e., by nationality or school,
then by artist's name when available), at a time when users became increasingly interested in content and subject. The intention is to publish subsequent volumes on the New Testament,
mythology, historical scenes, allegory, literary subjects, land-

scapes, and genre subjects, and to expand indexing to other media. ND1430.R63

Christian

Schiller, Gertrud. Ikonographie der christlichen Kunst. [3., durchgesehene Aufl.]. Gütersloh : Gütersloher Verlagshaus G. Mohn, 1990–1991. v. 5, pt. 1–2 : plates. (In progress). **BE102**

For Bd. 1–4 and annotation, see *Guide* BE207.

Contents: Bd. 5¹, Die Apokalypse des Johannes: Textteil (1990. ISBN 3-579-00261-9); Bd. 5², Bildteil (1991. ISBN 3-579-00262-7). N7830.S35

Hindu

Aryan, K. C. Encyclopedia of Indian art, references, symbols, evolution of Devanagari script = Rekhā. New Delhi : Rekha Prakashan, c1989. 159 p. : chiefly ill. (some col.). ISBN 81-900003-4-9. Rs200.00. **BE103**

First publ. in 1952; 2nd ed., 1966.

A small volume (chiefly illustrations), that is less an encyclopedia than a guide; nevertheless it fills a gap in the literature on Asian symbolism. The main reason for this edition was the author's "deep and abiding love for Indian culture."—*Pref.* The topical arrangement covers lettering and calligraphy (specimens from various periods and sources, including several examples of Sanskrit lettering), emblems, coats of arms and heraldic designs, designing (motifs, patterns, and images), ornaments and decoration (toys, flags, musical instruments, jewelry, headgear, etc.). Concludes with a short bibliography. N7301.A835

Stutley, Margaret. An illustrated dictionary of Hindu iconography. London ; Boston : Routledge & Kegan Paul, 1985. 175 p. : ill. ISBN 0-7100-9294-6. $36.95. **BE104**

Includes a six-page introduction, a 19-page essay on "English subjects and Sanskrit equivalents," and a five-page bibliography. Many entries illustrated with line drawings. To be used in conjunction with the author's unillustrated *Dictionary of Hinduism* (*Guide* BB513), J.N. Banerjea's *Development of Hindu iconography* (2nd ed., rev. and enl., 1956, *Guide* BE213; 3rd ed., rev. and enl., Columbia, Mo. : South Asia Books, 1986), and T. A. Gopinātha Rāu's *Elements of Hindu iconography* (*Guide* BE214; repr., N.Y. : Garland, 1981). N8195.A4S78

Art reproductions

Cashman, Norine D. Slide buyers' guide : an international directory of slide sources for art and architecture / ed. by Norine D. Cashman ; subject index by Mark M. Braunstein. 5th ed. Littleton, Colo. : Libraries Unlimited, 1985. 241 p. ISBN 0-87287-471-0. **BE105**

1st–4th eds. ed. by Nancy DeLaurier.

1st ed., 1970; 4th ed., 1980.

This edition lists 510 sources, current through mid-1984, compiled from responses to a questionnaire sent to some 1,000 presumed vendors, of whom roughly half were in the U.S. Listings give location, a profile of offerings, type of photography and production, documentation, purchase, and an evaluation based on guidelines used since 1979. Appendixes 1 and 2 list respondents no longer selling slides and nonrespondents; Appendix 3 is a bibliography of basic art history texts for which slide sets are available, naming the vendors. A 6th ed. was published in 1990.

§ A related title is Suzy Ticho's *Directory of artists slide registries* (N.Y. : American Council for the Arts, 1980), which provides a short history of the development of registries and obser-

vations on their use, followed by the listings. Registries are defined as "public repositories for current written and visual information about contemporary artists and their work, which contains slides, resumes and addresses."—*Introd.* An appendix lists nonfunctioning registries. N4040.V57C3

Restoration and conservation

International index of conservation research = Répertoire international de la recherche en conservation / ICCROM. Wash. : Smithsonian Institution, Conservation Analytical Laboratory, 1988. 142 p. : forms. ISBN 92-9077-080-5. **BE106**

" . . . the first attempt to summarize the ongoing research that has not yet been published . . . [by creating] a directory of professionals who share a concern for the conservation of cultural heritage."—*Pref.* Intended to encourage international collaboration by listing areas of expertise. Provides forms for the submission of information for future editions and for an eventual database (presumably to be maintained by the International Centre for the Study of the Preservation and Restoration of Cultural Property in conjunction with the Conservation Analytical Laboratory at the Smithsonian Institution). Arranged in 31 categories (media), each subdivided. Lacks name indexes, but includes codes to indicate affilation with some 170 institutions. CC135.I57

Legal aspects

Crawford, Tad. Legal guide for the visual artist. Rev. ed. N.Y. : Allworth Pr. ; Cincinnati : distr. by North Light Books, 1990. 213 p. : ill. ISBN 0-927629-00-3. $18.95. **BE107**

First published in 1977 and first revised in 1986; revisions in this edition are contained in a preliminary section, "Update," p.i–x. The 24 chapters cover copyright, moral rights, contracts, sales, taxes, estates, and related topics, and provide samples of typical legal documents. Concludes with a bibliography of 34 titles published over the past two decades. Topical and name index. Similar to Crawford's *Writer's legal guide* (*Guide* AA407). KF390.A7C73

Feldman, Franklin. Art law : rights and liabilities of creators and collectors / Franklin Feldman, Stephen E. Weil ; with the collaboration of Susan Duke Biederman. Boston : Little, Brown, c1986. 2 v. ISBN 0-316-09296-7 (v. 1). ISBN 0-316-09297-5 (v. 2). **BE108**

Successor to the author's *Art works: law, policy, practice* (N.Y. : Practicing Law Institute, c1974).

More technical than Ralph Lerner's *Art law* (below). Consists of 14 chapters on topics ranging from the right of expression to art as a "collectible" asset that present the text of pertinent cases that are themselves amplified by extensive footnotes. Excludes coverage of tax rules as they relate to artists. Two indexes: table of cases, table of statutes. KF390.A7F45

Lerner, Ralph E. Art law : the guide for collectors, investors, dealers, and artists / Ralph E. Lerner, Judith Bresler. N.Y. : Practising Law Institute, 1989. 766 p. : ill., forms. ISBN 0-87224-000-2. **BE109**

Also issued in 1988 as no. 254 in the "Patents, copyrights, trademarks and literary property course handbook" series (1064 p.).

Practical and well-organized; intended for investors, collectors, dealers, artists, appraisers, and museum directors. Has sections on dealers, artwork transactions, artists' rights, collectors, and tax and estate planning. Each section includes samples of typical legal forms used for specific art transactions and numerous footnotes citing laws. The preface mentions several sources published in the 1970s and 1980s, including Tad Crawford's *Legal guide for the visual artist* (above). Indexes of authorities (i.e., legal regulations and rulings) and topics.

§ See also John H. Merryman and Albert E. Elsen's *Law, ethics, and the visual arts* (Philadelphia : Univ. of Pennsylvania Pr., c1987).   KF390.A7L473

ARCHITECTURE

Bibliography

Harris, Eileen. British architectural books and writers, 1556–1785 / Eileen Harris assisted by Nicholas Savage. Cambridge ; N.Y. : Cambridge Univ. Pr., 1990. 571 p. : ill. ISBN 0-521-38551-2.   **BE110**
Taking Howard M. Colvin's *Biographical dictionary of British architects* (*Guide* BE294) as a model, the compiler treats "authors' books as [Colvin] did architects' buildings. Thus bibliographical descriptions of the works are preceded by an essay, which examines the author's publishing activities as a whole without necessarily discussing every item."—*Pref.* The main section, Writers and their books, is prefaced by introductory essays on books on the orders, books of designs and pattern-books, carpenters' manuals, measuring and price books, books on bridges, archaeological books, publishers and booksellers, and architectural engraving. Excluded are books on garden design and articles in periodicals and encyclopedias. The 950 entries include title, imprint date, collation and contents, editions, locations, and notes. Locates copies in major architectural libraries, including Avery Library (Columbia Univ.), Canadian Centre for Architecture, Royal Institute of British Architects, and Soane Museum. Concludes with a Chronological index of titles and editions and an index of names, subjects, and titles.
                                                   NA965.H37

Schimmelman, Janice Gayle. Architectural treatises and building handbooks available in American libraries and bookstores through 1800. Worcester, Mass. : American Antiquarian Society, 1986. [183 p.]. ISBN 0-912296-79-8.   **BE111**
Identifies 147 books, 65 of which are additions to Helen Park's *A list of architectural books available in America before the Revolution* (new ed., Los Angeles : Hennessey & Ingalls, 1973). The purpose "is twofold: to develop a list of European architectural books available in America through 1800, and to identify all eighteenth-century libraries and bookstores that either circulated or sold architectural books . . . [with the intention] to enhance, clarify, and expand Park's work by including materials available after the Revolution."—*p. 317.* The body of the work lists each title alphabetically by author and cites references unaltered from the original library or bookseller catalogs, concluding with bibliographic information and numbers from *Early American imprints* (*Guide* AA560 *note*), Charles Evans's *American bibliography* (*Guide* AA557), and Robert B. Winans's *A descriptive checklist of book catalogues separately printed in America, 1693–1800* (*Guide* AA122). Two appendixes: Publication dates and imprints of books cited, in order of number of references; Treatises listed by date of earliest American catalog reference.   Z5941.3.S2

Schultz, LeRoy G. Barns, stables, and outbuildings : a world bibliography in English, 1700–1983. Jefferson, N.C. : McFarland, c1986. 150 p. ISBN 0-89950-193-1. $35.00.   **BE112**
Covers Europe and America. 3,346 bibliographic citations are presented in chronological order within 14 categories, including particular types of barns, corn cribs, silos, barn conversions, barn art and barn poetry. The references are from a variety of monographs and journals, 100 of which are agriculture-

related. Includes an author index and a limited subject index.
                                                   Z5943.B35S38

Indexes

●**Architecture database** [computer file]. London : British Architectural Library, Royal Institute of British Architects, 1978– .   **BE113**
File size: 136,000 records. Updated monthly. Available online (DIALOG).
A machine-readable file that includes titles indexed in *Architectural periodicals index* (*Guide* BE257), 1978 to date, and books added to the collections of the British Architectural Library, 1984 to date.

Australian architectural periodicals index : APPI / comp. by the staff of the Reference Dept., Stanton Library [microform]. 1910–1983– . North Sydney, N.S.W. Australia : Stanton Library, c1986. ISSN 0817-2684.   **BE114**
Photoreproductions, arranged in one alphabet, of 20,000 handwritten index entries covering: subjects; building types, materials, and features; architects; and firms. Excludes product or technical material. Covers about 60 journals published in Australia and New Zealand, 1910–83.
§ More recent articles can be located in *ARCH*, the Australian architectural database (also developed by Stanton Library).

Avery index to architectural periodicals. Supplement 4–10 / Columbia University. Boston : G.K. Hall, 1985–1990.   **BE115**
For 2nd ed., 1973, and supplement 1–3, see *Guide* BE253.
Supplement 4 covers 1979–82; supplement 5, 1983–84; supplement 6, 1985; supplement 7, 1986; supplement 8, 1987; supplement 9, 1988; supplement 10, 1989. Each supplement includes a list of periodical titles and volumes indexed.
Since 1984, *Avery index* has been a program of the Getty Art History Information Program. It remains the primary architectural periodical index published in North America, despite the existence of two others with slightly overlapping coverage: *Architectural index* (Boulder, Colo. : 1950– ; annual), which indexes nine journals, and *Search : the periodical index for architecture, interior design, housing and construction* (Devon, Pa. : Search Publishing, 1988–), which indexes 21. Neither has an author index.
Also available in machine-readable form: Z5945.C653

●**Avery index to architectural periodicals** [computer file]. N.Y. : Avery Architectural and Fine Arts Library, Columbia Univ. , 1979– .   **BE116**
File size: 115,000+ records. Available online (RLIN, updated daily; DIALOG, as *Avery architecture index*, updated semiannually).
In 1989, some 8,000 retrospective records from supplement 3 (1977–78) of the printed version were added to the online file.

Bergeron, Claude. Index des périodiques d'architecture canadiens, 1940–1980 = Canadian architectural periodicals index, 1940–1980. Québec : Presses de l'Université Laval, 1986. 518 p. ISBN 2-7637-7090-8. $42.00. **BE117**
In English and French. Provides some 30,000 index entries for articles published 1940–80 in nine journals. The chief section is arranged by 12 broad building categories, gives full bibliographic information for articles cited, and is followed by building type, architect, place name, and author indexes. This complex arrangement resembles that of *Architectural periodicals index* (*Guide* BE257) and offers great versatility.
                                                   NA745.B37

The Burnham index to architectural literature. N.Y. : Garland, 1989. 10 v. ISBN 0-8240-2661-6 (v. 1). **BE118**

Photoreproductions of some 100,000 cards from an index maintained at the Ryerson and Burnham Libraries of the Art Institute of Chicago. This index was maintained until the mid-1960s and was the only index for architecture from 1919 until the *Avery index to architectural periodicals* (above) was begun in 1934. It indexes more than 200 serial titles (some retrospectively) and 600 monographs, many from the 19th century. Lists of both the serials and monographs precede the index. Index entries are by architect, firm, place and building name, and author, in one alphabet. Midwestern topics are emphasized.

Z5944.U5B87

Construction index. 87:1– . Chicago : ArchiText, c1987– . Quarterly. ISSN 0892-2047. $75.00. **BE119**

Subtitle: An annotated quarterly index of articles in the fields of building design and construction.

Indexes 43 American technical journals in the field of building construction, emphasizing building envelope topics. Arrangement is by subject, with 16 "Masterformat" divisions. Citations include brief annotations. Lacks an author index. The publisher sells photocopies of cited articles. Z7914.B9C62

Holmes, Michael. The country house described : an index to the country houses of Great Britain and Ireland. Winchester, U.K. : Saint Paul's Bibliographies in association with Victoria & Albert Museum, 1986. 328 p. : ill. ISBN 0-906795-39-7. £30.00. **BE120**

Aims "to provide a quick reference to the literature on individual country houses . . . held in the National Art Library at the Victoria and Albert Museum."—*Introd.* Covers not only books but county histories, individual guides, catalogs of collections, sales catalogs, and *Country life* articles up to 1982. Arrangement is alphabetical by name of country house (4,000 are listed), within England and Wales, Ireland, Scotland. Excludes a few royal residences. Includes a list of the 135 books indexed and a bibliography of works not indexed but of interest.

NA7562.H6

Index to historic preservation periodicals / National Trust for Historic Preservation Library of the University of Maryland, College Park ; gen. ed., Hye Yun Choe. Boston : G.K. Hall, c1988. 354 p. ISBN 0-8161-0474-3. $95.00. **BE121**

"A compilation of the monthly listing of articles and ephemera" *(Pref.)* issued by the National Trust for Historic Preservation Library, 1979–87. Articles are from international, national, regional, state, and local historic preservation organizations, as well as from popular and scholarly serials. The topical arrangement includes headings in architecture, law, design review, interiors, real estate, fund raising, and government policy. Contains a limited number of citations (about 5,000), assigns only one subject heading per citation, and provides very limited access by geographic location and none by author. A supplement (covering 1987–90) has been announced for early 1992.

Z1251.A2I54

Encyclopedias

Encyclopedia of architecture : design, engineering & construction / Joseph A. Wilkes, ed. in chief, Robert T. Packard, assoc. ed. N.Y. : Wiley, c1988–c1989. 5 v. : ill. ISBN 0-471-63351-8. $850.00. **BE122**

Substantial (more than 4,000 pages) and very current, compiled over a six-year period with the aim of serving "as the first source of information with sufficient coverage to satisfy the needs of the average reader."—*Pref.* Approximately 500 signed articles by some 400 contributors contain bibliographies and emphasize processes and technology but include as well entries on building types, styles, architectural education, and regulations. About 100 biographical entries emphasize 20th-century

architects, but overlap somewhat with *Macmillan encyclopedia of architects* (*Guide* BE271) and show some unevenness in selection. The pages are well laid out and illustrations ample and interesting. Introductory matter includes sections of Conversion factors, abbreviations and unit symbols and Acronyms and abbreviations. Vol. 5 includes a supplement of 23 entries and a 150-page index.

NA31.E59

Dictionaries

Leick, Gwendolyn. A dictionary of ancient Near Eastern architecture. London ; N.Y. : Routledge, 1988. 261 p. : ill. ISBN 0-415-00240-0. **BE123**

Contains 263 entries, most with bibliographical notes, that are accompanied by about 180 illustrations and five maps. Lacks an introduction. Concludes with an alphabetical list of entries and an index.

NA212.L45

McMullan, Randall. Dictionary of building. N.Y. : Nichols Pub., c1988. 262 p. : ill. ISBN 0-89397-319-X. $44.50. **BE124**

For annotation, see *Supplement* EJ38. TH9.M36

Directories

Catalog of national historic landmarks / comp. by the History Division, National Park Service. Wash. : U.S. Dept. of the Interior, 1987. 290 p. **BE125**

Superintendent of Documents classification: I 29.120.

The catalog for 1987 lists 1,811 properties and, unlike that for 1985, supplies an introduction that covers the designation process, criteria of national significance, ineligible properties and exceptions to exclusions, recognition and effects of designation, withdrawal of designation, and other regulations. Arranged alphabetically by state, then by building name. Each entry provides address, county, date, architect (if known), a one- or two-sentence description, and date of designation. Lacks an index.

E159.C33

Greeves, Lydia. The National Trust guide / Lydia Greeves & Michael Trinick. Rev. ed. N.Y. : Weidenfeld & Nicolson, 1990. 1 v. ISBN 1-55584-390-5. **BE126**

3rd ed., 1984 (*Guide* BE122).

This edition, substantially changed and rewritten, provides "a description of all major holdings in England, Wales, and Northern Ireland" (*p. xxvi*) and mentions two related publications given to members: *Properties of the National Trust* (3rd rev. ed., 1983) and *National Trust handbook for members and visitors* (1987–). Arranged alphabetically by site name, descriptions range from a paragraph to a full page (for prominent sites), many illustrated in color. A 12-page foreword by John Jules Norwich describes the Trust's goals and activities. Includes maps showing site locations (p. 354–369), a list of Trust properties omitted from the text (by county, p. 370–89), a page of useful addresses, and an index of people and site names. Excludes covenanted properties.

DA60.G746

Landmark yellow pages : where to find all the names, addresses, facts, and figures you need / National Trust for Historic Preservation, Diane Maddex, gen. ed. Wash. : Preservation Pr., 1990. 319 p. ISBN 0-89133-154-9. **BE127**

A revision and successor to *The brown book : a directory of preservation information* (Wash. : Preservation Pr., 1983).

Pt. I (All about preservation) is based on *The brown book*, and has been enlarged by the U.S. Committee, International Council of Monuments and Sites (US/ICOMOS). Chapters cover practical topics, including books, court cases, education programs, illustration sorces, local preservation contacts, periodicals, rehabilitation standards, and tax incentives. Pt. II (The preservation network) presents the National Trust's member organizations: state and local networks, the states and their territories, foreign countries. Index of sites, personal and institutional names, publications.   E159.L28

National register of historic places, 1966–1988 / National Conference of State Historic Preservation Officers, National Park Service, American Association for State and Local History. Wash. : The Service, c1989. 807 p. : ill. ISBN 0-942063-03-1. $89.95.   **BE128**

The first cumulative list of properties since 1979, listing 52,000 sites. The *Register,* "the nation's official list of cultural resources worthy of preservation ... is maintained by the National Park Service under the Secretary of the Interior. Expanded from earlier lists of resources of national significance [*Guide* BE228] ... now includes properties important in the history of communities and states as well as the nation."—*Introd.* Arrangement is alphabetical by state, then by county and building or site name, providing for each: address, date of designation, and codes for four criteria for inclusion. Front matter and cumulative list of properties have been compiled and edited by the American Association for State and Local History. Includes some statistical analysis of the listings.   E159.N3418

Handbooks

All about old buildings : the whole preservation catalog / ed. by Diane Maddex [for] National Trust for Historic Preservation. Wash. : Preservation Pr., c1985. 433 p. : ill. ISBN 0-89133-107-7. $39.95. ISBN 0-89133-108-5 (pbk.). $24.95.   **BE129**

A topically-organized handbook that is attractive, well-illustrated, and useful, with bibliographies in each of 15 chapters. Contents: Fugitive places; Preservation; Looking at the built environment; Form and function; Preservationists; Protecting the past; Taking action; Building roots; Rehabilitation and restoration; Adaptive use; Historic sites; Neighborhoods; Main streets; Paying for preservation; Education.   NA106.A44

Apperley, Richard. A pictorial guide to identifying Australian architecture : styles and terms from 1788 to the present / Richard Apperley, Robert Irving, Peter Reynolds ; photographs by Solomon Mitchell. North Ryde, N.S.W., Australia : Angus & Robertson Publishers, 1989. 297 p. : ill. ISBN 0-207-16201-8.   **BE130**

Lists and identifies "on the illustrations, the items that are indicators of each style."—*Foreword.* Arranged in six periods, 1788 to the present, in which buildings are classified by 66 styles. For each style, discusses distribution, style indicators, and style keys; provides photographs of many named buildings as examples, stating architect or firm and dates. Format is similar to John J.G. Blumenson's *Identifying American architecture : a pictorial guide to styles and terms 1600–1945* (2nd ed., rev. and enl., N.Y. : Norton, 1981). Glossary (12 p.); bibliography (3 p., current through 1987). Lacks an index to the many persons, places or building names cited in captions and definitions.   NA1600.A66

History

Repertorio delle cattedrali gotiche / a cura di Ernesto Brivio. Milano : Fabbrica del Duomo di Milano : Nuove edizioni Duomo, 1986. 2 v. (1009 p.) : ill.   **BE131**

"... developed as a basic source of knowledge about the social environment of Gothic cathedrals ... presents an architectural and artistic profile."—*Foreword.* Selective in that it is based on 101 responses to a questionnaire sent in 1986 to 245 individuals responsible for all known Gothic cathedrals. Ar-

rangement is by 19 countries, subdivided alphabetically by city; most entries are in Italian, some in French, German, or English. Data for buildings: historical "excursus" (approximately four pages per entry); building history; administration; technical and artistic management system; restoration problems; religious life; cultural life; bibliography; photography information. Vol. 2 concludes with an index of towns.   NA4830.R47

Biography

Contemporary architects / editors, Ann Lee Morgan and Colin Naylor. 2nd ed. Chicago : St. James Pr., 1987. 1038 p. : ill. ISBN 0-912289-26-0.   **BE132**

1st ed., 1980 (*Guide* BE295).

Resembles the previous edition, with each entry updated through the mid-1980s. Adds some 40 biographies and deletes some architects whose activity ceased before World War II.   NA680.C625

Doumato, Lamia. Architecture and women : a bibliography documenting women architects, landscape architects, designers, architectural critics and writers, and women in related fields working in the United States. N.Y. : Garland, 1988. 269 p., [20] p. of plates : ill. (Garland reference library of the humanities, vol. 886). ISBN 0-8240-4105-4.   **BE133**

The main section offers bibliographies of 130 American women architects in one alphabetical sequence, each listing subdivided by "Primary works" (as author) and "Secondary works" (as subject). Begins with a general bibliography listing manuscript and special collections, monographs, dissertations and theses, exhibition catalogs and reviews, and periodical articles published through the mid-1980s. Concludes with an index of topics, personal and institutional names, and places.   Z5944.U5D6886

Gray, Alexander Stuart. Edwardian architecture : a biographical dictionary / A. Stuart Gray ; photographs by Jean & Nicholas Breach. Iowa City : Univ. of Iowa Pr., c1986. 421 p. : ill. ISBN 0-87745-136-2.   **BE134**

Also publ. London : Duckworth, 1985.

"... it would be a mistake to see this book as merely an assemblage of fascinating detail ... It is biased in favour of London as against the provinces, in favour of public buildings as against country houses, in favour of classicism as against Arts and Crafts."—*Foreword.* The 70-page introduction has essays on 20 topics; the 348 biographical entries include ample photographs, lists of work, and brief bibliographical references from 12 British publications. Name index, with buildings cited under location. Alastair Service has published a survey of the same period, *Edwardian architecture : a handbook to building design in Britain, 1890–1914* (N.Y. : Oxford Univ. Pr., 1977).   NA968.5.E38G7

Harvey, John Hooper. English mediaeval architects : a biographical dictionary down to 1550 : including master masons, carpenters, carvers, building contractors, and others responsible for design / by John Harvey ; with contributions by Arthur Oswald. Rev. ed. Gloucester : A. Sutton, 1984. lxii, 479 p. [2] leaves of plates : ports. ISBN 0-86299-034-3. £30.00.   **BE135**

1st ed., 1954 (*Guide* BE296).

This edition incorporates corrections and additions; results of searches for more books and papers; a substantial amount of material gathered in newspapers, periodicals, and ephemera; information from archives now available in public repositories. 400 new "lives" have been added to the original 1,300. The preface describes at length aspects treated in the course of revision (illustration, the background, foreign influences, evidence, and bibliography). Includes: Key to Christian names ("to assist identification of masters"); Key to occupations; Appendixes (Portraits; Table of remuneration); Indexes (topographical and county); Chronological table (for the commencement of works); Subject index of buildings; General index. NA963.H37

Wright, Sylvia Hart. Sourcebook of contemporary North American architecture from postwar to postmodern. N.Y. : Van Nostrand Reinhold, c1989. 200 p. : ill. ISBN 0-442-29190-6. **BE136**

Contains "virtually all the information" found in Wright's *Highlights of recent American architecture: a guide to contemporary architects and their leading works completed 1945–1978* (Metuchen, N.J. : Scarecrow, 1982) "plus an additional 135 entries—most of them dating from the mid-1970s on—and five times as many photographs."—*Pref.* Much of the information on projects, awards, and bibliographic sources has been updated. Alphabetic entries for architects and firms are complemented by indexes for building type, building name, and geographic location. Superior to Les Krantz's *American architects: a survey of award-winning contemporaries and their notable works* (N.Y. : Facts on File, 1989), which is uneven in coverage and contains factual errors. NA703.W75

City planning

Bibliography

Schröder, Brigitte. Bibliographie zur deutschen historischen Städteforschung / bearb. von Brigitte Schröder und Heinz Stoob. Köln : Böhlau, 1986. v. 1–2 : ill. (Städteforschung. Reihe B, Handbücher, Bd. 1, etc.). ISBN 3-412-07685-6 (T. 1). (In progress). **BE137**

The initial volume contains 8,600 citations extending through the early 1980s, many for 19th-century titles. Front matter includes a list of individual towns named within each region or state, addresses for compilers, an abbreviations list, and list of journals cited. Vol. 1 is in two parts: general city history, subdivided by seven broad topics; bibliography of specific regions (East and West Prussia, Pomerania, Silesia, Saxony, Saxony-Anhalt, Thuringia, Berlin and Brandenburg, Mecklenburg, Hamburg, Schleswig-Holstein and Lübeck, Bremen, and Lower Saxony). Within the region or state, arrangement is alphabetical by city. For each citation in Pt. 1, codes indicate the general geographic area; for those in Pt. 2, codes indicate publication type, such as maps, inventory, or handbook, and citations are alphabetized by author within that category. DD91.S36

Indexes

Ekistic index of periodicals. v. 18, no. 104 (Jan.–June 1985)– . [Athens, Greece] : Athens Technological Organization, Athens Center of Ekistics, [1985–]. Semiannual. $100.00. **BE138**

Continues *Ekistic index* (*Guide* BE304a).

Format remains the same, with an increase in the number of journals indexed. Z5942.E38

Dictionaries

Venturi, Marco. Town planning glossary : 10,000 multilingual terms in one alphabet for European town planners = Stadtplanungsglossar = glossaire d'urbanisme = glosario de urbanismo = glossario di urbanistica. München ; N.Y. : Saur, c1990. 277 p. ISBN 88-7743-053-2. L50000. **BE139**

Also publ. Venezia : Arsenale, c1990.

A polyglot work, with 2,000 English, French, German, Italian, and Spanish entries arranged in one alphabet, giving the equivalents in the other languages. Intended to provide a common ground for planners. The foreword briefly describes the tendency toward frequent disparities between terms in the five languages and the compiler's attempt "to establish a semantic field" for terms. HT108.5.V46

Directories

Directory of planning and urban affairs libraries in the United States and Canada, 1990 / [Patricia Coatsworth, ed.]. [5th ed.]. Chicago : Council of Planning Librarians, c1990. 98 p. **BE140**

4th ed., 1980.

Arranged geographically by state or province and city. Has 261 listings, compared with 291 in the previous edition. Appendixes: Libraries listed in 1980 edition, now merged or defunct; Nonrespondents. Indexes of organizations and library contacts (names). Z675.C55D57

Landscape architecture

Bibliography

Desmond, Ray. Bibliography of British gardens. Winchester, Hampshire : St. Paul's Bibliographies, c1984. 318 p., 20 p. of plates : ill. ISBN 0-906795-15-X. £25.00. **BE141**

The bibliography, called "Catalogue of works," is arranged by site, and lists from one to 30 citations for each site. Includes a preface by John Harvey, a 14-page introduction, a 20-page bibliography of works consulted, 20 plates, a county index (arranged by seven regions, listing each property and its town), and an index to places depicted on Wedgwood dinner service. Complements Miles Hadfield's *British gardeners: a biographical dictionary* (London : Zwemmer, 1980). Z5996.5.G7D47

Powell, Antoinette Paris. Bibliography of landscape architecture, environmental design, and planning. Phoenix : Oryx, 1987. 312 p. ISBN 0-89774-250-8. $74.50. **BE142**

" . . . designed to be enhanced and updated . . . by using the MARC Data Base" (*Introd.*) to locate other sources. A brief thesaurus of terms is followed by an unannotated bibliography that is alphabetically arranged and by author and title indexes. To compile the bibliography, subject terms were chosen from *Library of Congress subject headings* for all pertinent English-language titles, without judgment as to value. Theses and dissertations, government publications, and serials are included; books with a geographic focus smaller than the entire U.S. are excluded. Z5996.A1P67

Encyclopedias

The Oxford companion to gardens / consultant editors, Sir Geoffrey Jellicoe, Susan Jellicoe ; executive editors, Patrick Goode, Michael Lancaster. Oxford ; N.Y. : Oxford Univ. Pr., 1986. 635 p. ISBN 0-19-866123-1. $40.25. **BE143**

Primarily concerned with "locating and describing gardens of all kinds . . . [and] touches upon the influences such as geography, climate, and ethnic and social factors that have conditioned gardens of all ages."—*Pref.* Includes brief biographies of principal designers and major patrons and excludes gardens which are neither representative of a trend nor outstanding in their design. Topics include places, concepts ("garden journalism," "ecology and gardens"), influences ("Linnaeus and his students"), plants, countries ("China" has six pages and some 20 cross-references), garden types ("hospital garden," "winter garden"), and organizations ("Garden History Society"). The alphabetical entries, by 174 contributors, constitute the body of the work and include illustrations and some color plates. The five-page bibliography is current through 1986.   SB469.25.O95

Dictionaries

Morrow, Baker H. A dictionary of landscape architecture. Albuquerque : Univ. of New Mexico Pr., c1987. 378 p. : ill. ISBN 0-8263-0943-7. $45.00. ISBN 0-8263-0944-5 (pbk.). $25.00.   **BE144**
International in scope, with entries in one alphabet for people, types of structures, techniques, regions and countries. A straightforward format, illustrated with line drawings and some photographs of landscape architects and sites, and incorporating an ample number of cross-references for technical terms. "Notes on sources" at the front serves as a bibliography.
SB469.25.M67

Handbooks

See also BE164.

American landscape architecture : designers and places / [ed. by William H. Tishler]. Wash. : Preservation Pr., c1989. 244 p. : ill. ISBN 0-89133-145-X. $10.95. **BE145**
The fifth volume in the "Building watchers series," intended to provide "an introduction to several centuries of the landscape tradition in America" (*Introd.*) by highlighting accomplishments. The 21 essays on designers are in chronological order ranging from Thomas Jefferson to those active until about 1960, while the 21 essays on topics include campuses, historic landscapes, national forests, parkways, and waterfronts. The 43 contributors are landscape architects. Includes a 12-page, up-to-date bibliography; index; and small, though numerous, illustrations.   SB470.53.A44

The traveler's guide to American gardens / ed. by Mary Helen Ray and Robert P. Nicholls. Chapel Hill : Univ. of North Carolina Pr., c1988. 375 p. : ill. ISBN 0-8078-1787-2. ISBN 0-8078-4214-1 (pbk.).   **BE146**
A revision and expansion of the same editors' *A guide to historic & significant gardens of America* (Athens, Ga. : AGEE Publishers, [1982]). Provides concise information and directions for visitors. Arrangement by state and city.   SB466.U6T7

PAINTING

Bibliography

See also BE33.

Parsons, Christopher. A bibliography of Salon criticism in Second Empire Paris / [comp. by] Christopher Parsons and Martha Ward. Cambridge ; N.Y. : Cambridge Univ. Pr., 1986. 288 p. ISBN 0-521-32149-2.   **BE147**
The 1,619 entries are arranged by Salon date, then alphabetically by author, and provide not only the bibliographic references but also the call number for the appropriate department at the Bibliothèque Nationale, Paris. Omits articles or caricatures that describe not works but other aspects of the Salon. The preface briefly discusses the history of Salon criticism. Indexes of authors and periodicals; bibliography of works consult-

ed. A related title appeared in 1991, *A bibliography of Salon criticism in Paris from the July monarchy to the Second Empire, 1831–1851,* ed. by Neil McWilliam (Cambridge : Cambridge Univ. Pr.).   Z5961.F7P37

Weisberg, Yvonne M. L. The realist debate : a bibliography of French realist painting, 1830–1885 / Yvonne M.L. Weisberg, Gabriel P. Weisberg. N.Y. : Garland, 1984. 213 p. (Garland reference library of the humanities, vol. 473). ISBN 0-8240-8994-4. $57.00.   **BE148**
About 500 well-annotated citations, organized in four main sections by publication type. These are then chronologically structured (through 1983), so that "the evolution of realism and the emergence of various theories" (*Introd.*) are illustrated. Includes standard author and subject indexes, as well as an introductory discussion of issues.   Z5949.F8W45

Catalogs

Subject catalogue of paintings in public collections. London : Visual Arts, c1989. v. 1–2. ISBN 0-9514166-0-X. (In progress).   **BE149**
Contents: v. 1, London : The National Gallery, the Wallace Collection, the Wellington Museum; v. 2, London : The Tate Gallery, Old Masters Collection.
A catalog of paintings in British collections open to the public. Neither of the first two volumes contains an explanation of the project's scope and timetable. In each, paintings are listed in a "Descriptive listing by artist," although in v. 1, descriptions are strictly textual, while in v. 2, briefer descriptions are accompanied by small black-and-white photographs of the paintings. Entries provide artist's name, dates, title of the work, medium and dimensions, and accession number. Both volumes have a subject index, based on nearly identical lists of some 60 headings, with centuries as subheadings. Vol.1 has an index of artists by alternate names, an index of persons in the paintings, and a topographical index. The volumes vary considerably in size (v. 1, 1400 p.; v. 2, 677 p.) and paper stock.   ND45.S94

Indexes

See also BE61.

Laing, Ellen Johnston. An index to reproductions of paintings by twentieth century Chinese artists. Eugene, Oregon : Univ. of Oregon, 1984. 530 p. (Asian studies publications series, no. 6).   **BE150**
Intended to supplement Laing's *Chinese paintings in Chinese publications, 1956–1968* (Ann Arbor : Univ. of Michigan, Center for Chinese Studies, 1969) and James F. Cahill's *An index of early Chinese painters and paintings* (*Guide* BE335) as well as earlier work by Osvald Sirén, which were limited to Imperial China. Covers 1912–80 and "includes the names of approximately 3500 traditional-style artists along with lists of their works, reproduced in some 264 monographs, books, journals and catalogues published from the 1920s to around 1980."—*Introd.* Arranged alphabetically by artist's name (also given in Chinese), and giving alternate names when known, birth and death dates, place of activity, education, positions held, bibliography, and list of paintings (in English, citing works in which a painting is illustrated). Begins with a list of short titles and a bibliography of books and journals indexed, and concludes with lists of collaborative works, institutional works, and alternate names.   ND1045.L35

Biography

Carpenter, Thomas H. Beazley addenda : additional references to *ABV, ARV²* & *Paralipomena* / comp. by Thomas H. Carpenter; with Thomas Mannack and Melanie Mendonça, at the Beazley Archive. 2nd ed. Oxford : Published for the British Academy by Oxford Univ. Pr., 1989. li, 481 p. ISBN 0-19-726069-1. **BE151**

Essential for use in conjunction with J.D. Beazley's *Attic black figure vase-painters* (Oxford : Clarendon, 1956; repr. N.Y. : Hacker Art Books, 1978), which provides definitive lists of vases by painters, groups, and classes. These "represent an ordered corpus of the most prolific and important source for studies in connoisseurship, iconography, pottery production and trade."—*Pref. to the first edition.* Incorporates "all material published in the first edition [Oxford : N.Y. : Oxford Univ. Pr., 1982, comp. by Lucilla Burn and Ruth Glynn] with references to published illustrations recorded from the material received in the Ashmolean Museum Library down to July 1987 . . . " as well as factual corrections and "new joins."—*Pref. to the second edition.* A related Beazley Archive database project is sponsored by the British Academy. NK4648.C26

Foskett, Daphne. Miniatures : dictionary and guide. Woodbridge, Suffolk : Antique Collectors' Club, c1987. 702 p. : ill. (some col.). ISBN 1-85149-063-9. **BE152**

Comprises, with revisions, the author's *Collecting miniatures* (Woodbridge, Eng. : Antique Collectors' Club, 1979) and *Dictionary of British miniature painters*, 1972 (*Guide* BE339).

Chapters from *Collecting miniatures* treat: Forming the collection; The early masters; Nine periods; Fakes, forgeries and facts. The index covers those chapters but omits material from the *Dictionary.* The bibliography is current only through the 1970s. ND1337.G7F465

Simon, Robin. The portrait in Britain and America : with a biographical dictionary of portrait painters 1680–1914. Boston : G.K. Hall ; Oxford : Phaidon Pr., 1987. 255 p. : ports. (some col.). ISBN 0-8161-8795-9. **BE153**

Equally divided between a critical history (including chapters on Poses and Practice) and biographical entries. The latter are selective, limited to 626 portraitists who worked in oils or crayons (pastel) and were primarily specialists, and give key biographical information and locations of some of the work. Bibliography is thorough and current through the mid-1980s. Index of names, techniques, and portrait titles. ND1314.S46

PRINTS AND ENGRAVINGS

Bibliography

Abrams, Leslie E. The history and practice of Japanese printmaking : a selectively annotated bibliography of English language materials. Westport, Conn. : Greenwood, 1984. 197 p. (Art reference collection, no. 5). ISBN 0-313-23188-5. $40.95. **BE154**

Lists 1,231 citations, 1861–1980, many giving descriptive annotations or citing reviews. Section headings: General work by period; Subjects depicted in prints; Types of prints; Techniques; Printmakers. Several other sections are devoted to Eastern and Western influences and collections. Concludes with a glossary of about 100 Japanese terms and author and subject indexes. Z5947.3.J30.A27

Mason, Lauris. Old master print references : a selected bibliography / comp. by Lauris Mason, Joan Ludman, Harriet P. Krauss. White Plains, N.Y. : Kraus Internat., c1986. 279 p. ISBN 0-527-62196-X. $70.00. **BE155**

Similar in format to the authors' *Print reference sources*, 2nd ed., 1979 (*Guide* BE347). References are to the work of some 900 artists, in 3,000 citations which "include catalogues raisonnés, checklists, articles in periodicals, listings in multivolume indices and . . . museum, exhibition and dealer catalogues."—*Introd.* Appears to be current through 1980, 1981, or 1982, using the Hogarth, Piranesi, and Dürer entries as samples. Z5947.3.E85M37

Indexes

Wilson, Raymond L. Index of American print exhibitions, 1882–1940. Metuchen, N.J. : Scarecrow, 1988. 906 p. ISBN 0-8108-2139-7. **BE156**

"The aim . . . is to make available a reference to individual prints and printmakers represented at the annual salons of the leading [print] societies."—*Pref.* Arrangement is chronological under the following societies: New York Etching Club, Chicago Society of Etchers, California Society of Etchers, Printmakers Society of California, Brooklyn Society of Etchers, Fine Prints of the Year, Fifty Prints of the Year, Panama-Pacific International Exposition, Victoria and Albert Museum, New York World's Fair [1939]. Artists index (p. 568–906) lists individual print titles under each name. NE507.W55

Handbooks

Gascoigne, Bamber. How to identify prints : a complete guide to manual and mechanical processes from woodcut to ink jet. [London] : Thames and Hudson, c1986. 1 v. (various pagings) : ill. (some col.). ISBN 0-500-23454-X. **BE157**

A handbook that was begun in order to answer the author's own needs as a print collector, and is "not concerned with artistic merit."—*Foreword.* Three main sections: The prints (manual prints, process prints, screenprints); Keys to identification; Reference (vocabulary, brief bibliography, "The Sherlock-Holmes approach," a sequence of questions). Glossary-index. NE850.G37

Goldman, Paul. Looking at prints, drawings, and watercolours : a guide to technical terms. London : British Museum Publications ; Malibu, Calif. : J. Paul Getty Museum, c1988. 64 p. : ill (some col.). ISBN 0-89236-148-4. $7.50. **BE158**

A small, durable guide, that grew out of two earlier books by the author and is superior to J.H.U. Brown's *A guide to collecting fine prints* (Metuchen, N.J. : Scarecrow, 1989). It is "directed at the person looking at traditional collections of prints . . . and hence deals only briefly with photomechanical processes and some modern development in original printmaking."—*Foreword.* Includes illustrations, many in color, and a brief bibliography. N33.G65

Printworld directory of contemporary prints and prices. 1st ed. (1982)– . [Bala-Cynwyd, Penn.] : Printworld, [c1982]– . Annual. ISSN 0734-2721. $35.00. **BE159**

For earlier editions, see *Guide* BE354.

Indexes: Print publishers; Printer/print workshops. The two-page list of paper abbreviations is very useful. NE491.P77

Biography

Contemporary graphic artists. v. 1–3. Detroit : Gale, c1986–1988. ISSN 0885-8462. $50.00.　**BE160**

　　Title page note: "a biographical, bibliographical, and critical guide to current illustrators, animators, cartoonists, designers, and other graphic artists."

　　Editor: Maurice Horn.

　　Ceased with v. 3, published in 1988.

　　Each biennial volume of *CGA* includes entries for 100 artists (primarily American), citing personal data and information on career, awards and honors, writings, films, exhibitions, and work in progress. Complements the editor's *World encyclopedia of cartoons* (1979–83).　　NC999.2.C65

Lister, Raymond. Prints and printmaking : a dictionary and handbook of the art in nineteenth-century Britain. London : Methuen, 1984. 385 p., [16] p. of plates : ill. ISBN 0-413-40130-8. £25.00.　**BE161**

　　The first third of the volume serves as a handbook, with discussion of different print techniques, a 20-page glossary, and a general bibliography (current through 1980); scope includes ephemera such as bottle labels. The dictionary proper excludes persons born after 1880, and includes a few important printers, printsellers, and publishers named on prints. For all persons, provides vital dates and places, media or processes used, subject categories, biographical details such as pupils, names of artists after whose work engravings were done, and bibliographical references.　　NE628.L54

SCULPTURE

Bibliography

Lyman, Thomas W. French Romanesque sculpture : an annotated bibliography / Thomas W. Lyman with Daniel Smartt. Boston : G.K. Hall, 1987. 450 p. : ill. ISBN 0-8161-8330-9.　**BE162**

　　The introduction describes the literature on Roman sculpture, calling it a pervasive "indigenous art." The bibliography (2,173 annotated entries) is presented within three periods: 1700–1900, 1900–44, and 1945 to the present. Each has an introduction and is subdivided for articles, books, and catalogs, each arranged in chronological order. Index to authors, names in annotations, reviewers' names, iconographic subjects, and places (such as churches).　　Z5954.F8L95

Catalogs

Souchal, François. French sculptors of the 17th and 18th centuries : the reign of Louis XIV : illustrated catalogue / [by] François Souchal, with the collaboration of Françoise de la Moureyre, Henriette Dumuis. Oxford : Cassirer ; London : distr. by Faber, 1977–1987. 3 v. : ill., geneal. tables (on lining papers), ports. ISBN 0-85181-062-4 (v. 1). £50.00.　**BE163**

　　Translated from the French by Elsie and George Hill.

　　Entries, arranged alphabetically, give a short biography and bibliography, then list the sculptor's works in chronological order with full data, but exclude extensive discussion of attribution or style. All three volumes list bibliographic sources and have an index of names, sites (numerous references for the pal-

ace and gardens of Versailles), and subjects. Vols. 1–2 include several pages of errata and addenda.　　NB546.S6813

Guidebooks

American battle monuments : a guide to military cemeteries and monuments maintained by the American Battle Monuments Commission / Elizabeth Nishiura, ed. Detroit : Omnigraphics, c1989. 469 p. : ill. ISBN 1-558888-12-8.　**BE164**

　　Based on information gathered by the Commission over a period of 65 years, and compiled from a series of pamphlets describing the sites. The monuments span "four continents, five wars and nearly 150 years of American military history . . . "—*Pref.* Sections: Introduction; American memorials and overseas military cemeteries; World War I cemeteries and memorials; World War II cemeteries and memorials (both World War sections arranged by country); Cemeteries and memorials of other American military efforts. Most entries include location, directions, hours, brief history, a photograph of the site, and a simple map. The index covers names of artists and architects, battles, historical figures, and locations.　　UB393.A45

Biography

Janson, H.W. An iconographic index to Stanislas Lami's *Dictionnaire des sculpteurs de l'Ecole française au dix-neuvième siècle* / H.W. Janson, with the editorial assistance of Judith Herschman. N.Y. : Garland, 1983. 218 p. (Garland reference library of the humanities, vol. 364). ISBN 0-8240-9399-2. $100.00 (est.).　**BE165**

　　Occasioned by the reprinting of Lami's *Dictionnaire* (Nendeln : Kraus Reprint, 1970; for original version and annotation, see *Guide* BE375). Begun in Fall 1976 by graduate students at Tulane Univ. and completed at the Graduate Center of the City Univ. of N.Y., the work has resulted in some 30,000 entries to cover all italicized entries from Lami's dictionary. Page numbers in entries refer to a list of works in the *Dictionnaire*. Titles of works are cited in the French form. Cross-references relate individual figures or components of sculpture groups.　　NB552.L333J36

Kjellberg, Pierre. Les bronzes du XIXe siècle : dictionnaire des sculpteurs. Paris : Editions de l'Amateur, [1987]. 684 p. : ill. (some col.).　**BE166**

　　Alphabetically arranged, entries include discussion, a facsimile signature, lists of manufacturers of individual works, museum holding works (France only), sales (international; current through 1986), and numerous photographs. The introductory section has excellent photographs of techniques used in bronze. Closes with a 27-page "Dictionnaire des fondeurs" and a two-page bibliography.　　NB1230.K57

Watson-Jones, Virginia. Contemporary American women sculptors. Phoenix : Oryx, 1986. 665 p. : ill. ISBN 0-89774-139-0.　**BE167**

　　"This book is about artists whose work is strong, vital, and often innovative."—*Introd.* For some 300 artists, gives basic information on education, individual and group exhibitions, public collections, awards, a select bibliography, gallery affiliations, artist's statement, artist's signature, and a photograph of one work. The artists range in age from 27 to 89. Two indexes are provided: geographic (by state) and media (30 categories).　　NB212.W37

BF

Applied Arts

GENERAL WORKS

The encyclopedia of arts and crafts : the international arts movement, 1850–1920 / Gillian Naylor . . . [et al.] ; Wendy Kaplan, consulting ed. N.Y. : E.P. Dutton, c1989. 192 p. : ill. (some col.). ISBN 0-525-24804-8. **BF1**

A handbook featuring eight chapters by specialists on interiors, architecture, furniture, textiles and wallpaper, glass, pottery, graphics, and metalwork. An introduction surveys the movement (1850–1920), and an afterword reviews Arts and Crafts influences through the 20th century. Includes ample illustrations, a skeletal chronology, 53 biographies (each a paragraph long), and index.　　　　NK1140.E54

Bibliography

The arts of Africa : an annotated bibliography. Atlanta : Crossroads Pr., [1986]– . Biennial. ISSN 1044-8640. $35.00.　　　　**BF2**

Derives from the acquisitions lists of the National Museum of African Art Branch Library, Washington. States as its purpose to cover "significant publications" (*Introd.*) and as its criteria substance and originality. In two main sections: General studies (grouped by 21 subjects) and Country and regional studies (Western, Central, Southern, Eastern, Northern Africa and African islands). Entries, including monographic and serial literature, are intended to be descriptive and informative; they include OCLC numbers when available. The main sections are followed by four others: Recommended titles on African art; OCLC numbers for serials cited in the bibliography; Author index; Subject index (objects, concepts, ethnic groups, museums, and individuals).

Biebuyck, Daniel P. The arts of Central Africa : an annotated bibliography. Boston : G.K. Hall, c1987. 300 p. (Reference publications in art history, [3]). ISBN 0-8161-8601-4.　　　　**BF3**

The third volume in a series intended to fill the gap in non-Western arts by reviewing both anthropological and art historical scholarship. Each volume cites books, periodical articles, dissertations, exhibition and sales catalogs. All will have indexes for authors, titles, and subjects (e.g., ethnic groups, media). Includes 1,920 citations, most with brief annotations, from publications in all languages. Covers overlapping ethnic units in neighboring countries.　　　　Z5961.Z28B53

Burt, Eugene C. Ethnoart : Africa, Oceania, and the Americas : a bibliography of theses and dissertations. N.Y. : Garland, 1988. 191 p. (Garland reference library of the humanities, vol. 840). ISBN 0-8240-7545-5. **BF4**

Compiled by consulting some 30 published sources, most of which are listed in the preface. The scope also encompasses "a few bachelor degree honors theses from British or Commonwealth universities."—*Pref.* Each title had to indicate that the topic related to the indigenous peoples of the regions covered

and that it "was primarily concerned with the visual arts, architecture, material culture, or archaeology . . . ." Covers late 19th century through April 1987, with a total of 1,022 citations. Arrangement of the five chapters follows that of *Ethnoarts index* (*Supplement* BF10), and is hierarchical within the chapters, based on geography, culture groupings, historical periods, and other factors. Four indexes: author, year of completion (in chronological order), institution granting the degree, and subject (including places).　　　　Z5956.P68B88

De Winter, Patrick M. European decorative arts, 1400–1600 : an annotated bibliography. Boston : G.K. Hall, c1988. 543 p. : 1 ill. ISBN 0-8161-8612-X.　　**BF5**

Intends "to select and call attention to a specialized body of literature . . . [and to present it] in such a manner that [it] will also be a useful tool for collectors."—*Introd.* Prefatory material offers an overview of the topic and of the various terms for "decorative arts." The 2,200 annotated references are arranged in a topical outline that provides great detail. Subjects are subdivided by form of publication (dictionaries and encyclopedias, surveys and histories, bibliographical guides, auction catalogs, collection catalogs, and exhibition catalogs), and for geographical and media groupings. Emphasizes titles 1960–86, including regional publications, most in Western languages, and cites English versions or translations.　　　　Z5956.D3D38

Hanson, Louise. The art of Oceania : a bibliography / Louise Hanson and F. Allan Hanson. Boston : G.K. Hall, [1984]. 539 p. (Reference publications in art history, [1]). ISBN 0-8161-8645-6.　　　　**BF6**

The first bibliography in a series described by the editor as reflecting increased interest in non-Western arts (see also Daniel Biebuyck's *The arts of Central Africa*, above). Incorporates monographs, catalogs, theses and dissertations, and periodical literature in five sections (Cross-region, Polynesia, Micronesia, Melanesia, Australia) which are then subdivided alphabetically by author. Entries include very short annotations. A sixth section lists sales catalogs alphabetically by city and gallery name. Indexes: personal names; titles; subjects.　　Z5961.A84H36

Stiverson, Cynthia Zignego. Architecture and the decorative arts : the A. Lawrence Kocher Collection of Books at the Colonial Williamsburg Foundation. West Cornwall, Conn. : Locust Hill Pr., 1989. 245 p. ISBN 0-933951-24-8. $30.00.　　　　**BF7**

A catalog of 462 titles listed alphabetically by author, giving full bibliographic citation, edition information, physical and binding description, pagination, bookplate and signature information, and association with Virginia. Includes a six-page list of publications by and about Kocher and index to titles, people, and owners.　　　　Z5941.S695

Current

Bibliography of American folk art for the year [. . .] / comp. by Eugene P. Sheehy, Rita G. Keckeissen, Edith C. Wise. [1987]– . N.Y. : Museum of American Folk Art, [1988?]– . Annual. ISSN 1046-9931.　　**BF8**

" . . . intended as an aid to scholars, collectors, students, and folk art enthusiasts at many levels of interest . . . is limited to separately-published works—books, pamphlets, and exhibition catalogues, plus a reasonably comprehensive listing of relevant auction catalogues."—*Introd.* Each issue covers imprints for only that year and does not repeat the date of publication. "American" refers only to North America north of Mexico. Categories covered include folk art of ethnic groups and religious sects as well as the various media. Folklore and folklife are excluded unless they relate specifically to folk art. Author-editor, title, and subject indexes.　　　　NK805.A1.B5

Design & applied arts index. v.1, pt. 1 (1988?)– . Burwash, England : Design Documentation, c1988– . Semiannual, cumulated triennially. ISSN 0953-0681.

BF9

Entries, which are annotated and include book and video reviews, are arranged by topics and designers' names in one alphabet; there is no access by author. Indexes 92 journals (as of 1989) but the publisher plans to expand the range and types of materials covered and hopes to index key journals retrospectively. Also known as *daai*; not to be confused with *Design index* (Evanston, Ill. : Design Information, 1982–83).

NK1160.D45

Ethnoarts index. v. 5, no. 1 (Jan.–Mar. 1987)– . [Seattle, Wash.] : Data Arts, c1987– . Quarterly. ISSN 0893-0120. ISSN 0893-0129. $35.00 (institutions).   **BF10**

Covers "indigenous peoples of Africa, Oceania, and the Americas . . . [and] endeavors to locate all publications relevant to the study of ethnoart published since July 1983 . . . [including] books, periodical articles, catalogs, book reviews, exhibition reviews, conference papers, theses and dissertations . . . "—*Using the Ethnoarts index*. Each issue includes an abbreviations list for journal titles, the bibliography (arranged by general subject and by region or hemisphere), and subject and author indexes. Entries are coded by region, include title translation if not in English, and may include a descriptive statement. A series of bibliographies has been derived from *Ethnoarts index*, entitled *Ethnoarts index supplemental publication*. The first four titles (1988–1990) included Oceanic art, African art, and Native American art.   N5310.7.T74

●**Ethnoarts index** [computer file]. Seattle, Wash. : Data Arts, 1983– .   **BF11**

Machine-readable version of *Ethnoarts index* (above).

Available online from publisher.

Serials indexed are listed in Eugene C. Burt's *Serials guide to ethnoart* (below).

Periodicals

Burt, Eugene C. Serials guide to ethnoart : a guide to serial publications on visual arts of Africa, Oceania, and the Americas. N.Y. : Greenwood, 1990. 368 p. (Art reference collection, no. 11). ISBN 0-313-27332-4.   **BF12**

A directory of serials that cover the indigenous arts of Africa, Oceania, and the Americas, developed from a database created by the author for *Ethnoarts index* (above). The main section, "Serial title database," cites 682 titles and has 20 categories of information (e.g., publisher's address, former title, ISSN, and the presence of book and exhibition reviews). A preface describes both the compiler's rationale and his system of grading individual titles and providing the nine appendixes. The latter group serial titles by general coverage, areas of geographic focus, indexing and abstracting services, ceased titles, and country of publication. Concludes with a rotated title keyword index.   N5310.7.B87

Dictionaries

Fleming, John. The Penguin dictionary of decorative arts / John Fleming and Hugh Honour. New ed. London : Viking, 1989. 935 p., [24] p. of plates : ill. (some col.). ISBN 0-670-82047-4. $40.00.   **BF13**

1st ed., 1977 (*Guide* BF103).

Includes new entries and revisions.   NK28

Biography

Contemporary designers / ed., Colin Naylor. 2nd ed. Chicago : St. James Pr., 1990. 641 p. : ill. ISBN 0-912289-69-4. $135.00.   **BF14**

1st ed., 1984 (*Guide* BF2).

This edition has photographs of better quality than the 1st ed. Size remains at 600 entrants who are currently active and "many who have died since 1970 but whose reputations remain essentially contemporary."—*Editor's note*. Entries are by 123 design critics and historians.   NK1166.C66

Folk artists biographical index / George H. Meyer, ed., George H. Meyer, Jr. and Katherine P. White, assoc. editors. Detroit : Gale, c1987. 496 p. ISBN 0-8103-2145-9. $40.00.   **BF15**

Subtitle: A guide to over 200 published sources of information on approximately 9,000 American folk artists from the seventeenth century to the present, including brief biographical information; a full bibliography of sources cited; art locator, ethnicity, geographic, media, and type of work indexes; and a directory of nearly 300 institutions where the works of the artists are located.

Published in association with the Museum of American Folk Art.

Uses a broad definition of folk art, with entries for craftsmen, businesses, or manufacturers. For each, provides artist's name; nickname, pseudonym, or variant spelling as pertinent; birth and death dates; period and place where the artist flourished; ethnicity; media; museums holding the artist's work (coded); reference to the published source of this information. Format is similar to that of *Artist biographies master index* (*Supplement* BE75). Indexes: Museums and collections, with list of artists represented; Ethnicity; Geography (by state and city); Media; Type of work (subjects).   NK805.F63

McKendry, Blake. A dictionary of folk artists in Canada from the 17th century to the present with inclusions of popular portrait, topographical, genre, religious, and decorative artists of the 17th, 18th, and 19th centuries. Elginburg, Ont. : B. McKendry, c1988. 287 p. ISBN 0-9693298-0-6 (pbk.).   **BF16**

For some 3,000 artists, entries provide dates or period of activity, place of activity, medium, a brief discussion, and references to bibliographic sources (listed at the end, current through 1987). An introduction includes definitions of folk art, primitive art, naive art, provincial art, and amateur art.   N6540.5.P7M38

Rosenak, Chuck. Museum of American Folk Art encyclopedia of twentieth-century American folk art and artists / Chuck and Jan Rosenak. N.Y. : Abbeville Pr., c1990. 416 p. : ill. (some col.). ISBN 1-55859-041-2.

BF17

An attractive encyclopedia that provides information about 257 artists working in various media. Much of the information was obtained during extensive interviews; the research materials assembled during compilation will eventually be accessible at the Museum. Entries cite biographical data, background on the artist's life, subjects and sources for images, materials and techniques, recognition or reputation, and footnotes. Each entry has a color photograph of the artist's work, augmented in the appendix by black-and-white portraits of many of the artists. Includes a listing of public collections in the U.S. holding folk art, a chronological list of major exhibitions, and a bibliography. Index of names, works of art, galleries and museums, organizations, and exhibition titles.   NK808.R6

CERAMICS AND GLASS

Bibliography

Guide to trade catalogs from the Corning Museum of Glass / The Corning Museum of Glass. N.Y. : Clearwater Pub. Co., 1987. 500 p. ISBN 0-88354-076-2. $95.00.
BF18

A bibliography of some 2,200 trade catalogs in the Museum's Rakow Library, intended to accompany *Trade catalogs from the Corning Museum of Glass* (N.Y. : Clearwater, 1987), a set of 5,000 microfiches reproducing those catalogs. They "are unparalleled resources for determining manufacturers' styles, patterns, dates of production and original costs . . . [and] provide primary source information for scholars researching glass . . . ."—*Pref.* They include related "design books, price lists, internal factory record books listing ware, and reprints."—*Introd.* Arranged by six broad categories, each divided into domestic and foreign lists: bottles and druggists' glassware; cut glass; flat glass; laboratory ware; lighting glassware and lamps; tableware. Within divisions, citations are alphabetical by factory name and provide: location; catalog title, date, and physical description; and fiche number. Many include annotations. Four indexes: company, geographical, chronological, subject.

§ Two related publications are *Trade catalogs at Winterthur : a guide to the literature of merchandising, 1750–1980* (N.Y. : Garland, 1984) and *Guide to architectural trade catalogs from Avery Library* [Columbia Univ.] (N.Y. : Clearwater, 1989).
Z6046.G84

Oppelt, Norman T. Southwestern pottery : an annotated bibliography and list of types and wares. 2nd ed., rev. and expanded. Metuchen, N.J. : Scarecrow, 1988. 325 p. : ill. ISBN 0-8108-2119-2.
BF19

1st ed. published as *Occasional publications in anthropology. Archaeology series*, no. 7 (Greeley : Museum of Anthropology, University of Northern Colorado, 1976).

Similar in format to Susan R. Strong's *History of American ceramics : an annotated bibliography* (*Guide* BF49). Pt. 1, the annotated bibliography, is arranged alphabetically and chronologically by author and includes books, theses, obscure journals such as *Highway salvage archaeology*, and regional series such as *Utah anthropological papers*. Pt. 2 is a "List of Southwestern pottery types and wares," which cites both published and unpublished examples, with dates, synonyms, illustrations, and references to descriptions. Index to site names and subjects. This edition incorporates revisions suggested by Southwesternists and adds 300 citations (and additional dates) for a total of 965, as well as some 1,240 type, ware, and variety names.
Z1208.S68O66

Weidner, Ruth Irwin. American ceramics before 1930 : a bibliography. Westport, Conn. : Greenwood, 1982. 279 p. (Art reference collection, no. 2). ISBN 0-313-22831-0.
BF20

Covers " . . . from the earliest colonial manufacture through about 1930, when styles, production methods and terminology changed . . . "—*Pref.* Lists about 90% of the nontechnical literature published through 1980—2,921 unannotated citations. Arranged by seven types of publications: Books and pamphlets; Conference proceedings and chapters from books; Catalogs from exhibitions, collections, and sales; Theses and dissertations; Federal, state, and municipal publications; Trade publications; Periodical articles. Includes a section of "Suggestions for additional research." Appendix: Guide to selected American clayworking, ceramics, china painting, and crockery journals before 1930. Indexes: author, subject. Should be used in conjunction with Susan R. Strong's *History of American ceramics : an annotated bibliography* (*Guide* BF49).
Z7179.W43

Encyclopedias

Cameron, Elisabeth. Encyclopedia of pottery & porcelain, 1800–1960. N.Y. : Facts on File, c1986. 366, [18] p. : ill. ISBN 0-8160-1225-3. $35.00.
BF21

Covers materials, techniques, styles, and movements of all nations. "Modern makers have been included only if they have produced work, other than as students, before 1960."—*About this book.* Entries range in length from a short paragraph to several pages (e.g., Doulton & Co.); many have bibliographical references. Includes numerous small illustrations, some cross-references between firm and personal names, and asterisks within entries to refer the reader to other personal name entries. Concludes with an 11-page abbreviations list that also serves as a partial, unannotated bibliography.
NK3920.C36

Godden, Geoffrey A. Encyclopaedia of British porcelain manufacturers. London : Barrie & Jenkins, 1988. [850] p. : ill. ISBN 0-7126-2100-8. £50.00.
BF22

Arranged alphabetically by marker's name. Provides photographs of representative objects and drawings of marks, along with biographical and production information. Introductory chapters cover basic types, characteristics of makers' marks and pattern numbers, and a list of manufacturers' names by decade of activity. Includes a list of identifying initials, an eight-page bibliography, and an index to names and terms. See also the author's *Encyclopedia of British pottery and porcelain marks* (*Guide* BF40).

Dictionaries

Atterbury, Paul,. The dictionary of Minton / Paul Atterbury and Maureen Batkin. Woodbridge [England] : Antique Collectors' Club, 1990. 370 p. : ill. ISBN 1-85149-073-6. £35.00.
BF23

The chief section defines a wide range of terms (e.g., "acid gold," "dishes," "trading"), followed by a 74-page section of biographies in which entries range in length from one line to a paragraph. Front matter includes a genealogical chart and a 13-page historical introduction. A select bibliography lists monographs, exhibition catalogs, and journals covering Minton (although individual periodical articles are omitted) and cites 16 exhibitions, 1851–1979. Two appendixes: marks and dating, and photographs from a 1933 factory promotional booklet.

Coysh, A. W. The dictionary of blue and white printed pottery 1780–1880 / A. W. Coysh and R. K. Henrywood. Woodbridge, [Suffolk] : Antique Collectors' Club, 1982–1989. 2 v. : ill. (some col.). ISBN 0-907462-06-5. $22.50 (v. 1). ISBN 1-85149-093-0. £25.00 (v. 2). **BF24**

Arranged alphabetically by manufacturer, subjects depicted in pottery designs, and type of object. Entries include literary and bibliographic references relating to the subject depicted. Excludes American examples. Appendixes: Index of potters' initial marks; Source books used by makers; Maps; Bibliography (current through 1981).

Vol. 2 (additional entries and supplemental information) functions as a supplement, incorporating previously unrecorded patterns discovered after publication of the basic volume. Arranged like the first volume, with the bibliography current through 1988. It somewhat extends the scope beyond 1880 as a result of increased interest in later wares.
NK4277

Sales

Ceramics and glass. 1990– . Lausanne, Switzerland : Éditions Vie Art Cité, 1990– . **BF25**

Editor: 1990– Sylvio Acatos.

Covers archeology, faience, glass, porcelain, pottery, stoneware, and terra cotta. Arrangement is within seven sections: Oriental; Occidental, ancient and medieval; Occidental, Renaissance and modern (subdivided by country); Near and Middle Eastern; Pre-Columbian American; African; 19th and 20th centuries. Entries provide name and description of each object, dimensions, maker when applicable, place and date of the sale, and sale price in three currencies. Includes some illustrations.

Handbooks

Bansal, Narottam P. Handbook of glass properties / Narottam P. Bansal and R.H. Doremus. Orlando, Fla. : Academic Pr., 1986. 680 p. : ill. ISBN 0-12-078140-9 : $160.00. **BF26**

For annotation, see *Supplement* EJ8.   TA450.B27

Rice, Prudence M. Pottery analysis : a sourcebook. Chicago : Univ. of Chicago Pr., c1987. 559 p. : ill. ISBN 0-226-71118-8. **BF27**

This substantial survey of the technical aspects of pottery addresses the subject "as a source of insights into people and cultures, and it is directed toward those with such interests : primarily to social scientists such as anthropologists, archaeologists, and ethnoarchaeologists."—*Pref.* Provides numerous diagrams and tables to illustrate chapters on history, raw materials used, properties of clays and their firing behavior, pottery manufacture and use, production and distribution, vessel functions, decoration and stylistic analysis, archaeological and ethnographic studies, description and characterization of pottery (color, mineralogical, chemical, and physical properties), special topics, and social topics. Bibliographic references are abundant. Concludes with a 15-page glossary, 55-page bibliography, and subject index.   NK3780.R53

History

McKearin, George S. American glass / George S. and Helen McKearin ; ill. with 2000 photographs and with 1000 drawings by James L. McCreery. N.Y. : Bonanza Books : Distr. by Crown Publishers, 1989. 634 p., [232] p. of plates : ill. ISBN 0-517-68237-0. **BF28**

Reprint. Originally publ.: New York : Crown, 1948.

A comprehensive survey.   NK5112.M26

COSTUME AND FASHION

Bibliography

African dress II : a selected and annotated bibliography / Ila M. Pokornowski . . . [et al.]. East Lansing : African Studies Center, Michigan State Univ., c1985. 316 p. : map. **BF29**

Lists 1,260 citations for books and articles that supplement those in Joanne Bubolz Eicher's *African dress : a select and annotated bibliography of Subsaharan countries* (East Lansing : African Studies Center, Michigan State Univ., 1970). Sections: The study of African dress; Resource materials for the study of African dress; Bibliography by six regions; Author index. Lacks a subject index.   Z5694.A4A47

Encyclopedias

Racinet, A. The historical encyclopedia of costumes. N.Y. : Facts on File, 1988. 320 p. : col. ill. ISBN 0-8160-1976-2. $40.00. **BF30**

For 1888 French ed. (6 v.), see *Guide* BF86. An edition with a selection of 92 plates was published in 1987 (N.Y. : Dover).

The earlier work "has been translated, re-organized, edited and re-designed to produce this book" (*Publisher's note*), removing material on furniture and ornaments and constructing a chronology. Quality of the color plates is excellent.

GT510.R3313

History

Boucher, François. 20,000 years of fashion : the history of costume and personal adornment / by François Boucher ; with a new chapter by Yvonne Deslandres. Expanded ed. N.Y. : H.N. Abrams, 1987. 459 p. : ill. (some col.). ISBN 0-8109-1693-2. **BF31**

1st ed., 1967 (*Guide* BF70) had title *Histoire du costume en Occident, de l'antiquité à nos jours.*

Published in Great Britain under the title: *A history of costume in the West.*

In addition to the new chapter on recent fashion, a general bibliography and glossary are included.   GT510.B6713

Biography

McDowell, Colin. McDowell's directory of twentieth century fashion. London : F. Muller, 1984. 320 p. : ill. (some col.). ISBN 0-584-11070-7. £20.00. **BF32**

The body of this directory consists of alphabetical entries for fashion designers of all nationalities, many with a photograph of the designer, and most illustrating the designer's work. It begins with five essays on 20th-century fashion, and concludes with: an essay on "The image makers"; a listing of autobiographies; information on fashion education, organizations, and awards; a 12-page glossary; and an index of personal names.   TT505.A1M37

Stegemeyer, Anne. Who's who in fashion. 2nd ed. N.Y. : Fairchild Publications, c1988. 243 p. : ill. (some col.). ISBN 0-87005-574-7. **BF33**

1st ed., 1980 (*Guide* BF93).

"Emphasis here is on designers with an established track record."—*Pref.* Includes portraits and examples of work. Unlike the previous edition, this one lists Americans and other nationalities in one alphabet.   TT505.A1S74

FURNITURE AND INTERIOR DESIGN

Bibliography

Decorative arts and household furnishings in America, 1650–1920 : an annotated bibliography / ed. by Kenneth L. Ames and Gerald W.R. Ward. Winterthur, Del. : Henry Francis du Pont Winterthur Museum ; Charlottesville : Distr. by the Univ. Pr. of Virginia, 1989. 392 p. ISBN 0-912724-19-6.　　　**BF34**

"... records the current state of scholarship in the field of historic furnishings."—*Introd.* Provides useful coverage of the material culture of domestic life. Chapters, compiled by 20 contributors, treat references and surveys, architecture, furniture, metals, ceramics and glass, textiles, timepieces, household activities and systems, and artisans and culture. Chapters begin with essays introducing the selective bibliographies, which are current through 1986 and have annotations that are for the most part not evaluative. An introduction covers previous bibliographies and the state of current scholarship, and highlights ten significant changes in recent decades. Index to authors and to titles of books and articles.　　　Z5956.D3D43

Makowski, Colleen Lahan. Quilting, 1915–1983 : an annotated bibliography. Metuchen, N.J. : Scarecrow, 1985. 157 p. : 1 ill. ISBN 0-8108-1813-2.　　　**BF35**

Cites 733 books, exhibition catalogs, periodical articles, nonprint media, and museum catalogs published through 1983 on American quilts. Entries are annotated. Index to titles, places, names, styles, and themes.　　　Z6153.Q54M34

Viaux, Jacqueline. Bibliographie du meuble : mobilier civil français. Supplément 1965–1985. Paris : Agence culturelle de Paris, 1988. 624 p. ISBN 2-906869-02-3.　　　**BF36**

For basic volume and annotation, see *Guide* BF97.

Includes holdings in French libraries.　　　Z5995.3.F7V52

Encyclopedias

Dictionary of English furniture makers 1660–1840 / ed. by Geoffrey Beard and Christopher Gilbert. [London] : Furniture History Society, 1986. 1046 p. [16] p. of plates : ill., facsims. ISBN 0-901286-18-4.　　　**BF37**

Covers all principal furniture trades and specialist branches, while ignoring fringe trades such as trunkmakers or coach builders, for a much more comprehensive listing than Ambrose Heal's *The London furniture makers from the Restoration to the Victorian era, 1660–1840* ... (*Guide* BF105). Several hundred members of the Furniture History Society working in 25 regional groups contributed to this work by evaluating listings in trade directories, insurance registers, and newspapers, and periodicals. The several thousand entries give dates, places of apprenticeship and later activity. An editor's explanation discusses types of sources and includes a one-page bibliography; an index of tradesmen and apprentices provides references to names not accorded individual entries but mentioned in other articles.　　　TS810.G7

Dictionaries

The Conran directory of design / ed. by Stephen Bayley. N.Y. : Villard Books, 1985. 255 p. : ill. (some col.). ISBN 0-394-54698-9. $40.00.　　　**BF38**

Consists of seven thematic chapters that emphasize product design, followed by 180 pages of alphabetical entries for persons and firms, terms, and events (e.g., major exhibitions). Biographical entries give dates and brief descriptions of the designer's work. Provides bibliographical information within the entries, a short general bibliography, and a list of design museums and organizations. Concludes with an index of products and designs.

§ A related title is John F. Pile's *Dictionary of 20th-century design* (N.Y. : Facts on File, 1990). A. Allen Dizik's *Concise encyclopedia of interior design*, 2nd ed. (N.Y. : Van Nostrand Reinhold, 1988) is very general and somewhat uneven.　　　NK1165.C6

Dictionary of furniture / [ed. by] Charles Boyce. N.Y. : Facts on File, c1985. 331 p. : ill. ISBN 0-8160-1042-0.　　　**BF39**

Repr. N.Y. : Holt, 1989.

A straightforward work that overstates its usefulness as "the most comprehensive listing in a single volume of terms ... in all countries and cultures" (*Foreword*), although it does incorporate a noticeable number of entries on Asian furniture. Entries for persons, styles, objects, and parts of furniture (some grouped, such as "finial" and "foot") in one alphabet with some cross-references, range in length from a few words to two pages, and have simple line drawings. Biographical entries cover persons born up to the early 1930s. Lacks an index, any bibliography, or bibliographic references.　　　NK2205.D5

Gloag, John. John Gloag's dictionary of furniture. Rev. and enl. ed. London : Unwin Hyman, 1990. 1 v. : ill. ISBN 0-04-440774-2.　　　**BF40**

Previous ed., 1969 (*Guide* BF104), had title: *Short dictionary of furniture.*

Rev. by Clive D. Edwards.

Revisions are limited to the Appendix (p. 814–828), which supplies some 85 additional terms ranging from adhesives to water beds and xylonite.　　　NK2270

Lewis, Philippa. Dictionary of ornament / Philippa Lewis & Gillian Darley. N.Y. : Pantheon Books, c1986. 319 p. : ill. ISBN 0-394-50931-5.　　　**BF41**

"... a survey of ornament, pattern and motifs in the applied arts and architecture ... The coverage is mainly of European and North American buildings and objects from the Renaissance to the present day, with reference, where relevant, to ancient and oriental sources and precedents."—*p. 5*. In one alphabet, the 1,020 entries include styles and personal names, with cross-references and small illustrations. Front matter includes a long, unannotated bibliography, and a ten-page "visual key" that groups motifs by type (plant, animal, human, linear and surface, architectural and decorative).　　　NK1165.L48

History

Sotheby's concise encyclopedia of furniture / gen. ed., Christopher Payne. N.Y. : Harper & Row, c1989. 208 p. : ill. (some col.). ISBN 0-06-016141-8. $49.95.　　　**BF42**

A chronological treatment that concludes with a chapter on "Modern times" and benefits from good color illustrations. Includes an index to names and styles; a one-page bibliography; a two-page "Anatomy of furniture," highlighting key terms for beds, chairs, and tables; and a six-page glossary.   NK2235.S68

METAL ARTS

Gold and silver

Encyclopedias

Rainwater, Dorothy T. Encyclopedia of American silver manufacturers. 3rd ed. rev. West Chester, Penn.: Schiffer Pub., c1986. 266 p.: ill. ISBN 0-88740-046-9 (pbk.). $19.95.   **BF43**

> 1st ed., 1966; 2nd ed., 1975.

> Entries, alphabetical by manufacturer's name, give location, diagram of the mark, a list of variants of the manufacturer's name or trademark (when pertinent), and one or more paragraphs describing the firm's activity. Sources for trademarks and dates include trade journals and related directories and indexes. Concludes with illustrations of nine unascribed marks, an alphabetical list of trade names and their companies, a key to unlettered marks, and a four-page glossary. Bibliography is current only to the mid-1970s. Lacks an index to names mentioned in the entries.   NK7112.R3

Dictionaries

Newman, Harold. An illustrated dictionary of silverware: 2,373 entries relating to British and North American wares, decorative techniques and styles, and leading designers and makers, principally from c1500 to the present. N.Y.: Thames and Hudson, 1987. 366 p., [16] p. of plates: ill. (some col.). ISBN 0-500-23456-6. $39.95.   **BF44**

> Includes "the many types of articles for domestic use... and the highly important fields of ware made for religious use."—*Pref.* Excludes silver jewelry, which is treated in the author's *An illustrated dictionary of jewelry* (*Guide* BF122) and "many other small portable objects of vertu." Emphasizes 17th–19th centuries. Alphabetical entries treat objects, styles, subjects depicted in silver, makers, and techniques. Entries range in length from one sentence to half a page, with a single bibliographic reference. Numerous small photographs and 16 color plates. No bibliography; no index to names or material cited in entries.   NK7104.N49

Biography

Culme, John. The directory of gold & silversmiths, jewellers, and allied traders, 1838–1914: from the London Assay Office registers. Woodbridge, Suffolk: Antique Collectors Club, 1987. 2 v. ISBN 0-907462-46-4 (set). £145.00.   **BF45**

> Contents: v. 1, The biographies; v. 2, The marks.

> Based upon information from the Makers' Marks Registers, Goldsmiths' Hall, London. Introductory material includes an essay, "Attitudes to old plate 1750–1900," a list of terms to describe trades, and an abbreviations list that has bibliographic references. The actual biographies (individuals and companies interfiled) are thorough in documentation; many are footnoted. The marks are photographs of 16,127 marks, which are accompanied by a name index.   NK7143.C924

Grimwade, Arthur. London goldsmiths 1697–1837: their marks and lives from the original registers at Goldsmiths' Hall and other sources. 3rd rev. and enl. ed. London: Faber and Faber, 1990. 773 p. ISBN 0-571-15238-4. £60.00.   **BF46**

> First publ. 1976; 2nd rev. ed., 1982.

> A solid contribution, with two sections: "Marks" provides many subsections (derived from categories found in goldsmiths' lists, the largest being the Goldsmiths' Hall registers) and small images; entries in "Lives" cite evidence of work, apprenticeships, addresses, existence of marks, and documentation. "Lives" refers to pertinent marks by number and uses asterisks to denote additional information in the addenda. An introduction describes the origins of the project, the plan, and the registers, with reference to Sir Ambrose Heal's *The London goldsmiths 1200–1800* (repr.: Newton Abbott: David & Charles, 1972). "Addenda to biographical dictionary" (p. 734–772) contains new material and concludes with a list of some 70 names found in John Culme's *The directory of gold and silversmiths 1838–1914* (above).   NK7144.L66G74

Kovel, Ralph M. Kovels' American silver marks / Ralph & Terry Kovel. N.Y.: Crown, c1989. 421 p.: ill. ISBN 0-517-56882-9. $40.00.   **BF47**

> Portions of this book originally appeared in Kovels' *A directory of American silver, pewter, and silver plate.*

> The introduction gives a brief history for 1640–1850 and 1850–1980. The extensive entries interfile initials with full personal and company names, making ample use of cross-references. Each entry gives dates of activity, city, bibliographic sources, and mark or monogram when pertinent. Closes with a bibliography of 160 books published through the mid-1980s.   NK7210.K68

RUGS

The Macmillan atlas of rugs & carpets / ed. by David Black. N.Y.: Macmillan, c1985. 255 p.: ill. (some col.), maps; 30 cm. ISBN 0-02-511120-5. $29.95.   **BF48**

> The body of the work is a gazetteer, arranged geographically with large sections on Turkey, the Caucasus, Persia, Turkoman tribes, and East Turkestan, and smaller sections on areas of Asia, Morocco, Europe, and North America. All include a simple outline map, and one or more color illustrations and description of a characteristic rug, along with text. Concludes with information on the buying and care of carpets, a four-page glossary of techniques and designs, a select bibliography, and an index.   NK2795.M25

COINS, MEDALS, AND CURRENCY

Cribb, Joe. The coin atlas: the world of coinage from its origins to the present day / Joe Cribb, Barrie Cook, Ian Carradice. N.Y.: Facts on File, c1990. 337 p.: ill. (some col.). ISBN 0-8160-2097-3. $40.00.   **BF49**

> With an introduction by the American Numismatic Association.

> Arranged by continent, then by country, providing an overview of the history of each nation's coinage. Maps are plentiful (totaling 100) and illustrations assist in identification of coins discussed. Glossary and bibliography are brief.   CJ59.C75

Room, Adrian. Dictionary of coin names. London; N.Y.: Routledge & K. Paul, 1987. 250 p.: ill. ISBN 0-7102-0646-1. £14.95.   **BF50**

> The introduction offers an explanation of "numismonymics," together with discussions of the use of multiple and/or colloquial names, the presence of portraits, geographical and his-

torical links to monarchs, and values. Entries give a skeletal history of each named coin. A majority of the entries are for foreign names. A "glossary" precedes the dictionary and functions as a small dictionary of technical terms.   CJ69.R66

POSTAGE STAMPS

Catalogs, dictionaries, etc.

Brookman, Lester G. The United States postage stamps of the 19th century. North Miami, Fla. : D.G. Phillips Pub. Co., [c1989]. 3 v. : ill. ISBN 1-87799-801-X (v. 1).
    BF51

First published as *The 19th century postage stamps of the United States* (*Guide* BF184). The current edition is a reprint of the 1966–67 ed. (N.Y. : H.L. Lindquist) and has some 450 new illustrations and additional material.   HE6185.U5B752

PHOTOGRAPHY

Bibliography

Films and videos on photography / comp. by Program for Art on Film, Direction des Musées de France. [N.Y.] : The Program, c1990. 114 p. ISBN 0-87099-573-1. **BF52**

Includes 511 entries, bringing together records from the *Critical inventory of films on art*, a database compiled by the Program for Art on Film, a joint venture of The Metropolitan Museum of Art and the J. Paul Getty Trust, and from the *Base audiart*, a database compiled by the Audiovisual Department of the Direction des Musées de France, Ministry of Culture and Communication, Paris.

Arrangement is alphabetical by title. The annotated entries provide information on series titles, length, black-and-white or color, date, country, language, distributors, production agency, and reviews and awards where pertinent. A names index lists film or video titles under filmmaker's name; the source index (alphabetical by title) is international.   TR147.F55

Gernsheim, Helmut. Incunabula of British photographic literature : a bibliography of British photographic literature, 1839–75, and British books illustrated with original photographs. London ; Berkeley, Calif. : Scolar Pr. in association with Derbyshire College of Higher Education, 1984. 159 p. : ill. ISBN 0-85967-657-9. £30.00.
    BF53

Serves as a *catalogue raisonné* or checklist restricted to the early period (up to 1875) and to the 638 titles that have original photographs (and their new editions). The preface provides a thorough explanation of technological changes and publishing characteristics during the four decades. Pt. 1 is the bibliography, chronologically arranged, Pt. 2 a bibliography of early British photographic literature. Pt. 3 lists photographic journals, almanacs, annuals, nonphotographic journals, and important essays. The appendix includes an outline of the historical use of three photography terms, and two indexes: photographers, and authors and artists.

§ A welcome complement to *The origins of photography*, 3rd. ed., rev., by the author and Alison Gernsheim (N.Y. : Thames and Hudson, 1988), first published in 1955 as *The history of photography*.   Z7134.G47

Heidtmann, Frank. Bibliographie der Photographie deutschsprachige Publikationen der Jahre 1839–1984 : Technik — Theorie — Bild = Bibliography of German-language photographic publications, 1839–1984 : technology — theory — visual. 2nd rev. and enl. ed. München : Saur, 1989. 2 v. ISBN 3-598-10829-X (set).
    BF54

First published as *Die deutsche Photoliteratur 1839–1978* (Münich : Saur, 1980).

Approaches the subject from a broad perspective, serving as a "national bibliography of photographic literature" and taking into account "the important technical aspects of photography, the social sciences side and above all the pictorial aspect of photography...."—*Pref.* Prefatory material in German and English. Vol. 1 contains a classified arrangement by subject (history, bibliography, practice, technology, techniques, genres, theory, etc.); v. 2 is a name and subject index. This edition, with 24,347 titles, is nearly 50% larger than the 1st, is current through 1984, and includes some new sections (e.g., illustrated children's books).   Z7134.H44

Johnson, William. Nineteenth-century photography : an annotated bibliography, 1839–1879. Boston : G.K. Hall, 1990. 962 p. : port. ISBN 0-8161-7958-1. $125.00. **BF55**

A current bibliography of some 21,000 annotated references to English-language books and articles from 60 periodicals—general interest as well as specialized—with a list of journals indexed. "... in addition to articles about photography ... contains examples of photographic practice during the period."—*Introd.* The compiler chose "broad and simple" subject headings such as "History : country" and "Exhibitions : country", which are subdivided by artist or author. The first 720 pages are the artist or author section, alphabetically arranged and providing substantial biographical information in some cases and simply dates and nationality in others. The following 220 pages are the topics section: Bibliography; Prehistory; History; Country; Apparatus or equipment [five categories]; Application or usage [nine categories]. Includes an author index, but lacks a title index. A second volume is planned to cover the period from 1880 through World War I.   Z7134.J64

Roosens, Laurent. History of photography : a bibliography of books / Laurent Roosens and Luc Salu. London ; N.Y. : Mansell, 1989. 446 p. ISBN 0-7201-2008-X. $63.00.
    BF56

A bibliography 25 years in the compilation that lists some 11,000 citations, current through the mid-1980s, in a dozen languages, including not only monographs but also company literature, dissertations, and exhibition catalogs, while excluding juvenile literature. The compilers examined most titles. Arrangement follows a structured format that includes topics, photographers, and types of publications in a single alphabet. Broad subjects or categories (e.g., History, Manuals) are subdivided by language. Listings for photographers give nationality and dates of birth and death, and are limited to photographers born before 1914. Within categories, citations are in chronological order and list all editions of a title, including reprints. Although otherwise selective, the work aims to be comprehensive for pre-1914 publications. Name index for photographers and authors.   Z7134.R66

Sennett, Robert S. The nineteenth-century photographic press : a study guide. N.Y. : Garland, 1987. 97 p. (Garland reference library of the humanities, vol. 694). ISBN 0-8240-8544-2.   **BF57**

The core of the work is a bibliography of 88 journals published between 1840 and the end of the century. Citations give pertinent dates and usually a one-line annotation. This is introduced by a seven-page overview of the birth and development of the press. Appendix: a geographic listing of journals by country. Index to names, subjects, book reviews, and exhibitions.

§ Recommended for use in conjunction with the author's *Photography and photographers to 1900 : an annotated bibliography* (N.Y. : Garland, 1985), which treats only books. For more thorough coverage, Laurent Roosens' *History of photography : a bibliography of books* (above) and William Johnson's

Nineteenth-century photography: an annotated bibliography (above) are recommended.   Z7134.S45

Indexes

Index to American photographic collections / Andrew H. Eskind and Greg Drake, editors ; comp. at the International Museum of Photography at George Eastman House. 2nd enlarged ed. Boston : G.K. Hall, 1990. 1 v. (various paging). ISBN 0-8161-0500-6.   **BF58**
    First ed., 1982 (*Guide* BF209), comp. by James McQuaid.
    This edition updates information for most of the original 400 collections and adds 140 new collections. Now provides cross-references and date(s) and/or nationality for a large number of the names. Some name listings show no holdings in the 540 collections, forming what amounts to a "not-collected" index within the index to collections. Collection entries now give the name of the contact person.   N4010.A1I5

Sales

The Artronix index : photographs at auction, 1952–1984 / ed. by Bhupendra Karia. N.Y. : Artronix, 1986. 1507 p. ISBN 0-935479-00-7. $2,000.00 (est.).   **BF59**
    A massive and unique compilation that is priced outside the reach of most libraries. Arrangement is alphabetical by photographer, preceded by a listing of photographers' names that is useful in verification. Includes a user's guide, list of photographic auctions, statistical overview of selected sales, and a chronology of photochemical and photomechanical processes and photosensitive materials.   TR6.5.A77

Handbooks

Haas, Ken. The location photographer's handbook : the complete guide for the out-of-studio shoot. N.Y. : Van Nostrand Reinhold, c1990. 427 p. : ill. ISBN 0-442-31948-7.   **BF60**
    Two introductory sections ("Preparing for the assignment" and "On the road") are followed by Country files, an alphabetical listing covering travel requirements, cultural mores, languages, transportation, and other essentials. A practical guide for any international traveller.   TR690.H27

Biography

Auer, Michèle. Encyclopédie internationale des photographes de 1839 à nos jours = Photographers encyclopaedia international 1839 to the present / Michèle Auer, Michel Auer. Hermance, Switzerland : Editions Camera obscura, c1985. 2 v. : ill. ISBN 2-903671-04-4 (set). 350F.   **BF61**
    Provides more than 1,600 biographies in English and French that are based on visits to some 600 of the photographers, on information obtained through agencies, and on published information. Entries cite key biographical information; most have a portrait of the photographer and/or an example of the work, a list of exhibitions, and a bibliography. Includes a useful two-page list of abbreviations (many specific to photography) and a 14-page chronology of the history of photography through 1985. Indexes of photographers by country (of which there are 44) and other names.   TR139.A94

Contemporary photographers / ed., Colin Naylor ; advisers, Ryszard Bobrowski . . . [et al.]. 2nd ed. Chicago : St. James Pr. ; Detroit : Distr. by Gale, 1988. 1145 p., [1] p. of plates : ill., ports. ISBN 0-912289-79-1.   **BF62**
    1st ed., 1982 (*Guide* BF222).
    This edition has 750 entrants (100 more than the previous edition), most updated through 1985–87. Some color photographs are included, the overall quality of photographs has been improved, and many entries contain new photographs. Does not delete entrants who died or ceased activity before 1940 (as does the 2nd edition of *Contemporary architects* [*Supplement* BE132]) or 1960 (as does the 2nd edition of *Contemporary artists* [*Supplement* BE78]); hence one finds entries for L. Hine (1874–1940), M. Nappelbaum (1869–1953), and E. Steichen (1879–1973).   TR139.C663

Edwards, Gary. International guide to nineteenth-century photographers and their works : based on catalogues of auction houses and dealers. Boston : G.K. Hall, c1988. 591 p. ISBN 0-8161-8938-2.   **BF63**
    The body of the work, an alphabetical listing by photographer, is preceded by a list of the 50 auction catalogs from which the listings are derived, with auction location and date. The entry for each photographer cites nationality, birth and death dates, inclusive dates of activity, processes used, formats (portraiture, genre, topography, documentary), geographic range (for topographic and documentary photographers), and location of studio. Attempts to distinguish (with "surnumbers") different people with the same name; this is in keeping with the compiler's statement that he was "more interested in uncovering basic information on obscure figures than obscure information on well-known figures."—*Pref.*   TR15.E48

Willis-Thomas, Deborah. An illustrated bio-bibliography of black photographers, 1940–1988. N.Y. : Garland, 1989. 483 p. : ill. (Garland reference library of the humanities, vol. 760). ISBN 0-8240-8389-X.   **BF64**
    A companion to the author's *Black photographers, 1840–1940: an illustrated bio-bibliography* (N.Y. : Garland, 1985). Arranged alphabetically, with entries for some 400 persons and studios. For half the photographers, gives only region and/or decade of activity; for others, provides birth date, a paragraph or two describing activity, a list of collections holding their work, a selected exhibitions list and bibliography, and one or more photographs. A general bibliography includes books, articles (with many incomplete citations), and exhibitions. No index.
    § Despite its weaknesses, makes a greater contribution to photography reference than *American photographers: an illustrated who's who among leading contemporary Americans* (N.Y. : Facts on File, 1989), and is useful in conjunction with Jeanne Moutoussamy-Ashe's *Viewfinders : black women photographers* (N.Y. : Dodd, Mead, 1986). For a thorough review of Willis-Thomas's work, see *Art libraries journal* 15, no.1 (1990): 37–39.   TR139.W55

BG

Theater and Performing Arts

GENERAL WORKS

Bibliography

Harris, Steve. Film, television, and stage music on phonograph records : a discography. Jefferson, N.C. : McFarland, c1988. 445 p. ISBN 0-89950-251-2. $49.95. **BG1**

For annotation, see *Supplement* BH145.   ML156.4.M6H3

Annuals

Black arts annual. 1987/88– . N.Y. : Garland, 1989– . Annual. ISSN 1042-7104. **BG2**

For annotation, see *Supplement* BE20.   NX512.3.A35B58

Directories

Handel's national directory for the performing arts. 4th ed. (1988?)– . Dallas : NDPA, c1988– . Annual. ISSN 0898-7955. **BG3**

Contents: v.1, Organizations and facilities; v.2, Educational institutions.

Formed by the merger of *National directory for the performing arts and civic centers* and *National directory for the performing arts/educational.*

In two parts: (1) performing arts institutions, arranged by state and city, then subdivided by Dance, Instrumental Music, Vocal music, Theatre performing arts, Series, Faculties, with an index for each category followed by a general index; and (2) educational institutions arranged by state with discussion of dance, music, and theater programs under each with an index. PN2289.H34

Slide, Anthony. Sourcebook for the performing arts : a directory of collections, resources, scholars, and critics in theatre, film, and television / comp. by Anthony Slide, Patricia King Hanson, and Stephen L. Hanson. N.Y. : Greenwood, 1988. 227 p. ISBN 0-313-24872-9. **BG4**

In three parts: (1) a listing by state of colleges and universities, libraries, historical societies with major holdings for research in theater, film, radio, and television; (2) a who's who of 200 leading academies, critics, archivists, historians, librarians, and scholars; (3) useful addresses of bookshops, organizations, journals, studios and production companies, networks. Topical index. PN2289.S55

Biography

Variety obituaries, 1905–1986 : including a comprehensive index. N.Y. : Garland, 1988–1989. 12 v. ISBN 0-8240-0835-9. $1,250.00. **BG5**

Project editors: Chuck Bartelt and Barbara Bergeron.

Contents: v. 1–10, 1905/28–1984/86; v. 11, Index; v. 12, 1987–88.

Reprint of the obituaries from *Variety* 1905–88 which appeared in news stories, editorials, and obituary columns covering the deaths of individuals connected with show business. Arranged chronologically by date of publication. Vol. 12, covering obituaries appearing 1987–88, has its own index.

PN1583.V35

Variety's who's who in show business / Mike Kaplan, ed. Rev. [i.e., 3rd] ed. N.Y. : Bowker, 1989. 412 p. ISBN 0-8352-2665-4. **BG6**

1st ed., 1983; rev. ed., 1985.

Now has 6,500 entries for "major talents and executives in film, television, music and the legitimate theatre."—*Pref.* Cut-off date is Nov. 30, 1988.   PN1583.V37

THEATER

Guides

Research guide to biography and criticism : world drama / ed. by Walton Beacham. Wash. : Research Pub., c1986. 742 p. ISBN 0-933833-06-7. $65.00. **BG7**

Like the companion volumes for fiction and poetry, this volume is "designed to assist students in narrowing and researching topics for term papers and essay exams, and to provide librarians with a tool which will help them lead students to valuable, accessible resources."—*Pref.* Treats 146 world dramatists, giving for each a chronology, select bibliography of the author's works, an overview of biographical sources, an evaluation of selected biographies, notes on autobiographical sources, an overview of critical sources, an evaluation of selected critical sources, and brief notes on additional sources. Includes an index of the names of all authors treated in this and the tow companion volumes.   Z5781.R47

Bibliography

Carpenter, Charles A. Modern drama scholarship and criticism, 1966–1980 : an international bibliography. Toronto ; Buffalo : Univ. of Toronto Pr., c1986. 587 p. ISBN 0-8020-2549-8. $75.00. **BG8**

For annotation, see *Supplement* BD87   Z5781.C37

Cavanagh, John. British theatre : a bibliography, 1901 to 1985. Mottisfont, Hampshire, England : Motley Pr., 1989. 510 p. (The Motley bibliographies, 1). ISBN 0-900281-01-4. $75.00. **BG9**

Planned as a sequel to J.F. Arnott and J.W. Robinson's *English theatrical literature, 1599–1900* (*Guide* BG24).

More than 9,300 books and pamphlets are listed topically within "three major divisions: A. Theatre, B. Drama, C. Music. Division A emphasizes performance, describes theatres, stage conditions and the lives and work of those actually engaged in production. Division B, while excluding the more literary aspects of the play, covers the history of dramatic genres and influences, and the lives and work of dramatists. Division C deals with music as an adjunct to dramatic theatre, and with musical

theatre, covering opera, operetta, and musical comedy."—*Pref.*
Author and subject indexes.   Z2014.D7C38

Evans, James E. Comedy, an annotated bibliography of
theory and criticism. Metuchen, N.J. : Scarecrow, 1987.
397 p. ISBN 0-8108-1987-2. $37.50.   **BG10**
    An annotated bibliography of about 3,000 English-
language materials (or of translation into English) published
through 1984. Topical arrangement: Comic theory before 1900
subdivided by period; Comic theory after 1900; Comic literature subdivided by country or genre (satire, farce, jokes). *See
also* item numbers are listed at the ends of sections, in many
cases too many to be helpful. Author index; personal subject
index.   Z5784.C6E94

Gray, John. Black theatre and performance : a pan-
African bibliography. N.Y. : Greenwood, 1990. 414 p.
(Bibliographies and indexes in Afro-American and African studies, no. 25). ISBN 0-313-26875-4.   **BG11**
    " . . . the user will find information on both oral and liter-
ary traditions ranging from African masquerades and New
World carnivals to the Travelling Theatres of Nigeria, protest
theatre in South Africa, and the literary dramas of Africa and
the Caribbean's literary elite."—*Introd.* Offers 4,000 books,
dissertations, archival materials, periodical and newspaper articles, films and videotapes in almost all languages arranged geographically or by individual playwright. Artist, title, subject and
author indexes. Appendix: Reference works; Regional list of
playwrights and theatre companies.   Z5784.B56G7

International bibliography of theatre. 1980– . [Brooklyn,
N.Y.] : Theatre Research Data Center, Brooklyn College, City Univ. of New York ; N.Y. : Distr. by the Publishing Center for Cultural Resources, [1982]– . Annual.
ISSN 0882-9446. $145.00.   **BG12**
    On cover: IBT.
    "Sponsored by the American Society for Theatre Research
and the International Association of Libraries and Museums of
the Performing Arts in cooperation with the International Federation for Theatre Research."—*Pref.*
    Represents "the first step toward the accumulation of a
wide-ranging databank of international theatre research references" (*Pref.*), with online access as a future goal. Full information is given in the "Classed entries" section, which is followed
by a subject index, an index of "document authors," and one of
"document content geography." A "Taxonomy of theatre" is intended as a guide to location of items in the classed list. With
1983, coverage became more international. Expanded subject
index; new geographical-chronological index.   Z6935.I53

Langhans, Edward A. Eighteenth century British and
Irish promptbooks : a descriptive bibliography. N.Y. :
Greenwood, 1987. 268 p. : ill. (Bibliographies and indexes in the performing arts, no. 6). ISBN 0-313-24029-9.
          BG13
    Offers "descriptions of over 380 British and Irish prompt-
books and related documents from the 18th century."—*Introd.*
Arranged alphabetically by author, then by title. Appendix A,
Prompters and annotators; bibliography, p.239–49. The topically arranged index includes headings such as "People named
in annotated copies" and "Play titles, subtitles, and alternate titles."   PN2593.L36

Samples, Gordon. The drama scholars' index to plays
and filmscripts : a guide to plays and filmscripts in selected anthologies, series, and periodicals. Metuchen,
N.J. : Scarecrow, 1986. v. 3. ISBN 0-8108-0699-1.   **BG14**
    For v. 1–2 and annotation, see *Guide* BG38.
    Vol.3 extends coverage through the end of 1983, with retro-
spective indexing to earlier relevant items not covered in v.1–2.
Cumulative list of anthologies, periodicals, and series indexed
by title in all three volumes.   Z5781.S17

Toro, Fernando de. Bibliografía del teatro hispanoamericano contemporáneo (1900–1980) / Fernando de Toro,
Peter Roster. Frankfurt am Main : Verlag Klaus Dieter
Vervuert, 1985. 2 v. (Editionen der Iberoamericana.
Reihe II, Bibliographische Reihe, 3). ISBN 3-921600-
35-9.   **BG15**
    Contents: v. 1, Original works published in journals, in
books, and in anthologies, and some translations; v. 2, Critical
works including histories, bibliographies, dissertations, reviews
and periodical articles and works of criticism.
    Both volumes arranged by author. Not indexed; nationali-
ty for author given in boldface at the end of each entry.
          Z1609.D7T67

Indexes

Hoffman, Herbert H. Recorded plays : indexes to dramatists, plays, and actors. Chicago : Amer. Lib. Assoc.,
1985. 139 p. ISBN 0-8389- 0440-8. $24.00 (est.).   **BG16**
    An index "to performances and headings of plays that have
been recorded on phonodiscs, audio cassettes or tapes, video
cassettes, and 16mm film."—*Pref.* 1,844 entries for some 700
different plays by 284 playwrights in 15 languages. Full information appears in the alphabetical author list, with title and
actor indexes. List of anthologies and directory of recording
companies.   PN1701.5.H64

Reviews

Selected theatre criticism / ed. by Anthony Slide. Metuchen, N.J. : Scarecrow, 1985–1986. 3 v.   ISBN
0-8108-1811-6 (v. 1).   **BG17**
    Contents: v. 1, 1900–19; v. 2, 1920–30; v. 3, 1931–50.
    Reprints in their entirety contemporary reviews of theater
productions, the latter "selected on the basis of their contemporary and historical importance, both in terms of critical and
popular regard."—*Pref., v.1.* Title arrangement within each volume, with index of critics and index of authors, actors, etc.
          PN2277.N5S44

Annuals

British theatre yearbook (New York, N.Y.). British theatre yearbook. 1989– . N.Y. : St. Martin's, c1989– . Annual. ISSN 1047-7101.   **BG18**
    Editor: 1989– , David Lemmon.
    A survey of the theatrical season for the London West End,
National Theatre, Royal Shakespeare Company, Outer London,
fringe and theatre clubs, regional theatre, touring companies. In
each section gives plays performed with cast list, the run, theatre, a short synopsis and a still. Index of plays.   PN2595.B75

Encyclopedias; Dictionaries

Bordman, Gerald Martin. The concise Oxford companion to American theatre. N.Y. : Oxford Univ. Pr., 1987.
451 p. ISBN 0-19-505121-1.   **BG19**
    The original volume (*Guide* BG56) has been reduced by
40% with some additional entries.   PN2220.B6

The Cambridge guide to world theatre / ed. by Martin
Banham. Cambridge [England] ; N.Y. : Cambridge
Univ. Pr., 1988. 1104 p. : ill. ISBN 0-521-26595-9.
          BG20

Covers dramatists, surveys of national developments, techniques. Emphasizes topics not adequately covered elsewhere: underrepresented areas (e.g., outside Europe and the U.S.), popular theater, popular entertainment. Articles are signed; longer articles have bibliographies. A review in *Booklist* (1 June 1989): 1701 concludes that "The *Cambridge guide* with its world view and wider, more inclusive definition of theatre, does offer new and/or expanded information compared with the Oxford [*companion to the theatre*; *Guide* BG63]. The majority of topics in the Cambridge guide are also covered in the Oxford."

PN2035.C27

Hodgson, Terry. The drama dictionary. N.Y. : New Amsterdam, c1988. 432 p. : ill. ISBN 0-941533-40-9. **BG21**
British title: *The Batsford dictionary of drama* (London : Batsford, 1988. 432 p.)
Offers lengthy definitions of terms used in the theater or by theater critics, with a bibliographic reference, and occasional illustrations. Cross-references; not indexed. PN1625.H64

Mendoza-López, Margarita. Teatro mexicano del siglo XX, 1900–1986 : catálogo de obras teatrales / Margarita Mendoza López, Daniel Salazar, Tomás Espinosa. México, D.F. : Instituto Mexicano del Seguro Social, c1987–c1989. 4 v. : ill., ports. ISBN 968-824-418-X (set). **BG22**
Contents: v. 1–2, A–Z; v. 3–4, A–Z.
Provides synopses and production information for plays listed alphabetically by author. PQ7189.M4

The Oxford companion to Canadian theatre / ed. by Eugene Benson and L.W. Conolly. Toronto ; N.Y. : Oxford Univ. Pr., 1989. 662 p. : ill. ISBN 0-19-540672-9. $50.00. **BG23**
Covers genres, plays, playwrights, theatres, criticism. Scholarly articles, signed. Topical index. PN2300.O94

Terms

An international dictionary of theatre language / Joel Trapido, gen. ed. ; Edward A. Langhans, ed. for Western theatre ; James R. Brandon, ed. for Asian theatre. Westport, Conn. : Greenwood, 1985. 1032 p. ISBN 0-313-22980-5. **BG24**
Definitions of 10,000 English and 5,000 foreign-language terms used in the English-speaking world. Excluded are terms from mass media, popular entertainment (circus, nightclubs) and words "adequately defined for our purposes in Webster's New Collegiate Dictionary."—*Guide*. For each term gives language if not English, definition, and reference to specific pages in works cited in the bibliography. Includes a short essay, brief history of theatre glossaries, and dictionaries. PN2035.I5

Lounsbury, Warren C. Theatre backstage from A to Z / Warren C. Lounsbury, Norman Boulanger. 3rd ed., rev. and expanded. Seattle : Univ. of Washington Pr., c1989. 213 p. : ill. ISBN 0-295-96829-X. ISBN 0-295-96828-1 (pbk.). **BG25**
1st ed., 1967; rev. ed., 1972 (*Guide* BG120).
Carries new material on sound, electronic control, and equipment, but retains articles on the older technology. Selected list of manufacturers and distributors. PN2091.M3L68

Directories

Howard, Diana. Directory of theatre resources : a guide to research collections and information services. 2nd ed. [London, England] : Library Association Information Services Group and the Society for Theatre Research, 1986. 144 p. ISBN 0-946347-08-5. **BG26**
1st ed., 1980.
Based on responses to a questionnaire. Pt.1, Public and private collections open to the public; pt.2, Societies and associations serving the theatre which provide information services. Geographical arrangement. PN2598.5.H68

Awards

Stevenson, Isabelle. The Tony Award : a complete listing, with a history of the American Theatre Wing / ed. by Isabelle Stevenson ; research consultant, Sonia Ediff. N.Y. : Crown, c1987. 197 p. : ill. ISBN 0-517-56664-8. **BG27**
1st issued 1980; updated 1984.
A year-by-year listing of all Tony Award nominees and winners. Index of winners. PN2270.A93S8

Handbooks

A guide to theatre in America / comp. and ed. by Lawrence S. Epstein. N.Y. : Macmillan, c1985. 443 p. ISBN 0-02-909670-7. $50.00. **BG28**
Provides directory information for a wide range of theater services and professional needs: agents, awards, councils and service organizations, critics, directors, facilities, festivals, colleges and schools, foundations, libraries, press agents, producers, suppliers, etc. Index of names and addresses of contact persons. PN2219.5.G8

History

American theatre companies / ed. by Weldon B. Durham. N.Y. : Greenwood, c1986–1989. 3 v. ISBN 0-313-20886-7 (v. 1). **BG29**
Contents: v. 1, 1749–1887; v. 2, 1888–1930; v. 3, 1931–86.
A "biographical" dictionary of resident acting companies and stock companies from 1749, with the first "significant" English-speaking company in the U.S., to 1986. Each entry gives a brief history including dates of founding and major seasons, locations, policies, critical assessment, personnel, repertory and bibliography (which includes both published and archival sources). The index covers play titles and names, although the names portion is incomplete. The arrangement is alphabetical with an appendix for a chronology of theatre companies and a list of theatre companies by state. PN2237.A43

Barnes, Philip. A companion to post-war British theatre. Totowa, N.J. : Barnes & Noble, c1986. 277 p. ISBN 0-389-20669-5. **BG30**
Offers entries for dramatists, directors, performers, theaters, stage companies, and terms. Many articles include quotations from critics or a personality's own statement about his or her craft. Suggested further readings for many topics. Index of plays mentioned in the text. PN2595.B28

Guernsey, Otis L. Curtain times : the New York theater, 1965–1987. N.Y. : Applause, c1987. 613 p. : ill. ISBN 0-

936839-24-4. $34.95. ISBN 0-936839-23-6 (pbk.).
$15.95.   **BG31**

Photographs by Martha Swope, drawings by Hirschfeld.

Narrative survey of each season, with critical analysis and
reporting. Index for playwright, title, actor or actress, director
or producer mentioned in the text.   PN2277.N5G8

Leiter, Samuel L. The encyclopedia of the New York
stage, 1920–1930 / Samuel L. Leiter, ed. in chief ; Holly
Hill, associate ed. Westport, Conn. : Greenwood, 1985.
2 v. (1331 p.). ISBN 0-313-23615-1. $145.00.   **BG32**

Aims "to provide a description of every legitimate theatre
production—play, musical, revue, revival—given in the New
York i.e., Manhattan professional theatre" (*Pref.*) during the period June 16, 1920–June 15, 1930. Entries are for plays only,
not performers, managers, etc. Each play is categorized by type,
and information is given regarding author, lyricist, director, designer, theater, opening date, length of run, etc., followed by
brief plot summary, critical reception (often with quotations
from reviews), and commentary. Appendixes include a calendar
of productions, a listing of plays by categories, awards, longest
running shows, list of critics cited, seasonal statistics, and theaters. Selected bibliography; index of proper names. Continued
by the author's *The encyclopedia of the New York stage,
1930–40* (1989. 1299 p. $145.00).   PN2277.N5L36

Mullin, Donald C. Victorian plays : a record of significant productions on the London stage, 1837–1901.
N.Y. : Greenwood, 1987. 444 p. (Bibliographies and indexes in the performing arts, no. 4). ISBN 0-313-24211-
9.   **BG33**

Provides production records for each play taken from original playbills giving title, playwright, first (or earliest known)
production date, revivals, principal players, names of characters, scene designers. Index of playwrights, adapters, translators.
A succeeding volume has been promised.   PN2596.L6M85

Theatre companies of the world / ed. by Colby H. Kullman and William C. Young. Westport, Conn. : Greenwood, 1986. 2 v. (979 p.). ISBN 0-313-21456-5. $95.00.
    BG34

Contents: v. 1, Africa, Asia, Australia and New Zealand,
Canada, Eastern Europe, Latin America, the Middle East, Scandinavia; v. 2, United States of America, Western Europe (excluding Scandinavia).

Nine editors with "specialized knowledge of the theatrical
tradition of a specific geographical area" (*Pref.*) have selected
the theatre companies to be included and with other contributors have written narrative essays which include name and address, brief history, significance, number of stages and seating
capacity, future plans. Vol.2 concludes with "Suggestions for
additional readings" and an index of names.   PN2052.T48

Wearing, J. P. The London stage, 1920–1929 : a calendar of plays and players. Metuchen, N.J. : Scarecrow,
1984. 3 v. ISBN 0-8108-1715-2. $95.00.   **BG35**

For coverage of earlier decades, see *Guide* BG89–91.

Continues to add about 4,000–5,000 productions per set of
volumes. The third volume is a title index and a general index
for performers, playwrights, production staff, etc.

§ The set covering 1930–39 was publ. in 1990.
    PN2596.L6W384

Biography

Highfill, Philip H. A biographical dictionary of actors,
actresses, musicians, dancers, managers & other stage
personnel in London, 1660–1800 / by Philip H. Highfill,
Jr., Kalman A. Burnim, and Edward A. Langhans. Carbondale : Southern Illinois Univ. Pr., [1987–1991]. v.
11–14 : illus. ISBN 0-8093-0518-6. $19.85 (v. 1). (In
progress).   **BG36**

For volumes 1–10 and annotation, see *Guide* BG96.

Contents: v. 11–14, Naso–Thynne.   PN2597.H5

Kosch, Wilhelm. Deutsches Theater-Lexikon : biographisches und bibliographisches Handbuch. Klagenfurt :
F. Kleinmayr, 1989. Lfg. 22.   **BG37**

For Lfg. 1–21 and annotation, see *Guide* BG99.

Contents: Lfg. 22, Schleuning–Schütz-Witt.   PN2035.K6

Morley, Sheridan. The great stage stars : distinguished
theatrical careers of the past and present. N.Y. : Facts on
File, 1986. 425 p., [44] p. of plates : ports. ISBN 0-
8160-1401-9.   **BG38**

Companion to David Shipman's *The great movie stars*
(*Guide* BG286).

Criterion: " . . . could the candidate for inclusion create advance booking at a theatre box office before the first night,
when appearing in a new and unknown play by a new and unknown author with an unknown supporting cast, and moreover
could he or she do so without relying on fame acquired in the
cinema or on television."—*Introd.* About 200 biographies,
mostly British, ranging in length from half a page to a page and
a half.   PN2597.M64

Notable women in the American theatre : a biographical
dictionary / ed. by Alice M. Robinson, Vera Mowry Roberts, and Milly S. Barranger. N.Y. : Greenwood, 1989.
993 p. ISBN 0-313-27217-4. $99.50.   **BG39**

Lengthy entries with a bibliography appended to each
sketch, for women influential and significant in the American
theatre. Appendixes list place of birth, profession. Cross-
references; topical index.   PN2285.N65

Peterson, Bernard L. Contemporary black American
playwrights and their plays : a biographical directory
and dramatic index. N.Y. : Greenwood, 1988. 625 p.
ISBN 0-313-25190-8. $75.00.   **BG40**

Covers some 700 black American "dramatists, screenwriters, radio and television scriptwriters, musical theatre collabo-
rators . . . written, produced, and/or published between 1950
and the present."—*Pref.* For each gives biographical information ranging from address to a brief sketch, then a list of plays
with one-sentence descriptions and first performance. Indexed.
    PS153.N5P43

———— Early black American playwrights and
dramatic writers : a biographical directory and catalog
of plays, films, and broadcasting scripts. N.Y. : Greenwood, c1990. 298 p. ISBN 0-313-26621-2.   **BG41**

Intends to be a "convenient source of information on approximately 218 pioneer black American playwrights, screenwriters, and other originators of dramatic works written and/or
produced in the United States and in Europe during the nineteenth century. Of these 218 playwrights, 136 are included in
the main directory, and 82 are included in two of the three appendixes in the back of this book."—*Pref.* For each, gives background, highlights of career, list of published or unpublished
works in anthologies, chronological list of individual works
(with synopses) and references to other material both primary
and secondary. Appendix: other early American playwrights
and their plays, additional musical librettists and brief descriptions of their shows. Chronology of plays and dramatic works

cited in this dictionary and classified by genre. Title index, organization index, and topical index. PS153.N5P44

Quién es quién en el teatro y el cine español e hispanoamericano. Barcelona, España : C.I.L.E.H., 1990. 2 v. (922 p.). ISBN 84-8741-100-2 (set). **BG42**

Lists directors, actors, and actresses, critics, dramatists, etc., giving very brief biographical information (usually profession, and often place and date of birth, date of death if deceased) and a chronology giving works and major events in the life. No publishing information is given for the works. Not indexed. PN2784.Q546

Sampson, Henry T. The ghost walks : a chronological history of blacks in show business, 1865–1910. Metuchen, N.J. : Scarecrow, 1988. 570 p. : ill. ISBN 0-8108-2070-6. $47.50. **BG43**

" . . . attempts to trace the development of black entertainment in the United States from its beginning, just at the end of the Civil War, to 1910."—*Pref.*

Chronological list of productions, sometimes with reviews, events, programs, letters, etc. Arranged by decade, each beginning with an introductory survey. Name index. Heavily indexed with black-and-white photographs of performers, sheet music covers, promotional literature, etc. PN2270.A35S25

Bibliography

Stage lives : a bibliography and index to theatrical biographies in English / comp. by George B. Bryan. Westport, Conn. : Greenwood, 1985. 368 p. (Bibliographies and indexes in the performing arts, no. 2). ISBN 0-3132-4577-0. $45.00. **BG44**

Intended to supplement J. P. Wearing's *American and British theatrical biography* (*Guide* BG109); *Performing arts biography master index* (2nd ed., Detroit : Gale, 1982); and Dennis La Beau's *Theatre, film and television biographies master index* (*Guide* BG20).

Provides reference to biographies for "any person whose life is or was connected with the living, non-mechanical theatre . . . ranging from 534 B.C. to the present."—*Introd.* English-language collective theatrical biographies, collective nontheatrical biographies, and individual biographies and autobiographies are indexed. Necrological annals list actors, directors, etc. by year of death. Z5781.S78

THE DANCE

Bibliography

Adamczyk, Alice J. Black dance : an annotated bibliography. N.Y. : Garland, 1989. 213 p. : ports. (Garland reference library of the humanities, vol. 558). ISBN 0-8240-8808-5. **BG45**

Based on collections of the New York Public Library Research Collections "documenting black dance in all of its forms."—*Introd.* 1,392 books, journal articles, and newspaper articles published in the Western hemisphere. An author listing with brief annotations. Subject index (e.g., terms such as Limbo, Cakewalk, or areas such as New Orleans). Z7514.D2A33

Forbes, Fred R. Dance : an annotated bibliography, 1965–1982. N.Y. : Garland, 1986. 261 p. (Garland reference library of the humanities, vol. 606). ISBN 0-8240-8676-7. $39.00. **BG46**

Aims to be "an annotated list of current references on dance in the areas of aesthetics, anthropology, education, history, literature, physiology, psychology and sociology" (*Pref.*) organized by topic. 1,166 numbered entries for books, articles, chapters, and dissertations, in English, published 1965–82. Author and subject indexes. Z7514.D2F58

Petermann, Kurt. Tanzbibliographie. Leipzig : Bibliographisches Institut, 1987. 1 v. ISBN 3-323-00021-8 (v. [6]). **BG47**

For Lfg. 1–30 and annotation, see *Guide* BG132.

Contents: Registerband ([1987]. 592 p.). Completes the set? Z7514.D2P44

Robinson, Doris. Music and dance periodicals : an international directory & guidebook. Voorheesville, N.Y. : Peri Pr., c1989. 382p. ISBN 0-961-7844-4-X. **BG48**

For annotation, see *Supplement* BH33. ML128.P24R58

Indexes

Studwell, William E. Ballet plot index : a guide to locating plots and descriptions of ballets and associated material / William E. Studwell and David A. Hamilton. N.Y. : Garland, 1987. 249 p. (Garland reference library of the humanities, vol. 756). ISBN 0-8240-8385-7. $40.00. **BG49**

Index to 54 books, all dealing with the ballet, for plots, illustrations, background, criticism, or analysis of individual ballets. Listing by title of the ballet, with composer index. GV1790.A1S77

MOTION PICTURES

Guides

Fisher, Kim N. On the screen : a film, television, and video research guide. Littleton, Colo. : Libraries Unlimited, 1986. 209 p. ISBN 0-87287-448-6. $35.00. **BG50**

Some 645 English-language reference books for those interested in motion pictures and television are listed by type of reference work (e.g., bibliographies, guides, dictionaries and encyclopedias, periodicals). The rest of the volume provides lists of research centers, archives, societies, and associations, arranged geographically. Useful annotations for all bibliographic or directory items. Author/title and subject indexes. Z5784.M9F535

Bibliography

Gebauer, Dorothea. Bibliography of national filmographies / comp. by Dorothea Gebauer with the assistance of the members of the Cataloguing Commission of the International Federation of Film Archives ; ed. by Harriet W. Harrison. Bruxelles : FIAF, c1985. 80 p. **BG51**

A country-by-country listing of filmographies. Aims "to include any reference work or tool, whether published or unpublished, which FIAF member archives have found helpful for their cataloging work" (*p.v*), and thus includes numerous items which are not, strictly speaking, national lists. Not indexed. Z5784.M9G42

Gray, John. Blacks in film and television : a Pan-African bibliography of films, filmmakers, and performers. N.Y. : Greenwood, 1990. 496 p. (Bibliographies and indexes in Afro-American and African studies, no. 27). ISBN 0-313-27486-X.   **BG52**

Based on collections at the New York Public Library: the Billy Rose Theatre Collection of the Performing Arts Research Center, and the Schomburg Center for Research in Black Culture.

About 6,000 books, dissertations, periodical and newspaper articles, films, video and audio tapes, and archival material for Africa, Europe, the Caribbean and Latin America, and the U.S. For Africa, includes material on "colonial and ethnographic film activity as well as works on indigenous African films and filmmaking" (*Introd.*), but does not include "television in an African context." For other countries concentrates on the black film tradition; for U.S. includes references to the African-American image in film. Appendix for film resources—e.g., archives, distributors, festivals, etc. Indexes for artist, title, subject, and author.   Z5784.M9G72

Manchel, Frank. Film study : an analytical bibliography. Rutherford, [N.J.] : Fairleigh Dickinson Univ. Pr. ; London : Associated Univ. Pr., c1990. 4 v. ISBN 0-8386-3186-X (v. 1). ISBN 0-8386-3412-5 (v. 2).   **BG53**

A revision and reworking of the author's *Film study : a resource guide* (*Guide* BG163).

Aims to present "six popular approaches to the study of cinema along with a practical analysis of selected books, materials, and information about motion picture rentals."—*Introd.* Extensive discussion of issues or genres (e.g., Stereotyping in film; Holocaust films) with annotated bibliography (mostly books) appended. Vol.4, appendixes and indexes, includes: production codes of producers, library and bookstore resources, indexes for book and film titles, authors, film personalities, subjects. Complicated arrangement, with a typeface that is difficult to read; still very useful.   Z5784.M9M34

Ross, Harris. Film as literature, literature as film : an introduction to and bibliography of film's relationship to literature. N.Y. ; London : Greenwood, 1987. 346 p. (Bibliographies and indexes in world literature, no. 10). ISBN 0-313-24595-9. £39.95.   **BG54**

Lists 2,500 articles and books published 1908–85 on the relationship of film to literature. Intended to be comprehensive, the bibliography omits film reviews, newspaper articles, foreign-language materials. A few citations include annotations, especially when the title is ambiguous. Author and subject indexes.   Z5784.M9

Schmidt, Nancy J. Sub-Saharan African films and filmmakers : an annotated bibliography = Films et cinéastes africains de la région Subsaharienne : une bibliographie commentée. London ; N.Y. : Zell, 1988. 401 p. ISBN 0-905450-32-9.   **BG55**

Preliminary ed., Bloomington : African Studies Program, Indiana Univ., 1986.

Almost 4,000 entries listed by author, subdivided by format: books, monographs, articles, reviews, and pamphlets, with short annotations. Excludes films by North American and South African filmmakers or about Africa by non-Africans. Indexes for actors/actresses, film festivals, film titles, filmmakers, countries divided by subject, general subject.   Z5784.M9S3

Writers' Program (New York, N.Y.). The film index : a bibliography. White Plains, N.Y. : Kraus Internat., 1985. v. 2–3. ISBN 0-527-29533-4 (v.2–3).   **BG56**

For v. 1 and annotation, see *Guide* BG181.

Contents: v. 2, The film as industry; v. 3, The film in society.

"Compiled by the Workers of the Writers' Program of the Work Projects Administration in the city of New York, 1935–1940, with the cooperation of the Museum of Modern Art, New York"—*t.p. of v. 2–3.*   Z5784.M9W75

Wulff, Hans Jürgen. Bibliographie der Filmbibliographien = Bibliography of film bibliographies / comp. and ed. by Hans Jürgen Wulff ; including a bibliography of

Slavic language film bibliographies, comp.by Andrzej Gwóźdź and Anna Wastkowska. München : New York : K.G. Saur, 1987. 326 p. ISBN 3-598-10630-0. $50.00.   **BG57**

Lists more than 1,000 bibliographies published as books, catalogs of individual library collections, pamphlets, articles and essays (and also parts of articles and essays) in English and in European languages, through 1985. Excludes almost all filmographies. Classified arrangement; *see also* references; author and subject indexes. "Retrospective, cumulative indexes to individual film journals," p. 64–70.   Z5784.M9W84

Periodicals

International film, radio, and television journals / ed. by Anthony Slide. Westport, Conn. : Greenwood, 1985. 428 p. ISBN 0-313-23759-X. $49.95.   **BG58**

The overwhelming majority of entries is for American and British periodicals, mainly from the field of film. Alphabetical listing; signed "profile" of each magazine, notes on publication history, and location of files. Appendixes list fan magazines, etc. Indexed.   Z5784.M9I485

Adaptations

Emmens, Carol A. Short stories on film and video. 2nd ed. Littleton, Colo. : Libraries Unlimited, 1985. 337 p. : ill. ISBN 0-87287-424-9. $25.00.   **BG59**

1st ed., 1978 (*Guide* BG170) had title: *Short stories on film.* Expands coverage for 1920–84 to about 1,375 entries.   PN1997.85.E45

Enser, A. G. S. Filmed books and plays : a list of books and plays from which films have been made, 1928–86. Rev. ed. Aldershot, Hampshire : Gower, c1987. 770 p. ISBN 0-566-03564-2. $55.00.   **BG60**

A revision of 1985 edition (*Guide* BG171) which covered 1928–83, adding new material.   Z5784.M9E563

Langman, Larry. Writers on the American screen : a guide to film adaptations of American and foreign literary works. N.Y. : Garland, 1986. 329 p. (Garland reference library of the humanities, vol. 658). ISBN 0-8240-9844-7.   **BG61**

". . . purpose is to present all the major and many of the minor writers, Americans as well as foreign, whose poems, short stories, plays and novels have been made into motion pictures."—*Pref.* Arranged by author, listing the written work followed by the title of the movie adaptation, date of release, and studio. Title index of both written work and movie titles. Enser's *Filmed books and plays* (above) and Langman overlap but Enser has more authors while Langman often has titles not covered by Enser.   Z5784.M9L28

Women writers, from page to screen / Jill Rubinson Fenton ... [et al.]. N.Y. : Garland, 1990. 483 p. (Garland reference library of the humanities, vol. 687). ISBN 0-8240-8529-9.   **BG62**

Aims to present "a comprehensive listing of more than two thousand two hundred British (English-speaking dominions included) and American feature films and television movies inspired by women's writings."—*Pref.* Cites novels, short fiction, nonfiction, and theatrical and biographical writings alphabetically by author; covers films, 1913–88. Title index.   PN1997.85.W58

Indexes

Film review index / ed. by Patricia King Hanson, Stephen L. Hanson. Phoenix : Oryx, 1986–1987. 2 v. ISBN 0-89774-153-6 (v.1). $58.50. ISBN 0-89774-331-8 (v.2). $58.50. **BG63**

Contents: v. 1, 1882–1949; v. 2, 1950–85.

Concentrates on "those pictures that have established themselves as being of continuing importance to film researchers," but includes various "minor films that could, at some point, become the object of certain highly specialized types of research due to their reflection of certain sociological trends or simply because they were extremely popular for a variety of reasons."—*Introd.* Emphasizes substantive reviews, mainly in fairly accessible sources, but including trade publication. Includes citations to selected books. Z5784.M9F513

Magill's cinema annual : cumulative indexes, 1982–1986 / ed. by Frank N. Magill. Pasadena, Calif. : Salem Pr., c1986. 258 p. ISBN 0-89356-405-2 (pbk.). **BG64**

Indexes five years of the annual volumes of *Magill's cinema annual* (*Guide* BG197): title, director, screenwriter, cinematographer, editor, art director, music, performer, subject. PN1993.3.M34

Magill's survey of cinema, foreign language films / ed. by Frank N. Magill. Englewood Cliffs, N.J. : Salem Pr., c1985. 8 v. ISBN 0-89356-243-2 (set). $330.00. **BG65**

Like the companion set for English-language films (*Guide* BG194a–196), offers signed essays on 700 outstanding films from throughout the world. Vol. 8 is an index. PN1995.9.F67M34

Catalogs and filmography

American Film Institute. Catalog of motion pictures produced in the United States : feature films, 1911–1920. Berkeley : Univ. of California Pr., 1988. 2 v. (1504 p.). ISBN 0-520-06301-5. $90.00. **BG66**

For other volumes of the American Film Institute catalog, see *Guide* BG200.

An alphabetical listing by title, with indexes for personal name, corporate name, chronology, genre, geographic name, subject and "Literary and dramatic source." The compilers consulted annuals, autobiographies, photographs, newspapers, and personal papers as well as film copies, copyright entries, etc., for credits and to augment the notes. PN1998.A57

Bergan, Ronald. The Holt foreign film guide / Ronald Bergan and Robyn Karney. N.Y. : Holt, 1989. 638 p. ISBN 0-8050-0991-4. $39.95. **BG67**

Publ. in U.K. as: *Bloomsbury foreign film guide* (London : Bloomsbury, 1988).

Includes "big box-office successes and movies which, irrespective of quality or current appeal, are representative of trends, fashions, styles, and developments." (*Introd.*) and which can be seen in the U.S. and Great Britain. Listed under British title with cross-references from American or original title. Gives for each: date of first release, country of origin, running time, color, production company, cast summary, any awards. No indexes. A 2nd ed., 1991, has been announced by Bloomsbury. PN1995.9.F67B4

Cyr, Helen W. A filmography of the Third World, 1976–1983 : an annotated list of 16mm films. Metuchen, N.J. : Scarecrow, 1985. 275 p. ISBN 0-8108-1768-3. **BG68**

Continues the author's *A filmography of the Third World* (1976).

Intended for teachers and students. Lists "films about the underdeveloped areas of the world . . . and also about the major ethnic minorities who live in the northern nations of North America and Europe."—*Foreword.* Geographically arranged, gives title, producer, date of publication, etc.

Continued by Cyr's *The Third World in film and video 1984–1990* (1991. 246 p.). HC59.7.C975

Drew, Bernard A. Motion picture series and sequels : a reference guide. N.Y. : Garland, 1990. 412 p. : ill. (Garland reference library of the humanities, vol. 1186). ISBN 0-8240-4248-4. **BG69**

Lists "some 906 English-language (or subtitle or dubbed) motion pictures beginning in the silent picture era which had one or more sequels."—*Introd.* The main entry is occasionally under the name of the book author (Dick Francis) or main character (James Bond) or first film of the series (*Night of the living dead*). One-sentence description of the series, titles of sequels, date, studio and director, and star(s). Title index.

PN1995.9.S29D66

Filmer, Alison J. Harrap's book of film directors and their films : a comprehensive guide from 1924 to the present day / Alison J. Filmer, Andre Golay. London : Harrap, 1989. 491 p. ISBN 0-245-54942-0. £14.95.

BG70

For the period 1924–89 tries to be a comprehensive listing of all feature film directors in the U.K. and the U.S. and foreign directors who have made at least one English-language film. Alphabetical by director's name with dates, nationality, and a chronological listing of all films (and date of release). Title index. PN1998.A2

Gifford, Denis. The British film catalogue, 1895–1985 : a reference guide. N.Y. : Facts on File, c1986. ca. 1000 p. ISBN 0-8160-1554-6. $75.00. **BG71**

Includes material in earlier work that covered 1895–1970 (*Guide* BG213).

A catalog of every film made in Great Britain and Ireland for entertainment regardless of whether it was released (not including television films). The listing is chronological within two sections, 1895–1970 and 1971–85, with an alphabetical index of film titles. For each film, gives: production details, director, cast and characters, screenplay author and source, summary, any awards. PN1998.G543

A guide to world cinema : covering 7,200 films of 1950–84 including capsule reviews and stills from the programmes of the National Film Theatre, London / ed. by Elkan Allan. London : Whittet Books in association with the British Film Institute ; Detroit : Distr. by Gale, 1985. 682 p. : ill. ISBN 0-905483-33-2. **BG72**

Reprints the notes (some "suitably doctored") from the monthly program booklet issued by Britain's National Film Theatre. Notes are critical in nature. Country of origin, date, and director are given; a still accompanies most entries. Arranged by title; index of directors. Many films predate the 1950 of the subtitle (which evidently refers to the dates of the NFT screenings). PN1995.G84

Halliwell, Leslie. Halliwell's film guide. 7th ed. N.Y. : Harper & Row, c1989. 1171 p. : ill. ISBN 0-06-016322-4. $50.00. **BG73**

4th ed., 1983 (*Guide* BG242); 6th ed., 1987.

Adds about 1,000 new entries and revisions.

PN1993.45.H27

Helt, Richard C. West German cinema since 1945 : a reference handbook / by Richard C. Helt and Marie E. Helt. Metuchen, N.J. : Scarecrow, 1987. 736 p., [16] p. of plates : ill. ISBN 0-8108-2053-6. $52.50. **BG74**

Covers "West German feature-length, commercial films produced between 1945 and early 1986" (*Pref.*) including those co-produced with directors from other countries. Alphabetical by German title; gives year of production, synopsis, credits, cast, length in minutes. Index of directors, actors and actresses; cross-reference from English to German title.

PN1993.5.G3H435

Library of Congress. Motion Picture, Broadcasting, and Recorded Sound Division. Early motion pictures : the paper print collection in the Library of Congress / by Kemp R. Niver ; ed. by Bebe Bergsten. Wash. : Motion Picture, Broadcasting, and Recorded Sound Division, Library of Congress : For sale by U.S. Govt. Print. Off., 1985. 509 p. : ill. ISBN 0-8444-0463-2. $24.00. **BG75**

A revision, expansion, and updating of of Niver's *Motion pictures from the Library of Congress paper print collection, 1894–1912 (Guide BG218).*

Superintendent of Documents classification: LC40.9:Ea7.

Serves as a guide to the more than 3,000 films restored from the paper print collection at the Library of Congress. Films are listed by title; information given includes copyright or distributor/producer, production credits, location and date of production, length, LC shelf location, summary, and notes. Indexes of credits (actors, camera operators, directors, scriptwriters, and authors) and of names/subjects. An important work for the film historian. Z5784.M9L5

Magliozzi, Ronald S. Treasures from the film archives : a catalog of short silent fiction films held by FIAF archives. Metuchen, N.J. : Scarecrow, 1988. 834 p. ISBN 0-8108-2180-X. **BG76**

"This catalogue is a list of holdings of the short silent fiction film in FIAF archives all over the world."—*Pref.* For each film, gives date, title, production company (and in later cases director and actors), and the archive. Arranged by country of production and year. Indexes for series title, animated title, performers, directors, production company. PN1995.75.M335

Museum of Modern Art (New York, N.Y.). The film catalog : a list of holdings in the Museum of Modern Art / general ed., Jon Gartenberg with Lee Amazonas . . . [et al.]. Boston : G.K. Hall, 1985. 443 p., [50] p. of plates : ill. ISBN 0-8161-0443-3. $60.00. **BG77**

"This catalog includes approximately 5,500 titles representing films acquired from 1935 through 1980 that had been entered into a computerized database by May 1985."—*Introd.* Title listing, with producer/director index. International coverage; cross-references from alternate titles. PN1993.4.M8

Nash, Jay Robert. The motion picture guide / Jay Robert Nash, Stanley Ralph Ross. Chicago : Cinebooks, 1985–1987. 12 v. (v. 1–9, 4181 p.; v. 10, 439 p.; v. 11–12, 3170 p.). ISBN 0-933997-00-0 (set). **BG78**

Contents: v. 1–9, 1927–84, comp. by Nash and Ross; v. 10, Silent film, 1910–36, comp. by Robert Connelly; v. 11–12, Index, comp. by Nash and Ross.

A title listing of 25,000 "English-speaking theatrically released feature films" (*Foreword*) with an additional 10,000 silent films. For all, gives title with variants and credits with date of release; for many, adds synopsis, genre note, and a rating for acting, directing, script, and technical achievement. Vol. 9 includes 1984 releases, p. 4006–4121, and a list of talkies the editors felt were of minor significance but which are included in the interest of completeness. Vols. 11–12 provide indexes of alternate titles, series, awards, and names. Kept up to date by annual supplements; beginning with 1986 annual suppl., each volume covers films of the previous year. PN1995.N346

Nowlan, Robert A. Cinema sequels and remakes, 1903–1987 / by Robert A. Nowlan and Gwendolyn Wright Nowlan. Jefferson, N.C. : McFarland, c1989. 954 p. : ill. ISBN 0-89950-314-4. $49.95. **BG79**

Includes "all films, silent or sound, from the genres of drama, action-adventure, romance, comedy, thriller which have at least one English-speaking sound remake or sequel."— *Introd.* Alphabetical arrangement by title. For each entry gives:

source of screenplay, year of release, production company, synopsis of original and remake or sequel, director, screenwriter, main characters and leading performers. Index for actors, writers, directors, song titles, etc.

§ Does not list as many film titles as Bernard A. Drew's *Motion picture series and sequels* (above) but the information included for a specific film is much more extensive.

PN1995.9.S29N69

Palmer, Scott. British film actors' credits, 1895–1987. Jefferson, N.C. : McFarland, c1988. 917 p. ISBN 0-89950-316-0. **BG80**

About 5,000 performers in motion pictures and some films made for television since 1895 alphabetically listed. Includes those who were born in the U.K. or the Commonwealth or worked in the U.K. Information for each performer: dates, brief characterization of most of the roles, list of films with dates. Not indexed. PN1998.2.P3

Sobański, Oskar. Polish feature films : a reference guide 1945–1985. West Cornwall, Conn. : Locust Hill Pr., 1987. 335 p. ISBN 0-933951-02-7. $35.00. **BG81**

Arranged in three parts: (1) 233 biobibliographies "of almost all Polish feature film directors who have made a noteworthy contribution to the feature film" (*Introd.*), for each giving background and a filmography; (2) Polish feature films, 1945–85: facts and figures; (3) Polish feature films by title, 1945–85. Name index. Index of English-language film titles with original Polish title. PN1998.S672

Turner, D. John. Canadian feature film index, 1913–1985 = Index des films canadiens de long métrage, 1913–1985 / D.J. Turner ; French text, Micheline Morisset. [Ottawa] : Public Archives Canada : National Film, Television, and Sound Archives, c1987. 816 p. ISBN 0-660-53364-2 (pbk.). $25.00. **BG82**

An "attempt to compile the principal credits of every Canadian feature film from 1913, when the first known feature [*Back to God's country*] was produced, to 1985."—*Introd.* The films are chronologically arranged by the date the film was shot. For each, gives: ". . . technical information related to the making of the film (film stock, laboratory, dialogue), then the principal participants (producers, directors, technicians, actors), the cost and running time followed by distribution and release information and lastly the Archives' holdings."—*User's guide.* Includes 1,222 films. Indexed by title, personal name, production company, etc. PN1998.T83

Library resources

International directory of film and TV documentation centres / ed. by Frances Thorpe. [3rd ed.]. Chicago : St. James Pr., c1988. 140 p. ISBN 0-912289-29-5. **BG83**

Rev. ed. of *FIAF directory of film and TV documentation sources* (Amsterdam : Netherlands Filmmuseum for the F.I.A.F., 1976); 2nd ed., 1980).

Lists 104 collections (40 new entries) from 40 countries: for each gives name and address, contact staff, budget, availability of copying facilities, holdings (including books, periodicals, correspondence, scripts, press books, stills, cuttings, typescripts, censorship records). PN1993.4.I57

Researcher's guide to British film & television collections / ed., Elizabeth Oliver. 2nd, rev. ed. [London] : British Universities Film & Video Council, [1985]. 176 p. : ill. **BG84**

1st ed., [1980].

New authors for the essays on Film research and Researching for a television series. Little change in glossary; additional archives and libraries desccribed; subject index.

PN1993.4.R47

Encyclopedias; Dictionaries

The BFI companion to the Western / ed. by Edward Buscombe. N.Y. : Atheneum, 1988. 432 p. : ill., map. ISBN 0-689-11962-3. **BG85**

Reprinted: N.Y. : DaCapo, 1991.

Heavily illustrated "panoramic history" of the Western, including definitions of terms, identification of characters, themes, biographies of filmmakers, actors and actresses, etc., and a guide to specific films. PN1995.9.W4B45

Bogle, Donald. Blacks in American films and television : an encyclopedia. N.Y. : Garland, 1988. 510 p. : ill. (Garland reference library of the humanities, vol. 604). ISBN 0-8240-8715-1. $60.00. **BG86**

Repr. : N.Y. : Simon & Schuster, 1989.

Concentrates on American films widely distributed, all black films made 1919–49, and major black-oriented series or mini-series on television, giving credits, synopses, and critical commentary. Alphabetical by title divided between movies and television; lengthy profiles of black actors, directors, dancers, etc. Name and title index. PN1995.9.N4B58

Cinegraph : Lexikon zum deutschsprachigen Film / hrsg. von Hans-Michael Bock ; [Redaktion, Frank Arnold . . . et al.]. München : Edition Text + Kritik, 1984– . **BG87**

Prefatory material in German and English.

A looseleaf "biographical and filmographical encyclopaedia, covering all categories of film-makers (directors, actors, technicians, publicists, etc.) in the German-speaking cinema . . . from the beginnings to the present. Also included are immigrants . . . and emigrés."—*Pref.* Arranged alphabetically; provides two- or three-page articles with secondary references and detailed filmographies. Supplemented and updated with additional pages on an irregular basis. PN1993.45.C455

Dictionnaire des personnages du cinéma / sous la direction de Gilles Horvilleur ; assisté de Philipe Carcassonne, Michel Chion et Jacques Fieschi. Paris : Bordas, 1988. 559 p., [48] p. of plates : ill. ISBN 2-04-016399-9. **BG88**

An extensively illustrated volume that presents signed essays both on named characters (e.g., Tarzan, Scarlett O'Hara, Medea) and specific types of characters (e.g., drunks, doctors, vamps or abstract ideas or places which have figured in films (New York, night). Some essays include bibliographic references. Actor and title indexes. PN1995.9.C36D53

Ensign, Lynne Naylor. The complete dictionary of television and film / Lynne Naylor Ensign and Robyn Eileen Knapton. N.Y. : Stein and Day, 1985. 256 p. ISBN 0-8128-2922-0. $35.00. **BG89**

An attempt to bring some standardization to the language—particularly the slang and jargon—of the film and television industries. Includes terms from silent film days as well as current terminology. Cross-references. Examples are sometimes cited, but in general, references to sources are not given. PN1992.18.E57

Handbook of American film genres / ed. by Wes D. Gehring. N.Y. : Greenwood, 1988. 405 p. ISBN 0-313-24715-3. $49.85. **BG90**

Essays by scholars on each genre (e.g., screwball comedy, social problem film, Western) covering development, themes, plot, settings, etc. with bibliographical overviews and notes. Indexed by topic. PN1993.5.U6H335

Haustrate, Gaston. Le guide du cinéma. Paris : Syros, c1984–c1988. 3 v. : ill. ISBN 2-901968-87-2 (set). 65.00F (v. 1). **BG91**

Contents: v. 1, 1895–1945 (1984. 192 p.); v. 2, 1946–67 (1984. 224 p.); v. 3. 1968–84 (1988. 272 p.).

Survey of cinema produced in a given country or region, together with discussions of filmmakers. Especially useful for Second- and Third-World countries. Title and director indexes in each volume. PN1997.8.H38

The international dictionary of films and filmmakers / ed., Christopher Lyon ; assistant ed. Susan Doll. Chicago : St. James Pr., 1984–1987. 5 v. ISBN 0-912289-09-0. $250.00. **BG92**

Contents: v. 1, Films, ed. Christopher Lyon and Susan Doll (1984); v. 2, Directors/filmmakers, ed. Christopher Lyon and James Vinson (1984); v. 3, Actors and actresses, ed. Christopher Lyon and James Vinson (1986); v.4, Writers and production artists, ed. Christopher Lyon and James Vinson (1987); v. 5, Title index, ed. Christopher Lyon and James Vinson (1987).

Tries to be truly international, covering films and filmmakers from the beginning. For each person, gives a brief biographical note, list of roles or films, bibliography, and a signed critical appraisal. The Title index covers all films in v.1–4 and provides cross-references for alternative or English-language titles. A major source of information.

A 2nd ed. began publication in 1990 with v.1, *Films*, ed. by Nicholas Thomas (1990. 1300 p. $95.00). PN1997.8.I58

Langman, Larry. Encyclopedia of American film comedy. N.Y. : Garland, 1987. 639 p. : ports. (Garland reference library of the humanities, vol. 744). ISBN 0-8240-8496-9. $50.00 (est.). **BG93**

A dictionary of comedy genres (screwball comedy, romantic humor), synopses and histories of representative films, fictional characters, and biographies of major comedy personalities (comedians, directors, screenwriters). Gives filmographies. Not indexed. PN1995.9.C55L34

Slide, Anthony. The American film industry : a historical dictionary. N.Y. : Greenwood, 1986. 431 p. ISBN 0-313-24693-9. **BG94**

More than 600 entries for "American producing and releasing companies, technological innovations, film series, industry terms, studios, genres, and organizations."—*Pref.* Cross-references; some bibliographic citations; index.

PN1993.5.U6S539

Dictionaries

Terms

Gartenberg, Jon. Glossary of filmographic terms = Lexique de termes filmographiques / FIAF ; Jon Gartenberg. Brussels, Belgium : Fédération internationale des archives du film, 1985. 141 p. **BG95**

Title and introductory matter also in French, German, Spanish and Russian.

Intended as "a useful reference for archive catalogers who in their daily work are confronted with credit terms appearing on films and in documentation sources."—*Introd.* Terms are grouped in a classified arrangement, and each term is given and defined (in parallel columns) in each of the five languages. Alphabetical index of terms in all five languages.

PN1993.45.G36

Konigsberg, Ira. The complete film dictionary. N.Y. : New American Library, c1987. 420 p. : ill. ISBN 0-453-00564-0. **BG96**

Defines technical terms in the production, business, technology, criticism, and historical development of film. Does not include words that could easily be looked up in a desk dictionary. Good illustrations. A review in *Reference books bulletin* (15 Jan. 1988): 840 concludes that this is "an excellent reference work for any library with a need for clear, concise definitions of movie terms for any level of expertise."   PN1993.45.K66

Singleton, Ralph S. Filmmakers dictionary. Beverly Hills, Calif. : Lone Eagle Pub., c1986. 188 p. ISBN 0-943728-08-8 (pbk.). $12.95.   **BG97**

Some 1,500 of the most "widely-used" (*Foreword*) terms in the motion picture and television industry. Brief definitions; occasionally gives derivation or pronunciation.

PN1993.45.S56

Directories and annuals

BFI film and television handbook / British Film Institute. 1990– . London : British Film Institute, 1990– . Annual.   **BG98**

Continues *BFI film and television yearbook*, 1983–1988/89.

Similar in scope and purpose to *Kemps international film and television yearbook* (*Guide* BG267), *International motion picture almanac* (*Guide* BG266), and *Variety international film guide* (1964–88 entitled *International film guide*; *Guide* BG265), but emphasizing British personalities and productions. The 1990 issue includes articles on current topics, as well as a directory of film and television production companies and support services, awards, festivals, bookshops, archives and libraries. General index.

Tavenas, Stéphane. Guide du cinéma européen / Stéphane Tavenas et François Volard, avec la collaboration de David Laloum. [Paris] : Editions Ramsay ; [S.l.] : Eurocinéma, c1989. 408 p. : ill. ISBN 2-85956-805-0. 380F.   **BG99**

Country-by-country chapters with subsections for lists of production and distribution companies (with brief histories or list of films produced), television stations, associations, and banks which are possible sources for financing. Name index.

PN1993.5.E8T38

Biography

International directory of cinematographers, set- and costume designers in film / International Federation of Film Archives (FIAF) ; ed. by Alfred Krautz. München ; N.Y. : Saur ; Detroit : Distr. by Gale, c1986–1988. v. 5–8. ISBN 3-598-21431-6. (In progress).   **BG100**

For v. 1–4 and annotation, see *Guide* BG275.

Contents: v. 5, Denmark, Finland, Norway, Sweden (from the beginnings to 1984), ed. Bujor T. Rîpeanu and Alfred Krautz (1986. 588 p.); v. 6, Supplementary volume: new entries, additions, corrections, 1978–1984 (Albania, Bulgaria, France, German Democratic Republic, Germany until 1945, Poland, Romania, Sweden, Yugoslavia), ed. Alfred Krautz (1986. 455 p.); v. 7, Italy (from the beginnings to 1986), ed., Eberhard Spiess and Alfred Krautz (1988. 666 p.); v. 8, Portugal, Spain (from the beginnings to 1988), ed. Rui Santana Brito and Alfred Krautz (1988. 439 p.).   PN1998.A1I55

World film directors / ed., John Wakeman. N.Y. : H.W. Wilson, 1987–1988. 2 v. : ports. ISBN 0-8242-0757-2. $90.00.   **BG101**

Contents: v.1, 1890–1945; v.2, 1945–88.

"This book provides introductions to the work and lives of about four hundred of the world's best-known film directors, from the beginning of cinema to the present."—*Pref.* Similar in orientation and presentation to *Twentieth century authors* (*Guide* BD107). Well-written articles covering career and popular and critical reputation, filmography, bibliography (brief) of

books and essays. Occasionally includes statements by the subject of the essay. Not indexed.

§ See also Geoff Andrew's *The film handbook* (Boston : G.K. Hall, 1990. 362 p.) for biographical and critical coverage of 200 directors.   PN1998.2.W67

RADIO AND TELEVISION

Guides

Cassata, Mary B. Television, a guide to the literature / by Mary Cassata and Thomas Skill. Phoenix : Oryx, 1985. 148 p. ISBN 0-89774-140-4.   **BG102**

A bibliographic essay in three sections: (1) Test patterns (overview of the field, historical development, reference sources); (2) The environment (processes and effects of television, news, politics); (3) Directions (the industry, criticism, collected works). Author, title, and subject indexes. A revised and expanded version of bibliographic essays that originally appeared in *Choice* 19 (1982): 548–597, 721–736, 1027–1036.

Z7711.C37

Bibliography

Hill, George H. Blacks on television : a selectively annotated bibliography / by George H. Hill and Sylvia Saverson Hill. Metuchen, N.J. : Scarecrow, 1985. 223 p. ISBN 0-8108-1774-8.   **BG103**

Consists of 2,800 entries for books, magazine and newspaper articles, and dissertations and theses on African-American involvement in television. Arranged by format, subdivided by topic (needs a detailed table of contents). Program and author/subject indexes. Appendix lists African-American owned television stations and cable companies and Emmy award winners.

Z1361.N39H53

TV genres : a handbook and reference guide / ed. by Brian G. Rose ; Robert S. Alley, advisory ed. Westport, Conn. : Greenwood, 1985. 453 p. ISBN 0-313-23724-7.   **BG104**

Central elements of 19 various formats or styles of television programming (documentary, game show, science fiction and fantasy) are each discussed in a chapter ending with a bibliographical survey, a short list of books and articles, and a videography. Chapters by specialists present a historical survey and an analysis of themes and issues. The videography cites about 10–15 shows of special interest in studying that genre.

PN1992.3.U5T88

Indexes

Variety television reviews, 1923–1988 : the first fifteen volumes of the series including a comprehensive index / ed. by Howard H. Prouty. N.Y. : Garland, 1989–1991. 15 v. ISBN 0-8240-2587-3 (v. 1).   **BG105**

Reprints all reviews in chronological order by issue date. Title, subject, name, local programming, and international programming indexes.   PN1992.3.U5V36

Catalogs and filmography

Annenberg School of Communications (University of Pennsylvania). Television Script Archive. Index to the Annenberg Television Script Archive / ed. by Sharon Black and Elizabeth Sue Moersh. Phoenix : Oryx, 1990. v. 1. ISBN 0-89774-553-1 (v. 1.). $115.00. (In progress).   **BG106**

Contents: v. 1, 1976–77.

Lists "2,477 cataloged records of the Annenberg Archive's holdings of prime-time episodic television scripts written in 1976 and 1977. Represented are 127 series with an additional 30 pilots that never developed into series."—*Introd.* Records are drawn from the Annenberg's online catalog, which in 1990 contained over 8,000 items. Each record indicates author, title, script date, air date, subject covered, and pagination, with notes as to any special features, such as cast and set lists, production numbers, or song lyrics. Arranged alphabetically by series name and chronologically within series. Author and subject indexes.   PN1992.16.A66

Einstein, Daniel. Special edition : a guide to network television documentary series and special news reports, 1955–1979. Metuchen, N.J. : Scarecrow, 1987. 1051 p. ISBN 0-8108-1898-1.   **BG107**

Commercial network documentary and news special programming is listed with brief annotation for each program giving date and subjects covered. Special section for documentary programming produced by David L. Wolper. Personality and personnel indexes. No subject approach.   PN1992.8.D6E56

Gianakos, Larry James. Television drama series programming : a comprehensive chronicle, 1982–1984. Metuchen, N.J. : Scarecrow, 1987. 830 p. ISBN 0-8108-1876-0.   **BG108**

Continues the author's *Television drama series programming . . . 1947/59–1980/82* (*Guide* BG298–301).

Updates listing to Jan. 31, 1985. Adds a new appendix for Western characters on American television. Cumulative title listing to the series.   PN1992.3.U5G532

Library of Congress. Motion Picture, Broadcasting, and Recorded Sound Division. 3 decades of television : a catalog of television programs acquired by the Library of Congress, 1949–1979 / comp. by Sarah Rouse and Katharine Loughney. Wash. : Library of Congress, 1989. 688 p. : ill. ISBN 0-8444-0544-2.   **BG109**

Lists by title some 1,400 programs acquired through Dec. 1979, giving production information, genre (e.g., Children's programs, Espionage, Social documentary), cast and credits, summary. Collecting has been active since 1949 from the Copyright Office and since the mid-1960s through acquisition. Genre or format index.   PN1992.9.L53

Marill, Alvin H. Movies made for television : the telefeature and the mini-series, 1964–1986. N.Y. : New York Zoetrope, c1987. 576 p. : ill. ISBN 0-918432-60-X. $29.95.   **BG110**

1st ed., 1984 (*Guide* BH303).

In alphabetical order with chronological index. More complete credit information than 1st ed.; 340 new entries. Television movies are defined as "films produced as separate, self-contained entries, not as episodes of continuing series."—*Introd.* Indexes of producers, directors, writers, and actors.   PN1992.8.F5M35

Parish, James Robert. The complete actors' television credits, 1948–1988 / by James Robert Parish and Vincent Terrace. 2nd ed. Metuchen, N.J. : Scarecrow, 1989–1990. 2 v. : ill. ISBN 0-8108-2204-0 (v. 1). ISBN 0-8108-2258-X (v. 2).   **BG111**

Revised edition of *Actors' television credits 1950–1972* (1973) and three supplements.

Contents: v. 1, Actors; v. 2, Actresses.

Listed by name of actor or actress. Includes all entertainment programs broadcast on network and cable TV and those made for syndication."—*Foreword.* Not indexed. Each volume gives a 30- to 40-page center spread of photographs.   PN1992.4.A2P3

Pratt, Douglas. The laser video disc companion : a guide to the best (and worst) laser video discs. N.Y. : New York Zoetrope, c1988. 447 p. ISBN 0-918432-86-3. $16.95.   **BG112**

Reviews of "domestic and imported laser video discs, most of which [were] released between 1984 and 1987."—*Introd.* Critical comments as well as plot summaries. Does not include cost, songs, etc. Not indexed.   PN1992.95.P7

Terrace, Vincent. Encyclopedia of television : series, pilots, and specials. N.Y. : New York Zoetrope, c1985–c1986. 3 v. : ill. ISBN 0-918432-69-3 (v. 1).   **BG113**

Contents: v. 1, 1937–73; v. 2, 1974–84; v. 3, Index.

Title listing of series, pilots, specials and experimental programs, alphabetically arranged. For each, gives cast and credits, story lines, running times, dates, networks. The index volume is a name listing of the producers, directors, performers, and writers with a full credit list, and the item number in the catalog for each work.   PN1992.9.T47

Woolery, George W. Animated TV specials : the complete directory to the first twenty-five years, 1962–1987. Metuchen, N.J. : Scarecrow, 1989. 542 p. : ill. ISBN 0-8108-2198-2.   **BG114**

Covers "all special animated television presentations aired on the various networks or syndicated extensively in the United States from 1962 through the 1986–1987 season . . . both prime-time and daytime programs."—*Pref.* Title listing, giving credits and annotation. Name and studio or distributor or production company indexes. Appendix: Holiday and topical animated TV specials, animated TV special series.   PN1992.8.S64W66

Dictionaries

McDonald, James R. The broadcaster's dictionary : dictionary of terms, directory of associations and government agencies, broadcasting techniques, solutions, and circuits. Broomfield, Colo. : Wind River Books, 1986. 198 p. : ill. ISBN 0-938023-00-4 (pbk.).   **BG115**

Briefly defines terms used in broadcast engineering, operations, and production. Appendixes contain directories of key associations and government agencies as well as a series of "tutorials" (e.g., schematic abbreviations, introduction to digital audio) aimed at nonengineering station personnel. Includes a short bibliography.   TK6544.M37 1986

History

Brooks, Tim. The complete directory to prime time TV stars, 1946–present. N.Y. : Ballantine Books, 1987. 1086 p. ISBN 0-345-32681-4 (pbk.).   **BG116**

Companion to *The complete directory to prime time TV shows* (*Supplement* BG117).

Regular performers on nighttime network series (which ran for at least four weeks) between 6:00 pm and midnight) are listed, giving birthplace and date, credits, and awards, with biographical notes for the biggest stars. Appendix for list of birthdays of the stars by month and day; list of birthplaces of stars with their names. Index of TV production.   PN1992.4.A2B76

Biography

Brooks, Tim. The complete directory to prime time network TV shows, 1946–present / Tim Brooks and Earle Marsh. 4th ed. N.Y. : Ballantine Books, 1988. 1063 p. : ill. ISBN 0-345-35610-1. $16.95.   **BG117**
    3rd ed., 1985 (*Guide* BG296).
    Companion to *The complete directory to prime time TV stars, 1946–present*, by Brooks (*Supplement* BG116).
    Adds programs through 15 April 1988.   PN1992.18.B68

BH

Music

GENERAL WORKS

Guides

Brockman, William S. Music : a guide to the reference literature. Littleton, Colo. : Libraries Unlimited, 1987. 254 p. ISBN 0-87287-526-1. $38.50.   **BH1**
    A guide to "the important current and retrospective sources of information on music [that] emphasizes, but is not restricted to, works in English."—*Pref.* Contains 841 annotated entries for general reference sources, general bibliographical sources, bibliographies of music literature, bibliographies of music, discographies, key journals, associations, and research centers. A very good overview of the literature. Author/title and subject indexes.   ML113.B85

Heintze, James R. Early American music : a research and information guide. N.Y. : Garland, c1990. 511 p. (Music research and information guides, vol. 13 ; Garland reference library of the humanities, vol. 1007). ISBN 0-8240-4119-4.   **BH2**
    An annotated bibliography of 1,959 books, articles, dissertations, papers, published sermons and discourses, catalogs, lists, directories, and other materials available for research on American music from its beginning to 1820. Within two large categories, General reference works and Historical studies, the listing is broken down into systematically arranged sections. Each section contains entries listed alphabetically by author; many are preceded by brief but bibliographically useful introductions. Author-title and subject indexes.
    § A related work is the author's *American music studies : a classified bibliography of master's theses* (Detroit : Information Coordinators, 1984), which contains 2,370 entries orrganized by topic.   ML120.U5H46

Phelps, Roger P. A guide to research in music education. 3rd ed. Metuchen, N.J. : Scarecrow, 1986. 368 p. : ill. ISBN 0-8108-1796-9.   **BH3**
    2nd ed., 1980 (*Guide* BH6).
    The content and bibliography for each chapter have been revised to reflect current trends; many chapters have been rewritten. Newly organized in 4 parts: The research problem, Methodologies, The research document, and Postscript. Covering the same area is *Research in music education : an introduction to systematic inquiry*, by Edward L. Rainbow and Hildegard C. Froehlich (N.Y. : Schirmer, 1987).   MT1.P5

Pruett, James W. Research guide to musicology / James W. Pruett and Thomas P. Slavens. Chicago : Amer. Lib. Assoc., 1985. 175 p. (Sources of information in the humanities, no. 4). ISBN 0-8389-0331-2. $20.00.   **BH4**
    Organized in two sections: the first an essay on the history and development of research in the field, and the second an annotated list of approximately 125 reference books and 16 periodicals.   ML3797.P78

Bibliography

Antônio, Irati. Bibliografia da música brasileira : 1977–1984 / [projeto e organização, Irati Antonio, Rita de Cássia Rodriques, Heloísa Helena Bauab]. São Paulo : Universidade de São Paulo, Escola de Comunicações e Artes, Serviço de Biblioteca e Documentação : Centro Cultural São Paulo, Divisão de Pesquisas, 1988. 275 p. (In progress).   **BH5**
    A bibliography of books, chapters from books, pamphlets, dissertations, theses, and articles on Brazilian music, published both in Brazil and abroad, 1977–84. Includes 2,239 author entries with bibliographies along with locations in seven Brazilian libraries. Subject and name indexes. Projected future volumes are to provide retrospective coverage up to 1976, as well as an ongoing bibliography of works published since 1985.
    ML120.B7A57

Baron, John H. Chamber music : a research and information guide. N.Y. : Garland, 1987. 500 p. (Music research and information guides, vol. 8 ; Garland reference library of the humanities, vol. 704). ISBN 0-8240-8346-6.   **BH6**
    An annotated bibliography of 1,600 items, most written after 1950. Entries are listed under six broad subjects, many with subdivisions. The most important works are listed first in each category; the remainder appear to be in random order. Helpful cross-references. Contains indexes by subjects, persons, authors, and chamber groups.   ML128.C4B37

Brookhart, Edward. Music in American higher education : an annotated bibliography. Warren, Mich. : Harmonie Park Pr., 1988. 245 p. : ill. (Bibliographies in American music, no. 10). ISBN 0-89990-042-9.   **BH7**
    An author bibliography of 1,300 items with brief, descriptive annotations on the history of music in American higher education. Entries are alphabetically arranged within general categories and cover publications from ca. 1830 to 1985. Author and subject indexes.   ML120.U5B77

Coover, James. Antiquarian catalogues of musical interest. London ; N.Y. : Mansell, 1988. 372 p. ISBN 0-7201-1979-0. $72.00.   **BH8**
    A listing of 5,531 catalogs, bulletins, and lists from 640 antiquarian dealers arranged alphabetically by firm. For each catalog, includes date of issue, form of publication if other than a catalog, specific title of the catalog, dealer's number, and the number of lots or pages. Informative introductory essay by Albi Rosenthal. Subject and place indexes.   ML152.C65

Damschroder, David. Music theory from Zarlino to Schenker : a bibliography and guide / by David Damschroder and David Russell Williams. Stuyvesant, N.Y. : Pendragon Pr., 1990. 522 p. : ill. (Harmonologia series, no. 4). ISBN 0-918728-99-1. $54.00. **BH9**

An alphabetical listing of approximately 200 theorists with introductory summary of their work, a bibliography of their published and unpublished treatises (with notes on the sources and available facsimiles and translations), and a bibliography of secondary literature. Coverage spans the history of Western music, from Glarean's *Isagoge in musicen* (1516) through Schoenberg's *Fundamentals of musical composition* (1967). A "Literature supplement" includes secondary works on more than one theorist. Topical, chronological, title, and name indexes. ML128.T5D27

Davis, Deta S. Computer applications in music : a bibliography. Madison, Wis. : A-R Editions, c1988. 537 p. (The computer music and digital audio series, v. 4). ISBN 0-89579-225-7. $49.95. **BH10**

International in scope. Lists 4,585 items alphabetically by author, or title if author is lacking, in 25 categories. Covers works published prior to mid-1986. English translations are provided for titles not in English, German, or French. Includes review citations and abstract citations when available. Index by author, with title entries for articles having no author. ML128.C62D4

Duckles, Vincent H. Music reference and research materials : an annotated bibliography / Vincent H. Duckles, Michael A. Keller. 4th ed. N.Y. : Schirmer ; London : Collier Macmillan, c1988. 714 p. ISBN 0-02-870390-1. **BH11**

Follows the same format as the 3rd ed., 1974 (*Guide* BH2). Includes over 3,000 entries. Revised and corrected 4th ed., due Spring 1992. ML113.D83

Folter, Siegrun H. Private libraries of musicians and musicologists : a bibliography of catalogs : with introduction and notes. Buren [The Netherlands] : F. Knuf, 1987. 261 p. : ill. (Auction catalogues of music, v. 7). ISBN 90-6027-411-3. ISBN 90-6027-394-X (pbk.). **BH12**

Lists 392 catalogs arranged by name of collector. Each entry includes title and publication information, libraries holding the catalog, contents, and annotations. Entries are limited to published catalogs from auction houses, dealers, exhibitions, privately printed and institutional catalogs, together with those published in monographs or articles. Chronological and dealer indexes. ML111.F64

Goodenberger, Jennifer. Subject guide to classical instrumental music. Metuchen, N.J. : Scarecrow, 1989. 163 p. ISBN 0-8108-2209-1. **BH13**

Guide to nonmusical subjects represented in the standard concert repertory, primarily from the 19th century. Musical compositions are listed under 208 subject categories, many of which are further subdivided. ML128.I65G59

Goodfellow, William D. Where's that tune? : an index to songs in fakebooks. Metuchen, N.J. : Scarecrow, 1990. 449 p. ISBN 0-8108-2391-8. **BH14**

Indexes 13,500 different songs in 64 fakebooks (collections "of music for which only the melody line, chord symbols, and words are written out."—*Pref.*). Includes a bibliography of the books indexed, as well as indexes by titles and composers. ML128.P63G66

Harvey, D. R. A bibliography of writings about New Zealand music published to the end of 1983. [Wellington, N.Z.] : Victoria Univ. Pr., 1985. 222 p. : ill. ISBN 0-86473-029-2 (pbk.). **BH15**

Contains "a comprehensive listing of all material pertaining to music and music-making in New Zealand, published in periodicals, or as monographs, or produced as dissertations."—*Introd.* Excludes material published in newspapers, reviews and notices of performances, and articles on recent popular music and Maori music. Entries are arranged alphabetically by author or title within larger subject categories, all of which are listed in the table of contents. Author and subject indexes. ML120.N53H3

Heskes, Irene. The resource book of Jewish music : a bibliographical and topical guide to the book and journal literature and program materials. Westport, Conn. : Greenwood, 1985. 302 p. (Music reference collection, no. 3). ISBN 0-313-23251-2. **BH16**

An annotated bibliography of 1,200 items intended to provide a "tool for the examination of Jewish music."—*Pref.* Entries consist of English-language books, periodicals, instruction manuals, music collections, and dance materials, and are arranged alphabetically by author under 16 categories. Cutoff date for inclusion is 1984. Author and topical indexes. ML128.J4H48

Krüger-Wust, Wilhelm J. Arabische Musik in europäischen Sprachen : eine Bibliographie. Wiesbaden : Harrassowitz, 1983. 124 p. ISBN 3-447-02339-2. **BH17**

Primarily an author listing of 2,100 books and articles published from the mid-19th century through the 1970s, with a few subject categories (e.g., recordings with European commentary listed under *Schallplatten*, subdivided by country). Contains an index by 30 broad subject terms. ML120.A7K8

Krummel, Donald William. Bibliographical handbook of American music. Urbana : Univ. of Illinois Pr., c1987. 269 p. ISBN 0-252-01450-2. $24.95. **BH18**

An annotated bibliographical guide to literature on many aspects of American music. The sources are systematically arranged in four broad categories: Chronological perspectives; Contextual perspective; Musical medium and genres; and Bibliographical forms. Critical, informative essays introduce each broad category which is then further subdivided systematically. Name and subject index. ML120.U5K78

Matsushita, Hitoshi. A checklist of published instrumental music by Japanese composers. Tokyo : Academia Music, c1989. 181 p. ISBN 4-87017-039-6. **BH19**

A checklist of published instrumental music written in Western notation by Japanese composers from the mid-19th century to the present. Includes 2,271 works by more than 350 composers published by 80 Japanese publishers. Each entry contains Japanese and English title with publication information. Genre index. ML128.I65M38

Pallay, Steven G. Cross index title guide to classical music. N.Y. : Greenwood, 1987. 206 p. (Music reference collection, no. 12). ISBN 0-313-25531-8. **BH20**

Contains more than 6,000 titles for vocal and instrumental compositions by 220 composers. Titles are listed under multiple and variant names (including the title under which the piece is most likely to be found in reference sources or catalogs), cross-indexed titles, and composer's name. Concludes with a list of composers, common thematic catalog numbers, and principal sources.

§ A companion, the author's *Cross index title guide to opera and operetta* (N.Y. : Greenwood, 1989. Music reference collection, no. 19), contains more than 5,500 titles of vocal and instrumental excerpts from approximately 1,400 operas and operettas by 535 composers. ML113.P34

Pierreuse, Bernard. Catalogue général de l'édition musicale en France : livres, méthodes et partitions de musique sérieuse en vente = General catalog of music publishing in France : books, methods, and scores of serious music on sale. Paris : Editions Jobert : Distribution, Editions musicales transatlantiques, 1984. 476 p. : ill. ISBN 2-903933-04-9. **BH21**

A listing of books, methods, and scores of serious music published in France and in print and available for sale as of 1982. Entries are arranged by subject and performance medium; a full list of subject headings appears at the front. Within each entry, listing is by composer, with title and publication information. Contains composer index, addresses of publishers, and list of exclusive agents in other countries. ML120.F7P5

Répertoire international des sources musicales = International inventory of musical sources. v. 1 (1960)– . Munich : G. Henle, 1960– . **BH22**

An ongoing major bibliographical series for pre-1800 source materials in music. For annotation, see *Guide* BH34. For Series C, *Directory of music research libraries*, see *Supplement* BH64.

Title also in German. Other title: *RISM*.

Additional contents: *Série alphabetique*, A/I/11, Addenda et corrigenda, A–F; Redaktion: Ilse und Jürgen Kindermann (1986). A/II, Music manuscripts, 1600–1800 (1986); 2 microfiches. *Série systématique*, B/III/3, The theory of music: Manuscripts from the Carolingian Era up to c.1500 in the Federal Republic of Germany (D-brd), by Michel Huglo and Christian Meyer (1986); B/IX/1, Hebrew notated manuscript sources up to circa 1840, by Israel Adler (1989); B/XI, Ancient Greek music theory: a catalogue raisonné of manuscripts, by Thomas J. Mathiesen (1988).

Smialek, William. Polish music : a research and information guide. N.Y. : Garland, 1989. 260 p. (Music research and information guides, vol. 12 ; Garland reference library of the humanities, vol. 1093). ISBN 0-8240-4614-5. **BH23**

An annotated bibliography of 600 books and articles published through 1987, organized roughly by *RILM* classification (see *Guide* BH102). The author chose the "most useful and important Polish writings in Western publications" (*Foreword*) and focused on the most readily available materials. Excludes Chopin for space reasons. Notes Western-language summaries of Polish works. Traces an item's publication if published both in the East and West. Discography, arranged by composer, for over 400 sound recordings. Index. ML120.P6S6

Tsuge, Gen'ichi. Japanese music : an annotated bibliography. N.Y. : Garland, 1986. 161 p. (Garland bibliographies in ethnomusicology, 2 ; Garland reference library of the humanities, vol. 472). ISBN 0-8240-8995-2. **BH24**

An annotated bibliography of 881 items in Western languages which appeared through 1983. Includes scholarly books, articles, review essays, bibliographies, discographies, as well as translations of songtexts, libretti, and synopses of dance-drama productions. Subject, name, and format indexes. ML120.J3T8

Warner, Thomas E. Periodical literature on American music, 1620–1920 : a classified bibliography with annotations. Warren, Mich. : Harmonie Park Pr., 1988. 644 p. (Bibliographies in American music, no. 11). ISBN 0-89990-034-8. **BH25**

Contains 5,348 entries drawn from over 600 periodicals, many with brief descriptive annotations. Organized by topics: research and reference materials; historical studies; theory and composition; ethnomusicology; organology; and special topics. Excludes Eskimo, American Indian, and folk music. Author and subject indexes. ML120.U5W18

Waters, William J. Music and the personal computer : an annotated bibliography. N.Y. : Greenwood, 1989. 175 p. (Music reference collection, no. 22). ISBN 0-313-26790-1. **BH26**

An author listing of 1,378 items organized in four parts: specific computers (seven products), nonspecific and other computers, music education, and books. Appendix of associations; author and subject indexes. ML128.C62W37

Books

Horn, David. The literature of American music in books and folk music collections : a fully annotated bibliography. Supplement 1 / by David Horn with Richard Jackson. Metuchen, N.J. : Scarecrow, 1988. 570 p. ISBN 0-8108-1997-X. **BH27**

Follows the same format as the basic volume (*Guide* BH22), with annotations for books published from mid-1975 to the end of 1980, as well as for a number of books overlooked in the original edition or included without annotations. Includes English-language material known to the compiler and judged to be of interest, with a representative sample of non-English titles. Contains 996 annotated entries and 323 unannotated pre-1981 entries. As in the basic volume, over two-thirds of the entries are devoted to folk and popular music. ML120.U5H7

Dissertations

Adkins, Cecil. Doctoral dissertations in musicology. Second series / ed. by Cecil Adkins and Alis Dickinson. 1st cumulative ed. Philadelphia : American Musicological Society ; [s.l.] : International Musicological Society, 1990. 177 p. **BH28**

7th North American ed., 2nd international ed., 1984 (*Guide* BH48).

A cumulation of interim editions, published annually beginning 1985. Contains 2,230 titles but does not supersede the 1984 ed. ML128.M8A42

Periodicals

Basart, Ann Phillips. Writing about music : a guide to publishing opportunities for authors and reviewers. Berkeley, Calif. : Fallen Leaf Pr., c1989. 588 p. (Fallen Leaf reference books in music, no. 11). ISBN 0-914913-10-7. **BH29**

Contains detailed information on editorial policies and publishing requirements of more than 430 current periodicals from 21 countries "that publish serious, informative, music-related articles and/or reviews in English."—*Pref.* Titles are listed alphabetically, with four indexes: Titles & organizations; Subject; Geographical; Type of materials reviewed. Concludes with list of titles considered but not included. ML128.P24B37

Bayerische Staatsbibliothek. Katalog der Musikzeitschriften : BSB-MuZ = Catalogue of music periodicals. München ; N.Y. : K.G. Saur, 1990. 242 p. ISBN 3-598-22241-6. **BH30**

A list of the 2,621 music periodicals in the collections of the Bavarian State Library in Munich. Entries are listed alphabetically under both corporate author and title, giving holdings information and call number. Indexed systematically in ten broad categories. ML136.M92B46

Fellinger, Imogen. Periodica musicalia (1789–1830) / im Auftrag des Staatlichen Instituts für Musikforschung Preussischer Kulturbesitz bearb. von Imogen Fellinger. Regensburg : G. Bosse, 1986. 1259 p. (Studien zur Musikgeschichte des 19. Jahrhunderts, Bd. 55). ISBN 3-7649-2182-X. **BH31**

A companion to Fellinger's *Verzeichnis der Musikzeitschriften des 19. Jahrhunderts* (*Guide* BH53). Contains a chronologically-arranged index to music in periodicals published 1789–1830. Includes some 250 titles, with each entry containing publication information, library repositories, and a listing by issue of the titles and page numbers for the compositions. Numerous indexes for text and music. ML117.F43

International music journals / ed. by Linda M. Fidler and Richard S. James. N.Y. : Greenwood, c1990. 544 p. ISBN 0-313-25004-9. **BH32**

A selective, alphabetical listing of over 160 journal titles, both ongoing and ceased, chosen as the profession's leading journals on the basis of their historical and contemporary significance. Annotations cover the physical properties of the journals, historical development, content profiles, critical assessment, and bibliography. Appendixes include similar descriptions for nine recent journals from the 1980s, and periodical indexes, as well as chronological, geographical, and subject listings. Index; cross-references. ML128.P24I6

Robinson, Doris. Music and dance periodicals : an international directory & guidebook. Voorheesville, N.Y. : Peri Pr., c1989. 382p. ISBN 0-961-7844-4-X. **BH33**

Provides comprehensive and international coverage of music and dance periodicals. Lists 1,867 currently published periodicals with descriptive annotations in 19 categories, including Reference; Musicology and ethnomusicology; Music industry; Musical instruments; Regional; Education; Classical; Religious and choral; Opera, theater, show music; Band; Composers and songwriters; Computer and electronic; Popular; Jazz and blues; Folk music; Dance; Sound; Miscellaneous; Unclassified. Five indexes: Title; Publisher & organization; Subject; Country of publication; ISSN. ML128.P24R58

Manuscripts and printed music

Bayerische Staatsbibliothek. Katalog der Musikdrucke : BSB-Musik. München ; N. Y. : K.G. Saur, 1988–1990. 17 v. ISBN 3-598-30560-5. **BH34**

An author-title catalog of printed music from the earliest publications through approximately 1974. In dictionary format, with main entries, added entries, and cross-references interfiled. Composer entries are subarranged by title; series title entries are further subarranged by titles of individual works. ML136.M92B42

Census-catalogue of manuscript sources of polyphonic music, 1400–1550 / comp. by the University of Illinois, Musicological Archives for Renaissance Manuscript Studies. [Rome] : American Institute of Musicology ; Neuhausen-Stuttgart : Hänssler-Verlag, 1979–1988. 5 v. (Renaissance Manuscript Studies, 1). ISBN 3-7751-0645-6 (v. 2). DM140.00. **BH35**

Contents: v. 1–3, A–U; v. 4, V–Z and supplement; v. 5, Cumulative bibliography and indexes.

Aims to list "all known manuscripts containing polyphonic music composed between 1400 and 1550."—*Introd., v. 4.* Excludes tablatures, manuscripts containing only anonymous "primitive" polyphony contained in *RISM*, B IV/3–4 (see *Guide* BH34), and most sources copied later than 1700. For each entry, includes siglum, manuscript designation, contents, composers, physical description, other historical information, and bibliography. Vol. 4 contains a supplement of additional and revised entries; v. 5, composer, geographical/institutional, geographical/chronological, and general indexes. ML169.8.R46

Guillo, Laurent. Catalogue de la musique imprimée avant 1801, conservée dans les bibliothèques de Lyon, Grenoble et la région. Grenoble : Agence de coopération régionale pour la documentation, 1986. 156 p. : ill. ISBN 2-85919-059-7. **BH36**

Contains bibliographical records for works by individual authors, collections from the 16th through 18th centuries, psalters, and other psalm collections held by 21 institutions in 11 cities outside Paris. Index of names includes composers, publishers, printers, engravers, and donors. Complements François Lesure's *Catalogue de la musique imprimée avant 1800 conservée dans les bibliothèques publiques de Paris* (*Guide* BH80). ML120.F7G84

Murray, Sterling E. Anthologies of music : an annotated index. Detroit : Information Coordinators, Inc., 1987. 178 p. (Detroit studies in music bibliography, no. 55). ISBN 0-89990-031-3. **BH37**

Indexes 33 anthologies (45 volumes), most published 1964–84. Broadens the coverage of Ruth B. Hilton's *An index to early music in selected anthologies* (*Guide* BH75). Includes anthologies which are arranged historically and contain complete movements or compositions, with special consideration given to readily accessible works. 3,532 entries by some 600 composers, arranged by author. Genre index. ML128.A7M87

Current

Music-in-print series. Began in 1974– . Philadelphia : Musicdata, Inc. Irregular. ISSN 0146-7883. **BH38**

For v. 1–6 and annotation, see *Guide* BH90.

Recently published additions, supplements, and new editions include: Arranger index (1987) and Supplement (1988) to v. 1, Sacred choral music in print; v. 2, Secular choral music in print (2nd ed., 1987) and Arranger index (1987); Supplement (1985) to v. 4, Classical vocal music in print; Supplement (1983) to v. 5, Orchestral music in print; Supplement (1984) to v. 6, String music in print; v. 7, Classical guitar music in print, ed. by Mijndert Jape (1989); Master composer index (1989), a composer and title index to the entire set.

Keyboard instruments

Hinson, Maurice. Guide to the pianist's repertoire. 2nd ed., rev. and enl. Bloomington : Indiana Univ. Pr., c1987. 856 p. ISBN 0-253-32656-7. **BH39**

1st ed., 1973 (*Guide* BH95).

Modestly enlarged, incorporating the 1979 supplement and new materials.

§ Two related works by the same author are *Pianist's reference guide* (Los Angeles : Alfred, 1987), an annotated bibliography of almost 1,000 books, dissertations, and theses relating to the piano repertory, and *Pianist's guide to transcriptions, arrangements, and paraphrases* (Bloomington : Indiana Univ. Pr., 1990), containing transcriptions by well-known composers and an index of transcriptions for one hand. ML128.P3H5

Indexes and abstracts

Crisp, Deborah. Bibliography of Australian music : an index to monographs, journal articles, and theses. Armidale [N.S.W.] : Australian Music Studies Project, 1982. 260 p. (Australian music studies, 1). ISBN 0-85834-429-7 (pbk.). $16.50. **BH40**

Contains 2,218 entries for published journal articles, monographs, and theses relating to Australian music and musicians, including aboriginal music and culture, which have "informative value to the scholar."—*Introd.* Covers works published by the end of 1981, with the earliest entry dating from 1790. Organized in two parts: Pt. 1, subject index, and Pt. 2, bibliographic listing by author. ML120.A86C74

Diamond, Harold J. Music analyses : an annotated guide to the literature. N.Y. : Schirmer : Maxwell Macmillan

International ; Toronto : Collier Macmillan Canada, c1991. 716 p. ISBN 0-02-870110-0.   **BH41**

An index to 4,655 analyses in books, periodicals, dissertations, and theses, of compositions by major composers. Entry is by commonly-known name of the composer, subarranged by title, with entries under "Anonymous" for medieval works. Most entries have brief descriptive annotations. Index of distinctive titles.   ML128.A7D5

Hassen, Marjorie. American Musicological Society : index to the *Papers, Bulletin,* and *Journal* 1936–1987 / comp. by Marjorie Hassen and Mark Germer. [Philadelphia] : American Musicological Society, 1990. 148 [i.e. 149] p.   **BH42**

Provides author-title access to the society's publications: *Papers* (1936–41), *Bulletin,* nos. 1–13 (1936–48), and *Journal,* v. 1–40 (1948–87). Organized in three sections: Articles, abstracts, and communications; Reviews; and Obituaries.   ML27.U58A5

●**Music index** [computer file]. Warren, Mich. : Harmonie Park Pr., 1981– .   **BH43**

Machine-readable version of *Music index* (*Guide* BH105).

Coverage: 1981–88. Updated annually. Available in CD-ROM (producer).

Review expected in *Notes,* March or June 1992.

Répertoire international de la presse musicale. Ann Arbor, Mich. : Univ. Microfilms International, c1988– . Irregular.   **BH44**

Other title: *RIPIM.*

This series will provide indexing for approximately 60 music periodicals from Western Europe and the U.S. published during the 18th, 19th, and early 20th centuries. The index for each is organized in two sections; the first contains a calendar or annotated listing of article titles for each issue, while the second contains a keyword-author index generated by computer from the calendar. Approximately a quarter of the indexes have been published to date.

●**RILM abstracts** / International Repertory of Music Literature [computer file]. N.Y. : RILM, 1970–84.   **BH45**

Machine-readable version of *RILM abstracts of music literature* (*Guide* BH102).

Coverage, currently 1970–84, to be extended to 1988 with next update. File size: 95,000 records. Available online as *Music literature international* (DIALOG) and in CD-ROM (NISC, Faxon).

Vol. 1–2, 1967–68, of printed version not available in machine-readable format. Review expected in *Notes,* March or June 1992.

Style manuals

Writing about music : a style sheet from the editors of *19th-century music* / D. Kern Holoman. Berkeley : Univ. of California Pr., c1988. 61 p. : music. ISBN 0-520-06382-1.   **BH46**

A style manual intended for publications in music, used by the editors and staff of the journal *19th-century music,* with examples from journal issues. Deviations from *The Chicago manual of style,* 13th ed. (*Guide* AA42) are noted.   ML63.W68

Encyclopedias

Ammer, Christine. The Harper dictionary of music. 2nd ed. N.Y. : Harper & Row, c1987. 493 p. : ill. ISBN 0-06-181020-7. $19.95.   **BH47**

1st ed., 1972 (*Guide* BH137), had title: *Harper's dictionary of music.*

Adheres to same format and scope as the prior edition. Expands coverage of early music and technological developments in sound reproduction, and includes more contemporary composers.   ML100.A48

Brockhaus Riemann Musiklexikon : in vier Bänden und einem Ergänzungsband / hrsg. von Carl Dahlhaus und Hans Heinrich Eggebrecht. Erw. Taschenbuchausgabe. Mainz : Schott ; München : Piper, c1989. 5 v. : ill. ISBN 3-7957-8301-1 (Schott). ISBN 3-492-18301-8 (Piper).   **BH48**

Contents: v. 1–4, A–Z; v. 5, Ergänzungsband A–Z.

Reprint of the 1978–79 ed. (*Guide* BH110) in paperback, with a supplementary volume incorporating new entries: popular, rock, and jazz composers and performers; timely topics such as "Frau und Musik"; and revised entries for more recent developments in many areas.   ML100.B85

Dictionnaire de la musique / sous la direction de Marc Vignal. Paris : Larousse, c1987. 882 p., 160 p. of plates : col. ill. ISBN 2-03-511306-1.   **BH49**

Presents 5,000 articles of varying length, alphabetically arranged, on persons (well-known composers, little-known composers connected to major figures, publishers, writers on music) and terms (geographical, form and genre, technical, etc.). Color illustrations arranged by topic.   ML100.D564

Dizionario enciclopedico universale della musica e dei musicisti : il lessico / diretto da Alberto Basso. Torino : UTET, c1983–c1984. 4 v. : ill. (some col.). ISBN 88-02-03732-9 (v. 1).   **BH50**
          ML100.D63

Dizionario enciclopedico universale della musica e dei musicisti : le biografie / diretto da Alberto Basso. Torino : UTET, c1985–1988. 8 v. : geneal. tables. ISBN 88-02-03930-5 (v. 1).   **BH51**

Successors to *La musica* (*Guide* BH126).

Accompanied by Appendice (1 v., c1990), which contains both names and terms and is meant to supplement the two-title set.

Together, these titles constitute the most important Italian encyclopedia of music. The dictionary portion contains terms arranged alphabetically, with extensive signed articles and bibliographies. The biographical portion offers signed articles on composers, arranged alphabetically, with worklists and bibliographies. Both parts have illustrations and cross-references.   ML105.D65

Griffiths, Paul. The Thames and Hudson encyclopaedia of 20th-century music. London ; N.Y. : Thames and Hudson, 1986. 207 p. ISBN 0-500-23449-3. $19.95.   **BH52**

A dictionary arrangement of entries, mostly brief, for names, terms, institutions, and trends in 20th-century music. A list of headings precedes the dictionary. Composer entries predominate (over 500), and generally contain a catalog of works (limited to those composed in the 20th century), principal publishers and/or record companies, and bibliographies. Cross-references, general bibliography, and chronology.   ML100.G85

Music printing and publishing / ed. by D.W. Krummel and Stanley Sadie. N.Y. : W.W. Norton, 1990. 615 p. : ill. ISBN 0-393-02809-7. $50.00.   **BH53**

Based on the article "Printing and publishing" in *The new Grove dictionary of music and musicians* (*Guide* BH129). The first section, "Music printing" by H. Edmund Poole, contains specialized text excised from the original article, as well as revisions and additions that treat recent developments. The second section consists of a dictionary of music publishers and printers, including those in *The new Grove*, supplemented by more than 150 additional entries. The final section is a glossary contributed by Stanley Boorman. ML112.M86

Die Musik in Geschichte und Gegenwart: allgemeine Enzyklopädie der Musik / Unter Mitarbeit zahlreicher Musikforscher des In– und Auslandes, hrsg. von Friedrich Blume. Kassel: Bärenreiter-Verlag, 1986. v. 17. **BH54**

For v.1–16, see *Guide* BH127.

Contents: v. 17, Register. Completes the set.

The long-awaited, indispensable index to this monumental encyclopedia is a single alphabetical listing of approximately 330,000 names and terms. A visual key further identifies major articles and headings in text illustrations, plates, musical examples, and errata. Cross-references. ML100.M92

The new Grove dictionary of American music / ed. by H. Wiley Hitchcock and Stanley Sadie. N.Y. : Grove's Dictionaries of Music, 1986. 4 v. : ill. ISBN 0-943818-36-2. $695.00. **BH55**

An important new work. Includes names and terms germane to the musical tradition of the U.S. Expands articles from *The new Grove* (*Guide* BH129) where appropriate, but adds many more on art music, varieties of popular music, the political and patriotic repertories, specifically American genres, music of the present day, etc. Standard music topics are treated in the American context. Signed articles, many with bibliographies, lists of works, and discographies. Many useful illustrations. List of contributors in v.4. ML101.U6N48

The new Harvard dictionary of music / ed. by Don Michael Randel. Cambridge, Mass. : Belknap Pr. of Harvard Univ. Pr., 1986. 942 p. : ill., music. ISBN 0-674-61525-5. $30.00. **BH56**

2nd ed., 1969 (*Guide* BH138), ed. by Willi Apel, had title: *Harvard dictionary of music*.

A new edition of this standard work, listing terms with definitions and language of origin. Continues to emphasize Western art music, with expanded coverage of non-Western music, popular music, and instruments from all cultures. Signed articles with bibliographies. Contributors are listed; cross-references. ML100.N485

The Norton/Grove concise encyclopedia of music / ed. by Stanley Sadie ; assistant ed., Alison Latham. N.Y. : W.W. Norton, 1988. 850 p. : ill. ISBN 0-393-02620-5. $40.00. **BH57**

A ready-reference work intended for the general reader. Uses *The new Grove* (*Guide* BH129) as its primary source, but offers expanded coverage of more recent events, and includes names or nicknames of individual works. Cross-references. ML100.N88

Pipers Enzyklopädie des Musiktheaters: Oper, Operette, Musical, Ballet / hrsg. von Carl Dahlhaus und dem Forschungsinstitut für Musiktheater der Universität Bayreuth unter Leitung von Sieghart Döhring. München : Piper, c1986–c1989. v. 1–3 : ill. ISBN 3-492-02411-4 (Bd. 1). (In progress). **BH58**

Contents: v. 1. Abbatini–Donizetti; v. 2. Donizetti–Henze; v. 3. Henze–Massine.

German-language encyclopedia of operas, operettas, musicals, and ballets focusing on works in the European tradition from its beginnings to the 20th century. To be complete in 8 v.: v. 1–5, main listing of works; v. 6, Register/Nachträge; v. 7–8, Sachteil. Vols. 1–5 will contain an alphabetical listing of composers or choreographers with their works subarranged chrono-

logically. Vol. 1 contains more than 1,000 titles for roughly 115 composers or choreographers. Each entry contains: birth and death information for the composer/choreographer, title of the work with its German translation if necessary, its text sources, librettists, first performance information, characters, orchestration, performance timings and stagings, background on the composition of the work, summary of contents, descriptive commentary, performance history, autograph and printed sources, and bibliography. Entries are signed; numerous illustrations (many in color). ML102.O6P5

Fact books and compendiums

Kupferberg, Herbert. The book of classical music lists. N.Y. : Penguin Books, c1988. 244 p. ISBN 0-14-011188-3. $8.95. **BH59**

Originally publ.: N.Y. : Facts on File, 1985.

Intends to present "... a book of musical lists consisting entirely of trivia and oddities."—*Pref.* Off-beat, but potentially useful. Numerous lists, including Metropolitan Opera ticket prices, musicians who left the Soviet Union, one-opera composers, etc. Indexes to composers and compositions. ML63.K88

Dictionaries

Ranade, Ashok D. Keywords and concepts, Hindustani classical music. New Delhi : Promilla & Co., 1990. 160 p. : ill. ISBN 81-85002-12-6. Rs200.00. **BH60**

Uses the thesaurus format to provide a conceptual overview to the subject. Arrangement is by systematic category in three major subdivisions: Music making; Technical and qualitative terms; and Musical instruments. All headwords are listed within their category at the head of the dictionary. Alphabetic index; bibliography. ML338.R257

Slonimsky, Nicolas. Lectionary of music. N.Y. : McGraw-Hill, c1989. 521 p. ISBN 0-07-058222-X. $22.95 (est.). **BH61**

A dictionary of music terms and phrases, composers, compositions, etc., with pithy, germane, and idiosyncratic definitions from a major writer on music. ML100.S637

Thomsett, Michael C. Musical terms, symbols, and theory : an illustrated dictionary. Jefferson, N.C. : McFarland, c1989. 277 p. : music. ISBN 0-89950-392-6. $39.95. **BH62**

Contains an alphabetical listing of terms with brief, elementary definitions. Also includes a list of instruments in five languages and an illustrated guide to musical notation. ML108.T46

Quotations

Crofton, Ian. A dictionary of musical quotations / comp. by Ian Crofton and Donald Fraser. N.Y. : Schirmer, 1985. 191 p. ISBN 0-02-906530-5. **BH63**

Brief quotations from literary works, composers' writings, newspaper articles, books on music, etc., organized under 291 headings, alphabetically arranged, with appropriate cross-references. Headings include composers and topics, and are listed in table of contents. Quotations, varying in number from one to more than 50, are arranged chronologically under each heading. Author and subject indexes. ML66.C86

Directories

Directory of music research libraries / Rita Benton, gen. ed. 2nd rev. ed. Kassel ; N.Y. : Bärenreiter, 1985. v. 5 : maps. (In progress). **BH64**
Constitutes Series C of the *International inventory of musical sources* (*RISM*); see *Guide* BH34 and *Supplement* BH22. For v. 1–4 see *Guide* BH151–152.
    Contents: v. 5, Czechoslovakia, Hungary, Poland, by James B. Moldovan. Yugoslavia, by Lilian Pruett (1985).
ML12.D615

Thorin, Suzanne E. International directory of braille music collections / comp. and ed. by Suzanne E. Thorin ; rev. and updated by Shirley Piper Emanuel. Wash. : National Library Service for the Blind and Physically Handicapped, Library of Congress, 1987. 41 p. ISBN 0-8444-0557-4 (pbk.). **BH65**
Superintendent of Documents classification: LC 19.2:IN8/3.
    Lists over 40 institutions, with entries arranged alphabetically by country, city, and organization. For each, gives description of the collection, institutional collecting and lending policies, and any products for the blind created by the institution. ML12.T5

Uscher, Nancy. The Schirmer guide to schools of music and conservatories throughout the world. N.Y. : Schirmer ; London : Collier Macmillan, c1988. 635 p. ISBN 0-02-873030-5. **BH66**
Lists the histories, curricula, special programs, tuition, admission requirements, and other information on some 750 music institutions with programs for training professional musicians. In two sections: U.S., arranged alphabetically by state; International, arranged alphabetically by country. Indexes of institutions, program areas, and instruments taught. ML12.U8

Handbooks

The musical woman : an international perspective. Westport, Conn. : Greenwood, 1984–[1990?]. v. 1–3 : ill. (In progress). **BH67**
Judith Lang Zaimont, ed. in chief; Catherine Overhauser and Jane Gottlieb, assoc. editors.
    Contents: v. 1, 1983; v. 2, 1984–85; v. 3, 1986–90.
    Planned as an ongoing series devoted to the achievements of women in music. Each vol. has two parts: a gazette of performances, festivals, commissions, films, new books, and other summary information; and a series of individual essays on various topics. ML82.M8

Music business

Baskerville, David. Music business handbook & career guide. 5th ed. Los Angeles : Sherwood Pub. Co., c1990. 541 p. : ill. **BH68**
3rd ed., 1982 (*Guide* BH174); 4th ed., 1985.
Follows the organization of the 3rd ed. ML3795.B33

Devriès, Anik. Dictionnaire des éditeurs de musique française / Anik Devriès, François Lesure. Genève : Minkoff, 1979–1988. v. 1–2 : ill. (Archives de l'édition musicale française, t. 4). ISBN 2-8266-0453-8 (set). 280F. (In progress). **BH69**
Contents: v. 1, Des origines à environ 1820 (2 v.); v. 2, De 1820 à 1914.

Contains names of publishers, printers, and dealers responsible for French music publications from the early 16th century. Entries are arranged alphabetically by French city, with the bulk of the entries under Paris. Where available, each entry contains brief biographical information, successive addresses, plate numbers, and bibliographical information. ML112.D45

Parkinson, John A. Victorian music publishers : an annotated list. Warren, Mich. : Harmonie Park Pr., 1990. 315 p., [1] leaf of plates : ill. (some col.). (Detroit studies in music bibliography, no. 64). ISBN 0-89990-051-8. **BH70**
A comprehensive list of British music publishers, 1830–1900. Includes roughly 750 firms, continuing Charles Humphries and William C. Smith's *Music publishing in the British Isles from the beginning until the middle of the nineteenth century* (*Guide* BH203), whose cutoff date was 1850. Lists more than 500 publishers alphabetically by firm name with known addresses, for each citing a representative example of the publisher's work. Annotations included for many entries. ML21.G7P3

Shemel, Sidney. This business of music / by Sidney Shemel and M. William Krasilovsky. Rev. and enl. 6th ed. N.Y. : Billboard Books, 1990. 688 p. : ill. ISBN 0-8230-7706-3. $27.50. **BH71**
3rd ed., 1982 (*Guide* BH175 *note*); 5th ed., 1985.
A compendium of useful information on contracts, copyrights, record production, music videos, agents and managers, performing-rights organizations, and other business practices specific to music. ML3790.S5

Wadhams, Wayne. Sound advice : the musician's guide to the record industry. N.Y. : Schirmer ; London : Collier Macmillan, c1990. 545 p. : ill. ISBN 0-02-872692-8. **BH72**
Nontechnical, covering the vocabulary commonly used by technicians and engineers working in recording studios, sound stages, and on location. Terms, with definitions, are organized in 15 categories, with key to categories given at the foot of each page. ML3790.W27

Chronologies, outlines, tables

Hall, Charles J. An eighteenth-century musical chronicle : events 1750–1799. N.Y. : Greenwood, 1990. 177 p. (Music reference collection, no. 25). ISBN 0-313-26576-3. **BH73**
A year-by-year chronology of political and social events, cultural history, musical events, biographical highlights, musical literature and compositions, etc. General musical index.
    § Similarly organized are the author's two additional volumes: *A nineteenth-century musical chronicle: events, 1800–1899* (N.Y. : Greenwood, 1989. 374 p.) and *A twentieth-century musical chronicle: events, 1900–1988* (N.Y. : Greenwood, 1989. 347 p.). ML195.H28

History

New Oxford history of music. Oxford ; N.Y. : Oxford Univ. Pr., 1986–1990. v. 6, 9 : music. ISBN 0-19-316329-2 (v. 2). $165.00. **BH74**
For earlier volumes and annotation, see *Guide* BH192.
    Contents: v. 6, Concert music (1630–1750), 1986; v. 9 Romanticism (1830–1890), 1990, both ed. by Gerald Abraham. Completes the original edition.
    Vol. 2, *Early medieval music up to 1300*, has been published in a 2nd ed., ed. by Richard Crocker and David Hiley, 1990; v.5, *Opera and church music, 1630–1750*, has been re-

printed with corrections and a revised bibliography, 1986; and reprinted with corrections have been v.3, *Ars nova and the Renaissance, 1300–1540*, 1986, and v.8, *The age of Beethoven, 1790–1830*, 1985. ML160.N44

Annuals

Computing in musicology : a directory of research. Oct. 1989– . Menlo Park, Calif. : Center for Computer Assisted Research in the Humanities, 1989– . Annual. **BH75**

Successor to the Center for Computer Assisted Research in the Humanities' *Directories of computer assisted research in musicology* (1985–87), this work is addressed "principally to musicologists seeking current information about research in progress, discussion of that research, and practical examples of applications."—*Pref.* (1989). Based on reports by readers, each issue covers current events, special topics, music printing, software, and other topics. ML73.D57

Biography

Biographical dictionary of Russian/Soviet composers / editors in chief, Allan Ho and Dmitry Feofanov. N.Y. : Greenwood, 1989. 739 p. ISBN 0-313-24485-5. **BH76**

An alphabetical listing of over 2,000 composers and others associated with music who were born in Russia or the U.S.S.R., were noteworthy émigrés, or were foreigners who settled and were influential in Russia. Each entry contains biographical information, worklists, bibliographies, discographies, and comments on style. Appendixes include a supplementary list of persons not included in the main listing and a discography for recordings cited. Name index and list of contributors. ML106.S68B56

Cohen, Aaron I. International encyclopedia of women composers. 2nd ed., rev. and enl. N.Y. : Books & Music USA, c1987. 2 v. (1151 p., [48] p. of plates) : ports. ISBN 0-9617485-2-4 (set). $125.00. **BH77**

1st ed., 1984 (*Guide* BH192).

Follows the format of the earlier edition, but has been expanded to include 6,196 historical and contemporary composers from all nationalities. Annotations focus on the composer's musical education, achievements, and works. Addendum at beginning of v. 1 lists names inadvertently omitted; v. 2 includes bibliography, photographs, appendixes, and discography. ML105.C7

Gilder, Eric. The dictionary of composers and their music : a listener's companion. New, rev. ed. N.Y. : Holt, Rinehart, and Winston, 1986. 592 p. ISBN 0-03-007177-1. $21.95. **BH78**

A compendium of factual information on the standard concert repertoire. The first part contains an alphabetical listing of 426 composers, 1300–1984, each entry giving the composer's dates, brief biographical information, and a chronological listing of musical works. The second part rearranges the information into a year-by-year survey showing composer dates and titles composed during that year. The third part contains a timeline with composers' dates. ML113.G4

Gray, John. Blacks in classical music : a bibliographical guide to composers, performers, and ensembles. N.Y. : Greenwood, c1988. 280 p. (Music reference collection, no. 15). ISBN 0-313-26056-7. $39.95. **BH79**

An author listing of books, articles, unpublished papers, recordings, and media performances documenting the "full range of black activity in classical music."—*Introd.* Organized topically with subdivisions under: General; Composers; Symphony

and concert artists; Concert and opera singers; Reference works; and Research centers. Artist and author indexes. ML128.B45G7

Greene, Frank. Composers on record : an index to biographical information on 14,000 composers whose music has been recorded. Metuchen, N.J. : Scarecrow, 1985. 604 p. ISBN 0-8108-1816-7. **BH80**

An index to 14,000 composers of "serious" music drawn from 66 discographies and record catalogs, and from the record collection at the University of Toronto. Each citation includes the composer's dates, national origin, and two types of indexing: to biographical information in basic reference books, and to discographies. Entries without indexing indicate composers found only in the collection at the University of Toronto. ML105.G78

Holmes, John L. Composers on composers. N.Y. : Greenwood, 1990. 189 p. ISBN 0-313-26602-6. **BH81**

Anecdotal quotations on 85 mainstream composers by other composers, arranged by the name of the composer under discussion. Notes and sources given. Composer index. ML90.H64

International who's who in music and musicians' directory. 12th ed. Cambridge, Eng. : [Melrose Press], 1990. 1 v. **BH82**

For earlier editions, see *Guide* BH205.

This edition contains 7,500 entries, over 3,000 listed for the first time, with updates for many of those previously listed. Most entries compiled from questionnaires. Appendixes contain lists of organizations and competitions. ML106.G7W4

Jacobs, Arthur. The Penguin dictionary of musical performers. London : Viking, 1990. 250 p. ISBN 0-670-80755-9. $35.00. **BH83**

Offers brief performance biographies for some 2,000 groups and individuals selected by the author and covering Western classical music, 1600 to the present. Index of 350 composers mentioned in the biographies. ML385.J32

Kutsch, K. J. Grosses Sängerlexikon / K.J. Kutsch, Leo Riemens. Bern : Francke, c1987. 2 v. (3452 columns) : geneal. table. ISBN 3-317-01638-8 (Deut. Bibl.). **BH84**

Contents: v. 1, A–L; v. 2, M–Z, Operas and operettas.

Contains biographies of singers from the last decades of the 16th century to the present. Some entries include a bibliography and, (if applicable), the singer's recording company. Appendix contains an alphabetical listing of operas and operettas with information on their first performance. Composer index. ML105.K83

LePage, Jane Weiner. Women composers, conductors, and musicians of the twentieth century : selected biographies. Metuchen, N.J. : Scarecrow, 1980–1988. 3 v. : ill. ISBN 0-8108-1298-3. **BH85**

Each volume contains entries for approximately 17 composers. Quotations from personal interviews are interwoven with biographical information. Entries conclude with lists of compositions, works in progress, discographies, and publisher addresses. ML82.L46

Tischler, Alice. A descriptive bibliography of art music by Israeli composers. Warren, Mich. : Harmonie Park Pr., 1988. 424 p. (Detroit studies in music bibliography, no. 62). ISBN 0-89990-045-3. **BH86**

Covers 63 composers selected according to the following criteria: "... (1) the date of 1910 as a starting-point, i.e., the beginning of organized musical activity in the newly-founded city of Tel Aviv; (2) composers who have won recognition in the musical life of Israel by having their works performed and/or published; and (3) those who have matured and are settled in their profession in Israel."—*Introd.* Excludes composers born after 1947. For each, gives brief overview of career, addresses, sources, and full information on individual compositions (including performance medium, first performances, etc.).

ML120.I75T57

Turner, Patricia. Dictionary of Afro-American performers : 78 RPM and cylinder recordings of opera, choral music, and song, c.1900–1949. N.Y. : Garland, 1990. 433 p., [24] p. of plates : ports. (Garland reference library of the humanities, vol. 590). ISBN 0-8240-8736-4.

BH87

Offers a single alphabetical listing of composers, vocalists (arranged by voice category), instrumentalists, operas and musicals, vocal groups, record companies, and spoken-word recordings. In a novel arrangement, the table of contents provides the systematic index to the list. Organization of the information in each entry differs by category, so annotations vary markedly from entry to entry. Compiled in part from the author's collection.

ML106.U3T87

Bibliography

Cowden, Robert H. Concert and opera singers : a bibliography of biographical materials. Westport, Conn. : Greenwood, 1985. 278 p. (Music reference collection, no. 5). ISBN 0-313-24828-1.

BH88

Contains information on 708 concert and opera singers who are the subject of an autobiography or biography, and who have entries or articles in one or more of ten major reference works or nine periodicals. In three sections: a bibliography, with annotations, of collective works; a bibliography of related works; and the bibliography arranged by individual singers. Additional reference sources are listed in Appendix I, while a very useful index to concert singers in *The new Grove* (*Guide* BH119) constitutes Appendix II. Overlaps considerably with Andrew Farkas's *Opera and concert singers : an annotated bibliography* (N.Y. : Garland, 1985).

§ A related work is the author's *Concert and opera conductors : a bibliography of biographical materials* (N.Y. : Greenwood, 1987), organized in the same manner as the above work, but with an appendix to conductors drawn from *Baker's biographical dictionary of musicians*, 7th ed. (*Guide* BH187).

ML128.B3C7

Floyd, Samuel A. Black music biography : an annotated bibliography / Samuel A. Floyd, Jr., Marsha J. Reisser. White Plains, N.Y. : Kraus Internat., c1987. 302 p. ISBN 0-527-30158-2.

BH89

Entries for 87 individuals include for each a "brief career vignette" followed by summaries of biographical books about the artists, including 147 monographs and 32 autobiographies. Some entries contain review citations culled from general indexes and selective discographies.

ML128.B3F6

Garland composer resource manuals. v. 1– . N.Y. : Garland, 1981– . Irregular.

BH90

A series on the most important composers from the Renaissance to the present day. Each volume contains annotated lists of writings in all major European languages about one or more composers, as well as lists of works, biographical sketches, guides to library resources, etc. To date, some 34 volumes have appeared. Each is individually authored, resulting in variation in quality among volumes. On the whole, a valuable resource.

§ A similar series is *Bio-bibliographies in music* (Westport, Conn. : Greenwood, 1984–); approximately 40 volumes have appeared.

Green, Richard D. Index to composer bibliographies. Detroit : Information Coordinators, 1985. 76 p. ISBN 0-89990-025-9.

BH91

A selective list of separately published bibliographies or bibliographical essays on 74 composers or 20th-century popular performing groups (e.g., the Beatles). Entries are drawn from

monographs and serial publications, and each entry is annotated. Particularly useful for pre-1949 coverage of major composers.

ML113.G793

Indexes

Bull, Storm. Index to biographies of contemporary composers. N.Y. : Scarecrow, 1987. v. 3. ISBN 0-8108-1930-9 (v. 3). (In progress).   **BH92**

For v. 1–2, see *Guide* BH211.

Follows the format of the earlier volumes, listing composers who meet the following criteria: still alive (1985), or born 1900 or later, or died 1950 or later regardless of birth date. Lists more than 13,500 composers, including 7,600 from v. 1–2 with additional information, and 5,900 new names. Indexes 98 reference works, half of them in English and almost all published after 1974.

ML105.B9

De Lerma, Dominique-René. Black music and musicians in *The new Grove dictionary of American music* and *The new Harvard dictionary of music* / Dominique-René de Lerma and Marsha J. Reisser. Chicago : Center for Black Music Research, Columbia College, c1989. 56 p. ISBN 0-929911-00-8.   **BH93**

A useful index of entries related to African-American music and musicians found in *The new Grove dictionary of American music* (*Supplement* BH55) and *The new Harvard dictionary of music* (*Supplement* BH56). Entries are arranged alphabetically within three sections: Individuals and ensembles; Subjects (taken directly from the dictionaries); and Authors of the articles. Each entry is coded for the presence of a bibliography, discography, musical example, or illustrations; length of the article is given in centimeters.

ML128.B45D445

MUSICAL FORMS

Opera

Anderson, James. The Harper dictionary of opera and operetta. 1st U.S. ed. N.Y. : Harper & Row, 1990. 691 p. ISBN 0-06-016488-3. $35.00.   **BH94**

Published in U.K. as *Bloomsbury dictionary of opera and operetta* (London : Bloomsbury Pub. Ltd., 1989).

A general guide to opera and operetta repertory, national aspects, audience practice, geographical considerations, etc., intended for general readers. Dictionary arrangement of name, title, and subject entries, with brief definitions and cross-references. Aims at currency, focusing on composers, opera titles, and contemporary performances rather than historical singers.

§ Another general guide on a smaller scale is Mary Hamilton's *A–Z of opera* (N.Y. : Facts on File, 1990), with approximately 850 entries and numerous illustrations. Plot summaries, historical overview, and recording information for 200 regularly-performed operas are provided in John Lazarus's *The opera handbook* (Boston : G.K. Hall, 1987).

ML102.O6A6

Annals of the Metropolitan Opera Guild : the complete chronicle of performances and artists : chronology 1883–1985. N.Y. : Metropolitan Opera Guild ; Boston : G.K. Hall, 1989. 1000 p. : ill. ISBN 0-8161-8903-X (set). $175.00.   **BH95**

Gerald Fitzgerald, ed. in chief.

Contains the "complete record of all performances by the company from October 1883 through June 1985."—*Pref.* 21,872 performances are grouped by their 100 seasons, including performances in New York and elsewhere. Vol. I contains the chronology of performance information; v. II, indexes of performances, composers and librettists, production artists, performing artists, locations, broadcast performances, and translations. Supersedes William Seltsam's *Metropolitan Opera annals* (*Guide* BH236) and its supplements.

ML1711.8.N3M38

Girardi, Michele. Il teatro La Fenice : cronologia degli spettacoli, 1792–1936 / Michele Girardi, Franco Rossi. Venezia : Albrizzi editore, 1989. 491 p. ISBN 88-7837-007-X. **BH96**

Lists 1,352 dramatic performances and concerts given in the Teatro La Fenice from its opening through 1936. Entries are organized by year, then by season, and each contains title, performers, and other relevant information. Indexes by names of operatic characters, other names, and titles.

ML1733.8.V4G57

Kobbé, Gustav. Kobbé's complete opera book / ed. and rev. by the Earl of Harewood. 10th ed. London : Bodley Head, 1987. 1404 p., [32] p. of plates : ill. ISBN 0-370-31017-9. £30.00. **BH97**

9th ed., 1976 (*Guide* BH243).

This edition adds approximately 20 new titles. MT95.K52

Kornick, Rebecca Hodell. Recent American opera : a production guide. N.Y. : Columbia Univ. Pr., c1991. 352 p. ISBN 0-231-06920-0. **BH98**

Contains information on 213 American opera/musical-theater works by approximately 120 composers. Most had their premiere after 1972 and were reviewed by major publications. Entries are organized by composer, and for each work provide brief assessment, summary of plot, production requirements, and citations to reviews. MT955.K82

Marco, Guy A. Opera : a research and information guide. N.Y. : Garland, 1984. 373 p. (Garland reference library of the humanities, vol. 468). ISBN 0-8240-8999-5. $45.00. **BH99**

A useful bibliography of 704 annotated entries dealing with the music and general literature. Most entries cite studies of individual composers, but other topics include reference works, historical studies, opera houses, international directories, production, specific countries, etc. Author-title and subject indexes. ML128.O4M28

The Metropolitan Opera encyclopedia : a comprehensive guide to the world of opera / ed. by David Hamilton ; contributors, Aliki Andris-Michalaros . . . [et al.]. N.Y. : Simon and Schuster, c1987. 415 p. : ill. (some col.). ISBN 0-671-61732-X. $35.00. **BH100**

A "guide to the world of opera, prepared under the auspices of the Metropolitan Opera Guild . . . and a compendium of information specifically related to the Metropolitan Opera, its history, repertory, and performers."—*Pref.* Alphabetical listing of operas, composers, librettists, performers, places, and terms. Includes 24 guest essays by prominent artists. ML102.O6M47

Pitou, Spire. The Paris Opéra : an encyclopedia of operas, ballets, composers, and performers. Westport, Conn. : Greenwood, c1983–1990. v. 1–3; in 4. ISBN 0-313-26218-7. (In progress). **BH101**

Contents: v. 1, Genesis and glory, 1671–1715; v. 2, Rococo and romantic, 1715–1815; v. 3, Growth and grandeur, 1815–1914 (2 v.)

An alphabetical listing of operas, ballets, singers, dancers, composers, choreographers, librettists, and scenarists connected with the Paris Opéra. Informative entries contain biographical information, synopses of dramatic action, asterisked cross-references to other articles, and bibliographies.

ML1727.8.P2P5

Sartori, Claudio. I libretti italiani a stampa dalle origini al 1800 : catalogo analitico con 16 indici. Cuneo : Bertola & Locatelli, c1990. v. 1–2. (In progress). **BH102**

Contents: v. 1, A–B; v. 2, C–D.

An extensive work which when complete will contain over 25,000 entries, with librettos listed by title. Entries vary in length depending on available information, but may include place of performance, librettist, composer, other personnel associated with the opera (impresarios, designers, choreographers, etc.), conductor, performers, singers, etc., and conclude with repositories identified by RISM sigla. ML136.A1S27

Studwell, William E. Opera plot index / William E. Studwell, David A. Hamilton. N.Y. : Garland, 1989. 466 p. (Garland reference library of the humanities, vol. 1099). ISBN 0-8240-4621-8. **BH103**

Indexes plots, descriptions, illustrations, historical background, criticism and analysis, musical themes, and bibliographical references for 2,900 operas and other works of musical theater from 169 books in 10 languages. Each entry gives the title of the work, the composer and date of first performance (if known), followed by codes giving the source indexed and its type of information. Composer index. ML128.O4S8

Musical theater

Bloom, Ken. American song : the complete musical theatre companion. N.Y. : Facts on File, c1985. 2 v. ISBN 0-87196-961-0. $95.00. **BH104**

A compilation of information on nearly 3,300 American musicals, 1900–84. Vol. I contains an alphabetical listing by title with performance information, composers, lyricists, song titles, casts, etc.; v. II contains indexes by songs and personal names, as well as a chronological list. Covers the same subject as David Hummel's *American musical theatre* (*Guide* BH253), but expands coverage to include non-New York performances, omits recordings, and offers more personal annotations.

ML128.M78B6

Diccionario de la zarzuela : biografias de compositores, argumentos y comentarios musicales sobre las principales zarzuelas del repertorio actual / R. Alier, X. Aviñoa, F.X. Mata. Madrid : Daimon, 1986. 386 p. : ill., ports. ISBN 968-6024-85-9. **BH105**

Focuses on some 100 composers of zarzuelas, primarily Spanish, as well as other individuals associated with the genre. Entries include biographical information, together with lengthy discussions of individual works for many composers. Concludes with a discography. ML102.Z3D53

Gänzl, Kurt. Gänzl's book of the musical theatre / Kurt Gänzl and Andrew Lamb. 1st American ed. N.Y. : Schirmer, 1989. 1353 p., [4] p. of plates : ill. ISBN 0-02-871941-7. $40.00. **BH106**

Publ. in U.K.: London : Bodley Head, 1988.

A companion to *The new Kobbé's complete opera book*, rev. ed. (*Guide* BH243) and its successor (*Kobbé's complete opera book, Supplement* BH97) for the light musical theater. Contains production and performance information, characters, and plot summaries for more than 300 musicals organized by country, then chronologically. Selection based on current performance availability, artistic or historic significance, and the authors' preferences. Includes discography and two indexes: Titles, authors, composers, and lyricists; and Song titles. MT95.G2

Green, Stanley. Broadway musicals, show by show. 3rd ed. Milwaukee, Wisc. : H. Leonard Books, 1990. 372 p. : ill. ISBN 0-88188-761-7 (pbk.). $16.95. **BH107**

1st ed., 1985; 2nd ed., 1987.

Contains information on approximately 300 shows presented both on and off Broadway, 1866–1975, arranged chronologically. For each, includes credits, brief description and history of the show, theater where it was performed, and photographs from the production. Criteria for inclusion were "length of run ... seminal importance, people involved, uniqueness of approach or subject matter, quality of score, and general acceptance as a significant work in the field."—*Pref.* ML1711.G735

Wildbihler, Hubert. The musical : an international annotated bibliography = eine internationale annotierte Bibliographie / by Hubert Wildbihler and Sonja Völklein. München ; N.Y. : Saur, 1986. 320 p. ISBN 3-598-10635-1. DM120.00.   **BH108**

Aims to present the "entire theoretical literature on the stage and film musical from its beginnings to 1986."—*Foreword.* Although international in focus, the majority of citations follow the development of the genre, and are from Anglo-American sources. Entries number 3,629 items in 5 categories: General reference works (100 items), Stage musical (1,100 items), Stage musical outside North America (220 items), Film musical (250 items), and People (1,850 items). List of sources consulted; author and subject indexes.   ML128.M78W56

Songs

Ewen, David. American songwriters. N.Y. : H.W. Wilson, 1987. 489 p. : ports. ISBN 0-8242-0744-0. $50.00.
                    BH109

Replaces the author's *Popular American composers* (1962) and *First supplement* (1972). Contains lengthy biographies of 90 composers and 50 lyricists or composer/lyricists, along with the performance history of some individual songs. Index to the 5,600 compositions mentioned. Summary bibliographical references.   ML390.E825

Hovland, Michael A. Musical settings of American poetry : a bibliography. Westport, Conn. : Greenwood, 1986. 531 p. (Music reference collection, no. 8). ISBN 0-313-22938-4.   **BH110**

Contains 5,800 settings by 2,100 composers of the poems of 99 prominent American authors. Selective coverage of collections and hymns; some discographies are listed. Composer and literary title index.   ML128.V7H67

Seaton, Douglass. The art song : a research and information guide. N.Y. : Garland, 1987. 273 p. (Music research and information guides, vol. 6 ; Garland reference library of the humanities, vol. 673). ISBN 0-8240-8554-X.
                    BH111

An annotated bibliography of 970 items, including monographs, journal articles, and dissertations published during the 20th century. Annotations are brief and summary; entries are organized in eight useful categories: general studies, individual composers, individual poets, aesthetics and analysis, texts and translations, performance, bibliographies, and sources. A brief historical overview of the art song precedes the bibliography. Name and subject indexes.   ML128.S3S33

Studwell, William E. Christmas carols : a reference guide. N.Y. : Garland, 1985. 278 p. ISBN 0-8240-8899-9.   **BH112**

Approximately 800 carols pertaining to Christmas and adjacent events from 171 anthologies are indexed. Each entry contains brief information on creator, place, and date for both text and music, along with pertinent supplementary notes. Title, person, and group indexes.   ML102.C3S9

Swanekamp, Joan. English ayres : a selectively annotated bibliography and discography. Westport, Conn. : Greenwood, 1984. 141 p. ISBN 0-313-23467-1. **BH113**

A specialized index in 28 sections, one on the "ayre" genre, the remainder on 27 individual composers. Each category is subdivided for literature, music, and recording, and many entries have brief annotations. It is necessary to consult the preface for the internal organization of the entries under music. Author and title indexes.   ML128.S3S9

Indexes

Havlice, Patricia Pate. Popular song index. Third supplement. Metuchen, N.J. : Scarecrow, 1989. 875 p. ISBN 0-8108-2202-4.   **BH114**

For 1st ed., 1975, and Suppl. 1–2, 1978–84, see *Guide* BH270.

Follows the plan of the basic volume and previous supplements. Indexes 181 song books published between 1979 and 1987, while picking up a few titles published earlier. Indexed by title, first line of song, and first line of chorus, plus a composer and lyricist index.   ML128.S3H4

Lax, Roger. The great song thesaurus / Roger Lax, Frederick Smith. 2nd ed., updated and expanded. N.Y. : Oxford Univ. Pr., 1989. 774 p. ISBN 0-19-505408-3. $75.00.   **BH115**

1st ed., 1984 (*Guide* BH264).

Follows the plan of the earlier edition, updating information on songs and awards through the mid-1980s. Contains an additional section listing key lines of many popular song lyrics with their titles.   ML128.S3L4

Choral music

DeVenney, David P. Nineteenth-century American choral music : an annotated guide. Berkeley, Calif. : Fallen Leaf Pr., 1987. 182 p. (Fallen Leaf reference books in music, no. 8). ISBN 0-914913-08-5 (pbk.).   **BH116**

"Lists choral music by composers who were active in the United States during the nineteenth century and died or ceased composing after the end of the First World War (ca. 1920)."—*Pref.* The 24 composers are arranged alphabetically, with an alphabetical subarrangement by titles of works. Brief annotations include publisher, repository, and other information. Contains an annotated bibliography of 134 items and several indexes by author, genre, etc.

§ A companion is the author's *Early American choral music: an annotated guide* (Berkeley, Calif. : Fallen Leaf Press, 1988), which lists choral music by 32 composers active from about 1670 to 1825.   ML128.C48D48

Jazz

Carl Gregor, *Duke of Mecklenburg.* International bibliography of jazz books / Carl Gregor Herzog zu Mecklenburg ; comp. with the assistance of Norbert Ruecker. Baden-Baden : Koerner, 1983–1988. v. 1–2. ISBN 3-87320-567-X (pbk. : v. 1). (In progress).   **BH117**

Revision and expansion of the author's *International jazz bibliography* and its two suppls. (*Guide* BH274).

Contents: v. 1, 1921–1949; v. 2, 1950–1959.

Planned to cover 1921–79 in 4 v. Vols. 1–2 contain 823 titles and 55 "phantom" titles. Entries, arranged alphabetically by author, with titles listed chronologically, contain references to *IJB* or its supplements, source of entry, and contributor. Several indexes and chronology.   ML128.J3C4

Jazz index. Jahrg. 1–7 (1983). [Frankfurt am Main [etc] : N. Ruecker], 1977–[c1987]. ISSN 0344-5399.
                    BH118

For annotation, see *Guide* BH281.
Ceased with v. 7, covering 1983.   ML128.J3J4

The new Grove dictionary of jazz / ed. by Barry Kernfeld. London : Macmillan ; N.Y. : Grove's Dictionaries of Music, 1988. 2 v. : ill. ISBN 0-333-39846-7 (set). $295.00.   **BH119**

A comprehensive dictionary covering all periods and styles of jazz from many countries. Although it draws on other Grove dictionaries, 90% of the material is newly written. Articles cover individuals, groups and bands, topics and terms, instruments, record companies and labels, and institutions; they are signed, and include bibliographies and selected discographies. Extensive bibliography on jazz and list of contributors in appendixes.   ML102.J3N48

Discography

Harrison, Max. The essential jazz records / Max Harrison, Charles Fox, and Eric Thacker. Westport, Conn. : Greenwood, 1984. v. 1. (Discographies, no. 12). ISBN 0-313-24674-2 (v. 1). (In progress).   **BH120**
Contents: v. 1, Ragtime to swing.

The first of two volumes intended to provide a selective, critical guide to recorded jazz. Organized chronologically, v. 1 covers the origins through the 1930s. The 250 signed entries each include recording information, performers, and a critical essay. Indexes of LP titles, tune titles, and musicians.   ML156.4.J3H33

Tulane University. William Ransom Hogan Jazz Archive. Catalog of the William Ransom Hogan Jazz Archive : the collection of seventy-eight RPM phonograph recordings / Howard-Tilton Memorial Library, Tulane University. Boston : G.K. Hall, 1984. 2 v. ISBN 0-8161-0434-4 (set).   **BH121**

Reproduces the author and title catalog cards for approximately 27,000 78-rpm recordings emphasizing New Orleans music and its origins.   ML156.2.T84

Electronic music

Tomlyn, Bo. Electronic music dictionary : a glossary of the specialized terms relating to the music and sound technology of today / by Bo Tomlyn & Steve Leonard. Milwaukee, Wisc. : H. Leonard Books, c1988. 77 p. ISBN 0-88188-904-0. $5.95.   **BH122**

Intended as a "practical, every-day glossary to the basic concepts of synthesizers, amplification, MIDI, computers and the physics of sound."—*Foreword.* Approximately 400 terms are listed alphabetically with definitions, references to related terms, and the general category or subject to which the term belongs in the context of electronic music.   ML102.E4T65

Folk and popular music

Bianco, David. Heat wave : the Motown fact book. Ann Arbor, Mich. : Pierian Pr., 1988. 524 p. : ill., ports. (Rock & roll reference series, no. 25). ISBN 0-87650-204-4.   **BH123**
Covers the history of the Motown recording company. Organized in eight sections: biographies of the major artists with discographies; year-by-year chronology of events; alphabetical listing and description of American and British labels issuing recordings by the company; discography of U.S. releases; discography of U.K. releases; indexes by performing artists, song titles, date, and record number for U.S. releases; the same for

U.K. releases; and Motown-related label discographies.   ML156.4.S6B5

Carr, Ian. Jazz : the essential companion / Ian Carr, Digby Fairweather, Brian Priestley. N.Y. : Prentice Hall, 1988. 562 p. : ports. ISBN 0-13-509274-4. $24.95.   **BH124**

Primarily a biographical dictionary of individuals, but also contains terms relevant to mainstream jazz from its beginnings through 1986. International in scope. Entries generally are brief, with discographies and bibliographical references, and are sometimes uneven, since all entries are written by one of the three author/musicians.   ML102.J3C32

Cooper, B. Lee. Rockabilly : a bibliographic resource guide / by B. Lee Cooper and Wayne S. Haney. Metuchen, N.J. : Scarecrow, 1990. 352 p. ISBN 0-8108-2386-1.   **BH125**

Focuses on a specific style of popular music of the 1950s by providing a bibliography of 1,945 books and periodical articles arranged by performer, with a separate discography of over 200 albums. Includes separate, additional bibliographies of books and periodicals on the genre in general. Author index.
                    ML128.R65C66

Encyclopedia of rock / [ed. by] Phil Hardy, Dave Laing ; additional material, Stephen Barnard, Don Perretta. N.Y. : Schirmer, 1988. 480 p. : ill. (some col.). ISBN 0-02-919562-4.   **BH126**
Updated and considerably expanded version of 1976 ed.

Contains roughly 2,000 entries for names of rock and rock-related individual and group performers, "backroom figures" (i.e., entrepreneurs and record producers), topics, recording companies, and types of media. Artists were chosen on the basis of chart success in the U.S. or the U.K., or the historical influence and artistic significance accorded them by the editors, who also determined the length of annotations. The latter give general biographic and artistic information, but lack bibliographies and discographies.   ML102.R6E5

Fuld, James J. The book of world-famous music : classical, popular, and folk. 3rd ed., rev. and enl. N.Y. : Dover, 1985. 714 p., [8] p. of plates : ill., music. ISBN 0-486-24857-7 (pbk.). $14.95.   **BH127**
Reprints the text of the 1971 ed. (*Guide* BH295), including the useful introduction containing a guide to bibliographical procedures, and the main text of historical information with musical themes. A supplement section (25 p.) adds new information and corrections.   ML113.F8

Gammond, Peter. The Oxford companion to popular music. Oxford [England] ; N.Y. : Oxford Univ. Pr., 1991. 739 p. ISBN 0-19-311323-6. £19.95 (est.). **BH128**
Aims to cover "all music that would not normally be found in a reference book on 'classical' or 'serious' music . . . and the essential elements and personalities concerned with popular song of all periods."—*Introd.* Dictionary arrangement of entries covers roughly 1850–1985, with emphasis on the English-speaking world. Many entries are lengthy, and some have bibliographies. Indexes: people and groups; shows and films; songs and albums.   ML102.P66G35

Helander, Brock. The rock who's who : a biographical dictionary and critical discography including rhythm-and-blues, soul, rockabilly, folk, country, easy listening, punk, and new wave. N.Y. : Schirmer ; London : Collier Macmillan, c1982. 686 p. ISBN 0-02-871250-1. ISBN 0-02-871920-4 (pbk.).   **BH129**
Provides a critical and historical discography of rock and soul recordings released in the U.S. from the mid-1950s through early 1982. Entries are arranged alphabetically by performer and contain a brief annotation on the group's or individual artist's career and performance history, followed by discography organized by date of recording. Each item includes

the album title, awards it received, label, number, and release date.   ML102.R6H5

Kaufmann, Walter. Selected musical terms of non-Western cultures : a notebook-glossary. Warren, Mich. : Harmonie Park Pr., 1990. 806 p. (Detroit studies in music bibliography, no. 65). ISBN 0-89990-039-9.
     BH130

Terms are listed alphabetically, giving country of origin, brief definitions, and source abbreviations. Sources include 321 items of varying currency, since the glossary was compiled over a 50-year period, albeit by a noted scholar.   ML108.K37

Nite, Norm N. Rock on almanac : the first four decades of rock 'n' roll : a chronology. N.Y. : Harper & Row, c1989. 532 p. : ill. ISBN 0-06-055166-6. $27.50. ISBN 0-06-096081-7 (pbk.). $14.95.   **BH131**

Compendium of information on rock from the 1940s through 1989. For each year, includes news and music highlights, artists and groups who debuted, monthly listing of popular songs in alphabetical order, top ten singles and albums, Grammy winners, Rock and Roll Hall of Fame inductions (beginning 1986), brief biographical facts on performers, rock movies, and motion picture Academy Awards. Numerous photographs and a glossary; indexes of performers and song titles.   ML3534.N58

Popular music : an annotated index of American popular songs. Detroit : Gale, c1974– .   **BH132**

Continues Nat Shapiro's *Popular music : an annotated index of American popular songs* (*Guide* BH308), published in 6 v., 1964–73, each of which covered a five-year period, 1920–69, and which was superseded by Shapiro and Bruce Pollock's *Popular music, 1920–1979 : a revised cumulation* (*Guide* BH308 *note*).

Contents: v. 7, 1970–74; v. 8, 1975–79; v. 9, 1980–84.

Annual, beginning with v. 10 (1985).

Entries are arranged alphabetically by title, each providing author, composer, publisher, and first or best-selling record, with indication of performer and recording company. For earlier coverage, Barbara Cohen-Stratyner's *Popular music, 1900–1919* (Detroit : Gale, 1988) follows the same format, but includes annotations covering historical data.   ML120.U5S5

Sandberg, Larry. The folk music sourcebook / Larry Sandberg and Dick Weissman. New, updated ed. N.Y. : Da Capo Pr., c1989. 272 p. : ill. ISBN 0-306-80360-7. $16.95.   **BH133**

Updates and expands the 1976 ed. (*Guide* BH307). New material is set in different type for easy identification. Introductory sectional overviews, bibliographies, and guides to resources comprise the new material.   ML12.S26

Stambler, Irwin. Encyclopedia of pop, rock & soul. Rev. ed. N.Y. : St. Martin's Pr., c1989. 881 p., [48] p. of plates : ill. ISBN 0-312-02573-4. $35.00.   **BH134**

1st ed., 1975.

An alphabetical listing of performers, both groups and individuals, with brief biographical information and summary essays on their work. Appendixes include chronological listings of record awards, Grammy winners, and Academy Award nominations and winners in music.   ML102.P66S8

Tyler, Don. Hit parade : an encyclopedia of the top songs of the jazz, depression, swing, and sing eras. N.Y. : Quill, c1985. 257 p. ISBN 0-688-05079-4. ISBN 0-688-06149-4 (pbk.). $12.95.   **BH135**

Year-by-year chronology of the most popular songs in the U.S., 1920–45. Selection was based on "Your hit parade" radio compilations, weekly charts from *Variety* and *Billboard*, and the "ASCAP all-time hit parade" of 16 songs chosen as the greatest hits, 1914–64. For each song, gives composer, lyricist, and brief annotation. Brief biographies of composers and lyri-

cists are appended. Indexes of names and song titles.   ML102.P66T9

Bibliography

Hoffmann, Frank W. The literature of rock, II, 1979–1983 : with additional material for the period 1954–1978 / by Frank Hoffmann and B. Lee Cooper ; with the assistance of Lee Ann Hoffmann. Metuchen, N.J. : Scarecrow, 1986. 2 v. (1097 p.). ISBN 0-8108-1821-3.   **BH136**

Continues Hoffmann's earlier work covering 1954–78 (*Guide* BH296), and includes some additional entries from that period. Arrangement is roughly chronological, subdivided by topic. Vol. II contains a "Related topics" listing that includes citations related to historical, social, and economic issues. Some brief annotations. Includes an index of names, titles, and subjects.   ML128.R6H62

Iwaschkin, Roman. Popular music : a reference guide. N.Y. : Garland, 1986. 658 p. (Garland reference library of the humanities, vol. 642). ISBN 0-8240-8680-5.
     BH137

Aims to cover the entire popular music field from the "beginnings of the genre to 1984" (*Introd.*), with some titles from 1985. Contains 4,744 entries in several sections: the music, biography, technical aspects, the music business, the product, and literary works. Includes a list of more than 500 periodicals. Many entries have brief annotations. Index.   ML128.P63I95

Popular music periodicals index : POMPI. No. 1–2 (Oct. 1984–Sept. 1986)– . London : British Library National Sound Archive, c1988– . Annual. ISSN 0951-1318.
     BH138

Annual, beginning with no. 5 (Oct. 1988–Sept. 1989); previous compilations, no. 1–2 (Oct. 1984–Sept. 1986); no. 3–4 (Oct. 1986–Sept. 1988).

Grew out of a local indexing project for the International Association for the Study of Popular Music (IASPM), U.K. branch. Currently indexes around 90 primarily English-language periodicals devoted to popular music and jazz.

Taylor, Paul. Popular music since 1955 : a critical guide to the literature. Boston. : G.K. Hall, 1985. 533 p. ISBN 0-8161-8784-3.   **BH139**

Intends "to provide a critical bibliographical guide to the literature of contemporary music published in English since 1955."—*Pref.* Includes 1,600 entries for monographs covering 1955–82, with some significant works 1983–84, arranged in broad categories for general works, social aspects, artistic aspects, business aspects, musical forms, lives and works, and fiction. Annotations are lengthy and informative. Also lists 200 periodicals. Author, title, and subject indexes.   ML128.P63T39

Discography

Aeppli, Felix. Heart of stone : the definitive Rolling Stones discography, 1962–1983. Ann Arbor, Mich. : Pierian Pr., 1985. 535 p. : ill. (Rock & roll reference series, 17). ISBN 0-87650-192-7. $39.50.   **BH140**

Aims to list in chronological order " . . . all musical recordings of the Rolling Stones that found their way onto record or film from July 1962 to December 31, 1983."—*Introd.* Includes all U.S. or U.K. releases, a few foreign albums not released in either country, and bootleg recordings up to June 30, 1984. Covers works by the group, as well as its individual members. Indexes in several categories.   ML156.7.R66A35

Cooper, B. Lee. A resource guide to themes in contemporary American song lyrics, 1950–1985. N.Y. : Greenwood, 1986. 458 p. ISBN 0-313-24516-9.   **BH141**

Lists more than 3,000 popular recordings organized by 15 social, political, and personal themes. A brief essay introducing each general theme is followed by subject subdivisions with record title/performer listings. Song title and recording artist indexes.   ML156.4.P6C66

Rust, Brian A. L. The complete entertainment discography, from 1897 to 1942 / Brian Rust and Allen G. Debus. 2nd ed. N.Y. : Da Capo Pr., c1989. 794 p. ISBN 0-306-76210-2. $85.00.   **BH142**

1st ed., 1973.

Updates and expands the 1st ed. Entries are organized by artists' names, including minstrel pioneers, vaudevillians, film stars, radio personalities, and actors and actresses, and are limited to artists of American birth or artists as well known in America as their native country. Excludes jazz and blues musicians, commercial dance bands, and selected major artists.   ML156.4.P6R88

———————— Jazz records, 1897–1942. 5th rev. and enl. ed. Chigwell, Essex : Storyville Publications, [1982]. 2 v. (1996 p.). ISBN 0-902391-04-6 (set).   **BH143**

Contains an alphabetical listing of performers heard on recordings of jazz music, dance music affiliated with jazz, and vocal recordings with jazz groups used as accompaniment made 1917–42, together with some ragtime recordings from 1897. Artist and title indexes.   ML156.4.J3R9

Spottswood, Richard K. Ethnic music on records : a discography of ethnic recordings produced in the United States, 1893 to 1942. Urbana : Univ. of Illinois Pr., c1990. 7 v. : ill. ISBN 0-252-01718-8 (set).   **BH144**

Contents: v. 1, Western Europe; v. 2, Slavic; v. 3, Eastern Europe; v. 4, Spanish, Portuguese, Philippine, Basque; v. 5, Mid-East, Far East, Scandinavian, English language, American Indian, international; v. 6, Artist and title indexes; v. 7, Record and matrix number indexes.

A comprehensive discography, produced with cooperation and assistance of the Library of Congress, of all foreign-language recordings produced in the U.S. and its possessions, 1893–1942, with a few exceptions. Over 130 record labels are represented. Entries are arranged by performer within 13 national or language groups. Detailed listing under each performer contains primary and secondary titles, instrumentation, date and place of recordings, master and release numbers.   ML156.4.F5S69

Music in motion pictures

Harris, Steve. Film, television, and stage music on phonograph records : a discography. Jefferson, N.C. : McFarland, c1988. 445 p. ISBN 0-89950-251-2. $49.95.   **BH145**

Lists 11,761 phonograph recordings of film (8,000 entries), television (1,800 entries), and stage music (1,200 entries) from the U.S. and Great Britain. Lists recordings from other countries only if they were presented or recorded in the U.S. or Britain. Includes original or adapted music issued through 1986. Tape formats, cylinders, and compact discs are not included. Entries are listed by title, and include date, composer credit, country of pressing, format, and label.   ML156.4.M6H3

Lynch, Richard Chigley. Movie musicals on record : a directory of recordings of motion picture musicals, 1927–1987. N.Y. : Greenwood, 1989. 445 p. (Discographies, no. 32). ISBN 0-313-26540-2.   **BH146**

Lists songs (approximately 6,500 titles) and singers on 666 commercial albums. Entries arranged alphabetically by film title, give the name of the production company, year of first release, original label and reissue information, composer, lyricist, musical conductor, cast members, and all the songs on the album. Concludes with a chronology of films, a performer index, and a technical index to composers, lyricists, and musical directors.

§ Similarly organized is the author's companion volume *Broadway on record*, (N.Y. : Greenwood, 1987. Discographies, no. 28), which covers 6,000 songs on 459 albums.   ML156.4.M6L9

Wescott, Steven D. A comprehensive bibliography of music for film and television. Detroit : Information Coordinators, 1985. 432 p. ISBN 0-89990-027-5.   **BH147**

Contains 6,340 entries, many with brief annotations, in five topical sections: History (3,000 entries), Individual composers (1,300 entries), Aesthetics (900 entries), Special topics, including performance on film and television, film music, and animated sound (1,000 entries), and Research (150 entries). An international compilation, representing publications by more than 3,700 authors in 28 countries and 18 languages. Index.   ML128.M7W47

Orchestral music

Kramer, Jonathan D. Listen to the music : a self-guided tour through the orchestral repertoire. N.Y. : Schirmer ; London : Collier Macmillan, c1988. 816 p. ISBN 0-02-871841-0. ISBN 0-02-871842-9 (pbk.).   **BH148**

"Based on program notes written for the Cincinnati Symphony Orchestra, 1980–89."

Aimed at the general listener, this work contains a series of essays on the orchestral music most often heard in the concert hall, on recordings, and on the radio, organized alphabetically by composer. Includes approximately 250 works by 52 composers.   MT125.K72

Stedman, Preston. The symphony : a research and information guide. N.Y. : Garland, 1990. v. 1. ISBN 0-8240-4447-9. (In progress).   **BH149**

A projected three-volume set. Vol. 1, an annotated bibliography of 931 books, articles, and dissertations on the 18th-century symphony, offers entries with brief, summary annotations, divided into three section: general resources (48 entries); the symphony (100); and national activities, including individual countries and composers (780). Further volumes are to cover the 19th and 20th centuries.

§ A complementary work is Jan LaRue's *Catalogue of 18th-century symphonies*, v.1, Thematic identifier (Bloomington : Indiana Univ. Pr., 1988), which lists incipits in alphabetic form for 16,558 symphonies, ca.1720–ca.1810, arranged alphabetically by key signature, then alphabetically within keys. Additional volumes will contain full musical notation.   ML128.S9S7

Symphony orchestras of the United States : selected profiles / ed. by Robert R. Craven. N.Y. : Greenwood, c1986. 521 p. ISBN 0-313-24072-8.   **BH150**

Lists approximately 125 leading symphony orchestras in the U.S. geographically by state and city. Signed entries give background information, chronology of music directors, bibliography, and mailing address.

§ A related work is the author's *Symphony orchestras of the world : selected profiles* (N.Y. : Greenwood, 1987. 468p.), covering 122 orchestras from 44 countries.   ML1211.S95

INSTRUMENTS

Adato, Joseph. The percussionist's dictionary : translations, descriptions, and photographs of percussion instruments from around the world / comp. and ed. by Joseph Adato and George Judy. Melville, N.Y. : Belwin-Mills Publ. Corp., c1984. 95 p. : ill. ISBN 0-910957-28-2 (pbk.). $8.95.   **BH151**

Contains brief definitions for approximately 600 terms commonly used in the performance of Western music. Terms are listed alphabetically in English. A second section offers photographs of unfamiliar instruments, while the third provides equivalent foreign terms and translations.   ML102.P4A3

Arnold, Corliss Richard. Organ literature : a comprehensive survey. 2nd ed. Metuchen, N.J. : Scarecrow, 1984. 2 v. : ill. ISBN 0-8108-1662-8 (v. 1).   **BH152**
1st ed., 1973.

Provides an "organized, comprehensive introduction to the vast literature for the organ and its development."—*Prelude.* Vol. 1 contains a historical survey of the literature, 1300–1970, organized geographically; v. 2, a listing of composers of organ music with brief biographical information and listing of works. Index in v. 1; alphabetical listing of German chorale titles with English translations and appropriate liturgical use in v. 2.   ML600.A76

Bildwörterbuch Musikinstrumente : Gliederung, Baugruppen, Bauteile, Bauelemente / Klaus Maersch . . . [et al.]. Lizenzausg. Mainz ; N. Y. : Schott, c1987. 218 p. : ill. ISBN 3-7957-0121-X. DM24.00.   **BH153**

Offers detailed drawings of instruments, with numbered parts each keyed to its German term. Instruments are systematically grouped into four families, with indexes by instrument name, structural function of part, and family classification.   ML102.I5B54

Fasman, Mark J. Brass bibliography : sources on the history, literature, pedagogy, performance, and acoustics of brass instruments. Bloomington, Ind. : Indiana Univ. Pr., 1990. 452 p. ISBN 0-253-32130-1.   **BH154**

Contains over 6,000 citations to sources related to brass instruments in four major categories: Reference and research materials; History and music literature; Pedagogy, study and technique; Acoustics and construction. Covers 1820–1988 (with a few entries from the late 18th century). Constitutes a compilation of relevant entries in English, German, French, or Italian from ten varied sources. Index of authors and subjects.   ML128.W5F3

Skei, Allen B. Woodwind, brass, and percussion instruments of the orchestra : a bibliographic guide. N.Y. : Garland, 1985. 271 p. (Garland reference library of the humanities, vol. 458). ISBN 0-8240-9021-7.   **BH155**

A selective, annotated bibliography of books, articles, and dissertations on wind and percussion instruments commonly heard in classical music. Indexes for subjects and for authors, editors, and translators.   ML128.W5S6

RECORDED MUSIC

Catalogs and discography

Duxbury, Janell R. Rockin' the classics and classicizin' the rock : a selectively annotated discography. Westport, Conn. : Greenwood, c1985. 188 p. (Discographies, no. 14). ISBN 0-313-24605-X.   **BH156**

Lists explicit borrowings and associations between rock music and classical music. The compiler defines rock music as containing a prominent beat and varying electronic instrumentation, while classical music refers to the standard repertory of Western classical music. Entries are listed by performer in several categories: rock versions of classic pieces, classical versions of rock pieces, etc. Updated by a *First supplement* (N.Y. : Greenwood, 1991. Discographies, no. 43).   ML156.4.R6D9

●**Music library** : musical sound recordings [computer file]. Dublin, Ohio : OCLC Online Computer Library Center, Inc.   **BH157**

File size: more than 400,000 records extracted from the OCLC database. Updated annually. Available in CD-ROM (producer).

Rosenberg, Kenyon C. A basic classical and operatic recordings collection for libraries. Metuchen, N.J. : Scarecrow, 1987. 255 p. ISBN 0-8108-2041-2.   **BH158**

Aims to provide librarians with a means for "creating or augmenting a nuclear classical and operatic recordings collection."—*Pref.* Recommends specific performances of the standard repertory, with entries arranged alphabetically by composer, subarranged by title under the author's genre terms. Gives record company, number, and performers, as well as ratings for budgetary considerations, technical recording characteristics, and appropriateness by type of library.

§ Similarly organized is the author's *A basic classical and operatic recordings collection on compact discs for libraries: a buying guide* (Metuchen, N.J. : Scarecrow, 1990), with an additional section containing the author's evaluation of current performing groups.   ML156.2.R7

Bibliography

Gray, Michael H. Classical music discographies, 1976–1988 : a bibliography. N.Y. ; London : Greenwood, 1989. [341] p. ISBN 0-313-25942-9. £38.75.   **BH159**

Aims to provide the first cumulative suppl. to v. 1 of *Bibliography of discographies* (*Guide* BH345), of which v. 4–5 were never published. Lists in one alphabetical sequence names and subjects for which discographies have appeared in books, articles, dissertations, and theses, as well as program notes. Considerably expands the entries for record labels and subjects. Index of names.   ML113

Dictionaries

White, Glenn D. The audio dictionary. Seattle : Univ. of Washington Pr., c1987. 291 p. : ill. ISBN 0-295-96527-4. ISBN 0-295-96528-2 (pbk.).   **BH160**

Terms, definitions and cross-references pertaining to sound recording, sound reinforcement, and musical acoustics. Appendixes contain a mixture of general advice and tabular information.   TK7881.4.W48

Reviews

Myers, Kurtz. Index to record reviews, 1984–1987: based on material originally published in *Notes, the quarterly journal of the Music Library Association*. Boston: G.K. Hall, 1989. 639 p. ISBN 0-8161-0482-4.　　**BH161**

　　Forms the 2nd and final supplement to the main volume and first supplement (*Guide* BH350–351), cumulating the reviews published in *Notes* through 1987.　　ML156.9.M89

BJ

Sports, Recreation, and Travel

SPORTS AND GAMES

Bibliography

Redekop, Paul. Sociology of sport: an annotated bibliography. N.Y.: Garland, 1988. 153 p. ISBN 0-8240-8464-0.　　**BJ1**

　　Covers journal literature and a limited number of books in both sports and sociology from the late 1960s to 1985. More than half the citations are descriptively annotated. List of periodicals reviewed. Author index marred by misspellings.
　　　　GV706.5.R43

Sport bibliography update = Bibliographie du sport mise á jour. v. 9–13. Ottawa, Ont.: Sport Information Resource Centre, 1983–1987. Annual.　　**BJ2**

　　Supplement to *Sport bibliography = Bibliographie du sport* (Ottawa: 1981–82. 8 v.). Both the basic set and the update volumes are especially sOCong in their coverage of specific sports. Covers journal literature, conference papers, monograph chapters, and master's theses and doctoral dissertations. Provides fairly comprehensive coverage of Western literature in the field, in English and other languages.
　　Publication in printed form ceased 1987; now available as:
　　　　GV571.S651

●**SPORT Discus** [computer file]. Gloucester, Ont.: Sport Information Resource Centre.　　**BJ3**
　　Coverage: monographs and theses, 1949– ; serials, 1975– . File size: 230,000 records. Updated semiannually. Available in CD-ROM (SilverPlatter).

　　Conflates entries in the 8 v. of *Sport bibliography = Bibliographie du sport* and the 5 v. of *Sport bibliography update = Bibliographie du sport mise à jour* (above) and provides continuing coverage of the literature indexed by those sources.

Current

Sport & leisure. v. 1, no. 1 (Spring 1989)– . Waterloo, Ont.: Univ. of Waterloo Pr., c1989– . Three times a year. ISSN 0838-4061. $95.00.　　**BJ4**

　　Surveys the sociological aspects of sport, recreation, and leisure, drawing from journals, monographs, conference papers, and dissertations; entries include detailed, well-written abstracts. Cites unpublished papers that can be difficult to locate, although the producer offers a photocopy service. Would profit from a more detailed index or a subject arrangement, and does not cumulate; but the excellence of its abstracts and comprehensiveness (many citations are not to be found elsewhere) make this work essential for research in the field.　　GV1.S6

Encyclopedias

Biographical dictionary of American sports: outdoor sports / ed. by David L. Porter. N.Y.: Greenwood, c1988. 728 p. ISBN 0-313-26260-8.　　**BJ5**

　　Brief, signed articles treat auto racing, communications and promotion, golf, horse racing, lacrosse, miscellaneous sports, skiing, soccer, speed skating, tennis, and track and field. Appendixes provide: an alphabetical list of entries with references to the appropriate sport; lists of entries classed by sport, by state of birth, and of women by sport (with cross-references to married names); major U.S. halls of fame; sports associations and organizations; and sites of Olympic Games. General index.
　　　　GV697.A1B49

Emery, David. The world sports record atlas / comp. by David Emery and Stan Greenberg. N.Y.: Facts on File, c1986. 192 p.: ill. (some col.). ISBN 0-8160-1378-0. ISBN 0-8160-1579-1 (pbk.).　　**BJ6**

　　Entries cover track and field (no relays, however), golf, soccer, tennis, squash, baseball, football, winter sports, racing, horse racing, mountaineering, ballooning, parachuting, channel swimming, long distance walking and running, weightlifting, boxing, fencing, and water sports. The writing is breezy and there are many illustrations, some in color. Especially noteworthy is the coverage of physiological responses and male-female differences. Individual and team final standings are given but there is no breakdown of those statistics or qualifying events.
　　　　GV741.E54

Markel, Robert. For the record: women in sports / by Robert Markel, Nancy Brooks, Susan Markel. N.Y.: World Almanac Publications: Distr. by Ballantine Books, 1985. 195 p.: ports. ISBN 0-345-32192-8 (pbk.). $8.95.　　**BJ7**

　　Sections on badminton, basketball, bowling, canoeing/kayaking, cycling, equestrian sports, fencing, field hockey, golf, gymnastics, ice skating, luge, rowing, skiing, softball, water sports, table tennis, tennis, track and field, triathlon, volleyball, and Women's Sports Foundation award winners each contain a brief introduction, brief biographies of a few leading figures in each sport, and statistics of that sport. Name index to the biographies.
　　　　GV697.A1M318

Sports encyclopedia North America / ed. by John D. Windhausen. Gulf Breeze, Fla.: Academic International Pr., 1987. v. 1. ISBN 0-87569-094-7. $32.00/vol. (In progress).　　**BJ8**

　　Proposes to be the "most complete reference guide to American and Canadian sports, present and past . . . both in the breadth of its subject entries and its insistence upon depth of coverage, including statistical information and reference aids."—*From the editor*. To be complete in 50 v.; three per year are planned. Relies heavily on information reprinted verbatim from various sports organizations. Entries include bibliographic references. Despite its promise of completeness, early volumes have no entries for, e.g., anabolic steroids, American College of Sports Medicine, attribution, attention, anxiety, Sparky Anderson.   GV581.S65

Rules

Sports rules encyclopedia / Jess R. White [ed.]. 2nd ed. Champaign, Ill. : Leisure Pr., c1990. 732 p. : ill. ISBN 0-88011-363-4.   **BJ9**

An alphabetic arrangement of amateur, major, and widely practiced sports (excluding activities using animals or mechanical devices as primary elements). Each entry includes a description of the governing body, rules, and two journals with publisher's address. Most rules are taken verbatim from the published official rules. Rules for some wheelchair sports are given. Appendixes list organizations concerned with sports for the handicapped and other sports organizations.   GV731.S75

Dictionaries

Palmatier, Robert A. Sports talk : a dictionary of sports metaphors / Robert A. Palmatier and Harold L. Ray. N.Y. : Greenwood, 1989. 227 p. ISBN 0-313-26426-0.   **BJ10**

More than 1,700 sports metaphors, giving for each: full, popular form of the expression; an illustration of correct grammatical usage; definition; the earliest date used, with probable source; the definition of the original sports term; a coded source of other works recognizing the source of the metaphor; and comparative and contrastive cross-references to other entries. Index is arranged by sport.   PE1689.P27

Wörterbuch der Sportwissenschaft : Deutsch, Englisch, Französisch = Dictionary of sport science : German, English, French / ed., Erich Beyer. Schorndorf : K. Hofmann, c1987. 770 p. : ill. ISBN 3-7780-3500-2.   **BJ11**

A polyglot dictionary on a German base that gives English and French equivalents in parallel columns, with indexes of French and English terms. The detailed entries discuss terms thoroughly and employ many synonyms for characteristics and attributes. Some cross-references embedded in the entries; extensive bibliography, chiefly of German-language sources.
GV567.W62

Quotations

Dictionary of sports quotations / comp. by Barry Liddle. London ; N.Y. : Routledge & K. Paul, 1987. 210 p. ISBN 0-7102-0785-9. $20.00.   **BJ12**

Arranged by sport. Cites sources of quotations. Author index.   GV706.8.D53

Maikovich, Andrew J. Sports quotations : maxims, quips and pronouncements for writers and fans. Jefferson, N.C. : McFarland, c1984. 168 p. ISBN 0-89950-100-1.
BJ13

Entries are arranged alphabetically by author within sections by sport. Profession is given for the author of each quotation. Name and subject indexes.   GV706.8.M34

Directories

International directory of sports organizations under the auspices of the International Association for Sports Information (IASI) / [ed. by] Rob Timmer, Josef Recla. Haarlem : De Vrieseborch, c1984. 429 p. : form. ISBN 90-6076-197-9.   **BJ14**

Lists international umbrella organizations, international nongovernmental and professional organizations, international sports federations, organizations representing special groups of people, national Olympic committees, and national documentation and information centers. Entries provide name and acronym, address, telephone, founding date, aim, executive officer(s), membership, and publications. Indexed by sport.
GV563.I748

Handbooks

American women in sport, 1887–1987 : a 100-year chronology / comp. by Ruth M. Sparhawk ... [et al.]. Metuchen, N.J. : Scarecrow, 1989. 149 p., [8] p. of plates : ill. ISBN 0-8108-2205-9.   **BJ15**

An introduction summarizing the history of women in sports is followed by a chronology in four sections: preorganizational era 1887–1916, the organizational years 1917–56, the competitive period 1957–71, and the Title IX era 1972–87. Treats recent well-known competitors rather than those that are more obscure. Black-and-white photographs; bibliography; list of organizations. Indexes of sports and names, the latter omitting married names.   GV583.A64

Handbook of social science of sport : with an international classified bibliography / ed. by Günther R.F. Lüschen and George H. Sage, with the assistance of Leila Sfeir. Champaign, Ill. : Stipes Pub. Co., c1981. 720 p. ISBN 0-87563-191-6.   **BJ16**

Provides an overview and bibliographic guide for a rapidly growing interdisciplinary field. An introductory section that discusses the nature of the field is followed by six subject sections (e.g., Cross-cultural and cross-national analysis of sport and games, Social problems and deviance in sport, Play, sport and personality), each in four parts that provide commentary and bibliography. A final section consists of an extensive international bibliography, in an arrangement that corresponds to the topical sections. An appendix lists sport and sport science organizations. Author and subject indexes.   GV706.5.H35

Individual sports

Baseball

The ballplayers : baseball's ultimate biographical reference / ed. by Mike Shatzkin ; managing ed., Stephen Holtje ; created and developed by Mike Shatzkin & Jim Charlton. N.Y. : Arbor House/William Morrow, c1990. 1230 p. : ill. ISBN 0-87795-984-6. $39.95.   **BJ17**

Includes about 6,000 20th-century players through 1989 and 1,000 19th-century players; special attention is given to the Negro League. Compiled from *The baseball encyclopedia*, *The sports encyclopedia : baseball* and *Total baseball* (all below). Entries include biographical and statistical information, stadiums, and descriptions of awards. Black-and-white photographs.
GV865.A1B323

The baseball encyclopedia : the complete and official record of major league baseball / Joseph L. Reichler, ed. 7th ed., rev., updated, and expanded. N.Y. : Macmillan ;

London : Collier Macmillan, 1988. 2875 p. ISBN 0-02-579030-7. **BJ18**

Provides statistics of team and individual player performance through the 1987 season. Includes a section on trades and surveys World Series and All-Star games. Appendixes list sources, decisions of special records committees, and major changes in professional rules. GV877.B27

Benson, Michael. Ballparks of North America : a comprehensive historical reference to baseball grounds, yards, and stadiums, 1845 to present. Jefferson, N.C. : McFarland, c1989. 475 p. : ill. ISBN 0-89950-367-5. $35.00. **BJ19**

Arranged alphabetically by city, then chronologically. Entries include league, first team to play in park, location, dimensions, seating capacity, attendance records. Extensive bibliography and good name index. Includes parks not covered in Philip J. Lowry's *Green cathedrals* (below). GV879.5.B46

Biographical dictionary of American sports : baseball / ed. by David L. Porter. N.Y. : Greenwood, 1987. 713 p. ISBN 0-313-23771-9. **BJ20**

Brief signed articles with short bibliographies treat 423 players, 27 managers, 6 umpires, and 61 executives. Appendixes list professional major leagues, Negro leagues, Hall of Fame members, and contributors. Special indexes by types, position, place of birth by state, and Negro League entries. Coverage not as extensive as *The ballplayers* (above). GV865.A1B55

Dickson, Paul. The Dickson baseball dictionary. N.Y. : Facts on File, c1989. 1 v. ISBN 0-8160-1741-7. $50.00 (est.). **BJ21**

Offers very readable definitions of nearly 5,000 baseball terms. Entries include origin and etymology, first usage with citations. Usage outside baseball, historic background, and cross-references included as applicable. Black-and-white photographs; bibliography. GV862.3.D53

James, Bill. The Bill James historical baseball abstract. Rev. ed. N.Y. : Villard Books, 1988. 723 p. : ill. ISBN 0-394-75805-6 (pbk.). $15.95. **BJ22**

Describes the careers of several hundred players in glib, breezy style. A statistics section, drawn from *The baseball encyclopedia* (above), *The sports encyclopedia : baseball* (6th ed., 1985) and Paul MacFarlane's *Daguerrotypes : Hall of Fame members and other immortals* (St. Louis : Sporting News, 1968), covers betting, baserunning, percentages, values, fielding, notes, and pitching, and is supplemented by compilations of trivia (e.g., drinking men, eyebrows). Glossary, bibliography, and index. GV863.A1J36

Lowry, Philip J. Green cathedrals. Cooperstown : Society for American Baseball Research, 1986. 157 p. : ill. ISBN 0-09-103721-8 (pbk.). **BJ23**

A roster of baseball stadiums, giving name, style of park, nickname or alternate name, occupants in chronological order, location, surface, dimensions, fences, former and current use, and phenomena of historical importance. Arranged by league; covers major and minor leagues, Negro League, home and neutral parks. Black-and-white photographs; bibliography. Lack of an index requires users to know the league associated with a particular ballpark. GV879.5.L69

Neft, David S. The sports encyclopedia : baseball / David S. Neft, Richard M. Cohen. 9th ed. N.Y. : St. Martin's Pr., c1989. 629 p. ISBN 0-312-026447 (pbk.). $16.95. **BJ24**

Team statistics for each league as well as data for individual batters and pitchers. Pennant, championship, and World Series statistics provided as are those for both annual and lifetime batting and pitching leaders. GV877.N43

Reichler, Joseph L. The baseball trade register. N.Y. : Macmillan ; London : Collier Macmillan, c1984. 567 p. ISBN 0-02-603110-8. **BJ25**

Has separate sections for the National and American Leagues (including earlier names and team locations), each with a player roster that lists date of trade, team acquired from and for whom exchanged, and a team listing that includes sections on manager/owner and best/worst trades. GV877.R375

Smith, Myron J. Baseball : a comprehensive bibliography. Jefferson, N.C. : McFarland, 1986. 915 p. : port. ISBN 0-89950-222-9. $55.00. **BJ26**

Lists monographs, government publications, theses and dissertations, yearbooks, some fiction and poetry, and articles from 365 journals. Sections, which begin with brief introductions, cover reference works, general works, history, special studies; professional leagues and teams; youth leagues, college, and amateur/semiprofessional play; rules and techniques; collective bibliography; and individual biography. Author and subject indexes. Z7514.B3S64

Total baseball / ed. by John Thorn and Pete Palmer, with David Reuther. N.Y. : Warner Books, c1989. 2294 p. ISBN 0-446-51389-X. $49.95. **BJ27**

Purports to correct omissions and errors in *The baseball encyclopedia* (6th ed., *Guide* BJ32). Includes an extensive introductory history of major league baseball by David Q. Voigt; team histories and listing of defunct clubs and leagues; postseason play, World Series, and All-Star games; 400 biographical sketches; a chronology of major events; mascots; scandals; umpires; awards and honors; black players. Other leagues, business, law, and the farm system are covered as well as Japanese, Caribbean, armed services, and women's baseball. Includes a large statistical compilation of players, umpires, coaches, and home-road statistics. Reprints professional rules. Extensive, briefly annotated bibliography. GV863.A1T68

Basketball

Biographical dictionary of American sports : basketball and other indoor sports / ed. by David L. Porter. N.Y. : Greenwood, 1989. 801 p. ISBN 0-313-26261-6. **BJ28**

More than half the 558 entries describe basketball figures, but people from bowling, boxing, diving, figure skating, gymnastics, ice hockey, swimming, weightlifting, wrestling, and miscellaneous sports are also included. Each entry is followed by a brief bibliography. Appendixes list players by category, position played, and state of birth; hall of fame members; conferences; women by sport; and ring names and real names of boxers. Index and list of contributors. GV697.A1B494

Football

Baldwin, Robert. College football records : Division I-A and the Ivy League, 1869–1984. Jefferson, N.C. : McFarland, c1987. 198 p. ISBN 0-89950-246-6. $25.95. **BJ29**

Provides statistics for 111 college and university Division I-A teams still active; arranged by conference, with a separate section for independent schools. Lists wins, losses, and ties against Division I and other opponents, total overall record, and total conference and bowl record. Entries give nickname, colors, location, stadium capacity, first year of football, year entered conference, number of conference championships. Appendixes give ranked summaries of various conference and bowl records. Index of nondivision and other opponents. Finding the entry for a Division I-A team requires knowledge of the conference in which it plays. GV950.B35

Biographical dictionary of American sports : football / ed. by David L. Porter. N.Y. : Greenwood, 1987. 763 p. ISBN 0-313-25771-X.   **BJ30**

Brief, signed biographies of 520 notable football figures, including players, coaches, executives, league administrators, rules developers, and promoters, arranged alphabetically. Each entry concludes with a brief bibliography. Appendixes list entries by category, position played, state of birth, collegiate and Professional Hall of Fame members, and conferences or leagues. Index and list of contributors.   GV939.A1B56

Martial arts

Nelson, Randy F. The martial arts : an annotated bibliography / Randy F. Nelson with Katherine C. Whitaker ; illus. by Forrest Williams and Jerry Lilly. N.Y. : Garland, 1988. 436 p. : ill. ISBN 0-8240-4435-5.   **BJ31**

Covers journal literature and monographs; some entries are annotated. Arranged by sections: general topics, specific forms of martial arts, other arts, weapons, and works prior to 1920.   Z7514.M37N44

Olympic games

Hugman, Barry J. The Olympic games : complete track and field results, 1896–1988 / Barry J. Hugman and Peter Arnold. N.Y. : Facts on File, c1988. [385] p. ISBN 0-8160-2120-1.   **BJ32**

" . . . the individual record[s] for every track and field competitor, by country, round by round, time, height, or distance achieved and medal won" (*Pref.*) are arranged chronologically by Olympic Game, then alphabetically. Each Olympic section is introduced by a narrative summarizing the highlights of those Games. Poorly reproduced black-and-white photographs; brief bibliography; no index.   GV1060.5.H84

Mallon, Bill. The Olympic record book. N.Y. : Garland, 1988. 522 p. ISBN 0-8240-2948-8.   **BJ33**

Lists overall Olympic records through the 24th Olympiad in Seoul, including most medals; most gold, silver, bronze; most years between medals; most appearances, etc. Also lists peripheral information such as speakers and torch bearers. The number of countries and athletes competing are given for each summer and winter Olympiad. No listing of team standings.   GV721.8.M34

Wallechinsky, David. The complete book of the Olympics. Rev. ed. N.Y. : Viking, 1988. 680 p., [54] p. of plates : ill. ISBN 0-670-82110-1. $35.00. ISBN 0-14-010771-1 (Penguin Books : pbk.). $12.95.   **BJ34**
1st ed., 1984 (*Guide* BJ27).
Covers through the 1984 Olympic Games in Los Angeles.   GV721.5.W25

Tennis

Lumpkin, Angela. A guide to the literature of tennis. Westport, Conn. : Greenwood, c1985. 235 p. ISBN 0-313-24492-8.   **BJ35**

Bibliographic essays on the history of the sport; history of championship players and performance; rules and administration; equipment, facilities, and travel; technique; players and teaching professionals; health and fitness; psychology; biography; children's books, humor, films; general works; periodicals; and promotional organizations. Appendixes list organizations, halls of fame, champions in various competitions. Subject and author indexes.   GV991.2.L85

Wrestling

Chapman, Mike. Encyclopedia of American wrestling. Champaign, Ill. : Leisure Pr., c1990. 533 p. : ill. ISBN 0-88011-342-1.   **BJ36**

Traces the history of wrestling in America and provides statistics on Olympic wrestling, world championships and other major world meets, AAU National Freestyle, U.S. Freestyle Senior Open, Greco-Roman Nationals, Collegiate Nationals, Midlands Championships, Junior Nationals, and Junior World Tournaments. Lists special honors and awards, halls of fame and biographical sketches of 78 members of the National Wrestling Hall of Fame through 1988. Brief bibliography. No index.   GV1198.12.C43

Other outdoor sports and recreation

Parks and protected areas

The complete guide to America's national parks : the official visitor's guide of the National Park Foundation : information on all 384 of America's national park areas. 1990–1991 ed. Wash. : The Foundation ; N.Y. : Distr. by Prentice Hall, 1990. 594 p. : ill. ISBN 0-9603410-6-4 (pbk.). $11.95.   **BJ37**
1st ed., 1979.

A guide to national parks, monuments, historic sites, preserves, etc., arranged by state. For each park gives name, address, telephone, name of superintendent, directions, visitor activities, any interesting features such as proximity to other parks, and reference to a "Climatable." The latter are graphs and charts for each park, showing temperature, precipitation, sunshine/cloudiness, and temperature means and extremes. Name index.   E160.C

International handbook of national parks and nature reserves / ed. by Craig W. Allin. N.Y. : Greenwood, 1990. 539 p. : ill., maps. ISBN 0-313-24902-4.   **BJ38**

National parks and nature reserves are described for 25 nations and one regional cluster (Argentina, Australia, Canada, Chile, Republic of China, Colombia, Federal Republic of Germany, Great Britain, Greece, Honduras, India, Indonesia, Japan, Kenya, Malaysia, New Zealand, Norway, Papua New Guinea, Peru, South Africa, Uganda, Union of Soviet Socialist Republics, United States, Venezuela, West Africa, and Zimbabwe). "Each of the chapters is written to a common outline. Each author addresses the history of park preservation, the natural values associated with parks and reserves, and the legal and administrative structures charged with park protection and management."—*Pref.* Bibliographies at the end of each chapter. Indexed.   SB481.I565

TRAVEL AND TOURISM

Bibliography

The traveler's reading guide : ready-made reading lists for the armchair traveler / Maggy Simony, ed. Rev., expanded ed. N.Y. : Facts On File, c1987. 831 p. ISBN 0-8160-1244-X. **BJ39**

". . . originally self-published as a three-volume paperback series" (*Pref.*), this edition "is intended to make it easier for armchair travelers, writers, teachers, travel professionals and the librarians who counsel them, to locate interesting background books, place-set novels and mysteries, travel memoirs, special guides, travel articles for the destination of choice."—*Notes.* Citations and brief annotations are arranged geographically by continent or region, then alphabetically by country or state. Headings under each place-name include guidebooks, background reading, history, novels, and travel articles (primarily from the *New York times* Sunday Travel section).

Z6004.T6T73

Dictionaries

Dervaes, Claudine. The travel dictionary. [New ed.]. Tampa, Fla. : Solitaire Pub., [c1990]. 307 p. ISBN 0-933143-16-8. $12.95. **BJ40**

Provides brief definitions for more than 2,800 terms, codes, acronyms, and abbreviations commonly used in the travel industry. Includes 19 sections (some 100 pages) of additional information, including metric conversion chart, comparative clothing size chart, world and U.S. time-zone tables, country currency codes, airport and airline codes, and communication and transportation codes. G155.A1D47

Metelka, Charles J. Dictionary of hospitality, travel, and tourism. 3rd ed. Albany, N.Y. : Delmar Publishers, c1990. 194 p. ISBN 0-8273-3496-6. **BJ41**

1st ed., 1981 (*Guide* BJ108); 2nd ed., 1986. Both had title: *The dictionary of tourism.*

Substantially augmented, now including definitions of some 2,700 terms and phrases related specifically to the travel industry. Two appendixes list organizations and governmental agencies involved in tourism, and journals and newsletters of the trade. G155.A1M443

Quotations

The travellers' dictionary of quotations : who said what, about where? / ed. by Peter Yapp. London ; Boston : Routledge & Kegan Paul, 1983. 1022 p. ISBN 0-7100-0992-5. $25.00. **BJ42**

A compilation of quotations "from the literature of travel, from letters and diaries, verse and song, history, fiction, journalism and drama."—*Introd.* Quotations, primarily in English, 15th century to the present, are arranged alphabetically by country. Source and date given for all quotations; asterisks identify entries from fiction. Special sections cover the earth, sun, moon, and universe. Indexes of places and peoples and of persons quoted. PN6084.P55T72

Directories

A guide to recreation, leisure, and travel for the handicapped. 1st ed.– . Toledo, Ohio : Resource Directories, c1985– . Biennial. ISSN 8756-2529. **BJ43**

For annotation, see *Supplement* CC109. GV183.5.G84

Hecker, Helen. Travel for the disabled : a handbook of travel resources and 500 worldwide access guides. Portland, Ore. : Twin Peaks Pr., c1985. 185 p. ISBN 0-933261-00-4. $9.95. **BJ44**

In 18 chapters, lists sources of information on all aspects of travel: travel agencies and clubs; modes of transportation; medical and respite services; accessible recreation spots; and travel books and magazines. A final bibliography contains citations to, and sources for, access guides in two sections, U.S. and foreign; includes information for obtaining these guides, many of them free. Geographical index. HV1568.6.H43

Worldwide travel information contact book. 1st ed. (1991–92)– . Detroit : Gale, c1991– . Biennial. ISSN 1051-6247. $69.50. **BJ45**

A comprehensive directory of addresses, telephone, telex, and fax numbers for more than 25,000 contacts in 309 countries or subdivisions of countries. Arranged by continent; countries listed alphabetically. Ten categories of information including tourism agencies at various governmental levels, recreational activities, transportation, and publications. Coverage is better for other countries, especially in Europe, than for the U.S.

Handbooks

Tourism's top twenty : fast facts on travel and tourism. [1988 ed.]. Boulder, Colo. : Business Research Division, Univ. of Colorado ; Wash. : U.S. Travel Data Center, c1987. 118 leaves. ISBN 0-89478-001-8. **BJ46**

1st ed., 1980; 2nd ed., 1984.

". . . a compilation of frequently requested facts and figures on travel, tourism, recreation and leisure."—*Introd.* 93 tables cover such topics as advertising, air travel, automobile travel, cities/ports, countries, hotels/motels, outdoor recreation, sports, and travel destinations. Primarily U.S. facts; covers all topics to the "top twenty." Information source listed with each table. Two appendixes: address of sources and state and territory abbreviations, and subject index. G155.A1T5928

Guidebooks

Braganti, Nancy L. The travelers' guide to European customs & manners : how to converse, dine, tip, drive, bargain, dress, make friends & conduct business while in Europe / Nancy L. Braganti and Elizabeth Devine. Deephaven, Minn. : Meadowbrook Books, c1984. 273 p. : ill. ISBN 0-88166-009-4 (pbk.). $5.95. **BJ47**
D909.B722

Chambers, Kevin. The travelers' guide to Asian customs & manners. Deephaven, Minn. : Meadowbrook Books ; N.Y. : Distr. by Simon & Schuster, c1988. 375 p. : ill. ISBN 0-88166-106-6. $7.95. ISBN 0-671-65888-3. **BJ48**

Entries, each 10–12 pages, arranged alphabetically by country, are designed to acquaint prospective travelers with cultural aspects of countries in Europe and Asia. Topics covered include: greetings, conversation, public manners, meals and foods, hotels and private homes, currency and tipping, business practices, holidays, transportation, legal matters and safety, and key phrases. DS12.C47

Hayes, Gregory. Going places : the guide to travel guides / Greg Hayes and Joan Wright. Harvard, Mass. : Harvard Common Pr., c1988. 772 p. ISBN 1-55832-007-5. $22.95. ISBN 1-55832-003-2 (pbk.). $14.95.   **BJ49**

"... comprehensive, though certainly not exhaustive, summary of the better travel guides available."—*Introd*. Provides bibliographic citations and annotations to a variety of travel guides, including specialty guides (e.g., photography, hiking, canoeing, and cycling). Arrangement is geographical by continent or region, then alphabetical by country. Four appendixes list phrase books, travel stores and mail order agents, travel book publishers, and travel newsletters and magazines. Detailed subject and geographic indexes.   Z6011.H37

C

SOCIAL AND BEHAVIORAL SCIENCES

CA

General Works

GUIDES

Li, Tze-chung. Social science reference sources : a practical guide. Rev. and enl. 2nd ed. N.Y. : Greenwood, 1990. 590 p. (Contributions in librarianship and information science, no. 68). ISBN 0-313-25539-3.   **CA1**
1st ed., 1980 (*Guide* CA4).
Contains 2,200 entries, compared to the earlier edition's 800. Geography is treated for the first time; business and economics, previously considered together, have been separated. Comparable in content and organization to *The social sciences* (below).   Z7161.A1L5

Rama Reddy, E. Social science information : some Indian sources. New Delhi : Affiliated East-West Pr., 1985. [169] p.   **CA2**
Begins with a survey of the development of the social science disciplines in India in the mid-20th century, followed by ten bibliographic chapters devoted to categories of publication: books, Indian newspapers, periodicals, dissertations, government publications, etc. A separate chapter describes the mission, activities, publications, and library collections of the Social Science Documentation Centre (founded by the Indian Council of Social Science). Defines the social sciences in the broadest possible terms; "Books," for example, describes the tools providing bibliographic access to India's publishing output, as well as statistics on production, language, and subject matter. Intended for Indian social scientists, but helpful to researchers from other countries interested in Indian scholarship and culture. A brief index is of limited use.   Z7161.A1R35

The social sciences : a cross-disciplinary guide to selected sources / gen. ed., Nancy L. Herron ; contributing authors, Cynthia Faries . . . [et al.]. Englewood, Colo. : Libraries Unlimited, 1989. 287 p. ISBN 0-87287-725-6. $36.00. ISBN 0-87287-777-9 (pbk.). $27.50.   **CA3**
An annotated bibliography of reference sources in the social sciences and related subjects. Arranged by discipline; each section opens with an introduction that defines its scope and bibliographic structure and suggests appropriate search strategies. Comparable to *Sources of information in the social sciences*, ed. by William H. Webb (below) but Herron treats the online databases Webb neglects. Author, title, subject index.   Z7161.S648

Sources of information in the social sciences : a guide to the literature / William H. Webb . . . [et al.]. 3rd ed. Chicago : Amer. Lib. Assoc., 1986. 777 p. ISBN 0-8389-0405-X. $45.00.   **CA4**
1st ed., 1964. A revision through 1985 of the 2nd ed. (1973; see *Guide* CA9) by Carl M. White and associates.

A review in *ARBA* (1987): 46 faults this edition for insufficient coverage of social science databases.   Z7161.S666

BIBLIOGRAPHY

Encyclopedia of public affairs information sources : a bibliographic guide to approximately 8,000 citations for publications, organizations, and other sources of information on nearly 300 subjects relating to public affairs / Paul Wasserman, James R. Kelly, and Desider L. Vikor, editors. Detroit : Gale, c1988. 303 p. ISBN 0-8103-2191-2. $125.00.   **CA5**

Designed for professionals, researchers, and librarians seeking factual information in the interdisciplinary field of public affairs. Its title notwithstanding, *EPAIS* is not an encyclopedia, since it contains no articles. The body of the work consists of alphabetically arranged subject headings (e.g., Acid rain, Child abuse, Hospices, Zoos), under which are listed sources by type (e.g., Abstract services, Indexes, Information systems; Associations and professional societies; Online databases; Research centers, institutes, clearinghouses). An alphabetical "Outline of contents" lists topical headings with cross-references.   Z7165.U5E53

Musmann, Klaus. Diffusion of innovations : a select bibliography / comp. by Klaus Musmann and William H. Kennedy. N.Y. : Greenwood, 1989. 250 p. (Bibliographies and indexes in sociology, no. 17). ISBN 0-313-26698-0.   **CA6**

Devoted to diffusion research, a study of the process by which a new concept or object is introduced to a social system. Unannotated citations to approximately 2,400 articles, books, dissertations, and research reports, published mainly during the 1970s and 1980s, are arranged in 14 chapters (e.g., Agriculture and related fields, Bibliographies and research methodologies, Technology).   Z7914.T247M87

Reading lists in radical social science / editorial coordinators, Mark Maier and Dan Gilroy. N.Y. : Monthly Review Pr. : Union for Radical Political Economics, c1982. 179 p. ISBN 0-85345-616-X.   **CA7**

1st ed., 1971; 2nd ed., 1974; and 3rd ed., 1977, had title *Reading lists in radical political economics*.

Study groups, teachers planning classes, and students seeking supplemental reading are the audiences for this fourth compilation of reading lists from social science courses taught from a socialist perspective. Submitted by teachers of introductory, upper division, and graduate courses, syllabi range from topical outlines with bibliographies to detailed course descriptions with synopses of lectures, course objectives, and annotated reading lists. Syllabi are arranged under broad topics: Marxism, women, labor, racism, etc. Usefulness in reference and collection development is limited by lack of an index.   Z7161.R36

Current

Applied social sciences index & abstracts : ASSIA. v. 1, no. 1– . London : Library Association, 1987– . Bimonthly, with an annual cumulation. ISSN 0950-2238. $756.00.   **CA8**

Intended for service professionals in such fields as youth work, race relations, and employment. Citations (with abstracts of 150 words or less) appear in alphabetical arrangement by topic. More than 500 English-language journals from 16 countries are indexed. A review in *Choice* 26 (Apr. 1989): 1299 finds little overlap with *PAIS* and *Social sciences index*

and praises especially the coverage of women's studies and anthropology.   Z7163.A66

A London bibliography of the social sciences. London : Mansell, [1987?]– . v. (In progress).   **CA9**

For basic set and suppl. for 1934–84, see *Guide* CA34.

Supplements 21–24 include books added to the British Library of Political and Economic Science and Edward Fry Library of International Law.   Z7161.L84

PAIS international in print. v. 1, no. 1 (Jan. 1991)– . N.Y. : Public Affairs Information Service, Inc., 1991– . Monthly, with every fourth issue being cumulative. ISSN 1051-4015.   **CA10**

Issued also in an annual cumulation.

Merges *Public Affairs Information Service bulletin* (1915–90) (*Guide* CA35) and *Foreign language index* (1972–90) (*Guide* CA33).   A13.P85

●**PAIS on CD-ROM** [computer file]. N.Y. : Public Affairs Information Service, Inc., 1986– .   **CA11**

Machine-readable version of *Public Affairs Information Service bulletin* (*Guide* CA35), (now *PAIS international in print*, above).

Available in CD-ROM format. Coverage: 1972– . Updated and cumulated quarterly.

●**Social sciences citation index** : compact disc edition [computer file]. Philadelphia, Pa. : Institute for Scientific Information, c1986– . ISSN 1044-6044.   **CA12**

Machine-readable version of *Social sciences citation index* (*Guide* CA36).

Multiple discs, each containing the equivalent of one year of *SSCI*. Also available online as *Social SciSearch* (BRS, DIALOG), covering 1972 and after, updated biweekly.

Periodicals

Liste mondiale des périodiques spécialisés dans les sciences sociales = World list of social science periodicals. [Paris] : Unesco, 1986. 7th ed.   **CA13**

5th ed., 1980 (*Guide* CA41); 6th ed., 1983.

This edition lists 892 new titles in a total of 3,515. Titles inactive for five years prior to June 30, 1986, have been deleted.   Z7163.L523

ENCYCLOPEDIAS

Filler, Louis. A dictionary of American social change. Malabar, Fla. : Krieger Pub. Co., 1982. 256 p. ISBN 0-89874-242-0. ISBN 0-89874-564-0 (pbk.).   **CA14**

1st ed. (1963) had title: *A dictionary of American social reform*.

Presents brief articles on issues, persons, court decisions, slogans, and cultural phenomena (e.g., Abrams *vs.* United States; Federal Theatre Project; Mailer, Norman; "Malefactors of great wealth"; Post-Watergate morality; Sacco-Vanzetti case). Witty and insightful, the entries do not claim objectivity. Articles added to this edition encompass the early years of the Reagan presidency, while those pertaining to earlier periods have been reprinted unchanged from the previous edition (although bibliographies have been updated). There are cross-references in the text (e.g., ABSCAM *see* Corruption) but no index. Set in very small type.   H41.F5

The social science encyclopedia / ed. by Adam Kuper and Jessica Kuper. London ; Boston : Routledge &

Kegan Paul, 1985. 916 p. : ill. ISBN 0-7102-0008-0. $75.00. **CA15**

Contains in one convenient volume more than 700 entries ranging in scope from the major disciplines (anthropology, economics) to issues (welfare state), theories (parapsychology), and significant individuals (Levi-Strauss, Machiavelli). Signed articles are alphabetically arranged with cross-references and suggested sources for further reading that often include classics. Includes a useful list of entries grouped by discipline or problem area. No indexes. H41.S63

DICTIONARIES

Koschnick, Wolfgang J. Standard dictionary of the social sciences = Standardwörterbuch für die Sozialwissenschaften. München ; N.Y. : K.G. Saur, 1984. v. 1 : ill. ISBN 3-598-10526-6 (v. 1). (In progress). **CA16**
Contents: v. 1, English-German.

A word book, primarily for the translation of English to German and secondarily for brief definitions, which are in German. Double-column pages; cross-references. H41.K68

DIRECTORIES

Current research in Britain : CRB. [1st. ed.](1984)– . Boston Spa, Wetherby, West Yorkshire : British Library Lending Division, c1985– . Frequency varies. **CA17**
Publishes an annual *Social sciences* volume; for annotation, see *Supplement* EA53. H62.5.G7C87

Directory of social science information courses = Répertoire des cours d'information dans les sciences sociales = Repertorio de cursos en información en ciencias sociales / prepared at Unesco by the Social and Human Sciences Documentation Centre and the Social Science Information and Documentation Committee of the International Federation for Documentation. Oxford ; N.Y. : Berg Publishers ; Paris, France : UNESCO ; N.Y. : Distr. by St. Martin's Pr., 1988. 167 p. ISBN 0-85496-240-9. $45.00 (est.). **CA18**
For students, social scientists, and information professionals. An international directory that lists major academic and practical courses and programs in information handling in the social sciences. Based on replies to a 1987 questionnaire, entries include such information as course level, admission requirements, and teaching methods. Introduction in English, French, and Spanish. Indexed by institution, country, contact person, and discipline. H61.9.D57

Répertoire mondial des institutions de sciences sociales = World directory of social science institutions / prepared by the Unesco Social Science Documentation Centre. [1977]– . Paris : UNESCO, 1977– . ISSN 0254-4660. **CA19**
3rd ed., 1982 (*Guide* CA74).

The 5th ed., 1990, provides descriptions of 2,088 institutions in 199 countries. For information about organizations concerned with peace or human rights research, see Unesco's companion publications, *World directory of peace research and training institutions* (*Supplement* CJ313) and *World directory of human rights teaching and research institutions* (*Supplement* CH1695). H62.A1R46

Selective inventory of social science information and documentation services = Inventaire sélectif des services d'information et de documentation en sciences sociales = Inventario selectivo de servicios de información y documentación en ciencias sociales / prepared by the Unesco Social and Human Sciences Documentation Centre. 3rd ed. N.Y. : Berg Publishers ; Paris, France : United Nations Educational, Scientific, and Cultural Organization, 1988. 680 p. ISBN 0-85496-270-0. $75.00 (est.). **CA20**
1st ed., 1981, and 2nd ed., 1985, had title: *Selective inventory of information services*.

Describes 894 organizations, arranged alphabetically under host country, that provide information to social science professionals. Personal name, subject, geographical area, and database indexes. H61.9.S45

Smallwood, Carol. Current issues resource builder : free and inexpensive materials for librarians and teachers. Jefferson, N.C. : McFarland, c1989. 402 p. ISBN 0-89950-388-8. $16.95. **CA21**
Designed to help teachers and librarians locate free or inexpensive resources (under $16.00). Section I combines issues (AIDS, smoking, terrorism) and formats (abstracts, large print, newsletters) in one alphabetical list. Under each heading are listed agencies, public and private, willing to provide material. Section II is an alphabetical list of organizations, with profiles that indicate purpose, examples of material provided, prices, and ordering aids. The review in *ARBA* 20 (1990): 39, notes that this compilation differs from *The educators guide* [to free materials] series (*Guide* AA531) in that it lists types, rather than specific titles, of materials. Z692.F73S6

HANDBOOKS

Marlin, John Tepper. Cities of opportunity : finding the best place to work, live, and prosper in the 1990's and beyond / by John Tepper Marlin with David Lampe . . . [et al.]. N.Y. : MasterMedia, c1988. 410 p. ISBN 0-942361-07-5. $24.95. ISBN 0-942361-06-7 (pbk.). $12.95. **CA22**
Delineates the economic environment and quality of life characteristic of 42 selected communities. Although there is a certain vagueness about the compiler's criteria, the cities were chosen primarily on the basis of economic strength, job opportunities, and large size, although variables such as weather, health facilities, and cultural attractions were also considered. Individual brief chapters treating each city are supplemented by others on smaller cities and on the best communities for specific populations (e.g., women, retirees). Designed to help with decisions about where to live, but useful to general readers desiring succinct information about these locations. HT123.M2985

Mullins, Carolyn J. A guide to writing and publishing in the social and behavioral sciences. Malabar, Fla. : R.E. Krieger Pub. Co., 1983. 431 p. ISBN 0-89874-643-4. **CA23**
1st ed., 1977 (*Guide* CA66).
A new preface in this reprint of the 1977 ed. calls attention to dated information. H91.M8

FOUNDATIONS AND PHILANTHROPIC ORGANIZATIONS

Guides

Krathwohl, David R. How to prepare a research proposal : guidelines for funding and dissertations in the social and behavioral sciences. 3rd ed. Syracuse, N.Y. : Distr. by Syracuse Univ. Pr., c1988. 302 p. : ill. ISBN 0-8156-8111-9. $29.95. ISBN 0-8156-8112-7 (pbk.). $14.95.
CA24

1st ed., 1965; 2nd ed., 1977.

Three times the length of the 2nd ed., this guide explores the aims of a research proposal, the problems and processes unique to particular research strategies (qualitative methods studies, predictive studies, etc.), and types of funding available. A final section, new to this edition, is intended for doctoral candidates (finding an advisor, preparing the proposal, applying to "small-grant programs," writing the dissertation) and beginning grant seekers. Appendixes (with bibliographies and sources of information) on foundation funding by state. Glossary and index.
HG177.K73

Directories

International

A Canadian directory to foundations. 6th ed. (1985)– . Toronto : Canadian Centre for Philanthropy, c1985– .
CA25

1st ed., 1966, had title: *Guide to foundations and granting agencies.*

Seventh ed. (1987) profiles 609 family, corporate, community and special interest foundations with grant programs available to Canadian individuals and charitable organizations. Information about foundations varies, often including source of funds, purpose, geographic scope, financial data, application procedure, and contact person. Indexes of foundation names, individuals, geographic location, and fields of interest.
AS911.A2C36

Fieldhouse, Arthur E. A directory of philanthropic trusts in New Zealand. 3rd ed. Wellington : New Zealand Council for Educational Research in association with J.R. McKenzie Trust Board, 1987. 126 p. ISBN 0-908567-65-0.
CA26

1st ed., 1964, and 2nd ed., 1978, had title: *Directory of philanthropic trusts.*

Descriptions of 179 trusts, listed under the following categories: general charitable purposes (trusts funding local projects are listed under the region served), education, health promotion, and conservation. Profiles include address, history, purpose and activities, disbursements, and application timetable and procedures. This edition excludes trusts that support activities outside New Zealand, includes trusts giving less than $1,000 yearly, and adds guidelines for prospective applicants. Alphabetical index of trusts.
HV515.5.F54

The Hague Club. Foundation profiles. 4th ed. [Netherlands] : Bernard van Leer Foundation, 1988. 55 p. **CA27**

1st ed., 1979.

Profiles 27 of the largest foundations in Europe and Israel, including origin, purpose, source of funds, annual expenditures, types of grants, restrictions, application procedures, trustees, and publications. List of chief executives.
HV41.H33

International encyclopedia of foundations / Joseph C. Kiger, ed. in chief. N.Y. : Greenwood, 1990. 355 p. ISBN 0-313-25983-6.
CA28

Presents essays on 145 of the most significant foundations in the world, excluding the U.S.; the preface provides a historical overview of European and Asian foundations. Profiles, some written by foundation officers, include history, structure, types of projects supported, cooperative projects with other organizations, publications, and sources of further information. Complements the more inclusive *International foundation directory* (below). Three appendixes: a chronological listing of foundations by date established; earlier names; and families associated with foundation giving. Index.
HV12.I58

International foundation directory. 4th ed., rev. and enl. Detroit : Gale ; London : Europa, 1986.
CA29

3rd ed., 1983 (*Guide* CA100).

Describes 770 international foundations and national foundations with a worldwide scope, 130 of them new to this edition. Introductions to the 1974 and 1983 editions are reprinted, providing a history of foundations from medieval times to the present.
HV7.I56

United States

America's new foundations. 5th ed. (1991)– . Rockville, Md. : Taft Group, c1990– . Annual. ISSN 1048-4965. $130.00.
CA30

1st ed., 1986, 2nd ed., 1988, and 3rd ed., 1989, had title: *America's newest foundations*; 4th ed., 1990.

Provides current contact information for more than 3,300 new foundations (for 5th ed., those founded since 1986) with total giving or assets above $100,000. New foundations are often overlooked due to their brief giving histories. Profiles are listed by state, in alphabetical order, and giving information that ranges from minimal (address and year started) to comprehensive (major grants given, recipients, and a catchall category, "Other things you should know"). An appendix lists foundations that appeared in the preceding edition but are no longer eligible for inclusion. Five indexes: foundations by grant and by recipient type, names of decision makers, recipient locations, and a list of all funders.
HV87.A6

Butler, Francis J. Foundation guide for religious grant seekers / Francis J. Butler & Catherine E. Farrell, co-editors. [3rd ed.]. Atlanta : Scholars Pr., [c1987]. 172 p. ISBN 1-55540-121-X (pbk.).
CA31

For annotation, see *Supplement* BB31.
BV774.5.B87

Corporate foundation profiles. 6th ed. N.Y. : Foundation Center, c1990. 742 p. ISBN 0-87954-336-1.
CA32

1st ed., 1980; 5th ed., 1988.

Describes 251 of the largest company-sponsored foundations in the U.S., 63 of them new to this edition. Provides information identical to that in *National directory of corporate giving*, also compiled by the Foundation Center (below), adding background information about each foundation and a detailed analysis of annual grant spending, including major recipients, percentage and dollar amount of support awarded to various types of projects, geographic distribution, etc. Pt. I lists foundations alphabetically, pt.II in descending order by total amount awarded. Three indexes: subject of grant, type of support, geographic.
HV89.C68

Directory of grants in the humanities. [1986]– . Phoenix : Oryx, c1986– . Annual. ISSN 0887-0551. $55.00.
CA33

Describes more than 3,000 funding programs from public and private sources supporting research and performance in the humanities and the visual and performing arts. Entries include each program's goals, restrictions, funding amounts, deadlines, and *Catalog of federal domestic assistance* number when appropriate. Like *Directory of research grants* (*Guide* CA105), this is a product of the *GRANTS* database (below), which is updated monthly and should be consulted for changes or additions to programs. AZ188.U5D56

Foundation grants to individuals / Stan Olson, ed.; Margaret Mary Feczko, assist. ed. 6th ed. N.Y. : Foundation Center, 1988. 306 p. ISBN 0-87954-048-6 (pbk.). $15.00. **CA34**

3rd ed., 1982 (*Guide* CA112).

This edition contains information on 1,233 private U.S. foundations. LB2336.F598

•**GRANTS** [computer file]. Phoenix : Oryx. **CA35**

Machine-readable version of *Directory of research grants* (*Guide* CA105).

Directory of research grants available from governmental, business, foundation, and private sources. Covers current year's data (file size 6,250 records); updated monthly. Available online (DIALOG).

Guide to corporate giving in the arts 4 / ed. by Robert Porter. N.Y. : ACA Books, c1987. 481 p. ISBN 0-915400-56-1. $60.00. **CA36**

Supersedes *Guide to corporate giving 3* (*Guide* CA114).

Profiles 505 corporations, 206 fewer than the previous edition. NX711.U5G84

Guide to federal funding for social scientists / prepared by the Consortium of Social Science Associations ; Susan D. Quarles, ed. N.Y. : Russell Sage Foundation, c1986. 382 p. ISBN 0-87154-699-X (pbk.). **CA37**

Designed to introduce scholars in the social sciences to more than 300 federal programs that provide research funding. Entries include application and review procedures, examples of funded projects, and indication of future directions. Though its financial information is dated, the handbook includes valuable discussions of ongoing cooperation with federal agencies, winning research proposals, and dissemination of results. Indexed by research topics and sources of fellowships and dissertation support. H62.5.U5G85

The national directory of arts & education support by business corporations / by Nancy A. Fandel and editors of the Washington Int'l Arts Letter. 3rd ed. Wash. : Washington International Arts Letter, 1988. 150 p. (Arts patronage series, no. 14). ISBN 0-912072-15-6. **CA38**

2nd ed., 1982 (*Guide* CA115).

This edition indicates for the first time, by an asterisk before the entry, corporations and businesses that directly support individual artists. NX711.U5N3

National directory of corporate giving / comp. by the Foundation Center. 1st ed.– . N.Y. : The Center, c1989– . **CA39**

Describes 1,551 firms that permitted publication of their gift-giving activities. Entries, arranged alphabetically by company, include general descriptions of the firms and their "giving mechanisms"; types of programs funded; limitations (e.g., geographic, type of recipient); and relevant publications. Six indexes: officers, donors, and trustees; geographic; type of support; subject; types of business; and corporation, foundation, and giving programs by name.

§ Two comparable publications include fewer than half the firms listed here: *Corporate 500 : the directory of corporate philanthropy* (*Guide* CA104) and *Guide to corporate giving in the arts 4* (above). HV89.N26

Search for security : the Access guide to foundations in peace, security, and international relations / ed. by Anne Allen. Wash. : Access, c1989. 191 p. : ill. **CA40**

Designed to assist both those seeking and those awarding grants in peace, security, and international relations. In four parts: (1) an analysis of fundings in these fields, including trends and changes in granting agencies; (2) profiles of 158 foundations, describing their priorities and providing guidelines for applicants and selected financial data; (3) information concerning U.S. government and government-funded organizations that award grants in these fields; (4) a list of foundations by activity funded, issues funded, and geographic region of concern. An appendix presents tables on the geographic preferences, amount given, assets, etc., of foundations. Index of foundations. JX1905.5.S43

Sternberg, Sam. National directory of corporate charity. San Francisco : Regional Young Adult Project, c1984. 598 p. ISBN 0-9606198-2-8 (pbk.). $80.00. **CA41**

An alphabetical list of U.S. corporations with annual revenues in excess of $200 million. Profile information complements that in *National directory of corporate giving* (above). While the latter is limited to corporations that have contributed to nonprofit organizations, Sternberg lists as well noncontributors and companies that support only directly useful technical research, suggesting that both are worth soliciting because they receive few competing requests. Indexes of companies by state and of support categories (e.g., Community arts, Film, Medical research). HG4028.C6S73

Australia

Philanthropic trusts in Australia. 5th ed. Hawthorn [Australia] : Australian Council for Educational Research, 1987. 168 p. ISBN 0-86431-009-9. **CA42**

1st ed., 1968 (*Guide* CA99); 4th ed., 1983.

This edition profiles 275 philanthropic trusts (all but 12 Australian), 17 fewer than the previous edition. Alphabetically arranged profiles include address, telephone, history, functions, amounts disbursed, and application information. Excluded are trusts disbursing less than $3,000 per year, those not wishing publicity, and those with local or exceedingly restricted beneficiaries. Index of subjects, scholarships, and institutions. HV473.A2P48

Handbooks

Carson, Emmett Devon. The charitable appeals fact book : how black and white Americans respond to different types of fund-raising efforts. Wash. : Joint Center for Political Studies, c1989. 60 p. ISBN 0-941410-83-8. ISBN 0-941410-84-6 (pbk.). **CA43**

Reports results of a 1985 Joint Center for Political Studies nationwide survey of 896 blacks and 916 whites. Consists of an introductory chapter summarizing the findings and seven chapters individually treating responses to the appeals of specific types of organizations (e.g., religious, educational). Data in tabular form indicates percentages of subjects who contributed after solicitation. Includes breakdowns by type of appeal, (e.g, letter, phone call, solicitation by acquaintances), race, age, economic status, demographic characteristics, and educational background. No index, but detailed table of contents. HV41.9.U5C37

The Foundation Center's user-friendly guide : grantseeker's guide to resources / comp. by Public Service staff of the Foundation Center, Anne Borland . . . [et al.] ; Judith B. Margolin, ed. N.Y. : The Center, c1990. 40 p. : ill. **CA44**

Responds to ten concerns of beginning grantseekers—e.g., researching appropriate funding sources, securing tax-exempt status for one's organization, writing a grant proposal. Annotated bibliography of relevant reference books, periodicals, and databases. Glossary.

Lefferts, Robert. Getting a grant in the 1990s : how to write successful grant proposals. N.Y. : Prentice Hall, c1990. 239 p. : ill. ISBN 0-13-313552-7. $12.95.   **CA45**
Previous ed., 1982 (*Guide* CA92) had title: *Getting a grant in the 1980s.*

Updates information on foundations and government funding sources and provides new chapters on applying marketing principles to grant proposals and on keeping a grant and getting it refunded. Bibliography of state and local foundation directories. Glossary; index.   HG177.5.U6L44

Park, Karin R. Publication grants for writers & publishers : how to find them, win them, and manage them / by Karin R. Park & Beth Luey. Phoenix : Oryx, 1991. 105 p. : ill. ISBN 0-89774-557-4. $29.95.   **CA46**
For annotation, see *Supplement* BD49.   Z283.P37

Read, Patricia. Foundation fundamentals : a guide for grantseekers. 3rd ed. N.Y. : Foundation Center, 1986. 239 p. : ill. ISBN 0-87954-100-8 (pbk.). $9.95.   **CA47**
1st ed., 1980, by Carol M. Kurzig (*Guide* CA91); rev. ed., 1981.

Thoroughly revised, with expanded bibliographies on all aspects of grant seeking. New to this edition is a list of national organizations that provide services to grant seekers.   HV41.9.U5R44

Renz, Loren. Foundations today : current facts and figures on private and community foundtions. 7th ed. [N.Y.] : Foundation Center, 1990. 39 p. ISBN 0-87954-339-6. $11.50.   **CA48**
1st ed., 1981; 6th ed., 1989.

Drawn from the Foundation Center's databases, this compendium contains statistical tables (mainly for the mid-1980s, but some going back to 1975) for assets of and awards by particular foundations and types of foundations, subjects supported, categories of recipients, and kinds of support. Includes a discussion of the history and types of foundations and trends in foundation giving.   HV85.F68

ASSOCIATIONS, SOCIETIES, AND ACADEMIES

International

Directory of European professional & learned societies = Répertoire des sociétés professionnelles et savantes en Europe. Ed. 4– . Beckenham, Kent, England : CBD Research, c1989– . Irregular.   **CA49**
Continues pt. 2 of *Directory of European associations* (*Guide* CA120).

Companion to *Directory of European industrial and trade associations* (Detroit : Gale, 1986). Provides information on professional, learned, scientific and technical associations in Europe (excluding the U.K. and Ireland), Iceland, Malta, and Cyprus. Arranged by topic (e.g., Napoleonic studies, robotics, tropical medicine), then by country. Entries include address, telephone and telex numbers, areas of interest, membership, activities, and publications. Subject index, classified directory of organizations, index of abbreviations of organizations, and alphabetical index of organizations.   HD6497.E85D57

World guide to scientific associations and learned societies / [ed., Michael Sachs]. 5th ed. München ; N.Y. : K. G. Saur, 1990. 672 p. ISBN 3-598-20530-9. $275.00.   **CA50**
4th ed., 1984 (*Guide* CA122).

Lists some 18,000 active national and international organizations in science, culture, and technology. Entries are arranged alphabetically by country and include the official name, address, numbers for telephone, telefacsimile, telex, and cable, official personnel listings, areas of activity, and publications. A special index to 12,000 association and society periodical titles has been added to this edition. Indexes by organization name and subject continue.   Q145.W9267

United States

Encyclopedia of associations. Regional, state, and local organizations. 1st ed. (1988–89)– . Detroit : Gale, c1987– . Biennial. ISSN 0894-2846. $469.00.   **CA51**
For parent publication, see *Guide* CA125.
Contents: v.1, Great Lakes states; v.2, Northeastern states; v.3, Middle Atlantic states; v.4, Western states; v.5, Southeastern states; v.6, Southwest and South Central states; v.7, Northwestern and Great Plains states.   AS22.E53

Great Britain

Directory of British associations & associations in Ireland. Ed. 4 (1974–5)– . Beckenham, Kent : CBD Research Ltd, 1974– .   **CA52**
For earlier eds. and annotations, see *Guide* CA151.
Ed. 1, 1965, and ed. 2, 1970, had title : *Directory of British associations.*

New to the 9th ed. and continued in the 10th ed. (1990) is a list of "Unverified and lost associations," about which information is solicited.

Secret societies

Hall, Manly Palmer. An encyclopedic outline of Masonic, Hermetic, Qabbalistic, and Rosicrucian symbolical philosophy : being an interpretation of the secret teachings concealed within the rituals, allegories, and mysteries of all ages. Los Angeles : Philosophical Research Society, 1977. [245] p., [42] leaves of plates (2 fold.) : ill. ISBN 0-89314-539-4. $27.50.   **CA53**
Repr. of subscriber's ed., (San Francisco : H.S. Crocker, 1928) with new preface and foreword.

Besides the topics in the title, the 45 chapters of this work, in rough chronological order, include other related topics (e.g., Gnosticism, alchemy, mathematical symbolism, and the symbolism of animals, plants, and the human body). Liberally illustrated. Bibliography of sources consulted; general index. Little of the information on the Masons and Rosicrucians can be easily found elsewhere. Useful for research in literature and the fine arts.   BF1411.H3

Mariel, Pierre. Dictionnaire des sociétés secrètes en Occident. [Paris : Culture, art, loisirs, 1971]. 478 p. : ill.   **CA54**

Devoted to secret societies throughout history that have nonmaterialistic concerns. Substantial entries on persons, organizations, key texts, and mystical topics are alphabetically arranged and include bibliographies. More selective than Arthur Preuss's *A dictionary of secret and other societies* (*Guide* CA167); resembles in scope Manly P. Hall's *An encyclopedic outline of Masonic, Hermetic, Qabbalistic and Rosicrucian symbolical philosophy* (above). No index, but terms defined elsewhere are underlined and page references to related articles appear at the beginning of entries.   HS12.M35

CB

Education

GENERAL WORKS

Guides

ARBA guide to education / comp. and ed. by Deborah J. Brewer. Littleton, Colo. : Libraries Unlimited, 1985. 232 p. ISBN 0-87287-490-7. $23.50.   **CB1**

Reprints 453 substantial critical annotations (many of them signed) selected from the more than 1,200 reviews of works in education published in *American reference books annual* 1970–85. Arranged in chapters citing specific kinds of reference works (e.g., indexes) or materials on special topics such as reading and special education. Coverage of database resources is incomplete: online versions of *Education index* and *Resources in education* are omitted (although *Current index to journals in education* is mentioned), and CD-ROM products are not discussed.   Z5811.A59

Berry, Dorothea M. A bibliographic guide to educational research. 3rd ed. Metuchen, N.J. : Scarecrow, 1990. 1 v. ISBN 0-8108-2343-8.   **CB2**

2nd ed., 1980 (*Guide* CB1).

Contains 1,050 entries, compared with 772 in the 2nd ed. 585 titles are new and 213 are new editions; 307 items listed in the 2nd ed. have been deleted. Entries for annual and biennial publications have been updated. Annotations have been rewritten and tend to be fuller; cross-references are used for the first time.   Z5811.B39

Buttlar, Lois. Education : a guide to reference and information sources. Englewood, Colo. : Libraries Unlimited, 1989. 258 p. (Reference sources in the social sciences series, no. 2). ISBN 0-87287-619-5. $27.50.   **CB3**

Describes more than 900 titles, including databases as well as printed sources. Almost all are in English and were published after 1980, with the exception of a few important works, such as unique bibliographies. Entries contain substantial annotations, some evaluative. Arranged in 20 chapters, most of which treat specific areas of the field (e.g., special education, educational administration, evaluation in education). Other chapters cover education periodicals, research centers and organizations, social science reference sources, and general reference works related to education. General index.   Z5811.B89

Freed, Melvyn N. The educator's desk reference (EDR) : a sourcebook of educational information and research / Melvyn N. Freed, author and ed. ; Robert K. Hess and Joseph M. Ryan, authors. N.Y. : American Council on Education, c1989. 536 p. : ill. ISBN 0-02-910740-7. **CB4**

A guide designed to assist professional educators in conducting research. Includes an annotated bibliography of 134 reference works; directories of journals, book publishers, and microcomputer software publishers, giving their specialties and guidelines for manuscript submission; lists of microcomputer software; reviews of standardized tests; guidelines for selection of appropriate research design, sampling techniques, and statis-

tical procedures; and descriptions of national and regional organizations. Because emphasis is "less on 'how to' and more on 'information lookup' " (*Pref.*), readers are referred to further sources of information. Cross-references; general index.   LB1028.27.U6F74

Bibliography

Parker, Franklin. Education in the People's Republic of China, past and present : an annotated bibliography / Franklin Parker, Betty June Parker. N.Y. : Garland, 1986. 845 p. (Reference books in international education, vol. 2 ; Garland reference library of social science, v. 281). ISBN 0-8240-8797-6.   **CB5**

Cites over 3,000 books, journal and newspaper articles, and other works covering both the Communist period and earlier years. Lists publications in several languages, but all annotations are in English. Arranged by subject, with some chronological subdivisions. Author and subject indexes.   Z5815.C54P37

The school administrator's resource guide / ed. by Katherine Clay. Phoenix : Oryx, 1988. 104 p. ISBN 0-89774-446-2 (pbk.).   **CB6**

An annotated bibliography, intended for principals, superintendents, and other educational administrators, of 550 journal articles, microfiche documents, books, and dissertations cited in the *ERIC*, *PsycInfo*, *Sociological abstracts*, and *Social SciSearch* databases, mostly between March 1982 and March 1987. Each of the nine chapters treats a major administrative function (e.g., Instructional leadership; School site management).   Z5814.M26S35

Science books for children : selections from *Booklist*, 1976–1983 / selected by Denise Murcko Wilms. Chicago : Amer. Lib. Assoc., 1985. 183 p. ISBN 0-8389-3312-2 (pbk.). $12.00.   **CB7**

Describes books reviewed favorably in *Booklist* (*Guide* AA446). Arranged in 14 subject sections. Author/title and subject indexes.   Z7401.S363

Higher education

Herring, Mark Youngblood. Ethics and the professor : an annotated bibliography, 1970–1985. N.Y. : Garland, 1988. 605. (Garland reference library of the humanities, vol. 742). ISBN 0-8240-8491-8.   **CB8**

Cites books and articles on moral law and the "action of that law in our educational realm."—*Pref.* Excludes reference and non-English language materials. Humorously worded table of contents and subdivisions. Author, title, and subject key word indexes.   Z5814.P73H47

Hines, Edward R. Higher education finance : an annotated bibliography and guide to research / Edward R. Hines, John R. McCarthy. N.Y. : Garland, 1985. 357 p. ISBN 0-8240-9054-3.   **CB9**

Covers 1970–83. Includes books, reports, studies, and articles from a list of core journals. Entries are numerically arranged, with full citations and annotations, in topical chapters on financing and fiscal support, general trends and economics, government support, external funding, student aid, institutional financial management, planning and budgeting, and reduction and retrenchment. Topic and author indexes; list of acronyms.   Z5815.U5H56

Rowland, A. Westley. Key resources on institutional advancement. San Francisco : Jossey-Bass Publishers, 1986. 251 p. ISBN 1-55542-014-1.   **CB10**

An annotated bibliography of important items that "significantly contributed to the basic foundation of the advancement field and to its growth and development."—*p. x*. Classic works are starred. Arranged in 13 topical chapters, including public relations, fund raising, institutional relations, government relations, and enrollment management. Indexes of subjects and names. Appendixes: statement of ethics for advancement professionals; annotated, alphabetical list of pertinent periodicals with addresses.   Z5815.U5R69

Sontz, Ann H. L. The American college president, 1636–1989 : a critical review and bibliography. N.Y. : Greenwood, c1991. 176 p. (Bibliographies and indexes in education, no. 10). ISBN 0-313-27325-1.   **CB11**

Updates Walter C. Eells and Ernest V. Hollis's *The college presidency, 1900–1960* (*Guide* CB33). Includes materials relevant to early academic presidencies as well as those since the 1960s to mirror "concerns of both historic and modern academic leaders."—*p.xxii*. Lists publications in four chapters: (1) bibliographies; (2) background sources (general treatises, alphabetical by author in broad subject categories); (3) biographies (alphabetical by institution, then by president) and (4) presidential works—the bulk of the work (same arrangement as chapter 3). Introductory material includes a short review essay, "Guide to the study of the academic presidency," and seven tables of statistical data. Author and subject indexes.

Z5814.U7S66

Occupational education

●**Resources in vocational education** : (RIVE) [computer file]. Berkeley, Calif. : National Center for Research in Vocational Education, 1978– .   **CB12**

File size: 14,000 records. Updated quarterly. Available online (BRS).

Includes descriptions of ongoing and recently completed research and development projects in vocational education. Describes federal and state exemplary curriculum development, staff development, and research projects.

Special education

The SpecialWare directory : a guide to software sources for special education. 1983– . Columbus, Ohio : LINC Associates, 1983– .   **CB13**

Lists more than 300 instructional, professional, and administrative software packages either designed for or deemed useful in special education. The directory section lists entries alphabetically and includes publisher, format, price, release date, version, hardware required, user population, curriculum area, applications, description, and citation for product review. Appendixes list product titles, publishers and distributors, and review sources. Indexes list titles by method of instruction, curriculum, hardware, input/output options, network, and special education administration.   LC3969.S64

Stein, Morris Isaac. Gifted, talented, and creative young people : a guide to theory, teaching, and research. N.Y. : Garland, 1986. lxvii, 465 p. (Garland reference library of social science, v. 120). ISBN 0-8240-9392-5.   **CB14**

An annotated bibliography of books, book chapters, articles, and conference and symposium papers, most published 1970–80 but including older classics and later works, representing the "major issues, orientations, research results, [and] curricular and instructional programs."—*Pref*. Intended to give graduate students and professional researchers a rapid survey of the field. Organized in chapters covering broad areas (e.g., Evaluation, Stimulating creativity); within chapters the arrangement varies, some alphabetical by author, some chronological, some thematic. Annotations contain "Suggestions for

further reading"; some annotations are detailed summaries as long as two pages. Author and subject indexes.   Z5815.U5S73

Sternlicht, Manny. Special education : a source book. N.Y. : Garland, 1987. 431 p. (Garland reference library of social science, v. 375 ; Garland reference library of social science. Source books on education, vol. 7). ISBN 0-8240-8524-8. $50.00.   **CB15**

An annotated bibliography of 1,001 sources, mostly journal articles. Organized by type of disability, with an additional chapter on mainstreaming. Author and subject indexes.

Z5814.S73S74

Teachers and teaching

Ayers, Jerry B. Teacher education program evaluation : an annotated bibliography and guide to research / Jerry B. Ayers, Mary F. Berney. N.Y. : Garland, 1990. 274 p. (Garland bibliographies in contemporary education, v. 10 ; Garland reference library of social science, v. 619). ISBN 0-8240-3537-2.   **CB16**

Intended for those planning the evaluation and subsequent redesign of teacher education programs, attempting to meet evaluation requirements, or seeking accreditation from official agencies. Cites with brief descriptive annotations 941 books, research reports, journal articles, dissertations, reviews of research, and essays. Nearly all were published 1976–March 1989, and were drawn from *Resources in education, Cumulative index to journals in education, Dissertation abstracts international,* or *Books in print*. Entries are grouped in seven chapters, each of which treats a major component of teacher education programs (e.g., Management and governance, Follow-up evaluation). Indexes of authors, titles, and subjects, and an index that relates citations to specific standards of the National Council for Accreditation of Teacher Education.   Z5814.T3A97

Handbook of research on teacher education / W. Robert Houston, ed. ; Martin Haberman, John Sikula, assoc. editors. N.Y. : Macmillan ; London : Collier Macmillan, c1990. 925 p. ISBN 0-02-901420-4.   **CB17**

A review of the literature in which experts "were asked not only to synthesize the most important research in their areas, but also to place it in a conceptual framework, to analyze trends, to summarize new directions, and to evaluate the potential for future research."—*Pref*. In 48 chapters divided among 9 sections on major areas such as Participants in teacher education, Curriculum of teacher education, and Teacher education in the curriculum areas. Extensive bibliography; name and subject indexes.   LB1715.H274

Powell, Marjorie. Teacher attitudes : an annotated bibliography and guide to research / Marjorie Powell, Joseph W. Beard. N.Y. : Garland, 1986. 457 p. (Garland bibliographies in contemporary education, v. 4 ; Garland reference library of social science, v. 199). ISBN 0-8240-9053-5. $45.00.   **CB18**

Contains more than 1,900 entries for journal articles, ERIC documents, and dissertations published from 1965 through June 1984. Arranged in seven topical sections, including Attitudes toward students, Attitudes toward teaching, Effects of teaching attitudes, and Reviews of research on teacher attitudes. Author, title, and subject indexes.   Z5815.U5P68

Other special topics

Boehnlein, Mary Maher. Children, parents, and reading : an annotated bibliography / comp. by Mary Maher Boehnlein and Beth Haines Hager for the Parents and Reading Committee. Newark, Del. : International Reading Association, 1985. 138 p. ISBN 0-87207-341-6 (pbk.). **CB19**

Designed for parents who want to improve children's reading skills and professionals who want to aid parents in doing this. In four sections: (1) Parents and reading, divided by educational level; (2) Professional and home/school involvement, divided by type of source; (3) Books and pamphlets for parents, and (4) Miscellaneous, listing periodicals for children and parents, audiovisual materials, booklists, and selection aids. Not indexed. Z5815.U5B63

Brooks, Ellen J. Learning to read and write : the role of language acquisition and aesthetic development : a resourcebook. N.Y. : Garland, 1986. 157 p. ISBN 0-8240-8800-X. **CB20**

Combines a brief text and a 245-item annotated bibliography, the latter constituting the book's value as a reference work. Author and subject indexes. LB1576.B783

Cooperative learning : a guide to research / Samuel Totten . . . [et al.]. N.Y. : Garland, 1991. 390 p. (Garland bibliographies in contemporary education, v. 12 ; Garland reference library of social science, v. 674). ISBN 0-8240-7222-7. **CB21**

An annotated bibliography of 818 works on the application of the various teaching strategies that fall under the rubric "cooperative learning." Cites items, dating from Dewey's writing in the early 1900s to the present, on uses at grade levels ranging from kindergarten through higher education. Describes books, essays, articles, dissertations, book reviews, nonprint media, reports and curricula. Topically arranged, with chapters on specific teaching strategies, instruction in individual subject areas, organizations, educational media, classroom environment, etc. Author and title indexes. Z5814.G84C66

Derivan, William J. Prevention education : a guide to research / William J. Derivan, Natalie Anne Silverstein. N.Y. : Garland, 1990. 282 p. (Garland bibliographies in contemporary education, v. 9 ; Garland reference library of social science, v. 524). ISBN 0-8240-3716-2. **CB22**

For annotation, see *Supplement* CC113. Z7164.N17D44

Fabiano, Emily. Index to tests used in educational dissertations. Phoenix : Oryx, 1989. 371 p. ISBN 0-89774-288-5. **CB23**

Indexes references to some 35,000 published and unpublished tests occurring in the 1938–80 volumes of *Dissertation abstracts international* and its predecessors. Index entries are drawn both from dissertation titles and from the abstracts. Access to the tests (sometimes difficult in the case of unpublished instruments) is facilitated by a section of the Preface that suggests ways of acquiring them. Indexes only *DAI*'s A section (Humanities and social sciences), hence dissertations in related fields (e.g., psychology) are not covered. In two parts: (1) Test title index, which lists instruments alphabetically and refers to *DAI* volume and page; (2) Keyword/names index, which contains three kinds of terms (topic keywords, author names, and test title acronyms) and refers to entries in the test title index. LB3051.F3

French, Joyce N. Adult literacy : a source book and guide. N.Y. : Garland, c1987. 435 p. (Garland reference library of social science, v. 346 ; Garland reference library of social science. Source books on education, vol. 14). ISBN 0-8240-8574-4. **CB24**

In two parts: a short overview of the field, and an annotated bibliography of 591 articles, books, and government documents. Author and subject indexes. Z5814.I3F73

Grambs, Jean Dresden. Sex differences and learning : an annotated bibliography of educational research, 1979–1989 / Jean Dresden Grambs, John C. Carr. N.Y. : Garland, 1991. 280 p. (Garland reference library of social science, v. 418 ; Garland bibliographies in contemporary education, v. 11). ISBN 0-8240-6641-3. $35.00. **CB25**

Contains 795 entries briefly describing research articles one could "reasonably expect to find . . . in a [university] library . . . ."—*Introd.* In 23 chapters with such titles as Cognitive styles/cognitive structures, Mathematics, and School attendance/ dropouts. Author and subject indexes.

Z5815.U5G73

High/low handbook : books, materials, and services for the problem reader / comp. and ed. by Ellen V. LiBretto. 2nd ed. N.Y. : Bowker, 1985. 264 p. : ill. ISBN 0-8352-2133-4. **CB26**

1st ed., 1981.

For "teachers, librarians, and others who must provide easy reading materials for disabled or reluctant teenage readers."—*Introd.* The second section has value as a reference tool, listing a "core collection" of 286 high interest/low reading level books and periodicals for disabled readers. Entries are arranged alphabetically by author and include price, fiction or nonfiction designation, reading grade level, interest grade level, and a critical annotation. An appendix presents an annotated listing of a core collection for reluctant readers. Title and subject indexes. Z1039.S5H54

Hladczuk, John. Comparative reading : an international bibliography / comp. by John Hladczuk and William Eller. N.Y. : Greenwood, 1987. 174 p. (Bibliographies and indexes in education, no. 4). ISBN 0-313-26004-4. **CB27**

Cites 1,947 sources, including periodical articles, books, government publications, dissertations, conference proceedings, and reports. Interdisciplinary in scope, containing entries related to psychological, sociological, historical, philosophical, and economic aspects of reading. In two parts: (1) International research, with sections treating national, world, regional, and cross-cultural research, and (2) Correlates of reading, with chapters on such subjects as "Correlates of learning to read," "Correlates of language," and "Correlates of the psychology of comparative reading." Author and subject indexes. Z5818.L3H58

———————— General issues in literacy/illiteracy : a bibliography / comp. by John Hladczuk, William Eller, and Sharon Hladczuk. N.Y. : Greenwood, 1990. 420 p. (Bibliographies and indexes in education, no. 8). ISBN 0-313-27327-8. **CB28**

Cites 4,085 journal articles, ERIC documents, books, dissertations, unpublished papers, proceedings, government documents and other materials. Attempts to be comprehensive but not exhaustive. Arranged topically in 37 chapters on subjects such as: Mathematical literacy, Economics of illiteracy, and Technology and literacy. Complements the compilers' *Literacy/illiteracy in the world*, (below) which contains many of the same titles, but emphasizes international and national research on literacy. Author and subject indexes. Z5814.I3H56

———————— Literacy/illiteracy in the world : a bibliography / comp. by John Hladczuk, William Eller, and Sharon Hladczuk. N.Y. : Greenwood, 1989. 201 p. (Bibliographies and indexes in education, no. 6). ISBN 0-313-26252-7. **CB29**

Has sections that list works on 126 specific countries, states of the U.S., world regions, and literacy worldwide, and on cross-national and cross-cultural studies. A companion to the author's *General issues in literacy/illiteracy* (above), which lists works dealing with 37 separate issues (e.g., job literacy, women and literacy), some not treated in the present volume; hence, the introduction suggests consulting both. Author and subject indexes.   Z5814.I3H57

Hunt, Thomas C. Religious schools in America : a selected bibliography / [comp. by] Thomas C. Hunt, James C. Carper, Charles R. Kniker. N.Y. : Garland, 1986. 391 p. ISBN 0-8240-8583-3.   **CB30**

Contains 1,181 entries on religiously affiliated elementary and secondary schools. Cites journal articles, books, dissertations and theses, reports and other works. Of 24 chapters, 17 deal with the schools of 17 individual religious groups. Other chapters treat such topics as court decisions on government aid to religious schools, state regulation of these schools, and statements about the schools by their supporters and public school educators. Author and subject indexes.   Z5814.C57H86

International biography of adult education / ed. by J.E. Thomas and Barry Elsey. Nottingham : Dept. of Adult Education, Univ. of Nottingham, c1985. 709 p. ISBN 1-85041-001-1.   **CB31**

Provides signed biographies of 200 18th–20th century figures who contributed to the field, some as professional adult educators, others as public leaders, writers, or scholars. International in scope, although there are more entries from the Commonwealth than the U.S. The biographies, alphabetically arranged, are typically one to three pages long and are followed by brief bibliographies. A "Thematic index" lists biographees arranged by areas of adult education, and a subject index locates articles on specific individuals.   LA2303.I615

Kelly, David H. Women's education in the Third World : an annotated bibliography / David H. Kelly, Gail P. Kelly. N.Y. : Garland, 1989. 478 p. ISBN 0-8240-8634-1.   **CB32**

Describes 1,188 journals, monographs, and books, including "many individual chapters hidden in books that didn't have women or education as their central concern."—*Introd.* Omits dissertations, unpublished reports, or conference papers. Further limited to "substantial research studies" on developing (rather than industrialized) countries, and to works in five languages: English (in which it attempts to be comprehensive), Portuguese, Spanish, French, and German. Most items were published in the 1970s and 1980s, though a few appeared earlier. Grouped into 15 topics, each subdivided by region and country, that relate to access to education, educational processes, and societal outcomes. Author and geographical indexes.   Z5815.D44K44

Malone, Cheryl Knott. Gender, unpaid labor, and the promotion of literacy : a selected, annotated bibliography. N.Y. : Garland, 1987. 148 p. (Garland reference library of social science, v. 401). ISBN 0-8240-8469-1.   **CB33**

Includes "materials on volunteers in schools, libraries, after school programs, higher education, and literacy campaigns."—*Introd.* 494 entries arranged chronologically 1946–86, then alphabetically by author. An introductory essay discusses "The gender dimension of literacy volunteer work." Author, subject, and title indexes.   Z7164.V65M34

McGee, Leo. Education of the black adult in the United States : an annotated bibliography / comp. by Leo McGee and Harvey G. Neufeldt. Westport, Conn. : Greenwood, 1985. 108 p. (Bibliographies and indexes in Afro-American and African studies, no. 4). ISBN 0-313-23473-6.   **CB34**

Spans the entire period from the arrival of blacks in 1619 to the present, divided into four eras, each covered by a chapter. A fifth chapter, General resources, treats sources not restricted to one of these periods. Annotations are nonevaluative and vary in length. Author and subject indexes.   LC2801.M27

Menendez, Albert J. School prayer and other religious issues in American public education : a bibliography. N.Y. : Garland, 1985. 168 p. (Garland reference library of social science, v. 291). ISBN 0-8240-8775-5.   **CB35**

Arranged in 21 chapters; cites 1,566 unannotated references to books, journal and newspaper articles, dissertations, and theses. Provides historical perspective on such issues as bible reading, teaching religion, religious elements in textbooks, grades in school. Author index, and a subject index that lists only states.   Z5815.U5M46

National Council of Teachers of English. Committee to Revise High Interest-Easy Reading. High interest easy reading : for junior and senior high school students / Dorothy Matthews, chair, and the Committee to Revise High Interest-Easy Reading of the National Council of Teachers of English. 5th ed. Urbana, Ill. : National Council of Teachers of English, c1988. 115 p. ISBN 0-8141-2096-2 (pbk.).   **CB36**

2nd ed., ed. by Marian E. White, 1972; 5th ed., 1988.

Suggests fiction and nonfiction books for students whose reading levels are significantly lower than their age levels. Useful for teachers, librarians, and other professionals, but intended to be a reference tool for the students as well, hence entries contain only brief bibliographic information and annotations describing content or plot, without evaluation or designation of age or interest levels. Arranged by subject, then alphabetically by author; author and title indexes.   Z1039.S5N4

Parker, Franklin. Education in England and Wales : an annotated bibliography / Franklin Parker, Betty June Parker. N.Y. : Garland, 1991. xcii, 531 p. (Reference books in international education, vol. 19 ; Garland reference library of social science, v. 581). ISBN 0-8240-5943-3.   **CB37**

Contains more than 2,000 briefly annotated entries for books, articles, and ERIC documents; excludes dissertations. Arranged into 13 chapters on subjects such as administration and higher education, but also on topics unique to the U.K. (e.g., Wales and Welsh language, Education Reform Act of 1988). Has introductory chapters on the history and structure of English and Welsh educational systems. Author and subject indexes.   Z5815.G5P37

Resources for educational equity : a guide for grades pre-kindergarten–12 / [ed. by] Merle Froschl, Barbara Sprung. N.Y. : Garland, 1988. 266 p. ISBN 0-8240-0443-4. $37.00.   **CB38**

A guide to materials used to educate students in attitudes of equality toward all races, sexes, and people with disabilities. Eleven chapters treat such topics as Early childhood education, Language arts and literature, and Teenage childbearing. Each chapter is written by an expert and contains a short essay followed by bibliographic entries with evaluative annotations. Author and subject indexes.   LC213.2.R47

Roberts, Patricia. Alphabet books as a key to language patterns : an annotated action bibliography. Hamden, Conn. : Library Professional Publications, 1987. 263 p. ISBN 0-208-02151-5.   **CB39**

Describes nearly 500 books recommended for use in developing children's language skills. Arranged by language patterns (e.g., alliteration, repetition, word association). An introductory chapter outlines the role of these patterns in developing skills. Author/title index.   Z2015.A44R62

Smith, Robert McCaughan. The independent learners' sourcebook : resources and materials for selected topics / Robert M. Smith, Phyllis M. Cunningham. Chicago : Amer. Lib. Assoc., 1987. 306 p. ISBN 0-8389-0459-9.   **CB40**

An annotated list of reference sources on 34 subjects, including, for most topics, reference books, introductory works, indexes, government publications, periodicals, databases, and

relevant organizations. Author-title and organizations indexes.
Z1035.1.S577

White, James P. Materials and strategies for the education of trainable mentally retarded learners. N.Y. : Garland, 1990. 348 p. (Garland reference library of social science, v. 476 ; Garland reference library of social science. Source books on education, vol. 24). ISBN 0-8240-6345-7. **CB41**

Essentially an annotated bibliography of articles, books, assessment instruments, and instructional materials. 15 chapters, each beginning with a brief outline, treat either the teaching of specific subjects or topics such as Assessment or Working with parents. Appendixes include an extensive list of relevant state-level public and private agencies, publishers, and suppliers, and microcomputer resources. General index. LC4601.W52

Woodward, Arthur. Textbooks in school and society : an annotated bibliography and guide to research / Arthur Woodward, David L. Elliott, Kathleen Carter Nagel. N.Y. : Garland, 1988. 176 p. (Garland bibliographies in contemporary education, v. 6 ; Garland reference library of social science, v. 405). ISBN 0-8240-8390-3. $25.00. **CB42**

Arranges 471 citations in two topical sections, Textbook producers and consumers and Evaluation and criticism of textbooks, preceded by introductions that provide an overview of the topics. Most of the citations were published 1975–87, but selected items from earlier years are included if they "made a lasting contribution to our knowledge of the area."—*Introd.* Subject and author indexes. Z5817.W64

Periodicals

Collins, Mary Ellen. Education journals and serials : an analytical guide. N.Y. : Greenwood, 1988. 355 p. ISBN 0-313-24514-2. **CB43**

Intended for professionals submitting manuscripts for publication or librarians developing collections. Attempts comprehensive coverage of journals in English, omitting only periodicals of marginal quality or limited interest. Includes newsletters, state and regional publications, and some titles from related disciplines. The 803 entries provide publishers' addresses and information on subscription costs, number of subscribers, availability of reprints, microform editions, coverage by print indexes and databases, target audiences, and type of manuscript selection (e.g., whether refereed, etc.). Most include descriptive, evaluative, or comparative annotations. In 39 chapters, most treating publications for specific education levels, curricular areas or topical areas (e.g., educational administration). Publisher, title, geographical, and subject indexes. Z5813.C64

Loke, Wing Hong. A guide to journals in psychology and education. Metuchen, N.J. : Scarecrow, 1990. 410 p. ISBN 0-8108-2327-6. **CB44**

Intended for prospective contributors. Describes 356 journals, arranged alphabetically by title, in structured format that gives for each title its focus, content, publisher, readership, circulation, cost, organizational affiliation, guidelines and prescribed style, preferred article length, and procedures for submission of manuscripts. Indexes of titles, editors, and publishers. BF76.8.L65

Indexes and abstracts

Business education index. 1940– . [Little Rock, Ark.] : Delta Pi Epsilon Fraternity, [1940]– . Annual. ISSN 0068-4414. **CB45**

Indexes approximately 50 journals, 2 yearbooks, the proceedings of Delta Pi Epsilon, dissertations, and other works. Covers the broad spectrum of business education, "with an emphasis on information systems (including business communications), business teacher education, and vocational education (primarily marketing education)."—*Editorial policy.* In two parts, an alphabetical author index and a topical subject index, both providing complete citations. The latter is preceded by an alphabetical table of topics and subtopics. Z5814.C7B85

Contents pages in education. v. 1, no. 1 (July 1986)– . [Abingdon, Oxfordshire] : Carfax Pub. Co., 1986– . Monthly. ISSN 0265-9220. **CB46**

Reprints the tables of contents of more than 600 journals, each monthly issue treating approximately 175 journals. Monthly issues also contain author and subject indexes and lists of journals cited in that issue and during the year. Cumulative indexes appear in the June and December issues and triennially. Z5813.C66

Current index to journals in education : CIJE : cumulated author index, 1969–1984 / ERIC. Phoenix : Oryx, 1985. 2218 p. ISBN 0-89774-235-4. **CB47**

A cumulated author index to all entries of the first 16 years of *Current index to journals in education [CIJE]* (*Guide* CB130). Like the author indexes of *CIJE*'s monthly issues, provides only titles and entry numbers. Z5813.C9364C8

●**Education index** [computer file]. Bronx, N.Y. : H.W. Wilson, 1983– . **CB48**

Machine-readable version of *Education index* (*Guide* CB131).

File size: 205,000 records. Available online (WILSONLINE, updated twice weekly), in CD-ROM (Wilson, updated quarterly), and on magnetic tape (Wilson).

Educational administration abstracts. v. 1 (Spring 1966)– . [College Station, Tex., etc. : Univ. Council for Educational Administration], 1966– . Quarterly, Jan. 1983–. ISSN 0013-1601. **CB49**

Frequency varies: 1966–82, three numbers per year; 1983– , quarterly. Publisher varies.

Abstracts 1,000 works per year, including books, articles from 120 journals, and other materials. International in scope; organized by broad subject areas (e.g., Administrative structure and processes, Curriculum), subdivided for areas such as Personnel selection and Administrative roles. Quarterly author and subject indexes cumulate annually. LB2805.E32

Educational technology abstracts. v. 1, no. 1– . [Abington, England] : Carfax Pub. Co., c1985– . ISSN 0266-3368. **CB50**

Frequency varies: v. 1–4 (1985–88), quarterly; v. 5 (1989)– , bimonthly.

Annually provides more than 600 signed abstracts (recent years have about 950) without evaluation, of books, book chapters, and articles drawn from 250 journals. Has six topical subdivisions: Design and planning, Teaching methods, Instructional media, Instructional resources, Learning, and Assessment and evaluation. Bimonthly author and subject indexes cumulate annually.

Educational Testing Service. Index to ETS research report series, 1948–1989 [microform]. 8th ed. Princeton, N.J. : ETS Archives, Educational Testing Service, 1990. [16] microfiches : negative. **CB51**

On t.p. of accompanying guide: *Index to ETS research report series and related publications, 1948–1989* / ed. by Gary D. Saretzky.

Provides access to 3,856 Educational Testing Service research studies and related publications. Four sets of microfiche cite documents by report number, author, title, and subject. Most entries contain abstracts. Includes a guide to the use of the

microfiche sets that tells how to obtain copies of the reports.
LB3051.E25I54

●**ERIC** [computer file]. Rockville, Md. : U.S. Dept. of Education, Educational Resources Information Center. **CB52**

Machine-readable version of *Resources in education* (*Guide* CB133) and *Current index to journals in education* (*Guide* CB130).

File size: 665,800 records. Available online (BRS, DIALOG, OCLC, EPIC, ORBIT, updated monthly); in CD-ROM (DIALOG OnDisc, 1966– , updated quarterly; OCLC as *ERIC retrospective files*, 1976–81; SilverPlatter as *ERIC on SilverPlatter*, 1966– , updated quarterly); and on magnetic tape (producer).

ERIC RIE cumulative index [microform]. 1968– . Springfield, Va. : Cincinnati Bell Information Systems. Annual. **CB53**

Publisher varies: through 1989, Alexandria, Va. : Computer Microfilm Corp.; 1990– , Springfield, Va. : Cincinnati Bell Information Systems.

Eye-legible headers read: *ERIC RIE cumulative [subject, author] index*, followed by inclusive date.

Cumulates in one source all indexing for *Resources in education* and its predecessor, *Research in education* (*Guide* CB132–133) from its inception in 1966. 6 indexes: (1) author, (2) title, (3) subject, (4) institution, (5) descriptor report, and (6) identifier report.

●**Exceptional child education abstracts** [computer file]. Reston, Va. : Council for Exceptional Children. **CB54**

Machine-readable version of *Exceptional child education resources* (below) and its predecessor *Exceptional child education abstracts* (v. 1–8, Apr. 1969–Winter 1977) (*Guide* CB63).

File size: 60,000 records. Updated monthly. Available online (BRS, DIALOG).

Contains citations with abstracts to published and unpublished literature on educationally handicapped and gifted children. Includes physical, mental, emotional, and learning disabilities. Emphasizes U.S. literature. Includes relevant citations from *Resources in education* (*Guide* CB133) and *Current index to journals in education* (*Guide* CB130).

Exceptional child education resources. v. 9 (Spring 1977)– . Reston, Va. : Council for Exceptional Children, 1977–78– . Quarterly. ISSN 0160-4309. $65.00. **CB55**

Continues *Exceptional child education abstracts*, v. 1–8 (Apr. 1969–Winter 1977) (*Guide* CB63).

Cites books, dissertations, ERIC microfiche, and more than 200 journals, abstracting all but the dissertations. Organized in two sections, Books and articles and Dissertations, with entries arranged numerically as they are entered into the database. Most entries also appear in the ERIC indexes, *Resources in education* (*Guide* CB133) and *Current index to journals in education* (*Guide* CB130). Author, title, and subject indexes. The indexes of the year's final issue are cumulative for the volume.
Z5814.C52E9

Higher education abstracts. v. 20, no. 1 (Fall 1984)– . Claremont, Calif. : Claremont Graduate School, c1984– . Quarterly. ISSN 0748-4364. $70.00 (institutions). **CB56**

Indexes about 150 journals and proceedings of many national conferences in higher education. Quarterly issues contain, besides author and subject indexes, sections on students, faculty, administration, and similar topics; the indexes cumulate in the fourth issue of each volume. With v. 20, supersedes *College student personnel abstracts* (v. 1–19, Oct. 1965–Summer 1984), which began as an abstracting journal focused on college student development and behavior. With the title

change, the scope has been broadened to include all issues relating to higher education.
Z5814.P8C66

Multicultural education abstracts. v. 1, no. 1– . [Abingdon, England] : Carfax Pub. Co., 1982– . Quarterly. ISSN 0260-9770. **CB57**

Each issue presents about 100 abstracts that are descriptive rather than evaluative of books, articles drawn from 400 journals, and materials not always easy to locate (e.g., conference reports, theses) on a broad range of topics. International in scope, with abstracts of books and journal articles in separate sections (the former including chapters). Quarterly author and subject indexes, cumulating annually. Most titles abstracted are available in a microfiche collection, *C O R E (Collected original resources in education*; Abingdon, England : Carfax, 1977–).

Reading abstracts. v. 1 (Apr. 1975)– . [La Jolla, Calif. : Essay Pr., 1974]– . Semi-annual. ISSN 0361-6118. $20.00. **CB58**

Indexes and abstracts 4,000 journal articles per year. Arranged by subject, subdivided into narrower topics. International in scope. Author, subject, and source publication indexes.
LB1050.R352

Encyclopedias

Concise encyclopedia of special education / ed., Cecil R. Reynolds, Elaine Fletcher-Janzen. N.Y. : Wiley, c1990. 1215 p. : ill. ISBN 0-471-51527-2. **CB59**

Essentially a condensation of Reynolds and Lester Mann's three-volume *Encyclopedia of special education* (below), intended to provide professionals and parents with a less expensive and less bulky desk book. Some 90% of the parent work's articles have been condensed and streamlined, others have been updated or completely rewritten, and new articles have been added. Nearly all entries on living persons have been deleted. Articles are alphabetically arranged and typically vary from a paragraph to two pages in length, followed by brief bibliographies and cross-references. General index. LC4007.E53

The encyclopaedia of educational media communications and technology / ed. by Derick Unwin and Ray McAleese. 2nd ed. N.Y. : Greenwood, 1988. 568 p. : ill. ISBN 0-313-23996-7. **CB60**

1st ed., 1978 (*Guide* CB144).

To stay current with extensive changes in the field (e.g., the growth of microcomputer applications), the editors have thoroughly updated the earlier edition, rewriting all substantial articles, adding 34 major new entries, and increasing short entries from 900 to 1,800 (despite the deletion of virtually all statistical definitions), and adding a subject index of 400 terms.
LB1042.5.E52

Encyclopedia of school administration & supervision / ed. by Richard A. Gorton, Gail T. Schneider, James C. Fisher. Phoenix : Oryx, 1988. 321 p. ISBN 0-89774-232-X. $74.50. **CB61**

Contains nearly 300 articles written by more than 200 specialists. Entries are arranged alphabetically and are short, typically one page, followed by bibliographies of three citations. A "Guide to related topics" groups article titles under such broad rubrics as School facilities, Community-school relations, and Curriculum areas and issues. In addition, each article contains three or four cross-references. A subject index also includes cross-references.
LB2805.E53

Encyclopedia of special education : a reference for the education of the handicapped and other exceptional children and adults / editors, Cecil R. Reynolds, Lester

Mann. N.Y.: Wiley, c1987. 3 v.: ill. ISBN 0-471-82858-0. $250.00. **CB62**

Articles by more than 400 experts on some 2,000 topics. Entries describe handicapping conditions, intervention and service delivery, educational and psychological tests, prominent workers in the field, laws and legislation, etc. Cross-references; name and subject indexes. Intended for intelligent general readers as well as professionals. A condensation, *Concise encyclopedia of special education* (above) is a less expensive, updated one-volume desk version for professionals and parents.

LC4007.E53

The international encyclopedia of education : research and studies / editors in chief, Torsten Husén, T. Neville Postlethwaite. Oxford ; N.Y.: Pergamon, 1985. 10 v.: ill. ISBN 0-08-028119-2 (set). $1750.00. **CB63**

For basic set, see *Guide* CB151.

Several titles published by Pergamon are based on articles extracted from the *Encyclopedia*, to which new articles have been added. Included are: *The international encyclopedia of teaching and teacher education*, ed. by Michael J. Dunkin (1987. 878 p. $75.00); *Economics of education : research and studies*, ed. by George Psacharopoulos (1987. 482 p. $60.00 est.); *Educational research, methodology, and measurement : an international handbook*, ed. by John P. Keeves (1988. 832 p. $125.00 est.); *The encyclopedia of comparative education and national systems of education*, ed. by T. Neville Postlethwaite (1988. 777 p. $95.00); *Lifelong education for adults : an international handbook*, ed. by Colin J. Titmus (1989. 590 p. $115.00 est.); *The international encyclopedia of educational technology* ed. by Michael Eraut (1989. 654 p. $105.00 est.); *The encyclopedia of human development and education : theory, research, and studies*, ed. by R. Murray Thomas (1989. 519 p. $110.00); *The international encyclopedia of educational evaluation*, ed. by Herbert J. Walberg and Geneva D. Haertel (1990. 796 p. $95.00 est.); *The foundations of students' learning*, ed. by Kevin Marjoribanks (1991. 349 p. $64.00); *The international encyclopedia of curriculum*, ed. by Arieh Lewy (1991. 1064 p. $150.00).

LB15.I569

The international encyclopedia of education : research and studies. Supplementary volume / editors in chief, Torsten Husén, T. Neville Postlethwaite. Oxford ; N.Y.: Pergamon, 1989– . v. 1– . ISBN 0-08-034974-9 (v. 1). $195.00. **CB64**

A planned series of periodic updates, each supplementary volume containing articles (Suppl. v. 1 contains 179) by experts charged to revise portions that "either needed expansion from the parent work or in which major new research or information was available."—*Pref.* Cross-references, both within the supplements and to articles in the basic set, are extensive. Name, subject, and contributor indexes. LB15.I569

International higher education : an encyclopedia / ed. by Philip G. Altbach. N.Y.: Garland, 1990. 2 v. (Garland reference library of social science, v. 506). ISBN 0-8240-4847-4. **CB65**

Presents 67 chapters by specialists, the first 16 devoted to timely topics in higher education today (e.g., women, strategic development, costs, academic freedom). The remainder focus on countries or regions, including the U.S. and Canada. Vol. 2 includes tables and charts, short bibliographies with each chapter, a list of contributors, and topic/name and country/region indexes. LB15.I59

Dictionaries

Barrow, Robin. A critical dictionary of educational concepts : an appraisal of selected ideas and issues in educational theory and practice / Robin Barrow, Geoffrey Milburn. 2nd ed. N.Y.: Teachers College Pr., Teachers College, Columbia Univ., 1990. 370 p. ISBN 0-8077-3058-0. **CB66**

Unlike dictionaries designed to be exhaustive or free of specific points of view, this work selects entries by "what we think important... so as to constitute a dictionary of ideas worth contemplating and examining... to explore and make sense of conflicting and sometimes confused or obscure ideas."—*Pref.* Contains 160 entries, typically one-half to three pages long, usually with references. Words in the text that have their own entries are printed in boldface; cross-references.

LB15.B29

A dictionary of reading and related terms / Theodore L. Harris and Richard E. Hodges, coeditors. Newark, Del. : International Reading Association, c1981. 382 p. : ill. ISBN 0-87207-944-9 (pbk.). $18.00. **CB67**

Defines a 5,400-term specialized vocabulary of reading instruction. Terms were drawn from scholarly and technical journals, specialized dictionaries, and glossaries. Some multiple definition entries are preceded by brief introductory essays. Appendix of equivalents for ambiguous or controversial English words as they are translated into French, Spanish, German, Danish, and Swedish. LB1049.98.D53

Ellington, Henry. Dictionary of instructional technology / comp. by Henry Ellington and Duncan Harris. London: Kogan Page ; N.Y.: Nichols Pub. Co., 1986. 189 p. : ill. ISBN 0-89397-243-6. $32.50. **CB68**

Defines 2,800 terms drawn from instructional technology, and from fields that "impinge upon or overlap" (*Introd.*) with it. Includes British and U.S. terms and those used in other English-speaking countries. Many clear, simple diagrams.

LB15.E42

Glossary of educational technology terms = Glosario de términos de tecnologia de la educación. Paris : UNESCO, c1986. 243 p. ISBN 9-23002-436-8 (pbk.). **CB69**

"Prepared by the Methods, Materials, and Techniques of Education Section, Unesco, for the International Bureau of Education."—*t.p.* LB15.G555

Glossary of educational technology terms = Glossaire des termes de technologie éducative. 2nd ed., rev. and enl. Paris : UNESCO, 1987. 263 p. ISBN 9-23002-517-8. **CB70**

1st ed., 1984. LB15.G555

Glossary of educational technology terms = Glossariĭ terminov po tekhnologii obrazovaniĩa. Paris : UNESCO, 1986. 239 p. ISBN 9-23002-437-6 (pbk.). **CB71**

"Prepared ... for the International Bureau of Education."—*t.p.*

Published in three versions, English/Spanish, English/French, English/Russian, each listing some 1,650 terms in two glossaries, one for each language, giving equivalent or correlative terms in the other. LB15.G555

A glossary of special education / ed. by Phillip Williams. Milton Keynes, England ; Philadelphia : Open Univ. Pr., 1988. 222 p. : ill. ISBN 0-335-15996-6. **CB72**

Attempts to provide "reasonably simple explanations of terms ... for teachers and parents ... and also for administrators. But it is not intended to offer detailed explanations for

219

experts."—*Introd.* British emphasis. Diagrams and photographs.   LC3986.G7

Gordon, Peter. A guide to English educational terms / Peter Gordon & Denis Lawton. N.Y. : Schocken Books, 1984. 220 p. ISBN 0-8052-3922-7.   **CB73**

A glossary of English education terms, intended to make the educational system of England (and Wales) "more comprehensible to students . . . some from overseas."—*Introd.* Some entries give historical background or bibliographic references. Contains an introduction to education in England and Wales and appendixes that include a list of acronyms, a short bibliography, and a list of Ministers of Education.   LB15.G62

Kelly, Leo J. Dictionary of special education and rehabilitation / Leo J. Kelly [and] Glenn A. Vergason. 2nd ed. Denver, Colo. : Love, 1985. 207 p. ISBN 0-89108-168-2.   **CB74**

Intended not as an "authoritative, exhaustive resource," but as "an understandable explanation of the terminology most commonly used . . . ."—*p. 1.* Contains 2,500 short definitions, typically of two to four lines, with phonetic pronunciations. Appendixes include lists of associations, periodicals in English, and sources of legal assistance. Cross-references.

LC3957.K445

Palmer, James C. Dictionary of educational acronyms, abbreviations, and initialisms / comp. and ed. by James C. Palmer and Anita Y. Colby ; ERIC Clearinghouse for Junior Colleges. 2nd ed. Phoenix : Oryx, 1985. 97 p. ISBN 0-89774-165-X (pbk.). $27.50.   **CB75**

1st ed., 1982 (*Guide* CB158)

This edition adds 1,995 entries, increasing its usefulness in a field that is prey to proliferating acronyms.   LB15.P35

Shafritz, Jay M. The Facts on File dictionary of education / Jay M. Shafritz, Richard P. Koeppe, Elizabeth W. Soper. N.Y. : Facts on File, c1988. 503 p. ISBN 0-8160-1636-4. $40.00.   **CB76**

Entries are of two basic types: "brief glossary descriptions," and "those that are given more comprehensive coverage, occasionally in the form of authors' comments and interpretations."—*Pref.* Besides entries that define terms, concepts, and practices, some identify individuals, court cases, publications, laws, organizations, and tests.   LB15.S43

Quotations

Dale, Edgar. The educator's quotebook. Bloomington, Ind. : Phi Delta Kappa Educational Foundation, c1984. 107 p. ISBN 0-87367-429-4 (pbk.).   **CB77**

Quotations are arranged under 51 alphabetical topics (e.g., Teaching, Potential, Democracy) two to 50 quotations per topic. No index or thesaurus, but a table of contents lists the 51 topics.   PN6081.D23

A teacher's treasury of quotations / comp. by Bernard E. Farber. Jefferson, N.C. : McFarland, c1985. 370 p. ISBN 0-89950-150-8. $39.95.   **CB78**

Arranged alphabetically by topic, the quotations represent many countries, cultures, and periods and portray differing points of view. Author and subject indexes.   PN6081.T4

Directories

Compton, Carolyn. A guide to 85 tests for special education. New ed. Belmont, Calif. : Fearon Education, c1990. 336 p. : ill. ISBN 0-8224-3585-3.   **CB79**

Prior eds.: *Guide to 65 tests for special education*, 1980; *Guide to 75 tests for special education*, 1984.

Describes psychological and educational tests used to assess students enrolled in or being considered for special education programs. Arranged by type of test in six sections: (1) Academic; (2) Perceptual, memory, and visual-motor skills; (3) Speech and language; (4) Bilingual (Spanish-English) language; (5) Gross and fine motor skills; (6) General intelligence tests and developmental scales. Entries describe test purpose, major areas tested, age or grade range, scoring, time involved, format, subtests, strengths, and limiting factors. Appendixes include: a glossary of testing terms and lists of tests for academic skills, cognitive processes, and reading, and of tests for preschool children. No index, but an alphabetical list of all 85 tests follows the table of contents.   LB1131.C5416

International

Academic year abroad. 15th ed. (1986–87)– . N.Y. : Institute of International Education, c1986– . Annual. ISSN 0893-0481.   **CB80**

Continues *The learning traveler* : v. 1, *U.S. college-sponsored programs abroad* (*Guide* CB199).

Its predecessor included only programs sponsored by American colleges and universities. *Academic year abroad* also describes programs offered by foreign universities, language schools, and other U.S. and foreign organizations.

LB2376.U46

Directory of educational documentation and information services = Répertoire des services de documentation et d'information pédagogiques. 5th ed. Paris : UNESCO, 1988.   **CB81**

1st ed., 1975; 4th ed., 1982.

Has separate sections for national, regional (e.g., Arab countries), and international agencies. Entries are arranged alphabetically within sections and list address, type of activities, population served, services given, collection size, publications, studies conducted, etc. Separate section gives addresses of member institutions of the International Bureau of Education. New with this edition is a section listing databases by country, with entries outlining the scope, timespan, size, etc., of each. Available in English, French, or Spanish versions.

LB1028.D484

Directory of educational research institutions = Répertoire des institutions de recherche en éducation / prepared by the International Bureau of Education. 2nd ed. Paris : UNESCO, 1986. 428 p. ISBN 9-23002-405-8 (pbk.).   **CB82**

Designed to facilitate direct contact with these organizations for researchers, administrators, and teacher trainers wanting to obtain documents which are not commercially available or are not yet published. Arranged in sections of national, regional (e.g., Latin America), and international institutions. Entries may be in English, French, or Spanish, and introductory material, directions for use, and indexes are in all three languages. Entries for institutions include address, year of creation, parent organization, staff size, type and functional objectives of research, monographic and periodical publications, study names, and surveys in preparation. A keyword index gives only entry numbers.   LB1028.D54

European faculty directory. 1st ed. (1991)– . London : Gale Research International, 1991– . Annual. ISSN 1053-640X.   **CB83**

A listing of approximately 300,000 faculty in nearly 1,400 institutions of postsecondary education in Europe. Information based on mailing lists from IBIS Information Services. Vol.1 contains a geographical arrangement of the colleges and universities and an alphabetical list of faculty with addresses; v.2 arranges faculty according to 96 academic disciplines.

L914.5.E95

International yearbook of educational and training technology / Association for Educational and Training Technology. 1976– . London : Kogan Page, [c1989]– . Annual.   **CB84**

Title varies: 1976–88, called *International yearbook of educational technology.*

A directory of centers for instructional technology, including universities, associations, foundations, research organizations consortia, etc. In four parts arranged by location: (1) international and regional (e.g., Middle East); (2) United Kingdom, (3) U.S. (arranged by state), and (4) other countries (by country). Entries give addresses and list areas of interest, services, publications, and related information. Includes institutional index and "Keyword Index," which lists subjects of interest (e.g., evaluation, interactive video) and refers to entries for organizations.

Vacation study abroad. 38th ed. (1988)– . N.Y. : Institute of International Education, c1987– . Annual. ISSN 1046-2104.   **CB85**

For earlier volumes and annotation, see *Guide* CB200.

Vol. 2 of the "Learning traveler" series.

Recent editions have added a "Worldwide" chapter describing programs operating in more than one world region. Added to other sections have been "More than one country" and "More than one city" listings.   LB2375.S8

Work, study, travel abroad : the whole world handbook. N.Y. : St. Martin's, 1972– . Biennial. $10.95.   **CB86**

1st–9th eds.(1972–1988) ed. by Marjorie Adoff Cohen; 10th– ed. by Del Franz. Published for the Council on International Educational Exchange.

Early eds. also have title *Whole world handbook.*

Provides introductory sections of general advice, followed by chapters on 11 regions of the world, including discussions of individual countries and brief descriptions of specific work, study, and travel programs. Beginning with the 10th ed. (1990), also includes comments by travelers. An appendix lists addresses of organizations offering high school programs. General index.   LB2376.W48

World list of universities = Liste mondiale des universités / International Association of Universities. 18th ed. N.Y. : Stockton Pr., 1990. 706 p. ISBN 0-935859-86-1.   **CB87**

Biennial issues are typically in two parts: (1) a list, alphabetical by country, of universities and other institutions of higher education, including, for some countries, national academic and student associations; (2) "international and regional organizations concerned with higher education."—*Explanatory note.* Appendixes include lists of contents for both sections, but there is no index. The 18th edition provides for the first time telephone, telefax, telex, and cable information. Explanatory text is in English and French. For universities, there are abbreviated lists of curricular and professional offerings, but the brevity of entries makes this primarily an address book.   LA225.W927

United States

Christo, Doris H. National directory of education libraries and collections. Westport, Conn. : Meckler, c1990. 269 p. ISBN 0-88736-621-X. $95.00.   **CB88**

An alphabetical listing by state and city. Entries include information on size and scope of holdings, special collections, personnel, and budget. A personal name list indicates title and institutional affiliation of staff members. Index includes library names, parent institutions, subject specializations, and names of special collections.   Z675.P3C48

Directory of ERIC information service providers / prepared by the Educational Resources Information Center (ERIC), ERIC Processing and Reference Facility. June 1986– . [Bethesda, Md.] : ERIC Processing and Reference Facility, 1986– .   **CB89**

Formed by merger of *Directory of ERIC microfiche collections,* which ceased 1983, and *Directory of ERIC search services,* which ceased 1981, both publ. Wash. : National Institute of Education, U.S. Dept. of Education.

Superintendent of Documents classification: ED 1.30/2:Ed 8/.

Lists more than 900 organizations that provide access to ERIC databases and related sources, including computerized searches, collections of ERIC microfiche, or collections of ERIC publications. Arranged geographically, with entries providing addresses and information on ERIC products held; copying, reading and computing equipment; and services (online searches, reproduction of fiche, etc.). Index of organizations.

LB1028.27.U6D57

Directory of state education agencies. 1982/1983– . [Wash.] : Council [of] Chief State School Officers, [1983]– . Annual. ISSN 0897-4462.   **CB90**

7th ed. (1988–89) provides information for states and possessions of the U.S., including: addresses of state education agencies, forms of school governance, addresses and telephone numbers of education associations and organizations, names and telephone numbers of officers of the Council of Chief State School Officers and coordinators of state projects sponsored by the Council, and national and regional officers of the U.S. Dept. of Education.

Guide to international education in the United States. 2nd ed– . Detroit : Gale, c1991– . Biennial. ISSN 1052-9586. $110.00.   **CB91**

1st ed., 1984 (*Guide* CB196) had title: *Global guide to international education.*

Contains twice as many entries (3,800) as the 1st ed. Three indexes found in the 1st ed. have been consolidated into a single subject and keyword index.

General

●**Educational directory online** : (EDOL) [computer file]. Shelton, Conn. : Market Data Retrieval, Inc.   **CB92**

Coverage: current. File size: 140,000 records. Updated semiannually. Available online (DIALOG) and on magnetic tape and in batch access (producer).

Contains information about U.S. educational institutions, including schools, school districts and dioceses, state departments of education, public libraries (main branches), and colleges and universities. Each record includes institution name, address, and telephone number; names of administrators; enrollment and budget data; and special facilities and services.

Higher education

A classification of institutions of higher education. 1987 ed. Princeton, N.J. : Carnegie Foundation for the Advancement of Teaching, c1987. 148 p. ISBN 0-931050-26-X (pbk.).   **CB93**

1st ed., 1973; rev. ed., 1976.

Classes 3,388 institutions and 128 central offices in one of ten categories: Research institutions I or II; Doctorate granting universities I or II; Comprehensive universities I or II; Liberal arts colleges I or II; Two-year community, junior, or technical colleges; and Professional schools or other specialized institutions. Criteria for categorization include range of baccalaureate and graduate programs, priority given to research, amount of federal support received, number of Ph.D.'s awarded, enrollment, and degree of selectivity. The first part lists colleges by classification and gives their average enrollment, the second lists them alphabetically and gives their classifications.   LA227.3.C5

The college price book. 1990– . Falls Church, Va. : Higher Education Publications, 1990– . Annual. **CB94**

Cover subtitle: *How to find an affordable college.*

Provides quick, factual guidance for initial selection of a college or university. Contains information on degree programs arranged by broad subject areas, locations, and costs, sizes of program and college, financial aid, and freshman academic achievement levels.   LB2342.C65

Directory of economic development programs at state colleges and universities. Wash. : American Association of State Colleges and Universities ; Lanham, Md. : Distr. by arrangement with Univ. Pub., 1989. 182 p. ISBN 0-88044-095-3. ISBN 0-88044-094-5 (pbk.).   **CB95**

Program entries provide description, structure, and contact person. Indexed by scope and audience, primary objective, and state and institution.   LC1085.2.D57

Directory of master's programs in foreign languages, foreign literatures, and linguistics. N.Y. : Modern Language Association of America, c1987. 173 p. ISBN 0-87352-169-2 (pbk.).   **CB96**

Lists locations, degrees offered, requirements, and special offerings of 538 programs. Arranged alphabetically, with program, geographic, and special program indexes.   PB38.U6D57

The . . . GIS guide to four-year colleges / by the editors of the Guidance Information System. 1988– . Boston : Educational Software Division/Trade and Reference Division, Houghton Mifflin Co., 1988– .   **CB97**

Based on the Guidance Information System (GIS) and a questionnaire which allows students to focus on college choice in six categories: setting, size, student body, type, cost, selectivity. The major section is an alphabetical list of college profiles including "complete data on each school as well as information on its setting, selectivity, admissions requirements, programs of study, and campus life."—*p.ix.* There is also a major directory of colleges arranged by baccalaureate degree programs.   L901.G5

Guide to American graduate schools. 6th ed., completely rev. N.Y. : Penguin Books, c1990. 1 v.   **CB98**

4th ed., 1982 (*Guide* CB227).

Ed. by Harold Doughty.

This edition contains descriptions of more than 1,100 institutions, all "surveyed once again for this sixth edition."—*Pref.*   L901.G834

A guide to graduate study in political science. 1972– . Wash. : American Political Science Association, 1972– . ISSN 0091-9632. $2.50.   **CB99**

Lists colleges and universities in the U.S. and Canada granting graduate degrees in political science, with descriptions of their masters and doctoral programs. Alphabetical by institution (in two groups—U.S., then Canada), each entry provides address, telephone number, tuition costs, application deadlines, requirements for admission and degrees, program description, and faculty list. A separate section provides a statistical summary for each institution (e.g., number of students admitted, women students, black students). Faculty and institution indexes.   JA88.U6G8

The index of majors. 1979/80– . N.Y. : College Entrance Examination Board. Annual. ISSN 0192-3242.   **CB100**

An extensive listing of undergraduate and graduate degree programs, listing approximately 3,000 colleges and universities in an alphabetical arrangement of more than 500 fields of study. Glossary of special types of programs. Lists of 17 types of special academic programs arranged by state and of colleges by state and by program level.   L901.C744

Lederman, Ellen. College majors : a complete guide from accounting to zoology. Jefferson, N.C. : McFarland, c1990. 122 p. ISBN 0-89950-462-0.   **CB101**

Describes college-level majors based on the Taxonomy and Classification of Instructional Programs in Higher Education of the Higher Education General Information Survey. Each major includes definition, degree levels offered, typical courses, related or complementary majors, needed abilities, and career possibilities.   LB2390.L43

Ohles, John F. Public colleges and universities / John F. Ohles and Shirley M. Ohles. N.Y. : Greenwood, c1986. 1014 p. (The Greenwood encyclopedia of American institutions , 9). ISBN 0-313-23257-1. $95.00.   **CB102**

A companion to the compilers' *Private colleges and universities* (*Guide* CB237). Provides sketches of 547 public colleges and universities and 31 state systems of higher education, based on information gleaned from a survey. Alphabetical arrangement by institution with cross-references. References follow each entry. Appendixes: Years founded, Location by states, Land-grant institutions, Specialized institutions. Indexes of personal and institutional names.   L901.O333

●**Peterson's college database** [computer file]. Princeton, N.J. : Peterson's Guides.   **CB103**

Machine-readable version of *Peterson's guide to four-year colleges* (19th ed.– , 1988–) and *Peterson's guide to two-year colleges* (19th ed.– , 1988–); for earlier title, *Peterson's annual guides to undergraduate study : guide to four-year colleges*, see *Guide* CB239.

Coverage: current. File size: 3,350 records. Updated annually. Available online (BRS, CompuServe, DIALOG, Dow Jones News/Retrieval) and in CD-ROM (SilverPlatter, Faxon).

Peterson's drug and alcohol programs and policies at four-year colleges / Janet Carney Schneider and Bunny Porter-Shirley, editors. Princeton, N.J. : Peterson's Guides, c1989. 445 p. : ill. ISBN 0-87866-731-8. $19.95.   **CB104**

Presents the results of the first national survey of responses to drug and alcohol use among accredited U.S. four-year colleges, 1988–89. Entries for 900 responding colleges are listed alphabetically in "Profiles of the colleges," giving for each: problem identification, support services, disciplinary action, contact person. Includes a comparative table of alcohol regulation. Appendixes include standards established by colleges attempting to eliminate drug and alcohol abuse and a list of organizations concerned with drugs and alcohol on campus.   HV5128.U5P48

●**Peterson's gradline** [computer file]. Princeton, N.J. : Peterson's Guides, 1990– .   **CB105**

Machine-readable version of *Peterson's annual guides to graduate study* (*Guide* CB238).

Covers current year's data (1,400 institutions, 26,000 graduate and professional programs); updated annually. Available online (DIALOG).

Peterson's guide to certificate programs at American colleges and universities / editors, George J. Lopos... [et al.]. Princeton, N.J.: Peterson's Guides, c1988. 343 p. ISBN 0-87866-741-5. $35.95. **CB106**

"The first comprehensive directory of certificate programs offered by the nation's four-year institutions of higher education."—*Foreword*. Arranged alphabetically by state, giving for each entry: contact personnel, costs, program, and enrollment requirements. L901.P4577

Peterson's national college databank : the college book of lists. 5th ed. Princeton, N.J.: Peterson's Guides, c1990. 1 v. ISBN 1-56079-020-2. $19.95. **CB107**

1st ed., 1979.

Provides numerous lists of colleges by a variety of parameters within 10 broad sections; for example, the section on campus life lists colleges with coed housing, with fraternities and sororities, with legal services for students, and with dress codes. Other sections are: general characteristics, enrollment, academics, admissions, entrance difficulty, expenses, financial aid, athletics, and unusual majors. Only college names and locations by state are given. The appendix provides a geographical list (by state) of colleges offering work opportunities to undergraduates. L901.N295

Rugg, Frederick E. Rugg's recommendations on the colleges. 8th ed., 1990–91. Sarasota, Fla.: Rugg's Recommendations. Annual. **CB108**

1st ed., 1980; 6th ed, 1989.

Lists recommended undergraduate programs (from a study of 600 colleges) for 39 fields of study. For each, colleges are listed with ratings ("most selective," "very selective," or "selective") and enrollment sizes. Colleges with programs in unusual categories (e.g., equestrian studies, Japanese studies) are listed in a "Miscellaneous majors" section. Concludes with a list of Average Scholastic Aptitude Test (SAT) scores (combined verbal and math) reported by colleges cited in the recommended programs section, listed alphabetically by college. Six appendixes list and categorize the colleges and provide planning aids (e.g., timetables, checklists).

Elementary and secondary education

The *Harvard independent* insider's guide to prep schools / ed. by Christopher J. Georges and James A. Messina, with members of the staff of the *Harvard Independent*. N.Y.: New American Library, c1987. 453 p. ISBN 0-452-25920-7 (pbk.). $9.95. **CB109**

Describes not so much the best schools as those with "interesting" programs where current Harvard undergraduates attended, some of whom either wrote school descriptions or provided information. The main body consists of two-page entries on 200 schools, most of them private, but a few public. Provides information on enrollment, selectivity, students' SAT scores, colleges attended by graduates, academic programs, social atmosphere, and dress code. Arrangement is alphabetical by state. Additional schools are briefly described in chapters on "Big preps," "New York preps," etc. There are also ranked listings of largest schools, most expensive and inexpensive institutions, highest and lowest student SAT scores, etc. Not indexed. L901.H364

Patterson's elementary education. v. 1 (1989)– . Mount Prospect, Ill.: Educational Directories Inc., c1989– . Annual. ISSN 1044-1417. **CB110**

Lists superintendents and addresses of public school districts, addresses of individual public elementary and middle (but not junior high) schools, and addresses of private and church-affiliated elementary and middle schools with as many

as 100 students. Similar in organization to *Patterson's American education* (*Guide* CB210), with arrangement by state, then community, then school type. Also lists officers of state education departments and boards. Appendixes give names and addresses of Catholic, Lutheran, and Adventist school district officials. L901.P33

Townsend, Kiliaen V. R. The boarding school guide: facts and figures on 231 leading schools throughout the United States. Athens, Ga.: Agee Publishers, c1989. 282 p.: maps. ISBN 0-935265-18-X. $16.50. **CB111**

An alphabetic listing of schools with more than 60 boarders, for each giving student data, costs and financial aid, admission requirements, academics, facilities, locale, etc. The volume begins with a geographic index, maps, and 27 tables that compare such variables as size of student body, foreign students, day students, and library size. L901.T69

Specialized education

Directory of college facilities and services for people with disabilities / ed. by Carol H. Thomas and James L. Thomas. 3rd ed. Phoenix: Oryx, 1991. 1 v. ISBN 0-89774-604-X. **CB112**

1st ed., 1983, called *Directory of college facilities and services for the handicapped* (*Guide* CB248).

This edition offers updated information for some 1,600 institutions in the U.S. and Canada. Also includes an alphabetical list of colleges and universities, an index of disabilities, and lists of organizations, clearinghouses and databases, printed sources, and grant programs. LC4812.6.D57

The Macmillan guide to correspondence study / comp. and ed. by Modoc Press, Inc. 3rd ed. N.Y.: Macmillan ; London: Collier Macmillan, c1988. 676 p. ISBN 0-02-921641-9. **CB113**

1st ed., 1983 (*Guide* CB235); 2nd ed., 1985.

Indicates subject areas available from accredited schools, courses offered, admission requirements and procedures, tuition and fees. Includes formal degree programs, professional noncredit courses, home-study programs, vocational programs, and computer-based programs. Comprehensive subject index to courses. L901.M26

The national guide to educational credit for training programs. Wash.: American Council on Education, [1980?]– . Irregular. ISSN 0275-4142. **CB114**

Intended to assist educational institutions in granting credit for courses offered by private industry and government agencies. Course entries are arranged alphabetically by the sponsoring organization and include location, length, dates, objective, learning outcomes, instruction outline, and credit recommendations. Appendixes: alphabetical list of evaluators and their institutional affiliations; index by subject to programs and sponsoring units.

Peterson's guide to colleges with programs for learning-disabled students / Charles T. Mangrum II and Stephen S. Strichart, editors. 2nd ed. Princeton, N.J.: Peterson's Guides, c1988. 398 p.: ill. ISBN 0-87866-689-3. $19.95. **CB115**

"... differentiates between colleges with specially designed programs for learning-disabled students and colleges that offer services that are available to LD students but that are not specifically designed for them."—*Foreword*. Includes two-year and four-year colleges in one alphabetical list of "Colleges with comprehensive programs." Contains a step-by-step guide to selecting a college for a learning-disabled student. Has a geographical index to listed colleges and a directory of organizations with additional information on programs and services for learning-disabled students. L901.P458

Spann, Milton G. The national directory of exemplary programs in developmental education / Milton G. Spann, Cynthia G. Thompson. Boone, N.C. : National Center for Developmental Education, Appalachian State Univ., c1986. 133 p.   **CB116**

Provides information concerning "165 programs in colleges and junior colleges which have reached a relatively mature level of operation and can serve as regional models and resources to . . . developing programs."—*Introd.* In five main lists: (1) exemplary parts of programs by state; (2) institutions having programs with specific kinds of exemplary components (e.g., counseling or tutoring); (3) names and addresses of the exemplary programs; (4) state information coordinators for developmental education and (5) samples of relevant legislation by state. No index.   LB1029.R4S55

Tests and measurements

The ETS Test Collection catalog / comp. by Test Collection, Educational Testing Service. Phoenix : Oryx, 1986–1991. v. 1–5. ISBN 0-89774-248-6 (v.1). $49.50. (In progress).   **CB117**

Contents: v. 1, Achievement tests and measurement devices; v. 2, Vocational tests and measurement devices; v. 3, Tests for special populations; v. 4, Cognitive aptitude and intelligence tests; v. 5, Attitude tests.

Describes the 16,250 tests and related instruments in the Educational Testing Service's collection. Includes research instruments that are hard to locate as well as commercially available standardized tests. Entries provide information on availability, source, age or grade level, subject descriptors or identifiers, and time required; abstracts treat the tests' uses and other characteristics. Arrangement is by ETS accession number, with author, title, and subject indexes.   LB3051.E79

●**ETS test collection** [computer file]. Princeton, N.J. : Educational Testing Service, 1950– .   **CB118**

File size: 9,000 records. Updated quarterly. Available online (BRS) and in batch access (producer).

Provides descriptions of standardized educational, aptitude, behavioral, and personality tests and evaluation instruments. Includes brief descriptions and information concerning availability.

Handbooks

Ambert, Alba N. Bilingual education : a sourcebook / Alba N. Ambert, Sarah E. Melendez. N.Y. : Garland, 1985. 340 p. ISBN 0-8240-9055-1.   **CB119**

Provides essays, a separate list of references, and an annotated bibliography for each of 11 chapters on the following aspects of bilingual education: (1) Program models; (2) Legal issues; (3) English as a second language; (4) Assessment; (5) Reading; (6) Bilingual special education; (7) Bilingual vocational education; (8) Program evaluation; (9) Parental involvement and participation; (10) Teachers and teacher training; and (11) Antibilingualism. Separate author and subject indexes and three appendixes: Curriculum materials resources—annotated bibliography; Organizations; and Journals list.   LC3731.A65

American Psychological Association. Standards for educational and psychological testing / American Educational Research Association, American Psychological Association, National Council on Measurement in Education. Wash. : American Psychological Association, c1985. 100 p. ISBN 0-912704-95-0 (pbk.).   **CB120**

For annotation, see *Supplement* EJ608.   LB3051.A693

Bilingual education and English as a second language : a research handbook, 1986–1987 / [ed. by] Alba N. Ambert. N.Y. : Garland, 1988. 457 p. (Garland reference library of social science, v. 464). ISBN 0-8240-6625-1.   **CB121**

Describes and analyzes 1986–87 research. Eleven chapters cover major areas such as assessment, legal issues, policy and program design, each written by an expert and containing a general analysis of the area, recommendations for future research, and an annotated bibliography. The latter list both 1986–87 and earlier citations, many of which also appear in the editor's *Bilingual education : a sourcebook* (above). Appendixes list multifunctional resource centers, organizations, information resources for professionals and students, and journals in the field. Author and subject indexes. A volume covering 1988–90 was published in 1991.   LC3731.B5467

Davis, William Edmund. Resource guide to special education : terms, laws, assessment procedures, organizations. 2nd ed. Boston : Allyn and Bacon, c1986. 317 p. ISBN 0-205-08546-6.   **CB122**

1st ed., 1980, had title: *Educator's resource guide to special education* (*Guide* CB137).

Features new to this edition include: a section explaining word roots, stems, prefixes, and suffixes used in special education; an extensive listing of computer terminology related to the field; substantially expanded treatment of terminology in other areas of special education; expanded and updated listing of organizations and agencies; expansion and updating of the section on legislation and litigation.   LC4007.D38

The education almanac / prepared and published by the National Association of Elementary School Principals. 1984–1987/88. Reston, Va. : NAESP, c1984–1987. ISSN 0747-5772. $20.00.   **CB123**

Cover title: Facts and figures about our nation's system of education.

Ceased publication with 1987/88 ed.

Ranges widely, presenting concisely statistics, historical background, a directory of organizations, descriptions of legislation and court cases, results of polls, descriptions of programs and innovations such as Head Start and Magnet Schools, excerpts from key documents, even jokes heard at education conventions. Neither as filled with statistics as *The teacher's almanac* (*Supplement* CB137) nor as systemically organized, but contains more on educational history and documents and on innovative programs.   LA210.E4375

Egelston, Roberta Riethmiller. Credits and careers for adult learners. Jefferson, N.C. : McFarland, c1985. 174 p. : forms. ISBN 0-89950-188-5 (pbk.). $19.95.   **CB124**

Suggests innovative programs for adults pursuing education beyond high school but outside the classroom. In two parts: (1) short chapters explaining nontraditional options for obtaining postsecondary credit, including descriptions of academic and vocational programs at selected institutions; (2) appendixes listing schools accepting high school equivalency or advanced placement examinations, plus institutions offering cooperative education programs or correspondence instruction. General index.   LC45.4.E34

Handbook of adult and continuing education / Sharan B. Merriam, Phyllis M. Cunningham, editors. San Francisco : Jossey-Bass Publishers, 1989. 718 p. ISBN 1-55542-161-X.   **CB125**

5th ed., 1970, had title *Handbook of adult education* (*Guide* CB166).

Unlike its predecessors, this edition is a review of the literature only and does not include directories or lists of information sources.   LC5215.H25

Handbook of educational ideas and practices / gen. ed., Noel Entwistle. London; N.Y.: Routledge, 1990. 1140 p.: ill. ISBN 0-415-02061-1. **CB126**

A summary of recent thinking, research findings, and innovative practices for practitioners. Not an encyclopedia; "rather, it samples a restricted number of topics and deals with them in more depth."—*Pref.* In four topical sections (Nature and function of education, Management and content of education, Learning environment, and Individual development) containing 101 chapters, most written by British experts with British orientations. Name and subject indexes. LB17.H267

Handbook of research on educational administration : a project of the American Educational Research Association / Norman J. Boyan, ed. N.Y.: Longman, c1988. 767 p. ISBN 0-582-28517-8. **CB127**

Summarizes 30 years of research. 33 chapters, each written by an expert, are arranged in five sections: The administrator; Organizations; Economics and finance; Politics and policy; and Special topics. Substantial bibliographies. Name and subject indexes. LB2805.H2864

Handbook of research on social studies teaching and learning / James P. Shaver, ed. N.Y.: Macmillan; Toronto: Collier Macmillan; N.Y.: Macmillan International, c1991. 661 p. ISBN 0-02-895790-3. $65.00. **CB128**

The "first handbook on social studies education [attempting] to provide a comprehensive view and analysis of research in the field."—*Pref.* Designed primarily for researchers, curriculum developers, and school administrators, and only secondarily for teachers. In eight sections (e.g., Issues of epistemology and methodology, The student in social studies education, Components of instruction), each containing several chapters written by experts. Name and subject indexes. LB1584.H275

Handbook of research on teaching / ed. by Merlin C. Wittrock. 3rd ed. N.Y.: Macmillan; London: Collier Macmillan, 1986. 1037 p. ISBN 0-02-900310-5. **CB129**

2nd ed., 1973, had title: *Second handbook of research on teaching* (*Guide* CB175).

Similar in purpose and organization to its predecessor, but contains new chapters on emerging areas of research such as cognitive processes. LB1028.H315

Handbook of special education : research and practice / ed. by Margaret C. Wang, Maynard C. Reynolds, Herbert J. Walberg. Oxford; N.Y.: Pergamon, c1987–1989. 3 v.: ill. ISBN 0-08-033383-4 (v. 1). $70.00 (est.). **CB130**

Contents: v. 1, Learner characteristics and adaptive education; v. 2, Mildly handicapped conditions; v. 3, Low incidence conditions.

Consists of 45 chapters that summarize the "well-confirmed knowledge" for the topic treated, covering first the research literature, then the "tested experience and practices of leading professionals," and finally recommending "improvements for effectively linking practice with the state of the art."—*Pref.* Does not cover the severely or profoundly handicapped, speech disorders, physical impairments, or chronic health problems. Extensive bibliographies; author and subject indexes in each volume. The editors have provided a synopsis, *Special education : research and practice : synthesis of findings* (below), which contains an epilogue in which the editors offer impressions, observations, and suggestions concerning the field, and which includes substantial bibliographies and author and subject indexes. LC3965.H263

Harrison, Charles Hampton. Public schools USA : a comparative guide to school districts. Charlotte, Vt.: Williamson Pub., c1988. 366 p. ISBN 0-913589-36-5. $17.95. **CB131**

Evaluates approximately 500 school districts in 52 metropolitan areas, basing evaluations on statistics gleaned from federal and state sources, accrediting agencies, other educational organizations, and on descriptive matter derived from responses to questionnaires. Criteria for ratings include expense per pupil, dropout rate, American College Test scores, percentage of graduates going to college, student-teacher ratio, teachers' salaries, and subjects in which advanced placement courses are offered. LA217.H375

International handbook of women's education / ed. by Gail P. Kelly. N.Y.; London: Greenwood, 1989. 1 v. ISBN 0-313-25638-1. £73.10. **CB132**

Summarizes the history, current status, and outcomes of women's education and its degree of equality to education for men. Focuses on the situations in 23 countries representing a range of social, political, and economic systems, industrial development, and wealth. In sections for major regions (e.g., Middle East), with individual chapters on each country by experts and a summary chapter by the editor. Contains statistical tables, extensive bibliography, and general index.

Prus, Joseph S. Handbook of certification and licensure requirements for school psychologists / Joseph S. Prus, Garry W. White, Anne Pendleton. 4th ed. Wash.: National Association of School Psychologists, 1987. 220, [16] p. ISBN 0-932955-06-1 (pbk.). **CB133**

1st ed., 1976, and 3rd ed., 1980–81, both ed. by T.J. Sewall, D.T. Brown, and J.C. Brantley, had title: *The handbook of certification/licensure requirements for school psychologists.*

Presents requirements of individual states. Intended for use by professionals seeking certification or licensure, students contemplating future employment, and personnel responsible for hiring or regulating school psychologists. Arranged alphabetically by state, the main section provides information on types and levels of certification available, educational and experiential requirements, examinations and the fees for them, the process of certification for in-state and out-of-state applicants, and addresses of persons or agencies to contact. Appendix summarizes in tabular form state certification requirements and processes and also outlines licensure requirements for private practice and related professional functions. LB3013.6.S48

Requirements for certification of teachers, counselors, librarians, administrators for elementary and secondary schools. Chicago: Univ. of Chicago Pr., 1935– . Annual. ISSN 1047-7071. **CB134**

49th ed., 1984–85 (*Guide* CB182) 54th ed., 1989–90.

Title varies.

Beginning with 54th ed., no longer lists requirements for junior college personnel.

Schmitz, Betty. Integrating women's studies into the curriculum : a guide and bibliography. Old Westbury, N.Y.: Feminist Pr., 1985. 192 p. ISBN 0-935312-36-6 (pbk.). $12.95. **CB135**

A guide for faculty and administrators in three parts: (1) Approaches to project management, covering assessment, design, planning, initiating and sustaining a project, and handling resistance to change; (2) The Northern Rockies program on women in the curriculum, providing brief histories of ten projects, giving for each the institutional background, inception, definition of the project, plan of action, short-term impact, future activities, and project director, and including a directory of 77 additional projects; (3) Bibliography and resources, citing, with annotations, books, articles, reports, programs, curriculum materials, organizations, and resources, 1978 to early 1984, arranged alphabetically by author. Directory of publishers; author and subject indexes. HQ1181.U5S36

Special education : research and practice : synthesis of findings / ed. by Margaret C. Wang, Maynard C. Reynolds, Herbert J. Walberg. Oxford; N.Y.: Pergamon, 1990. 223 p. ISBN 0-08-040238-0. $44.00. ISBN 0-08-040237-2 (pbk.). $19.00. **CB136**

Summary volume to *Handbook of special education* (above).

The editors of the *Handbook of special education*'s nine subsections have contributed chapters on their specialties, analyzing findings and implications for practice, research, and policy. A summary offers impressions, observations, and suggestions that relate to the entire field. Substantial bibliographies; author and subject indexes. LC3965.S65

The teacher's almanac. v.1 (1986/1987)– . N.Y. : Facts on File, c1986– . Annual. ISSN 0889-079X. $24.95.
CB137

A compendium of information about education, mostly in tabular form, aimed at the teaching profession (see sections on The teacher's year, State rankings, Teacher salaries and jobs, Profile of the teaching profession). Resembles *Education almanac* (*Supplement* CB123), but devotes more space to higher education, sports, and events of the previous year, less to the history of education, documents of education, and innovative programs. Sources are cited for the data. L101.U6T39

Weisenstein, Gregory R. Administrator's desk reference on special education / Gregory R. Weisenstein, Ruth Pelz. Rockville, Md. : Aspen Publishers, 1986. 254 p. : ill. ISBN 0-87189-357-6. **CB138**

A handbook of concise information for school administrators, emphasizing legal requirements and similar considerations related to such services. Placement of subject terms in page margins (in addition to their employment as section headings and subheadings) facilitates quick use. Designed as a desk reference for principals, but also of value for education libraries. LC3981.W38

Weller, Carol. Educators' desk reference for special learning problems / Carol Weller, Mary Buchanan. Boston : Allyn and Bacon, c1988. 373 p. ISBN 0-205-10299-9. **CB139**

Describes 229 educational methods, including techniques for each exceptionality and severity level, briefly outlining each method and its uses and referring to published sources for more detailed descriptions. Methods are indexed by title, author, source publications describing the method, intervention areas (e.g., mathematics, sensory disorders, therapy), and ages for which the method is appropriate. LC4704.W45

World education encyclopedia / ed. by George Thomas Kurian. N.Y. : Facts on File, c1988. 3 v. (1720 p.) : ill. ISBN 0-87196-748-0. $175.00. **CB140**

Describes the national education systems of 181 countries. Unusual organization groups nations into "major," "middle," or "minor" sections, based on how much information about their system was obtainable. Articles on individual countries range in length from 1 paragraph (Andorra) to 42 pages (the U.S.) At the ends of most articles are bibliographies. Appendixes contain 1984 Unesco statistics on national literacy rates, numbers of schools, expenditures per capita, etc. Indexed. LB15.W87

Yearbooks

Educational media and technology yearbook. v. 11 (1985)– . Littleton, Colo. : Libraries Unlimited, Inc., 1985– . Annual. ISSN 8755-2094. $47.50. **CB141**

For earlier volumes, see *Guide* CB179.

Title varies; through 1984, called *Educational media yearbook.*

Editors vary.

Sponsor varies; 1983–85, co-sponsored by Assocation for Educational Communications and Technology and American Society for Training and Development; beginning 1986, by Association for Educational Communications and Technology.

Still in six main sections, but these change; 16th ed. (1990) had: (1) The year in review, (2) Technology update, (3) Leadership profiles, (4) Organizations and associations in North America, (5) Graduate programs, (6) Mediagraphy. LB1028.3.E37

Special education yearbook. 1986– . Reston, Va. : Council for Exceptional Children, 1987– . Annual. **CB142**

Superintendent of Documents classification: ED 1.310/2. Vols. for 1986– distributed to depository libraries in microfiche.

"A product of the ERIC Clearinghouse on Handicapped and Gifted Children."—*t.p.*

A compendium of information on special education in the U.S. Content varies, but annual issues ordinarily include statistics for each state on children served, staffs and funding; directories of national government and association officials; lists of awards; and a section on early childhood special education. A "General information" section covers legislation, judicial decisions, and federal policies, and contains articles on trends, position papers, and reports issued by associations. Some sections include information on special education in Canada. No index. LC3981.S65

Biography

American Association of School Administrators. Who's who in educational administration. 1976/77– . Arlington, Va. : American Association of School Administrators, [1977]– . ISSN 0271-1613. **CB143**

"Roster of members, American Association of School Administrators."—*t.p.* For each person, gives current position, business address, and highest degree earned and institution. Arranged alphabetically by state, with a separate section listing foreign members. Alphabetical index of names that gives the state under which the member's entry is found. L13.A366

Nauman, Ann K. A biographical handbook of education : five hundred contributors to the field. N.Y. : Irvington Publishers, c1985. 237 p. ISBN 0-8290-0722-9 (pbk.). $19.50. **CB144**

Alphabetically arranged entries include dates of birth and death, nationality, profession, a short paragraph summarizing contributions and significance, and bibliography. Intended as "a jumping off point or ready reference" (*Introd.*) for those beginning research. LA2301.N38

Who's who in American education. 1988–1989– . Owings Mills, Md. : National Reference Institute : Distr. by Varied Print. Co., c1988– . Annual. ISSN 1046-7203. **CB145**

Nearly all entries are for classroom teachers nominated by their peers. Selection criteria include educational achievement, responsibilities representing substantial influence on education, publications, honors and awards, and leadership in professional organizations. Contains short, alphabetically arranged entries outlining education, positions held, professional activities, honors, research and publications, etc. Index lists names by state. Not to be confused with *Who's who in American education*, 1928–68 (*Guide* CB274). LA2311.W47

Statistics

American Council on Education. Fact book on higher education : 1989–90 / comp. by Charles J. Anderson [et al.]. N.Y. : American Council on Education : Macmillan, c1989. 287 p. : ill. **CB146**

Title varies: *Fact book for academic administrators*; *Fact book for academic administration*; *Fact book for higher education*; *F B : a fact book on higher education.*

Began publication 1959.

Continues the "tradition of compiling pertinent data on baseline trends in higher education."—*Introd.* For the first time, this edition includes a "Guide to sources," briefly describing some of the major data sources used in the *Fact book*, with the names and addresses of organizations providing data.

LA227.3.A44a

The condition of education. 1975– . Wash. : U.S. Dept. of Education, Office of Educational Research and Improvement, National Center for Education Statistics : : U.S. Govt. Print. Off., 1975– . Annual. ISSN 0098-4752. **CB147**

For earlier volumes, see *Guide* CB257.

Vols. for 1986–1988 by U.S. Department of Education, Office of Educational Research and Improvement, Center for Education Statistics; 1988– by the National Center for Education Statistics.

Superintendent of Documents classifications numbers: HE 19.314; ED 1.310/2; ED 1.109.

Beginning with 1988, issued in two volumes, *Elementary and secondary education* and *Postsecondary education*, each arranged by broad subject areas with subdivisions. The 1990 edition includes a three-year general index. L112.N377a

The condition of teaching : a state-by-state analysis, 1990. Princeton, N.J. : Carnegie Foundation for the Advancement of Teaching : Available from Princeton Univ. Pr., c1990. 330 p. ISBN 0-931050-39-1. **CB148**

Earlier editions: 1983, 1985, 1988.

A survey of the opinions of 21,000 elementary and secondary school teachers on a wide range of topics relating to the teaching profession. In two parts, National profile and State-by-state comparisons, each divided into eight sections that treat such subjects as teachers' attitudes and values, working conditions, and judgments concerning students and academic programs. Based on responses to the 203 questions in the Carnegie Foundation for the Advancement of Teaching's 1990 National Survey of Public School Teachers. Data are presented primarily in tabular form, with results of the 1987 National Survey adjacent to 1990. Brief narrative summaries highlight the findings. Index of tables. LB2832.2.C66

Gallup polls of attitudes toward education 1969–1984 : a topical summary / Stanley M. Elam, ed. Bloomington, Ind. : Phi Delta Kappa, c1984. 95 p. ISBN 0-87367-792-7 (pbk.). **CB149**

Based on Gallup's *Topical report : annual surveys of the public's attitudes toward the public schools, 1969–83.* Summarizes findings of the annual "Gallup polls of the public attitudes toward the public schools of the U.S.," (regularly published in the journal *Phi Delta Kappan*), and includes responses to a few other Gallup polls. The 1984 poll is reported in full. Answers to 400 questions are arranged in 38 categories such as Acceptance of education innovations, Testing, Drugs, alcohol, and smoking. No index, but a table of contents lists the categories. LA217.G35

Kindergarten programs and practices in public schools. Arlington, Va. : Educational Research Service, c1986. 123 p. : ill. **CB150**

Presents the results of a 1985 nationwide survey of a random sample of public school kindergarten teachers and principals, providing statistics on such topics as enrollment; number and characteristics of teachers; programs and practices; teachers and principals' opinions on goals, priorities, and other aspects of programs; etc. Findings are topically arranged in six categories: Demographics, The kindergarten pupil, Schedule of day, The kindergarten program, Kindergarten schedule of personnel, and Administrative concerns. No index, but the table of contents locates results for each question. LB1205.K56

National Education Association—Research. Rankings of the states. 1973– . [Washington] : National Education

Association—Research. Annual. ISSN 0077-4332. **CB151**

Provides tabular rankings, highest to lowest, of educational statistics by state in eight categories: Population, Enrollment and attendance, Faculty, General financial resources, Government revenue, School revenue, Governmental expenses, and School expenses. Some of the information was drawn from other National Education Association studies, U.S. government publications, and the "Survey of buying power" issues of *Sales and marketing management.* LA212.N36a

National School Boards Association. Survey of public education in the nation's urban school districts. [Wash. : National School Boards Association], 1979– . ISSN 0272-8656. $12.50. **CB152**

Spine title: *Triennial report—Council of Urban Boards of Education.*

Designed for school leaders, this work presents data on the finances, staffing, programs, etc., of 52 school districts, and on the educational, political, and social conditions and issues that affect them. Each of the nine sections (which have such titles as School district finances, The school board, and Federal issues) opens with a narrative description of current facts, statistics, and trends, followed by information in tabular form on individual school districts. A rich source of data not easily found elsewhere (e.g., districts using television programming technology, desegregation strategies, districts covered by bargaining laws, methods of debt financing). Detailed table of contents, but no index. LB2817.N33a

School law

Deskbook encyclopedia of American school law. 1980/81– . Rosemount, Minn. : Informational Research Systems, 1981– . Annual. **CB153**

Designed to provide educators and lawyers with a compilation of recent state and federal appellate court decisions. Topically arranged, with chapters on subjects such as Freedom of speech, Accidents, injuries and deaths, and Employment discrimination, subdivided into narrower topics. Contains appendixes citing recent Supreme Court cases and recently published law review articles, and presenting portions of the Constitution most frequently cited in education cases.

KF4114.D46

The yearbook of education law. 1988– . Topeka, Kan. : National Organization on Legal Problems of Education, c1988– . Annual. ISSN 1049-0264. **CB154**

Continues *Yearbook of school law* (*Guide* CB69), which ceased with the 1987 edition.

GUIDANCE

Stewart, Jayme. How to get into the college of your choice—and how to finance it. N.Y. : W. Morrow, 1991. 176 p. : ill. ISBN 0-688-09209-8. **CB155**

An outline and calendar of strategies in preparation for the college admission process. Sections on writing essays, personal statements, applications, follow-up letters, requests for recommendations, preparing questionnaires and applications, financial aid, informing administrators on learning disabilities. Appendixes include a list of resource books, preparation courses, examples of financial aid forms. LB2351.2.S77

Encyclopedias

The encyclopedia of careers and vocational guidance / William E. Hopke, ed. in chief. 8th ed. Chicago : J.G. Ferguson Pub. Co., c1990. 4 v. : ill. ISBN 0-89434-117-0 (set).   **CB156**

6th ed., 1984 (*Guide* CB284); 7th ed., 1987.

Contents: v. 1, Industry profiles; v. 2, Professional careers; v. 3, General and special careers; v. 4, Technicians' careers.

Now in 4 v. describing more major industries (76) and more occupations (nearly 1,000) than the 6th–7th eds., updating such matters as average salaries and employment prospects. Adds appendixes on assistance for the disabled and on training programs, internships, and apprenticeships. The format is essentially unchanged. An initial volume of industry profiles with other volumes containing career descriptions.   HF5381.E52

FELLOWSHIPS AND SCHOLARSHIPS

Dennis, Marguerite J. Dollars for scholars : Barron's complete college financing guide. N.Y. : Barron's, c1989. 248 p. : ill., forms. ISBN 0-8120-4155-0. $12.95.   **CB157**

A guide to sources of financial aid at state, federal, and international levels, giving addresses of institutions, organizations, and government offices, together with descriptions of assistance programs.   LB2337.4.D455

Education interface ... guide to pre-college foundation support. 1990– . Skillman, N.J. : Information Interface Institute, [1990?]– . Annual. ISSN 1048-3012.   **CB158**

Profiles 103 private philanthropic foundations that reserve a substantial portion of their resources to fund precollege programs. Entries range from one to four pages and indicate foundation assets, program preferences, persons to contact, application procedures and deadlines, and programs previously supported. Indexes list foundations by geographical preferences and by types of programs supported (e.g., advanced studies, college preparation).

Fellowship guide to western Europe / ed. by Gina Bria Vescovi. 7th ed. N.Y. : Council for European Studies, 1989. 113 p.   **CB159**

6th ed., 1985.

A list of grants from an international group of agencies. For each gives address, brief description, amount, deadlines, duration, eligibility. Corporate name index.   LB2339.E9F4

Financial aid for research, study, travel, and other activities abroad. 1990–1991– . San Carlos, Calif. : Reference Service Pr., 1990– . Biennial.   **CB160**

Entries arranged by level of study, type of award, and program title. States eligibility, special features, and limitations for each award. Indexed by title, sponsoring organization, geographic location, subject, and filing date. Annotated bibliography of financial aid directories.

Peterson's college money handbook. 6th ed. (1989)– . Princeton, N.J. : Peterson's Guides, c1988– . Annual. ISSN 0894-9395. $17.95.   **CB161**

A guide to the availability of financial aid at more than 1,700 U.S. undergraduate institutions. The main segment, Cost and aid profiles, is an alphabetical arrangement of institutions that gives summaries of undergraduate financial aid, need-based and non-need-based freshman awards, and addresses of financial aid officers. Contains glossary of pertinent terms, background information on applying for financial aid, and directories of both non-need and athletic scholarships.   LB2337.2.C65

Scholarships, fellowships & grants for programs abroad : a handbook of awards for US nationals for study or research abroad / [consulting ed., W. Wickremasinghe]. Houston, Tex. : American Collegiate Service, c1989. 299 p. ISBN 0-940937-02-6.   **CB162**

The main section has 374 entries on specific awards, arranged alphabetically by name of granting institution. Data provided includes person to contact; number, value, and duration of awards; fields of study; closing dates for applications; where tenable; and eligibility requirements. Another section briefly profiles host countries, giving their languages, religions, currency rates, academic years, required skills for awardees (such as knowledge of French), and sources of information in the host country. Appendixes provide information on various Fulbright awards. Four indexes: general, by country or region, by subject, and by level of studies.   LB2338.S36

ACADEMIC CUSTOMS

Costume and protocol

Sparks, Linda. American college regalia : a handbook / comp. by Linda Sparks and Bruce Emerton. N.Y. : Greenwood, 1988. 380 p. ISBN 0-313-26266-7.   **CB163**

For American colleges and universities with enrollment of 2,500 or more, indicates nickname, mascot, name of newspaper, colors, title of yearbook, fight song, and alma mater.   LB3630.S64

CC

Sociology

GENERAL WORKS

Guides

Aby, Stephen H. Sociology : a guide to reference and information sources. Littleton, Colo. : Libraries Unlimited, 1987. 231 p. (Reference sources in the social sciences series, [no. 1]). ISBN 0-87287-498-2. $36.00.   **CC1**

In three sections: (1) works of use to all social sciences; (2) individual social science resources of use to sociologists; (3) sociological sources, including general works and a section on resources especially useful in 22 subdivisions of sociology. Author-title index and cross-referenced subject index.   Z7164.S68A24

Bart, Pauline. The student sociologist's handbook / Pauline Bart, Linda Frankel. 4th ed. N.Y. : Random House, c1986. 291 p. ISBN 0-394-35109-6 (pbk.). $8.00.   **CC2**

3rd ed., 1981 (*Guide* CC1).

This edition describes more than 500 reference sources and journals. Materials on sex roles and the section on women's studies journals have been greatly expanded and a chapter added on Computers in sociological work.   HM68.B37

Bibliography

Berndt, Judy. Rural sociology : a bibliography of bibliographies. Metuchen, N.J. : Scarecrow, 1986. 177 p. ISBN 0-8108-1860-4.   **CC3**

Contains annotated entries for 434 English-language bibliographies published since 1970, arranged alphabetically by author in 16 chapters covering topics such as rural development, irrigation, overview studies, women, land tenure, and nomadism. Chapter headings provide the only subject access. Personal and corporate name, title, and geographic indexes.
Z7164.S688B47

Bono, Anna Maria. Bibliografia della sociologia italiana, 1975–1980. Milano, Italy : F. Angeli, c1984. 275 p. (Archivio italiano di sociologia, n. 5).   **CC4**

A continuation of two classified bibliographies from the same publisher covering earlier time periods: *Bibliografia della sociologia italiana 1969–1971*, ed. by Anna Bono, Piera Brustia, and Valeria Repaci (1978) and *Bibliografia della sociologia italiana 1972–1974*, ed. by Anna Bono (1979). Lists articles from all Italian sociological journals. Thematic organization (e.g., Marxism and society, sociology of work, terrorism). Author and journal index.   Z7164.S68B633

Brown, Samuel R. Finding the source in sociology and anthropology : a thesaurus-index to the reference collection. N.Y. : Greenwood, 1987. 269 p. (Finding the source, no. 1). ISBN 0-313-25263-7. $39.95.   **CC5**

An attempt to provide a quicker means of finding specific information than the usual annotated guide to reference sources. In two sections: (1) citations listed by broad subjects, then titles, with author and title/subtitle indexes following; and (2) the "thesaurus-index," which gives related terms and also refers users back to citations in section one. No annotations.
Z7164.S68B75

Bruhn, John G. Medical sociology : an annotated bibliography, 1972–1982 / John G. Bruhn, Billy U. Philips, Paula L. Levine. N.Y. : Garland, 1985. 779 p. (Garland bibliographies in sociology, v. 6 ; Garland reference library of social science, v. 243). ISBN 0-8240-8938-3.   **CC6**

Serves to update Theodor J. Litman's bibliography *The sociology of medicine and health care* (San Francisco : Boyd & Fraser, 1976) which cited literature published through 1971. Contains 1,949 annotated entries for books, articles, and government documents in 14 topical sections. Author and subject indexes.   Z6675.S53B78

Fritz, Jan M. The clinical sociology handbook. N.Y. : Garland, 1985. 292 p. (Garland bibliographies in sociology, v. 7 ; Garland reference library of social science, v. 134). ISBN 0-8240-9203-1.   **CC7**

Primarily an annotated bibliography of books, articles, book reviews, papers read at scholarly meetings, and unpublished manuscripts produced from 1931 through 1981. The entries comprise 13 chapters that treat specific areas (e.g., Community/environment, Policy analysis). Other chapters provide information on the Clinical Sociology Association, give addresses of other professional organizations, and list institutions with training programs in clinical sociology. Author index.   Z7164.S68F75

Ghorayshi, Parvin. The sociology of work : a critical annotated bibliography. N.Y. : Garland, 1990. 214 p. (Garland library of sociology, vol. 17 ; Garland reference library of social science, v. 591). ISBN 0-8240-3438-4.   **CC8**

An interdisciplinary and international bibliography of 405 selected books, articles, and reports, intended for students, academics, professionals, and general readers. In six subject chapters (e.g., Division of labor, Hazards of work, The trade union, industrial conflict, and the strike), divided into sections such as Union's power and Experience of unemployment. Author and subject indexes.   Z7164.I45G46

Kinloch, Graham Charles. Social stratification : an annotated bibliography. N.Y. : Garland, 1987. 357 p. (Garland library of sociology, vol. 11 ; Garland reference library of social science, v. 393). ISBN 0-8240-9805-6.   **CC9**

Emphasizes social science literature published 1960s–1980s. 1,744 numbered entries in six chapters cover general bibliographies and research trends, theoretical and conceptual issues, methodological issues, historical studies, the U.S., and societies outside the U.S.. Entries are alphabetical by author within subtopics. List of journals; author and subject indexes.   Z7164.S64K56

Viterbi, Mario. Bibliografi della sociologia italiana. (1945–1970) / Con un saggio di Filippo Barbano. Torino : Giappichelli, 1970. lxii, 319 p. (Pubblicazioni dell'Istituto di scienza politiche dell'Universit'a di Torino, no. 22.).   **CC10**

Viterbi and Filippo Barbano's *Bibliografia della sociologia italiana (1948–1958)* (*Guide* CC3) is the point of departure for this classified bibliography. Because of the dramatic increase in Italian sociological literature over the last decade, the author omitted articles on related disciplines, which were included in the earlier compilation. Arranged by topical chapters: e.g., sociology of communication, sociology of political phenomena, sociology of religion. A preface describes the historical development of Italian sociology. Author and subject indexes.
Z7164.S68V58

Current

Sociological abstracts. v. 1 (Jan./Oct. 1952/53)– . [San Diego, etc. : Sociological Abstracts, inc.], 1953– . 6 issues yearly. ISSN 0038-0202. $120.00.   **CC11**

For earlier volumes and annotation, see *Guide* CC16.

Co-sponsored by the International Sociological Association

Beginning with v.37 (1989), proceedings of association meetings are no longer published as *Conference abstracts supplement* sections within regular issues; they have the same title, but comprise the sixth issue of each volume, which formerly contained the annual cumulative indexes. The latter are still published separately, but without an issue number.   HM1.S67

●**Sociological abstracts** : (SA) [computer file]. San Diego, Calif. : Sociological Abstracts, Inc., 1963– .   **CC12**

Machine-readable version of *Sociological abstracts*, above.

File size: 250,000 records. Updated five times per year. Available online (BRS, DIALOG, Data-Star) and in CD-ROM as *Sociofile* (SilverPlatter), incorporating *Sociological abstracts* (*SA*), 1974– and *Social planning, policy & development abstracts* (*SOPODA*; *Guide* CC71 and *Supplement* CC28), 1980– ; updated every four months.

Periodicals

Lantz, Judith C. Cumulative index of sociology journals, 1971–1985. Wash. : American Sociological Association, c1987. 763 p.   **CC13**

Indexes eight American Sociological Association journals, including *American sociological review*, *Contemporary sociology*, and *Sociological theory*, plus *American journal of sociology* and *Social forces*. Cites articles, book reviews, and review essays, omitting notes and comments. In two sections, Author index and Subject index, the latter including both subject headings and keyword indexing in one alphabet. Both indexes give limited citations, containing only journal titles, dates, and pagination.   Z7164.S68L36

Dictionaries

Boudon, Raymond. A critical dictionary of sociology / Raymond Boudon and François Bourricaud. Chicago : Univ. of Chicago Pr., 1989. 438 p. : ill. ISBN 0-226-06728-9.   **CC14**

Translation of: *Dictionnaire critique de la sociologie* (Paris : Presses universitaires de France; 1st ed., 1982; 2nd ed., 1986).

A foreword describes the abridgment adopted for the English edition and lists excluded entries. The thematic index in the English edition gives page references omitted from the French edition. Includes introductions to the 1st and 2nd eds. Provides lengthy essays on subjects such as beliefs, Comte, ideologies, Marx, minorities, prophetism, and social control. Bibliographies follow each essay.   HM17.B6813

Terminology

Thematic list of descriptors—sociology = Liste thématique des descripteurs—sociologie / prepared on behalf of UNESCO by the International Committee for Social Science Information and Documentation. London ; N.Y. : Routledge, 1989. 475 p. ISBN 0-415-01779-3. ISBN 0-415-01776-9.   **CC15**

Companion to *International bibliography of sociology* (*Guide* CC15). For description, see *Supplement* CE16.
                                                        Z695.1.S63T48

Quotations

Bardis, Panos Demetrios. Dictionary of quotations in sociology. Westport, Conn. : Greenwood, 1985. 356 p. ISBN 0-313-23778-6.   **CC16**

Intends "to present the nature, origin, development, and current status of general sociological concepts through direct quotation."—*Pref.* Crosscultural, interdisciplinary, and historical in coverage, entries appear in chronological order under alphabetically arranged subject headings such as alienation, class struggle, ideology, methodology, power, division of labor, and violence. Each entry provides author, book title, and date of first publication. Bibliography; name and subject indexes.
                                                        HM17.B37

Directories

Selth, Jefferson P. Alternative lifestyles : a guide to research collections on intentional communities, nudism, and sexual freedom. Westport, Conn. : Greenwood, c1985. 133 p. (Bibliographies and indexes in sociology, no. 6). ISBN 0-313-24773-0.   **CC17**

Describes 36 collections in the U.S. which total 120,000 volumes, 15,000 periodicals, 125,000 audiovisual items, over 3 million photographs, and many ephemeral materials. Introductory pages to the three sections noted in the subtitle provide definitions and scope. Entries, which vary in length from two to ten pages and are arranged alphabetically by title, include address, phone, contact name, hours, general description, holdings, and bibliographic access. Alphabetical index of collections and institutions; geographical index of collections; and separate indexes for periodicals, names, and subjects.   HQ971.S45

Handbooks

Handbook of clinical sociology / ed. by Howard M. Rebach and John G. Bruhn. N.Y. : Plenum Pr., c1991. 410 p. : ill. ISBN 0-306-43559-4. ISBN 0-306-43579-9 (pbk.).   **CC18**

Intended for students, sociologists, instructors, and those in clinical disciplines. 22 essays each in four parts: covers definition and history; the common concerns of practitioners; practice in several settings; mental health settings and work with ethnic minorities, women, elderly, and substance abusers. 26 contributors; general index.   HM73.H315

Handbook of social science of sport : with an international classified bibliography / ed. by Günther R.F. Lüschen and George H. Sage, with the assistance of Leila Sfeir. Champaign, Ill. : Stipes Pub. Co., c1981. 720 p. ISBN 0-87563-191-6.   **CC19**

For annotation, see *Supplement* BJ16.   GV706.5.H35

Handbook of sociology / Neil J. Smelser, ed. Newbury Park, Calif. : Sage Publications, c1988. 824 p. ISBN 0-8039-2665-0. $89.95.   **CC20**

The first general handbook of sociology since Robert E. L. Faris's *Handbook of modern sociology* (Chicago : Rand McNally, 1964). Individual chapters by experts treat nearly all the discipline's major fields, discuss "problems and issues that have persisted in the field" (*Introd.*), and summarize recent trends in empirical research. Substantial bibliographies.   HM51.H249

SOCIAL CONDITIONS AND SOCIAL WELFARE

Bibliography

Biegel, David E. Social networks and mental health : an annotated bibliography / David E. Biegel, Ellen McCardle, Susan Mendelson. Beverly Hills, Calif. : Sage Publications, [1985]. 391 p. ISBN 0-8039-2420-8.   **CC21**

Lists 1,340 citations, mostly to journal articles, 1950–82, under five major headings: Overview and theory; Research—physical health; Research—mental health; Intervention; and Professional roles and policy. Entries are consecutively numbered and alphabetically arranged by author under various chapter subtopics. Author and subject indexes. Continued by:
                                                        Z6664.N5B54

Social support networks : a bibliography, 1983–1987 / comp. by David E. Biegel. N.Y. : Greenwood, 1989. 334 p. (Bibliographies and indexes in sociology, no. 15). ISBN 0-313-26604-2.   **CC22**

Updates Biegel's earlier bibliography (above) with 2,693 entries covering 1983–87. Each entry includes several keywords.   Z7164.S662S63

Social support and health : an annotated bibliography / John G. Bruhn . . . [et al.]. N.Y. : Garland, 1987. 504 p. (Garland library of sociology, vol. 13 ; Garland reference library of social science, v. 412). ISBN 0-8240-8348-2.
CC23

Presents 1,247 entries in 7 chapters covering social networks, physical health and rehabilitation, mental health, the life cycle, social and cultural factors, and applications. Entries, arranged alphabetically under subdivisions, provide brief summary, suggested audience, and type of material (literature review, research, case report, etc.) Emphasizes English-language publications of the 1980s; omits popular literature. Author and subject indexes.   RA418.S6495

Biography

American reformers / ed., Alden Whitman. N.Y. : H.W. Wilson, 1985. 930 p. : ports. ISBN 0-8242-0705-X. $65.00.   **CC24**

A work for students and general readers, giving "brief but incisive biographical sketches of the principal reformers in America from the seventeenth century to modern times."— *Pref.* Includes both moderate and radical reformers ("disturbers of the social peace") in 61 categories (e.g., abolition, anarchism, black rights, libraries, food reform/vegetarianism, women's rights, temperance). 508 signed entries, alphabetically arranged, include a photograph, biographical sketch, detailed endnotes, and location of the subject's papers, if known.
CT215.A67

Biographical dictionary of social welfare in America / Walter I. Trattner, ed. N.Y. : Greenwood, 1986. 897 p. ISBN 0-313-23001-3.   **CC25**

Emphasizes the doers and activists, not the philosophers or givers. Over 300 signed articles, each three to four pages in length and alphabetically arranged, provide birth and death dates; a summary of life, career, and contributions; and a selected bibliography of sources by and about the subject. Indicates location of the subject's papers, if known. Useful appendixes offer a chronology of significant events and a list of subjects by year and place of birth. List of contributors with affiliations; general index.   HV27.B57

Social work

Guides

Mendelsohn, Henry N. A guide to information sources for social work and the human services. Phoenix : Oryx, 1987. 136 p. ISBN -089774-338-5 (pbk.).   **CC26**

Clearly and concisely describes the organizaton of services in academic or large public libraries, and specific reference sources in social work and related disciplines, public documents, statistics, and law. Reviews database searching and sources for historical and current information. Includes an annotated list of 1200 social work and social welfare journals. Systematicallly approaches the research process and explains how to use sources noted. Detailed table of contents; general index.
HV91.M43

Bibliography

Li, Hong-Chan. Social work education II : a bibliography 1977–1987. Metuchen, N.J. : Scarecrow, 1989. v. 1–2. ISBN 0-8108-1108-1 (v. 1). ISBN 0-8108-2195-8 (v. 2).   **CC27**

A continuation of the compilers' 1978 volume (*Guide* CC67), which covered 1960–76. Contains approximately 2,800 entries, including some 20 new subject headings (e.g., Radical social work, Private practice, Homosexuality, Off-campus programs). Author index; a cumulative subject index covers both volumes.   Z7164.C4L49

•**Social planning/policy and development abstracts** : (SO-PODA) [computer file]. San Diego, Calif. : Sociological Abstracts, c1977/78– .   **CC28**

Machine-readable version of *Social planning, policy & development abstracts (Guide* CC71).

File size: 20,000 records. Updated semiannually. Available online (BRS, DIALOG [as part of *Sociological abstracts (SA)*, *Supplement* CC12]) and in CD-ROM as *Sociofile* (Silver-Platter) incorporating *Sociological abstracts (SA)*, (*Supplement* CC11), 1974– and *Social planning, policy & development abstracts (SOPODA)*, 1980– ; updated every four months.

Encyclopedias

Encyclopedia of social work / Anne Minahan, ed. in chief. 18th ed. Silver Spring, Md. : National Association of Social Workers, 1987. 2 v. ISBN 0-87101-142-5.
CC29

For earlier volumes, see *Guide* CC76.

Revises and updates the 1977 edition, called v. 17. Offers 225 topical articles, alphabetically arranged, that reflect the increasingly interdisciplinary nature of social work. Highlights implications "for social work practice, for ethnic, racial, and cultural minorities, and for women."—*Pref.* The Preface explains eight content areas, and a how-to-use section lists article titles, names of those in the biography section, and contributors. Approximately a third of the articles retain their titles from the 1977 edition, but new titles treat such topics as adolescent pregnancy, divorce and separation, homelessness, homosexuality, immigrants, purchasing social services, and workfare. The lengthy, signed articles conclude with source bibliographies and cross-references to other articles, and many provide reading lists. Each volume contains a general index to both volumes. Appendixes: (1) Code of ethics of the National Association of Social Workers; (2) Curriculum policy for the Master's degree and Baccalaureate degree programs in social work education; (3) NASW standards for the practice of clinical social work; and (4) Guide to sources of information on social welfare agencies. Kept up to date by: HV35.E6

Face of the nation, 1987 : statistical supplement to the 18th edition of the *Encyclopedia of social work* / Sumner M. Rosen, David Fanshel, and Mary E. Lutz, editors. Silver Spring, Md. : National Association of Social Workers, c1987. 124 p. : ill. ISBN 0-87101-142-5 (pbk.).
CC30

Presents data on various subjects covered in the 18th ed. (above). For teachers, students, and practitioners. 11 sections provide text, tables, and charts on demographics, employment, social indicators, child welfare, social welfare expenditures, and other topics. Sources of data are cited. Table of contents indicates section topic and lists tables and graphics. No index.
HV90.F33

Dictionaries

Barker, Robert L. The social work dictionary. 2nd ed. Silver Spring, Md.: National Association of Social Workers, NASW Pr., c1991. 287 p. ISBN 0-87101-190-5.   **CC31**
  1st ed., 1987.
  Contains brief entries for some 3,000 terms selected from major social work journals, textbooks, and the literature of related disciplines, reflecting various social work orientations and philosophy. Includes a chronology of significant social welfare events, 1750 BCE to the present, and National Association of Social Workers' code of ethics. Cross-references.   HV12.B37

Directories

Rao, Vijaya. World guide to social work education / comp. by Vijaya Rao ; ed. by Katherine A. Kendall. 2nd ed. N.Y.: Publ. by the Council on Social Work Education for the International Association of Schools of Social Work, c1984. 223 p. ISBN 0-87293-001-7 (pbk.).   **CC32**
  Previous ed., 1974, by Patricia J. Stickney and Rosa Perla Resnick (*Guide* CC90).
  An updated edition that retains the original purpose, to assist schools of social work, employers of social workers, and interested readers in assessing "the approximate comparability of social work qualifications" (*Pref.*) among countries. Describes 74 schools in 61 countries, 24 national and regional associations, and the International Association of Schools of Social Work. Countries and regions are listed alphabetically in each of the three sections: Schools, National associations, and Regional associations. No indexes.   HV11.R3125

Aging

Guides

Zito, Dorothea R. A guide to research in gerontology: strategies and resources / Dorothea R. Zito and George V. Zito. N.Y.: Greenwood, 1988. 130 p. ISBN 0-313-25904-6.   **CC33**
  A guide to resources and research in eight chapters, the first three providing an introduction to the field, research strategies, and an overview of the organization of information. The remaining five chapters give general discussions of handbooks, directories and encyclopedias, indexes and abstracts, agencies, computerized systems, and community resources. Appendixes include a reading list on aging, and lists of indexes and abstracts, journals, and selected databases. Subject index.
  Z7164.O4Z57

Bibliography

Aday, Ron H. Crime and the elderly: an annotated bibliography. N.Y.: Greenwood, 1988. 118 p. (Bibliographies and indexes in gerontology, no. 8). ISBN 0-313-25470-2.   **CC34**
  A bibliography of 361 entries in two main units: the first details crimes against the elderly and has chapters dealing with criminal justice, victims, abuse and neglect, etc.; the second treats the elderly as criminals, and has chapters dealing with old age, crime patterns, prisoners, etc. Pt. 3 lists other resources and information such as crime prevention programs for older persons. Includes sources published, for the most part, in the U.S. since 1970. Author and subject indexes.
  Z5703.4.A35A33

Bailey, William G. Human longevity from antiquity to the modern lab: a selected, annotated bibliography. N.Y.: Greenwood, 1987. 208 p. (Bibliographies and indexes in gerontology, no. 4). ISBN 0-313-25371-4. **CC35**
  A unique work that lists books and journal articles in 15 chapters covering topics such as health planning, rejuvenation, and biomedical research. Three appendixes include addresses of health centers and descriptions of research; addresses of U.S. health resorts, spas, and mineral baths; and science fiction novels and plays. Author and subject indexes.   Z6663.A3B28

Brazil, Mary Jo. Building library collections on aging: a selection guide and core list. Santa Barbara, Calif.: ABC-Clio, c1990. 174 p. ISBN 0-87436-559-7.   **CC36**
  In two main sections. The first, focusing on policy statements, selection criteria, and building a collection, lists book publishers, associations, federal offices, and other resources. The second, the "core list," occupying most of the book, contains bibliographies on 27 topics (e.g., alcohol and drug abuse, Alzheimer's disease, elder abuse, ethics and legal issues), subarranged by format (books, periodicals, videocassettes, etc.). Entries are annotated and listed alphabetically. General index.
  Z688.A58B7

Coyle, Jean M. Women and aging: a selected, annotated bibliography. N.Y.: Greenwood, 1989. 135 p. (Bibliographies and indexes in gerontology, no. 9). ISBN 0-313-26021-4.   **CC37**
  For annotation, see *Supplement* CC255.   Z7164.O4C68

Davis, Lenwood G. The black aged in the United States: a selectively annotated bibliography. Rev. and updated, 2nd ed. N.Y.: Greenwood, 1989. 277 p. (Bibliographies and indexes in Afro-American and African studies, no. 23). ISBN 0-313-25931-3.   **CC38**
  1st ed., 1980 (*Guide* CC97).
  Identical in format and arrangement to the 1st ed. Lists 633 titles published through 1987, expands coverage of dissertations and theses and articles, and of the topics aged abuse, alcoholism, crime, hypertension, mental health, and legal services. List of homes for the black aged extended to 1988.
  Z1361.N39D354

Dolan, Eleanor F. The mature woman in America: a selected annotated bibliography, 1979–1982 / comp. by Eleanor F. Dolan and Dorothy M. Gropp. Wash.: National Council on the Aging, 1984. 122 p. ISBN 0-910883-02-5 (pbk.).   **CC39**
  For annotation, see *Supplement* CC256.   Z7164.O4D64

Donavin, Denise Perry. Aging with style and savvy. Chicago: Amer. Lib. Assoc., 1990. 163 p.: ill. ISBN 0-8389-0526-9.   **CC40**
  Includes nonfiction, plays, film/videos, and fiction, most published after 1983. Ten chapters list nonfiction entries by topic (e.g., Family relations; Health, fitness and sex; Travel and recreation; Retirement; Humor and reflections; Poetry). Chapters on plays, films, and fiction follow. Some 280 annotated entries appear alphabetically by author under each subtopic. Lists 22 organizations and associations. General index.
  HQ1064.U5D665

Edwards, Willie M. Gerontology: a cross-national core list of significant works / Willie M. Edwards and Frances Flynn. Ann Arbor, Mich.: Institute of Gerontology, Univ. of Michigan, c1982. 365 p.   **CC41**
  Prior ed., 1978 (*Guide* CC99), had title: *Gerontology: a core list of significant works.*
  A greatly expanded edition, now international in scope, emphasizing Canada, the U.K., the U.S., and eight other developed nations. "The classification is based on the system devel-

oped for the earlier United States edition, but several new categories have been added (e.g., Geriatric medicine, Quality of life, Religion, Social work)."—*Introd.* Z7164.O4E39

Ethnicity and aging : a bibliography / comp. by Edward Murguia ... [et al.]. San Antonio, Tex. : Trinity Univ. Pr., c1984. 132 p. (Checklists in the humanities and education, 8). ISBN 0-939980-03-7. $15.00 (est.). **CC42**

Organizes 1,432 entries in six sections covering Multiethnic and general studies, Black Americans, Hispanic Americans, Native Americans, Asian and Pacific Americans, and European origin ethnic groups. Subarranged by topic with entries listed alphabetically by author. Most publications date from the 1970s and early 1980s. Includes only readily available materials; omits unpublished material and ephemera. Z7164.O4E85

Guttmann, David. European American elderly : an annotated bibliography. N.Y. : Greenwood, 1987. 122 p. (Bibliographies and indexes in gerontology, no. 6). ISBN 0-313-25583-0. **CC43**

Consists of 310 entries—books, articles, and government publications in English—arranged alphabetically by author under 24 topical sections included in 6 chapters. Publication dates range from the early 1970s to 1986. A seventh chapter contains a short list of other bibliographies; an appendix provides a list of related journal titles. Author and subject indexes. Z7165.U5G92

Harris, Diana K. Sociology of aging. 2nd ed. N.Y. : Harper & Row, c1990. 510 p. : ill. ISBN 0-06-042655-1. **CC44**

1st ed., 1985 (*Guide* CC103).

Revised and reorganized edition includes new topics (e.g., Elder abuse, The older criminal, Alzheimer's, Shopping bag women, Cryonics, The aging homosexual, and Emergency response systems) and more cross-cultural materials than the 1st ed. HQ1064.U5H27

Johnson, Tanya F. Elder neglect and abuse : an annotated bibliography / comp. by Tanya F. Johnson, James G. O'Brien, and Margaret F. Hudson. Westport, Conn. : Greenwood, 1985. 223 p. (Bibliographies and indexes in gerontology, no. 1). ISBN 0-313-24589-4. **CC45**

For each of 144 annotated entries, provides topics, methods, and conclusions, also giving profession of the first author, type of exposition, and issues addressed. An unannotated list of 144 entries follows, divided into sections for periodical articles, state publications, and federal publications. Entries arranged by author within each list. Coverage: 1975 to the present. Lists state agencies, offices, and organizations. Appendix includes Model Adult Protective Services Act. List of journal abbreviations; author index. Z7164.O4J56

Oriol, William E. Federal public policy on aging since 1960 : an annotated bibliography. N.Y. : Greenwood, 1987. 127 p. (Bibliographies and indexes in gerontology, no. 5). ISBN 0-313-25286-6. **CC46**

Covers 1960–86. Pt.1 (162 entries) covers general critiques and major themes. Pt.2 (589 entries) covers issues and programs (e.g., income and retirement, health and long term care, Older Americans Act, discrimination, minorities, consumer issues, women). Entries are arranged alphabetically by author under each heading. An appendix describes relevant congressional committees and lists national organizations. Author and subject indexes. Z7164.O4O74

Strange, Heather. Aging & cultural diversity : new directions and annotated bibliography / Heather Strange, Michele Teitelbaum & contributors. South Hadley, Mass. : Bergin & Garvey Publishers, 1987. 350 p. ISBN 0-89789-103-1. $29.95. **CC47**

Eight essays in Pt. 1 treat inter- and intra-cultural diversity. The annotated bibliography of Pt. 2 is in five chapters covering: General works; Ethnic, national, racial, or regional studies;

Comparative studies; Cross-cultural studies; and Bibliographies. Arranges entries alphabetically by author within each subtopic. Author and subject indexes. GN485.S77

Where do we come from? What are we? Where are we going? : an annotated bibliography of aging and the humanities / by Donna Polisar ... [et al.]. Wash. : Gerontological Society of America ; Galveston, Tex. : Moody Medical Library and Institute for the Medical Humanities, The Univ. of Texas Medical Branch, 1988. 150 p. : ill. ISBN 0-929596-01-3. **CC48**

Includes approximately 1,100 books, book chapters, articles, and dissertations, 1975–87, arranged alphabetically by author in six subject chapters. Topics include ethics, euthanasia, attitudes, history, images of aged, religious institutions, and legal rights and issues. Author and subject indexes.
Z7164.O4W46

Current

Abstracts in social gerontology. v. 33, no. 1 (Mar. 1990)– . Newbury Park, Calif. : Sage Publications, c1990– . Quarterly. ISSN 1047-4862. $98.00 (institutions). **CC49**

Continues *Current literature on aging* (*Guide* CC114), which ceased with v. 32 no. 4 (1989), and continues its volume numbering.

Publ. in cooperation with the National Council on the Aging, Inc.

●**AgeLine** [computer file]. Wash. : American Association of Retired Persons, National Gerontology Research Center, 1978– . **CC50**

File size: 28,000 records. Updated bimonthly. Available online (BRS, DIALOG).

Contains citations with abstracts to the journal, monograph, and report literature of social gerontology, focusing on social, psychological, and economic aspects of aging. Primarily U.S. coverage in English.

Periodicals

Hesslein, Shirley B. Serials on aging : an analytical guide. N.Y. : Greenwood, 1986. 176 p. ISBN 0-313-24709-9. **CC51**

Provides bibliographic citations and contents notes, often evaluative, for 376 serial titles. Most are published in the U.S., but some foreign titles are included. Titles are alphabetically arranged in 5 sections: General, Social gerontology, Health and biomedicine, Retirement and pensions, Statistics and reference tools. Title, subject, geographical, and publisher/organization indexes. Z7164.O4H47

Encyclopedias

The encyclopedia of aging / George L. Maddox, ed. in chief. N.Y. : Springer Pub. Co., c1987. 890 p. : ill. ISBN 0-8261-4840-9. **CC52**

Signed articles, alphabetically arranged, treat key topics in aging, legislation, government agencies, foundations, and membership organizations. Entries (typically two to three columns, some as long as 16—e.g., Social security) include Asian-American aged, Cell morphology, Demography, Congressional committees, Gray Panthers, Health care policy, Sexuality, and World Assembly on Aging. Separate list of headwords; tables, diagrams, and figures; list of 224 contributors. 128 pages of references; detailed general index. HQ1061.E53

Dictionaries

Harris, Diana K. Dictionary of gerontology. N.Y. : Greenwood, 1988. 201 p. ISBN 0-313-25287-4.   **CC53**

Contains statistical and research terms used in gerontology. Entries include bibliographies, cross-references, origin, and first usage. Name index.   HQ1061.H338

International glossary of social gerontology = Glosario internacional de gerontología social = Glossaire international de gérontologie sociale = Internationales Wörterverzeichnis für Sozialgerontologie / editors, Mary Jo Storey Gibson, Charlotte Nusberg. N.Y. : Van Nostrand Reinhold Co., c1985. lxx, 96 p. ISBN 0-442-24282-4.   **CC54**

Defines 287 terms in English, Spanish, French, and German (across four columns per page), arranged alphabetically by the English version. Introductory materials and the subject index are presented in all four languages.   HQ1061.I5348

Directories

Congregate care by county. Jan. 1989– . Phoenix : Oryx, c1989– . Semiannual. $150.00.   **CC55**

A directory of more than 6,800 continuing care retirement communities in the U.S. Arranged geographically by state and county, each entry contains the name of the institution, address and telephone, contact person, average monthly fees, type and number of nursing beds, etc. Indexed by type of facility and by type of ownership.   HD7287.92.U54C67

CPA world directory of old age / comp. by Gillian Crosby . . . [et al.]. Chicago : St. James Pr., 1989. 208 p. ISBN 1-55862-023-0.   **CC56**

Published for the Centre for Policy on Ageing, London.

International in scope. The greater part of the text (Pt.II) lists more than 150 countries giving for each a statistical summary of its aged population based on 1985 data (collected by survey) and a list of organizations (e.g., pressure groups, service providers, national gerontology institutes). An introductory section provides an overview of the world's aged population. Pt.I describes 35 international organizations devoted to the issues and concerns of the elderly. The index is an alphabetical list of all organizations included.   HV1451.C63

International directory of organizations in aging / American Association for International Aging. Wash. : The Association, 1988. 350 p.   **CC57**

Lists 264 organizations in 136 countries by region (Africa, Asia and the Pacific, Europe, Latin America and the Caribbean, and North America), then alphabetically by name under each country. Entries provide mission, constituency, member countries, priority concerns, activities, budgets, languages, and publications. Geographic and subject indexes.   HQ1061.I55

National continuing care directory : retirement communities with nursing care / ed. by Ann Trueblood Raper and Anne C. Kalicki (American Association of Homes for the Aging). 2nd ed. Wash. : American Association of Retired Persons ; Glenview, Ill. : Scott, Foresman and Co., c1988. 449 p. : ill. ISBN 0-673-24885-2 (Scott, Foresman : pbk.). $13.95.   **CC58**

1st ed., [1984] (*Guide* CC131).

Describes 366 facilities, following the same arrangement as the 1st ed.   HV1454.2.U6N37

National directory of educational programs in gerontology / David A. Peterson, David Bergstone, Joy C. Loben-

stine. Wash. : Association for Gerontology in Higher Education, 1987. [856] p.   **CC59**

Presents results of a survey by the Association of Gerontology in Higher Education to determine the extent of training in the field offered by American and Canadian institutions. In two main sections: (1) a brief tabular listing of all institutions surveyed providing little more than the number of courses and units each offers and of faculty involved; (2) one-page descriptions of each program including degrees offered, areas of specialty, course requirements, etc. In alphabetical order by state.

National directory of retirement facilities. 2nd ed. Phoenix : Oryx, 1988. 878 p. ISBN 0-89774-450-0. $175.00.   **CC60**

1st ed., 1979 (*Guide* CC130).

This revised edition, consolidated into one volume, includes more than 18,000 facilities (the 1st ed. listed 12,000).   HQ1063.N37

U.S. directory and source book on aging, 1989–90 / produced by American Association for International Aging, [ed., Susan Coombs-Ficke]. Silver Spring, Md. : Business Publishers, 1989. 374 p.   **CC61**

An interdisciplinary guide to government agencies, private voluntary organizations, corporations, foundations, and publishers. Lists organizations by state, then alphabetically by name. Separate lists for agencies, state offices, selected federal agencies, federal regional offices, and selected congressional committees. Entries provide mission, primary concerns, activities, structure, staffing, and finance. Eight-page list of acronyms; general index.   HV1450.U7

Handbooks

America's elderly : a sourcebook / ed. by Edward E. Duensing. New Brunswick, N.J. : Center for Urban Policy Research, c1988. 190 p. : ill. ISBN 0-88285-125-X. $25.00.   **CC62**

More than 200 graphs and tables in seven chapters that cover demographics, income and expenditures, employment and unemployment, health and health care, housing and homeownership, federal programs and expenditures, and social characteristics. Tables and figures indicate sources of data. No indexes.   HQ1064.U5A646

Encyclopedia of senior citizens information sources : a bibliographic guide to approximately 13,500 citations for publications, organizations, and other sources of information on nearly 300 subjects / Paul Wasserman, Barbara Koehler, and Yvonne Lev, editors. Detroit : Gale, c1987. 1 v. ISBN 0-8103-2192-0.   **CC63**

English-language sources, most published after 1980, organized by topic (e.g., alcoholism, counseling, day care, poverty, senility). Entries are arranged alphabetically by title within subcategories such as abstract services and indexes, associations and professional societies, bibliographies, directories, handbooks, online databases, and statistical sources. Cross-references; detailed table of contents.   Z7164.O4E53

Handbook of aging and the social sciences / editors, Robert H. Binstock and Linda K. George ; associate editors, Victor W. Marshall, George C. Myers, and James H. Schulz. 3rd ed. San Diego, Calif. : Academic Pr., c1990. 489 p. : ill. ISBN 0-12-099190-X.   **CC64**

2nd ed., 1985 (*Guide* CC119).

Follows the format of the 2nd ed. New chapters include: Diversity and heterogeneity; Old age pensions; Leisure and time use; Geographic distribution and migration; and Illness behavior.

§ Other titles in the "Handbooks of aging" series are: *Handbook of the biology of aging* (3rd ed., 1990), ed. by Edward L. Schneider and John W. Rowe and *Handbook of the psycholo-*

gy of aging (3rd ed., 1990), ed. by James E. Birren and K. Warner Schaie.   HQ1061.H336

Kouri, Mary K. Volunteerism and older adults. Santa Barbara, Calif. : ABC-Clio, c1990. 197 p. ISBN 0-87436-562-7.   **CC65**

Pt. 1 includes chapters on types of volunteerism, opportunities, locations, and keys to success. Pt. 2 describes organizations, professional societies, volunteer networks, books, bibliographies, directories, periodicals, newsletters, pamphlets, films, videos, and databases. Entries are alphabetical by name or author in each category. General index.   HN90.V64K68

Statistical handbook on aging Americans / ed. by Frank L. Schick. Phoenix : Oryx, 1986. 294 p. : ill. ISBN 0-89774-259-1.   **CC66**

Provides statistics on the economic and social problems of Americans over the age of 65. Compiled mostly from 1980–85 data published by U.S. government agencies. Contains 337 tables and charts in six topical areas: Demographics, Social characteristics, Health aspects, Employment conditions, Economic status, and Expenditures for the elderly. Sources are listed with tables and in an appended bibliography. Includes a guide to other sources for further study. Index.   HQ1064.U5S343

Weiss, David M. National guide to funding in aging / comp. and ed. by David M. Weiss, Diane E. Mahlmann ; Long Island University, Nassau County Department of Senior Citizen Affairs, the Foundation Center. N.Y. : The Center, 1987. 280 p. ISBN 0-87954-191-1 (pbk.). $35.00.   **CC67**

Describes 369 public and private sources of funding support and technical assistance. Four sections cover federal programs, state programs, foundations, and voluntary organizations. Entries provide donor(s), finances, purpose, types of support, limitations, application information, officers, etc. General index. A 2nd ed. was published in 1989.   HV1461.W42

Statistics

Vierck, Elizabeth. Fact book on aging. Santa Barbara, Calif. : ABC-Clio, c1990. 199 p. ISBN 0-87436-284-9.   **CC68**

"Over 1,500 statistical 'one liners.' "—*Pref.* 20 chapters cover geographic distribution, money, living arrangement, recreation, world records, native languages, crime, the senior market, etc. 13-page bibliography; general index.   HQ1064.U5V494

Alcoholism

Bibliography

Lobb, Michael L. Native American youth and alcohol : an annotated bibliography / Michael L. Lobb and Thomas D. Watts. N.Y. : Greenwood, 1989. 165 p. (Bibliographies and indexes in sociology, no. 16). ISBN 0-313-25618-7.   **CC69**

A 37-page introduction and review of the literature is followed by ten broad subject sections (e.g., accidental death, biomedical factors, gender, policy and prevention, urban vs. rural). Entries arranged by author in each chapter. Lengthy, descriptive abstracts; subject and author indexes.   Z1209.2.U5L6

Miletich, John J. Work and alcohol abuse : an annotated bibliography. N.Y. : Greenwood, 1987. 263 p. (Bibli-

ographies and indexes in sociology, no. 12). ISBN 0-313-25689-6.   **CC70**

Over 1,000 entries, numbered and arranged alphabetically by author in seven subject chapters: Definitions, identification, and diagnosis; Companies and management; Unions, safety, and employee dismissal; Government; Occupations; Women; and Counseling and treatment. Includes English-language books, articles, government publications, theses, dissertations, and conference proceedings, 1972–86. Separate author, subject, and company name indexes.   Z7164.C81M619

Nordquist, Joan. Substance abuse II : alcohol abuse : a bibliography. Santa Cruz, Calif. : Reference and Research Services, 1990. 68 p. (Contemporary social issues, no. 17.). ISBN 0-937855-32-4 (pbk.).   **CC71**

In ten sections, drawing from the last five years of the legal, social, political, and psychological literatures. Citations pertain to genetic, biological, and familial explanations for abuse; specific populations; violence and crime; the workplace; prevention and regulation; drunk-driving; and treatment. Sections list books followed by articles; entries are alphabetical by author within subsections. The final section lists resources: bibliographies, directories, organizations, and statistical sources. No indexes. See also *Supplement* CC114.

Page, Penny Booth. Alcohol use and alcoholism : a guide to the literature. N.Y. : Garland, 1986. 164 p. ISBN 0-8240-9020-9.   **CC72**

Intended for general readers or professionals. Includes English-language books, pamphlets, leaflets, and government publications, most from the mid-1970s to 1985; omits journal articles and audiovisual materials. Offers 405 consecutively numbered entries, arranged alphabetically by author, in 16 subject chapters that include: Effects on body; Treatment; Use among women; Alcohol and the fetus; and Traffic safety. Each chapter begins with an introductory paragraph and ends with cross-references. Two appendixes include alcohol-related periodicals and resource organizations; author and title indexes.   Z7721.P33

Watts, Thomas D. Black alcohol abuse and alcoholism : an annotated bibliography / Thomas D. Watts, Roosevelt Wright, Jr. N.Y. : Praeger, 1986. 265 p. ISBN 0-03-005713-2. $30.00.   **CC73**

Intended for students, practitioners, and professionals. Draws from social, economic, medical, and historical literature, 1943–85. 533 entries are arranged chronologically and include detailed informative annotations. Includes a list of social service and information organizations. Author and subject indexes.   Z7721.W37

Encyclopedias

O'Brien, Robert. The encyclopedia of alcoholism / Robert O'Brien and Morris Chafetz ; ed. by Glen Evans. 2nd ed. N.Y. : Facts on File, 1991. 346 p. : ill. ISBN 0-8160-1955-X.   **CC74**

1st ed., 1982 (*Guide* CC145).

Follows the same format as the earlier edition. Of more than 600 entries, 100 are new.   HV5035.O27

Directories

Moore, Jean. Roads to recovery : a national directory of alcohol and drug addiction treatment centers. N.Y. : Collier Books ; London : Collier Macmillan Publishers, c1985. 384 p. ISBN 0-02-059470-4 (pbk.). $17.95. **CC75**

Centers are arranged alphabetically by state in three sections (Eastern, Central/Southern, and Western), each entry giving center name, address, telephone, director, average patient census, minimum duration of treatment, cost, accreditation. Describes services and eligibility; excludes outpatient services. An appendix lists national organizations and agencies by state. Index of programs for specific groups (adolescents, men, women), but there are not other indexes. **RC564.73.M66**

National directory of drug abuse and alcoholism treatment and prevention programs. Rockville, Md. : National Institute on Alcohol Abuse and Alcoholism, [1989]. 370 p. (DHHS publication, no. [ADM] 89–1603). **CC76**
Previous ed., 1983 (*Guide* EK294)
Early eds. had title: *National directory of drug abuse and alcoholism treatment programs.* **HV5825.N323**

Children and youth

Guides

Haag, Enid E. Research guide for studies in infancy and childhood. N.Y. : Greenwood, 1988. 430 p. (Reference sources for the social sciences and humanities, no. 8). ISBN 0-313-24763-3. **CC77**
Section I reviews research strategy, describes 25 databases, and provides a brief bibliography of online searching materials, with 50 pages devoted to reference works, grouped by subject area. Section II offers subject bibliographies, with names of related databases, in broad categories (e.g., families, communication, social/cultural development), further subdivided by subject. Entries are alphabetical by title within each subtopic. Includes books, articles, and reports from psychology, social work, education, sociology, medicine, law, home economics, and the arts. Approximately 1,400 annotated entries. Separate author, title, and subject indexes. **Z7164.C5H3**

Washington, Valora. Black children and American institutions : an ecological review and resource guide / Valora Washington, Velma La Point. N.Y. : Garland, 1988. 432 p. ISBN 0-8240-8517-5. $67.00. **CC78**
An essay that examines African-American children in relation to schools, family, criminal justice, social services, and physical and mental health is followed by a bibliography, arranged by author with descriptive annotations. One section lists organizations with their activities and contact names, and describes seven organizations at greater length (e.g., Children's Defense Fund, National Urban League). Author/name and subject indexes. **Z1361.N39W34**

Bibliography

Black adolescence : current issues and annotated bibliography / by The Consortium for Research on Black Adolescence with Velma McBride Murry and assistance from Georgie Winter. Boston : G.K. Hall, 1990. 160 p. ISBN 0-8161-9080-1. **CC79**
Consists of 11 chapters, each in three parts: a literature review, a list of annotated references, and a list of additional references. Topics covered include psychosocial development, psychological and physical health, drug abuse, education, employment, sexuality, and family relationships. No index. **Z1361.N39B495**

De Young, Mary. Child molestation : an annotated bibliography. Jefferson, N.C. : McFarland, c1987. 176 p. ISBN 0-89950-243-1 (pbk.). $29.95. **CC80**
An introduction that defines child molestation is followed by 557 numbered entries from journals and books, listed alphabetically by author under topical sections (e.g., effects on children, prevention, treatment, sex rings, child pornography, legal issues). Also has sections for statistical studies, literature re-

views, and historical works. Each section is prefaced with a scope note. Covers early 1960s through 1986; draws from psychology, sociology, medicine, law, and other disciplines. Author, title, and subject indexes. **Z7164.S42D39**

Gouke, Mary Noel. One-parent children, the growing minority : a research guide / Mary Noel Gouke, Arline McClarty Rollins. N.Y. : Garland, 1990. 494 p. (Reference books on family issues, v. 14 ; Garland reference library of social science, v. 344). ISBN 0-8240-8576-0. **CC81**
Includes 1,142 abstracts of English-language scholarly books, journal articles, essays, and conference papers; also lists dissertations, but without abstracts. Covers research from the U.S. and many other countries, 1970–89. In 15 chapters, arranged by four major sections: types of families (e.g., fatherless, lesbian or gay, adoptive); circumstances of loss or absence (e.g., single-parenthood, employment, divorce); general aspects; and schools. Separate geographic, programs/projects/associations/institutions, author, and subject indexes. **Z7164.C5G68**

Nuba-Scheffler, Hannah. Infancy : a guide to research and resources / Hannah Nuba-Scheffler, Deborah Lovitky Sheiman, Kathleen Pullan Watkins. N.Y. : Garland, 1986. 182 p. (Garland reference library of social science, v. 324). ISBN 0-8240-8699-6. **CC82**
Addresses development from prenatal period to two years. Compiled for students, parents, and teachers. In 11 chapters (e.g., Physical, cognitive, and language development; Nutrition and health; Infant-family interaction; The exceptional infant; Play). Chapter 10 lists books for babies, chapter 11 includes an alphabetized list of organizations and publications. Chapters begin with introductory essays and conclude with annotated bibliographies, alphabetically arranged by author. Author and title indexes. **HQ774.N83**

Powell, Paul W. The great deceiver : seeing Satan for what he is. Nashville, Tenn. : Broadman Pr., c1988. 142 p. ISBN 0-8054-1957-8 (pbk.). $5.95. **CC83**
This edition offers essays and articles by 11 contributors on various aspects of child sexual abuse. The bibliography contains 310 entries for articles, books, booklets, and reports from Canada and the U.S. for 1980–85. **BT981.P68**

Sexual abuse of children in the 1980's : ten essays and an annotated bibliography / ed. by Benjamin Schlesinger. Toronto ; Buffalo : Univ. of Toronto Pr., c1986. 201 p. ISBN 0-8020-6622-4. **CC84**
1st ed., 1982 (*Guide* CC264).
Eleven authors contribute essays and articles on various aspects of child sexual abuse to this updated edition. Contains 310 entries for articles, books, booklets, and reports from Canada and the U.S. for 1980–85. **HQ72.C3S49**

Sheiman, Deborah Lovitky. Resources for middle childhood : a source book / Deborah Lovitky Sheiman, Maureen Slonim. N.Y. : Garland, 1988. 138 p. ISBN 0-8240-7777-6. **CC85**
Annotated bibliographies follow the six to eight pages of text in each chapter, covering various topics: physical, psychosocial, and cognitive development; family interactions; peer relationships; etc. A practical treatment of the subject for undergraduates, parents, and teachers. Focuses upon the six- to twelve-year old child (the elementary school years). Author and title indexes only. **HQ767.9.S48**

Watkins, Kathleen Pullan. Parent-child attachment : a guide to research. N.Y. : Garland, 1987. 190 p. (Reference books on family issues, v. 11 ; Garland reference library of social science, v. 388). ISBN 0-8240-8465-9. **CC86**
Written for professionals, parents, and general readers. Emphasizes attachment in infancy and early childhood; includes only English-language works. In 11 chapters, each begin-

ning with a topical essay on subjects such as theory, the adoptive family, prematurity, chronic illness, parents with disabilities, and single parenthood, followed by an annotated bibliography. Essays and bibliographies average eight pages each. Author and subject indexes.   BF723.A75W38

Encyclopedias

Clark, Robin E. The encyclopedia of child abuse / Robin E. Clark and Judith Freeman Clark. N.Y. : Facts on File, c1989. 328 p. : ill. ISBN 0-8160-1584-8.   **CC87**

For general readers and professionals. Draws from various disciplines (e.g., law, medicine, sociology, psychology, economics, and education); international in scope, although U.S. information predominates. Omits biographical information. A 17-page overview is followed by 200 pages of entries, alphabetically arranged and written by the compilers. Cross-references; some entries conclude with suggested readings. 15 appendixes include organizations, agencies, reporting procedures and statutes by state, types of immunity, and statistics. Bibliography; general index.   HV6626.5.C57

Encyclopedia of adolescence / ed. by Richard Lerner, Anne C. Petersen, Jeanne Brooks-Gunn. N.Y. : Garland, 1991. 2 v. : ill. ISBN 0-8240-4378-2 (set).   **CC88**

More than 200 signed entries by 233 specialists in the social sciences, sciences, and humanities, alphabetically arranged, each concluding with a bibliography and cross-references. Addresses subjects such as eating disorders, friendship, Hispanic adolescents, adolescent fathers, chronic illness, gay and lesbian youth, and suicide. List of contributors; subject index.

HQ796.E58

Directories

Fritsch, Ronald E. Directory of public and private programs for emotionally disturbed children and youth. Phoenix : Oryx, 1985. 336 p. ISBN 0-89774-199-4.

CC89

Describes public school systems, private day and residential schools, and other facilities offering specialized programs. Arranged by state, then alphabetically by organization. Entries provide names of contacts, addresses, information on physical plant, kinds of children served, tuition staff size and specialties, educational and therapy programs, etc. Has "Exceptionalities index," listing organizations by type of exceptionality served (e.g., mentally retarded) and "Psychopathological conditions treated index," classifying facilities by kinds of behavioral systems treated (e.g., alcohol abuse, depression).   HV3006.A4F75

International directory of youth bodies = Répertoire international des organismes de jeunesse = Repertorio internacional de organismos de juventud. 1990– . Paris : UNESCO, c1990– .   **CC90**

Describes 559 nonprofit governmental and private organizations in 123 countries. In two parts: (1) international, regional, and nongovernmental organizations, arranged alphabetically by organization; (2) national organizations, arranged alphabetically by country, subarranged by Governmental coordinating bodies and Governmental and non-governmental youth organizations, research centres, training centres, and information centres. Entries give address, short description of purpose, programs and activities, relationships to other organizations. Includes an alphabetical list of countries; a list of organizations; an index of interests coordinated by government bodies (e.g., Cultural activities) that lists countries that sponsor programs; and a similar index for programs of youth organizations and of centers for training, research, or information. In English, with French and Spanish prefaces.

Sherman, Barbara Smiley. Directory of residential treatment facilities for emotionally disturbed children. Phoenix : Oryx, 1985. 231 p. ISBN 0-89774-118-8.   **CC91**

Lists facilities by state, within which the arrangement is alphabetical by name. Entries give addresses, types of placement, children served (ages, diagnoses, etc.), tuition, setting (e.g., cottages in the country), social and rehabilitation services, educational and vocational services, and referral requirements. Indexes of institutions by type of placement, type of funding, and characteristics exhibited by children (e.g., autistic, drug abuse, hearing impaired).   RJ504.5.S54

Handbooks

Finkelhor, David. A sourcebook on child sexual abuse / David Finkelhor with Sharon Araji ... [et al.]. Beverly Hills : Sage Publications, c1986. 276 p. ISBN 0-8039-2748-7. ISBN 0-803-92749-5 (pbk.).   **CC92**

A review of research that summarizes findings on five topics: prevalence, high risk children, abusers, effects of abuse, and prevention. Bibliography; subject index.   HQ71.F52

Death and dying

Bibliography

Basford, Terry K. Near-death experiences : an annotated bibliography. N.Y. : Garland, 1990. 182 p. (Garland reference library of social science, vol. 481). ISBN 0-8240-6349-X.   **CC93**

A selective list, chronologically arranged, of 759 titles of books, articles, and dissertations published 1847–1975. In three sections: (1) Near-death experiences; (2) Death visions; (3) Analogues of near-death experiences. Author index.

Z6878.P8B37

Benson, Hazel B. The dying child : an annotated bibliography. N.Y. : Greenwood, 1988. 270 p. (Contemporary problems of childhood, no. 6). ISBN 0-313-24708-0.

CC94

In six main sections (General aspects, The young child, The adolescent, The family, Caregivers, and Physical care) with numerous subdivisions. 743 entries are arranged alphabetically by author within subchapters. Includes popular and professional journals, books, book chapters, conference reports, government publications, pamphlets, and dissertations, 1960–87. Omits foreign languages, speeches, and unpublished papers. All entries except dissertations have descriptive annotations. Six appendixes list children's books, audiovisuals, support organizations, wish-granting organizations, hospices, and reference tools. Author index; selective keyword subject index.

Z6671.52.T47B46

Death education : an annotated resource guide / Hannelore Wass ... [et al.]. Wash. : Hemisphere Pub. Corp., c1985. v. 2 (467 p.). ISBN 0-89116-321-2. $26.50 (est.).

CC95

Updates the 1980 publication, following the same format.

HQ1073.D42

McIntosh, John L. Research on suicide : a bibliography. Westport, Conn. : Greenwood, c1985. 323 p. (Bibliographies and indexes in psychology, no. 2). ISBN 0-313-23992-4. $35.00.   **CC96**

Includes English-language publications from the mid-1970s to early 1984. An introduction precedes each of the ten chapters, which are divided into subtopics and list entries alphabetically by author. Chapters cover theories, demography and epidemiology, prevention, ethics, postvention, etc. Author and subject indexes.   Z7615.M38

Poteet, G. Howard. Death and dying : a bibliography, 1950–1974 : supplement vol. 1 : suicide / by G. Howard Poteet and Joseph C. Santora. Troy, N.Y. : Whitson Pub. Co., 1978– . 166 p. ISBN 0-87875-108-4.   **CC97**
Z7204.D4P68

———— Death and dying : a bibliography, 1974–1978 / by G. Howard Poteet and Joseph C. Santora. Troy, N.Y. : Whitston Pub. Co., c1989. 520 p. ISBN 0-87875-351-6.   **CC98**

The two items above extend the scope and coverage of Poteet's 1976 bibliography for the 1950–74 period (*Guide* CC169) which excluded writings on suicide. The 1974–78 compilation includes fuller coverage of euthanasia as well as death, dying, and suicide. The latter volume now provides cross-references for the subject headings used in the section for periodical articles. Author index in each volume.
Z7204.D4P682

Simpson, Michael A. Dying, death, and grief : a critical bibliography. Pittsburgh : Univ. of Pittsburgh Pr., c1987. 259 p. ISBN 0-8229-3561-9.   **CC99**
4th ed., 1979 (*Guide* CC171).

Lists more than 1,700 books published 1979–87 alphabetically by title and rates them by a five-star system. Provides for some titles critical annotations that vary in length. Two "stop press" sections (books identified after the main section was written) follow the main book list, as do three additional unannotated bibliographies of books on murder, terrorism and the political uses of death, and nuclear holocaust and megadeath. A useful subject index arranges the main list and "stop press" entries into subject categories where they are listed in order of their rating. Author index.   Z5725.S55

Encyclopedias

Encyclopedia of death / ed. by Robert Kastenbaum and Beatrice Kastenbaum. Phoenix : Oryx, 1989. 295 p. : ill. ISBN 0-89774-263-X. $74.50.   **CC100**

Contains 131 lengthy, signed articles, aimed at students, academics, and general readers, on such topics as Rigor mortis, Grief counseling, and National Funeral Directors Association. Contributors are academicians from many disciplines, theologians, physicians, hospice directors, officials of associations, etc., who attempt to write "well-balanced entries with an objective tone," but have also been "invited to share their own experiences, beliefs, and suggestions."—*Introd.* Many articles are followed by lists of suggested readings and cross-references. Subject index.   HQ1073.E54

Evans, Glen. The encyclopedia of suicide / Glen Evans and Norman L. Farberow. N.Y. : Facts on File, c1988. 434 p. ISBN 0-8160-1397-7. $40.00.   **CC101**

Intended for both professionals and general readers; multidisciplinary in coverage. Consists of more than 500 entries, alphabetically arranged, on such topics as black Americans, college students, myths, and John Lennon. A third of the book is devoted to appendixes of detailed tabular data on U.S. suicide rates by sex, age, race, geographic area, marital status, month of occurrence, and method. An introductory essay reviews the history of suicide. Lists U.S. organizations specializing in suicide prevention and crisis, and a smaller number of Canadian, U.N., and international organizations. List of English-language periodicals; 14-page bibliography. Cross-references; general index.   HV6545.E87

Disabled

Bibliography

Fellendorf, George W. Bibliography on deafness : *The Volta review, American annals of the deaf, The teacher of the deaf.* Supplement, 1977–1979. Wash. : Alexander Graham Bell Association for the Deaf, c1980. 42 p. ISBN 0-88200-139-6.   **CC102**
For basic volume and annotation, see *Guide* CC179.

Provides updating through 1979, and now includes citations from the British journal, *The teacher of the deaf.* Author index.   Z5721.F4

Friedberg, Joan Brest. Accept me as I am : best books of juvenile nonfiction on impairments and disabilities / Joan Brest Friedberg, June B. Mullins, Adelaide Weir Sukiennik. N.Y. : Bowker, 1985. 363 p. : ill. ISBN 0-8352-1974-7.   **CC103**

Designed as a companion to Barbara Baskin and Karen Harris's *More notes from a different drummer* (N.Y. : Bowker, 1984) which surveyed juvenile fiction portraying disabled people, 1940–81. Treats nonfiction books to 1984. Divided into chapters describing works on specific disabilities. Alphabetically arranged entries give brief bibliographic information, specific disabilities treated, reading level, and evaluative annotations. Author, title, and subject indexes.   Z1037.9.F73

Ritter, Audrey L. A deafness collection : selected and annotated / comp. by Audrey L. Ritter and Karen A. Hopkins. Chicago : Association of Specialized & Cooperative Library Agencies, 1985. 186 p. ISBN 0-8389-6921-6 (pbk.).   **CC104**

T.p. note: National Technical Institute for the Deaf at Rochester Institute of Technology.

Claimed by the compilers to be the most comprehensive bibliography on deafness to date. Cites books, periodical articles, government publications, reports, and other materials, excluding dissertations. Annotations are "written in a generally descriptive and occasionally critical manner."—*Pref.* Arranged topically in 19 chapters on such subjects as Audiology, Multiply handicapped, and Sign language. General index.

Encyclopedias

Gallaudet encyclopedia of deaf people and deafness / John V. Van Cleve, ed. in chief. N.Y. : McGraw-Hill, c1987. 3 v. : ill. ISBN 0-07-079229-1. $300.00.   **CC105**

Contains 273 alphabetically arranged signed articles treating characteristics of the deaf, educational practices, specific individuals, organizations, periodicals, etc. Many entries are divided into sections and subsections ("Sign language" has 41 of them), and most include cross-references and bibliographies. General index.   HV2365.G35

Sardegna, Jill. The encyclopedia of blindness and vision impairment / Jill Sardegna and T. Otis Paul. N.Y. : Facts on File, c1991. 329 p. ISBN 0-8160-2153-8.   **CC106**

For annotation, see *Supplement* EK44.   RE91.S27

Directories

Directory of national information sources on handicapping conditions and related services / U.S. Department of Education, National Institute of Handicapped Research. [4th ed.]. Wash. : The Institute : For sale by the Supt. of Docs., U.S. Govt. Print. Off., [1986]. 366 p. **CC107**
3rd ed., 1982 (*Guide* CC194).

Superintendent of Documents classification: ED1.202:H 19/2/1986.

New to this edition are: a list of databases by subject; descriptions of 45 additional organizations; and a revised scheme of organization that replaces the previous division into two parts (national organizations and federal information sources) with sections for kinds of groups (e.g., advocacy organizations, federal government, professional organizations, facilities, schools, and clinics). **HV1553.D544**

Financial aid for the disabled and their families. 1988–1989– . Redwood City, Calif. : Reference Service Pr., 1988– . Biennial. ISSN 0898-9222. $35.00. **CC108**

Provides program descriptions and application information, organized by type of disability. Includes an annotated bibliography of general financial aid directories. Indexed by program title, sponsoring organization, geographic area, subject, and deadline date ("Calendar index"). **LB2337.2.F58**

A guide to recreation, leisure, and travel for the handicapped. 1st ed.– . Toledo, Ohio : Resource Directories, c1985– . Biennial. ISSN 8756-2529. **CC109**
Contents: v. 1, Recreation and sports; v. 2, Travel and transportation

Vol. 1 lists sports and recreation programs, equipment and information sources, in sections such as Sports and recreation organizations and Mobility vehicles for children and adults. Entries profile populations served, backgrounds and objectives, services, and publications. Appendixes list addresses of local chapters and regional representatives of sport and recreation associations. Four indexes: activities for adults, activities for children, activities by disability, and equipment by disability and activity. Vol. 2 provides information on accessibility in chapters on such topics as Transportation, Lodging, and Camps. An appendix lists addresses and telephones of state tourist agencies. **GV183.5.G84**

Handicapped funding directory : a guide to sources of funding in the United States for programs and services for the disabled / Richard M. Eckstein, researcher. 7th ed. Margate, Fla. : Research Grant Guides, 1990. 251 p. **CC110**
1st ed., 1980 (*Guide* CC195); 6th ed., (1988–89), 1988.

The word "handicapped" is to be dropped from the title in future editions. Appendixes include types of federal assistance and programs requiring circular coordination; also lists regional and local offices and federal information centers. Indexes: foundations and corporations; associations; area of interest; federal programs by agency. **HV1553.H35**

Hecker, Helen. Travel for the disabled : a handbook of travel resources and 500 worldwide access guides. Portland, Ore. : Twin Peaks Pr., c1985. 185 p. ISBN 0-933261-00-4. $9.95. **CC111**
For annotation, see *Supplement* BJ44. **HV1568.6.H43**

Statistics

Digest of data on persons with disabilities / prepared under contract to the Congressional Research Service, Library of Congress ; prepared by Mathematica Policy Research, Inc. ; John L. Czajka, principal investigator. Wash. : U.S. Dept. of Education, [1984]. 177 p. : ill. **CC112**
Superintendent of Documents classification: ED 1.2:D 26/3.

In five sections: (1) Prevalence of disabilities; (2) Characteristics of the disabled population (e.g., employment, living arrangements); (3) Federal programs (e.g., special education); (4) Individual impairments and chronic conditions: comparative data; and (5) State level data. Statistics are presented in tables and charts, with highlights and explanatory notes accompanying each table. Includes a complete list of tables and an Index matrix that cross-tabulates Disability indicators (e.g., chronic activity limitation) with Additional data items presented (e.g., age, diagnostic condition such as visual impairment, education level). **HV1553.D525**

Drug abuse

Bibliography

Derivan, William J. Prevention education : a guide to research / William J. Derivan, Natalie Anne Silverstein. N.Y. : Garland, 1990. 282 p. (Garland bibliographies in contemporary education, v. 9 ; Garland reference library of social science, v. 524). ISBN 0-8240-3716-2. **CC113**

An annotated bibliography of 611 works on prevention of drug and alcohol abuse, including books, articles, curriculum guides, teacher training materials, government publications, project evaluation guides, research reports, and other sources. In seven main categories (e.g., Prevention programs—school based, Curricula/material, Family systems). Appendixes list sources of information and resources and periodicals on drug and alcohol abuse. Author, title, and subject indexes.

Z7164.N17D44

Nordquist, Joan. Substance abuse I : drug abuse : a bibliography. Santa Cruz, Calif. : Reference and Research Services, 1989. 68 p. (Contemporary social issues, no. 16.). ISBN 0-93785-531-6 (pbk.). $15.00. **CC114**

Nine sections draw from the last three years of the legal, psychological, business, and social literatures. Citations pertain to specific populations, crime, the workplace, AIDS, treatment, legal aspects, and the drug war. Sections divided by format: books, pamphlets, and documents, or articles in periodicals and books. Entries are alphabetical by author in each subsection. A final section lists resources: bibliographies, guides, directories, statistical sources, and organizations. No indexes. See also *Supplement* CC71. **Z7164.N17N67**

Dictionaries

Fay, John. The alcohol/drug abuse dictionary and encyclopedia. Springfield, Ill. : Thomas, c1988. 167 p. ISBN 0-398-05491-6. **CC115**

Includes "language that extends from the coarse jargon of the illicit drug subculture to the complex dialect of pharmacology."—*Pref.* Headwords (130 p.) include: "anabolic steroid," "deterrence theory," "Mexican brown," "meprobamate," "nutmeg," "PCP." Appendix includes additional jargon arranged alphabetically under drug name or type; matched lists of generic and brand names; state agencies, drug poison information centers, and resource agencies; and six toll-free help-lines. Three-page bibliography. RC564.F39

Directories

Women's recovery programs : a directory of residential addiction treatment centers. Phoenix: Oryx, 1990. 339 p. ISBN 0-89774-584-1. **CC116**

Profiles some 1,200 residential and inpatient programs in the U.S. that treat drug, alcohol, and behavioral disorders in women. After two essays on women and addiction, the directory listings are arranged alphabetically by state and geographically within each state. Separate indexes for organization names, addictions/disorders, and treatment methods. List of abbreviations; one-page glossary of terms. RC564.73.W66

Homeless

Burt, Martha R. America's homeless : numbers, characteristics, and programs that serve them / Martha R. Burt, Barbara E. Cohen. Wash.: Urban Institute Pr.; Lanham, Md.: Distr. by Univ. Pr. of America, c1989. 176 p. (Urban Institute report, 89-3). ISBN 0-87766-471-4. ISBN 0-87766-472-2 (pbk.). **CC117**

From three Urban Institute research projects, brings together findings on the homeless, presenting statistics on their number, location, racial characteristics, nutrition, etc., and a summary of state and national programs intended for their assistance. Verbal descriptions are supplemented by numerous tables. No index, but a detailed table of contents includes a complete list of statistical tables. HV4505.B89

Hombs, Mary Ellen. American homelessness : a reference handbook. Santa Barbara, Calif.: ABC-Clio, c1990. 193 p. ISBN 0-87436-547-3. ISBN 0-87436-546-5. **CC118**

Presents an "organized overview of the wide variety of... resources and tools" (*Pref.*) for understanding the causes and characteristics of homelessness. In nine chapters, including a chronology, biographical sketches of advocates for the homeless, summaries of legislation and court cases, a directory of organizations, and an annotated bibliography of reference materials. Glossary; general index. HV4505.H647

Homelessness in the United States / ed. by Jamshid A. Momeni. N.Y.: Greenwood, 1989–1990. 2 v. : ill. ISBN 0-313-25566-0 (v. 1). ISBN 0-313-26792-8 (v. 2). **CC119**

Presents national, state, and local statistical data on the homeless, plus discussions and analyses of the problem. Vol. 1 contains 14 chapters, each by an expert, concerning homeless distributions, variations, trends, and characteristics in individual states and cities. Vol. 2 offers 11 chapters on varied topics such as drug abuse among the homeless, public policies for reducing homelessness, and a national overview of the problem. Many statistical tables. Both volumes have general indexes. HV4505.H656

Nordquist, Joan. The homeless in America : a bibliography. Santa Cruz, Calif.: Reference and Research Services, 1988. 64 p. ISBN 0-937855-23-5. $15.00. **CC120**

Contains approximately 500 entries from scholarly, technical, and popular sources, including recent books, journals, conference papers, and government publications. Arranged in topical categories (e.g., families, women, children, drugs, federal policies, mental health, legal issues), subdivided by format; entries in sections are alphabetical by author. Includes list of bibliographies, directories, and organization names. No indexes. Z7164.H72N67

Marriage and the family

Bibliography

Barnes, Grace M. Alcohol and the family : a comprehensive bibliography / comp. by Grace M. Barnes and Diane K. Augustino. N.Y.: Greenwood, 1987. 461 p. (Bibliographies and indexes in sociology, no. 9). ISBN 0-313-24782-X. **CC121**

Includes more than 6,000 books, book chapters, and journal articles from the social sciences and human services arranged alphabetically by author. Non-English entries include English translations of titles. Subject index. Z7721.B364

Benson-von der Ohe, Elizabeth. An annotated bibliography of U.S. scholarship on the history of the family / Elizabeth Benson-von der Ohe, Valmari M. Mason. N.Y.: AMS Pr., c1986. 194 p. ISBN 0-404-61606-2. **CC122**

Emphasizes journal articles, books, book chapters, and dissertations, 1975–83. Topical arrangement of entries, as outlined in table of contents; no subject index. Detailed, descriptive annotations are provided for more than half the entries. Name index. Z7164.M2B46

Black American families, 1965–1984 : a classified, selectively annotated bibliography / Walter R. Allen, ed. in chief; Richard A. English and Jo Anne Hall, associate editors. N.Y.: Greenwood, 1986. 480 p. (Bibliographies and indexes in Afro-American and African studies, no. 16). ISBN 0-313-25613-6. **CC123**

Lists 1,153 entries, arranged alphabetically by author. Provides subject descriptors for each reference; some include annotations and notes. Indexes: classified, keyword, co-author/co-editor. List of periodical titles and publishers. Lack of variation in typeface or size makes text difficult to use. Z1361.N39B5

Davis, Lenwood G. The black family in the United States : a revised, updated, selectively annotated bibliography. N.Y.: Greenwood, 1986. 234 p. (Bibliographies and indexes in Afro-American and African studies, no. 14). ISBN 0-313-25237-8. **CC124**

1st ed., 1978 (*Guide* CC364).

Contains over 650 entries and several new topics (e.g., abortion, genocide, polygamy, military families, racism, and sterilization). Author index. Z1361.N39D355

De Young, Mary. Incest : an annotated bibliography. Jefferson, N.C.: McFarland, c1985. 161 p. ISBN 0-89950-142-7 (pbk.). **CC125**

Focuses on professional journals and books, most from the last ten years, in 13 chapters covering the forms, effects, and treatment of incest. Includes statistical studies, book reviews, and a useful chapter on definitions. Entries are arranged alphabetically by author under chapter subheadings. Author and subject indexes. Z7164.S42D4

Engeldinger, Eugene A. Spouse abuse : an annotated bibliography of violence between mates. Metuchen, N.J.: Scarecrow, 1986. 317 p. ISBN 0-8108-1838-8. **CC126**

Lists scholarly and popular English-language books, articles, government publications, theses, dissertations, conference papers, directories, pamphlets, and handbooks through 1983; omits newspaper articles, films, and recordings. 1,783 entries, alphabetically arranged by author in a single listing. Name and subject indexes. Z5703.4.W53E53

●**Family resources database** [computer file]. Minneapolis : National Council on Family Relations, 1970– . **CC127**

Coverage: 1970– (nonjournal records); 1973– (journal articles). File size: 200,000 records. Updated monthly. Available online (BRS, Human Resource Information Network [HRIN]) and on magnetic tape (producer).

Provides coverage of the psychological and sociological literature relating to family studies. Journal citations correspond to those in *Inventory of marriage and family literature* (*Guide* CC216 *note*). Subsidiary files include Idea bank (works in progress), Human resources bank (bibliographic information about professionals available for consulting), and Family study centers (a directory of family life research agencies).

Family therapy : a bibliography, 1937–1986 / comp. by Bernard Lubin. N.Y. : Greenwood, 1988. 470 p. (Bibliographies and indexes in psychology, no. 4). ISBN 0-313-26172-5. **CC128**

A comprehensive work, intended for undergraduates and graduate students. Includes 6,167 cross-referenced entries, primarily journal articles, with some books and dissertations, arranged alphabetically by author. Author and subject indexes.
Z6665.7.F35F36

Gruber, Ellen J. Stepfamilies : a guide to the sources and resources. N.Y. : Garland, 1986. 122 p. ISBN 0-8240-8688-0. $28.00. **CC129**

Includes books and periodical articles, 1980–84. Within sections for professionals who work with parents or children, for parents, and for children and young adults, entries are alphabetical by author. Separate, brief list of audiovisual materials, organizations, and newsletters. Index of names and some broad subjects.
Z7164.M2G78

Kemmer, Elizabeth Jane. Violence in the family : an annotated bibliography. N.Y. : Garland, 1984. 192 p. (Garland reference library of social science, v. 182). ISBN 0-8240-9090-X. **CC130**

Covers periodical articles and books published in English, 1960–82, and includes contributions from many fields: psychology, social work, medicine, women's studies, law, criminology, nursing, and the popular press. 1,055 consecutively numbered entries are arranged alphabetically by author. Author and subject indexes.
Z7164.C5K46

Melina, Lois Ruskai. Adoption : an annotated bibliography and guide. N.Y. : Garland, 1987. 292 p. ISBN 0-8240-8942-1. $34.00. **CC131**

Includes English-language books and journals published after 1973 in sociology, social work, psychology, anthropology, education, psychiatry, child development, medicine, and law. Lists works readily available; intended for a wide audience. 845 cross-referenced entries are listed alphabetically by author in 13 topical chapters (e.g., Infant, special needs, intercountry, and minority adoption; Sealed records, proadoption issues, and termination of parent rights). Lists children's resources, education and training materials, and audiovisuals. Author and subject indexes.
Z7164.A23M44

Nofsinger, Mary M. Children and adjustment to divorce : an annotated bibliography. N.Y. : Garland, 1989. 1 v. (Garland reference library of social science, v. 554). ISBN 0-8240-4297-2. **CC132**

Contains three bibliographies, an audiovisual resource list, and an organizational resources list, each with an introduction. In the main bibliography of books and articles, arranged by author, entries indicate categories of professionals to whom the items would be of interest. Separate bibliographies for parents and for children and young adults follow. The audiovisual resources list, alphabetical by title, includes the audience level for each entry, from preschool to adult. Organizational resources

are listed alphabetically by name. Author, book title, user category, and subject indexes. Z7164.C5N66

Nordquist, Joan. Domestic violence : spouse abuse, marital rape. Santa Cruz, Calif. : Reference and Research Services, 1986. 64 p. ISBN 0-93785-507-3. **CC133**

A slim volume with very recent English-language, multidisciplinary coverage. Includes scholarly and general interest books, articles, pamphlets, and advocacy group publications. Section I covers domestic violence and spouse abuse, Section II marital rape. Entries are grouped by format and listed alphabetically by author. Section III lists bibliographies, directories, organizations, and periodical titles. No indexes.
HQ809.3.U6N67

Sadler, Judith DeBoard. Families in transition : an annotated bibliography. Hamden, Conn. : Archon Books, 1988. 251 p. ISBN 0-208-02180-9. **CC134**

Intended for a wide audience. An introduction provides statistical information and an overview. The bibliography lists 970 books, articles, and audiovisual materials, late 1970s–mid-1980s; a late additions list includes items as recent as 1987. Except for chapter 15 (audiovisuals), entries are grouped in 14 topical chapters, including Single parents, Adoptive and foster families, Parental kidnapping, Working parents and latchkey children, Works for children and youth, and Homosexual relationships. Entries are alphabetical by author within each chapter. Appendix lists addresses for associations and organizations. Separate indexes for subjects, authors, book titles, and article titles. Z5118.F2S23

Zollar, Ann Creighton. Adolescent pregnancy and parenthood : an annotated guide. N.Y. : Garland, 1990. 244 p. ISBN 0-8240-4295-6. **CC135**

A bibliography of 700 articles, book chapters, and books from the sociological and psychological literatures, plus an additional 87 references to holdings of the Data Archive on Adolescent Pregnancy and Pregnancy Prevention (DAAPPP). Arranged by 12 broad topical areas (e.g., Contraception, Sex education, Adolescent fathers, Legal issues), with no other subject access and no cross-references. Author index. Z7164.Y8Z64

Encyclopedias

DiCanio, Margaret. The encyclopedia of marriage, divorce, and the family. N.Y. : Facts on File, c1989. 607 p. ISBN 0-8160-1695-X. **CC136**

A comprehensive treatment of present-day family life in North America, presented through more than 500 entries on such subjects as living wills, throwaway children, bisexual spouses, and homeless families. Entries are alphabetically arranged, vary in length from a few lines to several pages, and include cross-references. Detailed index of authors, titles, and subjects; 32-page bibliography. Nine appendixes include: How to choose therapists, mental health agencies, and divorce attorneys; Sample antenuptial and living-together agreements; Directories of state child-care licensing and child-support enforcement agencies.
HQ9.D38

Dictionaries

Sauber, S. Richard. Family therapy : basic concepts and terms / S. Richard Sauber, Luciano L'Abate, Gerald R. Weeks. Rockville, Md. : Aspen Systems Corp., 1985. 181 p. ISBN 0-89443-556-6. **CC137**

An encyclopedic dictionary whose entries provide definitions, examples, sources, and references to uses of the term. A brief appendix describes professional organizations and publications. RC488.5.S27

Directories

The adoption directory / Ellen Paul, ed. Detroit : Gale, c1989. 515 p. ISBN 0-8103-2240-4. $55.00. **CC138**

Subtitle: The most comprehensive guide to family-building options, including state statutes on adoption, public and private adoption agencies, adoption exchanges, foreign requirements and adoption agencies, independent adoption services, foster parenting, biological alternatives, and support groups.

A comprehensive work, covering official policies, statutes, and agencies by state. Describes organizations that match children with families, foster care agencies and groups, support groups, and facilities providing biological alternatives such as in vitro fertilization and artificial insemination. Describes agencies and adoption criteria for Colombia, Guatemala, India, Korea, Philippines, and Taiwan. Includes glossary and list of suggested readings. Geographic, name, and subject indexes. HV875.55.A364

Posner, Julia L. CWLA's guide to adoption agencies : a national directory of adoption agencies and adoption resources. Wash. : Child Welfare League of America, c1989. 668 p. ISBN 0-87868-345-3. $15.95. **CC139**

Sections, arranged by state, list the following: public adoption programs/community resources; out-of-state agencies; and licensed private adoption agencies. Entries listed alphabetically in each category. Private agency entries provide information on cost, waiting period, requirements, and the children. An appendix lists agencies providing nationwide services. Based on data collected 1987–88. HV875.55.P67

Handbooks

Handbook of family measurement techniques / John Touliatos, Barry F. Perlmutter, Murray A. Straus, editors. Newbury Park, Calif. : Sage, 1990. 797 p. ISBN 0-8039-3121-2. **CC140**

Describes 976 instruments organized in five categories—(1) Dimensions of interaction; (2) Intimacy and family values; (3) Parenthood; (4) Roles and power; (5) Adjustment—and 16 subcategories. Entries are typically a page or less in length and provide brief descriptions of the variables measured, the instrument's content and procedures, reliability and validity, availability, and one to four references. Author and title indexes, and a Classification index, arranging entries by subcategories and by "primary interactants" (e.g., husband-wife, parent-child). For clinicians and researchers. HQ728.T68

Handbook of marriage and the family / ed. by Marvin B. Sussman and Suzanne K. Steinmetz. N.Y. : Plenum Pr., c1987. 915 p. : ill. ISBN 0-306-41967-X. **CC141**

Offers 30 signed articles by specialists in sociology, demography, history, social work, and psychology. Articles include many charts, tables, and figures and conclude with lengthy bibliographies. Topics include comparative perspectives, family theory, methodology, ethnicity, nontraditional family forms, gender roles, therapy, and voluntary childlessness. List of contributors; subject index. HQ518.H154

Klinman, Debra G. Fatherhood U.S.A : the first national guide to programs, services, and resources for and about fathers / Debra G. Klinman, Rhiana Kohl. N.Y. : Garland, 1984. 321 p. : ill. ISBN 0-8240-9011-X. ISBN 0-8240-9012-8 (pbk.). **CC142**

Five broad subject chapters cover health care, education, law, social and supportive services, and the workplace, and are divided into subchapters on, for example, programs for expec-

tant and new fathers, services for teen fathers, the gay fathers network, fathers' rights organizations, and parental leave policies. A sixth chapter lists books, films, videocassettes, and newsletters. Alphabetical and state indexes of programs and organizations; brief subject index. HQ756.K55

Poverty

Chalfant, H. Paul. Sociology of poverty in the United States : an annotated bibliography. Westport, Conn. : Greenwood, 1985. 187 p. (Bibliographies and indexes in sociology, no. 3). ISBN 0-313-23929-0. **CC143**

Cites 621 selected books, book chapters, and articles, most published 1970–early 1984. Entries are arranged in broad topical sections. Annotations are of substantial length. Author index. Z7164.C4C44

Feinberg, Renee. The feminization of poverty in the United States : a selected, annotated bibliography of the issues, 1978–1989 / Renee Feinberg, Kathleen E. Knox. N.Y. : Garland, 1990. 317 p. (Garland reference library of social science, v. 530). ISBN 0-8240-1213-5. **CC144**

Contains 18 chapters that treat such topics as families headed by women, children of poverty, comparable worth and pay equity, older women and poverty, women of color and poverty, and housing and homelessness. Each chapter includes several introductory paragraphs, usually with references to other sources. Z7164.C4F45

Nordquist, Joan. The feminization of poverty. Santa Cruz, Calif. : Reference and Research Services, 1987. 64 p. ISBN 0-93785-511-1. **CC145**

Three sections draw from the last ten years of feminist, economic, political, and activist literatures. Section I focuses on the labor force, comparable worth, sex discrimination in employment, poverty, and the family, Section II on the feminization of poverty, subdivided by topic. Entries are grouped by format and alphabetically arranged by author. Section III lists 15 bibliographies and 33 organizations. No indexes. HQ1381.N67

Sex and sexual behavior

Bibliography

Dynes, Wayne R. Homosexuality : a research guide. N.Y. : Garland, 1987. 853 p. ISBN 0-8240-8692-9. $47.00. **CC146**

Lists 4,858 annotated entries alphabetically by author under 24 main and 176 subtopics. Brief introductions provide useful context for the subtopics. International in scope; includes many materials in European languages. Emphasizes books and journal articles from major disciplines in the social sciences and humanities; omits fiction, poetry, drama, and most unpublished dissertations. Coverage from the 19th century to 1986. Subject and names index. Z7164.S42D96

Frayser, Suzanne G. Studies in human sexuality : a selected guide / Suzanne G. Frayser, Thomas J. Whitby. Littleton, Colo. : Libraries Unlimited, 1987. 442 p. ISBN 0-87287-422-2. $47.50. **CC147**

Provides citations, informative abstracts, and brief descriptions of content for 627 monographic works. Entries grouped by subject; anthropology, biology, history, law, literature, arts, medicine, politics, psychology, and sociology. Most titles were published in the last two decades, but early landmark works are also included. Indicates suggested reading level. The introduction includes an overview of the literature.

Z7164.S42F73

Maggiore, Dolores J. Lesbianism : an annotated bibliography and guide to the literature, 1976–1986. Metuchen, N.J. : Scarecrow, 1988. 150 p. ISBN 0-8108-2048-X. $18.50.   **CC148**

Includes entries for some 350 books, articles, and resources from fields such as social work, sociology, law, and women's studies. Excludes items that contain erroneous information or negative views of lesbians. In five topical sections: The individual lesbian; Minorities within a minority; Lesbian families; Oppression; and Special health issues. Entries are arranged alphabetically by author within each section; exemplary works are starred. Each section concludes with a list of related organizations. Section VI lists bookstores and publications. Separate author and title indexes.   Z7164.S42M33

Parker, William. Homosexuality bibliography. Second supplement, 1976–1982. Metuchen, N.J. : Scarecrow, 1985. 395 p. ISBN 0-8108-1753-5.   **CC149**

For basic work and first supplement, see *Guide* CC260–261.

Contains more than 3,500 entries, following the same arrangement as the first supplement.   Z7164.S42P34

Ridinger, Robert B. Marks. The homosexual and society : an annotated bibliography. N.Y. : Greenwood, c1990. 1 v. (Bibliographies and indexes in sociology, no. 18). ISBN 0-313-25357-9.   **CC150**

Entries treating homophobia (discrimination against, and irrational fear of, homosexual men and women) are arranged chronologically in seven categories: Adoption and foster care; Child custody; The military establishment; Employment discrimination; Censorship; Religion; and Police attitudes and actions. "The time span covered comprises some two thousand years of time."—*Pref.* Omits literature dealing with AIDSphobia and items issued after December 1987. General index.

Z7164.S42R5

Indexes

Potter, Clare. The lesbian periodicals index. Tallahassee, Fla. : Naiad Pr., 1986. 413 p. ISBN 0-930044-74-6 (pbk.).   **CC151**

Indexes 42 lesbian periodicals selected to reflect the political, cultural, racial, and class diversity within the lesbian community. Serves as a retrospective index, since all titles have ceased. In four sections: (1) Authors and subjects; (2) Lesbian writings (diary and journal entries, humor, satire, stories, poems); (3) Book reviews; and (4) Visual arts (cartoons, drawings, photographs, miscellaneous).   HQ75.6.U5P68

Encyclopedias

Encyclopedia of homosexuality / ed. by Wayne Dynes ; associate editors, Warren Johansson, William A. Percy ; with the assistance of Stephen Donaldson. N.Y. : Garland, 1990. 2 v. (1484 p.). ISBN 0-8240-6544-1.   **CC152**

A pioneering work written for a broad audience that offers more than 770 signed articles arranged alphabetically. A useful 22-page reader's guide provides an outline of major topics and disciplines, with relevant article titles. The preface explains the work's scope and structure and the difficulties inherent in defining homosexuality. List of contributors; detailed 66-page index of subjects and names; cross-references in the text.

HQ76.25.E53

Dictionaries

Kahn, Ada P. The A–Z of women's sexuality / Ada P. Kahn, Linda Hughey Holt. N.Y. : Facts on File, c1990. 362 p. : ill. ISBN 0-8160-1996-7.   **CC153**

Presents more than 2,000 alphabetically arranged definitions of terms pertaining to sexual behavior, reproduction, obstetrics, and gynecology. Includes many terms relating to male physiology and behavior. 24-page bibliography of books and articles alphabetically arranged by author within 47 subject categories. No statement of criteria for inclusion, preface, introduction, or table of contents. General index.   RG121.K218

Directories

Malinowsky, Harold Robert. International directory of gay and lesbian periodicals. Phoenix : Oryx, 1987. 226 p. ISBN 0-89774-297-4 (pbk.). $32.50 (est.).   **CC154**

Lists 1,924 periodicals by title. Full entries provide detailed publication and circulation information, advertising rates, subject index terms, and a descriptive paragraph. There are also brief entries for titles that have ceased, are nondeliverable, or for which only name and address were available. Cross-references; separate subject/geographic and publisher/editor indexes.   HQ76.25.M35

Handbooks

The Alyson almanac / a treasury of information for the gay and lesbian community. Boston : Alyson Publications, 1989. 208 p. : ill. ISBN 0-932870-19-8. $6.95.   **CC155**

Offers 25 chapters on a wide range of topics: history, books, films, organizations, awards, advice, health, safer sex, symbols, slang, church policies, congressional report cards, and 175 famous gays and lesbians. Some sections end with suggested reading lists; general index.   HQ76.25.A48

Curry, Hayden. A legal guide for lesbian and gay couples / by Hayden Curry & Denis Clifford ; ed. by Robin Leonard. 5th ed. Berkeley, Calif. : Nolo Pr., 1989. 1 v. (various pagings) : ill., forms. ISBN 0-87337-077-5 (pbk.). $17.95.   **CC156**

1st ed., 1980; 4th ed., 1986.

Completely revised and updated to reflect the latest changes in law; intended for general readers. In 12 chapters, treats contracts, housing, investments,, marriage, children, divorce, medical emergencies, estate planning, etc. The text and appendix include many sample forms and documents. The table of contents lists chapter headings and subtopics; separate table of contents for appendix. General index.   KF538.C87

Sexuality-related measures : a compendium / ed. and publ. by Clive M. Davis, William L. Yarber, Sandra L. Davis. Syracuse, N.Y. : C.M. Davis, c1988. 270 p. : ill. ISBN 0-9620581-0-6.   **CC157**

Designed for researchers and practitioners. Groups more than 100 measures by subject categories (e.g., abortion, aging, contraception, education, homosexuality, rape), subarranged by author. Most entries indicate instrument or scale, reliability, validity, scoring, and references; some include only a brief description of the measure. No indexes, but the table of contents includes cross-references.   HQ60.S53

Urbanization

Bibliography

Casper, Dale E. Urban America examined : a bibliography. N.Y. : Garland, 1985. 212 p. (Garland reference library of social science, v. 269). ISBN 0-8240-8815-8.
CC158

A topical arrangement of 2,070 entries on urban environment, ethnicity, socialism, politics, religion, transportation, and education. Entries are alphabetical by author within subsections. Includes scholarly books and journal articles, 1973–83. Geographic index; brief subject index. Z7164.U7C375

Coatsworth, Patricia A. An annotated bibliography and index covering CPL bibliographies 1–253, January 1979–December 1989 / Patricia A. Coatsworth, Mary Ravenhall, James Hecimovich. Chicago : Council of Planning Librarians, [1989]. 51 p. (CPL bibliography, no. 253.). ISBN 0-86602-253-8. **CC159**

For earlier series, see *Guide* CC274.

Number 177 (1986) was "A selected guide to abstracting and indexing sources and bibliographies relating to planning." Z7161.A1C63

Modern urban history research in Europe, USA, and Japan : a handbook / ed. by Christian Engeli and Horst Matzerath. Oxford ; N.Y. : Berg ; N.Y. : Distr. by St. Martin's Pr., 1989. 575 p. ISBN 0-85496-040-6. **CC160**

Pt. I is a survey of the development of the discipline and a state-of-the-art report on the research in each country, written by scholars of the country. Pt. II presents selective bibliographies of relevant works published in each country. Not indexed. HT113.M63

RACE AND ETHNIC RELATIONS

Bibliography

American ethnic revival : group pluralism entering America's third century / Jack Kinton, ed. Aurora, Ill. : Social Science and Sociological Resources, c1977. 203 p. **CC161**

Designed as a companion to Kinton's bibliography, *American ethnic groups and the revival of cultural pluralism* (*Guide* CC322). Consists of five theoretical essays and seven research studies, with accompanying notes. E184.A1A633

Cordasco, Francesco. The Italian emigration to the United States, 1880–1930 : a bibliographic register of Italian views, including selected numbers from the Italian Commissariat of Emigration, Bollettino dell'emigrazione / Francesco Cordasco and Michael Vaughn Cordasco. Fairview, N.J. : Junius-Vaughn Pr., 1990. 187 p. : facsims. ISBN 0-940198-05-3. $32.00. **CC162**

Consists of two main parts: a bibliography, arranged alphabetically by author, of 607 firsthand accounts of the immigrant experience, and 114 pages of reprints from the *Bollettino dell'emigrazione*, published by the Italian Commissariat of Emigration. Italian-language materials predominate. Includes a nine-page bibliography of publications, containing both English- and Italian-language materials on Italian emigration. Subject index for the bibliography of firsthand accounts. Z1361.I8C6594

———— The new American immigration : evolving patterns of legal and illegal emigration : a bibliography of selected references. N.Y. : Garland, 1987. 418 p. (Garland reference library of social science, v. 376). ISBN 0-8240-8523-X. **CC163**

Contains 2,328 entries, alphabetically arranged and some annotated, in four parts: (1) American immigration before 1865; (2) American immigration after 1865; (3) Illegal immigrants in the United States; (4) Miscellanea. Books (general interest and scholarly) and law journal and law review articles are included. The appendix reprints the introduction and recommendations of the report of the Select Commission on Immigration and Refugee Policy (*U.S. immigration policy and the national interest*, Wash. : The Commission, 1981). Authors and organizations index. Z7164.I3C58

Elkin, Judith Laikin. Latin American Jewish studies : an annotated guide to the literature / comp. by Judith Laikin Elkin and Ana Lya Sater. N. Y. : Greenwood , 1990. 238 p. (Bibliographies and indexes in ethnic studies, no. 4). ISBN 0-313-25936-4. **CC164**

For annotation, see *Supplement* BB131. Z6373.L3E44

Minorities in America. 1976–1978. University Park : Pennsylvania State Univ. Pr., c1985–1987. 3 v. ISSN 0748-2302. **CC165**

Continues Wayne Charles Miller's *A comprehensive bibliography for the study of American minorities* (*Guide* CC326).

Lists 21,000 additional items published 1976–78. Although organization follows that of the earlier bibliography, articles and dissertations are now included for all groups, and most entries are annotated. Author index only. Z1361.E4M57

Miska, John P. Canadian studies on Hungarians, 1886–1986 : an annotated bibliography of primary and secondary sources. Regina, Sask. : Canadian Plains Research Center, Univ. of Regina, 1987. 245 p. (Canadian plains bibliography, 1). ISBN 0-88977-034-4. $35.00.
CC166

For annotation, see *Supplement* DC145. Z1395.H94M57

Momeni, Jamshid A. Housing and racial/ethnic minority status in the United States : an annotated bibliography with a review essay. N.Y. : Greenwood, 1987. 310 p. (Bibliographies and indexes in sociology, no. 8). ISBN 0-313-24820-6. **CC167**

Presents 1,007 entries, annotated and alphabetically arranged by author in eight chapters. Topics covered include redlining, segregation and desegregation, renting and ownership, housing for the elderly, and homelessness. Books, articles, government publications, dissertations, and working papers are included. There are some housing differentials based on the 1980 census. Author and subject indexes. Z7164.H8M64

Viera, David J. The Portuguese in the United States : a bibliograpraphy [sic] (first supplement) / comp. by David J. Viera, Geoffrey L. Gomes, Adalino Cabral. Durham, N.H. : International Conference Group on Portugal, Dept. of History, Univ. of New Hampshire, [1989?]. 126 p. (Essays in Portuguese studies, no. 6.).
CC168

For basic work, 1976, by Leo Pap, see *Guide* CC330.

Arrangement follows basic work. Lists 1,270 additional items, concentrating on titles published after 1950. Approximately half the entries are in Portuguese, the remainder in English. Author index. E184.P8V5

Weinberg, Meyer. The education of poor and minority children : a world bibliography. Supplement, 1979–1985. N.Y. : Greenwood, 1986. 849 p. (Bibliographies and indexes in education, no. 3). ISBN 0-313-24880-X. **CC169**

For basic volume and annotation, see *Guide* CB55.

Adds 20,000 new entries. Z5814.E68W44

———————— Racism in the United States : a comprehensive classified bibliography. N.Y. : Greenwood, 1990. 682 p. (Bibliographies and indexes in ethnic studies, no. 2). ISBN 0-313-27390-1.   **CC170**

A 618-page bibliography whose 87 chapters cover a wide variety of topics (e.g., affirmative action, anti-Semitism, discrimination, I.Q. and race, sexism, tests and measurements, unemployment). Entries, arranged alphabetically by author, include books, periodical articles, government publications, letters to the editor, masters theses, and dissertations. An introduction analyzes racism. The only subject access is provided by the table of contents. No annotations; author index.

Z1361.E4W45

Woll, Allen L. Ethnic and racial images in American film and television : historical essays and bibliography / Allen L. Woll, Randall M. Miller. N.Y. : Garland, 1987. 408 p. (Garland reference library of social science, v. 308). ISBN 0-8240-8733-X.   **CC171**

Ten of the 12 chapters cover specific groups, an eleventh is devoted to a number of groups, and one is an introduction. Groups receiving major coverage: African Americans, Arabs, Asians, East Europeans and Russians, Germans, Hispanic Americans, Irish, Italians, Jews, and Native Americans. Gives lesser coverage to Africans, Armenians, Dutch, East Indians, Greeks, Hawaiians, Cajuns, Norwegians, Swedes, and Turks. Lists books, general and scholarly articles, dissertations, and filmographies. Indexes of authors, films and television shows, and subjects.   Z5784.M9W65

Periodicals

Ireland, Sandra L. Jones. Ethnic periodicals in contemporary America : an annotated guide. N.Y. : Greenwood, 1990. 222 p. (Bibliographies and indexes in ethnic studies, no. 3). ISBN 0-313-26817-7.   **CC172**

For annotation, see *Supplement* AE24.   Z6953.5.A1I74

Encyclopedias

Cashmore, Ernest. Dictionary of race and ethnic relations. 2nd ed. London : Routledge, 1988. 325 p. ISBN 0-415-02511-7.   **CC173**

1st ed., 1984 (*Guide* CC346).

The overall organization is retained, but there are new bibliographic references and updated information on events, key individuals, theories, and legislation.   GN496.C37

Dictionary of Afro-American slavery / ed. by Randall M. Miller and John David Smith. N.Y. : Greenwood, 1988. 866 p. : ill. ISBN 0-313-23814-6.   **CC174**

A short-entry encyclopedia of 297 signed articles and accompanying bibliographies that attempts to cover the "diverse aspects of the slavery experience in North America."—*Introd.* Designed both to be a comprehensive reference book, and to provide a synthesis of the scholarship of African-American slavery. Includes a chronology of slavery and a list of editors and contributors with institutional affiliations. Subject index.

E441.D53

Dictionary of American immigration history / ed. by Francesco Cordasco. Metuchen, N.J. : Scarecrow, 1990. 784 p. ISBN 0-8108-2241-5. $97.50.   **CC175**

For annotation, see *Supplement* DB61.   JV6450.D53

Directories

Minority organizations: a national directory. 3rd ed. Garrett Park, Md. : Garrett Park Pr., c1987. ISBN 0-8120-4830-1 (pbk.). $36.00.   **CC176**

2nd ed., 1982 (*Guide* CC355).

This edition provides information about 7,700 organizations and lists 2,800 organizations for which no current information was available.   E184.A1M544

Schorr, Alan Edward. Refugee and immigrant resource directory, 1990–1991. Juneau, Alaska : Denali Pr., c1990. 349 p. ISBN 0-938737-19-8. $37.50.   **CC177**

1st ed., 1987, had title: *Directory of services for refugees and immigrants.*

Provides names, addresses, telephone and fax numbers, and brief descriptions of 958 agencies, research centers, academic programs, and government agencies that "offer services or provide information policy analysis."—*Introd.* Appendixes include an essay on U.S. immigration and refugee policy, directories of the Immigration and Naturalization Service and of the U.N. High Commission for Refugees, chronologies of immigration policy, and statistical data. Six indexes: Organizational names, Contact persons, Services, Clientele, Religious affiliation, and Board of Immigration Appeals.   HV640.4.U54S365

Weaver, Jack W. Immigrants from Great Britain and Ireland : a guide to archival and manuscript sources in North America / comp. by Jack W. Weaver and DeeGee Lester. Westport, Conn. : Greenwood, 1986. 129 p. (Reference guides to archives and manuscript collections on immigrant culture, no. 1). ISBN 0-313-24342-5.   **CC178**

A companion to DeeGee Lester's *Irish research* (*Supplement* DC146). A directory of 389 repositories in the U.S. and Canada holding relevant unpublished materials; based on responses to questionnaires. For the few archives or manuscript repositories not answering, information was supplied from U.S. National Historical Publications Commission, *A guide to archives and manuscripts in the United States* (*Guide* DB73). Arrangement is geographical, each entry giving name, address, telephone, hours of access, copying facilities, description, published finding aids. Index for names of collections and ethnic groups.   Z1361.B74W43

World directory of minorities / ed. by the Minority Rights Groups ; regional introductions by Patrick Thornberry ; main compilers Miranda Bruce-Mitford ... [et al.]. Chicago : St. James Pr., [1990]. 427 p. : maps. ISBN 1-55862-016-8.   **CC179**

Describes 160 groups "numerically inferior to the rest of the population of a state, in a non-dominant position, whose members—being nationals of the state—possess ethnic, religious or linguistic characteristics differing from those of the rest of the population and show, if only implicitly, a sense of solidarity directed towards preserving their culture, traditions, religion or language."—*Pref.* Entries are arranged in 11 sections that reflect regions of the world: the U.S.S.R., Western and Northern Europe, Eastern Europe, South Asia, Oceania, etc. Entries in each section, arranged alphabetically, give for each group alternative names, location, population, percentage of total population, religion, and language and conclude with references for further reading. Information included was gathered from Minority Rights Group Reports, nongovernmental research organizations, and human rights groups. Appendixes of extracts of international documents on human rights. Maps accompany some entries. Subject index; cross-references.

HM131

Handbooks

Akiner, Shirin. Islamic peoples of the Soviet Union : with an appendix on the non-Muslim Turkic peoples of the Soviet Union : an historical and statistical handbook. 2nd ed. London ; N.Y. : KPI : Distr. by Routledge & Kegan Paul, 1986. 462 p. : maps. ISBN 0-7103-0188-X.   **CC180**
1st ed., 1983 (*Guide* CC349).
Retains the format of the 1st ed. Contains updated statistical information from the 1979 Soviet census as available. Entries on the Karaims and Tats have been revised.
DK34.M8A35

Arab American almanac. 3rd ed.– . Glendale, Calif. : News Circle Pub. Co., c1984– . Irregular. ISSN 0742-9576. $9.95.   **CC181**
The only publication of its kind. Three chapters list names and addresses of organizations, the press and other media, and religious institutions; a fourth, "Who's who," provides biographical information otherwise available only in a number of specialized sources. The remaining six chapters contain information found in basic encyclopedias. Detailed table of contents and index of names.   E184.A65A45

Armenian American almanac / Hamo B. Vassilian, ed. 2nd ed., completely rev. Glendale, Calif. : Armenian Reference Books Co., c1990. 402 p. ISBN 0-931539-14-7.   **CC182**
Subtitle: a guide to organizations, churches, print and nonprint media, libraries, Armenian studies, bookstores, Armenian schools, etc., and who is who in the medical, dental, health, and legal professions in the U.S.A. and Canada.
1st ed., 1985.
In three parts: (1) a directory, subdivided into nine topical sections, of 1,305 organizations, institutions, and cultural agencies, giving addresses and telephone numbers, and for many, annotations; (2) two alphabetical lists, the first of professionals by category (e.g., physicians, dentists, lawyers), the second an index to the names in the first, both giving addresses and telephone numbers; (3) an index to the entries in the first part, and two geographical indexes to the entire directory, one for the U.S., the other for Canada.   E184.A7A76

Directory of special programs for minority group members : career information services, employment skills banks, financial aid / [ed. by Willis L. Johnson]. [5th ed.]. [Garrett Park, Md. : Garrett Park Press], 1990. 1 v.   **CC183**
1st ed., 1973; 4th ed., 1986.
Defines minorities as Native Americans, African Americans, Hispanic Americans, and Asian Americans. Lists alphabetically 2,940 organizations, including colleges and universities, government and social service agencies, service clubs and programs, churches, etc. Addresses and annotations are provided for most entries. Includes a bibliography, a glossary of terms, and a general subject index.   HD5724.D56

Handbook on international migration / ed. by William J. Serow . . . [et al.]. N.Y. : Greenwood, 1990. 385 p. ISBN 0-313-26117-2.   **CC184**
Offers essays, accompanied by references, on 19 countries, including those with significant immigration (the U.S., Canada, Israel, Australia), sending countries (Jordan, Mexico, the Philippines, Turkey), and refugee havens (Pakistan, Nigeria). The Soviet Union and Eastern Europe are omitted. Although each essay is written by a specialist, all cover legal and public policy issues, analyze the demographic, social, and economic effects of international migration, and evaluate all data presented. Tables, charts, and graphs accompany the essays. List of selected references; subject index.   JV6035.H36

International handbook on race and race relations / ed. by Jay A. Sigler. N.Y. : Greenwood, 1987. 483 p. ISBN 0-313-24770-6.   **CC185**
Consists of 20 chapters, each devoted to a single country, including Australia, New Zealand, France, the Netherlands, West Germany, Japan, the U.S., Brazil, South Africa, and the Soviet Union. Notes and a bibliography accompany each chapter; 26 tables; summary bibliographic essay. An appendix describes racial/ethnic divisions in the countries included. Subject index.   HT1521.I485

Omond, Roger,. The apartheid handbook. 2nd ed. Harmondsworth, Middlesex, England ; N.Y. : Penguin Books, 1986. 282 p. : ill. ISBN 0-14-022749-0 (pbk.). $5.95.   **CC186**
1st ed., 1985.
Discusses apartheid policies in South Africa and their impact on daily life. Following an introduction describing the historical development of apartheid, the author groups information into chapters by subject (e.g., banning orders, "pass laws," race classification, housing, education), presenting it in question-and-answer format. Bibliography; general index and index of legislation.

Refugees in the United States : a reference handbook / ed. by David W. Haines. Westport, Conn. : Greenwood, 1985. 243 p. ISBN 0-313-24068-X.   **CC187**
In two parts: (1) Context and overview, consisting of three essays with accompanying bibliographies, on general issues; (2) The refugees, containing nine essays with accompanying bibliographies, covering the Chinese from Southeast Asia, Cubans, Haitians, Hmong, Khmer, Lao, Salvadoreans and Guatamalans, Soviet Jews, and the Vietnamese. Some survey data and demographic information in tables. 19-page annotated bibliography of books, articles, and government information, 1968–83. Subject index.   E184.A1R43

Atlases

Allen, James Paul. We the people : an atlas of America's ethnic diversity / James Paul Allen, Eugene James Turner. N.Y. : Macmillan, c1988. 315 p. : maps in color ; 29 x 43 cm. ISBN 0-02-901420-4. $85.00.   **CC188**
Graphically depicts in 111 full-color maps data from the 1980 census on ancestral origin(s). Text accompanying the maps presents historical perspective, including comparison with 1920 data but no analysis of current data. Three introductory chapters provide essential documentation and explain data and methodology. 66 possible ethnic origins are shown in nine broad categories: early North American, western European, northern European, eastern European, southern European, Middle Eastern, African, Middle and South American, and Asian and Pacific island. A final chapter presents general patterns. Extensive list of references. Appendixes provide tables of ethnic population data at state and county levels and reference maps of U.S. counties. Indexes to place names and ethnic populations.   G1201.E1A4

African Americans

Guides

Davis, Nathaniel. Afro-American reference : an annotated bibliography of selected resources. Westport, Conn. : Greenwood, 1985. 288 p. (Bibliographies and indexes in Afro-American and African studies, no. 9). ISBN 0-313-24930-X. **CC189**

A classed list of 642 entries alphabetically arranged by author within topic. Both interdisciplinary works and works describing any aspects of the African-American experience are included. Focuses on the U.S., but has a section on the black experience in the Caribbean, Central, and South America. Entries are annotated and the Library of Congress subject headings assigned to each book are noted. Title and subject indexes.
Z1361.N39D37

Images of blacks in American culture : a reference guide to information sources / ed. by Jessie Carney Smith ; foreword by Nikki Giovanni. N.Y. : Greenwood, 1988. 390 p. : ill. ISBN 0-313-24844-3. $49.95. **CC190**

Consists of chapters, each written by a specialist, concerning the image of African Americans in American culture—e.g., in music, art, film, television, children's books, toys. Includes sections on: Image of the black female and male, Collecting black Americana. Each chapter offers a historical survey of the topic and an extensive bibliography. Indexed. NX652.A37I43

Plunkett, Michael. Afro-American sources in Virginia : a guide to manuscripts. Charlottesville : Univ. Pr. of Virginia, 1990. 323 p. ISBN 0-8139-1252-0. **CC191**

Consists of 1,038 annotated entries alphabetically arranged in 22 sections, each covering a single repository. Collections of historical societies and of college and university libraries are described. Materials cited include plantation and church records, the archives of traditionally black colleges and universities, diaries, photographs, and the papers of politicians, businesses, and civil rights groups. Subject index.
Z1361.N39P496

Stevenson, Rosemary M. Index to Afro-American reference resources. N.Y. : Greenwood, 1988. 315 p. (Bibliographies and indexes in Afro-American and African studies, no. 20). ISBN 0-313-24580-0. **CC192**

In two main parts: a list of nearly 180 reference books, alphabetically arranged by title, and a classed index to the contents of the reference books. Covers the arts, social sciences, and humanities. Author and title index. Z1361.N39S77

Bibliography

Black immigration and ethnicity in the United States : an annotated bibliography / Center for Afroamerican and African Studies, the University of Michigan. Westport, Conn. : Greenwood, 1985. 170 p. (Bibliographies and indexes in Afro-American and African studies, no. 2). ISBN 0-313-24366-2. $29.95. **CC193**

Consists of 1,049 annotated entries alphabetically arranged in six sections: (1) Bibliographies and general surveys of literature, (2) General literature on immigration and ethnicity, (3) U.S. immigration legislation and policies, (4) Aspects of black immigration, (5) Studies of black immigrant groups, (6) Selected works on black immigration to Canada and Great Britain. Books, articles, dissertations, and government publications are included. Author and subject indexes. Z1361.N39B553

Davis, Lenwood G. A bibliographical guide to black studies programs in the United States : an annotated bibliography / comp. by Lenwood G. Davis and George Hill, with the assistance of Janie Miller Harris. Westport, Conn. : Greenwood, 1985. 120 p. (Bibliographies and indexes in Afro-American and African studies, no. 6). ISBN 0-313-23328-4. **CC194**

Contains 725 annotated entries, alphabetically arranged in four chapters: 79 major books and pamphlets providing a history and overview of the topic, 72 general works including titles on the development of black studies at large traditionally white universities, 68 dissertations, and 500 articles published in scholarly and general interest periodicals. Author index.
Z1361.N39D353

——————— Black-Jewish relations in the United States, 1752–1984 : a selected bibliography. Westport, Conn. : Greenwood, 1984. 130 p. (Bibliographies and indexes in Afro-American and African studies, no. 1). ISBN 0-313-23329-2. **CC195**

Lists 1,241 annotated entries alphabetically arranged in four sections: major books and pamphlets, general works, dissertations and theses, and articles. Sections are subdivided by topic, including: black anti-Semitism, Jews as slave owners, various African American leaders' opinions of Jews, black-Jewish relations in the civil rights movement, and black-Jewish relations in N.Y., California, Atlanta, Philadelphia, and New Jersey. The introduction provides a brief history of the topic. Author index. Z1361.N39D357

Herod, Agustina. Afro-American nationalism : an annotated bibliography of militant separatist and nationalist literature / Agustina and Charles C. Herod. N.Y. : Garland, 1986. 272 p. ISBN 0-8240-9813-7. **CC196**

In ten sections, 620 annotated entries published since 1945 are alphabetically arranged. Eight of the sections cover historical periods, the ninth treats definitions of black nationalism, and the tenth lists bibliographies. Among the viewpoints represented are Christian, Muslim, Marxist, integrationist, and separatist. Cross-references at the end of each chapter. A table of contents provides the only subject access; author index.
Z1361.N39H47

Hill, George H. Black media in America : a resource guide. Boston : G.K. Hall, c1984. 333 p. ISBN 0-8161-8610-3. **CC197**

Contains 4,049 entries divided by format: 317 monographs, theses, and dissertations; 342 journal articles; and 3,388 newspaper and magazine articles. Within each format, entries are subdivided by topic and arranged alphabetically by author. Topics include advertising, public relations, marketing, book and magazine publishing, and newspaper, radio, and television journalism. Three indexes: author/subject, radio stations, and television stations. Z5633.A37H55

Joyce, Donald F. Blacks in the humanities, 1750–1984 : a selected annotated bibliography. N.Y. : Greenwood, 1986. 209 p. (Bibliographies and indexes in Afro-American and African studies, no. 13). ISBN 0-313-24643-2. **CC198**

Annotated entries are arranged alphabetically and grouped by format in 12 chapters. Citations are drawn from bibliographies, indexes, union lists, encyclopedias, biographical dictionaries, and library catalogs. Most entries were published in the 20th century, although the earliest title cited appeared in 1750. Chapter topics include philosophy, religion, cultural and intellectual history, librarianship, folklore, linguistics, literary criticism, art and music. Subject and author-title indexes.
Z1361.N39J69

Michael, Colette Verger. Negritude : an annotated bibliography. West Cornwall, Conn. : Locust Hill Pr., 1988. 315 p. ISBN 0-933951-15-9. $35.00.   **CC199**

Consists of 972 entries for books, articles, and dissertations, mid-1950s to June 1987, alphabetically arranged in three sections: (1) selective listing of primary sources: novels, poetry, short stories, and drama, (2) anthologies and bibliographies; (3) secondary sources (annotated entries of literary criticism, dissertations, and sources for further research). Three indexes: journals, books, and names of subjects.   Z6520.N44M53

Miller, Joseph Calder. Slavery : a worldwide bibliography, 1900–1982. White Plains, N.Y. : Kraus Internat., 1985. 451 p. ISBN 0-527-63659-2. $40.00.   **CC200**

An outgrowth of the author's teaching bibliography; see *Guide* CC381.   Z7164.S6M543

Obudho, Robert A. Afro-American demography and urban issues : a bibliography / comp. by R.A. Obudho and Jeannine B. Scott. Westport, Conn. : Greenwood, 1985. 433 p. (Bibliographies and indexes in Afro-American and African studies, no. 8). ISBN 0-313-24656-4.   **CC201**

Consists of 5,234 entries, alphabetically arranged by author in eight chapters. Topics covered include bibliography, demography, urbanization, housing patterns, ghettoization, suburbanization, rural studies, and planning. Books, articles, dissertations, and government publications are listed. Libraries in the U.S. holding major collections in African-American studies are noted, and there is a list of periodicals consulted by the compilers. Author index.   Z1361.N39O29

Rice, Mitchell F. Health of black Americans from post reconstruction to integration, 1871–1960 : an annotated bibliography of contemporary sources / comp. by Mitchell F. Rice and Woodrow Jones, Jr. N.Y. : Greenwood, 1990. 206 p. (Bibliographies and indexes in Afro-American and African studies, no. 26). ISBN 0-313-26314-0.   **CC202**

A comprehensive annotated bibliography of the literature on "the condition of blacks [including] . . . patterns of mortality, morbidity and utilization behaviors of blacks from slavery to the mid-20th century . . . " that aims to provide "a fuller understanding of the history of health care inequities in the U.S."—*Introd.* In three chapters: 1871–1919, 1920–50, 1951–60. Entries give full bibliographic information, and there are subject and author indexes. A companion volume, *Black American health: an annotated bibliography*, comp. by Mitchell F. Rice and Woodrow Jones (N.Y. : Greenwood, 1987) treats the literature of the 1970s and 1980s.   RA448.5.N4R52

Southern, Eileen. African-American traditions in song, sermon, tale, and dance, 1600s–1920 : an annotated bibliography of literature, collections, and artworks / comp. by Eileen Southern and Josephine Wright. N.Y. : Greenwood, 1990. 365 p., [6] p. of plates : ill. ISBN 0-313-24918-0.   **CC203**

Lists 2,328 annotated entries, which are organized alphabetically by author under three headings (literature, artworks, or collections of tales and songs) and divided among five chapters; each devoted to a historical period. Bibliography of works consulted; three indexes: name, subdivided by authors and artists; subject, subdivided by literature and artworks; and songs, subdivided by first lines of choruses and first lines of verses.   Z5956.A47S68

Encyclopedias

Newton, Michael. The Ku Klux Klan : an encyclopedia / by Michael and Judy Ann Newton. N.Y. : Garland, c1991. 639 p., [32] p. of plates : ill. (Garland reference library of the social sciences, vol. 499). ISBN 0-8240-2038-3.   **CC204**

A short-entry encyclopedia whose entries cover topics, people, and organizations associated with the Ku Klux Klan from its inception in 1866 until the mid-1980s. The information was gathered from newspaper and wire service reports, general interest magazines, and books, all listed in a bibliography. Entries are arranged alphabetically and are linked to the bibliography. Four alphabetical lists of entries are designed to substitute for an index: a general list, a geographic list, an organization list, and a list of people. A preface provides a short history of the Klan.   HS2330.K63N49

Directories

Black Americans information directory. 1st ed. (1990–91)– . Detroit : Gale, c1990– . Biennial. ISSN 1045-8050. $69.00.   **CC205**

Contains 17 chapters that cover a variety of topics (e.g., awards, prizes, and honors; local, state, regional and national associations; governmental agencies and programs; the print and broadcast media; universities, libraries and research centers; videos). Scope notes describe the contents and arrangement of individual chapters. Addresses are included for all entries; contact persons and telephone numbers are supplied if available, and annotations accompany some 40–50% of the entries. The information was compiled from other Gale directories, government publications, unnamed directories and lists, questionnaire responses, or telephone inquiries. Combined name and keyword index.   E185.5.B513

The black resource guide. 1981– . Wash. : Ben Johnson, 1981– . Annual. ISSN 0882-0643. $30.00.   **CC206**

For 1983 national ed., see *Guide* CC415.

Published annually since 1981; this edition includes additional sections listing consultants, information processing companies, travel agencies, and alumni associations, but omits the section on celebrities.   E185.5.B565

Biography

Black leaders of the nineteenth century / ed. by Leon Litwack and August Meier. Urbana : Univ. of Illinois Pr., c1988. 344 p. : ports. ISBN 0-252-01506-1.   **CC207**

Arranged in 16 chapters that consist of biographies, 16–28 pages in length, treating such persons as: Nat Turner, Harriet Tubman, Blanche K. Bruce, and Robert Brown Elliot; and a bibliographic essay that provides references for further reading. Subject index.   E185.96.B535

Sammons, Vivian O. Blacks in science and medicine. N.Y. : Hemisphere Pub. Corp., c1990. 293 p. ISBN 0-89116-665-3. $40.00.   **CC208**

For annotation, see *Supplement* EA80.   Q141.B58

Statistics

Black Americans : a statistical sourcebook / Alfred N. Garwood, ed. 1990 ed. Boulder, Colo. : Numbers & Concepts, c1990. 340 p. ISBN 0-929960-03-3. ISBN 0-929960-02-5 (pbk.).   **CC209**

Seven chapters of tables cover basic demographics, vital statistics, education, politics and government, income and earnings, poverty and wealth, crime and justice; an eighth, Special topics, includes data on social security recipients, farm operators, and surveys of consumer expenditures. For purposes of comparison, data is categorized as "Black," "White," and "All races." Sources of data (originally published by U.S. government agencies) are noted at the end of each table. Includes a glossary of terms used and a subject index.   E185.86.B52

The metropolitan area fact book : a statistical portrait of blacks and whites in urban America / ed. by Katherine McFate. Wash. : Joint Center for Political Studies, 1988. 109 p. : maps. ISBN 0-941410-65-X. $8.95.   **CC210**

A compilation of demographic data about the 48 Standard Metropolitan Statistical Areas with a black population of more than 100,000. Tables present basic demographic data, and data on the numbers and percentages of suburban and urban blacks, labor force participation, income, earnings, home ownership, and poverty rates in each SMSA. Data on whites is included for comparison. All data is taken from the 1980 census; a list of the census volumes used as sources is found in the appendix. No index.   E185.86.M48

Statistical record of black America. 1st ed.– . Detroit : Gale, c1990– . Biennial. ISSN 1051-8002. $89.50.   **CC211**

A compendium of data, presented in tables and graphs, that illustrate aspects of African-American life: attitudes and values, business and economics, crime, law enforcement and justice, education, family, health and medical care, income, labor and employment, military affairs, politics, and elections, population, professions, sports and leisure, vital statistics. Data were originally published by agencies of the U.S. government or resulted from surveys conducted by academic researchers, public opinion polling organizations, or private research firms. Bibliography of sources; subject index.

Asian Americans

Dictionary of Asian American history / ed. by Hyung-Chan Kim. N.Y. : Greenwood, [1986]. 627 p. ISBN 0-313-23760-3.   **CC212**

In two sections: 15 essays (114 p.) by various authors and an encyclopedia containing 800 brief entries, all written by the editor. Seven of the essays treat the historical experience of Asian Americans and Pacific Islanders; the remainder deal with the place of Asian Americans in the "American social order."—*Pref.* The encyclopedia entries are accompanied by bibliographies and concentrate on the historical experiences of persons of Chinese, Japanese, Korean, Asian Indian, and Filipino ancestry, give some attention to refugees from Vietnam, Kampuchea, and Laos, and mention Pacific Islanders. Three appendixes: Select bibliography, Chronology of Asian American history, and 1980 Census data. Subject index.

E184.O6D53

Haseltine, Patricia. East and Southeast Asian material culture in North America : collections, historical sites, and festivals. N.Y. : Greenwood, 1989. 163 p. (Material culture directories, no. 3). ISBN 0-313-25343-9.   **CC213**

Describes 191 American and Canadian museums, historic sites, and cultural festivals of Chinese, Japanese, Korean, Hmong, Indonesian, Malaysian, Thai, and Vietnamese immigrant cultures. Arranged alphabetically by state or province, then by name of institution. Includes a list of material culture museums in east and southeast Asia, a glossary, and a bibliography. Index of institutions, general index.   E184.O6H37

Kim, Hyung-chan. Asian American studies : an annotated bibliography and research guide. N.Y. : Greenwood, 1989. 504 p. (Bibliographies and indexes in American history, no. 11). ISBN 0-313-26026-5.   **CC214**

Lists 3,396 books, periodical articles, theses, and dissertations in the social and behavioral sciences and the humanities relating to 22 ethnic groups in two broad sections: historical perspectives and contemporary perspectives, with appropriate subdivisions. Also included are three essays that attempt to place the Asian-American experience "within the context of American scholarship on immigration and emigration."—*Pref.* Author and subject indexes.   Z1361.O7K56

Native Americans

Bibliography

Johnson, Bryan R. The Blackfeet : an annotated bibliography. N.Y. : Garland, 1988. 231 p. (Garland reference library of social science, v. 441). ISBN 0-8240-0941-X.   **CC215**

Lists 1,186 items published 1843–1985, arranged alphabetically. Includes English and non-English scholarly and popular books, biographies, fiction, juvenile literature, periodical articles, theses, films, filmstrips, recordings, U.S. and some Canadian government publications, and manuscripts (21 collections in the U.S. and Canada). Author-subject index.   Z1210.S59J63

Kersey, Harry A. The Seminole and Miccosukee tribes : a critical bibliography. Bloomington : Indiana Univ. Pr., c1987. 102 p. ISBN 0-253-30662-0 : $5.95.   **CC216** 0-253-30662-0 (pbk.).

Consists of a 70-page bibliographic essay followed by a bibliography and index (called Alphabetical list and index). The latter lists the 249 titles discussed in the essay alphabetically by author; included are books, articles, and some dissertations. Government publications are omitted. Also includes a beginning reading list and a basic library collection.   Z1210.S5K47

Martin, M. Marlene. Ethnographic bibliography of North America, 4th edition. Supplement 1973–1987 / M. Marlene Martin and Timothy J. O'Leary. New Haven, Conn. : Human Relations Area Files Pr., 1990. 3 v. ISBN 0-87536-254-0 (set).   **CC217**

4th ed., 1975, by George P. Murdock and Timothy J. O'Leary (*Guide* CC453).

Contents: v. 1, Indexes; v. 2–3, Citations.

Contains 25,058 alphabetically arranged entries published from 1973 through 1987. Includes books, journal articles, ERIC documents, theses and dissertations, and U.S. and Canadian government publications. Subject, ethnic group, and author indexes.   Z1209.2.N67M87

Native American bibliography series. No. 1– . Metuchen, N.J. : Scarecrow, 1980– . Irregular. ISSN 1040-9629.   **CC218**

Contents: v. 1, *Bibliography of the Sioux*, by Jack W. Marken and Herbert T. Hoover (1980. 370 p.); v. 3, *Bibliography of the languages of native California, including closely related languages of adjacent areas*, by William Bright (1982. 234 p.); v. 4, *A guide to Cherokee documents in foreign archives*, by William L. Anderson and James A. Lewis (1983. 768 p.); v. 5, *A biobibliography of Native American writers, 1772–1924 : a supplement*, by Daniel F. Littlefield, Jr. and James W. Parins (1985. 350 p.); v. 6, *Bibliography of the Osage*, by Terry P. Wilson (1985. 172 p.); v. 7, *A guide to Cherokee documents in the northeastern*

United States, by Paul Kutsche (1986. 541 p.); v. 8, *In pursuit of the past : an anthropological and bibliographic guide to Maryland and Delaware*, by Frank W. Porter III (1986. 268 p.); v. 9, *The Indians of Texas : an annotated research bibliography*, by Michael L. Tate (1986. 514 p.); v. 10, *Bibliography of the Catawba*, by Thomas J. Blumer (1987. 575 p.); v. 11, *Bibliography of the Chickasaw*, by Anne Kelley Hoyt (1987. 230 p.); v. 12, *Kinsmen through time : an annotated bibliography of Potawatomi history*, by R. David Edmunds (1987. 237 p.); v. 13, *Bibliography of the Blackfoot*, by Hugh A. Dempsey and Lindsay Moir (1989. 255 p.); v. 14, *The upstream people : an annotated research bibliography of the Omaha tribe*, by Michael L. Tate (1991. 522 p.); v. 15, *Languages of the aboriginal southeast*, by Karen M. Booker (1991. 265 p.)

A series consisting of bibliographies of individual Native American tribes of North America and of general topics concerning Native Americans. The number of entries varies from about 1,500 to more than 6,000; some entries have annotations.

Parezo, Nancy J. Southwest Native American arts and material culture : a guide to research / Nancy J. Parezo, Ruth M. Perry, Rebecca Allen. N.Y. : Garland, 1991. 2 v. (1506 p.). (Garland reference library of the humanities, vol. 1337 ; Garland reference library of the humanities. Studies in ethnic art, vol. 1). ISBN 0-8240-7093-3. **CC219**

In three main parts: Pt. I, in v. 1, consists of scope notes, bibliographic sources, a list of journals and serials, a glossary of cultures (common and preferred names of Southwest groups), and a list of key terms in the field of material culture; Pt. II, divided A–N in v. 1, O–Z in v. 2, is a bibliography of 8,363 alphabetically arranged entries published 1844–1988, in which books and articles predominate, although museum catalogs and leaflets and some dissertations are included. Pt. III consists of two indexes, both in v. 2: a list of cultural groups subdivided by topic, and a subject index.　　Z1209.2.U52S686

Weist, Katherine M. An annotated bibliography of Northern Plains ethnohistory / by Katherine M. Weist and Susan R. Sharrock. Missoula, Mont. : Dept. of Anthropology, Univ. of Montana, [1985]. 299 p. : map. **CC220**

Contains 718 entries, alphabetically arranged, for books, articles, reports, memoirs, diaries, other historical accounts, and publications of the U.S. and Canadian governments covering the period 1690–1880. The most recent publication cited appeared in 1974. Every entry includes a list of descriptions. Major tribes covered: Blackfeet, Gros Ventre, Assiniboine, Plains Ojibwa, Crow, Cheyenne, Arapahoe, Teton Dakota. A map shows the territories of each group. The introduction consists of an essay and a bibliography of general and ethnographic sources. No table of contents; subject index.　　Z1209.2.G7W44

Welch, Thomas L. The Aztecs : a bibliography of books and periodical articles / comp. by Thomas L. Welch and René L. Gutiérrez. Wash. : Columbus Memorial Library, Organization of American States, 1987. 169 p. (Hipólito Unanue bibliographic series, 3). ISBN 0-8270-2611-0 (pbk.). **CC221**

Lists 778 books and 438 articles in Spanish or English, arranged alphabetically by author. Covers Aztec culture, including much on language. Title and subject indexes.

Z1210.A9W45

———— The Incas : a bibliography of books and periodical articles / comp. by Thomas L. Welch and René L. Gutiérrez. Wash. : Columbus Memorial Library, Organization of American States, 1987. 145 p. (Hipólito Unanue bibliographic series, 1). ISBN 0-8270-2555-6 (pbk.). **CC222**

Includes 401 articles are 715 books in Spanish or English, arranged by author. Title and subject indexes.　Z1210.I53W45

Periodicals

Littlefield, Daniel F. American Indian and Alaska native newspapers and periodicals / Daniel F. Littlefield, Jr., and James W. Parins. Westport, Conn. : Greenwood, 1986. v. 2–3. ISBN 0-313-23425-6 (set). **CC223**

For v. 1 and annotation, see *Guide* CC465.

Contents: v. 2, 1925–70; v. 3, 1971–85. Completes the set. Identical to v. 1 in arrangement and format. Vol. 2 has 500 titles; v. 3, 1,000 titles.　　PN4883.L57

Library resources

American Indian resource materials in the Western History Collections, University of Oklahoma / Donald L. DeWitt, ed. Norman, Okla. : Univ. of Oklahoma Pr., c1990. 272 p. ISBN 0-8061-2289-7. **CC224**

Consists of 1,056 entries that describe 269 manuscript collections, 96 collections of photographs, 20 oral histories, 165 microform sets, and 506 newspapers and periodicals, all held by the Western History Collections. In four sections: primary documentation, photography, oral histories, and holdings of the Library Division of the Collections. The preface provides a history of the Collections, and each section begins with a summary essay. Emphasizes history of the Western U.S., but includes materials on other regions and on Canada. Subject index.

E78.O45A69

Wolf, Carolyn E. Indians of North and South America : a bibliography based on the collection at the Willard E. Yager Library-Museum, Hartwick College, Oneonta, N.Y. : Supplement / by Carolyn E. Wolf and Nancy S. Chiang. Metuchen, N.J. : Scarecrow, 1988. 654 p. ISBN 0-8108-2127-3. **CC225**

For basic volume, see *Guide* CC460.

Lists 3,542 titles added to the collection between Spring 1976 and May 1987. OCLC numbers are included for monographs. Title and subject index.　　Z1209.W82

Encyclopedias

Klein, Barry T. Reference encyclopedia of the American Indian. 5th ed. West Nyack, N.Y. : Todd Publications, c1990. 1078 p. ISBN 0-915344-16-5. $95.00. **CC226**

Now in 1 v., in four sections: a directory with separate sections for the U.S. and Canada, a bibliography of about 4,000 in-print books, and a collective biography of some 2,000 Native Americans.　　E76.2.K5

Ruby, Robert H. A guide to the Indian tribes of the Pacific Northwest / by Robert H. Ruby and John A. Brown. Norman : Univ. of Oklahoma Pr., c1986. 289 p. : ill. ISBN 0-8061-1967-5. **CC227**

An alphabetically arranged short-entry encyclopedia designed for general readers. Entries vary in length, the shortest providing the name of the group, its alternative names, a paragraph or two of descriptive information, and a list of additional readings. The more extensive entries also provide information on population, locations, government, land claims, and contemporary life and culture. A pronunciation guide to tribal names is accompanied by references. Five detailed maps indicate historic lands, present-day reservations, locations of missions, of fur trading and military posts, and language families. Subject index.　　E78.N77R79

Directories

Frazier, Gregory W. The American Indian index : a directory of Indian country, USA / by Gregory W. Frazier ; ed. by Randolph J. Punley. Denver, Colo. : Arrowstar Pub., c1985. 320 p. ISBN 0-935151-39-7 (pbk.). $19.95. **CC228**

A directory listing interest groups, state and federal agencies, social service agencies, reservations, health and housing programs, festivals, arts and crafts sources, and publications. In 17 topical chapters, each subarranged by state or region with the entries alphabetically arranged. No index. E76.2.F7

Indian reservations : a state and federal handbook / comp. by the Confederation of American Indians. Jefferson, N.C. : McFarland, c1986. 329 p. ISBN 0-89950-200-8. $45.00. **CC229**

Provides descriptions of 278 reservations located in 31 states. Organized by state, with entries listed alphabetically in each state. Each entry includes the location of the reservation, notes its relationship with the federal and state governments, the location of the tribal headquarters, and the names of the tribes residing on the reservation. Additional information is provided on the land area, history, culture, government, population, economy, climate, availability of transportation, and recreation on each reservation. Name index. E93.I3828

Handbooks

Handbook of North American Indians / William C. Sturtevant, gen. ed. Wash. : Smithsonian Institution : for sale by the Supt. of Docs., U.S. Govt. Print. Off., 1978–1990. v. 4, 7, 11 : ill. (In progress). **CC230**

For earlier volumes and annotation, see *Guide* CC470.

Contents: v. 4, History of Indian-white relations, ed. by Wilcomb E. Washburn; v. 7, Northwest Coast, ed. by Wayne Suttles; v. 11, Great Basin, ed. by Warren L. D'Azevedo.

Identical to earlier volumes in arrangement and format. E77.H25

Biography

Waldman, Carl. Who was who in Native American history : Indians and non-Indians from early contacts through 1900. N.Y. : Facts on File, c1990. 410 p. : ill. ISBN 0-8160-1797-2. **CC231**

An alphabetically arranged short-entry collective biography. Entries include birth and death dates, if available, and alternative names, if appropriate. Illustrations and cross-references are provided. The appendix consists of an alphabetical list of tribes which lists the Native Americans, and a list of occupations, which notes the non-Indians. Sources are not noted and bibliographies or reading lists are omitted. No index. E89.W35

Atlases

Atlas of Great Lakes Indian history / ed. by Helen Hornbeck Tanner . . . [et al.] ; cartography by Miklos Pinther. Norman : Publ. for the Newberry Library by the Univ. of Oklahoma Pr., c1987. 224 p. : ill., maps in color ; 32 cm. (The civilization of the American Indian series, v. 174). ISBN 0-8061-1515-7. **CC232**

Contains 182 pages of text, 30 maps (many of which are two-page spreads), and 86 illustrations, covering the years 1400–1880. The maps illustrate such topics as vegetation, wars

of the 17th–19th centuries, locations of native villages at various periods, and location of reservations in the late 19th century. Includes a bibliographic essay and a select bibliography arranged alphabetically by author. Subject index. E78.G7A87

Ferguson, T. J. A Zuni atlas / by T.J. Ferguson and E. Richard Hart ; new cartography by Ronald Stauber and Troy Lucio. Norman : Univ. of Oklahoma Pr., c1985. 154 p. : ill. ; 32 cm. (The civilization of the American Indian series, v. 172). ISBN 0-8061-1945-4. **CC233**

Contains 44 maps showing landforms, geologic features, natural and mineral resources, climate, 16th-century villages, 19th-century areas of Zuni sovereignty, traditional hunting and grazing lands, religious sites, historical and current locations of reservations. All maps are accompanied by text, many by black-and-white photographs. There is a nine-page bibliography, arranged by topic. Two appendixes: Zuni land use sites and summary of land use by site. Subject index. G1496.E1F4

Waldman, Carl. Atlas of the North American Indian / Carl Waldman ; maps and illustrations by Molly Braun. N.Y. : Facts on File, c1985. 276 p. : ill. (some col.). ISBN 0-87196-850-9. **CC234**

In eight topical chapters (e.g., Ancient civilizations, Indian culture, The Indians and the explorers, The Indian wars, Indian land cessions, and Contemporary Indians). The 246 maps are surrounded by text and cover quarter- or half-pages. Includes reproductions of historical maps and maps produced for this volume. Illustrated with historical drawings and contemporary photographs. A chronology of explorers' contacts with the Indians, and an Indian language classification table are provided in the relevant chapters. Six appendixes: (1) a chronology of Indian history; (2) a list of tribes with their historical and contemporary locations; (3) federal and state reservations; (4) Indian bands in Canada; (5) major Indian place names; (6) a list of museums, historical and archaeological sites. Bibliography; subject index. E77.W195

Spanish-speaking Americans

Bibliography

Camarillo, Albert. Mexican Americans in urban society : a selected bibliography. Oakland, Calif. : Floricanto Pr., c1986. 296 p. ISBN 0-915745-12-7. $29.95. **CC235**

Offers 2,133 entries arranged alphabetically by author in topical chapters on art and theater, Chicana studies, culture and identity, employment, family, history, immigration, language, law and criminal justice, literature, mass media, politics, religion, social stratification, education, and general reference. Contains books, articles, dissertations and government publications published through 1983. Author index. Z1361.M4C38

Gutierrez, David. The Chicano public catalog : a collection guide for public libraries / comp. by David Gutierrez and Roberto G. Trujillo. Encino, Calif. : Floricanto Pr., c1987. 188 p. ISBN 0-915745-03-8. $39.00. **CC236**

Lists 487 annotated entries arranged alphabetically by author in topical chapters: general works, bibliographies, and periodicals in religion, the social sciences (including law), language, arts and music, literature, and history. English-language materials predominate. Author and title indexes. Z1039.M5G87

Latinos in the United States : a historical bibliography / Albert Camarillo, ed. Santa Barbara, Calif. : ABC-Clio, c1986. 332 p. ISBN 0-8743-6458-2. **CC237**

Consists of 1,325 citations previously listed in *America: history and life*, 1973–85 (see *Guide* DB47). In four categories: (1) Historiography and bibliography; (2) Colonization and settlement; (3) People from Mexico; and (4) People from the Carribean, Central America and South America. Author and subject indexes.   Z1361.S7L37

MacCorkle, Lyn. Cubans in the United States : a bibliography for research in the social and behavioral sciences, 1960–1983. Westport, Conn. : Greenwood, 1984. 227 p. (Bibliographies and indexes in sociology, no. 1). ISBN 0-313-24509-6.   **CC238**

Approximately 1,600 citations, alphabetically arranged by author in eight topical sections: economics, education, public administration, psychology, health, politics, sociology, and demography. Books, scholarly articles, dissertations, government reports, conference papers, and unpublished papers are listed. Author index.   Z1361.C85M32

Varona, Esperanza Bravo de. Cuban exile periodicals at the University of Miami Library : an annotated bibliography. Madison, Wis. : Secretariat, Seminar on the Acquisition of Latin American Library Materials, Memorial Library, Univ. of Wisconsin—Madison, c1987. 203 p. (Seminar on the Acquisition of Latin American Library Materials bibliography and reference series, 19). ISBN 0-917617-14-2 (pbk.).   **CC239**

Lists 665 alphabetically arranged entries giving for each a complete bibliographic citation and notes on frequency, language, and editors. Brief annotations accompany many entries. List of directors (i.e., publishers); a chronological index; a geographic index subdivided into city and country; and a subject index. The preface provides a brief history of publishing among Cuban émigrés.   Z1361.C85D4

Indexes

García-Ayvens, Francisco. Chicano anthology index : a comprehensive author, title, and subject index to Chicano anthologies, 1965–1987. Berkeley : Chicano Studies Library Publications Unit, Univ. of California, 1990. 1 v. ISBN 0-918520-13-4. $75.00.   **CC240**

Consists of 15,577 subject entries that index approximately 5,000 analytical and critical articles and creative writing in 280 anthologies published 1965–87. Entries are arranged alphabetically by author under each subject entry. Covers topics in the social sciences and the humanities, as well as poetry, song lyrics, short stories, and plays. English-language materials predominate. List of the anthologies indexed; notes on the compilation of the work; author and title index.   Z1361.M4G37

Directories

Caballero, Cesar. Chicano organizations directory / comp. by Cesar Caballero ; assisted by Susana Delgado [et al.]. N.Y. : Neal-Schuman, c1985. 221 p. ISBN 0-918212-65-0 (pbk.). $19.95 (est.).   **CC241**

A list of 378 civil rights, social service, cultural, political, and professional groups, and educational institutions, in two main parts: Chicano organizations, and Chicano studies departments and programs. Address, telephone, contact persons, and annotation are provided for each entry. Information was gathered by questionnaire. A short bibliography and a list of acronyms are included. Three indexes: geographic, divided into organizations and Chicano studies programs; subjects; and organizations.   E184.M5C26

Gonzales, Sylvia Alicia. Hispanic American voluntary organizations. Westport, Conn. : Greenwood, 1985. 267 p. ISBN 0-313-20949-9.   **CC242**

Contains approximately 200 entries, alphabetically arranged, listing Mexican-American, Puerto Rican, and Cuban-American associations and groups. Entries include history, goals, structure, activities, and sources consulted. Information

included was gathered by questionnaire. Three appendixes: (1) entries grouped by geographic location; (2) entries grouped by function or activity; (3) a chronology of general events, and events directly related to the organizations covered. Author and subject index.   E184.S75G65

Graham, Joe Stanley. Hispanic-American material culture : an annotated directory of collections, sites, archives, and festivals in the United States. N.Y. : Greenwood, 1989. 257 p. (Material culture directories, no. 2). ISBN 0-313-24789-7.   **CC243**

"Describes collections of artifacts, structures, and other aspects of the built environment, where Hispanics in the United States and its territories demonstrate components of material culture distinctive to Hispanics."—*Pref.* Includes descriptions of museum collections, holdings of historical societies and other public agencies, and sites listed on the National Register of Historical Places. Includes material on the Basques, but acknowledges that Basques are not Hispanics. A bibliography emphasizes titles in arts and crafts. Indexed only by name or type of artifact.   E184.S75G69

Handbooks

The Hispanic almanac. Edition two. N.Y. : Hispanic Policy Development Project, c1990. 203 p. : ill. (some col.).   **CC244**

In three sections: (1) brief narrative histories of Hispanic groups in the Western Hemisphere who have emigrated to the U.S.; (2) socioeconomic, demographic, and linguistic data for the entire Hispanic population in the U.S., with detailed and comparative analyses of four subgroups (Mexican Americans, Puerto Ricans, Cuban Americans, and other Hispanics); (3) detailed descriptive analysis of the 20 Standard Metropolitan Statistical Areas with the largest Hispanic populations. There is also a description of the voting behavior of Hispanic electorates. Information is presented in maps, tables, graphs, and text. Data was drawn from the U.S. census, and references are included in the text. Includes a spotty list of cultural organizations, communications and media organizations, and research institutes. The technical appendix describes preparation of the data. No index.   E184.S75H47

Biography

Meier, Matt S. Mexican American biographies : a historical dictionary, 1836–1987. N.Y. : Greenwood, 1988. 270 p. ISBN 0-313-24521-5.   **CC245**

A compilation of 270 biographical sketches, 200 of which treat living individuals. Sources of additional information are included with each entry. Appendixes list the biographees by field of endeavor and by state of residence. Index of names and organizations included in the entries.   E184.M5M454

Statistics

Schick, Frank Leopold. Statistical handbook on U.S. Hispanics / by Frank L. Schick and Renee Schick. Phoenix : Oryx, c1991. 1 v. ISBN 0-89774-554-X. $39.50.   **CC246**

Consists of eight chapters covering overall demographics, immigration and naturalization, social characteristics, education, health, politics and government, labor force participation, and economic conditions. Data are presented primarily in tables and charts, although some are represented by graphs or maps. Each chapter includes an overview of the data and references for further reading. The "List of sources" indicates that most of the data were originally published by U.S. agencies. Includes a list of the tables and charts, a glossary of terms, and a subject index. **E184.S75S27**

WOMEN

Guides

Carter, Sarah. Women's studies : a guide to information sources / Sarah Carter and Maureen Ritchie. Jefferson, N.C. : McFarland, 1990. 269 p. ISBN 0-89950-534-1. $39.95. **CC247**

A highly useful sourcebook that includes "all major woman-centered English-language reference works, monographic and serial."—*Introd.* 1,076 annotated entries with cross-references are arranged in three sections: General material (reference works, biographical dictionaries, women's sources); Women in the world (i.e., works relating to women of specific geographic areas); and Special subjects (e.g., Black women, Law and politics, Lesbians, Spirituality). Omits sources on children's literature and individual women writers. Detailed general index. **Z7961.C37**

Chapman, Anne. Feminist resources for schools and colleges : a guide to curricular materials. 3rd ed. N.Y. : Feminist Pr. at The City Univ. of New York, 1986. 190 p. ISBN 0-935312-35-8 (pbk.). $12.95. **CC248**

1st ed., 1973; 2nd ed., 1977. Editor varies.

Includes 445 annotated entries, 1975–84, alphabetically arranged by author or title within the major disciplines covered in the high school and undergraduate college curriculum. The first section lists 310 print resources, the second 135 audiovisual resources. Annotations are descriptive and evaluative. Omits biographies, novels, poetry, and drama. Eight-page directory of publishers and distributors; separate author/title indexes for print and audiovisual resources; combined subject index. **Z5817.C48**

Schuster, Marilyn R. Selected bibliography for integrating research on women's experience in the liberal arts curriculum / comp. by Marilyn Schuster and Susan Van Dyne. 6th ed. Northampton, Mass. : Smith College, 1988. 101 leaves. **CC249**

1st ed., 1983; 5th ed., 1986.

Compiled for teachers for instructional and research purposes. Multidisciplinary; organized by academic field, Afro-American studies to theater. In each section, lists citations alphabetically by author under two categories, Classroom use and Teacher preparation. Offset from typescript; some running heads obscured by spiral binding. No indexes. **HQ1181.U5OCS38**

Searing, Susan E. Introduction to library research in women's studies. Boulder, Colo. : Westview Pr., 1985. 257 p. ISBN 0-86531-267-2. $17.95. **CC250**

Pt. I describes the nature of women's studies, reviews basic research strategy, and explains use of card catalogs, periodical indexes, and interlibrary loan. Pt. II provides annotated lists of specific research tools, including: guides to research, bibliographies, indexes, library catalogs, guides to special collections, biographical sources, directories, microform sources, online sources, periodicals, guides, and handbooks. Three appendixes contain the Dewey Decimal and Library of Congress classification systems, and review essays from *Signs*, 1975–Summer 1984. **Z7961.S42**

Women in development : a resource guide for organization and action / ISIS Women's International Information and Communication Service. Philadelphia : New Society Publishers, c1984. 225 p. : ill. ISBN 0-86571-040-6. ISBN 0-86571-041-4 (pbk.). **CC251**

Essays focus on five issues: multinationals, rural development, health, education and communication, and migration and tourism. Subtopics include food production and appropriate technology. Resource lists follow each chapter and include organizations, reference tools, research centers, periodicals, and bibliographies. Numerous graphics and photographs, but no indexes. **HQ1240.5.D44W663**

Women's studies in Western Europe : a resource guide / ed. by Stephen Lehmann and Eva Sartori. Chicago : Association of College and Research Libraries, 1986. 129 p. (WESS occasional publication, no. 2). ISBN 0-8389-7037-0 (pbk.). **CC252**

Contains three essays: (1) Women's publishing in Europe, which includes lists of organizations, archives, databases, directories, publishers, journals, and bookstores for Europe as a whole and for 27 countries and geographic areas; (2) Women's studies education and research, including a list of related agencies by country; (3) The Fawcett Library and collection development issues, which includes a list of British libraries devoted exclusively to women's collections. Essays range in length from 10 to 15 pages and include resource lists. An appendix includes an alphabetical list of North American periodicals relevant to European women's studies. No indexes. **HQ1181.E85W66**

Bibliography

Ballou, Patricia K. Women : a bibliography of bibliographies. 2nd ed. Boston : G.K. Hall, c1986. 268 p. ISBN 0-8161-8729-0. $30.00. **CC253**

1st ed., 1980 (*Guide* CC498).

Revises and enlarges the 1st ed., eliminating superseded titles and including 1970–85 imprints. Adds many new topics, including incest, sexual harassment, peace, and mothers and daughters, and adds title and subject indexes. **Z7961.B32**

Cantor, Aviva. The Jewish woman, 1900–1985 : a bibliography / partially annotated by Aviva Cantor with 1983–1986 citations comp. by Ora Hamelsdorf. [2nd ed.]. Fresh Meadows, N.Y. : Biblio Pr., 1987. 193 p. ISBN 0-930395-04-2. **CC254**

Reprints the 1st ed., 1979 (*Guide* CC506) as Pt. I, and eight pages of corrections and additions to the 1st ed., which were issued as supplements in 1981 and 1982. Pt. II contains the second edition, which includes materials published 1980–85 and provides 11 pages of selected 1986 titles. Index of personal names. **Z7963.J4C36**

Coyle, Jean M. Women and aging : a selected, annotated bibliography. N.Y. : Greenwood, 1989. 135 p. (Bibliographies and indexes in gerontology, no. 9). ISBN 0-313-26021-4. **CC255**

Intended for practitioners, researchers, and older women. 622 numbered entries appear in 13 topical sections (e.g., Employment, Health, Retirement, Racial and ethnic groups, Policy issues, Housing). Subarranged by type of material, then alphabetically by author. Includes books, articles, films, documents, and dissertations. Subject and author indexes. **Z7164.O4C68**

Dolan, Eleanor F. The mature woman in America : a selected annotated bibliography, 1979–1982 / comp. by Eleanor F. Dolan and Dorothy M. Gropp. Wash. : National Council on the Aging, 1984. 122 p. ISBN 0-910883-02-5 (pbk.). **CC256**

An author listing of 423 entries that emphasize statistics and research and include books, articles, pamphlets, directories, guides, bibliographies, reports, government publications, and some unpublished papers. Subject index. **Z7164.O4D64**

Ferber, Marianne A. Women and work, paid and unpaid : a selected, annotated bibliography. N.Y. : Garland, 1987. 408 p. (Garland reference library of social science, v. 315). ISBN 0-8240-8690-2. $35.00.   **CC257**
    For annotation, see *Supplement* CH273.   Z7963.E7F47

Lent, John A. Women and mass communications : an international annotated bibliography. N.Y. ; Westport, Conn. : Greenwood, c1991. 481 p. (Bibliographies and indexes in women's studies, no. 11). ISBN 0-313-26579-8.   **CC258**
    Includes mass media (publishing, radio, magazines, television, newspapers, film, and video) as well as wire services, public relations, and advertising. Omits speeches and interpersonal communications. 3,235 entries represent published and unpublished literature, 1960–90. A preface provides a history of the literature, databases searched, and a detailed review of chapter content and background. The first chapter treats global and comparative perspectives, and the five remaining chapters focus on different regions of the world. Entries are alphabetically arranged by author. An appendix gives alphabetical lists of organizations and periodicals. Author and subject indexes.
                                                        Z5633.W65L45

Loeb, Catherine. Women's studies : a recommended core bibliography, 1980–1985 / Catherine R. Loeb, Susan E. Searing, Esther F. Stineman. Littleton, Colo. : Libraries Unlimited, 1987. 538 p. ISBN 0-87287-472-9. $55.00.   **CC259**
                                                         Z7963.F44L63

———— Women's studies : a recommended core bibliography, 1980–1985 / Catherine R. Loeb, Susan E. Searing, Esther F. Stineman. Abridged ed. Littleton, Colo. : Libraries Unlimited, 1987. 222 p. ISBN 0-87287-598-9. $23.50.   **CC260**
    Continues *Women's studies : a recommended core bibliography*, by Esther Stineman (*Guide* CC522).
    Extends coverage of the basic volume into 1985, including 1,211 English-language or translated works from small women's presses and university and trade publishers. Lists annotated entries alphabetically by author in 17 subject chapters, and in two chapters on reference sources and on periodicals (the latter describing nearly 60 feminist serials). Each chapter begins with an introduction. Includes addresses of publishers not listed in *Books in print* or *Ulrich's international periodicals directory*. Author, title, and subject indexes.
    The briefer version, intended for smaller libraries, focuses on items that are in print, from well-known publishers, of general subject interest, and lower priced. 645 entries.
                                                        Z7963.F44L63

Mumford, Laura Stempel. Women's issues : an annotated bibliography. Pasadena, Calif. : Salem Pr., c1989. 163 p. ISBN 0-89356-654-3. $40.00.   **CC261**
    Intended for high school and college students. An introduction provides context, background, definitions, and an annotated list of 12 general reference sources. The bibliography is divided into sections that include: History, politics, and education; Women's movement; Economics; Health issues and sexuality; Family, home, and relationships; Violence against women; and Religion and spirituality. Index of names.
                                                         Z7961.M85

Nordquist, Joan. Rape : a bibliography. Santa Cruz, Calif. : Reference and Research Services, 1990. 72 p. ISBN 0-93785-536-7 (pbk.).   **CC262**
    Ten sections cover various topics from the psychological, feminist, social, and legal literatures. Section I deals with types of rape and occurrences. Other sections include psychological impact, treatment, attitudes, race and class issues, rapists, pornography, prevention, and legal aspects. The first nine sections are each arranged by format: books, pamphlets, papers, and documents; or articles in periodicals and books. The tenth section lists resources: statistical sources, bibliographies, directories, and organizations. Entries are alphabetical by author and focus on the most recent five years. No indexes.
                                                        Z5703.R35.N67

Ogilvie, Marilyn Bailey. Women in science : antiquity through the nineteenth century : a biographical dictionary with annotated bibliography. Cambridge, Mass. : MIT Pr., c1986. 254 p. ISBN 0-262-15031-X. $25.00.   **CC263**
    For annotation, see *Supplement* EA78.   Q141.O34

Sellen, Betty-Carol. Feminists, pornography & the law : an annotated bibliography of conflict, 1970–1986 / Betty-Carol Sellen, Patricia A. Young. Hamden, Conn. : Library Professional Publications, 1987. 204 p. ISBN 0-208-02124-8.   **CC264**
    Contains six sections by type of resource: books, periodical articles, newspapers, nonprint media, unpublished material, and organizations. An introductory essay summarizes the conflict and provides a chronology. Each section contains an introductory scope note and lists entries alphabetically by author. Appendixes list publications which contain frequent references to the feminist antipornography movement and a chronology of newspaper articles. General index.   Z7164.P84S45

Sullivan, Kaye. Films for, by, and about women. Series II. Metuchen, N.J. : Scarecrow, 1985. 780 p. ISBN 0-8108-1766-7. $57.50.   **CC265**
    Lists some 3,200 films alphabetically by title. Updates the 1980 volume with the same title (*Guide* CC523) and follows its format, except the subject index includes the names of women and many new headings (e.g., Child custody, Children's rights, Adoption). The synopsis for each film includes credits, citation to a script or filmbook if available, whether the film is based on a book, and whether the film is sexually explicit.
                                                        PN1995.9.W6S95

Watson, G. Llewellyn. Feminism and women's issues : an annotated bibliography and research guide / G. Llewellyn Watson with the assistance of Janet P. Sentner. N.Y. : Garland, 1990. 2 v. (1710 p.). (Garland reference library of social science, v. 599). ISBN 0-8240-5543-8.   **CC266**
    Groups 7,364 citations, many without annotations, alphabetically by author into subject categories outlined in the table of contents, the only source of subject access. Journal articles from the 1960s and 1970s predominate.   Z7961.W37

Winter, Eugenia B. Psychological and medical aspects of induced abortion : a selective, annotated bibliography, 1970–1986. N.Y. : Greenwood, 1988. 162 p. (Bibliographies and indexes in women's studies, no. 7). ISBN 0-313-26100-8.   **CC267**
    Describes 500 works that are "either classics in the field or representational of the kind of writing being published . . . ."—*Pref.* Besides books and research articles, includes a number of films and audio and video recordings. Author, title, and subject indexes.   Z6671.2.A2W56

Current

Feminist collections. Madison, Wisc. : [Women's Studies Librarian-at-Large for The Univ. of Wisconsin System]. Quarterly. $38.00 (institutions).   **CC268**
    A quarterly survey of publications in women's studies. Regular sections include book reviews; essays on feminism and publishing; research exchange information; new periodicals, title changes, or cessations; and a list of books recently received. The last issue in each volume contains combined author and title index for entire volume.

New books on women and feminism. [No. 1] (June 1979)– . Madison, Wisc. : Memorial Library, Univ. of Wisconsin System, 1979– . Irregular. ISSN 0742-7123.
CC269

A bibliography of books and periodicals listed alphabetically by title within broad subject areas (e.g., anthropology, literature: poetry, religion/spirituality). Each issue provides author and subject indexes and an abbreviations list.

Women's studies index. 1989– . Boston : G.K. Hall, c1991– . Annual.   **CC270**

A selective author/subject index to relevant articles in a wide range of scholarly and popular periodicals, mainly American in origin. Includes concise instructions on use of the index, cross-references, and an alphabetical list of the 78 periodicals scanned.

Periodicals

Doughan, David. Feminist periodicals, 1855–1984 : an annotated critical bibliography of British, Irish, Commonwealth, and international titles / David Doughan, Denise Sanchez. N.Y. : New York Univ. Pr., 1987. 316 p. ISBN 0-8147-1798-5. $95.00.   **CC271**

A chronological listing of 920 primarily British journals 1855–1984, which "define themselves . . . as committed to improving the social, legal and economic position of women in relation to men," although many of the pre-1960 titles are "far more philanthropic than feminist in intention."—*Foreword.* Lists a few titles explicitly opposed to feminism, and some that appear to be feminist but are not. Entries include, when available, title, variant titles, editor, publisher, frequency, dates, locations, availability on microfilm. Has a brief introduction, list of abbreviations, explanation of entry format, and short bibliography. Name/title, subject, and chronological indexes.
Z7963.F44D68

Humphreys, Nancy K. American women's magazines : an annotated historical guide. N.Y. : Garland, 1989. 303 p. (Garland reference library of the humanities, vol. 789). ISBN 0-8240-7543-9.   **CC272**

"Women from three centuries, every geographical region, age, racial and class background, sexual preference, and ideology are represented by these periodicals."—*Introd.* In sections for alternative publications and mainstream publications. Pt. I covers 19th and early 20th century women's rights, as well as the feminist movement from the 1960s to present. Pt. II emphasizes mass market periodicals, covering 19th century ladies' magazines, 20th century women's magazines, women's pages in newspapers, and confession/romance magazines. 888 entries, alphabetically arranged by author in each subsection. Subject index.   Z6944.W6H85

Women in specific countries, regions, or ethnic groups

Brady, Anna. Women in Ireland : an annotated bibliography. N.Y. : Greenwood, 1988. 478 p. (Bibliographies and indexes in women's studies, no. 6). ISBN 0-313-24486-3. $45.00.   **CC273**

Restricted to women of Irish ancestry whose lives were spent primarily in Ireland, those strongly connected to Irish affairs, or well-known figures. Includes 2,312 books, book chapters, articles, theses, memoirs, travel accounts, pamphlets, and correspondence; excludes fiction, poetry, and most literary criticism and newspaper items. Covers from the early Celtic period to the present. Entries arranged by author under subject categories (e.g., biography and autobiography; religion and witchcraft;

revolutionary movements). English-language entries are annotated; author and subject indexes.   Z7964.I73B7

Bullwinkle, Davis. African women, a general bibliography, 1976–1985. N.Y. : Greenwood, 1989. 334 p. (African special bibliographic series, no. 9). ISBN 0-313-26607-7.   **CC274**

Entries are alphabetically arranged by author under 32 subject headings (e.g., Abortion, Cultural roles, Education and training, Employment and labor, Sexual mutilation/circumcision). Includes references not specific to a region or nation. No annotations. Appendixes include organizations, official names and capitals, and geographic and historical names. Author index.   Z7964.A3B84

———— Women of eastern and southern Africa : a bibliography, 1976–1985. N.Y. : Greenwood, 1989. 545 p. (African special bibliographic series, no. 11). ISBN 0-313-26606-9.   **CC275**

Lists entries by subject under regional and national headings; nations with a small number of entries are not divided by subject. Utilizes 34 subject headings (e.g., Apartheid and race relations, Bibliographies, Sex roles, Status of women). Lists entries alphabetically by author within each category. No annotations; author index.   Z7964.A337B84

———— Women of northern, western, and central Africa : a bibliography, 1976–1985. N.Y. : Greenwood, 1989. 601 p. (African special bibliographic series, no. 10). ISBN 0-313-26609-3.   **CC276**

Arranged by subject under regions or nations, using 33 subject subdivisions (e.g., Agriculture, Divorce, Equality and liberation, Religion and witchcraft, and Slavery). Nations with a small number of entries are not subdivided. Lists entries alphabetically by author within categories; no annotations. Author index.   Z7964.A3B85

Byrne, Pamela R. Women in the Third World : a historical bibliography / Pamela R. Byrne, Suzanne R. Ontiveros, editors. Santa Barbara, Calif. : ABC-Clio Information Services, c1986. 152 p. (ABC-Clio research guides, 15). ISBN 0-87436-459-0. $28.00.   **CC277**

Organizes 601 citations with abstracts into six chapters covering general topics and specific regions of the world (Africa, Asia, Middle East, Pacific Region, Latin America, and the West Indies). Entries, arranged alphabetically by author within chapters, include articles from ABC-Clio's database, 1970–85. A rotated subject index provides a descriptor profile for each entry, including subject, geographic, and biographical terms and dates. Includes cross-references. Separate author index.   Z7964.D44B96

Feinberg, Renee. The Equal Rights Amendment : an annotated bibliography of the issues, 1976–1985. N.Y. : Greenwood, 1986. 151 p. (Bibliographies and indexes in women's studies, no. 3). ISBN 0-313-24762-5. $29.95.
CC278

Documents the struggle for ERA ratification. Designed as sequel to Equal Rights Amendment Project's *The equal rights amendment* (*Guide* CC534) expanding coverage to include TV news and selective annotations. Includes over 700 entries from books, articles, government publications, and television news programs in 11 chapters covering public opinion, federal and state interpretations, employment, education, family and religion, military, ratification efforts, and more. Lists of organizations; subject and author indexes.   KF4758.A1F45

Fenton, Thomas P. Women in the Third World : a directory of resources / comp. and ed. by Thomas P. Fenton and Mary J. Heffron. Maryknoll, N.Y. : Orbis Books, c1987. 141 p. : ill. ISBN 0-88344-530-1 (pbk.). $9.95.
CC279

Five chapters cover organizations, books, periodicals, pamphlets and articles, and audiovisual materials. In each chapter, annotated entries are followed by brief entry lists and lists of information sources. Organization, individuals, title, geographical area, and subject indexes.   Z7964.D44F46

Frey, Linda. Women in western European history. First supplement : a select chronological, geographical, and topical bibliography / comp. and ed. by Linda Frey, Marsha Frey, and Joanne Schneider. N.Y. : Greenwood, 1986. lxv, 699 p. ISBN 0-313-25109-6.   **CC280**

Continues and updates earlier volumes (*Guide* CC561), following the same format. Of 6,505 entries, fewer than 100 are repeated from the earlier volumes, these being "either significant new editions or translations, or works previously cited in the second volume which also covered topics dealt with in the first volume."—*Pref.*   Z7961.F74

Gabaccia, Donna R. Immigrant women in the United States : a selectively annotated multidisciplinary bibliography. N.Y. : Greenwood, 1989. 325 p. (Bibliographies and indexes in women's studies, no. 9). ISBN 0-313-26452-X.   **CC281**

Cites books, articles, and dissertations in English concerning immigrants of all periods and geographic origins. Entries are arranged alphabetically by author within 12 chapters: Bibliography, General works, Migration, Family, Work, Working together, Body, Mind, Cultural change, Biography, Autobiography, Fiction. Each chapter begins with a page of introductory comment. Separate author, person, group, and subject indexes; no table of contents.   Z7164.I3G33

Green, Rayna. Native American women : a contextual bibliography. Bloomington : Indiana Univ. Pr., c1983. 120 p. ISBN 0-253-33976-6.   **CC282**

Contains 672 annotated entries, arranged alphabetically by author. A 20-page introduction surveys the topics. Although the earliest entry appeared in 1620, most titles listed were published since the 1920s. Books, periodicals, firms, audio recordings, dissertations and government publications are included. Chronological and subject indexes.   Z1209.2.N67G75

Harrison, Cynthia Ellen. Women in American history : a bibliography. Santa Barbara, Calif. : ABC-Clio , c1985. v. 2. ISBN 0-87436-260-1 (v. 1). $78.00.   **CC283**

For v. 1 and annotation, see *Guide* CC539.

Contains 3,700 abstracts drawn from *America: history and life* (*Guide* DB47). Covers 1978–84. Follows same arrangement as the first volume.   Z7962.H37

Kanner, Barbara. Women in English social history, 1800–1914 : a guide to research. N.Y. : Garland, 1987–1990. 3 v. (Garland reference library of social science, v. 155, 408–409). ISBN 0-8240-9168-X (v. 3).   **CC284**

Vols. 1 (6,000 entries) and 2 (5,000 entries) list books, periodical articles, critical reviews, theses, and dissertations on broad topics such as marriage and the family, sickness and health care, law, religion and spiritualism, and education (v. 1); and employment, philanthropy, crime and deviance, sexual issues, natural and social sciences, and women's rights (v. 2). In each section, entries are arranged chronologically, some with annotations. A 62-page general index is printed in both volumes. Vol. 3 contains 776 annotated entries in two sections, Introduction and Autobiographical writings. No subject or title indexes.   Z7964.G7K36

Kelly, David H. Women's education in the Third World : an annotated bibliography / David H. Kelly, Gail P. Kelly. N.Y. : Garland, 1989. 478 p. ISBN 0-8240-8634-1.   **CC285**

For annotation, see *Supplement* CB32.   Z5815.D44K44

Pandit, Harshida. Women of India : an annotated bibliography. N.Y. : Garland, 1985. 278 p. (Garland reference library of social science, vol. 152). ISBN 0-8240-9175-2.   **CC286**

An introductory essay reviews demographics and legal rights. 1,119 numbered entries are grouped by subject or format (legal status, social problems, art and culture, films, etc.) and arranged within categories alphabetically by author. Gives scope notes for each category. Author index.   Z7964.I5P36

Redfern, Bernice. Women of color in the United States : a guide to the literature. N.Y. : Garland, 1989. 156 p. ISBN 0-8240-5849-6.   **CC287**

A classed list of 636 annotated entries covering African Americans, Asian Americans, Hispanics, and Native Americans. Entries are arranged alphabetically by author within topics, which include biography, autobiography, education, employment, literature and the arts, history and politics. Includes books, essays, indexes, articles, and dissertations, most published since 1975. Author and subject indexes.   Z7964.U49R4

Stoner, K. Lynn. Latinas of the Americas : a source book. N.Y. : Garland, 1989. 692 p. (Garland reference library of social science, v. 363). ISBN 0-8240-8536-1.   **CC288**

"Includes both published and unpublished research on women in Spanish-, Portuguese-, and French-speaking Latin America, as well as on Hispanic American women in the United States."—*Pref.* 15 topical chapters, each consisting of an essay in English followed by a bibliography alphabetically arranged by author. Bibliographies cover 1977–86 and include works in English, Spanish, Portuguese, French, and other languages.   Chapters include such topics as biography, feminist studies, religion, development, law. Author, country/region, and subject indexes.   Z7964.L3S76

Women of color and Southern women : a bibliography of social science research 1975 to 1988. Memphis, Tenn. : Center for Research on Women, Memphis State Univ., c1988.   **CC289**

Women of color and Southern women : a bibliography of social science research 1975 to 1988. Supplement. 1989– . Memphis, Tenn. : Center for Research on Women, Memphis State Univ., c1988– . Annual.   **CC290**

Andrea Timberlake, ed.

Includes articles, books, newsletters, working papers, dissertations, and conference proceedings. Six main sections: Culture, Education, Employment, Family, Health, and Political activism/social movements, subarranged by ethnic group (African American, Asian American, Latina, Native American) with added categories for women of color and Southern women. Entries are listed alphabetically by author within subgroups. Relevant keywords from *A women's thesaurus* (*Supplement* CC300) appear with every entry. Author index; keyword index. The supplement follows the same format, adding 900 new citations.
          Z7964.U49W637

Encyclopedias

Ammer, Christine. The new A to Z of women's health : a concise encyclopedia. N.Y. : Facts on File, c1989. 472 p. : ill. ISBN 0-8160-2073-6. $29.95.   **CC291**

For annotation, see *Supplement* EK37.   RA778.A494

Handbook of American women's history / Angela Howard Zophy, ed., Frances M. Kavenik, associate ed. N.Y. : Garland, 1990. 736 p. (Garland reference library of the humanities, vol. 696). ISBN 0-8240-8744-5.   **CC292**

For annotation, see *Supplement* DB65.   HQ1410.H36

Tuttle, Lisa. Encyclopedia of feminism. N.Y. : Facts on File, 1986. 399 p. ISBN 0-8160-1424-8. $24.95. **CC293**

Intended for both readers new to and those familiar with feminism, this alphabetically arranged work covers "individuals, organizations, classic works, and specialized terminology."—*Introd.* Sample entries include: Bambara, Toni Cade; COYOTE; Seneca Falls; Gynarchy; Muslim feminists; Publishing; Separatism. Cross-references; 21-page bibliography.

HQ1115.T87

Women's studies encyclopedia / ed. by Helen Tierney. N.Y. : Greenwood, 1989–1990. v. 1–2. ISBN 0-313-26725-1. $59.95. (In progress). **CC294**

Contents: v. 1, Views from the sciences; v. 2, Literature, arts, and learning.

Vol. 1 contains some 240 articles, most signed, on the natural, behavioral, and social sciences, health and medicine, economics, linguistics, and political and legal sciences; v. 2 has 135 entries that emphasize women as producers of art, literature, and music. Both volumes are intended for general readers and emphasize the American experience, but v. 2 gives "greater attention . . . both to other Western and non-Western women than was possible in the first volume."—*Pref.* Some articles contain cross-references and many end with brief bibliographies. Both volumes have lists of consultants and contributors, general indexes, and select bibliographies. Sample entries: v. 1, Differential socialization, Osteoporosis, Rape; v. 2, Chicana writers, Fiber arts, Hagiography, Women's colleges. The third volume will treat women's history, religion, and philosophy.

HQ1115.W645

Dictionaries

A dictionary of sexist quotations / [comp. by] Simon James. Brighton, Sussex : Harvester Pr. ; Totowa, N.J. : Barnes & Noble, 1984. 206 p. ISBN 0-389-20501-X. **CC295**

The title is misleading; the work focuses on "the ancient rivalry between the sexes."—*Pref.* Contains 157 pages of quotations, very few contemporary, grouped alphabetically by topic, and a separate list of 105 topics, which include art, divorce, flattery, money, and virtue. Authors, sources, and dates are provided for most entries. Authors/sources and keyword indexes.

HQ1075.D52

Humm, Maggie. The dictionary of feminist theory. Columbus : Ohio State Univ. Pr., c1990. 278 p. ISBN 0-8142-0506-2. ISBN 0-8142-0507-0 (pbk.). **CC296**

Cross-cultural and international in scope, although focus is on Anglo-American and French theory. Each entry provides definitions, commentary, and references to the 28-page bibliography which follows. Preface includes sections on aims, definitions, issues, criteria, and design.

HQ1115.H86

Kramarae, Cheris. A feminist dictionary / Cheris Kramarae and Paula A. Treichler. London ; Boston : Pandora Pr., 1985. 587 p. ISBN 0-86358-060-2. $30.00. ISBN 0-86358-015-7 (pbk.). $15.00. **CC297**

"Places women at the center and rethinks language from that crucially different perspective."—*p.15.* A 22-page introduction, "Words on a feminist dictionary," provides useful background, rationale, and editorial information. Cross-referenced, English-language entries range in length from a few lines to several columns. Extensive 73-page bibliography.

HQ1115.K73

Maggio, Rosalie. The nonsexist word finder : a dictionary of gender-free usage. Phoenix : Oryx, 1987. 210 p. ISBN 0-89774-449-7 (pbk.). **CC298**

A glossary of words and phrases designed to assist writers in finding alternatives to sexist language. Suggested substitutes are given in italics and listed in order of usefulness. Appendix A, which the author suggests be read first, contains useful guidelines, rationale, and many examples. Appendix B contains eight short essays. Four-page bibliography. PE1689.M23

Terminology

Dickstein, Ruth. Women in LC's terms : a thesaurus of Library of Congress subject headings relating to women / ed. by Ruth Dickstein, Victoria A. Mills, and Ellen J. Waite. Phoenix : Oryx, 1988. 221 p. ISBN 0-89774-444-6. **CC299**

Lists more than 3,500 subject headings and cross-references pertaining to women, derived from a review of all the headings in the Dec. 1983 printing of *Library of Congress subject headings* (9th ed., *Guide* AB254). Terms are arranged in a main alphabetical list, then under the 11 sections prescribed in *A women's thesaurus* (below). Five appendixes: Free-floating subdivisions; Free-floating subdivisions used under classes of persons; Subdivision pattern headings for names of individual authors; Free-floating subdivisions used under names of persons; Library of Congress call numbers assigned to women and topics relating to women. Z695.1.W65D53

A women's thesaurus : an index of language used to describe and locate information by and about women / ed. by Mary Ellen S. Capek. N.Y. : Harper & Row, c1987. 1052 p. ISBN 0-06-015775-5. $14.95. ISBN 0-06-091552-8 (pbk.). $37.50. **CC300**

"A project of the National Council for Research on Women and the Business and Professional Women's Foundation."

A much-needed compilation, containing more than 5,000 terms recommended for indexing and subject cataloging of works relating to women. Terms are arranged in alphabetical, rotated, and hierarchical displays, and under 11 broad subject groups (e.g., History and social change; International women). Entries include references to broader, narrower, and related terms; variant forms; and scope notes. There are separate lists of "use/do not use" terms and of delimiters (generic search terms or proper nouns—e.g., historical periods, national and regional descriptors). An introductory section describes thesaurus construction and applications, form of entry, guidelines, etc. Provides rosters of contributors and members of the Thesaurus Task Force, cites the lists that were combined to form the thesaurus, and lists test sites. Brief bibliography.

Z695.1.W65W65

Directories

Directory of women's media. 1988– . Wash. : Women's Institute for Freedom of the Pr., c1988– . Annual. ISSN 1040-1156. $12.00. **CC301**

Two sections, Directory of media groups and Directory of media women and media-concerned women. The first includes entries, brief descriptions, and contact information for periodicals, publishers, news services, radio-TV, video and cable, film, music, art, theatre, public relations, advertising, distributors, media change organizations, bookstores and mail order, and library collections. The second provides names, affiliations, positions, and interests. Index of names arranged by zip code.

Directory of women's studies programs & library resources / ed. by Beth Stafford. Phoenix : Oryx, 1990. 154 p. ISBN 0-89774-507-8. **CC302**

Reflects data collected 1987–88 from U.S. colleges and universities. More than 400 entries, arranged by state and city, provide name, address, coordinator, descriptions of courses, degrees, library resources, names of women's studies faculty.

Indexes by institution, degree offered, library collections, and subject area.　　　　　　　　　　　　　　　HQ1181.U5D57

Schlachter, Gail A. Directory of financial aids for women, 1991–1992. San Carlos, Calif. : Reference Service Pr., 1991. 476 p. ISBN 0-918276-14-4. $50.00.
　　　　　　　　　　　　　　　　　　　　　　　CC303

2nd ed., 1982 (*Guide* CC587).
　　Revised and updated, adding approximately 400 new entries for a total of 1,818.　　　　　　　　　　LB2338.D564

Women scholars in women's studies / comp. by Women's Studies Progam, University of Illinois at Urbana-Champaign. Rev. ed. Champaign, Ill. : Committee on Institutional Cooperation, 1987. 173 p.　　　**CC304**
　　"Expands and updates the 1982 listing of women scholars active in women's studies at institutions affiliated with the Committee on Institutional Cooperation (CIC)."—*Introd.* Includes degrees, employment history, research interests, subjects taught, publications, and community involvement (the latter new to this edition). Entries are alphabetical and reflect data collected in 1985. Separate institution, disciplines and fields, and subject indexes.　　　　　　　　　HQ1181.U5W55

Women's movements of the world : an international directory and reference guide / ed. by Sally Shreir. Phoenix : Oryx, 1988. 384 p. ISBN 0-89774-508-6. $95.00.
　　　　　　　　　　　　　　　　　　　　　　　CC305
　　"A guide to the current status of women's issues and organizations throughout the world."—*Pref.* For each of 184 countries arranged in alphabetical order, provides an introductory section (including statistics) on key topics (e.g., political participation, education, marital and divorce rights, the workforce, contraception, and abortion), followed by an alphabetized list of "all major nationally-operating organizations and a selection of lesser groups."—*Introd.* Separate annotated list of 81 international organizations. Brief bibliography; no index.
　　　　　　　　　　　　　　　　　　　　　HQ1883.W63

Women's recovery programs : a directory of residential addiction treatment centers. Phoenix : Oryx, 1990. 339 p. ISBN 0-89774-584-1.　　　　　　　**CC306**
　　For annotation, see *Supplement* CC116.　　RC564.73.W66

Handbooks

Beere, Carole A. Gender roles : a handbook of tests and measures. N.Y. : Greenwood, c1990. 575 p. ISBN 0-313-26278-0.　　　　　　　　　　　　　　**CC307**
　　　　　　　　　　　　　　　　　　　　　　　HM253.B43

———————— Sex and gender issues : a handbook of tests and measures. N.Y. : Greenwood, 1990. 605 p. ISBN 0-313-27462-2.　　　　　　　　　**CC308**
　　These titles jointly constitute a revision of Beere's *Women and women's issues : a handbook of tests and measures*, 1979 (*Guide* CC574). *Gender roles* lists 211 titles in 11 chapters, updating for the period 1979–88 information concerning tests and measures related to gender roles (e.g., stereotypes, marital and parental roles, attitudes toward gender issues). *Sex and gender issues* lists 197 titles in nine chapters, updating for 1979–88 information concerning tests and measures related to sex and gender issues (e.g., heterosexuality, contraception, abortion, pregnancy). Both volumes are indexed.　　　BF692.B38

Every woman's legal guide : protecting your rights at home, in the workplace, and in the marketplace / by 28 lawyers and rights experts ; Barbara A. Burnett, consulting ed. Rev. ed. Garden City, N.Y. : Doubleday, c1985. 653 p. : ill. ISBN 0-385-18523-5. $19.95.　　**CC309**

Previous ed., 1983 (*Guide* CC575).
　　Revises the 1983 publication, following the same format.
　　　　　　　　　　　　　　　　　　　　　KF390.W6E83

International handbook of women's education / ed. by Gail P. Kelly. N.Y. ; London : Greenwood, 1989. 1 v. ISBN 0-313-25638-1. £73.10.　　　　　　**CC310**
　　For annotation, see *Supplement* CB132.

Miller, Casey. The handbook of nonsexist writing / Casey Miller and Kate Swift. 2nd ed. N.Y. : Harper & Row, c1988. 180 p. ISBN 0-06-181602-7. $15.95. ISBN 0-06-096238-0 (pbk.). $6.95.　　　**CC311**
　　For annotation, see *Supplement* AA57.　　PN218.M5

Chronologies

Clark, Judith Freeman. Almanac of American women in the 20th century. N.Y. : Prentice Hall, c1987. 274 p. : ill. ISBN 0-13-022658-0. ISBN 0-13-022641-6 (pbk.).
　　　　　　　　　　　　　　　　　　　　　　　CC312

　　Each of nine chapters covers one decade in this overview of U.S. women's history, 1900–87. Chronologies of events, brief biographies, and topic essays are interspersed. Events are categorized by topics such as education, reform, military, arts and culture, politics, and labor. Photographs; general index.
　　　　　　　　　　　　　　　　　　　　　HQ1420.C55

Biography

Jackson, Guida. Women who ruled. Santa Barbara, Calif. : ABC-Clio, c1990. 190 p. : ill. ISBN 0-87436-560-0.　　　　　　　　　　　　　　　**CC313**
　　An illustrated encyclopedia covering "all women rulers, de facto rulers, and constitutional monarchs, living or deceased, of the world's kingdoms, islands, empires, nations, and tribes since the beginning of recorded history."—*Pref.* An eight-page introduction provides historical context for regions of Africa, India and the Middle East, Central Asia, China and the Far East, Polynesia and the Western Hemisphere, and Europe. Includes a useful chronology of rulers by century. Entries, arranged alphabetically by ruler, begin with name, title, place of rule, and years of rule and vary in length from a short paragraph to several columns. Separate list of illustrations; six-page bibliography.　　　　　　　　　　　　　　　D107.J33

CD

Psychology and Psychiatry

GENERAL WORKS

Bibliography

Parsifal-Charles, Nancy. The dream : 4,000 years of theory and practice : a critical, descriptive, and encyclopedic bibliography. West Cornwall, Conn. : Locust Hill Pr., 1986. 2 v. (576 p.). ISBN 0-933951-07-8 (set). $59.95.   **CD1**

An annotated, evaluative bibliography of 700 significant books and monographs, arranged alphabetically by author. International in scope, including traditional and Third World societies. Material ranges from ancient and classical dreamworks, to modern dream chapbooks and rapid eye movement research. Indexes of subjects and personal names (i.e., individuals mentioned in the sources).   BF1078.P33

Riggar, T. F. Stress burnout : an annotated bibliography. Carbondale : Southern Illinois Univ., c1985. 299 p. ISBN 0-8093-1186-0.   **CD2**

Presents more than 1,000 entries, mostly journal articles but including books, in alphabetical order by author, with detailed annotations. An introduction defines and characterizes stress burnout and describes the organization and use of the book. A table of contents following the text takes the form of an outline index under the broad categories: Signs/symptoms, Causes/sources, and Coping strategies.   BF481.R53

White, James P. Materials and strategies for the education of trainable mentally retarded learners. N.Y. : Garland, 1990. 348 p. (Garland reference library of social science, v. 476 ; Garland reference library of social science. Source books on education, vol. 24). ISBN 0-8240-6345-7.   **CD3**

For annotation, see *Supplement* CB41.   LC4601.W52

Periodicals

Journals in psychology : a resource listing for authors. 2nd ed., rev. and expanded. Wash. : American Psychological Association, c1989. 118 p. ISBN 1-55798-047-0.   **CD4**

1st ed., 1988.

An alphabetical list of 233 English-language journals published in the U.S. Provides information on publishers, editors, editorial policy, notes for submission of articles, circulation, frequency, etc. Classified index. To be updated frequently.   BF76.8.J68

Loke, Wing Hong. A guide to journals in psychology and education. Metuchen, N.J. : Scarecrow, 1990. 410 p. ISBN 0-8108-2327-6.   **CD5**

For annotation, see *Supplement* CB44.   BF76.8.L65

Wang, Alvin Yafu. Author's guide to journals in the behavioral sciences. Hillsdale, N.J. : L. Erlbaum Associates, c1989. 481 p. ISBN 0-8058-0313-0.   **CD6**

Updates Allen Markle and Roger C. Rinn's *Author's guide to journals in psychology, psychiatry and social work* (*Guide* CD62).

Presents entries for 460 journals, alphabetically arranged by title, in a structured format that includes publication information, scope, editorial policies, style requirements, etc. Introduction defines coverage and entry formats.   BF76.8.W36

Abstract journals and indexes

A history of American psychology in notes and news, 1883–1945 : an index to journal sources / Ludy T. Benjamin, Jr. .. [et al.]. Millwood, N.Y. : Kraus Internat., c1989. 591 p. (Bibliographies in the history of psychology and psychiatry, 5). ISBN 0-527-06626-5.   **CD7**

Provides access to non-article information published in six journals—*Science* (1883–1945); *American journal of psychology* (1887–1945); *Psychological review* (1894–1903); *Psychological bulletin* (1904–45); *Journal of philosophy, psychology and scientific method* (1904–45); and *Journal of applied psychology* (1917–45). Includes detailed instructions for the appropriate use of this unique work of historical importance.   Z7201.H52

●**PsycLIT** [computer file]. Arlington, Va. : Amer. Psychological Assoc., 1967– .   **CD8**

Machine-readable version of *Psychological abstracts* (*Guide* CD69).

File size: 700,000 records. Available online as *PsycINFO* (BRS, DIALOG; updated monthly) and in CD-ROM (Silver-Platter, Abt Books, Faxon; updated quarterly).

Encyclopedias

Baker encyclopedia of psychology / ed. by David G. Benner. Grand Rapids, Mich. : Baker Book House, c1985. 1223 p. ([Baker reference library, 2]). ISBN 0-8010-3413-2. ISBN 0-8010-0865-4.   **CD9**

Offers signed entries of various lengths by experts; many have brief bibliographies and cross-references. Gives comprehensive coverage to topics in psychology, using language that is thoroughly professional but easily accessible to general readers. Although the preface characterizes the work as Christian in approach, the majority of the articles are neutral and factual. List of contributors; a "Category index" lists all headings under broad subjects.   BF31.B25

Concise encyclopedia of psychology / Raymond J. Corsini, ed. N.Y. : Wiley, c1987. 1242 p. ISBN 0-471010-68-5. $89.95.   **CD10**

A condensation of *Encyclopedia of psychology* (*Guide* CD83).

"Contains every entry in the *Encyclopedia of psychology* originally published in four volumes in 1984. In addition it contains several new entries . . . as well as updatings of several of the original articles"—*p. xxi.*   BF31.E553

Dictionary of behavioral science / comp. and ed. by Benjamin B. Wolman. 2nd ed. San Diego : Academic Pr., c1989. 370 p. : ill. ISBN 0-12-762455-4. ISBN 0-12-762456-2 (pbk.).   **CD11**

1st ed., 1973 (*Guide* CD102).

A revised and updated edition that omits the appendixes found in the 1st ed.   BF31.D48

Doctor, Ronald M. The encyclopedia of phobias, fears, and anxieties / Ronald M. Doctor and Ada P. Kahn. N.Y. : Facts on File, c1989. 487 p. ISBN 0-8160-1798-0.   **CD12**

Intended for both general readers and health care professionals. An alphabetic listing of more than 2,000 common psychological conditions; includes definitions, forms of therapy, outstanding individuals in the field, psychopharmacological information, and historical comments. Entries vary in length from 50 to more than 1,000 words and contain cross-references; many end with brief bibliographies. The work ends with a 40-page bibliography and subject index.   RC535.D63

The encyclopedic dictionary of psychology / ed. by Rom Harré and Roger Lamb. Cambridge, Mass. : MIT Pr., 1983. 718 p. : ill. ISBN 0-262-08135-0.   **CD13**

For main work, see *Guide* CD86.

From this work, the editors have selected materials which they have updated and supplemented and have reissued as four independent titles, all published by MIT Pr. in 1986: *Dictionary of developmental and educational psychology*; *Dictionary of physiological and clinical psychology*; *Dictionary of personality and social psychology*; and *Dictionary of ethnology and animal learning*.   BF31.E555

The Oxford companion to the mind / ed. by Richard L. Gregory, with the assistance of O.L. Zangwill. Oxford ; N.Y. : Oxford Univ. Pr., 1987. 856 p. : ill. ISBN 0-19-866124-X. $30.00.   **CD14**

Arranged alphabetically, covering a wide range of topics (e.g., Physiological bases of neurological function, Prominent individuals in psychology, Illusions, Aesthetics, Other cultures' ideas of mind, Computer intelligence). Focuses on psychology, with forays into philosophy, art, medicine, mythology. Definitions range in length from a few sentences to a few pages, with an index of topics and individuals buried in longer articles. Many entries have a brief bibliography; all are signed. Cross-references are provided only when further information is available, not to all related entries.   BF31.O94

Psychology and its allied disciplines / ed. by Marc H. Bornstein. Hillsdale, N.J. : L. Erlbaum Associates, 1984. 3 v. in 1 : ill. ISBN 0-89859-318-2. $74.95. ISBN 0-89859-319-0 (pbk.). $60.00.   **CD15**

Contents: v. 1, Psychology and the humanities; v. 2, Psychology and the social sciences; v. 3, Psychology and the natural sciences.

Offers 21 essays by specialists, including the relationship of psychology to art, literature, music, philosophy, religion, anthropology, education, history, political science, mathematics, physics, engineering, medicine, etc. Each essay has a substantial bibliography; each section has biographical notes on the authors. Author and subject indexes to themes and individuals treated within the essays.   BF38.P786

Roesch, Roberta. The encyclopedia of depression. N.Y. : Facts on File, c1991. 263 p. ISBN 0-8160-1936-3.   **CD16**

An alphabetic listing of entries on all aspects of depression varying in length from 50 to 1,000 words, with many cross-references. Appendixes include statistics, psychiatric drug information, and information sources (including selected treatment centers, self-help groups, publications and an extensive bibliography). Subject index. Intended for general readers.   RC537.R63

Treatments of psychiatric disorders : a task force report of the American Psychiatric Association. Wash. : The Association, 1989. 4 v. (3068 p.). ISBN 0-89042-205-2 (set). $235.00.   **CD17**

Provides comprehensive descriptions for treatments of disorders, encompassing diverse orientations and treatment variables. Covers multiple approaches, including pharmacologic, psychodynamic, behavioral, cognitive, family, individual, and group treatments, recognizing evolving knowledge and preferred treatments as well as acceptable alternatives. More than 400 pages of references. Vol. 4 is a 250-page author-subject index. A cautionary statement emphasizes this should not serve as a standard of care. Useful for graduate research and health professionals.   RC480.T69

Dictionaries

Campbell, Robert Jean. Psychiatric dictionary. 6th ed. N.Y. : Oxford Univ. Pr., 1989. 811 p. ISBN 0-19-505293-5.   **CD18**

5th ed., 1981 (*Guide* CD78).

Incorporates terms of the official *Diagnostic and statistical manual of mental disorders : DSM-III-R* of the American Psychiatric Association (*Supplement* CD29) but also includes older terms if they are more familiar or continue to be widely used. Useful list of abbreviations.   RC437.H5

Popplestone, John A. Dictionary of concepts in general psychology / John A. Popplestone and Marion White McPherson. N.Y. : Greenwood, 1988. 380 p. (Reference sources for the social sciences and humanities, no. 7). ISBN 0-313-23190-7.   **CD19**

Presents two- to three-page discussions that contain four elements (current definition, origin, references, and sources of additional information) for terms such as "achievement," "anger," and "fear of failure." Author and subject indexes.   BF31.P665

Reber, Arthur S. The Penguin dictionary of psychology. Harmondsworth, Middlesex, England ; N.Y. : Penguin Books, 1985. 848 p. : ill. ISBN 0-1405-1079-6 (pbk.). $7.95.   **CD20**

In a vocabulary of approximately 17,000 words, identifies 175 terms as major entries that receive extensive coverage of 200 words or more—" . . . terms that have (often unacknowledged) subtleties of usage or are controversial in their manner of usage or simply have meanings that are denotatively or connotatively complex."—*Pref.* Includes a list of authorities cited.   BF31.R43

Stone, Evelyn M. American psychiatric glossary. 6th ed. Wash. : American Psychiatric Pr., c1988. 143 p. ISBN 0-88048-275-3. $15.00 (est.).   **CD21**

5th ed., 1980 (*Guide* CD76) had title *A psychiatric glossary*.

This edition incorporates the revised nomenclature of *Diagnostic and statistical manual of mental disorders : DSM-III-R* of the American Psychiatric Association (*Supplement* CD29). Diagnostic terms are cross-referenced from older nomenclatures. Includes valuable lists of abbreviations, tables of commonly abused drugs, legal terms, psychological tests, research terms, and schools of psychiatry.   RC437.S76

Sutherland, N. S. The international dictionary of psychology. N.Y. : Continuum, c1989. 491 p. : ill. ISBN 0-8264-0440-5.   **CD22**

Brief definitions of technical terms used in psychology, which are intended to clarify the reading of professional articles and papers for general readers, although many definitions use terminology that is professionally sophisticated. Numerous cross-references, occasional diagrams. Appendixes constitute an atlas of the brain.   BF31.S83

Zusne, Leonard. Eponyms in psychology : a dictionary and biographical sourcebook. N.Y. : Greenwood, 1987. 339 p. ISBN 0-313-25750-7. **CD23**

Provides definitions, biographical origins, and bibliographic references for 852 eponyms—"the person after whom something is named and that which is named after a person"—*Pref.* Entries (e.g., Alzheimer's disease, Freudian slip) are alphabetically arranged. Includes a preface and a list of periodical and book title abbreviations used in citations. Name and subject index. BF31.Z87

Terms

Psychoanalytic terms and concepts / ed. by Burness E. Moore and Bernard D. Fine. [N. Y.] : American Psychoanalytic Association ; New Haven, Conn. : Yale Univ. Pr., c1990. 210 p. ISBN 0-300-04577-8. ISBN 0-300-04701-0 (pbk.). **CD24**

A greatly revised and expanded 3rd ed. of the compilers' *Glossary of psychoanalytic terms and concepts* (N.Y. : American Psychoanalytic Association, 1967) with short essays (150–2,000 words) on topics arranged alphabetically, with subsidiary terms defined and related. Useful cross-references; most entries end with brief bibliographies. Emphasizes, but is not limited to, Freudian framework. RC501.4.P79

Thesaurus of psychological index terms. 6th ed. / Alvin Walker, Jr., ed. Arlington, Va. : American Psychological Association, c1991. 332 p. ISBN 1-55798-111-6. **CD25**

1st ed., 1974; 5th ed., 1988.

Consists of controlled vocabulary used in indexing *Psychological abstracts* (*Guide* CD69), and for print and online retrieval. Terms include scope notes, cross-references, hierarchical relationships, and related terms. Z695.1.P7T48

Directories

Martin, Daniel R. A directory of credentials in counseling and psychotherapy / Daniel R. Martin and J. Richard Cookerly. Boston : G.K. Hall, c1989. 219 p. ISBN 0-8161-9062-3. **CD26**

An alphabetic listing of organizations that attempt to establish training and proficiency levels by credentials in counseling or psychotherapy in the U.S. Entries contain name of credentialing organization, individual's title, prerequisites, training, requirements, costs, and remarks. A glossary, legal requirements of individual states, a subject index, and credentials index are included. Useful for students, therapists, employers, and consumers. RC440.9.M37

Sherman, Barbara Smiley. Directory of residential treatment facilities for emotionally disturbed children. Phoenix : Oryx, 1985. 231 p. ISBN 0-89774-118-8. **CD27**

For annotation, see *Supplement* CC91. RJ504.5.S54

Stoloff, Michael L. Computer use in psychology : a directory of software / Michael L. Stoloff, James V. Couch. Wash. : American Psychological Association ; Hyattsville, Md. : Order from Order Dept., c1987. [95] p. ISBN 1-55798-029-2 (pbk.). **CD28**

Lists computer software useful for clinical and academic psychologists. Entries are alphabetical by title in four sections: Academic software, Clinical and applied software, Software for statistics and research, and Testing software. Each listing includes title, type of software, for academic software the course in which the software would be most useful, authors, publisher's address and telephone, program description, price, and hardware requirements. Indexed. BF79.5.S76

Handbooks

Diagnostic and statistical manual of mental disorders : DSM-III-R. 3rd ed., rev. Wash. : American Psychiatric Association, 1987. 567 p. ISBN 0-89042-018-1. $39.95. ISBN 0-89042-019-X. $29.95. **CD29**

1st ed., 1952; 3rd ed., 1980.

The original publication attempted to establish a glossary for describing diagnoses. This edition, translated into 13 languages, is viewed by mental health researchers and clinicians as the accepted classification system for disorders. Contains all diagnostic criteria plus systematic descriptions of disorders, using a numerical code system. Includes an explanation of the code system and instructions for its use, descriptions of disorders, glossary, classification history, alphabetic and numeric listing of diagnoses and indexes of symptoms, diagnoses, and codes. Essential for mental health professionals.

RC455.2.C4D54

International handbook of psychology / ed. by Albert R. Gilgen and Carol K. Gilgen. N.Y. : Greenwood, 1987. 629 p. : ill. ISBN 0-313-23832-4. $75.00. **CD30**

Separate chapters written by native psychologists describe the development of psychology since World War II in each of 29 countries in "Black Africa" (i.e., countries south of the Sahara). Arranged alphabetically by country. Profiles vary, as a standard format was not used, but typically include major trends and influences, future directions, and references. An overall introduction elaborates on "International perspectives in psychology." Includes name index, subject index, and a list of contributors with brief biographies. BF77.I62

Keith-Spiegel, Patricia. The complete guide to graduate school admission : psychology and related programs. Hillsdale, N.J. : L. Erlbaum Associates, 1990. 1 v. ISBN 0-8058-0637-7. ISBN 0-8058-0638-5 (pbk.). **CD31**

Practical information and advice, presented in 32 chapters covering five major perspectives: an overview of the graduate school "issues," factors and activities that enhance an applicant's chances, choices to be made, the actual application processes, and what to expect in the post-application period. Most of the text is in question-and-answer format. No index. Seven appendixes include a supplementary reading list, notes for selected student groups, and a guide to creating a résumé. Concludes with a list of references. BF77.K35

Krug, Samuel E. Psychware : a reference guide to computer-based products for behavioral assessment in psychology, education, and business. Kansas City, Mo. : Test Corp. of America ; Detroit : Distr. by Gale, c1984. 801 p. ISBN 0-9611286-5-8. $65.00. **CD32**

Designed to identify and describe computer-based products applicable to the assessment or modification of human behavior. Most products listed are described as computer-based interpretive instruments, not simple test-scoring devices. Listings are alphabetical by title and include name, supplier, product category, applications, sale restrictions, type/cost of service provided, and product description. Indexed by title, category, application, service, and supplier. BF39.5.K78

Treatises

Comprehensive textbook of psychiatry/V / editors, Harold I. Kaplan, Benjamin J. Sadock. 5th ed. Baltimore : Williams & Wilkins, c1989. 2 v. (2158, 71 p.) : ill. ISBN 0-683-04517-2. **CD33**

3rd ed., 1980 (*Guide* CD96); 4th ed., 1985.

Substantially revised from the 4th ed. with closer integration between basic and clinical sciences, an expanded geriatric psychiatry section, and a new section on neuroscience. All described disorders are consistent with DSM-III-R nosology (see *Supplement* CD29). Some 237 contributors in this edition. Bibliographic references accompany each section in 50 chapters. The volumes have identical subject indexes. Scholarly and comprehensive. RC454.C637

Biography

American Psychiatric Association. Biographical directory. Wash. : The Association, c1983– . **CD34**

For earlier volumes and annotation, see *Guide* CD125.

At head of title: Fellows and members of the American Psychiatric Association.

Latest volume includes a language section, which locates members by the languages used in their professional practice. Information provided is at the option of the member except for name, address, and initial membership year. RC326.A56

International directory of psychologists, exclusive of the U.S.A : a publication of the International Union of Psychological Science / ed., Kurt Pawlik. 4th ed. Amsterdam ; N.Y. : North-Holland ; N.Y. : Distr. by Elsevier, 1985. 1181 p. ISBN 0-444-87774-6. ISBN 0-444-87809-2 (pbk.). **CD35**

3rd ed., 1980 (*Guide* CD126).

This edition offers biographies of 36,000 psychologists from 48 countries in the Union and eight countries affiliated with the International Association for Cross-Cultural Psychology (Indonesia, Jamaica, Kenya, Kuwait, Malaysia, Nigeria, Saudi Arabia, and Singapore). Entries are alphabetically arranged by country. Also includes a section on the Union itself (history, functions, programs, publications, and affiliations) and the current status of the field in each country (with respect to major organizations, academic training, fields of research, etc.). BF30.I52

Women in psychology : a bio-bibliographic sourcebook / ed. by Agnes N. O'Connell and Nancy Felipe Russo. N.Y. : Greenwood, 1990. 1 v. ISBN 0-313-26091-5. **CD36**

Offers biographies of 36 women prominent in psychology. In five parts: (1) Overview, outlining the intent, selection process, biographical elements solicited, and potential use; (2) The women and their contributions, giving for each person: background, education, career, major contributions, evaluation, bibliography; (3) Awards and recognition; (4) Bibliographic resources; (5) Appendixes. The appendixes group biographees by birth year, by birthplace, and by major fields. General index. BF109.A1W65

Style manuals

Sternberg, Robert J. The psychologist's companion : a guide to scientific writing for students and researchers. 2nd ed. Cambridge ; N.Y. : Cambridge Univ. Pr. ; Leicester : British Psychological Society, c1988. 208 p. : ill. ISBN 0-521-34121-3. **CD37**

Rev. ed. of *Writing the psychology paper* (Woodbury, N.Y. : Barron's Education Series, Inc., 1977).

Treats the style and mechanics of papers being submitted for publication in journals in psychology. Ten chapters address such subjects as common misconceptions, misused words, annotated references, and guidelines for writing, evaluating, and submitting research papers for British and American journals. Includes sample typescript papers. General index. BF76.8.S73

Tests and measurements

American Psychological Association. Standards for educational and psychological testing / American Educational Research Association, American Psychological Association, National Council on Measurement in Education. Wash. : American Psychological Association, c1985. 100 p. ISBN 0-912704-95-0 (pbk.). **CD38**

Supersedes *Standards for educational and psychological tests* (rev. ed., 1974).

Intends to provide "criteria for the evaluation of tests, testing practices, and the effects of test use."—*Introd.* Addresses professionals' needs for ethically, scientifically, and clinically sound procedures. In four sections: (1) Technical standards for test construction and evaluation; (2) Professional standards for test use; (3) Standards for particular applications; and (4) Standards for administration. Each is divided into subsections that begin with textual explanations and definitions followed by individually numbered statements of standards. Includes a glossary of technical terms and a subject index referring to specific standards. LB3051.A693

Cumulative index to *Tests in microfiche*, 1975–1987 / cumulation produced by John C. Hepner. Princeton, N.J. : ETS Test Collection, c1988. 344 p. ISBN 0-88685-078-9. **CD39**

Cumulates the annual indexes to the first 13 annual sets of this collection, (sets A–M), indexing approximately 1,500 unpublished tests. Sequentially numbered entries provide citations and brief abstracts that describe the instruments' characteristics and uses. The volume's author, title, and subject indexes cite entry numbers. LB3051.T44

Dictionary of behavioral assessment techniques / ed. by Michel Hersen, Alan S. Bellack. N.Y. : Pergamon Pr., 1988. 519 p. ISBN 0-08-031975-0. $85.00. **CD40**

Presents signed articles that describe more than 300 professionally accepted techniques used to assess both behavioral disorders (e.g., depression, anxiety, phobias) and normal behaviors (assertiveness, cognition, social skills). Articles, alphabetically arranged, describe a variety of techniques (interviewing, rating scales, direct observation, self-reporting, etc.) and are structured alike under the headings Description, Purpose, Development, Psychometric characteristics, Clinical use, and Future directions. Each two- to four-page entry concludes with a short list of references. The text is preceded by a list of contributors and a "User's guide," the latter serving as a rudimentary subject index, listing each technique by "Focus of assessment" (i.e., the traits being assessed) and giving its "Assessment modality" or mode of evaluation (e.g., teacher rating, self-reported). Author index. BF176.5.D53

Directory of selected national testing programs / comp. by Test Collection, Educational Testing Service. Phoenix : Oryx, 1987. 280 p. ISBN 0-89774-386-5 (pbk.). **CD41**

Describes 220 programs conducted mainly for educational purposes, in areas such as admissions, licensing, certification, academic credit. Entries provide information on each test's content, purpose, and cost, plus dates given, registration, and agencies to contact. Arranged by test type (e.g., Selection/admission). Appendixes give addresses of relevant government agencies. LB3051.D56

The ETS Test Collection catalog / comp. by Test Collection, Educational Testing Service. Phoenix : Oryx, 1986–1991. v. 1–5. ISBN 0-89774-248-6 (v.1). $49.50. (In progress). **CD42**

For annotation, see *Supplement* CB117. LB3051.E79

●**ETS test collection** [computer file]. Princeton, N.J.: Educational Testing Service, 1950– .   **CD43**

For annotation, see *Supplement* CB118.

Fabiano, Emily. Index to tests used in educational dissertations. Phoenix: Oryx, 1989. 371 p. ISBN 0-89774-288-5.   **CD44**

For annotation, see *Supplement* CB23.   LB3051.F3

●**Mental measurements yearbook** [computer file]. Lincoln, Neb.: Buros Institute of Mental Measurements, Univ. of Nebraska—Lincoln, 1972– .   **CD45**

Machine-readable version of *Mental measurements yearbook*, ed. by Oscar K. Buros (*Guide* CD132).

File size: 1,800 published tests. Updated monthly. Available online (BRS).

O'Brien, Nancy P. Test construction: a bibliography of selected resources. N.Y.: Greenwood, 1988. 299 p. ISBN 0-313-23435-3. $39.95.   **CD46**

Cites 2,759 books, reports, journal articles, dissertations and ERIC documents published from the early 1900s through 1986. Very few of the works cited appear in other bibliographies on test construction. Citations are arranged by test type, following the classification scheme of the early *Mental measurements yearbooks* (*Guide* CD132). No annotations; author and subject indexes.   Z5814.E9O18

Tests: a comprehensive reference for assessments in psychology, education, and business / Richard C. Sweetland, Daniel J. Keyser, gen. editors. 2nd ed. Kansas City, Mo.: Test Corp. of America, c1986. 1122 p. ISBN 0-933701-05-5. ISBN 0-933701-06-3 (pbk.). ISBN 0-933701-03-9.   **CD47**

1st ed., 1983, and supplement, 1984 (*Guide* CD140).

Includes 600 new or revised tests and five additional indexes: out of print, hearing-impaired, physically impaired, foreign language availability, and publisher/distributor.   BF176.T43

Truch, Stephen. The WISC-R companion: a desk reference for the Wechsler scales. Seattle: Special Child Publications, c1989. 272 p.: ill. ISBN 0-87562-100-7. $44.50.   **CD48**

Intended for use by practicing school psychologists and those in training. In seven chapters, provides background information on intelligence and intelligence tests, WISC-R applications to reading, and interpretation of WISC-R test results, levels I–V. Includes bibliography, 14 appendixes, an index of figures, and an index of tables.   BF432.5.W42T78

PARAPSYCHOLOGY AND OCCULTISM

Berger, Arthur S. The encyclopedia of parapsychology and psychical research / Arthur S. Berger and Joyce Berger. N.Y.: Paragon House, 1991. 554 p. ISBN 1-55778-043-9. $45.00. ISBN 1-55778-358-6 (pbk.).   **CD49**

More than 1,400 entries in dictionary format cover individuals, movements, organizations, publications, phenomena, and terms. Longer entries have brief bibliographies. Focuses specifically on parapsychology (e.g., Catholic saints are characterized primarily by their parapsychological abilities). Three appendixes: countries, with a brief history and description of parapsychological study in each, including research centers, organizations, and journals; a "Country index," i.e., a list of the headwords in the encyclopedia arranged by country; and a comprehensive 40-page bibliography of journal articles and books.   BF1025.B47

Crabtree, Adam. Animal magnetism, early hypnotism, and psychical research, 1766–1925: an annotated bibliography. White Plains, N.Y.: Kraus Internat., c1988. 522 p. (Bibliographies in the history of psychology and psychiatry, 4). ISBN 0-527-20006-9.   **CD50**

A long introduction gives the history and background of animal magnetism. Entries are arranged chronologically from 1766, the date of publication of Mesmer's medical thesis, through 1925, when most publication on this subject ceased. The most significant items are annotated. Related subjects in parapsychology have been excluded. Separate indexes for subjects, titles, and personal names. A short glossary of terms, and references to newly published works, precede the main bibliography.   Z6878.A54C73

Encyclopedia of occultism & parapsychology / ed. by Leslie Shepard. 3rd ed. Detroit: Gale, c1991. 2 v. (2008 p.). ISBN 0-8103-4907-8 (set).   **CD51**

2nd ed., 1984 (*Guide* CD145).

Subtitle: A compendium of information on the occult sciences, magic, demonology, superstitions, spiritism, mysticism, metaphysics, psychical science, and parapsychology, with biographical notes and comprehensive indexes.

A thorough revision with hundreds of new items. Entries vary in length; some have bibliographies. A brief essay on "The recent evolution of occultism" including "Occultism and the media," introduces the work. Concludes with a general index and a topical index by broad categories (e.g., Animals, Demons, Gems, Gods, Plants, and Flowers).   BF1407E56

Kies, Cosette N. The occult in the western world: an annotated bibliography. Hamden, Conn.: Library Professional Publications, 1986. 233 p. ISBN 0-208-02113-2. $29.50.   **CD52**

In 13 chapters with subdivisions, lists works on traditional and modern witchcraft, magic, secret societies, psychics, ghosts, unidentified flying objects, astrology, prophecy, folklore, and general works. Chapters begin with introductory essays; there are annotations of varying length. Brief glossary; name and title indexes.   Z6876.K53

Man, myth & magic: the illustrated encyclopedia of mythology, religion, and the unknown / ed. in chief, Richard Cavendish; editorial board, C.A. Burland . . . [et al.]. New ed., ed. and comp. by Yvonne Deutch. N.Y.: Marshall Cavendish, 1983. 12 v. (3201 p.): ill. (some col.). ISBN 0-86307-041-8 (set). $349.50.   **CD53**

For annotation, see *Supplement* CF4.   BF1411.M25

Riland, George. The new Steinerbooks dictionary of the paranormal. N.Y.: Steinerbooks, c1980. 358 p. ISBN 0-8334-0719-8.   **CD54**

Nearly 2,800 brief alphabetical entries include terms from different ages, countries, cultures, religions, and cults. Useful in identifying unusual terms, obscure individuals, or unusual meanings for common terms.   BF1025.R5

White, Rhea A. Parapsychology: new sources of information, 1973–1989. Metuchen, N.J.: Scarecrow, 1990. 699 p. ISBN 0-8108-2385-3.   **CD55**

Intended to update and supplement Rhea White and Laura Dale's *Parapsychology: sources of information*, 1973 (*Guide* CD153).

An annotated selective bibliography of 643 items, arranged in 28 topical sections. Numbering continues from the earlier work; areas new to this version include Animal psi, Biographies, Near-death experiences, Reincarnation, Physics and psi, Children and psi, Books for young people. Reviews are cited; there are sections on such topics as Using general sources to get parapsychological information and The U.S. government and parapsychology. Includes a list of theses, a glossary of terms, and addresses of publishers not readily available.   Indexes by name, title, and subject.   Z6878.P8W47

CE

Anthropology and Ethnology

GUIDES

Bernard, H. Russell. Research methods in cultural anthropology. Newbury Park, Calif. : Sage Publications, c1988. 520 p. : ill. ISBN 0-8039-2977-3. $39.95. ISBN 0-8039-2978-1 (pbk.). $19.95.   **CE1**

A comprehensive treatment of research methodology in three sections: preparing for field research, collecting data, and analyzing data. Provides well-illustrated examples of both quantitative and non-quantitative techniques and includes discussion of commonly-used statistical techniques. Index; extensive bibliography.   GN345.B37

BIBLIOGRAPHY

Bibliographic guide to anthropology and archaeology. 1987– . Boston : G.K. Hall & Co., c1988– . Annual. ISSN 0896-8101. $165.00.   **CE2**

Supplements the Tozzer Library's *Author and subject catalogues of the Tozzer Library* (*Supplement* CE7). "Contains entries for books, serials, microforms, manuscripts, maps and video recordings" (*Introd.*) added to the Library's collections since June 1986. Main entry, title, and subject heading access in one alphabet.   Z5111.B47

Gravel, Pierre Bettez. Anthropological fieldwork : an annotated bibliography / Pierre Bettez Gravel and Robert B. Marks Ridinger. N.Y. : Garland, 1988. 241 p. ISBN 0-8240-6642-1.   **CE3**

An annotated bibliography of 700 entries focusing on "the practical aspects of fieldwork."—*Pref.* Covers journal articles, monographs, and museum literature in English, French, and German. Most citations are from the 20th century, with a few dating as early as 1800 for historical perspective. Entries are alphabetical by author; geographical and subject indexes.   Z5118.F44G7

General

Brown, Samuel R. Finding the source in sociology and anthropology : a thesaurus-index to the reference collection. N.Y. : Greenwood, 1987. 269 p. (Finding the source, no. 1). ISBN 0-313-25263-7. $39.95.   **CE4**

For annotation, see *Supplement* CC5.   Z7164.S68B75

Ferguson, R. Brian. The anthropology of war : a bibliography / R. Brian Ferguson with Leslie E. Farragher. N.Y. : Harry Frank Guggenheim Foundation, 1988. 361 p. (Occasional papers of the Harry Frank Guggenheim Foundation, no. 1).   **CE5**

A comprehensive bibliography of "non-modern warfare" (*Introd.*) that excludes warfare as carried on under the influence of the technical and political developments since 15th-century Europe. More than 5,000 citations are divided into 23 topical sections (e.g., Ecology, demography and war; Feud; Magic, religion, ritual and war; Raiding for slaves). No separate author or subject indexes. Complements and updates William T. Divale's *Warfare in primitive societies* (*Guide* CE6).   GN497.F47

Nordquist, Joan. Claude Levi-Strauss, a bibliography. Santa Cruz, Calif. : Reference and Research Services, 1987. 60 p. (Social theory, ISSN 0887-3577; no. 6.). ISBN 0-937855-10-3.   **CE6**

Bibliography of English-language works by and about Levi-Strauss. In four sections: (1) books by Levi-Strauss translated into English, with citations to reviews and critical essays; (2) essays by Levi-Strauss, with articles discussing the essays; (3) books in English about Levi-Strauss; and (4) selected articles (from books, 1970–87, and from journals, 1979–87) about his work. Includes a number of citations more recent than Francois and Claire Lapointe's *Claude Levi-Strauss and his critics* (*Guide* CE18).   Z8504.35.N6

Tozzer Library. Author and subject catalogues of the Tozzer Library [microform]. 2nd enl. ed. Boston : G.K. Hall, 1988. 8 v. (1122 microfiches) : negative. ISBN 0-8161-1731-4 (microfiche).   **CE7**

Supersedes: Harvard University. Peabody Museum of Archaeology and Ethnology. Library. *Catalogue : authors* and *Catalogue : subjects* (*Guide* CE12).

Contains entries for monographs and serials cataloged through 1986 and periodical articles through 1983. Continued, for cataloged entries after 1986, by *Bibliographic guide to anthropology and archaeology* (*Supplement* CE2) and for periodical articles after 1983, by *Anthropological literature* (*Supplement* CE9). Especially useful for its inclusion and indexing of journal articles, festschriften, and conference proceedings. The Author/title catalogue contains approximately 636,000 entries, the Subject catalogue approximately 702,600. The latter uses as headings terms specific to the discipline; a complete list is provided in *Tozzer Library index to anthropological subject headings* (*Guide* CE12a).

Current

Abstracts in anthropology. v. 1 (Feb. 1970)– . [Westport, Conn.] : Greenwood [etc.], [1970]– . ISSN 0001-3455.   **CE8**

For earlier volumes and annotation, see *Guide* CE26.

Frequency varies: 1970–86, quarterly; 1987– , 8 issues per year.

Several significant changes in format and coverage were introduced with v. 14 (1987). The frequency increased to eight issues in two volumes per year; the number of titles indexed increased by about 25%; the number of citations doubled; and the subject index begins to cumulate in each issue.   GN1.A15

Anthropological literature. v. 11, no. 1– . Cambridge, Mass. : Tozzer Library, Harvard Univ., c1989– . Quarterly. ISSN 0190-3373. $125.00.   **CE9**

For earlier volumes and annotation, see *Guide* CE28.

Vol. 6–10 (1984–88) published in microfiche. With v. 11 (1989), publication in printed format resumed.

Retains grouping of entries into five sections by topic, but has added a subject index. Also includes lists of authors, journals, and edited works and series indexed. For articles prior to 1983, see *Author and subject catalogues of the Tozzer Library* (*Supplement* CE7). Z5112.A573

Dissertations

Webber, Jonathan. Research in social anthropology, 1975–1980: a register of theses accepted for higher degrees at British universities, 1975–1980. London: Royal Anthropological Institute, 1983. 425 p. **CE10**

Alphabetical listing, by author, of 404 masters theses and doctoral dissertations in social anthropology, with abstracts. Five indexes: author; academic institution; country of research; peoples and cultures; and subject (from words in title). Thorough explanation of conventions used to compile entries; scope defined in preface. GN316.W42

Periodicals

Williams, John T. Anthropology journals and serials: an analytical guide. N.Y.: Greenwood, 1986. 182 p. ISBN 0-313-23834-0. **CE11**

Lists 404 currently published English-language serials, arranged in five sections: Archaeology, Cultural anthropology, Linguistics, Physical anthropology, and Indexes and abstracts. Each entry has two parts: bibliographic and subscription information, and an annotation that indicates scope, purpose, and format. Title, subject, and geographic indexes. Unique in the discipline for its depth of coverage. Z5112.W54

ENCYCLOPEDIAS

Dictionary of anthropology / ed. by Charlotte Seymour-Smith. Boston: G.K. Hall, 1986. 305p. ISBN 0-8161-8817-3. **CE12**

Contains some 950 entries for terms and concepts used primarily in cultural and social anthropology. Specifically excludes "the fields of linguistics, physical anthropology, archaeology and so on" (*Foreword*) and entries for specific ethnic groups. Includes brief entries for individual anthropologists born before 1920. Entries vary in length from a brief paragraph to several pages. Numerous cross-references to other entries and to the selected bibliography. GN11.D48

Encyclopedia of human evolution and prehistory / ed. by Ian Tattersall, Eric Delson and John Van Couvering. N.Y.: Garland, c1988. 603 p.: ill. (Garland reference library of the humanities, vol. 768). ISBN 0-8240-9375-5. $87.50. **CE13**

First encyclopedia to cover human (i.e., primate) evolution. Some 1,200 signed entries by 40 experts in the field range in length from brief paragraphs to ten-page essays and include many cross-references and brief bibliographies. Illustrated with numerous photographs, diagrams, tables, drawings, and maps. Access provided through Subject list by topic, arranged alphabetically and chronologically, and through heavily cross-referenced prefatory essay "Brief introduction to human evolution and prehistory." Also includes a "Classification of primates" and an evolutionary "Time chart." GN281.E53

Encyclopedia of world cultures / David Levinson, ed. in chief. Boston: G.K. Hall, c1991. v. 1. ISBN 0-8161-1808-6. (In progress). **CE14**

Contents: v. 1, North America, ed. by Timothy J. O'Leary and David Levinson.

Prepared under auspices of Human Relations Area Files, Inc., and expected to include more than 1,500 cultural groups. Descriptions of these 20th century cultures vary in length from several paragraphs to several pages. Each signed entry contains the following elements: culture name, ethnonym, history and cultural relations, settlements, economy, kinship, marriage and family, sociopolitical organization, religion and expressive culture, and bibliography. Each volume will also include: maps indicating current locations of cultures; filmography; list of extinct cultures of the region; ethnonym index; and glossary. To be complete in 10v. GN307.E53

DICTIONARIES

Pearson, Roger. Anthropological glossary. Malabar, Fla.: R.E. Krieger Pub. Co., 1985. 282 p. ISBN 0-89874-510-1. **CE15**

Defines approximately 4,500 terms used in cultural and physical anthropology, archaeology, and linguistics, including ethnic groups, archaeological sites, and geographical names. Definitions vary in length from two lines to an entire page. Contains more entries than *Encyclopedia of anthropology* (*Guide* CE38) and a number of terms not included in Charles Winick's *Dictionary of anthropology* (*Guide* CE40). Lacks illustrations. GN11.P43

Terminology

Thematic list of descriptors—anthropology = Liste thématique des descripteurs—anthropologie / prepared on behalf of UNESCO by the International Committee for Social Science Information and Documentation. London; N.Y.: Routledge, 1989. 522 p. ISBN 0-415-01776-9. **CE16**

Presents some 8,000 terms, and includes lists of geographic names, ethnic groups, and languages.

§ One of four similar lists, the others being *Thematic list of descriptors—economics* (*Supplement* CH12), *Thematic list of descriptors—political science* (*Supplement* CJ26), and *Thematic list of descriptors—sociology* (*Supplement* CC15), each intended to be used with the appropriate section of the "International bibliography of the social sciences" series, for anthropology (*Guide* CE29), economics (*Guide* CH36), political science (*Guide* CJ39), and sociology (*Guide* CC15). Each presents controlled vocabulary terms and cross-references used to index publications listed in the bibliographies in the series and to retrieve information from the parent database maintained by the International Committee for Social Science Information and Documentation. In two sections, alphabetical and thematic. The alphabetical list gives terms in English and French and indicates in which sections of the component bibliographies the terms are used. The thematic list is a coded hierarchical arrangement of English terms with French equivalents. All four thesauruses have lists of geographic terms. Z5111.A63T47

DIRECTORIES

American Anthropological Association. AAA guide. Wash.: American Anthropological Association, c1989– . $25.00 (members). **CE17**

Continues *Guide to departments of anthropology* (*Guide* CE46). Describes academic, museum, and research departments and government agencies in the U.S., Canada, and selected foreign countries and lists the Association's membership in two directories: an alphabetical listing of names and addresses and a listing by Association units of their respective members. A statistics section is based on numerical data provided in descriptions. Continues to list completed doctoral dissertations. Indexed by individuals in departments and by departments/ institutions.

YEARBOOKS

IWGIA yearbook. 1986– . Copenhagen, Denmark : International Work Group for Indigenous Affairs, 1987– . Annual.   **CE18**

Provides illustrated accounts of major events of the indigenous world. Each issue includes a section on developments in indigenous rights and surveys work of the International Work Group for Indigenous Affairs (IWGIA). The yearbook for 1988 includes an index to articles published in the *IWGIA newsletter* 1976–88.   GN380.I95

BIOGRAPHY

Biographical directory of anthropologists born before 1920 / gen. ed., Thomas L. Mann ; comp. by Library-Anthropology Resource Group (LARG). N.Y. : Garland, 1988. 245 p. : ill., port. (Garland reference library of the humanities, vol. 439). ISBN 0-8240-5833-X.   **CE19**

"For each person the entries include dates of birth and death, birthplace, profession, major contributions and published sources of biographical information."—*Pref.* Scope is international, and the discipline of anthropology is broadly defined. Since inclusion is based on the identification of a biographical source, omissions are possible. Includes tables listing number of entries by country of birth and by career and an index to subject words from the "Statement of contributions" fields.   Z5111.B56

Díaz Polanco, Héctor. Directorio de antropólogos latinoamericanos, México. México : Instituto Panamericano de Geografía e Historia : Para canje, ventas y distribución de publicaciones se atiende en Secretaría General del IPGH, 1985. 191 p. : ill. (In progress). **CE20**

First of a projected three-volume series that will cover Mexico, Central America and the Caribbean, and South America and will include professional anthropologists who live in Latin America and whose research is concerned with Latin America. Each entry includes professional affiliation, address, telephone, educational background, subject specialty, list of publications, and description of current research. Indexes by educational degree, subject specialty, research (topical), research (geographical), and research (historical period). GN41.6.D53

Directory of anthropologists and anthropological research in aging / a publication of [the] Association for Anthropology and Gerontology. 9th ed. Tampa, Fla. : Association for Anthropology and Gerontology, 1987. $4.00.   **CE21**

1st ed., 1971.

Biannual directory of the international membership of the Association of Anthropology and Gerontology. The 9th ed. has 287 entries; each includes professional affiliation and address, and some include telephone numbers and research and teaching interests. Research index; geographic/societal index.

Ray, Shyamal Kumar. Directory of scientific personnel of the Anthropological Survey of India : with life-sketches / Shyamal Kumar Ray and Ajay Kumar Srivas-

tav. Calcutta : Anthropological Survey of India, Ministry of Human Resource Development, Dept. of Culture, Govt. of India, 1988. v. 1 : ports. (In progress). **CE22**

"With a view to highlighting the achievements of members of both the scientific and technical staff of the Anthropological Survey of India, a project of compilation of their bibliographies and bio-data in several volumes was undertaken... "—*Pref.* Vol. 1 includes biographies and bibliographies of 26 staff members. Bibliographies cite books, papers, and reports, including unpublished papers presented at conferences, through 1985.
GN17.3.I4R39

Women anthropologists : a biographical dictionary / ed. by Ute Gacs ... [et al.]. N.Y. : Greenwood, 1988. 428 p. ISBN 0-313-24414-6. $55.00.   **CE23**

Contains four- to six-page signed biographies of 58 anthropologists from the past 100 years. A six-page introduction explains the criteria for selection. Each biography is followed by a list of works about and by the person. Supplementary information includes two appendixes (Fieldwork areas and Chronology of birth dates), an index, and brief biographical entries for contributors.   GN20.W63

ATLASES

Price, David H. Atlas of world cultures : a geographical guide to ethnographic literature. Newbury Park, Calif. : Sage Publications, c1989. 156 p. ; 29 cm. ISBN 0-8039-3240-5.   **CE24**

A combined ethnic atlas, bibliography, and guide intended to accompany the Human Relations Area Files (HRAF). The first section consists of 40 numbered maps on which are identifed the geographical locations of 3,500 cultural groups; the second is a 1,237-item bibliography of ethnographic studies concerning the groups. A final section, Culture index, links each culture group to its appropriate map, bibliographic entries, HRAF codes and listing (if any) in George P. Murdock's *Atlas of world cultures* (*Guide* CE52).   G1046.E1P7

THE AMERICAS

Handbooks

Handbook of Middle American Indians. Supplement. Austin : Univ. of Texas Pr., c1981–1986. v. 1–4 : ill. ISBN 0-292-77556-3 (v. 1). $55.00. (In progress). **CE25**

Contents: v. 1, Archaeology (*Guide* CE75); v. 2, Linguistics, Munro S. Edmonson, ed. (1984. 146 p.); v. 3, Literatures, Munro S. Edmonson, ed. (1985. 195 p.); v. 4, Ethnohistory, Ronald Spores, ed. (1986. 232 p.)   F1219.A76

CF

Mythology, Folklore, and Popular Culture

MYTHOLOGY

International

Encyclopedias; Dictionaries

Bauer, Wolfgang. Lexikon der Symbole : Mythen, Symbole und Zeichen in Kultur, Religion, Kunst und Alltag / Wolfgang Bauer, Irmtraud Dümotz, Sergius Golowin. 3. Aufl. München : Heyne, c1987. 557 p. : ill. ISBN 3-453-02451-6. DM14.80. **CF1**
1st ed., 1980.
Symbols are grouped in topical/geographic sections (e.g., Indian, Greek mythology, astrology, tarot), then arranged alphabetically by name of symbol with a line drawing or other illustration. Bibliographic references; index of names.
BF1623.S9B38

Cotterell, Arthur. The illustrated encyclopedia of myths & legends. London : Cassell, 1989. 260 p. : ill., maps. **CF2**
A section of brief introductory surveys of the mythology of specific countries or regions is followed by "Characters and concepts: an A–Z of myths" (the major portion of the book). A "Micropedia" consisting of "more than one thousand short entries alphabetically arranged" (*p.180*) treats names not dealt with in the previous section. Cross-references; brief list of works for further reading. Index of names and subjects. PZ8.1

Lurker, Manfred. Dictionary of gods and goddesses, devils and demons. London ; N.Y. : Routledge and K. Paul, 1987. 451 p. : ill. ISBN 0-7102-0877-4. $30.00. ISBN 0-7102-1106-6 (pbk.). $15.00. **CF3**
Translation of: *Lexikon der Götter und Dämonen* (Stuttgart : A. Kramer, 1984).
"... offers a conspectus of all the more important beings who have acquired 'personality' [in the sense of having had names bestowed on them] ... both in the pantheons of the classical cultures and in the world of religions of today; and the religious systems of the so-called 'primitive' races are also given their due place."—*Pref.* Arranged alphabetically by name; brief entries. Appendixes of functions, etc., and of symbols and motifs. Brief bibliography. BL303.L8713

Man, myth & magic : the illustrated encyclopedia of mythology, religion, and the unknown / ed. in chief, Richard Cavendish ; editorial board, C.A. Burland ... [et al.]. New ed., ed. and comp. by Yvonne Deutch. N.Y. : Marshall Cavendish, 1983. 12 v. (3201 p.) : ill. (some col.). ISBN 0-86307-041-8 (set). $349.50. **CF4**

A unique resource for topics and themes not usually covered in standard reference works. Interdisciplinary and comprehensive in scope, ranging from prehistory to the newest cults. Includes entries for deities, significant individuals, and cross-cultural themes (e.g., water, birds, human body) as well as religious movements (e.g., Vishnu, Voodoo, Zen). Many illustrations; easily understood by the general reader. Vol. 1 includes a series of long bibliographies on general subjects supplementing the short bibliographies that accompany each article throughout the work; v. 12 is a detailed general index.
BF1411.M25

Mercatante, Anthony S. The Facts on File encyclopedia of world mythology and legend. N.Y. : Facts on File, c1988. 807 p. : ill. ISBN 0-8160-1049-8. **CF5**
An A–Z listing of about 3,000 entries. Following the "entry name is a concise definition, usually followed by a longer encyclopedic detailed discussion. As an additional reference aid, citations of relevant art, music, films, and literature are provided."—*Author's pref.* Annotated bibliography; key to variant spellings; cultural and ethnic index; general index.
BL303.M45

Mythical and fabulous creatures : a source book and research guide / ed. by Malcolm South. N.Y. : Greenwood, 1987. 393 p. : ill. ISBN 0-313-24338-7. $49.95. **CF6**
"Although this work discusses some creatures invented by individual artists and writers, it mainly deals with creatures that have a place in folklore, myth, or history and have a body of traditional lore connected with them."—*Pref.* Pt. I describes 20 fabulous creatures in separate chapters: Birds and beasts, Human-animal composites, Creatures of darkness, and Giants and fairies. Their appearances in literature, history, and art are cited and their functions noted. A bibliography concludes each chapter. Pt. II, A miscellany and taxonomy, briefly discusses creatures not previously mentioned or given only passing attention earlier, and classifies some 145 creatures in five categories. There is a glossary of the more important creatures, a section of illustrations, a general bibliography, and a selective index.
GR825.M87

Walker, Barbara G. The woman's dictionary of symbols and sacred objects. San Francisco : Harper & Row, c1988. 563 p. : ill. ISBN 0-06-250922-5. $32.95. ISBN 0-06-250923-3 (pbk.). $19.95. **CF7**
Symbols are arranged by shapes (e.g., round and oval, three-way, multipointed) or by types (e.g., birds, rituals). Within each section entries are alphabetically arranged. Indexed by name of symbol and by subject.
CB475.W35

Wörterbuch der Mythologie. 1 Abteilung, Die alten Kulturvölker / unter Mitarbeit zahlreicher Fachgelehrter hrsg. von H.W. Haussig. Stuttgart : E. Klett, c1984–1988. v. 19–24 : ill. (In progress). **CF8**
For previously published parts and annotation, see *Guide* CF9.
The plan of the work as originally outlined designated the volumes as "Teil 1," etc.; when title pages and prefatory matter were issued "Teil" was changed to "Band" and some of the parts named in *Guide* CF9 were retitled. Vols. completed to date are made up of the following *Lieferungen*: Bd. 1, Götter und Mythen im Vorderen Orient (Lfg. 1–4); Bd. 2, Götter und Mythen im alten Europa (Lfg. 5–7, 9–10); Bd. 4 (originally designated as Teil 3), Götter und Mythen der kaukasischen und iranischen Völker (Lfg. 11–12, 17); Bd. 5, Götter und Mythen des indischen Subkontinents (Lfg. 8, 13–16, 18–19). Lfg. 20 completes Bd. 5 and begins Bd. 6, Götter und Mythen in Zentral-, Ost- und Südostasien; Lfg. 21–24 continue but do not complete Bd. 6. A newly designated Bd. 3, Götter und Mythen der Antike (dealing with Greek and Roman mythology) is still in preparation. A "Sonderabend: Die klassische chinesische Mythologie," announced for publication in 1986, seems not yet

to have appeared. Egidius Schmalzriedt is listed as principal editor beginning with Lfg. 20.   BL303.W63

Egyptian

Hart, George. A dictionary of Egyptian gods and goddesses. London ; Boston : Routledge & Kegan Paul, 1986. 229 p. : ill. ISBN 0-7102-0965-7. $12.95. ISBN 0-7102-0167-2 (pbk.). $8.00.   **CF9**

Intended to "be useful to undergraduates of Egyptology, religious studies or anthropology as a starting point or for quick reference."—*Pref.* Entries indicate the deities' functions and relationships and often refer to the iconography. Numerous line drawings; cross-references are signaled by use of italics in the text. Very brief bibliography; list of "Alternative rendering of divine names."   BL2450.G6H37

Greek and Roman

Bell, Robert E. Place-names in classical mythology : Greece. Santa Barbara, Calif. : ABC-Clio, c1989. 350 p. ISBN 0-87436-507-4. $50.00.   **CF10**

Intended as a companion to the author's *Dictionary of classical mythology* (*Guide* CF23). Aims "to organize into one book the geography of classical mythology. For the most part no attention is paid to historical events or individuals unless there are mythological associations (such as religious phenomena, foundation of temples, etc.)."—*Introd.* Articles, in dictionary arrangement, range from a few lines to several pages in length; most include a substantial amount of detail concerning mythological association. Modern names are given in parentheses in many entries, and there is an alphabetical list of modern names and their ancient equivalents. A "Guide to personae" indicates the articles in which various characters are mentioned. Brief bibliography.   DF16.B45

Grimal, Pierre. The dictionary of classical mythology / Pierre Grimal ; translated by A.R Maxwell-Hyslop. Oxford ; N.Y. : Blackwell, 1985. 603 p. : ill. ISBN 0-631-13209-0. $50.00.   **CF11**

Translation of *Dictionnaire de la mythologie grecque et romaine*, first publ. 1951 (4. éd. rev., 1969; *Guide* CF27).

A dictionary of names in classical mythology, with a summary of associated legends, relationship to other mythological figures, attributes, etc. The Greek form of the name is given in parentheses following the entry as appropriate. Bibliographic references keyed to specific articles appear on p. 471–515. Table of sources, genealogical tables, and a general index complete the volume in the parent work.

§ *A concise dictionary of classical mythology*, ed. by Stephen Kershaw (Oxford : Blackwell, 1990. 456 p.) is based on the Maxwell-Hyslop translation of Grimal's work. "Some of the minor supplementary variant myths have been deleted and a number of small extra entries have been added" (*Publisher's note*) and additional cross-references have been introduced, but the bibliographical apparatus, most of the genealogical tables, and the general index do not appear in the concise volume.   BL715.G713

Hunger, Herbert. Lexikon der griechischen und römischen Mythologie : mit Hinweisen auf das Fortwirken antiker Stoffe und Motive in der bildenden Kunst, Literatur und Musik des Abendlandes bis zur Gegenwart. 8., erw. Aufl. Wien : Hollinek, c1988. 557 p. : ill. ISBN 3-85119-230-3.   **CF12**

7th ed., 1975 (*Guide* CF29).

Bibliographies have been much expanded, some additions made to the lists of art works, and black-and-white illustrations

(mostly of indifferent quality) distributed throughout the text.   BL715.H86

Irish

Ellis, Peter Berresford. A dictionary of Irish mythology. Santa Barbara, Calif. : ABC-Clio, 1989. 240 p. ISBN 0-87436-553-8.   **CF13**

An A–Z arrangement of personal and place names, together with some terms, in Irish mythology. Cross-references; select bibliography. Covers much of the same ground as Smyth's *Guide to Irish mythology* (below), but each work includes entries not found in the other (and spellings of the same word frequently differ).   BL980.I7E45

Smyth, Daragh. A guide to Irish mythology. Dublin : Irish Academic Pr., c1988. 176 p. : ill. ISBN 0-7165-2434-1. ISBN 0-7165-2429-5 (pbk.).   **CF14**

A dictionary arrangement of personal and place-names and other terms from Irish mythology. An asterisk in the text indicates that the word has its own entry; sources are mentioned, and there is a brief listing thereof. Indexed.   BL900.S495

Oceanic

Craig, Robert D. Dictionary of Polynesian mythology. N.Y. : Greenwood, 1989. 409 p. : map. ISBN 0-313-25890-2.   **CF15**

Gods, goddesses, and ancient heroes are entered alphabetically by name, with occasional entries for objects and places connected with the myths. Cross-references; citations to sources; list of sources, p. xxix–xlvii; appendix of Categories of gods and goddesses; comprehensive index of all references to mythological characters.   BL2620.P6C7

Scandinavian

Lindow, John. Scandinavian mythology : an annotated bibliography. N.Y. : Garland, 1988. 593 p. (Garland folklore bibliographies, v. 13). ISBN 0-8240-9173-6. $25.00.   **CF16**

Aims "to offer easy access to the more important parts of the vast amount of scholarship on the subject, most of it in languages other than English."—*Introd.* Owing to the nature of past scholarship, the compiler has felt obliged to include "many works whose emphasis is on religion rather than the mythological corpus." Some 3,059 entries are arranged alphabetically by author with a detailed subject index. Annotations are descriptive, with only occasional value judgments.   Z7836.L58

Slavic

Kulikowski, Mark. A bibliography of Slavic mythology. Columbus, Ohio : Slavica Publishers, c1989. 137 p. ISBN 0-89357-203-9. $17.95.   **CF17**

"The scope of this bibliography is all written materials (books, dissertations, pamphlets, articles, and selections) from the earliest times up to and including 1981, published in all Slavic and major Western languages."—*Introd.* 805 items are listed alphabetically in sections devoted to primary and secondary sources. These citations, and a supplementary list of journals cited, include library locations. Author/title and subject indexes. Z7836.K85

FOLKLORE AND POPULAR CULTURE

General Works

Bibliography

Ashliman, D. L. A guide to folktales in the English language : based on the Aarne-Thompson classification system. N.Y. : Greenwood, 1987. 368 p. (Bibliographies and indexes in world literature, no. 11). ISBN 0-313-25961-5. $45.00. **CF18**

Intended "to help readers find reliable texts of any given folktale, not only in its best known version, but also in less familiar variants."—*Introd.* Arranged by the Aarne-Thompson tale type numbers, with an alphabetical index "where the titles of the best-known tales and key words from typical plots are located." Each entry gives a brief synopsis and indicates the tale's published title(s) and a published collection in which it can be found. Bibliography of folktale collections.

Z5983.F17A83

Azzolina, David S. Tale type- and motif-indexes : an annotated bibliography. N.Y. : Garland, 1987. 105 p. (Garland reference library of the humanities, vol. 565 ; Garland folklore bibliographies, v. 12). ISBN 0-8240-8788-7. $33.00. **CF19**

Designed "to give folklorists and reference librarians access to and background of a genre of a reference tool peculiar to the scholarly discussion of folklore."—*Introd.* 186 entries are arranged alphabetically by author and include books, journal articles, and unpublished dissertations and theses. Annotations are mainly descriptive, but often include references to related works and citations to reviews. Subject, geographic, and "Additional author" (joint authors, translators, etc.) indexes.

Z5983.L5A98

Carnes, Pack. Fable scholarship : an annotated bibliography. N.Y. : Garland, 1985. 382 p. (Garland reference library of the humanities, vol. 367 ; Garland folklore bibliographies, v. 8). ISBN 0-8240-9229-5. $40.00. **CF20**

An author listing of some 1,457 studies of "Aesopic" fables and closely related traditions. Includes books, articles, and dissertations mainly from the 1880–1982 period. Descriptive annotations. Indexes of names and subjects, fables, and tale types (by Perry number). Z5896.C37

Coleman, Earle Jerome. Magic : a reference guide. N.Y. : Greenwood, 1987. 198 p. ISBN 0-313-23397-7. **CF21**

Offers bibliographical essays on the history and psychology of magic, the art of conjuring, etc., as well as pertinent biographies and autobiographies. Appendixes: Selected dates in the history of conjuring; Directory of magic periodicals, research collections, dealers. Author and subject indexes.

GV1547.C595

Dicke, Gerd. Die Fabeln des Mittelalters und der frühen Neuzeit : ein Katalog der deutschen Versionen und ihrer lateinischen Entsprechungen / Gerd Dicke, Klaus Grubmüller. München : W. Fink, 1987. lxxii, 891 p. (Münstersche Mittelalter-Schriften, Bd. 60). ISBN 3-7705-2488-8. **CF22**

A listing of 655 fables arranged alphabetically by the main German word in the story, usually the name of an animal. Entries provide a brief summary of the fable, with abbreviated ci-

tations to: (1) Latin versions to 1500; (2) German versions to 1500; (3) German versions of the 16th century; and (4) versions in other languages to 1500. Each section is arranged chronologically and entries include references to related fables and to secondary sources. Indexes of manuscripts arranged by city, of authors and anonymous titles cited in the entries, and of subjects. Includes a concordance to Perry numbers. List of abbreviations (arranged by collections), individual titles, and secondary sources, p.773–819. PT179.D47

Internationale Volkskundliche Bibliographie = International folklore bibliography. 1979/80– . [S.l.] : Commission internationale des arts et traditions populaires, 1985– . ISSN 0074-9737. Irregular. **CF23**

For earlier volumes and annotation, see *Guide* CF49.

With "Jahre 1979 und 1980" (publ. 1985) an English-language subject index was added, together with a complete list of journals searched for the issue. With "Jahre 1981 und 1982" (publ. 1986) a French preface and index were added. Computerization of the bibliography was developed in conjunction with the Modern Language Association of America, and the possibility of attaching it as a subfile of the MLA bibliography (with improved subject indexing) is being explored. Z5982.I523

Neumann, Renate. Bibliographie zur Comic-Sekundärliteratur. Frankfurt am Main ; N.Y. : P. Lang, c1987. 267 p. ISBN 3-8204-1096-1. **CF24**

Lists primarily European books and articles in a classed arrangement, with name and title indexes. Z5956.C6N48

Dissertations

Kerst, Catherine Hiebert. Ethnic folklife dissertations from the United States and Canada, 1960–1980 : a selected annotated bibliography. Wash. : American Folklife Center, Library of Congress, 1986. 69 p. (Publications of the American Folklife Center, no. 12). **CF25**

Superintendent of Documents classification: LC 39.9:12.

A selective bibliography of dissertations, arranged by author. The compiler's definition of folklife emphasizes "traditional forms of ethnic folk culture."—*Pref.* Indexed by ethnic group and by state or province. Z5984.U6K47

Encyclopedias

Enzyklopädie des Märchens : Handwörterbuch zur histor. u. vergleichenden Erzählforschung / hrsg. von Kurt Ranke zusammen mit Hermann Bausinger ... [et al.] ; Red., Lotte Baumann ... [et al.]. Berlin ; N.Y. : de Gruyter, 1985–1990. v. 5–6. ISBN 3-11-006781-1 (v. 1). (In progress.) **CF26**

For Bd. 1–4 and annotation, see *Guide* CF54.

Contents: Bd. 5–6 (pub. in Lfg., 1985–90): Fortuna–Hyltén-Cavallius. GR72.E58

Guiley, Rosemary. The encyclopedia of witches and witchcraft. N.Y. : Facts on File, c1989. 421 p. : ill. ISBN 0-8160-1793-X. $45.00. **CF27**

Intends "to provide information pertaining to the evolution of witchcraft in Western civilization and its history, beliefs, practices, and adherents."—*Introd.* Short articles discuss contemporary and historical personages, practices, and folklore. Brief bibliography; general index. BF1566.G85

Dictionaries

The Penguin encyclopedia of horror and the supernatural / ed. by Jack Sullivan. N.Y. : Viking, 1986. 482 p. : ill. ISBN 0-670-80902-0. $29.95.　　　　　**CF28**

Signed articles by more than 60 contributors treat authors, terms, motion pictures, music, etc. "The main criteria for coverage are that the evocation of fear, whether supernatural or psychological, be the main or at least a major part of the artist's intent and that the work be either historically important or of enduring quality."—*Foreword*. British and American figures and topics predominate, but attention is given to practitioners of France, Germany, Russia, etc. Cross-references; bibliographies.　　　　　BF1407.P46

The Americas

Directory of popular culture collections / by Christopher D. Geist . . . [et al.]. Phoenix : Oryx, 1989. 234 p. ISBN 0-89774-351-2. $39.50.　　　　　**CF29**

Libraries with relevant collections are arranged by geographical area—state or province, then by city. For each gives address and phone number, names of curators, hours, restrictions and access requirements, and description of collections. Indexed by subject and by name of institution.　　E169.1.D54

Humor in America : a research guide to genres and topics / ed. by Lawrence E. Mintz. N.Y. : Greenwood, 1988. 241 p. ISBN 0-313-24551-7.　　　　　**CF30**

A state-of-the-art review of the various forms of humor (e.g., comic strip, standup comic, film), or topics of humor (e.g., political humor, racial and ethnic humor). Also included in each essay are lists of topics needing research, a checklist, and bibliographical survey. Names/titles index.　　PS430.H86

Scott, Randall W. Comic books and strips : an information sourcebook. Phoenix : Oryx, 1988. 152 p. ISBN 0-89774-389-X.　　　　　**CF31**

Lists and briefly annotates 1,033 books, periodicals, and library collections useful for the study of comics. In five main sections: (1) Core library collection; (2) Books about comics; (3) Books that reprint comics; (4) Periodicals and journals; (5) Library collections. Author, title, and subject indexes.

Z5956.C6S37

Directories

Bartis, Peter. Folklife sourcebook : a directory of folklife resources in the United States and Canada / prepared by Peter T. Bartis and Barbara C. Fertig. Wash. : American Folklife Center, Library of Congress, 1986. 152 p. (Publications of the American Folklife Center, no. 14). ISBN 0-8444-0521-3 (pbk.).　　　　　**CF32**

Superintendent of Documents classification: LC 39.9:14.

A directory of agencies and programs, organizations and institutions, college and university courses, archival holdings, serials, recording companies, and similar listings. Based on responses to a questionnaire. Not indexed.　　GR37.B37

Handbooks

The encyclopedia of American comics / ed. by Ron Goulart. N.Y. : Facts on File, 1990. 408 p., [16] p. of plates : ill. (some col.). ISBN 0-8160-1852-9. $39.25.

CF33

"The articles in this book are arranged alphabetically and fall into two basic categories: biographical entries on the people of the comics field (artists, creators, packagers, writers) and entries on the comic strips themselves."—*Introd.* Entries are signed and black-and-white illustrations appear throughout. General index.　　　　　PN6725.E64

Handbook of American popular culture / ed. by M. Thomas Inge. 2nd ed., rev. and enlarged. N.Y. : Greenwood, 1989. 3 v. ISBN 0-313-25406-0 (set). $150.00.

CF34

1st ed., 1978–81 (*Guide* CF90).

Although basically a revision of the 1st ed., "there have been many modifications. New subjects have been added, including chapters on business, catalogs, computers, dance, fashion, gardening, graffiti, musical theater, and the study of popular culture. Some articles have been completely recast; some are contributed by different authors. All others have been extensively revised and updated, with special attention given to recent bibliography."—*Introd.* Articles now appear in a single alphabetical sequence, Advertising to Women, with name and subject indexes at the end of v.3.

§ The essays on literary aspects of popular culture (e.g., best sellers, comic books, detective and mystery novels, pulps and dime novels, Westerns) were revised, expanded and separately published as *Handbook of American popular literature* (*Supplement* BD163) which serves as a companion volume.

E169.1.H2643

Europe

Yassif, Eli. Jewish folklore : an annotated bibliography. N.Y. : Garland, 1986. 341 p. (Garland folklore bibliographies, v. 10 ; Garland reference library of the humanities, vol. 450). ISBN 0-8240-9039-X. $35.00.　　**CF35**

Aims to provide "a critical summary of one hundred years of the study of Jewish folklore" (*Introd.*)—i.e., publications of ca.1872–1980. Concerned with studies of folklore, not collections of tales, etc. Lists and annotates 1,356 items in an author arrangement, with subject index. Does not include the study of East European Jewish culture because it was felt that that extensive area requires a separate bibliography.　　Z6374.F6Y37

Asia

The Yanagita Kunio guide to the Japanese folk tale / trans. and ed. by Fanny Hagin Mayer. Bloomington : Indiana Univ. Pr., [1986?]. 363 p. : maps, port. ISBN 0-253-36812-X. $27.50.　　　　　**CF36**

Translation of *Nihon mukashibanashi meii*, comp. under the supervision of Yanagita Kunio and ed. by Nihon Hōsō Kyōkai.

"Yanagita Kunio . . . started the movement to collect folk tales in Japan and led it for more than fifty years."—*Pref.* This motif index is in two parts: complete tales and derived or partial stories. Each part contains chapters on various themes (e.g., Marriage, Stepchildren) which in turn have entries for various tale types. Each entry includes a brief summary, geographical locations and variants, and a list of sources. Supplementary material consists of a complete bibliography of sources, a glossary, indexes of English and Japanese tales and titles, and geographical indexes with reference maps.　　GR340.N52213

HOLIDAYS

The folklore of American holidays / Hennig Cohen and Tristram Potter Coffin, editors. Detroit : Gale, c1987. 431 p. : music. ISBN 0-8103-2126-2. $78.00. **CF37**

As the subtitle indicates, this is "a compilation of more than 400 beliefs, legends, superstitions, proverbs, riddles, poems, songs, dances, games, plays, pageants, fairs, foods, and processions associated with over 100 American calendar customs and festivals." Includes bibliographical references and indexes. GT4803.F65

ETIQUETTE

Bibliography

Hodges, Deborah Robertson. Etiquette : an annotated bibliography of literature published in English in the United States, 1900 through 1987. Jefferson, N.C. : McFarland, c1989. 182 p. ISBN 0-89950-429-9. $39.95. **CF38**

Lists 1,075 books and periodical articles by author, with a title and subject index. A prefatory "Overview of the literature" provides a history of the genre. Z5877.H6

CG

Statistics and Demography

GENERAL WORKS

Guides

Haupt, Arthur. The Population Reference Bureau's population handbook / by Arthur Haupt and Thomas T. Kane. 2nd ed., International ed. Wash. : The Bureau, c1989. 74 p. : ill. ISBN 0-917136-10-1. **CG1**

On cover: A quick guide to population dynamics for journalists, policymakers, teachers, students, and other people interested in people.

1st ed., 1978.

Includes explanations of how to compute various demographic variables and their meanings. HB871.H357

Bibliography

Bibliography of IUSSP conference proceedings from 1927 to 1985 / ed. by Jacqueline Claude = Bibliographie des actes des congrès de l'union, 1927 à 1985. Liège, Belgium : Ordina Editions, 1987. 435 p. ISBN 2-87108-003-8 (pbk.). **CG2**

Supersedes an earlier volume covering 1947–73 (*Guide* CG7). Z7164.D3B593

Byerly, Greg. The baby boom : a selective annotated bibliography / Greg Byerly, Richard E. Rubin. Lexington, Mass. : Lexington Books, c1985. 238 p. ISBN 0-669-08903-6. **CG3**

Contains citations with descriptive annotations to more than 700 English-language works. The first chapter cites books, dissertations, ERIC documents, and government publications; the remaining chapters list journal articles reflecting the demographic, economic, marketing, sociological, and popular aspects of the subject. Includes a detailed index of authors, subjects, and periodicals cited. Z7164.S66B925

Gärtner, Karla. Bibliographie deutschsprachiger bevölkerungswissenschaftlicher Literatur, 1978–1984 / Karla Gärtner, Johannes Otto und Manfred Tölle. Wiesbaden : Bundesinstitut für Bevölkerungsforschung, 1986. 802 p. (Materialien zur Bevölkerungswissenschaft, Heft 48). **CG4**

For similar compilations covering earlier periods, see *Guide* CG4. Z7165.G3G37

Gerhan, David R. A retrospective bibliography of American demographic history from colonial times to 1983 / comp. by David R. Gerhan and Robert V. Wells. N.Y. : Greenwood, [1989]. 474 p. (Bibliographies and indexes in American history, no. 10). ISBN 0-313-23130-3. $65.00. **CG5**

For annotation, see *Supplement* DB9. Z7165.U5G43

Kurian, George Thomas. Sourcebook of global statistics. N.Y. : Facts on File, c1985. 413 p. ISBN 0-87196-063-X. **CG6**

A bibliographic guide that lists more than 200 sources of statistics whose focus is global. Each entry provides a bibliographic citation, list of contents, and an evaluative annotation. Includes books, annuals, monthlies, and irregular serials issued by official and private sources, national and international. Subject index. Z7551.K46

Statistics sources. [1st ed.]– . Detroit : Gale, c1962– . ISSN 0585-198X. **CG7**

For 9th ed., 1984, and annotation, see *Guide* CG72.

With the 10th ed., 1986, appears annually.

Beginning with the 12th edition, 1988, three new features were added: (1) a bibliography of sources cited in the entries, with the addresses of publishers; (2) a list of sources for unpublished statistical data; and (3) a directory of state agencies that make census information and other statistical data available to the public. Z7551.S83

Westfall, Gloria. Bibliography of official statistical yearbooks and bulletins. Alexandria, Va. : Chadwyck-Healey, 1986. 247 p. ISBN 0-859-64124-4. $75.00. **CG8**

Analyzes the contents of recent editions of official yearbooks and bulletins for countries of the world and dependencies; limited to publications wholly or partially in the Roman or Cyrillic alphabet. Gives complete bibliographic description for each title. Z7551.W47

Dictionaries

Marriott, F. H. C. A dictionary of statistical terms. 5th ed., prepared for the International Statistical Institute by F.H.C. Marriott. Burnt Mill, Harlow, Essex, England : Publ. for the International Statistical Institute by Longman Scientific & Technical ; N.Y. : Wiley, 1990. 223 p. ISBN 0-470-21349-3. $59.95.   **CG9**

For annotation, see *Supplement* EF11.   HA17.K4

Multilingual demographic dictionary. *Spanish.* Diccionario demográfico multilingüe. Version en espanol, 2a ed., a cargo de Guillermo A. Macció. Lieja, Bélgica : Ediciones Ordina, [1985]. 194 p. ISBN 2-87040-033-0.   **CG10**

For the 2nd ed. of the English version, see *Guide* CG37.

Produced "using four sources, namely the second editions of the French and English versions and the first edition of the Spanish version, and demographic terminology of the Spanish world coined in the last twenty years."—*Notes translation.*

HB849.2.M8418

Petersen, William. Dictionary of demography : multilingual glossary / William Petersen and Renee Petersen. Westport, Conn. : Greenwood, 1985. 259 p. ISBN 0-313-25139-8.   **CG11**

In two parts: (1) an alphabetic list of English demographic terms, with their equivalents in French, Spanish, Italian, German, Japanese, Chinese, and Russian; and (2) alphabetic lists in the other languages that refer to the English base list. The Japanese and Chinese lists are written in ideograms with romanized transliteration, and the Russian in the Cyrillic alphabet with romanized transliteration; these lists are alphabetized by the transliterated versions.   HB849.2.P468

———— Dictionary of demography : terms, concepts, and institutions / William Petersen and Renee Petersen. N.Y. : Greenwood, 1986. 2 v. (1154 p.) : map. ISBN 0-313-24134-1 (set).   **CG12**

Provides definitions of varying length for more than 1,400 demographic terms. Includes a bibliography of works cited in the definitions; a classified list of institutes, organizations, associations, and agencies concerned with demography; and a long subject index that includes references to the author's *Dictionary of demography: biographies* (*Supplement* CG18).   HB849.2.P47

Population terminology : English, French, Spanish = Terminologie de la population : français, anglais, espagnol = Terminología de población : español, inglés, francés. Wash. : World Bank, c1986. 27 p. ISBN 0-8213-0762-2 (pbk.).   **CG13**

A lexicon of population terminology in three sections: (1) English terms translated into French and Spanish; (2) French terms into English; and (3) Spanish terms into English. Short definitions for some of the terms are given in English in the first section.   HB849.2.P67

Directories

Statistical services directory. First ed., issue no. 1 (June 1982)–1983. Detroit : Gale, c1982–1983. ISSN 0732-6971.   **CG14**

1st ed., 1982–83 (*Guide* CG44).

1st ed. issued in three nos. with annual cumulation. 2nd ed. issued as a separate. No more published.

The original scheme to publish four times a year with the fourth issue being cumulative has been dropped; the 2nd ed. is a single volume.   HA37.U137

Handbooks

Müller, Georg P. Comparative world data : a statistical handbook for social science / Georg P. Müller with the collaboration of Volker Bornschier. Baltimore : Johns Hopkins Univ. Pr., c1988. 496 p. : ill. ISBN 0-8018-3734-0. ISBN 0-8018-3770-7 (with three 5.25" diskettes). ISBN 0-8018-3805-3 (with two 3.5" diskettes).   **CG15**

Contains statistical information and rankings for 51 variables for each of 128 countries. Country tables are arranged alphabetically and in a uniform format to allow for comparisons of one country with another on similar time periods, units of measure, decile and percentile rankings, country partners and rankings, and the predecessor nation in an ordered chain of countries. Citations to sources are available only in the long list of footnotes. Includes a statistical table of critical values. "For statistical investigations beyond the exploratory data analysis, the numerical information of this book is also available on PC-diskettes of the DOS-type."—*Appendix.* Suitable for graduate and advanced research.   HA155.M85

Showers, Victor. World facts and figures. 3rd ed. N.Y. : Wiley, c1989. 721 p. : ill. ISBN 0-471-85775-0.   **CG16**

Previous ed., 1979 (*Guide* CG60).

This significantly revised edition is divided into 11 main chapters and lists latitude and longitude for every city and for physiographic features.   G109.S52

Social indicators of development. Baltimore : Publ. for the World Bank, The Johns Hopkins Univ. Pr., 1988. 1 v. ISBN 0-8018-3831-2.   **CG17**

Incorporates statistical and demographic data compiled by World Bank countries or international agencies specializing in education, health, nutrition, etc. Arranged alphabetically by country with summary tables (for countries with populations greater than 1 million persons) which permit some comparative analysis.   HA155.S63

Biography

Petersen, William. Dictionary of demography : biographies / William Petersen and Renee Petersen. Westport, Conn. : Greenwood, 1985. 2 v. (1365 p.). ISBN 0-313-25137-1 (v. 1). ISBN 0-313-25138-X (v. 2).   **CG18**

An international collective biography of demographers born before 1930 and of those born after that date whose work promises to have lasting significance. Entries average eight to ten lines and include year of birth, affiliation, a brief list of publications, and the source of biographic information. Includes an extensive general index, a list of reference sources, and an index by nationality.   HB855.P47

COMPENDIUMS

International

Kurian, George Thomas. The new book of world rankings. 3rd ed. / updated by James Marti. N.Y. : Facts on File, c1991. 324 p. ISBN 0-8160-1931-2.   **CG19**

Previous ed., 1984 (*Guide* CG55).

This edition contains over 110 fewer criteria then were reported in the 2nd ed.   HA155.K87

World comparisons / editors of the Economist. N.Y.: Times Books, 1990. 254 p. : col. ill., map. ISBN 0-8129-1877-0. $29.95. **CG20**

Also published as: *The Economist book of vital world statistics.*

Provides data on 146 countries (those with population greater than 1 million or gross national product greater than $1 billion, in 15 general categories: Demography, Economic strength, Agriculture and food, Industry and energy, Commodities, Transport and communications, Government finance, Inflation and finance, Trade and balance of payments, Debt and aid, Employment, Education, Health, Family life, and Environment. Extensive use of tables, charts, and graphs. "Data are normally shown for the latest year, as indicated in each case."—*Notes.* Sources cited in section-by-section guide. No index. HC59.W634

World population profile. 1985– . [Wash.]: U.S. Dept. of Commerce, Bureau of the Census, 1986– . Annual. ISSN 0895-3341. **CG21**

Superintendent of Documents classification: C 3.205/3:WP– .

"Most of the statistics presented in this report are derived from information in the International Data Base compiled by the Center for International Research, U.S. Bureau of the Census."—*Appendix.* Arranged in broadly defined subject areas, the data represent the most current population estimates and projections the Center prepares on every country of the world and are based on the latest demographic information available for each individual country. Includes tables, a glossary, and an appendix showing the availabilty of demographic data. HA154.W65

World tables. Baltimore : publ. for the World Bank by the Johns Hopkins Univ. Pr., c1988. 4th ed. **CG22**

3rd ed., 1984 (*Guide* CG68).

Covers the period 1967–1987. HC59.W669

Zachariah, K. C. World population projections, 1987–88 : short- and long-term estimates / K.C. Zachariah, My T. Vu. Baltimore : publ. for the World Bank [by] John Hopkins Univ. Pr., c1988. 439 p. : chiefly tables. ISBN 0-8018-3673-5. **CG23**

Contains census and demographic estimates for individual countries, arranged in broad regional groupings. Includes appendixes listing sources of data for population, mortality, and fertility. HA155.Z33

Bibliography

European directory of non-official statistical sources. 1st ed. (1988)– . London: Euromonitor; Detroit : Gale, c1988– . Annual. ISSN 0953-0258. **CG24**

An index to more than 2,000 key nongovernmental publications (e.g., opinion surveys, forecasts) that provide statistics concerning markets, industries, and products for both individual countries of Europe and the continent as a whole. Stresses pan-European sources and those of the major European Economic Community nations (notably France, West Germany, and the U.K.) but includes selected materials from 12 other European countries. Arranged alphabetically by organization. Subject and geographic indexes, and an organization list arranged geographically. HA37.E914

The Americas

Statistical handbook on women in America / comp. and ed. by Cynthia Taeuber. Phoenix : Oryx, 1991. 385 p. : ill. ISBN 0-89774-609-0. **CG25**

Presents demographic, economic, social, and health status data in more than 400 tables and charts reproduced from federal statistical publications. Many cover the period through 1988, but some tables give projections and forecasts up to the year 2030. The appendix includes a guide to relevant information sources, a list of important telephone numbers at the Bureau of the Census, a glossary of demographic and statistical terms, a list of sources used in the book keyed to table numbers, and a subject index. HQ1420.T34

United States

Regional differences in America : a statistical sourcebook / Alfred N. Garwood, ed. Seattle, Wash. : Numbers & Concepts, c1988. 590 p. **CG26**

For annotation, see *Supplement* DB44. HA215.R43

USA by numbers : a statistical portrait of the United States. Wash. : Zero Population Growth, c1988. 164 p. : ill. ISBN 0-945219-00-8. $8.95. **CG27**

A compendium of data on social, economic, and environmental topics. Each of the 13 chapters contains a short essay and statistical tables covering varying time periods; for example, some historical tables give data from 1790, while some tables of forecasts project data to the year 2080. Chapter topics include Basic U.S. demographics, Adolescent sexuality and pregnancy, Abortion in America, The U.S. labor force, and other social issues. Includes maps and a list of sources from which the statistics were taken. There is no index, but the table of contents serves this purpose. HA214.U8

Guides

Guide to U.S. government statistics. 1990/91 ed. McLean, Va. : Documents Index, 1990. **CG28**

4th ed., 1973 (*Guide* CG100).

Prepared 1961– by J.L. Andriot.

Similar in scope to the 4th ed.; entries now include OCLC numbers. The index section has been expanded to include an agency index, an area index for the world, and an area index for the U.S. Z7554.U5G8

Bibliography

Guide to 1980 U.S. decennial census publications : detailed abstracts and indexes derived from the *American statistics index.* Bethesda, Md. : Congressional Information Service, c1986. 2 v. : ill. ISBN 0-88692-099-X (pbk.). **CG29**

As the subtitle indicates, these volumes are substantially reprinted from *American statistics index* (*Guide* CG108). Vol. 1, Index, provides detailed indexing by subject, geographic area, report number, title, and type of data, and v. 2, Abstracts, extensive abstracts of individual 1980 census publications.

HA37.U55G85

State and local statistics sources. 1st ed. (1990–91)– . Detroit : Gale, c1990– . Biennial. ISSN 1047-3394. $135.00. **CG30**

Subtitle: A subject guide to statistical data on states, cities, and locales.

Includes "information on demographic, socioeconomic, and business indicators for the states and local areas of the United States, the District of Columbia, Guam, Puerto Rico, and the Virgin Islands."—*Introd.* Information is arranged in alphabetical order by state, city, and other locations, then by broad subject areas. Appendixes include an annotated bibliography of nonprint sources of statistics and an annotated bibliography of the sources used in compilation. HA203.S7

Stratford, Juri. Guide to statistical materials produced by governments and associations in the United States / Juri Stratford and Jean Slemmons Stratford. Alexandria, Va. : Chadwyck-Healey, 1987. 279 p. ISBN 0-85964-127-9. $75.00. **CG31**

"An annotated bibliography providing subject access to the statistical contents of over seven hundred publications . . . from many federal agencies and the U.S. Congress, state agencies or state funded educational and/or research institutions, and nonprofit membership organizations representing a specific industry, profession or sector of the economy."—*Introd.* Arranged alphabetically by sponsoring agency or organization. Includes appendixes and title and subject indexes. Z7554.U5S8

United States. Bureau of the Census. Census catalog and guide. 1985– . Wash. : U.S. Dept. of Commerce, Bureau of the Census : For sale by the Supt. of Docs., U.S. Govt.Print.Off., [1985]– . Annual. **CG32**

Title varies: earlier eds. had title *Bureau of the Census catalog* (*Guide* CG101). Z7554.U5U32

Indexes

Schulze, Suzanne. Population information in twentieth century census volumes, 1900–1940. Phoenix : Oryx, 1985. 274 p. : maps. ISBN 0-89774-164-1. $82.00. **CG33**
Z7164.D3S45

————— Population information in twentieth century census volumes, 1950–1980. Phoenix : Oryx, 1988. 317 p. : maps. ISBN 0-89774-400-4. $82.00. **CG34**

These volumes continue *Population information in nineteenth century census volumes* (1983; *Guide* CG109) and continue its pattern of indexing. Entries for the 20th-century volumes analyze printed reports for the 12th through 20th decennial censuses. Full bibliographic information is given; entries are arranged by Dubester number (consecutive numbers assigned to volumes of the reports). Charts in the endpapers correlate some 40 population characteristics with the Dubester numbers. The entry for each volume gives location of tables in that volume.
Z7164.D3S46

Directories

Evinger, William R. Federal statistical data bases : a comprehensive catalog of current machine-readable and online files. Phoenix : Oryx, 1988. 670 p. ISBN 0-89774-255-9. $115.00. **CG35**

Complements *Directory of federal statistical data files*, 1981– (*Guide* CG111).

Describes with abstracts 2,500 government compiled statistical files, organized by department and agency. Each abstract provides a description of the contents, geographic coverage, date, technical characteristics of the file, accompanying documentation, related reports, an agency contact, and availability information. Title and subject indexes. HA37.U55E84

Handbooks

Almanac of the 50 states. 1985 ed.– . [Wellesley Hills, Mass.] : Information Publications, c1985– . Annual. ISSN 0887-0519. $45.00. **CG36**

In two parts: (1) statistical and demographic profiles of each of the 50 states, the District of Columbia, and the entire U.S., with tables of vital statistics, health, education, housing, government finance, etc.; (2) tables that rank the same areas according to 54 selected criteria such as population, households, doctors, hospitals, crime rate, etc. Sources of data are cited.
HA203.A5

Metro insights. 1987 ed.– . Lexington, Mass. : Regional Information Group, Data Resources, c1987– . Annual. **CG37**

Analyses and commentaries by experts concerning 100 major metropolitan areas of the U.S. Uniform format of the articles permits easy comparison. Includes tables and graphs, and details the industrial mix, population characteristics, and infrastructure of these areas. Appendixes. HC101.M43

Africa

Morrison, Donald George. Black Africa : a comparative handbook / Donald George Morrison, Robert Cameron Mitchell, John Naber Paden. 2nd ed. N.Y. : Paragon House : Irvington Publishers, c1989. 716 p. : ill. ISBN 0-88702-042-9. **CG38**

1st ed., 1972 (*Guide* DD98).

Updates the earlier edition to the late 1970s, revises the essays, and expands coverage to include Angola, Djibouti, Equatorial Guinea, Guinea-Bissau, Madagascar, Mozambique, Namibia, Swaziland, and Zimbabwe. No index, but this lack is compensated by an extensive table of contents and a list of tables and figures. Data are derived from the compilers' *Black Africa data base*, which is available from the publisher by subscription on diskettes. DT352.8.M67

Bibliography

Domschke, Eliane. The handbook of national population censuses : Africa and Asia / Eliane Domschke and Doreen S. Goyer. N.Y. : Greenwood, 1986. 1032 p. : ill. ISBN 0-313-25361-7. **CG39**

Describes censuses of population (most of them taken in the 20th century) for 55 African and 47 Asian countries. Gives for each country its statistical agency, its national repository (if known), and the main U.S. repository. Appendixes contain: (1) international population charts, showing, for example, country and major city population at five-year intervals beginning in 1945, and ranked tables for the latest population figures of major metropolitan areas; and (2) international topic charts, which provide summary census tables by broadly defined topics, also at five-year intervals beginning in 1945. A list of variant country names and capital cities is provided. There is no subject index, but the table of contents gives access by country. For a similar work by the same compilers covering Latin America, the Caribbean, North America, and Oceania, see *Guide* CG46. HA37.A33D65

Evalds, Victoria K. Union list of African censuses, development plans and statistical abstracts. Oxford, England : Zell, 1985. 232 p. ISBN 0-905450-20-5. **CG40**

Lists works published after 1945 and acquired as late as 1984, and shows holdings in 13 U.S. and Canadian research libraries. Z7554.A34E93

Albania

40 vjet Shqiperi socialiste = 40 years of socialist Albania. Tiranë : Shtëpia botuese "8 Nëntori", 1984. [160] p. : ill. **CG41**

Contains charts, tables and graphs that give national statistics, social indicators, industrial and agricultural production, trade, etc. English version; also published in Albanian and French. DR912.A14

Canada

Canadian statistics index. [v. 1] (1985)– . Toronto : Micromedia, [1985]– . Frequency varies. ISSN 0832-655X. $225.00 per yr. **CG42**

Microfiche edition, 1985– .
Includes some text in French. HA741

Hillman, Thomas A. Catalogue of census returns on microfilm, 1666–1891 = Catalogue de recensements sur microfilm, 1666–1891 / Thomas A. Hillman. Ottawa, Canada : Public Archives Canada : Available from Canadian Govt. Pub. Centre, Supply and Services Canada, c1987. 289 p. ISBN 0-660-53711-7 (pbk.). $21.60. **CG43**

Previous ed., covering 1666–1881, publ. 1981.

Lists Canadian census returns available on microfilm, with information for requesting them from the Public Archives of Canada through interlibrary loan. Within chapters for each province, entries are arranged alphabetically by subdistrict (towns, townships, and city wards) followed by census district (cities and counties). Each entry provides dates for which returns are available, and the microfilm reel numbers on which census returns are located. Z7554.C2H55

Bibliography

Guide to Statistics Canada data on women : target groups project. Ottawa : Statistics Canada, Housing, Family and Social Statistics, [1987]. 113 p. **CG44**

An index to statistical data treating women and women's issues that were originally listed separately in Statistics Canada's annual *Catalogue* (*Guide* CG168) and other of its publications. In three parts: (1) cataloged publications other than census materials, with a subject index; (2) other sources of information, arranged by topic and medium of dissemination (e.g., demographic and census information on computer tape) (3) a select bibliography of related materials (e.g., papers presented at conferences) which are available in the Statistics Canada library. Z7964.C36G83

Chile

Mamalakis, Markos. Historical statistics of Chile. Westport, Conn. : Greenwood, 1985–1989. v. 5–6. ISBN 0-313-20619-8 (v. 1). $50.00. **CG45**

For v.1–4 and annotation, see *Guide* CG172.
Contents: v. 5, Money, banking, and financial services; v.

6, Government services and public sector and a theory of services. HA1004.M35

China

10 percent sampling tabulation on 1982 population census of People's Republic of China. [Arlington, Va.] : PBIS, Foreign Broadcast Information Service, Joint Publications Research Service ; Springfield, Va. : National Technical Information Service, [1985]. 408 p. **CG46**

Results of the 1982 Sample Census arranged in 64 tables: population distribution, age, nationality, reproduction, education, industry, summary tables. Appendixes list China's major demographic figures, administrative division, and the method of the tabulation. Detailed table of contents in Chinese and English. HB3654.A3C54

China statistical abstract. 1988– . N.Y. : Praeger, 1989– . Irregular. ISSN 1050-351X. **CG47**

Also available in microform (Wash. : Congressional Information Service).

Based on statistics published by the Statistical Bureau of the People's Republic of China. Tables are arranged under 13 headings: General survey; Population and labor force; Agriculture; Industry; Transportation; Postal and telecommunications services; Investment in fixed assets; Finance, trade and price; People's livelihood; Education; Science; Culture; Public health and sports. Figures are current through 1987 with some retrospective coverage from 1978. Some figures are provisional; final counts are to be included in the *Statistical yearbook of China* (*Guide* CG181).

China statistical yearbook / State Statistical Bureau of the People's Republic of China. English ed. Hong Kong : International Centre for the Advancement of Science & Technology ; Beijing : China Statistical Information & Consultancy Service Centre, c1988– . **CG48**

Also publ.: N.Y. : Praeger, 1989– .

The volume for 1989 "contains national and provincial data in social and economic fields for . . . 1988, as well as major time series of national figures from 1949–1988 . . . a revised English language volume of the Chinese language edition *Zhongguo Tongji Nianjian 1989*, published by the State Statistical Bureau of the People's Republic of China."—*Pref.* A publisher's brochure adds that this is an improved English-language edition of *Statistical yearbook of China* (*Guide* CG181). Arranged in 18 sections covering demographics, finance and economics, industry and commerce, trade and tourism, education, and culture and health. A section of explanatory notes describes concepts, terms, and methodology. Detailed table of contents, but no index. HA4631.S83

Costa Rica

Censo de población, 1984. San José, Costa Rica : Ministerio de Gobernación y Policía, Impr. Nacional, 1987. 2 v. : ill. **CG49**

The results of the 1984 census, presented in 52 tables. Subdivided by major cities, provinces, counties, and districts, the tables show various types of demographic information: e.g., population, levels of education, types of occupations. Includes a subject index; a glossary of technical words, and graphs of selected data. HA801.5

Ecuador

Delaunay, Daniel. Demografía en el Ecuador: una bibliografía. Poblaciones de las parroquias, Ecuador, 1950–1982 / [Daniel Delaunay, Blanca Carrera, Juan León]. Quito: Centro Ecuatoriano de Investigación Geográfica, 1985. 16, 69 p.   **CG50**

Contains two distinct works: *Demografía en el Ecuador, una bibliografía* and *Poblaciones de las Parroquias, Ecuador 1950–1982* (a collection of demographic data). Compiled by the Ecuadorian Center for Geographic Investigation (CEDIG), the Scientific Office of the National Section of the Panamerican Institute of Geography and History (IPGH) as a part of the *Geografía basica del Ecuador*. Future volumes in this series are projected for migration, the demographic structure of the Ecuadorian population, and a map showing this geographic distribution.   HA1025.D45

Europe, Western

Harvey, Joan M. Statistics Europe: sources for social, economic, and market research. 5th ed. Beckenham, England: CBD Research, 1987. 320 p. ISBN 0-900246-36-7. £42.50.   **CG51**

4th ed., rev. and enl., 1981 (*Guide* CG204).

The shrinkage between the 4th and the 5th editions has been caused by "the economic climate which has deteriorated in many European countries and which has meant that the governments of some individual countries have had to restrict the number of official documents published and the government departments have been able to offer less assistance than previously; also, there appear to be fewer non-official publications issued at present"—*p. v.*   Z7554.E8H35

Great Britain

Mitchell, Brian. British historical statistics. Cambridge; N.Y.: Cambridge Univ. Pr., 1988. 886 p. ISBN 0-521-33008-4.   **CG52**

A cumulation and expansion of Mitchell's *Abstract of British historical statistics* (*Guide* CG227) and Mitchell and H.G. Jones's *Second abstract of British historical statistics* (*Guide* CG228). Emphasizes social and economic history. Most tables cover to about 1980.   HA1134.M58

Bibliography

Benjamin, Bernard. Population statistics: a review of UK sources. Aldershot, Eng.; Brookfield, Vt.: Gower Pub. Co., c1989. 355 p.: ill. ISBN 0-566-05731-X. $75.00.   **CG53**

"Intended to provide assistance to the many people in the different occupations or professions who are not continually immersed in population arithmetic but who from time to time need information on some aspects of population change and need guidance as to where to look for this information."—*p.1.* In addition to listing the sources of information, the work attempts to explain the methodology by which the data are derived, how the information should be interpreted, and how it may be used. Subject index.   HA37.G7B445

Maunder, W. F. Reviews of United Kingdom statistical sources. London; Pergamon, 1984–88. v. 16–25. (In progress).   **CG54**

For earlier volumes, see *Guide* CG235.

Contents: v. 16, Iron and steel, by David Heal, and Shipbuilding, by Anthony Slaven; v. 17, Weather, by B.W. Atkinson, and Water, by E.C. Penning-Rowsell and D.J. Parker; v. 18, Posts and telecommunications by Stuart Wall and Paul Nicholson; v. 19, Intellectual property rights, by Derek L. Bosworth; v. 20, Religion, by L.M. Barley, C.D. Field, B.A. Kosmin, and J.S. Nielson; v. 21, Finance, by Kate Phylaktis and Geraldine Kaye; v. 22, Printing and publishing, by W.D. McClelland; v. 23, Agriculture, by G.H. Peters and K.R. Clark; v. 24, Local government, by J.M. Gillespie; v. 25, Family planning, by Peter Selman.

Hungary

Fóti, Istvánné. Statisztikai adatforrások: bibliográfia, 1945–1985 = Sources of statistical data: bibliography, 1945–1985. Budapest: Központi Statisztikai Hivatal, Könyvtár és Dokumentációs Szolgálat, 1987. 431 p. ISBN 963-340-826-1. 155.00Ft.   **CG55**

For previous edition, covering 1945–74, see *Guide* CG242.

A bibliography of sources of statistical data, 1945–85.   Z7554.H8F67

India

Bibliography

Guide to official statistics. 3rd ed. New Delhi: Central Statistical Organisation, Dept. of Statistics, Ministry of Planning, Govt. of India; Delhi: Controller of Publications, 1987 [i.e. 1988]. 156 p.   **CG56**

1st ed., 1979 (*Guide* CG247); 2nd ed., 1985.

This edition in three parts: Social statistics, Economic statistics, and Public administration and electoral statistics. Appendixes contain lists of national sample survey reports, lists of publications, lists of abbreviations, etc.   Z7165.I6G78

Indonesia

Way, Peter O. Detailed statistics on the urban and rural population of Indonesia, 1950 to 2010. Wash.: Center for International Research, Bureau of the Census, [1984]. 416 p.   **CG57**

Distributed to depository libraries in microfiche.

Superintendent of Documents classification: C 3.2:St 2/16/Indone.

§ Several new volumes have been issued in the Center's series of population statistics for various countries of the world: this one on Indonesia, Pakistan (*Supplement* CG65), Israel (*Supplement* CG58), and the Philippines (*Supplement* CG68). Earlier volumes treated Cuba (*Guide* CG189), Mexico (*Guide* CG301), South Africa (*Guide* CG335), and Turkey (*Guide* CG358). Each contains "tables of selected demographic information including size of population and estimates of fertility, mortality and migration for the total urban and rural areas."—*Pref.* Each includes a glossary, technical notes, a list of major resources.   HA4605.W39

Israel

Roof, Michael K. Detailed statistics on the population of Israel by ethnic and religious group and urban and rural residence, 1950 to 2010. Wash. : Center for International Research, U.S. Bureau of the Census, [1984]. 780 p. **CG58**

Distributed to depository libraries in microfiche.
Superintendent of Documents classification: C 3.2:St 2/15.
For annotation, see *Supplement* CG57.   HA4560.R66

Latin America

Anuario estadístico de América Latina y el Caribe = Statistical yearbook for Latin America and the Caribbean. 1985– . [Santiago, Chile] : Economic Commission for Latin America and the Caribbean, 1986– . Annual. ISSN 0251-9445.   **CG59**

Continues *Statistical yearbook for Latin America* (*Guide* CG285).
In English and Spanish.   HA751.A58

Statistical abstract of Latin America for [date] / prepared by Committee on Latin American Studies, University of California at Los Angeles. [1st ed.] (1955)– . Los Angeles : The Univ., 1956– . Annual. ISSN 0081-4687. **CG60**

For earlier issues, see *Guide* CG286.
"Beginning with vol. 24 [1986], the editors have included alternative data in the form of partial tables from previous issues going back to vol. 17."—*Pref.* Endpapers give abbreviations, sources of information, and symbols.   HA935.S8

Statistical abstract of Latin America. Supplement. 10– . Los Angeles : UCLA Latin American Center Publications, Univ. of California, 1990– . Irregular.   **CG61**

For basic work and Suppl. [1–9], see *Guide* CG286.
Contents: [no. 10] Society and economy in Mexico (publ. 1990); [no. 11] United States-Mexico border statistics since 1990 (publ. 1990).

Bibliography

A guide to Latin American and Caribbean census material : a bibliography and union list / gen. ed., Carole Travis. Boston, Mass : G.K. Hall, 1990. 739 p. ISBN 0-8161-0497-2.   **CG62**

A bibliography of the many censuses in the region from the earliest times to 1979 (e.g., major national censuses of population, housing, and agriculture), and some early colonial records that are clearly forerunners of the modern census. Arranged chronologically by country are summaries of each census's general results and supplementary material and data; location of census reports is indicated in U.K. libraries. Index of names of countries, provinces, and towns.   Z7553.C3G85

Malaysia

Buku tahunan perangkaan Malaysia = Yearbook of statistics Malaysia. 1984– . Kuala Lumpur, Malaysia : Jabatan Perangkaan, 1985– . Annual. ISSN 0127-2624.   **CG63**

Offers comprehensive and timely data on the economic and social conditions of Malaysia, Peninsular Malaysia, Sabah, and Sarawak: population, climate, trade, transport, communi-

cation, tourism etc. Includes a map of population distribution.   HA1791.D45a

Mexico

Bibliography

Consejo Nacional de Población (Mexico). Catálogo de publicaciones : ordenado por tema y fecha de publicación. México : Consejo Nacional de Población, 1987. 20 p.   **CG64**

An index to the census publications issued by the National Council on Population (CNP). Arranged by types of census material, each section is further subdivided chronologically by dates of publication. The stated purpose is to help users identify which census materials may be purchased from the CNP and which may only be seen in the Documentation Center of the National Council of Population (CDCNP).   Z7164.D3C66

Pakistan

Finch, Glenda. Detailed statistics on the urban and rural population of Pakistan, 1950 to 2010 / by Glenda S. Finch, Paul R. Campbell, and James F. Spitler. Wash. : Center for International Research, U.S. Bureau of the Census, [1984]. 350 p.   **CG65**

Superintendent of Documents classification: C 3.2:St 2/16/Pakist.
Distributed to depository libraries in microfiche.
For annotation, see *Supplement* CG57.   HA4590.5.F56

Peru

Perú, compendio estadístico / Instituto Nacional de Estadística. Lima, Perú : El Instituto.   **CG66**

An abstract of statistics covering 18 subject areas (e.g., Population, Housing, Transportation, Agriculture, National accounts, Tourism). Footnotes list sources of data. In Spanish.   HA1051.P47

Perú en números. Lima, Perú : Cuánto S.A.   **CG67**

"A compendium of Peruvian statistics which covers a large variety of material from the national scene, with emphasis on economics, but also with full coverage of the physical characteristics of the country, and with many quantitative aspects of its social and cultural development."—*Preface* [translation]. In 22 topical chapters (e.g., Population, Education, Health, Labor, National accounts, Farming, Minerals and petroleum, Electricity and water, Public finance). Sources are cited for tables, which cover 20th-century data; contains many charts and satellite maps. Includes a subject index, a list of technical and ecological terms with definitions, a glossary of Spanish words with equivalents in English and French, a list of the principal sources of statistical information in Peru, and a directory of organizations that produce statistical information that gives local addresses and telephone numbers. Comparable in scope to *Statistical abstract of the United States* (*Guide* CG94).

Philippines

Kinsella, Kevin G. Detailed statistics on the urban and rural population of the Philippines, 1950 to 2010. Wash. : Center for International Research, U.S. Dept. of the Census, [1984]. 492 p.　　　　**CG68**
　　Superintendent of Documents classification: C 3.2:St 2/16/Philip.
　　For annotation, see *Supplement* CG57.　　HA4615.K56

Poland

Poland. Główny Urząd Statystyczny. Bibliografia wydawnictw Głównego Urzędu Statystycznego, 1968–1973 / opracowała Joanna Górska. Warszawa : Główny Urząd Statystyczny, 1976. 392 p. : ill.　　**CG69**
　　　　　　　　　　　　　　Z7554.P6G67

———— Bibliografia wydawnictw Głównego Urzędu Statystycznego, 1974–1980 / opracowała Joanna Górska. Warszawa : Główny Urząd Statystyczny, 1988. 277 p.　　**CG70**
　　For basic volume and annotation, see *Guide* CG325.
　　　　　　　　　　　　　　Z7554.P6P65

Sri Lanka

Srī Laṅkā saṅkhyāta nibandhaya = Ilaṅkaip puḷḷiviparat tokuppu = Statistical abstract of Sri Lanka. 1973–. Kolamba : Janalkhana hā Saṅkhyālēkhana Depārtamēntuva; Rajayē Prakāśana Karyāṃśayen miladī labāgata hǎka, 1975– . Annual. Rs.25.50.　　**CG71**
　　Continues *Statistical abstract of Ceylon* (*Guide* CG344).
　　Vols. for 1977– have English title: Statistical abstract of the Democratic Socialist Republic of Sri Lanka.
　　In English, Singhalese, and Tamil.　　HA1728.C43

Thailand

Annotated statistical bibliography. 1984/1986– . Bangkok : National Statistical Office, Office of the Prime Minister, 1986– . Annual.　　**CG72**
　　Lists "publications pertaining to statistics printed or published by various functional government agencies, as well as state enterprises ... "—*Pref.* Arranged by agency or ministry. No index, but a lengthy table of contents.

Union of Soviet Socialist Republics

Bibliography

Davydova, A. G. Literatura o narodonaselenii : bibliograficheskiĭ ukazatel : 1979–pervaia polovina 1983 g.g / [ukazatel literatury o narodonaselenii sostavlen A.G. Davydovoĭ] ; pod redaktsieĭ D.I. Valenteia, É.IU. Burnasheva. Moskva : "Mysl", 1987. 286 p.　　**CG73**
　　Previous ed., 1981, had title *Literatura o naselenii* (*Guide* CG367).
　　Presents 2,219 citations arranged in 21 chapters covering a variety of topics (e.g., Theoretical and applied demography, The census, Migration, Marriage and family, Economics, Law).

Each chapter is subdivided into narrower topics, with entries alphabetically arranged within sections. Monographs, journal articles, dissertations, conference proceedings are included. Entries are confined to Russian-language publications. Author index.　　Z7164.D3D295

Heleniak, Timothy E. Bibliography of Soviet statistical handbooks. Wash. : Center for International Research, U.S. Bureau of the Census, [1988]. 237 p. (CIR staff paper, no. 42).　　**CG74**
　　1979, 1980, and 1984 editions had title: *Bibliography of regional statistical handbooks in the U.S.S.R.*
　　The main volume lists "over 2,000 Soviet statistical handbooks known to have been published since the mid-1950's."—*Summary.* Includes regional, national, international and foreign trade publications. Six appendixes: (1) Geographical index; (2) Summary of Soviet national statistical handbooks, 1955–1988; (3) Summary of Soviet Republic statistical handbooks, 1955–1988; (4) Summary of Soviet regional handbooks, 1955–1988; (5) Number of Soviet statistical handbooks, by year and type, and percentage in the Center for International Research, (6) Number of Soviet statistical handbooks, by chapter and type, and percentage in CIR.
　　§ The 1989 update lists handbooks devoted to special topics (e.g., Agriculture, Women and children, Publishing, Plan fulfillment reports). Appendix 1 contains updated citations to titles included in the main volume, and three other appendixes update the summaries in the main volume.　　Z7165.S65H47

Research guide to the Russian and Soviet censuses / ed. by Ralph S. Clem. Ithaca : Cornell Univ. Pr., 1986. 323 p. ISBN 0-8014-1838-0.　　**CG75**
　　In two parts: (1) general and topical essays (accompanied by bibliographies) that analyze data across the five censuses (1897, 1926, 1959, 1970, 1979); (2) Index and guide to the Russian and Soviet census, 1897-1979, which describes briefly each of the five censuses and provides an annotated and translated list of all the tables in each census. Each volume has a table of contents; a keyword index provides detailed cross-references to all five censuses.　　HB3607.R43

CH

Economics

GENERAL WORKS

Bibliography

Classical political economy : a survey of recent literature / ed. by William O. Thweatt. Boston : Kluwer Academic Publishers, c1988. 275 p. : ill. ISBN 0-89838-229-7. $45.00 (est.).　　**CH1**
　　Contains signed bibliographic essays surveying publications on classical political economy over the past 30 years, covering Adam Smith, Malthus, David Ricardo, and John Stuart Mill in separate chapters, with accompanying commentary in separate sections. Other economists are discussed in the re-

maining chapters; a group of six (Longfield, James Mill, Senior, Bailey, Torrens, and Say), in "Classical reassessments," and several others in "Some developments in Marxian theory since Schumpeter." Author and subject indexes.   HB94.C42

Hacken, Richard D. Central European economic history from Waterloo to OPEC, 1815–1975 : a bibliography. N.Y. : Greenwood, 1987. 270 p. (Bibliographies and indexes in economics and economic history, no. 6). ISBN 0-313-25460-5.   **CH2**

    For annotation, see *Supplement* DC3.   Z7165.C42H33

Current

●**Economic literature index** [computer file]. Pittsburgh : American Economic Association, 1969– .   **CH3**

    File size: 124,000 records. Updated quarterly. Available online (DIALOG) and in CD-ROM as *EconLit* (SilverPlatter).

    Compiled from the index section of *Journal of economic literature* (*Guide* CH37) and *Index of economic articles* (*Guide* CH35). Cites articles in more than 300 economics journals (selectively abstracted since 1984) and selected books and dissertations.

Periodicals

Miller, A. Carolyn. Refereed and nonrefereed economic journals : a guide to publishing opportunities / comp. by A. Carolyn Miller and Victoria J. Punsalan ; with the assistance of Kenneth G. Rohm. N.Y. : Greenwood, 1988. 252 p. ISBN 0-313-25857-0.   **CH4**

    "Designed to aid prospective authors seeking publication opportunities in economic journals."—*Pref.* Lists and describes some 200 journals in economics and related disciplines that accept manuscripts in English, presenting bibliographic, review/refereeing, and manuscript submission information for each. Also included are lists of style manual publishers, refereed and nonrefereed journals, and a chart comparing journals' reviewing criteria. Geographic and affiliations/keywords indexes.   HB63.M54

Sichel, Beatrice. Economics journals and serials : an analytical guide / comp. by Beatrice Sichel and Werner Sichel. N.Y. : Greenwood, 1986. 285 p. (Annotated bibliographies of serials, no. 5). ISBN 0-313-23810-3. $45.00.   **CH5**

    Lists, describes, and evaluates 450 titles drawn from economics and related disciplines. Each entry is in three parts: (1) bibliographic information, also giving databases and indexes in which included; (2) a narrative description discussing scope, content, authority, and when applicable, comparing it to related publications; and (3) a discussion of format, special features, and the like. A brief chapter presents an annotated list of English-language economics indexes and abstracts. Geographical, publisher, and title indexes.   Z7164.E2S49

Book reviews

Business library review. 1990– . N.Y. : Gordon and Breach Science Publishers, 1990– . Quarterly.   **CH6**

    Combines *The Wall Street review of books* (*Guide* CH42), which ceased with v.15 (1990), and *Economics and business: an international annotated bibliography* (*Guide* CH30), which ceased with v.30 (1990) with reviews of monographs, computer software, and audiovisual materials in economics and business. The bulk of each issue consists of critical reviews by scholars of about 20–30 titles; the remaining section, "Selected titles,"

combines a list of titles included in the first section with brief annotations describing additional works, following the format of *Economics and business.* Unlike that publication, however, titles are arranged alphabetically rather than by broad subject area, and far fewer titles are covered.

Encyclopedias

Block, Walter. Lexicon of economic thought / Walter Block and Michael Walker. Vancouver, B.C., Canada : Fraser Institute, c1989. 390 p. ISBN 0-88975-081-5. ISBN 0-88975-077-7 (pbk.).   **CH7**

    Contains one- to three-page commentaries, presenting the views of market economists on some 176 economic and social topics, ranging from "Aboriginal rights—land claims" to "Zoning." Examples used in the commentaries are generally drawn from Canada, but the discussion transcends national issues. Indexed, but lacks a bibliography.   HB61.B574

The new Palgrave : a dictionary of economics / ed. by John Eatwell, Murray Milgate, Peter Newman. London : Macmillan ; N.Y. : Stockton Pr. ; Tokyo : Maruzen, 1987. 4 v. : ill. ISBN 0-935839-10-1. $750.00.   **CH8**

    Successor to *Palgrave's dictionary of political economy* (*Guide* CH59). Provides encyclopedic coverage of modern economic thought, with nearly 2,000 signed entries written by more than 900 prominent economists, historians, philosophers, mathematicians, and statisticians. Articles present diverse philosophies, ideologies, and methodologies and discuss their origin, historical development, and philosophical foundation. The 700 biographical entries exclude living economists born after 1915. Bibliographies accompany most entries. Appendixes list contributors and biographies included in the earlier *Palgrave* but omitted here, and subject entries classified under 53 fields of study. Analytical subject index.   HB61.N49

Dictionaries

Lee, Susan. Susan Lee's ABZs of economics. N.Y. : Poseidon Pr., c1987. 224 p. : ill. ISBN 0-671-55711-4. **CH9**

    Entries give clear, nontechnical definitions of key economic terms, include explanations of the ideas behind the terms and, in many instances, "a glimpse of how the ideas fit into public policy debates."—*Pref.* Illustrations. Intended for general readers rather than economists or students of economics.   HB61.L34

A lexicon of economics / ed. by Phyllis Deane and Jessica Kuper. London ; N.Y. : Routledge, 1988. 380 p. ISBN 0-415-00234-6.   **CH10**

    Some 130 brief signed essays, by university faculty in the U.K., U.S., Canada, Japan, and Europe, that define basic concepts and discuss key issues and prominent economists. Suggestions for further reading and *see also* references follow each essay. Serves as a useful supplement to the *McGraw-Hill dictionary of modern economics* (*Guide* CH55).   HB61.L427

Pass, Christopher. Harper dictionary of economics / Christopher Pass, Bryan Lowes, Leslie Davies. N.Y. : HarperPerennial, 1991. 562 p. ISBN 0-06-461017-9 (pbk.). $7.95.   **CH11**

    Published in U.K. as *Collins dictionary of economics* (London : Collins, 1988).

    Contains more than 1,700 clearly written definitions of key economic terms, descriptions of organizations, and biographies of major economists. Numerous cross-references; nearly 200 illustrations.   HB61.P39

Terminology

Thematic list of descriptors—economics / prepared on behalf of UNESCO by the International Committee for Social Science Information and Documentation. London ; N.Y. : Routledge, 1989. 1 v. ISBN 0-415-01777-7. **CH12**

Companion to *International bibliography of economics* (*Guide* CH36). For description, see *Supplement* CE16.
Z695.1.E2T45

Directories

Capie, Forrest. Directory of economic institutions. N.Y. : Stockton Pr., c1990. 472 p. ISBN 0-935859-41-1. $190.00. **CH13**

Lists by country some 350 economic research organizations. Level of information provided varies, but generally includes: name; address and telephone, telex, and fax numbers; name of parent organization; date founded/incorporated; names of top officials; nature; objectives; type(s) of funding; research interests; publications; and other activities. An "Addresses" section at the front serves as both directory and index of organizations by name; there is no other index. HB74.5.C37

Guide to graduate study in economics, agricultural economics, public administration, and doctoral programs in business administration in the United States and Canada / ed. by Wyn F. Owen and Douglas A. Ruby. 8th ed. Boulder, Colo. : Economics Institute, c1989. 503 p. ISBN 0-88036-016-X. $29.95. **CH14**

7th ed., 1984 (*Guide* CH64).

Title has varied: first publ. 1965 as *Graduate studies in economics*.

This edition describes 220 economics programs, 29 Ph.D. programs in business administration, and 14 programs in public administration. Also offers general information for prospective graduate students and additional information for foreign graduate students. HB74.8.G84

Meerhaeghe, Marcel Alfons Gilbert van. International economic institutions. 5th rev. ed. Dordrecht ; Boston : Kluwer Academic, 1987. 368 p. ISBN 90-247-3513-0. **CH15**

Translation of *International economische betrekkingen en instellingen*, first publ. 1964 (Leiden : H. E. Stenfert Krose); 1st English language ed., 1966; 4th ed., 1985.

Contains descriptions in three main sections (Introduction, World organizations, European organizations) of U.N., specialized, and regional agencies, of such international organizations as the International Monetary Fund and the World Bank, and of such European organizations as Benelux and the European Communities. Although descriptions of agencies in the introduction are generally no longer than a paragraph or two, entries in the other sections are considerably longer, usually discussing origins, objectives, organization, functions and operation, and containing an appraisal of the organization, selected statistics, and a bibliography. Appended are lists of articles from legal documents pertaining to each organization, and author and subject indexes. HF1411.M433

Handbooks

Frumkin, Norman. Guide to economic indicators. Armonk, N.Y. : M.E. Sharpe, c1990. 242 p. : ill. ISBN 0-87332-620-2 (pbk.). ISBN 0-87332-521-4. **CH16**

Provides basic descriptions (including where and when available, content, methodology, accuracy, relevance, and recent trends) for more than 50 economic indicators developed by the federal government, private sources, and international organizations. References to primary data sources are also given. Some entries contain charts or tables, but there is no index. HC103.F9

Lehmann, Michael B. The Dow Jones-Irwin guide to using the *Wall Street journal*. 3rd ed. Homewood, Ill. : Dow Jones-Irwin, c1990. 382 p. ISBN 1-55623-242-X. **CH17**

1st ed., 1984; 2nd ed., 1987.

Intends to "show the reader how to use *The Wall Street journal* to be your own economist" (*Pref.*), focusing on key economic indicators and describing what they measure, how they are computed, and when they appear in the *Journal*. Also explains how each indicator is used to track the economy and includes excerpts from *Journal* articles that illustrate the contexts in which specific statistics are used. Includes illustrations, index, appendixes (miscellaneous statistical indicators, alphabetical list of statistical series published in the *Journal*, statistical series in chapter order, and a list of statistical series according to the *Journal* publication schedule). HB3743.L44

Moore, Geoffrey Hoyt. International economic indicators : a sourcebook / Geoffrey H. Moore and Melita H. Moore. Westport, Conn. : Greenwood, 1985. 373 p. : ill. ISBN 0-313-21989-3. **CH18**

Provides detailed information concerning three categories of international economic indicators—leading, coincident, and lagging—for the seven largest industrial countries (U.S., U.K., Canada, West Germany, France, Italy, and Japan). A discussion of the development of these indicators is followed by country-by-country descriptions of economic indicators, and by monthly and quarterly data (1948–82), for individual countries and for multicountry indexes. Appendixes list current sources of international economic indicators, present chronologies of growth cycles in 13 countries, 1948–83, show the record of leading economic indicators for seven countries, and discuss the method of contruction of the composite indexes. An indicator series finding guide lists composite indexes, giving citations to pages on which descriptions and data are included. Statistics in the tables are updated by the monthly *International economic indicators*, published since June 1983 by Columbia University's Center for International Business Cycle Research. HC59.M62

World index of economic forecasts : including industrial tendency surveys and development plans / ed. by Robert Fildes with Thana Chrissanthaki. 3rd ed. N.Y. : Stockton Pr., c1988. 563 p. : ill. ISBN 0-566-02702-X. **CH19**

2nd ed., 1981 (*Guide* CH65).

Includes profiles of 329 organizations, many new to this edition. Also new is a signed essay on the state of the art of cyclical business and consumer surveys in 42 countries.
HB3730.W66

Biography

Blaug, Mark. Great economists before Keynes : an introduction to the lives & works of one hundred great economists of the past. Atlantic Highlands, N.J. : Humanities Pr. International, 1986. 286 p. : ports. ISBN 0-391-03381-6. **CH20**
HB76.B54

———— Great economists since Keynes : an introduction to the lives & works of one hundred modern economists. Totowa, N.J. : Barnes & Noble, 1985. 267 p. : ill. ISBN 0-389-20517-6. $32.50. **CH21**

Describes the careers and contributions of key economists. Entries are alphabetically arranged and include photographs or illustrations as well as biographical and academic information. Indexed by names (other than main entries) and subjects.

HB76.B55

Council of Economic Advisers (U.S.). Biographical directory of the Council of Economic Advisers / ed. by Robert Sobel and Bernard S. Katz. N.Y. : Greenwood, 1988. 301 p. ISBN 0-313-22554-0. **CH22**

Contains 4-to-5-page signed biographical essays concerning the 45 economists who have served on the Council of Economic Advisers (CEA) since its beginning in 1946. Arrangement is alphabetical rather than chronological, and the essays, which focus on professional careers prior to and during appointment to the CEA, include bibliographies. An appendix lists membership in the CEA by presidential administration. Indexed.

HC102.5.A2C68

Nobel laureates in economic sciences : a biographical dictionary / ed. by Bernard S. Katz. N.Y. : Garland, 1989. 339 p. (Garland reference library of the humanities, vol. 850). ISBN 0-8240-5742-2. **CH23**

Contains biographical essays on each of the recipients of the Nobel Prize in economic sciences since the award was first given in 1969. Entries, written by colleagues, are several pages long and generally include descriptions of the recipients' backgrounds and careers, main contributions, specific achievements for which the awards were given, and bibliographies of works by and about the laureates. A brief introduction describes the award itself and is followed by a list of recipients by year. Indexed.

HB76.N63

Who's who in economics : a biographical dictionary of major economists, 1700-1986 / ed. by Mark Blaug. 2nd ed. Cambridge, Mass. : MIT Pr., 1986. 935 p. ISBN 0-7450-0230-7. **CH24**

1st ed., 1983 (*Guide* CH67).

Expanded to cover four additional years (1982-86), with inclusion of living economists in this edition determined solely by frequency with which journal articles are cited, based on the *Social sciences citation index*.

HB76.W47

Atlases

The Economist atlas : the shape of the world today. London : Hutchinson Business, 1989. 384 p. : col. ill., maps in color ; 26 cm. ISBN 0-09-174235-8. £19.95. **CH25**

In three main parts: (1) world maps, grouped together by continent and subcontinent; (2) world comparisons, showing for 19 different categories (e.g., economic strength, foreign debt) maps, charts, and graphs that highlight relevant countries and statistics; and (3) a world encyclopedia that presents a brief overview of each country's economy and its economic history, as well as general information (official name, capital city, ethnic composition, religion, language, education, climate, currency, public holidays, and government). General and map indexes, but no introductory or explanatory sections. G1021.E36

Freeman, Michael J. Atlas of the world economy / Michael Freeman ; consulting ed., Derek Aldcroft. N.Y. : Simon & Schuster, c1991. 167 p. : ill. ISBN 0-13-050741-5. $40.00. **CH26**

For each of eight broad categories (population, agriculture, energy, industry, national income, transport and trade, labour, and multinationals) and subcategories, contains brief introductory comments accompanied by some 250 maps, charts, tables, and graphs, none in color. Short bibliography. HC59.F734

Statistics

Liesner, Thelma. One hundred years of economic statistics : United Kingdom, United States of America, Australia, Canada, France, Germany, Italy, Japan, Sweden. Rev. and expanded to 1987. N.Y. : Facts on File, c1989. 344 p. : col. ill. ISBN 0-8160-2344-1. $75.00. **CH27**

Rev. ed. of *Economic statistics, 1900-1983* (1985).

A compilation of key economic indicators, drawn primarily from official publications and arranged by country. Also includes analytical tables and charts that present composite data and growth triangles for all nine countries. Indexed.

HC106.L68

ECONOMIC CONDITIONS

International

Country report : an analysis of economic and political trends every quarter / EIU, the Economist Intelligence Unit. 1988-89- . London : The Unit, 1988- . Quarterly. **CH28**

Title varies: *Quarterly economic review; QER; Three-month economic review.*

Provides quarterly information on current political, economic, and business conditions in 165 countries of the world, grouped geographically into 92 regional reports. Typically treats the political scene; economic policy; domestic economy; foreign trade and payments; agriculture, construction, communications, and manufacturing; business news; and prospects. Supplements text with graphs, charts, and statistical appendixes, usually drawn from official national and international statistical sources. Available as a set; regional reports may also be purchased separately.

§ A companion series, *Country profile* (published annually; included with subscriptions to *Country report* and also available separately) provides more detailed coverage. Profiles are about 50 pages in length, offer background information arranged by such categories as national accounts, employment, tourism, and foreign trade, and include charts, graphs, maps, and select bibliographies.

●**ECONBASE** : time series & forecasts [computer file]. Bala Cynwyd, Pa. : The WEFA Group, 1948- . **CH29**

Coverage: varies, with earliest time series beginning in 1948. File size: 11,639 records, updated monthly. Available online (DIALOG).

Monthly, quarterly, and annual time series, covering such areas as economics, business conditions, finance, manufacturing, income distribution, prices, and national income. Includes international, national, regional, state, Metropolitan Statistical Area (MSA) and Consolidated Metropolitan Statistical Area (CMSA) data. Also provides two-year forecasts for some 1,100 major economic indicators.

Handbook of economic statistics / National Foreign Assessment Center. Wash. : The Center : For sale by the Supt. of Docs., U.S. Govt. Print. Off. Annual. ISSN 0195-9018. **CH30**

Superintendent of Documents classification: PrEx 3.10/7: .

Provides data for all Communist and selected non-Communist countries. Some 176 tables are grouped into the following categories: Graphic summary, Economic profile, Aggregative trends, Developed country trends, Soviet economic performance, Communist countries: commodity data, Energy, Agriculture, Minerals and metals, Chemicals and manufactured goods, Foreign trade and aid, and Transportation. Indexed, with an appendix of conversion factors.   HA155.U54a

World debt tables. Wash. : World Bank. Annual. ISSN 0253-2859. $125.00 (set).   **CH31**
Continues *External public debt.*
In two volumes. "Volume 1 contains analysis and commentary on recent developments in international lending to developing countries, together with summary debt tables for 107 countries, for selected regions, and for other analytical groups. Volume 2 contains statistical tables showing the external debt of each of the 107 countries that report public and publicly guaranteed debt under the World Bank's Debtor Reporting System."—*Pref.*   HJ8899.W672

World economic and business review. 1990– . Cambridge, Mass. : B. Blackwell, Inc. Annual. ISSN 0957-8099.   **CH32**
Attempts to give an annual survey of economic and business conditions in countries of the world. Entries, alphabetically arranged by country, are usually three pages in length and include a map, a signed essay reviewing the year's political and economic developments, key facts and indicators, and country profile tables. Each entry also features a business guide section, with brief information regarding the country's time zone, climate, entry requirements, health precautions, representation overseas, air and surface access, hotels, transportation and telecommunications, working hours and public holidays, and banking. Front matter includes tables of world currencies and world indicators, and an essay surveying world developments during the year. Country and territory index.   HC10.W7975

World economic outlook : a survey by the staff of the International Monetary Fund. May 1980– . Wash. : The Fund, [1980–]. Semiannual, Sept. 1984– . ISSN 0256-6877.   **CH33**
Frequency varies: annual, 1980–Apr. 1984.
Also called, 1981–1984: *Occasional paper* / International Monetary Fund.
Combines a review of world economic conditions with short- and medium-term (up to five years) economic projections. Slightly more than half the publication consists of chapters (supplemented by tables, charts, and supplementary notes) that discuss the economy in industrial and developing countries. A lengthy statistical appendix contains 53 tables, arranged under the following categories: output, inflation, financial policies, foreign trade, current account transactions, current account financing, external debt and debt service, and medium-term scenario. Not indexed.   HC10.W7979

Africa

Hodd, Michael. African economic handbook. London : Euromonitor, 1986. 335 p. : ill. ISBN 0-86338-088-3.   **CH34**
"Considers the economic structure of 47 African countries south of the Sahara, examines their economic performance over the past decade, and looks at their prospects for the next ten years."—*Introd.* The first chapter discusses Africa in a world context, the next four focus on regions (east, west, central, and southern) and the countries in each, reviewing their recent political record and economic strategy. The final chapter considers the outlook for the continent, its regions and countries. Statistical tables and charts throughout, with an appendix of comparative statistics. Not indexed.   HC800.H63

Asia

Asia Pacific : an investment guide. London, England : Euromoney Publications in association with Arthur Andersen & Co.... [et al.], 1990. 282 p. : ill. ISBN 1-85564-030-9. £88.00.   **CH35**
Presents profiles of 11 countries or territories (Australia, Hong Kong, Indonesia, Republic of Korea, Malaysia, New Zealand, the Philippines, Singapore, Taiwan, Thailand, and China), discussing for each its economy, foreign investment, capital markets, equity market, the corporate sector, regulatory environment, and tax and accounting practices. An introductory chapter considers the development of the Pacific Rim, while the final chapter describes the emerging markets in Laos and Vietnam. Numerous statistics, charts, graphs, photographs and other illustrations. Not indexed.   HG5702.A752

Asian economic handbook. London : Euromonitor, 1987. 272 p. : ill. ISBN 0-86338-141-3. £45.00.   **CH36**
"Presents an economic overview of the region as a whole within the context of the world economy; discusses recent economic growth and development by subregion and country; and assesses future growth and development"—*Foreword.* Numerous statistics, including a "Statistical factfile" chapter. Indexed.   HC412.A748

Boger, Karl. Postwar industrial policy in Japan : an annotated bibliography. Metuchen, N.J. : Scarecrow, 1988. 208 p. ISBN 0-8108-2080-3. $22.50.   **CH37**
Lists and describes briefly some 520 English-language books, journal articles, and U.S. and Japanese government publications covering the social and economic aspects of Japan's postwar industrial policy (primarily from a U.S. perspective). Arranged by broad subject category, with author/editor, title, and subject indexes. No newspaper or news magazine articles are included.   Z7165.J3B63

China trade and price statistics / State Statistical Bureau, People's Republic of China. N.Y. : Praeger, 1991. 181 p. ISBN 0-275-93846-8. $95.00.   **CH38**
1st ed., 1988, publ. 1987.
Presents tables of statistics in four sections: domestic trade, price indexes and average prices, foreign economic relations, and trade and tourism. Generally the statistics cover the early 1950s through 1988. Brief explanatory notes; not indexed.   HF3831.C476

Grummitt, Karsten. China economic handbook. London : Euromonitor ; Detroit : Distr. by Gale, 1986. 246 p. : ill. ISBN 0-86338-155-3. £45.00.   **CH39**
Takes as its starting point the foundation of the People's Republic of China in 1949 and ends with 1984–85. Two of the nine chapters focus on historical background (socialist economic development, the four modernizations), one discusses human resources, five consider specific economic activities (e.g., industry and energy), and one examines the new consumer markets. Statistics and charts throughout. Also includes a brief, unannotated bibliography; a directory of "useful addresses" (e.g., government ministries, foreign banks, trade organizations); and a statistical fact file. Indexed.   HC427.9.G77

The Pacific Basin : an economic handbook. London : Euromonitor, 1987. 204 p. : ill. ISBN 0-86338-139-1. £45.00.   **CH40**
Editor: Stuart W. Sinclair.
Surveys economic conditions, progress, and the future for the Pacific Basin, consisting of 34 East Asian countries and California. Chapters discuss the Pacific Basin, its composition, and its role in the world economy; political and economic issues; commodities and commodity trade; banking and capital markets; social issues; manufacturing; trade; and the future of the Pacific Basin. Each chapter includes country-specific sec-

tions and statistics. Also provides a statistical data file chapter, list of tables, and an index.   HC681.P26

Neri, Rita E. U.S./Japan foreign trade : an annotated bibliography of socioeconomic perspectives. N.Y. : Garland, 1988. 306 p. ISBN 0-8240-8471-3.   **CH41**

For 1970–87, lists and describes English-language monographs and periodical articles that discuss "socioeconomic aspects of Japanese society as well as the general and economic dynamics of U.S.-Japan trade relations"—*Pref.* Arrangement is by topical chapters and subchapters, then alphabetically by author. Author and subject indexes, plus separate indexes for book titles and periodical titles.   Z7165.J3N36

Schmidt, Marlis. Economic reforms in the People's Republic of China since 1979 : a bibliography of articles and publications in English-language magazines and newspapers. West Cornwall, Conn. : Locust Hill Pr., 1987. 177 p. ISBN 0-933951-10-8. $25.00.   **CH42**

Lists articles published in major economics and business newspapers and magazines treating economic changes that have taken place in China since 1979 under the leadership of Deng Xiaoping. Arrangement is by subject, employing the classification system used in *Journal of economic literature* (*Guide* CH37). Within sections, entries are arranged alphabetically by title of journal or newspaper, then chronologically. Author index.   Z7165.C6S35

Caribbean

Fraser, Peter D. Caribbean economic handbook / [by Peter D. Fraser and Paul Hackett]. London : Euromonitor, 1985. 241 p. : ill. ISBN 0-86338-089-1.   **CH43**

Following discussion of the Caribbean economy in a world context and an overview of the region, chapters focus on specific countries (Bahamas and Bermuda, Barbados, Cuba, Dominican Republic, Haiti, Jamaica, Puerto Rico, and Trinidad and Tobago). Separate chapters cover the smaller islands (Virgin Islands, Cayman Islands, Leeward Islands, Martinique and Guadeloupe, Netherlands Antilles, Turks and Caicos Islands, Windward Islands) and provide an economic outlook for the entire region. A statistical factfile, with most tables covering the 1970s through the mid-1980s, supplements the statistics and graphs in each of the chapters. List of tables, but no index.   HC151.F7

Central America

Central American economic handbook. London : Euromonitor, 1987. 172 p. : map. ISBN 0-86338-218-5.   **CH44**

Analyzes economic conditions and prospects in regional overview chapters (Central America in a world context, Regional interdependence, and Future outlook) and country-specific chapters covering Mexico, Costa Rica, El Salvador, Guatemala, Honduras, Nicaragua, and Panama. Statistical tables are found throughout, and a final chapter presents comparative economic and financial indicators for the past five to six years. List of tables; index.   HC141.C3785

Europe, Eastern

East European economic handbook. London : Euromonitor, 1985. 325 p. : ill. ISBN 0-86338-029-8. £45.00.   **CH45**

Although major political and economic changes have taken place since this title was published, it remains a source of useful background information. Following chapters in which the region's economic relationships with the rest of the world and the economic interrelationship of countries within the region are considered, individual chapters focus on the economies of Bulgaria, Czechoslovakia, the German Democratic Republic, Hungary, Poland, Romania, and Yugoslavia. Maps and many statistics appear throughout, and a separate chapter presents comparative economic statistics for all seven countries, generally for the early 1980s. List of tables; not indexed.   HC244.E216

Europe, Western

West European economic handbook. London : Euromonitor, 1987. 184 p. : ill. ISBN 0-86338-142-1.   **CH46**

"Examines the political, economic, and social structure of the European community and the other principal countries of Western Europe."—*Foreword.* Consists of 12 chapters, each focusing on a major theme relevant to economic development (e.g., industrial development, external trade patterns and flows.) Graphs and statistics throughout, with two statistical fact files. Indexed.   HC240.W42

Latin America

South American economic handbook. London : Euromonitor, 1986. 274 p. : ill. ISBN 0-86338-125-1.   **CH47**

For each of 11 countries, describes its land, people, political and economic structure, and, in most instances, agriculture, manufacturing, mining, transport and communications, foreign investment, foreign trade, and tourism. Includes maps and statistics. Additional chapters discuss South America's role in the world economy, the continent itself, and the economic outlook for South America and its major economies (Argentina, Brazil, Chile, Colombia, Peru, and Venezuela). Contains a statistical fact file chapter, lists of sources and tables, and an index.   HC165.S64

Oceania

Oceanic economic handbook. London : Euromonitor, c1990. 226 p. : ill. ISBN 0-86338-140-5.   **CH48**

Considers Oceania's role in the world economy and interdependence within the region, with separate chapters devoted to Australia, New Zealand, and the South Pacific islands. A final chapter considers the future of the region's trade development, economic development and growth, population and migration, and aid and investment. Contains many tables and statistics in each chapter, with a separate section of statistical tables. Indexed.   HC681.O32

Third World

Dictionary of development : Third World economy, environment, society / ed. by Brian W.W. Welsh & Pavel Butorin. N.Y. : Garland, 1990. 2 v. (1194 p.). (Garland reference library of social science, v. 487). ISBN 0-8240-1447-2. $150.00.   **CH49**

Describes major organizations, concepts, and issues relating to Third World development. Entries range from a sentence to a few pages, cross-references are numerous, and most of the longer entries contain brief bibliographies. A preliminary section, "Developing country indicators," presents demographic and economic statistics. Vol. 2 concludes with a list of national and international periodicals and newspapers devoted to development topics.   HC59.7.D513

Third World economic handbook. 2nd ed. London : Euromonitor : Distr. by Gale, 1989. 387 p. : ill. ISBN 0-86338-163-4. $80.00.   **CH50**

1st ed., 1982, by Stuart Sinclair.

Combines discussion of broad economic trends with more detailed consideration of regional issues in Latin America, Africa, West Asia, and South and East Asia. Contains charts and graphs, based on statistics issued by the U.N. and other international organizations. Six appendixes present statistics pertaining to demographics, economics, foreign trade, production, consumption, and infrastructure. Indexed.   HC59.7.S4668

Third World resource directory / ed. by Thomas P. Fenton and Mary J. Heffron. Maryknoll, N.Y. : Orbis Books, c1984. 283 p. : ill. ISBN 0-88344-509-3 (pbk.). $17.95.   **CH51**

Lists resources on "United States involvement in the affairs of Third World nations and peoples" (*Pref.*) in two principal sections, Areas (Third World, Africa, Asia and the Pacific, Latin America and Caribbean, Middle East) and Issues (food, human rights, militarism, transnational corporations, women). Each subsection lists organizations, printed resources (books, periodicals, pamphlets and articles), audiovisual resources, other resources. Entries for resources are annotated. Index of organizations; seven indexes (titles only) of resources by type (books, audiovisuals, etc.).   Z7164.U5T46

Union of Soviet Socialist Republics

Scrivener, Ronald. USSR economic handbook. London : Euromonitor ; Detroit : Distr. by Gale, 1986. 246 p. : ill. ISBN 0-86338-156-1.   **CH52**

No longer up-to-date (the most recent statistics are for 1985) but useful for background information. Includes an overview of the Soviet Union (land, people, economic growth, mining, etc.), followed by ten chapters that discuss Soviet economic history and growth, its economy in a world context, specific economic activities (e.g., finance and banking), the U.S.S.R. as a market for consumer goods, and its economic outlook. Five appendixes consist primarily of statistical tables, with lists of Soviet trade representatives in the U.K. and Sovet foreign trade organizations. List of tables; index.   HC336.25.S37

A study of the Soviet economy. Wash. : International Monetary Fund, c1991. 3 v. : ill. ISBN 92-64-13468-9. $100.00.   **CH53**

A detailed study, undertaken by the International Monetary Fund, Organization for Economic Co-operation and Development, and European Bank for Reconstruction and Development. Vol. 1 covers general economic and reform developments and macroeconomic policies and reform, v. 2 deals with systemic reforms, including prices, enterprises, foreign trade, foreign direct investment, finance, labor, and social policies; and v. 3 focuses on such sectoral issues as the environment, transportation, telecommunications, energy, manufacturing, and housing. A chapter on medium-term economic prospects and an unannotated bibliography are also included. Numerous statistical tables. Not indexed.   HC336.26.S78

United States

Government assistance almanac. 1985–86– . Wash. : Foggy Bottom Publications, c1985– . Annual. ISSN 0883-8690.   **CH54**

Compiled by J.R. Dumouchel, 1985– .

Provides information on federal assistance programs, both financial (direct payments, loans, etc.) and nonfinancial (advisory services, investigation of complaints, etc.), drawn from the *Catalog of federal domestic assistance* (*Guide* CH119). Condenses the profiles of individual programs found in the *Catalog*, adding both an introductory section on application strategies and tables that summarize funding of programs the previous year. Not needed by libraries that have the *Catalog*.   HC110.P63G69

ECONOMIC DEVELOPMENT

Dictionaries

Fry, Gerald. The international development dictionary / Gerald W. Fry, Galen R. Martin. Santa Barbara, Calif. : ABC-Clio, c1991. 445 p. ISBN 0-87436-545-7.   **CH55**

Entries, which combine paragraph-long current definitions and a "Significance" paragraph that discusses historical and current relevance, are arranged in four subject-oriented chapters: Development thinkers/theorists, leaders, and practitioners; Basic development concepts; Analytical concepts; and Development movements, projects, and organizations. Frequent cross-references, with an alphabetical list of terms, glossary of acronyms, bibliography, and detailed index.   HF1359.F79

Directories

Bartke, Wolfgang. The economic aid of the PR China to developing and socialist countries. 2nd, rev. and enl. ed. München ; N.Y. : K.G. Saur, 1989. 160 p. ISBN 3-598-10839-7.   **CH56**

At head of title: A publication of the Institute of Asian Affairs, Hamburg.

1st ed., 1975, had title: *China's economic aid.*

Focuses primarily on economic aid to developing countries, with a listing by country of some 700 projects. Entries generally include date of agreement, a brief description of the project, and a citation to the source (usually a press report) from which the information was obtained. Also includes separate chapters describing China's global aid in general terms (main regions of aid, suspension of aid, and cooperation with U.N. organizations), aid projects by category (medical aid, road construction, sports complexes, textile mills, factories, agricultural aid, and buildings), and China's aid to socialist countries. Military aid is specifically excluded. Not indexed.

Development aid : a guide to national and international agencies / researched and comp. by Eurofi (UK) Limited. London ; Boston : Butterworths ; Birmingham [England] ; N.Y. : Eurofi (UK), 1988. 587 p. : ill. ISBN 0-408-00991-8. £55.00.   **CH57**

In two main sections: (1) Multilateral aid agencies (e.g., U.N. Development Programme; African Development Bank) and (2) Bilateral aid donors, organized by continent and country. Entries, which may feature statistical tables and flow charts, generally include: origins, objectives, management, nature and scope of operations, methods of operations, funding characteristics, beneficiary countries, and contacts. Nongov-

ernment organizations are excluded. Not indexed.
HG3881.D43

The development directory : a guide to the international development community in the United States and Canada. 1988/89– . Madison, Conn. : Editorial PKG, c1988– . ISSN 1045-005X.   **CH58**
Imprint varies: 1990– , Detroit : Omnigraphics, Inc.
Presents international development directory information in two parts: Organizations and Individuals. The first lists organizations by type, location, sectors (fields of interest), and geographic area, categorizes organizational publications by sector and geographic area, and lists organizational personnel. The second presents biographical entries that include the individual's title, institutional affiliation, degrees, and publications. Indexes to individuals by sector and by geographic area.
HC60.D476

World development directory / comp. and ed. by Roger East, Miles Smith-Morris and Martin Wright for CIRCA, Cambridge International Reference on Current Affairs, Ltd. Chicago : St. James Pr., c1990. 568 p. ISBN 1-55862-067-2.   **CH59**
In three parts: (1) Intergovernmental organizations grouped by category (U.N. bodies; other global organizations; federations of financing institutions; regional intergovernmental organizations for Africa, the Americas, Asia-Pacific, Europe, and the Middle East/Arab world), each entry including: acronym; address, telephone, telex, and cable numbers; founding date; origin and aims; principal officials; structure; areas of operation; sources of finance; publications; and affiliates. (2) Official programs (statistics, distribution of overseas development assistance, and principal government agency/officer) and nongovernmental organizations (NGOs) involved in global development arranged by country. (3) Government agencies handling foreign assistance, branch offices of organizations listed in Pts. 1–2, and locally-based NGOs in developing countries (here called "south countries"). Also includes a list of NGOs classified by type and an index of country profiles and organizations.
HC60.W67

Handbooks

Social indicators of development. Baltimore : Publ. for the World Bank, The Johns Hopkins Univ. Pr., 1988. 1 v. ISBN 0-8018-3831-2.   **CH60**
For annotation, see *Supplement* CG17.   HA155.S63

ACCOUNTING

Bibliography

Brown, Lawrence D. Accounting research directory : the database of accounting literature / by Lawrence D. Brown, John C. Gardner, Miklos A. Vasarhelyi. 2nd updated and enl. ed. N.Y. : M. Wiener Pub., 1988. 583 p. ISBN 1-558-76003-2. $49.50.   **CH61**
A somewhat idiosyncratic bibliography, developed originally by merging two private databases, a citation index and an attribute index. In two sections: the first lists alphabetically by author articles published in six major accounting journals 1963–88; the second classifies the articles by four taxonomies (mode of reasoning, research method, school of thought, and treatment or subject area), with several coded subcategories for each. In addition a citation frequency index, based on the number of times a work has been cited since 1976, identifies articles

that are frequently cited. Glossary. For the serious researcher.
Z7164.C81B884

Dictionaries

Shim, Jae K. Encyclopedic dictionary of accounting and finance / Jae K. Shim and Joel G. Siegel. Englewood Cliffs, N.J. : Prentice Hall, c1989. 504 p. : ill. ISBN 0-13-275801-6. $49.50.   **CH62**
Contains clear and sometimes lengthy definitions (some more than two pages long), enhanced with formulas, charts, tables, checklists, and practical applications. Covers more than 500 topics in accounting and finance and approximately 100 topics in related fields. Indexed.   HF1001.S525

Siegel, Joel G. Dictionary of accounting terms / by Joel G. Siegel, Jae K. Shim. N.Y. : Barron's, c1987. 472 p. : ill. ISBN 0-8120-3766-9 (pbk.). $8.95.   **CH63**
Briefly defines more than 2,500 words and phrases drawn from all areas of accounting and from related fields of business and economics. Key accounting organizations are also included. Also features a brief list of acronyms and abbreviations, and compounded and present value tables.   HF5621.S54

Directories

Emerson's directory of leading U.S. accounting firms. 2nd ed. Redmond, Wash. : Big Eight Review, c1990. 381 p. ISBN 0-943945-05-4. $140.00.   **CH64**
Spine title: Directory of leading U.S. accounting firms.
1st ed., 1988.
Lists 3,000 firms with some 3,900 offices, and more than 14,000 key personnel and their functions. In three parts: (1) Key national firm information, providing besides directory information the number of U.S. and international offices and approximate U.S. and international revenues for each of the country's 13 largest accounting firms; (2) Office listings by state, including for each office address, telephone and fax numbers, up to nine staff members and their functions, number of professionals, indication of home or branch location, other firm locations, and firm functional and industry specializations; and (3) Alphabetical index to firms, listing home office first, followed by other offices in alphabetical order.   HF5616.U5E47

Handbooks

Accountants' handbook / ed. by D.R. Carmichael, Steven B. Lilien, Martin Mellman. 7th ed. N.Y. : Wiley, c1991. 1 v. (various pagings) : ill. ISBN 0-471-61979-5.   **CH65**
6th ed., 1981 (*Guide* CH146).
The two-volume, 45-chapter format of the 6th ed. has been condensed to a single volume containing 36 chapters, expanding coverage of financial and business accounting topics and adding several new chapters about specialized industries (e.g., regulated utilities and financial institutions) and areas (e.g., prospective financial statements, litigation counseling services). Indexed.   HF5621.A22

Ameiss, Albert P. Accountant's desk handbook / Albert P. Ameiss and Nicholas A. Kargas. 3rd ed. Englewood Cliffs, N.J. : Prentice Hall, c1988. 724 p. : ill. ISBN 0-13-001877-5.   **CH66**
2nd ed., 1981 (*Guide* CH147).
Emphasizes trends, techniques, and generally accepted accounting principles currently employed in business operations. Nearly twice the length of the previous edition, but now has only three sections: (1) Financial accounting, (2) Managerial ac-

counting, and (3) Standards, procedures, and reporting requirements. Indexed.   HF5635.A474

Plank, Tom M. Accounting desk book : the accountant's everyday instant answer book / Tom M. Plank, Douglas L. Blensly. 9th ed. Englewood Cliffs, N.J. : Prentice Hall, c1989. 772 p. ISBN 0-13-003559-9.   **CH67**

7th ed., 1983 (*Guide* CH148).

Originally ed. by William J. Casey.

The three sections of prior editions have been revised and updated, and nine new sections added, reflecting new accounting practices, standards, technology, and technical terminology.   HF5635.B668

Siegel, Joel G. Accounting handbook / Joel G. Siegel, Jae K. Shim. N.Y. : Barron's, c1990. 836 p. : ill. ISBN 0-8120-6176-4. $24.95.   **CH68**

Arranged in 12 sections by subject (e.g., financial accounting, government and nonprofit accounting) including a dictionary. Indexed, but lack bibliographies.   HF5635.S586

ADVERTISING AND PUBLIC RELATIONS

Bibliography

Williams, Emelda L. American advertising : a reference guide / Emelda L. Williams and Donald W. Hendon. N.Y. : Garland, 1988. 208 p. (Garland reference library of social science, v. 398). ISBN 0-8240-8490-X.   **CH69**

A briefly annotated bibliography of significant books and articles grouped by subject in four main chapters (Advertising overview, Institution of advertising, Creating the advertising, and Special types of advertising) and 24 subcategories. Most items included were published during the last 20 years, but a few "classics" date back to the early 1900s. Author index.   Z7164.C81W55

Dictionaries

Imber, Jane. Dictionary of advertising and direct mail terms / by Jane Imber and Betsy-Ann Toffler. N.Y. : Barron's, c1987. 514 p. : ill. ISBN 0-8120-3765-0 (pbk.). $8.95.   **CH70**

Offers "3,000 clear, informative definitions of key terms used in television, radio, print advertising, and direct mail campaigns" (*Cover*), including industry jargon, statistical and technical terminology, and descriptions of key professional associations and of such producers of industry information as the Audit Bureau of Circulations and A.C. Nielsen Co. Alphabetic arrangement, letter-by-letter; compound terms are alphabetized as single words. An appendix lists abbreviations and acronyms, and illustrates proofreading marks and their meanings as well as various print fonts.   HF5803.I46

Directories

National directory of corporate public affairs. 1st ed. (1983)– . Wash. : Columbia Books, 1983– . Annual. ISSN 0749-9736. $70.00.   **CH71**

In two sections: companies and people. The first lists 1,800 companies that maintain public affairs programs. Besides the usual corporate directory information, entries include when available: address of the firm's office in Washington,

D.C.; name and address of its political action committee, and money contributed by the PAC to political parties and candidates; name, address, and awards of the corporate foundation; company publications and their editors; and public affairs and related personnel at the head office, the Washington office, and elsewhere. The second section lists 12,000 corporate public affairs staff (including those in public relations, political action, corporate communications, regulatory affairs, and lobbying), giving for each: title, corporate affiliation, address, telephone, and if applicable, where registered as a lobbyist.   HD59.N24

Who's who in advertising. 1st ed. (1990–1991)– . Wilmette, Ill. : Marquis Who's Who, c1989– . ISSN 1049-1201.   **CH72**

Presents biographical sketches of some 17,500 advertising professionals from a variety of businesses, includng executives, creative directors, photographers, graphic artists, and copywriters, as well as prominent public relations specialists and marketing professionals. Besides standard biographical information, sketches list creative works, honors, and awards. Geographic and professional indexes.   HF6178.W48

Handbooks

Barban, Arnold M. Advertising media sourcebook / Arnold M. Barban, Donald W. Jugenheimer, Peter B. Turk. 3rd ed. Lincolnwood, Ill. : NTC Business Books, c1989. 122 p. : ill. ISBN 0-8442-3159-2.   **CH73**

1st ed. (Columbus, Ohio : Grid, Inc., [1975]) and 2nd ed. (N.Y. : Wiley, 1981) had title: *Advertising media sourcebook and workbook.*

Contains two-page descriptions, with reproductions of sample pages of major reference sources (categorized as media/marketing, media audience measurement, media cost sources and estimators, and media audience research estimators); includes a section of problems requiring the use of one or more of the sources described in the first section. Appendixes include a media calculation guide, a brief list of advertising media source contacts, and a glossary of advertising media terms. Indexed.   HF5826.5.A38

Dilenschneider, Robert L. The Dartnell public relations handbook : with a special section on the health care field / Robert L. Dilenschneider, Dan J. Forrestal. 3rd ed., rev. Chicago : Dartnell Corporation, c1987. 875 p. ISBN 0-85013-159-6.   **CH74**

2nd ed., 1979 (*Guide* CH175)

This edition has six main sections: (1) Public relations: an overview; (2) Public relations in the marketplace; (3) Public relations: special considerations; (4) Internal public relations; (5) Internal pubic relations: inside stories; and (6) Public relations for health care facilities. Contains photographs, case studies, annual lectures of the Foundation for Public Relations Research and Education (1981–86), and a bibliography. Indexed.   HD59.D28

Lesly's handbook of public relations and communications / ed. by Philip Lesly. 4th ed. Chicago, Ill. : Probus Pub. Co., c1991. 874 p. : ill. ISBN 1-55738-133-X. $39.95.   **CH75**

3rd ed., 1983, had title: *Lesly's public relations handbook* (*Guide* CH178).

This basic guide has been revised and expanded.   HM263.L46

BUSINESS

Guides

The basic business library : core resources / ed. by Bernard S. Schlessinger ; Rashelle S. Karp and Virginia S. Vocelli, associate editors. 2nd ed. Phoenix : Oryx, 1989. 278 p. ISBN 0-89774-451-9. $38.50.   **CH76**

1st ed., 1983 (*Guide* CH181).

Updated and revised. The bibliography now covers 1976–87. Indexed.   Z675.B8B37

Berle, Gustav. Business information sourcebook. N.Y. : Wiley, c1991. 374 p. ISBN 0-471-52976-1.   **CH77**

Intended primarily for business people rather than researchers. In six parts (Books; Periodicals; Directories; Government business references; Newsletters, association and corporate publications; and Electronics), most divided into sections by business activity or industry (e.g., accounting, beverage industry, confectionery), under which titles are listed alphabetically. Includes an assortment of reference, trade, and commercial publications. Entries are brief and generally limited to bibliographic citation, publisher's address, and price; a few include short descriptive annotations. Not indexed.   Z7164.C8B43

Encyclopedia of business information sources. 8th ed. (1991–92)– . Detroit : Gale, 1990– . Biennial with periodic supplement. ISSN 0071-0210.   **CH78**

5th ed., 1985 (*Guide* CH184); 7th ed., 1988.

Subtitle: A bibliographic guide to more than 21,000 citations covering over 1,000 subjects of interest to business personnel.

Expanded to include about 1,000 additional citations and more than 50 new topics (e.g., AIDS policy, facsimile systems, employee wellness programs); arrangement follows that of previous editions.   Z7164.C81E93

Hawbaker, A. Craig. Industry and company information : illustrated search strategy and sources / by A. Craig Hawbaker, Judith M. Nixon. Ann Arbor, Mich. : Pierian Pr., 1991. 172 p. : ill. ISBN 0-87650-287-7 (pbk.). $25.00.   **CH79**

A good basic introduction to industry and company research, with several illustrations of key reference sources, a library skills test, bibliography of additional sources, and title index.   HF5365.H38

Lavin, Michael R. Business information : how to find it, how to use it. Phoenix : Oryx, 1987. 299 p. : ill. ISBN 0-89774-157-9. $49.50.   **CH80**

A selective guide, particularly useful for its treatment of statistics, business and tax law, and trademarks, but including company and marketing information as well as business information for job hunters and consumers. Detailed coverage of major business information sources, enhanced by discussion of relevant business concepts and the inclusion of sample pages from some sources. Bibliographies; title and subject indexes. A 2nd ed. is to be published in late 1991.   HF5356.L36

Philcox, Phil. Executive's business information sourcebook. Englewood Cliffs, N.J.: Prentice Hall, c1990. 492 p. ISBN 0-13-29569-2-6. $39.95.   **CH81**

Lists and frequently annotates information sources (associations and organizations, databases, periodicals, books and directories) pertaining to 152 management topics. A cross-reference index follows the table of contents. Similar to, but far less inclusive than, *Encyclopedia of business information sources* (above), particularly in its coverage of specific industries.   HD30.35.P45

Scanlan, Jean M. Business online : the professional's guide to electronic information sources / Jean M. Scanlan, Ulla de Stricker, Anne Conway Fernald. N. Y. : Wiley, c1989. 368 p. : ill. ISBN 0-471-60838-6.   **CH82**

Combines an introduction to basic online searching and practical information about selecting hardware and vendors with descriptions of selected databases, grouped by subject (Company; News; Management, marketing and industry; Legal and tax; Accounting, economic and demographic; Patent and trademark). Discussion is enhanced by numerous examples, sample searches, and screen prints. CD-ROMs and electronic mail and messaging services receive brief coverage. Also includes a directory of online services, CD-ROM producers and distributors, gateways, and electronic mail services. Indexed.   HF5548.2.S2635

Strauss, Diane Wheeler. Handbook of business information : a guide for librarians, students, and researchers. Englewood, Colo. : Libraries Unlimited, 1988. 537 p. : ill. ISBN 0-87287-607-1. $42.00.   **CH83**

An introduction to basic business concepts and vocabulary as well as key publications and databases. The first eight chapters are format-specific; the rest focus on specific fields of business (e.g., accounting). Generously illustrated with excerpts from major reference works. 12 appendixes list, for example, business acronyms, free vertical file materials, and relevant government organizations and publications. Extensively indexed. Complements Lorna Daniells's *Business information sources* (*Guide* CH183) and Michael R. Lavin's *Business information: how to find it, how to use it* (above).   Z7164.C81S7796

Tudor, James. Macmillan directory of business information sources. London : Macmillan, 1987. [300] p. ISBN 0-333-38954-9. £35.00.   **CH84**

Aims "to provide guidance on both the published and organisational sources relevant to the needs of the non-professional business researcher."—*Pref.* Focus is on the U.K., and arrangement is by British Standard Industrial Classification codes (SICs); separate sections list foreign trade organizations in the U.K. and British trade publications. Alphabetical index to SICs and an index to organizational sources.   AA2.M4T549

Bibliography

Ball, Sarah. The directory of international sources of business information. London : Pitman ; Philadelphia : Distr. by Trans-Atlantic Publications, 1989. 698 p. ISBN 0-273-03047-7. £65.00.   **CH85**

"Covers business information sources with primary focus on companies, markets, finance, securities and economics"— *Introd.* Separate chapters contain directory listings for European business information brokers and Euro-Info centres, country data sources, industry data sources, online databases–background, and online databases–descriptions. Although print sources are listed, they are not described; the emphasis is on organizations and databases. Appendixes include directories of publishers of market research reports and database hosts and producers, a summary chart showing database country coverage and subject area, and international telephone codes and time differences. Not indexed.   HF54.5.B35

Slomanson, William R. International business bibliography. Buffalo, N.Y. : W.S. Hein, 1989. 407 p. ISBN 0-89941-665-9.   **CH86**

A comprehensive listing of English-language books published in the U.S. and elsewhere. Topical arrangement, subdivided by topic and country; entries within sections are alphabetical by title. Full bibliographic information. An appendix lists publishers.   Z7164.C8S52

Current

●**ABI/Inform** [computer file]. Louisville, Ky. : UMI/
Data Courier, [1971]– .   **CH87**
File size: 400,000+ records. Available online (DIALOG,
ORBIT, BRS, VU/TEXT, Data-Star, NEXIS, Dial Com,
Human Resource Information Network; updated weekly) and
in CD-ROM as *ABI/INFORM ondisc* (Univ. Microfilms Inter-
national, Faxon).

Indexes and abstracts articles from some 800 business and
management periodicals published worldwide. About half the
journals are indexed cover-to-cover, the others selectively. Abstracts are about 200 words long.

●**Business dateline** [computer file]. [Louisville, Ky.]:
UMI/Data Courier, 1985– .   **CH88**
File size: 30,000+ records. Available online (DIALOG,
BRS, Dow Jones News/Retrieval, VU/TEXT; updated weekly)
and in CD-ROM as *Business dateline ondisc* (Univ. Microfilms
International).

Contains the full text of articles from more than 180 regional business periodicals, newspapers, and business wire services. Useful for information on companies, individuals, and
products and services that might not be covered nationally.

●**Trade & industry index** [computer file]. Foster City,
Calif. : Information Access Co., 1981– .   **CH89**
File size: more than 3 million records. Updated weekly.
Available online (DIALOG).

Indexes and selectively abstracts some 300 trade and industry journals, 100 local and regional business publications,
and business and trade information from nearly 1,200 additional publications. A companion online database, *Trade and
industry ASAP*, contains citations and the full text of articles
from more than 200 of the major journals covered in *Trade and
industry index*.

Periodicals

Business journals of the United States / ed. by William
Fisher. N.Y.: Greenwood, 1991. 318 p. ISBN 0-313-
25292-0. $55.00.   **CH90**
Contains descriptions of more than 100 serials, arranged
alphabetically by title. The signed entries are in two parts: (1)
an essay tracing the history of the publication and describing its
current contents and special features; and (2) information such
as where indexed, availabilty of microform copy or reprints,
types of libraries where located and bibliographic notes (including title changes, volume and issue data, frequency and place of
publication, and editors). Three types of publishers are
represented—business school/university presses, professional
associations/societies, and commercial publishers. Some government publications are included, but some are omitted (e.g.,
Federal Reserve bulletin, *Survey of current business*); newsletters
and house organs are excluded. Three appendixes: a chronology of major U.S. business and economic events, with indication
of the years in which specific titles began publication; and lists
of journal titles by location and by type of publisher. Indexed.
Z7164.C81B978

Business serials of the U.S. government / Business Reference and Services Section, Reference and Adult Services
Division, Amer. Lib. Assoc. ; ed. by Priscilla C. Geahigan, Robert F. Rose. 2nd ed. Chicago : Amer. Lib. Assoc., 1988. 86 p. ISBN 0-8389-3349-1 (pbk.).   **CH91**
1st ed., 1978.
Arranged by broad subject categories: General, Economic
conditions, Demographics, International business, Industry,
Agriculture, Environment, Labor, Small business, Patents and
trademarks, Grants and contracts, Public finance, Taxation,
and Consumers. Entries include title, initial date of publica-

tion, frequency, previous title(s) and dates of publication, special features, Superintendent of Documents number, where indexed, and a paragraph-long descriptive and evaluative annotation.   Z7165.U5B88

Cabell, David W. E. Cabell's directory of publishing opportunities in business and economics. 4th ed. Beaumont, Tex. : Cabell Pub. Co., c1988. 3 v. (1436 p.).
ISBN 0-911753-03-8. $59.95.   **CH92**
2nd ed., 1981 (*Guide* CH210); 3rd ed., 1985.
Expanded to include more than 400 journals, the increased
coverage reflecting growing interest in global issues (with additional new journals from Australia, England, Europe, and other
countries) and in quantitative and economic topics. Indexed.
H91.C23

European directory of trade and business journals. London : Euromonitor, 1990. 339 p. ISBN 0-86338-339-4.
£135.   **CH93**
Lists and describes more than 2,000 major European journals concerned with Western European markets and industries.
A pan-European/international section is followed by separate
sections for 17 Western European countries. Entries, listed alphabetically in each section include: address; telephone, telex,
and fax numbers; year founded; language; frequency; editorial
content (often noting regularly published statistical data, market reports, and company rankings); readership; circulation; editor; and advertising manager. Title and subject indexes.

Dictionaries

A concise dictionary of business. Oxford ; N.Y. : Oxford
Univ. Pr., 1990. 401 p. ISBN 0-19-211667-3. $22.00
(est.). ISBN 0-19-285231-0 (pbk.). $7.00 (est.).   **CH94**
For business students and practitioners, with short definitions of terms and jargon in all fields of business and more selective coverage of economics and law.   HF1001.C63

Multinational enterprise : an encyclopedic dictionary of
concepts and terms / [comp.] by Ankie Hoogvelt with
Anthony G. Puxty ; consultant ed., John M. Stopford.
N.Y. : Nichols Pub., c1987. 261 p. ISBN 0-89397-249-5.
$50.00.   **CH95**
Clearly defines theoretical and technical terms drawn from
accounting, economics, finance, law, management, taxation,
and related fields; and includes descriptions of key international organizations. Numerous cross-references, three appendixes
(references, select list of bibliographies, and brief list of organizations), and an index of terms grouped under 13 broad categories (e.g., industry structure, international marketing).
HD2755.5.M8337

Quotations

A dictionary of business quotations / comp. by Simon
James and Robert Parker. N.Y. : Simon & Schuster,
1990. 172 p. ISBN 0-13-210154-8. $35.00.   **CH96**
Quotations are grouped under 215 topics. Entries cite the
person being quoted and the publication or other source in
which it first appeared. Author/source and keyword indexes.
PN6084.B87D54

A treasury of business quotations / [selected] by Michael
C. Thomsett. Jefferson, N.C. : McFarland, c1990. 218 p.
ISBN 0-89950-469-8. $29.95.   **CH97**
Contains some 2,000 quotations from business leaders,
philosophers, writers, and others, grouped under 117 broad
subjects. Quotations are numbered in sequence, and source

and publication date are given for each. Author and key word indexes. PN6084.B87T74

Directories

Business organizations, agencies, and publications directory. 3rd ed. (1986)– . Detroit : Gale, c1986– . Annual. ISSN 0888-1413. $275.00. **CH98**

Earlier vols. had title *Business organizations and agencies directory* (see *Guide* CH233).

With the 5th ed. (1990), revised, updated and expanded, including international as well as domestic coverage and adding fax and toll-free telephone numbers. Now organized in five categories (U.S. and international organizations, Government agencies and programs, Facilities and services, Research and educational facilities, Publications and information services) and 39 subcategories. Data for all but a handful of the subcategories are drawn from other Gale reference works, key government sources, and a few trade publications. Indexed. HF3010.B86

●**Dun's market identifiers online** : (DMI) [computer file].]. Parsippany, N.J. : Dun's Marketing Services. **CH99**

Entire file is reloaded quarterly. Available online (DIALOG).

A current directory, providing detailed information on 6.7 million business establishments with at least ten employees or $1 million in annual sales. As many as 40 searchable fields are presented (e.g., sales, number of employees, changes over time in sales or size of workforce, net worth, square footage, sales territory, type of ownership). Similar information can be found in companion databases: *Canadian Dun's market identifiers (CDMI)* (357,000 Canadian firms), *European Dun's market identifers (EDMI)* (1.8 million businesses in some 25 countries), and *International Dun's Market Identifiers (IDMI)* (2.4 million firms in 150 African, Asian, European, Central and South American, Middle Eastern, and Pacific Rim countries).

Bibliography

Directories in print. 6th ed. (1989)– . Detroit : Gale, c1989– . Annual. ISSN 0899-353X. $195.00. **CH100**

Continues *Directory of directories* (*Guide* CH256), which ceased with the 5th ed., 1988. Z5771.D55

Guide to American directories. Coral Springs, Fla. : B. Klein Publications, 1989. 12th ed. 498 p. ISBN 0-87340-006-2. $75.00. **CH101**

11th ed., 1982 (*Guide* CH257).

Subtitle: A guide to the major directories of the United States covering all trade, professional, and industrial categories. Z5771.G8

International

●**Directory of corporate affiliations** [computer file]. Wilmette, Ill. : National Register Publ. Co. **CH102**

Machine-readable version of *Directory of corporate affiliations* (*Guide* CH235) and *International directory of corporate affiliations* (1990/91).

Coverage: current. File size: 80,872 companies. Reloaded quarterly. Available online (DIALOG, Pergamon Financial Data Services).

Offers descriptive information on U.S. and multinational parent companies and their affiliates, divisions, and subsidiaries.

Directory of foreign firms operating in the United States. N.Y. : Simon & Schuster, Technical and Reference Book Division, 1989. 680 p. 6th ed. ISBN 0-8360-0031-5. $135.00. **CH103**

4th ed., 1978 (*Guide* CH391).

This edition "lists nearly 1600 foreign firms in 50 countries, and more than 2500 businesses in the U.S. which they own, wholly or in part."—*Introd.* Addresses of both foreign and American firms are given, as are, when available, telephone, telex and fax numbers, number of employees, and primary product or service. Percentage of foreign ownership of the American affiliates is frequently included.

HG4057.A21943

Directory of the world's largest service companies. 1990– . N.Y. : Moody's Investors Service and United Nations Centre on Transnational Corporations, c1990– . Annual. ISSN 1014-8507. $95.00. **CH104**

An annual survey of service companies, projected to appear in two series that will be published in alternate years. Series 1 (v. 1) offers detailed directorial, descriptive, and financial information concerning more than 200 firms in 14 alphabetically arranged industry categories. Each category includes a one-page introduction to the industry, ranked lists of the largest firms, and as many as 15 individual company profiles (the ten largest firms and others selected to provide geographical coverage.) Most profiles include address, industry designation, international standard industrial classification, directors, number of shareholders, ownership, description (history, structure, current products and markets), consolidated financial tables. Appendixes list publications of the U.N. Centre on Transnational Corporations and of Moody's Investors Service. Series 2, to provide similar coverage for 16 other service industry categories, is expected in late 1991.

Duns Europa. [1st ed.] (1990)– . High Wycombe, England : D & B Europe, Ltd., c1989– . ISSN 0957-5812. **CH105**

Issues for 1990– published in 3 vols.

Lists the largest companies in all 12 European Community countries, Austria, and Switzerland. Arrangement in v. 1–2 is by country, then alphabetically (in the language of the country) by company name. Entries include: DUNS number, address, telephone and telex numbers; list of principal directors and executives and numeric codes designating their functions; indication of exporter and/or importer status; name of parent company; nominal capital; number of employees; annual sales and percent of annual sales going to export; and net profit or loss. Vol. 3 contains ranked lists of the 10,000 largest companies and of the top 30% in each main business activity, statistical profiles (sales, SIC) by country and for Europe as a whole, company name and business activity indexes, and SIC and executive function code tables. A supplement indexes companies by principal SIC and country. Also available from the publisher on computer tape and diskette.

New ICC world directory of chambers of commerce = Nouvel annuaire mondial CCI des chambres de commerce. 1990 ed.– . Paris : International Chamber of Commerce ; [N.Y.] : ICC Publishing Corp.], 1990– . Irregular. $175.00. **CH106**

In English and French.

Lists more than 10,000 chambers of commerce throughout the world in three sections: (1) Chambers of commerce, (2) Binational chambers and chambers abroad; and (3) Regional associations of chambers of commerce. Each section is arranged by country, then alphabetically. Length of entries varies: some are limited to name and address, while others also give telephone, telex, and fax numbers; opening hours; year established; names of presidents and managing directors; number of members; and jurisdiction. Country indexes only. HF294.W73

Trade shows worldwide. 4th ed. (1990)– . Detroit : Gale, c1990– . Annual. ISSN 1046-4395. $170.00.   **CH107**

1st–3rd eds., 1985–88, had title: *Trade shows and professional exhibits directory* (see *Guide* CH741).

Now in three parts: (1) directory of ca.5,100 trade shows and exhibits (of which 2,000 are in foreign countries), presenting for each: 23 items of contact and descriptive information; (2) brief descriptions of 4,100 trade show sponsors and organizers; and (3) an overview of facilities, services, and information sources, including profiles of 540 conference and convention centers. Also features ranking lists (e.g., square feet/meters of exhibit space, number of hotel rooms needed for specific shows) and chronological, geographical, subject, and master indexes.

T394.T723

World chamber of commerce directory. 1989– . Loveland, Colo. : World Chamber of Commerce Directory, c1989– . Annual. ISSN 1048-2849. $24.00.   **CH108**

Lists U.S. chambers of commerce by state and city, giving mailing address, telephone and telex numbers, name of president, number of members, and local population. Similar information is provided for state boards of tourism, convention and visitors bureaus, economic development organizations, Canadian chambers of commerce, American chambers of commerce abroad, and foreign tourist information bureaus and chambers of commerce in the U.S. and abroad. Also lists members of Congress, key diplomats, U.S. and foreign embassy addresses, and the names and telephone numbers of U.S. Chamber of Commerce executives.

HF294.W75

WORLDSCOPE company profiles / by Center for International Financial Analysis and Research, Inc. [and] Wright Investors' Service. Bridgeport, Conn. : The Service, c1988– . $695.00.   **CH109**

An international listing of industrial, financial, and service firms that is made up of two independent sources:

(1) *WORLDSCOPE industrial company profiles* (5 v. $525.00. ISBN 0-944703-01-1), offering "complete, consistent, and comparative financial information" (*Introd.*) concerning 3,000 companies from 18 industries in 24 industrialized and emerging countries. Company profiles are listed geographically in v. 1–4: Asia/Africa/Australia, Europe, and North America (2 v.). Each profile is one page long and contains nearly 100 data elements, including general directory information, finanical data for the past six years, six-year financial ratios and growth rates, six-year per-share data and investment ratios, selected financial data in U.S. dollars, five-year annual growth rates, five-year averages of financial ratios, and accounting practices. Vol. 5 contains the user's guide, explanations of local practices in preparing financial statements, country and industry averages, worldwide company rankings, and tables of company rankings within countries, within industries and within countries by industry. Indexes of company names, countries, and industries.

(2) *WORLDSCOPE financial and service company profiles* (3 v. $245.00. ISBN 0-944703-02-X), which lists more than 1,000 firms, including commercial banks, savings and loans, real estate investment trusts, real estate companies, insurance companies, rental and leasing firms, securities brokers, and transportation and utilities. Vols. 1–2 are arranged geographically (Asia/Africa/Australia/Europe and North America); v. 3 contains a user's guide, industry averages, company rankings within country and industry, company rankings worldwide within industry, and indexes of companies, countries, and industries.

All three titles are drawn from *WORLDSCOPE*, a mainframe database maintained by the publisher, which is available on magnetic tape (publisher), online (CompuServe and the publisher) and in CD-ROM as *CD/Investment : international equities* (Lotus Development). Subsets of the mainframe database are available online (Dow Jones), and *Company profiles* on CD-ROM as *WORLDSCOPE profiles* (publisher).

Worldwide franchise directory. 1st ed.– . Detroit : Gale, c1991– . Irregular. ISSN 1056-456X. $129.50.   **CH110**

Provides information concerning some 1,574 franchising companies in 16 countries. Arranged by type of business in more than 80 categories, ranging from accounting/tax services to weight control. In addition to standard directory information, entries generally include: date founded and date began franchising; number of outlets; initial franchise fee and start-up costs; description of the business; type of franchise; equipment needed; support provided; franchise agreement information (terms of contract, renewal terms, sales royalty, selling a franchise, etc.); and source of profile. Also lists U.S. and foreign franchise consulting firms and trade associations. Master name and keyword, geographic, and personal name indexes.

United States

The corporate 1000. Mar. 1985– . Wash. : The Washington Monitor, Inc., c1985– . Quarterly. ISSN 0882-3227. $135.00.   **CH111**

Imprint varies: 1st quarter 1988– , N.Y. : Monitor Pub. Co.

A directory of manufacturers, service businesses, and utilities, all public companies; but beyond that, criteria for inclusion are vague: "revenue or asset figures are part of the criteria involved," but "other parameters, such as growth rate, media interest, and subscriber needs" (*Introd. note*) have also been considered. Arrangement is alphabetical, each entry including the address, telephone, telex and fax numbers for the corporate headquarters, a brief narrative description of the business, lists of officers and directors, and subsidiaries, divisions, and affiliates. Emphasis is on company executives rather than financial or statistical data. Indexed by parent company, subsidiary and division; by state; by industry (but not by SIC); and by the names of officers and directors. Companion volumes from the same publisher: *Financial 1000, International corporate 1000,* and *Over-the-counter 1000.*   HG4057.A15646

The corporate directory. 1989– . Gaithersburg, Md. : Cambridge Information Group Directories, 1988– . ISSN 1044-3525. $280.00.   **CH112**

Issued in 2 parts, 1989– .

Provides descriptions in alphabetic order of more than 10,000 publicly held corporations with at least $5 million in assets. Besides standard business directory information, each entry includes: stock data (52-week price range, numbers of outstanding shares and shareholders, shares held by officers and directors, and dividends); financial statistics (up to five years of sales, net income, earnings per share, and current assets and liabilities); and when applicable, *Fortune* and *Forbes* rankings. Also lists individuals, family groups, or businesses that own more that 5% of the company's stock, and percentage of ownership for each. A separate volume contains indexes: officers and directors, owners, subsidiary/parent, geographic, SIC, stock exchange, company rankings, and newly registered corporations.

HG4057.A156467

Corporate technology directory. U.S. ed. 1986– . Wellesley Hills, Mass. : Corporate Technology Information Services, c1986– . Annual. ISSN 0887-1930. $750.00.   **CH113**

Contents: v. 1, Indexes; v. 2–4, Corporate profiles, A–Z.

Describes more than 35,000 companies, subsidiaries, or divisions, public and private, of all sizes in the U.S. that manufacture or develop high technology products (advanced materials, automation, biotechnology, chemicals, computers, defense, manufacturing, medical, pharmaceuticals, photonics, services, software, subassemblies and components, telecommunications, test and measurement, and transportation). Company profiles generally include company name and address; telephone, telex, and fax numbers; executives and their departments (including research and development, marketing, purchasing, and personnel); type of ownership, date established, annual sales, and number of employees; and product codes, both SIC and those assigned by the publisher. The index volume contains indexes by firms and products. Index entries provide summary information about companies and refer to full entries in other volumes. A table converts SIC codes to CorpTech codes.

§ Available online (ORBIT) and in CD-ROM (in *SciTech reference plus* [Bowker]). Besides the printed and electronic versions, the publisher offers regional directories in printed form and on diskettes, and a hard card version. HG4057.A16

Directory of American firms operating in foreign countries. N.Y.: Uniworld Business Publications, 1987. 3 v. (1629 p.) 11th ed. ISBN 0-8360-0029-3. $175.00. **CH114**

10th ed., 1984 (*Guide* CH394).

This edition "lists more than 3,000 U.S. corporations which have over 22,500 subsidiaries and affiliates in 122 foreign countries."—*Introd.* HG4538.A1D5

Dun's directory of service companies. 1989– . Parsippany, N.J.: Dun's Marketing Services, c1989– . Annual. ISSN 1040-6395. $395.00. **CH115**

Lists the 50,000 largest U.S. public and private service enterprises—those that employ at least 50 people, have a headquarters or single location, and derive their primary income by providing services in such industries as repair, lodging, amusement and recreation, motion pictures, management consulting, engineering, accounting, and legal, health, and social services. Entries are similar to those in the *Million dollar directory* (*Guide* CH242), with which the publisher estimates an approximate 10% overlap. Indexed geographically and by SIC code. HD9981.3.D86

●**Dun's electronic business directory** [computer file]. Parsippany, N.J.: Dun's Marketing Services. **CH116**

Title formerly: *Dun's electronic yellow pages.*

Coverage current. Reloaded quarterly. Available online (DIALOG).

Presents summary directory information for 8.2 million U.S. businesses and business-related professionals, including primary and as many as 24 secondary SICs, employee size range, legal and organizational status, and the population of the city or town in which located. No printed counterpart.

●**Dun's million dollar directory** [computer file]. Parsippany, N.J.: Dun's Marketing Services. **CH117**

Machine-readable version of *Million dollar directory* (*Guide* CH242).

File size: 160,000 records. Entire file reloaded annually. Available online (DIALOG) and in CD-ROM as *Dun's million dollar disc* (producer).

Foster, Dennis L. The rating guide to franchises. Rev. ed. N.Y.: Facts on File, 1991. 236 p. ISBN 0-8160-2517-7. ISBN 0-8160-2517-7. $40.00. **CH118**

Combines descriptions and comparative ratings for more than 300 U.S. and Canadian franchises. Arranged by 16 broad industry categories, then alphabetically by name of franchise. Each profile includes: comparative ratings for industry and franchising experience, financial strength, training and services, fees and royalties, and satisfied franchisees; franchise overview and description; franchisee profile; projected earnings; franchisor's services; advertising; disputes and litigation; initial investment; contract highlights; fees and royalties; summary; and franchise highlights. Back matter includes a ranked list of the leading 350 franchise chains and franchisors and category indexes. A useful supplement to *Franchise opportunities handbook* (*Guide* CH239), which covers more franchises, but in less detail and without the ratings. HF5429.23.F676

Hoover's handbook : profiles of over 500 major corporations. 1991– . Austin, Tex.: The Reference Pr., c1990– . ISSN 1056-6279. **CH119**

Contains one-page profiles of 542 organizations, of which 29 are nonprofit or government agencies and the remainder are companies, public and private, U.S. and foreign. Information varies according to type of organization, but generally includes, in addition to standard directory data; overview; history; types of products and their brand names; current and historical financial statistics; rankings in published lists (e.g., *Fortune* 500); and major competitors. Includes a glossary, several categorized lists of the organizations included, and four indexes: profiles by industry, profiles by headquarters location, people, and companies and products.

National business telephone directory. 1st ed.– . Detroit: Published for Nicholas Pub. Co. by Gale, c1986– . Annual. ISSN 0891-3021. $95.00. **CH120**

Contains, in a single alphabetical list, addresses and telephone numbers for 429,000 establishments (i.e., corporate headquarters, plant, subsidiary, sales office, or retail location) with a minimum of 20 employees. HF5035.N284

National directory of minority-owned business firms. 1986 ed.– . Lombard, Ill.: Business Research Services, c1986– . Annual. ISSN 0886-3881. **CH121**

Originally publ. 1985 as: *National directory of minority and women-owned business firms.*

Lists approximately 35,000 firms, arranged by 4-digit SICs, then by state, city, and company name. Entries generally include the firm's name, address, telephone and fax numbers, name of contact person, date established, keyword business description, number of employees, and sales volume. Specialized information includes minority type and trading area designations, experience in government contracting, and the names of business/government agency references. Indicates firms located in Labor Surplus Area zip codes. Provides firm name and business description indexes and a list of 4-digit SICs. HD2346.U5N332

National directory of nonprofit organizations. 1st (1990)– . Rockville, Md.: The Taft Group, c1990– . $225.00. **CH122**

1st– issued in 2 v.

An alphabetical list of more than 140,000 nonprofit organizations with reported annual incomes over $100,000. Among the organizations included are nonprofit corporations; religious, educational, and charitable organizations; social and recreation clubs; fraternal beneficiary societies; and mutual insurance companies. Each entry includes name, address, and telephone; estimated range of annual income; Internal Revenue Service filing status; and a brief activity/mission description. Also features an IRS filing status table, and activity, income range, and geographic indexes. AS29.5.N38

National directory of women-owned business firms. 1986 ed.– . Lombard, Ill.: Business Research Services, Inc., c1986– . Annual. ISSN 0886-389X. **CH123**

A companion volume to *National directory of minority-owned business firms* (above), listing some 25,000 firms and following the same arrangement. HD2346.U5N333

●**Standard & Poor's register—corporate** [computer file]. N.Y.: Standard & Poor's Corp. **CH124**

Machine-readable version of *Standard & Poor's register of corporations, directors, and executives*, v. 1 (*Guide* CH247).

Coverage: current. File size: 55,000 records. Updated quarterly. Available online (CompuServe, DIALOG, LEXIS) and in CD-ROM (DIALOG).

Provides directory coverage of more than 145,000 public and private companies, subsidiaries, and affiliates.

•**TRINET company database** [computer file]. Parsippany, N.J. : TRINET, Inc. **CH125**

Coverage: current records, with file reloaded quarterly. File size: 200,000+ records. Available online (DIALOG, NEXIS).

For both public and private companies with 20 or more employees, provides directory, sales, and ownership information. Both single and multi-establishment firms are listed, but data for the latter are aggregate rather than establishment-specific. *TRINET U.S. businesses* (below) provides information on establishments.

•**TRINET U.S. businesses** [computer file]. Parsippany, N.J. : TRINET, Inc. **CH126**

Former title: *TRINET establishment database*; also called *X-Market*.

Coverage: current records, with file reloaded quarterly. File size: 400,000+ records. Available online (DIALOG, NEXIS, Control Data Corp.).

For public and private companies with at least 20 employees, provides directorial information, sales, share of market in percentage, headquarters or branch designation. Entries are specific to company establishments (i.e., headquarters or branch locales).

Ward's business directory of U.S. private and public companies. 1990– . Detroit : Gale, c1990– . Annual. ISSN 1048-8707. $995.00 (4 v. set). **CH127**

For earlier numbers, called *Ward's directory of [number] largest U.S. corporations*, see *Guide* CH248a.

Revised, reformatted, and expanded. Vols. 1–2 list alphabetically some 107,000 companies, giving up to 20 items of information for each (e.g., type of company, number of employees, sales, officers, SICs, and import/export designation). Vol. 3 provides a tabular list of companies arranged by zip code within state and also lists the 1,000 largest private and 1,000 largest public companies, the 1,000 largest employers, and has tabular analyses of companies by state, revenue per employee, and 4-digit SICs. Vol. 4 ranks companies by sales within 4-digit SICs. Company information in v. 3–4 is abbreviated and limited to address, telephone, type, sales, and number of employees; v. 4 also contains names of chief executive officers. Company name index includes primary SIC and assigned rank number.

HG4057

Financial and operating ratios

Industry norms and key business ratios. 1982–83 ed.– . [N. Y.] : Dun & Bradstreet Credit Services, 1983– . Annual. ISSN 8755-2396. **CH128**

The 1989/90 ed. provides composite financial information and 14 financial and operating ratios for the year of coverage for 800 lines of business, arranged by SIC. An appendix lists SIC codes by broad industry categories. Not as detailed as *RMA annual statement studies* (below), but useful for industries it does not cover. HF5681.R25I53

RMA annual statement studies. 1977– . Philadelphia : Robert Morris Associates, 1977– . Annual. **CH129**

Title formerly: Robert Morris Associates. *Annual statement studies*.

Provides composite financial data (current year plus five preceding years) for some 400 industries, including for each: assets, liabilities, and income data and 16 financial and operating ratios. Arranged by five broad industry categories (manufacturing; wholesaling; retailing; services; and not elsewhere classified; finance), then by industry group and SIC. Preliminary pages explain balance sheet and income data, define the ratios used, list the SICs included, and list and describe industries covered. A bibliography annotates sources that publish financial data for industries not covered. Indexed by industry.

Handbooks

The handbook of international business / ed. by Ingo Walter ; associate ed., Tracy Murray. 2nd ed. N.Y. : Wiley, c1988. 677 p. in various pagings : ill. ISBN 0-471-84234-6. **CH130**

1st ed., 1982 (*Guide* CH408).

Intended for practitioners, but useful in an academic setting. This edition, arranged in 23 chapters, omits the appendixes and all but one of the indexes from the 1st edition, but is supplemented and enhanced by a companion volume, *Handbook of international management* (below). HD2755.5.H37

Handbook of international management / ed. by Ingo Walter ; associate ed., Tracy Murray. N.Y. : Wiley, c1988. 1 v. (various pagings) : ill. ISBN 0-471-60674-X. **CH131**

Deals with "managerial issues confronting firms doing business internationally" (*Pref.*), treating such issues as marketing research, financial accounting, and technology transfer. In both volumes, chapters begin with an outline of topics, frequently contain charts and tables, and conclude with bibliographies; both are indexed. HD62.4.H36

Statistics

Business rankings annual / comp. by Brooklyn Public Library, Business Library Staff. 1989– . Detroit : Gale, c1989– . Annual. ISSN 1043-7908. $140.00. **CH132**

Continues: Business Library (Brooklyn Public Library). *Business rankings and salaries index*, 1st ed. (Detroit : Gale, 1988).

A collection of lists extracted from newspapers, periodicals, directories, statistical annuals, and other publications, arranged alphabetically by subject. Among the characteristics covered by the rankings are market shares for various products and the largest, most or least profitable, fastest-growing, or otherwise notable organizations or individuals. Each list begins with a brief description that identifies the characteristic being ranked, the criteria used, notes the total number of items in the original list, gives the first ten items from the original with a numeric value for each, and cites the source publication. Index of companies, individuals, organizations, and products. HG4050.B88

•**PTS international forecasts** [computer file]. Cleveland, Ohio : Predicasts, [1972?]– . **CH133**

Machine-readable version of *Worldcasts* (*Guide* CH208–209).

File size: 666,000 records. Updated monthly. Available online (Data-Star, DIALOG).

Combines the forecasts contained in the product and regional sections of *Worldcasts*, with the added advantage of monthly updates.

•**PTS U.S. forecasts** [computer file]. Cleveland, Ohio : Predicasts, 1972– . **CH134**

Machine-readable version of *Predicasts forecasts* (*Guide* CH207).

Covers July 1971– . File size: 467,000+ records. Updated monthly. Available online (Data-Star, DIALOG).

Updated more frequently than the printed counterpart.

History

Armstrong, John. Business documents: their origins, sources, and uses in historical research / John Armstrong and Stephanie Jones. London; N.Y.: Mansell, 1987. 251 p.: facsims. ISBN 0-7201-1846-8. $60.00 (est.).
CH135

Introduces 15 of the most typical and readily available British business documents, including prospectuses, bookkeeping records, and dealers and agency agreements. Each is covered in a separate chapter, with the text following a standard format: original purpose, sources, the information they contain, uses, cross-references to other documents, works using this source, the example, and notes. Sample documents are reproduced with varying degrees of legibility. Includes a bibliography, list of useful addresses, and index. HF5349.G7A76

Encyclopedia of American business history and biography. N.Y.: Facts on File, 1988–1990. v. 1–7. (In progress). **CH136**

Contents: The automobile industry, 1896–1920 / ed. by George S. May (1990); The automobile industry, 1920–1980 / ed. by George S. May (1989); Banking and finance to 1913 / ed. by Larry E. Schweikart (1990); Railroads in the age of regulation, 1900–1980 / ed. by Keith L. Bryant, Jr. (1988); Banking and finance, 1913–1989 / ed. by Larry E. Schweikart (1990); Iron and steel in the nineteenth century / ed. by Paul F. Paskoff (1989); Railroads in the nineteenth century / ed. by Robert L. Frey (1988).

Each volume combines biographical entries with articles discussing major companies, government and labor organizations, inventions, and legislation and legal decisions for the industry and period being covered. The signed entries range in length from one-half to ten or more pages; most include photographs and other illustrations, list publications and references, and note archives and unpublished documents. Indexed.

Geahigan, Priscilla C. U.S. and Canadian businesses, 1955 to 1987: a bibliography. Metuchen, N.J.: Scarecrow, 1988. 589 p. ISBN 0-8108-2186-9. **CH137**

Lists more than 4,000 titles concerned with business and corporate histories, biographies of business people, and nonprofit organizations. Cites primarily books published after 1954, but includes a few reprints from earlier years, some dissertations, company publications, and "substantial" periodical articles. Arranged by two-digit SIC, then by company or individual name. Indexed by company name, personal name, and author. Supplements *Studies in enterprise* (*Guide* CH277), which inspired it. Z7164.C81G32

Goodall, Francis. A bibliography of British business histories. Aldershot, England; Brookfield, Vt.: Gower, c1987. 638 p. ISBN 0-566-05307-1. $70.00. **CH138**

The main section lists works alphabetically by author, giving full bibliographic information for each title and noting the presence of indexes or illustrations, the name of the firm described, its primary SIC, and a code for the source library. Preliminary pages include an essay on the nature, new directions, and methodology of business history, the British standard industrial classification, a bibliography of business history bibliographies, libraries with business history collections, and a list of abbreviations. Company name and SIC indexes.
Z7165.G8G59

International directory of company histories / ed., Thomas Derdak. Chicago: St. James Pr., c1988–[1991]. v. 1–3. ISBN 0-912289-10-4 (v. 1). $95.00. (In progress). **CH139**

A set projected for 5 v. that aims to provide "accurate and detailed information on the historical development of 1,250 of the world's largest and most influential companies."—*Editor's note.* Each of the volumes published to date lists 250 companies, grouped by industry: v. 1, Advertising–Drugs; v. 2, Electrical and electronics–Food services and retailers; v. 3, Health and personal care–Materials. Vol. 4 is to cover Mining and metals–Retail, and v. 5, Rubber and tire–Waste. To be included, a firm must have annual sales of at least $2 billion, or be considered by the editors a leading influence in an industry or geographic region. Entries, generally two to three pages long, include the company's logo and legal name, address, telephone, ownership (public, private, government), date incorporated, number of employees, assets, and when applicable, exchange(s) on which its stock is traded. Lists subsidiaries and frequently cites sources for further reading. HD2721.I63

Manufacturing: a historiographical and bibliographical guide / David O. Whitten, ed., Bessie E. Whitten, assistant ed. N.Y.: Greenwood, 1990. 503 p. (Handbook of American business history, v. 1). ISBN 0-313-25198-3. $75.00. **CH140**

For each of 23 industries, includes a brief history, bibliographic essay, and bibliography of published and unpublished works. Chapters, written by scholars in business, economics, law, engineering, and social history, are grouped by broad industry category following the Enterprise Standard Industrial Classification (ESIC). More general works on U.S. business history are noted in the introduction. Thoroughly indexed.
HC103.M25

Nasrallah, Wahib. United States corporation histories: a bibliography, 1965–1985. N.Y.: Garland, 1987. 355 p. (Garland reference library of social science, v. 391). ISBN 0-8240-9847-1. $30.00. **CH141**

Contains "books, periodical articles, theses, dissertations, pamphlets and other company-produced literature, and corporate histories embedded in annual reports or fact sheets."—*Introd.* Arrangement is alphabetical by company name, with *see* references from popular names to legal company names, and *see also* references linking corporate name changes. Industry and author indexes. Z7164.T87N37

Orbell, John. A guide to tracing the history of a business. Aldershot; Brookfield, [Vt.]: Gower, c1987. 116 p. ISBN 0-566-05591-0 (pbk.). $35.00. **CH142**

Outlines the various information sources, including records of government agencies and associations, corporate reports on file, printed indexes, and personal records, for researching the history of British businesses. Includes an unannotated bibliography and the addresses of all record offices, libraries, museums, societies, and other organizations mentioned in the text. Indexed. HD2321.O7

Robinson, Richard. United States business history, 1602–1988: a chronology. N.Y.: Greenwood, 1990. 643 p. ISBN 0-313-26095-8. $55.00. **CH143**

"... designed to provide a basic calendar of representative events... in the evolution of U.S. business."—*Pref.* Contains descriptive historical data, arranged by year, then under categories of general news and business news. Significant individuals, specific companies, inventions, trade unions, and key business, economic, and social developments are included. Brief bibliography; detailed index. HC103.R595

Biography

Dictionary of business biography: a biographical dictionary of business leaders active in Britain in the period 1860–1980 / ed. by David J. Jeremy. London: Butterworths, 1984. v. 5 and suppl.: ill. ISBN 0-406-27340-5. **CH144**

For earlier volumes, see *Guide* CH280.
Contents: v. 5, S-Z; Suppl.: Indexes, contributors, errata. Completes the set. HC252.5.A2D53

Dictionary of Scottish business biography, 1860–1960 / editors, Anthony Slaven, Sydney Checkland ; associate editors, Sheila Hamilton . . . [et al.]. Aberdeen : Aberdeen Univ. Pr., 1986–1990. 2 v. : ill. ISBN 0-08-030398-6 (v. 1). £40.00. ISBN 0-08-030399-4 (v. 2).
CH145

Contents: v.1, The staple industries (496 p.); v.2, Processing, distribution, services (447 p.).

Offers signed biographical essays, grouped by industry. Each section begins with an introductory article tracing the history and development of the industry, followed by the biographies, listed alphabetically. Most are two to four pages long, include bibliographies of published and unpublished works, and frequently contain photographs or drawings. Each volume concludes with name and subject indexes.   HC252.5.A2D54

Ingham, John N. Contemporary American business leaders : a biographical dictionary / John N. Ingham and Lynne B. Feldman. N.Y. : Greenwood, 1990. 788 p. ISBN 0-313-25743-4.   **CH146**

Presents 116 biographies of the historically most significant business leaders, 1945 to the present. Emphasizes important business decisions rather than personal lives. Entries are generally several pages long, each including a bibliography of primary and secondary sources. Appendixes allow access by industry, company, place of business, place of birth, and black and women leaders. Indexed. A useful companion to John N. Ingham's *Biographical dictionary of American business leaders* (*Guide* CH281).   HC102.5.A2I534

Leavitt, Judith A. American women managers and administrators : a selective biographical dictionary of twentieth-century leaders in business, education, and government. Westport, Conn. : Greenwood, 1985. 317 p. ISBN 0-313-23748-4.   **CH147**

Entries treating 226 women are one to two pages long, and generally include bibliographies of works by and about the biographees. Appendix lists women "firsts," founders, presidents of colleges and universities, presidents of businesses, vice presidents of major corporations, and women in positions of national prominence. Indexed.   HC102.5.A2L37

●**Standard & Poor's register—biographical** [computer file]. N.Y., Standard & Poor's Corp.   **CH148**

Machine-readable version of *Standard & Poor's register of corporations, directors, and executives*, v. 2 (*Guide* CH247).

Coverage: current. File size: 790,000 records. Available online (DIALOG, LEXIS; updated semiannuallly) and in CD-ROM (DIALOG; updated quarterly).

Brief biographies of more than 70,000 active business executives.

Who's wealthy in America. Rockville, Md. : Taft Group, c1990– . Annual. $295.00.   **CH149**

Issued in two volumes, 1990– .

Vol. 1 lists individuals with an estimated net worth of at least $1 million. The brief entries, arranged alphabetically, may include name, address, and telephone; year of birth or age range; life-style indicators (e.g., ownership of art or a yacht, involvement in a business limited partnership); estimated net worth; alma mater(s); recent political contributions; and additional references. Vol. 2 lists people from v. 1 who are officers, directors, or 10% principal stockholders in publicly traded companies. Entries include name, address, and telephone; name of company/security; number of shares held; and nature of the individual's affiliation with the company. Also has insider stock/security, political contribution, and geographic indexes.
E154.7.W45

BUSINESS MANAGEMENT

Bibliography

Crimando, William. Staff training : an annotated review of the literature, 1980–1988 / William Crimando, T.F. Riggar. N.Y. : Garland, 1990. 341 p. (Research and information guides in business, industry, and economic institutions, 3). ISBN 0-8240-7385-1.   **CH150**

An annotated bibliography of scholarly and popular literature, published 1980–88, arranged in 22 chapters under five broad headings (Instructional systems, Assessment, Design, Implementation, and Follow-up). Each section begins with a definition, Glossary, and brief bibliographic essay discussing the sources and suggesting issues for further consideration. Citations to other works are included. Indexed by title and author.
Z5814.T4C75

Gunderson, Nels L. Pension funds : an annotated bibliography. Metuchen, N.J. : Scarecrow, 1990. 136 p. ISBN 0-8108-2328-4.   **CH151**

A selective list of books and journal articles published in the last 35–40 years, grouped by subject. Brief list of abbreviations; glossary; and author index.   Z7164.P4G85

Miller, Herbert A. Retirement benefit plans : an information sourcebook. Phoenix : Oryx, 1988. 207 p. (Oryx sourcebook series in business and management, 8). ISBN 0-89774-282-6.   **CH152**

Lists and sometimes annotates sources (i.e., those in chapters on surveys, promotional literature, periodicals, and miscellaneous sources including databases are annotated, those in the monographs and theses chapters are not). Includes a core library collection of nearly 50 titles and descriptions of relevant organizations. Author, title, and subject indexes.
Z7164.P4M54

Current

●**Management contents** [computer file]. Foster City, Calif. : Information Access Company, 1979– .   **CH153**

File size: 200,000+ records, updated monthly. Available online (BRS, Data-Star, ORBIT) and on magnetic tape.

Indexes and abstracts articles related to business and management from more than 120 English-language journals worldwide, together with proceedings, transactions, business course materials, newsletters, and research reports. Also available from the producer on computer tape.

Encyclopedias

Shafritz, Jay M. The Facts on File dictionary of personnel management and labor relations. 2nd ed., rev. and expanded. N.Y. : Facts on File, c1985. 534 p. : ill. ISBN 0-8160-1234-2.   **CH154**

1st ed., 1980 (*Guide* CH315) had title: *Dictionary of personnel management and labor relations*.

Revised and expanded, but with the same coverage of court cases, laws, organizations, journals, people, and personnel tests as well as terms. Appendixes list both the official and popular names of national unions with their acronyms and provide the text of the National Labor Relations Board style manual.
HF5549.A23S52

Dictionaries

Banki, Ivan S. Dictionary of administration and management : authoritative, comprehensive. Los Angeles, Calif. : Systems Research Institute, c1986. 1369 p. ISBN 0-912352-08-6. **CH155**

Pevious ed., 1981 (*Guide* CH308).

Revised and expanded, with brief definitions for more than 20,000 terms, concepts, and techniques; an extensive list of acronyms and abbreviations, and a bibliography. HD30.15.B36

Employee benefit plans : a glossary of terms / ed. by Debora J. Lyne. 7th ed. Brookfield, Wis. : International Foundation of Employee Benefit Plans, 1990. 174 p. ISBN 0-89154-407-0. $25.00. **CH156**

6th ed., ed. by June M. Lohman, 1987.

"Includes over 2,400 definitions derived from current Canadian and U.S. sources."—*Foreword.* Also contains a list of some 775 benefits-related acronyms and abbreviations. HD4928.N6E46

Johannsen, Hano. International dictionary of management / Hano Johannsen and G.T. Page. 4th ed. N.Y. : Nichols Pub., 1990. 359 p. ISBN 0-89397-358-0. $42.50. **CH157**

2nd ed., 1980 (*Guide* CH314), had title: *International dictionary of business*; 3rd ed., 1986.

Updated, revised, and expanded to include 6,500 entries, some with charts and diagrams and with numerous cross-references. Also features a directory of banks, trade unions, and professional and employers' associations. Two appendixes: time zones and the world's currencies. HD30.15.J64

Ott, J. Steven. The Facts on File dictionary of nonprofit organization management / J. Steven Ott and Jay M. Shafritz. N.Y. : Facts on File, c1986. 407 p. ISBN 0-8160-1282-2. **CH158**

"Presents a comprehensive set of definitions for terms and phrases related to the purpose, structures, functions, law, codes, ethics, and financing (especially fund raising) of nonprofit organizations."—*Pref.* Also defines relevant terms drawn from other fields of business and management. Includes charts and other illustrations and a brief, unannotated bibliography. HD62.6.O88

Statt, David A. The concise dictionary of management. [London] : Rutledge, 1991. [192] p. ISBN 0-415-05569-5. £9.99. **CH159**

Briefly defines basic management and organization terms from a British perspective. Some charts, numerous cross-references. HD31

Directories

Consultants and consulting organizations directory. Detroit : Gale, c1973– . ISSN 0196-1292. **CH160**

For earlier numbers and annotation, see *Guide* CH318.

Frequency varies: 2nd–7th eds., triennial; 8th ed.– , annual.

With the 10th ed., 1990, issued in 2 v.: v. 1 contains descriptive entries organized by subject in 12 sections, and v. 2 has four indexes: geographic, consulting activities, personal name, and consulting firms. HD69.C6C647

Directory of executive recruiters. Fitzwilliam, N.H. : Consultants News. ISSN 0090-6484. **CH161**

The 20th ed. (1991) contains listings in separate sections for retainer- and contingency-based executive recruiting firms. Entries generally include address, minimum salary level handled, names of key contacts, a brief description, codes for the management functions and industries handled, and the professional association affiliations considered by the firm to be important. Each section has its own function and industry indexes. Also has combined (retainer and contingency) geographic and key personnel indexes, appendixes (including a bibliography), and a series of signed essays intended for job candidates or clients of recruiting firms. HF5549.5.R44D58

International business travel and relocation directory. Detroit : Gale, c1981– . **CH162**

For earlier numbers and annotation, see *Guide* CH327.

The 5th ed. (1987) is revised and updated but otherwise similar in content and format to the preceding editions. HF5549.5.E45D56

Seminars directory. 1st ed. (1989)– . Detroit : Gale, c1988– . ISSN 1042-1866. $130.00. **CH163**

Subtitle to 2nd ed.: A descriptive guide to 8,000 public seminars and workshops in 20,000 locations, covering 2,000 subject areas of interest to business, industry, and government.

Lists and describes national and regional public seminars, workshops, and training programs, categorized under 35 major subject sections, such as management and communications. Entries include program title; vendor's name, address, and telephone; a brief description; length, cost, and location(s) of program; and remarks. Geographic and title indexes. HF5549.5.T7S392

The trainer's resource. 1981– . Amherst, Mass. : Human Resource Development Press. Annual, 1986– . **CH164**

Vols. for 1988– issued in 2 vols.

A directory of more than 500 programs for human resources training, education, and development. Arrangement is by broad subject category (e.g., management development, performance appraisal). Entries include: audience for whom intended, program description (outlining objectives and topics covered), delivery system (medium, length of program, recommended participant group size), instructional strategies, date introduced, recent users, cost, and contact organization's name, address, and telephone number. Subject, title, and vendor indexes. HD30.412.T73

Handbooks

The Dartnell personnel administration handbook / [ed.] by Wilbert E. Scheer. 3rd ed. Chicago : Dartnell Corp., 1985. 1124 p. : illus., ports. ISBN 0-85013-148-0. **CH165**

2nd ed., 1979 (*Guide* CH336).

Updated, revised, and expanded, covering over 500 topics in 13 chapters. Contains illustrations, charts, and sample forms. Indexed, but lacks a bibliography. HF5549.D3392

Handbook of human resources administration / [ed. by] Joseph J. Famularo. 2nd ed. N.Y. : McGraw-Hill, c1986. 1 v. (various pagings) : ill., forms. ISBN 0-07-019914-0. **CH166**

1st ed., 1972, had title: *Handbook of modern personnel management* (*Guide* CH337).

Revised and expanded to reflect changes in the law, attitudes, values, and life-style, with 80 signed chapters grouped by subject. Includes charts, diagrams, bibliographies, and an index. HF5549.H297

Thomsett, Michael C. The little black book of business statistics. N.Y. : American Management Association, c1990. 233 p. : ill. ISBN 0-8144-7731-3. **CH167**

Describes and illustrates how basic business statistics and graphs might be used in analyzing past events and the current business situation and in making predictions. Includes exercises, with answers in an appendix. Indexed.   HD30.27.T57

Secretary's handbooks

Taintor, Sarah Augusta. The secretary's handbook / Sarah Augusta Taintor and Kate M. Monro. 10th ed, rev. by Margaret D. Shertzer. N.Y. : Macmillan, c1988. 422 p. : ill. ISBN 0-02-610211-0. $17.95.   **CH168**
1st ed., 1929; 9th ed., 1978.

A standard handbook in two parts, the first treating grammar and good English, the second specific secretarial practices (e.g., filing, word processing, making travel arrangements), business letter writing and forms of address, sources of information for secretaries, and goals and advancement. Appendix of common signs and symbols; index.   HF5547.5.T29

Webster's New World secretarial handbook / prepared under the editorial supervision of *In Plain English, Inc.*. 4th ed. N.Y. : Webster's New World, c1989. 691 p. : ill. ISBN 0-13-949256-9. ISBN 0-13-949249-6 (pbk.) : $8.95.   **CH169**
New rev. ed. (i.e., 3rd), 1981 (*Guide* CH349).

Revised, expanded, and updated to reflect recent developments in word processing and microcomputer systems. In nine sections: The secretary today, Office correspondence, Record keeping, Special functions, Business English, Legal information, For the specialized secretary, Travel information, and General reference. Indexed.   HF5547.5.W39

COMMERCE

Seller's guide to government purchasing. 1st ed. (1991)– . Detroit : Gale, 1991– . Biennial. ISSN 1052-7443. $135.95.   **CH170**

In three sections. (1) A directory of more than 600 federal civilian and military agency headquarters and regional purchasing centers. (2) A directory of purchasing offices for all 50 states, the District of Columbia, U.S. Trust Territories, and the 100 largest cities and the 100 largest counties. Agency entries generally include: address, telephone, and name of contact person; products and services purchased; whether telephone and/or fax bids are accepted; forms required; and the availability of special programs for minority-, women-owned, and small business. (3) A bibliography of more than 600 printed and electronic information sources. Includes products and services index, a master index, "how-to" guidelines, and brief lists of trade and professional associations and of abbreviations.

Commodities

Chapman, Karen J. Commodities price locator. Phoenix : Oryx, 1989. 135 p. ISBN 0-89774-366-0. $45.00.   **CH171**

More than 150 government, trade, financial, and other serials that publish commodities price information are listed alphabetically by commodity and briefly annotated. An appendix lists databases (none of which appear in the mail list) that contain commodities prices. The emphasis is on cash ("spot") prices paid for commodities received rather than on commodities futures prices, which are not covered.   Z7164.C83C46

Commodity trading manual / [prepared by the Education and Marketing Services Department of the Chicago Board of Trade ; project ed., Christine Depp Stebbins].

[Chicago : Board of Trade of the City of Chicago, c1989]. 401 p. : ill. (some col.).   **CH172**

"A comprehensive textbook/reference guide on the futures industry covering topics from the historical development of futures markets to nuts-and-bolts description of the day-to-day operations of a futures exchange."—*Foreword*. Each of the major types of futures and options are described in separate chapters in which production, demand, world markets, futures markets, and price considerations are covered; an appendix lists contract specifications for all U.S. exchanges. Includes a bibliography, glossary, and index.   HG6049.C65

Friedman, Catherine. Commodity prices. 2nd ed. Detroit : Gale, c1991. 630 p. ISBN 0-8103-0499-6. $69.50.   **CH173**
1st ed., 1974 (*Guide* CH358)

Revised and expanded. Lists sources of prices (spot, cash, retail, and futures) for some 10,400 commodities, drawn from nearly 200 domestic and international trade publications and federal, state, and foreign government publications. Arranged alphabetically by commodity, usually giving for each: name of the commodity, source publication, time intervals for which price data are available, geographic area(s) covered, unit of measure in which the price is reported, type of price quoted, and the extent of historical price data included. An index of publishers lists the sources covered, giving frequency, subscription and single issue prices, and a brief description of the commodities prices included in addition to standard directory information.   Z7164.P94F74

Labys, Walter C. Primary commodity markets and models : an international bibliography. Aldershot, [England] ; Brookfield, Vt. : Avebury, c1987. 290 p. ISBN 0-566-05324-1. $80.00.   **CH174**

A guide to the "economics of primary commodity markets, their structure, the various forces influencing their short-term and long-term behavior, and the modeling of these markets for forecasting and policy analysis."—*Foreword*. A 40-page introductory essay on commodity analysis and modeling is followed by the bibliography, which groups entries alphabetically under broad subject categories and subcategories. Not indexed.
Z7164.C8L33

St. James world futures and options directory. 1991–92– . Chicago : St. James Pr., 1991– . Annual. $95.00.   **CH175**

A directory of more than 350 agricultural, financial, metal, petroleum, equity, and miscellaneous futures contracts and the 48 exchanges on which they are traded. The first section lists the exchanges; in addition to standard directory information, entries include a paragraph describing the exchange's structure and history, the titles and names of executives, types of contracts administered, number and types of members, the clearing organization, location of overseas offices, and the name and address of the overseeing regulatory agency. The next six sections list specific contracts, grouped by type of commodity, with entries giving the name of the exchange, the date trading began, contract specifications, delivery months, trading hours, maximum daily limit, last day of trading, delivery specifications, method of trading, commissions, and historical turnover and interest statistics. The last section lists the names and addresses of members of many of the exchanges as well as the types of commodities in which they specialize. Some U.S. exchanges do not provide membership listings. Not indexed. HG6024.A3S7

Consumerism

Directories

Consumer sourcebook. 6th ed. (1990/91). Detroit : Gale, c1989. 526 p. ISBN 0-8103-2997-2.   **CH176**
    4th ed., 1983 (*Guide* CH370).
    Subtitle: A subject guide to approximately 7,000 federal, state, and local government agencies and offices, national, regional, and grassroots associations and organizations, information centers, clearinghouses, and related consumer resources in the fields of general consumerism, aging, children and family, education, employment, energy and the environment, finance and money management, food and drug safety, funerals, government accountability, handicapped, health care, health promotion, housing and home improvements, insurance, legal services, mass communications, occupational safety and health, products and product safety, real estate, recreation and leisure, trade and commerce, transportation, travel and tourism, utilities, veterans.
    A directory, arranged by broad subject area (e.g., aging, insurance, utilities), for more than 7,300 organizations.
                    HC110.C63C638

Handbooks

Guide to European company information : EC countries. 4th ed. London : London Business School Information Service, 1990. 129 p. ISBN 0-9512201-1-X. £45.00.
                              CH177
For annotation, see *Supplement* CK124.   HD2844.5.G853

Foreign trade

Bibliography

Lutz, James M. Protectionism : an annotated bibliography with analytical introductions. Ann Arbor, Mich. : Pierian Pr., 1988. 207 p. ISBN 0-87650-249-4. $40.00.
                              CH178
    Considers the reappearance and rise of protectionism in the U.S. and other countries. Arranged by 11 subject-oriented chapters (e.g., Protectionism and the other industrialized states), with brief introductory essays, generally about three pages long, followed by annotated bibliographies of key English-language works. Includes a chronology of key dates relating to protectionism since World War II, a glossary of technical terms, and author and title indexes.   Z7164.T2L88

Żurawicki, Leon. Global countertrade : an annotated bibliography / Leon Żurawicki, Louis Suichmezian. N.Y. : Garland, 1991. 115 p. (Research and information guides in business, industry, and economic institutions, 5 ; Garland reference library of social science, v.716). ISBN 0-8240-4615-3.   **CH179**
    Lists and often annotates books, journal articles, and doctoral dissertations pertaining to countertrade (full or partial trade of one product or commodity for another). Emphasizes sources published since 1978, but includes a few earlier titles. Works "in some way significant" (*Intro.*) are annotated. Foreign publications are cited in their original language. Arranged by topical chapters, with author and subject indexes and appendixes that list doctoral dissertations and countertrade periodicals.   Z7164.C8Z87

Directories

Directory of foreign trade organizations in Eastern Europe : Bulgaria, Czechoslovakia, East Germany, Hungary, Poland, Romania, and the U.S.S.R. 2nd ed. San Francisco : International Trade Pr., 1989. 359 p. ISBN 0-926476-01-7. $125.00.   **CH180**
    Lists and describes more than 1,800 export/import organizations and other enterprises engaged in foreign trade activities, including chambers of commerce, banks, state committees, commercial agents, and embassies. Arrangement is by country, with a preliminary list of organizations grouped by standard international trade classification. Texts of selected International Chamber of Commerce publications are included. Indexed. A 3rd ed. was publ. 1990.   HF3500.7.A48D57

Loiry, William S. The U.S.-Eastern European trade sourcebook : an invaluable reference for doing business in Poland, Hungary, Czechoslovakia, Yugoslavia, Bulgaria, Romania, and Albania. Chicago : St. James Pr., 1991. 269 p. ISBN 1-55862-156-3.   **CH181**
    In two main parts: U.S. resources and East European resources. The first lists, in 13 classified sections (e.g., Advertising and promotion, Communication and shipping, Translators and interpreters) contacts, companies, and organizations; entries include brief descriptions of the services offered in addition to standard directory information. The second part has separate sections for each of the countries covered, each beginning with a single-page summary of the country's demographic, political, and economic conditions. The entries are generally limited to directory information. Also includes a 36-page "yellow pages" section in which some of the organizations from the first two parts are listed alphabetically. Not indexed.

———— The U.S.-Soviet trade sourcebook. Chicago : St. James Pr., 1991. 283 p. ISBN 1-55862-142-3.
                              CH182
    A directory in 14 sections covering organizations and individuals in consulting and trading, law, government, finance, insurance, and other fields. Entries generally include a brief description as well as name, address, telephone and fax numbers, and contact person. Appendixes list registered U.S.-Soviet joint ventures and major Soviet legislation and decrees affecting foreign trade. No indexes.

Handbooks

The Australian business and investment guide. Chicago : St. James Pr., 1987. 672 p. : ill. ISBN 0-912289-78-3. $55.00.   **CH183**
    In four main parts. Pt. 1, Current opinion, presents articles by political and industrial leaders on Australia's economy, politics, and foreign trade, and by others on lifestyle and humor. Pt. 2 focuses on the business climate, covering international business; new directions in business and investment; leading companies; legal, fiscal and industrial framework; the states and territories; and tourism and migration. Pt. 3 contains information about the publication's sponsors, and Pt. 4 is a business directory, divided by type of industry. Each industry segment begins with essays describing the current situation, followed by directory listings that frequently include brief narrative descriptions of organizations in addition to standard business directory information. All directory entries are indexed.
                           HF5292.A97

Brooke, Michael. Handbook of international trade / Michael Brooke and Peter Buckley. London : Macmillan, 1988. [500] p. ISBN 0-333-45333-6. £125.00.   **CH184**
    In eight topical sections: Strategic issues; Export and import; Licensing, franchising, and other contractural arrangements; Foreign investment; Key markets; Special industrial sec-

tors; Influence of treaty organisations; and Sources of information. The sections are divided into chapters, which frequently incorporate charts, statistics, and bibliographies. The emphasis is British. Indexes of: subjects; abbreviations; countries and regions; treaties, companies and other relevant organizations; and publications.   HF1008

International business handbook / V.H. (Manek) Kirpalani, ed. N.Y. : Haworth Pr., c1990. 667 p. : ill., map. (Haworth series in international business, #1). ISBN 0-86656-862-X. $79.95.   **CH185**

"Designed to inform succinctly about global trends, different regions and their consumer cultures and business customs, methods of entry, and global strategies."—*Pref.* Chapters, all by specialists, are signed. The first is a global overview, the last a consideration of the future; the remaining 15 treat specific countries or regions. Although style varies, chapters generally discuss 15 topics, presenting an overview of economic, physical, sociocultural, political, legal, technological, international, and other factors. Sources of information are also discussed, and each chapter concludes with a bibliography. Country/geographic area and name indexes.   HF1379.I567

Transportation

Bibliography

Trucksource. Alexandria, Va. : American Trucking Associations, Information Center, c1988– . Annual. ISSN 1044-1506.   **CH186**

An annotated bibliography in three parts: (1) Trucking fundamentals, containing entries categorized by format (bibliographies, databases, dictionaries, directories, periodicals, statistical sources, videos); (2) Trucking business, with entries grouped by business activity; and (3) Trucking and the law. Also includes a list of industry contacts and an index. A pamphlet listing American Trucking Associations staff specialists and their telephone numbers and areas of expertise is attached to the inside back cover.   HE5623.A45T73

Dictionaries

Transportation-logistics dictionary / Joseph L. Cavinato, ed. 3rd ed. Wash. : International Thomson Transport Pr., 1989. 312 p. ISBN 0-87408-050-9. $29.95.   **CH187**

More than 4,800 terms relating to systems, operations, equipment, personnel, organizations, and the history of transportation and logistics. A list of acronyms, summary of key legislation and regulations, and standard operational information (metric conversion formulas, state postal abbreviations, and U.S. and foreign time differences) are also included.   HE141.T69

Aviation

Hall, R. J. Dictionary of aviation / R.J. Hall and R.D. Campbell. Chicago : St. James Pr., c1991. 346 p. ISBN 1-55862-106-7. $45.00.   **CH188**

Contains brief definitions of English aeronautical terms as they are used in Europe and the U.S. Terms used only in the U.S. are so designated. Selective cross-references. Also features an extensive list of relevant acronyms and abbreviations.   TL509.H25

Miletich, John J. Airline safety : an annotated bibliography. N.Y. : Greenwood, 1990. 222 p. (Bibliographies

and indexes in psychology, no. 7). ISBN 0-313-27391-X. $45.00.   **CH189**

Lists and briefly describes some 650 books, journal articles, conference proceedings, government documents, and theses published 1960–90. Titles are listed alphabetically in 11 subject-oriented chapters (e.g., Collision avoidance, Airline deregulation). Includes a brief acronyms list and author and subject indexes.   HE9784.M56

Ships

Brodie, Peter R. Dictionary of shipping terms. London ; N.Y. : Lloyd's of London Pr., 1985. 155 p. ISBN 1-85044-069-7 (pbk.). £15.50.   **CH190**

Briefly defines terms used by ship owners and brokers, tramp and liner operators, freight forwarders, ship's agents, loading brokers, exporters, and importers. Intended for students and those new to the trade.   HE567.B68

Kludas, Arnold. Die Geschichte der deutschen Passagierschiffahrt. Hamburg : E. Kabel, c1986–1989. v. 1–4 : ill. (some col.). ISBN 3-8225-0037-2 (Bd. 1).   **CH191**

Contents: v. 1, Die Pionierjahre von 1850 bis 1890; v. 2, Expansion auf allen Meeren 1890 bis 1900; v. 3, Sprunghaftes Wachstum 1900 bis 1914; v. 4, Vernichtung und Wiedergeburt 1914 bis 1930.

A history of German passenger ship trade, 1850–1990. Contains photographs of ships with charts outlining their specifications and history. Indexed.   HE601.G3K58

Sullivan, Eric. The marine encyclopaedic dictionary. 2nd ed. London ; N.Y. : Lloyd's of London Pr., 1988. 470 p. ISBN 1-85044-127-8.   **CH192**

1st ed., Valletta, Malta : Gulf Publ., 1980.

Contains thousands of maritime and technical terms, expressions, and acronyms used by those in the business of shipping, navigation, marine insurance, maritime and commercial law, chartering and operation of ships, and general commerce. Definitions range in length from a phrase to a paragraph. Not illustrated.   HE567.S95

Annuals

Maritime services directory. 1989–1990– . San Diego, Calif. : Aegis Publications, c1989– . Annual. ISSN 1056-1692. $85.00.   **CH193**

Combines directory information with industry analysis and statistics in three main parts. Pt. I lists by broad category some 4,000 firms (shipbuilding and repair, marine products, professional service firms, vessel operation and marine services, and cargo handling and management). Entries vary but generally include: address, telephone and fax numbers; key personnel; and a brief description of the business. Some 100 national and regional associations and schools are also listed. Pt. II lists relevant regional and federal government agencies and personnel (with organization charts for many of the key federal agencies). Pt. III, Trends and statistics, contains data on government ship repair and construction programs, labor and materials price trends, oceanborne trade and container statistics, a vessel inventory report, and U.S. shipbuilding and repair assets. Includes a glossary of maritime terms and company and advertiser indexes.

Communications

Snow, Marcellus S. Telecommunication economics and international regulatory policy : an annotated bibliography / comp. by Marcellus S. Snow and Meheroo Jussawalla. N.Y. : Greenwood, 1986. 216 p. (Bibliographies and indexes in economics and economic history, no. 4). ISBN 0-313-25370-6. $39.95.   **CH194**

Offers 16 topical chapters in three parts. Pt. 1, Conceptual and theoretical background, addresses economic issues; Pt. 2, Technological, institutional, and legal framework, focuses on telecommunications; Pt. 3 Empirical, policy, and future studies; research agendas, combines economics and telecommunications. Emphasizes scholarly books and journal articles published in the late 1970s and the 1980s, although a few "classic" works published earlier are also included. Annotations are thorough and sometimes evaluative. Brief acronyms list; author and subject indexes.   Z5834.T4S56

Dictionaries

Machovec, George S. Telecommunications and networking glossary. Chicago : Library and Information Technology Association, 1990. 64 p. (LITA guides, 3). ISBN 0-8389-7476-7.   **CH195**

Contains brief, nontechnical definitions, intended for librarians, information managers, and students, of key terms and acronyms. Brief, selective bibliography.   TK5102.M33x

Mass media

Bibliography

Blum, Eleanor. Mass media bibliography : an annotated guide to books and journals for research and reference / Eleanor Blum and Frances Goins Wilhoit. 3rd ed. Urbana : Univ. of Illinois Pr., c1990. 344 p. ISBN 0-252-01706-4.   **CH196**

Title varies: 2nd ed., 1980, called *Basic books in the mass media* (*Guide* CH495).

Revised, updated, and expanded, with 1,947 entries for works published mainly 1980–87. Arranged by type of media (general communications, broadcasting, print, film, advertising and public relations) or by publication format (bibliographies, directories and handbooks, journals, and indexes). Author, title, and subject indexes.   Z5630.B55

Greenfield, Thomas Allen. Radio : a reference guide. N.Y. : Greenwood, 1989. 172 p. ISBN 0-313-22276-2.   **CH197**

Presents "an evaluative survey of available research materials."—*Pref.* An introduction that surveys the history of American broadcast radio is followed by eight topical chapters (Radio networks and station histories; Drama; News; Music; Comedy and variety; Sports; Miscellaneous subjects; and Organizations, collections, journals, and indexes). In each, a bibliographic essay, seven to 22 pages long, is followed by an unannotated bibliography. Generally, textbooks are excluded but dissertations are cited with some frequency. Indexed.   Z7224.U6G74

Lent, John A. Global guide to media & communications. München ; N.Y. : K.G. Saur, 1987. 145 p. ISBN 3-598-10746-3. $70.00.   **CH198**

Selectively lists and sometimes briefly annotates books, dissertations and theses, monographs, and some journal articles relating to mass media. Generally arranged by continent, then by country; the U.S. is omitted because "there are numerous bibliographies on the market."—*Pref.* Some parts of the bibliographies appeared first in 1975–78 issues of the *Journal of broadcasting*, but have been updated through 1984. Not indexed.   Z5630.L3984

McKerns, Joseph P. News media and public policy : an annotated bibliography. N.Y. : Garland, 1985. 171 p. (Public affairs and administration series, 11 ; Garland reference library of social science, v. 219). ISBN 0-8240-9004-7. $39.00.   **CH199**

A select, annotated list of philosophical, theoretical, and quantitative research and popular writings on the relationship between mass media and the government. Includes more than 700 items, arranged by subject in ten chapters. Author and subject indexes.   Z6944.G68M38

Müller, Werner. Children and families watching television : a bibliography of research on viewing processes / comp. by Werner Müller and Manfred Meyer. München ; N.Y. : K.G. Saur, 1985. 159 p. (Communication research and broadcasting, no. 7). ISBN 3-598-20206-7 (pbk.).   **CH200**

Lists and categorizes empirical research on the behavior of children (ranging in age from two to twelve) as "recipients" of television programs and their interactions with family and peers while viewing. Arranged in four parts: Bibliographies, introductory literature; Reception processes (with separate chapters for attention, comprehension, arousal and emotions, cognition, fantasy and reality, social perception, and media literacy); View situation (with chapters on viewing behavior, parental influence and the family, and peers); and Media action. Sources cited were published 1975–85 in English, French, or German. Author and subject indexes.   Z7164.C5M8413

Signorielli, Nancy. Role portrayal and stereotyping on television : an annotated bibliography of studies relating to women, minorities, aging, sexual behavior, health, and handicaps / comp. and ed. by Nancy Signorielli ; with the assistance of Elizabeth Milke and Carol Katzman. Westport, Conn. : Greenwood, 1985. 214 p. (Bibliographies and indexes in sociology, no. 5). ISBN 0-313-24855-9.   **CH201**

Research sponsored by the Corporation for Public Broadcasting.

A bibliography of articles in scholarly and popular journals, books, and U.S government publications, listed alphabetically by author in five sections: Women and sex-roles, Racial and ethnic minorities, Aging and age-roles, Sexual behavior and orientations, and Health and handicaps. Entries give citation and, when applicable, a description of the sample used in the research and an abstract of the results. Dissertations and conference proceedings excluded. Author and subject indexes.   Z7711.S53

———— Violence and terror in the mass media : an annotated bibliography / comp. by Nancy Signorielli and George Gerbner. N.Y. : Greenwood, 1988. 233 p. (Bibliographies and indexes in sociology, no. 13). ISBN 0-313-26120-2.   **CH202**

Lists and briefly annotates scholarly and popular periodical articles, books, government reports, and selected conference papers and dissertations published through Spring 1987. Four major subjects covered: violence and mass media content, violence and mass media effects, pornography, and terrorism. Author and subject indexes.   Z5633.V56S56

Snorgrass, J. William. Blacks and media : a selected, annotated bibliography, 1962–1982 / comp. by J. William Snorgrass and Gloria T. Woody. Tallahassee : Univ. Presses of Florida, c1985. 150 p. ISBN 0-8130-0810-7. $12.00.   **CH203**

Lists and briefly annotates "over 700 books, journal and magazine articles and other printed materials concerning blacks in America and their relationship to mass media."—*Pref.* Arranged in four broad categories—print media, broadcast media, advertising and public relations, and film and theater—then by type (books, chapters/sections in books, journal articles, magazine articles, other sources). Author and title index.

Z5633.A37S56

Encyclopedias

Hudson, Robert V. Mass media : a chronological encyclopedia of television, radio, motion pictures, magazines, newspapers, and books in the United States. N.Y.: Garland, 1987. 435 p. (Garland reference library of social science, v. 310). ISBN 0-8240-8695-3. **CH204**

Presents brief summaries of significant events in mass media history, 1638–1985. Events are arranged chronologically within periods (e.g., American Revolution, the Jazz Age), each period divided into sections by medium (books, broadsides, pamphlets; newspapers; magazines; motion pictures; and radio and television). An introductory essay, Trends in mass media history, precedes the chronology. Indexed.　　P92.U5H77

International encyclopedia of communications / Erik Barnouw, ed. in chief... [et al.]. N.Y. ; Oxford : Oxford Univ. Pr., c1989. 4 v. : ill. ISBN 0-19-504994-2. $350.00.　　**CH205**

"Published jointly with the Annenburg School of Communications, University of Pennsylvania."

Attempts to "define, reflect, summarize, and explain" (*Foreword*) the field of communications, interpreted broadly. Coverage extends from cuneiform tablets to communication satellites, and articles examine verbal and nonverbal communication, current communication processes, and the role and influence of the arts, science, commerce, historical events, and social activities in the diffusion of ideas. Signed entries are arranged alphabetically and frequently contain illustrations and brief bibliographies. In some instances, articles on related topics are clustered together under a single heading. Directory of contributors, topical guide, and analytical index in v. 4.

P87.5.I5

Dictionaries

The broadcast communications dictionary / Lincoln Diamant, ed. in chief. 3rd ed., rev. and expanded. N.Y. : Greenwood, 1989. 255 p. ISBN 0-313-26502-X.　**CH206**

2nd ed., 1978 (*Guide* CH513).

Coverage has been expanded to 6,000 terms and a brief bibliography of more detailed technical reference works has been included.　　PN1990.4.D5

Broadcast research definitions / National Association of Broadcasters ; ed. by James E. Fletcher. [3rd ed.]. Wash. : NAB, c1988. 75 p. ISBN 0-89324-039-7. **CH207**

2nd ed., 1970, had title: *Standard definitions of broadcast research terms.*

Contains brief, clear definitions of broadcasting, statistical, and technical terms, some with illustrations. No cross-references; brief bibliography.　　PN1992.18.B651

DeVito, Joseph A. The communication handbook : a dictionary. N.Y. : Harper & Row, c1986. 337 p. : ill. ISBN 0-06-041638-6 (pbk.).　　**CH208**

Briefly defines more than 2,000 terms, with extended essays on 100 additional terms relating to communication theory and practical communication tasks such as public speaking. Includes graphs, illustrations, and a list of the essays.　P87.5.D46

Weiner, Richard. Webster's New World dictionary of media and communications. N.Y. : Webster's New

World : Distr. by Prentice Hall Trade Sales, c1990. 533 p. ISBN 0-13-969759-4. $29.95.　　**CH209**

Briefly defines words from a variety of fields, including sales and advertising, broadcasting and publishing, and computers and computer graphics. Also lists and describes leading companies, and trade and professional associations.

P87.5.W45

Handbooks

International directory of telecommunications : market trends, companies, statistics, and personnel / consultant editors, Steven Roberts, Tony Hay. 3rd ed. Burnt Mill, Harlow, Essex, England : Longman, 1988. 319 p. ISBN 0-582-01890-0. £85.00.　　**CH210**

1st ed., 1984.

Twelve geographically-based chapters, covering more than 100 countries, present telecommunications statistics, describe the region's current situation (regulations, technological capabilities, market trends), and profile regulatory agencies and public and private companies that supply equipment or services. Profiles generally include address; telephone and telex; type of organization; parent company; activities; operational sites; sales; number of staff; and publications. Includes a glossary and five indexes: companies/organizations, product area, services, registered trade name, and personal name.　HE7621.I52

Steinberg, Cobbett. TV facts. Rev. and expanded ed. N.Y. : Facts on File, c1985. 541 p. ISBN 0-87196-312-4. $17.95.　　**CH211**

1st ed., 1980 (*Guide* CH520).

Format and contents follow those of the previous editions, with coverage extended in many sections to 1984–85.

PN1992.18.S75

FINANCE AND BANKING

Bibliography

Balachandran, M. A guide to statistical sources in money, banking, and finance. Phoenix : Oryx, 1988. 119 p. ISBN 0-89774-265-6. $45.00.　　**CH212**

A select, annotated bibliography, containing primarily serial reference sources that provide banking and monetary statistics. Arranged by broad geographic category (state, regional, national, foreign, and international), with databases listed in a separate section. Directory of publishers; subject and title indexes.　　Z7164.F5B23

Deuss, Jean. Banking in the U.S : an annotated bibliography. Metuchen, N.J. : Scarecrow, 1990. 164 p. ISBN 0-8108-2348-9. $22.50.　　**CH213**

Lists and annotates "basic books in the history, organization, regulation, and management of U.S. banks and banking."—*Introd.* Citations are arranged by subject in ten chapters; in all but the history chapter, only monographs published since 1984 are included. Two additional chapters list reference sources (bibliographies, dictionaries, and encyclopedias) and serials (indexes; directories, yearbooks, and annual reports; periodicals and newspapers; and services). Appendixes contain acronyms and abbreviations, a chronology of banking landmarks, and brief directory listings of regulatory agencies and trade associations. Author and title indexes.　Z7164.F5D48

Fisher, William Harvey. Financial journals and serials : an analytical guide to accounting, banking, finance, insurance, and investment periodicals. N.Y. : Greenwood,

1986. 201 p. (Annotated bibliographies of serials, no. 6). ISBN 0-313-24195-3. $37.50.   **CH214**

Lists more than 500 English-language titles, including scholarly journals, popular periodicals, newsletters, looseleaf services, association publications, and house organs. Entries, grouped under the topics in the subtitle, generally include (besides an evaluative annotation): date first published; title changes; frequency of publication; 1984–85 subscription prices for individuals and institutions; publisher's and editor's names and addresses; illustrations, advertisements, and indexes; manuscript selection policy; availability of reprints and sample issues; book reviews and special issues; where indexed; and target audience. Front matter includes a table of abbreviations and directories of indexes and abstracts, microform and reprint publishers, and databases. Geographic, title, publisher, and subject indexes.   Z7164.F5F53

Hulbert, Mark. The Hulbert guide to financial newsletters. 4th ed. N.Y. : New York Institute of Finance, 1991. 450 p. : ill. ISBN 0-13-441460-8.   **CH215**

Title varies: *Hulbert financial digest annual review of investment newsletters* (Reston, Va. : Reston Pub., 1985); *Second Hulbert financial digest almanac* (Wash. : Minerva, 1988).; *The Hulbert guide to financial newsletters* (3rd ed. Chicago : Probus, 1989).

Describes and evaluates 100 investment advisory newsletters, giving for each: address; telephone; name of editor; annual subscription; availability of telephone and money management services; a reproduction of the cover page; text that describes the publication and its investment philosophy; and a graph that compares the publication's investment performance with that of the Standard & Poor's 500 composite index. Rankings in the appendixes rate newsletters for their performance during specified time periods between 1980 and mid-1990 and risk-adjusted performance during the same period.   HG4529.H86

The individual investor's guide to investment publications. Chicago : International Pub. Corp., c1988. 269 p. ISBN 0-942641-07-8.   **CH216**

Lists newsletters and other serials "covering mutual funds, stocks, bonds, international investing, collectibles, real estate, financial planning, forecasting, and many other subjects . . . "—*Pref.* Section 1, arranged by investment category, lists and describes (but does not evaluate) 600 titles. Entries include: publisher and address; editor's name, background, and qualifications; editorial philosophy; publication description; format; frequency; average number of pages; subscription prices; circulation; date of first issue; and special publisher's offers. Alphabetical lists of titles and publishers are appended. Section 2 lists and gives addresses for some 800 additional publications, and lists 100 more that the editors were unable to confirm as still being published. Indexed.   Z7164.F5I52

Investment newsletters. N.Y. : Larimi Communications Associates, 1988. 436 p. ISBN 0-935224-46-7.   **CH217**

Alphabetically lists and describes, but does not evaluate, U.S. investment newsletters and advisory services. Entries typically include address, telephone, editor, type of readership, frequency, circulation, length and cost, topics covered, and types of releases and reports each newsletter would like to receive from corporate public relations and investor relations professionals.

Marshall, Marion B. Public finance : an information sourcebook. Phoenix : Oryx, 1987. 287 p. (Oryx sourcebook series in business management and management, no. 6). ISBN 0-89774-276-1.   **CH218**

Intended for those unfamiliar with the basic concepts or literature of the field. Lists and annotates sources, grouped by subject (e.g., theory, state and local fiscal policy, intergovernmental fiscal relations), and identifies and annotates 28 titles for a core library collection. Author, title, and subject indexes.   Z7164.P9555M38

Indexes

Chapman, Karen J. Investment statistics locator. Phoenix : Oryx, 1988. 182 p. ISBN 0-89774-367-9. $45.00.   **CH219**

Lists, in alphabetic order, market indicators and other investment statistics that are published regularly in 22 standard investment serials such as *Value line* and the *Wall Street journal.* Under each topic, entries are listed in order of frequency of issuance of the statistic being covered (e.g., sources that publish hourly reports of the Dow Jones Industrial Average precede those that publish weekly or monthly versions).   Z7164.C18C47

●**Investext** [computer file]. Boston : Thomson Financial Networks, Inc., 1982– .   **CH220**

File size: 1.4 million records. Updated weekly. Available online (DIALOG, Dow Jones News/Retrieval, INVESTEXT/ PLUS, Mead Data Central, NewsNet) and in CD-ROM (Information Access Co.).

Contains the full text of some 200,000 company and industry reports written by analysts at 120 brokerage houses, investment banks, and research firms. Coverage includes 15,000 publicly traded companies worldwide and more than 50 industry groups.

Encyclopedias

Colby, Robert W. The encyclopedia of technical market indicators / Robert W. Colby and Thomas A. Meyers. Homewood, Ill. : Dow Jones-Irwin, c1988. 581 p. : ill. ISBN 1-55623-049-4. $50.00.   **CH221**

For sophisticated investors or students. In two parts: (1) signed essays focusing on methods of evaluating technical market indicators, and (2) descriptions of more than 100 indicators of stock market performance (e.g., advance/decline divergence oscillator, confidence index, presidential election cycle), arranged alphabetically. Entries vary in length; most occupy at least half a page and frequently contain charts, graphs, and other illustrations. Appendix of indicator interpretation definitions; index.   HG4915.C56

Encyclopedia of investments / ed. in chief, Jack P. Friedman. 2nd ed. Boston : Warren, Gorham & Lamont, c1990. 964 p. : ill. ISBN 0-7913-0365-9. $98.00.   **CH222**
    1st ed., 1982 (*Guide* CH548).

Articles, written by experts, discuss 48 different types of investments, including both traditional investment mediums and nontraditional (e.g., horses, sports memorabilia). Articles follow standard format, covering basic characteristics, attractive features, potential risks, and tax consequences. The types of investors that typically choose the medium are described, and each chapter generally includes a glossary, a suggested reading list, and a directory of dealers and brokers. A separate section, Investment strategy, contains articles intended to provide "a unifying framework for assembling and assessing a portfolio."—*Pref.* Indexed.   HG4527.E5

Fraser, Robert. The world financial system. Burnt Mill, Harlow, Essex, England : Longman ; Phoenix : Oryx, c1987. 582 p. ISBN 0-89774-473-X.   **CH223**

In three parts. Pt. 1 discusses the evolution of the world financial system, covering such developments as the Marshall Plan, the formation of the International Monetary Fund (IMF), and Third World country indebtedness, providing numerous statistical tables and texts of significant agreements excerpted or printed in their entirety. Pt. 2, International economic organizations, lists some 50 organizations, grouped geographically under four headings (general, monetary, developmental, and trade), giving besides standard directory information, extensive discussion of the organization's background, objectives, membership, and structure. Pt. 3, U.N. declarations, lists, describes, and reprints the text of relevant U.N. declarations. Three appendixes: Independence, U.N. and IMF membership; Country nomenclature; Exchange rate movements 1970–86. Brief bibliography; index.   HG3881.F7118

Munn, Glenn G. Encyclopedia of banking & finance / Glenn G. Munn, F.L. Garcia, Charles J. Woelfel. 9th ed., rev. and expanded. Chicago : St. James Pr., 1991. 1097 p. : ill. ISBN 1-55862-141-5. $95.00.   **CH224**
   8th ed., 1983 (*Guide* CH553).
   Revised and expanded to cover technological and institutional changes and developments, with nearly 4,200 entries.
                                                     HG151.M8

Dictionaries

Banking terminology. 3rd ed. Wash. : Education Policy & Development, American Bankers Association, c1989. 409 p. ISBN 0-89982-360-2. $30.00 (est.).   **CH225**
   1st ed., 1981.
   Defines new terms and updates existing terminology in banking and financial services and such related fields as accounting, marketing and sales, and real estate. Numerous cross-references. Five appendixes: acronyms and abbreviations, common bank performance ratios, glossary of economic indicators, the addresses and telephone numbers of Federal Reserve banks by district, and the addresses and telephone numbers of other organizations and agencies useful to bankers.
                                                     HG151.B268

A desktop reference manual of compliance terms / Regulatory Compliance Associates, Inc. Rolling Meadows, Ill. : Bankers Publ. Co., 1990. 210 p. ISBN 1-55520-135-0 (pbk.).   **CH226**
   Defines major banking and regulatory terms, with a glossary of regulations, list of acronyms, and index.

Downes, John. Dictionary of finance and investment terms / John Downes, Jordan Elliot Goodman. 2nd ed. N.Y. : Barron's, c1987. 495 p. : ill. ISBN 0-8120-4631-5. $9.95.   **CH227**
   1st ed., 1985 (*Guide* CH547). A 3rd ed. is expected in 1991.
   Defines new terms and updates traditional vocabulary used for banking, corporate finance, and such investment mediums as stocks, bonds, mutual funds, commodities, and options, both domestic and worldwide.   HG151.D69

Fitch, Thomas P. Dictionary of banking terms / by Thomas P. Fitch ; consulting editors, Irwin Kellner, Donald G. Simonson, Ben Weberman. N.Y. : Barron's, c1990. 698 p. ISBN 0-8120-3946-7 (pbk.). $9.95. **CH228**
   Concise definitions of key terms and descriptions of government agencies and other organizations. Also includes tables and other illustrations and a list of abbreviations and acronyms.   HG151.F57

Jarrell, Howard R. Common stock newspaper abbreviations and trading symbols. Metuchen, N.J. : Scarecrow, 1989. 413 p. : ill. ISBN 0-8108-2255-5. $49.50.   **CH229**
   Lists Associated Press abbreviations, primary stock exchange/market on which traded, and ticker symbols for more than 6,300 companies selling common stock on the New York or American Stock Exchanges or traded in the over-the-counter National Association of Securities Dealers Automated Quotations (NASDAQ) market. Separate sections provide access by company name, AP newspaper abbreviation, and ticker symbol.

§ Supplement one (1991. $29.50. ISBN 0-8108-2119-1), covers some 2,400 changes and new listings that have occurred since the original volume was compiled.   HG4636.J37

Pessin, Allan H. The illustrated encyclopedia of the securities industry. N.Y. : New York Institute of Finance, c1988. 530 p. : ill. ISBN 0-13-450306-6. $59.95.   **CH230**
   Essentially a dictionary of investment and finance. Definitions range in length from a sentence to a few pages and frequently are supplemented by graphs, charts, or securities tables from newspaper financial pages.   HG4513.P463

———————— Still more words of Wall Street / Allan H. Pessin, Joseph A. Ross. Homewood, Ill. : Business One Irwin, c1990. 1 v. ISBN 1-55623-329-9.   **CH231**
   Continues the authors' *Words of Wall Street* (*Guide* CH554) and *More words of Wall Street* (1986). *More words* is an intermediate-level supplement to *Words*, focusing on more advanced terms and concepts, and *Still more words* contains even more advanced terminology and jargon, much of it international. The authors intend that the three titles be used together to provide a single approach to the vocabulary of the financial services industry, each title providing a different level of access.
                                                     HG4513.P467

Richards, Robert W. The Dow Jones-Irwin dictionary of financial planning. Homewood, Ill. : Dow Jones-Irwin, c1986. 377 p. ISBN 0-87094-612-9.   **CH232**
   Intended for both professionals and general readers, with definitions of more than 3,000 terms drawn from accounting, business law, estate planning, finance, insurance, investments, and related fields. A subject index groups terms by broad subject categories.   HG151.R52

Rosenberg, Jerry Martin. Dictionary of banking and financial services. 2nd ed. N.Y. : Wiley, c1985. 708 p. ISBN 0-471-83088-7. $34.95. ISBN 0-471-83133-6 (pbk.).   **CH233**
   1982 ed. (*Guide* CH556) had title: *Dictionary of banking and finance.*
   Has been revised to reflect the blurring of distinctions between banks and other financial institutions. Now contains 15,000 definitions, many attributed to sources listed in a brief "References" section at the back. The statistical and factual appendixes contained in the first edition have been deleted.
                                                     HG151.R67

———————— The investor's dictionary. N.Y. : Wiley, c1986. 513 p. ISBN 0-471-83678-8. ISBN 0-471-84567-1 (pbk.). $16.95.   **CH234**
   Contains approximately 8,000 entries, including traditional and more recent terms, foreign words and phrases commonly used in investment, abbreviations, acronyms, and symbols. Gives multiple senses for many terms, the most commonly used first. Numerous cross-references.   HG4513.R67

Scott, David Logan. Wall Street words. Boston : Houghton Mifflin Co., c1988. 404 p. : ill. ISBN 0-395-43747-4 ; 0-395-46777-2 (pbk.).   **CH235**
   Contains definitions of 3,600 terms, many supplemented by case studies. Also features 87 investment tips from experts, typical examples of technical analysis chart patterns, and a brief bibliography.   HG4513.S37

Shook, R. J. The Wall Street dictionary / R.J. Shook, R.L. Shook. N.Y. : New York Institute of Finance, c1990. 470 p. ISBN 0-13-950189-4.   **CH236**
   Briefly defines more than 5,000 financial, investment, and economic terms; includes jargon and slang.   HG151.S424

Terry, John V. Dictionary for business & finance. 2nd ed. Fayetteville : Univ. of Arkansas Pr., 1990. 399 p. ISBN 1-55728-169-6. ISBN 1-55728-170-X. **CH237**
1st ed., 1989.
Includes economic, legal, and statistical terms as well as those from accounting, banking, investment, insurance, management, marketing, and real estate. Definitions vary from brief sentences to a paragraph or more. Appendixes.
HF1001.T43

Thomsett, Michael C. Investment and securities dictionary. Jefferson, N.C. : McFarland, c1986. 328 p. : ill. ISBN 0-89950-225-3. $29.95. **CH238**
Repr. as: *Webster's New World investment and securities dictionary* (N.Y. : Webster's New World ; Dist. by Prentice-Hall Trade, 1988. ISBN 0-13-948175-3 [pbk.]. $8.95.)
Briefly defines or describes more than 2,000 investment terms, associations, government agencies, and key laws and regulations. Includes cross-references, charts and illustrations, a glossary, an abbreviations list, a guide to prospectus and offering documents, and a bond classification list. HG4513.T48

Walmsley, Julian. Dictionary of international finance. 2nd ed. N.Y. : Wiley, c1985. 222 p. : ill. ISBN 0-471-83654-0. **CH239**
1st ed., 1979 (*Guide* CH561).
Revised to reflect changes in the international finance market that have taken place since the 1st ed. Coverage of U.S. markets has also been broadened. HG151.W34

Directories

Asian finance directory. 1990– . Phoenix : Mead Ventures, c1989– . Annual. ISSN 1044-4718. $195.00.
CH240
A directory of banks, securities and insurance companies, leasing concerns and other groups, attorneys, consultants, accountants, and individual investors, listed alphabetically. Entries generally include address; telephone, fax, and telex numbers; names of key contacts; and general descriptive information. Brief, signed introductory essays precede the main section. Indexes by company name, country of owner/affiliate, state, and type of business.

The corporate finance bluebook. 1983– . N.Y. : Zehring Publ., c1983– . Annual. ISSN 0740-2546. **CH241**
Publisher varies; 19??– , Wilmette, Ill. : National Register Publ. Co./Macmillan Directory Div.
Lists some 5,200 public and private U.S. companies. In addition to standard business directory information, entries frequently include: sales estimates, assets and liabilities, net worth, assets of pension/profit sharing fund portfolio, key financial officers, and outside firms providing financial services. Detailed indexes: company name, private company name, companies by SIC, outside firms providing financial services (grouped by service category), geographical, and personnel.
HG4057.A15647

Directory of European banking and financial associations / comp. by Philip Molyneux. Chicago : St. James Pr. ; London : Woodhead-Faulkner, 1990. 217 p. ISBN 1-55862-077-X. $65.00. **CH242**
The main body of the work is a listing by country in which an overview of each country's banking, financial, and insurance systems is followed by a directory of associations and organizations. For each, the following are generally given: name (in vernacular with English translation); abbreviation; address; telephone, telex, and fax numbers; date founded; senior officials; branches; areas of interest; key area; specialist groups or sections; affiliations with other organizations; activities; membership; publications; other details. An introductory essay surveying trends in the financial services industry is followed by a di-

rectory of European regional financial institutions. Indexes of officials, organizations, and publications. K1066.D57

Directory of world stock exchanges / comp. by the Economist Publications. Baltimore : Johns Hopkins Univ. Pr., 1988. 469 p. : ill. ISBN 0-8018-3717-0. $89.50.
CH243
Combines standard directory listings (name, addresses, and telephone/telex/fax numbers) with other useful information (e.g., organization of the exchange, trading hours, types of securities traded and settlement procedures, taxation of income, special rules for foreign investors, technical publications and information sources). Entries frequently include histories of the exchanges (some with chronologies) and tables that show nominal and market value of shares traded, turnover of the exchange, and share price indexes for 1982–86. Arrangement is by country, then city. Not indexed; no glossary or other appendixes.
HG4551.D53

●**DISCLOSURE database** [computer file]. Bethesda, Md. : Disclosure, Inc., 1977– . **CH244**
Coverage: current. File size: 12,207 records. Updated weekly. Available online (ADP Data Services, BRS, CompuServe, Data-Star, DIALOG, Dow Jones News/Retrieval, Mead Data Central), in CD-ROM as *Compact D/SEC* (producer), and on magnetic tape (producer).
Contains financial and management information on some 12,000 publicly held companies, drawn from annual reports to shareholders and various filings with the Securities and Exchange Commission (e.g., registration and proxy statements, 10-K reports).

Financial planners and planning organizations directory : a reference guide to concerns and individuals engaged in advising and counseling on financial affairs / Steven Wasserman, Jacqueline Wasserman O'Brien, Judy Popp, editors. 2nd ed. Detroit : Omnigraphics, c1990. 977 p. ISBN 1-55888-278-2. $150.00. **CH245**
1st ed., 1987.
Lists 3,190 organizations, giving for each: address, telephone number, year founded, as many as ten areas of activity, and target audience. Background sketches of 4,450 planners are also included, with entries generally listing academic degrees; special licenses, certificates, or professional designations; and professional association memberships. Entries for organizations and individuals are interfiled within an arrangement by state and city. Begins with an introduction to the field of financial planning and key associations and concludes with personal name and organization indexes. An interim supplement is promised before the next edition. HG179.5.F56

Investment companies. 1944 ed.– . N.Y. : Arthur Wiesenberger & Co., 1944– . Annual. ISSN 0075-0271. $395.00. **CH246**
50th annual edition, 1990. 1157 p.
One of the most comprehensive sources on mutual funds and investment companies. In four parts; the first two contain general information on and discussion of the use of mutual funds to meet specific investment objectives. Pt. 3 contains single-page entries for mutual funds, including for each a description of its objective; composition of its portfolio; list of directors, investment manager(s), and other key personnel; a 10-year financial/statistical history; address and telephone; whether or not there is a sales charge; special services offered; and states in which the fund is qualified for sale. Provides similar information in Pt. 4, closed-end investment companies. Also contains a glossary, list of managers/advisors, and a companies index. Updated by two monthlies included with the service; *Management results* and *Current dividend record*, both of which provide current summary statistics on specific funds.
HG4530.I5

Nelson's directory of investment managers. 1st annual ed. (1988)– . Port Chester, N.Y. : Nelson Publications, c1988– . Annual. ISSN 0896-0143. $185.00. **CH247**

Detailed profiles of some 2,000 money management firms listed alphabetically, with up to 18 categories of data (e.g., Investment specialties, Decision-making process, Fees) in addition to standard directory information. Separate sections list firms geographically and by total assets managed, organization type, and area of specialization. Another section lists the most successful firms in descending order, based on 1-, 3-, and 5-year results. HG4907.N44

St. James mutual fund directory / Investment Company Institute. 1991– . Chicago : St. James Pr., 1991– . Annual. **CH248**

Contains summary data (name, address, telephone/fax numbers; year began; investment assets; minimum initial and subsequent investment; fees; and where to buy) for more than 2,900 mutual funds, grouped by investment objective categories. Also contains a glossary, a general discussion of mutual funds and their use, and an index. Less comprehensive than *Investment companies* (above), since closed-end funds (investment companies) are not included, and mutual fund listings exclude descriptions of portfolio composition and 10-year historical statistics. HG4530.S26

Thomson credit union directory. 1986– . Skokie, Ill. : Thomson Financial Information, c1991– . Annual. $54.95. **CH249**

Published 1986–90 as : *The Rand McNally credit union directory* (Chicago : Rand McNally, 1986–90).

Arranged alphabetically by state and city. Entries give address and telephone, managing officer, charter number and year established, number of members, routing number, and a financial summary; and when applicable, primary correspondent, automated clearinghouse code, and wire network participation. Includes an alphabetical list of credit unions; ranks the top 300 credit unions by total assets, shares, and loans; and provides general federal and state industry data. HG2037.R28

Thomson savings directory. v. 8 (1989)– . Skokie, Ill. : Thomson Financial Information, 1991– . Annual. **CH250**

Vol. 1–7 (also called eds. 1–7) published as : *The U.S. savings and loan directory* (Skokie, Ill. : Rand McNally, 1982–88).

Lists savings and loan institutions and savings banks by state and city. Structured entries include the following: legal name, type of charter, type of institution, membership in the U.S. League, location, membership code number, type of insurance for deposits, type of ownership, year established, number of employees, officers, financial data for the past two years, location of branches, routing number, and other operational data. Four preliminary reference sections list the institutions covered, present federal, state, and industry information, and list routing numbers and the savings institutions to which they are assigned.

Handbooks

The bankers' handbook / ed. by William H. Baughn, Thomas I. Storrs, Charls E. Walker. 3rd ed. Homewood, Ill. : Dow Jones-Irwin, c1988. 1347 p. : ill. ISBN 1-55623-043-5. **CH251**

Rev. ed., 1978 (*Guide* CH568).

"A basic reference on the subjects that are currently most important to performance in banking."—*Pref.* Contains 85 signed chapters arranged in 16 sections (e.g., financial management; the impact of monetary and fiscal policies on the banking system). Most of the chapters drawn from earlier editions have

been completely rewritten, and are enhanced by tables, charts, graphs, and other illustrations. Indexed. HG2491.B25

Berlin, Howard M. The handbook of financial market indexes, averages, and indicators. Homewood, Ill. : Dow Jones-Irwin, c1990. 262 p. : ill. ISBN 1-55623-125-3. **CH252**

Describes more than 200 measures of financial market performance worldwide. In nine chapters: the first discusses the mathematics of averages, indexes, and technical indicators; the next six focus on measures used with specific types of securities (U.S. stocks, notes and bonds, commodities, mutual funds, money and the dollar, foreign stocks); and the last two cover key technical indicators and unusual/amusing financial benchmarks. Entries frequently include charts and graphs but do not evaluate the effectiveness of the measures described. An appendix gives the names and addresses of domestic and international securities markets, and of selected banks and newspapers that maintain major market measures. Indexed. HG4636.B49

Downes, John. Barron's finance & investment handbook / John Downes, Jordan Elliot Goodman. 3rd ed. N.Y. : Barron's, c1990. 1234 p. : ill. ISBN 0-8120-6188-8. $24.95. **CH253**

1st ed., 1986.

Intended for general readers. In four parts: descriptions of 30 personal investment mediums, giving information on buying/selling/holding and risk, tax, and economic considerations; "how to" sections (e.g., reading annual reports and financial pages); a dictionary of finance and investment; and a ready reference section that lists organizations, companies, publications, and computer software and databases, and contains historical statistical data. Appendixes list titles for further reading, world currencies, and abbreviations and acronyms. All parts except the dictionary are indexed. HG173.D66

The financial analyst's handbook / ed. by Sumner N. Levine. 2nd ed. Homewood, Ill. : Dow Jones-Irwin, c1988. 1870 p. : ill. ISBN 0-87094-919-5. $80.00. **CH254**

1st ed., 1975 (*Guide* CH577).

Follows the purpose and arrangement of the first edition, but with chapters consolidated into a single volume and revised to reflect the many significant changes in finance, investments, and the economy since that edition was published. The essay on published information sources for this edition was written by Susan DiMattia. HG4521.F558

Handbook of financial markets and institutions / ed. by Edward I. Altman ; assoc. ed. Mary Jane McKinney. 6th ed. N.Y. : Wiley, c1987. 1197 p. in various pagings : ill. ISBN 0-471-81954-9. **CH255**

5th ed., 1981 (*Guide* CH569), had title *Financial handbook.*

Considerably revised, now covering domestic and international financial institutions and markets as well as investment theory and practice. Many chapters have been updated, the appendixes on the mathematics of finance and sources of investment information have been expanded, and sections added on investment banking, microcomputers and investments, the bond rating process, fixed income portfolios, high yield bonds, asset pricing models, and small business financing. No longer covers corporate finance; a companion volume, *The handbook of corporate finance* (N.Y. : Wiley, 1986) now treats that subject. Both volumes contain signed articles with bibliographies and are indexed. HG173.H33

Handbook of modern finance / ed., Dennis E. Logue. 2nd ed. Boston : Warren Gorham & Lamont, c1990. 1 v. (various pagings) : ill. ISBN 0-7913-0311-X. **CH256**

1st ed., 1984.

Offers 46 essays, written by experts, on the technical, analytical, and theoretical aspects of finance. The essays, which contain graphs, charts, and bibliographies, are presented in seven subject sections: Financial systems and markets; Security analysis, pricing, and portfolio management; Short-term financial management; Long-term financial management; Financial policy; Personal finance; and International dimensions. Indexed. HG173.H34

Hay, Tony. A guide to European financial centres. Chicago; London: St. James Pr., 1990. 289 p. ISBN 1-55862-140-7. £65.00. **CH257**

Provides general information, and discusses background, current trends, and future developments relating to western European financial institutions. Arranged by country. Each country chapter begins with a brief survey of the political structure and economy, followed by separate sections in which banking, insurance, the stock market, and laws and regulations pertaining to them are discussed. Statistics and lists of largest banks are frequently included. Also features lists of information sources, including relevant publications, reference libraries, and the name of the country's central statistics agency. Chapters conclude with a directory of key institutions. List of abbreviations with translations; general index and index of offices. Complements *Directory of European banking and financial associations* (Supplement CH242). HG3881.H39

Pratt's guide to venture capital sources. 8th ed. (1984)– . Wellesley Hills, Mass.: Capital Pub., c1984– . Annual. ISSN 0884-1616. **CH258**

8th ed., 1984 (*Guide* CH579).

The 14th edition (1990. 746 p.) is revised and expanded, the main part being a directory of over 800 venture capital firms in the U.S. and Canada, arranged by state and province. Company, name, and industry preference indexes. HG65.G83

Warfield, Gerald. The investor's guide to stock quotations and other financial listings. 3rd ed. N.Y.: Perennial Library, 1990. 254 p. ISBN 0-06-055196-8. $29.95. ISBN 0-06-096492-8 (pbk.). $10.95. **CH259**

An introduction discussing investing, brokers, and securities exchanges is followed by sections in which the most frequently traded securities (stocks, bonds, mutual funds, options, and futures) are covered. Each section deals with a specific investment medium and includes chapters that present the basics, describe trading in the security, reproduce sample quotation tables from the *Wall Street journal* and other newspapers, and discuss how to interpret them. Also includes appendixes (dollar/decimal equivalent of fractions, definitions of ratings by Moody's and Standard & Poor's), a glossary, and an index. Particularly useful for those who are new to investing or who need help in deciphering securities tables in newspapers. HG4636.W28

Statistics

The Dow Jones averages, 1885–1990 / ed. by Phyllis S. Pierce. Homewood, Ill.: Business One Irwin, c1991. 1 v. (unpaged). ISBN 1-55623-512-7. **CH260**

Following a nine-page chronology of the development of the Dow Jones averages, presents daily figures, beginning with the 14-stock average (combining railroads and industrials) in 1885 and ending with the daily 1990 averages for industrials, transportations, utilities, and bonds. Supersedes earlier volumes published in 1982 (*Guide* CH583) and 1986. HG4915.D6433

Prime rate archive & update service : a historical and ongoing service of changes in the prime rate. San Francisco, Calif.: Bank of America, World Information Services; Westport, Conn.: Meckler, c1990– . 1 v. (looseleaf): ill. ISBN 0-88736-620-1. $295.00. **CH261**

An introduction describing the prime interest rate and how it is determined is followed by a section that cites every change in the prime rate, January 1, 1939–July 31, 1989, giving for each the date on which the change took place and the prime rate itself. Subsequent sections covering briefer time periods (1935–49, 1950–59, 1960–69, 1970–79, 1980–84, 1985–89, and 1990) begin with commentary on the economy and actions of the Federal Reserve and their impact on the prime rate, and are followed by graphs depicting those changes. The last section is to be kept current by the publisher's *Prime rate update service*, which will be issued each time the prime rate changes. Lack of page numbers detracts from this work's usefulness. HG1623.U5P75

Statistical information on the financial services industry. 5th ed. Wash. : American Bankers Association, c1989. 1 v. (various pagings) : ill. **CH262**

A compilation of statistics drawn from government agencies, trade groups, and other sources. Tables are arranged in 13 sections by subject, under such broad headings as Economic trends, Consumer attitudes, Sources and uses of funds, Capital, Earnings, Structure, Payment systems, and International banking. Includes a summary conclusion, a list of members of Congress, and an unannotated bibliography. HG181.S795

INSURANCE

Bibliography

Weiner, Alan R. The insurance industry : an information sourcebook. Phoenix : Oryx, 1988. 278 p. (Oryx sourcebook series in business and management, 16). ISBN 0-89774-307-5. **CH263**

The first of two parts is an annotated bibliographic guide to print and nonprint English-language sources (excluding proceedings), arranged in seven chapters by broad subject areas (e.g., Insurance lines, Legal environment, Consumer guides, Careers), with subdivisions by form (e.g., statistics, handbooks). Annotations are not evaluative, but are "based, for the most part, on author and publisher introductions in the latest editions available."—*Introd.* A core list of titles—some too costly or specialized for general reference collections—concludes the section. The second part is an annotated directory of organizations, including associations, libraries, and database vendors. Author, title, and subject indexes. Z7164.I7W44

Dictionaries

Rubin, Harvey W. Dictionary of insurance terms. N.Y. : Barron's, c1987. 371 p. ISBN 0-8120-3772-3 (pbk.). $8.95. **CH264**

Contains brief definitions of 2,500 terms used in life, health, casualty, and other types of insurance, including those likely to be of interest to insurance consumers. Includes a brief list of abbreviations and acronyms. A 2nd ed. is to be published in 1991. HG8025.R83

Thomsett, Michael C. Insurance dictionary. Jefferson, N.C. : McFarland, c1989. 243 p. : ill. ISBN 0-89950-391-8. $29.95. **CH265**

An illustrated nontechnical glossary of insurance terms and phrases, with names and addresses of state insurance commissioners and Canadian provincial agencies. A brief acronyms list is included. HG151.T48

Directories

Rew, John. Directory of Lloyd's of London / John Rew, Charles Sturge, and Julian Sandys, editors. N.Y. : Stockton Pr., 1989. 279 p. ISBN 0-935859-75-6. $190.00.
CH266

Contains varying coverage in separate directory sections for Lloyd's underwriting agents, brokers, insurance companies, auditors, banks, solicitors, and syndicates. Also includes general information about Lloyd's (a brief history, organization charts, statistics). HG8601.Z9L657

Handbooks

Lybarger, Barbara E. An advocate's guide to surviving the SSI system : (with reference to the retirement, survivors' and disability system) / by Barbara E. Lybarger and Neil Onerheim. [1985 ed.]. [Boston] : Massachusetts Poverty Law Center, 1985. 491 p. : forms. **CH267**
Supplements *Social Security handbook* (*Guide* CH632).
Original title: *The Massachusetts SSI advocates' manual.*

A reference manual for advocates and attorneys who help Supplemental Security Income (SSI) claimants receive or keep their SSI and SSDI (Social Security Disability Insurance) benefits. Also useful for human services professionals and for academic libraries supporting degree programs in social work, gerontology, or law. Eight chapters describe SSI, Social Security retirement and disability insurance programs, the structure of the Social Security Administration, the advocate's role, eligibility, application process, appeals, and related benefits. Six appendixes include forms and sample letters, office addresses in Mass., medical abbreviations, etc.; eight-page general index. Although it emphasizes practice in Mass., the book's focus on federal programs makes it useful in other states. KF3649.L92

LABOR AND INDUSTRIAL RELATIONS

Bibliography

Annotated bibliography on clandestine employment. Geneva : International Labour Office, 1987. 132 p. (International labour bibliography, no. 2). ISBN 92-2-105726-7 (pbk.). 17.50F. **CH268**
Provides "a wide range of references on the issues which are of current concern, and often of controversy in many countries and on the various aspects, such as the nature, extent, and magnitude of clandestine employment, the characteristics of the enterprises and workers concerned, and the measures taken and results achieved."—*Foreword.* Some 213 monographs, journal articles, reports, and conference proceedings are arranged alphabetically by author. Since publications are in a variety of languages, entries designate language of text and frequently describe how publications may be obtained. Subject index. HD7802.A55

Bennett, J. D. Industrial relations : an international and comparative bibliography / comp. by John Bennett and Julian Fawcett for the British Universities Industrial Relations Association. London ; N.Y. : Mansell, 1985. 172 p. ISBN 0-7201-1787-9. **CH269**
An unannotated bibliography arranged by country, then by year of publication, on such topics as collective bargaining, labor economics, law, industrial conflict, and labor history. Works in English predominate, but some titles in French, Ger-

man, and Spanish are included. Lists mainly books and journal articles, but some pamphlets and government documents are included for countries for which little else is available. Author and subject indexes. Z7164.L1B454

Burnett, John. The autobiography of the working class : an annotated, critical bibliography / editors, John Burnett, David Vincent, David Mayall. N.Y. : New York Univ. Pr., 1984–1989. v. 2–3. ISBN 0-8147-1135-9.
CH270

For v. 1, see *Guide* CH648.
Contents: v. 2, 1900–1945; v. 3, Supplement, 1790–1945. Completes the set.

Vol. 2 contains 858 autobiographical entries with an additional 250 entries in the appendixes (miscellaneous, work, oral, military, political, collections, and diaries); v. 3 offers 204 main entries and 104 appendix entries drawn from new working-class autobiographies and from 19th- and early 20th-century printed works and manuscripts not previously covered. Indexes conform to those in v. 1. Z7164.L1B95

Buttel, Frederick H. Labor and the environment : an analysis of and annotated bibliography on workplace environmental quality in the United States / comp. by Frederick H. Buttel, Charles C. Geisler, and Irving W. Wiswall. Westport, Conn. : Greenwood, c1984. 148 p. ISBN 0-313-23935-5. $40.95. **CH271**
Contains two signed essays (Labor's stake in environmental quality and energy policy and Benefit-cost analysis: a labor-environmental concern), each accompanied by an annotated bibliography. Nearly 290 books, journal articles, and documents are described. Indexed. Z5863.P6B87

Dryden, Laurel. Employment creation policies and strategies : an annotated bibliography, 1980–86. Geneva : International Labour Office, 1987. 400 p. (International labour bibliography, no. 3.). ISBN 92-2-106173-6 (pbk.).
CH272

A bibliography in seven chapters (e.g., Economic policies, Direct employment creation) "each covering a different approach to the problem of reducing unemployment and creating employment opportunities."—*Introd.* Titles listed are drawn from research papers, government publications, articles, books, and conference proceedings published since 1980. Bibliographies in a separate chapter; indexes of authors, corporate authors, country/area, and titles. Z7164.L1D79

Ferber, Marianne A. Women and work, paid and unpaid : a selected, annotated bibliography. N.Y. : Garland, 1987. 408 p. (Garland reference library of social science, v. 315). ISBN 0-8240-8690-2. $35.00. **CH273**
Lists and critically annotates 1,031 monographs and journal articles, most published since 1960, but with a few classics and curiosities from earlier periods as well. Entries are arranged in nine major chapters—e.g., Economics of the family and Earnings and the female-male pay gap. The annotations are enhanced by codes indicating whether the emphasis is primarily on theory, methodology, empirical evidence, or policy issues, and whether a background in economics or mathematics is required. Author and subject indexes. Z7963.E7F47

Labor in America : a historical bibliography. Santa Barbara, Calif. : ABC-Clio Information Services, c1985. 307 p. (Clio bibliography series, no. 18). ISBN 0-87436-397-7. **CH274**
Lists with annotations some 2,865 articles published 1973–83 in journals in history and related fields. Arrangement is chronological in five chapters: early American, 1865–1900, 1900–45, 1945–82, and "multiperiod," for articles spanning two or more of the chronological categories. Within each chapter are several topical divisions, (e.g., economics and statistics of labor). Subject and author indexes, with lists of abbrevia-

tions, periodicals indexed, and contributing abstractors.

Z7164.L1L3

Labour information : a guide to selected sources. Geneva : International Labour Office, 1991. 231 p. (International labour bibliography, no. 8). ISBN 92-2-107274-6.
CH275

A core list of reference sources and I.L.O. publications. Pt. 1 lists and selectively annotates reference works by format (book selection, dictionaries and encyclopedias, directories, handbooks and atlases, legislative information and labor standards, and statistics); Pt. 2 focuses on current I.L.O. publications categorized by broad subject category (Employment, Training, Labor relations and administration, Working environment, Social security, Promotion of equality, and Workers' education) and subcategories. Nine appendixes list I.L.O. periodicals, serials, databases, and manuals and guides for librarians and documentalists. Index by title.   HD7802.A55

Periodicals

Hoerder, Dirk. The immigrant labor press in North America, 1840s–1970s : an annotated bibliography / ed. by Dirk Hoerder ; Christiane Harzig, assistant ed. N.Y. : Greenwood, 1987. 3 v. : ill. (Bibliographies and indexes in American history, no. 4, 7–8). ISBN 0-313-24638-6.
CH276

Contents: v.1, Migrants from northern Europe; v.2, Migrants from eastern and southeastern Europe; v.3, Migrants from southern and western Europe.

Includes about 2,170 titles in the categories of labor unions, radicalism, and reform; "periodicals expressing the radicalism of ethnic groups in agriculture are excluded, whereas papers of farmer-labor alliances are included."—*Chapter 1.* Arranged by ethnic group. Information for each group includes an introductory chapter on its history (concentrating on the working class) with a brief bibliography; an alphabetical listing of labor-related periodicals with detailed descriptions, including selected locations; and title, place, and chronological indexes for the periodicals. Each volume also has a combined title index.   Z6953.5.A1H63

Vocino, Michael C. Labor and industrial relations journals and serials : an analytical guide / comp. by Michael C. Vocino, Jr. and Lucille W. Cameron. N.Y. : Greenwood, 1989. 214 p. (Annotated bibliographies of serials, no. 14). ISBN 0-313-25986-0.   **CH277**

A selective bibliography of 346 currently published English language serials, including academic journals, representative trade union newsletters, and state and local government publications. Entries are arranged alphabetically, and contain up to 21 pieces of information including, besides standard serials directory information, the presence of a book review section, availability in microform or reprint, special issues, where indexed, target audience, and the availability of sample copies. An appendix lists titles not examined and therefore not included in the main section. Indexed geographically and by publisher, title, and subject.   Z7164.L1V6

Encyclopedias

Labor conflict in the United States : an encyclopedia / ed. by Ronald L. Filippelli. N.Y. : Garland, 1990. 609 p. ISBN 0-8240-7968-X.   **CH278**

Intended for students and general readers. Contains 254 alphabetically arranged entries, generally three to five pages long, with brief bibliographies. Covers significant strikes, lockouts, boycotts, and other labor conflicts, and also features a chronology of American labor history, a glossary, and a select

general bibliography. Entries are unsigned, but a list of contributors is given. Indexed.   HD5324.L32

Dictionaries

Roberts, Harold Selig. Roberts' dictionary of industrial relations. 3rd ed. Wash. : Bureau of National Affairs, c1986. 811 p. ISBN 0-87179-488-8. $65.00.   **CH279**

Rev. ed., 1971 (*Guide* CH709)

Preliminary ed., 1957–63, and 1966 ed. had title: *Dictionary of labor-management relations.*

Prepared by Industrial Relations Center, University of Hawaii at Manoa.

Revised and expanded. Contains 4,400 entries (600 new to the 3rd ed.), some 3,800 cross-references, and nearly 9,000 references to sources.   HD4839.R612

Directories

Conditions of work and quality of working life : a directory of institutions / ed. by Linda Stoddart assisted by Kristine Falciola. 2nd rev. ed. Geneva : International Labour Office, 1986. 306 p. ISBN 92-2-105328-8 (pbk.). 40.00F.   **CH280**

1st ed., 1981.

Lists 288 institutions concerned with the working environment (government agencies, trade unions, employers' organizations, research institutes, university departments) in 56 countries. Arrangement is geographical; regional and international organizations are followed by country listings. Entries generally include: name of the organization in the vernacular with its English translation, acronym, address and telephone, working language(s), date begun, type of organization, subject scope, financial support, budget (local currency and U.S. dollars), total staff, director(s), number of volumes, information services, training audience, training subjects, publications, and research. Personal name and acronym indexes.   HD7260.C64

Employers' organizations of the world / ed. by Martin Upham. Burnt Mill, Harlow, Essex, England : Longman ; Chicago : St. James Pr., 1990. 237 p. ISBN 1-55862-068-0. ISBN 0-582-06037-0. £70.00.   **CH281**

Lists key organizations by country with international organizations in a separate section. Each country section begins with a brief overview of pertinent economic, political, and industrial developments. Level of coverage varies, but organization entries generally include: address; telephone, telex and fax numbers; name of the president or director; total membership; aims and objectives; services to members; and publications. A brief list of acronyms and an index of major employers' organizations are also included.   HD6943.E559

Latin American labor organizations / ed. by Gerald Michael Greenfield and Sheldon L. Maram. N.Y. : Greenwood, 1987. 929 p. ISBN 0-313-22834-5. $125.00.
CH282

Provides basic information in English on the labor movement in Latin America. A brief introduction tracing its history from the mid-19th century is followed by 26 signed chapters, each devoted to a specific country. Included are all countries from Mexico southward in continental Latin America, Cuba, the Dominican Republic, Haiti, Jamaica, and Puerto Rico. Each chapter consists of three parts: a discussion of the development of the labor movement within the context of the country's history; a brief bibliography; and descriptions of the country's most important labor organizations, covering the origin, development, and activities of both active and defunct organizations. Three appendixes: a description of international labor organizations; chronologies of labor development by country; and a glossary of terms, people, and events, arranged by country. Thoroughly indexed.   HD6530.5.L38

Marsh, Arthur Ivor. Trade union handbook : a guide and directory to the structure, membership, policy, and personnel of the British trade unions. 4th ed. Aldershot, England ; Brookfield, Vt., : Gower, c1988. 387 p. : ill. ISBN 0-566-02749-6. $70.00.   **CH283**
   3rd ed., 1984 (*Guide* CH714).
   Coverage remains essentially the same, although the bibliography of trade union histories and the Citation Officer's list of trade unions have been omitted. The number of trade unions listed has been expanded to 402.   HD6663.M37

Trade unions of the world 1989–1990 / contributors: John Coggins . . . [et al.]. 2nd ed. Chicago : St. James Pr., 1989. 480 p. ISBN 0-582-03908-8. $85.00.   **CH284**
   1st ed., 1987.
   For each country, briefly discusses its political system, economy, and the status of trade unionism, followed by a list of individual trade unions in the country, giving for each its address, telephone and fax numbers; top officials; a description of its history and character; and its international affiliations. International and regional organizations of national trade union centers are listed in a separate section. Includes a select list of acronyms and an index of trade unions.

Handbooks

Fenton, Thomas P. Transnational corporations and labor : a directory of resources / comp. and ed. by Thomas P. Fenton and Mary J. Heffron. Maryknoll, N.Y. : Orbis Books, c1989. 166 p. : ill. ISBN 0-88344-635-9.
                                                   CH285
   Describes organizations, print, and nonprint sources that present pogressive labor activist views on transnational corporations and their impact on Third World economies, development, and people. Arranged by format in five chapters (Organizations, Books, Periodicals, Pamphlets and articles, and Audiovisual materials), with supplementary lists of books/periodicals and information sources frequently included at the end of each chapter. Indexed by organization name, individual name, and geographical area.   Z7164.U5F46

Kelly, Matthew A. Labor and industrial relations : terms, laws, court decisions, and arbitration standards. Baltimore : Johns Hopkins Univ. Pr., c1987. 200 p. ISBN 0-8018-3310-8. ISBN 0-8018-3311-6 (pbk.).
                                                   CH286
   Intended for students, scholars, and practitioners. In 3 main parts: a glossary; a compendium of labor legislation, describing and analyzing labor relations and protective labor legislation and pertinent court decisions; and a discussion of arbitration laws, court decisions, and standards. Includes a selective bibliography of reference works and principal texts. Indexed by terms and court decisions.   KF3369.K45

History

Marsh, Arthur Ivor. Historical directory of trade unions / Arthur Marsh and Victoria Ryan. Farnborough, Hants., England : Gower, c1987–1988. v. 3–4. ISBN 0-566-02160-9 (v.3). $83.50. (In progress).   **CH287**
   For v. 1–2 and annotation, see *Guide* CH702.
   Contents: v. 3, Transport and construction; v. 4, Textiles, printing, retail distribution and miscellaneous industries.
                                                   HD6664.M26

Statistics

International labour statistics : a handbook, guide, and recent trends / ed. by R. Bean. London ; N.Y. : Routledge, 1989. 306 p. ISBN 0-415-02179-0.   **CH288**
   Pt. 1, A guide to the use of labour statistics, contains signed essays on working population, unemployment, wages, consumer prices, labor costs, hours of work, trade union membership, and industrial disputes. The nature of data sources, cross-national trends, and potential pitfalls in interpreting statistics are discussed. Emphasis is on developed, capitalist countries that are members of OECD. Pt. 2 "provides a summary of key labour-market statistics, on an individual country basis, for 24 OECD and 20 other (including some Third World) countries."—*Pref.* An appendix offers membership information about trade secretariats affiliated with the International Confederation of Free Trade Unions. Indexed. Complements *Yearbook of labour statistics* (*Guide* CH724).   HD4826.I636

MANUFACTURING, RETAIL, SERVICE, AND WHOLESALE INDUSTRIES

Bibliography

Calantone, Roger J. Successful industrial product innovation : an integrative literature review / comp. by Roger J. Calantone and C. Anthony di Benedetto. N.Y. : Greenwood, c1990. 174 p. (Bibliographies and indexes in economics and economic history, no. 11). ISBN 0-313-27571-8. $45.00.   **CH289**
   Divided into six chapters, each treating one aspect of industrial product innovation, development, or marketing, and each beginning with a literature review of five to 16 pages, followed by an annotated bibliography. More than 450 books, articles, and conference proceedings (most published since 1978) are cited. Author and subject indexes.   HF5415.153.C35

Krismann, Carol. Quality control : an annotated bibliography through 1988. White Plains, N.Y. : Quality Resources, c1990. 482 p. ISBN 0-527-91659-5. $85.00.
                                                   CH290
   A brief introduction to quality control is followed by ten subject-oriented sections arranged according to a classification developed by the American Society for Quality Control Bibliography Committee. In each section, sources are grouped together by type; books published since 1931 are annotated and are followed by lists of journal articles (published mainly since 1980), dissertations, and audiovisual materials. Four appendixes: audiovisual materials, standards, associations, and education and training. Author, title, and topic indexes.
                                                   Z7914.Q3K74

Dictionaries

A historical dictionary of American industrial language / ed. by William H. Mulligan, Jr. N.Y. : Greenwood, c1988. 332 p. ISBN 0-313-24171-6.   **CH291**
   Brief definitions, drawn primarily from the period before World War I. An appendix lists terms by industry. Includes a list of contributors, bibliography, and index of institutions and people.   TS9.H57

Hunt, V. Daniel. Dictionary of advanced manufacturing technology. N.Y. : Elsevier, c1987. 431 p. : ill. ISBN 0-444-01208-7. **CH292**

A 52-page introduction is followed by brief definitions of terms (some accompanied by illustrations and photographs), including those relating to computer-aided design, manufacturing, process planning, robotics, machine vision, and communication and software interfaces. Also featured are directories of key organizations, a list of acronyms and abbreviations, a bibliography, and a directory of flexible manufacturing systems suppliers and users in the U.S. TS155.6.H85

Directories

Arpan, Jeffrey S. Directory of foreign manufacturers in the United States / Jeffrey S. Arpan, David A. Ricks. 4th ed. Atlanta : Publishing Services Division, College of Business Administration, Georgia State Univ., 1990. 437 p. ISBN 0-88406-219-8. $135.00. **CH293**
3rd ed., 1985 (*Guide* CH392).
This edition lists nearly 6,000 foreign-owned manufacturing firms in the U.S. HD9723.A76

Brands and their companies. 8th ed. (1990)– . Detroit : Gale, c1990– . Annual. ISSN 1047-6407. $320.00. **CH294**
1st–7th eds., 1976–89, had title *Trade names dictionary* (see *Guide* CH739).
Editor: 1990– Donna Wood.
Issued in two volumes. T223.V4A25

Brands and their companies. Supplement. 8th ed. (1990)– . Detroit : Gale, c1990– . Annual. ISSN 1047-6407. **CH295**
Continues *New trade names*, 1976–89 (14 v., see *Guide* CH739a).
Editor: 1990– Donna Wood.
Volume numbering for supplement corresponds with that of the parent title. T223.V4A255

Companies and their brands. 8th ed. (1990)– . Detroit : Gale, c1990– . Annual. ISSN 1047-6393. $320.00. **CH296**
1st–7th eds., 1976–89, had title *Trade names dictionary. Company index* (see *Guide* CH739).
Editor: 1990– Donna Wood.
Issued in two volumes. T223.V4A253

International brands and their companies. 2nd ed. (1991–92)– . Detroit : Gale, c1990– . Annual. ISSN 1050-8376. $240.00. **CH297**
Editor: 1990– : Donna Wood.
1st ed., 1988, had title *International trade names dictionary.*

International companies and their brands. 2nd ed. (1991–92)– . Detroit : Gale, c1990– . Annual. ISSN 1050-8384. $210.00. **CH298**
Editor: 1990– : Donna Wood.
1st ed., 1988, had title *International trade names company index.*
Brands and their companies alphabetically lists nearly 220,000 consumer brand names, giving for each a description of the product, company name, and a code for the source from which the information was taken. Company names (about 40,000 manufacturers and importers) are listed separately in the yellow pages at the end of v. 2, with entries including address, source code, and telephone number. *Companies and their brands* provides an alphabetical list of the 40,000 companies and the brand names attributed to them. Each company entry is followed by the firm's address and telephone number and an alphabetical listing of its trade names, collected from

printed sources and from information supplied by the company itself. Both directories are updated by *Brands and their companies: supplement*, which lists new consumer products introduced since the directories were published. Pt. 1 lists brands alphabetically, with a brief description of the product, manufacturer and importer, and in many instances, a code for the source from which the entry was taken. Pt. 2 lists corresponding company names, addresses, phone numbers, and brand names. *International brands and their companies* and *International companies and their brands* provide similar information for over 65,000 international consumer products and the nearly 15,000 manufacturers, importers, and distributors associated with them.

●**Trade names database** [computer file]. [Detroit] : Gale. **CH299**
Machine-readable version of *Brands and their companies* and *International brands and their companies* (above).
File size: 300,000 records. Coverage: current, file reloaded semiannually. Available online (DIALOG).
Lists some 280,000 U.S. and foreign consumer brand names and their owners or distributors. Each record contains the brand name, product description, company name, and in many instances, company address and telephone number and the source from which the information was taken.

Financial times industrial companies: chemicals. 1985–. Chicago : St. James Pr., c1985– . Annual. ISSN 0141-321X. **CH300**
Worldwide directory of the top 200 companies in the chemical, petrochemical, and pharmaceutical industries. Entries contain the name, address, and telephone number of corporate headquarters and, when applicable, the U.K. office; list of executives; description of the business; list of subsidiaries; discussion of company operations; and summary financial records, usually for the past three years. Includes an introductory essay on the chemical industry, comparative statistics, currency conversion rates, company abbreviations, and a glossary of financial terms. Product and company indexes.

●**Thomas register online** [computer file]. N.Y. : Thomas Pub. Co. **CH301**
Coverage: current; file reloaded semiannually. File size: 105,000 records. Available online (DIALOG) and in CD-ROM as *Thomas register ondisc* (DIALOG).
Machine-readable version of *Thomas' register of American manufacturers* and *Thomas' register catalog file* (*Guide* CH740).

●**Trademarkscan—federal** [computer file]. North Quincy, Mass. : Thomson & Thomson, [1884]– . **CH302**
Updated weekly. File size: 850,000 records. Available online (DIALOG).
Contains full-text records for all active and pending trademarks filed with the U.S. Patent and Trademark Office, and all inactive trademarks since October 1983. Each record includes the trademark; the serial/registration, U.S., and international classification numbers assigned to it; brief descriptions of the mark and the product or service it represents; and ownership and registration information. Searchers with DIALOGLINK software can also display or type the images of trademarks. Also available on compact disc.
§ A companion database, *Trademarkscan—state* (North Quincy, Mass. : Thomson & Thomson) allows the retrieval of similar information on trademarks filed with all 50 states and Puerto Rico since November 1986. The state file is updated biweekly.

U.S. manufacturers directory. Omaha, Neb. : American Business Directories, c1990. 2 v. (3160 p.) : ill. ISBN 0-945041-00-4. $495.00. **CH303**
Lists companies with at least ten employees, giving for each: name, address, telephone, employee size category, executive's name and code, SIC code(s), and sales volume code. A separate section lists manufacturers by state and city, large

manufacturers (100 or more employees) by state and city, and manufacturers by SIC code. Alphabetical cross-reference and manufacturing counts by SIC codes, state and 3-digit zip codes, and by county also included. HD9723.U27

Handbooks

Production handbook. 4th ed. [ed. by] John A. White. N.Y. : Wiley, c1987. 1 v. (various pagings) : ill. ISBN 0-471-86347-5. $78.50. **CH304**

3rd ed., 1972 (*Guide* CH743).

Revised to reflect new approaches and technologies in manufacturing, with more than 60 chapters grouped under the following categories: management, manpower, methods, machines, material, money, space, and systems. Charts, tables, and bibliographies frequently included. Indexed. TS155.P747

Industry analysis

Industry and development / United Nations Industrial Development Organization. 1985– . N.Y. : United Nations, 1985– . Annual. **CH305**

An annual review of the world industrial economy, with an assessment of the current situation and short-term forecasts. The issue for 1989/90 treats 13 manufacturing industries in depth, and a statistical annex presents current economic information for each of 161 countries. Statistics, tables, graphs. HC59.69.I53

Manufacturing USA. 1st ed.– . Detroit : Gale, c1989– . Annual. ISSN 1044-7024. $159.00. **CH306**

Editor, 1989– : Arsen J. Darnay.

Integrates statistics from the U.S. Bureau of the Census publications *Census of manufactures, County business patterns,* and other government publications with company information from *Ward's business directory of U.S. private and public companies* (*Supplement* CH127). Arrangement is by SIC, with 448 industries covered. Entries are three to four pages long and include graphs that chart industry shipments and employment and tables that present general statistics and indexes of change for the past seven years, as well as selected financial and operating ratios. A list of leading companies (giving address, chief executive officer, telephone, company type, sales, and employment) is followed by tables of input and output, product share details, and occupations employed. Summary state and regional data (including maps) are also present. Indexed by SIC, product, company, and occupation. Most useful to those lacking immediate access to the publications from which the data were taken, but convenient and handy for all libraries.

Mattera, Philip. Inside U.S. business : a concise encyclopedia of leading industries. [2nd] ed. Homewood, Ill. : Business One Irwin, c1991. 568 p. ISBN 1-55623-377-9. **CH307**

1st ed., 1987.

Contains 25 chapters on specific industries, arranged by broad category (communications, consumer goods and services, electronics, energy, finance, and heavy industry and transportation). Gives industry descriptions and histories, lists and profiles of leading companies, discussion of industry labor relations and a source guide that lists leading stock analysts and experts, trade associations, data sources and directories, online databases, trade publications, and books and reports. Indexed. HC106.8.M337

Panorama of EC industry. 1989– . Luxembourg : Office for Official Publications of the European Communities, 1988– . Annual. £14.70. **CH308**

For annotation, see *Supplement* CK129. HC241.2.P313

Standard industrial classification manual : 1987 / [prepared by the] Executive Office of the President, Office of Management and Budget. [Wash.] : The Office ; Springfield, Va. : For sale by National Technical Information Service, 1987. 705 p. **CH309**

For 1972 ed. and 1977 suppl., see *Guide* CH745; 1987 ed. supersedes all previous editions and supplements.

Previous ed. prepared by the Statistical Policy Division, United States Office of Management and Budget.

Also available from U.S. Govt. Print. Off. ($24.00).

Superintendent of Documents classification: PrEx 2.6/2:In 27/987.

Changes from the 1972 edition and the 1977 supplement reflect technological and industrial changes and expansion in the service sector. Titles, numeric codes, and industry descriptions are presented in 11 main divisions and numerous subsections. An alphabetic index lists all manufacturing and non-manufacturing industries and the codes assigned to each; an appendix gives conversion tables between the 1972/77 edition/supplement and the 1987 edition. HF1042.S73

U.S. industrial outlook : prospects for over 350 manufacturing and service industries. [31st annual ed.]. [Wash.] : U.S. Dept. of Commerce, International Trade Administration : for sale by the Supt. of Docs., U.S. Govt.Print.Off., 1990. 1 v. (various pagings) : ill. **CH310**

An essential reference source containing industry analyses and statistical data for both manufacturing and service industries. Arrangement is by ten broad industry categories (e.g., construction, information, communications), with subsections devoted to specific industries. Entries range from a single page to two or more, and usually include a general description, as well as discussion of U.S. production, foreign trade, the outlook for the current year, and long-term prospects. "Trends and forecasts" tables carry industry, product, and trade data and percent change for the current year and three years preceding. Information is specific to industries, not companies. Entries conclude with the name, office, and telephone number of the government specialist who wrote the report as well as a bibliography of additional references. An industry index lists SIC code(s) and page numbers. HC101.U55

MARKETING

Bibliography

Dickinson, John R. The bibliography of marketing research methods. 3rd ed. Lexington, Mass. : Lexington Books, c1990. 1025 p. ISBN 0-669-21697-6. $75.00. **CH311**

Contains 14,000 entries on market research, data collection, and data analysis drawn from marketing journals, handbooks, and conference proceedings, and from related disciplines. Entries are grouped by subject. Not annotated. Author and subject indexes. Z7164.M18D52

Marketing information : a professional reference guide / ed. by Jac L. Goldstucker ; comp. by Otto R. Echemendia, with the staff of the Business Publishing Division, Georgia State University. 2nd ed. Atlanta : Business Pub. Division, College of Business Administration, the Univ., 1987. 436 p. ISBN 0-88406-195-7. **CH312**

1st ed., 1982 (*Guide* CH755).

Although originally intended to be a biennial publication, only two editions have appeared to date. This 2nd ed. follows the plan of the first, with some additional subsections in the first part (e.g., consulting firms; the 300 largest advertising agencies) and additional indexing in the second.

HF5415.124.M37

Weekly, James K. Information for international marketing : an annotated guide to sources / comp. by James K. Weekly and Mary K. Cary. N.Y. : Greenwood, 1986. 170 p. (Bibliographies and indexes in economics and economic history, no. 3). ISBN 0-313-25440-0.   **CH313**

Lists and briefly annotates 195 items, including government publications, databases, periodical and newspaper indexes, and basic reference sources. Arranged by type of information (e.g., demographic data, methodological data, and political data and political risk assessments) or by format (bibliographies, directories, and indexes; dictionaries; databases), with some items listed in several sections. Appendixes present brief directory listings for publishers, state trade contacts, U.S. foreign service offices in foreign countries, foreign embassies in the U.S., the U.S. International Trade Administration, and international marketing journals. Indexed by title only.

Z7164.C8W4

Current

•**PTS marketing and advertising reference service** [computer file]. Cleveland, Ohio : Predicasts, 1985– . **CH314**

File size: 132,000 records. Updated daily. Available online (Data-Star, BRS, DIALOG).

Provides 300-word abstracts of articles from more than 110 trade, research, and consumer periodicals and newsletters dealing with the marketing and advertising of consumer goods and services. No printed counterpart.

Encyclopedias

Beacham's marketing reference / ed. by Walton Beacham, Richard T. Hise, Hale N. Tongren. Wash. : Research Pub., c1986. 2 v. (1045 p.). ISBN 0-933833-03-2 (set). $139.00.   **CH315**

An alphabetical arrangement of signed articles, written by experts, that treat both the theoretical and practical aspects of 212 marketing topics. Each article follows a standard format in which an overview of the concept is followed by examples, discussion of benefits, implementation, evaluation, and a conclusion. Small business applications are described, and relevant references, software, and databases identified. An index and appendix of software applications are also included.

HF5415.B379

Dictionaries

Baker, Michael John. Dictionary of marketing and advertising. 2nd ed. N.Y. : Nichols Pub., 1990. 271 p. ISBN 0-89397-371-8.   **CH316**

1st ed., 1984, had title: *Macmillan dictionary of marketing & advertising* (Guide CH758).

Revised and expanded, with the addition of technical terms particularly notable. British emphasis continues.

HF5415.B273

Dictionary of marketing terms / contributors, Paul F. Anderson . . . [et al.] ; ed., Peter D. Bennett. Chicago :

American Marketing Association, c1988. 220 p. ISBN 0-87757-194-5.   **CH317**

Signed definitions of terms, written individually or in pairs by experts in various fields of marketing. No illustrations, charts, or graphs. List of references.   HF5415.D4873

Ostrow, Rona. The dictionary of marketing / Rona Ostrow, Sweetman R. Smith. N.Y. : Fairchild Publications, c1988. 258 p. : ill. ISBN 0-87005-573-9.   **CH318**

Contains brief, nontechnical definitions of terms in such fields as marketing research, direct marketing, sales, wholesaling, retailing, and international marketing as well as descriptions of major marketing associations. Features some formulas, graphs, and charts.   HF5415.O76

Van Minden, Jack J. R. Dictionary of marketing research. Chicago : St. James Pr., c1987. 200 p. ISBN 0-912289-57-0.   **CH319**

Contains some 2,000 terms in applied and theoretical marketing research and related fields. In two parts: Pt. 1 is an index of terms; Pt. 2 contains definitions, arranged by subject in 7 chapters, which are divided into sections to allow terms to be grouped by concept. Appendixes include a checklist for marketing researchers and the ethical codes of key professional associations.   HF5415.2.V35

Directories

•**FINDEX** [computer file]. Bethesda, Md. : Cambridge Scientific Abstracts, [1973?]– .   **CH320**

Machine-readable version of *FINDex : the directory of market research reports, studies, and surveys* (Guide CH764).

File size: 12,500 records. Updated semiannually. Available online (DIALOG).

Palder, Edward L. The catalog of catalogs II : the complete mail-order directory. 2nd ed. Rockville, Md. : Woodbine House, 1990. 549 p. ISBN 0-933149-38-7. $14.95.   **CH321**

1st ed., 1987.

Lists some 12,000 sources for mail-order catalogs and travel information in over 600 subject areas. Arranged in 2 sections (Sources/products and Travel information), each divided by subject. Entries include company name and address, a brief description of the products/services offered, and a telephone number. Separate name indexes for products and travel information, with a combined subject index.   HF5466.P35

The sales prospecting & territory planning directory : the 4,000 richest organizations in North America / John C. Thomas, ed. N.Y. : Amacom, c1990. 653 p. ISBN 0-8144-7735-6. $120.00.   **CH322**

Lists more than 4,100 organizations (public and private companies and their divisions and affiliates, financial institutions, headquarters of foreign companies, nonprofit associations, and government agencies) with annual revenues greater than $250 million. In four parts, the most detailed being the alphabetical listing, which includes for each organization its address and telephone, type of business and organization, names of executives, number of employees, annual revenue, and assets. The other sections list organizations in rank order by revenue, geographically, and by industry.   HG4057.A464

Handbooks

Crispell, Diane. The insider's guide to demographic know-how : how to find, analyze, and use information about your customers. 2nd ed. Ithaca, N.Y. : American Demographics Pr., 1990. 291 p. : ill. ISBN 0-936889-07-1.   **CH323**

1st ed., 1988.

Aimed at those new to demographic research and its business applications. Combines essays, descriptions of sources (some highly specialized), and directories of the organizations issuing them. The essays, reprints of articles from *American demographics*, discuss the uses of demographics, the 1990 census, and Europe in 1992. Descriptions of sources and their publishers are arranged by type of issuing agency (federal government, private, etc.). The most useful parts of the appendix are a glossary, source and subject indexes, a bibliography of reprinted articles, and a list of the contributors and their affiliations; less useful is "Useful publications for additional information," basically a list of American Demographics publications.

HF5415.2.C757

Encyclopedia of telemarketing / ed. by Richard L. Bencin, Donald J. Jonovic. Englewood Cliffs, N.J. : Prentice Hall, c1989. 726 p. : ill. ISBN 0-13-275918-7.   **CH324**

Intended as a handbook for practitioners, emphasizing applications rather than theory. Consists of 30 chapters by specialists, treating specific aspects of telemarketing (e.g., organization and staffing, training, reporting systems, fund-raising telemarketing). Includes case histories, sample forms, and other illustrations. Appendixes include: detailed descriptions of key telemarketing associations, discussing their histories, mission statements, and goals; an annotated bibliography of telemarketing books (including the titles of individual chapters) and a categorized list of magazines, newspapers, and newsletters; descriptions of telephone peripheral equipment; and a glossary. Indexed.   HF5415.1263.B46

Japan marketing handbook. London : Euromonitor, 1988. 160 p. ISBN 0-86338-213-4.   **CH325**

Analyzes Japan's economy and major industries and the Japanese consumer market and discusses doing business in Japan, with coverage from the mid-1980s through the rest of the 20th century. "Statistics are provided separately at the end of the text, in a Fact File giving data on the country, its economy, and its consumers, and in an A to Z with key facts on 45 of Japan's major markets."—*Foreword.* Also contains a directory of government and government-related bodies, importers' associations, market research and consultancy firms, and newspapers. Indexed.   HF3826.5.J39

Statistics

Almanac of consumer markets. 1990–1991– . Ithaca, N.Y. : American Demographics Pr., c1989– . Biennial. ISSN 1045-5507.   **CH326**

Presents data concerning U.S. consumers—population, households, marital status and fertility, education, labor force, income, expenditures, health, wealth—in ten chapters, each devoted to roughly a decade in the age of the population, from less than five years of age to 75 and older. Each chapter begins with a one-page discussion of the characteristics of the population of greatest interest for marketing. Makes use of maps, graphs, tables, and some projections. Tables provide explanatory text and cite sources of data; much of the data are drawn from *American demographics* and publications of the Census Bureau, Bureau of Labor Statistics, and other government agencies. A short glossary defines technical terms widely used in demography. An appendix contains tables of income and expenditure for house-

holds not shown in the tables for age groups. Detailed table of contents; index.   HA203.A45

Canadian markets. 61st ed. (1986)– . Toronto : Financial Post Information Service, c1986– . Annual. ISSN 0832-2503.   **CH327**

Contains demographic, economic, and consumer sales data for Canada, its provinces, census metropolitan areas, divisions, and subdivisions. The most detailed information, presented in profiles of urban consumer regions with populations of at least 10,000, includes current estimates or most recent census figures for population (age, sex, marital status, families, mother tongue, level of schooling), housing, labor force, occupation, income, taxation, manufacturing industries, homes built, and building permits. The profiles also list the names of daily and community newspapers and television and radio stations. Other sections contain rankings, estimates, and projections of population, retail sales, and personal income. Also features a glossary, directory of industrial development bureaus, description of services offered by Statistics Canada, and general and advertisers indexes.

Consumer Europe. [Ed. 1]– . [London : Euromonitor], 1976– . Irregular.   **CH328**

For earlier vols., see *Guide* CH771.

Revised and expanded with the 8th ed. (1991). Although some new consumer products have been added, the most notable changes are the inclusion of data for the major countries of Eastern Europe, totals for the European Community, and comparisons between the European Community, Japan, and the U.S.   HD7022.C68

●**Donnelley demographics** / [computer file]. Stamford, Conn. : Donnelley Marketing Information Services (DMIS), 1980– .   **CH329**

File size: 16,039 records. Updated annual reloads. Available online (DIALOG).

Contains demographic data from the most recent decennial census as well as current estimates and five-year projections covering age, race, sex, marital status, families, households, housing, education, income, industry, and occupation. Summary U.S. data and data for states, counties, cities, zip codes, Metropolitan Statistical Areas (MSAs), Arbitron Areas of Dominant Influence (ADIs), and A.C. Nielsen Designated Marketing Areas (DMAs) are available.

The lifestyle market analyst. 1989– . Wilmette, Ill. : Standard Rate & Data Service, 1989– . Annual. $277.00.   **CH330**

Continues *Lifestyle marketplanner* (ceased 1988).

In four sections: (1) a market profiles section of two-page statistical profiles for 209 geographic markets (defined by the media rating firm Arbitron as an area of dominant influence—ADI), highlighting demographic characteristics and lifestyle interests for each; (2) a lifestyle profiles section, with four-page entries for 56 broad interest categories (e.g., avid book reading, motorcycles), showing demographic characteristics, other lifestyle interests pursued, and ADI locations; (3) a consumer segment profiles section that focuses on specific demographic characteristics and their ADI concentration; and (4) a list of consumer magazines and direct mail lists targeted to each lifestyle profile.   HF5415.33.U6L54

Market share reporter. 1st (1991)– . Detroit : Gale, 1991– . Annual. $165.00.   **CH331**

Contains market share statistics 1988–90, drawn from brokerage house reports included in the *INVESTEXT* database (*Supplement* CH220) and from periodicals. In the first chapter, entries deal with general interest and broad topics; subsequent chapters group entries by two-digit SIC categories. Within chapters, arrangement is by four-digit SIC, then successively by topic, alphabetically by title, and publication date. Entries generally include the topic, SIC, title, statistics, and the source from which the statistics were taken. Numerous pie charts and bar graphs. Four indexes: sources; place names; products, services, and issues; and company. An appendix lists three- and four-digit SICs covered.

The sourcebook of zip code demographics. 7th ed. (1990)– . [Fairfax, Va.] : CACI, c1990– . Annual. **CH332**

In two sections: residential and business. The residential section, arranged by state and then by zip code, includes population and age, demographic and buying power, income, and housing and socioeconomic profiles. Statistics are derived from the most recent published decennial census, other Bureau of the Census and Bureau of Economic Analysis data, and CACI projections. A market potential index, based on survey data, compares potential demand for specific consumer products/services in each zip code location to the U.S. average. The business section, extracted from *County business patterns* data files, shows the number of employees and the number of firms of the predominant SIC code for each zip code. Four appendixes: state summary data, SIC codes, county maps, and county FIPS codes. A companion volume from the same publisher, *Sourcebook of county demographics* (formerly *Sourcebook of demographics and buying power for every county in the USA*), contains similar information for each county in the U.S.

HA203.S66

The survey of buying power data service. [N.Y.] : Sales & Marketing Management Magazine, [1981]– . 1 v. (looseleaf) : ill. **CH333**

The 1990 issue contains over 900 pages of maps and statistics, including state and county outline maps; current population estimates (with breakdowns by age categories and sex); households (number, size, age of householder); effective buying income distribution; buying power indexes; and retail sales by 12 different store groups (e.g., eating and drinking places, drug stores). Data in most of the 21 sections are arranged geographically, by region, state, metro area and county, and TV market (area of dominant influence). Also includes comparisons with U.S. totals, ranked lists, and projections for metro, county, and TV markets for population, effective buying income, and sales. Similar to, but considerably more detailed than, the "Survey of buying power" issues of *Sales and marketing management magazine.*

HC110.C6S847

OCCUPATIONS

American salaries and wages survey : statistical data derived from more than 300 government, business & news sources / [ed. by] Arsen J. Darnay. Detroit ; London : Gale, 1991. clxx, 918 p. ISBN 0-8103-8042-0 (pbk.). $89.50. **CH334**

". . . a compilation of occupations and their corresponding salaries obtained from hundreds of federal and state government sources and from various trade associations and journals."—*Introd.* Arranged by occupational title in tabular format, with columns presenting: occupation/type/industry; geographic location to which the data refer; intervals at which the wage amount is paid, with codes for hourly, monthly , or annual; and the date and source from which the data were obtained. Front matter includes a detailed list of occupational classifications and a geographical outline of areas and occupations covered. Five appendixes: an annotated list of sources, a salary conversion table, American Chamber of Commerce Research Association cost of living index, abbreviations, and employment by occupation, 1988 and 2000. HD4975.A447

Codes of professional responsibility / ed. by Rena A. Gorlin. 2nd ed. Wash. : Bureau of National Affairs, c1990. 555 p. ISBN 0-87179-641-4. $55.00. **CH335**

Presents the official codes for 37 major professional associations, grouped in 3 categories: business, health, and law. For each organization, information generally includes: address and telephone, date founded, number of members, name of the ethics committee, and the title of its code of ethics; the organization's activities and goals, implementation and enforcement of the code, and development and sources of code; and the full text of the code itself. Also includes a resources section (organizational, periodical, bibliographic, and other resources on ethics) and indexes of issues, professions, and organizations. BJ1725.C57

Federal career directory : the U.S. government, find out why it's becoming the first choice! : career America. Wash. : U.S. Office of Personnel Management : For sale by U.S. Govt. Print. Off., [1990–]. 1 v. (looseleaf) : ill. (some col.), map. **CH336**

Intended for recent college graduates and others seeking information about federal employment opportunities and benefits. In 14 tabbed sections that include (besides descriptions of major government agencies, their employees, and the address and telephone numbers of their personnel offices) general information about training and development opportunities, special employment programs, employee benefits, federal pay and personnel classification systems, and an index of college majors employed by agencies. Also has a section of instructions on how to apply for federal employment. Photographs, organization charts, and other illustrations.

Job hunter's sourcebook. 1st ed.– . Detroit : Gale, 1991– . Biennial. ISSN 1053-1874. $49.95. **CH337**

Compiled in cooperation with the Career and Employment Information Center of the Detroit Public Library.

In two main parts: (1) Job-hunting information, organized by profession or occupation, in which 155 occupations are profiled, and descriptions of sources of employment information grouped under 7 broad categories (Help-wanted ads; Placement/job referral services; Employer directories; Networking lists; Handbooks and manuals; Employment agencies and executive search firms; and Other leads); and (2) General job-hunting information, which contains descriptions of reference works, newspapers, periodicals, audiovisual materials, and software and databases relating to 20 key topics. Also includes an essay on library resources and services for job hunters and an index to information sources. A companion to *Professional careers sourcebook* (below). HF5382.7.J62

Kocher, Eric. International jobs : where they are, how to get them : a handbook for over 500 career opportunities around the world. 3rd ed., rev. and expanded. Reading, Mass. : Addison-Wesley, c1989. 440 p. ISBN 0-201-51763-9. $12.95. **CH338**

Previous ed., 1984 (*Guide* CH781).

Revised and expanded, but following the same general format as the earlier edition. HF5382.7.K62 1989

Krantz, Les. The jobs rated almanac : 250 jobs!· N.Y. : World Almanac : Distr. by Ballantine Books, c1988. 349 p. : ill. ISBN 0-88687-307-X (pbk.). $14.95. **CH339**

Ranks 250 jobs by nine criteria (each assigned a different section): work environment, income, outlook, stress, travel opportunities, physical demands, extras, security, and where the jobs are. Within each section, jobs are listed alphabetically; a final section, "The big picture," contains an overall ranking of jobs. Not indexed. HF5382.5.U5K7

The national job bank, 1991 / managing ed., Carter Smith ; associate editors, Sharon L. Capen, Peter F. Weiss. 7th ed. Holbrook, Mass. : B. Adams, c1991. 1008 p. ISBN 1-55850-886-4. **CH340**

1st ed., 1979 (*Guide* CH782).

Expanded to include major employers in all 50 states and the District of Columbia. Arrangement is geographic, with an industry index subdivided by state. Also includes chapters on résumé writing and job winning strategies.　HF5382.5.U5N341

Professional careers sourcebook : an information guide for career planning. 1st ed.– . Detroit : Gale, c1990– . Biennial. ISSN 1045-9863. $69.95.　　**CH341**
　　Compiled in cooperation with InfoPLACE.
　　An "overview of the literature and professional organizations that aid career planning and related research for 111 careers requiring college degrees or specialized education."— *Introd.* The career profiles, grouped in ten major categories by professional type and then listed alphabetically, generally contain the following information: job descriptions; career guides; professional associations; standards/certification agencies; test guides; educational directories and programs; awards, scholarships, grants, and fellowships; basic reference guides and handbooks; professional and trade periodicals; professional meetings and conventions; and other sources of information. Also includes a master list of profiled careers, a directory of state occupational and professional licensing agencies, and lists of jobs ranked by employment outlook, security, stress, pay, working environment, and overall job quality. Indexed. Partially drawn from, but complementary to, U.S. Bureau of Labor Statistics, *Occupational outlook handbook* (*Guide* CH784).
　　　　　　　　　　　　　　HF5382.5.U5P76

REAL ESTATE

Bibliography

Burns, Grant. Affordable housing : a resource guide to alternative and factory-built homes, new technologies, and the owner-builder option. Jefferson, N.C. : McFarland, c1989. 186 p. ISBN 0-89950-419-1.　**CH342**
　　In two main parts. Pt. 1, a bibliography, groups annotated entries for English-language books, articles, reports, and government publications published mainly since 1980 in topical chapters (Housing crisis, Factory-built housing, Foreign factory-built housing, Owner-builders, Log houses, Reference books, and The mortgage). Many popular "how-to" publications are listed. Pt. 2 is a directory of resources, featuring an annotated list (with prices and addresses) of periodicals for owners, planners, and builders; addresses for and descriptions of key organizations and owner-builder schools; and directories of manufacturers and publishers. Includes a glossary and author/editor, title, and subject indexes.　　Z7914.D87B87

Clatanoff, Robert M. The valuation of industrial property : a classified annotated bibliography. Chicago : International Association of Assessing Officers, Research and Technical Service Dept., 1987. 75 p. ISBN 0-88329-144-4 (pbk.).　　**CH343**
　　A bibliography of more than 290 books and journal articles published in the U.S., England, Canada, Australia, and New Zealand. In four sections: Assessment and mass appraisal; Valuation; Appraisal of specific types of industrial property; Industrial taxation, location, and neighborhood effects. Annotations generally include the type(s) of property covered, whether a sample appraisal is included, the presence of illustrations or bibliographies, technique or approach used, and geographical area. Indicates publications not examined by the author. Also includes a bibliography of bibliographies, an author index, and a directory of serials cited.　　Z7164.V3C58

Harris, Laura A. The real estate industry : an information sourcebook. Phoenix : Oryx, 1987. 170 p. (Oryx sourcebook series in business and management, 5). ISBN 0-89774-262-1. $39.50.　　**CH344**

A select, annotated bibliography of books, journals, reference sources, and other publications. A core library collection of 135 titles, grouped by format (bibliographies, directories, etc.), is followed by a general literature section that contains a list of titles by broad subject categories, descriptions of 158 real estate journals, and "Other sources of information," which describes and provides addresses for associations, government agencies, special libraries, state real estate boards, and other organizations. Brief author, title, subject indexes. Complements the older but more inclusive *Real estate: a bibliography of the monographic literature*, by Peter D. Haikalis and Jean K. Freeman (*Guide* CH790).　　Z7164.L3H244

Nurcombe, Valerie J. International real estate valuation, investment, and development : a select bibliography / Valerie J. Nurcombe. N. Y. : Greenwood, 1987. 232 p. (Bibliographies and indexes in economics and economic history, no. 7). ISBN 0-313-26082-6.　　**CH345**
　　Lists without annotations nearly 3,800 scholarly and popular books and journal articles. Entries are grouped in subject-oriented chapters which frequently are subdivided geographically. Two appendixes: dictionaries and encyclopedias, and journals. Author and subject indexes.　　Z7164.L3N87

Dictionaries

Blankenship, Frank J. The Prentice Hall real estate investor's encyclopedia. Englewood Cliffs, N.J. : Prentice Hall, c1989. 539 p. : ill. ISBN 0-13-712837-1. ISBN 0-13-713827-X (pbk.). $24.95.　　**CH346**
　　Combines definitions of terms with examples of usage and investor advice. Charts, sample forms, and other illustrations are also included.　　HD1365.B55

The dictionary of real estate appraisal. 2nd ed. Chicago : American Institute of Real Estate Appraisers, c1989. 366 p. ISBN 0-911780-93-9. $28.50.　　**CH347**
　　1st ed., 1984.
　　Offers brief, clear definitions, with coverage of business, economic, legal, and quantitative terminology.　HD1387.D435

Reilly, John W. The language of real estate. 3rd ed. Chicago : Real Estate Education Co., c1989. 467 p. : ill. ISBN 0-88462-673-3. $24.95.　　**CH348**
　　1st ed., 1977 (*Guide* CH806).
　　Revised and expanded to include some 2,400 terms. Also includes a classified list of subjects, an abbreviations list, the full text of the realtor code of ethics, and a sample closing problem with illustrative forms.　　KF568.5.R44

Thomsett, Michael C. Real estate dictionary. Jefferson, N.C. : McFarland, c1988. 220 p. : ill. ISBN 0-89950-321-7. $29.95.　　**CH349**
　　Defines some 1,100 terms pertaining to commercial and residential real estate and investment and briefly describes relevant associations and regulatory agencies. Some charts and statistics, numerous *see also* references. Also includes owner/seller checklists, amortization and remaining balance tables, and a list of abbreviations.　　HD1365.T46

West, Bill W. Street talk in real estate / Bill W. West, Richard L. Dickinson. Alameda, Calif. : Unique Pub. Co., [1987]. 216 p. : ill. ISBN 0-934189-04-8 (pbk.). $9.95.　　**CH350**
　　Contains brief, practical, nontheoretical definitions of the "colloquial terminology commonly and frequently used by the many diverse groups involved with ordinary real estate transactions."—*Pref.*　　HD1365.W47

Directories

Directory of foreign investment in the U.S: real estate and business. 1st ed.– . Detroit : Gale, c1991– . Irregular. ISSN 1050-8694. $195.00. **CH351**

In two sections. Section 1 lists some 1,200 real estate properties—office buildings, commercial and industrial developments, apartment complexes, hotels, golf courses, country clubs, farm land—owned in a whole or in part by foreign enterprises. Arrangement is geographical by state and city; most listings are for large urban areas. Besides standard directory information, entries generally include the property's square footage, assessed value, number of stories, purchase date and price, joint owners/ventures, and current or planned use. Section 2 lists more than 10,000 foreign-owned businesses arranged by 3-digit SICs, with directory information for both the U.S. and foreign parent company, annual sales, number of employees, and sometimes purchase date and price, sellers, and joint owners/ventures. In both sections, percentage of foreign ownership is given when available for those properties and businesses that are only partially foreign-owned. Three indexes: foreign owners by country, geographic, alphabetic. HG4538.D58

European investment in U.S. and Canadian real estate directory. 1990– . Phoenix : Mead Ventures, c1990– . Annual. ISSN 1049-8508. $195.00. **CH352**

Lists European companies and their intermediaries in separate sections for the U.S. and Canada. Entries include name, address, telephone, fax, and telex numbers; name of parent company and its country affiliation; type(s) of business and type(s) of property; key contact(s); and general information. Also contains brief introductory essays, appendixes (foreign abbreviations, European diplomatic offices, and European chambers of commerce), and indexes—geographic by country or state/province; type of business; type of property; parent company; and country of owner/affiliate.

The real estate sourcebook. 9th ed. (1990)– . Wilmette, Ill. : National Register Pub. Co., Macmillan Directory Division, c1990– . Annual. ISSN 1049-0108. $269.00. **CH353**

Title varies; v.1–8 (1982–89) called *Directory of real estate investors.*

A "comprehensive guide to major investors, brokers, syndicators, developers, service firms, international investors, and sources of financial investment."—*Users guide.* Lists approximately 3,000 companies and organizations, grouped by type of business. Entries generally include address; telephone and fax numbers; line of business; key personnel; contact people for acquisitions and depositions; average purchase price/investment range; size of portfolio; investment structure; and geographic preference. Indexed by company name, property preference, investment range, geographical preference, company type, state/city, and personnel. HD1382.5.D57

Handbooks

Newell, James E. The St. James encyclopedia of mortgage & real estate finance : over 1,000 terms defined, explained and illustrated / James Newell, Albert Santi, Chip Mitchell. Chicago : St. James Pr., c1991. 575 p. : ill. ISBN 1-55738-123-2. **CH354**

Combines brief definitions and lengthy explanations for more than 2,000 terms, concepts, and organizations. Many cross-references and charts, sample forms, and other illustrations.

The real estate handbook / editors in chief, Maury Seldin, James H. Boykin. 2nd ed. Homewood, Ill. : Dow

Jones-Irwin, c1990. 1055 p. : ill. ISBN 0-87094-917-9. $70.00. **CH355**

1st ed., 1980 (*Guide* CH812).

This edition has 58 signed chapters, some illustrated or with bibliographies, organized into sections on real estate transactions, marketing, analysis, financing, and investment. Indexed. HD255.R38

Statistics

ULI market profiles. 1986– . Wash. : Urban Land Institute, c1986– . Annual. ISSN 0894-6108. $229.00 (nonmembers). **CH356**

Continues in part *Development review and outlook* (1983–84).

In two main parts: Market profiles and Market reports. The first contains signed chapters, generally seven to eight pages in length, each dealing in structured format with a specific city or metropolitan area. Discussion of the location's development climate is followed by consideration of real estate development in the residential, retail, office, industrial, and hotel sectors; an area development map; and statistical tables. The second part consists of two-page reports that selectively update information on real estate markets that have been covered in at least one of the previous editions. HD251.U45

SMALL BUSINESS

Handbook of small business data, 1988 / U.S. Small Business Administration, Office of Advocacy. Wash. : The Office : For sale by the Supt. of Docs., U.S. Govt. Print. Off., 1988. 344 p. : ill. **CH357**

The first four chapters describe various government and private sources of data on small business; subsequent chapters consist mainly of statistical tables covering employment, income, business failures, new incorporation, growth, financial ratios, and related topics. List of tables and brief glossary. Not indexed. HD2346.U5H37

Ryans, Cynthia C. Small business : an information sourcebook. Phoenix : Oryx, 1987. 286 p. (Oryx sourcebook series in business and management, no. 1). ISBN 0-89774-272-9. $45.00. **CH358**

Lists and briefly annotates titles pertaining to small business activities (e.g., strategic planning, marketing). Also included are a core list of 185 key reference sources, a directory of publishers, and several appendixes and indexes.

Z7164.C81R92

Small business sourcebook. 4th ed. Detroit : Gale, c1991. ISSN 0883-3397. $85.00. **CH359**

1st ed., 1983 (*Guide* CH198); 3rd ed., 1989.

Expanded and updated, now in 2 v. Vol. 1 has so-called "profiles" (two to 25 pages in length) of 194 specific businesses; v. 2 contains 39 general small business topics, directories and descriptions of sources of assistance offered by state organizations and federal government agencies, a glossary, and master index. The "profiles" do not focus on businesses themselves, but on sources of information about each business, generally grouped under the following categories: start-up information, primary associations, educational programs, reference works, statistical sources, trade periodicals, trade shows and conventions, franchises and business opportunities, information services, and other resources of interest. The general topics covered in v. 2 emphasize specific small business practices or operations (e.g., business plans and government procurement). Categories of sources are the same as those used in v. 1. The state listings section lists government, academic, and commercial agencies within the state (or Canadian province) that offer information and assistance, while the federal listings section covers 29 agencies and offices, including for many their regional, branch, and district offices.   HD2346.U5S66

CJ

Political Science

GENERAL WORKS

Guides

Holler, Frederick L. Information sources of political science. 4th ed. Santa Barbara, Calif. : ABC-Clio, c1986. 417 p. ISBN 0-87436-375-6. $65.00.   **CJ1**
3rd ed., 1980 (*Guide* CJ3).
A revised and greatly expanded edition. A special section on political reference theory and a typology index have been added.   Z7161.H64

Kalvelage, Carl. Bridges to knowledge in political science : a handbook for research / Carl Kalvelage, Albert P. Melone, Morley Segal. Pacific Palisades, Calif. : Palisades Publishers, c1984. 153 p. ISBN 0-913530-37-9 (pbk.). $6.95.   **CJ2**
A successor to *Research guide for undergraduates in political science* by Kalvelage, Segal, and Peter J. Anderson ([Morristown, N.J.] : General Learning Pr., [1972]) and *Research guide in political science* by Kalvelage and Segal (2nd ed., 1976). Both a practical introduction to research tools and a manual for conceptualizing, researching, and writing a paper. Most appropriate for undergraduates. Consists of chapters that treat steps in developing a research paper; e.g., chapter 1 discusses topics that have an economic emphasis and is divided into bibliographic sections (e.g., Economic regulation, Labor policy, Communication policy). Bibliographies are signed, generally not annotated, and limited to English-language publications. General index.
                                                         JA86.K34

York, Henry E. Political science : a guide to reference and information sources. Englewood, Colo. : Libraries Unlimited, 1990. 249 p. (Reference sources in the social sciences series, no. 4). ISBN 0-87287-794-9. $38.00. **CJ3**
Provides annotations for 805 major information sources in political science, its subdivisions, and related social science fields. Groups entries in six chapters: (1) General social science; (2) Social science disciplines; (3) General political science; (4) Political science by geographic area; (5) Political science by topic (e.g., international relations, human rights, peace and conflict); and (6) Public policy. Within chapters, entries are alphabetical under type of publication (e.g., bibliographies, directories, handbooks). Primarily covers English-language publications 1980–87, but serials are included regardless of beginning date. Excludes legal publications, guides to government documents, directories of government officials, texts of laws and

treaties, and state publications. Author/title and subject indexes.   Z7161.Y75

Bibliography

Bergerson, Peter J. Ethics and public policy : an annotated bibliography. N.Y. : Garland, 1988. 200 p. ISBN 0-8240-6632-4.   **CJ4**
Provides 330 citations to selected books, articles, and dissertations published over the last 25 years on ethics and public policy. An extensive introduction provides an overview of the subject and its literature. Entries are arranged in topical chapters (e.g., Ethics and state and local governments, Health care/medical/bio-scientific) and feature lengthy annotations, some a page long. Author index, but no subject index.   Z7161.A15B47

Black, J. L. Origins, evolution, and nature of the Cold War : an annotated bibliographic guide. Santa Barbara, Calif. : ABC-Clio, c1986. 173 p. (War/peace bibliography series, no. 19). ISBN 0-87436-391-8. $50.00.   **CJ5**
Cites English-language books, articles, and dissertations focusing on the Cold War. Topical chapters (e.g., History, Images of the enemy, American-Soviet relations, Regional influences and developments) are subdivided by topic. Annotations; numerous cross-references. Author index and subject index (divided into sections covering persons, regions, and topics).
                                                       Z6465.U5B53

Canadian review of studies in nationalism : bibliography = Revue canadienne des études sur le nationalisme : bibliographie. v. 1 (1974)–14 (1987). Charlottetown, P.E.I. : Univ. of Prince Edward Island, 1974–1987. ISSN 0317-7912.   **CJ6**
For annotation, see *Guide* CJ37.
Ceased with v.14 (1987).

International relations : a handbook on current theory / ed. by Margot Light and A.J.R. Groom. Boulder, Colo. : L. Rienner, 1985. 245 p. ISBN 0-931477-12-3. $25.00.
                                                         CJ7
Prior ed., 1978 (*Guide* CJ5), had title *International relations theory*, ed. by A.J.R. Groom and Christopher Mitchell.
A revised and updated version, consisting of 14 chapters, each a bibliographic essay by a contributing scholar, organized in two sections: (1) The paradigmatic debate (e.g., World society and human needs, Development and dependency) and (2) Partial theories (e.g., Power, Influence and authority, Psychological aspects). Each chapter concludes with a bibliography. Author index; notes on contributors.   JX1291.I56

Jodice, David A. Political risk assessment : an annotated bibliography. Westport, Conn. : Greenwood, 1985. 279 p. (Bibliographies and indexes in law and political science, no. 3). ISBN 0-313-24444-8. $35.00.   **CJ8**
Focuses "on the experience of political risk overseas, e.g., nationalizations, and restrictions on operations, and how American and foreign-based multinational companies and financial institutions have responded to these changes."—*Introd.* Following an essay giving an overview of the field, entries are alphabetically arranged within thematic chapters covering multinational corporations in world politics, sources of political risk, risk management and assessment, and reference sources for risk analysts. Emphasizes books and articles, 1970–83; lengthy annotations. Name index.   Z7164.E17J63

Messick, Frederic M. Primary sources in European diplomacy, 1914–1945 : a bibliography of published memoirs and diaries. N.Y. : Greenwood, [1987]. 221 p. : maps. (Bibliographies and indexes in world history, no. 6). ISBN 0-313-24555-X. $39.95.   **CJ9**

Includes people who held diplomatic or foreign service positions or functioned in that role, or those who witnessed international events or negotiations at first hand and wrote a published memoir or diary in a Western language. For each gives name, dates, a paragraph of explanation, and bibliographic citation. Nationality and subject indexes. Z2000.M395

Nagel, Stuart S. Basic literature in policy studies : a comprehensive bibliography. Greenwich, Conn. : Jai Pr., 1984. 453 p. ISBN 0-89232-367-1. $75.00. **CJ10**

Reprints, updates, and supplements bibliographies previously appearing in unspecified issues of *Policy studies journal* and adds several new bibliographies. In three parts: General aspects of policy studies, Specific policy problems, and Bibliographic syllabi for policy studies courses. The first two parts are divided into topical sections (e.g., selection). Contains sections on footnotes and bibliographies and special skills (e.g., interviewing and corresponding with public officials). The general index would be more useful if it included authors and titles for all the sources mentioned. Z7161.N24

Snyder, Louis Leo. Encyclopedia of nationalism. N.Y. : Paragon House, 1990. 445 p. ISBN 1-55778-167-2. $35.00. **CJ11**

An introductory essay defining and describing nationalism is followed by alphabetically arranged and cross-referenced entries that range in length from a paragraph to several pages and contain brief bibliographies. Coverage extends to nationalism (e.g., Quebec nationalism), nationalist groups (e.g., Irish Republican Army), concepts and topics (e.g., chauvinism), and individuals (e.g., Yasir Arafat). Bibliography; no index.

JC311.S5484

Bibliography of bibliography

Harmon, Robert B. Political science bibliographies. Metuchen, N.J. : Scarecrow, 1976. v. 2. ISBN 0-8108-0558-8 (v. 1). **CJ12**

For v. 1 and annotation, see *Guide* CJ35.

Contains 913 entries arranged alphabetically by topic, then by main entry, with author and title indexes. Z7161.A1H35

Indexes

Politics and religion : a bibliography selected from the ATLA religion database / ed. by Paul D. Petersen ; Ruth F. Frazer, gen. ed. 2nd rev. ed. Chicago : American Theological Library Association, 1984. 774 p. **CJ13**

Presents citations selected from the ATLA (American Theological Library Association) religion database that treat religion and its relationship with politics (e.g., church and state, politics and Islam, Zionism). Includes articles, conference proceedings, and essays in collections, 1949–84, and book reviews for titles published in the 1970s and 1980s. Citations are divided into three sections (each alphabetically arranged): (1) Subject index, (2) Author index (some with annotations), (3) Book review index. Z7776.72.P6

Encyclopedias

Beck, Reinhart. Sachwörterbuch der Politik. 2., erw. Aufl. Stuttgart : A. Kröner, c1986. 1101 p. ISBN 3-520-40002-2. **CJ14**

1st ed., 1977 (*Guide* CJ46).

A completely revised edition. 60 new entries reflect developments and problems in German and international politics (e.g., "Green" movement, women's movement). Now offers cross-references from names or acronyms of significant German and international political groups and persons to the entries that discuss those groups or persons. JA63.B4

The Blackwell encyclopaedia of political institutions / ed. by Vernon Bogdanor. Oxford ; N.Y. : Blackwell Reference, 1987. 667 p. ISBN 0-631-13841-2. $65.00. **CJ15**

Identifies and defines key concepts, terms, and individuals related to political institutions. Includes forms of political organization, types of political community, principal parties and movements, political terms, and important political thinkers of the past. Focuses on Western Europe and the U.S. but has a few items relevant to the Soviet Union and Eastern Europe (e.g., Nomenklatura, Politburo). Alphabetically arranged entries are signed, contain cross-references, and end with bibliographies. General index. There is some overlap with the companion title, *The Blackwell encyclopedia of political thought* (below).

JA61.B56

The Blackwell encyclopaedia of political thought / ed. by David Miller. Oxford and N.Y. : Blackwell, 1987. 570 p. ISBN 0-631-14011-5. $52.50. **CJ16**

Long entries, alphabetically arranged, provide a comprehensive approach to political ideas, doctrines, and theorists. Discusses ideologies in both historical and contemporary contexts. Emphasizes Western tradition but includes survey articles on Chinese, Hindu, and Islamic political thought. Articles contain cross-references, are signed, and end with bibliographies. General index. JA61.B57

Dictionary of modern political ideologies / M.A. Riff, ed. N.Y. : St. Martin's Pr., 1987. 226 p. ISBN 0-312-00928-3. $37.50. **CJ17**

Consists of 42 entries in alphabetic order that treat ideas "since the French and Industrial Revolutions" (*Introd.*) that have shaped and determined political behavior (e.g., the Cold War, the Enlightenment, Islamic fundamentalism, Zionism). The articles are written by specialists, chiefly British, contain cross-references, and end with brief bibliographies. The lack of an index will limit its usefulness. JA61.D53

Evans, Graham. The dictionary of world politics : a reference guide to concepts, ideas, and institutions / Graham Evans and Jeffrey Newnham. N.Y. : Simon & Schuster, 1990. 449 p. ISBN 0-13-210527-6. **CJ18**

Defines the key ideas, concepts, and institutions of world politics (e.g., deterrence, human rights) as well as more specialized terms (e.g., domino theory, no-first-use, SDI). Omits individuals unless they are associated with particular ideas or policies (e.g., Monroe doctrine, Schuman plan) and only includes 20th-century events of continued relevance (e.g., Bay of Pigs, Camp David accords). More than 600 entries, ranging in length from a paragraph to two pages, are alphabetically arranged and contain cross-references. Bibliography; no index. JA61.E85

Kurian, George Thomas. The encyclopedia of the Third World. 3rd ed. N.Y. : Facts on File, c1987. 3 v. (2342 p.) : ill. ISBN 0-8160-1118-4 (set). **CJ19**

Rev. ed., 1982 (*Guide* CJ212).

Incorporates changes up to June 1, 1986 and includes four new entries: Antigua and Barbuda, Belize, Brunei, and St. Kitts and Nevis. HC59.7.K87

Plano, Jack C. The international relations dictionary / Jack C. Plano, Roy Olton. 4th ed. Santa Barbara, Calif. : ABC-Clio, c1988. 446 p. ISBN 0-87436-477-9. $42.95. ISBN 0-87436-478-7 (pbk.). $18.00. **CJ20**

3rd ed., 1982 (*Guide* CJ58).

This edition includes a "guide to Major Concepts for quick and easy access to all of the terms included in the work."—*Pref.* JX1226.P55

Robertson, David. A dictionary of modern politics. Philadelphia : Taylor & Francis, c1985. 341 p. ISBN 0-85066-320-2. $34.00.　　**CJ21**

Key terms and concepts in political science, emphasizing ideas because they are the "enduring elements of political argument."—*Pref.* Includes concepts (e.g., public interest), political ideologies (e.g., Falangism), influential political thinkers (e.g., Durkheim), selected political parties of Western states (e.g., PCI). Entries are lengthy, contain cross-references, and are written in concise, effective style; but there is no index and no bibliography.　　JA61.R63

Smith, John William. The urban politics dictionary / John W. Smith, John S. Klemanski. Santa Barbara, Calif. : ABC-Clio, c1990. 613 p. ISBN 0-87436-533-3. ISBN 0-87436-534-1 (pbk.).　　**CJ22**

Covers approximately 600 terms relating to 20th-century urban politics and life (e.g., citizen advisory board, enterprise zone, gridlock, sinking fund), primarily in the U.S. and Canada. Alphabetically arranged entries include both a descriptive definition and a paragraph analyzing the term's historical and contemporary significance. Cross-references; suggested readings. General index.　　JS48.S65

Worldmark encyclopedia of the nations. 7th ed. N.Y. : Worldmark Pr. : J. Wiley, exclusive world distributor, c1988. 5 v. : maps (some col.). ISBN 0-471-62406-3. $285.00 (est.).　　**CJ23**

6th ed., 1984 (*Guide* CJ218).

Contents: v. 1, United Nations; v. 2, Africa; v. 3, Americas; v. 4, Asia & Oceania; v. 5, Europe.

Continues the five-volume plan of previous editions and their policy of revision and updating throughout.　　G63.W67

Dictionaries

Kleines politisches Wörterbuch. Neuausg. Berlin : Dietz, 1989. 1148 p. ISBN 3-320-01177-4.　　**CJ24**

3., überarb. Aufl., 1978 (*Guide* CJ55); 4., überarb. Aufl., 1983.

Reflects domestic and international changes resulting from the 11th meeting of the East German Communist Party and the 27th meeting of the Soviet Communist Party. Also includes terms used in Marxist-Leninist discourse and theory.　　JA63.K54

Kruschke, Earl R. The public policy dictionary / Earl R. Kruschke, Byron M. Jackson. Santa Barbara, Calif. : ABC-Clio, c1987. 159 p. (CLIO dictionaries in political science, 15). ISBN 0-87436-443-4.　　**CJ25**

Introduces basic concepts in U.S. public policy and public policy-making. Entries, alphabetically arranged within five broad topical chapters (Nature, Formulation, Implementation, Types, and Evaluation and impact) include both an up-to-date definition (often ending with cross-references) and a paragraph that describes the term's relevance. Bibliography; general index.　　H97.K78

Terminology

Thematic list of descriptors—political science = Liste thématique des descripteurs—science politique / prepared on behalf of UNESCO by the International Committee for Social Science Information and Documentation. London ; N.Y. : Routledge, 1989. 481 p. ISBN 0-415-01778-5.　　**CJ26**

Companion to *International bibliography of political science* (*Guide* CJ39). For description, see *Supplement* CE16.　　Z695.1.P63T48

Quotations

Political quotations : a collection of notable sayings on politics from antiquity through 1989 / Daniel B. Baker, ed. Detroit : Gale, c1990. 509 p. ISBN 0-8103-4920-5.　　**CJ27**

Some 4,000 quotations on political topics, dating from biblical times to the present, are chronologically arranged under 53 general subject headings (e.g., Democracy, Ethics in politics, War and peace). Each includes the source and the version in the original language if appropriate. Author and keyword indexes cite entry rather than page numbers.　　PN6084.P6P64

The wit & wisdom of politics / collected, compiled & arranged by Charles Henning. Golden, Colo. : Fulcrum, 1989. 305 p. ISBN 1-55591-043-2. $12.95.　　**CJ28**

Presents short quotations under 188 alphabetically arranged topics (e.g., Bureaucracy, Politicians, Vice presidents). Table of contents lists the topics. Index of persons quoted.　　PN6288.P6W57

Directories

Day, Alan J. Political parties of the world. 3rd ed. Chicago : St. James Pr., 1988. 776 p. ISBN 0-912289-94-5.　　**CJ29**

1st ed., 1980 (*Guide* CJ209); 2nd ed., 1984, was edited by Alan J. Day and Henry W. Degenhardt.

This edition contains substantially revised and updated material in both its country introductions and party descriptions. Has been expanded to incorporate a greater number of minor parties, for a total of 2,130 parties. The appendixes contain information on party organizations which are international in scope, and a long party name index.　　JF2051.D39

Directory of European political scientists / comp. and ed. by the Central Services, European Consortium for Political Research, University of Essex. 4th fully rev. ed. München ; N.Y. : Zell, 1985. 627 p. ISBN 0-905450-12-4.　　**CJ30**

3rd fully rev. ed., 1979 (*Guide* CJ64).

This edition covers more political scientists in Southern Europe, provides additional information for many listings, and has been expanded to 2,499 entries.　　JA84.E9D57

A guide to graduate study in political science. 1972– . Wash. : American Political Science Association, 1972– . ISSN 0091-9632. $2.50.　　**CJ31**

For annotation, see *Supplement* CB99.　　JA88.U6G8

Worldwide government directory, with international organizations. 1987–88– . Bethesda, Md. : National Standards Association, c1987– . Annual. ISSN 0894-1521. $325.00. $275.00 (pbk.).　　**CJ32**

Publ. by Cambridge Information Group Directories, 1988– .

A directory, organized by country, of government officials in 175 countries, followed by an alphabetical list of international organizations. An appendix contains maps.　　JF37.L345

Handbooks

Elections since 1945 : a worldwide reference compendium / gen. ed., Ian Gorvin. Burnt Mill, Harlow, Essex, England : Longman ; Chicago : St. James Pr., 1989. 420 p. : ill. ISBN 0-582-03620-8. **CJ33**

Describes trends in national presidential and legislative elections for sovereign states, 1945–88 or, in the case of former colonies, from the date of independence. Entries are alphabetical by country (plus a section for the European Parliament), and include electoral system, evolution of suffrage, principal political parties, and an electoral summary. Ranging in length from one to nine pages, entries vary as to completeness of information: some (e.g., U.K., France) contain charts, an electoral map, and many details while others (e.g., Canada, Romania) do not mention political leaders. A brief appendix explains proportional representation electoral systems. No index. Provides an overview and statistical trends, but for more details it is necessary to consult *Europa year book* (*Guide* CJ220), *Political handbook of the world* (*Guide* CJ222), and items such as *World encyclopedia of political systems & parties* (*Supplement* CJ136) and *Political parties of the world* (*Supplement* CJ29). JF1001.E378

Ethics, government, and public policy : a reference guide / ed. by James S. Bowman and Frederick A. Elliston. N.Y. : Greenwood, 1988. 341 p. : ill. ISBN 0-313-25192-4. **CJ34**

Considers "the ethical questions that affect government policy and administration."—*Introd.* Consists of 12 topical chapters containing essays (most including literature reviews and case studies) by scholars in governmental administration, in four sections covering: Analytical approaches; Ethical dilemmas and standards for public servants; Techniques and methods in ethical policy-making; and Studies of systemic issues in government. A final essay provides a comparative analysis of ethics, public policy, and public service. Bibliography; general index. JA79.E824

Munro, David. A world record of major conflict areas / David Munro, Alan J. Day. Sevenoaks [England] : Edward Arnold, 1990. [384] p. : maps. ISBN 1-55862-066-4. £35.00. **CJ35**

Describes 28 current areas of conflict, with chapters for each, in five sections: Africa, Middle East, Asia/Far East, Americas, and Europe. Includes not only widely known countries such as Afghanistan, but also less familiar regions such as East Timor. Chapters follow a standard format, beginning with a map and an introduction describing the historical background and current status of the conflict, together with a chronology, followed by sections outlining key personalities, important locations, and other ingredients such as organizations, treaties, ethnic groups, etc. Not indexed. D842

Political risk yearbook. 1987– . Syracuse, N.Y. : Political Risk Services, 1991– . **CJ36**

Publisher varies. 1987–1990, N.Y. : Frost & Sullivan.

Contents: v. 1, North and Central America; v. 2, Middle East and North Africa; v. 3, South America; v. 4, Sub-Saharan Africa; v. 5, Asia and the Pacific; v. 6, Europe: countries of the European Community; v. 7, Europe: outside the European Community.

Published annually in 7 v.

Developed by Political Risk Services for students, faculty, and researchers, this annual publication draws on data gathered from 250 country specialists throughout the world and provides probability forecasts on political and economic matters in addition to political, economic, and social data. Covers 85 countries that are internationally significant, alphabetically dividing each volume into sections by country. Each country report contains: an executive summary; update data (if available before publication); map and list of territorial and maritime disputes; fact sheet; background review; information on politically important individuals and organizations, the regime's stability,

level of turmoil, international investment restrictions, trade restrictions, economic policies; and a five-year political and economic forecast projecting three possible scenarios. No index.

Political scandals and causes célèbres since 1945 : an international reference compendium / contributors, Louis Allen ... [et al.]. Chicago : St. James Pr., [1991]. 478 p. ISBN 1-55862-009-5. **CJ37**

Brings together information on major political scandals since 1945 (e.g., Waldheim affair, Iran-Contra). Selection was based on the event being political in content or implication and being identifiable as a self-contained episode. Entries examine the evolution and impact of the scandal, provide a summary of the facts and leading interpretations, and put the episode into historical context. Entries are signed, contain cross-references and are arranged chronologically within alphabetically arranged country sections. Personal name index.

Revolutionary and dissident movements : an international guide / ed. by Henry W. Degenhardt. 2nd ed., rev. and updated. Burnt Mill, Harlow, Essex, England : Longman ; Detroit : Gale, 1988. 466 p. ISBN 0-582-00986-3. ISBN 0-8103-2056-8. **CJ38**

1st ed., 1983 (*Guide* CJ210), had title: *Political dissent: an international guide to dissidents, extra-parliamentary, guerilla and illegal political movements.*

Arranged alphabetically by country. Select bibliography; index. JC328.3.D43

Chronologies

Jessup, John E. A chronology of conflict and resolution, 1945–1985 / John E. Jessup. N.Y. : Greenwood, 1989. 942 p. ISBN 0-313-24308-5. **CJ39**

Briefly describes significant events relating to international and intranational conflicts, beginning with September 2, 1945 (shortly after the end of World War II), giving day, country, and an account of what transpired, typically ranging in length from less than a sentence to several sentences. Glossary of abbreviations. A 96-page general index has few subheadings; some headings are heavily posted. U42.J47

Biography

Rees, Philip. Biographical dictionary of the extreme right since 1890. N.Y. : Simon & Schuster, 1991. 418 p. ISBN 0-13-089301-3. **CJ40**

Contains nearly 500 entries, international in scope, alphabetically arranged, sketches typically ranging from one-half to a full page in length followed by several references. Besides political leaders, includes philosophers, novelists, others. The author's intent is to be "critical and evaluative" without "unwarranted judgment and polemic."—*Introd.* D412.6.R39

Atlases

Chaliand, Gérard. A strategic atlas : comparative geopolitics of the world's powers / Gérard Chaliand and Jean-Pierre Rageau. Rev. and updated, 1st Perennial Library ed. N.Y. : Harper & Row, 1990. 224 p. : some maps in color ; 20 x 26 cm. ISBN 0-06-055183-6. $29.95. ISBN 0-06-096434-0 (pbk). $17.95. **CJ41**

1st ed., 1983; 2nd ed., 1985.

Translation of: *Atlas stratégique.*

Treats cultural as well as the usual political, military, and economic factors, and pays careful attention to smaller, regional powers. Hence, a map of Nigeria charts tribal groups, and another entitled "Arab Muslim view of the world" shows Muslim-controlled regions, those with strong Muslim minorities, and their neighbors. In addition, contains not only maps with the usual Mercator projections, but also polar projections in order to convey the true size of oceans and to account for polar regions' not being barriers to missiles and nuclear submarines. Arranged topically, with chapters on such considerations as historical context, natural constraints (such as deserts), and security perceptions of individual nations. No index, but has a detailed table of contents.   G1046.F1C513

Freedman, Lawrence. Atlas of global strategy. N.Y.: Facts on File, c1985. 192 p. : ill. (some col.). ISBN 0-8160-1058-7.   **CJ42**

Not a straightforward reference work but a summary of the author's ideas on the world geopolitical situation as of 1985. Its reference value lies in its maps, which portray global strategic concerns and theories, including the polar areas. Especially useful may be those in the chapter on war since 1945, which describes even conflicts in small countries (e.g., revolution in Chad). List of illustrations and general index.   U42.F74

Leonard, R. L. World atlas of elections : voting patterns in 39 democracies / Dick Leonard and Richard Natkiel. London : The Economist Publications, c1986. 159 p.   **CJ43**

Presents voting patterns for the most recent elections (often supplemented by historical data) in an alphabetical arrangement by country. Graphs, tables, and maps are used to indicate main political parties, parties in power, electoral distribution, etc. Concludes with a section on the European Parliament and a "Stop press" supplement.   G1046.F9L4

NATIONAL POLITICS & GOVERNMENT

United States

Bibliography

Beede, Benjamin R. Military and strategic policy : an annotated bibliography. N.Y. : Greenwood, 1990. 334 p. (Bibliographies and indexes in military studies, no. 2). ISBN 0-313-26000-1.   **CJ44**

Cites with brief annotations 1,900 works on U.S. policy during the presidencies of Eisenhower through Reagan. In an essentially chronological arrangement, offers chapters on individual administrations and on the Vietnam confrontation, as well as chapters on bibliographies and other reference works and on general and comparative studies. Cites many of the documents reprinted in *U.S. national security policy and strategy : documents and policy proposals*, ed. by Sam C. Sarkesian with Robert A. Vitas (N.Y. : Greenwood, 1988).   Z1361.D4B4

Bowman, James S. Gubernatorial and presidential transitions : an annotated bibliography and resource guide / James S. Bowman and Ronald L. Monet. N.Y. : Garland, 1988. 113 p. (The public affairs and administration series, 19). ISBN 0-8240-7218-9. $37.00.   **CJ45**

Somewhat misnamed, this brief bibliography (211 entries) actually focuses on several aspects of gubernatorial and presidential government in the U.S. Annotated citations are listed alphabetically in topical chapters that cover: Transitions; Management, leadership, and executive functions; and Executive offices, staffing, and appointments. Includes articles, monographs, and dissertations published in the last 25 years. 16 appendixes, mainly tables, offer a variety of relevant information (e.g., state cabinet systems, the powers and duties of lieutenant

governors, dates in gubernatorial transitions). Author index.   Z1249.P7B68

Dillman, David L. Civil service reform : an annotated bibliography. N.Y. : Garland, 1987. 239 p. ISBN 0-8240-8480-2.   **CJ46**

Offers 539 annotated citations, emphasizing those that relate to the 1978 Civil Service Reform Act (CSRA). Includes English-language government documents, books, and articles published primarily 1976–86. Within six topical chapters (e.g., Historical perspective, Impetus for reform, State and local reform) entries are arranged alphabetically by author (excepting government documents which are chronological). Appendixes provide excerpts from key provisions of the CSRA and a list of organizations interested in civil service reform. Cross-references; author and subject indexes.   Z7164.C6D54

Johansen, Elaine. Political corruption : scope and resources : an annotated bibliography. N.Y. : Garland, 1990. 241 p. ISBN 0-8240-3529-1.   **CJ47**

Contains 914 entries (most annotated) to English-language articles, books, dissertations, government publications, law cases, and statutes, primarily from the last 20 years, on political corruption in the U.S. alone or in comparison with other countries. Excludes material on campaign finance and police corruption. Contains ten topical chapters (e.g., Legal writings, Business-government corruption, Public opinion and corruption) with entries arranged alphabetically. A general introduction explains the scope and framework of the book, and each chapter has its own brief introduction. General index.   Z7164.C94J64

Kaid, Lynda Lee. Political campaign communication : a bibliography and guide to the literature, 1973–1982 / by Lynda Lee Kaid and Anne Johnston Wadsworth. Metuchen, N.J. : Scarecrow, 1985. 217 p. ISBN 0-8108-1764-0.   **CJ48**

Continues *Political campaign communication* by Kaid [et al.] (*Guide* CJ83).

Includes nearly 2,500 entries for items published 1973–82. This volume excludes government documents, unpublished papers presented at meetings and conferences, and articles in popular magazines and newspapers and omits the French and German supplement, the annotated list of selected books, and the list of professional and scholarly organizations.   Z7164.R4K34

Indexes

Garza, Hedda. The Watergate investigation index : House Judiciary Committee hearings and report on impeachment. Wilmington, Del. : Scholarly Resources, 1985. 261 p. ISBN 0-8420-2186-8. $95.00.   **CJ49**
          KF27.J8

———— The Watergate investigation index : Senate Select Committee hearings and reports on presidential campaign activities. Wilmington, Del. : Scholarly Resources, 1982. 325 p. ISBN 0-8420-2175-2. $75.00.   **CJ50**

These volumes provide detailed indexes, respectively, to the 39 volumes of the hearings and report of the House Judiciary Committee on the resolution to impeach President Richard Nixon, and to the 26 volumes of the hearings (including public testimony, Executive Committee testimony, and exhibits) and the final report of the Senate Select Committee on Presidential Campaign Activities (Watergate Committee). The indexes include subjects, personal names, organizations, geographic names, and cross-references. Preceding the House index is a list of indictments brought by the Special Prosecutor; the Senate volume includes a list of Committee members and witnesses.

The Senate volume does not cover the two-volume appendix.

KF26.5.P7

Encyclopedias

Encyclopedia of U.S. government benefits : a complete, practical, and convenient guide to United States government benefits available to the people of America / ed. by Beryl Frank. New & completely rev. ed. N.Y. : Dodd, Mead, 1985. 518 p. : ill. ISBN 0-396-08438-9.   **CJ51**
New & rev. ed., 1981 (*Guide* CJ95).
Completely rewritten and updated. Retains format, scope, and coverage but omits cross-references found in 1981 edition.

JK424.E55

Filler, Louis. Dictionary of American conservatism. N.Y. : Philosophical Library, c1987. 380 p. ISBN 0-8022-2506-3. $29.95.   **CJ52**
Called by its author the first dictionary of conservatism, this work "defines past and present conservative concepts and illustrates their workings with examples and references" (-*Introd.*) and offers entries that describe persons and movements. Explains concepts from a conservative viewpoint (e.g., the entry for World War II says the number of conservatives with fascist tendencies was overestimated by "left-wing propagandists"). Alphabetically arranged.   JA84.U5F55

Findling, John E. Dictionary of American diplomatic history. 2nd ed., rev. and expanded. N.Y. : Greenwood, 1989. 674 p. : ill. ISBN 0-313-26024-9.   **CJ53**
1st ed., [1980] (*Guide* CJ96).
Expands coverage to mid-1988. About 100 entries have been added, a few dropped, and many revised. Adds the last two years of the Carter administration and seven years of the Reagan administration.   E183.7.F5

Plano, Jack C. The American political dictionary / Jack C. Plano, Milton Greenberg. 8th ed. N.Y. : Holt, Rinehart, and Winston, c1989. 608 p. ISBN 0-03-022932-4.   **CJ54**
7th ed., 1985 (*Guide* CJ98).
Revises and updates many entries; includes new terms.

JK9.P55

Renstrom, Peter G. The electoral politics dictionary / Peter G. Renstrom, Chester B. Rogers. Santa Barbara, Calif. : ABC-Clio , c1989. 365 p. ISBN 0-87436-517-1. ISBN 0-87436-518-X (pbk.).   **CJ55**
Contains 404 entries arranged alphabetically within seven topical chapters (e.g., Political parties), each of which begins with an overview of the material covered in the chapter. Focuses on ideas, terms, concepts, organizations, federal statutes, and court decisions relevant to electoral politics in the U.S. Entries feature a lengthy definition and a paragraph called "Significance" that gives historical perspective and puts the entry into a political context. Covers fewer topics, but in more depth, than Michael Young's *The American dictionary of campaigns and elections* (below). Cross-references. Name and subject index.   JK1971.R46

Shafritz, Jay M. The Dorsey dictionary of American government and politics. Chicago : Dorsey Pr., c1988. 661 p. : ill. ISBN 0-256-05639-0. $26.00. ISBN 0-256-05589-0 (pbk.). $18.00.   **CJ56**
Defines terms, phrases, and processes relevant to U.S. national, state, or local government and politics (e.g., Apportionment, General welfare clause, Primary). Also includes significant Supreme Court cases, laws, biographical sketches, political slang, scholarly journals, and professional associations. The more than 4,000 alphabetically arranged entries often cite bibliographic sources and occasionally include illustrations, sidebars, statistics, or lists. Among five appendixes are guides

to federal government publications and online databases relevant to U.S. government. Cross-references.   JK9.S42

Young, Michael L. The American dictionary of campaigns and elections. Lanham, Md. : Hamilton Pr., c1987. 246 p. ISBN 0-8191-5446-6. $29.95.   **CJ57**
Contains 725 entries that define and describe "the major notions, concepts, tools and terms associated with the contemporary American political campaign" (*Pref.*), arranged alphabetically within seven topical chapters (e.g., Polling and public opinion). Includes a bibliography and a subject index that is awkward to use because it refers to chapters rather than page or entry numbers. Entries end with cross-references. Has more but briefer entries than Peter G. Renstrom's *The electoral politics dictionary* (above).   JK1971.Y68

Dictionaries

Guide to federal government acronyms / ed. by William R. Evinger. Phoenix : Oryx, 1989. 279 p. ISBN 0-89774-458-6.   **CJ58**
Lists nearly 20,000 acronyms, initialisms, and abbreviations found in federal documents, regulations, publications, news releases, and other materials. In two parts: acronyms, initialisms, and abbreviations followed by their expanded forms; and a reverse list. The first part includes agency, organization, program, and budget names, position titles, laws and the legislative process, budgeting, agency products and services, names of agency computer systems, terms found in regulations, publication titles, names of surveys, and data collections. Also covers international organizations, programs, and activities in which the U.S. participates.   JK464

Directories

American lobbyists directory. Detroit : Gale, c1990– . $169.00.   **CJ59**
Subtitle: A guide to the more than 65,000 registered federal and state lobbyists and the businesses, organizations, and other concerns they represent.
Gives the names, addresses, and telephone numbers of businesses/organizations and their lobbyists. Entries are arranged by state (including District of Columbia), then alphabetically by sponsoring body. A section on federal lobbyists, printed on yellow paper for quick reference, precedes the state entries. Includes a list of federal and state disclosure offices. Lobbyists, organizations, and subject/specialty indexes. Excludes laws and rules governing registration of lobbyists but otherwise fills the gap left by the discontinuance with the 2nd ed., 1975, of *Directory of registered lobbyists and lobbyist legislation* (*Guide* CJ104). For federal lobbyists, see also *Washington representatives* (*Guide* CJ113).   JK1118.A65

Beacham's guide to key lobbyists : an analysis of their issues and impact / [executive ed., Walton Beacham ; senior ed., Margaret Roberts ; coordinating ed., C. Peter Kessler]. Wash. : Beacham Pub., 1989. 632 p. : ill. ISBN 0-933833-13-X. $195.00.   **CJ60**
Presents information on 125 key lobbyists in Washington—their organizations, issues, and influence. Alphabetically arranged profiles offer a photograph, personal data, organization data, and narrative descriptions of the lobbyist's employment history, lobbying activities, and organization. Three appendixes: Selected PAC contributions for 1987–88, 1987 honoraria paid to members of Congress, and Lobbyists grouped by issue areas. General index. For other directories of lobbyists, consult *Washington representatives* (*Guide* CJ113) or *American lobbyists directory* (above).   JK1118.B3924

Black elected officials / Joint Center for Political Studies. 1984– . N.Y.: UNIPUB, c1984– . Annual. ISSN 0882-1593.　　**CJ61**

Provides names, addresses, offices held, and date elected for government officials, including senators, representatives, judges, county and city officers, and members of school boards. Listed by state, then by categories of federal, state, or local offices. Contains a summary, including tables, of the number of African-American officials throughout the U.S. Index of names.　　E185.615.N29

Government programs and projects directory. 1st ed. (May 1983)– . Detroit: Gale, c1983– . Irregular. ISSN 0737-5255.　　**CJ62**

Lists U.S. federal government programs administered by "executive departments and independent agencies" (*Subtitle*)—e.g., Cancer Control Program, Skill Training Improvement Program, Food Stamp Program. Compiled from the *Catalog of federal domestic assistance* (*Guide* CH119), annual and other reports from sponsoring departments and agencies, questionnaire responses, and correspondence with federal public information agencies. Published in three issues per year, each consisting of approximately 400 entries alphabetically arranged by department and agency. Entries include name of program or project, sponsoring department or agency and its address, legislative authorization, program description, funding, and source of entry's information. Name and keyword index cumulates with each issue.　　JK404.G68

Guide to the American left. Kansas City, Mo.: Editorial Research Service, 1986– .　　**CJ63**

Lists more than 3,200 American organizations that "represent some form of sympathy with and/or interest in various forms of collectivism and/or liberalism and/or environmentalism and/or homosexual rights and/or other issues traditionally identified with 'left' political positions."—*Introd.* The main section, arranged by zip code, consists of one-line entries, each giving address and a two-letter code for the organization's chief concern (e.g., AN for antinuclear; MS for Marxist-socialist). Another section lists groups alphabetically, giving the zip codes under which addresses may be found in the main section. Also contains a bibliography of more than 900 citations, some with single-sentence annotations.

Guide to the American right. Kansas City, Mo.: Editorial Research Service, c1984– .　　**CJ64**

Lists some 3,500 American and Canadian organizations that "represent some form of protest against, opposition to, or concern about the threat of totalitarianism, collectivism and/or its various manifestations *as they see it*."—*Introd.* Like the companion publication (above), gives for each entry address and codes indicating the group's chief interests. The main section is arranged by zip code. Includes a substantial bibliography and an alphabetical index of organizations.　　HS2321.D57

National directory of corporate public affairs. 1st ed. (1983)– . Wash.: Columbia Books, 1983– . Annual. ISSN 0749-9736. $70.00.　　**CJ65**

For annotation, see *Supplement* CH71.　　HD59.N24

Political resource directory. National ed. Rye, N.Y.: Political Resource Directories, c1987– .　　**CJ66**

Covers people and organizations that offer products and services to the political community, primarily in the U.S. The main section lists organizations alphabetically, giving name, address, geographic region, areas of specialization, description of services, percentage of work that is political, and principal contacts. Indexes of organizations by state, specialization (e.g., polling, fundraising, press/public relations), and principal contact. Members of the American Association of Political Consultants are listed in a separate, color-coded section. Includes lists of

national and state Democratic and Republican organizations and of federal and state boards of election.　　JK2283.P65

Public interest profiles. Wash.: Foundation for Public Affairs, [c1977]– . Biennial.　　**CJ67**

Provides information on important public interest organizations (e.g., The Conference Board, Mothers Against Drunk Driving, Greenpeace, League of Women Voters). The 1988–89 ed. contains 250 entries in 12 topical chapters (e.g., Business/economic, Consumer/health, International affairs). Alphabetical entries range from two to five pages in length and offer details such as address, telephone, size of staff, budget, purpose, recent publications, board of directors, and funding sources. Includes assessments of effectiveness and political orientation derived from comments by both supporters and critics in newspapers and magazines. Features a 34-page introduction on the history, behavior, and role of interest groups in American politics. Organization and personal name indexes.　　JK1118.P79

U.S. agricultural groups: institutional profiles / ed. by William P. Browne and Allan J. Cigler. N.Y.: Greenwood, 1990. 274 p. ISBN 0-313-25088-X.　　**CJ68**

For annotation, see *Supplement* EH18.　　HD9005.U19

Watson, Cynthia Ann. U.S. national security policy groups: institutional profiles. N.Y.: Greenwood, 1990. 289 p. ISBN 0-313-25733-7.　　**CJ69**

Describes 135 not-for-profit, essentially educational groups that either are interested exclusively in national security or are large organizations with projects on related topics (e.g., disarmament, strategic defense). Entries, alphabetically arranged, vary in length from one to seven pages, and include the group's national headquarters, address, basic orientation or mission, origins, organization and funding, electoral politics (if it is active in this sphere), and policy concerns and tactics. General index.　　UA23.W364

Handbooks

Austin, Erik W. Political facts of the United States since 1789 / Erik W. Austin; with the assistance of Jerome M. Clubb. N.Y.: Columbia Univ. Pr., 1986. 518 p. ISBN 0-231-06094-7. $45.00.　　**CJ70**

For annotation, see *Supplement* DB70.　　E183.A97

The lobbying handbook / [collected] by John L. Zorack. Wash.: Professional Lobbying and Consulting Center, c1990. 1118 p.　　**CJ71**

Written for the practicing lobbyist, this definitive insider's guide provides advice and pertinent reference sources and documents. In 23 topical chapters (e.g., Getting around Capitol Hill, Lobbying strategy, House legislative procedure, Ethics and the lobbyist), many followed by an essay on the chapter's topic, usually written by a member of Congress. A final chapter offers 80 interviews on lobbying with members of Congress, congressional staff, professional lobbyists, and others. 19 appendixes contain helpful information and relevant documents (e.g., Constitution, Freedom of Information Act, government organization charts, forms of address and salutations). Includes figures and interviews indexes, a general index, and a bibliography.　　JK1118.L58

Wolfe, Gregory. Right minds: a sourcebook of American conservative thought. Chicago: Regnery Books, c1987. 245 p. ISBN 0-89526-583-4. $16.95.　　**CJ72**

In three parts: (1) a briefly annotated bibliography of American conservative writings; (2) short (typically one paragraph) biographies of American conservative thinkers, organized by historical era; and (3) an annotated guide to sources of information, including periodicals, think tanks and foundations, publishers, and collections of private papers. The bibliography is arranged topically in such categories as The American conservative tradition, The welfare state, Communism and ideology, and Crime and punishment. Contains a name index and a foreword by William F. Buckley (whose *National review* sponsored the work).   Z1249.C74W64

Executive Branch

Guides

Congressional Quarterly's guide to the presidency / Michael Nelson, ed. Wash. : Congressional Quarterly Inc., c1989. 1521 p. ISBN 0-87187-500-4. $137.50.   **CJ73**

This massive compendium of information on the origins, evolution, history, and present operation of the presidency also includes facts about the presidents and their families. Has seven sections (e.g., Origins and development of the presidency, Powers of the presidency, The chief executive and the federal government), subdivided into 37 chapters, each ending with footnotes and a selected bibliography. The useful appendix features tables (e.g., a list of cabinet members and officials for each presidential administration), charts (e.g., presidential approval ratings), and documents (e.g., Wilson's "Fourteen Points" speech). General index; cross-references.   JK516.C57

Bibliography

Cohen, Norman S. The American presidents : an annotated bibliography. Pasadena, Calif. : Salem Pr., c1989. 202 p. ISBN 0-89356-658-6. $40.00.   **CJ74**

Provides annotated citations for selected books. Following an introduction covering general bibliographies and studies are separate chapters on each president, George Washington through George Bush. Within chapters, entries are alphabetical by main entry. Author index. Complements Fenton S. Martin and Robert U. Goehlert's *American presidents* (below) and the series "Bibliographies of the presidents of the United States, 1789–1989" (Westport, Conn. : Meckler, 1988–).
        Z1249.P7C63

Goehlert, Robert. The Department of State and American diplomacy : a bibliography / Robert U. Goehlert, Elizabeth R. Hoffmeister. N.Y. : Garland, 1986. 349 p. ISBN 0-8240-8591-4.   **CJ75**

Presents 3,818 unannotated citations to English-language books, articles, dissertations, research reports, and selected documents (primarily 1945–84) covering the history, functions, organizations, structure, and procedures of the U.S. Department of State. An introduction lists State Department publications, guides to U.S. documents, and relevant bibliographies. In four major sections: (1) Topical (e.g., organization, functions, diplomacy); (2) Conduct of foreign policy; (3) Conduct of diplomacy by geographical area; (4) Biographical. Each section contains numerous subdivisions within which citations are alphabetically arranged by author. Author and subject indexes.
        Z6465.U5G63

————— The executive branch of the U.S. government : a bibliography / comp. by Robert U. Goehlert and Hugh Reynolds. N.Y. : Greenwood, 1989. 380 p. (Bibliographies and indexes in law and political science, no. 11). ISBN 0-313-26568-2.   **CJ76**

Lists over 4,000 unannotated citations to English-language monographs, articles, dissertations, and selected research reports (but not government publications) on the executive branch of the U.S. federal government, including the history, development, organization, procedures, rulings, and policies of individual departments. Specifically excludes items on the presidency and the executive office of the White House covered in Goehlert and Fenton S. Martin's *The American presidency* (below) A general chapter on the executive branch, public ad-

ministration, and bureaucracy is followed by chapters for each of the 13 executive departments (e.g., Defense, Education, Treasury) and the U.S. Postal Service. Alphabetically arranged within these chapters, most entries date 1945–85. Author and subject indexes.   Z7165.U5G56

Martin, Fenton S. The American presidency : a bibliography / Fenton S. Martin, Robert U. Goehlert. Wash. : Congressional Quarterly, c1987. 506 p. ISBN 0-87187-415-6. $75.00.   **CJ77**
        Z1249.P7M357

————— American presidents : a bibliography / Fenton S. Martin, Robert U. Goehlert. Wash. : Congressional Quarterly, c1987. 756 p. ISBN 0-87187-416-4. $125.00.   **CJ78**

Two complementary works, the first focusing on the history, development, powers and relationships of the office of the presidency, the other on the individual activities, policies, and accomplishments of the presidents themselves, from Washington through Reagan.

Presidency lists 8,567 unannotated citations in 13 topical chapters (e.g., The presidency and the law, The organization of the presidency, The presidency and foreign affairs). *Presidents* arranges 13,150 unannotated citations chronologically by president, then in five general categories: bibliographies, private life, public career, presidential years, and writings. Both titles include English-language books, articles, dissertations, essays, and research reports, 1885–1986, but exclude government publications; *Presidents* excludes the *Public papers of the presidents* series. Sources consulted by the compilers are listed in the introductions to each title; both have author and subject indexes.
        Z1249.P7M36

Menendez, Albert J. Religion and the U.S. presidency : a bibliography. N.Y. : Garland, 1986. 142 p. ISBN 0-8240-8718-6.   **CJ79**

Lists books, articles, dissertations, and theses relating to the religious beliefs of the U.S. presidents through Ronald Reagan, their relationships with religious communities, and their handling of church-state disputes. Separate chapters (alphabetically arranged) on individual presidents follow an introductory chapter citing general works. Each chapter includes a brief essay, often commenting on the major sources, and a list of unannotated entries (alphabetic by main entry). Author and subject indexes.   Z1249.P7M46

Archives

Burton, Dennis A. A guide to manuscripts in the Presidential Libraries / comp. and ed. by Dennis A. Burton, James B. Rhoads, Raymond W. Smock. College Park, Md. : Research Materials Corp., c1985. 451 p. : ill. ISBN 0-934-63100-X. $90.00.   **CJ80**

For annotation, see *Supplement* AB47.   CD3029.82.B87

Haines, Gerald K. A reference guide to United States Department of State special files. Westport, Conn. : Greenwood, c1985. 393 p. : ill. ISBN 0-313-22750-0.   **CJ81**

Describes the special "lot" files of the Department of State, 1940–59—working papers, drafts, notes, annotated memoranda, and other historically valuable documents on foreign policy—an important supplement to the Department's central files. Entries are arranged in 17 topical chapters (e.g., National security, Asia and the Pacific, Congressional relations), generally following State Department organization. Each entry gives title, content description, dates, amount and location of records, lot file and National Archives accession numbers, finding aids available, and access restrictions. Includes a list of abbreviations and three Department of State organization charts. File number and name/subject indexes.   CD3031

Schick, Frank Leopold. Records of the presidency : presidential papers and libraries from Washington to Reagan / by Frank L. Schick with Renee Schick and Mark Carroll. Phoenix : Oryx, 1989. 309 p. ISBN 0-89774-277-X. $39.50.   **CJ82**

Presents "the story of presidential papers from their origin to their place of deposit" and provides "a comprehensive guide to their contents and to bibliographic references to them."—*Introd.* In four parts: (1) agencies responsible for maintenance of presidential papers, legislation relating to presidential libraries, guides to presidential records, and presidential book collections at historic sites; (2) presidential papers in the Manuscript Division of the Library of Congress; (3) presidential papers in historical societies and special libraries; and (4) presidential libraries administered by the National Archives. Appendixes include tabular data on presidential libraries, lists of major presidential records collections and presidential historic sites, and an overview of the White House filing system. Bibliography; general index.   CD3029.82.S35

Veit, Fritz. Presidential libraries and collections. N.Y. : Greenwood, 1987. 152 p. ISBN 0-313-24996-2.   **CJ83**

Topical chapters discuss the development of presidential libraries, their fiscal impact, the nature of archival collections, the presidential libraries as a group; individually, the repositories of papers of presidents preceding Hoover; and the future of presidential libraries. Information on the libraries and repositories, which includes holdings, policies, services, programs, staff, and budget, was obtained through a questionnaire and from government publications. Appendixes provide statistics on the cost of presidential libraries, 1955–87, a copy of the questionnaire, and a list of organizations supporting presidential libraries. Bibliography; general index.   CD3029.82.V45

Quotations

The bully pulpit : quotations from America's presidents / ed. by Elizabeth Frost. N.Y. : Facts on File, c1988. 282 p. ISBN 0-8160-1247-4. $23.95.   **CJ84**

Contains approximately 3,000 quotations by U.S. presidents from George Washington to Ronald Reagan, chosen because of their "historic significance, intrinsic human interest, and colorful or eloquent language."—*Introd.* Quotations are alphabetical by topic (e.g., equality, law, the presidency), then chronological. Each entry includes the name of the president, source of the quote, and date. An appendix lists the presidents, birth and death dates, and dates in office. Bibliography; author and subject indexes.   E176.1.B925

Directories

Biographical directory of the United States executive branch, 1774–1989 / Robert Sobel, ed. in chief. N.Y. : Greenwood, 1990. 567 p. ISBN 0-313-26593-3.   **CJ85**

For earlier editions and annotation, see *Guide* CJ122.

This edition revised and updated through 1989.

E176.B578

United States. Dept. of State. Office of the Historian. Principal officers of the Department of State and United States chiefs of mission, 1778–1990 / United States Department of State. [Wash.] : U.S. Dept. of State, Office of the Historian, Bureau of Public Affairs : for sale by the Supt. of Docs., U.S. Govt. Print. Off., 1991. 219 p. (Department of State publication, 9825.).   **CJ86**

2nd ed., 1982 (*Guide* CJ111); new rev. ed., 1986; rev ed., 1988.

Superintendent of Documents classification: S 1.2:Of 2/1778–1990.

Updated through August 31, 1990. Beginning with the 1986 edition, information on major executive officers of the Department of State was rearranged and expanded. The work now features two major parts: (1) Principal officers of the Department of State, and (2) United States chiefs of mission. Appendixes include listings of the heads of the U.S. foreign assistance agencies, U.S. trade representatives, and directors of the U.S. Information Agency and the U.S. Arms Control and Disarmament Agency. Personal name index.   JX1706.A59U54

Handbooks

Historic documents on the presidency : 1776–1989 / [ed. by] Michael Nelson. Wash. : Congressional Quarterly, c1989. 1 v. ISBN 0-87187-518-7.   **CJ87**

Contains selected documents focusing on "the most memorable and significant activities of individual presidents."—*Pref.* Emphasizes the development of the presidency as an institution and the leadership role of the president. Documents are chronologically arranged and introduced by notes that place documents in both their contemporary setting and historical context and provide cross-references to other documents. General index.   JK511.H57

Zink, Steven D. Guide to the Presidential advisory commissions, 1973–1984. Alexandria, Va. : Chadwyck-Healey, 1987. 643 p. ISBN 0-85964-122-8. $75.00. **CJ88**

Describes 74 temporary presidential commissions and their work (including task forces, boards, etc.). Arranged by year, entries are systematic and succinct, and for each group list establishment and termination dates, sources of authority (e.g., specific public laws), functions, activities, recommendations, dates and places of meetings, names of members, and publications. For publications, gives title, classification or report number, abstract, and information on availability (the latter useful since nearly half these documents were not distributed through the GPO depository program). Title, subject, and personal name indexes. There are some errors; e.g., the National Commission on Libraries and Information Science is listed in the index but does not appear in the text.   JK468.C7Z56

Sourcebooks

Speeches of the American presidents / ed. by Janet Podell and Steven Anzovin. N.Y. : H.W. Wilson, 1988. 820 p. : ports. ISBN 0-8242-0761-0.   **CJ89**

Contains 180 major speeches of U.S. presidents, Washington to Reagan, delivered during their terms of office. Most are complete; a few that are very long are excerpted. Speeches were chosen to show how speechmaking has grown as a political tool or to illustrate each president's character and to cover important issues of his administration. In chronological order, sections on the presidents begin with brief notes describing the president and his speechmaking style; each speech is preceded by comments on its historical context, composition, and delivery. General index.   J81.C88

Biographical dictionaries

DeGregorio, William A. The complete book of U.S. presidents. 2nd ed. N.Y. : Dembner Books, c1989. 740 p. : ports. ISBN 0-942637-17-8. $29.95.   **CJ90**

1st ed., 1984 (*Guide* CJ123).

A revised edition that includes new information and is updated through George Bush.   E176.1.D43

Kane, Joseph Nathan. Facts about the presidents: a compilation of biographical and historical information. 5th ed. N.Y.: Wilson, 1989. 419 p.: ill. ISBN 0-8242-0774-2.   **CJ91**

    4th ed., 1981 (*Guide* CJ126)

    This edition updates information to March 1989.

                              E176.1.K3

Congress

Guides

Goehlert, Robert. Congress and law-making: researching the legislative process / Robert U. Goehlert and Fenton S. Martin. 2nd ed. Santa Barbara, Calif.: ABC-Clio; Oxford: Clio Pr., c1989. 306 p. ISBN 0-87436-509-0. $35.00.   **CJ92**

    1st ed., 1979 (*Guide* CJ132).

    Revised, reorganized, and considerably enlarged. Additional chapters cover: Federal legislation, Federal administrative law, The congressional budget process, Congressional support agencies, and Foreign affairs and treaties. New sections on committee membership and on how a bill goes through the legislative process. A subject index and a glossary have been added.   KF240.G63

Bibliography

A guide to research collections of former members of the United States House of Representatives, 1789-1987 / prepared under the direction of the Office for the Bicentennial of the United States, House of Representatives; Cynthia Pease Miller, ed. in chief. Wash.: The Office, 1988. 504 p.   **CJ93**

    Superintendent of Documents classification: Y 1.1/7:100-171.

    Provides information on historical papers, diaries and/or memoirs, and oral history collections relating to approximately 3,300 former members of the House of Representatives. Arranged alphabetically by name of representative, entries include birth and death dates, an abbreviation for state represented, and names of repositories along with their holdings, document dates, size of collection, and a brief collection description. Includes various supplementary materials: a list of representatives whose papers were not located; documentary publication projects relating to federal government history; addresses of repositories (alphabetical by state); a chronological table of the sessions of Congress; and a copy of the survey form sent to repositories. Lacks a list of collections by repository. A companion to *Guide to research collections of former United States senators, 1789-1982* (*Guide* CJ135).   CD3043.G84

Kennon, Donald R. The speakers of the U.S. House of Representatives: a bibliography, 1789-1984. Baltimore: Johns Hopkins Univ. Pr., c1986. 323 p. ISBN 0-8018-2786-8.   **CJ94**

    Lists 4,280 books, articles, dissertations, and manuscripts related to the lives and careers of 46 speakers of the House of Representatives (ending with Tip O'Neill) and to the office itself. A general section of works on the speakership, Congress, congressional history, and congressional research is followed by four chronological sections, each beginning with a brief list of works on the speakership and speakers of that period. The chronological sections are further subdivided into chapters on individual speakers, each including a short biographical sketch, a list of available manuscript collections of the speaker's papers, and a bibliography. Includes author and subject indexes.   Z7165.U5K45

Zwirn, Jerrold. Congressional publications and proceedings: research on legislation, budgets, and treaties. 2nd ed. Englewood, Colo.: Libraries Unlimited, 1988. 299 p. ISBN 0-87287-642-X. $27.50.   **CJ95**

    For annotation, see *Supplement* AG6.   JK1067.Z85

Directories

Bosnich, Victor W. Congressional voting guide: a ten year compilation of the 99th Congress. Wash.: V.W. Bosnich, c1987. 630 p. ISBN 0-9618958-0-2 (pbk.).   **CJ96**

    Compiles voting records, 1977-86, for members of the 99th Congress on selected "major votes" chosen by the compiler (e.g., Nicaraguan aid, South Africa sanctions, immigration reform). Divided into House and Senate sections, each beginning with a numbered list (in reverse chronological order) that provides a description of the proposed legislation (119 House Resolutions; 108 Senate Bills or Joint Resolutions) and the overall vote. Following each list are the voting records of individual members on the measures, arranged by state and district in the House section and by state and seniority in the Senate section; each record includes a brief biography and presidential support score. Name index.   JK1051.B67

Sharp, J. Michael. The directory of congressional voting scores and interest group ratings. N.Y.: Facts on File, c1988. 2 v. (1204 p.). ISBN 0-8160-1464-7.   **CJ97**

    Presents ratings of the voting records of members of Congress, 1947-85. Following a helpful introduction explaining the methodology and use of the work, alphabetically arranged entries for each member contain scores on four rating scales compiled by *Congressional Quarterly* (Conservative coalition, Party unity, Presidential support, Voting participation) and ratings by 11 interest groups (e.g., American Civil Liberties Union, National Taxpayers Union). Entries also include biographical data and the percentage of votes received in each election. An appendix lists members of each congress. No index.   JK1051.S555

Stubbs, Walter. Congressional committees, 1789-1982: a checklist. Westport, Conn.: Greenwood, 1985. 210 p. (Bibliographies and indexes in law and political science, no. 6). ISBN 0-313-24539-8.   **CJ98**

    For annotation, see *Supplement* AG15.   JK1029.S78

Handbooks

Congress & defense. 1988- . Palo Alto, Calif.: EW Communications, c1988- . ISSN 1045-5949. $2.20.   **CJ99**

    Attempts to indicate by presenting numerical data the relationship between the U.S. defense industry and individual members of Congress. The main section contains profiles of individual senators and representatives, giving for each the leading Department of Defense (DoD) contractors for his or her congressional district, leading weapons systems, leading DoD contractor political action committee donors, and votes on key defense-related issues. Appendixes give such data as state rankings by DoD total contracts, similar rankings for congressional districts and cities, a ranked list of DoD contractor-sponsored political action committees, and Senate and House defense voting records.   UC263.C63

Congress A to Z: CQ's ready reference encyclopedia. Wash.: Congressional Quarterly, c1988. 612 p.: ill., ports. ISBN 0-87187-447-4. $75.00.   **CJ100**

    Provides comprehensive information on the history, structure, personnel, and operations of the federal government's legislative branch. Written for a wide audience, the entries, alphabetically arranged, are of two types: (1) long essays (three to seven pages) on 30 broad subject areas (e.g., Budget process, Ethics, Seniority system) and (2) briefer entries giving definitions of specific terms, descriptions of congressional committees, and biographies of outstanding members of Congress. An extensive 75-page appendix contains factual and statistical data (e.g., historical lists of Speakers of the House of Representatives, Senate and House floor leaders, cases of expulsion), some miscellaneous information (e.g., how a bill becomes a law), and a bibliography.   Detailed table of contents; cross-references within entries; general index; and index of members of Congress.   JK1067.C67

Congress and the nation. [v. 1] (1945–1964)– . Wash. : Congressional Quarterly Service, 1965– . Quadrennial. ISSN 1047-1324. $135.00.   **CJ101**

For previous volumes and annotation, see *Guide* CJ152.

Contents: v. 4, 1973–76; v. 5, 1977–80; v. 6, 1981–84; v. 7, 1985–88.   KF49C65

Tiefer, Charles. Congressional practice and procedure : a reference, research, and legislative guide. N.Y. : Greenwood, 1989. 1046 p. ISBN 0-313-26355-8.   **CJ102**

An extensive and detailed work that treats both the procedures (i.e., rules and precedents) and practices (e.g., how an agenda is carried out) followed by Congress. Draws heavily from books and articles by members of Congress and political scientists. A lengthy selected bibliography is arranged by topics that correspond to sections of the text—e.g., Agenda setting and structuring House proceedings, Filibuster and cloture, Appropriations. General index. Serves as a valuable companion to the *Senate manual* (*Guide* CJ147), *Senate procedure* (*Guide* CJ148), and Lewis Deschler's *Deschler's precedents* (*Guide* CJ144) and *Deschler's procedure* (*Guide* CJ145).   KF4937.T54

Biography

Members of Congress since 1789. 3rd ed. Wash. : Congressional Quarterly, c1985. 186 p. ISBN 0-87187-335-4 (pbk.). $9.95.   **CJ103**

1st ed., 1977; 2nd ed., 1981.

Contains biographical data on all persons who have served in Congress from 1789 through the first session of the 99th Congress in 1985. In three sections: (1) statistics and summary data on members of Congress (e.g., age, religion); (2) very brief biographies of individual members of Congress; and (3) congressional statistics on sessions, party affiliations, and leaders. Select bibliography.

For more extensive biographies, see: JK1010.M45

United States. Congress. Biographical directory of the United States Congress, 1774–1989 : the Continental Congress, September 5, 1774, to October 21, 1788, and the Congress of the United States, from the First through the One Hundredth Congresses, March 4, 1789, to January 3, 1989, inclusive. Bicentennial ed. Wash. : U.S. Govt. Print. Off., 1989. 2104 p.   **CJ104**

Rev. ed., 1971, had title *Biographical directory of the American Congress, 1774–1971* (*Guide* CJ140).

Comp. and ed. under the direction of the Joint Committee on Printing, Congress of the U.S., ed. by Bruce A. Ragsdale and Kathryn Allamong Jacob.

A revised and corrected edition, updated through 1989. Many of the biographies now include short bibliographies. Closing date of compilation for this edition: June 30, 1988.   JK1010.A5

Congressional districts

Parsons, Stanley B. United States congressional districts, 1843–1883 / Stanley B. Parsons, William W. Beach, Michael J. Dubin. N.Y. : Greenwood, 1986. 225 p. : maps.   **CJ105**

——— United States congressional districts, 1883–1913 / Stanley B. Parsons, Michael J. Dubin, Karen Toombs Parsons. N.Y. : Greenwood, 1990. 439 p. : maps. ISBN 0-313-26482-1.   **CJ106**

Companions to Stanley B. Parsons's *United States congressional districts, 1788–1841* (*Guide* CJ154a). Provide a statistical description of congressional districts through tabular data and maps. Information on eight to fourteen variables (e.g., Percentage of African Americans in the population, Value of farm real estate) is alphabetically arranged by state within decades. Each volume has an introduction explaining methodology, a user's guide, and a table of congresses.   Material on individual congressmen is omitted from these volumes, since for these periods it is covered in *Biographical directory of the United States Congress* (*Supplement* CJ104) and other sources.

G1201.F7P353

Elections

Blake, Fay M. Verbis non factis : words meant to influence political choices in the United States, 1800–1980 / by Fay M. Blake and H. Morton Newman. Metuchen, N.J. : Scarecrow, 1984. 143 p. ISBN 0-8108-1688-1.   **CJ107**

Presents 1,062 U.S. political slogans (e.g., "Fifty-four forty or fight!", "Win with Willkie", "New Frontier") used 1800–1980 on banners, placards, bumper stickers, and buttons, and in campaign songs, speeches, cartoons, advertisements, and commercials. Slogans are listed chronologically and include year, candidate, political party, and at least one book in which the slogan appears. Many entries contain brief explanations of the use or derivation of the slogan. Bibliography; political party, personal name, and keyword indexes.   JK2261.B618

Campaign speeches of American presidential candidates, 1948–1984 / ed. & introduced by Gregory Bush. N.Y. : Ungar, c1985. 343 p. ISBN 0-8044-1137-9. $25.00.   **CJ108**

1st ed., 1976, covered 1928–72.

Presents 44 complete speeches by presidential candidates, 1948–84. Omits speeches 1928–44 that were included in the 1st ed. Includes the nomination acceptance speech and a representative campaign speech for both the Democratic and Republican candidates as well as representative campaign speeches for third-party candidates Henry A. Wallace (1948), J. Strom Thurmond (1948), George C. Wallace (1968), and John B. Anderson (1980). Groups speeches chronologically into election year chapters and begins each with a brief discussion of the major election issues. No index.   E743.C236

Congressional Quarterly's guide to U.S. elections. 2nd ed. Wash. : Congressional Quarterly Inc., c1985. 1308 p. ISBN 0-87187-339-7. $100.00.   **CJ109**

1st ed., 1975 (*Guide* CJ162).

Includes returns through 1984. Contains new sections on pre-1824 gubernatorial elections and gubernatorial and senatorial primaries since 1956.   JK1967.C662

Makinson, Larry. The price of admission : an illustrated atlas of campaign spending in the 1988 congressional elections / Larry Makinson ; [with the assistance of Ellen

Miller... et al.]. Wash., D C. : Center for Responsive Politics, c1989. 173 p. : ill., maps ; 28 cm.   **CJ110**

Presents findings about campaign spending through graphs and charts illustrating the 1988 U.S. congressional races. Concentrates on the relationship between money and votes, level of competition, advantages of incumbency, role of PACS, and stockpiling of campaign funds. An overview of trends, 1974–88, is followed by 1988 data grouped into Senate, House, regional, and state sections. Appendixes provide campaign spending indexes for Senate and House members which include their total receipts, PAC receipts, amount spent, amount opposition spent, and ending balance. General index.   JK1991.M25

Miller, Warren E. American national election studies data sourcebook, 1952–1986 / Warren E. Miller, Santa Traugott. Cambridge, Mass. : Harvard Univ. Pr., 1989. 375 p. ISBN 0-674-02636-5.   **CJ111**

Updates a work by the same title, published in 1980, that covered 1972–78. Now includes results of all 18 biennial studies of voter behavior conducted by the Center for Political Studies, Univ. of Michigan, 1952–86. Seven topical chapters (e.g., Social characteristics of the electorate, Positions on public policy issues), each begin with a descriptive introduction and contain tables with data such as age, education, party identification, issue preference. Contains a list of tables and a general introduction explaining the work. Data is also available on tape from the Interuniversity Consortium for Political and Social Research.   JK1967.M54

The people speak : American elections in focus. Wash. : Congressional Quarterly, Inc., 1990. 288 p. : ill. ISBN 0-87187-513-6. $35.00.   **CJ112**

Updates *Congressional Quarterly's guide to U.S. elections* (above), concentrating on 1984–88. In three parts: (1) Political parties (e.g., 1988 delegate selection, party conventions, nominee acceptance speeches); (2) Presidential elections (e.g., 1984 and 1988 results, 1988 electoral votes); (3) Congressional and gubernatorial elections (e.g., 1986 and 1988 results, off-year and special elections, 1985–89). Also contains a list of corrections to the *CQ guide*. General index.   JK1967.P39

Presidential elections since 1789. 4th ed. Wash. : Congressional Quarterly, c1987.   235 p. :   ill.   ISBN 0-87187-431-8 (pbk.). $11.95.   **CJ113**

3rd ed., 1983 (*Guide* CJ163).
Updated through the 1984 elections.   JK524.P68

Scammon, Richard M. America at the polls 2 : a handbook of American presidential election statistics, 1968–1984 / comp. and ed. by Richard M. Scammon and Alice V. McGillivray. Wash. : Elections Research Center, Congressional Quarterly, 1988. 594 p. : maps. ISBN 0-87187-452-0. $60.00.   **CJ114**

Continues *America at the polls*, 1965 (*Guide* CJ165) and follows the plan of that work.

Includes three new features: (1) a national summary of the popular and Electoral College vote for President, 1920–84; (2) population data and county outline maps for each state; and (3) a summary of Presidential preference primary elections by state and candidate, 1968–84.   JK524.S22

Thomas, G. Scott. The pursuit of the White House : a handbook of presidential election statistics and history. N.Y. : Greenwood, 1987. 485 p. ISBN 0-313-25795-7.   **CJ115**

In four sections: The elections, The candidates, The parties, The role of individual states. The first section groups presidential elections by historical period, giving a brief historical account of each followed by statistical tables that give regional breakdowns (east, south, midwest, west) for primaries, conventions, and general elections through 1984. The second presents brief profiles, alphabetically arranged, of presidential candidates, and charts of each candidate's presidential election record. The third offers party profiles, alphabetically arranged,

followed by charts that provide such information as the number of general elections won by the party's nominee. The last lists the states alphabetically, giving a brief description of the political role of each and tables of its voting record. Selected bibliography; general index. Less extensive than *Congressional Quarterly's guide to U.S. elections* (above), which covers gubernatorial, Senate, and House elections in addition to presidential.   JK524.T44

Political parties

Martis, Kenneth C. The historical atlas of political parties in the United States Congress, 1789–1989 / Kenneth C. Martis, author and ed. ; Ruth Anderson Rowles, cartographer ; Gyula Pauer, production cartographer. N.Y. : Macmillan ; London : Collier Macmillan, c1989. 518 p. : maps in color ; 34 x 46 cm. ISBN 0-02-920170-5.   **CJ116**

The second in a series designed to map the geographic patterns of political parties for each Congress. While Martis's *The historical atlas of United States congressional districts, 1789–1983* (*Guide* CJ154), presented maps showing district boundaries for the first 97 Congresses and listed the representatives from each district, this volume provides political affiliation/party for each district and member of Congress through the 100th Congress (1989). In four parts: (1) a descriptive introduction surveying the history of political parties, congressional elections, and political parties in Congress; (2) national political party maps for each Congress, showing political party affiliation by district and including pie charts of party percentages for House and Senate and lists of members of Congress with their district and party affiliations; (3) and (4) tables showing the sources that were checked to verify party affiliation. Bibliography; general index to Pt. 1 and personal name index to Pt. 2.   G1201.F9M26

National party conventions, 1831–1984. 4th ed. Wash. : Congressional Quarterly, c1987. 264 p. : ports. ISBN 0-87187-450-4 (pbk.). $10.25.   **CJ117**

3rd ed., 1983 (*Guide* CJ174).
Updated through 1984. New features include GOP primary rules, changes in the Democrats' nominating rules, and a brief summary of third-party election results.   JK2255.N374

Biography

American leaders, 1789–1987 : a biographical summary. Wash. : Congressional Quarterly, c1987. 427 p. ISBN 0-87187-413-X. $19.95.   **CJ118**

Lists every American president, vice president, governor, Supreme Court justice, and member of Congress from the first national government through 1987. The five chapters, one for each office, contain short entries listing birth and death dates, incumbency dates, party affiliation, state represented, other offices held, and relatives who held office. For each office, entries are alphabetically arranged (except for governors, who are by state), then chronologically, followed by an alphabetical name index. Appendixes include: (1) a table of political party affiliations in Congress and the presidency, arranged in reverse chronological order, listing the president and the numbers of members from the Democratic, Republican, and other parties during his incumbency; (2) a listing, in chronological order, of the sessions of Congress, their dates, and speakers of the House and presidents pro tempore of the Senate; and (3) a list of leaders of the House and Senate since 1899, including floor leaders and whips.   E176.A495

Biographical dictionary of the American left / ed. by Bernard K. Johnpoll and Harvey Klehr. Westport, Conn. : Greenwood, 1986. 493 p. ISBN 0-313-24200-3. **CJ119**

Brief biographies of 259 figures, intended to provide a "representative cross-section of the leadership of the American Left which will give scholars and general readers a sense of who was in charge in the various radical parties and from what social or ethnic stratum these parties drew their vitality."—*Introd*. Includes such diverse types as Communists, 1960s radicals, academic labor leaders, civil rights activists, etc. Entries are alphabetically arranged and give birthdate and place, other names used, year of immigration, occupations of the biographee and his or her father, political affiliation, major roles in and contributions to radical movements, and sometimes a bibliography. General index. HX84.A2B56

Justice, Keith L. Public office index. Jefferson, N.C. : McFarland, 1985. v. 1. ISBN 0-89950-137-0 (v. 1). $19.95. (In progress). **CJ120**

Contents: v. 1, U.S. presidents, vice presidents, cabinet members, Supreme Court justices.

A source for basic information about major U.S. officials. Following a chronological list of presidential administrations that gives incumbents and terms of office for cabinet positions are sections that give for presidents, vice presidents, cabinet members, and Supreme Court justices: (1) chronological succession lists and (2) biographical data (e.g., birth and death dates, age at and date of inauguration or appointment, retirement date and age, years of service), alphabetically arranged, for those in the lists. Personal name index. Content of forthcoming volumes has not been announced. JK7

State & Local Government

Bibliography

Goehlert, Robert. State legislatures : a bibliography / Robert U. Goehlert, Frederick W. Musto. Santa Barbara, Calif. : ABC-Clio, c1985. 229 p. ISBN 0-87436-422-1. $30.00 (est.). **CJ121**

Cites more than 2,500 scholarly English-language books, articles, dissertations, reports, and selected documents (excluding state documents) published 1945 through mid-1984 on the history, functions, organization, structure, and procedures of state legislatures. In two sections: (1) theoretical and empirical works arranged alphabetically by main entry within 25 topical chapters (e.g., Committees, Decision making, Reapportionment and redistricting); and (2) studies on individual legislatures grouped alphabetically by state. Author and subject indexes. Z7164.R4G574

State blue books, legislative manuals, and reference publications : a selective bibliography / Lynn Hellebust, ed. Topeka, Kan. : Government Research Service, c1990. 142 p. ISBN 0-9615227-7-1. **CJ122**

For annotation, see *Supplement* AG28.

Encyclopedias

Elliot, Jeffrey M. The state and local government political dictionary / Jeffrey M. Elliot, Sheikh R. Ali. Santa Barbara, Calif. : ABC-Clio, c1988. 325 p. ISBN 0-87436-417-5. ISBN 0-87436-512-0 (pbk.). **CJ123**

Defines 290 concepts and terms relevant to the institutions, processes, and policies of state and local government. Entries are arranged alphabetically within 11 topical chapters (e.g., Federal and state constitutions, Intergovernmental relations, Bureaucracy and civil service) and include descriptive definitions, cross-references, and a paragraph explaining the term's historical roots and contemporary importance. General index. JK2408.E44

Handbooks

The handbook of state legislative leaders. 1983/84– . Cambridge, Mass. : Ballinger, c1984– . Annual. ISSN 0743-0728. **CJ124**

Publisher varies; issued by State Legislative Leaders Foundation, 1985– .

Offers political and biographical information on every speaker, president, and majority and minority leader in the state legislatures. Each profile contains a photograph, district, address, telephone, years in office, party affiliation, staff, other political offices held, legislative priorities, and personal data (e.g., birth date, occupation, family, education, military service). Arranged by state; each state section includes state legislative session schedules, terms of office, party composition, committee rosters, and lists of major legislative agencies. Name index. A helpful complement to the directory information found in supplements to *Book of the states* on state legislative leadership, committees, and staff (*Guide* CJ195). JK2484.H27

Kane, Joseph Nathan. Facts about the states / editors, Joseph Nathan Kane, Steven Anzovin, Janet Podell. N.Y. : H.W. Wilson, 1989. 556 p. : ill. ISBN 0-8242-0407-7. $60.00. **CJ125**

Offers "the basic geographic, demographic, economic, political, and cultural facts about the fifty states of the Union, the District of Columbia, and Puerto Rico."—*Pref*. Data were drawn primarily from federal sources listed in the preface. Two sections: state entries in alphabetical order and comparative tables. Three bibliographies follow each state entry: the state in literature; guides to resources; and selected nonfiction sources. Comparative tables cover population, demography, geographic characteristics, education, and finance. Most data current to 1988. E180.K4

State government research directory : a descriptive guide to basic and applied research and data collection programs and activities sponsored and/or conducted by the government agencies of the 50 states, the District of Columbia, and the U.S. territories / Kay Gill and Susan E. Tufts, editors. Detroit : Gale, c1987. 349 p. ISBN 0-8103-1591-2. $225.00. **CJ126**

Offers information on research units sponsored by state government agencies. Alphabetically arranged by state names, with separate sections for each of the 50 states and the District of Columbia, followed by the U.S. territories. Within sections, entries are alphabetical and consist of name, address, telephone, date established, size and composition of staff, research descriptions, special facilities, publications and information services, and special remarks. Indexes of names, keywords, and agencies and of subjects. Q180.U5S78

State information book. 1980/1981–1987/1988. Rockville, Md. : INFAX Corp., [1980]–1988. Biennial. **CJ127**

For annotation, see *Guide* CJ200.

Editor: 1987–88, Gerry Jones.

Ceased with 1987/88 ed.; continued by *State yellow book* (below). JK2408.S73

State legislative sourcebook. 1986– . Topeka, Kan. : Government Research Service, c1985– . Annual. ISSN 0898-7297. $99.50. **CJ128**

Provides basic data and lists sources of information concerning state legislative operations. The 50 state chapters include such information as: legislative organization and process, legislators, session, interim study period, lobbying, and general state information. Bill status and bill room telephone numbers for each state are given in appendixes. Ends with a 37-page bibliography, Resource guide to influencing state legislatures. No index. JK2495.S689

State yellow book. N.Y. : Monitor Pub. Co., c1989– . $135.00. **CJ129**

Supersedes *State information book* (above).

Offers state profiles and personnel information for all 50 states and the District of Columbia, American Samoa, Guam, Puerto Rico, and the Virgin Islands. The first three sections give the names, titles, telephone numbers, and addresses of some 30,000 key executive, legislative, and judicial officials. A state profiles section provides a map, brief history, and selected details (e.g., military installations, county data), and an intergovernmental organization section lists national organizations of state officials. Subject index and name index which groups names alphabetically by state. JK2403.S77

States in profile : the state policy reference book. McConnellsburg, Pa. : Brizius & Foster and State Policy Research, Inc., [1990?]– . **CJ130**

Earlier editions, 1984–89, had title: *State policy data book.*

Features four types of current data relating to policy decisions of state governments: (1) State characteristics (e.g., population, age, composition, income); (2) Workloads and tax bases (e.g., number of school children, cars on the road); (3) Programs (e.g., spending per student); and (4) Program effectiveness (e.g., graduation rate). Compiled from various sources and presented in tabular form, data are grouped into 16 topical chapters (e.g., Education, Health, Transportation). Tables are listed in the table of contents and a cross-reference list compares them with those in the previous edition. Subject index.

Worldmark encyclopedia of the states : a practical guide to the geographic, demographic, historical, political, economic, and social development of the United States. 2nd ed. N.Y. : Worldmark Pr. : Wiley, c1986. 690 p. : maps (some col.). ISBN 0-471-83213-8. **CJ131**

1st ed., 1981 (*Guide* CJ201).

Revisions and updating throughout. E156.W67

Biography

Ritter, Charles F. American legislative leaders, 1850–1910 / Charles F. Ritter & Jon L. Wakelyn ; James H. Broussard, James Roger Sharp, and Nancy Weatherly Sharp, advisory editors. N.Y. : Greenwood, 1989. lxvii, 1090 p. ISBN 0-313-23943-6. **CJ132**

Profiles the 1,390 men who served as speakers of state or territorial houses of representatives in the U.S., 1850–1910. An introduction describes the shift from agrarian to industrial politics, the political economy and economic issues of the times, the evolution of legislatures, the leadership role of the speakers, and provides a statistical career profile for the speakers. The main body of the work consists of alphabetically arranged biographies containing personal and professional data (e.g., birth and death dates and locations, family, education, offices held), ending with a list of sources. Eight appendixes in tabular form list the speakers alphabetically by state, chronologically by years in office, by party membership, etc. Bibliography; name and subject index. E663.R57

Elections

Mullaney, Marie Marmo. American governors and gubernatorial elections, 1979–1987. Westport, Conn. : Meckler, c1988. [103] p. ISBN 0-88736-316-4. **CJ133**

A continuation of Roy Glashan's earlier volume covering 1775–1978 (*Guide* CJ204). JK2447.M85

Statistics

Stanley, Harold W. Vital statistics on American politics / by Harold W. Stanley and Richard G. Neimi. 2nd ed. Wash. : CQ Pr., 1990. 435 p. ISBN 0-87187-516-0 (pbk.). $18.95. **CJ134**

1st ed., 1988.

Contains more than 200 statistical tables, lists, and graphs gathered from a variety of sources. Topical chapters (e.g., Elections and campaigns, Congress, Interest groups, Social policy) include brief introductions and questions designed to test the reader's understanding of the statistics. The general introduction has a helpful section on the accuracy of published data. An appendix lists various definitions of U.S. regions and an annotated "Guide to references for political statistics" describes sources of additional information. General index. A teacher's manual is available from the publisher. Less detailed than *America votes* (*Guide* CJ157), *American public opinion data* (*Supplement* CJ229), and *Congressional Quarterly weekly report* (*Guide* CJ150). JK274.S74

General Works

Bibliography

Huck, Burkhardt J. Informationshandbuch internationale Beziehungen und Länderkunde = Information handbook international relations and area studies / Dietrich Seydel (Hrsg.) ; bearb. von Burkhardt J. Huck. Baden-Baden : Nomos, [1989]. 752 p. (Internationale Politik und Sicherheit, Bd. 26). ISBN 3-7890-1757-4. **CJ135**

For annotation, see *Supplement* DA57.

Encyclopedias

World encyclopedia of political systems & parties / ed. by George E. Delury. 2nd ed. N.Y. : Facts on File, c1987. 2 v. ISBN 0-8160-1539-2 (set). **CJ136**

1st ed., 1983 (*Guide* CJ216).

Contents: v. 1, Afghanistan–Luxembourg; v. 2. Madagascar–Zimbabwe, smaller countries and microstates, index.

Revised and updated to reflect political changes in individual countries in the intervening five years. JF2011.W67

Directories

The international directory of government. 1990– . London : Europa Publications Ltd., 1990– . Annual. ISSN 0956-0998. **CJ137**

Arranged alphabetically by country; for each country includes notes on the head of state, an explanation of the legislature, and directory information for government ministries, departments, agencies, and corporations, together with their ministers and key personnel. No index. Essentially taken from *Europa world year book* (*Supplement* CJ144).

Ó Maoláin, Ciarán. The radical right : a world directory. Burnt Mill, Harlow, Essex, England : Longman ; Santa Barbara, Calif. : Distr. by ABC-Clio, c1987. 500 p. ISBN 0-87436-514-7. $70.00. **CJ138**

Describes 3,000 organizations in 81 countries and four regions or possessions (e.g., Northern Ireland). The groups are as diverse as ultraright death squads and the Republican Party of the U.S. (the latter said to have a "mainstream conservative" orientation), but essentially they represent three overlapping strands: ultraconservative, anticommunist, and right-wing extremist. Each entry is introduced by a brief treatment of the country's political system, recent history, and the evolution of its far right. There follow a list of the country's active organizations, describing their orientation, history, leadership, policies, etc., a section, Defunct organizations, that gives brief descriptions or histories, and, for some nations, a section, Other organizations, that briefly mentions minor groups. Subject index.

HS2303.O18

Parliaments of the world : a comparative reference compendium. 2nd ed. N.Y.: Facts on File, c1986. 2 v. (1422 p.). ISBN 0-8160-1186-9 (set).   **CJ139**
　　1st ed., 1976 (Guide CJ211).
　　Prepared by the International Centre for Parliamentary Documentation of the Inter-Parliamentary Union.
　　Updated through June 1985, expanded to cover 83 parliaments, and now issued in 2 v. Consists of 15 sections (e.g., Parliament and its membership, Parliamentary procedure, Parliament and the media), many subdivided. Within sections, data relating to the parliaments is usually alphabetically arranged by country and presented in tabular form preceded by introductory text. Contains a list of the parliaments covered; omits bibliography included in 1st ed. Subject index.   JF501.P36

Handbooks

Cook, Chris. The Facts on File world political almanac. N.Y.: Facts on File, c1989. 453 p. ISBN 0-8160-1377-2. $29.95.   **CJ140**
　　A concise and convenient assemblage of facts on post-World War II political developments. Divided into sections covering such subjects as: Heads of state; Legislatures and constitutions; Treaties, alliances, and diplomatic agreements (arranged by country); Descriptions of countries, parties, and election results; Incidents of violence; and a Dictionary of events (such as Watergate and Bandung Conference).   D843.C5797

Mackie, Thomas T. The international almanac of electoral history / Thomas T. Mackie & Richard Rose. 3rd ed. Wash.: Congressional Quarterly Inc., c1990. 1 v. ISBN 0-87187-575-6. $60.00.   **CJ141**
　　2nd ed., 1982 (Guide CJ214).
　　Revises and updates information through 1989. Malta, included in the 1st ed. but not the 2nd, is restored. Excludes the appendix on European Community elections found in the 2nd ed.   JF1001.M17

World fact file / ed. by Roger East and the staff of CIRCA Reference. N.Y.: Facts on File, c1990. 607 p.: maps. ISBN 0-8160-2522-3.   **CJ142**
　　An international handbook covering the geography, history, constitution and government, international relations, economy, communications, education, and welfare of all the countries of the world. There is no subject index, but the uniformity of the text for each country and the alphabetical arrangement of country names facilitate the location of information. Includes a map and brief tables of data for many countries.   D843.W636

World government / gen. ed., Peter J. Taylor. N.Y.: Oxford Univ. Pr., 1990. 256 p.: ill. (some col.), maps. ISBN 0-19-520861-7.   **CJ143**
　　Surveys the field of political geography, concentrating on the nature of government and governing institutions throughout the world. Concepts treated in three thematic chapters covering sovereignty and territory, power within states, and relations between states are used to explore the history and current roles of governing institutions in chapters on various regions (e.g., Middle East, Southern Africa). Extensively illustrated with photographs and maps. Glossary; bibliography; general index.   JF51.W65

Yearbooks

The Europa world year book. London, England: Europa Publications Limited, c1989– .   **CJ144**
　　Represents a change of title for the Europa year book (Guide CJ220) beginning with the 1989 edition.
　　Still issued in 2v., with v.1 covering international organizations and the first group of alphabetically arranged country entries and v.2 the remainder of the country entries. Information covered remains substantially the same except the list of universities is no longer included.   JN1.E85

Registers

Da Graça, John V. Heads of state and government. N.Y.: New York Univ. Pr., 1985. 265 p. ISBN 0-8147-1778-0. $60.00.   **CJ145**
　　A register of leaders of 13 major international organizations and 500 present-day nations, provinces, regions, and territories. Arrangement is alphabetic by country; for each, a short historical note is followed by a list of leaders, chronological under the title of their office, their dates in office, family relationship where appropriate, political party affiliation, how the term of office ended if not by natural cause. The work lists some 10,000 leaders, but the absence of a personal name index limits its usefulness.   JF37.D3

Morby, John E. Dynasties of the world : a chronological and genealogical handbook. Oxford ; N.Y.: Oxford Univ. Pr., 1989. 254 p. ISBN 0-19-215872-4. $45.00.
　　　　　　　　　　　　　　　　　　　　　　CJ146
　　A register of major past and present dynasties and their lineage. Arranged by broad geographic area (e.g., Ancient Near East, Europe, Africa), further subdivided by country. For each dynasty, chronological tables list names of rulers, length of reign, relationship to previous rulers, and sobriquets. Also includes supplementary notes and brief bibliographies. Excludes dynasties where no reliable information is available (e.g., kingdom of Medes, most Hindu Indian royal lines). Name index.   CS27.M67

Truhart, Peter. Regents of nations : systematic chronology of states and their political representatives in past and present : a biographical reference book. München ; N.Y.: Saur, 1984. pt. 3/1. ISBN 3-598-10491-X. (In progress).   **CJ147**
　　For earlier numbers and annotation, see Guide CJ231.
　　Contents: pt.3/1, Central, eastern, and northern Europe.
　　　　　　　　　　　　　　　　　　　　　　JF37.T78

World guide to foreign services. Weissensberg, Federal Republic of Germany: World Guides Internationale Publikationen ; Detroit: Distr. by Gale, c1986. 838 p.
　　　　　　　　　　　　　　　　　　　　　　CJ148
　　Subtitle: a directory of ministries of foreign affairs, embassies, consulates, high commissions, missions, legations, delegations, and representations.
　　Added title page and introductory material in German. Title on added t.p.: Internationales Verzeichnis der Auswärtigen Dienste.
　　Lists "18,400 diplomatic and consular services of 170 states."—Pref. Arranged alphabetically by country, providing for each country the address, telephone and telex, office hours, and areas of jurisdiction for its foreign affairs ministry, embassies, consulates, and other foreign missions. Also includes the names of important representatives (e.g., ministers, ambassadors, attachés). No index.   JX1631.W67

Africa

Cook, Chris. African political facts since 1945 / Chris Cook and David Killingray. 2nd ed. N.Y. : Facts on File, c1991. 280 p. ISBN 0-8160-2418-9.   **CJ149**
> 1st ed., 1983 (*Guide* CJ238).
> Revised and updated through 1990.   DT30.C594

Ray, Donald Iain. Dictionary of the African left : parties, movements, and groups. Aldershot, England ; Brookfield, Vt. : Dartmouth, c1989. 273 p. ISBN 1-85521-014-2-. $70.00 (est.).   **CJ150**
> Describes socialist, communist, Marxist, left nationalist, left national liberation, left pan-Africanist, or anti-imperialist parties, movements, or other groups that aim to exercise power at the national or regional level. The main section is arranged alphabetically and gives, in outline form, each organization's establishment date, type (e.g., mass party), legal and political status (e.g., in exile, governing party), publications, orientation (e.g., left nationalist), strategy, history, and leadership. An introductory section provides a history of the African left and a chronology of left-governed states. Indexes acronyms of organizations and groups by country.   HX439.R38

Williams, Gwyneth. The dictionary of contemporary politics of southern Africa / Gwyneth Williams and Brian Hackland. London ; N.Y. : Routledge, 1988. 1 v. ISBN 0-415-00245-1.   **CJ151**
> Includes Angola, Botswana, Lesotho, Malawi, Mozambique, Namibia, South Africa, Swaziland, Tanzania, Zambia, and Zimbabwe. Alphabetically arranged entries cover political figures, political organizations, terms, events, and places. Entries vary in length from one sentence to two pages, have cross-references, and contain the name(s) of the relevant country or countries in parentheses. A list of entries by country and a brief bibliography follow the main body of the works. No index.   JQ2720.A127W55

Arab countries

Shimoni, Yaacov. Political dictionary of the Arab world. N.Y. : Macmillan, c1987. 520 p. ISBN 0-02-916422-2.   **CJ152**
> Rev. ed. of Shimoni and Evyatar Levine's *Political dictionary of the Middle East in the twentieth century* (*Guide* DE71).
> Published in cooperation with the Dayan Center for Middle Eastern and African Studies, Tel Aviv University.
> A Hebrew translation has appeared as *Leksikon politi shel ha-olam ha-'Arvi* (Yerushalyim : Keter, [1988]. 434 p.)
> Despite its title (and like its companion, *Political dictionary of the state of Israel, Supplement* CJ190), more encyclopedia than dictionary (for example, the article "Arab-Israeli conflict" is 38 pages long). Covers only the Arab portion of the Middle East; Israel, Iran, Turkey, and Cyprus are included only as they may be linked to Arab affairs. Covers the 20th century to the mid-1980s. Alphabetically arranged; no index.   DS37.S53

Asia

Political parties of Asia and the Pacific / Haruhiro Fukui, ed. in chief. Westport, Conn. : Greenwood, 1985. 2 v. (1346 p.). ISBN 0-313-21350-X (set).   **CJ153**
> Offers information on political parties and party-like organizations for 41 countries or political entities of Asia and the Pacific. Arranged alphabetically by country, each entry containing an essay on the country's political history, a bibliography, and an alphabetical list of political parties with descriptions. The latter are written by specialists, are signed, and often have brief bibliographies and cross-references. Three appendixes: (1) a chronology of political events, (2) a genealogy of parties, and (3) a typology of parties (e.g., listings by ideology, religion). Name index.   JQ39.A45P64

Ziring, Lawrence. The Asian political dictionary / Lawrence Ziring, C.I. Eugene Kim. Santa Barbara, Calif. : ABC-Clio, c1985. 438 p. : maps. (Clio dictionaries in political science, 10). ISBN 0-87436-368-3. $37.50. ISBN 0-87436-369-1 (pbk.). $15.00.   **CJ154**
> Covers contemporary politics, government, and foreign relations in 27 countries and territories in Asia. Entries are alphabetical within broad categories: Political geography, Political culture and ideology, Political parties and movements, Militarism and the armed forces, Modernization and development, diplomacy, and International relations and conflict. Each entry includes both a descriptive text, giving historical background (and often ending with cross-references), and a "Significance" section relating the entry to developments, ideologies, or history. Entries are preceded by an Asian countries index and followed by a general index.   DS31.Z57

Canada

Feigert, Frank B. Canada votes, 1935–1988. Durham : Duke Univ. Pr., 1989. 351 p. ISBN 0-8223-0894-0.   **CJ155**
> Reports results for Canadian national, provincial, and territorial elections, 1935–88. Divided into chapters corresponding to national, regional summary, and regional individual results, each with an introduction providing contextual information. Extensive tables include: numbers and percentages of votes received and seats won by year, province, and party; seats contested, retained, gained, and lost by year, province, and party; seats won by percentage point margins; voter turnout by year and province or territory; national election results by riding; and provincial and territorial election results. A list of tables precedes an introduction that explains the tables and the book's organization. Bibliography.   JL193.A54

Guide to Canadian ministries since confederation, July 1, 1867–February 1, 1982. [Ottawa] : Govt. of Canada, Privy Council Office, c1982. 326 p. ISBN 0-660-11156-X (pbk.). $15.50.   **CJ156**
> 1st publ., 1957; supplement, 1966; new ed., 1974.
> A chronological list of ministries, giving names and dates of service together with notes on formation and abolition of offices and departments. Name index.   JL97.G84

Mahler, Gregory S. Contemporary Canadian politics : an annotated bibliography, 1970–1987. N.Y. : Greenwood, 1988. 400 p. (Bibliographies and indexes in law and political science, no. 10). ISBN 0-313-25510-5.   **CJ157**
> Contains 3,738 entries for English and French books and articles published 1970–87 on contemporary Canadian politics. A general sources chapter is followed by 13 topical chapters (e.g., Regionalism and local politics; Political parties, ideology, and elections; The administrative process). Entries in each chapter are alphabetically arranged by author under separate sections for books and articles. Although the subtitle indicates entries are annotated, most are not; when annotations occur, they are brief. Keyword index.   Z1385.M35

Maillet, Lise. Provincial royal commissions and commissions of inquiry, 1867–1982 : a selective bibliography = Commissions royales provinciales et commissions d'enquête, 1867–1982 : bibliographie sélective / comp. by Lise Maillet. Ottawa : National Library of Canada,

1986. 254 p. ISBN 0-660-53123-2 (pbk.). $15.00 ($18.00 other countries).   **CJ158**

In English and French.

Facilitates identification and location of reports issued by 767 Canadian provincial royal commissions and commissions of inquiry on political, cultural, economic, or social problems. Unannotated entries are arranged by province, then chronologically. Each entry contains date and name of commission, name and bibliographic data for its report(s), names of chairman and commissioners, and library location symbols. Subject and name (of chairmen and commissioners) indexes. The National Library of Canada's *Symbols of Canadian libraries* is needed to interpret location symbols.   Z1373.3.M34

China

Bartke, Wolfgang. Biographical dictionary and analysis of China's party leadership, 1922–1988. München : K.G. Saur, 1990. 482 p. : ill. ISBN 3-598-10876-1.   **CJ159**

In two parts, the first consisting of alphabetically arranged biographies of the 1,094 members and alternates of the Central Committees of the Chinese Communist Party (CCP). Entries include photographs where available and such information as date and place of birth, education, military career, party career, visits abroad, posts held. Pt. 2 analyzes (primarily in tabular form) numerous aspects of the membership of both the Politburo (e.g., women members, age at time of election, military leadership, participation in the Long March) and the Central Committee (e.g, women members, purged members, provincial leaders, government cadres, nepotism). Appendixes supply a list of members and alternates organized by Central Committee number and a list of Congresses of the CCP. No index.   JQ1519.A5B3

————— China's new party leadership : biographies and analysis of the Twelfth Central Committee of the Chinese Communist Party / by Wolfgang Bartke and Peter Schier. Armonk, N.Y. : M.E. Sharpe, c1985. 289 p. : ports. ISBN 0-87332-281-9.   **CJ160**

Focuses on the 12th Congress of the Chinese Communist Party and the members of China's 12th Central Committee. In three parts: Pt. 1 in ten descriptive chapters covers the 12th Congress (e.g., political background, composition of the 12th Central Committee and its leading bodies). Pt. 2 contains alphabetically arranged biographies (arranged by Pinyin romanization) of the 210 full and 138 alternate members of the 12th Central Committee. Entries feature a photograph where available, brief personal data, and a listing of current and past Party positions. Pt. 3 offers lists of the central leadership of the People's Republic of China as of January 1, 1984, in sections covering the party, the state, and the military. As the cutoff date for biographical data is September 1, 1983, researchers will want to consult sources such as Bartke's *Who's who in the People's Republic of China*, 2nd ed. (*Supplement* AJ41) for more current information. No index.   JQ1519.A5B32

Directory of Chinese officials and organizations / Central Intelligence Agency, Directorate of Intelligence. Wash. : The Agency : Document Expediting (DOCEX) Project, Exchange & Gift Division, Library of Congress [distributor] ; Springfield, Va. : National Technical Information Service [distributor], 1986– .   **CJ161**

Superintendent of Documents classification: PrEx 3.10/7-13.

Merges *Directory of Chinese officials. National level organizations* (Wash. : National Foreign Assessment Center, 1980–[85]); .... *Provincial organizations* (1981–86); and .... *Scientific and educational organizations* (1981–85; 1979 ed., *Guide* CJ274, had title *Directory of Chinese scientific and educational officials*.)

Essentially a register of officials of the People's Republic of China that draws information primarily from Chinese press releases. In 17 sections (e.g., Judicial system, State bureaus, Military regions) with organization and personal name indexes. For biographical information, consult Wolfgang Bartke's *Who's who in the People's Republic of China* (*Supplement* AJ41).   JQ1507.D544

Hoover Institution on War, Revolution, and Peace. Unofficial documents of the Democracy Movement in Communist China, 1978–1981 = Chung-kuo min chu yun tung tzu liao : a checklist of Chinese materials in the Hoover Institution on War, Revolution and Peace / comp. by I-mu. Stanford, Calif. : East Asian Collection, Hoover Institution, 1986. 100 p. (Hoover Press bibliographical series, 67). ISBN 0-8179-2672-0 (pbk.).   **CJ162**

For annotation, see *Supplement* DE51.   Z31OC.U5H66

Europe

Cook, Chris. European political facts, 1918–84 / Chris Cook and John Paxton. New ed. N.Y. : Facts on File, 1986. 280 p. ISBN 0-8160-1301-2.   **CJ163**

1st ed., 1975 (*Guide* CJ283).

Updates information through 1984, but drops the chapters on: Economics, planning and nationalization; Trade unions; Education; and Press.   JN12.C643

Europe transformed : documents on the end of the Cold War / ed. by Lawrence Freedman. N.Y. : St. Martin's, 1990. 516 p. ISBN 0-312-05225-1.   **CJ164**

Presents the texts of treaties, agreements, journalistic accounts, and other statements that document the profound political changes in Eastern Europe that began in 1989 and continue to the present. In three chronologically arranged sections: (1) The critical agreements, beginning with a 1945 pact between Poland and the U.S.S.R., that provide the diplomatic framework; (2) Official proposals and draft materials for arms control negotiations; (3) Important proposals and statements by political leaders, including two of Gorbachev's landmark speeches. Detailed table of contents, but no index.   D849.F685

Marxist local governments in Western Europe and Japan / ed. by Bogdan Szajkowski. London : F. Pinter ; Boulder, [Colo.] : L. Rienner, 1986. 216 p. : ill., maps. ISBN 0-931477-25-5. $25.00. ISBN 0- 931477-26-3 (pbk.). $11.95.   **CJ165**

Consists mainly of chapters on individual countries, each written by an expert. Useful as a source for election statistics and, to a lesser degree, for bibliographies. General index.   JS3000.2.M37

Opfell, Olga S. Queens, empresses, grand duchesses, and regents : women rulers of Europe, A.D. 1328–1989. Jefferson, N.C. : McFarland, c1989. 282 p. : ports. ISBN 0-89950-385-3.   **CJ166**

Presents biographies of 39 European royal women, from the 14th century to the present, who were either sitting monarchs or regents with actual power. Entries are chronologically arranged, vary from four to eight pages in length, and include a portrait. Bibliography; name index.   D107.O64

Political and economic encyclopaedia of Western Europe / ed. by Frances Nicholson for Cambridge International Reference on Current Affairs (CIRCA) Limited. Chicago : St. James Pr., c1990. 411 p. : maps. ISBN 1-55862-072-9.   **CJ167**

Signed entries treat terms and concepts, political parties, trade unions, organizations, leading politicians, and natural resources. Focuses on the post-World War II period and regards Europe as extending from Iceland to Gibraltar and from Lapland to Cyprus but excludes former Soviet bloc countries, Yugoslavia, and Turkey. Entries are arranged alphabetically and contain cross-references; references to related entries are printed in boldface. General index.   JN94.A2P64

Rossi, Ernest E. The European political dictionary / Ernest E. Rossi, Barbara P. McCrea. Santa Barbara, Calif. : ABC-Clio, c1985. 408 p. : maps. (Clio dictionaries in political science, 7). ISBN 0-87436-046-3. $42.50. ISBN 0-87436-367-5 (pbk.). $15.00.   **CJ168**

Treats political developments within and among the major European powers (U.K., France, Federal Republic of Germany, and U.S.S.R.); also includes a section on Western European regionalism. For each, includes alphabetically arranged entries on major structures of government, national political parties and interest groups, political culture, recent election summaries, and principal government officials since World War II. Each entry has both a descriptive definition and an analysis of its significance. A geographic index precedes the body of the book, and a general index follows it. Cross-references.   JN12.R65

Western European political parties : a comprehensive guide / ed. and comp. by Francis Jacobs. Burnt Mill, Harlow, Essex, England : Longman ; Detroit : Distr. by Gale, c1989. 730 p. : maps. ISBN 0-8103-7482-X.   **CJ169**

Emphasizes political parties currently represented in national parliaments, providing up-to-date information (early 1989) obtained from the parties and through interviews with politicians and party secretariats. In three sections: (1) Countries of the European Community; (2) Other Western European democracies (excluding those with no political party system, such as Monaco, Andorra); (3) Western European political groups (e.g., European Parliament, Nordic Council). Description of the political institutions and systems and recent political history of each country is followed by an alphabetical list of parties, with addresses and telephone numbers of headquarters, party history, support, organization, policies and major personalities. Some countries (e.g., Italy, Spain, U.K.) have regional subsections. Name index.   JN94.A979W475

Who's who in European politics / [prepared by the Bowker-Saur Database Publishing Group]. London ; N.Y. : Bowker-Saur, 1990. 1 v. ISBN 0-8629-1911-8. £149.00.   **CJ170**

Current biographical information for more than 6,000 European political leaders in the 22 member states of the Council of Europe. Covers heads of state, members of governments or national legislatures, leaders of political parties or trade unions, and regional politicians. In two parts. Pt.1 consists of alphabetically arranged biographical entries that include nationality, party affiliation, personal data, positions held, professional career, publications, honors and awards, and address, if available. Pt. 2 is an alphabetical directory by country that lists the heads of state, government, legislature, political parties, regional government, and trade unions, and gives address, telephone, and fax, where available. No index.   D1070.W49

France

Biographical dictionary of French political leaders since 1870 / ed. by David S. Bell, Douglas Johnson, Peter Morris. N.Y. : Simon and Schuster, c1990. 463 p. ISBN 0-13-084690-2.   **CJ171**

Contains some 400 biographies of individuals important in French politics since 1870, featuring political, military, and union leaders, writers, and political philosophers. Varying in length from a few paragraphs to several pages, the entries, alphabetically arranged and signed, include cross-references and short bibliographies (some annotated) of books by or about the individual. Appendixes provide lists of French presidents, prime ministers, postwar union leaders, and Fifth Republic

party leaders. General index; notes on contributors (mainly British academicians).   DC342.B56

Germany, East

DDR Handbuch / wissenschaftliche Leitung, Hartmut Zimmermann, unter Mitarbeit von Horst Ulrich und Michael Fehlauer ; hrsg. vom Bundesministerium für innerdeutsche Beziehungen. 3., überarbeitete und erw. Aufl. Köln : Verlag Wissenschaft und Politik, c1985. 2 v. (1660 p.) : ill. ISBN 3-8046-8642-7 (set).   **CJ172**

2nd ed., 1979 (*Guide* CJ306).

Enlarged and updated through the middle of 1983.
          DD280.6.D37

Germany, West

Schramm, Friedrich Karl. Staatsbürgerlexikon : Grundbegriffe aus Politik, Recht und Wirtschaft im ABC. 6., völlig neu bearb. Aufl. Bonn : F. Dummler, [1968, c1969]. 264 p. : ill.   **CJ173**

5. Aufl., 1961, had title *Der Staatsbürger fragt* (*Guide* CJ316).

Revised and expanded to include concepts relating to politics, law, and economics.   JN3971.A92S37

Great Britain

Encyclopedias

Weigall, David. Britain & the world, 1815–1986 : a dictionary of international relations. N.Y. : Oxford Univ. Pr., 1987. 240 p., [12] p. of plates : maps. ISBN 0-19-520610-X. $29.95.   **CJ174**

For annotation, see *Supplement* DC118.   DA45.W45

Handbooks

Butler, David. British political facts, 1900–1985 / by David Butler and Gareth Butler. 6th ed. N.Y. : St. Martin's Pr., 1986. 536 p. ISBN 0-312-10467-7. $45.00.   **CJ175**

5th ed., 1980 (*Guide* CJ331).

This edition updates information to 1985.   JN231.B8

Political parties

British general election manifestos, 1959–1987 / comp. and ed. by F.W.S. Craig. 3rd ed. Aldershot, England : Parliamentary Research Services ; Aldershot, England ; Brookfield, Vt. : Dartmouth, 1990. 521 p. ISBN 0-900178-34-5. $67.00.   **CJ176**

2nd ed., 1975 (*Guide* CJ340).

Contains the texts of election manifestos for the Conservative, Labour, and Liberal parties, 1959–87; omits manifestos 1900–55 that were included in earlier editions. Appendixes provide a copy of the Tamworth Manifesto of 1834 and a list of separate manifestos relating to policy on Scotland and Wales, also for 1959–87.   JN1121.C73

Biography

The Blackwell biographical dictionary of British political life in the twentieth century / ed.by Keith Robbins. Oxford ; Cambridge, Mass.: Blackwell Reference, 1990. 449 p. : ill. ISBN 0-631-15768-9. £49.50. **CJ177**
For annotation, see *Supplement* DC112.   DA566.9.A1B57

Parliament

Handbooks

Waller, Robert. The almanac of British politics. 4th ed. London; N.Y.: Routledge, 1991. 640 p. : maps. ISBN 0-415-06434-1. £45.00. ISBN 0-415-00508-6 (pbk.). £19.99. **CJ178**
1st ed., 1983 (*Guide* CJ345); 3rd ed., 1987.
Updates information through 1987.   JN561.W28

Election statistics

Britain votes : a handbook of parliamentary election results / comp. and ed. by F.W.S. Craig. Altershot, England : Parliamentary Research Services : Gower Pub. Co. ; Brookfield, Vt. : Gower Pub. Co., 1977–1988. v. 1–4. (In progress). **CJ179**
Contents: v. 1, 1974–77; v. 2, 1974–79; v. 3, 1983; v. 4, 1983–87.
An interim cumulative supplement, following the same format, to the most recently published *British parliamentary election results* (*Guide* CJ346–350 and below); also intended to be used with the author's *British electoral facts* (below). New volumes are published following each general election.
JN1037.B76

Craig, Fred W. S. British electoral facts, 1832–1987. 5th ed. Aldershot, England : Parliamentary Research Services, Dartmouth ; Brookfield, Vt. : Gower, 1989. 210 p. ISBN 0-900178-30-2. $70.00 (est.). **CJ180**
Consists chiefly of tabular information grouped in categories: elections, by-elections, expenses, electorate, forfeited deposits, gains and losses, parties, postal voting, public opinion polls, women, European Parliament, local government, referendums, miscellaneous (e.g., unopposed returns, spoilt ballot papers), and appendixes (e.g., hours of poll, acts of Parliament, void elections). No index. Designed to be used in conjunction with the author's multivolume *British parliamentary election results* (*Guide* CJ346–350 and below) and *Britain votes* (above), each of which contains some unique information (e.g., *Results* gives votes by constituency, *Facts* offers reasons for elections and election timetables).   JN1037.C667

———— British parliamentary election results, 1832–1885. 2nd ed. Aldershot, England : Parliamentary Research Services, 1989. 746 p. ISBN 0-900178-26-4. **CJ181**
1st ed., 1977 (*Guide* CJ346).
Contains a new appendix with an analysis of voting in multimember seats at the general elections (1874 and 1880) directly following the introduction of the secret ballot. Omits tables and many appendixes found in the first edition, since that information is now available in the author's *British electoral facts* (above).   JN945

———— British parliamentary election results, 1885–1918. 2nd ed. Aldershot, England : Parliamentary

Research Services ; Brookfield, Vt. : Gower Pub., 1989. 676 p. ISBN 0-900178-27-2. **CJ182**
1st ed., 1974 (*Guide* CJ347).
Omits tables and some appendixes included in the first edition but now available in the author's *British electoral facts* (above).   JN1037.C68

British Commonwealth

The Commonwealth yearbook / Foreign and Commonwealth Office. 1987– . London : H.M.S.O., 1987– . Annual. £17.50. **CJ183**
Supersedes *A year book of the Commonwealth* (*Guide* CJ367) of which the last volume covered 1986.
Continues the scope of the preceding title, but drops sections on British representatives in other Commonwealth countries and Representatives in Britain of other Commonwealth countries, since this information may be found in *HM Diplomatic overseas reference list* and *The London diplomatic list.* Two new features: (1) a tabular presentation of non-Commonwealth representation in Commonwealth countries, Commonwealth representation in other Commonwealth countries, and Commonwealth representation in non-Commonwealth countries; and (2) tables providing economic, trade, finance, population, and social data.   JN248.C5912

Atlases

Waller, Robert. The atlas of British politics. London ; Dover, N.H. : Croom Helm, c1985. 205 p. ; 21 x 30 cm. ISBN 0-7099-3608-7. $28.00 (est.). ISBN 0-7099-3609-5 (pbk.). $13.95. **CJ184**
Intended as a successor to Michael Kinnear's *The British voter* (*Guide* CJ344) and a companion to Robert Waller's *The almanac of British politics* (*Guide* CJ345). Provides a geographical presentation of the political and social situation in the U.K. Contains 13 sections of maps beginning with a national section followed by regional sections (e.g., Greater London, Yorkshire, Wales). Each section (except Northern Ireland) consists of maps of parliamentary constituencies preceded by explanatory notes, showing election winners, party support, social class, housing, nonwhite voters, unemployment, car ownership, and educational level. Now somewhat dated, since information is based on the 1981 census and the results of the 1983 general election. No index.   G1812.21.F9W3

India

Singh, V. B. Elections in India : data handbook on Lok Sabha elections, 1952–85 / V.B. Singh, Shankar Bose. [2nd ed.]. New Delhi ; Beverly Hills, Calif. : Sage Publications, 1986. 784 p. ISBN 0-8039-9519-9. **CJ185**
1st ed., 1984 (*Guide* CJ373).
Updates election results through 1984.   JQ294.S565

Ireland

O'Clery, Conor. The dictionary of political quotations on Ireland, 1886–1987 : phrases make history here. Boston : G.K. Hall, [1987]. 232 p. ISBN 0-8161-8939-0. **CJ186**
For annotation, see *Supplement* DC151.   DA959.O25

Ireland, Northern

Flackes, William D. Northern Ireland, a political directory, 1966–88 / W.D. Flackes and Sydney Elliott. Belfast ; St. Paul, Minn. : Blackstaff Pr., 1989. 1 v. ISBN 0-85640-417-9. £14.95. ISBN 0-85640-418-7 (pbk.). £8.95.

CJ187

Previous ed., 1983 (*Guide* CJ332).

Revises and updates information through 1988. Review in *Choice* 27 (May 1990): 1472 notes "inconsistencies in the election statistics from the second edition to the third" and "the continued lack of an index and bibliography."

DA990.U46F487

Israel

Benvenisti, Meron. The West Bank handbook : a political lexicon / Meron Benvenisti with Ziad Abu-Zayed and Danny Rubinstein. Jerusalem, Israel : Jerusalem Post, c1986. 228 p., [15] p. of plates : maps.   **CJ188**

Translation of: *Leksikon Yehudah ye-Shomron.*

Intends "to acquaint those directly involved, namely Jews and Arabs living in the Holy Land, with the facts as well as with the institutions and agencies affecting their daily lives."—*Foreword.* Data are extracted from Benvenisti's *The West Bank data project: a survey of Israel's policies* (Wash. : American Enterprise Institute, 1984) and cover social, economic, institutional, legal, cultural, and political topics relating to the West Bank. Entries are alphabetical, range in length from a paragraph to several pages, and contain cross-references. Includes 15 maps and a detailed table of contents, but no index.

DS110.W47B47413

Mahler, Gregory S. Bibliography of Israeli politics. Boulder, Colo. : Westview Pr., 1985. 133 p. ISBN 0-8133-7042-6 (pbk.). $18.95.   **CJ189**

Treats the full breadth of Israeli political life and political culture, including the constitutional system, elections and parties, public opinion, political history, foreign relations, Zionism, the Palestinians, the West Bank and Gaza questions, etc. Contains 1,419 citations published through 1984, arranged alphabetically. A keyword index to entry numbers only.

Z3476.M3

Political dictionary of the State of Israel / Susan Hattis Rolef, ed. N.Y. : Macmillan ; London : Collier Macmillan, c1987. 351 p. : ill. ISBN 0-02-916421-4.   **CJ190**

A Hebrew translation has appeared as *Leksikon politi shel Medinat Yi'sra'el* (Yerushalayim : Keter, [1988]. 310 p.)

More encyclopedia than dictionary; entries range in length from a short paragraph to 17 pages (Arab-Israeli conflict). Contains 450 signed articles on all aspects of Israeli politics, including personalities, parties and other groups, political institutions, outstanding events, foreign policy, the media, etc. Some entries give historical background; some contain cross-references. Supersedes an earlier work, Yaacov Shimoni and Evyatar Levine's *Political dictionary of the Middle East in the twentieth century* (*Guide* DE71) and incorporates several articles from that volume. A companion to Shimoni's *Political dictionary of the Arab world* (*Supplement* CJ152).   DS126.5.P62

Italy

Pallotta, Gino. Dizionario della politica italiana. Roma : Newton Compton, 1985. 442 p. : ill. (Quest'Italia, 81).   **CJ191**

Previous ed., 1976 (*Guide* CJ384), had title: *Dizionario politicio e parlamentare italiano.*

Subtitle: i meccanismi della vita politica con la sua vasta terminologia specifica e quarant'anni di storia in uno strumento di lavoro e di consultazione per il giornalista, il parlamentare, il lettore di prosa politica, il cittadino.

Includes neologisms coined since the previous edition. Historical articles on such subjects as terrorism, pollution, and Italian political parties have been updated through 1985.

JN5451.P34

Japan

Who's who in Japanese government. [Tokyo] : I.C.A. of Japan Co., [1986]– . Y6500.   **CJ192**

Intended to provide "basic and up-to-date information for foreigners who are interested in politics per se or whose work brings them in contact with the Japanese government."—*Foreword.* Begins with a profile of the Japanese political and electoral system, followed by biographical entries for members of the lower and upper houses (House of Representatives and House of Councillors) of the Diet, each containing a photograph, directory of information, party, number of times elected, committee or ministry assignments, posts held, education, and date of birth. Includes a listing of standing, special, and select committees of both houses of the Diet and their membership; political party organization charts; ministry and agency organization charts; lists of ministry and agency officials; and important addresses and telephone numbers. Personal name index

JQ1651.W48

Latin America

Biographical dictionary of Latin American and Caribbean political leaders / ed. by Robert J. Alexander. N.Y. : Greenwood, 1988. 509 p. ISBN 0-313-24353-0. $75.00.   **CJ193**

Intended to complement *Political parties of the Americas* (*Guide* CJ246). Offers 450 sketches of political figures from the 19th and 20th centuries. Entries are lengthy, are signed, and include cross-references and bibliographies. Also included are a chronology of major events in the region, 1804–1985, and a list of biographies by country. Name index. Covers more countries and has fuller entries (though only about half the number) than *Who is who [in] government, politics, banking and industry : in Latin America* (below).   F1414.2.B48

Gunson, Phil. The dictionary of contemporary politics of South America / Phil Gunson, Andrew Thompson, and Greg Chamberlain. 1st American ed. N.Y. : Macmillan, 1989. [250] p. ISBN 0-02-913145-6. $45.00 (est.).   **CJ194**

Written by three British journalists as a guide to themes, events, and personalities in the politics of 20th-century South America. Headwords are usually in English with cross-references from the vernacular. Occasionally important cross-references are omitted (e.g., there is no reference from Malvinas to Falklands). Includes a partial list of entries by country. For earlier time periods, see Ernest E. Rossi and Jack C. Plano's topically arranged *The Latin American political dictionary* (*Guide* CJ394).   JL1851.A25G86

Handbook of political science research on Latin America : trends from the 1960s to the 1990s / ed. by David W. Dent. N.Y. : Greenwood, 1990. 448 p. ISBN 0-313-26446-5.   **CJ195**

Offers a synthesis of political science research on Latin America over the past 30 years. 16 chapters in the form of bibliographic essays by specialists on Latin America focus on a country or region and are grouped in two general sections, comparative politics and international relations. Includes English-and Spanish-language books, articles, government publications, and selected dissertations. Three appendixes: (1) a bibliography of reference works on Latin American politics; (2) data on macrotrends in political science research, 1960–85, from the *Handbook of Latin American studies* (*Guide* DB241); and (3) a listing of major research centers and institutes in Latin America and the Caribbean. Name and subject indexes.   JA84.L3H36

Ó Maoláin, Ciarán. Latin American political movements. N.Y. : Facts on File , 1985. 287 p. ISBN 0-8160-1410-8. $24.95.   **CJ196**

Presents "basic factual information on political parties and alliances, guerrilla movements, pressure groups, and other legal and illegal organizations."—*Introd.* Divided into sections covering 20 Latin American countries and Puerto Rico, each beginning with a brief summary of the country's political history, constitutional background, and recent election results. The entries that follow are alphabetical by vernacular name and feature information on leadership, structure, history, and policies. Name index. Complements but does not replace *Political parties of the Americas* (*Guide* CJ246), which covers more countries and is more descriptive.   JL969.A45O18

Radu, Michael. Latin American revolutionaries : groups, goals, methods / Michael Radu and Vladimir Tismaneanu. Wash. : Pergamon-Brassey's International Defense Publishers, c1990. 386 p. ISBN 0-08-037429-8. $50.00 (est.).   **CJ197**

Provides comprehensive coverage of leftist groups in Latin America. In two parts: Pt.1 analyzes violence, ideology, and revolution in Latin America; Pt.2 (the larger) is a handbook of revolutionary organizations in Latin America. Arranged alphabetically by organization name within country chapters. The entry for each group contains up to 16 categories of information (e.g., origins, membership, leadership, ideology, trends and assessment). Bibliography; name index.   JL966.R34

Who is who [in] government, politics, banking, and industry : in Latin America. N.Y. : Decade Media Books, Inc., c1989. 389 p.   **CJ198**

1st ed., 1984 (*Guide* CJ395), had title: *Who is who in government and politics in Latin America.*

This edition expands the number of entries to 1,600 to include about 600 individuals from banking and industry, and unlike the 1st ed., offers entries only in English. For political figures, readers should also consult *Biographical dictionary of Latin American and Caribbean political leaders* (above), which provides fewer but more detailed entries.   JL957.W47

Near East

Gresh, Alain. An A to Z of the Middle East / Alain Gresh and Dominique Vidal ; translated by Bob Cumming. London : Biddles Ltd. ; Atlantic Highlands, N.J. : Zed Books, 1990. 261 p., [3] p. of plates : ill., maps. ISBN 0-86232-880-2. ISBN 0-86232-881-0 (pbk.).   **CJ199**

For annotation, see *Supplement* DE20.   DS43.G7413

Political leaders of the contemporary Middle East and North Africa : a biographical dictionary / ed. by Bernard Reich. N.Y. : Greenwood, 1990. 557 p. ISBN 0-313-26213-6.   **CJ200**

Profiles 70 individuals who have made substantial contributions to and had lasting effects on the politics of the Middle East and North Africa since World War II. Lengthy entries (from four to twelve pages) are alphabetically arranged and contain essential biographical data (e.g., birth and death dates, education, career); a description and analysis of the person's development, programs, goals, methods, and significant contributions to politics; and a bibliography of books by and about the

individual (most in English). Written by specialists, the entries are signed and contain cross-references. Includes a list of the biographees by country, a chronology of important events in the region, and a bibliography of works on the political elite of the region. General index.   DS61.5.P65

Papua New Guinea

Papua New Guinea handbook, business and travel guide. 11th ed.–. Sydney, N.S.W. : Pacific Publications, 1985– . Irregular.   **CJ201**

9th ed., 1978, had title *Papua New Guinea handbook and travel guide* (*Guide* CJ408).

11th ed. revised and updated through 1984.
    DU740.A2P32a

South Africa

Davies, Robert H. The struggle for South Africa : a reference guide to movements, organizations, and institutions / Robert Davies, Dan O'Meara, Sipho Dlamini. New ed., rev. and updated. London ; Atlantic Highlands, N.J. : Zed Books, 1988. 2 v. : ill. ISBN 0-86232-760-1 (v. 1). ISBN 0-86232-761-X (pbk. : v. 1).   **CJ202**

1st ed., 1984 (*Guide* CJ415).

Contains two new chapters, one at the end of each volume, that cover developments from early 1983 to August 1987.
    JQ1931.D38

Gastrow, Shelagh. Who's who in South African politics. 3rd rev. ed. London ; N.Y. : Zell, 1990. 368 p. : ports. ISBN 0-905450-37-X. £45.00.   **CJ203**

1st ed., 1985; 2nd ed., 1987.

Offers alphabetically arranged biographies of 131 key figures in contemporary South African politics (e.g., Mangosuthu Buthelezi, Frederik De Klerk, Nelson Mandela, Desmond Tutu). Each profile contains a photograph, basic biographical information, the biographee's political history and views, and a list of sources. An introduction describes recent (1989–90) political changes in South Africa as well as historical events that influenced these leaders. Includes a list of individuals profiled in the 1st and 2nd eds. but excluded from the 3rd. No index.
    DT1774.G37

Sri Lanka

Peiris, H. A. Political parties in Sri Lanka since independence : a bibliography. New Delhi : Navrang, 1988. 161 p. ISBN 81-7013-027-1. Rs140.00.   **CJ204**

Lists English-language books, periodical articles, theses, dissertations, party manifestos, and seminar and conference papers on political parties in Sri Lanka from its independence in 1848 through 1984. Excludes election literature, parliamentary debates, and newspaper articles. In three sections: (1) historical essays on majority, minority, and leftist parties; (2) aims and limitations of the work as well as sources for further research; and (3) an annotated bibliography. The 487 entries in the bibliography are grouped into reference, general, and political party categories, then arranged alphabetically by main entry. Personal author index.   Z7164.P8P45

Union of Soviet Socialist Republics

Laird, Roy D. A Soviet lexicon : important concepts, terms, and phrases / Roy D. Laird, Betty A. Laird. Lexington, Mass. : Lexington Books, c1988. 201 p. ISBN 0-669-16739-8. $10.95. **CJ205**

Defines words, concepts, and phrases commonly used in Soviet studies (e.g., apparatchik, glasnost, Politburo, revisionism), excluding most geographical and personal names. Begins with an essay describing the Soviet economic, political, and social system. The entries, alphabetically arranged, often include the Cyrillic equivalents. Three appendixes offer a historical list of full and candidate members of the Politburo, the Soviet constitution, and the rules of the Communist party. Cross-references. DK266.3.L27

The Tauris Soviet directory : the elite of the USSR today / comp. by Romolo Cichero. London : I.B. Tauris, c1989. 713 p. ISBN 1-85043-090-X. **CJ206**

For annotation, see *Supplement* AJ100. DK37.4.T38

Zimbabwe

Johnstone, I. J. Zimbabwean political material published in exile, 1959–1980 : a bibliography. Harare : National Archives, 1987. 31 p. **CJ207**

Lists materials published in exile by the Zimbabwe liberation movement, 1959–80. Excludes books, articles by Zimbabweans in non-Zimbabwean serials and monographs, Zimbabwean political material published inside Rhodesia, and non-political material. General index. Z3578.J64

Mitchell, Diana. African nationalist leaders in Zimbabwe who's who 1980. Independence souvenir ed. Salisbury, Zimbabwe : D. Mitchell, c1980. 106 p., [10] p. of plates : ill. ISBN 079740511X. **CJ208**

1st ed., 1977 (*Guide* CJ441), had title: *African nationalist leaders in Rhodesia who's who.*

This edition has chapters featuring biographies of the 20 first ministers, five selected deputy ministers, and two selected members of Parliament. Includes lists of military commanders, members of the Senate and House of Assembly by constituency. No index. DT2914.M58

PUBLIC ADMINISTRATION

American public administration : a bibliographical guide to the literature / Gerald E. Caiden ... [et al.]. N.Y. : Garland, 1983. 201 p. (The public affairs and administration series, 3). ISBN 0-82409-152-3. $30.00. **CJ209**

Lists basic reference sources, leading journals, and significant books, but excludes government publications and journal articles. An introductory essay describing the scope of the field is followed by chapters including: (1) annotated citations for relevant abstracts, indexes, and continuing bibliographies; (2) annotated citations for professional journals; and (3) unannotated citations for selected books. Within chapters, entries are alphabetically arranged by main entry within subdivisions for subject or type of publication. Author index, journal title index, and index of abstracts, indexes, and continuing bibliographies. Z7164.A2A53

Chandler, Ralph C. The public administration dictionary / Ralph C. Chandler, Jack C. Plano. 2nd ed. Santa Barbara, Calif. : ABC-Clio, c1988. 430 p. ISBN 0-87436-498-1. ISBN 0-87436-499-X (pbk.). **CJ210**

1st ed., 1982 (*Guide* CJ47a).
An updated and expanded edition. JA61.C47

Coleman, James R. Public administration desk book / James R. Coleman and Robert E. Dugan. Newton, Mass. : Government Research Publications, c1990. 270 p. ISBN 0-931684-12-9. $35.00 (est.). **CJ211**

Intended as a guide for practitioners, researchers, and students of American public administration. Divided into chapters covering reference tools or providing information on: (1) People and organizations; (2) Statistics; (3) Terminology, research, and publishing; (4) Abstracts, indexes and periodicals; (5) Electronic information; (6) Law and reporter services; and (7) Associations and institutes. Entries are annotated and are alphabetically arranged within topical chapter subdivisions. Appendixes include a list of books for a basic public administration library and a list of other guides to public administration information. Title and subject indexes. Z7164.A2C59

Dynes, Patrick S. Program evaluation : an annotated bibliography / Patrick S. Dynes, Mary K. Marvel. N.Y. : Garland, 1987. 241 p. (The public affairs and administration series, 17 ; Garland reference library of social science, v. 172). ISBN 0-8240-9146-9. $44.00. **CJ212**

Focuses on program evaluation as it relates to public administration. Lists selected books and articles published 1970–1985, arranged in four categories: Overviews of program evaluation, Methodology, Organization and management, and Utilization. Entries treat a wide range of issues (e.g., program design, standards and ethics, experimental methods, communicating results) and applications in politics, personnel administration, organization theory, decision making, administrative leadership, budgeting, regulation, management, and legislation. A brief but helpful introduction defines program evaluation, gives criteria for selection, describes the organization of the book, and suggests sources for further information. Excludes newspaper articles, government publications, occasional papers, and some dissertations. Author index. Z7164.A2D95

Grasham, W. E. Canadian public administration: bibliography = Administration publique canadienne: bibliographie / comp. by W. E. Grasham [and] Germain Julien. Toronto : Institute of Public Administration of Canada, c1972. 261 p. **CJ213**

Kept up to date by supplements issued at three- to five-year intervals.

In English and French. Contains unannotated citations to books, articles, dissertations, and government publications, 1930–71. The classified arrangement presents subject chapters (e.g., Municipal administration, Public finance, Administrative sectors) subdivided for more specific topics. Within each section, English language entries are followed by French entries, both arranged alphabetically. No index. Z7165.C2G7

Handbook of public administration / James L. Perry, ed. San Francisco : Jossey-Bass, 1989. 660 p. ISBN 1-55542-128-8. **CJ214**

Written primarily for professional public administrators; attempts to communicate "the accumulated body of knowledge ... covering the problems and situations that confront [them] at all levels of government and in all types of services."—*Pref.* Each of the 43 chapters treats a specific role, function, or aspect of the field and is written by an expert. Bibliographies conclude each chapter. Name and subject indexes. JF1351.H276

Handbook of public administration / ed. by Jack Rabin, W. Bartley Hildreth, Gerald J. Miller. N.Y. : M. Dekker, c1989. 1095 p. : ill. (Public administration and public policy, 35). ISBN 0-8247-7964-9. **CJ215**

A detailed review of the literature of public administration, intended more for students or scholars than the practically-oriented *Handbook of public adminstration* (above). Contains 13 topical sections (e.g., Public budgeting and financial management, Policy sciences, Public law and regulation), each containing a chronological essay describing major concepts, theories, and applications and a "great ideas" essay consisting of the five most significant ideas or concepts. The lengthy essays are signed and have individual bibliographies. General index.

JF1351.H275

Holzer, Marc. Public sector productivity : a resource guide / Marc Holzer, Arie Halachmi. N.Y. : Garland, 1988. 166 p. ISBN 0-8240-9458-1.   **CJ216**
Cites literature (mostly 1980–87) and organizations focusing on productivity improvement, primarily in the public sector. A lengthy introduction giving an overview of the topic is followed by five chapters of alphabetically arranged entries for books, reports, articles, periodicals and newsletters, and organizations. All entries are annotated except those for articles, which list keywords instead. Title index. Lack of a subject index or classified arrangement limits usefulness.

JF1525.P67H65

Jreisat, Jamil E. Administration and development in the Arab world : an annotated bibliography / Jamil E. Jreisat, Zaki R. Ghosheh. N.Y. : Garland, 1986. 259 p. ISBN 0-8240-8593-0.   **CJ217**
Intends to examine "the literature on administration, human resources, and development in the Arab world" (*Introd.*), with emphasis on contemporary societies and internal affairs of the 21 member countries of the Arab League, but excluding their foreign policies and international relations. English-language books, articles, and dissertations, 1970–85, are listed in four topical chapters plus a dissertation chapter subdivided by topic. The introduction includes a list of English-language journals cited in the text and another of Arabic-language journals focusing on administration and development. Author and country indexes.   Z7165.A67J73

Martin, Daniel. The guide to the foundations of public administration. N.Y. : Dekker, c1989. 454 p. (Public administration and public policy, 37). ISBN 0-8247-8284-4.   **CJ218**
Serves as " . . . an annotated bibliographic guide to the development of the literature in public administration" (*Pref.*), emphasizing English-language articles, books, government publications, court cases, and legislation. In two parts, The emergence and impacts of public administration and The internal operation of public administration, each arranged in topical chapters that begin with a background paragraph, contain chronologically arranged and annotated citations, and end with a continuing concerns essay and notes. Emphasizes "formative" literature rather than the frequently cited works found in Howard E. McCurdy's *Public administration* (below). Offers an introduction and a final essay of concluding observations. Name and subject indexes.   Z7164.A2M27

McCurdy, Howard E. Public administration : a bibliographic guide to the literature. N.Y. : M. Dekker, c1986. 311 p. (Public administration and public policy, 29). ISBN 0-8247-7518-X. $29.75.   **CJ219**
Limited to monographs, this self-styled guide begins with two long essays, one on recent trends in public administration, the other on the history of the development of the field. There follows a list of the 181 most frequently cited books in public administration, in alphabetic order by author or title, with a lengthy review of each that summarizes the work's reputation and its contribution to the field; an unannotated list of monographs in classed order that includes the titles in the preceding part; and at the end, an index. Not for casual users, and not successful as a guide, since its principal section is highly selec-

tive, includes only monographs, and is in alphabetic rather than classed order.   Z7164.A2M29

Murin, William F. Delivering government services : an annotated bibliography / William F. Murin, Judith Pryor. N.Y. : Garland, 1988. 315 p. ISBN 0-8240-6618-9.   **CJ220**
Contains 926 annotated citations to English-language books, articles, and reports on delivery systems for services provided by local and county levels of government. Specifically excluded are trade journal and newspaper articles; most references are from the past 20 years. Entries are arranged in seven broad topical chapters (some with further subdivisions), then alphabetically by main entry. Subject and author indexes.

Z7164.L8M96

Payad, Aurora T. Organization behavior in American public administration : an annotated bibliography. N.Y. : Garland, 1986. 264 p. (The public affairs and administration series, 15). ISBN 0-8240-8685-6.   **CJ221**
Particularly useful, since it focuses on organization behavior in public administration; earlier bibliographies emphasized the private sector. Sections deal with: Organizational behavior in government; The ecology of public organizations (e.g., budgetary strategies and constraints, technology and office modernization); Individual behavior; Intergroup and intragroup behavior; and Managerial behavior. Includes journal articles, books, book chapters, reviews, and dissertations, 1940–84, although most were published 1974–84. List of professional associations; author and subject indexes.   Z7164.A2P39

Public administration in the Third World : an international handbook / ed. by V. Subramaniam. N.Y. : Greenwood, 1990. 447 p. : ill. ISBN 0-313-24730-7.
          CJ222
Describes the evolution, structure, and processes of public administration for selected Third World countries. Chapters on individual countries by specialists; the editor adds an introduction, a conclusion describing features common to all the countries, and an appendix discussing the sociohistorical characteristics of the countries' middle classes. Extensive bibliography; name and subject indexes.   JF60.P86

Shafritz, Jay M. The Facts on File dictionary of public administration. N.Y. : Facts on File, c1985. 610 p. ISBN 0-8160-1266-0. $29.95.   **CJ223**
Brief entries in alphabetic order treat all aspects of public administration: terms, concepts, processes and practices, significant individuals and organizations, statutes and judicial decisions, journals. Although a roster of 24 contributors is given, entries are unsigned. Some entries end with brief bibliographies, some of which include legal citations. Entries contain cross-references, but there is no index.   JA61.S54

Thésaurus multilingue international en administration publique = Multilingual international thesaurus of public administration = Tesauro multilingue internacional de administración pública / [sous la direction de Jean-Marc Alain et Jorge Avilés]. Montreal : Corporation de l'encyclopédie d'administration publique = Corporation for the Encyclopedia of Public Administration, 1987–1988. 2 v.   **CJ224**
In French, English, and Spanish.
Seven sections, including a Thematic Thesaurus, which divides the field into 15 themes, (e.g., Public policy, Organization, and Personnel administration), which are subdivided in turn into 116 subthemes, augmented by other descriptors, and arranged hierarchically. Other sections include a conventional alphabetic thesaurus and a permuted alphabetic index of descriptors. The sections attempt to show relationships among the themes, subthemes, and descriptors by the use of diagrams and a system of numerical codes to which the various indexes refer.   Z695.1.P79T43

PARLIAMENTARY PROCEDURE

Davidson, Henry A. Handbook of parliamentary procedure / [by] Henry A. Davidson. 2nd ed. N.Y. : Ronald Pr. Co., [1968, c1955]. 300 p.   **CJ225**

1st ed., 1955 (*Guide* CJ442).

A revised edition, with expanded definitions of terms and discussions of procedures.   JF515.D32

Robert, Henry M. Robert's rules of order. Modern ed., completely rev. / by Darwin Patnode. Nashville : T. Nelson, c1989. 155 p. ISBN 0-8407-7184-3. ISBN 0-8407-7199-1.   **CJ226**

Based on Robert's original edition (1876). Attempts to retain his style and content while modernizing the work for current use. For a more detailed version, see *The Scott, Foresman Robert's rules of order newly revised* (below).   JF515.R692

———————— The Scott, Foresman Robert's rules of order newly revised. 1990 ed., a new and enl. ed. / by Sarah Corbin Robert. Glenview, Ill. : Scott, Foresman, c1990. 706 p. ISBN 0-673-38735-6. $18.95. ISBN 0-673-38734-8 (pbk.).   **CJ227**

8th ed., 1981 (*Guide* CJ445).

Expanded, revised, updated, and reset in larger type.
                JF515.R692

Sturgis, Alice. Standard code of parliamentary procedure. 3rd ed., new and rev. N.Y. : McGraw-Hill, c1988. 275 p. ISBN 0-07-062399-6. $15.95.   **CJ228**

2nd ed., 1966, had title *Sturgis standard code of parliamentary procedure* (*Guide* CJ446).

Revised to clarify wording, minimize gender bias, eliminate rarely used motions, and validate "tabling" a motion. New chapters contain often-asked questions and answers and a guide to dealing with disapproved or obsolete motions. Also adds appendixes covering principal rules governing motions, incidental motions, and chief purposes of motions. The appendix on labor organizations has been omitted.   JF515.S88

PUBLIC OPINION

American public opinion data [microform]. 1981– . [Louisville, Ky. : Opinion Research Service, 1981–]. Annual. ISSN 0885-6893.   **CJ229**

American public opinion index. 1981– . Louisville, Ky. : Opinion Research Service, [1981]– . Annual. ISSN 0740-8978.   **CJ230**

Two works designed to be used together. The *Index* is a subject index to questions asked in nonproprietary public opinion polls with scientifically drawn random samples. From 1981 through 1984, it indexed only questions about the opinions of respondents, but since 1985 has also included behavioral questions. Questions, listed under alphabetically arranged topics, include response categories offered, polling group, and date of the poll. Ends with a section giving the full names, addresses, and phone numbers for the organizations conducting the polls, when the poll was released, the sample size, the poll method, the poll universe, and the special topic of the poll, if applicable. The companion microfiche *Data* contains tabulated responses to most of the questions listed in the *Index*, the exact question wording, and detailed information about polling methodology for most of the polls. Arrangement is alphabetical by polling organization as given in the *Index*.   HM261.A463

Gilbert, Dennis A. Compendium of American public opinion. N.Y. : Facts on File, c1988. 438 p. : ill. ISBN 0-8160-1619-4. $60.00.   **CJ231**

A selection of results of polls conducted primarily from 1984 through 1986. Findings were originally disseminated via newspapers, journals, reports, press releases, and broadcasts. In 20 chapters, each treating a broad area (e.g., Foreign Policy, Health, Women). Contains numerous graphic representations of poll results. Sources are cited, but there is no index.
                HN90.P8G56

Index to international public opinion. 1978/79– . Westport, Conn. : Greenwood, [1980]– . ISSN 0193-905X.
                CJ232

For earlier volumes and annotation, see *Guide* CJ449.

Beginning with the 1980/81 volume, the three sections noted in *Guide* CJ449 became: (1) Single nation surveys; (2) Multinational surveys; (3) World surveys. Arrangement within these sections and content of entries remains substantially the same.   HM261.I552

Lake, Celinda C. Public opinion polling : a handbook for public interest and citizen advocacy groups / Celinda C. Lake with Pat Callbeck Harper. Wash. : Island Pr., c1987. 166 p. ISBN 0-933280-32-7. $19.95.   **CJ233**

Prepared for the Montana Alliance for Progressive Policy.

Presents information on (1) how to plan, administer, and analyze a poll and (2) how to analyze the sampling, interpretation, and question-wording of polls conducted by others. Topical chapters (e.g., Questionnaire wording and construction; Interviewing; Sampling) proceed step-by-step through the polling process and feature tips for success, checklists, and possible problems. Includes an annotated bibliography and several appendixes (e.g., sample questionnaires, grids, and tabulations, a case study, and a glossary of terms). Subject index. A software package, *POLLSTART*, is also available.   HM261.L18

Niemi, Richard G. Trends in public opinion : a compendium of survey data / Richard G. Niemi, John Mueller, Tom W. Smith. N.Y. : Greenwood, 1989. 325 p. ISBN 0-313-25426-5.   **CJ234**

A collection of survey data that facilitates comparisons of public opinions over time, covering 1972–88 with some results from earlier years. Features the annual General Social Surveys (GSS) conducted by the National Opinion Research Center of the Univ. of Chicago but also reports on surveys from a number of other organizations. Topical chapters (e.g., The role of women, Race relations, International affairs) begin with a summary of the survey trends on that topic and a list of references. The data tables which follow include the survey question with the GSS mnemonic code if applicable, month and year of the survey, the percentage of responses for each answer, the number of respondents, and an abbreviation for the survey source (full source names are given in the introduction). Index of GSS mnemonics and a subject index.   HN90.P8N53

Opinions. Detroit : Gale, c1990– . Quarterly with annual cumulations. $129.00.   **CJ235**

Volumes carry in the title the year designation, e.g. Opinions '90.

Brings together highlights from a wide variety of recent public opinion polls covering numerous topics (e.g., attitudes toward abortion, chances of a recession, time spent at malls). Entries are grouped within alphabetically arranged subject categories such as advertising, environment, and taxes, and include description, results, extracts (often presented graphically), details (e.g., when and by whom conducted), and bibliographic citation for each poll. An appendix provides names, addresses, and telephone numbers of organizations conducting the polls. General index.

Walden, Graham R. Public opinion polls and survey research : a selective annotated bibliography of U.S. guides and studies from the 1980s. N.Y. : Garland,

1990. 306 p. (The public affairs and administration series, 24). ISBN 0-8240-5732-5.   **CJ236**

Entries are arranged alphabetically in topical chapters (e.g., Sampling, Interviewing, Questions) and cite instructional guides, handbooks, reference works, textbooks, research studies, and evaluative and critical studies by American authors published in the U.S. Generally limited to 1980s publications although all relevant U.S. dissertations, 1941 to date, are incorporated. Specifically excludes newspaper articles, reviews of journals, book reviews, university occasional papers, most proceedings, master's theses, and mass market periodicals. Concludes with an unannotated addendum, eight appendixes (e.g., acronyms, bibliographic sources, organizations), an author index, and a selective keyword index.   Z7164.P956W34

Wood, Floris W. An American profile : opinions and behavior, 1972–1989 / Floris W. Wood, ed. ; chronology of world events, 1972–1989 by Edward Weilant. Detroit : Gale, c1990. 1065 p. ISBN 0-8103-7723-3.   **CJ237**

Subtitle: opinion results on 300 high-interest issues derived from the General Social Survey conducted by the National Opinion Research Center.

Extracts data from the General Social Surveys (GSS) carried out annually 1972–89 (except 1979 and 1981) by the National Opinion Research Center of the Univ. of Chicago. 305 questions are grouped in three major sections: (1) Demography (e.g., How many children have you ever had?), (2) Opinions (e.g., Would you be for or against sex education in the public schools?), (3) Behavior (e.g., How often do you spend a social evening with friends?). For each question, separate tables provide results by total population, gender, age, and race, and include year of the survey, percentage of responses for each answer, and number of respondents. The tables are preceded by "A chronology of world events, 1972–1989" and followed by seven appendixes (e.g., a listing of questions and their corresponding GSS variable name; U.S. crime index, 1972–88; U.S. unemployment rate, 1972–88). Keyword index. Data is also available on tape through the Roper Center for Public Opinion Research or the Interuniversity Consortium for Political and Social Research. Similar data may be found in Richard G. Niemi's *Trends in public opinion* (above).   HN90.P8A52

COMMUNISM AND SOCIALISM

Bibliography

Communism in the world since 1945 : an annotated bibliography / Susan K. Kinnell, ed. Santa Barbara, Calif. : ABC-Clio, c1987. 415 p. ISBN 0-87436-169-9. $85.00.   **CJ238**

A bibliography of 4,151 entries on communism in all parts of the world since World War II, drawn from the publisher's databases for *America : history and life* and *Historical abstracts.* Arranged by geographic region, with entries in each region alphabetical by author. Most entries "cover the political history of the larger communist countries and socialist nations as well as the McCarthy era in the United States and the impact of communism in Southeast Asia."—*p.xi.* Lengthy author and subject indexes; lists of periodicals, abstractors, acronyms, abbreviations.   Z7164.S67C594

Haynes, John Earl. Communism and anti-communism in the United States : an annotated guide to historical writings. N.Y. : Garland, 1987. 321 p. ISBN 0-8240-8520-5. $47.00.   **CJ239**

Focuses on the Communist Party of the U.S., with some material on its splinter groups; omits studies of theoretical Marxism unless they deal directly with the American Communist movement. Anti-communism is treated only so far as it opposed the American movement. Primarily concerned with the period from the party's founding shortly after the Bolshevik Revolution through its near-disintegration in the mid-50s, although some items deal with the pro-Bolshevik movements out of which American communism developed, and some with the 1960s and 1970s. Contains 2,086 citations for books, published and unpublished essays, articles, dissertations, and theses, most of which are scholarly or historical in nature. Arranged in 37 chapters covering such subjects as Communism and the churches and Espionage. Author index.   Z7164.S67H4

Kahan, Vilém. Bibliography of the Communist International (1919–1979). Leiden ; N.Y. : E.J. Brill, 1990. v. 1. ISBN 90-04-09320-6 (v. 1). (In progress).   **CJ240**

Designed to be a three-volume bibliography of publications by and about the Communist International (Comintern) that have been published in more than 20 European languages. Based on several published bibliographies and the catalogs and holdings of 15 research institutions. Vol. 1 offers 3,186 unannotated entries grouped in sections by form (Bibliographies; Reference books, yearbooks; Documents and other primary sources; Memoirs; Literature on the Comintern—books and pamphlets published 1919–79 and periodical articles 1943–79). Entries are arranged alphabetically by main entry except for documents and materials relating to Comintern meetings, plenums, and congresses, which are arranged chronologically. Titles published in languages other than German, French, Italian, Spanish, and Portuguese have been translated into English or French. Includes summaries of Comintern congresses and Executive Committee plenums, chronologies of congresses and meetings, and lists of Comintern members and candidates. Author index. Vol. 2 will list publications of and studies on organizations affiliated with the Comintern (e.g., Communist Youth International) and v. 3 will cover the national Communist parties that were members of the Comintern. When complete, will be more comprehensive than Witold S. Sworakowski's *The Communist International and its front organizations* (*Guide* CJ481).   Z7164.S67K34

Lubitz, Wolfgang. Trotsky bibliography : a classified list of published items about Leon Trotsky and Trotskyism. 2nd, totally rev. and expanded ed. München ; N.Y. : K.G. Saur, 1988. 581 p. ISBN 3-598-10754-4.   **CJ241**

1st ed., 1982 (*Guide* CJ482).

Enlarged by some 1,750 items through addition of 1,900 new citations and deletion of 150 from the 1st ed. Now employs a classified arrangement.   Z8886.5.L8

Encyclopedias

Draper, Hal. The Marx-Engels cyclopedia / by Hal Draper ; with the assistance of the Center for Socialist History. N.Y. : Schocken Books, 1985–1986. v. 2–3. ISBN 0-8052-3909-X (v. 1).   **CJ242**

For v. 1 and annotation, see *Guide* CJ491.

Contents: v. 2, The Marx-Engels register: a complete bibliography of Marx and Engels' individual writings; v. 3, The Marx-Engels glossary: a glossary to the chronicle and register, and index to the glossary. Completes the set.

Vol. 3 is both a dictionary describing the importance of all proper names (e.g., people, organizations, parties, places, periodicals) referred to in v. 1–2 and an index to names. It also includes a personal name index (excluding Marx and Engels) to v. 3.   HX39.5.D69

Encyclopedia of the American left / ed. by Mari Jo Buhle, Paul Buhle, Dan Georgakas. N.Y. : Garland, 1990. 928 p. : ill. (Garland reference library of social sciences, v. 502). ISBN 0-8240-3713-8. $95.00.   **CJ243**

For annotation, see *Supplement* DB62.   HX86.E58

Dictionaries

Carver, Terrell. A Marx dictionary. Totowa, N.J.: Barnes & Noble Books, 1987. 164 p. ISBN 0-389-20684-9.   **CJ244**

Intended for students and general readers. The body of the book consists of 16 short chapters, each treating one of the major Marxian concepts "that need careful explanation before his works can be grasped and criticized adequately" (*Pref.*) and an introductory chapter tying them together. Other terms are explained in the context of these 16, and readers are directed toward specific terms by an "Entry finder" section that refers to the appropriate chapter, and by a general index. The 16 key terms are printed in upper case when they occur in the text. Includes a bibliographic essay.   HX17.C37

Handbooks

Hobday, Charles. Communist and Marxist parties of the world. Burnt Mill, Harlow, Essex, England: Longman; Santa Barbara, Calif.: Distr. by ABC-Clio, 1986. 529 p. ISBN 0-582-90264-9. £48.00.   **CJ245**

In three parts: (1) an essay on the rise and evolution of the world communist movement, including international Marxist organizations, conferences and front organizations; (2) descriptions of Marxist and communist parties arranged alphabetically within broad geographic areas, the largest and most important treated in greater detail; (3) classification of parties according to affiliation (e.g., "pro-Soviet parties," "pro-Chinese parties"), a selection of important party documents, (e.g., *The communist manifesto*, *The Brezhnev doctrine*, and the *"Eurocommunist" declaration*), and a selected bibliography of important communist and Marxist material. Personal name index.   HX40.H567

Biography

Biographical dictionary of Marxism / ed. by Robert A. Gorman. Westport, Conn.: Greenwood, 1986. 388 p. ISBN 0-313-24851-6. $55.00.   **CJ246**

Describes the careers and theories of more than 200 Marxist philosophers from 45 countries, including extensive treatment of Third World Marxists who "have retooled Marxism for the postcolonial liberation struggles without . . . altering its philosophical base."—*Pref.* Does not include nonmaterialist (i.e., nonorthodox) Marxists, who are treated by the editor's *Biographical dictionary of neo-Marxism* (below), to which the present volume provides references. Five entries describe groups of theorists. Biographies are arranged alphabetically; each is followed by a short bibliography. An appendix lists subjects by nationality, which facilitates the relating of theorists and movements to national and regional cultures. General index.   HX23.B568

Biographical dictionary of neo-Marxism / ed. by Robert A. Gorman. Westport, Conn.: Greenwood, 1985. 463 p. ISBN 0-313-23513-9. $55.00.   **CJ247**

Surveys some 200 nonmaterialist Marxists, complementing *Biographical dictionary of Marxism* (above), which treats materialists. Ten additional entries treat groups, movements, or journals. The articles were written by "scholars with an intimate interest in and knowledge of a particular entrant."—*Pref.* Not complete, since some subjects (mostly East Europeans) were omitted at their own request, and others asked that some information be excluded. Entries, alphabetically arranged, are followed by two-part bibliographies of primary and secondary works. The index associates key terms with their originators, permitting readers to trace the "source and meaning of technical words and phrases that have turned many radical journals

into lexical nightmares." An appendix lists subjects by nationality.   HX23.B57

Lazić, Branko M. Biographical dictionary of the Comintern / by Branko Lazitch in collaboration with Milorad M. Drachkovitch. New, rev., and expanded ed. Stanford, Calif.: Hoover Institution Pr., 1986. 532 p. ISBN 0-8179-8401-1.   **CJ248**

1st ed., 1973 (*Guide* CJ498).

Adds 35 new biographies (bringing the total to 753) and 77 more pseudonyms. Also modifies 229 of the original biographies, supplying corrections or additions.   HX23.L35

Quotations

Brassey's Soviet and communist quotations / comp. and ed. by Albert L. Weeks. Wash.: Pergamon-Brassey's, c1987. 387 p. ISBN 0-08-034488-7. $50.00.   **CJ249**

A "comprehensive . . . compilation of major statements whose ideas drive the Soviet Union today . . . the words that reflect and have shaped the world view of the Soviet Union."— *Pref.* Includes pronouncements by Marx, Stalin, Gorbachev, etc., as well as by lesser-known figures (among whom are obscure officers whose statements may have been used by leaders to send signals the leaders did not wish attributed to themselves). Much material is drawn from official publications (e.g., *Pravda, Military thought*) and from transcripts of official radio broadcasts. The 2,117 quotations are arranged in 17 chapters (e.g., Class and class warfare, Foreign policy), each of which is further subdivided. Quotations vary in length. The index is arranged by chapter.   HX73.B7

ARMED FORCES

Bibliography

Current

Current military & political literature. Oxford: Military Pr., c1989– .   **CJ250**

Continues *Current military literature* (*Guide* CKJ513), which ceased with the volume covering 1984.

Provides citations, some with abstracts, to articles and occasional papers drawn from an international list of periodicals in the fields of international relations, strategic studies, military-political science and history, theory and conduct of military action, peace studies, and conflict resolution. Entries are arranged in classed order with cross-references. Author, source, and geographical indexes in each issue; the first issue of each volume has a list of titles scanned with publishers' addresses.

Current world affairs: a quarterly bibliography. v. 14, no. 1 (Spring 1990)– . Alexandria, Va.: John C. Damon, c1990– . Quarterly. ISSN 1050-4850. $146.00.   **CJ251**

Continues *Quarterly strategic bibliography* (*Guide* CJ514), which ceased with v. 13 (1989).

Cites periodical articles, government documents, research reports, and monographs that relate to the U.S. and world affairs (e.g., foreign policy, arms control, environmental protection). Arranged by form (periodicals, congressional documents, books, other documents) and indexed by subject; contains a list of periodicals consulted and a glossary.   Z1361.D4Q37

Periodicals

Unsworth, Michael. Military periodicals : United States and selected international journals and newspapers. N.Y. : Greenwood, 1990. 404 p. ISBN 0-313-25920-8. **CJ252**

Presents historical sketches of selected periodicals (primarily American) that have influenced the armed forces and military thought of the U.S. In three sections, each alphabetically arranged by periodical title: Long profiles (of the more prominent journals), Short profiles (of the less prominent), and Multiple-edition profiles (of journals having special editions, supplements, etc.). Also contains an appendix listing journals by subject, a chronology, and a general index.   Z6723.U57

Encyclopedias

Kohn, George C. Dictionary of wars. N.Y. : Facts on File, c1986. 586 p. ISBN 0-8160-1005-6.   **CJ253**
For annotation, see *Supplement* DA21.   D25.A2K63

Taylor, Michael John Haddrick. Encyclopedia of the world's air forces. N.Y. : Facts on File, 1988. 211 p. : col. ill. ISBN 0-8160-2004-3.   **CJ254**

Describes the air forces of 150 nations, indicating air bases, number of specific models of planes, number of personnel, etc. Discusses the purposes of the force (e.g., for Benin, transport and liaison) and the world events and national conditions that have affected them. Short, fact-filled entries, arranged alphabetically by country, are followed by an appendix describing the speed, range, armaments, etc., for each type of aircraft, thus facilitating assessment of a nation's air strength. Includes a glossary and an index to specific models of aircraft.   UG628.T39

Dictionaries

Brassey's multilingual military dictionary = Brassey's dictionnaire multilingue militaire = Brassey's, diccionario polígloto militar = Brassey's, Militär-Wörterbuch in sechs Sprachen = [Brassi, mnogoîazychnyĭ voennyĭ slovar'] = [Qāmūs Brāysīs al-' askarī al-muta'addid al-lughāt]. London ; Wash. : Brassey's Defence Publishers, 1987. 815 p. ISBN 0-08-027032-8 (pbk.). $45.00. **CJ255**

Designed to meet "the general needs of the service user and to provide the basic military vocabulary for a wide variety of situations in which direct word-for-word translation is required in an Army, Navy, or Air Force context."—*Introd.* Gives French, Spanish, German, Russian, and Arabic equivalents in a base list of 6,960 American English terms, with separate indexes for each language that refer to the base list. The Russian and Arabic indexes use Cyrillic and Arabic alphabets; there is also a brief index of British English. Appendixes give terms for ranks, units/formations, numerals/notation, tools, etc.   U25.B66

Dobenik, Richard H. Dictionnaire technique de la marine : anglais-français et français-anglais / Richard H. Dobenik et Gregory W. Hartline. Paris : Maison du dictionnaire, c1989. 646, [17] p. of plates : ill. ISBN 2-85608-031-6. 450F.   **CJ256**
Added title page in English: *Naval technical dictionary.* Prefatory material in French and in English.

Presents 35,000 naval terms (e.g., drop anchor, mutiny, rudder, submarine) arranged alphabetically in two sections, French-English and English-French. Appendixes include illustrations with relevant terminology provided in English and French and a table of naval ranks used by the U.S., British, Canadian, Belgian, French, and NATO navies. Bibliography.   V24.D63

Dupuy, Trevor Nevitt. Dictionary of military terms : a guide to the language of warfare and military institutions / comp. by Trevor N. Dupuy, Curt Johnson, Grace P. Hayes. N.Y. : H.W. Wilson, 1986. 237 p. ISBN 0-8242-0717-3.   **CJ257**

Intends to provide military professionals with the first comprehensive dictionary in the field, offering 2,500 concise definitions pertaining to all aspects of modern and historical military and naval affairs. Includes basic military terms (e.g., attack) that were omitted from the *Department of Defense dictionary of military and associated terms* (*Guide* CJ521). Neglects such lexicographic concerns as etymology in favor of a strict concern for "military meanings and derivations ... including those that enjoy popular usage."—*Introd.*   U24.D87

Gutzman, Philip C. Dictionary of military, defense contractor & troop slang acronyms. Santa Barbara, Calif. : ABC-Clio, c1990. 392 p. ISBN 0-87436-589-9.   **CJ258**
Includes initialisms and abbreviations as well as acronyms. Alphabetically arranged.   U26.G88

International code name directory. 3rd ed. (1984)– . Newtown, Conn. : Forecast International/DMS, Inc., 1983– . Annual. ISSN 0883-2803.   **CJ259**
Title varies: some issues called *DMS international code name handbook*, *DMS international code name directory*, or *Code name directory. International.*

Place and publisher vary; some issues published in Greenwich, Conn., by DMS, Inc.

Designed to provide industry and government officials with a comprehensive listing of all past and current aerospace and defense code names and acronyms assigned by foreign governments and industries, including Warsaw Pact nations. An alphabetical listing, letter-by-letter, with succinct definitions, several words to two lines in length. Cross-references to other publications. Appendixes list entries in this volume and in the 1983 *DMS code name handbook.*   U26.C568

Luttwak, Edward. The dictionary of modern war / Edward Luttwak and Stuart Koehl. N.Y. : HarperCollins, c1991. 680 p. ISBN 0-06-270021-9. $45.00.   **CJ260**

Presents some 1,100 detailed yet concise entries defining concepts, organizations, weapons, military technologies, methods of warfare, negotiations, and treaties. Intended as a reference source and a readable guide for both experts and general readers. Too short to be an encyclopedia, but more than a dictionary because it "explains and does not merely describe its contents . . . ." (*Introd.*) and includes its authors' opinions (e.g., statements as to whether a weapon really works). Alphabetically arranged, with extensive cross-references. A glossary lists popular names of weapon systems and vehicles and their nationalities. Not illustrated.   U24.L93

Robertson, David. Guide to modern defense and strategy : a complete description of the terms, tactics, organizations and accords of today's defense. Detroit : Gale, c1987. 324 p. ISBN 0-8103-5043-2.   **CJ261**

Intended to go further "than the standard dictionary in that the entries are not confined to mere definitions. The main aim ... is to set out the policy implications and theoretical arguments that lie behind the concepts and the physical specifications."—*Pref.* Alphabetically arranged entries, typically from one-half to two pages in length, define not only standard technical terms, but also such popular or colloquial usages as "Dr. Strangelove, " "McNamara," and "Blue Water Navy." Extensive cross-referencing, including the use of boldface for terms within entries that are themselves the subjects of entries. Table of abbreviations.   U24.R63

Shafritz, Jay M. The Facts on File dictionary of military science / Jay M. Shafritz, Todd J.A. Shafritz, David B. Robertson. N.Y. : Facts on File, c1989. 498 p. ISBN 0-8160-1823-5. **CJ262**

Focuses on the strategy, tactics, and technology of warfare, but "does not ignore peripheral yet critical concerns such as logistics, law, administration, or history." Aimed at both professionals and concerned citizens, but "essential for any commissioned or noncommissioned officer . . . [containing] the vocabulary of his or her profession and brief discussions of all its major strategic doctrines or concerns."—*Pref.* Entries vary in length from two words to half a page. Some entries end with bibliographies, and cross-references are used liberally; those that refer to other entries are printed in upper case. U24.S47

Quotations

Royle, Trevor. A dictionary of military quotations. N.Y. : Simon & Schuster, 1989. 210 p. ISBN 0-13-210113-0. **CJ263**

Contains 3,500 quotations ranging from the classical period to the present, including those ascribed not only to political and military leaders, but to writers, academics, ordinary foot soldiers, etc. Entries appear under 351 numbered topics, in five sections: (1) Famous leaders; (2) Specific wars or battles; (3) Functional divisions of the armed forces (e.g., infantry, communications) and characteristics of the armed forces of specific nations; (4) The military life; and (5) The results of war (e.g., death, victory). Author and subject indexes. U102.R784

Handbooks

Conway's all the world's fighting ships, 1947–1982 / [ed., Robert Gardiner ; contributors, Norman Friedman . . . et al.]. Annapolis, Md. : Naval Institute Pr., c1983. 2 v. : ill. ISBN 0-87021-923-5 (set). **CJ264**

In other editions, coverage varies: 1860–1905 (publ. 1979); 1906–21 (publ. 1985); 1922–46 (publ. 1980).

Describes the fleets of 143 countries: Pt. 1, The Western powers, with sections on NATO and pro-Western powers; Pt. 2, The Warsaw Pact and non-aligned nations, with sections on Africa, Asia, neutral Europe, Latin America, Middle East, and the Warsaw Pact. Entries for each country follow a standard format, beginning with a general introduction, followed by a description of fleet strength in 1947. The description of post-1947 additions to the fleet is subdivided by ship type, with separate sections for major surface ships (e.g., aircraft carriers, destroyers). For each class of ship, gives detailed information on dimensions, personnel, armament, sensors, engines, etc., and the launch dates and current status of individual vessels. For larger classes both photographs and diagrams may supplement the text. Index by ship name. V765.C663

The Naval Institute guide to combat fleets of the world / ed. by Bernard Prézelin ; English language version prepared by A.D. Baker III. 8th English language edition. Annapolis, Md. : Naval Institute Pr., c1990. 962 p. ill. ISBN 0-87021-250-8. $120.00. **CJ265**

Translation of *Flottes de combat.*

This guide to the naval programs of 167 nations with navies, coast guards, or paramilitary maritime forces "describes all naval vessels, large and small, in service and under construction, as well as naval aircraft and weapons systems and sensors."—*Introd.* Arranged alphabetically by nation. Lists equipment, physical specifications, performance capabilities, and personnel requirements, and estimates each navy's number of personnel. Includes tables of terms and abbreviations and conversion tables for measurements. An index lists full names

of individual ships. 3,700 photos and line drawings.
VA40.L11e

The nuclear weapons world : who, how & where / ed. by Patrick Burke. Westport, Conn. : Greenwood, 1988. 383 p. : ill. ISBN 0-313-26590-9. **CJ266**

A handbook of information on the official nuclear weapons states and organizations of the world, in seven chapters covering the U.S., Soviet Union, U.K., France, People's Republic of China, NATO, and Warsaw Pact. Each chapter has two cross-referenced parts, the first describing the decision-making organizations (e.g., committees, agencies, contractors) and their decision-making processes, the second containing alphabetically arranged biographies of decision-makers. Each chapter ends with a list of references. Name and subject indexes. U264.N84

Individual countries

United States

Bibliography

Champion, Brian. Advanced weapons systems : an annotated bibliography of the cruise missile, MX missile, laser and space weapons, and stealth technology. N.Y. : Garland, 1985. 206 p. ISBN 0-8240-8793-3. **CJ267**

Intended for a wide audience, from general readers to those with a substantial background in science and technology. The citations, mostly to scholarly and professional journals and newspapers, are arranged in individual chapters on specific weapons. Within chapters, organization is chronological to show how particular weapons systems have developed. Author and subject indexes. Z6724.W4C47

Fredriksen, John C. Shield of republic, sword of empire : a bibliography of United States military affairs, 1783–1846. N.Y. : Greenwood, [1990]. 433 p. (Bibliographies and indexes in American history, no.15). ISBN 0-313-25384-6. **CJ268**

For annotation, see *Supplement* DB8. Z1249.M5F73

Lawrence, Robert M. Strategic Defense Initiative : bibliography and research guide. Boulder, Colo. : Westview Pr. ; London : Mansell, 1987. 352 p. ISBN 0-8133-7229-1. $18.50. **CJ269**

Less a research guide than a literature survey, this work's chief value lies in its bibliographies that cite some 1,000 items. 84 key citations (with substantial abstracts) occur in chapters summarizing writings favoring SDI, those opposing it, and works providing technical background. Includes a glossary of acronyms and terminology. UG743.L38

Military history of the United States : an annotated bibliography / Susan K. Kinnell, ed. Santa Barbara, Calif. : ABC-Clio, c1986. 333 p. ISBN 0-87436-474-4. **CJ270**

Covers the entire span of American military history, from the earliest colonial militia to 1985, treating major wars with signed abstracts, the military in peacetime, and social implications of the armed forces. Included are books reviewed in at least one major historical journal, articles published 1974– 85, and dissertations. Arranged chronologically. Subject and author indexes. See also annotation for *Supplement* CJ302.
Z1249.M5M54

Research guides in military studies. N.Y. : Greenwood, 1988–1990. v. 1–3. (In progress). **CJ271**

Contents: no. 1, The peacetime army, 1900–1941, by Marvin Fletcher (1988. 177 p.); no. 2, Special operations and elite units 1939–1988, by Roger A. Beaumont (1988. 243 p.); no. 3,

The late 19th century U.S. Army, 1865–1898 : a research guide, by Joseph G. Dawson III (1990. 252 p.).

Aims "to catalogue, survey and appraise the substantial body of contemporary and historical literature that taken together depicts both the scale and the importance of this stage in the evolution of the U.S. Army."—*Series foreword*, in no. 3. Each volume covers about 1,100–1,200 books, articles, and dissertations in a topical arrangement, with two- to three-sentence annotations. Author and subject indexes (with some omissions). Appendixes usually give chronology, Army personnel, etc.

Dictionaries

Noel, John Vavasour. Naval terms dictionary / by John V. Noel, Jr. and Edward L. Beach. 5th ed. Annapolis, Md. : Naval Institute Pr., c1988. 316 p. ISBN 0-87021-571-X. $15.95.   **CJ272**

4th ed., 1978 (*Guide* CJ566).

Adds words that have become part of normal usage since the 4th ed. and deletes "some outmoded expressions, including slang and normal words that have no special naval association. Acronyms, except those that have entered the language in their own right . . . have been deleted, because they are included in the *Dictionary of naval abbreviations* [Annapolis, Md. : U.S. Naval Institute, 1970], compiled by Bill Wedertz."—*Pref.* Appendixes explaining designations of ships, aircraft, and other equipment and the ranking structure for personnel have been dropped.   V23.N6

The United States Army : a dictionary / ed. by Peter Tsouras, Bruce W. Watson, Susan M. Watson. N.Y. : Garland, 1990. 898 p. ISBN 0-8240-5348-6.   **CJ273**

In two major sections: (1) 28 pages of acronyms; and (2) definitions of words, with extensive cross-referencing and, for each entry, one or two references to publications (including government publications giving official definitions).   UA25.U49

The United States Navy : a dictionary / ed. by Bruce W. Watson and Susan M. Watson. N.Y. : Garland, 1991. 948 p. (Garland reference library of social sciences, vol. 695). ISBN 0-8240-5538-1.   **CJ274**

Intended for serious researchers. Defines major terms "currently in use" (*Introd.*) during the period since World War II, with emphasis on recent vocabulary. Entries are arranged alphabetically, each followed by a short list of references. Extensive use of cross-references. Two lists of acronyms, one for major types of ships.   V23.U64

Waldman, Harry. The dictionary of SDI. Wilmington, Del. : Scholarly Resources, 1988. 182 p. : ill. ISBN 0-8420-2281-3. ISBN 0-8420-2295-3 (pbk.).   **CJ275**

" . . . nearly 800 items are defined in the areas of ballistic missile defense, arms control, research and development, countermoves to defense, Soviet capabilities, the roles of U.S. allies, personalities in the field, SDI software and hardware."—*Introd.* Most definitions are brief, although some are a page or more in length. Numerous drawings, diagrams, charts, and tables.   UG743.W35

Directories

Directory of military bases in the U.S. Phoenix : Oryx, 1991. 197 p. ISBN 0-89774-531-0.   **CJ276**

Ed. by William R. Evinger.

" . . . the only single source to comprehensively list the Army, Navy, Air Force, Marines, Coast Guard, National Guard, Reserve, and Joint Service Installations, as well as Department of Defense agencies, military camps and stations, recruiting offices, and command headquarters offices."—*Introd.*

The main section lists bases/installations alphabetically by state and city. Brief entries indicate the facility's address and size, telephone numbers of key officers, number of personnel, expenditures, major units, history, and services for personnel and their families (e.g., housing, commissaries, recreational opportunities). Index of bases; appendix of facilities that are candidates for possible closing or realignment.   UA26.A26

United States Navy and Marine Corps bases, domestic / Paolo E. Coletta, ed., K. Jack Bauer, assoc. ed. Westport, Conn. : Greenwood, 1985. 740 p. ISBN 0-313-23133-8.   **CJ277**
VA67.U55

United States Navy and Marine Corps bases, overseas / Paolo E. Coletta, ed., K. Jack Bauer, associate ed. Westport, Conn. : Greenwood, 1985. 459 p. ISBN 0-313-24504-5.   **CJ278**

These publications list by location in alphabetical order all "important and historically significant . . . bases and facilities, extant and extinct. Each entry discusses the form and function of the base or facility and gives something of its history and development."—*Pref. Bases, domestic* treats bases and facilities within U.S. boundaries, *Bases, overseas,* those in other countries.   VA67.U554

Handbooks

Estes, Kenneth W. The Marine officer's guide. 5th ed. Annapolis, Md. : Naval Institute Pr., c1985. 523 p. : ill. ISBN 0-87021-408-X. $24.95.   **CJ279**

4th ed., 1977, by Robert Debs Heinl (*Guide* CJ571).

Updated "to reflect service reorganizations and changes in public law."—*Pref.*   VE153.E85

Decorations and insignia

The Congressional Medal of Honor : the names, the deeds. Forest Ranch, Calif. : Sharp & Dunnigan Publications, 1984. 1105 p., [1] leaf of plates : 1 col. ill. ISBN 0-918495-01-6. $27.50.   **CJ280**

Lists recipients of the medal from its foundation during the Civil War through the Vietnam conflict. Short entries giving accounts of the acts of bravery that led to each bestowal are organized by military campaign in reverse chronological order. There is also a list arranged by state from which the recipient enlisted. Name index.   UB433.C65

Biography

Brown, Russell K. Fallen in battle : American general officer combat fatalities from 1775. N.Y. : Greenwood, 1988. 243 p. ISBN 0-313-26242-X.   **CJ281**

Gives brief biographical data, career highlights, and circumstances of death of each military or naval general officer killed in battle or its aftermath, from colonial times through Vietnam. Includes Confederate fatalities. Contains statistical tables.   E181.B886

Union of Soviet Socialist Republics

Encyclopedias

Polmar, Norman. Guide to the Soviet navy. 4th ed. Annapolis, Md.: Naval Institute Pr., c1986. 536 p.: ill. (some col.). ISBN 0-87021-240-0. $38.95. **CJ282**
3rd ed., 1983 (*Guide* CJ606).

This edition emphasizes weapons and electronics while continuing detailed description of other components of the Soviet Navy. VA573.P598 1986

Soviet military encyclopedia. Fort Belvoir, Va.: Air Force Intelligence Agency, [1988]. v. 1A–B, 2A–B. (In progress). **CJ283**
Contents: v. 1A, A–Ar'yergard; v. 1B, As–Byuro; v. 2A, Vavilon–Voyna za pfal'tsskoye nasledstvo 1688–97; v. 2B, Voyna i revolyutsiya–Grazhdanskaya voyna v severnoy amerike.

No more published?
Translation of *Sovetskaĭa voennaĭa entsiklopediĭa* (*Guide* CJ529). U24.S69

INTELLIGENCE AND ESPIONAGE

Becket, Henry S. A. The dictionary of espionage: spook-speak into English. N.Y.: Stein and Day, 1986. 203 p. ISBN 0-8128-3068-7. $17.95. **CJ284**
A helpful guide, alphabetically arranged, to the language of the espionage community, defining terms such as "access permit," "disinformation," and "paper merchant." Cross-references; bibliography of printed sources consulted. UB270.B35

Constantinides, George C. Intelligence and espionage: an analytical bibliography. Boulder, Colo.: Westview Pr., 1983. 559 p. ISBN 0-86531-545-0. $55.00 (est.). **CJ285**

The main portion of the book offers descriptive and evaluative annotations for some 500 English-language books on the intelligence process and the history of intelligence, arranged alphabetically by author, with cross-references. Covers 17th–20th centuries, with emphasis on the latter. Preceding the annotated list is an "intelligence category index" that cites works from the annotated list by topic (e.g., American intelligence—World War II, Censorship and economic warfare, Photographic intelligence). Combined glossary and abbreviations list; title and subject/author indexes. Z6724.I7C66

O'Toole, G. J. A. The encyclopedia of American intelligence and espionage: from the Revolutionary War to the present. N.Y.: Facts on File, c1988. 539 p.: ill. ISBN 0-8160-1011-0. $39.95. **CJ286**
The five major types of articles treat: American intelligence organizations; the role of intelligence in the principal wars of American history; subjects of importance in American intelligence history (e.g., cryptology); events, and individuals. Some of the other entries further explicate the major articles. Entries are arranged alphabetically and vary in length from a paragraph to 16 pages (Vietnam War). Articles include cross-references. Extensive bibliography; general index. UB271.U5O85

Rocca, Raymond G. Bibliography on Soviet intelligence and security services / Raymond G. Rocca and John J. Dziak with the staff of the Consortium for the Study of

Intelligence. Boulder, Colo.: Westview Pr., 1985. 203 p. ISBN 0-8133-7048-5 (pbk.). $16.00. **CJ287**
The compilers (experts with government and teaching experience) attempt to provide scholars and policy analysts with "an analytic aid for research and teaching about Soviet intelligence and its role in both Soviet domestic politics and contemporary world affairs."—*Foreword*. Citations (many annotated) to more than 500 books, articles, and government documents are arranged in five sections: (1) Selected bibliographies and other reference works, (2) Russian/Soviet accounts, (3) Defector/first hand accounts, (4) Secondary accounts, and (5) Congressional and other government documents. Author/source and title indexes. Z6724.I7R6

United States intelligence: an encyclopedia / ed. by Bruce W. Watson, Susan M. Watson, Gerald W. Hopple. N.Y.: Garland, 1990. 792 p. ISBN 0-8240-3713-8. **CJ288**

"Intended for the serious researcher of the U.S. Intelligence Community" (*Introd.*); entries treat major terms, persons, and organizations since World War II. Lists of acronyms and major weapon systems, a chronology, and a bibliography are followed by the alphabetical list of entries, which contain cross-references and end with bibliographies. Ends with appendixes containing 25 relevant executive and congressional statements issued since 1941. JK468.I6U57

ARMS CONTROL & PEACE RESEARCH

Bibliography

Arms control, disarmament and international security. 1987– . Claremont, Calif.: Regina Books, c1988– . Annual. ISSN 0899-6547. $29.95. **CJ289**
Annual bibliography sponsored by the Center for the Study of Armament and Disarmament, California State Univ., Los Angeles, and The Arms Control Association, Washington, D.C. Begins with citations for 1987. Z6464.D6A76

Atkins, Stephen E. Arms control and disarmament, defense and military, international security, and peace: an annotated guide to sources, 1980–1987. Santa Barbara, Calif.: ABC-Clio, c1989. 411 p. ISBN 0-87436-488-4. $37.50. **CJ290**
Presents annotated citations for 1,596 monographs, hearings, papers, and reports (mostly English-language) published 1980–87. Within topical chapters (Arms control and disarmament, Defense and military, International security, and Peace) entries are alphabetically arranged by type of material (e.g., bibliographies, guidebooks, hearings, newsletters). Author/title and subject indexes. Z6464.D6A85

Canada and international peace and security: a bibliography: covering materials from January 1985 through December 1989 = Le Canada, la paix et la sécurité internationales: une bibliographie: comrenanat des documents de janvier 1985 à décembre 1989. Ottawa: Canadian Institute for International Peace and Security = Institut canadien pour la paiz et la sécurité internationales, 1990. 434 p. ISBN 0-660-55772-X. **CJ291**
Provides access to both French- and English-language literature on "international peace and security from a Canadian perspective."—*Pref.* Focuses primarily on arms control, disarmament, defense, and conflict resolution in more than 10,000 articles, government publications, theses, dissertations, conference papers, and organization newsletters, 1985 through 1989. Entries are alphabetical by main entry under alphabetically arranged subject headings (e.g., Arms race, Espionage, Nuclear

winter). Introductory material, headings, and subject headings lists are in English and French; the citations are in the language of publication. Annual updates are planned. Author index.

Z6464.Z9C32

Doenecke, Justus D. Anti-intervention : a bibliographical introduction to isolationism and pacifism from World War I to the early cold war. N.Y. : Garland, 1987. 421 p. ISBN 0-8240-8482-9. **CJ292**

Contains citations to 1,581 books, articles, dissertations, and primary sources on the opposition of both isolationists and pacifists to U.S. overseas involvement from World War I to the mid-1950s. Entries (most briefly annotated) are organized in five topical chapters featuring general works, World War I and its aftermath, the 1920s to the mid-1950s, opinion-making, and groups and leaders. Within chapters, entries are chronologically or topically subdivided, then listed alphabetically by main entry. Includes a detailed table of contents and indexes by author, topic, and personal name. Z6465.U5D62

Fenton, Thomas P. Third World struggle for peace with justice : a directory of resources / comp. and ed. by Thomas P. Fenton and Mary J. Heffron. Maryknoll, N.Y. : Orbis Books, c1990. 1 v. ISBN 0-88344-660-X. $9.95. **CJ293**

Provides access to readily available English-language material related to peace efforts in the Third World. Begins with a helpful introduction explaining definitions, selection criteria, geographic scope, political orientation, and format. Entries are divided into five chapters: Organizations, Books, Periodicals, Pamphlets and articles, and Audiovisuals. Chapters are subdivided into annotated entries, supplementary lists, and further information sources (each alphabetically arranged). Organization, personal author, title, geographic area, and subject indexes. Z7164.U5F45

Gay, William. The nuclear arms race / William Gay and Michael Pearson. Chicago : Amer. Lib. Assoc., 1987. 289 p. (The last quarter century, no. 1). ISBN 0-8389-0467-X (pbk.). $29.95. **CJ294**

Covers the major issues and literature of the nuclear arms race. Eight topical chapters provide historical background, describe consequences, and discuss deterrence and alternatives to the arms race and nuclear warfare. Each chapter summarizes the relevant issues in an essay and contains an extensive bibliography, often with annotations. The appendix serves as a guide to conducting further research on the topic. Includes a glossary, author-title index, and subject index. Z6724.A9G39

Green, Marguerite. Peace archives : a guide to library collections of the papers of American peace organizations and of leaders in the public effort for peace. Berkeley, Calif. : World Without War Council, 1986. 66 p. **CJ295**

Brings together information on library collections containing papers of American peace organizations and of individuals active in peace efforts. Developed by the Historians Project of the World Without War Council. 30 major collections are listed alphabetically by institution name, giving address, telephone, director, description of the collection and its holdings, services available for researchers, and services provided for donors. An additional section lists with locations 72 individual peace collections (alphabetic by name). Appendixes give the archival methods of 27 peace organizations, a summary of the standards for record keeping and archiving used by the Swarthmore College Peace Collection, and a bibliography. No index.

Z6464.Z9G74

Hartley, Keith. The economics of defense, disarmament, and peace : an annotated bibliography / Keith Hartley, Nick Hooper. Aldershot, England ; Brookfield, Vt. : E. Elgar, c1990. 1 v. (unpaged). ISBN 1-85278-051-7.

CJ296

Attempts to provide access to literature on economic aspects of defense, disarmament, and peace published 1960–89, although some items prior to 1960 appear in a separate section. Contains 2,318 entries (many annotated, some listing tables of contents) for English-language books, articles, and selected government documents. Entries, in 14 topical chapters (e.g., General studies, Developing countries, Terrorism) are listed by date; then alphabetically by author. Author and keyword indexes. A review in *Choice* 28 (Feb. 1991) : 3077 terms the work "disappointing" and notes shortcomings. Z6464.D6H37

Meulen, Jacob ter. From Erasmus to Tolstoy : the peace literature of four centuries : Jacob ter Meulen's bibliographies of the peace movement before 1899 / Jacob ter Meulen ; ed., with an introduction by Peter van den Dungen. N.Y. : Greenwood, c1990. 145 p. (Bibliographies and indexes in law and political science, no. 14). ISBN 0-313-26827-4. **CJ297**

Lists in chronological order nearly 4,000 titles published from the beginning of printing until the end of the 19th century. In two sections, 1480–1776 and 1776–1898, each with its own author index. A reprinting of two titles published in limited editions: *Bibliography of the peace movement before 1899 (provisional lists)* = *Bibliographie du mouvement de la paix avant 1899 (liste provisoires)* (Hague : Library of the Palace of Peace, 1934) and *Bibliography of the peace movement before 1899 (provisional lists, 1480–1776)* = *Bibliographie du mouvement de la paix avant 1899 (listes provisoires periode 1480–1776)* (Hague : Library of the Palace of Peace, 1936). This version adds a 50-page introduction which has its own general index.

Z6464.Z9M38

Musto, Ronald G. The peace tradition in the Catholic Church : an annotated bibliography. N.Y. : Garland, 1987. 590 p. (Garland reference library of social science, v. 339). ISBN 0-8240-8584-1. $67.00. **CJ298**

Serves as a detailed (1,485 entries), critically annotated bibliography for the author's earlier study, *The Catholic peace tradition* (Maryknoll, N.Y. : Orbis Books, 1986). Entries cover Catholic church history from apostolic times to the present, and include books, articles, tracts, papal bulls, and dissertations in English, French, German, Italian, Spanish, Portuguese, and Latin up to November 1986. Arranged by broad chronological classification (e.g., Peace in the New Testament, The era of the Crusades) and subdivided by topic. Indexes of titles; authors, editors, and translators; and proper names. Z7838.P54M87

Ridinger, Robert B. Marks. The Peace Corps : an annotated bibliography. Boston : G.K. Hall, c1989. 366 p. ISBN 0-8161-8912-9. **CJ299**

Contains annotated citations to selected literature by and about the Peace Corps, 1961–86, including government and Peace Corps publications, books, articles, memoirs, dissertations, and videotapes. In three sections: (1) Creation and development of the agency and its programs, (2) Individual country programs, and (3) Roles and influence of returned volunteers. Sections one and three are alphabetic by main entry, section two alphabetic by country. Appendixes list Peace Corps directors, 1961–86, and periodicals published by the Peace Corps (alphabetic by country). Subject and name index; no author index. Z7164.P3R53

Scrivener, David. Bibliography of arms control verification / David Scrivener and Michael Sheehan. Aldershot, England : Dartmouth Pub. Co. ; Brookfield, Vt. : Gower Pub., c1990. 161 p. ISBN 1-85521-044-4. $37.00. **CJ300**

Cites books, book chapters, journal articles, reports, dissertations, proceedings, yearbooks, newspaper articles, and government publications on verification of compliance with arms control agreements. Consists of a general introductory overview followed by four chapters: General issues in arms control verification, Compliance issues and compliance diplomacy, Verification aspects of arms control negotiations and agreements, and Arms control verification in Soviet writings. Chapters 2, 3, and

4 are topically subdivided. Detailed table of contents, but no index.   Z6724.A73S38

UNIDIR repertory of disarmament research / United Nations Institute for Disarmament Research. 1990– . N.Y. : United Nations, 1990– .   **CJ301**

An updated and revised version of *Repertory of disarmament research* (*Guide* CJ614).

Drawn from the U.N. Institute for Disarmament Research's (UNIDIR) computerized Research Institute Data Base. This edition focuses on research institutes and their activities. In two parts: Pt. 1, Research institutes, a directory of 730 research institutes and organizations (alphabetically arranged by country) gives name, acronym, address, description, date established, type of organization and activities, sources of funding, languages used, staff, periodical publications, research activities, and references to recent publications. Includes alphabetical lists of institutes by country and city and by name, an alphabetical index of periodical publications of the institutes, a subject index to research projects, and a personal name index. Pt. 2, Publications, features unannotated citations for 1988–90 publications of the institutes included in Pt. 1. Arranged alphabetically within topical divisions (e.g., Arms race, Nuclear weapons and disarmament). Includes author index. An appendix provides a questionnaire used to update UNIDIR's Data Base.   Z6464.D6U43

Abstract journals

Peace research abstracts journal. v. 1 (June 1964)– . Oakville, Ont. [etc.] : Canadian Peace Research Institute, 1964– . ISSN 0031-3599.   **CJ302**

Provides abstracts of books, journal articles, conference papers, government publications, and other materials, grouping them in ten major areas (e.g., International organizations, Pairs of nations and crisis areas) with subsections (e.g., U.N. General Assembly, France and Germany). Each monthly issue treats only part of the field, sometimes considering portions of several major areas; a year's issues may not cover the entire field. Monthly issues have author indexes, but subject indexes are found only in an annual cumulative index, which consists of: (1) authors; (2) a "Complete subject index" that cites entry numbers for all items treating a topic, and (3) a "Primary code index" that lists only the works for which the topic is the principal focus. The latter is especially useful to pinpoint the most relevant entries when topics in the subject index are heavily posted.   JX1901.P38

Encyclopedias

Ali, Sheikh Rustum. The peace and nuclear war dictionary. Santa Barbara, Calif. : ABC-Clio , c1989. 294 p. ISBN 0-87436-531-7.   **CJ303**

Like *The arms control, disarmament, and military security dictionary* (below), this book is designed to be used as a supplementary resource for college courses. Thus, its "over 300 entries, arranged alphabetically, have been systematically selected and organized to complement most standard works on the subject."—*Pref.* Headwords overlap with those of Elliot and Reginald; each concise definition is followed by a paragraph on the historical and contemporary significance of the concept. Extensive cross-references; subject index.   U263.A434

Elliot, Jeffrey M. The arms control, disarmament, and military security dictionary / Jeffrey M. Elliot, Robert Reginald. Santa Barbara, Calif. : ABC-Clio, c1989. 349 p. ISBN 0-87436-430-2. ISBN 0-87436-532-5 (pbk.).   **CJ304**

Designed as a supplementary resource for college classes, hence organized by subject areas that "parallel chapter topics in most reading books in the field" (*Pref.*) rather than alphabetically. The 268 entries, typically a page in length, overlap with those in Sheikh Rustum Ali's *The peace and nuclear war dictionary* (above). The subject arrangement makes the general index essential. Extensive cross-references and copious notes.   JX1974.E55

Seeley, Robert A. The handbook of non-violence : including Aldous Huxley's *An encyclopedia of pacifism*. Westport, Conn. : L. Hill ; Great Neck, N.Y. : Lakeville Pr., c1986. 344 p. ISBN 0-88208-208-6. ISBN 0-88208-209-4 (pbk.).   **CJ305**

Reprints and updates Aldous Huxley's *An encyclopedia of pacifism* (N.Y.; London : Harper, 1937) and adds Seeley's *Handbook of nonviolence*. Huxley's alphabetically arranged *Encyclopedia* has entries for terms, concepts, and organizations related to nonviolence and pacifism—e.g., armaments race, sanctions, Peace Pledge Union (PPU), War Resisters International (WRI)—and has cross-references, a general index, and two new appendixes that provide updated information on the PPU and the WRI. Seeley's *Handbook* is also alphabetical with cross-references and concentrates on more recent terminology, organizations, and individuals (e.g., nuclear free zones, Bishops' Pastoral Letter, Helen Caldicott). Bibliography; list of groups that work for peace (with addresses) but no index.   JX1952.S43

World encyclopedia of peace / honorary ed. in chief, Linus Pauling, exec. eds., Ervin Laszlo, Jong Youl Yoo. Oxford ; N.Y. : Pergamon Pr., 1986. 4 v. ISBN 0-08-032685-4. $300.00.   **CJ306**

Contents: v. 1–2, A–Z; v. 3, Treaties, chronology of the peace movement, Nobel peace prize laureates; v. 4, Peace institutes and organizations, bibliography, journals, indexes.

Vols. 1–2 consist of signed articles arranged alphabetically within 18 categories (e.g., Theories of aggression, conflict, and war; The East-West conflict; Feminism and peace; Peace education). This arrangement makes necessary frequent cross-references and requires referral to the name and subject indexes in v. 4. Articles vary in length from two to six pages and conclude with bibliographies.   JX1944.W67

Quotations

Larson, Jeanne. Seeds of peace : a catalogue of quotations / comp. by Jeanne Larson & Madge Micheels-Cyrus. Philadelphia : New Society Publishers, c1986. 276 p. ISBN 0-86571-098-8. ISBN 0-86571-099-6 (pbk.).   **CJ307**

Presents some 1,600 quotations on peace, war, and nonviolence. In five sections: (1) Waging war; (2) The lighter side of a serious subject; (3) Patriotism; (4) Bumperstickers, buttons, T-shirts, and graffiti; and (5) Waging peace. Longer sections are subdivided. Quotes the compilers feel contain sexist language are starred. Authors are cited (where known) but sources are not always given. Author index.   PN6084.P45L3

Directories

The ACCESS resource guide : an international directory of information on war, peace, and security / William H. Kincade and Priscilla B. Hayner, editors. 1988 ed. Cambridge, Mass. : Ballinger Pub. Co., c1988. 238 p. : ill. ISBN 0-88730-260-2. ISBN 0-88730-262-9 (pbk.).   **CJ308**

A directory of 657 international organizations concerned with research on war, peace, and security. Entries list name, address, telephone, contact person, purpose, subject areas or specialization, and publications. Arranged alphabetically by country; nearly half the entries are for organizations in the U.S. Indexes include a guide to publications, an organizational locator by topic, an organizational locator by product or service, a general index of organizations, and an index of U.S. organizations by state.   U104.A36

The international peace directory / ed. by T. Woodhouse (University of Bradford, School of Peace Studies). Plymouth, U.K.: Northcote House, 1988. 189 p. ISBN 0-7463-0379-3 (pbk.).   **CJ309**

Lists "the organizations which concern themselves with the promotion of peaceful relationships and constructive resolution of conflicts, whether within or between states, and at either the practical or academic and theoretical levels."—*p.19*. The 584 entries, arranged alphabetically within country name, contain information compiled from questionnaire responses. The standardized format for each entry lists the name, address, telephone, membership and affiliations, meeting times and publication, etc. Indexes include: lists of other directories and guides, bibliographies, a guide to current periodicals, organizations identified by issues covered and membership type, and an alphabetical index of organizations.   JX1905.5.I58

Meyer, Robert S. Peace organizations, past and present: a survey and directory. Jefferson, N.C.: McFarland, c1988. 266 p.: ill. ISBN 0-89950-340-3. $24.95.   **CJ310**

Offers profiles of 92 peace organizations (primarily U.S.). Following a chapter describing historical peace efforts, information on the organizations is presented in three sections: (1) Personal, focusing on friendship, pacifism, service, understanding, unity; (2) Instructional, emphasizing knowledge and action in research, publishing, education; (3) Structural, aiming for world unity, organization, federation, citizenship, justice, law, and order. The entries, from one to five pages in length, usually cover the group's history, aims, efforts, and accomplishments. Included in the eight appendixes are a copy of the survey form, the U.N. Universal Declaration of Human Rights, and the Delhi Declaration of the Five Continent Peace Initiative. Bibliography; general index.   JX1905.5.M48

Peace movements of the world / ed. by Alan J. Day. Burnt Mill, Harlow, Essex, England: Longman; Phoenix: Distr. by Oryx, [1986]. 398 p. ISBN 0-89774-438-1.   **CJ311**

Lists peace movements, chiefly post-1945, in seven categories: international, Western Europe, North America, the Pacific region, Asia and the Indian Ocean, other regions (e.g., Middle East, Africa, Latin America and the Caribbean). Entries, in structured format, give address, aims and objectives, formation, activities, membership, publications, and where appropriate, affiliations. Based on information used to compile *Keesing's contemporary archives* (*Guide* DA195). Indexes of movements and publications.   JX1905.5.P426

Peace resource book / from the Institute for Defense & Disarmament Studies. Cambridge, Mass.: Ballinger Pub. Co., c1986–c1988. 3 v.   **CJ312**

A greatly expanded successor to *American peace directory* (Cambridge, Mass.: Ballinger, 1984), intended for those active in arms control, disarmament, and world peace. In three parts: (1) Peace issues and strategies, offering introductory essays describing the world military system, arms control negotiations, and peace movements; (2) (the major section) Directory of U.S. peace groups, consisting of a user's guide and lists of national peace groups and peace-oriented programs (arranged alphabetically with descriptive information), national and local peace organizations (arranged alphabetically and by zip code), members of Congress by state and congressional district, and national peace organizations by focus, constituency, and structure; (3) Guide to peace-related literature, a topical, annotated bibliography of books, articles, government publications, and pamphlets

with an author index and a publisher/distributor address list.   JX1905.5.A64

World directory of peace research and training institutions = Répertoire mondial des institutions de recherche et de formation sur la paix / prepared at UNESCO by the Social and Human Sciences Documentation Centre and the Division of Human Rights and Peace. 6th ed. Deddington, Oxford; N.Y.: Berg; Paris: UNESCO, 1988. 271 p. ISBN 0-85496-156-9. $49.95. ISBN 92-3-102486-8 (pbk.: UNESCO).   **CJ313**

Sixth ed. of: *World directory of peace research institutions*, 5th ed., rev. 1984.

Expanded to include training and information institutions.   JX1904.5.W67

Handbooks

Menos, Dennis. Arms control fact book. Jefferson, N.C.: McFarland, c1985. 140 p. ISBN 0-89950-158-3. ISBN 0-89950-180-X (pbk.). $15.95.   **CJ314**

A nontechnical guide to arms control "intended to help the layman understand the basic issues underlying arms control, its accomplishments to date, and the challenges for the future."—*Pref.* Individual sections feature: encyclopedic entries of significant terms; descriptions of arms control organizations; reference data (e.g., acronyms, chronology, legislation); and a bibliography. General index.   JX1974.7.M45

Biography

Abrams, Irwin. The Nobel Peace Prize and the laureates: an illustrated biographical history, 1901–1987. Boston: G.K. Hall, c1988. 269 p.: ports. ISBN 0-8161-8609-X.   **CJ315**

Essays on the origins and development, mechanics, and evaluation of the prize are followed by profiles of the recipients. In four chronological sections (each beginning with a historical overview); the chronologically arranged profiles are 2,000–3,000 words in length, describe the lives and peace activities of the laureates, provide bibliographies of primary and secondary sources (some briefly annotated), and include portraits. Among the appendixes are Alfred Nobel's will and listings of the laureates by category and country. The second printing includes the 1988 award. General index.   JX1962.A2A25

Biographical dictionary of modern peace leaders / ed. in chief, Harold Josephson. Westport, Conn.: Greenwood, 1985. 1133 p. ISBN 0-313-22565-6.   **CJ316**

Offers signed entries on "individuals [from 41 countries] who either contributed to the organized peace effort or who influenced others to question wars and organized violence."—*Introd.* Most biographees are from the U.S. or Europe and lived in the 19th and 20th centuries; all are now deceased. Entries, one to three pages long, are alphabetically arranged, cross-referenced, and contain: (1) an introductory paragraph with biographical data; (2) a discussion of the person's work, thought, and activities related to peace; and (3) a bibliography of works by and about the individual and the location of manuscript collections. Includes an introductory essay, a chronology of the peace movement, and an appendix grouping the biographees by their national affiliation. General index. A companion to Warren F. Kuehl's *Biographical dictionary of internationalists* (*Guide* CJ76); the two works cross-reference each other.   JX1962.A2B56

CK

Law

GENERAL WORKS

Guides

Berring, Robert C. Bob Berring's commando legal research [video recording]. Los Angeles : Legal Star Communications, 1989. 6 videocassettes (314 min.) : B&W ; 3/4 in. **CK1**

Contents: Tape 1, Introduction to cases (53 min.); Tape 2, Case finding (48 min.); Tape 3, Statutes & administrative materials (49 min.); Tape 4, Secondary sources (54 min.); Tape 5, Shepard's & online research (47 min.); Tape 6, Research strategies (63 min.)

Appropriate for law schools, law firms, and university libraries. KF240.B471

Cohen, Morris L. Finding the law : an abridged edition of *How to find the law,* 9th ed / by Morris L. Cohen, Robert C. Berring, Kent C. Olson. St. Paul, Minn. : West Pub. Co., 1989. 570 p. : ill. ISBN 0-314-54587-5. **CK2**

Abridged edition of *How to find the law,* 9th ed. (below). Aimed at instructional needs; appropriate for undergraduates or paralegals. KF240.C5382

——————— How to find the law / by Morris Cohen, Robert C. Berring, and Kent C. Olson. 9th ed. St. Paul, Minn. : West Pub. Co., 1989. 716 p. : ill. ISBN 0-314-53318-4. **CK3**

A standard text, substantially revised and updated, with many chapters rewritten to include computer-based research methods and sources. Appendixes: (1) state legal research guides and bibliographies; (2) state primary legal resources; (3) West's regional reporters; (4) sources of federal agency rules and regulations; (5) subject guide to selected looseleaf services. Name, title, and subject indexes. KF240.C538

Corbin, John. Find the law in the library : a guide to legal research. Chicago : Amer. Lib. Assoc., 1989. 327 p. : ill. ISBN 0-8389-0502-1. $35.00 (est.). **CK4**

Intends to provide "practicing librarians and library school students with a reference tool that introduces them to legal research techniques...." A basic introduction to legal research is followed by sections on the family, the community, business organizations, and the elderly. KF240.C63

Elias, Stephen. Legal research : how to find and understand the law / by Stephen Elias ; editors, Katherine M. Galvin, Ralph Warner. Berkeley, Calif. : Nolo Pr., 1982. 229 p. : ill. ISBN 0-917316-39-8 (pbk.). $12.95. **CK5**

Intended for general readers. Explains the basic procedures of legal research, concentrating on materials for statutory and case law. Succinct explanations, with examples and many illustrations. A good basic guide. KF240.E35

Jacobstein, J. Myron. Fundamentals of legal research / by J. Myron Jacobstein and Roy M. Mersky. 5th ed. Westbury, N.Y. : Foundation Pr., 1990. 734 p. ISBN 0-88277-794-7. **CK6**

3rd ed., 1985 (*Guide* CK5); [4th ed.], 1987.

Continues the general arrangement of the previous edition. Several chapters have been revised to reflect the use of computerized sources, and a chapter has been added on legal citation form. KF240.J3

Legal research made easy : a roadmap through the law library maze / produced by Nolo Press and Legal Star Communications ; producer, David B. Feldman ; director, James Wooden ; writers, Robert C. Berring, Ralph Warner [videorecording]. Berkeley, Calif. : Nolo Pr., 1990. 1 videocassette (145 min.) : sd., col. ISBN 0-87337-138-0. **CK7**

A 2½-hour VHS videocassette whose purpose is to teach the use of basic legal research sources. Follows a hypothetical question through a sequence of research steps in appropriate sources. Clear, concise definitions and descriptions. A 42-page handbook accompanies the cassette. KF240

Manual of law librarianship : the use and organization of legal literature / ed. by Elizabeth M. Moys. 2nd ed. Boston : G.K. Hall, 1986. [915] p. ISBN 0-8161-1854-X. $65.00. **CK8**

For annotation, see *Supplement* AB58. Z675.L2M27

Matthews, Elizabeth W. The law library reference shelf : annotated subject guide / by Elizabeth W. Matthews ; with the assistance of Peggy Jans. Buffalo, N.Y. : W.S. Hein, 1988. 127 p. ISBN 0-89941-645-4. **CK9**

An annotated list of legal and nonlegal reference titles recommended for law library ready reference collections. Arranged by broad topic. KF1.M33

Olson, Kent C. Practical approaches to legal research / Kent C. Olson, Robert C. Berring. N.Y. : Haworth Pr., c1988. 150 p. ISBN 0-86656-253-2. ISBN 0-86656-853-0 (pbk.). $14.95. **CK10**

Intended for librarians, covering basic legal sources. Informal; often humorous. KF240.O37

The process of legal research : successful strategies / Christina L. Kunz... [et al.]. 2nd ed. Boston : Little, Brown, c1989. 424 p. : ill. ISBN 0-316-50715-6. **CK11**

A guide aimed at law students and paralegals. Chapters, arranged by types of legal materials, feature numerous sample pages from the sources described and self-teaching elements (e.g., problem sets and worked-out examples of the research process). KF240.P76

Specialized legal research / Leah F. Chanin, gen. ed. ; with contributions from Joseph James Beard... [et al.]. Boston : Little, Brown, c1987– . 1 v. (looseleaf). ISBN 0-316-13625-5. **CK12**

Contains 12 chapters, each describing the primary and secondary literature in a legal specialty (e.g., immigration, banking, copyright, securities regulation). Topical index; general bibliography. KF240.S69

Wren, Christopher G. The legal research manual : a game plan for legal research and analysis / Christopher G. Wren, Jill Robinson Wren. 2nd ed. Madison, Wis. : A-R Editions, c1986. 242 p. ISBN 0-89579-210-9 (pbk.). **CK13**

Emphasizes research procedures rather than bibliography. Arranged by type of material; subject index. KF240.W7

Bibliography

Bander, Edward J. Searching the law / [comp.] by Edward J. Bander, Frank Bae, Francis R. Doyle. Dobbs Ferry, N.Y. : Transnational Publishers, c1987. 324 p. ISBN 0-941320-27-8. $45.50.   **CK14**

A bibliography of monographs, periodicals, and bibliographies important in legal research, arranged by topic. Many topical sections conclude with lists of New York state legal texts. Author index.   KF240.B265

Encyclopedia of legal information sources : a bibliographic guide to approximately 19,000 citations for publications, organizations, and other sources of information on 460 law-related subjects / ed. by Paul Wasserman, Gary McCann, Patricia Tobin. Detroit : Gale, c1988. 634 p. ISBN 0-8103-0245-4.   **CK15**

A topical list, arranged according to a 460-item "Outline of contents," of selected legal titles published in the U.S. since 1980. Contains a mix of scholarly, practical, and general reader's titles. A particularly useful section, "States," lists primary and secondary state legal materials alphabetically by state.   KF1.E53

The international law list. 1937– . London : L. Corper-Mordaunt & Co., 1937– . Annual.   **CK16**

A directory of attorneys and law firms, arranged geographically by country, then by city. U.S. entries are by state, then city. For each firm, gives directory information and lists individual attorneys, areas of practice, and representative clients. Includes law societies, bar associations, and patent offices.

International legal books in print, 1990–1991 : an annotated bibliography / ed., Michael D. Chapman. London ; N.Y. : Bowker-Saur, 1990. 2 v. ISBN 0-86291-856-1 (set). £180.00.   **CK17**

Contents: v. 1, Author/title; v. 2, Subjects/publishers.

A comprehensive bibliography of 20,000 English-language titles published or distributed in the U.K., Western Europe, and the Commonwealth. Vol.1 arranged alphabetically, with authors and titles interfiled; v.2 arranged by 2,000 topical headings. Some entries are annotated.   K38.I58

●**LEXIS** [computer file]. Dayton, Ohio : Mead Data Central.   **CK18**

Available online by subscription through the producer. Updated continuously.

A collection of more than 120 machine-readable files, searchable by full text, in the fields of general law (federal and state case reports, statutes, legal journals, state law publications, legislative publications, treatises, directories, etc.), specialized law (admiralty law, banking law, military law, tax law, etc.), U.K. and Commonwealth law, French law, and specialized services (e.g., Shepard's Citations, private client files). Contains more than 7 million records.

Recent titles in law for the subject specialist. v. 5 (1988)– . Ann Arbor, Mich. : Ward & Associates, 1988– . Quarterly.   **CK19**

Continues in part *National legal bibliography* (Guide CK33), which ceased 1988(?).

Comp. and ed. by Margaret Goldblatt & Peter Ward.

A quarterly compilation of titles drawn from: (1) *Catalog of current law titles* (Supplement CK24); (2) *Lawyer's monthly catalog* (Supplement CK27); (3) *Catalog of new foreign and international law titles* (Supplement CK25). Arranged by 23 legal topics (e.g., Banking and securities, Torts, Resource and environment), each topic published in a separate binder. Topical sections may be purchased individually.

Szladits, Charles. A bibliography on foreign and comparative law : books and articles in English, 1978–1983. Dobbs Ferry, N.Y. : Oceana for the Parker School of Foreign and Comparative Law, Columbia Univ., 1989. 5 v. ISBN 0-379-14040-3. $450.00.   **CK20**
K38.S98

——— Szladits' bibliography on foreign and comparative law : books and articles in English, 1984–1986 / comp. and annotated by Vratislav Pechota. Dobbs Ferry, N.Y. : published for the Parker School of Foreign and Comparative Law, Columbia Univ. in the city of New York by Oceana, 1990. 2 v. ISBN 0-379-14068-3 (v. 1). ISBN 0-379-14069-1 (v. 2).   **CK21**

For basic work, 1955, and supplements covering 1953–59 (1962), 1960–65 (1968), 1966–71 (1975), and 1972–77 (1982), see *Guide* CK12.

Continues the classified arrangement of earlier volumes. Beginning with the 1978–83 suppl., the final volume contains geographic and name indexes. Coverage of the 1984–86 suppl. expanded to include non-common law systems and all foreign legal systems.

●**WESTLAW** [computer file]. St. Paul, Minn. : West Publ. Co.   **CK22**

Available by contract through the producer. Updated continuously.

A collection of more than 100 machine-readable files in several categories: federal databases (statutes, regulations, administrative law, case law), state databases from all 50 states, topical materials (administrative law, bankruptcy law, intellectual property law, tort law, etc.), texts of law reviews and legal journals, and specialized materials. Subject searching is enhanced by a subject classification scheme, West Digest Topic and Key Number System.

Bibliography of bibliography

Legal bibliography index. 1978– . Baton Rouge, La. : Publications Institute, Paul M. Hebert Law Center, Louisiana State Univ. [etc.], 1978– . Annual. ISSN 0270-2878.   **CK23**

Editors: 1978– W. S. Chiang and L. E. Dickson.

A subject index to bibliographies appearing in legal publications. In five sections: (1) List of subject headings; (2) List of bibliography titles published regularly (i.e., serial bibliographies separately published or appearing in journals); (3) Serial titles featuring bibliography sections regularly; (4) General bibliographies (i.e., bibliographies treating the law in general); (5) Subject bibliographies. Excludes bibliographies in languages other than English.   KF1.L43

Current

Catalog of current law titles. no.1 (1989)– . Ann Arbor, Mich. : Ward and Associates, 1990– . Bimonthly. ISSN 1044-2987. $215.00.   **CK24**

Continues in part *National legal bibliography* (Guide CK33), which ceased 1988(?).

Previously published (1989–90) by W. S. Hein & Co., Buffalo, N.Y.

Lists books, journals, and other materials currently published and of interest in the development of law collections. Excludes journal articles. Arranged by jurisdiction (region or country), then by subject. Author and title indexes. Produced from the publisher's machine-readable database, *National legal bibliography*.   KF4.C395

Catalog of new foreign and international law titles. v. 1, no. 1 (Jan./Feb. 1989)– . Ann Arbor, Mich. : Ward and

Associates, [1989]– . Bimonthly. ISSN 1043-4852. $210.00. **CK25**

Continues in part *National legal bibliography* (*Guide* CK33), which ceased 1988(?).

Lists recent acquisitions by some 50 academic, law firm, and government libraries. Covers all forms of material except journal articles. Arranged by jurisdiction (regions followed by countries), then by subject. Author and title indexes. K40.C38

DeLashmitt, Eleanor. Annuals and surveys appearing in legal periodicals : an annotated listing. Littleton, Colo. : F.B. Rothman, 1987– . 1 v. (looseleaf). ISBN 0-8377-2033-8 (looseleaf). **CK26**

An annotated list of more than 90 annuals and surveys of the law appearing in U.S. and selected Canadian periodicals, arranged in three sections: State surveys, Federal court surveys, and Subject-specific surveys. KF8.D45

Lawyer's monthly catalog. no. 1 (1989)– . Ann Arbor, Mich. : Ward and Associates, Jan./Feb. 1990– . Bimonthly. ISSN 1044-7660. $205.00. **CK27**

Continues in part *National legal bibliography* (*Guide* CK33), which ceased 1988(?).

Lists federal and state government publications of interest to the legal profession. Arranged by jurisdiction, then by subject. Corporate name and detailed subject indexes. Produced from the publisher's machine-readable database, *National legal bibliography.*

Reynolds, Thomas H. Foreign law : current sources of codes and basic legislation in jurisdictions of the world / Thomas H. Reynolds, Arturo A. Flores. Littleton, Colo. : F. Rothman, 1989–1990. v. 1–2 (looseleaf). (In progress). **CK28**

Contents: v. 1, The Western hemisphere; v. 2, Western and Eastern Europe and the European Communities. Vol. 3, Africa, Asia, and Australia (to be publ. 1991).

Provides comprehensive information on official and unofficial sources for the texts of foreign laws, including citations to legislation and the existence of English translations. Arranged alphabetically by geographic jurisdiction. To be updated annually. K38.R49

United States

Martin, Fenton S. The U.S. Supreme Court : a bibliography / Fenton S. Martin, Robert U. Goehlert. Wash. : Congressional Quarterly, c1990. 594 p. ISBN 0-87187-554-3. $175.00. **CK29**

An unannotated bibliography of books, articles, dissertations, essays, and research reports in two major sections: (1) activities of the Supreme Court, arranged in 14 topical areas; (2) materials on individual justices, arranged alphabetically by name. Excludes government publications. Citations are drawn from a number of fields in the social sciences and humanities. An excellent introduction surveys selected research sources. Author and subject indexes. KF8741.A1M37

Individual states

Doyle, Francis R. Searching the law, the states : a selective bibliography of state practice materials in the 50 states. Dobbs Ferry, N.Y. : Transnational, c1989. 525 p. ISBN 0-941320-47-2. $65.00. **CK30**

A bibliography of books used in the practice of law in each of the 50 states, arranged by state, then alphabetically by subject. Introductory matter includes a subject heading list. KF1.D69

Nyberg, Cheryl. Subject compilations of state laws, 1985–1988 : an annotated bibliography. Urbana, Ill. : C. Boast and C. Nyberg, 1989. 544 p. ISBN 0-9616293-1-2. **CK31**

For earlier compilations covering 1960–79 and 1979–83, see *Guide* CK55–56.

Continues the scope and arrangement of the earlier compilations. KF1.N94

Australia

Legal research : materials and methods / by Enid Campbell ... [et al.]. 3rd ed. North Ryde, N.S.W. : Law Book Co., 1988. 326 p. ISBN 0-455-20802-6. ISBN 0-455-20803-4 (pbk.). **CK32**

1st ed., 1967; 2nd ed., 1979.

A general guide to legal research and legal and nonlegal materials relevant to the law in Australia. Includes a useful chapter on Australian legal citation form. KTA.L44

Canada

Canadian guide to uniform legal citation. 2nd ed. Toronto : Carswell, 1988. 162, 172 p. ISBN 0-459-32401-2. $29.95. ISBN 0-459-32391-1 (pbk.). **CK33**

Title on added t.p.: Manuel canadien de la référence juridique.

Text in English and French.

Intends "to provide a comprehensive system of reference for the citation of legal materials in general use in the Canadian legal community."—*Introd.* Provides rules and examples for citing legal sources in both French and English. Arranged by form of publication (e.g., legislation, cases, secondary materials). Includes chapters on British, French, and international materials. Appendixes list courts, administrative tribunals, periodicals. Subject index. KE259C35

The Canadian law list. 1883– . Agincourt, Ont. : Canada Law Book [etc.]. Annual. ISSN 0084-8573. **CK34**

A comprehensive directory, arranged geographically, of barristers and solicitors, federal and provincial judicial and government personnel, bar associations, and educational associations. Has sections for law departments in corporations, foreign firms, and patent specialists. Index of individuals.

Tang, Chin-Shih. Guide to legal citation and sources of citation aid : a Canadian perspective. 2nd ed. Don Mills, Ont. : De Boo, c1988. 369 p. ISBN 0-88820-297-0. $25.00. **CK35**

Provides rules and examples for citing Canadian, British, and American legal sources. Arranged by form (e.g., cases, legislation, secondary sources). Appendixes include an alphabetical list of common abbreviations of law reports and a list of courts by country. Topical index. KE259T36

Yogis, John. Legal writing and research manual / John A. Yogis and Innis M. Christie. 3rd ed. / by Michael J. Iosipescu. Toronto ; Boston : Butterworths, c1988. 199 p. ISBN 0-409-81154-8. **CK36**

An excellent guide to Canadian legal research sources. Arranged by type of material, then by geographic jurisdiction. Discusses U.K. legal sources. Subject index; useful appendixes (e.g., suggested citation formats, subject reporters, abbreviations). KE250.Y64

China

Johnson, Constance A. Chinese law : a bibliography of selected English-language materials. Wash. : Far Eastern Law Division, Law Library of Congress, 1990. 138 p.   **CK37**

Intended as a continuation of Jeannette L. Pinard's *The People's Republic of China : a bibliography of selected English-language legal materials*, 1985 ed. (*Guide* CK64).

A selective bibliography, arranged by 46 subject categories, of legal materials in English on laws of the PRC, mid-1985–mid-1989. Includes journal articles and monographs, but generally excludes newspaper articles.

Kenworthy, James L. A guide to the laws, regulations, and policies of the People's Republic of China on foreign trade and investment. Buffalo, N.Y. : W.S. Hein, 1989. 189 p. ISBN 0-89941-701-9.   **CK38**

A selective bibliography intended as a guide to locating the texts of Chinese laws and regulations. Consists of: (1) a citation guide to sources where the texts of laws are published; (2) a topical listing of Chinese laws and regulations that gives title, date of promulgation, and citations to translations; (3) a selective bibliography of compilations, books, and journal articles, the latter arranged by topic.   KQK.C5K37

Germany

Kearley, Timothy. Charles Szladits' guide to foreign legal materials : German / by Timothy Kearley, Wolfram Fischer. 2nd rev. ed. Dobbs Ferry, N.Y. : Oceana, 1990. 318 p. ISBN 0-379-11755-X.   **CK39**

For similar compilations covering other countries of Western Europe, see *Guide* CK68–69, CK84.

Rev. ed. of pt. 2 of Szladits' *Guide to foreign legal materials : French, German, Swiss* (*Guide* CK69).

A comprehensive guide for English-speaking researchers to the legal literature of West Germany. Includes a general introduction to the German legal system and full bibliographic citations to primary and secondary materials in the major branches of German law. Emphasizes traditional scholarly works rather than those aimed at practitioners or students. Includes works published through the end of 1987. Although legal materials from the German Democratic Republic (East Germany) are excluded, an introduction discusses the legal implications of reunification. Extensive author-title and subject indexes; appendixes of legal abbreviations, publishers' addresses, and an especially helpful list of English-language titles.   KK76.K42

Great Britain

Hines, W. D. English legal history : a bibliography and guide to the literature / W.D. Hines ; with contributions by R.W. Ireland, P.J. Rawlings, C.P. Rodgers. N.Y. : Garland, 1990. 201 p. (Garland reference library of the humanities, vol. 1011). ISBN 0-8240-4299-9.   **CK40**

For annotation, see *Supplement* DC102.   KD532.A1H56

Selden Society. A centenary guide to the publications of the Selden Society. London : The Society, 1987. 242 p., 7 leaves of plates : ports.   **CK41**

Provides detailed summaries of publications of the Society. In three parts, the first two comprising the Introduction (The Society's first hundred years, 1887–1987, and Survey of the Society's projects and publications). The third part consists of a survey of the range and scope of publications of the Society, including its *Supplementary series, Occasional publications*, published lectures, and pamphlets. Name and subject indexes.   KD456.S4A162

Jewish

Rakover, Nahum. The multi-language bibliography of Jewish law. Jerusalem : Jewish Legal Heritage Society, [1990]. 871, 39 p.   **CK42**

Title on added t.p.: *Bibliyografyah rav-leshonit la-mishpaṭ ha-'Ivri*.

Cites books, monographs, journals, festschriften, encyclopedias, and dissertations in languages other than Hebrew. Arranged by broad topic, then alphabetical by author. Indexes in Hebrew and English to subjects, authors, place names, and rabbinical scholars.   Z6374.L4R35

Weisbard, Phyllis Holman. Jewish law : bibliography of sources and scholarship in English / comp. by Phyllis Holman Weisbard, David Schonberg. Littleton, Colo. : F.B. Rothman, 1989. 558 p. ISBN 0-8377-1350-1.   **CK43**

A comprehensive topical bibliography of materials in English on Jewish law. Author and subject indexes.   Z6374.L4W45

Korea, North

Cho, Sung Yoon. Law and legal literature of North Korea : a guide. Wash. : Library of Congress : For sale by the Supt. of Docs., U.S. Govt. Print. Off., 1988. 256 p. ISBN 0-8444-0584-1.   **CK44**

Contians 1,015 entries, arranged under 16 broad topics, for books, articles, book reviews, and chapters or parts of books, most published 1945–83 (with some items as late as 1986), in Korean, Japanese, and English. Index of names.   KQS.L27C46

Luxembourg

Krieger, Georges. Bibliographie juridique luxembourgeoise / Georges Krieger, Dean Spielmann, Cl. Graas-Lorang. Bruxelles : Editions Nemesis, 1989. 266 p.   **CK45**

An unannotated bibliography of monographs and articles arranged by topic, then alphabetical by author. Entries are preceded by introductory essays on legal history and specific areas of the law. Author and subject indexes.

Nepal

Shiwakoti, Shesh Raj. Law bibliography. Kathmandu : S.R. Shiwakoti, 1985. 56 p. (Nepal-bibliography series, no. 1).   **CK46**

Consists of citations to monographs, periodicals, and unpublished materials on the law and legal system of Nepal. Topical arrangement; brief annotations.   KPK.A1S54

Nigeria

Nigerian legal periodicals : a subject index, 1946–1988 / comp. by the Library Staff, Nigerian Institute of Advanced Legal Studies. Lagos : The Institute, 1989. 109 p. (NIALS law series, no. 4.). ISBN 978-2353-16-7 (pbk.).   **CK47**

Topical arrangement. Author index.

Papua New Guinea

Creech, Heather. A guide to legal research in Papua New Guinea / by Heather Creech. Sydney : Law Book Co., 1990. 226 p. : ill. ISBN 0-455-20922-7.   **CK48**

A guide to finding and using legal materials relating to Papua New Guinea. Arranged by type of material. Each section concludes with a chart summarizing the points covered by the section. Appendixes include a table of treaties, a checklist of laws, suggested titles for a basic law collection, and a legal directory.

Union of Soviet Socialist Republics

Butler, William Elliott. Soviet law. 2nd ed. Stoneham, Mass. : Butterworths Legal Publishers, 1988. 430 p. ISBN 0-88063-255-0.   **CK49**

Contains chapters on the history and sources of current Soviet law and discusses basic principles governing specific areas of law (e.g., taxation, criminal law, family law, collective farm law). Includes a discussion of the role of the Communist Party in the Soviet legal system. Topical index; list of additional readings. English translations of most of the documents cited may be found in: KM.B88 S69

Basic documents on the Soviet legal system / comp., translated, and ed. by W.E. Butler. 2nd ed. N.Y. : Oceana, 1990. 1 v. ISBN 0-379-20978-0. $75.00. ISBN 0-379-20979-9 (pbk.). $35.00.   **CK50**

A documentary supplement to the author's *Soviet law* (above). Contains English translations of selected Soviet legislation concerning state structure, the legal system, the economic system, and foreign relations. Table of contents, but no topical index.   KM.B38

Kavass, Igor I. Soviet law in English : research guide and bibliography, 1970–1987. Buffalo, N.Y. : W.S. Hein, 1988. 653 p. ISBN 0-89941-631-4.   **CK51**

Cites 1,600 general works, monographs, and articles. Sections: (1) an extensive essay on researching Soviet law; (2) an unannotated topical bibliography preceded by a list of subject headings; and (3) an annotated bibliography of the sources indexed in the topical section, arranged alphabetically by author.   KM.K38

USSR legal materials / Vratislav Pechota, gen. ed. ; Peter J. Pettibone, ed. [Ardsley-on-Hudson, N.Y.] : Transnational Juris Publications ; [London] : Graham & Trotman/Martinus Nijhoff, 1990– .   **CK52**

Contains the text in English translation of Soviet laws of importance to the conduct of trade and investment. Official translations are used where available. Tables of contents, but no topical index.

Indexes

CIS federal register index. Bethesda, Md. : Congressional Information Service, c1984– . $595.00.   **CK53**

Frequency: weekly, with interim cumulations about every five weeks and semiannual cumulations.

An index to the *Federal register* (*Guide* CK212). In three parts: Subjects and names; Code of Federal Regulations section numbers; Agency docket numbers.   KF70.A2

Index to legal books. N.Y. : Bowker, c1988– . 6 v. (looseleaf). ISBN 0-8352-2652-2.   **CK54**

Merges the indexes of more than 800 recent treatises covering all aspects of U.S. and international law. More than 1 million entries with cross-references, arranged by 58 subject categories.   KF1.I54

●**Index to legal periodicals** [computer file]. Bronx, N.Y. : H.W. Wilson, c1981– .   **CK55**

Machine-readable version of *Index to legal periodicals* (*Guide* CK170).

File size: about 130,000 records. Available online (WILSONLINE, LEXIS, WESTLAW, updated twice weekly), in CD-ROM (Wilson, Faxon, updated quarterly), and on magnetic tape (Wilson).

An index to more than 500 legal publications, including major law reviews, bar and specialty journals, yearbooks, institutes, and government publications.

Index to periodical articles related to law : thirty year cumulation, v. 1–30 (1958–1988) / editors, Roy M. Mersky, J. Myron Jacobstein ; compilers, Gary R. Hartman, Daniel W. Martin. Dobbs Ferry, N.Y. : Glanville, 1989. 4 v.   **CK56**

For basic index and 10-year cumulation, see *Guide* CK171.

Cumulates the entries from v. 1–30 (1958–88) in 4 v.: v. 1–2, Subject index; v. 3–4, Author index.   KF8.I57

Legal journals index. v. 1 (1986)– . Hebden Bridge, West Yorkshire : Legal Information Resources Ltd., 1986– . Monthly, with quarterly and annual cumulations. ISSN 0950-4206.   **CK57**

An index by subject, author, case, legislation, and book reviews to 165 law and law-related journals published in the U.K.   K33.L45

●**Legal resource index** [computer file]. Foster City, Calif. : Information Access Co., 1980– .   **CK58**

Machine-readable version of *Current law index* (*Guide* CK164).

File size: about 400,000 records. Updated monthly. Available online (BRS, DIALOG, LEXIS, WESTLAW) and in CD-ROM as *Legal Trac* (Producer).

An index to more than 800 U.S. legal publications, including major law reviews, bar and specialty journals, and legal newspapers, and to selected legal publications from other English-speaking countries.

Encyclopedias

Encyclopedia of the American judicial system : studies of the principal institutions and processes of law / Robert J. Janosik, ed. N.Y. : Scribner, c1987. 3 v. (1420 p.). ISBN 0-684-17807-9. $225.00.   **CK59**

" . . . accessible to a wide audience . . . layperson, university student, and academic researcher not trained in the ways of the law library."—*Pref.* Contains 88 signed articles in six categories: Legal history, Substantive law, Institutions and personnel, Process and behavior, Constitutional law and issues, Methodology. Articles end with citations to relevant cases and select bibliographies. Alphabetical list of articles; subject index.   KF154.E53

The guide to American law : everyone's legal encyclopedia. St. Paul [Minn.] : West Pub. Co., c1983–c1985. v. 9–12 : ill. (some col.), ports. ISBN 0-314-73224-1. $990.00.   **CK60**

For v.1–8, see *Guide* CK145.

Contents: v. 9–10, Remission–Zoning; v. 11, Appendix; v. 12, Index. Completes the set.

The index volume includes (1) a list of signed articles; (2) a list of cases cited; (3) a table of popular names for statutes; and

(4) a list of specific topics. Kept up to date by annual supplements. KF154.G85

Witt, Elder. Congressional Quarterly's guide to the U.S. Supreme Court. 2nd ed. Wash. : Congressional Quarterly Inc., c1990. 1060 p. : ill. ISBN 0-87187-502-0. $149.00. **CK61**
1st ed., 1979 (*Guide* CK141).
Revised and expanded, retaining the organization of the 1st ed. Covers developments in constitutional history and law, 1979–90. Subject and case indexes are more detailed. A section of "Documents and texts" and an appendix reprint such texts as the Judiciary Act of 1789 and contain a glossary and a list of acts of Congress held unconstitutional by the Court.
KF8742.W567

Dictionaries

Bieber, Doris M. Bieber's dictionary of legal abbreviations : reference guide for attorneys, legal secretaries, paralegals, and law students. 3rd ed. / by Mary Miles Prince. Buffalo, N.Y. : W.S. Hein Co., 1988. 584 p. ISBN 0-89941-630-6. **CK62**
Rev. ed. of: *Dictionary of legal abbreviations used in American law books*, 2nd ed., 1985.
The most concise and complete reference work for legal abbreviations, containing more than 20,000 domestic and international abbreviations, acronyms and symbols found in historic and contemporary legal literature. KF246.B46

Garner, Bryan A. A dictionary of modern legal usage. N.Y. : Oxford Univ. Pr., 1987. 587 p. ISBN 0-19-504377-4. $35.00. **CK63**
Intends to "allow readers to resolve at a glance the myriad questions of grammar and style that arise in legal writing."—*Introd.* Besides brief definitions, includes articles on usage, word formation, and spelling, and a classified list of articles.
KF156.G367

Leonard, Robin. Family law dictionary : marriage, divorce, children & living together / by Robin D. Leonard and Stephen R. Elias. 2nd national ed. Berkeley, Calif. : Nolo Pr., 1990. 224 p. ISBN 0-87337-129-1. $13.95. **CK64**
1st ed., 1988.
Intended for general readers. Provides definitions for more than 500 terms and phrases. KF503.6.L46

Sloane, Richard. The Sloane-Dorland annotated medical-legal dictionary. St. Paul, Minn. : West Pub. Co., c1987. 787 p. : ill. ISBN 0-314-93512-6. **CK65**
For annotation, see *Supplement* EK87. RA1017.S56

Words and phrases legally defined. 3rd ed. London : Butterworths, 1988–1990. 4 v. ISBN 0-406-08040-2 (set). **CK66**
2nd ed., Toronto : R. De Boo, c1963–65.
Includes judicial, statutory, and textbook definitions, emphasizing British sources but including Australian, Canadian, New Zealand, and in this edition, American references. Updated by annual cumulative supplements. KD313.W67

Foreign terms

Dutch

Sinke, Marjorie J. Legal language : US-Dutch legal concepts on business and tax law : a glossary. Deventer, The Netherlands ; Boston : Kluwer Law and Taxation Publishers, c1990. 212 p. ISBN 90-6544-450-5. **CK67**
Arranged by topic, then by Dutch word or phrase, with English equivalents. K52.D8S57

Polyglot

Moreno, Federico B. Philippine law dictionary : words and phrases in Philippine law : legally and judicially defined and accepted. 3rd ed. Manila : Vera-Reyes : Distr. by Jacobo & Sons, 1988. 1020 p. ISBN 971-15-1014-6.
CK68
A comprehensive dictionary of words and phrases in four languages: English, Spanish, Philipino, and Latin. Includes words and phrases that have been legally and judicially defined and form a part of Philippine law and jurisprudence.
KPM.A1M84

Spanish

Torres, Arturo L. Latin American legal abbreviations : a comprehensive Spanish/Portuguese dictionary with English translations / comp. by Arturo L. Torres and Francisco Avalos. N.Y. : Greenwood, 1989. 604 p. ISBN 0-313-26200-4. **CK69**
Provides approximately 75,000 legal abbreviations from Spanish-speaking Latin America, Brazil, and Spain. Entries, alphabetical by abbreviation, give the full phrase in Spanish or Portuguese, the country of origin, and an English translation.
KG25.T67

Quotations

Gerhart, Eugene C. Quote it! Memorable legal quotations : data, epigrams, wit, and wisdom from legal and literary sources. N.Y. : C. Boardman Co., 1969. 766 p. ISBN 0-87632-001-9. **CK70**
Quotations, arranged by subject, from legal and literary sources on law and legal philosophy. Opens with an index of topics; author index and concordance. Author, source, and date given for quotations. K58.G46

———— Quote it II : a dictionary of memorable legal quotations : data, epigrams, wit and wisdom from legal and literary sources. Buffalo, N.Y. : W.S. Hein Co., 1988. 553 p. ISBN 0-89941-576-8. **CK71**
Continues *Quote it* (above). Subject headings from approximately 300 to more than 1,000. Headings are idiosyncratic; many entries are not strictly on legal topics. K58.G47

Shrager, David S. The quotable lawyer / David S. Shrager and Elizabeth Frost. N.Y. : Facts on File, c1986. 373 p. : ill. ISBN 0-8160-1184-2. $24.95. **CK72**
Provides 2,600 quotations from legal and nonlegal sources, arranged alphabetically by topic, then chronologically. Author, source and date are cited for each quotation. Author and sub-

ject indexes, the latter including cross-references to related topics. K58.S5

Directories

Canada legal directory. 1911– . Toronto : J.H. Wharton, 1911– . Annual. ISSN 0315-8322. **CK73**

Editor: 1911–58, R.A. Wharton; 1959– , J.H. Wharton.

An alphabetical listing of law firms by city. For each province, gives a comprehensive list of courts, officials, judicial districts, and law societies. Separate lists of individual lawyers and corporation counsel. KA82

Directory of law libraries in the British Isles. 3rd ed., ed. by Christine Miskin. Hebden Bridge : Publ. for the British and Irish Association of Law Librarians by Legal Information Resources, 1988. 121 p. ISBN 1-87036-902-5 (pbk.). **CK74**

Covers England, Scotland, Northern Ireland, the Republic of Ireland, the Channel Islands, and the Isle of Man, with entries arranged alphabetically by town in each region. Indexes by name of institution, contact person, type of organization, and special collections. Z675.L2

Directory of state court clerks & county courthouses. 1990 ed.– . Wash. : WANT Pub. Co., c1989– . Annual. ISSN 1042-4172. $59.00. **CK75**

A state-by-state list of clerks of appellate, trial, and county courts. Includes lists of state attorneys general and their staffs. A separate section includes Canadian federal court, provincial court, and enforcement officials.

Guide to foreign law firms / [prepared by the American Bar Association, Section of International Law and Practice ; ed. by Howard B. Hill and James R. Silkenat]. Chicago : The Association, c1988. 209 p. ISBN 0-89707-390-8. **CK76**

Arranged geographically by region, then by country. Entries are brief, giving firm name, address, telephone, and partners. Excludes foreign offices of U.S. firms. K68.G85

Judicial staff directory. 1986– . Mt. Vernon, Va. : Congressional Staff Directory, Ltd., 1986– . Annual. $45.00. **CK77**

Editors: 1986– C. B. Brownson and Anna L. Brownson.

Lists more than 10,000 individuals in the federal justice system: judges and staff of the Supreme Court and of circuit, district, and bankruptcy courts; and U.S. attorneys and marshals in the Department of Justice. Includes biographies, maps of court jurisdictions, an index of names, and an index of judges by year of appointment and by appointing President.

KF8700.A19J83

King, Kamla J. BNA's directory of state courts, judges, and clerks : a state-by-state listing / comp. by Kamla J. King and Judith Springberg with the BNA Library staff. 3rd ed. Wash. : BNA Books, 1990. 445 p. ISBN 0-87179-670-8. **CK78**

A directory of appellate courts of general jurisdiction in the 50 states plus the District of Columbia, American Samoa, Guam, Puerto Rico, and the Virgin Islands.

The directory for each state is preceded by an organization chart. Finding aids include indexes of personal names and geographic jurisdictions and a list of state-level administrators.

KF8700.A19K56

●**The Martindale-Hubbell law directory on CD-ROM** [computer file]. N.Y. : Bowker Electronic Pub., 1990– . **CK79**

Machine-readable version of *Martindale-Hubbell law directory* (below).

File size: about 750,000 records. Updated annually. Available in CD-ROM (producer).

Lists more than 750,000 lawyers, law firms, corporate legal departments, banks, and special services in the U.S., Canada and overseas. Search fields include state, city, county, name of attorney or firm, law school, fields of law, etc.

The Martindale-Hubbell law directory. 63rd year (1931)– . Summit, N.J. : Martindale-Hubbell Law Directory, Inc., 1931– . Annual. ISSN 0191-0221. $255.00. **CK80**

For previous volumes, see *Guide* CK187.

With the 123rd year, expanded from 8 v. to 16 v. annually. Vol. 1–13 cover the U.S. and Canada, organized by city and state (for Canada, by province), subdivided into sections for practice profiles and professional biographies. Vol. 14, published separately as *Martindale-Hubbell international law directory. Canadian & international lawyers*, continues the annual numbering of the earlier set. Vols. 15–16, expanded from v. 8 of the earlier set, are published separately as *Martindale-Hubbell law digest*, contain summaries of laws of the 50 states of the U.S., the District of Columbia, Puerto Rico, the Virgin Islands, ten provinces of Canada, and 58 foreign countries, and continue the annual numbering of the earlier set. Still contains no single alphabetical list of lawyers, but one is promised for the 124th annual issue. KF190.H813

National directory of black law firms. 1988 inaugural ed.– . Philadelphia : M.L. Williams Pub. Co., [c1988]– . Annual. ISSN 0896-8780. $39.95. **CK81**

In three sections—Minority law firms, Sole practitioners, and Employed attorneys—each arranged alphabetically. Indexes: geographical and areas of practice.

Want's Federal-state court directory. 1984 ed.– . Wash. : WANT Pub. Co., c1984– . Annual. ISSN 0742-1095. $12.95. **CK82**

Provides address and telephone for federal judges and clerks, U.S. attorneys, U.S. magistrates, probation officers, and federal administrative law judges. For all 50 states, gives the same information for judges of state supreme courts and their clerks, attorneys general, and secretaries of state. Also has a directory for major Canadian courts. Includes state court organization charts, a guide to the federal court system, and a glossary. KF8700.A19F42

Worldwide government directory, with international organizations. 1987–88– . Bethesda, Md. : National Standards Association, c1987– . Annual. ISSN 0894-1521. $325.00 . $275.00 (pbk.). **CK83**

For annotation, see *Supplement* CJ32. For each country, identifies the country's highest court and lists its chief officers.

JF37.L345

Handbooks

Codes of professional responsibility / ed. by Rena A. Gorlin. 2nd ed. Wash. : Bureau of National Affairs, c1990. 555 p. ISBN 0-87179-641-4. $55.00. **CK84**

For annotation, see *Supplement* CH335 BJ1725.C57

Crawford, Tad. Legal guide for the visual artist. Rev. ed. N.Y. : Allworth Pr. ; Cincinnati : distr. by North Light Books, 1990. 213 p. : ill. ISBN 0-927629-00-3. $18.95. **CK85**

For annotation, see *Supplement* BE107. KF390.A7C73

Feldman, Franklin. Art law : rights and liabilities of creators and collectors / Franklin Feldman, Stephen E. Weil ; with the collaboration of Susan Duke Biederman.

Boston : Little, Brown, c1986. 2 v. ISBN 0-316-09296-7 (v. 1). ISBN 0-316-09297-5 (v. 2). **CK86**
For annotation, see *Supplement* BE108.   KF390.A7F45

The legal researcher's desk reference 1990 / comp. and ed. by Arlene L. Eis. Teaneck, N.J. : Infosources Publishing, 1990. 325 p. ISBN 0-939486-18-0.   **CK87**
Title varies: 1982–84, called *The law librarian's professional desk reference and diary*; 1986–89?, called *Lawyer's diary and desk reference*.
A directory of federal and state agencies, bar and law-related associations, selected international organizations, law schools in the U.S. and Canada, and library suppliers. Includes tables, charts, maps.   KF240.E52

Lerner, Ralph E. Art law : the guide for collectors, investors, dealers, and artists / Ralph E. Lerner, Judith Bresler. N.Y. : Practising Law Institute, 1989. 766 p. : ill., forms. ISBN 0-87224-000-2.   **CK88**
For annotation, see *Supplement* BE109.   KF390.A7L473

Prince, Mary Miles. Bieber's dictionary of legal citations : reference guide for attorneys, legal secretaries, paralegals, and law students. 3rd ed. Buffalo, N.Y. : W.S. Hein, 1988. 316 p. ISBN 0-89941-664-0.   **CK89**
2nd ed., 1986, had title: *Bieber's current American legal citations*.
Intended to assist readers in properly citing American legal authorities; a companion to *A uniform system of citation* (the "Bluebook"; Cambridge, Mass. : Harvard Law Review Association, 1986). Provides examples of citation forms for statutes, case reports, law reviews, looseleaf services, treatises, etc.   KF246.B45

A reference guide to the United States Supreme Court / advisors, Richard S. Kay, Robert C. Khayat, James W. Zirkle ; gen. ed., Stephen P. Elliott. N.Y. : Facts on File, c1986. 476 p. : ill., ports. ISBN 0-8160-1018-8. $50.00.   **CK90**
Contains commentary on major issues considered by the Court, summaries of landmark cases, and biographies of the justices. Appendixes include tabular data on the justices and their decisions. Bibliography; topical index.   KF8742.R45

West's legal desk reference / William P. Statsky . . . [et al.]. St. Paul : West Pub. Co., [1991]. 1514 p. : ill., map. ISBN 0-314-48146-X. ISBN 0-314-79997-4 (pbk.).   **CK91**
A handbook of useful legal information that includes (1) a legal dictionary and usage guide; (2) bibliographies of legal specialties (topics, foreign countries, states); (3) information on state court systems; (4) citations to selected U.S. statutes and U.S. Supreme Court cases; (5) biographies of U.S. Supreme Court justices; (6) the "biography" of a litigation (documents, strategies, skills); (7) the text of the U.S. Constitution; (8) tables, charts, and directories. Index.   KF387.W49

Biography

Martindale-Hubbell bar register of preeminent lawyers in the United States, Canada, and other countries. 1990– . Summit, N.J. : Martindale-Hubbell, c1990– . Annual. ISSN 1051-5518.   **CK92**
A collective biography of some 7,000 eminent members of the bar in the U.S., Canada, and abroad. Arranged geographically and by specialty.   KF190.B37

STATUTES

United States

Hui, Y. H. United States food laws, regulations, and standards. 2nd ed. N.Y. : Wiley, c1986. 2 v. : ill. ISBN 0-471-84846-8 (set). $150.00 (est.).   **CK93**
For annotation, see *Supplement* EH31.   KF3875.H8

Indexes

Code of federal regulations index. 1988– . N.Y. : Bowker, c1988– . Annual.   **CK94**
An index to the *Code* (*Guide* CK210) that is more timely and thorough than the index published with the *Code* itself. Indexes of titles, topics, and keywords; includes statutory authority tables.   KF70.A34C6

Texts

Smith, Robert Ellis. Compilation of state and federal privacy laws. 1988 ed. Wash. : Privacy Journal, c1988. 105 p.   **CK95**
Contains 1989 suppl. bound in at the back of the book.
Cites and describes more than 650 state and federal laws affecting confidentiality of personal information. Arranged by topic (e.g., criminal records, credit reporting, school records), subarranged by state.   KF1262.A3

CRIMINOLOGY

Guides

Lutzker, Marilyn. Criminal justice research in libraries : strategies and resources / Marilyn Lutzker and Eleanor Ferrall. N.Y. : Greenwood, 1986. 167 p. ISBN 0-313-24490-1.   **CK96**
Useful for both experienced and novice researchers. Includes a discussion of the organization of information in criminal justice, research design and control, and bibliographic searching, including computer database searching. Presents suggested research sources, special areas of research, and lists of useful subject headings and directories.   Z5703.4.C73L87

Bibliography

Berens, John F. Criminal justice documents : a selective, annotated bibliography of U.S. government publications since 1975. N.Y. : Greenwood, 1987. 236 p. (Bibliographies and indexes in law and political science, no. 7). ISBN 0-313-25183-5.   **CK97**
Contains 1,094 entries arranged by broad topical categories. Author, subject, geographic, and association/organization indexes.   Z5703.4.C73B47

Radelet, Michael L. Capital punishment in America : an annotated bibliography / Michael L. Radelet, Margaret

Vandiver. N.Y. : Garland, 1988. 243 p. ISBN 0-8240-1623-8. **CK98**

Lists books, articles, congressional publications, and U.S. Supreme Court cases, most published since 1972. Arranged by form of publication, then alphabetically by author. Topical index. Z5703.4.C36R3

Current

Document retrieval index : DRI / U.S. Department of Justice, National Institute of Justice [microform]. 1972–1978– . Wash. : U.S. Dept. of Justice, Law Enforcement Assistance Administration, National Institute of Law Enforcement and Criminal Justice, [1979]– . **CK99**

An index to national and international documents on all aspects of criminal justice. Author, title, and subject indexes; thesaurus of subject terms. Z7164.P76D63

Encyclopedias

The encyclopedia of police science / ed., William G. Bailey. N.Y. : Garland, 1989. [734 p.]. ISBN 0-8240-6627-8. **CK100**

Contains 143 signed articles, alphabetically arranged and ranging in length from two to seven pages. Most have individual bibliographies. Appendixes include a bibliography of police history and a bibliography of bibliographies. General index and index of legal cases. HV7901.E53

Encyclopedia of world crime : criminal justice, criminology, and law enforcement dictionary / [ed. in chief] Jay Robert Nash. Wilmette, Ill. : CrimeBooks, 1989– . 6 v. ISBN 0-923582-00-2 (set). **CK101**

Contents: v. 1–4, A–Z and suppl.; v. 5, Dictionary; v. 6, Index.

Consists of more than 50,000 unsigned articles with bibliographies on all aspects of crime and law enforcement in all countries. The dictionary volume contains 20,000 terms. Indexed by names and subjects. A general bibliography of 25,000 entries is cross-referenced to articles in v.1–4. HV6017.E54

Fay, John. The police dictionary and encyclopedia. Springfield, Ill. : C.C. Thomas, c1988. 370 p. ISBN 0-398-05494-0. **CK102**

Gives concise definitions for a wide range of terms used in law enforcement. Appendixes include felony definitions and sentence limits by state, capital offenses and method of execution by state, social security number index, and a bibliography. HV7901.F39

Handbook on crime and delinquency prevention / ed. by Elmer H. Johnson. N.Y. : Greenwood, 1987. 402 p. ISBN 0-313-24023-X. **CK103**

Written for the theorist and practitioner. Consists of 14 lengthy, signed essays, each with footnotes and an annotated bibliography. Also includes a 10-page annotated supplementary bibliography, an 18-page list of national, state, and local organizations, biographical notes on contributors, and an index. HV7431.H373

Kurian, George Thomas. World encyclopedia of police forces and penal systems. N.Y. : Facts on File, c1989. 582 p. : ill. ISBN 0-8160-1019-6. **CK104**

Describes the national law enforcement and penal systems of 183 countries of the world. Entries are two to three pages long and are arranged by country. Concludes with information on Interpol, a world police directory, a bibliography, and an index. HV7901.K87

Directories

A world directory of criminological institutes / comp. and ed. by Carla Masotti Santoro. 5th ed. Rome, Italy : United Nations Interregional Crime and Justice Research Institute, 1990. 661 p. ISBN 92-9078-009-6. **CK105**

Lists 400 criminological organizations in 72 countries, giving for each: name, address, history, method of governance, types of activities, staff, finances, and publications. HV6024.5.W67

INTERNATIONAL LAW

Guides

Guide to international legal research / the George Washington journal of international law and economics. Stoneham, Mass. : Butterworth Legal Publishers, 1990. 400 p. **CK106**

1981 ed. (*Guide* CK282) had title: *Research tips in international law.*

Originally publ. in *The George Washington journal of international law and economics,* 20, no. 1–2 (1986).

A guide to basic sources for international law. Includes a bibliography arranged by source, with sections on: Primary sources (codified law and case law), Secondary sources (serial and analytical tools), and Research tools (practice, research, and reference sources). JX1297.G84

Digests and collections

Berger, Vincent. Case law of the European Court of Human Rights. Sarasota, Fla. : UNIFO, c1989. [340 p.]. ISBN 0-89111-026-7. **CK107**

Excellent synopses of 117 cases decided by the Court. A foreword discusses the nature and force of Court decisions. Bibliographies. KJC5132.A52B47

From Helsinki to Vienna : basic documents of the Helsinki process / ed. by Arie Bloed. Dordrecht ; Boston : M. Nijhoff in co-operation with the Europa Institute, Utrecht ; Norwell, Mass. : distr. by Kluwer Academic Publishers, c1990. 285 p. ISBN 0-7923-0851-4. **CK108**

Contains the text of all substantive documents signed or adopted by meetings of the Conference on Security and Cooperation in Europe, including the Bonn Conference of 1990. The documents, arranged chronologically, are preceded by a survey of the basic features of the CSCE and of developments at follow-up meetings since the Helsinki Accords of 1975. Select bibliography; subject index. JX1393.C65F544

The Seven-power summit : documents from the summits of industrialized countries, 1975–1989 / comp. and ed. by Peter I. Hajnal. Millwood, N.Y. : Kraus Internat., c1989. 491 p. : ill. ISBN 0-527-37319-2. **CK109**

A sourcebook containing political and economic declarations, formal communiques, chairman's summaries, and press releases. Subject index, list of acronyms, and bibliography. A *Supplement—documents from the 1990 summit,* covering the Houston summit, was published in 1991. HF1352.S48

Encyclopedias

Encyclopedia of human rights / [comp. by] Edward Lawson. N.Y.: Taylor & Francis, c1991. 1907 p. ISBN 0-8002-8003-2.   **CK110**

Provides an overview of human rights in 150 countries and includes the full texts of treaties, conventions and declarations, reports on concepts of human rights and fundamental freedoms, and lists information on intergovernmental and nongovernmental organizations. Includes a 100-page bibliography prepared by the Human Rights Internet Documentation Center. Entries include cross-references; subject index.   JC571.E67

TREATIES

Collections and indexes

Treaties and alliances of the world. 5th ed. / ed. by Nicholas Rengger. Burnt Mill, Harlow, Essex, England: Longman; Detroit: Distr. by Gale, 1990. 579 p.: ill., maps. ISBN 0-582-05733-7. £68.00. ISBN 0-8103-9914-8.   **CK111**

3rd ed., 1981 (*Guide* CK357).

This edition presents significant changes in organization and content. The body of the work continues to consist of concise summaries of the principal extant treaties and alliances. The order of sections has been rearranged, a division into parts established, and certain maps and charts deleted. Three analytical and interpretive chapters have been added: (1) the role and function of treaties in the contemporary international system; (2) a summary of principal events of the last five years, with a discussion of their international implications; (3) a discussion of "covert alliances"—i.e., tacit agreements on various aspects of international politics. The bibliography has been considerably expanded. Index of subjects, agreements, organizations, and abbreviations.   JX4165

Union of Soviet Socialist Republics

A calendar of Soviet treaties, 1974–1980 / [ed. by] George Ginsburgs. Dordrecht; Boston: M. Nijhoff Publ.; Hingham, Mass.: Distr. [by] Kluwer Academic Publishers, 1987. 666 p. (Law in Eastern Europe, no. 33). ISBN 90-247-3628-5.   **CK112**

For compilations covering 1917–57 and 1958–73, see *Guide* CK387–388.

This volume covers agreements to which the U.S.S.R was a party, 1974–80.   KJC510.A15L39

CONSTITUTIONS

United States

Bibliography of original meaning of the United States Constitution / prepared by the faculty and students at the University of San Diego School of Law. [Wash.?]: U.S. Dept. of Justice, Office of Legal Policy, Federal Justice Research Program: [Supt. of Docs., U.S. Govt. Print. Off., distributor, 1988]. 287 p.   **CK113**

Superintendent of Documents classification: J 1.20/2:C 76/2.

Lists references to records of framing and ratification debates, related documents, works of contemporary and modern commentators, and U.S. Supreme Court cases. No annotations.   KF4546.A1B53

Chandler, Ralph C. The constitutional law dictionary: vol. 1, Individual rights, suppl. 1: Ralph C. Chandler, Richard A. Enslen, Peter G. Renstrom. Santa Barbara, Calif.: ABC-Clio, c1987. 138 p. (Clio dictionaries in political science, v. 8). ISBN 0-87436-484-1 (v. 1). $45.00.   **CK114**

For parent publication, see *Guide* CK401.

Suppl. 1 covers the 1983–84, 1984–85, and 1985–86 terms of the Supreme Court.   KF4548.5.C47

The dynamic Constitution: a historical bibliography / Suzanne Robitaille Ontiveros, ed. Santa Barbara, Calif.: ABC-Clio, c1986. 343 p. (ABC-Clio research guides, 19). ISBN 0-87436-470-1.   **CK115**

Consists of 1,370 citations to articles, books, and dissertations; article citations have annotations. Arranged chronologically, then by form of publication, then alphabetically by author. Subject and author indexes.   KF4541.D95

Encyclopedia of the American Constitution / Leonard W. Levy, ed. in chief. N.Y.: Macmillan, c1986. 4 v. ISBN 0-02-918610-2. $320.00.   **CK116**

"... organizes in readable form an epitome of all that is known and understood on the subject of the Constitution by the nation's specialist scholars."—*Introd.* More than 2,000 signed articles, arranged alphabetically and liberally cross-referenced, covering doctrinal concepts, individuals, judicial decisions, legislation, and historical periods. Articles vary in length; many include bibliographies. Appendixes of documents, chronologies, a glossary, and case name and topical indexes. An excellent source; for all libraries.   KF4548.E53

Hall, Kermit. A comprehensive bibliography of American constitutional and legal history: Supplement, 1980–1987. Millwood, N.Y.: Kraus Internat., c1991. 2 v. (956 p.). ISBN 0-527-37414-9.   **CK117**

For basic work covering 1986–1979, see *Guide* CK403.

Adds about 4,000 entries, continuing the topical arrangement of the main work. Cites numerous titles on the Bicentennial of the U.S. Constitution.   KF4541.H34

Reams, Bernard D. The Constitution of the United States: a guide and bibliography to current scholarly research / by Bernard D. Reams, Jr. and Stuart D. Yoak. Dobbs Ferry, N.Y.: Oceana, c1987. 545 p. ISBN 0-379-20888-1. $65.00.   **CK118**

An unannotated bibliography of essays, articles, books, and government publications arranged by branch of government and by constitutional amendment.   KF4546.A1R4

INTERNATIONAL ORGANIZATIONS

Directories

Fredland, Richard A. A guide to African international organisations. London; N.Y.: Zell, 1990. [432] p.: ill., maps. ISBN 0-905450-90-6. £35.00.   **CK119**

Provides information concerning nearly 500 international organizations that have appeared in the African continent during the 20th century. Eight sections, including background, analysis of international organizations, directory, biographical data and chronology, tables and appendixes, maps, bibliography. Subject index. JX1995.F67

European communities

Guides

Mathijsen, P. S. R. F. A guide to European Community law. 5th ed. London : Sweet & Maxwell, 1990. [330] p. ISBN 0-421-42810-4 (pbk.). £19.50. **CK120**

1st ed., 1972; 4th ed., 1985.

A general introduction to laws governing the European Community, with chapters on history, institutions, policies, and external relations. Each chapter cites source materials and has a bibliography. A detailed table of contents permits location of treaties, secondary legislation, and U.K. national legislation implementing European Community laws. Subject index.

Thomson, Ian. The documentation of the European communities : a guide. London ; N. Y. : Mansell, 1989. 382 p. ISBN 0-7201-2022-5. $63.00. **CK121**

Describes the current range of publications produced by organs of the European Community, including primary and secondary legislation and explanatory and background materials. In two parts: an introduction to the EC and its publications; individual chapters on organs of the EC (e.g., European Parliament, Council of Ministers, Court of Justice), providing for each a description of its structure and a list of pubications. Appendixes include lists of depository libraries, information offices, and online services, as well as a table of regularly published series with references to their discussion in the text. General subject index. Z7165.E8T47

Bibliography

●**CELEX** [computer file]. Brussels, Belgium : Commission of the European Communities. **CK122**

File size: 113,000 records in each of seven languages (Danish, Dutch, English, French, German, Greek, Italian). Updated weekly. Available online (Mead Data Central, producer) and in CD-ROM as *JUSTIS CD-ROM* (Context Ltd., Global Transactions).

A machine-readable version of *Official journal of the European Communities.* Full-text searchable, containing documents relating to European Community law, in three files: Legislative file (treaties, agreements and other legal acts, legislation); Case-law file (judgments delivered by the Court of Justice and opinions of the Advocates-General); Preparatory documents file (preparatory legislation). Also called *Communitatis Europae lex.*

Encyclopedias

Toth, A. G. The Oxford encyclopaedia of European Community law. Oxford : Clarendon Pr. ; N.Y. : Oxford Univ. Pr., 1990. v. 1. ISBN 0-19-825589-6 (set). $120.00. (In progress). **CK123**

Contents: v. 1, Institutional law. To be complete in 3 v.

An authoritative guide to the definition and interpretation of all aspects of European Community law. When complete, will treat institutional law, substantive law, and social policy, providing references to relevant cases, acts, and treaties. Vol. 1 deals with Community institutions, including courts, the Directorate General, the European Parliament, the Commission and Council, and committees. Entries, arranged alphabetically, each commonly consist of a brief statement of definition followed by a more detailed description, cross-references, and a brief bibli-

ography. A list of entries at the beginning of the volume serves as an index. Includes tables of cases, acts, treaties, international agreements, and U.K. statutes. KJE926.T67

Directories

Guide to European company information : EC countries. 4th ed. London : London Business School Information Service, 1990. 129 p. ISBN 0-9512201-1-X. £45.00. **CK124**

1st ed., 1988.

For each of the 12 European Community countries, lists and annotates information sources by format (directories, online databases, CD-ROMs and diskettes, newspapers and magazines, and other services). Preliminary sections list normal business hours, major industrial centers, language, currency, number of public and private companies, number and location of stock exchanges, legal types of companies, and filing requirements and public access to company records. Other sections include a listing of pan-European information sources, a directory and descriptions of company accounts/credit reporting agencies, a brief bibliography, and title and format indexes.

HD2844.5.G853

Handbooks

The Arthur Andersen European community sourcebook : the most comprehensive, authoritative reference guide ever assembled on the European market / Arthur Andersen & Co. ; Iain P.A. Stitt, consulting ed.; John J. McGonagle, Jr., ed. Chicago : Triumph Books, 1991. 499 p. ISBN 0-9624436-4-6. $95.00. **CK125**

Intended to serve as "a comprehensive guide to the Single Market Program and the vast array of information sources available."—*Introd.* In five parts: (1) The European Community and the single market of 1991, considers both the EC's history and key institutions, strategies, and legislation; (2) Profiles of the European Community member states, includes in addition to standard background information, data on establishing businesses and business taxation practices in each member country; (3) Sources on EC 1992 by topic (e.g., employment and labor, regulation of business and competition); (4) Sources on EC 1992 by industry, with information on 11 different industry sectors; and (5) Appendixes and indexes, with eight appendixes (e.g., bibliographies, lists of acronyms and abbreviations, contact directories), an index of associations and organizations, and a general subject index. HC241.2.A755

Rosenberg, Jerry Martin. The new Europe 1992 : an A to Z compendium on the European Community. Wash. : Bureau of National Affairs, 1991. 206 p. : ill. ISBN 0-87179-669-4. **CK126**

Defines or describes more than 2,500 terms, organizations, and publications pertaining to the European Community, with numerous cross-references. An introduction describes the EC's structure; also included are a chronology of events since the EC's creation in 1957 through October 1990, and an index of major subjects. HC241.2.R59

Setting up a company in the European Community : a country by country guide / comp. by Brebner and Co., International Division. Phoenix : Oryx, 1989. 251 p. ISBN 0-89774-601-5. **CK127**

For each of the 12 member countries of the European Community, lists and describes the requirements for establishing private and public companies, including: documents, registration requirements, capital requirements, ownership, management, formation expenses and taxation, and fundamental legislative texts. Not indexed.   KJE2448.S47

Yearbooks

1992 : the single market handbook. London : Euromonitor, 1990. 222 p. ISBN 0-86338-355-6. £95.00.   **CK128**

A handy compilation, dealing with Europe 1992, in 4 parts. Sect. 1, 1992 and beyond, is a series of essays on the impact of new legislation, covering such areas as trade controls, advertising, media, and foreign relations. Sect. 2 traces the history of the single market, the role and policy-making instruments of the Commission of European Communities, and reprints with explanations relevant extracts from legislation pertaining to 1992. Sect. 3 describes organizations, publications, and databases relating to doing business in the single market. Sect. 4, Statistical masterfile, is a collection of economic projections prepared by Euromonitor, the European Community, government agencies, trade associations, and other organizations. Appendixes list specific documents and other titles for further reading. Indexed.
HC241.2.A618

Panorama of EC industry. 1989– . Luxembourg : Office for Official Publications of the European Communities, 1988– . Annual. £14.70.   **CK129**

Describes the current situation for more than 125 European manufacturing and service industries. Major trends are identified, and production, foreign trade, and other statistics are presented. Most analyses include a forecast and outlook section. A macroeconomic outlook for Europe and an index are also included.   HC241.2.P313

United Nations system

Osmańszyk, Edmund Jan. The encyclopedia of the United Nations and international agreements. 2nd ed. London ; N.Y. : Taylor & Francis, 1990. 1 v. ISBN 0-85066-833-6. $340.00.   **CK130**

1st ed., 1985 (*Guide* CK482).

Revised and updated, retaining the arrangement of the previous edition. Indexes: (1) an analytical index with 13,000 entries; (2) an index of 3,000 agreements, conventions, and treaties.   JX1977.O8213

CL

Geography

GENERAL WORKS

Guides

Information sources in cartography / editors, C.R. Perkins, R.B. Parry. London ; N.Y. : Bowker-Saur, c1990. 540 p. : ill., maps. ISBN 0-408-02458-5. ISBN 0-87071-361-2 (pbk.).   **CL1**

International in scope; arranges current and retrospective sources in a "sensible logical sequence to reflect a contemporary overview of a range of cartographic concerns"—*Introd.* 30 chapters with references, in five parts: General; History of cartography; Map production; Map librarianship; Types of mapping, map use and promotion. Appendixes include lists of cartographic periodicals, geographical arrangement of cartographic societies, and map publishers. Detailed subject and name indexes; list of contributors.   Z6021.I53

Bibliography

A bibliography of geographic thought / comp. by Catherine L. Brown and James O. Wheeler. N.Y. : Greenwood, 1989. 520 p. (Bibliographies and indexes in geography, no. 1). ISBN 0-313-26899-1.   **CL2**

Rev. and expanded ed. of Wheeler's *Bibliography on geographic thought, 1950–1982* (Athens : Univ. of Georgia, Dept. of Geography, 1983).

A comprehensive bibliography of approximately 6,000 English-language journal articles and 600 books on the history, philosophy, and methodology of geography. Books are listed in the first chapter alphabetically by author; articles are divided into nine chapters by topic, then listed alphabetically by author. Separate author, subject, and biographical indexes, but the subject index covers only citations in the chapter Subdisciplines in geography.   Z6001.B5814

Encyclopedia of geographic information sources. U.S. volume / Jennifer Mossman, ed. 4th ed. Detroit : Gale, c1987. 437 p. ISBN 0-8103-0410-4. $100.00.   **CL3**

3rd ed., 1978 (*Guide* CL18).

Significantly changes focus from previous editions, which were international in scope; now comprehensively covers U.S. only. "Work [is] already in progress on an interedition supplement to the U.S. volume and a companion volume with international coverage."—*Introd.* Index of regions, states, and cities in one alphabet, with cities also listed under each state.
HF5343.E53

Lee, David R. Women and geography : a comprehensive bibliography. Boca Raton, Fla. : David Lee, Department of Geography, Florida Atlantic Univ., [1986?]. 1 v. (various pagings). **CL4**

Includes "works appearing in a known geography publication which make reference to women or gender issues" and "works dealing with women which are written by individuals identified as geographers... irrespective of where they appear."—*Introd.* Emphasizes English-language titles. Arranged alphabetically by author with personal name and subject indexes. Updated by supplements for 1988, 1989, 1990. Z6001.L43

Current

●**GEOBASE** [computer file]. Norwich, England : Elsevier/Geo Abstracts, 1980– . **CL5**

Machine-readable version of *Geographical abstracts. Human geography* and *Geographical abstracts. Physical geography* (both below) and their predecessors.

File size: 350,000 records. Updated monthly. Available online (DIALOG).

Also contains relevant records from *International development abstracts* (*Guide* CH124), *Geological abstracts* (Norwich Eng. : GeoAbstracts Ltd., 1977–) and *Ecological abstracts* (*Supplement* EC23).

Geographical abstracts. Human geography. 1989– . Norwich [England] : Elsevier/Geo Abstracts, 1989– . Monthly. $333.00. **CL6**
GF1.G47

Geographical abstracts. Physical geography. Norwich, [England] : Elsevier/Geo Abstracts, c1989– . $434.75. **CL7**

For preceding title, *Geo abstracts*, see *Guide* CL57.

In 1986, *Geo abstracts*, pts. A, B, E, and G changed title to *Geographical abstracts*, pts. A, B, E, and G, and *Geo abstracts*, pts. C, D, and F changed title to *Geographical abstracts*, pts. C, D, and F. In 1989, pts. A, B, E, and G merged to form *Geographical abstracts. Physical geography* and pts. C, D, and F merged to form *Geographical abstracts. Human geography*.

The subject arrangement of the earlier titles has been retained. Each issue has a regional index, and regional and author indexes cumulate annually. GB54.5.G46

Indexes

National Geographic index, 1888–1988. [Wash.] : National Geographic Society, 1989. 1215 p. : ill. (some col.). ISBN 0-87044-764-5. $24.95. **CL8**

Compiled to commemorate the 100th anniversary of the National Geographic Society and publication of the *National geographic* magazine. Contains a brief chronology of milestones in the history of the Society and a list of winners of Society medals and awards. The index proper, more than 1,000 pages, has author, title, and subject entries, with photographs in color and symbols to identify books, maps, and television programs. G1.N27

Encyclopedias

Modern geography : an encyclopedic survey / ed. by Gary S. Dunbar. N.Y. : Garland, 1990. 219 p. (Garland reference library of the humanities, vol. 1197). ISBN 0-8240-5343-5. **CL9**

Contains approximately 400 signed entries for "personalities, institutions, major concepts, subfields and the evolution of the discipline" (*Introd.*) of geography, 1890 to the present. Biographical entries cite major publications and biographies; other

entries include brief bibliographies. Major terms and concepts only are defined; reference is made to appropriate subject dictionaries for other definitions. Cross-references; index of personal names. G63.M57

Dictionaries

Cartographical innovations : an international handbook of mapping terms to 1900 / ed. by Helen M. Wallis and Arthur H. Robinson. [Tring, Herts.] : Publ. by Map Collector Publications in association with the International Cartographic Association, 1987. 353 p. : ill. ISBN 0-906430-04-6. **CL10**

"Documents a wealth of innovative ideas and concepts which led to the advance of the art, craft and science of mapmaking in the past. The book covers all aspects of the field ranging from types of maps to concepts and from techniques of production to those of symbolization."—*Foreword.* International in scope. Contains 191 entries in eight sections: Types of maps; Maps of human occupation and activities; Maps of natural phenomena; Reference systems and geodetic concepts; Symbolism; Techniques and media; Methods of duplication; and Atlases. Entries are alphabetical within section; each entry includes a definition (citing *Multilingual dictionary of technical terms in cartography* [Wiesbaden : F. Steiner, c1973] where appropriate), a description of its innovative aspects, and bibliographical references. 25 black-and-white photographs illustrate significant entries. General index. GA102.2.C37

The encyclopaedic dictionary of physical geography / ed. by Andrew Goudie . . . [et al.]. Oxford ; N.Y. : Blackwell, 1985. 528 p. : ill. ISBN 0-631-13292-9. $60.00. **CL11**

Contains more than 2,000 entries consisting of both short definitions and longer signed articles from the discipline and its subdivisions, including biogeography, climatology, geomorphology, hydrology, and quaternary studies. Longer definitions include brief bibliographies. Extensive cross-references and index. GB10.E53

Small, R. J. A modern dictionary of geography / John Small and Michael Witherick. 2nd ed. London ; N.Y. : E. Arnold : Distr. by Routledge, Chapman and Hall, 1989. 247 p. : ill. ISBN 0-340-49318-6. ISBN 0-340-49317-8 (pbk.). **CL12**

1st ed., 1986.

This edition reflects recent changes in the discipline. 2,000 entries, including 100 new and many revised from the 1st ed., cover both human and physical geography. 1135 illustrations and maps. Terms limited to those likely to be encountered by advanced high school and undergraduate students; excludes highly specialized, unusual, and local terms, as well as those covered in standard college dictionaries. G63.S53

Quotations

Wheeler, James O. Dictionary of quotations in geography / comp. by James O. Wheeler and Francis M. Sibley. N.Y. : Greenwood, 1986. 257 p. ISBN 0-313-24196-1. **CL13**

Uses quotations, "many by the most prominent American geographers of this century," to describe a wide range of views on geography, to review the development of geographic thought, and "to characterize a variety of themes as the discipline has evolved."—*Pref.* Five sections, including four that cover the main traditions of American geography (earth science, man-land, area studies, and spatial) and one on other aspects. Sections are subdivided topically, and quotations arranged chronologically within topics. Quotations are drawn primarily from the major American geographical journals, listed in "Sources cited."   G63.W47

Directories

Guide to departments of geography in the United States and Canada. 1984–1985– . [Wash. : Association of American Geographers], 1984– . Annual. ISSN 0882-1542.   **CL14**

1968/69–1983/84 (*Guide* CL102) had title: *Guide to graduate departments of geography in the United States and Canada.*

Expanded to include government agencies, research institutions, and private companies that employ geographers, 1988–89; two-year institutions with geography courses, 1989–90; directory of Association of American Geographers members, 1990–91. Lists theses and dissertations completed during the previous year. Departmental specialties, name, and geographic indexes.   G76.5.U5G8

Orbis geographicus = Adressar géographique du monde = World directory of geography = Geographisches Weltadressbuch. 1952– . Wiesbaden : F. Steiner, 1952– . Irregular.   **CL15**

For annotation, see *Guide* CL103.

6th ed., 1988/92, comp. and ed. in cooperation with the International Geographical Union by Eckart Ehlers.

With the 6th ed., format and organization changed. Entries arranged alphabetically by country; within country, the following structure is used: national committees and IGU, geographical societies, central institutions and academies, departments of geography and their members, agencies engaged in geography, and agencies engaged in cartography. Information current to 1988; personal name index.   G67.W92

Handbooks

Boyer, Rick. Places rated almanac : your guide to finding the best places to live in America / Richard Boyer & David Savageau. All new ed. N.Y. : Prentice HallTravel, c1989. 421 p. : ill., maps. ISBN 0-13-677006-1. $16.95.   **CL16**

Previous ed., 1985 (*Guide* CL87).

Arranged like earlier editions, but expanded to include 333 metropolitan areas. A new appendix (Metropolitan place finder) lists smaller cities and towns considered to lie within metropolitan areas. Includes population estimates for 1989.

HN60.B69

Cities of the United States / ed. by Diane L. Dupois. Detroit : Gale, 1988–1990. 4 v. : ill. ISBN 0-8103-2500-4.   **CL17**

Contents: v. 1, The South (1988. 403 p.); v. 2, The West (1989. 344 p.); v. 3, The Midwest (1990. 447 p.); v. 4, The Northeast (1990. 415 p.).

Offers comprehensive current descriptions of selected major cities, one to five per state. Arrangement is alphabetical by state, then by city. Concise "State in brief" and "City in brief" overviews are followed by detailed descriptions of cities, each including introduction, geography and climate, history, population profile, municipal government, economy, education and research, health care, recreation, convention facilities, transportation, and communications. Illustrated with black-and-white photographs and general maps of each state and urban area. Index cumulates with each volume.

HT123.C49677

Cities of the world : a compilation of current information on cultural, geographical, and political conditions in the countries and cities of six continents, based on the

Department of State's "Post reports". 3rd ed. Detroit : Gale, c1987. 4 v.   **CL18**

Previous ed., 1982 (*Guide* CL88).

Contents: v. 1, Africa; v. 2, The Western Hemisphere (exclusive of the United States); v. 3, Europe and the Mediterranean Middle East; v. 4, Asia, the Pacific, and the Asiatic Middle East; Cumulative index.

This edition expanded to provide information on 451 major cities and 2,865 other cities in 140 countries; contains illustrations and maps.   G153.4.C56

Fitzpatrick, Gary L. Direct-line distances—international edition / by Gary L. Fitzpatrick and Marilyn J. Modlin. Metuchen, N.J. : Scarecrow, 1986. 275 p. : maps. ISBN 0-8108-1872-8.   **CL19**

G109.F53

———— Direct-line distances—United States edition / by Gary L. Fitzpatrick and Marilyn J. Modlin. Metuchen, N.J. : Scarecrow, 1986. 275 p. : maps. ISBN 0-8108-1871-X.   **CL20**

Taken together, these volumes consist of tables of distances between 1,001 cities, towns, and other selected geographic places. The international edition includes only 120 U.S. cities and gives distances in kilometers; the U.S. edition includes 312 U.S. cities and gives distances in miles. Distances are computed mathematically and recorded as "geodesic" distances (roughly equivalent to "air miles"); the introduction explains the computational methodology. Alphabetical list of cities with coordinates and reference maps that locate cities.   G109.F54

Shanks, Thomas G. The American atlas : U.S. longitudes & latitudes, time changes and time zones. 5th ed., expanded. San Diego, Calif. : ACS Publications, 1990. 617 p. ISBN 0-935127-13-5.   **CL21**

QB205.U37

———— The international atlas : world latitudes, longitudes, and time changes. 2nd ed. San Diego, Calif. : ACS Publications, c1988. 426, [1] p. ISBN 0-935127-03-8.   **CL22**

American atlas covers only the U.S.; *International atlas* excludes U.S. place-names. Each title functions as a gazetteer of 100,000 cities and towns; both are arranged alphabetically by country or state, then by place-name. For each place-name, gives county code, then latitude and longitude coordinates to the minute. Designed to aid astrologers in calculating birthplace distance from Greenwich and birth hour in sidereal time, so only populated places are listed (no physical features). Index to geographic place-names also provides variant forms of county names. Most changes in various editions deal with improved techniques in calculating historical time for astrological purposes.   QB205.U373

Thomas, G. Scott. The rating guide to life in America's small cities. Buffalo, N.Y. : Prometheus Books, c1990. 538 p. : map. ISBN 0-87975-600-4 (pbk.). $16.95. **CL23**

Presents ratings based on a 20-point distribution, high to low, for 219 micropolitan areas (populations of 15,000–50,000). Ten chapters cover lifestyle factors (e.g., Climate, Economics, Education, Sophistication, Health care, Housing). For each factor, presents national ratings, then lists micropolitan areas alphabetically within states, with assigned scores. Sources of data are given. Concludes with "report card" summaries of scores for each micropolitan area, alphabetically listed by state. Glossary of terms; subject index to tables of national rankings. A companion to *Places rated almanac* (*Supplement* CL16), which ranks metropolitan areas.

HA214.T46

Biography

Geographers: biobibliographical studies. v. 1–12. [London] : Mansell, 1977–1988. **CL24**
Ceased with v. 12 (1988); for annotation, see *Guide* CL106.
Z6001.G425

Tooley, R. V. Tooley's dictionary of mapmakers. Supplement. N.Y. : A.R. Liss, c1985. 116 p. : ill., maps, ports. ISBN 0-8451-1703-3. **CL25**
For basic work and annotation, see *Guide* CL108.
"This Supplement adds approximately four thousand names to the Dictionary."—*Foreword.* GA198.T66

GAZETTEERS

General

Chambers world gazetteer : an A–Z of geographical information / ed. by David Munro. 5th ed. Edinburgh : Chambers ; Cambridge ; N.Y. : Cambridge Univ. Pr., 1988. 733 p., 112 p. of plates : ill. (some col.). ISBN 1-85296-200-3. **CL26**
Previous ed., 1965, called *Chambers's world gazetteer and geographical dictionary* (*Guide* CL110).
Contains more than 20,000 place names. Includes, for many entries, a current geographical description and brief history, as well as location (including coordinates), area, and population. Uses Pinyin romanization for Chinese place names. Provides a small uncluttered map with each country entry in addition to the maps by John Bartholomew & Son, appended as a 120-page "World atlas." Introductory pages explain inclusion criteria and give a sample entry and other notes. G103.5.C44

CIS foreign gazetteers [of the] USBGN [microform]. [Wash.] : Congressional Information Service, [1987]. 1500 microfiches : negative, maps. **CL27**
A republication in microform of the gazetteers published by the U.S. Defense Mapping Agency, containing geographic names approved by the U.S. Board on Geographic Names. (For earlier versions of gazetteers published in printed format, see *Guide* CL119.) The basic microform set contains 181 volumes, consisting of the most recent editions of the gazetteers as of May 1987; the supplement (Group 2 in the microform set) contains 22 country updates plus the current edition of *Gazetteer of conventional names* (3rd ed., Wash. : Defense Mapping Agency, 1988). The printed guide that accompanies the microform set lists gazetteers in the set and is keyed to the microfiche numbers.

Foreign gazetteers of the U.S. Board on Geographic Names [guide]. [Wash.] : Congressional Information Service, [1987]. 12 p. **CL28**
Cover title. Serves as index to *CIS foreign gazetteers of the USBGN* (above).

Webster's new geographical dictionary. Springfield, Mass. : Merriam-Webster, c1988. 1376 p., [2] p. of plates : maps. ISBN 0-87779-446-4. **CL29**
For previous ed., 1984, see *Guide* CL121.
The authority for place names used in cataloging by the Library of Congress. This edition continues to use Wade-Giles romanization for Chinese place names without cross-references from Pinyin versions. G103.5.W42

United States

The national gazetteer of the United States of America. [Wash.] : U.S. Govt. Print. Off. ; Alexandria, Va. : for sale by the Distribution Branch, U.S. Geological Survey, 1983–1990. 7 v. : maps. (Geological Survey professional paper, 1200). (In progress). **CL30**
For early volumes and annotation, see *Guide* CL128.
Contents: New Jersey (1983); Delaware (1983); Kansas (1984); Arizona (1986); Indiana (1988); South Dakota (1989); North Dakota (1990).
Also published in a concise edition: E154.N3

The national gazetteer of the United States of America : United States concise 1990 / prep. by the U.S. Geological Survey in cooperation with the U.S. Board on Geographic Names. Wash. : U.S. Govt. Print. Off. ; Denver, Co. : For sale by the Books and Open-File Reports Section, U.S. Geological Survey, 1990. 526 p. : col. maps. **CL31**
Superintendent of Documents classification: I 19.16:1200-US.
A condensed version of *The national gazetteer of the United States of America* (above). Includes about 45,000 entries for populated places, administrative areas, and major physical features. Provides official name, feature type, elevation, county and state location, and geographic coordinates. Brief glossary.
E154.N38

Africa

Kirchherr, Eugene C. Place names of Africa, 1935–1986 : a political gazetteer. Metuchen, N.J. : Scarecrow, 1987. 136 p. : maps. ISBN 0-8108-2061-7. **CL32**
A political gazetteer of African territories in four parts: general introduction, place names of the principal African states and adjacent islands, supplementary notes and maps, selected bibliography. Place names are listed alphabetically based on common spellings of territorial names with variant spellings included. Entries give both the common name and the official title of each state, cross-references, and map locations. Supplemental notes; list of maps; bibliography arranged by types of sources. Updates Kirchherr's *Abyssinia to Zimbabwe : a guide to the political units of Africa in the period 1947–1978*, 3rd ed., (Athens : Ohio Univ. Center for Interntional Studies, 1979).
DT31.K53

Great Britain

Bartholomew gazetteer of places in Britain / comp. by Oliver Mason. Rev. and repr. Edinburgh : J. Bartholomew, 1986. 270, 120 p. : maps in color. ISBN 0-7028-0731-1. **CL33**
1st ed., 1977, had title: *Bartholomew gazetteer of Britain* (*Guide* CL156).
This edition updates the statistical section to include data for all places with more than 5,000 inhabitants (England) or 2,000 (Scotland and Wales), according to 1981 census; population estimates as of 1984 are also listed. Includes postal code area maps.
DA640.B26

GEOGRAPHICAL NAMES AND TERMS

General Works

Names & nicknames of places & things / ed. by Laurence Urdang. Boston : G.K. Hall, c1987. 327 p. ISBN 0-8161-8780-0. $39.95.   **CL34**

A selective compilation of "names and nicknames as might qualify for consideration as being universal or, at least, important."—*Foreword.* Geographic names are interspersed with names of buildings, foods, institutions, modes of transportation, in a single alphabet. Well indexed.   G105.N36

United States

Place guide / ed. by Donna Andriot . . . [et al.]. 1990 ed. McLean, Va. : Documents Index, c1990. 561 p.   **CL35**

An alphabetical list of place names in the U.S., giving county and state for each. Compiled from U.S. Census Bureau publications. A preface describes various political subdivisions within states and lists abbreviations.   E155.P63

United States Board on Geographic Names. Decisions on geographic names in the United States. Wash. : Dept. of the Interior, 1963– .   **CL36**

For earlier numbers and annotation, see *Guide* CL201.

Frequency varies; annual, 1990– .

Superintendent of Documents classifications: I 33.5/2: .
    E154.U54a

Canada

Répertoire toponymique du Québec : 1987 / Commission de toponymie. Québec : Gouvernement du Québec, c1987. 1900 p., [2] leaves of plates : maps.   **CL37**

1st ed., 1969; 2nd ed., 1979.

Over 93,000 place names. Indicates type of feature, administrative division, latitude and longitude coordinates, and sheet number (1:50,000 map series) for location.   F1051.4.R47

ATLASES

Guides

Ehrenberg, Ralph E. Scholars' guide to Washington, D.C. for cartography and remote sensing imagery : (maps, charts, aerial photographs, satellite images, cartographic literature, and geographic information systems) / Ralph E. Ehrenberg ; ed., Zdeněk V. David. Wash. : Smithsonian Institution Pr., 1987. 385 p. (Scholars' guide to Washington, D.C., no. 12). ISBN 0-87474-406-7. ISBN 0-87474-407-5 (pbk.).   **CL38**

Superintendent of Documents classification: SI 1.20:Sch 6/7.

Provides comprehensive information on location, collections, organization and accessibility for institutions in Washington, D.C. metropolitan area. Arranges 180 sources of cartographic information in 11 sections, four for research collections and seven for organizations. The entry for each source includes address and telephone, number of volumes, scope of collec-

tions, and hours of service; additional information may include collection history, facilities description, special events, and access information. Contains six appendixes, five indexes, and short bibliography. Three appendixes provide information on Map stores; Housing, transportation, and other services; and Federal government holidays. Indexes include personal names, subjects, geographic headings (one each for maps and remote sensing imagery), and names of organizations and institutions.
    GA193.U5E37

Bibliography and indexes

American Geographical Society of New York. Index to maps in books and periodicals : third supplement. Boston : G.K. Hall, 1987. 668 p. : ill. ISBN 0-8161-0458-1.   **CL39**

For basic volume and supplement 1–2, see *Guide* CL259.

Covers 1976–86 and includes 12,200 entries. Format remains the same.   Z6028.A5

Bibliographie cartographique internationale. 1936–75. Paris : A. Colin [etc.], 1938–1975. ISSN 0067-6934.   **CL40**

For early volumes and annotation, see *Guide* CL297.

Ceased, 1975.

"Publiée sous les auspices du Comité national francais de géographie et de l'Union géographique internationale."
    Z6021.B5

British Library. Catalogue of cartographic materials in the British Library, 1975–1988. London ; N.Y. : Saur, 1989. 3 v. (1201 p.). ISBN 0-86291-765-4 (set). £360.00.   **CL41**

For basic set and supplement, see *Guide* CL260–261.

"The British Library Catalogue of Cartographic Materials contains bibliographic records for atlases, single-sheet maps, map series, maritime charts, plans, globes and related reference materials acquired by the British Library Map Library since 1974."—*Explanatory note.* Includes records for current map accessions to the Manuscripts Collection and for remote-sensing and digital cartographic databases throughout the U.K. Vol. 1–2 contain the author/title index, v. 3 the geographic names and subject indexes.   Z6028.B854

A guide to Civil War maps in the National Archives. Wash. : National Archives, National Archives and Records Administration, 1986. 139 p. : ill. ISBN 0-911333-36-3.   **CL42**

For annotation, see *Supplement* DB36.   Z1242.G85

Walsh, Jim. Maps contained in the publications of the American bibliography, 1639–1819 : an index and checklist. Metuchen, N.J. : Scarecrow, 1988. 367 p. ISBN 0-8108-2193-1. $37.50.   **CL43**

In three parts: an "index and checklist of all map separates and maps contained in books" (*Introd.*) (1) in Charles Evans's *American bibliography*, 1639–1800 (*Guide* AA557), arranged by Evans numbers; (2) in Ralph R. Shaw and Richard H. Shoemaker's *American bibliography*, 1801–1819 (*Guide* AA567), arranged by Shaw-Shoemaker numbers; and (3) six indexes. Indexes by date of publication, place of publication, personal or corporate name, book title, map title, and geographic name.   Z6027.U5W35

Directories

Cobb, David A. Guide to U.S. map resources / comp. by David A. Cobb ; regional editors, Brent Allison ... [et al.]. 2nd ed. Chicago : Amer. Lib. Assoc., 1990. 495 p. ISBN 0-8389-0547-0. **CL44**
1st ed., 1986.
Provides directory and access information, size, holdings and collection strengths for 974 U.S. map collections at a wide variety of institutions: academic, geoscience, private, public and governmental. Entries are arranged alphabetically by state, then by city and institution. 13 tables for collection size, classification systems, preservation techniques, public access policies, equipment and staff, and collection strengths. Three appendixes list addresses for federal and state mapping and cartographic information agencies. Indexes by library/institution, collection strengths, and personal names.   GA193.U5C62

International directory of tactile map collections / Frank Kurt Cylke, Judith M. Dixon, managing editors. [The Hague, Netherlands?] : Section of Libraries for the Blind, International Federation of Library Associations and Institutions ; [Wash.] : National Library Service for the Blind and Physically Handicapped. Library of Congress, 1985. 19 p. ISBN 0-8444-0506-X.   **CL45**
The first international directory describing collections of maps intended for the visually handicapped. Arranged alphabetically by country, then city; organizations are listed alphabetically under city. Entry includes address of institution, description of collections, and availability of maps, whether for sale or for loan. Alphabetical list of organizations.   GA135.I57

World directory of map collections / comp. by the Section of Geography and Map Libraries ; ed. by John A. Wolter (gen. ed.), Ronald E. Grim, and David K. Carrington. 2nd ed. München ; N.Y. : K.G. Saur, 1986. 405 p. (IFLA publications, 31). ISBN 0-86291-296-2.   **CL46**
1st ed., 1976 (*Guide* CL303).
A directory of major map collections as of 1980–82 containing 670 entries from 65 countries. Lists "national libraries and archives, principal geographical, cartographical and historical society and institute collections, the collections of military geographical institutes or departments, and all other map collections, archives, or libraries of special significance."—*Pref.* More selective for countries with published national directories of map collections (Australia, Canada, Federal Republic of Germany, France, Netherlands, U.K., U.S.). Detailed information on each collection lists location, history, size, reference services, access policies, reproduction facilities, classification, specializations, and publications.   GA192.W67

World mapping today / [ed. by] R.B. Parry, C.R. Perkins ; graphic indexes prepared by Cartographic Unit, Department of Geography, Portsmouth Polytechnic, U.K. London ; Boston : Butterworths, 1987. 583 p. : maps. ISBN 0-408-02850-5. £125.00.   **CL47**
Systematically lists maps (primarily series), atlases and gazetteers of the world and its continents and countries. Introductory matter treats the state of world mapping, map acquisition, map evaluation, maps and remote sensing, digital mapping, and future trends in digital mapping. Entries are arranged by continent then listed alphabetically by country. Each country entry includes a brief description of that country's mapping activities, addresses of mapping agencies, and bibliographies of maps, atlases, and other cartographic sources available as of approximately 1984–86. Does not include commercial road and tourist maps. 122 graphic indexes to major series. Brief glossary, geographical index, and publishers index.   GA105.3.W67

Handbooks

Larsgaard, Mary Lynette. Map librarianship : an introduction. 2nd ed. Littleton, Colo. : Libraries Unlimited, 1987. 382 p. : ill. ISBN 0-87287-537-7. $43.50.   **CL48**
For annotation, see *Supplement* AB57.   Z692.M3L37

The map catalog : every kind of map and chart on earth and even some above it / Joel Makower, ed., Cathryn Poff, Laura Bergheim, assoc. editors. 2nd ed., rev. and expanded. N.Y. : Random House, c1990. 364 p. : ill. (some col.). ISBN 0-394-58326-4. $27.50. ISBN 0-679-72767-1 (pbk.). $16.95.   **CL49**
1st ed., 1986.
A compilation of "information about the many types of maps available, the major sources of each map type, and descriptions or examples of the map products available from each source."—*Introd.* Chapters include Travel maps; Maps of specific areas; Boundary maps; Scientific maps; History through maps; Utility and service maps; Water maps; Sky maps; Images as maps; and Atlases and globes. Includes information on map accessories, software and organizations. Numerous illustrations, some in color, provide examples of each type of map. Contains cross-references and a comprehensive index. Five appendixes list addresses for state, federal and foreign map agencies, map stores, and libraries. A sixth appendix defines selected cartographic terms.   Z6028.M23

General

Esselte kartor (Firm). Earth book world atlas. Boulder, Colo. : Graphic Learning International Pub., c1987. 327 p. : ill. (some col.), maps in color ; 34 cm. ISBN 0-87746-100-7. $65.00.   **CL50**
In three sections: Encyclopedia of the earth, The world in maps, Index. The heavily illustrated encyclopedia section presents current topics from the physical and biological sciences clustered around environmental themes of air, water, earth and fire. World in maps section covers regions, not individual states and countries; a new mapping technique depicts landscape, especially vegetation, as the map base rather than the more traditional political or relief base. The index includes approximately 57,000 place names; brief glossary.   G1021.E784

Goode, J. Paul. Goode's world atlas / ed., Edward B. Espenshade, Jr. ; sr. consultant, Joel L. Morrison. 18th ed. Chicago : Rand McNally, c1990. 367 p. : maps in color ; 29 cm. ISBN 0-528-83128-3.   **CL51**
16th ed., 1983 (*Guide* CL307).
Twenty new thematic maps update the world economic situation, U.S. health and economic conditions, information on the Soviet Union, and ethnic situation in the Middle East and Caribbean. List of source materials and index by subject to thematic maps have been added.   G1021.G6

Kidron, Michael. The new state of the world atlas / Michael Kidron and Ronald Segal. [2nd ed.], rev. and updated. N.Y. : Simon & Schuster, c1987. [167] p. : 57 maps in color ; 25 cm. ISBN 0-671-64554-4. $22.95. ISBN 0-671-64555-2 (pbk.). $12.95.   **CL52**
1st ed., 1981 (*Guide* CL312).
The 3rd printing (1987, [2nd ed.] rev. and updated) drops the four-page chart, The state of the world. Some data updated to 1986. A new edition is expected in 1991.   G1021.K46

Maps on file. N.Y. : Facts on File, c1981– . 2 v. (looseleaf) : maps ; 30 cm. ISBN 0-8160-1685-2.   **CL53**
For annotation, see *Guide* CL315.

Additions, especially to the thematic section, bring the total of maps to more than 430 in two looseleaf volumes.

G1046.A1M16

National Geographic Society (U.S.). National Geographic atlas of the world. 6th ed. Wash. : National Geographic Society, 1990. (133, 136 p.) : col. ill., maps in color ; 47 cm. ISBN 0-87044-398-4. $59.95.   **CL54**

5th ed., 1981 (*Guide* CL318).

Published in a year of significant changes in world political geography. Maps in this edition show, e.g., Yemen unified, Germany unified (but with two capitals on some sheets), and southeast Asian country of Myanmar (Burma). Includes a fold-out map of the world using the recently adopted Robinson projection, and a number of spacecraft images of the earth and the planets. Indexes more than 150,000 place names.   G1021.N38

Peters, Arno. Peters atlas of the world. N.Y. : Harper & Row, 1990. 188, [39] p. : ill. (som col.), maps in color ; 35 cm. ISBN 0-06-016540-5. $50.00.   **CL55**

Includes 43 shaded-relief and 246 thematic maps. Relief is shown with a combination of shading, spot heights, and photography of relief models; color indicates vegetation, not relief. Thematic maps cover the usual subjects (Precipitation, Languages, Economic growth) and some not so usual (The direction of writing, Monogamy/polygamy, a series on Sport). Lists sources of data used in thematic section. Maps use an equal area representation (Peters projection); illustrates areal significance of equatorial regions. Index includes both local and relevant English forms of place names.   G1021.P4

Rand McNally and Company. The new international atlas = Der neue internationale Atlas = El nuevo atlas internacional = Le nouvel atlas international = O nôvo atlas internacional. Anniversary ed. Chicago : Rand McNally, c1991. 320, 200 p. : col. ill., maps in color ; 39 cm. ISBN 0-528-83413-4.   **CL56**

For 1980 ed., see *Guide* CL326.

Some data updated to 1988–89, but does not depict politico-geographical changes in Europe and Asia of 1990 (e.g., Germany, Yemen, Myanmar). Format remains the same.

G1021.R23

The Times atlas of the world. 8th comprehensive ed. N.Y. : Times Books, 1990. [245], 225 p. : col. ill., maps in color ; 46 cm. ISBN 0-8129-1874-6.   **CL57**

6th ed., 1980 (*Guide* CL336).

This edition offers 47 pages of prefatory information; graphic size comparisons of contintents, oceans, river drainage basins, islands, and inland water bodies; eight pages of world thematic mapping; and an index that includes more than 210,000 place names and continues to provide latitude and longitude coordinates.   G1021.T55

National and regional

United States

Andriot, John L. Township atlas of the United States. McLean, Va. : Documents Index, c1987. 969 p. : 29 cm.   **CL58**

2nd ed., 1979 (*Guide* CL341).

Updated to include information from the 1980 census. Provides more detail by showing subdivisions on separate county maps. Includes a seven-page explanation of the Public Land Surveys and merges incorporated and unincorporated place name index with township index. Does not include Alaska or Hawaii.   G1201.F7A5

Rand McNally and Company. Standard highway mileage guide. 1934– . Chicago : Rand McNally & Co., 1934– . Irregular.   **CL59**

In the most recent edition, mileage charts list distances between 530 ("key point") major and medium-sized U.S. and Canadian cities. Alphabetical index to key point cities. The atlas section includes 135 pages of indexed highway maps by state and region and 47 urban vicinity maps and designates key point cities in bright green circles.   G1201.P1R3

Thorndale, William. Map guide to the U.S. federal censuses, 1790–1920 / William Thorndale and William Dollarhide. Baltimore : Genealogical Pub. Co., 1987. 420 p. : maps ; 23 x 30 cm. ISBN 0-8063-1188-6. $49.95.   **CL60**

Shows U.S. county boundary maps for the census decades superimposed on modern county boundaries. Gives background information on each census, including census availability for each county.   G1201.F7T5

Handbooks

Thompson, Morris Mordecai. Maps for America : cartographic products of the U.S. Geological Survey and others. 3rd ed. Reston, Va. : U.S. Geological Survey, 1987. 265 p. : ill. (some col.).   **CL61**

2nd ed., 1981 (*Guide* CL346).

Superintendent of Documents classification: I 19.2:M32/12/987.

"The third edition . . . is intended primarily to replenish the supply of copies of the book, but it also contains a number of changes to correct or update the text."—*Foreword.* The most significant changes occur in sections on digital cartographic data.   GA405.T46

Americas

Coe, Michael D. Atlas of ancient America / by Michael Coe, Dean Snow, and Elizabeth Benson. N.Y. : Facts on File, c1986. 240 p. : col. ill. ISBN 0-8160-1199-0.   **CL62**

A heavily illustrated work, discussing physical, cultural, and political aspects of the indigenous population of the Americas, arranged in more or less broad geographical sections. Bibliography; gazetteer; index by subject for text and illustrative material.   E61.C66

Canada

Canada. Energy, Mines and Resources Canada. The national atlas of Canada. 5th ed. Ottawa : Energy, Mines and Resources Canada, 1985– . 9 p. : folded maps in color ; 46 X 40 cm.; in box, 49 X 47 cm.   **CL63**

4th ed., 1974 (*Guide* CL363).

"The fifth edition of the National Atlas of Canada is a serial publication of separate maps to be published over a period of time. The subject matter is organized into 44 separately titled and numbered realms of information . . . which encompass all aspects of geographical information relating to Canada."—*Pref.* Most maps at a scale of 1:7,500,00. Also issued in French under title: *L'atlas national du Canada.*   G1115

Ethiopia

Ethiopian Mapping Agency. Geography Division. National atlas of Ethiopia / [prepared and comp. by Geography Division]. Addis Ababa : Ethiopian Mapping Authority, 1988. 76 [i.e. 156] p. : ill., maps in color ; 39 cm.

CL64

Natural conditions, socioeconomic activities, and historical development are depicted in 76 color maps, most at a scale of 1:5,000,000. Government, international, and educational institutions provided sources of data; information is current to 1984. Maps are accompanied by charts, tables and explanatory text. Index to place names. G2505.E8

Israel

Israel. Agaf ha-medidot. Atlas of Israel : cartography, physical and human geography. 3rd ed. (English-Hebrew). Tel-Aviv : Survey of Israel ; N.Y. : Macmillan, 1985. [7], 40 [i.e. 160], 80 p. : maps in color; 50 cm. ISBN 0-02-905950-X. $175.00. **CL65**

1st ed., 1956–64 (*Guide* CL391); 2nd ed., 1970 (*Guide* CL392).

Includes 40 double-page plates of bilingual maps (Hebrew and English) in color, portraying climatic, population, and economic aspects. Gives special attention to urban geography; new maps cover Jerusalem, Haifa, Tel-Aviv and 13 medium-sized and small towns. 80 pages of text in English, with numerous tables, provide supplementary information. Although listed as a 3rd ed., does not replace two older editions, each of which has special strengths. G2235.I77

D

HISTORY AND AREA STUDIES

DA

General History

GENERAL WORKS

Guides

Fritze, Ronald H. Reference sources in history : an introductory guide / Ronald H. Fritze, Brian E. Coutts, Louis A. Vyhnanek. Santa Barbara, Calif. : ABC-Clio, 1990. 319 p. ISBN 0-87436-164-8. $49.00.   **DA1**

"... designed to provide an introduction to the major reference works for all periods of history and for all geographical areas."—*Pref.* Intended to extend Helen J. Poulton's *A historian's handbook* (*Guide* DA2). Cites mainly English-language materials, arranged by format (bibliographies, newspaper lists, archives and manuscript guides) subdivided geo-

graphically or by period, with lengthy, well-written annotations. Strongest for Europe and North America, but includes major reference works on Asian, African and Latin American history. Indexed by broad field (e.g., Ethnic studies, Medieval studies), and by author and title.   Z6201.F72

Bibliography

Air and space history : an annotated bibliography / ed. by Dominick A. Pisano and Cathleen S. Lewis. N.Y. : Garland, 1988. 571 p. : ill. (Garland reference library of the humanities, vol. 834). ISBN 0-8240-8543-4. $75.00.   **DA2**

Sponsored by the National Air and Space Museum, Smithsonian Institution.

Curators of the Museum have assembled "a selective, annotated bibliography of international dimensions to give the beginning (or advanced) researcher access to the best literature of the field."—*Introd.* 1,768 items (books, articles, government documents, and technical reports), mostly in English, are arranged topically with a brief essay at the beginning of each section explaining the organization and rationale for selection. Cross-references; author index.   Z5060.A44

Henige, David P. Serial bibliographies and abstracts in history : an annotated guide. Westport, Conn. : Greenwood, 1986. 220 p. (Bibliographies and indexes in world history, no. 2). ISBN 0-313-25070-7. $35.00.   **DA3**

An alphabetical listing by title of some 874 items, with subject index. Aims to list relatively current bibliographies published serially, usually at least every two years. History is broadly interpreted to include works "which address in whole or part *any* aspect of the past."—*Pref.* Descriptive annotations.   Z6201.A1H45

King, H. G. R. Atlantic Ocean. Oxford ; Santa Barbara, Calif. : Clio Pr., c1985. 250 p. (World bibliographical series, v. 61). ISBN 1-85109-004-5. £30.00. **DA4**

Aims to treat man's activity in the Atlantic region, Atlantic Ocean nature and wildlife, and aspects of islands or island groups not already covered by a volume in this series. 913 entries, mostly for English-language books published up to early 1985, with some government documents and periodical articles, and including works of the imagination. Author/title/subject index. Z6004.P6K5

Munro, D. J. Microforms for historians : a finding-list of research collections in London libraries. London : Institute of Historical Research, 1991. 110 p. **DA5**

Based on responses to a survey designed to identify microforms of collections or groups of materials held by libraries in the Greater London area. The 1,200 items are arranged by broad subject areas. Title index; provenance index (owners of original material); name and subject index. D13

Current

Falk, Joyce Duncan. Searching *America : History and life* (*AHL*) and *Historical abstracts* (*HA*) on DIALOG / Joyce Duncan Falk and Susan K. Kinnell. Rev. 1987. Santa Barbara, Calif. : ABC-Clio, c1987. 31 p. ISBN 0-87436-091-9 (pbk.). **DA6**

1st ed., 1980.

Intended as an aid to searching the machine-readable versions of *Historical abstracts* (*Guide* DA19–21) and *America : history and life* (*Guide* DB47; *Supplement* DB17). It includes *List of periodicals (rev. 1986) surveyed for* America : history and life *and* Historical abstracts, which has been separately published and updated to 1987 (Santa Barbara : 1987. 29 p.) and is a listing by title of journals indexed, with years of coverage and a two-letter code representing the country of publication. D20.F26

Historical abstracts five year index : v. 31–35, 1980–84. Santa Barbara, Calif. : ABC-Clio, 1986. 2 v. **DA7**

For annotation and earlier indexes, see *Guide* DA20–21.

In 2 v. corresponding to the abstracts: Pt. A, Modern history; Pt. B, 20th century. Rotated subject index; author index. A cumulated index for v.36–40 (1985–89) has been announced.

Dissertations

Kuehl, Warren F. Dissertations in history, 1970–June 1980 : an index to dissertations completed in history departments of United States & Canadian universities. Santa Barbara, Calif. : ABC-Clio, c1985. 466 p. ISBN 0-87436-356-X. $58.50. **DA8**

For volumes covering 1873–June 1970, see *Guide* DA26.

Unlike the earlier volumes, this one follows the topical arrangement of *Recently published articles* (*Guide* DA23). Also new to this volume is the inclusion of numbers for ordering copies from University Microfilms International. Author and subject indexes. Z6201.K82

Periodicals

Fyfe, Janet. History journals and serials : an analytical guide. N.Y. : Greenwood, 1986. 351 p. (Annotated bibliographies of serials : a subject approach, no. 8). ISBN 0-313-23999-1. **DA9**

Limited to English-language journals with international reputations or "general or specialized interest" from which completed questionnaires were received, plus local history serials

"of interest to more than a few enthusiasts . . . aimed primarily at helping the librarian select journals for a library and the historian to select journals for personal reading or submission of manuscripts."—*Pref.* Topical listings, with complete publishing information and annotations. Arranged in 35 geographical and topical sections, indexed by title and geographical area. Directory of publishers. Z6956.G6F94

Historical periodicals directory / Eric H. Boehm, Barbara H. Pope, and Marie S. Ensign, eds. Santa Barbara, Calif. : ABC-Clio, c1986. v. 5. **DA10**

For v. 1–4 and annotation, see *Guide* DA31.

Contents: v. 5, Australia and New Zealand (1986. 227 p.). Completes the set.

Vol. 5 includes cumulative title and subject/geographic indexes. Z6205.H654

Historiography

The Blackwell dictionary of historians / ed. by John Cannon . . . [et al]. N.Y. : Blackwell Reference, 1988. 480 p. ISBN 0-631-14708-X. $45.00. **DA11**

Also publ.: Oxford : Blackwell Reference, 1988.

Contains articles on terms, movements, historiography of particular countries, and "450 biographical entries which indicate the scholarly reputation of historians, the circumstances in which they worked, and the extent to which their work has subsequently been confirmed or refuted."—*Pref.* Includes about 50 entries for living historians. Most articles are two to three paragraphs in length and often end with a list of principal publications and secondary works. Entries are signed with the initials of contributing scholars, most of them British. Indexed. D14.B58

Cook, Chris. Dictionary of historical terms. 2nd ed. N.Y. : Peter Bedrick Books, 1990. 350 p. ISBN 0-87226-331-2. $34.95. **DA12**

1st ed., 1983 (*Guide* DA41). 2nd ed. also published as *Macmillan dictionary of historical terms* (London : Macmillan Reference, 1989).

Mainly an updating with a few new terms, such as "perestroika," or with a sentence or two added to cover the 1980s in such articles as those for "PLO" and "ZAPU," or the addition of a death date (e.g., Harold Macmillan's death date added in the article "Wind of change"). No index. D9.C67

Dictionnaire des sciences historiques / publié sous la direction de André Burguière. Paris : Presses universitaires de France, c1986. 693 p. ISBN 2-13-039361-6. **DA13**

A dictionary of broad topics (e.g., Africa, Bourgeoisie, Women, Revolution) with discussion of how they have been treated by French historians. Each article has a short bibliography of fairly recent materials (a few publications from the 1980s are included). Numerous page-length articles on noted French and German historians (e.g, Bloch, Froissart, Monod). Not indexed. D9.D57

Great historians from antiquity to 1800 : an international dictionary / Lucian Boia, ed. in chief. N.Y. : Greenwood, [1989]. 417 p. ISBN 0-313-24517-7. $65.00. **DA14**

Sponsored by the Commission on the History of Historiography of the International Commission on the Historical Sciences.

Two criteria for inclusion were: " 'absolute' merit of those individuals in the development of universal historiography and their significance within each national culture."—*Pref.* Signed articles are arranged by country or geographical area, e.g. Austrian, African, Southeast Asian, Islamic. Each entry covers the subject's life and contributions and includes a short bibliography of secondary works. Indexes of historians, subjects.

D14.G74

Lawton, Henry. The psychohistorian's handbook. N.Y. : Psychohistory Pr., c1988. 241 p. ISBN 0-914434-27-6.

DA15

Both a guide to psychohistory research and a bibliography of books and articles leading the researcher deeper into the field. The overview of the field cites major journals and associations, and considers such aspects as training, methodology, types of psychohistory, getting published, and teaching psychohistory. An appendix lists "Notable psychohistorical work." No index. D16.16.L38

Richardson, R. C. The study of history : a bibliographical guide. Manchester : Manchester Univ. Pr. ; N.Y. : Distr. by St. Martin's Pr., c1988. 98 p. ISBN 0-7190-1881-1. $35.00. **DA16**

A listing of books and articles on historiography arranged by broad period, then topically. Predominantly English-language materials with a scattering of French citations. "Concentrates on *modern* historians' views on the development of history; it does not list and evaluate the primary sources themselves."—*Pref.* Cross-references; author/editor/compiler index. Z6208.H5R53

Ritter, Harry. Dictionary of concepts in history. Westport, Conn. : Greenwood, 1986. 490 p. (Reference sources for the social sciences and humanities, no. 3.). ISBN 0-313-22700-4. $55.00. **DA17**

About 100 "key concepts of contemporary historical analysis" (*Pref.*) are discussed in short essays (e.g., Feudalism, Alienation, New history). For each, gives a short definition; historical development, usage, and evolution of the term; and sources of additional information. Cross-references; subject index.

D13.R49

Fellowships, grants, etc.

Grants, fellowships & prizes of interest to historians. [Wash.] : American Historical Association, Institutional Services Program, 1987– . Annual. **DA18**

Continues *Grants and fellowships of interest to historians* (*Guide* DA40), last published in 1986.

The 1989/90 edition is updated to contain over 300 listings for organizations. The title was changed to reflect a new section : Books, essays, and article awards and prizes.

D16.25.G69

Encyclopedias; Dictionaries

Dupuy, R. Ernest. The encyclopedia of military history from 3500 B.C. to the present / R. Ernest Dupuy and Trevor N. Dupuy. 2nd rev. ed. N.Y. : Harper & Row, c1986. 1524 p. : ill., maps. ISBN 0-06-181235-8. $39.95.

DA19

Previous ed., 1977 (*Guide* DA43).

Publ. in U.K. by Jane's, London.

Addendum, p. 1346–1400, covers events and developments 1975–84; otherwise, the text remains the same except for a few corrections. Separate index to addendum. D25.A2D8

Gurney, Gene. Kingdoms of Asia, the Middle East, and Africa : an illustrated encyclopedia of ruling monarchs from ancient times to the present. N.Y. : Crown, c1986. 438 p. : ill. ISBN 0-517-55256-6. **DA20**

A heavily illustrated survey of the history of dynasties and monarchies of each country, for all periods. Indexed by name of ruler. DS32.G87

Kohn, George C. Dictionary of wars. N.Y. : Facts on File, c1986. 586 p. ISBN 0-8160-1005-6. **DA21**

Intended to be a concise but comprehensive source for the major wars, revolutions, and rebellions, 2000 BCE to the present. The author defines war as "overt, armed conflict . . . between states . . . or between parties, factions, or people in the same state." Of primary concern in this work "is the military information, though political, social, and cultural influences are often specified."—*Pref.* Entries, arranged alphabetically, give the name(s) of the conflict, dates, how it began, opponents, leaders, concise descriptions or summaries of events, and outcome or significance. A geographic index is arranged by country, region, or polity, then chronologically. Name index.

D25.A2K63

Laffin, John. Brassey's battles : 3,500 years of conflict, campaigns, and wars from A–Z. London ; Wash. : Brassey's Defence Publishers, 1986. 484 p. : ill., maps. ISBN 0-08-031185-7. $30.00 (est.). **DA22**

Treats about 7,000 battles in dictionary arrangement. In general, follows the principle of "the more recent the event the longer the entry . . . . Recent conflicts deserve greater space if only because it is difficult for the average reader to find adequate consolidated information about events which are still in the news."—*Introd.* Includes various engagements not in David Eggenberger's *Dictionary of battles* (*Guide* DA44), but entries tend to be much less detailed in Brassey's table of "Major wars and their battles," p. 1–23. D25.A2L23

Chronologies, outlines, tables

Johnson, David E. From day to day : a calendar of notable birthdays and events / by David E. Johnson. Metuchen, N.J. : Scarecrow, 1990. 850 p. ISBN 0-8108-2354-3. **DA23**

Compiled to "present chronologically the highlights in history of each day of the year, and consider which noteworthy events occurred and which famous persons were born on the day."—*Pref.* At the beginning of each month discusses the name of the month and its length, followed by the list of events and the list of birthdays, each in chronological order. Over 15,000 entries with name index. A review in *Booklist* 87(15 Feb. 1991):1248 finds that "*From Day to Day* covers western history, American pop culture, and sports so extensively that it is a welcome addition to this body of literature." CT105.J64

Steinberg, S. H. Historical tables, 58 B.C.–A.D. 1985. 11th ed., updated by John Paxton. N.Y. : Garland, 1986. 277 p. ISBN 0-8240-8951-0. **DA24**

10th ed., 1979 (*Guide* DA60).

The medieval section has been enlarged and 1972–75 revised. Extends coverage to 1979, with a few tables summarizing events to 1985. D11.S83

Wetterau, Bruce. The New York Public Library book of chronologies. N.Y. : Prentice Hall, c1990. 634 p. ISBN 0-13-620451-1. $29.95. **DA25**

Provides 250 chronologies arranged by broad topic (e.g., under "Technology" are chronologies for prehistoric tools, clocks, photography, development of ships, the quest for speed). Boxes within some of the chronologies give added information, usually lists such as winners of Nobel prizes, British prime ministers, U.S. Supreme Court justices. Name index. D11.W47

Atlases

The Harper atlas of world history. N.Y. : Harper & Row, c1987. 340 p. : ill. (some col.), col. maps. ISBN 0-06-181884-4. $29.95.   **DA26**

Published in U.K. as: *Collins atlas of world history* (London : Collins, 1987. 340 p.).

Translation of: *Le grand livre de l'histoire du monde* (Paris : Hachette, 1986.)

Presents graphs, maps, reproductions, chronologies, texts, and photographs from the period of the Rift Valley to about 1986/87, with in some cases projections to the year 2000. Scales vary. The addition of a table of contents would be of great help; topical index. An update through 1989 was announced for publication in 1991.   G1030.G68513

Martin Greenwald Associates. Historical maps on file. N.Y. : Facts on File, c1984. 1 v. [looseleaf]) : 30 cm. ISBN 0-87196-708-1. $145.00 (without binder); $300.00 (with binder).   **DA27**

The 323 black-and-white maps were designed to be photocopied, hence are very simple, without much detail, and concentrate on depicting one aspect or historical development. Maps vary in size from about 6 $\frac{1}{4}$ x 4 $\frac{1}{2}$" to 6 x 8 $\frac{1}{2}$", and cover from the Ice Age to after the Korean War. Arranged by period or geographic area. 29-page index for geographical names.

§ *Time lines on file* (N.Y. : Facts on File, 1988. 300 p. $145.00), another looseleaf service, has about 200 charts giving time lines in world, European and American history, with separate displays for religion and ideas, culture and the arts, and science and technology.   G1030.M37

Natkiel, Richard. Atlas of maritime history / Richard Natkiel, Antony Preston. N.Y. : Facts on File, c1986. 256 p. : ill., maps in color ; 28 cm. ISBN 0-8160-1132-X.   **DA28**

Published in U.K. as *The Weidenfeld atlas of maritime history* (London : Weidenfeld and Nicolson, 1986).

Offers textual commentary with maps, drawings, and photographs covering from the Phoenicians to maritime trade in the 1980s. Emphasizes naval battles, explorations, and the evolving patterns of trade and commerce. Two-page glossary. Index of topics and names of people, places, and ships.

G1059.N3

Rand McNally atlas of world history / [gen. ed., R.I. Moore ; assoc. editors, Mark Greengrass and Bernard Wasserstein]. Rev. and updated 1987. Chicago : Rand McNally, [c1987]. 191 [i.e. 192] p.) : maps in color; 31 cm. ISBN 0-528-83288-3. $18.95.   **DA29**

1st ed., 1957; other eds., 1965 (*Guide* DA69), 1981.

Now includes some 88 maps from 23 contributors. Covers up to 1945, with a few later maps (e.g., Movement within the U.S. 1940–1970, Middle East since 1945). Textual comment for each map ends with "Suggestions for further reading." Place-names used in the maps conform to contemporary usage, so there is an index to reconcile the names. Topical index for maps and text.   G1030.R36

The Times atlas of world history / ed. by Geoffrey Barraclough. 3rd ed. / ed. by Norman Stone, repr. with rev. Maplewood, N.J. : Hammond Incorporated, c1989. 358 p. : col. ill., maps in color; 37 cm. ISBN 0-7230-0304-1. $85.00.   **DA30**

Rev. ed., 1984 (*Guide* DA71).

Plates show considerable revision especially in the prehistoric and post-1945 sections (e.g., the chapter "Origins of man" is totally revised and rewritten). The chronology is updated to 1989.   G1030.T54

ARCHAEOLOGY AND ANCIENT HISTORY

Guides

Woodhead, Peter. Keyguide to information sources in archaeology. London ; N.Y. : Mansell, 1985. 219 p. ISBN 0-7201-1745-3. $36.00.   **DA31**

A discussion of archaeological research, its relationship to other disciplines, and forms of archaeological literature is followed by an annotated bibliography of reference sources, topically arranged. The third part lists an archaeological organization for each country. Index of names, titles, and subjects.

CC120.W66

Bibliography

British archaeological abstracts. v. 1 (Apr. 1968)– . London : Council for British Archaeology, 1968– . Semiannual. ISSN 0007-0270.   **DA32**

Vol. 1, no. 1 preceded by an issue called v. 0 dated Autumn 1967.

Indexes journals for materials about archaeology in Great Britain and Ireland to 1600 CE. With the demise in 1981 of the *Archaeological bibliography for Great Britain and Ireland* (*Guide* DC249) this work assumed coverage of all articles on archaeology in 350 British and Irish periodicals as well as 360 other serials. Although coverage is now international, emphasis is still strongly British. Topical arrangement within a generally chronological framework. An index by name and topic appears in the second issue of each year.

§ The Council also issued *Archaeological site index to radiocarbon dates for Great Britain and Ireland* (London, 1971).

DA90.B82

Sovetskaia arkheologicheskaia literatura : bibliografiia, 1986–1989 / sostaviteli T.N. Zadneprovskaia, R.Sh. Levina, L.M. Vseviov. Leningrad : "Nauka," Leningradskoe otd-nie, 1986–89. v. [7–8]. (In progress).   **DA33**

For earlier volumes and annotation, see *Guide* DA92.

1976/78 and subsequent volumes have subtitle: *Bibliograficheskii ukazatel'*.

Contents: 1976–78, ed. T.N. Zadneprovskaia, R.Sh. Levina, L.M. Vseviov (1986. 383 p.); 1979–1981, ed. R.Sh. Levina, T.N. Zadneprovskaia, L.M. Vseviov (1989. 471 p.).

Z5131.Z33

Swedish archaeology. 1976–1980– . [Stockholm, Sweden] : Svenska arkeologiska samfundet, [c1983]– . Quinquennial.   **DA34**

Continues *Swedish archaeological bibliography* (*Guide* DA93), which ceased with 1971/75.

1976/80– , comp. Aake Hyehstrand and Pontus Hellström. 112 p.

Offers bibliographical essays by Swedish scholars discussing trends in the fields of archaeology with citations to the works discussed ending each essay. Citations to works on Nordic archaeology are now incorporated into *Nordic archaeological abstracts* (vol. covering 1971– publ. 1974– ; annual), but the references to classical archaeology remain in *Swedish archaeology*.   Z5111.S86

Encyclopedias; Dictionaries

Dictionnaire de la préhistoire / directeur de la publication, André Leroi-Gourhan. Paris : Pr. universitaires de France, c1988. 1222 p. (16 p. of plates) : ill. ISBN 2-13-041459-1. 495 F.   **DA35**

Contains definitions of terms and descriptions of the most important sites, together with entries for names of early cultures, prehistoric periods, etc. Signed articles, most of which end with one to three bibliographical references. See also *Encyclopedia of human evolution and prehistory* (*Supplement* CE13).
GN710.D53

Reallexikon der Assyriologie, unter Mitwirkung zahlreicher Fachgelehrter / hrsg. von Erich Ebeling . . . und Bruno Meissner. Berlin und Leipzig : W. de Gruyter & Co., 1987–1990. v. 7$^{1/2-7/8}$: ill. (In progress).   **DA36**

For annotation and earlier volumes, see *Guide* DA105. Vol. 6 was completed with fasc. 7/8.

Contents: v. 7$^{1/2-7/8}$, Libanukšabaš–Medizin (completes the volume).   DS69.1.R4

Atlases

Past worlds : the Times atlas of archaeology. Maplewood, N.J. : Hammond, [1988]. 319 p. : col. ill., maps in color ; 27 x 37 cm. ISBN 0-7230-0306-8. $85.00.   **DA37**

Intended to be a companion volume to *The Times atlas of world history* (*Guide* DA71).

Also called *Hammond past worlds.*

A handsome presentation through maps, photographs, charts and drawings of "world history, from the beginnings of human life down to the emergence of the modern world" (*Introd.*), i.e., from about 16 million BCE to 1800 CE. Representative sites or cultures are pictured within six broad chronological divisions. Includes a 10-page comparative chronology, a glossary of terms, an extensive name and subject index, and a short bibliography for each map.

§ Similar to *The world atlas of archaeology* (below), in that both are handsome volumes with much thought given to visual presentation, but each addresses areas or sites not covered by the other. While *Past worlds* employs a chronological framework with more attention to the European world, the geographical framework of the *World atlas* covers all areas more comprehensively.   G1046.E15P3

Roaf, Michael. Cultural atlas of Mesopotamia and the ancient Near East. N.Y. : Facts on File, c1990. 238 p. : ill. (some col.), maps in color. ISBN 0-8160-2218-6. $45.00.   **DA38**

Maps, text, photographs, and drawings "describe the highlights of human achievement . . . against the background of the geography of the region" (*Pref.*) from the early farmers of 12000 BCE to the last empires of 330 BCE. Chronological framework; glossary; gazetteer.   DS69.5.R63

The world atlas of archaeology. Boston : G.K. Hall, c1985. 423 p. : col. ill., maps in color ; 37 cm. ISBN 0-8161-8747-9. $65.00.   **DA39**

English edition of *Le grand atlas de l'archéologie* (Paris : Encyclopaedia Universalis, 1985).

Brief chronological surveys within a geographical arrangement, with photographs, maps, and line drawings. Covers from "The origin of man and his first habitats" (under Africa) through "Industrial archaeology" (under Modern period—a catch-all section and the only one that is not geographical). Bibliography (p. 394–403); glossary; index by topic.
G1046.E15W6

General histories

The Cambridge ancient history / ed. by John Boardman . . . [et al.]. 2nd ed. London ; N.Y. : Cambridge Univ. Pr., 1982–88. v. 3^3, 4, 8 : ill., maps. (In progress).   **DA40**

For previously published volumes and annotation, see *Guide* DA112.

Contents: v. 3, pt. 3, The expansion of the Greek world, eighth to sixth century B.C. / ed. John Boardman, N.G.L. Hammond (2nd ed., 1982. 530 p.); v. 4, Persia, Greece and the Western Mediterranean c.525–479 B.C. / ed. John Boardman . . . [et al.]. (2nd ed., 1988. 960 p. $105.00); and plates to v. 4, ed. John Boardman (called new ed. 1988. 264 p. $67.50); v. 8, Rome and the Mediterranean to 133 B.C., ed. A.E. Astin et al. (2nd ed., 1989. 625 p.).   D57.C252

Classical antiquities

Encyclopedias

Civilization of the ancient Mediterranean : Greece and Rome / ed. by Michael Grant and Rachel Kitzinger. N.Y. : Scribner's, c1988. 3 v. (1980 p.) : ill. ISBN 0-684-17594-0. $195.00.   **DA41**

Some 100 signed articles arranged topically within broad subject areas—e.g., Political and social life—with articles thereunder on topics such as folklore, athletes, and medicine. Each article is thorough and well written and concludes with a substantive bibliography. Coverage is from 1000 BCE to the fifth century CE. Index; chronology.   DE59.C55

Classical scholarship : a biographical encyclopedia / ed. by Ward W. Briggs and William M. Calder III. N.Y. : Garland, 1990. 396 p. : ports. (Garland reference library of the humanities, vol. 928). ISBN 0-8240-8448-9. $110.00.   **DA42**

Presents biographies of some 50 outstanding scholars active in the "modern period" of 1977–86, "whose lives amounted to more than just bibliographies."—*Pref.* For each classicist there is a signed essay describing career and importance to the field, with a photograph or portrait. Appended to each is a bibliography of the subject's books and articles, and sources subdivided into Autobiography, Bibliography, Biography, Letters, Papers. Chronological list of biographies; list of contributors.
PA83.C58

Handbooks

Grant, Michael. The Roman emperors : a biographical guide to the rulers of imperial Rome, 31 BC–AD 476. 1st U.S. ed. N.Y. : Scribner's, 1985. 367 p. : ill. ISBN 0-684-18388-9. $25.00.   **DA43**

A chronological presentation of the lives and backgrounds of 92 Roman emperors to 476 CE. Very readable biographies. Includes genealogical tables; portraits from coins caused to be minted by the emperors; list of Latin technical terms. Index to maps and plans.   DG274.G73

Chronologies

Lauffer, Siegfried. Daten der griechischen und römischen Geschichte. München : Deutscher Taschenbuch Verlag, [1987]. 444 p. ISBN 3-423-03275-8. **DA44**

Arranged by year within two broad sections: Greece 5000–30 BCE; Rome 5000 BCE–500 CE. For each year, gives a sentence identifying each major event. Indexes for personal names and for places and topics. DE86.L37x

Atlases

Atlas of classical history / ed. by Richard J. A. Talbert. London : Croom Helm ; N.Y. : Macmillan, c1985. 217 p. : 26 cm. ISBN 0-02-933110-2. **DA45**

Reissued: London : Routledge, [1988].

" . . . a volume in which lucid maps [offer] the high school student and the undergraduate a reasonably comprehensive, up-to-date, and scholarly coverage of classical history down to the time of Constantine, accompanied by modest elucidation of the material and by some suggestions for further reading."— *Pref.* Covers Greek and Roman history from Troy and Knossos to the Roman Empire in 314 CE. The black-and-white maps, though small, are very clear. Many city maps. The text is brief, in many cases good mainly for identification, a skeletal history, or verification of a few key dates. Suggestions for further reading, p.179–89. Place name index with name, page, and coordinates. G1033.A833

MEDIEVAL AND RENAISSANCE

Bibliography

Toronto medieval bibliographies. Toronto : Univ. of Toronto Pr., 1986–88. v. 10–11. (In progress). **DA46**

For numbers 1–9, see *Guide* DA156.

Contents: no. 10, Chaucer, a bibliographical introduction, by John Leyerle and Anne Quick ([1986]. 321 p.); no. 11, Medieval Christian literary imagery : a guide to interpretation, R.E. Kaske ([1988]. 247 p.)

Encyclopedias

Bergin, Thomas Goddard. Encyclopedia of the Renaissance / Thomas G. Bergin, Jennifer Speake. N.Y. : Facts on File, c1987. 454 p., [32] p. of plates : ill. (some col.). ISBN 0-8160-1315-2. **DA47**

Brief articles on all aspects of the Renaissance (the period of 1300–1620 in Europe) in alphabetical arrangement, with cross-references. A bibliography for further reading is divided into primary and secondary materials. Includes a chronological table with columns for politics and secular events, religion, emperors, kings and princes. CB361.B43

Broughton, Bradford B. Dictionary of medieval knighthood and chivalry. N.Y. : Greenwood, 1986–1988. 2 v. ISBN 0-313-24552-5. $67.95 (v.1). ISBN 0-313-25347-1. $55.00 (v.2). **DA48**

Contents: v. 1, Concepts and terms (597 p.); v. 2, People, places, and events (774 p.)

Intended "to help students understand the background of some of the literary works they were reading in medieval literature courses."—*Acknowledgments.* Provides definitions, explanations, or identification of ideas and concepts, major figures, social customs and mores, events, and information a knight was expected to know (e.g. conduct, weapons, feast days, currency). Concentrates on England and France, 1050–1400. Most entries include reference to a specific title in a numbered bibliography of 394 books and articles. Topical index for each volume. CR4505.B76

Dictionary of the Middle Ages / Joseph R. Strayer, ed. in chief. N.Y. : Scribner's, c1985–1989. v. 6–13 : ill. ISBN 0-684-19073-7. $70.00/vol. **DA49**

For v. 1–5 and annotation, see *Guide* DA164.

Contents: v. 6–12, Grosseteste–Zwartnoc; v. 13, Index. Completes the set.

The index offers entries for people, places, and concepts; it includes cross-references but does not "entirely replace the existing system of parenthetical and blind-entry headings and *see also* references at the end of the articles." —*Accessus*. There is a list of contributors with titles of articles written by each; an errata list for v.1–12; and a discussion of the treatment and alphabetizing of particular languages (e.g., Arabic), titles (e.g., anonymous works), or topics (e.g., law). D114.D5

Lexikon des Mittelalters / [hrsg. von Robert Auty . . . et al.]. München ; Zürich : Artemis-Verlag, [1984–1990]. Bd. 3¹⁻¹⁰–5⁶. (In progress). **DA50**

For earlier volumes and annotation, see *Guide* DA165.

Contents: Bd. 3–5, Lfg. 6, Codex Wintoniensis–Konrad.

Bd. 3 and 4 are each complete in 10 Lieferungen. D101.5.L49

The Middle Ages : a concise encyclopaedia / general ed., H.R. Loyn. N.Y. : Thames and Hudson, 1989. 352 p. : ill. maps. ISBN 0-500-25103-7. $39.95. **DA51**

"The overriding aim throughout has been to provide both beginner and specialist with a single volume that presents a summary of current thought on the key protagonists, events and themes relating to the history of Europe from c.400 to c.1500."—*p.[5]*. Entries for individuals, battles, events, and sites are brief, usually only a paragraph; the "theme" articles (e.g., Jews, Climate, Handwriting) are several columns in length and are signed. Most articles have at least one bibliographic citation. Not indexed. Very useful for ready reference; good illustrations. CB351.M565

Directories

Répertoire international des médiévistes = International directory of medievalists. 6th ed. Paris ; N.Y. : Saur, 1987. 2 v. (1259 p.). ISBN 3-598-10683-1. **DA52**

5th ed., 1979 (*Guide* AJ55).

Compiled by the Institut de Recherche et d'Histoire des Textes.

A list of the "scientific activities" of some 5,000 "medievalists worldwide from 1974 to 1980."—*Pref.* Subject index by broad fields refers by item number to entry for biographee. A 7th ed. was published in 1990 ([Tournhout, Belgium] : Brepols). D112.R512

Byzantine studies

The Oxford dictionary of Byzantium / Alexander P. Kazhdan, ed. in chief. N.Y. : Oxford Univ. Pr., 1991. 3 v. (li, 2232 p.) : ill., maps. ISBN 0-19-504652-8. **DA53**

Prepared at Dumbarton Oaks, Washington, D.C.

A major reference source for information on Byzantine "saints, patriarchs, all emperors, writers, places, fiscal and administrative concepts" (*Pref.*) of the 4th–15th centuries, including few classical authors with focus "on the transmission and knowledge of their writings in Byzantium." Over 100 contributors; emphasizes interdisciplinary coverage. Major survey articles (with cross-references designated by small capitals) and many shorter articles on lesser topics. Special attention to everyday life: e.g., articles on diet, the family, gesture, emotions. Bibliographical notes at the end of articles include references to the most recent scholarship, to the best editions of texts, and to major studies. Illustrations include photographs of art works, buildings, etc., and there are maps and genealogies. No index.

DF521.O93

Crusades

Riley-Smith, Jonathan Simon Christopher. The atlas of the Crusades. N.Y. : Facts on File, 1990. 192 p. : col. ill., maps ; 29 cm. ISBN 0-8160-2186-4. $40.00.   **DA54**

A chronological presentation with narrative supplemented by colored maps, photographs, and drawings. Chronology; glossary; place-name index with some subject entries and cross-references.   G1034.R5

MODERN

Bibliography

Bibliographies in history / foreword by Eric H. Boehm. Santa Barbara, Calif. : ABC-Clio, c1988. 2 v. ISBN 0-87436-521-X. $137.50.   **DA55**

Contents: v. 1, [U.S. and Canada]; v. 2, [Rest of the world].

Reprints citations with abstracts retrieved by searching the databases used to generate *Historical abstracts* (*Guide* DA19–21) and *America: history and life* (*Guide* DB47) under the terms "Bibliography" and "Bibliographies." Most entries are from the 1970s and 1980s, but a few date from 1965 to 1969.

§ Other bibliographies drawn from the *HA* and *AHL* databases, all published in Santa Barbara, Calif. by ABC-Clio: *Africa since 1914 : a historical bibliography* (*Guide* DD3); *American maritime history : a bibliography* (1986. 260 p. $31.50.); *The American presidency : a historical bibliography* (*Guide* CJ117); *The American South : a historical bibliography* (1986. 2 v. $127.50); *Communism in the world since 1945 : an annotated bibliography* (*Supplement* CJ238); *The dynamic Constitution : a historical bibliography* (*Supplement* CK115); *Global terrorism : a historical bibliography* (1986. 168 p. $40.00); *The great depression : a historical bibliography* (*Guide* DB112); *Historiography : an annotated bibliography of journal articles, books, and dissertations* (1987. 2 v. $85.00); *Labor in America : a historical bibliography* (*Supplement* CH274); *Latin American politics : a historical bibliography* (*Guide* CJ393); *Latinos in the United States : a historical bibliography* (*Supplement* CC237); *The Middle East in conflict : a historical bibliography* (*Guide* DE47); *Military history of the United States : an annotated bibliography* (1986. 333 p.); *People in history : an index to U.S. and Canadian biographies in history journals and dissertations* (1988. 2 v. $147.00); *People in world history : an index to biographies in history journals and dissertations covering all countries of the world except Canada and the U.S.* (1989. 2 v. $175.00); *Sino-Soviet conflict : a historical bibliography* (*Guide* DC542); *Women in American history : a bibliography* (*Supplement* CC283); *Women in the Third World : a historical bibliography* (*Supplement* CC277).

All these titles employ SPIndex, a rotated index of names and topics that refers to citation numbers in the bibliographic list.   Z1236.B48

Edelheit, Abraham J. The Jewish world in modern times : a selected, annotated bibliography / Abraham J. Edelheit and Hershel Edelheit. Boulder, Colo. : Westview ; London, England : Mansell, 1988. 569 p. ISBN 0-8133-0572-1. $65.00.   **DA56**

Companion to the compilers' *Bibliography on Holocaust literature* (*Supplement* DA81).

Designed to "place modern Jewish history into both universal and local contexts."—*p. iv.* English-language books, pamphlets, and articles are arranged topically within two sections: Pt. I, The Jewish world [listing general discussions]; Pt. II, The Jewish community [subdivided geographically]. Includes a brief introductory essay surveying Jewish history since the 1650s. Author, title, and subject indexes.   Z6372.E25

Huck, Burkhardt J. Informationshandbuch internationale Beziehungen und Länderkunde = Information handbook international relations and area studies / Dietrich Seydel (Hrsg.) ; bearb. von Burkhardt J. Huck. Baden-Baden : Nomos, [1989]. 752 p. (Internationale Politik und Sicherheit, Bd. 26). ISBN 3-7890-1757-4.   **DA57**

A classed arrangement of handbooks, encyclopedias and dictionaries, bibliographies, databases (and directories of databases), journals, and guides to government publications. Indexes of authors, sponsoring bodies, titles, and geographical areas.

Novaia istoriia : ukazatel' literatury, izdannoĭ v SSSR na russkom iazyke, 1917–1940 / [sostaviteli I.I. Korndorf ... et al.]. Moskva : Izd-vo Moskovskogo universiteta, 1986–1988. v. 2, pt. 1–2.   **DA58**

For chast I, see *Guide* DA185.

Contents: chast II, vyp. 1, Vtoroĭ period noveĭsheĭ istorii, 1871–1918 gg.; chast II, vyp. 2, Vtoroĭ period novoĭ istorii, 1871–1918 gg.

Continues the series covering writings on modern history published 1917–40.   Z6204.N683

Encyclopedias; Dictionaries

Brownstone, David M. Dictionary of 20th-century history / David M. Brownstone, Irene M. Franck. N.Y. : Prentice Hall, c1990. 444 p. ISBN 0-13-209883-0. $24.95.   **DA59**

"... our main aim has been to identify and briefly discuss the central events, people, movements, ideas and discoveries of the twentieth century. Our main focus has been on political, military, economic, religious, scientific and medical matters."—*Pref.* A few cultural topics are included but the publishers plan to issue a dictionary for 20th-century culture. Most entries are one paragraph long, giving identification or definition and a brief history, though a few entries are quite lengthy (e.g., nearly two columns on AIDS). Events covered are as recent as Ivan Boesky and the insider trading scandal (1986), but the country entries are more current; for example, coverage for the Philippines extends to December 1989. No bibliography; cross-references.

§ See also S.R. Gibbons, *A handbook of modern history* (London : Longmans, 1986. 271 p.) which is an alphabetical arrangement of about 450 articles on world history since 1870. Indexed.   D419.B76

Chronologies

Chase's annual events. 1984 (27th year)– . Chicago: Contemporary Books, c1983– . $29.95. **DA60**

Subtitle: An almanac and survey of the year: a calendar of holidays, holy days, national and ethnic days, seasons, astronomical phenomena, festivals and fairs, anniversaries, birthdays, special events and traditional observances of all kinds, the World over.

Formerly: *Chase's calendar of annual events*, 1958–83.

The 1990 edition covers some 9,000 events in a chronological arrangement. Besides the categories listed in the subtitle, includes significant historical events from the past 50 years, presidential proclamations, names and addresses of sponsoring organizations, and birthdays of famous people. Special tables of hurricanes, time zones, major awards, and an anniversary gift list. Well indexed. GT4803.C48

Annuals and current surveys

Facts on file five year index, 1981–1985. N.Y.: Facts on File [etc.], 1986. 1021 p. **DA61**

For earlier cumulations of the index and a description to the weekly news digest, see *Guide* DA193.

●**Facts on File news digest CD-ROM** [computer file]. N.Y.: Facts on File, 1980– . **DA62**

Machine-readable version of *Facts on file: world news digest with index* (*Guide* DA193).

Disk covering 1980–90, $695.00 for Facts on File subscribers, $795.00 for others; annual update, $195.00.

Full text of printed version. Updated annually.

Atlases

Atlas of modern world history / editorial advisers Haydn Middleton, Derek Heater. Oxford: Oxford Univ. Pr., c1989. [64] p.: ill. (some col.), maps in color, facsims. (some col.), ports. (some col.). ISBN 0-19-831677-1. £7.95. **DA63**

Begins with the unification of Italy, but covers mostly 20th-century history to the "Victims of wars 1945–1985." Small maps with brief captions; time line 1900–80. Most maps concentrate on a single feature. Cross-references to related sections; not indexed. G1030

Friesel, Evyatar. Atlas of modern Jewish history. Rev. from the Hebrew ed. N.Y.: Oxford Univ. Pr., 1990. 159 p.: col. ill., maps in color; 31 cm. ISBN 0-19-505393-1. $49.95. **DA64**

Revised and updated from Hebrew edition, Aṭlas Karṭa le-toldot 'Am Yiśra'el ba-zeman he-ḥadash, 1983.

Offers maps, charts, and drawings portraying Jewish history in the world from the late 19th century to the 1980s. Concentrates on demography and history, but economic, ideological and religious developments are also featured. Four-page bibliography; index of geographical names; general index of other names. G1030.F6513

The World Wars

Bibliography

Enser, A. G. S. A subject bibliography of the First World War: books in English, 1914–1987. [Aldershot, England]; Brookfield, Vt.: Gower, [1990]. 412 p. ISBN 0-566-05619-4. $69.95. **DA65**

Companion to *A subject bibliography of the Second World War...* (below). A topical arrangement of books, including memoirs, published 1914–87. Cross-references are used sparingly. Author and anonymous title indexes; list of subject headings used. Z6207.E8E58

———— A subject bibliography of the Second World War, and aftermath: books in English, 1975–1987. [Aldershot, England]; Brookfield, Vt.,: Gower, c1990. 287 p. ISBN 0-566-05736-0. **DA66**

Continues the author's *A subject bibliography of the Second World War: books in English 1939–1974* (*Guide* DA201) and supersedes its continuation covering 1975–83 (1985).

Adds an additional 1,600 titles, including a section under each country on the aftermath of the war. Arrangement is by subject as in earlier volumes and there is a list of headings at the end of the volume. Author index. Z6207.W8E56

Law, Derek G. The Royal Navy in World War Two: an annotated bibliography. [London]: Greenhill Books, [1988]. 305 p. ISBN 1-85367-002-2. £25.00. **DA67**

Cites books published in English up to 1987, topically arranged in four sections: (1) Campaign histories; (2) Allied unit histories; (3) The Axis forces; (4) Technical studies and miscellanea. Emphasis is on the "operational histories, campaign histories and biographies of the Royal Navy, the Dominion Navies, and the other Allied Navies" (*Scope notes*), although there are sections for art, literature, etc. Extensive cross-references; author, title and ship name indexes. Z6207.W8L38

Neue Forschungen zum Ersten Weltkrieg : Literaturberichte und Bibliographien von 30 Mitgliedstaaten der "Commission internationale d'histoire militaire comparée" / Herausgeber, Jürgen Rohwer. Koblenz: Bernard & Graefe, c1985. 406 p. (Schriften der Bibliothek für Zeitgeschichte, Bd. 25). ISBN 3-7637-0231-8. **DA68**

A state-of-the-art account of research as of 1989/90 on World War I, for "as many countries as possible with a select bibliography."—*Pref.* For some countries the author includes a brief survey of that country's participation in the war. Author/editor index. D522.42.N48

Noffsinger, James Philip. World War I aviation books in English: an annotated bibliography. Metuchen, N.J.: Scarecrow, 1987. 305 p., [16] p. of plates: ill. ISBN 0-8108-1951-1. **DA69**

An author listing of more than 1,650 books and government publications in English, most with short annotations. A brief subject index includes references to items relating to specific squadrons or units. Z6207.E8N64

Sbrega, John J. The war against Japan, 1941–1945: an annotated bibliography. N.Y.: Garland, 1989. 1050 p. ISBN 0-8240-8940-5. **DA70**

Lists English-language books, articles, novels, and documents (including declassified military reports) issued through 1987. Arrangement is by broad subject, subdivided topically. All aspects are included—diplomatic, political, economic, military, social and cultural, religious. Author and subject indexes; chronology. Z6207.W8S299

Smith, Myron J. World War II at sea : a bibliography of sources in English, 1974–1989. Metuchen, N.J. : Scarecrow, 1990. 304 p. ISBN 0-8108-2260-1. $32.50. **DA71**

Constitutes a supplement to the compiler's 1976 bibliography (*Guide* DA207). Provides citations for some 3,600 books, articles, and documents in English, including some earlier works inadvertently omitted from the 1976 compilation.

Z6207.W8S572

Tutorow, Norman E. War crimes, war criminals, and war crimes trials : an annotated bibliography and source book / comp. and ed. by Norman E. Tutorow with the special assistance of Karen Winnovich. N.Y. : Greenwood, [1986]. 548 p. (Bibliographies and indexes in world history, 4). ISBN 0-313-24412-X. **DA72**

A classified bibliography of 4,500 items mainly relating to war crimes of World War II and the subsequent war crimes trials, but including sections for earlier war crimes, general background, and subsidiary topics. Aims to be "representative" rather than exhaustive, with an admitted emphasis on American materials (books, periodical articles, and government documents). Author and subject index. Z6464.W33T87

Woodward, David R. America and World War I : a selected annotated bibliography of English-language sources / David R. Woodward, Robert Franklin Maddox. N.Y. : Garland, 1985. 368 p. (Wars of the United States, vol. 6 ; Garland reference library of social science, v. 259). ISBN 0-8240-8939-1. **DA73**

A classified, briefly annotated bibliography of more than 2,000 items, with author and subject indexes. Encompasses works which examine the war's impact on society as well as those relating to military operations. Z6207.E8W67

Encyclopedias

Bruce, A. P. C. An illustrated companion to the First World War. London ; N.Y. : Joseph, 1989. 424 p. : ill., maps. ISBN 0-7181-2781-1. £19.95. **DA74**

An alphabetical arrangement of some 800 entries, mainly political, military, and biographical with 200 contemporary photographs, most of them drawn from the collections of the Imperial War Museum, London. Chronology; short bibliography; not indexed. For general collections. D521.B7

Hogg, Ian V. Encyclopaedia of the Second World War / by Ian V. Hogg & Bryan Perrett. [Novato, Calif.] : Presidio Pr., c1989. 447 p. : ill., maps. ISBN 0-89141-362-6. $40.00. **DA75**

A general dictionary of "personalities, campaigns, battles, events, warships, aircraft, land warfare weapons, electronic warfare, intelligence, abbreviations, and operational codenames."—*Pref.* Short articles give a person's career during the war, summary of a battle, definition of term or abbreviation, location of a place name. Three-page bibliography; cross-references. Lacks an index. D740.H64

Wheal, Elizabeth-Anne. A dictionary of the Second World War / Elizabeth-Anne Wheal, Stephen Pope and James Taylor. London : Grafton, [1989]. 541, [46] p., [24] p. of plates : ill., maps. ISBN 0-246-13391-0. **DA76**

Includes articles on "actions and events, personalities and politics, men and machines . . . [as well as] comprehensive generic entries for each major war theatre and on the armed forces and decisive weapons of the combatants"—*How to use this book.* Cross-references within articles, no index. Appendix of chronologies. Useful for quick reference. D743.W

Chronologies, outlines, tables

Gray, Randal. Chronicle of the First World War / Randal Gray and Christopher Argyle. N.Y. : Facts on File, 1990. v. 1. ISBN 0-8160-2139-2 (v. 1). (In progress). **DA77**

Contents: v. 1, 1914–16 (420 p. $40.00).

A chronology arranged in nine parallel columns, each column (with subheading) representing a military site or theater of war: The Western front, Home fronts, Eastern front, African operations, Southern fronts, Turkish fronts, Sea war, International events, Air war. Tables give statistics for important military operations and for the overall war. A glossary defines wartime terminology and abbreviations, and there are maps of fronts and battles, a bibliography (p. 309–13) arranged by topic, and an index to main events. D523.G634

Atlases

Pitt, Barrie. The chronological atlas of World War II / Barrie and Frances Pitt. London : Macmillan, c1989. 178 p. : some maps in color ; 36 x 27 cm. ISBN 0-671-68880-4. **DA78**

Published in U.S. as *The month-by-month atlas of World War II.*

Offers a month-by-month account of the war, emphasizing "the panorama of the war . . . so that not only could the progress of each individual compaign and battle be followed, but also their relationship to the whole global conflict."—*Author's note.* For each month, a double-page spread gives: a world map showing advances and contractions in the territory controlled by the Germans and Japanese; more detailed maps for specific battles; and a summary of military events. Also includes essays on compaigns (e.g., Barbarossa, D-Day) or political history (e.g., The world in Autumn 1945). Index of place names divided by Eastern, European and Middle Eastern, and Pacific fronts; index of political and military names and events. G1038.P6

The Times atlas of the Second World War / ed. by John Keegan. London : Times Books ; N.Y. : Harper & Row, c1989. 254 p. : ill. (some col.), some maps in color ; 37 cm. ISBN 0-06-016178-7. $50.00. **DA79**

Covers the war in maps, charts, photographs, and brief essays, beginning with Europe after the First World War and continuing through 1945. The arrangement is roughly chronological, then area by area. Besides military aspects, sections for The world war economies, The casualties, Resistance in Eastern Europe. One-page bibliography, glossary of personal names, lists of abbreviations and of battles (locating them); index of place names (referring to specific maps); chronology for each area. G1038.T6

Holocaust

Cargas, Harry J. The Holocaust : an annotated bibliography. 2nd ed. Chicago : Amer. Lib. Assoc., 1985. 196 p. ISBN 0-8389-0433-5. $27.95 (est.). **DA80**

1st ed., Haverford, Pa. : Catholic Library Assoc., 1977.

Contains critical annotations in classified arrangement of approximately 500 books published in English in the U.S. Includes a chapter on "Researching the Holocaust, guidance for students." Regional indexes by nation and by concentration camp; index by author and title. Compiler calls himself "a post-Auschwitz Catholic." Z6374.H6C37

Edelheit, Abraham J. Bibliography on Holocaust literature / Abraham J. Edelheit and Hershel Edelheit. Boulder, Colo. : Westview Pr., 1986. 842 p. ISBN 0-8133-7233-X. $80.00. **DA81**

Contains 9,014 entries for English-language books, periodicals, and pamphlets; selected book entries are annotated. Entries are arranged chronologically by four periods and in classified order within periods. Detailed table of contents; index of authors. Z6374.H6E33

———————— Bibliography on Holocaust literature. Supplement / Abraham J. Edelheit and Hershel Edelheit. Boulder, Colo. : Westview Pr., 1990. 684 p. ISBN 0-8133-0896-8. **DA82**

Contains 5,637 additional English-language entries arranged in the same order as the 1986 work. To the historical sections of the original work, it adds sections on: Reflections on the Holocaust, The Holocaust in literature and art, Distorting the Holocaust, Historiography, Dissertations, Bibliographies, Guides. Detailed table of contents, glossary, author/title index, subject index. Z6374.H6E33

Encyclopedia of the Holocaust / Yisrael Gutman, ed. in chief. N.Y. : Macmillan, c1990. 4 v. : ill., maps. ISBN 0-02-896090-4 (set). **DA83**

Offers 100 signed articles, clearly written, with short bibliographies. Includes entries for "individual names, major events, the countries involved, the concentraton camps, the ghettos, the extermination camps and murder sites, political movements and trends and resistance movements."—*Pref.* Also covers antecedents (e.g., Antisemitism, Protocols of the Elders of Zion) and the postwar impact (Psychology of Holocaust survivors, Museum and memorial institutes). Alphabetical arrangement with subject index. Glossary; chronology; table giving estimates of Jewish victims by country; sentences resulting from the Nuremberg trials. D804.3.E53

Fortunoff Video Archive for Holocaust Testimonies. Guide to Yale University Library Holocaust video testimonies. N.Y. : Garland, 1990. v. 1. ISBN 0-8240-6043-1 (v. 1). (In progress). **DA84**

This first volume describes 255 accounts of "videotape witnesses of the Holocaust (survivors, liberators, bystanders) from the initial persecution in 1933 to the liberation of the camps in 1945."—*Pref.* Each interviewee is identified only by initial of last name. For each entry gives interviewer, date, place and number of interviews; length; brief summary; and format. Subject index. D804.3.F67

Gilbert, Martin. Atlas of the Holocaust. Oxford ; N.Y. : Pergamon, 1988. 256 p. : ill. ; 25 cm. ISBN 0-08-036761-5 (pbk.). $17.95 (est.). **DA85**

Presents 314 maps that "show in chronological sequence, the destruction of each of the main Jewish communities of Europe, as well as acts of resistance and revolt, avenues of escape and rescue, and the fate of individuals."—*Introd.* Many of the maps show locations of Jewish communities in regions of Europe with indication of the number of Jews killed in specific towns and villages. An 8-½ page list of sources includes the map number for each (but the alphabetical arrangement of the sources means that the accompanying map numbers are not in sequence). Index by name of concentration camp or mass murder site. Basically a reprint with a few corrections of *Macmillan atlas of the Holocaust* (N.Y. : Macmillan; London : Michael Joseph, 1982. 256 p.). G1797.21.E29G58

The Holocaust : an annotated bibliography and resource guide / ed. by David M. Szonyi. [Hoboken, N.J.] : Ktav Pub. House for the National Jewish Resource Center, New York, c1985. 396 p. ISBN 0-88125-057-0. $29.50. ISBN 0-88125-058-9 (pbk.). $16.95. **DA86**

Identifies and annotates a wealth of material: primary and secondary print sources, audiovisual materials, music, exhibits, education centers, U.S. and Canadian memorials and landmarks, survivor groups, resources for religious services, and

funding sources for research and programming. Arranged in classified order, but there is no index.

§ See also Martin Sable's *Holocaust studies : a directory and bibliography of bibliographies* (Greenwood, Fla. : Penkeville, [1987]. 115 p.) for a listing with addresses of relevant organizations, associations, information and research centers, government agencies, libraries and archives, schools and universities, monuments and sculptures. Z6374.H6H65

Laska, Vera. Nazism, resistance & Holocaust in World War II : a bibliography. Metuchen, N.J. : Scarecrow, 1985. 183 p. ISBN 0-8108-1771-3. $20.00. **DA87**

Cites over 1,900 books relating to resistance to Nazi occupiers, Jewish and non-Jewish victims, partisans, war crimes, art and photography, and literature within 13 categories. Some entries are annotated, others rely on subtitle for indication of content. Author index. Z6374.H6L37

Skirball, Sheba F. Films of the Holocaust : an annotated filmography of collections in Israel. N.Y. : Garland, [1990]. 273 p., [8] p. of plates : ill. (Garland filmographies, 2 ; Garland reference library of social science, v. 463). ISBN 0-8240-5847-X. **DA88**

Sponsored by the Steven Spielberg Jewish Film Archive, Jerusalem.

An inventory of films and videotapes in libraries and archives in Jerusalem and Tel Aviv, including newsreels, television clips, commercially produced films, etc. Arranged by title, with a separate listing by date for untitled films. Subject index; language index.

§ See also Charles Lawrence Gellert's *The Holocaust, Israel and the Jews : motion pictures in the National Archives* (Wash. : Publ. for NARA by National Archives Trust Fund Board, 1989. 117 p. $17.00). About 600 films are listed, described and indexed. D804.3.S59

DB

The Americas

UNITED STATES

Guides to research

Prucha, Francis Paul. Handbook for research in American history : a guide to bibliographies and other reference works. Lincoln : Univ. of Nebraska Pr., c1987. 289 p. ISBN 0-8032-3682-4. $21.95 ; $9.95 (pbk.). **DB1**

"The purpose of this handbook is to introduce beginning historians to the help that awaits them in the reference sections of the library."—*Introd.* Pt. 1 features essays on types and formats of reference books (e.g., library catalogs, periodical indexes and abstracts, databases, book review indexes, government publications guides, and bibliographies). Pt. 2 covers individual disciplines (e.g., foreign affairs, women, local history, religion, economics). Some 1,500 works are described and annotated. Emphasis is on more recent publications. Author, title, subject index. A major guide for historians.   Z1236.P78

Bibliography

See also Diaries; Letters in Section BD.

America on film and tape : a topical catalog of audiovisual resources for the study of United States history, society, and culture / Howard B. Hitchens, general ed. ; Vidge Hitchens, associate ed. Westport, Conn. : Greenwood, [1985]. 392 p. (Bibliographies and indexes in American history, no. 3). ISBN 0-313-24778-1.   **DB2**

A topically arranged listing of 16mm films, 35mm slide sets, audio cassettes, video recordings, and filmstrips for secondary and post-secondary students. Feature films are included only if available for educational use. Each entry indicates title, format, sound or silent, color or black-and-white, distributor, date, length, and a brief description. List of distributors with addresses; list of titles.   E169.1.A471873

American studies : an annotated bibliography / ed. by Jack Salzman on behalf of the American Studies Association. Cambridge ; N.Y. : Cambridge Univ. Pr., [1986]. 3 v. (2058 p.). ISBN 0-521-32555-2. $175.00.   **DB3**

Expands and updates *American studies: an annotated bibliography of works on the civilization of the United States* (Wash. : U.S. Information Agency, 1982), to include books written through 1983. Arranged under 11 broad topics, each beginning with a preface which is a bibliographical essay on relevant reference works, followed by an annotated listing of studies grouped according to smaller topics. Unfortunately, there is no outline of the arrangement. Author, title, subject indexes in v. 3. A supplement covering 1984–88 was published by Cambridge Univ. Pr. (1085 p.) in 1990.   Z1361.C6A436

Church and state in America : a bibliographical guide / ed. by John F. Wilson. N.Y. : Greenwood, 1986–c1987. 2 v. ISBN 0-313-25236-X (v.1). ISBN 0-313-25914-3 (v.2).   **DB4**

Contents: v. 1, The colonial and early national periods (433 p.); v. 2, The Civil War to the present day (452 p.).

Sponsored by the Princeton Project of Church and State.

In signed bibliographical essays devoted mostly to historical periods, with additional chapters on education, law, and gender relations, the compilers cite books, articles, bibliographies, and primary sources of the last 25 years (with a few older materials). Index for authors and subjects cited in the essays but not for the bibliographies that follow the essays, which include additional citations.   Z7776.72.C48

Coletta, Paolo Enrico. A selected and annotated bibliography of American naval history. Lanham, Md. : Univ. Pr. of America, c1988. 523 p. ISBN 0-8191-7111-5. $39.50.   **DB5**

A revision and updating of Coletta's *A bibliography of American naval history*, 1981 (*Guide* DB23). More than 60% of the entries from the previous edition were dropped to make room for more recent ones. Now includes more than 4,600 entries with cutoff date of 1987. The subject index has been expanded, but references to specific ships are now in the author index. An appendix lists Secretaries of the Navy and Chiefs of Naval Operations. The earlier volume will still be useful for older materials.   Z1249.N3C64

Dare, Philip N. American communes to 1860 : bibliography. N.Y. : Garland, 1990. 203 p. (Sects and cults in America. Bibliographical guides, v. 12 ; Garland reference library of social science, v. 347). ISBN 0-8240-8572-8.   **DB6**

More than 1,900 books, articles, and archival materials are grouped by name of commune or utopian society, with a brief historical note for each community. The volume begins with a

listing of bibliographies and general works on communal movements. Topical index.

Continued by: Z7164.C69D37

Miller, Timothy. American communes, 1860–1960 : a bibliography. N.Y. : Garland, 1990. 583 p. (Sects and cults in America. Bibliographical guides, v. 13 ; Garland reference library of social science, v. 402). ISBN 0-8240-8470-5 (series).   **DB7**

An alphabetical listing of communes, giving for each a brief description (usually a paragraph) followed by a list of secondary works and any published primary material available— e.g., periodicals issued by the commune or works by a leader. The bibliographies list mostly English-language books and articles, plus a few theses. A separate chapter contains an annotated list of other bibliographical works and research aids. Name index of authors of works cited, communes, and those associated with the history and development of any commune.

                    Z7164.C69M54

Fredriksen, John C. Shield of republic, sword of empire : a bibliography of United States military affairs, 1783–1846. N.Y. : Greenwood, [1990]. 433 p. (Bibliographies and indexes in American history, no.15). ISBN 0-313-25384-6.   **DB8**

Serves as a companion to Fredricksen's *Free trade and sailor's rights* (1985. 399 p.)

A topical arrangement of 6,783 books, articles, and some state and federal publications covering the period from the Revolution through the Mexican War. In five sections: (1) a general overview of the period; (2) U.S. Army; (3) U.S. Navy; (4) Militia, Canada, Indians; (5) biographies. Subsections for wars and battles, and for contemporary accounts. Cross-references; indexes of authors/titles and subjects.

                    Z1249.M5F73

Gerhan, David R. A retrospective bibliography of American demographic history from colonial times to 1983 / comp. by David R. Gerhan and Robert V. Wells. N.Y. : Greenwood, [1989]. 474 p. (Bibliographies and indexes in American history, no. 10). ISBN 0-313-23130-3. $65.00.   **DB9**

Demographic history is broadly defined to include both quantitative data and "the values people attach to their behavior."—*Pref.*. Divided into six sections (subdivided "early," "19th century," and "recent"): General background; Marriage and fertility; Health and death; Migration, pluralism, and local patterns; Family and demographic history; Population, economics, politics, and society. The compilers exclude diaries, letters, and memoirs, and cite 20th-century academic journals sparingly. Each section begins with commentary followed by the bibliography. Indexed by author, geographic area, and major subject grouping (e.g., ethnic, religious, occupation). A second volume is to deal with the post-1983 era.

                    Z7165.U5G43

A guide to the sources of United States military history : Supplement II / ed. by Robin Higham and Donald J. Mrozek. Hamden, Conn. : Archon Books, 1986. 332 p. ISBN 0-208-02072-1. $42.50.   **DB10**

For original ed., ed. by Higham (1975) and Suppl. I, ed. by Higham and Mrozek (1981), see *Guide* DB28.

Surveys publications of 1978–83; continues the numbering of the first supplement. Not indexed.   Z1249.M5G83

Guide to the study of United States history outside the U.S., 1945–1980 / ed. by Lewis Hanke . . . [et al.]. White Plains, N.Y. : Kraus Internat., [1985]. 5 v. ISBN 0-527-36717-6. $418.00.   **DB11**

Edited "with the assistance of many historians in many lands. Sponsored by the American Historical Association & the University of Massachusetts, Amherst."—*t.p.*

Contents: v. 1, Introductory material, perspectives, essays and reports; Africa through China; v. 2–3, Essays and reports :

Colombia through Venezuela; author index; v. 4–5, Bibliography.

Intended to "inform historians of the U.S. of the studies made by foreign scholars . . . [show them] new sources and fresh perspectives on their own history, and . . . help broaden their views. It should also foster communication between historians in the U.S. and abroad."—*p. 2.* Pt. 1 (v. 1–3) contains essays contributed by foreign specialists on U.S. history describing the teaching and research carried out in their countries between the end of World War II and 1980. Also includes essays describing archival materials in the various countries relating to any aspect of U.S. history. Pt. 2 (v. 4–5) is a classified annotated bibliography of 3,100 books, articles and dissertations, published abroad, arranged topically within period divisions. Author index; detailed table of contents. No subject index.

E175.8.G85

Havlice, Patricia Pate. Oral history : a reference guide and annotated bibliography. Jefferson, N.C. : McFarland, c1985. 140 p. ISBN 0-89950-138-9 (pbk.). $18.95. **DB12**

An annotated bibliography of 773 books and periodical articles from the 1950s through late 1983. Africa and Europe are covered but emphasis is on North America. Author listing with subject index. Z6201.H38

Historical documentary editions, 1988 : a list of documentary publications supported by the National Historical Publications and Records Commission. Wash. : The Commission, [1988]. 77 p. : ill. **DB13**
1st ed., 1986.

Listing of editions, either in paper or microfilm, which have been published with NPRC support since 1986. For each gives name of editor or project director, title, publisher, price, ISBN, and a brief description of contents. Title arrangement with broad subject index. Includes a list of publishers' addresses. Z1236.H66

Lincove, David A. The Anglo-American relationship : an annotated bibliography of scholarship, 1945–1985 / comp. and annotated by David A. Lincove and Gary R. Treadway. N.Y. : Greenwood, [1988]. 415 p. (Bibliographies and indexes in world history, no. 14). ISBN 0-313-25845-7. $49.95. **DB14**

Lists books, essays, articles, and British and American doctoral dissertations accepted or published 1945–85 that treat interaction between the U.S. and Great Britain or Canada, 1783–1945. In two sections: (1) Social and cultural interaction, subdivided by topic (excluding literary criticism, art, and music), and (2) Diplomatic and military relations, subdivided by period (excluding legal sources). Annotations; author and subject indexes. Z6465.U5L56

Meckler's bibliographies of battles and leaders. Westport, Conn. : Meckler, 1990–1991. v. 1–7. (In progress). **DB15**

Contents: v. 1, The battle of Antietam and the Maryland Campaign of 1862: a bibliography, by D. Scott Hartwig ([1990]. 129 p. $39.00); v. 2, The central Pacific campaign, 1943–1944: a bibliography, by James T. Controvich ([1990]. 152 p. $35.00); v. 3, American warplanes 1908–1988: a bibliography, by Myron J. Smith, Jr. (1991. 900 p. $55.00); v. 4, The battle of Pearl Harbor: a bibliography, by Myron J. Smith, Jr. (1991. 210 p. $55.00); v. 5, The battles of Coral Sea and Midway, May–June 1942: a bibliography, by Myron J. Smith, Jr. (1991. 169 p. $55.00); v. 6, The Falklands/Malvinas campaign: a bibliography, by Eugene L. Rasor (1991); v. 7, The battle of Jutland: a bibliography, by Eugene L. Rasor (1991).

An ambitious series of bibliographies covering armed conflicts and military leaders. Arrangement and type and quality of indexing vary from volume to volume. Included are "books, memoirs, monographs, periodical/journal articles, documents,

theses and dissertations, and several newspapers."—*Series editor's foreword.*

Palmer, Gregory. A guide to Americana : the American collections of the British Library. London ; N.Y. : K.G. Saur, [1988]. 252 p. : ill., facsims. (Great collections and collectors, 1). ISBN 0-86291-475-2. $60.00. **DB16**

Describes the kinds of books, pictures, maps, music, government publications, newspapers, and manuscripts in the American collection, and discusses the finding aids available at the Library. An appendix includes such lists as Files of American newspapers published before 1820 in the British Library and American publishers depositing books in the British Library 1850–1950. Z792.B863P34

Current

America, history and life. v. 26, no. 1– . Santa Barbara, Calif. : ABC-Clio, c1989– . Five no. a year. ISSN 0002-7065. **DB17**
For earlier volumes, see *Guide* DB47.

Now issued in five parts: issues 1–4 contain abstracts and citations for articles, book reviews, and dissertations, while issue 5 is the annual index. Also cites reviews of films, videos and nonprint media.

§ A manual for searching the database is now available: *Searching* America: history and life (AHL) *and* Historical abstracts (HA) *on DIALOG*, by Joyce Duncan Falk and Susan K. Kinnell (*Supplement* DA6). Z1236.A482

Manuscripts

Directory of archives and manuscript repositories in the United States / National Historical Publications and Records Commission. 2nd ed. Phoenix : Oryx, 1988. 853 p. ISBN 0-89774-475-6. $55.00. **DB18**
1st ed., 1978 (*Guide* DB72).

"The second edition of the *Directory* . . . is a revision of the 1978 edition and includes descriptions of approximately 1,400 repositories not described in the earlier volume, as well as updated entries for previously listed institutions."—*Pref.* Based on the results of questionnaires, telephone calls and site visits, now includes some 4,225 repositories in the U.S., Puerto Rico, and the Virgin Islands. Repository and subject indexes.
CD3020.D49

Index to personal names in the *National union catalog of manuscript collections*, 1959–1984. Alexandria, Va. : Chadwyck-Healey, [1988]. 2 v. ISBN 0-89887-037-2. $450.00. **DB19**
Ed. under the supervision of Harriet Ostroff.

Cumulates all personal name entries (including family names) used in the indexes of *NUCMC* (*Guide* DB64) through 1984. Item numbers in italics refer to descriptions of major collections. Z6620.U5I53

Researcher's guide to archives and regional history sources / ed. by John C. Larsen. Hamden, Conn. : Library Professional Publications, [1988]. 167 p. ISBN 0-20802-144-2. $27.50. **DB20**

A general introduction designed to "help the researcher whose work requires the use of archival records, for resources which go beyond printed library materials [by] identifying basic procedures and tools."—*Pref.* 14 essays, each written by an experienced archivist, deal with such topics as archival sources, ethics and archives, oral histories, preservation, reference tools. CD3021.R47

Smith, Allen. Directory of oral history collections. Phoenix : Oryx, 1988. 141 p. ISBN 0-89774-322-9. $74.50.
DB21

Based on responses to questionnaires sent to Oral History Association members and to institutions listed in library and oral history directories. Arranged geographically, covering some 500 oral history collections in the U.S. Subject and interviewee indexes. Describes some collections not treated in Alan Meckler and Ruth McMullin's *Oral history collections* (*Guide* DB63) but the latter includes a section on foreign repositories and has fuller descriptions and better indexing. Z6208.O7S54

Szucs, Loretto Dennis. The archives : a guide to the National Archives field branches / by Loretto Dennis Szucs & Sandra Hargreaves Luebking. Salt Lake City, Utah : Ancestry Pub., 1988. 340 p. : ill. ISBN 0-916489-23-X. $35.95.
DB22

The 11 National Archives Field Branches were established to preserve and make available "original records created by field offices of federal agencies" as well as to house and make available, on microfilm or microfiche, records from the National Archives of the decennial censuses 1790–1910, U.S. diplomatic missions, "large bodies of material relating to Indian affairs, the Revolutionary and Civil Wars, German records captured at the end of World War II, and territorial papers."—*Introd.* Section 1 describes each field office, giving brief summaries of its distinctive holdings, services, and activities. Section 2 lists holdings in common, and Section 3 provides an administrative history and listing of each record group held by a branch office, arranged alphabetically (e.g., Census, Bureau of; Centers for Disease Control; Courts, District), with indications of printed guides. Includes descriptions of record groups, microfilm call numbers, bibliographies, illustrations. Excludes the National Archives itself, the National Records Center in Suitland, Md., and the newest branch in Anchorage, Ak. Indexed by agency, title of finding aid, and some topics. A very useful guide that also discusses how to use the archives.

§ For notes on the contents and a discussion of presidential libraries, see Dennis A. Burton, *A guide to manuscripts in the presidential libraries* (*Supplement* AB47); Frank Schick, *Records of the presidency* (*Supplement* CJ82); and Fritz Veit, *Presidential libraries and collections* (*Supplement* CJ83). For guides to the records of the U.S. House of Representatives and Senate, see *Guide to research collections of former members of the U.S. House of Representatives 1789–1987* (*Supplement* CJ93); *Guide to research collections of former U.S. Senators 1789–1982* (*Guide* CJ135). CD3026

United States. National Archives and Records Administration. Guide to the National Archives of the United States / new pref. by Frank B. Evans. Wash. : The Archives, 1987. 896 p. ISBN 0-911333-23-1. **DB23**

Reprint. Issued in 1974 by the body under its earlier name: National Archives and Record Service.

"Except for this Preface, the new Foreword and an appendix describing the record groups newly assigned to the National Archives between 1970 and 1977 the text of the 1974 guide [*Guide* DB70] has been reproduced without modification."—*Foreword.* Appendix D lists 20 record groups added 1970–77; these are not included in the index. CD3023.U53

———— Microfilm resources for research : a comprehensive catalog. Wash. : The Archives, [1990]. 118 p. ISBN 0-911333-34-7 (pbk.). $5.00. **DB24**

Continues U.S. National Archives and Records Service's *Catalog of National Archives microfilm publications* (*Guide* DB69) and supersedes the National Archives' *Microfilm resources for research* (1986).

Microfilm issued since publication of the latter are marked with a symbol, and a few titles have been dropped (e.g., T721–T722, T958–T963), a practice that will be followed in forthcoming editions. Organization is based on that in the National Archives' *Guide to the National Archives of the United*

States (above); there are indexes by keyword and title, and lists by record group number and microfilm number.

§ The National Archives also issues more detailed catalogs that give reel-by-reel descriptions of microfilm sets. Some cover specific topics (e.g., *Diplomatic records*, 1986; *Federal court records*, 1987); geographic areas (e.g., *New England regional catalog*, 1986; *The South and Southwest regional catalog*, 1986); or ethnic groups (e.g., *American Indians*, 1984; *Black studies*, 1984). CD3026

17th and 18th centuries

Kallich, Martin. British poetry and the American Revolution : a bibliographical survey of books and pamphlets, journals and magazines, newspapers, and prints, 1755–1800. Troy, N.Y. : Whitston Pub. Co., 1988. 2 v. (1731 p.). ISBN 0-87875-318-4 (set). $150.00. **DB25**
For annotation, see *Supplement* BD244. Z2014.P7K34

Wehmann, Howard H. A guide to pre-federal records in the National Archives / comp. by Howard H. Wehmann ; rev. by Benjamin L. DeWhitt. Wash. : National Archives and Records Administration, 1989. 375 p. ISBN 0-911333-75-4. $25.00. **DB26**
Superintendent of Documents classification: AE 1.108:P91.

Describes the "holdings of the National Archives that relate directly to, or were created during, the period before the Constitution went into effect on March 4, 1779."—*Pref.* Each record group and series is discussed with indications of organization, brief history, availability on microform (and reel numbers) and any finding aid. Subject index for names, offices, places and a few topics. CD3045.W44

19th century

Venzon, Anne Cipriano. The Spanish-American War : an annotated bibliography. N.Y. : Garland, 1990. 255 p. (Garland reference library of the humanities, vol. 1120 ; Wars of the United States, vol. 11). ISBN 0-8240-7974-4. **DB27**

Cites books, articles, government publications, and a few dissertations in English published 1898–1986 on the Spanish-American War, including the Philippine-American War. Arranged by broad topics, subdivided for books and articles. Includes fiction and music; most articles have brief annotations. Author and subject indexes. Z1243.V45

Civil War

Bibliography

Cole, Garold. Civil War eyewitnesses : an annotated bibliography of books and articles, 1955–1986. Columbia, S.C. : Univ. of South Carolina Pr., c1988. 351 p. ISBN 0-87249-545-0. $29.95. **DB28**

Lists 1,400 books, collected essays, memoirs, autobiographies, popular and scholarly periodical articles. In three parts: 1) The North, 2) The South, 3) Anthologies and studies, with subdivisions for military, civilian and foreign accounts. Index of authors, editors, titles, troops by state, battles, places mentioned, and a few subjects (e.g., recreation, vices, character, effect of war on soldiers). Z1242.C78

Murdock, Eugene Converse. The Civil War in the North : a selective annotated bibliography. N.Y. : Garland, 1987. 764 p. (Wars of the United States, v. 9 ; Garland reference library of social science, v. 254). ISBN 0-8240-8941-3. $58.00. **DB29**

A topical listing of some 5,600 books and articles believed to be widely available. Annotated; author and subject indexes.

Z1242.M87

Parrish, T. Michael. Confederate imprints : a bibliography of Southern publications from secession to surrender / by T. Michael Parrish & Robert M. Willingham, Jr. Austin, Tex. : Jenkins Pub. Co. ; Katonah, N.Y. : G.A. Foster, [ca. 1984]. 991 p., [132] p. of plates : ill. ISBN 0-86307-12-3. **DB30**

Expands and revises the earlier compilations by Marjorie Crandall (1955) and Richard Harwell (1957) (*Guide* DB97–98).

Aims to list "any book, pamphlet, broadside, map, piece of sheet music, pictorial print, newspaper, magazine or other serial publication, published in Confederate-held territory . . . [including] official imprints: national, state and local government publications, as well as army, militia, or other military publications."—*Introd.* Divided into official publications (arranged by state) and nonofficial publications (arranged by topic). Location symbols; table of cross-references from the 5,121 Crandall and Harwell entry numbers to the 9,497 entries in this volume. Index of authors, titles, and broad subjects.

Z1242.5.P37

Manuscripts and archives

Library of Congress. Manuscript Division. Civil War manuscripts : a guide to collections in the Manuscript Division of the Library of Congress / comp. by John R. Sellers. Wash. : Library of Congress : For sale by the Supt. of Docs., U.S. Govt. Print. Off., 1986. 391 p. : ill. ISBN 0-8444-0381-4. **DB31**

Superintendent of Documents classification: LC4.2:C49.

The collections consist mainly of personal papers (as opposed to government records held by the National Archives). The guide lists and briefly describes materials dealing directly in whole or in part with the Civil War. Listing is by name of the individual or agency whose papers are described. Subject index. Does not include materials in other parts of the library.

Z1242.L48

Neagles, James C. Confederate research sources : a guide to archive collections. Salt Lake City, Utah : Ancestry Pub., c1986. 286 p. : ill. ISBN 0-916489-11-6. ISBN 0-916489-16-7 (pbk.). **DB32**

Intended to help the researcher "track down information about his confederate ancestor whether in a state archive, the National Archives in Washington, D.C., or in a state or other genealogical library."—*Introd.* Offers descriptions of archives and lists of publications. Z1242.N3

Encyclopedias; Dictionaries

Boatner, Mark Mayo. The Civil War dictionary / by Mark Mayo Boatner III ; maps and diagrams by Allen C. Northrop and Lowell I. Miller. Rev. ed. N.Y. : McKay, c1988. 974 p. : ill., maps. ISBN 0-8129-1726-X. $29.95. **DB33**

1st ed., 1959 (*Guide* DB103).

Boatner has updated the bibliography to the early 1960s, otherwise there is little change from previous printings. Still about half biographical. E468.B7

Historical times illustrated encyclopedia of the Civil War / Patricia L. Faust, ed. N.Y. : Harper & Row, c1986. 849 p. : ill. ISBN 0-06-181261-7. $39.95. **DB34**

The 2,100 signed articles are strongly biographical, but include entries for newspapers, battles, towns, organizations, and weapons. Illustrated with photographs and maps. According to *Booklist* 83 (1987): 1108, "Readers familiar with other single-volume works on the Civil War such as [Mark M.] Boatner's *The Civil War dictionary* [*Guide* DB103; rev. ed., above] and *Civil War almanac* [exec. ed., John S. Bowman. N.Y. : Facts on File, 1983. 400 p.] will find that this book combines the best features of each . . . . At this price, [it] is a good value."

E468.H57

Biography

Sifakis, Stewart. Who was who in the Civil War. N.Y. : Facts on File, c1988. 766 p. : ill. ISBN 0-8160-1055-2. ISBN 0-8160-0055-2. $45.00. **DB35**

Some 2,500 entries deal with principal Union and Confederate military figures, together with politicians, activists, journalists, artists, medical personnel, diplomats and foreign observers, and engineers. Each entry includes sources for further information, if available. Concludes with a monthly chronology, list of officers who received thanks of the U.S. Congress, select annotated bibliography. Indexed. E467.S56

Atlases

A guide to Civil War maps in the National Archives. Wash. : National Archives, National Archives and Records Administration, 1986. 139 p. : ill. ISBN 0-911333-36-3. **DB36**

1st ed., 1964, had title: *Civil War maps in the National Archives.*

Lists about 8,000 Civil War maps, charts, and plans housed in the Cartographic and Architectural Branch of the National Archives. Pt. 1 describes all maps by Record Group number. Pt. 2 deals with maps of "exceptional interest" (*p. 73*); these are arranged by state and are described in more detail. Added to this edition are maps of Record Group 109, War Department Collection of Confederate Records. Index for place names and for cartographers. Z1242.G85

Library of Congress. Geography and Map Division. Civil War maps : an annotated list of maps and atlases in the Library of Congress / comp. by Richard W. Stephenson. 2nd ed. Wash. : Library of Congress, 1989. 410 p. : maps (some col.). ISBN 0-8444-0598-1. **DB37**

1st ed., 1961.

Superintendent of Documents classification: LC 1.12/2:C49.

" . . . expanded to include descriptions of 2,240 maps and charts and 76 atlases and sketch books in the Geography and Map Division [and] . . . 162 maps from the collections of the Manuscript Division."—*Pref.* Arranged by geographical area (i.e., the nation as a whole, then state). Title and general indexes. Z6027.U5L5

20th century

Historical dictionary of the New Deal : from inauguration to preparation for war / ed. by James S. Olson. Westport, Conn. : Greenwood, [1985]. 611 p. ISBN 0-313-23873-1. $65.00. **DB38**

Offers articles on persons, agencies, terms, slogans, etc., relative to U.S. domestic policy during the 1933–40 period. Contributed articles are signed, others are by the editor. One or more bibliographic references for each article. Also has a chronology, a select bibliography of New Deal programs, and a list of New Deal acronyms. Indexed by subject.   E806.H58

Kyvig, David E. New day/New Deal : a bibliography of the Great American Depression, 1929–1941 / comp. by David E. Kyvig and Mary-Ann Blasio with contributions by Dawn Corley. N.Y. : Greenwood, 1988. 306 p. (Bibliographies and indexes in American history, no. 9). ISBN 0-313-26027-3. $45.00.   **DB39**

Cites 4,600 books, articles, dissertations in classed arrangement subdivided by format. Separate section for biographies. Cutoff date is early 1987. Indexed by author with reference to topical number.   Z1244.K95

Olson, James Stuart. Historical dictionary of the 1920s : from World War I to the New Deal, 1919–1933. N.Y. : Greenwood, 1988. 420 p. ISBN 0-313-25683-7. $55.00.   **DB40**

Offers brief articles, alphabetically arranged, on "the most prominent individuals, social movements, organizations, legislation, treaties, political events, and ideas of the era" (*Pref.*) in the U.S., with emphasis on individuals and events. Each article ends with at least one bibliographical reference. Detailed index, chronology, and topically arranged bibliography of books and articles on the period.   E784.O44

Regional and local

Filby, P. William. A bibliography of American county histories. Baltimore : Genealogical Pub., 1985. 449 p. ISBN 0-8063-1126-6. $24.95.   **DB41**

Aims to replace Clarence S. Peterson's *Consolidated bibliography of county histories in fifty states in 1961* (Baltimore : 1961). Listing is by state, then by county, giving full bibliographic information. Not indexed.   Z1250.F54

Neagles, James C. The Library of Congress : a guide to genealogical and historical research / by James C. Neagles ; assisted by Mark C. Neagles. Salt Lake City, Utah : Ancestry Pub., c1990. 381 p. : ill. ISBN 0-916489-48-5.   **DB42**

Discusses major subject areas in the Library of Congress collections, but emphasizes genealogical and historical resources. Includes helpful background material, cites many bibliographies, and provides LC call numbers. Useful for genealogists and reference librarians.   Z1250.N4

Reference guides to state history and research. N.Y. : Greenwood, [1982–1991]. 5 v. (In progress).   **DB43**

Contents: A guide to the history of Louisiana, ed. by Light Townsend Cummins and Glen Jeansonne (1982. 298 p.); ... Massachusetts, ed. by Martin Kaufman, John W. Ifkovic, and Joseph Carvalho III (1988. 313 p.); ... Texas, ed. by Light Townsend Cummins and Alvin R. Bailey, Jr. (1988. 307 p.); ... Florida, ed. by Paul S. George (1989. 300 p.); ... California, ed. by Doyce R. Nunis, Jr. and Gloria Ricci Lothrop (1989. 309 p.); ... Illinois, ed. by John Hoffman (1991. 349 p.)

Intended for researchers of state and local history. Volumes follow a standard pattern: Pt. I, Historical essays, presents chapters arranged by periods or topics (urban, women's, oral history), written by specialists and designed to cover "major sources and interpretations ... while surveying the major historical literature, including books, articles, and dissertations"—*Introd., Massachusetts.* Pt. II, Archives and sources, describes major archival repositories of the state's history. Subject index. Some volumes include a chronology of the state's history; all give brief biographical accounts of the contributors. See also *A bibliography of state bibliographies, 1970–1982*, comp. by David W. Parish (*Supplement* AG27).

Regional differences in America : a statistical sourcebook / Alfred N. Garwood, ed. Seattle, Wash. : Numbers & Concepts, c1988. 590 p.   **DB44**

Information drawn from census publications, surveys, and polls (especially Gallup polls) is organized by broad topic (e.g., Health and vital statistics; Transportation; Income, poverty, subsidy, and wealth; Education, the arts, culture, recreation). Data is presented in tables most of which cover 1982–85, with a few beginning as early as 1970. Glossary of terms; subject index.   HA215.R43

Shearer, Benjamin F. State names, seals, flags, and symbols : a historical guide / Benjamin F. Shearer and Barbara S. Shearer. N.Y. : Greenwood, [1987]. 239 p., [20] p. of plates : ill. (some col.). ISBN 0-313-24559-2.   **DB45**

Origins of state names and symbols (e.g., mottoes, seals, flowers, trees, birds, songs) are arranged alphabetically by state under the type of symbol. Selected bibliography of state histories.   E155.S44

Steiner, Michael. Region and regionalism in the United States : a source book for the humanities and social sciences / Michael Steiner, Clarence Mondale. N.Y. : Garland, 1988. 495 p. (Garland reference library of social science, v. 204). ISBN 0-8240-9048-9.   **DB46**

A topical arrangement of 1,652 books, articles and essays on cultural regions as a concept and as an object of study. Headnotes to each section or subsection; annotations. Author index only.   Z1247.S73

Stephens, W. B. Sources for U.S. history : nineteenth-century communities. Cambridge [England] ; N.Y. : Cambridge Univ. Pr., 1991. 558 p. ISBN 0-521-35315-7.   **DB47**

Presents a discussion of archival, statistical, and historical sources for "research into the history of individual nineteenth-century U.S. communities, large and small. The book is arranged topically (covering demography, ethnicity and race, land use and settlement, religion, education, politics and local government, industry, trade and transportation, and poverty, health and crime)."—*Adv.* Includes a very useful section on the use of primary sources. Topical index.

Similar in scope to Stephens' *Sources for English local history* (*Guide* DC327).   E180.S74

Young, Arthur P. Cities and towns in American history : a bibliography of doctoral dissertations. N.Y. : Greenwood, [1989]. 438 p. (Bibliographies and indexes in American history, no. 13). ISBN 0-313-26588-7.   **DB48**

Lists 4,314 doctoral dissertations through 1987, identified in *Comprehensive dissertation index* (*Guide* AH15), that treat the urban experience. "All subject areas—culture, economics, education, ethnicity, health, politics, religion, and social structure—are reflected in the compilation ... " (*Pref.*) if they have a historical orientation. Pt. I lists dissertations by state, then city; cities with more than 25 entries are subdivided by topic, and New York City by neighborhood, borough, and street. Pt. II lists works by topic (e.g., cultural and intellectual life, labor). Gives University Microfilms order numbers when available, but omits references to *Dissertation abstracts international.* Author and subject indexes.   Z7164.U7Y7

New England

Bibliographies of New England history / prepared by the Committee for a New England Bibliography. Hanover, N.H. : Univ. Pr. of New England, [1986–89]. v. 6–8. (In progress).   **DB49**

For v. 1–5 and annotation, see *Guide* DB121.

Contents: v. 6, Connecticut, ed. by Roger Parks (571 p.); v. 7, New England, ed. by Roger Parks (259 p.); v. 8, New England: additions to the six state bibliographies, ed. by Roger Parks (776 p.).

Publisher varies.

Vol. 6 follows the plan of other state volumes with 1984 the cutoff date (but including many 1985 titles). Items with NUC entries for library locations are marked with a cross.

Vol. 7 "contains entries that pertain to the history of the region and to more than one New England state. It also includes writings about the Northeastern United States in which New England is prominently mentioned and works on certain subjects in the American past that are nearly synonymous with New England: [e.g.,] Puritan history."—*Introd.* Citations to books, pamphlets, journal articles, and doctoral dissertations (and a few master's essays) are topically arranged. Although the cutoff date is December 31, 1987, some 1988 and 1989 titles are included. Index of authors, editors, compilers, and subjects. Also of interest is a historiographic essay, "Reassessing the local history of New England," by David D. Hall and Alan Taylor.

Vol. 8 "lists additions and corrections to the state bibliographies and updates them through 1987 with additional entries for 1988 and early 1989."—*Introd.* Plans call for additional volumes in 1994 or 1995 with updating and corrections.

Z1251.E1N454

The encyclopedia of New England / ed. by Robert O'Brien with Richard D. Brown. N.Y.: Facts on File, c1985. 613 p.: ill., maps. ISBN 0-87196-759-6.　**DB50**

Concerned with the states of Connecticut, Maine, Massachusetts, New Hampshire, Rhode Island, and Vermont. Includes entries for historical works, cultural institutions and developments, geographical topics, statistical and political information, and more general themes as they relate to New England. Dictionary arrangement with cross-references and select bibliography.　　　　F2.E43

The South

Brown, Catherine L. The urban South: a bibliography. N.Y.: Greenwood, 1989. 455 p. (Bibliographies and indexes in American history, no. 12). ISBN 0-313-26154-7.　　　　**DB51**

Lists 7,370 books and pamphlets, periodical articles, theses, and doctoral dissertations concerned with cities, towns, Indian settlements, ghost towns, etc. in the South (West Virginia to Oklahoma, Texas to Maryland). Arranged by format subdivided by broad topic (e.g., Archaeology, Artisans and crafts, History and geography). Does not give *Dissertation abstracts* references for dissertations. Geographic index, subject index.

Z7164.U7B69

Encyclopedia of Southern culture / Charles Reagan Wilson & William Ferris, coeditors; Ann J. Abadie & Mary L. Hart, assoc. editors. Chapel Hill: Univ. of North Carolina Pr., c1989. 1634 p.: ill. ISBN 0-8078-1823-2. $49.95.　　　　**DB52**

Sponsored by The Center for the Study of Southern Culture, Univ. of Mississippi.

Signed, short articles, with bibliographies, are arranged under broader topics (e.g., "We shall overcome" under Black life; Stoicism under Philanthropy; Northern under History and manners; Jonathan Daniels under Media). Cross-references; index of contributors; general index. An excellent survey.

F209.E53

O'Brien, Robert. The encyclopedia of the South / ed. by Robert O'Brien with Harold H. Martin. N.Y.: Facts on File, c1985. 583 p.: ill. ISBN 0-87196-728-6.　**DB53**

The South here includes Alabama, Arkansas, Florida, Georgia, Kentucky, Louisiana, Maryland, Mississippi, Missouri, North and South Carolina, Tennessee, Texas, Virginia, and West Virginia. Offers short-entry articles on people, institutions, cities, states, events, and products, with longer essays on

tourism, railroads, tobacco, ragtime, architecture, etc. Surprisingly little coverage of religious denominations and of those topics (e.g. red clay, dialects) that make the region distinctive. Topical index, some cross-references. Appendix of counties with county seats, state statistics for 1970 and 1980, list of governors, and three pages of bibliography. Not as useful as *The encyclopedia of Southern history* (*Guide* DB124) or *Encyclopedia of Southern culture* (above).　　　　F207.7.O27

The Midwest

Carpenter, Allan. The encyclopedia of the Midwest / by Allan Carpenter; contributor, Randy Lyon. N.Y.: Facts on File, c1989. 544 p.: ill. ISBN 0-8160-1660-7. $35.00.　　　　**DB54**

Treats the states of Illinois, Indiana, Iowa, Michigan, Minnesota, Missouri, Ohio, and Wisconsin by presenting "information of the widest variety" (*Pref.*), including local events, institutions, statistics, etc., in alphabetical arrangement. Cross-references; general index. Brief bibliography, p. 505–506.

F351.C33

The West

Beck, Warren A. Historical atlas of the American West / by Warren A. Beck and Ynez D. Haase. Norman: Univ. of Oklahoma Pr., c1989. [156p.]; 32 cm. ISBN 0-8061-2193-9. $29.95.　　　　**DB55**

Presents 78 black-and-white maps with discussion on facing pages. Covers 17 Western states from Texas to Canada "along the hundredth meridian and westward."—*Pref.* Bibliography of works used for each map. Index mainly of names. Appendix: Spanish-American land grants—Lower Rio Grande Valley, west of the Nueces River, Texas.　　　G1381.S1B4

Carpenter, Allan. The encyclopedia of the Central West / by Allan Carpenter; editorial assistant, Carl Provorse. N.Y.: Facts on File, c1990. 544 p.: ill. ISBN 0-8160-1661-5. $35.00.　　　　**DB56**

Covering Colorado, Kansas, Montana, Nebraska, New Mexico, North Dakota, Oklahoma, South Dakota, Texas, and Wyoming, the work presents in a dictionary arrangement information on people, places, colleges and universities, native American groups, and topics (Adobe architecture, Agriculture—pueblo) relating specifically to this region. State entries describe population, archeology, etc. of that state. Short bibliography; topical index.

§ From the same editor and publisher, *The encyclopedia of the far West* (1991) covers Alaska, Arizona, California, Hawaii, Idaho, Nevada, Oregon, Utah, Washington, and the U.S. territories in the Pacific (e.g., Guam).　　　　F351.C325

Mattes, Merrill J. Platte River road narratives: a descriptive bibliography of travel over the great central overland route to Oregon, California, Utah, Colorado, Montana, and other western states and territories, 1812–1866. Urbana: Univ. of Illinois Pr., c1988. 632 p.: 1 map. ISBN 0-252-01342-5. $95.00.　　**DB57**

"... attempts to identify, describe and evaluate all known substantive central overland accounts [focusing on the Platte River and its major tributaries between the Missouri River and South Pass] during the half-century prior to the advent of the transcontinental railroad, with a resultant total of two thousand entries."—*Pref.* Arranged by year, then alphabetically by traveler's name. Index in six columns: name of traveler, year/sex, narrative form with a rating, places of departure and arrival, Missouri River crossing, item number.　　Z1251.W5M37

Thrapp, Dan L. Encyclopedia of frontier biography. Glendale, Calif.: A.H. Clark Co., 1988. 3 v. ISBN 0-87062-191-2. $175.00.   **DB58**

Short biographic sketches of all "who came to attention through the significance of their deeds or simply were of interest in some connection with the evolving drama" (*Introd.*)—trappers, traders, cowboys, scouts, explorers, miners, heroes, desperadoes, etc. Omits people in the mining industry and those noted only through "formal and declared wars." Each entry gives dates, brief biography, significance or influence, and sources for further research. Indexed by topic, names, locations, Indian tribes, occupations.   F596.T515

Townley, John M. The trail west : a bibliography-index to western American trails, 1841–1869. Reno, Nev.: Jamison Station Pr., [1988]. 309 p.: maps. ISBN 0-913381-05-5.   **DB59**

Begins with the first California-bound settlers in 1841 and ends with the completion of the transcontinental railroad in 1869. Includes staging and freight lines and the telegraph. The main portion of the work is an alphabetical listing of diaries, recollections, books, articles, theses, and maps, with complete bibliographical information. Indexes refer to the author's name in the main section: Chronological index by year, Subject index, Trail segment index. For this last index, the trails have been divided into 42 geographical segments; each segment is listed with the author's names, subdivided by year.   Z1251.W5T68

Valk, Barbara G. BorderLine : a bibliography of the United States-Mexico borderlands. Los Angeles : UCLA Latin American Center Publications ; Riverside : UC MEXUS, Univ. of California Consortium on Mexico and the United States, c1988. 711 p. ISBN 0-87903-112-3. $150.00.   **DB60**

Based on a MARC-formatted database operating as a subfile of ORION, UCLA's online cataloging system. Many of the references and abstracts were supplied by faculty, students, and librarians at universities in the Southwest. Arrangement is topical, covering Arizona, California, New Mexico, Texas, Baja California, Chihuahua, Coahuila, Nuevo Léon, Sonora, Tamaulipas. Most materials were published 1960–85, and include books, government documents, conference proceedings, theses and dissertations, unpublished papers, maps, films and other audiovisual materials. Each citation is listed only once with no cross-references, but scope notes appear in the table of contents. Author index.   Z1251.M44V35

Encyclopedias; Dictionaries

Dictionary of American immigration history / ed. by Francesco Cordasco. Metuchen, N.J.: Scarecrow, 1990. 784 p. ISBN 0-8108-2241-5. $97.50.   **DB61**

Entries, varying in length from a paragraph to a long essay, are arranged alphabetically and cover a broad range of topics relating to immigration: ethnic groups, individuals, societies, legislation, and conceptual themes (e.g., assimilation, pluralism, ethnicity). Includes Canada. Entries end with brief bibliographies of one to three items. The introduction provides a brief history of immigration law. Cross-references; select bibliography.   JV6450.D53

Encyclopedia of the American left / ed. by Mari Jo Buhle, Paul Buhle, Dan Georgakas. N.Y.: Garland, 1990. 928 p.: ill. (Garland reference library of social sciences, v. 502). ISBN 0-8240-3713-8. $95.00.   **DB62**

A dictionary arrangement of articles treating "that segment of society which has sought fundamental changes in the economic, political and cultural systems" (*Introd.*), but also including political parties, conventions, organizations, issues, literature, etc., from about 1870 to the early to mid-1980s. The signed articles are based on primary sources and include one to

five bibliographic citations. Indexes of names and subjects.   HX86.E58

Encyclopedia USA : the encyclopedia of the United States of America past & present / ed. by R. Alton Lee. Gulf Breeze, Fla.: Academic International Pr., c1983–1990. v. 1–12. ISBN 0-87569-076-9 (set). (In progress).   **DB63**

Editor varies.

Contents: v. 1–12, AAA (Agriculture Adjustment Administration)–Closely watched trains.

Attempts to "produce an encyclopedia that will encompass all major facts, events, personalities, and institutions important in American life ... those of most interest and use to a wide readership .... Designed primarily for the general public from the beginning researcher to the specialist in any field who needs an authoritative statement on a topic not in his specialty ...."—*From the editor*. The articles are clear, very readable, seem to cover the topic adequately, are signed, and end with brief bibliographies. Although the contributors are not of wide repute, the overall product is scholarly and workmanlike.   E156.E52

Findling, John E. Dictionary of American diplomatic history. 2nd ed., rev. and expanded. N.Y.: Greenwood, 1989. 674 p.: ill. ISBN 0-313-26024-9.   **DB64**

For annotation, see *Supplement* CJ53.   E183.7.F5

Handbook of American women's history / Angela Howard Zophy, ed., Frances M. Kavenik, associate ed. N.Y.: Garland, 1990. 736 p. (Garland reference library of the humanities, vol. 696). ISBN 0-8240-8744-5.   **DB65**

Signed articles, alphabetically arranged, with appended bibliographies on concepts, events, organizations, and people. Cross-references; subject index.   HQ1410.H36

Historical dictionary of North American archaeology / Edward B. Jelks, ed., Juliet C. Jelks, assistant ed. N.Y.: Greenwood, 1988. 760 p. ISBN 0-313-24307-7. $95.00.   **DB66**

An alphabetical arrangement of more than 1,800 entries for prehistoric cultures, archaeological sites, and major artifact types. Bibliography, p. [555]–705.   E77.9.H57

Directories

Cockrell, Philip C. Directory of historical consultants / comp. and ed. by Philip C. Cockrell for the National Council on Public History. [Massachusetts?] : The Council, 1988. 61 p.   **DB67**

Related to a 1981 ed. (Washington : National Coordinating Committee for the Promotion of History. 91 p.), ed. by Page Putnam Miller.

Lists individuals and firms whose members have been formally trained as historians. For each, gives name and address, names of staff, examples of previous experience. Services category index; geographic index; consultant name index.

E172.C63

Directory of historical organizations in the United States and Canada. 13th ed.– . Nashville, Tenn.: AASLH Pr., American Association for State and Local History, c1986– . Biennial. $79.95.   **DB68**

Eds. 1–12 had title: *Directory of historical societies and agencies in the United States and Canada* (*Guide* DB141).

The indexing has been much expanded to include lists of groups and organizations with special interests or affiliations, such as "historic person," "archaeology," "pioneer." New appendix: Historical and archaeological areas administered by the National Park Service.   E172.D5

Handbooks

The American history sourcebook / Joel Makower, ed. N.Y.: Prentice Hall, c1988. 548 p.: ill. ISBN 0-13-027491-7. $40.00. ISBN 0-13-027483-6 (pbk.). $22.95. **DB69**

A directory of about 3,000 museums, historical societies, and libraries, giving for each address, phone number (usually), hours, access, and a brief description of the content of the collection. Arrangement is alphabetical within state. Appendixes: Key dates in American history, and an "American history bibliography" giving an alphabetical list of bibliographies, manuals, and guides. Organization name and subject indexes.
Z1236.A5144

Austin, Erik W. Political facts of the United States since 1789 / Erik W. Austin; with the assistance of Jerome M. Clubb. N.Y.: Columbia Univ. Pr., 1986. 518 p. ISBN 0-231-06094-7. $45.00. **DB70**

A collection of selected data, chiefly in tabular form, with emphasis on politics and government at the national level. Includes sections on: National leadership; State politics; Parties and elections; Foreign affairs; Armed forces; Wealth, revenue, taxation, and public expenditure; and Demographics. Tables can be located from the table of contents, but lack of an index limits the item's usefulness for quick reference. Sources of the data are cited at the end of the work.
E183.A97

Eleuterio-Comer, Susan K. Irish American material culture: a directory of collections, sites, and festivals in the United States and Canada. N.Y.: Greenwood, 1988. 107 p. (Material culture directories, no. 1). ISBN 0-313-24731-5. $35.00. **DB71**

Pt. 1 offers a directory of some 90 museums, libraries, historical societies, archives, and centers in the U.S. and Canada. Pt. 2 is a listing of 44 sites taken mainly from the *National register of historic places* (1976) plus a few in Canada. Pt. 3 lists 27 festivals in the U.S. and Canada, with brief historic descriptive notes. An appendix lists relevant museums and "folk parks" in Ireland. Based on responses to a questionnaire. Indexed by the name of organization and topic. There is some overlap with DeeGee Lester's *Irish research* (*Supplement* DC146), but the latter covers only printed material.
E184.I6E43

Chronologies

Carruth, Gorton. The encyclopedia of American facts & dates. 8th ed. N.Y.: Harper & Row, c1987. 1006 p. ISBN 0-06-181143-2. $29.95. **DB72**

7th ed., 1979 (*Guide* DB145).

Updated to include events of 1986 and provided with a more detailed index.
E174.5.C3

Gordon, Lois G. American chronicle: six decades in American life, 1920–1980 / Lois Gordon, Alan Gordon. N.Y.: Atheneum, 1987. 565 p.: ill., ports. ISBN 0-689-11899-6; $39.95. 0-689-11901-1 (pbk.); $16.95. **DB73**

A chronology presenting in columnar form for each year: Facts and figures, In the news, Deaths, Quotes, Ads, Radio and television, The arts, Science and technology, Sports, Fashion, and a "Kaleidoscope" which aims to give the flavor of the year by listing, e.g., food prices, new words. At the beginning of each decade a brief narrative describes trends and presents vital, economic, social, and consumer statistics. Not indexed.
E169.1.G665

Gross, Ernie. This day in American history. N.Y.: Neal-Schuman, c1990. 477 p. ISBN 1-55570-046-2. $49.95. **DB74**

A chronology containing some 11,000 entries arranged by date. "Each day's listings begin with the earliest date available."—*Pref.* Includes both people chosen for their "impact on American life through their positions or actions—U.S. presidents and vice presidents and their wives, Supreme Court justices, key legislators, inventors and pioneers, military and business leaders, scientists and doctors, artists, sports figures, and entertainment personalities..." and "scientific inventions and geographical discoveries, landmark government actions, manmade and natural disasters." The index of names and events could be more extensive: some place-names mentioned in the text, and all professions, are omitted. Intended for "the harried newswriter and other print and media professionals, speechwriters, planners of special events, teachers and students, the general reader."
E174.5.G76

Biography

American historians, 1866–1912 / ed. by Clyde N. Wilson. Detroit: Gale, c1986. 427 p.: ill., ports. (Dictionary of literary biography, v. 47). ISBN 0-8103-1725-7. **DB75**

For volumes covering other periods, see *Guide* DB177–DB178. For other volumes in series, see *Guide* BD416 and *Supplement* BD52.

Treats the "more important American writers of history whose first works were published between the end of the Civil War and 1912."—*Foreword.* Profiles 50 American historians, most writing about the U.S., emphasizing their careers in history. Bibliography of primary and secondary works, location of papers, and a supplementary reading list. No subject index. An appendix features two articles on historiography of the Civil War.
E175.45.A483

Historians of the American frontier: a bio-bibliographical sourcebook / ed. by John R. Wunder. N.Y.: Greenwood, 1988. 814 p. ISBN 0-313-24899-0. **DB76**

Signed essays treat 57 historians, giving for each a biography, themes treated, analysis of work, and bibliography of writings by and (often) about the historian. Index of titles cited in the bibliographies and of topics.
E175.45.H57

Atlases

Ferrell, Robert H. Atlas of American history / Robert H. Ferrell, Richard Natkiel. N.Y.: Facts on File, c1987. 192 p.: ill., maps in color; 28 cm. ISBN 0-8160-1028-5. **DB77**

Arranged by broad periods (e.g., The Colonial era, Founding a nation, Expansion and Civil War, Imperial democracy, The two World Wars, America in a divided world). For each period, a short essay of three to five pages is followed by maps, photographs, and drawings. Index by topic to text and illustrations. A 1990 updated printing (192 p. $19.95 pbk.) adds 1988 election results.

§ A review in *Wilson library bulletin* 62 (Jan. 1988): 97–98 states that there are "enough faulty facts to shake one's confidence... [otherwise] a fine supplement to [Kenneth T.] Jackson's textless, unillustrated, strictly black-and-white *Atlas of American history* [*Guide* DB160]."
G1201.S1F4

Martis, Kenneth C. The historical atlas of political parties in the United States Congress, 1789–1989 / Kenneth C. Martis, author and ed.; Ruth Anderson Rowles, cartographer; Gyula Pauer, production cartographer.

N.Y. : Macmillan ; London : Collier Macmillan, c1989. 518 p. : maps in color ; 34 x 46 cm. ISBN 0-02-920170-5.　　**DB78**

For annotation and companion volumes on districts and votes, see *Supplement* CJ116.　　　G1201.F9M26

National Geographic Society (U.S.). Historical atlas of the United States. Wash. : National Geographic Society, c1988. 289 p. : ill. ; 47 cm. ISBN 0-87044-747-5. $75.00.　　**DB79**

Heavily illustrated with reproductions of paintings, charts, graphs, photographs, maps with relevant text, chronologies, and time lines. An accompanying portfolio contains 18 maps for regions and for the entire U.S. The presentation in six major areas (The land, People, Boundaries, Economy, Networks, Communities) is interspersed with five chronological sections: 1400–1606, 1607–1788, 1789–1860, 1861–1916, 1917–88. The illustrative material is very well chosen and clearly presented, but since much of it runs across or up to the inner margin, the book can never be satisfactorily rebound. The bibliography cites sources for the illustrations and text of each page and the consultants used. Topical index for illustrations and text.

§ Two extremely useful specialized atlases expand coverage for women and ethnic groups: James P. Allen and Eugene J. Turner, *We the people : an atlas of America's ethnic diversity* (*Supplement* CC188) and Barbara G. Shortridge, *Atlas of American women* (N.Y. : Macmillan ; London : Collier Macmillan, c1987).　　　G1201.S1N3

CANADA

Bibliography

Barrett, Jane R. A bibliography of works on Canadian foreign relations, 1981–1985 / comp. by Jane R. Barrett with Jane Beaumont and Lee-Anne Broadhead. Toronto : Canadian Institute of International Affairs, c1987. 157 p. ISBN 0-919084-57-5 (pbk.).　　**DB80**

Continuation of series begun by Donald M. Page and covering 1945–70, 1971–75 (*Guide* DB186), and 1976–80 ([1982]). Covers books, parts of books, collections, and government publications issued 1981–85. Follows an arrangement similar to the earlier volumes. Personal name and subject indexes.

Z6465.C2B37

Black, J. L. Soviet perception of Canada, 1917–1987 : an annotated bibliographic guide. Kingston, Ont., Canada : R.P. Frye, c1989. 2 v. in 1 [242 p.]. (The Centre for Canadian Soviet Studies bibliographic series, no. 1). ISBN 0-919741-94-0.　　**DB81**

In two parts: Pt. 1 is "a list of all books, articles from periodical literature, chapters in books, and dissertations written in the USSR about Canada since 1917" (*Introd.*), arranged by format; Pt. 2 is a listing by date of Soviet newspapers reporting on Canada, 1945–87. Author index for each part.　Z6465.C2B58

Day, Alan Edwin. Search for the Northwest Passage : an annotated bibliography. N.Y. : Garland, 1986. 632 p. (Garland reference library of social science, v. 186). ISBN 0-8240-9288-0.　　**DB82**

"The search for a passage by the northwest is traced in print from the late fifteenth-century voyages of the Cabots . . . to the voyage of a Royal Canadian Mounted Police schooner through the passage in both directions in the early 1940s."— *Pref.* A section of general works is followed by a chronological arrangement of entries for the various voyages and expeditions. 5,160 entries, indexed by author.　Z6016.N67D39

Metropolitan Toronto Library. Canadian History Dept. A bibliography of Canadiana : being items in the Metropolitan Toronto Library relating to the early history and development of Canada : second supplement / ed. by Sandra Alston ; assisted by Karen Evans. Toronto : Metropolitan Toronto Library Board, 1985–1989. 4 v. : ill., facsims. ISBN 0-88773-029-9.　　**DB83**

For basic work and 1st suppl., see *Guide* DB191.

Contents: v. 1, 1512–1800 (1989. 352 p.); v. 2, 1801–49 (1985. 839 p.); v. 3, 1850–57 (1989. 910 p.); v. 4, Indexes (1989. 717 p.)

The second suppl. adds 3,254 titles received by the Library since 1959. The arrangement is by imprint date; index in each volume. Vol. 4 is a cumulative index to v. 1–3 and covers names of individuals and corporate bodies, titles, places of publication, printers and publishers, subjects, maps and plans, illustrations in separate sections.　Z1365.T64

Waterston, Elizabeth. The travellers, Canada to 1900 : an annotated bibliography of works published in English from 1577 / Elizabeth Waterston ; with Ian Easterbrook, Bernard Katz, and Kathleen Scott. Guelph, Ontario, Canada : Univ. of Guelph, 1989. 321 p. [13] leaves of plates : ill. ; 28 cm.　　**DB84**

A listing of about 700 travelers' accounts that cover more than one region of Canada. Each entry gives full title, birth and death dates of the author, collation, publishing information for first edition, microfiche number if available from the Canadian Institute for Historical Microreproduction, and an annotation summarizing the content. Author/title index; topical index. The topical index includes sections for places, climatic conditions, institutions, people, social customs, language patterns, health care, modes of transportation, native tribes. The extensive secondary bibliography includes sections for: Bibliographies, collections and histories; Reference books; Articles, books and dissertations on Canadian travel and exploration literature to 1900; Books and dissertations on other travel and exploration literature to 1900.　Z1382.W37

Dissertations

Dossick, Jesse J. Doctoral research on Canada and Canadians, 1884–1983 = Thèses de doctorat concernant le Canada et les Canadiens, 1884–1983. Ottawa : National Library of Canada, 1986. 559 p. ISBN 0-660-53227-1. $38.75.　　**DB85**

More than 12,000 items on Canadian topics from Canadian, U.S., and British institutions. Subject arrangement, with author index. An introductory note to each subject gives statistical information on dissertations in that field. The name index includes the microfilm number of dissertations filmed by the National Library.

§*Sub-doctoral theses on Canada accepted by universities in the United Kingdom & Ireland 1899–1986*, by Elspeth Reid ([Edinburgh] : British Association for Canadian Studies, 1987. 10 p. C$5) lists dissertations not included by Dossick as well as nondoctoral theses and theses submitted for the Fellowship of the Library Association. Covers all fields related to Canada, topically arranged, with author index.　Z1365.D67

Manuscripts and archives

Union list of manuscripts in Canadian repositories : supplement 1981–1982 = Catalogue collectif des manuscrits conservés dans les dépôts d'archives canadiens : supplément 1981–1982 / Robert S. Gordon, dir. ; Peter Yurkiw, ed., Andrée Lavoie, assistant editor. Ottawa : Public Archives Canada : [Sold by] Canadian Govt. Publ. Centre, Supply and Services Canada, 1985. 616 p. ISBN 0-660-53090-2. **DB86**

For main set and previous supplement, see *Guide* DB197.

Cooperative project of the Public Archives of Canada and the Humanities Research Council of Canada.

This 4th suppl. (with 9,000 contributions from 73 institutions) represents new acquisitions between 1 Dec. 1980 and 31 Dec. 1982. CD3622.A2U54

Encyclopedias

Bercuson, David Jay. The Collins dictionary of Canadian history : 1867 to the present / David J. Bercuson and J. L. Granatstein. Toronto : Collins, 1988. 270 p. : ill. ISBN 0-00-217758-7. $24.95. **DB87**

An alphabetical arrangement of 1,600 articles covering "people, institutions, and events [together with] key terms to answer the most commonly asked queries about our collective past."—*Pref.* Short entries with cross-references indicated by small capitals. Chronology in five parallel columns: Major political events; Major social, economic and industrial events; Science and technology; Artistic and cultural events; Sporting events. Appendix of statistical tables and maps. Not indexed. F1033.B488

The Canadian encyclopedia. 2nd ed. Edmonton : Hurtig, c1988. 4 v. (2736 p.) : ill. (some col.), col. maps, ports. ISBN 0-88830-326-2 (set). $175.00. **DB88**

Editor in chief, James H. Marsh.

1st ed., 1985.

Includes entries for all aspects of Canadian life—e.g., places, people, political themes, flora and fauna, historical background, ethnic groups, titles of literary works. Signed articles by specialists, many with short bibliographies. General index; excellent illustrations. This edition adds much new material, updates statistics to incorporate 1986 census figures, and expands the index. A supplementary volume is planned. F1006.C35

Atlases

Historical atlas of Canada / R. Cole Harris, ed. ; Geoffrey J. Matthews, cartographer/designer. Toronto ; Buffalo, N.Y. : Univ. of Toronto Pr., [1987–1990]. v. 1, 3 : col. ill., maps in color ; 38 cm. ISBN 0-8020-2495-5. $100.00. (In progress). **DB89**

Published in separate English and French editions.

Contents: v. 1, From the beginning to 1800 ([1987]. 198 p.); v. 2, The nineteenth century (announced for 1992); v. 3, Addressing the twentieth century, 1891–1961 ([1990]. 197p.).

"Our aim was to use the latest research in historical geography, history, and related disciplines to present the social and economic evolution of Canada."—*Foreword.* Vol. 1 presents maps, drawings, and charts for the prehistorical period, with subsequent periods treated under geographical divisions; e.g., The Atlantic realm, Inland expansion, The St. Lawrence settlements, The Northwest, and ending with Canada in 1800. Notes for each plate list primary and secondary sources. Vol. 3 has two sections: The great transformation 1891–1929, and Crisis and response, 1930s–1961. The 66 plates "examine Canadian's

past through specific groups and individuals in specific times and places."—*Pref.* Within each section the maps are presented chronologically but each features multivariables. Source is given for each map and there are often suggestions for further reading. G1116.S1H5

LATIN AMERICA

General Works

Bibliography

A bibliography of Latin American bibliographies, 1980–1984 : social sciences and humanities / Lionel V. Loroña, ed. Metuchen, N.J. : Scarecrow, 1987. 223 p. ISBN 0-8108-1941-4. $25.00. **DB90**

For annotation, see *Supplement* AA8. Z1601.A2G76

Delorme, Robert. Latin America, 1983–1987 : a social science bibliography. N.Y. : Greenwood, [1988]. 391 p. (Bibliographies and indexes in sociology, no. 14). ISBN 0-313-26406-6. **DB91**

Continues Delorme's two earlier compilations covering 1967–79 and 1979–83 (*Guide* DB221–222).

Lists more than 3,900 books, essays, and periodical articles in English and Spanish. Arrangement is by geographical region or country, subdivided as (1) books and monographs and (2) articles and chapters. Author and subject indexes.

Z7165.L3D4395

Garst, Rachel. Bibliografía anotada de obras de referencia sobre Centroamérica y Panamá en el campo de las ciencias sociales. San José, Costa Rica : Instituto de Investigaciones Sociales, Universidad de Costa Rica ; [S.l.] : Friends World College, Latin American Center, 1983. 2 v. (662 p.). **DB92**

Spanish and English language books and journals addressing socioeconomic and political study of the area, 1968–82, are listed by region or country, subdivided by topic. Annotated; subject, author, and title indexes. Appendix lists relevant libraries. Z7165.C4G37

Grieb, Kenneth J. Central America in the nineteenth and twentieth centuries : an annotated bibliography. Boston : G.K. Hall, c1988. 573 p. ISBN 0-8161-8130-6. $95.00. **DB93**

Lists books (including codification of laws and compilations of documents and treaties) for the period 1810–1980 on Guatamala, Honduras, El Salvador, Nicaragua, Costa Rica, and Belize, in Spanish and English. Indicates library locations. Annotations are well written and balanced. Author and subject indexes. Z1437.G74

Latin American studies : a basic guide to sources / Robert A. McNeil, ed. ; Barbara G. Valk, associate ed. 2nd ed., rev. and enl. Metuchen, N.J. : Scarecrow, 1990. 458 p. ISBN 0-8108-2236-9. **DB94**

1st. ed., 1978 (*Guide* DB228), had title: *Latin American bibliography.*

A complete revision but still a basic handbook for researchers, compiled by a group of librarians. Discusses major Latin American library collections in Great Britain, Europe, and the U.S., and describes how to use them; indicates major bibliographies available (subject, national, and personal) and notes other kinds of reference sources (e.g., dictionaries, newspapers, etc., including nonprint resources such as databases, visual materials). Ends with a discussion of career development in the field and lists institutions with Latin American programs, opportunities for study abroad, societies, conferences, travel guides. Subject and author/title indexes.   Z1601.L324

Nordquist, Joan. Current Central American-U.S. relations. Santa Cruz, Calif. : Reference and Research Services, 1987. 68 p. (Contemporary social issues : a bibliographic series, no. 5). ISBN 0-93785-509-X. $15.00.   **DB95**

An annotated bibliography developed for use by undergraduates. Lists books, articles, government publications, and pamphlets. Appendix of religious organizations and periodicals, with addresses.   F1436.C4N670

Research guide to Central America and the Caribbean / Kenneth J. Grieb, ed. in chief. Madison, Wis. : Univ. of Wisconsin Pr., 1985. 431 p. ISBN 0-299-10050-2. $35.00.   **DB96**

Signed contributions describe major archives or discuss areas for future research on various topics. Topical index. A major resource for scholars.   Z1595.R47

Yale University. Library. Guide to Latin American pamphlets from the Yale University Library : selections from 1600–1900 / ed. by Lofton Wilson ; comp. by Lisa Browar, Anna Fernicola, Miryam A. Ospina. N. Y. : Clearwater Pub. Co., c1985. 7 v. ISBN 0-88354-060-6 (set). $590.00.   **DB97**

Lists more than 6,300 pamphlets for Mexico, 2,000 for Peru, and 1,325 for the rest of Central and South America. Principally concerned with social, political, and economic history, 17th–20th centuries. Each geographical part is divided into subject, author, and imprint date sections.   Z1431.Y34

Manuscripts and archives

Archives nationales (France). Guide des sources de l'histoire de l'Amérique latine et des Antilles dans les archives françaises. Paris : Archives nationales : Diffusé par la Documentation française, 1984. 711 p., [8] p. of plates : col. ill. ISBN 2-86000-104-2. 390F.   **DB98**

Forms part of the series *Guides to the sources of the history of the nations* (*Guide* DB259).

A list of inventories covering materials, 18th century to about 1952, for: Archives nationales, Archives départementales et communales, Archives of ministries (e.g., Relations extérieures, Defense, Economie et des finances), Archives parlementaires, Archives des Chambres de Commerce, Bibliothèque nationale, Archives missionaires, and some private collections. For each, gives address, brief history and terms of access, finding aids, and detailed inventories. Appendix lists ministers, secretaries of state, colonial administrators for the French colonies in the Antilles, and government representatives in territorial Latin America. Not indexed.   Z1610.F72

Encyclopedias; Dictionaries

The Cambridge encyclopedia of Latin America and the Caribbean / gen. eds., Simon Collier, Harold Blakemore, Thomas E. Skidmore. Cambridge ; N. Y. : Cambridge Univ. Pr., 1985. 456 p. : ill. (some col.). ISBN 0-521-26263-1. $42.50.   **DB99**

Provides discussion of all of Latin America and the Caribbean within six topical sections: Physical environment, The economy, The peoples, History, Politics and society, Culture, each subdivided and with short bibliographies appended to each signed subsection. Heavily illustrated with maps, photographs, charts. Subject index. A review in *TLS* 16 May 1986, 522, concludes that the encyclopedia provides "a very valuable means to help understand the issues facing Latin America and the Caribbean, to see all dimensions of this continent's past and present, and to appreciate the nature of both its enormous problems and its enormous potential."   F1406.C36

Latin American historical dictionaries / A. Curtis Wilgus, gen. ed. Metuchen, N.J. : Scarecrow, 1987–1991. v. 7, 16, 22. (In progress).   **DB100**

For annotation and other volumes, see *Guide* DB274.

Contents: v. 7, Chile, by Salvatore Bizzarro (2nd ed., 1987); v. 16, Costa Rica, by Theodore S. Creedman (2nd ed., 1991); v. 22, Cuba, by Jaime Suchlick. (1988).

South America, Central America, and the Caribbean. 1st ed. (1986)– . London : Europa Publications Ltd., 1985– . Biennial. ISSN 0268-0661.   **DB101**

3rd ed. publ. in 1991.

Covers 43 countries and territories. In three parts: (1) Background to the region, which includes essays by scholars on such topics as Church and politics in Latin America, The politics of cocaine in Latin America, Ecology in Latin America; (2) Country surveys, featuring "historical and economic essays written by experts on the country, statistical surveys, directory and bibliography" (*Foreword*); (3) The region, which lists regional organizations, major commodities, research institutes, bibliography of periodical titles. Index to regional organizations. Contributors are mainly British, with a few Americans represented.   F1401.S68

General Works

Directories

Bray, David B. A directory of Latin American studies in the United States / David B. Bray and Richard E. Greenleaf with the assistance of Bruce D. Tobias. [New Orleans, La.] : Roger Thayer Stone Center for Latin American Studies, Tulane Univ. for the Consortium of Latin American Studies Programs, [1986]. 243 p.   **DB102**

Aims to provide "description and analysis of the programs in Latin American studies in 111 institutions of higher education in the United States ... through a mailed questionnaire."—*Introd.* For each, gives address, directors, courses offered, faculty, degrees offered, library description, overseas opportunities, and student support. Not indexed.

F1409.95.U6B73

Directorio latinoamericano : socio-económico, político, académico = Latin American directory. Quito, Ecuador : EDIEC Latina, c1985. 4 v.   **DB103**

Contents: v. 1, México y Centro América; v. 2, Caribe y Brasil; v. 3, Group Andino; v. 4, Cono sur y extrarregionales.

Contains "15,000 names of institutions and personalities, mass media, governments, companies, chambers of commerce, labour unions, inter-regional organizations, academic centers, political parties, and a variety of different Latin American associations, and also the names of its leaders."—*Foreword*. Arranged by country, then by type of organization; for each entry, gives name of organization, address, title or name of person in charge, and occasionally phone numbers. Vol. 4 covers organizations in other countries of interest to Latin America (e.g., branches of Latin American banks, university departments, government offices). Lists of countries and topics used.

F1406.5.D57

Fenton, Thomas P. Latin America and Caribbean : a directory of resources / comp. and ed. by Thomas P. Fenton and Mary J. Heffron. Maryknoll, N.Y. : Orbis Books ; London : Zed Books, c1986. 142 p. : ill. ISBN 0-88344-529-8 (pbk.). $9.95.   **DB104**

An expansion of the Latin American and Caribbean chapters in *Third World resource directory* (*Supplement* CH51).

A directory of organizations, news services, etc., together with a bibliography of books, periodicals, pamphlets, articles, audiovisual materials concerned with human rights in the region. Indexes for organizations, individuals, titles, geographic areas, and subjects. Z1601.F46

Manual para las relaciones Europeo-Latinoamericanas = Handbook for European-Latin American relations. Madrid : Instituto de Relaciones Europeo-Latino-americanas, c1987. 772 p. ISBN 84-393-9310-8. $50.00.
DB105

Compiled by Brigitte Farenholtz and Wolfgang Grenz.
In English and Spanish.

Offers directory information based on questionnaire responses from about 500 organizations—academic, government, business, religious, technical—with interests in one or more Latin American countries. Includes short biographies of individuals. Arranged by country, then by city (using Spanish form of name). Indexed by personal name, region, subject, institution, and acronym. An appendix lists diplomatic missions, periodical publications, banks, cultural institutes, and organizations in Austria, Switzerland, and Sweden. AS97.M3

National directory of Latin Americanists : biographies of 4,915 specialists / comp. in the Hispanic Division of the Library of Congress. 3rd ed. / ed. by Inge Maria Harman. Wash. : Library of Congress : For sale by the Supt. of Docs., U.S. Govt. Print. Off., 1985. 1011 p. ISBN 0-8444-0491-8. **DB106**

1st ed., 1966.
Superintendent of Documents classification: LC 1.2:L34.

Provides information on active Latin Americanists, based on responses to questionnaires. Index by subject specialty and by geographical area. A fourth edition has been announced (1991).

§ The European equivalent is *Latinoamericanistas en Europa 1990 : registro biobibliografico*, comp. by Jean Stroom (Amsterdam : Centrum voor Studie in Dokumentatie van Latijns Amerika, [1990]. 240 p.). F1409.8.A2N37

Tinker guide to Latin American and Caribbean policy and scholarly resources in metropolitan New York / ed. by Ronald G. Hellman & Beth Kempler Pfannl. [N.Y.] : Bildner Center for Western Hemisphere Studies, Graduate School and Univ. Center, City Univ. of New York, c1988. 217 p. ISBN 0-929972-00-7. ISBN 0-929972-01-5 (pbk.). **DB107**

Lists 212 organizations and collections interested in public policy, international relations, and social sciences. For each gives name, address, phone number, and activities and collections related to Latin American and the Caribbean. Appendix lists bookstores, publishers, and scholars at the City University of New York interested in this subject. Name and subject indexes. F1409.95.U6T56

Histories

The Cambridge history of Latin America / ed. by Leslie Bethell. Cambridge [England] ; N.Y. : Cambridge Univ. Pr., 1985–1990. v. 3–5, 7 : ill. ISBN 0-521-23223-6 (v. 1). (In progress). **DB108**

For v. 1 (in 2 v., now designated [v. 1–2]), see *Guide* DB281.

Contents: v. 3, From independence to c.1870 (1985. 945 p.); v. 4–5, c.1870–1930 (1986. 2 v.); v. 7, Latin America since 1930 : Mexico, Central America and the Caribbean (1990. 775 p.). Vol. 8, Latin America since 1930 : Spanish America, is scheduled for publication in 1991.

Cambridge Univ. Pr. has republished parts or chapters of various of these volumes under new titles: e.g., *Colonial Spanish America* (1987) is taken from v.1–2; *The independence of Latin America* (1987) is from part of v.3; *Central America since independence* (1991) reissues chapters from v.3, 5, 7; *Latin America : economy and society 1870–1930* (1989) is part of v.4; *Colonial Brazil* (1987) and *Brazil: empire and republic 1822–1930* (1989) are reprints of chapters from v.1–2, 3 and 5 respectively. F1410.C1834

Argentina

Horvath, Laszlo. Peronism and the three Perons : a checklist of material on Peronism and on Juan Domingo, Eva, and Isabel Peron, and their writings, in the Hoover Institution library and archives and in the Stanford University Libraries. Stanford, Calif. : Hoover Institution, Stanford Univ., c1988. 170 p. (Hoover Press bibliography, 71). ISBN 0-8179-2712-3 (pbk.). $16.95.
DB109

A checklist of books, pamphlets, offprints, and archival material at Stanford. Arranged in four sections: (1) Works on peronism and on Don Domingo Peron; (2) Works on Eva Peron; (3) Works on Isabel Peron; (4) All published writings of the three Perons at Stanford. Not indexed. Z1630.3.H67

Bolivia

Yeager, Gertrude Matyoka. Bolivia. Oxford ; Santa Barbara, Calif. : Clio Pr., c1988. 228 p. : map. (World bibliographical series, v. 89). ISBN 1-85109-066-5. $60.00.
DB110

Offers 816 annotated entries for books, government reports, periodical articles, and dissertations. Topically arranged in 36 sections. Author/title/subject indexes. Z1641.Y43

Brazil

Bibliography

Bryant, Solena V. Brazil / Solena V. Bryant, comp. ; ed. by Sheila R. Herstein. Oxford ; Santa Barbara, Calif. : Clio Pr., c1985. 244 p. : map. (World bibliographical series, v. 57). ISBN 1-85109-000-2. $60.00. **DB111**

Presents 802 annotated entries for books, essays, and articles arranged in 36 topical sections. Emphasizes English-language materials published in the 1970s and early 1980s. Author/title/subject index. Z1671.B78

Corrêa, Carlos Humberto. Catálogo das dissertações e teses dos cursos de pós-graduação em História, 1973–1985. Florianópolis : Editora da UFSC [Universita Fed. de Santa Catarina], 1987. 400 p. **DB112**

A university-by-university listing of 770 theses completed in history at 14 Brazilian universities 1973–85. Author, advisor, and subject indexes. Z1686.C59

Hartness, Ann. Brazil in reference books, 1965–1989 : an annotated bibliography. Metuchen, N.J. : Scarecrow, 1991. 351 p. ISBN 0-8108-2400-0. **DB113**

Aims to satisfy the "need for reference materials to provide bibliographic data, define terms, locate places, identify individuals and supply statistics."—*Introd.* Books, pamphlets, reprints, annuals, and whole issues of journals are arranged by broad topic, subdivided by format, geographic area, or subtopic as needed. Cites reference material at the regional, country, state, and city levels. Annotations indicate scope of the work. Author and subject indexes. A very useful compilation.

Z1671.H38

Library resources

France. Ministère des affaires étrangères. Archives. Guide des sources de l'histoire du Brésil aux archives du Ministère français des affaires étrangères / Pascal Even. Paris : Publications de l'I.H.E.A.L., 1987. 63 p. : ill. (Travaux & mémoires de l'Institut des hautes études de l'Amérique latine, 38 ; Travaux & mémoires de l'Institut des hautes études de l'Amérique latine. Collection "Textes & documents", 1).   **DB114**

Lists files of materials relevant to Brazil in the Archives. Appendix lists French representatives to Brazil. Not indexed.

Z1699.F73

Encyclopedias

Dicionário histórico-biográfico brasileiro, 1930–1983 / coordenação de Israel Beloch e Alzira Alves de Abreu. Rio de Janeiro-RJ : Forense-Universitária : FINEP, 1984. v. 4 : ports.   **DB115**

For v. 1–3 and annotation, see *Guide* DB313.

Contents: v. 4, Peris–Zup. Completes the set.

This last volume includes "Bibliografía geral," p.[3593]–3631, and two pages of corrections.   F2504.D53

Donato, Hernâni. Dicionário das batalhas brasileiras. São Paulo : Instituição Brasileira de Difusão Cultural, [1987], c1986. 542 p. (Biblioteca "Estudos brasileiros", 15).   **DB116**

Cover title: Dos conflitos com indígenas ás guerrilhas políticas urbanas e rurais.

Includes a list of popular names of battles, a chronology, surveys of wars, and a short-entry dictionary of people, battles, places, etc.   F2522.D66

Chile

Blakemore, Harold. Chile. Oxford ; Santa Barbara, Calif. : Clio Pr., c1988. 197 p., [2] p. of plates : maps. (World bibliographical series, v. 97). ISBN 1-85109-026-6. $50.00.   **DB117**

Presents 642 annotated entries for books and longer periodical articles topically arranged in 29 sections. Most are English-language works although Spanish-language materials are included where there is little or no coverage of the topic in English. Emphasizes recent publications. Author, title, and subject indexes.   Z1701.B56

Colombia

Davis, Robert H. Colombia. Oxford ; Santa Barbara, Calif. : Clio Pr., c1990. 204 p. : map. (World bibliographical series, v. 112). ISBN 1-85109-093-2. $60.00.   **DB118**

Intends to present "a good representative sample for an English-language reader" (*Pref.*) with a preference for materials of the last 25 years. About 660 annotated entries, arranged topically. Indexed by author, title, and subject.   Z1731.D38

Ecuador

Corkill, David. Ecuador. Oxford ; Santa Barbara, Calif. : Clio Pr., c1989. 155 p. : map. (World bibliographical series, v. 101). ISBN 1-85109-069-X. $45.00.   **DB119**

A topical arrangement of 557 annotated entries for books and articles in Spanish and English. Indexed by author, title, and subject.   Z1761.C67

El Salvador

Woodward, Ralph Lee. El Salvador. Oxford ; Santa Barbara, Calif. : Clio Pr., c1988. 213 p. : map. (World bibliographical series, v. 98). ISBN 1-85109-073-8. $60.00.   **DB120**

" . . . guide to the most significant publications in the field with annotations that should help the reader to identify both the scope and utility of individual items."—*Introd.* Cites 659 books and articles (mainly in English with some Spanish) plus a few theses and dissertations. Topically arranged in 40 sections. Author/title/subject index.   Z1491.W66

Guyana

Chambers, Frances. Guyana. Oxford ; Santa Barbara, Calif. : Clio Pr., c1989. 206 p. : map. (World bibliographical series, v. 96). ISBN 1-85109-070-3. $55.00.   **DB121**

Provides 606 annotated entries for books, periodical articles, and government publications, topically arranged. Author, title, and subject indexes.   Z1791.C48

Honduras

Danby, Colin. Honduras bibliography and research guide / Colin Danby, Richard Swedberg. Cambridge, Mass. : Central American Information Office, [1984]. 333 p. ISBN 0-942328-06-X (pbk.).   **DB122**

A topical listing of books, essays and chapters, government publications, articles, and a few unpublished papers on Honduran history, statistics, economy, society, the state, and U.S. policy toward Honduras. Each section and subsection begins with a brief overview pointing out the standard works. List of major periodicals and organizations with addresses; author index.

Z1471.D35

Enciclopedia histórica de Honduras : obra fundamental de información y consulta e imprescindible auxiliar pedagógico para maestros, padres de familia y estudiantes de todos los niveles / editada bajo la dirección de Ramiro Colindres Ortega . . . [et al.]. Tegucigalpa, D.C., Honduras, C.A. : Graficentro Editores, 1988. v. 1 : ill. (In progress).   **DB123**

Contents: v. 1. Honduras precolombina. Período colonial.

A heavily illustrated encyclopedia intended for use in schools and the home. Vol. 1 is in 5 topical sections: Honduras precolombina (1500 a. de C./1502 d. de C.); Colapso del Imperio Maya; Período colonial (1502–1821); Le iglesia y la cultura colonial; L'empira y la Soberanía nacional. No index in v. 1.

F1506.E53

Mexico

Beltrán Bernal, Trinidad. Bibliografía histórica del Estado de México / Trinidad Beltrán Bernal, Eliva Montes de Oca N. [Zinacantepec, Edo. de México] : El Colegio Mexiquense, [1989–1990]. 2 v.   **DB124**

An annotated listing of books, articles, government publications, and pamphlets. Arranged by period up to the 1940s, with subdivisions for topics such as archaeology, literature, history, economics. Author index. Vol.2 is a supplement to v.1, listing materials omitted therefrom but following the same arrangement.   F1301.B441

Enciclopedia de México / director, José Rogelio Alvarez. Ciudad de México : Enciclopedia de México : Secretaría de Educación Pública, 1987–1988. 14 v. (8460 p.) : ill. ISBN 968-6234-00-4 (set).   **DB125**

1st ed., 1977.

An extensive encyclopedia that covers people, institutions, places, and topics. Indexes at the end of v. 14 for authors of articles and broad topics (referring to titles of articles instead of volume and page number)—e.g., academias, artisanias y arte popular, cocina, ciudad, villas y municipios, and personas. The last section is subdivided by profession and by century.

F1204.E46

Flores Villela, Carlos Arturo. México, la cultura, el arte y la vida cotidiana. México, D.F. : Coordinación de Humanidades, Universidad Nacional Autónoma de México, 1990. 2 v. (561 p.). (Cuadernos del CIIH. Serie fuentes, 7).   **DB126**

Almost 7,000 references are arranged in 51 broad headings (e.g., Architecture, Literature, Kitsch, Urbanism, Chicanos) with subsections for categories such as general works, theory, biographies. Cites books and articles. Author index.

F1210.M49

Musacchio, Humberto. Diccionario enciclopédico de México. México, D.F. : A. Léon, Editor, [1989]. 4 v. : ill. (some col.). ISBN 968-61-0593-X (set).   **DB127**

Short articles about people, places, organizations, journals, and newspapers, together with longer articles on topics such as political parties or education. Special emphasis on art and the cinema. Alphabetical arrangement. Lacks an index or cross-references.   F1204.M95

Bibliography

Guía internacional de investigaciones sobre México / el Colegio de la Frontera Norte = International guide to research on Mexico / Center for U.S.-Mexican Studies, University of California, San Diego. 1986– . Tijuana, Baja California, México : El Colegio ; La Jolla, Calif. : The Center, 1986– . Annual. ISSN 0883-7740.   **DB128**

Formed by merger of *International inventory of current Mexico-related research* (Los Angeles : Center for U.S.-Mexican studies, Univ. of California, San Diego and Univ. of California consortium on Mexico and the U.S., v. 1–4, 1982–84; v. 1 had title *Current research inventory*) and *Estudios fronterizos México-Estados Unidos : directorio general de investigadores* (Tijuana : Centro de Estudios Fronterizos del Norte de México, no. 1–2, 1982–84).

" . . . focuses on unpublished research in progress at hundreds of sites around the world."—*Editor's note.* Based on responses to questionnaires, each entry includes name, address, and phone number of investigator; title and abstract of project with beginning and ending dates; and funding source(s). Topical arrangement; concentrates on social sciences and humani-

ties. Indexes for: researcher, topics (in both Spanish and English), and organizations and institutions.   F1225.5.G84

Nicaragua

Sandinista Nicaragua : an annotated bibliography with analytical introductions / by Neil Snarr and associates. Ann Arbor, Mich. : Pierian Pr., 1989–1990. 2 v. ISBN 0-87650-255-9 (v. 1). $40.00.   **DB129**

Contents: Pt. 1, Revolution, religion, and social policy: an annotated bibliography with analytical introductions (1989. 188 p.); Pt. 2, Economy, politics, and foreign policy: an annotated bibliography with analytical introductions (1990. 191 p.)

Chapters signed by scholars address various topics of the ten years of Sandinista Nicaragua. Critical introductions and lengthy annotated bibliography form each chapter. Lists English and some Spanish books, with a few government publications and periodical articles. Author and title indexes in each volume. Appended in v. 2 is a chronology of 20th-century Nicaragua.   Z1487.P65S26

Paraguay

Nickson, R. Andrew. Paraguay. Oxford ; Santa Barbara, Calif. : Clio Pr., c1987. 212 p. : map. (World bibliographical series, v. 84). ISBN 1-85109-028-2. $45.00.   **DB130**

Offers 600 annotated entries organized into 33 topical chapters. Cross-references; indexed by author, title, and subject.   Z1821.N53

Peru

Diccionario histórico y biográfico del Perú, siglos XV–XX / dirección, producción, revisión, ilustración, epígrafes, diagramación y edición, Carlos Milla Batres. Lima, Perú : Editorial Milla Batres, 1986. 9 v. : ill.   **DB131**

An encyclopedia of Peruvian history with a preponderance of biographical entries. Some living persons are included; bibliography appended to many articles.

Supplemented by *Diccionario histórico biográfico de los conquistadores del Perú*, comp. José Antonio del Busto Duthurburu (Lima : Librería Studium Ediciones, 1986–87. v. 1–2, in progress), which gives information on the Spanish conquerors with reference to chronicles and secondary sources.

F3404.D53

Fisher, John Robert. Peru. Oxford ; Santa Barbara, Calif. : Clio Pr., c1989. 193 p. : map. (World bibliographical series, v. 109). ISBN 1-85109-100-9. $58.00.   **DB132**

A selective annotated bibliography of 705 recent publications in English (with some in Spanish): books, U.N. publications, and a few articles. Topically arranged in 31 sections. Cross-references; author, title, and subject indexes. Z1851.F57

Peru. Archivo General de la Nación. Guía del archivo histórico. Lima, Perú : Archivo General de la Nación : Fondo del Libro del B.I.P., 1987. 44 p., [2] leaves of plates : ill.   **DB133**

Descriptions of files in the Archivo, focusing on those from 1708 till about 1940. A few contain material as late as 1985.

CD4223.P47

Suriname

Hoefte, Rosemarijn. Suriname. Oxford ; Santa Barbara, Calif. : Clio Pr., 1990. 227 p. : map. (World bibliographical series, v. 117). ISBN 1-85109-103-3. £37.00. **DB134**
     A topical listing of 731 books and a few journal articles in English, Spanish, German, French, and Dutch. Indexed by author, title and subject.

Uruguay

Finch, M. H. J. Uruguay / Henry Finch ; with the assistance of Alicia Casas de Barrán, compilers. Oxford ; Santa Barbara, Calif. : Clio Pr., c1989. 232 p. : map. (World bibliographical series, v. 102). ISBN 1-85109-098-3. $60.00. **DB135**
     Offers 667 annotated entries arranged in 34 topical sections. Covers River Plate area. Indexed by author, title, and subject. Theses and dissertations on Uruguay, p. xxvii–xxix; this section not indexed.   Z1881.F56

Venezuela

Bibliography

Lovera De-Sola, R. J. Guía para el estudio de la historia de Venezuela. Caracas : Academia Nacional de la Historia, 1982. 217 p. (Biblioteca de la Academia Nacional de la Historia. Estudios, monografías y ensayos, 23). **DB136**
     The 700 annotated entries for reference materials include bibliographies and guides for the study of Latin American as well as Venezuelan history, together with historical encyclopedias, chronologies, collections of documents, and archival guides. An author listing of books, pamphlets, periodicals and articles. Not indexed.   Z1926.L68

Sullivan, William M. Dissertations and theses on Venezuelan topics, 1900–1985. Metuchen, N.J. : Scarecrow, 1988. 274 p. ISBN 0-8108-2017-X. **DB137**
     An annotated listing of master's theses and doctoral dissertations accepted in the U.S., Canada, the U.K., France, Austria, Venezuela, Germany, and Belgium, arranged by broad topics. Author and subject indexes.   Z1911.S84

Waddell, D. A. G. Venezuela. Oxford, England ; Santa Barbara, Calif. : Clio Pr., c1990. 206 p. : map. (World bibliographical series, v. 110). ISBN 1-85109-106-8. $59.00. **DB138**
     Presents 800 annotated entries in a topical arrangement. Indexed by author, title, and subject.   Z1911.W33

Encyclopedias

Diccionario de historia de Venezuela. Caracas, Venezuela : Fundacíon Polar, 1988 [i.e. 1989]. 3 v. ISBN 980-6100-16-6 (set). **DB139**
     A scholarly encyclopedia covering Venezuela from pre-Conquest up to about 1985/6 and offering an alphabetical arrangement of 10,000 entries for people, places, events, institutions, historiography, and similar topics. Articles are signed with initials; most have bibliographies of books and articles, and cross-references to related articles. Appendixes list chronicles and travelers' accounts, rulers and administrators, bishops,

administrative divisions, oil towns, treaties, etc. Authoritative but not indexed.   F2304.D43

ISLANDS OF THE CARIBBEAN AND WEST ATLANTIC

General works

Hughes, Roger. The Caribbean : a basic annotated bibliography for students, librarians and general readers. London : Commonwealth Institute Library Services, 1987. 71 p. (Commonwealth bibliographies, no. 6). ISBN 0-946140-32-4. £2.50. **DB140**
     "... a selective list of the main publications available ... including a short annotation to indicate the level and coverage of the publication."—*Introd.* Subdivided under the headings Caribbean experience, Lifestyle, Communication, Education, Arts. Index by name of island. Covers only books and documents.   Z1501

Provost, Foster. Columbus : an annotated guide to the study on his life and writings, 1750 to 1988. Detroit : Publ. for the John Carter Brown Library by Omnigraphics, 1991. 225 p. ISBN 1-55888-157-3. **DB141**
     A topically arranged bibliography of about 800 books and articles on Columbus (editions of primary source materials, biographies of Columbus, works concerning Columbus' ships, etc.). Literary works are excluded. Annotations emphasize scope and purpose. Indexes of authors/editors and anonymous titles, of persons and places treated in the bibliography and of topics. Cross-references.   Z8187.P76

Bahamas

Boultbee, Paul G. The Bahamas. Oxford ; Santa Barbara, Calif. : Clio Pr., c1989. 195 p. : map. (World bibliographical series, v. 108). ISBN 1-85109-102-5. $57.00. **DB142**
     Offers 703 annotated entries for books, articles, and a few government documents, topically arranged in 35 sections. Author/title/subject index.   Z1503.B68

Barbados

Potter, Robert B. Barbados / Robert B. Potter, Graham M.S. Dann, compilers. Oxford ; Santa Barbara, Calif. : Clio Pr., c1987. 356 p. : map. (World bibliographical series, v. 76). ISBN 1-85109-022-3. $70.00. **DB143**
     Lists books, theses, and articles deemed significant and readily available in large libraries or through interlibrary loan. 958 annotated entries are arranged in broad categories. Author, title, and subject indexes.   Z1561.B3P67

Cuba

Chilcote, Ronald H. Cuba, 1953–1978 : a bibliographic guide to the literature / ed. and comp. by Ronald H. Chilcote with Sheryl Lutjens. White Plains, N.Y. : Kraus Internat., c1986. 2 v. ISBN 0-527-16824-6. **DB144**

Similar in plan to Lambros Comitas' *The complete Caribbeana* (*Guide* DB408). Offers a comprehensive, classed listing of books, periodical articles, pamphlets, and dissertations. Principal sections include: Structure of society; Culture; Politics; Economics; International affairs; Periodization of the revolution; Revolutionary leadership. The latter has separate extensive sections for Ché Guevara and Fidel Castro, listing their speeches and writings as well as works about them. English translations of Spanish titles are given in brackets. Appendix: Annotated list of Cuban newspapers. Author index, but no detailed subject approach. Z1511.C48

Pérez, Louis A. Cuba : an annotated bibliography. N.Y. : Greenwood, 1988. 301 p. (Bibliographies and indexes in world history, no. 10). ISBN 0-313-26162-8. $45.00. **DB145**

Consists of 1,120 annotated entries in topical arrangement, including English and Spanish books, articles, and journals. Author/title/subject indexes. Z1511.P43

———— A guide to Cuban collections in the United States. N.Y. : Greenwood, 1991. 179 p. (Reference guides to archival and manuscript sources in world history, no. 1). ISBN 0-313-26858-4. $39.95. **DB146**

Emphasizes "collections of substantial and varied holdings... [but] exceptions have been made... where records deal with a particularly critical period in Cuban history or if the records are related to persons involved in these events in some important fashion."—*Introd.* Arranged by state, then by repository. For each, gives for each address and brief description of each file. A "Collection index" provides access from names of individual record files. Subject index. Z1525.P44

Dominica

Myers, Robert A. Dominica. Oxford ; Santa Barbara, Calif. : Clio Pr., c1987. 190 p. : map. (World bibliographical series, v. 82). ISBN 1-85109-031-2. $55.00. **DB147**

Offers 93 items, mostly in English but a few in French or Caribe, including books, articles and chapters. Author/title/subject index.

§ The same author has compiled a comprehensive bibliography, *Resource guide to Dominica 1493–1986* (New Haven, Conn. : HRAF, 1987. 3 v. [649 l.]), which includes archival materials, films, recordings, paintings, and photographs as well as books, articles, theses, etc., with a name and subject index. Z1561.D65M93

Dominican Republic

Rutinel Domínguez, Ulises. Diccionario histórico dominicano / Ulises Rutinel Domínguez, Manuel Darío De León. Santo Domingo : Editora Universitaria, 1986. 365 p. : ill., maps, ports. (Collección Historia y sociedad, 69 ; Publicaciones de la Universidad Autónoma de Santo Domingo, 499). **DB148**

Offers short entries for places, subjects, and people. Includes a list of prelates 1510–1986, governors 1492–1821, presidents and governors 1844–1990, and reproduction of significant documents. Not indexed; although there are interesting maps and illustrations, they are not well produced. F1932.R875

Schoenhals, Kai P. Dominican Republic. Oxford ; Santa Barbara, Calif. : Clio Pr., c1990. 210 p. : map. (World

bibliographical series, v. 111). ISBN 1-85109-110-6. $62.50. **DB149**

Arranges 913 annotated entries for books, articles, dissertations, and government publications (e.g., *Congressional record*)—mostly English- and Spanish-language materials in 40 sections. Author/title/subject indexes. Z1536.S36

Grenada

Schoenhals, Kai P. Grenada. Oxford : Clio Pr., 1991. 179 p. : ill., 1 map. (World bibliographical series, 119.). ISBN 1-85109-126-2. £37.95. **DB150**

Citations to 793 books, dissertations and periodical articles are arranged by topic. Author/title/subject index.

Haiti

Lawless, Robert. Haiti : a research handbook / by Robert Lawless ; with contributions from Ilona Maria Lawless... [et al.]. N.Y. : Garland, 1990. [354] p. (Garland reference library of social science, v. 546). ISBN 0-8240-6543-3. **DB151**

Intended for both specialists and general readers. Cites 2,040 books, journal articles, dissertations, and masters essays in a numbered topical arrangement (e.g., History—general or by period, Fiction, Health, AIDS, Butterflies, Mammalogy). Each section begins with a bibliographic essay of two to four pages that emphasizes published materials widely available in major libraries. Includes a list of Creole language item numbers and an author index. Expanded from Lawless' *Bibliography on Haiti : English and Creole items* (Gainsville, Fla. : Center for Latin American Studies, Univ. of Florida, 1985. 146p. Caribbean Migration Program, Occasional paper no.6). Z1531.L39

Puerto Rico

Cevallos, Elena E. Puerto Rico / Elena E. Cevallos, comp. ; ed. by Sheila R. Herstein. Oxford ; Santa Barbara, Calif. : Clio Pr., c1985. 193 p. : map. (World bibliographical series, v. 52). ISBN 0-903450-89-5. £28.50. **DB152**

Consists of 605 annotated entries for books, government publications, and articles, topically arranged. For the "non-specialist, English speaking reader."—*Introd.* Most entries are in English, except for Spanish-language materials which are classics or the only available source. Except for classic works, publications date from 1970 to about 1984. Emphasis on economics and politics. Author/title/subject index. F1958.Z99C48

Fowlie-Flores, Fay. Annotated bibliography of Puerto Rican bibliographies. N.Y. : Greenwood, 1990. 167 p. (Bibliographies and indexes in ethnic studies, no. 1). ISBN 0-313-26124-5. **DB153**

Lists, in topical arrangement, book or pamphlet-length bibliographies published (some in mimeographed form) in Spanish or English up to 1988. Annotations are two to three sentences in length, usually descriptive. Author/title/subject indexes. Z1551.F69

Trinidad and Tobago

Chambers, Frances. Trinidad and Tobago / Frances Chambers, comp. ; ed. by Sheila Herstein. Oxford ; Santa Barbara, Calif. : Clio Pr., c1986. 213 p. : map. (World bibliographical series, v. 74). ISBN 1-85109-020-7. **DB154**

A selective list of some 640 entries from books, journal articles, and a few government documents. Topical arrangement. Annotations, author/title/subject index. Z1561.T7C43

DC

Europe

GENERAL WORKS

Bibliography

Conlon, Pierre M. Le siècle des lumières : bibliographie chronologique. Genève : Droz, 1986–1990. v. 4–7. (Histoire des idées et critique littéraire, vol. 239, 250, 266, 282.). (In progress). **DC1**

For annotation, see *Supplement* AA113.   Z7128.E55C66

Ferguson, Chris D. Europe in transition : a select, annotated bibliography of the twelfth-century renaissance. N.Y. : Garland, 1989. 156 p. (Garland reference library of the humanities, vol. 875). ISBN 0-8240-3722-7. **DC2**

A topical arrangement of books, articles, and dissertations, most published since World War II and preponderantly in English, French, and German (but with a few in Spanish and Italian) "that examine the major social, political, cultural and economic currents."—*Pref.* Annotations are usually a paragraph in length, and there is a good discussion of bibliographies. Indexes of authors and of persons as subjects.   Z2000.F45

Hacken, Richard D. Central European economic history from Waterloo to OPEC, 1815–1975 : a bibliography. N.Y. : Greenwood, 1987. 270 p. (Bibliographies and indexes in economics and economic history, no. 6). ISBN 0-313-25460-5. **DC3**

Lists 5,300 monographs, bibliographies, dissertations, and articles from journals and festschriften, grouped in five broad categories (Economic conditions, Agriculture, Industry, Business and commerce, and Finance) subdivided geographically and chronologically. German-speaking and mixed-language areas of central Europe are covered; non-German-speaking areas are not. Concerned with secondary rather than primary source materials published in Western languages, particularly English and German. Cross-references; author index.   Z7165.C42H33

Krewson, Margrit B. The German-speaking countries of Europe : a selective bibliography. 2nd ed., rev. and enl.
Wash. : Library of Congress, 1989. 318 p. ISBN 0-8444-0650-3.   **DC4**

1st ed., 1985.

Superintendent of Documents classification: LC 43.9:G31.

"Intends to provide researchers and students with a current guide to sources on the German-speaking countries of Europe: Austria, the Federal Republic of Germany, the German Democratic Republic, Liechtenstein, and Switzerland."—*Introd.* Preference is given to English-language books and documents published in the 1980s, although publications of the 1970s and publications in German are also among the 1,485 items cited. Arranged by broad topic under country. LC call numbers are given. Indexed by main entry.

§ The Library of Congress has also published *The economies of the German-speaking countries of Europe : a selective bibliography*, comp. by Margrit Krewson and Stephan H. Lindner (Wash. : 1986. 98p.).   Z2000.K73

Messick, Frederic M. Primary sources in European diplomacy, 1914–1945 : a bibliography of published memoirs and diaries. N.Y. : Greenwood, [1987]. 221 p. : maps. (Bibliographies and indexes in world history, no. 6). ISBN 0-313-24555-X. $39.95.   **DC5**

For annotation, see *Supplement* CJ9.   Z2000.M395

Sheehan, Michael M. Domestic society in medieval Europe : a select bibliography / comp. by Michael M. Sheehan and Jacqueline Murray. Toronto : Pontifical Institute of Mediaeval Studies, c1990. 57 p. ISBN 0-88844-413-3.   **DC6**

"… intended to provide preliminary orientation for the study of medieval European demography and kinship, family and marriage, various special groups, related to the family, or excluded from it and the attitudes of the population to each of these institutions and groups."—*Pref.* 453 well-chosen entries are topically arranged, each with a very brief annotation (usually a phrase) and a note indicating the time period covered. Index of authors and editors.   Z7164.M2S46

Taylor, Barry. European economic and social history, 1450–1789. Manchester ; N.Y. : Manchester Univ. Pr. ; N.Y. : Distr. by St. Martin's Pr., c1989. 303 p. ISBN 0-7190-1948-6.   **DC7**

Published in U.K. as: *Society and economy in early modern Europe, 1450–1789 : a bibliography of post-war research*.

Concentrates on English-language publications, 1945–87, but includes a few older classics and a sprinkling of French, German, Spanish, and Italian works. Topical arrangement of books (noting reviews), articles, and essays, with brief annotations, often critical. Extensive cross-references; topographical and author/editor indexes.   HC240.T356

Zophy, Jonathan W. An annotated bibliography of the Holy Roman Empire. N.Y. : Greenwood, [1986]. 398 p. (Bibliographies and indexes in world history, no. 3). ISBN 0-313-24028-0. $65.00.   **DC8**

A classed listing of more than 3,000 items that includes sections for rulers, relations with the church, the nobility, the peasantry, economic and social history, etc. Annotations are brief. Author and subject indexes.   Z2236.Z66

Library resources

Cook, Chris. Sources in European political history / Chris Cook and Geoff Pugh. N.Y. : Facts on File, [1987–89]. v. 1–3. ISBN 0-8160-1016-1. $35.00. (In progress).   **DC9**

Contents: v. 1, The European left. (237 p. $35.00); v. 2, Diplomacy and international affairs (190 p.); v. 3, War and resistance.

U.K. ed. published by Macmillan; v.2 of that edition has title, *Diplomacy and imperialism.*

Intends to locate and describe unpublished personal papers of major Western European political figures of the 19th and 20th centuries. Similar in arrangement to Cook's *Sources in British political history* (*Guide* DC287)—i.e., alphabetical under personal name, each entry giving dates, very brief biographical information, location of manuscripts and papers. Occasionally, a citation will mention an inventory or cite published papers. Vol. 1 describes "over 1,000 individuals active in socialist, labour, radical and revolutionary movements in Europe . . . from the Revolution of 1848 through to the end of the Second World War in 1945."—*Introd.* Excludes the Eastern European, Irish, and British left. Vol. 2 adds "private papers of a further 1,000 individuals active in European diplomacy and international affairs . . . broadly from 1870 . . . to 1945." Figures from Britain and Ireland are again excluded. Thus far, not indexed.   Z2000.C57

Higbee, Joan Florence. Scholars' guide to Washington, D.C. for southwest European studies : France, Italy (including Ancient Rome), Malta, Portugal, Spain, the Vatican / Joan Florence Higbee; ed., Zdenek V. David. Wash. : Wilson Center Pr. ; Lanham, Md. : distr. by Univ. Pr. of America, 1989. 475 p. (Scholars' guide to Washington, D.C., 13). ISBN 0-943875-12-9. $45.00. ISBN 0-943875-11-0 (pbk.). $24.95.   **DC10**

Similar to other guides in the series—e.g., for Central and East European studies (*Guide* DC14) and for Northwest Europe (*Guide* DC15). Describes about 500 organizations, government agencies (including embassies), library collections, museums, academic programs and departments, noting their resources and any finding aids, along with pertinent directory information (address, phone number, hours, etc.). Appendixes: directory of bookstores in the Washington area; housing and travel information; government holidays. Indexes: Oral histories and personal papers; Artists; Library subject strengths; Subject; Organizations and institutions.   Z2000.H5

Handbooks

Cook, Chris. The Longman handbook of modern European history, 1763–1985 / Chris Cook and John Stevenson. London ; N.Y. : Longman, [1987]. 435 p. : maps. ISBN 0-582-48585-1. ISBN 0-582-48584-3 (pbk.) : £17.95.   **DC11**

Offers "chronological, statistical and tabular information . . . biographies of important individuals, a glossary of commonly used historical terms and a topic bibliography . . . . The coverage of the volume is European-wide in its broadest sense, including events in Russia, the Balkans and Scandinavia."—*Pref.* Complements Cook and Stevenson's *Longman handbook of modern British history, 1714–1980* (*Guide* DC306).   D299.C627

EASTERN AND SOUTHEASTERN EUROPE

Bibliography

Church and state in postwar eastern Europe : a bibliographical survey / comp. by Paul Mojzes. N.Y. : Greenwood, [1987]. 109 p. (Bibliographies and indexes in religious studies, no. 11). ISBN 0-313-24002-7.   **DC12**

"The subject of this bibliography is the literature on the relationship between Soviet and Eastern European churches and the societies in which they have existed since the end of World War II. Covered are Albania, Bulgaria, Czechoslovakia, East Germany, Hungary, Poland, Romania, and Yugoslavia."—*Pref.* Two survey chapters on the mutual relations between the churches and society are followed by country sections listing books and articles. Author, title, and subject indexes.   Z7776.72.C5

Horak, Stephan M. Russia, the USSR, and Eastern Europe : a bibliographic guide to English language publications, 1981–1985. Littleton, Colo. : Libraries Unlimited, 1987. 273 p. ISBN 0-87287-561-X. $32.50.   **DC13**

For earlier volumes, see *Guide* DC23–24.

Adds another 1,000 English, American, and Canadian publications; also cites reviews.   Z2483.H543

——— The Soviet Union and Eastern Europe : a bibliographic guide to recommended books for small and medium-sized libraries and school media centers. Littleton, Colo. : Libraries Unlimited, 1985. 373 p. ISBN 0-87287-469-9. $27.50.   **DC14**

". . . offers 1,555 titles which should aid librarians in small and medium-sized public libraries and media centers and librarians of high schools, junior colleges, and four-year colleges in assisting students and especially teachers in the development of curricula, classroom instruction, and reading lists to enhance the learning process."—*Introd.* Lists English-language materials in classed arrangement, with author/short title index. Annotations and references to reviews.   Z2491.H59

Dictionaries

Political and economic encyclopaedia of the Soviet Union and Eastern Europe / ed. by Stephen White. Harlow, Essex : Longman ; Chicago : St. James Pr., 1990. 328 p. : maps. ISBN 1-5586-2070-2. £65.00.   **DC15**

Articles on the political and economic background of each country, political parties, leaders, and topics (e.g., women, sports) are alphabetically arranged. Emphasizes the most recent period up to March 31, 1990. Articles are signed with the initials of the contributors. Chronology, 1945–90. Cross-references; index for topics. Useful because of its currency.   JN96.A2P64

The Balkans

Jessup, John E. Balkan military history : a bibliography. N.Y. : Garland, 1986. 478 p. (Military history bibliographies, vol. 8). ISBN 0-8240-8963-4. $66.00.   **DC16**

Bibliographical essays on Balkan military history during chronological periods from the late 14th century through 1984. Each essay is followed by a bibliography of the works cited. Author and subject indexes.   Z2851.M5J47

List of British diplomatic records for Balkan history, 1879–1905 : from general correspondence, classes FO 32 (Greece), FO 103 (Montenegro), FO 104 (Roumania), FO 105 (Serbia), FO 78 (Turkey). Sofia : Centre international d'information sur les sources de l'histoire balkanique et méditerranéenne, 1984. 278 p. (Balcanica. II, Inventaires et catalogues, v. 4).   **DC17**

Detailed listing (arranged under Public Record Office class, then chronologically) giving volume number, statement of content, and repository in the Balkans of microfilm copies. Name and geographical area indexes.   Z6465.G7L53

Südost-Institut München. Bibliothek. Bestandskatalog der Bibliothek des Südost-Instituts München / Gerhard Seewann, unter Mitarbeit von Gerda Bartl und Wilma Kömives. München : R. Oldenbourg, 1990. v. 1.

(Südosteuropa-Bibliographie. Ergänzungsband, 1). ISBN 3-486-55031-4. (In progress). **DC18**

Contents: v. 1, Druckschriften 1529–1945 (840 p.); v. 2, Periodica (in preparation).

A topical arrangement under geographical area, after a general section. Strongest for materials on the countries that make up the Balkans. Authors, editors, titles index. Z2483.S85

ALBANIA

Bland, William B. Albania. Oxford ; Santa Barbara, Calif. : Clio Pr., c1988. 290 p. : map. (World bibliographical series, v. 94). ISBN 1-85109-037-1. $65.00. **DC19**

A topical arrangement of 893 books and a few articles in English, French, Albanian, and German. "In the annotations information has often been provided concerning the institutional affiliation of the authors."—*Introd.* Indexes for authors, titles, and subjects. Z2886.B54

Daniel, Odile. Albanie, une bibliographie historique. Paris : Editions du Centre national de la recherche scientifique, [1985]. 616 p. ISBN 2-222-03236-9. 335F. **DC20**

A topically arranged bibliography covering all periods of Albanian history up to 1945. Cites Western-language materials (books, articles, and some essays) and within 24 libraries locates at least one copy of each item. Author index and index to journals cited. Z2886.D36

ARMENIA

Armen, Garbis. Historical atlas of Armenia = Hayastani patmakan atlas / text, Garbis Armen ; editing, Vrej-Armen Artinean ; maps and design, Hamo Abdalian. N.Y. : Armenian National Education Committee, c1987. 50 p. text, 51 p. maps : ill., maps in color ; 23 x 35 cm. ISBN 0-9617933-0-9 (pbk.). **DC21**

In Armenian and English.

Maps depict geographical, historical, and cultural aspects of Armenia's past, with brief text and photographs. Covers 3000 BCE to ca.1975, including the Armenian diaspora.

G2157.61.S1A7

Avakian, Anne M. Armenia and the Armenians in academic dissertations : Supplement one : a bibliography. Berkeley, Calif. : Professional Pr. : Distr. by A.M. Avakian, c1987. 53 p. **DC22**

Supplements a list publ. 1974 (*Guide* DC72).

An author listing of 386 masters theses and doctoral dissertations, including a few omitted from the previous list. Only Western-language titles are included. Topical index.

Z3461.A85

AUSTRIA

Bibliography

Malina, Peter. Bibliographie zur österreichischen Zeitgeschichte, 1918–1985 : eine Auswahl / Peter Malina, Gustav Spann. Wien : Verlag für Geschichte und Politik, 1985. 107 p. (Politische Bildung [Vienna, Austria], Hft. 47–50). **DC23**

Replaces an earlier bibliography published in 1978 (*Guide* DC79). Extends coverage to 1985, within the same arrangement, etc. Z2120.3.M35

Österreichische historische Bibliographie, 1945–1964 = Austrian historical bibliography. Salzburg : W. Neugebauer ; Santa Barbara, Calif. : Clio Pr., 1985. **DC24**

Provides the same type of coverage, in similar arrangement, as the annuals for the later period (*Guide* DC84). A *Register = index* (629 p.), providing both author and subject indexes, was publ. 1985. Z2116.O47

Österreichische historische Bibliographie, fünf-Jahres-Register, 1980–84 = Austrian historical bibliography, five-year-index : 1980–1984. Graz : W. Neugebauer ; Santa Barbara, Calif. : ABC-Clio, c1989. 793 p. ISBN 3-85376-096-1. **DC25**

For the series and earlier *Register* volumes, see *Guide* DC84.

Author index, p. 12–125; subject, personal name and place index, p. 126-193. Z2116.O48

Rausch, Wilhelm. Bibliographie zur Geschichte der Städte Österreichs. Linz/Donau : Österreichischer Arbeitskreis für Stadtgeschichtsforschung, 1984. 329 p., [2] leaves of plates : 1 map. ISBN 3-900387-31-1. OS1450.00. **DC26**

More than 4,250 citations to books, dissertations, essays, and articles on the cities, towns, and states of Austria (including Südtirol) are arranged alphabetically by geographic area with author index. Z2123.R38

Salt, Denys. Austria / comp., Denys Salt, with the assistance of Arthur Farrand Radley. Oxford ; Santa Barbara, Calif. : Clio Pr., c1986. 318 p., [1] leaf of plates : 1 map. (World bibliographical series, v. 66). ISBN 1-85109-009-6. $52.25. **DC27**

Intends to provide a "broad and representative spectrum" (*Introd.*) of English- and German-language books and articles. 847 entries with good annotations in topical arrangement. Author/title/subject index. Chart of Austrian rulers.

Z2101.S27

Wunschheim, Johannes. Bibliographie zur oberösterreichischen Geschichte, 1981–1985. Linz : Oberösterreichisches Landesarchiv, 1987. 311 p. ISBN 3-900313-42-3. **DC28**

For earlier volumes and annotation see *Guide* DC80–81.

Z2124.V66W86

Dictionaries

Die Habsburger : ein biographisches Lexikon / hrsg. von Brigitte Hamann. München : Piper, c1988. 447 p. : ill. (some col.), geneal. tables, ports. ISBN 3-492-03163-3. **DC29**

A somewhat popular account, giving brief facts (family relationship, birth, dates, burial place) followed by a biographical sketch written by a scholar and signed with initials. Genealogies; cross-references. Not indexed. DB36.3.H3H32

Kleindel, Walter. Die Chronik Österreichs. 2., durchgesehene Aufl. Dortmund : Chronik Verlag, 1985. 648 p. : ill., maps, ports. **DC30**
  A history of Austria, 5000 BCE–1984 CE, presented as short newspaper articles. Heavily illustrated. Chronological arrangement; name and subject indexes. Appendix of population and economic statistics, and lists of prime ministers and presidents, prime ministers, and mayors of Vienna. A 3., durchgesehene Aufl., was published in 1989 (672 p.). DB38.K5

BELGIUM

Hendrickx, Jean-Pierre. Répertoire des mémoires de licence et des thèses de doctorat présentés dans les départements d'histoire contemporaine des universités belges. Louvain : Editions Nauwelaerts, 1986. v. 1. (In progress). **DC31**
  Contents: t. l, 1945–1975 (214 p.).
  Topical arrangement with author and subject indexes. Almost all theses listed deal with Belgium in some way. DH403.C42

Heyse, Micheline. Bibliografie van de geschiedenis van België, 1914–1940 = Bibliographie de l'histoire de Belgique, 1914–1940 / Micheline Heyse, Romain van Eenoo. Brussel : Nauwelaerts, 1986. 410 p. **DC32**
  Continues and follows the arrangement of J. de Belder and J. Hannes, *Bibliografie van de geschiedenis van België, 1865–1914 (Guide* DC87). DH403.C42

Riley, Raymond Charles. Belgium. Oxford ; Santa Barbara, Calif. : Clio Pr., c1989. 271 p. (World bibliographical series, v. 104). ISBN 1-85109-099-1. **DC33**
  Cites 819 books and articles, published from earliest times to the present day, "encompassing those territories that eventually came to be Belgium."—*Pref.* Topically arranged; author, title, and subject indexes. "Theses and dissertations on Belgium," p. xxix–xxxviii. Z2401.R55

BULGARIA

Bibliography

Crampton, R. J. Bulgaria. Oxford ; Santa Barbara, Calif. : Clio Pr., c1989. 232 p. (World bibliographical series, v. 107). ISBN 1-85109-104-1. $65.00. **DC34**
  Lists 794 books and a few articles (mostly in English) topically arranged. Author, title, and subject indexes. Z2896.C7

Voenna istoriĭa na Bŭlgariĭa, 681–1945 : bibliografiĭa / [sŭstav. L. Venkova-Ilieva . . . et al. ; pod red. na Liliĭana Venkova-Ilieva i Petŭr At. Petrov]. Sofiĭa : Voen. izd., 1977–1987. 2 v. **DC35**
  A bibliography of works on Bulgarian military history for 681–1945, mostly in Bulgarian. Cites materials published from 1850s to 1972. Vol. 1 covers books, collections of documents, albums of pictures and drawings; v.2 lists articles from 119 journals. Topically arranged (mostly in chronological sections); annotations; indexed for authors and anonymous titles. Z2898.M5

Encyclopedias

Entsiklopediĭa Bŭlgariĭa / [glav. redaktor Vladimir Georgiev]. Sofiĭa : BAN, 1984–1988. v. 4–6 : ill., maps (some col.). (In progress). **DC36**
  For earlier volumes and annotation, see *Guide* DC105.
  Contents: v. 4–6, M–Tu. DR53.E57

Information Bulgaria : a short encyclopaedia of the People's Republic of Bulgaria / ed. by the Bulgarian Academy of Science ; translated by Sofia Press Agency. Oxford ; N.Y. : Pergamon Pr., 1985. 976 p., [40] p. of plates : ill. (some col.). ISBN 0-08-031853-3. $120.00 (est.). **DC37**
  "Articles assembled and edited by the Bulgarian Academy of Sciences."—*Introd.*
  Entries cover all subjects, (e.g., mass media, economics, armed forces), and include statistics current to about 1982. Intends to offer a "Bulgarian view of Bulgarians." Topical index. DR53.I54

CYPRUS

Megalē Kypriakē enkyklopaideia / [genikē euthynē ekdosēs Antros Paulidēs]. Leukōsia, Kypros : Philokypros, 1984–1991. 14 v. : ill. (some col.). **DC38**
  Addresses Cyprus and its relations to the world outside as well as flora and fauna, personalities, events, history, etc., within the island (e.g., the article on Egypt discusses Cyprus under the Ptolomies, that on Adonis addresses cult sites on Cyprus). DS54.A3M44

Richter, Heinz A. Greece and Cyprus since 1920 : bibliography of contemporary history = Griechenland und Zypern seit 1920 : Bibliographie zur Zeitgeschichte. Heidelberg : Wissenschaftlicher Verlag Nea Hellas, c1984. 437 p. **DC39**
  For annotation, see *Supplement* DC142. Z2300.3.R5

CZECHOSLOVAKIA

Jilek, Heinrich. Bibliographie zur Geschichte und Landeskunde der Böhmischen Länder von den Anfängen bis 1948 : Publikationen der Jahre 1850 bis 1975. Köln : Böhlau, 1986–1988. v. 1–2. (Ostmitteleuropa in Vergangenheit und Gegenwart, 19/I, 19/II). ISBN 3-412-01885-6 (Bd. 1). (In progress). **DC40**
  Offers 23,884 numbered entries for books and articles in a topical arrangement for all fields of history, including the history of literature, publishing, art, and music. Vol.3 (which will complete the set) is to be an index of authors and editors, anonymous works, and personal and place names. Z2131.J54

Short, David. Czechoslovakia. Oxford ; Santa Barbara, Calif. : Clio Pr., c1986. 409 p. : map. (World bibliographical series, v. 68). ISBN 1-85109-011-8. $80.00. **DC41**
  Consists of 1,000 annotated entries, mostly English-language books, topically arranged. Author/title/subject index. Z2131.S5

DENMARK

Holtermann, Henrik. Danish foreign policy : literature in languages other than Danish, 1979–1986. Copenhagen : Danish Institute of International Studies : Association of Danish Lawyers and Economists Pub. Dept., 1988. 109 p. ISBN 87-7318-363-6.　　**DC42**

A classified listing of 831 books, articles, documents, chapters, and dissertations that the "user might reasonably expect to find in large university, public, or government libraries."— *Introd.* Covers political, economic, and military aspects, as well as "Danish participation in European and Nordic cooperation," and home rule in Greenland. Includes a few references to 1987 publications and some forthcoming ones. Author index.　　Z6465.D4H64

Miller, Kenneth E. Denmark. Oxford ; Santa Barbara, Calif. : Clio Pr., c1987. 216 p. : map. (World bibliographical series, v. 83). ISBN 1-85109-042-8. $55.00.　　**DC43**

A selective (730 items) bibliography of books and a few articles, mostly in English, arranged topically. A chapter is devoted to basic materials on Greenland and the Faroe Islands. Cross-references; author/title/subject index.　　Z2561.M55

FINLAND

Paloposki, Toivo J. Quellenkunde zur Geschichte Finnlands. Wiesbaden : Harrassowitz, 1988. 145 p. (Veröffentlichungen des Osteuropa-Institutes München. Reihe Geschichte, Bd. 55). ISBN 3-447-02768-1.　**DC44**

A discussion of resources and guides to Finnish archives. Arranged by subject, e.g., Reichsrat, Archive der Kirche und der Pfarrgemeinden, Die Presse. Not indexed.　　Z2520.P35

Suomen historiallinen bibliografia = Finsk historisk bibliografi = Bibliografie historique finlandaise, 1971–1980. Helsinki, 1988. 755 p. (Suomen historiallinen seura. Käsikirjoja, 11). (In progress).　　**DC45**

Constitutes v. 6 of the set; for v. 1–5 and annotation, see *Guide* DC127.

Comp. by Tuula Rantanen and Raija Mankki.

Follows the plan of the earlier volumes.　　Z2520.S94

Uppslagsverket Finland. Helsingfors : Schildt, [1982–1985]. 3 v. : ill. ISBN 951-50-0267-2 (v. 1). **DC46**

A heavily illustrated national encyclopedia covering all areas of Finnish life—politics, history, culture, biography, etc. Alphabetical arrangement; not indexed. Suppl. in v. 3 includes some new articles and additions to earlier ones, but consists mostly of cross-references to the main body of the work.　　DL1007.U66

FRANCE

Bibliography

French Revolution

Bibliography

Caldwell, Ronald J. The era of the French Revolution : a bibliography of the history of western civilization, 1789–1799. N.Y. : Garland, c1985. 2 v. ISBN 0-8240-8794-1.　　**DC47**

Companion to the author's *The era of Napoleon* (*Supplement* DC61).

" . . . a partly annotated topical listing of 42,420 books, articles, theses, and dissertations on the general and national history of Europe and the Western hemisphere" (*Pref.*) in the period of the French Revolution. "Since it is principally a bibliography of writings on history, it includes only the most important works published during the Revolution." Relatively few annotations. Cross-references; detailed table of contents; index of names and subjects.　　Z2178.C34

Dallet, Sylvie. Filmographie mondiale de la Révolution française / Sylvie Dallet, Francis Gendron. Montreuil : Centre d'action culturelle de Montreuil, c1989. 229 p. : ill. ISBN 2-907468-07-3. 130F.　　**DC48**

An international list of films with production information and plot summary for each. Very inclusive, embracing films with only a few scenes on the Revolution, e.g., *Singin' in the rain.* Arrangement is by year of release, then by country name (in French), and finally alphabetical by title. Indexed by title and by country.　　DC149.5.D35

Fierro, Alfred. Bibliographie de la Révolution française, 1940–1988. Paris : Références, c1989. 2 v. (1334 p.). ISBN 2-908302-10-1.　　**DC49**

An extensive bibliography (31,960 books and articles) on the French Revolution published since André Monglond's *La France révolutionnaire et impériale* (*Guide* DC147) and Gerard Walter's *Répertoire de l'histoire de la Révolution française* (*Guide* DC150). Mainly French- and English-language materials in topical arrangement; long sections on biography and local history. Indexes for authors and for names and places.

DC148.Z9F465

Archives

France. Archives nationales. Guide des papiers privés d'époque révolutionnaire / par Françoise Hildesheimer. Paris : Archives nationales : Documentation française [distributor], 1987. 301 p. ISBN 2-86000-132-8. 100F.　　**DC50**

In two parts: (1) a listing by name of collections of papers of persons (e.g., Danton, Marie Antoinette) prominent during the French Revolution, with archival location and brief description of contents; (2) Archives départementales, communales et hospitalières, listing by *département* and then by repository with indications of holdings of papers. Name index for the second part.　　CD1192.A2F74

Dictionaries

Chronicle of the French Revolution, 1788–1799. London : Chronicle Publications ; N. Y. : Distr. [by] Prentice Hall, c1989. 703 p. : ill. (some col.). ISBN 0-13-133729-7. $55.00. **DC51**

Originally published as: *Chronique de la Révolution* (Paris : Éd. Chronique, 1988).

On the verso of each double-page spread is a chronology of five to eight days, with the rest of the space devoted to "articles relating in the manner of a newspaper, in simple and direct style, not only the political facts, but also the daily life of the French."—*Foreword.* Heavily illustrated. Short essays scattered throughout (on cream-colored paper) provide historical perspective (e.g., The France of Louis XVI; Year I of liberty; The Gerondist and Montagnard conventions). An appendix lists government personnel, 1788–99; table of illustrations. Index for people, places, and "principal revolutionary themes." DC148.C47

A critical dictionary of the French Revolution / ed. by François Furet and Mona Ozouf ; transl. by Arthur Goldhammer. Cambridge, Mass. : Belknap Pr. of Harvard Univ. Pr., 1989. 1063 p., [32] p. of plates : ill. (some col.). ISBN 0-674-17728-2. $85.00. **DC52**

Translation of *Dictionnaire critique de la Révolution française* ([Paris] : Flammarion, [1988]).

A summary of contemporary scholarship presented as a collection of essays arranged in five groups: Events, Actors, Institutions and creations, Ideas, Historians and commentators. Short bibliographies; cross-references. Indexes by theme and proper name to name of article; alphabetical listing of articles within the sections. Good illustrations in color. DC148.D5313

Dictionnaire historique de la Révolution française / publié sous la direction scientifique de Jean-René Suratteau et François Gendron ; comité de rédaction, Jean-Paul Bertaud . . . [et al.]. 1re éd. Paris : Pr. universitaires de France, c1989. 1132 p.; maps. ISBN 2-13-042522-4. **DC53**

At head of title: Albert Soboul.

Offers signed articles, with bibliographies, on the French Revolution, including biographies, events, cities, and topics, such as Administration locales, Musique. Index of names as subjects. Includes an essay on the historiography of the Revolution and a chronology with events divided by topics in parallel columns (e.g., Politiques et religions, Literature et philosophie). DC147.D52

Jones, Colin. The French Revolution : a companion. London ; N.Y. : Longman, [1988]. 473 p. ISBN 0-582-49418-4. **DC54**

Published in U.K. as: *The Longman companion to the French Revolution.*

A quick reference guide that includes: chronologies, biographical dictionary, glossary, explanation of calendar, government machinery, political groups and parties, statistical tables portraying social and economic data, select bibliography, and subject index.

§ A similar quick reference guide is John Paxton's *Companion to the French Revolution* (N.Y. : Facts on File, [1988]. 231 p.) DC148.J57

Manceron, Claude. La Révolution française / Claude Manceron, avec la collaboration d'Anne Manceron. Paris : Renaudot : Diffusion Stendhal, c1989. 2 v. ISBN 2-87742-008-5. 230F. (In progress). **DC55**

Contents: v. [1], Dictionnaire biographique (571 p. 230F); v. [2], Dictionnaire général (385 p.).

Each volume presents an alphabetical arrangement of brief articles. Cross-references; no bibliography. DC147.M36

Tulard, Jean. Histoire et dictionnaire de la Révolution française : 1789–1799 / par Jean Tulard, Jean-François Fayard, Alfred Fierro. Paris : R. Laffont, c1987. 1213 p.; maps. ISBN 2-221-04588-2. 120F. **DC56**

A quick-reference handbook giving brief discussions of events, a chronology, tables of conversion for Gregorian and revolutionary calendars, a dictionary of short entries for people and topics, a historiography, and a filmography. Topical index. DC147.T85

Biography

Caratini, Roger. Dictionnaire des personnages de la Révolution. [Paris] : Le Préaux Clercs, c1988. 576 p. : ill. ISBN 2-7144-2232-2. 195F. **DC57**

Offers short biographical notices of some 3,000 people involved in the French Revolution, 1789–95. Chronology; brief bibliography. DC147.C37

Atlases

Atlas de la Révolution française / sous la direction de Serge Bonin et Claude Langlois. Paris : Editions de l'École des hautes études en sciences sociales, [1987–1990]. 5 v. : ill. (some col.), some maps in color ; 30 cm. ISBN 2-7132-0894-7 (v. 1). **DC58**

Contents: v. 1, Routes et communications, dir. Guy Arbellot and Bernard Lepetit ([1987]. 91 p.); v. 2, L'enseignement, 1760–1815, dir. Dominique Julia ([1987]. 104 p.); v. 3, L'armée et la guerre, dir. Jean-Paul Bertaud, Daniel Reichel ([1989]. 79 p.); v. 4, Le territoire (1) : Réalités et représentations, dir. Daniel Nordman, Marie-Vic Ozouf-Marignier ([1990]. 106 p.). v. 5, Le territoire (2): les limites administratives, dir. Daniel Nordman, Marie-Vic Ozouf-Marignier. Each part 120F.

Maps, tables, charts, and text portray the Revolution and often the Napoleonic era to 1815 or 1820. Detailed list of sources and good bibliography in each volume. DC148.A84

Since 1789

Echard, William E. Foreign policy of the French Second Empire : a bibliography. N.Y. : Greenwood, [1988]. 416 p. (Bibliographies and indexes in world history, no. 12). ISBN 0-313-23799-9. $75.00. **DC59**

A topical bibliography of books, articles, and dissertations published between the mid-1880s and the mid-1980s in English, French, German, Italian, or Spanish on the French world role and foreign policy together with general studies of major diplomatic history topics "where French interest was paramount, or, in some instances, peculiar."—*Pref.* Author and subject indexes. To be used with a *Select bibliography of the French Second Empire* (not yet published) and *Historical dictionary of the French Second Empire* (*Supplement* DC75). Z6465.F7E26

Evleth, Donna. France under the German occupation, 1940–1944 : an annotated bibliography. N.Y. : Greenwood, 1991. 220 p. (Bibliographies and indexes in world history, no. 20). ISBN 0-313-27474-6. **DC60**

Arranged under seven headings with appropriate subdivisions: Vichy France; Daily life in France under the Occupation; Collaboration and the collaborationists outside the government; The resistance; The position of the Communists; The liberation; The purge. Annotations consist of a brief identification of the author plus a sentence (with citation) from one or more reviews. The final two chapters offer brief discussions of newspapers published during the period in France and a guide to major French archives. Author, reviewer, and subject indexes.   Z6207.W8E84

Napoleonic era

Bibliography

Caldwell, Ronald J. The era of Napoleon : a bibliography of the history of western civilization, 1799–1815. N.Y. : Garland, 1991. 2 v. (1447 p.). (Garland reference library of the humanities, vol. 1097). ISBN 0-8240-5644-2. $210.00.   **DC61**
Companion to the author's *The era of the French Revolution: a bibliography of the history of Western civilization, 1789–1799* (*Supplement* DC47).
"... a topical, partially annotated, listing of 48,136 books, articles, and doctoral dissertations and theses on the general and national history of Europe and the Western Hemisphere in this period."—*Pref.* Cites works published up to 1986, arranged topically under six broad headings: v. 1, General history; France; Biography of Napoleonic France; Local history of Napoleonic France; v. 2, National history of Europe; National history of the Americas. Author/subject index.   Z5579.6.C35

Horward, Donald D. Napoleonic military history : a bibliography. N.Y. : Garland, 1986. 689 p. (Military history bibliographies, vol. 9). ISBN 0-8240-9058-6. $74.00.
                                                             DC62
In 24 chapters, Horward and contributing scholars deal with specific wars, campaigns, and military activities in particular countries or regions during the Napoleonic era. A bibliographic essay introduces each section. Lacks an index.
                                                       Z2181.M5H67

Meyer, Jack Allen. An annotated bibliography of the Napoleonic era : recent publications, 1945–1985. N.Y. : Greenwood, 1987. 288 p. (Bibliographies and indexes in world history, no. 8). ISBN 0-3132-4901-6. $45.00.
                                                             DC63
Companion to Owen Connelly's *Historical dictionary of Napoleonic France, 1799–1815* (*Supplement* DC66).
Scholarship since World War II is cited under broad topics (e.g., Napoleon) with subdivisions (e.g., Napoleon's family). Excludes journal articles. Annotations are intended to be a "rough guide to the contents of the volume."—*Introd.* Author/editor index only.   Z2179.M49

Encyclopedias

Dictionnaire Napoléon / sous la direction de Jean Tulard. [2nd ed.]. [Paris] : Fayard, [1989]. 1866 p., [16] p. of plates : ill. (some col.). ISBN 2-213-02035-3. 950F.
                                                             DC64
1st ed., 1987.
Signed articles offer coverage of major topics (e.g. continental blockade, conscription) and biographies of major and some minor figures; each usually ends with a brief bibliography. An "Index thématique" groups articles under broad topics (e.g. Mémoires [auteurs de], Nourriture). More comprehensive than *Historical dictionary of Napoleonic France* (below). This edition adds a supplementary section, p. 1761–1855, for new articles on people and subjects (e.g., list of Sous-préfectures, Mikhail Sokolniki). The Index thématique prints the new entries in italics.   DC147.D53

Haythornthwaite, Philip J. The Napoleonic source book. London : Arms and Armour, 1990. 414 p. : ill., maps. ISBN 0-85368-969-5.   **DC65**
Pt. I is a chronological narrative of the Napoleonic wars and their treaties. Pt. II surveys weaponry and tactics "which would be familiar to every capable company officer of the period."—*Introd.* Pt. III offers a country-by-country review of military participation. Pt. IV gives brief biographical descriptions of the leading military participants. Pt. V discusses Napoleonic literature and art. Pt. VI, Miscellanea, provides lists and charts—e.g., the calendar, expenses, measurements, colors. Pt. VII is a glossary of military terms in use at the time. Each section includes bibliographies of representative works, usually books. Subject index to broader topics.
§ Much of the same material is included in David G. Chandler's *Dictionary of the Napoleonic Wars* (*Guide* DC17), but Haythornthwaite's work treats military matters more extensively and is heavily illustrated with reproductions of prints, drawings, pictures of medals, portraits, maps.   DC151.H32

Historical dictionary of Napoleonic France, 1799–1815 / ed. by Owen Connelly. Westport, Conn. : Greenwood, 1985. 586 p. ISBN 0-313-21321-6.   **DC66**
Emphasis is on Napoleon's Empire, its "events, politics, economy and economic developments, society and its evolution, and the institutions and culture of the era."—*Pref.* Brief articles are included on campaigns and battles but the reader is referred to David G. Chandler's *Dictionary of the Napoleonic War* (*Guide* DC17) for fuller information. Topical articles (e.g., a satellite kingdom such as Naples or women) and biographical articles (for writers, artists, actors, scientists prominent in the period) provide good coverage, give a list of secondary references and end with a list of related entries. Some entries, (e.g., Campaigns; Spain: ministers) provide a list of the names of articles relating to that topic. Chronology, 1768–1840; general bibliography subdivided by topic; topical index.
§ Note that *An encyclopedia of Napoleon's Europe* by Alan Palmer (*Guide* DC18) tries to address the period 1797–1815 in Europe as a whole, so that, in addition to political and military matters, it includes entries for major writers (such as Jane Austen or William Blake) who lived during the period but may not have commented on the war or on Napoleon, and for issues such as the slave trade or the Enclosure Act. Illustrated with black-and-white reproductions of portraits, paintings, maps, etc.   DC201.H673

Archives and manuscripts

Archives nationales (France). État des inventaires / publié sous la direction de Jean Favier. Paris : Archives nationales : Diffusé par La Documentation française, 1985–1986. v. 1, 4. ISBN 2-86000-067-4 (t. 1). 150F. (In progress).   **DC67**
Contents: v. 1, L'Ancien Régime (1985. 283 p. 150F); v. 4, Fonds divers (1986. 315 p. 160F). To be complete in 4 v.
Lists registers, indexes and other finding aids, and similar research tools for French public archives as of January 1, 1983. Arranged by major chronological periods, subdivided by *série*.
                                                             CD1196

———————— État général des fonds / publié sous la direction de Jean Favier. Paris : Archives nationales : Diffusé par La Documentation française, 1988. v. 5.   **DC68**
For v. 1–4 and annotation, see *Guide* DC161.
Contents: v. 5, 1940–58, Fonds conservé à Paris (1988. 468p. 220F.)
Vol. 5 extends coverage of vols. 2 and 4 for archives in Paris, thereby excluding the Centre des Archives Contemporaines at Fontainebleau. Includes an extensive list of members of French cabinets, 1940–58.

§ The papers of the Minutier Central des Notaires de Paris described in v. 4 have been treated in more detail and by special subject in publications issued by the Archives Nationales: *Documents du Minutier central des notaires de Paris. Inventaires après décès,* comp. by Madeleine Jurgens (v. 1, 1483–1547. Paris, 1982; in progress); *Ronsard et ses amis,* comp. by Madeleine Jurgens (1985. 442 p.); *Histoire de l'art au XVIe siècle, 1540–1600* (1985–86. 2 v). Another portion of the Archives Nationales receiving its own published guide is: *L'administration parisienne à la veille de la Révolution: délibérations du Bureau de la Ville de Paris, 1784–1790: inventaire des minutes H(2)...* (1989. 137 p.).   **CD1196**

———————— Guide des papiers des ministres et secrétaires d'État de 1871 à 1974 / par Chantal de Tourtier-Bonazzi et François Pourcelet. 2e éd. rev. et augm. Paris : Archives nationales : Diffusé par la Documentation française, 1984. 282 p. ISBN 2-86000-099-2. 130F.   **DC69**

1st ed., 1978.

Cabinet ministers are listed alphabetically; for each, gives a biographical sketch followed by descriptions of any papers in national, departmental, and private archives, mentioning any finding aids and noting terms of access.   **CD1196**

État des inventaires des archives départementales, communales et hospitalières au 1er janvier 1983 / par les Services d'archives départementaux et communaux et le Service technique de la Direction des archives de France. Paris : Archives nationales : Diffusé par la Documentation française, 1984. 2 v. (1275 p.). ISBN 2-86000-097-6 (v. 1). 390F (set).   **DC70**

Supersedes *État des inventaires...,* 1938, and its *Supplément,* 1955 (*Guide* DC162).

Covers departmental, regional, and private papers on deposit in those archives, listing for each the inventories and other finding aids available as of January 1, 1983. In two parts: (1) general aids arranged by historical period and subject; (2) aids listed by department. Appendix for list of laws, statutes, etc. applying to archives, and a list of chief archivists.

CD1192.A2E72

France. Ministère des affaires étrangères. Etat général des inventaires des archives diplomatiques. Paris : Impr. nationale, 1987. 249 p. ISBN 2-11-086039-1.   **DC71**

A catalog of inventories of archives of diplomatic and consular posts that also includes descriptions of the records of the French occupation of Germany and Austria after World War II.

CD1201

France. Ministère des relations extérieures. Archives et documentation. Les archives du Ministère des relations extérieures depuis les origines : histoire et guide : suivis d'une étude des sources de l'histoire des affaires étrangères dans les dépôts parisiens et départementaux. Paris : Impr. nationale, 1984–1985. 2 v. : ill. ISBN 2-11-085246-1 (set).   **DC72**

Pt. 1 is a history of the Archives of the Ministère, discussing the applicable laws, the development, relevant finding aids and bibliographies, general organization, and staffing. Pt. 2 is the guide to individual files, indicating their organization, dates covered, size, and a summary list of finding aids. Pt. 3 describes related files in other archives and libraries in Paris, such as Bibliothèque Nationale, Archives de la Marine, Bibliothèque de la Sorbonne. An appendix in v. 2 gives names and terms of ministers, secretaries and undersecretaries. Names and subject indexes for each volume.   **CD1201**

Guide des centres de documentation en histoire ouvrière et sociale / sous la responsabilitié de Michel Dreyfus. Paris : Editions ouvrières, 1983. v. 1. ISBN 2-7082-2360-7. 80.00F. (In progress).   **DC73**

A directory of libraries, parties, centers of research, museums, and government agencies giving address, hours, telephone, brief history, catalogs of holdings, conditions of access, and list of publications. Indexes of personal names, periodical publications, organizations.   Z7164.T7G83

Dictionaries

Historical dictionary of France from the 1815 restoration to the Second Empire / ed. by Edgar Leon Newman ; Robert Lawrence Simpson, assistant ed. N.Y. : Greenwood, c1987. 2 v. (1241 p.). ISBN 0-313-22751-9. $135.00.   **DC74**

Consists of 950 articles by 75 scholars that cover the period from the end of the reign of Napoleon Bonaparte to the beginning of that of Louis Napoleon and deal with movements, cultural life, influences, and political figures. List of references and related articles at the end of each article. Chronology; general index.   DC256.H57

Historical dictionary of the French Second Empire, 1852–1870 / ed. by William E. Echard. Westport, Conn. : Greenwood, c1985. 829 p. ISBN 0-313-21136-1.   **DC75**

About 350 entries by contributing scholars, plus unsigned articles written by the editor with bibliographies and references to related articles. Chronology. A detailed index complements the dictionary arrangement.   DC276.H57

Historical dictionary of the Third French Republic, 1870–1940 / Patrick H. Hutton, ed. in chief ; Amanda S. Bourque and Amy J. Staples, asst. eds. N.Y. : Greenwood, [1986]. 2 v. ISBN 0-313-22080-8. $125.00.   **DC76**

With "over 750 entries written largely by American scholars, the volume scans all aspects of French civilization between 1870 and 1940" (*Pref.*) for political, social, economic, and cultural issues. Many articles are quite extensive, especially 24 interpretive essays. Each article is signed and includes a short bibliography and a list of related articles. Appendix: Entries classified by topic; Presidents and premiers of the Third Republic. Topical index.   DC337.H57

Chronologies

Jouette, André. Toute l'histoire par les dates et les documents : chronologie de l'histoire de France et regards sur le monde. Paris : Perrin, 1989. 973 p. ISBN 2-262-00697-0. 250F.   **DC77**

A chronology presented in three main columns: (1) In France, (2) Outside France, (3) Civilization, science and technology. A fourth column gives quotations, facts, lists, etc., relevant to the year(s) covered in the other columns. Prehistoric times through 18th century treated in 80 pages. Appendix for genealogies, lists, calendars, reprinting of texts, etc. Index from name of event, place, or person to the date in the chronology section.

Atlases

Atlas historique de la France / préface de Pierre Miquel ; [conçu, écrit et réalisé par Édimages]. [Paris] : Plon, c1985. 150 p. : maps in color ; 30 cm. ISBN 2-259-01317-1. 185F.   **DC78**

Colored maps with textual commentary are arranged by period from prehistoric time to that of the European Community.

List of maps. "Chronologie de l'histoire de France," p. 7–39, gives, in columns, political, military, and international events.

§ A less elegantly produced (in black-and-white) but often clearer work is the *Atlas de géographie historique de la France et de la Gaule, de la conquête césarienne à nos jours*, by Stéphane Sinclair (Paris: SEDES, [1985]. 260 p.), which includes an index of names of places and people and a bibliography of sources.　　　G1844.21.S1A8

Reverdy, Georges. Atlas historique des routes de France. Paris: Presses de l'École nationale des ponts et chaussées, c1986. 182 p.: some maps in color; 38 cm. ISBN 2-85978-090-4.　　　**DC79**

Reproduces maps of the roads in France with explanatory text and notes on the cartographers. Arranged chronologically in five parts: (1) Jusqu'en 1550; (2) 1550–1750; (3) 1750–1800; (4) 1800–1900; (5) De 1900 à nos jours [i.e., to 1986]. One-page index of geographical names.　　　G1844.21.P2R4

GERMANY

Bibliography

Dahlmann, F. C. Dahlmann-Waitz Quellenkunde der deutschen Geschichte: Bibliographie der Quellen und der Literatur zur deutschen Geschichte. Register zu Band 1 und 2. 10. Aufl. unter Mitwirkung zahlreicher Gelehrter hrsg. im Max-Planck-Institut für Geschichte von Hermann Heimpel und Herbert Geuss. Stuttgart: A. Hiersemann, 1985. 1 v. ISBN 3-7772-8519-6.　**DC80**
Index to *Guide* DC181.　　　Z2236.D34

──────── Dahlmann-Waitz Quellenkunde der deutschen Geschichte: Bibliographie der Quellen und der Literatur zur deutschen Geschichte. 10. Aufl. unter Mitwirkung zahlreicher Gelehrter hrsg. im Max-Planck-Institut für Geschichte von Hermann Heimpel und Herbert Geuss. Stuttgart: A. Hiersemann, 1985–[1990]. v. 3, 6, 7. ISBN 3-7772-8519-6 (v.1). (In progress).　**DC81**
For earlier parts and annotation, see *Guide* DC181.
Contents: v. 3, Abschnitt 125–136 (Lfg. 52, 53, 55–57) (complete); v. 6, Abschnitt 275–279 (Lfg. 51, 54, 58) (complete); v. 7, Abschnitt 280–371 (Lfg. 59–66).　　Z2236.D34

Dotzauer, Winfried. Das Zeitalter der Glaubensspaltung (1500–1618). Darmstadt: Wissenschaftliche Buchgesellschaft, 1987. 182 p. (Quellenkunde zur deutschen Geschichte der Neuzeit von 1500 bis zur Gegenwart, Bd. 1).　　　**DC82**
A topical listing of the principal sources for the history of the Reformation. Each section concludes with a brief discussion of the documents, ending with references to other bibliographies, e.g., Dahlmann-Waitz (*Guide* DC180). An appendix lists documentary sources for this period for non-German countries. Indexed by title, compiler or editor, and subject.　　　Z2237.5.D66x

Henning, Herzeleide. Bibliographie Friedrich der Grosse, 1786–1986: das Schrifttum des deutschen Sprachraums und der Übersetzungen aus Fremdsprachen / bearb. von Herzeleide und Eckart Henning. Berlin; N.Y.: W. de Gruyter, 1988. 511 p. ISBN 3-11-009921-7. DM292.00.　　　**DC83**
In two sections: primary sources arranged by format, and secondary literature arranged by topic. Includes German-language material only; indexed by author and by cited personal and place names.　　　Z8397.13.H46

to 1600

Willemsen, Carl Arnold. Bibliographie zur Geschichte Kaiser Friedrichs II. und der letzten Staufer. München: Monumenta Germaniae Historica, [1986]. 205 p. (Monumenta Germaniae historica: Hilfsmittel, 8). ISBN 3-88612-019-3.　　　**DC84**
A scholarly bibliography of books, articles, essays, and dissertations concerning Friedrich II (1194–1250) and later Staufen family members. Arranged by format; name indexes.　　　Z2237.W54

20th century

See also in DA sections World Wars; Holocaust.

Detwiler, Donald S. West Germany: the Federal Republic of Germany / Donald S. Detwiler, Ilse E. Detwiler. Oxford; Santa Barbara, Calif.: Clio Pr., c1987. 353 p. (World bibliographical series, v. 72). ISBN 1-85109-017-7.　　　**DC85**
Covers post-1945 West Germany including West Berlin. About 500 entries with lengthy annotations which cite about another 500 titles. Includes English and German publications. Author/title/subject index.　　　Z2240.3.D37

Paul, Barbara Dotts. The Germans after World War II: an English-language bibliography. Boston: G.K. Hall, [1990]. 190 p. ISBN 0-8161-8994-3.　　　**DC86**
Annotated bibliography of books and articles, government publications, doctoral dissertations, motion pictures, and filmstrips on Germany, 1945–48. In 9 sections: German experiences, Foreign observers, Civilian relief efforts, Journal articles, Fiction by Germans, Non-German fiction, Films about Germany, Historical studies, Bibliographies. Author/title index.　　　Z2240.3.P38

Snyder, Louis Leo. The Third Reich, 1933–1945: a bibliographical guide to German national socialism. N.Y.: Garland, 1987. 284 p. (Canadian review of studies in nationalism, v. 7; Garland reference library of social science, v. 384). ISBN 0-8240-8463-2. $42.00.　　**DC87**
A selection of citations to 850 books and articles mostly in English, but some in German. Topical arrangement. Annotations provide a brief summary of contents; asterisks appear before those entries considered most important. Introduction to each chapter is an overview of the research on that topic. Author index.　　　Z2241.N27S65

Sperling, Walter. Landeskunde DDR: eine kommentierte Auswahlbibliographie: Ergänzungsband, 1978–1983. München; N.Y.: K.G. Saur, 1984. 623 p. ISBN 3-598-21135-X.　　　**DC88**
Cites 4,323 books, essays, and articles on East Germany, mainly German-language publications with a few English titles. Arranged by topic: e.g., Wirtschaft, Die brandenburgische Bezirke, Bildung und Wissenschaft. Each section has an introductory overview. Indexes for author, title and subject.
§ The period up to 1978 is covered by *Landeskunde DDR: eine annotierte Auswahlbibliographie*, comp. by Walter Sperling (München: Verlag Documentation, 1978. 456 p. Bibliographien zur regionalen Geographic und Landerkunde, 1).　　　Z2250.S65

Wallace, Ian. East Germany: the German Democratic Republic. Oxford; Santa Barbara, Calif.: Clio Pr., c1987. 293 p.: map. (World bibliographical series, v. 77). ISBN 1-85109-023-1. $51.50.　　　**DC89**
Presents topically arranged entries for books, articles, essays, and a few documents on all aspects of East Germany since 1945. Nothing on pre-World War II Germany or West Germa-

ny is included unless it has great significance for East Germany. Well annotated; author/title/subject index. Z2250.W34

Guides to records

Deutsche Wirtschaftsarchive : Nachweis historischer Quellen in Unternehmen, Kammern und Verbänden der Bundesrepublik Deutschland / hrsg. im Auftrag der Gesellschaft für Unternehmensgeschichte e.V. von Klara van Eyll . . . [et al.]. 2., völlig neu bearb. Aufl. Stuttgart : F. Steiner Verlag Wiesbaden, 1987–88. 2 v. ISBN 3-515-04556-2. **DC90**
1st ed., 1978–83.
Contents: Bd. 1 [without special title] (471 p.); Bd. 2, Kreditwirtschaft (557 p.).
Describes archives in companies, banks, and foundations. For each, indicates address, archivist, contents, hours, and any finding aids. Name and place indexes, plus an index to branch names by broad topic in each volume. HC282.2.D48

Frohn, Axel. Guide to inventories and finding aids of German archives at the German Historical Institute, Washington, D.C / Axel Frohn, with the assistance of Anne Hope. Wash. : German Historical Institute, 1989. 84 p. (Reference guides of the German Historical Institute, no. 2). **DC91**
A listing of published inventories and finding aids arranged alphabetically by city, then by the name of the archive. Index for names of archives and for titles. Appendixes cover a few archives in Austria and Switzerland and a list of guides from *Guides to German records microfilmed at Alexandria, Va.* (*Guide* DC210). CD1229.F76

Encyclopedias

The encyclopedia of the Third Reich / ed. by Christian Zentner and Friedemann Bedürftig ; English translation ed. by Amy Hackett. N.Y. : Macmillan ; London : Collier Macmillan, c1991. 2 v. : ill. ISBN 0-02-897500-6 (set). $175.00. **DC92**
Translation of *Grosse Lexikon des Dritten Reiches* (München : Sudwest Verlag, 1985. 686 p.)
A richly illustrated dictionary of the people, organizations, jargon (e.g., "blood sacrifice," "final solution"), events, movements, politics, culture, etc., of German history 1933–45. 22 overview essays (e.g., Women in the Third Reich, Concentration camps, Opposition, Attempts to assassinate Hitler) are designed to provide context and link the shorter articles together. The more than 3,000 entries, signed by German historians, are alphabetically arranged. Cross-references; subject index. The topical bibliography, p. 1083–1103, has been updated for the N.Y. edition, especially with English-language titles (which are starred). DD256.5.G76313

Handbooks

Overesch, Manfred. Chronik deutscher Zeitgeschichte : Politik, Wirtschaft, Kultur / [Manfred] Overesch, [Friedrich Wm.] Saal. Düsseldorf : Droste, c1986. v. 3, pt. 1–2. ISBN 3-7700-0571-6 (Bd. 1). **DC93**
For v. 1–2 and annotation, see *Guide* DC225.
Contents: Bd. 3¹, Das besetze Deutschland 1945–1947; Bd. 3², Das besetze Deutschland 1948–1949. DD232.O9

Taylor, James. The Third Reich almanac / James Taylor and Warren Shaw. N.Y. : World Almanac, c1987.

392 p., [21] p. of plates : ill. ISBN 0-88687-363-0. $24.95. **DC94**
Published in England as *A dictionary of the Third Reich* (London : Grafton, 1987).
An alphabetical dictionary of people, parties, events, government organizations, concentration camps, battles, military units, etc., intended for the general reader. Includes chronologies, maps, charts, photographs. Not indexed; cross-references. Some odd choices of headings: "Diary of Anne Frank" but no entry or cross-reference under "Frank"; "Cinema in the Third Reich" with no cross-reference from "film" or "motion pictures," though the term "film" is used in the preface. A section of quotations give source but not page. Brief bibliography.
§ Overlaps with Louis Leo Snyder's *Encyclopedia of the Third Reich* (*Guide* DC229), in that both give chronologies and cover the same people, battles, events, etc., though with varying amounts of information. Snyder also lacks an index but has a much longer bibliography. DD256.5.T283

Biography

Biographisches Lexikon zur Weimarer Republik / hrsg. von Wolfgang Benz und Hermann Graml. München : C.H. Beck, c1988. 392 p. ISBN 3-406-32988-8. DM58. **DC95**
Signed articles (Adenauer to Zweig) of about one column each, with bibliographical references to primary and secondary works and location of archives. Appendix gives government leaders in each administration, 1919–33, and a chronology for the Weimar Republic, 1918–33. CT1062.B56

Weber, Wolfgang. Biographisches Lexikon zur Geschichtswissenschaft in Deutschland, Österreich und der Schweiz : die Lehrstuhlinhaber für Geschichte von den Anfängen des Faches bis 1970. 2., durchgesehene und durch ein Vorwort erg. Aufl. Frankfurt am Main ; N.Y. : P. Lang, c1987. 697 p. ISBN 3-8204-1051-1. **DC96**
Limited to historians in Germany, Austria, and Switzerland who achieved an academic position during the years 1800–1970. Offers much information about career and educational background but nothing about publications, although each entry includes a short bibliography of other sources. DD86.5.W43

Atlases

Freeman, Michael J. Atlas of Nazi Germany / Michael Freeman ; consulting ed., Tim Mason. N.Y. : Macmillan, c1987. 205 p. : ill. (some col.), some maps in color. ISBN 0-02-910681-8. **DC97**
Also published: London : Croom Helm, 1987.
Diagrams, charts, tables, maps, photographs, and historical summaries are used "to provide a graphic presentation of the outward face and inward structures of the Third Reich and, where applicable, the manner of their evolution."—*Introd.* Topical index. DD256.5.F73354

Hilgemann, Werner. Atlas zur deutschen Zeitgeschichte, 1918–1968 / Werner Hilgemann ; Kartografie, Jürgen Taufmann. München : Piper, c1984. 207 p. : ill., maps (chiefly in col.) ; 20 x 26 cm. ISBN 3-492-02460-2. DM48.00. **DC98**
A chronological framework for maps and text on facing tables illustrates the history of Germany 1918–68. Arranged in five sections: Das Ende des Kaiserreiches (1918); Die Weimarer Republik (1919–33); Das Dritte Reich (1933–45); Deutschland unter Besatzungsmächten (1945–49); Bundesrepublik Deutsch-

land und Sowjetische Besatzungszone DDR (1949–58). Ends with a chronology of the period. Not indexed. **G1911.S1H5**

GIBRALTAR

Shields, Graham J. Gibraltar. Oxford ; Santa Barbara, Calif. : Clio Pr., c1987. 100 p. (World bibliographical series, v. 87). ISBN 1-85109-045-2. $27.50. **DC99**
A selective bibliography (260 entries) of books, government publications, maps, and British dissertations. Clear and frequently critical annotations. Author, title, and subject indexes. **Z2704.G44S56**

GREAT BRITAIN

Bibliography

British military history / Gerald Jordan, ed. N.Y. : Garland, 1988. 586 p. (Military history bibliographies, vol. 10 ; Garland reference library of the humanities, vol. 715). ISBN 0-8240-8450-0. **DC100**
A supplement to Robin Higham's *Guide to the sources of British military history* (*Guide* DC237), updating that work to about 1984. An excellent introduction to reference materials begins each chapter. Not indexed.
§ In the same series and also extremely useful is *British naval history since 1815 : a guide to the literature* by Eugene L. Rasor (N.Y. : Garland, 1990. 841 p. Military history bibliographies, 13), covering naval and maritime history of Great Britain and the British Empire since 1815. Also not indexed. **Z2021.M5H54**

Hartigan, Maureen. The history of the Irish in Britain : a bibliography. [London : The Irish in British History Group, 1986]. 85 p. ISBN 0-9510945-0-5. **DC101**
Lists books, articles, and some theses and conference papers on all aspects of the contact. Works range from general histories to local studies and autobiographies, but exclude novels and government publications. Alphabetically arranged by author with subject and chronological period indexes. Two bibliographical articles, The Irish in other parts of the world and Some general studies on migration, are appended but not indexed. **Z2027.I75H37**

Hines, W. D. English legal history : a bibliography and guide to the literature / W.D. Hines ; with contributions by R.W. Ireland, P.J. Rawlings, C.P. Rodgers. N.Y. : Garland, 1990. 201 p. (Garland reference library of the humanities, vol. 1011). ISBN 0-8240-4299-9. **DC102**
The intended audience for this compilation of essays and bibliographies is "from a variety of backgrounds, coming afresh to the study of legal history."—*Introd.* Three bibliographical essays—for the medieval period, for 1485–1815, and for criminal justice and punishment (including a short section on crime literature)—discuss collections of the law, commentaries and secondary works, procedures and traditions, court records, the legal profession; "significant gaps in the published work" are noted. The concluding two essays—Periodicals and periodical indexes, Introduction to bibliography—survey the most important periodicals, library catalogs, and other reference works. Bibliography with complete citations for all titles discussed. **KD532.A1H56**

Jackson, Paul. British sources of information : a subject guide and bibliography. London ; N.Y. : Routledge &

Kegan Paul, 1987. 526 p. ISBN 0-7102-0696-8. $79.50. **DC103**
In three sections: (1) a bibliography of books "recognized as useful introductions or as authoritative studies on a given topic" (*Pref.*), subdivided for specific subject areas (e.g., Government and administration—cabinet); (2) periodicals, journals, and magazines "which provide general or specific coverage of major topics"; (3) sources of information (e.g., organizations and institutions "which stock information on particular fields," films, videocassettes, audiovisual aids). Appendix of addresses and suppliers: publishers, distributors of films, video workshops. No index. **Z2001.J33**

Perks, Robert. Oral history : an annotated bibliography. London : British Library National Sound Archive, 1990. [200] p. ISBN 0-7123-0505-X (pbk.). £12.95. **DC104**
Lists 2,132 "books, pamphlets, periodicals, articles, catalogs and published recordings about, based on or using oral history, together with relevant coverage of related topics like sound archives and reminiscent therapy."—*Introd.* Intended to be comprehensive for the U.K. and selective for the rest of the world. Materials cited were published 1945–89. Arranged alphabetically by author; cross-references; topical index.

20th century

Catterall, Peter. British history, 1945–1987 : an annotated bibliography. Oxford ; Cambridge, Mass. : B. Blackwell, 1991. 843 p. ISBN 0-631-17049-9. $200.00. **DC105**
First publ. 1990.
A classified bibliography of books, articles, and some British and American theses published through 1989 (with a few from 1990). Includes special sections for Scotland, Wales, and Northern Ireland. "The objective in researching this bibliography, as well as demonstrating the areas where further research is required, has been to establish the range and quality of the material available."—*Pref.* Headnotes discuss scholarship; cross-references link sections together. Good annotations, often including citations to related works. Author and subject indexes. Complements *Bibliography of British history* (*Guide* DC231) and, like those volumes, should be a starting point for research in the period. **Z2020.3.C37**

Havighurst, Alfred F. Modern England, 1901–1984. 2nd ed. Cambridge ; N.Y. : Cambridge Univ. Pr. for the North American Conference on British Studies, [1987]. 109 p. ISBN 0-521-30974-3. **DC106**
1st ed., 1976 (*Guide* DC282).
"The selection of books and articles here presented rests upon a comprehensive search of historical literature published before 1984, though a few important items published in 1984 are included. Of the major aspects of English life only literature per se is excluded."—*Pref.* A new category "Labour history" has been added. Arranged by broad topics subdivided by format (e.g., printed sources, surveys, monographs). Occasional annotations; author/editor/translator index. **Z2020.H38**

Guides to records

Foster, Janet. British archives : a guide to archive resources in the United Kingdom / Janet Foster & Julia Sheppard. 2nd ed. N.Y. : Stockton Pr., 1989. lviii, 834 p. ISBN 0-93585-974-8. $100.00. **DC107**
For annotation, see *Supplement* AB50. **CD1040.F67**

Guides to sources for British history based on the National Register of Archives. London : H.M.S.O., [1986–1990]. v. 5–8. (In progress). **DC108**

For v. 1–4 and annotation, see *Guide* DC294.

At head of title: Royal Commission on Historical Manuscripts.

Contents: v. 5, Private papers of British colonial governors 1782–1900 (66 p.); v. 6, Papers of British churchmen 1780–1940 (96 p.); v. 7, Papers of British politicians 1782–1900 (125 p.); v. 8, Records of British business and industry, 1760–1914: textiles and leather (130 p.).

Vol. 5 treats senior officials of the Colonial Office as well as British colonial governors. Vol. 6 lists locations of papers of "over 800 churchmen and women... selected on the basis of their significance for the study of British ecclesiastical history.... Colonial churchmen and missionaries have not been included except where their papers illustrate a substantial part of their careers spent at home."—*Introd.* Vol. 7 excludes those papers cited in v. 1 (*Papers of British Cabinet ministers 1782–1900*). "The main focus is on members of the House of Commons and House of Lords... also private secretaries of senior politicians, political hostesses, party managers, national agents, political journalists, local politicians... who left a significant quantity of political papers."—*Introd.* Vol. 8 "... describes the records of 1200 textile, clothing and leather firms in Great Britain and Northern Ireland between 1760 and 1914."—*Introd.* Arranged alphabetically by name of individual or firm under type of industry (e.g., wool, lace, leather). Index of businesses and geographical index.   CD1042.A2.G8

Record repositories in Great Britain : a geographical directory / the Royal Commission on Historical Manuscripts. [8th ed]. London : H.M.S.O., [1987]. 35 p. ISBN 0-11-440210-8 (pbk.).   **DC109**

1st ed., 1964; 7th ed., 1982.

"A total of 234 repositories are noticed with details of a further twenty-four dependent institutions."—*Pref.* Each entry gives address, hours, telephone, and facilities for providing photographs or microfilm. Arranged alphabetically under city; indexed by name of repository.   CD1040.G73

Riden, Philip. Record sources for local history. London : B.T. Batsford, 1987. 253 p. ISBN 0-7134-4726-5. £17.95.   **DC110**

A "guide to classes of the public records which can be searched reasonably expeditiously and profitably for local studies" (*Pref.*), "setting out what is available, where it is likely to be found and what finding aids exist."—*p. 9.* The chapters follow a chronological arrangement, beginning with the Middle Ages and ending with a discussion of "Local material amongst the modern records of central government." Topical index. Very helpful for students or beginning researchers; complements W.B. Stephens, *Sources for English local history* (*Guide* DC327).   Z2023.R53

Surveys of historical manuscripts in the United Kingdom : a select bibliography. 2nd impression. London : H.M.S.O., [1990, c1989]. 20 p. ISBN 0-11-887529-9 (pbk.). £1.50.   **DC111**

Comp. by Christopher Kitching.

"This bibliography aims to bring together details of nationwide surveys of historical records."—*Pref.* Excluded are guides to individual repositories, guides to papers of an individual or a "narrow locality," standard or general bibliographies which might have a chapter devoted to archival research. Arranged by broad topic, e.g., Business, Ecclesiastical. Cites books, articles, annual lists, typescripts, specific reports on file in the National Register of Archives and individuals currently gathering information when this bibliography was compiled. Not indexed.

Encyclopedias; Dictionaries

The Blackwell biographical dictionary of British political life in the twentieth century / ed.by Keith Robbins. Oxford ; Cambridge, Mass. : Blackwell Reference, 1990. 449 p. : ill. ISBN 0-631-15768-9. £49.50.   **DC112**

Offers "succinct summaries of the careers of leading figures in twentieth-century British political life, together with concise estimates of their stature and significance."—*Editor's introd.* Political life is interpreted broadly: besides party leaders, "front-rank" politicians, and prominent civil servants, includes newspaper publishers and editors, archbishops, trade union leaders, and scientists; biographies range from Gilbert Murray to Rupert Murdock. Signed articles with bibliographies, many including a photograph. Subject index.   DA566.9.A1B57

The Cambridge historical encyclopedia of Great Britain and Ireland / ed., Christopher Haigh. Cambridge ; N.Y. : Cambridge Univ. Pr., 1985. 392 p. : ill. (some col.). ISBN 0-521-25559-7.   **DC113**

Signed articles are organized within a chronological framework, with an overview introducing each period. Emphasis is on political, diplomatic, economic, social, and economic history. In the margins are definitions, identifications (of events, of documents), etc., that relate to the broader articles. Heavily illustrated with photographs, drawings, and maps, well-chosen and well-placed in the text. "Who's who," giving brief biographies, p. 338–73; "Further reading," p. 374–76. Cross- references; subject index.   DA34.C28

The Cambridge illustrated dictionary of British heritage / ed. by Alan Isaacs and Jennifer Monk. Cambridge ; N.Y. : Cambridge Univ. Pr., [1986]. 484 p. : ill. ISBN 0-521-30214-5.   **DC114**

Intended for foreigners or those not well acquainted with England. Provides short descriptions or definitions of terms and topics not always easily found in similar works (e.g., Arts and Crafts movement, Arts Council of Great Britain, Arundel Castle, Ascot races). Heavily illustrated with small black-and-white photographs and drawings. Select bibliography, p. 480–83. Not indexed.   DA110.C254

Lines, Clifford John. Companion to the Industrial Revolution / Clifford Lines ; consultant ed., Barrie Trinder. N.Y. : Facts on File, c1990. 262 p. : ill. ISBN 0-8160-2157-0.   **DC115**

"In addition to essential information about industrial and technological developments and the people who made these possible, [the dictionary] also includes organizations and events which affected the lives of working people."—*Introd.* Short articles of one to three paragraphs identify, define, or briefly describe; most end with one bibliographic citation for a relevant study and/or a site open to the public. Cross-references; not indexed. A chronology, 1702–1867, is arranged in columns for Industry, Transport, Society. Maps and charts for age distribution in 1841, canals and railways, coalfields and industrial regions in 1820, etc.   HC254.5.L72

The Plantagenet encyclopedia : an alphabetical guide to 400 years of English history / ed. by Elizabeth Hallam. N.Y. : Grove Weidenfeld, c1990. 224 p. : ill. (some col.), maps. ISBN 0-8021-1289-7. $32.95 : £25.00.   **DC116**

Publ. in U.K. : London : Weidenfeld and Nicolson.

Designed as a companion to three chronicles translated and edited by Hallam: *The Plantagenet chronicles* (London : Weidenfeld & Nicolson ; Markham, Ont. : Viking, 1987. 352p.), *Chronicles of the age of chivalry* (London : Weidenfeld & Nicolson, 1987 ; publ. in the U.S. as *Four gothic kings*, N.Y. : Weidenfeld & Nicolson, 1987. 320p.), and *The chronicles of the Wars of the Roses*, N.Y. : Weidenfeld & Nicolson, 1988. 320p.). The set covers English history from before the coronation of Henry II in 1154 to the death of Richard III in 1485.

A lavishly illustrated dictionary of short entries identifying places, giving short biographies of notables, and treating a few subjects (e.g., Travel) or government bodies (e.g., Parliament). Each article ends with specific citations to one or more of the chronicles. Includes a 2½-page bibliography, a list of manuscripts, and an index of names.   DA225.P54

Victorian Britain : an encyclopedia / Sally Mitchell, ed. .. [et al.]. N.Y. : Garland, 1988. 986 p. : ill. (Garland reference library of social science, v. 438). ISBN 0-8240-1513-4. $125.00.   **DC117**

Intends to provide an "overview and point of departure" for the study of "persons, events, institutions, topics, groups, and artifacts in Great Britain between 1837 and 1901."—*Pref.* Arranged alphabetically, the signed articles end with bibliographies of sources. A seven-page annotated bibliography of key reference sources concludes the dictionary. Cross-references; general index. Chronology, p. xi–xxi.   DA550.V53

Weigall, David. Britain & the world, 1815–1986 : a dictionary of international relations. N.Y. : Oxford Univ. Pr., 1987. 240 p., [12] p. of plates : maps. ISBN 0-19-520610-X. $29.95.   **DC118**

"Intended... as a standard work of reference on British foreign policy and international relations."—*Pref.* Features historical and biographical entries (e.g., Boer War, Winston Churchill, every British foreign secretary since 1815); definitions of terms and concepts used in diplomacy and foreign relations (e.g., Balkanization, Reparations); and extended articles on bilateral relations between Britain and major powers (e.g., France, Germany). Entries are arranged alphabetically, contain cross-references, and many end with short bibliographies; they are followed by a chronological table giving events and treaties of British significance and a map section.   DA45.W45

Handbooks

Cook, Chris. British historical facts, 1688–1760 / Chris Cook and John Stevenson. N.Y. : St. Martin's Pr., 1988. 252 p. ISBN 0-312-02106-2. $35.00.   **DC119**

Publ. in U.K. : Houndsmill, Basingstoke : Macmillan.

Covers the period between the compilers' similar compilations for 1603–88 and 1760–1830; see *Guide* DC303–304.   DA498.C66

———————— The Longman handbook of modern British history, 1714–1987 / Chris Cook and John Stevenson. 2nd ed. London ; N.Y. : Longman, [1988]. 418 p. ISBN 0-582-01328-3. ISBN 0-582-01329-1 (pbk.). £18.95.   **DC120**

1st ed., 1983 (*Guide* DC306).

Existing tables have been updated to 1985–87, 24 new tables added—e.g., Chancellors of the Exchequer, European elections (for the European Parliament)—and a few dropped (e.g., Slum clearance). Subject index. A few additions to the bibliography.   DA470.C65

Mitchell, Brian. British historical statistics. Cambridge ; N.Y. : Cambridge Univ. Pr., 1988. 886 p. ISBN 0-521-33008-4.   **DC121**

For annotation, see *Supplement* CG52.   HA1134.M58

Chronology

Handbook of British chronology / ed. by E.B. Fryde ... [et al.]. 3rd ed. London : Royal Historical Society, 1986. 605 p. ISBN 0-86193-106-8.   **DC122**

2nd ed., 1961, comp. by F.M. Powicke and Fryde (*Guide* DC308).

A heavily revised edition which incorporates recent scholarship; tables updated to 1985. Bibliographical guide to the lists of English officeholders, p. xxiii–xxxix.   DA34.P6

Annuals and current surveys

Keesing's UK record. Harlow, U.K. : Longman, 1988– . ISSN 0952-195X. £70.00.   **DC123**

6 times a year.

Each issue begins with a calendar of principal events that provides textual comment on major ones. The focus is on "events occurring in the UK and on the UK's external relations, based on constant monitoring of the press, official sources and other information sources."—*Inside front cover.* The index of names and subjects cumulates semiannually, then annually.   JN101.K5

Biography

Who's who in British history / ed. Geoffrey Treasure. London : Shepheard-Walwyn ; Chicago : St. James Pr., 1988–1990. v. 1, 4–5 : maps. (In progress).   **DC124**

Contents: v. 1, *Who's who in Roman Britain and Anglo-Saxon England*, by Richard A. Fletcher ([1989]. 245 p.); v. 4, *... Tudor England*, by C.N.R. Routh, rev. and enl. Peter Holmes (1990. 476 p.; 1st ed., *Who's who in history*, v. 4, 1964); v. 5, *... Stuart England*, by C.P. Hill, rev. and enl. by Hill (1988. 466 p.; 1st ed., *Who's who in history*, v. 3, 1965). Announced for publication are volumes for early Hanoverian Britain (to 1789) and for Victorian Britain.

Biographical essays, very readable and well-researched, are arranged chronologically in order to give a picture of an age. Each essay concludes with a reference to an original source in translation or a good secondary work. Glossary; maps; and, in some volumes, genealogical charts. A brief subject index in each volume also refers from variant names to the page number of the form chosen by the author.

Atlases

Atlas of British social and economic history since c. 1700 / ed. by Rex Pope. N.Y. : Macmillan, [1989]. [250] p.; ill.; maps. ISBN 0-02-897341-0. $75.00.   **DC125**

Publ. in U.K. : London : Routledge.

Chapters, written by scholars, on particular topics, (e.g., The textile and chemical industries, Demographic changes) discuss British social and economic history and development through a narrative summary followed by a graphic presentation using maps with extensive explanatory text. "The different sections of the Atlas contain roughly equal proportions of maps and supporting text."—*Introd.* Notes at the end of each section provide bibliographies of source materials; suggestions for further reading, p. 236–245; topical index. Does not include Ireland.   HC253.A86

Atlas of industrializing Britain 1780–1914 / ed. by John Langton and R.J. Morris. London ; N.Y. : Methuen, [1986]. 246 p. ; 26 cm. ISBN 0-416-30290-4. ISBN 0-416-30300-5 (pbk.).   **DC126**

The social and economic history of the Industrial revolution in England, Scotland, and Wales, presented through maps, graphs, and detailed explanations. Arranged under 31 headings, such as The physical environment, Population, Wages, Wind and water power, Religion, and Electoral system. Sources of maps, p. 228–235; bibliography, p. 236–246. Not indexed.

G1812.21.G1A8

Atlas of the English civil war / Peter Newman. N.Y.: Macmillan, 1985. 126 p.; 26 cm. ISBN 0-02-906540-2.
DC127

Simultaneously published: London : Croom Helm, c1985.

In 56 maps, with text on facing pages, depicts campaigns and battles of the English Civil War, 1642–51, plus a few maps that show the state of the country overall. Scotland and Ireland are included. Chronological arrangement; index for geographical and personal names. G1812.21.S4N42

Jones, Barri. An atlas of Roman Britain / Barri Jones and David Mattingly. Cambridge, Mass.: Blackwell, 1990. 341 p.: ill., maps. ISBN 0-631-13791-2. $150.00.
DC128

Narrative description, heavily illustrated with maps, photographs and tables, beginning with Britain before the Conquest and ending with "The Saxon inheritors." Arrangement of the 12-page bibliography is coordinated with the chapters. Indexed by place and topic. G1812.21.S2J6

Manley, John. Atlas of prehistoric Britain. N.Y.: Oxford Univ. Pr., 1989. 160 p.: some maps in color; 31 cm. ISBN 0-19-520807-2. **DC129**

Publ. in U.K.: Oxford : Phaidon.

A popular work in which photographs, maps, drawings, and text "depict the principal concentration of major prehistoric monuments in Britain and Ireland."—*Pref.* Topical index.

GN805.M36

British Empire and Commonwealth

Atlas of the British Empire / [ed., C.A. Bayly; contributors, Alan Atkinson... et al.]. N.Y.: Facts on File, c1989. 256 p.: ill. (some col.). ISBN 0-8160-1995-9. $40.00. **DC130**

Also publ.: London : Macdonald, 1989.

"... organized not only to show the rise and subsequent decline of British dominance but also to analyse and map the evolution of the states and peoples of the modern world as they interacted, traded and fought with the British over 400 years."—*Introd.* Narrative discussion copiously illustrated with maps, photographs of art objects and places, etc. Begins with World politics and trade in the 15th century and ends with The Commonwealth today. Index by topic, place and personal name. DA16.A8

Burdett, Anita L. P. Summary guide to the archive and manuscript collections relevant to the former British colonial territories in the United Kingdom / Anita L.P. Burdett for the Joint Copyists Standing Committee of the Commonwealth Archivists' Association. London : Commonwealth Archivists Association, 1988. 97 p.
DC131

Intends to provide a "list of all known accessible repositories with relevant collections" (*Introd.*) relating to colonies of the British Empire in libraries or archives in the U.K. Does not inventory the Public Record Office, regimental museums, or repositories in the Republic of Ireland. Excludes materials on Canada, Australia, New Zealand, and Kenya because separate studies for those countries were planned. For each repository gives address, major publications describing the collection, examples of documents held, and other useful details including travel tips and backgound notes on the institution. Intended to update *Guide to manuscript sources for the history of Latin America and the Caribbean* (*Guide* DB258) and Noel Matthews and M. Doreen Wainwright's *Guide to manuscripts and documents in the British Isles relating to Africa* (*Guide* DD96). Indexes to repositories and geographical locations.

§ The same organization has issued *Commonwealth sources in British official records : Colonial and Dominion Offices* (1985. 93 p.), describing the relevant classes in Public Record Office, London; Australian National Library, Public Archives Canada; Public Archives Bahamas. Also indicates availability of microfilm. Z2021.C7B87

Palmegiano, Eugenia M. The British Empire in the Victorian press, 1832–1867 : a bibliography. N.Y.: Garland, 1987. 234 p. (Themes in European expansion, vol. 8; Garland reference library of social science, vol. 389). ISBN 0-8240-9802-1. $42.00. **DC132**

Contains 3,000 entries drawn from 50 popular London-based magazines. Author index; broad subject index. Includes checklist of 37 magazines treating imperial matters exclusively or extensively. Z2021.C7P32

University of London. Institute of Commonwealth Studies. Library. Theses in progress in Commonwealth studies : a cumulative list, November, 1989. [London]: Univ. of London, Institute of Commonwealth Studies, [1989?]. 57 p. **DC133**

"This list now contains all titles believed to be still in progress noted to October 1989."—*Introd.* Supersedes all previous editions (e.g., those published 1970–86). "Commonwealth studies is defined as study on the Commonwealth or Empire or on any other current or former constituent countries, together with countries formerly under British protection." Excludes studies on Great Britain, the U.S., or Egypt. Arranged alphabetically under geographic areas. Z200.9.U55

Regional and local

Historic towns : maps and plans of towns and cities in the British Isles. [N.Y.]: Oxford Univ. Pr. in conjunction with Historic Towns Trust, 1989. v. 3. (In progress).
DC134

For v. 1–2 and annotation, see *Guide* DC330.

Contents: The City of London from prehistoric times to c. 1520, ed. Mary D. Lobel (99 p., [20] p. of plates.)

The British atlas of historic towns series is a project of the International Commission for the History of Towns and the British Committee of Historic Towns.

Vol.3 offers a collection of essays by scholars describing London at various periods (e.g., The prehistoric background, The central Middle Ages 800–1270). These are followed by seven maps: The situation of London [showing principal roads]; The London area in pre-Roman times; Roman London; City of London c.1270; c.1520 [used as the base map]; The Wards c.1520; The parishes c.1520. The gazetteer is keyed to the c.1270 and c.1520 maps.

Victoria history of the counties of England. London : Oxford Univ. Pr., 1986–1990. 14 v.: ill. (In progress).
DC135

For annotation and contents of previous volumes, see *Guide* DC328.

Contents:

General introduction: supplement 1970–90, C.R. Elrington. 1990. 67 p.

Cambridge and the Isle of Ely: v. 9, A.P.M. Wright and C.P. Lewis. 1989;

Chester: v. 1, Physique, prehistory, Roman, Anglo-Saxon and Domesday, B.E. Harris. 1987;

Essex: Bibliography supplement, Frank Sansbury. 1987;

Gloucester: v. 4, The City of Gloucester, ed. N.M. Herbert. 1988;

Middlesex: v. 9, Hampstead and Paddington parishes, T.F.T. Baker. 1989;

Oxford: v. 12, Wooten Hundred (South) including Woodstock, Alan Crossley. 1990;

Shropshire: v. 4, Agriculture, G.C. Baugh. 1989;

Somerset: Extracts from v. 3 (Huish Episcopi, Langport and Somerton), R.J.E. Bush and R.W. Dunning. 1983;

Stafford: v. 14, Lichfield, M.W. Greenslade. 1990;

Sussex: v. 6, pt. 2, Bramber Rape (Northwestern part) including Horsham, T.P. Hudson. 1986; v. 6, pt. 3, Bramber Rape (Northeastern part) including Crawley New Town, T.P. Hudson. 1987;

Wiltshire: v. 13, South-West Wiltshire, D.A. Crowley. 1987;

Yorkshire, East Riding: v. 6, The Borough and Liberties of Beverley, K.J. Allison. 1989.

The *General introduction* supplement lists by county the contents of the volumes published since 1970 and indexes by author and title the articles in each volume.

West, John. Town records. [Chichester, Sussex] : Phillimore, [1983]. 366 p., [16] p. of plates : ill. ISBN 0-85033-472-1. £20.00.   **DC136**

A companion to John West's *Village records* (*Guide* DC329). All the 375 towns here discussed had borough status in 1971. Serves as a handbook identifying documentary materials available for the study of English towns. Place name index.   DA690.A1W47

London

The London encyclopaedia / ed. by Ben Weinreb and Christopher Hibbert. [1984 ed.]. London : Macmillan London, [1984]. 1029 p. : ill. ISBN 0-333-30024-6. £24.00.   **DC137**

" ... the record of [London's] streets and buildings, people and events."—*Introd.* Intended to revise and extend Henry B. Wheatley's *London, past and present* (London : J. Murray ; N.Y. : Scribner & Welford, 1891) and Peter Cunningham's *A handbook for London, past and present* (London : John Murray, 1849). Most articles are about a paragraph in length, although some for major buildings (e.g., the Tower of London) and topics (e.g., Road transport) are quite extensive. Good, well-chosen black-and-white illustrations; indexes of people and topics. A special typeface is used for headwords for buildings or gardens that no longer exist or survive in a much different form. Published at intervals, most recent being 1991.   DA677.L86

Marcan, Peter. Greater London local history directory and bibliography : a borough by borough guide to local history organisations, their activities, and publications, 1983–1987. [High Wycombe] : P. Marcan Publications, 1988. 83 p. ISBN 0-9510289-8-7 (pbk). £15.00.   **DC138**

A continuation of Marcan's *London's local history* (1983; reprinted with corrections, 1985) which listed publications by borough. This volume, also arranged by borough, lists and describes organizations, local history museums and societies, oral history groups, etc. For each, gives address, description (including activities), and a list of publications 1983–87, including any newsletter or journal. A final section presents organizations and societies which cover all of London. Not indexed.

§ See also P.J. Atkins, *The directories of London, 1677–1977* (London : Mansell, 1990. 732 p. ill. £60) for a description and history of the various types of directories and useful explanations of their research value.

Scotland

Donnachie, Ian L. Companion to Scottish history : from the Reformation to the present / Ian Donnachie and George Hewitt. N.Y. : Facts on File, 1990. 245, 17p.; maps, charts. ISBN 0-8160-2398-0.   **DC139**

Publ. in U.K. : London : B.J. Batsford, [1989].

Covers people, events, themes, and topics beginning with the 16th century, placing less emphasis on 20th-century Scotland. Copious cross-references; bibliographies follow most articles. Chronology; statistical tables; genealogies; 18 pages of maps.   DA757.9.D68

Stevenson, David. Scottish texts and calendars : an analytical guide to serial publications / David and Wendy B. Stevenson. London : Royal Historical Society ; Edinburgh : Scottish History Society, 1987. 233 p. (Guides and handbooks, no. 14 ; Scottish History Society. 4th ser., 23). ISBN 0-86193-111-4. £15.00.   **DC140**

A companion to Edward Mullin's *Texts and calendars* for England and Wales (*Guide* DC239–240).

Lists primary sources published in series from 43 private societies in Scotland. Occasional brief annotations. Topical index, but no author or editor index. Updates and partially replaces Charles Sanford Terry's *Catalogue of the publications of Scottish historical and kindred clubs and societies... 1780–1908* (*Guide* DC336) and Cyril Matheson's *Catalogue... 1908–1927* (*Guide* DC337).   DA750.S25

Wales

Jones, Philip Henry. A bibliography of the history of Wales [microform] / comp. for the History and Law Committee of the University of Wales Board of Celtic Studies, by Philip Henry Jones. 3rd ed. Cardiff : Univ. of Wales Pr., 1989. 21 microfiches.   **DC141**

2nd ed., 1962 (*Guide* DC342).

This microfiche edition cites 22,000 works in classed arrangement. Does not cover prehistoric or Roman Wales. The accompanying guide includes a list of abbreviations, classification chart, and instructions. A supplement of two fiche is promised for records that were not available for inclusion in July 1988, with an author index for the supplement.   Z2081.W229

GREECE

Richter, Heinz A. Greece and Cyprus since 1920 : bibliography of contemporary history = Griechenland und Zypern seit 1920 : Bibliographie zur Zeitgeschichte. Heidelberg : Wissenschaftlicher Verlag Nea Hellas, c1984. 437 p.   **DC142**

History is here defined broadly to include economics, art, education, etc. In three sections: Greece's contemporary history; Greek communism, socialism and trade unionism; Contemporary history of Cyprus. Sections are subdivided by period, then by format; e.g., bibliographies, documents, memoirs and diaries, articles in periodicals. All Western languages are included. Index of personal and corporate names.   Z2300.3.R5

HUNGARY

Guide to research and scholarship in Hungary / ed. by Márton Tolnai, Péter Vas-Zoltán ; [trans. by Barbara Harasztos ; English text ed. by Gloria Deák]. Budapest : Akadémiai Kiadó ; Bloomington : Distr. by Indiana Univ. Pr., c1988. 2 v. (1127 p.). ISBN 0-253-32718-0. $75.00. **DC143**

At head of title: International Research and Exchanges Board/American Council of Learned Societies—Hungarian Academy of Sciences, Commission on the Humanities and Social Sciences.

The history and present state (as of 1985/86) of Hungarian scholarly research is reviewed in two sections: (1) a series of ten signed essays on the development of individual areas of Hungarian scholarship, including philosophy, language, history, medicine, science, and technology; and (2) a directory of research institutions in Hungary, including the Hungarian Academy of Sciences, university and college departments and institutes, industrial research units, museums, archives, and libraries. Entries list name, address, telephone, principal scientists and staff, recent publications, and research programs. Alphabetic index by research unit. Q180.H8G85

Guide to the archives of Hungary / [ed. by Péter Balázs]. Budapest : Archival Board, Ministry of Culture, 1976. 229 p., [7] leaves of plates : 7 ill. ISBN 963-03-0279-9. **DC144**

Extensive descriptions of about 65 archives, giving general statements about major collections, rules of access, and address, and citing printed guides. The Magyar Országos Levéltár and the Új Magyar Köponti Levéltár are treated first, followed by the regional archives and special archives (including church archives) in alphabetical order. Not indexed. CD1170.G84

Miska, John P. Canadian studies on Hungarians, 1886–1986 : an annotated bibliography of primary and secondary sources. Regina, Sask. : Canadian Plains Research Center, Univ. of Regina, 1987. 245 p. (Canadian plains bibliography, 1). ISBN 0-88977-034-4. $35.00. **DC145**

Monographs, periodicals and newspapers, theses, book reviews, and research papers, topically arranged in two sections: (1) Writings about Hungary and the Magyars; (2) Writings by and about Hungarian Canadians (the larger portion). Includes brief descriptions of archival collections of Hungarian material. Author/title/subject index. Z1395.H94M57

IRELAND

Bibliography

Lester, DeeGee. Irish research : a guide to collections in North America, Ireland, and Great Britain. N.Y. : Greenwood, [1987]. 348 p. (Bibliographies and indexes in world history, no. 9). ISBN 0-313-24664-5. **DC146**

A companion to Jack W. Weaver and DeeGee Lester's *Immigrants from Great Britain and Ireland* (*Supplement* CC178). Covers all aspects of Irish life in the U.K., U.S., Canada, Northern Ireland, and Eire by describing book collections of university and college libraries and publishing efforts of organizations. Based on responses to a questionnaire. Entries, arranged alphabetically under geographic headings, describe the institution and its library, giving for the latter contents, access, special services, address, and telephone. Organization and subject index. Appendixes: Bookstores and bookdealers; Irish local newspapers. Overlaps somewhat with Susan Eleuterio-Comer's *Irish American material culture* (*Supplement* DB71), since both

include publications, but the latter concentrates on the U.S. and focuses more fully on festivals, historic sites, objects, and audio and video tapes. Z2031.L47

Shannon, Michael Owen. Irish Republic. Oxford ; Santa Barbara, Calif. : Clio Pr., c1986. 404 p. : map. (World bibliographical series, v. 69). ISBN 1-85109-014-2. **DC147**

A "sampling of some of the better or more popular general works on Ireland" (*Introd.*) after 1922. 1,459 books and a few articles published through 1985 are topically arranged. Author/title/subject index. Z2031.S53

Writings on Irish history. 1984– . Dublin : Irish Committee of Historical Sciences, 1986– . Annual. **DC148**

Title of 1984 edition: *Writings on Irish history 1984 incorporating addenda from 1973–1983.*

Continues *Writings on Irish history* 1979–1983, which appeared in microfiche (*Guide* DC378), and follows the same arrangement. With the volume covering 1985 an author index has been added. Z2041W75

Manuscripts and archives

Directory of Irish archives / ed. by Seamus Helferty & Raymond Refaussé. [Dublin] : Irish Academic Pr., [1988]. 112 p. ISBN 0-7165-2433-3. ISBN 0-7165-2432-5 (pbk.). **DC149**

Based on responses to a questionnaire. For each of 155 repositories gives name, address, phone, hours, published or in-house guides, and name of major collections. County and subject indexes. CD1101.D57

Prochaska, Alice. Irish history from 1700 : a guide to sources in the Public Record Office. [London] : British Records Association, 1986. 96 p. (Archives and the user, no. 6). ISBN 0-900222-07-7. £6.75. **DC150**

Offers brief descriptions of record classes, arranged by Public Record Office number, in two main sections: Summary of classes of public records 1750–1950 which contain material of relevance to Irish history; Classes of records related entirely to Irish affairs. Indexed by subject and agency. Z2041.P76

Quotations

O'Clery, Conor. The dictionary of political quotations on Ireland, 1886–1987 : phrases make history here. Boston : G.K. Hall, [1987]. 232 p. ISBN 0-8161-8939-0. **DC151**

Publ. in Ireland as: *Phrases make history here* (Dublin : O'Brien Pr., 1986).

A chronological arrangement of "telling phrases . . . touching on the great issues and arguments of the day, the political and social preoccupations and passing distractions."—*Introd.* Notes with each quotation identify the speaker, date, and situation in which the statement was made. Introductory chapters discuss key issues and outline important political developments. Indexes of speakers and subjects. DA959.O25

Chronology

Doherty, J. E. A chronology of Irish history since 1500 / J.E. Doherty, D.J. Hickey. Savage, Md. : Barnes & Noble, 1990. 395 p. ISBN 0-389-20895-7. £58.20. **DC152**

A companion to the same authors' *A dictionary of Irish history since 1800* (*Guide* DC383).

Publ. in Ireland : [Dublin] : Gill and Macmillan, [1989].

Although coverage begins with 1500, the emphasis is on the 19th and 20th centuries to Nov. 30, 1988. History is interpreted broadly to include religious, social, cultural and sporting events as well as military and political affairs. Extensive subject index.   DA910.D66

General histories

A new history of Ireland / ed. by T. W. Moody, F. X. Martin, F. J. Byrne. Oxford : Clarendon Pr. ; N.Y. : Oxford Univ. Pr., 1987–89. v. 2, 5¹ : ill. (In progress).
DC153

For a note on the series and other volumes published thus far, see *Guide* DC386.

Contents: v. 2, Medieval Ireland, 1169–1534, ed. Art Cosgrove (1987. 982 p. £75.00); v. 5, pt. 1, Ireland under the Union, 1801–70, ed. W.E. Vaughan (1985. 850 p. £75.00).
DA912.N48

ITALY

Bibliography

Antonini, R. Bibliografia dell'Italia antica : epigrafia, linguistica e scienze ausiliarie, 1950–1984 / R. Antonini, L. Del Tutto Palma, S. Renzetti Marra. Urbino : Università degli studi di Urbino, 1985. 2 v. (Quaderni dell'Istituto di linguistica dell'Università degli studi di Urbino, 3).   **DC154**

T. I is a bibliography of general works: periodicals, catalogs, festschriften, guides to museums. T. II, Epigrafia—linguistica, archeologia, storia, bibliografia, offers subject listings subdivided by geographical area. The arrangement within each section is chronological by date of publication, then by author. 9,400 articles, reviews, monographs and essays are cited. Indexes of authors and reviewers at end of t. I cover both volumes.   Z2357.A58

Coppa, Frank J. Modern Italian history : an annotated bibliography / comp. by Frank J. Coppa and William Roberts. N.Y. : Greenwood, c1990. 226 p.; ill. (Bibliographies and indexes in world history, no. 18). ISBN 0-313-24812-5.   **DC155**

Intended as a companion to *Dictionary of modern Italian history* (*Guide* DC403). Books, journals, and dissertations in English and Italian are arranged under seven headings: (1) General and reference works; (2) Monographic studies encompassing more than one period; (3) Eighteenth century, 1700–1796; (4) Risorgimento, 1796–1861; (5) Liberal Italy, 1861–1922; (6) Fascist Italy, 1922–1945; (7) Italian republic, 1945 to the present. Annotations are succinct but capture the scope of contents. Author and subject indexes.   Z2358.C67

Archives

Bibliografia dell'Archivio centrale dello Stato, 1953–1978 / a cura di Sandro Carocci . . . [et al.] ; coordinamento di Maura Piccialuti Caprioli. Roma : Ministero per i beni culturali e ambientali, : Distribuzione e vendita, Istituto poligrafico e zecca dello Stato Libreria dello Stato, 1986. 457 p. (Pubblicazioni degli archivi di Stato. Sussidi, 1).   **DC156**

A bibliography of monographs, articles, biographies, editions, etc., whose authors made use of documents in the state archives. Arrangement is alphabetical; each entry gives complete bibliographic information for the published work and a list of documents used in the Archivio. Pt. 1 covers 1953–68 and is an expanded version of Costanzo Casucci's "Saggio di bibliografia dell'Archivio Centrale dello Stato (1953–1968)," *Rassegna degli Archivi di Stato* 31 (1971): 335–96. Pt. 2 adds publications for the 1969–78 period. About 80% of the journals covered are Italian, the rest English, German, and French. Indexes of documents, subjects, and year of publication.
Z2360.B33

Guida generale degli archivi di Stato italiani / direttori, Piero D'Angiolini, Claudio Pavone. Roma : Ministero per i beni culturali e ambientali, Ufficio centrale per i beni archivistici, 1986. v. 3. (In progress).   **DC157**

For v. 1–2 and annotation, see *Guide* DC401.

Contents: v. 3, N–R (1986).   CD1424.G84

Encyclopedias

Enciclopedia dell'antifascismo e della Resistenza. Milano : La pietra, 1987–c1989. v. 5–6 : ill.   **DC158**

For earlier volumes and annotation, see *Guide* DC404.

Contents: v. 5–6, R–Z. Completes the set.

Vol. 6 includes an appendix of 400 articles (p. 473–573) but does not duplicate the articles published in the 1971 Appendice. A list of authors with the titles of the articles each wrote appears at the end of v.6.   DG571.A2E5

LATVIA

Latvijas padomju enciklopēdija / [redakcijas koļēģija E. Āboliņš, et al. ; P. Jērāns, galvenais redaktors]. Rīga : Galvenā enciklopēdiju redakcija, 1981–1988. 10 v. in 12 : ill. (some col.).   **DC159**

For v. 1–3 and annotation, see *Guide* DC410.

Contents: v. 4–10, Hait–Zvīgule. Vol. 5 and 10 each issued in 2 volumes. Vol. 10, pt. 2, is a supplement to the set, with personal name and geographic name indexes.   AE35.5.L37

LITHUANIA

Lietuviškoji tarybinė enciklopedija. Papildymai A-Ž / [vyriausiasis redaktorius J. Zinkus]. Vilnius : Vyriausioji enciklopedijų redakcija, 1985. 640 p. : ill.   **DC160**

For the main set, see *Guide* DC417.

Title from colophon: Litovskaiā sovetskaiā ēntsiklopediiā.

Contains: (1) new articles on topics not covered "for one reason or another" (*Pref.*) in the earlier volumes (some reflecting more recent developments, but many others covering topics that date well before 1975), and (2) supplementary material to articles in the main set (marked with an asterisk).

AE35.55.L54

Lithuania : an encyclopedic survey / [ed. in chief, Jonas Zinkus ; contributors, Tadas Adomonis . . . et al.]. Vilnius : Encyclopedia Publishers, 1986. 431 p. : ill.   **DC161**
    Some 50 scholars have contributed to chapters that survey Lithuanian science, folk art, literature and art, public health, etc. Statistics are current to about 1983. Heavily illustrated; not indexed. A picture of Lithuania by Lithuanians.

DK511.L2L478

Šešplaukis, Alfonsas. Lituanica collections in European research libraries : a bibliography. Chicago : Lithuanian Research and Studies, 1986. 215 p. ISBN 0-918920-05-1 (pbk.).   **DC162**
    The bibliography is based on the collections of Dr. Vilius Gaigalaitis, Professor Eduard Hermann, Professor Ernst Fraenkel, and Petras Klimas.
    Based on four collections (one still in a private library) this topically arranged listing of books in any language (mostly 20th-century with some 19th-century publications) treats all aspects of Lithuania. Author and subject indexes.

DK511.L2S475

Tarybú Lietuvos enciklopedija / [TLE redakciné kolegija, J. Antanavičius . . . et al., J. Zinkus (pirmininkas)]. Vilnius : Vyriausioji enciklopedijų redakcija, 1985–1988. 4 v. : ill. (some col.).   **DC163**
    Successor to *Mužoji Lietuviškoji Tarybiné enciklopedija* (1975) and draws information from *Lietuviškoji tarybiné enciklopedija* (*Guide* DC417).
    Title on spine: *TLE*. Title from colophon: *Ėntsiklopediıa Sovetskoĭ Litvy.*
    An alphabetically arranged encyclopedia covering all aspects of Lithuanian life, history, culture and economy. Material from the earlier works is considerably revised and updated; articles tend to be of a less political nature, and there are fewer entries for party functionaries and other officials; place-names are included. Émigrés continue to be represented.

AE35.55.T37

MALTA

Thackrah, John Richard. Malta. Oxford ; Santa Barbara, Calif. : Clio Pr., c1985. 163 p., [1] leaf of plates : map. (World bibliographical series, v. 64). ISBN 1-85109-007-X. $50.00.   **DC164**
    Offers 588 annotated entries for primarily English-language materials, topically arranged in 35 sections. Indexed by author, title, subject.

Z2375.T47

NETHERLANDS

Bibliography

King, Peter. The Netherlands / Peter King and Michael Wintle, compilers. Oxford ; Santa Barbara, Calif. : Clio Pr., c1988. 308 p. (World bibliographical series, v. 88). ISBN 1-85109-041-X. $70.00.   **DC165**
    A selective bibliography (1,025 entries) of Dutch- and English-language books, topically arranged. Author, title, and subject indexes; cross-references.

Z2431.K56

Krewson, Margrit B. The Netherlands and Northern Belgium, a selective bibliography of reference works. Rev. ed. Wash. : Library of Congress, 1989. 152 p.   **DC166**
    A revision and expansion of *The Netherlands, a selective bibliography of reference works,* 1986.
    Superintendent of Documents classification: LC 1.12/2:N38.
    Based on collections at the Library of Congress. Lists books and government publications (most published in the 1980s, with a few from the 1970s) in a broad topical arrangement. Includes studies, reference works, histories, and travel accounts, in Dutch, English, French, and German. Appendix of institutions concerned with the Netherlands and northern Belgium; indexed by main entry.

Z2431.K73

NORWAY

Gjønnes, Svein Tore. Norsk historisk bibliografi 1916–1945. Oslo : Universitetsbiblioteket i Oslo, 1988. 470 p. (Skrifter (Universitetsbiblioteket i Oslo), 16). ISBN 82-7000-144-9.   **DC167**
    Lists 4,563 books and articles, mostly in Norwegian, with some in French, German, English, Swedish, or Danish, on the history of Norway, 1916–45. Topical arrangement; name index.

Z2606.G58

Hill, Dennis Auburn. Norwegian local history : a bibliography of material in the collections of the Memorial Library, University of Wisconsin-Madison. Jefferson, N.C. : McFarland, c1989. 125 p. ISBN 0-89950-377-2. $35.00.   **DC168**
    An unannotated list of books in the DL576 and DL596 classes of the University of Wisconsin Library. In addition, place names and personal names were searched in the card catalog bringing the total to about 1,300 entries. Arranged alphabetically by place-name, then by title. Cross-references; names index.

Z2613.H54

Sather, Leland B. Norway / Leland B. Sather, comp. ; ed. by Hans H. Wellisch. Oxford, England ; Santa Barbara, Calif. : Clio Pr., c1986. 293 p. : map. (World bibliographical series, v. 67). ISBN 1-85109-010-X. $46.95.   **DC169**
    Offers 942 annotated entries arranged in 41 sections covering from the Vikings to the present. Indexed by author, title, and subject.

Z2591.S28

Schiötz, Eiler H. Utlendingers reiser i Norge. En bibliografi. Oslo : Universitetsforlaget, [1986]. v. 2 (595 p.) : illus. (Norsk bibliografisk bibliotik, 54).   **DC170**
    For v. 1 and annotation, see *Guide* DC437.
    Contents: Bd. 2, Itineraria Norvegica . . . [until 1900] and Supplementer. Completes the set.
    Offers supplementary material in three parts: (1) books not listed in the 1970 volume; (2) list of foreign painters in Norway before 1900; (3) additional information concerning books in the earlier volume. Index of names, geographic areas, historical periods, and nationalities, and of books on the Lapps. Two additional indexes of privately printed books, and books on hunting and angling cover both volumes.

Z2606.S32

POLAND

Bibliography

Kanka, August Gerald. Poland : an annotated bibliography of books in English. N.Y. : Garland, 1988. 395 p. (Garland reference library of the humanities, v. 743). ISBN 0-8240-8492-6. $47.00. **DC171**

" . . . attempts to be the most exhaustive and the most comprehensive list of works in the English language."—*Pref.* A topical listing of books, government publications written by individuals, and pamphlets. Excluded are articles, translations of literary works by Poles, and government statistical materials. Author and title indexes. Z2526.K28

Lerski, Jerzy J. Jewish-Polish coexistence, 1772–1939 : a topical bibliography / comp. by George J. Lerski and Halina T. Lerski. N.Y. : Greenwood, [1986]. 230 p. (Bibliographies and indexes in world history, no. 5). ISBN 0-313-24758-7. **DC172**

Lists 3,000 books, pamphlets, and articles in scholarly journals on the relations between the Jews and the rest of the people living in Poland, 1772–1939. The citations are arranged alphabetically within 34 topical sections, e.g., Economics, Jews in Polish literature, Town communities and shtetls. Author index only. Z6373.P7L47

Wielewinski, Bernard. Doctoral dissertations and masters theses regarding Polish subjects, 1900–1985 : an annotated bibliography. Boulder, Colo. : East European Monographs ; N.Y. : Distr. by Columbia Univ. Pr., 1988. 200 p. (East European monographs, no. 235). ISBN 0-88033-132-1. $30.00. **DC173**

Published jointly with the Commission on History and Archives of the Polish National Catholic Church.

An author listing of theses accepted in U.S., Canada, and Great Britain. Subject, title, discipline, and school indexes. Z2526.W54

Atlases

The historical atlas of Poland / [editors, Władysław Czapliński and Tadeusz Ładogórski ; authors, Irena Gieysztorowa . . . et al. ; translator, Maria Paczyńska]. Warszawa : Państwowe Przedsiębiorstwo Wyd. Kartograficzynch, 1986. 54, 56 p. : maps in color ; 31 cm. ISBN 83-7000-037-1. zł320.00. **DC174**

Translation of *Atlas historyczny Polski.*

Contains 54 pages of maps in color followed by 39 pages of explanatory material. Covers from the early stone age to about 1975, with roughly half the maps devoted to 800–1600. Index of places.

§ A less authoritative English-language publication, Iwo Pogonowski's *Poland: a historical atlas* (N.Y. : Hippocrene Books, 1987. 321p. $27.50) depicts Poland from prehistoric times to the 1980s in black-and-white maps. Tables of dynasties, chronology, bibliography, index by subject and placename. Gives a few statistics (e.g., number of Holocaust victims). G1951.S1P33

PORTUGAL

Marques, Alfredo Pinheiro. Guia de história dos Descobrimentos e expansão portuguesa : estudos. Lisboa : Biblioteca Nacional, [1987]. 188 p. **DC175**

A topical arrangement of books and articles concerning Portuguese discoveries and expansion through 18th centuries. Most citations are to Portuguese-language materials, although some are in French, English, and Spanish. Not indexed; cross-referenced to related sections. DP583.M36

Marques, António Henrique R. de Oliveira. Guia do estudante de história medieval portuguesa. 3a. ed. Lisboa : Editorial Estampa, 1988. 294 p. **DC176**

2nd ed., 1979 (*Guide* DC462).

Most sections have been updated to include entries up to about 1987.

Unwin, P. T. H. Portugal. Oxford ; Santa Barbara, Calif. : Clio Pr., c1987. 269 p. (World bibliographical series, v. 71). ISBN 1-85109-016-9. $50.50. **DC177**

An annotated, topically arranged bibliography of 787 English-language books and some articles. Author, title, subject index. Z2711.U59

ROMANIA

Deletant, Andrea. Romania / Andrea Deletant, Dennis Deletant, compilers. Oxford ; Santa Barbara, Calif. : Clio Pr., c1985. 236 p., [1] leaf of plates : map. (World bibliographical series, v. 59). ISBN 1-85109-002-9. $38.00. **DC178**

A topically arranged bibliography of primarily English-language books, but including French, German and Romanian publications when there is no equivalent English-language work. 797 annotated entries index by author, title and subject. DR205.Z99D44

SCANDINAVIA

Dictionary of Scandinavian history / ed. by Byron J. Nordstrom. Westport, Conn. : Greenwood, [1986]. 703 p. ISBN 0-313-22887-6. $75.00. **DC179**

Articles deal with Denmark, Finland, Iceland, Norway, and Sweden, together with some information on the Faroe Islands and Greenland. About 400 entries with bibliographic references, signed by contributors. Appendixes include lists of monarchs, prime ministers, chronology, etc. An index by topic complements the alphabetical arrangement. DL43.D53

Directory of Scandinavian studies in North America / Robert B. Kvavik, ed. Madison, Wis. : Publ. for the Society for the Advancement of Scandinavian Study by Grote Deutsch, 1989. 280 p. **DC180**

A state-of-the-art discussion of Scandinavian studies in America in the humanities, language, history, and the social sciences, and of relevant resources in America libraries. Directory of departments, programs, instructors and professors. Plans call for new editions every ten years. PT7037.N67D5

Guide to Nordic bibliography / general ed., Erland Munch-Petersen. [Copenhagen] : Nord, c1984. 235 p. : ill. ISBN 87-7303-080-5. Kr.195.00. **DC181**

An excellent guide, produced in collaboration by lecturers at five library schools in Denmark, Norway, Iceland, Sweden, and Finland. In two parts: (1) essays on each country's history, language, computerized library and information systems, and national bibliographic systems; (2) annotated entries for retrospective and current national bibliographies and for more than 800 author and subject bibliographies in print, microform, or online, arranged by UDC. The second part is indexed by author and title.

A *Supplement* (1988–) extends coverage, includes sections on changes to the national bibliographies, adds some bibliographies published before 1983 that were omitted from the earlier work, and includes recommended bibliographies of Nordic authors and composers. Z2551.G84

SPAIN

Bibliography

Aguilar Piñal, Francisco. Bibliografía de estudios sobre Carlos III y su época. Madrid : Consejo Superior de Investigaciones Científicas, 1988. 428 p. ISBN 84-00-06906-4. **DC182**

Companion to *Bibliografia de autores del siglo XVIII* (*Supplement* BD322).

A topically arranged bibliography of 18th-century Spain, including coverage of architecture, painting, and literature as well as economic affairs and social life. Lists 8,176 books, articles, and pamphlets in Spanish, English, German, and French. Author index.

Cadenas y Vicent, Vicente de. Bibliografía del Emperador Carlos V. Madrid : Instituto Salazar y Castro (C.S.I.C.), 1986. 245 p. ISBN 84-00-06330-9. **DC183**

A long bibliographical essay (p. 5–36) is followed by a bibliography of books, documents, and articles arranged by author. Mostly Spanish and Italian works with some in German and French. No index.

García Durán, Juan. La guerra civil española, fuentes : archivos, bibliografía y filmografía. Barcelona : Crítica, c1985. 443 p. **DC184**

In three parts: (1) archivos, colecciones, bibliografías, museos; (2) bibliografías, antologías, indices de publicaciones periodicas; (3) filmes, filmstecas, filmografías. Geographical arrangement. Listings are extensive, in the case of archives describing the files of records. List of pseudonyms with real name. Not indexed. Z2700.G33

Ruhl, Klaus-Jörg. Der spanische Bürgerkrieg : Literaturbericht und Bibliographie. München : Bernard & Graefe, [1988]. Bd. 2. (Schriften der Bibliothek für Zeitgeschichte, N.F., Bd. 26). ISBN 3-7637-0224-5. DM56.00. (In progress). **DC185**

For Bd. 1, see *Guide* DC484.

Contents: Bd. 2, Der militärische Konflikt (225p.).

Extends the earlier volume's coverage of publications on the political conflict through 1986–87, adding citations for economic and military topics. Author index to Bd. 2. Z2700.R83

Shields, Graham J. Spain. Oxford ; Santa Barbara, Calif. : Clio Pr., c1985. 340 p. : map. (World bibliographical series, v. 60). ISBN 1-85109-003-7. **DC186**

A selected, annotated bibliography of 982 books and periodical articles. Emphasizes recently published English-language material. The annotations often include references to related titles. Topical arrangement; author/title/subject index. DP17.Z99S54

Manuscripts and archives

Spain. Inspección Tecnica de Archivos. Guía de los archivos estatales españoles : guía del investigador / Ministerio de Cultura, Dirección General de Bellas Artes y Archivos, Subdirección General de Archivos, Inspección Tecnica de Archivos. 2a. ed. Madrid : Ministerio de Cultura, 1984. 244 p. : ill. ISBN 84-505-0652-2. **DC187**

1st ed., 1977.

Describes government and other historical archives; for each gives name, address, size, outline of contents, any printed descriptions. Appendix lists archives by geographical area, functionaries in the archive, and archives by type. Not indexed. CD1850.S67

Encyclopedias

Historical dictionary of modern Spain, 1700–1988 / Robert W. Kern, ed. in chief, Meredith D. Dodge, associate ed. N.Y. : Greenwood, [1990]. 697 p. : ill.; maps. ISBN 0-313-25971-2. **DC188**

Offers signed articles by scholars from the U.S., Britain, Spain, Canada, and Latin America in areas of politics, government, diplomacy, institutions, culture, society, and the military. Gives little attention to the Spanish Civil War because of the coverage by *Historical dictionary of the Spanish Civil War 1936–1939* ed. by James W. Cortada (*Guide* DC492). "The objective of this dictionary is not to provide definitive, detailed history for Spain, but to offer a quick reference on a broad range of material for those interested in basic information."— *Pref*. Bibliographic references with each article; cross-references; subject index; chronology of Spanish history; selected bibliography. Very useful. DP192.H57

SWEDEN

Sather, Leland B. Sweden / Leland B. Sather, Alan Swanson, compilers ; ed. by Hans H. Wellisch. Oxford : Clio, 1987. 370 p. : 1 map. (World bibliographical series, 80.). ISBN 1-85109-035-5. $70.00. **DC189**

1,015 entries, arranged in 44 topical sections; lists books and some articles, mostly in English but including significant works by Swedish scholars. Cross-references; author/title/subject index. Z2640.3

Svensk historisk bibliografi 1971–1975 : systematisk förteckning över skrifter och uppsatser som rör Sveriges historia utkomna fråm och med 1971 till och med 1975 = Swedish historical bibliography 1971–1975 : publications concerning Swedish history from 1971–1975 / [Marie-Louise Bachman, Yvonne Hirdman, Lillemor Lundstrom och Mayre Lehtilä-Olsson; red. av Yvonne Hirdman]. Stockholm : Almqvist & Wiksell International, 1987. 551 p. ISBN 91-22-01164-1. **DC190**

Continues the coverage and arrangement of the earlier volumes (*Guide* DC497). DL648.S93

SWITZERLAND

Meier, Heinz K. Switzerland / Heinz K. Meier, Regula A. Meier, compilers. Oxford ; Santa Barbara, Calif. : Clio Pr., c1990. 409 p. (World bibliographical series, v. 114). ISBN 1-85109-107-6. **DC191**

A bibliography of 974 annotated entries, arranged by topic, with chapters on major periodicals, reference books, and bibliographies. Intends to provide "a representative sample of works available in each of the subject areas."—*Introd.* Most titles cited are in English, but a good number are in French, German, or Italian. Author, title, and subject indexes. Z2771.M45

TURKEY

Tuğlac, Pars. Çağdaş Türkiye. Istanbul : Cem Yayınevi, 1987–1989. 3 v. (1978 p.) : ill. (some col.), ports. **DC192**

An encyclopedia devoted to Atatürk and Turkey at the time of Atatürk. Heavily illustrated; bibliographies end many of the articles. Each volume has its own index, mainly for personal names. DR576.T84

Witherell, Julian W. The Republic of Turkey : an American perspective : a guide to U.S. official documents and government-sponsored publications. Wash. : Library of Congress : For sale by the Supt. of Docs., U.S. Govt. Print. Off., 1988. 211 p., [1] leaf of plates : map. ISBN 0-8444-0587-6. **DC193**

Superintendent of Documents classification: LC 1.6/4:T84.

" . . . records a selection [i.e. 1,702] of publications on Turkey issued by or for agencies of the U.S. government in the period 1919–1986."—*Pref.* Arranged topically; includes Library of Congress call number or library location if not in L.C. Does not include classified documents, Congressional bills and resolutions, preliminary or program reports on government contracts. Author/title/subject index. Z6465.U5W56

UNION OF SOVIET SOCIALIST REPUBLICS

Bibliography

Egan, David R. Russian autocrats from Ivan the Great to the fall of the Romanov dynasty : an annotated bibliography of English language sources to 1985 / by David R. Egan and Melinda A. Egan. Metuchen, N.J. : Scarecrow, 1987. 512 p. ISBN 0-8108-1958-9. **DC194**

Aims to provide a comprehensive listing of English-language monographs, chapters from general works, essays, articles, memoirs, letters, and doctoral dissertations, plus a selection of reviews. Includes translations from French, German and Russian. Annotations, some quite lengthy, are descriptive. Asterisks are "provided for sources that focus upon one or more monarchs and are comprehensive, scholarly, or unique in some way."—*Introd.* Arranged chronologically by tsar, with an author index and a subject index arranged alphabetically by ruler. Items in the "General" section are not indexed. Z2506.E35

A guide to scholarly resources on the Russian Empire and the Soviet Union in the New York metropolitan area / the Social Science Research Council ; comp. by Robert A.

Karlowich. Armonk, N.Y. : M.E. Sharpe, c1990. 312 p. ISBN 0-87332-619-9. $45.00. **DC195**

Sponsored by the Bibliography, Information Retrieval and Documentation Subcommittee of the Joint Committee on Soviet Studies of the Social Science Research Council and the American Council of Learned Societies.

Intended to supplement Steven A. Grant and John H. Brown's *The Russian Empire and the Soviet Union : a guide to manuscripts and archival materials in the United States* (*Guide* AB118a).

Based on responses to a questionnaire sent to libraries and archives within a 50-mile radius of the New York Public Library; thus, institutions such as Princeton University and the U.S. Military Academy are included. For each is given: address, phone, contact person if available, hours, access, facilities, brief history, holdings (often in some detail), any special features, citations to catalogs and bibliographies. Index of names of collections, subjects, and contents of collections. Z2491.G86

Istoriia dorevoliutsionnoĭ Rossii v dnevnikakh i vospominaniiakh : [annotirovannyĭ ukazatel' knig i publikatsii v zhurnalakh / sostaviteli G.A. Glavatskikh . . . et al. ; nauchnoe rukovodstvo, red. i vvedenie P.A. Zaĭonchkovskogo]. Moskva : Kniga, 1985–1988. v. 4^3–5^2. **DC196**

For other volumes and annotation, see *Guide* DC532.

Contents: t. 4, ch. 3–4, 1895–1917 (completes the volume); t. 5, ch. 1, Literatura; t. 5, ch. 2, Dopolmenuak t. 1–5 (completes the volume).

T. 5, ch. 1 deals specifically with seven authors: Pushkin, Saltykov-Shedrin, Tolstoi, Chekov, Blok, Gorkii, and Maiakovskii. These writers were omitted in the earlier volumes because they were already subjects of comprehensive bibliographies; the compilers have reconsidered and feel the set would be incomplete without citations to memoirs relating to them. T. 5, ch. 2 is a supplement to v.1–4^1, following the same arrangement as the earlier volumes; it also includes a consolidated table of contents for the full set, telling where the same section heads appear in each volume. Each volume includes its own author and place or ethnic group indexes. Z2506.I87

Archives and manuscripts

Bakhmeteff Archive of Russian and East European History and Culture. Russia in the twentieth century : the catalog of the Bakhmeteff Archive of Russian and East European History and Culture / the Rare Book and Manuscript Library, Columbia University. Boston : G.K. Hall, 1987. 187 p. ISBN 0-8161-0462-X. **DC197**

Lists more then 900 collections pertaining to people and institutions of late 19th- and 20th-century Eastern Europe and Russia. Arranged alphabetically by author with descriptions of contents and indication of extent of collection and access (but not of provenance). Index of names and subjects. CD1739.N483B35

Bolkhovitinov, N. N. Russia and the United States : an analytical survey of archival documents and historical studies / Nikolai Nikolaevich Bolkhovitinov ; trans. and ed. by J. Dane Hartgrove. [Armonk, N.Y. : M.E. Sharpe, c1986]. 79 p. ISBN 0-87332-414-5 (pbk.). $15.00 (est.). **DC198**

Also issued as *Soviet studies in history*, 25, no. 2 (1986).

Translation of *Rossiia i SShA* (Moscow : INION AN SSSR, 1984).

A discussion of the archival guides and a survey of the holdings of the state archives and of major libraries in Moscow and Leningrad, plus a summary of research in the U.S.S.R. on U.S.-Russian relations. Selected bibliography of finding aids,

and of English- and Russian-language material. Not indexed.
Z6465.U5B64

Gosudarstvennye arkhivy SSSR : spravochnik / V.N. Avtokratov, F.M. Vaganov (predsedatel redkollegii) ... et al. ; sostaviteli N.M. Andreeva ... I.V. Volkova (otvetstvennyĭ sostavitel) ... [et al.]. Moskva : "Mysl'", 1989. 2 v. **DC199**

Updates and replaces the 1956 guide produced by Glavnoe Arkhivnoe Upravlenie (*Guide* DC557).

A guide to using the Soviet state archives. Entries are arranged by republic; each gives address, phone, description of holdings, and citations to finding aids. Index of proper names. Not as extensive as Patricia Grimsted's *Archives and manuscript repositories in the USSR* (*Guide* AB155–156 and below) but lists archives not yet included in her surveys.
CD1711.G66

Grimsted, Patricia Kennedy. Archives and manuscript repositories in the USSR. Ukraine and Moldavia. Princeton, N.J. : Princeton Univ. Pr., c1988. v. 1 : map. ISBN 0-691-05391-X (v.1). $125.00. (In progress).
DC200

A companion to the compiler's earlier volumes for Moscow and Leningrad (*Guide* AB156), and for Estonia, Latvia, Lithuania, and Belorussia (*Guide* AB155). To be in two parts: "Book 1 [the volume at hand] provides a bibliography of general reference literature relating to archives and manuscript collections in both union republics, followed by a comprehensive directory of archives and other manuscript repositories with bibliographies of their respective finding aids. Book 2, to be published later, will present a historical survey of the development of archives and recordkeeping practices in Ukraine and Moldavia."—*Pref.* Format follows that of previous volumes.
CD1735.U4G75

——————— A handbook for archival research in the USSR. [N.Y.?] : International Research and Exchanges Board ; [Wash.] : Kennan Institute for Advanced Russian Studies, c1989. 430 p. **DC201**

"The aim ... is to provide an updated general orientation for the beginning researcher, with selected bibliographic leads for further reference."—*Pref.* Discusses the state administration of the archives in U.S.S.R, their general arrangement, access, how to prepare for on-site use, and duplication services. Also includes a bibliographical essay on reference aids and a directory of major archives, libraries, and manuscript repositories in Moscow and Leningrad, as well as state archives of the other republics. The latter gives for each: address, staff, brief description of holdings, and published guides and finding aids. General index. A necessity for anyone planning research in the U.S.S.R.

§ An earlier work by Grimsted discusses bibliographies of archival literature, with emphasis on repositories in Moscow and Leningrad: *Recent Soviet archival literature: a review and preliminary bibliography of selected reference aids* (Wash. : Kennan Institute for Advanced Russian Studies, 1987. 122 p. Occasional paper 8).
CD1711.G68

Hartley, Janet M. Guide to documents and manuscripts in the United Kingdom relating to Russia and the Soviet Union. London ; N.Y. : Mansell, [1987]. 526 p. ISBN 0-7201-1805-0. $90.00. **DC202**

The result of "a three-year research project undertaken at the School of Slavonic and East European Studies, University of London, from 1982 to 1985."—*Introd.* Information is based mainly on responses to questionnaires sent to libraries, museums, record offices, and professional, religious and cultural organizations; many repositories were also visited. Geographical arrangement with address, finding aids and brief descriptions. Indexed.
Z2491.H37

Hoover Institution on War, Revolution, and Peace. Guide to the collections in the Hoover Institution archives relating to Imperial Russia, the Russian revolutions and civil war, and the first emigration / comp. by Carol A. Leadenham. Stanford, Calif. : Hoover Institution Pr., Stanford Univ., c1986. 208 p. (Hoover Press bibliographical series, 68). ISBN 0-8179-2681-X. $18.95.
DC203

A guide to one of the great Western repositories concentrating on 20th-century Russian political, diplomatic, and military affairs, gathered from émigrés, relief workers, Russian consulates in Germany, Tsarist military officers, government officials, and embassies in France. The archives also include motion pictures, films, posters, and art works. Collections are listed alphabetically, with notes on size and content, within period or broad category (e.g., Mongolia, Relief agencies). Indexed by subject.
Z2510.H66

The study of Russian history from British archival sources / ed. by Janet M. Hartley. London ; N.Y. : Mansell, [1986]. 184 p. ISBN 0-7201-1784-4. $45.00. **DC204**

Reprints 11 papers read at a conference at the School of Slavonic and East European Studies, University of London, April 1984, intended to demonstrate "the richness and variety of sources in Britain for the study of Anglo-Russian and Anglo-Soviet relations and Russian and Soviet history and to show how these sources could be used as a basis for scholarly research."—*Introd.* Some papers discuss specific archives (e.g., the Leeds Russian Archives), in others particular topics (e.g., Britons in 17th-century Russia). Not indexed.
DK3.S88

Encyclopedias; Handbooks

The Blackwell encyclopedia of the Russian Revolution / ed. by Harold Shukman. Oxford ; N.Y. : Blackwell, 1988. 418 p. : ill., ports. ISBN 0-631-15238-5. $65.00.
DC205

Treats organizations, events, and individuals important in Russian history, 1860s–1921. Contributors are mostly British. Pt. 1 is arranged basically in chronological chapters (unsigned) with cross-references in the text, each article ending with suggestions for further reading. Pt. 2, a biographical dictionary, deals with fewer people than *Dictionary of the Russian Revolution* (below), since here coverage begins with the roots of the revolution; no bibliographies in this part. Topical index. Heavily illustrated.
DK265.B54

De Mowbray, Stephen. Key facts in Soviet history. Boston : G.K. Hall, c1990. v. 1. ISBN 0-8161-1820-5 (v. 1). (In progress). **DC206**

Simultaneously published under title: *A chronology of Soviet history* (London : Pinter, 1990–).

Contents: v. 1, 1917 to 22 June 1941 (386 p.).

Emphasizes internal political developments, but devotes some attention to economic, social, and military history, and a few references to developments in the arts and sciences. Offers a chronological listing of events with several paragraphs describing each. "The aim has been to produce an uncluttered text based on secondary sources which would be fully accessible to the non-specialist reader" and the editor has therefore "dispensed with footnotes altogether."—*Introd.* The "List of sources" (p. 361–375) is extensive and includes material in the Public Record Office, parliamentary papers, books and newspapers. Index of personal and geographic names.
DK266.D39

Dictionary of the Russian Revolution / George Jackson, ed. in chief ; Robert Devlin, assistant ed. N.Y. : Greenwood, 1989. 704 p. : ill. ISBN 0-313-21131-0. $75.00.
DC207

Approximately 300 signed articles on "revolutionary leaders and governing institutions ... social classes and social problems, workers, peasants, the agrarian question, the national question, the army, the navy, and the trade unions . . . [and] national minorities.—*Pref.* Articles include bibliographic citations and cross-references. Contributors are mostly American. Much broader in coverage of the Revolution than *The Blackwell encyclopedia of the Russian Revolution* (above), but not as extensive for the earlier period. Chronology, 1898–1922. Name and subject indexes.   DK265.D49

The modern encyclopedia of Russian and Soviet history / ed. by Joseph L. Wieczynski. [Gulf Breeze, Fla.] : Academic International Pr., [1986]–1990. v. 40–53. ISBN 0-87569-064-5. (In progress).   **DC208**
    For v. 1–39 and annotation, see *Guide* DC571.
    Contents: v.40–54, Trubetskoi–Supplement: Wilno. V. 46 covers Zemstvo Agricultural policy–Zyriane, Supplement: Abakan–Archives in the Soviet Union.
    With v. 46 begins a supplement designed to cover topics previously omitted, especially material on the history and development of cites and towns, articles for the *Great Soviet encyclopedia* (*Guide* AC71), and biographies of people who died since publication of earlier volumes. Note especially v. 46–47, which include discussion of archives in the Soviet Union, in the Union Republics, and in Tsarist Russia.
    § Also being published is: *The modern encyclopedia of religions in Russia and the Soviet Union*, ed. Paul D. Steeves (Gulf Breeze, Fla. : Academic International Pr. 1988–).
    DK36.M55

Directories

A scholars' guide to humanities and social sciences in the Soviet Union : the Academy of Sciences of the USSR and the academies of sciences of the Union republics / American Council of Learned Societies-Soviet Academy of Sciences Commission on the Humanities and Social Sciences; [ed. by Blair A. Ruble and Mark H. Teeter]. Armonk, N.Y. : M.E. Sharpe, c1985. 310 p. ISBN 0-87332-335-1.   **DC209**
    Publ. in U.K. : [London], Longman.
    A comprehensive survey of the humanities and social sciences institutions of the Soviet Academy of Sciences and the academies of the various Union republics, giving for each a historical sketch, notes on structure, staff, areas of research, library facilities or collections, and publications. There is also information on "Contacts and cooperation" for each academy or institute, and a bibliography of writings about the institution. "This *Guide* is organized according to the administrative hierarchy of the Academy of Sciences of the USSR and the academies of sciences of the Union republics, which in Russian is alphabetical within each segment of the Academy. We have realphabetized in English in each Academy subdivision but have otherwise preserved the Soviet structure."—*p. xi.* Detailed table of contents; indexes by subject, city, and administrator.   AS258.S36

Regional and local

Bibliographia studiorum uralicorum, 1917–1987 = Uralistiikan tutkimuksen bibliografia = Bibliography on Uralic studies / [bibliografian toimitusneuvosto, Esko Häkli, puheenjohtaja, Helsinki . . . et al. ; V.A. Vinogradov, puheenjohtaja, Moskova . . . et al.]. Helsinki : Suomalaisen Kirjallisuuden Seura, 1988. v. 1. ISBN 951-717-545-0 (v. 1). (In progress).   **DC210**
    Contents: v. 1, Archaeology (397 p.) Future volumes are to include Ethnology and folklore, Linguistics, Literary studies.
    Also publ.: Moskva : Akademiia nauk SSSR, 1988– .
    Joint project of Akademiia Nauk SSSR and Suomen Akatemian ja Neuvostoliiton. Vol. 1 lists monographs, essays, journals, abstracts of conferences, and dissertations written by So-

viet or Finnish scholars 1917–87 on this part of western Russia. Topical arrangement within geographical areas or period divisions. Index in Russian for names of authors, compilers, and editors; indexes in Russian and English for subjects.
    Z7045.A16

Encyclopedia of Ukraine / ed. by Volodymyr Kubijovyč. Toronto ; Buffalo : Univ. of Toronto Pr., c1984–c1988. v. 1–2 : ill. ISBN 0-8020-3362-8 (set). (In progress).   **DC211**
    Published for the Canadian Institute of Ukrainian Studies, the Shevchenko Scientific Society and the Canadian Foundation for Ukrainian Studies.
    Contents: v.1–2, A–K. To be complete in 4v.
    Translation and revision of *Entsyklopediia ukraïnoznavstva* (1949–73).
    Covers all areas of Ukrainian studies, including information on Ukrainians living outside the U.S.S.R. Some long survey articles (e.g., Anthropology, Botany); much biographical information. Longer articles are signed and usually give bibliographical references. Handsome illustrations.   DK508.E613

Ukrainskaĩa Sovetskaĩa Sotsialisticheskaĩa Respublika : ėntsiklopedicheskiĭ spravochnik / [glavnaĩa redaktsionnaĩa kollegiĩa Babiĭ B.M., Babichev F.S. (glavnyĭ redaktor USĖ, predsedatel' redkollegii) . . . et al.]. Kiev : Glav. red. Ukrainskoĭ Sov. ėntsiklopedii, 1987. 513 p., [75] p. of plates : ill. (some col.).   **DC212**
    Russian ed. of *Ukraïns'ka Radĩans'ka Sotsialistychna Respublika*, 1986.
    A single-volume encyclopedia, covering 500 BCE–1986, published and translated in the Ukraine. Articles treat broad topics, such as history or culture. Heavily illustrated.
    DK508.A4U4717

University of Toronto. Library. Ucrainica at the University of Toronto Library : a catalogue of holdings / comp. by Paul Robert Magocsi with the assistance of Nadia Odette Diakun. Toronto ; Buffalo : Univ. of Toronto Pr., c1985. 2 v. (1845 p.). ISBN 0-8020-3430-6 (pbk.). $80.00 (set).   **DC213**
    About 11,000 titles published up to 1980 held by the University of Toronto Library are topically arranged in 31 chapters with 80 subdivisions. Covers "all materials in whatever language or form that deal in some way in the Ukraine or which are produced by individuals working within a Ukrainian historical and cultural environment."—*Introd.* Not indexed.
    Z2514.U5U55

Wynar, Bohdan S. Ukraine : a bibliographic guide to English-language publications. Englewood, Colo. : Ukrainian Academic Pr., 1990. 406 p. ISBN 0-87287-761-2. $85.00.   **DC214**
    A bibliography of 1,084 English-language books, theses, pamphlets, essays, and articles, with critical annotations that often cite reviews. Subsumed in the annotations are citations to other works in English or Ukrainian. Arrangement is topical, well divided, even for individual authors in the "Literature" section. Author/title/subject index (with subject headings in boldface).   Z2514.U5W9

Atlases

Magocsi, Paul R. Ukraine, a historical atlas / Paul Robert Magocsi ; Geoffrey J. Matthews, cartographer. Toronto ; Buffalo : Univ. of Toronto Pr., c1985. 25 [i.e. 59] p. : maps in color. ISBN 0-8020-3428-4. ISBN 0-8020-3429-2 (pbk.).   **DC215**
    Reprinted with a few revisions, 1987.
    Text and maps on facing pages cover "the present-day Ukrainian Soviet Socialist Republic and the Ukrainian ethnolinguistic territory" (*Pref.*) from the time of the Greek colonies

through World War II. Very clear presentation.

G2151.S1M34

Milner-Gulland, R. R. Cultural atlas of Russia and the Soviet Union / by Robin Milner-Gulland with Nikolai Dejevsky. N.Y. : Facts on File, 1989. 240 p. : ill. (some col.), some maps in color ; 31 cm. ISBN 0-8160-2207-0. $40.00. **DC216**

U.K. edition entitled: *Atlas of Russia and the Soviet Union* (Oxford : Phaidon, 1989).

Essentially a narrative history of Russia and the Soviet Union up to 1985, heavily illustrated with maps, diagrams, and photographs. A final section gives "a concise geographical and cultural 'portrait' in maps, words and pictures of each of the republics . . . so as to give the reader a sense of its location within the USSR, its people, its resources, its past and its individuality."—*p.185*. A chronological table, 800–1979, is presented in parallel columns for: Politics and rulers; Religion; International relations; Territorial expansion; Art and architecture; Learning, science and literature. Bibliography arranged by themes; glossary; list of illustrations; gazetteer; index by topic.

DK32.M62

YUGOSLAVIA

Enciklopedija Slovenije / [glavni urednik Marjan Javornik]. Ljubljana : Mladinska knjiga, 1987–1989. v. 1–3 : ill. (some col.). (In progress). **DC217**

Contents: v.1–3: A–Hab.

A good regional encyclopedia, well illustrated, with signed articles and brief bibliographies. Includes statistics up to 1985; most articles are current to the early or mid-1980s.

DR1357.5.E52

Horton, John J. Yugoslavia. Rev. and expanded ed. Oxford ; Santa Barbara, Calif. : Clio Pr., c1990. 279 p. (World bibliographical series, v. 1). ISBN 1-85109-105-X. **DC218**

1st ed., 1977 (*Guide* DC584).

Offers 921 annotated entries, mostly English-language publications, topically arranged in 42 sections. Many more references are subsumed in the annotations. About half the entries appear to be new to this edition. Indexed by author, title, and subject.

Z2951.H67

Terry, Garth M. Yugoslav history : a bibliographic index to English-language articles. Cotgrave, Nottingham : Astra Pr., 1985. 141 p. (Bibliography of southeast European history, v. 1). ISBN 0-946134-04-9. $14.55. **DC219**

Attempts to list "all articles on the history—in its broadest sense—of Yugoslavia contained in *Festschriften*, conference proceedings, collected papers and journals in the English language from 1945 to 1985."—*Introd.* Includes areas such as diplomacy, economics, intellectual life, religious development as well as history. Topically arranged in four main sections: (1) General; (2) To 1945; (3) 1945– ; (4) History of the Yugoslav republics. List of subject headings; name index for authors, compilers, editors, translators, and any other person mentioned in an entry.

Z2956.T47

DD

Africa

GENERAL WORKS

Bibliography

Lauer, Joseph J. American and Canadian doctoral dissertations and master's theses on Africa, 1974–1987 / comp. by Joseph J. Lauer, Alfred Kagan & Gregory V. Larkin. Atlanta : Crossroads Pr., Emory Univ., c1989. 1 v. (377 p.). ISBN 0-918456-63-0. $75.00. **DD1**

Cumulates the annual lists in *ASA news* (v.14 no.1, Jan./ Mar. 1981–89; sponsored by the African Studies Association) and serves as a continuation of Michael Sims and Alfred Kagan's compilation for 1886–1974 (*Guide* DD33).

Z3501.L33

Library resources (including archives)

Guides to the sources for the history of the nations. 3rd series, North Africa, Asia and Oceania = Guides des sources de l'histoire des nations. 3ème série, Afrique du Nord, Asie et Océanie. München ; N.Y. : K.G. Saur, 1986–91. v. 7–9. (In progress). **DD2**

For annotation, see *Supplement* DD15. CD941.G85

South, Aloha. Guide to non-federal archives and manuscripts in the United States relating to Africa. London ; N.Y. : Zell, 1989. 2 v. (1250 p.). ISBN 0-905450-55-8 (set). £120.00. **DD3**

Companion to the compiler's *Guide to federal archives relating to Africa* (*Guide* DD44).

Based on answers received from questionnaires sent to repositories in the U.S., this listing of archives by state, then city gives for each: address, name of collection and size, and a description of each file or collection (microforms, sound recordings, motion pictures, and photographs are often included). Africa here includes North Africa and the outlying islands. Alphabetical list of repositories; topical index. CD3002.S68

Dictionaries

Africa / ed. by Sean Moroney. Rev. and updated ed. N.Y. : Facts on File, [1989]. 2 v. (1208 p.) : ill., maps. ISBN 0-8160-1623-2 (set). **DD4**

At head of title: Handbooks to the modern world.

First publ. London : Anthony Blond, 1962.

This edition completely revised, expanded, and updated. Country surveys are followed by short articles organized into three large areas: Political affairs, Economic affairs, and Social affairs. Signed articles; subject index.   DT3.A243

African historical dictionaries. 1st ed. Metuchen, N.J. : Scarecrow, 1987–90. v. 40–46, 48.   **DD5**
  Contents: v. 40, Nigeria, A. Oyewole (1987. 391 p.); v. 41, Ivory Coast, R.J. Mundt (1987. 246 p.); v. 42, Republic of Cape Verde, R. Lobban and M. Halter (1988. 171 p.); v. 43, Zaire, F.S. Bobb (1988. 349 p.); v. 44, Botswana, F. Morton, A. Murray, J. Ramsey (1989. 216 p.); v. 45, Tunisia, K.J. Perkins (1989. 234 p.); v. 46, Zimbabwe, R.K. Rasmussen, S.C. Rubert (1990. 502 p.); v. 48, Cameroon, M. DeLancey (1990. 297 p.).

African historical dictionaries. 2nd ed. Metuchen, N.J. : Scarecrow, 1987–88. v. 4, 7, 9, 11, 13, 16, 20–22. **DD6**
  For other volumes in the series, see *Guide* DD46.
  Contents: v. 4, Gambia, H.A. Gailey (1987. 176 p.); v. 7, Benin, S. Decalo (1987. 349 p.); v. 9, Togo, S. Decalo (1987. 331 p.); v. 11, Mali, P. J. Imperato (1986. 359 p.); v. 13, Chad, S. Decalo (1987. 532 p.); v. 16, Guinea (formerly Guinea/Conakry) (1987. 204 p.); v. 20, Niger, S. Decalo (1989. 234 p.); v. 21, Equatorial Guinea, M. Liniger-Goumaz (1988. 238 p.); v. 22, Republic of Guinea-Bissau, R. Lobban, J. Forrest (1988. 210 p.).

Stewart, John. African states and rulers : an encyclopedia of native, colonial, and independent states and rulers past and present. Jefferson, N.C. : McFarland, c1989. 395 p. ISBN 0-89950-390-X. $45.00.   **DD7**
  Covers African countries (including North Africa) and outlying islands, giving for each: name of country, dates for that name, location, capital, names earlier and later under which the country existed, very brief history, list of rulers with dates. Cross-references from common to official names of the country. Personal name index. A brief review in *Library journal* 114, no.9 (15 May 1989):66 concludes the work is an "indispensable addition to collections for specialists and generalists either for biography or the chronology of various African political entities."   DT31.S786

Directories

International guide to African studies research = Études africaines : guide international de recherches / comp. by Philip Baker. 2nd fully rev. and expanded ed. London ; N.Y. : Zell, 1987. 264 p. ISBN 0-905450-25-6. $72.00.
                              DD8
  Rev. ed., 1975, had title *International guide to African research studies* (*Guide* DD59).
  Published for the International African Institute, London.
  Adds some 600 new entries, bringing the total to about 1,100 institutes, research centers, etc. Inclusion of phone numbers is a new feature. Indexes by institution; scholar; subjects of research; specialization by region, country, or ethnic group.
                              DT19.8.I58

Zell, Hans M. The African studies companion : a resource guide & directory. London ; N.Y. : Zell, 1989. 165 p. (Hans Zell resource guides, no. 1). ISBN 0-905450-80-9. £48.00.   **DD9**
  Includes some 667 "annotated listings of the major reference tools; bibliographies and continuing sources; journals and magazines; major libraries and documentation centres; publishers with African studies lists; dealers and distributors of African studies associations; foundations and donor agencies supporting African studies research or which are active in Africa; and awards and prizes in African studies."—*Pref.* Name index. Appendix of abbreviations and acronyms in African studies.
                              DT19.8.Z45

General history

The Cambridge history of Africa / gen. editors, J. D. Fage and Roland Oliver. Cambridge ; N.Y. : Cambridge Univ. Pr., 1986. v. 7 : ill. ISBN 0-521-20981-1 (v. 3). $48.00.   **DD10**
  For preceding volumes and annotation, see *Guide* DD60.
  Contents: v. 7, 1905–40, ed. Andrew Roberts (1063 p.) Completes the set.   DT20.C28

Atlases

Freeman-Grenville, G. S. P. The new atlas of African history. N.Y. : Simon & Schuster, c1991. 144 p. ; 30 cm. ISBN 0-13-612151-9.   **DD11**
  A much expanded version of Freeman-Grenville's *Modern atlas of African history* (London : R. Collings, 1976. 63 p.)
  Two color maps for all of Africa, covering prehistoric times to 1990. Almost all of the 103 maps show relief and have accompanying explanatory text. Index to place-names and subjects.   G2446.S1F73

AFRICA, EAST

Ofcansky, Thomas P. British East Africa, 1856–1963 : an annotated bibliography. N.Y. : Garland, 1985. 474 p. (Themes in European expansion, v. 7 ; Garland reference library of social science, v. 158). ISBN 0-8240-9164-7. $99.00.   **DD12**
  An annotated bibliography of 3,086 books and pamphlets, mostly in English, on British East Africa generally together with sections for Kenya, Uganda, Tanganyika, and Zanzibar. Includes special headings for exploration, religion, agriculture, education, Mau Mau revolt, medicine, slavery, and wildlife. Author index.   Z3516.O33

Thurston, Anne. Guide to archives and manuscripts relating to Kenya and East Africa in the United Kingdom. London ; N.Y. : Zell, 1991. 2 v. (1196 p.). ISBN 0-905450-47-7 (set). £120.00.   **DD13**
  Contents: v. 1, Official records (617 p.); v. 2, Non-official archives and manuscripts (579 p.)
  A detailed listing of papers of nine official repositories (Public Record Office, Foreign and Commonwealth Office, India Office, Post Office, Royal Botanic Gardens, etc.) and a large number of university, religious, public libraries, and record office repositories. Arranged alphabetically under geographic headings. Topical index to both volumes in v. 2 with cross-references for variant names.   Z3587.T48

AFRICA, NORTHERN

García-Arenal, Mercedes. Repertorio bibliográfico de las relaciones entre la península Ibérica y el Norte de África, siglos XV–XVI : fuentes y bibliográfia / Mercedes García-Arenal, Miguel Ábgel de Bunes, Victoria Aguilar. Madrid : Consejo Superior de Investigaciones Científicas, Instituto de Filología, 1989. 303 p. ISBN 84-00-06950-1.   **DD14**
  Citations to 97 Castilian and Portuguese-language sources written between 1415 and 1610, published and in manuscript,

are followed by a secondary bibliography of 725 books, chapters, and articles. Not indexed. DT197.5.S7G37

Guides to the sources for the history of the nations. 3rd series, North Africa, Asia and Oceania = Guides des sources de l'histoire des nations. 3ème série, Afrique du Nord, Asie et Océanie. München ; N.Y. : K.G. Saur, 1986–91. v. 7–9. (In progress). **DD15**

For v. 1–6 and annotation, see *Guide* DE16

At head of title: International Council on Archives.

Contents: v. 7, Guía de fuentes para la historia de Asia en España, by Luis Sanchez Belda (1987. 242 p.); v. 8, Quellen zur Geschichte Afrikas, Asiens und Ozeaniens im Österreichischen Staatsarchiv bis 1919 (1986. 273 p.); v. 9, Sources of the history of Africa, Asia, Australia and Oceania in Hungary (with a supplement: Latin America) (1991. 451 p.). CD941.G85

AFRICA, SOUTH OF THE SAHARA

Cooperative Africana Microform Project (U.S.). CAMP catalog. 1985 cumulative ed. Chicago : Cooperative Africana Microform Project and the Center for Research Libraries [etc.], [1986]. 642 p. **DD16**

For 1977 cumulative edition and 1981 cumulative suppl., see *Guide* DD7.

Supersedes all earlier editions and is cumulative to May 1985. Quality of some of the reproductions is very poor.

Z3509.C66

Fenton, Thomas P. Africa : a directory of resources / comp. and ed. by Thomas P. Fenton and Mary J. Heffron. Maryknoll, N.Y. : Orbis Books, c1987. 144 p. : ill. ISBN 0-88344-532-8 (pbk.). $9.95. **DD17**

An updated and greatly expanded version of the corresponding chapter in *Third World resource directory* (*Supplement* CH51).

Cites organizations, publishers, books and pamphlets, and audiovisual materials that focus primarily on Africa south of the Sahara. Indexes for organizations and author, title, and geographic area. Z3501.F45

Scheven, Yvette. Bibliographies for African studies, 1970–1986. London ; N.Y. : Zell, 1988. 615 p. ISBN 0-905450-33-7. $100.00. **DD18**

Cumulates the compiler's earlier volumes for 1970–75, 1976–79, and 1980–83 (*Guide* DD82–84), adding new materials published through 1986. Z3501.S34

Shavit, David. The United States in Africa : a historical dictionary. N.Y. : Greenwood, [1989]. 298 p. ISBN 0-313-25887-2. **DD19**

Brief entries treat persons, institutions, and events concerning Africa south of the Sahara and adjacent islands. Index of names and a few subjects; list of individuals by profession and occupation. Appendix: Chiefs of American diplomatic missions in Africa 1863–1988 (arranged alphabetically by personal name). A companion to Shavit's *The United States in the Middle East* (*Supplement* DE22) and *The United States in Asia* (*Supplement* DE3). DT38.1.S53

U.S. imprints on Sub-Saharan Africa / African Section, African and Middle Eastern Division, Research Services. v. 1 (1985)– . Wash. : Library of Congress : For sale by the Supt. of Docs., U.S. Govt. Print. Off., 1986– . Biennial, 1988/89– . ISSN 0888-2878. **DD20**

Subtitle: a guide to publications cataloged at the Library of Congress.

Each biennial issue has a combined numeric designation (i.e. 1988/89 is called v. 4/5).

Superintendent of Documents classification: LC 41.12/2.

Focuses on monographs which have been cataloged and therefore includes material published before 1985. Each issue is an author listing of about 1,200 titles with a title index. The majority of the titles are in English; a few works of belles-lettres are included. Appendix: List of publishers' and distributors' addresses. Z3509.U18

AFRICA, SOUTHERN

Böhmer, Elizabeth W. Left-radical movements in South Africa and Namibia 1900–1981 : a bibliographical and historical study. Cape Town : South African Library, 1986. 2 v. (liv, 1249 p.). ISBN 0-86968-055-2 (set). £48.10. **DD21**

Lists some 7,350 books and pamphlets, journal and newspaper articles, theses, and research reports, and court cases available in South African libraries. The compiler includes banned materials if she had been able to get permission to see them. Arranged topically in five main divisions: Africa, Southern Africa, South Africa, Lesotho (coverage not as thorough), and Namibia. Library locations (mostly in South African libraries) are included at the end of each entry. Addenda: List of banned persons, organizations and periodicals; Consolidated alphabet of all persons listed in terms of the Suppression of Communism Act to 30 June 1983. Indexes for subjects, names as subject, periodicals, and court cases. HN801.Z9R33

Southern African update. v. 1, no. 1 (Apr. 1986)– . [Braamfontein, South Africa] : Univ. of the Witwatersrand Library, c1986– . Semiannual. ISSN 0258-9168. **DD22**

Subtitle: "A bibliographical survey."

A survey of publications on South Africa, arranged in chapters by topic. The first three chapters are bibliographic essays, new to the series; the others are annotated bibliographies updating chapters previously published. Topics covered are mostly political (e.g., Trade unions, International pressure against apartheid). Southern Africa is defined as Zambia and Mozambique south. Author index.

AFRICA, WEST

Archives du Sénégal. Guide des archives de l'Afrique occidentale française / Saliou Mbaye. Dakar : Archives du Sénégal, 1990. 205 p. **DD23**

Describes the archives for Senegal, Mauritania, Sudan, Guinea, Ivory Coast, Upper Volta, Niger, and Dahomey. Includes a bibliography of works whose authors used the archives. Reprints laws and regulations concerning the archives. Topic and name index. CD2491.S38S25

Fage, J. D. A guide to original sources for precolonial western Africa published in European languages. Madison, Wis. : African Studies Program, Univ. of Wisconsin-Madison, c1987. 192 p. : map. (Studies in African sources, 2). ISBN 0-942615-01-8. $20.00. **DD24**

A chronological listing of books, parts of collections, and articles concerning published sources on Western Africa, Senegal to Angola, from about mid-15th century to the 19th century. For each entry, gives a brief annotation identifying the author, area, or purpose. Index for author; for editor, compiler, translator, or commentator; and for geographical area. Z3516.5.F34

ALGERIA

Maynadies, Michel. Bibliographie algérienne : répertoire des sources documentaires relatives à l'Algérie. Alger : Office des publications universitaires, c1989. 336 p.
DD25

Cites 1,133 books and series, arranged topically following a general section. Concentrates on bibliographies, periodical indexes, encyclopedias, journals, catalogs, and inventories of the 19th and 20th centuries, published up to 1982. Some annotations; author and anonymous title indexes. Locates copies at Paris (Bibliothèque Nationale) and in Algeria (Bibliothèque universitaire d'Alger and Bibliothèque de l'Institut des Sciences Économiques de l'Université d'Alger). Z3681.M38

Ruhe, Ernstpeter. Algerien-Bibliographie ; Publikationen aus der Bundesrepublik Deutschland, Österreich und der Schweiz 1962–1989. Wiesbaden : Harrassowitz, 1990. 181 p. ISBN 3-447-03039-9. DM48.00. **DD26**

German-language publications on Algeria are arranged by broad topics (e.g., Wirtschaft, Literatur, Naturwissenschaft), subdivided into slightly less broad topics (e.g., Biologie). Covers 1,262 books and pamphlets. Author index. Z3681.R84

BOTSWANA

Lekaukau, T. M. A guide to the public archives of Botswana. [Botswana] : Botswana National Archives, [1984]. v. 1. (In progress). **DD27**
Contents: v. 1, 1885–1965 (41 p.).

A historical survey of the archives and of administrative departments, together with an outline of the contents of the National Archives. CD2491.B6L45

CAMEROON

DeLancey, Mark. Cameroon / Mark W. DeLancey, Peter J. Schraeder, compilers. Oxford ; Santa Barbara, Calif. : Clio Pr., c1986. 201 p., [1] leaf of plates. (World bibliographical series, v. 63). ISBN 1-85109-006-1. $55.00.
DD28

A topical arrangement of 502 annotated entries for articles, books, and a few government publications. Although English-language materials are stressed, a few German and French citations are also included. Author/title/subject index. Z3761.D45

DJIBOUTI

Aubry, Marie-Christine. Djibouti : bibliographie fondamentale (domaine francophone). Paris : L'Harmattan, 1990. 168 p. : maps. ISBN 2-7384-0818-4. **DD29**

Much expanded from *Bibiographie de la RDD* (Djibouti: Centre Culturel Arthur Rimbaud, 1980. 77 p.). An alphabetical listing of about 1,600 books, chapters, articles in periodicals and newspapers, proceedings, and a few government publications. Topically arranged in four sections: Vues d'ensemble; La nature; Les hommes; Visions litteraires. Some entries have annotations. Location in a library in Djibouti or France is given for each item. Index by names, and by sponsoring body for anonymous works. List of periodicals indexed is quite extensive and includes locations. DT411.22A9

EGYPT

Annual Egyptological bibliography. Late reviews AEB 1947–1984 / comp. by L.M.J. Zonhoven ; with the collaboration of A. Egberts and W. Hovestreydt. Leiden : International Association of Egyptologists in cooperation with the Nederlands Instituut voor het Nabije Oosten, [1989]. 74 p. **DD30**

Book reviews that appeared after the annual publication of the *Annual Egyptological bibliography* (see *Guide* DD115) are listed by *AEB* citation number. An earlier list appended to *AEB* 1973 (published 1977) is incorporated into this volume. Beginning with *AEB* 1985 (published 1989), there will be a section of late reviews at the end of each annual volume. Z3656.L37

Lexikon der Ägyptologie / Hrsg. von Wolfgang Helck und Eberhard Otto. Wiesbaden : Harrassowitz, 1985–1990. v. 6^4–7^3. ISBN 3-447-01441-5 (v. 1/1). (In progress). **DD31**

For v. 1–6^3 and annotation, see *Guide* DD121.
Contents: v. 6^{4-9}, Thinnis–Zypresse (completes the volume); v. 7^{1-3}, Nachträge, Korrekturen, und Indices (in progress).

The *Nachträge* thus far includes a list of abbreviations, Addenda et correginda, Allgemeiner index, and the beginning of the Urtsnämen index. DT58.L49

Makar, Ragai N. Egypt. Oxford ; Santa Barbara, Calif. : Clio Pr., c1988. 306 p. (World bibliographical series, v. 86). ISBN 1-85109-039-8. $70.00. **DD32**

Presents 1,022 annotated entries for books and some articles and documents, mostly in English (95%). All periods are covered, but emphasis is on the medieval and modern periods. Indexes for author, title, and subject. Chronology; glossary. Z3651.M34

EQUATORIAL GUINEA

Liniger-Goumaz, Max. Guinea Ecuatorial : bibliografía general. Berne : Commission nationale suisse pour l'Unesco, 1985. v. 5. **DD33**

For v. 1–4 and annotation, see *Guide* DD124.
Contents: v. 5, Volumen recapitulativo (referencias 1–8125). 264 p. Completes the set.

Includes indexes to v. 2–5 (with item numbers in v. 5 in italics): geographical and subject; movements, organizations, and parties; names as subjects. Z3937.L56

ETHIOPIA

Milkias, Paulos. Ethiopia : a comprehensive bibliography. Boston : G.K. Hall, c1989. 694 p. : ill. ISBN 0-8161-9066-6. $75.00. **DD34**

" . . . covers almost all materials on Ethiopia, not only in English but also in Amharic, Tigrigna, Oromic, German, Italian, French, and to a lesser extent, in Russian, Greek, Dutch, and Swedish."—*Pref.* Cutoff date is 1988. Almost 19,300 numbered entries (for books, pamphlets, periodical articles, and government publications) are listed by broad topic with author index. Because of the lack of a subject index and the many spelling errors, other bibliographies of Ethiopia are still needed. Z3521.M55

GAMBIA

Gamble, David P. The Gambia. Oxford ; Santa Barbara, Calif. : Clio Pr., c1988. 135 p. (World bibliographical series, v. 91). ISBN 1-85109-068-1. $45.00.   **DD35**

A topical arrangement of 334 annotated entries, mainly for English-language publications (with some in French). Includes classic works as well as most current. Author/title/subject indexes.   Z3735.G319

———————— A general bibliography of the Gambia up to 31st December 1977. San Francisco : D.P. Gamble, [1987]. 185 leaves. (Gambian studies, no. 18).   **DD36**
Z3735.G33

———————— A general bibliography of the Gambia, Supplement II, 1978–1982. San Francisco : D.P. Gamble, [1987]. 404 leaves. (Gambian studies, no. 19).   **DD37**
Supplements to the 1979 bibliography by the same title (see *Guide* DD132).

Suppl. I contains 935 entries in topical arrangement, including materials that were printed in a supplement (but not indexed) in the 1979 work, items omitted from it, and titles that have been revised or enlarged. Name index; list of corrigenda.

Suppl. II contains 2,450 books, newspaper and journal articles, government reports, theses, and mimeographed materials, mostly in English but with a smattering of titles in other languages, in topical arrangement. Based on visits to libraries in California, Banjul and Fajara, Belfast, Liverpool, and London. Name index.   Z3735.G33

GHANA

Sarfoh, Joseph A. Population, urbanization, and rural settlement in Ghana : a bibliographic survey. N.Y. : Greenwood, 1987. 124 p. (African special bibliographic series, no. 8). ISBN 0-313-26073-7.   **DD38**

An unannotated listing by format of 1,344 books, articles, theses, documents, and conference papers, published in English or French. Author index.   Z7164.D3S33

GUINEA-BISSAU

Galli, Rosemary E. Guinea-Bissau. Oxford ; Santa Barbara, Calif. : Clio Pr., 1990. 180 p. : map. (World bibliographical series, v. 121). ISBN 1-85109-108-4. £30.00.   **DD39**

Cites books, articles, and government publications in English and Portuguese (with a few in German and French), arranged by topic. Indexed by author, title, and subject (in a few instances the numbers are slightly off). Separate listings of 12 theses on Guinea-Bissau.   Z3878.G34

IVORY COAST

Borremans, Raymond. Le grand dictionnaire encyclopédique de la Côte d'Ivoire. Abidjan : Nouvelles Editions africaines, [1986–c1988]. v. 1–4 : ill. (some col.), maps, ports. ISBN 2-7236-0733-X (v. 1). (In progress).   **DD40**
Contents: v. 1–4, A–M.

Heavily illustrated. Consists mostly of short articles on places, people, flora and fauna, geographical features, and on topics such as "Art, African." Longer articles (e.g., Abidjan, Alester [a fish], Animism) have short bibliographies.
DT545.15.B67

LIBYA

Lawless, Richard I. Libya. Oxford ; Santa Barbara, Calif. : Clio Pr., c1987. 243 p. : map. (World bibliographical series, v. 79). ISBN 1-85109-033-9. $65.00.
DD41

The 626 annotated entries are mostly for English-language publications, though some French, German, and Italian materials are included. Emphasizes most recently published books, articles, and dissertations. Topical arrangement. Author/title/subject index.   Z3971.L39

Witherell, Julian W. Libya, 1969–1989 : an American perspective : a guide to U.S. official documents and government-sponsored publications. Wash. : Library of Congress : For sale by the Supt. of Docs., U.S. Govt. Print. Off., 1990. 180 p. : map. (Near East series, no. 4).
DD42
Superintendent of Documents classification: LC 41.9: L61.

Topical arrangement for a "selection of publications on Libya issued by or for agencies of the U.S. government since 1969 . . . including reports on its agriculture, commerce, economic situation, labor force, petroleum industry, and politics and government."—*Pref.* Most of the 669 documents are housed in the Library of Congress, with a few from the Dept. of State Library, Pentagon Library, Air University and Air Force libraries. Omits classified materials, Congressional bills and resolutions, but does include JPRS reports. Author/title/subject index.   DT215.W57

MAURITANIA

Robert, Dieter. Recueils bibliographiques concernant la Mauritanie. 2nd ed. Nouakchott : D. Robert, [1985]. 252 p. in various pagings.   **DD43**
1st ed., 1984–85.
Contents: Liste sommaire d'ouvrages concernant la Mauritanie (5 p.); Recueil bibliographique d'intérêt général concernant la Mauritanie (60 p.); Recueil d'études sectorielles . . . (126 p.); Recueil d'études traitant des régions administratives et géographiques . . . (58 p.).

An extensive listing of books, chapters, articles, and research reports. Topical arrangement within each section; not indexed.   Z7165.M37R63

MOROCCO

La grande encyclopédie du Maroc / [rédacteur en chef, Daniel Vaxelaire]. Rabat : Distribution exclusive par GEM en collaboration avec Gruppo Walk Over, Bergamo, Italie, c1986–1987 [i.e. 1986–1988]. 12 v. : ill. (some col.).   **DD44**
Ed. by Mustapha Sehimi, with the participation of Me. Ahmed Rída Guedira, councillor to S.M. Hassan II.
Contents: v. 1, Institutions; v. 2, Economie et finances; v. 3, Géographie physique et géologie; v. 4, Flore et végétation; v. 5, Culture, arts et traditions (v. 1); v. 6, Culture, arts et traditions (v. 2); v. 7, Agriculture et pêche; v. 8, Histoire; v. 9,

Géographie humaine; v. 10, Faune; v. 11, Sports et loisirs. Education; v. 12, Index.

Short articles, heavily illustrated, covering all aspects of Moroccan life. The last volume is an index to the set. An appendix to v. 1 gives the 1972 amended Constitution.

DT305.G73

MOZAMBIQUE

Darch, Colin. Mozambique / comp. [by] Colin Darch, with the assistance of Calisto Pacheleke, in association with the Centro de Estudos Africanos, Universidade Eduardo Mondlane. Oxford ; Santa Barbara, Calif. : Clio Pr., c1987. 360 p., [1] leaf of plates : 1 map. (World bibliographical series, v. 78). ISBN 1-85109-025-8. $70.00.
DD45

A topical arrangement of 735 books, documents, articles and essays, mostly in English but a few in French, German, Portuguese, Swahili, and Shangaan. Cross-references; author/title/subject index.
Z3881.D37

NAMIBIA

Scheven, Yvette. Namibia bibliographies. Urbana-Champaign, [Ill.] : Y. Scheven, [1985]. 16, [9] p. **DD46**

Cumulates the Namibia entries in Scheven's *Bibliographies for African studies* (*Guide* DD82–85) together with any other recent bibliographies the compiler could trace, into an annotated bibliography of books, articles, and bibliographic essays arranged by keyword. Author index and index by year of publication, 1884–1985. An appendix (9 p.) describes coverage of Africa in DIALOG databases.
Z3771.S33

NIGER

Université de Niamey. Institut de recherches en sciences humaines. Service de la documentation. Catalogue des thèses et mémoires /[Saïdou Harouna]. Niamey : IRSH, 1985. 94 p.
DD47

An alphabetical author listing of 545 master's essays and dissertations in the Institute library from any university in Europe, the U.S., or Africa relating to Niger.
Z3707.U58

NIGERIA

Myers, Robert A. Nigeria. Oxford ; Santa Barbara, Calif. : Clio Pr., c1989. 462 p. : map. (World bibliographical series, v. 100). ISBN 1-85109-083-5. $80.00.
DD48

A topical arrangement of 1,150 annotated entries for books, dissertations, articles, and government publications. Emphasizes English-language materials, but significant works in German and French are also cited. Author/title/subject indexes. Annotations often list additional references (which are included in the index).
Z3597.M94

Le Nigeria contemporain / sous la direction de Daniel C. Bach. Paris : Editions du Centre national de la recherche scientifique, 1986. 336 p., [20] p. of plates : ill. maps. ISBN 2-222-03717-4. 150F.
DD49

Offers surveys written by specialists on all aspects of Nigeria (e.g., history, culture, urbanization). Pt. 2 is a union list of Nigerian periodicals in collections in Belgium, France, and Switzerland. Pt. 3 is a topical bibliography of 1,538 books, articles, and theses in French. Author index to the bibliography.
DT515.22.N533

RWANDA

Hertefelt, Marcel d'. Société, culture et histoire du Rwanda : encyclopédie bibliographique 1863–1980/87 / Marcel d'Hertefelt, Danielle de Lame. Tervuren, Belgique : Musée royal de l'Afrique centrale, 1987. 2 v. (1849 p.).
DD50

An author or anonymous title listing of books, essays, and articles published 1863–1987 concerning Rwanda in areas of social and cultural anthropology, archeology, history, sociology, demography, politics, economics, education, linguistics, oral tradition, literature, musicology, and religion. Annotations, some quite lengthy; each citation concludes with a symbol denoting a holding library. Subject index.

§ Supplementing Hertefelt is *Documentation sur le Rwanda : catalogue du centre de documentation du Ministère du Plan* (Kigali : The Centre, 1988. 140 leaves).
Z3721.H47

SOMALIA

Carboni, Fabio. Bibliografia somala : primo contributo. [Rome] : Ministero degli affari esteri, Dipartimento per la cooperazione allo sviluppo : Comitato tecnico linguistico per l'Università somala, [1983]. 309 p. (Studi somali, 4).
DD51

A classed arrangement of some 7,500 books, articles, and government publications, mostly in English and Italian. Author, subject, and place name indexes.
Z3526.C37

Somalia / Mark W. DeLancey . . . [et al.] compilers. Oxford ; Santa Barbara, Calif. : Clio Pr., c1988. 191 p., [1] leaf of plates : map. (World bibliographical series, v. 92). ISBN 1-85109-038-X. $43.50.
DD52

The 584 annotated entries are mainly for books, but some articles, documents, and dissertations on Somalia are included. Emphasizes recent publications and those in English, though Italian materials are cited when needed to fill a gap. Topical arrangement. Indexes for author, title, and subject.
Z3526.S65

SOUTH AFRICA

Kalley, Jacqueline A. South Africa under apartheid : a select and annotated bibliography. Westport, Conn. : Meckler, c1989. 544 p. ISBN 0-88736-506-X. $45.00.
DD53

Published in South Africa: Pietermaritzburg : Shuter & Shooter in association with Institute of Social and Economic Research, Rhodes University, 1987 (Occasional paper 31).

An author listing of 1,123 articles, books, government publications, and book reviews offering a representative sampling of South Africa under apartheid. Annotations are deliberately non-evaluative. Author and subject indexes.

§ See also Sherman A. Pyatt's *Apartheid : a selective annotated bibliography, 1979–1987* (N.Y. : Garland, 1990. 169 p.)
Z3608.R3K34

Lulat, Y. G.-M. U.S. relations with South Africa : an analytical survey and annotated bibliography. Boulder, Colo. : Westview Pr., 1989–1991. 2 v. ISBN 0-8133-7138-4 (v. 1). $28.50. **DD54**

Contents: v. 1, Books, documents, reports, and monographs [including citations to ERIC documents]; v. 2, Periodical literature and guide to sources of current information.

Some 4,500 items published in English up to 1990 are arranged by format and subdivided by topic, then further subdivided for full and partial annotations. A full annotation includes the author's institutional affiliation, contents, and occasionally reviews. The first part of v. 2 is a listing by D.J. Bertuca of sources of current information. Each volume has its own index for organizations, authors, subjects, and for v. 2, periodical titles. Z6465.U5L84

South African Library. Guide to the South African manuscript collections in the South African Library, Cape Town. 4th ed. Pretoria : State Archives Service, 1989. 1 v. **DD55**

1st ed., 1977.

A classed list (by shelf mark) of manuscripts, typescripts, and other unpublished material of interest to scholars of South African history. For each, gives terminal dates and description of the file, including finding aids, accessibility, size, brief biographical details, and summary of contents. Index for authors, subject, corporate bodies, anonymous titles.

§ A similar publication is *Guide to accessions in the Cape Archives Depot, Cape Town* (10th ed. 1990. 488 p.; 1st ed. 1978), citing unpublished documents "which originated with private persons and organisations and which reflect aspects of the political, cultural, social and economic history of the Cape since the seventeenth century."—*Pref.*

For government archives, see *Guide to arranged archives in the Cape Archives Depot* (2nd ed. Pretoria, 1986. 2 v.; 1st ed. 1982).

For microfilms or archival materials found in English, French, Dutch, and South African archives, see *Guide to microfilms in the Cape Archives Depot, Cape Town*, comp. by M. Potgieter ([Pretoria] : Government Archives Service, 1988. 43 l.)

Stultz, Newell Maynard. South Africa : an annotated bibliography with analytical introductions. Ann Arbor, Mich. : Pierian Pr., 1989. 191 p. (Resources on contemporary issues, 3). ISBN 0-87650-254-0 (pbk.). $40.00. **DD56**

A selective, annotated bibliography of books and articles on South Africa since 1860. Arranged in topical chapters, each opening with an analytical essay which offers a survey, a context, and a definition. Author and title indexes; glossary; chronology, 1899–1987. DT779.9.S75

SUDAN

Wawa, Yosa H. Southern Sudan : a select bibliography / by Yosa H. Wawa, Amal Eisa El-Fadil, Fatima Shalaby Sid Ahmed. Khartoum : Univ. of Khartoum, Institute of African Studies, Library & Documentation, 1988. 138 leaves. **DD57**

Title on added t.p.: Janūb al-Sūdān.

English, French, Arabic books and pamphlets, theses, conference proceedings, government publications, journal articles, and press releases are listed under broad topics (e.g., Education, Language, Politics, Anthropology, History, Administration, Socio-economic affairs). No annotations, although contents of conference proceedings are listed. Author and subject indexes. Z3665.W39

ZIMBABWE

A concise encyclopedia of Zimbabwe / ed. by Denis Berens in association with Donatus Bonde and Albert Bruno Plangger. [Gweru, Zimbabwe] : Mambo Pr., [1988]. 444 p. : ill. (some col.). ISBN 0-86922-441-7. **DD58**

Attempts "to cover, within a limited framework, flora and fauna, history and geography, religion and culture, economics, politics, and social life."—*Pref.* Alphabetical arrangement of entries, with longer essays (called "focus" articles) at the end of some letters; e.g., following entries for the letter C occurs "Focus on churches." Similar essays treat Education, International relations, Law, Literature, Publishing, Sports, and Trade unionism. Occasionally an article concludes with a bibliographical reference. Appendix for statistics, with 1986 most recent. DT962.C64

Encyclopedia Zimbabwe. Harare, Zimbabwe : Quest Pub., 1987. 431 p., 40 p. of plates : ill. (some col.), some maps in color. ISBN 0-908306-04-0. ISBN 0-908306-05-9 (pbk.). **DD59**

An alphabetical arrangement of articles covering all aspects of Zimbabwe life and culture—flora and fauna, leading people, and topics such as agriculture, economics, constitution, education. Population figures for 1982. Besides plates there are many line drawings. The subject index lists titles of articles under broad topics and subdivisions. DT962.E53

Johnstone, I. J. Zimbabwean political material published in exile, 1959–1980 : a bibliography. Harare : National Archives, 1987. 31 p. **DD60**

For annotation, see *Supplement* CJ207. Z3578.J64

DE

Asia

GENERAL WORKS

Bibliography

De Silva, Daya. The Portuguese in Asia : an annotated bibliography of studies on Portuguese colonial history in Asia, 1498–c.1800. Zug, Switzerland : IDC, 1987. 313 p. (Bibliotheca Asiatica, 22). ISBN 3-300-00006-8. **DE1**

An annotated listing of 2,773 books, pamphlets, and articles in European languages, with emphasis on published primary source material. Excluded is literature unless it is significant "in terms of the development of historiography of Portuguese Asia."—*Introd.* Arranged under five broad subjects subdivided by geographic area: Travel and description; Conquest: expansion and decline; Religion: encounter, confrontation and conversion; Economic foundations; Impact on Asian society. Index of authors, editors, translators, compilers, etc. 1,000 of the titles cited in the bibliography and considered scarce are available on microfiche from IDC.   Z3001.D32

Gotthold, Julia J. Indian Ocean / Julia J. Gotthold, comp., with the assistance of Donald W. Gotthold. Oxford ; Santa Barbara, Calif. : Clio Pr., c1988. 329 p., [1] leaf of plates : map. (World bibliographical series, v. 85). ISBN 1-85109-034-7. $70.00.   **DE2**

Offers 804 annotated entries for books, articles, atlases, maps, and bibliographies on the Indian Ocean, including the Red Sea and the Persian Gulf. Broad subject arrangement with appropriate subdivisions; mostly English-language titles with a few in French. Author/title/subject index.   Z3499.G67

Shavit, David. The United States in Asia : a historical dictionary. N.Y. : Greenwood, 1990. 620 p. ISBN 0-313-26788-X.   **DE3**

Companion to Shavit's *The United States in Africa* (*Supplement* DD19) and *The United States in the Middle East* (*Supplement* DE22).

" . . . attempts to be comprehensive, including all persons, institutions, and events that brought the U.S. in contact with Asia."—*Pref.* All of Asia is included except the Middle East. Short articles with bibliographies appended. Brief chronology; bibliographic essays; cross-references; topical index.

DS33.4.U6S46

Library resources (including archives)

Pearson, J. D. A guide to manuscripts and documents in the British Isles relating to South and South-East Asia. London ; N.Y. : Mansell, 1989. v. 1. ISBN 0-7201-1961-8 (v. 1). $108.00 (est.). (In progress).   **DE4**

A supplement to M.D. Wainwright and Noel Matthews's *A guide to Western manuscripts and documents in the British Isles relating to South and South East Asia* (*Guide* DE17).

Contents: v. 1, London (319 p.).

Based on visits to repositories and on published and unpublished lists and articles. Vol. 1 describes changes in locations and additions to collections, and includes information concerning India Office holdings in the British Library (but is not so detailed as either Amar Kaur Jasbir Singh, *A guide to source materials in the India Office Library and Records for the history of Tibet, Sikkim and Bhutan 1765–1950* [*Supplement* DE29] or India Office Library and Records, *A general guide to the India Office Records*, ed. by Martin Moir [*Supplement* DE32]). Also lists finding aids and publications where blocks of manuscripts are printed. Topical index.   CD1048.A8P43

Encyclopedias; Handbooks

Asian historical dictionaries. Metuchen, N.J. : Scarecrow, 1989–1991. v. 1–3. (In progress).   **DE5**

Contents: v. 1, Vietnam, William J. Duiker (1989. 269 p.); v. 2, Bangladesh, Craig Baxter and Syedur Rahman (1989. 144 p.); v. 3, Pakistan, Shahid Javed Burki (1991. 254 p.).

Replaces *Historical and cultural dictionaries of Asia* (*Guide* DE20), and resembles two other series by the same publisher: *African historical dictionaries* (*Supplement* DD5 and DD6) and *Latin American historical dictionaries* (*Guide* DB274). Each volume begins with a short survey on the history and economics of the country, followed by short entries for people, events, and places in alphabetical sequence. Brief bibliography at end; no indexing.

Encyclopedia of Asian history / Ainslie T. Embree, ed. in chief. N.Y. : Scribner's ; London : Collier Macmillan, c1988. 4 v. : ill. ISBN 0-684-18619-5. $335.00.   **DE6**

Prepared under the auspices of the Asia Society.

Signed articles by scholars, well-written and informative, are aimed toward a non-specialist audience. Asia is defined as covering Iran to the Philippines and excludes the U.S.S.R except for the Central Asian republics. Most of the articles include short bibliographies of English-language works. Features a synoptic outline; numerous *see* and *see also* references; topical index; directory of contributors. Black-and-white photographs and maps are well chosen and clearly reproduced.   DS31.E53

Directories

Fenton, Thomas P. Asia and Pacific : a directory of resources / comp. and ed. by Thomas P. Fenton and Mary J. Heffron. Maryknoll, N.Y. : Orbis Books, c1986. 137 p. ISBN 0-88344-528-X (pbk.).   **DE7**

Updates and expands the Asia and Pacific chapter of the *Third World resource directory* (*Supplement* CH51).

Lists, with annotations, books, organizations, periodicals, pamphlets and articles, audiovisuals, news services, etc., which aim to promote fundamental reform in the designated areas. Arranged by format. Indexes by name, title, and geographical area.   Z3001.F46

NEAR AND MIDDLE EAST

Bibliography

See also BB126.

Bibliographie der Deutschsprachigen Arabistik und Islamkunde : von den Anfängen bis 1986 nebst Literatur über die arabischen Länder der Gegenwart. Frankfurt am Main : Institut für Geschichte der Arabisch-Islamischen Wissenschaften an der Johann Wolfgang Goethe-Universität, 1990. v. 1. (Veröffentlichungen des Institutes für Geschichte der Arabisch-Islamischen Wissenschaften. Reihe A, Texte und Studien, Bd. 3). (In progress).   **DE8**

Contents: v. 1, Allgemeines und Hilfsmittel der Forschung, hrsg. von Fuat Sezgin (308 p.).

To be in 8 v. covering all areas and topics relative to the Islamic world (language, literature, history, medicine, art, geography, religion, etc.), concluding with an author/title/subject index. Vol. 1 is the general volume and includes entries for general bibliographies, major journals, festschriften, bibliographies relating to scholars, guides to papyrology, publishers, the press, manuscripts and archives, etc. Citations are mainly to German publications, most of them issued in the 20th century, but with some 18th- and 19th-century publications included. Major reviews are cited.   DS61.9.B53

Gardner, J. Anthony. The Iraq-Iran war : a bibliography. Boston : G.K. Hall, 1989. 124 p. ISBN 0-8161-8997-8. $56.00.   **DE9**

"First published 1988 by Mansell Publishing Limited"— *t.p. verso.*

Provides more than 500 citations to books, articles, filmed interviews and feature length films, documentaries, and some essays and documents in many languages, including Persian and Arabic, published to the end of 1986. Arranged topically under broad headings such as Background, Domestic impact, Conflict in the Gulf, Literature and films of war. Focuses on the

1980–87 conflict. Annotated; no cross-references or detailed subject index; author and title indexes. Z3366.G36

Internationale Jahresbibliographie Südwestasien = International annual bibliography South West Asia : SWA. Jahrg. 1 (1985)– . Osnabrück : F. Dietrich, 1988– . Annual. **DE10**

Editors, 1988– , Otto and Wolfram Zeller.

Based on the collection of the Univ. of Tübingen. A subject listing of books, articles, book reviews, festschriften, and conference proceedings. Southwest Asia is here understood to cover from India to the Sudan. Similar in organization and appearance to *IBZ* (*Guide* AE222); the topical headings are listed in a subject index under 16 broad fields. An index of authors and reviewers refers to the appropriate subject heading. DS44.Z99I58

Khoury, Fawzi. National union catalog of Middle Eastern microforms / comp. by Fawzi W. Khoury and Rachel Simon. Seattle, Wash. : Univ. of Washington Libraries, 1989. 77 p. **DE11**

At head of title: Middle East Microfilming Project.

Planned "to inform interested people of those libraries in the United States which hold microforms of serials which are either published in the Middle East or have the Middle East as their main subject."—*Introd.* Arranged alphabetically by title; each entry includes "imprint, frequency, language, and the holdings of the first-mentioned library which has the largest holdings of the title." Holdings of the Center for Research Libraries are included. Z3013.5.K46

McLachlan, K. S. A bibliography of the Iran-Iraq borderland / Keith McLachlan & Richard N. Schofield. Wisbech : Middle East & North African Studies, 1987. 383 p. ISBN 0-906559-21-9. £26.00. **DE12**

Based on the collection developed at the School of Oriental and African Studies at the Univ. of London, this is an extensive listing of books, essays, dissertations, government publications, and maps in Western languages. Topical arrangement (e.g., Geography, Geology, Geomorphology, International relations, Modern history). Appendix lists relevant materials in the India Office and the Public Record Office. Addendum for recent publications or for works indvertently omitted. Author index only. Z3366.I55M2

Middle East and Islam : a bibliographical introduction : supplement, 1977–1983 / ed. by Paul Auchterlonie. Zug, Switzerland : IDC, c1986. 244 p. (Bibliotheca Asiatica, 20). ISBN 3-300-00001-7. **DE13**

Supplements the basic 1979 publication (*Guide* DE27), following the same guidelines for inclusion, arrangement, indexing, etc. For some areas very little information has been published, hence these chapters were omitted (e.g., Arabic mathematics and astronomy, Berber studies). New chapters have been added on Hadīth literature, International relations, and Islam in East Africa. Z3013.M48

Ponko, Vincent. Britain in the Middle East, 1921–1956 : an annotated bibliography. N.Y. : Garland, 1990. 513 p. (Themes in European expansion, v. 9 ; Garland reference library of social science, v. 357). ISBN 0-8240-8551-5. **DE14**

Lists publications "dealing in some way with the British presence in the Middle East from about 1921 to the period of the 1956 Suez Canal crisis."—*Pref.* The Middle East is defined as encompassing Iran, Iraq, Jordan, Israel, Egypt, and the Arabian peninsula. Topical arrangement of books and documents, with extensive annotations and cross-references. There is a separate list of doctoral dissertations accepted in the U.S., 1980–87 (in no order), and an appendix of periodical articles, 1980–88, arranged by year of publication; entries in these sections are not included in the author index. Z3014.R44P66

Silverburg, Sanford R. United States foreign policy and the Middle East/North Africa : a bibliography of twentieth-century research / Sanford R. Silverburg, Bernard Reich. N.Y. : Garland, 1990. 407 p. (Garland reference library of social science, v. 570). ISBN 0-8240-4613-7. **DE15**

Concentrates on English-language books, essays, articles, dissertations, master's essays, NTIS reports, and government documents that treat the relationship between the U.S. and the Middle East and North Africa (defined as from Turkey and Iran to South Yemen and Morocco). 3,676 numbered items, arranged alphabetically by author, with a subject index. Z3515.S55

Stavrou, Theofanis George. Russian travelers to the Christian East from the twelfth to the twentieth century / Theofanis G. Stavrou and Peter R. Weisensel. Columbus, Ohio : Slavica Publishers, 1986. li, 925 p. ISBN 0-89357-157-1. $39.95. **DE16**

Lists "pilgrims' accounts, officers' memoirs, ambassadors' reports, scholars' monographs, newspaper articles" (*Pref.*), 1106–1914, although works in the latter two categories are included only if they describe the experiences on a journey, and were originally written in Russian, or if the author was a Russian national or in Russian service (e.g., naval officers). The Christian East covers the countries under the "geographical jurisdiction of the Eastern Patriarchs of Constantinople, Alexandria, Antioch and Jerusalem." The books and articles are arranged chronologically by the first date in the travel account. Very full annotations describe the context and identify the author. Glossary of terms; author and topic index. Gives locations from *Slavic Cyrillic union catalog* (*Guide* AA1050) and for several Finnish libraries, the Bibliothèque Nationale, the British Library, and St. Vladimir's Seminary in N.Y. Z3014.D45S73

Dissertations

Saliba, M. Arab Gulf States : doctoral dissertations & graduate theses in English, French & German (1881–1981). [Antélias, Lebanon] : M. Saliba, 1983. 171 p. (Middle East bibliographical serials, 1). **DE17**

Aims "to identify all dissertations and theses written in English, French, and German in fields of history, geography, politics, economics, law, social studies, arts, sciences, etc. and [which] are directly concerned with the following states: Iraq, Saudi Arabia, Kuwait, United Arab Emirates, Bahrain, Oman, Qatar, North and South Yemen."—*Introd.* Arranged alphabetically by country, with author and subject indexes. Z3026.S235

Selim, George Dimitri. American doctoral dissertations on the Arab world : supplement August 1981–December 1987. Wash. : Library of Congress : For sale by the Supt. of Docs., U.S. Govt. Print. Off., 1989. 265 p. ISBN 0-8444-0619-8. **DE18**

For earlier compilation and supplement, see *Guide* DE61–62.

Superintendent of Documents classification: LC 41.2:Arl/975–81/supp.

Lists U.S. and Canadian dissertations 1981–1987, plus any pre-1981 titles omitted from the earlier volumes. Subject and title keyword index. Z3013.S43

Encyclopedias; Dictionaries

The Cambridge encyclopedia of the Middle East and North Africa / executive ed., Trevor Mostyn ; advisory ed., Albert Hourani. Cambridge ; N. Y. : Cambridge Univ. Pr., 1988. 504 p. : ill. (some col.). ISBN 0-521-32190-5. $39.50.　　　　　**DE19**

Companion to *Cambridge atlas of the Middle East and North Africa* (Supplement DE26).

Offers an overview of various subject areas for the region: e.g., history, quick survey by major periods; culture, including religion, literature, arts, music, Islamic science, Islamic law; economics, with statistics as current as 1986. Pt. 5 is a survey of individual countries, Mauritania to Afghanistan to Somalia. The volume ends with "peoples without a country," e.g., Kurds, Armenians, Palestinians. Suggestions for further reading. Subject index.　　　　　DS44.C37

Gresh, Alain. An A to Z of the Middle East / Alain Gresh and Dominique Vidal ; translated by Bob Cumming. London : Biddles Ltd. ; Atlantic Highlands, N.J. : Zed Books, 1990. 261 p., [3] p. of plates : ill., maps. ISBN 0-86232-880-2. ISBN 0-86232-881-0 (pbk.).　**DE20**

Translation and updating of *Les cent portes du Proche-orient* (Paris : Autrement, 1986).

Covers countries, people, events, movements, and problems relating to the Middle East. 112 alphabetically arranged entries, generally concentrating on the last half of the 20th century, average two pages in length, and combine description with analysis. Includes a chronology of events (through Iraq's invasion of Kuwait, August 2, 1990), maps, tables, and 13 appendixes of important documents (e.g., The Balfour Declaration, Camp David Framework). Bibliography; personal name index. Less comprehensive than Lawrence Ziring's *The Middle East political dictionary* (Guide CJ401), Yaacov Shimoni's *Political dictionary of the Arab World* (Supplement CJ152), or *Political dictionary of the State of Israel*, ed. by Susan H. Rolef (Supplement CJ190).　　　　　DS43.G7413

The Middle East / ed. by Michael Adams. N.Y. : Facts on File, 1987. 865 p. : maps. ISBN 0-8160-1268-7. $45.00.　　　　　**DE21**

At head of title: *Handbooks to the modern world.*

An overview by 41 English- and American-trained scholars giving basic information on each country, 34 pages of comparative statistics, and essays on the region (e.g., Zionism and the Arab question, Foreign aid and investment, Archaeology). North Africa is not included except for Libya. Subject index.　　　　　DS44.H35

Shavit, David. The United States in the Middle East : a historical dictionary. N.Y. : Greenwood, [1988]. 441 p. ISBN 0-313-25341-2.　　　　　**DE22**

Provides "information about persons, institutions, and events that affected the relationships between the United States and the Middle East" (*Pref.*), Morocco to Afghanistan. Most entries are single paragraphs, followed by bibliographic references. Appendix: Chiefs of American diplomatic missions in the Middle East, 1831–1986. A companion to Shavit's *The United States in Africa* (Supplement DD19) and *The United States in Asia* (Supplement DE3).　　　　　DS63.2.U5S384

Directories

Middle East : a directory of resources / comp. and ed. by Thomas P. Fenton and Mary J. Heffron. Maryknoll, N.Y. : Orbis Books, c1988. 144 p. : ill. ISBN 0-88344-533-6 (pbk.).　　　　　**DE23**

Updates and expands a chapter in *Third World resource directory* (Supplement CH51).

Covers the Middle East and North Africa as a region, as well as the individual countries. "We situate our study in this 'radical' political context."—*Introd.* Cites organizations, books and pamphlets, and audiovisual materials. Index for organizations, individuals, titles, and geographical areas.

Z3014.P64M53

Middle East organizations in Washington, D.C. 4th ed. Wash. : Middle East Institute, c1989. 95 p. ISBN 0-916808-34-3. $9.00.　　　　　**DE24**

1st ed., 1985; 3rd ed., 1987.

A directory of 135 human rights groups, information services, development agencies, research centers, political action committees, cultural associations, publishers, and religious organizations "that offer public programs on the Middle East."—*Introd.* Alphabetical within two sections: Principal, Significant. For each organization gives name, address, date established, brief description, officers, publications.　　DS41.W35

Chronologies

Rahman, H. U. A chronology of Islamic history, 570–1000 CE. Boston : G.K. Hall, [1989]. 181 p., [6] p. of plates : ill. ISBN 0-7201-1982-0. $60.00 (est.).　**DE25**

Published in London by Mansell.

From the birth of the Prophet to the expeditions of Mahmud of Ghazna into India. Short articles describe the events, the people involved, and the exact locations. Index by name of person or place.　　　　　DS38.3.R35

Atlases

The Cambridge atlas of the Middle East and North Africa / [ed. by] Gerald Blake, John Dewdney, Jonathan Mitchell. Cambridge ; N.Y. : Cambridge Univ. Pr., 1987. 124 p. : maps in color ; 26 x 36 cm. ISBN 0-521-24243-6.　　　　　**DE26**

Companion to *Cambridge encyclopedia of the Middle East and North Africa* (Supplement DE19).

A topical presentation of 58 maps with text, tables, and some statistics (e.g., Soils, Irrigation, Ottoman Empire to 1556, World oil movements). Each chapter ends with a list of key references. Most maps treat the whole region. No indexes.

G2205.C3

Karta (Firm). Atlas of the Middle East / ed. by Moshe Brawer ; prepared by Carta, Jerusalem. N.Y. : Macmillan ; London : Collier Macmillan, c1988. 140 p. : maps in color ; 29 cm. ISBN 0-02-905271-8. $50.00.　**DE27**

Companion to *Political dictionary of the Arab world* (Supplement BD1097) and *Political dictionary of the state of Israel* (Supplement CJ190).

Covers from Turkey to Iran to Sudan to Libya. Arranged in 2 parts: (1) The region (with maps, narrative, and tables on geology, climate, flora and fauna, population, oil, etc.), (2) The countries, which treats political, cultural, and historic life of each nation. Current in its coverage to 1988. Bibliography and list of further readings. Index to geographical names.

G2205.K33

ASIA, SOUTH

Bibliography

Dogra, R. C. Catalogue of the early printed books on South Asia : from 1586 to 1864, held in the Library of the School of Oriental and African Studies, University of London. New Delhi : Aditya Prakashan, [1988]. 231, [21] p.; ill. ISBN 81-85179-08-5. Rs250.00. **DE28**

Lists more than 1,130 titles arranged by date of publication with author, brief title, and language indexes. Includes reproductions of some title pages. Z3185.D64

Library resources (including archives)

Amar Kaur Jasbir Singh. A guide to source materials in the India Office Library and Records for the history of Tibet, Sikkim and Bhutan 1765–1950. [London] : British Library, 1988. 187 p. **DE29**

Primarily a guide to archives (both official and private) held in the India Office, but also offers information on the Office's maps, drawings, and printed books. Brief notes on other archival sources; index by topic. Z6005.H6A

Directory of South Asian library resources in the UK and the Republic of Ireland / ed. by S. Gunasingam. [London] : South Asia Library Group, 1988. 182 p. ISBN 0-9513593-0-4 (pbk.). **DE30**

Based on replies to a questionnaire. Gives operating details of each library (hours, address, staff members, admission, etc.), relevant catalogs, and an overview of the South Asian material. Geographic arrangement. Index of libraries; index to language collections. DS336.D58

India Office Library and Records. A brief guide to biographical sources / India Office Library and Records; [comp. by] Ian A. Baxter. 2nd ed. London : British Library, 1990. 59 p. ISBN 0-7123-0637-4 (pbk.). £5.95. **DE31**

1st ed., 1979.

Tries to identify records available in the India Office Library (e.g., passenger lists, city directories, lists of awards for military honors), which could be used to glean biographical information. Arranged by category, e.g. chaplains, medical or veterinary officers. For each record gives series, file, and document number with a very brief contents note. The 2nd ed. provides corrections and a few additions. The India Office Library is now part of the British Library. Z5305.I5I53

———— A general guide to the India Office Records / Martin Moir. [London] : British Library, 1988. 331 p. : ill. ISBN 0-7123-0629-3. **DE32**

Now a part of the British Library, the collections of the India Office (formerly the East India Company) were until recently part of the Foreign and Commonwealth Office. This work presents information on the administrative background of the Office followed by a descriptive inventory of the archives. Does not totally supersede William Foster's *Guide to the India Office Records 1600–1858* (London : Eyre and Spottiswoode, 1919) for the earlier period. Indexed. CD1052.I4I53

Encyclopedias

The Cambridge encyclopedia of India, Pakistan, Bangladesh, Sri Lanka, Nepal, Bhutan, and the Maldives / ed., Francis Robinson. Cambridge ; N.Y. : Cambridge Univ. Pr., [1989]. 520 p. : ill. ISBN 0-521-33451-9. **DE33**

A heavily illustrated encyclopedia intended for the general reader, and topically arranged under broad headings: Land; Peoples; History to independence; Politics; Foreign relations; Economics; Religion; Societies; Culture. Statistics are current to about 1983, although references in the bibliographies are as recent as 1986–87. Topical index. DS334.9..C36

Atlases

Dutt, Ashok K. Atlas of South Asia : fully annotated / Ashok K. Dutt, M. Margaret Geib. Boulder, Colo. : Westview Pr., 1987. 231 p. : ill. ; 28 cm. ISBN 0-8133-0044-4. ISBN 0-8133-0045-2 (pbk.). **DE34**

Updates the authors' *India in maps* (Dubuque, Iowa : Kendall/Hunt, 1976. 124 p.)

Even though the emphasis is on India, some treatment is given to Pakistan, Bangladesh, Sri Lanka, Nepal, and Bhutan. Surveys Indian history, politics, sociology, and agriculture through text, charts, and maps. Topical arrangement; seven-page bibliography. No index. G2260.D8

ASIA, SOUTHEAST

ASEAN : a bibliography / project co-ordinator, Patricia Lim ; contributors, IDE, Tokyo . . . [et al.]. Singapore : Institute of Southeast Asian Studies, 1984. 487 p. **DE35**
Z3221.A72

ASEAN : a bibliography, 1981–85 / project co-ordinator, Patricia Lim Pui Huen ; ed. by Ajita Thuraisingham ; with contributions from Violeta V. Encarnacion . . . [et al.]. Singapore : Institute of Southeast Asian Studies, 1988. 532 p. : ill. **DE36**

Based on the collection at the Institute of Southeast Asian Studies, the basic bibliography lists 6,300 books, articles, theses, official publications, conference papers, press releases, and radio monitoring reports with some archival materials and unpublished seminar and conference reports. All languages are represented, with the focus more on the region of Southeast Asia than on individual countries. Employs a topical arrangement with author index.

The 1988 compilation adds an additional 6,397 items, follows the same arrangement, and gathers the same type of material from the Library of the Institute. Z3221.A722

Lim, Patricia Pui Huen. The Malay world of Southeast Asia : a select cultural bibliography. Singapore : Programme on the Cultural Heritage of Southeast Asia, Institute of Southeast Asian Studies, c1986. 456 p. ISBN 9971-988-36-4. £32.00. **DE37**

The Malay world comprises Brunei, Indonesia, Singapore, Thailand, Malaysia, and the Philippines. Topical arrangement, emphasizing culture (e.g., history, anthropology, literature, sociology, political science), subdivided by geographical area or time period. Lists 5,327 books, articles and dissertations, most published mid-1960s to 1983, with a few as late as 1986. Author index. Z3221.L547

Research on Southeast Asia : a catalogue of doctoral dissertations, 1981–1986 : economics, education, literature, political science, religion. Ann Arbor, Mich. : Univ. Microfilms International, 1986. 41 p.   **DE38**

Broad topical listing of dissertations completed in U.S. and Canadian universities and available from Univ. Microfilms International. Author index.

§ For dissertations completed in Great Britain and Ireland see *Theses on South-East Asia 1965–1985 accepted by universities in the United Kingdom and Ireland,* comp. by Helen L. Stephens ([Hull, England] : Centre for South-East Asian Studies, [1986]. 74 p.), which also includes Papua New Guinea. Muriel Charras and Brigitte Renard-Clamagirand have made a similar compilation for France: *Les thèses françaises sur l'Asie du Sud-Est depuis 1980* (Paris : AFRASE, 1986. 50 p.)

Z3221.R47

The-Mulliner, Lian. Southeast Asia microforms project resources : draft listing. Athens, Ohio : Ohio Univ. Libraries, 1989. 16 p.   **DE39**

A "preliminary attempt to list materials owned by SEAM [Southeast Asia Microforms Project] or which SEAM members are permitted to use."—*Pref.* The materials are available through the Center for Research Libraries. Listing is by country and includes theses and dissertations, microform sets, newspapers, and gazettes. Not indexed.

§ See also *A checklist of Southeast Asian newspapers and other research materials in microform held by the Center for Research Libraries,* comp. Daniel F. Doeppers (Madison : Univ. of Wisconsin, Center for International Studies, 1989. 15 p. Bibliography series, 1).

ASIA, EAST

Bibliography

Harvard-Yenching Library. Catalogues of the Harvard-Yenching Library. N.Y. : Garland, 1986. 72 v. ISBN 0-8240-8133-1 (v. 1).   **DE40**

Half title: Chinese and Japanese catalogues of the Harvard-Yenching Library.

Contents: Chinese catalogue: v. 1–28, Author/title; v. 29–38, Subjects; v. 39, Serial records, Newspapers; Japanese catalogue: v. 1–22, Author/title; v. 23–33, Subjects.

A reproduction of the catalog cards of the largest university library for East Asian research. Vol. 39, the Serials volume in the Chinese catalog portion, covers both Chinese and Japanese serials (including newspapers), giving holdings through March 1986, and cross-references to variant titles.   Z881.H35H37

AFGHANISTAN

Nursai, Ata M. Bibliographie zur Afghanistan-Literatur 1960–1987. Köln : Bundesinstitut für Ostwissenschaftliche und Internationale Studien, c1988. 360 p.   **DE41**

A topical arrangement of books, documents, essays, and occasional articles held by libraries in West Germany. Much of the material is in English but German, French, and Russian publications are also included. A 40-page author index was issued separately (1989).   Z3016.N87

Otto, Ingeborg. Die Beziehungen Afghanistans zur Sowjetunion : eine Auswahlbibliographie = The relationship between Afghanistan and the Soviet Union : a selected bibliography / Ingeborg Otto, Marianne Schmidt-Dumont. Hamburg : Deutsches Übersee-Institut, Übersee-Dokumentation, Referat Vorderer Orient, 1988. 90 p. (Dokumentationsdienst Moderner Orient.

Reihe A, 15 ; Near and Middle East documentation service. Series A, 15).   **DE42**

Lists articles, government publications, books, and pamphlets, in English and German, on Russian/Soviet contact with emphasis on the Soviet intervention. Topical arrangement; each entry gives a German library location. Author index.

Z3016.O87

Witherell, Julian W. Afghanistan : an American perspective : a guide to U.S. official documents and government-sponsored publications. Wash. : Library of Congress, 1986. 158 p. (Near East series, no. 3).   **DE43**

For sale by Supt. of Docs., U.S. Govt. Print. Off.

" . . . records a selection of publications on Afghanistan issued by or for the United States government from the time of initial official contacts between the two nations in the 1920s to 1984."—*Pref.* 631 items in classed arrangement; author/subject index.   Z3016.W58

BANGLADESH

Rājjāka, Moḥ Ābadura. Bangladesh : a select general bibliography. [Rajshahi] : Razzaque, [1987]. 239 p. : map.
DE44

A topical listing of almost 1,000 books, including a few non-English titles and journal articles. Modelled on the Clio Press "World bibliography series." Author/title/subject index.

Z3186.R34

BHUTAN

Dogra, Ramesh C. Bhutan. Oxford ; Santa Barbara, Calif. : Clio, [1990]. [150] p. : 1 map. (World bibliographical series, v. 116). ISBN 1-85109-128-9. £25.00.
DE45

Offers 402 English-language citations to books and a few articles and documents relating to Bhutan from the English period to the current era. Topical arrangement; annotated. Chronology for 500 BCE–1987; tables of rulers and dignitaries; brief glossary. Author/title/subject index.

BURMA

Burma, a study guide. Wash. : Wilson Center Pr. ; Lanham, Md. : Distr. in North America by UPA Inc., c1988. 59, ca.150 p. ISBN 0-943875-40-4. $37.50.   **DE46**

Contents: Burma studies worldwide, ed. by Ronald A. Morse and Helen L. Loerke; Burma, a selective guide to scholarly resources, ed. by Anita Hibler and William P. Tuchrello; Burma, a selective guide to periodical literature (1970–1986), ed. by Anita Hibler and William P. Tuchrello.

Intended to be used with F. J. Shulman's *Burma: an annotated bibliographical guide to international dissertation research* (below) and Patrick M. Mayerchak's *Scholar's guide to Washington D.C. for Southeast Asian studies* (*Guide* DE120). The first section contains reports arranged by country summarizing research on Burma. The selective guide is an updating of an earlier publication, with 340 new entries, including 19th-century material and works in Burmese. The guide to periodical literature includes 1,618 citations arranged in alphabetical order by author. The latter two sections have their own topical indexes.

Z3216.B86

Shulman, Frank Joseph. Burma : an annotated bibliographical guide to international doctoral dissertation research, 1898–1985. Lanham, Md. : Univ. Pr. of America ; Wash. : Wilson Center, c1986. 247 p. ISBN 0-8191-5458-X. ISBN 0-8191-5459-8 (pbk.). **DE47**

About 700 entries in classed arrangement. Author and subject indexes. Z3216.S55

CHINA

Bibliography

See also BB104.

University of London. School of Oriental and African Studies. Library. Western books on China published up to 1850 in the Library of the School of Oriental and African Studies, University of London : a descriptive catalogue / John Lust. London : Bamboo, 1987. [336] p. : ill. **DE48**

A classified listing of 1,283 books and pamphlets on China, eastern central Asia including Tibet, Manchuria and Mongolia, Taiwan, and Hong Kong. For each entry, gives a transcription of the title page, annotation, indication of a major catalog where cited—e.g., *NUC*, British Museum *Catalogue*, Henri Cordier's *Bibliotheca sinica* (*Guide* DE151), Tōyō Bunko in Tokyo. Author and title indexes; "Supplementary subject index." Z3101

Dictionaries

O'Neill, Hugh B. Companion to Chinese history. N.Y. : Facts on File, c1987. 397 p. : maps. ISBN 0-87196-841-X. ISBN 0-8160-1825-1 (pbk.). **DE49**

Aims "to provide basic information on several hundred topics and a number of individuals."—*Introd.* Many articles are quite lengthy and include bibliographic references. Five-page chronology, 1506–1985. Cross-references; not indexed. DS705.O63

General histories

The Cambridge history of China / gen. editors, Denis Twitchett and John K. Fairbank. Cambridge [Eng.] ; N.Y. : Cambridge Univ. Pr., 1986–88. v. 1, 7^1, 13^2, 14^1. ISBN 0-521-21447-5. (In progress). **DE50**

For previously published volumes and annotation, see *Guide* DE180.

Contents: v. 1, The Ch'in and Han Empires, 221 B.C.–A.D. 220 / ed. Denis Twitchett and Michael Loewe (1986); v. 7, pt. 1, The Ming Dynasty 1368–1644 / ed. Frederick W. Mote and Denis Twitchett (1988); v. 13, pt. 2, Republican China 1912–1949 / ed. John K. Fairbank and Albert Feuerwerker (1988); v. 14, The People's Republic, pt. 1: The emergence of Revolutionary China 1949–1965 / ed. Roderick MacFarquhar and John K. Fairbank (1987).

The Nationalist era in China, 1927–1949, by Lloyd Eastman (1990) is taken from v. 13, pt. 2.

Many of these volumes have been translated into Chinese and published in the People's Republic. DS735.C3145

Post-1945

Hoover Institution on War, Revolution, and Peace. Unofficial documents of the Democracy Movement in Communist China, 1978–1981 = Chung-kuo min chu yun tung tzu liao : a checklist of Chinese materials in the Hoover Institution on War, Revolution and Peace / comp. by I-mu. Stanford, Calif. : East Asian Collection, Hoover Institution, 1986. 100 p. (Hoover Press bibliographical series, 67). ISBN 0-8179-2672-0 (pbk.). **DE51**

A checklist of materials relevant to the democracy movement in the People's Republic of China, 1978–82, divided into sections featuring two collections of the Hoover Institution, a microfilm set from Oxford's Bodleian Library, and a 15-volume compilation of reprints published by the Institute for the Study of Chinese Communist Problems, Taipei. Includes unofficial journals, pamphlets, Democracy Wall papers, and miscellaneous underground publications. Titles within each collection are alphabetically arranged according to Wade-Giles romanization and give title, place of publication, and publisher in Chinese and holdings and location information in English. Preceding the checklist are a foreword, a review of the collections, and a chronology of the events of the democracy movement. No index. Z31OC.U5H66

Lieberthal, Kenneth. A research guide to central party and government meetings in China, 1949–1986 / Kenneth G. Lieberthal, Bruce J. Dickson. Rev. and expanded ed. Armonk, N.Y. : M.E. Sharpe, c1989. lvi, 339 p. ISBN 0-87332-492-7. $50.00. **DE52**

1st ed., 1976 (*Guide* DE178).

Increases the number of meetings from 298 to 513, and includes some missed in the 1st ed. Scope and presentation remain the same. Sources of information include U.S. government translation services (e.g., JPRS) as well as Chinese print media. Index to meeting summaries. JQ1519.A5L474

Mackerras, Colin. The Cambridge handbook of contemporary China / by Colin Mackerras and Amanda Yorke. Cambridge, U.K. ; N.Y. : Cambridge Univ. Pr., 1991. 266 p. : ill. ISBN 0-521-38342-0. ISBN 0-521-38755-8 (pbk.). $40.00. **DE53**

Focuses on the People's Republic of China, with occasional mention of Taiwan and Hong Kong. Includes: surveys of the history, economics, population, minority nationals, culture and society, etc.; biographies of one-half to one column in length; a 58-page chronology, 1900–April 1990, divided into categories such as foreign affairs, economics, natural disasters, births and deaths; an annotated bibliography of English-language books arranged by broad categories; gazetteer; topical index. Cut-off date is April 30, 1990. Very useful. DS706.M24

Müller, Meike. China nach Mao : Auswahlbibliographie = China after Mao : a selected bibliography. Hamburg : Deutsches Übersee-Institut, Referat Asien und Südpazifik, 1987. 239 p. (Dokumentationsdienst Asien. Reihe A, 19). ISBN 3-922852-16-5. **DE54**

Table of contents, introductory material and subject headings in German and English.

Cites some 1,300 books, essays, and periodical articles selected for their focus "on reforms in the areas of domestic and foreign policy, economic planning and development strategy. Publications on geography, history, law and the constitution, population and society, health and culture were included, too."—*Pref.* Classed arrangement. Most entries are annotated, with library locations, usually in Germany, but including a few European libraries outside Germany. Author index.

Z3108.A5M85

HONG KONG

Research material for Hong Kong studies / ed. by Alan Birch, Y.C. Jao, and Elizabeth Sinn. [Hong Kong] : Centre of Asian Studies, Univ. of Hong Kong, 1984. [340 p.] : ill. (Centre of Asian Studies bibliographies and research guides, no. 23). **DE55**

Consists of papers presented at a conference called to assess the current state of research materials, institutions, and studies of Hong Kong. Thus the article on reference materials points out the major sources but also notes lacunae—e.g., a bibliography of literary works set in Hong Kong, updating H. Anthony Rydings's *A Hong Kong union catalogue* (*Guide* DE183). The article on institutions covers contents of and access to the Public Record Office in Hong Kong, the Hongkong and Shanghai Bank Corporation, the Hungon-to Memorial Library, and the Information Services Department of the government. Not indexed. DS796.H74R47

Scott, Ian. Hong Kong. Oxford ; Santa Barbara, Calif. : Clio Pr., c1990. 248 p. : map. (World bibliographical series, v. 115). ISBN 1-85109-089-4. $40.00. **DE56**

Since the audience is expected to be general readers, focus is on books, articles, and a few government publications in English. 838 citations arranged by topic. Cross-references; author, title, subject indexes. Z3107.H7S36

INDIA

Bibliography

Riddick, John F. Glimpses of India : an annotated bibliography of published personal writings by Englishmen, 1583–1947. N.Y. : Greenwood, 1989. 195 p. (Bibliographies and indexes in world history, no. 15). ISBN 0-313-25661-6. **DE57**

Offers 580 entries, arranged by period (e.g., 1583–1740, 1740–1818, 1920–47), for published memoirs, autobiographies, collections of personal letters, diaries and journals, travel narratives. Coverage is wider than India since many accounts include other parts of South Asia (e.g., Nepal, Tibet, Afghanistan, Burma). Annotations give a brief note identifying the author and a description of the contents. Name index. Z3206.R5

Saha, Santosh C. Indo-U.S. relations, 1947–1988 : a guide to information sources. N.Y. : P. Lang, [1990]. 213 p. (American university studies., vol. 95). ISBN 0-8204-1354-2. **DE58**

Following an overview of relations between the U.S. and India 1947–89, describes relevant portions of presidential archives and related holdings in the Detroit Public Library and the United Nations Library. These are complemented by a bibliography of books, journal articles, newspaper articles, and economic documents from U.S. government agencies. Author and subject indexes. Z6465.U5S24

Thomas, Timothy N. Indians overseas : a guide to source materials in the India Office Records for the study of Indian emigration, 1830–1950. London : British Library, 1985. 97 p. : ill. ISBN 0-7123-0043-0 (pbk.). £10.00. **DE59**

An introductory essay on the historical background 1830–1950 (p. 1–27) is followed by an inventory of "the official records relating to Indian emigration and Indians overseas... of the principal London offices responsible for British government in India and Burma (the East India Company, the Board of Control, the India Office and the Burma Office) [and] proceedings of the Government of India and the provincial govern-

ments, which are copied to London for information."—*p. 32.* Arranged by record group. Appendix of brief descriptions of other archives. Not indexed. Z7164.I3T48

Tōyō Bunko (Japan). A classified catalogue of books on the section XII, India, in the Tōyō Bunko (II) acquired during the years 1951–1982 / ed. by the Seminar on South and South-East Asian History. Tokyo : Tōyō Bunko (The Oriental Library), 1987. 371 p. **DE60**

Lists books, monographic series, and pamphlets added to the Oriental Library in Tokyo 1957–82. Since acquisition date is the criterion, older materials are also represented. Mostly English-language materials, with some German and Sanskrit. India here includes Nepal, Bhutan and Ceylon. Author index.

Encyclopedias

Chopra, Pran Nath. Encyclopaedia of India / P.N. Chopra, Prabha Chopra. Delhi : Agam Prakashan, 1988. 2 v. (628 p., [44] p. of plates) : ill., maps, ports. **DE61**

Intends to be the standard encyclopedia of India, with articles on people, places, companies and industries, religions, arts, fairs and festivals, mathematics, etc. For each topic, information is meant to be current through 1981. Short bibliographies end most articles. Includes a gazetteer of India, giving population figures from the Census of 1981 and a chronology, 4000 BCE–1986. Index of article titles under broad topics, e.g., Books, Castes.

§ For the findings of the last 150 years on Indian archaeology of the prehistory, protohistory and ancient periods, see *Encyclopaedia of Indian archaeology*, ed. by A. Ghosh, sponsored by the Indian Council of Historical Research (Leiden : Brill, 1990. 2 v. $228.57). DS405.C47

Mehra, Parshotam. A dictionary of modern Indian history, 1707–1947. Delhi ; N.Y. : Oxford Univ. Pr., 1987. 823 p. : maps. ISBN 0-19-561552-2. **DE62**

About 400 alphabetically arranged entries cover places, events, leaders, parties, etc. Some articles are lengthy and all end with a brief bibliography of one to nine entries. Cross-references; topical index. Appendix includes chronology, glossary of Indian terms, list of governors general and viceroys, 1774–1947. DS433.M33

Saletore, Rajaram Narayan. Encyclopaedia of Indian culture. Atlantic Highlands, N.J. : [distr. by] Humanities Pr. ; New Delhi : Sterling Publishers, 1985. v. 5 : ill. ISBN 0-391-02282-2 (v. 1). **DE63**

For v. 1–4 (1981–84) and annotation, see *Guide* DE205. A 2nd rev. ed. (New Delhi : Sterling Publ.) began in 1985.

Contents: v. 5, V–Z (1985). Completes the set. DS423.S218

General histories

The new Cambridge history of India / [gen. ed., Gordon Johnson ; assoc. editors, C.A. Bayly and John F. Richards]. Cambridge ; N.Y. : Cambridge Univ. Pr., 1987–1990. v. 1¹⁻², 2¹⁻², 3¹, 4¹ : maps; ill. (In progress). **DE64**

1st ed., 1922–37, had title *Cambridge history of India* (*Guide* DE207).

Contents: v. 1, The mughals and their contemporaries: pt. 1, The Portuguese in India, by M.N. Pearson (1987. 178 p.), pt. 2, Vijayanagara, by Burton Stein (1989. 156 p.); v. 2, Indian states and their transition to colonialism: pt. 1, Indian society and the making of the British Empire, by C.A. Bayly (1988. 230 p.), pt. 2, Bengal, the British bridgehead, by P.J. Marshall (1987. 195 p.); v. 3, The Empire and the beginning of modern society: pt. 1, Socio-religious reform movements in British India, by Kenneth W. Jones (1989. 243 p.); v. 4, The evolution of contemporary South Asia: pt. l, The politics of India since independence, by Paul R. Brass (1990. 357 p.).

The plan of the new edition is to divide Indian history beginning with the 16th century into "four overlapping chronological volumes, each containing about eight short books on individual themes or subjects."—*General editor's pref.* Each volume is a monograph written by a specialist on an aspect of Indian history; some include bibliographies, others bibliographic essays.   DS436.N47

INDOCHINA

Ruscio, Alain. La première guerre d'Indochine, 1945–1954 : bibliographie. Paris : L'Harmattan, c1987. 286 p. ISBN 2-85802-831-1.   **DE65**
Books and periodical articles in French and English, arranged by topic. No pagination is given in the bibliographic citations. Personal name and "thèmatique" index.   Z3226.R87

INDONESIA

Dengel, Holk H. Annotated bibliography of new Indonesian literature on the history of Indonesia. Stuttgart : F. Steiner Verlag Wiesbaden, 1987. 114 p. (Beiträge zur Südasienforschung, Bd. 113). ISBN 3-515-04988-6 (pbk.).   **DE66**
An alphabetical listing of books on Indonesia written by Indonesians, 1970–86, with emphasis on the "struggle for independence, regional history and biographies of important Indonesians."—*Introd.* Annotations describe contents and provide English translations of the titles. Subject index arranged under three headings: Ancient history, History of 16th–19th centuries, Modern history. Appendix lists "books published by Indonesia's National Archives to which the author had no access."

§ For an extensive bibliography on the modern period, see *The Indonesian economy and politics, 1963–1986* by Melanie S. Arief (Jakarta : Institute for Development Studies, 1987 373 p.).   DS634.D46

IRAN

Bibliography

Berghe, Louis van den. Bibliographie analytique de l'archéologie de l'Iran ancien : supplément 2, 1981–1985. Leuven : Peeters, 1987. 102 p.   **DE67**
For original volume and Supplement 1, see *Guide* DE222.
Adds publications of 1981–85, plus a few items previously omitted.   Z3369.A8B47

Ghanī, Sīrūs. Iran and the West : a critical bibliography. London ; N.Y. : Kegan Paul ; N. Y. : Distr. by Methuen, Routledge & Kegan Paul, 1987. 967 p. ISBN 0-7103-0243-6.   **DE68**
Based on a personal collection of works on Persia published in the 19th and 20th centuries, mainly in English. Alphabetically arranged in four sections: (A) History, politics, and travel; (B) Literature, religion, science, language including fiction with an Eastern setting; (C) Arts, archaeology, books of illustrations, photography albums, art sale catalogs; (D) Pam-

phlets, articles, journals, occasional papers, museum catalogs, newspaper and news magazine articles. Author index.
                                                        Z3366.G46

Navabpour, Reza. Iran. Oxford ; Santa Barbara, Calif. : Clio Pr., c1988. 308 p. : map. (World bibliographical series, v. 81). ISBN 1-85109-036-3. $52.00.   **DE69**
Offers 1,787 annotated entries for books, articles, essays in English. Priority was given to titles in print and those "which can reasonably be expected to be found in the Middle East sections of universities or large public libraries."—*Introd.* Author/title/subject index; cross-references.   Z3366.N37

Nawabi, Y. M. A bibliography of Iran : a catalogue of books and articles on Iranian subjects, mainly in European languages. [Tehran] : Cultural Studies & Research Institute, 1987. v. 7. (In progress).   **DE70**
For earlier volumes, see *Guide* DE228.
Contents: v. 7, Linguistics (1004 p.).
Cites over 10,000 books and articles on Old, Middle, and Modern Iranian languages and dialects. The chapters devoted to Avestan, old Persian, and Pahlavi are revised from v. 1. An "Addendum on Persian language and literature" is a supplement to that section in v. 2.   Z3366.N38

Encyclopedias

Encyclopædia Iranica / ed. by Ehsan Yarshater. London ; Boston : Routledge & Kegan Paul, 1986–1990. v 2^2–4^8. ISBN 0-7100-9099-4 (v. 1). $300.00. (In progress). **DE71**
For annotation and earlier parts, see *Guide* DE232.
Contents: v. 2, fasc. 2–v. 4, fasc. 8: Anthropology–Carpets XIV. Each volume complete in eight fascicles.   DS253.E53

ISRAEL

See also CJ189, CJ190, and BB8.

Korsch, Boris. Soviet publications on Judaism, Zionism, and the State of Israel, 1984–1988 : an annotated bibliography. N.Y. : Garland, 1990. 126 p. (Garland reference library of social science, vol. 482). ISBN 0-8240-4108-9.   **DE72**
An author listing of 386 books, pamphlets, journal articles, and theses designed to demonstrate "the unity of party- and government-inspired attitudes and the homogeneity of these antagonistic conditions."—*Pref.* Annotated. Reviews are listed separately under the author of the book being reviewed. Index for authors and reviewers; list of journals cited. Addendum for an additional 20 titles.   Z6366.K67

JAPAN

Bibliography

Catalogue of books in English on Japan, 1945–1981 / [comp. by The Japan Foundation]. [Tokyo] : The Foundation, 1986. 726 p.   **DE73**
Lists some 9,000 books published 1945–81 in humanities, social sciences, art, and the history of science. Entries were drawn from collections of the National Diet Library, the Japan Foundation Library and from lists in the *Bibliography of Asian studies* (*Guide* DE8). Classified arrangement with indexes for authors and titles.

§ A much shorter listing of English-language books is *Japan reading guide : a select list of books on Japan with annotations* (Tokyo : International House of Japan Library, 1986. [109] p.), a topical arrangement of 300 basic books on Japan. Also provides a list of government publications and periodicals in English. For general readers.   Z3306.C34

Catalogue of books on Japan translated from the Japanese into English, 1945–1981 = Eiyaku Nihon kankei hōbun tosho mokuroku / [comp. by The Japan Foundation] ; henshū Kokusai Kōryū Kikin]. Tokyo : The Foundation, 1988. 109 p.   **DE74**

A classified arrangement of books identified while compiling *Catalogue of books in English on Japan 1945–1981* (above). Entry indicates title of the Japanese original. Author and title indexes.   Z3301.C38

International studies in Japan : a bibliographic guide / ed. by Sadao Asada. Tokyo : Japan Association of International Relations, c1988. 241 p.   **DE75**

"A project of the Japan Association of International Relations."—*t.p.*   Based on: *Sengo Nihon no kokusai seijigaku* (Tokyo : 1979).

Companion to: DS881.96.I58

Japan and the world, 1853–1952 : a bibliographic guide to Japanese scholarship in foreign relations / ed. by Sadao Asada. N.Y. : Columbia Univ. Pr., c1989. 462 p. ISBN 0-231-06690-2.   **DE76**

"A project of the Japan Association of International Relations."—*t.p.*

Translates, revises, and much expands the chapter on Japanese diplomatic relations in *Sengo Nihon no kokusai seijigaku* (Tokyo : hatsubai Yūhikaku, 1979). Scholars discuss the "range and content of what Japanese historians have been writing during the past forty years . . . in the field of international studies both historical and theoretical" (*Pref.*) on the period 1853 through the Allied Occupation (1945–52). At the end of each chapter is a bibliography of the books, articles, archives, and personal papers discussed. Cutoff date is 1986–87. Author and subject indexes.   Z3308.R4J36

Nagao, Philip M. Japanese local histories in the Library of Congress : a bibliography. Wash. : Library of Congress : For sale by the Supt. of Docs., U.S. Govt. Print. Off., 1988. 324 p. : maps. ISBN 0-8444-0543-4.   **DE77**

Superintendent of Documents classification: LC 17.9:J27.

Consists of 2,848 entries for local history materials cataloged by the Library of Congress 1958–80, arranged by prefectural division. A map of Japan at the beginning of each division shows the location of the prefecture and a second map shows the chief roads and towns in the prefecture. Title index in romanized characters. Entries are in Japanese characters except for author, date of publication, and LC classification.   Z3309.N3413

Shulman, Frank Joseph. Japan. Oxford ; Santa Barbara, Calif. : Clio Pr., c1989. 873 p. : maps. (World bibliographical series, v. 103). ISBN 1-85109-074-6. $139.50.   **DE78**

Provides 1,615 annotated entries for books, with special emphasis on those published in the 1970s and 1980s. Topical arrangement. Cross-references; author, title, and subject indexes.   Z3301.S475

Handbooks

De Mente, Boye. Everything Japanese. Lincolnwood, Ill. : Passport Books, c1989. 319 p. : ill., map. ISBN 0-8442-8513-7. $27.95.   **DE79**

A dictionary of terms, movements, people, commercial companies, notable geographic features, etc., of interest to a foreigner concerned with Japan. Includes a listing of English-language materials arranged by publisher (with address).

§ *An English dictionary of Japanese culture* by Nobuyuki Honna and Bates Hoffer (Tokyo : Yuhikaka Publ., 1986. 349 p. ill.) concentrates on Japanese customs and culture. Arranged by Japanese term; Japanese and English language definitions of about a paragraph are given on facing pages.   DS821.D46

KOREA

McFarland, Keith D. The Korean War, an annotated bibliography. N.Y. : Garland, 1986. 463 p. ISBN 0-8240-9068-3.   **DE80**

A classified bibliography of more than 2,300 English-language items, including books, articles, theses, and government publications. Author and subject indexes; chronology.   Z3319.K6M38

Summers, Harry G. Korean War almanac. N.Y. : Facts on File, c1990. 330 p. : ill. ISBN 0-8160-1737-9. $24.95.   **DE81**

Covers the Korean War by means of the following sections: (1) Essays on the setting: Geographical realities, Historical realities, The two Koreas; (2) Chronology 1950–1953; and (3) a dictionary in a single alphabet of short entries on people, places, battles, military groups, and topics. The dictionary is the largest section, each entry concluding with suggestions for further reading. Selected bibliography arranged by author; cross-references; topical index.   DS918.S86

LAOS

Sage, William W. Laos : a bibliography / comp. by William W. Sage and Judith A.N. Henchy. Singapore : Institute of Southeast Asian Studies, 1986. 253 p. (Library bulletin, Institute of Southeast Asian Studies, no. 16). ISBN 9971-988-26-7.   **DE82**

Based on Sage's own collection and that of the Institute, meant to supplement Pierre-Bernard Lafont's *Bibliographie du Laos* (*Guide* DE280).

An extensive listing of mostly English-language (with some French, Vietnamese, and Lao) materials published 1975–84, arranged by topic (including refugees and resettlement). Covers books, pamphlets, articles, government and international agency reports, mimeographed papers, and radio monitoring services. Subject and author indexes.   Z3228.L3S24

MACAO

Edmonds, Richard L. Macau. Oxford ; Santa Barbara, Calif. : Clio Pr., c1989. lv, 110 p. : map. (World bibliographical series, v. 105). ISBN 1-85109-090-8. $45.00.   **DE83**

Includes "almost all available English or French references as well as a considerable number of Portuguese items" (*Introd.*) and a few selected Chinese publications. Lists 381 books, articles and documents, topically arranged with cross-references and an author/title/subject index.   Z3107.M24E35

MALAYSIA

Malaysian studies : archaeology, historiography, geography, and bibliography / John A. Lent and Kent Mulliner, editors. [De Kalb, Ill.] : Northern Illinois Univ., Center for Southeast Asian Studies : Distr. by the Cellar Bookshop, Detroit, 1985. 240 p. (Northern Illinois University. Center for Southeast Asian Studies. Occasional paper, no. 11.). **DE84**

Presents state-of-the-art papers and surveys, with bibliographies. DS592.M348

MONGOLIA

Information Mongolia : the comprehensive reference source of the People's Republic of Mongolia (MPR) / comp. and ed. by the Academy of Sciences, MPR. Oxford ; N.Y. : Pergamon Pr., 1990. 505 p., [45] p. of plates : ill., some maps in color. ISBN 0-08-036193-5. $240.00. **DE85**

B. Lhamsüren, ed. in chief.

"... offers encyclopaedic coverage of all aspects of contemporary Mongolian life within a detailed historical framework ... beginning with a background survey of the land and people and their history from ancient times right up to the present day."—*Pref.* Arranged by topics within broad categories (e.g., Industry under National economy or Written literature under Mongolian culture). Each broad topical section ends with a bibliography; most references are in Russian or Mongolian. Heavily illustrated with photographs, charts, and maps. Directory; chronology; subject index. Last chapter: MPR in figures. DS798.I54

NEPAL

Whelpton, John. Nepal / John Whelpton, comp., with the assistance of Lucette Boulnois ... [et al.]. Oxford ; Santa Barbara, Calif. : Clio Pr., c1990. 294 p. : map. (World bibliographical series, v. 38). ISBN 0-903450-68-2. $75.00. **DE86**

Lists 917 works, mainly books with a few articles and essays. Mostly English-language materials, but some in French, German, or Nepalese. Topical arrangement; annotations. Cross-references; author/title/subject index. Z3210.W45

PAKISTAN

Bhatty, K. M. Annotated bibliography of social research in Pakistan. Peshawar : Pakistan Academy for Rural Development, [1986]. 141 p., [1] leaf of plates : col. ill. **DE87**

A topical arrangement under 18 subjects of 540 annotated entries for organization and government publications, articles, mimeographs and typewritten research reports, and a few books. Author index. Z7165.P3B43

Taylor, David D. Pakistan. Oxford ; Santa Barbara, Calif. : Clio Pr., c1990. 255 p., [1] leaf of plates : map. (World bibliographical series, v. 10). ISBN 1-85109-081-9. $70.00. **DE88**

Lists 797 English-language books and a few articles, topically arranged and annotated. Chronology; list of heads of state. Author, title, and subject indexes; cross-references. Z3196.T39

SAUDI ARABIA

American and Canadian doctoral dissertations on the Kingdom of Saudi Arabia, 1935–1987 / comp. by Abdullah N. al-Subaiy. [Wash. : Saudi Arabian Educational Mission], 1987. 276 p. **DE89**

Using Univ. Microfilms database searches and individual institution lists, the compiler has amassed a list of 789 dissertations on Saudi Arabia, 1935–87. Arranged by broad subject (e.g., accounting, agriculture, biology, communications), then by year and alphabetically by author. Author index in the front of the volume. Z3026.A647

Clements, Frank. Saudi Arabia. Rev. and expanded ed. Oxford ; Santa Barbara, Calif. : Clio Pr., c1988. 354 p. : map. (World bibliographical series, v. 5). ISBN 1-85109-067-3. $55.00. **DE90**

1st ed., 1979 (*Guide* DE303).

Updated through 1986. Z3026.C57

Philipp, Hans-Jürgen. Saudi Arabia : bibliography on society, politics, economics = Saudi-Arabien : Bibliographie zu Gesellschaft, Politik, Wirtschaft : Literatur seit dem 18. Jahrhundert in westeuropäischen Sprachen mit Standortnachweisen. München ; N.Y. : Saur, 1989. v. 2 (634 p.). (Bibliographies on regional geography and area studies = Bibliographien zur regionalen Geographie und Landeskunde, 7). ISBN 3-598-21137-6 (v. 2). **DE91**

For v. 1, see *Guide* DE304.

Title page, table of contents, introduction, and index in English and German.

Arrangement and criteria for selection are the same as in v. 1; also continues the item numbering. Adds 5,540 references for materials which have appeared since 1983, including reprints and new editions. Three-fourths of the citations are in English. Indexes for v. 2 only: subject, author, editor. Z3026.P48

SINGAPORE

Quah, Stella R. Singapore / Stella R. Quah, Jon S.T. Quah, compilers. Oxford ; Santa Barbara, Calif. : Clio Pr., c1988. 258 p. : maps. (World bibliographical series, v. 95). ISBN 1-85109-071-1. $52.50. **DE92**

Includes English-language "works dealing with Singapore as the only, or the major topic" (*Introd.*), published 1980–88, except for a few significant older materials. Lists 764 books and articles in a topical arrangement. Author, title, and subject indexes. Z3285.Q33

SRI LANKA

Rupesinghe, Kumar. Ethnic conflict and human rights in Sri Lanka : an annotated bibliography / Kumar Rupesinghe & Berth Verstappen. London ; N.Y. : Zell ; Oslo : Publ. for the International Peace Research Institute, 1989. 565 p. ISBN 0-905450-65-5. £45.00. **DE93**

"The purpose of this bibliography is to record the literature concerning the escalating phase of the internal conflict in Sri Lanka, with an emphasis on the period 1983–88."—*Introd.* A topical listing with good annotations of 2,311 books, pamphlets, government publications, articles, and documents of or-

ganizations. Author, subject, and geographical indexes.
          Z3211.R855

Samaraweera, Vijaya. Sri Lanka. Oxford ; Santa Barbara, Calif. : Clio Pr., c1987. 194 p. : map. (World bibliographical series, v. 20). ISBN 0-903450-33-X. $40.50.
          DE94

An annotated list of books, government publications, and periodical articles. Topical arrangement with author/title/subject index.   Z3211.S26

SYRIA

Seccombe, Ian J. Syria. Oxford ; Santa Barbara, Calif. : Clio Pr., c1987. 341 p. : map. (World bibliographical series, v. 73). ISBN 1-85109-018-5. $65.00.   **DE95**

An annotated bibliography of 903 books, government publications, and articles, primarily in English but some in French, German, or Italian. Emphasis is on history, politics, and archaeology. Author, title, subject indexes.   Z3481.S43

TAIWAN

Lee, Wei-chin. Taiwan. Oxford ; Santa Barbara Calif. : Clio Pr., c1990. 247 p. : map. (World bibliographical series, v. 113). ISBN 1-85109-091-6. $69.00.   **DE96**

A topical listing of 825 books, articles, doctoral dissertations, and government publications, most of them in English and published after 1980. Cross-references; author, title, subject indexes.   Z3116.L44

Republic of China yearbook. 1989– . Taipei, Taiwan, R.O.C.: Kwang Hwa Pub. Co., 1989– . Annual. ISSN 1013-0942. $44.50.   **DE97**

Surveys events and developments of the year, with chapters on language, history, central government, political parties, science and industry, etc., each chapter ending with a short bibliography and a listing of relevant institutions, organizations, government agencies, etc. Appendix: Who's who in the R.O.C.; Chronology, January 1911–June 1987; Constitution; The Republic of China in figures; National holidays; Directory of legislators; Diplomatic representatives. Topical index.
          DS798.92.R46

TIBET

Bibliography of Tibetan studies / comp. by Hallvard Kåre Kuløy, Yoshiro Imaeda. Narita-shi Chiba-ken, Japan : Naritasan Shinshōji, 1986. 735 p. (Monograph series of Naritasan Institute for Buddhist studies, 2).
          DE98

Amasses 11,822 entries to produce a comprehensive bibliography of books and articles, in all languages, "published up to (and including) 1975, and which deal with 'Tibetan' civilisation: all aspect of 'Tibetan'-speaking people and followers of Mahāyāna Buddhism . . . and in the strictly cultural, linguistic and ethnical context."—p. v. Author arrangement, with cross-references to variant form of name, etc., but no index.
          Z3107.T5B53

Pinfold, John R. Tibet. Oxford ; Santa Barbara, Calif. : Clio Pr., c1991. 158 p. : map. (World bibliographical series, v. 128.). ISBN 1-85109-158-0.   **DE99**

Intended for the general reader or the first-time researcher in Tibetan studies. Cites 559 titles, mostly in English, of books and articles, with brief annotations. Author, title, and brief subject indexes.   DS786.P56

VIETNAM

Library of Congress. Vietnamese holdings in the Library of Congress. Supplement, 1979–1985 / comp. by A. Kohar Rony. Wash. : The Library : For sale by the Supt. of Docs., U.S. Govt. Print. Off., 1987. 167 p. ISBN 0-8444-0564-7.   **DE100**

For original compilation, see *Guide* DE320.

Superintendent of Documents classification: LC 1.12/2:V67/3/supp./979-85.

Follows the same arrangement and criteria for selection, adding an additional 1,927 items.   Z3228.V5L52

Peake, Louis A. The United States in the Vietnam War, 1954–1975 : a selected annotated bibliography. N.Y. : Garland, 1986. 406 p. (Wars of the United States, vol. 4 ; Garland reference library of social science, vol. 256). ISBN 0-8240-8946-4.   **DE101**

More than 1,500 English-language items in classed arrangement, including books, articles, government publications, films, and recordings. Author and subject indexes; chronology; glossary; four-page list of addenda.   Z3226.P43

Wittman, Sandra M. Writing about Vietnam : a bibliography of the literature of the Vietnam Conflict. Boston : G.K. Hall, c1989. 385 p. : ill. ISBN 0-8161-9083-6.
          DE102

An annotated listing by genre of novels, narratives, poetry, drama, short stories, literary criticism, dissertations, periodicals, and teaching materials published 1954–88 on the Vietnam conflict. Author/title index.   Z3226.W58

Bibliography

Butler, Deborah A. American women writers on Vietnam : unheard voices : a selected annotated bibliography. N.Y. : Garland, 1990. 312 p. (Garland reference library of the humanities, vol. 1278). ISBN 0-8240-3528-3.   **DE103**

Intends "not only to highlight women's writing on the Vietnam War itself, but to make clear the ideas, events, and personalities that women focused on, even if these were not always about the female experience nor even the Vietnam War directly."—*Pref.* 781 books, articles, chapters, and dissertations, published 1954–87 are arranged by format (novels, autobiographies, journalism, etc.) subdivided by period, with descriptive annotations. Author, title, and subject index.
          Z1227.B88

Harnly, Caroline D. Agent Orange and Vietnam : an annotated bibliography. Metuchen, N.J. : Scarecrow, 1988. 401 p. ISBN 0-8108-2174-5.   **DE104**

Expanded from the author's *Agent Orange and the Vietnam veteran* (Monticello, Ill. : Vance Bibliographies, 1985).

An annotated listing of journal articles, government publications (federal and state), reports of international organizations, and a few books arranged under five broad headings (some subdivided): Ethical and political issues; Effects on Vietnam's ecology; Health costs; Disposal of Agent Orange; Effects on Vietnam veterans. Author index.

§ Another specialized bibliography on the Vietnam War is *Stress, strain, and Vietnam : an annotated bibliography of two decades of psychiatric and social science literature reflecting the effect of the war on the American soldier*, by Norman M. Camp,

Robert H. Stretch, and William C. Marshall (N.Y.: Greenwood, 1988. 315 p. $45.95). Z6724.C5H38

Johnson, Victoria E. Vietnam on film and television: documentaries in the Library of Congress. [Wash.: Library of Congress], 1989. 77 p. **DE105**

An alphabetical listing by title of the holdings of the Motion Picture, Broadcasting and Recorded Sound Division of the Library of Congress, excluding fiction films and television news broadcasts. About 400 works are included, with cross-references from episode titles to series titles. Name and subject indexes. An appendix gives a brief description of a collection of 16mm film from the Embassy of South Vietnam now in the Library of Congress. Z3228.V5J64

Dictionaries

Dictionary of the Vietnam War / ed. by James S. Olson. N.Y.: Greenwood, 1988. 585 p.: maps. ISBN 0-313-24943-1. $65.00. **DE106**

An encyclopedia with "brief descriptive essays on most people, legislation, military operations, and controversies important to American participation in the Vietnam War."—*Pref.* Articles not written by Olson are signed with the contributor's name. Most articles have short bibliographies. Cross-references; subject index. Appendix of tables showing population in South Vietnam and of minority groups in South Vietnam; glossary of acronyms and slang; select bibliography; chronology.

§ See also *Words of the Vietnam War* by Gregory R. Clark (*Supplement* AD41). DS557.7.D53

DF

Australia and New Zealand

GENERAL WORKS

Bloomfield, Valerie. Resources for Australian and New Zealand studies: a guide to library holdings in the United Kingdom. London: Australian Studies Centre: British Library, 1986. 284 p. ISBN 0-7123-0122-4. **DF1**

Aims " to provide a guide to the holdings of printed and audiovisual materials in the United Kingdom relating to Australia and New Zealand."—*Introd.* Manuscripts and archives are excluded because they are treated by Phyllis Mander-Jones's *Manuscripts in the British Isles relating to Australia, New Zealand and the Pacific* (*Guide* DF3). Based on responses to a questionnaire and on personal visits. Covers 172 libraries and institutions, giving for each: name and address, hours, access, lending policies, details of holdings, and any publications about the library. Arranged alphabetically under name of city. Index of names, subjects and categories (e.g. maps, information retrieval services, audiovisual materials). Z4009.B54

AUSTRALIA

Australians: a historical library. Broadway, N.S.W., Australia: Fairfax, Syme & Weldon, 1987. 11 v.: ill. (some col.), maps, ports. ISBN 0-949288-09-8 (set). **DF2**

General editors: Alan D. Gilbert and K.S. Inglis for v. 1–5, Frank Crowley and Peter Spearritt for v. 6–10. Chairman of the Management Committee: Oliver MacDonagh.

Contents: v. 1, Australians to 1788, ed., D.J. Mulvaney and J. Peter White (476 p.); v. 2, Australians 1838, ed. Alan Atkinson and Marian Aveling (474 p.); v. 3, Australians 1888, ed. Graeme Davison, J.W. McCarty and Ailsa McLeary (474 p.); v. 4, Australians 1938, ed. Bill Gammage and Peter Spearritt; oral history coord., Louise Douglas (474 p.) v. 5, Australians from 1939, ed. Ann Curthoys, A.W. Martin, and Tim Rowse (474 p.) v. 6, Australians: a historical atlas, ed. J.C.R. Camm and John McQuilton; cartographic ed., Trevor W. Plumb (290 p., 40 cm.); v. 7, Australians: events and places, ed. Graeme Aplin, S.G. Foster and Michael McKernan (476 p.); v. 8, Australians: a historical dictionary, ed. Graeme Aplin, S.G. Foster, Michael McKernan (462 p.); v. 9, Australians: a guide to sources, ed. D.H. Borchardt and Victor Crittenden (473 p.); v. 10, Australians: historical statistics, ed., Wray Vamplew (470 p.); v. 11, Australians: the guide and index (83 p.).

Written to commemorate the bicentenary of European settlement in Australia, each volume is intended to stand alone and has its own index, but all are meant to complement each other. The set is composed of five historical volumes, of which three are "slice" volumes (i.e., describing a single year); the others are reference volumes. General index (v. 11 unites the individual indexes). DU96.A87

Bassett, Jan. The concise Oxford dictionary of Australian history. Melbourne: Oxford Univ. Pr., 1986. 276 p. ISBN 0-19-554422-6. £8.95. **DF3**

Reprinted with corrections, 1987.

Includes entries for "the principal people, institutions, places, ideas, movements, events, artifacts, and documents generally considered to be historically significant in Australia's history to 1975."—*Pref.* About 550 short articles. Not indexed. DU90.B38

Brown, Robin. Collins milestones in Australian history / Robin Brown; ed. by Richard Appleton. Sydney: W. Collins; Boston: G.K. Hall, 1986. 835 p. ISBN 0-8161-8820-3. **DF4**

Offers chronological tables with parallel columns for: History, politics, economics, law; Science, technology, transport, discovery; Arts; Religion, learning; Sport; Historia dignum (other memorable events). Index of persons, places, subjects, titles of work, etc.

§ A similar, though less extensive, dictionary is *Great events in Australia's history from discovery to the present* ([Frenchs Forest, N.S.W.]: Child, [1988]. 462 p.) which covers the period up to 1988. Each year encompasses two pages and offers a list of some seven to nine events with one or two explained more fully, often with an illustration. Subject index includes references to the illustrations. DU110.B76

Ferguson, John Alexander. Bibliography of Australia: addenda, 1784–1850. Canberra: National Library of Australia, 1986. 706 p. ISBN 0-642-99307-6. **DF5**

Includes titles omitted from v. 1–4 and addenda in v. 2–4 of the author's *Bibliography of Australia* (1941–69, 7 v.; *Guide* DF6). Arranged chronologically with general author/title/subject index. Z4011.F47

NEW ZEALAND

Guides

Wood, G. A. Studying New Zealand history. Dunedin, New Zealand : Univ. of Otago Pr., [1988]. 118 p. ISBN 0-908569-44-0.   **DF6**

1st ed., 1973, had title *A guide for students of New Zealand history* (*Guide* DF15).

A very useful guide for students and researchers that discusses libraries and archives, finding aids for various types of material (e.g., printed reference works, theses, primary sources, official documents, and records), and offers advice on writing a thesis. Author/title index.   Z4116.W66

Bibliography

Bagnall, Austin Graham. New Zealand national bibliography to the year 1960. Wellington : Govt. Printer, 1985. v. 5.   **DF7**

For annotation, see *Supplement* AA164.   Z4101.B28

New Zealand foreign policy, 1945–1985 : a bibliography / comp. by John Henderson ... [et al.] assisted by Robert Barton ... [et al.]. Wellington, N.Z. : N.Z. Institute of International Affairs, 1986. 82 p. ISBN 0-908772-02-5 (pbk.).   **DF8**

Based on an earlier edition by Kay Cijffers (Wellington, N.Z. : Institute of International Affairs, 1980?) covering 1945–79.

An author listing of books, articles, and official documents from New Zealand, Australia, South East Asia, Europe, the U.K. and U.S., and, for the last five years, from the U.S.S.R. Not indexed.   Z6465.N45N49

Dissertations

Mosen, Norah D. Theses on the history of New Zealand. Supplement, 1968–1982. [Palmerston North, N.Z.] : Massey Univ., 1985. 128 p. (Massey University Library series, no 18).   **DF9**

Supplements the earlier compilation by Margaret Rodger (*Guide* DF21). Includes "theses on New Zealand history accepted for degrees in Australia, Great Britain, New Zealand, and the United States of America, and research essays accepted for New Zealand degrees."—*Pref.* 757 theses are arranged by broad topics, with cross-references. Author and subject indexes. The two-page supplement at the end is included in the index.   Z4116.R6

Encyclopedias; Handbooks

The illustrated encyclopedia of New Zealand / ed. in chief Gordon McLauchlan. Updated ed. Auckland, N.Z. : D. Bateman, [1989]. 1448 p. : ill. ISBN 1-86953-007-1.   **DF10**

"Originally published in 52 parts by Windsor Watt Ltd., Auckland. This updated one-volume edition first published in 1989 by David Bateman."—*verso of t.p.*

Bears a striking resemblance to the 1984 *Bateman New Zealand encyclopedia* (*Guide* DF24) since all material (including most of the illustrations) from that volume is incorporated here. The new publication is more heavily illustrated, includes extended and updated articles, and some additional entries

(mainly biographies). Most articles are current to mid-1980. The chronology now covers through 1988, some of the charts (e.g., religious professions, occupations) were dropped, and the index is now alphabetical instead of by broad topics.   DU405.I55

Chronologies

The New Zealand book of events / devised and ed. by Bryce Fraser. [Auckland, N.Z.] : Reed Methuen, [1986]. 448 p. : ill. ISBN 0-474-00123-7.   **DF11**

Offers a series of chronologies presented in chapters (e.g., Aviation, Trade and protection, Farming, Women, The visual arts). At the end of each chapter is a general reading list. Index of people, places, and subjects.   DU420.N48

DG

Oceania

GENERAL WORKS

Bibliography

Fry, Gerald. Pacific Basin and Oceania / Gerald W. Fry, Rufino Mauricio, compilers. Oxford ; Santa Barbara, Calif. : Clio Pr., c1987. 468 p. : map. (World bibliographical series, v. 70). ISBN 1-85109-015-0. $55.00.   **DG1**

Lists 1,178 English-language books and periodical articles, most of them published 1975–85, with a few earlier works "of enduring value or special interest."—*Introd.* Arrangement is by broad topic; the annotations are meant to be evaluative and descriptive. Covers Melanesia, Micronesia, and Polynesia; specific countries (e.g., Australia, Indonesia) are not included because they are accorded separate volumes in this series. The compilers made an effort to include "a sizable portion of indigenous publications." Author/title/subject index.   Z4501.F79

Goetzfridt, Nicholas J. Micronesia, 1975–1987 : a social science bibliography / comp. by Nicholas J. Goetzfridt and William L. Wuerch. N.Y. : Greenwood, 1989. 194 p. : ill. (Bibliographies and indexes in anthropology, no. 5). ISBN 0-313-26852-5. $39.95.   **DG2**

Extends Mac Marshall and James D. Nason's *Micronesia 1944–1974* (*Guide* CE112) with a further 1,849 entries.   Z5116.G63

Graham, Theresa. A finding aid to reference books in South Pacific studies. Auckland, N.Z. : Auckland Univ. Library, 1988. 48 p. (Bibliographical bulletin, University of Auckland. Library, 15).   **DG3**

Concerned with "research publications held in the New Zealand & Pacific Collection in the General Library [of Auckland University]."—*p. iv.* A bibliography of bibliographies, directories, encyclopedias, manuscript guides, and atlases arranged by format with bibliographies subdivided by subject or geographical area. Not indexed. **DV17.G73**

Guides to the sources for the history of the nations. 3rd series, North Africa, Asia and Oceania = Guides des sources de l'histoire des nations. 3ème série, Afrique du Nord, Asie et Océanie. München ; N.Y. : K.G. Saur, 1986–91. v. 7–9. (In progress). **DG4**

For annotation, see *Supplement* DD15. **CD941.G85**

Hamnett, Judith D. A guide to films about the Pacific Islands. [Honolulu, Hawaii] : Pacific Islands Studies Program, Center for Asian and Pacific Studies, Univ. of Hawaii at Manoa, 1986. 148 p. **DG5**

Lists films and videocassettes in three sections: 1) Pacific Islands excluding Hawaii; 2) Hawaii; 3) Pacific Islands films available outside the U.S. Excluded are films and videos whose sole purpose is entertainment. Each entry includes name of film, country or culture, length, format, color or black-and-white, year of release, producer, distributor, and a brief annotation. List of producers' names and addresses. Not indexed.

§ A more narrowly focused compilation is the New Zealand Film Archive's *Maori and Pacific films from New Zealand 1901–1984* (Wellington : New Zealand Film Archive, 1984). **DU28.2.H36**

Pacific Island studies : a survey of the literature / Miles M. Jackson, ed. in chief. N.Y. : Greenwood, [1986]. 244 p. (Bibliographies and indexes in sociology, no. 7). ISBN 0-313-23528-7. **DG6**

Based on the collection of the library of the University of Hawaii, Manoa, the guide provides "a concise synthesis of the significant literature" (*Pref.*) on history, political change, popular accounts, language, and sources of information (e.g., newspapers and journals). Presented as a series of bibliographic essays on Polynesia subdivided for Pacific Islands and Hawaii, Micronesia, Melanesia, and Australian aboriginal studies with a list of full citations at the end of each. Subject/author index. A second volume is planned to cover reference sources, subject bibliographies, directories, dictionaries, atlases and gazetteers, statistical compendia, and handbooks. **Z4501.P33**

Thompson, Anne-Gabrielle. The Southwest Pacific : an annotated guide to bibliographies, indexes and collections in Australian libraries. Canberra : Research School of Pacific Studies, the Australian National Univ. in association with the Academy of Social Sciences in Australia, 1986. 127 p. (Aids to research series, no. A/6). ISBN 0-86784-832-7. **DG7**

Lists reference materials on the Southwest Pacific: Fiji, New Caledonia, Papua New Guinea, the Solomon Islands, and Vanuatu (formerly New Hebrides). Includes sections for general and subject bibliographies, thesis catalogs, and guides to archives and manuscripts, to newspaper and journal articles, to official publications, to holdings of special libraries, and to serial publications. Author and subject indexes. **DU3.T56**

Where the whalers went : an index to the Pacific ports and islands visited by American whalers (and some other ships) in the 19th century / ed. by Robert Langdon. Canberra : Pacific Manuscripts Bureau, Research School of Pacific Studies, Australian National Univ., 1984. 298 p. : ill., maps. ISBN 0-86784-471-X. **DG8**

Supersedes *Thar she went...* (Canberra : Pacific Manuscripts Bureau, Research School of Pacific Studies, The Australian National University, 1979).

A bibliography of logbooks kept by 19th century American whaling, trading, and naval ships with ports of call in Australia, New Zealand, and the Pacific Islands. Arranged by place and date; each entry gives precise dates, captain/logkeeper, and citation to microfilm number if reproduced in the New England Microfilming Project sponsored by the Pacific Manuscripts Bureau. Index of captains/logkeepers.

§ Francis X. Hezel's *Foreign ships in Micronesia : compendium of ship contacts in the Caroline and Marshall Islands 1521–1885* (Saipan, Marian Is. : publ. in cooperation with the Trust Territory Historic Preservation Office and the U.S. Heritage Conservation and Recreation Service, 1979) gives chronological listings for Palau, Yap, Truk, Ponape, Kosrai, Marshalls and Carolines. **SH382.6.W44**

Encyclopedias

Political and economic encyclopaedia of the Pacific / ed. by Gerald Segal. Chicago : St. James Pr. ; Burnt Mill, Harlow, Essex, England : Longman, [1989]. 293 p. ISBN 1-55862-033-8. **DG9**

Offers signed articles on countries, parties, people, and topics which "cover bilateral and multilateral issues in the field of security, economics, ideology, culture and resources."—*Introd.* Emphasizes post-1945 developments. Index includes title of each article; under country, the names of other related articles; and cross-references for variant forms of names.

HN930.7.A8P6

Handbooks

Pacific islands yearbook / ed. by Norman & Ngaire Douglas. 16th ed. North Ryde, N.S.W., Australia : Angus & Robertson Publishers in assoc. with Nationwide NW Party Ltd., [1989]. 717 p. : ill., maps. ISBN 0-207-16114-3. **DG10**

Continues: *Pacific Island year book and who's who*, ed. 1–15 (1932–84).

With this edition, reorganized and re-edited. The country sections are now first with many "personalities" dropped and only major office holders included. Also dropped is the trade directory for each country, since the compilers found it very incomplete. Added are names, addresses, and phone numbers for most important government, diplomatic, and international organizations and officials, and an expanded section for accomodations in each country. Pacific chronology, ca.35,000 BCE–1989. Index of islands.

PAPUA NEW GUINEA

Butler, Alan. A New Guinea bibliography. Waigani : Univ. of Papua New Guinea Pr., 1984–1987. v. 1–4. (In progress). **DG11**

Vol. 3–4 comp. by Alan Butler and Gary Cummings.

Available from University Bookshop, University of Papua New Guinea.

Based on the New Guinea collection at Michael Somare Library, University of Papua New Guinea. A topical listing of all books, pamphlets, theses, reports, government documents, seminar papers, journals, etc., either published in New Guinea or which deal with Papua New Guinea or Irian Jayan topics. Cut-off date is 1983, with a few 1984 titles. Journal articles are omitted with the intention of listing them in a future bibliography. To be complete in 5 v.; v. 5 is to include the indexes.

Z4811.B88

McConnell, Fraiser. Papua New Guinea. Oxford ; Santa Barbara, Calif. : Clio Pr., [1988]. 378 p. : map. (World bibliographical series, v. 90). ISBN 1-85109-030-4. $55.00. **DG12**

A bibliography of published works (primarily books, with some series and government publications) issued before April

1987. Topical arrangement with good annotations; indexed by author and subject.   DU740.A12P261

DH

Arctic and Antarctic

PHILIPPINES

Richardson, Jim. Philippines. Oxford ; Santa Barbara, Calif. : Clio Pr., c1989. 372 p. : map. (World bibliographical series, v. 106). ISBN 1-85109-077-0. $65.00.
DG13
The compiler offers "a fully annotated listing of selected books, articles and other materials on every major aspect of the Philippines and its people . . . [seeking to] reflect cultural diversity [yet provide a] fair balance between major geographical regions"—*Introd.* 955 entries in topical arrangement; titles listed are in English or Pilipino (the national language). Author, title, and subject indexes.   Z3296.R53

SAMOA

Pereira, Janet Aileen. A check list of selected material on Samoa. Western Samoa : Samoan History Writing Project, Univ. of the South Pacific, Extension Centre, 1983. v. 1–2. (In progress).   **DG14**
Contents: v. 1, General bibliography (437 p.); v. 2, Agriculture (112 p.).
A topical bibliography of books, articles, government publications, manuscripts and archives; coverage is predominantly of Western Samoa. Name index in each volume.   Z4891.P47

SOLOMON ISLANDS

Edridge, Sally. Solomon Islands bibliography to 1980. Suva, Fiji : Institute of Pacific Studies, the Univ. of the South Pacific, 1985. 476 p. : map. ISBN 0-908702-03-5.
DG15
Also issued by Alexander Turnbull Lib, Wellington, N.Z. and the Solomon Islands Natl. Lib, Honiara.
A retrospective bibliography of "books, pamphlets and periodical articles published within the Solomon Islands, or relating to those Islands. Works published by Solomon Islanders are included regardless of subject."—*Introd.* Classed arrangement with author and title/subject indexes.   Z4898.E37

BIBLIOGRAPHY

King, H. G. R. The Arctic. Oxford ; Santa Barbara, Calif. : Clio Pr., c1989. 272 p. : map. (World bibliographical series, v. 99). ISBN 1-85109-072-X. $65.00.
DH1
A topical/geographical arrangement of 935 entries for English-language books and government publications, and for the major periodicals in any language. Author, title, subject indexes.   Z6005.P7K56

[Knight, Russell W.]. Australian Antarctic bibliography. [Tasmania] : Institute of Antarctic and Southern Ocean Studies, Univ. of Tasmania, [1988]. 463 p. ISBN 0-85901-370-7.   **DH2**
"This bibliography comprises material relating to the Australian Antarctic Territory, the subantarctic islands, Heard, Macquarie, and McDonald, and the waters in close proximity to those geographical areas."—*Pref.* Classed arrangement of books, articles, and research reports, mostly in English but some in Russian. For items appearing in *Antarctic bibliography* (*Guide* DH1) reference is made to the annotations in that publication. Not indexed.   Z6005.P7K

Minion, Robin. 20th century Canadian arctic expeditions / comp. by Robin Minion and Marion Saffran. Edmonton, Alta. : Boreal Institute for Northern Studies, Univ. of Alberta, [1986]. 116 p. (BINS bibliographical series, 29). ISBN 0-919058-64-7.   **DH3**
An annotated bibliography of 304 books, articles, theses, essays, and government publications, arranged by author with author, title, and geographical area indexes.
§ Minion's *Nineteenth century expeditions in the Arctic and Canada* from the same publisher ([1984]. 97 p. BINS bibliographical series, 4), includes 255 books, government publications, and articles, for 19th century accounts. Indexes for authors, geographical names, titles, and expedition leaders and ships.   F1090.5.M56

ENCYCLOPEDIAS; HANDBOOKS

Headland, Robert. Chronological list of Antarctic expeditions and related historical events. Cambridge ; N.Y. : Cambridge Univ. Pr., [1989]. 730 p. : ill. ISBN 0-521-30903-4.   **DH4**
Based on Brian Roberts's "Chronological list" published in the *Polar record* of the Scott Polar Research Institute, v. 9 (1958): 97–134, 191–239.
Aims to record "as concisely as possible the history of discovery, exploration, exploitation, mapping, scientific investigation, administration . . . in Antarctic regions."—*p. 2.* A chronological list of about 2,800 expeditions and events, giving for each: nationality, purpose, leader, and brief annotations containing other details; this section constitutes most of the work.

Bibliography of Antarctic chronology, p. 604–21, gives sources of further information. Index of personal and place names, ship names, and institutions.   G860.H36

Stewart, John. Antarctica : an encyclopedia. Jefferson, N.C. : McFarland, c1990. 2 v. (1193 p.). ISBN 0-89950-470-1 (set). $135.00.   **DH5**
    "Incorporating geographical features, expeditions, people, scientific subjects, and entries of general interest" (*Pref.*), offers thorough coverage of the continent (south of 60°) for the "average reader." Short articles define, identify, locate, or describe a wide variety of topics relating to Antarctica, even discussing churches, fossils, penguins, stamps, etc. Alphabetical arrangement. Copious cross-references; chronology; list of expeditions. A bibliography, p. 1173–93, cites 420 books with some annotations.   G855.S74

E

SCIENCE, TECHNOLOGY, AND MEDICINE

EA

General Works

GUIDES

Chen, Ching-chih. Scientific and technical information sources. 2nd ed. Cambridge, Mass. : MIT Pr., c1987. 824 p. ISBN 0-262-03120-5. $55.00.   **EA1**

1st ed., 1977 (*Guide* EA2).

An essential guide to current sources of information in science and technology, " . . . intended primarily as a basic one-volume reference guide for science and engineering information professionals and their assistants and as a textbook for library and information science school students."—*Pref.* The new edition has been revised and expanded to 5,300 sources, many

published 1980–86. Arranged by type of material (e.g. handbook, directory, manual), then by subject. Many entries are annotated and include critical notes and citations to both scientific and library reviewing sources. Complete name and title indexes.   Z7401.C48

Encyclopedia of physical sciences and engineering information sources / Steven Wasserman, Martin A. Smith, and Susan Mottu, editors. Detroit : Gale, c1989. 736 p. ISBN 0-8103-2498-9.   **EA2**

Subtitle: a bibliographic guide to approximately 16,000 citations for publications, organizations, and other sources of information on 425 subjects relating to the physical sciences and engineering.

Citations are organized under topical subject headings, often narrowly defined, which are subdivided by type of source (e.g., abstract services, directories, statistics sources, databases). Individual citations include the bibliographic description or address, telephone, and publication or subscription price. Information sources are frequently repeated under related subject headings. An outline of contents serves as a guide to subjects and related terms. No index.   Z7401.E56

Hurt, Charlie Deuel. Information sources in science and technology. Englewood, Colo. : Libraries Unlimited, 1988. 362 p. ISBN 0-87287-581-4. $29.50. ISBN 0-87287-582-2 (pbk.). $21.50.   **EA3**

This selective bibliography provides a basic introduction to the literature of science, medicine, and technology. Some 2,000 English-language reference works are arranged in 17 subject chapters. Within each chapter, entries are grouped by form or type of material (e.g., abstracts, dictionaries, atlases). Annotated entries include descriptive and critical comments about each publication. Author/title and subject indexes. Similar in scope and content to Harold Robert Malinowsky and Jeanne

M. Richardson's *Science and engineering literature*, 3rd ed., 1980 (*Guide* EA5).   Z7401.H85

Parker, C. C. Information sources in science and technology : a practical guide to traditional and online use / C.C. Parker, R.V. Turley. 2nd ed. London ; N.Y. : Butterworths, 1986. 328 p. : ill. ISBN 0-408-01467-9. £25.00.   **EA4**
   1st ed., 1975.
   A selective guide to current information sources which also discusses strategies for finding and using information. Addressed to librarians, scientists, engineers, and students, this combination bibliography and reader's advisor is particularly useful for its description of British sources and research methods. Name and subject index.   Q224.P37

Smith, Robert V. Graduate research : a guide for students in the sciences. 2nd ed. N.Y. : Plenum Pr., c1990. 292 p. : ill. ISBN 0-306-43465-2. $24.95.   **EA5**
   1st ed., 1984 (*Guide* EA7).
   Offers an expanded and updated overview of the issues confronting graduate students in the sciences. Topics range from the principles of research and professional ethics to time management and grantsmanship. The section about libraries is brief, but does mention online catalogs and computerized literature searching.   Q180.55.M4S58

Walford, Albert John. Walford's guide to reference material / ed. by A. J. Walford ; with the collaboration of Marilyn Mulley and Priscilla Schlicke, and with the assistance of Charles A. Crossley. 5th ed. Metuchen, N. J. ; N. Y. : K. G. Saur, 1989–90. v. 1–2. ISBN 3-598-10905-9 (v.1). ISBN 0-85365-539-1 (v.2). (In progress).
                                                        EA6
   For annotation, see *Supplement* AA67.

BIBLIOGRAPHY

Powell, Russell H. Core list of books and journals in science and technology / ed. by Russell H. Powell and James R. Powell, Jr. Phoenix : Oryx, 1987. 134 p. ISBN 0-89774-275-3. $35.00.   **EA7**
   A selective bibliography of some 1,500 English-language publications, emphasizing recent imprints, standard editions of textbooks, and current serials used in college and advanced educational programs. Titles are organized in ten subject sections: agriculture, astronomy, biology, chemistry, computer science, engineering, geology, mathematics, physics, reference. A complete bibliographic citation is given for each entry, plus a critical annotation for books. Indexed by author or editor, title, and subject.   Z7401.P778

Current

Science and technology annual reference review. 1989– . Phoenix : Oryx, c1989– . Annual. ISSN 1041-2557. $74.50.   **EA8**
   Ed. by H. Robert Malinowsky.
   Also referred to as *STARR*.
   Reviews a broad range of scientific and technical reference publications, including textbooks, manuals, directories, and bibliographies. The signed reviews range from 200 to 500 words, with some 600 or more reviews per volume. Title, author, subject, and type of library indexes. Complements the science section of *American reference books annual* (*Guide* AA476).   Z7401.S357

●**Scientific and technical books and serials in print** [computer file]. N.Y. : Bowker, 1990– .   **EA9**
   Machine-readable version of *Scientific and technical books and serials in print* (*Guide* EA29).
   File size: about 200,000 records. Available online (ORBIT, BRS, DIALOG, updated monthly) and in CD-ROM as part of *SciTech reference plus* (*Supplement* EA10).
   A standard source for scientific and technical books and serials, providing multiple access points to some 130,000 books and 18,000 serials.

●**SciTech reference plus** [computer file]. [N.Y.] : Bowker, c1989– .   **EA10**
   Available in CD-ROM (Bowker). Updated annually.
   Represents the merger of five scientific and technical information sources and databases: (1) *American men & women of science* (*Guide* EA221); (2) science and technology citations from *Books in print* (*Guide* AA590); (3) *Directory of American research and technology* (*Supplement* EA62); (4) scientific and technical periodicals from *Ulrich's international periodicals directory* (*Supplement* AE8); and (5) *Corporate technology directory* (*Corptech*) on a CD-ROM compact disc. Sources are searched individually or in combination by various search criteria such as name, keyword, or address. A variety of formatted displays and printouts is possible.

General and juvenile

Kennedy, DayAnn M. Science & technology in fact and fiction : a guide to children's books / DayAnn M. Kennedy, Stella S. Spangler, Mary Ann Vanderwerf. N.Y. : Bowker, c1990. 319 p. ISBN 0-8352-2708-1.   **EA11**
   An annotated guide to children's literature for ages up to 11 years that arranges entries for some 500 recommended works of fiction and nonfiction under the two broad categories of science and technology. Each entry includes a complete bibliographic description, a summary of the work, and evaluative comments on the literary and scientific qualities of the book. Indexed by author, title, illustrator, subject, and reading level.
                                                      Z7401.K46

————— Science & technology in fact and fiction : a guide to young adult books / DayAnn M. Kennedy, Stella S. Spangler, Mary Ann Vanderwerf. N.Y. : Bowker, c1990. 363 p. ISBN 0-8352-2710-3.   **EA12**
   Similar in purpose and arrangement to the author's guide to children's books (above), this evaluative bibliography reviews fiction and non fiction titles for reading levels grade 3 to 12+. Excludes works about the life sciences. Author, title, subject, and reading level indexes.   Z7401.K46

Richter, Bernice. The Museum of Science and Industry basic list of children's science books, 1973–1984 / comp. by Bernice Richter and Duane Wenzel. Chicago : Amer. Lib. Assoc., 1985. 154 p. ISBN 0-8389-3294-0. $9.75.
                                                      EA13
   "This bibliography of science trade literature is an extension of the Museum of Science and Industry's Kresge Library and its annual Children's Science Book Fair."—*Pref.* Some 1,100 entries include bibliographic description; contents summary; reading level; evaluative rating; citations to reviews. Appendixes list publishers, adult sourcebooks, children's science magazines, and review journals. Author and title indexes.
   Updated by: Z7401.R49

The Museum of Science and Industry basic list of children's science books. Chicago : Amer. Lib. Assoc., c1985– . Annual.   **EA14**
                                                      Z7401.M87

Wolff, Kathryn. AAAS science book list, 1978–1986 / comp. and ed. by Kathryn Wolff, Susan M. O'Connell, and Valerie J. Montenegro. Wash. : American Association for the Advancement of Science, 1986. 568 p. (AAAS publication, 85–24). ISBN 0-87168-315-6. **EA15**

"A selected and annotated list of science and mathematics books which supplements the *AAAS science book list* [*Guide* EA31] and the *AAAS science book list supplement* [*Guide* EA33] for secondary school students, college undergraduates, teachers, and nonspecialist readers."—*t.p.* Based on reviews published in *Science books & films* (*Guide* EA32). Arranged by Dewey Decimal Classification. Author index; title and subject index.
Q181.A1A68

Translations

Consolidated index of translations into English II : 1967–1984 cumulation of *Translations register-index*. Chicago : National Translations Center, 1986. 3 v. ISBN 0-935599-17-7 (pbk. : set). $450.00. ISBN 0-935599-21-5 (microfiche). $300.00. **EA16**

Updates the 1969 ed. (*Guide* EA38) which covered 1953–66.

Cover title (all volumes): CITE II.

Cumulates information previously listed in *Translations register-index* (*Guide* EA39) for 250,000 translations of scientific and technical articles originally published in journals and serials. Listing is alphabetical by title of journal, then year of publication, volume, issue, and pages. CODEN, ISSN, and a source for obtaining copy are indicated in each entry. Directory of sources appears in each volume. Z7403.C79

World translations index : a joint publication of International Translations Centre [and] Centre national de la recherche scientifique in cooperation with the National Translations Center at the John Crerar Library of the University of Chicago. Vol. 1, no. 1– . Delft, Netherlands : International Translations Centre, 1987– . Ten no. a year. ISSN 0259-8264. **EA17**

Formed by the merger of *Translations register-index* (*Guide* EA39), which ceased with v. 20, 1986, and *World transindex* (*Guide* EA42), which ceased with v. 9, 1986. Z7403.W95

Periodicals

Gascoigne, Robert Mortimer. A historical catalogue of scientific periodicals, 1665–1900 : with a survey of their development. N.Y. : Garland, 1985. 205 p. (Garland reference library of the humanities, v. 583). ISBN 0-8240-8752-6. **EA18**

A companion to Robert M. Gascoigne's *A historical catalogue of scientists and scientific books*, 1984 (*Guide* EA228a). Pt. 1 contains citations to some 900 scientific periodicals, arranged chronologically by subject. Pts. 2–3 analyze and review the development of periodical literature for the sciences. Bibliography of sources; general index by author, title, and place. More selective than Henry C. Bolton's *Catalogue of scientific and technical periodicals 1665–1895* (*Guide* EA47). Z7403.G3

Bibliography

Linda Hall Library. Serials holdings in the Linda Hall Library [as of April 30] 1989. Kansas City, Mo. : The Library, 1989. 800 p. **EA19**

First issued 1967; previous ed., 1986.

An alphabetical arrangement of some 24,000 serial titles at the library through April 1989. Holdings information and frequent cross-references make this a useful directory for the identification and location of scientific and technical serial publications. Z7403.L65a

Union list of scientific serials in Canadian libraries / comp. and ed. in the Library of the National Research Council. [1st ed.]– . Ottawa : The Library, 1957– . Biennial, 1967– . ISSN 0082-7657. **EA20**

At head of title: National Research Council Canada. Conseil national de recherches Canada. Title on added t.p.: *Catalogue collectif des publications scientifiques dans les bibliothèques canadiennes.*

Lists more than 65,000 scientific, technical, and medical serial titles representing the holdings of 294 Canadian libraries. Entries are arranged by title and include complete bibliographic description and holdings information. The file "is available for online searching on CISTI's [Canada Institute for Scientific and Technical Information] CAN/OLE system (Union File) and on DOBIS."—*Pref.* Z7403.U3425

Japanese

Kokuritsu Kokkai Toshokan (Japan). Directory of Japanese scientific periodicals, 1988 / National Diet Library. Tokyo : The Library, 1989. 2271 p. **EA21**

Previous ed., 1974 (*Guide* EA54).

A comprehensive, classified listing of current serials published in Japan in science, medicine, agriculture, and technology. Entries include title in Japanese, romanized Japanese, and Western language; publisher name and address; price; language of text; and ISSN. Indexes by romanized and Western-language title and by editor and publisher. Z7403.J312

Abbreviations

Report series codes dictionary / Eleanor J. Aronson, ed. 3rd ed. Detroit : Gale, c1986. 647 p. ISBN 0-8103-2147-5. $175.00. **EA22**

2nd ed., 1973, had title: *Dictionary of report series codes* (*Guide* EA60).

Subtitle: A guide to more than 20,000 alphanumeric codes used to identify technical reports, arranged both by code and by corporate author.

Section 1 is arranged alphabetically by report code series and Section 2 by the name of the issuing organization. The "information is derived from the unclassified and unlimited cataloging records of the National Technical Information Service (NTIS), the Office of Scientific and Technical Information (OSTI) under the Department of Energy (DOE), the Defense Technical Information Center (DTIC), and the National Aeronautics and Space Administration (NASA), as received in NTIS during the period 1979–May 1985."—*Introd.* Previous edition contains information about report codes prior to 1979, hence will continue to be useful. Z6945.A2R45

INDEXES AND ABSTRACT JOURNALS

●**Applied science & technology index** [computer file]. N.Y. : H.W. Wilson, 1983– . **EA23**

Machine-readable version of *Applied science and technology index* (*Guide* EA66).

File size: 300,000 records. Available online (BRS, WIL-

SONLINE, updated twice weekly), in CD-ROM (Wilson, updated quarterly), and on magnetic tape (Wilson).

Indexes some 335 English-language periodicals, Oct. 1983 to the present. Besides searching by subject words, the electronic versions provide multiple approaches, including article authors and titles. User guides available.

●**Current contents on diskette** [computer file]. Philadelphia : Institute for Scientific Information, 1989– . **EA24**
Machine-readable version of *Current contents* (*Guide* EA67).

Coverage: current. Updated weekly. Available from publisher on diskette formatted for IBM, MacIntosh, or NEC.

Available for six of the *Current contents* sections: (1) Agriculture, biology & environmental sciences; (2) Clinical medicine; (3) Engineering, technology & applied sciences; (4) Life sciences; (5) Physical, chemical & earth sciences; (6) Social & behavioral sciences. The contents pages of some 4,500 periodical titles may be browsed or searched by means of a variety of access points such as author, title keyword, and journal title. Article abstracts are scheduled to be included in 1991/92. Information on weekly diskettes does not cumulate. User's guide.

●**Current contents search** [computer file]. Philadelphia : Institute for Scientific Information. **EA25**
Machine-readable version of the seven printed sections of *Current contents* (*Guide* EA67).

Coverage: current (the most recent three to four months). Updated weekly. Available online (BRS, DIALOG) and on magnetic tape (Institute for Scientific Information).

Provides access by author, author's address, title keywords, and journal title to the table of contents of some 6,500 current journals.

●**General science index** [computer file]. N.Y. : H.W. Wilson, 1984– . **EA26**
Machine-readable version of *General science index* (*Guide* EA68).

File size: 150,000 records. Available online (BRS, WILSONLINE, updated twice weekly), CD-ROM (Wilson, updated quarterly), magnetic tape (Wilson).

Indexes 111 English-language science periodicals, from May 1984 to date, offering approaches (including searches by article author and title and by journal name) that are not possible in the printed version. User documentation.

Index to scientific book contents : ISBC. Philadelphia : Institute for Scientific Information, c1986– . Quarterly with annual cumulations. $990.00. **EA27**
Indexes chapters from multiauthored scientific books and books that are part of multiauthored series. Disciplines covered include the life sciences and clinical medicine, the physical sciences, and agriculture. Complete descriptive entries for works are arranged by code number; access is provided through indexes to author/editor, book and chapter title keywords, author affiliation, and geographic location of author. A unique index to information generally unavailable from most other abstracting and indexing sources. Z7401.I37

●**NTIS bibliographic database** [computer file]. Springfield, Va. : National Technical Information Service, 1964– . **EA28**
File size: more than 1.5 million records. Available online (BRS, CAN/OLE, Data-Star, DIALOG, ORBIT, OCLC EPIC, STN, updated biweekly) on CD-ROM (DIALOG, SilverPlatter, Faxon, updated with replacement disks quarterly), and on magnetic tape (NTIS).

Corresponds in large part to *Government reports announcements & index*, *Government reports annual index*, and their predecessors (*Guide* EA78–80). Cites federally produced or sponsored technical reports, machine-readable data files, software, translations, and licensable government inventions as

well as references to some foreign government research publications.

●**Science citation index. Compact disc edition** [computer file]. Philadelphia : Institute for Scientific Information, 1980– . **EA29**
Machine-readable version of *Science citation index* (*Guide* EA72).

Coverage: 1980– , one disk per year. Current disk updated quarterly.

Searchable by author, title keyword, journal title, address, and cited author. Permits Boolean searching and truncation, and features displays of references from the current citations and retrieval of related records through common citation patterns. User guide.

Science citation index. Philadelphia : Institute for Scientific Information. **EA30**
For earlier volumes and annotation, see *Guide* EA72.

Five-year cumulations have been published for 1980–84 and 1985–89. A 1945–54 cumulation covers a period not previously indexed. Z7401.S365

●**SCISEARCH** [computer file]. Philadelphia : Institute for Scientific Information, 1974– . **EA31**
Machine-readable version of *Science citation index* (*Guide* EA72).

File size: 8 million records. Updated weekly. Available online (DataStar, DIALOG) and on magnetic tape (publisher).

Covers some 4,500 periodicals in science, medicine, and technology indexed in *Science citation index* plus some additional periodicals listed in *Current contents* (*Guide* EA67). *SCISEARCH* user guide available from the publisher.

ENCYCLOPEDIAS AND HANDBOOKS

Composite index for CRC handbooks. 3rd ed. Boca Raton, Fla. : CRC Pr., 1990. 3 v. ISBN 0-8493-0284-6. $1,200.00. **EA32**
1st ed., 1971; 2nd ed., 1977.

This work "provides access to information and data contained in over 140,000 pages from 317 handbook volumes [comprising 298 separate titles] published by CRC press [dating from 1969 through 1990]. Indexes from these volumes have been merged to form a single, unified composite index."—*Pref.* The 1st ed. indexed 10 volumes, the 2nd ed. indexed 58. This edition indexes most of the volumes published since 1977, and a few before that, and includes the 71st ed. (1990) of the *CRC handbook of chemistry and physics*. A CD-ROM edition, which is a machine-readable version of the entire contents of the printed edition and allows searching combined terms with Boolean operators, is included with the printed edition. Regular supplements are planned, the first of which is nearly finished; these will include updates of the CD-ROM edition. In spite of its high price, this work and its companion CD-ROM are essential to the efficient use of the CRC press publications and give users full access to the subject content of all volumes, including those not held locally. QD65.C74

Encyclopedia of physical science and technology / Robert A. Meyers, ed. Orlando, Fla. : Academic Pr., c1987. 15 v. : ill. ISBN 0-12-226901-2. $2,500 (set). **EA33**
Signed articles by specialists begin with a table of contents, glossary, and introductory definition of the subject. Technical levels of the articles vary, but most are more sophisticated than those in *McGraw-Hill encyclopedia of science & technology* (*Supplement* EA38), and some are at a much higher technical level. Because the titles of articles can be somewhat idiosyncratic, it will generally be necessary to consult the index (v. 15) to

find information. Articles have cross-references and include bibliographies.

Kept up to date by: Q123.E497

Encyclopedia of physical science and technology yearbook. 1989– . San Diego, Calif.: Academic Pr., c1989– . Annual. ISSN 0898-9842. $185.00.   **EA34**
Q123.E4973

The Facts on File scientific yearbook. 1985– . N.Y.: Facts on File, c1985– . Annual. ISSN 0883-0800. $29.95.   **EA35**

Well-illustrated articles report on current, popular topics in science. Glossary of terms; index to names and topics. Useful for secondary school students and general readers, but lacks bibliographies or sources for additional reading.   Q9.F32

Geigy scientific tables / ed. by C. Lentner. 8th, rev. and enl. ed. [West Caldwell, N.J.]: Ciba-Geigy [Corp.], c1984–90. v. 3–5: ill. ISBN 0-914168-50-9. (In progress).   **EA36**

For v. 1–2 and annotation, see *Guide* EA92.

Contents: v. 3, Physical chemistry, composition of blood, hematology, somatometric data.; v. 4, Biochemistry, metabolism of xenobiotics, inborn errors of metabolism, pharmacogenetics and ecogenetics; v. 5, Heart and circulation.

QP33.5.G4513

●**McGraw-Hill CD-ROM science and technical reference set** [computer file]. N.Y.: McGraw-Hill, Reference Technology, Inc., Fulcrum Technologies, Inc., c1987.   **EA37**

Machine-readable version of *McGraw-Hill concise encyclopedia of science and technology*, 1983 (*Guide* EA96) and *McGraw-Hill dictionary of scientific and technical terms*, 3rd ed., 1984 (*Guide* EA120).

Available in CD-ROM (McGraw-Hill).

Combines 7,300 articles from the *Encyclopedia* and more than 100,000 terms from the *Dictionary*. This version is word and phrase searchable and supports graphics software for illustrations.

McGraw-Hill encyclopedia of science & technology. 6th ed. N.Y.: McGraw-Hill, c1987. 20 v.: ill. ISBN 0-07-079292-5. $1600.00.   **EA38**

5th ed., 1982 (*Guide* EA96).

The new edition of this comprehensive encyclopedia "explores all important developments and achievements since 1982."—*Pref.* Expanded to 20 volumes, with 28 of the 77 major subject areas revised; 7,700 signed articles and 15,000 illustrations, some in color. Many brief, definitional articles have been replaced in favor of longer, more comprehensive treatment of subjects. All article bibliographies were reviewed and revised. Vol. 20 contains a list of contributors, scientific notation schemes, and analytic and topical indexes. A 7th ed. is scheduled for Spring 1992.

§ The publisher has derived other works from this edition: *Computer science source book* (1988. 370 p.); *Fluid mechanics source book* (1988. 274 p.); *McGraw-Hill concise encyclopedia of science and technology* (2nd ed., 1989. 2200 p.); *McGraw-Hill encyclopedia of the geological sciences* (2nd ed., 1988. 722 p.); *Meteorology source book* (1988. 304 p.); *Physical chemistry source book* (1988. 406 p.); *Spectroscopy source book* (1988. 288 p.).   Q121.M3

Van Nostrand's scientific encyclopedia / Douglas M. Considine, ed. 7th ed. N.Y.: Van Nostrand Reinhold, 1989. 2v. (3180 p.): ill. ISBN 0-442-21750-1 (set). $175.00.   **EA39**

6th ed., 1983 (*Guide* EA99).

The new edition of this standard encyclopedia is conveniently published in two volumes. Although emphasis is on short, concise entries, longer, frequently signed articles are included, many with revised and updated bibliographies. Over

3,000 black-and-white illustrations; some 500 tabular summaries. Now includes an extensive alphabetic index of terms.

Q121.V3

DICTIONARIES

General

Barnhart, Robert K. The American Heritage dictionary of science / Robert K. Barnhart; with Sol Steinmetz, managing ed. Boston: Houghton Mifflin, c1986. 740 p.: ill. ISBN 0-395-48367-0. $19.95.   **EA40**

Originally publ. 1986 as *Hammond Barnhart dictionary of science.*

"... designed to support the student in his or her introduction to a first systematic study of the physical and biological sciences."—*Pref.* Defines more than 15,000 words and phrases; definitions indicate subject, and may give derivative or variant forms, a pronunciation key for difficult words, notes about related terms, examples of usage, and word etymologies. Black-and-white line illustrations. A useful, nontechnical source for a variety of scientific disciplines.   Q123.B35

Cambridge dictionary of science and technology / gen. ed. Peter M.B. Walker. Cambridge; N.Y.: Cambridge Univ. Pr., [1990]. 1008 p. ISBN 0-521-39441-4. $39.50.   **EA41**

Rev. ed., 1975, had title: *Dictionary of science and technology* (*Guide* EA117).

British ed., 1988, had title: *Chambers science and technology dictionary.*

Defines 45,000 terms in 100 scientific and technical areas. Short definitions identify a field of specialty for each term and often refer to related headwords. British spelling and usage. Appendixes contain tables of chemical formulas, chemical elements, SI conversion factors, physical constants, animal and plant classifications, SI units, geological eras, paper sizes, and a periodic table. The work is "useful both to the layman and to the professional but will not replace the expert's own specialist dictionaries."—*Pref.* Compact size and sturdy binding make this a good choice for smaller library collections.   Q123.C482

Durbin, Paul T. Dictionary of concepts in the philosophy of science. N.Y.: Greenwood, 1988. 362 p. (Reference sources for the social sciences and humanities, no. 6). ISBN 0-313-22979-1. $59.95.   **EA42**

Summarizes 100 basic controversies in philosophy of science. Topics are arranged alphabetically, with historical and contemporary issues discussed in encyclopedia-length articles. Excellent bibliographies. Accessible to advanced undergraduate and graduate students and educated general readers.

Q174.7.D87

Emiliani, Cesare. Dictionary of the physical sciences: terms, formulas, data. N.Y.: Oxford Univ. Pr., c1987. 365 p.: ill. ISBN 0-19-503651-4. $35.00. ISBN 0-19-503652-2 (pbk.). $19.95.   **EA43**

A convenient compilation of terms, formulas, and data for the disciplines of physics, chemistry, the geological sciences (including related areas in biology), and cosmology (astronomy and astrophysics). Definitions are arranged alphabetically, and often include useful formulas, diagrams, or references to one of the 70 supplementary data tables. A separate bibliography of sources is provided for the tables and illustrations.   Q123.E46

McGraw-Hill dictionary of scientific and technical terms / Sybil P. Parker, ed. in chief. 4th ed. N.Y.: McGraw-

Hill, c1989. 2088, 49 p. : ill. ISBN 0-07-045270-9. $95.00. **EA44**

3rd ed., 1984 (*Guide* EA120).

Brief definitions (now including pronunciation) are given for 100,100 terms, an increase of 7,600 over the previous edition. Entries note field of interest, acronyms, synonyms, and abbreviations. Small black-and-white line drawings and photographs illustrate some 3,000 terms. U.S. customary, SI, and metric units are used. The appendix includes a selection of standard tables and charts: the periodic table, fundamental constants, etc. as well as a biographical listing of noted historical and modern scientists. Continues to be the principal English-language dictionary for science and technology.

Q123.M34

Abbreviations

Murith, Jean. Dictionnaire des abréviations & acronymes scientifiques, techniques, économiques = Dictionary of scientific, technical & economic abbreviations & acronyms. Paris : Lavoisier ; Cambridge, Mass. : Distr. by Lavoisier Pub., c1984. 407 p. ISBN 2-85206-235-6. **EA45**

French and English uses are listed for some 33,000 alphabetically arranged acronyms and abbreviations. Q179.M8

Foreign terms

Czech

Anglicko-český technický slovník / [hlavní redaktorka Blanka Kutinová ; odpovea7dná redaktorka Libuse Malinová]. 4., nezměněné vyd. Praha : SNTL-Nakl. technické literatury, 1985. 1026 p. **EA46**

1st ed., 1969; 3rd ed., 1982.

Lists 78,000 English terms from all branches of engineering and technology with their Czech equivalents. T10.A57

Česko-anglický technický slovník / [autori Zd. Bazant ... et al. ; hlavní redaktorka Blanka Kutinová]. 4., nezměněné vyd. Praha : SNTL-Nakl. technické literatury, 1986. 944 p. **EA47**

Title on added t.p.: *Czech-English technical dictionary*.

1st ed., 1963; 3rd ed., 1983.

A companion volume to the English-Czech dictionary (above). T10.C44

French

Harrap's French and English science dictionary / consultant ed., D.E. Hathway. London : Harrap, 1985. 320, 302 p. ISBN 0-245-54072-5. £17.50. **EA48**

Arranges about 20,000 terms in the physical and life sciences in two sections, English-French and French-English. Entries note the discipline associated with the term and give brief definitions when necessary for clarification. Medical and pharmaceutical terms and taxonomic names are excluded.

Q123.H265

Japanese

Intā Puresu kagaku gijutsu 25-mango daijiten / [executive ed. Kabe Jun'ichi ; ed. Fujioka Keisuke]. Dai 1-han. Tōkyō : Intā Puresu, 1983. 2 v. ISBN 4-87087-001-0 (set). Y88000. **EA49**

Colophon title: *Inter Press dictionary of science and engineering*.

Contents: v. 1, Japanese-English; v. 2, English-Japanese.

This massive dictionary, with more than 100,000 headwords in each volume, is especially strong in engineering and technology. Lacks any English introduction or explanation.

T10.I57

Polyglot

Dictionary of scientific and technical terminology / A.S. Markov... [et. al.]. The Hague ; Boston : Martinus Nijhoff ; Hingham, Mass. : Distr. by Kluwer Boston, 1984. 496 p. ISBN 90-201-1667-3. **EA50**

A five-language polyglot dictionary of 9,000 terms, arranged alphabetically by English term with equivalents in other languages. German, French, Dutch, and Russian indexes.

T10.D564

Portuguese

Fürstenau, Eugênio. Novo dicionário de termos técnicos inglês-português. 15a. ed. São Paulo, Brasil : Editora Globo, [1989]. 2 v. (1413 p.) : ill. ISBN 85-250-0251-8. **EA51**

5th ed., 1974 (*Guide* EA152); 13th ed., 1986.

About 30,000 terms are new or revised, including words from such rapidly growing fields as astronautics, nuclear physics, and computer sciences. T10.F87

Spanish

Thomann, Arthur E. Elsevier's dictionary of technology : English-Spanish = Elsevier diccionario de tecnología : inglés-español. Amsterdam ; N.Y. : Elsevier, 1990. 2 v. ISBN 0-444-88069-0. **EA52**

Includes some 250,000 terms drawn from such fields as metallurgy, mining, drilling, engineering, electronics, and management. Prefers internationally accepted forms of Spanish terms, but gives geographical indications when local forms are used. T10.T46

DIRECTORIES

Current research in Britain : CRB. [1st. ed.](1984)– . Boston Spa, Wetherby, West Yorkshire : British Library Lending Division, c1985– . Frequency varies. **EA53**

Supersedes *Research in British universities, polytechnics and colleges*, 1979/80–1984 (*Guide* EA176).

Each edition is in 4 v.: *Physical sciences* (annual, two parts); *Biological sciences* (annual, two parts); *Social sciences* (annual); *The humanities* (biennial).

Provides information on more than 60,000 research projects at some 300 British institutions. The main arrangement is by institutional and departmental code numbers; within code numbers, listings are in alphabetical order by the name of the principle investigator and include the names of all researchers, a brief description of the project, project dates, sponsors, and publications. Departmental addresses and the names of department heads are also included. Institution/department index.

H62.5.G7C87

Directory of technical and scientific directories : a world bibliographic guide to medical, agricultural, industrial, and natural science directories. 5th ed. Burnt Mill, Harlow, Essex, England : Longman ; Phoenix : Oryx, 1988. 1 v. ISBN 0-582-00602-3.   **EA54**

1st–4th eds. had title: *Directory of scientific directories*.

Listings are relatively current, since all were published within the past six years. New to this edition are technical encyclopedias, dictionaries, and handbooks. Indexes: author/editor/compiler; directory title; publisher (with address).

Z7405.D55D57

European research centres : a directory of scientific, technological, agricultural and biomedical laboratories. 8th ed. Burnt Mill, Harlow, Essex, England : Longman ; Detroit : Distr. by Gale, 1990. 2 v. (1751 p.). ISBN 0-582-06124-5. $545.00.   **EA55**

5th ed., 1982 (*Guide* EA171); 7th ed., 1988.

Lists more than 17,000 research centers from 31 countries. Entries are grouped by country, then alphabetically by name. Listings typically include official name, address, telephone and telex numbers, contact person, activities, annual expenditures, and publications. Subject and organization name indexes.

Q180.E9

European sources of scientific and technical information. 8th ed. Burnt Mill, Harlow, Essex, England : Longman ; Detroit : Gale, 1989. 375 p. ISBN 0-582-03379-9.   **EA56**

5th ed., 1981 (*Guide* EA172); 7th ed., 1986.

The format of previous editions is retained. Some 1,400 western and eastern European organizations are arranged by country within 25 topical or subject headings. Organization name and subject indexes. A 9th ed. is due in 1991.

T10.65.E8E84

Libraries, information centers and databases in science and technology : a world guide = Bibliotheken, Informationszentren und Datenbasen für Wissenschaft und Technik : ein internationales Verzeichnis. 1st ed.– . München ; N.Y. : K.G. Saur, 1984– . Biennial. ISSN 0176-7593. $195.00.   **EA57**

A directory of 14,000 scientific and technical libraries, information and documentation centers, and data bank producers in 141 countries. Entries are arranged by country and include name in original language, address, telephone, year founded, director, collecting interests, holdings, online and loan services. Some 300 databases are briefly described. Name and subject indexes. Similar information is found in *World guide to libraries* (*Guide* AB46).

Z675.T3L56

Longman guide to world science and technology. v. 1 (1982)– . London ; N.Y. : Longman ; Detroit : Distr. by Gale, 1982– . Irregular.   **EA58**

Contents: v. 1, *Science and technology in the Middle East* (1982); v. 2, *... in Latin America* (1983); v. 3, *... in China* (1984); v. 4, *... in Japan* (1984); v. 5, *... in the USA* (1986); v. 6, *... in the USSR* (1988); v. 7, *... in France and Belgium* (1988); v. 8, *... in Eastern Europe* (1988); v. 9, *... in Scandinavia* (1989); v. 10 *... in Africa* (1989); v. 11, *... in Australasia, Antarctica and the Pacific Islands* (1990); [v. 12], *... in India, Pakistan, Bangladesh and Sri Lanka* (1990); [v. 13], *... in the Federal Republic of Germany* (1990).

A series of individually authored volumes reporting on the current state of the scientific and technical enterprise in various countries. Volumes vary in organization and style, but generally provide detailed reviews of the development, current activities, and research programs of official governmental bureaus, semiofficial agencies, private-sector industrial organizations,

and professional associations. Addresses and some statistical data are given. Subject and organization indexes.

Scientific and technical organizations and agencies directory / Margaret Labash Young, ed. 2nd ed. Detroit : Gale, c1987. 2 v. (1670 p.). ISBN 0-8103-2103-3. $185.00 (set).   **EA59**

1st ed., 1985 (*Guide* EA177).

Expanded to include 15,000 U.S., Canadian, and international organizations in the physical and applied sciences and engineering. Entries are grouped in 19 chapters based on type of organization (e.g., federal government agencies, state agencies, standards organizations). Name and keyword indexes.

Q145.S36

World guide to scientific associations and learned societies / [ed., Michael Sachs]. 5th ed. München ; N. Y. : K. G. Saur, 1990. 672 p. ISBN 3-598-20530-9. $275.00.   **EA60**

For annotation, see *Supplement* CA50.   Q145.W9267

SOCIETIES AND CONGRESSES

Publications

British Library. Document Supply Centre. Index of conference proceedings. ICP 256 (Jan. 1989)– . Boston Spa, U.K. : The Centre, 1989– . Monthly, with annual cumulation. ISSN 0144-7556. ISSN 0305-5183.   **EA61**

Supersedes: British Library. Lending Division. *Index of conference proceedings received*, 1973–88 (*Guide* EA189).

Coverage extends to all conference publications regardless of subject, language, or format with the exception of audiovisual material. About 18,000 titles are added each year. The arrangement is alphabetical by keyterms which are derived from the conference title and/or sponsoring agency. Within a heading, entries are arranged by the date of the meeting. Information for each conference consists of title, sponsor, date, meeting location, and Document Supply Centre identifier code.

§ A 25-year cumulation (1964–88) is available in microfiche. A CD-ROM version of the series entitled *Boston Spa conferences* (Boston Spa: Document Supply Centre) is scheduled for release in 1991.   Z5051.B862

LABORATORIES

Directory of American research and technology / ed. by Jaques Cattell Press. 20th ed. (1986)– . N.Y. : Bowker, c1986– . Annual. ISSN 0886-0076. $259.95.   **EA62**

Title varies: 19th ed. (1985) had title *Industrial research laboratories of the United States* (*Guide* EA196).

Listings cover nongovernmental facilities currently active in basic and applied research, including the development of products and processes. Of the 11,322 organizations in the 1991 edition, 6,544 are parent companies listed alphabetically by name and 4,768 are subsidiaries listed under a parent company entry. Each entry includes name, address, telephone, executive officers, professional staff, and research and development interests. Geographic, personnel, and research and development classification indexes.

§ The *Directory* is available online from Pergamon Infoline and in CD-ROM as part of *SciTech reference plus* (*Supplement* EA10).   T176.I65

Directory of federal laboratory & technology resources : a guide to services, facilities, and expertise / prepared by the Center for the Utilization of Federal Technology, U.S. Dept. of Commerce, National Technical Information Service. Springfield, Va. : The Service : For sale by the National Technical Information Service, 1986/87– . Biennial. $39.00. **EA63**

Continues *Directory of federal technology resources* (1984). Superintendent of Documents classification: C 51.19/2-2: . Available in machine-readable form online from BRS.

Lists some 1,000 federal government research centers, testing facilities, laboratories, and special technology centers which will share expertise, equipment, or facilities with commercial businesses and universities. Information includes name, address, telephone, contact person, and description of facility. Indexed by subject, state, facility name, and government agency. T21.D57

Directory of testing laboratories / comp. by ASTM. Philadelphia : American Society for Testing and Materials, c1987– . ISSN 0895-7886. $40.00 (members); $50.00 (non-members). **EA64**

Continues: American Society for Testing and Materials, *Directory of testing laboratories, commercial-institutional*, 6th ed., 1982 (*Guide* EA195).

A geographic listing of about 1,000 commercial testing laboratories in the U.S. and Canada, with some listings for foreign laboratories. In addition to name, address, and telephone, provides information on the laboratory's specialty, equipment, testing capabilities, and staff. Name and field/specialty indexes. TA416.5.U6D55

MUSEUMS

Danilov, Victor J. America's science museums. N.Y. : Greenwood, c1990. 483 p. ISBN 0-313-25865-1. $65.00. **EA65**

The nature, history, facilities, collections, and programs of 480 scientific and technologic museums and related institutions such as botanic gardens, zoos, and observatories are described. Institutions are selected for their stature in the field, speciality, age, or novelty. Entries are organized in 12 subject categories. The introduction to each category reviews the development and present state of the particular type of science museum. Selected bibliography and name index. Lacks a geographical index. Q105.U5D36

SCIENTIFIC ILLUSTRATION

Council of Biology Editors. Scientific Illustration Committee. Illustrating science : standards for publication. Bethesda, Md. : The Council, c1988. 296 p. : ill. (some col.). ISBN 0-914340-05-0. $49.95. **EA66**

A style manual which aims to "develop specific standards and guidelines for publication of illustrated scientific materials."—*Pref.* Chapters review illustration techniques emphasizing standards of reproduction and publication. Glossary of graphic arts terms, annotated bibliography, and topics index. Q222.C68

The Guild handbook of scientific illustration / ed. by Elaine R.S. Hodges . . . [et al.]. N.Y. : Van Nostrand Reinhold, c1989. 575 p., [12] p. of plates : ill. (some col.). ISBN 0-442-23681-6. $70.00. **EA67**

Sponsored by the Guild of Natural Science Illustrators.

A comprehensive review, with more than 600 black-and-white and color illustrations, of the principles and techniques of scientific illustration. An appendix lists sources for artist's materials and equipment, degree programs, professional organizations, business information, and a bibliography. Subject index and index to illustrators. Q222.G85

HISTORY OF SCIENCE

Bibliography

Batschelet, Margaret. Early American scientific and technical literature : an annotated bibliography of books, pamphlets, and broadsides. Metuchen, N.J. : Scarecrow, 1990. 136 p. ISBN 0-8108-2318-7. **EA68**

Offers 833 annotated citations to works published in the U.S., 1665–1799. Entries are arranged by date within three sequences: medical; technical science; nature and physical science. Author and subject indexes. Z7402.B38

Harkanyi, Katalin. The natural sciences and American scientists in the revolutionary era : a bibliography. N.Y. : Greenwood, 1990. 510 p. (Bibliographies and indexes in American history, no. 17). ISBN 0-313-26547-X. $65.00. **EA69**

An extensive bibliography of primary and secondary works including monographs, serials, pamphlets, and documentary sources concerning science and scientists of the American revolutionary period, 1760–89. Entries are arranged alphabetically under nine topics and often include descriptive annotations. Appendixes give biographical details of scientists. Subject index. Arrangement and typography are drawbacks to effective use. Z7405.H6H37

Isis cumulative bibliography 1976–1985 : a bibliography of the history of science formed from *Isis* critical bibliographies 101–110 indexing literature published from 1975 through 1984 / ed. by John Neu. Boston : G.K. Hall in conjunction with the History of Science Society, c1989. 2 v. ISBN 0-8161-9058-5 (v. 1). $62.50. ISBN 0-8161-9069-0 (v. 2). $62.50. **EA70**

For earlier cumulations, see *Guide* EA206–207.

Contents: v. 1, Persons and institutions. (587 p.); v. 2, Subjects, periods and civilizations (911 p.).

This second supplement to the original 1913–65 series continues to cumulate references from the critical bibliographies published annually in *Isis.* Z7405.H6I2

Chronologies

Asimov, Isaac. Asimov's chronology of science and discovery. N.Y. : Harper & Row, c1989. 707 p. : col. ill. ISBN 0-06-015612-0. $29.95. **EA71**

Chronicles scientific, medical, and technical discoveries and achievements from the advent of human bipedality in 4,000,000 BCE to the greenhouse effect in 1988. Written for a general readership, this year by year historical record emphasizes developments of interest to a modern American audience. Index of names and subjects. No bibliography or list of works consulted. Q125.A765

Hellemans, Alexander. The timetables of science : a chronology of the most important people and events in the history of science / Alexander Hellemans and Bryan

Bunch. N.Y. : Simon and Schuster, c1988. 656 p. ISBN 0-671-62130-0. $29.95.　　　　**EA72**

On t.p. the registered trademark symbol "TM" in superscript follows "science" in the title.

Chronologically organized tables record events, discoveries, and inventions from the time of the appearance of hominids to 1988. Each table's entries are grouped under headings such as astronomy, physics, earth sciences, and medicine. Short overviews of major scientific periods and brief information inserts in the tables themselves provide historical context. The timetable format promotes examination of simultaneous events, but limits the amount of information conveyed. Name and topical indexes.　　　　Q125.H557

Mount, Ellis. Milestones in science and technology : the ready reference guide to discoveries, inventions, and facts / by Ellis Mount and Barbara A. List. Phoenix : Oryx, 1987. 141 p. ISBN 0-89774-260-5. $27.50.　　**EA73**

An alphabetically arranged selection of 1,000 significant topics in science and technology from the prehistoric period to 1987. "Topics cover basic discoveries as well as practical inventions, and range from relativity and genetics to the electric motor and DDT."—*Foreword.* Each entry gives a brief description of the topic, and includes dates, relevant persons, and a source for additional reading. Indexes by personal name, date, place, and field of study. Annotated bibliography of references.　　　　Q199.M68

Parkinson, Claire L. Breakthroughs : a chronology of great achievements in science and mathematics, 1200–1930. Boston : G.K. Hall, c1985. 576 p. : ill. ISBN 0-8161-8706-1.　　　　**EA74**

Events and accomplishments important for the development of western science are listed chronologically in 9 categories: astronomy, biology, chemistry, earth sciences, health sciences, mathematics, meteorology, physics, and supplemental topics. Each event is described briefly, referring to important figures, published works, and the subsequent influence or use of the development. Subject and name indexes, the latter enhanced with birth/death dates, nationality, and alternate names. Bibliography of original and secondary sources. Useful for college libraries and history of science collections; more specialized than *Asimov's chronology of science and discovery* or Alexander Hellemans's *The timetables of science* (both above).　　　　Q125.P327

BIOGRAPHY

American men & women of science. 17th ed. (1989–90). N.Y. : Bowker, c1989. 8 v.　　　　**EA75**

15th ed., 1982 (*Guide* EA221); 16th ed., 1986.

Includes approximately 127,000 U.S. and Canadian scientists, 3,831 new to this edition. Established criteria for inclusion remain unchanged from previous editions. Index (v. 8) lists individual names by specialty within 10 major discipline groups: Agricultural and forest sciences; Biological sciences; Chemistry; Computer sciences; Engineering; Environmental, earth and marine sciences; Mathematics; Medical and health sciences; Physics and astronomy; Other professional fields. Included in the CD-ROM source *SCITECH reference plus* (*Supplement* EA10).　　　　Q141.A474

Dictionary of scientific biography : Supplement II / Frederic L. Holmes, ed. in chief. N.Y. : Scribner, [1990]. 2 v. ISBN 0-684-18294-7. $160.00.　　　　**EA76**

For basic set and *Suppl. I*, see *Guide* EA227.

Also issued as v. 17–18 of the *Dictionary of scientific biography.*

Published under the auspices of the American Council of Learned Societies.

Maintains the principles of selection and subject scope developed for the original work, but extends coverage to scientists active during the 20th century. The majority of the 445 biographees died between 1970 and 1981. All biographical essays are signed and include bibliographies of original and secondary works. Name and topics index and list of scientists by field in v. 2.　　　　Q141.D5

National Academy of Sciences (U.S.). Biographical memoirs. v. 1– . Wash. : National Academy of Sciences, 1877– . Irregular. ISSN 0077-2933.　　　　**EA77**

Deceased members of the National Academy of Sciences are the subjects of biographical essays written by colleagues. Articles include a portrait and bibliography of the subject's published scientific work. Recent volumes have a cumulative index to the series.　　　　Q141.N2

Ogilvie, Marilyn Bailey. Women in science : antiquity through the nineteenth century : a biographical dictionary with annotated bibliography. Cambridge, Mass. : MIT Pr., c1986. 254 p. ISBN 0-262-15031-X. $25.00.　　　　**EA78**

Includes some 200 women who made significant contributions to science prior to 1910. Biographical entries vary in length from a few lines to several pages. All listings include references to the extensive bibliography of sources. Name index.　　　　Q141.O34

Royal Society (Great Britain). Biographical memoirs of fellows of the Royal Society. v. 1 (1955)– . London : Royal Society of London, 1955– . ISSN 0080-4606.　　　　**EA79**

Vol. 26 (1980) includes a subject index (i.e., by biographee), for *Obituary notices* (v. 1–9; 1932–54; *Guide* EA233) and *Biographical memoirs* (v. 1–26; 1955–80; *Guide* EA234); v. 35 (1990) includes a similar index for *Biographical memoirs* (v. 27–35; 1981–90).　　　　Q41.R9

Sammons, Vivian O. Blacks in science and medicine. N.Y. : Hemisphere Pub. Corp., c1990. 293 p. ISBN 0-89116-665-3. $40.00.　　　　**EA80**

Presents biographical information, based on published sources, for more than 1,500 living and deceased individuals who have contributed to the development of science, medicine, and technology, focusing on contributions by African Americans in the U.S. Entries are brief, in who's who style, but include citations to the source material. Extensive bibliography. A very useful index to biographees is arranged by such categories as occupation, discipline, or invention, and notes "first black" and "first (black or white)" achievements.　　　　Q141.B58

Who's who in frontiers of science and technology. 2nd ed. Chicago : Marquis Who's Who, c1985. 1 v.　　　　**EA81**

Continues *Who's who in frontier science and technology,* 1984 (*Guide* EA236).

Uses the same format and selection as the earlier title. Includes approximately 14,000 scientists and technologists currently working in North America. Fields and subspecialities index.

Who's who in science in Europe. 6th ed. London : Longman ; Detroit : Distr. by Gale, 1989. 4 v. (2500 p.). ISBN 0-582-04737-4. £450.00.　　　　**EA82**

4th ed., 1984 (*Guide* EA237); 5th ed., 1987.

Contents: v. 1, United Kingdom; v. 2–3, European Community countries, A–Z; v. 4, Non-EC countries and Eastern Europe.

Expanded to include approximately 55,000 scientists and engineers from Europe (excluding the U.S.S.R.), most entries being revised from previous editions. Each volume has two sections: biographical entries for each country in alphabetic order by surname; subject specialty index arranged by country. Lacks comprehensive name index. Q141.W52

Indexes

Elliott, Clark A. Biographical index to American science : the seventeenth century to 1920. N.Y. : Greenwood, 1990. 300 p. (Bibliographies and indexes in American history, no. 16). ISBN 0-313-26566-6. $55.00. **EA83**

Supplements in part the author's *Biographical dictionary of American science: the seventeenth through the nineteenth centuries* (*Guide* EA228).

Biographical entries have been compiled from standard biographical directories, dictionaries, and indexes for 2,850 American scientists deceased prior to 1920; for lesser-known individuals information is drawn from sources such as obituaries and local histories. Principal focus is on the natural and physical sciences, but some engineers, inventors, and physicians are included if relevant to the development of American science. Entries are arranged alphabetically by name and include year of birth and death, scientific field, occupation, any references in the *National union catalog of manuscript collections*, 1959–84 (*Guide* DB64), and citations to sources of additional information. Index of names by scientific field. Q141.E373

Herzenberg, Caroline L. Women scientists from antiquity to the present : an index : an international reference listing and biographical directory of some notable women scientists from ancient to modern times. West Cornwall, Conn. : Locust Hill Pr., 1986. 200 p. ISBN 0-933951-01-9. $30.00. **EA84**

Identifies 2,500 women who worked in or contributed to the development of science, medicine, engineering, and technology. Brief alphabetical listings provide name, birth and death dates or date of activity, nationality, field of work, and reference to the bibliography of sources. Index of names by specialty and field of work. Q141.H475

Pelletier, Paul A. Prominent scientists : an index to collective biographies. 2nd ed. N.Y. : Neal-Schuman, c1985. 356 p. ISBN 0-918212-78-2. $34.95. **EA85**

1st ed., 1980 (*Guide* EA240).

Coverage extended to 12,211 scientists, with citations from 262 sources published primarily 1960–83. Q141.P398

PATENTS

Phillips, John B. Directory of patent depository libraries / originally comp. by John B. Phillips ; recompiled, rev., and ed. by James A. Arshem. 1st ed., rev. "f", including changes through September 1989. [Wash.?] : Patent and Trademark Office, U.S. Dept. of Commerce, Patent Depository Library Program, [1988]. 179 [i.e. 251] l. : charts. **EA86**

1st ed., 1986.

A geographic listing of all U.S. patent depository libraries; describes the staff, collections, and services available for public use. Z675.D4P55

Rimmer, Brenda M. International guide to official industrial property publications. 2nd ed. London : British Library, Science Reference and Information Service, 1988– . 1 v. (loose-leaf) : ill. ISBN 0-7123-0754-0. **EA87**

1st ed. (1985) had title: *Guide to official industrial property publications*.

This handbook describes the official literature that records patents, designs, and trademarks for some 50 nations and international patenting authorities. The principles of industrial property registration are described in an introductory chapter. Invaluable information is included about the historical development of patent systems and contemporary legislation and publications. Subject/title index. T210.R545

STANDARDS

Index and directory of industry standards. Englewood, Colo. : Information Handling Services ; Irvine, Calif. : distr. by Global Engineering Documents, c1991. 7 v. ISBN 0-89847-008-0. $550.00 (set). **EA88**

Previous edition in 4 v., 1989–90.

Contents: v. 1, U. S. standards (Subject index); v. 2, U. S. standards (Numeric index); v. 3–4, International and non-U. S. national standards (Subject index A–Z); v. 5, International and non-U. S. national standards (Numeric index); v. 6, DIN German standards (Subject index); v. 7, DIN German standards (Numeric listing).

Lists over 138,000 standards from some 400 national and international standards developing organizations.

§ The online machine-readable file, *IHS international standards & specifications* (DIALOG) and the CD-ROM product, *Worldwide standards service* (Englewood, Co. : Information Handling Services, 1991–) correspond in part to the printed index. T59.2.U6I15

Ricci, Patricia. Standards : a resource and guide for identification, selection, and acquisition / by Patricia L. Ricci and Linda Perry. St. Paul, Minn. : Stirtz, Bernards & Co., 1990. iii, 239 p. **EA89**

A convenient inventory of national and international governmental and industrial organizations that develop voluntary standards and specifications. Additional features of the directory include listings of libraries, standards vendors, consultants, standards newsletters, and a bibliography of standards publications. Subject and name indexes. T59.R35

Standards activities of organizations in the United States / prepared for Office of Product Standards Policy, National Bureau of Standards ; Robert B. Toth, ed. Gaithersburg, Md. : U.S. Dept. of Commerce, National Bureau of Standards ; Wash., [1984]. 591 p. (NBS special publication, 681). **EA90**

Supersedes *Directory of United States standardization activities* (1975), ed. by Sophie Chumas (*Guide* EA257).

A directory to more than 750 federal, state, and nongovernmental agencies and organizations that produce mandatory and voluntary standards. In this edition, information about standards vendors, libraries, and union lists of standards repositories has been added. Individual entries include name, address, telephone, and a summary of the scope and activities of the organization. Indexes by subject field and acronym/initials. QC100.U57

EB

Astronomy

GENERAL WORKS

Bibliography

Danko, Steven I. Black holes : an annotated bibliography, 1975–1983. Metuchen, N.J. : Scarecrow, 1985. 282 p. ISBN 0-8108-1836-1. $25.00.　　**EB1**

Offers 1,182 annotated entries to English-language works on black holes, extending the earlier bibliography, *Black holes, 1970–74* (London : Institution of Electrical Engineers, 1974. 83 p.). Entries are organized by year within the categories: books, popular journal articles, technical journal articles, conference reports, government reports, academic dissertations, nonprint media, and newspaper articles. Author and title indexes.

Z5154.S8D36

Freitag, Ruth S. Halley's comet : a bibliography. Wash. : Library of Congress : For sale by the Supt. of Docs., U.S. Govt. Print. Off., 1984. 555 p. : ill. ISBN 0-8444-0459-4. $26.00.　　**EB2**

Superintendent of Documents classification: LC 33.9/2:H15.

An extensive bibliography that lists works about the history, popular reaction to, and scientific study of Halley's comet. Most entries cite "books, parts of books, pamphlets and reports, and articles in journals, selected newspapers, conference proceedings, encyclopedias, and other collections" (*Pref.*), but personal recollections, letters, fiction, drama, music, and early broadsides and news sheets are also included. The 3,235 entries are alphabetically arranged by main entry; many are annotated and cite additional sources. Locations and call numbers at the Library of Congress or other North American and European libraries are provided. Bibliography of sources; a list of perihelion dates for the appearance of the comet (1404 BCE–1986); name and topical indexes.　　Z5154.H2F74

Indexes; Abstract journals

●**Physics briefs** [computer file]. N.Y. : American Institute of Physics, 1979– .　　**EB3**

For annotation, see *Supplement* EG3.

Sky and telescope cumulative index : volumes 1–70, 1941 November–1985 December / comp. by Judith Lola Bausch. Cambridge, Mass. : Sky Pub. Corp., c1988. 297 p. ISBN 0-933346-49-2.　　**EB4**

For a note on the monthly publication, see *Guide* EB20.

Five separate cumulative indexes (title, author, department and features, topic and celestial object, and special supplement) were prepared from the annual indexes of the journal.

Encyclopedias

Encyclopedia of astronomy and astrophysics / Robert A. Meyers, ed. ; Steven N. Shore, scientific consultant. San Diego, Calif. : Academic Pr., c1989. 807 p. : ill. ISBN 0-12-226690-0. $49.95.　　**EB5**

Contains 41 signed essays, many derived from *Encyclopedia of physical science and technology* (*Supplement* EA33), arranged alphabetically by topic. Each includes a glossary and short bibliography. There are over 300 black-and-white photographs and illustrations, numerous tables, and a general subject index. Intended for a broad audience, but most useful to those with some knowledge of the subject, since there are variations in coverage and style. Reviewed in *Sky and telescope* 79 (Feb. 1990): 169–70.　　QB14.E53

The international encyclopedia of astronomy / ed. by Patrick Moore. N.Y. : Orion Books, c1987. 464 p. : ill. (some col.). ISBN 0-517-56179-4. $40.00.　　**EB6**

Seven longer essays on the universe, the "big bang," space exploration, interstellar matter, moons, pulsars, and superclusters are interspersed in an alphabetic arrangement of about 2,500 short articles. Most articles are signed and many are illustrated with diagrams, charts, and photographs; many biographical entries include portraits. A four-page supplement has standard data about stellar objects. No index. Useful as a general reference to both historic and contemporary developments in astronomy and astrophysics.　　QB14.I58

Dictionaries

The Facts on File dictionary of astronomy / ed. by Valerie Illingworth. 2nd ed. N.Y. : Facts on File, 1985. 437 p. : ill. ISBN 0-8160-1357-8. $24.95.　　**EB7**

1st ed., 1979 (*Guide* EB25).

Published in U.K. as *Macmillan dictionary of astronomy*.

"Entries in the first edition have been updated, often extensively, and over 250 entries have been added, bringing the total to more than 2300."—*Pref.*　　QB14.F3

Heck, André. Acronyms & abbreviations in astronomy, space sciences, & related fields. Strasbourg, France : Observatoire Astronomique, 1990. 218 p. (Publication spéciale du C.D.S., no. 15). ISBN 2-908064-13-8.　　**EB8**

An alphabetical list of some 15,000 acronyms and abbreviations with their parent terms for organizations, procedures, equipment, etc., in astronomy, space sciences, and several related disciplines in the physical sciences and engineering. Prepared as a complement to the author's directory, *Astronomy, space sciences, and related organizations of the world : A.Sp.Sc.R.O.W.* (Strasbourg, France : Observatoire Astronomique, 1991. 2 v.). No index.　　QB14.H42

Room, Adrian. Dictionary of astronomical names. London ; N.Y. : Routledge, 1988. 282 p. : ill. ISBN 0-415-01298-8. $27.50. ISBN 0-7102-1115-5.　　**EB9**

Describes origins of the names for about 600 astronomical objects. Two lengthy appendixes list the names of lunar craters and minor planets (asteroids). Includes a short astronomical glossary and select bibliography of sources. No index.

QB14.R66

Directories

Earth and astronomical sciences research centres: a world directory of organizations and programmes / consultant ed., Jennifer M. Fitch. Burnt Mill, Harlow, Essex, England : Longman ; Detroit : Distr. by Gale, 1984. 742 p. ISBN 0-582-90020-4. **EB10**
For annotation, see *Supplement* EE17. QE40.E25

Handbooks

Kronk, Gary W. Comets : a descriptive catalog. Hillside, N.J. : Enslow Publ., [1984]. 331 p. ISBN 0-89490-071-4 (pbk.). $22.50. **EB11**
Provides details about the discovery, magnitude, and physical characteristics of some 650 comets observed from 371 BCE to 1982 CE. In two sections: long-period and non-period comets arranged by date; and short-period comets arranged alphabetically by proper name. Precise orbital information is not supplied. Brief reference list and index by comet name.
QB722.K76

Zombeck, Martin V. Handbook of space astronomy and astrophysics. 2nd ed. Cambridge ; N.Y. : Cambridge Univ. Pr., 1990. 440 p. ISBN 0-521-34550-2. $75.00. **EB12**

1st ed., 1982.
A diversified reference work using tables, graphs, charts, and formulas drawn from sources in classical astronomy, astrophysics, physics, geophysics, and mathematics. Although intended for the practicing astronomer and astrophysicist, it is a useful general compilation of the most recent data for astrophysical quantities and events. Short bibliographies for each chapter and a general topical index. QB136.Z65

History

The general history of astronomy / gen. ed., Michael A. Hoskin. Cambridge ; N.Y. : Cambridge Univ. Pr., 1984–1989. v.2, pt. A; v.4, pt. A.: ill. ISBN 0-521-24254-1 (v.2). ISBN 0-521-24256-8 (v.4). (In progress). **EB13**
Contents: v. 2, René Taton and Curtis Wilson [eds.], *Planetary astronomy from the Renaissance to the rise of astrophysics* : Pt. A. *Tycho Brahe to Newton*; v. 4, Owen Gingerich [ed.], *Astrophysics and twentieth-century astronomy to 1950* : Pt. A.
Published under the auspices of the International Astronomical Union and the International Union for the History and Philosophy of Science.
Written for non-specialist readers, this set when complete will survey the development of astronomy from earliest times to the mid-1950s. Each volume consists of essays of 15–20 pages written by historians of astronomy, and includes short bibliographies and a volume index. QB15.G38

Biography

The biographical dictionary of scientists: astronomers / general ed., David Abbott. N.Y. : P. Bedrick Books, 1984. 204 p. : ill. ISBN 0-911745-80-7. $28.00. **EB14**
Presents 200 alphabetically arranged articles about historical figures as well as modern scientists. Few illustrations and no portraits. Includes a name and topics index and a glossary of

astronomical terms. No principles for selection are given, articles are unsigned, and there is no bibliography. QB35.B56

Atlases

The Cambridge atlas of astronomy / ed. by Jean Audouze and Guy Israël. 2nd ed. Cambridge ; N.Y. : Cambridge Univ. Pr., c1988. 431 p. : ill. (some col.). ISBN 0-521-36360-8. $90.00. **EB15**
1st ed., 1985.
Translation of *Grand atlas de l'astronomie.*
Signed essays by 26 French astronomers and scientists are organized in five main sections: The sun; The solar system; Stars and the galaxy; Extragalactic domain; Scientific perspective. Heavily illustrated with photographs, satellite imagery, maps, and diagrams. Glossary, reading list, and alphabetic index of topics and objects supplement the text. A general astronomy encyclopedia for the educated reader, containing more scientific detail and greater coverage of extra-solar system bodies and phenomena than Patrick Moore's *The new atlas of the universe* (below). QB65.G6813

Moore, Patrick. The new atlas of the universe. N.Y. : Crown, c1984. 271 p. : ill. (some col.). ISBN 0-517-55500-X. $24.95. **EB16**
Title varies: 1st ed., 1970 (*Guide* EB54) called *The atlas of the universe*; rev. ed., 1974, called *The concise atlas of the universe.*
Completely revised from earlier editions, this atlas, intended for general readers, has four sections: The development of astronomy; The solar system; The outer universe; Into the future. A short introductory text precedes each pictorial feature. A catalog of stellar objects, glossary, "Beginner's guide to the heavens," and subject index complete the atlas. Many illustrations, photographs, maps, and charts are in color. The detailed maps of planetary surfaces, seasonal star maps, and list of constellations are useful. QB44.2.M66

STARS

Norton, Arthur P. Star atlas and reference handbook (epoch 2000.0). 18th ed. rev. under the editorship of Ian Ridpath. Burnt Mill, Harlow, Essex, England : Longman Scientific & Technical ; N.Y. : Wiley, 1989. 179 p. : ill. ISBN 0-470-21460-0. $34.95. **EB17**
17th ed., 1978 (*Guide* EB56).
At head of title: Norton's 2000.0.
The familiar features of this standard atlas of practical astronomy have been retained, but all maps have been redrawn to standard epoch 2000.0. Map projections have been standardized and computer-verified. The reference section has been rewritten and expanded; "the emphasis is on reference information and practical observing advice that is often difficult to obtain elsewhere."—*Pref.* Includes a glossary and a subject index to the reference handbook. No bibliography. QB65.N7

Tirion, Wil. Uranometria 2000.0 / Wil Tirion, Barry Rappaport, George Lovi. Richmond, Va. : Willmann-Bell, 1987–88. 2 v. ISBN 0-943396-14-X (v. 1). $39.95. ISBN 0-943396-15-8 (v. 2). $39.95. **EB18**
Contents: v. 1, The northern hemisphere to -6°; v. 2, The southern hemisphere to +6°.
A computer-plotted atlas that records some 332,000 stars and 10,300 deep sky objects. Data were compiled to 9.5 magnitude from several highly respected celestial atlases and catalogs: *Bonner Durchmusterung (BD)* of the Universitäts-Sternwarte zu Bonn (Bonn : A. Marcus, 1859–1903. 4 v.); *Bonner Durchmusterung: Südliche Teil (SBD)*, 2nd ed. rev., (Bonn: Dümmler, 1951); *Cordoba Durchmusterung (CoD)* of the Observatorio As-

tronomico of the Universidad Nacional de Córdoba (Buenos Aires, 1892–1932. 5 v.); and Jack W. Sulentic and William G. Tifft's *The revised new general catalogue of nonstellar astronomical objects* (Tucson : Univ. of Arizona Pr., 1973). Includes an introductory essay and a selective bibliography on the history of celestial cartography by George Lovi. The compact size, highly legible and well-labeled charts, and comprehensive coverage make this an important stellar atlas.   QB65.T55

CHRONOLOGY

Fitzpatrick, Gary L. International time tables. Metuchen, N.J. : Scarecrow, 1990. 106 p., [2] p. of plates : col. maps. ISBN 0-8108-2341-1. $25.00.   **EB19**

Tables are arranged by country, and allow for 12- and 24-hour forms of notation, standard and advanced time periods, multiple time zones, and the effect of the International Dateline. Notes on use, examples, and several maps help to make this an excellent source for libraries.   QB211.F56

EC

Biological Sciences

GENERAL WORKS

Guides

Information sources in the life sciences / ed., H.V. Wyatt. 3rd ed. London ; Boston : Butterworths, 1987. 191 p. ISBN 0-408-11472-X. £30.00.   **EC1**

2nd ed., 1971 (*Guide* EC1), had title: *The use of biological literature*, ed. by R.T. Bottle and H.V. Wyatt.

"A number of chapters have been omitted or completely changed in this new edition."—*Pref.* The major divisions in this edition are: Current awareness; Searching by computer; Abstracts, indexes and bibliographies; Major research databases; Guides to the literature; Biochemical sciences; Microbiology; Biotechnology; Genetics; Zoology; Ecology; Botany; and History of biology. Index to major formats, subjects, and book titles.   QH303.6.I54

Magel, Charles R. Keyguide to information sources in animal rights. London : Mansell ; Jefferson, N.C. : McFarland, 1989. 267 p. ISBN 0-89950-405-1. $60.00.   **EC2**

In three main parts: a general overview of the literature, an annotated bibliography of 335 works arranged chronologically, and a list of selected organizations concerned with animal rights. A "literature cited" section lists approximately 1,000 additional articles and books. Appendixes include a declaration on animal rights and a brief list of magazines and journals. Indexed.   Z7164.C45M36

Nicholas, Robin. Immunology, an information profile / Robin and David Nicholas. London ; N.Y. : Mansell, c1985. 216 p. : ill. ISBN 0-7201-1724-0. $36.00.   **EC3**

In three parts: (1) topical coverage of history, organizations, conferences, and literature of the field; (2) a list of 529 bibliographic sources; (3) a directory of more than 800 organizations and database hosts. Index to titles and subjects.   QR182.N53

Indexes; Abstract journals

●**BioBusiness** [computer file]. Philadelphia : BIOSIS, 1984– .   **EC4**

File size: 285,000 records. Updated monthly. Available online (BRS, Data-Star, DIALOG).

Covers the business aspects of biological and biomedical research, especially in the areas of agriculture, food technology, bioengineering, pharmaceutics, and other fields with substantial economic impact. International coverage drawn from journals, books, trade and business pubications (such as the *Wall Street journal*), newsletters, and conference proceedings. Patents are included, especially in the pharmaceutical area.

●**Biological & agricultural index** [computer file]. N.Y. : H.W. Wilson, 1983– .   **EC5**

Machine-readable version of *Biological & agricultural index* (*Guide* EC7).

File size: 275,000 records. Updated twice weekly. Available online (BRS, WILSONLINE) and in CD-ROM (Wilson).

Draws from 202 journals of relatively high circulation. Especially good for undergraduates.

●**BIOSIS previews** [computer file]. Philadelphia : BIOSIS, 1969– .   **EC6**

Machine-readable version of the combined *Biological abstracts* (*Guide* EC10) and *Biological abstracts/RRM* (*Guide* EC8).

File size: more than 8 million records. Updated weekly. Available online (BRS, CAN/OLE, Data-Star, DIALOG, STN International), in CD-ROM (producer), and on diskette or magnetic tape (producer).

Draws from more than 9,000 publications, including books, journal articles, conference proceedings, patents, meeting announcements. Coverage is very broad, including substantial nonclinical medical publications. Records that mention chemical substances are combined with CAS Registry Numbers in *BIOSIS previews/RN* (available through STN International). A current awareness version, *BioExpress*, includes the latest eight weeks of *BIOSIS previews* without abstracts (available through Life Sciences Network).

●**CSA life sciences collection** [computer file]. Bethesda, Md. : Cambridge Scientific Abstracts, c1978– .   **EC7**

Machine-readable version of abstracting journals issued by the publisher, each also available as a stand-alone database: *Animal behavior abstracts*; *Biochemistry abstracts : amino-acid, peptide, and protein*; *Biochemistry abstracts: biological membranes*; *Biochemistry abstracts: nucleic acids*; *Biotechnology research abstracts*; *Calcified tissues abstracts*; *Chemoreception abstracts*; *Ecology abstracts*; *Endocrinology abstracts*; *Entomology abstracts*; *Genetics abstracts*; *Immunology abstracts*; *Marine biotechnology abstracts*; *Microbiology abstracts : algology, mycology, and protozoology*; *Microbiology abstracts : industrial and applied microbiology*; *Neurosciences abstracts*; *Oncogenes and growth factors abstracts*; *Virology and AIDS abstracts*.

Dates of coverage vary. File size: about 1.2 million records, updated monthly. Available online (BRS, DIALOG) and in CD-ROM as *Compact Cambridge life sciences* (publisher). CD-ROM version covers 1982 to the present and is updated quarterly.

Provides good coverage of many applied and basic fields in the sciences, including biotechnology; genetic engineering, and clinical applications, Covers journal articles, reports, books, and conference proceedings.

●**Current awareness in biological sciences**: (CABS) [computer file]. Oxford : Pergamon, 1982– . **EC8**

File size: 1.2 million records. Updated monthly. Available online (BRS, ORBIT, Pergamon Infoline).

Citations covering a mix of basic biological and clinical/medical subjects, collected from more than 2,500 journals.

Encyclopedias

Encyclopedia of human biology / [ed. by] Renato Dulbecco. San Diego, Calif. : Academic Pr., 1991. 8 v. ISBN 0-12-226751-6 (v. 1). **EC9**

Contains more than 600 articles, averaging about nine pages each, by more than 700 contributors. The topics covered encompass all biological fields relating to humans, including anthropology, behavior, biochemistry, biophysics, cytology, ecology, evolution, genetics, immunology, neurosciences, pharmacology, physiology, and toxicology. Vol. 8 contains the subject index and cross-index of related articles. A major survey work on human biology. QP11.E53

Magill's survey of science. Life science series / ed. by Frank N. Magill, consulting ed., Laura L. Mays Hoopes. Pasadena, Calif. : Salem Pr., c1991. 6 v. (liv, 2763, cxlii p.). ISBN 0-89356-612-8. $400.00. **EC10**

Contents: v. 1, A–Central and peripheral nervous system functions; v. 2, Central metabolism regulation–Eukaryotic transcriptional control; v. 3, Positive and negative eukaryotic transcriptional control–Mammalian hormones; v. 4, Hormones and behavior–Muscular contraction; v. 5, Muscular contraction and relaxation–Sexual reproduction in plants; v. 6, Reproductive behavior and mating–X inactivation and the Lyon hypothesis.

An alphabetic arrangement of about 350 signed short essays (usually about eight pages long) on selected major topics in the life sciences (e.g., Reproductive behavior, Neurotransmitters, Ribosomes, Systematics). Each essay has sections of principal terms, summary of the phenomenon, methods of study, context, bibliography, and cross-references. Each volume begins with a table of contents and ends with alphabetical and topical lists of essay headings. Vol. 6 contains a comprehensive index of subject terms. No illustrations or diagrams. This work is most suitable as an undergraduate or secondary school resource. QH307.2.M34

Milner, Richard. The encyclopedia of evolution : humanity's search for its origins. N.Y. : Facts on File, c1990. 481 p. ISBN 0-8160-1472-8. **EC11**

Quirky and aimed at a popular audience, but of interest to all libraries for the variety of off-beat information its 500 entries contain. Emphasizes human evolution, includes biographies of many well-known researchers, and treats topics as diverse as "Planet of the apes" and "Minium's dead cow quarry" (a Miocene deposit in Kansas). Illustrations include photographs, circus posters, cartoons. Indexed. GN281.M53

Singleton, Paul. Dictionary of microbiology and molecular biology / Paul Singleton, Diana Sainsbury. 2nd ed. Chichester [West Sussex] ; N.Y. : Wiley, c1987. 1019 p. : ill. (some col.). ISBN 0-471-91114-3. $113.00. **EC12**

Rev. ed. of 1978 ed. (*Guide* EC31), which had title *Dictionary of microbiology*.

Very complete, with nearly 15,000 entries that vary in length from one line to more than three pages, often with citations to sources. Terms are defined "in a way which reflects their actual usage."—*Pref.* Appendixes include metabolic path-

way charts, a bibliography of major sources, and a key to journal title abbreviations used in the entries. QR9.S56

Dictionaries

Chambers biology dictionary / ed., Peter M.B. Walker. Cambridge ; N.Y. : Chambers : Cambridge Univ. Pr., c1989. 324 p. : ill. ISBN 1-85296-152-X. ISBN 1-85296-153-8 (pbk.). **EC13**

Offers definitions, nearly all less than 100 words in length, of some 10,000 words and phrases, plus more than 100 short special articles (many illustrated) on important or difficult topics. Uses British spelling. Some controversial terms, recently introduced, such as "protoctista" and "undulipodia," are excluded. Cross-references. QH302.5.C47

The dictionary of cell biology / ed. by J.M. Lackie and J.A.T. Dow. London : Academic Pr., c1989. 262 p. ISBN 0-12-432560-2. **EC14**

Offers more than 4,000 entries, which include most of the commonly used terms, although some controversial terms (e.g., "protoctista" and "undulipodia") are omitted. Definitions vary in length from about ten words to 250, averaging around 40. Uses British spelling. Some 27 tables of families of terms are interspersed; a list of these is given at the beginning. No illustrations. QH575.D53

Dictionary of immunology / ed. by W.J. Herbert, P.C. Wilkinson, D.I. Stott. 3rd ed. Oxford ; Boston : Blackwell Scientific ; St. Louis, Mo. : Blackwell Mosby Book Distributors, 1985. 240 p. : ill. ISBN 0-632-00984-5 (pbk.). **EC15**

2nd ed., 1977 (*Guide* EC25).

"Our aim . . . has been to include a range of terms wide enough to satisfy the needs of any biologist, clinician or biochemist who requires easy reference to current immunological usage."—*Pref.* 300 entries are new and about 100 have been deleted since the 2nd ed. Maximum entry length about 200 words; approximately 2,000 entries. QR180.4.D53

The Facts on File dictionary of biology / ed. by Elizabeth Tootill. Rev. and expanded ed. N.Y. : Facts On File, c1988. 326 p. : ill. ISBN 0-8160-1865-0. **EC16**

2nd ed., 1981 (*Guide* EC33).

This edition exhibits many changes that attempt to account for rapidly developing fields such as biotechnology and AIDS research. Definitions are well written and longer than those in many comparable dictionaries. QH13.F35

International dictionary of medicine and biology / editorial board, E. Lovell Becker . . . [et al.] ; consulting ed., Alexandre Manuila ; ed. in chief, Sidney I. Landau. N.Y. : Wiley, c1986. 3 v. (3200 p.). ISBN 0-471-01849-X. $395.00. **EC17**

For annotation, see *Supplement* EK48. R121.I58

Lawrence, Eleanor. Henderson's dictionary of biological terms. 10th ed. N.Y. : Wiley, 1989. 637 p. : ill. ISBN 0-470-21446-5. **EC18**

9th ed., 1979 (*Guide* EC24).

This edition contains over 22,000 entries, including expanded definitions and many new terms. Acronyms and biochemical terms are included; British spelling. Appendixes contain structural formulae of important biochemical compounds and outline classifications of the various kingdoms and phyla. QH302.5.H65

Directories

The directory of North American fisheries and aquatic scientists / Beth D. McAleer, ed. 2nd ed. Bethesda, Md. : American Fisheries Society, c1987. 363 p. ISBN 0-913235-40-7.   **EC19**

1st ed., 1984.

Consists of several lists arranged by scientist's name, geographic location (state, province, or country), area of expertise, and type of professional activity. About 20% larger than the 1st ed.   SH203.D57

Life sciences organizations and agencies directory / Brigitte T. Darnay, Margaret Labash Young, editors. Detroit : Gale, c1988. 864 p. ISBN 0-8103-1826-1. $155.00.   **EC20**

Over 7,600 entries, arranged into 18 chapters, cover agricultural sciences, veterinary sciences, biology, and biotechnology. Each entry gives name, address, telephone, officers, publications, meetings, etc. Six of the 18 chapters are based on material from other Gale directories. Indexed.   QH321.L54

Handbooks

CRC handbook of microbiology / editors, Allen I. Laskin, Hubert A. Lechevalier. 2nd ed. Boca Raton, Fla. : CRC Pr., c1987–c1988. v. 8–9; v. 9 in two parts. : ill. ISBN 0-8493-7200-3 (set).   **EC21**

For earlier volumes, see *Guide* EC40.

Contents: v. 8, Toxins and enzymes (1987); v. 9A, Antibiotics (1988); v. 9B, Antimicrobial inhibitors (1988). Completes the set.

References are listed at the end of each section. Each volume has taxonomic and subject indexes, but there is no general index. An abbreviated edition (below) has title: *Practical handbook of microbiology*.   QR6.C2

Practical handbook of microbiology / ed. by William M. O'Leary. Boca Raton, Fla. : CRC Pr., c1989. 681 p. : ill. ISBN 0-8493-3704-6.   **EC22**

A condensed version of the most useful sections of *CRC handbook of microbiology* (above), covering bacteria, mycoplasmas, fungi, and viruses, and including both the table of contents and index from the parent work.   QR72.5.P73

ECOLOGY

Ecological abstracts. 1990– . [Norwich, Eng. : Geo Abstracts Ltd.]. Monthly. ISSN 0305-196X. £12.00.   **EC23**

This service abstracts about 700 journals as well as books, conference proceedings, reports, and dissertations. Combines with *Geographical abstracts* (*Supplement* CL7 and CL6), *International development abstracts* (*Guide* CH124) and other databases to form the *GEOBASE* database (*Supplement* CL5).   QH540.E27

NATURAL HISTORY

Encyclopedias

Lincoln, Roger J. The Cambridge illustrated dictionary of natural history / R.J. Lincoln and G.A. Boxshall. Cambridge ; N.Y. : Cambridge Univ. Pr., 1987. 413 p. : ill. ISBN 0-521-30551-9. $24.95.   **EC24**

Based in part on the authors' *Dictionary of ecology, evolution and systematics* (*Guide* EC47). "The major taxonomic groups . . . are included, down to the level of order. For flowering plants, vertebrate animals and the economically more important insect groups, the coverage extends further, to include families."—*Pref.* Many common names are included, but only as cross-references to higher taxa. Defines virtually no organismal body parts. Includes about 700 small but clear stippled black-and-white drawings and some maps and charts.

§ Appropriate for both scientifically literate general readers and undergraduates, but both this work and *The Oxford dictionary of natural history* (below) are useful compendiums of terms even for specialists. The two works overlap less than 50%, the *Oxford* being somewhat more scholarly.   QH13.L56

The Oxford dictionary of natural history. Oxford ; N.Y. : Oxford Univ. Pr., 1985. 688 p. ISBN 0-19-217720-6. $45.00.   **EC25**

An alphabetic arrangement of about 14,000 entries, most less than 100 words in length. Intended primarily for students and amateur naturalists, this is nevertheless a good compilation of terms in common use by the several disciplines that make up the general field of natural history (e.g., earth and atmospheric sciences, genetics, taxonomy, elementary cell biology). No diagrams or illustrations.   QH13.O9

Annuals

Audubon wildlife report. 1985–1989/1990. N.Y. : National Audubon Society, c1985–c1990. Annual. ISSN 0885-6044.   **EC26**

Published: Orlando, Fla. : Academic Pr., 1987; San Diego, Calif. : Academic Pr., 1988–90.

Ceased in 1990.

Each volume contains chapters by specialists on major problems, issues, and developments affecting fish and wildlife resources, a chapter on a featured agency, and chapters on species selected annually for each report (14 in 1988–89). A good source for information on the organization of, and important personnel in, governmental agencies concerned with the environment. Index to subjects.   QL84.2.A9

BOTANY

General Works

Guides

Davis, Elisabeth B. Guide to information sources in the botanical sciences. Littleton, Colo. : Libraries Unlimited, 1987. 175 p. ISBN 0-87287-439-7. $32.50.   **EC27**

Arranged by subject. "The purpose of this guide is to provide a useful survey of information sources for students, librarians, avocational and professional botanists."—*Pref.* Excludes agriculture, horticulture and gardening. Index to titles, authors, and major subjects. Z5351.D38

Dictionaries

The American Horticultural Society encyclopedia of garden plants / ed. in chief, Christopher Brickell ; horticultural consultant, John Elsley. N.Y. : Macmillan, 1989. 608 p. : col. ill. ISBN 0-02-557920-7. $49.95. **EC28**

" ... offers both amateur and professional horticulturists a wealth of theoretical and practical information on ... over 8,000 [plants]."—*Foreword*. The plants are grouped systematically in the dictionary section, where their characteristics and cultivation are described, while in the catalog section they are arranged by size, color, and season of interest along with about 4,000 excellent color photographs. The dictionary serves as an index to the catalog and there is a separate index to common names. SB403.2.A46

Mabberley, D. J. The plant-book. Cambridge ; N.Y. : Cambridge Univ. Pr., 1987. 706 p. ISBN 0-521-34060-8 (pbk.). **EC29**

Subtitle: A portable dictionary of the higher plants utilising Cronquist's *An integrated system of classification of flowering plants* (1981) and current botanical literature arranged largely on the principles of editions 1–6 (1896/97–1931) of Willis's *A dictionary of the flowering plants and ferns.*

An update of J.C. Willis's *Dictionary of flowering plants and ferns*, 8th ed., 1973 (*Guide* EC146). Attempts "to present all currently accepted generic and family names of flowering plants (including gymnosperms), ferns (and other Pteridophyta), as well as a wide range of English names encountered in the literature."—*Pref.* About 100 primary sources and 230 major botanical periodicals are also listed. QK11.M29

Handbooks

Plants in danger : what do we know? / Stephen D. Davis ... [et al.]. Gland, Switzerland : International Union for Conservation of Nature and Natural Resources, 1986. 461 p. : ill. ISBN 2-88032-707-5 (pbk.). **EC30**

A comprehensive guide to literature on endangered plant species from around the world, including the U.S., listed alphabetically by country. The data sheet for each country includes, when they exist, citations to checklists and floras, field guides, information sources on threatened plants, laws protecting plants, voluntary organizations, botanic gardens, useful addresses and a section called "Additional references." Annotations are very brief or nonexistent. Appendixes provide a list of additional general and regional references, a geographical index to these, and a list of the dates when each country implemented the various global conservation conventions. Index only to countries, islands, and island groups mentioned in the text. QK86.A1P58

Takhtadzhîan, A. L. Floristic regions of the world. Berkeley : Univ. of California Pr., c1986. 522 p. : maps. ISBN 0-520-04027-9. **EC31**

Translation of *Floristicheskie oblasti Zemli.*

A description of the five floristic kingdoms and 35 regions of the world. Appendix gives a distribution list of orders and families. Extensive bibliography arranged by floristic kingdom. Index is primarily of plant names and some important geographic locations. QK101.T313

Flora

Clapham, A. R. Flora of the British Isles / A.R. Clapham, T.G. Tutin, D.M. Moore. 3rd ed. Cambridge ; N.Y., : Cambridge Univ. Pr., 1987. 688 p. : ill. ISBN 0-521-30985-9. **EC32**

2nd ed., 1962 (*Guide* EC134).

Arranged taxonomically, with a synopsis of the classification provided as a preface, along with a key to families. Provides authoritative coverage of each plant's natural history, including chromosome number, physical description, variability, habitat, and associated species. Illustrations are confined to fruits and seeds. Appendixes include a table of authorship of families, notes on the plant life forms, and a glossary. Index to vernacular names and to scientific names of families, genera, and species. QK306.C57

Hickey, Michael. 100 families of flowering plants / Michael Hickey & Clive King. 2nd ed. Cambridge ; N.Y. : Cambridge Univ. Pr., 1988. 619 p. : ill. ISBN 0-521-33049-1. ISBN 0-521-33700-3 (pbk.). **EC33**

A taxonomically arranged guide to differences between 100 important plant families (of the 300–400 now living). Each family is first treated generally, then detailed descriptions are given of one or two representative genera. Also contains additional natural history information on each family. Index of families and genera with a few vernacular group names (e.g., grass and rose families). References are confined to 25 listed at the end. QK495.A1H53

Fungi

Fungi on plants and plant products in the United States / David F. Farr ... [et al.]. St. Paul, Minn. : American Phytopathological Society, 1989. 1252 p. (Contributions from the U.S. National Fungus Collections, no. 5). ISBN 0-89054-099-3. **EC34**

Provides host-fungus, fungus, host, and host common name indexes, as well as a list of authors of the scientific names. SB733.F9815

Rossman, Amy Y. A literature guide for the identification of plant pathogenic fungi / Amy Y. Rossman, Mary E. Palm, and Linda J. Spielman. St. Paul, Minn. : American Phytopathological Society, 1987. 252 p. (Contributions from the U.S. National Fungus Collections, no. 1). ISBN 0-89054-080-2 (pbk.). **EC35**

In two sections, the first listing general references to major groups and the second providing an alphabetical listing of genera. Z5356.F97R67

Trees

Preston, Richard Joseph. North American trees : exclusive of Mexico and tropical Florida. 4th ed. Ames : Iowa State Univ. Pr., 1989. 407 p. : ill. ISBN 0-8138-1171-6. ISBN 0-8138-1172-4 (pbk.). **EC36**

2nd ed., 1961 (*Guide* EC161).

A taxonomic arrangement of both native and commonly planted exotic species. A general introduction is followed by a key to the genera, then by a general description of each major family, with a key to each of its species and detailed descriptions of them, with illustrations of key features and small distribution maps. Index to common names and to genera as main headings with species as subheadings: e.g., Cupressus; arizonica, bakeri, goveniana, etc. Changes from the 3rd ed. lie mainly in nomenclature and accepted species designations, as well as in

improvements in the distribution maps and key descriptions.
QK110.P74

Sinclair, Wayne A. Diseases of trees and shrubs / by Wayne A. Sinclair, Howard H. Lyon, and Warren T. Johnson. Ithaca, N.Y. : Comstock Pub. Associates, 1987. 574 p. : col. ill. ISBN 0-8014-1517-9.   **EC37**

Provides a description of each disease and its causal agent, with a bibliography of some 2,000 references. Very fine photographs in color; index of common and scientific names of plants and fungi. Very useful.   SB762.S56

ZOOLOGY

General Works

Bibliography

Baker, Sylva. Endangered vertebrates : a selected, annotated bibliography, 1981–1988. N.Y. : Garland, 1990. 197 p. ISBN 0-8240-4796-6.   **EC38**

A list of about 1,000 vertebrates which, following a general sources section, are arranged taxonomically from mammals to fishes. An appendix lists organizations concerned with endangered species and includes their publications. Indexes to common names, scientific names, authors, and geographic areas.
Z7996.V4B35

Abstract journals and indexes

•**Zoological record online** [computer file]. Philadelphia : BIOSIS, 1978– .   **EC39**

Machine-readable version of *The zoological record*, 1978 to the present (*Guide* EC183).

File size: 800,000 records. Updated monthly. Available online (DIALOG) and on magnetic tape (producer).

More up-to-date and generally easier to search than the printed version. Worldwide in scope; records are drawn from some 6,000 journals and consist mainly of systematic and taxonomic information about all living and extinct animals, divided into 27 groups. Records contain basic bibliographic data and include subject headings and systematic classification for each animal. No abstracts.

Dictionaries

Gozmany, László. Seven-language thesaurus of European animals. London : Chapman and Hall, 1990. 2 v. ISBN 0-412-37280-0. $475.00.   **EC40**

Vol. 1 contains 12,026 scientific names, listed alphabetically by genus or suprageneric category, of vertebrate and invertebrate animals, including insects and protozoa, which have vernacular names in at least two of six modern languages (English, German, French, Hungarian, Spanish, and Russian). The scientific name is considered the 7th language. Beneath each scientific name is a list of vernacular synonyms in each of the other languages in which they exist. Vol. 1 also contains a dictionary of the zoological taxa designations in each language (plus Latin) and an outline of the taxonomy used. Vol. 2 contains indexes to the first key word of the vernacular names in each language.   QL353.G69

Handbooks

The official World Wildlife Fund guide to endangered species of North America / [managing ed., David W. Lowe, editors, John R. Matthews, Charles J. Moseley]. Wash. : Beacham Pub., c1990. 2 v. : ill. (some col.). ISBN 0-933833-17-2 (set). $195.00.   **EC41**

Contents: v. 1, Plants, mammals; v. 2, Birds, reptiles, amphibians, fishes, mussels, crustaceans, snails, insects, & arachnids.

An exceptional work that attempts to "consolidate information on native plants and animals that have been placed on the list of threatened and endangered species.... "—*Pref.* Each species is described in about two pages, which include: a brief physical description; behavior; habitat; historic and current distribution; an essay on conservation and recovery; a brief bibliography; a small black-and-white photograph, generally poor in quality; a diagrammatic distribution map; and contacts for further information. Appendixes include lists of U.S. Fish and Wildlife Service and National Marine Fisheries Service offices, State Heritage Programs, Bureau of Land Management and National Forest Service offices, National Wildlife Refuges, and state-by-state occurrence of each endangered species. Index to common and scientific names.   QL84.2.O35

Treatises

Halstead, Bruce W. Poisonous and venomous marine animals of the world. 2nd rev. ed. Princeton, N.J. : Darwin Pr., c1988. 1168 p., 288 p. of plates : ill. (some col.). ISBN 0-87850-050-2.   **EC42**

1st ed., 1965–70 (Wash. : U.S. Govt. Print Off. 3v.)

Authoritative and exhaustive coverage of marine biotoxicology. Taxonomic arrangement of well over 500 species, with an exceptional set of plates. Citations are listed at the end of each chapter and in a brief list at end. Personal name and subject indexes.   RA1255.H35

Pennak, Robert W. Fresh-water invertebrates of the United States : protozoa to mollusca. 3rd ed. N.Y. : Wiley, c1989. 628 p. : ill. ISBN 0-471-63118-3.   **EC43**

1st ed., 1953; 2nd ed., 1978.

Chapters for each major group, in taxonomic order, Protozoa to Pelecypoda. Insects are included. Each chapter has a taxonomic key to members of the group and gives general descriptions of the group's biological characteristics, taxonomy, ecology, and techniques of culture and preservation. References are at the end of each chapter. The appendix lists and defines reagents, solutions, and laboratory items mentioned more than once in the text. Index to subjects and to scientific and common names.   QL141.P45

Amphibians and reptiles

Ernst, Carl H. Turtles of the world / Carl H. Ernst and Roger W. Barbour. Wash. : Smithsonian Institution Pr., c1989. 313 p., 16 p. of plates : ill. (some col.). ISBN 0-87474-414-8.   **EC44**

Primarily a guide to identification of the 257 turtle species now living, presented in 12 chapters, one for each family. Good bibliography and glossary; adequate illustrations. Indexes of terminology and of scientific and common names.
QL666.C5E77

Obst, Fritz Jürgen. The completely illustrated atlas of reptiles and amphibians for the terrarium / Fritz Jürgen Obst, Klaus Richter, Udo Jacob ; English-language ed., Jerry G. Walls. Neptune City, N.J. : T.F.H. Publications, c1988. 830 p. : ill. (some col.). ISBN 0-86622-958-2. $125.00. **EC45**

Translation of *Lexikon der Terraristik und Herpetologie* (Hannover : Land-buch Verlag, 1984).

Athough not comprehensive, an impressive information source for domestic reptiles and amphibians. Over 1,500 excellent full-color photographs and hundreds of drawings are included. Indexed. SF459.A45O27

Birds

Check-list of North American birds : the species of birds of North America from the Arctic through Panama, including the West Indies and Hawaiian Islands / prepared by the Committee on Classification and Nomenclature of the American Ornithologists' Union. 6th ed. [Wash.] : The Union, 1983. 877 p. : port., maps. ISBN 0-943610-32-X. **EC46**

1st ed., 1889; 5th ed., 1957.

Taxonomic arrangement. Includes AOU numbers for each species, and lists species which have been introduced. Index of scientific and common names. QL681.C52

Clark, William S. A field guide to hawks, North America. Boston : Houghton Mifflin, 1987. 198 p. : ill., maps. (The Peterson field guide series, 35). ISBN 0-395-36001-3. $19.95. ISBN 0-395-44112-9 (pbk.). $13.95. **EC47**

"Sponsored by the National Audubon Society and the National Wildlife Federation."

A taxonomic arrangement of species of the U.S. and Canada only. A prefatory chapter treats the general topography of hawks. Provides a good description of each of 39 species, including sexual differences, both flight and stationary identification marks, geographic distribution, and behavior. An unusual feature of this guide is the set of photographs of virtually all the species, many both in flight and at rest. At the end are a list of over 400 references indexed by both species and topics, and a general index to genera as main headings, to species as subheadings, and to common names. 24 plates in color. QL696.F3C59

Ehrlich, Paul R. The birder's handbook : a field guide to the natural history of North American birds : including all species that regularly breed north of Mexico / Paul R. Ehrlich, David S. Dobkin, Darryl Wheye. N.Y. : Simon & Schuster, c1988. 785 p. : ill. ISBN 0-671-62133-5. ISBN 0-671-65989-8 (pbk.). $14.95. **EC48**

In two parts: (1) taxonomically arranged essays treating nearly 650 species; (2) brief essays on aspects of their natural history. Separate subject, author, and scientific/common name indexes and a guide to essay topics. Extensive bibliography. QL681.E37

Handbook of the birds of Europe, the Middle East and North Africa : the birds of the Western Palearctic / Stanley Cramp, chief ed. .. [et al.]. Oxford ; N.Y. : Oxford Univ. Pr., 1977–1988. v. 1–5 : ill. (some col.). ISBN 0-19-857505-X (v. 2). £25.00 (v. 2). (In progress). **EC49**

Contents: v. 1, Ostrich to ducks (1977); v. 2, Hawks to bustards (1980); v. 3, Waders to gulls (1983); v. 4, Terns to woodpeckers (1985); v. 5, Tyrant flycatchers to thrushes (1988). To be complete in 7 v.

Provides excellent descriptions of more than 2,700 species (through v.5). Each species is described by field characters habitat, distribution, movements, food, behavior, voice, breeding and detailed external morphology. Each volume has a separate index to scientific names as well as indexes to common English, French, and German names. Full-color illustrations are distributed through each volume with color plates of eggs at the end, along with an extensive list of cited references. Each later volume has a section of corrections to earlier volumes. Nonpasser-

ine species are covered in v. 1–4, passerines in v. 5–7. QL690.A1H25

Howard, Richard. A complete checklist of the birds of the world / Richard Howard, Alick Moore. 2nd ed. [Orlando, Fla.] : Academic Pr., 1991. 701 p. ISBN 0-12-356910-9. **EC50**

Previous ed., 1980 (*Guide* EC209).

Arranged taxonomically with an outline of the taxonomy provided as a preface. References for each group are presented as a separate section, in taxonomic order, prior to the checklist. Index to genera and species. QL677.H75

Johnsgard, Paul A. Hawks, eagles & falcons of North America : biology and natural history. Wash. : Smithsonian Institution Pr., c1990. 403 p., [31] p. of plates : ill. (some col.), maps. ISBN 0-87474-682-5. **EC51**

Begins with several chapters on general aspects of ecology and behavior, followed by a taxonomic arrangement of chapters on each species with distribution maps. Appendixes contain a taxonomic key to species, origins of both common and scientific names, a glossary, and field identification marks. A separate section at the end cites about 7,700 references. Indexed.

QL696.F3J6

Lever, Christopher. Naturalized birds of the world / Christopher Lever ; illustrations by Robert Gillmor. Burnt Mill, Harlow, Essex, England : Longman Scientific & Technical ; N.Y. : Wiley, 1987. 615 p. : ill. ISBN 0-470-20789-2. **EC52**

Taxonomic arrangement of about 140 species. "Each species account is a monograph on an individual bird" whose collective intent is to describe "when, where, how and by whom various birds now living in the wild state were introduced, and what effects for good or ill, they have had on the native biota."—*Pref.* Indexed by common and scientific names and by geographic location. Provides small natural and naturalized distribution maps for each species. Bibliography of about 2,000 references. QL677.4.L49

Miller, Melanie Ann. Birds : a guide to the literature. N.Y. : Garland, 1986. 887 p. (Garland reference library of the humanities, vol. 680). ISBN 0-8240-8710-0. **EC53**

An annotated bibliography of literature about birds, 1800–1984, readily accessible in libraries. Nearly 2,000 individual works are listed, as well as major periodicals and organization publications. Index of authors and anonymous titles.

Z5331.M54

Mountfort, Guy. Rare birds of the world : a Collins/ICBP handbook. Lexington, Mass. : S. Greene Pr., 1989. 1 v. ISBN 0-8289-0719-6. **EC54**

Lists about 1,000 species in a geographic arrangement with a taxonomic arrangement in each geographic group. Appendix I gives a systematic list of the species with vernacular and scientific names, endangered status, zoogeographic region, and range of distribution; Appendix II lists those birds presumed to have gone extinct since 1600 (about 100). Separate indexes of scientific and vernacular names. QL676.7.M68

Palmer, Ralph S. ed. Handbook of North American birds. New Haven, Conn. : Yale Univ. Pr., 1988. v. 4–5. ISBN 0-300-01902-5 (v. 2). **EC55**

For v. 1–3, see *Guide* EC211.

Contents: v. 4–5, Diurnal raptors. Completes the set.

An exceptional, very thorough standard ornithological work. Intended to be comprehensible by general readers, hence unfamiliar terminology and concepts are kept to a minimum. For each species, gives detailed textual description of both sexes, as well as of any known subspecies, including field identification marks, voice, habitat, distribution, banding status, reproduction, survival, general habits and food. Vol. 4 has its own index, v. 5 an index for both volumes and a list of literature cited in both volumes. Illustrations consist of a few simple ink drawings and distribution maps.   QL681.P35

Mammals

Burton, John A. The Collins guide to the rare mammals of the world / John A. Burton with the assistance of Vivien G. Burton. Lexington, Mass. : S. Greene Pr. ; N.Y. : Distr. by Viking Penguin, 1988. 240 p. : ill. (some col.), maps. ISBN 0-8289-0658-0.   **EC56**

A taxonomically arranged listing of the most threatened mammalian species. Verso pages have several one-paragraph descriptions of individual species, recto pages have color drawings of many of these species and distribution maps. A brief bibliography and a checklist of the species and their threatened status appear as appendixes. Index to genera and vernacular names.   QL706.8.B87

Grzimek's encyclopedia of mammals. N.Y. : McGraw-Hill, 1989. 5 v. ISBN 0-07-909508-9 (set). $500.00 (est.).   **EC57**

Translation of *Grzimeks Enzyklopädie Säugetiere.*

Offers more complete coverage of each mammalian group than *Grzimek's animal life encyclopedia* (*Guide* EC187) but retains its general high quality, although the lack of adequate references in both works detract from their value. Arranged by subclasses and orders; each category includes an introduction, information on phylogeny and evolution of the group, detailed information about many species, and bibliographies. Good for summary accounts of the basic biology of each group and of selected individual species. Excellent photographs, although many are double page spreads in which detail is lost in the gutter. Index in each volume, but no general index.
    QL701.G7913

Institute of Laboratory Animal Resources (U.S.). Committee on Care and Use of Laboratory Animals. Guide for the care and use of laboratory animals. Rev. 1985. Bethesda, Md. : U.S. Dept. of Health and Human Services, Public Health Service, National Institutes of Health, 1985. 83 p. (NIH publication, no. 85-23.). **EC58**

1st ed., 1963, had title: *Guide for laboratory animal facilities and care.*

Superintendent of Documents classification: HE20.3008:-An 5/985.

Divided into five topical chapters and meant to serve, in conjunction with other applicable federal laws, regulations, and policies, as a guide to the operation of institutional animal facilities and programs. Each chapter ends with a list of references. Appendixes include a substantial selected bibliography, certifying organizations, federal laws, and Public Health Service policy and government principles on care and use of animals. See also Trevor B. Poole, ed., *The UFAW handbook on the care and management of laboratory animals* (*Supplement* EH29).
    SF406.G8

Lever, Christopher. Naturalized mammals of the world. London ; N.Y. : Longman, 1985. 487 p. : ill. ISBN 0-582-46056-5. £45.00.   **EC59**

Describes when, where, why, how, and by whom the various alien mammals now living in the wild throughout the world were introduced, how they subsequently became naturalized, and what effects they have had on native biota and vice versa. Indexes to common and scientific names. Extensive bibliography. Tables of species listed by country in appendix.
    QL86.L48

Orders and families of recent mammals of the world / ed. by Sydney Anderson, J. Knox Jones, Jr. ; sponsored by the American Society of Mammalogists. N.Y. : Wiley,

1984. 686 p. : ill. ISBN 0-471-08493-X. $50.00 (est.).
    EC60

Arranged taxonomically by orders and families with a chapter for each major grouping. Each order or family is described by its general characteristics, habits, habitats, recent distribution, recent genera, geologic range and major fossil groups. Index to common and scientific names and a separate section of about 1,700 references to works cited in the text.
    QL703.O73

BACTERIOLOGY

Bergey's manual of systematic bacteriology. Baltimore : Williams & Wilkins, c1989. v. 4 : ill. ISBN 0-683-04108-8 (v. 1).   **EC61**

For earlier volumes and annotation, see *Guide* EC243.

Vol. 3 ed. by James T. Staley; v. 4 ed. by Stanley T. Williams. Completes the set.

Intends to aid in bacterial identification and to indicate relationships between various bacteria. Divided into various taxonomic "sections" or chapters, each by specialists, which are based on general characteristics of each major taxonomic grouping. Light and electron micrographs are interspersed. Each volume has a separate extensive bibliography and an index to scientific names of the bacteria within that volume. Vol. 4 has a cumulative index.   QR81.B46

BIOCHEMISTRY

Data for biochemical research / Rex M.C. Dawson . . . [et al.]. 3rd ed. Oxford : Clarendon Pr., 1986. 580 p. : ill. ISBN 0-19-855358-7. $49.95.   **EC62**

2nd ed., 1969 (*Guide* EC252).

Attempts to supply information of potential use to a majority of biochemists in a form sufficiently concise to be kept in the laboratory. Considerably expanded over the 2nd ed. Index mainly to chemical terms.   QP520.D37

Stenesh, J. Dictionary of biochemistry and molecular biology. 2nd ed. N.Y. : Wiley, c1989. 525 p. ISBN 0-471-84089-0.   **EC63**

1st ed., 1975 (*Guide* EC259).

Contains 4,000 more entries than the 12,000 in the 1st ed., mainly in the addition of names of compounds. Entries are direct rather than inverted, (e.g., "First law of cancer biochemistry" rather than "Cancer biochemistry, first law"). Cross-references.   QP512.S73

ENTOMOLOGY

Torre-Bueno, José Rollin de la. The Torre-Bueno glossary of entomology / comp. by Stephen W. Nichols ; including Supplement A by George S. Tulloch ; managing ed., Randall T. Schuh. Rev. ed. N.Y. : New York Entomological Society in cooperation with the American Museum of Natural History, 1989. 840 p.   **EC64**

1st ed., 1937, called *A glossary of entomology* (*Guide* EC263); 2nd ed., 1960, by George S. Tulloch, called *Torre-Bueno's glossary of entomology* (*Guide* EC264).

A greatly expanded edition: cross-references are extensive, more than one sense of a term is given where necessary, and the number and length of definitions have both been increased. Includes a bibliography and an ordinal classification. Anatomical plates and other figures used in earlier editions have been deleted. Computerization of the file will permit more frequent updates. The standard source for terminology in entomology.

QL462.3.T67

GENETICS

King, Robert C. A dictionary of genetics / Robert C. King, William D. Stansfield. 4th ed. N.Y.: Oxford Univ. Pr., 1990. 496 p. ISBN 0-19-506370-8. ISBN 0-19-506371-6 (pbk.).   **EC65**

3rd ed., 1985 (*Guide* EC275).

This edition contains some 6,000 entries for terms in both classical and molecular genetics. Appendixes give a chronology of events in the history of genetics, a list of major journals, a classification of organisms, and a list of domesticated species.

QH427.K55

Maclean, Norman. Dictionary of genetics & cell biology. N.Y.: New York Univ. Pr., 1987. 422 p.: ill. ISBN 0-8147-5438-4. $60.00.   **EC66**

Contains both basic and specialized terms. Definitions are brief and clear, similar in length to those in J.M. Lackie and J.A.T. Dow's *The dictionary of cell biology* (*Supplement* EC14). Uses British spelling and the controversial classification of Lynn Margulis's *Five kingdoms* (San Francisco: W.H. Freeman, 1982; 2nd ed., 1988). A good companion to R.C. King and W.D. Stansfield's *A dictionary of genetics* (above).

QH427.M33

McKusick, Victor A. Mendelian inheritance in man: catalogs of autosomal dominant, autosomal recessive, and X-linked phenotypes. 9th ed. Baltimore: Johns Hopkins Univ. Pr., 1990. clxxv, 2028 p. ISBN 0-8018-4041-4.   **EC67**

Available both in printed and machine-readable versions; the printed version is derived from the machine-readable file.

This compilation of research on genetic disease is probably the best available. The printed version is well indexed, but the machine-readable version is more current and provides indexing for all keywords. The machine-readable version is available online through the Welch Medical Library of Johns Hopkins Univ., where, in combination with the *Genome data base (GDB)*, it gives mapping, linkage, and additional bibliographic data as well as a list of experts on various genetic diseases.

Z6675.M4M33

VIROLOGY

Fraenkel-Conrat, Heinz. The viruses: catalogue, characterization, and classification. N.Y.: Plenum Pr., c1985. 266 p., [2] p. of plates: ill. ISBN 0-306-41766-9.   **EC68**

Three sections: animal (including protozoan) viruses, plant viruses, and prokaryote (bacteria and blue-green algae) phage. Attempts "to list most if not all well established and studied viruses in alphabetical order...."—*Pref.* Animal and plant viruses are listed by common and scientific name and prokaryote phage by name or by identifying letters and/or numbers, or by host. Each virus is classified, as appropriate, to group, genus, family, and subfamily. Fairly complete descriptions of each family or major group are included with citations to the list of references at the end of each section. Provides good illustrations of most families or groups, mainly by electron micrographs of negatively stained specimens. No index.

QR394.F73

Hull, Roger. Virology: directory & dictionary of animal, bacterial, and plant viruses / Roger Hull, Fred Brown, Chris Payne. N.Y.: Stockton Pr.; London: Macmillan, 1989. 1 v. ISBN 0-935859-59-4. $79.00.   **EC69**

The authors "have attempted to list most, if not all, viruses of vertebrates, invertebrates, plants and bacteria."—*Introd.* A combined directory and dictionary section lists the "names of viruses and their higher order taxa as well as terms which are commonly used in the virological literature." Many entries include references to recent reviews and papers. The directory portion also includes appendixes, of which several (A–E) list viral isolates from various insect species and one (F) gives a list of nearly 2,000 known bacteriophage isolates. No separate index.

QR358.H85

ED

Chemistry

GENERAL WORKS

Guides

Maizell, Robert E. How to find chemical information: a guide for practicing chemists, educators, and students. 2nd ed. N.Y.: J. Wiley, c1987. 402 p.: ill. ISBN 0-471-86767-5. $55.00 (est.).   **ED1**

1st ed., 1979 (*Guide* ED4).

A major revision and expansion, with much greater coverage of key reference tools such as *Chemical abstracts* (*Guide* ED22), Beilstein (*Guide* ED90), and Gmelin (*Guide* ED87).

QD8.5.M34

Schulz, Hedda. From CA to CAS ONLINE. N.Y.: VCH, c1988. 227 p.: ill. ISBN 0-89573-815-5.   **ED2**

Translation of *Von CA bis CAS ONLINE* (Weinheim; Deerfield Beach, Fla.: VCH, c1985).

This guide to *Chemical abstracts* and its online version is a very useful starting point for anyone needing to use the single most important source of information in chemistry and related fields. Users will need to consult Chemical Abstracts Service documents for the most recent changes in the online system (e.g., for information on the software package "STN Express," which facilitates searching *CAS Online*).   QD9.S3813

Wiggins, Gary. Chemical information sources. N.Y.: McGraw-Hill, 1991. 352 p.: ill. ISBN 0-07-9099394.   **ED3**

"... a textbook designed to give to the chemist, librarian, or student the command of the chemical literature which is needed to successfully solve most chemical information problems... the material found herein will lay a solid foundation upon which to build toward mastery of the vast domain of chemical information science."—*Pref.* Contains helpful and detailed information on the use of reference sources, and is particularly strong on the use of the Chemical Abstracts online file (*CA FILE*) as made available through STN International. A unique feature is a Pro-Cite database included with the book on a 3 1/2-inch MS-DOS disk; the database includes records for over 2,150 sources (bibliographic information and index terms) which can be searched for sources on particular topics, using the Pro-Cite search-only software which is also included with the book on a second 3 1/2-inch disk. This database contains records for printed reference works, online databases, and software, including many reference sources not discussed in the parent work. An ASCII version of the database may be obtained from the author. Printed text is indexed, but does not have entries for all titles mentioned.   Z699.5.C5W54

Bibliography

Cole, William A. Chemical literature, 1700–1860 : a bibliography with annotations, detailed descriptions, comparisons, and locations. London ; N.Y. : Mansell, 1988. 582 p. ISBN 0-7201-1967-7. $250.00 (est.).   **ED4**

An elaborate descriptive bibliography that follows largely (but not entirely) the precepts of Philip Gaskell's *A new introduction to bibliography* (*Guide* AA4). The wealth of detail makes this work an important addition to collections where much use is made of Henry Carrington Bolton's *A select bibliography of chemistry 1492–[1902]* (*Guide* ED10), Denis I. Duveen's *Bibliotheca alchemica et chemica* (*Guide* ED11), or *Bibliotheca chemica* by John Ferguson (*Guide* ED12).   Z5522.C73

Periodicals

Chemical Abstracts Service source index : 1907–1989 cumulative. [Columbus, Ohio] : American Chemical Society, [1990].   **ED5**

For a discussion of the previous cumulation, see *Guide* ED17.

Also known as *CASSI*.

This cumulation contains information on 68,000 serial and nonserial source publications; including cross-references, there are about 125,000 entries.   Z5523.A52

Indexes and abstract journals

●**CA search** / Chemical Abstracts Service [computer file]. Columbus, Ohio : The Service, [1967]– .   **ED6**

Machine-readable version of *Chemical abstracts* (*Guide* ED22).

File size: more than 9 million records. Available online (BRS, CAN/OLE, Data-Star, DIALOG, ORBIT, STN; most vendors update biweekly).

Versions available through different online services differ substantially in their indexing features and in the period of years for which full abstracts are available. This important database is very complex, and may require sophisticated search techniques; it is important to study the database information available from the online service being used before starting a search.

Dictionaries

Bennett, H. Concise chemical and technical dictionary. 4th enl. ed. N.Y. : Chemical Pub. Co., c1986. 1271 p. : ill. ISBN 0-8206-0204-3.   **ED7**

3rd ed., 1974 (*Guide* ED35).

A significantly enlarged edition, containing more than 85,000 terms.   QD5.B4

Compendium of chemical terminology : IUPAC recommendations / comp. by Victor Gold . . . [et al.]. Oxford ; Boston : Blackwell Scientific, 1987. 456 p. : ill. ISBN 0-632-01765-1. ISBN 0-632-01767-8 (pbk.).   **ED8**

At head of title: International Union of Pure and Applied Chemistry.

A dictionary of terms compiled from material published up to the end of 1985 by the Physical, Inorganic, Organic, Macromolecular, and Analytical Chemistry divisions of IUPAC. Contains brief definitions, some with diagrams or formulas, and references to IUPAC source documents and other sources. Cross-references; related entries in definitions are italicized.   QD5.C455

Hackh, Ingo W. D. Grant & Hackh's chemical dictionary : American, international, European, and British usage. 5th ed. / completely rev. and ed. by Roger Grant, Claire Grant. N.Y. : McGraw-Hill, c1987. 641 p. : ill. ISBN 0-07-024067-1. $69.50.   **ED9**

4th ed., 1969 (*Guide* ED40).

"Containing the words generally used in chemistry, and many of the terms used in the related sciences of physics, medicine, engineering, biology, pharmacy, astrophysics, agriculture, mineralogy, etc. Based on recent scientific literature."—*t.p.* Although the number of entries remains about 55,000, only half are taken unchanged from the previous edition; the remainder have been modified or are new. New entries deal with new materials and revised nomenclature; some classes of older entries such as traditional plant-derived medicines have been winnowed. Internationally accepted terminology or symbols (from IUPAC) are starred.   QD5.H3

Hawley's condensed chemical dictionary. 11th ed. / rev. by N. Irving Sax and Richard J. Lewis. N.Y. : Van Nostrand Reinhold, c1987. 1288 p. : ill. ISBN 0-442-28097-1.   **ED10**

10th ed., 1981 (*Guide* ED36).

This edition includes CAS Registry Numbers and an expanded listing of trade names.   QD5.C5

Handbooks

Barin, Ihsan. Thermochemical data of pure substances. Weinheim, Federal Republic of Germany ; N.Y. : VCH, c1989. 2 v. ISBN 0-89573-866-X.   **ED11**

"In collaboration with Fried Sauert, Ernst Schultze-Rhonof, Wang Shu Sheng."—*t.p.*

A compilation of thermodynamic data for some 2,400 pure substances that complements *JANAF thermochemical tables* (below), which were compiled for the U.S. Air Force and are concerned chiefly with substances related to propulsion, fuels, combustion, etc. The present work includes many additional elements and compounds of importance to metallurgy and other fields. Data are given for room temperature, for 300°K, and where possible are graduated in 100°K increments to 5,000°K. Data are given in SI units, and sources are cited; critically evaluated data are used when available. Thermodynamic functions are included; the layout of the tables corresponds to conventions used in standard works such as the *JANAF tables*. Apart from some 100 organic substances, these tables contain data on chemical elements and on inorganic compounds of two, three, or four elements; primary arrangement of the tables is in alphabetical order of the first element in the chemical formula. Six introductory sections discuss basic thermodynamic principles and explain how the tables were compiled and how they can be used, with examples.   QD511.8.B369

Comprehensive coordination chemistry : the synthesis, reactions, properties & applications of coordination compounds / ed. in chief, Sir Geoffrey Wilkinson. Oxford ; N.Y. : Pergamon, 1987. 7 v. : ill. ISBN 0-08-026232-5 (set). $2200.00. **ED12**

Contents: v. 1, Theory & background; v. 2, Ligands; v. 3, Main group & early transition elements; v. 4, Middle transition elements; v. 5, Late transition elements; v. 6, Applications; v. 7, Indexes.

An encyclopedic collection of signed, authoritative articles including tabular data and literature references. The index volume contains subject and formula indexes, and an index of review articles and specialist texts. QD474.C65

CRC handbook of laboratory safety. 3rd ed., ed. by A. Keith Furr. Boca Raton, Fla. : CRC Pr., c1990. 704 p. : ill. ISBN 0-8493-0353-2. **ED13**

2nd ed., 1971 (*Guide* ED81).

Completely rewritten. "Not primarily intended for the safety and health specialist, but . . . to guide research personnel in working with safety and health professionals to implement effective health and safety programs in their facilities."—*Foreword.* Gives much more emphasis to disposal of chemical and other hazardous wastes, and covers newer topics such as recombinant DNA laboratories that were not mentioned in the previous edition. References in the text direct readers to generalized source documents rather than specialized technical articles. QD51.H27

Emsley, J. The elements. Oxford : Clarendon Pr. ; N.Y. : Oxford Univ. Pr., 1988. 264 p. ISBN 0-19-855238-6. $37.50. ISBN 0-19-855237-8 (pbk.). $13.50. **ED14**

Lists the elements in alphabetical order. Each two-page entry gives chemical and physical properties including radii, electronegativity, standard reduction potential, oxidation states, melting and boiling points, thermodynamic properties, density, conductivities, lattice structures, nuclear properties including NMR, electronic configuration, ionization energies, and principal atomic lines, as well as other significant data. Each entry also gives a brief statement of chemical properties, sources, and uses; history of discovery and origin of the element's name; abundance on Earth; and biological role, if any. A key at the beginning of the book explains the properties listed, giving units used, conversion factors to other common units, and sources for the data. Tables at the back list 16 of the properties both in order of the elements and in numerical order of the property. A very convenient handbook. QD466.E48

JANAF thermochemical tables. 3rd ed. N.Y. : American Institute of Physics, c1986. 2 v. (1856 p.). ISBN 0-88318-473-7. **ED15**

Issued as: *Journal of physical and chemical reference data*, v. 14, suppl. no. 1 (1985).

Combines material revised and updated from the 2nd ed., 1971 (*Guide* ED67) with the four supplements published in the *Journal of physical and chemical reference data* (1974, 1975, 1978, and 1982) and with previously unpublished tables. All tables are now in SI units and "notation has been made consistent with current international recommendations."—*Foreword.* Gives thermodynamic properties of about 1,800 substances. QC100.U573

Kaye, G. W. C. Tables of physical and chemical constants and some mathematical functions. 15th ed. London ; N.Y. : Longman, 1986. 477 p. : ill. ISBN 0-582-46354-8. £17.50. **ED16**

For annotation, see *Supplement* EG12. QC61.K3

Lefèvre, M. J. First aid manual for chemical accidents. 2nd English-language ed. / rev. by Shirley A. Conibear. N.Y. : Van Nostrand Reinhold, c1989. 261 p. ISBN 0-442-20490-6. **ED17**

1st English ed., 1980.

Chapters describe symptoms of poisoning and first aid measures in cases of inhalation, ingestion, skin contact, and eye contact; within each of these chapters are numbered sections on groups of chemical compounds having the same symptoms and treatment procedures. A chemical index gives the section number for each chapter and the CAS Registry Number of each particular compound. Appendixes include general instructions in case of poisoning by unknown chemicals, and a glossary of commercial and common pesticide names. RC963.3.L4313

The Merck index : an encyclopedia of chemicals, drugs, and biologicals / Susan Budavari, ed. 11th (centennial) ed. Rahway, N.J. : Merck, 1989. 1 v. (various pagings) : ill. ISBN 0-911910-28-X. **ED18**

10th ed., 1983 (*Guide* ED77).

Significant changes include addition of a "Therapeutic category and biological activity index," and deletion of the "Organic name reactions" section. RS51.M4

●**The Merck index online** / comp. by Merck & Company [computer file]. Rahway, N.J. : Merck & Co. **ED19**

File size: 10,300 records. Updated semiannually. Available online (BRS, DIALOG). Contains textual, numeric, and bibliographic data.

Includes full text of the latest edition of *Merck index* (above), with additional entries added or revised since publication of that edition.

Official methods of analysis of the Association of Official Analytical Chemists / ed. by Kenneth Helrich. 15th ed. Arlington, Va. : The Association, 1990. 684 p. : ill. ISBN 0-935584-42-0. $215.00. **ED20**

Of more than 1,800 methods in this edition, 143 are new and 81 revised or updated from those in the 14th ed., 1984 (*Guide* ED64). CAS Registry Numbers are now included where applicable. Supplemented annually by *Changes in official methods of analysis* (1946– ; repr. from *Journal of the Association of Official Analytical Chemists*); the purchase price includes five annual supplements. QD75.O444

Sax, N. Irving. Dangerous properties of industrial materials / N. Irving Sax and Richard J. Lewis, Sr. 7th ed. N.Y. : Van Nostrand Reinhold, c1989. 3 v. ISBN 0-442-28020-3 (set). **ED21**

6th ed., 1984 (*Guide* ED80).

The first volume of this extensively revised edition contains (besides signed articles on toxicology, carcinogenesis, and genetic toxicology) bibliographic citations, and indexes to the chemical substance entries which make up the other two volumes. Over 3,500 entries have been added. T55.3.H3S3

Shugar, Gershon J. Chemical technicians' ready reference handbook / Gershon J. Shugar, Jack T. Ballinger. 3rd ed. N.Y. : McGraw-Hill, c1990. 889 p. : ill. ISBN 0-07-057183-X. **ED22**

2nd ed., 1981 (*Guide* ED65).

Expanded and revised to include more information on instrumental analysis and calibration. QD61.S58

Standard methods for the examination of water and wastewater / prepared and published jointly by American Public Health Association, American Water Works Association, Water Pollution Control Federation. 17th ed. Wash. : APHA, c1989. 1 v. (various pagings) : ill. ISBN 0-87553-161-X. **ED23**

16th ed., 1985 (*Guide* ED63).

"The organization . . . reflects a commitment to develop and retain a permanent numbering system. New numbers have been assigned to all sections, and numbers unused in the present edition have been reserved for future use."—*Pref.* Several of the sections have been substantially revised. TD380.S8

Style manuals

The ACS style guide : a manual for authors and editors / Janet S. Dodd, ed. ; Marianne C. Brogan, advisory ed. Wash. : American Chemical Society, 1986. 264 p. : ill. ISBN 0-8412-0917-0. $24.95. ISBN 0-8412-0943-X (pbk.). $14.95.　　**ED24**

A complete revision and substantial expansion of the *Handbook for authors of papers in American Chemical Society publications* (3rd ed., 1978; *Guide* ED85), this style manual is more general in outlook than the previous editions, going beyond ACS house style requirements and "stressing those principles and practices that are desirable throughout the scientific literature."—*Foreword*. Other changes include the addition of chapters on machine-readable manuscripts and oral presentations in science, and an overview of the chemical literature.

QD8.5.A25

Biography

The Nobel Prize winners : chemistry / ed. by Frank N. Magill. Pasadena, Calif. : Salem Pr., c1990. 3 v. (1246 p.) : ill. ISBN 0-89356-561-X (set). $210.00. **ED25**

A collection of articles on Nobel Prize winners in chemistry, arranged chronologically from the first prize through 1989. Articles follow a fixed pattern and include a picture of the chemist; summaries of the award presentation, the Nobel lecture, and the critical reception of the award; a biography of the prize winner; and a brief bibliography. Unlike the series in chemistry issued by the Nobelstiftelsen (*Guide* ED127) these volumes do not include the full texts of presentation speeches or Nobel lectures, but the additional material they include makes this a useful source for the history of chemistry which both supplements and updates Edward Faber's *Nobel prize winners in chemistry, 1901–1961* (*Guide* ED126). Vol. 1 includes an overview of the history of the Nobel Prize in chemistry, and each volume has an alphabetical list of prize winners. The index includes names, subjects, and institutions mentioned in the articles, and nationalities of the prize winners.　QD35.N64

INORGANIC

Block, B. Peter. Inorganic chemical nomenclature : principles and practice / B. Peter Block, Warren H. Powell, W. Conard Fernelius. Wash. : American Chemical Society, 1990. 210 p. : ill. ISBN 0-8412-1697-5. ISBN 0-8412-1698-3 (pbk.).　　**ED26**

" . . . concerned with the nomenclature of all substances except those that have carbon as a central atom and contain carbon-to-carbon bonds. Its purpose is to provide the reader with a basic understanding of the principles currently in use for naming such substances and the background necessary for searching much of the older literature."—*Pref*. Includes references; indexed.　QD149.B59

●**Gmelin formula index** [computer file]. [Berlin?] : Gmelin-Institut für Anorganische Chemie der Max-Planck-Gesellschaft.　　**ED27**

Available online (STN). Updated annually.

An index to *Gmelins Handbuch der anorganischen Chemie* (*Guide* ED87), this database allows searching by molecular formula, element count, compound class identifier, and other controlled text, as well as by words from the *Handbuch* abstracts. Search results include volume and page number in the *Handbuch*, which must be consulted for full information, although an abstract can also be retrieved online.

Nomenclature of inorganic chemistry : recommendations 1990 / issued by the Commission on the Nomenclature of Inorganic Chemistry and ed. by G.J. Leigh. Oxford [England] ; Boston : Blackwell Scientific, 1990– . v.1 : ill. ISBN 0-632-02319-8. ISBN 0-632-02494-1 (pbk.). (In progress).　　**ED28**

Part I, a general expansion of the 2nd ed., 1971 (*Guide* EB88), "expounds the basic principles of inorganic chemical nomenclature. . . . Part II and subsequent volumes will deal with specialized areas of nomenclature, and some of the eventual contents have already appeared in *Pure and applied chemistry*."—*Introd*. " . . . the level of Part I should be such that its general principles will not be undermined, and . . . it should retain its currency for many years. Part II, more specialized, will appear in the near future, and, by its nature, will probably require more frequent revision."—*Pref*. This edition appears in an instructional format rather than as a series of numbered rules as in past editions; it provides numerous examples and the text is more coherent and discursive. Also new are two introductory chapters: Chapter 1 gives a concise history of inorganic chemical nomenclature, and Chapter 2 summarizes "the usages of inorganic nomenclature" and is intended to be used in conjunction with other chapters. Indexed.　QD149.N66

ORGANIC

Dictionary of organic compounds : supplement. 1st (1983)– . N.Y. : Chapman and Hall, 1983– . Annual. ISSN 0264-1100.　　**ED29**

For the parent work, 5th ed., 1982, and for earlier supplements, see *Guide* ED98.

The 5th annual suppl. (1987) is in 2 volumes, of which the second is a cumulative index to suppl. 1–5. The 7th and subsequent suppl. cumulate indexing from the 6th suppl. onward.

§ Chapman and Hall are issuing several titles and series that are complementary and provide information on a very wide range of organic compounds. These consist of *Dictionary of organic compounds* (*Guide* ED98) and its supplements, including the present work; *Dictionary of organometallic compounds* (*Guide* ED99) and its supplements (below); dictionaries of alkaloids, antibiotics, drugs, and organophosphorus compounds (below); and sourcebooks on amino acids and peptides and on carbohydrates (below). The data in these works (except for the sourcebooks) are drawn together and supplemented in the online file *HEILBRON* (below).

Dictionary of organometallic compounds : Supplement. 1st (1984)– . London ; N.Y. : Chapman and Hall, 1985– . Annual. ISSN 0265-8372.　　**ED30**

For the parent work, see *Guide* ED99.

Substances are in order alphabetically by the metallic element. Indexes by molecular formula and CAS Registry Number. The 5th annual suppl. is in 3 volumes, of which the second and third are cumulative indexes to suppl. 1–5; one of these is a cumulative structure index, the first structure index since the parent work was published in 1984. The 7th and subsequent suppl. will cumulate indexing from the 6th suppl. onwards.

QD411.D53

Dictionary of alkaloids / editorial board: G.A. Cordell . . . [et al.] ; comp. and ed. by I.W. Southon, J. Buckingham. London ; N.Y. : Chapman and Hall, 1989. 2 v. : ill. ISBN 0-412-24910-3 (set). $1295.00.　**ED31**

RS431.A53D53

Dictionary of antibiotics and related substances / ed. by B.W. Bycroft. London ; N.Y. : Chapman and Hall, 1988. 944 p. : ill. ISBN 0-412-25450-6. $620.00.　　**ED32**

RS431.A6D53

Dictionary of drugs : chemical data, structures, and bibliographies / editors, J. Elks, C.R. Ganellin. London ; N.Y.: Chapman and Hall, 1990. 2 v.: ill. ISBN 0-412-27300-4 (set). $1250.00. **ED33**
RS51.D479

Dictionary of organophosphorus compounds / ed. and comp. by R.S. Edmundson. London ; N.Y.: Chapman and Hall, c1988. 1347 p.: ill. ISBN 0-412-25790-4. $575.00. **ED34**

These four dictionaries, part of a series being issued by this publisher, complement *Dictionary of organic compounds* and *Dictionary of organometallic compounds* (above). The coverage of each dictionary is substantially discrete, for the most part not duplicating that of the more comprehensive works, or of one another. See also the series of sourcebooks (below).
QD412.P1E36

Amino acids and peptides / ed. by J.S. Davies. London ; N.Y.: Chapman and Hall, 1985. 430 p. ISBN 0-412-26950-3. $80.00. **ED35**
QP561.A48

Carbohydrates / ed. by P.M. Collins ; principal contributor, V.R.N. Munasinghe. London ; N.Y.: Chapman and Hall, 1987. 719 p.: ill. ISBN 0-412-26960-0. $155.00. **ED36**

Part of the "Chapman and Hall chemistry sourcebooks" series, these works (which despite the series title are dictionaries of organic substances) contain material drawn for the most part from the publisher's dictionaries of organic compounds. Some entries do not occur in those dictionaries, and some are revised. Substances are listed alphabetically by chemical name, and there are indexes of names, molecular formulas, and CAS Registry Numbers. QP701.C294

●**HEILBRON** [computer file]. London : Chapman & Hall Ltd. **ED37**
Available online (DIALOG). Updated semiannually.

Drawn primarily from the producer's series of dictionaries of organic compounds: *Dictionary of organic compounds* and supplements (*Guide* ED98 and above), *Dictionary of organometallic compounds* and supplements (*Guide* ED99 and above), *Dictionary of alkaloids* (above), *Dictionary of antibiotics and related substances* (above), and *Dictionary of organophosphorus compounds* (above). The online file contains additional information not in the dictionaries. Full text is searchable, as is numerical data (e.g., melting point, density, optical rotation). Includes more than 200,000 substances.

●**Beilstein online** [computer file]. [Berlin?] : Beilstein Institute. **ED38**
File size: 1.6 million records. Available online (DIALOG, STN). Updated irregularly.

Includes data on organic compounds from the *Handbuch der organischen Chemie* and suppl. I–IV, covering literature 1830–1959 (see *Guide* ED90), and from the Beilstein collection of excerpts drawn from the primary literature, 1960–79, which has not yet been critically reviewed but will eventually appear in suppl. V. The database is being released in several steps. "By 1991 we plan to have the complete literature from 1830–1980 available online."—*Beilstein brief*, No. 2 (1989). As with the printed *Handbuch*, the online file contains preparative information and data on the compounds in addition to bibliographic citations; numerical data are searchable.

Dean, John Aurie. Handbook of organic chemistry. N.Y.: McGraw-Hill, c1987. 1 v. (various pagings): ill. ISBN 0-07-016193-3. $64.50. **ED39**
A compilation of numerical information in tabular form, designed to meet the needs of organic chemists. Includes a brief introduction to organic nomenclature. The main table includes basic properties and Beilstein references for 4,000 organic compounds; other tables give physical properties, thermodynamic

properties, and spectroscopic data for some of the these compounds and for inorganic compounds considered to be useful to organic chemists. Also has chapters giving useful data for laboratory manipulations, data on polymers, rubbers, fats, oils and waxes, and miscellaneous data (e.g., conversion factors). Indexed. QD251.2.D43

EE

Earth Sciences

GENERAL WORKS

Guides

Information sources in the earth sciences / [ed. by] David N. Wood, Joan E. Hardy, and Anthony P. Harvey. 2nd ed. London ; N.Y.: Bowker-Saur, c1989. 518 p. ISBN 0-408-01406-7. **EE1**
Rev. ed. of: David N. Wood's *Use of earth sciences literature*, 1973 (*Guide* EE2).

For this completely revised edition, 19 librarians and earth scientists contributed detailed bibliographic essays. Introductory chapters describing the general nature of primary and secondary literature in the earth sciences are followed by reviews of reference sources, textbooks, and special format materials for specific earth sciences subdisciplines. Topical index with some title entries. Z6031.I55

Encyclopedias

Fairbridge, Rhodes Whitmore, series ed. Encyclopedia of earth sciences. N.Y.: Van Nostrand Reinhold, 1986–[1989?]. v. 10–11, 14–[16]: ill. **EE2**
For earlier volumes, see *Guide* EE5.

According to the publisher, plans for future volumes have been cancelled.

Contents: v. 10, *Encyclopedia of structural geology and plate tectonics*, ed. by Carl Seyfert (912 p. 1987. $114.95); v. 11, *Encyclopedia of climatology*, ed. by R.W. Fairbridge (1088 p. 1986. $109.95); v. 14, *Encyclopedia of field and general geology*; [v. 15] *Encyclopedia of solid earth geophysics* (*Supplement* EE6); [v. 16] *Encyclopedia of igneous and metamorphic petrology* (*Supplement* EE43).

Magill's survey of science. Earth science series / ed. by Frank N. Magill. Pasadena, Calif.: Salem Pr., c1990. 5 v.: ill. ISBN 0-89356-606-3 (set). $400.00. **EE3**
Part of the "Magill survey of sciences" series, this set contains 377 signed articles by 130 contributors. All major aspects of the earth sciences are surveyed, including geology, paleontology, geochemistry, hydrology, oceanography, atmospheric sciences, and astronomy. The alphabetically arranged articles are written for general readers and organized for ease of use, with definitions of pertinent terms and short annotated bibliographies. Few tables, charts, or illustrations. Each volume con-

tains a complete table of contents and topical index for the set. Glossary of terms and comprehensive index in v. 5. A more general source than R.W. Fairbridge's *Encyclopedia of earth sciences* (above). QE28.M33

Dictionaries

The concise Oxford dictionary of earth sciences / ed. by Ailsa Allaby and Michael Allaby. Oxford ; N.Y. : Oxford Univ. Pr., 1990. 410 p. ISBN 0-19-866146-0. $39.95.
EE4

Some 6,000 alphabetically organized headwords from all disciplines in the earth sciences are defined and explained. Brief, two- to three-sentence definitions include biographical entries for important figures and cross-references to terms defined elsewhere in the dictionary. Prepared by 33 contributors and advisors, with about a third of the terms drawn from *The Oxford dictionary of natural history* (*Supplement* EC25). Useful bibliography of sources. QE5.C66

GEOLOGY

Bibliography

●**Geological reference file** : (GeoRef) [computer file]. Alexandria, Va. : American Geological Institute, GeoRef Information System, 1961– . **EE5**

Coverage: North American geology, 1785– ; other areas of the world, 1933– . File size: 1.5 million records. Available online (CAN/OLE, DIALOG, ORBIT, STN; updated monthly), in CD-ROM as *GeoRef* (SilverPlatter; updated quarterly), and on magnetic tape (producer).

Corresponds to the printed versions of *Bibliography and index of geology* (*Guide* EE31), *Bibliography of North American geology* (*Guide* EE32), *Bibliography and index of geology exclusive of North America* (*Guide* EE30), and *Geophysical abstracts* (*Guide* EE67). Includes books, serials, maps, reports, and U.S. and Canadian dissertations. Search fields include author, source, subject, geographic descriptor, map coordinate. *GeoRef thesaurus and guide to indexing* (*Supplement* EE12) is needed for effective searching.

Encyclopedias

The encyclopedia of solid earth geophysics / ed. by David E. James. N.Y. : Van Nostrand Reinhold, c1989. 1328 p. : ill. (Encyclopedia of earth sciences, [v. 15]). ISBN 0-442-24366-9. $132.95. **EE6**

Surveys recent research in solid earth geophysics, drawing from specialities in physics, geology, and the space sciences with the intent of integrating that research with classical geophysics. Some 160 signed topical essays, alphabetically arranged, treat both introductory and technical issues and incorporate formulas, tables, diagrams, maps, cross-references, and short bibliographies. Written by specialists but accessible to a wide audience including students and knowledgeable general readers. Author and subject indexes. QE501.E58

McGraw-Hill encyclopedia of the geological sciences / Sybil P. Parker, ed. in chief. 2nd ed. N.Y. : McGraw-Hill, 1988. 722 p. : ill. ISBN 0-07-045500-7. $85.00.
EE7

1st ed., 1978 (*Guide* EE11).

Contains 520 signed articles that explore a broad range of topics in the earth sciences and include cross-references and brief bibliographies. Articles were drawn from *McGraw-Hill encyclopedia of science and technology* (6th ed., 1987; see *Supplement* EA38). Numerous black-and-white illustrations, tables, and charts. Subject index. QE5.M29

Dictionaries

Bates, Robert Latimer. Glossary of geology / Robert L. Bates and Julia A. Jackson, editors. 3rd ed. Alexandria, Va. : American Geological Institute, c1987. 788 p. ISBN 0-913312-89-4. $69.95. **EE8**

2nd ed., 1980 (*Guide* EE78).

Brief entry definitions. Coverage has been expanded to 37,000 headwords, with many new entries added for the fields of carbonate sedimentology, hydrogeology, marine geology, mineralogy, ore deposits, plate tectonics, and snow and ice. Terms and definitions recommended in the North American Stratigraphical Code (1983) are included. Syllabication and accents are given for headwords. List of references cited at end. No index. QE5.B38

Challinor, John. Challinor's dictionary of geology / ed. by Antony Wyatt. 6th ed. Cardiff : Univ. of Wales Pr. ; N.Y. : Oxford Univ. Pr., 1986. 374 p. ISBN 0-19-520505-7. $19.95. ISBN 0-19-520506-5 (pbk.). $9.95.
EE9

5th ed., 1978 (*Guide* EE80), had title: *A dictionary of geology*.

Definitions in this standard British work are longer than those in Robert L. Bates and Julia A. Jackson's *Glossary of geology* (above) and employ quotations from the geological literature to show usage. Classified index of terms. QE5.C45

Lexicon of geologic names of the United States for 1968–1975 / by Gwendolyn W. Luttrell... [et al.]. Wash. : U.S. Govt. Print. Off., 1981. 342 p. (U.S. Geological Survey bulletin, 1520). **EE10**

For previous editions, see *Guide* EE83–86.

Superintendent of Documents classification: I 19.3:1520.

"A compilation of the new geologic names introduced into the literature from 1968–1975 in the United States, its possessions, the Trust Territory of the Pacific Islands, and the Panama Canal Zone."—*t.p.*

Continued by: QE75.B9

Lexicon of new formal geologic names of the United States, 1976–1980 / by Gwendolyn W. Luttrell, Marilyn L. Hubert, and Virginia M. Jussen. Wash. : U.S. Govt. Print. Off. ; Alexandria, Va. : For sale by the Distribution Branch, U.S. Geological Survey, 1986. 191 p. (U.S. Geological Survey bulletin, 1564). **EE11**

Superintendent of Documents classification: I 19.3:1524.

"A compilation of the new geologic names introduced into the literature from 1976 to 1980 in the United States, Puerto Rico, Panama Canal Zone, and American Samoa."—*t.p.*
QE75.B9

Terminology

GeoRef thesaurus and guide to indexing. 5th ed. / Ruth H. Shimomura, ed. Alexandria, Va. : American Geological Institute, c1989. 731 p. : ill. ISBN 0-913312-98-3. $75.00. **EE12**

1st ed., 1977; 4th ed., 1986.

A guide "to the index terms used in *GeoRef* (*Guide* EE31 note and *Supplement* EE5). It includes term relationships, usage notes, dates of addition, indexing rules, guidelines for searching, and lists of systematic and other terms."—*Introd.*

This edition contains 20,242 terms, of which 4,284 are new. Essential for using the printed *Bibliography and index of geology* (*Guide* EE31) as well as the electronic versions of the database. Z695.1.G43G46

Foreign language and multilingual

French

Michel, Jean Pierre. Dictionary of earth science, English-French, French-English = Dictionnaire des sciences de la terre, anglais-français, français-anglais / ed. by J. P. Michel, Rhodes W. Fairbridge. N.Y. : Masson Pub. USA, c1980. 411 p. ISBN 0-89352-076-4. **EE13**

Provides both current and obsolete terminology in geology and physical geography for both languages. The sizeable vocabulary list makes this dictionary suitable for students and professional users. QE5.M52

Russian

Timofeev, Petr Petrovich. Anglo-russkiĭ geologicheskiĭ slovar' : okolo 52,000 terminov / P.P. Timofeev, M.N. Alekseev, T.A. Sofiano ; pod redaktsieĭ P.P. Timofeeva i M.N. Alekseeva. Moskva : "Russkiĭ iʾazyk", 1988. 540 p. ISBN 5-200-00284-2. 7.10 rub. **EE14**

Title on added t.p.: *English-Russian dictionary of geology*.

Gives Russian equivalents for about 52,000 English terms, with explanations or definitions in Russian provided for some words. Alphabetic arrangement, with supplementary tables in English and Russian for geological time periods and paleomagnetic reversals. QE5.T547

Multilingual

Multilingual thesaurus of geosciences / ed. by G.N. Rassam, J. Gravesteijn, R. Potenza ; sponsored by the International Council of Scientific and Technical Information (ICSTI) and International Union of Geological Sciences (IUGS). N.Y. : Pergamon, c1988. lii, 516 p. ISBN 0-08-036431-4. **EE15**

Lists some 5,000 terms in six languages: English, French, German, Italian, Russian, and Spanish. The base list, in English, identifies terms by a reference number and by subject field; indexes in all six languages refer to the base list. There is also an index by subject field. Z695.1.G43M84

Nederlands Geologisch Mijnbouwkundig Genootschap. Geological nomenclature / Royal Geological and Mining Society of the Netherlands ; ed. by W.A. Visser. The Hague ; Boston : M. Nijhoff, 1980. 540 p. ISBN 90-247-2403-1. **EE16**

1st ed., 1959 (*Guide* EE97).

This edition has been expanded to more than 7,000 terms and subject coverage broadened. As with earlier editions, a principal list on an English base is followed by indexes to Dutch, French, German, and for the first time, Spanish. Also lists terms that lack English equivalents, some synonyms in languages other than the five of the text, and obsolete or antiquated terms. 14 supplementary geological data tables. QE5.N413

Directories

Earth and astronomical sciences research centres : a world directory of organizations and programmes / consultant ed., Jennifer M. Fitch. Burnt Mill, Harlow, Essex, England : Longman ; Detroit : Distr. by Gale, 1984. 742 p. ISBN 0-582-90020-4. **EE17**

Lists some 3,500 governmental, industrial, and academic laboratories, national geological and meteorological agencies, observatories, and professional societies. Entries are arranged alphabetically by country. In addition to name, address, and telephone, the entries frequently include the name of the director, size of staff, a description of activities, and brief list of publications. Organization name and subject indexes. QE40.E25

Tinsley, Elizabeth J. Worldwide directory of national earth-science agencies and related international organizations / comp. by E.J. Tinsley and Joyce P. Hollander. Alexandria, Va. : Distribution Branch, Text Products Section, U.S. Geological Survey [distributor], 1984. 102 p. : maps. (U.S. Geological Survey circular, 934). **EE18**

For 1981 ed. and annotation, see *Guide* EE103.

Subtitle: a listing of governmental earth-science agencies and selected major international organizations whose functions are similar to those of the U.S. Geological Survey.

Superintendent of Documents classification: I 19.4/2:934.

Entries have been updated through November 1983. QE23.T56

History

Sarjeant, William Antony S. Geologists and the history of geology : an international bibliography from the origins to 1978. Supplement, 1979–1984 and additions. Malabar, Fla. : R.E. Krieger Pub. Co., 1987. 2 v. ISBN 0-89874-939-5. $162.50. **EE19**

For main set (1980) and annotation, see *Guide* EE108.

Contents: v. 1, Bibliography; v. 2, Index.

This suppl. includes some 7,100 new references and 1,548 brief biographies. The index volume contains an appendix listing women geologists identified in the main set and the suppl. Z6031.S28

Thompson, Susan J. A chronology of geological thinking from antiquity to 1899. Metuchen, N.J. : Scarecrow, 1988. 320 p. ISBN 0-8108-2121-4. $29.50. **EE20**

Descriptions of discoveries, ideas, and significant findings in the history of geology, collected from some 200 primary and secondary sources, briefly paraphrased, and arranged in chronological order. Although not a comprehensive survey, the work provides an overview of the development of geological thought. Useful bibliography of sources. Name index. QE11.T47

Guide-books

Union list of geologic field trip guidebooks of North America / comp. and ed. by the Geoscience Information Society Guidebooks Committee, Charlotte Derksen, chair. 5th ed. Alexandria, Va. : American Geological Institute, in cooperation with the Geoscience Information Society, c1989. 223 p. ISBN 0-913312-97-5. **EE21**

1st ed., 1968, had title *Geologic field trip guidebooks of North America, a union list incorporating monographic titles*; 4th ed., 1986.

Alphabetically organized by the name of the sponsoring society, organization, conference, government agency, or commercial source responsible for the guidebook. Includes guidebooks for field trips scheduled through 1985. Within each corporate entry, guidebooks are listed chronologically, followed by library holdings. Includes a directory of participating libraries and their services and geographic and stratigraphic indexes to the guidebooks. Useful for college and university library collections. QE45.G48

CRYSTALLOGRAPHY

World directory of crystallographers and of other scientists employing crystallographic methods. 7th ed. Boston : Publ. for the International Union of Crystallography by D. Reidel Pub. Co., 1986. **EE22**
1st ed., 1957; 6th ed., 1981.

An international directory of scientists with active interests in crystallography. Lists 8,968 scientists from 69 countries. Entries are arranged alphabetically by country and include: name and title; institutional address; birth date; highest academic degree awarded and granting university; present position; telephone; major fields of interest. Index by personal name. QD903.5.W6

GLACIOLOGY

Elsevier's dictionary of glaciology in four languages : English (with definitions), Russian (with definitions), French, and German / comp. by V.M. Kotlyakov and N.A. Smolyarova. Amsterdam ; N.Y. : Elsevier, 1990. 336 p. ISBN 0-444-88671-0. **EE23**

All types of glaciological phenomena (atmospheric, glacial, sea, river, lake, and ground ice; snow cover; and paleoglaciology) are defined. Terms from closely related disciplines such as physics, meteorology, and geocryology are included. The base list contains about 1,200 English headwords with accompanying definitions. Russian, French, and German language indexes are keyed to the main section. Useful introductory essay on the development of glaciological science and terminology. GB2401.E57

HYDROLOGY

Bibliography

●**Selected water resources abstracts** : (SWRA) [computer file]. Reston, Va. : U.S. Geological Survey, Water Resources Information Center, 1967– . **EE24**
For annotation, see *Supplement* EJ34.

Van der Leeden, Frits. Geraghty & Miller's groundwater bibliography. 4th ed. Plainview, N.Y. : Water Information Center, Inc., c1987. 381 p. ISBN 0-912394-20-X. **EE25**
1st ed., 1971 (*Guide* EE128), had title: *Ground water : a selected bibliography*; 3rd ed., 1983.

Expanded to 5,000 entries to accommodate new developments in the field. A general section contains citations to bibliographies, textbooks, and serial titles, while the subject section is arranged by topic and includes journal articles, reports, documents, and specialized monographs. No index. Z7935.V35

Dictionaries

Elsevier's dictionary of environmental hydrogeology : in English, French, and German / comp. by Hans-Olaf Pfannkuch. Amsterdam ; N.Y. : Elsevier, 1990. 332 p. ISBN 0-444-87269-8. **EE26**
Previous ed., 1969 (*Guide* EE130), had title *Elsevier's dictionary of hydrogeology in three languages.*

Expanded to 5,422 terms to include new areas of interest and interdisciplinary nature of the subject. English words are alphabetically arranged and are followed by French and German equivalents. Some definitions are provided for clarification. French and German term indexes refer to the English section. Bibliography of sources. GB1003.E47

METEOROLOGY

Directories

Curricula in the atmospheric, oceanic and related sciences. 1984– . Boston : American Meteorological Society, 1984– . Biennial. $25.00. **EE27**
Issues for 1963/64–73 had title: *Curricula in the atmospheric sciences*; for 1974–83: *Curricula in the atmospheric and oceanographic sciences.*

A directory of American and Canadian college and university programs in atmospheric science and in closely related oceanic and other sciences. Alphabetically arranged listings include: course and degree offerings, financial aid sources, research grants and contracts in effect, faculty, and information on recently completed theses and dissertations. Alphabetic, geographic, and degree indexes to universities and colleges; faculty index.

Climatology

Hatch, Warren L. Selective guide to climatic data sources. Rev. ed. Wash. : U.S. Dept. of Commerce, National Oceanic and Atmospheric Administration, National Environmental Satellite, Data, and Information Service, 1988. 1 v. (various pagings). (Key to meteorological records documentation, no. 4.11). **EE28**
1969 ed., *Guide* EE164.

Published and unpublished climatalogical data sources are grouped alphabetically by title within five categories: (1) Current serial publications; (2) Marine publications; (3) Decennial and intermittent publications; (4) Special publications including atlases; (5) Data catalogs and indexes. An essential reference for locating detailed U.S. climate information. Indexed by climatologic element. Z6685.U64

Pearce, E. A. The Times Books world weather guide / by E.A. Pearce and Gordon Smith. 2nd ed. N.Y. : Times Books/Random House, 1990. 1 v. ISBN 0-8129-1881-9. $17.95. **EE29**
Published in U.K. as *World weather guide.*
1st ed., 1984.

A convenient compilation of climatic information, largely unchanged from the 1st ed. Climate summaries and data tables are arranged by continent, then country, and for some larger countries, by region. Tables for the several representative stations in each country include latitude, longitude, and altitude of the station; monthly maximum and minimum temperatures in Fahrenheit and Celsius scales; relative humidity; and precipitation. British Meteorological Office publications are the principal source for the climatic data. Helpful introduction, glossary, country maps, and geographic index. QC982.P43

Ruffner, James A. The weather almanac : a reference guide to weather, climate, and air quality in the United States and its key cities, comprising statistics, principles, and terminology / James A. Ruffner and Frank E. Bair, editors. 5th ed. Detroit : Gale, c1987. 811 p. : ill. ISBN 0-8103-1497-5. $110.00. **EE30**
4th ed., 1984 (*Guide* EE159).
Updates data series from earlier editions, with special reports on recent unusual weather phenomena in the United States. QC983.R83

The weather handbook : a summary of climatic conditions and weather phenomena for selected cities in the United States and around the world / ed. by McKinley Conway and Linda L. Liston. Rev. ed. 1990. Norcross, Ga. : Conway Data, 1990. 548 p. : ill., maps. ISBN 0-910436-29-0. $39.95. **EE31**
1st ed., 1963.
A compilation of basic climatic data covering 250 U.S. cities and more than 600 foreign cities. Other features include small-scale state maps with weather risk profiles, U.S. summary climatic maps, charts of unusual weather phenomena, and a list by country of major weather-related disasters. Indexed by city. QC982.W38

World weather records, 1961–1970. Wash. : Environmental Data and Information Service, 1981–82. v. 3, 6. (In progress). **EE32**
For earlier volumes, see *Guide* EE154.
Contents: v. 3, West Indies, South and Central America (1982); v. 6, Islands of the world (1981).
Continued by: QC982.W6

World weather records, 1971–80. Wash. : National Climatic Data Center, 1987–89. v. 1–2. (In progress). **EE33**
Contents: v. 1, North America (1989); v. 2, Europe (1987).
Continues statistical series from previous editions (*Guide* EE152–154) with some additional stations. QC982.W6

MINERALOGY

Dictionaries

Read, Peter G. Dictionary of gemmology. 2nd ed. London ; Boston : Butterworth Scientific, 1988. 266 p. : ill. ISBN 0-408-02925-0. $49.95. **EE34**
1st ed., 1982.
A compact, alphabetical listing which provides "concise descriptions of the principal gem materials, as well as definitions of associated scientific terms and brief working explanations of the many types of gemmological instruments."—*Pref.* Some black-and-white illustrations, crystal system diagrams, and a data appendix. TS722.R43

Handbooks

Handbook of mineralogy / John W. Anthony . . . [et al.]. Tucson, Ariz. : Mineral Data Pub., c1990. v. 1. ISBN 0-9622097-0-8 (v. 1). $82.50. (In progress). **EE35**
Contents: v. 1. Elements, sulfides, sulfosalts.
To be complete in 5 v. Projected contents: v. 2, Silica, silicates; v. 3, Halides, hydroxides, oxides; v. 4, Arsenates, phosphates, uranates, vanadates; v. 5, Borates, carbonates, sulfates.

This substantial set will "gather in convenient form the data crucial to identification of all mineral species and . . . provide relatively up-to-date references containing information central to the definition of each species."—*Introd.* Alphabetically arranged entries record: physical, chemical, crystal, X-ray powder, and optical properties; occurrence and distribution; history of name; type specimen information; and bibliographic references for each mineral species. A specialist's source important for college and university library collections. No illustrations or index. QE366.8.H36

Nickel, Ernest H. Mineral reference manual / Ernest H. Nickel, Monte C. Nichols. N.Y. : Van Nostrand Reinhold, c1991. 250 p. : ill. ISBN 0-442-00344-7. **EE36**
An alphabetical listing of "all valid mineral species [that] includes the name, formula, current status, crystal system, appearance, hardness, measured and calculated density, type locality, mineral classification, a reference to the origin of the name, an indication of related species, and selected literature references."—*Introd.* Short, condensed entry format is useful for quick reference by students, and for field and laboratory use. No index. QE372.2.N53

Roberts, Willard Lincoln. Encyclopedia of minerals / Willard Lincoln Roberts, Thomas J. Campbell, George Robert Rapp, Jr. 2nd ed. N.Y. : Van Nostrand Reinhold, c1990. 979 p., 48 p. of plates : ill. (some col.). ISBN 0-442-27681-8. **EE37**
1st ed., 1974 (*Guide* EE199).
This desk reference for mineralogical data has been expanded to 3,200 alphabetically arranged entries, many rewritten in light of new research and technological developments. QE355.R6

Meteorites

Graham, A. L. Catalogue of meteorites : with special reference to those represented in the collection of the British Museum (Natural History) / by A.L. Graham, A.W.R. Bevan and R. Hutchison. 4th ed., rev. and enl. Tucson, Ariz. : Univ. of Arizona Pr., 1985. 460 p. ISBN 0-8165-0912-3. $50.00. **EE38**
3rd ed., 1966 (*Guide* EE203).
". . . this edition incorporates and expands the information published in the third edition (1966) and its appendix (1977). It includes the names of all well-authenticated meteorites known up to January 1984, even if no material has been preserved."—*Introd.* Contains entries for 2,611 meteorites of which 1,435 are represented in the collection of the British Museum (Natural History). Classified lists of meteorites by country and by type serve as indexes to the alphabetically arranged entries. QB755.G73

OCEANOGRAPHY

Bibliography

●**Oceanic abstracts** : (OC) [computer file]. Bethesda, Md. : Cambridge Scientific Abstracts, 1964– . **EE39**
Machine-readable version of *Oceanic abstracts* (*Guide* EE216).
File size: 214,500 records. Updated bimonthly. Available online (DIALOG), and as part of *CSA life sciences collection* from BRS, DIALOG), on CD-ROM as part of *Pollution/ toxicology CD-ROM* (Compact Cambridge, Faxon), and on magnetic tape (producer).

Indexes literature since 1964 in oceanography, marine sciences, and related subjects in meteorology, geophysics, environmental sciences, and engineering.

Biography

U.S. ocean scientists & engineers: 1987 directory. Wash. : American Geophysical Union, c1987. 179 p. **EE40**
Expanded version of *U.S. directory of marine scientists*, 1982 (*Guide* EE224).
A directory to some 6,600 American scientists and engineers teaching or working in marine science. Data was gathered by questionnaire in 1986. Individual entries are brief, listing name, current business address and telephone, and specializations. Entries are arranged in 3 sections: alphabetic; geographic by state and current employer; area of specialization.
GC10.D57

PALEONTOLOGY

Directories

International Paleontological Association. Directory of paleontologists of the world / [comp.] by Rex A. Doescher. 5th ed. [Wash.] : International Paleontological Association, 1989. 447 p. ISBN 0-9622577-0-2. **EE41**
2nd ed., 1968 (*Guide* EE250); 4th ed., 1984.
Alphabetic listings for some 7,600 paleontologists include name, address, telephone, and subject specialties. Geographic and taxonomic specialty indexes. QE707.A2I61

Handbooks

Kuhn-Schnyder, Emil. Handbook of paleozoology / Emil Kuhn-Schnyder, Hans Rieber. Baltimore : Johns Hopkins Univ. Pr., c1986. 394 p. : ill. ISBN 0-8018-2837-6. $35.00. **EE42**
Translation of *Paläozoologie*.
A selective guide that aims "to provide students with a well-illustrated, condensed introduction to the systematics of fossil animals."—*Foreword*. Entries are arranged by taxon and include morphological and ecological data and numerous illustrations. Appendixes include charts of temporal distribution of fossil groups and of geologic periods, and a tabular summary of the classificiation system. Indexes of subjects and of genera and species. QE761.K8413

PETROLOGY

The encyclopedia of igneous and metamorphic petrology / ed. by D.R. Bowes. N.Y. : Van Nostrand Reinhold, c1989. 666 p. : ill. (Encyclopedia of earth sciences, [v. 16]). ISBN 0-442-20623-2. $112.95. **EE43**
In 250 signed articles, provides detailed information on the mineralogical, chemical, and physical nature of igneous and metamorphic rock types as well as more general information on their formation, location, and investigation. Articles contain short bibliographies and cross-references as well as formulas, illustrations, charts, and tables. Author and subject indexes.
QE461.E56

International Union of Geological Sciences. Subcommission on the Systematics of Igneous Rocks. A classification of igneous rocks and glossary of terms / ed. by Roger W. Le Maitre . . . [et al]. Oxford ; Boston : Blackwell, 1989. 193 p. ISBN 0-632-02593-X. £19.95 (est.). **EE44**
A revised classification scheme approved after 20 years of deliberation and study. In two main sections: (1) classification scheme and nomenclature for igneous rocks with a summary of all published IUGS recommendations; (2) glossary of 1,586 rock names and related terms including description of properties, original source for the name, type locality, and references to additional sources of information about the rock type. Includes an extensive bibliography, appendixes on the history of the Subcommission's work, and a wall chart illustrating the classification scheme. QE461.I547

Mitchell, Richard Scott. Dictionary of rocks. N.Y. : Van Nostrand Reinhold, c1985. 228 p., [4] p. of plates : ill. (some col.). ISBN 0-442-26328-7. $29.95. **EE45**
Physical properties of rocks and histories of the origin and use of rock names are given from some 4,000 alphabetically arranged rock types. Meteoritics, natural organic materials, and gemstones are included. Includes black-and-white and color plates of specimens, a glossary of terms, and a bibliography.
QE423.M58

EF

Mathematics

GENERAL WORKS

Bibliography

Anderson, Nancy D. French mathematical seminars : a union list. 2nd ed. Providence, R.I. : American Mathematical Society, 1989. 178 p. ISBN 0-8218-0129-5. $23.00. **EF1**
1st ed., 1978.
A bibliography of proceedings of French mathematical seminars that includes library locations. Designed to "provide a means for librarians to verify the existence of published French mathematical seminars."—*Pref.* This edition includes 95 new seminar titles plus additional cross-references; first edition entries have been "corrected, revised, and augumented." Arranged alphabetically by the form most frequently cited in the literature. Entries include, as appropriate, sponsoring body, inclusive publication dates, variant titles, cross-references to former and later titles, series title and numeration, titles of individual volumes, library cataloging entry, *Mathematical reviews* references, publisher name and address, and holdings of almost 100 academic libraries in the U.S. and Canada. Z6655.A53

[Omega]—bibliography of mathematical logic / ed. by Gert H. Müller in collaboration with Wolfgang Lenski.

Berlin; N.Y.: Springer-Verlag, c1987. 6 v. ISBN 0-387-17457-5 (set). $1078.00. **EF2**

Contents: v. 1, Classical logic; v. 2, Non-classical logics; v. 3, Model theory; v. 4, Recursion theory; v. 5, Set theory; v. 6, Proof theory and constructive mathematics.

A comprehensive compilation of significant works in mathematical logic, 1879–1985. Each volume is in four sections: subject index, author index, source index, and miscellaneous indexes. Bibliographic citations to books, journal articles, and proceedings papers are contained in the alphabetical author index; cross-references are included. The subject index is arranged according to a subject classification scheme similar to those used in *Mathematical reviews* (*Guide* EF19) and *Zentralblatt für Mathematik und ihre Grenzgebiete* (*Guide* EF21); within subject classes, author/title entries are arranged chronologically, then by author; complete citations are given in the author index. The source index contains full title and publishing information for journals, series, proceedings, and collections that are cited in abbreviated form in the author index.

Z6654.M26O47

Sachs, Lothar. A guide to statistical methods and to the pertinent literature = Literatur zur Angewandten Statistik. Berlin; N.Y.: Springer-Verlag, 1986. 212 p. ISBN 0-387-16835-4. **EF3**

A guide to intermediate statistical methods designed for students, professional statisticians, and nonprofessional users of statistics. An alphabetical subject index, composed of title keywords and subject headings for journal articles and book contents, refers the user to entries in the bibliography section, which contains 1,449 citations. Coverage is through 1985.

Z6654.M33S23

Indexes and abstract journals

Current mathematical publications. v. 7 (Jan. 10, 1975)– . [Providence, R.I.]: American Mathematical Society, 1975– . Every three weeks, Nov. 25, 1983– . ISSN 0361-4794. $297.00. **EF4**

Continues *Contents of contemporary mathematical journals and new publications*, (v. 4–6, 1972–74) and assumes its numbering.

Indexes the current mathematical literature, both periodical and monographic. Items are arranged by the AMS classification, so may appear in several sections. Each issue contains an author index plus cumulative author and key subject indexes. Most items will eventually be included in *Mathematical reviews* (*Guide* EF19). Z6653.C85

●**Mathematics abstracts** : (MATH) [computer file]. Karlsruhe (Germany) : Fachinformationszentrum Karlsruhe GmbH (FIZ Karlsruhe), 1972– . **EF5**

Machine-readable version of *Zentralblatt für Mathematik und ihre Grenzgebiete* (*Guide* EF21).

Coverage: 1972– . File size: 700,000 records. Available online, updated monthly (STN) and in CD-ROM as *Compact-MATH*, 1985– , updated annually (Springer-Verlag).

●**MathSci** [computer file]. Providence, R.I. : American Mathematical Society, 1959– . **EF6**

Coverage: Mathematical literature, 1959– ; statistical literature, 1902– . File size: 800,000 records. Available online, updated monthly (BRS, DIALOG, CompuServe, EasyNet, STN) and in CD-ROM as *MathSci disc*, updated semiannually (SilverPlatter).

Provides comprehensive coverage of research literature in mathematics and statistics and select coverage of literature in related fields that contain statistical and mathematical applications. The online version contains records from *Mathematical reviews*, 1959– (*Guide* EF19); *Current mathematical publications*, 1985– (*Supplement* EF4); *Current index to statistics*, 1980– (*Guide* EF16); *Index to statistics and probability* (The Tukey index), 1910–68; *Computing reviews*, 1984– (*Guide* EJ226 note); *ACM guide to computing literature*, 1986–89 (*Guide* EJ226); and *Technical reports in computer science*, 1954– . Abstracts and reviews are included for *Mathematical reviews*, 1980– . The CD-ROM version contains records from the *Mathematical reviews* and *Current mathematical publications* subfiles only, 1981– .

Encyclopedias

Encyclopedia of mathematics : an updated and annotated translation of the Soviet "Mathematical encyclopaedia" / [managing ed., M. Hazewinkel]. Dordrecht ; Boston : Reidel ; Norwell, Mass. : Distr. by Kluwer Academic Publ., c1988–1990. v. 1–6. ISBN 1-55608-010-7. $149.00/vol. (In progress). **EF7**

A translation of *Matematicheskaia éntsiklopediia* (Moskva : 1977–85. 5 v.) with updating and editorial comment, to be complete in 10 v. including index. Contains three levels of entries: general survey articles on main topics; more specialized articles on concrete problems, techniques, and results; and brief definitions. Most articles include bibliographies, cross-references, and classification numbers in the scheme developed by the American Mathematical Society. QA5.M3713

Encyclopedia of statistical sciences / editors in chief, Samuel Kotz, Norman L. Johnson. N.Y.: Wiley, c1985–1989. v. 6–9 : ill. ISBN 0-471-05544-1 (set). $868.00. **EF8**

For v. 1–5 and annotation, see *Guide* EF22.

Contents: v. 6–9, Multivariate analysis–Z. Completes the set. QA276.14.E5

Encyclopedia of statistical sciences : Supplement volume / editors in chief, Samuel Kotz, Norman L. Johnson ; associate ed., Campbell B. Read. N.Y.: Wiley, 1989. 289 p. ISBN 0-471-81274-9. $65.00. **EF9**

Contains full, detailed articles for topics not covered in the basic set, plus additional cross-references. Includes cumulative index for basic set and supplement. QA276.14E5

Encyclopedic dictionary of mathematics / by the Mathematical Society of Japan ; ed. by Kiyosi Itô. 2nd ed. Cambridge, Mass.: MIT Pr., c1987. 4 v. (2148 p.) : ill. ISBN 0-262-09026-0. $350.00. **EF10**

1st ed., 1977 (*Guide* EF28).

Translation of *Iwanami sūgaku jiten*.

An English version of the 3rd Japanese edition (1985). "Intended to be a compact, up-to-date source of information comprising, as completely as possible, all significant results in all fields of our Science, pure and applied, from the elementary to the advanced level."—*Foreword*. Contains 450 articles on broad mathematical subjects, with extensive subdivisions and literature references, including some biographical entries. Vol. 4 contains appendixes (tables of formulas, numerical tables, lists of journals and publishers, tables of special notations, systematic and alphabetic lists of articles, and lists of contributors and translators), as well as name and detailed subject indexes. QA5.I8313

Dictionaries

Marriott, F. H. C. A dictionary of statistical terms. 5th ed., prepared for the International Statistical Institute by F.H.C. Marriott. Burnt Mill, Harlow, Essex, England : Publ. for the International Statistical Institute by Longman Scientific & Technical ; N.Y.: Wiley, 1990. 223 p. ISBN 0-470-21349-3. $59.95. **EF11**

4th ed., 1982 (*Guide* CG34).

Includes about "400 new entries, based on a study of the literature over the past ten years."—*Pref.* HA17.K4

Tietjen, Gary L. A topical dictionary of statistics. N.Y. : Chapman and Hall, 1986. 171 p. ISBN 0-412-01201-4. $22.50. **EF12**

Attempts "to offer more than the usual string of isolated and independent definitions: it provides also the context, applications, and related terminology."—*Pref.* Intended for statistcans, students, scientists, and other users of statistics. Divided into 15 well-organized topical chapters with references. Includes an index. QA276.14.T54

Foreign terms

Russian

Lohwater, A. J. A.J. Lohwater's Russian-English dictionary of the mathematical sciences / ed. by R.P. Boas. 2nd ed., rev. and expanded / with the assistance of Alana I. Thorpe. Providence, R.I. : American Mathematical Society, c1990. 343 p. ISBN 0-8218-0133-3. $50.00. ISBN 0-8218-0133-3 (pbk.). $35.00. **EF13**

1st ed., 1961 (*Guide* EF38).

A comprehensive dictionary that provides English equivalents for some 15,000 Russian terms, reflecting current usage in mathematics. "The vocabulary has been extensively enlarged and brought up to date, although it retains some obsolete terms that may be needed by users who have to consult older literature."—*Pref.* This edition adds stress markings on Russian words and contains a revised brief Russian grammar section with appendixes that contain noun declensions, verb conjugations, list of numerals, and root list. QA5.L64

Handbooks

Bronshteĭn, I. N. Handbook of mathematics / I. N. Bronshtein, K. A. Semendyayev ; English translation ed. by K. A. Hirsch. 3rd rev. ed. Frankfurt : Verlag Harri Deutsch ; N.Y. : Van Nostrand Reinhold [distributor], 1985. 973 p. : ill. ISBN 0-442-21171-6. $45.95. **EF14**

This English translation is based on the 19th and 20th German editions of the standard handbook, *Taschenbuch der Mathematik*. The 19th ed. (Leipzig : Teubner, 1979) represented a major revision undertaken by a team of mathematicians primarily from the Karl Marx Univ. of Leipzig; the 20th German edition (Leipzig : Teubner, 1981) was basically a reprint of the 19th. The original version, *Spravochnik po matematike : dlia inzhenerov i uchashchikhsia vtuzov*, was published in Russian (6th ed., Moskva : Gos. izd-vo tekhniko-teoret. lit-ry, 1956).

Provides in-depth coverage of all aspects of mathematics, including analysis, probability theory, and mathematical information processing. Useful for students, teachers, and mathematicians. Organized in broad subject sections that contain definitions, equations, and tables. Includes bibliography and subject index. QA40.B869

Spanier, Jerome. An atlas of functions / Jerome Spanier, Keith B. Oldham. Wash. : Hemisphere Pub. Corp., c1987. 700 p. : ill. (some col.). ISBN 0-89116-573-8. $149.95. **EF15**

A useful compendium concerning groups of functions, in 64 chapters. The data are presented in a standardized format that includes notation, behavior, definitions, special cases, interrelationships, expansions, particular values, numerical values, approximations, operations of the calculus, complex argument, generalizations, cognate functions, and related topics.

Contains extensive tables and more than 180 multicolored computer-generated graphs. Includes appendixes of general algorithms and of useful data (e.g., conversion factors, units, constants, and Greek alphabet). Bibliography; subject and symbol indexes. Valuable to researchers, teachers, and students. QA331.S685

Zwillinger, Daniel. Handbook of differential equations. Boston : Academic Pr., c1989. 673 p. : ill. ISBN 0-12-784390-6. $49.95. **EF16**

A compilation of "the most important and widely applicable methods for solving and approximating differential equations" (*Introd.*) that is "... designed to serve as both a reference book and as a complement to a text on differential equations ... [while also being] useful for the practicing engineer or scientist who solves differential equations on an occasional basis."—*Pref.* Assumes a basic understanding of differential equations. Includes extensive literature references for each technique and an index to named differential equations. QA371.Z88

Tables

Compendiums

Selected tables in mathematical statistics. Providence, R.I. : American Mathematical Society, 1985–88. v. 9–11. (In progress). **EF17**

For v. 1–8 and annotation, see *Guide* EF77.

Vols. issued jointly by the Institute of Mathematical Statistics and the American Mathematical Society.

Continues the scope of the first eight volumes. QA276.25.S43

Biography

Women of mathematics : a biobibliographic sourcebook / ed. by Louise S. Grinstein and Paul J. Campbell. N.Y. : Greenwood, 1987. 292 p. ISBN 0-313-24849-4. $55.00. **EF18**

Contains 43 essays about important women mathematicians from ancient times to the present. Written primarily by women mathematicians, each essay includes biographical information, a detailed discussion of the individual's mathematical work, and a bibliography of works by and about the individual. Broader in scope than either L.M. Osen's *Women in mathematics* (Cambridge, Mass. : MIT Pr., 1974) or T. Perl's *Math equals: biographies of women mathematicians + related activities* (Menlo Park, Calif. : Addison-Wesley, 1978), both of which emphasize biographical rather than mathematical information. QA28.W66

EG

Physics

GENERAL WORKS

Bibliography

Behrens, Heinrich. Datensammlungen in der Physik = Data compilations in physics / H. Behrens, G. Ebel. Karlsruhe : Fachinformationszentrum Energie, Physik, Mathematik, 1985. 623 p. in various pagings. (Physik Daten. Physics data, no. 3–5).   **EG1**

Cumulates, revises, and extends the four earlier volumes in the series (*Guide* EG4), indexing about 3,600 data compilations.   Z7405.T3B44

Abstract journals and indexes

●**INSPEC** / Institution of Electrical Engineers [computer file]. Piscataway, N.J. : INSPEC Marketing Dept., IEEE Service Center, [1969]– .   **EG2**

File size: 3.5 million records. Updated monthly. Available online (BRS, CAN/OLE, Data-Star, DIALOG) and on magnetic tape (producer).

Provides access to literature on physics, electrical engineering and electronics, control theory and technology, computing and control engineering. Records correspond to those in the printed INSPEC databases *Science abstracts: Sec. A, Physics abstracts* (*Guide* EG10), *Sec. B, Electrical & electronics abstracts* (*Guide* EJ200) and *Sec. C, Computer & control abstracts* (*Guide* EJ201), and *IT focus : update on information technology.*

●**Physics briefs** [computer file]. N.Y. : American Institute of Physics, 1979– .   **EG3**

Machine-readable form of *Physics briefs* (*Guide* EG9).

File size: 1.1 million records. Updated semimonthly. Available online (STN).

Covers all topics in physics, astronomy, astrophysics, and related fields.

Encyclopedias

Encyclopedia of physics / ed. by Rita G. Lerner, George L. Trigg. 2nd ed. N.Y. : VCH, 1990. 1408 p. : ill. ISBN 0-89573-752-3.   **EG4**

Retaining the format of the 1st ed., 1981 (*Guide* EG13), this edition is expanded by about 20% in order to include developments in physics over the past decade in fields such as high-temperature superconductors, chaos theory, scanning tunneling microscopy, etc.   QC5.E545

Handbuch der Physik. Berlin ; N.Y. : Springer-Verlag, 1988. v. 55. ISSN 0085-140X.   **EG5**

For v. 1–54 and annotation, see *Guide* EG19.

Contents: v. 55, General index. Completes the set, although v. 43 was never issued and only part 1 of v. 5 was published.

Subject headings in the index volume are organized by topical group, as were the volumes in the series: (1) Mathematical methods; (2) Principles of theoretical physics; (3) Mechanical and thermal behaviour of matter; (4) Electric and magnetic behaviour of matter; (5) Optics; (6) X-rays and corpuscular rays; (7) Atomic and molecular physics; (8) Nuclear physics; (9) Cosmic rays; (10) Geophysics; (11) Astrophysics. Also includes an index of contributors and a listing of all volumes in the series, with chapters and contributors.   QC21.H327

Dictionaries

Lord, M. P. Macmillan dictionary of physics. London : Macmillan, 1986. [331] p. : ill. ISBN 0-333-39066-0. £29.95. ISBN 0-333-42377-1 (pbk.). £8.95.   **EG6**

Brief definitions with cross-references. Includes some formulas, illustrations, and tables of SI units.   QC5.L67

Handbooks

CRC handbook of laser science and technology / ed., Marvin J. Weber. Boca Raton, Fla. : CRC Pr., c1986–1987. v. 3–5. ISBN 0-8493-3501-9. (In progress?).   **EG7**

For v. 1–2 and annotation, see *Guide* EG38.

Contents: v. 3, Optical materials, pt. 1: Nonlinear optical properties/radiation damage; v. 4, Optical materials, pt. 2: Properties; v. 5, Optical materials, pt. 3: Applications, coatings, and fabrication.   TA1675.L38

Lasers / ed., Marvin J. Weber. Boca Raton, Fla. : CRC Pr., 1990. v. 1. (CRC handbook of laser science and technology. Supplement, 1). ISBN 0-8493-3506-X. (In progress).   **EG8**

Updates *CRC handbook of laser science and technology* (above).

Contents: v.1, Lasers.   TA1675.L378

A physicist's desk reference / Herbert L. Anderson, ed. in chief. N.Y. : American Institute of Physics, c1989. 356 p. : ill. ISBN 0-88318-629-2. ISBN 0-88318-610-1 (pbk.).   **EG9**

lst ed., 1981 (*Guide* EG36), had title *AIP 50th anniversary physics vade mecum.*

Chapters have been expanded and updated, adding, e.g., material on high temperture superconductors. Several chapters have been significantly revised, and the index expanded.   QC61.P49

Style manuals

American Institute of Physics. AIP style manual / prepared under the direction of the AIP Publication Board. 4th ed. N.Y. : American Institute of Physics, 1990. 64 p. : ill. ISBN 0-88318-642-X. $10.00.   **EG10**

3rd ed., 1978, had title *Style manual for guidance in the preparation of papers for journals published by the American Institute of Physics and its member societies.*

" . . . presents advice which, if followed, should result in the preparation of clear, concise, and well organized manuscripts eminently suitable for submission to any physics or astronomy journal editor's office."—*Pref.*   QC5.45.A45

Tables

Browne, Edgardo. Table of radioactive isotopes / Edgardo Browne and Richard B. Firestone ; Virginia S. Shirley, ed. N.Y. : Wiley, c1986. 1 v. (various pagings) : ill. ISBN 0-471-84909-X. $59.95.   **EG11**

A compendium of data for all known radioactive isotopes, derived in part from the related compendium *Table of isotopes* (ed. by Charles Michael Lederar and Virginia S. Shirley; *Guide* EG48), the journal *Nuclear data sheets*, and other sources. The compilers have "tried to satisfy the ever increasing demand for *adopted* properties for *all* radiations emitted by nuclei. We have therefore included tables of adopted properties, which were derived from experimental data plus reliable calculations (e.g. continuous radiation spectra), along with those based on statistical analyses of existing experimental data alone.... We further calculated other derived adopted properties (e.g. average photon energies per disintegration) for which we sensed strong user demand."—*Pref.* As with the *Table of isotopes,* the main table is ordered by mass number and subordered by atomic number.   QD601.2.B76

Kaye, G. W. C. Tables of physical and chemical constants and some mathematical functions. 15th ed. London ; N.Y. : Longman, 1986. 477 p. : ill. ISBN 0-582-46354-8. £17.50.   **EG12**

14th ed., 1974 (*Guide* EG46).

"Originally compiled by G.W.C. Kaye and T.H. Laby ; now prepared under the direction of an editorial committee."—*t.p.*

Most of the mathematical tables have been dropped from this edition since pocket calculators have rendered them obsolete. Some new sections have been added, including wavelength standards, cosmic rays, atomic radii, calorific values of fuels, nuclear fusion, and radioactive series.   QC61.K3

Biography

The Nobel Prize winners : physics / ed. by Frank N. Magill. Pasadena, Calif. : Salem Pr., c1989. 3 v. (1364 p.) : ports. ISBN 0-89356-557-1 (set). $210.00.   **EG13**

For physics, observes the scope and arrangement of the same series for chemistry (*Supplement* ED25) from the first prize through 1988. The full texts of the Nobel lectures are published in the series in physics issued by the Nobelstiftelsen (*Guide* EG53).   QC25.N63

EH

Agricultural Sciences

AGRICULTURE

Guides

Information sources in agriculture and food science / ed., G.P. Lilley. London ; Boston : Butterworths, 1981. 603 p. ISBN 0-408-10612-3. £28.00.   **EH1**

In two parts: (1) general topics such as use of libraries, general abstracts and indexes, computerized bibliographic sources, and statistical sources; (2) more specialized areas such as food science, soils, farming, animal production and veterinary science. 18 contributors including the editor. Indexed.

S494.5.I47I53

Morgan, Bryan. Keyguide to information sources in agricultural engineering. London ; N.Y. : Mansell, 1985. 209 p. ISBN 0-7201-1720-8. $36.00.   **EH2**

In three parts: a survey of agricultural engineering and its literature, an annotated bibliography of sources of information, and organizational sources of information. International in scope; emphasis is on U.K. publications. Cross-references; index.   Z5074.E6M67

Bibliography

International union list of agricultural serials. Wallingford, U.K. : C.A.B. International, c1990. 767 p. ISBN 0-85198-661-7.   **EH3**

"Gives details of 11,567 publications coming from 129 different countries, with titles in 53 languages. The entries were derived from a database . . . created and maintained by [the National Agricultural Library]."—*Foreword.* A conflation of the lists of serials indexed by the machine-readable databases *AGRICOLA, AGRIS,* and *CAB abstracts.* Entries are arranged alphabetically by title. Each entry includes code for country of publication, and one or more subject codes. Includes a key to country and subject codes.   Z5076

Jensen, Richard D. Agricultural and animal sciences journals and serials : an analytical guide / comp. by Richard D. Jensen, Connie Lamb, and Nathan M. Smith. Westport, Conn. : Greenwood, 1986. 211 p. ISBN 0-313-24331-X.   **EH4**

Provides bibliographic information and descriptive annotations for 362 selected English-language research journals and other serials, covering the subject areas of agricultural economics, agronomy, animal science, fisheries, forestry, horticulture, and veterinary science. The target audience is indicated for each title. Geographical, publishers, subject, and title indexes.   Z5073.J46

Indexes

●**AGRICOLA** : (AGRIcultural OnLine Access) [computer file]. Beltsville, Md. : U.S. National Agricultural Library, 1970– . **EH5**

Includes records from *Bibliography of agriculture* (*Guide* EH30) and *National Agricultural Library catalog* (*Guide* EH9) and citations with abstracts from the Food and Nutrition Information Center (FNIC) at the U.S. National Agricultural Library.

File size: 2.5 million records. Updated monthly. Available online (BRS, DIALOG), in CD-ROM (OCLC, SilverPlatter, Abt Books, Faxon), and on magnetic tape (producer).

The database records are from journals (90%) and monographs and are worldwide in scope, about 30% from Western European, Slavic, Oriental, and African languages. Titles are given in English as well as in the original language. Beginning 1985, all materials are indexed using the *CAB Thesaurus* (*Supplement* EH5). The serials indexed are listed in *International union list of agricultural serials* (*Supplement* EH3). Only FNIC indexed materials include abstracts.

●**AGRIS** : (International information system for the agricultural sciences and technology) [computer file]. Rome : Food and Agriculture Organization of the United Nations (FAO), AGRIS Coordinating Centre, 1975– . **EH6**

Machine-readable version of *Agrindex* (Rome : AGRIS Coordinating Centre, FAO, 1975–).

File size: 1.6 million records. Updated monthly. Available online (DIALOG [non-U.S. literature only]), in CD-ROM (Faxon, SilverPlatter), and on magnetic tape (producer).

Comparable in scope to *AGRICOLA* (above) and supplements its coverage of non-English literature. About 10% of the records include abstracts. All titles are in English as well as the original language. The serials indexed are listed in *International union list of agricultural serials* (*Supplement* EH3) and in the *AGRIS serials list* (Rome : AGRIS Coordinating Centre, 1983–).

●**Biological & agricultural index** [computer file]. N.Y. : H.W. Wilson, 1983– . **EH7**

For annotation, see *Supplement* EC5.

Abstract journals

●**CAB abstracts** [computer file]. Wallingford, Eng. : C.A.B. International, 1973– . **EH8**

Machine-readable version of 52 abstracting journals published by C.A.B. International (for partial list, see *Guide* EH35).

File size: about 3 million records (most with abstracts). Updated monthly. Available online (BRS, CAN/OLE, DataStar, DIALOG, STN) and in CD-ROM (SilverPlatter, EBSCO, Faxon, producer). Portions also available in CD-ROM (see below).

Provides worldwide coverage of about 10,000 agricultural journals and monographs. Indexed, like *AGRICOLA* (*Supplement* EH5), using *CAB thesaurus* (*Supplement* EH5). The serials indexed are listed in *International union list of agricultural serials* (*Supplement* EH3).

§ C.A.B. International is producing three CD-ROM databases that constitute subsets of *CAB abstracts*. *VETCD* contains 300,000 records and includes citations and abstracts from *Index veterinarius* (*Guide* EH76) and *Veterinary bulletin* (*Guide* EH78), 1972 to the present. *BEASTCD* complements *VETCD* but covers the production side of animal science for the same period. *TREECD* includes *Forestry abstracts* (*Guide* EH97) from 1939 to the present as well as *Forest products abstracts*

(1978–) and *Agroforestry abstracts* (1988–). These CDs are updated annually.

Encyclopedias

The Oxford companion to gardens / consultant editors, Sir Geoffrey Jellicoe, Susan Jellicoe ; executive editors, Patrick Goode, Michael Lancaster. Oxford ; N.Y. : Oxford Univ. Pr., 1986. 635 p. ISBN 0-19-866123-1. $40.25. **EH9**

For annotation, see *Supplement* BE143. SB469.25.O95

Dictionaries

Dalal-Clayton, D. B. Black's agricultural dictionary. 2nd ed. London : A. & C. Black, 1985. 432 p. : ill. ISBN 0-7136-2679-8. £15.00. **EH10**

1st ed., 1981 (*Guide* EH42).

Many entries expanded, revised and added. "Not only is the dictionary a complete coverage of the numerous terms used by farmers and agricultural scientists, but eighteen pages are devoted towards listing, and explaining, several hundred important abbreviations, acronyms and initials."—*Foreword.* Especially good for unusual British terms (e.g., "Batology, the study of brambles"). Many cross-references; British spelling.

S411.D245

Holliday, Paul. A dictionary of plant pathology. Cambridge ; N.Y. : Cambridge Univ. Pr., 1989. 369 p. ISBN 0-521-33117-X. **EH11**

Concerned with diseases of commercial crops, listing "the authoritative names of all important pathogens and many minor ones."—*Pref.* Besides definitions of terms, provides brief descriptions of each disease species, along with citations to major research papers. Common names of the diseases are listed under the name of the plant species they infect (e.g., "Cowpea chlorotic mottle"). Similarly, the plant species that each pathogen infects is listed beneath the pathogen name. Definitions of pathogen genera and species are very technical.

SB728.H65

Soule, James. Glossary for horticultural crops / James Soule ; sponsored by the American Society for Horticultural Science. N.Y. : Wiley, c1985. 898 p. : ill. ISBN 0-471-88499-5. $40.00 (est.). **EH12**

Provides "ready access to technical terms over a broad spectrum of the plant and plant-related sciences."—*Pref.* In six main sections: Horticultural crops, Morphology and anatomy, Horticultural taxonomy and plant breeding, Horticultural physiology and crop ecology, Propagation, nursery handling, soils, crop production, and Postharvest handling and marketing. Line drawings; indexes of terms and crops. SB317.58.S68

Thesaurus of agricultural organisms, pests, weeds, and diseases / ed. by Derwent Publications Ltd., Literature Division with the assistance of CIBA-GEIGY SA. London ; N.Y. : Chapman and Hall, 1990. 2 v. ISBN 0-442-30422-6. **EH13**

An alphabetically arranged index and cross-reference to the Latin names, keywords, and most frequently used synonyms and common names of weeds, pests and disease microorganisms as well as crop species. "For each organism there is a MAIN ENTRY, consisting of an approved Latin name, followed by one or two HIGHER TAXA in parentheses."—*Pref.* Vol. 2 has a separate index of about 23,000 inverted species names (including main entries and synonyms). Common names are given in English, French and German. Indispensable for agricultural libraries. Z695.1.A4T52

Terminology

CAB thesaurus. 1990 ed. Wallingford, U.K. : C.A.B. International, 1990. 2 v. ISBN 0-85198-685-4 (v. 1). ISBN 0-85198-686-2 (v. 2). ISBN 0-85198-687-0 (pbk.). £100.00. **EH14**

The basic source used in indexing the databases *AGRICOLA* (*Supplement* EH5) and *CAB abstracts* (*Supplement* EH8). Each entry is followed by a list, where appropriate, of nonpreferred terms, broader terms, narrower terms, and related terms. An excellent resource for anyone indexing agricultural literature and essential for those using either *AGRICOLA* or *CAB abstracts*. Available both in printed form and on magnetic tape. Z699.5.A5T4

Organizational and biographical directories

Agricultural information resource centers : a world directory 1990 / Rita C. Fisher... [et al.]. Urbana, Ill. : IAALD, CTA, 1990. 641 p. ISBN 0-9624052-0-5. **EH15**

A directory of "3,971 information resource centers that have agriculture-related collections and/or information services. Agriculture is defined in the broadest sense ranging from production agriculture to basic research and including related sciences and social sciences."—*Introd.* Arranged by country, then by city and parent institution or, for Australia, Canada, U.S.S.R. and the U.S., by state, province, or Soviet Socialist Republic (SSR), then by city and parent institution. Indexes: country; city (for selected countries); institution (includes current, former, and variant names of the parent institutions); and subject. S494.5.I47A47

Directory of technical and scientific directories : a world bibliographic guide to medical, agricultural, industrial, and natural science directories. 5th ed. Burnt Mill, Harlow, Essex, England : Longman ; Phoenix : Oryx, 1988. 1 v. ISBN 0-582-00602-3. **EH16**

For annotation, see *Supplement* EA54. Z7405.D55D57

Horticultural research international : directory of horticultural research institutes and their activities in 63 countries. 4th ed. Wageningen : International Society for Horticultural Science, 1986. 903 p. : maps. ISBN 90-6605-332-1. fl.315. **EH17**

1st ed., 1966; 3rd ed., 1981.

"This edition includes 16,650 scientists at 1,250 institutes...."—*Pref.* Arranged alphabetically by country, giving for each a survey of horticultural research institutions and information on local conditions (rainfall and hours of sunshine, for example). Individual research institutes, including names of researchers and research projects, are listed by city. Two indexes: names and places, names of research workers.

U.S. agricultural groups : institutional profiles / ed. by William P. Browne and Allan J. Cigler. N.Y. : Greenwood, 1990. 274 p. ISBN 0-313-25088-X. **EH18**

Intended "as a reference guide for those interested in the role of agricultural interests in American national politics"; provides "profiles of over 100 private organizations that are most likely to gain the greatest attention from those who observe, study, and participate in agriculture policy-making."—*Pref.* An additional list of about 100 major groups is provided

as an appendix. Index to groups and persons mentioned in the text. HD9005.U19

Handbooks

Crop protection chemicals reference : CPCR. 1st ed.– . N.Y. : Chemical and Pharmaceutical Pub. Corp., c1985– . ISSN 0884-5115. $49.95. **EH19**

Complete text of product labels with a variety of indexes: brand name, manufacturer, common and chemical name, product category, crop and noncrop use, pest use, and product label by company. SB950.9.C76

Handbook of pesticide toxicology / Wayland J. Hayes, Jr., Edward R. Laws, Jr., editors. San Diego, Calif. : Academic Pr., 1991. 3 v. ISBN 0-12-334160-4. $400.00. **EH20**

Contents: v. 1, General principles; v. 2–3, Pesticides in humans.

Covers in signed chapters the toxicology of more than 250 insecticides, herbicides and fungicides. Indexed. RA1270.P4H36

Herbicide handbook of the Weed Science Society of America / Herbicide Handbook Committee, N.E. Humburg, chairman ; S.R. Colby... [et al.]. 6th ed. Champaign, Ill. : The Society, 1989. 301 p. : ill. ISBN 0-911733-13-2. **EH21**

1st ed., 1967, under the Society's earlier name, Weed Society of America, had title: *Herbicide handbook*; 5th ed., 1983.

"Includes information on herbicides and a few other chemicals such as safeners, modifiers, and extenders for herbicides... and plant growth regulators. There are sections on herbicide and weed control references, terms and definitions, Advanced Wiswesser and Wiswesser Line Notations... soil terminology, abbreviations and symbols, addresses of herbicide manufacturers... pronunciation guide for common names and... section of mathematical conversions...."—*Pref.* Data on herbicides and other chemicals are arranged alphabetically by common name or code number. Three indexes: Trademarks and chemicals by company; Index of chemical names; Index of common and product names, and code numbers. SB611.H43

Lorenzi, Harri. Weeds of the United States and their control / Harri J. Lorenzi, Larry S. Jeffery. N.Y. : Van Nostrand Reinhold, c1987. 355 p., [34] p. of plates : ill. (some col.). ISBN 0-442-25884-4. $69.95. **EH22**

Describes and illustrates over 300 plants. Each entry, on a separate page, provides the botanical description of a particular weed, describes its habitat, and suggests methods for its control. Each entry also includes a small-scale distribution map that gives a general indication where a specific weed may be found. Numbers preceding species names refer to illustrations in a color plates section. An introductory chapter describes weed identification and different kinds of weed control methods. Glossary of botanical terms; index. SB612.A2L67

Nyvall, Robert F. Field crop diseases handbook. 2nd ed. N.Y. : Van Nostrand Reinhold, c1989. 817 p. ISBN 0-442-26722-3. **EH23**

Arranged by crop name with separate chapters for each, Alfalfa to Wild rice. Diseases caused by bacteria, fungi, mycoplasmas, nematodes, rickettsias, viroids, and viruses are described for each species as appropriate. Bibliography with each chapter; index to both common and scientific name of each disease. SB731.N94

Schultz, LeRoy G. Barns, stables, and outbuildings : a world bibliography in English, 1700–1983. Jefferson,

N.C. : McFarland, c1986. 150 p. ISBN 0-89950-193-1. $35.00.   **EH24**
For annotation, see *Supplement* BE112.   Z5943.B35S38

Westcott, Cynthia. Westcott's plant disease handbook. 5th ed. / rev. by R. Kenneth Horst. N.Y. : Van Nostrand Reinhold, c1990. 953 p., [6] p. of plates : ill. (some col.). ISBN 0-442-31853-7.   **EH25**
1st ed., 1950; 4th ed., 1979.
A compendium on diseases of plants grown in gardens or in the home in the continental U.S. The backbone of the handbook, in Chapter 4, is the list of diseases arranged under an alphabetical list of more than 1,200 host plants. Includes indexes of common and scientific names of host plants, names of pathogens, and common names of more than 2,400 diseases. Select bibliography.   SB731.W47

ANIMAL SCIENCE

Guides

Gibb, Mike. Keyguide to information sources in veterinary medicine. London ; N.Y. : Mansell, 1990. 459 p. : ill. ISBN 0-7201-2018-7. $81.00.   **EH26**
Pt. I, "Survey of veterinary medicine and its literature," provides "a narrative survey of the kinds of information sources available with some discussion of their use in practice."—*Introd.* Pt. II consists of a bibliography of 1,782 entries with sections on general works, large animals, small animals, and specialties. Most entries contain brief annotations. Emphasis is on English-language works. Pt. III, "Directory of organizations," includes national veterinary associations, selected libraries, online databases and publishers. International in scope; index.   SF610.8.G53

Dictionaries

Concise veterinary dictionary / [consultant editors, Christopher M. Brown, D.A. Hogg, D.F. Kelly]. Oxford ; N.Y. : Oxford Univ. Pr., 1988. 890 p. : ill. ISBN 0-19-854208-9. $24.75.   **EH27**
Covers "all the major fields in veterinary science . . . . For . . . agricultural and veterinary students, veterinary assistants and practitioners, . . . research workers . . . in fields related to veterinary science."—*Pref.* Cross-references; line drawings.   SF609.C66

Handbooks

The Merck veterinary manual : a handbook of diagnosis, therapy, and disease prevention and control for the veterinarian / Clarence M. Fraser, ed. . . . [et al.]. 6th ed. Rahway, N.J. : Merck, 1986. 1677 p. : ill. ISBN 0-911910-53-0.   **EH28**
5th ed., 1979 (*Guide* EH86).
In this ed., "nearly all of the text that is not actually new has been extensively revised . . . " and the prescription section "has been replaced by a part entitled Pharmacology, and by short discussions on principles of therapy in the introductory portions of the sections relating to the anatomical systems."—*Foreword.*   SF748.M47

The UFAW handbook on the care and management of laboratory animals / ed. by Trevor B. Poole ; editorial assistant, Ruth Robinson. 6th ed. London : Longman ;

N.Y. : Churchill Livingstone, 1986. 1 v. ISBN 0-582-40911-X. $39.00.   **EH29**
5th ed., 1976 (*Guide* EH87).
Has "come to be regarded as the standard work in the field."—*Foreword.* Far more complete than Institute of Laboratory Animal Resources *Guide for the care and use of laboratory animals* (*Supplement* EC58) in its treatment of individual species. This edition, completely rewritten, is about 30% larger than the 5th ed.   SF406.U55

FOOD SCIENCE

Food science and technology abstracts. v. 1 (Jan. 1969)– . [Shinfield, Eng.] : International Food Information Service, 1969– . Monthly. ISSN 0015-6574.   **EH30**
The printed version of the *FSTA* database (available online through CAN/OLE, Data-Star, DIALOG, ORBIT, STN, and in CD-ROM through SilverPlatter). "Increasing by up to 20,000 records per year, *FSTA* covers articles on the basic food sciences, food products and food processes published in more than 2,000 journals in 40 languages, as well as information from patents, books, conference proceedings, legislative papers, etc."—*Foreword.* Each issue has 21 topical sections (e.g., Basic food science; Biotechnology; Food hygiene and toxicology; Cereals and bakery products; Standards, laws and regulations; Patent literature). Author and subject indexes; separate listing of abstracts concerning food safety.   TP368.F678

Hui, Y. H. United States food laws, regulations, and standards. 2nd ed. N.Y. : Wiley, c1986. 2 v. : ill. ISBN 0-471-84846-8 (set). $150.00 (est.).   **EH31**
1st ed., 1979.
Intends "to provide a basic understanding of the major food regulatory agencies in the U.S. and of the regulations they promulgate concerning food inspections, standards, specifications, and related matters."—*Pref.* Includes chapters on the Food and Drug Administration, the U.S. Dept. of Agriculture, medical fraud, the postal service, and food transportation. Each volume contains the tables of contents of both volumes; an index for both volumes is found in each volume.   KF3875.H8

Igoe, Robert S. Dictionary of food ingredients. 2nd ed. N.Y. : Van Nostrand Reinhold, c1989. 225 p. ISBN 0-442-31927-4.   **EH32**
For annotation, see *Supplement* EK101.   TX551.I26

Lewis, Richard J., *Sr.* Food additives handbook. N.Y. : Van Nostrand Reinhold, c1989. 592 p. ISBN 0-442-20508-2.   **EH33**
Designed to serve the information needs of the food chemicals industry; covers direct and indirect additives, packaging materials components, pesticides added directly or as residue, and selected animal drugs. Entries list substances in alphabetical order, giving for each descriptive data (CAS Registry Numbers, molecular formula and weight, physical properties, synonyms) information relating to use in food (purpose, where used, relevant regulations, potential hazards, standards, recommendations), safety profiles, and toxocity data. Four indexes: purpose served in foods, food type, CAS number, synonym. References cite CODEN, volume, page, and year; list of journals by CODEN.   RA1270.F6L49

HOME ECONOMICS

Food and cookery

Guides

Green, Syd. Keyguide to information sources in food science and technology. London ; N.Y. : Mansell, 1985. 231 p. ISBN 0-7201-1748-8. $45.00 (est.). **EH34**

Pt. I, "Food science and technology and their literature," provides a narrative account of the major sources of information and the structure of this literature; Pt. II is an annotated bibliography of sources of information; Pt. III, "Directory of selected organizations," is international in scope. Detailed table of contents. Index of names, subjects, organizations, and geographic areas. TP370.5.G76

Prytherch, Raymond John. Food, cookery, and diet : an information guide / Ray Prytherch, Suzanne Stanley. Aldershot, Hants, England ; Brookfield, Vt. : Gower, c1989. 109 p. : ill. ISBN 0-566-03568-5. $21.95. **EH35**

Arranged by subject categories: basic references; background; professional catering; training, education and careers; home cooking; and healthy eating and special diets. Subject index. Z7914.F63P79

Handbooks

Newman, Jacqueline M. Melting pot : an annotated bibliography and guide to food and nutrition information for ethnic groups in America. N.Y. : Garland, 1986. 194 p. ISBN 0-8240-4326-X. **EH36**

In ten chapters, eight treating ethnic groups: African Americans, Hispanic Americans, Chinese Americans, Japanese Americans, other Asian Americans, Indian Americans, Middle Eastern Americans, and "mixed ethnic references." East Europeans and Russians are omitted. Each chapter has three parts: an introduction, references (citations from medical, health, and nutrition journals) and "resources for recipes" (cookbooks). Chapter 1 provides an overview of American food preferences and nutritional habits, and Chapter 10, tables of food compositions. No index. Z7914.F63N48

EJ

Engineering

GENERAL WORKS

Guides

Information sources in engineering / ed., L.J. Anthony. 2nd ed. London ; Boston : Butterworths, 1985. 579 p. : ill. ISBN 0-408-11475-4. $95.00 (est.). **EJ1**

Rev. ed. of *Use of engineering literature*, 1976, ed. by K.W. Mildren (*Guide* EJ4).

The first ten chapters discuss primary sources (e.g., report literature, patents, standards, translations) and secondary sources (abstracts, indexes, bibliographies, online services). 18 subject fields are examined in detail, including: fluid mechanics, stress analysis, automotive engineering, electronics, computers, and public health engineering. Index of subjects, organizations, and information services. T10.7.I54

Indexes

●**COMPENDEX** [computer file]. N.Y. : Engineering Information, Inc., 1969– . **EJ2**

Machine-readable equivalent of *Engineering index* (*Guide* EJ9).

File size: 2.1 million records. Updated monthly. Available online (BRS, CAN/OLE, STN) and on magnetic tape (producer).

Covers engineering and technical literature published throughout the world.

§Also available is *COMPENDEX PLUS*, which combines *COMPENDEX* with *Ei engineering meetings* database. Coverage: 1970– . File size: 2.5 million records. Available online (Data-Star, DIALOG, ORBIT), in CD-ROM (DIALOG, Faxon, producer), and on magnetic tape (producer).

Institutional and biographical directories

Directory of technical and scientific directories : a world bibliographic guide to medical, agricultural, industrial, and natural science directories. 5th ed. Burnt Mill, Harlow, Essex, England : Longman ; Phoenix : Oryx, 1988. 1 v. ISBN 0-582-00602-3. **EJ3**

For annotation, see *Supplement* EA54. Z7405.D55D57

Who's who in engineering. 3rd ed.– . N.Y. : American Association of Engineering Societies [etc.], 1977– . ISSN 0149-7537. **EJ4**

5th ed., 1982 (*Guide* EJ18); 6th ed., 1985; 7th ed., 1988.

Concise entries, with geographic and subject specialization indexes.   TA139.E37

Who's who in technology / Amy L. Unterberger, ed. 6th ed. Detroit : Gale, c1989. 2 v. ISBN 0-8103-4950-7 (set).
                                                                EJ5
4th ed., 5 v., 1984 (*Guide* EJ20) had title: *Who's who in technology today*: 5th ed., 7 v., 1986.
Contents: v. 1, Biographies; v. 2, Indexes.
Publisher varies.
Contains more than 38,000 entries for North Americans, with a separate obituary section listing persons from the 5th ed. who died between 1986 and 1988. Indexes: geographic; employer; technical discipline (corresponding to the general categories from the 5th ed.); expertise (with designations chosen by the biographees).   T39.W5

Handbooks

Eshbach, Ovid W. Eshbach's handbook of engineering fundamentals. 4th ed., ed. by Byron D. Tapley; managing ed., Thurman R. Poston. N.Y. : Wiley, c1990. 1 v. (various pagings) : ill. ISBN 0-471-89084-7. $79.95.   **EJ6**
3rd ed., 1975 (*Guide* EJ27) had title: *Handbook of engineering fundamentals*.
Among the changes in this edition: a strong emphasis on computers and computer technology, including a new chapter on computers and computer science, and the incorporation of computer applications into other chapters; the chapter on aerodynamics and astrodynamics has been expanded to two separate chapters; the section on engineering economics has been substantially revised. Other additions include "the adoption of the international standard units throughout and the revision of the references to cite current literature."—*Pref.* Indexed.
                                                                TA151.E8

Materials

ASM engineered materials reference book / comp. by the editorial staff, Reference Publications, ASM International. Metals Park, Ohio : ASM International, c1989. 517 p. : ill. ISBN 0-87170-350-5. $87.00.   **EJ7**
Consists of tables and phase diagrams without text on "composites, ceramics, engineering or high-performance plastics, and electronic materials."—*Pref.* Appendixes: references; guide to general information sources; directory of composites laboratories and information centers; directory of composites manufacturers, suppliers, and services; international standards-issuing organizations; and universities with faculties in polymer science and in ceramics. No index.   TA403.4.A84

Bansal, Narottam P. Handbook of glass properties / Narottam P. Bansal and R.H. Doremus. Orlando, Fla. : Academic Pr., 1986. 680 p. : ill. ISBN 0-12-078140-9 : $160.00.   **EJ8**
Tables and graphs predominate, with a minimum of text. Silicate glasses are treated more thoroughly than nonsilicate glasses. The authors have critically evaluated the literature relating to thermal, electrical, mechanical, transport, and other related properties for a variety of different glasses. Chapters contain extensive bibliographies; short subject index.
                                                                TA450.B27

Brady, George S. Materials handbook : an encyclopedia for managers, technical professionals, purchasing and production managers, technicians, supervisors, and foremen / George S. Brady, Henry R. Clauser. 13th ed.

N.Y. : McGraw Hill, c1991. 1 v. ISBN 0-07-007074-1. $74.50.   **EJ9**
12th ed., 1956 (*Guide* EJ32).
Covers more than 15,000 minerals, animal and plant substances, and commercial and engineering materials. Uses, production methods, and trade names are included for common items. Most entries are shorter than half a page. The special chapter on structure and properties of materials includes charts, tables, and a glossary of terms. Uses both SI and U.S. customary units. Subject index is very important because the main text has no cross-references.   TA402.B73

Encyclopedia of materials science and engineering / ed. in chief, Michael B. Bever. Oxford : Pergamon ; Cambridge, Mass. : MIT Pr., 1986. 8 v. : ill. ISBN 0-262-02231-1. $1,950.00.   **EJ10**
Contents: v. 1–7, A–Z; v. 8, Systematic outline of the encyclopedia.
Although this work's 1,580 articles stress theory and practice, the treatment is not exhaustive. All the articles contain bibliographies, but indexes are found only in v.8, which also contains a systematic outline that readers should consult first. Indexes to authors of articles, cited authors, and acronyms, and an extensive subject index.   TA402.E53

Encyclopedia of materials science and engineering : Supplementary volume / ed., Robert W. Cahn ; senior advisory ed., Michael B. Bever. Oxford ; N.Y. : Pergamon Pr., 1988–[1990]. v. 1–[2] : ill. ISBN 0-08-032521-1 (v. 1). $240.00. ISBN 0-08-036196-X (v. 2). (In progress).
                                                                EJ11
Each supplement contains some new articles as well as those which replace or update entries form the parent *Encyclopedia* (above). Numerous cross-references. Suppl. 2 cumulates the subject index and the systematic subject outline. Additional supplement volumes will also have cumulative indexes.
                                                                TA402.E53

Engineered materials handbook / prepared under the direction of the ASM International Handbook Committee ; Theodore J. Reinhart, technical chairman. Metals Park, Ohio : ASM International, c1987–c1990. v. 1–3 : ill. ISBN 0-87170-279-7 (v. 1). (In progress).   **EJ12**
Contents: v. 1, Composites (1987); v. 2, Engineering plastics (1988); v. 3, Adhesives and sealants (1990).
Designed to be similar in comprehensiveness to the multivolume *Metals handbook* (9th ed., *Guide* EJ351 and *Supplement* EJ86; 10th ed., *Supplement* EJ87). Engineered materials include composites, plastics, adhesives, sealants, ceramics, and glasses. Gives current and practical information for choosing, utilizing, and evaluating these materials; includes numerous charts and graphs. Each volume has its own subject index and a separate glossary of terms.   TA403.E497

Materials data sources / comp. for the Materials Group, the Institution of Mechanical Engineers, and sponsored by the Institute of Metals . . . [et al.]. London : Mechanical Engineering Publications Limited for the Institution of Mechanical Engineers, 1987. 111 p. ISBN 0-85298-636-X.   **EJ13**
Gen. ed., P.T. Houldcroft.
Lists sources of data rather than the data proper. In four main sections: Metals and alloys; Refractories, ceramics, glasses and hardmetals; Polymers and composites; and Timber. Within each section are listed published data (books and standards) and useful organizations. Chapters on databases and materials selectors, and higher educational establishments (U.K. universities and polytechnics) complete the volume. Appendixes: Addresses of standards organizations (an international listing); Joining and adhesive bonding consumables (with two entries). This edition "will be updated within two years."—*Foreword.*   TA403.6M36

METADEX [computer file]. Materials Park, Ohio : Materials Information, ASM International, 1966– .
EJ14

Machine-readable version of *ASM review of metal literature* (*Guide* EJ329), *Metals abstracts* (*Guide* EJ332), *Alloys index* (1974–), *Steels supplement to Metals abstracts* (1983–84), and *Steels alert* (1985).

File size: 755,000 records. Updated monthly. Available online (CAN/OLE, Data-Star, DIALOG, STN), in CD-ROM as part of *METADEX collection* (DIALOG, Faxon), and on magnetic tape (producer).

The CD-ROM version includes *Metals abstracts* and *Engineered materials abstracts* (1986–).

AERONAUTICAL AND SPACE ENGINEERING

Aerospace database [computer file]. N.Y. : American Institute of Aeronautics and Astronautics, 1962– . **EJ15**

Machine-readable version of *International aerospace abstracts* (*Guide* EJ49) and *Scientific and technical aerospace reports (STAR)* (*Guide* EJ50).

File size: 1.7 million records. Updated semimonthly. Available online (DIALOG), in CD-ROM (DIALOG, Faxon), and on magnetic tape (producer).

Drawn from the worldwide literature on aerospace and related technology. The CD-ROM version from DIALOG provides coverage from the mid-1980s.

Cambridge air and space dictionary / gen. ed. P.M.B. Walker. Cambridge ; N.Y. : Cambridge Univ. Pr., c1990. 216 p. : ill. ISBN 0-521-39439-2. ISBN 0-521-39763-4 (pbk.). **EJ16**

Published in the U.K. under title: *Chambers air and space dictionary*.

Offers more than 6,000 terms, emphasizing aeronautics, astronomy, space, and radar, but including some abbreviations and terms in engineering, physics, telecommunications, and acoustics. An unusual feature consists of 66 "special articles" enclosed in separate panels to allow a fuller description of such topics as cosmic rays, navigation systems, and planets. Alphabetical entries include symbols, abbreviations, phrases, and numerous *see* references. An appendix contains a table of specifications for jet fuels. TL509.C35

BIOTECHNOLOGY

The biotechnology directory. 3rd ed. (1986)– – . N.Y. : Stockton Pr., 1986– . Annual. $150.00. **EJ17**

Continues: *The international biotechnology directory*, ed. by J. Coombs (N.Y. : Nature Press, 1983).

Publisher varies: 1983–85, Nature Pr.; 1986– , Stockton Pr.

A directory, organized geographically, of organizations, information services (databases, abstracting services, journals, newsletters), societies, and companies. Listings of companies include products and areas of research. Indexes include a buyers' guide directory of products, research, and services.
TP248.3.I56

Crafts-Lighty, A. Information sources in biotechnology. 2nd ed. London : Macmillan, 1985. [350] p. ISBN 0-943818-18-4 (pbk.). £40.00. **EJ18**

1st ed., 1983.

A useful introduction and guide to the literature of biotechnology, especially needed given the nature of the field, which ranges over topics such as biochemistry, molecular biology, chemical engineering, microbiology, and genetics. After a first chapter, "What is biotechnology? The science and the business," and a second that is an overview of types of sources, nine chapters discuss different types of sources, including not only the usual sources of scientific literature but also trade periodicals, patents, market surveys, and corporate directories. Includes a chapter on organizations related to biotechnology, and a concluding chapter on providing library and information services in biotechnology. Indexed. Z7914.B33C7

Walker, John M. The language of biotechnology : a dictionary of terms / John M. Walker and Michael Cox ; Allan Whitaker, contributor. Wash. : American Chemical Society, 1988. 255 p. : ill. ISBN 0-8412-1489-1. ISBN 0-8412-1490-5 (pbk.). **EJ19**

Taking "biotechnology" to mean "the practical application of biological systems to the manufacturing and service industries and to the management of the environment," including "the wide spectrum of related disciplines that must come together to commercialize a biological process," the authors seek "to define routinely used specialized language in the various areas of biotechnology."—*Pref.* Definitions are usually of paragraph length; some illustrations and equations are used. Cross-references. TP248.16.W35

CHEMICAL ENGINEERING

Plastics

Encyclopedia of polymer science and engineering / editorial board, Herman F. Mark . . . [et al.] ; ed. in chief, Jacqueline I. Kroschwitz. 2nd ed. N.Y. : Wiley, c1985–1990. v. 4–17, suppl. and index : ill. ISBN 0-471-89540-7 (v. 1). $200.00 (est.). **EJ20**

For v. 1–3 and annotation, see *Guide* EJ102.

Contents: v. 4–17, Composites, Fabrication–Zwitterionic polymerization. Supplement (1989); Index (1990). Completes the set.

The suppl. volume contains 33 articles (Acid-base interaction to Vinyl chloride polymers) but no index. The index volume has 13 additional supplementary articles (Asphaltic materials to Processing aids) and the subject index for all 17 v. of the main work and for the suppl. TP1087.E46

Information sources in polymers and plastics / ed., R. T. Adkins. London ; N.Y. : Bowker-Saur, c1989. 313 p. ISBN 0-408-02027-X. $70.00. **EJ21**

The editor stresses international coverage of the topics, drawing chapter authors from industry, universities, and libraries. Pt. 1 treats specific categories such as serials, books, patents, theses, and online databases. Pt. 2 discusses individual subjects such as polymer structure and nomenclature, rubber coatings and adhesives, and new developments in polymers. Pt. 3 emphasizes national and regional sources. Indexed.
Z5524.P7I54

Polymer handbook / ed. by J. Brandrup, E.H. Immergut. 3rd ed. N.Y. : Wiley, c1989. 1 v. (various pagings) : ill. ISBN 0-471-81244-7. $150.00. **EJ22**

2nd ed., 1975 (*Guide* EJ100).

Uses data compilations of chapter length to summarize information for synthetic polymers, polysaccharides and derivatives, and oligomers. Contains 30% more data than the 2nd edition. Short subject index. QD388.P65

Society of the Plastics Industry. Plastics engineering handbook of the Society of the Plastics Industry / [ed.

by] Michael L. Berins. 5th ed. N.Y.: Van Nostrand Reinhold, 1991. 1 v. ISBN 0-442-31799-9. **EJ23**

4th ed., 1976 (*Guide* EJ107).

Designed to be a state-of-the-art compilation. Chapters 1 through 3 include a glossary of terms and a description of classes of plastics. Chapters describe current types of processing (including machinery and equipment) as well as secondary processing methods. Contains numerous graphs, tables, line drawings, and photographs. Glossary terms are not listed in the subject index. TP1130.S58

CIVIL ENGINEERING

Handbooks

Civil engineer's reference book / ed. by L.S. Blake ; with specialist contributors. 4th ed. London ; Boston : Butterworths, 1989. 1 v. (various pagings) : ill. ISBN 0-408-01208-0. $140.00. **EJ24**

3rd ed., 1975 (*Guide* EJ110).

Chapters 1–10 discuss basic principles (e.g., strength of materials, engineering surveying, rock mechanics and rock engineering); chapters 11–44 give current design and construction practices (e.g., practical steel work, bridges, water supplies, offshore construction); chapter 45 treats units, conversion, and symbols. Includes references and bibliographies in all chapters except the last. Subject index. TA151.C58

The surveying handbook / ed. by Russell C. Brinker, Roy Minnick. N.Y.: Van Nostrand Reinhold, c1987. 1270 p. : ill. ISBN 0-442-21423-5. **EJ25**

Chapters are illustrated with figures and tables, together with worked-out examples of calculations. Discusses surveys for land, mining, routes, construction, and public lands. Includes chapters on land litigation and courtroom techniques; also contains addresses of state registration agencies. Indexed. TA555.S87

Environment and environmental problems

General works

Indexes and abstract journals

●**Enviroline** [computer file]. N.Y.: Bowker A & I Publ., 1971– . **EJ26**

Machine-readable version of *Environment abstracts* (*Guide* EJ122).

File size: 120,000 records. Updated monthly. Available online with coverage beginning 1971 (DIALOG, ORBIT), in CD-ROM with coverage beginning 1988 as part of *Enviro/energyline abstracts plus* (producer), and on magnetic tape (producer).

Emphasizes environmental and natural resources literature selected from more than 5,000 publications. The CD-ROM version covers both *Energy information abstracts* (1976–) and *Acid rain abstracts* (1985–).

●**Pollution abstracts** [computer file]. Bethesda, Md.: Cambridge Scientific Abstracts, 1970– . **EJ27**

Machine-readable version of *Pollution abstracts* (*Guide* EJ125).

File size: 145,000 records. Updated bimonthly. Available

online (Data-Star, DIALOG), in CD-ROM as part of *Pollution/toxicology CD-ROM* (producer), and on magnetic tape (producer).

Includes both technical and nontechnical publications.

Dictionaries

Allaby, Michael. Dictionary of the environment. 3rd ed. N. Y.: New York Univ. Pr., 1989. 423 p. ISBN 0-8147-0591-X. $55.00. **EJ28**

2nd ed., 1983 (*Guide* EJ126)

Extensively revised from the earlier ed. Lists acronyms, abbreviations, phrases, and some personal names and contains numerous cross-references. Some terms omitted from the 2nd ed. have been restored in the 3rd ed. QH540.4.A44

Directories

United Nations. ACCIS guide to United Nations information sources on the environment / prepared by the Advisory Committee for the Co-ordination of Information Systems (ACCIS), in collaboration with the Programme Activity Centre of the International Environmental Information System (INFOTERRA PAC) of the United Nations Environment Programme (UNEP). N.Y.: United Nations, 1988. 141 p. ISBN 92-1-100339-3. **EJ29**

Separate sections describe the organizations within the U.N., or related to it or any of its administrative units, that relate to the environment; environment-related directories produced by ACCIS or depository U.N. libraries; and, in a series of annexes at the end, addresses of national sources of U.N. environmental information and information about some U.N. online databases. Indexed. TD169.5.U55

Handbooks

Allegri, Theodore H. Handling and management of hazardous materials and wastes. N.Y.: Chapman and Hall, 1986. 458 p. : ill. ISBN 0-412-00751-7. $45.00. **EJ30**

Discusses "the safe and legal handling of hazardous materials and waste from the manufacturer's plant through the storage, transportation and distribution channels to the user, and, ultimately, to the disposal of the product or waste materials."—*Pref.* Practices are based on U.S. laws and regulations. There are chapters on asbestos, polychlorinated biphenyls (PCBs), acid rain, oil spills, handling radioactive waste, the Code of Federal Regulations, Superfund, and Toxic Substances Control Act. Includes a glossary of terms and appendixes giving information about U.S. Environmental Protection Administration regional asbestos coordinators and state solid and hazardous waste agencies. Indexed. T55.3.H3A45

Standard handbook of environmental engineering / [ed. by] Robert A. Corbitt. N.Y.: McGraw-Hill, c1990. 1281p. : ill. ISBN 0-07-013158-9. $89.50. **EJ31**

Although "oriented toward the needs of practicing environmental engineers," this work is also "intended to serve as a single-volume reference for other engineers, architects, planners, corporate managers, elected officials, lawyers, students, and others seeking insight into environmental engineering technology."—*Pref.* Six of the nine chapters (all by teams of authors) are longer than 100 pages: Environmental engineering; Air quality control; Water supply, wastewater disposal; Stormwater management; Solid waste; and Hazardous waste. Three shorter chapters describe Environmental legislation and regulations, Air and water quality standards, and Environmental assessment. Numerous tables and figures. SI and U.S. customary units are used throughout. Indexed.　　TD145.S72

Air pollution

Air pollution / ed. by Arthur C. Stern. 3rd ed. N.Y. : Academic Pr., 1986. v. 6–8 : ill. ISBN 0-12-666601-6 (v. 1). (In progress).　　**EJ32**

For basic set, called v. 1–5, see *Guide* EJ148.

Contents: v. 6, Supplement to Air pollutants, their transformation, transport, and effects; v. 7, Supplement to Measurements, monitoring, surveillance, and engineering control; v. 8, Supplement to Management of air quality.

Information in v. 1–5 has been revised and brought up to date in v. 6–8. Prefaces in v. 6–8 include charts showing how the supplements augment the corresponding chapters in the 2nd ed. (3 v., 1968) and the 3rd ed.　　TD883.S83

Miller, E. Willard. Environmental hazards : air pollution : a handbook for reference / E. Willard Miller, Ruby M. Miller. Santa Barbara, Calif. : ABC-Clio, c1989. 250 p. ISBN 0-87436-528-7.　　**EJ33**

The principal sections are an annotated bibliography that lists some 400 works and an introduction that discusses various causes of air pollution. Contains a chronology of significant events, biographical sketches of major researchers, and a listing of relevant U.S. laws.　　HC110.A4M55

Water resources and water pollution

●**Selected water resources abstracts** : (SWRA) [computer file]. Reston, Va. : U.S. Geological Survey, Water Resources Information Center, 1967– .　　**EJ34**

Machine-readable version of *Selected water resources abstracts* (*Guide* EJ155).

File size: 214,000 citations. Available online (DIALOG, updated monthly) and on CD-ROM as *Water resources abstracts* (National Information Services Corp., updated quarterly) and as *Selected water resources abstracts* (OCLC/SilverPlatter, updated quarterly).

Beginning in 1967/68, this source indexes and abstracts the water resources literature published in the physical, life, and social sciences, in related branches of engineering, and in the legal literature.

Van der Leeden, Frits. The water encyclopedia / Frits van der Leeden, Fred L. Troise, David Keith Todd. 2nd ed. Chelsea, Mich. : Lewis Publishers, c1990. 808 p. : ill., maps. ISBN 0-87371-120-3. $125.00.　　**EJ35**

1st ed., 1970 (*Guide* EJ163).

This comprehensive statistical sourcebook on water and all its related aspects was compiled from a wide variety of governmental and private information sources. Substantially revised and expanded from the 1st ed. More than 700 tables, maps, charts, and diagrams are arranged in 11 chapters covering climate, hydrology, surface and ground water, water use, water quality, environmental problems, water management, water resources agencies, legislation, constants, and conversion factors. Subject index.　　TD351.V36

Structural engineering

Manual of steel construction : allowable stress design. 9th ed. Chicago : American Institute of Steel Construction, 1989. 1 v. (various pagings) : ill.　　**EJ36**

8th ed., 1980 (*Guide* EJ173).

This volume treats one method of design; the new companion title (below) offers a different type of design procedure. Arrangement in sections is continued from the 8th ed.; the section of Miscellaneous data and mathematical tables is repeated in the companion volume. Contains numerous tables, graphs, and worked examples expressed in U.S. customary units. Indexed.　　TA684.A51

Manual of steel construction : load & resistance factor design. [Chicago] : American Institute of Steel Construction, c1986. 1 v. (various pagings) : ill.　　**EJ37**

Organization is similar to the companion title above. Features graphs, tables, and solved problems; uses U.S customary units throughout. The chapter on miscellaneous data and mathematical tables is printed both here and in the companion volume. Indexed.　　TA684.L558

McMullan, Randall. Dictionary of building. N.Y. : Nichols Pub., c1988. 262 p. : ill. ISBN 0-89397-319-X. $44.50.　　**EJ38**

Emphasizes the vocabulary of current building practice, as found in "modern specifications, technical standards, reports and product literature...."—*Pref.* Excludes classical terms not presently used and specialized "masonry and carpentry... terms which deserve complete books of their own." Cross-references, *see also* references, and comparison references are ample, and distinctions are noted between British and American usage. Not illustrated, except for 11 pages of simple line drawings of some of the basics of construction.　　TH9.M36

Means estimating handbook. Kingston, Mass. : R.S. Means Co., c1990. 905 p. : ill. ISBN 0-87629-177-9. $89.95.　　**EJ39**

Senior editor: Jeffrey M. Goldman.

Directed primarily to architects, builders and engineers. Consists of 16 sections covering topics such as concrete, masonry, metals, mechanical, electrical, finishes, wood, and plastic. Each section is arranged similarly: a general overview; charts; tables and worked-out examples for estimating needed data; a check list of named items; and final reminders. Prices are omitted. Conversion tables and abbreviations appear in an appendix. Subject index.　　TH435.M42

National Fire Protection Association. Fire protection handbook. 16th ed. Quincy, Mass. : National Fire Protection Association, 1986. 1 v. : ill. ISBN 0-87765-315-1.　　**EJ40**

15th ed., [1981] (*Guide* EJ181).

Contains much revised material and three new sections: Education for fire protection; Hazardous wastes and materials; Fire modeling and analysis. Indexed.　　TH9150.F47

Structural engineering handbook / ed. by Edwin H. Gaylord, Jr., Charles N. Gaylord. 3rd ed. N.Y. : McGraw-Hill, c1990. 1 v. (various pagings) : ill. ISBN 0-07-023188-5. $84.50.　　**EJ41**

2nd ed., 1979 (*Guide* EJ175)

Extensively revised. "The 30 sections have been written by 45 contributors. They have presented their material in ready-to-use form wherever possible.... Derivations of formulas are omitted in all but a few instances and many worked-out examples are given."—*Pref.* Indexed.　　TA635.S77

Wood engineering handbook / Forest Products Laboratory. 2nd ed. Englewood Cliffs, N.J. : Prentice Hall, c1990. 1 v. (various pagings) : ill. ISBN 0-13-963745-1. $59.95.　　**EJ42**

Rev. ed. of *Wood handbook*, 1974 (*Guide* EJ185).

Chapters are written by specialists. Discusses woods of commercial importance in the U.S., including some imported varieties. Chapters cover commercial lumber, wood preservation, insulation board, plywood, and other applications. Illustrated with figures, tables, and photographs. A glossary precedes the subject index.   TA419.W78

ELECTRICAL AND ELECTRONIC ENGINEERING

Guides

Ardis, Susan. A guide to the literature of electrical and electronics engineering / Susan B. Ardis ; ed. by Jean M. Poland. Littleton, Colo. : Libraries Unlimited, 1987. 190 p. ISBN 0-87287-474-5. $37.50.   **EJ43**

Cites the usual types of reference sources (handbooks, indexes, dictionaries, databases), together with more specialized categories such as patents, standards, data compilations, newsletters, and product literature. Entries give full bibliographic data and a short annotation. Subjects not covered are robotics, CAD/CAM, appliance repair, electrical wiring, and electrical construction. Author and title index.   Z5832.A83

Abstract journals

●**INSPEC** / Institution of Electrical Engineers [computer file]. Piscataway, N.J. : INSPEC Marketing Dept., IEEE Service Center, [1969]– .   **EJ44**

For annotation, see *Supplement* EG2.

Encyclopedias

Encyclopedia of electronics / Stan Gibilisco, Neil Sclater. 2nd ed. Blue Ridge Summit, Pa. : TAB Professional and Reference Books, c1990. 960 p. : ill. ISBN 0-8306-3389-8. $69.50.   **EJ45**

Descriptive entries treat electronics, electrical engineering, and some areas of computer science. Physical sciences, mathematics, and statistics are represented to a limited extent. Cross-references are plentiful; many line drawings and tables. Indexed.   TK7804.E47

Dictionaries

Institute of Electrical and Electronics Engineers. IEEE standard dictionary of electrical and electronics terms / Frank Jay, ed. in chief. 4th ed. N.Y. : Institute of Electrical and Electronics Engineers, c1988. 1270 p. : ill. ISBN 1-55937-000-9. $65.00.   **EJ46**

3rd ed., 1984 (*Guide* EJ203).

Over 24,000 terms and phrases in this edition.   TK9.I478

Weik, Martin H. Fiber optics standard dictionary. 2nd ed. N.Y. : Van Nostrand Reinhold, c1989. 366 p. : ill. ISBN 0-442-23387-6. $35.95.   **EJ47**

Rev. ed. of *Fiber optics and lightwave communications standard dictionary*, 1981.

The author has taken care to make his definitions consistent with the standards from national, international, federal, and business sources. An appendix gives very recent entries that could not be included in the main work.   TK5102.W45

Handbooks

Electronics engineer's reference book / ed. by F.F. Mazda ; with specialist contributors. 6th ed. London ; Boston : Butterworths, 1989. 1 v. (various pagings) : ill. ISBN 0-408-00590-4. $135.00.   **EJ48**

5th ed., 1983 (*Guide* EJ215).

Includes six new chapters on application-specific integrated circuits, computer-aided design techniques, digital system analysis, software engineering, local area networks, and integrated services digital network (ISDN). Indexed.   TK7825.E36

IES lighting handbook / John E. Kaufman, ed., Jack F. Christensen, assoc. ed. N.Y. : Illuminating Engineering Society of North America, c1984–1987. 2 v. : ill. (some col.). ISBN 0-87995-015-3 (v. 1). ISBN 0-87995-024-2 (v. 2).   **EJ49**

6th ed., 1981 (*Guide* EJ218)

Contents: 1984 reference volume; 1987 applications volume. (Volumes unnumbered but designated by year).

Each volume is now revised on its own cycle; the separate reference and applications volumes comprise the 2 v. of the handbook. Individual chapters contain figures, tables, photographs, and references. The subject index in each volume covers both volumes.   TK4161.I37

Computer science

Guides

Computing information directory : a comprehensive guide to the computing literature / comp. and ed. by Darlene Myers Hildebrandt. 7th ed. Colville, Wash. : Hildebrandt, Inc., c1990. 543 p.   **EJ50**

1985 ed. (*Guide* EJ230).

An extensive guide to the computer science literature, providing bibliographic information at title or article level, depending on the focus of a particular section. Sections: Computing journals; University computing center newsletters; Books, biblios, special issues; Dictionaries and glossaries; Indexing and abstracting services; Software resources; Review resources; Hardware resources; Directories, encyclopedias, and handbooks; Computer languages; ACM SIG proceedings; Standards bibliography; Career and salary trends bibliography; Expansion to the Library of Congress Classifications System; and Publishers' addresses. Detailed subject index.

Bibliography

Artificial intelligence : bibliographic summaries of the select literature / Henry M. Rylko, compiling ed. Lawrence, Kan. : Report Store, c1985. v. 2. ISBN 0-916313-04-2 (set). $150.00.   **EJ51**

For v. 1, see *Guide* EJ227. Vol. 2 completes the set.

Vol. 2 contains bibliographic entries, detailed annotations, and comprehensive contents information on 237 titles, including research reports, books, and conference proceedings, 1976–85. Includes a list of artificial intelligence-related periodicals, author and subject indexes, and a guide to the subject index.   Z7405.A7A77

The artificial intelligence compendium : abstracts and index to research on AI theory and applications, 1954–1987. N.Y. : Scientific DataLink, c1988. 5 v. ISBN 0-913251-40-2.   **EJ52**

lst ed., 1985 (*Guide* EJ231) had title: *The Scientific Data-Link index to artificial intelligence research, 1954–1984.*

Contents: v. 1, Abstracts I; v. 2, Abstracts II; v. 3, Author and title indices; v. 4, Subject index I, A–Men; v. 5, Subject index II, Met–Z.

Follows the format of the 1st ed. and contains nearly twice the number of entries. Covers the literature through 1987, now including technical reports and dissertations from 24 research centers, both academic and industrial. Contains more titles in the areas of applied artificial intelligence, computer vision, and pattern recognition.   Q334.A77

Cortada, James W. A bibliographic guide to the history of computing, computers, and the information processing industry. N.Y. : Greenwood, 1990. 644 p. (Bibliographies and indexes in science and technology, no. 6). ISBN 0-313-26810-X. $65.00.   **EJ53**

Intended "to serve as a general introduction to the literature of the industry. Cast in historical terms, it provides an annotated list of published materials describing the history of the industry as well as items of importance to those interested in the general topic."—*Pref.* Organized in chapters with numerous subheadings by topic and historical period. Includes all entries in Cortada's *An annotated bibliography on the history of data processing* (*Guide* EJ229).   Z5640.C67

Indexes and abstracts

●**Compuscience** [computer file]. Eggenstein-Leopoldshafen, Germany : FIZ Karlsruhe, 1972– . **EJ54**

File size: about 100,000 records. Available online, updated monthly (STN).

Provides coverage of the literature of computer science, computer technology, and information processing; includes citations to journal articles, conference papers, reports, theses, and preprints. Contains records from *ACM guide to computing literature*, 1977– (*Guide* EJ226) and *Computing reviews*, 1977– (*Guide* EJ226 note). Also has records from the computer science section of *MATH* [computer file], 1972– (Supplement EJ54).

Computer literature index. v. 10, no. 1 (Apr. 1980)– . [Phoenix] : Applied Computer Research, 1980– . Quarterly, with annual cumulation. ISSN 0270-4846. $175.00.   **EJ55**

Continues *Quarterly bibliography of computers and data processing*, v. 1–9 (1971–80).

An index to literature in "computer-related trade publications, general business and management periodicals, and publications of computer and management-oriented professional societies and organizations."—*Guide to use.* Designed for computer users and individuals in computer-related professions. Presents an alphabetical subject arrangement of entries with brief abstracts; extensive cross-references. Includes author and publisher indexes that cumulate annually.   QA76.Q3

Microcomputer index. Santa Clara, Calif. : Microcomputer Information Services, 1980– . Quarterly, Mar. 1989– . ISSN 8756-7040. $140.00.   **EJ56**

Issues for Mar. 1989– have title: *Micro computer index.*

An index to microcomputing-related articles in approximately 75 popular computing magazines. Entries include abstracts and are divided into eight sections: Software reviews, Hardware reviews, Book reviews, Buyer and vendor guides, New product announcements, Program listings, Columns and letters, and Feature articles. Includes author, company, product, and subject indexes; annual cumulative indexes.   QA75.5.M5

●**Microcomputer index** [computer file]. Medford, N.J. : Learned Information, Inc., 1981– .   **EJ57**

Machine-readable version.

File size: 75,000 records. Updated monthly. Available online (DIALOG).

Encyclopedias

Encyclopedia of artificial intelligence / Stuart C. Shapiro, ed. in chief, David Eckroth, managing ed. N.Y. : Wiley, c1987. 2 v. (1219 p.) : ill. ISBN 0-471-80748-6 (set). $195.00.   **EJ58**

Attempts to define "the discipline of Artificial Intelligence (AI) by bringing together the core of knowledge from all its fields and related disciplines."—*Foreword.* Designed primarily for the AI professional. Contains some 260 alphabetically arranged articles that are written by experts and include bibliographies. The work has more than 450 tables and figures, numerous cross-references, and an index.   Q335.E53

Encyclopedia of computer science and technology / executive editors, Jack Belzer, Albert G. Holzman, Allen Kent. N.Y. : M. Dekker, [1975]–[1990]. v. 1–23 : ill. ISBN 0-8247-2251-5 (v. 1). $150.00 (per vol.). (In progress).   **EJ59**

Contents: v. 1–14, A–Z; v. 16, author and subject indexes to v. 1–15; v. 15 and v. 17– are supplements that continue the numbering of the main set.

Contains an alphabetical arrangement of detailed articles covering a wide range of topics (e.g., specific programming languages, corporations, leading figures, systems, mathematical and computational concepts, applications). Articles are written by experts and have extensive bibliographies. Intended to be "scholarly and exhaustive, yet straightforward, so that most articles will be comprehensible to the newcomer and stimulating to the informed specialist as well."—*Pref.* Vol. 1–14 contain 277 articles and are kept up to date by supplementary volumes and by a companion title *Encyclopedia of microcomputers* (below).   QA76.15.E5

Encyclopedia of microcomputers / executive editors, Allen Kent, James G. Williams ; administrative ed., Rosalind Kent. N.Y. : M. Dekker, c1988–1991. v. 1–8 : ill. ISBN 0-8247-2700-2 (v. 1). $160.00 (per vol.). (In progress).   **EJ60**

Contents: v. 1–8, Access methods–Hypertext.

Intended as a companion to the *Encyclopedia of computer science and technology* (above), it closely parallels the format and subject treatment of that title. Presents an alphabetical arrangement of detailed articles, covering the "broad spectrum of microcomputer knowledge ... aimed at the needs of microcomputer hardware specialists, programmers, systems analysts, engineers, operations researchers and mathematicians."—*Pref.* Articles are written by specialists and include bibliographies. To be complete in 12 v. plus supplements.   QA76.15.E52

Dictionaries

Dictionary of computing. 3rd ed. Oxford ; N.Y. : Oxford Univ. Pr., 1990. 510 p. ISBN 0-19-853825-1. $39.95.   **EJ61**

1st ed., 1983 (*Guide* EJ237); 2nd ed., 1987.

Gen. ed.: Valerie Illingworth.

Of more than 4,500 terms, 550 are new to this edition, reflecting the substantial advances in the field since the 2nd ed. Designed for use by "students and teachers of computer science and of all subjects in which computing plays a part."—*Pref.* Entries range from basic to complex concepts; definitions are understandable and written by practitioners. The subject coverage is extensive, ranging from algorithms and programming

languages to information technology and legal aspects of computing. Includes extensive cross-references; in definitions, asterisks are used to indicate words that have their own entries.
QA76.15.D526

Hordeski, Michael F. The illustrated dictionary of microcomputers. 3rd ed. Blue Ridge Summit, Pa. : TAB Professional and Reference Books, 1990. 442 p. ISBN 0-8306-7368-7. $28.95. ISBN 0-8306-3368-5 (pbk.). $18.60. **EJ62**
1st ed., 1978, had title *The illustrated dictionary of microcomputer terminology*; 2nd ed., 1986.
Comprehensive and useful for anyone who works with microcomputers. Presents an alphabetical arrangement of more than 9,500 terms in all aspects of microcomputing, including software, hardware, desktop publishing, word processing, networking, and graphics. Definitions are clearly written and complemented by extensive illustrations. TK7885.H67

Longley, Dennis. Van Nostrand Reinhold dictionary of information technology / Dennis Longley and Michael Shain. 3rd ed. N.Y. : Van Nostrand Reinhold, c1989. 566 p. : ill. ISBN 0-442-23685-9. **EJ63**
1st ed., 1982, had title *Dictionary of information technology*.
Designed to provide accurate, up-to-date definitions for terms in the emerging discipline of information technology. Contains some 7,800 entries (1,800 more than the 2nd ed.) with short and informative definitions, some illustrations, and extensive cross-references. Includes extended entries for a few important topics in the field, such as artificial intelligence, computer security, machine translation, and desktop publishing. QA76.15.L63

Rosenberg, Jerry Martin. Dictionary of artificial intelligence and robotics. N.Y. : Wiley, c1986. 203 p. ISBN 0-471-84982-0. ISBN 0-471-84981-2 (pbk.). $14.95. **EJ64**
Useful for experts and general readers. Where multiple definitions occur for the same term the broadest definition is listed first. Contains abbreviations, acronyms, and symbols. Some entries not currently used have been retained for historical reasons. Q334.6.R67

———————— Dictionary of computers, informational processing, and telecommunications. 2nd ed. N.Y. : Wiley, 1987. 734 p. ISBN 0-471-85558-8. $34.95. ISBN 0-471-85559-6 (pbk.). $18.95. **EJ65**
1st ed., 1984 (*Guide* EJ244) had title: *Dictionary of computers, data processing, and telecommunications*.
Provides concise definitions for more than 12,000 computer terms, 2,000 of which are new in this edition. Includes cross-references and an appendix of Spanish and French equivalents for many terms.

Directories

The software encyclopedia. N.Y. : Bowker, c1985– . $190.00. **EJ66**
Describes more than 21,000 microcomputer software packages. Entries in the Title index are arranged alphabetically and include title, subtitle, version, series, authors, grade level, release date, hardware compatibility, microprocessor type, operating system requirements, languages, memory requirements, publisher, cost, and a descriptive annotation. In the System compatibility/applications index, packages are organized by major operating systems, then by specific applications. A Publishers index is also included. QA76.753.S67

Handbooks

The handbook of artificial intelligence / ed. by Avron Barr, Paul R. Cohen, and Edward A. Feigenbaum. Reading, Mass. : Addison-Wesley Pub. Co., c1989. v. 4 : ill. ISBN 0-86576-004-7 (set). $90.00. (In progress). **EJ67**
For v. 1–3 and annotation, see *Guide* EJ241.
Contents: v. 4, Blackboard systems, Cooperative distributed problem solving, Fundamentals of expert systems, Natural language understanding, Knowledge-based software engineering, Qualitative physics, Knowledge-based simulation, Computer vision update.
Eight chapters by experts; some update information in earlier volumes, others discuss new topics. Unlike the first three volumes, the "bulk of every chapter is devoted to issues, principles, and theory."—*Pref.* Includes bibliography and name and subject indexes. Q335.H36

Handbook of theoretical computer science / ed. by Jan van Leeuwen. Amsterdam ; N.Y. : Elsevier ; Cambridge, Mass. : MIT Pr., 1990. 2 v. : ill. ISBN 0-444-88075-5 (set). $250.00. **EJ68**
Contents: v. A, Algorithms and complexity; v. B, Formal models and semantics.
Designed to provide computer science professionals and students with an overview of the field of theoretical computer science, this handbook "attempts to offer an in-depth view of the field of Theoretical Computer Science as a whole, by a comprehensive exposition of the scientific advances in this area."—*Pref.* Presents 37 chapters, written by experts, with extensive bibliographies. Each volume has a separate subject index. QA76.H279

Radio and television

Weik, Martin H. Communications standard dictionary. 2nd ed. N.Y. : Van Nostrand Reinhold, c1989. 1219 p. : ill. ISBN 0-442-20556-2. $59.95. **EJ69**
1st ed., 1983 (*Guide* EJ262).
This edition contains more than 3,600 more terms and definitions than the 1st ed. Terms have been selected from the technical literature. TK5102.W437

ENERGY

General works

Handbook of energy systems engineering : production, and utilization / ed. by Leslie C. Wilbur. N.Y. : Wiley, c1985. 1775 p. : ill. ISBN 0-471-86633-4. $105.00. **EJ70**
Consists of 18 chapters written by specialists. Discusses coal, nuclear, petroleum, and gas technology, hydroelectric and solar power, geothermal energy. Contains a chapter on guides to available codes, standards, and reference materials. Subject index. TJ163.9.H35

Information sources in energy technology / ed., L.J. Anthony. London ; Boston : Butterworths, 1988. 324 p. ISBN 0-408-03050-X. £32.00. **EJ71**
Sixteen chapters written by the editor and other specialists are presented in three parts: (1) Energy in general; (2) Fuel technology (combustion, steam and boiler plant . . . electrical energy, energy conservation, energy and the environment); and (3) Specific energy sources (solid, liquid, and gaseous fuels, solar and geothermal energy, alternative energy sources). Ex-

tensive bibliographies with each chapter. Indexed.

TJ163.17.I54

Weber, R. David. Energy update : a guide to current reference literature. San Carlos, Calif. : Energy Information Pr., 1991. 455 p. ISBN 0-9628518-5-X.   **EJ72**

Continues the author's *Energy information guide*, 1982–84, 3 v. (*Guide* EJ276).

Chapters cover environmental impact, energy in general, energy conservation, solar energy, other alternative energy, electric power, nuclear power, fossil fuels, coal, petroleum, and natural gas. Entries are annotated. Purposely omitted are: periodical titles from the earlier compilation if the title and format are unchanged; references written entirely in languages other than English; items dealing with areas outside the U.S. Separate indexes for authors, titles, subjects, and government publication numbers. Supplements are planned at four-year intervals.

Atlases

Cuff, David J. The United States energy atlas / David J. Cuff, William J. Young. 2nd ed. N.Y. : Macmillan ; London : Collier Macmillan, c1985. 387 p. : ill. (some col.). ISBN 0-02-691240-6. $85.00.   **EJ73**

1st ed., 1980 (*Guide* EJ278).

Retains the general arrangement of the first edition, with three major divisions and a glossary of terms. Includes a new chapter on ocean energy, and new essays on such topics as the Strategic Petroleum Reserve and the importance of tax policy to wind power investments.   TJ163.25.U6C83

HEATING AND REFRIGERATION

ASHRAE handbook. Atlanta : American Society of Heating, Refrigerating and Air Conditioning Engineers, c1987– .   **EJ74**

For earlier volumes, see *Guide* EJ280.

Contents of parts and dates of most recent issues: *Equipment* (1988); *Fundamentals* (1989); *Refrigeration systems and applications* (1990); *Heating, ventilating, and air-conditioning applications* (1991). All parts are available in two editions; an SI edition, and an I-P (inch-pound) units edition.

TH7015.A74

INDUSTRIAL ENGINEERING

Handbook of human factors / [ed. by] Gavriel Salvendy. N.Y. : Wiley, c1987. 1874 p. : ill. ISBN 0-471-88015-9. $95.00.   **EJ75**

Gives "information about the effective design and use of systems requiring the interaction among human, machine (computer), and environment."—*Pref.* 68 chapters contributed by international specialists include bibliographies. General areas discussed include: human factors function; human factors fundamentals; functional analysis; job organization design; equipment and workplace design; environmental design; design for health and safety; design of selection and training systems; performance modeling; system evaluation; human factors in the design and use of computing systems; and selected applications of human factors in computer systems. Indexed.   TA166.H275

Instrumentation reference book / ed. by B.E. Noltingk with specialist contributors. London ; Boston : Butter-

worths, 1988. 1 v. (various pagings) : ill. ISBN 0-408-01562-4. £72.00.   **EJ76**

A collection of signed articles grouped into five parts: (1) Mechanical measurements; (2) Measurement of temperature and chemical composition; (3) Electrical and radiation measurements; (4) Instrumentation systems; (5) Further scientific and technical information. A sixth part, Directories and commercial information, provides information on British suppliers of instrumentation. The articles offer authoritative introductions to different aspects of scientific instrumentation, with references to the scientific literature. Indexed.   QC53.I574

International encyclopedia of robotics : applications and automation / Richard C. Dorf, ed. in chief ; Shimon Y. Nof, consulting ed. N.Y. : Wiley, c1988. 3 v. : ill. ISBN 0-471-87868-5 (set). $410.00.   **EJ77**

"... defines the discipline and the practice of robotics by bringing together the core of knowledge and practice from the field and all closely related fields. The *Encyclopedia* is written primarily for the professional who seeks to understand and use robots and automation."—*Pref.* Articles include bibliographies and cross-references. Indexed.   TJ210.4.I57

MECHANICAL ENGINEERING

Dictionaries

Nayler, G. H. F. Dictionary of mechanical engineering. 3rd ed. London ; Boston : Butterworths, 1985. 394 p. ISBN 0-408-01505-5. $80.00.   **EJ78**

2nd ed., 1975, by J.L. and G.H.F. Nayler (*Guide* EJ302).

This edition contains more entries on engineering design and manufacture than the 2nd ed. Abbreviations, initialisms, and symbols occur at the beginning of the entries for each letter. Definitions generally are concise, with *see* and *see also* references. A few graphs and line drawings are used to enhance the brief definitions. Retains practically all the entries from preceding editions.   TJ9.N28

Handbooks

Marks' standard handbook for mechanical engineers. 9th ed. N.Y. : McGraw-Hill, 1987. ISBN 0-07-004127-X : $104.50.   **EJ79**

8th ed., 1978 (*Guide* EJ318), had title *Standard handbook for mechanical engineers.*

Contains a new chapter on robots and robotics. As in the previous edition, dual units—International System (SI), and U.S. Customary System (USCS)—have been retained. Contains bibliographic references at the beginning of chapters. Indexed.   TJ151.S82

Mechanical engineers' handbook / ed. by Myer Kutz. N.Y. : Wiley, c1986. 2316 p. : ill. ISBN 0-471-08817-X. $72.00 (est.).   **EJ80**

Purposely omits mathematical tables. Stresses manufacturing engineering and research management, plus the traditional treatments of energy and power. Includes chapters on engineers' liability, patents, sources of mechanical engineering information, and online databases. Numerous charts, diagrams, tables, and graphs. Subject index.   TJ151.M395

Shock and vibration handbook / ed. by Cyril M. Harris. 3rd ed. N.Y. : McGraw-Hill, c1988. 1 v. (various pagings) : ill. ISBN 0-07-026801-0. $75.00.   **EJ81**

2nd ed., 1976 (*Guide* EJ311).

A comprehensive treatment prepared by 60 specialists, this edition includes 50% new or revised material. Worked examples of problems appear in many chapters. Included are chapters on packaging design and effects of shock and vibration on man. Subject index. TA355.S5164

Standard handbook of machine design / editors in chief, Joseph E. Shigley, Charles R. Mischke. N.Y. : McGraw-Hill, c1986. 1 v. (various pagings) : ill. ISBN 0-07-056892-8. $96.00. **EJ82**

Contains 47 chapters written by specialists. "Mathematical and statistical formulas and tabulations . . . are not included in this handbook."—*Pref.* Indexed. TJ230.S8235

Tool and manufacturing engineers handbook : a reference book for manufacturing engineers, managers, and technicians. 4th ed. / revised under the supervision of the SME Publications Committee in cooperation with the SME Technical Divisions. Dearborn, Mich. : Society of Manufacturing Engineers, c1985–c1988. v. 3–5 : ill. ISBN 0-87263-085-4. **EJ83**

For v. 1–2 and annotation, see *Guide* EJ319.

Charles Wick, ed. in chief, v. 2–4; Raymond F. Veilleux, staff ed., v. 5.

Contents: v. 3, Materials, finishing, and coating (1985); v. 4, Quality control and assembly (1987); v. 5, Manufacturing management (1988). Completes the set. TS176.T63

Welding handbook. 8th ed. Miami, Fla. : American Welding Society, c1987–1991. v. 1–2 : ill. (some col.). ISBN 0-87171-281-4 (v. 1). (In progress). **EJ84**

7th ed., 1976–84, 5 v. (*Guide* EJ307).

Contents: v. 1, Welding technology, ed. by Leonard P. Conner; v. 2, Welding processes, ed. by R.L. O'Brien. To be complete in 3 vols.

Most chapters contain bibliographies as well as illustrations, drawings, and tables. Vol. 1 gives basic information (e.g., joining and cutting processes, physics of welding, welding metallurgy, residual stresses, distortion). Indexed. TS227.W387

MINING AND METALLURGICAL ENGINEERING

Handbooks

Handbook of corrosion data / ed. by Bruce D. Craig. Metals Park, Ohio : ASM International, c1989. 683 p. : ill. ISBN 0-87170-361-0. **EJ85**

Designed to give users " a starting point to quickly and easily assess the recent literature on metals in corrosive environments."—*Pref.* In two parts: Corrosion of metals and alloys; Corrosion media. The latter category generally refers to specific compounds. Numerous charts and tables. TA462.H37

Metals handbook / prepared under the direction of the ASM Handbook Committee. 9th ed. Metals Park, Ohio : American Society for Metals, 1985–c1989. v. 9–17 : ill. ISBN 0-87170-007-7 (v. 1). **EJ86**

For v. 1–8 and annotation, see *Guide* EJ351.

Contents: v. 9, Metallography and microstructures (1985); v. 10, Materials characterization (1986); v. 11, Failure analysis and prevention (1986); v. 12, Fractography (1987); v. 13, Corrosion (1987); v. 14, Forming and forging (1988); v. 15, Casting (1988); v. 16, Machining (1989); v. 17, Nondestructive evalua-

tion and quality control (1989). Completes the set. TA459.M43

Metals handbook / prepared under the direction of the ASM International Handbook Committee. 10th ed. Materials Park, Ohio : ASM International, 1990. v. 1–2 : ill. ISBN 0-87170-377-7 (v. 1). $118.00. ISBN 0-87170-378-5 (v. 2). (In progress). **EJ87**

9th ed., 17 v., 1978–89 (above).

Contents: v. 1, Properties and selection—irons, steels, and high-performance alloys (1990); v. 2, Properties and selection—nonferrous alloys and special-purpose materials (1990).

The thorough treatment of topics is continued in this edition. Vol. 1 contains 14 new articles, 10 that have been rewritten entirely, and 29 that have had major revisions. There are new articles on superalloys; strategic materials availability and supply; and recycling of iron, steel, and superalloys. Each volume is indexed separately. TA459.M43

Woldman's engineering alloys / ed. by John P. Frick. 7th ed. Materials Park, Ohio : ASM International, 1990. 1459 p. ISBN 0-87170-408-0. $128.00. **EJ88**

Lists alloys from 23 countries under trade names, followed by the producer's name, alloy composition, properties and applications. In this edition obsolete alloys that were listed only by name in the 6th ed. now have complete entries and the designation "obsolete." Over 5,000 new alloys have been added and 12,000 entries revised. TA483.W64

PETROLEUM ENGINEERING

Bibliography

Pearson, Barbara C. Guide to the petroleum reference literature / Barbara C. Pearson and Katherine B. Ellwood. Littleton, Colo. : Libraries Unlimited, 1987. 193 p. ISBN 0-87287-473-7. $45.00. **EJ89**

Most chapters contain short annotated entries and full bibliographic information, but in the database chapter, one title is described per page. International sources are included. Although the emphasis is primarily on English-language material issued since 1978, some of the older "classic" titles have been listed also. Author/title index; subject index. Z6972.P33

EK

Medical and Health Sciences

MEDICINE

Guides

Handbook of medical library practice / Louise Darling, ed., David Bishop, Lois Ann Colaianni, associate editors. 4th ed. Chicago : Medical Library Association, 1988. v. 3 : ill. ISBN 0-912176-21-0.   **EK1**
For v. 1–2, see *Guide* EK4.
Contents: v. 3, Health science librarianship and administration. Completes the set.   Z675.M4H33

Haselbauer, Kathleen J. A research guide to the health sciences : medical, nutritional, and environmental. N.Y. : Greenwood, 1987. 655 p. : ill. (Reference sources for the social sciences and humanities, no. 4). ISBN 0-313-25530-9. $49.95.   **EK2**
Cites more than 2,000 sources in four broad categories: General works, Basic sciences supporting clinical medicine, Social aspects of the health sciences, and Medical specialties. Intended for researchers at all levels, with emphasis on the needs of students and those working outside their specialty. Critical and evaluative annotations, many of them lengthy, compare similar sources. Cross-references are numerous. Indexed by author, title, and subject.   Z6658.H35

Lingle, Virginia A. How to find information about AIDS / Virginia A. Lingle, M. Sandra Wood. N.Y. : Haworth Pr., c1988. 130 p. ISBN 0-86656-752-6.   **EK3**
Intended for both health professionals and general readers; provides "an inexpensive resource to key access points" (*Introd.*) of AIDS information. Covers most aspects of AIDS, with a clinical emphasis; popular literature is generally excluded. Sections: organizational resources, health departments, research institutions, grant funding sources and federal agencies, hotlines, databases, print sources, and audiovisual producers. General index of titles, organizations, and people; geographic index.   RC607.A26L56

Strickland-Hodge, Barry. Medical information : a profile / Barry Strickland-Hodge and Barbara Allan. White Plains, N.Y. : Knowledge Industry Publications, 1986. 145 p. ISBN 0-86729-163-X. $35.00 (est.).   **EK4**
A survey of the major types of medical information sources. Provides a list of printed and other sources, shows how searches can be carried out, and discusses techniques for organizing information retrieved during online searches. Intended to be a practical guide, aimed at those beginning medical research. Emphasis on British sources.   Z6658.S92

Zito, Dorothea R. A guide to research in gerontology : strategies and resources / Dorothea R. Zito and George

V. Zito. N.Y. : Greenwood, 1988. 130 p. ISBN 0-313-25904-6.   **EK5**
For annotation, see *Supplement* CC33.   Z7164.O4Z57

Bibliography

AIDS : acquired immune deficiency syndrome. [1st ed.]– . Phoenix : Oryx, c1985– . ISSN 0899-9449.   **EK6**
Editor: 1985– D.A. Tyckoson.
Frequency varies: annual, 1985–1987; semiannual, 1988– .
This highly selective bibliography provides current, fully annotated references to English-language articles from the general literature, including journals, newspapers, and some monographs. Key sources are printed in boldface. Useful to students, general readers, teachers, and academic, public, and high school librarians. Author and subject index.   Z6664.A27A36

Bruhn, John G. Medical sociology : an annotated bibliography, 1972–1982 / John G. Bruhn, Billy U. Philips, Paula L. Levine. N.Y. : Garland, 1985. 779 p. (Garland bibliographies in sociology, v. 6 ; Garland reference library of social science, v. 243). ISBN 0-8240-8938-3.   **EK7**
For annotation, see *Supplement* CC6.   Z6675.S53B78

Cordasco, Francesco. American medical imprints, 1820–1910 : a checklist of publications illustrating the history and progress of medical science, medical education, and the healing arts in the United States : a preliminary contribution. Totowa, N.J. : Rowman & Littlefield ; Fairview, N.J. : Junius-Vaughn Pr., 1985. 2 v. ISBN 0-8476-7338-3 (set). $195.00.   **EK8**
Continues *Early American medical imprints... 1668–1820*, by Robert B. Austin (*Guide* EK30).
A "systematic and enumerative bibliography ... intended as a functional checklist" that includes "any item which could legitimately be related to the medical arts and their progress in the U.S."—*Introd.* Contains 36,612 entries arranged chronologically by decade of publication; within decades, entries are arranged alphabetically by author, then by date of publication. Each entry includes a transcription of the work's title page; for most items, only the principal pagination is given. Shows one to four library locations. Some items are annotated, and there is an index of names. Introductory material includes "A handlist of selected bibliographies, catalogues and related reference materials." An appendix, "Wood's library of standard medical authors" (a checklist of 100 medical textbooks published in N.Y. by William Wood & Co. from the 1870s to the 1890s), was originally published in *AB bookman's weekly* 73 (1984): 3333–56.   Z6661.U5C67

Current bibliographies in medicine / National Library of Medicine. [Bethesda, Md.] : The Library ; [Wash. : Sold by Supt. of Docs., U.S. Govt. Print. Off., 1988– . $26.00.   **EK9**
Superintendent of Documents classification: HE20.3615/2.
Continues in part *Literature search/National Library of Medicine* (*Guide* EK19) which ceased in 1987; in 1989 absorbed the National Library of Medicine's "Specialized bibliography series." "Each bibliography ... covers a distinct subject area of biomedicine and is intended to fulfill a current awareness function."—*Pref.* Approximately 20 bibliographies are published per year. Contains citations to articles indexed for MEDLARS. A list of currently available bibliographies appears each month in *Index medicus* (*Guide* EK52).

Encyclopedia of health information sources / Paul Wasserman, ed. ; Suzanne Grefsheim, assoc. ed. Detroit : Gale, c1987. 483 p. ISBN 0-8103-2135-1. $135.00.   **EK10**

Subtitle: a bibliographic guide to approximately 13,000 citations for publications, organizations, and other sources of information on more than 450 health-related subjects.

Intended as a starting point to locate information on health and medical subjects. Includes all types of information sources, listed alphabetically under each subject. International in scope. Detailed table of contents and cross-references. No index.

Z6658.E54

Handbook of bioengineering / co-editors, Richard Skalak, Shu Chien. N.Y. : McGraw-Hill, c1987. 1 v. (various pagings) : ill. ISBN 0-07-057783-8. **EK11**

"The purpose of this handbook is to collect, in one place, authoritative summary accounts of the various topics that comprise the field of bioengineering."—*Pref.* 41 signed chapters by experts include references to the primary literature. Indexed.

R856.H36

Learning AIDS. 2nd ed. (1989)– . N.Y. : American Foundation for AIDS Research : Distr. by Bowker, c1989– . Annual. ISSN 1043-8564. **EK12**

1st ed. (1988) had title: *AIDS information resources directory.*

Reviews and evaluates more than 1,700 AIDS/HIV educational resources of all types. Intended to be a first step in identifying suitable materials for a particular audience. Arranged by 21 target audiences. Entries include bibliographic description, reviewer comments, price, and ordering information.

RC607.A26A34747

National Library of Medicine (U.S.). A catalogue of seventeenth century printed books in the National Library of Medicine / comp. by Peter Krivatsky. Bethesda, Md. : National Library of Medicine, 1989. 1315 p. (NIH publication, no. 89–2619). **EK13**

Superintendent of Documents classification: HE 20.3614:Se 8.

For some 13,300 books printed 1601–1700, "... monographs, dissertations and corresponding program disputations, broadsides, pamphlets and serials" (*Introd.*), provides title page transcription, physical description, and reference to standard bibliographies. Entries are alphabetical by author, editor, compiler, occasionally by corporate body, and in a few instances by title. Most authors' names are in vernacular form with cross-references to latinized or other names. There is no index, but the National Library of Medicine's History of Medicine Division maintains indexes of printers, publishers, and vernacular imprints.

§ Complements earlier catalogs of pre-19th century holdings of NLM: *A catalogue of incunabula and manuscripts in the Army Medical Library,* by Dorothy M. Schulllian and Francis E. Sommer, 1948? (*Guide* EK39); *A catalogue of sixteenth century printed books in the National Library of Medicine,* comp. by Richard J. Durling, 1967 (*Guide* EK29); *A catalogue of incunabula and sixteenth century books in the National Library of Medicine: first supplement,* comp. by Peter Krivatsky, 1971 (*Guide* EK40); and *A short title catalogue of eighteenth century printed books in the National Library of Medicine,* comp. by John R. Blake (1979). Z6659.N38

Olson, James Stuart. The history of cancer : an annotated bibliography. N.Y. : Greenwood, 1989. 426 p. (Bibliographies and indexes in medical studies, no. 3). ISBN 0-313-25889-9. **EK14**

A comprehensive bibliography that emphasizes the documents in the history of the etiology, manifestations, diagnosis, and treatment of cancer, and on persons with distinguished careers in cancer research and treatment. Citations to approximately 3,000 articles are arranged in 30 categories. Helpful cross-references; author and subject index. RC262.O47

Rees, Alan M. The consumer health information source book / by Alan M. Rees and Catherine Hoffman. 3rd ed. Phoenix : Oryx, 1990. 210 p. ISBN 0-89774-408-X. $39.50. **EK15**

2nd ed., 1984 (*Guide* EK28).

"This edition represents a substantial revision, with more than 90 percent of the content new."—*Pref.* Z6673.R43

Sir William Osler : an annotated bibliography with illustrations / ed. by Richard L. Golden, Charles G. Roland. San Francisco : Norman Pub., 1988. 214 p. : ill. (Norman bibliography series, no. 1). ISBN 0-930405-00-5. $85.00. **EK16**

Rev. and updated ed. of Maude E. Abbott's *Classified and annotated bibliography of Sir William Osler's publications,* 2nd ed. (Montreal : The Medical Museum, McGill Univ., 1939).

Contains 1,493 citations, some with annotations, arranged chronologically in 11 categories. This edition includes a checklist of Osler's papers published under his pseudonym (Egerton Yorrick Davis) and a list of editions, printings, and translations of *The principles of medicine.* Z8647.8.S55

Thornton, John Leonard. Thornton's medical books, libraries, and collectors : a study of bibliography and the book trade in relation to the medical sciences / ed. by Alain Besson. 3rd rev. ed. Aldershot, Eng. ; Brookfield, Vt. : Gower, c1990. 417 p. : ill. ISBN 0-566-05481-7. **EK17**

An introductory history of the literature of medicine from the earliest times through the 19th century. A separate chapter treats medical writings before the invention of printing. Medical literature of the 20th century is included in chapters on growth of the medical periodical literature and medical libraries of today. Intends "to record the chief writings of every prominent medical author and to chart the growth and development of medical bibliography."—*Introd.* Includes a bibliography and indexes of personal and institutional names, journal titles, and subjects. Z286.M4T47

West, Ruth. Alternative medicine : a bibliography of books in English / comp. by Ruth West and Joanna E. Trevelyan. London ; N.Y. : Mansell, 1985. 210 p. ISBN 0-7201-1721-6. $33.00 (est.). **EK18**

Lists more than 2,000 books relating to certain major systems for the treatment of illness. Entries are arranged alphabetically by author within broad subject categories (e.g., homeopathy, herbal medicine, naturopathy, clinical nutrition, osteopathy, chiropractic, Chinese medicine, acupuncture). Includes textbooks, manuals, reference books, pamphlets, mostly from Britain and the U.S. Some brief annotations; subject index.

Z6665.P49W47

Winter, Eugenia B. Psychological and medical aspects of induced abortion : a selective, annotated bibliography, 1970–1986. N.Y. : Greenwood, 1988. 162 p. (Bibliographies and indexes in women's studies, no. 7). ISBN 0-313-26100-8. **EK19**

For annotation, see *Supplement* CC267. Z6671.2.A2W56

Audiovisual materials

●**AVLINE** [computer file]. Bethesda, Md. : U.S. National Library of Medicine, 1975– . **EK20**

Machine-readable version of *National Library of Medicine audiovisuals catalog* (below).

File size: 20,000 records. Updated weekly. Available online (MEDLARS).

Contains bibliographic records for audiovisual materials, and since 1988, to microcomputer software catalogued by NLM. Includes primarily English-language material available in the U.S. and Canada.

Health media review index / Jill E. Provan, Joy W. Hunter, editors. Metuchen, N.J. : Scarecrow, 1985. 844 p. ISBN 0-8108-1739-X. $59.50. **EK21**

Subtitle: a guide to reviews and descriptions of commercially-available nonprint material for the medical, mental, allied health, human service, and related counselling professions.

Provides excerpts and often includes several different critical reviews published 1980–83. Does not duplicate reviews cited in *AVLINE* (above) and the *National Library of Medicine audiovisuals catalog* (below), nor audiovisual reviews from journals and databases devoted to the review of software. Lists programs that have won awards. RA440.55.H44

Health media review index, 1984–86 / Deborah J. McCalpin, ed.; Jill E. Provan, Joy W. Hunter, contributing editors. Metuchen, N.J. : Scarecrow, 1988. 751 p. ISBN 0-8108-2172-9. **EK22**

Supplement to *Health media review index* (above).

Includes abstracts of reviews and descriptions of more than 3,000 audiovisual products and computer software programs. RA440.55.H44

National Library of Medicine (U.S.). National Library of Medicine audiovisuals catalog. Bethesda, Md. : National Library of Medicine ; Wash. : For sale by the Supt. of Docs., U.S. Govt. Print. Off., 1977– . Quarterly, with the fourth issue being the annual cumulation. ISSN 0149-9939. **EK23**

Superintendent of Documents classification: HE 20.3609/ 4: .

Provides bibliographic citations to audiovisual materials, and since 1988 to microcomputer software, catalogued by the National Library of Medicine. Provides access to both monographs and serials by name and title and by subject, includes a section concerning procurement, and an appendix covering audiovisual serials. Citations to these materials are also available through the *AVLINE* database (above). R835.U49b

Periodicals

●**SERLINE** : (SERials onLINE) [computer file]. Bethesda, Md. : U. S. National Library of Medicine. **EK24**

Machine-readable version of *List of journals indexed in Index medicus* (Guide EK42), *Index of NLM serial titles* (Guide EK44), and *List of serials indexed for online users* (1983–).

File size: 74,000 records. Updated monthly. Available online (MEDLARS).

Provides bibliographic information for all serial titles catalogued by the National Library of Medicine. Gives location information for approximately a third of the titles.

Vaillancourt, Pauline M. Cancer journals and serials : an analytical guide. N.Y. : Greenwood, 1988. 259 p. ISBN 0-313-24055-8. **EK25**

Provides full bibliographic descriptions for some 400 titles that devote a significant portion of their content to cancer, appear at least once per year, and are published for the most part in English. Where applicable, annotations give the International Cancer Research Data Bank (ICRDB) ranking (last made available in 1981). Publisher, geographic, subject, and sponsor indexes. Z6664.C2V343

Government publications

Chitty, Mary Glen. Federal information sources in health and medicine : a selected annotated bibliography / comp. by Mary Glen Chitty with the assistance of Natalie Schatz. N.Y. : Greenwood, 1988. 306 p. (Bibliographies and indexes in medical studies, no. 1). ISBN 0-313-25530-X. **EK26**

Lists "about 1200 government publications and 100 databases from some 90 federal agencies, institutes and information centers."—*Pref.* Consists of subject bibliographies in the medical and health sciences fields, including many depository titles. Entries are numbered and include author, title, document availability, publication date, and Superintendent of Documents and NTIS numbers but not GPO stock number or format. Appendixes of discontinued publications and addresses of major federal agencies. Indexes of keywords in titles, database names, agencies, and subjects. Z6658.C445

Library catalogs

●**CATLINE** : (CATalog onLINE) [computer file]. Bethesda, Md. : U.S. National Library of Medicine, 1966– . **EK27**

Machine-readable version of *National Library of Medicine current catalog* (Guide EK33).

File size: 655,000 records. Updated weekly. Available online (MEDLARS)

Contains bibliographic records for monographs and serials catalogued for the collection of the National Library of Medicine.

Indexes and Abstract journals

AIDS bibliography. v. 1, no. 1 (Jan. 1988 through Mar. 1988)– . Bethesda, Md. : National Library of Medicine ; Wash. : For sale by the Supt. of Docs., U.S. Govt. Print. Off., [1988]– . ISSN 1052-0287. **EK28**

Frequency varies: quarterly, 1988; monthly, 1989– .

Superintendent of Documents classification: HE 20.3615/ 3: .

Continues in part *Literature search/National Library of Medicine* (Guide EK19), discontinued in 1987. In that series, 17 bibliographies on Acquired Immunodeficiency Syndrome (AIDS) were published between 1983 and 1987. Consists of citations from the National Library of Medicine's *AIDSLINE* (below), *CATLINE* (above), and *AVLINE* (Supplement EK20) databases. Citations are arranged by publication type in three sections: (1) journal articles, listed under alphabetically arranged subject headings and subheadings; (2) monographs, arranged alphabetically by author or editor, and (3) audiovisuals, alphabetically by title. The June and Dec. issues contain an additional section that lists all new serial titles on AIDS added during the previous six months. Z6664.A27A39

●**AIDSLINE** [computer file]. Bethesda, Md. : U. S. National Library of Medicine, 1980– . **EK29**

Machine-readable version of *AIDS bibliography* (above).

File size: 25,000 records. Updated three times per month. Available online (Data-Star, DIALOG, MEDLARS) and in CD-ROM (SilverPlatter).

Provides comprehensive coverage on all AIDS-related topics from 1980 to the present. Citations are drawn from several databases: *MEDLINE* (below), *Health planning and administration* (below), *CANCERLIT* (below), *CATLINE* (above), and *AVLINE* (Supplement EK20).

●**CANCERLIT** [computer file]. Bethesda, Md.: U.S. National Cancer Institute, International Cancer Information Center, 1963– . **EK30**

File size: 700,000 records. Updated monthly. Available online (BRS, DIALOG, MEDLARS), in CD-ROM (Aries, Compact Cambridge, Faxon), and in CD-ROM as part of *CANCER-CD* and *OncoDisc*.

Provides international coverage of the literature pertaining to all aspects of cancer, including epidemiology, pathology, treatment, and research, from a variety of source documents. From 1963 to 1967, this database was the machine-readable version of *Carcinogenesis abstracts* and *Cancer therapy abstracts*. Since 1983, most citations to journals have been derived from *MEDLINE* (below).

●**EMBASE** [computer file]. Amsterdam: Excerpta Medica/EMBASE Publ. Group, 1974– . **EK31**

Machine-readable version of *Excerpta medica* (*Guide* EK63).

File size: more than 4 million records, with abstracts. Updated weekly. Available online (BRS, Data-Star, DIALOG), in CD-ROM (SilverPlatter), and on diskette and magnetic tape (producer).

Indexes more than 3,500 journals, providing access to biomedical literature on human medicine and related areas of the biological sciences. International in scope; 55% of the journals indexed are published in Europe. Approximately 25% of citations added annually do not appear in the printed version.

●**Health planning and administration** : (HEALTH) [computer file]. Bethesda, Md.: U.S. National Library of Medicine, 1975– . **EK32**

File size: 477,000 records. Updated monthly. Available online (BRS, DIALOG, MEDLARS) and in CD-ROM (CD Plus, SilverPlatter).

Provides bibliographic coverage of the international literature on health care delivery, including administration, management, finances, and planning. Approximately 30% of citations have abstracts. Citations are drawn from *MEDLINE* (below), from *Hospital literature index* (*Guide* EK59), and from material submitted by the National Health Planning Information Center since 1983.

●**MEDLINE** [computer file]. Bethesda, Md.: National Library of Medicine, 1966– . **EK33**

Machine-readable file, corresponding to *Index medicus* (*Guide* EK52), and in part to *Index to dental literature* (*Guide* EK190) and *International nursing index* (*Guide* EK215).

File size: 6 million records. Updated weekly. Available online (BRS, Data-Star, DIALOG, MEDLARS, STN), and in CD-ROM (SilverPlatter, Aries, CD Plus, DIALOG, EBSCO, Bureau of Electronic Publishing, Compact Cambridge).

Provides bibliographic access to the international biomedical literature. Indexes more than 3,900 biomedical journals published in the U.S and abroad and chapters and articles from selected monographs, 1976–81. Abstracts are available for approximately 60% of the citations.

Style manuals

American Medical Association manual of style. 8th ed. / Cheryl Iverson, chair . . . [et al.]. Baltimore: Williams & Wilkins, c1989. 377 p.: ill. ISBN 0-683-04351-X. **EK34**

Title varies: 1st ed., 1962, called *AMA stylebook*; [6th ed., 1976] called *Stylebook: editorial manual*; 7th ed., 1981, called *Manual for authors and editors*. Compiler varies.

Presents guidelines for medical authors and editors in writing and preparing articles for publication. Offers advice on style, usage, nomenclature, statistics, and mathematical composition; also considers types of articles, fraud and plagiarism, grammar, the publishing process, online resources, sexist lan-

guage, and duplicate publication. An appendix lists virus names. Indexed. R119.A533

Huth, Edward J. How to write and publish papers in the medical sciences. 2nd ed. Baltimore: Williams & Wilkins, c1990. 252 p. ISBN 0-683-04272-6. ISBN 0-683-04271-8 (pbk.). **EK35**

1st ed., 1982.

"19 chapters describe all the steps in writing and publishing a paper."—*Introd.* Punctuation, abbreviation, citation, formats for references, etc. are those specified in the author's *Medical style and format: an international guide for authors, editors and publishers* (Phildelphia: ISI Press, 1987). Includes a chapter on how to search the medical literature. 4 appendixes, including a list of "Journals in the 'Uniform requirements' agreement as of September 1989." Index. R119.H87

Encyclopedias

The American Medical Association encyclopedia of medicine / medical ed., Charles B. Clayman. N.Y.: Random House, c1989. 1184 p.: ill. ISBN 0-394-56528-2. $39.95. **EK36**

Produced in response to growing public interest in health care, and to provide wider understanding of the language of medicine. The main section (more than 5,000 entries) includes symptoms, disorders, anatomy and physiology, medical tests, surgical procedures, and drugs, and is illustrated by flow charts, diagrams, etc. References in the text that refer to headwords of other articles are italicized. Also has a directory of self-help organizations and a drug glossary that cross-references brand and generic drug names and gives page numbers for related entries. General index. RC81.A2A52

Ammer, Christine. The new A to Z of women's health : a concise encyclopedia. N.Y.: Facts on File, c1989. 472 p.: ill. ISBN 0-8160-2073-6. $29.95. **EK37**

Revised edition of Ammer's *The A to Z of women's health* (1983).

Entries cover a broad range of topics related to women's health, emphasizing all aspects of reproduction and sexuality. Also discusses alternative health issues such as herbal remedies and astrological birth control. An appendix acts as a subject index, grouping related entries under 18 major topics (e.g., pregnancy and childbirth, cancer); an additional appendix provides addresses of related associations and organizations. Cross-references. RA778.A494

The encyclopedia of aging / George L. Maddox, ed. in chief. N.Y.: Springer Pub. Co., c1987. 890 p.: ill. ISBN 0-8261-4840-9. **EK38**

For annotation, see *Supplement* CC52. HQ1061.E53

Encyclopedia of medical devices and instrumentation / John G. Webster, ed. in chief. N.Y.: Wiley, c1988. 4 v. (3022 p.): ill. ISBN 0-471-82936-6 (set). $425.00 (est.). **EK39**

An alphabetically arranged collection of over 250 articles by experts, providing a comprehensive treatment of the contributions of engineering, physics, and computers to the various areas of medicine. Broader than the title would indicate, the work covers not only devices and instrumentation, but also the scientific basis for medical biotechnology, including articles on topics such as blood rheology, statistical methods, and biomechanics of scoliosis. Articles include many illustrations and substantial bibliographies of the primary literature. Cross-references; index. R856.A3E53

Encyclopedia of neuroscience / ed. by George Adelman. Boston : Birkhäuser, 1987. 2 v. : ill. ISBN 0-8176-3335-9 (set).   **EK40**

The first general encyclopedia in the field, with some 700 signed entries varying in length from several hundred words to several pages, and covering all clinical and basic aspects of neuroscience for both specialists and general readers. Both volumes begin with a list of all entries and end with an appendix of illustrations of the gross anatomy of the brain and name and subject indexes. Vol. 2 has two additional appendixes: a discussion of the use of animals in neuroscience research and concise biographies of contributors to neuroscience, 300 BCE to 1950.   RC334.E53

The Oxford companion to medicine / ed. by John Walton, Paul B. Beeson, Ronald Bodley Scott. Oxford ; N.Y. : Oxford Univ. Pr., 1986. 2 v. : ill. ISBN 0-19-261191-7. $63.25.   **EK41**

Contains essays that vary in length, some historical, some contemporary, on disciplines, specialties, and topics affecting the practice of medicine. Includes biographical entries and short definitions of selected medical terms. Essays are signed and include bibliographies. Appendixes give abbreviations and full names for major medical and related qualifications.   R121.O88

Physics in medicine & biology encyclopedia : medical physics, bioengineering, and biophysics / ed., T.F. McAinsh. Oxford ; N.Y. : Pergamon, 1986. 2 v. (980 p.) : ill. ISBN 0-08-026497-2. $175.00.   **EK42**

Includes more than 200 signed comprehensive articles with bibliographies. Articles are predominantly clinical in nature; topics demanding a highly mathematical treatment have been omitted. A classified list, grouping material into broad fields, precedes the alphabetical list of articles. Glossary; author and subject index. Intended for "the reader who has a basic grounding in physics, but no particular knowledge of the specific topic under discussion."—*Foreword*.   R895.A3P47

Rodin, Alvin E. Medicine, literature & eponyms : an encyclopedia of medical eponyms derived from literary characters / Alvin E. Rodin and Jack D. Key. Malabar, Fla. : R.E. Krieger Pub. Co., 1989. 345 p. : ill. ISBN 0-89464-2774. $39.50.   **EK43**

Defines over 350 medical eponyms derived from literary characters; among the sources are mythology, fables, and cartoons. Each entry includes a synopsis of the medical condition, a description of the associated literary character and of how specific characteristics correspond to symptoms of the condition, further literary references to the medical state, and other related material. A list of references to both the literary character and the medical condition appear with each entry. Subject index.   R121.R62

Sardegna, Jill. The encyclopedia of blindness and vision impairment / Jill Sardegna and T. Otis Paul. N.Y. : Facts on File, c1991. 329 p. ISBN 0-8160-2153-8.   **EK44**

The basic guide aimed at both professionals and general readers; treats all aspects of blindness, including health issues, education, adaptive aids, and organizations. Over 500 entries include both brief definitions and main articles (one to two pages in length), some of which include short lists of references. Provides an extensive bibliography and a subject and name index. Appendixes give addresses of companies, organizations, and schools, and list databases and services related to blindness and vision impairment; five tables provide statistical information related to eye injuries and diseases in the U.S., containing data for 1978–79.   RE91.S27

Wynbrandt, James. The encyclopedia of genetic disorders and birth defects / James Wynbrandt and Mark D.

Ludman. N.Y. : Facts on File, c1991. 426 p. : ill. ISBN 0-8160-1926-6.   **EK45**

Presents some 600 articles written for both health care professionals and general readers. Entries for disorders, selected on the basis of incidence and historical and clinical importance, discuss prognosis, prevalence, mode of inheritance, and the availability of both carrier screening and prenatal diagnosis; many include addresses of private organizations which can provide further information. Also included are brief discussions of subjects and terminology related to genetic disorders and congenital anomalies. Appendixes provide statistics and tables on congenital malformations and infant mortality, addresses for federal organizations and other associations in the U.S., support groups in the U.K., and Canadian organizations. Bibliography; subject and name index; numerous cross-references.
    RB155.5.W96

Dictionaries

Churchill's illustrated medical dictionary. N.Y. : Churchill Livingstone, 1989. 2120 p. : ill. ISBN 0-443-08691-5. $31.95.   **EK46**

Some 100,000 entries, with "extensive coverage given to vocabulary... from medical research, advanced diagnostic technology and innovations in health care."—*Pref.* Pronunciations (for more than 32,000 terms) and some usage notes (for 750). Includes biographical data for eponymous terms.
    R121.I58

Firkin, Barry G. Dictionary of medical eponyms / B.G. Firkin and J.A. Whitworth. Carnforth, U.K. ; Park Ridge, N.J. : Parthenon Pub. Group, 1987. 591 p. : ill. ISBN 0-940813-15-7. $48.00.   **EK47**

Offers explanations of approximately 2,300 eponyms currently used in internal medicine; in general, eponymous terms from subspecialities have been excluded. Each entry includes a brief definition of the term, and provides biographical information about the person from whose name the term is derived; some entries include a photograph or portrait. Although the orientation is Australian, these terms are used in most English-speaking countries. Includes some cross-references, but there is no index. The introduction provides a brief list of reference sources, but individual entries do not provide bibliographic citations.   R121.F535

International dictionary of medicine and biology / editorial board, E. Lovell Becker... [et al.] ; consulting ed., Alexandre Manuila ; ed. in chief, Sidney I. Landau. N.Y. : Wiley, c1986. 3 v. (3200 p.). ISBN 0-471-01849-X. $395.00.   **EK48**

An unabridged dictionary of medicine and closely allied biological sciences, offering some 159,000 definitions and 30,000 etymologies. In addition to the standard current terminology from the various disciplines and specialties, it also includes many terms of historical interest.   R121.I58

Lorenzini, Jean A. Medical phrase index : a one-step reference to the terminology of medicine. 2nd ed. Oradell, N.J. : Medical Economics Books, c1989. 948 p. ISBN 0-87489-539-1.   **EK49**

1st ed., 1978 (*Guide* EK99).

This updated edition includes new "terms used in reference to AIDS... organ donors... computer terms, and additional language relating to radiation oncology... and nuclear medicine."—*Pref.*   R123.L84

Stedman, Thomas Lathrop. Stedman's medical dictionary. 25th ed. Baltimore : Williams & Wilkins, c1990. 95, 1784 p. : ill. ISBN 0-683-07916-6. $38.95.   **EK50**

24th ed., 1982 (*Guide* EK101).

"Making *Stedman's* easier to use and easier to read has been a major focus in the preparation of the edition . . . . Noteworthy updating occurred in the terminologies of molecular biology, immunology, infectious diseases, endocrinology, genetics, and psychiatry and psychology . . . . Four appendices, 'Comparative Temperature Scales,' 'Temperature Equivalents,' 'Weights and Measures,' and 'Laboratory Reference Range Values,' have been revised and updated to include SI units and equivalents."—*Pref.* R121.S8

Willeford, George. Webster's New World medical word finder. 4th ed. N.Y.: Prentice-Hall, c1987. 433 p. ISBN 0-13-947326-2 (pbk.). $11.95. **EK51**

3rd ed., 1983 (*Guide* EK100) had title: *Medical word finder.*

This edition has an enlarged vocabulary, arranged in seven sections. "Two parts are of special note: Section II contains the phonetic/correct spelling of often used medical words . . . Section VIII lists commonly used proprietary drugs and corresponding generic terms."—*Pref.* R123.W47

Specialized dictionaries

Dictionary of obstetrics and gynecology / comp. by the editorial staff of *Pschyrembel Klinisches Wörterbuch*; managing ed., Christoph Zink. Berlin; N.Y.: W. de Gruyter, 1988. 277 p.: ill. (some col.). ISBN 0-89925-533-7. $27.00 (est.). **EK52**

English translation of *Pschyrembel Wörterbuch Gynäkologie und Gerburtshilfe* (1987), which supplemented and augmented *Pschyrembel's Klinisches Wörterbuch* (1986).

"This English version is primarily to be understood as the translation of a reference book which has its origins in the German scientific tradition. Nevertheless, also aspects specific to English-speaking countries have been included."—*Pref.* More than 2,600 entries are arranged alphabetically (except for plural forms). Derivation is given for words of Greek or Latin origin. Includes biographical entries. More than 400 illustrations, some in color; large number of tables and charts. Medical abbreviations have their own entries; general abbreviations are in an "Abbreviations list" (*p.xi*). Copious use of cross-references. RG45.P7813

Dictionary of visual science / [ed. by] David Cline, Henry W. Hofstetter, John R. Griffin. 4th ed. Radnor, Pa.: Chilton, c1989. 820 p.: ill. ISBN 0-8019-7862-9. $55.00. **EK53**

1st ed., 1960; 3rd ed., 1980.

A comprehensive dictionary providing succinct definitions for terms in all fields of visual science, including anatomy and physiology of the eye, optics, and ocular pharmacology. Includes entries for syndromes with ocular manifestations. Compound and eponymous terms are listed alphabetically under the noun ("artificial light" under "light," "Harada's disease" under "disease"), and pronunciation is given for more difficult terms. An appendix lists terms, symbols and abbreviations, and there are reference tables related to visual science. RE21.D42

Goodwin, Diana M. A dictionary of neuropsychology. N.Y.: Springer-Verlag, c1989. 325 p. ISBN 0-387-97123-8. **EK54**

Intends "to provide a cross-referenced, alphabetical listing of terms, common medical abbreviations, diseases, symptoms, syndromes, brain structures and locations, and test instruments used in neuropsychology and their neuropsychological interpretation . . . . Some historical information is included as well as current basic neuropsychological knowledge."—*Pref.* QP360.G66

Magalini, Sergio I. Dictionary of medical syndromes / Sergio I. Magalini, Sabina C. Magalini, Giovanni de

Francisci. 3rd ed. Philadelphia: Lippincott, c1990. 1042 p. ISBN 0-397-50882-4. $59.50. **EK55**

2nd ed., 1981 (*Guide* EK109).

Many new entries have been added and some older ones deleted. References which accompany entries have been updated. RC69.M33

Rosen, Fred S. Dictionary of immunology / Fred S. Rosen, Lisa A. Steiner, Emil R. Unanue. N.Y.: Stockton Pr.; London: Macmillan, 1989. 223 p.: ill. ISBN 0-935859-58-6. $50.00. **EK56**

"Draws from the vocabulary of molecular biology, cell biology and genetics as well as from immunology itself . . . . Many of the definitions are long and contain considerable detail."—*Introd.* May be useful to readers with little background in immunology. QR180.4.R67

Foreign terms

Dictionary of medicine: English-German: containing about 55,000 terms / comp. by Jürgen Nöhring. Amsterdam; N.Y.: Elsevier, 1984. 708 p. ISBN 0-444-99641-9. $90.00 (est.). **EK57**

"Terms have been selected from all branches of medicine [with the] aim . . . to serve as a practical source . . . intended not only for physicians . . . and specialists, but also students of medicine and . . . ancillary staff."—*Pref.* R121.N63

Dictionary of medicine: German-English: containing about 75,000 terms / comp. by Jürgen Nöhring. Amsterdam; N.Y.: Elsevier, 1987. 846 p. ISBN 0-444-98982-X. $150.00 (est.). **EK58**

"In preparing this edition the terminology of the English-German volume has been revised and . . . some new terms have been added."—*Pref.* R121.N63

Ruiz Torres, Francisco. Diccionario de términos médicos, inglés-español, español-inglés. 6a ed., rev. y ampliada. Madrid: Editorial Alhambra, c1989. 880 p. ISBN 84-205-1306-7. **EK59**

1st ed., 1957; 5th ed., 1986.

A revision and expansion of the 5th ed. Offers brief Spanish-language definitions of English medical terms and a separate section of Spanish medical terms with English equivalents (not definitions). R121.R93

Directories

International

Directory of technical and scientific directories: a world bibliographic guide to medical, agricultural, industrial, and natural science directories. 5th ed. Burnt Mill, Harlow, Essex, England: Longman; Phoenix: Oryx, 1988. 1 v. ISBN 0-582-00602-3. **EK60**

For annotation, see *Supplement* EA54. Z7405.D55D57

United States

Congregate care by county. Jan. 1989– . Phoenix: Oryx, c1989– . Semiannual. $150.00. **EK61**

For annotation, see *Supplement* CC55.

HD7287.92.U54C67

Directory of health care professionals / American Hospital Association. 1990 ed.– . Chicago: The Association,

c1990– . Annual. ISSN 1049-9253. $100.00 (members).
EK62

Lists over 150,000 names, titles, addresses, and telephone numbers of health care professionals in U.S. hospitals. Arranged in separate alphabetical sections for state, city, and hospital. Other sections list health care systems headquarters professionals and names organized by job function in different job categories. A companion to the American Hospital Association's *AHA Guide to the health care field* (*Guide* EK127).   R712.A1D49

●**DIRLINE** : (Directory of Information Resources Online) [computer file]. Bethesda, Md. : U.S. National Library of Medicine.   **EK63**

File size: 16,000 records. Updated quarterly. Available online (MEDLARS).

Lists primarily U.S. organizations that provide information services in areas related to health sciences: government agencies, information centers, professional societies, voluntary and self-help agencies. Records provide organization name, address and telephone numbers, description of the organization, and types of services provided.

Encyclopedia of medical organizations and agencies / Anthony T. Kruzas, Kay Gill, and Robert Wilson, editors. 2nd ed. Detroit : Gale, c1987. 975 p. ISBN 0-8103-0324-8. $180.00.   **EK64**

1st ed., 1983 (*Guide* EK136).

Subtitle: a subject guide to more than 11,000 medical societies, professional and voluntary associations, foundations, research institutes, federal and state agencies, medical and allied health schools, information centers, data base services, and related health care organizations.

This edition adds a large number of agencies, computer-based information services, and a keyword index. Derived from *Encyclopedia of associations* (*Guide* CA125).   R712.A1U5

National health directory / John T. Grupenhoff, ed. ; Betty Farley, assoc. ed. [14th ed.]. Rockville, Md., : Aspen Systems Corp., 1990. lxxvii, 651 p. : ill., maps. ISBN 0-8342-0171-2.   **EK65**

9th ed., 1985 (*Guide* EK139); [13th ed.], 1989.

Additions made in recent years include: a listing of key staff of standing committees and subcommittees of Congress and of state legislative committees that deal with health-related issues and legislation; listing of officials of state, city and county health agencies; congressional district maps; organization charts for agencies.

Handbooks

AIDS information sourcebook / ed. by H. Robert Malinowsky and Gerald J. Perry. 3rd ed., 1991–92. Phoenix : Oryx, 1991. 300 p. ISBN 0-8977-4598-1.   **EK66**

1st ed., 1988; 2nd ed., 1989–90.

In four parts: (1) Chronology, listing events in the AIDS epidemic, June 1981–Jan. 1991; (2) Directory, listing approximately 1,000 facilities in the U.S. and Canada, arranged alphabetically by state or province, then by city and name of facility; (3) Bibliography, including citations to periodical articles, bibliographies, books, pamphlets, etc.; (4) an appendix containing selected statistical tables and a glossary of brief, nontechnical definitions.   RC607.A26A3475

The American Medical Association family medical guide / editors, Jeffrey R.M. Kunz, Asher J. Finkel. Rev. ed. N.Y. : Random House, c1987. 832 p. : ill. (some col.). ISBN 0-394-55582-1.   **EK67**

1st ed., 1982 (*Guide* EK67).

This revised and updated edition continues the philosophy of preventive medicine and care of the first edition.   RC81.A543

Fry, John. Disease data book / John Fry, Gerald Sandler, David Brooks. Lancaster, England ; Boston : MTP Pr., c1986. 405 p. : ill. ISBN 0-85200-922-4. $40.00 (est.).   **EK68**

For each of 22 important medical conditions and problems, including high blood pressure, diabetes, epilepsy, etc., the same set of questions (what is it? who gets it when? what happens? what to do?) is posed, answers are given to each, and the nature, course, prognosis and outcome of these conditions is described. Index.   RC55.F75

Griffith, H. Winter. Complete guide to medical tests. Tucson, Ariz. : Fisher Books, c1988. 932 p. ISBN 1-55561-011-0 (pbk.). $17.95.   **EK69**

A comprehensive guide for general readers that contains descriptions of more than 400 physician-ordered medical tests, with an additional section on do-it-yourself tests. Although entries are arranged by most common test name, the table of contents provides access by test type (e.g., Blood gases and electrolytes). Has sections on "Before the test" (purpose, risks, precautions, etc.) and "Test" (what the patient will see and hear, equipment used, etc.), and includes advice on post-test care and interpretation of results. Provides a glossary of medical terms, a subject index, various appendixes, and a brief list of related titles.   RC71.3.G75

Handbook of biomedical engineering / ed. by Jacob Kline. San Diego : Academic Pr., c1988. 733 p. : ill. ISBN 0-12-415145-0.   **EK70**

" . . . presents in one place authoritative summary accounts of the important areas in which significant advances have been made because of biomedical engineering . . . it concentrates on . . . an in-depth description of the most important currently used systems and materials."—*Pref.* 27 signed chapters include numerous references. Indexed.   R856.H37

Iturralde, Mario P. Dictionary and handbook of nuclear medicine and clinical imaging. Boca Raton, Fla. : CRC Pr., c1990. 564 p. ISBN 0-8493-3233-8.   **EK71**

Designed to bridge the gap between highly specialized sources and general science dictionaries. The first part, a dictionary of brief definitions, also includes various lists (e.g., terms used to describe anatomical positions and planes, common abbreviations). The accompanying handbook consists of tables on subjects such as: properties of elements and radioisotopes, radionuclides and radiopharmaceuticals; radioactive decay; radiation dosimetry; Reference Man; SI units for the measurement of radioactivity and ionizing radiation; physical constants and conversion factors. The handbook includes a subject index.   RC78.7.D53I88

The Merck manual of geriatrics / William B. Abrams, and Robert Berkow, editors ; Andrew J. Fletcher, assistant ed. Rahway, N.J. : Merck Sharp & Dohme Research Laboratories, 1990. 1267 p. : ill. ISBN 91-1-091032-8.   **EK72**

Covers "all aspects of disease and the clinical management of elderly patients . . . [following] the tradition set by the *Merck manual* [*Guide* EK87] . . . ."—*Pref.* Provides information on common problems among older patients, treatment approaches specific to the elderly, normal changes and diseases or disorders arranged by organ systems. Emphasizes age-related concerns, and treats epidemiological, social, ethical, financial, and legal issues specific to the elderly. Includes expected laboratory values and other data unique to the older population. Numerous cross-references in both text and index; in the index, page numbers in boldface signify major discussions of the topics.   RC952.55.M555

History

Erlen, Jonathon. The history of the health care sciences and health care, 1700–1980 : a selective annotated bibliography / Jonathon Erlen. N.Y. : Garland, 1984. 1028 p. (Garland reference library of the humanities, vol. 398). ISBN 0-8240-9166-3.   **EK73**

Contains 5,004 entries with descriptive annotations; arranged alphabetically by topic. Includes English-language books, journal articles, government documents, unpublished masters' theses and Ph.D. dissertations. Author index. Intended for researchers and students.   Z6660.8.E74

McGrew, Roderick E. Encyclopedia of medical history / Roderick E. McGrew, with the collaboration of Margaret P. McGrew. N.Y. : McGraw-Hill, c1985. 400 p. ISBN 0-07-045087-0. $34.95.   **EK74**

Intends "to provide an easily accessible historical treatment of important medical topics.—*Pref.* Includes 103 essays, each with a bibliography of additional readings. Topical entries are arranged in alphabetical order. No biographical articles, but individuals' contributions to medical science are discussed in the essays. Index.   R133.M34

Rutkow, Ira M. The history of surgery in the United States, 1775–1900. San Francisco : Norman Pub., 1988. v. 1 : ill. (Norman surgery series, no. 2). ISBN 0-930405-02-1 (v. 1). (In progress).   **EK75**

Contents: v. 1, Textbooks, monographs, and treatises.

An annotated bibliography to be complete in 4 v. Vol. 1 lists 552 works "written by surgeons living in the U.S."—*Introd.* Most entries are either first editions of textbooks or the initial printing of a treatise or monograph. For each work includes a summary. Brief biographical sketches of authors. Includes 130 reproductions from various cited works and a short-title list of all items found in the volume. Name/subject index.   Z6666.R87

Biography

Nobel laureates in medicine or physiology : a biographical dictionary / ed. by Daniel M. Fox, Marcia Meldrum, and Ira Rezak. N.Y. : Garland, c1990. 595 p. (Garland reference library of the humanities, vol. 852). ISBN 0-8240-7892-6.   **EK76**

Contains scholarly biographical articles on prize winners, 1901–89. Articles are signed and "written to be accessible to students and general readers as well as to specialists in medical science and history."—*Pref.* Following a brief chronological listing, entries are arranged alphabetically by laureates' names. Index of laureates and scientists named in the articles, including names occurring in bibliographies appended to each article. No subject index.   R134.N63

Sammons, Vivian O. Blacks in science and medicine. N.Y. : Hemisphere Pub. Corp., c1990. 293 p. ISBN 0-89116-665-3. $40.00.   **EK77**

For annotation, see *Supplement* EA80.   Q141.B58

Bibliography

Morton, Leslie T. A bibliography of medical and biomedical biography / Leslie T. Morton and Robert J. Moore. Aldershot, England : Scolar Pr. ; Brookfield, Vt., : Gower Pub. Co., c1989. 208 p. ISBN 0-85967-797-4. $75.00.   **EK78**

Begun as a 3rd ed. of John L. Thornton's *A select bibliography of medical biography* (2nd ed., 1970; *Guide* EK160), this work is broader in scope, including biographical references to over 1,600 individuals in the biomedical sciences as well as in clinical medicine and surgery. Lists only English-language publications and provides references to biographies published in book form, to entries in *Dictionary of scientific biography,* (*Guide* EA227), *Biographical memoirs of Fellows of the Royal Society* (*Guide* EA234), *Obituary notices of Fellows of the Royal Society* (*Guide* EA233), *Biographical memoirs* (of the National Academy of Sciences) (*Supplement* EA77), and selected periodical references. An initial section of individual biographies is alphabetic by biographee, giving nationality, field, and notable accomplishments; location of archival material is also indicated. A list of collective biographies follows, usually giving a brief description of the work, while a third section provides a short list of books on the history of medicine and related works, arranged by subject. Indexed by discipline; biographees are listed within each discipline by birth date.   Z6660.5.M67

International

Medical sciences international who's who. 3rd ed. Burnt Mill, Harlow, Essex, England : Longman ; Detroit : Gale, 1987.   **EK79**

2nd ed., 1985 (*Guide* EK164) had title: *International medical who's who: a biographical guide in the biomedical sciences.*

Provides information on approximately 8,000 biomedical scientists from more than 90 countries. Vol. 1 gives individual profiles in alphabetical order; v. 2 presents a listing of experts in 14 subject areas, by country. Subject areas include anatomy and physiology, biochemistry, biophysics, molecular biology, dental sciences, immunology and transplantation, clinical medicine and neoplasia. A companion to *Medical research centres* (*Guide* EK124).   R134.I57

BIOETHICS

●**BIOETHICSLINE** [computer file]. Wash. : Center for Bioethics, Kennedy Institute of Ethics, Georgetown Univ., 1973– .   **EK80**

Machine-readable version of *Bibliography of bioethics* (*Guide* EK185).

File size: more than 29,000 records. Updated bimonthly. Available online (MEDLARS).

Provides bibliographic citations to all areas of biomedical ethics, including genetic intervention, abortion, professional ethics, and related public policy and legal issues. Sources indexed include other indexes (both online and print) and more than 70 journals and newspapers.

BioLaw. 1986– . Frederick, Md. : Univ. Publications of America, c1986– . Annual.   **EK81**

Editors: 1986–   James F. Childress [et al.].

Loose-leaf; updated between editions.

Each annual consists of 2 v.: v. 1, Resource manual, contains essays on biological, medical and health care issues with ethical and legal implications; v. 2 includes updates and special sections on laws, regulations, court cases, etc. Each update comes with a cumulative subject index covering both volumes and a cumulative index to court cases. A microfiche supplement containing the original source documents is available.

DENTISTRY

Guides

Clennett, Margaret A. Keyguide to information sources in dentistry / Margaret A. Clennett. London ; N.Y. : Mansell, 1985. 287 p. : ill. ISBN 0-7201-1747-X (U.S.). $30.00 (est.).   **EK82**

Offers "the information worker or non-dental researcher an overview of the major sources in the field as a whole, and in specialized subject areas."—*Introd.* Pt.I, "Survey of dentistry and its literature," includes a chapter on the history of dentistry. Pt.II contains a bibliography of 666 annotated entries, and Pt.III a directory of organizations. Index.   RK28.7.C55

Kowitz, Aletha. Basic dental reference works. [9th ed.]. Chicago : Bureau of Library Services, American Dental Association, 1990. 23 p.   **EK83**

5th ed., 1983 (*Guide* EK186); 8th ed., 1989.

An "annotated listing of 131 titles . . . [intended] to provide a guide to the most pertinent works that the dental reference librarian and others who use the dental literature cannot work without."—*Pref.*   RK56.K69

Bibliography

Kowitz, Aletha. Dentistry journals and serials : an analytical guide. Westport, Conn. : Greenwood, 1985. 226 p. (Annotated bibliographies of serials, no. 3). ISBN 0-313-24363-8.   **EK84**

"Dental journals have proliferated since 1839 while the literature of related fields has also done so. The result is an extensive list of titles of widely varied styles and depths of content."—*Pref.* Includes 645 titles with descriptive annotations, arranged alphabetically by title. Geographical, publishers, and classified titles indexes.   Z6668.K68

Dictionaries

Fairpo, Jenifer E. H. Heinemann dental dictionary. 3rd ed. [London] : Heinemann Medical, 1987. 311 p. ISBN 0-433-10704-9. £15.95. ISBN 0-433-10703-0 (pbk.). £8.50.   **EK85**

Rev. ed. of *Heinemann modern dictionary for dental students*, 2nd ed., 1973.

A major revision that provides brief definitions of terms, including many obsolete terms from early dental literature. American terms are included, although the clinical terminology is based on the *British standard glossary of dental terms* (British Standard 4492; London: BSI, 1983). This edition omits pronunciations and illustrations included in earlier editions. Anatomical charts of the head and neck show arteries, muscles, nerves, and veins; an appendix lists dental periodicals, with country of origin and frequency of publication.   RK27

Harty, F. J. Concise illustrated dental dictionary / F.J. Harty, R. Ogston. Bristol : Wright, 1987. [304] p. : ill. ISBN 0-7236-0788-5. £9.95.   **EK86**

Offers brief definitions for a comprehensive range of dental terminology, including both common and more exotic terms. Designed to be an aid to practitioners, dental students, and dental surgery assistants. Includes cross-references and line drawings illustrating anatomical features and dental instruments. Appendixes include a chronological table of the development

and eruption of the teeth, and addresses of selected dental schools and national dental organizations.   RK27

MEDICAL JURISPRUDENCE

Sloane, Richard. The Sloane-Dorland annotated medical-legal dictionary. St. Paul, Minn. : West Pub. Co., c1987. 787 p. : ill. ISBN 0-314-93512-6.   **EK87**

Definitions of medical terms, taken from *Dorland's illustrated medical dictionary* (*Guide* EK96), are combined with "judicial interpretations of the same terms . . . drawn from court opinions, the testimony of medical experts, and extracts of lawyers' briefs found in those opinions."—*Pref.*   RA1017.S56

NURSING

Bibliography

Directory of educational software for nursing. 1987– . N.Y. : National League for Nursing, c1987– . Annual.   **EK88**

Intended for educators and others responsible for the selection and purchase of computer-assisted instruction (CAI) software for use in nursing. Divides CAI programs into two sections: those which use microcomputers, and those which use both microcomputers and videodisc players. Lengthy entries provide detailed description and evaluation, and information concerning hardware requirements, price, preview policy, warranty, published reviews, and support after purchase. Indexed by topic, mode of instructional style, and publisher (including address and telephone number). Glossary of terms; bibliography.

Indexes, Abstract journals

●**Nursing & allied health database** [computer file]. Glendale, Calif. : CINAHL Corp., 1983– .   **EK89**

Machine-readable version of *Cumulative index to nursing & allied health literature* (*Guide* EK214).

File size: more than 106,000 records. Updated monthly. Available online (BRS, Data-Star, DIALOG) and in CD-ROM (CD Plus, Compact Cambridge, SilverPlatter, Faxon).

Indexes more than 330 English-language nursing, allied health, and biomedical journals, publications of the American Nurses' Association and the National League for Nursing, nursing dissertations, and new books.

Encyclopedias

Miller, Benjamin Frank. Encyclopedia and dictionary of medicine, nursing, and allied health / by Benjamin F. Miller and Claire Brackman Keane. 4th ed. Philadelphia : Saunders, 1987. 1427 p. : ill. ISBN 0-03-011507-8.   **EK90**

3rd ed., 1983 (*Guide* EK220).

This edition expands coverage to include entries for individual nursing diagnoses and for conceptual models of nursing.   R121.M65

Dictionaries

Mosby's medical, nursing, and allied health dictionary. 3rd ed. Managing ed., Walter D. Glanze; revision ed., Kenneth N. Anderson; consulting ed. and writer, Lois E. Anderson. St. Louis : Mosby, 1990. [1652] p. ISBN 0-8016-3227-7. **EK91**

1st ed., 1983 (*Guide* EK222), and 2nd ed., 1986, had title: *Mosby's medical & nursing dictionary*.

This edition has an added emphasis on allied health professions, with new categories of entries in physical therapy, occupational therapy, and respiratory care. "Word roots have been added to the principal entries, to aid in understanding complex medical terminology."—*Foreword*.   R121M89

Directories

Allen, Sallie T. The directory of black nursing faculty : baccalaureate and higher degree programs. Lisle, Ill. : Tucker Publications, 1988. 169 p.   **EK92**

Provides brief biographical data for African-American nursing faculty teaching in baccalaureate or degree programs accredited by the National League for Nursing. Arranged by state, then by institution. Gives for each biographee: highest degree, RN, title, position or rank, telephone, educational background, areas of teaching and research, professional and community interests. Institutions with no African-American faculty are noted. A second section functions as an index by name, noting institution and state where employed.   RT79.A38

Guide to programs in nursing in four-year colleges and universities : baccalaureate and graduate programs in the United States and Canada / ed. by Barbara K. Redman, Linda K. Amos ; managing ed., Ruth Lamothe. N.Y. : American Council on Education/Macmillan Pub. Co., c1987. 472 p. ISBN 0-02-901490-5. $90.00.   **EK93**

Provides information on the more than 600 nursing education programs in the U.S. and Canada, including faculty research activities and admission and graduation requirements. Organized by state and province; each entry provides information about the institution and the programs offered, including library facilities and affiliations with health care facilities. Indexed by type of program and institution.   RT79.G85

Biography

American nursing : a biographical dictionary / ed. by Vern L. Bullough, Olga Maranjian Church, Alice P. Stein. N.Y. : Garland, 1988. 358 p., [24] p. of plates : ill. ISBN 0-8240-8540-X.   **EK94**

Contains long entries for 175 women and 2 men who "made a significant contribution to nursing" (*Intro.*), and who died or were born prior to 1890. Entries include bibliographies. Indexed by decade of birth, first nursing school attended, area of interest or accomplishment, and state and country of birth. Covers much the same ground as *Dictionary of American nursing biography* (below). Of the individuals in these sources, 109 appear in both, but each provides unique information.   RT34.A44

Dictionary of American nursing biography / Martin Kaufman, ed. in chief. N.Y. : Greenwood, 1988. 462 p. ISBN 0-313-24520-7.   **EK95**

Companion to *Dictionary of American medical biography* (*Guide* EK169).

Contains "196 biographical sketches of persons who were important in the history of American nursing" (*Pref.*) and who died prior to January 31, 1987. For each individual, includes biographical data, summary of contributions to nursing, and a list of writings and references. Appendixes list persons by place of birth, state where prominent, and specialty or occupation. Indexed by personal name, organization, place, and special subject.   RT34.D53

NUTRITION

Guides

Szilard, Paula. Food and nutrition information guide. Littleton, Colo. : Libraries Unlimited, 1987. 358 p. : ill. ISBN 0-87287-457-5. $37.50.   **EK96**

A selection of predominantly English-language materials (most published during the last ten years) on human nutrition, dietetics, and food sciences and technology. Materials on animal nutrition are omitted unless considered useful for those interested in human nutrition. Contains publications from commercial publishers and international organizations (including FAO and WHO), and government publications. Most citations are annotated. Under topical headings, citations are arranged alphabetically. Detailed table of contents and extensive subject index. Intended for students, professionals, researchers, and librarians.   Z5776.N8S94

Encyclopedias

The Columbia encyclopedia of nutrition / the Institute of Human Nutrition, Columbia University College of Physicians and Surgeons ; comp. and ed. by Myron Winick... [et al.]. N.Y. : G.P. Putnam, c1988. 349 p. : ill. ISBN 0-399-13298-8. $19.95.   **EK97**

Provides authoritative summaries of current knowledge for selected major topics in nutrition, in language readily comprehensible by general readers. Entries vary in length from a half page to several pages, and cover a wide variety of topics (e.g., osteoporosis, obesity, cholesterol, nutrition in the workplace, seaweed). Indexed by subject.   QP141.C69

Garrison, Robert H. The nutrition desk reference / Robert H. Garrison, Jr., and Elizabeth Somer. 2nd ed. New Canaan, Conn. : Keats, c1990. 306 p. : ill. ISBN 0-87983-523-0. $34.95. ISBN 0-87983-488-9 (pbk.). $15.95.   **EK98**

Directed at health professionals and interested general readers. Combines basic nutritional information and recent nutritional research findings in six sections, each dealing with a major dietary topic: Dietary factors, Vitamin and mineral research, The relationships between nutrition and cancer, Cardiovascular disease, Other diseases, and Drugs. Separate section of dietary recommendations. List of figures and tables, glossary, and index.   QP141.G33

Modern nutrition in health and disease / ed. by Maurice E. Shils, Vernon R. Young. 7th ed. Philadelphia : Lea & Febiger, 1988. 1694 p. : ill. ISBN 0-8121-0984-8.   **EK99**

6th ed., 1980 (*Guide* EK236).

This edition includes "20 new chapters or major subsections and 68 new authors .... Additional space is devoted to trace elements, vitamin-like compounds, ... diet and drug interactions, nutrition and diet in relation to behavioral, neurologic, and rheumatic disorders."—*Pref.*   QP141.M64

Tver, David F. The nutrition and health encyclopedia / David F. Tver and Percy Russell. 2nd ed. N.Y. : Van

Nostrand Reinhold, c1989. 639 p. : ill. ISBN 0-442-23397-3.   **EK100**

1st ed., 1981.

This edition of this comprehensive dictionary contains 150 revised definitions and 86 new terms. Entries, which vary in length from short definitions to several pages, are arranged alphabetically and cover a wide range of nutritional topics. Food entries give a description of the food and its caloric value; includes food tables with nutritional values. 13 appendixes are included, such as a table of nutritive values, and height/weight ranges of men and women.   QP141.T88

Handbooks

Igoe, Robert S. Dictionary of food ingredients. 2nd ed. N.Y. : Van Nostrand Reinhold, c1989. 225 p. ISBN 0-442-31927-4.   **EK101**

1st ed., 1983.

Intended for those who work with foods. Each entry in the initial "Ingredients" section is defined according to functions, properties and applications; chemical formulations and usage levels are provided where applicable, and there are many cross-references. The second section, "Ingredients categories," groups principal ingredients and provides collective information, often in tabular form, on their properties and the relationship of their component ingredients. A final section reprints six parts of the Code of Federal Regulations, listing food ingredients and their U.S. approved status. An extensive bibliography is included. This edition includes additional ingredients and provides expanded information for ingredients previously listed.   TX551.I26

National Research Council (U.S.). Committee on Diet and Health. Diet and health : implications for reducing chronic disease risk / Committee on Diet and Health, Food and Nutrition Board, Commission on Life Sciences, National Research Council. Wash. : National Academy Pr., 1989. 749 p. : ill. ISBN 0-309-03994-0.   **EK102**

Discusses the complex relationship between dietary intake and chronic disease, and attempts to formulate dietary guidelines. Pt. 1 contains an introduction, definitions and methodology, Pt. 2 discusses evidence relating to chronic diseases, with chapters on individual dietary components, Pt. 3 describes the impact of dietary patterns on chronic diseases, with chapters on major diseases, and Pt. 4 provides an overall assessment, conclusions, and recommendations. Comprehensive index.   RC108.N38

PHARMACOLOGY

Guides

Andrews, Theodora. Guide to the literature of pharmacy and the pharmaceutical sciences. Littleton, Colo. : Libraries Unlimited, 1986. 383 p. ISBN 0-87287-420-6. $37.50.   **EK103**

A comprehensive bibliography of 958 entries covering the entire field of pharmacy and the pharmaceutical sciences. Annotations are descriptive and evaluative. Pt. I emphasizes reference works. Pt. II, "Source material by subject area," lists standard treatises and textbooks in pharmacy practice, industrial and physical pharmacy, medicinal chemistry and pharmacognosy, pharmacology and toxicology, cosmetics, perfumes and flavors, and drug abuse. Pt. III covers computerized databases and provides a list of currently published periodicals.   Z6675.P5A56

Information sources in pharmaceuticals / ed., W.R. Pickering. London ; N.Y. : Bowker-Saur, c1990. 566 p. : ill. ISBN 0-408-02518-2.   **EK104**

Describes the pharmaceutical literature, including online databases, throughout the different stages of the pharmaceutical process. Considers the role of drug companies, relevant national associations, and the World Health Organization. Examines the "information scenario" in the U.S., Western Europe, Japan, Australia, South America, Africa, and China. Companion to *Information sources in the medical sciences (Guide* EK5).   RS56.I54

Snow, Bonnie. Drug information : a guide to current resources. Chicago : Medical Library Association, c1989. 243 p. ISBN 0-912176-24-5. $32.00.   **EK105**

Provides an introduction to a wide selection of relevant printed and online sources and discusses common problems in the provision of information concerning drugs. Background information on pharmacological terminology, legal and regulatory issues, and marketing and business data is given. Also included are a detailed contents listing, a keyword index, a glossary that defines pharmaceutical and information science terminology used in the text, and practicum exercises.   Z6675.P5S64

Bibliography

Cocaine : an annotated bibliography / Carlton E. Turner... [et al.]. Jackson, Miss. : Research Institute of Pharmaceutical Sciences, Univ. of Mississippi, and Univ. Pr. of Mississippi, c1988. 2 v. ISBN 0-87805-382-4 (set).   **EK106**

Vol.1 is a two-part bibliography of the scientific literature on cocaine, including social and historical aspects of cocaine use, arranged alphabetically by author. Pre-1950 citations (1855–1949) lack annotations and are indexed by author only; 1950–1986 citations are annotated and indexed by both author and subject. Vol.2 contains author and subject indexes.   Z6663.C63C63

Periodicals

WHO drug information. v. 1, no. 1– . Geneva : World Health Organization, c1987– . Four issues yearly. ISSN 1010-9609.   **EK107**

Provides an overview of topics relating to drug development and regulation that are of current relevance. Includes lists of proposed and recommended International Nonproprietary Names for Pharmaceutical Substances (INN) and changes to WHO's "Model list of essential drugs."

Dictionaries

Dictionary of alkaloids / editorial board: G.A. Cordell... [et al.] ; comp. and ed. by I.W. Southon, J. Buckingham. London ; N.Y. : Chapman and Hall, 1989. 2 v. : ill. ISBN 0-412-24910-3 (set). $1295.00.   **EK108**

For annotation, see *Supplement* ED31.   RS431.A53D53

Dictionary of antibiotics and related substances / ed. by B.W. Bycroft. London ; N.Y. : Chapman and Hall, 1988. 944 p. : ill. ISBN 0-412-25450-6. $620.00.   **EK109**

For annotation, see *Supplement* ED32.   RS431.A6D53

Dictionary of drugs : chemical data, structures, and bibliographies / editors, J. Elks, C.R. Ganellin. London ;

N.Y.: Chapman and Hall, 1990. 2 v.: ill. ISBN 0-412-27300-4 (set). $1250.00.   **EK110**

For annotation, see *Supplement* ED33.   RS51.D479

Dictionary of pharmacy / [ed. in chief, Julian H. Fincher]. Columbia, S.C.: Univ. of South Carolina Pr., c1986. 374 p. ISBN 0-87249-444-6.   **EK111**

Includes approximately 6,000 brief definitions, mainly from the pharmaceutical and pharmacological sciences, but also many from general medicine. Cross-references and 45 pages of appendixes.   RS51.D48

Negwer, Martin. Organic-chemical drugs and their synonyms: (an international survey). 6th rev. and enl. ed. N.Y.: VCH Publishers, c1987. 3 v. ISBN 0-89573-550-4 (set). $250.00 (est.).   **EK112**

Rev. and enl. ed. and English translation of: *Organisch-chemische Arzneimittel und ihre Synonyma*, 5th ed.

This 1st English ed. includes "9,040 organo-chemical drugs which are chemically unified by molecular formula definition, and more than 80,000 synonyms."—*Pref.* Arrangement of drugs and their synonyms is "by the concept of incremental molecular formulas" (*Introd.*) in two columns per page. Entries include CAS Registry Number, structural formula, references, synonyms, and use. Group, CAS number, and synonym indexes.   R551.N428

Handbooks

Briggs, Gerald G. Drugs in pregnancy and lactation: a reference guide to fetal and neonatal risk / Gerald G. Briggs, Roger K. Freeman, Sumner J. Yaffe. 3rd ed. Baltimore: Williams & Wilkins, c1990. 732 p. ISBN 0-683-01059-X.   **EK113**

1st ed., 1983 (*Guide* EK252); 2nd ed., 1986.

Many drug monographs in this edition have been "extensively revised.... For example, cocaine... the antineoplastic agents, and most of the vitamin products...."—*Pref.*   RG627.6.D79B75

Drug evaluations / prepared by the American Medical Association, Department of Drugs, Division of Drugs and Technology in cooperation with the American Society for Clinical Pharmacology and Therapeutics. Chicago: American Medical Association, c1986. 6th ed. ISSN 0898-7467.   **EK114**

5th ed., 1983, (*Guide* EK250) had title *AMA Drug Evaluations.*

For this revised edition, the "original goal is unaltered: To provide... up-to-date, unbiased information on the clinical use of drugs."—*Pref.*

Drugs available abroad. 1991– . Detroit: Medical Economics Co., Gale, c1991– . Annual. ISSN 1051-7723. $89.95 (single issue).   **EK115**

Subtitle: Guide to therapeutic drugs available and approved outside the U.S.

Lists more than 1,000 therapeutic drugs in use in Australia, Canada, Central America, South Africa, Western Europe, and elsewhere that have not been approved by the Food and Drug Administration, hence are not yet available in the U.S. Arranged alphabetically by generic name, entries include such information as countries where the drug is available, its release date, FDA approval status, and equivalent U.S. drug therapy. Indexes: drug action, clinical indications, manufacturer, country where used, drug name. Appendixes: directories of manufacturers and regulatory authorities. Includes a survey of the drug approval process in various countries. Regular updates are planned.   RS51.D78

Handbook of nonprescription drugs. 8th ed. Wash.: American Pharmaceutical Association, c1986. 741 p. ISBN 0-917330-54-4.   **EK116**

7th ed., 1982 (*Guide* EK258).

This revised edition includes a new chapter on antipyretic drug products, a new section on sports medicine, and expanded information on nutritional supplements, asthma, contact lenses, and oral health care products.   RM671.A1H34

Martindale, William. The extra pharmacopoeia. 29th ed. / ed. by James E.F. Reynolds... [et al.]. London: Pharmaceutical Pr., 1989. 1896 p. ISBN 0-85369-210-6. $195.00.   **EK117**

1st ed., 1883; 28th ed., 1982. Compiled since 1933 by the editorial staff of the Royal Pharmaceutical Society of Great Britain.

Provides "concise reports on the actions and uses of most of the world's drugs and medicines... " and reflects recent developments in therapeutics.... Based on published information. It is not a book of standards."—*Pref.* International in scope, covering prescription and nonprescription drugs. In three parts: (1) Monographs on drugs and ancillary substances, containing data on approximately 4,000 substances in 72 chapters; (2) Supplementary drugs and other substances, containing information on new and investigational drugs and obsolescent drugs still of interest (3) Formulas of British proprietary medicines. Includes a directory of manufacturers. General index of 62,000 entries.   RS141.3.M4

The Merck index: an encyclopedia of chemicals, drugs, and biologicals / Susan Budavari, ed. 11th (centennial) ed. Rahway, N.J.: Merck, 1989. 1 v. (various pagings): ill. ISBN 0-911910-28-X.   **EK118**

For annotation, see *Supplement* ED18.   RS51.M4

●**The Merck index online** / comp. by Merck & Company [computer file]. Rahway, N.J.: Merck & Co.   **EK119**

For annotation, see *Supplement* ED19.

Ophthalmic drug facts: ODF / editorial panel: Jimmy D. Bartlett, N. Rex Ghormley, Siret D. Jaanus, J. James Rowsey, Thom J. Zimmerman. St. Louis: Facts and Comparisons Division, J.B. Lippincott, c1989. 226 p. ISBN 0-932686-66-4.   **EK120**

A comprehensive work that includes prescription and nonprescription products and intends "to provide reliable and objective ophthalmic drug information."—*Pref.* 12 chapters, organized according to therapeutic use, group comparable drugs to provide comparative information. Additional chapters treat dosage forms, routes of administration, systemic drugs, and investigational drugs. A cost index provides wholesale price ratios. Selected bibliographies; many cross-references. An index lists generic, brand, and group names, and many synonyms. Appendixes: "Excipient glossary"; "Manufacturer index."   RE994.O64

Dispensatories and pharmacopoeias

British pharmacopoeia 1988 / pub. on the recommendation of the Medicines Commission pursuant to the Medicines Act 1968. [14th ed.]. London: H.M.S.O., 1988. 2 v.: ill. ISBN 0-11-320837-5.   **EK121**

[13th ed.], 1980 (*Guide* EK274).

Vol. 1 of this edition contains 2,100 monographs for medicinal and auxiliary substances; v. 2 comprises the formulary (which has been substantially revised and is contained in a section entitled "Formulated preparations"), has sections on blood products, immunological products, radiopharmaceutical preparations, and surgical materials, and contains the index for both volumes.   RS141.3.B8

National drug code directory / prepared by Drug Listing Branch, Center for Drugs and Biologics. 1985 ed. [i.e., 8th ed.]. [Wash.]: U.S. Dept. of Health and Human Services, Public Health Service, Food and Drug Administration, 1985. v. 1. (In progress).   **EK122**
7th ed., 1982 (*Guide* EK275).
This edition includes the FDA approved new drug application numbers required since 1984 by the FDA's Drug Product Verification Compliance Program. Supplements list products which have been added, changed, or discontinued.   RS53.N35

World Health Organization. The international pharmacopoeia = Pharmacopoea internationalis. 3rd ed. Geneva: World Health Organization, 1986. v. 3. ISBN 92-4-154215-2. (In progress).   **EK123**
For v. 1–2 and annotation, see *Guide* EK283.
Contents: v. 3, Quality specifications.
Vol. 3 contains specifications for quality control of pharmaceutical preparations. To be complete in 5 v.

PUBLIC HEALTH

A dictionary of epidemiology / ed. for the International Epidemiological Association by John M. Last. 2nd ed. N. Y.: Oxford Univ. Pr., 1988. 141 p.: ill. ISBN 0-19-505480-6. ISBN 0-19-505481-4 (pbk.).   **EK124**
1st ed., 1983 (*Guide* EK288).
Many definitions are new or revised; includes a bibliography.   RA651.D53

National directory of drug abuse and alcoholism treatment and prevention programs. Rockville, Md.: National Institute on Alcohol Abuse and Alcoholism, [1989]. 370 p. (DHHS publication, no. [ADM] 89–1603).   **EK125**
For annotation, see *Supplement* CC76.   HV5825.N323

Rice, Mitchell F. Health of black Americans from post reconstruction to integration, 1871–1960: an annotated bibliography of contemporary sources / comp. by Mitchell F. Rice and Woodrow Jones, Jr. N.Y.: Greenwood, 1990. 206 p. (Bibliographies and indexes in Afro-American and African studies, no. 26). ISBN 0-313-26314-0.   **EK126**
For annotation, see *Supplement* CC202.   RA448.5.N4R52

TOXICOLOGY

Guides

Wexler, Philip. Information resources in toxicology. 2nd ed. N.Y.: Elsevier, c1988. 510 p. ISBN 0-444-01214-1.   **EK127**
1st ed., 1982 (*Guide* EK296)
An expanded and updated edition. Scope has been widened to reflect the growing interdisciplinary nature of the field, and to provide more international coverage, with a "finer subdivision of categories within toxicology."—*Pref.*
RA1193.4.W49

Bibliography

Toxic and hazardous materials : a sourcebook and guide to information sources / ed. by James K. Webster. N.Y.: Greenwood, 1987. 431 p. (Bibliographies and indexes in science and technology, no. 2). ISBN 0-313-24575-4.   **EK128**
"Interdisciplinary in scope and content. [12] chapters cover every aspect of the subject—from technical and engineering topics to legal matters to public policy concerns."—*Pref.* Chapter 1, "General sources of information," may be of special interest to librarians. Most material published 1980 onward. Index.   Z7914.S17T69

●**TOXLINE** [computer file]. Bethesda, Md.: U.S. National Library of Medicine, Toxicology Information Program, 1965– .   **EK129**
File size: 2.5 million records. Updated monthly. Available online (BRS, MEDLARS) and in CD-ROM (SilverPlatter) and as part of *Pollution/toxicology CD-ROM*.
Provides information on the adverse effects of drugs and other chemicals. Composed of a number of subfiles with varying dates of coverage, most of which are also available individually in printed or machine-readable form: *Environmental mutagen information center file*, *Environmental teratology information center file*, *Pesticides abstracts* (1968–8l; *Guide* EK297), *Toxicity bibliography*, etc. Almost all bibliographic records include abstracts, as well as CAS Registry Numbers.

Encyclopedias

Hodgson, Ernest. Dictionary of toxicology / Ernest Hodgson, Richard B. Mailman, Janice E. Chambers. N.Y.: Van Nostrand Reinhold, c1988. 395 p.: ill. ISBN 0-442-31842-1. $73.95.   **EK130**
Designed as an introduction to the field for students and for scientists in other disciplines. Most entries relate directly to toxicology, but others provide background information that might be needed by toxicologists. Bibliography.   RA1211.H69

Handbooks

Dreisbach, Robert Hastings. Handbook of poisoning: prevention, diagnosis & treatment / Robert H. Dreisbach, William O. Robertson. 12th ed. Norwalk, Conn.: Appleton & Lange, 1987. 589 p.: ill. ISBN 0-8385-3643-3.   **EK131**
11th ed., 1983 (*Guide* EK298).
This edition " . . . has been substantially revised and includes the following new features: Sections on diagnosis and treatment revised and updated to reflect the latest procedures in use in emergency rooms and poison centers; sections on water and electrolyte balance and acidosis simplified for easier use in emergencies; significant reorganization of the section on agricultural poisons, with the addition of many new compounds; addition of an index to tables following the table of contents; reference lists restricted to useful recent articles plus essential older ones."—*Pref.*   RA1211.D7

Index

§ This computer-prepared index lists authors (personal and corporate) in Roman typeface, titles in italic, and subjects in bold. Authors and titles cited in annotations or notes are indexed. Numerals file before the letter A. Titles beginning *U.S.* file at the beginning of the letter U with other U acronyms and abbreviations; author entries are spelled out ("United States") and so filed. Interfiled are "catalog" and "catalogue", "encyclopedia" and "encyclopaedia"; names beginning "Mc" and "Mac"; and "St." and "Saint."

10 percent sampling tabulation on 1982 population census of People's Republic of China, CG46
100 families of flowering plants, Hickey, Michael, EC33
12,000 words, AD32
1981–1985 supplement to Crime fiction, 1749–1980, Hubin, Allen J., BD105
1992, CK128
The 19th century postage stamps of the United States, Brookman, Lester G., BF51

20,000 years of fashion, Boucher, François, BF31
20th century Canadian arctic expeditions, Minion, Robin, DH3

3 decades of television, Library of Congress. Motion Picture, Broadcasting, and Recorded Sound Division, BG109

40 vjet Shqiperi socialiste = 40 years of socialist Albania, CG41

50 biografías de figuras dominicanas, Clase, Pablo, AJ46
550 books on Buddhism, BB122

6,000 words, AD32

9,000 words, AD32

An A to Z of the Middle East, Gresh, Alain, CJ199, DE20
The A to Z of women's health, Ammer, Christine, CC291, EK37
The A–Z guide to tracing ancestors in Britain, Markwell, F. C., AK33
A–Z of opera, Hamilton, Mary, BH94
The A–Z of women's sexuality, Kahn, Ada P., CC153
AAA guide, American Anthropological Association, CE17
AAAS science book list, 1978–1986, Wolff, Kathryn, EA15
ABEPI, AJ93
ABI/Inform, CH87
ABI/INFORM ondisc, CH87
Access (Organization : Washington, D.C.). *Search for security*, CA40
The ACCESS resource guide, CJ308
ACCIS guide to United Nations information sources on the environment, United Nations, EJ29
ACM guide to computing literature, EF6, EJ54

The ACS style guide, ED24
AGP, AG29
AGRIS, EH3, EH6
AGRIS serials list, EH6
AHA guide to the health care field, American Hospital Association, EK62
AIP 50th anniversary physics vade mecum, EG9
AIP Publication Board. *AIP style manual*, EG10
AIP style manual, American Institute of Physics, EG10
A.J. Lohwater's Russian-English dictionary of the mathematical sciences, Lohwater, A. J., EF13
AKL, BE74
ALA world encyclopedia of library and information services, AB11
ALA yearbook of library and information services, AB11
AMA stylebook, EK34
ARBA guide to education, CB1
ARBA guide to library science literature, 1970–1983, AB1
ASEAN, DE35, DE36
ASHRAE handbook, EJ74
ASM engineered materials reference book, EJ7
ASM Handbook Committee. *Metals handbook*, EJ86
ASM International. *Engineered materials handbook*, EJ12
—— *Handbook of corrosion data*, EJ85
—— *Metals handbook*, EJ86, EJ87
ASM review of metal literature, EJ14
Abad Nebot, Francisco. *Diccionario de lingüística de la escuela española*, BC11
Abate, Frank R. *Loanwords dictionary*, AD65
—— *Mottoes*, BD62
Abbott, David. *The biographical dictionary of scientists: astronomers*, EB14
Abbott, Maude E. *Classified and annotated bibliography of Sir William Osler's publications*, EK16
Abbreviations, AD9, EB8
Abbreviations, Wall, C. Edward, AD9
Abdalian, Hamo. *Historical atlas of Armenia = Hayastani patmakan atlas*, DC21
Abernethy, Peter L. *English novel explication. Supplement*, BD241
Abingdon Bible handbook, Blair, Edward Payson, BB47
Āboliņš, E. *Latvijas padomju enciklopēdija*, DC159
Abortion, CC267, EK19
Abrams, Irwin. *The Nobel Peace Prize and the laureates*, CJ315

Abrams, Leslie E. *The history and practice of Japanese printmaking*, BE154
Abrams, M. H. *A glossary of literary terms*, BD31
Abrams, William B. *The Merck manual of geriatrics*, EK72
Abreu, Alzira Alves de. *Dicionário histórico-biográfico brasileiro, 1930–1983*, DB115
Abreu, Maria Isabel. *Latin American writers*, BD334
Abse, Joan. *The art galleries of Britain and Ireland*, BE49
Abstract of British historical statistics, Mitchell, Brian, CG52, DC121
Abstracting and indexing, Rowley, Jennifer E., AB86
Abstracting services *see under topic*, subhead **Abstract journals; Indexes and abstracting services**
Abstracts in anthropology, CE8
Abstracts in social gerontology, CC49
Abu-Zayed, Ziad. *The West Bank handbook*, CJ188
Aby, Stephen H. *Sociology*, CC1
Abyssinia to Zimbabwe, Kirchherr, Eugene C., CL32
Academia Republicii Populare Romîne. *Dicționarul limbii române*, AD148
Academia Republicii Socialiste România. *Bibliografia românească modernă, 1831–1918*, AA177
—— *Dicționarul limbii române*, AD148
—— *Publicațiunile periodice românești (ziare, gazete, reviste)*, AE63
Academic American encyclopedia, AC3
Academic year abroad, CB80
Académie des sciences d'outre-mer. *Hommes et destins*, AJ54
Académie française. *Dictionnaire de l'Académie française*, AD90
Académie royale des sciences, des lettres et des beaux-arts de Belgique. *Biographie nationale*, AJ38
Academy of the Social Sciences in Australia. *The Southwest Pacific*, DG7
Acatos, Sylvio. *Ceramics and glass*, BF25
Accept me as I am, Friedberg, Joan Brest, CC103
Accessions list, Brazil and Uruguay, Library of Congress. Library of Congress Office, Rio de Janeiro, AA90, AA197
Accountant's desk handbook, Ameiss, Albert P., CH66
Accountants' handbook, CH65

Accounting
  bibliography, CH61
  dictionaries, CH62, CH63
  directories, CH64
  handbooks, CH65, CH66, CH67, CH68
Accounting desk book, Plank, Tom M., CH67
Accounting handbook, Siegel, Joel G., CH68
Accounting research directory, Brown,
  Lawrence D., CH61
Achtemeier, Paul J. *Harper's Bible dictionary*,
  BB51
Achtert, Walter S. *MLA handbook for writers of
  research papers*, AH1
——— *The MLA style manual*, AA53
Acid rain abstracts, EJ26
Acquired immunodeficiency syndrome *see* AIDS
  (Disease)
*Acquisitions management and collection
  development in libraries*, Magrill, Rose Mary,
  AB67
Acquisitions work in libraries, AB63, AB64,
  AB65, AB66, AB67, AB68, AB69
*Acronyms & abbreviations in astronomy, space
  sciences, & related fields*, Heck, André, EB8
Actors' television credits 1950–1972, Parish,
  James Robert, BG111
Adamczyk, Alice J. *Black dance*, BG45
Adams, Charles J. *The encyclopedia of religion*,
  BB25
Adams, Michael. *The Middle East*, DE21
Adato, Joseph. *The percussionist's dictionary*,
  BH151
Aday, Ron H. *Crime and the elderly*, CC34
*Addenda y corrigenda o volumen
  complementario del tomo primero del Manual
  del librero hispanoamericano de Antonio
  Palau y Dulcet*, Palau Claveras, Agustín,
  AA185
Adelman, George. *Encyclopedia of
  neuroscience*, EK40
Adey, David. *Companion to South African
  English literature*, BD286
Adkins, Cecil. *Doctoral dissertations in
  musicology. Second series*, BH28
Adkins, R. T. *Information sources in polymers
  and plastics*, EJ21
*Administration and development in the Arab
  world*, Jreisat, Jamil E., CJ217
*Administration parisienne à la veille de la
  Révolution*, Archives nationales (France),
  DC68
Administrators, CH147
*Administrator's desk reference on special
  education*, Weisenstein, Gregory R., CB138
Ado, Anatoliĭ Vasil'vich. *Novaia istoriia*, DA58
Adolescent pregnancy and parenthood, Zollar,
  Ann Creighton, CC135
Adomonis, Tadas. *Lithuania*, DC161
Adoption, CC131, CC138, CC139
Adoption, Melina, Lois Ruskai, CC131
The adoption directory, CC138
Adresar pisaca Jugoslavije, BD360
Adult education, CB124
  guides, CB40
  handbooks, CB125
Adult literacy, French, Joyce N., CB24
Advanced manufacturing technology, CH292
Advanced weapons systems, Champion, Brian,
  CJ267
Advertising and public relations
  bibliography, CH69
  biography, CH72
  databases, CH314
  dictionaries, CH70, CH316
  directories, CH72
  handbooks, CH73, CH74, CH75
Advertising media sourcebook, Barban, Arnold
  M., CH73
Advertising media sourcebook and workbook,
  CH73
An advocate's guide to surviving the SSI system,
  Lybarger, Barbara E., CH267
Aeppli, Felix. *Heart of stone*, BH140

Aeronautical and space engineering
  abbreviations, EB8
  databases, EJ15
  dictionaries, EJ16
  history
    bibliography, DA2
Aerospace database, EJ15
Affordable housing, Burns, Grant, CH342
Afghanistan
  bibliography, DE41, DE43
  foreign relations, DE42
Afghanistan, Witherell, Julian W., DE43
Africa
  bibliography, DD1
  bibliography of bibliography, AA71
  biography, AJ29
  dictionaries, DD5, DD6
  economic conditions, CH34
  foreign relations, DD19
  gazetteers, CL32
  guides, DD9
  handbooks, DD4, DD9
  history
    atlases, DD11
    general histories, DD10
    library resources, DD2, DD3, DD15, DG4
  politics and government, CJ149, CJ150, DD7
  statistics
    bibliography, CG40
    handbooks, CG39
Africa, DD4
——— Fenton, Thomas P., DD17
Africa, East
  guides to records, DD13
  history
    bibliography, DD12
Africa, Northern
  atlases, DE26
  history
    bibliography, DD14
    encyclopedias, DE19
Africa since 1914, DA55
Africa, South of the Sahara, DD17
  bibliography, DD16, DD18
  biography, AJ29
  filmography, BG55
  history
    bibliography, DD20
Africa, Southern
  history
    bibliography, DD21, DD22
  politics and government, CJ151
  statistics, CG38
Africa, West
  history
    bibliography, DD24
    manuscripts and archives, DD23
African-American art, BE20, BG2
African-American children, CC78
African-American literature, BD190, BD191
African American literature, BG40
African-American literature, CC203
  bibliography, BD185, BD186, BD188
  biography, BD187, BD188, BD189
African-American music, CC203
African-American religion, BB78, BB80
*African-American traditions in song, sermon,
  tale, and dance, 1600s–1920*, Southern,
  Eileen, CC203
African-American women, CC287, CC289,
  CC290
African Americans
  bibliography, CC38, CC73, CC79, CC123,
    CC124, CC189, CC193, CC194, CC195,
    CC196, CC197, CC198, CC199, CC201,
    CC203
  biography, AJ22, CC207
    indexes, AJ23
  by occupation or profession
    art, BE20, BG2, CC190
    authorship, BD185
    education, EK92
    law, CK81

  literature, BD181
  mass media, CH203
  medicine, CC208, EA80, EK77
  motion pictures, BG52, BG86
  music, BH79, BH87, BH89, BH93
  performing arts, CC190
  photographers, BF64
  politics and government, CJ61
  radio and television, BG103
  science and technology, CC208, EA80,
    EK77
  television, BG86
  theater, BG41, BG43
  directories, CC205, CC206
  education
    bibliography, CB34
    guides, CC192
    health care, CC202, EK126
    manuscripts and archives, CC191
    statistics, CC209, CC210, CC211
African dress, Eicher, Joanne Bubolz, BF29
African dress II, BF29
African economic handbook, Hodd, Michael,
  CH34
African historical dictionaries, DD5, DD6
*African language materials in the Boston
  University Libraries*, BC57
African languages, BC57, BC58
African literature
  bibliography, BD186, BD372, BD373,
    BD374
  encyclopedias, BD376
  indexes, BD375
  women authors, BD372
African literatures in the 20th century, BD376
*African nationalist leaders in Rhodesia who's
  who*, Cary, Robert, CJ208
——— Mitchell, Diana, CJ208
*African nationalist leaders in Zimbabwe who's
  who 1980*, Mitchell, Diana, CJ208
African political facts since 1945, Cook, Chris,
  CJ149
African states and rulers, Stewart, John, DD7
African studies, DD8
The African studies companion, Zell, Hans M.,
  DD9
*African women, a general bibliography,
  1976–1985*, Bullwinkle, Davis, CC274
African writers (French), BD302
Afrikaans language, AD68
Afro-American demography and urban issues,
  Obudho, Robert A., CC201
Afro-American nationalism, Herod, Agustina,
  CC196
Afro-American reference, Davis, Nathaniel,
  CC189
The Afro-American short story, Yancy, Preston
  M., BD191
Afro-American sources in Virginia, Plunkett,
  Michael, CC191
Afro-Americans *see* African Americans
AgeLine, CC50
Agency catalogue, AG39
Agent Orange and the Vietnam veteran, Harnly,
  Caroline D., DE104
Agent Orange and Vietnam, Harnly, Caroline
  D., DE104
Aging; *see also* Retirement homes
  bibliography, CC34, CC35, CC36, CC37,
    CC38, CC39, CC40, CC41, CC42, CC43,
    CC44, CC45, CC46, CC47, CC48, CC255,
    CC256
    current, CC49
  databases, CC50
  dictionaries, CC53, CC54
  directories, CC55, CC56, CC57, CC58,
    CC59, CC60, CC61, CE21, EK61
  encyclopedias, CC52, EK38
  guides, CC33, EK5
  handbooks, CC62, CC63, CC64, CC65,
    CC67, EK72
  periodicals, CC51
  statistics, CC66, CC68

Aging & cultural diversity, Strange, Heather, CC47
Aging with style and savvy, Donavin, Denise Perry, CC40
AGRICOLA, EH3, EH6, EH8, EH14, EH5
Agricultural and animal sciences journals and serials, Jensen, Richard D., EH4
Agricultural information resource centers, EH15
Agriculture
  databases, EC5, EH5, EH6, EH7, EH8
  dictionaries, EH10, EH12
    terminology, EH14
  directories, CJ68, EC20, EH15, EH17, EH18
  guides, EH1, EH2
  periodicals, EH3, EH4
Agrindex, EH6
Agroforestry abstracts, EH8
Aguayo Nayle, L. Rosa. *Archivo biográfico de España, Portugal e Iberoamérica*, AJ93
——— *Indice biográfico de España, Portugal e Iberoamérica = Indice biográfico de Espanha, Portugal e Ibero-América = Spanish, Portuguese and Latin American biographical index*, AJ94
Aguilar, Victoria. *Repertorio bibliográfico de las relaciones entre la península Ibérica y el Norte de África, siglos XV–XVI*, DD14
Aguilar Piñal, Francisco. *Bibliografía de autores españoles del siglo XVIII*, BD322
——— *Bibliografía de estudios sobre Carlos III y su época*, DC182
Ahmed, Fatima Shalaby Sid. *Southern Sudan*, DD57
AIDS, EK6
AIDS bibliography, EK29, EK28
AIDS (Disease), EK3, EK6, EK12, EK28, EK29, EK66
AIDS information resource directory, EK12
AIDS information sourcebook, EK66
AIDSLINE, EK28, EK29
Air and space history, DA2
Air forces, CJ254
Air pollution
  guides, EJ33
  handbooks, EJ32
Air pollution, EJ32
Airline safety, Miletich, John J., CH189
Aissing, Alena. *Russian dictionaries*, AD155
Akadémiai kislexikon, AC15
Akademie der Wissenschaften. *Deutsches Wörterbuch*, AD105
Akademie der Wissenschaften der DDR. *Etymologisches Wörterbuch des Deutschen*, AD111
——— *Goethe-Wörterbuch*, BD298
Akademie der Wissenschaften in Göttingen. *Goethe-Wörterbuch*, BD298
Akademiia nauk SSSR. *Svodnyĭ katalog knig na inostrannykh ĭazykakh, izdannykh v Rossii v XVIII veke, 1701–1800*, AA180
——— *Uralistiikan tutkimuksen bibliografia*, DC210
Akimova, E. A. *Istoriia dorevoliutsionnoĭ Rossii v dnevnikakh i vospominaniiakh*, DC196
Akiner, Shirin. *Islamic peoples of the Soviet Union*, CC180
Akkadisches Handwörterbuch, Soden, Wolfram von, AD73
Alain, Jean-Marc. *Thésaurus multilingue international en administration publique = Multilingual international thesaurus of public administration = Tesauro multilingue internacional de administración pública*, CJ224
Albania
  bibliography, AA85
  history
    bibliography, DC19, DC20
  statistics, CG41
Albania, Bland, William B., DC19
Albanian literature, BD351
Albanie, une bibliographie historique, Daniel, Odile, DC20

Albrecht, Günter. *Lexikon deutschsprachiger Schriftsteller*, BD293
Alcohol and the family, Barnes, Grace M., CC121
Alcohol use and alcoholism, Page, Penny Booth, CC72
The alcohol/drug abuse dictionary and encyclopedia, Fay, John, CC115
Alcoholism, CC70
  bibliography, CB22, CC69, CC71, CC72, CC73, CC113, CC121
  dictionaries, CC115
  directories, CC75, CC76, CC116, CC306, EK125
  encyclopedias, CC74
Aldcroft, Derek Howard. *Atlas of the world economy*, CH26
Alden, John Eliot. *European Americana*, AA78
Aleksakhina, I. V. *Russkie sovetskie pisateli—poèty*, BD355
Alekseev, M. N. *Anglo-russkiĭ geologicheskiĭ slovar'*, EE14
Alexander, Robert Jackson. *Biographical dictionary of Latin American and Caribbean political leaders*, AJ77, CJ193
Alexander Graham Bell Association for the Deaf. *Bibliography on deafness*, CC102
Algeria
  bibliography, DD25
  biography, AJ30
  history
    bibliography, DD26
Algerien-Bibliographie, Ruhe, Ernstpeter, DD26
Ali, Ahmed. *al-Qur'ān*, BB70
Ali, Sheikh Rustum. *The peace and nuclear war dictionary*, CJ303, CJ304
——— *The state and local government political dictionary*, CJ123
Alier Aixalà, Roger. *Diccionario de la zarzuela*, BH105
Alkaloids, ED31, EK108
Alkire, Leland G. *Periodical title abbreviations*, AE12
——— *The writer's advisor*, BD44
All about old buildings, BE129
Allaby, Ailsa. *The concise Oxford dictionary of earth sciences*, EE4
Allaby, Michael. *The concise Oxford dictionary of earth sciences*, EE4
——— *Dictionary of the environment*, EJ28
——— *The Oxford dictionary of natural history*, EC25
Allan, Barbara. *Medical information*, EK4
Allan, Elkan. *A guide to world cinema*, BG72
Allegri, Theodore H. *Handling and management of hazardous materials and wastes*, EJ30
Allen, Anne. *Search for security*, CA40
Allen, G. G. *Guide to the availability of theses II*, AB97
Allen, James Paul. *We the people*, CC188, DB79
Allen, Louis. *Political scandals and causes célèbres since 1945*, CJ37
Allen, Mark. *The essential Chaucer*, BD252
Allen, R. E. *The pocket Oxford dictionary of current English*, AD57
Allen, Rebecca. *Southwest Native American arts and material culture*, CC219
Allen, Richard F. *Teatro hispanoamericano*, BD337
Allen, Sallie T. *The directory of black nursing faculty*, EK92
Allen, Walter Recharde. *Black American families, 1965–1984*, CC123
Allen County Public Library. *Periodical source index*, AK10
Allenbach, J. *Biblia patristica*, BB101
Alley, Brian. *Biographical sources*, AJ2
Alley, Robert S. *TV genres*, BG104
Allgemeines Künstlerlexikon, BE74

Allin, Craig W. *International handbook of national parks and nature reserves*, BJ38
Allis, Jeanette B. *West Indian literature*, BD284
Allison, Antony Francis. *A catalogue of Catholic books in English printed abroad or secretly in England, 1558–1640*, BB115
——— *The contemporary printed literature of the English Counter-Reformation between 1558 and 1640*, BB115
Allison, Brent. *Guide to U.S. map resources*, CL44
Alloys, EJ88
Alloys index, EJ14
Allusions, AD22, BD32, BD35, BD38, BD46
  bibliography, BD2
Allusions—cultural, literary, biblical, and historical, AD22, BD32
Almanac of American women in the 20th century, Clark, Judith Freeman, CC312
The almanac of British politics, Waller, Robert, CJ178
Almanac of consumer markets, CH326
Almanac of the 50 states, CG36
Almanacs *see* **Fact books and compendiums**
Alphabet books as a key to language patterns, Roberts, Patricia, CB39
Alphabetischer Katalog 1501–1840, Bayerische Staatsbibliothek, AA26
Alpher, Joseph. *Encyclopedia of Jewish history*, BB138
Alston, R. C. *A bibliography of the English language from the invention of printing to the year 1800*, BC17
Alston, Sandra. *A bibliography of Canadiana*, DB83
Altbach, Philip G. *International higher education*, CB65
Alter, Robert. *The literary guide to the Bible*, BB56
Alternative lifestyles, Selth, Jefferson P., CC17
Alternative medicine, West, Ruth, EK18
Alternative publications, AA48
Alternatives in print, AA48
Altfranzösisches Wörterbuch, Tobler, Adolf, AD102
Althochdeutsches Wörterbuch, AD103
Altman, Edward I. *Handbook of financial markets and institutions*, CH255
Alvarez Noguera, José Rogelio. *Enciclopedia de México*, DB125
The Alyson almanac, CC155
Amacom. *The sales prospecting & territory planning directory*, CH322
Amar Kaur Jasbir Singh. *A guide to source materials in the India Office Library and Records for the history of Tibet, Sikkim and Bhutan 1765–1950*, DE29, DE4
Amazonas, Lee. *The film catalog*, BG77
Ambert, Alba N. *Bilingual education*, CB119, CB121
——— *Bilingual education and English as a second language*, CB121
Ambry, Margaret. *Almanac of consumer markets*, CH326
Ameiss, Albert P. *Accountant's desk handbook*, CH66
America and World War I, Woodward, David R., DA73
America at the polls 2, Scammon, Richard M., CJ114
America, history and life, CC237, CC283, CJ270, DA6, DA55, DB17
America on film and tape, DB2
America votes, CJ134
American advertising, Williams, Emelda L., CH69
American and British theatrical biography, Wearing, J. P., BG44
American and Canadian doctoral dissertations and master's theses on Africa, 1886–1974, Kagan, Alfred, DD1
——— Sims, Michael, DD1

American and Canadian doctoral dissertations and master's theses on Africa, 1974–1987, Lauer, Joseph J., DD1

American and Canadian doctoral dissertations on the Kingdom of Saudi Arabia, 1935–1987, DE89

American Anthropological Association. *AAA guide,* CE17

American architects, Krantz, Les, BE136

American art annual, BE93

American art auctions, 1785–1942, Lancour, Harold, BE67

American artists, Castagno, John, BE96, BE97

American artists' materials suppliers directory, Katlan, Alexander W., BE55

American Association for International Aging. *International directory of organizations in aging,* CC57

American Association for State and Local History. *Directory of historical organizations in the United States and Canada,* DB68

—— *National register of historic places, 1966–1988,* BE128

American Association for the Advancement of Science. *AAAS science book list, 1978–1986,* EA15

American Association of Homes for the Aging. *National continuing care directory,* CC58

American Association of Political Consultants. *Political resource directory,* CJ66

American Association of School Administrators. *Who's who in educational administration,* CB143

The American atlas, Shanks, Thomas G., CL21

American authors, 1600–1900, BD55

American Bar Association. *Guide to foreign law firms,* CK76

American battle monuments, BE164

American Battle Monuments Commission. *American battle monuments,* BE164

American Bibliographical Center. *America, history and life,* DB17

American bibliography, Evans, Charles, AA79, BE111, CL43

—— Shaw, Ralph R., AA81

—— Shaw, Ralph Robert, AA79, CL43

—— Shoemaker, Richard H., AA79, AA81, CL43

American bibliography, a preliminary checklist, 1801 to 1819, Newton, Frances P., AA81

American biographical archive, AJ20

American book trade directory, AB22

American ceramics before 1930, Weidner, Ruth Irwin, BF20

American Chemical Society. *The ACS style guide,* ED24

—— *CA search,* ED6

—— *The language of biotechnology,* EJ19

American Chemical Society. Chemical Abstracts Service. *Source index,* ED5

American chronicle, Gordon, Lois G., DB73

American collections of the British Library, DB16

The American college president, 1636–1989, Sontz, Ann H. L., CB11

American college regalia, Sparks, Linda, CB163

American communes, 1860–1960, Miller, Timothy, DB7

American communes to 1860, Dare, Philip N., DB6

American Council for the Arts. *Money for artists,* BE54

American Council of Learned Societies. *Dictionary of scientific biography,* EA76

—— *A guide to scholarly resources on the Russian Empire and the Soviet Union in the New York metropolitan area,* DC195

American Council on Education. *Fact book on higher education,* CB146

American Demographics, CH323

American Dental Association. *Basic dental reference works,* EK83

American diaries, Arksey, Laura, BD183, BD184, BD250

—— Pries, Nancy, BD184

—— Reed, Marcia, BD184

The American dictionary of campaigns and elections, Young, Michael L., CJ55, CJ57

American doctoral dissertations on the Arab world : supplement August 1981–December 1987, Selim, George Dimitri, DE18

American drama, BD172, BD230

American Educational Research Association. *Handbook of research on educational administration,* CB127

—— *Standards for educational and psychological testing,* CB120, CD38

American ethnic groups and the revival of cultural pluralism, Kinton, Jack F., CC161

American ethnic press, AE27

American ethnic revival, CC161

American fiction
 awards, BD177
 bibliography, BD175
  historical, BD173
 bibliography of bibliography, BD176
 handbooks, BD174
 indexes, BD177

The American film industry, Slide, Anthony, BG94

American Film Institute. *Catalog of motion pictures produced in the United States,* BG66

American Fisheries Society. *The directory of North American fisheries and aquatic scientists,* EC19

American Folklife Center. *Folklife sourcebook,* CF32

American Foundation for AIDS Research. *Learning AIDS,* EK12

American Geographical Society of New York. *Index to maps in books and periodicals,* CL39

American Geological Institute. *Union list of geologic field trip guidebooks of North America,* EE21

American glass, McKearin, George S., BF28

American governors and gubernatorial elections, 1775–1978, Glashan, Roy R., CJ133

American governors and gubernatorial elections, 1979–1987, Mullaney, Marie Marmo, CJ133

American heritage dictionary, AD164

The American heritage dictionary of Indo-European roots, AD10

The American Heritage dictionary of science, Barnhart, Robert K., EA40

The American heritage illustrated encyclopedic dictionary, AD4

The American Heritage Larousse Spanish dictionary, AD164

American historians, 1866–1912, DB75

American Historical Association. *Grants, fellowships & prizes of interest to historians,* DA18

—— *Guide to the study of United States history outside the U.S., 1945–1980,* DB11

The American history sourcebook, DB69

American homelessness, Hombs, Mary Ellen, CC118

The American Horticultural Society encyclopedia of garden plants, EC28

American Hospital Association. *AHA guide to the health care field,* EK62

—— *Directory of health care professionals,* EK62

American humor magazines and comic periodicals, AE14

American imprints on art through 1865, Schimmelman, Janice Gayle, BE13

American Indian and Alaska native newspapers and periodicals, Littlefield, Daniel F., CC223

The American Indian index, Frazier, Gregory W., CC228

American Indian resource materials in the Western History Collections, University of Oklahoma, CC224

American Indians, DB24

American Institute of Parliamentarians. *Standard code of parliamentary procedure,* CJ228

American Institute of Physics. *AIP style manual,* EG10

—— *A physicist's desk reference,* EG9

—— *Physics briefs,* EB3, EG3

American Journalism Historians Association. *Guide to sources in American journalism history,* AF19

American journalism history, Sloan, W. David, AF20

American landscape architecture, BE145

American leaders, 1789–1987, CJ118

American legislative leaders, 1850–1910, Ritter, Charles F., CJ132

American library and book trade annual, AB43

American library annual, AB43

American Library Association. *ALA world encyclopedia of library and information services,* AB11

—— *Alternative publications,* AA48

—— *Anglo-American cataloguing rules,* AB79

—— *Business serials of the U.S. government,* CH91

—— *Directory of government document collections & librarians,* AG2

—— *Directory of library & information professionals,* AB39, AB40

—— *A directory of oral history tapes of librarians in the United States and Canada,* AB37

—— *Find the law in the library,* CK4

—— *Guide to official publications of foreign countries,* AG1

—— *Guide to the publications of interstate agencies and authorities,* AG26

—— *The library trustee,* AB71

—— *The Museum of Science and Industry basic list of children's science books,* EA14

American Library Association. Collection Management and Development Committee. *Guidelines for collection development,* AB63

American Library Association. Subcommittee on Guidelines for Collection Development. *Guide for written collection policy statements,* AB63

American library directory, AB22, AB21

American library history, Davis, Donald G., AB2

—— Harris, Michael H., AB2

American literary magazines, BD159

American literary publishing houses, 1900–1980. Trade and paperback, AA50

American literature; *see also* **African-American literature**
 Asian-American writers, BD192
 bibliography, BD151, BD152, BD156, BD157, BD158
 biography, BD150, BD153, BD169, BD171
 criticism, BD161
 guides, BD149, BD200, BD201
 handbooks, BD162, BD163
 history, BD167
 outlines, BD165, BD166
 periodicals, BD159
 regional literature
  South, BD154, BD155
 Spanish-American writers, BD193
 women authors, BD168, BD199

American lobbyists directory, CJ60, CJ59

American magazine journalists, 1741–1850, AF21

American magazine journalists, 1850–1900, AF22

American magazine journalists, 1900–1960, AF23

American maritime history, DA55

American mass-market magazines, AE15

American Mathematical Society. *Current mathematical publications,* EF4

—— *Selected tables in mathematical statistics,* EF17

American Medical Association. *American Medical Association manual of style*, EK34
—— *Drug evaluations*, EK114
The American Medical Association encyclopedia of medicine, EK36
The American Medical Association family medical guide, EK67
American Medical Association manual of style, EK34
American medical imprints, 1820–1910, Cordasco, Francesco, EK8
American men & women of science, EA10, EA75
American Meteorological Society. *Curricula in the atmospheric, oceanic and related sciences*, EE27
American music studies, Heintze, James R., BH2
American musical theatre, Hummel, David, BH104
American Musicological Society. *American Musicological Society*, BH42
American Musicological Society, Hassen, Marjorie, BH42
American national election studies data sourcebook, 1952–1986, Miller, Warren E., CJ111
American nursing, EK94
American orators before 1900, BD148
American Ornithologists' Union. *Check-list of North American birds*, EC46
American peace directory, CJ312
American periodicals 1741–1900, Heath, Trudy, AE77, AE78
—— Hoornstra, Jean, AE77, AE78
American periodicals : series I, 1741–1800, AE78
American periodicals: series I, 1741–1900, AE77
American periodicals : series II, 1800–1850, AE78
American photographers, BF64
American Phytopathological Society. *A literature guide for the identification of plant pathogenic fungi*, EC35
American playwrights since 1945, BD172
American poetry, BH110
  bibliography, BD178, BD179
  biography, BD171
  criticism, BD182
  indexes, BD180, BD181
The American political dictionary, Plano, Jack C., CJ54
American Political Science Association. *A guide to graduate study in political science*, CB99, CJ31
American popular culture, BD163
The American presidency, DA55
—— Goehlert, Robert, CJ76
—— Martin, Fenton S., CJ76, CJ77
The American presidents, Cohen, Norman S., CJ74
American presidents, Goehlert, Robert, CJ74
—— Martin, Fenton S., CJ74, CJ78
An American profile, Wood, Floris W., CJ237
American Psychiatric Association. *Biographical directory*, CD34
—— *Diagnostic and statistical manual of mental disorders*, CD18, CD21, CD29
—— *Treatments of psychiatric disorders*, CD17
American psychiatric glossary, Stone, Evelyn M., CD21
American Psychological Association. *Standards for educational and psychological testing*, CB120, CB120, CD38
American public administration, CJ209
American Public Health Association. *Standard methods for the examination of water and wastewater*, ED23
American public opinion data, CJ134, CJ230, CJ229
American public opinion index, CJ229, CJ230

American reference books annual, AB1, AB44, CB1, EA8
American reformers, AJ21, CC24
American salaries and wages survey, CH334
American social change, CA14
American Society for Clinical Pharmacology and Therapeutics. *Drug evaluations*, EK114
American Society for Horticultural Science. *Glossary for horticultural crops*, EH12
American Society for Information Science. *Directory of library & information professionals*, AB39
American Society for Metals. *ASM engineered materials reference book*, EJ7
American Society for Testing and Materials. *Directory of testing laboratories, commercial-institutional*, EA64
American Society for Theatre Research. *International bibliography of theatre*, BG12
American Society for Training and Development. *Educational media and technology yearbook*, CB141
American Society of Heating, Refrigerating and Air-Conditioning Engineers. *ASHRAE handbook*, EJ74
American Society of Mammalogists. *Orders and families of recent mammals of the world*, EC60
American Sociological Association. *Cumulative index of sociology journals, 1971–1985*, CC13
American song, Bloom, Ken, BH104
American songwriters, Ewen, David, BH109
The American South, DA55
American statistics index, CG29
American studies, AB28, DB3
American studies, DB3
American Studies Association. *American studies*, DB3
American theatre companies, BG29
American Theatre Wing. *The Tony Award*, BG27
American Theological Library Association. *Index to book reviews in religion*, BB20, BB21
—— *Politics and religion*, BB15, CJ13
American Trucking Associations. *Trucksource*, CH186
American warplanes 1908–1988, Smith, Myron J., DB15
American Water Works Association. *Standard methods for the examination of water and wastewater*, ED23
American Welding Society. *Welding handbook*, EJ84
American wit and humor, AE14
American women artists, past and present, Tufts, Eleanor, BE95
American women in sport, 1887–1987, BJ15
American women managers and administrators, Leavitt, Judith A., CH147
American women writers on Vietnam, Butler, Deborah A., BD198, DE103
American women's magazines, Humphreys, Nancy K., CC272
American writers since 1900, Vinson, James, BD169
American writers to 1900, Vinson, James, BD169
Americas
  atlases, CL62
  directories, CE20
  history
    bibliography, AA78
America's elderly, CC62
America's homeless, Burt, Martha R., CC117
America's new foundations, CA30
America's science museums, Danilov, Victor J., EA65
Amerika-Gedenkbibliothek/Berliner Zentralbibliothek. *Künstler der jungen Generation*, BE80
Ames, Kenneth L. *Decorative arts and household furnishings in America, 1650–1920*, BF34

Amino acids and peptides, ED35
Ammer, Christine. *The A to Z of women's health*, CC291, EK37
—— *The Harper dictionary of music*, BH47
—— *The new A to Z of women's health*, CC291, EK37
Amos, Ashley Crandell. *Old English word studies*, BC18
Amos, Linda K. *Guide to programs in nursing in four-year colleges and universities*, EK93
Amos, William. *The originals*, BD95
Amphibians and reptiles, EC45
Amune, Stephen A. *Retrospective index to Nigerian doctoral dissertations and masters theses, 1895–1980*, AH16
Anatomy of wonder, BD109
Ancestry's red book, AK4
Ancient history *see* **Archaeology and ancient history**
And so to bed, Havlice, Patricia Pate, BD250
Anderson, Bernhard W. *The books of the Bible*, BB63
Anderson, Charles J. *Fact book on higher education*, CB146
Anderson, Herbert Lawrence. *A physicist's desk reference*, EG9
Anderson, James. *The Harper dictionary of opera and operetta*, BH94
Anderson, Kenneth. *Mosby's medical, nursing, and allied health dictionary*, EK91
Anderson, Lois E. *Mosby's medical, nursing, and allied health dictionary*, EK91
Anderson, Nancy D. *French mathematical seminars*, EF1
Anderson, Paul F. *Dictionary of marketing terms*, CH317
Anderson, Peter J. *Research guide for undergraduates in political science*, CJ2
Anderson, Peter M. *A structural atlas of the English dialects*, BC30
Anderson, Robert Ralph. *Frühneuhochdeutsches Wörterbuch*, AD104
Anderson, Sydney. *Orders and families of recent mammals of the world*, EC60
Anderson, William L. *A guide to Cherokee documents in foreign archives*, CC218
Andreeva, N. M. *Gosudarstvennye arkhivy SSSR*, AB36, DC199
Andrew, Geoff. *The film handbook*, BG101
Andrews, B. G. *The Oxford companion to Australian literature*, BD276
—— *The Oxford literary guide to Australia*, BD274
Andrews, John. *William Shakespeare*, BD269
Andrews, Robert. *The concise Columbia dictionary of quotations*, BD57
Andrews, Theodora. *Guide to the literature of pharmacy and the pharmaceutical sciences*, EK103
Andriot, Donna. *Place guide*, CL35
Andriot, John L. *Guide to U.S. government statistics*, CG28
—— *Township atlas of the United States*, CL58
Andris-Michalaros, Aliki. *The Metropolitan Opera encyclopedia*, BH100
Anglicko-český technický slovník, EA46
Angliĭsko-bŭlgarski rechnik, Rankova, Mariía, AD79
Anglo-American cataloguing rules, AB79
The Anglo-American relationship, Lincove, David A., DB14
Anglo-Irish literature, BD270
Anglo-Norman dictionary, AD62
Anglo-Norman Text Society. *Anglo-Norman dictionary*, AD62
Anglo-russkiĭ geologicheskiĭ slovar', Timofeev, Petr Petrovich, EE14
Animal behavior abstracts, EC7
Animal magnetism, early hypnotism, and psychical research, 1766–1925, Crabtree, Adam, CD50

Animal rights, Keyguide to information sources in, EC2

Animal science
dictionaries, EH27
directories, EC20
guides, EH26
handbooks, EH28
periodicals, EH4

Animated TV specials, Woolery, George W., BG114

Annals of American literature, 1602–1983, Ludwig, Richard M., BD165

Annals of English drama, 975–1700, Harbage, Alfred, BD232

Annals of English literature, BD165

Annals of English verse, 1770–1835, Jackson, J. R. de J., BD243

Annals of the Metropolitan Opera Guild, BH95

Annenberg School of Communications (University of Pennsylvania). Television Script Archive. Index to the Annenberg Television Script Archive, BG106

An annotated bibliography and index covering CPL bibliographies 1–253, January 1979–December 1989, Coatsworth, Patricia A., CC159

The annotated bibliography of Canada's major authors, BD277

Annotated bibliography of new Indonesian literature on the history of Indonesia, Dengel, Holk H., DE66

An annotated bibliography of North American doctoral dissertations on Old English language and literature, Pulsiano, Phillip, BC24, BD207

An annotated bibliography of Northern Plains ethnohistory, Weist, Katherine M., CC220

Annotated bibliography of Puerto Rican bibliographies, Fowlie-Flores, Fay, DB153

Annotated bibliography of social research in Pakistan, Bhatty, K. M., DE87

Annotated bibliography of Southern American English, McMillan, James B., BC23

An annotated bibliography of the Holy Roman Empire, Zophy, Jonathan W., DC8

An annotated bibliography of the Napoleonic era, Meyer, Jack Allen, DC63

Annotated bibliography of theses and dissertations . . . May 1973 to April 1983, AH17

An annotated bibliography of U.S. scholarship on the history of the family, Benson-von der Ohe, Elizabeth, CC122

An annotated bibliography of works on daily newspapers in Canada, 1914–1983 = Une bibliographie annotée des ouvrages portant sur les quotidiens canadiens, 1914–1983; Gordon Rabchuk, indexation, Sotiron, Minko, AF4

Annotated bibliography on clandestine employment, CH268

Annotated bibliography on the history of data processing, Cortada, James W., EJ53

An annotated critical bibliography of feminist criticism, Humm, Maggie, BD20

An annotated critical bibliography of Jacobean and Caroline comedy, Corbin, Peter, BD233
—— Sedge, Douglas, BD233

An annotated critical bibliography of John Milton, Patrides, C. A., BD259

An annotated guide to current national bibliographies, Bell, Barbara L., AA70

Annotated statistical bibliography, CG72

Annuaire des cotes international, BE64, BE65

Annuaire des cotes international = International art price annual, BE58

Annual bibliography of Victorian studies, BD212

Annual catalogue of Australian publications, AA87

Annual Egyptological bibliography. Late reviews AEB 1947–1984, DD30

The annual exhibition record of the Pennsylvania Academy of the Fine Arts, BE66

Annual statement studies, CH129

Annuals and surveys appearing in legal periodicals, DeLashmitt, Eleanor, CK26

Die anonym erschienenen autobiographischen Schriften des neunzehnten Jahrhunderts, Hänsel, Markus, AJ57

Anonymes 1501–1800, Bibliothèque Nationale (France), AA14

Anonyms and pseudonyms
Bulgaria, AA34
international, AA31, AA32
Mexico, AA35
United States and Gt. Brit., AA33

Antanavičius, J. Tarybú Lietuvos enciklopedija, DC163

Antarctic see **Arctic and Antarctic**

Antarctic bibliography, DH2

Antarctica, Stewart, John, DH5

Anthologies of music, Murray, Sterling E., BH37

Anthony, John W. Handbook of mineralogy, EE35

Anthony, L. J. Information sources in energy technology, EJ71
—— Information sources in engineering, EJ1

Anthropological fieldwork, Gravel, Pierre Bettez, CE3

Anthropological glossary, Pearson, Roger, CE15

Anthropological literature, CE7, CE9

Anthropological Survey of India. Directory of scientific personnel of the Anthropological Survey of India, CE22

Anthropology and ethnology
abstract journals, CE8
atlases, CE24
bibliography, CC5, CE3, CE4
Americas, CE25
current, CE8, CE9
biography, CE19, CE20, CE21, CE22, CE23
directories, CE17
Americas, CE20
dissertations, CE10
encyclopedias, CE12, CE14
guides, CE1
handbooks, CE25
library catalogs, CE2, CE7
periodicals, CE11
terminology, CE16

Anthropology journals and serials, Williams, John T., CE11

The anthropology of war, Ferguson, R. Brian, CE5

Anti-evolution, McIver, Tom, BB6

Anti-intervention, Doenecke, Justus D., CJ292

Anti-Semitism, BB128, CC195

Antibiotics, ED32, EK109

Antiquarian catalogues of musical interest, Coover, James, BH8

Antisemitism, BB128

Antonini, R. Bibliografia dell'Italia antica, DC154

Antônio, Irati. Bibliografia da música brasileira, BH5

Anuario bibliográfico, AA159

Anuario bibliográfico de historia del pensamiento ibero e iberoamericano, BA8

Anuario bibliográfico dominicano, AA103

Anuario bibliográfico ecuatoriano, AA104

Anuario bibliográfico hondureño, AA137

Anuario estadístico de América Latina y el Caribe = Statistical yearbook for Latin America and the Caribbean, CG59

Anzovin, Steven. Facts about the states, CJ125
—— Speeches of the American presidents, CJ89

Apartheid, CC186, CJ202, DD53

Apartheid, Pyatt, Sherman A., DD53

The apartheid handbook, Omond, Roger,, CC186

Apel, Willi. Harvard dictionary of music, BH56

Apéndice a la Bibliografía guatemalteca, Figueroa Marroquín, Horacio, AA136

Apocrypha and pseudepigrapha of the Old Testament in English, BB40

Appel, Marsha C. Illustration index VI, 1982–1986, BE31

Apperley, Richard. A pictorial guide to identifying Australian architecture, BE130

Appleton, George. The Oxford book of prayer, BB72

Appleton, Richard. Collins milestones in Australian history, DF4

Applied arts
bibliography, BF6
by country or region
Oceania, BF6

Applied science & technology index, EA23

Applied social sciences index & abstracts, CA8

Arab American almanac, CC181

Arab Americans, CC181

The Arab bibliography of Libya, AA155

Arab countries; see also names of individual countries
bibliography, CJ217, DE17
biography
bibliography, AJ31
dissertations, DE18
encyclopedias, CJ152

Arab Gulf states, Saliba, M., DE17

Arab-Israeli conflict, CJ188

Arabic biographical dictionaries, Auchterlonie, Paul, AJ31

Arabic language, AD69, AD70, AD71

Arabische Musik in europäischen Sprachen, Krüger-Wust, Wilhelm J., BH17

Araji, Sharon. A sourcebook on child sexual abuse, CC92

Arãjs, E. Latviešu periodika, AE57

Arbeitsgemeinschaft Schweizer Familiennamen. Familiennamenbuch der Schweiz = Répertoire des noms de famille suisses = Register of Swiss surnames, AK45

ARCH, BE114

Archaeological bibliography for Great Britain and Ireland, DA32

Archaeological site index to radiocarbon dates for Great Britain and Ireland, DA32

Archaeology and ancient history
atlases, DA37, DA38, DA39
bibliography
current, DA34
by country or region
classical, DA42
North America, DB66
U.S.S.R., DA33
encyclopedias, DA35, DA36
general histories, DA40
guides, DA31

Architectural index, BE115

Architectural periodicals index, BE113, BE117

Architectural treatises and building handbooks available in American libraries and bookstores through 1800, Schimmelman, Janice Gayle, BE111

Architecture
bibliography, BE110, BF7
biography, BE122, BE132, BE134, BE135, BE136
by country or region
Australia, BE130
Gt. Brit., BE120, BE134, BE135
Ireland, BE120
Middle East, BE123
United States, BE125, BF7
bibliography, BE111
by period
ancient, BE123
databases, BE113
encyclopedias, BE122
history, BE130, BE131
indexes, BE114, BE115, BE118, BE119, BE120
Canada, BE117

library resources, BE51
preservation, BE121, BE129
Architecture and the decorative arts, Stiverson, Cynthia Zignego, BF7
Architecture and women, Doumato, Lamia, BE133
Architecture database, BE113
Archives; *see also* under names of individual countries and topics, subhead **Manuscripts and archives**
  bibliography, DB24
  dictionaries, AB73
  directories, AB46
  handbooks, AB74
  United States, DB20
The archives, Szucs, Loretto Dennis, AB49, DB22
Archives and manuscript repositories in the USSR, Grimsted, Patricia Kennedy, AB36, DC199
Archives and manuscript repositories in the USSR. Ukraine and Moldavia, Grimsted, Patricia Kennedy, AB52, DC200
Archives biographiques françaises, AJ50
Les archives du Ministère des relations extérieures depuis les origines, France. Ministère des relations extérieures. Archives et documentation, DC72
Archives du Sénégal. *Bulletin bibliographique des Archives du Sénégal*, AA182
—— *Guide des archives de l'Afrique occidentale française*, DD23
Archives nationales du Sénégal. *Bibliographie du Sénégal*, AA182
Archives nationales (France). *Administration parisienne à la veille de la Révolution*, DC68
—— *État des inventaires*, DC67
—— *État des inventaires des archives départementales, communales et hospitalières au 1er janvier 1983*, DC70
—— *État général des fonds*, DC68
—— *Guide des papiers des ministres et secrétaires d'État de 1871 à 1974*, DC69
—— *Guide des recherches sur l'histoire des familles*, AK23
—— *Guide des sources de l'histoire de l'Amérique latine et des Antilles dans les archives françaises*, DB98
Archives of American Art. *The card catalog of the manuscript collections of the Archives of American Art. Supplement 1981–1984*, BE32
Archivio biografico italiano, AJ74
Archivio centrale dello Stato (Italy). *Bibliografia dell'Archivio centrale dello Stato, 1953–1978*, DC156
Archivo biográfico de España, Portugal e Iberoamérica, AJ93
The Arctic, King, H. G. R., DH1
Arctic and Antarctic
  bibliography, DH1, DH2, DH3
  chronologies, DH4
  encyclopedias, DH5
Ardis, Susan. *A guide to the literature of electrical and electronics engineering*, EJ43
Argentina
  bibliography, AA86
  biography, AJ32
  history
    library resources, DB109
Argueta, Mario. *Diccionario de escritores hondureños*, BD342
Argyle, Christopher. *Chronicle of the First World War*, DA77
Arief, Melanie S. *The Indonesian economy and politics, 1963–1986*, DE66
Arkib Negara Malaysia. *Panduan rekod-rekod kerajaan persekutuan di Arkib Negara Malaysia*, AG45
Arksey, Laura. *American diaries*, BD183, BD184, BD250
ARLIS M/O/Q, BE51

Armed forces; *see also* Military history; Naval warfare; and under names of countries
  acronyms, CJ258
  bibliography
    current, CJ250, CJ251
    dictionaries, CJ260, CJ261
    handbooks, CJ264, CJ266
    periodicals, CJ252
    quotations, CJ263
Armen, Garbis. *Historical atlas of Armenia = Hayastani patmakan atlas*, DC21
Armenia, DC21, DC22
Armenia and the Armenians in academic dissertations, Avakian, Anne M., DC22
Armenian American almanac, CC182
Armenian Americans, CC182
Armentier, Louis. *Dictionnaire de la théorie et de l'histoire littéraires du XIXe siècle à nos jours*, BD33
Arms control and disarmament, defense and military, international security, and peace, Atkins, Stephen E., CJ290
Arms control and peace research
  abstracts, CJ302
  archives, CJ295
  bibliography, BB117, CJ289, CJ290, CJ291, CJ292, CJ293, CJ294, CJ296, CJ297, CJ298, CJ300, CJ301
  biography, CJ315, CJ316
  compendiums, CJ314
  directories, CA40, CJ301, CJ308, CJ309, CJ310, CJ311, CJ312
  encyclopedias, CJ303, CJ304, CJ305, CJ306
  quotations, CJ307
Arms Control Association (Washington, D.C.). *Arms control, disarmament and international security*, CJ289
Arms control, disarmament and international security, CJ289
The arms control, disarmament and military security dictionary, Elliot, Jeffrey M., CJ303, CJ304
—— Reginald, Robert, CJ303
Arms control fact book, Menos, Dennis, CJ314
Armstrong, John. *Business documents*, CH135
Armstrong, Julia I. *The index of paintings sold in the British Isles during the nineteenth century*, BE61
Arnaldi, Francesco. *Latinitatis Italicae Medii Aevi inde ab a. CDLXXVI usque ad a. MXXII Lexicon imperfectum cura et studio... Addenda, fasc. 6 (In Bulletin Du Cange, v. 44/45; 1985)*, AD138
—— *Novum glossarium mediae latinitatis*, AD141
Arnim, Max. *Internationale Personalbibliographie, 1944–1975*, AA4
Arnold, Corliss Richard. *Organ literature*, BH152
Arnold, Frank. *Cinegraph*, BG87
Arnold, Peter. *The Olympic games*, BJ32
Arnott, J. F. *English theatrical literature, 1599–1900*, BG9
Arny, Rose. *Forthcoming books*, AA83
Aronson, Eleanor J. *Report series codes dictionary*, EA22
Arpan, Jeffrey S. *Directory of foreign manufacturers in the United States*, CH293
Årsbibliografi över Sveriges offentliga publikationer, AG47
Arshem, James A. *Directory of patent depository libraries*, EA86
Art : a history of painting, sculpture, architecture, Hartt, Frederick, BE72
Art and archaeology technical abstracts, BE16
Art and architecture in Central Europe, 1550–1620, Kaufmann, Thomas DaCosta, BE8
The art and architecture of Islam: 650–1250, Ettinghausen, Richard, BE73
—— Grabar, Oleg, BE73
The art and architecture of the Indian subcontinent, Harle, J. C., BE73

Art and architecture thesaurus, BE45
Art & architecture thesaurus, BE44
Art & artists of South Africa, Esmé Berman, BE85
The art galleries of Britain and Ireland, Abse, Joan, BE49
Art index, BE17
Art information, Jones, Lois Swan, BE2
Art Institute of Chicago. *The Burnham index to architectural literature*, BE118
—— *Index of art sales catalogs, 1981–1985*, BE60
Art law, Feldman, Franklin, BE108, CK86
—— Lerner, Ralph E., BE108, BE109, CK86, CK88
Art literature international, BE23
Art literature international (RILA), BE22
Art museums, BE30
Art museums of the world, BE47
The art of Oceania, Hanson, Louise, BF6
Art research methods and resources, Jones, Lois Swan, BE2
Art sales from early in the eighteenth century to early in the twentieth century, Graves, Algernon, BE61
The art song, Seaton, Douglass, BH111
Artbibliographies modern, BE18
Arte Chicano, Goldman, Shifra M., BE5
The Arthur Andersen European community sourcebook, CK125
The Arthurian encyclopedia, BD138
The Arthurian handbook, Lacy, Norris J., BD139
Arthurian romances, BD204
Articles on women writers, Schwartz, Narda Lacey, BD199
Artificial intelligence, EJ51, EJ52, EJ58, EJ64, EJ67
Artificial intelligence, EJ51
The artificial intelligence compendium, EJ52
Artikler i bøger, AA102
Artinian, Vrej-Armen. *Historical atlas of Armenia = Hayastani patmakan atlas*, DC21
Artist biographies master index, BE80, BE88, BF15, BE75
Artists, BE74, BE75, BE78, BE80, BE81, BE84, BE86, BE90, BE92, BE93, BE94
  filmography, BE76
  legal status, laws, etc., BE107, BE108, BE109, CK85, CK86, CK88
  recordings, BE76
Artists and galleries of Australia, Germaine, Max, BE82
Artists as illustrators, Castagno, John, BE97
The artists file, New York Public Library, BE84
The artist's handbook of materials and techniques, Mayer, Ralph, BE69
Artists in quotation, La Cour, Donna Ward, BE46
Artists' marks, BE100
Artists' signatures, BE96, BE98, BE99
ARTnews international directory of corporate art collections, BE52
The Artronix index, BF59
The arts of Africa, BF2
The arts of Central Africa, Biebuyck, Daniel P., BF3, BF6
Artspeak, Atkins, Robert, BE43
Aryan, K. C. *Encyclopedia of Indian art, references, symbols, evolution of Devanagari script = Rekhā*, BE103
Aryan language, AD72
Aryanpur, Manoochehr. *Farhang-i nuvīn-i payvastah-i Fārsī–Ingilīsī va Ingilīsī–Fārsī*, AD144
Āryānpūr Kāshānī, 'Abbās. *Farhang-i nuvīn-i payvastah-i Fārsī–Ingilīsī va Ingilīsī–Fārsī*, AD144
ASA news, DD1
Asada, Sadao. *International studies in Japan*, DE75
—— *Japan and the world, 1853–1952*, DE75, DE76

Ashe, Geoffrey. *The Arthurian encyclopedia*, BD138
—— *The Arthurian handbook*, BD139
Ashley, Michael. *Science fiction, fantasy, and weird fiction magazines*, BD122
Ashliman, D. L. *A guide to folktales in the English language*, CF18
Asia
  directories, DE7
  economic conditions, CH36
  encyclopedias, DE5
  foreign relations, DE3
  handbooks, DE5
  history
    bibliography, DE1
    encyclopedias, DE6
    library resources, DD2, DD15, DG4
  politics and government, CJ154
  statistics
    handbooks, CG39
Asia and Pacific, Fenton, Thomas P., DE7
Asia, East
  history
    bibliography
      library catalogs, DE40
  material culture, CC213
Asia Pacific, CH35
Asia Society, DE6
—— *Encyclopedia of Asian history*, DE6
Asia, South
  bibliography, DE28, DE32
  history
    atlases, DE34
    encyclopedias, DE33
  library resources, DE30
  manuscripts and archives, DE4
Asia, Southeast
  bibliography, DE65
    dissertations, DE38
  history
    bibliography, DE35, DE36, DE37
    library resources, DE39
  languages, BC59, BC60, BD382
  manuscripts and archives, DE4
  material culture, CC213
Asian American literature, Cheung, King-Kok, BD192
Asian American studies, Kim, Hyung-chan, CC214
Asian Americans
  bibliography, CC214
  encyclopedias, CC212
  material culture, CC213
Asian economic handbook, CH36
Asian finance directory, CH240
Asian historical dictionaries, DE5
The Asian political dictionary, Ziring, Lawrence, CJ154
Asimov, Isaac. *Asimov's chronology of science and discovery*, EA71, EA74
Asimov's chronology of science and discovery, Asimov, Isaac, EA71, EA74
Aslib. *Aslib directory of information sources in the United Kingdom*, AB26
—— *Index to theses with abstracts accepted for higher degrees by the universities of Great Britain and Ireland and the Council for National Academic Awards*, AH11
—— *Online bibliographic databases*, AB95
Aslib directory of information sources in the United Kingdom, AB26
Association for Anthropology and Gerontology. *Directory of anthropologists and anthropological research in aging*, CE21
Association for Documentary Editing. *Editing documents and texts*, AA59
—— *A guide to documentary editing*, AA54, BD13
Association for Educational and Training Technology. *International yearbook of educational and training technology*, CB84

Association for Educational Communications and Technology. *Educational media and technology yearbook*, CB141
Association of American Geographers. *Guide to departments of geography in the United States and Canada*, CL14
Association of College and Research Libraries. *Books for college libraries*, AA62
—— *Women's studies in Western Europe*, CC252, CC252
Association of Official Analytical Chemists. *Official methods of analysis of the Association of Official Analytical Chemists*, ED20
Association of Research Libraries. *Preservation guidelines in ARL libraries*, AB105, AB105
—— *Preservation organization and staffing*, AB106
—— *Preservation planning program*, AB104
Association periodicals, AE22
Associations, societies and academies
  directories
    Great Britain, CA52
    international, CA49, CA50, EA60
    United States, CA51, DB68
    U.S.S.R., DC209
  periodicals, AE22
The Assyrian dictionary, University of Chicago. Oriental Institute, AD74
Assyrian dictionary, University of Chicago. Oriental Institute, AD75
Assyro-Babylonian language, AD73, AD74, AD75
Astronomy
  abbreviations, EB8
  abstract journals, EB4
  atlases, EB15, EB16
  biography, EB14
  databases, EB3, EG3
  dictionaries, EB7, EB9
  directories, EB10, EE17
  encyclopedias, EB5, EB6
  handbooks, EB12
  history, EB13
Astronomy, space sciences, and related organizations of the world, EB8
Astrophysics
  databases, EB3, EG3
  encyclopedias, EB5
  handbooks, EB12
Atanasova, Teodora. *Angliĭsko-bŭlgarski rechnik*, AD79
Atiyeh, George Nicholas. *The Near East national union list*, AA25
Atkins, Beryl T. *Robert-Collins dictionnaire français-anglais, anglais-français*, AD95
Atkins, P.J. DC138
Atkins, Robert. *Artspeak*, BE43
Atkins, Stephen E. *Arms control and disarmament, defense and military, international security, and peace*, CJ290
Atkinson, Alan. *Atlas of the British Empire*, DC130
Atkinson, Frank. *Dictionary of literary pseudonyms*, AA33
Atlanta constitution, AJ7
Atlanta constitution [index], AF13
Atlantic Ocean, DA4
Atlantic Ocean, King, H. G. R., DA4
Atlas de géographie historique de la France et de la Gaule, de la conquête césarienne à nos jours, Sinclair, Stéphane, DC78
Atlas de la Révolution française, DC58
Atlas des formes linguistiques des textes littéraires de l'ancien français, Dees, Anthonij, BC3
Atlas historique de la France, DC78
Atlas historique des routes de France, Reverdy, Georges, DC79
Atlas historyczny Polski, DC174
Aṭlas Karṭa le-toldot 'Am Yiśra'el ba-zeman he-ḥadash, DA64
L'atlas national du Canada, CL63

Atlas of American history, Ferrell, Robert H., DB77
—— Jackson, Kenneth T., DB77
Atlas of American women, DB79
Atlas of America's ethnic diversity, CC188
Atlas of ancient America, Coe, Michael D., CL62
The atlas of British politics, Waller, Robert, CJ184
Atlas of British social and economic history since c. 1700, DC125
Atlas of classical history, DA45
An atlas of functions, Spanier, Jerome, EF15
Atlas of global strategy, Freedman, Lawrence, CJ42
Atlas of Great Lakes Indian history, CC232
Atlas of industrializing Britain 1780–1914, DC126
Atlas of Israel, Israel. Agaf ha-medidot, CL65
Atlas of maritime history, Natkiel, Richard, DA28
Atlas of modern Jewish history, Friesel, Evyatar, DA64
Atlas of modern world history, DA63
Atlas of Nazi Germany, Freeman, Michael J., DC97
Atlas of prehistoric Britain, Manley, John, DC129
An atlas of Roman Britain, Jones, Barri, DC128
Atlas of South Asia, Dutt, Ashok K., DE34
Atlas of the British Empire, DC130
The atlas of the Crusades, Riley-Smith, Jonathan Simon Christopher, DA54
Atlas of the English civil war, DC127
Atlas of the Holocaust, Gilbert, Martin, DA85
Atlas of the Middle East, Karṭa (Firm), DE27
Atlas of the North American Indian, Waldman, Carl, CC234
The atlas of the universe, Moore, Patrick, EB16
Atlas of the world, CL55
Atlas of the world economy, Freeman, Michael J., CH26
Atlas of world cultures, Murdock, George Peter, CE24
—— Price, David H., CE24
Aṭlas Yiśra'el. Atlas of Israel, CL65
Atlas zur deutschen Zeitgeschichte, 1918–1968, Hilgemann, Werner, DC98
Atlas zur Kirchengeschichte, BB107
Atlases
  archaeology, DA39
  bibliography, AA79, CL40, CL43, CL47
  directories, CL47
  general, CL22, CL50, CL51, CL52, CL53, CL54, CL55, CL56, CL57
  handbooks, CL49
  historical, DA26, DA27, DA29
    Germany, DC98
    Gt. Brit., DC126
    Ukraine, DC215
  indexes, CL39
Atterbury, Paul. *The dictionary of Minton*, BF23
Attic black figure vase-painters, Beazley, J. D., BE151
Aublet, Robert. *Nouveau guide de généalogie*, AK21
Aubry, Marie-Christine. *Djibouti*, DD29
Auchterlonie, Paul. *Arabic biographical dictionaries*, AJ31
—— *Middle East and Islam*, DE13
Auction records, AA44
The audio dictionary, White, Glenn D., BH160
Audiovisual materials
  directories, AA84, AA125
  encyclopedias, CB60
  lists and indexes, EK23
Audouze, Jean. *The Cambridge atlas of astronomy*, EB15
Audubon wildlife report, EC26

Auer, Michel. *Encyclopédie internationale des photographes de 1839 à nos jours = Photographers encyclopaedia international 1839 to the present*, BF61

Auer, Michèle. *Encyclopédie internationale des photographes de 1839 à nos jours = Photographers encyclopaedia international 1839 to the present*, BF61

Augustino, Diane K. *Alcohol and the family*, CC121

Aulestia, Gorka. *Basque-English dictionary*, AD76

—— *English-Basque dictionary*, AD77

Austin, Erik W. *Political facts of the United States since 1789*, CJ70, DB70

Austin, Robert B. *Early American medical imprints . . . 1668–1820*, EK8

Australia
  bibliography, AA87
  biography, AJ33, AJ34
  government publications, AG30
    bibliography, AG29
  history, DF2
    bibliography, AA88, DF5
    chronologies, DF4
    dictionaries, DF3
  library resources, DF1

Australian Antarctic bibliography, [Knight, Russell W.], DH2

Australian architectural periodicals index, BE114

Australian artists' index, McDonald, Jan, BE82

The Australian business and investment guide, CH183

The Australian concise Oxford dictionary of current English, AD53

Australian dictionary of biography, AJ34, AJ33

Australian government publications, AG29

Australian literary criticism, 1945–1988, Ross, Robert L., BD275

Australian literature
  bibliography, BD275
  encyclopedias, BD276
  handbooks, BD274

Australian national bibliography, 1901–1950, AA87

The Australian national dictionary, AD54

Australian National University. *The Southwest Pacific*, DG7

—— *Where the whalers went*, DG8

The Australian pocket Oxford dictionary, AD55

—— Johnston, Grahame, AD55

Australian words and their origins, AD54

Australians, DF2

Austria
  biography, AJ35, AJ36, AJ37, DC29
  dissertations, AH5
  history, DC30
    bibliography, DC23, DC24, DC27, DC28
      current, DC25
    local
      bibliography, DC26

Austria, Salt, Denys, DC27

Auswahlbibliographie zum Studium der anglistischen Sprachwissenschaft, Höhlein, Helga, BC20

Author and subject catalogues of the Tozzer Library, Tozzer Library, CE2, CE7, CE9

Author's guide to journals in psychology, psychiatry and social work, Markle, Allen, CD6

—— Rinn, Roger C., CD6

Author's guide to journals in the behavioral sciences, Wang, Alvin Yafu, CD6

Authorship, BD44, BD49, CA46

The autobiography of the working class, Burnett, John, CH270

Automated library systems, AB87, AB88

The automobile industry, 1896–1920, May, George S., CH136

The automobile industry, 1920–1980, May, George S., CH136

Auty, Robert. *Lexikon des Mittelalters*, DA50

Avakian, Anne M. *Armenia and the Armenians in academic dissertations*, DC22

Avalos, Francisco. *Latin American legal abbreviations*, CK69

Avereintsev, Sergeĭ Sergeevich. *Filosofskiĭ éntsiklopedicheskiĭ slovar'*, BA15

Avery index to architectural periodicals, BE118, BE116

Avery index to architectural periodicals. Supplement 4–10, BE115

Aves, King, Warren B., EC54

Aviation, CH188, CH189, DA69

Avilés, Jorge. *Thésaurus multilingue international en administration publique = Multilingual international thesaurus of public administration = Tesauro multilingue internacional de administración pública*, CJ224

Aviñoa, Xosé. *Diccionario de la zarzuela*, BH105

Avis, Walter. *Writings on Canadian English, 1792–1975*, BC21

AVLINE, EK21, EK23, EK28, EK29, EK20

Avtokratov, V. N. *Gosudarstvennye arkhivy SSSR*, AB36, DC199

Axelsen, Jens. *The standard Danish-English, English-Danish dictionary = Dansk-engelsk, engelsk-dansk ordbok*, AD84

Ayers, Jerry B. *Teacher education program evaluation*, CB16

Ayto, John. *The Longman register of new words*, AD33

The Aztecs, Welch, Thomas L., CC221

Azzolina, David S. *Tale type- and motif-indexes*, CF19

The BFI companion to the Western, BG85

BFI film and television handbook, BG98

BNA Library (Washington, D.C.). *BNA's directory of state courts, judges, and clerks*, CK78

BNA's directory of state courts, judges, and clerks, King, Kamla J., CK78

BNB on CD-ROM, AA132

The BRITS index, AH10

Babichev, F. S. *Ukrainskaĭa Sovetskaĭa Sotsialisticheskaĭa Respublika*, DC212

Babiĭ, B. M. *Ukrainskaĭa Sovetskaĭa Sotsialisticheskaĭa Respublika*, DC212

The baby boom, Byerly, Greg, CG3

Baby boom generation, CG3

Bach, Daniel. *Le Nigeria contemporain*, DD49

Bachmann, Horst. *Konkordanz zum Novum Testamentum Graece von Nestle-Aland*, BB60

Backgrounds to restoration and eighteenth-century English literature, Spector, Robert Donald, BD211

Bacteriology, EC61

Badawi, El-Said M. *A dictionary of Egyptian Arabic*, AD69

Bae, Frank. *Searching the law*, CK14

Bagnall, Austin Graham. *New Zealand national bibliography to the year 1960*, AA164, DF7

Bahamas, DB142

The Bahamas, Boultbee, Paul G., DB142

Baiculescu, George. *Publicaţiunile periodice româneşti (ziare, gazete, reviste)*, AE63

Bailey, Joyce Waddell. *Handbook of Latin American art = Manual de arte latinoamericano : a bibliographic compilation*, BE6

Bailey, William G. *The encyclopedia of police science*, CK100

—— *Guide to popular U.S. government publications*, AG7

—— *Human longevity from antiquity to the modern lab*, CC35

Baillie, Laureen. *American biographical archive*, AJ20

—— *British biographical archive*, AJ64

Bain, Robert. *Fifty southern writers after 1900*, BD155

—— *Fifty southern writers before 1900*, BD154

Bair, Frank E. *The weather almanac*, EE30

Baird, Lorrayne Y. *Bibliography of Chaucer, 1964–1973*, BD253

Baird-Lange, Lorrayne Y. *A bibliography of Chaucer, 1974–1985*, BD253

Bajec, Anton. *Slovar slovenskega knjižnega jezika*, AD162

Baker, A. D. *Combat fleets of the world*, CJ265

Baker, Daniel B. *Political quotations*, CJ27

Baker, John Hamilton. *A centenary guide to the publications of the Selden Society*, CK41

Baker, Michael John. *Dictionary of marketing and advertising*, CH316

Baker, Philip. *International guide to African studies research = Études africaines : guide international de recherches*, DD8

Baker, Sylva. *Endangered vertebrates*, EC38

Baker encyclopedia of psychology, CD9

Baker's biographical dictionary of musicians, BH88, BH88

Bakhmeteff Archive of Russian and East European History and Culture. *Russia in the twentieth century*, DC197

Bakró-Nagy, Marianne Sz. *Uralisches etymologisches Wörterbuch*, AD172

Balachandran, M. *A guide to statistical sources in money, banking, and finance*, CH212

Balázs, Péter. *Guide to the archives of Hungary*, DC144

Baldwin, Robert. *College football records*, BJ29

Balkan military history, Jessup, John E., DC16

Balkans
  history
    bibliography, DC16, DC18
    manuscripts and archives, DC17

Ball, Sarah. *The directory of international sources of business information*, CH85

Ballad scholarship, Richmond, W. Edson, BD248

Ballads, BD248

Ballet plot index, Studwell, William E., BG49

Ballinger, Jack T. *Chemical technicians' ready reference handbook*, ED22

Ballou, Patricia K. *Women*, CC253

Ballparks of North America, Benson, Michael, BJ19

The ballplayers, BJ20, BJ17

Balteau, J. *Dictionnaire de biographie française*, AJ51

Balz, Horst Robert. *Theologische Realenzyklopädie*, BB91

Bander, Edward J. *Searching the law*, CK14

Banerjea, J. N. *Development of Hindu iconography*, BE104

Bangladesh, DE44; *see also* **Pakistan**

Bangladesh, Rājjāka, Moḥ Ābadura, DE44

Banham, Martin. *The Cambridge guide to world theatre*, BG20

Bank, David. *British biographical index*, AJ65

The bankers' handbook, CH251

Banki, Ivan S. *Dictionary of administration and management*, CH155

Banking *see* **Finance and banking**

Banking and finance, 1913–1989, Schweikart, Larry E., CH136

Banking and finance to 1913, Schweikart, Larry E., CH136

Banking in the U.S, Deuss, Jean, CH213

Banking terminology, CH225

Banks, Olive. *The biographical dictionary of British feminists*, AJ61

Bannānukrom hāēng chāt = Thai national bibliography, AA195

Bansal, Narottam P. *Handbook of glass properties*, BF26, EJ8

Barbados, DB143

Barbados, Potter, Robert B., DB143

Barban, Arnold M. *Advertising media sourcebook*, CH73

Barbano, Filippo. *Bibliografi della sociologia italiana. (1945–1970)*, CC10

Barbosa, Clarita S. *Compilation of graduate theses, 1983–1984*, AH17

Barbour, Roger William. *Turtles of the world*, EC44

Bardis, Panos Demetrios. *Dictionary of quotations in sociology*, CC16

Barin, Ihsan. *Thermochemical data of pure substances*, ED11

Barker, Robert L. *The social work dictionary*, CC31

Barkhudarov, S. G. *Slovar' russkogo ĩazyka XI-XVII vv*, AD151

Barnard, Stephen. *Encyclopedia of rock*, BH126

Barnes, Grace M. *Alcohol and the family*, CC121

Barnes, Philip. *A companion to post-war British theatre*, BG30

Barnhart, Clarence Lewis. *The third Barnhart dictionary of new English*, AD36

Barnhart, David K. *The Barnhart dictionary companion—index, 1982–1985*, AD34

Barnhart, Robert K. *The American Heritage dictionary of science*, EA40
—— *The Barnhart dictionary of etymology*, AD11
—— *The third Barnhart dictionary of new English*, AD36

The Barnhart dictionary companion, AD34

The Barnhart dictionary companion—index, 1982–1985, Barnhart, David K., AD34

The Barnhart dictionary of etymology, AD11

Barnhart dictionary of new English, AD36

Barnouw, Erik. *International encyclopedia of communications*, CH205

Barns, BE112, EH24

Barns, stables, and outbuildings, Schultz, LeRoy G., BE112, EH24

Baron, John H. *Chamber music*, BH6

Barr, Avron. *The handbook of artificial intelligence*, EJ67

Barraclough, Geoffrey. *The Times atlas of world history*, DA30

Barranger, Milly S. *Notable women in the American theatre*, BG39

Barrett, Jane R. *A bibliography of works on Canadian foreign relations, 1981–1985*, DB80

Barron, Neil. *Anatomy of wonder*, BD109
—— *Fantasy literature*, BD110
—— *Horror literature*, BD111

Barron's finance & investment handbook, Downes, John, CH253

Barrow, Robin. *A critical dictionary of educational concepts*, CB66

Barrows, Floyd D. *A dictionary of obituaries of modern British radicals*, AJ62

Bart, Pauline. *The student sociologist's handbook*, CC2

Barteczko, Ewa. *Polskie wydawnictwa informacyjne 1945–1981*, AA63

Bartelt, Chuck. *Variety obituaries, 1905–1986*, BG5

Bartholomew gazetteer of places in Britain, CL33

Bartholomew gazetteers of Britain, CL33

Bartis, Peter. *Folklife sourcebook*, CF32

Bartke, Wolfgang. *Biographical dictionary and analysis of China's party leadership, 1922–1988*, CJ159
—— *China's new party leadership*, CJ160
—— *The economic aid of the PR China to developing and socialist countries*, CH56
—— *Who's who in the People's Republic of China*, AJ41, CJ160, CJ161

Bartl, Gerda. *Bestandskatalog der Bibliothek des Südost-Instituts München*, DC18

Bartlett, Jimmy D. *Ophthalmic drug facts*, EK120

Barton, Robert. *New Zealand foreign policy, 1945–1985*, DF8

Bartz, Bettina. *Internationales Bibliotheks-Handbuch = World guide to libraries*, AB20

Barua, B.P. *Directory of Indian public libraries*, AB30

Barzun, Jacques. *A catalogue of crime*, BD101
—— *European writers*, BD54

Basart, Ann Phillips. *Writing about music*, BH29

Base audiart, BF52

Baseball, BJ17, BJ18, BJ19, BJ20, BJ21, BJ22, BJ23, BJ24, BJ25, BJ26, BJ27

Baseball, Smith, Myron J., BJ26

The baseball encyclopedia, BJ17, BJ22, BJ18

The baseball trade register, Reichler, Joseph L., BJ25

Basford, Terry K. *Near-death experiences*, CC93

Basic books in the mass media, CH196

The basic business library, CH76

A basic classical and operatic recordings collection for libraries, Rosenberg, Kenyon C., BH158

A basic classical and operatic recordings collection on compact discs for libraries: a buying guide, Rosenberg, Kenyon C., BH158

Basic dental reference works, Kowitz, Aletha, EK83

Basic documents on the Soviet legal system, CK50

Basic literature in policy studies, Nagel, Stuart S., CJ10

Baskerville, David. *Music business handbook & career guide*, BH68

Basketball, BJ28

Basking, Barbara. *More notes from a different drummer*, CC103

Basque-English dictionary, Aulestia, Gorka, AD76

Basque language, AD76, AD77, BC51

Bassan, Fernande. *French language and literature*, BC38, BD308

Bassett, Jan. *The concise Oxford dictionary of Australian history*, DF3

Basso, Alberto. *Dizionario enciclopedico universale della musica e dei musicisti : il lessico*, BH50
—— *Dizionario enciclopedico universale della musica e dei musicisti : le biografie*, BH51

Bateman New Zealand encyclopedia, DF10

Bates, Robert Latimer. *Glossary of geology*, EE8, EE9

Batkin, Maureen. *The dictionary of Minton*, BF23

Batschelet, Margaret. *Early American scientific and technical literature*, EA68

The Batsford dictionary of drama, BG21

Battaglia, Salvatore. *Grande dizionario della lingua italiana*, AD128

The battle of Antietam and the Maryland Campaign of 1862, Hartwig, D. Scott, DB15

The battle of Jutland, Rasor, Eugene L., DB15

The battle of Pearl Harbor, Smith, Myron J., DB15

Battles, DA22

The battles of Coral Sea and Midway, May–June 1942, Smith, Myron J., DB15

Bauab, Heloísa Helena. *Bibliografia da música brasileira*, BH5

Bauer, K. Jack. *United States Navy and Marine Corps bases, domestic*, CJ277
—— *United States Navy and Marine Corps bases, overseas*, CJ278

Bauer, Wolfgang. *Lexikon der Symbole*, CF1

Baughn, William Hubert. *The bankers' handbook*, CH251

Baumbach, Lydia. *Studies in Mycenaean inscriptions and dialect, 1953–1964*, BC55
—— *Studies in Mycenaean inscriptions and dialect, 1965–1978*, BC55

Baumgarten, Rolf. *Bibliography of Irish linguistics and literature, 1942–71*, BC54

Baumgartner, Charles. *Dictionnaire de spiritualité*, BB85

Bausch, Judith Lola. *Sky and telescope cumulative index*, EB4

Bausinger, Hermann. *Enzyklopädie des Märchens*, CF26

Baxter, Angus. *In search of your British & Irish roots*, AK30
—— *In search of your German roots*, AK24

Baxter, Ian A. *A brief guide to biographical sources*, DE31

Bayerische Akademie der Wissenschaften. *Mittellateinisches Wörterbuch bis zum ausgehenden 13. [i.e. dreizehnten] Jahrhundert*, AD140
—— *Neue deutsche Biographie*, AJ59

Bayerische Staatsbibliothek. *Alphabetischer Katalog 1501–1840*, AA26
—— *Katalog der Musikdrucke*, BH34
—— *Katalog der Musikzeitschriften*, BH30
—— *Verzeichnis der im deutschen Sprachbereich erschienenen Drucke des XVI. Jahrhunderts*, AA119

Baylen, Joseph O. *Biographical dictionary of modern British radicals*, AJ8, AJ62

Bayley, Stephen. *The Conran directory of design*, BF38

Bayly, C. A. *Atlas of the British Empire*, DC130
—— *The new Cambridge history of India*, DE64

Beach, Edward Latimer. *Naval terms dictionary*, CJ272

Beach, William W. *United States congressional districts, 1843–1883*, CJ105

Beacham, Walton. *Beacham's guide to key lobbyists*, CJ60
—— *Beacham's marketing reference*, CH315
—— *Research guide to biography and criticism*, BD15, BG7

Beacham's guide to key lobbyists, CJ60

Beacham's marketing reference, CH315

Beal, Peter. *Index of English literary manuscripts*, BD215

Beals, Alan R. *Sources of information in the social sciences*, CA4

Bean, R. *International labour statistics*, CH288

Beard, Geoffrey W. *Dictionary of English furniture makers 1660–1840*, BF37

Beard, Joseph J. *Specialized legal research*, CK12

Beard, Joseph W. *Teacher attitudes*, CB18

Beard, Robert. *Bibliography of morphology, 1960–1985*, BC1

Beasley, Jerry C. *Check list of prose fiction published in England, 1740–1749*, BD238

BEASTCD, EH8

Beat generation, BD157

Beaudiquez, Marcelle. *Inventaire général des bibliographies nationales rétrospectives = Retrospective national bibliographies : an international directory*, AA76

Beaumarchais, Jean-Pierre de. *Dictionnaire des littératures de langue française*, BD312

Beaumont, Jane. *A bibliography of works on Canadian foreign relations, 1981–1985*, DB80

Beaumont, Roger A. *Special operations and elite units 1939–1988*, CJ271

Beazley, J. D. *Attic black figure vase-painters*, BE151
—— *Beazley addenda*, BE151

Beazley addenda, Carpenter, Thomas H., BE151

Beazley Archive. *Beazley addenda*, BE151

Becela, Lidia. *Kto jest kim w Polsce*, AJ87

Beck, Reinhart. *Sachwörterbuch der Politik*, CJ14

Beck, Warren A. *Historical atlas of the American West*, DB55

Becker, E. Lovell. *International dictionary of medicine and biology*, EC17, EK48

Becket, Henry S. A. *The dictionary of espionage*, CJ284

Beckson, Karl E. *Literary terms*, BD34

Bedürftig, Friedemann. *The encyclopedia of the Third Reich*, DC92

—— *Grosse Lexikon des Dritten Reiches,* DC92

Beeching, Cyril Leslie. *A dictionary of eponyms,* AD12

Beede, Benjamin R. *Military and strategic policy,* CJ44

Beere, Carole A. *Gender roles,* CC307
—— *Sex and gender issues,* CC308
—— *Women and women's issues,* CC307, CC308

Beeson, Paul B. *The Oxford companion to medicine,* EK41

Behavioral sciences *see* **Social and behavioral sciences**

Behrens, Heinrich. *Datensammlungen in der Physik = Data compilations in physics,* EG1

Beilstein, Friedrich. *Handbuch der organischen Chemie,* ED38

Beilstein online, ED38

Belder, J. de. *Bibliografie van de geschiedenis van België,* DC32

Belgian writers, BD303

Belgium
bibliography, DC31
biography, AJ38
history
bibliography, DC32, DC33

Belgium, Riley, Raymond Charles, DC33

Bell, Barbara L. *An annotated guide to current national bibliographies,* AA70

Bell, David Scott. *Biographical dictionary of French political leaders since 1870,* CJ171

Bell, Herbert W. *How to get your book published,* AA49

Bell, James. *New and comprehensive gazetteer of England and Wales,* AK29

Bell, Maureen. *A biographical dictionary of English women writers, 1580–1720,* BD223

Bell, Robert E. *Place-names in classical mythology,* CF10

Bellack, Alan S. *Dictionary of behavioral assessment techniques,* CD40

Bellamy, Joyce M. *Dictionary of labour biography,* AJ63

Belle, Gilbert van. *Johannine bibliography 1966–1985,* BB41

Beloch, Israel. *Dicionário histórico-biográfico brasileiro, 1930–1983,* DB115

Beltrán Bernal, Trinidad. *Bibliografía histórica del Estado de México,* DB124

Belzer, Jack. *Encyclopedia of computer science and technology,* EJ59

Bencin, Richard L. *Encyclopedia of telemarketing,* CH324

Benedict, John T. *Tool and manufacturing engineers handbook,* EJ83

Benét's reader's encyclopedia, BD24

Benin, Decalo, S., DD6

Benjamin, Bernard. *Population statistics,* CG53

Benjamin, Ludy T. *A history of American psychology in notes and news, 1883–1945,* CD7

Benner, David G. *Baker encyclopedia of psychology,* CD9

Bennett, H. *Concise chemical and technical dictionary,* ED7

Bennett, J. D. *Industrial relations,* CH269

Bennett, James R. *A bibliography of stylistics and related criticism, 1967–83,* BD140

Bennett, Peter D. *Dictionary of marketing terms,* CH317

Bennett, Richard J. *A brief guide to centres of international lending and photocopying,* AB98

Bennett, Scott. *Victorian periodicals,* AE43

Benn's media directory. International, AE1

Benn's media directory. United Kingdom, AE44

Benn's press directory, AE1, AE44

Benskin, Michael. *A linguistic atlas of late mediaeval English,* BC31

Benson, Elizabeth P. *Atlas of ancient America,* CL62

Benson, Eugene. *The Oxford companion to Canadian theatre,* BG23

Benson, Hazel B. *The dying child,* CC94

Benson, Michael. *Ballparks of North America,* BJ19

Benson, Morton. *An English-SerboCroatian dictionary,* AD158
—— *SerboCroatian-English dictionary,* AD159

Benson-von der Ohe, Elizabeth. *An annotated bibliography of U.S. scholarship on the history of the family,* CC122

Bentley, Elizabeth Petty. *County courthouse book,* AK15
—— *The genealogist's address book,* AK16

Benton, Rita. *Directory of music research libraries,* BH64

Benvenisti, Meron. *The West Bank data project,* CJ188
—— *The West Bank handbook,* CJ188

Benz, Wolfgang. *Biographisches Lexikon zur Weimarer Republik,* DC95

Bercuson, David Jay. *The Collins dictionary of Canadian history,* DB87

Berens, Denis. *A concise encyclopedia of Zimbabwe,* DD58

Berens, John F. *Criminal justice documents,* CK97

Bergan, Ronald. *The Holt foreign film guide,* BG67

Berger, Arthur S. *The encyclopedia of parapsychology and psychical research,* CD49

Berger, Bruno. *Deutsches Literatur-Lexikon,* BD291

Berger, Joyce. *The encyclopedia of parapsychology and psychical research,* CD49

Berger, Marilyn. *Répertoire des dossiers documentaires traitant de l'art et de l'architecture dans les régions représentées á la section ARLIS M/O/Q = Directory of vertical file collections on art and architecture represented by ARLIS M/O/Q,* BE51

Berger, Sidney E. *Medieval English drama,* BD229

Berger, Vincent. *Case law of the European Court of Human Rights,* CK107

Bergeron, Barbara. *Variety obituaries, 1905–1986,* BG5

Bergeron, Claude. *Index des périodiques d'architecture canadiens, 1940–1980 = Canadian architectural periodicals index, 1940–1980,* BE117

Bergerson, Peter J. *Ethics and public policy,* CJ4

Bergey, D. H. *Bergey's manual of systematic bacteriology,* EC61

Bergey's manual of systematic bacteriology, EC61

Berghe, Louis van den. *Bibliographie analytique de l'archéologie de l'Iran ancien,* DE67

Bergheim, Laura. *The map catalog,* CL49

Bergin, Thomas Goddard. *Encyclopedia of the Renaissance,* DA47

Bergsten, Bebe. *Early motion pictures,* BG75

Bergstone, David. *National directory of educational programs in gerontology,* CC59

Berins, Michael L. *Plastics engineering handbook of the Society of the Plastics Industry,* EJ23

Berkow, Robert. *The Merck manual of geriatrics,* EK72

Berkowitz, Luci. *Thesaurus Linguae Graecae canon of Greek authors and works,* BD367

Berle, Gustav. *Business information sourcebook,* CH77

Berlin, Howard M. *The handbook of financial market indexes, averages, and indicators,* CH252

Bernard, Annick. *Guide de l'utilisateur des catalogues des livres imprimés de la Bibliothèque Nationale,* AA15

Bernard, Gildas. *Les familles protestantes en France,* AK22

—— *Guide des recherches sur l'histoire des familles,* AK23

Bernard, H. Russell. *Research methods in cultural anthropology,* CE1

Berndt, Judy. *Rural sociology,* CC3

Bernet, Charles. *Dictionnaire du français parlé,* AD97

Berney, Mary F. *Teacher education program evaluation,* CB16

Berrian, Brenda F. *Bibliography of African women writers and journalists,* BD372
—— *Bibliography of women writers from the Caribbean,* BD282

Berring, Robert C. *Bob Berring's commando legal research,* CK1
—— *Finding the law,* CK2
—— *How to find the law,* CK3
—— *Legal research made easy,* CK7
—— *Practical approaches to legal research,* CK10

Berry, Dorothea M. *A bibliographic guide to educational research,* CB2

Bertaud, Jean Paul. *Dictionnaire historique de la Révolution française,* DC53

Besemer, Susan P. *From museums, galleries, and studios,* BE76

Besserman, Lawrence L. *Chaucer and the Bible,* BD254

Besson, Alain. *Thornton's medical books, libraries, and collectors,* EK17

Best, Richard I. *Bibliography of Irish philology and manuscript literature,* BC54

Best American short stories, BD177

Best encyclopedias, Kister, Kenneth F., AC7

Bestandskatalog der Bibliothek des Südost-Instituts München, Südost-Institut München. Bibliothek, DC18

Bethell, Leslie. *The Cambridge history of Latin America,* DB108

Bettelheim, Anton. *Neue österreichische Biographie ab 1815,* AJ36

Bevan, A. W. R. *Catalogue of meteorites,* EE38

Bever, Michael B. *Encyclopedia of materials science and engineering,* EJ10, EJ11

Beyer, Erich. *Wörterbuch der Sportwissenschaft,* BJ11

Die Beziehungen Afghanistans zur Sowjetunion, Otto, Ingeborg, DE42

Bezzel, Irmgard. *Verzeichnis der im deutschen Sprachbereich erschienenen Drucke des XVI. Jahrhunderts,* AA119

Bhattacharya, Ram Shankar. *Encyclopedia of Indian philosophies,* BA13

Bhatty, K. M. *Annotated bibliography of social research in Pakistan,* DE87

Bhutan, DE29, DE45

Bhutan, Dogra, Ramesh C., DE45

Bianco, David. *Heat wave,* BH123

Bible
Apocrypha
bibliography, BB42
atlases, BB68, BB69
bibliography, BB41, BB43, BB44
reference works, BB79
commentaries, BB56, BB63, BB64, BB65, BB66, BB67
computer programs, BB53
concordances, BB54, BB59, BB60, BB61
dictionaries, BB48, BB49, BB52
encyclopedias, BB22, BB46, BB50, BB51, BB54, BB55, BB57, BB58
handbooks, BB47
indexes, BB45
pronunciation, BB52
quotations, BB62
versions, BB36, BB37, BB38, BB39, BB40

Biblia patristica, BB101

Biblio, Lorenz, Otto H., AA115

BiblioData (Firm). *Fulltext sources online,* AE76

Bibliografi della sociologia italiana. (1945–1970), Viterbi, Mario, CC10

Bibliografi over Danmarks offentlige publikationer, AA102

Bibliografía anotada de obras de referencia sobre Centroamérica y Panamá en el campo de las ciencias sociales, Garst, Rachel, DB92

Bibliografia brasileira, AA89

Bibliografia brasileira : catalogo de teses, AH6

Bibliografia czasopism polskich wydanych poza granicami Kraju od września 1939 roku = World index of Polish periodicals published outside of Poland since September 1939, Kowalik, Jan, AE62

Bibliografia da música brasileira, Antônio, Irati, BH5

Bibliografía de autores españoles del siglo XVIII, Aguilar Piñal, Francisco, BD322

Bibliografía de estudios sobre Carlos III y su época, Aguilar Piñal, Francisco, DC182

Bibliografía de la literatura hispánica, Simón Díaz, José, BD325

Bibliografía de la literatura uruguaya, Welch, Thomas L., BD350

Bibliografía de la poesía española del siglo XIX (1801–1850), Rokiski Lázaro, Gloria, BD328

Bibliografia de linguística portuguesa, BC46

Bibliografía del Emperador Carlos V, Cadenas y Vicent, Vicente de, DC183

Bibliografía del teatro hispanoamericano contemporáneo (1900–1980), Toro, Fernando de, BG15

Bibliografia della linguistica italiana, Hall, Robert Anderson, BC41

Bibliografia della sociologia italiana, 1975–1980, Bono, Anna Maria, CC4

Bibliografia dell'Archivio centrale dello Stato, 1953–1978, DC156

Bibliografia dell'Italia antica, Antonini, R., DC154

Bibliografia di bibliografie, edizioni italiane del XVI secolo, Bosco, Giovanna, AA7

Bibliografía guatemalteca, Valenzuela, Gilberto, AA136

Bibliografía histórica del Estado de México, Beltrán Bernal, Trinidad, DB124

Bibliografía hondureña, AA137

Bibliografia kombëtare e librit që botohet në RPS të Shqipërisë, AA85

Bibliografía mexicana, AA159

Bibliografía nacional, AA172

Bibliografia polska, Estreicher, Karol Józef Teofil, AA173

Bibliografia polska 1901–1939 = Polish bibliography 1901–1939, AA173

Bibliografia polska XIX stulecia, Estreicher, Karol Józef Teofil, AA174

Bibliografia românească modernă, 1831–1918, AA177

Bibliografia româneasca veche 1508–1830, AA177

Bibliografia României, AA178

Bibliografia selectiva de Ca lingua portuguesa, Ferreiva, José de Azevedo, BC46

Bibliografia slovenských kníh, 1901–1918, Fedor, Michal, AA97

Bibliografía sobre el español del Caribe hispánico, BC48

Bibliografia somala, Carboni, Fabio, DD51

Bibliografia wydawnictw ciągłych = Bibliography of Polish serials, AE60

Bibliografia wydawnictw Głównego Urzędu Statystycznego, 1968–1973, Poland. Główny Urząd Statystyczny, CG69

Bibliografia wydawnictw Głównego Urzędu Statystycznego, 1974–1980, Poland. Główny Urząd Statystyczny, CG70

Bibliograficky katalog ČSSR, AA100

Bibliografický katalog ČSSR. České knihy, AA99

Bibliografie van de geschiedenis van België, Belder, J. de, DC32

―――― Hannes, J., DC32

Bibliografie van de geschiedenis van België, 1914–1940 = Bibliographie de l'histoire de Belgique, 1914–1940, Heyse, Micheline, DC32

Bibliografija Jugoslavije. Zbirke i monografske serije, AA203

Bibliografija rasprava, članaka i književnih radova, Jugoslavenski leksikografski zavod, AE82

Bibliographia dramatica et dramaticorum, Meyer, Reinhart, BD295

Bibliographia studiorum uralicorum, 1917–1987 = Uralistiikan tutkimuksen bibliografia = Bibliography on Uralic studies, DC210

Bibliographic guide to anthropology and archaeology, CE7, CE2

A bibliographic guide to educational research, Berry, Dorothea M., CB2

Bibliographic guide to microform publications, AA29

A bibliographic guide to the history of computing, computers, and the information processing industry, Cortada, James W., EJ53

Bibliographic input standards, OCLC, AA77

The bibliographic instruction-course handbook, Wheeler, Helen Rippier, AB103

A bibliographical guide to black studies programs in the United States, Davis, Lenwood G., CC194

A bibliographical guide to Spanish American literature, Rela, Walter, BD330

Bibliographical handbook of American music, Krummel, Donald William, BH18

Bibliographical Society of America. *Bibliography of American literature*, BD151

Bibliographie algérienne, Maynadies, Michel, DD25

Bibliographie analytique de l'archéologie de l'Iran ancien, Berghe, Louis van den, DE67

Bibliographie analytique des biographies collectives imprimées de la France contemporaine, Fierro, Alfred, AJ53

Bibliographie cartographique internationale, CL40

Bibliographie de la France, AA116, AA117

Bibliographie de la presse classique, 1600–1789, Sgard, Jean, AE34

Bibliographie de la RDD, DD29

Bibliographie de la Révolution française, 1940–1988, Fierro, Alfred, DC49

Bibliographie de l'humanisme des anciens Pays-Bas, Gerlo, Aloïs, BA9

―――― Vervliet, Hendrik D. L., BA9

Bibliographie de l'humanisme des anciens Pays-Bas, avec un répertoire bibliographique des humanistes et poètes néo-latins, BA9

Bibliographie der Autobiographien, Jessen, Jens Christian, AJ60

Bibliographie der Deutschsprachigen Arabistik und Islamkunde, DE8

Bibliographie der Filmbibliographien = Bibliography of film bibliographies, Wulff, Hans Jürgen, BG57

Bibliographie der Hispanistik in der Bundesrepublik Deutschland, Österreich und der deutschsprachigen Schweiz, Heydenreich, Titus, BC51

Bibliographie der lokalen Alternativpresse, Rösch-Sondermann, Hermann, AE39

Bibliographie der nationalen Bibliographien = Bibliographie mondiale des bibliographies nationales = A world bibliography of national bibliographies, Domay, Friedrich, AA74

Bibliographie der Photographie deutschsprachige Publikationen der Jahre 1839–1984, Heidtmann, Frank, BF54

Bibliographie der Zeitschriften des deutschen Sprachgebietes bis 1900, Kirchner, Joachim, AE38

Bibliographie deutschsprachiger bevölkerungswissenschaftlicher Literatur, 1978–1984, Gärtner, Karla, CG4

Bibliographie du Laos, Lafont, Pierre-Bernard, DE82

Bibliographie du meuble, Viaux, Jacqueline, BF36

Bibliographie du Sénégal, AA182

Bibliographie du sport mise à jour, BJ2, BJ3

Bibliographie du Zaire, AA206

Bibliographie Friedrich der Grosse, 1786–1986, Henning, Herzeleide, DC83

Bibliographie hellénique, Legrand, Emile, AA134

Bibliographie juridique luxembourgeoise, Krieger, Georges, CK45

Bibliographie linguistique de l'ancien occitan (1960–1982), Klingebiel, Kathryn, BC35, BD309

Bibliographie nationale, AA161

Bibliographie nationale de la principauté de Monaco, 1761–1986, Lavagna, Paul, AA160

Bibliographie Nationale de Madagascar, AA156

Bibliographie nationale française depuis 1975 sur CD-ROM, AA116

Bibliographie nationale française. Livres, AA117

Bibliographie signalétique des écrits académiques disponibles au Centre de bibliographie rwandaise, Université nationale du Rwanda. Centre de bibliographie rwandaise, AH19

Bibliographie signalétique du latin des chrétiens, Sanders, Gabriel, BC43

Bibliographie zur Afghanistan-Literatur 1960–1987, Nursai, Ata M., DE41

Bibliographie zur Aussprache des Latein, Steitz, Lothar, BC44

Bibliographie zur Comic-Sekundärliteratur, Neumann, Renate, CF24

Bibliographie zur deutschen historischen Städteforschung, Schröder, Brigitte, BE137

Bibliographie zur Geschichte der Städte Österreichs, Rausch, Wilhelm, DC26

Bibliographie zur Geschichte Kaiser Friedrichs II. und der letzten Staufer, Willemsen, Carl Arnold, DC84

Bibliographie zur Geschichte und Landeskunde der Böhmischen Länder von den Anfängen bis 1948, Jilek, Heinrich, DC40

Bibliographie zur lateinischen Wortforschung, BC42

Bibliographie zur oberösterreichischen Geschichte, 1981–1985, Wunschheim, Johannes, DC28

Bibliographie zur österreichischen Zeitgeschichte, 1918–1985, Malina, Peter, DC23

Bibliographien zur Philosophie, BA4

Bibliographies for African studies, Scheven, Yvette, DD46

Bibliographies for African studies, 1970–1986, Scheven, Yvette, DD18

Bibliographies in history, DA55

Bibliographies of New England history, DB49

Bibliographische Berichte, AA3

Bibliographischer Wegweiser der philosophischen Literatur, Totok, Wilhelm, BA3

Bibliography; *see also* under topic, subhead **Bibliography**
bibliography, AA3, AA4
guides, AA1, AA2
national and trade, AA70
  bibliography, AA74, AA76, AA77
  developing countries, AA75
universal, AA9

Bibliography and index of English verse printed 1476–1558, Ringler, William A., BD246

Bibliography and index of geology, EE5, EE12

Bibliography and index of geology exclusive of North America, EE5

Bibliography and index of mainland Southeast Asian languages and linguistics, Huffman, Franklin E., BC59

Bibliography for the study of magazines, Schacht, John H., AE18

Bibliography of African women writers and journalists, Berrian, Brenda F., BD372

Bibliography of agriculture, EH5

A bibliography of American county histories, Filby, P. William, DB41

Bibliography of American folk art for the year [. . .], BF8

Bibliography of American literature, Blanck, Jacob, BD151

A bibliography of American naval history, Coletta, Paolo Enrico, DB5

A bibliography of ancient Ephesus, Oster, Richard, BB7

Bibliography of arms control verification, Scrivener, David, CJ300

Bibliography of Asian studies, DE73

Bibliography of Australia, Ferguson, John Alexander, AA87

Bibliography of Australia : addenda, 1784–1850, Ferguson, John Alexander, AA88, DF5

Bibliography of Australian music, Crisp, Deborah, BH40

Bibliography of bibliographies of the languages of the world, Troike, Rudolph C., BC6

Bibliography of bioethics, EK80

A bibliography of British business histories, Goodall, Francis, CH138

Bibliography of British gardens, Desmond, Ray, BE141

Bibliography of British history, DC105

Bibliography of British literary bibliographies, Howard-Hill, T. H., BD202

Bibliography of British newspapers, AF7

A bibliography of Canadiana, Metropolitan Toronto Library. Canadian History Dept, DB83

Bibliography of Chaucer, 1964–1973, Baird, Lorrayne Y., BD253

A bibliography of Chaucer, 1974–1985, Baird-Lange, Lorrayne Y., BD253

The bibliography of contemporary American fiction, 1945–1988, McPheron, William, BD176

Bibliography of criticism on English and French literary translations in Canada, Mezei, Kathy, BD306

Bibliography of discographies, BH159

Bibliography of doctoral dissertations, AH13

Bibliography of film bibliographies, BG57

A bibliography of geographic thought, CL2

Bibliography of German Expressionism, Robert Gore Rifkind Center for German Expressionist Studies, BE29

A bibliography of Indian bibliographies, 1961–1980, Kochukoshy, K. K., AA5

A bibliography of Iran, Nawabi, Y. M., DE70

Bibliography of Irish linguistics and literature, 1942–71, Baumgarten, Rolf, BC54

Bibliography of Irish philology and manuscript literature, Best, Richard I., BC54

Bibliography of Israeli politics, Mahler, Gregory S., CJ189

Bibliography of IUSSP conference proceedings from 1927 to 1985, CG2

Bibliography of landscape architecture, environmental design, and planning, Powell, Antoinette Paris, BE142

A bibliography of Latin American bibliographies, Gropp, Arthur E., AA8, DB90

A bibliography of Latin American bibliographies, 1980–1984, AA8, DB90

The bibliography of marketing research methods, Dickinson, John R., CH311

"Bibliography of Mauritius . . . ", AA158

A bibliography of medical and biomedical biography, Morton, Leslie T., EK78

Bibliography of medieval drama, Stratman, Carl J., BD229

A bibliography of military name lists from pre-1675 to 1900, Horowitz, Lois, AK5

Bibliography of modern Icelandic literature in translation, Mitchell, Philip M., BD300

Bibliography of modern Icelandic literature in translation. Supplement, 1971–1980, Ober, Kenneth H., BD300

Bibliography of morphology, 1960–1985, Beard, Robert, BC1

Bibliography of national filmographies, Gebauer, Dorothea, BG51

Bibliography of North American geology, EE5

Bibliography of official statistical yearbooks and bulletins, Westfall, Gloria, CG8

Bibliography of Old Spanish texts, BD323

Bibliography of original meaning of the United States Constitution, CK113

Bibliography of Polish serials, AE60

Bibliography of published articles on American Presbyterianism, 1901–1980, Parker, Harold M., BB111

Bibliography of religion in the South, Lippy, Charles H., BB4

A bibliography of Salon criticism in Paris from the July monarchy to the Second Empire, 1831–1851, McWilliam, Neil, BE147

A bibliography of Salon criticism in Second Empire Paris, Parsons, Christopher, BE147

Bibliography of semiotics, 1975–1985, Eschbach, Achim, BC2

A bibliography of Slavic mythology, Kulikowski, Mark, CF17

Bibliography of Soviet statistical handbooks, Heleniak, Timothy E., CG74

A bibliography of state bibliographies, 1970–1982, Parish, David W., AG27

A bibliography of stylistics and related criticism, 1967–83, Bennett, James R., BD140

A bibliography of the architecture, arts, and crafts of Islam by Sir K.A.C. Creswell, C.B.E. Second supplement, Jan. 1972 to Dec. 1980 (with omissions from previous years), Pearson, J. D., BE11

Bibliography of the architecture, arts, and crafts of Islam to 1st Jan. 1960, Creswell, K. A. C., BE11

Bibliography of the Blackfoot, Dempsey, Hugh A., CC218

——— Moir, Lindsay, CC218

Bibliography of the Catawba, Blumer, Thomas J., CC218

Bibliography of the Chickasaw, Hoyt, Anne Kelley, CC218

Bibliography of the Communist International (1919–1979), Kahan, Vilém, CJ240

A bibliography of the English language from the invention of printing to the year 1800, Alston, R. C., BC17

Bibliography of the history of art, BE21, BE22, BE19

A bibliography of the history of Wales [microform], Jones, Philip Henry, DC141

A bibliography of the Iran-Iraq borderland, McLachlan, K. S., DE12

Bibliography of the languages of native California, Bright, William, CC218

Bibliography of the Osage, Wilson, Terry P., CC218

Bibliography of the peace movement before 1899, Meulen, Jacob ter, CJ297

A bibliography of the periodical literature on the Acts of the Apostles, 1962–1984, Mills, Watson E., BB43

Bibliography of the Sioux, Hoover, Herbert T., CC218

——— Marken, Jack W., CC218

Bibliography of the Summer Institute of Linguistics, Philippines, 1953–1984, Cook, Marjorie, BC61

Bibliography of Tibetan studies, DE98

Bibliography of Ukrainian literature in English and French, Piaseckyj, Oksana, BD359

Bibliography of women & literature, Boos, Florence Saunders, BD152

Bibliography of women writers from the Caribbean, Berrian, Brenda F., BD282

A bibliography of works on Canadian foreign relations, 1981–1985, Barrett, Jane R., DB80

A bibliography of writings about New Zealand music published to the end of 1983, Harvey, D. R., BH15

A bibliography of writings for the history of the English language, Fisiak, Jacek, BC19

Bibliography of writings on the English language, Kennedy, A. G., BC25

Bibliography on deafness, Fellendorf, George W., CC102

A bibliography on foreign and comparative law, Szladits, Charles, CK20

Bibliography on geographic thought, Wheeler, James O., CL2

Bibliography on Haiti, Lawless, Robert, DB151

Bibliography on Holocaust literature, Edelheit, Abraham J., DA81

Bibliography on Holocaust literature. Supplement, Edelheit, Abraham J., DA82

Bibliography on portraiture, Heppner, Irene, BE7

Bibliography on Soviet intelligence and security services, Rocca, Raymond G., CJ287

Biblioteca Centrală Universitară Bucureşti. *Teze de doctorat,* AH18

Biblioteca Nacional de Honduras. *Anuario bibliográfico hondureño,* AA137

Biblioteca Nacional de México. *Bibliografía mexicana,* AA159

Biblioteca Nacional Rubén Darío. *Nicaraguan national bibliography, 1800–1978 = Bibliografía nacional nicaragüense, 1800–1978,* AA165

Biblioteca Nacional (Spain). *Catalogo general de Incunables en bibliotecas españolas,* AA40

——— *Catálogo general de libros impresos, 1982–1987,* AA11

——— *Catálogo general de libros impresos, hasta 1981,* AA10

Bibliotecas para la Gente. *Spanish-language reference books,* AA66

Biblioteka Jagiellońska. *Katalog czasopism polskich Biblioteki Jagiellońskiej,* AE61

Biblioteka Kombëtare (Albania). *Bibliografia kombëtare e librit që botohet në RPS të Shqipërisë,* AA85, AA85

Biblioteka Narodowa (Poland). *Bibliografia polska 1901–1939 = Polish bibliography 1901–1939,* AA173

——— *Bibliografia wydawnictw ciągłych = Bibliography of Polish serials,* AE60

Biblioteka Narodowa (Poland). Dział Informacji i Udostępniania Zbiorów. *Polskie wydawnictwa informacyjne 1945–1981,* AA63

Bibliotekscentralen (Denmark). *Dansk Bogfortegnelse [for aarene],* AA101

Bibliotheca alchemica et chemica, Duveen, Denis I., ED4

Bibliotheca chemica, Ferguson, John, ED4

Bibliotheca Hertziana, Max-Planck-Institut. *Kataloge der Bibliotheca Hertziana in Rom (Max-Planck-Institut),* BE24

Bibliotheca lexicologiae Medii Aevi, Tremblay, Florent A., BC45

Bibliothèque de documentation internationale contemporaine (France). *L'emigration russe,* AE64

Bibliothèque Nationale (France). *Anonymes 1501–1800,* AA14

——— *Bibliographie nationale française depuis 1975 sur CD-ROM,* AA116

——— *Bibliographie nationale française. Livres,* AA117, AA117

——— *Catalogue général des livres imprimés, 1897–1959,* AA12

——— *Catalogue général des livres imprimés. Auteurs, collectivités-auteurs, anonymes, 1970–1979. Série en caractères non latins,* AA13

—— *Catalogue général des périodiques du début du XVIIe siècle à 1959. Fichier alphabetique des titres*, AE33

—— *Catalogues des livres imprimés de la Bibliothèque Nationale*, AA15

—— *Les publications en série éditées au Sénégal, 1856–1982*, AE68

Bibliothèque Nationale (Madagascar). *Bibliographie Nationale de Madagascar*, AA156

Bibliothèque Nationale (Malagasy Republic). *Bibliographie Nationale de Madagascar*, AA156

Bibliothèque royale Albert Ier. *Répertoire des catalogues de ventes de livres imprimés*, AA44

Bibliothèque universitaire de Tananarive. *Bibliographie Nationale de Madagascar*, AA156

al-Bibliyūghrāfiyā al-qawmīyah al-Tūnisīyah, AE70

al-Bibliyūghrāfiyā al-waṭanīyah al-Sūrīyah, AA192

al-Bibliyūghrāfiyā al-waṭanīyah al-Sūrīyah al-rāji'ah, AA193

al-Bibliyūghrāfiyā al-waṭanīyah al-Urdunnīyah, AA152

al-Bibliyūghrāfiyah al-'Arabīyah al-Lībīyah, AA155

al-Bibliyūghrāfiyah al-waṭanīyah al-'Irāqīyah, AA143

Bibljografija nazzjonali ta' Malta = Malta national bibliography, AA157

Bieber, Davis M. *Bieber's current American legal citations*, CK89

Bieber, Doris M. *Bieber's dictionary of legal abbreviations*, CK62

Bieber's current American legal citations, Bieber, Davis M., CK89

—— Prince, Mary Miles, CK89

Bieber's dictionary of legal abbreviations, Bieber, Doris M., CK62

Bieber's dictionary of legal citations, Prince, Mary Miles, CK89

Biebuyck, Daniel P. *The arts of Central Africa*, BF3, BF6

Biegel, David E. *Social networks and mental health*, CC21, CC22

—— *Social support networks*, CC22

Bietenholz, Peter G. *Contemporaries of Erasmus*, BA26

Bildwörterbuch Musikinstrumente, BH153

Bilingual education, CB119, CB121

Bilingual education, Ambert, Alba N., CB119, CB121

Bilingual education and English as a second language, CB121

The Bill James historical baseball abstract, James, Bill, BJ22

Billick, David J. *Lexical studies of medieval Spanish texts*, BC49

Bingel, Marie Agnes. *Künstler der jungen Generation*, BE80

Bingham, Jane M. *Writers for children*, BD83

Binstock, Robert H. *Handbook of aging and the social sciences*, CC64

Bio-bibliographies in music, BH90

A bio-bibliography of German-American writers, 1670–1970, Ward, Robert Elmer, BD170

A biobibliography of native American writers, 1772–1924, Littlefield, Daniel F., BD196, BD197, CC218

—— Parins, James W., CC218

BioBusiness, EC4

Biochemistry, EC62, EC63

Biochemistry abstracts : amino-acid, peptide, and protein, EC7

Biochemistry abstracts : biological membranes, EC7

Biochemistry abstracts : nucleic acids, EC7

Bioethics, EK80, EK81

BIOETHICSLINE, EK80

BioExpress, EC6

Biográf Szerkesztőség. *Magyar ki kicsoda 1990*, AJ70

Biografisch woordenboek van Nederland, AJ82

Biogramy uczonych polskich, AJ85

Biographical dictionary and analysis of China's party leadership, 1922–1988, Bartke, Wolfgang, CJ159

A biographical dictionary of actors, actresses, musicians, dancers, managers & other stage personnel in London, 1660–1800, Highfill, Philip H., BG36

Biographical dictionary of American business leaders, Ingham, John N., CH146

Biographical dictionary of American cult and sect leaders, Melton, J. Gordon, BB34

Biographical dictionary of American journalism, AF24

Biographical dictionary of American science, Elliott, Clark A., EA83

Biographical dictionary of American sports : baseball, BJ20

Biographical dictionary of American sports : basketball and other indoor sports, BJ28

Biographical dictionary of American sports : football, BJ30

Biographical dictionary of American sports : outdoor sports, BJ5

Biographical dictionary of British architects, Colvin, Howard M., BE110

The biographical dictionary of British feminists, Banks, Olive, AJ61

Biographical dictionary of contemporary Catholic American writing, BD150

A biographical dictionary of English women writers, 1580–1720, BD223

Biographical dictionary of French political leaders since 1870, CJ171

Biographical dictionary of Hispanic literature in the United States, Kanellos, Nicolás, BD195

Biographical dictionary of internationalists, Kuehl, Warren F., CJ316

A biographical dictionary of Irish writers, BD271

Biographical dictionary of Latin American and Caribbean political leaders, AJ77, CJ193

Biographical dictionary of Marxism, CJ247, CJ246

Biographical dictionary of modern British radicals, Baylen, Joseph O., AJ8, AJ62

—— Gossman, Norbert J., AJ8, AJ62

Biographical dictionary of modern European radicals and socialists, AJ8

Biographical dictionary of modern peace leaders, CJ316

Biographical dictionary of neo-Marxism, CJ246, CJ247

Biographical dictionary of Russian/Soviet composers, BH76

A biographical dictionary of science fiction and fantasy artists, Weinberg, Robert E., BD128, BE89

The biographical dictionary of scientists: astronomers, EB14

Biographical dictionary of social welfare in America, CC25

Biographical dictionary of the American Congress, 1774–1971, CJ104

Biographical dictionary of the American Congress, 1774–1989, Jacob, Kathryn Allamong, CJ104

—— Ragsdale, Bruce A., CJ104

Biographical dictionary of the American left, CJ119

Biographical dictionary of the Comintern, Lazić, Branko M., CJ248

Biographical dictionary of the extreme right since 1890, Rees, Philip, CJ40

A biographical dictionary of the Soviet Union, 1917–1988, Vronskaya, Jeanne, AJ49, AJ99

Biographical dictionary of women artists in Europe and America since 1850, Dunford, Penny, BE79

Biographical directory, American Psychiatric Association, CD34

Biographical directory of anthropologists born before 1920, CE19

Biographical directory of clergy, BB108

Biographical directory of fellows and members of the American Psychiatric Association, CD34

Biographical directory of the American Congress, CJ105, CJ106

Biographical directory of the Council of Economic Advisers, Council of Economic Advisers (U.S.), CH22

Biographical directory of the governors of the United States, 1983–1988, Mullaney, Marie Marmo, AJ27

Biographical directory of the United States Congress, 1774–1989, United States. Congress, CJ104

Biographical directory of the United States executive branch, 1774–1989, CJ85

A biographical handbook of education, Nauman, Ann K., CB144

Biographical index to American science, Elliott, Clark A., EA83

Biographical memoirs, National Academy of Sciences (U.S.), EA77

Biographical memoirs of Fellows of the Royal Society, EK78

—— Royal Society (Great Britain), EA79

Biographical memoirs of the National Academy of Sciences, EK78

A biographical register, 1788–1939, Gibbney, H. J., AJ34

Biographical sources, Graves, Diane J., AJ2

Biographie nationale, Académie royale des sciences, des lettres et des beaux-arts de Belgique, AJ38

Biographies of Inuit artists, BE77

Biographisches Lexikon zur Geschichte der böhmischen Länder, AJ43

Biographisches Lexikon zur Geschichtswissenschaft in Deutschland, Österreich und der Schweiz, Weber, Wolfgang, DC96

Biographisches Lexikon zur Weimarer Republik, DC95

Biography
bibliography, AJ2, AJ3, BD15
by occupation or profession
authors, AJ14, AJ15, BD53
journalists, AF26
medievalists, AJ18, DA52
military leaders
France, AJ52
indexes, AF12, AJ4, AJ5, AJ6, AJ7
international, AJ1, AJ8, AJ9, AJ10, AJ11, AJ12
contemporary, AJ16, AJ17

Biography and genealogy master index, BE75

BioLaw, EK81

Biological abstracts, EC6

Biological abstracts/RMM, EC6

Biological & agricultural index, EC5, EH7

Biological sciences
biography, EC19
databases, EC4, EC5, EC6, EC7, EC8, EH7
dictionaries, EC13, EC15, EC16, EC17, EC18, EJ19, EK48
directories, EC20
encyclopedias, EC9, EC10
guides, EC1, EC2

Biomedical engineering, EK11, EK39, EK70

BIOSIS previews, EC6

BIOSIS previews/RN, EC6

Biotechnology, EJ17, EJ18

Biotechnology, EJ19

The biotechnology directory, EJ17

Biotechnology research abstracts, EC7

Birch, Alan. *Research material for Hong Kong studies*, DE55

The birder's handbook, Ehrlich, Paul R., EC48

Birds, EC46, EC47, EC48, EC49, EC50, EC51, EC52, EC54, EC55
bibliography, EC53
Birds, Miller, Melanie Ann, EC53
Birkett, Patricia. *Checklist of parish registers, 1986 = Répertoire de registres paroissiaux, 1986,* AK20
Birney, Alice L. *The literary lives of Jesus,* BB74, BD1
Birren, James E. *Handbook of the psychology of aging,* CC64
Bishop, David. *Handbook of medical library practice,* AB56, EK1
Bishops *see* **Popes, cardinals, bishops**
Bits, bytes & biblical studies, Hughes, John J., BB53
Bits & bytes review, BB53
Black, David. *The Macmillan atlas of rugs & carpets,* BF48
Black, J. L. *Origins, evolution, and nature of the Cold War,* CJ5
—— *Soviet perception of Canada, 1917–1987,* DB81
Black, Patricia. *Répertoire des dossiers documentaires traitant de l'art et de l'architecture dans les régions représentées à la section ARLIS M/O/Q = Directory of vertical file collections on art and architecture represented by ARLIS M/O/Q,* BE51
Black, Sharon. *Index to the Annenberg Television Script Archive,* BG106
Black adolescence, CC79
Black Africa, Morrison, Donald George, CG38
Black Africa data base, CG38
Black African literature in English. 1977–1981 supplement, Lindfors, Bernth, BD373
Black African literature in English, 1982–1986, Lindfors, Bernth, BD374
The black aged in the United States, Davis, Lenwood G., CC38
Black alcohol abuse and alcoholism, Watts, Thomas D., CC73
Black American families, 1965–1984, CC123
Black American women in literature, Glikin, Ronda, BD185
Black American women novelists, Werner, Craig Hansen, BD190
Black Americans, CC209
Black Americans information directory, CC205
Black arts annual, BE20, BG2
Black authors, Newby, James Edward, BD188
Black biographical dictionaries, 1790–1950, AJ22
Black biography, 1790–1950, AJ23
Black children and American institutions, Washington, Valora, CC78
Black dance, Adamczyk, Alice J., BG45
Black elected officials, CJ61
The black family in the United States, Davis, Lenwood G., CC124
Black holes, EB1
Black holes, Danko, Steven I., EB1
Black holes, 1970–74, EB1
Black holiness, Jones, Charles Edwin, BB80
Black immigration and ethnicity in the United States, CC193
Black-Jewish relations in the United States, 1752–1984, Davis, Lenwood G., CC195
Black leaders of the nineteenth century, CC207
Black media in America, Hill, George H., CC197
Black music and musicians in The new Grove dictionary of American music and The new Harvard dictionary of music, De Lerma, Dominique-René, BH93
Black music biography, Floyd, Samuel A., BH89
Black photographers, 1840–1940, Willis-Thomas, Deborah, BF64
The black resource guide, CC206
Black studies, DB24
Black theatre and performance, Gray, John, BG11

Black theology, Evans, James H., BB78
The Blackfeet, Johnson, Bryan R., CC215
Black's agricultural dictionary, Dalal-Clayton, D. B., EH10
Blacks and media, Snorgrass, J. William, CH203
Blacks in American films and television, Bogle, Donald, BG86
Blacks in classical music, Gray, John, BH79
Blacks in film and television, Gray, John, BG52
Blacks in science and medicine, Sammons, Vivian O., CC208, EA80, EK77
Blacks in the humanities, 1750–1984, Joyce, Donald F., CC198
Blacks on television, Hill, George H., BG103
The Blackwell biographical dictionary of British political life in the twentieth century, CJ177, DC112
The Blackwell dictionary of historians, DA11
The Blackwell encyclopaedia of political institutions, CJ15
The Blackwell encyclopaedia of political thought, CJ15, CJ16
The Blackwell encyclopedia of the Russian Revolution, DC207, DC205
Blahynka, Milan. *Čeští spisovatelé 20. století,* BD352
Blain, Virginia. *The feminist companion to literature in English,* BD228
Blair, Edward Payson. *Abingdon Bible handbook,* BB47
—— *The illustrated Bible handbook,* BB47
Blake, Fay M. *Verbis non factis,* CJ107
Blake, Gerald Henry. *The Cambridge atlas of the Middle East and North Africa,* DE26
Blake, John R. *A short title catalogue of eighteenth century printed books in the National Library of Medicine,* EK13
Blake, L. S. *Civil engineer's reference book,* EJ24
Blake, N. F. *Index of printed Middle English prose,* BD205
Blake, Robert. *The dictionary of national biography, 1981–1985,* AJ66
Blakemore, Harold. *The Cambridge encyclopedia of Latin America and the Caribbean,* DB99
—— *Chile,* DB117
Blanck, Jacob. *Bibliography of American literature,* BD151
Bland, William B. *Albania,* DC19
Blandy, Susan Griswold. *Library instruction for librarians,* AB102
Blankenship, Frank J. *The Prentice Hall real estate investor's encyclopedia,* CH346
Blasio, Mary-Ann. *New day/New Deal,* DB39
Blatt, Franz. *Novum glossarium mediae latinitatis,* AD141
Blaug, Mark. *Great economists before Keynes,* CH20
—— *Great economists since Keynes,* CH21
—— *Who's who in economics,* CH24
Bleiler, Everett Franklin. *Science-fiction, the early years,* BD123
—— *Supernatural fiction writers,* BD127
Bleiler, Richard. *Science-fiction, the early years,* BD123
Blensly, Douglas L. *Accounting desk book,* CH67
Blind
encyclopedias, CC106, EK44
library resources, BH65, CL45
Bloch, R. Howard. *A new history of French literature,* BD314
Block, B. Peter. *Inorganic chemical nomenclature,* ED26
Block, David. *A directory of vendors of Latin American library materials,* AB18
Block, Walter. *Lexicon of economic thought,* CH7
Bloed, A. *From Helsinki to Vienna,* CK108
Blogie, Jeanne. *Répertoire des catalogues de ventes de livres imprimés,* AA44

Bloom, Harold. *The new Moulton's library of literary criticism,* BD217
—— *Twentieth-century British literature,* BD227
Bloom, Ken. *American song,* BH104
Bloomfield, Valerie. *Resources for Australian and New Zealand studies,* DF1
Bloomsbury dictionary of opera and operetta, BH94
Bloomsbury dictionary of quotations, BD58
Bloomsbury foreign film guide, BG67
Bloomsbury good word guide, AD23
Bloomsbury guide to English literature, BD220
A Bloomsbury iconography, Richardson, Elizabeth P., BD213
Bluhm, R. K. *Bibliography of British newspapers,* AF7
Blum, Eleanor. *Mass media bibliography,* CH196
Blume, Friedrich. *Die Musik in Geschichte und Gegenwart,* BH54
Blumenson, John J. G. *Identifying American architecture,* BE130
Blumer, Thomas J. *Bibliography of the Catawba,* CC218
Blumhofer, Edith Waldvogel. *Twentieth-century evangelicalism,* BB75
The boarding school guide, Townsend, Kiliaen V. R., CB111
Boardman, John. *The Cambridge ancient history,* DA40
Boards of trade, CH108
Boas, Ralph Philip. *A.J. Lohwater's Russian-English dictionary of the mathematical sciences,* EF13
Boatner, Mark Mayo. *The Civil War dictionary,* DB33, DB34
Bob Berring's commando legal research, Berring, Robert C., CK1
Bobb, F. S. *Zaire,* DD5
Bobrowski, Ryszard. *Contemporary photographers,* BF62
Bock, Hans-Michael. *Cinegraph,* BG87
Boehm, Eric H. *Bibliographies in history,* DA55
—— *Historical periodicals directory,* DA10
Böhmer, Elizabeth W. *Left-radical movements in South Africa and Namibia 1900–1981,* DD21
Boehnlein, Mary Maher. *Children, parents, and reading,* CB151
Böni, Otto. *Schriftstellerinnen und Schriftsteller der Gegenwart,* BD301
Boëthius, Bertil. *Svenskt biografiskt lexikon,* AJ96
Böttcher, Kurt. *Lexikon deutschsprachiger Schriftsteller,* BD293
Bogdanor, Vernon. *The Blackwell encyclopaedia of political institutions,* CJ15
Bogdanov, Ivan. *Rechnik na bŭlgarskite psevdonimi,* AA34
Boger, Karl. *Postwar industrial policy in Japan,* CH37
Bogle, Donald. *Blacks in American films and television,* BG86
Bogus, Ronald J. *The complete rhyming dictionary and poet's craft book,* AD38
Bohatta, Hanns. *Neue österreichische Biographie ab 1815,* AJ36
The bohemian register, Hickey, Morgen, BD157
Boia, Lucian. *Great historians from antiquity to 1800,* DA14
Boîadzhiev, Simeon. *Rechnik na bŭlgarskiĭa ezik,* AD80
Bold, Alan Norman. *Scotland,* BD272
—— *Who was really who in fiction,* BD96
Boletín bibliográfico da Biblioteca Nacional, AA89
Boletín ISBN, Venezuela, AA198
Bolivia, DB110
Bolivia, Yeager, Gertrude Matyoka, DB110
Bolkhovitinov, N. N. *Russia and the United States,* DC198
Boller, Paul F. *They never said it,* BD59

Bollettino dell'emigrazione, CC162
Bol'shoĭ anglo-russkiĭ slovar', AD152
Bolton, Henry C. *Catalogue of scientific and technical periodicals 1665–1895*, EA18
Bolton, Henry Carrington. *A select bibliography of chemistry 1492–[1902]*, ED4
Bond, Otto Ferdinand. *The University of Chicago Spanish dictionary*, AD165
Bonde, Donatus. *A concise encyclopedia of Zimbabwe*, DD58
Bonin, Serge. *Atlas de la Révolution française*, DC58
Bonk, Wallace John. *Building library collections*, AB64
Bono, Anna Maria. *Bibliografia della sociologia italiana, 1975–1980*, CC4
Book illustration, BE97
The book of classical music lists, Kupferberg, Herbert, BH59
The book of Jewish books, BB129
The book of saints, BB96
Book of the states, CJ124
Book of vital world statistics, CG20
The book of world-famous music, Fuld, James J., BH127
Book reviews
  by subject
    literature, BD210
    religion, BB19, BB20, BB21
    science and technology, EA8
Book selection
  colleges, AA62
  guides, AA60, AA61, AB18, AB69
  reference books, AA63, AA64, AA65, AA66, AA67, EA6, EA8
Book selection, Spiller, David, AB69
Booker, Karen M. *Languages of the aboriginal southeast*, CC218
Books
  history
    dictionaries, AA47
Books for college libraries, AA62
Books in print, AA82, CB16, EA10
Books in print plus, AA82
The books of the Bible, BB63
Booksellers and bookselling, AB18
  directories
    United States, AB22
Boos, Florence Saunders. *Bibliography of women & literature*, BD152
Borchardt, C. F. A. *South African theological bibliography = Suid-Afrikaanse teologiese bibliografie*, BB18
Borchardt, D. H. *Guide to the availability of theses*, AB97
BorderLine, Valk, Barbara G., DB60
Bordman, Gerald Martin. *The concise Oxford companion to American theatre*, BG19
Boreal Institute for Northern Studies. *20th century Canadian arctic expeditions*, DH3
Bork, Inge. *The Wuerttemberg emigration index*, AK13
Borland, Anne. *The Foundation Center's user-friendly guide*, CA44
Bornschier, Volker. *Comparative world data*, CG15
Bornstein, Marc H. *Psychology and its allied disciplines*, CD15
Borremans, Raymond. *Le grand dictionnaire encyclopédique de la Côte d'Ivoire*, DD40
Bosco, Giovanna. *Bibliografia di bibliografie, edizioni italiane del XVI secolo*, AA7
Bose, Shankar. *Elections in India*, CJ185
Bosnich, Victor W. *Congressional voting guide*, CJ96
Boss, Richard W. *The library manager's guide to automation*, AB87
Bossuat, Robert. *Manuel bibliographique de la littérature française du Moyen Age de Robert Bossuat. Troisième supplément, 1960–1980*, BD310
Boston, Ray. *The newspaper press in Britain*, AF9

Boston globe, AJ7
Boston globe [index], AF13
Boston Spa conferences, EA61
Botany
  dictionaries, EC28, EC29
  guides, EC27
  handbooks, EC30, EC31
Botswana, DD27
Botswana, Morton, F., DD5
——— Murray, A., DD5
——— Ramsey, J., DD5
Botterweck, G. Johannes. *Theological dictionary of the Old Testament*, BB48
——— *Theologisches Wörterbuch zum Alten Testament*, BB49
Bottle, Robert Thames. *The use of biological literature*, EC1
Boucher, François. *20,000 years of fashion*, BF31
——— *Histoire du costume en Occident*, BF31
Boudon, Raymond. *A critical dictionary of sociology*, CC14
Boulanger, Grégoire. *Schriftstellerinnen und Schriftsteller der Gegenwart*, BD301
Boulanger, Norman. *Theatre backstage from A to Z*, BG25
Boultbee, Paul G. *The Bahamas*, DB142
Bourque, Amanda S. *Historical dictionary of the Third French Republic, 1870–1940*, DC76
Bourricaud, François. *A critical dictionary of sociology*, CC14
Bouscarle, Marie-Elisabeth. *Les publications en série éditées au Sénégal, 1856–1982*, AE68
Bowes, D. R. *The encyclopedia of igneous and metamorphic petrology*, EE43
The Bowker annual library and book trade almanac, AB22, AB43
The Bowker annual of library and book trade information, AB43
Bowker international serials database update, AE10
Bowman, James S. *Ethics, government, and public policy*, CJ34
——— *Gubernatorial and presidential transitions*, CJ45
Bowman, John S. *Civil War almanac*, DB34
Bowman, Mary Ann. *Library and information science journals and serials*, AB8
Boxshall, Geoffrey A. *The Cambridge illustrated dictionary of natural history*, EC24
——— *A dictionary of ecology, evolution and systematics*, EC24
Boy, Joachim. *Nationalbibliographien Schwarzafrikas*, AA71
Boyan, Norman J. *Handbook of research on educational administration*, CB127
Boyce, Charles. *Dictionary of furniture*, BF39
——— *Shakespeare A to Z*, BD267
Boyer, Rick. *Places rated almanac*, CL16, CL23
Boykin, James H. *The real estate handbook*, CH355
Boylan, Henry. *A dictionary of Irish biography*, AJ73
Bracken, James K. *Reference works in British and American literature*, BD200
Bradley, Susan. *Archives biographiques françaises*, AJ50
Brady, Anna. *Women in Ireland*, CC273
Brady, Anne. *A biographical dictionary of Irish writers*, BD271
Brady, George S. *Materials handbook*, EJ9
Braganti, Nancy L. *The travelers' guide to European customs & manners*, BJ47
Braille music collections, International directory of, BH65
Brandon, James R. *An international dictionary of theatre language*, BG24
Brandrup, J. *Polymer handbook*, EJ22
Brands and their companies, CH299, CH294
——— Wood, Donna, CH295, CH296, CH297, CH298
Brands and their companies: supplement, CH294, CH296, CH297, CH298, CH295

Branford, Jean. *A dictionary of South African English*, AD56
Branford, William. *The South African pocket Oxford dictionary*, AD57
Brass bibliography, Fasman, Mark J., BH154
Brassey's battles, Laffin, John, DA22
Brassey's multilingual military dictionary = Brassey's dictionnaire multilingue militaire = Brassey's, diccionario polígloto militar = Brassey's, Militär-Wörterbuch in sechs Sprachen = [Brassi, mnogoĭazychnyĭ voennyĭ slovar'] = [Qāmūs Brāysīs al-'askarī al-muta'addid al-lughāt], CJ255
Brassey's Soviet and communist quotations, CJ249
Bratkowsky, Joan Gloria. *Yiddish linguistics*, BC34
Braun, Molly. *Atlas of the North American Indian*, CC234
Braun, Wilhelm. *Etymologisches Wörterbuch des Deutschen*, AD111
Braunmüller, Kurt. *Deutsch-Skandinavisch im Vergleich*, BC32
Braunmüller, A. R. *The Cambridge companion to English Renaissance drama*, BD235
Braunstein, Mark Mathew. *Slide buyers' guide*, BE105
Brautigam, Patsy Fowler. *Interlibrary loan policies directory*, AB100
Brawer, Moshe. *Atlas of the Middle East*, DE27
Bray, David B. *A directory of Latin American studies in the United States*, DB102
Brazil, Mary Jo. *Building library collections on aging*, CC36
Brazil
  bibliography, AA89, AA90, AA197, AH6
  foreign relations, DB114
  handbooks, DB116
  history
    bibliography, DB111, DB113
    dissertations, DB112
    encyclopedias, DB115
    library resources, DB114
Brazil, Bryant, Solena V., DB111
Brazil. Biblioteca Nacional. *Bibliografia brasileira*, AA89
Brazil : empire and republic 1822–19930, DB108
Brazil in reference books, 1965–1989, Hartness, Ann, DB113
Brazilian literature
  bibliography, BD319
  encyclopedias, BD318
  guides, BC47, BD317
Brazilian literature, Foster, David William, BD319
Brazilian poetry, BD320
Breach, Jean. *Edwardian architecture*, BE134
Breach, Nicholas. *Edwardian architecture*, BE134
Breakthroughs, Parkinson, Claire L., EA74
Brebner and Co. *Setting up a company in the European Community*, CK127
Brednich, Rolf Wilhelm. *Enzyklopädie des Märchens*, CF26
Brekke, Elaine. *Directory of librarians in international development*, AB38
Bresler, Judith. *Art law*, BE109, CK88
Brewer, Annie M. *Dictionaries, encyclopedias, and other word-related books*, AD67
Brewer, Deborah J. *ARBA guide to education*, CB1
Brewer, Ebenezer Cobham. *Brewer's dictionary of phrase and fable*, BD46
Brewer's dictionary of phrase and fable, Brewer, Ebenezer Cobham, BD46
Briamonte, Nino. *Saggio di bibliografia sui problemi storici, teorici e pratici della traduzione*, BC16
Bricka, Carl Frederik. *Dansk biografisk leksikon*, AJ45

Brickell, Christopher. *The American Horticultural Society encyclopedia of garden plants*, EC28

Bridges to knowledge in political science, Kalvelage, Carl, CJ2

A brief guide to biographical sources, India Office Library and Records, DE31

A brief guide to centres of international lending and photocopying, AB98

Brieger, Gert H. *Nobel prize winners*, AJ11

Briggs, Asa. *The Longman encyclopedia*, AC5

Briggs, Gerald G. *Drugs in pregnancy and lactation*, EK113

Briggs, Ward W. *Classical scholarship*, DA42

Bright, William. *Bibliography of the languages of native California*, CC218

Brinker, Russell C. *The surveying handbook*, EJ25

Brinker-Gabler, Gisela. *Lexikon deutschsprachiger Schriftstellerinnen, 1800–1945*, BD288

Brinson, H. F. *Engineered materials handbook*, EJ12

Britain in the Middle East, 1921–1956, Ponko, Vincent, DE14

Britain & the world, 1815–1986, Weigall, David, CJ174, DC118

Britain votes, CJ179

—— Craig, Fred W. S., CJ180

British Academy. *Dictionary of medieval Latin from British sources*, AD139

—— *A lexicon of Greek personal names*, AK50

British and American utopian literature, 1516–1985, Sargent, Lyman Tower, BD239

British and Irish Association of Law Librarians. *Directory of law libraries in the British Isles*, CK74

British archaeological abstracts, DA32

British architectural books and writers, 1556–1785, Harris, Eileen, BE110

British Architectural Library. *Architecture database*, BE113

British archives, Foster, Janet, AB50, AK28, DC107

British Association for Mycenaean Studies. *Studies in Mycenaean inscriptions and dialect, 1965–1978*, BC55

The British atlas of historic towns, DC134

British authors before 1800, BD55

British authors of the nineteenth century, BD55

British biographical archive, AJ64

British biographical index, AJ65

British Committee of Historic Towns. *Historic towns*, DC134

British Council. *British writers. Supplement*, BD226

British East Africa, 1856–1963, Ofcansky, Thomas P., DD12

British electoral facts, Craig, Fred W. S., CJ179, CJ181, CJ182

British electoral facts, 1832–1987, Craig, Fred W. S., CJ180

British Empire and Commonwealth, DC130

The British Empire in the Victorian press, 1832–1867, Palmegiano, Eugenia M., DC132

British English, A to Zed, Schur, Norman W., AD26

British fiction, 1750–1770, Raven, James, BD238

British film actors' credits, 1895–1987, Palmer, Scott, BG80

The British film catalogue, 1895–1985, Gifford, Denis, BG71

British Film Institute. *The BFI companion to the Western*, BG85

—— *BFI film and television handbook*, BG98

British gardeners, Hadfield, Miles, BE141

British general election manifestos, 1959–1987, CJ176

British historical facts, 1688–1760, Cook, Chris, DC119

British historical statistics, Mitchell, Brian, CG52, DC121

British history, 1945–1987, Catterall, Peter, DC105

British Library. *BNB on CD-ROM*, AA132

—— *The British Library general catalogue of printed books, 1976 to 1982*, AA18

—— *The British Library general catalogue of printed books, 1982 to 1985*, AA19

—— *The British Library general catalogue of printed books, 1986 to 1987*, AA20

—— *The British Library general catalogue of printed books 1988 to 1989*, AA21

—— *The British Library general catalogue of printed books to 1975*, AA16, AA17

—— *The British Library general subject catalogue, 1975 to 1985*, AA23

—— *Catalogue of books from the Low Countries 1601–1621 in the British Library*, AA163

—— *Catalogue of books printed in Spain and of Spanish books printed elsewhere in Europe before 1601 now in the British Library*, AA187

—— *Catalogue of cartographic materials in the British Library, 1975–1988*, CL41

—— *Catalogue of seventeenth century Italian books in the British Library*, AA146

—— *Current British journals: a bibliographic guide*, AE45

—— *The eighteenth century short title catalogue 1990*, AA128

—— *Serials in the British Library*, AE46, AE46

—— *Short-title catalogue of books printed in Italy and of Italian books printed in other countries from 1465 to 1600 now in the British Library. Supplement*, AA147

—— *Short-title catalogue of books printed in the German-speaking countries and of German books printed in other countries from 1455 to 1600 now in the British Library. Supplement*, AA118

—— *The South Asia and Burma retrospective bibliography (SABREB)*, AA92

—— *Subject index of modern books acquired, 1971–1975*, AA22

British Library. Dept. of Manuscripts. *Index of manuscripts in the British Library*, AA36

The British library directory, AB27

British Library. Document Supply Centre. *Index of conference proceedings*, EA61

The British Library general catalogue of printed books, 1976 to 1982, British Library, AA18

The British Library general catalogue of printed books, 1982 to 1985, British Library, AA19

The British Library general catalogue of printed books, 1986 to 1987, British Library, AA20

The British Library general catalogue of printed books 1988 to 1989, British Library, AA21

The British Library general catalogue of printed books to 1975, British Library, AA16, AA17

The British Library general subject catalogue, 1975 to 1985, British Library, AA23

British Library of Political and Economic Science. *A London bibliography of the social sciences*, CA9

British literary magazines, BD203

British military history, DC100

British Museum. Department of Printed Books. *Catalogue of books printed in Spain and of Spanish books printed elsewhere in Europe before 1601 now in the British Library*, AA187

British Museum. Dept. of Printed Books. *General catalogue of printed books*, BD243

British Museum (Natural History). *Catalogue of meteorites*, EE38

British naval history since 1815, Rasor, Eugene L., DC100

British newspapers and periodicals, 1641–1700, Nelson, Carolyn, AA131, AE41

—— Seccombe, Matthew, AA131

British parliamentary election results, Craig, Fred W. S., CJ179, CJ180

British parliamentary election results, 1832–1885, Craig, Fred W. S., CJ181

British parliamentary election results, 1885–1918, Craig, Fred W. S., CJ182

British parliamentary election statistics, Craig, Fred W. S., CJ180

British pharmacopoeia 1988, EK121

British poetry and the American Revolution, Kallich, Martin, BD244, DB25

British political facts, 1900–1985, Butler, David, CJ175

British sources of information, Jackson, Paul, DC103

British standard glossary of dental terms, EK85

British Standards Institution. *Universal decimal classification = Classification décimale universelle = Dezimalklassifikation*, AB83, AB83

British theatre, Cavanagh, John, BG9

British theatre yearbook, BG18

British Universities Film & Video Council. *Researcher's guide to British film & television collections*, BG84

British Universities Industrial Relations Association. *Industrial relations*, CH269

British women writers, BD224

British women's diaries, Huff, Cynthia Anne, BD251

British words on tape, AA125

British writers. Supplement, BD226

Brivio, Ernesto. *Repertorio delle cattedrali gotiche*, BE131

Brix, Michel. *Guide bibliographique des études d'histoire de la littérature française*, BD307

The broadcast communications dictionary, CH206

Broadcast research definitions, CH207

The broadcaster's dictionary, McDonald, James R., BG115

Broadcasting *see* **Mass media; Radio and television**

Broadhead, Lee-Anne. *A bibliography of works on Canadian foreign relations, 1981–1985*, DB80

Broadway musicals, show by show, Green, Stanley, BH107

Broadway on record, Lynch, Richard Chigley, BH146

Brockhaus Enzyklopädie, AC12

Brockhaus Enzyklopädie in zwanzig Bänden, AC12

Brockhaus Riemann Musiklexikon, BH48

Brockman, William S. *Music*, BH1

Broderick, Dorothy M. *Building library collections*, AB64

Brodie, Peter R. *Dictionary of shipping terms*, CH190

Brogan, Marianne C. *The ACS style guide*, ED24

Brogan, T. V. F. *English versification*, BD129

—— *Verseform*, BD129

Bromiley, Geoffrey William. *The international standard Bible encyclopedia*, BB55

—— *Theological dictionary of the New Testament*, BB58

Bronshteĭn, I. N. *Handbook of mathematics*, EF14

Les bronzes du XIXe siècle, Kjellberg, Pierre, BE166

Brooke, Michael. *Handbook of international trade*, CH184

Brookhart, Edward. *Music in American higher education*, BH7

Brooklyn College. *International bibliography of theatre*, BG12

Brookman, Lester G. *The 19th century postage stamps of the United States*, BF51

—— *The United States postage stamps of the 19th century*, BF51

Brooks, David. *Disease data book*, EK68

Brooks, Ellen J. *Learning to read and write*, CB20

Brooks, Nancy. *For the record*, BJ7

Brooks, Tim. *The complete directory to prime time network TV shows, 1946–present*, BG117

—— *The complete directory to prime time TV stars, 1946–present*, BG116

Brooks-Gunn, Jeanne. *Encyclopedia of adolescence*, CC88

Brottman, May. *The LIRT library instruction handbook*, AB101

Broughton, Bradford B. *Dictionary of medieval knighthood and chivalry*, DA48

Brower, Keith H. *Contemporary Latin American fiction*, BD339

Brown, Archie. *The Soviet Union*, AJ98

Brown, Carleton. *Index of Middle English verse*, BD205, BD246

Brown, Catherine L. *A bibliography of geographic thought*, CL2

—— *The urban South*, DB51

Brown, Charles N. *Science fiction, fantasy & horror*, BD120

—— *Science fiction in print*, BD120

Brown, Christopher M. *Concise veterinary dictionary*, EH27

Brown, Douglas T. *Handbook of certification/licensure requirements for school psychologists*, CB133

Brown, Fred. *Virology*, EC69

Brown, Gene. *Handbook of American-Jewish literature*, BD194

Brown, J. H. U. *A guide to collecting fine prints*, BE158

Brown, John Arthur. *A guide to the Indian tribes of the Pacific Northwest*, CC227

Brown, John H. *The Russian Empire and the Soviet Union*, DC195

Brown, Lawrence D. *Accounting research directory*, CH61

Brown, Marjorie J. *Online bibliographic databases*, AB95

Brown, Michelle P. *A guide to western historical scripts from antiquity to 1600*, AA39

Brown, Raymond Edward. *The new Jerome biblical commentary*, BB67

Brown, Richard D. *The encyclopedia of New England*, DB50

Brown, Robin. *Collins milestones in Australian history*, DF4

Brown, Russell K. *Fallen in battle*, CJ281

Brown, Samuel R. *Finding the source in sociology and anthropology*, CC5, CE4

The brown book, BE127

Browne, Edgardo. *Table of radioactive isotopes*, EG11

Browne, William Paul. *U.S. agricultural groups*, CJ68, EH18

Brownson, Anna L. *Judicial staff directory*, CK77

Brownson, Charles Bruce. *Judicial staff directory*, CK77

Brownstone, David M. *Dictionary of 20th-century history*, DA59

Bruccoli, Matthew Joseph. *First printings of American authors*, BD156

Bruce, A. P. C. *An illustrated companion to the First World War*, DA74

Bruce-Mitford, Miranda. *World directory of minorities*, CC179

Bruhn, John G. *Handbook of clinical sociology*, CC18

—— *Medical sociology*, CC6, EK7

—— *Social support and health*, CC23

Brun, Christophe. *Dictionnaire des maréchaux de France*, AJ52

Bruntjen, Scott. *A checklist of American imprints*, AA80

Brussell, Eugene E. *Webster's New World dictionary of quotable definitions*, BD68

Bryan, George B. *Stage lives*, BG44

Bryant, Bonita. *Guide for written collection policy statements*, AB63

Bryant, E. T. *Music librarianship*, AB54

Bryant, Keith L. *Railroads in the age of regulation, 1900–1980*, CH136

Bryant, Solena V. *Brazil*, DB111

Bryer, Jackson R. *Sixteen modern American authors*, BD161

Buchanan, Mary. *Educators' desk reference for special learning problems*, CB139

Der Buchdruck im 15. Jahrhundert, Corsten, Severin, AA45

Buckingham, J. *Dictionary of alkaloids*, ED31, EK108

Buckley, Peter. *Handbook of international trade*, CH184

Budavari, Susan. *The Merck index*, ED18, EK118

Buddhism; *see also* **Zen Buddhism**
 bibliography, BA2, BB12, BB122, BB123
 encyclopedias, BA12, BB23

Büchler, Edeltrud. *Deutsche Sprache im Reformationszeitalter*, BC33

Bürger, Erich. *Dictionary of information science*, AB14

Bürgisser, Max. *Etymologisches Wörterbuch der deutschen Sprache*, AD112

Buhle, Mari Jo. *Encyclopedia of the American left*, CJ243, DB62

Buhle, Paul. *Encyclopedia of the American left*, CJ243, DB62

Building library collections, Curley, Arthur, AB64

Building library collections on aging, Brazil, Mary Jo, CC36

Buildings
 conservation and restoration, BE129
 indexes, BE121
 dictionaries, BE124, EJ38

Buja, Maureen E. *Italian Renaissance poetry*, BD315

Bujas, Željko. *Hrvatsko ili srpsko-engleski enciklopedijski rječnik*, AD160

Buku tahunan perangkaan Malaysia = Yearbook of statistics Malaysia, CG63

Bulgaria
 bibliography, AA91
 encyclopedias, DC37
 history
  bibliography, DC34, DC35
  encyclopedias, DC36

Bulgaria, Crampton, R. J., DC34

Bulgarian language, AD78, AD79, AD80

Bŭlgarska akademiia na naukite. *Entsiklopediia Bŭlgariia*, DC36

—— *Information Bulgaria*, DC37

Bŭlgarska entsiklopediia (Firm). *Entsiklopediia Bŭlgariia*, DC36

Bŭlgarski etimologichen rechnik, AD78

Bull, Edvard. *Norsk biografisk leksikon*, AJ83

Bull, Storm. *Index to biographies of contemporary composers*, BH92

Bullard, Roger Aubrey. *Mercer dictionary of the Bible*, BB57

Bulletin bibliographique des Archives du Sénégal, Archives du Sénégal, AA182

Bulletin of bibliography, AA9

Bulletin signalétique d'information administrative, AG35

Bullock, Alan. *The Harper dictionary of modern thought*, AC4

Bullough, Vern L. *American nursing*, EK94

Bullwinkle, Davis. *African women, a general bibliography, 1976–1985*, CC274

—— *Women of eastern and southern Africa*, CC275

—— *Women of northern, western, and central Africa*, CC276

The bully pulpit, CJ84

Bunch, Bryan H. *The timetables of science*, EA72

Bundy, Alan L. *Directory of Australian academic libraries*, AB25

Bunes Ibarra, Miguel Angel de. *Repertorio bibliográfico de las relaciones entre la península Ibérica y el Norte de África, siglos XV–XVI*, DD14

Burdett, Anita L. P. *Summary guide to the archive and manuscript collections relevant to the former British colonial territories in the United Kingdom*, DC131

Burguière, André. *Dictionnaire des sciences historiques*, DA13

Burke, Patrick. *The nuclear weapons world*, CJ266

Burkett, Nancy H. *Black biography, 1790–1950*, AJ23

Burkett, Randall K. *Black biography, 1790–1950*, AJ23

Burland, C. A. *Man, myth & magic*, BB29, CD53, CF4

Burma, AA92, DE46, DE47

Burma, Shulman, Frank Joseph, DE46, DE47

Burma, a study guide, DE46

Burn, Lucilla. *Beazley addenda*, BE151

Burnashev, Elgizar IUsupovich. *Literatura o narodonaselenii*, CG73

Burnett, Barbara A. *Every woman's legal guide*, CC309

Burnett, John. *The autobiography of the working class*, CH270

The Burnham index to architectural literature, BE118

Burnham Library of Architecture. *The Burnham index to architectural literature*, BE118

Burnim, Kalman A. *A biographical dictionary of actors, actresses, musicians, dancers, managers & other stage personnel in London, 1660–1800*, BG36

Burnout, CD2

Burns, Grant. *Affordable housing*, CH342

Buros, Oscar Krisen. *Mental measurements yearbook*, CD45

Burrington, Douglas. *East Germany*, DC89

Burrows, Sandra. *Checklist of indexes to Canadian newspapers = Liste de contrôle des index de journaux canadiens*, AF14

Burt, Eugene C. *Erotic art*, BE4

—— *Ethnoart*, BF4

—— *Ethnoarts index*, BF4, BF12

—— *Serials guide to ethnoart*, BF10, BF11, BF12

Burt, Martha R. *America's homeless*, CC117

Burton, Dennis A. *A guide to manuscripts in the Presidential Libraries*, AB47, AB49, CJ80, DB22

Burton, John A. *The Collins guide to the rare mammals of the world*, EC56

Burton, Vivien G. *The Collins guide to the rare mammals of the world*, EC56

Buscombe, Edward. *The BFI companion to the Western*, BG85

Bush, Gregory. *Campaign speeches of American presidential candidates, 1948–1984*, CJ108

Business; *see also* **Corporations; International business enterprises**
 annuals, CH32, CH129
 bibliography, CH86, CH358, CH359
  Canada, CH137
  United States, CH137
 biography, CH144, CH145, CH146, CH147, CH149
 book reviews, CH6
 databases, CH87, CH88, CH89, CH99, CH102, CH116, CH117, CH124, CH126, CH148
 dictionaries, CH94, CH237
 directories, CH98
  Australia, CH183
  Gt. Brit., CH84
  international, CH85, CH110
  United States, CH118, CH121, CH123
 encyclopedias, CH307
 guides, CH76, CH77, CH78, CH79, CH80, CH81, CH83, CH84, CH85

handbooks, CH130
history, CH135, CH138, CH140, CH142, CH143
periodicals, CH90, CH91, CH92, CH93
quotations, CH96, CH97
statistics, CH132
Business and Professional Women's Foundation. *A women's thesaurus*, CC300
Business dateline, CH88
Business documents, Armstrong, John, CH135
Business education, CB45
Business education index, CB45
Business information, Lavin, Michael R., CH80, CH83
Business information sourcebook, Berle, Gustav, CH77
Business information sources, Daniells, Lorna, CH83
Business journals of the United States, CH90
Business Library (Brooklyn Public Library). *Business rankings and salaries index*, CH132
—— *Business rankings annual*, CH132
Business library review, CH6
Business management
biography, CH147
databases, CH153
dictionaries, CH155, CH159
directories, CH161, CH162, CH163, CH164
encyclopedias, CH157
handbooks, CH131, CH165, CH167
Business online, Scanlan, Jean M., AB96, CH82
Business organizations, agencies, and publications directory, CH98
Business organizations and agencies directory, CH98
Business rankings and salaries index, Business Library (Brooklyn Public Library), CH132
Business rankings annual, CH132
Business ratios, CH128, CH129
Business Research Services (Ill.). *National directory of minority-owned business firms*, CH121
—— *National directory of women-owned business firms*, CH123
Business serials of the U.S. government, CH91
Busto Duthurburu, José Antonio del. *Diccionario histórico biográfico de los conquistadores del Perú*, DB131
Butler, Alan. *A New Guinea bibliography*, AA169, DG11
Butler, David. *British political facts, 1900–1985*, CJ175
Butler, Deborah A. *American women writers on Vietnam*, BD198, DE103
Butler, Francis J. *Foundation guide for religious grant seekers*, BB31, CA31
Butler, Gareth. *British political facts, 1900–1985*, CJ175
Butler, William Elliott. *Basic documents on the Soviet legal system*, CK50
—— *Soviet law*, CK49
Butorin, Pavel. *Dictionary of development*, CH49
Buttel, Frederick H. *Labor and the environment*, CH271
Buttlar, Lois. *Education*, CB3
Bycroft, B. W. *Dictionary of antibiotics and related substances*, ED32, EK109
Byerly, Greg. *The baby boom*, CG3
Bynagle, Hans E. *Philosophy*, BA1
Byrne, F. J. *A new history of Ireland*, DC153
Byrne, Mary. *Eureka!*, AD13
Byrne, Pamela R. *Women in the Third World*, CC277
Byzantine studies, DA53

CA search, ED6
CAB abstracts, EH3, EH14, EH8
CAB thesaurus, EH5, EH8, EH14
CACI, Inc. *The sourcebook of zip code demographics*, CH332
CAMP catalog, Cooperative Africana Microform Project (U.S.), DD16

CCCC bibliography of composition and rhetoric, BD142
CCLM literary magazine directory, AE21, BD160
CD-ROM databases, AB89
CD-ROMs in print, AB90
CD/Investment, CH109
CDMARC bibliographic, AA24
CELEX, CK122
CIRCA Ltd. *Political and economic encyclopaedia of Western Europe*, CJ167
CIRCA Reference (Firm). *World fact file*, CJ142
CIS federal register index, CK53
CIS foreign gazetteers [of the] USBGN, CL27
CIS index to presidential executive orders & proclamations, AG20
CIS index to presidential executive orders & proclamations : Supplement, AG21
CIS index to unpublished U.S. House of Representatives committee hearings, AG13
CIS index to unpublished U.S. House of Representatives committee hearings, 1833–1936, AG16
CIS index to unpublished U.S. Senate committee hearings, AG13, AG17, AG18
CIS index to U.S. executive branch documents, 1789–1909, AG22
CIS index to U.S. Senate executive document & reports, AG12
CIS index to U.S. Senate executive documents and reports, AG13
CIS U.S. congressional committee hearings index, AG13, AG19
CIS U.S. congressional committee prints index, AG13
CIS U.S. serial set index, AG13
CPA world directory of old age, CC56
CPL bibliography, Council of Planning Librarians, CC159
CRC handbook of laboratory safety, ED13
CRC handbook of laser science and technology, EG7
CRC handbook of microbiology, EC21
CSA life sciences collection, EE39, EC7
CWLA's guide to adoption agencies, Posner, Julia L., CC139
Caballero, Cesar. *Chicano organizations directory*, CC241
Cabell, David W. E. *Cabell's directory of publishing opportunities in business and economics*, CH92
Cabell's directory of publishing opportunities in business and economics, Cabell, David W. E., CH92
Cabral, Adalino. *The Portuguese in the United States*, CC168
Cadenas y Vicent, Vicente de. *Bibliografía del Emperador Carlos V*, DC183
Çağdaş Türkiye, Tuğlac, Pars, DC192
Cahill, James F. *An index of early Chinese painters and paintings*, BE150
Cahn, R. W. *Encyclopedia of materials science and engineering*, EJ11
Cahner, Max. *Diccionari etimològic i complementari de la llengua catalana*, AD81
Caiden, Gerald E. *American public administration*, CJ209
Calantone, Roger J. *Successful industrial product innovation*, CH289
Calcified tissue abstracts, EC7
Calder, William M. *Classical scholarship*, DA42
Caldwell, Ronald J. *The era of Napoleon*, DC47, DC61
—— *The era of the French Revolution*, DC47, DC61
Caldwell-Wood, Naomi. *Checklist of bibliographies appearing in the Bulletin of bibliography 1897–1987*, AA9
A calendar of Soviet treaties, 1974–1980, CK112

California State University, Los Angeles. *Arms control, disarmament and international security*, CJ289
Call, Jerry. *Census-catalogue of manuscript sources of polyphonic music, 1400–1550*, BH35
Camarillo, Albert. *Latinos in the United States*, CC237
—— *Mexican Americans in urban society*, CC235
Cambridge air and space dictionary, EJ16
The Cambridge ancient history, DA40
The Cambridge atlas of astronomy, EB15
The Cambridge atlas of the Middle East and North Africa, DE19, DE26
Cambridge bibliography of English literature, BD243
Cambridge biographical dictionary, AJ1
The Cambridge companion to English Renaissance drama, BD235
Cambridge dictionary of science and technology, EA41
The Cambridge encyclopedia, AC1
The Cambridge encyclopedia of India, Pakistan, Bangladesh, Sri Lanka, Nepal, Bhutan, and the Maldives, DE33
The Cambridge encyclopedia of language, Crystal, David, BC7
The Cambridge encyclopedia of Latin America and the Caribbean, DB99
The Cambridge encyclopedia of the Middle East and North Africa, DE26, DE19
Cambridge guide to English literature, BD218
The Cambridge guide to literature in English, BD218
The Cambridge guide to the museums of Britain and Ireland, Hudson, Kenneth, BE49
The Cambridge guide to world theatre, BG20
The Cambridge handbook of American literature, BD162
The Cambridge handbook of contemporary China, Mackerras, Colin, DE53
The Cambridge historical encyclopedia of Great Britain and Ireland, DC113
The Cambridge history of Africa, DD10
The Cambridge history of China, DE50
Cambridge history of India, DE64
The Cambridge history of Judaism, BB137
The Cambridge history of Latin America, DB108
The Cambridge history of Renaissance philosophy, BA19
The Cambridge history of Russian literature, BD357
The Cambridge illustrated dictionary of British heritage, DC114
The Cambridge illustrated dictionary of natural history, Lincoln, Roger J., EC24
Cambridge International Reference on Current Affairs, Ltd. *World development directory*, CH59
Cambridge Scientific Abstracts, Inc. *CSA life sciences collection*, EC7
Cameron, Angus. *Old English word studies*, BC18
Cameron, Elisabeth. *Encyclopedia of pottery & porcelain, 1800–1960*, BF21
Cameron, Lucille W. *Labor and industrial relations journals and serials*, CH277
Cameroon, DD28
Cameroon, DeLancey, Mark, DD5, DD28
Camion, Jean. *Dictionnaire des homonymes de la langue française*, AD89
Camp, Norman M. *Stress, strain, and Vietnam*, DE104
Camp, Roderic Ai. *Who's who in Mexico today*, AJ80
Campaign speeches of American presidential candidates, 1948–1984, CJ108
Campbell, Enid Mona. *Legal research*, CK32
Campbell, Paul J. *Women of mathematics*, EF18

Campbell, Paul R. *Detailed statistics on the urban and rural population of Pakistan, 1950 to 2010*, CG65

Campbell, R. D. *Dictionary of aviation*, CH188

Campbell, Robert Jean. *Psychiatric dictionary*, CD18

Campbell, Thomas J. *Encyclopedia of minerals*, EE37

Canada
  atlases, CL63
  bibliography, AA93, DB81, DB83
  biography, AJ39
  encyclopedias, DB88
  foreign relations, DB80
  government publications
    bibliography, AG31, CJ158
  history
    atlases, DB89
    bibliography, DB84, DH3
    encyclopedias, DB87
    manuscripts and archives, AK20, DB86
    registers, CJ156
  place-names, CL37
  politics and government, CJ156, CJ157, CJ213
  statistics, CG42, CG44, CH327

Canada and international peace and security, CJ291

Canada. Energy, Mines and Resources Canada. *The national atlas of Canada*, CL63

Canada Institute for Scientific and Technical Information. *Union list of scientific serials in Canadian libraries*, EA20

Canada legal directory, CK73

Canada votes, 1935–1988, Feigert, Frank B., CJ155

Canadian Centre for Philanthropy. *A Canadian directory to foundations*, CA25

A Canadian directory to foundations, CA25

Canadian Dun's market identifiers (CDMI), CH99

The Canadian encyclopedia, DB88

Canadian feature film index, 1913–1985 = Index des films canadiens de long métrage, 1913–1985, Turner, D. John, BG82

Canadian fiction, BD281

Canadian guide to uniform legal citation, CK33

Canadian Institute for International Peace and Security. *Canada and international peace and security*, CJ291

The Canadian law list, CK34

Canadian Library Association. *Canadian periodical index, 1920–1937*, AE81
——— *Interlibrary loan directory*, AB99

Canadian literature
  bibliography, BD277, BD279, BD305, BD306
  biography, BD153
  handbooks, BD280
  manuscripts and archives, BD278

Canadian markets, CH327

Canadian men and women of the time, Morgan, H. J., AJ39

Canadian Peace Research Institute. *Peace research abstracts journal*, CJ302

Canadian periodical index, 1920–1937, AE81

Canadian public administration: bibliography = Administration publique canadienne: bibliographie, Grasham, W. E., CJ213

Canadian review of studies in nationalism, CJ6

Canadian serials directory = Répertoire des publications sériées canadiennes, AE29

Canadian statistics index, CG42

Canadian studies on Hungarians, 1886–1986, Miska, John P., CC166, DC145

Canadian translations = Traductions canadiennes, AA30

Canadian who's who index, 1898–1984, McMann, Evelyn de R., AJ39

Canadian writers (French), BD304

Canadiana 1867–1900, monographs, AA93

Cancer, EK14, EK25

CANCER-CD, EK30

Cancer journals and serials, Vaillancourt, Pauline M., EK25

Cancer therapy abstracts, EK30

CANCERLIT, EK29, EK30

Canfield, D. Lincoln. *The University of Chicago Spanish dictionary*, AD165

Cankar, Izidor. *Slovenski biografski leksikon*, AJ103

Cannon, John Ashton. *The Blackwell dictionary of historians*, DA11

Cantor, Aviva. *The Jewish woman, 1900–1985*, CC254

Cantrell, Karen. *Funding for museums, archives, and special collections*, BE53

Cape Archives Depot. *Guide to accessions in the Cape Archives Depot, Cape Town*, DD55
——— *Guide to arranged archives in the Cape Archives Depot*, DD55
——— *Guide to microfilms in the Cape Archives Depot, Cape Town*, DD55

Capek, Mary Ellen S. *A women's thesaurus*, CC299, CC300

Capen, Sharon L. *The national job bank, 1991*, CH340

Capie, Forrest. *Directory of economic institutions*, CH13

Capital punishment in America, Radelet, Michael L., CK98

Caratini, Roger. *Dictionnaire des personnages de la Révolution*, DC57

Carbohydrates, ED36

Carboni, Fabio. *Bibliografia somala*, DD51

Carcassonne, Philippe. *Dictionnaire des personnages du cinéma*, BG88

Carcinogenesis abstracts, EK30

The card catalog of the manuscript collections of the Archives of American Art. Supplement 1981–1984, Archives of American Art, BE32

Cardinale, Susan. *Women and the literature of the seventeenth century*, AA130

Cardinals *see* **Popes, cardinals, bishops**

Career America, CH336

Cargas, Harry J. *The Holocaust*, DA80

Cargill, Jennifer S. *Biographical sources*, AJ2

Caribbean
  biography, AJ40
  directories, DB104
  economic conditions, CH43
  encyclopedias, DB99
  handbooks, DB101
  history
    bibliography, DB140
    manuscripts and archives, DB96
  politics and government, AJ77, CJ193

The Caribbean, Hughes, Roger, DB140

Caribbean economic handbook, Fraser, Peter D., CH43

Caribbean literature, BD282, BD283, BD284, BD285
  bibliography, BD186

Caribbean writing, Hughes, Roger, BD284

Carl Gregor, *Duke of Mecklenburg*. *International bibliography of jazz books*, BH117
——— *International jazz bibliography*, BH117

Carlos V, DC183

Carmichael, D. R. *Accountants' handbook*, CH65

Carnegie Foundation for the Advancement of Teaching. *The condition of teaching*, CB148

Carnes, Pack. *Fable scholarship*, CF20

Carocci, Sandro. *Bibliografia dell'Archivio centrale dello Stato, 1953–1978*, DC156

Carpenter, Allan. *The encyclopedia of the Central West*, DB56
——— *The encyclopedia of the Midwest*, DB54

Carpenter, Charles A. *Modern drama scholarship and criticism, 1966–1980*, BD87, BG8

Carpenter, Joel A. *Twentieth-century evangelicalism*, BB75

Carpenter, Thomas H. *Beazley addenda*, BE151

Carper, James C. *Religious schools in America*, CB30

Carr, Ian. *Jazz*, BH124

Carr, John Charles. *Sex differences and learning*, CB25

Carradice, Ian. *The coin atlas*, BF49

Carratelli, Giovanni Pugliese. *Enciclopedia dell'arte antica, classica e orientale*, BE34

Carrera, Blanca. *Demografía en el Ecuador*, CG50

Carrington, David K. *World directory of map collections*, CL46

Carroll, Mark. *Records of the presidency*, CJ82

Carruth, Gorton. *The encyclopedia of American facts & dates*, DB72

Carson, Emmett Devon. *The charitable appeals fact book*, CA43

Carter, Sarah. *Women's studies*, CC247

Cartographical innovations, CL10

Cartography
  bibliography, CL41
  dictionaries, CL10
  guides, CL1

Carver, Terrell. *A Marx dictionary*, CJ244

Cary, Mary K. *Information for international marketing*, CH313

Cary, Robert. *African nationalist leaders in Rhodesia who's who*, CJ208

Casa editrice Valentino Bompiani. *Dizionario Bompiani degli autori di tutti i tempi e di tutte le letterature*, BD53

Casas de Barrán, Alicia. *Uruguay*, DB135

Case law of the European Court of Human Rights, Berger, Vincent, CK107

Cashman, Norine D. *Slide buyers' guide*, BE105

Cashmore, Ernest. *Dictionary of race and ethnic relations*, CC173

Caskey, Jefferson D. *Index to poetry in popular periodicals, 1960–1964*, BD180

Casper, Dale E. *Urban America examined*, CC158

Cassata, Mary B. *Television, a guide to the literature*, BG102

CASSI, ED5

Cassidy, Frederic Gomes. *Dictionary of American regional English*, AD52

Castagno, John. *American artists*, BE96, BE97
——— *Artists as illustrators*, BE97
——— *European artists*, BE98

Castillo, Carlos. *The University of Chicago Spanish dictionary*, AD165

Caswell, Lucy Shelton. *Guide to sources in American journalism history*, AF19

Catalan language, AD81, BC51

Catalogue : [authors and subjects], Harvard University. Peabody Museum of Archaeology and Ethnology. Library, CE7

Catalogue collectif des périodique du début du XVIIe siècle à 1939, AE33

Catalogue collectif des publications scientifiques dans les bibliothèques canadiennes, EA20

Catalogue de la musique imprimée avant 1801, conservée dans les bibliothèques de Lyon, Grenoble et la région, Guillo, Laurent, BH36

Catalogue de la musique imprimée dans les bibliothèques publiques de Paris, Lesure, Francois, BH36

Catalogue des thèses et mémoires /[Saïdou Harouna], Université de Niamey. Institut de recherches en sciences humaines. Service de la documentation, DD47

Catalogue général de l'édition musicale en France, Pierreuse, Bernard, BH21

Catalogue général des livres imprimés, 1897–1959, Bibliothèque Nationale (France), AA12

Catalogue général des livres imprimés. Auteurs, collectivités-auteurs, anonymes, 1970–1979. Série en caractères non latins, Bibliothèque Nationale (France), AA13

Catalogue général des ouvrages en langue française, 1926–1929, AA115

Catalogue général des périodiques du début du XVIIᵉ siècle à 1959. Fichier alphabetique des titres, Bibliothèque Nationale (France), AE33

Catalogue générale de la librarie francaise, 1840–1925, Lorenz, Otto H., AA115

Catalogue of 18th-century symphonies, LaRue, Jan, BH149

Catalogue of books from the Low Countries 1601–1621 in the British Library, British Library, AA163

Catalogue of books in English on Japan, 1945–1981, DE73

Catalogue of books on Japan translated from the Japanese into English, 1945–1981 = Eiyaku Nihon kankei hōbun tosho mokuroku, DE74

A catalogue of books printed in Hong Kong, [year], AA138

Catalogue of books printed in Spain and of Spanish books printed elsewhere in Europe before 1601 now in the British Library, British Library, AA187

Catalogue of cartographic materials in the British Library, 1975–1988, British Library, CL41

The catalog of catalogs II, Palder, Edward L., CH321

A catalogue of Catholic books in English printed abroad or secretly in England, 1558–1640, Allison, Antony Francis, BB115

Catalogue of census returns on microfilm, 1666–1891 = Catalogue de recensements sur microfilm, 1666–1891, Hillman, Thomas A., CG43

Catalog of copyright entries. Fourth series. Part two, serials and periodicals, AE14

A catalogue of crime, Barzun, Jacques, BD101

Catalog of current law titles, CK19, CK24

A catalogue of English books printed before 1801 held by the University Library at Göttingen, Jefcoate, Graham, AA129

Catalog of federal domestic assistance, CH54, CJ62

A catalogue of incunabula and manuscripts in the Army Medical Library, Schullian, Dorothy, EK13

—— Sommer, Francis E., EK13

A catalogue of incunbula and sixteenth century books in the National Library of Medicine, Krivatsky, Peter, EK13

Catalogue of meteorites, Graham, A. L., EE38

Catalog of motion pictures produced in the United States, American Film Institute, BG66

Catalog of National Archives microfilm publications, United States. National Archives and Records Service, DB24

Catalog of national historic landmarks, BE125

Catalog of new foreign and international law titles, CK19, CK25

Catalogue of scientific and technical periodicals 1665–1895, Bolton, Henry C., EA18

Catalogue of seventeenth century Italian books in the British Library, British Library, AA146

A catalogue of seventeenth century printed books in the National Library of Medicine, National Library of Medicine (U.S.), EK13

A catalogue of sixteenth century printed books in the National Library of Medicine, Durling, Richard J., EK13

Catalogue of the early printed books on South Asia, Dogra, R. C., DE28

Catalogue of the Erasmus collection in the City Library of Rotterdam, Gemeentebibliotheek Rotterdam, BA27

Catalogue of the publications of Scottish historical and kindred clubs and societies, Matheson, Cyril, DC140

—— Terry, Charles Sanford, DC140

Catalog of the Rübel Asiatic Research Collection, Harvard University Fine Arts Library, Harvard University. Fine Arts Library, BE25

Catalogue of the United Kingdom official publications (UKOP), AG37

Catalog of the William Ransom Hogan Jazz Archive, Tulane University. William Ransom Hogan Jazz Archive, BH121

Cataloging
  codes
    United States, AB79, AB80
    manuals, AB75, AB76
      MARC formats, AB77
  special subjects
    audiovisual materials, AB78

Cataloging with copy, Taylor, Arlene G., AB75

Catálogo colectivo del patrimonio bibliográfico español, AA188

Catálogo das dissertações e teses dos cursos de pós-graduação em História, 1973–1985, Corrêa, Carlos Humberto, DB112

Catalogo de autores y obras anonimas de la Biblioteca Nacional de Madrid, AA10, AA11

Catálogo de publicaciones, Consejo Nacional de Población (Mexico), CG64

Catálogo de seudónimos, anagramas, iniciales y otros alias usados por escritores mexicanos y extranjeros que han publicado en México, Ruiz Castañeda, María del Carmen, AA35

Catalogo de teses, AH6

Catalogo dei periodici italiani, Maini, Roberti, AE55

Catalogo general de Incunables en bibliotecas españolas, Biblioteca Nacional (Spain), AA40

Catálogo general de libros impresos, 1982–1987, Biblioteca Nacional (Spain), AA11

Catálogo general de libros impresos, hasta 1981, Biblioteca Nacional (Spain), AA10

Catalogues des livres imprimés de la Bibliothèque Nationale, Bibliothèque Nationale (France), AA15

Catalogues of the Harvard-Yenching Library, Harvard-Yenching Library, DE40

Cates, Jo A. *Journalism*, AF17

Catholic Church. *The New American Bible. Revised New Testament*, BB37

The Catholic novel, Menendez, Albert J., BD92

The Catholic peace tradition, Musto, Ronald G., BB117, CJ298

Catholic reference books, BB116

Catholicism in early modern history, BB119

CATLINE, EK28, EK29, EK27

Catterall, Peter. *British history, 1945–1987*, DC105

Cavanagh, John. *British theatre*, BG9

Cavendish, Richard. *Man, myth & magic*, BB29, CD53, CF4

Cavinato, Joseph L. *Transportation-logistics dictionary*, CH187

Cedergreen Bech, Svend. *Dansk biografisk leksikon*, AJ45

Celtic language and literature
  faculty
    directories, BC28

Censimento delle edizioni italiane del XVI secolo, AA148

Censo de población, 1984, CG49

Census catalog and guide, United States. Bureau of the Census, CG32

Census-catalogue of manuscript sources of polyphonic music, 1400–1550, BH35

Census of manufactures, CH306

Census of modern Greek literature, Philippides, Dia Mary L., BD368

Censuses
  atlases
    United States, AK3, CL60
  bibliography
    Africa, CG40
    Canada, CG43
    Caribbean, CG62
    Latin America, CG62
    Russia, CG75
    United States, CG29
    U.S.S.R., CG74, CG75

Les cent portes du Proche-orient, CJ199, DE20

A centenary guide to the publications of the Selden Society, Selden Society, CK41

Center for Arts Information. *Money for artists*, BE54

Center for Bibliographical Studies (Uppsala, Sweden). *Swedish imprints 1731–1833*, AA190

Center for Computer Assisted Research in the Humanities. *Computing in musicology*, BH75

Center for International Financial Analysis and Research (Princeton, N.J.). *WORLDSCOPE company profiles*, CH109

Center for International Research (U.S.). *Detailed statistics on the population of Israel by ethnic and religious group and urban and rural residence, 1950 to 2010*, CG58

—— *Detailed statistics on the urban and rural population of Indonesia, 1950 to 2010*, CG57

—— *Detailed statistics on the urban and rural population of Pakistan, 1950 to 2010*, CG65

—— *Detailed statistics on the urban and rural population of the Philippines, 1950 to 2010*, CG68

Center for Research Libraries (U.S.). *Soviet serials currently received at the Center for Research Libraries*, AE66

Center for Socialist History (Berkeley, Calif.). *The Marx-Engels cyclopedia*, CJ242

Central America
  economic conditions, CH44
  foreign relations, DB95
  handbooks, DB101
  history
    bibliography, DB92, DB93
    manuscripts and archives, DB96

Central America in the nineteenth and twentieth centuries, Grieb, Kenneth J., DB93

Central America since independence, DB108

Central American economic handbook, CH44

Central American Information Office (Cambridge, Mass.). *Honduras bibliography and research guide*, DB122

Central European economic history from Waterloo to OPEC, 1815–1975, Hacken, Richard D., CH2, DC3

The central Pacific campaign, 1943–1944, Controvich, James T., DB15

Centre d'analyse et de documentation patristiques (France). *Biblia patristica*, BB101

Centre for Policy on Ageing (London, England). *CPA world directory of old age*, CC56

Centre national de la recherche scientifique (France). *Albanie, une bibliographie historique*, DC20

—— *Guide des centres de documentation en histoire ouvrière et sociale*, DC73

—— *World translations index*, EA17

Centro de Investigaciones Literarias Españolas e Hispanoamericanas. *Quién es quién en el teatro y el cine español e hispanoamericano*, BG42

Centro di studi filosofici di Gallarate. *Dizionario dei filosofi del Novecento*, BA23

Centro nazionale d'informazioni bibliografiche (Italy). *Indice generale degli incunaboli delle biblioteche d'Italia*, AA42

Ceramics and glass, BF28
  bibliography, BF19, BF20
  catalogs, BF18
  dictionaries, BF23
  encyclopedias, BF21, BF22, BF24
  handbooks, BF26, BF27, EJ8
  marks and monograms, BF22
  price guides, BF25

Ceramics and glass, BF25

Česko-anglický technický slovník, EA47

Čeští spisovatelé 19. a počátku 20. století, BD352

Čeští spisovatelé 20. století, BD352

Cevallos, Elena E. *Puerto Rico*, DB152

Ceylon *see* **Sri Lanka**

Chad, Decalo, S., DD6

Chadwyck-Healey France S.A.R.L. *Catalogue général des périodiques du début du XVIIe siècle à 1959. Fichier alphabetique des titres*, AE33

Chafetz, Morris E. *The encyclopedia of alcoholism*, CC74

Chalfant, H. Paul. *Sociology of poverty in the United States*, CC143

Chaliand, Gérard. *A strategic atlas*, CJ41

Chall, Leo P. *Sociological abstracts*, CC11

Challinor, John. *Challinor's dictionary of geology*, EE9

Challinor's dictionary of geology, Challinor, John, EE9

Chamber music, Baron, John H., BH6

Chamberlain, Bobby J. *Portuguese language and Luso-Brazilian literature*, BC47, BD317

Chamberlain, Greg. *The dictionary of contemporary politics of South America*, CJ194

Chambers, Frances. *Guyana*, DB121

—— *Trinidad and Tobago*, DB154

Chambers, Janice E. *Dictionary of toxicology*, EK130

Chambers, Kevin. *The travelers' guide to Asian customs & manners*, BJ48

Chambers 20th century dictionary, AD7

Chambers biology dictionary, EC13

Chambers English dictionary, AD7

Chambers of commerce, CH106, CH108

Chambers world gazetteer, CL26

Chambers's twentieth century dictionary of the English language, AD7

Chametzky, Jules. *Handbook of American-Jewish literature*, BD194

Champion, Brian. *Advanced weapons systems*, CJ267

Champion, Larry S. *The essential Shakespeare*, BD260

Chan, Lois Mai. *Immroth's guide to the Library of Congress classification*, AB81

Chand, Dinesh. *Directory of periodicals published in India, 1986–87*, AE50

Chandler, David G. *Dictionary of the Napoleonic war*, DC6

—— *Dictionary of the Napoleonic Wars*, DC65

Chandler, Ralph C. *The constitutional law dictionary : vol. 1, Individual rights, suppl. 1*, CK114

—— *The public administration dictionary*, CJ210

Changes in official methods of analysis, ED20

Chanin, Leah F. *Specialized legal research*, CK12

Chapman, Anne. *Feminist resources for schools and colleges*, CC248

Chapman, Dorothy Hilton. *Index to poetry by black American women*, BD181

Chapman, Karen J. *Commodities price locator*, CH171

—— *Investment statistics locator*, CH219

Chapman, Michael D. *International legal books in print, 1990–1991*, CK17

Chapman, Mike. *Encyclopedia of American wrestling*, BJ36

Chapman, Robert L. *New dictionary of American slang*, AD40

Characters in 20th-century literature, Harris, Laurie Lanzen, BD10

Characters in literature, BD10, BD95, BD96, BD97, BD174

The charitable appeals fact book, Carson, Emmett Devon, CA43

Charité, J. *Biografisch woordenboek van Nederland*, AJ82

Charles Szladits' guide to foreign legal materials, Kearley, Timothy, CK39

Charlesworth, James H. *The New Testament apocrypha and pseudepigrapha*, BB42

—— *The Old Testament pseudepigrapha*, BB40

Charlton, James. *The ballplayers*, BJ17

Charras, Muriel. *Les thèses françaises sur l'Asie du Sud-Est depuis 1980*, DE38

Chase, Helen M. *Chase's annual events*, DA60

Chase, William D. *Chase's annual events*, DA60

Chase's annual events, DA60

Chase's calendar of annual events, DA60

Chaucer, G.
  bibliography, BD252, BD253, BD254, BD255, BD257
  dictionaries, BD256

Chaucer, a bibliographical introduction, Leyerle, John, BD257, DA46

—— Quick, Anne Wenley, DA46

Chaucer and the Bible, Besserman, Lawrence L., BD254

The Chaucer bibliographies, BD255

A Chaucer name dictionary, De Weever, Jacqueline, BD256

Chaucer's General prologue to the Canterbury tales, Eckhardt, C. D., BD255

Chaucer's lyrics and Anelida and Arcite, Peck, R. A., BD255

Chaucer's Romaunt of the rose and Boece, Treatise on the astrolabe, Equatorie of the planetis, lost works, and Chaucerian apocrypha, Peck, R. A., BD255

Chaudhuri, Brahma. *A comprehensive bibliography of Victorian studies*, BD212

Chavda, P. *Who's who, Indian personages*, AJ72

Check list of English prose fiction, 1700–1739, McBurney, William Harlin, BD238

Check-list of North American birds, EC46

Check list of prose fiction published in England, 1740–1749, Beasley, Jerry C., BD238

A check list of selected material on Samoa, Pereira, Janet Aileen, DG14

Checkland, S. G. *Dictionary of Scottish business biography, 1860–1960*, CH145

A checklist of American imprints, AA80

Checklist of bibliographies appearing in the Bulletin of bibliography 1897–1987, AA9

Checklist of indexes to Canadian newspapers = Liste de contrôle des index de journaux canadiens, Burrows, Sandra, AF14

Checklist of parish registers, 1986 = Répertoire de registres paroissiaux, 1986, National Archives of Canada. Manuscript Division, AK20

A checklist of published instrumental music by Japanese composers, Matsushita, Hitoshi, BH19

A checklist of Southeast Asian newspapers and other research materials in microform held by the Center for Research Libraries, Doeppers, Daniel F., DE39

Checklist of United States public documents, 1789–1909, AG22

Chemical abstracts, ED2, ED6

Chemical Abstracts Service source index, ED5

Chemical elements, ED14

Chemical engineering, ED22

Chemical industry, CH300

Chemical information sources, Wiggins, Gary, ED3

Chemical literature, 1700–1860, Cole, William A., ED4

Chemical Rubber Company. *CRC handbook of laser science and technology*, EG7

Chemical technicians' ready reference handbook, Shugar, Gershon J., ED22

Chemistry; see also Biochemistry
  analytic, ED20
  bibliography, ED4
  biography, ED25
  databases, ED6, ED19, ED27, ED37, ED38, EK119
  dictionaries, ED7, ED8, ED9, ED10
  guides, ED1, ED2, ED3

  handbooks, ED14, ED18, ED19, ED22, EK118, EK119
  inorganic, ED26, ED27, ED28
  organic, ED29, ED30, ED31, ED32, ED33, ED34, ED35, ED36, ED37, ED38, ED39, EK108, EK109, EK110
  periodicals, ED5
  style manuals, ED24
  tables, ED16, EG12

Chemistry, Nobelstiftelsen, Stockholm, ED25

Chemoreception abstracts, EC7

Chen, Ching-chih. *Scientific and technical information sources*, EA1

Cheung, King-Kok. *Asian American literature*, BD192

Chevalier, Tracy. *Contemporary poets*, BD131

—— *Twentieth-century children's writers*, BD82

Chiang, Nancy S. *Indians of North and South America*, CC225

Chiang, Win-Shin S. *Legal bibliography index*, CK23

Chiarmonte, Paula L. *Women artists in the United States*, BE79, BE91

Chicago Board of Trade. *Commodity trading manual*, CH172

Chicago guide to preparing electronic manuscripts, University of Chicago. Press, AA58

Chicago tribune, AJ7

Chicago tribune [index], AF13

Chicano anthology index, García-Ayvens, Francisco, CC240

Chicano literature, BD193

Chicano organizations directory, Caballero, Cesar, CC241

Chicano periodical index, BE5

The Chicano public catalog, Gutierrez, David, CC236

Chicano thesaurus, BE5

Chielens, Edward E. *American literary magazines*, BD159

Chien, Shu. *Handbook of bioengineering*, EK11

Chilcote, Ronald H. *Cuba, 1953–1978*, DB144

Child abuse, CC80, CC87, CC92

Child molestation, De Young, Mary, CC80

Child Welfare League of America. *CWLA's guide to adoption agencies*, CC139

Children and adjustment to divorce, Nofsinger, Mary M., CC132

Children and families watching television, Müller, Werner, CH200

Children and youth, CC85
  bibliography, CC77, CC79, CC80, CC81, CC82, CC84, CC86, CC94
  directories, CC89, CC90, CC91, CD27
  encyclopedias, CC88

Children, parents, and reading, Boehnlein, Mary Maher, CB19

Children's authors and illustrators, Nakamura, Joyce, BD78

Children's books in print, AA82

Children's literature, BD78
  bibliography, BD77, CB36, EA13
  biographies of authors, BD80, BD82, BD83
  directories, BD73
  handbooks, BD74, BD75, BD76
  indexes, BD79, BD81

Childress, James F. *BioLaw*, EK81

—— *The Westminster dictionary of Christian ethics*, BB92

Chile
  bibliography
    current, AA94
  government publications, AG32
  history
    bibliography, DB117
  statistics, CG45

Chile, Blakemore, Harold, DB117

Chilvers, Ian. *The Oxford dictionary of art*, BE38

China; see also Taiwan
  bibliography, AA95, AA194

biography, CJ159
  contemporary, AJ41, AJ42, CJ160
directories, CJ161
economic conditions, CH38, CH39, CH42
economic relations, CH56
history
  bibliography, CJ162, DE48, DE51
  by period
    post-1945, CJ159, CJ162, DE51, DE52, DE53, DE54
  dictionaries, DE49
  general histories, DE50
  library resources, BB104
politics and government, CJ159, CJ161
statistics, CG46, CG47, CG48, CH38
China economic handbook, Grummitt, Karsten, CH39
China nach Mao, Müller, Meike, DE54
China statistical abstract, CG47
China statistical yearbook, CG48
China trade and price statistics, CH38
China's new party leadership, Bartke, Wolfgang, CJ160
Chinese language, AD82
Chinese law, Johnson, Constance A., CK37
Chinese newspapers in the Library of Congress, Library of Congress, AF6
Chinese paintings in Chinese publications, 1956–1968, Laing, Ellen Johnston, BE150
Chinese religion in Western languages, Thompson, Laurence G., BB12
Chion, Michel. *Dictionnaire des personnages du cinéma*, BG88
Chitty, Mary Glen. *Federal information sources in health and medicine*, EK26
Chivalry, DA48
Cho, Sung Yoon. *Law and legal literature of North Korea*, CK44
Choe, Hye Yun. *Index to historic preservation periodicals*, BE121
Choice, BG102
Cholakova, Kristalina. *Rechnik na bŭlgarskiia ezik*, AD80
Chopra, H. R. *Directory of library and information science schools in India*, AB31
Chopra, Prabha. *Encyclopaedia of India*, DE61
Chopra, Pran Nath. *Encyclopaedia of India*, DE61
Choquette, Diane. *New religious movements in the United States and Canada*, BB2
Choral music, BH116
Chrissanthaki, Thana. *World index of economic forecasts*, CH19
Christensen, Jack F. *IES lighting handbook*, EJ49
Christian antiquities, BB94, BB95
Christian communication, Soukup, Paul A., BB82
Christian ethics, BB92
Christian literary imagery, BB81, BD3
Christian religion, BB94, BB95
  bibliography, BB11
  by country or region
    United States, BB84
      Southern states, BB24
  church history and expansion, BB86, BB100
    atlases, BB107
    encyclopedias, BB102
  dictionaries, BB136
  encyclopedias, BB85, BB86, BB87, BB89
  library resources, BB104
  symbolism, BB73
Christian Science monitor [index], AF13
Christianity in China, BB104
Christie, I. M. *Legal writing and research manual*, CK36
Christmann, Hans Helmut. *Altfranzösisches Wörterbuch*, AD102
Christmas carols, Studwell, William E., BH112
Christo, Doris H. *National directory of education libraries and collections*, CB88
Chronicle of the First World War, Gray, Randal, DA77

Chronicle of the French Revolution, 1788–1799, DC51
Chronicles of the age of chivalry, Hallam, Elizabeth M., DC116
The chronicles of the Wars of the Roses, Hallam, Elizabeth M., DC116
Chronik deutscher Zeitgeschichte, Overesch, Manfred, DC93
Die Chronik Österreichs, Kleindel, Walter, DC30
The chronological atlas of World War II, Pitt, Barrie, DA78
Chronological list, Roberts, Brian, DH4
Chronological list of Antarctic expeditions and related historical events, Headland, Robert, DH4
A chronological outline of American literature, Rogal, Samuel J., BD166
A chronology of conflict and resolution, 1945–1985, Jessup, John E., CJ39
A chronology of English literature, Gray, Martin, BD221
A chronology of geological thinking from antiquity to 1899, Thompson, Susan J., EE20
A chronology of Irish history since 1500, Doherty, J. E., DC152
A chronology of Islamic history, 570–1000 CE, Rahman, H. U., DE25
Chuguev, Vladimir. *A biographical dictionary of the Soviet Union, 1917–1988*, AA194
Chung-hua min kuo ch'u pan t'u shu mu lu, AA194
Chung-kuo pao k'an ta ch'üan, AE30
Church, Olga Maranjian. *American nursing*, EK94
Church and state, BB15, CJ13
  Europe, East and Southeast
    bibliography, BB76, DC12
Church and state in America, DB4
Church and state in postwar eastern Europe, BB76, DC12
The church librarian's handbook, McMichael, Betty, AB59
Church libraries, AB59
Church of England, BB77
Churchill's illustrated medical dictionary, EK46
Ciba-Geigy, S.A. *Thesaurus of agricultural organisms, pests, weeds, and diseases*, EH13
Cichero, Romolo. *The Tauris Soviet directory*, AJ100, CJ206
Cigler, Allan J. *U.S. agricultural groups*, CJ68, EH18
Cimbala, Diane J. *Biographical sources*, AJ2
CINAHL, EK89
Cinegraph, BG87
Cinema *see* Motion pictures
Cinema sequels and remakes, 1903–1987, Nowlan, Robert A., BG79
Cities; *see also* Urbanization
  bibliography, CC158
    Austria, DC26
    United States, DB48
  economic conditions, CA22
  handbooks, CL17, CL18, CL23
  statistics, CG37
Cities and towns in American history, Young, Arthur P., DB48
Cities of opportunity, Marlin, John Tepper, CA22
Cities of the United States, CL17
Cities of the world, CL18
The City of London from prehistoric times to c.1520, Lobel, Mary D., DC134
City planning
  bibliography, BE137, BE138, CC159
  dictionaries, BE139
  libraries, BE140
Civil engineering, EJ24, EJ25
Civil engineer's reference book, EJ24
Civil service reform, Dillman, David L., CJ46
Civil War almanac, Bowman, John S., DB34
The Civil War dictionary, Boatner, Mark Mayo, DB33, DB34

Civil War eyewitnesses, Cole, Garold, DB28
The Civil War in the North, Murdock, Eugene Converse, DB29
Civil War manuscripts, Library of Congress. Manuscript Division, DB31
Civil War maps, Library of Congress. Geography and Map Division, DB37
Civilization of the ancient Mediterranean, DA41
Claiborne, Robert. *The roots of English*, AD14
Clandestine employment, Annotated bibliography on, CH268
Clapham, A. R. *Flora of the British Isles*, EC32
Clark, Gregory R. *Words of the Vietnam War*, AD41
Clark, John Owen Edward. *Word perfect*, AD24
Clark, Judith Freeman. *Almanac of American women in the 20th century*, CC312
——— *The encyclopedia of child abuse*, CC87
Clark, P. F. *A dictionary of ecology, evolution and systematics*, EC24
Clark, Robin E. *The encyclopedia of child abuse*, CC87
Clark, William S. *A field guide to hawks, North America*, EC47
Clase, Pablo. *50 biografías de figuras dominicanas*, AJ46
Classical and medieval literature criticism, BD17
Classical antiquities, DA41
  atlases, DA45
  bibliography, BD365
  chronologies, DA44
Classical instrumental music, BH13
Classical literature
  bibliography, BD365
  biography, BD364
  collections, BD369
  criticism, BD17
  handbooks, BD366
  history, BD370
Classical music discographies, 1976–1988, Gray, Michael H., BH159
Classical philology, BB53, DA42
Classical political economy, CH1
Classical scholarship, DA42
——— Halton, Thomas P., BD365
Classification, AB81, AB82, AB83
Classification and index of the world's languages, Voegelin, Charles, BC15
——— Voegelin, Florence, BC15
A classification of igneous rocks and glossary of terms, International Union of Geological Sciences. Subcommission on the Systematics of Igneous Rocks, EE44
A classification of institutions of higher education, CB93
Classified and annotated bibliography of Sir William Osler's publications, Abbott, Maude E., EK16
A classified catalogue of books on the section XII, India, in the Tōyō Bunko (II) acquired during the years 1951–1982, Tōyō Bunko (Japan), DE60
Classified state bibliography of linguistic research on Indian languages, Geetha, K. R., BC56
Clatanoff, Robert M. *The valuation of industrial property*, CH343
Claude, Jacqueline. *Bibliography of IUSSP conference proceedings from 1927 to 1985*, CG2
Claude Levi-Strauss, a bibliography, Nordquist, Joan, CE6
Claude Levi-Strauss and his critics, Lapointe, Claire, CE6
——— Lapointe, Francois, CE6
Clauser, Henry R. *Materials handbook*, EJ9
Clavis scriptorum Graecorum at Latinorum, LaRue, Rodrigue, BC45
Clay, Katherine. *The school administrator's resource guide*, CB6

Clayman, Charles B. *The American Medical Association encyclopedia of medicine*, EK36

Cleeve, Brian Talbot. *A biographical dictionary of Irish writers*, BD271

—— *Dictionary of Irish writers*, BD271

Clem, Ralph S. *Research guide to the Russian and Soviet censuses*, CG75

Clements, Frank. *Saudi Arabia*, DE90

Clements, Patricia. *The feminist companion to literature in English*, BD228

Clennett, Margaret A. *Keyguide to information sources in dentistry*, EK82

Cleveland, Ana D. *Introduction to indexing and abstracting*, AB85

Cleveland, Donald B. *Introduction to indexing and abstracting*, AB85

Clifford, Denis. *A legal guide for lesbian and gay couples*, CC156

Climatology, EE28, EE29, EE31, EE32, EE33
handbooks, EE30

Cline, Cheryl. *Women's diaries, journals, and letters*, BD249

Cline, David. *Dictionary of visual science*, EK53

The clinical sociology handbook, Fritz, Jan M., CC7

Clubb, Jerome M. *Political facts of the United States since 1789*, CJ70, DB70

Clubbe, John. *The English romantic poets*, BD247

Coatsworth, Patricia A. *An annotated bibliography and index covering CPL bibliographies 1–253, January 1979–December 1989*, CC159

—— *Directory of planning and urban affairs libraries in the United States and Canada, 1990*, BE140

Cobb, David A. *Guide to U.S. map resources*, CL44

Cocaine, EK106

Cockrell, Philip C. *Directory of historical consultants*, DB67

Cockton, Peter. *Subject catalogue of the House of Commons Parliamentary papers, 1801–1900*, AG42

Code name directory, CJ259

Code of federal regulations index, CK94

Codes of professional responsibility, CH335, CK84

Codlin, Ellen M. *Aslib directory of information sources in the United Kingdom*, AB26

Coe, Michael D. *Atlas of ancient America*, CL62

Coffin, Tristram Potter. *The folklore of American holidays*, CF37

Cofrestri plwyf Cymru = Parish registers of Wales, Williams, C. J., AK48

Coggins, John. *Trade unions of the world 1989–1990*, CH284

Coggins, R. J. *A dictionary of Biblical interpretation*, BB50

Cohen, Aaron I. *International encyclopedia of women composers*, BH77

Cohen, Barbara E. *America's homeless*, CC117

Cohen, Hennig. *The folklore of American holidays*, CF37

Cohen, Marjorie Adoff. *Work, study, travel abroad*, CB86

Cohen, Morris L. *Finding the law*, CK2

—— *How to find the law*, CK2, CK3

Cohen, Norman S. *The American presidents*, CJ74

Cohen, Paul R. *The handbook of artificial intelligence*, EJ67

Cohen, Ralph. *New literary history international bibliography of literary theory and criticism*, BD8

Cohen, Richard M. *The sports encyclopedia*, BJ24

Cohen, Susan Sarah. *Antisemitism*, BB128

Cohen-Stratyner, Barbara. *Popular music, 1900–1919*, BH132

The coin atlas, Cribb, Joe, BF49

Coins, medals, currency; *see also* **Money catalogs, dictionaries, etc.**, BF49, BF50

Colaianni, Lois Ann. *Handbook of medical library practice*, AB56, EK1

Colby, Anita Y. *Dictionary of educational acronyms, abbreviations, and initialisms*, CB75

Colby, Robert W. *The encyclopedia of technical market indicators*, CH221

Colby, S. R. *Herbicide handbook of the Weed Science Society of America*, EH21

Cold War, CJ5, CJ164

Coldham, Peter Wilson. *The complete book of emigrants*, AK19

Cole, Garold. *Civil War eyewitnesses*, DB28

Cole, Sylvia. *The Facts on File dictionary of twentieth-century allusions*, BD35

Cole, William A. *Chemical literature, 1700–1860*, ED4

Colee, C. M. *Union list of Victorian serials*, AE73

Colegio de la Frontera Norte (Tijuana, Baja California Norte, Mexico). *Guía internacional de investigaciones sobre México*, DB128

Coleman, Earle Jerome. *Magic*, CF21

Coleman, James R. *Public administration desk book*, CJ211

Coletta, Paolo Enrico. *A bibliography of American naval history*, DB5

—— *A selected and annotated bibliography of American naval history*, DB5

—— *United States Navy and Marine Corps bases, domestic*, CJ277

—— *United States Navy and Marine Corps bases, overseas*, CJ278

Colgrave, Bertram. *Early English manuscripts in facsimile*, BD214

Colin, Jean-Paul. *Dictionnaire de l'argot*, AD98

Colindres O., Ramiro. *Enciclopedia histórica de Honduras*, DB123

Collected works of Erasmus, Erasmus, Desiderius, BA26

Collecting miniatures, Foskett, Daphne, BE152

Collective nouns and group terms, AD28

Collective settlements, DB7

College Art Association of America. *Répertoire international de la littérature de l'art*, BE22

The College Board index of majors, CB100

College costs, CB94

College Entrance Examination Board. *The index of majors*, CB100

College football records, Baldwin, Robert, BJ29

College majors, Lederman, Ellen, CB101

College money handbook, CB161

The college presidency, 1900–1960, Eells, Walter C., CB11

—— Hollis, Ernest V., CB11

The college price book, CB94

College student personnel abstracts, CB56

Collegium Carolinum. *Biographisches Lexikon zur Geschichte der böhmischen Länder*, AJ43

Collier, Simon. *The Cambridge encyclopedia of Latin America and the Caribbean*, DB99

Collinge, N. E. *An encyclopaedia of language*, BC8

Collins, James T. *An Indonesian-English dictionary*, AD126

Collins, Mary. *The new dictionary of theology*, BB118

Collins, Mary Ellen. *Education journals and serials*, CB43

Collins, P. M. *Carbohydrates*, ED36

Collins atlas of world history, DA26

Collins CoBUILD English language dictionary, AD8

The Collins dictionary of Canadian history, Bercuson, David Jay, DB87

Collins dictionary of economics, CH11

The Collins guide to the rare mammals of the world, Burton, John A., EC56

Collins milestones in Australian history, Brown, Robin, DF4

Collins-Robert French-English, English-French dictionary, AD95

Colombia, DB118

Colombia, Davis, Robert H., DB118

Colonial Brazil, DB108

Colonial British Caribbean newspapers, Pactor, Howard S., AF5

Colonial Spanish America, DB108

Colonial Williamsburg Foundation. *Architecture and the decorative arts*, BF7

The Columbia encyclopedia of nutrition, EK97

Columbia Granger's guide to poetry anthologies, BD11

The Columbia Granger's index to poetry, Hazen, Edith P., BD11

Columbia literary history of the United States, BD167

Columbia University. *Avery index to architectural periodicals*, BE116

—— *Avery index to architectural periodicals. Supplement 4–10*, BE115

—— *The Columbia encyclopedia of nutrition*, EK97

—— *Russia in the twentieth century*, DC197

Columbus, Provost, Foster, DB141

Columbus, C., DB141

Columbus Memorial Library. *The Aztecs*, CC221

—— *The Incas*, CC222

Colvin, Howard M. *Biographical dictionary of British architects*, BE110

Comaromi, John P. *Dewey decimal classification and relative index*, AB82

Combat fleets of the world, Baker, A. D., CJ265

—— Prézelin, Bernard, CJ265

Comedy, BG10, BG93

Comedy, an annotated bibliography of theory and criticism, Evans, James E., BG10

Comets, EB2, EB11

Comets, Kronk, Gary W., EB11

Comic books and strips, CF24, CF31, CF33

Comic books and strips, Scott, Randall W., CF31

Comitas, Lambros. *The complete Caribbeana*, DB144

Commando legal research, Bob Berring's, CK1

Commerce, CH182

Commission on the Humanities and Social Sciences. *Guide to research and scholarship in Hungary*, DC143

—— *A scholars' guide to humanities and social sciences in the Soviet Union*, DC209

Committee for a New England Bibliography. *Bibliographies of New England history*, DB49

Committee on Institutional Cooperation. *Women scholars in women's studies*, CC304

Commodities, CH171, CH172, CH173, CH174, CH175

Commodities price locator, Chapman, Karen J., CH171

Commodity prices, Friedman, Catherine, CH173

Commodity trading manual, CH172

Common knowledge, Grote, David, BD38

Common stock newspaper abbreviations and trading symbols, Jarrell, Howard R., CH229

Commonwealth Agricultural Bureaux. *CAB thesaurus*, EH14

Commonwealth Archivists' Association. *Summary guide to the archive and manuscript collections relevant to the former British colonial territories in the United Kingdom*, DC131

Commonwealth national bibliographies, AA73, AA72

Commonwealth of Nations, AA72, AA73

Commonwealth retrospective national bibliographies, AA72, AA73

Commonwealth sources in British official records, DC131

The Commonwealth yearbook, CJ183

Communes, DB6, DB7

Communication
bibliography, BB82, CH198
dictionaries, CH208, CH209
encyclopedias, CH205
The communication handbook, DeVito, Joseph A., CH208
Communications standard dictionary, Weik, Martin H., EJ69
Communism and anti-communism in the United States, Haynes, John Earl, CJ239
Communism and Christianity, BB76, DC12
Communism and socialism
bibliography, CJ238, CJ239, CJ240
biography, CJ159, CJ160, CJ246, CJ247, CJ248
encyclopedias, CJ243, DB62
handbooks, CJ245
quotations, CJ249
Communism in the world since 1945, DA55, CJ238
Communist and Marxist parties of the world, Hobday, Charles, CJ245
The Communist International and its front organizations, Sworakowski, Witold S., CJ240
Communitatis Europae lex, CK122
Compact Cambridge life sciences, EC7
Compact D/SEC, CH244
CompactMATH, EF5
Companies and their brands, CH296
——— Wood, Donna, CH294, CH295, CH297, CH298
Companion to Chinese history, O'Neill, Hugh B., DE49
A companion to post-war British theatre, Barnes, Philip, BG30
Companion to Scottish history, Donnachie, Ian L., DC139
Companion to South African English literature, BD286
Companion to the Industrial Revolution, Lines, Clifford John, DC115
A companion to the medieval theatre, BD89
Comparative dictionary of Ge'ez (Classical Ethiopic), Leslau, Wolf, AD86
Comparative literature, BD27, BD47, BD48
Comparative reading, Hladczuk, John, CB27
Comparative world data, Müller, Georg P., CG15
COMPENDEX, EJ2
COMPENDEX PLUS, EJ2
Compendium of American public opinion, Gilbert, Dennis A., CJ231
Compendium of chemical terminology, ED8
Compilation of graduate theses, 1983–1984, Barbosa, Clarita S., AH17
——— Mata, Maria Nena R., AH17
Compilation of graduate theses prepared in the Philippines, Philippines. National Science Development Board, AH17
Compilation of state and federal privacy laws, Smith, Robert Ellis, CK95
The complete actors' television credits, 1948–1988, Parish, James Robert, BG111
The complete book of emigrants, Coldham, Peter Wilson, AK19
The complete book of the Olympics, Wallechinsky, David, BJ34
The complete book of U.S. presidents, DeGregorio, William A., CJ90
The complete Caribbeana, Comitas, Lambros, DB144
A complete checklist of the birds of the world, Howard, Richard, EC50
The complete dictionary of television and film, Ensign, Lynne Naylor, BG89
The complete directory to prime time network TV shows, 1946–present, Brooks, Tim, BG117
The complete directory to prime time TV shows, BG116
The complete directory to prime time TV stars, 1946–present, Brooks, Tim, BG116

The complete entertainment discography, from 1897 to 1942, Rust, Brian A. L., BH142
The complete film dictionary, Konigsberg, Ira, BG96
The complete guide to America's national parks, BJ37
The complete guide to graduate school admission, Keith-Spiegel, Patricia, CD31
Complete guide to medical tests, Griffith, H. Winter, EK69
The complete rhyming dictionary and poet's craft book, Wood, Clement, AD38
The completely illustrated atlas of reptiles and amphibians for the terrarium, Obst, Fritz Jürgen, EC45
Composers, BH76, BH78, BH80, BH81, BH85, BH86, BH92
bibliography, BH90
bibliography of bibliography, BH91
Composers on composers, Holmes, John L., BH81
Composers on record, Greene, Frank, BH80
Composite index for CRC handbooks, EA32
A comprehensive bibliography for the study of American minorities, Miller, Wayne Charles, CC165
A comprehensive bibliography of American constitutional and legal history, Hall, Kermit, CK117
A comprehensive bibliography of English-Canadian short stories, 1950–1983, Weiss, Allan Barry, BD281
A comprehensive bibliography of music for film and television, Wescott, Steven D., BH147
A comprehensive bibliography of Victorian studies, BD212
A comprehensive bibliography of Yugoslav literature in English, 1593–1980, Mihailovich, Vasa D., BD361
Comprehensive coordination chemistry, ED12
A comprehensive etymological dictionary of the Hebrew language for readers of English, Klein, Ernest David, AD118
A comprehensive survey of Persian bibliographies in the world, AA6
Comprehensive textbook of psychiatry/V, CD33
Compton, Carolyn. *A guide to 85 tests for special education*, CB79
Compuscience, EJ54
Computer and control abstracts, EG2, EJ44
Computer applications in music, Davis, Deta S., BH10
Computer assisted instruction, EK88
Computer-Kondordanz zum Novum Testamentum Graece, BB60
Computer literature index, EJ55
Computer music, BH10, BH26, BH75
Computer-readable data bases, AB91
Computer science
bibliography, EJ53
databases, EG2, EJ44, EJ54
dictionaries, EJ61, EJ63, EJ65
encyclopedias, EJ59
guides, EJ50
handbooks, EJ68
indexes, EJ55
Computer science source book, EA38
Computer software, CB13, CD28, CD32
Computer use in psychology, Stoloff, Michael L., CD28
Computers see Microcomputers
Computers and literature, Rudall, B. H., BD16
Computing in musicology, BH75
Computing information directory, EJ50
Computing reviews, EF6, EJ54
Comrie, Bernard. *The world's major languages*, BC10
Concert and opera conductors, Cowden, Robert H., BH88
Concert and opera singers, Cowden, Robert H., BH88
The concise AACR2, 1988 revision, Gorman, Michael, AB80

Concise chemical and technical dictionary, Bennett, H., ED7
The concise Columbia dictionary of quotations, Andrews, Robert, BD57
The concise Columbia encyclopedia, AC5, AC2
Concise dictionary of American biography, AJ24
A concise dictionary of business, CH94
A concise dictionary of classical mythology, Kershaw, Stephen, CF11
A concise dictionary of Indian philosophy, Grimes, John A., BA17
The concise dictionary of management, Statt, David A., CH159
A concise dictionary of military biography, Windrow, Martin, AJ13
Concise encyclopedia of interior design, Dizik, A. Allen, BF38
The concise encyclopedia of Islam, Glasse, Cyril, BB127
Concise encyclopedia of psychology, CD10
Concise encyclopedia of special education, CB62, CB59
The concise encyclopedia of western philosophy and philosophers, BA11
A concise encyclopedia of Zimbabwe, DD58
A concise English-Hungarian dictionary, Országh, László, AD124
A concise Hungarian-English dictionary, Magay, Tamás, AD123
Concise illustrated dental dictionary, Harty, F. J., EK86
The concise Oxford companion to American theatre, Bordman, Gerald Martin, BG19
The concise Oxford dictionary of Australian history, Bassett, Jan, DF3
Concise Oxford dictionary of current English, Sykes, J. B., AD53
The concise Oxford dictionary of earth sciences, EE4
The concise Oxford dictionary of English etymology, AD15
The concise Oxford dictionary of literary terms, BD31
The concise Scots dictionary, AD59
Concise veterinary dictionary, EH27
A concordance to Middle English metrical romances, Saito, Toshio, BD209
Concrete poetry, McCullough, Kathleen, BD130
Condensed chemical dictionary, ED10
The condition of education, CB147
The condition of teaching, CB148
Conditions of work and quality of working life, CH280
Confederación Española de Centros de Estudios Locales. *Dialectología hispánica y geografía lingüística en los estudios locales (1920–1984)*, BC53
Confederate imprints, Crandall, Marjorie, DB30
——— Parrish, T. Michael, DB30
Confederate research sources, Neagles, James C., AK6, DB32
Confederation of American Indians. *Indian reservations*, CC229
Conference on College Composition and Communication (U.S.). *CCCC bibliography of composition and rhetoric*, BD142
Confraternity of Christian Doctrine. *The New American Bible. Revised New Testament*, BB37
Congregate care by county, CC55, EK61
The Congregationalists, Youngs, J. William T., BB114
Congress A to Z, CJ100
Congress and law-making, Goehlert, Robert, CJ92
Congress and the nation, CJ101
Congress & defense, CJ99
Congressional committees, 1789–1982, Stubbs, Walter, AG15, CJ98

Congressional Information Service. *CIS federal register index*, CK53

—— *CIS foreign gazetteers [of the] USBGN*, CL27

—— *CIS index to presidential executive orders & proclamations*, AG20

—— *CIS index to presidential executive orders & proclamations : Supplement*, AG21

—— *CIS index to unpublished U.S. House of Representatives committee hearings, 1833–1936*, AG16

—— *CIS index to unpublished U.S. Senate committee hearings*, AG17, AG18

—— *CIS index to U.S. executive branch documents, 1789–1909*, AG22

—— *CIS index to U.S. Senate executive document & reports*, AG12

—— *CIS U.S. congressional committee hearings index*, AG19

—— *Congressional masterfile 1*, AG13

—— *Congressional masterfile 2*, AG14

—— *Foreign gazetteers of the U.S. Board on Geographic Names*, CL28

—— *Guide to 1980 U.S. decennial census publications*, CG29

Congressional masterfile 1, AG13

Congressional masterfile 2, AG14

The Congressional Medal of Honor, CJ280

Congressional practice and procedure, Tiefer, Charles, CJ102

Congressional publications and proceedings, Zwirn, Jerrold, AG6, CJ95

Congressional Quarterly, inc. *Congress A to Z*, CJ100

Congressional Quarterly weekly report, CJ134

Congressional Quarterly's guide to the presidency, CJ73

Congressional Quarterly's guide to the U.S. Supreme Court, Witt, Elder, CK61

Congressional Quarterly's guide to U.S. elections, CJ112, CJ115, CJ109

Congressional voting guide, Bosnich, Victor W., CJ96

Conibear, Shirley A. *First aid manual for chemical accidents*, ED17

Conlon, Pierre M. *Le siècle des lumières*, AA113, DC1

Connelly, Owen. *Historical dictionary of Napoleonic France, 1799–1815*, DC63, DC66

Connor, Billie M. *Ottemiller's index to plays in collections*, BD86

Connor, Leonard P. *Welding handbook*, EJ84

Conolly, L. W. *The Oxford companion to Canadian theatre*, BG23

Conquest, John. *Trouble is their business*, BD102

Conran, Terence. *The Conran directory of design*, BF38

The Conran directory of design, BF38

Consejo Nacional de Población (Mexico). *Catálogo de publicaciones*, CG64

Conservation *see* **Fine arts—restoration and conservation**

Conservatism, AE26, CJ52, CJ72

Considine, Douglas M. *Van Nostrand's scientific encyclopedia*, EA39

Consolidated bibliography of county histories in fifty states in 1961, Peterson, Clarence S., DB41

Consolidated index of translations into English II, EA16

Consortium for the Study of Intelligence. *Bibliography on Soviet intelligence and security services*, CJ287

Consortium of Latin American Studies Programs. *A directory of Latin American studies in the United States*, DB102

Consortium of Social Science Associations. *Guide to federal funding for social scientists*, CA37

Constantinides, George C. *Intelligence and espionage*, CJ285

The Constitution of the United States, Reams, Bernard D., CK118

The constitutional law dictionary : vol. 1, Individual rights, suppl. 1, Chandler, Ralph C., CK114

Constitutions

United States, CK113, CK114, CK115, CK116, CK117, CK118

Construction index, BE119

Consultants and consulting, CH160

Consultants and consulting organizations directory, CH160

Consumer Europe, CH328

The consumer health information source book, Rees, Alan M., EK15

Consumer sourcebook, CH176

Consumerism, CH176, CH326

Contemporaries of Erasmus, BA26

Contemporary American business leaders, Ingham, John N., CH146

Contemporary American women sculptors, Watson-Jones, Virginia, BE79, BE167

Contemporary architects, BF62, BE132

Contemporary artists, BF62, BE78

Contemporary authors autobiography series, AJ14

Contemporary authors bibliographical series, AJ15

Contemporary authors of the German-speaking countries of Europe, Krewson, Margrit B., BD287

Contemporary black American playwrights and their plays, Peterson, Bernard L., BG40

Contemporary Canadian politics, Mahler, Gregory S., CJ157

Contemporary designers, BF14

Contemporary dramatists, BD88

Contemporary graphic artists, BE160

Contemporary Latin American fiction, Brower, Keith H., BD339

Contemporary novelists, BD93

Contemporary photographers, BF62

Contemporary poets, BD131

The contemporary printed literature of the English Counter-Reformation between 1558 and 1640, Allison, Antony Francis, BB115

Contemporary quotations, BD66

Contemporary Turkish writers, Mitler, Louis, BD383

Contento, William. *Index to crime and mystery anthologies*, BD103

—— *Index to science fiction anthologies and collections*, BD120

—— *Science fiction, fantasy & horror*, BD120

Contents of contemporary mathematical journals and new publications, EF4

Contents pages in education, CB46

The Continuum dictionary of women's biography, AJ9

The contributors' index to the Dictionary of national biography, 1885–1901, Fenwick, Gillian, AJ67

Controversial issues in librarianship, Herring, Mark Youngblood, AB3

Controvich, James T. *The central Pacific campaign, 1943–1944*, DB15

Conway, H. McKinley. *The weather handbook*, EE31

Conway's all the world's fighting ships, 1947–1982, CJ264

Cook, Barrie. *The coin atlas*, BF49

Cook, Chris. *African political facts since 1945*, CJ149

—— *British historical facts, 1688–1760*, DC119

—— *Dictionary of historical terms*, DA12

—— *European political facts, 1918–84*, CJ163

—— *The Facts on File world political almanac*, CJ140

—— *The Longman handbook of modern British history, 1714–1987*, DC120

—— *The Longman handbook of modern European history, 1763–1985*, DC11

—— *Macmillan dictionary of historical terms*, DA12

—— *Sources in European political history*, DC9

Cook, Elizabeth. *550 books on Buddhism*, BB122

Cook, John. *A guide to commonwealth government information sources*, AG30

Cook, Marjorie. *Bibliography of the Summer Institute of Linguistics, Philippines, 1953–1984*, BC61

Cook, Michael L. *Mystery, detective, and espionage fiction*, BD104

Cookbooks, EH36

Cookerly, J. Richard. *A directory of credentials in counseling and psychotherapy*, CD26

Coombs, J. *The international biotechnology directory*, EJ17

Coombs-Ficke, Susan. *U.S. directory and source book on aging, 1989–90*, CC61

Cooper, B. Lee. *The literature of rock, II, 1979–1983*, BH136

—— *A resource guide to themes in contemporary American song lyrics, 1950–1985*, BH141

—— *Rockabilly*, BH125

Cooperative Africana Microform Project (U.S.). *CAMP catalog*, DD16

Cooperative learning, CB21

Coordinating Council of Literary Magazines (U.S.). *Directory of literary magazines*, AE21, BD160

Coover, James. *Antiquarian catalogues of musical interest*, BH8

Coppa, Frank J. *Modern Italian history*, DC155

Copping, Debbie A. *Ford list of British parliamentary papers, 1974–1983, together with specialist commentaries*, AG43

Copy preparation, AA53, AA54, AA55, AA56, AA57, AA58, BC26, BC27, BD13, CC311, EK35

bibliography, AA59

Corbin, John. *Find the law in the library*, CK4

Corbin, John Boyd. *Acquisitions management and collection development in libraries*, AB67

Corbin, Peter. *An annotated critical bibliography of Jacobean and Caroline comedy*, BD233

Corbitt, Robert A. *Standard handbook of environmental engineering*, EJ31

Cordasco, Francesco. *American medical imprints, 1820–1910*, EK8

—— *Dictionary of American immigration history*, CC175, DB61

—— *The Italian emigration to the United States, 1880–1930*, CC162

—— *The new American immigration*, CC163

Cordasco, Michael Vaughn. *The Italian emigration to the United States, 1880–1930*, CC162

Cordell, Geoffrey A. *Dictionary of alkaloids*, ED31, EK108

Core list of books and journals in science and technology, Powell, Russell H., EA7

Corkill, David. *Ecuador*, DB119

Corley, Dawn. *New day/New Deal*, DB39

Cornejo A., Manuel. *Publicaciones oficiales de Chile, 1973–1983*, AG32

Corning Museum of Glass. *Guide to trade catalogs from the Corning Museum of Glass*, BF18

Cornish, Graham P. *Religious periodicals directory*, BB3

Corns, Thomas N. *Computers and literature*, BD16

Corominas, Joan. *Diccionari etimològic i complementari de la llengua catalana*, AD81

The corporate 1000, CH111

The corporate directory, CH112

The corporate finance bluebook, CH241

Corporate foundation profiles, CA32

Corporate technology directory, EA10, CH113

Corporation for Public Broadcasting. *Role portrayal and stereotyping on television,* CH201

Corporations
  art collections, BE52
  bibliography, CH141
  charitable contributions, CA39, CA41
  databases, CH109, CH125
  directories, CH103, CH109, CH112, CH113, CH114, CH115, CH119, CH139
    United States, CH111, CH127
  Europe, CH105
  foreign ownership, CH351
  history, CH139
  public relations, CH71, CJ65
Corporations, foreign, CH293
Corporations, nonprofit, CH122, CH158
Corpus Christianorum. Lingua patrum, BC43
Corrêa, Carlos Humberto. *Catálogo das dissertações e teses dos cursos de pós-graduação em História, 1973–1985,* DB112
Correspondence schools, CB113
Corrosion and anticorrosives, EJ85
Corsini, Raymond J. *Concise encyclopedia of psychology,* CD10
Corsten, Severin. *Der Buchdruck im 15. Jahrhundert,* AA45
—— *Lexikon des gesamten Buchwesens,* AA46
Cortada, James W. *Annotated bibliography on the history of data processing,* EJ53
—— *A bibliographic guide to the history of computing, computers, and the information processing industry,* EJ53
—— *Historical dictionary of the Spanish Civil War 1936–1939,* DC188
Cortelazzo, Manlio. *Dizionario etimologico della lingua italiana,* AD131
Cosgrove, Art. *A new history of Ireland,* DC153
Costa Rica, CG49
Costa Rica. *Censo de población, 1984,* CG49
Costinescu, Mariana. *Dicţionarul limbii române literare vechi, 1640–1780,* AD147
Costume and fashion
  bibliography, BF29
  biography, BF32, BF33
  encyclopedias, BF30
  history, BF31
Côte d'Ivoire *see* **Ivory Coast**
Coteanu, Ion. *Dicţionarul limbii române,* AD148
Cotterell, Arthur. *The illustrated encyclopedia of myths & legends,* CF2
Cottrill, Tim. *Science fiction and fantasy series and sequels,* BD112
Couch, James V. *Computer use in psychology,* CD28
Council for British Archaeology. *British archaeological abstracts,* DA32
Council for Exceptional Children. *Exceptional child education abstracts,* CB54
—— *Exceptional child education resources,* CB55
Council of Biology Editors. Scientific Illustration Committee. *Illustrating science,* EA66
Council of Economic Advisers (U.S.). *Biographical directory of the Council of Economic Advisers,* CH22
Council of Planning Librarians. *An annotated bibliography and index covering CPL bibliographies 1–253, January 1979–December 1989,* CC159
—— *CPL bibliography,* CC159
Council of Societies for the Study of Religion. *Directory of departments and programs of religious studies in North America,* BB32
Council of State Governments. *Interstate compacts and agencies,* AG26
Council of Urban Boards of Education. *Survey of public education in the nation's urban school districts,* CB152

Council on International Educational Exchange. *Work, study, travel abroad,* CB86
The country house described, Holmes, Michael, BE120
Country profile, CH28
Country report, CH28
County business patterns, CH332
—— United States. Bureau of the Census, CH306
County courthouse book, Bentley, Elizabeth Petty, AK15
Coutts, Brian E. *Reference sources in history,* DA1
Couty, Daniel. *Dictionnaire des littératures de langue française,* BD312
The cover story index, 1960–1989, AE75
Cowden, Robert H. *Concert and opera conductors,* BH88
—— *Concert and opera singers,* BH88
Cox, Michael. *The language of biotechnology,* EJ19
Coyle, Jean M. *Women and aging,* CC37, CC255
Coysh, A. W. *The dictionary of blue and white printed pottery 1780–1880,* BF24
Crabtree, Adam. *Animal magnetism, early hypnotism, and psychical research, 1766–1925,* CD50
Crafts, BF1
Crafts-Lighty, A. *Information sources in biotechnology,* EJ18
Craig, Bruce D. *Handbook of corrosion data,* EJ85
Craig, Fred W. S. *Britain votes,* CJ179, CJ180
—— *British electoral facts,* CJ179, CJ181, CJ182
—— *British electoral facts, 1832–1987,* CJ180
—— *British general election manifestos, 1959–1987,* CJ176
—— *British parliamentary election results,* CJ179, CJ180
—— *British parliamentary election results, 1832–1885,* CJ181
—— *British parliamentary election results, 1885–1918,* CJ182
—— *British parliamentary election statistics,* CJ180
Craig, Robert D. *Dictionary of Polynesian mythology,* CF15
Craigie, William A. Sir. *A dictionary of the older Scottish tongue,* AD60
Cramp, Stanley. *Handbook of the birds of Europe, the Middle East and North Africa,* EC49
Crampton, R. J. *Bulgaria,* DC34
Crandall, Marjorie. *Confederate imprints,* DB30
Craven, Robert R. *Symphony orchestras of the United States,* BH150
Craven, Toni. *Harper's Bible pronunciation guide,* BB52
Crawford, Tad. *Legal guide for the visual artist,* BE107, BE109, CK85, CK88
—— *Writer's legal guide,* BE107, CK85
Crawford, Walt. *MARC for library use,* AB77
Creative literature of Trinidad and Tobago, Wharton-Lake, Beverly D., BD285
Credit unions, CH249
Credits and careers for adult learners, Egelston, Roberta Riethmiller, CB124
Cree, Jan. *Directory of special libraries in Australia,* AB24
Creech, Heather. *A guide to legal research in Papua New Guinea,* CK48
Creel, Austin B. *Guide to Indian philosophy,* BA7
Creswell, K. A. C. *Bibliography of the architecture, arts, and crafts of Islam to 1st Jan. 1960,* BE11
Cribb, Joe. *The coin atlas,* BF49
Crimando, William. *Staff training,* CH150
Crime and the elderly, Aday, Ron H., CC34

Criminal justice documents, Berens, John F., CK97
Criminal justice research in libraries, Lutzker, Marilyn, CK96
Criminology; *see also* **Police**
  bibliography, CC34, CK97, CK99
  dictionaries, CK101
  directories, CK105
  encyclopedias, CK100, CK101, CK103
  guides, CK96
Crisp, Deborah. *Bibliography of Australian music,* BH40
Crispell, Diane. *The insider's guide to demographic know-how,* CH323
A critical bibliography of writings on Judaism, Griffiths, David B., BB132
A critical dictionary of educational concepts, Barrow, Robin, CB66
A critical dictionary of sociology, Boudon, Raymond, CC14
A critical dictionary of the French Revolution, DC52
Critical guide to Catholic reference books, McCabe, James Patrick, BB116
Critical inventory of films on art, BF52
Critical review of books in religion, BB19
Critical survey of drama, BD230
Critical survey of literary theory, BD18
Croatoserbian-English encyclopedic dictionary, AD160
Croft, P. J. *Index of English literary manuscripts,* BD215
Crofton, Ian. *A dictionary of musical quotations,* BH63
Cronjé, Ulrich Jerome. *Groot woordeboek,* AD68
Crop protection chemicals reference, EH19
Crosby, Gillian. *CPA world directory of old age,* CC56
Crosman, Christopher. *From museums, galleries, and studios,* BE76
Cross index title guide to classical music, Pallay, Steven G., BH20
Cross index title guide to opera and operetta, Pallay, Steven G., BH20
Crossley, Charles A. *Walford's guide to reference material,* AA67, EA6
Crouch, Archie R. *Christianity in China,* BB104
Crowley, F. K. *Australians,* DF2
Crumb, Lawrence N. *The Oxford Movement and its leaders,* BB77
Crusades, DA54
Crystal, David. *The Cambridge encyclopedia of language,* BC7
—— *A dictionary of linguistics and phonetics,* BC12
Crystallography, EE22
Cuadra directory of databases, AB92
Cuba
  history
    bibliography, DB144, DB145
    manuscripts and archives, DB146
Cuba, Pérez, Louis A., DB145
Cuba, 1953–1978, Chilcote, Ronald H., DB144
Cuban exile periodicals at the University of Miami Library, Varona, Esperanza Bravo de, CC239
Cuban literature, BD340, BD341
Cubans in the United States, MacCorkle, Lyn, CC238
Cuff, David J. *The United States energy atlas,* EJ73
Culme, John. *The directory of gold and silversmiths 1838–1914,* BF46
—— *The directory of gold & silversmiths, jewellers, and allied traders, 1838–1914,* BF45
Cults, BB2, BB34
Cultural atlas of Mesopotamia and the ancient Near East, Roaf, Michael, DA38
Cultural atlas of Russia and the Soviet Union, Milner-Gulland, R. R., DC216

Cummings, Gary. *A New Guinea bibliography*, AA169, DG11

Cummings, Paul. *Dictionary of contemporary American artists*, BE92

Cumulative bibliography of Victorian studies, 1976–1980, BD212

Cumulative index of sociology journals, 1971–1985, Lantz, Judith C., CC13

Cumulative index to journals in education, CB16

Cumulative index to nursing & allided health literature, EK89

Cumulative index to Tests in microfiche, 1975–1987, CD39

Cumulative record of exhibition catalogues, Rutledge, Anna Wells, BE66

Cunningham, Peter. *A handbook for London, past and present*, DC137

Cunningham, Phyllis M. *Handbook of adult and continuing education*, CB125

—— *The independent learners' sourcebook*, CB40

Curley, Arthur. *Building library collections*, AB64

Currency *see* **Coins, medals, currency**

Current awareness in biological sciences, EC8

Current bibliographies in medicine, EK9

Current biography, AJ17

Current biography. Cumulated index, 1940–1985, AJ16

Current British journals: a bibliographic guide, AE45

Current Central American-U.S. relations, Nordquist, Joan, DB95

Current contents, EA25, EA31

Current contents on diskette, EA24

Current contents search, EA25

Current dividend record, CH246

Current index to journals in education, CB1, CB52, CB54, CB47

Current index to statistics, EF6

Current Indian periodicals in English, Gidwani, N. N., AE50

—— Navalani, K., AE50

Current issues resource builder, Smallwood, Carol, CA21

Current law index, CK58

Current literature on aging, CC49

Current mathematical publications, EF6, EF4

Current military literature, CJ250

Current military & political literature, CJ250

Current research in Britain, CA17, EA53

Current research inventory, DB128

Current world affairs, CJ251

Curricula in the atmospheric, oceanic and related sciences, EE27

Curry, Hayden. *A legal guide for lesbian and gay couples*, CC156

Curtain times, Guernsey, Otis L., BG31

Cutolo, Vicente Osvaldo. *Nuevo diccionario biografico argentino*, AJ32

Cyclopedia of literary characters II, BD97

Cylke, Frank Kurt. *International directory of tactile map collections*, CL45

Cypess, Sandra Messinger. *Women authors of modern Hispanic South America*, BD331

Cyprus, AA96, DC38

Cyr, Helen W. *A filmography of the Third World, 1976–1983*, BG68

—— *The Third World in film and video*, BG68

Cytology, EC14, EC66

Czajka, John L. *Digest of data on persons with disabilities*, CC112

Czapliński, Władysław. *The historical atlas of Poland*, DC174

Czech and Slovak literature in English, Kovtun, George J., BD353

Czech-English technical dictionary, EA47

Czech language, AD83, EA46, EA47

Czech literature, BD352, BD353

Czechoslovakia
   bibliography, AA97, AA98, AA99
   current, AA100
   biography, AJ43, AJ44
   history
      bibliography, DC40, DC41

Czechoslovakia, Short, David, DC41

Członkowie Polskiej Akademii Nauk, Krzyzanowska, Jadwiga, AJ86

D & B Europe. *Duns Europa*, CH105

daai, BF9

DDR Handbuch, CJ172

Diasle, Faitelson-Weiser, Silvia, BC50

DMI, CH99

DMS code name handbook, CJ259

Da Graça, John V. *Heads of state and government*, CJ145

Daemmrich, Horst S. *Themes & motifs in western literature*, BD47

Daemmrich, Ingrid. *Themes & motifs in western literature*, BD47

Daftar majalah Indonesia yang telah mempunyai ISSN, Zulkarjono, Maesarah, AE52

Daguerrotypes : Hall of Fame members and other immortals, MacFarlane, Paul, BJ22

Dahl, Svend. *Dansk biografisk leksikon*, AJ45

Dahlhaus, Carl. *Brockhaus Riemann Musiklexikon*, BH48

—— *Pipers Enzyklopädie des Musiktheaters*, BH58

Dahlmann, F. C. *Dahlmann-Waitz Quellenkunde der deutschen Geschichte*, DC80, DC81

Dahlmann-Waitz Quellenkunde der deutschen Geschichte, Dahlmann, F. C., DC80, DC81

Daily, Jay Elwood. *Encyclopedia of library and information science*, AB12

Dalal-Clayton, D. B. *Black's agricultural dictionary*, EH10

Dalby, David. *Language map of Africa and the adjacent islands*, BC58

—— *A thesaurus of African languages*, BC58

Dale, Doris Cruger. *A directory of oral history tapes of librarians in the United States and Canada*, AB37

Dale, Edgar. *The educator's quotebook*, CB77

Dale, Laura. *Parapsychology*, CD55

D'Aleo, Richard J. *FEDfind*, AG3

Dalil al-matbuat al-miṣriyah, 1940–1956, AA105

Dallet, Sylvie. *Filmographie mondiale de la Révolution française*, DC48

Damschroder, David. *Music theory from Zarlino to Schenker*, BH9

Danby, Colin. *Honduras bibliography and research guide*, DB122

Dance, Daryl Cumber. *Fifty Caribbean writers*, BD283

Dance
   bibliography, BG45, BG46, BG47
   encyclopedias, BH58
   indexes, BG49
   periodicals, BG48, BH33

Dance, Forbes, Fred R., BG46

Dangerous properties of industrial materials, Sax, N. Irving, ED21

D'Angiolini, Piero. *Guida generale degli archivi di Stato italiani*, DC157

Dania polyglotta, AA102

Daniel, Odile. *Albanie, une bibliographie historique*, DC20

Daniells, Lorna. *Business information sources*, CH83

Danilov, Victor J. *America's science museums*, EA65

Danish foreign policy, Holtermann, Henrik, DC42

Danish language, AD84

Danko, Steven I. *Black holes*, EB1

Dann, Graham. *Barbados*, DB143

Dansk anmeldelsesindeks, AA102

Dansk artikelindeks. Aviser og tidsskrifter, AA102

Dansk billedfortegnelse, AA102

Dansk biografisk leksikon, AJ45

Dansk bogfortegnelse, AA102, AA102

Dansk Bogfortegnelse [for aarene], AA101

Dansk lydfortegnelse, AA102

Dansk musikfortegnelse, AA102

Dansk periodicafortegnelse, AA102

Danske grammofonplader og kassetteband, AA102

Dār al-Kutub al-Qaṭarīyah. *Qā'imat al-intāj al-fikrī al-Qaṭarī li-'ām*, AA176

Darch, Colin. *Mozambique*, DD45

Dare, Philip N. *American communes to 1860*, DB6

Darley, Gillian. *Dictionary of ornament*, BF41

Darling, Louise. *Handbook of medical library practice*, AB56, EK1

Darling, Pamela W. *Preservation planning program*, AB104

Darnay, Arsen J. *American salaries and wages survey*, CH334

—— *Manufacturing USA*, CH306

Darnay, Brigitte T. *Life sciences organizations and agencies directory*, EC20

Dars, Celestine. *Subject catalogue of paintings in public collections*, BE149

The Dartnell personnel administration handbook, CH165

The Dartnell public relations handbook, Dilenschneider, Robert L., CH74

Data base alert, AB93

Data base directory, AB93

Data for biochemical research, EC62

Database directory, AB93

Databases
   aeronautical and space engineering, EJ15
   agriculture, EC5, EH5, EH6, EH7, EH8
   architecture, BE113
   bibliography
      France, AA116
   bibliography, national, AA151
      Finland, AA109
      Norway, AA167
   biological sciences, EC4, EC5, EC6, EC7, EC8, EH7
   book trade, AB22
   business, AB96, CH82, CH87, CH88, CH89, CH99, CH102, CH109, CH116, CH117, CH124, CH125, CH126, CH148, CH153, CH299, CH301, CH314, CH320
   census data, CH329
   chemistry, ED6, ED19, ED27, ED37, ED38, EK119
   computer science, EJ54, EJ57
   current events, DA62
   directories, AB89, AB90, AB91, AB92, AB93, AB94, AB95, CG35
   economics, CH3, CH29, CH133, CH134
   education, CB12, CB48, CB52, CB54, CB92, CB103, CB105, CB118, CD43
   engineering, EJ2
   environment and environmental problems, EJ26, EJ27
   finance and banking, CH220, CH244
   fine arts, BE16, BE18, BE21, BE23, BE63
   general, AC3
   geography, CL5
   geology, EE5
   government publications, AG13, AG14, AG37
   guides, AB96, CH82
   history, DA62
   language and literature, BD9
   law, CK18, CK22, CK55, CK58, CK79, CK122
   librarianship and library resources, AB21, AB22, AB40
   library and information science, AB6
   marketing, CH329
   mathematics, EF5, EF6
   medical and health sciences, EK80
   medicine, EK20, EK24, EK27, EK29, EK30, EK31, EK32, EK33, EK63

metals, EJ14
music, BH43, BH45, BH157
newspapers, AF13
nursing, EK89
oceanography, EE39
patents and trademarks, CH302
periodicals, AE9
physics, EB3, EG2, EG3, EJ44
psychology, CD45
religion, BB16, BB17, BB21
science and technology, EA9, EA10, EA23,
  EA24, EA25, EA26, EA28, EA29, EA31,
  EA37
  directories, EA57
social and behavioral sciences, EA24
sociology, CC12, CC28, CC50, CC127
statistics and demography, CG35
toxicology, EK129
water resources and water pollution, EE24,
  EJ34
zoology, EC39
Daten der griechischen und römischen
  Geschichte, Lauffer, Siegfried, DA44
Datensammlungen in der Physik = Data
  compilations in physics, Behrens, Heinrich,
  EG1
Datta, Amaresh. Encyclopaedia of Indian
  literature, BD377
David, Jack. The annotated bibliography of
  Canada's major authors, BD277
David, Zdeněk V. Scholars' guide to
  Washington, D.C. for cartography and remote
  sensing imagery, CL38
—— Scholars' guide to Washington, D.C. for
  southwest European studies, DC10
Davidson, Henry A. Handbook of
  parliamentary procedure, CJ225
Davies, J. G. A new dictionary of liturgy and
  worship, BB89
—— The new Westminster dictionary of
  liturgy and worship, BB89
—— The Westminster dictionary of worship,
  BB89
Davies, J. S. Amino acids and peptides, ED35
Davies, Leslie. Harper dictionary of economics,
  CH11
Davies, Robert H. The struggle for South Africa,
  CJ202
Davies, William David. The Cambridge history
  of Judaism, BB137
Davis, Charles Hargis. Library and information
  science, AB7
Davis, Clive M. Sexuality-related measures,
  CC157
Davis, Deta S. Computer applications in music,
  BH10
Davis, Donald G. American library history,
  AB2
—— ARBA guide to library science literature,
  1970–1983, AB1
Davis, Elisabeth B. Guide to information
  sources in the botanical sciences, EC27
Davis, Lenwood G. A bibliographical guide to
  black studies programs in the United States,
  CC194
—— The black aged in the United States,
  CC38
—— The black family in the United States,
  CC124
—— Black-Jewish relations in the United
  States, 1752–1984, CC195
Davis, Nathaniel. Afro-American reference,
  CC189
Davis, Robert H. Colombia, DB118
Davis, Sandra L. Sexuality-related measures,
  CC157
Davis, Stephen D. Plants in danger, EC30
Davis, William Edmund. Resource guide to
  special education, CB122
Davydova, A. G. Literatura o narodonaselenii,
  CG73
Dawson, Joseph G. The late 19th century U.S.
  Army, 1865–1898, CJ271

Dawson, R. M. C. Data for biochemical
  research, EC62
Day, Alan Edwin. Search for the Northwest
  Passage, DB82
Day, Alan J. Peace movements of the world,
  CJ311
—— Political parties of the world, CJ29, CJ33
—— A world record of major conflict areas,
  CJ35
De Francisci, Giovanni. Dictionary of medical
  syndromes, EK55
De Kock, W. J. Dictionary of South African
  biography, AJ92
De la Croix, Horst. Gardner's art through the
  ages, BE71
De Lerma, Dominique-René. Black music and
  musicians in The new Grove dictionary of
  American music and The new Harvard
  dictionary of music, BH93
De Luise, Alexandra A. Historical bibliography
  of art museum serials from the United States
  and Canada, BE30
De Mente, Boye. Everything Japanese, DE79
De Mowbray, Stephen. Key facts in Soviet
  history, DC206
De Silva, Daya. The Portuguese in Asia, DE1
De Stricker, Ulla. Business online, AB96, CH82
De Vendittis, Luigi. La letteratura italiana,
  BD316
De Weever, Jacqueline. A Chaucer name
  dictionary, BD256
De Winter, Patrick M. European decorative
  arts, 1400–1600, BF5
De Young, Mary. Child molestation, CC80
—— Incest, CC125
Deaf, CC102, CC104, CC105
A deafness collection, Ritter, Audrey L., CC104
De'ak, Gloria. Guide to research and
  scholarship in Hungary, DC143
Dean, John Aurie. Handbook of organic
  chemistry, ED39
Deane, Phyllis. A lexicon of economics, CH10
Dearman, John Andrew. Harper's Bible
  pronunciation guide, BB52
Death and dying
  bibliography, CC93, CC94, CC95, CC96,
    CC97, CC98, CC99
  encyclopedias, CC100
Death and dying, Poteet, G. Howard, CC97
Death and dying : a bibliography, 1974–1978,
  Poteet, G. Howard, CC98
Death education, CC95
Debates and proceedings of the British
  parliaments, Jones, David Lewis, AG36
Debus, Allen G. The complete entertainment
  discography, from 1897 to 1942, BH142
Decalo, S. Benin, DD6
—— Chad, DD6
—— Niger, DD6
—— Togo, DD6
Deccan College Post-graduate and Research
  Institute. An encyclopaedic dictionary of
  Sanskrit on historical principles, AD156
Decisions on geographic names in the United
  States, United States Board on Geographic
  Names, CL36
Decorative arts, BE103, BF5, BF7, BF9, BF13,
  BF34, BF41
Decorative arts and household furnishings in
  America, 1650–1920, BF34
Decrees of the ecumenical councils, BB98
Deering, Catherine M. Union list of American
  studies periodicals in UK libraries, AB28
Dees, Anthonij. Atlas des formes linguistiques
  des textes littéraires de l'ancien français,
  BC39
Defense Marketing Services, Inc. International
  code name directory, CJ259
Degenhardt, Henry W. Political dissent, CJ38
—— Political parties of the world, CJ29
—— Revolutionary and dissident movements,
  CJ38

—— Treaties and alliances of the world,
  CK111
DeGeorge, R.T. Philosopher's guide, BA1
DeGregorio, William A. The complete book of
  U.S. presidents, CJ90
Dehlinger, Christel. Metzler Philosophen
  Lexikon, BA25
Dejevsky, Nikolai J. Cultural atlas of Russia
  and the Soviet Union, DC216
Del Tutto Palma, L. Bibliografia dell'Italia
  antica, DC154
DeLancey, Mark. Cameroon, DD5, DD28
—— Somalia, DD52
DeLashmitt, Eleanor. Annuals and surveys
  appearing in legal periodicals, CK26
Delaunay, Daniel. Demografía en el Ecuador,
  CG50
—— Poblaciones de las parroquias, Ecuador,
  1950–1982, CG50
Deletant, Andrea. Romania, DC178
Deletant, Dennis. Romania, DC178
Delgado, Susana. Chicano organizations
  directory, CC241
Delivering government services, Murin, William
  F., CJ220
Della Corte, Francesco. Dizionario degli
  scrittori greci e latini, BD364
DeLoach, Charles. The quotable Shakespeare,
  BD266
Delorme, Robert. Latin America, 1983–1987,
  DB91
Delson, Eric. Encyclopedia of human evolution
  and prehistory, CE13
Delury, George E. World encyclopedia of
  political systems & parties, CJ136
Democracy movement in Communist China,
  CJ162, DE51
Demografía en el Ecuador, Delaunay, Daniel,
  CG50
Demography see Statistics and demography
Demougin, Jacques. Dictionnaire historique,
  thématique et technique des littératures,
  BD25
Dempsey, Hugh A. Bibliography of the
  Blackfoot, CC218
Dengel, Holk H. Annotated bibliography of new
  Indonesian literature on the history of
  Indonesia, DE66
Denmark
  bibliography, AA102
    19th and 20th centuries, AA101
  biography, AJ45, AJ91
  foreign relations, DC42
  history
    bibliography, DC43
Denmark, Miller, Kenneth E., DC43
Dennis, Marguerite J. Dollars for scholars,
  CB157
Dent, David W. Handbook of political science
  research on Latin America, CJ195
Dentistry
  dictionaries, EK85, EK86
  guides, EK82, EK83
  periodicals, EK84
Dentistry journals and serials, Kowitz, Aletha,
  EK84
Denvir, Bernard. The Thames and Hudson
  encyclopaedia of Impressionism, BE33
Department of Defense dictionary of military
  and associated terms, CJ257
The Department of State and American
  diplomacy, Goehlert, Robert, CJ75
Depression, CD16, DB39
Derdak, Thomas. International directory of
  company histories, CH139
Derivan, William J. Prevention education,
  CB22, CC113
Derksen, Charlotte. Union list of geologic field
  trip guidebooks of North America, EE21
Dermineur, Bernard. Catalogue général des
  ouvrages en langue française, 1926–1929,
  AA115
Dervaes, Claudine. The travel dictionary, BJ40

Derwent Publications, Ltd. *Thesaurus of agricultural organisms, pests, weeds, and diseases*, EH13

Deschler, Lewis. *Deschler's precedents*, CJ102

—— *Deschler's procedure*, CJ102

Deschler's precedents, Deschler, Lewis, CJ102

Deschler's procedure, Deschler, Lewis, CJ102

A descriptive bibliography of art music by Israeli composers, Tischler, Alice, BH86

A descriptive checklist of book catalogues separately printed in America, 1693–1800, Winans, Robert B., BE111

Desgraves, Louis. *Répertoire bibliographique des livres imprimés en France au XVIIe siècle*, AA112

—— *Répertoire bibliographique des livres imprimés en France au XVIIIe siècle*, AA114

Design, BF9, BF14

Design & applied arts index, BF9

Design index, BF9

Deskbook encyclopedia of American school law, CB153

A desktop reference manual of compliance terms, CH226

Deslandres, Yvonne. *20,000 years of fashion*, BF31

Desmond, Ray. *Bibliography of British gardens*, BE141

Detailed statistics on the population of Israel by ethnic and religious group and urban and rural residence, 1950 to 2010, Roof, Michael K., CG58

Detailed statistics on the urban and rural population of Indonesia, 1950 to 2010, Way, Peter O., CG57

Detailed statistics on the urban and rural population of Pakistan, 1950 to 2010, Finch, Glenda, CG65

Detailed statistics on the urban and rural population of the Philippines, 1950 to 2010, Kinsella, Kevin G., CG68

Detective and mystery fiction, BD101, BD102, BD103, BD104, BD105, BD107, BD108

Detroit Public Library. *Job hunter's sourcebook*, CH337

Detwiler, Donald S. *West Germany*, DC85

Deubert, K. *Guide to the availability of theses II*, AB97

Deuss, Jean. *Banking in the U.S*, CH213

Deutch, Yvonne. *Man, myth & magic*, BB29, CD53, CF4

Deutsch-Skandinavisch im Vergleich, Braunmüller, Kurt, BC32

Deutsche Akademie der Wissenschaften zu Berlin. *Mittellateinisches Wörterbuch bis zum ausgehenden 13. [i.e. dreizehnten] Jahrhundert*, AD140

Deutsche Bibliographie-aktuell-CD-ROM, AA123

Deutsche Bibliographie. Hochschulschriften-Verzeichnis, AA122

Deutsche Bibliographie. Wöchentliches Verzeichnis, AA122

Deutsche Bibliographie. Wöchentliches Verzeichnis. Neuerscheinungen Sofortdienst (CIP), AA122

Deutsche Bibliographie. Zeitschriften-Verzeichnis, AE40

Deutsche Bibliothek (Frankfurt am Main, Germany). *Deutsche Bibliographie-aktuell-CD-ROM*, AA123

—— *Deutsche Bibliographie. Zeitschriften-Verzeichnis*, AE40

—— *Deutsche Nationalbibliographie und Bibliographie der im Ausland erschienenen deutschsprachigen Veröffentlichungen. Amstblatt. [. . .] Verzeichnis*, AA122

Deutsche literarische Zeitschriften, 1880–1945, Dietzel, Thomas, AE35, AE36

Die deutsche Literatur des Mittelalters, BD289

Deutsche Morgenländische Gesellschaft. *Wörterbuch der klassischen arabischen Sprache*, AD71

Deutsche Nationalbibligraphie, AA122

Deutsche Nationalbibliographie und Bibliographie der im Ausland erschienenen deutschsprachigen Veröffentlichungen. Amstblatt. [. . .] Verzeichnis, AA122

Die deutsche Photoliteratur 1839–1978, BF54

Deutsche Sprache im Reformationszeitalter, Pasierbsky, Fritz, BC33

Deutsche Wirtschaftsarchive, DC90

Die deutschen Literatur-Zeitschriften, 1815–1850, AE36

Die deutschen Literatur-Zeitschriften, 1850–1880, Estermann, Alfred Adolph, AE36

Die deutschen Literature-Zeitschriften, 1850–1880, Estermann, Alfred Adolph, AE35

Deutscher, Thomas Brian. *Contemporaries of Erasmus*, BA26

Deutscher biographischer Index, Koch, Hans-Albrecht, AJ56

Deutsches biographisches Archiv, AJ55

Deutsches biographisches Jahrbuch, Ihme, Heinrich, AJ58

Deutsches Literatur-Lexikon, Kosch, Wilhelm, BD291

Deutsches Literaturarchiv (Germany). *Deutsche literarische Zeitschriften, 1880–1945*, AE35

Deutsches Theater-Lexikon, Kosch, Wilhelm, BG37

Deutsches Wörterbuch, Grimm, Jacob, AD105

—— Mackensen, Lutz, AD114

—— Wahrig, Gerhard, AD107

Developing countries *see* **Third world**

Developing library and information center collections, Evans, G. Edward, AB65

Development aid, CH57

The development directory, CH58

Development of Hindu iconography, Banerjea, J. N., BE104

Development review and outlook, CH356

DeVenney, David P. *Early American choral music*, BH116

—— *Nineteenth-century American choral music*, BH116

Devine, Elizabeth. *The travelers' guide to European customs & manners*, BJ47

DeVito, Joseph A. *The communication handbook*, CH208

Devlin, Robert James. *Dictionary of the Russian Revolution*, DC207

Devriès, Anik. *Dictionnaire des éditeurs de musique française*, BH69

Dewdney, John C. *The Cambridge atlas of the Middle East and North Africa*, DE26

Dewey, Melvil. *Dewey decimal classification and relative index*, AB82

Dewey decimal classification and relative index, Dewey, Melvil, AB82

DeWhitt, Benjamin L. *A guide to pre-federal records in the National Archives*, DB26

DeWitt, Donald L. *American Indian resource materials in the Western History Collections, University of Oklahoma*, CC224

Di Benedetto, C. Anthony. *Successful industrial product innovation*, CH289

Di Berardino, Angelo. *Dizionario patristico e di antichità cristiane*, BB102

Diagnostic and statistical manual of mental disorders, CD29

—— American Psychiatric Association, CD18, CD21

Diakun, Nadia Odette. *Ucrainica at the University of Toronto Library*, DC213

Dialectología hispánica y geografía lingüística en los estudios locales (1920–1984), Viudas Camarasa, Antonio, BC53

Diamant, Lincoln. *The broadcast communications dictionary*, CH206

Diamond, Harold J. *Music analyses*, BH41

Diaries and letters

American, BD183, BD184, BD249

bibliography, BD250

British, BD216, BD249, BD251

Díaz Polanco, Héctor. *Directorio de antropólogos latinoamericanos, México*, CE20

DiCanio, Margaret. *The encyclopedia of marriage, divorce, and the family*, CC136

Diccionari etimològic i complementari de la llengua catalana, Corominas, Joan, AD81

Diccionario biobibliográfico de escritores contemporaneos de México, BD343

Diccionario biográfico del Ecuador, Pérez Pimentel, Rodolfo, AJ48

Diccionario de escritores hondureños, Argueta, Mario, BD342

Diccionario de escritores mexicanos, siglo XX, BD343

Diccionario de escritores uruguayos, Rela, Walter, BD348

Diccionario de historia de Venezuela, DB139

Diccionario de hombres y mujeres ilustres de Puerto Rico y de hechos históricos, Reynal, Vicente, AJ90

Diccionario de la zarzuela, BH105

Diccionario de lingüística de la escuela española, Abad Nebot, Francisco, BC11

Diccionario de literatura uruguaya, BD347

Diccionario de términos médicos, inglés-español, español-inglés, Ruiz Torres, Francisco, EK59

El diccionario del español chicano = The dictionary of Chicano Spanish, Galván, Roberto A., AD169

El diccionario del español de Tejas, AD169

Diccionario del español medieval, Heidelberger Akademie der Wissenschaften, AD168

—— Müller, Bodo, AD168

Diccionario demográfico multilingüe, CG10

Diccionario enciclopédico de México, Musacchio, Humberto, DB127

Diccionario etimológico español e hispánico, García de Diego, Vicente, AD166

Diccionario histórico biográfico de los conquistadores del Perú, Busto Duthurburu, José Antonio del, DB131

Diccionario histórico dominicano, Rutinel Domínguez, Ulises, DB148

Diccionario histórico y biográfico del Perú, siglos XV–XX, DB131

Dicionário das batalhas brasileiras, Donato, Hernâni, DB116

Dicionário de poetas contemporâneos, Igreja, Francisco, BD320

Dicionário de termos técnicos inglês-português, EA51

Dicionário histórico-biográfico brasileiro, 1930–1983, DB115

Dicke, Gerd. *Die Fabeln des Mittelalters und der frühen Neuzeit*, CF22

Dickinson, A. T. *Dickinson's American historical fiction*, BD173

Dickinson, Alis. *Doctoral dissertations in musicology. Second series*, BH28

Dickinson, John R. *The bibliography of marketing research methods*, CH311

Dickinson, Richard L. *Street talk in real estate*, CH350

Dickinson's American historical fiction, Dickinson, A. T., BD173

Dickson, Bruce J. *A research guide to central party and government meetings in China, 1949–1986*, DE52

Dickson, Lance E. *Legal bibliography index*, CK23

Dickson, Paul. *The Dickson baseball dictionary*, BJ21

Dickson, Roy. *The directory of Caribbean personalities in Britain and North America*, AJ40

The Dickson baseball dictionary, Dickson, Paul, BJ21

Dickstein, Ruth. *Women in LC's terms*, CC299

Dictionaries
bibliography, AD67
Dictionaries, encyclopedias, and other word-related books, AD67
Dicţionarul limbii române, AD148
Dicţionarul limbii române literare vechi, 1640–1780, Costinescu, Mariana, AD147
Dictionary and handbook of nuclear medicine and clinical imaging, Iturralde, Mario P., EK71
Dictionary catalog of the Research Libraries, New York Public Library. Research Libraries, AA27
Dictionary for business & finance, Terry, John V., CH237
Dictionary of 20th-century design, Pile, John F., BF38
Dictionary of 20th-century history, Brownstone, David M., DA59
Dictionary of accounting terms, Siegel, Joel G., CH63
Dictionary of administration and management, Banki, Ivan S., CH155
Dictionary of advanced manufacturing technology, Hunt, V. Daniel, CH292
Dictionary of advertising and direct mail terms, Imber, Jane, CH70
Dictionary of African historical biography, Lipschutz, Mark R., AJ29
Dictionary of Afro-American performers, Turner, Patricia, BH87
Dictionary of Afro-American slavery, CC174
Dictionary of Albanian literature, Elsie, Robert, BD351
Dictionary of alkaloids, ED37, ED31, EK108
A dictionary of American and British euphemisms, Holder, R. W., AD44
Dictionary of American biography, AJ24
Dictionary of American biography. Comprehensive index, AJ26
Dictionary of American biography. Supplement eight, AJ25
Dictionary of American children's fiction, 1859–1959, Helbig, Alethea, BD74
Dictionary of American children's fiction, 1960–1984, Helbig, Alethea, BD75
Dictionary of American conservatism, Filler, Louis, CJ52
Dictionary of American diplomatic history, Findling, John E., CJ53, DB64
Dictionary of American immigration history, CC175, DB61
Dictionary of American literary characters, BD174
Dictionary of American nursing biography, EK94, EK95
Dictionary of American regional English, AD52
Dictionary of American slang, Flexner, Stuart Berg, AD40
—— Wentworth, Harold, AD40
A dictionary of American social change, Filler, Louis, CA14
A dictionary of American social reform, CA14
A dictionary of ancient Near Eastern architecture, Leick, Gwendolyn, BE123
Dictionary of anthropology, CE12
—— Winick, Charles, CE15
Dictionary of antibiotics and related substances, ED37, ED32, EK109
*Dictionary of archival terminology =
Dictionnaire de terminologie archivistique : English and French, with equivalents in Dutch, German, Italian, Russian and Spanish,* AB73
Dictionary of artificial intelligence and robotics, Rosenberg, Jerry Martin, EJ64
Dictionary of Asian American history, CC212
Dictionary of astronomical names, Room, Adrian, EB9
A dictionary of Australian colloquialisms, Wilkes, G. A., AD58
Dictionary of aviation, Hall, R. J., CH188

Dictionary of banking and financial services, Rosenberg, Jerry Martin, CH233
Dictionary of banking terms, Fitch, Thomas P., CH228
Dictionary of behavioral assessment techniques, CD40
Dictionary of behavioral science, CD11
The dictionary of Bible and religion, BB22
A dictionary of Biblical interpretation, BB50
Dictionary of biochemistry, Stenesh, J., EC63
Dictionary of biochemistry and molecular biology, Stenesh, J., EC63
The dictionary of blue and white printed pottery 1780–1880, Coysh, A. W., BF24
A dictionary of book history, Feather, John, AA47
Dictionary of borrowed words, AD65
Dictionary of Brazilian literature, BD318
The dictionary of British and American homophones, Williams, Stephen N., AD31
A dictionary of British and American women writers, 1660–1800, BD168
The dictionary of British book illustrators and caricaturists, 1800–1914, Houfe, Simon, BE97
Dictionary of British children's fiction, Helbig, Alethea, BD76
Dictionary of British literary characters, BD174
Dictionary of British miniature painters, Foskett, Daphne, BE152
Dictionary of building, McMullan, Randall, BE124, EJ38
Dictionary of business biography, CH144
A dictionary of business quotations, CH96
The dictionary of cell biology, EC14
—— Dow, J. A. T., EC66
—— Lackie, J. M., EC66
Dictionary of changes in meaning, Room, Adrian, AD19
A dictionary of Christian ethics, Macquarrie, John, BB92
Dictionary of Christianity in America, BB84
The dictionary of classical mythology, Grimal, Pierre, CF11
Dictionary of coin names, Room, Adrian, BF50
Dictionary of collective nouns and group terms, Sparkes, Ivan George, AD28
The dictionary of composers and their music, Gilder, Eric, BH78
Dictionary of computers, data processing, and telecommunications, Rosenberg, Jerry Martin, EJ65
Dictionary of computers, informational processing, and telecommunications, Rosenberg, Jerry Martin, EJ65
Dictionary of computing, EJ61
Dictionary of concepts in general psychology, Popplestone, John A., CD19
Dictionary of concepts in history, Ritter, Harry, DA17
Dictionary of concepts in the philosophy of science, Durbin, Paul T., EA42
Dictionary of contemporary American artists, Cummings, Paul, BE92
The dictionary of contemporary politics of South America, Gunson, Phil, CJ194
The dictionary of contemporary politics of southern Africa, Williams, Gwyneth, CJ151
Dictionary of demography : biographies, Petersen, William, CG18
Dictionary of demography : multilingual glossary, Petersen, William, CG11
Dictionary of demography : terms, concepts, and institutions, Petersen, William, CG12
Dictionary of development, CH49
Dictionary of developmental and educational psychology, CD13
Dictionary of drugs : chemical data, structures, and bibliographies, ED33, EK110
Dictionary of earth science, English-French, French-English = Dictionnaire des sciences de la terre, anglais-français, français-anglais, Michel, Jean Pierre, EE13

A dictionary of ecology, evolution and systematics, Boxshall, Geoffrey A., EC24
—— Clark, P. F., EC24
—— Lincoln, Roger J., EC24
Dictionary of educational acronyms, abbreviations, and initialisms, Palmer, James C., CB75
A dictionary of Egyptian Arabic, Hinds, Martin, AD69
A dictionary of Egyptian gods and goddesses, Hart, George, CF9
Dictionary of English furniture makers 1660–1840, BF37
A dictionary of epidemiology, EK124
A dictionary of eponyms, Beeching, Cyril Leslie, AD12
The dictionary of espionage, Becket, Henry S. A., CJ284
Dictionary of ethnology and animal learning, CD13
The dictionary of feminist theory, Humm, Maggie, CC296
Dictionary of finance and investment terms, Downes, John, CH227
A dictionary of folk artists in Canada from the 17th century to the present with inclusions of popular portrait, topographical, genre, religious, and decorative artists of the 17th, 18th, and 19th centuries, McKendry, Blake, BF16
Dictionary of food ingredients, Igoe, Robert S., EH32, EK101
Dictionary of foreign terms, Mawson, C. O. Sylvester, AD66
Dictionary of furniture, BF39
Dictionary of gemmology, Read, Peter G., EE34
A dictionary of genetics, King, Robert C., EC65, EC66
—— Stansfield, William D., EC66
Dictionary of genetics & cell biology, Maclean, Norman, EC66
Dictionary of German-American creative writers, Ward, Robert Elmer, BD170
Dictionary of gerontology, Harris, Diana K., CC53
Dictionary of gods and goddesses, devils and demons, Lurker, Manfred, CF3
Dictionary of Hinduism, Stutley, Margaret, BE104
Dictionary of historical terms, Cook, Chris, DA12
Dictionary of hospitality, travel, and tourism, Metelka, Charles J., BJ41
Dictionary of immunology, EC15
—— Herbert, W. J., EK56
—— Rosen, Fred S., EK56
—— Wilkinson, P. C., EK56
Dictionary of Indian philosophical concepts, Singh, B.N, BA17
Dictionary of information science, Bürger, Erich, AB14
Dictionary of information technology, Longley, Dennis, EJ63
—— Shain, Michael, EJ63
Dictionary of instructional technology, Ellington, Henry, CB68
Dictionary of insurance terms, Rubin, Harvey W., CH264
Dictionary of international finance, Walmsley, Julian, CH239
A dictionary of Irish biography, Boylan, Henry, AJ73
A dictionary of Irish history since 1800, Doherty, J. E., DC152
—— Hickey, D. J., DC152
A dictionary of Irish mythology, Ellis, Peter Berresford, CF13
Dictionary of Irish writers, Cleeve, Brian Talbot, BD271
Dictionary of jargon, Green, Jonathon, AD42
A dictionary of Jewish Palestinian Aramaic of the Byzantine period, Sokoloff, Michael, AD119

Dictionary of labor-management relations, CH279

Dictionary of labour biography, Bellamy, Joyce M., AJ63

A dictionary of landscape architecture, Morrow, Baker H., BE144

Dictionary of legal abbreviations, CK62

Dictionary of library and educational technology, Rosenberg, Kenyon C., AB16

A dictionary of linguistics and phonetics, Crystal, David, BC12

Dictionary of literary biography, DB75, BD52

Dictionary of literary pseudonyms, Atkinson, Frank, AA33

A dictionary of literary quotations, Stephens, Meic, BD67

Dictionary of literary themes and motifs, BD48

The dictionary of marketing, Ostrow, Rona, CH318

Dictionary of marketing and advertising, Baker, Michael John, CH316

Dictionary of marketing research, Van Minden, Jack J. R., CH319

Dictionary of marketing terms, CH317

Dictionary of mechanical engineering, Nayler, G. H. F., EJ78

Dictionary of medical eponyms, Firkin, Barry G., EK47

Dictionary of medical syndromes, Magalini, Sergio I., EK55

Dictionary of medicine, EK57, EK58

Dictionary of medieval knighthood and chivalry, Broughton, Bradford B., DA48

Dictionary of medieval Latin from British sources, Latham, R. E., AD139

A dictionary of Mexican American proverbs, Glazer, Mark, BD344

Dictionary of microbiology and molecular biology, Singleton, Paul, EC12

Dictionary of military, defense contractor & troop slang acronyms, Gutzman, Philip C., CJ258

A dictionary of military quotations, Royle, Trevor, CJ263

Dictionary of military terms, Dupuy, Trevor Nevitt, CJ257

The dictionary of Minton, Atterbury, Paul, BF23

A dictionary of modern critical terms, BD36
—— Fowler, Roger, BD31

Dictionary of modern French literature, Dolbow, Sandra W., BD313

A dictionary of modern Indian history, 1707–1947, Mehra, Parshotam, DE62

Dictionary of modern Italian history, DC155

A dictionary of modern legal usage, Garner, Bryan A., CK63

Dictionary of modern political ideologies, CJ17

A dictionary of modern politics, Robertson, David, CJ21

The dictionary of modern war, Luttwak, Edward, CJ260

A dictionary of musical quotations, Crofton, Ian, BH63

A dictionary of narratology, Prince, Gerald, BD40

Dictionary of national biography, AJ64, AJ67

The dictionary of national biography, 1981–1985, AJ66

Dictionary of national biography. Supplement, AJ71

Dictionary of naval abbreviations, Wedertz, Bill, CJ272

A dictionary of neuropsychology, Goodwin, Diana M., EK54

A dictionary of obituaries of modern British radicals, Barrows, Floyd D., AJ62

A dictionary of obscenity, taboo & euphemism, McDonald, James,, AD46

Dictionary of obstetrics and gynecology, EK52

Dictionary of Old English, BC18, AD63

Dictionary of organic compounds, ED37, ED29

Dictionary of organometallic compounds, ED37, ED30

Dictionary of organophosphorus compounds, ED37, ED34

Dictionary of ornament, Lewis, Philippa, BF41

Dictionary of personality and social psychology, CD13

Dictionary of personnel management and labor relations, CH154

Dictionary of pharmacy, EK111

Dictionary of Philippine biography, Manuel, E. Arsenio, AJ84

A dictionary of philosophy, Lacey, A. R., BA16

Dictionary of physiological and clinical psychology, CD13

A dictionary of plant pathology, Holliday, Paul, EH11

The dictionary of political quotations on Ireland, 1886–1987, O'Clery, Conor, BD63, CJ186, DC151

Dictionary of Polynesian mythology, Craig, Robert D., CF15

Dictionary of problem words and expressions, Shaw, Harry, AD27

Dictionary of quotable definitions, BD68

Dictionary of quotations in geography, Wheeler, James O., CL13

Dictionary of quotations in sociology, Bardis, Panos Demetrios, CC16

Dictionary of Qur'ānic terms and concepts, Mir, Mustansir, BB71

Dictionary of race and ethnic relations, Cashmore, Ernest, CC173

A dictionary of reading and related terms, CB67

The dictionary of real estate appraisal, CH347

Dictionary of religion and philosophy, MacGregor, Geddes, BB28

Dictionary of report series codes, EA22

Dictionary of rocks, Mitchell, Richard Scott, EE45

Dictionary of Russian abbreviations, Scheitz, Edgar, AD154

Dictionary of Russian literature since 1917, Kasack, Wolfgang, BD356

Dictionary of Scandinavian history, DC179

Dictionary of scientific and technical terminology, EA50

Dictionary of scientific biography, EK78, EA76

Dictionary of Scottish business biography, 1860–1960, CH145

The dictionary of SDI, Waldman, Harry, CJ275

A dictionary of secret and other societies, Preuss, Arthur, CA54

A dictionary of sexist quotations, CC295

Dictionary of shipping terms, Brodie, Peter R., CH190

Dictionary of signatures & monograms of American artists, Falk, Peter H., BE97, BE99

Dictionary of South African biography, AJ92

A dictionary of South African English, Branford, Jean, AD56

The dictionary of South African painters and sculptors, including Namibia, Ogilvie, Grania, BE85

Dictionary of special education and rehabilitation, Kelly, Leo J., CB74

Dictionary of sports quotations, BJ12

A dictionary of statistical terms, Marriott, F. H. C., CG9, EF11

A dictionary of stylistics, Wales, Katie, BD141

Dictionary of the African left, Ray, Donald Iain, CJ150

Dictionary of the environment, Allaby, Michael, EJ28

A dictionary of the Jewish-Christian dialogue, BB136

Dictionary of the liturgy, Lang, Jovian, BB120

Dictionary of the Middle Ages, DA49

Dictionary of the Napoleonic war, Chandler, David G., DC66

Dictionary of the Napoleonic Wars, Chandler, David G., DC65

A dictionary of the older Scottish tongue, Craigie, William A. Sir, AD60

Dictionary of the physical sciences, Emiliani, Cesare, EA43

A dictionary of the print trade in Ireland, 1550–1775, Munter, Robert, AA51

Dictionary of the Russian Revolution, DC205, DC207

A dictionary of the Second World War, Wheal, Elizabeth-Anne, DA76

A dictionary of the Third Reich, Taylor, James, DC94

Dictionary of the Vietnam War, DE106

Dictionary of toxicology, Hodgson, Ernest, EK130

Dictionary of translated names and titles, Room, Adrian, BD50

A dictionary of true etymologies, Room, Adrian, AD20

Dictionary of twentieth-century Cuban literature, BD340

Dictionary of uncommon words, AD35

Dictionary of visual science, EK53

Dictionary of wars, Kohn, George C., CJ253, DA21

Dictionary of women artists, Petteys, Chris, BE79

The dictionary of world politics, Evans, Graham, CJ18

Dictionnaire alphabétique et analogique de la langue française, Robert, Paul, AD93

Dictionnaire biographique de militants nationalistes algériens, Stora, Benjamin, AJ30

Dictionnaire critique de la révolution française, DC52

Dictionnaire critique de la sociologie, CC14

Dictionnaire de biographie française, AJ51

Dictionnaire de l'Académie française, AD90

Dictionnaire de l'argot, Colin, Jean-Paul, AD98

Dictionnaire de la musique, BH49

Dictionnaire de la mythologie grecque et romaine, CF11

Dictionnaire de la préhistoire, DA35

Dictionnaire de la théorie et de l'histoire littéraires du XIXe siècle à nos jours, Armentier, Louis, BD33

Dictionnaire de spiritualité, BB85

Dictionnaire des abréviations & acronymes scientifiques, techniques, économiques = Dictionary of scientific, technical & economic abbreviations & acronyms, Murith, Jean, EA45

Dictionnaire des auteurs de langue française en Amérique du Nord, Hamel, Réginald, BD304

Dictionnaire des éditeurs de musique française, Devriès, Anik, BH69

Dictionnaire des homonymes de la langue française, Camion, Jean, AD89

Dictionnaire des littératures de langue française, Beaumarchais, Jean-Pierre de, BD312

Dictionnaire des maréchaux de France, AJ52

Dictionnaire des personnages de la Révolution, Caratini, Roger, DC57

Dictionnaire des personnages du cinéma, BG88

Dictionnaire des philosophes antiques, BA22

Dictionnaire des sciences historiques, DA13

Dictionnaire des sculpteurs de l'Ecole française au dix-neuvième siècle, Lami, Stanislas, BE165

Dictionnaire des sociétés secrètes en Occident, Mariel, Pierre, CA54

Dictionnaire du français parlé, Bernet, Charles, AD97

Dictionnaire historique de la Révolution française, DC53

Dictionnaire historique des argots française, Esnault, Gaston, AD98

Dictionnaire historique, thématique et technique des littératures, BD25

Dictionnaire international des termes littéraires, Escarpit, Robert, BD37

Dictionnaire Napoléon, DC64

Dictionnaire technique de la marine, Dobenik, Richard H., CJ256

Diet and health, National Research Council (U.S.). Committee on Diet and Health, EK102

Dietzel, Thomas. *Deutsche literarische Zeitschriften, 1880–1945*, AE35, AE36

Differential equations, EF16

Diffusion of innovations, Musmann, Klaus, CA6

Digest of data on persons with disabilities, CC112

Dilenschneider, Robert L. *The Dartnell public relations handbook*, CH74

Dillman, David L. *Civil service reform*, CJ46

Diplomacy, CJ9, CJ53, DB64, DC5

Diplomatic and consular service, CJ148

Diplomatic records, DB24

Diplomatics, AA39

Direct-line distances—international edition, Fitzpatrick, Gary L., CL19

Direct-line distances—United States edition, Fitzpatrick, Gary L., CL20

Direct mail terms, CH70

Direction des archives de France. *État des inventaires des archives départementales, communales et hospitalières au 1er janvier 1983*, DC70

Direction des Musées de France. *Films and videos on photography*, BF52

Director of artists slide registries, Ticho, Suzy, BE105

Directories
    bibliography
        United States, CH100, CH101

Directories in print, CH100

The directories of London, 1677–1977, DC138

Directorio de antropólogos latinoamericanos, México, Díaz Polanco, Héctor, CE20

Directorio latinoamericano, DB103

Directory of African museums, BE48

Directory of American firms operating in foreign countries, CH114

Directory of American libraries with genealogy or local history collections, Filby, P. William, AK17

Directory of American research and technology, EA10, EA62

Directory of American silver, pewter, and silver plate, Kovel, Ralph M., BF47

Directory of American studies librarians in the UK, AB28

Directory of anthropologists and anthropological research in aging, CE21

Directory of archives and manuscript repositories in the United States, DB18

Directory of Australian academic libraries, AB25

The directory of black nursing faculty, Allen, Sallie T., EK92

Directory of British associations & associations in Ireland, CA52

The directory of Caribbean personalities in Britain and North America, AJ40

Directory of Chinese officials and organizations, CJ161

Directory of Chinese scientific and educational officials, CJ161

Directory of college facilities and services for people with disabilities, CB112

The directory of congressional voting scores and interest group ratings, Sharp, J. Michael, CJ97

Directory of corporate affiliations, CH102, CH102

A directory of credentials in counseling and psychotherapy, Martin, Daniel R., CD26

Directory of departments and programs of religious studies in North America, BB32

Directory of directories, CH100

Directory of economic development programs at state colleges and universities, CB95

Directory of economic institutions, Capie, Forrest, CH13

Directory of educational documentation and information services = Répertoire des services de documentation et d'information pédagogiques, CB81

Directory of educational research institutions = Répertoire des institutions de recherche en éducation, CB82

Directory of educational software for nursing, EK88

Directory of ERIC information service providers, CB89

Directory of ERIC microfiche collections, CB89

Directory of ERIC search services, CB89

Directory of European banking and financial associations, CH257, CH242

Directory of European political scientists, CJ30

Directory of European professional & learned societies = Répertoire des sociétés professionnelles et savantes en Europe, CA49

Directory of executive recruiters, CH161

Directory of federal laboratory & technology resources, EA63

Directory of financial aids for women, 1991–1992, Schlachter, Gail A., CC303

Directory of foreign firms operating in the United States, CH103

Directory of foreign investment in the U.S, CH351

Directory of foreign manufacturers in the United States, Arpan, Jeffrey S., CH293

Directory of foreign trade organizations in Eastern Europe, CH180

The directory of gold and silversmiths 1838–1914, Culme, John, BF46

The directory of gold & silversmiths, jewellers, and allied traders, 1838–1914, Culme, John, BF45

Directory of government document collections & librarians, AG2

Directory of grants in the humanities, CA33

Directory of health care professionals, EK62

Directory of historical consultants, Cockrell, Philip C., DB67

Directory of historical organizations in the United States and Canada, DB68

Directory of historical societies and agencies in the United States and Canada, DB68

Directory of Indian public libraries, AB30

Directory of information resources online, EK63

The directory of international sources of business information, Ball, Sarah, CH85

Directory of investment managers, CH247

Directory of Irish archives, DC149

Directory of Japanese scientific periodicals, 1988, Kokuritsu Kokkai Toshokan (Japan), EA21

A directory of Latin American studies in the United States, Bray, David B., DB102

Directory of law libraries in the British Isles, CK74

Directory of librarians in international development, AB38

Directory of libraries in Zimbabwe, Dube, S. R., AB23

Directory of library and information science schools in India, AB31

Directory of library & information professionals, AB39, AB40

Directory of literary magazines, AE21, BD160

Directory of Lloyd's of London, Rew, John, CH266

Directory of master's programs in foreign languages, foreign literatures, and linguistics, BD42, CB96

Directory of military bases in the U.S, CJ276

Directory of museums in Africa = Répertoire des musées en Afrique, BE48

The directory of museums & living displays, Hudson, Kenneth, BE50

Directory of music research libraries, BH64

Directory of national information sources on handicapping conditions and related services, CC107

The directory of North American fisheries and aquatic scientists, EC19

Directory of online databases, AB92

Directory of oral history collections, Smith, Allen, DB21

A directory of oral history tapes of librarians in the United States and Canada, Dale, Doris Cruger, AB37

Directory of paleontologists of the world, International Paleontological Association, EE41

Directory of patent depository libraries, Phillips, John B., EA86

Directory of periodicals online, AE2

Directory of periodicals published in India, 1986–87, Susheel Kaur, AE50

A directory of philanthropic trusts in New Zealand, Fieldhouse, Arthur E., CA26

Directory of planning and urban affairs libraries in the United States and Canada, 1990, BE140

Directory of popular culture collections, CF29

Directory of portable databases, AB94

Directory of public and private programs for emotionally disturbed children and youth, Fritsch, Ronald E., CC89

Directory of publishing opportunities in business and economics, CH92

A directory of rare book and special collections in the United Kingdom and the Republic of Ireland, AB29

Directory of real estate investors, CH353

Directory of registered lobbyists and lobbyist legislation, CJ59

Directory of research grants, CA33, CA35

Directory of residential treatment facilities for emotionally disturbed children, Sherman, Barbara Smiley, CC91, CD27

Directory of Scandinavian studies in North America, DC180

Directory of scientific and technical libraries in India, Kalia, D. R., AB34

Directory of scientific directories, EA54, EH16, EJ3, EK60

Directory of scientific personnel of the Anthropological Survey of India, Ray, Shyamal Kumar, CE22

Directory of Scottish newspapers, Ferguson, Joan P. S., AF8

Directory of selected national testing programs, CD41

Directory of services for refugees and immigrants, CC177

Directory of social science information courses = Répertoire des cours d'information dans les sciences sociales = Repertorio de cursos en información en ciencias sociales, CA18

Directory of South Asian library resources in the UK and the Republic of Ireland, DE30

Directory of special and research libraries in India, AB32

Directory of special libraries and information sources in Indonesia 1985 = Direktori perpustakaan khusus dan sumber informasi di Indonesia 1985, AB35

Directory of special libraries in Australia, Cree, Jan, AB24

Directory of special programs for minority group members, CC183

Directory of state court clerks & county courthouses, CK75

Directory of state education agencies, CB90

Directory of statistical data files, CG35

Directory of technical and scientific directories, EA54, EH16, EJ3, EK60

Directory of testing laboratories, EA64

Directory of testing laboratories, commercial-institutional, American Society for Testing and Materials, EA64

Directory of the world's largest service companies, CH104

Directory of theatre resources, Howard, Diana, BG26

Directory of United States standardization activities, EA90

A directory of vendors of Latin American library materials, Block, David, AB18

Directory of women's media, CC301

Directory of women's studies programs & library resources, CC302

Directory of world Jewish press and publications, AE3

Directory of world museums, Hudson, Kenneth, BE50

Directory of world stock exchanges, CH243

Dirkschnieder, Edmund. *Deutsche Sprache im Reformationszeitalter,* BC33

DIRLINE, EK63

Disabled; *see also* **Special education**
  bibliography, CC103
  directories, BJ43, CB112, CC107, CC108, CC109, CC110
  handbooks, BJ44, CC111
  statistics, CC112

Disarmament *see* **Arms control and peace research**

Disciunari rumantsch grischen, Società Retorumantscha, AD149

DISCLOSURE database, CH244

Discovery and exploration, DC175, DH3

Disease data book, Fry, John, EK68

Diseases of trees and shrubs, Sinclair, Wayne A., EC37

Dissertation abstracts international, CB16, CB23, CD44

Dissertations
  bibliography
    by subject
      Africa, DD1
      anthropology and ethnology, CE10
      Arab countries, DE18
      Armenia, DC22
      Belgium, DC31
      Brazil, DB112
      Burma, DE47
      cities, DB48
      Commonwealth, DC133
      English language, BC24, BD207
      fine arts, BE12
      folklore, CF25
      history, DA8
      Irish literature, BD270
      library and information science, AB7
      music, BH28
      New Zealand, DF9
      Niger, DD47
      Poland, DC173
      Saudi Arabia, DE89
      Southeast Asia, DE38
      Venezuela, DB137
    national
      Arab countries, DE17
      Austria, AH5, AH9
      Brazil, AH6
      Canada, AH7, DB85, DE18
      Germany, AH8, AH9
      Gr. Brit., AH11
      Gt. Brit., AH10
      Hungary, AH12
      India, AH13
      Ireland, AH11
      Morocco, AH14
      Nigeria, AH15, AH16
      Philippines, AH17
      Romania, AH18
      Switzerland, AH9
      United States, DE18
    bibliography of bibliography, AB97, AH4
    manuals, AH1, AH2, AH3

Dissertations and theses on Venezuelan topics, 1900–1985, Sullivan, William M., DB137

Dissertations in history, 1970–June 1980, Kuehl, Warren F., DA8

Distance tables, CL19, CL20

Divale, William T. *Warfare in primitive societies,* CE5

Divorce, CC132

Dixon, Judith M. *International directory of tactile map collections,* CL45

Dizik, A. Allen. *Concise encyclopedia of interior design,* BF38

Dizionario biografico degli Italiani, AJ75

Dizionario Bompiani degli autori di tutti i tempi e di tutte le letterature, BD53

Dizionario degli scrittori greci e latini, BD364

Dizionario dei filosofi del Novecento, BA23

Dizionario della politica italiana, Pallotta, Gino, CJ191

Dizionario enciclopedico universale della musica e dei musicisti : il lessico, BH50

Dizionario enciclopedico universale della musica e dei musicisti : le biografie, BH51

Dizionario etimologico della lingua italiana, Cortelazzo, Manlio, AD131

Dizionario patristico e di antichità cristiane, BB102

Dizionario politicio e parlamentare italiano, Pallotta, Gino, CJ191

Djibouti, DD29

Djibouti, Aubry, Marie-Christine, DD29

Dlamini, Sipho. *The struggle for South Africa,* CJ202

Dobenik, Richard H. *Dictionnaire technique de la marine,* CJ256

Dobkin, David S. *The birder's handbook,* EC48

Dobrée, Bonamy. *The Oxford history of English literature,* BD222

Doctor, Ronald M. *The encyclopedia of phobias, fears, and anxieties,* CD12

Doctoral dissertations and masters theses regarding Polish subjects, 1900–1985, Wielewinski, Bernard, DC173

Doctoral dissertations in musicology. Second series, Adkins, Cecil, BH28

Doctoral research on Canada and Canadians, 1884–1983 = Thèses de doctorat concernant le Canada et les Canadiens, 1884–1983, Dossick, Jesse J., DB85

Document retrieval index, CK99

La documentation administrative, AG34

The documentation of the European communities, Thomson, Ian, CK121

Documentation sur le Rwanda, DD50

Documents du Minutier central des notaires de Paris. Inventaire après décès, Jurgens, Madeleine, DC68

Dodd, Janet S. *The ACS style guide,* ED24

Dodge, Meredith D. *Historical dictionary of modern Spain, 1700–1988,* DC188

Döhring, Sieghart. *Pipers Enzyklopädie des Musiktheaters,* BH58

Doenecke, Justus D. *Anti-intervention,* CJ292

Doeppers, Daniel F. *A checklist of Southeast Asian newspapers and other research materials in microform held by the Center for Research Libraries,* DE39

Doescher, Rex A. *Directory of paleontologists of the world,* EE41

Dogra, R. C. *Catalogue of the early printed books on South Asia,* DE28

Dogra, Ramesh C. *Bhutan,* DE45

Doherty, J. E. *A chronology of Irish history since 1500,* CJ152

—— *A dictionary of Irish history since 1800,* DC152

Doke, Clement Martyn. *English-Zulu Zulu-English dictionary,* AD177

Dolan, Eleanor F. *The mature woman in America,* CC39, CC256

Dolbow, Sandra W. *Dictionary of modern French literature,* BD313

Doll, Susan. *The international dictionary of films and filmmakers,* BG92

Dollarhide, William. *Map guide to the U.S. federal censuses, 1790–1920,* AK3, CL60

Dollars for scholars, Dennis, Marguerite J., CB157

Domay, Friedrich. *Bibliographie der nationalen Bibliographien = Bibliographie mondiale des bibliographies nationales = A world bibliography of national bibliographies,* AA74

Domestic society in medieval Europe, Sheehan, Michael M., DC6

Domestic violence, Nordquist, Joan, CC133

Dominica, DB147

Dominica, Myers, Robert A., DB147

Dominican Republic
  bibliography, AA103
  biography, AJ46, AJ47
  history
    bibliography, DB149
    encyclopedias, DB148

Dominican Republic, Schoenhals, Kai P., DB149

Domschke, Eliane. *The handbook of national population censuses,* CG39

Donaldson, Stephen. *Encyclopedia of homosexuality,* CC152

Donato, Hernâni. *Dicionário das batalhas brasileiras,* DB116

Donavin, Denise Perry. *Aging with style and savvy,* CC40

Donnachie, Ian L. *Companion to Scottish history,* DC139

Donnelley demographics, CH329

Donner, Herbert. *Hebräisches und aramäisches Handwörterbuch über das Alte Testament,* AD117

Donohue, Joseph. *English drama of the nineteenth century,* BD231

Doremus, R. H. *Handbook of glass properties,* BF26, EJ8

Dorf, Richard C. *International encyclopedia of robotics,* EJ77

The Dorsey dictionary of American government and politics, Shafritz, Jay M., CJ56

Dossick, Jesse J. *Doctoral research on Canada and Canadians, 1884–1983 = Thèses de doctorat concernant le Canada et les Canadiens, 1884–1983,* DB85

Dotzauer, Winfried. *Das Zeitalter der Glaubensspaltung (1500–1618),* BB99, DC82

Doughan, David. *Feminist periodicals, 1855–1984,* AE42, CC271

Doughty, Harold. *Guide to American graduate schools,* CB98

Douglas, Auriel. *Webster's New World best book of aphorisms,* BD60

Douglas, Ngaire. *Pacific islands yearbook,* DG10

Douglas, Norman. *Pacific islands yearbook,* DG10

Douglas, R. G. S. *Directory of libraries in Zimbabwe,* AB23

Doumato, Lamia. *Architecture and women,* BE133

Dow, J. A. T. *The dictionary of cell biology,* EC14, EC66

Dow, Susan L. *State document checklists,* AG25

The Dow Jones averages, 1885–1990, CH260

The Dow Jones-Irwin dictionary of financial planning, Richards, Robert W., CH232

The Dow Jones-Irwin guide to using the Wall Street journal, Lehmann, Michael B., CH17

Downes, John. *Barron's finance & investment handbook,* CH253

—— *Dictionary of finance and investment terms,* CH227

Doyle, Francis R. *Searching the law,* CK14

—— *Searching the law, the states,* CK30

Drabble, Margaret. *The Oxford companion to English literature,* BD219

Drachkovitch, Milorad M. *Biographical dictionary of the Comintern,* CJ248

Drake, Greg. *Index to American photographic collections,* BF58

Drama
  bibliography, BD84
  biography, BD88
  criticism, BD88
  indexes, BD85, BD86, BG14
The drama dictionary, Hodgson, Terry, BG21
The drama scholars' index to plays and filmscripts, Samples, Gordon, BG14
Draper, Hal. *The Marx-Engels cyclopedia*, CJ242
The dream, Parsifal-Charles, Nancy, CD1
Dreams, CD1
Dreisbach, Robert Hastings. *Handbook of poisoning*, EK131
Drenikoff, Iván. *Impresos venezolanos del siglo XIX*, AA199
Drew, Bernard A. *Motion picture series and sequels*, BG69, BG79
Dreyfus, Michel. *Guide des centres de documentation en histoire ouvrière et sociale*, DC73
Drosdowski, Günther. *Das Grosse Wörterbuch der deutschen Sprache in 6 Bänden*, AD106
Drost, Jerome. *Themes and settings in fiction*, BD90
Drozda, Tom. *Tool and manufacturing engineers handbook*, EJ83
Drug abuse
  bibliography, CB22, CC113, CC114
  dictionaries, CC115
  directories, CB104, CC75, CC76, CC116, CC306, EK125
Drug and alcohol programs and policies at four-year colleges, CB104
Drug evaluations, EK114
Drug information, Snow, Bonnie, EK105
Drugs, EK112, EK114, EK122; *see also* Pharmacology
  encyclopedias, ED33, EK110
  guides, EK105
  handbooks, EK113, EK115, EK116, EK120
Drugs available abroad, EK115
Drugs in pregnancy and lactation, Briggs, Gerald G., EK113
Drury, Francis K. W. *Drury's guide to best plays*, BD84
Drury's guide to best plays, Drury, Francis K. W., BD84
Dryden, Laurel. *Employment creation policies and strategies*, CH272
Du Rietz, Gun-Britt. *Swedish imprints 1731–1833*, AA190
Du Rietz, Rolf. *Swedish imprints 1731–1833*, AA190
Duarte i Montserrat, Carles. *Diccionari etimològic i complementari de la llengua catalana*, AD81
Dube, S. R. *Directory of libraries in Zimbabwe*, AB23
Dubin, Michael J. *United States congressional districts, 1843–1883*, CJ105
——— *United States congressional districts, 1883–1913*, CJ106
Duchesne, Alain. *L'obsolète*, AD101
Duckles, Vincent H. *Music reference and research materials*, BH11
Dudenredaktion (Bibliographisches Institut). *Das Grosse Wörterbuch der deutschen Sprache in 6 Bänden*, AD106
——— *The Oxford-Duden German dictionary*, AD109
Dümotz, Irmtraud. *Lexikon der Symbole*, CF1
Duensing, Edward. *America's elderly*, CC62
Duffy, Bernard K. *American orators before 1900*, BD148
Dugan, Robert E. *Public administration desk book*, CJ211
Duke Biederman, Susan. *Art law*, BE108, CK86
Dulbecco, Renato. *Encyclopedia of human biology*, EC9
Dumouchel, J. Robert. *Government assistance almanac*, CH54

Dumuis, Henriette. *French sculptors of the 17th and 18th centuries*, BE163
Dunbar, Gary S. *Modern geography*, CL9
Duncan, Evan M. *Principal officers of the Department of State and United States chiefs of mission, 1778–1990*, CJ86
Dunford, Penny. *Biographical dictionary of women artists in Europe and America since 1850*, BE79
Dunhouse, Mary Beth. *International directory of children's literature*, BD73
Dunkin, Michael J. *The international encyclopedia of teaching and teacher education*, CB63
Dun's directory of service companies, CH115
Dun's electronic business directory, CH116
Duns Europa, CH105
Dun's market identifiers online, CH99
Dun's million dollar directory, CH117
Dun's million dollar disc, CH117
Dupois, Diane L. *Cities of the United States*, CL17
Dupuy, R. Ernest. *The encyclopedia of military history from 3500 B.C. to the present*, DA19
Dupuy, Trevor Nevitt. *Dictionary of military terms*, CJ257
——— *The encyclopedia of military history from 3500 B.C. to the present*, DA19
Durbin, Paul T. *Dictionary of concepts in the philosophy of science*, EA42
Durham, Weldon B. *American theatre companies*, BG29
Durling, Richard J. *A catalogue of sixteenth century printed books in the National Library of Medicine*, EK13
Dutch households in U.S. population censuses, 1850, 1860, 1870, Swierenga, Robert P., AK43
Dutch language, AD85
Dutt, Ashok K. *Atlas of South Asia*, DE34
Duveen, Denis I. *Bibliotheca alchemica et chemica*, ED4
Duxbury, Janell R. *Rockin' the classics and classicizin' the rock*, BH156
Dwinarto, Sudarisman. *Directory of special libraries and information sources in Indonesia 1985 = Direktori perpustakaan khusus dan sumber informasi di Indonesia 1985*, AB35
Dworkin, Steven Norman,. *Lexical studies of medieval Spanish texts*, BC49
The dying child, Benson, Hazel B., CC94
Dying, death, and grief, Simpson, Michael A., CC99
The dynamic Constitution, DA55, CK115
Dynasties of the world, Morby, John E., AK2, CJ146
Dynes, Patrick S. *Program evaluation*, CJ212
Dynes, Wayne R. *Encyclopedia of homosexuality*, CC152
——— *Homosexuality*, CC146
Dziak, John J. *Bibliography on Soviet intelligence and security services*, CJ287
Dzwonkoski, Peter. *American literary publishing houses, 1900–1980. Trade and paperback*, AA50

EPAIS, CA5
ERIC, CB6, CB52
ERIC Clearinghouse for Junior Colleges. *Dictionary of educational acronyms, abbreviations, and initialisms*, CB75
ERIC Clearinghouse on Handicapped and Gifted Children. *Special education yearbook*, CB142
ERIC on SilverPlatter, CB52
ERIC retrospective files, CB52
ERIC RIE cumulative index, CB53
ESTC, AA128
ESTC (Project). *The eighteenth century short title catalogue 1990*, AA128
ETS test collection, CB118, CD43
The ETS Test Collection catalog, CB117, CD42

Eadie, Bruce. *The Harper dictionary of modern thought*, AC4
Eagleson, Robert D. *A Shakespeare glossary*, BD265
Eakins, Rosemary. *Picture sources UK*, BE70
Earls, Irene. *Renaissance art*, BE41
Early American choral music, DeVenney, David P., BH116
Early American imprints, BE111
Early American medical imprints . . . 1668–1820, Austin, Robert B., EK8
Early American music, Heintze, James R., BH2
Early American scientific and technical literature, Batschelet, Margaret, EA68
Early and rare books, AA40, AA41, AA42, AA43, AA44, AA45, AB29
Early black American playwrights and dramatic writers, Peterson, Bernard L., BG41
Early English books, AA130
Early English drama, Everyman to 1580, White, D. Jerry, BD234
Early English manuscripts in facsimile, BD214
Early modern English lexicography, Schäfer, Jürgen, AD2
Early motion pictures, Library of Congress. Motion Picture, Broadcasting, and Recorded Sound Division, BG75
Earth and astronomical sciences research centres, EB10, EE17
Earth book world atlas, Esselte kartor (Firm), CL50
Earth sciences
  dictionaries, EE4
  encyclopedias, EE3
  guides, EE1
East, Roger. *World development directory*, CH59
——— *World fact file*, CJ142
East and Southeast Asian material culture in North America, Haseltine, Patricia, CC213
East European economic handbook, CH45
East Germany, Wallace, Ian, DC89
Easter, Gerry. *American biographical archive*, AJ20
Easterbrook, Ian. *The travellers, Canada to 1900*, DB84
Easterling, P. E. *Greek literature*, BD370
Eatwell, John. *The new Palgrave*, CH8
Ebel, Gerhard. *Datensammlungen in der Physik = Data compilations in physics*, EG1
Ebeling, Erich. *Reallexikon der Assyriologie, unter Mitwirkung zahlreicher Fachgelehrter*, DA36
Echard, William E. *Foreign policy of the French Second Empire*, DC59
——— *Historical dictionary of the French Second Empire, 1852–1870*, DC75
Echemendia, Otto R. *Marketing information*, CH312
Echols, John M. *An Indonesian-English dictionary*, AD126
Eckhardt, C. D. *Chaucer's General prologue to the Canterbury tales*, BD255
Eckroth, David. *Encyclopedia of artificial intelligence*, EJ58
Eckstein, Richard M. *Handicapped funding directory*, CC110
Ecological abstracts, EC23
Ecology, EC23
Ecology abstracts, EC7
ECONBASE, CH29
EconLit, CH3
The economic aid of the PR China to developing and socialist countries, Bartke, Wolfgang, CH56
Economic development
  bibliography, CH42
  dictionaries, CH55
  directories, CH56, CH57, CH58, CH59
  education, CB95
  library resources directories, AB38
  yearbooks, CH28, CH305

Economic forecasting, CH19, CH33, CJ36
  databases, CH29, CH133, CH134
Economic history, CH33
Economic indicators, CG17, CH16, CH17,
  CH18, CH60
Economic literature index, CH3
*Economic reforms in the People's Republic of
  China since 1979,* Schmidt, Marlis, CH42
Economic statistics, 1900–1983, Liesner,
  Thelma, CH27
Economics; *see also* **Economic development;**
  under names of individual countries,
  subhead **Economic conditions**
  annuals, CH32
  atlases, CH25, CH26, DC126
  bibliography, CH1
  biography, CH20, CH21, CH22, CH23,
    CH24
  book reviews, CH6
  databases, CH3, CH29
  dictionaries, CH9, CH10, CH11
    abbreviations, EA45
  directories, CH13, CH15
  education, CH14
  encyclopedias, CH7, CH8
  periodicals, CH4, CH5, CH92
  statistics, CH27
  terminology, CH12
*Economics and business : an international
  annotated bibliography,* CH6
Economics journals and serials, Sichel,
  Beatrice, CH5
*The economics of defense, disarmament, and
  peace,* Hartley, Keith, CH27
Economics of education : research and studies,
  Psacharopoulos, George, CB63
*The economies of the German-speaking
  countries of Europe : a selective bibliography,*
  Krewson, Margrit B., DC4
——— Lindner, Stephan H., DC4
The Economist atlas, CH25
The Economist book of vital world statistics,
  CG20
Economist Intelligence Unit (Great Britain).
  Country report, CH28
Economist Publications (Firm). *Directory of
  world stock exchanges,* CH243
Ecuador
  bibliography, AA104
  biography, AJ48
  history
    bibliography, DB119
  statistics
    bibliography, CG50
Ecuador, Corkill, David, DB119
Edelheit, Abraham J. *Bibliography on
  Holocaust literature,* DA81
——— *Bibliography on Holocaust literature.
  Supplement,* DA82
——— *The Jewish world in modern times,*
  BB130, DA56
Edelheit, Hershel. *Bibliography on Holocaust
  literature,* DA81
——— *Bibliography on Holocaust literature.
  Supplement,* DA82
——— *The Jewish world in modern times,*
  BB130, DA56
Ediff, Sonia. *The Tony Award,* BG27
Edimages (Firm). *Atlas historique de la France,*
  DC78
Editing *see* **Copy preparation**
Editing documents and texts, Luey, Beth, AA59
Editorial Research Service (Kansas City, Mo.).
  Guide to the American right, CJ64
Editors, BD171
Le edizioni italiane del XVI secolo, AA148
Edmonds, Richard L. *Macau,* DE83
Edmonson, Munro S. *Linguistics,* CE25
——— *Literatures,* CE25
Edmunds, R. David. *Kinsmen through time,*
  CC218
Edmundson, R. S. *Dictionary of
  organophosphorus compounds,* ED34

Edridge, Sally. *Solomon Islands bibliography to
  1980,* DG15
Education
  abstract journals, CB49, CB53, CB57
  acronyms, CB75
  bibliography, CB1
    by country or region
      China, CB5
      Gt. Brit., CB37
  biography, CB31, CB143, CB144, CB145
  databases, CB48, CB52, CB103
  dictionaries, CB68, CB69, CB70, CB71,
    CB73, CB76
  directories, CB82, CB114
    databases, CB92
    international, CB81, CB85, CB91
    nursing, EK93
    United States, CB90
      elementary and secondary, CB109,
        CB110, CB111, CB131
  encyclopedias, CB61, CB63, CB64, CB140
  guides, CB2, CB3, CB4
  handbooks, CB123, CB126, CB127
  indexes, CB47
  library resources
    United States, CB88
  periodicals, CB43, CB44, CD5
    indexes, CB46
  public opinion, CB149
  quotations, CB77, CB78
  software, CB13
  statistics, CB123, CB137, CB147, CB150,
    CB151, CB152
  tests and measurements, CB120, CD38
Education, Buttlar, Lois, CB3
The education almanac, CB123
Education, higher
  abstract journals, CB56
  databases, CB105
  directories, CB83, CB89, CB93, CB98,
    CB102, CB106
  encyclopedias, CB65
  statistics, CB146
  yearbooks, CB146
Education in England and Wales, Parker,
  Franklin, CB37
*Education in the People's Republic of China,
  past and present,* Parker, Franklin, CB5
Education index, CB1, CB48
*Education interface . . . guide to pre-college
  foundation support,* CB158
Education journals and serials, Collins, Mary
  Ellen, CB43
The education of poor and minority children,
  Weinberg, Meyer, CC169
*Education of the black adult in the United
  States,* McGee, Leo, CB34
Educational administration abstracts, CB49
Educational directory online, CB92
Educational equity, CB38
Educational media and technology yearbook,
  CB141
Educational media yearbook, CB141
*Educational research, methodology, and
  measurement : an international handbook,*
  Keeves, John P., CB63
**Educational Resources Information Center
  (U.S.).** *Current index to journals in education,*
  CB47
——— *Directory of ERIC information service
  providers,* CB89
——— *ERIC,* CB52
Educational technology
  abstract journals, CB50
  encyclopedias, CB60
  yearbooks, CB84, CB141
Educational technology abstracts, CB50
Educational Testing Service. *Cumulative index
  to Tests in microfiche,* 1975–1987, CD39
——— *Directory of selected national testing
  programs,* CD41
——— *ETS test collection,* CB118, CD43

——— *The ETS Test Collection catalog,* CB117,
  CD42
——— *Index to ETS research report series,
  1948–1989,* CB51
The educator's desk reference (EDR), Freed,
  Melvyn N., CB4
*Educators' desk reference for special learning
  problems,* Weller, Carol, CB139
The educators guide to free materials, CA21
The educator's quotebook, Dale, Edgar, CB77
*The Edward Deming Andrews Memorial Shaker
  Collection,* Henry Francis du Pont
  Winterthur Museum, BB113
Edwardian architecture, Gray, Alexander
  Stuart, BE134
——— Service, Alastair, BE134
Edwards, A. S. G. *Index of printed Middle
  English prose,* BD205
Edwards, Clive. *John Gloag's dictionary of
  furniture,* BF40
Edwards, Gary. *International guide to
  nineteenth-century photographers and their
  works,* BE59, BF63
Edwards, Willie M. *Gerontology,* CC41
Edzard, Dietz Otto. *Reallexikon der
  Assyriologie, unter Mitwirkung zahlreicher
  Fachgelehrter,* DA36
*The Eerdmans analytical concordance to the
  Revised Standard Version of the Bible,*
  Whitaker, Richard E., BB61
The Eerdmans Bible dictionary, BB46
Egan, David R. *Russian autocrats from Ivan the
  Great to the fall of the Romanov dynasty,*
  DC194
Egan, Melinda A. *Russian autocrats from Ivan
  the Great to the fall of the Romanov dynasty,*
  DC194
Egberts, A. *Annual Egyptological bibliography.
  Late reviews AEB 1947–1984,* DD30
Egelston, Roberta Riethmiller. *Credits and
  careers for adult learners,* CB124
Eggebrecht, Hans Heinrich. *Brockhaus
  Riemann Musiklexikon,* BH48
Egle, Kārlis. *Latviešu periodika,* AE57
Egypt
  bibliography, AA105
  dictionaries, DD31
  history
    bibliography, DD30, DD32
Egypt, Makar, Ragai N., DD32
Egyptian gods and goddesses, CF9
Ehrenberg, Ralph E. *Scholars' guide to
  Washington, D.C. for cartography and remote
  sensing imagery,* CL38
Ehresmann, Donald L. *Fine arts,* BE1
Ehrlich, Eugene. *The Harper dictionary of
  foreign terms,* AD66
——— *Mene, Mene, Tekel,* BB62
Ehrlich, Paul R. *The birder's handbook,* EC48
Ei engineering meetings, EJ2
Eichelberger, Ursula. *Zitatenlexikon,* BD69
Eicher, Joanne Bubolz. *African dress,* BF29
Eichholz, Alice. *Ancestry's red book,* AK4
*Eighteenth century British and Irish
  promptbooks,* Langhans, Edward A., BG13
An eighteenth-century musical chronicle, Hall,
  Charles J., BH73
Eighteenth century short title catalogue, AG36
*The eighteenth century short title catalogue
  1990,* AA128
Einstein, Daniel. *Special edition,* BG107
Eis, Arlene L. *The legal researcher's desk
  reference 1990,* CK87
Eisler, Rudolf. *Wörterbuch der philosophischen
  Begriffe,* BA18
Ekistic index of periodicals, BE138
Ekpaideutikē Hellēnikē Enkyklopaideia, AC13

Eksteen, Louis Cornelis. *Groot woordeboek*, AD68

El-Fadil, Amal Eisa. *Southern Sudan*, DD57

El Salvador, DB120

El Salvador, Woodward, Ralph Lee, DB120

Elam, Stanley Munson. *Gallup polls of attitudes toward education 1969–1984*, CB149

Elder neglect and abuse, Johnson, Tanya F., CC45

Election statistics
    Canada, CJ155
    Gt. Brit., CJ179, CJ180, CJ181, CJ182
    India, CJ185
    international, CJ43
    United States, CJ109, CJ111, CJ112, CJ113, CJ114, CJ115
        state and local, CJ133

Elections, CJ141

Elections in India, Singh, V. B., CJ185

Elections since 1945, CJ33

The electoral politics dictionary, Renstrom, Peter G., CJ55, CJ57

Electrical and electronic abstracts, EG2, EJ44

Electrical and electronic engineering; *see also*
    Computer science; Radio and television
    databases, EG2, EJ44
    dictionaries, EJ46
    encyclopedias, EJ45
    guides, EJ43
    handbooks, EJ48, EJ49

Electronic encyclopedia, AC3

Electronic music, BH122

Electronic music dictionary, Tomlyn, Bo, BH122

Electronics engineer's reference book, EJ48

The elements, Emsley, J., ED14

Elements of Hindu iconography, Gopināthā Rāu, T. A., BE104

Elenchus of Biblica, BB45

Eleuterio-Comer, Susan K. *Irish American material culture*, DB71, DC146

Eliade, Mircea. *The encyclopedia of religion*, BB25

Elias, Stephen. *Family law dictionary*, CK64
—— *Legal research*, CK5

Elkin, Judith Laikin. *Latin American Jewish studies*, BB131, CC164

Elks, J. *Dictionary of drugs : chemical data, structures, and bibliographies*, ED33, EK110

Eller, William. *Comparative reading*, CB27
—— *General issues in literacy/illiteracy*, CB28, CB29
—— *Literacy/illiteracy in the world*, CB28, CB29

Ellington, Henry. *Dictionary of instructional technology*, CB68

Elliot, Jeffrey M. *The arms control, disarmament and military security dictionary*, CJ303, CJ304
—— *The state and local government political dictionary*, CJ123

Elliott, Clark A. *Biographical dictionary of American science*, EA83
—— *Biographical index to American science*, EA83

Elliott, David L. *Textbooks in school and society*, CB42

Elliott, Emory. *Columbia literary history of the United States*, BD167

Elliott, Stephen P. *A reference guide to the United States Supreme Court*, CK90

Elliott, Sydney. *Northern Ireland, a political directory, 1966–88*, CJ187

Ellis, James. *English drama of the nineteenth century*, BD231

Ellis, Peter Berresford. *A dictionary of Irish mythology*, CF13

Elliston, Frederick. *Ethics, government, and public policy*, CJ34

Ellwood, Katherine B. *Guide to the petroleum reference literature*, EJ89

Elsbree, John J. *Dictionary of library and educational technology*, AB16

Elsen, Albert E. *Law, ethics, and the visual arts*, BE109, CK88

Elsevier's concise Spanish etymological dictionary, Gómez de Silva, Guido, AD167

Elsevier's dictionary of environmental hydrogeology, EE26

Elsevier's dictionary of glaciology in four languages, EE23

Elsevier's dictionary of hydrogeology in three languages, EE26

Elsevier's dictionary of technology, Thomann, Arthur E., EA52

Elsevier's Russian-English dictionary, Macura, Paul, AD153

Elsey, Barry. *International biography of adult education*, CB31

Elsie, Robert. *Dictionary of Albanian literature*, BD351

Elsley, John. *The American Horticultural Society encyclopedia of garden plants*, EC28

Emanuel, Shirley P. *International directory of braille music collections*, BH65

EMBASE, EK31

Embree, Ainslie Thomas. *Encyclopedia of Asian history*, DE6

Emerson, James C. *Emerson's directory of leading U.S. accounting firms*, CH64

Emerson's directory of leading U.S. accounting firms, CH64

Emerton, Bruce. *American college regalia*, CB163

Emery, David. *The world sports record atlas*, BJ6

L'emigration russe, AE64

L'émigration russe en Europe, Volkoff, Anne Marie, AE71

Émigré literature, AE71, CC239

Emiliani, Cesare. *Dictionary of the physical sciences*, EA43

Emmens, Carol A. *Short stories on film and video*, BG59

Emmons, Glenroy. *Spanish literature, 1500–1700*, BD324

Emmons, Marilyn C. *Spanish literature, 1500–1700*, BD324

Emotionally disturbed, CC89

Emotionally disturbed children, CC91, CD27

Employee benefit plans, CH156

Employers' organizations of the world, CH281

Employment creation policies and strategies, Dryden, Laurel, CH272

Emsley, J. *The elements*, ED14

Enciclopedia de México, DB125

Enciclopedia del Novecento, AC16

Enciclopedia dell'antifascismo e della Resistenza, DC158

Enciclopedia dell'arte antica, classica e orientale, BE34

Enciclopedia filosofia, BA23

Enciclopedia hispanica, AC17

Enciclopedia histórica de Honduras, DB123

Enciclopedia universale dell' arte, BE35

Enciklopedija Slovenije, DC217

The encyclopaedic dictionary of physical geography, CL11

An encyclopaedic dictionary of Sanskrit on historical principles, AD156

Encyclopedia and dictionary of medicine, nursing, and allied health, Miller, Benjamin Frank, EK90

Encyclopaedia Britannica, Inc. *Enciclopedia hispanica*, AC17

Encyclopedia buying guide, AC7

Encyclopædia Iranica, DE71

Encyclopedia of adolescence, CC88

The encyclopedia of aging, CC52, EK38

The encyclopedia of alcoholism, O'Brien, Robert, CC74

Encyclopedia of American business history and biography, CH136

The encyclopedia of American comics, CF33

The encyclopedia of American facts & dates, Carruth, Gorton, DB72

Encyclopedia of American film comedy, Langman, Larry, BG93

Encyclopedia of American humorists, BD153

The encyclopedia of American intelligence and espionage, O'Toole, G. J. A., CJ286

The encyclopedia of American religions, Melton, J. Gordon, BB30

Encyclopedia of American silver manufacturers, Rainwater, Dorothy T., BF43

Encyclopedia of American wrestling, Chapman, Mike, BJ36

Encyclopedia of anthropology, CE15

Encyclopedia of architecture, BE122

Encyclopedia of artificial intelligence, EJ58

The encyclopedia of arts and crafts, BF1

Encyclopedia of Asian history, DE6

Encyclopedia of associations, EK64, AE22

Encyclopedia of associations. Regional, state, and local organizations, CA51

Encyclopedia of astronomy and astrophysics, EB5

Encyclopedia of Australian art, McCulloch, Alan, BE82

Encyclopedia of banking & finance, Munn, Glenn G., CH224

The encyclopedia of blindness and vision impairment, Sardegna, Jill, CC106, EK44

Encyclopaedia of British porcelain manufacturers, Godden, Geoffrey A., BF22

Encyclopedia of British pottery and porcelain marks, Godden, Geoffrey A., BF22

An encyclopedia of British women writers, BD225

Encyclopedia of business information sources, CH81, CH78

The encyclopedia of careers and vocational guidance, CB156

The encyclopedia of child abuse, Clark, Robin E., CC87

The encyclopedia of comparative education and national systems of education, Postlethwaite, T. Neville, CB63

Encyclopedia of computer science and technology, EJ59

Encyclopedia of death, CC100

The encyclopedia of depression, Roesch, Roberta, CD16

Encyclopedia of early Christianity, BB86

Encyclopedia of earth sciences, EE6, EE43
—— Fairbridge, Rhodes Whitemore, EE3
—— Fairbridge, Rhodes Whitmore, series ed, EE2

The encyclopedia of Eastern philosophy and religion, BA12, BB23

The encyclopaedia of educational media communications and technology, CB60

Encyclopedia of electronics, EJ45

The encyclopedia of evolution, Milner, Richard, EC11

Encyclopedia of feminism, Tuttle, Lisa, CC293

Encyclopedia of frontier biography, Thrapp, Dan L., DB58

The encyclopedia of genetic disorders and birth defects, Wynbrandt, James, EK45

Encyclopedia of geographic information sources. U.S. volume, CL3

Encyclopedia of German-American genealogical research, Smith, Anna Pszczan-Czaja, AK24
—— Smith, Clifford Neal, AK24

Encyclopedia of health information sources, EK10

Encyclopedia of homosexuality, CC152

Encyclopedia of human biology, EC9

Encyclopedia of human evolution and prehistory, CE13

Encyclopedia of human rights, CK110

The encyclopedia of igneous and metamorphic petrology, EE43

Encyclopaedia of India, Chopra, Pran Nath, DE61

Encyclopedia of Indian art, references, symbols, evolution of Devanagari script = Rekhā, Aryan, K. C., BE103

Encyclopaedia of Indian culture, Saletore, Rajaram Narayan, DE63
Encyclopaedia of Indian literature, BD377
Encyclopedia of Indian philosophies, BA13
Encyclopedia of investments, CH222
The encyclopaedia of Islam, BB125
Encyclopedia of Jewish history, BB138
An encyclopaedia of language, BC8
Encyclopedia of legal information sources, CK15
Encyclopedia of library and information science, AB12
The encyclopedia of marriage, divorce, and the family, DiCanio, Margaret, CC136
Encyclopedia of materials science and engineering, EJ10, EJ11
Encyclopedia of mathematics, EF7
Encyclopedia of medical devices and instrumentation, EK39
Encyclopedia of medical history, McGrew, Roderick E., EK74
Encyclopedia of medical organizations and agencies, EK64
Encyclopedia of microcomputers, EJ59, EJ60
The encyclopedia of military history from 3500 B.C. to the present, Dupuy, R. Ernest, DA19
Encyclopedia of minerals, Roberts, Willard Lincoln, EE37
An encyclopaedia of Napoleon's Europe, Palmer, Alan, DC66
Encyclopedia of nationalism, Snyder, Louis Leo, CJ11
Encyclopedia of neuroscience, EK40
The encyclopedia of New England, DB50
Encyclopedia of occultism, Spence, Lewis, CD51
Encyclopedia of occultism & parapsychology, CD51
Encyclopedia of pacifism, Huxley, Aldous, CJ305
The encyclopedia of parapsychology and psychical research, Berger, Arthur S., CD49
The encyclopedia of phobias, fears, and anxieties, Doctor, Ronald M., CD12
Encyclopedia of physical science and technology, EA33
Encyclopedia of physical science and technology yearbook, EA34
Encyclopedia of physical sciences and engineering information sources, EA2
Encyclopedia of physics, EG5, EG4
The encyclopedia of police science, CK100
Encyclopedia of polymer science and engineering, EJ20
Encyclopedia of pop, rock & soul, Stambler, Irwin, BH134
Encyclopedia of pottery & porcelain, 1800–1960, Cameron, Elisabeth, BF21
Encyclopaedia of psychic science, Fodor, Nandor, CD51
Encyclopedia of public affairs information sources, CA5
The encyclopedia of religion, BB25
Encyclopedia of religion and ethics, Hastings, James, BB25
Encyclopedia of religion in the South, BB24
Encyclopedia of rock, BH126
Encyclopedia of school administration & supervision, CB61
Encyclopedia of senior citizens information sources, CC63
Encyclopedia of social work, CC29
The encyclopedia of solid earth geophysics, EE6
Encyclopedia of Southern culture, DB53, DB52
The encyclopedia of Southern history, DB53
Encyclopedia of special education, CB62
—— Mann, Lester, CB59
—— Reynolds, Cecil R., CB59
Encyclopedia of statistical sciences, EF8, EF9
The encyclopedia of suicide, Evans, Glen, CC101
The encyclopedia of technical market indicators, Colby, Robert W., CH221

Encyclopedia of telemarketing, CH324
Encyclopedia of television, Terrace, Vincent, BG113
Encyclopedia of the American Constitution, CK116
Encyclopedia of the American judicial system, CK59
Encyclopedia of the American left, CJ243, DB62
Encyclopedia of the American religious experience, BB26
The encyclopedia of the Central West, Carpenter, Allan, DB56
Encyclopedia of the Holocaust, DA83
The encyclopedia of the Midwest, Carpenter, Allan, DB54
The encyclopedia of the New York stage, 1920–1930, Leiter, Samuel L., BG32
Encyclopedia of the Renaissance, Bergin, Thomas Goddard, DA47
Encyclopaedia of the Second World War, Hogg, Ian V., DA75
The encyclopedia of the South, O'Brien, Robert, DB53
The encyclopedia of the Third Reich, DC92
Encyclopedia of the Third Reich, Snyder, Louis Leo, DC94
The encyclopedia of the Third World, Kurian, George Thomas, CJ19
The encyclopedia of the United Nations and international agreements, Osmańszyk, Edmund Jan, CK130
Encyclopedia of the world's air forces, Taylor, Michael John Haddrick, CJ254
Encyclopedia of twentieth-century journalists, Taft, William H., AF25
Encyclopedia of Ukraine, DC211
The encyclopedia of unbelief, BB27
Encyclopedia of U.S. government benefits, CJ51
The encyclopedia of witches and witchcraft, Guiley, Rosemary, CF27
Encyclopedia of world art, BE35
Encyclopedia of world crime, CK101
Encyclopedia of world cultures, CE14
Encyclopedia of world literature in the 20th century, BD376, BD26
Encyclopedia universalis, AC10
Encyclopædia Universalis (Firm). *Le grand atlas des littératures*, BD28
Encyclopedia USA, DB63
Encyclopedia Zimbabwe, DD59
Encyclopedias
  American and English, AC1, AC2, AC4, AC5, AC6
  bibliography, AD67
  databases, AC3
  foreign language
    Czech, AC9
    French, AC10, AC11
    German, AC12
    Greek, AC13
    Hebrew, AC14
    Hungarian, AC15
    Spanish, AC17, AC18
    Ukranian, DC211
  guides, AC7
  indexes, AC8
Encyclopedic dictionary of accounting and finance, Shim, Jae K., CH62
Encyclopedic dictionary of mathematics, EF10
The encyclopedic dictionary of psychology, CD13
Encyclopedic dictionary of semiotics, BC9
Encyclopedic dictionary of yoga, Feuerstein, Georg, BB124
An encyclopedic outline of Masonic, Hermetic, Qabbalistic, and Rosicrucian symbolical philosophy, Hall, Manly Palmer, CA53, CA54
Encyclopédie internationale des photographes de 1839 à nos jours = Photographers encyclopaedia international 1839 to the present, Auer, Michèle, BF61
Encyclopédie philosophique universelle, BA14

Endangered species, EC26, EC30, EC38, EC41, EC54, EC56
Endangered vertebrates, Baker, Sylva, EC38
Energy, EJ70, EJ71, EJ72, EJ73
Energy information abstracts, EJ26
Energy information guide, Weber, R. David, EJ72
Energy update, Weber, R. David, EJ72
Engeldinger, Eugene A. *Spouse abuse*, CC126
Engeli, Christian. *Modern urban history research in Europe, USA, and Japan*, CC160
Engels, F., CJ242
Engelstoft, Povl. *Dansk biografisk leksikon*, AJ45
Engineered materials abstracts, EJ14
Engineered materials handbook, EJ12
Engineering; *see also* specific branches of engineering, e.g., **Civil engineering**
  databases, EJ2
  guides, EJ1
  handbooks, EJ6
  institutional and biographical directories, EJ5
  materials, ED21, EJ7, EJ9, EJ10, EJ11, EJ12, EJ13
    databases, EJ14
Engineering index, EJ2
Englantilais-suomalainen koulusanakirja, Wuolle, Aino, AD88
Englesko-srpskohrvatski rečnik, AD158
English, Richard A. *Black American families, 1965–1984*, CC123
English and American drama of the nineteenth century, BD231
English as a second language, CB119, CB121
English ayres, Swanekamp, Joan, BH113
English-Basque dictionary, Aulestia, Gorka, AD77
English-Czech dictionary, Hais, Karel, AD83
English-Czech technical dictionary, EA46
An English dictionary of Japanese culture, Hoffer, Bates, DE79
—— Honna, Nobuyuki, DE79
English drama
  bibliography, BD229, BD230, BD231, BD232, BD233, BD234
  handbooks, BD235
English drama of the nineteenth century, Ellis, James, BD231
English fiction
  bibliography, BD236, BD237, BD238, BD240
  criticism, BD241
  handbooks, BD242
English-German contrastive linguistics, Markus, Manfred, BC22
An English-Hausa dictionary, Newman, Roxana Ma, AD116
English language
  abbreviations, AD9
  Americanisms, CH291
  atlases, BC30, BC31
  bibliography, AD2, BC17, BC18, BC20, BC21, BC23, BC24, BC25, BD207
  composition, BD143, BD144, BD147
  dictionaries, AD35, AD95
    abridged, AD8
      American, AD4, AD5
      English, AD7
    Anglo-Norman, AD62
    Anglo-Saxon, AD63
    bibliography, AD1
    etymology, AD10, AD11, AD13, AD14, AD15, AD16, AD17, AD19, AD20, AD21
    foreign words and phrases, AD65, AD66
    Middle English, AD64
    obscene words, AD46
    pronunciation, AD37
    regional and dialect
      American, AD52
      Australian, AD53, AD54, AD55, AD58
      English, AD26
      Scottish, AD59, AD60, AD61
      South African, AD56, AD57

unabridged
American, AD3
English, AD6
euphemisms, AD44, AD47
faculty
directories, BC28
grammar
bibliography, BC22
handbooks, BC26, BC27, BC29
history
bibliography, BC19
homophones, AD31
idioms and usage, AD18, AD22, AD23, AD24, AD25, AD27, AD28, AD29, AD30, BD32
jargon, AD42
new words, AD32, AD33, AD34, AD36
rhymes
dictionaries, AD38, AD39
slang
dictionaries, AD41, AD42, AD43, AD44, AD48
American, AD40, AD45
synonyms and antonyms, AD49, AD50, AD51

English-language dictionaries, 1604–1900, O'Neill, Robert Keating, AD1
English legal history, Hines, W. D., CK40, DC102
English literature; *see also* Irish literature
bibliography, BD152
18th century, BD210, BD211
19th century, BD212
20th century, BD213, BD226
Old and Middle English, BD205, BD206, BD209
Restoration, BD211
to 1700, BD236
bibliography of bibliography, BD202
biography, BD223, BD224, BD226, BD227
criticism, BD164, BD217
20th century, BD227
dictionaries, BD164
encyclopedias, BD218, BD219, BD220
faculty
directories, BC28
guides, BD149, BD200, BD201
history, BD217, BD222
manuscripts and archives, BD214, BD215
outlines, BD221
periodicals, BD203
women authors, BD168, BD225, BD228
English mediaeval architects, Harvey, John Hooper, BE135
English-Norwegian dictionary = Engelsk-norsk ordbok, Kirkeby, Willy, AD143
English novel explication. Supplement, BD241
English poetry
bibliography, BD243, BD244, BD245, BD246, BD247, DB25
English poetry of the Second World War, Reilly, Catherine W., BD245
English Renaissance prose fiction, 1500–1660, Harner, James L., BD236
The English romantic poets, BD247
English-Russian dictionary of geology, EE14
An English-SerboCroatian dictionary, Benson, Morton, AD158
English theatrical literature, 1599–1900, Arnott, J. F., BG9
—— Robinson, J. W., BG9
English versification, Brogan, T. V. F., BD129
English-Zulu Zulu-English dictionary, Doke, Clement Martyn, AD177
Enlightenment, AA113, DC1
Ensayo de un repertorio bibliográfico venezolano, Villasana, Angel Raúl, AA200
Enser, A. G. S. *Filmed books and plays,* BG60
—— *A subject bibliography of the First World War,* DA65
—— *A subject bibliography of the Second World War, and aftermath,* DA66

—— *A subject bibliography of the Second World War: books in English, 1939–1974,* DA65, DA66
Ensign, Lynne Naylor. *The complete dictionary of television and film,* BG89
Ensign, Marie. *Historical periodicals directory,* DA10
Ensk-íslensk orðabók, AD125
Enslen, Richard A. *The constitutional law dictionary : vol. 1, Individual rights, suppl. 1,* CK114
Entomology, EC64
Entomology abstracts, EC7
Entsiklopediia Bŭlgariia, DC36
ha-Entsiklopedyah ha-Yiśre'elit ha-kelalit, AC14
Entsyklopediia ukraïnoznavstva, DC211
Entwistle, Noel James. *Handbook of educational ideas and practices,* CB126
Enviro/energyline abstracts plus, EJ26
Enviroline, EJ26
Environment abstracts, EJ26
Environment and environmental problems, EC26
databases, EJ26, EJ27
dictionaries, EJ28
directories, EJ29
handbooks, EJ31
Environmental hazards, Miller, E. Willard, EJ33
Environmental mutagen information center file, EK129
Environmental policy
United States, CH271
Environmental teratology information center file, EK129
Enzyklopädie des Märchens, CF26
Ephesus, BB7
Epics *see* Romances, epics, etc.
Epidemiology, EK124
Eponyms, AD12, EK43, EK47
Eponyms in psychology, Zusne, Leonard, CD23
Eppard, Philip B. *First printings of American authors,* BD156
Epstein, Lawrence S. *A guide to theatre in America,* BG28
The Equal Rights Amendment, Feinberg, Renee, CC278
Equatorial Guinea, DD33
Equatorial Guinea, Liniger-Goumaz, M., DD6
The era of Napoleon, Caldwell, Ronald J., DC47, DC61
The era of the French Revolution, Caldwell, Ronald J., DC47, DC61
Erasmus, Desiderius. *Collected works of Erasmus,* BA26
Erasmus, D., BA26, BA27
Eraut, Michael. *The international encyclopedia of educational technology,* CB63
Erbse, Hartmut. *Lexikon des frühgriechischen Epos,* BD25
Eren, Hasan. *Türkçe sözlük,* AD171
Erlen, Jonathon. *The history of the health care sciences and health care, 1700–1980,* EK73
Ernst, Carl H. *Turtles of the world,* EC44
Erotic art, Burt, Eugene C., BE4
Escarpit, Robert. *Dictionnaire international des termes littéraires,* BD37
Eschbach, Achim. *Bibliography of semiotics, 1975–1985,* BC2
—— *Semiotik-Bibliographie I,* BC2
—— *Zeichen, Text, Bedeutung,* BC2
Eschbach-Szabó, Viktoria. *Bibliography of semiotics, 1975–1985,* BC2
Escritores de la diáspora cubana, Maratos, Daniel C., BD341
Eshbach, Ovid W. *Eshbach's handbook of engineering fundamentals,* EJ6
Eshbach's handbook of engineering fundamentals, Eshbach, Ovid W., EJ6
Eskind, Andrew H. *Index to American photographic collections,* BF58
Esmé Berman. *Art & artists of South Africa,* BE85

Esnault, Gaston. *Dictionnaire historique des argots française,* AD98
Espenshade, Edward Bowman. *Goode's world atlas,* CL51
Espinosa, Tomás. *Teatro mexicano del siglo XX, 1900–1986,* BD345, BG22
Espionage, CJ284, CJ285, CJ286, CJ287
fiction, BD106
Esposito, Anthony. *British biographical index,* AJ65
Esselte kartor (Firm). *Earth book world atlas,* CL50
The essential Chaucer, Allen, Mark, BD252
The essential jazz records, Harrison, Max, BH120
The essential Milton, Klemp, P. J., BD258
The essential Shakespeare, Champion, Larry S., BD260
Estermann, Alfred Adolph. *Die deutschen Literatur-Zeitschriften, 1850–1880,* AE36
—— *Die deutschen Literatur-Zeitschriften, 1850–1880,* AE35
Estes, Kenneth W. *The Marine officer's guide,* CJ279
Estimating handbook, EJ39
Estreicher, Karol Józef Teofil. *Bibliografia polska,* AA173
—— *Bibliografia polska XIX stulecia,* AA174
Estudios fronterizos México-Estados Unidos, DB128
État des inventaires, Archives nationales (France), DC67
État des inventaires des archives départementales, communales et hospitalières au 1er janvier 1983, DC70
État général des fonds, Archives nationales (France), DC68
État général des inventaires des archives diplomatiques, France. Ministère des affaires étrangères, DC71
Ethics, BB92, CB8
Ethics and public policy, Bergerson, Peter J., CJ4
Ethics and the professor, Herring, Mark Youngblood, CB8
Ethics, government, and public policy, CJ34
Ethiopia
atlases, CL64
bibliography, AA106, DD34
Ethiopia, Milkias, Paulos, DD34
Ethiopian language, AD86
Ethiopian Mapping Agency. Geography Division. *National atlas of Ethiopia,* CL64
Ethiopian publications, AA106
Ethnic and native Canadian literature, Miska, John P., BD279
Ethnic and native Canadian literature 1850–1979, BD279
Ethnic and racial images in American film and television, Woll, Allen L., CC171
Ethnic conflict and human rights in Sri Lanka, Rupesinghe, Kumar, DE93
Ethnic folklife dissertations from the United States and Canada, 1960–1980, Kerst, Catherine Hiebert, CF25
Ethnic music on records, Spottswood, Richard K., BH144
Ethnic periodicals in contemporary America, Ireland, Sandra L. Jones, AE24, CC172
Ethnic press, AE16, AE24, AE27, CC172
The ethnic press in the United States, AE16
Ethnicity and aging, CC42
Ethnoart, Burt, Eugene C., BF4
Ethnoarts index, BF10, BF11, BF4, BF12
Ethnoarts index supplemental publication, BF10
Ethnographic bibliography of North America, Murdock, George Peter, CC217
—— O'Leary, Timothy J., CC217
Ethnographic bibliography of North America, 4th edition. Supplement 1973–1987, Martin, M. Marlene, CC217
Ethnohistory, Spores, Ronald, CE25

Ethnology *see* **Anthropology and ethnology**
Etiquette, CF38
Etiquette, Hodges, Deborah Robertson, CF38
Ettinghausen, Richard. *The art and architecture of Islam: 650–1250,* BE73
Etymologisches Wörterbuch der deutschen Sprache, Kluge, Friedrich, AD112
Etymologisches Wörterbuch des Altindoarischen, Mayrhofer, Manfred, AD157
Etymologisches Wörterbuch des Deutschen, AD111
Eureka!, Byrne, Mary, AD13
Eurofi (UK) Limited. *Development aid,* CH57
The Europa world year book, CJ144
Europa year book, CJ33, CJ144
Europe
 foreign relations, CJ9, DB105, DC5
 government publications, AG33
 history
  archival sources, DC9
  bibliography, CH2, DC2, DC3, DC4, DC6, DC7
  library resources, DC10
  Middle Ages, DA51
 politics and government, CJ163, CJ164, CJ168, CJ170
  archival sources, DC9
Europe, East and Southeast
 bibliography, DC13, DC14, DC197
 biography, AJ49
 directories, CH180
 economic conditions, CH45, CH181
 history
  encyclopedias, DC15
Europe in transition, Ferguson, Chris D., DC2
Europe transformed, CJ164
Europe, Western
 economic conditions, CH46
 politics and government, CJ165, CJ167
 statistics
  bibliography, CG51
European American elderly, Guttmann, David, CC43
European Americana, AA78
European artists, Castagno, John, BE98
European authors, 1000–1900, BD55
European Bank for Reconstruction and Development. *A study of the Soviet economy,* CH53
European Communities, CK128
 directories, CH177, CK124
 economic conditions, CH177, CK124
 encyclopedias, CK123
 guides, CK107, CK120, CK121
 handbooks, CK125, CK126, CK127
 yearbooks, CH308, CK129
European Consortium for Political Research. *Directory of European political scientists,* CJ30
European Court of Human Rights. *Case law of the European Court of Human Rights,* CK107
European decorative arts, 1400–1600, De Winter, Patrick M., BF5
European directory of non-official statistical sources, CG24
European directory of trade and business journals, CH93
European Dun's market identifiers, CH99
European economic and social history, 1450–1789, Taylor, Barry, DC7
European faculty directory, CB83
European investment in U.S. and Canadian real estate directory, CH352
European-Latin American relations, DB105
The European political dictionary, Rossi, Ernest E., CJ168
European political facts, 1918–84, Cook, Chris, CJ163
European political scientists, CJ30
European research centres, EA55
European sources of scientific and technical information, EA56

European writers, BD54
Evalds, Victoria K. *Union list of African censuses, development plans and statistical abstracts,* CG40
Evangelical Lutheran Church in America. *Biographical directory of clergy,* BB108
—— *Yearbook,* BB109
Evangelicalism, BB75
Evangelisches Kirchenlexikon, BB87
Evans, Charles. *American bibliography,* AA79, BE111, CL43
Evans, G. Edward. *Developing library and information center collections,* AB65
Evans, Glen. *The encyclopedia of alcoholism,* CC74
—— *The encyclopedia of suicide,* CC101
Evans, Graham. *The dictionary of world politics,* CJ18
Evans, Hilary. *Picture researcher's handbook,* BE68
Evans, Ivor H. *Brewer's dictionary of phrase and fable,* BD46
Evans, James E. *Comedy, an annotated bibliography of theory and criticism,* BG10
Evans, James H. *Black theology,* BB78
Evans, Karen. *A bibliography of Canadiana,* DB83
Evans, Mary. *Picture researcher's handbook,* BE68
Even, Pascal. *Guide des sources de l'histoire du Brésil aux archives du Ministère français des affaires étrangères,* DB114
Everton, George B. *Handy book for genealogists,* AK4
Every woman's legal guide, CC309
Everyman's English pronouncing dictionary, Jones, Daniel, AD37
Everything Japanese, De Mente, Boye, DE79
Evinger, William R. *Directory of military bases in the U.S.,* CJ276
—— *Federal statistical data bases,* CG35
—— *Guide to federal government acronyms,* CJ58
Evleth, Donna. *France under the German occupation, 1940–1944,* DC60
Evolution, BB6, CE13, EC11
Ewen, David. *American songwriters,* BH109
—— *Popular American composers from revolutionary times to the present,* BH109
Exceptional child education abstracts, CB54, CB55, CB54
Exceptional child education resources, CB55
Excerpta medica, EK31
The executive branch of the U.S. government, Goehlert, Robert, CJ76
Executive recruiters, CH161
Executives
 United States, CH111
Executive's business information sourcebook, Philcox, Phil, CH81
An exegetical bibliography of the New Testament, Wagner, Günter, BB44
Exemplary programs in developmental education, CB116
Exhaustive concordance of the Bible, Strong, James, BB59
Exhibitions, CH107
Expressionism, BE29
External public debt, CH31
The extra pharmacopoeia, Martindale, William, EK117
Eyll, Klara van. *Deutsche Wirtschaftsarchive,* DC90

FIAF Cataloguing Commission. *Bibliography of national filmographies,* BG51
Die Fabeln des Mittelalters und der frühen Neuzeit, Dicke, Gerd, CF22
Faber, Edward. *Nobel prize winners in chemistry, 1901–1961,* ED25
The Faber dictionary of euphemisms, Holder, R. W., AD44

Fabian, Bernhard. *A catalogue of English books printed before 1801 held by the University Library at Göttingen,* AA129
—— *Deutsches biographisches Archiv,* AJ55
Fabiano, Emily. *Index to tests used in educational dissertations,* CB23, CD44
Fable scholarship, Carnes, Pack, CF20
Fables, CF22
Face of the nation, 1987, CC30
Fact book on aging, Vierck, Elizabeth, CC68
Fact book on higher education, American Council on Education, CB146
Fact books and compendiums, AC20
Facts about the presidents, Kane, Joseph Nathan, CJ91
Facts about the states, Kane, Joseph Nathan, CJ125
Facts and figures about our nation's system of education, CB123
The Facts on File dictionary of astronomy, EB7
The Facts on File dictionary of biology, EC16
The Facts on File dictionary of classical, biblical, and literary allusions, BD35
The Facts on File dictionary of education, Shafritz, Jay M., CB76
The Facts on File dictionary of military science, Shafritz, Jay M., CJ262
The Facts on File dictionary of nonprofit organization management, Ott, J. Steven, CH158
The Facts on File dictionary of personnel management and labor relations, Shafritz, Jay M., CH154
The Facts on File dictionary of public administration, Shafritz, Jay M., CJ223
The Facts on File dictionary of twentieth-century allusions, Cole, Sylvia, BD35
The Facts on File encyclopedia of word and phrase origins, Hendrickson, Robert, AD16
The Facts on File encyclopedia of world mythology and legend, Mercatante, Anthony S., CF5
Facts on file five year index, 1981–1985, DA61
Facts on File news digest CD-ROM, DA62
The Facts on File scientific yearbook, EA35
The Facts on File world political almanac, Cook, Chris, CJ140
Fage, J. D. *The Cambridge history of Africa,* DD10
—— *A guide to original sources for precolonial western Africa published in European languages,* DD24
Fahlbusch, Erwin. *Evangelisches Kirchenlexikon,* BB87
Fairbank, John King. *The Cambridge history of China,* DE50
Fairbridge, Rhodes Whitemore. *Encyclopedia of earth sciences,* EE3
Fairbridge, Rhodes Whitmore. *Dictionary of earth science, English-French, French-English = Dictionnaire des sciences de la terre, anglais-français, français-anglais,* EE13
Fairbridge, Rhodes Whitmore, series ed. *Encyclopedia of earth sciences,* EE2
Fairpo, C. Gavin. *Heinemann dental dictionary,* EK85
Fairpo, Jenifer E. H. *Heinemann dental dictionary,* EK85
Fairweather, Digby. *Jazz,* BH124
Faitelson-Weiser, Silvia. *Diasle,* BC50
Fakebooks, an index to songs in, BH14
Falciola, Kristine. *Conditions of work and quality of working life,* CH280
Falk, Byron A. *Personal name index to "The New York times index," 1975–1989 supplement,* AF12
Falk, Joyce Duncan. *Searching America: history and life,* DB17
—— *Searching America: history and life (AHL) and Historical abstracts (HA) on DIALOG,* DA6

Falk, Peter H. *The annual exhibition record of the Pennsylvania Academy of the Fine Arts*, BE66

—— *Dictionary of signatures & monograms of American artists*, BE97, BE99

—— *Who was who in American art*, BE93, BE99

Falk, Valerie R. *Personal name index to "The New York times index," 1975–1989 supplement*, AF12

The Falklands/Malvinas campaign, Rasor, Eugene L., DB15

Fallen in battle, Brown, Russell K., CJ281

Familiennamenbuch der Schweiz = Répertoire des noms de famille suisses = Register of Swiss surnames, AK45

Families in transition, Sadler, Judith DeBoard, CC134

Les familles protestantes en France, Bernard, Gildas, AK22

Family *see* **Marriage and the family**

Family historian's enquire within, Markwell, F. C., AK33

Family history and local history in England, Hey, David, AK32

Family law dictionary, Leonard, Robin, CK64

Family resources database, CC127

Family therapy, CC128

—— Sauber, S. Richard, CC137

The famine immigrants, AK11

Famularo, Joseph J. *Handbook of human resources administration*, CH166

Fandel, Nancy A. *The national directory of arts & education support by business corporations*, CA38

Fang, Anna J. *International guide to library and information science education*, AB19

Fang, Josephine Riss. *International guide to library and information science education*, AB19

Fanshel, David. *Face of the nation, 1987*, CC30

Fantasy for children, Lynn, Ruth Nadelman, BD77

Fantasy literature *see* **Science fiction, fantasy, and Gothic literature**

Fantasy literature, BD110

Fantasy literature for children and young adults, Lynn, Ruth Nadelman, BD77

Farber, Bernard E. *A teacher's treasury of quotations*, CB78

Farberow, Norman L. *The encyclopedia of suicide*, CC101

Farenholtz, Brigitte. *Manual para las relaciones Europeo-Latinoamericanas = Handbook for European-Latin American relations*, DB105

Farhang-i kitābhā-yi Fārsī, Mudabbirī, Maḥmūd, AA142

Farhang-i nuvīn-i payvastah-i Fārsī–Ingilīsī va Ingilīsī–Fārsī, Āryānpūr Kāshānī, 'Abbās, AD144

Faries, Cynthia. *The social sciences*, CA3

Faris, Robert E. L. *Handbook of modern sociology*, CC20

Farkas, Andrew. *Opera and concert singers*, BH88

Farley, Betty. *National health directory*, EK65

Farm buildings, BE112, EH24; *see also* **Stables**

Farmer, David Hugh. *The Oxford dictionary of saints*, BB97

Farr, David F. *Fungi on plants and plant products in the United States*, EC34

Farr, Dennis. *The Oxford dictionary of art*, BE38

Farragher, Leslie E. *The anthropology of war*, CE5

Farrell, Catherine E. *Foundation guide for religious grant seekers*, BB31, CA31

Fascism, DC158

Fashion *see* **Costume and fashion**

Fasman, Mark J. *Brass bibliography*, BH154

Fatherhood U.S.A., Klinman, Debra G., CC142

Faulhaber, Charles. *Bibliography of Old Spanish texts*, BD323

Faust, Patricia L. *Historical times illustrated encyclopedia of the Civil War*, DB34

Favier, Jean. *État des inventaires*, DC67

—— *État général des fonds*, DC68

Fawcett, Julian. *Industrial relations*, CH269

Fay, John. *The alcohol/drug abuse dictionary and encyclopedia*, CC115

—— *The police dictionary and encyclopedia*, CK102

Fayard, Jean-François. *Histoire et dictionnaire de la Révolution française*, DC56

Feather, John. *A dictionary of book history*, AA47

Feczko, Margaret Mary. *Foundation grants to individuals*, CA34

Feder, Yon. *ha-Entsiḳlopedyah ha-Yiśre'elit ha-kelalit*, AC14

Federal career directory, CH336

Federal court records, DB24

Federal information sources in health and medicine, Chitty, Mary Glen, EK26

Federal public policy on aging since 1960, Oriol, William E., CC46

Federal register, CK53

Federal statistical data bases, Evinger, William R., CG35

FEDfind, D'Aleo, Richard J., AG3

Fedor, Michal. *Bibliografia slovenských kníh, 1901–1918*, AA97

Fehlauer, Michael. *DDR Handbuch*, CJ172

Feigenbaum, Edward A. *The handbook of artificial intelligence*, EJ67

Feigert, Frank B. *Canada votes, 1935–1988*, CJ155

Feinberg, Renee. *The Equal Rights Amendment*, CC278

—— *The feminization of poverty in the United States*, CC144

Fekete, Márton. *Prominent Hungarians*, AJ69

Feldman, Franklin. *Art law*, BE108, CK86

Feldman, Lynne B. *Contemporary American business leaders*, CH146

Feldman, Paula R. *The wordworthy computer*, BD12

Fellendorf, George W. *Bibliography on deafness*, CC102

Fellhauer, Ruth. *550 books on Buddhism*, BB122

Fellinger, Imogen. *Periodica musicalia (1789–1830)*, BH31

—— *Verzeichnis der Musikzeitschriften des 19. Jahrhunderts*, BH31

Fellowship guide to western Europe, CB159

Fellowships and scholarships, CB157, CB159, CB161, CB162, CC108; *see also* **Grants-in-aid**

Feminism, BD20, CC248, CC264, CC266, CC269, CC297

    dictionaries, CC296

    encyclopedias, CC293

    periodicals, AE42, CC271

Feminism and women's issues, Watson, G. Llewellyn, CC266

Feminist collections, CC268

The feminist companion to literature in English, Blain, Virginia, BD228

A feminist dictionary, Kramarae, Cheris, CC297

Feminist literary criticism, Frost, Wendy, BD20

Feminist periodicals, 1855–1984, Doughan, David, AE42, CC271

Feminist resources for schools and colleges, Chapman, Anne, CC248

—— Froschl, Merle, CC248

Feminists, AJ61

Feminists, pornography & the law, Sellen, Betty-Carol, CC264

The feminization of poverty, Nordquist, Joan, CC145

The feminization of poverty in the United States, Feinberg, Renee, CC144

Fennica, AA109

Fenton, Jill. *Women writers, from page to screen*, BG62

Fenton, Thomas P. *Africa*, DD17

—— *Asia and Pacific*, DE7

—— *Latin America and Caribbean*, DB104

—— *Middle East*, DE23

—— *Third World resource directory*, CH51

—— *Third World struggle for peace with justice*, CJ293

—— *Transnational corporations and labor*, CH285

—— *Women in the Third World*, CC279

Fenwick, Gillian. *The contributors' index to the Dictionary of national biography, 1885–1901*, AJ67

Feofanov, Dmitry. *Biographical dictionary of Russian/Soviet composers*, BH76

Ferber, Marianne A. *Women and work, paid and unpaid*, CC257, CH273

Ferguson, Chris D. *Europe in transition*, DC2

Ferguson, Everett. *Encyclopedia of early Christianity*, BB86

Ferguson, F. S. *A short-title catalogue of books printed in England, Scotland, & Ireland and of English books printed abroad, 1475–1640*, AA127

Ferguson, Joan P. S. *Directory of Scottish newspapers*, AF8

Ferguson, John. *Bibliotheca chemica*, ED4

Ferguson, John Alexander. *Bibliography of Australia*, AA87

—— *Bibliography of Australia : addenda, 1784–1850*, AA88, DF5

Ferguson, R. Brian. *The anthropology of war*, CE5

Ferguson, Sinclair B. *New dictionary of theology*, BB88

Ferguson, T. J. *A Zuni atlas*, CC233

Fernald, Anne Conway. *Business online*, AB96, CH82

Fernández-Caballero, Carlos F. S. *The Paraguayan bibliography*, AA170

Fernández-Caballero, Marianne. *The Paraguayan bibliography*, AA170

Fernelius, W. Conard. *Inorganic chemical nomenclature*, ED26

Ferrall, Eleanor. *Criminal justice research in libraries*, CK96

Ferreiva, José de Azevedo. *Bibliografia selectiva de Ca lingua portuguesa*, BC46

Ferrell, Robert H. *Atlas of American history*, DB77

Ferris, William R. *Encyclopedia of Southern culture*, DB52

Ferrua, Antonio. *Note al Thesaurus linguae latinae*, AD135

—— *Note al Thesaurus linguae latinae : addenda et corrigenda*, AD134

Fertig, Barbara C. *Folklife sourcebook*, CF32

Festschriften

    bibliography, AA28

    by subject

        fine arts, BE9

Festschriften in art history, 1960–1975, Lincoln, Betty Woelk, BE9

Feuerstein, Georg. *Encyclopedic dictionary of yoga*, BB124

Feuerwerker, Albert. *The Cambridge history of China*, DE50

Fiber optics and lightwave communications standard dictionary, Weik, Martin H., EJ47

Fiber optics standard dictionary, Weik, Martin H., EJ47

Fiction

    bibliography, BD90, BD91, BD92

    biobibliography, BD94

    biography, BD93

    criticism, BD93, BD99, BD100

    fairy tales, CF26

    indexes, BD98

Fidler, Linda M. *International music journals*, BH32

Fieg, Eugene C. *Religion journals and serials*, BB14

Field crop diseases handbook, Nyvall, Robert F., EH23

A field guide to hawks, North America, Clark, William S., EC47

Fieldhouse, Arthur E. *A directory of philanthropic trusts in New Zealand*, CA26

Fielding, Mantle. *Mantle Fielding's dictionary of American painters, sculptors & engravers*, BE94

Fierro, Alfred. *Bibliographie analytique des biographies collectives imprimées de la France contemporaine*, AJ53

—— *Bibliographie de la Révolution française, 1940–1988*, DC49

—— *Histoire et dictionnaire de la Révolution française*, DC56

Fieschi, Jacques. *Dictionnaire des personnages du cinéma*, BG88

Fifty Caribbean writers, BD283

Fifty southern writers after 1900, BD155

Fifty southern writers before 1900, BD154

Figueroa Marroquín, Horacio. *Apéndice a la Bibliografía guatemalteca*, AA136

al-Fihris al-waṭanī lil-maṭbūʿāt al-ʿIrāqīyah, AA143

Fiji Islands, AA107

Fiji national bibliography, AA107

Filby, P. William. *A bibliography of American county histories*, DB41

—— *Directory of American libraries with genealogy or local history collections*, AK17

—— *Germans to America*, AK12

—— *Passenger and immigration lists bibliography, 1538–1900*, AK8

Fildes, Robert. *World index of economic forecasts*, CH19

Filin, Fedot Petrovich. *Slovar' russkikh narodnykh govorov*, AD150

—— *Slovar' russkogo îazyka XI–XVII vv*, AD151

Filippelli, Ronald L. *Labor conflict in the United States*, CH278

Filler, Louis. *Dictionary of American conservatism*, CJ52

—— *A dictionary of American social change*, CA14

Film and television handbook, BG98

Film as literature, literature as film, Ross, Harris, BG54

The film catalog, Museum of Modern Art (New York, N.Y.), BG77

Film genres, BG90

The film handbook, Andrew, Geoff, BG101

The film index, Writers' Program (New York, N.Y.), BG56

Film review index, BG63

Film study, Manchel, Frank, BG53

Film, television, and stage music on phonograph records, Harris, Steve, BG1, BH145

Filmed books and plays, Enser, A. G. S., BG60

Filmer, Alison J. *Harrap's book of film directors and their films*, BG70

Filmmakers dictionary, Singleton, Ralph S., BG97

Filmographie mondiale de la Révolution française, Dallet, Sylvie, DC48

A filmography of the Third World, 1976–1983, Cyr, Helen W., BG68

Films and videos on photography, BF52

Films for, by, and about women. Series II, Sullivan, Kaye, CC265

Films of the Holocaust, Skirball, Sheba F., DA88

Filosofskiĭ ēntsiklopedicheskiĭ slovar', BA15

Filov, V. A. *Svodnyĭ katalog knig na inostrannykh îazykakh, izdannykh v Rossii v XVIII veke, 1701–1800*, AA180

Finance and banking
annuals, CH129
bibliography, CH213
databases, CH220, CH244

dictionaries, CH62, CH225, CH226, CH227, CH228, CH231, CH232, CH233, CH234, CH235, CH236, CH237, CH239
directories, CH119, CH240, CH241, CH245, CH247, CH250, CH257
 Europe, CH242
encyclopedias, CH223, CH224, CH230
handbooks, CH251, CH253, CH254, CH255, CH256, CH258, CH259
indexes, CH219
periodicals, CH214, CH217
statistics, CH212, CH260, CH262

Financial 1000, CH111

Financial aid for research, study, travel, and other activities abroad, CB160

Financial aid for the disabled and their families, CC108

The financial analyst's handbook, CH254

Financial journals and serials, Fisher, William Harvey, CH214

Financial market indexes, averages, and indicators, CH252

Financial planners, CH245

Financial planners and planning organizations directory, CH245

Financial Post Information Service. *Canadian markets*, CH327

Financial times industrial companies: chemicals, CH300

Financial times international yearbook, CH300

Finch, Glenda. *Detailed statistics on the urban and rural population of Pakistan, 1950 to 2010*, CG65

Finch, M. H. J. *Uruguay*, DB135

Fincher, Julian H. *Dictionary of pharmacy*, EK111

Find the law in the library, Corbin, John, CK4

FINDEX, CH320

A finding aid to reference books in South Pacific studies, Graham, Theresa, DG3

Finding the law, Cohen, Morris L., CK2

Finding the source in sociology and anthropology, Brown, Samuel R., CC5, CE4

Findling, John E. *Dictionary of American diplomatic history*, CJ53, DB64

Fine, Bernard D. *Glossary of psychoanalytic terms and concepts*, CD24

—— *Psychoanalytic terms and concepts*, CD24

Fine arts
 art reproductions, BE105
 bibliography, BE6, BE8, BE11, BE12, BE13, BE14, BE21, BE22, BE23
  current, BE16, BE19
 biography, BE74, BE75, BE77, BE80, BE81, BE82, BE83, BE84, BE85, BE87, BE88, BE90, BE93, BE94
 by country or region
  Africa, BF3
   bibliography, BF2
  China, BE87
   indexes, BE150
  Europe, BE8, BE41
  Germany, BE39
  India, BE103
  Italy, BE24, BE41
  Japan, BE42, BE100
  Latin America, BE6
  Namibia, BE85
  South Africa, BE85
  United States
   manuscripts and archives, BE32
   prints and engravings, BE156
   Spanish-speaking Americans, BE5
 criticism, BE147
 databases, BE16, BE18, BE21, BE23
 dictionaries, BE42, BE43
 directories, BE55, BE57
 encyclopedias, BE34, BE36, BE37, BE38, BE39, BE40, BE41, BE81
 exhibition catalogs, BE66, BE67
 guides, BE1, BE2
 handbooks, BE69

 history, BE71, BE72, BE73
  bibliography, BE9
 indexes, BE17, BE31, BE67
 influence studies, BE15
 library catalogs, BE24, BE25, BE28
 library resources, BE51
 manuscripts and archives, BE32
 quotations, BE46
 restoration and conservation, BE106
 sales, BE58, BE59, BE60, BE61, BE62, BE64, BF63
  databases, BE63
 symbolism, BB73
  Christian, BE101, BE102
  Hindu, BE103, BE104
 thesauruses, BE44

Fine arts, Ehresmann, Donald L., BE1

Finke, Horst-Dieter. *Bibliographischer Wegweiser der philosophischen Literatur*, BA3

Finkel, Asher J. *The American Medical Association family medical guide*, EK67

Finkelhor, David. *A sourcebook on child sexual abuse*, CC92

Finkelstein, Louis. *The Cambridge history of Judaism*, BB137

Finland
 bibliography, AA108, AA110, AA181, DC181
  databases, AA109
 biography, AJ91
 encyclopedias, DC46
 history
  bibliography, DC45
  manuscripts and archives, DC44

Finlands nationalbibliografi, AA109

Finnish language, AD87, AD88

The Finnish national bibliography, AA109

Finnish national bibliography, AA110

Fire protection handbook, National Fire Protection Association, EJ40

Firestone, Richard B. *Table of radioactive isotopes*, EG11

Firkin, Barry G. *Dictionary of medical eponyms*, EK47

First aid manual for chemical accidents, Lefèvre, M. J., ED17

A first dictionary of linguisitics and phonetics, BC12

The first Gothics, Frank, Frederick S., BD114

First printings of American authors, BD156

First stop, Ryan, Joe, AC8

First supplement to A comprehensive bibliography of Yugoslav literature in English, 1981–1985, Mihailovich, Vasa D., BD362

Fischer, August. *Wörterbuch der klassischen arabischen Sprache*, AD71

Fischer, Wolfram. *Charles Szladits' guide to foreign legal materials*, CK39

Fischer-Schreiber, Ingrid. *The encyclopedia of Eastern philosophy and religion*, BA12, BB23

Fisher, Benjamin Franklin. *The Gothic's Gothic*, BD113

Fisher, James C. *Encyclopedia of school administration & supervision*, CB61

Fisher, John H. *The essential Chaucer*, BD252

Fisher, John Robert. ¨ *eru*, DB132

Fisher, Kim N. *On ˍne screen*, BG50

Fisher, Rita C. *Aˍricultural information resource centers*, EH15

Fisher, William Harvey. *Business journals of the United States*, CH90

—— *Financial journals and serials*, CH214

Fisheries, EC19

Fisiak, Jacek. *A bibliography of writings for the history of the English language*, BC19

Fitch, Jennifer M. *Earth and astronomical sciences research centres*, EB10, EE17

Fitch, Thomas P. *Dictionary of banking terms*, CH228

Fitzgerald, Gerald. *Annals of the Metropolitan Opera Guild*, BH95

Fitzmyer, Joseph A. *The new Jerome biblical commentary*, BB67

Fitzpatrick, Gary L. *Direct-line distances—international edition*, CL19

—— *Direct-line distances—United States edition*, CL20

—— *International time tables*, EB19

Five kingdoms, Margulis, Lynn, EC66

Fjioka, Keisuke. *Intā Puresu kagaku gijutsu 25-mango daijiten*, EA49

Flackes, William D. *Northern Ireland, a political directory, 1966–88*, CJ187

Fleming, John. *The Penguin dictionary of decorative arts*, BF13

Fletcher, Andrew J. *The Merck manual of geriatrics*, EK72

Fletcher, James E. *Broadcast research definitions*, CH207

Fletcher, Katy. *Spy fiction*, BD106

Fletcher, Marilyn P. *Reader's guide to twentieth-century science fiction*, BD119

Fletcher, Marvin. *The peacetime army, 1900–1941*, CJ271

Fletcher, Richard A. *Who's who in Roman Britain and Anglo-Saxon England*, DC124

Fletcher-Janzen, Elaine. *Concise encyclopedia of special education*, CB59

Flexner, Stuart Berg. *Dictionary of American slang*, AD40

—— *The Random House dictionary of the English language*, AD3

—— *The Random House thesaurus*, AD50

Flora, Joseph M. *Fifty southern writers after 1900*, BD155

—— *Fifty southern writers before 1900*, BD154

Flora, EC32, EC33

Flora of the British Isles, Clapham, A. R., EC32

Flores, Arturo A. *Foreign law*, CK28

Flores Villela, Carlos Arturo. *México, la cultura, el arte y la vida cotidiana*, DB126

Floristic regions of the world, Takhtadzhīan, A. L., EC31

Floyd, Samuel A. *Black music biography*, BH89

Fluid mechanics source book, EA38

Flynn, Francis. *Gerontology*, CC41

Fodor, Nandor. *Encyclopaedia of psychic science*, CD51

Folk and popular music, BH27, BH123, BH125, BH127, BH128, BH130, BH132, BH133, BH134, BH135

  bibliography, BH136, BH137, BH138, BH139

  discography, BH141, BH142, BH144

Folk art, BF3, BF4, BF8, BF10, BF11, BF12, BF15, BF16, BF17

Folk artists biographical index, BF15

The folk music sourcebook, Sandberg, Larry, BH133

Folklife sourcebook, Bartis, Peter, CF32

Folklore and popular culture

  bibliography, CF18, CF19, CF20, CF21, CF22, CF23, CF24

  by region

    Canada, CF32

    Japan, BD381, CF36

    United States, BD163, CF29, CF30, CF32, CF34

  dictionaries, CF28

  dissertations, CF25

  encyclopedias, CF26

  indexes, CF19

  thematic indexes, CF18

The folklore of American holidays, CF37

Folktales in the English language, A guide to, CF18

Folter, Siegrun H. *Private libraries of musicians and musicologists*, BH12

The Fontana biographical companion to modern thought, AC4

The Fontana dictionary of modern thought, AC4

Food additives handbook, Lewis, Richard J., Sr, EH33

Food and cookery, EH32, EK96, EK101; *see also* **Nutrition**

  guides, EH34, EH35

Food and nutrition information guide, Szilard, Paula, EK96

Food, cookery, and diet, Prytherch, Raymond John, EH35

Food science, CK93, EH1, EH30, EH31, EH33, EK100

Food science and technology abstracts, EH30

Football, BJ29, BJ30

For the record, Markel, Robert, BJ7

Forbes, Fred R. *Dance*, BG46

Forbes, Patricia. *Harrap's concise French-English dictionary = dictionnaire anglais-français*, AD94

Ford list of British parliamentary papers 1965–1974, AG43

Ford list of British parliamentary papers, 1974–1983, together with specialist commentaries, AG43

Foreign gazetteers of the U.S. Board on Geographic Names, CL27, CL28

Foreign investment in the U.S, CH351

Foreign language index, CA10

Foreign law, Reynolds, Thomas H., CK28

Foreign manufacturers in the United States, CH293

Foreign policy of the French Second Empire, Echard, William E., DC59

Foreign ships in Micronesia, Hezel, Francis X., DG8

Foreign study, CB80, CB85, CB160

Foreign trade; *see also* **International business enterprises**

  bibliography, CH178, CH179

  directories, CH180, CH181

  handbooks, CH183, CH184, CH185

Forest products abstracts, EH8

Forest Products Laboratory (U.S.). *Wood engineering handbook*, EJ42

Forestry abstracts, EH8

Forrest, J. *Republic of Guinea-Bissau*, DD6

Forrestal, Dan J. *The Dartnell public relations handbook*, CH74

Forster, Antonia. *Index to book reviews in England, 1749–1774*, BD210

Forster, Merlin H. *Vanguardism in Latin American literature*, BD332

Forthcoming books, AA82, AA83

Fortunoff Video Archive for Holocaust Testimonies. *Guide to Yale University Library Holocaust video testimonies*, DA84

Foskett, Daphne. *Collecting miniatures*, BE152

—— *Dictionary of British miniature painters*, BE152

—— *Miniatures*, BE152

Foster, David William. *Brazilian literature*, BD319

—— *Handbook of Latin American literature*, BD329

Foster, Dennis L. *The rating guide to franchises*, CH118

Foster, Janet. *British archives*, AB50, AK28, DC107

Foster, Mamie Marie Booth. *Southern black creative writers, 1829–1953*, BD187

Foster, William. *Guide to the India Office records 1600–1858*, DE32

Fóti, Istvánné. *Statisztikai adatforrások*, CG55

Foundation Center. *Corporate foundation profiles*, CA32

—— *The Foundation Center's user-friendly guide*, CA44

—— *Foundation grants to individuals*, CA34

—— *Foundations today*, CA48

—— *National directory of corporate giving*, CA39

—— *National guide to funding in aging*, CC67

The Foundation Center's user-friendly guide, CA44

Foundation fundamentals, Read, Patricia, CA47

Foundation grants to individuals, CA34

Foundation guide for religious grant seekers, Butler, Francis J., BB31, CA31

Foundation profiles, The Hague Club, CA27

Foundations and philanthropic organizations

  compendiums, CA48

  directories, CA28, CA29, CA32, CA34, CA39

    Australia, CA42

    Canada, CA25

    international, CA26

    United States, BE53, CA30, CA38, CA40, CB158

  handbooks, CA44, CA45, CA47

  international, CA27

The foundations of students' learning, Marjoribanks, Kevin, CB63

Foundations today, Renz, Loren, CA48

Four gothic kings, Hallam, Elizabeth M., DC116

Fowler, Roger. *A dictionary of modern critical terms*, BD31, BD36

Fowlie-Flores, Fay. *Annotated bibliography of Puerto Rican bibliographies*, DB153

—— *Index to Puerto Rican collective biography*, AJ89

Fox, Charles. *The essential jazz records*, BH120

Fox, Daniel M. *Nobel laureates in medicine or physiology*, EK76

Fraenkel, Josef. *The Jewish press of the world*, AE3

Fraenkel-Conrat, Heinz. *The viruses*, EC68

Fraker, Anne T. *Religion and American life*, BB9

France

  bibliography, AA114

    16th century, AA111

    17th century, AA112

    19th and 20th centuries, AA115

    current, AA116, AA117

  biography, AJ50, AJ51, AJ53, AJ54, CJ171

  foreign relations, DB114, DC59

    manuscripts and archives, DC72

  government officials, DC69

  government publications, AG34, AG35

  history

    19th century

      encyclopedias, DC74

    atlases, DC78, DC79

    bibliography, DC60

      Napoleonic era, DC61, DC63

      since 1789, DC59, DC75, DC76

    chronologies, DC77

    encyclopedias, DC66

    manuscripts and archives, DC67, DC68, DC70, DC71, DC73

    military history, DC62, DC65

      biography, AJ52

    politics and government, CJ171, DC69

France. Archives nationales. *Guide des papiers privés d'époque révolutionnaire*, DC50

France. Direction des bibliothèques, des musées et de l'information scientifique et technique. *La documentation administrative*, AG34

France. Direction générale des enseignements supérieurs et de la recherche. *La documentation administrative*, AG34

France. Ministère des affaires étrangères. *Etat général des inventaires des archives diplomatiques*, DC71

France. Ministère des affaires étrangères. Archives. *Guide des sources de l'histoire du Brésil aux archives du Ministère français des affaires étrangères*, DB114

France. Ministère des relations extérieures. Archives et documentation. *Les archives du Ministère des relations extérieures depuis les origines*, DC72

La France révolutionnaire et impériale,
Monglond, André, DC49
France under the German occupation,
1940–1944, Evleth, Donna, DC60
Franchise opportunities handbook, CH118
La francité canadienne, Sabourin, Conrad,
BC40
Franck, Irene M. *Dictionary of 20th-century*
history, DA59
Frank, Beryl. *Encyclopedia of U.S. government*
benefits, CJ51
Frank, Frederick S. *The first Gothics,* BD114
—— *Gothic fiction,* BD115
—— *Guide to the Gothic,* BD116
—— *Through the pale door,* BD117
Frank, Ruth S. *The book of Jewish books,*
BB129
Frankel, Linda. *The student sociologist's*
handbook, CC2
Franklin, Benjamin. *Dictionary of American*
literary characters, BD174
Franz, Del. *Work, study, travel abroad,* CB86
Französisches etymologisches Wörterbuch,
Wartburg, Walther von, AD96
Fraser, Bryce. *The New Zealand book of events,*
DF11
Fraser, Clarence M. *The Merck veterinary*
manual, EH28
Fraser, Donald. *A dictionary of musical*
quotations, BH63
Fraser, P. M. *A lexicon of Greek personal*
names, AK50
Fraser, Peter D. *Caribbean economic*
handbook, CH43
—— *Central American economic handbook,*
CH44
Fraser, Robert. *The world financial system,*
CH223
Frayser, Suzanne G. *Studies in human*
sexuality, CC147
Frazer, Ruth F. *Politics and religion,* BB15,
CJ13
Frazier, Gregory W. *The American Indian*
index, CC228
Fredericksen, Burton B. *The index of paintings*
sold in the British Isles during the nineteenth
century, BE61
Frederiksen, Elke. *Women writers of Germany,*
Austria, and Switzerland, BD294
Fredland, Richard A. *A guide to African*
international organisations, CK119
Fredriksen, John C. *Free trade and sailors'*
rights, CJ268, DB8
—— *Shield of republic, sword of empire,*
CJ268, DB8
Free trade and sailors' rights, Fredriksen, John
C., CJ268, DB8
Freed, Melvyn N. *The educator's desk reference*
(EDR), CB4
Freedman, Lawrence. *Atlas of global strategy,*
CJ42
—— *Europe transformed,* CJ164
Freeman, Jean K. *Real estate,* CH344
Freeman, Michael J. *Atlas of Nazi Germany,*
DC97
—— *Atlas of the world economy,* CH26
Freeman, Morton S. *A handbook of problem*
words & phrases, AD25
Freeman, Roger K. *Drugs in pregnancy and*
lactation, EK113
Freeman, Thomas Walter. *Geographers:*
biobibliographical studies, CL24
Freeman-Grenville, G. S. P. *Modern atlas of*
African history, DD11
—— *The new atlas of African history,* DD11
Freitag, Ruth S. *Halley's comet,* EB2
French, Joyce N. *Adult literacy,* CB24
French-Canadian authors, Kandiuk, Mary,
BD305
French feminist criticism, Gelfand, Elissa D.,
BD311
French language
atlases, BC39

bibliography, BC38, BD308
Canadian French, BC40
dictionaries, AD89, AD90, AD91, AD92,
AD93
bilingual, AD94, AD95, EA48
etymology, AD96
new words, AD100
Old–17th century, AD102
slang, AD97, AD98
synonyms, AD99
obsolete words, AD101
French language and literature, Bassan,
Fernande, BC38, BD308
French literature
bibliography, BC38, BD308
medieval, BD310
criticism, BD311
dictionaries, BD312
encyclopedias, BD313
guides, BD307
history, BD314
French mathematical seminars, Anderson,
Nancy D., EF1
French Revolution, DC51
atlases, DC58
bibliography, DC47, DC49
biography, DC57
encyclopedias, DC52, DC53, DC55
filmography, DC48
handbooks, DC54, DC56
manuscripts and archives, DC50
The French Revolution, Jones, Colin, DC54
French Romanesque sculpture, Lyman, Thomas
W., BE162
French sculptors of the 17th and 18th centuries,
Souchal, François, BE163
French Second Empire, 1852–1870, DC75
Frenzel, Elisabeth. *Motive der Weltliteratur,*
BD27
Fresh-water invertebrates of the United States,
Pennak, Robert W., EC43
Frey, Linda. *Women in western European*
history. First supplement, CC280
Frey, Marsha. *Women in western European*
history. First supplement, CC280
Frey, Robert L. *Railroads in the nineteenth*
century, CH136
Frick, John P. *Woldman's engineering alloys,*
EJ88
Frickx, Robert. *Lettres françaises de Belgique,*
BD303
Fried, Lewis. *Handbook of American-Jewish*
literature, BD194
Friedberg, Joan Brest. *Accept me as I am,*
CC103
Friedman, Catherine. *Commodity prices,*
CH173
Friedman, Jack P. *Encyclopedia of investments,*
CH222
Friedman, Norman. *Conway's all the world's*
fighting ships, 1947–1982, CJ264
Friedrich, Gerhard. *Theological dictionary of*
the New Testament, BB58
Friedrich der Grosse, Bibliographie, DC83
Friesel, Evyatar. *Atlas of modern Jewish history,*
DA64
Frings, Theodor. *Althochdeutsches Wörterbuch,*
AD103
Fritsch, Ronald E. *Directory of public and*
private programs for emotionally disturbed
children and youth, CC89
Fritz, Jan M. *The clinical sociology handbook,*
CC7
Fritze, Ronald H. *Reference sources in history,*
DA1
Froehlich, Hildegard C. *Research in music*
education, BH3
Froelke, Ruth. *The Wuerttemberg emigration*
index, AK13
Frohn, Axel. *Guide to inventories and finding*
aids of German archives at the German
Historical Institute, Washington, D.C, DC91

From CA to CAS ONLINE, Schulz, Hedda,
ED2
From day to day, Johnson, David E., DA23
From Erasmus to Tolstoy, Meulen, Jacob ter,
CJ297
From Helsinki to Vienna, CK108
From museums, galleries, and studios, Besemer,
Susan P., BE76
From radical left to extreme right, Skidmore,
Gail, AE26
Frontier and pioneer life, DB76
Froschl, Merle. *Feminist resources for schools*
and colleges, CC248
—— *Resources for educational equity,* CB38
Frost, Elizabeth. *The bully pulpit,* CJ84
—— *The quotable lawyer,* CK72
Frost, Pandora Kerr. *Chambers English*
dictionary, AD7
Frost, Wendy. *Feminist literary criticism,* BD20
Frühneuhochdeutsches Wörterbuch, AD104
Frumkin, Norman. *Guide to economic*
indicators, CH16
Fry, Gerald. *The international development*
dictionary, CH55
—— *Pacific Basin and Oceania,* DG1
Fry, John. *Disease data book,* EK68
Fryde, E. B. *Handbook of British chronology,*
DC122
Fryer, Deborah J. *The Columbia Granger's*
index to poetry, BD11
Fuchs, Reimar Walter. *Der Buchdruck im 15.*
Jahrhundert, AA45
Fürstenau, Eugênio. *Novo dicionário de termos*
técnicos inglês-portugues, EA51
Fukui, Haruhiro. *Political parties of Asia and*
the Pacific, CJ153
Fuld, James J. *The book of world-famous music,*
BH127
Fulltext sources online, AE76
Fulton, Richard D. *Union list of Victorian*
serials, AE73
Fund raising, CA43
Fundamentals of legal research, Jacobstein, J.
Myron, CK6
Fundamentals of musical composition,
Schoenberg, Arnold, BH9
Funding for museums, archives, and special
collections, BE53
Fungi, EC34, EC35
Fungi on plants and plant products in the
United States, EC34
Furet, François. *A critical dictionary of the*
French Revolution, DC52
Furlani, Silvio. *Archivio biografico italiano,*
AJ74
Furniture
bibliography, BF34, BF36
biography, BF37
dictionaries, BF39, BF40, BF41
encyclopedias, BF37, BF42
Furniture History Society. *Dictionary of*
English furniture makers 1660–1840, BF37
Furr, A. Keith. *CRC handbook of laboratory*
safety, ED13
Futures see Commodities
Fyfe, Janet. *History journals and serials,* DA9

GAO masterfile, United States. General
Accounting Office, AG23
GAO masterfile, 1976–1989, AG23
The . . . GIS guide to four-year colleges, CB97
Gabaccia, Donna R. *Immigrant women in the*
United States, CC281
Gacs, Ute. *Women anthropologists,* CE23
Gänzl, Kurt. *Gänzl's book of the musical*
theatre, BH106
Gänzl's book of the musical theatre, Gänzl,
Kurt, BH106
Gärtner, Karla. *Bibliographie deutschsprachiger*
bevölkerungswissenschaftlicher Literatur,
1978–1984, CG4
Gailey, H. A. *Gambia,* DD6

Gale, Steven H. *Encyclopedia of American humorists*, BD153
Gale directory of publications, AE23
Gale directory of publications and broadcast media, AE23
Gale international directory of publications, AE4
Gale Research Company. *Twentieth-century literary criticism*, BD19
Galerstein, Carolyn L. *Women writers of Spain*, BD326
Gall, Ernst. *Reallexikon zur deutschen Kunstgeschichte*, BE39
Gallaudet encyclopedia of deaf people and deafness, CC105
Galli, Rosemary E. *Guinea-Bissau*, DD39
Gallup polls of attitudes toward education 1969–1984, CB149
Gallup polls of the public attitudes toward the public schools of the U.S, CB149
Gal'perin, Il'ïà Romanovich. *Bol'shoĭ anglo-russkiĭ slovar'*, AD152
Galván, Roberto A. *El diccionario del español chicano = The dictionary of Chicano Spanish*, AD169
Galvin, Katherine M. *Legal research*, CK5
Gambia, DD35, DD36, DD37
Gambia, Gailey, H. A., DD6
The Gambia, Gamble, David P., DD35
Gamble, David P. *The Gambia*, DD35
—— *A general bibliography of the Gambia, Supplement II, 1978–1982*, DD37
—— *A general bibliography of the Gambia up to 31st December 1977*, DD36
Gammond, Peter. *The Oxford companion to popular music*, BH128
Ganellin, C. R. *Dictionary of drugs : chemical data, structures, and bibliographies*, ED33, EK110
Ganly, John. *Serials for libraries*, AA68
Ganz, Arthur F. *Literary terms*, BD34
García, Barbara M. *The University of Chicago Spanish dictionary*, AD165
Garcia, F. L. *Encyclopedia of banking & finance*, CH224
García, Miguel Angel. *Anuario bibliográfico hondureño*, AA137
García-Arenal, Mercedes. *Repertorio bibliográfico de las relaciones entre la península Ibérica y el Norte de África, siglos XV–XVI*, DD14
García-Ayvens, Francisco. *Chicano anthology index*, CC240
García Craviotto, Francisco. *Catalogo general de Incunables en bibliotecas españolas*, AA40
García de Diego, Carmen. *Diccionario etimológico español e hispánico*, AD166
García de Diego, Vicente. *Diccionario etimológico español e hispánico*, AD166
García Durán, Juan. *La guerra civil española, fuentes*, DC184
Gardens, BE141, BE146
  encyclopedias, BE143, EH9
Gardiner, Robert. *Conway's all the world's fighting ships, 1947–1982*, CJ264
Gardner, Helen. *Gardner's art through the ages*, BE71
Gardner, J. Anthony. *The Iraq-Iran war*, DE9
Gardner, John Consaul. *Accounting research directory*, CH61
Gardner's art through the ages, Gardner, Helen, BE71
Garg, Gaṅgā Rām. *International encyclopaedia of Indian literature*, BD378
Garland, Henry B. *The Oxford companion to German literature*, BD290
Garland, Mary. *The Oxford companion to German literature*, BD290
Garland composer resource manuals, BH90
The Garland Shakespeare bibliographies, BD261
Garlant, Julia. *Latin American bibliography*, DB94

Garner, Bryan A. *A dictionary of modern legal usage*, CK63
Garraty, John Arthur. *Dictionary of American biography. Supplement eight*, AJ25
Garrison, Robert H. *The nutrition desk reference*, EK98
Garst, Rachel. *Bibliografía anotada de obras de referencia sobre Centroamérica y Panamá en el campo de las ciencias sociales*, DB92
Gartenberg, Jon. *The film catalog*, BG77
—— *Glossary of filmographic terms = Lexique de termes filmographiques*, BG95
Garwood, Alfred N. *Almanac of the 50 states*, CG36
—— *Black Americans*, CC209
—— *Regional differences in America*, CG26, DB44
Garza, Hedda. *The Watergate investigation index*, CJ49, CJ50
Garzanti comprehensive Italian-English, English-Italian dictionary, Hazon, Mario, AD130
Gascoigne, Bamber. *How to identify prints*, BE157
Gascoigne, Robert Mortimer. *A historical catalogue of scientific periodicals, 1665–1900*, EA18
—— *A historical catalogue of scientists and scientific books*, EA18
Gaskell, Philip. *A new introduction to bibliography*, ED4
Gastrow, Shelagh. *Who's who in South African politics*, CJ203
Gates, Henry Louis. *Black biography, 1790–1950*, AJ23
Gates, Jean Key. *Guide to the use of libraries and information sources*, AB9
Gaudet, Franceen. *Checklist of indexes to Canadian newspapers = Liste de contrôle des index de journaux canadiens*, AF14
Gavrilenko, N. V. *Gosudarstvennye (natsional'nye) bibliograficheskie ukazateli sotsialisticheskikh stran*, AA77
Gay, William. *The nuclear arms race*, CJ294
Gaylord, Charles N. *Structural engineering handbook*, EJ41
Gaylord, Edwin Henry. *Structural engineering handbook*, EJ41
Gazetteer of conventional names, CL27
Gazetteers, CL26, CL27, CL28, CL29
Geahigan, Priscilla C. *Business serials of the U.S. government*, CH91
—— *U.S. and Canadian businesses, 1955 to 1987*, CH137
Gebauer, Dorothea. *Bibliography of national filmographies*, BG51
Geddes, C. L. *Guide to reference books for Islamic studies*, BB126
Geer, Gary. *Dictionary of American literary characters*, BD174
Geetha, K. R. *Classified state bibliography of linguistic research on Indian languages*, BC56
Gehring, Wes D. *Handbook of American film genres*, BG90
Geib, M. Margaret. *Atlas of South Asia*, DE34
Geils, Peter. *Gesamtverzeichnis des deutschsprachigen Schrifttums (GV), 1700–1910*, AA120
Geiriadur Prifysgol Cymru, AD173
Geisler, Charles C. *Labor and the environment*, CH271
Geist, Christopher D. *Directory of popular culture collections*, CF29
Gelb, Ignace J. *Assyrian dictionary*, AD75
Gelfand, Elissa D. *French feminist criticism*, BD311
Gellert, Charles Lawrence. *The Holocaust, Israel and the Jews*, DA88
Gemeentebibliotheek Rotterdam. *Catalogue of the Erasmus collection in the City Library of Rotterdam*, BA27
Gems, EE34

Gender roles, Beere, Carole A., CC307
Gender, unpaid labor, and the promotion of literacy, Malone, Cheryl Knott, CB33
Gendron, Francis. *Dictionnaire historique de la Révolution française*, DC53
—— *Filmographie mondiale de la Révolution française*, DC48
A genealogical handbook of German research, Jensen, Larry O., AK24, AK25
Genealogical resources in English repositories, Moulton, Joy Wade, AK34
The genealogist's address book, Bentley, Elizabeth Petty, AK16
Genealogy
  Canada, AK20
  France, AK21, AK22, AK23
  Germany, AK12, AK24, AK25, AK27
  Gt. Brit., AK29
    guides, AK30, AK31, AK32, AK34, AK35
    handbooks, AK33
    indexes, AK19
  international, AK1
  Ireland, AK30, AK38, AK39, AK40, AK41
  Jewish, AK42
  Netherlands, AK43
  Scotland, AK44
  Switzerland, AK45
  United States
    bibliography, AK5, AK8
    directories, AK15, AK16, AK17, AK18
    guides, AB49, AK4, AK6, AK7, DB22, DB32, DB42
    indexes, AK9, AK10
  Wales, AK29, AK46, AK47, AK48
Genealogy for librarians, Harvey, Richard, AK31
A general bibliography of the Gambia, Supplement II, 1978–1982, Gamble, David P., DD37
A general bibliography of the Gambia up to 31st December 1977, Gamble, David P., DD36
General catalogue of printed books, British Museum. Dept. of Printed Books, BD243
A general guide to the India Office Records, India Office Library and Records, DE4, DE32
—— Moir, Martin, DE4
The general history of astronomy, EB13
General issues in literacy/illiteracy, Eller, William, CB29
—— Hladczuk, John, CB28, CB29
—— Hladczuk, Sharon, CB29
General science index, EA26
Genetic disorders and birth defects, EK45
Genetics, EC65, EC66, EC67
Genetics abstracts, EC7
Genome data base, EC67
Gentz, William H. *The dictionary of Bible and religion*, BB22
Geo abstracts, CL6, CL7
GEOBASE, EC23, CL5
Geographers: biobibliographical studies, CL24
Geographical abstracts, EC23
Geographical abstracts. Human geography, CL6
Geographical abstracts. Physical geography, CL7
Geographical names and terms, BD50, CL34, CL35, CL36; *see also* under individual countries, subhead **Place-names**
Geography
  abstract journals, CL6, CL7
  bibliography, CL2, CL3, CL41
  biography, CL4, CL24, CL25
  databases, CL5
  dictionaries, CL10, CL12
  directories, CL14, CL15
  encyclopedias, CL9, CL11
  handbooks, CJ125
  indexes, CL8
  quotations, CL13
Geological nomenclature, Nederlands Geologisch Mijnbouwkundig Genootschap, EE16

Geological reference file, EE5
Geological Survey (U.S.). *The national gazetteer of the United States of America*, CL30, CL31
Geologists and the history of geology, Sarjeant, William Antony S., EE19
Geology
  biography, EE19
  databases, EE5
  dictionaries, EE8, EE9, EE10, EE11
    polyglot, EE13, EE15, EE16
    terminology, EE12
  directories, EB10, EE17, EE18
  encyclopedias, EE7, EE43
  guidebooks, EE21
  history, EE19
  sourcebooks, EE20
Geophysical abstracts, EE5
Geophysics, EE6
GeoRef, EE5, EE12
GeoRef thesaurus and guide to indexing, EE5, EE12
Georgakas, Dan. *Encyclopedia of the American left*, CJ243, DB62
George, John H. *They never said it*, BD59
George, Linda K. *Handbook of aging and the social sciences*, CC64
The George Washington journal of international law and economics, CK106
Georges, Christopher J. *The Harvard independent insider's guide to prep schools*, CB109
Georgescu, Magdalena. *Dicţionarul limbii române literare vechi, 1640–1780*, AD147
Georgia State University. *Marketing information*, CH312
Georgiev, Vladimir Ivanov. *Bŭlgarski etimologichen rechnik*, AD78
—— *Entsiklopediîa Bŭlgariîa*, DC36
Geoscience Information Society. *Union list of geologic field trip guidebooks of North America*, EE21
Geraghty & Miller's groundwater bibliography, Van der Leeden, Frits, EE25
Gerbner, George. *Violence and terror in the mass media*, CH202
Gerdts, William H. *The National Museum of American Art's index to American art exhibition catalogues*, BE67
Gerhan, David R. *A retrospective bibliography of American demographic history from colonial times to 1983*, CG5, DB9
Gerhardstein, Virginia Brokaw. *Dickinson's American historical fiction*, BD173
Gerhart, Eugene C. *Quote it II*, CK71
—— *Quote it! Memorable legal quotations*, CK70
Gerlo, Aloïs. *Bibliographie de l'humanisme des anciens Pays-Bas*, BA9
Germaine, Max. *Artists and galleries of Australia*, BE82
German-American literature, BD170
German-American names, Jones, George Fenwick, AK49
German drama, BD295, BD296
German fiction, BD297
German Historical Institute (Washington, D.C.). *Guide to inventories and finding aids of German archives at the German Historical Institute, Washington, D.C*, DC91
German immigrants, Zimmerman, Gary J., AK14
German language
  bibliography, BC33
  dictionaries, AD103, AD104, AD105, AD106, AD107, AD108
    bibliography, BC32
    bilingual, AD109, AD110
    etymology, AD111, AD112
    slang, AD113
    usage, AD114
  grammar
    bibliography, BC22, BC32

German literature
  bibliography, BD287
  biography, BD293, BD294
  dictionaries, BD290
  dictionaries of authors and literature, BD288, BD289, BD291, BD292
  periodicals, AE36, AE36
The German-speaking countries of Europe, Krewson, Margrit B., DC4
The German stage, 1767–1890, Richel, Veronica C., DC296
The Germans after World War II, Paul, Barbara Dotts, DC86
Germans in the United States, AK13, AK14
Germans to America, AK14, AK12
Germany
  archival sources, DC90
  bibliography
    18th–19th centuries, AA120
    20th century, AA121
    current, AA122, AA123
    early, AA26, AA118, AA119
  biography, AJ55, AJ56, AJ57, AJ58, AJ59, DC95
    bibliography, AJ60
  history
    20th century, DA87, DC95
    atlases, DC97, DC98
    bibliography, DC80, DC81, DC84
      20th century, DC86, DC87, DC92
    chronologies, DC93
    encyclopedias, DC94
    guides to records, DC91
    handbooks, DC93
    oral history, BE137
Germany, East
  bibliography, DC89
    20th century, DC88
  politics and government, CJ172
Germany, West
  history
    bibliography, DC85
  politics and government, CJ173
Germer, Mark. *American Musicological Society*, BH42
Gernsheim, Alison. *The history of photography*, BF53
—— *The origins of photography*, BF53
Gernsheim, Helmut. *The history of photography*, BF53
—— *Incunabula of British photographic literature*, BF53
—— *The origins of photography*, BF53
Gerontology *see* Aging; Old age pensions
Gerontology, Edwards, Willie M., CC41
Gerow, Edwin. *Guide to Indian philosophy*, BA7
Gervasi, Anne. *Handbook for small, rural, and emerging public libraries*, AB55
Gesamtkatalog der Wiegendrucke, AA42, AA41
Gesamtverzeichnis des deutschsprachigen Schrifttums ausserhalb des Buchhandels (GVB), 1966–1980, AA121
Gesamtverzeichnis des deutschsprachigen Schrifttums (GV), 1700–1910, AA120
Gesamtverzeichnis deutschsprachiger Hochschulschriften (GVH), 1966–1980, AH8
Gesamtverzeichnis österreichischer Dissertationen, AH5
Die Geschichte der deutschen Passagierschiffahrt, Kludas, Arnold, AK26, CH191
Gesellschaft für Unternehmensgeschichte. *Deutsche Wirtschaftsarchive*, DC90
Gesenius, Wilhelm. *Hebräisches und aramäisches Handwörterbuch über das Alte Testament*, AD117
Getting a grant in the 1980s, CA45
Getting a grant in the 1990s, Lefferts, Robert, CA45
Getty Art History Information Program. *Art and architecture thesaurus*, BE45
—— *Art & architecture thesaurus*, BE44

—— *Bibliography of the history of art*, BE19
—— *The index of paintings sold in the British Isles during the nineteenth century*, BE61
Geuss, Herbert. *Dahlmann-Waitz Quellenkunde der deutschen Geschichte*, DC80, DC81
Geyer, Douglas W. *Index to book reviews in religion*, BB20
Ghana, AA124, DD38
Ghana national bibliography bi monthly, AA124
Ghanī, Sīrūs. *Iran and the West*, DE68
Ghatage, Amrit Madhav. *An encyclopaedic dictionary of Sanskrit on historical principles*, AD156
Ghisalberti, Alberto Maria. *Dizionario biografico degli Italiani*, AJ75
Ghorayshi, Parvin. *The sociology of work*, CC8
Ghormley, N. Rex. *Ophthalmic drug facts*, EK120
The ghost walks, Sampson, Henry T., BG43
Ghūshah, Zakī Rātib. *Administration and development in the Arab world*, CJ217
Gianakos, Larry James. *Television drama series programming*, BG108
Gibaldi, Joseph. *MLA handbook for writers of research papers*, AH1
—— *The MLA style manual*, AA53
Gibb, Hamilton Alexander Rosskeen,. *The encyclopaedia of Islam*, BB125
Gibb, Mike. *Keyguide to information sources in veterinary medicine*, EH26
Gibbney, H. J. *A biographical register, 1788–1939*, AJ34
Gibbons, S. R. *A handbook of modern history*, DA59
Gibilisco, Stan. *Encyclopedia of electronics*, EJ45
Gibraltar, DC99
Gibraltar, Shields, Graham J., DC99
Gibson, Mary Jo Storey. *International glossary of social gerontology = Glosario internacional de gerontología social = Glossaire international de gérontologie sociale = Internationales Wörterverzeichnis für Sozialgerontologie*, CC54
Giddings, Robert. *Who was really who in fiction*, BD96
Gidwani, N. N. *Current Indian periodicals in English*, AE50
Gieysztorowa, Irena. *The historical atlas of Poland*, DC174
Gifford, Denis. *The British film catalogue, 1895–1985*, BG71
Gifted children, CB14
Gifted, talented, and creative young people, Stein, Morris Isaac, CB14
Gilbert, Alan D. *Australians*, DF2
Gilbert, Christopher,. *Dictionary of English furniture makers 1660–1840*, BF37
Gilbert, Dennis A. *Compendium of American public opinion*, CJ231
Gilbert, Martin. *Atlas of the Holocaust*, DA85
—— *Macmillan atlas of the holocaust*, DA85
Gilder, Eric. *The dictionary of composers and their music*, BH78
Gilgen, Albert R. *International handbook of psychology*, CD30
Gilgen, Carol K. *International handbook of psychology*, CD30
Gill, Kay. *Encyclopedia of medical organizations and agencies*, EK64
—— *State government research directory*, CJ126
Gillie, Christopher. *Longman companion to English literature*, BD220
Gillmor, Robert. *Naturalized birds of the world*, EC52
Gilroy, Dan. *Reading lists in radical social science*, CA7
Gimson, A. C. *Everyman's English pronouncing dictionary*, AD37

Ginsburgs, George. *A calendar of Soviet treaties, 1974–1980,* CK112
Girardi, Michele. *Il teatro La Fenice,* BH96
Gjønnes, Svein Tore. *Norsk historisk bibliografi 1916–1945,* DC167
Glaciology, EE23
Gladkova, T. L. *L'emigration russe,* AE64
Glanze, Walter D. *Mosby's medical, nursing, and allied health dictionary,* EK91
Glareanus, Henricus. *Isagoge in musicen,* BH9
Glashan, Roy R. *American governors and gubernatorial elections, 1775–1978,* CJ133
Glass see **Ceramics and glass**
Glasse, Cyril. *The concise encyclopedia of Islam,* BB127
Glavatskikh, G. A. *Istoriia dorevoliutsionnoǐ Rossii v dnevnikakh i vospominaniiakh,* DC196
Glazer, Mark. *A dictionary of Mexican American proverbs,* BD344
Glazier, Ira A. *The famine immigrants,* AK11
—— *Germans to America,* AK12
Glikin, Ronda. *Black American women in literature,* BD185
Glimpses of India, Riddick, John F., DE57
Glixon, David M. *Allusions—cultural, literary, biblical, and historical,* AD22, BD32
Gloag, John. *John Gloag's dictionary of furniture,* BF40
—— *Short dictionary of furniture,* BF40
Global countertrade, Żurawicki, Leon, CH179
Global guide to international education, CB91
Global guide to media & communications, Lent, John A., CH198
Global terrorism, DA55
Glossary for horticultural crops, Soule, James, EH12
Glossary of art, architecture and design since 1945, Walker, John A., BE43
Glossary of educational technology terms = Glosario de términos de tecnologia de la educación, CB69
Glossary of educational technology terms = Glossaire des termes de technologie éducative, CB70
Glossary of educational technology terms = Glossariǐ terminov po tekhnologii obrazovaniia, CB71
A glossary of entomology, Torre-Bueno, José Rollin de la, EC64
Glossary of filmographic terms = Lexique de termes filmographiques, Gartenberg, Jon, BG95
Glossary of geology, Bates, Robert Latimer, EE8, EE9
—— Jackson, Julia A., EE9
A glossary of literary terms, Abrams, M. H., BD31
Glossary of psychoanalytic terms and concepts, Fine, Bernard D., CD24
—— Moore, Burness E., CD24
A glossary of special education, CB72
Glossolalia, BB83
Gmelin formula index, ED27
Gmelins Handbuch der anorganischen Chemie, ED27
Godden, Geoffrey A. *Encyclopaedia of British porcelain manufacturers,* BF22
—— *Encyclopedia of British pottery and porcelain marks,* BF22
Goebel, Ulrich. *Frühneuhochdeutsches Wörterbuch,* AD104
Goehlert, Robert. *The American presidency,* CJ76, CJ77
—— *American presidents,* CJ74, CJ78
—— *Congress and law-making,* CJ92
—— *The Department of State and American diplomacy,* CJ75
—— *The executive branch of the U.S. government,* CJ76
—— *State legislatures,* CJ121
—— *The U.S. Supreme Court,* CK29

Goehring, James E. *The Eerdmans analytical concordance to the Revised Standard Version of the Bible,* BB61
Goethe, J. W. von, BD298, BD299
Goethe-Wörterbuch, BD298
Goetz, J. A. *IEEE standard dictionary of electrical and electronics terms,* EJ46
Goetzfridt, Nicholas J. *Micronesia, 1975–1987,* DG2
Gözaydın, Nevzat. *Türkçe sözlük,* AD171
Going places, Hayes, Gregory, BJ49
Golay, Andre. *Harrap's book of film directors and their films,* BG70
Gold, Victor. *Compendium of chemical terminology,* ED8
Gold and silver plate
  American, BF43, BF47
  English, BF45, BF46
Goldblatt, Margaret A. *Recent titles in law for the subject specialist,* CK19
Golden, Richard L. *Sir William Osler,* EK16
Goldman, Jeffrey M. *Means estimating handbook,* EJ39
Goldman, Paul. *Looking at prints, drawings, and watercolours,* BE158
Goldman, Shifra M. *Arte Chicano,* BE5
Goldstucker, Jac L. *Marketing information,* CH312
Golowin, Sergius. *Lexikon der Symbole,* CF1
Gomes, Geoffrey L. *The Portuguese in the United States,* CC168
Gómez de Silva, Guido. *Elsevier's concise Spanish etymological dictionary,* AD167
Gómez F., Héctor. *Publicaciones oficiales de Chile, 1973–1983,* AG32
Gonzales, Sylvia Alicia. *Hispanic American voluntary organizations,* CC242
Goodall, Francis. *A bibliography of British business histories,* CH138
Goode, J. Paul. *Goode's world atlas,* CL51
Goode, Patrick. *The Oxford companion to gardens,* BE143, EH9
Goodenberger, Jennifer. *Subject guide to classical instrumental music,* BH13
Goode's world atlas, Goode, J. Paul, CL51
Goodfellow, William D. *Where's that tune?,* BH14
Goodfriend, Joyce D. *The published diaries and letters of American women,* BD184
Goodman, Jordan Elliot. *Barron's finance & investment handbook,* CH253
—— *Dictionary of finance and investment terms,* CH227
Goodrick, Edward W. *The NIV exhaustive concordance,* BB59
Goodwin, Diana M. *A dictionary of neuropsychology,* EK54
Gopinātha Rāu, T. A. *Elements of Hindu iconography,* BE104
Gordon, Alan. *American chronicle,* DB73
Gordon, Lois G. *American chronicle,* DB73
Gordon, Peter. *A guide to English educational terms,* CB73
Gordon, Robert S. *Union list of manuscripts in Canadian repositories,* DB86
Gordon, W. Terrence. *Semantics,* BC3
Gorenflo, Roger M. *Verzeichnis der bildenden Künstler von 1880 bis heute,* BE88
Goring, Rosemary. *Cambridge biographical dictionary,* AJ1
Gorlin, Rena A. *Codes of professional responsibility,* CH335, CK84
Gorman, G. E. *Black theology,* BB78
—— *Church and state in postwar eastern Europe,* BB76, DC12
—— *Guide to current national bibliographies in the Third World,* AA75
—— *Theological and religious reference materials,* BB79
Gorman, Kathleen. *Editing documents and texts,* AA59
Gorman, Lyn. *Theological and religious reference materials,* BB79

Gorman, Michael. *Anglo-American cataloguing rules,* AB79
—— *The concise AACR2, 1988 revision,* AB80
Gorman, Robert A. *Biographical dictionary of Marxism,* CJ246
—— *Biographical dictionary of neo-Marxism,* CJ247
Górska, Joanna. *Bibliografia wydawnictw Głównego Urzędu Statystycznego, 1968–1973,* CG69
—— *Bibliografia wydawnictw Głównego Urzędu Statystycznego, 1974–1980,* CG70
Gorton, Richard A. *Encyclopedia of school administration & supervision,* CB61
Gorvin, Ian. *Elections since 1945,* CJ33
Gorzny, Willi. *Deutscher biographischer Index,* AJ56
—— *Deutsches biographisches Archiv,* AJ55
—— *Gesamtverzeichnis des deutschsprachigen Schrifttums (GV), 1700–1910,* AA120
—— *Gesamtverzeichnis deutschsprachiger Hochschulschriften (GVH), 1966–1980,* AH8
Gossman, Norbert J. *Biographical dictionary of modern British radicals,* AJ8, AJ62
Gosudarstvennye arkhivy SSSR, AB36, DC199
Gosudarstvennye (natsional'nye) bibliograficheskie ukazateli sotsialisticheskikh stran, Kuznetsova, T. R., AA77
Gothic fiction, Frank, Frederick S., BD115
Gothic literature see **Science fiction, fantasy, and Gothic literature**
The Gothic's Gothic, Fisher, Benjamin Franklin, BD113
Gotthold, Donald W. *Indian Ocean,* DE2
Gotthold, Julia J. *Indian Ocean,* DE2
Goudie, Andrew. *The encyclopaedic dictionary of physical geography,* CL11
Gouke, Mary Noel. *One-parent children, the growing minority,* CC81
Goulart, Ron. *The encyclopedia of American comics,* CF33
Goulet, Richard. *Dictionnaire des philosophes antiques,* BA22
Government assistance almanac, CH54
Government programs and projects directory, CJ62
Government publications; see also under individual countries, subhead **Government publications**
  databases, AG13, AG14
  Europe, AG33
  guides, AG1
  international bibliography, AG39
  library resources, AG2
Government publications, Great Britain. Stationery Office, AG39, AG40, AG41
Government publications monthly list, Great Britain. Stationery Office, AG40, AG41
Government reference books, AG10, AG8
Government reference serials, AG8
—— Schwarzkopf, LeRoy C., AG10
Government research directory, CJ126
Government Research Service. *State legislative sourcebook,* CJ128
Governors, CJ45, CJ133
Goyer, Doreen S. *The handbook of national population censuses,* CG39
Gozmany, László. *Seven-language thesaurus of European animals,* EC40
Graas-Lorang, Cl. *Bibliographie juridique luxembourgeoise,* CK45
Grabar, Oleg. *The art and architecture of Islam: 650–1250,* BE73
Graduate research, Smith, Robert V., EA5
Graff, Carol. *The dictionary of South African painters and sculptors, including Namibia,* BE85
Graham, A. L. *Catalogue of meteorites,* EE38
Graham, Bessie. *The reader's adviser,* AA60
Graham, Joe Stanley. *Hispanic-American material culture,* CC243

Graham, Theresa. *A finding aid to reference books in South Pacific studies*, DG3

Grambs, Jean Dresden. *Sex differences and learning*, CB25

Graml, Hermann. *Biographisches Lexikon zur Weimarer Republik*, DC95

Gran enciclopedia Rialp, AC18

Granatstein, J. L. *The Collins dictionary of Canadian history*, DB87

Grand allusions, Webber, Elizabeth, AD22, BD32

Le grand atlas de l'archéologie, DA39

Grand atlas de l'astronomie, Moore, Patrick, EB15

Le grand atlas des littératures, BD28

Le grand dictionnaire des synonymes, Macé, Pierre-Antoine, AD99

Le grand dictionnaire encyclopédique de la Côte d'Ivoire, Borremans, Raymond, DD40

Grand livre de l'histoire du monde, DA26

Grande dizionario della lingua italiana, Battaglia, Salvatore, AD128

La grande encyclopédie, AC11

La grande encyclopédie du Maroc, DD44

Granger, Edith. *Index to poetry*, BD11

Granger's index to poetry, BD132, BD133

Granić, Gordana. *Adresar pisaca Jugoslavije*, BD360

Grant, Claire. *Grant & Hackh's chemical dictionary*, ED9

Grant, Michael. *Civilization of the ancient Mediterranean*, DA41
—— *The Roman emperors*, DA43

Grant, Roger L. *Grant & Hackh's chemical dictionary*, ED9

Grant, Steven A. *The Russian Empire and the Soviet Union*, DC195

Grant & Hackh's chemical dictionary, Hackh, Ingo W. D., ED9

GRANTS, CA35

GRANTS [computer file], CA33

Grants, fellowships & prizes of interest to historians, DA18

Grants-in-aid, CB162; *see also* **Foundations and philanthropic organizations**
> **by subject**
>> **fine arts**, BE54, BE56
>> **history**, DA18
>> **religion**, BB31, CA31
>> **women**, CC303
> **databases**, CA35
> **directories**, CA33, CA37, CB159, CC108, CC110
> **guides**, AH2, BD49, CA24, CA44, CA46

Graphic arts, BE160, BF9

Grasham, W. E. *Canadian public administration: bibliography = Administration publique canadienne: bibliographie*, CJ213

Graur, Alexandru. *Dicționarul limbii române*, AD148

Gravel, Pierre Bettez. *Anthropological fieldwork*, CE3

Graves, Algernon. *Art sales from early in the eighteenth century to early in the twentieth century*, BE61

Graves, Diane J. *Biographical sources*, AJ2

Gravesteijn, J. *Multilingual thesaurus of geosciences*, EE15

Gray, Alexander Stuart. *Edwardian architecture*, BE134

Gray, John. *Black theatre and performance*, BG11
—— *Blacks in classical music*, BH79
—— *Blacks in film and television*, BG52

Gray, Martin. *A chronology of English literature*, BD221

Gray, Michael H. *Classical music discographies, 1976–1988*, BH159

Gray, Randal. *Chronicle of the First World War*, DA77

Great Britain
> **annuals and current surveys**, DC123

> **armed forces**, DA67
> **atlases**, CJ184
> **bibliography**, DC103
>> **17th and 18th centuries**, AA128, AA129, AA130, AA131
>> **19th and 20th centuries**, AA126, AA133
>> **before 1640**, AA127
>> **current**, AA132
> **biography**, AJ62, AJ63, AJ64, AJ65, AJ66, AJ67, AJ68, CH270
> **directories**, DC103
> **foreign relations**, CJ174, DC17, DC118, DE14
>> **bibliography**, DB14
> **gazetteers**, CL33
> **government publications**
>> **bibliography**, AG38
>> **catalogs and indexes**, AG40, AG41, AG42
>> **databases**, AG37
>> **parliamentary publications**, AG36
>> **select lists**, AG43
> **history**
>> **atlases**, DC125, DC126, DC127, DC128, DC129, DC134
>> **bibliography**, CC284, CK40, DC102, DC104
>>> **16th and 17th centuries**, AG38, BB115
>>> **18th and 19th centuries**, DC115
>>> **20th century**, DC105, DC106
>> **biography**, CJ177, DC112
>> **British Empire and Commonwealth**, DC130, DC131, DC132
>> **chronologies**, DC122
>> **dictionaries**, DC124
>> **encyclopedias**, DC113, DC116, DC117
>> **guides to records**, DC109, DC110, DC111
>>> **regional**, DC110
>> **handbooks**, DC114, DC119, DC120
>> **manuscripts and archives**, AB50, AK28, DC107, DC108
>> **regional**, AK37, DC135, DC136, DC138
> **maritime history**, DA28
> **military history**, DC100
> **politics and government**
>> **atlases**, CJ184
>> **biography**, CJ177, DC112
>> **Commonwealth**, CJ183
>> **handbooks**, CJ175
>> **statistics**, CG52, DC119, DC121
>>> **bibliography**, CG53, CG54

Great Britain. Foreign and Commonwealth Office. *The Commonwealth yearbook*, CJ183

Great Britain. Her Majesty's Stationery Office. *HMSO agency catalogue*, AG39
—— *HMSO annual catalogue*, AG41

Great Britain. Parliament
> **handbooks**, CJ178

Great Britain. Public Record Office. *Irish history from 1700*, DC150

Great Britain. Royal Commission on Historical Manuscripts. *Guides to sources for British history based on the National Register of Archives*, DC108
—— *Record repositories in Great Britain*, DC109

Great Britain. Stationery Office. *Government publications*, AG39, AG40, AG41
—— *Government publications monthly list*, AG40, AG41
—— *UKOP*, AG37

Great Britons, Oxbury, Harold, AJ68

The great deceiver, Powell, Paul W., CC83

The great depression, DA55

Great economists before Keynes, Blaug, Mark, CH20

Great economists since Keynes, Blaug, Mark, CH21

Great historians from antiquity to 1800, DA14

Great lives from history. Twentieth century series, AJ10

The great movie stars, Shipman, David, BG38

The great song thesaurus, Lax, Roger, BH115

The great stage stars, Morley, Sheridan, BG38

Greater London local history directory and bibliography, Marcan, Peter, DC138

Greece
> **bibliography**, AA134
>> **current**, AA135
> **history**, DA41
>> **bibliography**, DC39, DC142
> **place-names**, CF10

Greece and Cyprus since 1920, Richter, Heinz A., DC39, DC142

Greek and Latin authors, 800 B.C.–A.D. 1000, BD55

Greek language, AD115, BC55

Greek literature, BD367, BD368

Greek literature, BD370

Greek national bibliography, AA135

Green, Jonathon. *Dictionary of jargon*, AD42
—— *Newspeak*, AD42

Green, Laura R. *Money for artists*, BE54

Green, Marguerite. *Peace archives*, CJ295

Green, Rayna. *Native American women*, CC282

Green, Richard D. *Index to composer bibliographies*, BH91

Green, Stanley. *Broadway musicals, show by show*, BH107

Green, Syd. *Keyguide to information sources in food science and technology*, EH34

Greenberg, Martin Harry. *Index to crime and mystery anthologies*, BD103
—— *Science fiction and fantasy series and sequels*, BD112

Greenberg, Milton. *The American political dictionary*, CJ54

Greenberg, Stan. *The world sports record atlas*, BJ6

Greene, Frank. *Composers on record*, BH80

Greenfield, Gerald Michael. *Latin American labor organizations*, CH282

Greenfield, Thomas Allen. *Radio*, CH197

Greenleaf, Richard E. *A directory of Latin American studies in the United States*, DB102

Greeves, Lydia. *The National Trust guide*, BE126

Grefsheim, Suzanne. *Encyclopedia of health information sources*, EK10

Gregor, Bernd. *Etymologisches Wörterbuch der deutschen Sprache*, AD112

Gregory, Richard L. *The Oxford companion to the mind*, CD14

Grenada, DB150

Grenada, Schoenhals, Kai P., DB150

Grenz, Wolfgang. *Manual para las relaciones Europeo-Latinoamericanas = Handbook for European-Latin American relations*, DB105

Gresh, Alain. *An A to Z of the Middle East*, CJ199, DE20

Grieb, Kenneth J. *Central America in the nineteenth and twentieth centuries*, DB93
—— *Research guide to Central America and the Caribbean*, DB96

Griffin, John R. *Dictionary of visual science*, EK53

Griffith, H. Winter. *Complete guide to medical tests*, EK69

Griffiths, David B. *A critical bibliography of writings on Judaism*, BB132

Griffiths, Paul. *The Thames and Hudson encyclopaedia of 20th-century music*, BH52

Grim, Ronald E. *World directory of map collections*, CL46

Grimal, Pierre. *The dictionary of classical mythology*, CF11

Grimes, John A. *A concise dictionary of Indian philosophy*, BA17

Grimm, Jacob. *Deutsches Wörterbuch*, AD105

Grimm, Wilhelm. *Deutsches Wörterbuch*, AD105

Grimsted, Patricia Kennedy. *Archives and manuscript repositories in the USSR*, AB36, DC199

—— *Archives and manuscript repositories in the USSR. Ukraine and Moldavia,* AB52, DC200

—— *A handbook for archival research in the USSR,* AB10, DC201

—— *Recent Soviet archival literature,* AB10, DC201

Grimwade, Arthur. *London goldsmiths 1697–1837,* BF46

Grinstein, Louise S. *Women of mathematics,* EF18

Gröber, Gustav. *Grundriss der romanischen Philologie,* BC36

Grønlandsk avis- og tidsskrift-index, AA102

Groom, A. J. R. *International relations,* CJ7

—— *International relations theory,* CJ7

Groos, Arthur. *Medieval Christian literary imagery,* BB81, BD3

Groot woordeboek, Kritzinger, Matthys Stefanus Benjamin, AD68

Gropp, Arthur E. *A bibliography of Latin American bibliographies,* AA8, DB90

Gropp, Dorothy M. *The mature woman in America,* CC39, CC256

Gross, Ernie. *This day in American history,* DB74

Der grosse Brockhaus, AC12

Das grosse Buch der Österreicher, Kleindel, Walter, AJ35

Grosse Lexikon des Dritten Reiches, Bedürftig, Friedemann, DC92

—— Zentner, Christian, DC92

Das Grosse Wörterbuch der deutschen Sprache in 6 Bänden, AD106

Grosses Sängerlexikon, Kutsch, K. J., BH84

Grote, David. *Common knowledge,* BD38

Ground water, EE25

Groyser verterbukh fun der Yidisher shprakh = Great dictionary of the Yiddish language, AD174

Gruber, Ellen J. *Stepfamilies,* CC129

Grubmüller, Klaus. *Die Fabeln des Mittelalters und der frühen Neuzeit,* CF22

Gründer, Karlfried. *Historisches Wörterbuch der Philosophie,* BA18

Grummitt, Karsten. *China economic handbook,* CH39

Grundriss der Geschichte der Philosophie, BA20

Grundriss der romanischen Philologie, Gröber, Gustav, BC36

Grundy, Isobel. *The feminist companion to literature in English,* BD228

Grupenhoff, John T. *National health directory,* EK65

Grzeszczuk, Stanisław. *Katalog czasopism polskich Biblioteki Jagiellońskiej,* AE61

Grzimek, Bernhard. *Grzimek's animal life encyclopedia,* EC57

—— *Grzimek's encyclopedia of mammals,* EC57

Grzimek's animal life encyclopedia, Grzimek, Bernhard, EC57

Grzimek's encyclopedia of mammals, EC57

The Guardian index, AF16

Guatemala, AA136

Gubernatorial and presidential transitions, Bowman, James S., CJ45

Günümüz Türkiyesinde kim kimdir = Who's who in Turkey, AJ97

Guernsey, Otis L. *Curtain times,* BG31

La guerra civil española, fuentes, García Durán, Juan, DC184

Güterbock, Hans Gustav. *The Hittite dictionary of the Oriental Institute of the University of Chicago,* AD122

Guia bibliográfica de la literatura hispano-americana desde siglo XIX hasta 1970, Rela, Walter, BD330

Guía de archivos y bibliotecas, AB51

Guia de história dos Descobrimentos e expansão portuguesa, Marques, Alfredo Pinheiro, DC175

Guía de los archivos estatales españoles, Spain. Inspección Tecnica de Archivos, DC187

Guía de publicações seriadas brasileiras, AE28

Guía del archivo histórico, Peru. Archivo General de la Nación, DB133

Guia do estudante de história medieval portuguesa, Marques, António Henrique R. de Oliveira, DC176

Guía internacional de investigaciones sobre México, DB128

Guía para el estudio de la historia de Venezuela, Lovera De-Sola, R. J., DB136

Guida generale degli archivi di Stato italiani, DC157

Guidance, CB156, CD26

Guidance Information System. *The . . . GIS guide to four-year colleges,* CB97

Guide bibliographique des études d'histoire de la littérature française, Brix, Michel, BD307

Guide de l'utilisateur des catalogues des livres imprimés de la Bibliothèque Nationale, Bernard, Annick, AA15

Guide des archives de l'Afrique occidentale française, Archives du Sénégal, DD23

Guide des centres de documentation en histoire ouvrière et sociale, DC73

Guide des papiers des ministres et secrétaires d'État de 1871 à 1974, Archives nationales (France), DC69

Guide des papiers privés d'époque révolutionnaire, France. Archives nationales, DC50

Guide des recherches sur l'histoire des familles, Bernard, Gildas, AK23

Guide des revues et des journaux marocains courants, AA161

Guide des sources de l'histoire de l'Amérique latine et des Antilles dans les archives françaises, Archives nationales (France), DB98

Guide des sources de l'histoire du Brésil aux archives du Ministère français des affaires étrangères, France. Ministère des affaires étrangères. Archives, DB114

Le guide du cinéma, Haustrate, Gaston, BG91

Guide du cinéma européen, Tavenas, Stéphane, BG99

A guide for students of New Zealand history, Wood, G. A., DF6

Guide for the care and use of laboratory animals, Institute of Laboratory Animal Resources (U.S.). Committee on Care and Use of Laboratory Animals, EC58

Guide for written collection policy statements, American Library Association. Subcommittee on Guidelines for Collection Development, AB63

Guide to 1980 U.S. decennial census publications, CG29

A guide to 85 tests for special education, Compton, Carolyn, CB79

Guide to A linguistic atlas of late mediaeval English, BC31

Guide to accessions in the Cape Archives Depot, Cape Town, Cape Archives Depot, DD55

A guide to African international organisations, Fredland, Richard A., CK119

Guide to American directories, CH101

—— Klein, Barry T., CH101

Guide to American graduate schools, CB98

The guide to American law, CK60

Guide to American poetry explication, BD182

A guide to Americana, Palmer, Gregory, DB16

Guide to architectural trade catalogs from Avery Library, BF18

Guide to archives and manuscripts relating to Kenya and East Africa in the United Kingdom, Thurston, Anne, DD13

Guide to arranged archives in the Cape Archives Depot, Cape Archives Depot, DD55

Guide to Buddhist philosophy, Inada, Kenneth K., BA2, BB123

Guide to Buddhist religion, Reynolds, Frank E., BA2, BB123

Guide to Canadian ministries since confederation, July 1, 1867–February 1, 1982, CJ156

A guide to Cherokee documents in foreign archives, Anderson, William L., CC218

—— Lewis, James A., CC218

A guide to Cherokee documents in the northeastern United States, Kutsche, Paul, CC218

Guide to Chinese religion, Yu, David C., BB13

A guide to Civil War maps in the National Archives, CL42, DB36

A guide to collecting fine prints, Brown, J. H. U., BE158

A guide to commonwealth government information sources, Cook, John, AG30

Guide to corporate giving in the arts 4, CA36

A guide to Cuban collections in the United States, Peréz, Louis A., DB146

Guide to current British periodicals in the humanities and social sciences, AE47

Guide to current national bibliographies in the Third World, Gorman, G. E., AA75

Guide to departments of anthropology, CE17

Guide to departments of geography in the United States and Canada, CL14

A guide to documentary editing, Kline, Mary-Jo, AA54, BD13

Guide to documents and manuscripts in the United Kingdom relating to Russia and the Soviet Union, Hartley, Janet M., DC202

Guide to economic indicators, Frumkin, Norman, CH16

A guide to English educational terms, Gordon, Peter, CB73

A guide to European Community law, Mathijsen, P. S. R. F., CK120

Guide to European company information, CH177, CK124

A guide to European financial centres, Hay, Tony, CH257

Guide to federal archives relating to Africa, South, Aloha, DD3

Guide to federal funding for social scientists, CA37

Guide to federal government acronyms, CJ58

A guide to films about the Pacific Islands, Hamnett, Judith D., DG5

A guide to folktales in the English language, Ashliman, D. L., CF18

Guide to foreign law firms, CK76

Guide to foreign legal materials, Szladits, Charles, CK39

A guide to government monographs, reports, and research works, Kenya National Archives, AG44

Guide to graduate study in economics, agricultural economics, public administration, and doctoral programs in business administration in the United States and Canada, CH14

A guide to graduate study in political science, CB99, CJ31

A guide to historic and significant gardens of America, Nicholls, Robert P., BE146

—— Ray, Mary Helen, BE146

Guide to Indian philosophy, Potter, Karl H., BA7

A guide to information sources for social work and the human services, Mendelsohn, Henry N., CC26

Guide to information sources in the botanical sciences, Davis, Elisabeth B., EC27

Guide to international education in the United States, CB91

Guide to international legal research, CK106

Guide to inventories and finding aids of German archives at the German Historical Institute, Washington, D.C, Frohn, Axel, DC91

A guide to Irish mythology, Smyth, Daragh, CF14

A guide to Irish parish registers, Mitchell, Brian, AK38

A guide to Jewish genealogical research in Israel, Sack, Sallyann Amdur, AK42

A guide to journals in psychology and education, Loke, Wing Hong, CB44, CD5

A guide to Latin American and Caribbean census material, CG62

Guide to Latin American pamphlets from the Yale University Library, Yale University. Library, DB97

Guide to legal citation and sources of citation aid, Tang, Chin-Shih, CK35

A guide to legal research in Papua New Guinea, Creech, Heather, CK48

A guide to literary criticism and research, Stevens, Bonnie Klomp, BD23

Guide to manuscript sources for the history of Latin America and the Caribbean, DC131

Guide to manuscripts and documents in the British Isles relating to Africa, Matthews, Noel, DC131

——— Wainwright, M. Doreen, DC131

A guide to manuscripts and documents in the British Isles relating to South and South-East Asia, Pearson, J. D., DE4

A guide to manuscripts in the Presidential Libraries, Burton, Dennis A., AB47, AB49, CJ80, DB22

Guide to microfilms in the Cape Archives Depot, Cape Town, Cape Archives Depot, DD55

A guide to MLA documentation, Trimmer, Joseph, AH1

Guide to modern defense and strategy, Robertson, David, CJ261

Guide to New Zealand information sources, AA64

Guide to non-federal archives and manuscripts in the United States relating to Africa, South, Aloha, DD3

Guide to Nordic bibliography, AA181, DC181

Guide to official publications of foreign countries, AG1

Guide to official statistics, CG56

A guide to original sources for precolonial western Africa published in European languages, Fage, J. D., DD24

Guide to popular U.S. government publications, Bailey, William G., AG7

——— Schwarzkopf, LeRoy C., AG7

A guide to pre-federal records in the National Archives, Wehmann, Howard H., DB26

Guide to programs in nursing in four-year colleges and universities, EK93

A guide to recreation, leisure, and travel for the handicapped, BJ43, CC109

Guide to reference books for Islamic studies, Geddes, C. L., BB126

Guide to reference works for the study of the Spanish language and literature and Spanish American literature, Woodbridge, Hensley Charles, BD321

Guide to research and scholarship in Hungary, DC143

A guide to research collections of former members of the United States House of Representatives, 1789–1987, AB49, DB22, CJ93

Guide to research collections of former United States senators, 1789–1982, AB49, CJ93, DB22

A guide to research in gerontology, Zito, Dorothea R., CC33, EK5

A guide to research in music education, Phelps, Roger P., BH3

A guide to scholarly resources on the Russian Empire and the Soviet Union in the New York metropolitan area, DC195

Guide to schools and departments of religion and seminaries in the United States and Canada, BB33

A guide to source materials in the India Office Library and Records for the history of Tibet, Sikkim and Bhutan, 1765–1950, Amar Kaur Jasbir Singh, DE4, DE29

Guide to sources in American journalism history, AF1, AF19

——— American Journalism Historians Association, AF19

Guide to special issues and indexes of periodicals, AE17

Guide to statistical materials produced by governments and associations in the United States, Stratford, Juri, CG31

A guide to statistical methods and to the pertinent literature = Literatur zur Angewandten Statistik, Sachs, Lothar, EF3

A guide to statistical sources in money, banking, and finance, Balachandran, M., CH212

Guide to Statistics Canada data on women, CG44

Guide to the American ethnic press, Wynar, Lubomyr Roman, AE27

Guide to the American left, CJ63

Guide to the American right, CJ64

Guide to the archives of Hungary, DC144

Guide to the archives of international organizations, AB45

Guide to the availability of theses, Borchardt, D. H., AB97

Guide to the availability of theses II, Allen, G. G., AB97

Guide to the collections in the Hoover Institution archives relating to Imperial Russia, the Russian revolutions and civil war, and the first emigration, Hoover Institution on War, Revolution, and Peace, DC203

Guide to the contents of the Kenya National Archives, Kenya National Archives, AG44

The guide to the foundations of public administration, Martin, Daniel, CJ218

Guide to the Gothic, Frank, Frederick S., BD116

Guide to the India Office records 1600–1858, Foster, William, DE32

A guide to the Indian tribes of the Pacific Northwest, Ruby, Robert H., CC227

Guide to the languages of the world, Ruhlen, Merritt, BC15

A guide to the laws, regulations, and policies of the People's Republic of China on foreign trade and investment, Kenworthy, James L., CK38

Guide to the Library of Congress classification, Immroth, John Philip, AB81

A guide to the literature of electrical and electronics engineering, Ardis, Susan, EJ43

Guide to the literature of pharmacy and the pharmaceutical sciences, Andrews, Theodora, EK103

A guide to the literature of tennis, Lumpkin, Angela, BJ35

Guide to the National Archives of the United States, United States. National Archives and Records Administration, DB23

——— United States. National Archives and Records Service, DB24

Guide to the petroleum reference literature, Pearson, Barbara C., EJ89

Guide to the pianist's repertoire, Hinson, Maurice, BH39

Guide to the Presidential advisory commissions, 1973–1984, Zink, Steven D., CJ88

A guide to the public archives of Botswana, Lekaukau, T. M., DD27

Guide to the publications of interstate agencies and authorities, AG26

Guide to the sources of British military history, Higham, Robin D. S., DC100

A guide to the sources of United States military history : Supplement II, DB10

Guide to the South African manuscript collections in the South African Library, Cape Town, South African Library, DD55

Guide to the Soviet navy, Polmar, Norman, CJ282

Guide to the study of United States history outside the U.S., 1945–1980, DB11

Guide to the use of libraries and information sources, Gates, Jean Key, AB9

A guide to the world's languages, Ruhlen, Merritt, BC15

A guide to theatre in America, BG28

Guide to theses and dissertations, Reynolds, Michael M., AH4

A guide to tracing the history of a business, Orbell, John, CH142

Guide to trade catalogs from the Corning Museum of Glass, BF18

Guide to U.S. government statistics, CG28

Guide to U.S. map resources, Cobb, David A., CL44

A guide to western historical scripts from antiquity to 1600, Brown, Michelle P., AA39

A guide to Western manuscripts and documents in the British Isles relating to South and South East Asia, Matthews, Noel, DE4

——— Wainwright, M. Doreen, DE4

A guide to world cinema, BG72

Guide to world science and technology, EA58

The guide to writers conferences, BD43

A guide to writing and publishing in the social and behavioral sciences, Mullins, Carolyn J., CA23

Guide to Yale University Library Holocaust video testimonies, Fortunoff Video Archive for Holocaust Testimonies, DA84

Guidebooks, BJ47, BJ48
    bibliography, BJ49

Guidelines for collection development, American Library Association. Collection Management and Development Committee, AB63

Guides to German records microfilmed at Alexandria, Va, DC91

Guides to sources for British history based on the National Register of Archives, DC108

Guides to the sources for the history of the nations. 3rd series, North Africa, Asia and Oceania = Guides des sources de l'histoire des nations. 3ème série, Afrique du Nord, Asie et Océanie, DD2, DD15, DG4

Guides to the sources of the history of the nations, DB98

The Guild handbook of scientific illustration, EA67

Guild of Natural Science Illustrators (U.S.). *The Guild handbook of scientific illustration*, EA67

Guiley, Rosemary. *The encyclopedia of witches and witchcraft*, CF27

Guillo, Laurent. *Catalogue de la musique imprimée avant 1801, conservée dans les bibliothèques de Lyon, Grenoble et la région*, BH36

Guinard, Madeleine. *Le grand dictionnaire des synonymes*, AD99

Guinea, DD6

Guinea-Bissau, Galli, Rosemary E., DD39

Guinea Ecuatorial, Liniger-Goumaz, Max, DD33

Guineau-Bissau, DD39

Guldan, Ernst. *Kataloge der Bibliotheca Hertziana in Rom (Max-Planck-Institut)*, BE24

Gulsoy, Joseph. *Diccionari etimològic i complementari de la llengua catalana*, AD81

Gunasingam, S. *Directory of South Asian library resources in the UK and the Republic of Ireland*, DE30

Gunderson, Nels L. *Pension funds*, CH151

Gunson, Phil. *The dictionary of contemporary politics of South America*, CJ194

Guralnik, David Bernard. *Webster's New World dictionary of American English*, AD5

Gurney, Gene. *Kingdoms of Asia, the Middle East, and Africa*, DA20

Guthrie, Paul. *Scandinavian biographical archive*, AJ91

Gutierrez, David. *The Chicano public catalog*, CC236

Gutiérrez, René L. *The Aztecs*, CC221
—— *The Incas*, CC222

Gutman, Israel. *Encyclopedia of the Holocaust*, DA83

Gutter life and language in the early "street" literature of England, Henke, James T., AD43

Guttmann, David. *European American elderly*, CC43

Gutzman, Philip C. *Dictionary of military, defense contractor & troop slang acronyms*, CJ258

Guy, Patricia A. *Women's poetry index*, BD132

Guyana, DB121

Guyana, Chambers, Frances, DB121

HLAA, BE6

HM diplomatic overseas reference list, CJ183

HMSO agency catalogue, Great Britain. Her Majesty's Stationery Office, AG39

HMSO annual catalogue, AG41

HMSO monthly catalogue, AG40

Haag, Enid E. *Research guide for studies in infancy and childhood*, CC77

Haas, Ken. *The location photographer's handbook*, BF60

Haase, Ynez D. *Historical atlas of the American West*, DB55

Haberman, Martin. *Handbook of research on teacher education*, CB17

Die Habsburger, DC29

Hacken, Richard D. *Central European economic history from Waterloo to OPEC, 1815–1975*, CH2, DC3

Hackett, Amy. *The encyclopedia of the Third Reich*, DC92

Hackett, Paul. *Caribbean economic handbook*, CH43

Hackh, Ingo W. D. *Grant & Hackh's chemical dictionary*, ED9

Hackland, Brian. *The dictionary of contemporary politics of southern Africa*, CJ151

Hadfield, Miles. *British gardeners*, BE141

Häkkinen, Kaisa. *Nykysuomen sanakirja*, AD87

Häkli, Esko. *Bibliographia studiorum uralicorum, 1917–1987 = Uralistiikan tutkimuksen bibliografia = Bibliography on Uralic studies*, DC210

Hänsel, Markus. *Die anonym erschienenen autobiographischen Schriften des neunzehnten Jahrhunderts*, AJ57

Haerinck, E. *Bibliographie analytique de l'archéologie de l'Iran ancien*, DE67

Haertel, Geneva D. *The international encyclopedia of educational evaluation*, CB63

Hagelweide, Gert. *Literatur zur deutschsprachigen Presse*, AE37

Hager, Beth Haines. *Children, parents, and reading*, CB19

Hagiography see **Saints**

Hague Club. *Foundation profiles*, CA27

Haig, Judith Giblin. *Dictionary of American literary characters*, BD174

Haigh, Christopher. *The Cambridge historical encyclopedia of Great Britain and Ireland*, DC113

Haikalis, Peter D. *Real estate*, CH344

Hain, Ludwig. *Repertorium bibliographium*, AA42

Haines, David W. *Refugees in the United States*, CC187

Haines, Gerald K. *A reference guide to United States Department of State special files*, CJ81

Hairston, Maxine. *The Scott, Foresman handbook for writers*, BC26, BC27

Hais, Karel. *English-Czech dictionary*, AD83
—— *Velký anglicko-český slovník*, AD83

Haiti, DB151

Haiti, Lawless, Robert, DB151

Hajnal, Peter I. *The Seven-power summit*, CK109

Halachmi, Arie. *Public sector productivity*, CJ216

Hall, Charles J. *An eighteenth-century musical chronicle*, BH73
—— *A nineteenth-century musical chronicle*, BH73
—— *A twentieth-century musical chronicle*, BH73

Hall, Halbert W. *Science fiction and fantasy book review index, 1980–1984*, BD125
—— *Science fiction and fantasy reference index, 1878–1985*, BD124
—— *Science fiction magazines*, BD122

Hall, J. L. *Online bibliographic databases*, AB95

Hall, Jo Anne. *Black American families, 1965–1984*, CC123

Hall, Kermit. *A comprehensive bibliography of American constitutional and legal history*, CK117

Hall, Manly Palmer. *An encyclopedic outline of Masonic, Hermetic, Qabbalistic, and Rosicrucian symbolical philosophy*, CA53, CA54

Hall, R. J. *Dictionary of aviation*, CH188

Hall, Robert Anderson. *Bibliografia della linguistica italiana*, BC41

Hallam, Elizabeth M. *Chronicles of the age of chivalry*, DC116
—— *The chronicles of the Wars of the Roses*, DC116
—— *Four gothic kings*, DC116
—— *The Plantagenet chronicles*, DC116
—— *The Plantagenet encyclopedia : an alphabetical guide to 400 years of English history*, DC116
—— *The Wars of the Roses*, DC116

Halley's comet, Freitag, Ruth S., EB2

Halliwell, Leslie. *Halliwell's film guide*, BG73

Halliwell's film guide, Halliwell, Leslie, BG73

Halstead, Bruce W. *Poisonous and venomous marine animals of the world*, EC42

Halter, M. *Republic of Cape Verde*, DD5

Halton, Thomas P. *Classical scholarship*, BD365

Hamann, Brigitte. *Die Habsburger*, DC29

Hamel, Réginald. *Dictionnaire des auteurs de langue française en Amérique du Nord*, BD304

Hamelsdorf, Ora. *The Jewish woman, 1900–1985*, CC254

Hamilton, David. *The Metropolitan Opera encyclopedia*, BH100

Hamilton, David A. *Ballet plot index*, BG49
—— *Opera plot index*, BH103

Hamilton, Mary. *A–Z of opera*, BH94

Hamilton, Sheila. *Dictionary of Scottish business biography, 1860–1960*, CH145

Hamilton-Edwards, Gerald Kenneth Savery. *In search of Welsh ancestry*, AK46

Hamm, Charles. *Census-catalogue of manuscript sources of polyphonic music, 1400–1550*, BH35

Hammond Barnhart dictionary of science, EA40

Hammond past worlds, DA37

Hamnett, Judith D. *A guide to films about the Pacific Islands*, DG5

Han yü ta tz'u tien, AD82

Han yü ta tz'u tien pien che wei yüan hui. Han yü ta tz'u tien, AD82

Han yü ta tz'u tien pien tsuan ch'u. Han yü ta tz'u tien, AD82

Hancock, Ian F. *International English usage*, AD29

Handbook for AACR2 1988 revision, Maxwell, Margaret, AB79

Handbook for academic authors, Luey, Beth, AA56

A handbook for archival research in the USSR, Grimsted, Patricia Kennedy, AB10, DC201

Handbook for authors of papers in American Chemical Society publications, ED24

A handbook for London, past and present, Cunningham, Peter, DC137

Handbook for research in American history, Prucha, Francis Paul, DB1

Handbook for small, rural, and emerging public libraries, Gervasi, Anne, AB55

Handbook of adult and continuing education, CB125

Handbook of aging and the social sciences, CC64

Handbook of American business history, CH140

Handbook of American film genres, BG90

Handbook of American-Jewish literature, BD194

Handbook of American popular culture, BD163, CF34

Handbook of American popular literature, BD163

Handbook of American women's history, CC292, DB65

The handbook of artificial intelligence, EJ67

Handbook of bioengineering, EK11

Handbook of biomedical engineering, EK70

Handbook of British chronology, DC122

Handbook of business information, Strauss, Diane Wheeler, CH83

Handbook of certification and licensure requirements for school psychologists, Prus, Joseph S., CB133

Handbook of certification/licensure requirements for school psychologists, Brown, Douglas T., CB133

Handbook of clinical sociology, CC18

The handbook of corporate finance, CH255

Handbook of corrosion data, EJ85

Handbook of differential equations, Zwillinger, Daniel, EF16

Handbook of economic statistics, CH30

Handbook of educational ideas and practices, CB126

Handbook of energy systems engineering, EJ70

Handbook of engineering fundamentals, EJ6

Handbook of English and Celtic studies in the United Kingdom and Republic of Ireland, BC28

Handbook of family measurement techniques, CC140

The handbook of financial market indexes, averages, and indicators, Berlin, Howard M., CH252

Handbook of financial markets and institutions, CH255

Handbook of glass properties, Bansal, Narottam P., BF26, EJ8

Handbook of human factors, EJ75

Handbook of human resources administration, CH166

The handbook of international business, CH130

Handbook of international management, CH131

Handbook of international trade, Brooke, Michael, CH184

Handbook of laser science and technology, EG7

Handbook of Latin American art = Manual de arte latinoamericano : a bibliographic compilation, BE6

Handbook of Latin American literature, BD329

Handbook of Latin American studies, CJ195

Handbook of literary research, Miller, R. H., BD14

Handbook of marriage and the family, CC141

Handbook of mathematics, Bronshteĭn, I. N., EF14

Handbook of medical library practice, AB56, EK1

Handbook of Middle American Indians. Supplement, CE25

Handbook of mineralogy, EE35

Handbook of modern finance, CH256

A handbook of modern history, Gibbons, S. R., DA59

Handbook of modern personnel management, CH166

Handbook of modern sociology, Faris, Robert E. L., CC20

The handbook of national population censuses, Domschke, Eliane, CG39

The handbook of non-violence, Seeley, Robert A., CJ305

Handbook of nonprescription drugs, EK116

The handbook of nonsexist writing, Miller, Casey, AA57, CC311

Handbook of North American birds, Palmer, Ralph S. ed, EC55

Handbook of North American Indians, CC230

Handbook of organic chemistry, Dean, John Aurie, ED39

Handbook of paleozoology, Kuhn-Schnyder, Emil, EE42

Handbook of parliamentary procedure, Davidson, Henry A., CJ225

Handbook of pesticide toxicology, EH20

Handbook of poisoning, Dreisbach, Robert Hastings, EK131

Handbook of political science research on Latin America, CJ195

A handbook of problem words & phrases, Freeman, Morton S., AD25

Handbook of public administration, CJ214, CJ215

Handbook of research on educational administration, CB127

Handbook of research on social studies teaching and learning, CB128

Handbook of research on teacher education, CB17

Handbook of research on teaching, CB129

Handbook of semiotics, Nöth, Winfried, BC14

Handbook of small business data, 1988, CH357

Handbook of social science of sport, BJ16, CC19

Handbook of sociology, CC20

Handbook of space astronomy and astrophysics, Zombeck, Martin V., EB12

Handbook of special education, CB130

The handbook of state legislative leaders, CJ124

Handbook of the biology of aging, Rowe, John W., CC64

—— Schneider, Edward L., CC64

Handbook of the birds of Europe, the Middle East and North Africa, EC49

Handbook of the psychology of aging, Birren, James E., CC64

—— Schaie, K. Warner, CC64

Handbook of theoretical computer science, EJ68

Handbook on crime and delinquency prevention, CK103

Handbook on international migration, CC184

A handbook to literature, Holman, C. Hugh, BD39

—— Thrall, William Flint, BD39

Handbuch der bibliographischen Nachschlagewerke, Totok, Wilhelm, AA2

Handbuch der Geschichte der Philosophie, Totok, Wilhelm, BA21

Handbuch der organischen Chemie, Beilstein, Friedrich, ED38

Handbuch der Physik, EG5

Handel's national directory for the performing arts, BG3

Handicapped *see* **Disabled**

Handicapped funding directory, CC110

Handling and management of hazardous materials and wastes, Allegri, Theodore H., EJ30

Handwriting, AA39

Handy book for genealogists, Everton, George B., AK4

Haney, Wayne S. *Rockabilly,* BH125

Han'guk sŏmok, AA153

Hanke, Lewis. *Guide to the study of United States history outside the U.S., 1945–1980,* DB11

Hanna, Archibald. *A mirror for the nation,* BD175

Hannan, M. *Standard Shona dictionary,* AD161

Hannes, J. *Bibliografie van de geschiedenis van België,* DC32

Hannesson, Jóhann S. *Ensk-íslensk oŕabók,* AD125

Hanson, F. Allan. *The art of Oceania,* BF6

Hanson, Louise. *The art of Oceania,* BF6

Hanson, Patricia King. *Film review index,* BG63

—— *Sourcebook for the performing arts,* BG4

Hanson, Stephen L. *Film review index,* BG63

—— *Sourcebook for the performing arts,* BG4

Hapsburg, House of, DC29

Harap, Louis. *Handbook of American-Jewish literature,* BD194

Harasztos, Barbara. *Guide to research and scholarship in Hungary,* DC143

Harbage, Alfred. *Annals of English drama, 975–1700,* BD232

Harbrace college handbook, BC29

Hardison, O. B. *The Princeton handbook of poetic terms,* BD137

Harduf, David Mendel. *Transliterated English-Yiddish dictionary = Ţransliterirţer English-Yidisher yerţerbukh,* AD175

—— *Transliterated Yiddish-English dictionary = Ţransliterirţer Yidish-Englisher yerţerbukh,* AD176

Hardy, Joan E. *Information sources in the earth sciences,* EE1

Hardy, Phil. *Encyclopedia of rock,* BH126

Hare, John. *Dictionnaire des auteurs de langue française en Amérique du Nord,* BD304

Harewood, George Henry Hubert Lascelles,. *Kobbé's complete opera book,* BH97

Harkanyi, Katalin. *The natural sciences and American scientists in the revolutionary era,* EA69

Harle, J. C. *The art and architecture of the Indian subcontinent,* BE73

The Harlem Renaissance and beyond, Roses, Lorraine Elena, BD189

Harman, Inge Maria. *National directory of Latin Americanists,* DB106

Harmon, Robert B. *Political science bibliographies,* CJ12

Harmon, William. *A handbook to literature,* BD39

Harner, James L. *English Renaissance prose fiction, 1500–1660,* BD236

—— *Literary research guide,* BD149

Harnly, Caroline D. *Agent Orange and the Vietnam veteran,* DE104

—— *Agent Orange and Vietnam,* DE104

Harouna, Saïda. *Catalogue des thèses et mémoires /[Saïdou Harouna],* DD47

Harper, F. John. *Political scandals and causes célèbres since 1945,* CJ37

Harper, Pat Callbeck. *Public opinion polling,* CJ233

The Harper atlas of the Bible, BB68

The Harper atlas of world history, DA26

Harper dictionary of economics, Pass, Christopher, CH11

The Harper dictionary of foreign terms, Mawson, C. O. Sylvester, AD66

The Harper dictionary of modern thought, AC4

The Harper dictionary of music, Ammer, Christine, BH47

The Harper dictionary of opera and operetta, Anderson, James, BH94

Harper's Bible commentary, BB64

—— Neil, William, BB64

Harper's Bible dictionary, BB64, BB51

Harper's Bible pronunciation guide, BB52

Harrap's book of film directors and their films, Filmer, Alison J., BG70

Harrap's concise French-English dictionary = dictionnaire anglais-français, AD94

Harrap's French and English science dictionary, EA48

Harré, Rom. *The encyclopedic dictionary of psychology,* CD13

Harris, Cyril M. *Shock and vibration handbook,* EJ81

Harris, Diana K. *Dictionary of gerontology,* CC53

—— *Sociology of aging,* CC44

Harris, Eileen. *British architectural books and writers, 1556–1785,* BE110

Harris, Janie Miller. *A bibliographical guide to black studies programs in the United States,* CC194

Harris, Karen. *More notes from a different drummer,* CC103

Harris, Laura A. *The real estate industry,* CH344

Harris, Laurie Lanzen. *Characters in 20th-century literature,* BD10

Harris, Michael H. *American library history,* AB2

Harris, N. D. C. *Dictionary of instructional technology,* CB68

Harris, Richard Colebrook. *Historical atlas of Canada,* DB89

Harris, Steve. *Film, television, and stage music on phonograph records,* BG1, BH145

Harris, Theodore Lester. *A dictionary of reading and related terms,* CB67

Harrison, Charles Hampton. *Public schools USA,* CB131

Harrison, Cynthia Ellen. *Women in American history,* CC283

Harrison, Harriet. *Bibliography of national filmographies,* BG51

Harrison, Max. *The essential jazz records,* BH120

Harrod, Leonard Montague. *Harrod's librarians' glossary of terms used in librarianship, documentation and the book crafts, and reference book,* AB15

Harrod's librarians' glossary of terms used in librarianship, documentation and the book crafts, and reference book, Harrod, Leonard Montague, AB15

Harry Frank Guggenheim Foundation. *The anthropology of war,* CE5

Hart, E. Richard. *A Zuni atlas,* CC233

Hart, George. *A dictionary of Egyptian gods and goddesses,* CF9

Hartgrove, J. Dane. *Russia and the United States,* DC198

Hartigan, Maureen. *The history of the Irish in Britain,* DC101

Hartley, Janet M. *Guide to documents and manuscripts in the United Kingdom relating to Russia and the Soviet Union,* DC202

—— *The study of Russian history from British archival sources,* DC204

Hartley, Keith. *The economics of defense, disarmament, and peace,* CJ296

Hartline, Gregory W. *Dictionnaire technique de la marine,* CJ256

Hartman, Donald K. *Themes and settings in fiction,* BD90

Hartman, Gary R. *Index to periodical articles related to law,* CK56

Hartness, Ann. *Brazil in reference books, 1965–1989,* DB113

Hartt, Frederick. *Art : a history of painting, sculpture, architecture,* BE72

Hartwig, D. Scott. *The battle of Antietam and the Maryland Campaign of 1862,* DB15

Harty, F. J. *Concise illustrated dental dictionary,* EK86

Harvard dictionary of music, Apel, Willi, BH56

The Harvard independent insider's guide to prep schools, CB109

Harvard University. Fine Arts Library. *Catalog of the Rübel Asiatic Research Collection, Harvard University Fine Arts Library,* BE25

—— *Iconographic index to Old Testament subjects represented in photographs and slides of paintings in the visual collections, Fine Arts Library, Harvard University,* BE101

Harvard University. Peabody Museum of Archaeology and Ethnology. Library. *Catalogue : [authors and subjects],* CE7

Harvard-Yenching Library. *Catalogues of the Harvard-Yenching Library,* DE40

Harvey, Anthony P. *Information sources in the earth sciences,* EE1

Harvey, D. R. *A bibliography of writings about New Zealand music published to the end of 1983,* BH15

Harvey, Joan M. *Statistics Europe,* CG51

—— *Walford's guide to current British periodicals in the humanities and social sciences,* AE47

Harvey, John Hooper. *English mediaeval architects,* BE135

Harvey, Paul. *The Oxford companion to classical literature,* BD366

—— *The Oxford companion to English literature,* BD219

Harvey, Richard. *Genealogy for librarians,* AK31

Harwell, Richard Barksdale. *More confederate imprints,* DB30

Harzig, Christiane. *The immigrant labor press in North America, 1840s–1970s,* CH276

Haselbauer, Kathleen J. *A research guide to the health sciences,* EK2

Haseltine, Patricia. *East and Southeast Asian material culture in North America,* CC213

Hassen, Marjorie. *American Musicological Society,* BH42

Hastings, James. *Encyclopedia of religion and ethics,* BB25

Hatch, Warren L. *Selective guide to climatic data sources,* EE28

Hathway, D. E. *Harrap's French and English science dictionary,* EA48

Hattaway, Michael. *The Cambridge companion to English Renaissance drama,* BD235

Haupt, Arthur. *The Population Reference Bureau's population handbook,* CG1

Hausa language, AD116

Haussig, Hans Wilhelm. *Wörterbuch der Mythologie. 1 Abteilung, Die alten Kulturvölker,* CF8

Haustrate, Gaston. *Le guide du cinéma,* BG91

Havighurst, Alfred F. *Modern England, 1901–1984,* DC106

Havlice, Patricia Pate. *And so to bed,* BD250

—— *Oral history,* DB12

—— *Popular song index. Third supplement,* BH114

Hawbaker, A. Craig. *Industry and company information,* CH79

Hawks, eagles & falcons of North America, Johnsgard, Paul A., EC51

Hawley, Gessner Goodrich. *Hawley's condensed chemical dictionary,* ED10

Hawley's condensed chemical dictionary, ED10

Hay, Tony. *A guide to European financial centres,* CH257

—— *International directory of telecommunications,* CH210

Hayes, Grace P. *Dictionary of military terms,* CJ257

Hayes, Gregory. *Going places,* BJ49

Hayes, Wayland J. *Handbook of pesticide toxicology,* EH20

Hayner, Priscilla B. *The ACCESS resource guide,* CJ308

Haynes, John Earl. *Communism and anti-communism in the United States,* CJ239

Haythornthwaite, Philip J. *The Napoleonic source book,* DC65

Hazardous substances, ED21, EJ30, EK128

Hazen, Edith P. *The Columbia Granger's index to poetry,* BD11

Hazewinkel, Michiel. *Encyclopedia of mathematics,* EF7

Hazon, Mario. *Garzanti comprehensive Italian-English, English-Italian dictionary,* AD130

—— *Il Nuovo dizionario Hazon Garzanti,* AD130

Headland, Robert. *Chronological list of Antarctic expeditions and related historical events,* DH4

Heads of state, CJ145, CJ147, CJ166, DA43, DD7

biography, CC313

directories, CJ32, CK83

genealogy, AK2, CJ146

Heads of state and government, Da Graça, John V., CJ145

Heal, Ambrose. *The London furniture makers from the Restoration to the Victorian era,* BF37

—— *The London goldsmiths 1200–1800,* BF46

Healey, Antonette. *Microfiche concordance to Old English,* AD63

Health media review index, EK21

Health media review index, 1984–86, EK22

Health of black Americans from post reconstruction to integration, 1871–1960, Rice, Mitchell F., CC202, EK126

Health planning and administration, EK29, EK32

Health sciences *see* **Medicine**

Heart of stone, Aeppli, Felix, BH140

Heat wave, Bianco, David, BH123

Heater, Derek. *Atlas of modern world history,* DA63

Heath, Trudy. *American periodicals 1741–1900,* AE77, AE78

Heating and refrigeration, EJ74

Hebel, Udo J. *Intertextuality, allusion, and quotation,* BD2

Hebräisches und aramäisches Handwörterbuch über das Alte Testament, Gesenius, Wilhelm, AD117

Hebrew incunabula in public collections, Offenberg, A. K., AA43

Hebrew language, AD117, AD118, AD119, AD120

Hebrew Union College-Jewish Institute of Religion. *Judaica Americana,* BB135

Hebrew Union College-Jewish Institute of Religion. American Jewish Periodical Center. *Jewish newspapers and periodicals on microfilm,* AE5

Hecimovich, James. *An annotated bibliography and index covering CPL bibliographies 1–253, January 1979–December 1989,* CC159

Heck, André. *Acronyms & abbreviations in astronomy, space sciences, & related fields,* EB8

Hecker, Helen. *Travel for the disabled,* BJ44, CC111

Heesakkers, Chris L. *Bibliographie de l'humanisme des anciens Pays-Bas, avec un répertoire bibliographique des humanistes et poètes néo-latins,* BA9

Heffron, Mary J. *Africa,* DD17

—— *Asia and Pacific,* DE7

—— *Latin America and Caribbean,* DB104

—— *Middle East,* DE23

—— *Third World resource directory,* CH51

—— *Third World struggle for peace with justice,* CJ293

—— *Transnational corporations and labor,* CH285

—— *Women in the Third World,* CC279

Heggie, Grace F. *Canadian periodical index, 1920–1937,* AE81

Heidelberger Akademie der Wissenschaften. *Diccionario del español medieval,* AD168

—— *Goethe-Wörterbuch,* BD298

Heidtmann, Frank. *Bibliographie der Photographie deutschsprachige Publikationen der Jahre 1839–1984,* BF54

HEILBRON, ED37

Heimpel, Hermann,. *Dahlmann-Waitz Quellenkunde der deutschen Geschichte,* DC80, DC81

Heinemann dental dictionary, Fairpo, Jenifer E. H., EK85

Heinemann modern dictionary for dental students, EK85

Heinl, Robert Debs. *The Marine officer's guide,* CJ279

Heintze, James R. *American music studies,* BH2

—— *Early American music,* BH2

Helander, Brock. *The rock who's who,* BH129

Helbig, Alethea. *Dictionary of American children's fiction, 1859–1959,* BD74

—— *Dictionary of American children's fiction, 1960–1984,* BD75

—— *Dictionary of British children's fiction,* BD76

Helck, Wolfgang. *Lexikon der Ägyptologie,* DD31

Heleniak, Timothy E. *Bibliography of Soviet statistical handbooks,* CG74

Helferty, Seamus. *Directory of Irish archives,* DC149

Hellebust, Lynn. *State blue books, legislative manuals, and reference publications,* AG28, CJ122

Hellemans, Alexander. *The timetables of science,* EA72, EA74

Hellēnikē vivliographia, AA135

—— Papadopoulos, Thōmas I., AA134

Hellman, Ronald G. *Tinker guide to Latin American and Caribbean policy and scholarly resources in metropolitan New York,* DB107

Helrich, Kenneth. *Official methods of analysis of the Association of Official Analytical Chemists,* ED20

Helt, Marie E. *West German cinema since 1945,* BG74

Helt, Richard C. *West German cinema since 1945,* BG74

Henchy, Judith A. N. *Laos,* DE82

Henderson, John,. *New Zealand foreign policy, 1945–1985,* DF8

Henderson, Lesley. *Twentieth-century romance and historical writers,* BD121

Henderson's dictionary of biological terms, Lawrence, Eleanor, EC18

Hendon, Donald W. *American advertising,* CH69

Hendrickson, Robert. *The Facts on File encyclopedia of word and phrase origins,* AD16

Hendrickx, Jean-Pierre. *Répertoire des mémoires de licence et des thèses de doctorat présentés dans les départements d'histoire contemporaine des universités belges,* DC31

Henige, David P. *Serial bibliographies and abstracts in history,* DA3

Henke, James T. *Gutter life and language in the early "street" literature of England,* AD43

Hennessee, Don A. *Nineteenth-century American drama,* BD231

Henning, Charles. *The wit & wisdom of politics,* CJ28

Henning, Eckart. *Bibliographie Friedrich der Grosse, 1786–1986,* DC83

—— *Taschenbuch für Familiengeschichtsforschung,* AK27

Henning, Herzeleide. *Bibliographie Friedrich der Grosse, 1786–1986,* DC83

Henry Francis du Pont Winterthur Museum. *The Edward Deming Andrews Memorial Shaker Collection,* BB113

Henry Sweet Society for the History of Linguistic Ideas. *Renaissance linguistics archive, 1350–1700,* BC5

Henrywood, R. K. *The dictionary of blue and white printed pottery 1780–1880*, BF24

Hepner, John C. *Cumulative index to Tests in microfiche, 1975–1987*, CD39

Heppner, Irene. *Bibliography on portraiture*, BE7

Herbert, Patricia. *South-East Asia*, BC60, BD382

Herbert, W. J. *Dictionary of immunology*, EC15, EK56

Herbicide handbook of the Weed Science Society of America, EH21

Herbicides, EH21

Hermann, Ursula,. *Deutsches Wörterbuch*, AD107

Hermeneia, BB65

Herod, Agustina. *Afro-American nationalism*, CC196

Herod, Charles C. *Afro-American nationalism*, CC196

Herrero Mediavilla, Victor. *Archivo biográfico de España, Portugal e Iberoamérica*, AJ93

—— *Indice biográfico de España, Portugal e Iberoamérica = Indice biográfico de Espanha, Portugal e Ibero-América = Spanish, Portuguese and Latin American biographical index*, AJ94

Herring, Mark Youngblood. *Controversial issues in librarianship*, AB3

—— *Ethics and the professor*, CB8

Herron, Nancy L. *The social sciences*, CA1, CA3

Hersen, Michel. *Dictionary of behavioral assessment techniques*, CD40

Herstein, Sheila R. *Brazil*, DB111

—— *Puerto Rico*, DB152

—— *Trinidad and Tobago*, DB154

Hertefelt, Marcel d'. *Société, culture et histoire du Rwanda*, DD50

Herzenberg, Caroline L. *Women scientists from antiquity to the present*, EA84

Herzog August Bibliothek. *Verzeichnis der im deutschen Sprachbereich erschienenen Drucke des XVI. Jahrhunderts*, AA119

Heskes, Irene. *The resource book of Jewish music*, BH16

Hess, Robert K. *The educator's desk reference (EDR)*, CB4

Hesse, Gritta. *Künstler der jungen Generation*, BE80

Hesslein, Shirley B. *Serials on aging*, CC51

Hewitt, George. *Companion to Scottish history*, DC139

Hey, David. *Family history and local history in England*, AK32

Heydenreich, Ludwig Heinrich. *Reallexikon zur deutschen Kunstgeschichte*, BE39

Heydenreich, Titus. *Bibliographie der Hispanistik in der Bundesrepublik Deutschland, Österreich und der deutschsprachigen Schweiz*, BC51

Heyse, Micheline. *Bibliografie van de geschiedenis van België, 1914–1940 = Bibliographie de l'histoire de Belgique, 1914–1940*, DC32

Hezel, Francis X. *Foreign ships in Micronesia*, DG8

Hibbert, Christopher. *The London encyclopaedia*, DC137

Hickey, D. J. *A chronology of Irish history since 1500*, DC152

—— *A dictionary of Irish history since 1800*, DC152

Hickey, Michael. *100 families of flowering plants*, EC33

Hickey, Morgen. *The bohemian register*, BD157

Hickman, Mary J. *The history of the Irish in Britain*, DC101

Higbee, Joan Florence. *Scholars' guide to Washington, D.C. for southwest European studies*, DC10

High interest easy reading, National Council of Teachers of English. Committee to Revise High Interest-Easy Reading, CB36

High technology industries, CH113

Higham, Robin D. S. *Guide to the sources of British military history*, DC100

—— *A guide to the sources of United States military history : Supplement II*, DB10

Higher education abstracts, CB56

Higher education finance, Hines, Edward R., CB9

Highfill, Philip H. *A biographical dictionary of actors, actresses, musicians, dancers, managers & other stage personnel in London, 1660–1800*, BG36

Highlights of recent American architecture, Wright, Sylvia Hart, BE136

High/low handbook, CB26

Higton, A. A. *Dictionary of antibiotics and related substances*, ED32, EK109

Hildebrandt, Darlene Myers. *Computing information directory*, EJ50

Hildesheimer, Françoise. *Guide des papiers privés d'époque révolutionnaire*, DC50

Hildreth, W. Bartley. *Handbook of public administration*, CJ215

Hilfinger, Ann. *Vietnam War literature*, BD158

Hilgemann, Werner. *Atlas zur deutschen Zeitgeschichte, 1918–1968*, DC98

Hill, C. P. *Who's who in Stuart England*, DC124

Hill, Dennis Auburn. *Norwegian local history*, DC168

Hill, George H. *A bibliographical guide to black studies programs in the United States*, CC194

—— *Black media in America*, CC197

—— *Blacks on television*, BG103

Hill, Holly. *The encyclopedia of the New York stage, 1920–1930*, BG32

Hill, Howard B. *Guide to foreign law firms*, CK76

Hill, Marnesba D. *Escritores de la diáspora cubana*, BD341

Hill, Samuel S. *Encyclopedia of religion in the South*, BB24

Hill, Sylvia Saverson. *Blacks on television*, BG103

Hillman, Thomas A. *Catalogue of census returns on microfilm, 1666–1891 = Catalogue de recensements sur microfilm, 1666–1891*, CG43

Hiltbrunner, Otto. *Bibliographie zur lateinischen Wortforschung*, BC42

Hilton, Ruth B. *An index to early music in selected anthologies*, BH37

Himalayas, DE29

Hinds, Martin. *A dictionary of Egyptian Arabic*, AD69

Hinduism, BA12, BB23, BE104

Hines, Edward R. *Higher education finance*, CB9

Hines, W. D. *English legal history*, CK40, DC102

Hinson, Maurice. *Guide to the pianist's repertoire*, BH39

—— *Pianist's guide to transcriptions, arrangements, and paraphrases*, BH39

—— *Pianist's reference guide*, BH39

Hinton, Frances. *The Continuum dictionary of women's biography*, AJ9

Hirdman, Yvonne,. *Svensk historisk bibliografi 1971–1975*, DC190

Hirose, Nobuko. *Japanese art signatures*, BE100

Hirsch, K. A. *Handbook of mathematics*, EF14

Hise, Richard T. *Beacham's marketing reference*, CH315

The Hispanic almanac, CC244

Hispanic-American material culture, Graham, Joe Stanley, CC243

Hispanic American voluntary organizations, Gonzales, Sylvia Alicia, CC242

Hispanic Policy Development Project. *The Hispanic almanac*, CC244

Hispanic rare books of the Golden Age (1470–1699) in the Newberry Library of Chicago and in selected North American libraries, Laurenti, Joseph L., AA189

Histoire de l'art au XVIe siècle, 1540–1600, DC68

Histoire du costume en Occident, Boucher, François, BF31

Histoire et dictionnaire de la Révolution française, Tulard, Jean, DC56

Historians, DA11, DA14, DB67, DB75

Austria, DC96

Germany, DC96

Switzerland, DC96

A historian's handbook, Poulton, Helen, DA1

Historians of the American frontier, DB76

Historic documents on the presidency : 1776–1989, CJ87

Historic preservation periodicals, BE121

Historic sites, BE125, BE126, BE127, BE128

Historic towns, DC134

Historic Towns Trust. *Historic towns*, DC134

Historical abstracts, DA6, DA55

Historical abstracts five year index, DA7

Historical atlas of Armenia = Hayastani patmakan atlas, Armen, Garbis, DC21

Historical atlas of Canada, DB89

The historical atlas of Poland, DC174

The historical atlas of political parties in the United States Congress, 1789–1989, Martis, Kenneth C., CJ116, DB78

Historical atlas of the American West, Beck, Warren A., DB55

Historical atlas of the United States, National Geographic Society (U.S.), DB79

The historical atlas of United States congressional districts, 1789–1983, Martis, Kenneth C., CJ116, DB78

Historical bibliography of art museum serials from the United States and Canada, Klos, Sheila M., BE30

A historical catalogue of scientific periodicals, 1665–1900, Gascoigne, Robert Mortimer, EA18

A historical catalogue of scientists and scientific books, Gascoigne, Robert Mortimer, EA18

A historical dictionary of American industrial language, CH291

Historical dictionary of France from the 1815 restoration to the Second Empire, DC74

An historical dictionary of German figurative usage, Spalding, Keith, AD110

Historical dictionary of modern Spain, 1700–1988, DC188

Historical dictionary of Napoleonic France, 1799–1815, DC66

—— Connelly, Owen, DC63

Historical dictionary of North American archaeology, DB66

Historical dictionary of the 1920s, Olson, James Stuart, DB40

Historical dictionary of the French Second Empire, DC59

Historical dictionary of the French Second Empire, 1852–1870, DC75

Historical dictionary of the New Deal, DB38

Historical dictionary of the Spanish Civil War 1936–1939, Cortada, James W., DC188

Historical dictionary of the Third French Republic, 1870–1940, DC76

Historical directory of trade unions, Marsh, Arthur Ivor, CH287

Historical documentary editions, 1988, DB13

The historical encyclopedia of costumes, Racinet, A., BF30

Historical maps on file, Martin Greenwald Associates, DA27

Historical periodicals directory, DA10

Historical statistics of Chile, Mamalakis, Markos, CG45

Historical tables, 58 B.C.–A.D. 1985, Steinberg, S. H., DA24
Historical times illustrated encyclopedia of the Civil War, DB34
Historiography, DA55
Historiography and historical method
  bibliography, DA16
  encyclopedias, DA17
  France, DA13
  United States, DB75
Historisches Wörterbuch der Philosophie, BA18
History and area studies
  abstract journals and indexes, DA3
  atlases, DA26, DA29, DA30, DA37
  bibliography, DA5
    current, DA6, DA7
  bibliography of bibliography, DA3, DA55
  by period
    archaeology and ancient history
      bibliography, DD30
    medieval and Renaissance
      bibliography, DA46, DC6
      directories, AJ18, DA52
      encyclopedias, DA47, DA48, DA49, DA50
    modern; *see also* **Holocaust; World Wars**
      annuals and current surveys, DA61
      atlases, DA63
      bibliography, CC160, DA58
      databases, DA62
      dictionaries, AJ10
  chronologies, DA24, DA25, DA60
  chronologies, outlines, tables, DA27
  chronologies, outlines, tasks, DA23
  dictionaries, DA12, DA20, DA22
  dissertations, DA8
  fellowships, grants, etc., DA18
  guides, DA1
  historiography and historical method, DA13
  periodicals, DA3, DA9, DA10
The history and practice of Japanese printmaking, Abrams, Leslie E., BE154
History journals and serials, Fyfe, Janet, DA9
History of American ceramics, Strong, Susan R., BF19, BF20
History of American literature, Walker, Marshall, BD169
A history of American psychology in notes and news, 1883–1945, CD7
History of art, Janson, H. W., BE72
The history of cancer, Olson, James Stuart, EK14
A history of costume in the West, BF31
The history of photography, Gernsheim, Alison, BF53
—— Gernsheim, Helmut, BF53
History of photography, Roosens, Laurent, BF56, BF57
The history of surgery in the United States, 1775–1900, Rutkow, Ira M., EK75
The history of the health care sciences and health care, 1700–1980, Erlen, Jonathon, EK73
The history of the Irish in Britain, Hartigan, Maureen, DC101
Hit parade, Tyler, Don, BH135
Hitchcock, H. Wiley. *The new Grove dictionary of American music*, BH55
Hitchens, Howard B. *America on film and tape*, DB2
Hitchens, Vidge. *America on film and tape*, DB2
The Hittite dictionary of the Oriental Institute of the University of Chicago, University of Chicago. Oriental Institute, AD122
Hittite etymological dictionary, Puhvel, Jaan, AD121
Hittite language, AD121, AD122
Hixon, Donald L. *Nineteenth-century American drama*, BD231
Hladczuk, John. *Comparative reading*, CB27
—— *General issues in literacy/illiteracy*, CB28, CB29

—— *Literacy/illiteracy in the world*, CB28, CB29
Hladczuk, Sharon. *General issues in literacy/illiteracy*, CB28, CB29
—— *Literacy/illiteracy in the world*, CB28, CB29
Ho, Allan Benedict. *Biographical dictionary of Russian/Soviet composers*, BH76
Hoad, T. F. *The concise Oxford dictionary of English etymology*, AD15
Hobday, Charles. *Communist and Marxist parties of the world*, CJ245
Hochstadt, Jenny. *African language materials in the Boston University Libraries*, BC57
Hodd, Michael. *African economic handbook*, CH34
Hodek, Břetislav. *Velký anglicko-český slovník*, AD83
Hodes, Franz. *Internationale Personalbibliographie, 1944–1975*, AA4
Hodges, Deborah Robertson. *Etiquette*, CF38
Hodges, Elaine R. S. *The Guild handbook of scientific illustration*, EA67
Hodges, John Cunyus. *Harbrace college handbook*, BC29
Hodges, Richard E. *A dictionary of reading and related terms*, CB67
Hodgson, Ernest. *Dictionary of toxicology*, EK130
Hodgson, Terry. *The drama dictionary*, BG21
Hodoş, Nerva. *Publicaţiunile periodice româneşti (ziare, gazete, reviste)*, AE63
Hoefte, Rosemarijn. *Suriname*, DB134
Höhlein, Helga. *Auswahlbibliographie zum Studium der anglistischen Sprachwissenschaft*, BC20
Hoerder, Dirk. *The immigrant labor press in North America, 1840s–1970s*, CH276
Hoffer, Bates. *An English dictionary of Japanese culture*, DE79
Hoffman, Catherine. *The consumer health information source book*, EK15
Hoffman, Herbert H. *Hoffman's index to poetry*, BD133
—— *Recorded plays*, BG16
Hoffman, Hester Rosalyn Jacoby. *The reader's adviser*, AA60
Hoffmann, Frank W. *The literature of rock, II, 1979–1983*, BH136
Hoffmann, Lee Ann. *The literature of rock, II, 1979–1983*, BH136
Hoffman's index to poetry, Hoffman, Herbert H., BD133
Hoffmeister, Elizabeth R. *The Department of State and American diplomacy*, CJ75
Hoffner, Harry A. *The Hittite dictionary of the Oriental Institute of the University of Chicago*, AD122
Hofmann, Theodore. *Index of English literary manuscripts*, BD215
Hofmann Cortesi, Livio. *I segreti dell'inglese*, AD129
Hofstetter, Eleanore O. *The twentieth-century German novel*, BD297
Hofstetter, Henry William. *Dictionary of visual science*, EK53
Hogg, D. A. *Concise veterinary dictionary*, EH27
Hogg, Ian V. *Encyclopaedia of the Second World War*, DA75
Holder, R. W. *A dictionary of American and British euphemisms*, AD44
—— *The Faber dictionary of euphemisms*, AD44
Hole, Maureen. *Bibliography of criticism on English and French literary translations in Canada*, BD306
Holidays, CF37
Hollander, Joyce P. *Worldwide directory of national earth-science agencies and related international organizations*, EE18
Holler, Frederick L. *Information sources of political science*, CJ1

Holliday, Paul. *A dictionary of plant pathology*, EH11
Hollier, Denis. *A new history of French literature*, BD314
Hollis, Ernest V. *The college presidency, 1900–1960*, CB11
Holman, C. Hugh. *A handbook to literature*, BD39
Holmes, Frederic Lawrence. *Dictionary of scientific biography*, EA76
Holmes, John L. *Composers on composers*, BH81
Holmes, Michael. *The country house described*, BE120
Holocaust, DA80, DA83, DA84, DA85, DA86, DA87, DA88
  bibliography, DA81, DA82
The Holocaust, DA86
—— Cargas, Harry J., DA80
The Holocaust, Israel and the Jews, Gellert, Charles Lawrence, DA88
Holocaust studies, Sable, Martin, DA86
Holoman, D. Kern. *Writing about music*, BH46
Holt, John G. *Bergey's manual of systematic bacteriology*, EC61
Holt, Linda Hughey. *The A–Z of women's sexuality*, CC153
The Holt foreign film guide, Bergan, Ronald, BG67
Holtermann, Henrik. *Danish foreign policy*, DC42
Holtje, Stephen. *The ballplayers*, BJ17
Holtus, Günter. *Lexikon der Romanistischen Linguistik*, BC36
Holtze, Sally Holmes. *Sixth book of junior authors & illustrators*, BD80
The Holy Bible, BB39
Holy Roman Empire, DC8
Holzer, Marc. *Public sector productivity*, CJ216
Holzman, Albert George. *Encyclopedia of computer science and technology*, EJ59
Hombs, Mary Ellen. *American homelessness*, CC118
Homeless, CC117, CC118, CC119, CC120
The homeless in America, Nordquist, Joan, CC120
Homelessness in the United States, CC119
Hommes et destins, AJ54
The homosexual and society, Ridinger, Robert B. Marks, CC150
Homosexuality, CC146, CC150, CC152, CC154, CC155, CC156
  bibliography, CC149
Homosexuality, Dynes, Wayne R., CC146
Homosexuality bibliography. Second supplement, 1976–1982, Parker, William, CC149
Honduran literature, BD342
Honduras
  bibliography, AA137
  history
    bibliography, DB122
    encyclopedias, DB123
Honduras bibliography and research guide, Danby, Colin, DB122
Hong Kong
  bibliography, AA138
  history
    bibliography, DE56
  library resources, DE55
Hong Kong, Scott, Ian, DE56
Hong Kong government gazette, AA138
A Hong Kong union catalogue, Rydings, H. Anthony, DE55
Honigsblum, Bonnie Birtwistle. *A manual for writers of term papers, theses, and dissertations*, AH3
Honna, Nobuyuki. *An English dictionary of Japanese culture*, DE79
Honour, Hugh,. *The Penguin dictionary of decorative arts*, BF13
Hoogvelt, Ankie M. M. *Multinational enterprise*, CH95

Hooper, Nick. *The economics of defense, disarmament, and peace,* CJ296

Hoornstra, Jean. *American periodicals 1741–1900,* AE77, AE78

Hooton, Joy W. *The Oxford companion to Australian literature,* BD276

Hoover, Herbert T. *Bibliography of the Sioux,* CC218

Hoover Institution on War, Revolution, and Peace. *Guide to the collections in the Hoover Institution archives relating to Imperial Russia, the Russian revolutions and civil war, and the first emigration,* DC203

—— *Peronism and the three Perons,* DB109

—— *Unofficial documents of the Democracy Movement in Communist China, 1978–1981 = Chung-kuo min chu yun tung tzu liao : a checklist of Chinese materials in the Hoover Institution on War, Revolution and Peace,* CJ162, DE51

Hoover's handbook, CH119

Hope, Anne. *Guide to inventories and finding aids of German archives at the German Historical Institute, Washington, D.C,* DC91

Hopke, William E. *The encyclopedia of careers and vocational guidance,* CB156

Hopkins, Karen A. *A deafness collection,* CC104

Hopple, Gerald W. *United States intelligence,* CJ288

Horak, Stephan M. *Russia, the USSR, and Eastern Europe,* DC13

—— *The Soviet Union and Eastern Europe,* DC14

Horden, John. *Index of English literary manuscripts,* BD215

Hordeski, Michael F. *The illustrated dictionary of microcomputer terminology,* EJ62

—— *The illustrated dictionary of microcomputers,* EJ62

Horn, David. *The literature of American music in books and folk music collections,* BH27

Horn, Maurice. *World encyclopedia of cartoons,* BE160

Horowitz, Lois. *A bibliography of military name lists from pre-1675 to 1900,* AK5

Horror fiction, BD113, BD127

Horror literature, BD111

Horst, R. Kenneth. *Westcott's plant disease handbook,* EH25

Horticultural research international, EH17

Horton, John J. *Yugoslavia,* DC218

Horvath, Laszlo. *Peronism and the three Perons,* DB109

Horvilleur, Gilles. *Dictionnaire des personnages du cinéma,* BG88

Horward, Donald D. *Napoleonic military history,* DC62

Hoskin, Michael A. *The general history of astronomy,* EB13

Hospital literature index, EK32

Hospitals, EK62

Hotaling, Edward R. *Shakespeare and the musical stage,* BD268

Houfe, Simon. *The dictionary of British book illustrators and caricaturists, 1800–1914,* BE97

Houghton, Walter Edwards. *The Wellesley index to Victorian periodicals, 1824–1900,* AE80

Houldcroft, P. T. *Materials data sources,* EJ13

Houlden, J. L. *A dictionary of Biblical interpretation,* BB50

Houlette, Forrest. *Nineteenth-century rhetoric,* BD143

Hourani, Albert Habib. *The Cambridge encyclopedia of the Middle East and North Africa,* DE19

Housing
    bibliography, CC167, CH342
    directories, CH342

Housing and racial/ethnic minority status in the United States, Momeni, Jamshid A., CC167

Houston, W. Robert. *Handbook of research on teacher education,* CB17

Hovestreydt, W. *Annual Egyptological bibliography. Late reviews AEB 1947–1984,* DD30

Hovland, Michael A. *Musical settings of American poetry,* BH110

The how-to-do-it manual for small libraries, AB70

How to find an affordable college, CB94

How to find chemical information, Maizell, Robert E., ED1

How to find information about AIDS, Lingle, Virginia A., EK3

How to find the law, Cohen, Morris L., CK2, CK3

How to get into the college of your choice—and how to finance it, Stewart, Jayme, CB155

How to get your book published, Bell, Herbert W., AA49

How to identify prints, Gascoigne, Bamber, BE157

How to prepare a research proposal, Krathwohl, David R., CA24

How to write and publish papers in the medical sciences, Huth, Edward J., EK35

Howard, Diana. *Directory of theatre resources,* BG26

Howard, Richard. *A complete checklist of the birds of the world,* EC50

Howard-Hill, T. H. *Bibliography of British literary bibliographies,* BD202

Howatson, M. C. *The Oxford companion to classical literature,* BD366

Hoyt, Anne Kelley. *Bibliography of the Chickasaw,* CC218

Hrvatski biografski leksikon, AJ102

Hrvatsko ili srpsko-engleski enciklopedijski rječnik, Bujas, Željko, AD160

Huang, Han-chu. *Chinese newspapers in the Library of Congress,* AF6

Hubert, Marilyn L. *Lexicon of new formal geologic names of the United States, 1976–1980,* EE11

Hubin, Allen J. *1981–1985 supplement to Crime fiction, 1749–1980,* BD105

Huck, Burkhardt J. *Informationshandbuch internationale Beziehungen und Länderkunde = Information handbook international relations and area studies,* CJ135, DA57

Hudson, Kenneth. *The Cambridge guide to the museums of Britain and Ireland,* BE49

—— *The directory of museums & living displays,* BE50

—— *Directory of world museums,* BE50

Hudson, Margaret F. *Elder neglect and abuse,* CC45

Hudson, Robert V. *Mass media,* CH204

Hügel, Hans-Otto. *Deutsche literarische Zeitschriften, 1880–1945,* AE35

Huff, Cynthia Anne. *British women's diaries,* BD251

Huffman, Franklin E. *Bibliography and index of mainland Southeast Asian languages and linguistics,* BC59

Hughes, John J. *Bits, bytes & biblical studies,* BB53

Hughes, Roger. *The Caribbean,* DB140

—— *Caribbean writing,* BD284

Hugman, Barry J. *The Olympic games,* BJ32

Hui, Y. H. *United States food laws, regulations, and standards,* CK93, EH31

Hulbert, Mark. *The Hulbert guide to financial newsletters,* CH215

Hulbert financial digest annual review of investment newsletters, CH215

The Hulbert guide to financial newsletters, Hulbert, Mark, CH215

Hules, Virginia T. *French feminist criticism,* BD311

Hull, Roger. *Virology,* EC69

Human biology, Encyclopedia of, EC9

Human engineering, EJ75

Human evolution and prehistory, CE13

Human longevity from antiquity to the modern lab, Bailey, William G., CC35

Human relations *see* **Personnel management**

Human Relations Area Files, Inc. *Atlas of world cultures,* CE24

Human rights, CK110

Humanism, BA9, BD5

Humanities
    directories
        Gt. Brit., CA17, EA53
        Hungary, DC143
    periodicals
        Gt. Brit., AE47
    research grants, CA33

Humanities and social sciences in the Soviet Union, DC209

Humanities Research Council of Canada. *Union list of manuscripts in Canadian repositories,* DB86

Humburg, N. E. *Herbicide handbook of the Weed Science Society of America,* EH21

Humm, Maggie. *An annotated critical bibliography of feminist criticism,* BD20

—— *The dictionary of feminist theory,* CC296

Hummel, David. *American musical theatre,* BH104

Humor in America, CF30

Humphrey-Smith, Cecil R. *The Phillimore atlas and index of parish registers,* AK29

Humphreys, Nancy K. *American women's magazines,* CC272

Humphries, Charles. *Music publishing in the British Isles,* BH70

Hungarian language, AD123, AD124

Hungary
    bibliography, AA139, CC166, DC145
    biography, AJ69
        contemporary, AJ70
    dissertations, AH12
    manuscripts and archives, DC144
    statistics, CG55

Hunger, Herbert. *Lexikon der griechischen und römischen Mythologie,* CF12

Hunt, Thomas C. *Religious schools in America,* CB30

Hunt, V. Daniel. *Dictionary of advanced manufacturing technology,* CH292

Hunter, Joy W. *Health media review index,* EK21

—— *Health media review index, 1984–86,* EK22

Hunter, Rosemary. *The Oxford literary guide to Australia,* BD274

Hunting the snark, Peters, Robert, BD136

Hurt, Charlie Deuel. *Information sources in science and technology,* EA3

Husband, Janet. *Sequels,* BD91

Husband, Jonathan F. *Sequels,* BD91

Husén, Torsten. *The international encyclopedia of education,* CB63, CB64

Hutchins, Geraldine L. *Science fiction and fantasy book review index, 1980–1984,* BD125

Hutchison, Robert. *Catalogue of meteorites,* EE38

Huth, Edward J. *How to write and publish papers in the medical sciences,* EK35

—— *Medical style and format,* EK35

Hutton, Patrick H. *Historical dictionary of the Third French Republic, 1870–1940,* DC76

Huxley, Aldous. *Encyclopedia of pacifism,* CJ305

Hydrology, EE25, EE26

Hypnosis, CD50

IASLIC (Association). *Directory of special and research libraries in India,* AB32

IBEPI, AJ94

IBN, Lobies, Jean-Pierre, AJ6

IBZ, DE10

IEEE standard dictionary of electrical and electronics terms, Institute of Electrical and Electronics Engineers, EJ46

IES lighting handbook, EJ49

IFLA International Office for UBC. *Commonwealth national bibliographies*, AA72

—— *Commonwealth retrospective national bibliographies*, AA73

IFLA Office for International Lending. *A brief guide to centres of international lending and photocopying*, AB98

IIC abstracts, BE16

IMS . . . Ayer directory of publications, AE23

IMS . . . directory of publications, AE23

ISSN, publicações periódicas brasileiras, AE28

IT focus: update on information technology, EG2, EJ44

IWGIA yearbook, CE18

I-mu. *Unofficial documents of the Democracy Movement in Communist China, 1978–1981 = Chung-kuo min chu yun tung tzu liao : a checklist of Chinese materials in the Hoover Institution on War, Revolution and Peace*, CJ162, DE51

IBT, BG12

Iceland
  bibliography, AA181, DC181
  biography, AJ91

Icelandic language, AD125

Icelandic literature, BD300

Iconclass, Waal, H. van de, BE101

Iconographic index to Old Testament subjects represented in photographs and slides of paintings in the visual collections, Fine Arts Library, Harvard University, Roberts, Helene E., BE101

An iconographic index to Stanislas Lami's Dictionnaire des sculpteurs de l'Ecole française au dix-neuvième siècle, Janson, H. W., BE165

Identifying American architecture, Blumenson, John J. G., BE130

Igoe, Robert S. *Dictionary of food ingredients*, EH32, EK101

Igreja, Francisco. *Dicionário de poetas contemporâneos*, BD320

Ihme, Heinrich. *Deutsches biographisches Jahrbuch*, AJ58

Ikonographie der christlichen Kunst, Schiller, Gertrud, BE102

Illingworth, Valerie. *Dictionary of computing*, EJ61

—— *The Facts on File dictionary of astronomy*, EB7

Illuminating Engineering Society of North America. *IES lighting handbook*, EJ49

The illustrated Bible handbook, Blair, Edward Payson, BB47

An illustrated bio-bibliography of black photographers, 1940–1988, Willis-Thomas, Deborah, BF64

An illustrated companion to the First World War, Bruce, A. P. C., DA74

Illustrated dictionary & concordance of the Bible, BB54

An illustrated dictionary of Hindu iconography, Stutley, Margaret, BE104

An illustrated dictionary of jewelry, Newman, Harold, BF44

The illustrated dictionary of microcomputer terminology, Hordeski, Michael F., EJ62

The illustrated dictionary of microcomputers, Hordeski, Michael F., EJ62

An illustrated dictionary of silverware, Newman, Harold, BF44

The illustrated encyclopedia of myths & legends, Cotterell, Arthur, CF2

The illustrated encyclopedia of New Zealand, DF10

The illustrated encyclopedia of the securities industry, Pessin, Allan H., CH230

Illustrating science, Council of Biology Editors. Scientific Illustration Committee, EA66

Illustration index VI, 1982–1986, Appel, Marsha C., BE31

The illustrator in America, Reed, Roger, BE97

—— Reed, Walter, BE97

Illustrators, BE97

Imaeda, Yoshiro. *Bibliography of Tibetan studies*, DE98

Images of blacks in American culture, CC190

Imaginary people, Pringle, David, BD10

Imai, Mitsunori. *A concordance to Middle English metrical romances*, BD209

Imber, Jane. *Dictionary of advertising and direct mail terms*, CH70

Immergut, E. H. *Polymer handbook*, EJ22

The immigrant labor press in North America, 1840s–1970s, Hoerder, Dirk, CH276

Immigrant women in the United States, Gabaccia, Donna R., CC281

Immigrants from Great Britain and Ireland, Lester, DeeGee, DC146

—— Weaver, Jack W., AK36, CC178, DC146

Immigration, AK9, AK11, AK12, AK13, AK14, AK36, CC162, CC163, CC175, CC177, CC178, CC193, CC281, DB61, DE59

Immroth, John Philip. *Guide to the Library of Congress classification*, AB81

Immroth's guide to the Library of Congress classification, Chan, Lois Mai, AB81

Immunology, EC3, EC15, EK56

Immunology abstracts, EC7

Immunology, an information profile, Nicholas, Robin, EC3

Imperato, P. J. *Mali*, DD6

Impresos venezolanos del siglo XIX, Drenikoff, Iván, AA199

Impressionism, BE33

Imprimeurs & libraires parisiens du XVIe siècle, Renouard, Philippe, AA52

Imps, Paul. *Trésor de la langue française*, AD91

In Plain English, Inc. *Webster's New World secretarial handbook*, CH169

In pursuit of the past, Porter, Frank W., CC218

In search of Welsh ancestry, Hamilton-Edwards, Gerald Kenneth Savery, AK46

In search of your British & Irish roots, Baxter, Angus, AK30

In search of your German roots, Baxter, Angus, AK24

Inada, Kenneth K. *Guide to Buddhist philosophy*, BA2, BB123

The Incas, Welch, Thomas L., CC222

Incest, De Young, Mary, CC125

Incunabula
  union lists, AA40, AA41, AA42, AA43

Incunabula of British photographic literature, Gernsheim, Helmut, BF53

The independence of Latin America, DB108

The independent learners' sourcebook, Smith, Robert McCaughan, CB40

The index and abstract directory, AE74

Index and directory of industry standards, EA88

Index des périodiques d'architecture canadiens, 1940–1980 = Canadian architectural periodicals index, 1940–1980, Bergeron, Claude, BE117

An index-dictionary of Chinese artists, collectors, and connoisseurs with character identification by modified stroke count, Seymour, Nancy N., BE87

Index medicus, EK9, EK33

Index of American print exhibitions, 1785–1940, Wilson, Raymond L., BE67

Index of American print exhibitions, 1882–1940, Wilson, Raymond L., BE156

Index of art sales catalogs, 1981–1985, BE60

Index of art sales catalogs, 1981–1985. SCIPIO, BE63

Index of conference proceedings, British Library. Document Supply Centre, EA61

Index of conference proceedings received, EA61

An index of early Chinese painters and paintings, Cahill, James F., BE150

Index of economic articles, CH3

Index of English literary manuscripts, BD215

The index of majors, CB100

Index of manuscripts in the British Library, British Library. Dept. of Manuscripts, AA36

Index of Middle English verse, Brown, Carleton, BD205, BD246

—— Robbins, Russell H., BD205, BD246

Index of NLM serial titles, EK24

The index of paintings sold in the British Isles during the nineteenth century, BE61

—— Getty Art History Information Program, BE61

Index of printed Middle English prose, Lewis, Robert E., BD205

Index of printers, publishers, and booksellers, Morrison, Paul G., AA130

Index scriptorum novus mediae latinitatis, AD142

Index to Afro-American reference resources, Stevenson, Rosemary M., CC192

Index to American periodicals of the 1700's, AE77

Index to American periodicals of the 1800's, AE78

Index to American photographic collections, BF58

Index to Best American short stories and O. Henry prize stories, White, Ray Lewis, BD177

Index to biographies of contemporary composers, Bull, Storm, BH92

Index to book reviews in England, 1749–1774, Forster, Antonia, BD210

Index to book reviews in religion, BB16, BB20, BB21

Index to children's plays in collections, 1975–1984, Trefny, Beverly Robin, BD81

Index to composer bibliographies, Green, Richard D., BH91

Index to crime and mystery anthologies, Contento, William, BD103

Index to dental literature, EK33

An index to early music in selected anthologies, Hilton, Ruth B., BH37

Index to ETS research report series, 1948–1989, Educational Testing Service, CB51

Index to fairy tales, 1978–1986, including folklore, legends, and myths in collections, Ireland, Norma Olin, BD98

Index to historic preservation periodicals, BE121

Index to international public opinion, CJ232

Index to legal books, CK54

Index to legal periodicals, CK55

Index to maps in books and periodicals, American Geographical Society of New York, CL39

Index to periodical articles related to law, CK56

Index to personal names in the National union catalog of manuscript collections, 1959–1984, DB19

Index to plays in periodicals, 1977–1987, Keller, Dean H., BD85

Index to poetry, Granger, Edith, BD11

Index to poetry by black American women, Chapman, Dorothy Hilton, BD181

Index to poetry in popular periodicals, BD180

Index to poetry in popular periodicals, 1960–1964, Caskey, Jefferson D., BD180

Index to Puerto Rican collective biography, Fowlie-Flores, Fay, AJ89

Index to record reviews, 1984–1987, Myers, Kurtz, BH161

Index to religious periodical literature, BB20

An index to reproductions of paintings by twentieth century Chinese artists, Laing, Ellen Johnston, BE150

Index to science fiction anthologies and collections, Contento, William, BD120

Index to scientific book contents, EA27

INDEX

Index to Spanish American collective biography, Mundo Lo, Sara de, AJ78
Index to statistics and probability, EF6
Index to tests used in educational dissertations, Fabiano, Emily, CB23, CD44
Index to the Annenberg Television Script Archive, Annenberg School of Communications (University of Pennsylvania). Television Script Archive, BG106
Index to the Wilson authors series, BD55
Index to theses with abstracts accepted for higher degrees by the universities of Great Britain and Ireland and the Council for National Academic Awards, AH11
Index to women of the world from ancient to modern times, Ireland, Norma Olin, AJ5
Index veterinarius, EH8
Indexing, AB85, AB86
India
  bibliography, AA65, DE32
  bibliography of bibliography, AA5
  biography, AJ71, AJ72, DE31
  emigration and immigration, DE59
  foreign relations, DE58
  history, DE64
    bibliography, DE57, DE60
    encyclopedias, DE61, DE62, DE63
  library resources, DE31
  politics and government, CJ185
  statistics
    bibliography, CG56
India Office Library and Records. *A brief guide to biographical sources*, DE31
—— *A general guide to the India Office Records*, DE4, DE32
—— *A guide to source materials in the India Office Library and Records for the history of Tibet, Sikkim and Bhutan 1765–1950*, DE29
Indian library directory, AB33
Indian national bibliography, AA5
Indian Ocean, DE2
Indian Ocean, Gotthold, Julia J., DE2
Indian reference sources, Sharma, H. D., AA65
Indian reservations, CC229
Indians of North America *see* **Native Americans**
Indians of North and South America, Wolf, Carolyn E., CC225
The Indians of Texas, Tate, Michael L., CC218
Indians overseas, Thomas, Timothy N., DE59
Indic languages, BC56
Indic literature, BD377, BD378
Indice alfabético de títulos-materias, correcciones, conexiones y adiciones del Manual del librero hispanoamericano de Antonio Palau y Dulcet, Palau Claveras, Agustín, AA186
Indice biográfico de España, Portugal e Iberoamérica = Indice biográfico de Espanha, Portugal e Ibero-América = Spanish, Portuguese and Latin American biographical index, AJ94
Indice generale degli incunaboli delle biblioteche d'Italia, AA42
Indigenous peoples, CE18
The individual investor's guide to investment publications, CH216
An Indo-European comparative dictionary, Mann, Stuart E., AD72
Indo-European language *see* **Aryan language**
Indo-U.S. relations, 1947–1988, Saha, Santosh C., DE58
Indochinese War, DE65
Indonesia
  bibliography, AA140, AA141, AE51
  history
    bibliography, DE66
  statistics, CG57
The Indonesian economy and politics, 1963–1986, Arief, Melanie S., DE66
An Indonesian-English dictionary, Echols, John M., AD126
Indonesian language, AD126

Industrial accidents, ED17
Industrial relations *see* **Labor and industrial relations**
Industrial relations, Bennett, J. D., CH269
Industrial research laboratories of the United States, EA62
Industrial Revolution, DC115
Industries
  history, CH140
  manuscripts and archives
    Gt. Brit., DC108
Industry and company information, Hawbaker, A. Craig, CH79
Industry and development, CH305
Industry norms and key business ratios, CH128
Infancy, Nuba-Scheffler, Hannah, CC82
InfoPLACE (Career information center). *Professional careers sourcebook*, CH341
Information Bulgaria, DC37
Information for international marketing, Weekly, James K., CH313
Information Interface Institute. *Education interface . . . guide to pre-college foundation support*, CB158
Information Mongolia, DE85
Information networks, CH195
Information resources in the arts, Shipley, Lloyd W., BE57
Information resources in toxicology, Wexler, Philip, EK127
Information sources in agriculture and food science, EH1
Information sources in biotechnology, Crafts-Lighty, A., EJ18
Information sources in cartography, CL1
Information sources in energy technology, EJ71
Information sources in engineering, EJ1
Information sources in pharmaceuticals, EK104
Information sources in polymers and plastics, EJ21
Information sources in science and technology, Hurt, Charlie Deuel, EA3
—— Parker, C. C., EA4
Information sources in the earth sciences, EE1
Information sources in the life sciences, EC1
Information sources in the medical sciences, EK104
Information sources of political science, Holler, Frederick L., CJ1
Informationshandbuch internationale Beziehungen und Länderkunde = Information handbook international relations and area studies, Huck, Burkhardt J., CJ135, DA57
Inge, M. Thomas. *Handbook of American popular culture*, CF34
—— *Handbook of American popular literature*, BD163
Ingham, John N. *Biographical dictionary of American business leaders*, CH146
—— *Contemporary American business leaders*, CH146
Inglis, Kenneth Stanley. *Australians*, DF2
Inorganic chemical nomenclature, Block, B. Peter, ED26
Inside U.S. business, Mattera, Philip, CH307
The insider's guide to demographic know-how, Crispell, Diane, CH323
INSPEC, EG2, EJ44
Institut de l'information scientifique et technique (France). *Bibliography of the history of art*, BE19
Institut de recherche et d'histoire des textes (France). *Répertoire international des médiévistes = International directory of medievalists*, AJ18, DA52
Institut russkogo îazyka (Akademiîa nauk SSSR). *Slovar' russkogo îazyka XI-XVII vv*, AD151
Institut russkogo îazyka (Akademiîa nauk SSSR). Slovarnyĭ sektor. *Slovar' russkikh narodnykh govorov*, AD150

Inštitut za slovenski jezik (Slovenska akademija znanosti in umetnosti). *Slovar slovenskega knjižnega jezika*, AD162
Institute for Antiquity and Christianity. *The Eerdmans analytical concordance to the Revised Standard Version of the Bible*, BB61
Institute for Defense and Disarmament Studies (U.S.). *Peace resource book*, CJ312
Institute for European-Latin American Relations. *Manual para las relaciones Europeo-Latinoamericanas = Handbook for European-Latin American relations*, DB105
Institute for Scientific Information. *Science citation index*, EA30
—— *Science citation index. Compact disc edition*, EA29
—— *Social sciences citation index*, CA12
Institute of Asian Affairs (Hamburg, Germany). *Who's who in the People's Republic of China*, AJ41
Institute of Electrical and Electronics Engineers. *IEEE standard dictionary of electrical and electronics terms*, EJ46
Institute of Laboratory Animal Resources (U.S.). Committee on Care and Use of Laboratory Animals. *Guide for the care and use of laboratory animals*, EC58
Institute of Mathematical Statistics. *Selected tables in mathematical statistics*, EF17
Institute of Metals. *Materials data sources*, EJ13
Institute of Southeast Asian Studies. *Laos*, DE82
Institution of Electrical Engineers. *INSPEC*, EG2, EJ44
Institution of Mechanical Engineers (Great Britain). *Materials data sources*, EJ13
Institutional advancement, CB10
Instituto Bibliográfico Mexicano. *Bibliografía mexicana*, AA159
Instituto Brasileiro de Informação em Ciência e Tecnologia. *Guia de publicações seriadas brasileiras*, AE28
Instituto "Miguel de Cervantes.". *Bibliografía de autores españoles del siglo XVIII*, BD322
Instituto Nacional de Estadística (Peru). *Perú, compendio estadístico*, CG66
Instituto Profesional de Santiago. *Publicaciones oficiales de Chile, 1973–1983*, AG32
Instituto Tecnológico Autónomo de México. *Las publicaciones periódicas mexicanas*, AE58
Instructional technology, CB68
Instrumental music, BH13
Instrumentation reference book, EJ76
Insurance
  dictionaries, CH264, CH265
  directories, CH266
  guides, CH263
Insurance dictionary, Thomsett, Michael C., CH265
The insurance industry, Weiner, Alan R., CH263
Intā Puresu kagaku gijutsu 25–mango daijiten, EA49
Integrating women's studies into the curriculum, Schmitz, Betty, CB135
Intelligence and espionage, Constantinides, George C., CJ285
Intelligence service, CJ285; *see also* **Espionage**
  United States, CJ286, CJ288
  U.S.S.R., CJ287
Interior design, BF34, BF38
Interlibrary loan, AB97, AB98, AB99, AB100
Interlibrary loan directory, AB99
Interlibrary loan policies directory, Morris, Leslie R., AB100
International aerospace abstracts, EJ15
International African Institute. *International guide to African studies research = Études africaines : guide international de recherches*, DD8

The international almanac of electoral history, Mackie, Thomas T., CJ141

International Art Alliance. *ARTnews international directory of corporate art collections,* BE52

International art auctions, BE64

International art price annual, BE58

International Association for Sports Information. *International directory of sports organizations under the auspices of the International Association for Sports Information (IASI),* BJ14

International Association of Egyptologists. *Annual Egyptological bibliography. Late reviews AEB 1947–1984,* DD30

International Association of Libraries and Museums of the Performing Arts. *International bibliography of theatre,* BG12

International Association of Schools of Social Work. *World guide to social work education,* CC32

International Association of Universities. *World list of universities = Liste mondiale des universites,* CB87

International Astronomical Union. *The general history of astronomy,* EB13

The international atlas, Shanks, Thomas G., CL22

International bibliography of jazz books, Carl Gregor, *Duke of Mecklenburg,* BH117

International bibliography of political science, CJ26

International bibliography of sociology, CC15

International bibliography of the social sciences, CE16

International bibliography of theatre, BG12

International biography of adult education, CB31

The international biotechnology directory, Coombs, J., EJ17

International brands and their companies, CH299, CH297

—— Wood, Donna, CH294, CH295, CH296

International Bureau of Education. *Directory of educational documentation and information services = Répertoire des services de documentation et d'information pédagogiques,* CB81

—— *Directory of educational research institutions = Répertoire des institutions de recherche en éducation,* CB82

International business bibliography, Slomanson, William R., CH86

International business enterprises, CH285

International business handbook, CH185

International business travel and relocation directory, CH162

International Cartographic Association. *Cartographical innovations,* CL10

International Centre for Parliamentary Documentation. *Parliaments of the world,* CJ139

International Centre for the Study of the Preservation and the Restoration of Cultural Property. *International index of conservation research = Répertoire international de la recherche en conservation,* BE106

International Chamber of Commerce. *New ICC world directory of chambers of commerce = Nouvel annuaire mondial CCI des chambres de commerce,* CH106

International code name directory, CJ259

International Commission for the History of Towns. *Historic towns,* DC134

International Committee for Social Science Information and Documentation. *Thematic list of descriptors—anthropology = Liste thématique des descripteurs—anthropologie,* CE16

—— *Thematic list of descriptors—economics,* CH12

—— *Thematic list of descriptors—political science = Liste thématique des descripteurs—science politique,* CJ26

—— *Thematic list of descriptors—sociology = Liste thématique des descripteurs—sociologie,* CC15

International Committee of Historical Sciences. *Great historians from antiquity to 1800,* DA14

International companies and their brands, CH298

—— Wood, Donna, CH294, CH295, CH296, CH297, CH298

International Conference Group on Portugal. *The Portuguese in the United States,* CC168

International corporate 1000, CH111

International Council for Bird Preservation. *Rare birds of the world,* EC54

International Council of Scientific and Technical Information. *Multilingual thesaurus of geosciences,* EE15

International Council on Archives. *Guides to the sources for the history of the nations. 3rd series, North Africa, Asia and Oceania = Guides des sources de l'histoire des nations. 3ème série, Afrique du Nord, Asie et Océanie,* DD2, DD15, DG4

—— *Modern archives administration and records management,* AB74

The international critical commentary on the Holy Scriptures of the Old and New Testaments, BB66

International development abstracts, EC23

The international development dictionary, Fry, Gerald, CH55

International dictionary of art and artists, BE81

The international dictionary of films and filmmakers, BG92

International dictionary of management, Johannsen, Hano, CH157

International dictionary of medicine and biology, EC17, EK48

The international dictionary of psychology, Sutherland, N. S., CD22

An international dictionary of theatre language, BG24

The international dictionary of women's biography, AJ9

International directory of archives = Annuaire international des archives, AB46

International directory of braille music collections, Thorin, Suzanne E., BH65

International directory of children's literature, Dunhouse, Mary Beth, BD73

International directory of cinematographers, set- and costume designers in film, BG100

International directory of company histories, CH139

International directory of corporate affiliations, CH102

International directory of film and TV documentation centres, BG83

International directory of gay and lesbian periodicals, Malinowsky, Harold Robert, CC154

The international directory of government, CJ137

International directory of organizations in aging, CC57

International directory of psychologists, exclusive of the U.S.A, CD35

International directory of sports organizations under the auspices of the International Association for Sports Information (IASI), BJ14

International directory of tactile map collections, CL45

International directory of telecommunications, CH210

International directory of youth bodies = Répertoire international des organismes de jeunesse = Repertorio internacional de organismos de juventud, CC90

International Dun's market identifiers (IDMI), CH99

International economic indicators, Moore, Geoffrey Hoyt, CH18

International economic institutions, Meerhaeghe, Marcel Alfons Gilbert van, CH15

The international encyclopedia of astronomy, EB6

International encyclopedia of communications, CH205

The international encyclopedia of curriculum, Lewy, Arieh, CB63

The international encyclopedia of education, CB63, CB64

The international encyclopedia of educational evaluation, Haertel, Geneva D., CB63

—— Walberg, Herbert J., CB63

The international encyclopedia of educational technology, Eraut, Michael, CB63

International encyclopedia of foundations, CA28

International encyclopaedia of Indian literature, Garg, Gaṅgā Rām, BD378

International encyclopedia of robotics, EJ77

The international encyclopedia of teaching and teacher education, Dunkin, Michael J., CB63

International encyclopedia of women composers, Cohen, Aaron I., BH77

International English usage, Todd, Loreto, AD29

International Environmental Information System (United Nations Environment Programme). *ACCIS guide to United Nations information sources on the environment,* EJ29

International Epidemiological Association. *A dictionary of epidemiology,* EK124

International Federation for Documentation. *Directory of social science information courses = Répertoire des cours d'information dans les sciences sociales = Repertorio de cursos en información en ciencias sociales,* CA18

International Federation for Theatre Research. *International bibliography of theatre,* BG12

International Federation of Film Archives. *Glossary of filmographic terms = Lexique de termes filmographiques,* BG95

—— *International directory of cinematographers, set- and costume designers in film,* BG100

—— *Treasures from the film archives,* BG76

International Federation of Library Associations and Institutions. *Guide to the availability of theses II,* AB97

—— *International directory of tactile map collections,* CL45

—— *Inventaire général des bibliographies nationales rétrospectives = Retrospective national bibliographies : an international directory,* AA76

—— *World directory of map collections,* CL46

International film guide, BG98

International film, radio, and television journals, BG58

International folklore bibliography, CF23

International Food Information Service. *Food science and technology abstracts,* EH30

International foundation directory, CA29

International Geographical Union. *Orbis geographicus = Adressar géographique du monde = World directory of geography = Geographisches Weltadressbuch,* CL15

International glossary of social gerontology = Glosario internacional de gerontología social = Glossaire international de gérontologie sociale = Internationales Wörterverzeichnis für Sozialgerontologie, CC54

International guide to African studies research = Études africaines : guide international de recherches, DD8

International guide to library and information science education, AB19

International guide to nineteenth-century photographers and their works, Edwards, Gary, BE59, BF63

International guide to official industrial property publications, Rimmer, Brenda M., EA87

International handbook of national parks and nature reserves, BJ38

International handbook of psychology, CD30

International handbook of women's education, CB132, CC310

International handbook on race and race relations, CC185

International higher education, CB65

International index of conservation research = Répertoire international de la recherche en conservation, BE106

International information system for the agricultural sciences and technology, EH6

International Institute for Conservation of Historic and Artistic Works. *Art and archaeology technical abstracts*, BE16

International inventory of current Mexico-related research, DB128

International inventory of musical sources, BH64

International jazz bibliography, Carl Gregor, Duke of Mecklenburg, BH117

International jobs, Kocher, Eric, CH338

International Labour Office. *Annotated bibliography on clandestine employment*, CH268

—— *Employment creation policies and strategies*, CH272

—— *Labour information*, CH275

International labour statistics, CH288

International law, CK106
  bibliography, CK25
  digests and collections, CK108, CK109
  encyclopedias, CK110

The international law list, CK16

International legal books in print, 1990–1991, CK17

International medical who's who, EK79

International Monetary Fund. *A study of the Soviet economy*, CH53

—— *World economic outlook*, CH33

International motion picture almanac, BG98

International Museum of Photography at George Eastman House. *Index to American photographic collections*, BF58

International music journals, BH32

International nursing index, EK33

International organisations and overseas agencies publications, AG39

International organisations catalogue, AG39

International organisations publications, AG39

International organizations; *see also* **European communities; United Nations**
  bibliography
    current, AG39
  directories, CJ32, CK83, CK119
  manuscripts and archives, AB45

International Paleontological Association. *Directory of paleontologists of the world*, EE41

The international peace directory, CJ309

The international pharmacopoeia = Pharmacopoea internationalis, World Health Organization, EK123

International proverb scholarship, Mieder, Wolfgang, BD70

International real estate valuation, investment, and development, Nurcombe, Valerie J., CH345

International relations
  bibliography, CJ7
  directories, CA40
  encyclopedias, CJ20
  guides, CJ135, DA57

International relations, CJ7

The international relations dictionary, Plano, Jack C., CJ20

International relations theory, Groom, A. J. R., CJ7

—— Mitchell, Christopher, CJ7

International Repertory of Music Literature. *RILM abstracts*, BH45

International repertory of the literature of art, BE22

International Research and Exchanges Board. *Guide to research and scholarship in Hungary*, DC143

—— *A handbook for archival research in the USSR*, AB10, DC201

The international standard Bible encyclopedia, BB55

International Statistical Institute. *A dictionary of statistical terms*, CG9, EF11

International studies in Japan, DE75

International subscription agents, Perryman, Wayne R., AB68

International time tables, Fitzpatrick, Gary L., EB19

International trade names company index, CH294, CH295, CH296, CH297, CH298

International trade names dictionary, CH294, CH295, CH296, CH297, CH298

International Translations Centre. *Journals in translation*, AE13

—— *World translations index*, EA17

International Union for the Scientific Study of Population. *Bibliography of IUSSP conference proceedings from 1927 to 1985*, CG2

International union list of agricultural serials, EH5, EH6, EH8, EH3

International Union of Crystallography. *World directory of crystallographers and of other scientists employing crystallographic methods*, EE22

International Union of Geological Sciences. *Multilingual thesaurus of geosciences*, EE15

International Union of Geological Sciences. Subcommission on the Systematics of Igneous Rocks. *A classification of igneous rocks and glossary of terms*, EE44

International Union of Psychological Science. *International directory of psychologists, exclusive of the U.S.A*, CD35

International Union of Pure and Applied Chemistry. *Compendium of chemical terminology*, ED8

International Union of the History and Philosophy of Science. *The general history of astronomy*, EB13

International vital records handbook, Kemp, Thomas Jay, AK1

International who's who in music and musicians' directory, BH82

International Work Group for Indigenous Affairs. *IWGIA yearbook*, CE18

International yearbook of educational and training technology, CB84

International yearbook of educational technology, CB84

Internationale Bibliographie der Festschriften von den Anfängen bis 1979, Leistner, Otto, AA28

Internationale Jahresbibliographie Südwestasien = International annual bibliography South West Asia : SWA, DE10

Internationale Personalbibliographie, 1944–1975, AA4

Internationale Volkskundliche Bibliographie = International folklore bibliography, CF23

Internationaler Nekrolog, AJ4

Internationales Bibliotheks-Handbuch = World guide to libraries, AB20

Interstate compacts and agencies, Council of State Governments, AG26

Intertextuality, allusion, and quotation, Hebel, Udo J., BD2

Introduction to automation for librarians, Saffady, William, AB88

Introduction to cataloging and classification, Wynar, Bohdan S., AB76

Introduction to classical scholarship, McGuire, Martin, BD365

Introduction to indexing and abstracting, Cleveland, Donald B., AB85

Introduction to library research in women's studies, Searing, Susan E., CC250

Introduction to reference work, Katz, William A., AB107

Introduction to United States public documents, Morehead, Joe, AG6, CJ95

Inuit art, BE77

Inventaire chronologique des éditions parisiennes du XVIe siècle, Moreau, Brigitte, AA111

Inventaire général des bibliographies nationales rétrospectives = Retrospective national bibliographies : an international directory, AA76

Inventare des Goethe- und Schiller-Archivs, BD299

Inventory of marriage and family literature, CC127

Invertebrates, EC43

Investext, CH220

Investment, CH222, CH246
  bibliography, CH215
  dictionaries, CH238
  directories, CH247
  encyclopedias, CH230
  handbooks, CH253
  indexes, CH219
  periodicals, CH216, CH217

Investment and securities dictionary, Thomsett, Michael C., CH238

Investment companies, CH246

Investment Company Institute (U.S.). *St. James mutual fund directory*, CH248

Investment newsletters, CH217

Investment statistics locator, Chapman, Karen J., CH219

The investor's dictionary, Rosenberg, Jerry Martin, CH234

The investor's guide to stock quotations and other financial listings, Warfield, Gerald, CH259

Ionescu, Alexandru Sadi. *Publicațiunile periodice românești (ziare, gazete, reviste)*, AE63

Ionov, E. P. *Pisateli Moskvy*, BD358

Iordan, Iorgu. *Dicționarul limbii române*, AD148

Iosipescu, Michael. *Legal writing and research manual*, CK36

Iran
  bibliography, AA142
  bibliography of bibliography, AA6
  encyclopedias, DE71
  history
    bibliography, DE9, DE12, DE67, DE68, DE69, DE70

Iran, Navabpour, Reza, DE69

Iran and the West, Ghani, Sīrūs, DE68

Iranian literature, BD379

Iraq, AA143, DE9, DE12

The Iraq-Iran war, Gardner, J. Anthony, DE9

Iraqi national bibliography, AA143

Ireland, Norma Olin. *Index to fairy tales, 1978–1986, including folklore, legends, and myths in collections*, BD98

—— *Index to women of the world from ancient to modern times*, AJ5

Ireland, Sandra L. Jones. *Ethnic periodicals in contemporary America*, AE24, CC172

Ireland
  bibliography
    current, AA144
  biography, AJ73
  government publications
    parliamentary publications, AG36
  history
    bibliography, DC147, DC148

chronology, DC152
encyclopedias, DC113
general histories, DC153
manuscripts and archives, DC150
quotations, BD63, CJ186, DC151
library resources, DC146
manuscripts and archives, DC146, DC149
politics and government, BD63, CJ186, DC151
Ireland, Northern
newspapers, AF10
politics and government, CJ187
Irish American material culture, Eleuterio-Comer, Susan K., DB71, DC146
Irish Americans, DB71
Irish books in print & Leabhair Gaeilge i gCló, AA144
Irish Committee of Historical Sciences. *Writings on Irish history*, DC148
Irish family history, Yurdan, Marilyn, AK41
Irish history from 1700, Prochaska, Alice, DC150
Irish in Britain, DC101
Irish in British History Group. *The history of the Irish in Britain*, DC101
Irish language
bibliography, BC54
dictionaries, AD127
Irish literature
bibliography, BC54
biography, BD271
dissertations, BD270
Irish records, Ryan, James G., AK40
Irish Republic, Shannon, Michael Owen, DC147
Irish research, Lester, DeeGee, DB71, DC146
Iron and steel in the nineteenth century, Paskoff, Paul F., CH136
Irregular serials and annuals, AE8, AE9
Irving, Robert. *A pictorial guide to identifying Australian architecture*, BE130
Isaacs, Alan. *The Cambridge illustrated dictionary of British heritage*, DC114
Isagoge in musicen, Glareanus, Henricus, BH9
Isis cumulative bibliography 1976–1985, EA70
ISIS (Organization). *Women in development*, CC251
Islam
bibliography, BB126, DE8, DE13
chronology, DE25
encyclopedias, BB125, BB127
statistics, CC180
Islamic art, BE11
Islamic peoples of the Soviet Union, Akiner, Shirin, CC180
Isotopes, EG11
Israël, Guy. *The Cambridge atlas of astronomy*, EB15
Israel
atlases, CL65
bibliography, AA145
history
atlases, DA64
bibliography, BB134, DE72
politics and government, CJ188, CJ189
encyclopedias, CJ190
statistics, CG58
Israel. Agaf ha-medidot. *Atlas of Israel*, CL65
Israeli books in print, AA145
Istituto centrale per il catalogo unico delle biblioteche italiane e per le informazioni bibliografiche. *Le edizioni italiane del XVI secolo*, AA148
Istituto della Enciclopedia italiana. *Enciclopedia del Novecento*, AC16
Istituto di studi rinascimentali (Ferrara, Italy). *Renaissance linguistics archive, 1350–1700*, BC5
Istoriia dorevoliutsionnoĭ Rossii v dnevnikakh i vospominaniiakh, DC196

Iswanti, Setya. *Directory of special libraries and information sources in Indonesia 1985 = Direktori perpustakaan khusus dan sumber informasi di Indonesia 1985*, AB35
Italian Americans, CC162
The Italian emigration to the United States, 1880–1930, Cordasco, Francesco, CC162
Italian language
bibliography, BC41
dictionaries, AD128
bilingual, AD129, AD130
etymology, AD132
synonyms, AD133
Italian literature, BD316
Italian poetry, BD315
Italian Renaissance poetry, Buja, Maureen E., BD315
Italy
bibliography, AA7, AA146, AA147, AA148, AA149
biography, AJ74, AJ75
history
bibliography, DC154, DC155, DC156
manuscripts and archives, DC156, DC157
politics and government, CJ191
Iter Italicum, Kristeller, Paul Oskar, AA37
Itineraria Norvegica, DC170
Itō, Kiyosi. *Encyclopedic dictionary of mathematics*, EF10
Iturralde, Mario P. *Dictionary and handbook of nuclear medicine and clinical imaging*, EK71
Iverson, Cheryl. *American Medical Association manual of style*, EK34
Ivory Coast, DD40
Ivory Coast, Mundt, R. J., DD5
Iwanami sūgaku jiten, EF10
Iwaschkin, Roman. *Popular music*, BH137
Izdatel'stvo "Sovetskaia éntsiklopediia". *Filosofskiĭ éntsiklopedicheskiĭ slovar'*, BA15

J-BISC, AA151
J. Paul Getty Trust. *Art & architecture thesaurus*, BE44
JANAF thermochemical tables, ED11, ED15
JNRC: Journal of the Nepal Research Centre, AA162
Jaanus, Siret D. *Ophthalmic drug facts*, EK120
Jackson, Byron M. *The public policy dictionary*, CJ25
Jackson, George D. *Dictionary of the Russian Revolution*, DC207
Jackson, Guida. *Women who ruled*, CC313
Jackson, J. R. de J. *Annals of English verse, 1770–1835*, BD243
Jackson, Julia A. *Glossary of geology*, EE8, EE9
Jackson, K. David. *Vanguardism in Latin American literature*, BD332
Jackson, Kenneth T. *Atlas of American history*, DB77
Jackson, Miles M. *Pacific Island studies*, DG6
Jackson, Paul. *British sources of information*, DC103
Jackson, Richard. *The literature of American music in books and folk music collections*, BH27
Jackson, Virginia. *Art museums of the world*, BE47
Jackson, W. T. H. *European writers*, BD54
Jackson, William A. *A short-title catalogue of books printed in England, Scotland, & Ireland and of English books printed abroad, 1475–1640*, AA127
Jacob, André. *Encyclopédie philosophique universelle*, BA14
Jacob, Kathryn Allamong. *Biographical dictionary of the American Congress, 1774–1989*, CJ104
Jacob, Udo. *The completely illustrated atlas of reptiles and amphibians for the terrarium*, EC45
Jacobean drama, Studies in, BD233
Jacobs, Arthur. *The Penguin dictionary of musical performers*, BH83

Jacobs, Francis. *Western European political parties*, CJ169
Jacobsen's . . . painting and bronze price guide, BE62
Jacobstein, J. Myron. *Fundamentals of legal research*, CK6
——— *Index to periodical articles related to law*, CK56
Jamaica, AA150
Jamaican national bibliography, AA150
James, Bill. *The Bill James historical baseball abstract*, BJ22
James, David E. *The encyclopedia of solid earth geophysics*, EE6
James, Richard S. *International music journals*, BH32
James, Simon R. *A dictionary of business quotations*, CH96
——— *A dictionary of sexist quotations*, CC295
Jan Smuts House (Johannesburg, South Africa). *Southern African update*, DD22
Janosik, Robert J. *Encyclopedia of the American judicial system*, CK59
Jans, Peggy. *The law library reference shelf*, CK9
Janson, Anthony F. *History of art*, BE72
Janson, H. W. *History of art*, BE72
——— *An iconographic index to Stanislas Lami's Dictionnaire des sculpteurs de l'Ecole française au dix-neuvième siècle*, BE165
Jao, Y. C. *Research material for Hong Kong studies*, DE55
Japan
bibliography, DE73
databases, AA151
biography, AJ76, CJ192
economic conditions, CH325
bibliography, CH37
economic relations, CH40
foreign relations, DE75, DE76
handbooks, DE79
history
bibliography, DE74, DE75, DE76, DE77, DE78
politics and government, CJ165, CJ192
Japan, Shulman, Frank Joseph, DE78
Japan and the world, 1853–1952, DE76
Japan Association of International Relations. *International studies in Japan*, DE75
Japan Foundation. *Catalogue of books in English on Japan, 1945–1981*, DE73
——— *Catalogue of books on Japan translated from the Japanese into English, 1945–1981 = Eiyaku Nihon kankei hōbun tosho mokuroku*, DE74
Japan Library Association. *J-BISC*, AA151
Japan marketing handbook, CH325
Japan reading guide, DE73
Japanese art signatures, Self, James, BE100
Japanese language, EA49
Japanese literature, BD380
Japanese local histories in the Library of Congress, Nagao, Philip M., DE77
Japanese music, Tsuge, Gen'ichi, BH24
Japonisme, Weisberg, Gabriel P., BE15
Jarboe, Betty. *Obituaries*, AJ3
Jarrell, Howard R. *Common stock newspaper abbreviations and trading symbols*, CH229
Jarzyńska, Joanna. *Polskie wydawnictwa informacyjne 1945–1981*, AA63
Jason, Philip K. *Nineteenth century American poetry*, BD178
Javornik, Marjan. *Enciklopedija Slovenije*, DC217
Jay, Frank. *IEEE standard dictionary of electrical and electronics terms*, EJ46
Jazz
bibliography, BH117, BH138
biography, BH124
dictionaries, BH124
discography, BH120, BH121, BH143
encyclopedias, BH119
indexes, BH118

Jazz, Carr, Ian, BH124
Jazz index, BH118
Jazz records, 1897–1942, Rust, Brian A. L., BH143
Jedin, Hubert. *Atlas zur Kirchengeschichte*, BB107
Jefcoate, Graham. *A catalogue of English books printed before 1801 held by the University Library at Göttingen*, AA129
Jeffery, Larry S. *Weeds of the United States and their control*, EH22
Jelks, Edward B. *Historical dictionary of North American archaeology*, DB66
Jelks, Juliet C. *Historical dictionary of North American archaeology*, DB66
Jen, Hseo-chin. *Chinese newspapers in the Library of Congress*, AF6
Jens, Walter. *Kindlers neues Literatur Lexikon*, BD29
Jensen, Larry O. *A genealogical handbook of German research*, AK24, AK25
Jensen, Richard D. *Agricultural and animal sciences journals and serials*, EH4
Jērāns, P. *Latvijas padomju enciklopēdija*, DC159
Jeremy, David J. *Dictionary of business biography*, CH144
Jerusalem, the Holy City, Purvis, James D., BB8
Jessen, Jens Christian. *Bibliographie der Autobiographien*, AJ60
Jessup, John E. *Balkan military history*, DC16
—— *A chronology of conflict and resolution, 1945–1985*, CJ39
Jesus Christ, BB74, BD1
Jeudy, Colette. *Les manuscrits classiques latins des bibliothèques publiques de France*, AA38
Jewish autobiographies and biographies, Zubatsky, David S., AJ19
Jewish-Christian dialogue, BB136
Jewish-Christian relations, Shermis, Michael, BB11
Jewish folklore, Yassif, Eli, CF35
Jewish heritage in America, Karkhanis, Sharad, BB133
Jewish law, Weisbard, Phyllis Holman, CK43
Jewish literature, BD194
Jewish music, The resource book of, BH16
Jewish newspapers and periodicals on microfilm, Hebrew Union College-Jewish Institute of Religion. American Jewish Periodical Center, AE5
Jewish-Polish coexistence, 1772–1939, Lerski, Jerzy J., DC172
Jewish press and publications, AE3
The Jewish press of the world, Fraenkel, Josef, AE3
Jewish serials of the world, Singerman, Robert, AE7
The Jewish woman, 1900–1985, Cantor, Aviva, CC254
The Jewish world in modern times, Edelheit, Abraham J., BB130, DA56
Jews
  biography, AJ19
  languages
    bibliography, BC37
Jews in Latin America, BB131, CC164
Jews in Poland, DC172
Jews in the United States, BB133, BB135, CC195
Jilek, Heinrich. *Bibliographie zur Geschichte und Landeskunde der Böhmischen Länder von den Anfängen bis 1948*, DC40
Job hunter's sourcebook, CH337
The jobs rated almanac, Krantz, Les, CH339
Jodice, David A. *Political risk assessment*, CJ8
Joffe, Judah Achilles. *Groyser verterbukh fun der Yidisher shprakh = Great dictionary of the Yiddish language*, AD174
Joginder Singh. *Indian library directory*, AB33

Johannesburg (South Africa). Public Library. *Southern African material in anthologies of English literature in the Strange Library of Africana*, BD375
Johannine bibliography 1966–1985, Belle, Gilbert van, BB41
Johannsen, Hano. *International dictionary of management*, CH157
Johansen, Elaine. *Political corruption*, CJ47
Johansson, Eve. *Official publications of Western Europe*, AG33
Johansson, Warren. *Encyclopedia of homosexuality*, CC152
John Carter Brown Library. *Columbus*, DB141
—— *European Americana*, AA78
John Gloag's dictionary of furniture, Gloag, John, BF40
Johnpoll, Bernard K. *Biographical dictionary of the American left*, CJ119
Johnsgard, Paul A. *Hawks, eagles & falcons of North America*, EC51
Johnson, Bryan R. *The Blackfeet*, CC215
Johnson, Constance A. *Chinese law*, CK37
Johnson, Curt. *Dictionary of military terms*, CJ257
Johnson, David E. *From day to day*, DA23
Johnson, Douglas W. J. *Biographical dictionary of French political leaders since 1870*, CJ171
Johnson, Elmer Hubert. *Handbook on crime and delinquency prevention*, CK103
Johnson, Gordon. *The new Cambridge history of India*, DE64
Johnson, Julia. *Film review index*, BG63
Johnson, Norman Lloyd. *Encyclopedia of statistical sciences*, EF8, EF9
Johnson, Tanya F. *Elder neglect and abuse*, CC45
Johnson, Victoria E. *Vietnam on film and television*, DE105
Johnson, Warren T. *Diseases of trees and shrubs*, EC37
Johnson, William. *Nineteenth-century photography*, BF55, BF57
Johnson, William A. *Thesaurus Linguae Graecae canon of Greek authors and works*, BD367
Johnson, Willis L. *Directory of special programs for minority group members*, CC183
Johnston, Grahame. *The Australian pocket Oxford dictionary*, AD55
Johnstone, I. J. *Zimbabwean political material published in exile, 1959–1980*, CJ207, DD60
Joint Center for Political Studies (U.S.). *Black elected officials*, CJ61
—— *The metropolitan area fact book*, CC210
Joint Committee on the Union List of Serials. *New serial titles*, AE72
Joint Steering Committee for Revision of AACR. *Anglo-American cataloguing rules*, AB79
Jones, Barri. *An atlas of Roman Britain*, DC128
Jones, Charles Edwin. *Black holiness*, BB80
Jones, Colin. *The French Revolution*, DC54
Jones, Daniel. *Everyman's English pronouncing dictionary*, AD37
Jones, David Lewis. *Debates and proceedings of the British parliaments*, AG36
Jones, George Fenwick. *German-American names*, AK49
Jones, Gerry. *State information book*, CJ127
Jones, H. G. *Second abstract of British historical statistics*, CG52, DC121
Jones, J. Knox. *Orders and families of recent mammals of the world*, EC60
Jones, Lois Swan. *Art information*, BE2
—— *Art research methods and resources*, BE2
Jones, Philip Henry. *A bibliography of the history of Wales [microform]*, DC141
Jones, Stephanie. *Business documents*, CH135
Jones, Woodrow. *Health of black Americans from post reconstruction to integration, 1871–1960*, CC202, EK126

Jonovic, Donald J. *Encyclopedia of telemarketing*, CH324
Jordan, Frank. *The English romantic poets*, BD247
Jordan, Gerald. *British military history*, DC100
Jordan, AA152
Josephson, Harold. *Biographical dictionary of modern peace leaders*, CJ316
Jost, Jean E. *Ten Middle English Arthurian romances*, BD204
Jouette, André. *Toute l'histoire par les dates et les documents*, DC77
Journal of economic literature, CH3
Journal of the Association of Official Analytical Chemists, ED20
Journalism
  bibliography, AE37, AF18
  biography, AF21, AF22, AF23, AF24, AF25, AF26
  guides, AF17
  history, AF19, AF20
Journalism, Cates, Jo A., AF17
The journalist's bookshelf, Wolseley, Roland Edgar, AF18
Journals in psychology, CD4
Journals in translation, AE13
Joyce, Donald F. *Blacks in the humanities, 1750–1984*, CC198
J.R. McKenzie Trust. *A directory of philanthropic trusts in New Zealand*, CA26
Jreisat, Jamil E. *Administration and development in the Arab world*, CJ217
Judaica Americana, Singerman, Robert, BB135
Judaism
  bibliography, BB11, BB129, BB132, BB133, BB134, DE72
  dictionaries, BB136
  history, BB137
    bibliography, BB130, DA56
    encyclopedias, BB138
Judeo-Romance linguistics, Wexler, Paul, BC37
Judicial staff directory, CK77
Judy, George. *The percussionist's dictionary*, BH151
Jugenheimer, Donald W. *Advertising media sourcebook*, CH73
Jugoslavenski bibligrafski institut. *Bibliografija Jugoslavije. Zbirke i monografske serije*, AA203
Jugoslavenski leksikografski zavod. *Bibliografija rasprava, članaka i književnih radova*, AE82
Julien, Germain. *Canadian public administration: bibliography = Administration publique canadienne: bibliographie*, CJ213
Jung, Václav. *Slovník anglicko-česky*, AD83
Jungian literary criticism, 1920–1980, Meurs, Jos van, BD6
Jurgens, Madeleine. *Documents du Minutier central des notaires de Paris. Inventaires après décès*, DC68
—— *Ronsard et ses amis*, DC68
Jussawalla, Meheroo. *Telecommunication economics and international regulatory policy*, CH194
Jussen, Virginia M. *Lexicon of new formal geologic names of the United States, 1976–1980*, EE11
Justice, Keith L. *Public office index*, CJ120
—— *Science fiction, fantasy, and horror reference*, BD118

Kabe, Jun'ichi. *Intā Puresu kagaku gijutsu 25–mango daijiten*, EA49
Kagan, Alfred. *American and Canadian doctoral dissertations and master's theses on Africa, 1886–1974*, DD1
—— *American and Canadian doctoral dissertations and master's theses on Africa, 1974–1987*, DD1
Kahan, Vilém. *Bibliography of the Communist International (1919–1979)*, CJ240

Kahler, Dorothy. *Problems in literary research*, BD149

Kahn, Ada P. *The A–Z of women's sexuality*, CC153

—— *The encyclopedia of phobias, fears, and anxieties*, CD12

Kaid, Lynda Lee. *Political campaign communication*, CJ48

Kalia, D. R. *Directory of scientific and technical libraries in India*, AB34

Kalicki, Anne C. *National continuing care directory*, CC58

Kállay, István. *Kandidátusi és doktori disszertációk*, AH12

Kalley, Jacqueline A. *South Africa under apartheid*, DD53

Kallich, Martin. *British poetry and the American Revolution*, BD244, DB25

Kallsen, Margarita. *Paraguay . . . años de bibliografía*, AA171

Kalvelage, Carl. *Bridges to knowledge in political science*, CJ2

—— *Research guide for undergraduates in political science*, CJ2

—— *Research guide in political science*, CJ2

Kandidátusi és doktori disszertációk, Kállay, István, AH12

Kandiuk, Mary. *French-Canadian authors*, BD305

Kane, Joseph Nathan. *Facts about the presidents*, CJ91

—— *Facts about the states*, CJ125

Kane, Thomas T. *The Population Reference Bureau's population handbook*, CG1

Kanellos, Nicolás. *Biographical dictionary of Hispanic literature in the United States*, BD195

Kanka, August Gerald. *Poland*, DC171

Kanner, Barbara. *Women in English social history, 1800–1914*, CC284

Kaplan, Harold I. *Comprehensive textbook of psychiatry/V*, CD33

Kaplan, Mike. *Variety's who's who in show business*, BG6

Kaplan, Wendy. *The encyclopedia of arts and crafts*, BF1

Karg-Gasterstädt, Elisabeth. *Althochdeutsches Wörterbuch*, AD103

Kargas, Nicholas A. *Accountant's desk handbook*, CH66

Karia, Bhupendra. *The Artronix index*, BF59

Karkhanis, Sharad. *Jewish heritage in America*, BB133

Karlowich, Robert A. *A guide to scholarly resources on the Russian Empire and the Soviet Union in the New York metropolitan area*, DC195

Karmī, Ḥasan Sa'īd. *al-Mughni al-akbar*, AD70

Karney, Robin. *The Holt foreign film guide*, BG67

Karno, Howard L. *A directory of vendors of Latin American library materials*, AB18

Karp, Rashelle S. *The basic business library*, CH76

Karst, Kenneth L. *Encyclopedia of the American Constitution*, CK116

Karṭa (Firm). *Atlas of the Middle East*, DE27

Kasack, Wolfgang. *Dictionary of Russian literature since 1917*, BD356

Kaske, Robert Earl. *Medieval Christian literary imagery*, BB81, BD3, DA46

Kastenbaum, Beatrice. *Encyclopedia of death*, CC100

Kastenbaum, Robert. *Encyclopedia of death*, CC100

Katalog czasopism polskich Biblioteki Jagiellońskiej, Biblioteka Jagiellońska, AE61

Katalog der Musikdrucke, Bayerische Staatsbibliothek, BH34

Katalog der Musikzeitschriften, Bayerische Staatsbibliothek, BH30

Katalog majalah terbitan Indonesia, Perpustakaan Nasional (Indonesia), AA140, AE51

Katalog surat kabar, Perpustakaan Nasional (Indonesia), AF11

Katalog terbitan Indonesia selama pendudukan Jepang, 1942–1945 = Catalogue of Indonesian publications during Japanese occupation, 1942–1945, Perpustakaan Nasional (Indonesia), AA141

Kataloge der Bibliotheca Hertziana in Rom (Max-Planck-Institut), Bibliotheca Hertziana, Max-Planck-Institut, BE24

Katlan, Alexander W. *American artists' materials suppliers directory*, BE55

Katz, Bernard. *The travellers, Canada to 1900*, DB84

Katz, Bernard S. *Biographical directory of the Council of Economic Advisers*, CH22

—— *Nobel laureates in economic sciences*, CH23

Katz, Ellen L. *Socrates*, BA29

Katz, Linda Sternberg. *Magazines for libraries*, AA69

Katz, William A. *The how-to-do-it manual for small libraries*, AB70

—— *Introduction to reference work*, AB107

—— *Magazines for libraries*, AA69

—— *Reference and information services*, AB107

Katzinger, Willibald. *Bibliographie zur Geschichte der Städte Österreichs*, DC26

Katzman, Carol. *Role portrayal and stereotyping on television*, CH201

Kaufman, John E. *IES lighting handbook*, EJ49

Kaufman, Martin. *Dictionary of American nursing biography*, EK95

Kaufmann, Thomas DaCosta. *Art and architecture in Central Europe, 1550–1620*, BE8

Kaufmann, Walter. *Selected musical terms of non-Western cultures*, BH130

Kavass, Igor I. *Soviet law in English*, CK51

Kavenik, Frances M. *Handbook of American women's history*, CC292, DB65

Kay, Richard S. *A reference guide to the United States Supreme Court*, CK90

Kaye, G. W. C. *Tables of physical and chemical constants and some mathematical functions*, ED16, EG12

Kazhdan, A. P. *The Oxford dictionary of Byzantium*, DA53

Keane, Claire Brackman. *Encyclopedia and dictionary of medicine, nursing, and allied health*, EK90

Kearley, Timothy. *Charles Szladits' guide to foreign legal materials*, CK39

Keckeissen, Rita G. *Bibliography of American folk art for the year [. . .]*, BF8

Keeble, N. H. *Handbook of English and Celtic studies in the United Kingdom and Republic of Ireland*, BC28

Keegan, John. *The Times atlas of the Second World War*, DA79

Keene, James A. *Planning, equipping, and staffing a document reprographic service*, AB109

Keesing's UK record, DC123

Keeves, John P. *Educational research, methodology, and measurement : an international handbook*, CB63

Keith-Spiegel, Patricia. *The complete guide to graduate school admission*, CD31

Keller, Dean H. *Index to plays in periodicals, 1977–1987*, BD85

Keller, Michael A. *Music reference and research materials*, BH11

Kellman, Herbert. *Census-catalogue of manuscript sources of polyphonic music, 1400–1550*, BH35

Kellner, Irwin. *Dictionary of banking terms*, CH228

Kelly, D. F. *Concise veterinary dictionary*, EH27

Kelly, David H. *Women's education in the Third World*, CB32, CC285

Kelly, Gail Paradise. *International handbook of women's education*, CB132, CC310

—— *Women's education in the Third World*, CB32, CC285

Kelly, J. N. D. *The Oxford dictionary of Popes*, BB121

Kelly, James R. *Encyclopedia of public affairs information sources*, CA5

Kelly, Leo J. *Dictionary of special education and rehabilitation*, CB74

Kelly, Matthew A. *Labor and industrial relations*, CH286

Kemmer, Elizabeth Jane. *Violence in the family*, CC130

Kemp, Louis Ward. *The museum*, BE10

Kemp, Thomas Jay. *International vital records handbook*, AK1

Kemps international film and television yearbook, BG98

Kendadamath, G. C. *Indian reference sources*, AA65

Kendall, Katherine A. *World guide to social work education*, CC32

Kennan Institute for Advanced Russian Studies. *A handbook for archival research in the USSR*, AB10, DC201

Kennedy, A. G. *Bibliography of writings on the English language*, BC25

Kennedy, DayAnn M. *Science & technology in fact and fiction*, EA11, EA12

Kennedy, James R. *Library research guide to religion and theology*, BB1

Kennedy, William H. *Diffusion of innovations*, CA6

Kennon, Donald R. *The speakers of the U.S. House of Representatives*, CJ94

Kent, Allen. *Encyclopedia of computer science and technology*, EJ59

—— *Encyclopedia of library and information science*, AB12

—— *Encyclopedia of microcomputers*, EJ60

Kent, Rosalind. *Encyclopedia of microcomputers*, EJ60

Kenworthy, James L. *A guide to the laws, regulations, and policies of the People's Republic of China on foreign trade and investment*, CK38

Kenya, AG44

Kenya National Archives. *A guide to government monographs, reports, and research works*, AG44

—— *Guide to the contents of the Kenya National Archives*, AG44

Kenyan periodicals directory, AE56

Kermode, Frank. *The literary guide to the Bible*, BB56

Kern, Robert W. *Historical dictionary of modern Spain, 1700–1988*, DC188

Kernchen, Dagmar. *Handbuch der bibliographischen Nachschlagewerke*, AA2

Kernchen, Hans-Jürgen. *Handbuch der bibliographischen Nachschlagewerke*, AA2

Kernfeld, Barry Dean. *The new Grove dictionary of jazz*, BH119

Kersey, Ethel M. *Women philosophers*, BA24

Kersey, Harry A. *The Seminole and Miccosukee tribes*, CC216

Kershaw, Stephen. *A concise dictionary of classical mythology*, CF11

Kerst, Catherine Hiebert. *Ethnic folklife dissertations from the United States and Canada, 1960–1980*, CF25

Kessler, Eckhard. *The Cambridge history of Renaissance philosophy*, BA19

Kessler, Peter. *Beacham's guide to key lobbyists*, CJ60

Key, Jack D. *Medicine, literature & eponyms*, EK43

Key facts in Soviet history, De Mowbray, Stephen, DC206

Key resources on institutional advancement, Rowland, A. Westley, CB10

Keyguide to information sources in agricultural engineering, Morgan, Bryan, EH2

Keyguide to information sources in animal rights, Magel, Charles R., EC2

Keyguide to information sources in archaeology, Woodhead, Peter, DA31

Keyguide to information sources in dentistry, Clennett, Margaret A., EK82

Keyguide to information sources in food science and technology, Green, Syd, EH34

Keyguide to information sources in museum studies, Woodhead, Peter, BE3

Keyguide to information sources in veterinary medicine, Gibb, Mike, EH26

Keyser, Daniel J. *Tests,* CD47

Keywords and concepts, Hindustani classical music, Ranade, Ashok D., BH60

Kharlakova, Ivanka. *Angliĭsko-bŭlgarski rechnik,* AD79

Khayat, Robert C. *A reference guide to the United States Supreme Court,* CK90

Khoury, Fawzi. *National union catalog of Middle Eastern microforms,* DE11

Kidd, John. *Jungian literary criticism, 1920–1980,* BD6

Kidron, Michael. *The new state of the world atlas,* CL52

Kiell, Norman. *Psychoanalysis, psychology, and literature, a bibliography,* BD4

Kies, Cosette N. *The occult in the western world,* CD52

Kiffer, Mary E. *Current biography. Cumulated index, 1940–1985,* AJ16

Kiger, Joseph Charles. *International encyclopedia of foundations,* CA28

Kilgour, Heather. *Bibliography of the Summer Institute of Linguistics, Philippines, 1953–1984,* BC61

Kilian, Jansie. *South African theological bibliography = Suid-Afrikaanse teologiese bibliografie,* BB18

Killingray, David. *African political facts since 1945,* CJ149

Kim, C. I. Eugene. *The Asian political dictionary,* CJ154

Kim, David U. *Policies of publishers,* AB66

Kim, Hyung-chan. *Asian American studies,* CC214

—— *Dictionary of Asian American history,* CC212

Kincade, William H. *The ACCESS resource guide,* CJ308

Kind words, Neaman, Judith S., AD47

Kindergarten programs and practices in public schools, CB150

Kindlers neues Literatur Lexikon, BD29

King, Clive John. *100 families of flowering plants,* EC33

King, H. G. R. *The Arctic,* DH1

—— *Atlantic Ocean,* DA4

King, Kamla J. *BNA's directory of state courts, judges, and clerks,* CK78

King, Peter. *The Netherlands,* DC165

King, Robert C. *A dictionary of genetics,* EC65, EC66

King, Warren B. *Aves,* EC54

Kingdoms of Asia, the Middle East, and Africa, Gurney, Gene, DA20

Kings and rulers *see* **Heads of state**

Kingsmill, Allison. *Old English word studies,* BC18

Kinloch, Graham Charles. *Social stratification,* CC9

Kinnell, Susan K. *Communism in the world since 1945,* CJ238

—— *Military history of the United States,* CJ270

—— *Searching America: history and life,* DB17

—— *Searching America: history and life (AHL) and Historical abstracts (HA) on DIALOG,* DA6

Kinsella, Kevin G. *Detailed statistics on the urban and rural population of the Philippines, 1950 to 2010,* CG68

Kinsmen through time, Edmunds, R. David, CC218

Kinton, Jack F. *American ethnic groups and the revival of cultural pluralism,* CC161

—— *American ethnic revival,* CC161

Kirchherr, Eugene C. *Abyssinia to Zimbabwe,* CL32

—— *Place names of Africa, 1935–1986,* CL32

Kirchner, Joachim. *Bibliographie der Zeitschriften des deutschen Sprachgebietes bis 1900,* AE38

Kirkeby, Willy. *English-Norwegian dictionary = Engelsk-norsk ordbok,* AD143

Kirkpatrick, D. L. *Contemporary dramatists,* BD88

—— *Contemporary novelists,* BD93

—— *Reference guide to American literature,* BD169

—— *Twentieth-century children's writers,* BD82

—— *Twentieth-century romance and historical writers,* BD121

Kirkpatrick, Diane. *Gardner's art through the ages,* BE71

Kirpalani, V. H. *International business handbook,* CH185

Kirschstein, Bettina. *Wörterbuch der mittelhochdeutschen Urkundensprache,* AD108

Kissinger, Warren S. *Lives of Jesus,* BB74, BD1

Kister, Kenneth F. *Best encyclopedias,* AC7

—— *Kister's concise guide to best encyclopedias,* AC7

Kister's concise guide to best encyclopedias, Kister, Kenneth F., AC7

Kitching, Christopher. *Surveys of historical manuscripts in the United Kingdom,* DC111

Kittel, Gerhard. *Theological dictionary of the New Testament,* BB58

Kitzinger, Rachel. *Civilization of the ancient Mediterranean,* DA41

Kjellberg, Pierre. *Les bronzes du XIXe siècle,* BE166

Klauser, Theodor. *Reallexikon für Antike und Christentum,* BB94, BB95

Klehr, Harvey. *Biographical dictionary of the American left,* CJ119

Klein, Barry T. *Guide to American directories,* CH101

—— *Reference encyclopedia of the American Indian,* CC226

Klein, Bernard. *Guide to American directories,* CH101

Klein, Ernest David. *A comprehensive etymological dictionary of the Hebrew language for readers of English,* AD118

Klein, Leonard S. *Encyclopedia of world literature in the 20th century,* BD26

Kleindel, Walter. *Die Chronik Österreichs,* DC30

—— *Das grosse Buch der Österreicher,* AJ35

Kleines politisches Wörterbuch, CJ24

Klemanski, John S. *The urban politics dictionary,* CJ22

Klemp, P. J. *The essential Milton,* BD258

Klenicki, Leon. *A dictionary of the Jewish-Christian dialogue,* BB136

Klever, W. N. A. *Repertorium der Nederlandse wijsbegeerte,* BA10

Kline, Jacob. *Handbook of biomedical engineering,* EK70

Kline, Mary-Jo. *A guide to documentary editing,* AA54, BD13

Klingebiel, Kathryn. *Bibliographie linguistique de l'ancien occitan (1960–1982),* BC35, BD309

Klinman, Debra G. *Fatherhood U.S.A,* CC142

Kloesel, Christian J. W. *English novel explication. Supplement,* BD241

Klos, Sheila M. *Historical bibliography of art museum serials from the United States and Canada,* BE30

Kloth, Karen. *A catalogue of English books printed before 1801 held by the University Library at Göttingen,* AA129

Kludas, Arnold. *Die Geschichte der deutschen Passagierschiffahrt,* AK26, CH191

Kluge, Friedrich. *Etymologisches Wörterbuch der deutschen Sprache,* AD112

Knapton, Robyn. *The complete dictionary of television and film,* BG89

[Knight, Russell W.]. *Australian Antarctic bibliography,* DH2

Knights and knighthood, DA48

Knihopis českých a slovenských tisku od doby nejstarsí až do konce XVIII stoleí, AA98

Kniker, Charles R. *Religious schools in America,* CB30

Književna zajednica Novog Sada. *Adresar pisaca Jugoslavije,* BD360

Knowledge Industry Publications, Inc. *Database directory,* AB93

Knox, Bernard MacGregor Walker. *Greek literature,* BD370

Knox, Helen. *Harrap's concise French-English dictionary = dictionnaire anglais-français,* AD94

Knox, Kathleen. *The feminization of poverty in the United States,* CC144

Kobbé, Gustav. *Kobbé's complete opera book,* BH97

Kobbé's complete opera book, BH106

—— Kobbé, Gustav, BH97

Koch, Hans-Albrecht. *Deutscher biographischer Index,* AJ56

Koch, Uta. *Deutscher biographischer Index,* AJ56

Kocher, Eric. *International jobs,* CH338

Kochukoshy, K. K. *A bibliography of Indian bibliographies, 1961–1980,* AA5

Koehl, Stuart L. *The dictionary of modern war,* CJ260

Koehler, Barbara. *Encyclopedia of senior citizens information sources,* CC63

Kömives, Wilma. *Bestandskatalog der Bibliothek des Südost-Instituts München,* DC18

Koeppe, Richard P. *The Facts on File dictionary of education,* CB76

Kössler, Franz. *Verzeichnis von Programm-Abhandlungen deutscher, österreichischer und schweizerischer Schulen der Jahre 1825–1918,* AH9

Kohl, Benjamin G. *Renaissance humanism, 1300–1550,* BD5

Kohl, Rhiana. *Fatherhood U.S.A,* CC142

Kohlenberger, John R. *The NIV exhaustive concordance,* BB59

Kohlschmidt, Werner. *Reallexikon der deutschen Literaturgeschichte,* BD292

Kohn, George C. *Dictionary of wars,* CJ253, DA21

Kohut, David R. *Women authors of modern Hispanic South America,* BD331

Kokuritsu Kokkai Toshokan (Japan). *Directory of Japanese scientific periodicals, 1988,* EA21

Kokusai Kōryū Kikin. *Catalogue of books on Japan translated from the Japanese into English, 1945–1981 = Eiyaku Nihon kankei hōbun tosho mokuroku,* DE74

Kolin, Philip C. *American playwrights since 1945,* BD172

Koller, Angelika. *Deutscher biographischer Index,* AJ56

Kolov, S. P. *Pisateli Moskvy,* BD358

Kolumbić, Nikica. *Hrvatski biografski leksikon,* AJ102

Komjáthy, Miklósné. *Magyar könyvészet, 1921–1944,* AA139

Komonchak, Joseph A. *The new dictionary of theology*, BB118

Konigsberg, Ira. *The complete film dictionary*, BG96

Konkordanz zum Novum Testamentum Graece von Nestle-Aland, BB60

Kopanev, A. I. *Svodnyĭ katalog knig na inostrannykh ĭazykakh, izdannykh v Rossii v XVIII veke, 1701–1800*, AA180

Koran, BB71

Korea, AA153

Korean national bibliography, AA153

Korean War, DE80, DE81

Korean War almanac, Summers, Harry G., DE81

The Korean War, an annotated bibliography, McFarland, Keith D., DE80

Korkmaz, Alâaddin. *Yeni Türk ansiklopedisi*, AC19

Korndorf, I. I. *Novaĭa istoriĭa*, DA58

Kornick, Rebecca Hodell. *Recent American opera*, BH98

Korsch, Boris. *Soviet publications on Judaism, Zionism, and the State of Israel, 1984–1988*, BB134, DE72

Kosch, Wilhelm. *Deutsches Literatur-Lexikon*, BD291

—— *Deutsches Theater-Lexikon*, BG37

Koschnick, Wolfgang J. *Standard dictionary of the social sciences = Standardwörterbuch für die Sozialwissenschaften*, CA16

KOTI, AA110

Kotliākov, Vladimir Mikhaĭlovich. *Elsevier's dictionary of glaciology in four languages*, EE23

Kotz, Samuel. *Encyclopedia of statistical sciences*, EF8, EF9

Kouri, Mary K. *Volunteerism and older adults*, CC65

Kovel, Ralph M. *Directory of American silver, pewter, and silver plate*, BF47

—— *Kovels' American silver marks*, BF47

Kovel, Terry H. *Kovels' American silver marks*, BF47

Kovels' American silver marks, Kovel, Ralph M., BF47

Kovtun, George J. *Czech and Slovak literature in English*, BD353

Kowalik, Jan. *Bibliografia czasopism polskich wydanych poza granicami Kraju od września 1939 roku = World index of Polish periodicals published outside of Poland since September 1939*, AE62

Kowitz, Aletha. *Basic dental reference works*, EK83

—— *Dentistry journals and serials*, EK84

Kramarae, Cheris. *A feminist dictionary*, CC297

Kramer, Jonathan D. *Listen to the music*, BH148

Krantz, Les. *American architects*, BE136

—— *The jobs rated almanac*, CH339

Krasilovsky, M. William. *This business of music*, BH71

Krathwohl, David R. *How to prepare a research proposal*, CA24

Krause, Gerhard. *Theologische Realenzyklopädie*, BB91

Krauss, Harriet P. *Old master print references*, BE155

Krautz, Alfred. *International directory of cinematographers, set- and costume designers in film*, BG100

Krawc, Alfred. *International directory of cinematographers, set- and costume designers in film*, BG100

Krewson, Margrit B. *Contemporary authors of the German-speaking countries of Europe*, BD287

—— *The economies of the German-speaking countries of Europe : a selective bibliography*, DC4

—— *The German-speaking countries of Europe*, DC4

—— *The Netherlands, a selective bibliography of reference works*, DC166

—— *The Netherlands and Northern Belgium, a selective bibliography of reference works*, DC166

Krieg, Noel R. *Bergey's manual of systematic bacteriology*, EC61

Krieger, Georges. *Bibliographie juridique luxembourgeoise*, CK45

Krismann, Carol. *Quality control*, CH290

Kristeller, Paul Oskar. *Iter Italicum*, AA37

Kritzinger, Matthys Stefanus Benjamin. *Groot woordeboek*, AD68

Krivatsky, Peter. *A catalogue of incunabula and sixteenth century books in the National Library of Medicine*, EK13

—— *A catalogue of seventeenth century printed books in the National Library of Medicine*, EK13

Kronk, Gary W. *Comets*, EB11

Kroschwitz, Jacqueline I. *Encyclopedia of polymer science and engineering*, EJ20

Krüger-Wust, Wilhelm J. *Arabische Musik in europäischen Sprachen*, BH17

Krug, Samuel E. *Psychware*, CD32

Krummel, Donald William. *Bibliographical handbook of American music*, BH18

—— *Music printing and publishing*, BH53

Kruschke, Earl R. *The public policy dictionary*, CJ25

Kruzas, Anthony Thomas. *Encyclopedia of medical organizations and agencies*, EK64

Krzyzanowska, Jadwiga. *Członkowie Polskiej Akademii Nauk*, AJ86

Kto jest kim w Polsce, AJ87

The Ku Klux Klan, Newton, Michael, CC204

Kubiĭovych, Volodymyr. *Encyclopedia of Ukraine*, DC211

Kuehl, Warren F. *Biographical dictionary of internationalists*, CJ316

—— *Dissertations in history, 1970–June 1980*, DA8

Künstler der jungen Generation, Hesse, Gritta, BE80

Küpper, Heinz. *Pons Wörterbuch der deutschen Umgangssprache*, AD113

Kuhn, Sherman M. *Middle English dictionary*, AD64

Kuhn-Schnyder, Emil. *Handbook of paleozoology*, EE42

Kulikowski, Mark. *A bibliography of Slavic mythology*, CF17

Kullman, Colby H. *Theatre companies of the world*, BG34

Kuløy, Hallvard Kåre. *Bibliography of Tibetan studies*, DE98

Kumar, P. S. G. *Directory of library and information science schools in India*, AB31

Kumar, Surender. *Directory of scientific and technical libraries in India*, AB34

Kungnip chungang Tosŏgwan (Seoul, Korea). *Taehan Min'guk ch'ulp'anmul ch'ongmongnok*, AA153

Kunitz, Joseph M. *Poetry explication*, BD182

Kunstgeschichte in Festschriften, Rave, Paul, BE9

Die Kunstliteratur, Schlosser, Julius, Ritter von, BE14

Kunz, Christina L. *The process of legal research*, CK11

Kunz, Jeffrey R. M. *The American Medical Association family medical guide*, EK67

Kuo li chung yang t'u shu kuan (China). *Chung-hua min kuo ch'u pan t'u shu mu lu*, AA194

Kuper, Adam. *The social science encyclopedia*, CA15

Kuper, Jessica. *A lexicon of economics*, CH10

—— *The social science encyclopedia*, CA15

Kupferberg, Herbert. *The book of classical music lists*, BH59

Kurath, Hans. *Middle English dictionary*, AD64

Kurian, George Thomas. *The encyclopedia of the Third World*, CJ19

—— *The new book of world rankings*, CG19

—— *Sourcebook of global statistics*, CG6

—— *World education encyclopedia*, CB140

—— *World encyclopedia of police forces and penal systems*, CK104

Kurikka, Jussi. *Suomen aikakauslehdistön bibliografia 1782–1955 = Bibliografi över Finlands tidskriftslitteratur 1782–1955 = Bibliography of Finnish periodicals, 1782–1955*, AE31

Kurzgefasstes etymologisches Wörterbuch des Altindischen, Mayrhofer, Manfred, AD157

Kutinova, Blanka. *Anglicko-český technický slovník*, EA46

—— *Česko-anglický technický slovník*, EA47

Kutsch, K. J. *Grosses Sängerlexikon*, BH84

Kutsche, Paul. *A guide to Cherokee documents in the northeastern United States*, CC218

al-Kutub al-'Arabīyah allaī nushirat fī miṣrbayna amay 1926–1940, Nuṣayr, 'Āydah Ibrāhīm, AA105

al-Kutub al-'Arabīyah allatī nushirat fī Miṣr fī al-qarn al-tāsi' 'ashar, Nuṣayr, 'Āydah Ibrāhīm, AA105

al-Kutub al-'Arabīyah allatī nushirat fī miṣrbayna 1900–1925, Nuṣayr, 'Āydah Ibrāhīm, AA105

Kutz, Myer. *Mechanical engineers' handbook*, EJ80

Kuznetsova, T. R. *Gosudarstvennye (natsional'nye) bibliograficheskie ukazateli sotsialisticheskikh stran*, AA77

Kvasil, Bohumil. *Malá československá encyklopedie*, AC9

Kvavik, Robert B. *Directory of Scandinavian studies in North America*, DC180

Kypriakē vivliographia, AA96

Kyvig, David E. *New day/New Deal*, DB39

The LIRT library instruction handbook, AB101

La Cour, Donna Ward. *Artists in quotation*, BE46

La Moureyre-Gavoty, Françoise de. *French sculptors of the 17th and 18th centuries*, BE163

La Point, Velma. *Black children and American institutions*, CC78

L'Abate, Luciano. *Family therapy*, CC137

LaBeau, Dennis. *Theatre, film and television biographies master index*, BG44

Labor and industrial relations
   bibliography, CH268, CH269, CH270, CH272, CH274, CH275
   by country or region
      Gt. Brit., CH270, CH283, CH287
      Latin America, CH282
   dictionaries, CH279
   directories, CH280
   encyclopedias, CH278
   guides, CH275
   handbooks, CH285, CH286
   history, CH287
   periodicals, CH276, CH277
   statistics, CH288

Labor and industrial relations, Kelly, Matthew A., CH286

Labor and industrial relations journals and serials, Vocino, Michael C., CH277

Labor and the environment, Buttel, Frederick H., CH271

Labor conflict in the United States, CH278

Labor in America, DA55, CH274

Laboratories
   directories, EA62, EA63, EA64
   handbooks, ED13

Laboratory animals, EC58, EH29

Labour information, CH275

Laby, T. H. *Tables of physical and chemical constants and some mathematical functions*, ED16, EG12

Labys, Walter C. *Primary commodity markets and models*, CH174

Lacey, A. R. *A dictionary of philosophy*, BA16

Lackie, J. M. *The dictionary of cell biology*, EC14, EC66

Lacy, Norris J. *The Arthurian encyclopedia*, BD138

——— *The Arthurian handbook*, BD139

Ładogórski, Tadeusz. *The historical atlas of Poland*, DC174

Laffin, John. *Brassey's battles*, DA22

Lafont, Pierre-Bernard. *Bibliographie du Laos*, DE82

Lafrance, Yvon. *Les présocratiques*, BA6

Laing, Dave. *Encyclopedia of rock*, BH126

Laing, Ellen Johnston. *Chinese paintings in Chinese publications, 1956–1968*, BE150

——— *An index to reproductions of paintings by twentieth century Chinese artists*, BE150

Laird, Betty A. *A Soviet lexicon*, CJ205

Laird, Roy D. *A Soviet lexicon*, CJ205

Lake, Celinda C. *Public opinion polling*, CJ233

Laloum, David. *Guide du cinéma européen*, BG99

Lamarche, Rolande. *La francité canadienne*, BC40

Lamb, Andrew. *Gänzl's book of the musical theatre*, BH106

Lamb, Connie. *Agricultural and animal sciences journals and serials*, EH4

Lamb, Roger. *The encyclopedic dictionary of psychology*, CD13

Lambert, Sheila. *Printing for Parliament, 1641–1700*, AG38

Lame, Danielle de. *Société, culture et histoire du Rwanda*, DD50

Lami, Stanislas. *Dictionnaire des sculpteurs de l'Ecole française au dix-neuvième siècle*, BE165

Lamothe, Ruth. *Guide to programs in nursing in four-year colleges and universities*, EK93

Lampe, David. *Cities of opportunity*, CA22

Lancaster, Michael. *The Oxford companion to gardens*, BE143, EH9

Lancour, Harold. *American art auctions, 1785–1942*, BE67

——— *Encyclopedia of library and information science*, AB12

Landau, Sidney I. *International dictionary of medicine and biology*, EC17, EK48

Landeskunde DDR, Sperling, Walter, DC88

Landis, Dennis Channing. *European Americana*, AA78

Landmark yellow pages, BE127

Landscape architecture, BE142
  biography, BE145
  encyclopedias, BE143, BE144, EH9

Lane, Dermot A. *The new dictionary of theology*, BB118

Lane, Nancy D. *A guide to commonwealth government information sources*, AG30

Lang, Carl Ludwig. *Deutsches Literatur-Lexikon*, BD291

Lang, Jovian. *Dictionary of the liturgy*, BB120

Langdon, Robert. *Thar she went*, DG8

——— *Where the whalers went*, DG8

Langhans, Edward A. *A biographical dictionary of actors, actresses, musicians, dancers, managers & other stage personnel in London, 1660–1800*, BG36

——— *Eighteenth century British and Irish promptbooks*, BG13

——— *An international dictionary of theatre language*, BG24

Langlois, Claude. *Atlas de la Révolution française*, DC58

Langman, Larry. *Encyclopedia of American film comedy*, BG93

——— *Writers on the American screen*, BG61

Langosch, Karl. *Die deutsche Literatur des Mittelalters*, BD289

Langton, John. *Atlas of industrializing Britain 1780–1914*, DC126

Language map of Africa and the adjacent islands, Dalby, David, BC58

The language of biotechnology, Walker, John M., EJ19

The language of real estate, Reilly, John W., CH348

Language teaching
  bibliography, CB39
  directories, BD42, CB96

Languages, modern, BD9

Languages of the aboriginal southeast, Booker, Karen M., CC218

Lantz, Judith C. *Cumulative index of sociology journals, 1971–1985*, CC13

Laos, DE82

Laos, Sage, William W., DE82

Lapointe, Claire. *Claude Levi-Strauss and his critics*, CE6

Lapointe, Francois. *Claude Levi-Strauss and his critics*, CE6

Larkin, Gregory V. *American and Canadian doctoral dissertations and master's theses on Africa, 1974–1987*, DD1

Larousse, Pierre. *Petit Larousse illustré, 1990*, AD92

Larousse (Firm). *La grande encyclopédie*, AC11

Larsen, John C. *Researcher's guide to archives and regional history sources*, DB20

Larsgaard, Mary Lynette. *Map librarianship*, AB57, CL48

Larson, Jeanne. *Seeds of peace*, CJ307

LaRue, Jan. *Catalogue of 18th-century symphonies*, BH149

LaRue, Rodrigue. *Clavis scriptorum Graecorum at Latinorum*, BC45

The laser video disc companion, Pratt, Douglas, BG112

Lasers, EG7, EG8

Lasers, EG8

Laska, Vera. *Nazism, resistance & Holocaust in World War II*, DA87

Laskin, Allen I. *CRC handbook of microbiology*, EC21

Lass, Abraham Harold. *The Facts on File dictionary of twentieth-century allusions*, BD35

Last, John M. *A dictionary of epidemiology*, EK124

Laszlo, Ervin. *World encyclopedia of peace*, CJ306

The late 19th century U.S. Army, 1865–1898, Dawson, Joseph G., CJ271

Late reviews AEB 1947–1984, DD30

Latham, Alison. *The Norton/Grove concise encyclopedia of music*, BH57

Latham, R. E. *Dictionary of medieval Latin from British sources*, AD139

Latin America
  bibliography, AA8, DB90
    current, AA154
  biography and indexes, AJ77, AJ78, AJ93, CJ193
  directories, DB101, DB102, DB103, DB104, DB106, DB107
  economic conditions, CH47
    bibliography, DB91
  encyclopedias, DB99, DB100
  foreign relations, DB105
  handbooks, DB101
  history
    bibliography, DB94, DB97
    histories and sourcebooks, DB108
    manuscripts and archives, DB98
  periodicals, AE69
  politics and government, AJ77, CJ193, CJ194, CJ195, CJ196, CJ197, CJ198
    bibliography, DB91
  statistics, CG59, CG60, CG61

Latin America, 1983–1987, Delorme, Robert, DB91

Latin America and Caribbean, Fenton, Thomas P., DB104

Latin America : economy and society 1870–1930, DB108

Latin American Bibliographic Foundation (Redlands, Calif.). *Nicaraguan national bibliography, 1800–1978 = Bibliografia nacional nicaragüense, 1800–1978*, AA165

Latin American bibliography, Garlant, Julia, DB94

Latin American historical dictionaries, DB100

Latin American Jewish studies, Elkin, Judith Laikin, BB131, CC164

Latin American labor organizations, CH282

Latin American legal abbreviations, Torres, Arturo L., CK69

Latin American library materials, AB18

Latin American literary authors, Zubatsky, David S., BD333

Latin American literature
  biography, BD334
  guides, BD321, BD329

Latin American political dictionary, Plano, Jack C., CJ194

——— Rossi, Ernest E., CJ194

Latin American political movements, Ó Maoláin, Ciarán, CJ196

Latin American politics, DA55

Latin American revolutionaries, Radu, Michael, CJ197

Latin American studies, DB94

Latin American writers, BD334

Latin and Greek elements in English words, AD13

Latin language
  bibliography, BC43, BC45
  dictionaries, AD134, AD135, AD136, AD137
    etymology, BC42
    medieval, AD138, AD139, AD140, AD141, AD142
    pronunciation, BC44

Latin literature, BD371

Latinas of the Americas, Stoner, K. Lynn, CC288

Latinitatis Italicae Medii Aevi inde ab a. CDLXXVI usque ad a. MXXII Lexicon imperfectum cura et studio . . . Addenda, fasc. 6 (In Bulletin Du Cange, v. 44/45; 1985), Arnaldi, Francesco, AD138

Latinos in the United States, DA55, CC237

Latourette, Kenneth Scott. *Atlas zur Kirchengeschichte*, BB107

Latvia, DC159

Latviešu periodika, AE57

Latvijas padomju enciklopēdija, DC159

Lauer, Joseph J. *American and Canadian doctoral dissertations and master's theses on Africa, 1974–1987*, DD1

Lauffer, Siegfried. *Daten der griechischen und römischen Geschichte*, DA44

Laurenti, Joseph L. *Hispanic rare books of the Golden Age (1470–1699) in the Newberry Library of Chicago and in selected North American libraries*, AA189

Lavagna, Paul. *Bibliographie nationale de la principauté de Monaco, 1761–1986*, AA160

Lavin, Michael R. *Business information*, CH80, CH83

Law, Derek G. *The Royal Navy in World War Two*, DA67

Law; *see also* International law; Medical jurisprudence; School law
  abbreviations, CK62
  bibliography, CK14, CK15, CK17, CK19, CK20, CK21, CK28
    Canada, CK36
    China, CK37
    current, CK24, CK27
    Germany, CK39
    Gt. Brit., CK40, CK41, DC102
    Jewish, CK42, CK43

Korea, North, CK44
Luxembourg, CK45
Nepal, CK46
Papua New Guinea, CK48
United States
   individual states, CK30, CK31
U.S.S.R., CK49, CK51, CK52
bibliography of bibliography, CK23
biography, CK92
citation form, CK89
databases, CK18, CK22, CK55, CK58, CK79, CK122
dictionaries, CK63, CK64, CK66
  foreign terms
    Dutch, CK67
    polyglot, CK68
    Portuguese, CK69
    Spanish, CK69
directories, CK16, CK34, CK73, CK75, CK76, CK77, CK78, CK79, CK80, CK81, CK82, CK87, CK92
encyclopedias
  United States, CK59, CK60
guides, CK1, CK2, CK3, CK4, CK5, CK6, CK7, CK9, CK10, CK11, CK12, CK13, CK32, CK35
guides for authors, CK33
handbooks, CK91
indexes, CK53, CK54, CK56, CK57, CK94
periodicals, CK26
quotations, CK70, CK71, CK72
Law and fine arts, BE108, BE109, CK86, CK88
Law and legal literature of North Korea, Cho, Sung Yoon, CK44
Law bibliography, Shiwakoti, Shesh Raj, CK46
Law, ethics, and the visual arts, Elsen, Albert E., BE109, CK88
—— Merryman, John H., BE109, CK88
Law libraries
  directories, CK74
  handbooks, AB58, CK8
The law library reference shelf, Matthews, Elizabeth W., CK9
Lawless, Richard I. *Libya,* DD41
Lawless, Robert. *Bibliography on Haiti,* DB151
—— *Haiti,* DB151
Lawrence, Eleanor. *Henderson's dictionary of biological terms,* EC18
Lawrence, Robert M. *Strategic Defense Initiative,* CJ269
Laws, Edward R. *Handbook of pesticide toxicology,* EH20
Lawson, Edward. *Encyclopedia of human rights,* CK110
Lawton, Denis. *A guide to English educational terms,* CB73
Lawton, Henry. *The psychohistorian's handbook,* DA15
Lawyer's monthly catalog, CK19, CK27
Lax, Roger. *The great song thesaurus,* BH115
Lazarus, John. *The opera handbook,* BH94
Lazić, Branko M. *Biographical dictionary of the Comintern,* CJ248
Le Maitre, R. W. *A classification of igneous rocks and glossary of terms,* EE44
Leabhair Gaeilge i gCló, AA144
Leadenham, Carol A. *Guide to the collections in the Hoover Institution archives relating to Imperial Russia, the Russian revolutions and civil war, and the first emigration,* DC203
Learning AIDS, EK12
Learning disabled, CB115
Learning to read and write, Brooks, Ellen J., CB20
The learning traveler, CB80
Leavitt, Judith A. *American women managers and administrators,* CH147
Lechevalier, Hubert A. *CRC handbook of microbiology,* EC21
Lecker, Robert. *The annotated bibliography of Canada's major authors,* BD277
Leclère, Christian. *Dictionnaire de l'argot,* AD98

Lectionary of music, Slonimsky, Nicolas, BH61
Lederer, Charles Michael. *Table of isotopes,* EG11
Lederman, Ellen. *College majors,* CB101
Lee, David R. *Women and geography,* CL4
Lee, R. Alton. *Encyclopedia USA,* DB63
Lee, Susan. *Susan Lee's ABZs of economics,* CH9
Lee, Tanya H. *-ologies & -isms,* AD35
Lee, Wei-chin. *Taiwan,* DE96
Leeuwen, Jan van. *Handbook of theoretical computer science,* EJ68
Lefèvre, M. J. *First aid manual for chemical accidents,* ED17
Lefferts, Robert. *Getting a grant in the 1990s,* CA45
Left-radical movements in South Africa and Namibia 1900–1981, Böhmer, Elizabeth W., DD21
Legal bibliography index, CK23
A legal guide for lesbian and gay couples, Curry, Hayden, CC156
Legal guide for the visual artist, Crawford, Tad, BE107, BE109, CK85, CK88
Legal Information Resources Ltd. *Legal journals index,* CK57
Legal journals index, CK57
Legal language, Sinke, Marjorie J., CK67
Legal research, CK32
—— Elias, Stephen, CK5
Legal research made easy, CK7
The legal research manual, Wren, Christopher G., CK13
The legal researcher's desk reference 1990, CK87
Legal resource index, CK58
Legal Star Communications. *Legal research made easy,* CK7
Legal writing and research manual, Yogis, John, CK36
Legrand, Emile. *Bibliographie hellénique,* AA134
Leguay, Thierry. *L'obsolète,* AD101
Lehmann, Michael B. *The Dow Jones-Irwin guide to using the Wall Street journal,* CH17
Lehmann, Stephen. *Women's studies in Western Europe,* CC252
Leich, Harold M. *Russian imperial government serials on microfilm in the Library of Congress,* AE65
Leick, Gwendolyn. *A dictionary of ancient Near Eastern architecture,* BE123
Leigh, Carol. *Southern African material in anthologies of English literature in the Strange Library of Africana,* BD375
Leigh, G. J. *Nomenclature of inorganic chemistry,* ED28
Leistner, Otto. *Internationale Bibliographie der Festschriften von den Anfängen bis 1979,* AA28
Leiter, Samuel L. *The encyclopedia of the New York stage, 1920–1930,* BG32
Lekaukau, T. M. *A guide to the public archives of Botswana,* DD27
Leksikon politi shel ha-olam ha-'Arvi, CJ152
Leksikon politi shel Medinat Yi'sra'el, CJ190
Leḳsiḳon Yehudah ye-Shomron, CJ188
Lemmon, David. *British theatre yearbook,* BG18
Lengenfelder, Helga. *Internationales Bibliotheks-Handbuch = World guide to libraries,* AB20
Lenski, Wolfgang. *[Omega]—bibliography of mathematical logic,* EF2
Lent, John A. *Global guide to media & communications,* CH198
—— *Malaysian studies,* DE84
—— *Women and mass communications,* CC258
Lentner, Cornelius. *Geigy scientific tables,* EA36
Leo, John R. *Guide to American poetry explication,* BD182

León, Juan. *Demografía en el Ecuador,* CG50
León, Manuel Darío de. *Diccionario histórico dominicano,* DB148
Leonard, Harold. *The film index,* BG56
Leonard, R. L. *World atlas of elections,* CJ43
Leonard, Robin. *Family law dictionary,* CK64
—— *A legal guide for lesbian and gay couples,* CC156
Leonard, Steve. *Electronic music dictionary,* BH122
Leonard's annual price index of art auctions, BE62
LePage, Jane Weiner. *Women composers, conductors, and musicians of the twentieth century,* BH85
Lerner, Ralph E. *Art law,* BE108, BE109, CK86, CK88
Lerner, Richard M. *Encyclopedia of adolescence,* CC88
Lerner, Rita G. *Encyclopedia of physics,* EG4
Leroi-Gourhan, André. *Dictionnaire de la préhistoire,* DA35
Lerski, Halina T. *Jewish-Polish coexistence, 1772–1939,* DC172
Lerski, Jerzy J. *Jewish-Polish coexistence, 1772–1939,* DC172
The lesbian periodicals index, Potter, Clare, CC151
Lesbianism, CC148, CC151, CC154, CC155, CC156
Lesbianism, Maggiore, Dolores J., CC148
Leslau, Wolf. *Comparative dictionary of Ge'ez (Classical Ethiopic),* AD86
Lesly, Philip. *Lesly's handbook of public relations and communications,* CH75
Lesly's handbook of public relations and communications, CH75
Lesly's public relations handbook, CH75
Lessico etimologico italiano, Pfister, Max, AD132
Lester, DeeGee. *Immigrants from Great Britain and Ireland,* AK36, CC178, DC146
—— *Irish research,* DB71, DC146
Lesure, Francois. *Catalogue de la musique imprimée dans les bibliothèques publiques de Paris,* BH36
—— *Dictionnaire des éditeurs de musique française,* BH69
La letteratura italiana, De Vendittis, Luigi, BD316
Lettres françaises de Belgique, Frickx, Robert, BD303
L'étude des auteurs classiques latins aux XIe et XIIe siècles, Munk Olsen, B., BD371
Lev, Yvonne. *Encyclopedia of senior citizens information sources,* CC63
Lever, Christopher. *Naturalized birds of the world,* EC52
—— *Naturalized mammals of the world,* EC59
Leverenz, Jon M. *The new international atlas = Der neue internationale Atlas = El nuevo atlas internacional = Le nouvel atlas international = O nôvo atlas internacional,* CL56
Lévi-Strauss, C., CE6
Levina, R. Sh. *Sovetskaîa arkheologicheskaîa literatura,* DA33
Levine, Evyatar. *Political dictionary of the Middle East in the twentieth century,* CJ152, CJ190
Levine, Paula L. *Medical sociology,* CC6, EK7
Levine, Sumner N. *The financial analyst's handbook,* CH254
Levinson, David. *Encyclopedia of world cultures,* CE14
Levy, Leonard Williams. *Encyclopedia of the American Constitution,* CK116
Lewin, Albert E. *The thesaurus of slang,* AD45
Lewin, Esther. *The thesaurus of slang,* AD45
Lewis, Cathleen S. *Air and space history,* DA2
Lewis, James A. *A guide to Cherokee documents in foreign archives,* CC218
Lewis, Philippa. *Dictionary of ornament,* BF41

Lewis, Richard J.,. *Dangerous properties of industrial materials*, ED21
—— *Hawley's condensed chemical dictionary*, ED10
Lewis, Richard J., Sr. *Food additives handbook*, EH33
Lewis, Robert E. *Index of printed Middle English prose*, BD205
Lewy, Arieh. *The international encyclopedia of curriculum*, CB63
Lexical studies of medieval Spanish texts, Billick, David J., BC49
Lexicon of economic thought, Block, Walter, CH7
A lexicon of economics, CH10
Lexicon of geologic names of the United States for 1968-1975, EE10
A lexicon of Greek personal names, AK50
Lexicon of new formal geologic names of the United States, 1976-1980, EE11
Lexikon der Ägyptologie, DD31
Lexikon der Götter und Dämonen, CF3
Lexikon der griechischen und römischen Mythologie, Hunger, Herbert, CF12
Lexikon der Kunst, BE36, BE37
Lexikon der östlichen Weisheitslehren, BA12, BB23
Lexikon der Romanistischen Linguistik, BC36
Lexikon der russischen Literatur ab 1917, BD356
Lexikon der Symbole, Bauer, Wolfgang, CF1
Lexikon der Terraristik und Herpetologie, EC45
Lexikon der Weltliteratur, Wilpert, Gero von, BD30
Lexikon des frühgriechischen Epos, Snell, Bruno, AD115
Lexikon des gesamten Buchwesens, AA46
Lexikon des Mittelalters, DA50
Lexikon deutschsprachiger Schriftsteller, BD293
Lexikon deutschsprachiger Schriftstellerinnen, 1800-1945, Brinker-Gabler, Gisela, BD288
Lexikon missionstheologischer Grundbegriffe, BB105
Lexique étymologique de l'irlandais ancien, Vendryes, Joseph, AD127
LEXIS, CK18
Leyerle, John. *Chaucer, a bibliographical introduction*, BD257, DA46
Lhamsüren, B. *Information Mongolia*, DE85
Lhéritier, Andrée. *Manuel de bibliographie*, AA1
Li, Hong-Chan. *Social work education II*, CC27
Li, Tze-chung. *Social science reference sources*, CA1
The librarian's companion, Wertsman, Vladimir, AB13
Librarians in international development, AB38
Librarianship and library resources; see also
   Library catalogs
   bibliography, AB38
   biography, AB37, AB39, AB40, AB41
   collection development, AB63, AB64, AB65, AB67
   databases, AB40
   dictionaries, AB15, AB16
   directories, AB20
      Australia, AB24, AB25
      Gt. Brit., AB26, AB27, AB28, AB29, DC202, DE30
      India, AB30, AB32, AB33, AB34
      Indonesia, AB35
      Ireland, AB29, DE30
      Mexico, AB51
      Pakistan, AB42
      United States, AB21, AB22, AK17
      Zimbabwe, AB23
   guides
      Gt. Brit., DC204, DF1
      Hungary, DD2, DD15, DG4
      international, AB46
      United States, CJ83, DC195
   handbooks, AB13
   handbooks of usage, AB9

   history
      bibliography, AB2
      Moldavian, AB52, DC200
      Ukraine, AB52, DC200
      U.S.S.R., AB52, DC200
      yearbooks, AB43
Libraries, information centers and databases in science and technology, EA57
Library administration, AB70, AB71, AB72
Library and information science
   acronyms, AB17
   bibliography, AB1, AB3, AB5, AB6, AB7, AB44
      China, AB53
   book reviews, AB44
   dictionaries, AB14, EJ63
   directories, CA18
   encyclopedias, AB11, AB12
   guides, AB4
   handbooks, AB62
   periodicals, AB8
   study and teaching, AB19
Library and information science, AB7
Library and information science annual, AB44
Library and information science in China, Wei, Karen T., AB53
Library and information science journals and serials, Bowman, Mary Ann, AB8
Library and Information Technology Association. *Telecommunications and networking glossary*, CH195
Library and resource center in Christian education, McMichael, Betty, AB59
Library-Anthropology Resource Group (Chicago, Ill.). *Biographical directory of anthropologists born before 1920*, CE19
Library Association. *Walford's guide to reference material*, AA67, EA6
Library Association of Australia. *Directory of special libraries in Australia*, AB24
Library Association. Rare Books Group. *A directory of rare book and special collections in the United Kingdom and the Republic of Ireland*, AB29
Library catalog of the Metropolitan Museum of Art, New York, Metropolitan Museum of Art (New York, N.Y.). Library, BE26, BE27, BE28
Library catalogs, AA10, AA11, AA12, AA13, AA14, AA15, AA16, AA17, AA18, AA19, AA20, AA21, AA22, AA23, AA24, AA27
Library education, AB31
Library instruction, AB101, AB102, AB103
Library instruction for librarians, Roberts, Anne F., AB102
Library Instruction Round Table (American Library Association). *The LIRT library instruction handbook*, AB101
Library literature, AB6
The library manager's guide to automation, Boss, Richard W., AB87
Library of Congress. *Afghanistan*, DE43
—— *American doctoral dissertations on the Arab world : supplement August 1981-December 1987*, DE18
—— *Bibliographic guide to microform publications*, AA29
—— *Chinese law*, CK37
—— *Chinese newspapers in the Library of Congress*, AF6
—— *Czech and Slovak literature in English*, BD353
—— *Digest of data on persons with disabilities*, CC112
—— *International directory of braille music collections*, BH65
—— *International directory of tactile map collections*, CL45
—— *Japanese local histories in the Library of Congress*, DE77
—— *Law and legal literature of North Korea*, CK44, CK44
—— *Libya, 1969-1989*, DD42

—— *Major studies & issue briefs of the Congressional Research Service*, AG9
—— *National directory of Latin Americanists*, DB106
—— *National union catalog. Books*, AA24
—— *The Near East national union list*, AA25
—— *The Netherlands and Northern Belgium, a selective bibliography of reference works*, DC166
—— *New serial titles*, AE72, AE72
—— *Respectfully quoted*, BD65
—— *Russian imperial government serials on microfilm in the Library of Congress*, AE65, AE65
—— *U.S. imprints on Sub-Saharan Africa*, DD20
—— *USMARC format for bibliographic data*, AB77
—— *Vietnamese holdings in the Library of Congress. Supplement, 1979-1985*, DE100, DE100
The Library of Congress, Neagles, James C., AK7, DB42
Library of Congress. Geography and Map Division. *Civil War maps*, DB37
Library of Congress. Library of Congress Office, Rio de Janeiro. *Accessions list, Brazil and Uruguay*, AA90, AA197
Library of Congress. Manuscript Division. *Civil War manuscripts*, DB31
Library of Congress. Motion Picture, Broadcasting, and Recorded Sound Division. *3 decades of television*, BG109
—— *Early motion pictures*, BG75
Library of Congress subject headings, CC299
Library reference plus, AB21, AB22
Library research guide to religion and theology, Kennedy, James R., BB1
Library science annual, AB44
Library Service of Fiji. *Fiji national bibliography*, AA107
The library trustee, AB71
I libretti italiani a stampa dalle origini al 1800, Sartori, Claudio, BH102
LiBretto, Ellen V. *High/low handbook*, CB26
Libri Walliae, Rees, Eiluned, AA202
Libros argentinos. ISBN, AA86
Libros chilenos ISBN, AA94
Libros en venta en Hispanoamérica y España, AA154
Libya, AA155, DD41, DD42
Libya. *al-Bibliyūghrāfiyah al-'Arabīyah al-Lībīyah*, AA155, AA155
Libya, Lawless, Richard I., DD41
Libya, 1969-1989, Witherell, Julian W., DD42
Liddle, Barry. *Dictionary of sports quotations*, BJ12
Lidman, Mark J. *Studies in Jacobean drama, 1973-1984*, BD233
Lieberthal, Kenneth. *A research guide to central party and government meetings in China, 1949-1986*, DE52
Liesner, Thelma. *Economic statistics, 1900-1983*, CH27
—— *One hundred years of economic statistics*, CH27
Lietuviškoji tarybinė enciklopedija, DC163
Lietuviškoji tarybinė enciklopedija. Papildymai A-Ž, DC160
Life sciences organizations and agencies directory, EC20
Lifelong education for adults : an international handbook, Titmus, Colin J., CB63
The lifestyle market analyst, CH330
Lifestyle marketplanner, CH330
Light, Margot. *International relations*, CJ7
Lighting, EJ49
Lilien, Steven B. *Accountants' handbook*, CH65
Lilley, George P. *Information sources in agriculture and food science*, EH1
Lilly, Jerry. *The martial arts*, BJ31
Lim, Patricia Pui Huen. *ASEAN*, DE35, DE36

—— *The Malay world of Southeast Asia*, DE37

Lincoln, Betty Woelk. *Festschriften in art history, 1960–1975*, BE9

Lincoln, Roger J. *The Cambridge illustrated dictionary of natural history*, EC24

—— *A dictionary of ecology, evolution and systematics*, EC24

Lincove, David A. *The Anglo-American relationship*, DB14

Linda Hall Library. *Serials holdings in the Linda Hall Library [as of April 30] 1989*, EA19

Lindemann, Erika. *Longman bibliography of composition and rhetoric*, BD144

Linder, Robert Dean. *Dictionary of Christianity in America*, BB84

Lindfors, Bernth. *Black African literature in English. 1977–1981 supplement*, BD373

—— *Black African literature in English, 1982–1986*, BD374

Lindner, Stephan H. *The economies of the German-speaking countries of Europe : a selective bibliography*, DC4

Lindow, John. *Scandinavian mythology*, CF16

Lindsell, Sheryl L. *Proofreading and editing for word processors*, AA55

Lines, Clifford John. *Companion to the Industrial Revolution*, DC115

Lingle, Virginia A. *How to find information about AIDS*, EK3

A linguistic atlas of late mediaeval English, McIntosh, Angus, BC31

Linguistic atlases
  England, BC30, BC31
  Wales, BC31

Linguistics, Edmonson, Munro S., CE25

Linguistics and philology
  bibliography, BC1, BC5, BC6
  databases, BD9
  dictionaries, BC11, BC12, BC13
  encyclopedias, BC7, BC8, BC10
  manuals, BC15
  morphology, BC1

Liniger-Goumaz, M. *Equatorial Guinea*, DD6

Liniger-Goumaz, Max. *Guinea Ecuatorial*, DD33

Linton, David. *The newspaper press in Britain*, AF9

Lippy, Charles H. *Bibliography of religion in the South*, BB4

—— *Encyclopedia of the American religious experience*, BB26

—— *Religious periodicals of the United States*, BB5

Lipschutz, Mark R. *Dictionary of African historical biography*, AJ29

Lisäyksiä Fredrik Wilhelm Pippingin bibliografiaan Luettelo suomeksi präntätyistä kirjoista = Tillägg till Förteckning öfver i tryck utgifna skrifter på finska av Fredrik Wilhelm Pippin, AA108

List, Barbara A. *Milestones in science and technology*, EA73

A list of architectural books available in American before the Revolution, Park, Helen, BE111

List of British diplomatic records for Balkan history, 1879–1905, DC17

List of journals indexed in Index medicus, EK24

List of serials indexed for online users, EK24

Liste mondiale des périodiques spécialisés dans les sciences sociales = World list of social science periodicals, CA13

Listen to the music, Kramer, Jonathan D., BH148

Lister, Raymond. *Prints and printmaking*, BE161

Liston, Linda L. *The weather handbook*, EE31

Literacy, CB20, CB24, CB29, CB33
  bibliography, CB28

Literacy/illiteracy in the world, Eller, William, CB28

—— Hladczuk, John, CB28, CB29

—— Hladczuk, Sharon, CB28

Literary characters *see* **Characters in literature**

The literary guide to the Bible, BB56

Literary history of the United States, Spiller, Robert E., BD167

The literary lives of Jesus, Birney, Alice L., BB74, BD1

Literary manuscripts at the National Library of Canada = Les manuscrits littéraires à la Bibliothèque nationale du Canada, BD278

Literary market place, AB22

Literary research guide, Harner, James L., BD149

—— Patterson, Margaret, BD149

Literary terms, Beckson, Karl E., BD34

Literatur zur deutschsprachigen Presse, Hagelweide, Gert, AE37

Literatura o narodonaselenii, Davydova, A. G., CG73

Literatura uruguaya, Rela, Walter, BD349

Literatura uruguaya : tablas cronologicas, 1835–1985, Rela, Walter, BD349

Literature
  applications of computers, BD12
  awards, BD45, BD56
  bibliography, BD4, BD7, BD8, BD52
  biographies of authors, BD52, BD54, BD55
  criticism, BD8, BD18, BD19, BD20, BD21, BD22, BD23
  databases, BD9
  dictionaries, BD31, BD33, BD34, BD36, BD37, BD39
  encyclopedias, BD24, BD25, BD26, BD27, BD28, BD30
  guides, BD14, BD44
  handbooks, BD46, BD50
  influence studies, BD51
  periodicals, AE21, BD160
  research methods, BD12, BD14, BD15, BD16

Literature Bureau (Zimbabwe). *Standard Shona dictionary*, AD161

A literature guide for the identification of plant pathogenic fungi, Rossman, Amy Y., EC35

The literature of American music in books and folk music collections, Horn, David, BH27

The literature of rock, II, 1979–1983, Hoffmann, Frank W., BH136

Literature search/National Library of Medicine, EK9, EK28

Literatures, Edmonson, Munro S., CE25

Literaturpsychologie, 1945–1987, Pfeiffer, Joachim, BD7

Lithuania
  bibliography, DC162
  encyclopedias, DC161
  history
    encyclopedias, DC160, DC163

Lithuania, DC161

Lithuanian Research and Studies Center (Chicago, Ill.). *Lituanica collections in European research libraries*, DC162

Litman, Theodor J. *The sociology of medicine and health care*, CC6, EK7

The little black book of business statistics, Thomsett, Michael C., CH167

Littlefield, Daniel F. *American Indian and Alaska native newspapers and periodicals*, CC223

—— *A biobibliography of native American writers, 1772–1924*, BD196, BD197, CC218

Lituanica collections in European research libraries, Šešplaukis, Alfonsas, DC162

Liturgics, BB89, BB120

Litwack, Leon F. *Black leaders of the nineteenth century*, CC207

Lives of Jesus, Kissinger, Warren S., BB74, BD1

Livros disponíveis, AA175

Lloyd's of London, CH266

Lo, Chu-feng. *Han yü ta tz'u tien*, AD82

Loanwords dictionary, AD65

Lobb, Michael L. *Native American youth and alcohol*, CC69

Lobban, R. *Republic of Cape Verde*, DD5

—— *Republic of Guinea-Bissau*, DD6

The lobbying handbook, CJ71

Lobbyists, CJ59, CJ60, CJ71

Lobel, Mary D. *The City of London from prehistoric times to c.1520*, DC134

Lobestine, Joy C. *National directory of educational programs in gerontology*, CC59

Lobies, Jean-Pierre. *IBN*, AJ6

The local historian's encyclopedia, Richardson, John, AK37

The location photographer's handbook, Haas, Ken, BF60

Location register of twentieth-century English literary manuscripts and letters, BD216

Lochar, Ruth. *Internationales Bibliotheks-Handbuch = World guide to libraries*, AB20

Loe, Mary. *The LIRT library instruction handbook*, AB101

Loeb, Catherine. *Women's studies*, CC259, CC260

Log-books, DG8

Logue, Dennis E. *Handbook of modern finance*, CH256

Lohwater, A. J. *A.J. Lohwater's Russian-English dictionary of the mathematical sciences*, EF13

—— *Russian-English dictionary of the mathematical sciences*, EF13

Loiry, William S. *The U.S.-Eastern European trade sourcebook*, CH181

—— *The U.S.-Soviet trade sourcebook*, CH182

Loke, Wing Hong. *A guide to journals in psychology and education*, CB44, CD5

Lomelí, Francisco A. *Chicano literature*, BD193

Lommatzsch, Erhard. *Altfranzösisches Wörterbuch*, AD102

London, DC134, DC137

London Assay Office. *The directory of gold & silversmiths, jewellers, and allied traders, 1838–1914*, BF45

A London bibliography of the social sciences, CA9

The London diplomatic list, CJ183

The London encyclopaedia, DC137

The London furniture makers from the Restoration to the Victorian era, Heal, Ambrose, BF37

The London goldsmiths 1200–1800, Heal, Ambrose, BF46

London goldsmiths 1697–1837, Grimwade, Arthur, BF46

London, past and present, Wheatley, Henry B., DC137

London School of Economics and Political Science. *A London bibliography of the social sciences*, CA9

The London stage, 1920–1929, Wearing, J. P., BG35

Long Island University. *National guide to funding in aging*, CC67

Longley, Dennis. *Dictionary of information technology*, EJ63

—— *Van Nostrand Reinhold dictionary of information technology*, EJ63

Longman bibliography of composition and rhetoric, BD142, BD144

Longman companion to English literature, Gillie, Christopher, BD220

The Longman companion to the French Revolution, DC54

Longman companion to Victorian fiction, Sutherland, John, BD242

Longman dictionary and handbook of poetry, Myers, Jack Elliott, BD134

Longman dictionary of applied linguistics, Richards, Jack C., BC13

INDEX

The Longman encyclopedia, AC5
Longman guide to world science and technology, EA58
Longman handbook of modern British history, 1714–1980, DC11
The Longman handbook of modern British history, 1714–1987, Cook, Chris, DC120
The Longman handbook of modern European history, 1763–1985, Cook, Chris, DC11
The Longman register of new words, Ayto, John, AD33
Longman synonym dictionary, AD49
Looking at prints, drawings, and watercolours, Goldman, Paul, BE158
Lopos, George J. *Peterson's guide to certificate programs at American colleges and universities,* CB106
Lord, M. P. *Macmillan dictionary of physics,* EG6
Lorenz, Otto H. *Biblio,* AA115
—— *Catalogue générale de la librairie francaise, 1840–1925,* AA115
Lorenzi, Harri. *Weeds of the United States and their control,* EH22
Lorenzini, Jean A. *Medical phrase index,* EK49
Loroña, Lionel V. *A bibliography of Latin American bibliographies, 1980–1984,* AA8, DB90
Los Angeles times, AJ7
Los Angeles times [index], AF13
Lottes, Wolfgang. *The contemporary printed literature of the English Counter-Reformation between 1558 and 1640,* BB115
Lougheed, W. C. *Writings on Canadian English, 1976–1987,* BC21
Loughney, Katharine. *3 decades of television,* BG109
Lounsbury, Warren C. *Theatre backstage from A to Z,* BG25
Lovera De-Sola, R. J. *Guía para el estudio de la historia de Venezuela,* DB136
Lovi, George. *Uranometria 2000.0,* EB18
Loving, Elizabeth. *Picture sources UK,* BE70
Lowe, David W. *The official World Wildlife Fund guide to endangered species of North America,* EC41
Lowes, Bryan. *Harper dictionary of economics,* CH11
Lowry, Philip J. *Green cathedrals,* BJ23
Loyn, H. R. *The Middle Ages,* DA51
Lubin, Bernard. *Family therapy,* CC128
Lubitz, Wolfgang. *Trotsky bibliography,* CJ241
Lucio, Troy. *A Zuni atlas,* CC233
Ludman, Joan. *Old master print references,* BE155
Ludman, Mark D. *The encyclopedia of genetic disorders and birth defects,* EK45
Ludwig, Karola. *Lexikon deutschsprachiger Schriftstellerinnen, 1800–1945,* BD288
Ludwig, Richard M. *Annals of American literature, 1602–1983,* BD165
Luebking, Sandra Hargreaves. *The archives,* AB49, DB22
Lüschen, Günther. *Handbook of social science of sport,* BJ16, CC19
Luettelo suomeksi präntätyistä kirjoista .., Pipping, F. W., AA108
Luey, Beth. *Editing documents and texts,* AA59
—— *Handbook for academic authors,* AA56
—— *Publication grants for writers & publishers,* BD49, CA46
Lugt, Frits. *Répertoire des catalogues des ventes publiques,* BE61
Lukman, Franc Ksaver. *Slovenski biografski leksikon,* AJ103
Lulat, Y. G.-M. *U.S. relations with South Africa,* DD54
Lumpkin, Angela. *A guide to the literature of tennis,* BJ35
Lunsford, Ronald F. *Research in composition and rhetoric,* BD147
Lurker, Manfred. *Dictionary of gods and goddesses, devils and demons,* CF3

Lust, John. *Western books on China published up to 1850 in the Library of the School of Oriental and African Studies, University of London,* DE48
Lutherans, BB108, BB109
Lutjens, Sheryl. *Cuba, 1953–1978,* DB144
Luttrell, Gwendolyn Lewise Werth. *Lexicon of geologic names of the United States for 1968–1975,* EE10
—— *Lexicon of new formal geologic names of the United States, 1976–1980,* EE11
Luttwak, Edward. *The dictionary of modern war,* CJ260
Lutz, Bernd. *Metzler Philosophen Lexikon,* BA25
Lutz, James M. *Protectionism,* CH178
Lutz, Mary E. *Face of the nation, 1987,* CC30
Lutzker, Marilyn. *Criminal justice research in libraries,* CK96
Lybarger, Barbara E. *An advocate's guide to surviving the SSI system,* CH267
Lyman, Thomas W. *French Romanesque sculpture,* BE162
Lynch, Richard Chigley. *Broadway on record,* BH146
—— *Movie musicals on record,* BH146
Lyne, Debora J. *Employee benefit plans,* CH156
Lynn, Ruth Nadelman. *Fantasy for children,* BD77
—— *Fantasy literature for children and young adults,* BD77
Lyon, Christopher. *The international dictionary of films and filmmakers,* BG92
Lyon, Howard H. *Diseases of trees and shrubs,* EC37
Lyon, Randy. *The encyclopedia of the Midwest,* DB54

MARC for library use, Crawford, Walt, AB77
MLA handbook, AA53
MLA handbook for writers of research papers, Gibaldi, Joseph, AH1
MLA international bibliography, BD9
The MLA style manual, Achtert, Walter S., AA53
Mabberley, D. J. *The plant-book,* EC29
McAinsh, T. F. *Physics in medicine & biology encyclopedia,* EK42
McAleer, Beth D. *The directory of North American fisheries and aquatic scientists,* EC19
McAleese, Ray. *The encyclopaedia of educational media communications and technology,* CB60
Macao, DE83
Macau, Edmonds, Richard L., DE83
McBurney, William Harlin. *Check list of English prose fiction, 1700–1739,* BD238
McCabe, Gerard B. *The smaller academic library,* AB62
McCabe, James Patrick. *Critical guide to Catholic reference books,* BB11
McCaffery, Larry. *Postmodern fiction,* BD94
McCalpin, Deborah J. *Health media review index, 1984–86,* EK22
McCann, Gary. *Encyclopedia of legal information sources,* CK15
McCardle, Ellen Steele. *Social networks and mental health,* CC21
McCarthy, John R. *Higher education finance,* CB9
Macció, Guillermo. *Diccionario demográfico multilingüe,* CG10
McConnell, Fraiser. *Papua New Guinea,* DG12
MacCorkle, Lyn. *Cubans in the United States,* CC238
McCormick, Donald. *Spy fiction,* BD106
McCrea, Barbara P. *The European political dictionary,* CJ168
McCulloch, Alan. *Encyclopedia of Australian art,* BE82

McCullough, Kathleen. *Concrete poetry,* BD130
McCurdy, Howard E. *Public administration,* CJ218, CJ219
MacDonagh, Oliver. *Australians,* DF2
McDonald, Archie P. *Encyclopedia USA,* DB63
McDonald, James,. *A dictionary of obscenity, taboo & euphemism,* AD46
McDonald, James R. *The broadcaster's dictionary,* BG115
McDonald, Jan. *Australian artists' index,* BE82
McDowell, Colin. *McDowell's directory of twentieth century fashion,* BF32
McDowell's directory of twentieth century fashion, McDowell, Colin, BF32
Macé, Pierre-Antoine. *Le grand dictionnaire des synonymes,* AD99
McFarland, Keith D. *The Korean War, an annotated bibliography,* DE80
MacFarlane, Paul. *Daguerrotypes : Hall of Fame members and other immortals,* BJ22
McFate, Katherine. *The metropolitan area fact book,* CC210
McGee, Leo. *Education of the black adult in the United States,* CB34
McGillivray, Alice V. *America at the polls 2,* CJ114
McGonagle, John J. *The Arthur Andersen European community sourcebook,* CK125
McGraw-Hill CD-ROM science and technical reference set, EA37
McGraw-Hill concise encyclopedia of science and technology, EA37, EA38
McGraw-Hill dictionary of art, BE37
McGraw-Hill dictionary of modern economics, CH10
McGraw-Hill dictionary of scientific and technical terms, EA37, EA44
McGraw-Hill encyclopedia of science & technology, EA33, EE7, EA38
McGraw-Hill encyclopedia of the geological sciences, EA38, EE7
MacGregor, Geddes. *Dictionary of religion and philosophy,* BB28
McGrew, Margaret P. *Encyclopedia of medical history,* EK74
McGrew, Roderick E. *Encyclopedia of medical history,* EK74
McGuire, Martin. *Introduction to classical scholarship,* BD365
Machalka-Felser, Rautgundis. *Bibliographie zur Geschichte der Städte Österreichs,* DC26
Machinery, EJ82
Machovec, George S. *Telecommunications and networking glossary,* CH195
McIntosh, Angus. *A linguistic atlas of late mediaeval English,* BC31
McIntosh, John L. *Research on suicide,* CC96
Macintyre, J. E. *Dictionary of organometallic compounds,* ED30
McIver, Tom. *Anti-evolution,* BB6
McKearin, George S. *American glass,* BF28
McKearin, Helen. *American glass,* BF28
McKendry, Blake. *A dictionary of folk artists in Canada from the 17th century to the present with inclusions of popular portrait, topographical, genre, religious, and decorative artists of the 17th, 18th, and 19th centuries,* BF16
Mackensen, Lutz. *Deutsches Wörterbuch,* AD114
McKerns, Joseph P.,. *Biographical dictionary of American journalism,* AF24
—— *News media and public policy,* CH199
Mackerras, Colin. *The Cambridge handbook of contemporary China,* DE53
Mackie, Thomas T. *The international almanac of electoral history,* CJ141
McKinney, Mary Jane. *Handbook of financial markets and institutions,* CH255
McKinstry, E. Richard. *The Edward Deming Andrews Memorial Shaker Collection,* BB113
McKirahan, R.D. *Plato and Socrates,* BA29

McKusick, Victor A. *Mendelian inheritance in man,* EC67

McLachlan, K. S. *A bibliography of the Iran-Iraq borderland,* DE12

McLauchlan, Gordon. *The illustrated encyclopedia of New Zealand,* DF10

McLean, Janice W. *Consultants and consulting organizations directory,* CH160

Maclean, Norman. *Dictionary of genetics & cell biology,* EC66

McLeish, Kenneth. *The Penguin companion to the arts in the twentieth century,* BE83

Macleod, Iseabail. *Scoor-oot,* AD61

McMann, Evelyn de R. *Canadian who's who index, 1898–1984,* AJ39

McManners, John. *The Oxford illustrated history of Christianity,* BB100

McMichael, Betty. *The church librarian's handbook,* AB59

—— *Library and resource center in Christian education,* AB59

McMillan, James B. *Annotated bibliography of Southern American English,* BC23

The Macmillan atlas of rugs & carpets, BF48

Macmillan atlas of the holocaust, Gilbert, Martin, DA85

Macmillan dictionary of historical terms, Cook, Chris, DA12

Macmillan dictionary of physics, Lord, M. P., EG6

The Macmillan dictionary of quotations, BD61

The Macmillan dictionary of women's biography, AJ9

Macmillan directory of business information sources, Tudor, James, CH84

Macmillan encyclopedia of architects, BE122

The Macmillan guide to correspondence study, CB113

McMullan, Randall. *Dictionary of building,* BE124, EJ38

McMullin, Ruth. *Oral history collections,* DB21

McNeil, Barbara. *Artist biographies master index,* BE75

McNeil, R. A. *Latin American studies,* DB94

McNerney, Kathleen. *Women writers of Spain,* BD326

McPheron, William. *The bibliography of contemporary American fiction, 1945–1988,* BD176

McPherson, Marion White. *Dictionary of concepts in general psychology,* CD19

Macquarrie, John. *A dictionary of Christian ethics,* BB92

—— *The Westminster dictionary of Christian ethics,* BB92

McRoberts, J. Paul. *Shakespeare and the medieval tradition,* BD262

Macura, Paul. *Elsevier's Russian-English dictionary,* AD153

McWilliam, Neil. *A bibliography of Salon criticism in Paris from the July monarchy to the Second Empire, 1831–1851,* BE147

Madagascar, AA156

Maddex, Diane. *All about old buildings,* BE129

—— *Landmark yellow pages,* BE127

Maddox, George L. *The encyclopedia of aging,* CC52, EK38

Maddox, Robert Franklin. *America and World War I,* DA73

Maersch, Klaus. *Bildwörterbuch Musikinstrumente,* BH153

Magalini, Sabina C. *Dictionary of medical syndromes,* EK55

Magalini, Sergio I. *Dictionary of medical syndromes,* EK55

Magay, Tamás. *A concise English-Hungarian dictionary,* AD124

—— *A concise Hungarian-English dictionary,* AD123

Magazines, Paine, Fred K., AE18

Magazines for libraries, Katz, William A., AA69

Magazines of the American South, Riley, Sam G., AE20

Magel, Charles R. *Keyguide to information sources in animal rights,* EC2

Maggio, Rosalie. *The nonsexist word finder,* CC298

Maggiore, Dolores J. *Lesbianism,* CC148

Magic, Coleman, Earle Jerome, CF21

Magill, Frank Northen. *Critical survey of drama,* BD230

—— *Critical survey of literary theory,* BD18

—— *Cyclopedia of literary characters II,* BD97

—— *Great lives from history. Twentieth century series,* AJ10

—— *Magill's cinema annual,* BG64

—— *Magill's survey of cinema, foreign language films,* BG65

—— *Magill's survey of science. Earth science series,* EE3

—— *Magill's survey of science. Life science series,* EC10

—— *The Nobel Prize winners : chemistry,* ED25

—— *The Nobel Prize winners : physics,* EG13

Magill's cinema annual, BG64

Magill's survey of cinema, foreign language films, BG65

Magill's survey of science. Earth science series, EE3

Magill's survey of science. Life science series, EC10

Magliozzi, Ronald S. *Treasures from the film archives,* BG76

Magnusson, Magnus. *Cambridge biographical dictionary,* AJ1

Magocsi, Paul R. *Ucrainica at the University of Toronto Library,* DC213

—— *Ukraine, a historical atlas,* DC215

Magril, Rose Mary. *Building library collections,* AB64

Magrill, Rose Mary. *Acquisitions management and collection development in libraries,* AB67

Magyar-angol kéziszótár, Országh, László, AD123

Magyar ki kicsoda 1990, AJ70

Magyar könyvészet, 1921–1944, AA139

Magyar nemzeti bibliográfia, AE48

Ma'had al-Idārah al-'Āmmah (Riyadh, Saudi Arabia). Markaz al-Wathā'iq. Qism al-Matbū'āt al-Rasmīyah. *al-Matbū'āt al-rasmīyah fī al-Mamlakah al-'Arabīyah al-al-Sa'ūdīyah,* AG46

Mahler, Gregory S. *Bibliography of Israeli politics,* CJ189

—— *Contemporary Canadian politics,* CJ157

Mahlmann, Diane E. *National guide to funding in aging,* CC67

Mahoney, Dennis J. *Encyclopedia of the American Constitution,* CK116

Maier, Mark. *Reading lists in radical social science,* CA7

Maikovich, Andrew J. *Sports quotations,* BJ13

Mail-order business, CH321

Maillet, Lise. *Provincial royal commissions and commissions of inquiry, 1867–1982,* AG31, CJ158

Mailman, Richard B. *Dictionary of toxicology,* EK130

Maini, Roberti. *Catalogo dei periodici italiani,* AE55

Maizell, Robert E. *How to find chemical information,* ED1

Major studies & issue briefs of the Congressional Research Service, AG9

Makar, Ragai N. *Egypt,* DD32

Makerere University. Library. *Uganda national bibliography,* AA196

Makinson, Larry. *The price of admission,* CJ110

Makower, Joel. *The American history sourcebook,* DB69

—— *The map catalog,* CL49

Makowski, Colleen Lahan. *Quilting, 1915–1983,* BF35

Malá československá encyklopedie, AC9

Malatesta, Edward. *St. John's Gospel, 1920–1965,* BB41

The Malay world of Southeast Asia, Lim, Patricia Pui Huen, DE37

Malaysia, DE84

   biography, AJ79

   goverment publications, AG45

   statistics, CG63

Malaysian studies, DE84

Malclès, Louise-Noëlle. *Manuel de bibliographie,* AA1

Mali, Imperato, P. J., DD6

Malina, Peter. *Bibliographie zur österreichischen Zeitgeschichte, 1918–1985,* DC23

Malinova, Libuse. *Anglicko-český technický slovník,* EA46

Malinowsky, Harold Robert. *AIDS information sourcebook,* EK66

—— *International directory of gay and lesbian periodicals,* CC154

—— *Science and engineering literature,* EA3

—— *Science and technology annual reference review,* EA8

Mallon, Bill. *The Olympic record book,* BJ33

Malone, Cheryl Knott. *Gender, unpaid labor, and the promotion of literacy,* CB33

Malta, AA157, DC164

Malta, Thackrah, John Richard, DC164

Malta national bibliography, AA157

Mamalakis, Markos. *Historical statistics of Chile,* CG45

Mammals, EC56, EC57, EC59, EC60

Man, myth & magic, BB29, CD53, CF4

Management see **Business management**

Management contents, CH153

Management results, CH246

Manceron, Anne. *La Révolution française,* DC55

Manceron, Claude. *La Révolution française,* DC55

Manchel, Frank. *Film study,* BG53

Mander Jones, Phyllis. *Manuscripts in the British Isles relating to Australia, New Zealand and the Pacific,* DF1

Mangrum, Charles T. *Peterson's guide to colleges with programs for learning-disabled students,* CB115

Manley, John. *Atlas of prehistoric Britain,* DC129

Mann, Lester. *Encyclopedia of special education,* CB59, CB62

Mann, Michael. *A thesaurus of African languages,* BC58

Mann, Stuart E. *An Indo-European comparative dictionary,* AD72

Mann, Thomas L. *Biographical directory of anthropologists born before 1920,* CE19

Mannack, Thomas. *Beazley addenda,* BE151

Manser, Martin H. *Bloomsbury good word guide,* AD23

Mantle Fielding's dictionary of American painters, sculptors & engravers, Fielding, Mantle, BE94

Manual del librero hispanoamericano, Palau y Dulcet, Antonio, AA185, AA186

Manual for authors and editors, EK34

A manual for writers of term papers, theses, and dissertations, Turabian, Kate L., AH3

Manual of law librarianship, AB58, CK8

Manual of steel construction, EJ36, EJ37

A manual of the writings in Middle English, 1050–1500, BD208, BD206

Manual para las relaciones Europeo-Latinoamericanas = Handbook for European-Latin American relations, DB105

Manuel, E. Arsenio. *Dictionary of Philippine biography,* AJ84

Manuel bibliographique de la littérature française du Moyen Age de Robert Bossuat. Troisième supplément, 1960–1980, Vielliard, Françoise, BD310
Manuel de bibliographie, Malclès, Louise-Noëlle, AA1
Manufacturing, CH140
Manufacturing, retail, service, and wholesale industries
 classification, CH309
Manufacturing, retail, service, and wholesale industries
 databases, CH301
 dictionaries, CH291, CH292
 directories, CH303
 handbooks, CH304
 statistics, CH306
Manufacturing USA, CH306
Manuila, Alexandre. *International dictionary of medicine and biology,* EC17, EK48
Manuscripts
 ancient, medieval, and Renaissance, AA39
  catalogs, BD371
   bibliography, AA36, AA37
   union lists, AA38
 editing, AA54, BD13
 guides
  by location
   Canada, DB86
   France, DC73
   Gt. Brit., DC111
   United States, DB18, DB19
  by subject
   history, DB23
   literature, BD216
Manuscripts in the British Isles relating to Australia, New Zealand and the Pacific, Mander Jones, Phyllis, DF1
Les manuscrits classiques latins des bibliothèques publiques de France, Jeudy, Colette, AA38
Maori and Pacific films from New Zealand 1901–1984, New Zealand Film Archive, DG5
The map catalog, CL49
Map collections, AB57, CL38, CL41, CL44, CL45, CL46, CL48
Map guide to the U.S. federal censuses, 1790–1920, Thorndale, William, AK3, CL60
Map librarianship, Larsgaard, Mary Lynette, AB57, CL48
Maps *see* **Atlases**
Maps contained in the publications of the American bibliography, 1639–1819, Walsh, Jim, AA79, CL43
Maps for America, Thompson, Morris Mordecai, CL61
Maps on file, CL53
Maram, Sheldon L. *Latin American labor organizations,* CH282
Maratos, Daniel C. *Escritores de la diáspora cubana,* BD341
Marcan, Peter. *Greater London local history directory and bibliography,* DC138
Marco, Guy A. *Music librarianship,* AB54
—— *Opera,* BH99
Marcuse, Michael J. *A reference guide for English studies,* BD201
Margolin, Judith B. *The Foundation Center's user-friendly guide,* CA44
Margulis, Lynn. *Five kingdoms,* EC66
Mariel, Pierre. *Dictionnaire des sociétés secrètes en Occident,* CA54
Marill, Alvin H. *Movies made for television,* BG110
Marine biotechnology abstracts, EC7
The marine encyclopaedic dictionary, Sullivan, Eric, CH192
Marine engineering, EE40
The Marine officer's guide, Estes, Kenneth W., CJ279
—— Heinl, Robert Debs, CJ279
Maritime services directory, CH193

Marjoribanks, Kevin. *The foundations of students' learning,* CB63
Mark, H. F. *Encyclopedia of polymer science and engineering,* EJ20
Mark, Yudel. *Groyser verterbukh fun der Yidisher shprakh = Great dictionary of the Yiddish language,* AD174
Markel, Robert. *For the record,* BJ7
Markel, Susan. *For the record,* BJ7
Marken, Jack W. *Bibliography of the Sioux,* CC218
Market profiles, CH356
Market share reporter, CH331
Marketing
 bibliography, CH311, CH313
 databases, CH314, CH320, CH329
 dictionaries, CH316, CH317, CH318, CH319
 directories, CH321
 encyclopedias, CH315
 guides, CH312
 handbooks, CH313, CH323, CH325
 statistics, CH326, CH327, CH328, CH330, CH331, CH333
Marketing information, CH312
Markle, Allen. *Author's guide to journals in psychology, psychiatry and social work,* CD6
Markov, A. S. *Dictionary of scientific and technical terminology,* EA50
Marks, Claude. *World artists 1980–1990,* BE90
Marks, Lionel S. *Marks' standard handbook for mechanical engineers,* EJ79
Marks' standard handbook for mechanical engineers, EJ79
Markus, Manfred. *English-German contrastive linguistics,* BC22
Markwell, F. C. *The A–Z guide to tracing ancestors in Britain,* AK33
—— *Family historian's enquire within,* AK33
Marlin, John Tepper. *Cities of opportunity,* CA22
Marques, Alfredo Pinheiro. *Guia de história dos Descobrimentos e expansão portuguesa,* DC175
Marques, António Henrique R. de Oliveira. *Guia do estudante de história medieval portuguesa,* DC176
Márquez Acevedo, Sergio. *Catálogo de seudónimos, anagramas, iniciales y otros alias usados por escritores mexicanos y extranjeros que han publicado en México,* AA35
Marriage and the family; *see also* **Divorce**
 bibliography, CC81, CC121, CC122, CC123, CC124, CC128, CC129, CC130, CC134, CC138
 databases, CC127
 dictionaries, CC137
 directories, CC142
 encyclopedias, CC136
 handbooks, CC139, CC140, CC141
Marriott, F. H. C. *A dictionary of statistical terms,* CG9, EF11
Marsden, Lucy E. *Guide to New Zealand information sources,* AA64
Marsden, Peter H. *Auswahlbibliographie zum Studium der anglistischen Sprachwissenschaft,* BC20
Marsh, Arthur Ivor. *Historical directory of trade unions,* CH287
—— *Trade union handbook,* CH283
Marsh, Earle. *The complete directory to prime time network TV shows, 1946–present,* BG117
Marsh, James H. *The Canadian encyclopedia,* DB88
Marsh, Peter E. *Biographical dictionary of modern European radicals and socialists,* AJ8
Marshall, Alice Kahler. *Pen names of women writers,* AA31
Marshall, Joan K. *Serials for libraries,* AA68
Marshall, Mac. *Micronesia 1944–1974,* DG2
Marshall, Marion B. *Public finance,* CH218

Marshall, William C. *Stress, strain, and Vietnam,* DE104
Marshallsay, Diana. *Ford list of British parliamentary papers, 1974–1983, together with specialist commentaries,* AG43
Marti, James. *The new book of world rankings,* CG19
The martial arts, Nelson, Randy F., BJ31
Martin, Daniel. *The guide to the foundations of public administration,* CJ218
Martin, Daniel R. *A directory of credentials in counseling and psychotherapy,* CD26
Martin, Daniel W. *Index to periodical articles related to law,* CK56
Martin, F. X. *A new history of Ireland,* DC153
Martin, Fenton S. *The American presidency,* CJ76, CJ77
—— *American presidents,* CJ74, CJ78
—— *Congress and law-making,* CJ92
—— *The U.S. Supreme Court,* CK29
Martin, Galen R. *The international development dictionary,* CH55
Martin, Harold H. *The encyclopedia of the South,* DB53
Martin, Jochen. *Atlas zur Kirchengeschichte,* BB107
Martin, M. Marlene. *Ethnographic bibliography of North America, 4th edition. Supplement 1973–1987,* CC217
Martin Greenwald Associates. *Historical maps on file,* DA27
Martindale, William. *The extra pharmacopoeia,* EK117
Martindale-Hubbell bar register of preeminent lawyers in the United States, Canada, and other countries, CK92
Martindale-Hubbell international law directory. Canadian & international lawyers, CK80
Martindale-Hubbell law digest, CK80
The Martindale-Hubbell law directory, CK80
The Martindale-Hubbell law directory on CD-ROM, CK79
Martínez, Julio A. *Chicano literature,* BD193
—— *Dictionary of twentieth-century Cuban literature,* BD340
Martinez, Nancy C. *Poetry explication,* BD182
Marting, Diane E. *Spanish American women writers,* BD335
—— *Women writers of Spanish America,* BD336
Martis, Kenneth C. *The historical atlas of political parties in the United States Congress, 1789–1989,* CJ116, DB78
—— *The historical atlas of United States congressional districts, 1789–1983,* CJ116, DB78
Marvel, Mary K. *Program evaluation,* CJ212
A Marx dictionary, Carver, Terrell, CJ244
The Marx-Engels cyclopedia, Draper, Hal, CJ242
Marx, K., CJ242
Marxism, CJ244
Marxist local governments in Western Europe and Japan, CJ165
Mašek, Petr. *Příspěvky ke knihopisu,* AA98
Mason, Francis K. *A concise dictionary of military biography,* AJ13
Mason, Lauris. *Old master print references,* BE155
Mason, Oliver. *Bartholomew gazetteer of places in Britain,* CL33
Mason, Tim. *Atlas of Nazi Germany,* DC97
Mason, Valmari M. *An annotated bibliography of U.S. scholarship on the history of the family,* CC122
Mass media, CH209; *see also* **Radio and television**
 bibliography, AE15, BG102, CC197, CC258, CH196, CH198, CH199, CH200, CH201, CH202, CH203
 dictionaries, CH207
 directories, AE1, AE44
 encyclopedias, CH204, CH205

handbooks, CH210
Mass media, Hudson, Robert V., CH204
Mass media bibliography, Blum, Eleanor, CH196
Massachusetts Poverty Law Center. *An advocate's guide to surviving the SSI system*, CH267
Master index to subject encyclopedias, AC8
Masterplots II, BD97
Mata, F. X. *Diccionario de la zarzuela*, BH105
Mata, Maria Nena R. *Compilation of graduate theses, 1983–1984*, AH17
al-Maṭbūʿāt al-rasmīyah fī al-Mamlakah al-ʿArabīyah al-al-Saʿūdīyah, Maʿhad al-Idārah al-ʿĀmmah (Riyadh, Saudi Arabia). Markaz al-Wathāʾiq. Qism al-Maṭbūʿāt al-Rasmīyah, AG46
Matejíc, Mateja. *A comprehensive bibliography of Yugoslav literature in English, 1593–1980*, BD361
Matematicheskaĭa ėnt͡siklopedii͡a, EF7
Materials and strategies for the education of trainable mentally retarded learners, White, James P., CB41, CD3
Materials data sources, EJ13
Materials handbook, Brady, George S., EJ9
Materials science and engineering, EJ10
MATH, EF5, EJ54
Math equals, Perl, T., EF18
Mathematica Policy Research, Inc. *Digest of data on persons with disabilities*, CC112
Mathematical logic, EF2
Mathematical reviews, EF1, EF4, EF6
Mathematical statistics, EF3, EF8, EF9, EF12, EF17
Mathematics
  bibliography, EF6
  biography, EF18
  congresses and meetings, EF1
  databases, EF5, EF6
  dictionaries, EF13
  encyclopedias, EF7, EF10
  handbooks, EF14, EF15
  indexes, EF4
Mathematics abstracts, EF5
Matheson, Cyril. *Catalogue of the publications of Scottish historical and kindred clubs and societies*, DC140
Mathijsen, P. S. R. F. *A guide to European Community law*, CK120
MathSci, EF6
MathSci disc, EF6
Matson, Patricia. *Bibliography of criticism on English and French literary translations in Canada*, BD306
Matsushita, Hitoshi. *A checklist of published instrumental music by Japanese composers*, BH19
Mattera, Philip. *Inside U.S. business*, CH307
Mattes, Merrill J. *Platte River road narratives*, DB57
Matthews, Dorothy. *High interest easy reading*, CB36
Matthews, E. *A lexicon of Greek personal names*, AK50
Matthews, Elizabeth W. *The law library reference shelf*, CK9
Matthews, Geoffrey J. *Historical atlas of Canada*, DB89
—— *Ukraine, a historical atlas*, DC215
Matthews, John R. *The official World Wildlife Fund guide to endangered species of North America*, EC41
Matthews, Noel. *Guide to manuscripts and documents in the British Isles relating to Africa*, DC131
—— *A guide to Western manuscripts and documents in the British Isles relating to South and South East Asia*, DE4
Mattingly, David. *An atlas of Roman Britain*, DC128
The mature woman in America, Dolan, Eleanor F., CC39, CC256

Matzerath, Horst. *Modern urban history research in Europe, USA, and Japan*, CC160
Maunder, W. F. *Reviews of United Kingdom statistical sources*, CG54
Mauricio, Rufino. *Pacific Basin and Oceania*, DG1
Mauritania, DD43
Mauritius, AA158
Mauritius. Archives Department. "*Bibliography of Mauritius . . .*", AA158
Mauser, Wolfram. *Literaturpsychologie, 1945–1987*, BD7
Mawson, C. O. Sylvester. *Dictionary of foreign terms*, AD66
—— *The Harper dictionary of foreign terms*, AD66
Maxwell, Margaret. *Handbook for AACR2 1988 revision*, AB79
May, George S. *The automobile industry, 1896–1920*, CH136
—— *The automobile industry, 1920–1980*, CH136
Mayall, David. *The autobiography of the working class*, CH270
Mayer, Fanny Hagin. *The Yanagita Kunio guide to the Japanese folk tale*, BD381, CF36
Mayer, Ralph. *The artist's handbook of materials and techniques*, BE69
Mayerchak, Patrick M. *Scholar's guide to Washington D.C. for Southeast Asian studies*, DE46
Maynadies, Michel. *Bibliographie algérienne*, DD25
Mayrhofer, Manfred. *Etymologisches Wörterbuch des Altindoarischen*, AD157
—— *Kurzgefasstes etymologisches Wörterbuch des Altindischen*, AD157
Mays, James Luther. *Harper's Bible commentary*, BB64
Mazda, F. F. *Electronics engineer's reference book*, EJ48
Maze-Sencier, Geneviéve. *Dictionnaire des maréchaux de France*, AJ52
Mbaye, Saliou. *Guide des archives de l'Afrique occidentale française*, DD23
Mead Data Central, Inc. *LEXIS*, CK18
Means estimating handbook, EJ39
Mechanical engineering
  dictionaries, EJ78
  handbooks, EJ79, EJ80, EJ81, EJ83, EJ84
Mechanical engineers' handbook, EJ80
Meckler, Alan. *Oral history collections*, DB21
Meckler's bibliographies of battles and leaders, DB15
Medals *see* Coins, medals, currency
Medical books, libraries, and collectors, Thornton, John Leonard, EK17
Medical ethics, EK81
Medical information, Strickland-Hodge, Barry, EK4
Medical jurisprudence, CK65, EK87
Medical libraries, AB56, EK1
Medical Library Association. *Handbook of medical library practice*, AB56, EK1
Medical phrase index, Lorenzini, Jean A., EK49
Medical research centres, EK79
Medical sciences international who's who, EK79
Medical sociology, Bruhn, John G., CC6, EK7
Medical style and format, Huth, Edward J., EK35
Medical tests, EK69
Medical word finder, EK51
Medicine
  audiovisual materials
    databases, EK20
  bibliography, EK8, EK10, EK13, EK15, EK16, EK17, EK21, EK22
    audiovisual materials, EK23
    government publications, EK26
  bibliography of bibliography, EK9
  biography, CC208, EA80, EK76, EK77, EK79
    bibliography, EK78

  databases, EK30, EK31, EK32, EK33
  dictionaries, EC17, EK43, EK46, EK47, EK48, EK49, EK50, EK51, EK52, EK55, EK59, EK91
    foreign terms, EK57, EK58
  directories
    United States, EK64, EK65
      databases, EK63
  encyclopedias, EK36, EK41, EK42, EK90
  guides, EK2, EK4
  handbooks, EK67
  history
    bibliography, EK73, EK75
    surveys, EK74
  library catalogs
    databases, EK27
  periodicals
    databases, EK24
  style manuals, EK34, EK35
Medicine, literature & eponyms, Rodin, Alvin E., EK43
Medieval Christian literary imagery, Kaske, Robert Earl, BB81, BD3, DA46
Medieval drama, BD89
Medieval English drama, Berger, Sidney E., BD229
Medieval literature, BB81, BD3, BD17, DA46; *see also* **Romances, epics, etc.**
Medieval rhetoric, Murphy, James Jerome, BD145
MEDLINE, EK29, EK30, EK32, EK33
Mednikova, Ė. M. *Bol'shoĭ anglo-russkiĭ slovar'*, AD152
Meer, Willemina van der. *Gesamtverzeichnis des deutschsprachigen Schrifttums ausserhalb des Buchhandels (GVB), 1966–1980*, AA121
Meerhaeghe, Marcel Alfons Gilbert van. *International economic institutions*, CH15
Megalē Kypriakē enkyklopaideia, DC38
Mehra, Parshotam. *A dictionary of modern Indian history, 1707–1947*, DE62
Meier, August. *Black leaders of the nineteenth century*, CC207
Meier, Emil. *Familiennamenbuch der Schweiz = Répertoire des noms de famille suisses = Register of Swiss surnames*, AK45
Meier, Heinz K. *Switzerland*, DC191
Měier, M. S. *Novai͡a istorii͡a*, DA58
Meier, Matt S. *Mexican American biographies*, CC245
Meier, Regula A. *Switzerland*, DC191
Meinecke, Michael. *A bibliography of the architecture, arts, and crafts of Islam by Sir K.A.C. Creswell, C.B.E. Second supplement, Jan. 1972 to Dec. 1980 (with omissions from previous years)*, BE11
Meissner, Bruno. *Akkadisches Handwörterbuch*, AD73
—— *Reallexikon der Assyriologie, unter Mitwirkung zahlreicher Fachgelehrter*, DA36
Meissner, Günter. *Allgemeines Künstlerlexikon*, BE74
Melcher, Florian. *Disciunari rumantsch grischen*, AD149
Meldrum, Marcia. *Nobel laureates in medicine or physiology*, EK76
Melendez, Sarah E. *Bilingual education*, CB119
Melina, Lois Ruskai. *Adoption*, CC131
Mellman, Martin. *Accountants' handbook*, CH65
Melone, Albert P. *Bridges to knowledge in political science*, CJ2
Melting pot, Newman, Jacqueline M., EH36
Melton, J. Gordon. *Biographical dictionary of American cult and sect leaders*, BB34
—— *The encyclopedia of American religions*, BB30
Melzer, Annabelle. *Shakespeare on screen*, BD264
Members of Congress since 1789, CJ103
Memphis State University. *Women of color and Southern women*, CC289

Memphis State University. Center for Research on Women. *Women of color and Southern women*, CC290

Mendelian inheritance in man, McKusick, Victor A., EC67

Mendelsohn, Henry N. *A guide to information sources for social work and the human services*, CC26

Mendelson, Susan. *Social networks and mental health*, CC21

Mendenhall, Doris A. *The index of paintings sold in the British Isles during the nineteenth century*, BE61

Mendonça, Melanie. *Beazley addenda*, BE151

Mendoza-López, Margarita. *Teatro mexicano del siglo XX, 1900–1986*, BD345, BG22

Mene, Mene, Tekel, Ehrlich, Eugene, BB62

Menendez, Albert J. *The Catholic novel*, BD92
—— *Religion and the U.S. presidency*, CJ79
—— *School prayer and other religious issues in American public education*, CB35
—— *The subject is murder*, BD107

Menos, Dennis. *Arms control fact book*, CJ314

Mental health, CC23, CC91, CD27

Mental illness, CD29

Mental measurements yearbook, CD46, CD45

Mental retardation, CB41, CD3

Mercatante, Anthony S. *The Facts on File encyclopedia of world mythology and legend*, CF5

Mercer dictionary of the Bible, BB57

The Merck index, ED18, EK118

The Merck index online, ED19, EK119

Merck manual, EK72

The Merck manual of geriatrics, EK72

The Merck veterinary manual, EH28

Merker, Paul. *Reallexikon der deutschen Literaturgeschichte*, BD292

Merle, Gabriel. *Les mots nouveaux apparus depuis 1985*, AD100

Merriam, Sharan B. *Handbook of adult and continuing education*, CB125

Merryman, John H. *Law, ethics, and the visual arts*, BE109, CK88

Mersky, Roy M. *Fundamentals of legal research*, CK6
—— *Index to periodical articles related to law*, CK56

Messick, Frederic M. *Primary sources in European diplomacy, 1914–1945*, CJ9, DC5

Messina, James A. *The Harvard independent insider's guide to prep schools*, CB109

METADEX, EJ14

METADEX collection, EJ14

Metal arts, BF43, BF45, BF46

Metallurgical engineering *see* **Mining and metallurgical engineering**

Metals, EJ14, EJ86, EJ87

Metals abstracts, EJ14

Metals handbook, EJ12, EJ86, EJ87

Metaphor, BC4, BD146

Metaphor, Noppen, J. P. van, BC4, BD146
—— Shible, Warren, BC4, BD146

Metelka, Charles J. *Dictionary of hospitality, travel, and tourism*, BJ41

Meteorites, EE38

Meteorology, EE27

Meteorology source book, EA38

Metherell, David. *Scandinavian biographical archive*, AJ91

Methodist union catalog, pre-1976 imprints, Rowe, Kenneth E., BB110

Methodists, BB110

Metro insights, CG37

The metropolitan area fact book, CC210

Metropolitan Museum of Art (New York, N.Y.). Library. *Library catalog of the Metropolitan Museum of Art, New York*, BE26, BE27, BE28

Metropolitan opera annals, Seltsam, William, BH95

The Metropolitan Opera encyclopedia, BH100

Metropolitan Opera Guild. *Annals of the Metropolitan Opera Guild*, BH95
—— *The Metropolitan Opera encyclopedia*, BH100

Metropolitan Toronto Library. Canadian History Dept. *A bibliography of Canadiana*, DB83

Mette, Hans Joachim. *Lexikon des frühgriechischen Epos*, AD115

Metzeltin, Michael. *Lexikon der Romanistischen Linguistik*, BC36

Metzler Philosophen Lexikon, BA25

Meulen, Jacob ter. *Bibliography of the peace movement before 1899*, CJ297
—— *From Erasmus to Tolstoy*, CJ297

Meurs, Jos van. *Jungian literary criticism, 1920–1980*, BD6

Mével, Jean-Pierre. *Dictionnaire de l'argot*, AD98

Mexican American biographies, Meier, Matt S., CC245

Mexican Americans *see* **Spanish-speaking Americans**

Mexican Americans in urban society, Camarillo, Albert, CC235

Mexican autobiography, Woods, Richard Donovon, AJ81, BD346

Mexican literature, BD343, BD345, BG22

Mexico
  bibliography, AA159
  biography
    bibliography, AJ81, BD346
    contemporary, AJ80
  encyclopedias, DB125, DB127
  history
    bibliography, CC221, DB60, DB124, DB126, DB128
    manuscripts and archives, AB51
  statistics
    indexes, CG64

México, la cultura, el arte y la vida cotidiana, Flores Villela, Carlos Arturo, DB126

Meyer, George H. *Folk artists biographical index*, BF15

Meyer, George H., Jr. *Folk artists biographical index*, BF15

Meyer, Jack Allen. *An annotated bibliography of the Napoleonic era*, DC63

Meyer, Manfred. *Children and families watching television*, CH200

Meyer, Mary Keysor. *Meyer's directory of genealogical societies in the U.S.A. and Canada*, AK18

Meyer, Reinhart. *Bibliographia dramatica et dramaticorum*, BD295

Meyer, Robert S. *Peace organizations, past and present*, CJ310

Meyer, Ronald. *Nineteenth-century Russian literature in English*, BD354

Meyer, Rudolf. *Hebräisches und aramäisches Handwörterbuch über das Alte Testament*, AD117

Meyers, Robert A. *Encyclopedia of astronomy and astrophysics*, EB5
—— *Encyclopedia of physical science and technology*, EA33

Meyers, Thomas A. *The encyclopedia of technical market indicators*, CH221

Meyer's directory of genealogical societies in the U.S.A. and Canada, Meyer, Mary Keysor, AK18

Mezei, Kathy. *Bibliography of criticism on English and French literary translations in Canada*, BD306

Michael, Colette Verger. *Negritude*, CC199

Michaelis dicionário prático, AD146

Micheels-Cyrus, Madge. *Seeds of peace*, CJ307

Michel, Jean Pierre. *Dictionary of earth science, English-French, French-English = Dictionnaire des sciences de la terre, anglais-français, français-anglais*, EE13

Michel, Suzanne P. *Répertoire des ouvrages imprimés en langue italienne au XVIIe siècle conservés dans les bibliothèques de France*, AA149

Micro computer index, EJ56

Microbiology, EC12, EC21, EC22

Microbiology abstracts : algology, mycology and protozoology, EC7

Microbiology abstracts : industrial and applied microbiology, EC7

Microcomputer index, EJ56, EJ57

Microcomputers, BH26, EJ60, EJ66
  abstract journals, EJ56
  databases, EJ57
  dictionaries, EJ62

Microfiche concordance to Old English, AD63
—— Healey, Antonette, AD63
—— Venezky, Richard L., AD63

Microfilm resources for research, United States. National Archives and Records Administration, DB24
—— United States. National Archives and Records Service, DB24

Microforms and reproductions, AA29, AB110, DA5

Microforms for historians, Munro, D. J., DA5

Micrographics, Saffady, William, AB110

Micronesia, DG2

Micronesia 1944–1974, Marshall, Mac, DG2
—— Nason, James D., DG2

Micronesia, 1975–1987, Goetzfridt, Nicholas J., DG2

The Middle Ages, DA51

Middle East, DE14, DE15, DE22

The Middle East, DE21

Middle East, DE23

Middle East and Islam, DE13

The Middle East in conflict, DA55

Middle East Libraries Committee. *Union catalogue of Persian serials & newspapers in British libraries*, AE53

Middle East Microform Project (U.S.). *National union catalog of Middle Eastern microforms*, DE11

Middle East organizations in Washington, D.C, DE24

The Middle East political dictionary, Ziring, Lawrence, CJ199, DE20

Middle English dictionary, AD63, AD63, AD64

Middle English romance, Rice, Joanne A., BD208

Middleton, Haydn. *Atlas of modern world history*, DA63

Middlewestern states, DB54, DB56

Mieder, Wolfgang. *International proverb scholarship*, BD70
—— *The Prentice-Hall encyclopedia of world proverbs*, BD71

Migration, CC184

Mihailovich, Vasa D. *A comprehensive bibliography of Yugoslav literature in English, 1593–1980*, BD361
—— *First supplement to A comprehensive bibliography of Yugoslav literature in English, 1981–1985*, BD362

Miki, Kunihiro. *A concordance to Middle English metrical romances*, BD209

Milburn, G. *A critical dictionary of educational concepts*, CB66

Mildren, K. W. *Use of engineering literature*, EJ1

Milestones in science and technology, Mount, Ellis, EA73

Miletich, John J. *Airline safety*, CH189
—— *Work and alcohol abuse*, CC70

Milgate, Murray. *The new Palgrave*, CH8

Military and strategic policy, Beede, Benjamin R., CJ44

Military bases, CJ276, CJ277, CJ278

Military history
  bibliography, CJ268, DB8, DB15, DC16

by country
  Balkans
    bibliography, DC16
    Brazil, DB116
    Bulgaria, DC35
    France, DC62
    Gt. Brit., DC100
    United States, BE164, DB10
  encyclopedias, CJ253, DA19, DA21
  quotations, CJ263
Military history of the United States, DA55, CJ270
Military periodicals, Unsworth, Michael, CJ252
Military science
  bibliography, CJ44
    current, CJ250
  biography, AJ13
  dictionaries, CJ255, CJ256, CJ257, CJ259, CJ260, CJ261, CJ262
  encyclopedias, CJ283
Milke, Elizabeth. *Role portrayal and stereotyping on television*, CH201
Milkias, Paulos. *Ethiopia*, DD34
Milla Batres, Carlos. *Diccionario histórico y biográfico del Perú, siglos XV–XX*, DB131
Miller, A. Carolyn. *Refereed and nonrefereed economic journals*, CH4
Miller, Benjamin Frank. *Encyclopedia and dictionary of medicine, nursing, and allied health*, EK90
Miller, Casey. *The handbook of nonsexist writing*, AA57, CC311
Miller, Cynthia Pease. *A guide to research collections of former members of the United States House of Representatives, 1789–1987*, CJ93
Miller, David. *The Blackwell encyclopaedia of political thought*, CJ16
Miller, E. Willard. *Environmental hazards*, EJ33
Miller, Ellen S. *The price of admission*, CJ110
Miller, Eugene G. *Writers and philosophers*, BD51
Miller, Gerald. *Handbook of public administration*, CJ215
Miller, Herbert A. *Retirement benefit plans*, CH152
Miller, Jeanne. *Bibliography of the Summer Institute of Linguistics, Philippines, 1953–1984*, BC61
Miller, Joseph Calder. *Slavery*, CC200
Miller, Kenneth E. *Denmark*, DC43
Miller, Lynn. *Bibliography of women & literature*, BD152
Miller, Melanie Ann. *Birds*, EC53
Miller, R. H. *Handbook of literary research*, BD14
Miller, Randall M. *Dictionary of Afro-American slavery*, CC174
—— *Ethnic and racial images in American film and television*, CC171
Miller, Ruby M. *Environmental hazards*, EJ33
Miller, Sally M. *The ethnic press in the United States*, AE16
Miller, Stephen T. *Mystery, detective, and espionage fiction*, BD104
Miller, Timothy. *American communes, 1860–1960*, DB7
Miller, Warren E. *American national election studies data sourcebook, 1952–1986*, CJ111
Miller, Wayne Charles. *A comprehensive bibliography for the study of American minorities*, CC165
Million dollar directory, CH117
Mills, J. J. *Guide to current national bibliographies in the Third World*, AA75
Mills, Victoria A. *Women in LC's terms*, CC299
Mills, Watson E. *A bibliography of the periodical literature on the Acts of the Apostles, 1962–1984*, BB43
—— *Directory of departments and programs of religious studies in North America*, BB32

—— *Mercer dictionary of the Bible*, BB57
—— *Speaking in tongues*, BB83
Milner, Anthony Crothers. *South-East Asia*, BC60, BD382
Milner, Richard. *The encyclopedia of evolution*, EC11
Milner-Gulland, R. R. *Cultural atlas of Russia and the Soviet Union*, DC216
Milton, J., BD258, BD259
Mináč, Vladimír. *Slovenský biografický slovník*, AJ44
Minahan, Anne. *Encyclopedia of social work*, CC29
Mineral reference manual, Nickel, Ernest H., EE36
Mineralogy, EE35, EE36, EE37
Miniature painters, BE152
Miniatures, Foskett, Daphne, BE152
Mining and metallurgical engineering, EJ87
Minion, Robin. *20th century Canadian arctic expeditions*, DH3
—— *Nineteenth century expeditions in the Arctic and Canada*, DH3
Minnick, Roy. *The surveying handbook*, EJ25
Minion, Robin *see* Race and minority relations
Minorities in America, CC165
Minority organizations: a national directory, CC176
Minority-owned business firms, CH121, CH123
Minority Rights Group. *World directory of minorities*, CC179
Minton Ltd., BF23
Mintz, Lawrence E. *Humor in America*, CF30
Minutes, Presbyterian Church (U.S.A.). General Assembly, BB112
Mir, Mustansir. *Dictionary of Qur'ānic terms and concepts*, BB71
A mirror for the nation, Hanna, Archibald, BD175
Mischke, Charles R. *Standard handbook of machine design*, EJ82
Miska, John P. *Canadian studies on Hungarians, 1886–1986*, CC166, DC145
—— *Ethnic and native Canadian literature*, BD279
Miskin, Christine. *Directory of law libraries in the British Isles*, CK74
—— *Legal journals index*, CK57
Mission handbook, BB106
Missions, BB105, BB106
Mitchell, Brian. *Abstract of British historical statistics*, CG52, DC121
—— *British historical statistics*, CG52, DC121
—— *A guide to Irish parish registers*, AK38
—— *A new genealogical atlas of Ireland*, AK38, AK39
—— *Second abstract of British historical statistics*, CG52, DC121
Mitchell, Chip. *The St. James encyclopedia of mortgage & real estate finance*, CH354
Mitchell, Christopher. *International relations theory*, CJ7
Mitchell, Diana. *African nationalist leaders in Rhodesia who's who*, CJ208
—— *African nationalist leaders in Zimbabwe who's who 1980*, CJ208
Mitchell, James. *The Random House encyclopedia*, AC6
Mitchell, Jonathan. *The Cambridge atlas of the Middle East and North Africa*, DE26
Mitchell, Philip M. *Bibliography of modern Icelandic literature in translation*, BD300
Mitchell, Richard Scott. *Dictionary of rocks*, EE45
Mitchell, Robert Cameron. *Black Africa*, CG38
Mitchell, Sally. *Victorian Britain*, DC117
Mitchell, Solomon. *A pictorial guide to identifying Australian architecture*, BE130
Mitler, Louis. *Contemporary Turkish writers*, BD383
—— *Ottoman Turkish writers*, BD384

Mittellateinisches Wörterbuch bis zum ausgehenden 13. [i.e. dreizehnten] Jahrhundert, AD140
Mochedlover, Helene G. *Ottemiller's index to plays in collections*, BD86
Mock, David B. *A dictionary of obituaries of modern British radicals*, AJ62
Modern archives administration and records management, AB74
Modern atlas of African history, Freeman-Grenville, G. S. P., DD11
A modern dictionary of geography, Small, R. J., CL12
Modern drama scholarship and criticism, 1966–1980, Carpenter, Charles A., BD87, BG8
The modern encyclopedia of religions in Russia and the Soviet Union, Steeves, Paul D., DC208
The modern encyclopedia of Russian and Soviet history, DC208
Modern England, 1901–1984, Havighurst, Alfred F., DC106
Modern geography, CL9
Modern Hebrew-English dictionary, Zilkha, Avraham, AD120
Modern Humanities Research Association. *Anglo-Norman dictionary*, AD62
Modern Italian history, Coppa, Frank J., DC155
Modern Language Association of America. *Directory of master's programs in foreign languages, foreign literatures, and linguistics*, BD42, CB96
—— *MLA handbook for writers of research papers*, AH1
—— *The MLA style manual*, AA53
—— *Victorian periodicals*, AE43
Modern Language Association of America. Middle English Group. *A manual of the writings in Middle English, 1050–1500*, BD206
Modern nutrition in health and disease, EK99
Modern proverbs and proverbial sayings, Whiting, Bartlett Jere, BD72
Modern Spanish and Portuguese literatures, BD327
Modern urban history research in Europe, USA, and Japan, CC160
Modlin, Marilyn J. *Direct-line distances—international edition*, CL19
—— *Direct-line distances—United States edition*, CL20
Moed-Van Walraven, C. *Hebrew incunabula in public collections*, AA43
Moersh, Elizabeth Sue. *Index to the Annenberg Television Script Archive*, BG106
Moir, Lindsay. *Bibliography of the Blackfoot*, CC218
Moir, Martin. *A general guide to the India Office Records*, DE4, DE32
Mojzes, Paul. *Church and state in postwar eastern Europe*, BB76, DC12
Molecular biology, EC12, EC63
Molyneux, Philip. *Directory of European banking and financial associations*, CH242
Momeni, Jamshid A. *Homelessness in the United States*, CC119
—— *Housing and racial/ethnic minority status in the United States*, CC167
Monaco, AA160
Mondale, Clarence C. *Region and regionalism in the United States*, DB46
Le Monde, AF15
Monet, Ronald L. *Gubernatorial and presidential transitions*, CJ45
Money, CH212
Money for artists, Green, Laura R., BE54
Money to work, BE56
Monfrin, J. *Manuel bibliographique de la littérature française du Moyen Age de Robert Bossuat. Troisième supplément, 1960–1980*, BD310

Monglond, André. *La France révolutionnaire et impériale*, DC49
Mongolia, DE85
Monk, Jennifer. *The Cambridge illustrated dictionary of British heritage*, DC114
Monro, Kate M. *The secretary's handbook*, CH168
Montana Alliance for Progressive Policy. *Public opinion polling*, CJ233
Montenegro, Valerie J. *AAAS science book list, 1978–1986*, EA15
Montes de Oca N., Elvia. *Bibliografía histórica del Estado de México*, DB124
Montgomery, Michael. *Annotated bibliography of Southern American English*, BC23
The month-by-month atlas of World War II, DA78
Monthly catalog—U.S. Congressional serial set supplement, AG11
Monuments, BE164
Moody, David. *Scottish family history*, AK44
Moody, Marilyn K. *Using government publications*, AG5
Moody, T. W. *A new history of Ireland*, DC153
Moore, Alick. *A complete checklist of the birds of the world*, EC50
Moore, Burness E. *Glossary of psychoanalytic terms and concepts*, CD24
—— *Psychoanalytic terms and concepts*, CD24
Moore, D. M. *Flora of the British Isles*, EC32
Moore, Geoffrey Hoyt. *International economic indicators*, CH18
Moore, Jean. *Roads to recovery*, CC75
Moore, Melita H. *International economic indicators*, CH18
Moore, Patrick. *The atlas of the universe*, EB16
—— *Grand atlas de l'astronomie*, EB15
—— *The international encyclopedia of astronomy*, EB6
—— *The new atlas of the universe*, EB16
Moore, Rachelle. *Women authors of modern Hispanic South America*, BD331
Moore, Robert J. *A bibliography of medical and biomedical biography*, EK78
Moran, Michael G. *Research in composition and rhetoric*, BD147
Morby, John E. *Dynasties of the world*, AK2, CJ146
More confederate imprints, Harwell, Richard Barksdale, DB30
More notes from a different drummer, Basking, Barbara, CC103
—— Harris, Karen, CC103
More words of Wall Street, CH231
Moreau, Brigitte. *Inventaire chronologique des éditions parisiennes du XVIe siècle*, AA111
Morehead, Joe. *Introduction to United States public documents*, AG6, CJ95
Moreno, Federico B. *Philippine law dictionary*, CK68
Morgan, Ann Lee. *Contemporary architects*, BE132
Morgan, Bryan. *Keyguide to information sources in agricultural engineering*, EH2
Morgan, H. J. *Canadian men and women of the time*, AJ39
Morgan, Jean. *Consumer sourcebook*, CH176
Moritz, A. F. *The Oxford illustrated literary guide to Canada*, BD280
Moritz, Theresa Anne. *The Oxford illustrated literary guide to Canada*, BD280
Morley, Sheridan. *The great stage stars*, BG38
Morocco, AA161, AH14, DD44
Morocco. *Bibliographie nationale*, AA161, AA161
Moroney, Sean. *Africa*, DD4
Morris, Helen. *The reader's catalog*, AA61
Morris, Leslie R. *Interlibrary loan policies directory*, AB100
Morris, Mary. *Morris dictionary of word and phrase origins*, AD17

Morris, Peter. *Biographical dictionary of French political leaders since 1870*, CJ171
Morris, R. J. *Atlas of industrializing Britain 1780–1914*, DC126
Morris, William. *Morris dictionary of word and phrase origins*, AD17
Morris dictionary of word and phrase origins, Morris, William, AD17
Morrison, Donald George. *Black Africa*, CG38
Morrison, John J. *Short-title catalogue of books printed in England, Scotland, Ireland, Wales, and British America, and of English books printed in other countries, 1641–1700*, AA131
Morrison, Paul G. *Index of printers, publishers, and booksellers*, AA130
Morrow, Baker H. *A dictionary of landscape architecture*, BE144
Morton, F. *Botswana*, DD5
Morton, Leslie T. *A bibliography of medical and biomedical biography*, EK78
Mosby's medical and nursing dictionary, EK91
Mosby's medical, nursing, and allied health dictionary, EK91
Moseley, Charles J. *The official World Wildlife Fund guide to endangered species of North America*, EC50
Moseley, William W. *Spanish literature, 1500–1700*, BD324
Mosen, Norah D. *Theses on the history of New Zealand. Supplement, 1968–1982*, DF9
Moser, Charles A. *The Cambridge history of Russian literature*, BD357
Mossman, Jennifer. *Encyclopedia of geographic information sources. U.S. volume*, CL3
—— *Pseudonyms and nicknames dictionary*, AA32
Mostyn, Trevor. *The Cambridge encyclopedia of the Middle East and North Africa*, DE19
Le mot juste, AD66
The motion picture guide, Nash, Jay Robert, BG78
Motion picture series and sequels, Drew, Bernard A., BG69, BG79
Motion pictures; *see also* **Performing arts**
bibliography, BG51, BG52, BG53, BG54, BG55, BG56
   adaptations, BG59, BG60, BG61, BG62
   bibliography of bibliography, BG57
biography, BG100, BG101
by country or region
   Africa, BG52
catalogs and filmography, BG51, BG66, BG67, BG68, BG69, BG70, BG71, BG72, BG73, BG74, BG75, BG76, BG77, BG78, BG79, BG80, BG81, BG82, CC265
dictionaries, BG85, BG88, BG89
   terms, BG95, BG96, BG97
directories, BG98, BG99
encyclopedias, BG86, BG87, BG92, BG93, BG94
guides, BG50
handbooks, BG90
indexes, BG14
   reviews and criticism, BG65
library resources, BG83, BG84
periodicals, BG58
reviews and criticism, BG64
   indexes, BG63
surveys, BG91
Motion pictures from the Library of Congress paper print collection, 1894–1912, BG75
Motive der Weltliteratur, Frenzel, Elisabeth, BD27
The Motown fact book, BH123
Les mots nouveaux apparus depuis 1985, AD100
Mottoes, BD62
Mottu, Susan. *Encyclopedia of physical sciences and engineering information sources*, EA2
Moulton, Joy Wade. *Genealogical resources in English repositories*, AK34
Mount, Ellis. *Milestones in science and technology*, EA73

—— *University science and engineering libraries*, AB60
Mountfort, Guy. *Rare birds of the world*, EC54
Moutoussamy-Ashe, Jeanne. *Viewfinders: black women photographers*, BF64
Movie musicals on record, Lynch, Richard Chigley, BH146
Movies made for television, Marill, Alvin H., BG110
Moys, Elizabeth M. *Manual of law librarianship*, AB58, CK8
Mozambique, DD45
Mozambique, Darch, Colin, DD45
Mrozek, Donald J. *A guide to the sources of United States military history: Supplement II*, DB10
Mudabbirī, Maḥmūd. *Farhang-i kitābhā-yi Fārsī*, AA142
Müller, Bodo. *Diccionario del español medieval*, AD168
Müller, G. H. *[Omega]—bibliography of mathematical logic*, EF2
Müller, Georg P. *Comparative world data*, CG15
Müller, Gerhard. *Theologische Realenzyklopädie*, BB91
Mueller, James R. *The New Testament apocrypha and pseudepigrapha*, BB42
Mueller, John E. *Trends in public opinion*, CJ234
Müller, Karl. *Lexikon missionstheologischer Grundbegriffe*, BB105
Müller, Meike. *China nach Mao*, DE54
Müller, Werner. *Children and families watching television*, CH200
al-Mughni al-akbar, Karmī, Ḥasan Saʿīd, AD70
Muʿjam al-lughah al-ʿArabīyah al-Miṣrīyah, AD69
Mullaney, Marie Marmo. *American governors and gubernatorial elections, 1979–1987*, CJ133
—— *Biographical directory of the governors of the United States, 1983–1988*, AJ27
Mulley, Marilyn. *Walford's guide to reference material*, AA67, EA6
Mulligan, William H. *A historical dictionary of American industrial language*, CH291
Mullin, Donald C. *Victorian plays*, BG33
Mullin, Edward. *Texts and calendars: an analytical guide to serial publications*, DC140
Mulliner, K. *Malaysian studies*, DE84
Mullins, Carolyn J. *A guide to writing and publishing in the social and behavioral sciences*, CA23
Mullins, June B. *Accept me as I am*, CC103
The multi-language bibliography of Jewish law, Rakover, Naḥum, CK42
Multicultural education abstracts, CB57
Multilingual thesaurus of geosciences, EE15
Multinational enterprise, CH95
Mumford, Laura Stempel. *Women's issues*, CC261
Munasinghe, V. R. N. *Carbohydrates*, ED36
Munch-Petersen, Erland. *Guide to Nordic bibliography*, AA181, DC181
Mundo Lo, Sara de. *Index to Spanish American collective biography*, AJ78
Mundt, R. J. *Ivory Coast*, DD5
Munford, William Arthur. *Who was who in British librarianship, 1800–1985*, AB41
Munk Olsen, B. *L'étude des auteurs classiques latins aux XIe et XIIe siècles*, BD371
Munn, Glenn G. *Encyclopedia of banking & finance*, CH224
Munro, D. J. *Microforms for historians*, DA5
Munro, David,. *Chambers world gazetteer*, CL26
—— *A world record of major conflict areas*, CJ35
Munter, Robert. *A dictionary of the print trade in Ireland, 1550–1775*, AA51
Murdock, Eugene Converse. *The Civil War in the North*, DB29

Murdock, George Peter. *Atlas of world cultures*, CE24
—— *Ethnographic bibliography of North America*, CC217
Murguia, Edward. *Ethnicity and aging*, CC42
Murin, William F. *Delivering government services*, CJ220
Murith, Jean. *Dictionnaire des abréviations & acronymes scientifiques, techniques, économiques = Dictionary of scientific, technical & economic abbreviations & acronyms*, EA45
Murphy, James Jerome. *Medieval rhetoric*, BD145
Murphy, Roland Edmund. *The new Jerome biblical commentary*, BB67
Murray, A. *Botswana*, DD5
Murray, James. *New English dictionary on historical principles*, AD6
Murray, Sterling E. *Anthologies of music*, BH37
Murray, Tracy. *The handbook of international business*, CH130
—— *Handbook of international management*, CH131
Murry, Velma McBride. *Black adolescence*, CC79
Musacchio, Humberto. *Diccionario enciclopédico de México*, DB127
The museum, BE10
Museum of American Folk Art. *Bibliography of American folk art for the year [. . .]*, BF8
—— *Folk artists biographical index*, BF15
—— *Museum of American Folk Art encyclopedia of twentieth-century American folk art and artists*, BF17
Museum of American Folk Art encyclopedia of twentieth-century American folk art and artists, Rosenak, Chuck, BF17
The Museum of Modern Art artists scrapbooks microform, BE84
Museum of Modern Art (New York, N.Y.). *The film catalog*, BG77
—— *The film index*, BG56
The Museum of Science and Industry basic list of children's science books, EA14
The Museum of Science and Industry basic list of children's science books, 1973–1984, Richter, Bernice, EA13
Museum of Science and Industry (Chicago, Ill.). *The Museum of Science and Industry basic list of children's science books*, EA14
—— *The Museum of Science and Industry basic list of children's science books, 1973–1984*, EA13
Museums, BE47, BE53; *see also* **Art museums; Exhibitions**
bibliography, BE10
directories, BE48, BE49, BE50, CC213, DB69
guides to research, BE3
Music; *see also* **Electronic music**
bibliography, BH5, BH7, BH8, BH12, BH13, BH15, BH16, BH17, BH18, BH19, BH20, BH21, BH22, BH23, BH24, BH25, BH27
music, manuscript and published, BH34, BH35, BH36, BH37, BH38, BH69
biography, BH50, BH51, BH76, BH77, BH81, BH82, BH83, BH84, BH85, BH86, BH92, BH109
by country or region
Australia, BH40
Brazil, BH5
France, BH21, BH69
Japan, BH19, BH24
New Zealand, BH15
Poland, BH23
Spain, BH105
chronologies, BH73
databases, BH43, BH45
dictionaries, BH50, BH51, BH60, BH61, BH62, BH72
directories, BH64, BH65
discography, BH156

dissertations, BH28
encyclopedias, BH47, BH48, BH49, BH50, BH51, BH52, BH54, BH55, BH56, BH57
fact books and compendiums, BH59
guides, BH1, BH2, BH4, BH11
handbooks, BH72
music business, BH71
history, BH74
indexes and abstracts, BH37, BH40, BH41, BH42, BH44
periodicals, BG48, BH29, BH30, BH31, BH32, BH33
quotations, BH63
Music, Brockman, William S., BH1
Music analyses, Diamond, Harold J., BH41
Music and dance periodicals, Robinson, Doris, BG48, BH33
Music and the personal computer, Waters, William J., BH26
Music business, BH72
Music business handbook & career guide, Baskerville, David, BH68
Music education, BH3, BH66
Music in American higher education, Brookhart, Edward, BH7
Music in motion pictures, BG1, BH145, BH146, BH147
Music-in-print series, BH38
Music index, BH43
Music, Jewish, BH16
Music librarianship, Bryant, E. T., AB54
Music libraries, AB54
Music library, BH157
Music literature international, BH45
Music printing and publishing, BH53
Music publishers, BH70
Music publishing in the British Isles, Humphries, Charles, BH70
—— Smith, William C., BH70
Music reference and research materials, Duckles, Vincent H., BH11
Music theory from Zarlino to Schenker, Damschroder, David, BH9
La musica, BH50, BH51
The musical, Wildbihler, Hubert, BH108
Musical instruments, BH151, BH152, BH153, BH154, BH155
Musical settings of American poetry, Hovland, Michael A., BH110
Musical terms, symbols, and theory, Thomsett, Michael C., BH62
Musical theater, BH98, BH104, BH105, BH106, BH107, BH108
discography, BG1, BH145
encyclopedias, BH58
The musical woman, BH67
Die Musik in Geschichte und Gegenwart, BH54
Musik-lexikon, Riemann, Hugo, BH48
Musmann, Klaus. *Diffusion of innovations*, CA6
Musto, Frederick W. *State legislatures*, CJ121
Musto, Ronald G. *The Catholic peace tradition*, BB117, CJ298
—— *The peace tradition in the Catholic Church*, BB117, CJ298
Mutual funds, CH246, CH248
Mužoji Lietuviškoj i Tarybinė enciklopedija, DC163
Myers, Allen C. *The Eerdmans Bible dictionary*, BB46
Myers, Bernard Samuel. *Encyclopedia of world art*, BE35
Myers, Jack Elliott. *Longman dictionary and handbook of poetry*, BD134
Myers, Kurtz. *Index to record reviews, 1984–1987*, BH161
Myers, Robert A. *Dominica*, DB147
—— *Nigeria*, DD48
Mystery, detective, and espionage fiction, Cook, Michael L., BD104
Mystery fiction *see* **Detective and mystery fiction**
Mythical and fabulous creatures, CF6

Mythology
by country or region
Egypt, CF9
Greek and Roman, CF10, CF11, CF12
Irish, CF13, CF14
Oceanic, CF15
Scandinavia, CF16
Slavic, CF17
dictionaries, CF1, CF3, CF5, CF7, CF8
encyclopedias, BB29, CD53, CF2, CF4, CF6
NCJRS document retrieval index, CK99
NTIS bibliographic database, EA28
Nagao, Philip M. *Japanese local histories in the Library of Congress*, DE77
Nagar, Murari Lal. *TULIP*, AE49
Nagar, Sarla Devi. *TULIP*, AE49
Nagel, Kathleen Carter. *Textbooks in school and society*, CB42
Nagel, Stuart S. *Basic literature in policy studies*, CJ10
Nairn, Bede. *Australian dictionary of biography*, AJ33
Nakamura, Joyce. *Children's authors and illustrators*, BD78
—— *Writers for young adults*, BD78
Names
geographical *see* **Geographical names and terms**
Names
personal, BD50, DB19
German, AK49
Greek, AK50
Names & nicknames of places & things, CL34
Namibia, DD46
Namibia bibliographies, Scheven, Yvette, DD46
Napoleon, DC64, DC65, DC66
Napoleonic military history, Horward, Donald D., DC62
The Napoleonic source book, Haythornthwaite, Philip J., DC65
Nappo, Tommaso. *Archivio biografico italiano*, AJ74
Narodna biblioteka (Serbia). *Srpska bibliografija*, AA204
Narodna in univerzitetna knjižnica v Ljubljani. *Slovenska bibliografija. Knjige*, AA205
Národní knihovna v Praze. *Bibliografický katalog ČSSR. České knihy*, AA99
Narratology, A dictionary of, BD40
Nash, Jay Robert. *Encyclopedia of world crime*, CK101
—— *The motion picture guide*, BG78
Nasjonalbibliografiske data 1962–1990, AA167
Nason, James D. *Micronesia 1944–1974*, DG2
Nasrallah, Wahib. *United States corporation histories*, CH141
Nasri, William Z. *Encyclopedia of library and information science*, AB12
National Academy of Sciences (U.S.). *Biographical memoirs*, EA77
National Agricultural Library catalog, EH5
National Archives of Canada. Manuscript Division. *Checklist of parish registers, 1986 = Répertoire de registres paroissiaux, 1986*, AK20
National Art Library (Great Britain). *The country house described*, BE120
National Association of Broadcasters. *Broadcast research definitions*, CH207
National Association of Elementary School Principals (U.S.). *The education almanac*, CB123
National Association of School Psychologists. *Handbook of certification and licensure requirements for school psychologists*, CB133
National Association of Social Workers. *Encyclopedia of social work*, CC29
—— *Face of the nation, 1987*, CC30
The national atlas of Canada, Canada. Energy, Mines and Resources Canada, CL63

National atlas of Ethiopia, Ethiopian Mapping Agency. Geography Division, CL64

National Audubon Society. *Audubon wildlife report*, EC26

—— *A field guide to hawks, North America*, EC47

National bibliographic indexes of the Socialist countries, AA77

National business telephone directory, CH120

National cemeteries, BE164

National Center for Research in Vocational Education (U.S.). *Resources in vocational education*, CB12

National Conference of State Historic Preservation Officers. *National register of historic places, 1966–1988*, BE128

National continuing care directory, CC58

National Council for Research on Women (U.S.). *A women's thesaurus*, CC300

National Council of Teachers of English. Committee to Revise High Interest-Easy Reading. *High interest easy reading*, CB36

National Council on Family Relations. *Family resources database*, CC127

National Council on Measurement in Education. *Standards for educational and psychological testing*, CB120, CD38

National Council on Public History (U.S.). *Directory of historical consultants*, DB67

National Council on the Aging. *Abstracts in social gerontology*, CC49

National criminal justice document retrieval index, CK99

National Diet Library (Japan). *J-BISC*, AA151

The national directory of arts & education support by business corporations, CA38

National directory of black law firms, CK81

National directory of corporate charity, Sternberg, Sam, CA41

National directory of corporate giving, CA32, CA41, CA39

National directory of corporate public affairs, CH71, CJ65

National directory of drug abuse and alcoholism treatment and prevention programs, CC76, EK125

National directory of education libraries and collections, Christo, Doris H., CB88

National directory of educational programs in gerontology, CC59

The national directory of exemplary programs in developmental education, Spann, Milton G., CB116

National directory of Latin Americanists, DB106

The national directory of magazines, AE25

National directory of minority and women-owned business firms, CH121, CH123

National directory of minority-owned business firms, CH121

National directory of newsletters and reporting services, AF2

National directory of nonprofit organizations, CH122

National directory of retirement facilities, CC60

National directory of women-owned business firms, CH123

National drug code directory, EK122

National Education Association—Research. *Rankings of the states*, CB151

National Film, Television and Sound Archives (Canada). *Canadian feature film index, 1913–1985 = Index des films canadiens de long métrage, 1913–1985*, BG82

National Film Theatre (London, England). *A guide to world cinema*, BG72

National Fire Protection Association. *Fire protection handbook*, EJ40

The national gazetteer of the United States of America, CL30, CL31

National Geographic atlas of the world, National Geographic Society (U.S.), CL54

National Geographic index, 1888–1988, CL8

National Geographic Society (U.S.). *Historical atlas of the United States*, DB79

—— *National Geographic atlas of the world*, CL54, CL54

—— *National Geographic index, 1888–1988*, CL8

The national guide to educational credit for training programs, CB114

National guide to funding in aging, Weiss, David M., CC67

National health directory, EK65

National Institute of Handicapped Research (U.S.). *Digest of data on persons with disabilities*, CC112

—— *Directory of national information sources on handicapping conditions and related services*, CC107

National Institute on Alcohol Abuse and Alcoholism (U.S.). *National directory of drug abuse and alcoholism treatment and prevention programs*, CC76, EK125

National Institutes of Health (U.S.). *Guide for the care and use of laboratory animals*, EC58

National Jewish Resource Center (U.S.). *The Holocaust*, DA86

The national job bank, 1991, CH340

National League for Nursing. *Directory of educational software for nursing*, EK88

National legal bibliography, CK19, CK24, CK25, CK27

National Library of Australia. *Australian government publications*, AG29

—— *Australian national bibliography, 1901–1950*, AA87

National Library of Canada. *Canadian translations = Traductions canadiennes*, AA30

—— *Canadiana 1867–1900, monographs*, AA93

—— *Checklist of indexes to Canadian newspapers = Liste de contrôle des index de journaux canadiens*, AF14

—— *Interlibrary loan directory*, AB99

National Library of Jamaica. *Jamaican national bibliography*, AA150

National Library of Medicine audiovisuals catalog, EK20, EK21

National Library of Medicine current catalog, EK27

National Library of Medicine (U.S.). *AIDS bibliography*, EK28

—— *A catalogue of seventeenth century printed books in the National Library of Medicine*, EK13

—— *Current bibliographies in medicine*, EK9

—— *National Library of Medicine audiovisuals catalog*, EK23

National Library of Wales. *Cofrestri plwyf Cymru = Parish registers of Wales*, AK48

—— *Libri Walliae*, AA202

National Museum of American Art (U.S.). *The National Museum of American Art's index to American art exhibition catalogues*, BE67

The National Museum of American Art's index to American art exhibition catalogues, Yarnall, James L., BE67

National Opinion Research Center. *An American profile*, CJ237

National Organization on Legal Problems of Education. *The yearbook of education law*, CB154

National parks *see* **Parks and protected areas**

National party conventions, 1831–1984, CJ117

National Reference Institute (U.S.). *Who's who in American education*, CB145

National Referral Center (U.S.). *Information resources in the arts*, BE57

National register of historic places, DB71

National register of historic places, 1966–1988, BE128

National Research Council of Canada. *Union list of scientific serials in Canadian libraries*, EA20

National Research Council (U.S.). Committee on Diet and Health. *Diet and health*, EK102

National School Boards Association. *Survey of public education in the nation's urban school districts*, CB152

National Science Library (Canada). *Union list of scientific serials in Canadian libraries*, EA20

National security, CA40, CJ44, CJ69

National Standards Association (U.S.). *Worldwide government directory, with international organizations*, CJ32, CK83

National Technical Institute for the Deaf. *A deafness collection*, CC104

National Trust for Historic Preservation in the United States. *All about old buildings*, BE129

—— *Landmark yellow pages*, BE127

The National Trust guide, Greeves, Lydia, BE126

National Trust handbook for members and visitors, BE126

National union catalog. Books, AA24

National union catalog of manuscript collections—indexes, DB19

National union catalog of Middle Eastern microforms, Khoury, Fawzi, DE11

National Wildlife Federation. *A field guide to hawks, North America*, EC47

Nationalbibliographien Schwarzafrikas, Boy, Joachim, AA71

Nationalism, CC196, CJ11

Native American bibliography series, CC218

Native American literature, BD196, BD197

Native American women, Green, Rayna, CC282

Native American youth and alcohol, Lobb, Michael L., CC69

Native Americans
  atlases, CC232, CC233, CC234
  bibliography, CC69, CC215, CC216, CC217, CC218, CC219, CC220, CC225, CC282
  biography, CC231
  directories, CC228
  encyclopedias, CC226, CC227, DB66
  handbooks, CC230
  library resources, CC224
  periodicals, CC223
  reservations, CC229

Natkiel, Richard. *Atlas of American history*, DB77

—— *Atlas of maritime history*, DA28

—— *World atlas of elections*, CJ43

Natural history, EC24, EC25, EC26

The natural sciences and American scientists in the revolutionary era, Harkanyi, Katalin, EA69

Naturalized birds of the world, Lever, Christopher, EC52

Naturalized mammals of the world, Lever, Christopher, EC59

Nault, Clifford A. *Annals of American literature, 1602–1983*, BD165

Nauman, Ann K. *A biographical handbook of education*, CB144

Nauta, Paul. *International guide to library and information science education*, AB19

Navabpour, Reza. *Iran*, DE69

The Naval Institute guide to combat fleets of the world, CJ265

Naval science, CJ256

Naval technical dictionary, CJ256

Naval terms dictionary, Noel, John Vavasour, CJ272

Naval warfare, CJ264, DA71

Navalani, K. *Current Indian periodicals in English*, AE50

Navia, Luis E. *Pythagoras*, BA28

—— *Socrates*, BA29

Navies, CJ265
  dictionaries, CJ274

Nawabi, Y. M. *A bibliography of Iran*, DE70

Nayler, G. H. F. *Dictionary of mechanical engineering*, EJ78

Naylor, Colin. *Contemporary architects*, BE132

—— *Contemporary artists*, BE78
—— *Contemporary designers*, BF14
—— *Contemporary photographers*, BF62
Naylor, Gillian. *The encyclopedia of arts and crafts*, BF1
Nazism, resistance & Holocaust in World War II, Laska, Vera, DA87
Neagles, James C. *Confederate research sources*, AK6, DB32
—— *The Library of Congress*, AK7, DB42
Neagles, Mark C. *The Library of Congress*, AK7, DB42
Neaman, Judith S. *Kind words*, AD47
Near and Middle East
   atlases, DE26
   bibliography, DE8, DE12
   biography, CJ200
   directories, DE23, DE24
   encyclopedias, DE21
   history
      atlases, DE27
      bibliography, DE10, DE11, DE13
      encyclopedias, DE19
   politics and government, CJ199, DE20
Near-death experiences, Basford, Terry K., CC93
The Near East national union list, AA25
Nederlands Geologisch Mijnbouwkundig Genootschap. *Geological nomenclature*, EE16
Nederlands Instituut voor het Nabije Oosten. *Annual Egyptological bibliography. Late reviews AEB 1947–1984*, DD30
Neft, David S. *The sports encyclopedia*, BJ24
Negritude, Michael, Colette Verger, CC199
Negwer, Martin. *Organic-chemical drugs and their synonyms*, EK112
Neil, William. *Harper's Bible commentary*, BB64
Nelson, Carolyn. *British newspapers and periodicals, 1641–1700*, AA131, AE41
—— *Short-title catalogue of books printed in England, Scotland, Ireland, Wales, and British America, and of English books printed in other countries, 1641–1700*, AA131
Nelson, Michael. *Congressional Quarterly's guide to the presidency*, CJ73
—— *Historic documents on the presidency : 1776–1989*, CJ87
Nelson, Randy F. *The martial arts*, BJ31
Nelson's directory of investment managers, CH247
Nepal, AA162, DE86
Nepal, Whelpton, John, DE86
Nepal Research Centre. *Nepalese national bibliography for [year]*, AA162
Nepalese national bibliography for [year], AA162
Neri, Rita E. *U.S./Japan foreign trade*, CH40
Netherlands
   bibliography, DC166
      17th–19th centuries, AA163
   biography, AJ82
   history
      bibliography, DC165
The Netherlands, King, Peter, DC165
The Netherlands, a selective bibliography of reference works, Krewson, Margrit B., DC166
The Netherlands and Northern Belgium, a selective bibliography of reference works, Krewson, Margrit B., DC166
Neu, John. *Isis cumulative bibliography 1976–1985*, EA70
Der neue Brockhaus, AC12
Neue deutsche Biographie, AJ59
Neue Forschungen zum Ersten Weltkrieg, DA68
Neue österreichische Biographie ab 1815, AJ36
Neuerscheinunger Sofortdienst (CIP), AA123
Neufeldt, Harvey G. *Education of the black adult in the United States*, CB34
Neufeldt, Victoria. *Webster's New World dictionary of American English*, AD5

Neumann, Renate. *Bibliographie zur Comic-Sekundärliteratur*, CF24
Neurology, EK40
Neuropsychology, EK54
Neurosciences abstracts, EC7
The new A to Z of women's health, Ammer, Christine, CC291, EK37
The New American Bible. Revised New Testament, BB37
The new American immigration, Cordasco, Francesco, CC163
New and comprehensive gazetteer of England and Wales, Bell, James, AK29
The new Arthurian encyclopedia, BD138
The new atlas of African history, Freeman-Grenville, G. S. P., DD11
The new atlas of the universe, EB15
—— Moore, Patrick, EB16
The new book of world rankings, Kurian, George Thomas, CG19
New books on women and feminism, CC269
New Cambridge bibliography of English literature, AE73
The new Cambridge history of India, DE64
The new comprehensive American rhyming dictionary, Young, Sue, AD39
New day/New Deal, Kyvig, David E., DB39
New Deal, DB38, DB39
A new dictionary of American slang, Chapman, Robert L., AD40
A new dictionary of liturgy and worship, Davies, J. G., BB89
New dictionary of theology, BB88
The new dictionary of theology, BB118
New dictionary of Arthurian encyclopedia... *New England regional catalog*, DB24
New England states, DB50
New English Bible, BB38
New English dictionary on historical principles, Murray, James, AD6
The new Europe 1992, Rosenberg, Jerry Martin, CK126
A new genealogical atlas of Ireland, Mitchell, Brian, AK38, AK39
The new Grove dictionary of American music, BH93, BH55
The new Grove dictionary of jazz, BH119
The new Grove dictionary of music and musicians, BH55, BH57, BH88
New guide to government publications, Newsome, Walter L., AG7
New Guinea *see* **Papua New Guinea**
A New Guinea bibliography, Butler, Alan, AA169, DG11
The new Harvard dictionary of music, BH93, BH56
A new history of French literature, BD314
A new history of Ireland, DC153
New ICC world directory of chambers of commerce = Nouvel annuaire mondial CCI des chambres de commerce, CH106
The new international atlas = Der neue internationale Atlas = El nuevo atlas internacional = Le nouvel atlas international = O nôvo atlas internacional, Rand McNally and Company, CL56
New international dictionary of acronyms in library and information science and related fields, Sawoniak, Henryk, AB17
A new introduction to bibliography, Gaskell, Philip, ED4
The new Jerome biblical commentary, BB67
The new Kobbé's complete opera book, BH106
New literary history international bibliography of literary theory and criticism, Cohen, Ralph, BD8
New Malaysian who's who, AJ79
The new Moulton's library of literary criticism, BD217
New Oxford history of music, BH74
The new Palgrave, CH8
New products, CH289
New pseudonyms and nicknames, AA32

New religious movements in the United States and Canada, Choquette, Diane, BB2
New serial titles, AE72
The new state of the world atlas, Kidron, Michael, CL52
The new Steinerbooks dictionary of the paranormal, Riland, George, CD54
The New Testament apocrypha and pseudepigrapha, Charlesworth, James H., BB42
New trade names, CH294, CH295, CH296, CH297, CH298
The new Westminster dictionary of liturgy and worship, BB89
New York Public Library. *The artists file*, BE84
—— *Bibliographic guide to microform publications*, AA29
—— *The New York Public Library book of chronologies*, DA25
—— *The New York Public Library desk reference*, AC20
The New York Public Library book of chronologies, Wetterau, Bruce, DA25
The New York Public Library desk reference, AC20
New York Public Library. Research Libraries. *Dictionary catalog of the Research Libraries*, AA27
New York times, AF12, AJ7
New York times [index], AF13
New York times obituary index (Westport, Conn.), AJ7
New Zealand
   bibliography, AA164, DF7, DF9
   chronology, DF11
   encyclopedias, DF10
   foreign relations, DF8
   history
      guides, DF6
   library resources, DF1
The New Zealand book of events, DF11
New Zealand Council for Educational Research. *A directory of philanthropic trusts in New Zealand*, CA26
New Zealand Film Archive. *Maori and Pacific films from New Zealand 1901–1984*, DG5
New Zealand foreign policy, 1945–1985, DF8
New Zealand information sources, AA64
New Zealand national bibliography to the year 1960, Bagnall, Austin Graham, AA164, DF7
Newby, James Edward. *Black authors*, BD188
Newell, James E. *The St. James encyclopedia of mortgage & real estate finance*, CH354
Newman, Edgar Leon. *Historical dictionary of France from the 1815 restoration to the Second Empire*, DC74
Newman, H. Morton. *Verbis non factis*, CJ107
Newman, Harold. *An illustrated dictionary of jewelry*, BF44
—— *An illustrated dictionary of silverware*, BF44
Newman, Jacqueline M. *Melting pot*, EH36
Newman, John. *Vietnam War literature*, BD158
Newman, P. R. *Atlas of the English civil war*, DC127
Newman, Peter K. *The new Palgrave*, CH8
Newman, Roxana Ma. *An English-Hausa dictionary*, AD116
Newnham, Jeffrey. *The dictionary of world politics*, CJ18
News media and public policy, McKerns, Joseph P., CH199
Newsletters, AF2, AF3, CH215, CH217
Newsletters directory, AF2
Newsletters in print, AF2
Newsmakers, AJ17
Newsome, Walter L. *New guide to government publications*, AG7
Newspaper abstracts ondisc, AF13
The newspaper press in Britain, Linton, David, AF9

Newspapers
    bibliography, AE4
        Canada, AE23, AF4
        China, AE30, AF6
        Gt. Brit., AE41, AF7, AF9
        Indonesia, AF11
        Ireland, AE54
        Jewish, AE3, AE5
        Nigeria, AE59
        Persian, AE53
        Scotland, AE67
        United States, AE23, AE27
    databases, AF13
    directories, AE1, AE44
    indexes
        Canada, AF14
        France, AF15
        Gt. Brit., AF16
        United States, AF1, AF12, AF13
    union lists
        Caribbean, AF5
        Ireland, Northern, AF10
        Scotland, AF8
Newspeak, Green, Jonathon, AD42
Newton, Frances P. *American bibliography, a preliminary checklist, 1801 to 1819*, AA81
Newton, Judy Ann. *The Ku Klux Klan*, CC204
Newton, Michael. *The Ku Klux Klan*, CC204
Nicaragua, AA165, DB129
Nicaraguan national bibliography, 1800–1978 = Bibliografía nacional nicaragüense, 1800–1978, AA165
Nicholas, David. *Immunology, an information profile*, EC3
Nicholas, Robin. *Immunology, an information profile*, EC3
Nicholls, Ann. *The Cambridge guide to the museums of Britain and Ireland*, BE49
—— *The directory of museums & living displays*, BE50
Nicholls, C. S. *The dictionary of national biography, 1981–1985*, AJ66
Nicholls, David. *Biographical dictionary of modern European radicals and socialists*, AJ8
Nicholls, Robert P. *A guide to historic and significant gardens of America*, BE146
—— *The traveler's guide to American gardens*, BE146
Nichols, Monte C. *Mineral reference manual*, EE36
Nichols, Stephen W. *The Torre-Bueno glossary of entomology*, EC64
Nicholson, Frances. *Political and economic encyclopaedia of Western Europe*, CJ167
Nickel, Ernest H. *Mineral reference manual*, EE36
Nickson, R. Andrew. *Paraguay*, DB130
Niedersächsische Staats- und Universitätsbibliothek Göttingen. *A catalogue of English books printed before 1801 held by the University Library at Göttingen*, AA129
Niemi, Richard G. *Trends in public opinion*, CJ234, CJ237
—— *Vital statistics on American politics*, CJ134
Nigarishī jāmi bar jahān-i kitābshināsī-yi Īrān, Tasbīhī, Gulām 'Husayn, AA6
Niger, DD47
Niger, Decalo, S., DD6
Nigeria, DD48, DD49
Nigeria, Myers, Robert A., DD48
—— Oyewole, A., DD5
Le Nigeria contemporain, DD49
Nigerian Institute of Advanced Legal Studies. *Nigerian legal periodicals*, CK47
Nigerian legal periodicals, CK47
Nigerian universities dissertation abstracts (NUDA), AH15
Nihon mukashibanashi meii, BD381, CF36
Nine thousand words, AD32
Nineteenth-century American choral music, DeVenney, David P., BH116

Nineteenth-century American drama, Hennessee, Don A., BD231
—— Hixon, Donald L., BD231
Nineteenth century American poetry, Jason, Philip K., BD178
Nineteenth century expeditions in the Arctic and Canada, Minion, Robin, DH3
A nineteenth-century musical chronicle, Hall, Charles J., BH73
The nineteenth-century photographic press, Sennett, Robert S., BF57
Nineteenth-century photography, Johnson, William, BF55, BF57
Nineteenth-century rhetoric, Houlette, Forrest, BD143
Nineteenth-century Russian literature in English, Proffer, Carl R., BD354
Nineteenth century short title catalogue, AA133
Nishiura, Elizabeth. *American battle monuments*, BE164
Nite, Norm N. *Rock on almanac*, BH131
Nitsch, Kazimierz. *Słownik staropolski*, AD145
The NIV exhaustive concordance, Goodrick, Edward W., BB59
Niver, Kemp R. *Early motion pictures*, BG75
Nixon, Judith M. *Industry and company information*, CH79
Nobel laureates in economic sciences, CH23
Nobel laureates in literature, BD56
Nobel laureates in medicine or physiology, EK76
The Nobel Peace Prize and the laureates, Abrams, Irwin, CJ315
Nobel prize winners, AJ11
The Nobel Prize winners : chemistry, ED25
Nobel prize winners in chemistry, 1901–1961, Faber, Edward, ED25
The Nobel Prize winners : physics, EG13
Nobel prizes, AJ11, BD56, CJ315, EK76
Nobelstiftelsen, Stockholm. *Chemistry*, ED25
—— *Physics*, EG13
Nöhring, Jürgen. *Dictionary of medicine*, EK57, EK58
Noel, John Vavasour. *Naval terms dictionary*, CJ272
Nöldeke, Theodor. *Wörterbuch der klassischen arabischen Sprache*, AD71
Nöth, Winfried. *Handbook of semiotics*, BC14
Nof, Shimon Y. *International encyclopedia of robotics*, EJ77
Noffsinger, James Philip. *World War I aviation books in English*, DA69
Nofsinger, Mary M. *Children and adjustment to divorce*, CC132
Nolo Press. *Legal research made easy*, CK7
Noltingk, B. E. *Instrumentation reference book*, EJ76
Nomenclature of inorganic chemistry, ED28
Nonbook materials, Weihs, Jean, AB78
The nonsexist word finder, Maggio, Rosalie, CC298
Nonsexist writing, The handbook of, AA57, CC311
Noppen, J. P. van. *Metaphor*, BC4, BD146
Nordic archaeological abstracts, DA34
Nordquist, Joan. *Claude Levi-Strauss, a bibliography*, CE6
—— *Current Central American-U.S. relations*, DB95
—— *Domestic violence*, CC133
—— *The feminization of poverty*, CC145
—— *The homeless in America*, CC120
—— *Rape*, CC262
—— *Substance abuse I : drug abuse*, CC114
—— *Substance abuse II : alcohol abuse*, CC71
Nordstrom, Byron J. *Dictionary of Scandinavian history*, DC179
Norman, Buford. *The wordworthy computer*, BD12
Norse, Old *see* Icelandic language
Norsk biografisk leksikon, AJ83
Norsk bokfortegnelse, 1971–75, AA166

Norsk historisk bibliografi 1916–1945, Gjønnes, Svein Tore, DC167
North, John S. *The Waterloo directory of Irish newspapers and periodicals, 1800–1900*, AE54
—— *The Waterloo directory of Scottish newspapers and periodicals, 1800–1900*, AE67
North American Conference on British Studies. *Modern England, 1901–1984*, DC106
North American trees, Preston, Richard Joseph, EC36
Northern Ireland, a political directory, 1966–88, Flackes, William D., CJ187
Northern Ireland newspapers, 1737–1987, AF10
Northwest Passage, DB82
Norton, Arthur P. *Star atlas and reference handbook (epoch 2000.0)*, EB17
The Norton/Grove concise encyclopedia of music, BH57
Norway
    bibliography
        19th–20th centuries, AA166
        databases, AA167
    biography, AJ83
    history
        bibliography, DC167, DC169, DC170
        local history, DC168
Norway, Sather, Leland B., DC169
Norwegian language, AD143
Norwegian local history, Hill, Dennis Auburn, DC168
Notable women in the American theatre, BG39
Note al Thesaurus linguae latinae, Ferrua, Antonio, AD135
Note al Thesaurus linguae latinae : addenda et corrigenda, Ferrua, Antonio, AD134
Nourie, Alan. *American mass-market magazines*, AE15
Nourie, Barbara. *American mass-market magazines*, AE15
Nouveau guide de généalogie, Aublet, Robert, AK21
Novaĭa istoriĭa, DA58
The novels of World War Two, Paris, Michael, BD237
Novo dicionário de termos técnicos inglês-português, Fürstenau, Eugênio, EA51
Novum glossarium mediae latinitatis, AD141
Nowlan, Gwendolyn Wright. *Cinema sequels and remakes, 1903–1987*, BG79
Nowlan, Robert A. *Cinema sequels and remakes, 1903–1987*, BG79
Nuba-Scheffler, Hannah. *Infancy*, CC82
The nuclear arms race, Gay, William, CJ294
Nuclear data sheets, EG11
Nuclear medicine, EK71
Nuclear warfare, CJ294
Nuclear weapons, CJ266
The nuclear weapons world, CJ266
NUDA, AH15
Nuessel, Frank H. *Theoretical studies in Hispanic linguistics (1960–)*, BC52
Nuevo diccionario biografico argentino, AJ32
Nuevo repertorio bibliográfico venezolano, Villasana, Angel Raúl, AA200
Numerical lists and schedule of volumes, AG11
Il Nuovo dizionario Hazon Garzanti, AD130
Nurcombe, Valerie J. *International real estate valuation, investment, and development*, CH345
Nursai, Ata M. *Bibliographie zur Afghanistan-Literatur 1960–1987*, DE41
Nursing
    biography, EK94, EK95
    databases, EK89
    dictionaries, EK91
    directories, EK93
    encyclopedias, EK90
    faculty
        directories, EK92
Nursing & allied health database, EK89
Nursing education, EK88

Nursing homes, CC58
Nuṣayr, 'Āydah Ibrāhīm. *al-Kutub al-'Arabīyah allatī nushirat fī miṣrbayna amay 1926–1940*, AA105
—— *al-Kutub al-'Arabīyah allatī nushirat fī Miṣr fī al-qarn al-tāsi' 'ashar*, AA105
—— *al-Kutub al-'Arabīyah allatī nushirat fī miṣrbayna 1900–1925*, AA105
Nusberg, Charlotte. *International glossary of social gerontology = Glosario internacional de gerontología social = Glossaire international de gérontologie sociale = Internationales Wörterverzeichnis für Sozialgerontologie*, CC54
Nutrition, EH32, EH36, EK101
  encyclopedias, EK97, EK98, EK99, EK100
  guides, EH34, EK96
  handbooks, EK102
The nutrition and health encyclopedia, Tver, David F., EK100
The nutrition desk reference, Garrison, Robert H., EK98
Nyberg, Cheryl. *Subject compilations of state laws, 1985–1988*, CK31
Nykysuomen sanakirja, Häkkinen, Kaisa, AD87
Nyvall, Robert F. *Field crop diseases handbook*, EH23

OCLC. *Bibliographic input standards*, AB77
—— *United States Newspaper Program national union list*, AF1
Ober, Kenneth H. *Bibliography of modern Icelandic literature in translation. Supplement, 1971–1980*, BD300
Obermeyer-Marnach, Eva. *Österreichisches biographisches Lexikon 1815–1950*, AJ37
Oberösterreichisches Landesarchiv. *Bibliographie zur oberösterreichischen Geschichte, 1981–1985*, DC28
Obituaries, Jarboe, Betty, AJ3
Obituary index, AJ7
Obituary notices of Fellows of the Royal Society, EK78
—— Royal Society of London, EA79
O'Brien, Geoffrey. *The reader's catalog*, AA61
O'Brien, Jacqueline Wasserman. *Financial planners and planning organizations directory*, CH245
O'Brien, James G. *Elder neglect and abuse*, CC45
O'Brien, Nancy P. *Test construction*, CD46
O'Brien, R. L. *Welding handbook*, EJ84
O'Brien, Robert. *The encyclopedia of alcoholism*, CC74
—— *The encyclopedia of New England*, DB50
—— *The encyclopedia of the South*, DB53
Observatoire de Strasbourg. *Acronyms & abbreviations in astronomy, space sciences, & related fields*, EB8
L'obsolète, Duchesne, Alain, AD101
Obst, Fritz Jürgen. *The completely illustrated atlas of reptiles and amphibians for the terrarium*, EC45
Obudho, Robert A. *Afro-American demography and urban issues*, CC201
Ocampo, Aurora M. *Diccionario de escritores mexicanos, siglo XX*, BD343
The occult in the western world, Kies, Cosette N., CD52
Occultism, CD51, CD52, CD54
Occupational education, CB12
Occupations, CB156, CH334, CH336, CH337, CH338, CH339, CH340
Oceania, DG8
  bibliography, AA168, DG1, DG3, DG6, DG7
  biography, DG10
  economic conditions, CH48
  encyclopedias, DG9
  filmography, DG5
  guides, DG7
  handbooks, DG10

history
  library resources, DD2, DD15, DG4
Oceanic abstracts, EE39
Oceanic economic handbook, CH48
Oceanography
  biography, EE40
  databases, EE39
  directories, EE27
O'Clery, Conor. *The dictionary of political quotations on Ireland, 1886–1987*, BD63, CJ186, DC151
O'Connell, Agnes N. *Women in psychology*, CD36
O'Connell, Susan M. *AAAS science book list, 1978–1986*, EA15
Österreichische historische Bibliographie, 1945–1964 = Austrian historical bibliography, DC24
Österreichische historische Bibliographie, fünf-Jahres-Register, 1980–84 = Austrian historical bibliography, five-year-index : 1980–1984, DC25
Österreichisches biographisches Lexikon 1815–1950, AJ37
Ofcansky, Thomas P. *British East Africa, 1856–1963*, DD12
Offenberg, A. K. *Hebrew incunabula in public collections*, AA43
Office practice, CH168, CH169
Official journal of the European Communities, CK122
Official methods of analysis of the Association of Official Analytical Chemists, ED20
Official publications of Western Europe, AG33
The official World Wildlife Fund guide to endangered species of North America, EC41
Officiel des arts, BE64
Ofori, Patrick E. *Retrospective index to Nigerian doctoral dissertations and masters theses, 1895–1980*, AH16
Ogbondah, Chris W. *The press in Nigeria*, AE59
Ogilvie, Grania. *The dictionary of South African painters and sculptors, including Namibia*, BE85
Ogilvie, Marilyn Bailey. *Women in science*, CC263, EA78
Ogston, R. *Concise illustrated dental dictionary*, EK86
Ohles, John F. *Public colleges and universities*, CB102
Ohles, Shirley M. *Public colleges and universities*, CB102
Olbrich, Harald. *Lexikon der Kunst*, BE36
Old age pensions, CH152
Old and Middle English language studies, Tajima, Matsuji, BC25
Old English word studies, Cameron, Angus, BC18
Old master print references, Mason, Lauris, BE155
The Old Testament pseudepigrapha, BB40
Olderr, Steven. *Olderr's young adult fiction index*, BD79
Olderr's fiction index, BD79
Olderr's young adult fiction index, BD79
Oldham, Keith B. *An atlas of functions*, EF15
O'Leary, Stella. *Classical scholarship*, BD365
O'Leary, Timothy J. *Encyclopedia of world cultures*, CE14
—— *Ethnographic bibliography of North America*, CC217
—— *Ethnographic bibliography of North America, 4th edition. Supplement 1973–1987*, CC217
O'Leary, William M. *Practical handbook of microbiology*, EC21, EC22
Oliver, Elizabeth. *Researcher's guide to British film & television collections*, BG84
Oliver, Roland Anthony. *The Cambridge history of Africa*, DD10
-ologies & -isms, AD35
Olson, James Stuart. *Dictionary of the Vietnam War*, DE106

—— *Historical dictionary of the 1920s*, DB40
—— *Historical dictionary of the New Deal*, DB38
—— *The history of cancer*, EK14
Olson, Kent C. *Finding the law*, CK2
—— *How to find the law*, CK3
—— *Practical approaches to legal research*, CK10
Olson, Stan. *Foundation grants to individuals*, CA34
Olton, Roy. *The international relations dictionary*, CJ20
Olympic Games, BJ32, BJ33, BJ34
The Olympic games, Hugman, Barry J., BJ32
The Olympic record book, Mallon, Bill, BJ33
O'Malley, John W. *Catholicism in early modern history*, BB119
O'Malley, William T. *Anglo-Irish literature*, BD270
Ó Maoláin, Ciarán. *Latin American political movements*, CJ196
—— *The radical right*, CJ138
O'Meara, Dan. *The struggle for South Africa*, CJ202
[Omega]—bibliography of mathematical logic, EF2
Omond, Roger,. *The apartheid handbook*, CC186
On the screen, Fisher, Kim N., BG50
OncoDisc, EK30
Oncogenes and growth factors abstracts, EC7
One hundred years of economic statistics, Liesner, Thelma, CH27
One-parent children, the growing minority, Gouke, Mary Noel, CC81
O'Neil, Rosanna M. *Cataloging with copy*, AB75
O'Neill, Hugh B. *Companion to Chinese history*, DE49
O'Neill, Robert Keating. *English-language dictionaries, 1604–1900*, AD1
Onerheim, Neil. *An advocate's guide to surviving the SSI system*, CH267
Onions, C. T. *Oxford dictionary of English etymology*, AD15
—— *A Shakespeare glossary*, BD265
Online bibliographic databases, AB95
Online searching, EK4
Onofrei, Neonila. *Bibliografia românească modernă, 1831–1918*, AA177
Ontiveros, Suzanne R. *The dynamic Constitution*, CK115
—— *Women in the Third World*, CC277
O'Pecko, Michael T. *The twentieth-century German novel*, BD297
Opera, BH94, BH95, BH96, BH97, BH98, BH101, BH102
  encyclopedias, BH58, BH100
  guides, BH99
  plots, BH103
Opera, Marco, Guy A., BH99
Opera and concert singers, Farkas, Andrew, BH88
The opera handbook, Lazarus, John, BH94
Opera plot index, Studwell, William E., BH103
Opfell, Olga S. *Queens, empresses, grand duchesses, and regents*, CJ166
Ophthalmic drug facts, EK120
Ophthalmology, EK53, EK120; *see also* Vision
Opinion Research Service (U.S.). *American public opinion data*, CJ229
—— *American public opinion index*, CJ230
Opinions, CJ235
Opitz, Glenn B. *Mantle Fielding's dictionary of American painters, sculptors & engravers*, BE94
Opitz, Helmut. *Internationales Bibliotheks-Handbuch = World guide to libraries*, AB20
Oppelt, Norman T. *Southwestern pottery*, BF19
Oral history, AB37, DA84, DB12, DB21, DC104
Oral history, Havlice, Patricia Pate, DB12
—— Perks, Robert, DC104

Oral history collections, McMullin, Ruth, DB21
—— Meckler, Alan, DB21
Orbell, John. *A guide to tracing the history of a business*, CH142
Orbis geographicus = Adressar géographique du monde = World directory of geography = Geographisches Weltadressbuch, CL15
Orchestral music, BH148, BH149
Ordbok öfver svenska språket, Svenska akademien, AD170
Orders and families of recent mammals of the world, EC60
Oreggioni, Alfredo F. *Diccionario de literatura uruguaya*, BD347
Organ literature, Arnold, Corliss Richard, BH152
Organic-chemical drugs and their synonyms, Negwer, Martin, EK112
Organisation for Economic Co-operation and Development. *A study of the Soviet economy*, CH53
Organisch-chemische Arzneimittel und ihre Synonyma, EK112
Organization behavior in American public administration, Payad, Aurora T., CJ221
Organometallic compounds, ED30
Organophosphorus compounds, ED34
The originals, Amos, William, BD95
Origins, evolution, and nature of the Cold War, Black, J. L., CJ5
The origins of photography, Gernsheim, Alison, BF53
—— Gernsheim, Helmut, BF53
Oriol, William E. *Federal public policy on aging since 1960*, CC46
Ornament, Dictionary of, BF41
Orozco Tenorio, José. *Las publicaciones periódicas mexicanas*, AE58
Orr, Leonard. *Research in critical theory since 1965*, BD21
Országh, László. *A concise English-Hungarian dictionary*, AD124
—— *Magyar-angol kéziszótár*, AD123
Országos Széchényi Könyvtár. *Magyar könyvészet, 1921–1944*, AA139
—— *Magyar nemzeti bibliográfia*, AE48
Ortamo, Anna-Maija. *Suomen aikakauslehdistön bibliografia 1956–1977 = Bibliografi över Finlands tidskriftslitteratur 1956–1977 = Bibliography of Finnish periodicals, 1956–1977*, AE32
Osborne, Harold. *The Oxford dictionary of art*, BE38
Osen, L. M. *Women in mathematics*, EF18
Osiobe, Stephen A. *Nigerian universities dissertation abstracts (NUDA)*, AH15
Osmańczyk, Edmund Jan. *The encyclopedia of the United Nations and international agreements*, CK130
Ośrodek Informacji Naukowej (Polska Akademia Nauk). *Biogramy uczonych polskich*, AJ85
Ossorguine-Bakounine, Tatiana. *L'emigration russe*, AE64
Oster, Richard. *A bibliography of ancient Ephesus*, BB7
Ostrow, Rona. *The dictionary of marketing*, CH318
Oswald, Arthur. *English mediaeval architects*, BE135
O'Toole, G. J. A. *The encyclopedia of American intelligence and espionage*, CJ286
Ott, J. Steven. *The Facts on File dictionary of nonprofit organization management*, CH158
Ottemiller, John H. *Ottemiller's index to plays in collections*, BD86
Ottemiller's index to plays in collections, Ottemiller, John H., BD86
Otto, Eberhard. *Lexikon der Ägyptologie*, DD31
Otto, Ingeborg. *Die Beziehungen Afghanistans zur Sowjetunion*, DE42

Otto, Johannes. *Bibliographie deutschsprachiger bevölkerungswissenschaftlicher Literatur, 1978–1984*, CG4
Ottoman Turkish writers, Mitler, Louis, BD384
Oughton, Marguerita. *Geographers: biobibliographical studies*, CL24
Ousby, Ian. *The Cambridge guide to literature in English*, BD218
Outward signs, West, Edward N., BB73
Over-the-counter 1000, CH111
Overesch, Manfred. *Chronik deutscher Zeitgeschichte*, DC93
Owen, S. G. *The Oxford companion to medicine*, EK41
Owen, Wyn F. *Guide to graduate study in economics, agricultural economics, public administration, and doctoral programs in business administration in the United States and Canada*, CH14
Oxbridge directory of newsletters, AF3
Oxbury, Harold. *Great Britons*, AJ68
The Oxford book of prayer, BB72
The Oxford companion to American theatre, BG19
Oxford companion to art, BE38
The Oxford companion to Australian literature, Wilde, W. H., BD276
The Oxford companion to Canadian theatre, BG23
The Oxford companion to classical literature, Howatson, M. C., BD366
The Oxford companion to English literature, Drabble, Margaret, BD219
The Oxford companion to gardens, BE143, EH9
The Oxford companion to German literature, Garland, Henry B., BD290
The Oxford companion to medicine, EK41
The Oxford companion to popular music, Gammond, Peter, BH128
Oxford companion to the decorative arts, BE38
The Oxford companion to the literature of Wales, BD273
The Oxford companion to the mind, CD14
Oxford companion to twentieth-century art, BE38
The Oxford dictionary of art, BE38
The Oxford dictionary of Byzantium, DA53
Oxford dictionary of English etymology, Onions, C. T., AD15
The Oxford dictionary of natural history, EE4, EC25
The Oxford dictionary of Popes, Kelly, J. N. D., BB121
The Oxford dictionary of saints, Farmer, David Hugh, BB97
The Oxford-Duden German dictionary, AD109
The Oxford encyclopaedia of European Community law, Toth, A. G., CK123
Oxford English: a guide to the language, BC29
The Oxford English dictionary, AD2, AD63, AD6
The Oxford history of English literature, BD222
The Oxford illustrated history of Christianity, BB100
The Oxford illustrated literary guide to Canada, Moritz, A. F., BD280
The Oxford literary guide to Australia, BD274
Oxford Movement, BB77
The Oxford Movement and its leaders, Crumb, Lawrence N., BB77
Oxford Russian-English dictionary, AD153
Oyewole, A. *Nigeria*, DD5
Ozouf, Mona. *A critical dictionary of the French Revolution*, DC52

PAIS, CA8
PAIS international in print, CA10
PAIS on CD-ROM, CA11
PERSI, AK10
POMPI, BH138
PTS international forecasts, CH133
PTS marketing and advertising reference service, CH314

PTS newsletter database, AB89
PTS U.S. forecasts, CH134
Pacheleke, Calisto. *Mozambique*, DD45
The Pacific Basin, CH41
Pacific Basin and Oceania, Fry, Gerald, DG1
Pacific Collection accession list, AA168
Pacific Collection legal deposit accessions, AA168
Pacific Island studies, DG6
Pacific island year book and who's who, DG10
Pacific islands yearbook, DG10
Pacific Publications (Firm). *Papua New Guinea handbook, business and travel guide*, CJ201
Pacific region, DE7
Pacific Rim countries, CH35, DG9
Packard, Robert T. *Encyclopedia of architecture*, BE122
Packard, William. *The poet's dictionary*, BD135
Packer, J. I. *New dictionary of theology*, BB88
Pactor, Howard S. *Colonial British Caribbean newspapers*, AF5
Paden, John N. *Black Africa*, CG38
Page, G. Terry. *International dictionary of management*, CH157
Page, James A. *Selected black American, African, and Caribbean authors*, BD186
Page, Penny Booth. *Alcohol use and alcoholism*, CC72
Paine, Fred K. *Magazines*, AE18
Paine, Nancy E. *Magazines*, AE18
Painting
 bibliography, BE147
 France, BE148
 biography, BE151, BE153
 by country or region
  Gt. Brit., BE153
 catalogs, BE149
 indexes, BE150
Paisey, David. *Short-title catalogue of books printed in the German-speaking countries and of German books printed in other countries from 1455 to 1600 now in the British Library. Supplement*, AA118
Pakistan
 bibliography, DE87
 history
  bibliography, DE88
 statistics, CG65
Pakistan, Taylor, David D., DE88
Paläozoologie, EE42
Palau Claveras, Agustín. *Addenda y corrigenda o volumen complementario del tomo primero del Manual del librero hispanoamericano de Antonio Palau y Dulcet*, AA185
—— *Indice alfabético de títulos-materias, correcciones, conexiones y adiciones del Manual del librero hispanoamericano de Antonio Palau y Dulcet*, AA186
Palau y Dulcet, Antonio. *Manual del librero hispanoamericano*, AA185, AA186
Palder, Edward L. *The catalog of catalogs II*, CH321
Palen, Roberta. *Guide to the publications of interstate agencies and authorities*, AG26
Paleography, AA39
Paleontology, EE41, EE42
Pallay, Steven G. *Cross index title guide to classical music*, BH20
—— *Cross index title guide to opera and operetta*, BH20
Pallotta, Gino. *Dizionario della politica italiana*, CJ191
—— *Dizionario politicio e parlamentare italiano*, CJ191
Palm, Mary Egdahl. *A literature guide for the identification of plant pathogenic fungi*, EC35
Palmatier, Robert A. *Sports talk*, BJ10
Palmegiano, Eugenia M. *The British Empire in the Victorian press, 1832–1867*, DC132
Palmer, Alan. *An encyclopaedia of Napoleon's Europe*, DC66
Palmer, Eileen C. *Index to children's plays in collections, 1975–1984*, BD81

Palmer, Gregory. *A guide to Americana*, DB16

Palmer, James C. *Dictionary of educational acronyms, abbreviations, and initialisms*, CB75

Palmer, Pete. *Total baseball*, BJ27

Palmer, Ralph S. ed. *Handbook of North American birds*, EC55

Palmer, Scott. *British film actors' credits, 1895–1987*, BG80

Paloposki, Toivo J. *Quellenkunde zur Geschichte Finnlands*, DC44

Panagiotou, Nikos. *Kypriakē vivliographia*, AA96

Pandit, Harshida. *Women of India*, CC286

Panduan rekod-rekod kerajaan persekutuan di Arkib Negara Malaysia, Arkib Negara Malaysia, AG45

Panorama of EC industry, CH308, CK129

Pantzer, Katharine F. *A short-title catalogue of books printed in England, Scotland, & Ireland and of English books printed abroad, 1475–1640*, AA127

Pap, Leo. *Portuguese in the United States*, CC168

Papadopoulos, Thōmas I. *Hellēnikē vivliographia*, AA134

Paprikoff, George I. *Works of Bulgarian emigrants*, AA91

Papua New Guinea
  bibliography, AA169, DG11, DG12
  politics and government, CJ201

Papua New Guinea, McConnell, Fraiser, DG12

Papua New Guinea handbook, business and travel guide, CJ201

Paquet, Léonce. *Les présocratiques*, BA6

Paraguay
  bibliography, AA170, AA171
  history
    bibliography, DB130

Paraguay, Nickson, R. Andrew, DB130

Paraguay . . . años de bibliografía, AA171

The Paraguayan bibliography, Fernández-Caballero, Carlos F. S., AA171

Parapsychology, BB29, CD49, CD51, CD53, CD55, CF4

Parapsychology, Dale, Laura, CD55

—— White, Rhea A., CD55

Parent-child attachment, Watkins, Kathleen Pullan, CC86

Parezo, Nancy J. *Southwest Native American arts and material culture*, CC219

Parfitt, George A. E. *A biographical dictionary of English women writers, 1580–1720*, BD223

Parins, James W. *American Indian and Alaska native newspapers and periodicals*, CC223

—— *A biobibliography of native American writers, 1772–1924*, BD196, BD197, CC218

Paris, Michael. *The novels of World War Two*, BD237

Paris, AA111

The Paris Opéra, Pitou, Spire, BH101

Parish, David W. *A bibliography of state bibliographies, 1970–1982*, AG27

Parish, James Robert. *Actors' television credits 1950–1972*, BG111

—— *The complete actors' television credits, 1948–1988*, BG111

The parish churches and nonconformist chapels of Wales, Rawlins, Bert J., AK47

Parish registers of Wales, Williams, C. J., AK47

Park, Helen. *A list of architectural books available in American before the Revolution*, BE111

Park, Karin R. *Publication grants for writers & publishers*, BD49, CA46

Parker, Betty June. *Education in England and Wales*, CB37

—— *Education in the People's Republic of China, past and present*, CB5

Parker, C. C. *Information sources in science and technology*, EA4

Parker, Franklin. *Education in England and Wales*, CB37

—— *Education in the People's Republic of China, past and present*, CB5

Parker, Harold M. *Bibliography of published articles on American Presbyterianism, 1901–1980*, BB111

Parker, R. H. *A dictionary of business quotations*, CH96

Parker, Sybil P. *McGraw-Hill dictionary of scientific and technical terms*, EA44

—— *McGraw-Hill encyclopedia of the geological sciences*, EE7

Parker, William. *Homosexuality bibliography. Second supplement, 1976–1982*, CC149

Parker School of Foreign and Comparative Law. *A bibliography on foreign and comparative law*, CK20

—— *Szladits' bibliography on foreign and comparative law*, CK21

Parkinson, Claire L. *Breakthroughs*, EA74

Parkinson, John A. *Victorian music publishers*, BH70

Parks, Roger N. *Bibliographies of New England history*, DB49

Parks and protected areas, BJ37, BJ38

Parliamentary procedure, CJ225, CJ226, CJ227, CJ228

Parliaments of the world, CJ139

Parrish, T. Michael. *Confederate imprints*, DB30

Parrish, William. *World directory of crystallographers and of other scientists employing crystallographic methods*, EE22

Parry, Robert B. *Information sources in cartography*, CL1

—— *World mapping today*, CL47

Parsifal-Charles, Nancy. *The dream*, CD1

Parsons, Christopher. *A bibliography of Salon criticism in Second Empire Paris*, BE147

Parsons, Karen Toombs. *United States congressional districts, 1883–1913*, CJ106

Parsons, Stanley B. *United States congressional districts, 1788–1841*, CJ105, CJ106

—— *United States congressional districts, 1843–1883*, CJ105

—— *United States congressional districts, 1883–1913*, CJ106

Pasierbsky, Fritz. *Deutsche Sprache im Reformationszeitalter*, BC33

Paskoff, Paul F. *Iron and steel in the nineteenth century*, CH136

Pass, Christopher. *Harper dictionary of economics*, CH11

Passenger and immigration lists bibliography, 1538–1900, Filby, P. William, AK8

Passenger and immigration lists index. Supplement, AK9

Passenger lists, AK9, AK11, AK12

Past worlds, DA37

Patents, EA86, EA87

Patnode, Darwin. *Robert's rules of order*, CJ226

Patrides, C. A. *An annotated critical bibliography of John Milton*, BD259

Patrology
  bibliography, BB101, BB103, BC43
  encyclopedias, BB102

Patrology, Quasten, Johannes, BB103

Patterson, Charles D. *ARBA guide to library science literature, 1970–1983*, AB1

Patterson, Margaret. *Literary research guide*, BD149

Patterson's American education, CB110

Patterson's elementary education, CB110

Pauer, Gyula. *The historical atlas of political parties in the United States Congress, 1789–1989*, CJ116, DB78

Paul, Barbara Dotts. *The Germans after World War II*, DC86

Paul, Ellen. *The adoption directory*, CC138

Paul, Shalom M. *Illustrated dictionary & concordance of the Bible*, BB54

Paul, T. Otis. *The encyclopedia of blindness and vision impairment*, CC106, EK44

Paulidēs, Antros. *Megalē Kypriakē enkyklopaideia*, DC38

Pauling, Linus. *World encyclopedia of peace*, CJ306

Pavone, Claudio. *Guida generale degli archivi di Stato italiani*, DC157

Pawlik, Kurt. *International directory of psychologists, exclusive of the U.S.A*, CD35

Paxton, John. *European political facts, 1918–84*, CJ163

—— *Historical tables, 58 B.C.–A.D. 1985*, DA24

Payad, Aurora T. *Organization behavior in American public administration*, CJ221

Payne, Chris. *Virology*, EC69

Payne, Christopher. *Sotheby's concise encyclopedia of furniture*, BF42

Payne, Mark. *Central American economic handbook*, CH44

Peace *see* **Arms control and peace research**

The peace and nuclear war dictionary, Ali, Sheikh Rustum, CJ303, CJ304

Peace archives, Green, Marguerite, CJ295

Peace Corps, CJ299

The Peace Corps, Ridinger, Robert B. Marks, CJ299

Peace movements of the world, CJ311

Peace organizations, past and present, Meyer, Robert S., CJ310

Peace research abstracts journal, CJ302

Peace resource book, CJ312

The peace tradition in the Catholic Church, Musto, Ronald G., BB117, CJ298

The peacetime army, 1900–1941, Fletcher, Marvin, CJ271

Peake, Louis A. *The United States in the Vietnam War, 1954–1975*, DE101

Pearce, E. A. *The Times Books world weather guide*, EE29

Pearson, Barbara C. *Guide to the petroleum reference literature*, EJ89

Pearson, J. D. *A bibliography of the architecture, arts, and crafts of Islam by Sir K.A.C. Creswell, C.B.E. Second supplement, Jan. 1972 to Dec. 1980 (with omissions from previous years)*, BE11

—— *A guide to manuscripts and documents in the British Isles relating to South and South-East Asia*, DE4

Pearson, Michael. *The nuclear arms race*, CJ294

Pearson, Roger. *Anthropological glossary*, CE15

Pechota, Vratislav. *Szladits' bibliography on foreign and comparative law*, CK21

—— *USSR legal materials*, CK52

Peck, Jeffrey M. *New literary history international bibliography of literary theory and criticism*, BD8

Peck, R. A. *Chaucer's lyrics and Anelida and Arcite*, BD255

—— *Chaucer's Romaunt of the rose and Boece, Treatise on the astrolabe, Equatorie of the planetis, lost works, and Chaucerian apocrypha*, BD255

Peiris, H. A. *Political parties in Sri Lanka since independence*, CJ204

Pelican history of art, BE73

Pelletier, Paul A. *Prominent scientists*, EA85

Pelou, Pierre. *La documentation administrative*, AG34

Pelz, Ruth. *Administrator's desk reference on special education*, CB138

Pen names of women writers, Marshall, Alice Kahler, AA31

Penco, Wilfredo. *Diccionario de literatura uruguaya*, BD347

Pendleton, Anne. *Handbook of certification and licensure requirements for school psychologists*, CB133

The Penguin companion to the arts in the twentieth century, McLeish, Kenneth, BE83

The Penguin dictionary of decorative arts, Fleming, John, BF13

The Penguin dictionary of foreign terms and phrases, AD66

The Penguin dictionary of musical performers, Jacobs, Arthur, BH83

The Penguin dictionary of psychology, Reber, Arthur S., CD20

The Penguin encyclopedia of horror and the supernatural, CF28

Pennak, Robert W. *Fresh-water invertebrates of the United States,* EC43

Pennsylvania Academy of the Fine Arts. *The annual exhibition record of the Pennsylvania Academy of the Fine Arts,* BE66

Pension funds, Gunderson, Nels L., CH151

Pentecostal movement, BB80

People in history, DA55

People in world history, DA55

The people speak, CJ112

The People's Republic of China, Pinard, Jeannette L., CK37

Pequeño Larousse, AD164

The percussionist's dictionary, Adato, Joseph, BH151

Percy, William A. *Encyclopedia of homosexuality,* CC152

Pereira, Janet Aileen. *A check list of selected material on Samoa,* DG14

Pérez, Louis A. *Cuba,* DB145

—— *A guide to Cuban collections in the United States,* DB146

Pérez Pimentel, Rodolfo. *Diccionario biográfico del Ecuador,* AJ48

Performing arts; *see also* **Dance; Motion pictures; Radio and television; Theater arts**
 annuals, BE20, BG2
 biography, BG5, BG6
 directories, BE57, BG3, BG4

Performing arts biography master index, BG44

Periodica musicalia (1789–1830), Fellinger, Imogen, BH31

Periodical directories and bibliographies, AE19

Periodical literature on American music, 1620–1920, Warner, Thomas E., BH25

Periodical source index, AK10

Periodical title abbreviations, AE12

Periodicals; *see also* **Ethnic press;** under specific topics, subhead **Periodicals**
 abbreviations, AE12
 bibliography, AE2, AE4, AE6, AE8, AE10, AE11, AE18
  Brazil, AE28
  Canada, AE23, AE25, AE29
  China, AE30
  Finland, AE31, AE32
  France, AE33, AE34
  Germany, AE35, AE36, AE40
  Gt. Brit., AE46
   19th century and after, AE43, AE73
   before 1800, AE41
   current, AE45
  Hungary, AE48
  India, AE49, AE50
  Indonesia, AA140, AE51, AE52
  Ireland, AE54
  Italy, AE55
  Jewish, AE3, AE5, AE7
  Kenya, AE56
  Latvia, AE57
  Mexico, AE58
  Nigeria, AE59
  Persian, AE53
  Poland, AE60, AE61, AE62
  Romania, AE63
  Russia and the U.S.S.R., AE65, AE66
  Scotland, AE67
  Senegal, AE68
  Tunisia, AE70
  United States, AE14, AE15, AE20, AE23, AE25, AE27
   government publications, AG10
  Yugoslavia, BD363

bibliography of bibliography, AE19
databases, AE9, AE76
directories, AE1, AE44
guides for authors, BH29
indexes
 bibliography, AE74
 Canada, AE17, AE81
 United States and Gt. Brit., AE17, AE75, AE77, AE78, AE79, AE80
 Yugoslavia, AE82
selection, AA68, AA69
translations, AE13
union lists
 Canada, AE73, EA20
 Middle East, AA25
 United States, AE72, AE73

Periódicos brasileiros de ciência e tecnologia, AE28

Periódicos brasileiros de cultura, Rio de Janeiro. Instituto Brasileiro de Bibliografia e Documentação, AE28

Periódicos y revistas españolas e hispanoamericanas, AE69

Perkins, Agnes. *Dictionary of American children's fiction, 1859–1959,* BD74

—— *Dictionary of American children's fiction, 1960–1984,* BD75

—— *Dictionary of British children's fiction,* BD76

Perkins, C. R. *Information sources in cartography,* CL1

—— *World mapping today,* CL47

Perkins, K. J. *Tunisia,* DD5

Perks, Robert. *Oral history,* DC104

Perl, T. *Math equals,* EF18

Perlmutter, Barry F. *Handbook of family measurement techniques,* CC140

Peronism and the three Perons, Horvath, Laszlo, DB109

Perpustakaan Nasional (Indonesia). *Katalog majalah terbitan Indonesia,* AA140, AE51

—— *Katalog surat kabar,* AF11

—— *Katalog terbitan Indonesia selama pendudukan Jepang, 1942–1945 = Catalogue of Indonesian publications during Japanese occupation, 1942–1945,* AA141

Perrett, Bryan. *Encyclopaedia of the Second World War,* DA75

Perretta, Don. *Encyclopedia of rock,* BH126

Perry, Gerald J. *AIDS information sourcebook,* EK66

Perry, James L. *Handbook of public administration,* CJ214

Perry, Linda. *Standards,* EA89

Perry, Ruth M. *Southwest Native American arts and material culture,* CC219

Perryman, Wayne R. *International subscription agents,* AB68

Persia *see* **Iran**

Persian language, AD144, DE70

Persian literature, Storey, C. A., BD379

Persian serials and newspapers in British libraries, AE53

Personal name index to "The New York times index," 1975–1989 supplement, Falk, Byron A., AF12

Personalidades dominicanas, AJ47

Personnel management, CH154, CH164, CH165, CH166

Peru
 bibliography, AA172
 history
  archival sources, DB133
  bibliography, CC222, DB132
  encyclopedias, DB131
 statistics, CG66, CG67

Peru, Fisher, John Robert, DB132

Peru. Archivo General de la Nación. *Guía del archivo histórico,* DB133

Perú, compendio estadístico, CG66

Perú en números, CG67

Pesante, Alessandra. *Bibliografia di bibliografie, edizioni italiane del XVI secolo,* AA7

Pessin, Allan H. *The illustrated encyclopedia of the securities industry,* CH230

—— *Still more words of Wall Street,* CH231

Pesticides, EH19, EH20

Pesticides abstracts, EK129

Petermann, Kurt. *Tanzbibliographie,* BG47

Peters, Arno. *Peters atlas of the world,* CL55

Peters, Robert. *Hunting the snark,* BD136

Peters, Susanne. *Directory of museums in Africa = Répertoire des musées en Afrique,* BE48

Peters atlas of the world, Peters, Arno, CL55

Petersen, Anne C. *Encyclopedia of adolescence,* CC88

Petersen, Paul D. *Politics and religion,* BB15, CJ13

Petersen, Renee. *Dictionary of demography : biographies,* CG18

—— *Dictionary of demography : multilingual glossary,* CG11

—— *Dictionary of demography : terms, concepts, and institutions,* CG12

Petersen, Toni. *Art and architecture thesaurus,* BE45

—— *Art & architecture thesaurus,* BE44

Petersen, William. *Dictionary of demography : biographies,* CG18

—— *Dictionary of demography : multilingual glossary,* CG11

—— *Dictionary of demography : terms, concepts, and institutions,* CG12

Peterson, Bernard L. *Contemporary black American playwrights and their plays,* BG40

—— *Early black American playwrights and dramatic writers,* BG41

Peterson, Clarence S. *Consolidated bibliography of county histories in fifty states in 1961,* DB41

Peterson, David A. *National directory of educational programs in gerontology,* CC59

Peterson's annual guides to graduate study, CB105

Peterson's annual guides to undergraduate study : guide to four-year colleges, CB103

Peterson's college database, CB103

Peterson's college money handbook, CB161

Peterson's drug and alcohol programs and policies at four-year colleges, CB104

Peterson's gradline, CB105

Peterson's guide to certificate programs at American colleges and universities, CB106

Peterson's guide to colleges with programs for learning-disabled students, CB115

Peterson's guide to four-year colleges, CB103

Peterson's guide to two-year colleges, CB103

Peterson's national college databank, CB107

Petit Larousse illustré, 1990, AD92

Petroleum engineering, EJ89

Petrology, EE43, EE44, EE45

Petrov, Petŭr At. *Voenna istoriia na Bŭlgariia, 681–1945,* DC35

Petrović, Milomir. *Srpska bibliografija,* AA204

Petrunoff, Vance T. *Directory of foreign trade organizations in Eastern Europe,* CH180

Petteys, Chris. *Dictionary of women artists,* BE79

Pevsner, Nikolaus. *Pelican history of art,* BE73

Pfannkuch, Hans-Olaf. *Elsevier's dictionary of environmental hydrogeology,* EE26

Pfannl, Beth Kempler. *Tinker guide to Latin American and Caribbean policy and scholarly resources in metropolitan New York,* DB107

Pfeifer, Wolfgang. *Etymologisches Wörterbuch des Deutschen,* AD111

Pfeiffer, Joachim. *Literaturpsychologie, 1945–1987,* BD7

Pfister, Max. *Lessico etimologico italiano,* AD132

Pflüger, Lou. *Schriftstellerinnen und Schriftsteller der Gegenwart,* BD301

Pflug, Günther. *Lexikon des gesamten Buchwesens*, AA46

Pharmacology
  bibliography, EK107
  dictionaries, EK111, EK112
  dispensatories and pharmacopoeias, EK117, EK121, EK122, EK123
  guides, EK104, EK105
  handbooks, EK113, EK115, EK116
Pharmacy, EK103
Phelps, Roger P. *A guide to research in music education*, BH3
Phi Delta Kappa, CB149
Philanthropic trusts in Australia, CA42
Philcox, Phil. *Executive's business information sourcebook*, CH81
Philipp, Hans-Jürgen. *Saudi Arabia*, DE91
Philippides, Dia Mary L. *Census of modern Greek literature*, BD368
Philippine languages, BC61
Philippine law dictionary, Moreno, Federico B., CK68
Philippine national bibliography, AH17
Philippines, AJ84, CG68, DG13
Philippines, Richardson, Jim, DG13
Philippines. National Science Development Board. *Compilation of graduate theses prepared in the Philippines*, AH17
Philips, Billy U. *Medical sociology*, CC6, EK7
The Phillimore atlas and index of parish registers, AK29
Phillips, John B. *Directory of patent depository libraries*, EA86
Philosopher's guide, DeGeorge, R.T, BA1
Die Philosophie des 17. Jahrhunderts, Schobinger, Jean-Pierre, BA20
Philosophy
  bibliography, BA3
    Greece, BA6
    India, BA7
    Latin America, BA8
    Netherlands, BA10
    Spain, BA8
  biography, BA23, BA24, BA25
  dictionaries, BA17, BA18
  encyclopedias, BA11, BA13, BA14, BA15, BA16, BA22, BB28
  guides, BA1
  history, BA19, BA20
    bibliography, BA21
  periodicals, BA5
Philosophy, Bynagle, Hans E., BA1
Philosophy and literature, BD51
Philosophy journals and serials, Ruben, Douglas H., BA5
Philosophy of science, EA42
Phobias, fears, and anxieties, CD12
Photographs at auction, 1952–1984, BF59
Photography, BF60
  auction records, BF59
  bibliography, BF52, BF53, BF54, BF55, BF56, BF57, BF64
  biography, BF61, BF62, BF64
  directories, BF58
  indexes, BE59, BF58, BF63
Photography and photographers to 1900, Sennett, Robert S., BF57
Phrases make history here, BD63, CJ186, DC151
Physical chemistry source book, EA38
A physicist's desk reference, EG9
Physics
  bibliography, EG1
  biography, EG13
  databases, EB3, EG2, EG3, EJ44
  dictionaries, EG6
  encyclopedias, EG4, EG5
  handbooks, EG9
  style manuals, EG10
  tables, ED16, EG12
Physics, Nobelstiftelsen, Stockholm, EG13
Physics abstracts, EG2, EG2, EJ44
Physics briefs, EB3, EG3

Physics in medicine & biology encyclopedia, EK42
Physics vade mecum, EG9
Pianist's guide to transcriptions, arrangements, and paraphrases, Hinson, Maurice, BH39
Pianist's reference guide, Hinson, Maurice, BH39
Piano music, BH39
Piaseckyj, Oksana. *Bibliography of Ukrainian literature in English and French*, BD359
Piccialuti Caprioli, Maura. *Bibliografia dell'Archivio centrale dello Stato, 1953–1978*, DC156
Pickering, W. R. *Information sources in pharmaceuticals*, EK104
A pictorial guide to identifying Australian architecture, Apperley, Richard, BE130
Picture researcher's handbook, Evans, Hilary, BE68
Picture sources UK, BE68, BE70
Pictures, BE68
Pierce, Peter. *The Oxford literary guide to Australia*, BD274
Pierce, Phyllis S. *The Dow Jones averages, 1885–1990*, CH260
Pierreuse, Bernard. *Catalogue général de l'édition musicale en France*, BH21
Piggott, Michael. *A guide to commonwealth government information sources*, AG30
Pike, Douglas. *Australian dictionary of biography*, AJ33
Pile, John F. *Dictionary of 20th-century design*, BF38
Pinard, Jeannette L. *The People's Republic of China*, CK37
Pinchemel, Phillipe. *Geographers: biobibliographical studies*, CL24
Pinfold, John R. *Tibet*, DE99
Pinther, Miklos. *Atlas of Great Lakes Indian history*, CC232
Pipers Enzyklopädie des Musiktheaters, BH58
Pipping, F. W. *Luettelo suomeksi präntätyistä kirjoista ..*, AA108
Pisano, Dominick. *Air and space history*, DA2
Pisateli Moskvy, Ionov, E. P., BD358
Pitou, Spire. *The Paris Opéra*, BH101
Pitt, Barrie. *The chronological atlas of World War II*, DA78
Pitt, Frances. *The chronological atlas of World War II*, DA78
Pittàno, Giuseppe. *Sinonimi e contrari*, AD133
Place guide, CL35
Place-names *see* **Geographical names and terms**; under specific countries, subhead **Place-names**
Place-names in classical mythology, Bell, Robert E., CF10
Place names of Africa, 1935–1986, Kirchherr, Eugene C., CL32
Places rated almanac, Boyer, Rick, CL16, CL23
Plangger, Albert B. *A concise encyclopedia of Zimbabwe*, DD58
Plank, Tom M. *Accounting desk book*, CH67
Planning, equipping, and staffing a document reprographic service, Keene, James A., AB109
Planning library facilities, Stephenson, Mary Sue, AB72
Plano, Jack C. *The American political dictionary*, CJ54
—— *The international relations dictionary*, CJ20
—— *Latin American political dictionary*, CJ194
—— *The public administration dictionary*, CJ210
The plant-book, Mabberley, D. J., EC29
Plant diseases, EC35, EC37, EH11, EH13, EH23, EH25
Planta, Robert de. *Disciunari rumantsch grischen*, AD149
The Plantagenet chronicles, Hallam, Elizabeth M., DC116

The Plantagenet encyclopedia : an alphabetical guide to 400 years of English history, DC116
Plants in danger, EC30
Plastics, EJ20, EJ21, EJ23
Plastics engineering handbook of the Society of the Plastics Industry, Society of the Plastics Industry, EJ23
Plato and Socrates, McKirahan, R.D, BA29
Platt, John Talbot. *Longman dictionary of applied linguistics*, BC13
Platt, Suzy. *Respectfully quoted*, BD65
Platte River road narratives, Mattes, Merrill J., DB57
Play production and dramatic technique, BG25
Plunkett, Michael. *Afro-American sources in Virginia*, CC191
Poblaciones de las parroquias, Ecuador, 1950–1982, Delaunay, Daniel, CG50
The pocket Oxford dictionary of current English, Allen, R. E., AD57
Podell, Janet. *Facts about the states*, CJ125
—— *Speeches of the American presidents*, CJ89
Poetics, BD137
Poetry; *see also* **Versification**
  bibliography, BD129, BD130, BD131
  dictionaries, BD134, BD136, BD137
  handbooks, BD135
  indexes, BD11, BD132, BD133
Poetry by American women, 1975–1989, Reardon, Joan, BD179
Poetry explication, Kunitz, Joseph M., BD182
—— Martinez, Nancy C., BD182
The poet's dictionary, Packard, William, BD135
Poff, Cathryn. *The map catalog*, CL49
Pogonowski, Iwo. *Poland, a historical atlas*, DC174
Poisoning *see* **Toxicology**
Poisonous and venomous marine animals of the world, Halstead, Bruce W., EC42
Pokornowski, Illa M. *African dress II*, BF29
Poland, Jean M. *A guide to the literature of electrical and electronics engineering*, EJ43
Poland
  bibliography, AA173, AA174, DC171, DC173
  biography, AJ85, AJ86, AJ87, AJ88
  history
    atlases, DC174
  statistics, CG69, CG70
Poland, Kanka, August Gerald, DC171
Poland, a historical atlas, Pogonowski, Iwo, DC174
Poland. Główny Urząd Statystyczny. *Bibliografia wydawnictw Głównego Urzędu Statystycznego, 1968–1973*, CG69
—— *Bibliografia wydawnictw Głównego Urzędu Statystycznego, 1974–1980*, CG70
Polar record, Scott Polar Research Institute, DH4
Police, CK100, CK102, CK104
The police dictionary and encyclopedia, Fay, John, CK102
Policies of publishers, Kim, David U., AB66
Policy studies journal, CJ10
Polisar, Donna. *Where do we come from? What are we? Where are we going?*, CC48
Polish feature films, Sobański, Oskar, BG81
Polish language, AD145
Polish music, Smialek, William, BH23
Political and economic encyclopaedia of the Pacific, DG9
Political and economic encyclopaedia of the Soviet Union and Eastern Europe, DC15
Political and economic encyclopaedia of Western Europe, CJ167
Political campaign communication, Kaid, Lynda Lee, CJ48
Political consultants, CJ66
Political corruption, Johansen, Elaine, CJ47
Political dictionary of the Arab world, Shimoni, Yaacov, CJ152, CJ190, CJ199, DE20, DE27

Political dictionary of the Middle East in the twentieth century, Levine, Evyatar, CJ152, CJ190
—— Shimoni, Yaacov, CJ152, CJ190
Political dictionary of the State of Israel, CJ190
—— Rolef, Susan Hattis, CJ152, CJ199, DE20, DE27
Political dissent, Degenhardt, Henry W., CJ38
Political ethics, CJ4, CJ34
Political facts of the United States since 1789, Austin, Erik W., CJ70, DB70
Political handbook of the world, CJ33
Political leaders of the contemporary Middle East and North Africa, CJ200
Political parties, CJ138
  Africa, CJ150
  Asia, CJ153, CJ204
  Europe, Western, CJ169
  Gt. Brit., CJ176
  international, CJ29
  Latin America, CJ196
  Oceania, CJ153
  United States, CJ108, CJ116, CJ117, DB78
Political parties in Sri Lanka since independence, Peiris, H. A., CJ204
Political parties of Asia and the Pacific, CJ153
Political parties of the Americas, AJ77, CJ193, CJ196
Political parties of the world, Day, Alan J., CJ29, CJ33
Political quotations, CJ27
Political quotations on Ireland, 1886–1987, BD63, CJ186, DC151
Political resource directory, CJ66
Political risk assessment, Jodice, David A., CJ8
Political risk yearbook, CJ36
Political scandals and causes célèbres since 1945, CJ37
Political science; *see also* under names of countries, subhead **Politics and government**
  atlases, CJ41, CJ42
  bibliography, CJ4, CJ8, CJ10
  bibliography of bibliography, CJ12
  chronologies, CJ39
  compendiums, CJ140
  dictionaries, CJ22, CJ24, CJ25
  directories, CJ30, CJ32, CJ137, CK83
  education
    directories, CB99, CJ31
  encyclopedias, CJ14, CJ15, CJ16, CJ17, CJ18, CJ21, CJ23, CJ136
  guides, CJ1, CJ2, CJ3
  handbooks, CJ33, CJ34, CJ36, CJ38, CJ139, CJ141, CJ142, CJ143
  quotations, CJ27, CJ28
  terminology, CJ26
  yearbooks, CJ144
Political science, York, Henry E., CJ3
Political science bibliographies, Harmon, Robert B., CJ12
Political slogans, CJ107
Politics and religion, BB15, CJ13
Pollard, Alfred W. *A short-title catalogue of books printed in England, Scotland, & Ireland and of English books printed abroad, 1475–1640*, AA127, AG36
Pollner, Clausdirk. *Auswahlbibliographie zum Studium der anglistischen Sprachwissenschaft*, BC20
Pollock, Bruce. *Popular music*, BH132
—— *Popular music, 1920–1979*, BH132
Pollution abstracts, EJ27, EJ27
Pollution/toxicology CD-ROM, EE39, EJ27, EK129
Polmar, Norman. *Guide to the Soviet navy*, CJ282
Polska Akademia Nauk. *Słownik staropolski*, AD145
Polska Akademia Umiejętności, Krakow. *Polski słownik biograficzny*, AJ88
Polski słownik biograficzny, Polska Akademia Umiejętności, Krakow, AJ88

Polskie wydawnictwa informacyjne 1945–1981, Barteczko, Ewa, AA63
Polymer handbook, EJ22
Polymers, EJ20, EJ21, EJ22
Ponko, Vincent. *Britain in the Middle East, 1921–1956*, DE14
Pons Wörterbuch der deutschen Umgangssprache, Küpper, Heinz, AD113
Pontifical Institute of Mediaeval Studies. *Dictionary of Old English*, AD63
Pontificio Istituto biblico. *Elenchus of Biblica*, BB45
Poole, Trevor B. *The UFAW handbook on the care and management of laboratory animals*, EC58, EH29
Poortman, J. J. *Repertorium der Nederlandse wijsbegeerte*, BA10
Pope, Barbara H. *Historical periodicals directory*, DA10
Pope, Rex. *Atlas of British social and economic history since c. 1700*, DC125
Pope, Stephen. *A dictionary of the Second World War*, DA76
Popes, cardinals, bishops, BB121
Popp, Judy. *Financial planners and planning organizations directory*, CH245
Popplestone, John A. *Dictionary of concepts in general psychology*, CD19
Popular American composers from revolutionary times to the present, Ewen, David, BH109
Popular music, BH132
—— Iwaschkin, Roman, BH137
—— Shapiro, Nat, BH132
Popular music, 1900–1919, Cohen-Stratyner, Barbara, BH132
Popular music, 1920–1979, Pollock, Bruce, BH132
—— Shapiro, Nat, BH132
Popular music periodicals index, BH138
Popular music since 1955, Taylor, Paul, BH139
Popular song index. Third supplement, Havlice, Patricia Pate, BH114
Popular U.S. government publications, AG7
Population
  bibliography, CG2, CG4
  compendiums, CG21
  dictionaries, CG13
Population forecasting, CG23
Population information in twentieth century census volumes, 1900–1940, Schulze, Suzanne, CG33
Population information in twentieth century census volumes, 1950–1980, Schulze, Suzanne, CG34
The Population Reference Bureau's population handbook, Haupt, Arthur, CG1
Population statistics, Benjamin, Bernard, CG53
Population terminology, CG13
Population, urbanization, and rural settlement in Ghana, Sarfoh, Joseph A., DD38
Porter, David L. *Biographical dictionary of American sports : baseball*, BJ20
—— *Biographical dictionary of American sports : basketball and other indoor sports*, BJ28
—— *Biographical dictionary of American sports : football*, BJ30
—— *Biographical dictionary of American sports : outdoor sports*, BJ5
Porter, Frank W. *In pursuit of the past*, CC218
Porter, Robert. *Guide to corporate giving in the arts 4*, CA36
Porter-Shirley, Bunny. *Peterson's drug and alcohol programs and policies at four-year colleges*, CB104
The portrait in Britain and America, Simon, Robin, BE153
Portraits, BE7, BE153
Portsmouth Polytechnic. *World mapping today*, CL47
Portugal
  bibliography, DC177
    current, AA175

  biography, AJ93
  history, DC175
    bibliography, DC176, DD14, DE1
Portugal, Unwin, P. T. H., DC177
The Portuguese in Asia, De Silva, Daya, DE1
The Portuguese in the United States, Pap, Leo, CC168
The Portuguese in the United States, Viera, David J., CC168
Portuguese language
  bibliography, BC46, BC51
  dictionaries
    bilingual, AD146, EA51
  guides, BC47, BD317
Portuguese language and Luso-Brazilian literature, Chamberlain, Bobby J., BC47, BD317
Portuguese literature
  bibliography, BC51
  criticism, BD327
  guides, BC47, BD317
Posner, Julia L. *CWLA's guide to adoption agencies*, CC139
Post report, United States. Dept. of State, CL18
Postage stamps, BF51
Postlethwaite, T. Neville. *The encyclopedia of comparative education and national systems of education*, CB63
—— *The international encyclopedia of education*, CB63, CB64
Postmodern fiction, BD94
Poston, Thurman R. *Eshbach's handbook of engineering fundamentals*, EJ6
Postwar industrial policy in Japan, Boger, Karl, CH37
Poteet, G. Howard. *Death and dying*, CC97
—— *Death and dying : a bibliography, 1974–1978*, CC98
Potenza, R. *Multilingual thesaurus of geosciences*, EE15
Potter, Clare. *The lesbian periodicals index*, CC151
Potter, Karl H. *Guide to Indian philosophy*, BA7
Potter, Robert B. *Barbados*, DB143
Pottery analysis, Rice, Prudence M., BF27
Poulton, Helen. *A historian's handbook*, DA1
Pourcelet, François. *Guide des papiers des ministres et secrétaires d'État de 1871 à 1974*, DC69
Poverty, CC143, CC144, CC145
Powell, Antoinette Paris. *Bibliography of landscape architecture, environmental design, and planning*, BE142
Powell, David. *The wisdom of the novel*, BD64
Powell, James R. *Core list of books and journals in science and technology*, EA7
Powell, Marjorie. *Teacher attitudes*, CB18
Powell, Paul W. *The great deceiver*, CC83
Powell, Russell H. *Core list of books and journals in science and technology*, EA7
Powell, Warren H. *Inorganic chemical nomenclature*, ED26
Practical approaches to legal research, Olson, Kent C., CK10
A practical guide to graduate research, Stock, Molly, AH2
Practical handbook of microbiology, EC22
—— O'Leary, William M., EC21
Praktisches Lexikon der Spiritualität, BB90
Pratt, Douglas. *The laser video disc companion*, BG112
Pratt, Stanley E. *Pratt's guide to venture capital sources*, CH258
Pratt's guide to venture capital sources, CH258
Prayers, BB72
Precollege foundation support, CB158
La première guerre d'Indochine, 1945–1954, Ruscio, Alain, DE65
Preminger, Alex. *The Princeton handbook of poetic terms*, BD137
The Prentice-Hall encyclopedia of world proverbs, Mieder, Wolfgang, BD71

Prentice Hall guide to English literature, BD220
The Prentice Hall real estate investor's encyclopedia, Blankenship, Frank J., CH346
Presbyterian Church (U.S.A.). General Assembly. *Minutes*, BB112
Presbyterians, BB111, BB112
Preservation guidelines in ARL libraries, AB105
Preservation organization and staffing, AB106
Preservation planning program, Darling, Pamela W., AB104
Preservation work in libraries, AB104, AB105, AB106
Presidential advisory commissions, 1973–1984, CJ88
Presidential elections since 1789, CJ113
Presidential executive orders and proclamations, AG20, AG21
Presidential libraries and collections, Veit, Fritz, AB49, CJ83, DB22
Presidents, AG24, CJ73, CJ74, CJ77, CJ78, CJ79, CJ87, CJ91, CJ108
  bibliography, CJ45
  manuscripts and archives, AB47, CJ80, CJ82
  quotations, CJ84
  speeches, CJ89
Les présocratiques, Paquet, Léonce, BA6
The press in Nigeria, Ogbondah, Chris W., AE59
Pressure groups, CJ67, CJ68, EH18
Preston, Antony. *Atlas of maritime history*, DA28
Preston, Richard Joseph. *North American trees*, EC36
Preuss, Arthur. *A dictionary of secret and other societies*, CA54
Prevention education, Derivan, William J., CB22, CC113
Prévost, Michel. *Dictionnaire de biographie française*, AJ51
Prézelin, Bernard. *Combat fleets of the world*, CJ265
Pribić, Rado. *Nobel laureates in literature*, BD56
Price, David H. *Atlas of world cultures*, CE24
The price of admission, Makinson, Larry, CJ110
Pries, Nancy. *American diaries*, BD183, BD184
Priestley, Brian. *Jazz*, BH124
Primary commodity markets and models, Labys, Walter C., CH174
Primary sources in European diplomacy, 1914–1945, Messick, Frederic M., CJ9, DC5
Prime rate archive & update service, CH261
Primo catalog collettivo delle biblioteche italiane, AA148
Prince, Gerald. *A dictionary of narratology*, BD40
Prince, Mary Miles. *Bieber's current American legal citations*, CK89
  —— *Bieber's dictionary of legal abbreviations*, CK62
  —— *Bieber's dictionary of legal citations*, CK89
Princeton encyclopedia of poetry and poetics, BD137
The Princeton handbook of poetic terms, BD137
Principal officers of the Department of State and United States chiefs of mission, 1778–1990, United States. Dept. of State. Office of the Historian, CJ86
Pringle, David. *Imaginary people*, BD10
Printing and publishing
  bibliography, AA48
  biography, AA51, AA52
  dictionaries, AA47
  directories
    bibliography, AA48
    United States, AB22
  encyclopedias, AA46
  handbooks, AA49, AB13, BD49, CA46
  history, AA50
Printing for Parliament, 1641–1700, AG38

Prints and engravings
  bibliography, BE155
  biography, BE161
  by country or region
    Japan, BE154
  guides, BE158
  handbooks, BE157, BE159, BE161
  indexes, BE156
Prints and printmaking, Lister, Raymond, BE161
Printworld directory of contemporary prints and prices, BE159
Prinz, Otto. *Mittellateinisches Wörterbuch bis zum ausgehenden 13. [i.e. dreizehnten] Jahrhundert*, AD140
Příspěvky ke knihopisu, Voit, Petr, AA98
Pritchard, James Bennett. *The Harper atlas of the Bible*, BB68
Private libraries of musicians and musicologists, Folter, Siegrun H., BH12
Prize stories, BD177
Prizewinning literature, Strachan, Anne, BD45
Problem words and expressions, AD27
Problems in literary research, Kahler, Dorothy, BD149
The process of legal research, CK11
Prochaska, Alice. *Irish history from 1700*, DC150
Production handbook, CH304
Professional careers sourcebook, CH337, CH341
Professional ethics, CH335, CK84
Proffer, Carl R. *Nineteenth-century Russian literature in English*, BD354
Program evaluation, Dynes, Patrick S., CJ212
Program for Art on Film (New York, N.Y.). *Films and videos on photography*, BF52
Prominent Hungarians, Fekete, Márton, AJ69
Prominent scientists, Pelletier, Paul A., EA85
Proofreading and editing for word processors, Lindsell, Sheryl L., AA55
Properties of the National Trust, BE126
Protectionism, Lutz, James M., CH178
Protestantism, BB87
Prouty, Howard H. *Variety television reviews, 1923–1988*, BG105
Provan, Jill. *Health media review index*, EK21
  —— *Health media review index, 1984–86*, EK22
Provençal language, BC35, BD309
Proverbs
  bibliography, BD70
  collections, BD71, BD72, BD344
Provincial royal commissions and commissions of inquiry, 1867–1982, Maillet, Lise, AG31, CJ158
Provorse, Carl. *The encyclopedia of the Central West*, DB56
Provost, Foster. *Columbus*, DB141
Prucha, Francis Paul. *Handbook for research in American history*, DB1
Pruett, James W. *Research guide to musicology*, BH4
Pruett, Nancy Jones. *Scientific and technical libraries*, AB61
Prus, Joseph S. *Handbook of certification and licensure requirements for school psychologists*, CB133
Pryor, Judith. *Delivering government services*, CJ220
Prytherch, Raymond John. *Food, cookery, and diet*, EH35
  —— *Harrod's librarians' glossary of terms used in librarianship, documentation and the book crafts, and reference book*, AB15
  —— *Sources of information in librarianship and information science*, AB4
Przewodnik bibliograficzny, AA173
Psacharopoulos, George. *Economics of education : research and studies*, CB63
Pschyrembel, Willibald. *Dictionary of obstetrics and gynecology*, EK52

Pschyrembel Wörterbuch Gynäkologie und Gerburtshilfe, EK52
Pschyrembel's Klinisches Wörterbuch, EK52
Pseudonyms *see* Anonyms and pseudonyms
Pseudonyms and nicknames dictionary, AA32
Psychiatric dictionary, Campbell, Robert Jean, CD18
Psychiatry
  biography, CD34
  dictionaries, CD18, CD21
  encyclopedias, CD17
  terminology, CD29
  treatises, CD33
Psychical research, CD50
Psychoanalysis, CD24
Psychoanalysis, psychology, and literature, a bibliography, Kiell, Norman, BD4
Psychoanalytic terms and concepts, CD24
The psychohistorian's handbook, Lawton, Henry, DA15
Psychohistory, DA15
Psychological abstracts, CD8, CD25
Psychological and medical aspects of induced abortion, Winter, Eugenia B., CC267, EK19
The psychologist's companion, Sternberg, Robert J., CD37
Psychology
  biography, CD35, CD36
  dictionaries, CD19, CD20, CD22, CD23
  encyclopedias, CD9, CD10, CD12, CD13, CD14, CD15
  graduate study, CD31
  guides for authors, CD37
  history
    indexes, CD7
  indexes, CD8
  periodicals, CB44, CD4, CD5
    guides for authors, CD6
  software, CD28, CD32
  surveys, CD30
  terminology, CD25
  tests and measurements, CB120, CD38
Psychology and its allied disciplines, CD15
Psychology and literature, BD4, BD6, BD7
Psychotherapy, CC128, CD26
Psychware, Krug, Samuel E., CD32
PsycINFO, CB6, CD8
PsycLIT, CD8
Public administration, CJ212, CJ215, CJ216, CJ218, CJ220, CJ221, CJ222
  bibliography, CJ209
  Canada, CJ213
  dictionaries, CJ224
  encyclopedias, CJ210, CJ223
  guides, CJ211, CJ219
  handbooks, CJ214
Public administration, McCurdy, Howard E., CJ218, CJ219
Public administration desk book, Coleman, James R., CJ211
The public administration dictionary, Chandler, Ralph C., CJ210
Public administration in the Third World, CJ222
Public Affairs Information Service. *PAIS international in print*, CA10
  —— *PAIS on CD-ROM*, CA11
Public Affairs Information Service bulletin, CA10
Public Archives Canada. *Canadian feature film index, 1913–1985 = Index des films canadiens de long métrage, 1913–1985*, BG82
Public Archives of Canada. *Union list of manuscripts in Canadian repositories*, DB86
Public colleges and universities, Ohles, John F., CB102
Public finance, CH218
Public finance, Marshall, Marion B., CH218
Public interest profiles, CJ67
Public libraries, AB55
Public office index, Justice, Keith L., CJ120

Public opinion
  bibliography, CJ236
  indexes, CJ230
  polls, CB148, CB149, CJ229, CJ231, CJ232, CJ233, CJ234, CJ235, CJ237
Public opinion polling, Lake, Celinda C., CJ233
Public opinion polls and survey research, Walden, Graham R., CJ236
Public papers of the presidents of the United States, United States. President, AG24
The public policy dictionary, Kruschke, Earl R., CJ25
Public relations handbook, CH74
Public schools, CB131
Public schools USA, Harrison, Charles Hampton, CB131
Public sector productivity, Holzer, Marc, CJ216
Publicaciones oficiales de Chile, 1973–1983, AG32
Las publicaciones periódicas mexicanas, Orozco Tenorio, José, AE58
Publication grants for writers & publishers, Park, Karin R., BD49, CA46
Les publications en série éditées au Sénégal, 1856–1982, Bibliothèque Nationale (France), AE68
Publicaţiunile periodice româneşti (ziare, gazete, reviste), AE63
The published diaries and letters of American women, Goodfriend, Joyce D., BD184
Publishers and publishing, AB66
Publishers, distributors, and wholesalers of the United States, AB22
Publishing opportunities in business and economics, CH92
Puccio, Joseph A. *Serials reference work,* AB108
Puerto Rico
  bibliography of bibliography, DB153
  biography, AJ89, AJ90
  history
    bibliography, DB152
Puerto Rico, Cevallos, Elena E., DB152
Pugh, Geoff. *Sources in European political history,* DC9
Puhvel, Jaan. *Hittite etymological dictionary,* AD121
Pulsiano, Phillip. *An annotated bibliography of North American doctoral dissertations on Old English language and literature,* BC24, BD207
Pult, Chasper. *Disciunari rumantsch grischen,* AD149
Punley, Randolph J. *The American Indian index,* CC228
Punsalan, Victoria J. *Refereed and nonrefereed economic journals,* CH4
Purcell, Gary R. *Reference sources in library and information services,* AB5
Purchasing, CH170
The pursuit of the White House, Thomas, G. Scott, CJ115
Purvis, James D. *Jerusalem, the Holy City,* BB8
Pusat Dokumentasi dan Informasi Ilmiah (Indonesia). *Directory of special libraries and information sources in Indonesia 1985 = Direktori perpustakaan khusus dan sumber informasi di Indonesia 1985,* AB35
Pusat Dokumentasi Ilmiah Nasional (Indonesia). *Directory of special libraries and information sources in Indonesia 1985 = Direktori perpustakaan khusus dan sumber informasi di Indonesia 1985,* AB35
Puxty, Anthony G. *Multinational enterprise,* CH95
Pyatt, Sherman A. *Apartheid,* DD53
Pythagoras, Navia, Luis E., BA28

Qā'imat al-intāj al-fikrī al-Qaṭarī li-'ām, AA176
Qatar, AA176
Quah, Jon S. T. *Singapore,* DE92
Quah, Stella R. *Singapore,* DE92
Quality control, CH290

Quality control, Krismann, Carol, CH290
Quarles, Susan D. *Guide to federal funding for social scientists,* CA37
Quarterly bibliography of computers and data processing, EJ55
Quasten, Johannes. *Patrology,* BB103
Québec (Province). *Répertoire toponymique du Québec,* CL37
Queens, empresses, grand duchesses, and regents, Opfell, Olga S., CJ166
Queen's University (Kingston, Ont.). *Writings on Canadian English, 1976–1987,* BC21
Quellenkunde zur Geschichte Finnlands, Paloposki, Toivo J., DC44
Quemada, B. *Trésor de la langue française,* AD91
Quick, Anne Wenley. *Chaucer, a bibliographical introduction,* BD257, DA46
Quién es quién en el teatro y el cine español e hispanoamericano, BG42
Quién es quién en Venezuela, AJ101
Quilting, 1915–1983, Makowski, Colleen Lahan, BF35
The quotable lawyer, Shrager, David S., CK72
The quotable Shakespeare, DeLoach, Charles, BD266
Quotations, BD57, BD58, BD59, BD60, BD61, BD64, BD65, BD66, BD67, BD68, BD266, CB78
  bibliography, BD2
  by subject
    armed forces, CJ263
    arms control and peace research, CJ307
    business, CH96, CH97
    education, CB77
    fine arts, BE46
    geography, CL13
    music, BH63
    political science, CJ27, CJ28, CJ84
    sociology, CC16
    sports and games, BJ12, BJ13
    travel and tourism, BJ42
    U.S.S.R., CJ249
    women, CC295
  German, BD69
  Irish, BD63, CJ186, DC151
Quote it II, Gerhart, Eugene C., CK71
Quote it! Memorable legal quotations, Gerhart, Eugene C., CK70
al-Qur'ān, BB70

RAA, BE19
RAMP (Program). *Modern archives administration and records management,* AB74
—— *Planning, equipping, and staffing a document reprographic service,* AB109
RILA, BE9, BE19, BE21, BE22, BE23
RILM abstracts, BH45
RIPIM, BH44
RISM, BH22, BH64
RSANB, 1926–1958, AA184
Rabchuk, Gordon. *An annotated bibliography of works on daily newspapers in Canada, 1914–1983 = Une bibliographie annotée des ouvrages portant sur les quotidiens canadiens, 1914–1983; Gordon Rabchuk, indexation,* AF4
Rabin, Jack. *Handbook of public administration,* CJ215
Race and ethnic relations
  atlases, CC188
  bibliography, CC161, CC162, CC165, CC167, CC169, CC170, CC171
  directories, CC176, CC179
  education, CB38
  encyclopedias, CC173
  handbooks, CC183, CC185, CC187
Racinet, A. *The historical encyclopedia of costumes,* BF30
Racism in the United States, Weinberg, Meyer, CC170

Radelet, Michael L. *Capital punishment in America,* CK98
The radical right, Ó Maoláin, Ciarán, CJ138
Radicalism, AE26, CJ119
Radicals and socialists, Biographical dictionary of modern European, AJ8
Radio, Greenfield, Thomas Allen, CH197
Radio and television; *see also* **Mass media; Performing arts**
  archival sources, BG106
  bibliography, BG102, BG103, BG104, CC197, CH197, CH200, CH201, CH202
  biography, BG116
  catalogs and filmography, BG107, BG108, BG109, BG110, BG111, BG112, BG113, BG114, BG117
  dictionaries, BG115, CH206, CH207, EJ69
  directories, AE1, AE44, BG4, BG98
  handbooks, CH211
  history, BG116
  indexes
    reviews, BG105
  periodicals, BG58
Radler, Rudolf. *Kindlers neues Literatur Lexikon,* BD29
Radley, Arthur Farrand. *Austria,* DC27
Radu, Michael. *Latin American revolutionaries,* CJ197
Rageau, Jean-Pierre. *A strategic atlas,* CJ41
Ragsdale, Bruce A. *Biographical dictionary of the American Congress, 1774–1989,* CJ104
Rahman, H. U. *A chronology of Islamic history, 570–1000 CE,* DE25
Rai, Priya Muhar. *Sikhism and the Sikhs,* BB140
Railroads in the age of regulation, 1900–1980, Bryant, Keith L., CH136
Railroads in the nineteenth century, Frey, Robert L., CH136
Rainbow, Edward L. *Research in music education,* BH3
Rainwater, Dorothy T. *Encyclopedia of American silver manufacturers,* BF43
Raja Rammohun Roy Library Foundation. *Directory of Indian public libraries,* AB30
Rājjāka, Moḥ Ābadura. *Bangladesh,* DE44
Rakover, Naḥum. *The multi-language bibliography of Jewish law,* CK42
Rama Reddy, E. *Social science information,* CA2
Ramsaran, Susan. *Everyman's English pronouncing dictionary,* AD37
Ramsey, J. *Botswana,* DD5
Ramson, W. S. *The Australian national dictionary,* AD54
Ranade, Ashok D. *Keywords and concepts, Hindustani classical music,* BH60
Rand McNally and Company. *The new international atlas = Der neue internationale Atlas = El nuevo atlas internacional = Le nouvel atlas international = O nôvo atlas internacional,* CL56
—— *Standard highway mileage guide,* CL59
Rand McNally atlas of world history, DA29
The Rand McNally credit union directory, CH249
Randel, Don Michael. *The new Harvard dictionary of music,* BH56
Randolph, Ruth Elizabeth. *The Harlem Renaissance and beyond,* BD189
The Random House dictionary of the English language, AD3
The Random House encyclopedia, AC6
The Random House thesaurus, AD50
The Random House thesaurus of slang, AD45
Ranke, Kurt. *Enzyklopädie des Märchens,* CF26
Rankings of the states, National Education Association—Research, CB151
Rankova, Mariîa. *Angliĭsko-bŭlgarski rechnik,* AD79
Rao, Vijaya. *World guide to social work education,* CC32

Rape, CC133, CC262

Rape, Nordquist, Joan, CC262

Raper, Ann Trueblood. *National continuing care directory,* CC58

Rapp, George Robert. *Encyclopedia of minerals,* EE37

Rappaport, Barry. *Uranometria 2000.0,* EB18

Rare birds of the world, Mountfort, Guy, EC54

Rasmussen, Carl. *Zondervan NIV atlas of the Bible,* BB69

Rasmussen, R. Kent. *Dictionary of African historical biography,* AJ29

—— *Zimbabwe,* DD5

Rasor, Eugene L. *The battle of Jutland,* DB15

—— *British naval history since 1815,* DC100

—— *The Falklands/Malvinas campaign,* DB15

Rassam, Ghassan N. *Multilingual thesaurus of geosciences,* EE15

The rating guide to franchises, Foster, Dennis L., CH118

The rating guide to life in America's small cities, Thomas, G. Scott, CL23

Rausch, Wilhelm. *Bibliographie zur Geschichte der Städte Österreichs,* DC26

Rave, Paul. *Kunstgeschichte in Festschriften,* BE9

Raven, James. *British fiction, 1750–1770,* BD238

Ravenhall, Mary. *An annotated bibliography and index covering CPL bibliographies 1–253, January 1979–December 1989,* CC159

Rawat, Prem Singh. *Directory of periodicals published in India, 1986–87,* AE50

Rawlins, Bert J. *The parish churches and nonconformist chapels of Wales,* AK47

Rawson, Hugh. *Wicked words,* AD48

Ray, Donald Iain. *Dictionary of the African left,* CJ150

Ray, Harold Lloyd. *Sports talk,* BJ10

Ray, Mary Helen. *A guide to historic and significant gardens of America,* BE146

—— *The traveler's guide to American gardens,* BE146

Ray, Nisith Ranjan. *Dictionary of national biography. Supplement,* AJ71

Ray, Shyamal Kumar. *Directory of scientific personnel of the Anthropological Survey of India,* CE22

Rayez, André. *Dictionnaire de spiritualité,* BB85

Read, Campbell B. *Encyclopedia of statistical sciences,* EF9

Read, Patricia. *Foundation fundamentals,* CA47

Read, Peter G. *Dictionary of gemmology,* EE34

The reader's adviser, AA60

The reader's catalog, AA61

Reader's Digest family word finder, AD50

Reader's Digest illustrated encyclopedic dictionary, AD4

Readers' guide abstracts, AE79

A reader's guide to contemporary literary theory, Selden, Raman, BD22

A reader's guide to Japanese literature, Rimer, J. Thomas, BD380

Readers' guide to periodical literature, AE79, BD180

Reader's guide to twentieth-century science fiction, BD119

Reading, CB27, CB67
 bibliography, CB19
 indexes and abstracts, CB58

Reading abstracts, CB58

Reading lists in radical social science, CA7

Real estate, CH356
 bibliography, CH343, CH344, CH345
 dictionaries, CH346, CH347, CH348, CH349, CH350
 directories, CH352
 foreign ownership, CH351
 handbooks, CH344, CH354, CH355

Real estate, Freeman, Jean K., CH344

—— Haikalis, Peter D., CH344

Real estate dictionary, Thomsett, Michael C., CH349

The real estate handbook, CH355

The real estate industry, Harris, Laura A., CH344

The real estate sourcebook, CH353

The realist debate, Weisberg, Yvonne M. L., BE148

Reallexikon der Assyriologie, unter Mitwirkung zahlreicher Fachgelehrter, DA36

Reallexikon der deutschen Literaturgeschichte, BD292

Reallexikon für Antike und Christentum, BB94, BB95

Reallexikon zur byzantinischen Kunst, Wessel, Klaus, BE40

Reallexikon zur deutschen Kunstgeschichte, BE39

Reams, Bernard D. *The Constitution of the United States,* CK118

Reardon, Joan. *Poetry by American women, 1975–1989,* BD179

Rebach, Howard M. *Handbook of clinical sociology,* CC18

Reber, Arthur S. *The Penguin dictionary of psychology,* CD20

Recent American opera, Kornick, Rebecca Hodell, BH98

Recent Soviet archival literature, Grimsted, Patricia Kennedy, AB10, DC201

Recent titles in law for the subject specialist, CK19

Recently published articles, DA8

Rechnik na bŭlgarskiia ezik, AD80

Rechnik na bŭlgarskite psevdonimi, Bogdanov, Ivan, AA34

Reckendorf, Hermann. *Wörterbuch der klassischen arabischen Sprache,* AD71

Recla, Josef. *International directory of sports organizations under the auspices of the International Association for Sports Information (IASI),* BJ14

Record repositories in Great Britain, DC109

Record sources for local history, Riden, Philip, DC110

Recorded music; *see also* under topics, subhead
 Discography
 catalogs and discography, BH156, BH158
 bibliography, BH159
 databases, BH157
 dictionaries, BH160
 reviews, BH161

Recorded plays, Hoffman, Herbert H., BG16

Records of the presidency, Schick, Frank Leopold, AB49, CJ82, DB22

Recueils bibliographiques concernant la Mauritanie, Robert, Dieter, DD43

Rédei, Károly. *Uralisches etymologisches Wörterbuch,* AD172

Redekop, Paul. *Sociology of sport,* BJ1

Redfern, Bernice. *Women of color in the United States,* CC287

Redgrave, G. R. *A short-title catalogue of books printed in England, Scotland, & Ireland and of English books printed abroad, 1475–1640,* AA127, AG36

Redman, Barbara Klug. *Guide to programs in nursing in four-year colleges and universities,* EK93

Rée, Jonathan. *The concise encyclopedia of western philosophy and philosophers,* BA11

Reed, Marcia. *American diaries,* BD183, BD184

Reed, Roger. *The illustrator in America,* BE97

Reed, Walter. *The illustrator in America,* BE97

Rees, Alan M. *The consumer health information source book,* EK15

Rees, Eiluned. *Libri Walliae,* AA202

Rees, Nigel. *Why do we say— ?,* AD18

Rees, Philip. *Biographical dictionary of the extreme right since 1890,* CJ40

Refereed and nonrefereed economic journals, Miller, A. Carolyn, CH4

Reference and information services, Katz, William A., AB107

Reference encyclopedia of the American Indian, Klein, Barry T., CC226

A reference guide for English studies, Marcuse, Michael J., BD201

Reference guide to American literature, BD169

A reference guide to the United States Supreme Court, CK90

A reference guide to United States Department of State special files, Haines, Gerald K., CJ81

Reference guides to state history and research, DB43

Reference sources in history, Fritze, Ronald H., DA1

Reference sources in library and information services, Purcell, Gary R., AB5

Reference work in libraries, AB107, AB108; *see also* **Online searching**

Reference works in British and American literature, Bracken, James K., BD200

Reformation, BA26, BB99, DC82

Reformers, AJ21, CC24

Refugee and immigrant resource directory, 1990–1991, Schorr, Alan Edward, CC177

Refugees, CC177

Refugees in the United States, CC187

Refussé, Raymond. *Directory of Irish archives,* DC149

Regents of nations, Truhart, Peter, CJ147

Reginald, Robert. *The arms control, disarmament and military security dictionary,* CJ303, CJ304

Region and regionalism in the United States, Steiner, Michael, DB46

Regional differences in America, CG26, DB44

Regional, state, and local organizations, CA51

Regional Young Adult Project (U.S.). *National directory of corporate charity,* CA41

Register und Auswertung zur 22. Auflage des etymologischen Wörterbuch von Friedrich Kluge, Seebold, Elmar, AD112

Regulatory Compliance Associates, Inc. *A desktop reference manual of compliance terms,* CH226

Reich, Bernard. *Political leaders of the contemporary Middle East and North Africa,* CJ200

—— *United States foreign policy and the Middle East/North Africa,* DE15

Reichenberger, Kurt. *Das spanische Drama im Goldenen Zeitalter,* BD338

Reichenberger, Roswitha. *Das spanische Drama im Goldenen Zeitalter,* BD338

Reichler, Joseph L. *The baseball encyclopedia,* BJ18

—— *The baseball trade register,* BJ25

Reichmann, Oskar. *Frühneuhochdeutsches Wörterbuch,* AD104

Reid, Daniel G. *Dictionary of Christianity in America,* BB84

Reid, Elspeth. *Sub-doctoral theses on Canada accepted by universities in the United Kingdom & Ireland 1899–1986,* DB85

Reilly, Catherine W. *English poetry of the Second World War,* BD245

Reilly, John M. *Twentieth-century crime and mystery writers,* BD108

Reilly, John W. *The language of real estate,* CH348

Reinhart, Theodore J. *Engineered materials handbook,* EJ12

Reisser, Marsha J. *Black music and musicians in The new Grove dictionary of American music and The new Harvard dictionary of music,* BH93

—— *Black music biography,* BH89

Rela, Walter. *A bibliographical guide to Spanish American literature,* BD330

—— *Brazilian literature,* BD319

—— *Diccionario de escritores uruguayos,* BD348

—— *Guia bibliográfica de la literatura hispano-americana desde siglo XIX hasta 1970,* BD330

—— *Literatura uruguaya,* BD349

—— *Literatura uruguaya : tablas cronologicas, 1835–1985,* BD349

Religion
  bibliography, BB10, BB18
    reference works, BB79
  biography, BB34, BB35
  book reviews
    indexes, BB20, BB21
  by country
    Canada, BB30
    China, BB12, BB13
    South Africa, BB18
    United States, BB9, BB26, BB30, BB34
      Southern states, BB4
  databases, BB16, BB17, BB21
  directories, BB30
  encyclopedias, BB22, BB25, BB26, BB27, BB28, BB29, BB88, BB91, BB118, CD53, CF4
  guides, BB1
  periodicals, BB3, BB5, BB14

Religion and American life, BB9

Religion and education, CB35

Religion and the U.S. presidency, Menendez, Albert J., CJ79

Religion index, BB21

Religion index one, BB21

Religion index one : periodicals, BB16

Religion index two : multi-author works, BB16

Religion indexes, BB16

Religion indexes [computer file], BB21

Religion journals and serials, Fieg, Eugene C., BB14

Religious and theological abstracts, BB17

Religious books and serials in print, BB10

Religious education, BB32, BB33

Religious & inspirational books & serials in print, BB10

Religious periodicals directory, Cornish, Graham P., BB3

Religious periodicals of the United States, Lippy, Charles H., BB5

Religious schools in America, Hunt, Thomas C., CB30

Remedial education, CB26, CB36, CB116

Renaissance, BE41
  bibliography, BD5
  biography, BA26

Renaissance art, Earls, Irene, BE41

Renaissance humanism, 1300–1550, Kohl, Benjamin G., BD5

Renaissance linguistics archive, 1350–1700, BC5

Renaissance philosophy, BA19

Renard-Clamagirand, Brigitte. *Les thèses françaises sur l'Asie du Sud-Est depuis 1980,* DE38

Rengger, Nicholas J. *Treaties and alliances of the world,* CK111

Renouard, Philippe. *Imprimeurs & libraires parisiens du XVIe siècle,* AA52

—— *Inventaire chronologique des éditions parisiennes du XVIe siècle,* AA111

Renstrom, Peter G. *The constitutional law dictionary : vol. 1, Individual rights, suppl. 1,* CK114

—— *The electoral politics dictionary,* CJ55, CJ57

Renz, Loren. *Foundations today,* CA48

Renzetti Marra, S. *Bibliografia dell'Italia antica,* DC154

Répertoire bibliographique des livres imprimés en France au XVIIe siècle, AA112

Répertoire bibliographique des livres imprimés en France au XVIIIe siècle, AA112

—— Desgraves, Louis, AA114

Répertoire d'art et d'archéologie, BE19, BE22, BE21

Répertoire d'art et d'archéologie [computer file], BE21

Répertoire de l'histoire de la Révolution française, Walter, Gerard, DC49

Répertoire des catalogues de ventes de livres imprimés, Blogie, Jeanne, AA44

Répertoire des catalogues des ventes publiques, Lugt, Frits, BE61

Répertoire des dossiers documentaires traitant de l'art et de l'architecture dans les régions représentées á la section ARLIS M/O/Q = Directory of vertical file collections on art and architecture represented by ARLIS M/O/Q, BE51

Répertoire des mémoires de licence et des thèses de doctorat présentés dans les départements d'histoire contemporaine des universités belges, Hendrickx, Jean-Pierre, DC31

Répertoire des ouvrages imprimés en langue italienne au XVIIe siècle conservés dans les bibliothèques de France, Michel, Suzanne P., AA149

Répertoire des publications officielles (séries et périodiques), AG35

Répertoire des thèses et mémoires, 1953–1984, AH14

Répertoire international de la littérature de l'art, BE19, BE21, BE23, BE22

Répertoire international de la presse musicale, BH44

Répertoire international des médiévistes = International directory of medievalists, AJ18, DA52

Répertoire international des sources musicales = International inventory of musical sources, BH22

Répertoire mondial des institutions de sciences sociales = World directory of social science institutions, CA19

Répertoire toponymique du Québec, CL37

Repertorio bibliográfico de las relaciones entre la península Ibérica y el Norte de África, siglos XV–XVI, García-Arenal, Mercedes, DD14

Repertorio delle cattedrali gotiche, BE131

Repertorium bibliographium, Hain, Ludwig, AA42

Repertorium der Nederlandse wijsbegeerte, Poortman, J. J., BA10

Repertorium doctoraalscripties 1981–1985, BE12

Repertory of disarmament research, CJ301

Report series codes dictionary, EA22

Reprography, AB109, AB110

Reptiles *see* **Amphibians and reptiles**

Republic of Cape Verde, Halter, M., DD5

—— Lobban, R., DD5

Republic of China yearbook, DE97

Republic of Guinea-Bissau, Forrest, J., DD6

—— Lobban, R., DD6

The Republic of Turkey, Witherell, Julian W., DC193

Requirements for certification of teachers, counselors, librarians, administrators for elementary and secondary schools, CB134

Research Clearinghouse and Curriculum Integration Project on Women of Color and Southern Women. *Women of color and Southern women,* CC289

Research guide for studies in infancy and childhood, Haag, Enid E., CC77

Research guide for undergraduates in political science, Anderson, Peter J., CJ2

—— Kalvelage, Carl, CJ2

—— Segal, Morley, CJ2

Research guide in political science, Kalvelage, Carl, CJ2

—— Segal, Morley, CJ2

Research guide to biography and criticism, BD15, BG7

Research guide to Central America and the Caribbean, DB96

A research guide to central party and government meetings in China, 1949–1986, Lieberthal, Kenneth, DE52

Research guide to musicology, Pruett, James W., BH4

A research guide to the health sciences, Haselbauer, Kathleen J., EK2

Research guide to the Russian and Soviet censuses, CG75

Research guides in military studies, CJ271

Research in British universities, polytechnics and colleges, CA17, EA53

Research in composition and rhetoric, BD147

Research in critical theory since 1965, Orr, Leonard, BD21

Research in education, CB53

Research in ministry, BB16

Research in music education, Froehlich, Hildegard C., BH3

—— Rainbow, Edward L., BH3

Research in social anthropology, 1975–1980, Webber, Jonathan, CE10

Research Libraries Group, Art and Architecture Program. *SCIPIO,* BE63

Research Library on African Affairs (Accra, Ghana). *Ghana national bibliography bi monthly,* AA124

Research material for Hong Kong studies, DE55

Research methods in cultural anthropology, Bernard, H. Russell, CE1

Research on Southeast Asia, DE38

Research on suicide, McIntosh, John L., CC96

Research tips in international law, CK106

Researcher's guide to archives and regional history sources, DB20

Researcher's guide to British film & television collections, BG84

—— British Universities Film & Video Council, BG84

Resnick, Rosa Perla. *World guide to social work education,* CC32

The resource book of Jewish music, Heskes, Irene, BH16

Resource guide to special education, Davis, William Edmund, CB122

A resource guide to themes in contemporary American song lyrics, 1950–1985, Cooper, B. Lee, BH141

Resources for Australian and New Zealand studies, Bloomfield, Valerie, DF1

Resources for educational equity, CB38

Resources for middle childhood, Sheiman, Deborah Lovitky, CC85

Resources in education, CB1, CB16, CB52, CB53, CB54

Resources in vocational education, CB12

Respectfully quoted, BD65

Restle, Marcell. *Reallexikon zur byzantinischen Kunst,* BE40

Retirement benefit plans, Miller, Herbert A., CH152

Retirement homes, CC60

A retrospective bibliography of American demographic history from colonial times to 1983, Gerhan, David R., CG5, DB9

Retrospective index to Nigerian doctoral dissertations and masters theses, 1895–1980, Ofori, Patrick E., AH16

Retrospektivnaía gosudarstvennaía bibliografiía SSSR, Semenovker, B. A., AA179

Reuther, David. *Total baseball,* BJ27

Reverdy, Georges. *Atlas historique des routes de France,* DC79

Reviews of United Kingdom statistical sources, Maunder, W. F., CG54

The revised English Bible with the Apocrypha, BB38

La Révolution française, Manceron, Claude, DC55

Revolutionary and dissident movements, CJ38

Revolutions in American lives, Wells, Robert V., CG5, DB9

Rew, John. *Directory of Lloyd's of London,* CH266

Rey, Alain. *Dictionnaire alphabétique et analogique de la langue française,* AD93
—— *Dictionnaire des littératures de langue française,* BD312

Reyes, Caroline. *Sears list of subject headings,* AB84

Reynal, Vicente. *Diccionario de hombres y mujeres ilustres de Puerto Rico y de hechos históricos,* AJ90

Reynolds, Cecil R. *Concise encyclopedia of special education,* CB59
—— *Encyclopedia of special education,* CB59, CB62

Reynolds, Frank E. *Guide to Buddhist religion,* BA2, BB123

Reynolds, Hugh. *The executive branch of the U.S. government,* CJ76

Reynolds, James E. F. *The extra pharmacopoeia,* EK117

Reynolds, Maynard Clinton. *Handbook of special education,* CB130
—— *Special education,* CB136

Reynolds, Michael M. *Guide to theses and dissertations,* AE4

Reynolds, Peter L. *A pictorial guide to identifying Australian architecture,* BE130

Reynolds, Thomas H. *Foreign law,* CK28

Rezak, Ira. *Nobel laureates in medicine or physiology,* EK76

Rézeau, Pierre. *Dictionnaire du français parlé,* AD97

Rhoads, James Berton. *A guide to manuscripts in the Presidential Libraries,* AB47, CJ80

Rhodes, Dennis E. *Catalogue of books printed in Spain and of Spanish books printed elsewhere in Europe before 1601 now in the British Library,* AA187

Rhodes, Philip. *The Oxford companion to medicine,* EK41

Rhodesia *see* **Zimbabwe**

Ribbe, Wolfgang. *Taschenbuch für Familiengeschichtsforschung,* AK27

Ricci, Patricia. *Standards,* EA89

Rice, Joanne A. *Middle English romance,* BD208

Rice, Mitchell F. *Health of black Americans from post reconstruction to integration, 1871–1960,* CC202, EK126

Rice, Prudence M. *Pottery analysis,* BF27

Richards, J. F. *The new Cambridge history of India,* DE64

Richards, Jack C. *Longman dictionary of applied linguistics,* BC13

Richards, Peter G. *Ford list of British parliamentary papers, 1974–1983, together with specialist commentaries,* AG43

Richards, Robert W. *The Dow Jones-Irwin dictionary of financial planning,* CH232

Richardson, Elizabeth P. *A Bloomsbury iconography,* BD213

Richardson, Jeanne M. *Science and engineering literature,* EA3

Richardson, Jim. *Philippines,* DG13

Richardson, John. *The local historian's encyclopedia,* AK37

Richardson, R. C. *The study of history,* DA16

Richel, Veronica C. *The German stage, 1767–1890,* BD296

Richmond, W. Edson. *Ballad scholarship,* BD248

Richter, Bernice. *The Museum of Science and Industry basic list of children's science books,* EA14
—— *The Museum of Science and Industry basic list of children's science books, 1973–1984,* EA13

Richter, Heinz A. *Greece and Cyprus since 1920,* DC39, DC142

Richter, Klaus. *The completely illustrated atlas of reptiles and amphibians for the terrarium,* EC45

Ricks, David A. *Directory of foreign manufacturers in the United States,* CH293

Riddick, John F. *Glimpses of India,* DE57

Riden, Philip. *Record sources for local history,* DC110

The Rider encyclopedia of Eastern philosophy and religion, BA12, BB23

Ridinger, Robert B. Marks. *Anthropological fieldwork,* CE3
—— *The homosexual and society,* CC150
—— *The Peace Corps,* CJ299

Ridpath, Ian. *Star atlas and reference handbook (epoch 2000.0),* EB17

Rieber, Hans. *Handbook of paleozoology,* EE42

Riemann, Hugo. *Musik-lexikon,* BH48

Riemens, Leo. *Grosses Sängerlexikon,* BH84

Riff, M. A. *Dictionary of modern political ideologies,* CJ17

Riggar, T. F. *Staff training,* CH150
—— *Stress burnout,* CD2

Right and left (Political science), CJ40, CJ52, CJ63, CJ64, CJ72, CJ138, CJ150; *see also* **Conservatism; Fascism; Radicalism** biography, CJ119 encyclopedias, CJ243, DB62 periodicals, AE26

Right minds, Wolfe, Gregory, CJ72

Riland, George. *The new Steinerbooks dictionary of the paranormal,* CD54

Riley, Raymond Charles. *Belgium,* DC33

Riley, Sam G. *American magazine journalists, 1741–1850,* AF21
—— *American magazine journalists, 1850–1900,* AF22
—— *American magazine journalists, 1900–1960,* AF23
—— *Magazines of the American South,* AE20

Riley-Smith, Jonathan Simon Christopher. *The atlas of the Crusades,* DA54

Rimer, J. Thomas. *A reader's guide to Japanese literature,* BD380

Rimmer, Brenda M. *International guide to official industrial property publications,* EA87

Rinderknecht, Carol. *A checklist of American imprints,* AA80

Ringgren, Helmer. *Theological dictionary of the Old Testament,* BB48
—— *Theologisches Wörterbuch zum Alten Testament,* BB49

Ringler, William A. *Bibliography and index of English verse printed 1476–1558,* BD246

Rinn, Roger C. *Author's guide to journals in psychology, psychiatry and social work,* CD6

Rio de Janeiro. Instituto Brasileiro de Bibliografia e Documentação. *Periódicos brasileiros de cultura,* AE28

Riou, Yves-François. *Les manuscrits classiques latins des bibliothèques publiques de France,* AA38

Ripley, Gordon. *Canadian serials directory = Répertoire des publications sériées canadiennes,* AE29

Ritchie, John. *Australian dictionary of biography,* AJ33

Ritchie, Maureen. *Women's studies,* CC247

Ritter, Audrey L. *A deafness collection,* CC104

Ritter, Charles F. *American legislative leaders, 1850–1910,* CJ132

Ritter, Harry. *Dictionary of concepts in history,* DA17

Ritter, Joachim. *Historisches Wörterbuch der Philosophie,* BA18

Rivas Dugarte, Rafael Angel. *Bibliografía sobre el español del Caribe hispánico,* BC48

RMA annual statement studies, CH128, CH129

Roads to recovery, Moore, Jean, CC75

Roaf, Michael. *Cultural atlas of Mesopotamia and the ancient Near East,* DA38

Robbins, Ceila Dame. *Mottoes,* BD62

Robbins, Keith. *The Blackwell biographical dictionary of British political life in the twentieth century,* CJ177, DC112

Robbins, Russell H. *Index of Middle English verse,* BD205, BD246

Robert, Dieter. *Recueils bibliographiques concernant la Mauritanie,* DD43

Robert, Henry M. *Robert's rules of order,* CJ226
—— *The Scott, Foresman Robert's rules of order newly revised,* CJ227

Robert, Paul. *Dictionnaire alphabétique et analogique de la langue française,* AD93

Robert, Sarah Corbin. *The Scott, Foresman Robert's rules of order newly revised,* CJ227

Robert-Collins dictionnaire français-anglais, anglais-français, AD95

Robert Gore Rifkind Center for German Expressionist Studies. *Bibliography of German Expressionism,* BE29

Robert Morris Associates. *RMA annual statement studies,* CH129

Roberts, A. D. *Dictionary of antibiotics and related substances,* ED32, EK109

Roberts, Anne F. *Library instruction for librarians,* AB102

Roberts, Brian. *Chronological list,* DH4

Roberts, Harold Selig. *Roberts' dictionary of industrial relations,* CH279

Roberts, Helene E. *Iconographic index to Old Testament subjects represented in photographs and slides of paintings in the visual collections, Fine Arts Library, Harvard University,* BE101

Roberts, Patricia. *Alphabet books as a key to language patterns,* CB39

Roberts, Steven. *International directory of telecommunications,* CH210

Roberts, Vera Mowry. *Notable women in the American theatre,* BG39

Roberts, Willard Lincoln. *Encyclopedia of minerals,* EE37

Roberts, William. *Modern Italian history,* DC155

Roberts' dictionary of industrial relations, Roberts, Harold Selig, CH279

Robert's rules of order, Robert, Henry M., CJ226

Robertson, David. *A dictionary of modern politics,* CJ21
—— *Guide to modern defense and strategy,* CJ261

Robertson, David B. *The Facts on File dictionary of military science,* CJ262

Robertson, Jack. *Twentieth-century artists on art,* BE76, BE86

Robertson, William O. *Handbook of poisoning,* EK131

Robinson, Alice M. *Notable women in the American theatre,* BG39

Robinson, Arthur Howard. *Cartographical innovations,* CL10

Robinson, Doris. *Music and dance periodicals,* BG48, BH33

Robinson, Francis. *The Cambridge encyclopedia of India, Pakistan, Bangladesh, Sri Lanka, Nepal, Bhutan, and the Maldives,* DE33

Robinson, J. W. *English theatrical literature, 1599–1900,* BG9

Robinson, Judith Schiek. *Subject guide to U.S. government reference sources,* AG4

Robinson, Mairi. *The concise Scots dictionary,* AD59

Robinson, Richard. *United States business history, 1602–1988,* CH143

Robinson, Ruth. *The UFAW handbook on the care and management of laboratory animals,* EH29

Robitaille, Denis. *Theses in Canada,* AH7

Robotics, EJ64, EJ77

Rocca, Raymond G. *Bibliography on Soviet intelligence and security services,* CJ287

Rock music, BH126, BH129, BH131, BH134 catalogs and discography, BH140, BH156

Rock on almanac, Nite, Norm N., BH131

The rock who's who, Helander, Brock, BH129

Rockabilly, Cooper, B. Lee, BH125
Rockin' the classics and classicizin' the rock, Duxbury, Janell R., BH156
Rocky Mountain states, DB56
Rodale, Jerome I. *The synonym finder*, AD49
Rodger, Margaret D. *Theses on the history of New Zealand*, DF9
Rodin, Alvin E. *Medicine, literature & eponyms*, EK43
Rodrigues, Rita de Cássia. *Bibliografia da música brasileira*, BH5
Roesch, Roberta. *The encyclopedia of depression*, CD16
Rösch-Sondermann, Hermann. *Bibliographie der lokalen Alternativpresse*, AE39
Rogal, Samuel J. *A chronological outline of American literature*, BD166
Rogers, Chester B. *The electoral politics dictionary*, CJ55
Rogers, Colin Darlington. *Tracing your English ancestors*, AK35
Rogers, D. M. *The contemporary printed literature of the English Counter-Reformation between 1558 and 1640*, BB115
Roget's II, AD51
Roh, Jae Min. *Selected black American, African, and Caribbean authors*, BD186
Rohm, Kenneth G. *Refereed and nonrefereed economic journals*, CH4
Rohwer, Jürgen. *Neue Forschungen zum Ersten Weltkrieg*, DA68
Rokiski Lázaro, Gloria. *Bibliografía de la poesía española del siglo XIX (1801–1850)*, BD328
Roland, Charles G. *Sir William Osler*, EK16
Role portrayal and stereotyping on television, Signorielli, Nancy, CH201
Rolef, Susan Hattis. *Political dictionary of the State of Israel*, CJ152, CJ190, CJ199, DE20, DE27
Rollins, Arline McClarty. *One-parent children, the growing minority*, CC81
Rollins, Stephen J. *Scientific and technical libraries*, AB61
Roman Catholic church; see also Patrology
  bibliography, BB115, BB116
  history
    guides, BB119
    papal and conciliar documents, BB98
    peace research, BB117, CJ298
The Roman emperors, Grant, Michael, DA43
Romance languages, BC37
Romances, epics, etc., BD138, BD139, BD204, BD208
Romania
  bibliography, AA177
    current, AA178
    dissertations, AH18
  history
    bibliography, DC178
Romania, Deletant, Andrea, DC178
Romanian language, AD147, AD148
Romansh language, AD149
Rome, DA41, DA43
Ronsard et ses amis, Jurgens, Madeleine, DC68
Rony, A. Kohar. *Vietnamese holdings in the Library of Congress. Supplement, 1979–1985*, DE100
Roof, Michael K. *Detailed statistics on the population of Israel by ethnic and religious group and urban and rural residence, 1950 to 2010*, CG58
Room, Adrian. *Dictionary of astronomical names*, EB9
—— *Dictionary of changes in meaning*, AD19
—— *Dictionary of coin names*, BF50
—— *Dictionary of translated names and titles*, BD50
—— *A dictionary of true etymologies*, AD20
Roosens, Laurent. *History of photography*, BF56, BF57
The roots of English, Claiborne, Robert, AD14

Roper, Michael. *Planning, equipping, and staffing a document reprographic service*, AB109
Rose, Brian Geoffrey. *TV genres*, BG104
Rose, Richard. *The international almanac of electoral history*, CJ141
Rose, Robert F. *Business serials of the U.S. government*, CH91
Rosen, Fred S. *Dictionary of immunology*, EK56
Rosen, Sumner M. *Face of the nation, 1987*, CC30
Rosenak, Chuck. *Museum of American Folk Art encyclopedia of twentieth-century American folk art and artists*, BF17
Rosenak, Jan. *Museum of American Folk Art encyclopedia of twentieth-century American folk art and artists*, BF17
Rosenberg, Jerry Martin. *Dictionary of artificial intelligence and robotics*, EJ64
—— *Dictionary of banking and financial services*, CH233, CH233
—— *Dictionary of computers, data processing, and telecommunications*, EJ65
—— *Dictionary of computers, informational processing, and telecommunications*, EJ65
—— *The investor's dictionary*, CH234
—— *The new Europe 1992*, CK126
Rosenberg, Kenyon C. *A basic classical and operatic recordings collection for libraries*, BH158
—— *A basic classical and operatic recordings collection on compact discs for libraries: a buying guide*, BH158
—— *Dictionary of library and educational technology*, AB16
Roses, Lorraine Elena. *The Harlem Renaissance and beyond*, BD189
Ross, Harris. *Film as literature, literature as film*, BG54
Ross, Joseph A. *Still more words of Wall Street*, CH231
Ross, Robert L. *Australian literary criticism, 1945–1988*, BD275
Ross, Stanley Ralph. *The motion picture guide*, BG78
Rossi, Ernest E. *The European political dictionary*, CJ168
—— *Latin American political dictionary*, CJ194
Rossman, Amy Y. *A literature guide for the identification of plant pathogenic fungi*, EC35
Roster, Peter. *Bibliografía del teatro hispanoamericano contemporáneo (1900–1980)*, BG15
Rothman, Fred B. *Foreign law*, CK28
Rothwell, Kenneth S. *Shakespeare on screen*, BD264
Rothwell, William. *Anglo-Norman dictionary*, AD62
Rouse, Sarah. *3 decades of television*, BG109
Roussel, M. *Les présocratiques*, BA6
Routh, C. N. R. *Who's who in Tudor England*, DC124
The Routledge dictionary of quotations, BD57
Rovira, Carmen. *Sears list of subject headings*, AB84
Rowe, John W. *Handbook of the biology of aging*, CC64
Rowe, Kenneth E. *Methodist union catalog, pre-1976 imprints*, BB110
Rowland, A. Westley. *Key resources on institutional advancement*, CB10
Rowles, Ruth Anderson. *The historical atlas of political parties in the United States Congress, 1789–1989*, CJ116, DB78
Rowley, Jennifer E. *Abstracting and indexing*, AB86
Rowsey, J. James. *Ophthalmic drug facts*, EK120
Royal Institute of British Architects. *Architecture database*, BE113

The Royal Navy in World War Two, Law, Derek G., DA67
Royal Pharmaceutical Society of Great Britain. *The extra pharmacopoeia*, EK117
Royal Society (Great Britain). *Biographical memoirs of fellows of the Royal Society*, EA79
Royal Society of London. *Obituary notices of fellows of the Royal Society*, EA79
Royal Statistical Society. *Reviews of United Kingdom statistical sources*, CG54
Royle, Trevor. *A dictionary of military quotations*, CJ263
Ruben, Douglas H. *Philosophy journals and serials*, BA5
Rubert, S. C. *Zimbabwe*, DD5
Rubin, Harvey W. *Dictionary of insurance terms*, CH264
Rubin, Richard. *The baby boom*, CG3
Rubinstein, Danny. *The West Bank handbook*, CJ188
Ruble, Blair A. *A scholars' guide to humanities and social sciences in the Soviet Union*, DC209
Ruby, Douglas A. *Guide to graduate study in economics, agricultural economics, public administration, and doctoral programs in business administration in the United States and Canada*, CH14
Ruby, Robert H. *A guide to the Indian tribes of the Pacific Northwest*, CC227
Rudall, B. H. *Computers and literature*, BD16
Ruecker, Norbert. *International bibliography of jazz books*, BH117
Rüterswörden, Udo. *Hebräisches und aramäisches Handwörterbuch über das Alte Testament*, AD117
Ruffner, Frederick G. *Allusions—cultural, literary, biblical, and historical*, AD22, BD32
Ruffner, James A. *The weather almanac*, EE30
Rugg, Frederick E. *Rugg's recommendations on the colleges*, CB108
Rugg's recommendations on the colleges, Rugg, Frederick E., CB108
Rugs, BF48
Ruh, Kurt. *Die deutsche Literatur des Mittelalters*, BD289
Ruhe, Ernstpeter. *Algerien-Bibliographie*, DD26
Ruhl, Klaus-Jörg. *Der spanische Bürgerkrieg*, DC185
Ruhlen, Merritt. *Guide to the languages of the world*, BC15
—— *A guide to the world's languages*, BC15
Ruiz Castañeda, María del Carmen. *Catálogo de seudónimos, anagramas, iniciales y otros alias usados por escritores mexicanos y extranjeros que han publicado en México*, AA35
Ruiz Torres, Francisco. *Diccionario de términos médicos, inglés-español, español-inglés*, EK59
Rupesinghe, Kumar. *Ethnic conflict and human rights in Sri Lanka*, DE93
Rupp, Heinz. *Deutsches Literatur-Lexikon*, BD291
Ruppert, James. *Guide to American poetry explication*, BD182
Rural sociology, Berndt, Judy, CC3
Ruscio, Alain. *La première guerre d'Indochine, 1945–1954*, DE65
Russell, Percy,. *The nutrition and health encyclopedia*, EK100
Russia and the United States, Bolkhovitinov, N. N., DC198
Russia and the U.S.S.R.
  bibliography, AA179, DC13, DC197
    18th century, AA180
  biography, DC194
  encyclopedias, DC208
  government publications, AE65
  history
    archival sources, DC204
    library resources, DC195

statistics, CG75
Russia in the twentieth century, Bakhmeteff Archive of Russian and East European History and Culture, DC197
Russia, the USSR, and Eastern Europe, Horak, Stephan M., DC13
Russian autocrats from Ivan the Great to the fall of the Romanov dynasty, Egan, David R., DC194
Russian dictionaries, Aissing, Alena, AD155
Russian emigrant literature, AE64
Russian emigration, AE64
The Russian Empire and the Soviet Union, Brown, John H., DC195
—— Grant, Steven A., DC195
Russian-English dictionary of the mathematical sciences, Lohwater, A. J., EF13
Russian imperial government serials on microfilm in the Library of Congress, Library of Congress, AE65
Russian language
  dictionaries, AD150, AD151
    abbreviations, AD154
    bibliography, AD155
    bilingual, AD152, AD153, EF13
Russian literature
  bibliography, BD355, DC196
  biography, BD358
  encyclopedias, BD356
  history, BD357
  translations, BD354
Russian travelers to the Christian East from the twelfth to the twentieth century, Stavrou, Theofanis George, DE16
Russische Abkürzungen, Scheitz, Edgar, AD154
Russkaïa émigratsiïa, AE64
Russkaïa obshchestvennaïa biblioteka imeni I.S. Turgeneva (Paris, France). *L'emigration russe,* AE64
Russkie sovetskie pisateli—poèty, BD355
Russo, Nancy Felipe. *Women in psychology,* CD36
Rust, Brian A. L. *The complete entertainment discography, from 1897 to 1942,* BH142
—— *Jazz records, 1897–1942,* BH143
Ruszkiewicz, John J. *The Scott, Foresman handbook for writers,* BC26, BC27
Rutinel Domínguez, Ulises. *Diccionario histórico dominicano,* DB148
Rutkow, Ira M. *The history of surgery in the United States, 1775–1900,* EK75
Rutledge, Anna Wells. *Cumulative record of exhibition catalogues,* BE66
Rwanda, DD50
Ryan, Halford Ross. *American orators before 1900,* BD148
Ryan, James G. *Irish records,* AK40
Ryan, Joe. *First stop,* AC8
Ryan, Joseph M. *The educator's desk reference (EDR),* CB4
Ryan, Victoria. *Historical directory of trade unions,* CH287
Ryans, Cynthia C. *Small business,* CH358
Rydbeck, Jan. *Svensk historisk bibliografi 1951–1960,* DC190
Rydings, H. Anthony. *A Hong Kong union catalogue,* DE55
Ryle, Anne. *-ologies & -isms,* AD35
Rylko, Henry M. *Artificial intelligence,* EJ51

SCIPIO, BE63
SCONUL Advisory Committee on American Studies. *Directory of American studies librarians in the UK,* AB28
SDI, CJ275
SFFRI, BD124
SOPODA, CC12
SOPODA [computer file], CC28
STARR, EA8
Saal, Friedrich Wilhelm. *Chronik deutscher Zeitgeschichte,* DC93
Sable, Martin. *Holocaust studies,* DA86

Sabourin, Conrad. *La francité canadienne,* BC40
Sabzwari, Ghaniul Akram. *Who's who in library and information science in Pakistan,* AB42
Sachs, Lothar. *A guide to statistical methods and to the pertinent literature = Literatur zur Angewandten Statistik,* EF3
Sachs, Michael. *World guide to scientific associations and learned societies,* CA50, EA60
Sachwörterbuch der Politik, Beck, Reinhart, CJ14
Sack, Sallyann Amdur. *A guide to Jewish genealogical research in Israel,* AK42
Sadie, Stanley. *Music printing and publishing,* BH53
—— *The new Grove dictionary of American music,* BH55
—— *The Norton/Grove concise encyclopedia of music,* BH57
Sadler, Judith DeBoard. *Families in transition,* CC134
Sadock, Benjamin J. *Comprehensive textbook of psychiatry/V,* CD33
Sächsische Akademie der Wissenschaften zu Leipzig. *Althochdeutsches Wörterbuch,* AD103
Saffady, William. *Introduction to automation for librarians,* AB88
—— *Micrographics,* AB110
Saffran, Marion A. *20th century Canadian arctic expeditions,* DH3
Sagar, H. L. *Who's who, Indian personages,* AJ72
Sage, George Harvey. *Handbook of social science of sport,* BJ16, CC19
Sage, William W. *Laos,* DE82
Saggio di bibliografia sui problemi storici, teorici e pratici della traduzione, Briamonte, Nino, BC16
Saha, Santosh C. *Indo-U.S. relations, 1947–1988,* DE58
Sainsbury, Diana. *Dictionary of microbiology and molecular biology,* EC12
St. Augustine's Abbey (Ramsgate, England). *The book of saints,* BB96
The St. James encyclopedia of mortgage & real estate finance, Newell, James E., CH354
St. James mutual fund directory, CH248
St. James world futures and options directory, CH175
St. John's Gospel, 1920–1965, Malatesta, Edward, BB41
Saints, BB96, BB97
Saito, Toshio. *A concordance to Middle English metrical romances,* BD209
SALALM bibliography and reference series, AA8, DB90
Salazar, Daniel. *Teatro mexicano del siglo XX, 1900–1986,* BD345, BG22
Salem, James M. *Drury's guide to best plays,* BD84
Sales catalog index project input on-line. *SCIPIO,* BE63
Sales & marketing management magazine, CH333
The sales prospecting & territory planning directory, CH322
Saletore, Rajaram Narayan. *Encyclopaedia of Indian culture,* DE63
Saliba, M. *Arab Gulf states,* DE17
Salon criticism in the Second Empire Paris, A bibliography, BE147
Salt, Denys. *Austria,* DC27
Salu, Luc. *History of photography,* BF56
Salvador *see* **El Salvador**
Salvendy, Gavriel. *Handbook of human factors,* EJ75
Salzman, Jack. *American studies,* DB3
—— *The Cambridge handbook of American literature,* BD162
Samaraweera, Vijaya. *Sri Lanka,* DE94

Samardžić, Radovan. *Srpska bibliografija,* AA204
Samkhya: a dualist tradition in Indian philosophy, BA13
Sammons, Vivian O. *Blacks in science and medicine,* CC208, EA80, EK77
Samoa, DG14
Samples, Gordon. *The drama scholars' index to plays and filmscripts,* BG14
Sampson, Henry T. *The ghost walks,* BG43
Samuels, M. L. *A linguistic atlas of late mediaeval English,* BC31
SANB: South African national bibliography, AA184
Sanchez, Denise. *Feminist periodicals, 1855–1984,* AE42, CC271
Sandberg, Larry. *The folk music sourcebook,* BH133
Sanders, Gabriel. *Bibliographie signalétique du latin des chrétiens,* BC43
Sandinista Nicaragua, DB129
Sandler, Gerald. *Disease data book,* EK68
Sandys, Julian. *Directory of Lloyd's of London,* CH266
Sanskrit language, AD156, AD157
Santi, Albert. *The St. James encyclopedia of mortgage & real estate finance,* CH354
Santora, Joseph C. *Death and dying,* CC97
—— *Death and dying : a bibliography, 1974–1978,* CC98
Santoro, Carla Masotti. *A world directory of criminological institutes,* CK105
Santoso, Wartini. *Katalog majalah terbitan Indonesia,* AA140
—— *Katalog surat kabar,* AF11
Sanz, María Teresa. *Publicaciones oficiales de Chile, 1973–1983,* AG32
Sardegna, Jill. *The encyclopedia of blindness and vision impairment,* CC106, EK44
Sarel, Baruch. *A comprehensive etymological dictionary of the Hebrew language for readers of English,* AD118
Saretzky, Gary D. *Index to ETS research report series, 1948–1989,* CB51
Sarfoh, Joseph A. *Population, urbanization, and rural settlement in Ghana,* DD38
Sargent, Lyman Tower. *British and American utopian literature, 1516–1985,* BD239
Sarjeant, William Antony S. *Geologists and the history of geology,* EE19
Sarkesian, Sam C. *U.S. national security policy and strategy,* CJ44
Sarkissian, Adele. *Children's authors and illustrators,* BD78
Sartori, Claudio. *I libretti italiani a stampa dalle origini al 1800,* BH102
Sartori, Eva. *Women's studies in Western Europe,* CC252
Sater, Ana Lya. *Latin American Jewish studies,* BB131, CC164
Sather, Leland B. *Norway,* DC169
—— *Sweden,* DC189
Satué, Angel. *Diccionari etimològic i complementari de la llengua catalana,* AD81
Sauber, S. Richard. *Family therapy,* CC137
Saudi Arabia
  bibliography, DE89
  government publications, AG46
  history, DE90, DE91
Saudi Arabia, Clements, Frank, DE90
—— Philipp, Hans-Jürgen, DE91
Saul, Pauline A. *The A–Z guide to tracing ancestors in Britain,* AK33
Saunders, John Beecroft. *Words and phrases legally defined,* CK66
Savage, Nicholas. *British architectural books and writers, 1556–1785,* BE110
Savageau, David. *Places rated almanac,* CL16
Saveleva, E. A. *Svodnyĭ katalog knig na inostrannykh ïazykakh, izdannykh v Rossii v XVIII veke, 1701–1800,* AA180
Savez književnika Jugoslavije. Adresar pisaca Jugoslavije, BD360

Saville, John. *Dictionary of labour biography*, AJ63

Savings institution directory, CH250

Sawoniak, Henryk. *New international dictionary of acronyms in library and information science and related fields*, AB17

Sax, N. Irving. *Dangerous properties of industrial materials*, ED21

—— *Hawley's condensed chemical dictionary*, ED10

Sbrega, John J. *The war against Japan, 1941–1945*, DA70

Scammon, Richard M. *America at the polls 2*, CJ114

Scandals, CJ37

Scandinavia
bibliography, AA181, DC181
biography, AJ91
encyclopedias, DC179
history
bibliography, DC180

Scandinavian biographical archive, AJ91

Scandinavian languages, BC32, BC32

Scandinavian mythology, Lindow, John, CF16

Scanlan, Jean M. *Business online*, AB96, CH82

Scanlon, George T. *A bibliography of the architecture, arts, and crafts of Islam by Sir K.A.C. Creswell, C.B.E. Second supplement, Jan. 1972 to Dec. 1980 (with omissions from previous years)*, BE11

Schacht, John H. *Bibliography for the study of magazines*, AE18

Schäfer, Jürgen. *Early modern English lexicography*, AD2

Schaie, K. Warner. *Handbook of the psychology of aging*, CC64

Schatz, Natalie. *Federal information sources in health and medicine*, EK26

Scheer, Wilbert E. *The Dartnell personnel administration handbook*, CH165

Scheitz, Edgar. *Dictionary of Russian abbreviations*, AD154

—— *Russische Abkürzungen*, AD154

Schels, Christa. *Vocabulary, English-Somali, Somali-English*, AD163

Schenk, Trudy. *The Wuerttemberg emigration index*, AK13

Schepper, Marcus de. *Bibliographie de l'humanisme des anciens Pays-Bas, avec un répertoire bibliographique des humanistes et poètes néo-latins*, BA9

Scheven, Yvette. *Bibliographies for African studies*, DD46

—— *Bibliographies for African studies, 1970–1986*, DD18

—— *Namibia bibliographies*, DD46

Schick, Frank Leopold. *Records of the presidency*, AB49, CJ82, DB22

—— *Statistical handbook on aging Americans*, CC66

—— *Statistical handbook on U.S. Hispanics*, CC246

Schick, Renee. *Records of the presidency*, CJ82

—— *Statistical handbook on U.S. Hispanics*, CC246

Schier, Peter. *China's new party leadership*, CJ160

Schiller, Gertrud. *Ikonographie der christlichen Kunst*, BE102

Schiller, J. C. F. von, BD299

Schimmelman, Janice Gayle. *American imprints on art through 1865*, BE13

—— *Architectural treatises and building handbooks available in American libraries and bookstores through 1800*, BE111

Schiötz, Eiler H. *Utlendingers reiser i Norge. En bibliografi*, DC170

The Schirmer guide to schools of music and conservatories throughout the world, Uscher, Nancy, BH66

Schlachter, Gail A. *Directory of financial aids for women, 1991–1992*, CC303

—— *Reference sources in library and information services*, AB5

Schlesinger, Benjamin. *Sexual abuse of children in the 1980's*, CC84

Schlessinger, Bernard S. *The basic business library*, CH76

Schlicke, Priscilla. *Walford's guide to reference material*, AA67, EA6

Schlosser, Julius, Ritter von. *Die Kunstliteratur*, BE14

Schlueter, June. *An encyclopedia of British women writers*, BD225

Schlueter, Paul. *An encyclopedia of British women writers*, BD225

Schmid, Bona. *I segreti dell'inglese*, AD129

Schmidt, Marlis. *Economic reforms in the People's Republic of China since 1979*, CH42

Schmidt, Nancy J. *Sub-Saharan African films and filmmakers*, BG55

Schmidt-Dumont, Marianne. *Die Beziehungen Afghanistans zur Sowjetunion*, DE42

Schmidt-Künsemüller, Friedrich Adolf. *Lexikon des gesamten Buchwesens*, AA46

Schmitt, Charles B. *The Cambridge history of Renaissance philosophy*, BA19

Schmitt, Christian. *Lexikon der Romanistischen Linguistik*, BC36

Schmitt, Otto. *Reallexikon zur deutschen Kunstgeschichte*, BE39

Schmitz, Betty. *Integrating women's studies into the curriculum*, CB135

Schmuck, Hilmar. *Gesamtverzeichnis des deutschsprachigen Schrifttums ausserhalb des Buchhandels (GVB), 1966–1980*, AA121

—— *Gesamtverzeichnis des deutschsprachigen Schrifttums (GV), 1700–1910*, AA120

Schneider, Edward L. *Handbook of the biology of aging*, CC64

Schneider, Gail T. *Encyclopedia of school administration & supervision*, CB61

Schneider, Janet Carney. *Peterson's drug and alcohol programs and policies at four-year colleges*, CB104

Schneider, Joanne. *Women in western European history. First supplement*, CC280

Schneider, Johannes. *Mittellateinisches Wörterbuch bis zum ausgehenden 13. [i.e. dreizehnten] Jahrhundert*, AD140

Schneider, Marshall J. *Modern Spanish and Portuguese literatures*, BD327

Schnuttgen, Hildegard. *A bibliography of Chaucer, 1974–1985*, BD253

Schobinger, Jean-Pierre. *Grundriss der Geschichte der Philosophie*, BA20

—— *Die Philosophie des 17. Jahrhunderts*, BA20

Schöffer, Ivo. *Biografisch woordenboek van Nederland*, AJ82

Schoenbaum, S. *Annals of English drama, 975–1700*, BD232

Schoenberg, Arnold. *Fundamentals of musical composition*, BH9

Schoenhals, Kai P. *Dominican Republic*, DB149

—— *Grenada*, DB150

Schofield, Richard N. *A bibliography of the Iran-Iraq borderland*, DE12

A scholars' guide to humanities and social sciences in the Soviet Union, DC209

Scholars' guide to Washington, D.C. for cartography and remote sensing imagery, Ehrenberg, Ralph E., CL38

Scholar's guide to Washington D.C. for Southeast Asian studies, Mayerchak, Patrick M., DE46

Scholars' guide to Washington, D.C. for southwest European studies, Higbee, Joan Florence, DC10

Scholarships, fellowships & grants for programs abroad, CB162

Scholze, Werner. *The Oxford-Duden German dictionary*, AD109

Schonberg, David. *Jewish law*, CK43

School administration and supervision, CB61

The school administrator's resource guide, CB6

School law, CB153, CB154

School prayer and other religious issues in American public education, Menendez, Albert J., CB35

School psychologists, CB133

Schoonees, Pieter Cornelis. *Groot woordeboek*, AD68

Schorr, Alan Edward. *Refugee and immigrant resource directory, 1990–1991*, CC177

Schorta, Andrea. *Disciunari rumantsch grischen*, AD149

Schraeder, Peter J. *Cameroon*, DD28

Schrag, Calvin O. *Women philosophers*, BA24

Schramm, Friedrich Karl. *Staatsbürgerlexikon*, CJ173

Schriftstellerinnen und Schriftsteller der Gegenwart, BD301

Schröder, Brigitte. *Bibliographie zur deutschen historischen Städteforschung*, BE137

Schröer, Helmut. *Handbuch der Geschichte der Philosophie*, BA21

Schütz, Christian. *Praktisches Lexikon der Spiritualität*, BB90

Schuh, Randall T. *The Torre-Bueno glossary of entomology*, EC64

Schuhmacher, Stephan. *The encyclopedia of Eastern philosophy and religion*, BA12, BB23

Schullian, Dorothy. *A catalogue of incunabula and manuscripts in the Army Medical Library*, EK13

Schultz, LeRoy G. *Barns, stables, and outbuildings*, BE112, EH24

Schulz, Hedda. *From CA to CAS ONLINE*, ED2

Schulze, Suzanne. *Population information in twentieth century census volumes, 1900–1940*, CG33

—— *Population information in twentieth century census volumes, 1950–1980*, CG34

Schur, Norman W. *British English, A to Zed*, AD26

Schuster, Marilyn R. *Selected bibliography for integrating research on women's experience in the liberal arts curriculum*, CC249

Schwade, Arcadio. *Shintō-bibliography in western languages*, BB139

Schwartz, Narda Lacey. *Articles on women writers*, BD199

Schwarz, C. M. *Chambers English dictionary*, AD7

Schwarz-Mackensen, Gesine. *Deutsches Wörterbuch*, AD114

Schwarzkopf, LeRoy C. *Government reference serials*, AG10

—— *Guide to popular U.S. government publications*, AG7

Schweiger, Anneliese. *Bibliographie zur Geschichte der Städte Österreichs*, DC26

Schweikart, Larry E. *Banking and finance, 1913–1989*, CH136

—— *Banking and finance to 1913*, CH136

Schweizerische Gesellschaft für Familienforschung. *Familiennamenbuch der Schweiz = Répertoire des noms de famille suisses = Register of Swiss surnames*, AK45

Sciattara, Diane. *Serials for libraries*, AA68

Science abstracts, EG2, EJ44

Science and engineering literature, Malinowsky, Harold Robert, EA3

—— Richardson, Jeanne M., EA3

Science and technology
bibliography, EA2, EA4, EA15
current, EA8
general and juvenile, CB7, EA7, EA11, EA12, EA13
biography, CC208, CC263, EA75, EA76, EA77, EA78, EA79, EA80, EA81, EA82, EA83, EA84, EA85, EK77
databases, EA4, EA9, EA10, EA23, EA24, EA25, EA26, EA28, EA29, EA31, EA37
dictionaries, EA40, EA41, EA44

abbreviations, EA45
foreign terms
Czech, EA46, EA47
French, EA45, EA48
Japanese, EA49
polyglot, EA50
Portuguese, EA51
Spanish, EA52
general, EA42, EA43
directories, EA54, EA59, EH16, EJ3, EK60
Europe, EA55, EA56
Gt. Brit., CA17, EA53
Hungary, DC143
encyclopedias, EA33, EA34, EA35, EA38, EA39
guides, EA1, EA3, EA5
handbooks, EA36
history, EA73
bibliography, EA68, EA69, EA70
chronologies, EA71, EA72, EA74
encyclopedias, EA71
indexes, EA27, EA30, EA32
museums, EA65
periodicals
bibliography, EA18, EA19, EA20
Japanese, EA21
reviews of research, EA58
societies and congresses, EA61
Science and technology annual reference review, EA8
Science books & films, EA15
Science books for children, CB7
Science citation index, EA31, EA30
Science citation index. Compact disc edition, EA29
Science fiction and fantasy book review index, 1980–1984, Hall, Halbert W., BD125
Science fiction and fantasy reference index, 1878–1985, BD124
Science fiction and fantasy research index, BD124
Science fiction and fantasy series and sequels, Cottrill, Tim, BD112
Science fiction book review index, BD124
Science fiction, fantasy, and Gothic literature
bibliography, BD109, BD110, BD111, BD112, BD113, BD114, BD115, BD116, BD117, BD118, BD119, BD120, BD121
biography, BD127
book reviews, BD126
book reviews and criticism, BD125
illustration, BD128, BE89
indexes, BD123, BD124
periodicals, BD122
Science fiction, fantasy, and horror reference, Justice, Keith L., BD118
Science fiction, fantasy, and weird fiction magazines, Tymn, Marshall B., BD122
Science fiction & fantasy book review annual, BD126
Science fiction, fantasy & horror, BD120
Science fiction in print, Brown, Charles N., BD120
Science fiction magazines, Hall, Halbert W., BD122
Science-fiction, the early years, Bleiler, Everett Franklin, BD123
Science fiction writers, BD127
Science & technology in fact and fiction, Kennedy, DayAnn M., EA11, EA12
Scientific and technical aerospace reports, EJ15
Scientific and technical books and serials in print, EA9
Scientific and technical information sources, Chen, Ching-chih, EA1
Scientific and technical libraries, Pruett, Nancy Jones, AB61
Scientific and technical organizations and agencies directory, EA59
Scientific DataLink index to artificial intelligence research, EJ52
Scientific illustration, EA66, EA67
Scientific libraries, AB60, AB61, EA57

SciSearch, EA29, EA31
SciTech reference plus, CH113, EA62, EA75, EA10
Sclater, Neil. *Encyclopedia of electronics*, EJ45
Scoor-oot, Stevenson, James A. C., AD61
Scotland
biography, CH145
government publications
parliamentary publications, AG36
history
bibliography, DC140
encyclopedias, DC139
newspapers, AF8
Scotland, Bold, Alan Norman, BD272
Scott, David H. *Mene, Mene, Tekel*, BB62
Scott, David Logan. *Wall Street words*, CH235
Scott, Ian. *Hong Kong*, DE56
Scott, Kathleen. *The travellers, Canada to 1900*, DB84
Scott, Randall W. *Comic books and strips*, CF31
Scott, Ronald Bodley. *The Oxford companion to medicine*, EK41
The Scott, Foresman handbook for writers, Hairston, Maxine, BC26, BC27
The Scott, Foresman Robert's rules of order newly revised, CJ226
—— Robert, Henry M., CJ227
Scott-Kilvert, Ian. *British writers. Supplement*, BD226
Scott Polar Research Institute. *Polar record*, DH4
Scottish family history, Moody, David, AK44
Scottish language, AD59, AD60, AD61
Scottish literature, BD272
Scottish texts and calendars, Stevenson, David, DC140
Scrivener, David. *Bibliography of arms control verification*, CJ300
Scrivener, Ronald. *USSR economic handbook*, CH52
Sculpture
bibliography, BE162
biography, BE165, BE166, BE167
by country or region
France, BE162, BE163, BE166
catalogs, BE163
Scuola normale superiore (Italy). *Bibliografia di bibliografie, edizioni italiane del XVI secolo*, AA7
Seals of Chinese painters and collectors of the Ming and Ch'ing periods, Wang, Chi-chien, BE42
Search, BE115
Search for security, CA40
Search for the Northwest Passage, Day, Alan Edwin, DB82
Searching America: history and life, Falk, Joyce Duncan, DB17
—— Kinnell, Susan K., DB17
Searching America: history and life (AHL) and Historical abstracts (HA) on DIALOG, Falk, Joyce Duncan, DA6
Searching the law, Bander, Edward J., CK14
Searching the law, the states, Doyle, Francis R., CK30
Searing, Susan E. *Introduction to library research in women's studies*, CC250
—— *Women's studies*, CC259, CC260
Sears, Jean L. *Using government publications*, AG5
Sears, Minnie Earl. *Sears list of subject headings*, AB84
Sears list of subject headings, Sears, Minnie Earl, AB84
Seaton, Douglass. *The art song*, BH111
Sebeok, Thomas Albert. *Encyclopedic dictionary of semiotics*, BC9
Secchia, Pietro. *Enciclopedia dell'antifascismo e della Resistenza*, DC158
Seccombe, Ian J. *Syria*, DE95
Seccombe, Matthew. *British newspapers and periodicals, 1641–1700*, AA131, AE41

Second abstract of British historical statistics, Jones, H. G., CG52, DC121
—— Mitchell, Brian, CG52, DC121
Second Barnhart dictionary of new English, AD36
Second Hulbert financial digest almanac, CH215
Secret societies, CA53, CA54
The secretary's handbook, Taintor, Sarah Augusta, CH168
Secretary's handbooks, CH168, CH169
Securities, CH238
Sedge, Douglas. *An annotated critical bibliography of Jacobean and Caroline comedy*, BD233
Seebold, Elmar. *Etymologisches Wörterbuch der deutschen Sprache*, AD112
—— *Register und Auswertung zur 22. Auflage des etymologischen Wörterbuch von Friedrich Kluge*, AD112
Seeds of peace, Larson, Jeanne, CJ307
Seeley, Robert A. *The handbook of non-violence*, CJ305
Seewann, Gerhard. *Bestandskatalog der Bibliothek des Südost-Instituts München*, DC18
Segal, Gerald. *Political and economic encyclopaedia of the Pacific*, DG9
Segal, Morley. *Bridges to knowledge in political science*, CJ2
—— *Research guide for undergraduates in political science*, CJ2
—— *Research guide in political science*, CJ2
Segal, Ronald. *The new state of the world atlas*, CL52
I segreti dell'inglese, Hofmann Cortesi, Livio, AD129
Sehimi, Mustapha. *La grande encyclopédie du Maroc*, DD44
Seibt, Betty Kay. *Handbook for small, rural, and emerging public libraries*, AB55
Seigneuret, Jean-Charles. *Dictionary of literary themes and motifs*, BD48
Selden, Raman. *A reader's guide to contemporary literary theory*, BD22
Selden Society. *A centenary guide to the publications of the Selden Society*, CK41
Seldin, Maury. *The real estate handbook*, CH355
A select bibliography of chemistry 1492–[1902], Bolton, Henry Carrington, ED4
Select bibliography of medical biography, Thornton, John Leonard, EK78
Select bibliography of the French Second Empire, DC59
A selected and annotated bibliography of American naval history, Coletta, Paolo Enrico, DB5
Selected bibliography for integrating research on women's experience in the liberal arts curriculum, Schuster, Marilyn R., CC249
Selected black American, African, and Caribbean authors, Page, James A., BD186
Selected musical terms of non-Western cultures, Kaufmann, Walter, BH130
Selected tables in mathematical statistics, EF17
Selected theatre criticism, BG17
Selected water resources abstracts, EE24, EJ34, EE24, EJ34
Selective guide to climatic data sources, Hatch, Warren L., EE28
Selective inventory of information services, CA20
Selective inventory of social science information and documentation services = Inventaire sélectif des services d'information et de documentation en sciences sociales = Inventario selectivo de servicios de información y documentación en ciencias sociales, CA20
Self, James. *Japanese art signatures*, BE100

Selim, George Dimitri. *American doctoral dissertations on the Arab world : supplement August 1981–December 1987*, DE18

Sellen, Betty-Carol. *Feminists, pornography & the law*, CC264

Sellers, John R. *Civil War manuscripts*, DB31

Seller's guide to government purchasing, CH170

Selth, Jefferson P. *Alternative lifestyles*, CC17

Seltsam, William. *Metropolitan opera annals*, BH95

Semantics, BC3

Semantics, Gordon, W. Terrence, BC3

Semendīaev, K. A. *Handbook of mathematics*, EF14

Semenovker, B. A. *Retrospektivnaīa gosudarstvennaīa bibliografiīa SSSR*, AA179

Le semestriel des arts, BE65, BE64

Seminar on South and South-east Asian History. *A classified catalogue of books on the section XII, India, in the Tōyō Bunko (II) acquired during the years 1951–1982*, DE60

Seminars directory, CH163

The Seminole and Miccosukee tribes, Kersey, Harry A., CC216

Semiotics, BC2, BC9, BC14

Semiotik-Bibliographie I, Eschbach, Achim, BC2

Senate executive documents and reports, AG12

Senate manual, CJ102

Senate procedure, CJ102

Senegal, AA182, AE68

Sengo Nihon no kokusai seijigaku, DE75, DE76

Senior citizens information sources, CC63

Sennett, Robert S. *The nineteenth-century photographic press*, BF57

—— *Photography and photographers to 1900*, BF57

Sentner, Janet P. *Feminism and women's issues*, CC266

Sequels, Husband, Janet, BD91

The Serbian bibliography : books, 1868–1944, AA204

Serbian literature, BD363

Serbo-Croatian language, AD158, AD159, AD160

SerboCroatian-English dictionary, Benson, Morton, AD159

Serial bibliographies and abstracts in history, Henige, David P., DA3

Serial publications, AB108

The serials directory, AE6

Serials for libraries, Ganly, John, AA68

Serials guide to ethnoart, Burt, Eugene C., BF10, BF11, BF12

Serials holdings in the Linda Hall Library [as of April 30] 1989, Linda Hall Library, EA19

Serials in the British Library, AE46

Serials on aging, Hesslein, Shirley B., CC51

Serials reference work, Puccio, Joseph A., AB108

Serle, Geoffrey. *Australian dictionary of biography*, AJ33

SERLINE, EK24

Serow, William J. *Handbook on international migration*, CC184

Service, Alastair. *Edwardian architecture*, BE134

Service companies, CH115

Service industries, CH104

Šešplaukis, Alfonsas. *Lituanica collections in European research libraries*, DC162

Sethi, Ātmarāma. *Indian library directory*, AB33

Setting up a company in the European Community, CK127

Seven-language thesaurus of European animals, Gozmany, László, EC40

The Seven-power summit, CK109

Sex and gender issues, Beere, Carole A., CC308

Sex and sexual behavior, CC83, CC84, CC157
  bibliography, CC125, CC147, CC308
  dictionaries, CC153

Sex differences and learning, Grambs, Jean Dresden, CB25

Sexual abuse of children in the 1980's, CC84

Sexuality-related measures, CC157

Seydel, Dietrich. *Informationshandbuch internationale Beziehungen und Länderkunde = Information handbook international relations and area studies*, CJ135, DA57

Seymour, Nancy N. *An index-dictionary of Chinese artists, collectors, and connoisseurs with character identification by modified stroke count*, BE87

Seymour-Smith, Charlotte. *Dictionary of anthropology*, CE12

Sfeir, Leila. *Handbook of social science of sport*, BJ16, CC19

Sgard, Jean. *Bibliographie de la presse classique, 1600–1789*, AE34

Shadily, Hassan. *An Indonesian-English dictionary*, AD126

Shafritz, Jay M. *The Dorsey dictionary of American government and politics*, CJ56

—— *The Facts on File dictionary of education*, CB76

—— *The Facts on File dictionary of military science*, CJ262

—— *The Facts on File dictionary of nonprofit organization management*, CH158

—— *The Facts on File dictionary of personnel management and labor relations*, CH154

—— *The Facts on File dictionary of public administration*, CJ223

Shafritz, Todd J. A. *The Facts on File dictionary of military science*, CJ262

Shain, Michael. *Dictionary of information technology*, EJ63

—— *Van Nostrand Reinhold dictionary of information technology*, EJ63

Shakers, BB113

Shakespeare, BD263

Shakespeare A to Z, Boyce, Charles, BD267

Shakespeare and the medieval tradition, McRoberts, J. Paul, BD262

Shakespeare and the musical stage, Hotaling, Edward R., BD268

A Shakespeare glossary, Onions, C. T., BD265

Shakespeare on screen, Rothwell, Kenneth S., BD264

Shakespeare, W.
  bibliography, BD260, BD261, BD262, BD263
  dictionaries, BD265
  filmography, BD264
  handbooks, BD267
  quotations, BD266
  stage productions, BD268
  surveys, BD269

Shanks, Thomas G. *The American atlas*, CL21

—— *The international atlas*, CL22

Shannon, Michael Owen. *Irish Republic*, DC147

Shapiro, Michael Steven. *The museum*, BE10

Shapiro, Nat. *Popular music*, BH132

—— *Popular music, 1920–1979*, BH132

Shapiro, Stuart Charles. *Encyclopedia of artificial intelligence*, EJ58

Sharma, H. D. *Indian reference sources*, AA65

Sharp, J. Michael. *The directory of congressional voting scores and interest group ratings*, CJ97

Sharrock, Susan R. *An annotated bibliography of Northern Plains ethnohistory*, CC220

Shatzkin, Mike. *The ballplayers*, BJ17

Shaver, James P. *Handbook of research on social studies teaching and learning*, CB128

Shavit, David. *The United States in Africa*, DD19, DE3, DE22

—— *The United States in Asia*, DD19, DE3, DE22

—— *The United States in the Middle East*, DD19, DE3, DE22

Shaw, Debora. *Library and information science*, AB7

Shaw, Graham. *The South Asia and Burma retrospective bibliography (SABREB)*, AA92

Shaw, Harry. *Dictionary of problem words and expressions*, AD27

Shaw, Ralph R. *American bibliography*, AA81

Shaw, Ralph Robert. *American bibliography*, AA79, CL43

Shaw, Warren. *The Third Reich almanac*, DC94

Shcherbakova, T. P. *Svodnyĭ katalog knig na inostrannykh īazykakh, izdannykh v Rossii v XVIII veke, 1701–1800*, AA180

Shearer, Barbara Smith. *State names, seals, flags, and symbols*, DB45

Shearer, Benjamin F. *State names, seals, flags, and symbols*, DB45

Sheehan, Michael. *Bibliography of arms control verification*, CJ300

Sheehan, Michael M. *Domestic society in medieval Europe*, DC6

Sheehan, Steven. *The artist's handbook of materials and techniques*, BE69

Sheehy, Eugene P. *Bibliography of American folk art for the year [. . .]*, BF8

Sheiman, Deborah Lovitky. *Infancy*, CC82

—— *Resources for middle childhood*, CC85

Shelley, Bruce L. *Dictionary of Christianity in America*, BB84

Shemel, Sidney. *This business of music*, BH71

Shepard, Leslie. *Encyclopedia of occultism & parapsychology*, CD51

Shepherd, Simon. *A biographical dictionary of English women writers, 1580–1720*, BD223

Sheppard, Jocelyn. *The bibliography of contemporary American fiction, 1945–1988*, BD176

Sheppard, Julia. *British archives*, AB50, AK28, DC107

Sherman, Barbara Smiley. *Directory of residential treatment facilities for emotionally disturbed children*, CC91, CD27

Shermis, Michael. *Jewish-Christian relations*, BB11

Shertzer, Margaret D. *The secretary's handbook*, CH168

Sherwood, P. A. *A concise Hungarian-English dictionary*, AD123

Shible, Warren. *Metaphor*, BC4, BD146

Shield of republic, sword of empire, Fredriksen, John C., CJ268, DB8

Shields, Graham J. *Gibraltar*, DC99

—— *Spain*, DC186

Shigley, Joseph Edward. *Standard handbook of machine design*, EJ82

Shils, Maurice E. *Modern nutrition in health and disease*, EK99

Shim, Jae K. *Accounting handbook*, CH68

—— *Dictionary of accounting terms*, CH63

—— *Encyclopedic dictionary of accounting and finance*, CH62

Shimomura, Ruth H. *GeoRef thesaurus and guide to indexing*, EE12

Shimoni, Yaacov. *Political dictionary of the Arab world*, CJ152, CJ190, CJ199, DE20, DE27

—— *Political dictionary of the Middle East in the twentieth century*, CJ152, CJ190

Shintō-bibliography in western languages, Schwade, Arcadio, BB139

Shintoism, BB139

Shipley, Lloyd W. *Information resources in the arts*, BE57

Shipman, David. *The great movie stars*, BG38

Ships and shipping, AK26, CH191
  annuals, CH193
  dictionaries, CH190, CH192

Shirley, Virginia S. *Table of isotopes*, EG11

—— *Table of radioactive isotopes*, EG11

Shiwakoti, Shesh Raj. *Law bibliography*, CK46

Shmelev, D. N. *Slovar' russkogo īazyka XI-XVII vv*, AD151

Shock and vibration handbook, EJ81

Shoemaker, Richard H. *American bibliography,* AA79, AA81, CL43

Shona language, AD161

Shook, R. J. *The Wall Street dictionary,* CH236

Shook, Robert L. *The Wall Street dictionary,* CH236

Shore, Steven N. *Encyclopedia of astronomy and astrophysics,* EB5

Short, David. *Czechoslovakia,* DC41

Short dictionary of furniture, Gloag, John, BF40

Short stories, BD97

Short stories on film and video, Emmens, Carol A., BG59

Short story criticism, BD99

Short-title catalogue of book printed in the Netherlands and Belgium, AA163

A short-title catalogue of books printed in England, Scotland, & Ireland and of English books printed abroad, 1475–1640, Pollard, Alfred W., AA127, AG36

—— Redgrave, G. R., AG36

Short-title catalogue of books printed in England, Scotland, Ireland, Wales, and British America, and of English books printed in other countries, 1641–1700, Wing, Donald Goddard, AA130, AA131, AG36

Short-title catalogue of books printed in Italy .., AA146

Short-title catalogue of books printed in Italy and of Italian books printed in other countries from 1465 to 1600 now in the British Library. Supplement, British Library, AA147

Short-title catalogue of books printed in the German-speaking countries and of German books printed in other countries from 1455 to 1600 now in the British Library. Supplement, British Library, AA118

A short title catalogue of eighteenth century printed books in the National Library of Medicine, Blake, John R., EK13

Shorter Aslib directory of information sources in the United Kingdom, AB26

Shortridge, Barbara G. DB79

Showers, Victor. *World facts and figures,* CG16

Shrager, David S. *The quotable lawyer,* CK72

Shreir, Sally. *Women's movements of the world,* CC305

Shugar, Gershon J. *Chemical technicians' ready reference handbook,* ED22

Shukman, Harold. *The Blackwell encyclopedia of the Russian Revolution,* DC205

Shulman, Frank Joseph. *Burma,* DE46, DE47

—— *Japan,* DE78

Sibley, Francis M. *Dictionary of quotations in geography,* CL13

Sichel, Beatrice. *Economics journals and serials,* CH5

Sichel, Werner. *Economics journals and serials,* CH5

Le siècle des lumières, Conlon, Pierre M., AA113, DC1

Siegel, Joel G. *Accounting handbook,* CH68

—— *Dictionary of accounting terms,* CH63

—— *Encyclopedic dictionary of accounting and finance,* CH62

Sierra Leone bibliography, AA183

Sierra Leone. Library Board. *Sierra Leone publications,* AA183

Sierra Leone publications, Sierra Leone. Library Board, AA183

Sieveking, Paul. *British biographical archive,* AJ64

Siewart, John. *Mission handbook,* BB106

Sifakis, Stewart. *Who was who in the Civil War,* DB35

Sigler, Jay A. *International handbook on race and race relations,* CC185

Signorielli, Nancy. *Role portrayal and stereotyping on television,* CH201

—— *Violence and terror in the mass media,* CH202

Sikhism, BB140

Sikhism and the Sikhs, Rai, Priya Muhar, BB140

Sikkim, DE29

Sikula, John P. *Handbook of research on teacher education,* CB17

Silkenat, James R. *Guide to foreign law firms,* CK76

Silver, Carole G. *Kind words,* AD47

Silver plate *see* **Gold and silver plate**

Silverburg, Sanford R. *United States foreign policy and the Middle East/North Africa,* DE15

Silverstein, Natalie Anne. *Prevention education,* CB22, CC113

Silverwork, BF44, BF47

Similes dictionary, BD41

Simms, Michael. *Longman dictionary and handbook of poetry,* BD134

Simon, Rachel. *National union catalog of Middle Eastern microforms,* DE11

Simon, Robin. *The portrait in Britain and America,* BE153

Simón Díaz, José. *Bibliografía de la literatura hispánica,* BD325

Simoni, Anna. *Catalogue of books from the Low Countries 1601–1621 in the British Library,* AA163

Simonson, Donald G. *Dictionary of banking terms,* CH228

Simony, Maggy. *The traveler's reading guide,* BJ39

Simpson, J. A. *The Oxford English dictionary,* AD6

Simpson, James Beasley. *Simpson's contemporary quotations,* BD66

Simpson, Michael A. *Dying, death, and grief,* CC99

Simpson, Robert Lawrence. *Historical dictionary of France from the 1815 restoration to the Second Empire,* DC74

Simpson's contemporary quotations, Simpson, James Beasley, BD66

Sims, Michael. *American and Canadian doctoral dissertations and master's theses on Africa, 1886–1974,* DD1

Sims-Williams, Ursula. *Union catalogue of Persian serials & newspapers in British libraries,* AE53

Sinclair, John. *Collins CoBUILD English language dictionary,* AD8

Sinclair, Stéphane. *Atlas de géographie historique de la France et de la Gaule, de la conquête césarienne à nos jours,* DC78

Sinclair, Stuart W. *The Pacific Basin,* CH41

—— *Third World economic handbook,* CH50

Sinclair, Wayne A. *Diseases of trees and shrubs,* EC37

Singapore, DE92

Singapore, Quah, Stella R., DE92

Singerman, Robert. *Jewish serials of the world,* AE7

—— *Judaica Americana,* BB135

Singers, BH84, BH88

Singh, B.N. *Dictionary of Indian philosophical concepts,* BA17

Singh, L. M. P. *Indian reference sources,* AA65

Singh, Ramji. *Indian reference sources,* AA65

Singh, V. B. *Elections in India,* CJ185

Singleton, Paul. *Dictionary of microbiology and molecular biology,* EC12

Singleton, Ralph S. *Filmmakers dictionary,* BG97

Sinke, Marjorie J. *Legal language,* CK67

Sinn, Elizabeth. *Research material for Hong Kong studies,* DE55

Sino-Soviet conflict, DA55

Sinonimi e contrari, Pittàno, Giuseppe, AD133

Sir William Osler, EK16

Six thousand words, AD32

Sixteen modern American authors, BD161

Sixth book of junior authors & illustrators, BD80

Sjöberg, Åke W. *The Sumerian dictionary of the University Museum of the University of Pennsylvania,* AD74

Skalak, Richard. *Handbook of bioengineering,* EK11

Skapura, Robert. *The cover story index, 1960–1989,* AE75

Skei, Allen B. *Woodwind, brass, and percussion instruments of the orchestra,* BH155

Skidmore, Gail. *From radical left to extreme right,* AE26

Skidmore, Thomas E. *The Cambridge encyclopedia of Latin America and the Caribbean,* DB99

Skill, Thomas. *Television, a guide to the literature,* BG102

Skinner, Quentin. *The Cambridge history of Renaissance philosophy,* BA19

Skirball, Sheba F. *Films of the Holocaust,* DA88

Sky and telescope cumulative index, EB4

Slaby, Wolfgang A. *Konkordanz zum Novum Testamentum Graece von Nestle-Aland,* BB60

Slaven, Anthony. *Dictionary of Scottish business biography, 1860–1960,* CH145

Slavens, Thomas P. *Research guide to musicology,* BH4

Slavery, CC174, CC200

Slavery, Miller, Joseph Calder, CC200

Slide, Anthony. *The American film industry,* BG94

—— *International film, radio, and television journals,* BG58

—— *Selected theatre criticism,* BG17

—— *Sourcebook for the performing arts,* BG4

Slide buyers' guide, Cashman, Norine D., BE105

Slingerland, Jean Harris. *The Wellesley index to Victorian periodicals, 1824–1900,* AE80

Šljivić–Šimšić, Biljana. *SerboCroatian-English dictionary,* AD159

Sloan, W. David. *American journalism history,* AF20

Sloane, David E. E. *American humor magazines and comic periodicals,* AE14

Sloane, Richard. *The Sloane-Dorland annotated medical-legal dictionary,* CK65, EK87

The Sloane-Dorland annotated medical-legal dictionary, Sloane, Richard, CK65, EK87

Slomanson, William R. *International business bibliography,* CH86

Slonim, Maureen. *Resources for middle childhood,* CC85

Slonimsky, Nicolas. *Lectionary of music,* BH61

Slovak literature, BD353

Slovar' russkikh narodnykh govorov, Institut russkogo iazyka (Akademiia nauk SSSR). Slovarnyi sektor, AD150

Slovar' russkogo iazyka XI-XVII vv, AD151

Slovar slovenskega knjižnega jezika, Inštitut za slovenski jezik (Slovenska akademija znanosti in umetnosti), AD162

Slovenia, DC217

Slovenian language, AD162

Slovenska bibliografija. Knjige, AA205

Slovenská národná bibliografia. Seria A: Knihy, AA100

Slovenski biografski leksikon, AJ103

Slovenský biografický slovník, AJ44

Slovník anglicko-česky, Jung, Václav, AD83

Słownik staropolski, Polska Akademia Nauk, AD145

Small, R. J. *A modern dictionary of geography,* CL12

Small business, CH357

Small business, Ryans, Cynthia C., CH358

Small business sourcebook, CH359

The smaller academic library, AB62

Smallwood, Carol. *Current issues resource builder,* CA21

Smartt, Daniel. *French Romanesque sculpture,* BE162

Smelser, Neil J. *Handbook of sociology,* CC20

Smethurst, J. M. *The eighteenth century short title catalogue 1990,* AA128

Smialek, William. *Polish music,* BH23

Smith, Allen. *Directory of oral history collections,* DB21

Smith, Ann G. *A biographical register, 1788–1939,* AJ34

Smith, Anna Pszczan-Czaja. *Encyclopedia of German-American genealogical research,* AK24

Smith, C. G. *The Times Books world weather guide,* EE29

Smith, Carter. *The national job bank, 1991,* CH340

Smith, Christine M. *Historical bibliography of art museum serials from the United States and Canada,* BE30

Smith, Clifford Neal. *Encyclopedia of German-American genealogical research,* AK24

Smith, Frederick. *The great song thesaurus,* BH115

Smith, Hilda L. *Women and the literature of the seventeenth century,* AA130

Smith, Jessie Carney. *Images of blacks in American culture,* CC190

Smith, John David. *Dictionary of Afro-American slavery,* CC174

Smith, John William. *The urban politics dictionary,* CJ22

Smith, Martin A. *Encyclopedia of physical sciences and engineering information sources,* EA2

Smith, Muriel Holland. *Harrap's concise French-English dictionary = dictionnaire anglais-français,* AD94

Smith, Myron J. *American warplanes 1908–1988,* DB15
—— *Baseball,* BJ26
—— *The battle of Pearl Harbor,* DB15
—— *The battles of Coral Sea and Midway, May–June 1942,* DB15
—— *World War II at sea,* DA71

Smith, Nathan M. *Agricultural and animal sciences journals and serials,* EH4

Smith, Nigel. *Legal journals index,* CK57

Smith, Robert Ellis. *Compilation of state and federal privacy laws,* CK95

Smith, Robert McCaughan. *The independent learners' sourcebook,* CB40

Smith, Robert V. *Graduate research,* EA5

Smith, Sweetman R. *The dictionary of marketing,* CH318

Smith, Tom W. *Trends in public opinion,* CJ234

Smith, William C. *Music publishing in the British Isles,* BH70

Smith-Morris, Miles. *World development directory,* CH59

Smithsonian Institution. *International index of conservation research = Répertoire international de la recherche en conservation,* BE106

Smits, Donald Wytze. *World directory of crystallographers and of other scientists employing crystallographic methods,* EE22

Smitten, Jeffrey R. *English novel explication. Supplement,* BD241

Smock, Raymond. *A guide to manuscripts in the Presidential Libraries,* AB47, CJ80

Smolyarova, N. A. *Elsevier's dictionary of glaciology in four languages,* EE23

Smyth, Daragh. *A guide to Irish mythology,* CF14

Snarr, Neil. *Sandinista Nicaragua,* DB129

Snell, Bruno. *Lexikon des frühgriechischen Epos,* AD115

Snorgrass, J. William. *Blacks and media,* CH203

Snow, Bonnie. *Drug information,* EK105

Snow, Dean R. *Atlas of ancient America,* CL62

Snow, Marcellus S. *Telecommunication economics and international regulatory policy,* CH194

Snow, Peter. *The United States: a guide to library holdings in the UK,* AB28

Snyder, Louis Leo. *Encyclopedia of nationalism,* CJ11
—— *Encyclopedia of the Third Reich,* DC94
—— *The Third Reich, 1933–1945,* DC87

Sobański, Oskar. *Polish feature films,* BG81

Sobel, Robert. *Biographical directory of the Council of Economic Advisers,* CH22
—— *Biographical directory of the United States executive branch, 1774–1989,* CJ85

Soboul, Albert. *Dictionnaire historique de la Révolution française,* DC53

Social and behavioral sciences
  abstracts, CA8
  bibliography, CA5, CA7
    current, CA9, CA10, CA11
  databases, CA12, EA24
  dictionaries, CA16
  directories, CA18, CA20
    Gt. Brit., CA17, EA53
    Hungary, DC143
  encyclopedias, CA15, CD11
  guides, CA1, CA2, CA3, CA4
  handbooks, CA23
  indexes, CA8
  periodicals, CA13
    Gt. Brit., AE47
  guides for authors, CD6

Social conditions and social welfare, CC21, CC22, CC25

Social indicators of development, CG17, CH60

Social networks and mental health, Biegel, David E., CC21, CC22

Social planning, policy & development abstracts, CC12

Social planning/policy and development abstracts, CC28

The social science encyclopedia, CA15

Social science information, Rama Reddy, E., CA2

Social science reference sources, Li, Tze-chung, CA1

Social Science Research Council (U.S.). *A guide to scholarly resources on the Russian Empire and the Soviet Union in the New York metropolitan area,* DC195

The social sciences, CA3
—— Herron, Nancy L., CA1

Social sciences citation index, CH24, CA12

Social sciences index, CA8

Social SciSearch, CA12, CB6

Social security, CH267

Social stratification, Kinloch, Graham Charles, CC9

Social studies teaching and learning, CB128

Social support and health, CC23

Social support networks, CC22

Social work
  databases, CC28
  dictionaries, CC31
  encyclopedias, CC29, CC30
  guides, CC26

The social work dictionary, Barker, Robert L., CC31

Social work education, CC27, CC32

Social work education II, Li, Hong-Chan, CC27

Società Retorumantscha. *Disciunari rumantsch grischen,* AD149

Societatea de Științe Filologice din Republica Socialistă România. *Bibliografia românească modernă, 1831–1918,* AA177

Société, culture et histoire du Rwanda, Hertefelt, Marcel d', DD50

Société d'histoire et d'épistémologie des sciences du langage. *Renaissance linguistics archive, 1350–1700,* BC5

Society and economy in early modern Europe, 1450–1789, Taylor, Barry, DC7

Society for the Advancement of Scandinavian Study (U.S.). *Directory of Scandinavian studies in North America,* DC180

Society for Theatre Research. *Directory of theatre resources,* BG26

Society of Biblical Literature. *Harper's Bible commentary,* BB64
—— *Harper's Bible dictionary,* BB51
—— *Harper's Bible pronunciation guide,* BB52

Society of Genealogists (Great Britain). *Cofrestri plwyf Cymru = Parish registers of Wales,* AK48

Society of Manufacturing Engineers. *Tool and manufacturing engineers handbook,* EJ83

Society of the Plastics Industry. *Plastics engineering handbook of the Society of the Plastics Industry,* EJ23

Sociofile, CC12

Sociofile [computer file], CC28

Sociological abstracts, CB6, CC11, CC12

Sociological abstracts [computer file], CC28

Sociology
  abstract journals, CC11
  bibliography, CC4, CC5, CC7, CC9, CC10, CE4
    current, CC11
  databases, CC12
  dictionaries, CC14
  guides, CC1, CC2
  handbooks, CC18, CC20
  periodicals
    indexes, CC13
  quotations, CC16
  terminology, CC15

Sociology, Aby, Stephen H., CC1

Sociology of aging, Harris, Diana K., CC44

The sociology of medicine and health care, Litman, Theodor J., CC6, EK7

Sociology of poverty in the United States, Chalfant, H. Paul, CC143

Sociology of sport, Redekop, Paul, BJ1

The sociology of work, Ghorayshi, Parvin, CC8

Socrates, BA29

Socrates, Navia, Luis E., BA29

Soden, Wolfram von. *Akkadisches Handwörterbuch,* AD73
—— *Reallexikon der Assyriologie, unter Mitwirkung zahlreicher Fachgelehrter,* DA36

Sörenson, Sören. *Ensk-íslensk orðabók,* AD125

Sofiano, T. A. *Anglo-russkiĭ geologicheskiĭ slovar',* EE14

The software encyclopedia, EJ66

Sokoloff, Michael. *A dictionary of Jewish Palestinian Aramaic of the Byzantine period,* AD119

Solé, Carlos A. *Latin American writers,* BD334

Solomon Islands, DG15

Solomon Islands bibliography to 1980, Edridge, Sally, DG15

Somali language, AD163

Somalia, DD51, DD52

Somalia, DD52

Somer, Elizabeth. *The nutrition desk reference,* EK98

Sommer, Elyse. *Similes dictionary,* BD41

Sommer, Francis E. *A catalogue of incunabula and manuscripts in the Army Medical Library,* EK13

Sommer, Mike. *Similes dictionary,* BD41

Songs, BH109, BH111, BH112, BH113
  indexes, BH104, BH114, BH115

Sonntag, Paula Rumbaugh. *Encyclopedia of world literature in the 20th century,* BD26

Sontz, Ann H. L. *The American college president, 1636–1989,* CB11

Sood, R. P. *Directory of periodicals published in India, 1986–87,* AE50

Soper, Elizabeth W. *The Facts on File dictionary of education,* CB76

Sotheby's concise encyclopedia of furniture, BF42

Sotheby's encyclopedia of porcelain, BF23

Sotiron, Minko. *An annotated bibliography of works on daily newspapers in Canada, 1914–1983 = Une bibliographie annotée des ouvrages portant sur les quotidiens canadiens, 1914–1983; Gordon Rabchuk, indexation,* AF4

Souchal, François. *French sculptors of the 17th and 18th centuries,* BE163

Soukup, Paul A. *Christian communication,* BB82

Soule, James. *Glossary for horticultural crops,* EH12

Sound advice, Wadhams, Wayne, BH72

Source index, American Chemical Society. Chemical Abstracts Service, ED5

Sourcebook for the performing arts, Slide, Anthony, BG4

Sourcebook of contemporary North American architecture from postwar to postmodern, Wright, Sylvia Hart, BE136

Sourcebook of county demographics, CH332

Sourcebook of demographics and buying power for every county in the USA, CH332

Sourcebook of global statistics, Kurian, George Thomas, CG6

The sourcebook of zip code demographics, CH332

A sourcebook on child sexual abuse, Finkelhor, David, CC92

Sources for English local history, Stephens, W. B., DC110

Sources for U.S. history, Stephens, W. B., DB47

Sources in European political history, Cook, Chris, DC9

Sources of information in librarianship and information science, Prytherch, Raymond John, AB4

Sources of information in the social sciences, CA4

—— Webb, William H., CA3

—— White, Carl Milton, CA4

Sources of serials, AE9

South, Aloha. *Guide to federal archives relating to Africa,* DD3

—— *Guide to non-federal archives and manuscripts in the United States relating to Africa,* DD3

South, Malcolm. *Mythical and fabulous creatures,* CF6

South Africa; *see also* **Apartheid**
  bibliography, AA184
  biography, AJ92
    contemporary, CJ203
  foreign relations, DD54
  history
    bibliography, DD53, DD55, DD56
  politics and government, CJ202

South Africa, Stultz, Newell Maynard, DD56

South Africa. State Archives Service. *Guide to the South African manuscript collections in the South African Library, Cape Town,* DD55

South Africa under apartheid, Kalley, Jacqueline A., DD53

South African bibliography to the year 1925, AA184

South African Library. *Guide to the South African manuscript collections in the South African Library, Cape Town,* DD55

South African literature, BD286

The South African pocket Oxford dictionary, AD57

South African theological bibliography = Suid-Afrikaanse teologiese bibliografie, BB18

South America, Central America, and the Caribbean, DB101

South American economic handbook, CH47

South and Southwest regional catalog, DB24

The South Asia and Burma retrospective bibliography (SABREB), Shaw, Graham, AA92

South Asia Library Group. *Directory of South Asian library resources in the UK and the Republic of Ireland,* DE30

South-East Asia, BC60, BD382

South Pacific bibliography, AA168

Southeast Asia microforms project resources, The-Mulliner, Lian, DE39

Southeast Asian literature, BC60, BD382

Southern, Eileen. *African-American traditions in song, sermon, tale, and dance, 1600s–1920,* CC203

Southern African material in anthologies of English literature in the Strange Library of Africana, Strange Library of Africana, BD375

Southern African update, DD22

Southern American English, BC23

Southern black creative writers, 1829–1953, Foster, Mamie Marie Booth, BD187

Southern states, DB51
  encyclopedias, BB24, DB52, DB53
  religion
    bibliography, BB4

Southern Sudan, Wawa, Yosa H., DD57

Southon, I. W. *Dictionary of alkaloids,* ED31, EK108

Southwest Native American arts and material culture, Parezo, Nancy J., CC219

The Southwest Pacific, Thompson, Anne-Gabrielle, DG7

Southwestern pottery, Oppelt, Norman T., BF19

Sovetskaĭa arkheologicheskaĭa literatura, DA33

Soviet intelligence and security services, CJ287

Soviet law, Butler, William Elliott, CK49

Soviet law in English, Kavass, Igor I., CK51

A Soviet lexicon, Laird, Roy D., CJ205

Soviet military encyclopedia, CJ283

Soviet perception of Canada, 1917–1987, Black, J. L., DB81

Soviet publications on Judaism, Zionism, and the State of Israel, 1984–1988, Korsch, Boris, BB134, DE72

Soviet serials currently received at the Center for Research Libraries, Center for Research Libraries (U.S.), AE66

The Soviet Union, AJ98

The Soviet Union and Eastern Europe, Horak, Stephan M., DC14

Space astronomy and astrophysics, EB12

Space engineering *see* **Aeronautical and space engineering**

Spahn, Theodore Jurgen. *From radical left to extreme right,* AE26

Spain
  bibliography, AA186
    early, AA187, AA188, AA189
    general, AA185
  biography, AJ93, AJ94
    contemporary, AJ95
  history
    bibliography, DC182, DC183, DC186
    encyclopedias, DC188
    manuscripts and archives, DC187
  periodicals, AE69

Spain, Shields, Graham J., DC186

Spain. Inspección Tecnica de Archivos. *Guía de los archivos estatales españoles,* DC187

Spalding, Keith. *An historical dictionary of German figurative usage,* AD110

Spangler, Stella S. *Science & technology in fact and fiction,* EA11, EA12

Spanier, Jerome. *An atlas of functions,* EF15

Der spanische Bürgerkrieg, Ruhl, Klaus-Jörg, DC185

Das spanische Drama im Goldenen Zeitalter, Reichenberger, Kurt, BD338

Spanish-American drama, BD337

Spanish-American fiction, BD339

Spanish-American literature, BD193
  bibliography, BD282, BD325, BD331, BD332, BD333, BD335, BD336
  biography, BD195
  dictionaries, BD344
  guides, BD330

The Spanish-American War, Venzon, Anne Cipriano, DB27

Spanish American women writers, BD335

Spanish and Spanish-American literature, Woodbridge, Hensley Charles, BD321

Spanish Civil War, DC185

Spanish drama, BD338

Spanish language
  bibliography, BC48, BC49, BC51, BC52
    regional and dialect, BC53
  dictionaries, EK59
    bilingual, AD164, AD165, AD167, EA52
    etymology, AD166, AD167
    indexes, BC50
    medieval–18th century, AD168
    regional and dialect, AD169
  guides, BD321

Spanish-language reference books, AA66

Spanish literature
  bibliography, BC51, BD322, BD323, BD324, BD325, BD326
  biography, BD326
  criticism, BD327
  guides, BD321

Spanish literature, 1500–1700, Moseley, William W., BD324

Spanish poetry, BD328

Spanish-speaking Americans
  bibliography, CC235, CC236, CC237, CC238, CC239, CC288
  biography, AJ28, CC245
  directories, CC241, CC242
  handbooks, CC244
  indexes, CC240
  material culture, CC243
  statistics, CC246

Spann, Gustav. *Bibliographie zur österreichischen Zeitgeschichte, 1918–1985,* DC23

Spann, Milton G. *The national directory of exemplary programs in developmental education,* CB116

Sparhawk, Ruth M. *American women in sport, 1887–1987,* BJ15

Sparkes, Ivan George. *Dictionary of collective nouns and group terms,* AD28

Sparks, Linda. *American college regalia,* CB163

Speake, Jennifer. *Encyclopedia of the Renaissance,* DA47

The speakers of the U.S. House of Representatives, Kennon, Donald R., CJ94

Speaking in tongues, BB83

Spearritt, Peter. *Australians,* DF2

Special collections in college and university libraries, AB48

Special edition, Einstein, Daniel, BG107

Special education, CB59
  abstract journals, CB55
  bibliography, CB15
  databases, CB54
  dictionaries, CB72, CB74
  encyclopedias, CB62
  handbooks, CB122, CB130, CB136, CB138, CB139, CB142

Special education, CB136

—— Sternlicht, Manny, CB15

Special education yearbook, CB142

Special issues and indexes of periodicals, AE17

Special operations and elite units 1939–1988, Beaumont, Roger A., CJ271

Specialized legal research, CK12

The SpecialWare directory, CB13

Spector, Robert Donald. *Backgrounds to restoration and eighteenth-century English literature,* BD211

Spectroscopy source book, EA38

Speech and rhetoric
  bibliography, BD142, BD143, BD144, BD145, BD147
  biography, BD148

Speeches of the American presidents, CJ89

Spence, Lewis. *Encyclopedia of occultism,* CD51

Sperling, Walter. *Landeskunde DDR,* DC88

Spielman, Linda June. *A literature guide for the identification of plant pathogenic fungi,* EC35

Spielmann, Dean. *Bibliographie juridique luxembourgeoise,* CK45

Spiess, Eberhard. *International directory of cinematographers, set- and costume designers in film,* BG100

Spiller, David. *Book selection,* AB69

Spiller, Robert E. *Literary history of the United States,* BD167

Spinelli, Donald C. *French language and literature,* BC38, BD308

Spirituality, BB90, BB93

Spitler, James F. *Detailed statistics on the urban and rural population of Pakistan, 1950 to 2010,* CG65

Spores, Ronald. *Ethnohistory,* CE25

Sport bibliography, BJ3

Sport bibliography update, BJ2, BJ3

Sport bibliography update = Bibliographie du sport mise à jour, BJ2

SPORT Discus, BJ3

Sport Information Resource Centre. *Sport bibliography update = Bibliographie du sport mise à jour,* BJ2

—— *SPORT Discus,* BJ3

Sport & leisure, BJ4

Sports and games; *see also* individual sports
  abstract journals, BJ4
  bibliography, BJ1
  biography, BJ28
  dictionaries, BJ10
    polyglot, BJ11
  directories, BJ14
  encyclopedias, BJ5, BJ6, BJ8
  handbooks, BJ16, CC19
  quotations, BJ12, BJ13
  rules, BJ9

The sports encyclopedia, Neft, David S., BJ24

The sports encyclopedia : baseball, BJ17, BJ22

Sports encyclopedia North America, BJ8

Sports quotations, Maikovich, Andrew J., BJ13

Sports rules encyclopedia, BJ9

Sports talk, Palmatier, Robert A., BJ10

Spottswood, Richard K. *Ethnic music on records,* BH144

Spouse abuse, CC133

Spouse abuse, Engeldinger, Eugene A., CC126

Spravochnik po matematike, EF14

Springberg, Judith. *BNA's directory of state courts, judges, and clerks,* CK78

Sprug, Joseph W. *Index to fairy tales, 1978–1986, including folklore, legends, and myths in collections,* BD98

Sprung, Barbara. *Resources for educational equity,* CB38

Spy fiction, McCormick, Donald, BD106

Squitier, Karl A. *Thesaurus Linguae Graecae canon of Greek authors and works,* BD367

Sri Lanka
  bibliography, CJ204, DE94
  history, DE93
  statistics, CG71

Sri Lanka, Samaraweera, Vijaya, DE94

Srī Laṅkā saṅkhyāta nibandhaya = Ilaṅkaip puḷḷiviparat tokuppu = Statistical abstract of Sri Lanka, CG71

Srivastav, Ajay Kumar. *Directory of scientific personnel of the Anthropological Survey of India,* CE22

Śródka, Andrzej. *Biogramy uczonych polskich,* AJ85

Srpska bibliografija, AA204

Srpska književna periodika 1768–1941, BD363

Staatliches Institut für Musikforschung Preussischer Kulturbesitz. *Periodica musicalia (1789–1830),* BH31

Staatsbürgerlexikon, Schramm, Friedrich Karl, CJ173

Stables, BE112, EH24

Stade, George. *European writers,* BD54

Stadler, Wolfgang. *Lexikon der Kunst,* BE37

Staff training, Crimando, William, CH150

Stafford, Beth. *Directory of women's studies programs & library resources,* CC302

Stage lives, BG44

Stambler, Irwin. *Encyclopedia of pop, rock & soul,* BH134

Stammler, Wolfgang. *Die deutsche Literatur des Mittelalters,* BD289

—— *Reallexikon der deutschen Literaturgeschichte,* BD292

Standard code of parliamentary procedure, Sturgis, Alice, CJ228

The standard Danish-English, English-Danish dictionary = Dansk-engelsk, engelsk-dansk ordbok, AD84

Standard definitions of broadcast research terms, CH207

Standard dictionary of the social sciences = Standardwörterbuch für die Sozialwissenschaften, Koschnick, Wolfgang J., CA16

Standard directory of newsletters, AF3

The standard Finnish-English English-Finnish dictionary, Wuolle, Aino, AD88

Standard handbook for mechanical engineers, EJ79

Standard handbook of environmental engineering, EJ31

Standard handbook of machine design, EJ82

Standard highway mileage guide, Rand McNally and Company, CL59

Standard industrial classification manual, CH309

Standard methods for the examination of water and wastewater, ED23

Standard & Poor's register—biographical, CH148

Standard & Poor's register—corporate, CH124

Standard Shona dictionary, Hannan, M., AD161

Standards, EA88, EA89, EA90

Standards, Ricci, Patricia, EA89

Standards activities of organizations in the United States, EA90

Standards for educational and psychological testing, American Psychological Association, CB120, CD38

The Stanford companion to Victorian fiction, Sutherland, John, BD242

Stanford University. Libraries. *Peronism and the three Perons,* DB109

Stanley, Harold W. *Vital statistics on American politics,* CJ134

Stanley, Suzanne. *Food, cookery, and diet,* EH35

Stansfield, Geoffrey. *Keyguide to information sources in museum studies,* BE3

Stansfield, William D. *A dictionary of genetics,* EC65, EC66

Stanton Library (North Sydney, N.S.W.). *Australian architectural periodicals index,* BE114

Staples, Amy J. *Historical dictionary of the Third French Republic, 1870–1940,* DC76

Star atlas and reference handbook (epoch 2000.0), Norton, Arthur P., EB17

Stars, EB17, EB18

State and local government
  bibliography, AG28, CJ122, CJ220
  handbooks, CJ126

The state and local government political dictionary, Elliot, Jeffrey M., CJ123

State and local statistics sources, CG30

State blue books, legislative manuals, and reference publications, AG28, CJ122

State court clerks and county courthouses, CK75

State document checklists, Dow, Susan L., AG25

State government research directory, CJ126

State information book, CJ129, CJ127

State Legislative Leaders Foundation (U.S.). *The handbook of state legislative leaders,* CJ124

State legislative sourcebook, CJ128

State legislatures, Goehlert, Robert, CJ121

State Library (South Africa). *RSANB, 1926–1958,* AA184

State names, seals, flags, and symbols, Shearer, Benjamin F., DB45

State policy data book, CJ130

State yellow book, CJ129

States in profile, CJ130

Statistical abstract of Ceylon, CG71

Statistical abstract of Latin America for [date], CG60

Statistical abstract of Latin America. Supplement, CG61

Statistical abstract of Sri Lanka, CG71

Statistical abstract of the United States, CG67

Statistical handbook on aging Americans, CC66

Statistical handbook on U.S. Hispanics, Schick, Frank Leopold, CC246

Statistical handbook on women in America, CG25

Statistical information on the financial services industry, CH262

Statistical record of black America, CC211

Statistical services directory, CG14

Statistical yearbook of China, CG48

Statistics and demography
  bibliography, CG2, CG5, CG6, CG8, DB9
  biography, CG18
  compendiums, CG15, CG16, CG19, CG20, CG21, CG22, CH30, CH332
    bibliography, CG7
  dictionaries, CG9, CG10, CG11, CG12, CG13, EF11
  directories, CG14
  guides, CG1
  handbooks, CH323

Statistics Canada. *Guide to Statistics Canada data on women,* CG44, CG44

Statistics Europe, Harvey, Joan M., CG51

Statistics sources, CG7

Statisztikai adatforrások, Fóti, Istvánné, CG55

Statliga publikationer, årsbibliografi, AG47

Státní knihovna ČSR. *Bibliografický katalog ČSSR. České knihy,* AA99

Statsky, William P. *West's legal desk reference,* CK91

Statt, David A. *The concise dictionary of management,* CH159

Statutes
  United States, CK95

Staub, Kurt Hans. *Der Buchdruck im 15. Jahrhundert,* AA45

Stauber, Ronald. *A Zuni atlas,* CC233

Stavrou, Theofanis George. *Russian travelers to the Christian East from the twelfth to the twentieth century,* DE16

Stebbins, Christine Depp. *Commodity trading manual,* CH172

Stedman, Preston. *The symphony,* BH149

Stedman, Thomas Lathrop. *Stedman's medical dictionary,* EK50

Stedman's medical dictionary, Stedman, Thomas Lathrop, EK50

Steels alert, EJ14

Steels supplement to Metals abstracts, EJ14

Steeves, Paul D. *The modern encyclopedia of religions in Russia and the Soviet Union,* DC208

Stegemeyer, Anne. *Who's who in fashion,* BF33

Stehle, Dorothy. *The Near East national union list,* AA25

Stein, Alice P. *American nursing,* EK94

Stein, Gordon. *The encyclopedia of unbelief,* BB27

Stein, Jess M. *The Random House encyclopedia,* AC6

—— *The Random House thesaurus,* AD50

Stein, Morris Isaac. *Gifted, talented, and creative young people,* CB14

Steinberg, Cobbett. *TV facts,* CH211

Steinberg, S. H. *Historical tables, 58 B.C.–A.D. 1985,* DA24

Steiner, Lisa A. *Dictionary of immunology,* EK56

Steiner, Michael. *Region and regionalism in the United States,* DB46

Steinmetz, Sol. *The American Heritage dictionary of science,* EA40

—— *The Barnhart dictionary of etymology,* AD11

—— *The third Barnhart dictionary of new English,* AD36

Steinmetz, Suzanne K. *Handbook of marriage and the family,* CC141

Steinmeyer, Elias von. *Althochdeutsches Wörterbuch,* AD103

Steitz, Lothar. *Bibliographie zur Aussprache des Latein,* BC44

Stenesh, J. *Dictionary of biochemistry,* EC63

—— *Dictionary of biochemistry and molecular biology,* EC63

Stepfamilies, Gruber, Ellen J., CC129

Stephens, Helen L. *Theses on South-East Asia 1965–1985,* DE38

Stephens, Meic. *A dictionary of literary quotations,* BD67

—— *The Oxford companion to the literature of Wales,* BD273

Stephens, W. B. *Sources for English local history,* DC110

—— *Sources for U.S. history,* DB47

Stephenson, Mary Sue. *Planning library facilities,* AB72

Stephenson, Richard W. *Civil War maps,* DB37

Stern, Arthur C. *Air pollution,* EJ32

Stern, Ephraim. *Illustrated dictionary & concordance of the Bible,* BB54

Stern, Irwin. *Dictionary of Brazilian literature,* BD318

—— *Modern Spanish and Portuguese literatures,* BD327

Sternberg, Robert J. *The psychologist's companion,* CD37

—— *Writing the psychology paper,* CD37

Sternberg, Sam. *National directory of corporate charity,* CA41

Sternlicht, Manny. *Special education,* CB15

Stetler, Susan L. *Cities of the world,* CL18

Steven Spielberg Jewish Film Archive. *Films of the Holocaust,* DA88

Stevens, Bonnie Klomp. *A guide to literary criticism and research,* BD23

Stevenson, David. *Scottish texts and calendars,* DC140

Stevenson, Isabelle. *The Tony Award,* BG27

Stevenson, James A. C. *Scoor-oot,* AD61

Stevenson, John. *British historical facts, 1688–1760,* DC119

—— *The Longman handbook of modern British history, 1714–1987,* DC120

—— *The Longman handbook of modern European history, 1763–1985,* DC11

Stevenson, Rosemary M. *Index to Afro-American reference resources,* CC192

Stevenson, Wendy B. *Scottish texts and calendars,* DC140

Stewart, Jayme. *How to get into the college of your choice—and how to finance it,* CB155

Stewart, John. *African states and rulers,* DD7

—— *Antarctica,* DH5

Stewart, Larry L. *A guide to literary criticism and research,* BD23

Stickney, Patricia J. *World guide to social work education,* CC32

Still more words of Wall Street, Pessin, Allan H., CH231

Stineman, Esther. *Women's studies,* CC259, CC260

Stitt, Iain P. A. *The Arthur Andersen European community sourcebook,* CK125

Stiverson, Cynthia Zignego. *Architecture and the decorative arts,* BF7

Stock, Molly. *A practical guide to graduate research,* AH2

Stock exchanges, CH229, CH243

Stocks, CH221, CH252, CH259

Stoddart, L. *Conditions of work and quality of working life,* CH280

Stoloff, Michael L. *Computer use in psychology,* CD28

Stone, Evelyn M. *American psychiatric glossary,* CD21

Stone, Louise W. *Anglo-Norman dictionary,* AD62

Stone, Norman. *The Times atlas of world history,* DA30

Stoner, K. Lynn. *Latinas of the Americas,* CC288

Stoob, Heinz. *Bibliographie zur deutschen historischen Städteforschung,* BE137

Stopford, John M. *Multinational enterprise,* CH95

Stora, Benjamin. *Dictionnaire biographique de militants nationalistes algériens,* AJ30

Storey, C. A. *Persian literature,* BD379

Storrs, Thomas I. *The bankers' handbook,* CH251

Stott, D. I. *Dictionary of immunology,* EC15

Stout, Harry S. *Dictionary of Christianity in America,* BB84

Strachan, Anne. *Prizewinning literature,* BD45

Strange, Heather. *Aging & cultural diversity,* CC47

Strange Library of Africana. *Southern African material in anthologies of English literature in the Strange Library of Africana,* BD375

A strategic atlas, Chaliand, Gérard, CJ41

Strategic Defense Initiative, CJ269, CJ275

Strategic Defense Initiative, Lawrence, Robert M., CJ269

Stratford, Jean Slemmons. *Guide to statistical materials produced by governments and associations in the United States,* CG31

Stratford, Juri. *Guide to statistical materials produced by governments and associations in the United States,* CG31

Stratman, Carl J. *Bibliography of medieval drama,* BD229

Straus, Murray Arnold. *Handbook of family measurement techniques,* CC140

Strauss, Diane Wheeler. *Handbook of business information,* CH83

Strauss, Gerhard. *Lexikon der Kunst,* BE36

Strayer, Joseph Reese. *Dictionary of the Middle Ages,* BD229

Street talk in real estate, West, Bill W., CH350

Ştrempel, Gabriel. *Bibliografia românească modernă, 1831–1918,* AA177

Stress burnout, Riggar, T. F., CD2

Stress, strain, and Vietnam, Camp, Norman M., DE104

—— Marshall, William C., DE104

—— Stretch, Robert H., DE104

Stretch, Robert H. *Stress, strain, and Vietnam,* DE104

Strichart, Stephen S. *Peterson's guide to colleges with programs for learning-disabled students,* CB115

Strickland-Hodge, Barry. *Medical information,* EK4

Strong, James. *Exhaustive concordance of the Bible,* BB59

Strong, Susan R. *History of American ceramics,* BF19, BF20

Stropnicky, Sabine. *Deutsch-Skandinavisch im Vergleich,* BC32

Strosetzki, Christoph. *Bibliographie der Hispanistik in der Bundesrepublik Deutschland, Österreich und der deutschsprachigen Schweiz,* BC51

Stroynowski, Juliusz. *Who's who in the socialist countries of Europe,* AJ49

A structural atlas of the English dialects, Anderson, Peter M., BC30

Structural engineering, BE124, EJ36, EJ37, EJ38, EJ39, EJ40, EJ41, EJ42

Structural engineering handbook, EJ41

The struggle for South Africa, Davies, Robert H., CJ202

Strumpf, Michael. *Webster's New World best book of aphorisms,* BD60

Stubbs, Walter. *Congressional committees, 1789–1982,* AG15, CJ98

Student aid, CB157

The student sociologist's handbook, Bart, Pauline, CC2

Studer, Heinrich. *Neue österreichische Biographie ab 1815,* AJ36

Studies in enterprise, CH137

Studies in human sexuality, Frayser, Suzanne G., CC147

Studies in Jacobean drama, 1973–1984, Lidman, Mark J., BD233

Studies in Mycenaean inscriptions and dialect, 1953–1964, Baumbach, Lydia, BC55

Studies in Mycenaean inscriptions and dialect, 1965–1978, Baumbach, Lydia, BC55

Studies of Chinese religion, Thompson, Laurence G., BB12

Studwell, William E. *Ballet plot index,* BG49

—— *Christmas carols,* BH112

—— *Opera plot index,* BH103

The study of history, Richardson, R. C., DA16

The study of Russian history from British archival sources, DC204

A study of selected English critical terms from 1650–1800, Watson, Edward A., BD164

A study of the Soviet economy, CH53

Studying New Zealand history, Wood, G. A., DF6

Stultz, Newell Maynard. *South Africa,* DD56

Sturge, Charles. *Directory of Lloyd's of London,* CH266

Sturgis, Alice. *Standard code of parliamentary procedure,* CJ228

Sturgis standard code of parliamentary procedure, CJ228

Sturm, Heribert. *Biographisches Lexikon zur Geschichte der böhmischen Länder,* AJ43

Sturtevant, William C. *Handbook of North American Indians,* CC230

Stutley, Margaret. *Dictionary of Hinduism,* BE104

—— *An illustrated dictionary of Hindu iconography,* BE104

Style manual for guidance in the preparation of papers for journals published by the American Institute of Physics and its member societies, EG10

Style manuals, AA58; *see also* **Copy preparation**
  medicine, EK34
  music, BH46
  science and technology, ED24, EG10, EK34

Stylebook: editorial manual, EK34

Stylistics, BD140, BD141

Sub-doctoral theses on Canada accepted by universities in the United Kingdom & Ireland 1899–1986, Reid, Elspeth, DB85

Sub-Saharan African films and filmmakers, Schmidt, Nancy J., BG55

al-Subaiy, Abdullah Nasir. *American and Canadian doctoral dissertations on the Kingdom of Saudi Arabia, 1935–1987,* DE89

A subject bibliography of the First World War, Enser, A. G. S., DA65

A subject bibliography of the Second World War, and aftermath, Enser, A. G. S., DA66

A subject bibliography of the Second World War: books in English, 1939–1974, Enser, A. G. S., DA65, DA66

Subject catalogue of paintings in public collections, BE149

Subject catalogue of the House of Commons Parliamentary papers, 1801–1900, Cockton, Peter, AG42

Subject compilations of state laws, 1985–1988, Nyberg, Cheryl, CK31

Subject guide to Books in print, AA82

Subject guide to classical instrumental music, Goodenberger, Jennifer, BH13

Subject guide to forthcoming books, AA83
Subject guide to government reference books,
Wynkoop, Sally, AG4
*Subject guide to U.S. government reference
sources,* Robinson, Judith Schiek, AG4
Subject headings
anthropology, CE16
economics, CH12
political science, CJ26
schedules, AB84
sociology, CC15
*Subject index of modern books acquired,
1971–1975,* British Library, AA22
The subject is murder, Menendez, Albert J.,
BD107
Subramaniam, Venkateswarier. *Public
administration in the Third World,* CJ222
Subscription agents, AB68
Substance abuse I : drug abuse, Nordquist,
Joan, CC114
Substance abuse II : alcohol abuse, Nordquist,
Joan, CC71
Successful industrial product innovation,
Calantone, Roger J., CH289
Sudan, DD57
Südost-Institut München. Bibliothek.
*Bestandskatalog der Bibliothek des Südost-
Instituts München,* DC18
Suichmezian, Louis. *Global countertrade,*
CH179
Suicide, CC96, CC101
Sukiennik, Adelaide Weir. *Accept me as I am,*
CC103
Sullivan, Alvin. *British literary magazines,*
BD203
Sullivan, Eric. *The marine encyclopaedic
dictionary,* CH192
Sullivan, Howard A. *French language and
literature,* BC38, BD308
Sullivan, Jack. *The Penguin encyclopedia of
horror and the supernatural,* CF28
Sullivan, Kaye. *Films for, by, and about women.
Series II,* CC265
Sullivan, William M. *Dissertations and theses
on Venezuelan topics, 1900–1985,* DB137
Sulzer, Jack. *Guide to the publications of
interstate agencies and authorities,* AG26
Sumerian *see* **Assyro-Babylonian**
*The Sumerian dictionary of the University
Museum of the University of Pennsylvania,*
AD74
*Summary guide to the archive and manuscript
collections relevant to the former British
colonial territories in the United Kingdom,*
Burdett, Anita L. P., DC131
Summer Institute of Linguistics—Philippines.
*Bibliography of the Summer Institute of
Linguistics, Philippines, 1953–1984,* BC61
Summers, Harry G. *Korean War almanac,*
DE81
Sundermeier, Theo. *Lexikon
missionstheologischer Grundbegriffe,* BB105
Suomalais-englantilainen sanakirja, Wuolle,
Aino, AD88
Suomalaisen Kirjallisuuden Seura.
Nykysuomen sanakirja, AD87
*Suomen aikakauslehdistön bibliografia
1782–1955 = Bibliografi över Finlands
tidskriftsliteratur 1782–1955 = Bibliography
of Finnish periodicals, 1782–1955,* Kurikka,
Jussi, AE31
*Suomen aikakauslehdistön bibliografia
1956–1977 = Bibliografi över Finlands
tidskriftsliteratur 1956–1977 = Bibliography
of Finnish periodicals, 1956–1977,* Takkala,
Marketta, AE32
Suomen Akatemia. *Bibliographia studiorum
uralicorum, 1917–1987 = Uralistiikan
tutkimuksen bibliografia = Bibliography on
Uralic studies,* DC210
*Suomen historiallinen bibliografia = Finsk
historisk bibliografi = Bibliografie historique
finlandaise, 1971–1980,* DC45

Suomen kirjallisuus, AA109
*Suomen kirjallisuus = Finlands litteratur = The
Finnish national bibliography,* AA110
Supernatural fiction writers, BD127
Suratteau, Jean-René. *Dictionnaire historique
de la Révolution française,* DC53
Suriname, DB134
Suriname, Hoefte, Rosemarijn, DB134
Surnames *see* **Names—personal**
The survey of buying power data service, CH333
Survey of English dialects, BC30
*Survey of public education in the nation's urban
school districts,* National School Boards
Association, CB152
Surveying, EJ25
The surveying handbook, EJ25
*Surveys of historical manuscripts in the United
Kingdom,* DC111
Susan Lee's ABZs of economics, Lee, Susan,
CH9
Susheel Kaur. *Directory of periodicals published
in India, 1986–87,* AE50
Sussman, Marvin B. *Handbook of marriage and
the family,* CC141
Sutherland, John. *Longman companion to
Victorian fiction,* BD242
——— *The Stanford companion to Victorian
fiction,* BD242
Sutherland, N. S. *The international dictionary
of psychology,* CD22
Svensk bok-katalog [för aren]. 1971/75, AA191
Svensk historisk bibliografi 1951–1960,
Rydbeck, Jan, DC190
Svensk historisk bibliografi 1971–1975, DC190
Svenska akademien. *Ordbok öfver svenska
språket,* AD170
Svenska arkeologiska samfundet. *Swedish
archaeology,* DA34
Svenskt biografiskt lexikon, AJ96
Sveriges statliga publikationer. *Bibliografi,*
AG47
*Svodnyĭ katalog knig na inostrannykh
īazykakh, izdannykh v Rossii v XVIII veke,
1701–1800,* AA180
Swanekamp, Joan. *English ayres,* BH113
Swanson, Alan. *Sweden,* DC189
Swedberg, Richard. *Honduras bibliography and
research guide,* DB122
Sweden
bibliography, AA191
18th–19th centuries, AA190
biography, AJ91, AJ96
history, DC190
bibliography, DC189
Sweden, Sather, Leland B., DC189
Swedish Archaeological bibliography, DA34
Swedish archaeology, DA34, DA34
*Swedish government publications, annual
bibliography,* AG47
Swedish imprints 1731–1833, AA190
Swedish language, AD170
Sweetland, Richard C. *Tests,* CD47
Swierenga, Robert P. *Dutch households in U.S.
population censuses, 1850, 1860, 1870,* AK43
Swift, Kate. *The handbook of nonsexist writing,*
AA57, CC311
Swiss literature, BD301
Switzerland, DC191
Switzerland, Meier, Heinz K., DC191
Sworakowski, Witold S. *The Communist
International and its front organizations,*
CJ240
Sykes, J. B. *Concise Oxford dictionary of
current English,* AD53
——— *The Oxford-Duden German dictionary,*
AD109
*Symbols and sacred objects, The woman's
dictionary of,* CF7
The symphony, Stedman, Preston, BH149
Symphony orchestras, BH150
Symphony orchestras of the United States,
BH150
Symphony orchestras of the world, BH150

Syndromes, EK55
The synonym finder, Rodale, Jerome I., AD49
Syria, AA192, AA193, DE95
Syria, Seccombe, Ian J., DE95
The Syrian national bibliography, AA192
Szajkowski, Bogdan. *Marxist local governments
in Western Europe and Japan,* CJ165
Szczawiński, Paweł. *Biogramy uczonych
polskich,* AJ85
Szelle, Béla. *Akadémiai kislexikon,* AC15
Szepsi Csombor Kör (London, England).
Prominent Hungarians, AJ69
Szilard, Paula. *Food and nutrition information
guide,* EK96
Szladits, Charles. *A bibliography on foreign and
comparative law,* CK20
——— *Guide to foreign legal materials,* CK39
——— *Szladits' bibliography on foreign and
comparative law,* CK21
*Szladits' bibliography on foreign and
comparative law,* Szladits, Charles, CK21
Szonyi, David M. *The Holocaust,* DA86
Szucs, Loretto Dennis. *The archives,* AB49,
DB22
Szymanek, Bogdan. *Bibliography of
morphology, 1960–1985,* BC1

TULIP, Nagar, Murari Lal, AE49
Table of isotopes, Lederer, Charles Michael,
EG11
——— Shirley, Virginia S., EG11
Table of radioactive isotopes, Browne, Edgardo,
EG11
*Tables of physical and chemical constants and
some mathematical functions,* Kaye, G. W.
C., ED16, EG12
Tactile map collections, CL45
Taehan Min'guk ch'ulp'anmul ch'ongmongnok,
AA153
Taeuber, Cynthia Murray. *Statistical handbook
on women in America,* CG25
Taft, William H. *Encyclopedia of twentieth-
century journalists,* AF25
Taft Group (Washington, D.C.). *America's new
foundations,* CA30
——— *National directory of nonprofit
organizations,* CH122
Taintor, Sarah Augusta. *The secretary's
handbook,* CH168
Taiwan, DE96, DE97; *see also* **China**
Taiwan, Lee, Wei-chin, DE96
Tajima, Matsuji. *Old and Middle English
language studies,* BC25
Takkala, Marketta. *Suomen aikakauslehdistön
bibliografia 1782–1955 = Bibliografi över
Finlands tidskriftslitteratur 1782–1955 =
Bibliography of Finnish periodicals,
1782–1955,* AE31
——— *Suomen aikakauslehdistön bibliografia
1956–1977 = Bibliografi över Finlands
tidskriftslitteratur 1956–1977 = Bibliography
of Finnish periodicals, 1956–1977,* AE32
Talbert, Richard J. A. *Atlas of classical history,*
DA45
Tale type- and motif-indexes, Azzolina, David
S., CF19
*Tanakh : a new translation of the Holy
Scriptures according to the traditional Hebrew
text,* BB36
Tang, Chin-Shih. *Guide to legal citation and
sources of citation aid,* CK35
Tanner, Helen Hornbeck. *Atlas of Great Lakes
Indian history,* CC232
Tanner, Norman P. *Decrees of the ecumenical
councils,* BB98
Tansey, Richard G. *Gardner's art through the
ages,* BE71
Tanzbibliographie, Petermann, Kurt, BG47
Taoism, BA12, BB23
Tapley, Bryon D. *Eshbach's handbook of
engineering fundamentals,* EJ6

Tarbert, Gary C. *Periodical directories and bibliographies,* AE19

Tarrab, Elca. *La francité canadienne,* BC40

Tarybú Lietuvos enciklopedija, DC163

Tasbīhī, Gulām 'Husayn. *Nigarishī jāmi bar jahān-i kitābshināsī-yi Īrān,* AA6

Taschenbuch für Familiengeschichtsforschung, AK27

Tate, Michael L. *The Indians of Texas,* CC218
—— *The upstream people,* CC218

Tattersall, Ian. *Encyclopedia of human evolution and prehistory,* CE13

Taufmann, Jürgen. *Atlas zur deutschen Zeitgeschichte, 1918–1968,* DC98

The Tauris Soviet directory, AJ100, CJ206

Tavenas, Stéphane. *Guide du cinéma européen,* BG99

Tavoni, Mirko. *Renaissance linguistics archive, 1350–1700,* BC5

Taylor, Arlene G. *Cataloging with copy,* AB75
—— *Introduction to cataloging and classification,* AB76

Taylor, Barry. *European economic and social history, 1450–1789,* DC7
—— *Society and economy in early modern Europe, 1450–1789,* DC7

Taylor, David D. *Pakistan,* DE88

Taylor, James,. *A dictionary of the Second World War,* DA76
—— *A dictionary of the Third Reich,* DC94
—— *The Third Reich almanac,* DC94

Taylor, Michael John Haddrick. *Encyclopedia of the world's air forces,* CJ254

Taylor, Paul. *Popular music since 1955,* BH139

Taylor, Peter J. *World government,* CJ143

Taylor, Wendell Hertig. *A catalogue of crime,* BD101

Teacher attitudes, Powell, Marjorie, CB18

Teacher education program evaluation, Ayers, Jerry B., CB16

The teacher's almanac, CB123, CB137

Teachers and teaching, CB8, CB17, CB18, CB78, CB129, CB145, CB148
education, CB16

A teacher's treasury of quotations, CB78

Teaching aids, CA21

Teatro hispanoamericano, Allen, Richard F., BD337

Il teatro La Fenice, Girardi, Michele, BH96

Teatro mexicano del siglo XX, 1900–1986, Mendoza-López, Margarita, BD345, BG22

Technical libraries, AB60, AB61, EA57

Technical reports, EA22

Technical reports in computer science, EF6

Teenage parents, CC135

Teenage pregnancy, CC135

Teeter, Mark H. *A scholars' guide to humanities and social sciences in the Soviet Union,* DC209

Teitelbaum, Michele. *Aging & cultural diversity,* CC47

Tejomurty, A. *Directory of library and information science schools in India,* AB31

Telecommunication, CH195, CH210

Telecommunication economics and international regulatory policy, Snow, Marcellus S., CH194

Telecommunications and networking glossary, Machovec, George S., CH195

Telemarketing, CH324

Television *see* **Radio and television**

Television, a guide to the literature, Cassata, Mary B., BG102

Television drama series programming, Gianakos, Larry James, BG108

Ten Middle English Arthurian romances, Jost, Jean E., BD204

Ten percent sampling tabulation on 1982 population census of People's Republic of China, CG46

Tennis, BJ35

Tepper, Michael. *The famine immigrants,* AK11

Terrace, Vincent. *The complete actors' television credits, 1948–1988,* BG111
—— *Encyclopedia of television,* BG113

Terry, Charles Sanford. *Catalogue of the publications of Scottish historical and kindred clubs and societies,* DC140

Terry, Garth M. *Yugoslav history,* DC219

Terry, John V. *Dictionary for business & finance,* CH237

Teschner, Richard V. *El diccionario del español chicano = The dictionary of Chicano Spanish,* AD169

Test construction, O'Brien, Nancy P., CD46

Tests, CD47

Tests and measurements, CB23, CB79, CB117, CB120, CC140, CD38, CD39, CD40, CD41, CD42, CD44, CD45, CD46, CD47, CD48
databases, CB118, CD43

Tests in microfiche, CD39

Textbooks in school and society, Woodward, Arthur, CB42

Textiles, BF35

Texts and calendars: an analytical guide to serial publications, Mullin, Edward, DC140

Teze de doctorat, AH18

Thacker, Eric. *The essential jazz records,* BH120

Thackrah, John Richard. *Malta,* DC164

Thailand, AA195, CG72

The Thames and Hudson encyclopaedia of 20th-century music, Griffiths, Paul, BH52

The Thames and Hudson encyclopaedia of Impressionism, Denvir, Bernard, BE33

Thar she went, Langdon, Robert, DG8

The Hague Club. *Foundation profiles,* CA27

The-Mulliner, Lian. *Southeast Asia microforms project resources,* DE39

Theater arts; *see also* **Musical theater; Performing arts**
annuals, BG18
awards, BG27
bibliography, BD87, BG8, BG9, BG10, BG11, BG12, BG13, BG14, BG15
biography, BG6, BG36, BG37, BG38, BG39, BG41, BG42, BG43
bibliography, BG44
by country or region
Latin America, BG15, BG42
Mexico, BD345, BG22
Spain, BG42
dictionaries, BD345, BG21, BG22, BG30
terms, BG24
directories, BG4, BG26, BG34
North America, BG28
discography, BG16
encyclopedias, BG19, BG20, BG23
guides, BG7
history, BG29, BG31, BG32, BG33, BG34, BG43
Gt. Brit., BG30, BG35
indexes, BG16
reviews, BG17

Theatre backstage from A to Z, Lounsbury, Warren C., BG25

Theatre companies of the world, BG34

Theatre, film and television biographies master index, LaBeau, Dennis, BG44

Théâtre noir, Waters, Harold A., BD302

Thematic list of descriptors—anthropology = Liste thématique des descripteurs—anthropologie, CE16

Thematic list of descriptors—economics, CH12

Thematic list of descriptors—political science = Liste thématique des descripteurs—science politique, CJ26

Thematic list of descriptors—sociology = Liste thématique des descripteurs—sociologie, CC15

Themes and settings in fiction, Hartman, Donald K., BD90

Themes & motifs in western literature, Daemmrich, Horst S., BD47

Theological and religious reference materials, Gorman, G. E., BB79

Theological dictionary of the New Testament, BB58

Theological dictionary of the Old Testament, Botterweck, G. Johannes, BB48

Theological seminaries, BB33

Theologische Realenzyklopädie, BB91

Theologisches Wörterbuch zum Alten Testament, Botterweck, G. Johannes, BB49

Theoretical studies in Hispanic linguistics (1960–), Nuessel, Frank H., BC52

Thermochemical data of pure substances, Barin, Ihsan, ED11

Thermochemistry, ED15

Thesaurus Linguae Graecae, BD369

Thesaurus Linguae Graecae canon of Greek authors and works, Berkowitz, Luci, BD367

Thesaurus linguae latinae, AD134, AD136, AD137

Thésaurus multilingue international en administration publique = Multilingual international thesaurus of public administration = Tesauro multilingue internacional de administración pública, CJ224

A thesaurus of African languages, Mann, Michael, BC58

Thesaurus of agricultural organisms, pests, weeds, and diseases, EH13

Thesaurus of psychological index terms, CD25

The thesaurus of slang, Lewin, Esther, AD45

Les thèses françaises sur l'Asie du Sud-Est depuis 1980, Charras, Muriel, DE38
—— Renard-Clamagirand, Brigitte, DE38

Theses in Canada, Robitaille, Denis, AH7

Theses in progress in Commonwealth studies, University of London. Institute of Commonwealth Studies. Library, DC133

Theses on South-East Asia 1965–1985, Stephens, Helen L., DE38

Theses on the history of New Zealand, Rodger, Margaret D., DF9

Theses on the history of New Zealand. Supplement, 1968–1982, Mosen, Norah D., DF9

They never said it, Boller, Paul F., BD59

The third Barnhart dictionary of new English, AD36

Third French Republic, 1870–1940, DC76

Third Reich, DC92, DC94, DC97

The Third Reich, 1933–1945, Snyder, Louis Leo, DC87

The Third Reich almanac, Taylor, James, DC94

Third World, AA75, CC277, CH49, CH50, CH51, CJ19, CJ222, CJ293

Third World economic handbook, CH50

The Third World in film and video, Cyr, Helen W., BG68

Third World resource directory, DB104, DD17, DE7, DE23, CH51

Third World struggle for peace with justice, Fenton, Thomas P., CJ293

This business of music, Shemel, Sidney, BH71

This day in American history, Gross, Ernie, DB74

Thomann, Arthur E. *Elsevier's dictionary of technology,* EA52

Thomas, Carol H. *Directory of college facilities and services for people with disabilities,* CB112

Thomas, Edmund J. *Writers and philosophers,* BD51

Thomas, G. Scott. *The pursuit of the White House,* CJ115
—— *The rating guide to life in America's small cities,* CL23

Thomas, J. E. *International biography of adult education,* CB31

Thomas, James L. *Directory of college facilities and services for people with disabilities,* CB112

Thomas, John C. *The sales prospecting & territory planning directory,* CH322

Thomas, R. J. *Geiriadur Prifysgol Cymru,* AD173

Thomas, Stephen B. *The yearbook of education law,* CB154

Thomas, Timothy N. *Indians overseas,* DE59

Thomas' register of American manufacturers and Thomas' register catalog file, CH301

Thomas register ondisc, CH301

Thomas register online, CH301

Thomason tracts, AA130

Thompson, Andrew. *The dictionary of contemporary politics of South America,* CJ194

Thompson, Anne-Gabrielle. *The Southwest Pacific,* DG7

Thompson, Cynthia G. *The national directory of exemplary programs in developmental education,* CB116

Thompson, Laurence G. *Chinese religion in Western languages,* BB12
—— *Guide to Chinese religion,* BB13
—— *Studies of Chinese religion,* BB12

Thompson, Morris Mordecai. *Maps for America,* CL61

Thompson, Susan J. *A chronology of geological thinking from antiquity to 1899,* EE20

Thomsett, Michael C. *Insurance dictionary,* CH265
—— *Investment and securities dictionary,* CH238
—— *The little black book of business statistics,* CH167
—— *Musical terms, symbols, and theory,* BH62
—— *Real estate dictionary,* CH349
—— *A treasury of business quotations,* CH97

Thomson, Ian. *The documentation of the European communities,* CK121

Thomson credit union directory, CH249

Thomson savings directory, CH250

Thorin, Suzanne E. *International directory of braille music collections,* BH65

Thorn, John. *Total baseball,* BJ27

Thornberry, Patrick. *World directory of minorities,* CC179

Thorndale, William. *Map guide to the U.S. federal censuses, 1790–1920,* AK3, CL60

Thornton, John Leonard. *Medical books, libraries, and collectors,* EK17
—— *Select bibliography of medical biography,* EK78
—— *Thornton's medical books, libraries, and collectors,* EK17

Thornton's medical books, libraries, and collectors, Thornton, John Leonard, EK17

Thorpe, Alana I. *A.J. Lowhater's Russian-English dictionary of the mathematical sciences,* EF13

Thorpe, Frances. *International directory of film and TV documentation centres,* BG83

Thorson, James L. *Reader's guide to twentieth-century science fiction,* BD119

Thrall, William Flint. *A handbook to literature,* BD39

Thrapp, Dan L. *Encyclopedia of frontier biography,* DB58

Through the pale door, Frank, Frederick S., BD117

Thư mục quốc gia, AA201

Thuraisingham, Ajita. *ASEAN,* DE36

Thurston, Anne. *Guide to archives and manuscripts relating to Kenya and East Africa in the United Kingdom,* DD13

Thweatt, William O. *Classical political economy,* CH1

Tibet, DE29, DE98, DE99

Tibet, Pinfold, John R., DE99

Ticho, Suzy. *Director of artists slide registries,* BE105

Tiefer, Charles. *Congressional practice and procedure,* CJ102

Tierney, Helen. *Women's studies encyclopedia,* CC294

Tietjen, Gary L. *A topical dictionary of statistics,* EF12

Timberlake, Andrea. *Women of color and Southern women,* CC289, CC290

Time
conversion tables, EB19

Time lines on file, DA27

The Times atlas of the Second World War, DA79

The Times atlas of the world, CL57

The Times atlas of world history, DA37, DA30

The Times Books world weather guide, Pearce, E. A., EE29

Times (London), AJ7

The timetables of science, Hellemans, Alexander, EA72, EA74

Timmer, Rob. *International directory of sports organizations under the auspices of the International Association for Sports Information (IASI),* BJ14

Timofeev, Petr Petrovich. *Anglo-russkiĭ geologicheskiĭ slovar',* EE14

Tinker guide to Latin American and Caribbean policy and scholarly resources in metropolitan New York, DB107

Tinsley, Elizabeth J. *Worldwide directory of national earth-science agencies and related international organizations,* EE18

Tirion, Wil. *Uranometria 2000.0,* EB18

Tischler, Alice. *A descriptive bibliography of art music by Israeli composers,* BH86

Tishler, William H. *American landscape architecture,* BE145

Tismaneanu, Vladimir. *Latin American revolutionaries,* CJ197

Titmus, Colin J. *Lifelong education for adults : an international handbook,* CB63

Toase, Charles A. *Bibliography of British newspapers,* AF7

Tobias, Bruce D. *A directory of Latin American studies in the United States,* DB102

Tobin, Patricia. *Encyclopedia of legal information sources,* CK15

Tobler, Adolf. *Altfranzösisches Wörterbuch,* AD102

Todd, David Keith. *The water encyclopedia,* EJ35

Todd, Janet M. *British women writers,* BD224
—— *A dictionary of British and American women writers, 1660–1800,* BD168

Todd, Loreto. *International English usage,* AD29

Tölle, Manfred. *Bibliographie deutschsprachiger bevölkerungswissenschaftlicher Literatur, 1978–1984,* CG4

Toffler, Betsy-Ann. *Dictionary of advertising and direct mail terms,* CH70

Togo, Decalo, S., DD6

Tolnai, Márton. *Guide to research and scholarship in Hungary,* DC143

Tomlyn, Bo. *Electronic music dictionary,* BH122

Tommila, Päivi. *Suomen aikakauslehdistön bibliografia 1956–1977 = Bibliografi över Finlands tidskriftslitteratur 1956–1977 = Bibliography of Finnish periodicals, 1956–1977,* AE32

Tongren, Hale N. *Beacham's marketing reference,* CH315

The Tony Award, Stevenson, Isabelle, BG27

Tool and manufacturing engineers handbook, EJ83

Tooley, R. V. *Tooley's dictionary of mapmakers. Supplement,* CL25

Tooley's dictionary of mapmakers. Supplement, Tooley, R. V., CL25

Tootill, Elizabeth. *The Facts on File dictionary of biology,* EC16

A topical dictionary of statistics, Tietjen, Gary L., EF12

Topical report: annual surveys of the public's attitudes toward the public schools, 1969–83, CB149

Toro, Fernando de. *Bibliografía del teatro hispanoamericano contemporáneo (1900–1980),* BG15

Toronto medieval bibliographies, DA46

Torre-Bueno, José Rollin de la. *A glossary of entomology,* EC64
—— *The Torre-Bueno glossary of entomology,* EC64

The Torre-Bueno glossary of entomology, Torre-Bueno, José Rollin de la, EC64

Torre-Bueno's glossary of entomology, Tulloch, George S., EC64

Torres, Arturo L. *Latin American legal abbreviations,* CK69

Total baseball, BJ17, BJ27

Toth, A. G. *The Oxford encyclopaedia of European Community law,* CK123

Toth, Robert B. *Standards activities of organizations in the United States,* EA90

Totok, Wilhelm. *Bibliographischer Wegweiser der philosophischen Literatur,* BA3
—— *Handbuch der bibliographischen Nachschlagewerke,* AA2
—— *Handbuch der Geschichte der Philosophie,* BA21

Totten, Samuel. *Cooperative learning,* CB21

Touliatos, John. *Handbook of family measurement techniques,* CC140

Tourism *see* **Travel and tourism**

Tourism's top twenty, BJ46

Tourtier-Bonazzi, Chantal de. *Guide des papiers des ministres et secrétaires d'État de 1871 à 1974,* DC69

Toute l'histoire par les dates et les documents, Jouette, André, DC77

Town planning glossary, Venturi, Marco, BE139

Town records, West, John, DC136

Townley, John M. *The trail west,* DB59

Townsend, Kiliaen V. R. *The boarding school guide,* CB111

Township atlas of the United States, Andriot, John L., CL58

Toxic and hazardous materials, EK128

Toxicity bibliography, EK129

Toxicology
bibliography, EK128
databases, EK129
encyclopedias, EK130
guides, EK127
handbooks, ED17, EH20, EK131

TOXLINE, EK129

Tōyō Bunko (Japan). *A classified catalogue of books on the section XII, India, in the Tōyō Bunko (II) acquired during the years 1951–1982,* DE60

Tozzer Library. *Anthropological literature,* CE9
—— *Author and subject catalogues of the Tozzer Library,* CE2, CE7, CE9

Tozzer Library index to anthropological subject headings, CE7

Tracing your English ancestors, Rogers, Colin Darlington, AK35

Trade catalogs at Winterthur, BF18

Trade catalogs from the Corning Museum of Glass, BF18

Trade & industry index, CH89

Trade names database, CH299

Trade names dictionary, CH294, CH295, CH296, CH297, CH298

Trade shows and professional exhibits directory, CH107

Trade shows worldwide, CH107

Trade union handbook, Marsh, Arthur Ivor, CH283

Trade unions, CH283, CH284, CH287

Trade unions of the world 1989–1990, CH284

Trademarks, CH294, CH295, CH296, CH297, CH298
databases, CH299, CH302

Trademarkscan—federal, CH302

Trademarkscan—state, CH302

The trail west, Townley, John M., DB59

The trainer's resource, CH164

Translating, BC16

Translations, AA30, AE13
  literature
    French, BD306
  science and technology, EA16, EA17

Translations register-index, EA16, EA17

Transliterated English-Yiddish dictionary = Ṭransliṭerirṭer English-Yidisher verṭerbukh, Harduf, David Mendel, AD175

Transliterated Yiddish-English dictionary = Ṭransliṭerirṭer Yidish-Englisher verṭerbukh, Harduf, David Mendel, AD176

Transnational corporations and labor, Fenton, Thomas P., CH285

Transportation, CH187

Transportation-logistics dictionary, CH187

Trapido, Joel. *An international dictionary of theatre language*, BG24

Trattner, Walter I. *Biographical dictionary of social welfare in America*, CC25

Trauger, Susan C. *Bibliography of German Expressionism*, BE29

Traugott, Santa. *American national election studies data sourcebook, 1952–1986*, CJ111

Travel and tourism; *see also* **Guidebooks**
  bibliography, BJ39
  dictionaries, BJ40, BJ41
  directories, BJ45
  handbooks, BJ46
  quotations, BJ42

The travel dictionary, Dervaes, Claudine, BJ40

Travel for the disabled, Hecker, Helen, BJ44, CC111

Travelers' accounts
  Near and Middle East, DE16

The traveler's guide to American gardens, BE146

The travelers' guide to Asian customs & manners, Chambers, Kevin, BJ48

The travelers' guide to European customs & manners, Braganti, Nancy L., BJ47

The traveler's reading guide, BJ39

The travellers, Canada to 1900, Waterston, Elizabeth, DB84

The travellers' dictionary of quotations, BJ42

Travis, Carole. *A guide to Latin American and Caribbean census material*, CG62

Treadway, Gary R. *The Anglo-American relationship*, DB14

Treasure, Geoffrey. *Who's who in British history*, DC124

Treasures from the film archives, Magliozzi, Ronald S., BG76

A treasury of business quotations, CH97

Treaties
  collections and indexes, CK111
    United States, AG12
    U.S.S.R., CK112

Treaties and alliances of the world, CK111

Treatments of psychiatric disorders, CD17

TREECD, EH8

Trees, EC36, EC37

Trefny, Beverly Robin. *Index to children's plays in collections, 1975–1984*, BD81

Treichler, Paula A. *A feminist dictionary*, CC297

Tremblay, Florent A. *Bibliotheca lexicologiae Medii Aevi*, BC45

Trends in public opinion, Niemi, Richard G., CJ234, CJ237

Trepanier, Peter. *Répertoire des dossiers documentaires traitant de l'art et de l'architecture dans les régions représentées à la section ARLIS M/O/Q = Directory of vertical file collections on art and architecture represented by ARLIS M/O/Q*, BE51

Trésor de la langue française, Imps, Paul, AD91

Trevelyan, Joanna E. *Alternative medicine*, EK18

Tribhuvan University. *Nepalese national bibliography for [year]*, AA162

Trigg, George L. *Encyclopedia of physics*, EG4

Trimmer, Joseph. *A guide to MLA documentation*, AH1

Trinder, Barrie Stuart. *Companion to the Industrial Revolution*, DC115

TRINET company database, CH125

TRINET establishment database, CH126

TRINET U.S. businesses, CH125, CH126

Trinick, Michael. *The National Trust guide*, BE126

Trinidad and Tobago, BD285, DB154

Trinidad and Tobago, Chambers, Frances, DB154

Troike, Rudolph C. *Bibliography of bibliographies of the languages of the world*, BC6

Troise, Fred L. *The water encyclopedia*, EJ35

Trombley, Stephen. *The Harper dictionary of modern thought*, AC4

Trotsky bibliography, Lubitz, Wolfgang, CJ241

Trotsky, L., CJ241

Trouble is their business, Conquest, John, BD102

Trousson, Raymond. *Lettres françaises de Belgique*, BD303

Truch, Stephen. *The WISC-R companion*, CD48

Trucking, CH186

Trucksource, CH186

Truhart, Peter. *Regents of nations*, CJ147

Trujillo, Roberto G. *The Chicano public catalog*, CC236

Tsouras, Peter. *The United States Army*, CJ273

Tsuge, Gen'ichi. *Japanese music*, BH24

Tucker, John Mark. *American library history*, AB2

Tudor, James. *Macmillan directory of business information sources*, CH84

Türkçe sözlük, Eren, Hasan, AD171

Tufts, Eleanor. *American women artists, past and present*, BE95

Tufts, Susan E. *State government research directory*, CJ126

Tuğlac, Pars. *Çağdaş Türkiye*, DC192

Tulane University. William Ransom Hogan Jazz Archive. *Catalog of the William Ransom Hogan Jazz Archive*, BH121

Tulard, Jean. *Dictionnaire Napoléon*, DC64

—— *Histoire et dictionnaire de la Révolution française*, DC56

Tulloch, George S. *The Torre-Bueno glossary of entomology*, EC64

—— *Torre-Bueno's glossary of entomology*, EC64

Tunisia, AE70

Tunisia, Perkins, K. J., DD5

Turabian, Kate L. *A manual for writers of term papers, theses, and dissertations*, AH3

Turk, Peter B. *Advertising media sourcebook*, CH73

Turkey
  biography, AJ97
  encyclopedias, AC19
  history
    bibliography, DC193
    encyclopedias, DC192

Turkish language, AD171

Turkish literature, BD383, BD384

Turley, Raymond Victor. *Information sources in science and technology*, EA4

Turner, Carlton E. *Cocaine*, EK106

Turner, D. John. *Canadian feature film index, 1913–1985 = Index des films canadiens de long métrage, 1913–1985*, BG82

Turner, Eugene J. *We the people*, CC188, DB79

Turner, George W. *The Australian concise Oxford dictionary of current English*, AD53

—— *The Australian pocket Oxford dictionary*, AD55

Turner, Patricia. *Dictionary of Afro-American performers*, BH87

Turtles, EC44

Turtles of the world, Ernst, Carl H., EC44

Tutin, Thomas Gaskell. *Flora of the British Isles*, EC32

Tutorow, Norman E. *War crimes, war criminals, and war crimes trials*, DA72

Tuttle, Lisa. *Encyclopedia of feminism*, CC293

TV facts, Steinberg, Cobbett, CH211

TV genres, BG104

Tver, David F. *The nutrition and health encyclopedia*, EK100

Twelve thousand words, AD32

Twentieth-century artists on art, Robertson, Jack, BE76, BE86

Twentieth century authors, BD55

Twentieth-century British literature, BD227

Twentieth-century children's writers, BD82

Twentieth-century crime and mystery writers, BD108

Twentieth-century evangelicalism, Blumhofer, Edith Waldvogel, BB75

The twentieth-century German novel, O'Pecko, Michael T., BD297

Twentieth-century literary criticism, Gale Research Company, BD19

A twentieth-century musical chronicle, Hall, Charles J., BH73

Twentieth-century romance and historical writers, BD121

Twentieth-century short story explication, Walker, Warren S., BD100

Twitchett, Denis Crispin. *The Cambridge history of China*, DE50

Twomey, Michael W. *Medieval Christian literary imagery*, BB81, BD3

Tyckoson, David A. *AIDS*, EK6

Tyler, Don. *Hit parade*, BH135

Tymn, Marshall B. *Science fiction, fantasy, and weird fiction magazines*, BD122

Tynan, Daniel J. *Biographical dictionary of contemporary Catholic American writing*, BD150

UCLA Latin American Center. *Statistical abstract of Latin America for [date]*, CG60

UCLA Latin American Center Publications (Firm). *Statistical abstract of Latin America. Supplement*, CG61

The UFAW handbook on the care and management of laboratory animals, EH29

—— Poole, Trevor B., EC58

U.K. Serials Group. *Current British journals: a bibliographic guide*, AE45

UKOP, Great Britain. Stationery Office, AG37

ULI market profiles, CH356

UMI article clearinghouse, AE11

U.S. agricultural groups, CJ68, EH18

U.S. and Canadian businesses, 1955 to 1987, Geahigan, Priscilla C., CH137

U.S. directory and source book on aging, 1989–90, CC61

U.S. directory of marine scientists, EE40

The U.S.-Eastern European trade sourcebook, Loiry, William S., CH181

U.S. imprints on Sub-Saharan Africa, DD20

U.S. industrial outlook, CH310

U.S. manufacturers directory, CH303

U.S. national security policy and strategy, CJ44

—— Sarkesian, Sam C., CJ44

—— Vitas, Robert A., CJ44

U.S. national security policy groups, Watson, Cynthia Ann, CJ69

U.S. ocean scientists & engineers: 1987 directory, EE40

U.S. relations with South Africa, Lulat, Y. G.-M, DD54

The U.S. savings and loan directory, CH250

The U.S. savings institutions directory, CH250

The U.S.-Soviet trade sourcebook, Loiry, William S., CH182

The U.S. Supreme Court, Martin, Fenton S., CK29

USA by numbers, CG27

USMARC format for bibliographic data, AB77
USSR economic handbook, Scrivener, Ronald, CH52
USSR legal materials, CK52
Ucrainica at the University of Toronto Library, University of Toronto. Library, DC213
Ueberweg, Friedrich. *Grundriss der Geschichte der Philosophie,* BA20
Uganda, AA196
Uganda national bibliography, AA196
Uglow, Jennifer S. *The Continuum dictionary of women's biography,* AJ9
Uhlan, Miriam. *Guide to special issues and indexes of periodicals,* AE17
Ukraine, Wynar, Bohdan S., DC214
Ukraine, a historical atlas, Magocsi, Paul R., DC215
Ukrainian literature, BD359
Ukrainskaia Sovetskaia Sotsialisticheskaia Respublika, DC212
Ullmann, Manfred. *Wörterbuch der klassischen arabischen Sprache,* AD71
Ulrich, Carolyn Farquhar. *Ulrich's international periodicals directory,* AE8
Ulrich, Horst. *DDR Handbuch,* CJ172
Ulrich's international periodicals directory, AE9, EA10, AE8
Ulrich's plus, AE9
Ulrich's quarterly, AE9, AE10
Ulrich's update, AE10
Unanue, Emil R. *Dictionary of immunology,* EK56
Unbelief, BB27
Underground press
 Germany, AE39
Unesco-ICOM Documentation Centre. *Directory of museums in Africa = Répertoire des musées en Afrique,* BE48
UNIDIR repertory of disarmament research, CJ301
A uniform system of citation, CK89
Union académique internationale. *Index scriptorum novus mediae latinitatis,* AD142
―――― *Novum glossarium mediae latinitatis,* AD141
Union catalogue of Persian serials & newspapers in British libraries, AE53
Union for Radical Political Economics. *Reading lists in radical social science,* CA7
Union list of African censuses, development plans and statistical abstracts, Evalds, Victoria K., CG40
Union list of American studies periodicals in UK libraries, Deering, Catherine M., AB28
Union list of geologic field trip guidebooks of North America, EE21
Union list of manuscripts in Canadian repositories, DB86
Union list of scientific serials in Canadian libraries, EA20
Union list of Victorian serials, Fulton, Richard D., AE73
Union of Soviet Socialist Republics; *see also* **Russia and the U.S.S.R.**
 armed forces
  encyclopedias, CJ282, CJ283
 atlases, DC216
 bibliography, DC14
 biography, AJ98, AJ99, DC205, DC207
  contemporary, AJ100, CJ206
 commerce, CH182
 dictionaries, CJ205
 economic conditions, CH52, CH53
 foreign relations, DC198, DE42
 history
  atlases, DC215
  bibliography, DC196
  chronologies, DC206
  encyclopedias, DC15, DC205, DC207
  manuscripts and archives, AB36, DC198, DC199, DC203
  regional and local, DC211, DC213, DC214
   Ukraine, DC212

 manuscripts and archives, AB10, DC198, DC201, DC202
 minorities, CC180
 statistics, CC180, CG74
  bibliography, CG73
 statutes, CK50
UNISIST (Program). *Modern archives administration and records management,* AB74
―――― *Planning, equipping, and staffing a document reprographic service,* AB109
United Church of Christ, BB114
United Nations, AB45, CK130
United Nations. *ACCIS guide to United Nations information sources on the environment,* EJ29, EJ29
United Nations. Centre on Transnational Corporations. *Directory of the world's largest service companies,* CH104
United Nations Industrial Development Organization. *Industry and development,* CH305
United Nations Institute for Disarmament Research. *UNIDIR repertory of disarmament research,* CJ301
United States
 armed forces
  bibliography, AK5, CJ271, DB15
  dictionaries, CJ272, CJ273
  handbooks, CJ99
  officers, CJ281
 atlases, AA79, CL21, CL43, CL58, CL59
  handbooks, CL61
 audiovisual resources, DB2
 bibliography, DB3
  19th century, AA80, AA81
  current, AA82, AA83
  databases, AA82
  regional, AG27
 biography, AJ20, AJ24, AJ25, AJ26, AJ27
  reformers, AJ21, CC24
 commerce, CH182
 economic conditions, CH310
 economic relations, CH40
 elections, CJ107
 emigration and immigration, CC175, DB61
 encyclopedias, DB63
 executive branch
  bibliography, CJ74, CJ79
  biography, CJ77, CJ78, CJ85, CJ90, CJ91
  directories, CJ85
  guides, CJ73
  indexes, AG22
  manuscripts and archives, CJ82
  sourcebooks, CJ87
 foreign relations, CJ53, CJ69, CJ81, CJ251, DB64, DB95, DC198, DD19, DD54, DE3, DE15, DE22, DE58
  bibliography, DB14
 gazetteers, CL30, CL31
 government publications
  bibliography, AG4, AG7, AG8, CG31, DD42, DE43
   executive branch, AG20, AG21, AG24
  Congressional Committee hearings, AG16, AG17, AG18
  congressional publications, AG6, CJ95
  guides, AG5
  handbooks, AG3
  indexes
   executive branch, AG22
   interstate agencies, AG26
  state publications
   bibliography, AG25, AG28, CJ122
 history
  atlases, DB77, DB79
  bibliography, BD175, DB11
   current, DA6, DB17
  by period
   17th and 18th centuries, DB26
   19th century, AK6, AK6, CJ268, CL42, DB8, DB27, DB28, DB29, DB31, DB32, DB33, DB34, DB36, DB37

   20th century, DA59, DA73, DB38, DB39, DB40, DB73, DE101
    American Revolution, BD244, DB25
    Civil War, DB35
  chronologies, DB72, DB73, DB74
  directories, DB67
  guides, DB1
  library resources, DB69
  manuscripts and archives, AB49, CJ81, DB11, DB18, DB20, DB22, DB23, DB24, DB26, DB69
  regional and local, AK7, DB20, DB41, DB42, DB43, DB45, DB46, DB47
   Middle West, DB54, DB56
   New England, DB49
   Rocky Mountain states, DB56
   South, DB51, DB52
   West, DB55, DB57, DB58, DB59, DB60, DB76
  sources, DB13
 judicial branch, CK59
 legislative branch
  biography, CJ104
  voting records, CJ99
 library resources, AB48
 maritime history, DA28
 naval history, DB5
 place-names, CL35
 politics and government, CJ56, CJ102
  acronyms, CJ58
  bibliography, CJ46, CJ47, CJ48, CJ76
  biography, CJ118, CJ120
  compendiums, CJ70, DB70
  directories, CJ62, CJ66, CJ86
  encyclopedias, CJ51, CJ53, CJ54, CJ55, CJ57, DB64
  indexes, CJ49, CJ50
  quotations, CJ84
  statistics, CJ134
 state and local government
  bibliography, CJ121
  biography, CJ124, CJ132
  dictionaries, CJ123
  handbooks, CJ124, CJ125, CJ126, CJ127, CJ128, CJ129, CJ130, CJ131
 statistics
  20th century, CG33, CG34
  bibliography, CG5, CG30, CG31, DB9
  compendiums, CG26, CG27, DB44
  directories, CG35
  guides, CG28
  handbooks, CG36
The United States: a guide to library holdings in the UK, Snow, Peter, AB28
United States. Army, CJ271
The United States Army, CJ273
United States Board on Geographic Names. *CIS foreign gazetteers [of the] USBGN,* CL27
―――― *Decisions on geographic names in the United States,* CL36
―――― *Foreign gazetteers of the U.S. Board on Geographic Names,* CL28
―――― *The national gazetteer of the United States of America,* CL30, CL31
United States. Bureau of the Census. *Census catalog and guide,* CG32
―――― *County business patterns,* CH306
United States business history, 1602–1988, Robinson, Richard, CH143
United States. Congress
 bibliography, AG11, CJ93, CJ94
 biography, CJ103, CJ104
 committee hearings, AG19
 committees, AG15, CJ98
 congressional districts, CJ105, CJ106
 election statistics, CJ112
 guides, CJ92
 handbooks, CJ100, CJ101
 publications, AG6, AG12, CJ95
 voting records, CJ96, CJ97
United States. Congress. *Biographical directory of the United States Congress, 1774–1989,* CJ104

United States congressional districts,
1788–1841, Parsons, Stanley B., CJ105,
CJ106
United States congressional districts,
1843–1883, Parsons, Stanley B., CJ105
United States congressional districts,
1883–1913, Parsons, Stanley B., CJ106
United States congressional serial set catalog,
AG11
United States corporation histories, Nasrallah,
Wahib, CH141
United States. Dept. of State, CJ75
United States. Dept. of State. *Post report,* CL18
United States. Dept. of State. Office of the
Historian. *Principal officers of the*
Department of State and United States chiefs
of mission, 1778–1990, CJ86
The United States energy atlas, Cuff, David J.,
EJ73
United States food laws, regulations, and
standards, Hui, Y. H., CK93, EH31
United States foreign policy and the Middle
East/North Africa, Silverburg, Sanford R.,
DE15
United States. General Accounting Office.
GAO masterfile, AG23
The United States in Africa, Shavit, David,
DD19, DE3, DE22
The United States in Asia, Shavit, David,
DD19, DE3, DE22
The United States in East Asia, DA55
The United States in the Middle East, Shavit,
David, DD19, DE3, DE22
The United States in the Vietnam War,
1954–1975, Peake, Louis A., DE101
United States intelligence, CJ288
United States. Marine Corps, CJ277, CJ278,
CJ279
United States-Mexico borderlands, DB60
United States. National Archives and Records
Administration. *Guide to the National*
Archives of the United States, DB23
—— *Microfilm resources for research,* DB24
United States. National Archives and Records
Service. *Catalog of National Archives*
microfilm publications, DB24
—— *Guide to the National Archives of the*
United States, DB24
—— *Microfilm resources for research,* DB24
United States Naval Institute. *The Naval*
Institute guide to combat fleets of the world,
CJ265
United States. Navy, CJ274, CJ277, CJ278
The United States Navy, CJ274
United States Navy and Marine Corps bases,
domestic, CJ277
United States Navy and Marine Corps bases,
overseas, CJ277, CJ278
United States Newspaper Program. *United*
States Newspaper Program national union
list, AF1
United States Newspaper Program national
union list, AF1
The United States postage stamps of the 19th
century, Brookman, Lester G., BF51
United States. President. *Public papers of the*
presidents of the United States, AG24
United States. Supreme Court, CK29, CK61,
CK90
United States Travel Data Center. *Tourism's*
top twenty, BJ46
Universal decimal classification = Classification
décimale universelle = Dezimalklassifikation,
AB83
Universidad Iberoamericana. *Guía de archivos*
y bibliotecas, AB51
Universidade Eduardo Mondlane.
Mozambique, DD45
Universidade Nova de Lisboa. *Bibliografia de*
linguística portuguesa, BC46
Universit'a di Torino. *Bibliografi della*
sociologia italiana. (1945–1970), CC10

Universität Bayreuth. *Pipers Enzyklopädie des*
Musiktheaters, BH58
Universität Münster. *Konkordanz zum Novum*
Testamentum Graece von Nestle-Aland, BB60
Université de Niamey. Institut de recherches
en sciences humaines. Service de la
documentation. *Catalogue des thèses et*
mémoires /[Saïdou Harouna], DD47
Université nationale du Rwanda. Centre de
bibliographie rwandaise. *Bibliographie*
signalétique des écrits académiques
disponibles au Centre de bibliographie
rwandaise, AH19
Universitetsbiblioteket i Oslo. *Norsk*
bokfortegnelse, 1971–75, AA166
Universities and colleges
admission, CB155, CD31
bibliography, CB11
curricula, CB100, CB106
United States, CB101
directories, CB87, CB97, CB102, CB107,
CB108, CB115
United States, CB94, CB101
finance, CB9
fund raising, CB10
insignia, CB163
Universities Federation for Animal Welfare.
The UFAW handbook on the care and
management of laboratory animals, EH29
University and college libraries, AB48
University of Bradford. *The international peace*
directory, CJ309
University of California Consortium on Mexico
and the United States. *Guía internacional de*
investigaciones sobre México, DB128
University of California, Los Angeles.
Statistical abstract of Latin America for
[date], CG60, CG60
—— *Statistical abstract of Latin America.*
Supplement, CG61
University of California, San Diego. *Guía*
internacional de investigaciones sobre
México, DB128
University of Chicago. *The University of*
Chicago Spanish dictionary, AD165
University of Chicago. Oriental Institute. *The*
Assyrian dictionary, AD74
—— *Assyrian dictionary,* AD75
—— *The Hittite dictionary of the Oriental*
Institute of the University of Chicago, AD122
University of Chicago. Press. *Chicago guide to*
preparing electronic manuscripts, AA58
The University of Chicago Spanish dictionary,
AD165
University of Colorado, Boulder. *Tourism's top*
twenty, BJ46
University of Connecticut. Consortium for
Research on Black Adolescence. *Black*
adolescence, CC79
University of Hawaii at Manoa. Industrial
Relations Center. *Roberts' dictionary of*
industrial relations, CH279
University of Hawaii at Manoa. Pacific Islands
Studies Program. *A guide to films about the*
Pacific Islands, DG5
University of Illinois at Urbana-Champaign.
Census-catalogue of manuscript sources of
polyphonic music, 1400–1550, BH35
—— *Women scholars in women's studies,*
CC304
University of London. *Studies in Mycenaean*
inscriptions and dialect, 1965–1978, BC55
University of London. Institute of
Commonwealth Studies. Library. *Theses in*
progress in Commonwealth studies, DC133
University of London. School of Oriental and
African Studies. *Catalogue of the early*
printed books on South Asia, DE28
University of London. School of Oriental and
African Studies. Library. *Western books on*
China published up to 1850 in the Library of
the School of Oriental and African Studies,
University of London, DE48

University of Maryland, College Park. *Index to*
historic preservation periodicals, BE121
University of Massachusetts at Amherst. *Guide*
to the study of United States history outside
the U.S., 1945–1980, DB11
University of Michigan. Center for
Afroamerican and African Studies. *Black*
immigration and ethnicity in the United
States, CC193
University of Nottingham. *International*
biography of adult education, CB31
University of Papua New Guinea. *A New*
Guinea bibliography, AA169, DG11
University of Pennsylvania. *The Sumerian*
dictionary of the University Museum of the
University of Pennsylvania, AD74
University of Prince Edward Island. *Canadian*
review of studies in nationalism, CJ6
University of Regina. *Canadian studies on*
Hungarians, 1886–1986, CC166, DC145
University of San Diego. *Bibliography of*
original meaning of the United States
Constitution, CK113
University of the South Pacific. *A check list of*
selected material on Samoa, DG14
—— *South Pacific bibliography,* AA168
University of the Witwatersrand. *Southern*
African update, DD22
University of Toronto. *Dictionary of Old*
English, AD63
University of Toronto. Library. *Ucrainica at*
the University of Toronto Library, DC213
University of Wales. *A bibliography of the*
history of Wales [microform], DC141
University of Wales. Board of Celtic Studies.
Geiriadur Prifysgol Cymru, AD173
University of Wisconsin System. *Feminist*
collections, CC268, CC268
—— *New books on women and feminism,*
CC269
University science and engineering libraries,
Mount, Ellis, AB60
Unofficial documents of the Democracy
Movement in Communist China, 1978–1981
= Chung-kuo min chu yun tung tzu liao : a
checklist of Chinese materials in the Hoover
Institution on War, Revolution and Peace,
Hoover Institution on War, Revolution, and
Peace, CJ162, DE51
Unpublished U.S. Senate committee hearings on
microfiche, AG17
Unsworth, Michael. *Military periodicals,* CJ252
Unterberger, Amy L. *Who's who in technology,*
EJ5
Unwin, Derick. *The encyclopaedia of*
educational media communications and
technology, CB60
Unwin, P. T. H. *Portugal,* DC177
Upham, Martin. *Employers' organizations of*
the world, CH281
Uppslagsverket Finland, DC46
The upstream people, Tate, Michael L., CC218
Upton, Clive. *Word maps,* BC30
Uralic languages, AD172
Uralic peoples, DC210
Uralisches etymologisches Wörterbuch, Rédei,
Károly, AD172
Uralistiikan tutkimuksen bibliografia,
Akademiia nauk SSSR, DC210
Uranometria 2000.0, Tirion, Wil, EB18
Urban, Bernd. *Literaturpsychologie,*
1945–1987, BD7
Urban America examined, Casper, Dale E.,
CC158
Urban Institute. *America's homeless,* CC117
Urban Land Institute. *ULI market profiles,*
CH356
The urban politics dictionary, Smith, John
William, CJ22
The urban South, Brown, Catherine L., DB51
Urbanization, CC158, CC160, CJ22; *see also*
Cities

Urdang, Laurence. *Allusions—cultural, literary, biblical, and historical,* AD22, BD32
—— *Loanwords dictionary,* AD65
—— *Mottoes,* BD62
—— *Names & nicknames of places & things,* CL34
—— *-ologies & -isms,* AD35
Urmson, J. O. *The concise encyclopedia of western philosophy and philosophers,* BA11
Uruguay, AA90, AA197, DB135
Uruguay, Finch, M. H. J., DB135
Uruguayan literature, BD347, BD348, BD349, BD350
Uscher, Nancy. *The Schirmer guide to schools of music and conservatories throughout the world,* BH66
The use of biological literature, Bottle, Robert Thames, EC1
—— Wyatt, H. V., EC1
Use of earth sciences literature, Wood, David Norris, EE1
Use of engineering literature, Mildren, K. W., EJ1
Using government publications, Sears, Jean L., AG5
U.S./Japan foreign trade, Neri, Rita E., CH40
Utlendingers reiser i Norge. En bibliografi, Schiötz, Eiler H., DC170
Utopias, BD239, DB6

Vacation study abroad, CB85
Vaganov, F. M. *Gosudarstvennye arkhivy SSSR,* AB36, DC199
Vaillancourt, Pauline M. *Cancer journals and serials,* EK25
Valentei, D. I. *Literatura o narodonaselenii,* CG73
Valenzuela, Gilberto. *Apéndice a la Bibliografía guatemalteca,* AA136
—— *Bibliografía guatemalteca,* AA136
Valk, Barbara G. *BorderLine,* DB60
—— *Latin American studies,* DB94
Vallet-Petit, Catherine. *A strategic atlas,* CJ41
Vallinkoski, J. *Suomen historiallinen bibliografia = Finsk historisk bibliografi = Bibliografie historique finlandaise, 1971–1980,* DC45
The valuation of industrial property, Clatanoff, Robert M., CH343
Value line, CH219
Valynseele, Joseph. *Dictionnaire des maréchaux de France,* AJ52
Van Cleve, John V. *Gallaudet encyclopedia of deaf people and deafness,* CC105
Van Couvering, John A. *Encyclopedia of human evolution and prehistory,* CE13
Van den Dungen, Peter. *From Erasmus to Tolstoy,* CJ297
Van der Leeden, Frits. *Geraghty & Miller's groundwater bibliography,* EE25
—— *The water encyclopedia,* EJ35
Van Dyne, Susan R. *Selected bibliography for integrating research on women's experience in the liberal arts curriculum,* CC249
Van Minden, Jack J. R. *Dictionary of marketing research,* CH319
Van Nostrand Reinhold dictionary of information technology, Longley, Dennis, EJ63
Van Nostrand's scientific encyclopedia, EA39
Van Uytfanghe, Marc. *Bibliographie signalétique du latin des chrétiens,* BC43
VanArsdel, Rosemary T. *Victorian periodicals,* AE43
Vanderwerf, Mary Ann. *Science & technology in fact and fiction,* EA11, EA12
Vandiver, Margaret. *Capital punishment in America,* CK98
Vanguardism in Latin American literature, Forster, Merlin H., BD332
Vann, J. Don. *Victorian novels in serial,* BD240
—— *Victorian periodicals,* AE43
Variety international film guide, BG98

Variety obituaries, 1905–1986, BG5
Variety television reviews, 1923–1988, BG105
Variety's who's who in show business, BG6
Varona, Esperanza Bravo de. *Cuban exile periodicals at the University of Miami Library,* CC239
Vas-Zoltán, Péter. *Guide to research and scholarship in Hungary,* DC143
Vasarhelyi, Miklos A. *Accounting research directory,* CH61
Vassilian, Hamo B. *Armenian American almanac,* CC182
Vaxelaire, Daniel. *La grande encyclopédie du Maroc,* DD44
Veigl, Hans. *Das grosse Buch der Österreicher,* AJ35
Veilleux, Raymond F. *Tool and manufacturing engineers handbook,* EJ83
Veit, Fritz. *Presidential libraries and collections,* AB49, CJ83, DB22
Velký anglicko-český slovník, Hais, Karel, AD83
Vendryes, Joseph. *Lexique étymologique de l'irlandais ancien,* AD127
Venezky, Richard L. *Microfiche concordance to Old English,* AD63
Venezuela
bibliography, AA198, AA199, AA200, DB137
biography, AJ101
guides, DB136
history
bibliography, DB138
encyclopedias, DB139
Venezuela, Waddell, D. A. G., DB138
Venkova-Ilieva, Liliana. *Voenna istoriia na Bŭlgariia, 681–1945,* DC35
Venture capital sources, CH258
Venturi, Marco. *Town planning glossary,* BE139
Venzon, Anne Cipriano. *The Spanish-American War,* DB27
Verbis non factis, Blake, Fay M., CJ107
Vergason, Glenn A. *Dictionary of special education and rehabilitation,* CB74
Verseform, Brogan, T. V. F., BD129
Versification, BD129
Verstappen, Berth. *Ethnic conflict and human rights in Sri Lanka,* DE93
Vertebrates, EC38
Vertical files (libraries), BE51
Vervliet, Hendrik D. L. *Bibliographie de l'humanisme des anciens Pays-Bas,* BA9
Verzeichnis der bildenden Künstler von 1880 bis heute, BE88
Verzeichnis der im deutschen Sprachbereich erschienenen Drucke des XVI. Jahrhunderts, AA119
Verzeichnis der Musikzeitschriften des 19. Jahrhunderts, Fellinger, Imogen, BH31
Verzeichnis von Programm-Abhandlungen deutscher, österreichischer und schweizerischer Schulen der Jahre 1825–1918, Kössler, Franz, AH9
Vescovi, Gina Bria. *Fellowship guide to western Europe,* CB159
VETCD, EH8
Veterinary bulletin, EH8
Veterinary medicine *see* **Animal science**
Viaux, Jacqueline. *Bibliographie du meuble,* BF36
Victoria and Albert Museum. *The country house described,* BE120
Victoria history of the counties of England, DC135
Victorian Britain, DC117
Victorian fiction, The Stanford companion to, BD242
Victorian music publishers, Parkinson, John A., BH70
Victorian novels in serial, Vann, J. Don, BD240
Victorian periodicals, AE43
Victorian plays, Mullin, Donald C., BG33

Victorian serials, AE73
Victorian studies, A comprehensive bibliography of, BD212
Vidal, Dominique. *An A to Z of the Middle East,* CJ199, DE20
Vidal Sassoon International Center for the Study of Antisemitism (Universiṭah ha-'Ivrit bi-Yerushalayim). *Antisemitism,* BB128
Vielliard, Françoise. *Manuel bibliographique de la littérature française du Moyen Age de Robert Bossuat. Troisième supplément, 1960–1980,* BD310
Viera, David J. *The Portuguese in the United States,* CC168
Vierck, Elizabeth. *Fact book on aging,* CC68
Vietnam, AA201, DE100
Vietnam on film and television, Johnson, Victoria E., DE105
Vietnam War, BD158, BD198, DE101, DE102, DE103, DE104
dictionaries, AD41
encyclopedias, DE106
filmography, DE105
Vietnam War literature, Newman, John, BD158
Vietnamese holdings in the Library of Congress. Supplement, 1979–1985, Library of Congress, DE100
Viewfinders : black women photographers, Moutoussamy-Ashe, Jeanne, BF64
Vignal, Marc. *Dictionnaire de la musique,* BH49
Vikor, Desider L. *Encyclopedia of public affairs information sources,* CA5
Village records, West, John, DC136
Villasana, Angel Raúl. *Ensayo de un repertorio bibliográfico venezolano,* AA200
—— *Nuevo repertorio bibliográfico venezolano,* AA200
Viller, Marcel. *Dictionnaire de spiritualité,* BB85
Vince, Ronald W. *A companion to the medieval theatre,* BD89
Vincent, David. *The autobiography of the working class,* CH270
Vinogradov, V. A. *Bibliographia studiorum uralicorum, 1917–1987 = Uralistiikan tutkimuksen bibliografia = Bibliography on Uralic studies,* DC210
Vinson, James. *American writers since 1900,* BD169
—— *American writers to 1900,* BD169
—— *Contemporary dramatists,* BD88
—— *Contemporary novelists,* BD93
—— *International dictionary of art and artists,* BE81
—— *The international dictionary of films and filmmakers,* BG92
Violence and terror in the mass media, Signorielli, Nancy, CH202
Violence in the family, Kemmer, Elizabeth Jane, CC130
Virology, EC68, EC69
Virology, Hull, Roger, EC69
Virology and AIDS abstracts, EC7
The viruses, Fraenkel-Conrat, Heinz, EC68
Vision, EK53
Visser, W. A. *Geological nomenclature,* EE16
Vital statistics on American politics, Stanley, Harold W., CJ134
Vitas, Robert A. *U.S. national security policy and strategy,* CJ44
Viterbi, Mario. *Bibliografi della sociologia italiana. (1945–1970),* CC10
Vitošević, Dragiša. *Srpska književna periodika 1768–1941,* BD363
Viudas Camarasa, Antonio. *Dialectología hispánica y geografía lingüística en los estudios locales (1920–1984),* BC53
Viviano, Benedict. *Illustrated dictionary & concordance of the Bible,* BB54
Vivliographikē Hetaireia Kyprou. *Kypriakē vivliographia,* AA96

Vivliographikē Hetaireia tēs Hellados. *Hellēnikē vivliographia*, AA135

Vocabulary, English-Somali, Somali-English, Schels, Christa, AD163

Vocational guidance, CH341

Vocelli, Virginia S. *The basic business library*, CH76

Vocino, Michael C. *Labor and industrial relations journals and serials*, CH277

Voegelin, Charles. *Classification and index of the world's languages*, BC15

Voegelin, Florence. *Classification and index of the world's languages*, BC15

Völklein, Sonja. *The musical*, BH108

Voenna istoriīa na Bŭlgariīa, 681–1945, DC35

Voennoistoricheska biblioteka (Institut za voenna istoriīa). *Voenna istoriīa na Bŭlgariīa, 681–1945*, DC35

Voisin, Russell L. *The new international atlas = Der neue internationale Atlas = El nuevo atlas internacional = Le nouvel atlas international = O nôvo atlas internacional*, CL56

Voit, Petr. *Příspěvky ke knihopisu*, AA98

Volard, François. *Guide du cinéma européen*, BG99

Volkoff, Anne Marie. *L'émigration russe en Europe*, AE71

Volkova, I. V. *Gosudarstvennye arkhivy SSSR*, AB36, DC199

Volunteer workers, CB33, CC65

Volunteerism and older adults, Kouri, Mary K., CC65

Von CA bis CAS ONLINE, ED2

Vorster, W. S. *South African theological bibliography = Suid-Afrikaanse teologiese bibliografie*, BB18

Vronskaya, Jeanne. *A biographical dictionary of the Soviet Union, 1917–1988*, AJ49, AJ99

Vsesoīūznyĭ nauchno-issledovatel'skiĭ institut dokumentovedeniīa i arkhivnogo dela (Soviet Union). *Gosudarstvennye arkhivy SSSR*, AB36, DC199

Vseviov, L. M. *Sovetskaīa arkheologicheskaīa literatura*, DA33

Vu, My T. *World population projections, 1987–88*, CG23

Vyhnanek, Louis Andrew. *Reference sources in history*, DA1

Vyriausioji enciklopedijų redakcija (Lithuania). *Tarybū Lietuvos enciklopedija*, DC163

WHO drug information, EK107

The WISC-R companion, Truch, Stephen, CD48

Wa-Ei taishō Nihon bijutsu yōgo jiten = A dictionary of Japanese art terms, bilingual "Japanese & English", BE42

Wa-Ei Taishō Nihon Bijutsu Yōgo Jiten Henshū Iinkai. *Wa-Ei taishō Nihon bijutsu yōgo jiten = A dictionary of Japanese art terms, bilingual "Japanese & English"*, BE42

Waal, H. van de. *Iconclass*, BE101

Waddell, D. A. G. *Venezuela*, DB138

Wadhams, Wayne. *Sound advice*, BH72

Wadsworth, Anne Johnston. *Political campaign communication*, CJ48

Wagner, Günter. *An exegetical bibliography of the New Testament*, BB44

Wagonheim, Sylvia Stoler. *Annals of English drama, 975–1700*, BD232

Wahrig, Gerhard. *Deutsches Wörterbuch*, AD107

Wainwright, M. Doreen. *Guide to manuscripts and documents in the British Isles relating to Africa*, DC131

—— *A guide to Western manuscripts and documents in the British Isles relating to South and South East Asia*, DE4

Waiser, Joni. *Theses in Canada*, AH7

Waite, Ellen J. *Women in LC's terms*, CC299

Waitz, Georg,. *Dahlmann-Waitz Quellenkunde der deutschen Geschichte*, DC80, DC81

Wakefield, Gordon S. *The Westminster dictionary of Christian spirituality*, BB93

Wakelyn, Jon L. *American legislative leaders, 1850–1910*, CJ132

Wakeman, John. *World film directors*, BG101

Walberg, Herbert J. *Handbook of special education*, CB130

—— *The international encyclopedia of educational evaluation*, CB63

—— *Special education*, CB136

Walden, Graham R. *Public opinion polls and survey research*, CJ236

Waldman, Carl. *Atlas of the North American Indian*, CC234

—— *Who was who in Native American history*, CC231

Waldman, Harry. *The dictionary of SDI*, CJ275

Wales, Katie. *A dictionary of stylistics*, BD141

Wales, AA202, DC141

Walford, Albert John. *Walford's guide to current British periodicals in the humanities and social sciences*, AE47

—— *Walford's guide to reference material*, AA67, EA6

Walford's guide to current British periodicals in the humanities and social sciences, AE47

Walford's guide to reference material, Walford, Albert John, AA67, EA6

Walker, Alvin. *Thesaurus of psychological index terms*, CD25

Walker, Barbara G. *The woman's dictionary of symbols and sacred objects*, CF7

Walker, Charls E. *The bankers' handbook*, CH251

Walker, John A. *Glossary of art, architecture and design since 1945*, BE43

Walker, John M. *The language of biotechnology*, EJ19

Walker, Marshall. *History of American literature*, BD169

Walker, Michael. *Lexicon of economic thought*, CH7

Walker, Peter M. B. *Cambridge air and space dictionary*, EJ16

—— *Cambridge dictionary of science and technology*, EA41

—— *Chambers biology dictionary*, EC13

Walker, Warren S. *Twentieth-century short story explication*, BD100

Walker, William O. *Harper's Bible pronunciation guide*, BB52

Wall, C. Edward. *Abbreviations*, AD9

—— *Periodical title abbreviations*, AE12

The Wall Street dictionary, Shook, R. J., CH236

Wall Street journal, CH17, CH219

Wall Street journal [index], AF13

The Wall Street review of books, CH6

Wall Street words, Scott, David Logan, CH235

Wallace, Ian. *East Germany*, DC89

Wallechinsky, David. *The complete book of the Olympics*, BJ34

Wallen, Denise. *Funding for museums, archives, and special collections*, BE53

Waller, Robert. *The almanac of British politics*, CJ178

—— *The atlas of British politics*, CJ184

Wallis, Helen. *Cartographical innovations*, CL10

Wallmannsberger, Josef. *English-German contrastive linguistics*, BC22

Walls, Jerry G. *The completely illustrated atlas of reptiles and amphibians for the terrarium*, EC45

Walmsley, Julian. *Dictionary of international finance*, CH239

Walne, Peter. *Dictionary of archival terminology = Dictionnaire de terminologie archivistique : English and French, with equivalents in Dutch, German, Italian, Russian and Spanish*, AB73

—— *Modern archives administration and records management*, AB74

Walsh, Gretchen. *African language materials in the Boston University Libraries*, BC57

Walsh, Jim. *Maps contained in the publications of the American bibliography, 1639–1819*, AA79, CL43

Walter, Gerard. *Répertoire de l'histoire de la Révolution française*, DC49

Walter, Ingo. *The handbook of international business*, CH130

—— *Handbook of international management*, CH131

Walton, John Nicholas. *The Oxford companion to medicine*, EK41

Wang, Alvin Yafu. *Author's guide to journals in the behavioral sciences*, CD6

Wang, Chi-chien. *Seals of Chinese painters and collectors of the Ming and Ch'ing periods*, BE42

Wang, Margaret C. *Handbook of special education*, CB130

—— *Special education*, CB136

Want's Federal-state court directory, CK82

War, CJ35, CJ260, DA22
   bibliography, CE5
   encyclopedias, CJ253, DA21

The war against Japan, 1941–1945, Sbrega, John J., DA70

War crimes, war criminals, and war crimes trials, Tutorow, Norman E., DA72

Ward, Gerald W. R. *Decorative arts and household furnishings in America, 1650–1920*, BF34

Ward, Martha. *A bibliography of Salon criticism in Second Empire Paris*, BE147

Ward, Peter D. *Recent titles in law for the subject specialist*, CK19

Ward, Robert Elmer. *A bio-bibliography of German-American writers, 1670–1970*, BD170, BD170

—— *Dictionary of German-American creative writers*, BD170

Ward's business directory of U.S. private and public companies, CH306, CH127

Warfare in primitive societies, Divale, William T., CE5

Warfield, Gerald. *The investor's guide to stock quotations and other financial listings*, CH259

Warner, Ralph E. *Legal research*, CK5

—— *Legal research made easy*, CK7

Warner, Thomas E. *Periodical literature on American music, 1620–1920*, BH25

Warnke, Frank J. *The Princeton handbook of poetic terms*, BD137

The Wars of the Roses, Hallam, Elizabeth M., DC116

Wartburg, Walther von. *Französisches etymologisches Wörterbuch*, AD96

Washington, Valora. *Black children and American institutions*, CC78

Washington post, AJ7

Washington post [index], AF13

Washington representatives, CJ59, CJ60

Washington State University. *Directory of librarians in international development*, AB38

Wass, Hannelore. *Death education*, CC95

Wasserman, Paul. *Consultants and consulting organizations directory*, CH160

—— *Consumer sourcebook*, CH176

—— *Encyclopedia of business information sources*, CH78

—— *Encyclopedia of health information sources*, EK10

—— *Encyclopedia of legal information sources*, CK15

—— *Encyclopedia of public affairs information sources*, CA5

—— *Encyclopedia of senior citizens information sources*, CC63

—— *Statistics sources*, CG7

Wasserman, Steven R. *Encyclopedia of physical sciences and engineering information sources*, EA2

—— *Financial planners and planning organizations directory,* CH245

Wasserstein, Stephen. *The reader's catalog,* AA61

Wasson, Tyler. *Nobel prize winners,* AJ11

The water encyclopedia, Van der Leeden, Frits, EJ35

Water Pollution Control Federation. *Standard methods for the examination of water and wastewater,* ED23

Water resources abstracts, EE24, EJ34

Water resources and water pollution databases, EE24, EJ34

handbooks, ED23, EJ35

The Watergate investigation index, Garza, Hedda, CJ49, CJ50

The Waterloo directory of Irish newspapers and periodicals, 1800–1900, North, John S., AE54

The Waterloo directory of Scottish newspapers and periodicals, 1800–1900, North, John S., AE67

Waterloo directory of Victorian periodicals, AE67

Waterloo directory of Victorian periodicals, 1824–1900, AE54

Waterloo directory series of newspapers and periodicals, AE67

Waters, Harold A. *Théâtre noir,* BD302

Waters, William J. *Music and the personal computer,* BH26

Waterston, Elizabeth. *The travellers, Canada to 1900,* DB84

Watkins, Calvert. *The American heritage dictionary of Indo-European roots,* AD10

Watkins, Kathleen Pullan. *Infancy,* CC82

—— *Parent-child attachment,* CC86

Watson, Bruce W. *The United States Army,* CJ273

—— *United States intelligence,* CJ288

—— *The United States Navy,* CJ274

Watson, Cynthia Ann. *U.S. national security policy groups,* CJ69

Watson, Edward A. *A study of selected English critical terms from 1650–1800,* BD164

Watson, G. Llewellyn. *Feminism and women's issues,* CC266

Watson, Susan M. *The United States Army,* CJ273

—— *United States intelligence,* CJ288

—— *The United States Navy,* CJ274

Watson-Jones, Virginia. *Contemporary American women sculptors,* BE79, BE167

Watts, Thomas D. *Black alcohol abuse and alcoholism,* CC73

—— *Native American youth and alcohol,* CC69

Watts-Williams, J. *Cofrestri plwyf Cymru = Parish registers of Wales,* AK48

Waugh, Charles. *Science fiction and fantasy series and sequels,* BD112

Wawa, Yosa H. *Southern Sudan,* DD57

Way, Peter O. *Detailed statistics on the urban and rural population of Indonesia, 1950 to 2010,* CG57

We the people, Allen, James Paul, CC188, DB79

—— Turner, Eugene J., DB79

Weapons systems, CJ267

Wearing, J. P. *American and British theatrical biography,* BG44

—— *The London stage, 1920–1929,* BG35

Weather see **Climatology**

The weather almanac, Ruffner, James A., EE30

The weather handbook, EE31

Weaver, Jack W. *Immigrants from Great Britain and Ireland,* AK36, CC178, DC146

Webb, William H. *Sources of information in the social sciences,* CA3, CA4

Webber, Elizabeth. *Grand allusions,* AD22, BD32

Webber, Jonathan. *Research in social anthropology, 1975–1980,* CE10

Weber, Heidi. *Longman dictionary of applied linguistics,* BC13

Weber, Marvin J.,. *CRC handbook of laser science and technology,* EG7

—— *Lasers,* EG8

Weber, R. David. *Energy information guide,* EJ72

—— *Energy update,* EJ72

Weber, Wolfgang. *Biographisches Lexikon zur Geschichtswissenschaft in Deutschland, Österreich und der Schweiz,* DC96

Weberman, Ben. *Dictionary of banking terms,* CH228

Webster, Duane. *Preservation planning program,* AB104

Webster, James K. *Toxic and hazardous materials,* EK128

Webster, John G. *Encyclopedia of medical devices and instrumentation,* EK39

Webster's biographical dictionary, AJ12

Webster's dictionary of English usage, AD30

Webster's new biographical dictionary, AJ12

Webster's new geographical dictionary, CL29

Webster's New World best book of aphorisms, Douglas, Auriel, BD60

Webster's New World dictionary of American English, AD5

Webster's New World dictionary of media and communications, Weiner, Richard, CH209

Webster's New World dictionary of quotable definitions, BD68

Webster's New World dictionary of the American language, AD5

Webster's New World medical word finder, Willeford, George, EK51

Webster's New World secretarial handbook, CH169

Webster's third new international dictionary, AD32

Webster's word histories, AD21

Wecken, Friedrich. *Taschenbuch für Familiengeschichtsforschung,* AK27

Wedertz, Bill. *Dictionary of naval abbreviations,* CJ272

Wedgeworth, Robert. *ALA world encyclopedia of library and information services,* AB11

Weed Science Society of America. *Herbicide handbook of the Weed Science Society of America,* EH21

Weeds, EH13, EH22

Weeds of the United States and their control, Lorenzi, Harri, EH22

Weekly, James K. *Information for international marketing,* CH313

Weeks, Albert Loren. *Brassey's Soviet and communist quotations,* CJ249

Weeks, Gerald R. *Family therapy,* CC137

Wehmann, Howard H. *A guide to pre-federal records in the National Archives,* DB26

Wei, Karen T. *Library and information science in China,* AB53

Weidner, Ernst. *Reallexikon der Assyriologie, unter Mitwirkung zahlreicher Fachgelehrter,* DA36

Weidner, Ruth Irwin. *American ceramics before 1930,* BF20

Weigall, David. *Britain & the world, 1815–1986,* CJ174, DC118

Weihs, Jean. *Nonbook materials,* AB78

Weik, Martin H. *Communications standard dictionary,* EJ69

—— *Fiber optics and lightwave communications standard dictionary,* EJ47

—— *Fiber optics standard dictionary,* EJ47

Weil, Stephen E. *Art law,* BE108, CK86

Weilant, Edward. *An American profile,* CJ237

Weinberg, Meyer. *The education of poor and minority children,* CC169

—— *Racism in the United States,* CC170

Weinberg, Robert E. *A biographical dictionary of science fiction and fantasy artists,* BD128, BE89

Weiner, Alan R. *The insurance industry,* CH263

Weiner, E. S. C. *The Oxford English dictionary,* AD6

Weiner, Richard. *Investment newsletters,* CH217

—— *Webster's New World dictionary of media and communications,* CH209

Weinreb, Ben. *The London encyclopaedia,* DC137

Weinreich, Beatrice. *Yiddish language and folklore,* BC34

Weinreich, Uriel. *Yiddish language and folklore,* BC34

Weisbard, Phyllis Holman. *Jewish law,* CK43

Weisberg, Gabriel P. *Japonisme,* BE15

—— *The realist debate,* BE148

Weisberg, Yvonne M. L. *Japonisme,* BE15

—— *The realist debate,* BE148

Weisensel, Peter R. *Russian travelers to the Christian East from the twelfth to the twentieth century,* DE16

Weisenstein, Gregory R. *Administrator's desk reference on special education,* CB138

Weiss, Allan Barry. *A comprehensive bibliography of English-Canadian short stories, 1950–1983,* BD281

Weiss, David M. *National guide to funding in aging,* CC67

Weiss, Peter F. *The national job bank, 1991,* CH340

Weissman, Dick. *The folk music sourcebook,* BH133

Weist, Katherine M. *An annotated bibliography of Northern Plains ethnohistory,* CC220

Weitzel, Rolf. *Handbuch der bibliographischen Nachschlagewerke,* AA2

Welch, Thomas L. *The Aztecs,* CC221

—— *Bibliografía de la literatura uruguaya,* BD350

—— *The Incas,* CC222

Welding, EJ84

Welding handbook, EJ84

Weller, Carol. *Educators' desk reference for special learning problems,* CB139

The Wellesley index to Victorian periodicals, 1824–1900, AE80

Wellisch, Hans H. *Norway,* DC169

—— *Sweden,* DC189

Wells, Robert V. *A retrospective bibliography of American demographic history from colonial times to 1983,* CG5, DB9

—— *Revolutions in American lives,* CG5, DB9

Wells, Stanley W. *Shakespeare,* BD263

Welsh, Brian W. W. *Dictionary of development,* CH49

Welsh Academy. *The Oxford companion to the literature of Wales,* BD273

Welsh County Archivists' Group. *Cofrestri plwyf Cymru = Parish registers of Wales,* AK48

Welsh language, AD173

Welsh literature, BD273

Wentworth, Harold. *Dictionary of American slang,* AD40

Wenzel, Duane. *The Museum of Science and Industry basic list of children's science books,* EA14

—— *The Museum of Science and Industry basic list of children's science books, 1973–1984,* EA13

Werkgroep Repertorium Doctoraalscripties. *Repertorium doctoraalscripties 1981–1985,* BE12

Werner, Craig Hansen. *Black American women novelists,* BD190

Wertsman, Vladimir. *The librarian's companion,* AB13

Wescott, Steven D. *A comprehensive bibliography of music for film and television,* BH147

Wessel, Klaus. *Reallexikon zur byzantinischen Kunst*, BE40

West, Bill W. *Street talk in real estate*, CH350

West, Edward N. *Outward signs*, BB73

West, John. *Town records*, DC136

—— *Village records*, DC136

West, Ruth. *Alternative medicine*, EK18

The West Bank data project, Benvenisti, Meron, CJ188

The West Bank handbook, Benvenisti, Meron, CJ188

West European economic handbook, CH46

West German cinema since 1945, Helt, Richard C., BG74

West Germany, Detwiler, Donald S., DC85

West India Reference Library (Jamaica). *Jamaican national bibliography*, AA150

West Indian literature, Allis, Jeanette B., BD284

West Indies, DB98

Westcott, Cynthia. *Westcott's plant disease handbook*, EH25

Westcott's plant disease handbook, Westcott, Cynthia, EH25

Westendorf, Wolfhart. *Lexikon der Ägyptologie*, DD31

Westerman, Cheryl I. *The writer's advisor*, BD44

Western books on China published up to 1850 in the Library of the School of Oriental and African Studies, University of London, University of London. School of Oriental and African Studies. Library, DE48

Western European political parties, CJ169

Western states, DB55, DB57

Westfall, Gloria. *Bibliography of official statistical yearbooks and bulletins*, CG8

—— *Guide to official publications of foreign countries*, AG1

WESTLAW, CK22

The Westminster dictionary of Christian ethics, BB92

The Westminster dictionary of Christian spirituality, BB93

The Westminster dictionary of worship, Davies, J. G., BB89

West's legal desk reference, CK91

Wetterau, Bruce. *The New York Public Library book of chronologies*, DA25

Wexler, Paul. *Judeo-Romance linguistics*, BC37

Wexler, Philip. *Information resources in toxicology*, EK127

Whaling ships, DG8

Wharton, J. H. *Canada legal directory*, CK73

Wharton, R. A. *Canada legal directory*, CK73

Wharton-Lake, Beverly D. *Creative literature of Trinidad and Tobago*, BD285

Wheal, Elizabeth-Anne. *A dictionary of the Second World War*, DA76

Wheatley, Henry B. *London, past and present*, DC137

Wheeler, Brian K. *A field guide to hawks, North America*, EC47

Wheeler, Helen Rippier. *The bibliographic instruction-course handbook*, AB103

Wheeler, James O. *A bibliography of geographic thought*, CL2

—— *Bibliography on geographic thought*, CL2

—— *Dictionary of quotations in geography*, CL13

Whelpton, John. *Nepal*, DE86

Where do we come from? What are we? Where are we going?, CC48

Where the whalers went, DG8

Where's that tune?, Goodfellow, William D., BH14

Wheye, Darryl. *The birder's handbook*, EC48

Whitaker, Allan. *The language of biotechnology*, EJ19

Whitaker, Cathy Seitz. *Alternative publications*, AA48

Whitaker, Katherine C. *The martial arts*, BJ31

Whitaker, Richard E. *The Eerdmans analytical concordance to the Revised Standard Version of the Bible*, BB61

Whitaker's books in print, AA126

Whitby, Thomas J. *Studies in human sexuality*, CC147

White, Carl Milton. *Sources of information in the social sciences*, CA4

White, D. Jerry. *Early English drama, Everyman to 1580*, BD234

White, David Allen. *Shakespeare A to Z*, BD267

White, Garry W. *Handbook of certification and licensure requirements for school psychologists*, CB133

White, Glenn D. *The audio dictionary*, BH160

White, James P. *Materials and strategies for the education of trainable mentally retarded learners*, CB41, CD3

White, Jess R. *Sports rules encyclopedia*, BJ9

White, John A. *Production handbook*, CH304

White, Katherine P. *Folk artists biographical index*, BF15

White, Linda. *English-Basque dictionary*, AD77

White, Ray Lewis. *Index to Best American short stories and O. Henry prize stories*, BD177

White, Rhea A. *Parapsychology*, CD55

White, Stephen. *Political and economic encyclopaedia of the Soviet Union and Eastern Europe*, DC15

Whiting, Bartlett Jere. *Modern proverbs and proverbial sayings*, BD72

Whitman, Alden. *American reformers*, AJ21, CC24

Whitten, Bessie E. *Manufacturing*, CH140

Whitten, David O. *Manufacturing*, CH140

Whitworth, Judith A. *Dictionary of medical eponyms*, EK47

Who is who in government and politics in Latin America, CJ198

Who is who [in] government, politics, banking, and industry, CJ198

Who is who [in] government, politics, banking and industry : in Latin America, AJ77, CJ193

Who was really who in fiction, Bold, Alan Norman, BD96

Who was who in American art, Falk, Peter H., BE93, BE99

Who was who in British librarianship, 1800–1985, Munford, William Arthur, AB41

Who was who in Native American history, Waldman, Carl, CC231

Who was who in the Civil War, Sifakis, Stewart, DB35

Whole preservation catalog, BE129

Whole world handbook, CB86

Who's wealthy in America, CH149

Who's who among Hispanic Americans, AJ28

Who's who in advertising, CH72

Who's who in American education, CB145

Who's who in British history, DC124

Who's who in China: current leaders, CJ160, AJ42

Who's who in economics, CH24

Who's who in educational administration, American Association of School Administrators, CB143

Who's who in engineering, EJ4

Who's who in European politics, CJ170

Who's who in fashion, Stegemeyer, Anne, BF33

Who's who in frontier science and technology, EA81

Who's who in frontiers of science and technology, EA81

Who's who in history, DC124

Who's who in Japan, AJ76

Who's who in Japanese government, CJ192

Who's who in librarianship in Pakistan, AB42

Who's who in library and information science in Pakistan, Sabzwari, Ghaniul Akram, AB42

Who's who in Mexico today, Camp, Roderic Ai, AJ80

Who's who in religion, BB35

Who's who in Roman Britain and Anglo-Saxon England, Fletcher, Richard A., DC124

Who's who in science in Europe, EA82

Who's who in South African politics, Gastrow, Shelagh, CJ203

Who's who in Spain, AJ95

Who's who in spy fiction, BD106

Who's who in Stuart England, Hill, C. P., DC124

Who's who in technology, EJ5

Who's who in technology today, EJ5

Who's who in the People's Republic of China, Bartke, Wolfgang, AJ41, CJ160, CJ161

Who's who in the press, AF26

Who's who in the socialist countries of Europe, AJ49

Who's who in Tudor England, Routh, C. N. R., DC124

Who's who in Turkey, AJ97

Who's who in writers, editors & poets, United States & Canada, BD171

Who's who, Indian personages, AJ72

Why do we say— ?, Rees, Nigel, AD18

Wick, Charles. *Tool and manufacturing engineers handbook*, EJ83

Wicked words, Rawson, Hugh, AD48

Wickremasinghe, W. *Scholarships, fellowships & grants for programs abroad*, CB162

Wieczynski, Joseph L. *The modern encyclopedia of Russian and Soviet history*, DC208

Wielewinski, Bernard. *Doctoral dissertations and masters theses regarding Polish subjects, 1900–1985*, DC173

Wiggins, Gary. *Chemical information sources*, ED3

Wigoder, Geoffrey. *A dictionary of the Jewish-Christian dialogue*, BB136

—— *Illustrated dictionary & concordance of the Bible*, BB54

Wilbur, Leslie C. *Handbook of energy systems engineering*, EJ70

Wilcox, Laird M. *Guide to the American left*, CJ63

—— *Guide to the American right*, CJ64

Wildbihler, Hubert. *The musical*, BH108

Wilde, W. H. *The Oxford companion to Australian literature*, BD276

Wildhaber, Robert. *Internationale Volkskundliche Bibliographie = International folklore bibliography*, CF23

Wildlife, EC26

Wildlife refuges *see* **Parks and protected areas**

Wilgat, Janina. *Bibliografia polska 1901–1939 = Polish bibliography 1901–1939*, AA173

Wilhoit, Frances Goins. *Mass media bibliography*, CH196

Wilkas, Lenore. *International subscription agents*, AB68

Wilkes, G. A. *A dictionary of Australian colloquialisms*, AD58

Wilkes, Joseph A. *Encyclopedia of architecture*, BE122

Wilkinson, Geoffrey,. *Comprehensive coordination chemistry*, ED12

Wilkinson, P. C. *Dictionary of immunology*, EC15, EK56

Willard E. Yager Library-Museum. *Indians of North and South America*, CC225

Willeford, George. *Webster's New World medical word finder*, EK51

Willemsen, Carl Arnold. *Bibliographie zur Geschichte Kaiser Friedrichs II. und der letzten Staufer*, DC84

Willenberg, Gabi. *Bibliography of semiotics, 1975–1985*, BC2

William Shakespeare, BD269

Williams, C. J. *Cofrestri plwyf Cymru = Parish registers of Wales*, AK48

—— *Parish registers of Wales*, AK47

Williams, David Russell. *Music theory from Zarlino to Schenker*, BH9

Williams, Emelda L. *American advertising*, CH69

Williams, Forrest. *The martial arts*, BJ31

Williams, Gwyneth. *The dictionary of contemporary politics of southern Africa*, CJ151

Williams, James G. *Encyclopedia of microcomputers*, EJ60

Williams, John T. *Anthropology journals and serials*, CE11

Williams, Martha E. *Computer-readable data bases*, AB91

Williams, Moelwyn I. *A directory of rare book and special collections in the United Kingdom and the Republic of Ireland*, AB29

Williams, Peter W. *Encyclopedia of the American religious experience*, BB26

Williams, Phillip. *A glossary of special education*, CB72

Williams, Stephen N. *The dictionary of British and American homophones*, AD31

Willingham, Robert Marion. *Confederate imprints*, DB30

Willis-Thomas, Deborah. *Black photographers, 1840–1940*, BF64

—— *An illustrated bio-bibliography of black photographers, 1940–1988*, BF64

Wilms, Denise Murcko. *Science books for children*, CB7

Wilpert, Gero von. *Lexikon der Weltliteratur*, BD30

Wilson, Charles Reagan. *Encyclopedia of Southern culture*, DB52

Wilson, Clyde Norman. *American historians, 1866–1912*, DB75

Wilson, Craig A. *Policies of publishers*, AB66

Wilson, Frank Percy. *The Oxford history of English literature*, BD222

Wilson, John Frederick. *Church and state in America*, DB4

Wilson, Lofton. *Guide to Latin American pamphlets from the Yale University Library*, DB97

Wilson, Raymond L. *Index of American print exhibitions, 1785–1940*, BE67

—— *Index of American print exhibitions, 1882–1940*, BE156

Wilson, Robert. *Encyclopedia of medical organizations and agencies*, EK64

Wilson, Samuel. *Mission handbook*, BB106

Wilson, Terry P. *Bibliography of the Osage*, CC218

Winans, Robert B. *A descriptive checklist of book catalogues separately printed in America, 1693–1800*, BE111

Windhausen, John D. *Sports encyclopedia North America*, BJ8

Windrow, Martin. *A concise dictionary of military biography*, AJ13

Wing, Donald Goddard. *Short-title catalogue of books printed in England, Scotland, Ireland, Wales, and British America, and of English books printed in other countries, 1641–1700*, AA130, AA131, AG36

Winick, Charles. *Dictionary of anthropology*, CE15

Winick, Myron. *The Columbia encyclopedia of nutrition*, EK97

Winkler, Paul W. *Anglo-American cataloguing rules*, AB79

Winnovich, Karen. *War crimes, war criminals, and war crimes trials*, DA72

Winship, Michael. *Bibliography of American literature*, BD151

Winter, Eugenia B. *Psychological and medical aspects of induced abortion*, CC267, EK19

Winter, Georgie. *Black adolescence*, CC79

Wintle, Michael J. *The Netherlands*, DC165

The wisdom of the novel, Powell, David, BD64

Wise, Edith C. *Bibliography of American folk art for the year [. . .]*, BF8

Wiswall, Irving W. *Labor and the environment*, CH271

Wit and humor, BD153, CF30; *see also* American wit and humor

The wit & wisdom of politics, CJ28

Witchcraft, CF27

Witherell, Julian W. *Afghanistan*, DE43

—— *Libya, 1969–1989*, DD42

—— *The Republic of Turkey*, DC193

Witherick, M. E. *A modern dictionary of geography*, CL12

Witt, Elder. *Congressional Quarterly's guide to the U.S. Supreme Court*, CK61

Witt, Maria. *New international dictionary of acronyms in library and information science and related fields*, AB17

Wittman, Sandra M. *Writing about Vietnam*, BD158, DE102

Wittrock, M. C. *Handbook of research on teaching*, CB129

Wižďálková, Bedřiška. *Příspěvky ke knihopisu*, AA98, AA98

Wöffen, Angela. *Lexikon deutschsprachiger Schriftstellerinnen, 1800–1945*, BD288

Woelfel, Charles J. *Encyclopedia of banking & finance*, CH224

Woerner, Gert. *The encyclopedia of Eastern philosophy and religion*, BA12, BB23

Wörterbuch der deutschen Gegenwartssprache, AD106

Wörterbuch der klassischen arabischen Sprache, AD71

Wörterbuch der mittelhochdeutschen Urkundensprache, AD108

Wörterbuch der Mythologie. 1 Abteilung, Die alten Kulturvölker, CF8

Wörterbuch der philosophischen Begriffe, Eisler, Rudolf, BA18

Wörterbuch der Sportwissenschaft, BJ11

Woldman's engineering alloys, EJ88

Wolf, Carolyn E. *Indians of North and South America*, CC225

Wolfe, Gregory. *Right minds*, CJ72

Wolfert, Marion. *German immigrants*, AK14

Wolff, John U. *An Indonesian-English dictionary*, AD126

Wolff, Kathryn. *AAAS science book list, 1978–1986*, EA15

Woll, Allen L. *Ethnic and racial images in American film and television*, CC171

Wollheim, William. *The book of Jewish books*, BB129

Wolman, Benjamin B. *Dictionary of behavioral science*, CD11

Wolseley, Isabel. *The journalist's bookshelf*, AF18

Wolseley, Roland Edgar. *The journalist's bookshelf*, AF18

Wolter, John Amadeus. *World directory of map collections*, CL46

The woman's dictionary of symbols and sacred objects, Walker, Barbara G., CF7

Women; *see also* Feminism
  bibliography, BD249, CC37, CC39, CC248, CC254, CC255, CC256, CC258, CC259, CC260, CC261, CC264, CC266, CC269, CC280, CC282, CC289, CC290, CC307, CC308
    bibliography of bibliography, CC253
    current, CC268
    women in specific countries or regions
      Africa, BD372, CC274, CC275, CC276
      Caribbean, BD282
      India, CC286
      Ireland, CC273
      Latin America, CC288
      Third World, CB32, CC277, CC279, CC285
      United States, BD184, CC144, CC278, CC281, CC283, CC288, CC292, DB65
  biography, AJ9, AJ61, BA24, CC287, CC313
    indexes, AJ5
  by occupation or profession
    anthropology, CE23
    architecture, BE133
    authorship, AA31, BD132, BD152, BD168, BD179, BD181, BD185, BD190, BD198, BD199, BD223, BD224, BD228, BD282, BD288, BD326, BD331, BD372, BG62, DE103
    business, CH147
    fine arts, BE79, BE91, BE95, BE167
    geography, CL4
    literature, BD189, BD225, BD335, BD336
    mass media, CC301
    mathematics, EF18
    music, BH67, BH77, BH85
    politics, CJ166
    science, CC263, EA78
    science and technology, EA84
    sports, BJ7, BJ15
    theater, BG39
  chronologies, CC312
  dictionaries, CC297, CC298
  directories, CC303, CC304, CC305
  economic conditions, CC145
  economic status, CC257, CH273
  education, CB32, CB132, CC285, CC310
  encyclopedias, CC294
  guides, CC247, CC250
  handbooks, AA57, CC309, CC311
  health care, CC291, EK37
    directories, CC116, CC306
  history
    bibliography, CC284
  indexes, CC270
  legal rights, CC309
  motion pictures, CC265
  periodicals, CC272
  quotations, CC295
  statistics, CG25, CG44
  terminology, CC299, CC300
  women in specific countries or regions
    Third World, CC251

Women, Ballou, Patricia K., CC253

Women and aging, Coyle, Jean M., CC37, CC255

Women and geography, Lee, David R., CL4

Women and literature, BD152

Women and mass communications, Lent, John A., CC258

Women and the literature of the seventeenth century, Smith, Hilda L., AA130

Women and women's issues, Beere, Carole A., CC307, CC308

Women and work, paid and unpaid, Ferber, Marianne A., CC257, CH273

Women anthropologists, CE23

Women artists in the United States, Chiarmonte, Paula L., BE79, BE91

Women authors of modern Hispanic South America, Cypess, Sandra Messinger, BD331

Women composers, BH77

Women composers, conductors, and musicians of the twentieth century, LePage, Jane Weiner, BH85

Women in American history, DA55

—— Harrison, Cynthia Ellen, CC283

Women in development, CC251

Women in English social history, 1800–1914, Kanner, Barbara, CC284

Women in Ireland, Brady, Anna, CC273

Women in LC's terms, Dickstein, Ruth, CC299

Women in mathematics, Osen, L. M., EF18

Women in psychology, CD36

Women in science, Ogilvie, Marilyn Bailey, CC263, EA78

Women in the Third World, DA55

—— Byrne, Pamela R., CC277

—— Fenton, Thomas P., CC279

Women in western European history. First supplement, Frey, Linda, CC280

Women of color and Southern women, CC289, CC290

Women of color in the United States, Redfern, Bernice, CC287

Women of eastern and southern Africa, Bullwinkle, Davis, CC275

Women of India, Pandit, Harshida, CC286
Women of mathematics, EF18
Women of northern, western, and central Africa, Bullwinkle, Davis, CC276
Women-owned business firms, CH121, CH123
Women philosophers, Kersey, Ethel M., BA24
Women scholars in women's studies, CC304
Women scientists from antiquity to the present, Herzenberg, Caroline L., EA84
Women who ruled, Jackson, Guida, CC313
Women writers, from page to screen, BG62
Women writers of Germany, Austria, and Switzerland, BD294
Women writers of Spain, BD326
Women writers of Spanish America, BD336
Women's diaries, journals, and letters, Cline, Cheryl, BD249
Women's education in the Third World, Kelly, David H., CB32, CC285
Women's Institute for Freedom of the Press. *Directory of women's media*, CC301
Women's issues, Mumford, Laura Stempel, CC261
Women's movements of the world, CC305
Women's poetry index, Guy, Patricia A., BD132
Women's recovery programs, CC116, CC306
Women's sexuality, CC153
Women's studies, CB135, CC249, CC250, CC252, CC268, CC302
Women's studies, Carter, Sarah, CC247
—— Loeb, Catherine, CC259, CC260
Women's studies encyclopedia, CC294
Women's studies in Western Europe, CC252
Women's studies index, CC270
A women's thesaurus, CC300
—— Capek, Mary Ellen S., CC299
Wong, John. *Asian economic handbook*, CH36
Wood, Clement. *The complete rhyming dictionary and poet's craft book*, AD38
—— *Wood's unabridged rhyming dictionary*, AD38
Wood, David Norris. *Information sources in the earth sciences*, EE1
—— *Use of earth sciences literature*, EE1
Wood, Donna. *Brands and their companies*, CH294, CH295, CH296, CH297, CH298
—— *Companies and their brands*, CH294, CH295, CH296, CH297, CH298
—— *International brands and their companies*, CH294, CH295, CH296
—— *International companies and their brands*, CH294, CH295, CH296, CH297, CH298
Wood, Floris W. *An American profile*, CJ237, CJ237
Wood, G. A. *A guide for students of New Zealand history*, DF6
—— *Studying New Zealand history*, DF6
Wood, M. Sandra. *How to find information about AIDS*, EK3
Wood, Patrick W. *Checklist of bibliographies appearing in the Bulletin of bibliography 1897–1987*, AA9
Wood, EJ42
Wood engineering handbook, EJ42
Wood handbook, EJ42
Woodbridge, Hensley Charles. *Guide to reference works for the study of the Spanish language and literature and Spanish American literature*, BD321
—— *Spanish and Spanish-American literature*, BD321
Woodhead, Peter. *Keyguide to information sources in archaeology*, DA31
—— *Keyguide to information sources in museum studies*, BE3
Woodhouse, Tom. *The international peace directory*, CJ309
Woods, Richard Donovon. *Mexican autobiography*, AJ81, BD346

Wood's unabridged rhyming dictionary, Wood, Clement, AD38
Woodward, Arthur. *Textbooks in school and society*, CB42
Woodward, David R. *America and World War I*, DA73
Woodward, Ralph Lee. *El Salvador*, DB120
Woodwind, brass, and percussion instruments of the orchestra, Skei, Allen B., BH155
Woodworth, David. *Current British journals: a bibliographic guide*, AE45
Woody, Gloria T. *Blacks and media*, CH203
Woolery, George W. *Animated TV specials*, BG114
Woordenboek der nederlandsche taal, AD85
Word maps, Upton, Clive, BC30
Word perfect, Clark, John Owen Edward, AD24
Word processing, AA55
Words and phrases legally defined, CK66
Words of the Vietnam War, Clark, Gregory R., AD41
Words of Wall Street, CH231
Words on tape, AA84
The wordworthy computer, Feldman, Paula R., BD12
Work, CC8
Work and alcohol abuse, Miletich, John J., CC70
Work environment, CH271, CH280
Work, study, travel abroad, CB86
Working class
by country or region
Gt. Brit., CH270
Workplace environmental quality in the United States, CH271
Works of Bulgarian emigrants, Paprikoff, George I., AA91
The World Almanac guide to good word usage, AD23
World artists 1980–1990, BE90
The world atlas of archaeology, DA37, DA39
World atlas of elections, Leonard, R. L., CJ43
World authors, BD55
World Bank. *World debt tables*, CH31
—— *World tables*, CG22
World book encyclopedia, BE31
World chamber of commerce directory, CH108
World collectors annuary, BE65
World comparisons, CG20
World debt tables, CH31
World development directory, CH59
A world directory of criminological institutes, CK105
World directory of crystallographers and of other scientists employing crystallographic methods, EE22
World directory of human rights teaching and research institutions, CA19
World directory of map collections, CL46
World directory of minorities, CC179
World directory of peace research and training institutions, CA19
World directory of peace research and training institutions = Répertoire mondial des institutions de recherche et de formation sur la paix, CJ313
World directory of peace research institutions, CJ313
World directory of social science institutions, CA19
World economic and business review, CH32
World economic outlook, CH33
World education encyclopedia, CB140
World encyclopedia of cartoons, Horn, Maurice, BE160
World encyclopedia of peace, CJ306
World encyclopedia of police forces and penal systems, Kurian, George Thomas, CK104
World encyclopedia of political systems & parties, CJ33, CJ136
World fact file, CJ142
World facts and figures, Showers, Victor, CG16
World film directors, BG101

The world financial system, Fraser, Robert, CH223
World futures and options directory, CH175
World government, CJ143
World guide to foreign services, CJ148
World guide to libraries, AB20
World guide to scientific associations and learned societies, CA50, EA60
World guide to social work education, Rao, Vijaya, CC32
—— Resnick, Rosa Perla, CC32
—— Stickney, Patricia J., CC32
World Health Organization. *The international pharmacopoeia = Pharmacopoea internationalis*, EK123
—— *WHO drug information*, EK107
World index of economic forecasts, CH19
World list of social science periodicals, CA13
World list of universities = Liste mondiale des universites, CB87
World mapping today, CL47
World population profile, CG21
World population projections, 1987–88, Zachariah, K. C., CG23
A world record of major conflict areas, Munro, David, CJ35
The world sports record atlas, Emery, David, BJ6
World tables, CG22
World transindex, EA17
World translations index, EA17
World War I aviation books in English, Noffsinger, James Philip, DA69
World War II at sea, Smith, Myron J., DA71
World wars
atlases, DA78, DA79
bibliography, DA65, DA66, DA67, DA68, DA69, DA70, DA71, DA73, DA87, DC60
chronologies, DA77
dictionaries, DA74
encyclopedias, DA75, DA76, DC158
fiction, BD237
guides, DA68
World weather records, 1961–1970, EE32
World weather records, 1971–80, EE33
World Wildlife Fund. *The official World Wildlife Fund guide to endangered species of North America*, EC41
World Without War Council. *Peace archives*, CJ295
Worldcasts, CH133
Worldmark encyclopedia of the nations, CJ23
Worldmark encyclopedia of the states, CJ131
The world's major languages, BC10
WORLDSCOPE company profiles, CH109
WORLDSCOPE financial and service company profiles, CH109
WORLDSCOPE industrial company profiles, CH109
WORLDSCOPE profiles\CD, CH109
Worldwide directory of national earth-science agencies and related international organizations, Tinsley, Elizabeth J., EE18
Worldwide franchise directory, CH110
Worldwide government directory, with international organizations, CJ32, CK83
Worldwide travel information contact book, BJ45
Wren, Christopher G. *The legal research manual*, CK13
Wren, Jill Robinson. *The legal research manual*, CK13
Wrestling, BJ36
Wright, David F. *New dictionary of theology*, BB88
Wright, Joan. *Going places*, BJ49
Wright, Josephine R. B. *African-American traditions in song, sermon, tale, and dance, 1600s–1920*, CC203
Wright, Martin. *World development directory*, CH59
Wright, Roosevelt. *Black alcohol abuse and alcoholism*, CC73

Wright, Sylvia Hart. *Highlights of recent American architecture*, BE136
——— *Sourcebook of contemporary North American architecture from postwar to postmodern*, BE136
Wright Investors' Service. *WORLDSCOPE company profiles*, CH109
The writer's advisor, BD44
Writers and philosophers, Thomas, Edmund J., BD51
Writers conferences, BD43
Writers for children, BD83
Writers for young adults, Nakamura, Joyce, BD78
Writer's legal guide, Crawford, Tad, BE107, CK85
Writers on the American screen, Langman, Larry, BG61
Writers' Program (New York, N.Y.). *The film index*, BG56
Writing about music, BH46
——— Basart, Ann Phillips, BH29
Writing about Vietnam, Wittman, Sandra M., BD158, DE102
Writing the psychology paper, Sternberg, Robert J., CD37
Writings on Canadian English, 1792–1975, Avis, Walter, BC21
Writings on Canadian English, 1976–1987, Lougheed, W. C., BC21
Writings on Irish history, DC148
Wuerch, William L. *Micronesia, 1975–1987*, DG2
The Wuerttemberg emigration index, Schenk, Trudy, AK13
Wulff, Hans Jürgen. *Bibliographie der Filmbibliographien = Bibliography of film bibliographies*, BG57
Wunder, John R. *Historians of the American frontier*, DB76
Wunschheim, Johannes. *Bibliographie zur oberösterreichischen Geschichte, 1981–1985*, DC28
Wuolle, Aino. *Englantilais-suomalainen koulusanakirja*, AD88
——— *The standard Finnish-English English-Finnish dictionary*, AD88
——— *Suomalais-englantilainen sanakirja*, AD88
Wyatt, Antony. *Challinor's dictionary of geology*, EE9
Wyatt, H. V. *Information sources in the life sciences*, EC1
——— *The use of biological literature*, EC1
Wyczynski, Paul. *Dictionnaire des auteurs de langue française en Amérique du Nord*, BD304
Wynar, Bohdan S. *Introduction to cataloging and classification*, AB76
——— *Ukraine*, DC214
Wynar, Lubomyr Roman. *Guide to the American ethnic press*, AE27
Wynbrandt, James. *The encyclopedia of genetic disorders and birth defects*, EK45
Wynkoop, Sally. *Subject guide to government reference books*, AG4
Wynne-Davies, Marion. *Prentice Hall guide to English literature*, BD220

X-Market, CH126
X/Toll, CH125

Yaffe, Sumner J. *Drugs in pregnancy and lactation*, EK113
Yale, D. E. C. *A centenary guide to the publications of the Selden Society*, CK41
Yale University. Library. *Guide to Latin American pamphlets from the Yale University Library*, DB97
Yale University Library Holocaust video testimonies, DA84
The Yanagita Kunio guide to the Japanese folk tale, BD381, CF36

Yancy, Preston M. *The Afro-American short story*, BD191
Yapp, Peter. *The travellers' dictionary of quotations*, BJ42
Yar-Shater, Ehsan. *Encyclopædia Iranica*, DE71
Yarber, William L. *Sexuality-related measures*, CC157
Yarnall, James L. *The National Museum of American Art's index to American art exhibition catalogues*, BE67
Yassif, Eli. *Jewish folklore*, CF35
Ybarra-Frausto, Tomás. *Arte Chicano*, BE5
Yeager, Gertrude Matyoka. *Bolivia*, DB110
A year book of the Commonwealth, CJ183
Yearbook, Evangelical Lutheran Church in America, BB109
The yearbook of education law, CB154
Yearbook of labour statistics, CH288
Yearbook of school law, CB154
Yeni Türk ansiklopedisi, AC19
Yiddish language
  bibliography, BC34
  dictionaries, AD174
    bilingual, AD175, AD176
Yiddish language and folklore, Weinreich, Beatrice, BC34
——— Weinreich, Uriel, BC34
Yiddish linguistics, Bratkowsky, Joan Gloria, BC34
Yoak, Stuart D. *The Constitution of the United States*, CK118
Yoga, BB124
Yogi, Stan. *Asian American literature*, BD192
Yogis, John. *Legal writing and research manual*, CK36
York, Henry E. *Political science*, CJ3
Yorke, Amanda. *The Cambridge handbook of contemporary China*, DE53
Young, Arthur P. *Cities and towns in American history*, DB48
Young, Margaret Labash. *Life sciences organizations and agencies directory*, EC20
——— *Scientific and technical organizations and agencies directory*, EA59
Young, Margaret Walsh. *Cities of the world*, CL18
Young, Michael L. *The American dictionary of campaigns and elections*, CJ55, CJ57
Young, Patricia A. *Feminists, pornography & the law*, CC264
Young, Sue. *The new comprehensive American rhyming dictionary*, AD39
Young, Vernon R. *Modern nutrition in health and disease*, EK99
Young, Virginia G. *The library trustee*, AB71
Young, William C. *Theatre companies of the world*, BG34
Young, William J. *The United States energy atlas*, EJ73
Young adult fiction index, BD79
Youngs, J. William T. *The Congregationalists*, BB114
Yu, Chŏng-nyŏl. *World encyclopedia of peace*, CJ306
Yu, David C. *Guide to Chinese religion*, BB13
Yugoslav history, Terry, Garth M., DC219
Yugoslav literature in English, BD361
Yugoslavia
  bibliography, AA203, AA204
    current, AA205
  biography, AJ102, AJ103
  history
    bibliography, DC218, DC219
Yugoslavia, Horton, John J., DC218
Yugoslavian language *see* **Serbo-Croatian language**
Yugoslavian literature, BD360, BD361, BD362
Yurdan, Marilyn. *Irish family history*, AK41
Yurkiw, Peter. *Union list of manuscripts in Canadian repositories*, DB86

Zachariah, K. C. *World population projections, 1987–88*, CG23
Zafren, Herbert Cecil. *Jewish newspapers and periodicals on microfilm*, AE5
Zaimont, Judith Lang. *The musical woman*, BH67
Zaĭonchkovskiĭ, Petr Andreevich. *Istoriia dorevoliutsionnoĭ Rossii v dnevnikakh i vospominaniiakh*, DC196
Zaire, AA206
Zaire, Bobb, F. S., DD5
Zak, Louise Allen. *English drama of the nineteenth century*, BD231
Zangwill, O. L. *The Oxford companion to the mind*, CD14
Zarzuela, Diccionario de la, BH105
Zeichen, Text, Bedeutung, Eschbach, Achim, BC2
Das Zeitalter der Glaubensspaltung (1500–1618), Dotzauer, Winfried, BB99, DC82
Zell, Hans M. *The African studies companion*, DD9
Zeller, Otto. *IBN*, AJ6
——— *Internationale Jahresbibliographie Südwestasien = International annual bibliography South West Asia : SWA*, DE10
Zeller, Wolfram. *Internationale Jahresbibliographie Südwestasien = International annual bibliography South West Asia : SWA*, DE10
Zen Buddhism, BA12, BB23
Zentner, Christian. *The encyclopedia of the Third Reich*, DC92
——— *Grosse Lexikon des Dritten Reiches*, DC92
Zentralblatt für Mathematik und ihre Grenzgebiete, EF5 '
Zero Population Growth, Inc. *USA by numbers*, CG27
Zgraon, Florentina. *Dicţionarul limbii române literare vechi, 1640–1780*, AD147
Zhongguo guojia shumu, AA95
Zhongguo Tongii Nianjian, CG48
Zilkha, Avraham. *Modern Hebrew-English dictionary*, AD120
Zimbabwe
  bibliography, CJ207, DD60
  biography, CJ208
  encyclopedias, DD58
  history, DD59
  politics and government, CJ207, CJ208, DD60
Zimbabwe, Rasmussen, R. Kent, DD5
——— Rubert, S. C., DD5
Zimbabwean political material published in exile, 1959–1980, Johnstone, I. J., CJ207, DD60
Zimmerman, Gary J. *German immigrants*, AK14
Zimmerman, Thom J. *Ophthalmic drug facts*, EK120
Zimmermann, Hartmut. *DDR Handbuch*, CJ172
Zink, Christoph. *Dictionary of obstetrics and gynecology*, EK52
Zink, Steven D. *Guide to the Presidential advisory commissions, 1973–1984*, CJ88
Zinkus, Jonas. *Lietuviškoji tarybinė enciklopedija. Papildymai A-Ž*, DC160
——— *Lithuania*, DC161
——— *Tarybū Lietuvos enciklopedija*, DC163
Ziring, Lawrence. *The Asian political dictionary*, CJ154
——— *The Middle East political dictionary*, CJ199, DE20
Zirkle, James W. *A reference guide to the United States Supreme Court*, CK90
Zitatenlexikon, BD69
Zito, Dorothea R. *A guide to research in gerontology*, CC33, EK5
Zito, George V. *A guide to research in gerontology*, CC33, EK5

Zollar, Ann Creighton. *Adolescent pregnancy and parenthood*, CC135

Zolli, Paolo. *Dizionario etimologico della lingua italiana*, AD131

Zombeck, Martin V. *Handbook of space astronomy and astrophysics*, EB12

Zondervan NIV atlas of the Bible, Rasmussen, Carl, BB69

Zonhoven, L. M. J. *Annual Egyptological bibliography. Late reviews AEB 1947–1984*, DD30

Zoological record online, EC39

Zoology, EC26, EC39, EC40

Zophy, Angela Marie Howard. *Handbook of American women's history*, CC292, DB65

Zophy, Jonathan W. *An annotated bibliography of the Holy Roman Empire*, DC8

Zorack, John L. *The lobbying handbook*, CJ71

Zubatsky, David S. *Jewish autobiographies and biographies*, AJ19

―――― *Latin American literary authors*, BD333

Zulkarjono, Maesarah. *Daftar majalah Indonesia yang telah mempunyai ISSN*, AE52

Zulu language, AD177

A Zuni atlas, Ferguson, T. J., CC233

Żurawicki, Leon. *Global countertrade*, CH179

Zusne, Leonard. *Eponyms in psychology*, CD23

Zwillinger, Daniel. *Handbook of differential equations*, EF16

Zwirn, Jerrold. *Congressional publications and proceedings*, AG6, CJ95